Encyclopedia of
MANAGEMENT

5th Edition

Encyclopedia of
MANAGEMENT

5th Edition

Edited by Marilyn M. Helms, D.B.A.

THOMSON

GALE

Detroit • New York • San Francisco • San Diego • New Haven, Conn. • Waterville, Maine • London • Munich

Encyclopedia of Management, 5th ed.

Marilyn M. Helms, D.B.A., Editor

Project Editor
Julie A. Gough

Editorial
Virgil Burton
Miranda Ferrara
Linda Hall
Lynn Pearce
Holly Selden

Composition and Electronic Prepress
Evi Seoud

Manufacturing
Wendy Blurton

LIBRARY OF CONGRESS CATALOGING-IN-PUBLICATION DATA

Encyclopedia of management / edited by Marilyn M. Helms.—5th ed.
    p. cm.
    Includes bibliographical references and index.
    ISBN 0-7876-6556-8 (hardcover : alk. paper)
    1. Industrial management—Encyclopedias. I. Helms, Marilyn M., 1962-

    HD30.15.E49 2006
    658'.003—dc22   2005018546

This title is also available as an e-book.
ISBN 1-4144-0478-6
Contact your Thomson Gale sales representative for ordering information.

Printed in the United States of America
10 9 8 7 6 5 4 3 2

The fifth edition of the *Encyclopedia of Management* presents a completely refreshed look at the vast and continually evolving field of management. Through 303 essays, readers will encounter thousands of terms, issues, and concepts such as:

- Aggregate Planning

- Apprenticeship Programs

- Balanced Scorecard

- Benchmarking

- Coalition Building

- Ethics

- Globalization

- Hypothesis Testing

- Inventory Management

- Japanese Management

- Lean Manufacturing and Just-in-Time Production

- Management Awards

- Mission and Vision Statements

- Organization Theory

- Outsourcing and Offshoring

- Pioneers of Management

- Project Management

- Quality of Work Life

- Time-Based Competition

- Virtual Organizations

- Women and Minorities in Management

- World-Class Manufacturer

- Zero-Sum Game

The *Encyclopedia of Management's* essays offer a unique starting point for individuals seeking comprehensive information that can't be adequately conveyed through brief dictionary-like definitions. Placed into context, and enhanced by background data as well as graphics and statistics, the topics covered in this volume are of both current and enduring interest.

ADDITIONAL FEATURES

- Contents are arranged alphabetically from A to Z in one volume

- One comprehensive tiered index simplifies accessibility

- Cross-references abound to help readers locate information

- Many essays written by acclaimed experts in their fields

- "Further Reading" sections provide source suggestions for further study

- Graphs, charts, and tables

- Math formulas illustrate concepts and models

Composed by subject matter specialists and business writers, under the guidance of an expert advisory panel headed by Dr. Marilyn M. Helms of Dalton State College, *EoM* represents a substantial contribution to business and management reference. Students, scholars, and business practitioners alike will find a wealth of information in this fully revised source.

152583

PREFACE

The *Encyclopedia of Management, 5th Edition* is an alphabetical reference book covering a comprehensive slate of management concepts. Last published in 2000, this fully revised work represents the latest management theories and practices. Each essay has been revised and new essays have been added to reflect the current state of management. The *Encyclopedia's* essays represent an authoritative treatment of the entire field of management, encompassing all the current theories and functional areas of this vast and growing discipline. For the management student, manager, business practitioner, reference librarian, or anyone interested in a better understanding of a business management term or concept, the *Encyclopedia* should be a first-stop for general information as well as a link to other management concepts, related terms, references, and electronic databases and information sources. It is designed to be a desk reference for everyday business management needs.

Still another use of the *Encyclopedia* is in a deeper understanding of one or more key functional areas of management. By using the book as a systematic or a programmed reading of entries in selected categories or cluster areas, the reader can obtain a more thorough, in-depth understanding of key functional areas of management. By reading all the essays for the terms under each heading in the "Guide to Functional-Area Readings", individuals with a limited business background, a specialty in another management functional area, or a liberal arts education background can gain a broad, general familiarity with the entire scope of the management discipline today in one easy-to-use reference source.

The field of management is an extremely broad discipline that draws upon concepts and ideas from the physical and social sciences, particularly mathematics, philosophy, sociology, and psychology. Within business, the field of management includes terms and ideas also common to marketing, economics, finance, insurance, transportation, accounting, computer technologies, information systems, engineering, and business law.

Management has applications in a wide variety of settings and is not limited to business domains. Management tools, as well as the art and science of management, find applications wherever any effort must be planned, organized, or controlled on a significant scale. This includes applications in government, the cultural arts, sports, the military, medicine, education, scientific research, religion, not-for-profit agencies, and in the wide variety of for-profit pursuits of service and manufacturing. Management takes appropriate advantage of technical developments in all the fields it serves.

The growth of the discipline of management has also led to specialization or compartmentalization of the field. These specialties of management make learning and study easier, but at the same time make broad understanding of management more difficult. It is particularly challenging to the entrepreneur and the small business owner to master the subject areas, yet this group is compelled to excel at all management functions to further their businesses' success. Management specialties have grown to such an extent it is difficult for any single manager to fully know what management is all about. So rapid have been the strides in recent years in such subjects as decision making, technology, the behavioral sciences, management information systems, and the like, to say nothing of proliferating legislative and governmental regulations affecting business, that constant study and education is required of all managers just to keep current on the latest trends and techniques. Thus, managers and executives need a comprehensive management desktop reference source to keep up-to-date. Having the management essays in one comprehensive encyclopedia saves valuable research time in locating the information.

In the growing age of specialists, there is a growing lack of generalists. Typically, a business manager spends a large percentage of their career developing a great familiarity and proficiency in a specialized field, such as sales, production, procurement, or accounting. The manager develops a very specialized knowledge in this area but may develop only a peripheral knowledge of advances in other areas of management. Yet as these individuals are promoted from a specialist-type position up the organizational chart to a more administrative or generalist supervisory or leadership position, the person with newly enlarged responsibilities suddenly finds that their horizon must extend beyond the given specialty. It must now include more than just a once-superficial understanding of all aspects of managing, including purchasing, manufacturing, advertising and selling, international management, quantitative techniques, human resources management, public relations, research and development, strategic planning, and management information systems. The need for broader management understanding and comprehension continues to increase as individuals are promoted.

The *Encyclopedia of Management* has had, as its goal, to bridge this gap in understanding and to offer every executive, executive-aspirant, management consultant, and educator and student of management, both comprehensive and authoritative information on all the theories, concepts, and techniques that directly impact the job of management. Building on the solid reputation established in prior editions, this thoroughly updated reference source strives to make specialists aware of the other functional areas of the management discipline and to give the top manager or administrator who occupies the general manager position new insights into the work of the specialists whom he or she must manage or draw upon in the successful management of others. In addition, the *Encyclopedia* proposes to make all practitioners aware of the advances in management science and in the behavioral sciences. These disciplines touch upon all areas of specialization because they concern the pervasive problems of decision-making and interpersonal relations.

USER'S GUIDE AND COMPILATION

REFERENCE, PLUS A PLANNED READING PROGRAM. The information in the *Encyclopedia* is accessible in two forms. First, through the traditional A-to-Z compilation, the reader readily has the quick answer to an immediate question or concise background information on any aspect of the field of management. As a handy desktop reference, the information is readily accessible. Second, and of more lasting importance, as a planned reading program for in-depth pursuit of any of the functional areas of management—the reader's own M.B.A., if you will. This program is set forth in the **"Guide to Functional-Area Readings"** located at the end of the frontmatter.

CROSS-REFERENCING AND SPECIAL FEATURES. The arrangement of the essays on a strictly alphabetical basis, rather than by subject categories, makes for extremely rapid and convenient information retrieval. At the same time, the extensive cross-referencing makes it easy to pursue a major area of interest in any depth of study desired. **"See-title"** cross-references serve to guide the reader directly toward the location of essays that may be recognized by more than one commonly used term. (For example, upon turning to "E-commerce" the see-title cross-reference would direct the reader to turn to "Electronic Commerce".)

Special features found within the essays include the following:

- **"See Also"** references, included at the end of many essays, refer the reader to further topics of closely related interest.

- **Charts, graphs, tables, and formulae** are included as illustrative examples whenever appropriate.

- **Further Reading** sections are included at the end of most entries. The bibliographic and URL citations point the reader toward a variety of suggested sources for further study and research.

INDEX. Supporting the easy-to-use, extensive system of cross-references, is a comprehensive index at the back of the *Encyclopedia*. The **Index** contains alphabetical references to the following as mentioned in the essays: important or unusual terms; names of companies, institutions, organizations, and associations; key governmental agencies; specific legislation; relevant court cases; names of prominent or historical individuals; titles of groundbreaking literature; and significant studies.

COMPREHENSIVE COVERAGE AND COMPILATION METHOD. Every effort has been made to achieve comprehensiveness in choice and coverage of subject matter. The 303 essays frequently go far beyond mere definitions and referrals to other sources. They are in-depth treatments, discussing background, subject areas, current applications, and schools of thought. In addition, information may be provided about the kinds of specialists who use the term in a given organization, the degree of current acceptance, and the possibilities for the future as the subject undergoes further development and refinement. Longer essays frequently provide charts, graphs, or examples to aid in understanding the topic.

All essays were written by recognized scholars, practitioners, and authorities in the field, including business management professors, other business professors, M.B.A. and doctoral research students, researchers, practitioners, reference librarians, and professional business writers. Additionally, all essays were vetted by the editor for accuracy, originality, and currency. The authors of all essays followed the editorial process specified for providing the reader an initial overview of the topic followed by information on the variety of management problems the information can be used to solve. Thus, if the reader has little knowledge of a term, after referring to the *Encyclopedia of Management, 5th Ed.,* he or she will be in possession of the basics of the subject—objective, scope, implementation, current usage in practice, and expected future usage. With this information, the reader will then be in a position to ask the right kind of questions of specialists and technicians to make sure that the firm (or department, or unit, or agency, etc.) is taking full advantage of the opportunity the term presents.

Marilyn M. Helms
D.B.A., CFPIM, CIRM

ABOUT THE EDITOR
AND ADVISORY BOARD

At the heart of the *Encyclopedia of Management's* editorial process was the Advisory Board. The Board team included a management professor, business reference librarians, and a freelance business writer and entrepreneur. This team of scholars and specialists, in addition to their teaching, research, writing and service work, found time to devote their expertise to the *EoM*. Their work began in developing and defining the list of management topics essential for inclusion. In addition to authoring a number of essays, they also assisted in selecting other qualified writers to contribute in their areas of management expertise. A brief biography of the editor and advisory board members is presented below.

DR. MARILYN M. HELMS is the Sesquicentennial Endowed Chair and a Professor of Management at Dalton State College (DSC), Dalton, Georgia. She works closely with the area business community on research projects, seminars, and training programs. Helms teaches production and operations management classes as well as classes in quality management and entrepreneurship. She held the UC Foundation and George Lester Nation Professor of Management at the University of Tennessee at Chattanooga from 1987 to 2000 where she also directed the Institute for Women as Entrepreneurs.

Helms holds a Doctorate of Business Administration Degree from the University of Memphis (TN). She is a Certified Fellow in Production and Inventory Management (CFPIM) and a Certified Integrated Resources Manager (CIRM) of the American Production and Inventory Control Society (APICS). She also teaches certification review courses for APICS and serves as Educational Director for the local Tri-State

Chapter of APICS. Dr. Helms is a Certified Quality Manager certified by the American Society for Quality.

She has published over 200 articles in periodicals including the *Production and Inventory Management Journal; Transportation Quarterly; European Business Review; Journal of Information Systems Education; International Journal of Benchmarking for Quality Management and Technology; The TQM Magazine; Industrial Management; Quality Progress; Industrial Management; and the Operations Management Review.*

Dr. Helms is a frequent manuscript and book reviewer, writes business cases and authors ancillaries and study guides for production and operations management textbooks. She also writes a business column for the Sunday *Dalton Daily Citizen* newspaper. She has received grants from the U.S. Department of Education, the Coleman Foundation, and the Southern Regional Education Board to develop new curricula and outreach programs. She serves on the editorial board of several academic peer-reviewed journals.

Dr. Helms has also directed and taught study abroad programs in Tokyo, Japan; Manchester Business School and at Kings College-Kensington (London); Cairns and Sydney, Australia; Monterrey, Mexico; Dublin and Galway, Ireland; and Moscow and St. Petersburg, Russia. She was awarded the Fulbright Teaching and Research Award and taught at the University of Coimbra, Portugal from April to June 2000.

She is a member of numerous professional organizations including the Academy of Management, the Academy of Entrepreneurship, the Decision Sciences Institute, the American Society for Competitiveness, and the American Production and Inventory Control Society. Her current research interests include entrepreneurship by women, manufacturing strategy, and supply chain management.

Helms has local and regional consulting experience and has spoken to international and national groups including the Decision Sciences Institute, the American Production and Inventory Control Society, and the Academy of Management. Her current research interests include women entrepreneurs, international competitiveness issues, corporate boards and leadership.

Dr. Helms comments on the *EoM*:

Even though the computer is always on and I can search the Internet for any topic, the most efficient way to find business management information is to start with the *EoM*. If a colleague mentions a business management term I need to be more familiar with, I consult the *EoM* and encourage my students to do the same. Even in the Internet age, I use a number of encyclopedias for their ease of use and comprehensive nature. You can be up-to-date on a subject in just a few minutes. It's the most effective way to start a research project. The essays in the *EoM* are also helpful to managers studying for certification and credentialing examinations. They offer a quick review. I am especially proud of the readings guide by subject area. I'd encourage all readers to read the *Emerging Topics in Management* selection of essays.

DR. R. ANTHONY (TONY) INMAN holds a Doctorate in Business Administration in Management from the University of Memphis (1988), an M.B.A. from the University of North Alabama (1983), and a Bachelor's degree from the University of Mississippi (1973).

Dr. Inman is the Ruston Building and Loan Professor of Management at Louisiana Tech University. Before assuming this professorship in 1997 he was an Associate Professor of Management at Louisiana Tech. Dr. Inman has taught courses in graduate and undergraduate Production/Operations Management, undergraduate Total Quality Management and undergraduate Purchasing. He has been a member of graduate faculty since 1990.

Dr. Inman has business experience as a former Materials Supervisor for Intex Plastics, as a Production Control Supervisor for Spun Steel, and as an Inventory Analyst for ITT Telecommunications.

Widely published in his field, his articles have appeared in journals such as *Production & Inventory Management Journal, Decision Sciences, International Journal of Production Research, International Journal of Operations and Production Management, and Production Planning and Control.* He has served on the editorial boards of *Production & Inventory Management Journal, Production Planning and Control, and Southern Business and Economic Journal.*

Dr. Inman is a Certified Fellow in Production and Inventory Management (CFPIM) through the American Production and Inventory Control Society (APICS). He is also an Academic Jonah as recognized by the Goldratt Institute. He was ranked 17th nationally in the article "POM Research Productivity in U.S. Business Schools," by S.T. Young, B.C. Baird, and M.E. Pullman, as published in the *Journal of Operations Management* volume 14 no.1, March 1996. He is a recipient of the Shingo Prize for Excellence in Manufacturing: Shingo Prize Research Award for 1993, for "Determining the Critical Elements of Just-In-Time Implementation," in *Decision Sciences* volume 23 no.1, January/February 1992. He was recently given the Louisiana Tech University Foundation Professor Award for 2005.

Dr. Inman comments on the EOM:

Even as one of the authors, I continually find the *Encyclopedia of Management* to be a helpful tool for those times when I need to quickly "brush up" on a topic. It should be even more useful for students and practitioners. I frequently recommend it to students who need an understandable overview of a difficult subject. My biggest problem in using the book is in finding it (I'm not sure where it is at this moment), as it is constantly on loan.

The addition of current topics and the deletion of obsolete ones required a thorough analysis by a number of management experts. New entries plus the updating of the retained topics challenged us to find not only those most knowledgeable in their fields but those with the ability to convey their knowledge in a brief but thorough and understandable manner. I think we have succeeded quite well!

JUDITH (JUDY) NIXON is a librarian at the Krannert Library of Management and Economics at Purdue University in West Lafayette, Indiana. Judith has a B.S. degree from Valparaiso University in Indiana and a M.L.S. from the University of Iowa. Prior to working at the Krannert Library she worked at the University of Arizona as a business librarian, and a librarian at the Consumer and Family Sciences Library at Purdue. Nixon is a frequent advisor on business reference sources. Her published articles have appeared in periodicals such as the *Journal of Business and Finance Librarianship*. As a librarian, Judith is both the head of the free-standing business library and leads a team of three business reference librarians as well as six support staff. She assists undergraduates through Ph.D.-level graduate students with their research projects as well as answers a broad range of business questions from data source needs to beginning search strategies and techniques. She works closely with a number of business faculty members including the tax law area. She instructs upper level accounting students in the use of the online tax service. She teaches classes on library use for a number of business groups. In addition, her library assists with business research needs for the entire Purdue University, and technology students in particular. Her research interests include: using data to evaluate collection needs, team building, and economic collection. She also manages the Krannert Special Collection of historic economic books.

Judith shares her thoughts about the *EOM, 5th edition:*

The *Encyclopedia of Management* is a valuable first stop for research on the broad range of topics in the field of management. The essays are concise, accurate and readable. In addition, each essay has a very concise list of the most useful books, articles and websites so the reader can get a quick start on the research process. This new edition, the first since 2000, will be welcomed by librarians and researchers. We keep it at the reference desk and use it frequently.

LAURIE COLLIER HILLSTROM is a noted freelance writer with the Northern Lights Writers Group. Laurie received an MBA from the University of Michigan and is co-founder of Northern Lights Writers Group, an editorial services firm based in Michigan. She has authored or edited award-winning reference books on a wide range of subjects, including business and industry, biography, American history, and international environmental issues. Publications include *Encyclopedia of Small Business (2001), The World's Environments (2003), War in the Persian Gulf Reference Library (2004), and The Industrial Revolution in America (2005).*

Laurie comments on the *EOM:*

This completely updated edition of the *Encyclopedia of Management* features new entries on topics that managers must understand to succeed in business today. From the latest developments in Affirmative Action legislation to the intricacies of Flexible Spending Accounts, and from the emerging technology of Radio-Frequency Identification to the time-saving potential of Handheld Computers and Instant Messaging, *EoM* provides managers with up-to-date information on a wide variety of current business issues.

The editor would also like to thank Julie Gough, editorial coordinator of the *EoM* at Thomson Gale for her effort in coordinating this project and offering her expertise and guidance.

John Alvis, Ph.D., CPA
George M. Clark Professor of Accounting
University of Tennessee at Chattanooga

Tim Barnett, D.B.A., SPHR
Professor of Management, Department of Management
    and Information Systems
Mississippi State University

Rebecca Bennett, D.B.A.
Associate Professor of Management, Department
    of Management and Information Systems
Louisiana Tech University

James J. Cochran, Ph.D.
Assistant Professor, Department of Marketing and Analysis
Louisiana Tech University

Sheila Delacroix, M.L.S.
Reference and Instruction Librarian
University of Tennessee at Chattanooga

Michael Doumpos, Ph.D.
Lecturer, Department of Production Engineering
    and Management
Technical University of Crete, Greece

Scott Droege, Ph.D.
Assistant Professor of Management
Western Kentucky University

Debbie D. DuFrene, Ed.D.
Professor, Department of General Business
Stephen F. Austin State University

Badie Farah, Ph.D.
Professor of Computer Information Systems and M.S.I.S.
    Program Advisor
Eastern Michigan University

J. Bryan Fuller, Ph.D.
Assistant Professor, Department of Management
    and Information Systems
Louisiana Tech University

Diane Franz, Ph.D., CPA
Professor and Chair, Department of Accounting
University of Toledo

Dawn Malone Gaymer, M.B.A.
Assistant Dean of Graduate Programs, College of Business
Eastern Michigan University

Evangelos Grigoroudis, Ph.D.
Lecturer, Department of Production Engineering
    and Management
Technical University of Crete, Greece

Debbie Hausler
President
Debsway Inc., Farmington, MI

Marilyn Helms, D.B.A., CFPIM, CIRM
Sesquicentennial Endowed Chair and Professor
    of Management
Dalton (GA) State College

Laurie Collier Hillstrom
Freelance Writer
Northern Lights Writers Group

R. Anthony Inman, D.B.A.
Ruston Building & Loan Professor of Management,
    Department of Management and Information Systems
Louisiana Tech University

Hal P. Kirkwood, Jr., M.L.S.
Associate Professor, Coordinator of Instruction, Management
    and Economics Library
Purdue University

Kriaki Kosmidou, Ph.D.
Adjunct Professor, Department of Production Engineering
    and Management
Technical University of Crete, Greece

Patricia A. Lanier, D.B.A.
Assistant Professor of Management, Department
    of Management
University of Louisiana at Lafayette

Theresa Liedtka, M.L.S.
Dean, Lupton Library
University of Tennessee, Chattanooga

Laura E. Marler, M.B.A.
Research Assistant, Department of Management
    and Information Systems, College of Administration
    and Business
Louisiana Tech University

Wendy Mason
Freelance Writer
Farmington Hills, MI

Judith M. Nixon, M.L.S.
Professor of Libraries and Librarian, Management
    & Economics Library
Purdue University

Eugenia Petridou, Ph.D.
Associate Professor of Management, Department of Economics
Aristotle University of Thessaloniki, Greece

Gerhard Plenert, Ph.D., CPIM
President, Institute of World Class Management
Carmichael, CA

Bill Prince, M.L.S., M.A.T. History
Associate Professor and Head of Reference Service,
    Lupton Library
University of Tennessee at Chattanooga

Nancy Ryan Prince, Ed.D.
Adjunct Professor of Education
University of Tennessee at Chattanooga

Mildred Golden Pryor, Ph.D.
Professor of Management
Texas A & M University-Commerce

Betty Jane Punnett, Ph.D.
Professor of International Business and Management,
    Department of Management Studies
University of the West Indies, Cave Hill Campus, Barbados

Matthew Ross, M.B.A.
Associate Marketing Manager
Playcore Inc., Chattanooga TN

Marcia J. Simmering, Ph.D.
Assistant Professor of Management, Department
    of Management and Information Systems
College of Administration and Business
Louisiana Tech University

Andrea Anderson Schurr, M.L.S.
Assistant Professor and Head of Access Services,
    Lupton Library
University of Tennessee, Chattanooga

Joanie Sompayrac, M.B.A., CPA
UC Foundation Associate Professor of Accounting,
    and Assistant Director, University Honors
University of Tennessee, Chattanooga

Charalambos Spathis, Ph.D.
Assistant Professor of Economics
Aristotle University of Thessaloniki, Greece

Joo-Seng Tan, Ph.D.
Visiting Scholar, Cornell University, School of Hotel
    Administration and Associate Professor of Business
Associate Professor of Management and Director of Programs,
    Center for Cultural Intelligence, Nanyang Technological
    University, Singapore

G. Steve Taylor, Ph.D.
Professor of Management, Department of Management and
    Information Systems, College of Business and Industry
Mississippi State University

Joe G. Thomas, Ph.D.
Professor of Management, Management and Marketing
    Department
Middle Tennessee State University

Monica C. Turner, M.L.S.
Reference Assistant, Management & Economics Library
Purdue University

Mark Vonderembse, Ph.D.
Professor of Information Operations and Technology
    Management
University of Toledo (OH)

Fraya Wagner-Marsh, D.B.A., SPHR
Professor and Department Head, Management Department
Eastern Michigan University

Bruce A. Walters, Ph.D.
Assistant Professor of Management, Department
    of Management and Information Systems
Louisiana Tech University

Rhoda Wilburn
Freelance Writer
Pinckney, MI

Diana J. Wong-MingJi, Ph.D.
Associate Professor of Management
Eastern Michigan University

Constantin Zopounidis, Ph.D.
Professor of Financial Management and Operations Research,
    Director of the Financial Engineering Laboratory
    and Department Chair, Department of Production
    Engineering and Management
Technical University of Crete, Greece

Eighteen functional-area reading curricula are outlined below. Items listed beneath each heading represent titles of specific essays in the *EoM*.

1. CORPORATE PLANNING AND STRATEGIC MANAGEMENT

Aggregate Planning
Brainstorming
Business Continuity Planning
Business Plan
Capacity Planning
Decision Making
Decision Rules and Decision Analysis
Decision Support Systems
Diversification Strategy
Divestment
Downsizing and Rightsizing
Economies of Scale and Economies of Scope
Exporting and Importing
Franchising
Free Trade Agreements and Trading Blocs
Futuring
Gap Analysis
Generic Competitive Strategies
Globalization
Goals and Goal Setting
Group Decision Making
Location Strategy
Macroenvironmental Forces
Make-or-Buy Decisions
Manufacturing Resources Planning
Market Share
Mergers and Acquisitions
Miles and Snow Typology
Multiple-Criteria Decision Making
New Product Development

Open and Closed Systems
Operations Strategy
Opportunity Cost
Order-Winning and Order-Qualifying Criteria
Porter's 5-Forces Model
Product Life Cycle and Industry Life Cycle
Production Planning and Scheduling
Strategic Planning Failure
Strategic Planning Tools
Strategy Formulation
Strategy Implementation
Strategy in the Global Environment
Strategy Levels
SWOT Analysis
Synergy
Zero-Based Budgeting

2. EMERGING TOPICS IN MANAGEMENT

Activity-Based Costing
Affirmative Action
Angels and Venture Capitalists
Artificial Intelligence
Assessment Centers
Balanced Scorecard
Bar Coding and Radio Frequency Identification
Business Continuity Planning
Business Process Reengineering
Cafeteria Plan—Flexible Benefits
Cellular Manufacturing
Chaos Theory
Coalition Building
Complexity Theory
Concurrent Engineering
Consulting
Contingency Approach to Management
Contingent Workers

Service Process Matrix
Simulation
Statistical Process Control and Six Sigma
Statistics
Systems Analysis
Systems Design, Development, and Implementation
Technology Transfer
Warehousing and Warehouse Management
World-Class Manufacturer

13. PERFORMANCE MEASURES AND ASSESSMENT

Activity-Based Costing
Balance Sheets
Balanced Scorecard
Benchmarking
Break-Even Point
Budgeting
Cash Flow Analysis and Statements
Continuous Improvement
Cost Accounting
Cost-Volume-Profit Analysis
Cycle Time
Debt vs. Equity Financing
Due Diligence
Effectiveness and Efficiency
Executive Compensation
Financial Issues for Managers
Financial Ratios
Forecasting
Gap Analysis
Goals and Goal Setting
Management Audit
Management Control
Management Information Systems
Market Share
Multiple-Criteria Decision Making
Nepotism
Order-Winning and Order-Qualifying Criteria
Performance Measurement
Pricing Policy and Strategy
Profit Sharing
Simulation
Stakeholders
Value Analysis
Value Chain Management
Value Creation
Vendor Rating
Zero-Based Budgeting
Zero Sum Game

14. PERSONAL GROWTH AND DEVELOPMENT FOR MANAGERS

The Art and Science of Management
Body Language
Brainstorming

Coalition Building
Communication
Consulting
Contingency Approach to Management
Continuing Education and Lifelong Learning Trends
Continuous Improvement
Creativity
Customer Relationship Management
Delegation
Diversity
Empathy
Employee Assistance Programs
Empowerment
Entrepreneurship
Facilitator
Feedback
Goals and Goal Setting
Group Dynamics
Intrapreneurship
Knowledge Workers
Leadership Styles and Bases of Power
Listening
Managing Change
Meeting Management
Mentoring
Morale
Motivation and Motivation Theory
Multimedia
Organizing
Participative Management
Personality and Personality Tests
Planning
Popular Press Management Books
Problem Solving
Professional Readings for Managers
Profit Sharing
Reactive vs. Proactive Change
Resumes and Cover Letter Trends
Safety in the Workplace
Sensitivity Training
Spirituality in Leadership
Strategic Planning Tools
Stress
Succession Planning
SWOT Analysis
Teams and Teamwork
Time Management
Trends in Organizational Change
Value Creation

15. PRODUCTION AND OPERATIONS MANAGEMENT

Activity-Based Costing
Aggregate Planning
Bar Coding and Radio Frequency Identification
Benchmarking
Break-Even Point

Bundled Goods and Services
Business Process Reengineering
Cellular Manufacturing
Computer-Aided Design and Manufacturing
Computer-Integrated Manufacturing
Concurrent Engineering
Continuous Improvement
Cost-Volume-Profit Analysis
Decision Rules and Decision Analysis
Decision Support Systems
Distribution and Distribution Requirements Planning
Domestic Management Societies and Associations
Economic Census
Five S Framework
Flexible Manufacturing
Focused Factory
Forecasting
Government-University-Industry Partnerships
Industrial Relations
International Management Societies and Associations
Inventory Management
Inventory Types
Japanese Management
Layout
Lean Manufacturing and Just-in-Time Production
Location Strategy
Logistics and Transportation
Maintenance
Make-or-Buy Decisions
Management Awards
Manufacturing Resources Planning
Market Share
New Product Development
Operations Management
Operations Scheduling
Operations Strategy
Order-Winning and Order-Qualifying Criteria
Outsourcing and Offshoring
Participative Management
Poka-Yoke
Popular Press Management Books
Porter's 5-Forces Model
Production Planning and Scheduling
Productivity Concepts and Measures
Product-Process Matrix
Program Evaluation and Review Technique
    and Critical Path Method
Project Management
Purchasing and Procurement
Quality and Total Quality Management
Quality Gurus
Reverse Supply Chain Logistics
Robotics
Safety in the Workplace
Service Factory
Service Industry
Service Operations
Service Process Matrix

Simulation
Statistical Process Control and Six Sigma
Statistics
Supply Chain Management
Synergy
Teams and Teamwork
Technological Forecasting
Technology Management
Technology Transfer
Theory of Constraints
Time-Based Competition
Warehousing and Warehouse Management
World-Class Manufacturer

16. QUALITY MANAGEMENT AND TOTAL QUALITY MANAGEMENT

Communication
Customer Relationship Management
Domestic Management Societies and Associations
Five S Framework
Gap Analysis
Goals and Goal Setting
Innovation
International Management Societies and Associations
Japanese Management
Management Awards
Manufacturing Resources Planning
Marketing Research
Operations Strategy
Opportunity Cost
Order-Winning and Order-Qualifying Criteria
Outsourcing and Offshoring
Participative Management
Popular Press Management Books
Productivity Concepts and Measures
Professional Readings for Managers
Quality and Total Quality Management
Quality Gurus
Quality of Work Life
Statistical Process Control and Six Sigma
Strategic Planning Tools
Teams and Teamwork
Value Analysis
Value Creation
Vendor Rating
World-Class Manufacturer

17. SUPPLY CHAIN MANAGEMENT

Activity-Based Costing
Business Process Reengineering
Capacity Planning
Cellular Manufacturing
Coalition Building
Communication
Competitive Advantage
Competitive Intelligence

Computer Networks
Computer-Integrated Manufacturing
Conflict Management and Negotiation
Customer Relationship Management
Cycle Time
Decision Support Systems
Distribution and Distribution Requirements Planning
Economies of Scale and Economies of Scope
Effectiveness and Efficiency
Electronic Commerce
Electronic Data Interchange and Electronic
    Funds Transfer
Enterprise Resource Planning
Expert Systems
Group Dynamics
Industrial Relations
Inventory Management
Inventory Types
Joint Ventures and Strategic Alliances
Lean Manufacturing and Just-in-Time Production
Location Strategy
Logistics and Transportation
Make-or-Buy Decisions
Manufacturing Resources Planning
Market Share
Multiple-Criteria Decision Making
New Product Development
Operations Management
Operations Scheduling
Operations Strategy
Organic Organizations
Organizing
Poka-Yoke
Problem Solving
Process Management
Product Design
Product Life Cycle and Industry Life Cycle
Production Planning and Scheduling
Productivity Concepts and Measures
Product-Process Matrix
Purchasing and Procurement
Quality and Total Quality Management
Reverse Supply Chain Logistics
Risk Management
Span of Control
Stakeholders
Teams and Teamwork
Vendor Rating
Warehousing and Warehouse Management

18. TRAINING AND DEVELOPMENT

Apprenticeship Programs
Artificial Intelligence
Assessment Centers
Autonomy

Business Continuity Planning
Concurrent Engineering
Conflict Management and Negotiation
Consulting
Contingency Approach to Management
Continuing Education and Lifelong Learning Trends
Continuous Improvement
Corporate Social Responsibility
Creativity
Delegation
Domestic Management Societies and Associations
Downsizing and Rightsizing
Employee Evaluation and Performance Appraisals
Employee Handbook and Orientation
Goals and Goal Setting
Government-University-Industry Partnerships
Group Decision Making
Human Resource Management
Innovation
Instant Messaging
International Cultural Differences
International Management Societies and Associations
Job Analysis
Knowledge Management
Knowledge Workers
Listening
Management and Executive Development
Management Audit
Marketing Communication
Meeting Management
Mission and Vision Statements
Morale
Motivation and Motivation Theory
Multimedia
Multiple-Criteria Decision Making
Organizational Culture
Organizational Learning
Organizing
Participative Management
Personality and Personality Tests
Popular Press Management Books
Problem Solving
Professional Readings for Managers
Project Management
Safety in the Workplace
Sensitivity Training
Simulation
Stress
Succession Planning
SWOT Analysis
Teams and Teamwork
Training Delivery Methods
Videoconferencing
Virtual Organizations
Women and Minorities in Management
Work-Life Balance

A

ACQUISITIONS

SEE: Mergers and Acquisitions

ACTIVITY-BASED COSTING

To support compliance with financial reporting requirements, a company's traditional cost-accounting system is often articulated with its general ledger system. In essence, this linkage is grounded in cost allocation. Typically, costs are allocated for either valuation purposes (i.e., financial statements for external uses) or decision-making purposes (i.e., internal uses) or both. However, in certain instances costs also are allocated for cost-reimbursement purposes (e.g., hospitals and defense contractors).

The traditional approach to cost-allocation consists of three basic steps: accumulate costs within a production or nonproduction department; allocate nonproduction department costs to production departments; and allocate the resulting (revised) production department costs to various products, services, or customers. Costs derived from this traditional allocation approach suffer from several defects that can result in distorted costs for decision-making purposes. For example, the traditional approach allocates the cost of idle capacity to products. Accordingly, such products are charged for resources that they did not use. Seeking to remedy such distortions, many companies have adopted a different cost-allocation approach called activity-based costing (ABC).

WHAT IS ACTIVITY-BASED COSTING?

In contrast to traditional cost-accounting systems, ABC systems first accumulate overhead costs for each organizational activity, and then assign the costs of the activities to the products, services, or customers (cost objects) causing that activity. As one might expect, the most critical aspect of ABC is activity analysis. Activity analysis is the processes of identifying appropriate output measures of activities and resources (cost drivers) and their effects on the costs of making a product or providing a service. Significantly, as discussed in the next section, activity analysis provides the foundation for remedying the distortions inherent in traditional cost-accounting systems.

TRADITIONAL COST-ACCOUNTING SYSTEMS VERSUS ABC

Geared toward compliance with financial reporting requirements, traditional cost-accounting systems often allocate costs based on single-volume measures such as direct-labor hours, direct-labor costs, or machine hours. While using a single volume measure as an overall cost driver seldom meets the cause-and-effect criterion desired in cost allocation, it provides a relatively cheap and convenient means of complying with financial reporting requirements.

In contrast to traditional cost-accounting systems, ABC systems are not inherently constrained by the tenets of financial reporting requirements. Rather, ABC systems have the inherent flexibility to provide special reports to facilitate management decisions regarding the costs of activities undertaken to design, produce, sell, and deliver a company's products or services. At the heart of this flexibility is the fact that ABC systems focus on accumulating costs via several key activities, whereas traditional cost allocation focuses on accumulating costs via organizational units. By focusing on specific activities, ABC systems provide superior cost allocation information—especially when costs are caused by non-volume-based cost drivers. Even so, traditional cost-accounting systems will continue to be used to satisfy conventional financial reporting requirements. ABC systems will continue to supplement, rather than replace, traditional cost-accounting systems.

IMPLEMENTATION

In most cases, a company's traditional cost-accounting system adequately measures the direct costs of products and services, such as material and labor. As a result, ABC implementation typically focuses on indirect costs, such as manufacturing overhead and selling, general, and administrative costs. Given this focus, the primary goal of ABC implementation is to reclassify most, if not all, indirect costs (as specified by the traditional cost-accounting system) as direct costs. As a result of these reclassifications, the accuracy of the costs is greatly increased.

According to Ray H. Garrison and Eric W. Noreen, there are six basic steps required to implement an ABC system:

1. Identify and define activities and activity pools

2. Directly trace costs to activities (to the extent feasible)

3. Assign costs to activity cost pools

4. Calculate activity rates

5. Assign costs to cost objects using the activity rates and activity measures previously determined

6. Prepare and distribute management reports

COSTS AND BENEFITS

While ABC systems are rather complex and costly to implement, Charles T. Horngren, Gary L. Sundem, and William O. Stratton suggest that many companies, in both manufacturing and nonmanufacturing industries, are adopting ABC systems for a variety of reasons:

1. Margin accuracy for individual products and services, as well as customer classifications, is becoming increasingly difficult to achieve given that direct labor is rapidly being replaced with automated equipment. Accordingly, a

company's shared costs (i.e., indirect costs) are becoming the most significant portion of total cost.

2. Since the rapid pace of technological change continues to reduce product life cycles, companies do not have time to make price or cost adjustments once costing errors are detected.

3. Companies with inaccurate cost measurements tend to lose bids due to over-costed products, incur hidden losses due to under-costed products, and fail to detect activities that are not cost-effective.

4. Since computer technology costs are decreasing, the price of developing and operating ABC systems also has decreased.

In 2004 John Karolefski cited the following benefits realized by foodservice distributors and restaurants that have converted to activity-based costing practices:

1. Understanding the true costs and productivity of capital equipment

2. Understanding which products are most profitable and where to focus sales efforts

3. More accurate pricing and determination of minimum order size

4. Less time, money, and effort spent on the wrong products

Implementation costs are an obstacle to some, who feel that ABC is just a fad or will show little benefit. According to Karolefski, "ABC works better if it's kept simple" (2004, pp. 18). Nevertheless, when implemented properly ABC yields benefits to the company, its business partners, and to consumers.

ACTIVITY-BASED MANAGEMENT

In order to manage costs, a manager should focus on the activities that give rise to such costs. Accordingly, given the activity focus of ABC, managers should implement ABC systems in order to facilitate cost management. Using ABC systems to improve financial management is called activity-based management (ABM). The goal of ABM is to improve the value received by customers and, in doing so, to improve profits.

The key to ABM success is distinguishing between value-added costs and non-value-added costs. A value-added cost is the cost of an activity that cannot be eliminated without affecting a product's value to the customer. In contrast, a non-value-added cost is the cost of an activity that can be eliminated without diminishing value. Some value-added costs are always necessary, as long as the activity that drives such costs is performed efficiently. However, non-value-added costs should always be minimized because they are assumed to be unnecessary. Examples of non-valued-added activities include storing and handling inventories; transporting raw materials or partly finished products, such as work-in-process inventory items, from one part of the plant to another; and redundancies in production-line configurations or other activities. Oftentimes, such non-value activities can be reduced or eliminated by careful redesign of the plant layout and the production process.

SEE ALSO: Cost Accounting; Inventory Management; Inventory Types; Process Management; Quality and Total Quality Management; Time-Based Competition

Michael S. Luehlfing
Revised by Wendy H. Mason

FURTHER READING:

Brimson, James A. *Activity Accounting: An Activity-Based Costing Approach.* New York: Wiley, 1997.

Cokins, Gary. "ABC Can Spell a Simpler, Coherent View of Costs." *Computing Canada* 24, no. 32 (September 1998): 34–35.

Cokins, Gary. "Why Is Traditional Accounting Failing Managers?" *Hospital Material Management Quarterly* 20, no. 2 (November 1998): 72–80.

Daly, John L. *Pricing for Profitability: Activity-Based Pricing for Competitive Advantage.* New York: Wiley, 2001.

Dolan, Pat, and Karen I. Schreiber. "Getting Started With ABC." *Supply House Times* 40, no. 4 (June 1997): 41–52.

Garrison, Ray H., and Eric W. Noreen. *Managerial Accounting.* 9th ed. Boston: Irwin McGraw-Hill, 1999.

Hicks, Douglas T. *Activity-Based Costing: Making It Work for Small and Mid-Sized Companies.* 2nd ed. New York: Wiley, 2002.

Horngren, Charles T., Gary L. Sundem, and William O. Stratton. *Introduction to Management Accounting.* 11th ed. Upper Saddle River, NJ: Prentice Hall, 1999.

Karolefski, John. "Time Is Money: How Much Are Your Customers Costing You?" *Food Logistics* 15 June 2004, 18.

Lindahl, Frederick W. "Activity-Based Costing Implementation and Adaptation." *Human Resource Planning* 20, no. 2 (1997): 62–66.

AFFIRMATIVE ACTION

Affirmative action is a descriptive phrase for policies and programs designed to correct the effects of past discrimination and increase the representation of historically disadvantaged groups, including women and African Americans. Affirmative action plans exist in the private and public sectors and involve the hiring of job applicants, the selection of contractors for government projects, and the admission of students to undergraduate and graduate educational institutions. Some employers, educational institutions, and government agencies are legally required by executive order to have affirmative action plans. Others may be ordered to develop affirmative action plans as part of a court finding that they have discriminated against individuals or groups. Still others voluntarily develop such plans because they believe it is good public policy, or that it provides them with a competitive advantage.

ORIGINS AND DEVELOPMENT OF AFFIRMATIVE ACTION

Although the roots of affirmative action in the United States go back to the nineteenth century, modern affirmative action plans originated with executive orders issued by Presidents John F. Kennedy, Lyndon B. Johnson, and Richard M. Nixon in the 1960s. Executive Order 11246, signed by President Johnson in 1965, required government agencies, contractors, and subcontractors to undertake affirmative action to remedy past discrimination in education, training, and employment. In 1969 President Nixon further strengthened affirmative action through Executive Order 11478, which required government contractors to develop goals for increasing the representation of historically disadvantaged groups and timetables for achieving them.

As amended in subsequent years, these executive orders eventually required all government agencies and contractors with annual contracts of $10,000 or more to undertake affirmative action. They also required agencies and contractors with 50 employees and government business of $50,000 or more to have written affirmative action plans. These written plans must include a utilization analysis, which compares the composition of the entity's workforce to the proportion of women and minorities in the available labor market. If underutilization is found, the agency or contractor must set specific goals and timetables for remedying the "imbalance" and develop specific plans for how this will be done. The use of affirmative action plans expanded greatly in the twenty years after the executive orders. Because most educational institutions and large organizations receive money and/or do business with the government, affirmative action plans are very common.

TYPES OF AFFIRMATIVE ACTION

In the employment context, affirmative action plans should be distinguished from equal employment opportunity (EEO) programs. EEO efforts focus on the process involved in hiring and promoting employees and attempt to ensure that there is a level playing field for all involved. Conversely, affirmative action programs focus on the outcomes of recruiting, hiring, and promotion processes, and involve additional efforts to increase the proportion of women and minorities that are hired and promoted.

There are various types of affirmative action plans. Some plans simply try to increase the number of applicants from underrepresented groups. Such plans, which are sometimes called "pure" plans or "opportunity enhancement" plans, involve proactive efforts to locate and recruit a larger number of individuals from the affected groups. Other affirmative action plans can be termed "limited preference" or "tiebreak" plans. They go a step further than pure affirmative action plans by considering race or gender as a "plus" factor when evaluating the qualifications of applicants who essentially are equally qualified. Finally, the most aggressive affirmative action plans are "strong preferential treatment" or "quota" plans. In these plans, qualified members of a disadvantaged group may be preferred to more highly qualified individuals who are not in the affected group. Generally speaking, the more aggressive the affirmative action strategy employed, the more likely it is to generate challenges and the more difficult it is to defend legally.

Affirmative action plans are quite controversial and have been the subject of hundreds of lawsuits, several of which have gone to the U.S. Supreme Court. Lawsuits filed by those who believe they have been unfairly treated by affirmative action plans usually are called "reverse discrimination" lawsuits. Although the courts generally have agreed that affirmative action is legal if it meets certain criteria, court decisions in the 1990s and early 2000s seemed to reflect a trend toward restricting the more aggressive types of affirmative action programs, which may include preferences based on race or gender. Affirmative action is certain to be a contentious issue for years to come.

SEE ALSO: Discrimination; Diversity

Tim Barnett

FURTHER READING:

Gomez-Mejia, Luis R., David B. Balkin, and Robert L. Cardy. *Managing Human Resources.* 4th ed. Upper Saddle River, NJ: Pearson/Prentice Hall, 2004.

Heilman, M. E., McCullough, W. F., & Gilbert, D. "The Other Side of Affirmative Action: Reactions of Nonbeneficiaries to Sex-Based Preferential Selection." *Journal of Applied Psychology* 81, no. 4 (1996): 346–357.

Kovach, Kenneth A., David A. Kravitz, and Allen A. Hughes. "Affirmative Action: How Can We Be So Lost When We Don't Even Know Where We Are Going?" *Labor Law Journal* 55, no. 1 (2004): 53–62.

Naff, Katherine C. "From Bakke to Grutter and Gratz: The Supreme Court as a Policymaking Institution." *The Review of Policy Research* 21, no. 3 (2004): 405–427.

Office of Federal Contract Compliance Programs. U.S. Department of Labor, Employment Standards Administration, Office of Federal Contract Compliance Programs. Available from <http://www.dol.gov/esa/ofccp>.

AGGREGATE PLANNING

Aggregate planning is the process of developing, analyzing, and maintaining a preliminary, approximate schedule of the overall operations of an organization. The aggregate plan generally contains targeted sales forecasts, production levels, inventory levels, and customer backlogs. This schedule is intended to satisfy the demand forecast at a minimum cost. Properly done, aggregate planning should minimize the effects of shortsighted, day-to-day scheduling, in which small amounts of material may be ordered one week, with an accompanying layoff of workers, followed by ordering larger amounts and rehiring workers the next week. This longer-term perspective on resource use can help minimize short-term requirements changes with a resulting cost savings.

In simple terms, aggregate planning is an attempt to balance capacity and demand in such a way that costs are minimized. The term "aggregate" is used because planning at this level includes all resources "in the aggregate;" for example, as a product line or family. Aggregate resources could be total number of workers, hours of machine time, or tons of raw materials. Aggregate units of output could include gallons, feet, pounds of output, as well as aggregate units appearing in service industries such as hours of service delivered, number of patients seen, etc.

Aggregate planning does not distinguish among sizes, colors, features, and so forth. For example, with automobile manufacturing, aggregate planning would consider the total number of cars planned for not the individual models, colors, or options. When units of aggregation are difficult to determine (for example, when the variation in output is extreme) equivalent units are usually determined. These equivalent units could be based on value, cost, worker hours, or some similar measure.

Aggregate planning is considered to be intermediate-term (as opposed to long- or short-term) in nature. Hence, most aggregate plans cover a period of three to 18 months. Aggregate plans serve as a foundation for future short-range type planning, such as production scheduling, sequencing, and loading.

The master production schedule (MPS) used in material requirements planning (MRP) has been described as the aggregate plan "disaggregated."

Steps taken to produce an aggregate plan begin with the determination of demand and the determination of current capacity. Capacity is expressed as total number of units per time period that can be produced (this requires that an average number of units be computed since the total may include a product mix utilizing distinctly different production times). Demand is expressed as total number of units needed. If the two are not in balance (equal), the firm must decide whether to increase or decrease capacity to meet demand or increase or decrease demand to meet capacity. In order to accomplish this, a number of options are available.

Options for situations in which demand needs to be increased in order to match capacity include:

1. **Pricing.** Varying pricing to increase demand in periods when demand is less than peak. For example, matinee prices for movie theaters, off-season rates for hotels, weekend rates for telephone service, and pricing for items that experience seasonal demand.

2. **Promotion.** Advertising, direct marketing, and other forms of promotion are used to shift demand.

3. **Back ordering.** By postponing delivery on current orders demand is shifted to period when capacity is not fully utilized. This is really just a form of smoothing demand. Service industries are able to smooth demand by taking reservations or by making appointments in an attempt to avoid walk-in customers. Some refer to this as "partitioning" demand.

4. **New demand creation.** A new, but complementary demand is created for a product or service. When restaurant customers have to wait, they are frequently diverted into a complementary (but not complimentary) service, the bar. Other examples include the addition of video arcades within movie theaters, and the expansion of services at convenience stores.

Options which can be used to increase or decrease capacity to match current demand include:

1. **Hire/lay off.** By hiring additional workers as needed or by laying off workers not currently required to meet demand, firms can maintain a balance between capacity and demand.

2. **Overtime.** By asking or requiring workers to work extra hours a day or an extra day per week, firms can create a temporary increase in capacity without the added expense of hiring additional workers.

3. **Part-time or casual labor.** By utilizing temporary workers or casual labor (workers who are considered permanent but only work when needed, on an on-call basis, and typically without the benefits given to full-time workers).

4. **Inventory.** Finished-goods inventory can be built up in periods of slack demand and then used to fill demand during periods of high demand. In this way no new workers have to be hired, no temporary or casual labor is needed, and no overtime is incurred.

5. **Subcontracting.** Frequently firms choose to allow another manufacturer or service provider to provide the product or service to the subcontracting firm's customers. By subcontracting work to an alternative source, additional capacity is temporarily obtained.

6. **Cross-training.** Cross-trained employees may be able to perform tasks in several operations, creating some flexibility when scheduling capacity.

7. **Other methods.** While varying workforce size and utilization, inventory buildup/backlogging, and subcontracting are well-known alternatives, there are other, more novel ways that find use in industry. Among these options are sharing employees with counter-cyclical companies and attempting to find interesting and meaningful projects for employees to do during slack times.

AGGREGATE PLANNING STRATEGIES

There are two pure planning strategies available to the aggregate planner: a level strategy and a chase strategy. Firms may choose to utilize one of the pure strategies in isolation, or they may opt for a strategy that combines the two.

LEVEL STRATEGY. A level strategy seeks to produce an aggregate plan that maintains a steady production rate and/or a steady employment level. In order to satisfy changes in customer demand, the firm must raise or lower inventory levels in anticipation of increased or decreased levels of forecast demand. The firm maintains a level workforce and a steady rate of output when demand is somewhat low. This allows the firm to establish higher inventory levels than are currently needed. As demand increases, the firm is able to continue a steady production rate/steady employment level, while allowing the inventory surplus to absorb the increased demand.

A second alternative would be to use a backlog or backorder. A backorder is simply a promise to deliver the product at a later date when it is more readily available, usually when capacity begins to catch up with diminishing demand. In essence, the backorder is a device for moving demand from one period to another, preferably one in which demand is lower, thereby smoothing demand requirements over time.

A level strategy allows a firm to maintain a constant level of output and still meet demand. This is desirable from an employee relations standpoint. Negative results of the level strategy would include the cost of excess inventory, subcontracting or overtime costs, and backorder costs, which typically are the cost of expediting orders and the loss of customer goodwill.

CHASE STRATEGY. A chase strategy implies matching demand and capacity period by period. This could result in a considerable amount of hiring, firing or laying off of employees; insecure and unhappy employees; increased inventory carrying costs; problems with labor unions; and erratic utilization of plant and equipment. It also implies a great deal of flexibility on the firm's part. The major advantage of a chase strategy is that it allows inventory to be held to the lowest level possible, and for some firms this is a considerable savings. Most firms embracing the just-in-time production concept utilize a chase strategy approach to aggregate planning.

Most firms find it advantageous to utilize a combination of the level and chase strategy. A combination strategy (sometimes called a hybrid or mixed strategy) can be found to better meet organizational goals and policies and achieve lower costs than either of the pure strategies used independently.

TECHNIQUES FOR AGGREGATE PLANNING

Techniques for aggregate planning range from informal trial-and-error approaches, which usually utilize simple tables or graphs, to more formalized and advanced mathematical techniques. William Stevenson's textbook *Production/Operations Management* contains an informal but useful trial-and-error process for aggregate planning presented in outline form. This general procedure consists of the following steps:

1. Determine demand for each period.

2. Determine capacity for each period. This capacity should match demand, which means it may require the inclusion of overtime or subcontracting.

3. Identify company, departmental, or union policies that are pertinent. For example, maintaining a certain safety stock level, maintaining a reasonably stable workforce, backorder policies, overtime policies, inventory level policies, and other less explicit rules such as the nature of employment with the individual industry, the possibility of a bad image, and the loss of goodwill.

4. Determine unit costs for units produced. These costs typically include the basic production costs (fixed and variable costs as well as direct and indirect labor costs). Also included are the costs associated with making changes in capacity. Inventory holding costs must also be considered, as should storage, insurance, taxes, spoilage, and obsolescence costs. Finally, backorder costs must be computed. While difficult to measure, this generally includes expediting costs, loss of customer goodwill, and revenue loss from cancelled orders.

5. Develop alternative plans and compute the cost for each.

6. If satisfactory plans emerge, select the one that best satisfies objectives. Frequently, this is the plan with the least cost. Otherwise, return to step 5.

An example of a completed informal aggregate plan can be seen in Figure 1. This plan is an example of a plan determined utilizing a level strategy. Notice that employment levels and output levels remain constant while inventory is allowed to build up in earlier periods only to be drawn back down in later periods as demand increases. Also, note that backorders are utilized in order to avoid overtime or subcontracting. The computed costs for the individual variables of the plan are as follows:

Output costs:
  Regular time = $5 per unit
  Overtime = $8 per unit
  Subcontracted = $12 per unit
Other costs:
  Inventory carrying cost = $3 per unit per period applied to average inventory
  Backorders = $10 per unit per period
Cost of aggregate plan utilizing a level strategy:
Output costs:
  Regular time = $5 × 1,500 = $7,500
  Overtime = $8 × 0 = 0
  Subcontracted = $10 × 0 = 0
Other costs:
  Inventory carrying cost = $3 × 850 = $2,400
  Backorders = $10 × 100 = $1,000
  Total cost = $10,900

A second example, shown in Figure 2, presents the same scenario as in Figure 1 but demonstrates the use of a combination strategy (i.e., a combination of level and chase) to meet demand and seek to minimize costs. For this example, let's assume that company

Figure 1

Period		1	2	3	4	5	6
Forecast		100	150	300	300	500	150
Output							
	Regular	250	250	250	250	250	250
	Overtime						
	Subcontract						
Output-forecast		150	100	-50	-50	-250	100
Inventory							
	Beginning	0	150	250	200	150	0
	Ending	15ა	250	200	150	0	100
	Average	75	200	225	175	75	50
Backlog	0	0	0	0	0	100	0

Cost of aggregate plan utilizing a level strategy:

Output:
```
Regular time       = $ 5  X  1500  = $7500
Overtime           = $ 8  X     0  =     0
Subcontracted      = $10  X     0  =     0
Inventory carrying cost = $ 3  X  850  =  2550
Backorders         = $10  X   100  =  1000
```
Total Cost $11050

---

policy prevents us from utilizing backorders and limits our plan to no more than 50 units of overtime per period. Notice that the regular output level is constant, implying a level workforce, while overtime and sub-contracting are used to meet demand on a period by period basis (chase strategy). One will notice that the cost of the combination plan is slightly lower than the cost of the level plan.

```
Output costs:
    Regular time = $5 × 1,200 = $6,000
    Overtime = $8 × 100 = 800
    Subcontracted = $12 × 250 = 2,500
Other costs:
    Inventory carrying cost = $3 × 325 = 975
    Backorders = $10 × 0 = 0
    Total cost = $10,275
```

MATHEMATICAL APPROACHES TO AGGREGATE PLANNING

The following are some of the better known mathematical techniques that can be used in more complex aggregate planning applications.

LINEAR PROGRAMMING. Linear programming is an optimization technique that allows the user to find a maximum profit or revenue or a minimum cost based on the availability of limited resources and certain limitations known as constraints. A special type of linear programming known as the Transportation Model can be used to obtain aggregate plans that would allow balanced capacity and demand and the minimization of costs. However, few real-world aggregate planning decisions are compatible with the linear assumptions of linear programming. *Supply Chain Management: Strategy, Planning and Operation,* by Sunil Chopra and Peter Meindl, provides an excellent example of the use of linear programming in aggregate planning.

MIXED-INTEGER PROGRAMMING. For aggregate plans that are prepared on a product family basis, where the plan is essentially the summation of the plans for individual product lines, mixed-integer programming may prove to be useful. Mixed-integer programming can provide a method for determining the number of units to be produced in each product family.

LINEAR DECISION RULE. Linear decision rule is another optimizing technique. It seeks to minimize total production costs (labor, overtime, hiring/lay off, inventory carrying cost) using a set of cost-approximating functions (three of which are quadratic) to obtain a single quadratic equation. Then, by using calculus, two linear equations can be derived from the quadratic equation, one to be used to plan the output for each period and the other for planning the workforce for each period.

MANAGEMENT COEFFICIENTS MODEL. The management coefficients model, formulated by E.H. Bowman, is based on the suggestion that the production rate for

Figure 2

Period		1	2	3	4	5	6
Forecast		100	150	300	300	500	150
Output							
	Regular	200	200	200	200	200	200
	Overtime				50	50	
	Subcontract					250	
Output-forecast		100	50	-100	-50	0	50
Inventory							
	Beginning	0	100	150	50	0	0
	Ending	100	150	50	0	0	50
	Average	50	125	100	25	0	25
Backlog	0	0	0	0	0	0	0

```
Output:
        Regular time    = $ 5  X  1200 = $6000
        Overtime        = $ 8  X   100 =   800
        Subcontracted   = $12  X   250 =  3000
Inventory carrying cost = $ 3  X   325 =   975
Backorders              = $10  X     0 =     0

Total Cost                             $10775
```

any period would be set by this general decision rule:

$$P_t = aW_{t-1} - bI_{t-1} + cF_{t+1} + K, \text{ where}$$

P_t = the production rate set for period t
W_{t-1} = the workforce in the previous period
I_{t-1} = the ending inventory for the previous period
F_{t+1} = the forecast of demand for the next period
$a, b, c,$ and K are constants

It then uses regression analysis to estimate the values of $a, b, c,$ and K. The end result is a decision rule based on past managerial behavior without any explicit cost functions, the assumption being that managers know what is important, even if they cannot readily state explicit costs. Essentially, this method supplements the application of experienced judgment.

SEARCH DECISION RULE. The search decision rule methodology overcomes some of the limitations of the linear cost assumptions of linear programming. The search decision rule allows the user to state cost data inputs in very general terms. It requires that a computer program be constructed that will unambiguously evaluate any production plan's cost. It then searches among alternative plans for the one with the minimum cost. However, unlike linear programming, there is no assurance of optimality.

SIMULATION. A number of simulation models can be used for aggregate planning. By developing an aggregate plan within the environment of a simulation model, it can be tested under a variety of conditions to find acceptable plans for consideration. These models can also be incorporated into a decision support system, which can aid in planning and evaluating alternative control policies. These models can integrate the multiple conflicting objectives inherent in manufacturing strategy by using different quantitative measures of productivity, customer service, and flexibility.

FUNCTIONAL OBJECTIVE SEARCH APPROACH. The functional objective search (FOS) system is a computerized aggregate planning system that incorporates a broad range of actual planning conditions. It is capable of realistic, low-cost operating schedules that provide options for attaining different planning goals. The system works by comparing the planning load with available capacity. After management has chosen its desired actions and associated planning objectives for specific load conditions, the system weights each planning goal to reflect the functional emphasis behind its achievement at a certain load condition. The computer then uses a computer search to output a plan that minimizes costs and meets delivery deadlines.

AGGREGATE PLANNING IN SERVICES. For manufacturing firms the luxury of building up inventories during periods of slack demand allows coverage of an anticipated time when demand will exceed capacity. Services cannot be stockpiled or inventoried so they do not have this option. Also, since services are considered "perishable," any capacity that goes unused is essentially wasted. An empty hotel room or an empty seat on a flight cannot be held and sold later, as can a manufactured item held in inventory.

Service capacity can also be very difficult to measure. When capacity is dictated somewhat by machine capability, reasonably accurate measures of capacity are not extremely difficult to develop. However, services generally have variable processing requirements that make it difficult to establish a suitable measure of capacity.

Historically, services are much more labor intensive than manufacturing, where labor averages 10 percent (or less) of total cost. This labor intensity can actually be an advantage because of the variety of service requirements an individual can handle. This can provide quite a degree of flexibility that can make aggregate planning easier for services than manufacturing.

WHAT'S NEW IN AGGREGATE PLANNING. Rudy Hung, in his *Production and Inventory Management Journal* article entitled "Annualized Hours and Aggregate Planning," presents a new, useful idea for aggregate planning called Annualized Hours (AH). Under AH, employees are contracted to work for a certain number of hours (say 1,800 hours) per year, for a certain sum of money. Employees can be asked to put in more hours during busy periods and fewer hours in slow periods. Typically, employees receive equal monthly or weekly payments so that hourly workers in effect have gained salaried status. Overtime is paid only when employees have worked beyond their annual hours.

AH is also known as flexiyear, as it can be seen as an extension of flextime, in which employees can vary their work hours within limits. This concept is used almost exclusively in Europe, particularly in the United Kingdom. The Scandinavian pulp and paper industries pioneered AH in the mid-1970s. Around that time, some West German firms, particularly those in the retail industry, also used AH.

AH gives employers much flexibility. AH serves to cut labor costs by offering employees an annual sum less than their previous annual earnings with overtime. Even though their total earnings may fall, their average earnings per hour would remain the same or even rise. Effective earnings could rise even more so if the employer is unable to consume all contracted hours. Employees have greater income security with no worries about layoffs. There is also increased morale because blue-collar workers are now salaried.

Another development affecting aggregate planning is postponement. This refers to delaying the "finish" of a product until the moment of sale. Firms that rely on the postponement strategy, such as PC-maker Dell Inc. or clothing franchise Benetton Group Sp.A., depend upon the availability of aggregate inventories of components that can be assembled to order shortly after, or even immediately, as an order is taken.

SEE ALSO: Capacity Planning; Planning; Simulation

R. Anthony Inman

FURTHER READING:

Chopra, Sunil and Peter Meindl. *Supply Chain Management: Strategy, Planning, and Operation.* Upper Saddle River, NJ: Pearson Prentice Hall, 2004.

Dejonckheere, J., S.M. Disney, M. Lambrecht, and D.R. Towill. "The Dynamics of Aggregate Planning." *Production Planning & Control* 14, no. 6, (2003): 497–516.

Finch, Byron J. *Operations Now.* Boston: McGraw-Hill Irwin, 2004.

Hung, Rudy. "Annualized Hours and Aggregate Planning." *Production and Inventory Management Journal* 38, no. 4 (1997).

Iyer, Ananth V., Vinayak Deshpande, and Zhengping Wu. "A Postponement Model for Demand Management." *Management Science* 49, no. 8, (2003): 983–1002.

Stevenson, William J. *Production Operations Management.* Boston: McGraw-Hill Irwin, 2004.

ANGELS AND VENTURE CAPITALISTS

SMALL BUSINESS FINANCE

The United States Small Business Administration (SBA) estimates that, as of 2003, there were approximately 23.7 million small businesses in the United States. The SBA defines a small business as "an independent business having fewer than 500 employees." Small businesses represent over 99 percent of all employers, and they employ more than half of all private sector employees. Moreover, small businesses employ about 40 percent of all high-tech personnel such as scientists, computer workers and engineers. These firms create anywhere from 60 percent to 80 percent of net new jobs each year, and they represent 97 percent of all exporters of goods. Small business create more than 50 percent of the private gross domestic product, and they pay about 45 percent of the total United States private payroll.

Clearly, small businesses play an important role in our business economy. It is important to note, however, that two-thirds of new small businesses survive at least two years, and about half survive at least four years. Owners of about one-third of the firms that closed said that their firm was successful at closure. Major factors contributing to a firm's success include an ample supply of capital, the fact that a firm is large enough to have employees, the owner's higher level of education, and the owner's reason for starting the firm in the first place, such as freedom for family life or wanting to be one's own boss.

As noted above, a firm's supply of capital is often a major factor in the firm's ability to survive. Consequently, business owners place a substantial emphasis on finding sources of funding for their business. Capital is typically defined as any asset that can be used to generate resources for the business. Capital for most businesses is generally comprised of some combination of cash, inventory and fixed assets.

PLANNING FOR A FIRM'S CAPITAL NEEDS

When starting a business, business owners typically need three types of capital—working capital, fixed capital and expansion capital. Working capital supports a business' short-term operations, and it represents a business' short-term source of funds. It may be used to purchase inventory, pay bills, or take care of other unexpected emergencies. Fixed capital represents those funds that a business needs to purchase land, buildings, equipment, machinery, furniture or other fixed assets that will be used in the business. While working capital supports the business' short-term needs, fixed capital supports the business' more permanent needs. Businesses need expansion capital when they seek to finance growth, expansion, or other long-term initiatives.

SOURCES OF CAPITAL

As business owners assess their needs for all types of capital, they must also assess what sources of capital are available to them. Conventional wisdom has often noted that many start-up businesses tend to secure their capital from the four F's: founders, families, friends and fools. This humorous observation, while bearing a nugget of truth, merely scratches the surface when looking at all of the sources of financing available to businesses in need of capital.

Some businesses owners choose to finance their businesses with debt. Debt financing is capital that a business owner has borrowed and must repay with interest. Debt financing may include traditional bank loans, credit card debt, lines of credit, unsecured loans, financing from commercial finance companies, insurance policy loans, securing trade credit and Small Business Administration Loans.

Many business owners, however, are uncomfortable with debt, and they choose to pursue sources of equity financing. With equity financing, the people or entities who contribute capital to a business do so in exchange for a share of ownership in the business. The business owner gives the equity investor a share of ownership in the business since the equity investor is assuming the primary risk of losing his or her funds in the business. If the business fails, all of the equity investors lose their investments. If the business succeeds, the founders and equity investors share in the benefits.

The types of equity investors that business owners typically pursue include themselves (via their personal savings), family members and friends, partners, shareholders, angels and venture capital investors.

ANGELS

Angels tend to be wealthy individuals, many times themselves entrepreneurs, who invest in new businesses in return for equity ownership interests in these new businesses. It is important to note, however, that angels do not make these investments out of the kindness of their hearts. Angels tend to be extremely savvy business men and women who seek to take calculated risks with business ventures that might enable them to generate tremendous gains when the businesses in which they invest "take off." Angels represent an outstanding source of financing for businesses that have grown too large to be financed by family and friends, but are still too small to attract the attention of venture capitalists.

Angels fill a substantial need in the capital market for young businesses. Typically, angels will finance new businesses with capital needs in the range $10,000 to $2 million.

ANGEL-HUNTING TIPS

1. Business angels are looking for investments capable of achieving a return of 20 percent or more, so make sure you can achieve this before you waste time chasing investors.

2. Angels tend to invest locally, so start your search within a 50-mile radius of your business premises.

3. Concentrate on successful individuals within your industry since angels prefer to look for investments in industries they know something about.

4. Use any contacts and networks you may have.

5. It may take six months to a year to find the right investor and another three to six months to negotiate the deal. Don't pressure investors—they may walk away.

6. The first meeting is the most important because business angels tend to place emphasis on the entrepreneur and management

team and how well they will be able to work with them.

Joanie Sompayrac

FURTHER READING:

Karlsgaard. "Dollars from Heaven: A Choir of Angels Bedevils the VCs." *Forbes,* 1 June 1998, 23.

APPRENTICESHIP PROGRAMS

Apprenticeship programs involve on-the-job training coupled with in-class support for students before they directly enter the workforce. Apprenticeships also are called dual-training programs because participants receive training both in the workplace and at school. Apprenticeship programs have proven extremely effective in smoothly transferring school-related skills to pragmatic workforce application.

THE GERMAN MODEL

Apprenticeship programs were first developed in Germany, where they have received worldwide attention. As Gitter and Scheuer note: "The comprehensive German apprenticeship system is often seen as a model for an improved school-to-work transition" (1997). Perhaps the reason the German model is so successful is the commitment of time both parties invest in the apprenticeship—usually three or more years. This commitment recognizes apprenticeship as a critical educational and training crossroad.

Also contributing to the acceptance of the German model, the Federal Ministry of Education regulates each occupation's training requirements and the ultimate rewarding of completion certification to apprentices. It also provides the framework for the working agreements between apprentices and employers.

Wages for apprentices generally are one-third of the standard employment rate in a given occupation. These wages are fixed across companies regionally through collective agreement of participating employers.

Rainer Winkelmann identifies three hallmark features of the German apprenticeship model: "it is company-based, it relies on voluntary participation by firms, and it generates portable, occupation-specific skills" (1996). Additionally, apprenticeships are funded by the individual companies involved, rather than through state funding or payroll taxation. Actual pay varies greatly according to the nature of the apprenticeship.

Traditionally, apprentices must find their own apprenticeships. In Germany, this often is accomplished through the potential apprentice's own personal connections or initiative. Additionally, Germany's Federal Employment Agency helps to place applicants with firms seeking apprentices. A range of Web sites are available that provide databases of employers offering apprenticeships, searchable by occupation. Though apprenticeships are in no way guaranteed, the vast majority of Germans have participated in an apprenticeship. Indeed, 71 percent of the German labor force had undergone a formal apprenticeship in 1991. Moreover, this figure is misleadingly low, since it does not include those Germans participating in alternative on-the-job training in specialized training schools for health care professionals, hotel workers, or civil servants.

APPRENTICESHIPS VS. INTERNSHIPS

Apprenticeships differ from the internship model more commonly practiced in the United States and Canada. Internships offer essentially minor workplace exposure over a comparatively short time. The internship is seen as merely augmenting the more important coursework. The nature of the internship may not even be set by the employer; instead, it might be determined by the educational institution with the goodwill of the host company. The benefit to the employer in an internship is often negligible, with the long-range benefit of a better qualified employment pool. If the intern contributes to the organization in more than a superficial way, it is an added benefit rather than an expected outcome, although having an intern pool does allow a company to prescreen potential new employees before hiring them permanently. Finally, the internship tends to be an isolated, short-term project as opposed to the four- to five-year commitment of most apprenticeship programs.

In many respects, apprenticeships are the diametric opposite of internships (see Table 1). In an apprenticeship, the work-related experience is central, with the company, rather than the educational institution, determining the terms of study. In apprenticeships, the coursework is coequal (rather than supplemental) to the on-the-job training. In apprenticeships, the employer expects to receive an immediate tangible benefit from the work carried out by the apprentice, in addition to the long-range benefit of a better qualified employment pool.

BENEFITS OF THE GERMAN MODEL

Gitter and Scheuer credit apprenticeship for the fact that, "with the exception of those with a postsecondary education, the unemployment rates in the United States are more than double those in Germany

Table 1 Differences Between Apprenticeships and Internships		
	Apprenticeships	**Internships**
On-the-job training	coequal to coursework	supplemental coursework
Time frame	4 to 5 years	6 months to a year
Training designer	employer	educational institution
Benefit to employer	tangible	coincidental
Procurement	individual participant	educational institution

for groups with a comparable education" (1997). Couch identified increased earnings for those participating in apprenticeship programs. In all, as Gitter summarizes, "The apprenticeship-trained worker is more likely to earn more money, work more hours per year, and rise to supervisory status than are workers who have learned the trade through other methods" (1994).

EUROPEAN CRITIQUES OF THE GERMAN SYSTEM

Germany has the longest history of apprenticeships, but it is not alone in its application. Several other European nations also have embraced the concept, most notably in Switzerland, Austria, Denmark, and in recent years, Great Britain. Yet, not all Europeans have embraced apprenticeships. Indeed, the apprenticeship system has come under attack within the European Union. As Roy Harrison indicated, the issue focuses on "the degree to which vocational qualifications should be harmonised at a European level" (1997).

While defenders of the apprenticeship system point to the tangential skills and work-related benefits of the model, they fail to address European-wide concerns that employers would favor the apprenticeship model, thus showing a preference for citizens of nations like Germany and Austria that support the system on a wide scale. Thus, in 1995 the European Council of Ministers met to discuss the difficulties imposed by the German model. In particular, the ministers expressed concern that apprenticeships disrupted the European goal of eliminating preferences for employees from one EU nation over another. The ministers, as Harrison explains, "stressed that a European area in qualifications and training cannot be established while countries continue to distrust the quality and value of each others' qualifications" (1997).

GREAT BRITAIN'S APPROACH

In 1995 Great Britain introduced Modern Apprenticeship. Modern Apprenticeship added flexibility into the program, with no set duration of training as a requisite for government funding. This helped to make apprenticeship more palatable to employers. Additionally, Great Britain does not nationally legislate apprenticeship as do other European countries. Rather, guidelines are sent out from the Department of Education and Skills that are left to open interpretation from varying geographic and occupational sectors.

While a small number of British apprentices obtain employment directly from an employer, most are directed through the government Learning and Skills Councils. Oftentimes, it is the training provider intermediary, rather than the employer, who conducts the assessment of the apprentice. However, complex requirements for receiving government funding for apprenticeship programs are often daunting to the private sector. Therefore many of the apprenticeships in Great Britain involve government-supported training programs and areas of occupation.

APPRENTICESHIP IN THE UNITED STATES

Even as apprenticeships have begun to come under debate in Europe, they have begun to gain wider acceptance in the United States. The apprenticeship programs taking root in the United States remain uncoordinated and hosted by a wide variety of sources. Some are sponsored by German companies themselves. For example, Siemens, the Munich-based multinational, has apprenticeship programs associated with its plants in Lake Mary, Florida; Franklin, Kentucky; and Wendell, North Carolina. Similarly, the Robert Bosch Corporation has set up apprenticeship programs linked to its Charleston, South Carolina, facility. Other German companies also have brought in apprenticeship programs in full or in part to their U.S. operations.

Other apprenticeship programs are sponsored by non-German companies. For example, Illinois-based Castwell Products (a division of Citation Corporation) runs an apprenticeship program for its foundry. As with several other U.S. apprenticeship programs, applicants come from the factory floor—not from secondary school. Nonetheless, the apprenticeship program imitates the German model in most other respects. Castwell's participants undergo a four-year apprenticeship involving eight college courses related to their work, and a rotation every six months for on-the-job training under a different tutor.

Other U.S. apprenticeship programs are cooperative efforts between secondary schools and companies, coordinated through trade associations. Such programs are not accurate representations of the German model, but tend to be modifications inspired by the European apprenticeship system. For example, the Tooling and Manufacturing Association of Park Ridge, Illinois, jointly set up apprenticeship programs with local high schools and manufacturing firms. The on-the-job training is coordinated with job-related coursework at the high school and culminates either in an associate's degree through the summer internship courses, or entry into the Illinois Institute of Technology's four-year manufacturing technology program at a junior standing. Bethany Paul, the association's apprenticeship manager, points to its success, indicating that "in Illinois only 17 percent of students finish college compared with over 90 percent who finish their four-year apprenticeship program."

Finally, in some U.S. apprenticeship programs governmental agencies have tried to plant the seeds for growing apprenticeship systems directly patterned on the German model. For example, the Rhode Island Departments of Labor and Education coordinated with the Rhode Island Teachers Union and private industry to send representatives directly to Germany and Switzerland to study their apprenticeship models. On their return in 1998, Rhode Island set in place a state-coordinated pilot apprenticeship program involving on-the-job training coordinated with business and technical coursework. In four to five years, the program culminated in a bachelor's degree.

Similarly, the Oklahoma Department of Human Services brought together local chambers of commerce, private companies, and public education organizations to form IndEx, a coordinating body for Tulsa-based apprenticeship programs. Unlike other vocational training, the IndEx programs are actual apprenticeships leading high-school juniors through four years of both academic and on-the-job training with pay for both studies and work training. As an incentive, the organization offers a $1,200 bonus for maintaining a 3.1 grade point average or better (Rowley, et al.).

Yet despite the growing interest from a variety of quarters in apprenticeship programs in the United States, problems exist. Germany has provided apprenticeships of some sort since the Middle Ages. This has led to a cultural receptivity to apprenticeships that may not be as readily transferable to the United States. As Gitter and Scheuer (1997) note, "the key to Germany's success is the country's social consensus on the importance of workforce training for youths." In the end, that consensus may not be easily transferred to the United States.

Issues regarding insurance and liability are arguably much greater factors in the heavily litigious U.S. workplace. German, Austrian, and Danish child-labor laws do not view apprenticeships as child labor because the apprenticeship systems are so deeply entrenched into the cultural understanding of education in those countries. By contrast, in the United States, where apprenticeships are a new idea, no such clear differentiation exists separating firms employing middle-school-age apprentices from companies employing inexpensive and illegal child labor. Additionally, in Germany teachers view apprenticeships as normal. In the United States, teachers may feel threatened by the implication that traditional U.S. education (data notwithstanding) does not prepare students for jobs.

Perhaps the greatest potential impediment to the widespread acceptance of apprenticeships may come from the way in which such programs are seen by labor unions in the United States. In Germany, union ranks are filled with members who learned their occupations through apprenticeships. Moreover, considerably greater labor-management cooperation characterizes the German workplace than in the United States. U.S. labor leaders are likely to be suspicious of apprenticeship programs as a management ploy to employ non-unionized, underpaid student workers. Indiana, for instance, was forced to scrap, for these very reasons, a state-sponsored apprenticeship initiative when local steel unions opposed the program. Still, labor can be supportive as well. Wisconsin passed a state law establishing apprenticeship programs with the full cooperation of the AFL-CIO.

Apprenticeship systems have a long history of successful school-to-work transition in Germany. The German model has achieved considerable success in several other nations such as Austria and Switzerland. Though somewhat modified, it has also achieved success in variant forms in Denmark and Great Britain, although practiced by a considerably more limited number of apprentices and employers. Since the early 1990s the German apprenticeship model has achieved growing attention in the United States. To date, U.S. apprenticeships have been both limited and relatively uncoordinated. Still, the initial programs sponsored both by private and state organizations seem promising, though they face several potential obstacles

SEE ALSO: Continuing Education and Lifelong Learning Trends; Training Delivery Methods

David A. Victor
Revised by Deborah Hausler

FURTHER READING:

"Apprenticeship Program Shows A European Flair." *Tooling & Production*, October 1998, 37–38.

Buechtemann, Christoph F., Juergen Schupp, and Dana Soloff. "Roads to Work: School-to-Work Transition Patterns in Germany and the United States." *Industrial Relations Journal* 24, no. 2 (1993): 97–111.

Filipczak, Bob. "Apprenticeships From High Schools to High Skills." *Training,* April 1992, 23–29.

Gitter, Robert J. "Apprenticeship-Trained Workers: United States and Great Britain." *Monthly Labor Review,* April 1994, 38–43.

Gitter, Robert J., and Markus Scheuer. "U.S. and German Youths: Unemployment and the Transition from School to Work." *Monthly Labor Review,* March 1997, 16–20.

Hamilton, Stephen F. "Prospects for an America-Style Youth Apprenticeship System." *Educational Researcher,* April 1993, 11–16.

Harrison, Roy. "Easing Border Controls for Vocational Training." *People Management,* 18 December 1997, 41.

Lightner, Stan, and Edward L. Harris. "Legal Aspects of Youth Apprenticeships: What You Should Know." *Tech Directions,* November 1994, 21–25.

"Manufacturers Cultivate 'Home-Grown' Employees." *Tooling & Production,* July 1997, 31.

Organisation for Economic Co-operation and Development. *OECD Employment Outlook.* Paris: OECD, 1994.

Philbin, Matthew L. "Castwell 'Grew Its Own' Maintenance MVP's." *Modern Casting,* May 1997, 44–47.

Rowley, Wayne, Terry Crist, and Leo Presley. "Partnerships for Productivity." *Training and Development,* January 1995, 53–55.

Steedman, Hilary. "Five Years of the Modern Apprenticeship Initiative: An Assessment Against Continental European Models." *National Institute Economic Review,* October 2001, 75.

Winkelmann, Rainer. "Employment Prospects and Skill Acquisition of Apprenticeship-Trained Workers in Germany." *Industrial and Labor Relations Review,* July 1996, 658–672.

THE ART AND SCIENCE OF MANAGEMENT

One of the enduring questions in the field of management is whether it is an art or a science. Webster's College Dictionary defines an art as "skill in conducting any human activity" and science as "any skill or technique that reflects a precise application of facts or a principle." Reflected in the differences in these definitions is the use of precision in science, in that there is a particular, prescribed way in which a manager should act. Thus, management as a science would indicate that in practice, managers use a specific body of information and facts to guide their behaviors, but that management as an art requires no specific body of knowledge, only skill. Conversely, those who believe management is an art are likely to believe that there is no specific way to teach or understand management, and that it is a skill borne of personality and ability. Those who believe in management as an art are likely to believe that certain people are more predisposed to be effective managers than are others, and that some people cannot be taught to be effective managers. That is, even with an understanding of management research and an education in management, some people will not be capable of being effective practicing managers.

FOUNDATIONS OF THE MANAGEMENT AS A SCIENCE PERSPECTIVE

Practicing managers who believe in management as a science are likely to believe that there are ideal managerial practices for certain situations. That is, when faced with a managerial dilemma, the manager who believes in the scientific foundation of his or her craft will expect that there is a rational and objective way to determine the correct course of action. This manager is likely to follow general principles and theories and also by creating and testing hypotheses. For instance, if a manager has a problem with an employee's poor work performance, the manager will look to specific means of performance improvement, expecting that certain principles will work in most situations. He or she may rely on concepts learned in business school or through a company training program when determining a course of action, perhaps paying less attention to political and social factors involved in the situation.

Many early management researchers subscribed to the vision of managers as scientists. The scientific management movement was the primary driver of this perspective. Scientific management, pioneered by Frederick W. Taylor, Frank and Lillian Gilbreth, and others, attempted to discover "the one best way" to perform jobs. They used scientific processes to evaluate and organize work so that it became more efficient and effective. Scientific management's emphasis on both reducing inefficiencies and on understanding the psychology of workers changed manager and employee attitudes towards the practice of management. See Exhibit 1 for a summary of the principles of scientific management.

FOUNDATIONS OF THE MANAGEMENT AS AN ART PERSPECTIVE

Practicing managers who believe in management as an art are unlikely to believe that scientific principles and theories will be able to implemented in actual managerial situations. Instead, these managers are likely to rely on the social and political environment surrounding the managerial issue, using their own knowledge of a situation, rather than generic rules, to determine a course of action. For example, as a contrast

Exhibit 1

Frederick W. Taylor's Principles of Scientific Management

1. Managers must study the way that workers perform their tasks and understand the job knowledge (formal and informal) that workers have, then find ways to improve how tasks are performed.

2. Managers must codify new methods of performing tasks into written work rules and standard operating procedures.

3. Managers should hire workers who have skills and abilities needed for the tasks to be completed, and should train them to perform the tasks according to the established procedures.

4. Managers must establish a level of performance for the task that is acceptable and fair and should link tit to a pay system that reward workers who perform above the acceptable level.

to the example given previously, a manager who has a problem with an employee's poor work performance is likely to rely on his or her own experiences and judgment when addressing this issue. Rather than having a standard response to such a problem, this manager is likely to consider a broad range of social and political factors, and is likely to take different actions depending on the context of the problem.

Henry Mintzberg is probably the most well-known and prominent advocate of the school of thought that management is an art. Mintzberg is an academic researcher whose work capturing the actual daily tasks of real managers was ground breaking research for its time. Mintzberg, through his observation of actual managers in their daily work, determined that managers did not sit at their desks, thinking, evaluating, and deciding all day long, working for long, uninterrupted time periods. Rather, Mintzberg determined that mangers engaged in very fragmented work, with constant interruptions and rare opportunities to quietly consider managerial issues. Thus, Mintzberg revolutionized thinking about managers at the time that his work was published, challenging the prior notion that managers behaved rationally and methodically. This was in line with the perspective of management as an art, because it indicated that managers did not necessarily have routine behaviors throughout their days, but instead used their own social and political skills to solve problems that arose throughout the course of work.

Another scholar that promoted the notion of management as an art was David E. Lilienthal, who in 1967 had his series of lectures titled *Management: A Humanist Art* published. In this set of published lectures, Lilienthal argues that management requires more than a mastery of techniques and skills; instead, it also requires that managers understand individuals and their motivations and help them achieve their goals. Lilienthal believed that combining management and leadership into practice, by not only getting work done but understanding the meaning behind the work, as effective managerial behavior. Thus, he promoted the idea of the manager as a motivator and facilitator of others. This manager as an artist was likely to

respond differently to each employee and situation, rather than use a prescribed set of responses dictated by set of known guidelines.

Another proponent of the management as art school of thought is Peter Drucker, famed management scholar who is best known for developing ideas related to total quality management. Drucker terms management "a liberal art," claiming that it is such because it deals with the fundamentals of knowledge, wisdom, and leadership, but because it is also concerned with practice and application. Drucker argues that the discipline (i.e., the science) of management attempts to create a paradigm for managers, in which facts are established, and exceptions to these facts are ignored as anomalies. He is critical of the assumptions that make up the management paradigm, because these assumptions change over time as society and the business environment change. Thus, management is more of an art, because scientific "facts" do not remain stable over time.

ART AND SCIENCE IN MANAGEMENT RESEARCH

Noted researcher Thomas Kuhn, in his book *The Structure of Scientific Revolutions,* addresses issues associated with the state of current scientific research and the opportunities for scientific discovery. Kuhn, in his previous editions of this text, drew distinctions between mature and immature fields of study. In mature fields of study, many of the central questions of that field have been answered, and strong consensus exists among researchers regarding the fundamental assumptions of that field. Conversely, in immature fields of study, there is still a great deal of debate on major questions in the field, and gains in knowledge come sporadically. In many ways, management is an immature science. While its foundations in psychology, sociology, and other related areas give it a long and rich history, the nature of the areas of study renders it immature. That is, due to the difficulties of studying human behavior in a number of disparate settings, the study of management is still very young when compared to other fields of research (e.g., in the physical sciences). In fact, many scholars have argued that the social sciences (e.g., management research) suffer from envy of the physical sciences, in which "truths" are able to be determined through research. As such, social sciences researchers may strive to create a more "scientific" approach to their fields in order to grant them more legitimacy.

Despite its relative immaturity, some consistent answers have been developed in the field of management. In many ways this is due to the increased sophistication of management research. However, there are still a number of research gaps in management; despite our increased knowledge in some areas, there is still a great deal of disagreement and confusion in other areas. In these circumstances, the practice of management is likely to be dictated by the perspective of management as an art. Because there are no hard and fast rules in certain circumstances, individual managers' experiences and skills must guide them.

Today, much of the management research conducted in academic institutions blends the notion of management as an art and as a science. Some of these trends in management research that have pushed the field in either direction—namely increased statistical sophistication and the emphasis on contextual influences—are described below.

INCREASED STATISTICAL SOPHISTICATION. As computer technology continues to improve, the ability of management researchers to conduct sophisticated statistical analyses has also been enhanced. Powerful statistical computing packages are now readily available for desktop computers, allowing for high-speed analysis of complex statistical models. Additionally, new statistical modeling techniques, such as structural equations modeling, have gained footing in management research. Thus, management researchers are now better able to empirically test more complex research hypotheses, and management as a science is perpetuated.

The improvement in researchers' ability to analyze statistics more quickly has resulted in an increase in information about theories of management. Practicing managers may now know of certain relationships that have received strong support through decades of empirical research. Such "truths" may become guiding principles that practicing managers see as ideal solutions to a variety of situations. For instance, numerous empirical studies over several recent decades have supported the relationship between appropriate goal setting and higher work performance. This relationship has been tested in a variety of situations, with a number of contextual influences present, yet the statistical relationship holds in nearly all of them. Thus, a practicing manager may see this body of empirical research and, in a work situation, see the benefits of goal setting on performance as a scientific ideal. He or she may then implement

goal setting in a number of practical situations, bolstered by the confidence afforded by decades of research supporting such actions.

Meta-analysis, in particular, is a methodological procedure that has contributed significantly to the study of management. Meta-analysis is a statistical technique that allows a researcher to combine findings from multiple studies, correct for errors in study design, and determine an "average" statistical relationship among variables. Meta-analysis first gained a foothold in management research in studies of the validity of selection techniques for different jobs in different organizations. Before the application of meta-analysis to research on the validity of different selection techniques, there was a belief in the situational specificity of these selection methods. That is, studies of the accuracy of selection techniques in predicting subsequent job performance had such disparate results that academics concluded that validity of a standardized test, for example, would differ dramatically in each selection situation (e.g., with different job applicants, in different organizations, in different geographic regions). This myth was dispelled, however, with the application of meta-analysis to the results of the collected body of research on the validity of selection methods. The use of meta-analysis established that the differences in findings were due primarily to limitations of research design, such as small sample size, unreliability of measures, and other correctable problems. When meta-analysis was applied to this group of studies, they were combined to determine that validates of selection techniques were general across jobs and organizations. Thus, the use of meta-analysis helped to establish that cognitive ability tests and structured interviews were highly valid selection methods in nearly every job.

Meta-analysis has now been applied to many different areas of management research, including training, recruitment, fairness, and many other topics. Additionally, there have been a number of refinements to the statistical corrections used in meta-analysis. This increased acceptance of and use of meta-analysis in management research supports the notion of management as a science. Meta-analysis provides for "truths" in management—relationships between variables that hold strong regardless of the people or situation involved. For instance, one consistent finding is that structured selection interviews, ones in which applicants are asked the same set of predetermined questions, and in which responses are evaluated using the same criteria, are a more valid predictor of future job performance than are unstructured interviews, in which applicants are asked different questions and responses are evaluated using different criteria. Meta-analysis has been used to establish this finding, and thus a practicing manager may use this information as a scientific "fact" when conducting selection interviews.

CONTEXTUAL INFLUENCES. While improvements in management researchers' ability to conduct statistical analysis in their studies has promoted the notion of management as a science, in some ways it has also promoted management as an art. Because of the capability to statistically analyze and interpret larger, more complex models of behavior, researchers are now testing models with this increased complexity. In particular, there is an increased emphasis on contextual influences. That is, rather than focusing solely on how behaviors are linked to outcomes, many researchers now include individual, social, and political variables in research models to have a richer understanding of behavior. Thus, there are more complex recommendations that can be made from recent research, rather than basic "truths."

For example, one of the most prominent areas of contextual research in recent years is in person-organization fit. Person-organization fit is a part of the attraction-selection-attrition model that suggests that certain types of individuals are attracted to particular organizations, selected by those organizations, and either adapt to become an effective part of the organization, or leave if they do not fit with the organization. Person-organization fit (p-o fit) is the notion that the particular skills, attitudes, values, and preferences of an individual employee should fit with those of the organization in order for that employee to have high job satisfaction and performance. The p-o fit model indicates that this fit is likely to be as important as an assessment of applicants' abilities when hiring. Previous models of selection emphasized a strict interpretation of applicant skills, with the use of valid selection tests as most important. However, the p-o fit model indicates that, even if skills and abilities have been appropriately measured, that hiring the applicant with the best skills is not always the best course of action, but that hiring an individual who fits into the culture of the organization could be more advantageous.

This move towards including contextual influences in management research models promotes the notion of management as an art. Rather than indicating that there are specific principles and guidelines that can guide management practice, it suggests that managerial behavior should change based on the social and political context of the situation.

ART AND SCIENCE IN MANAGEMENT EDUCATION AND DEVELOPMENT

Management education and development, which attempt to prepare today's managers for organizational challenges, are guided by both the notion of management as an art and as a science. The approach to management education and development is likely to differ dramatically depending on the belief one has as to the nature of the practice of management. The perspective of management as an art assumes to some extent that a manager has a disposition or experiences that guide him or her in managerial decisions and activities. Thus, with this perspective, many managers may be successful without any formal education or training in management. The perspective of management as a science, however, would indicate that management skills can be taught through an understanding of theory and principles of management. Many of today's educational institutions and workplaces blend the notion of management as a science and an art in their approach to preparing employees for management.

Primarily, formal management education for practicing managers, such as with bachelors and masters degrees, emphasizes the science of management. Management education in today's universities primarily emphasizes management as a science. Textbooks are used in management courses for bachelors' degrees, and these texts emphasize many of the consistent findings of many decades of management research. And, as these degrees increase in popularity, it is likely that more practicing managers will have a set of established management ideals with which they operate.

While formal management education may promote management as a science, many development efforts support the notion of management as an art. To cultivate management talent, organizations offer mentoring, overseas experiences, and job rotation. These activities allow managers to gain greater social and political insight and thus rely on their own judgment and abilities to improve their management style. Much of mentoring involves behavior modeling, in which a protégé may learn nuances of managerial behavior rather than a set of specific guidelines for managing. Overseas experiences are likely to involve a great deal of manager adaptation, and the general rules by which a manager might operate in one culture are likely to change when managing workers in other countries. Finally, job rotation is a technique that requires a manager to work in a variety of settings. Again, this encourages a manager to be flexible and adaptive, and likely rely more on his or her personal skill in managing.

The foundations of management as an art and management as a science are evident in today's educational institutions and work organizations. Management as a science was primarily influenced by researchers in the area of scientific management, such as Frederick Taylor, and continues today in much of the empirical research on management issues. Management as an art has been influenced by scholars such as Henry Mintzberg and Peter Drucker, and is often evident in complex theories of management. Many scholars and practitioners blend art and science to more effectively cultivate managerial talent. This is evident in recent theories of management, research in workplaces, and education and development of managers.

SEE ALSO: Management Science; Management Thought; Organizational Behavior; Research Methods and Processes; Statistics

Marcia J. Simmering

FURTHER READING:

Appley, Lawrence A. *Management in Action: The Art of Getting Things Done through People.* American Management Association, 1956.

DuBrin, Andrew J. *Essentials of Management.* 6th ed. Peterborough, Ontario: Thomson South-Western, 2003.

Drucker, Peter F. *The Essential Drucker.* New York, NY: Harper Collins Publishers, 2001.

Jones, Gareth R., and George, Jennifer M. *Contemporary Management.* 4th ed. New York, NY: McGraw-Hill Irwin, 2006.

Kuhn, Thomas S. *The Structure of Scientific Revolutions.* 3rd ed. Chicago, IL: The University of Chicago Press, 1996.

Lilienthal, David E. *Management: A Humanist Art.* New York, NY: Colombia University Press, 1967.

Mintzberg, Henry. "The Manager's Job: Folklore and Fact." *Harvard Business Review,* July-August 1975, 56–62.

————. *The Nature of Managerial Work.* New York: Harper & Row, 1973.

Rue, Leslie W., and Byars, Lloyd L. *Management: Skills and Applications.* 10th ed. New York, NY: McGraw-Hill Irwin, 2003.

Williams, Chuck. *Management.* Cincinnati, OH: South-Western College Publishing, 2000.

ARTIFICIAL INTELLIGENCE

Artificial intelligence (AI) refers to computer software that exhibits intelligent behavior. The term "intelligence" is difficult to define, and has been the subject of heated debate by philosophers, educators, and psychologists for ages. Nevertheless, it is possible to enumerate many important characteristics of intelligent behavior. Intelligence includes the capacity to learn, maintain a large storehouse of knowledge, utilize commonsense reasoning, apply analytical abilities, discern relationships between facts, communicate ideas to others and understand communications from others, and perceive and make sense of the world around us. Thus, artificial intelligence systems are computer programs that exhibit one or more of these behaviors.

AI systems can be divided into two broad categories: knowledge representation systems and machine learning systems. Knowledge representation systems, also known as expert systems, provide a structure for capturing and encoding the knowledge of a human expert in a particular domain. For example, the knowledge of medical doctors might be captured in a computerized model that can be used to help diagnose patient illnesses.

MACHINE LEARNING SYSTEMS

The second category of AI, machine learning systems, creates new knowledge by finding previously unknown patterns in data. In contrast to knowledge representation approaches, which model the problem-solving structure of human experts, machine learning systems derive solutions by "learning" patterns in data, with little or no intervention by an expert. There are three main machine learning techniques: neural networks, induction algorithms, and genetic algorithms.

NEURAL NETWORKS. Neural networks simulate the human nervous system. The concepts that guide neural network research and practice stem from studies of biological systems. These systems model the interaction between nerve cells. Components of a neural network include neurons (sometimes called "processing elements"), input lines to the neurons (called dendrites), and output lines from the neurons (called axons).

Neural networks are composed of richly connected sets of neurons forming layers. The neural network architecture consists of an input layer, which inputs data to the network; an output layer, which produces the resulting guess of the network; and a series of one or more hidden layers, which assist in propagating. This is illustrated in Figure 1.

During processing, each neuron performs a weighted sum of inputs from the neurons connecting to it; this is called activation. The neuron chooses to fire if the sum of inputs exceeds some previously set threshold value; this is called transfer.

Inputs with high weights tend to give greater activation to a neuron than inputs with low weights. The weight of an input is analogous to the strength of a synapse in a biological system. In biological systems, learning occurs by strengthening or weakening the synaptic connections between nerve cells. An artificial neural network simulates synaptic connection strength by increasing or decreasing the weight of input lines into neurons.

Neural networks are trained with a series of data points. The networks guess which response should be given, and the guess is compared against the correct answer for each data point. If errors occur, the weights into the neurons are adjusted and the process repeats itself. This learning approach is called backpropagation, and is similar to statistical regression.

Neural networks are used in a wide variety of business problems, including optical character recognition, financial forecasting, market demographics trend assessment, and various robotics applications.

Figure 1

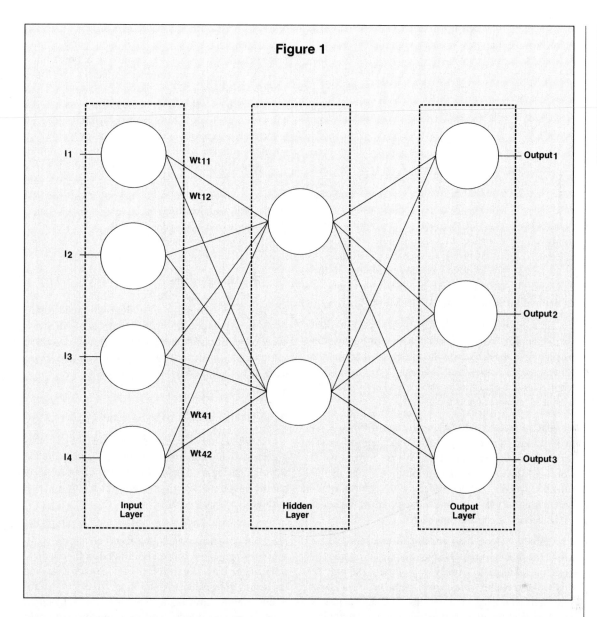

INDUCTION ALGORITHMS. Induction algorithms form another approach to machine learning. In contrast to neural networks, which are highly mathematical in nature, induction approaches tend to involve symbolic data. As the name implies, these algorithms work by implementing inductive reasoning approaches. Induction is a reasoning method that can be characterized as "learning by example." Unlike rule-based deduction, induction begins with a set of observations and constructs rules to account for these observations. Inductive reasoning attempts to find general patterns that can fully explain the observations. The system is presented with a large set of data consisting of several input variables and one decision variable. The system constructs a decision tree by recursively partitioning data sets based on the variables that best distinguish between the data elements. That is, it attempts to partition the data so that each partition contains data with the same value for a decision variable. It does this by

selecting the input variables that do the best job of dividing the data set into homogeneous partitions. For example, consider Figure 2, which contains the data set pertaining to decisions that were made on credit loan applications.

Figure 2
Artificial Intelligence &
Expert Systems

	Salary	Credit History	Current Assets	Loan Decision
a)	High	Poor	High	Accept
b)	High	Poor	Low	Reject
c)	Low	Poor	Low	Reject
d)	Low	Good	Low	Accept
e)	Low	Good	High	Accept
f)	High	Good	Low	Accept

An induction algorithm would infer the rules in Figure 3 to explain this data.

Figure 3

If the credit history is good, then accept the loan application

If the credit history is poor and current assets are high, then accept the loan application

If the credit history is poor and current assets are low, then reject the loan application

---

As this example illustrates, an induction algorithm is able to induce rules that identify the general patterns in data. In doing so, these algorithms can prune out irrelevant or unnecessary attributes. In the example above, salary was irrelevant in terms of explaining the loan decision of the data set.

Induction algorithms are often used for data mining applications, such as marketing problems that help companies decide on the best market strategies for new product lines. Data mining is a common service included in data warehouses, which are frequently used as decision support tools.

GENETIC ALGORITHMS. Genetic algorithms use an evolutionary approach to solve optimization problems. These are based on Darwin's theory of evolution, and in particular the notion of survival of the fittest. Concepts such as reproduction, natural selection, mutation, chromosome, and gene are all included in the genetic algorithm approach.

Genetic algorithms are useful in optimization problems that must select from a very large number of possible solutions to a problem. A classic example of this is the traveling salesperson problem. Consider a salesman who must visit n cities. The salesperson's problem is to find the shortest route by which to visit each of these n cities exactly once, so that the salesman will tour all the cities and return to the origin. For such a problem there are $(n-1)!$ possible solutions, or $(n-1)$ factorial. For six cities, this would mean $5 \times 4 \times 3 \times 2 \times 1 = 120$ possible solutions. Suppose that the salesman must travel to 100 cities. This would involve 99! possible solutions. This is such an astronomical number that if the world's most powerful computer began solving such a problem at the time that the universe had begun and worked continuously on it since, it would be less than one percent complete today!

Obviously, for this type of problem a brute strength method of exhaustively comparing all possible solutions will not work. This requires the use of heuristic methods, of which the genetic algorithm is a prime example. For the traveling salesperson problem, a chromosome would be one possible route through the cities, and a gene would be a city in a particular sequence on the chromosome. The genetic algorithm would start with an initial population of chromosomes (routes) and measure each according to a fitness function (the total distance traveled in the route). Those with the best fitness functions would be selected and those with the worst would be discarded. Then random pairs of surviving chromosomes would mate, a process called crossover. This involves swapping city positions between the pair of chromosomes, resulting in a pair of child chromosomes. In addition, some random subset of the population would be mutated, such that some portion of the sequence of cities would be altered. The process of selection, crossover, and mutation results in a new population for the next generation. This procedure is repeated through as many generations as necessary in order to obtain an optimal solution.

Genetic algorithms are very effective at finding good solutions to optimization problems. Scheduling, configuration, and routing problems are good candidates for a genetic algorithm approach. Although genetic algorithms do not guarantee the absolute best solution, they do consistently arrive at very good solutions in a relatively short period of time.

AI IN THE TWENTY-FIRST CENTURY

Artificial intelligence systems provide a key component in many computer applications that serve the world of business. In fact, AI is so prevalent that many people encounter such applications on a daily basis without even being aware of it.

One of the most ubiquitous uses of AI can be found in network servers that route electronic mail. Expert systems are routinely utilized in the medical field, where they take the place of doctors in assessing the results of tests like mammograms or electrocardiograms. Neural networks are commonly used by credit card companies, banks, and insurance firms to help detect fraud. These AI systems can, for example, monitor consumer spending habits, detect patterns in the data, and alert the company when uncharacteristic patterns arise. Genetic algorithms serve logistics planning functions in airports, factories, and even military operations, where they are used to help solve incredibly complex resource-allocation problems. And perhaps most familiar, many companies employ AI systems to help monitor calls in their customer service call centers. These systems can analyze the emotional tones of callers' voices or listen for specific words, and route those calls to human supervisors for follow-up attention.

Although computer scientists have thus far failed to create machines that can function with the complex intelligence of human beings, they have succeeded in creating a wide range of AI applications that make people's lives simpler and more convenient.

SEE ALSO: Expert Systems

Michel Mitri
Revised by Rhoda L. Wilburn

FURTHER READING:

Dhar, V., and R. Stein. *Seven Methods for Transforming Corporate Data into Business Intelligence.* Upper Saddle River, NJ: Prentice Hall, 1997.

"Hot Topics: Artificial Intelligence." BBC Online. Available from <http://www.bbc.co.uk/science/hottopics/ai/>.

Kahn, Jennifer. "It's Alive! From Airport Tarmacs to Online Job Banks to Medical Labs, Artificial Intelligence Is Everywhere." *Wired,* March 2002. Available from <http://www.wired.com/wired/archive/10.03/everywhere.html>.

Menzies, Tim. "21st Century AI: Proud, Not Smug." *IEEE Intelligent Systems,* May/June 2003.

Norvig, P., and S. Russell. *Artificial Intelligence: A Modern Approach.* Upper Saddle River, NJ: Prentice Hall, 2002.

Van, Jon. "Computers Gain Power, But It's Not What You Think." *Chicago Tribune,* 20 March 2005.

ASSESSMENT CENTERS

An assessment center is a process used to make personnel decisions in which participants engage in a variety of exercises and have their performance evaluated by multiple assessors. The goal of an assessment center is to simulate job tasks so that an applicant can demonstrate skills or characteristics that would be effective on the job.

According to the International Task Force on Assessment Center Guidelines, assessment centers:

- Conduct job analyses of relevant behaviors

- Classify participants' behaviors into meaningful and relevant categories

- Use techniques that are designed to provide information for evaluating the dimensions previously determined by the job analysis

- Involve multiple assessment techniques, such as tests, interviews, questionnaires, sociometric devices, and simulations

- Include a sufficient number of job-related simulations, allowing opportunities to observe the candidate's behavior related to each competency/dimension being assessed

- Utilize several assessors to evaluate each participant

- Employ thoroughly trained assessors

- Provide a means for assessors to record their observations of participants' behavior as it occurs

- Involve the preparation of an assessor's report

- Base the integration of behaviors on the pooling of assessors' information, or upon a statistical integration process validated in accordance with professionally accepted standards.

Behavioral dimensions that are frequently measured in assessment centers include planning and organizing, leadership, oral communication, tolerance for stress, and initiative. Participants have their performance on these and similar dimensions evaluated while they engaging in two or more of the following activities over a one- or two-day period:

- In-basket exercises, in which participants respond to a series of administrative problems that simulate typical managerial tasks

- Leaderless group discussions, in which a group of participants without an assigned leader must arrive at a group solution to a specified problem within a given time period

- Role-plays, in which participants are involved in a simulation of a situation that could occur on the job

- Interviews, in which participants typically are questioned about how they have handled particular work situations in the past and how they would respond to specific work situations in the future

- Management games, in which participants must work cooperatively to meet mental or physical challenges

Evaluations of assessment center participants can be used for employee selection decisions (hiring and promotion), and to help identify training and development needs. The most common use of assessment centers is to evaluate participants' management potential. When used for selection or promotion decisions, the emphasis is on identifying participants who do well on essential job performance dimensions. When used for training and development purposes, the focus is on identifying participant deficiencies on critical job dimensions. The feedback and employee development suggestions that result from an assessment form the basis for training programs that are designed to correct performance problems. For organizations, assessment centers can serve as needs assessment programs that identify employee development and hiring needs.

Early versions of assessment centers were used by the military in the 1940s. The first use of an assessment center in an industrial setting was in the 1950s, when AT&T used the process in an attempt to evaluate participants' potential for managerial success. The results of this early assessment center application were encouraging, and assessment center use increased following AT&T's apparent success. According to one study by Gaugler, Rosenthal, Thornton, and Bentson, by 1987 more than 2,000 organizations, including Pepsico, IBM, Rubbermaid, and the FBI, used assessment centers to select and promote managers.

As the use of assessment centers increased during the 1960s and 1970s, researchers identified several ways in which their utility as a personnel selection tool could be improved. In 1973, Bender suggested that companies should undertake validation studies to ensure that assessment centers actually predicted managerial success. He also pointed out that assessors should be more thoroughly trained before they evaluated assessment center participants.

In an attempt to encourage uniformity and professionalism in assessment center practices, the Task Force on Assessment Center Guidelines published *Guidelines and Ethical Considerations for Assessment Center Operations* in 1989. These guidelines were updated in 2000 and endorsed by the International Congress on Assessment Center Methods. They spell out the essential elements of assessment centers and provide recommendations regarding the content of assessor training, information participants should receive before beginning the assessment center, data usage, and validation methods. In addition, these guidelines provide a standard for judging assessment center practices employed by organizations.

The preponderance of research evidence indicates that, when designed and conducted in a manner consistent with professional guidelines, assessment centers are valid predictors of future promotions and job performance. Additional research suggests that assessment centers have less adverse impact on women and minorities than many other commonly used selection tools, and courts generally have upheld the use of properly designed assessment centers.

The primary criticism of assessment centers is that they are very expensive in terms of both development and implementation, which makes their use infeasible for many small organizations. Other researchers question the convergent and discriminant validity of the measurement of behavioral dimensions in assessment centers. One method used to overcome the expense problem is to videotape the candidates' performance and have the assessors evaluate them later. This avoids costs and problems related to the logistics of assembling candidates and assessors. Another technique is to use "situational judgment tests," or written simulation tests. Candidates either choose the best course of action from a selection of choices or provide a written course of action. Research indicates that situational judgment tests are good predictors of job performance.

SEE ALSO: Employee Evaluation and Performance Appraisals; Employee Recruitment Planning; Employee Screening and Selection

Tim Barnett
Revised by Judith M. Nixon

FURTHER READING:

Beagrie, Scott. "How to Cut It at Assessment Centres." *Personnel Today,* 5 October 2004.

Bender, J.M. "What Is 'Typical' of Assessment Centers?" *Personnel* 50, no. 4 (1973): 50–57.

Gatewood, Robert D., and Hubert S. Field. *Human Resource Selection.* 6th ed. Mason, OH: South-Western College Publishing, 2004.

Gaugler, B.B., D.B. Rosenthal, G.C. Thornton, III, and C. Bentson. "Meta-Analysis of Assessment Center Validity." *Journal of Applied Psychology* 72 (1987): 493–511.

The International Congress on Assessment Center Methods. Available from <http://www.assessmentcenters.org>.

Joiner, D.A. "Assessment Centers: What's New?" *Public Personnel Management* 31, no. 2 (2002): 179–185.

———. "Guidelines and Ethical Considerations for Assessment Center Operations: International Task Force on Assessment Center Guidelines." *Public Personnel Management* 29, no. 3 (2000): 315–331.

Lievens, F., and R.J. Klimoski. "Understanding the Assessment Center Process: Where Are We Now?" In *International Review of Industrial and Organizational Psychology.* ed. C.L. Cooper and I.T. Robertson. Chichester, United Kingdom: John Wiley & Sons, Ltd.

McDaniel, M.A., F.P. Morgeson, E.B. Finnegan, M.A. Campion, and E.P. Braverman. "Use of Situational Judgment Tests to Predict Job Performance: A Clarification of the Literature." *Journal of Applied Psychology* 86 (2001): 730–740.

Spychalski, A.C., M.A. Quiñones, B.B. Gaugler, and K. Pohley. "A Survey of Assessment Center Practices in Organizations in the United States." *Personnel Psychology* 50 (1997): 71–90.

Woehr, D.J. and W. Arthur, Jr. "The Construct-Related Validity of Assessment Center Ratings: A Review and Meta-Analysis of the Role of Methodological Factors." *Journal of Management* 29, no. 2 (2003): 231–258.

ATTRIBUTION THEORY

Attribution theory is intended to help a person understand the causes of human behavior, be it their own or someone else's. The basis of attribution theory is that people want to know the reasons for the actions that they and others take; they want to attribute causes to behaviors they see rather than assuming that these behaviors are random. This allows people to assume some feeling of control over their own behaviors and over situations. Psychologist Fritz Heider (1896–1988) first developed attribution theory in his 1958 book *The Psychology of Interpersonal Relations*. Heider proposed that what people perceived and believed about what they saw dictated how they would act, even if their beliefs about what they perceived were invalid.

Heider's proposed theory of attribution was further developed by psychologist Bernard Weiner and colleagues in the 1970s and 1980s, and this new theoretical framework has been used primarily in current attribution research. A final development to attribution theory was provided by psychologist Harold Kelley, who examined how consistency, distinctiveness, and consensus could be used by individuals to establish the validity of their perceptions.

Attributions are critical to management because perceived causes of behavior may influence managers' and employees' judgments and actions. For instance, managers must often observe employee performance and make related judgments. If a manager attributes an employee's poor performance to a lack of effort, then the outcome is likely to be negative for that employee; he or she may receive a poor performance appraisal rating or even be terminated from the job. Conversely, if a manager perceives that an employee's poor performance is due to a lack of skill, the manager may assign the employee to further training or provide more instruction or coaching. Making an inaccurate judgment about the causes of poor performance can have negative repercussions for the organization.

Attributions also may influence employee motivation. Employees who perceive the cause of their success to be outside of their control may be reluctant to attempt new tasks and may lose motivation to perform well in the workplace. Conversely, employees who attribute their success to themselves are more likely to have high motivation for work. Thus, understanding attributions that people make can have a strong effect on both employee performance and managerial effectiveness.

ATTRIBUTION PROCESS AND THE CAUSES OF BEHAVIOR

Attribution is considered to be a three-stage process. First, the behavior of an individual must be observed. Second, the perceiver must determine that the behavior they have observed is deliberate. That is, the person being observed is believed to have behaved intentionally. Finally, the observer attributes the observed behavior to either internal or external causes.

Internal causes are attributed to the person being observed, while external causes are attributed to outside factors. The two internal attributions one can make are that a person's ability or a person's effort determined the outcome. Task difficulty and luck are the external causes of behavior. When perceiving behavior, an observer will make a judgment as to which of these factors is the cause of behavior. However, when making a determination between internal and external causes of behavior, the perceiver must examine the elements of consistency, distinctiveness, and consensus.

Consistency describes whether the person being observed behaves the same way when faced with the same set of circumstances. If the person being observed acts the same way in the same type of situation, consistency is high; if they act differently each time, then consistency is low. Distinctiveness is whether the observed person acts the same way in different types of situations. If the person being observed exhibits the same behavior in a variety of contexts, then distinctiveness is low; if they have different behavior depending on the context, then distinctiveness is high. Finally, consensus is the degree to which other people, if in the same situation, would behave similarly to the person being observed. If the observer sees others acting the same way that the person being perceived acts, then consensus is high. However, if others behave differently in the type of situation, then consensus is low. Consistency, distinctiveness, and consensus are evaluated when observing behavior, and then a judgment about an internal versus external cause of behavior is made. When consistency, distinctiveness, and consensus are all high, the perceiver concludes that there is an external cause of behavior. When consistency is high, distinctiveness is low, and consensus is low, the perceiver will attribute the cause of behavior to internal factors.

To better understand consistency, distinctiveness, and consensus, consider a workplace example. Nancy, a manager, has assigned a team of employees to develop a custom sales training program for a client. As the project progresses, Nancy continues to see problems in the work produced by Jim, one of the team members. In order to determine why Jim's performance is not satisfactory, Nancy first considers consistency, or whether Jim has performed poorly on other similar team projects. A review of his past performance appraisals indicates that he has not had prior performance problems when creating custom sales training programs. This would lead Nancy to conclude that there was an external cause of the poor performance. Second, Nancy considers distinctiveness; she wants to know if Jim has performed poorly on different types of tasks. Again, in checking Jim's performance reviews, she finds that when he is on a team to accomplish a different type of task, such as developing a selection interview, he has excelled. This further points to an external cause of Jim's poor performance. Finally, Nancy assesses consensus, or the behavior of others in this similar task. In asking the team members about their experiences with the current project, she finds that many of them have had difficulty in developing this custom sales training program. Thus, all indicators point to Jim's poor performance being caused by an external factor, such as a difficult task or a demanding client. Based on this attribution, Nancy may explore ways in which to minimize the negative effects of the external factors on Jim's performance rather than attempting to influence his level of effort or ability.

The prior example illustrated how consistency, distinctiveness, and consensus might point toward an external cause. However, these three factors also may lead an observer to attribute behavior to an internal cause, such as the observed person's effort or ability. Nancy, the observer from the previous example, also has experienced difficulties with a secretary named Kelly. Another manager has complained to Nancy that Kelly has not completed work on time and turns in work full of errors. Nancy observes Kelly for several days and finds that, when given work by this particular manager, Kelly continues to perform poorly, which indicates an internal cause (i.e., high consistency). Second, when performing work for other managers on other tasks, Kelly continues to do substandard work; this is distinctiveness, and it again points to an internal cause. Finally, Nancy observes that when other secretaries perform the work assigned by the manager who complained about Kelly, they are able to successfully perform their duties in a timely manner. This is consensus, and it also points to an internal cause. Based on these observations, Nancy can attribute Kelly's poor performance to an internal cause, or namely to Kelly's own lack of skill or effort.

FUNDAMENTAL ATTRIBUTION ERROR AND SELF-SERVING BIAS

People make attributions every day. However, these attributions are not always correct. One common problem in assigning cause is called the fundamental attribution error. This is the tendency of a person to overestimate the influence of personal factors and underestimate the influence of situational factors when assessing someone else's behavior. That is, when observing behavior, a person is more likely to assume that another person's behavior is primarily caused by them and not by the situation. In the workplace, this may mean that managers are more likely to assume that employees' poor performance is due to a lack of ability or effort rather than to task difficulty or luck. The fundamental attribution error, while prominent in North America, is not as common across the rest of the world. In other cultures, such as in India,

the fundamental attribution error is the opposite; people assume that others are more influenced by situation than by personal factors. Thus, while one can assume this error to be present in American managers' perceptions, this may not be the case for managers from other cultures.

As described previously, when a person perceives their own success or failure versus perceiving the success or failure of others, they assign one or more causes: effort, ability, task difficulty, or luck. Effort and ability are internal causes, and task difficulty and luck are external causes. Some researchers argue that it is human nature to have a self-serving bias, which is the tendency to credit one's own successes to internal factors and one's own failure to external factors. Thus, a common assessment of a person's own success might be: "I got a raise because I'm very skilled at my job" (ability), or "I was promoted because of all of the hours I've put into the job" (effort). Common assessments of a person's own failure might be: "I didn't finish the project on time because the deadline was unreasonable for the amount of work required" (task difficulty), or "I didn't make the sale because someone else happened to speak to the client first" (luck). Coupled with the fundamental attribution error, the self-serving bias indicates that people tend to make different attributions about their own successes and failures than the successes and failures of others.

While some researchers argue that the self-serving bias is widespread across most humans in most cultures, others argue that this is not so. Results from a meta-analysis (a method that statistically combines results of multiple empirical research studies) published in 2004 by Mezulis, Abramson, Hyde, and Hankin aimed to address this issue. In examining more than 500 published research studies, some of the results of this meta-analysis indicated that, in general, there were no differences between men and women in their self-serving biases; men and women were just as likely to make self-serving attributions. Additionally, these researchers found that the United States and other Western nations (Canada, the United Kingdom, Australia, New Zealand, and Western Europe) had a strong self-serving bias, which was more pronounced than in most other cultures on other continents. However, despite these strength-related differences, the researchers found that there was a positive self-serving bias in all cultures studied. Within the United States, there were no meaningful differences in self-serving bias among different racial and ethnic groups; no one race was more likely than the others to be more susceptible to this self-serving bias. The general conclusion of Mezulis and her colleagues was that there is a universal self-serving attributional bias that exists across gender, race, and even nation.

Attribution theory was developed to explain how people understand the causes of human behavior, be it their own or someone else's. Managers often act based on their attributions and may act inappropriately if attributions are not valid. Managers who are aware of the attributional process, the types of internal and external attributions, and the presence of the fundamental attribution error and the self-serving bias can better understand their own and others' behavior.

Marcia J. Simmering

FURTHER READING:

Heider, Fritz. *The Psychology of Interpersonal Relations.* New York: Wiley, 1958.

Jones, E.E., D.E. Kanouse, H.H. Kelley, R.E. Nisbett, S. Valins, and B. Weiner, eds. *Attribution: Perceiving the Causes of Behavior.* Morristown, NJ: General Learning Press, 1972.

Kelley, H.H. "Attribution in Social Interaction." In *Attribution: Perceiving the Causes of Behavior.* ed. E.E. Jones, et al. Morristown, MJ: General Learning Press, 1972.

Mezulis, Amy H., Lyn Y. Abramson, Janet S. Hyde, and Benjamin L. Hankin. "Is There a Universal Positivity Bias in Attributions? A Meta-Analytic Review of Individual, Developmental, and Cultural Differences in Self-Serving Attributional Bias." *Psychological Bulletin* 130, no. 5 (2004): 711–747.

AUTONOMY

Autonomy is the degree to which a job provides an employee with the discretion and independence to schedule their work and determine how it is to be done. Higher levels of autonomy on the job have been shown to increase job satisfaction, and in some cases, motivation to perform the job. In traditional organizations, only those employees at higher levels had autonomy. However, new organizational structures, such as flatter organizations, have resulted in increased autonomy at lower levels. Additionally, many companies now make use of autonomous work teams. Autonomy in the workplace can have benefits for employees, teams, managers, and the company as a whole, but it also may have drawbacks. Information regarding both the pros and cons of autonomy for these groups is discussed below.

EMPLOYEE AUTONOMY

According to job design theories, increased autonomy should make employees feel a greater responsibility for the outcomes of their work, and therefore have increased work motivation. Research indicates that when employees have greater levels of autonomy, their personality traits (specifically conscientiousness and extroversion) have a stronger impact on job performance. Thus, by giving employees more autonomy, they are better able to use their personal attributes to contribute to job performance.

Unfortunately, too much autonomy can lead to employee dissatisfaction. Each individual has a different level of need for autonomy in their job. Some workers prefer more direction from a manager and feel uncomfortable with autonomy; they may not want to exert effort or take the responsibility of having their name solely associated with a task, project, or product. Additionally, if employees are not well-equipped—either in training or in personality—to exercise autonomy, it may result in workplace tension and poor performance. Finally, when given autonomy, workers may believe that they have authority somewhat equal to that of their direct supervisor. This may cause them to resent the extra responsibility or feel that their pay should be increased. A related concern is that managers may feel marginalized when employee autonomy increases, particularly when there is a change to a traditional work environment. Managers may feel that by giving employees autonomy, they no longer contribute as much to the organization or that their jobs may be at stake.

MANAGERIAL AUTONOMY

Managers tend to have increased autonomy in organizations that are more decentralized. In such organizations, managers have more latitude to make decisions regarding the work of employees and even personnel decisions. For example, managers with increased autonomy may be able to assign merit raises to the employees in their unit at their discretion. As with employee autonomy, this freedom can result in feelings of motivation and satisfaction for the manager, who may be in a better position to reward and motivate employees. However, as with employee autonomy, managers who have autonomy may not be equipped to handle it. If managers make poor decisions, this may be harmful to employees and the organization as a whole. Using the example of autonomy in deciding pay raises, a manager may give merit pay increases that are significantly higher than those in other work units, which may cause problems across the organization.

TEAM AUTONOMY

In recent years, many organizations have made use of teams in the workplace, many of which operate autonomously. Self-managed work teams are those in which a supervisor gives little direction to the team, and the team members manage themselves. The success of such teams depends greatly on the team members, including their professional capabilities and their ability to work together. Oftentimes, such autonomous teams can greatly enhance an organization's ability to be creative, flexible, and innovative. However, as with individuals, too much autonomy in a team can reduce productivity. When individuals work too independently, their lack of communication and monitoring of one another may result in poor team performance. Additionally, without supervision the team may pursue goals that are different from those of the organization. Thus, periodic meetings and supervision from a manager may be necessary to avoid problems associated with too much autonomy.

AUTONOMY AND THE ORGANIZATION

The autonomy of employees and managers is often dictated by an organization's structure and culture; traditional, bureaucratic organizations often have little autonomy, but newer, more organic structures rely on autonomy, empowerment, and participation to succeed. Employee autonomy is believed to have minimized some of the relational barriers between superiors and subordinates. Therefore, autonomy may improve workplace functions through the ideas and suggestions of employees, and foster relationships with a greater degree of trust between management and employees. However, increased autonomy in the organization also may create disparity among units through different work practices and rules. In the worst case, increased autonomy may allow some employees to engage in unethical behavior. Thus, a certain amount of oversight is necessary in organizations to prevent wrongdoing that may go unnoticed when there are high levels of autonomy.

In conclusion, autonomy generally is a positive attribute for employees, managers, teams, and organizations as a whole. Employees typically desire autonomy, and its introduction can increase motivation and satisfaction. However, because too much autonomy can have organizational drawbacks, care should be taken when increasing it.

SEE ALSO: Empowerment

Marcia J. Simmering

FURTHER READING:

Gómez-Mejía, Luis R., David B. Balkin, and Robert L. Cardy. *Managing Human Resources.* 4th ed. Upper Saddle River, NJ: Prentice Hall, 2004.

Hackman, J.R., and G.R. Oldham. "Motivation through the Design of Work: Test of a Theory." *Organizational Behavior and Human Performance* 16 (1976): 250–279.

B

BALANCE SHEETS

The balance sheet, also known as the statement of financial position, is a snapshot of a company's financial condition at a single point in time. It presents a summary listing of a company's assets, liabilities, and owners' equity. The balance sheet is prepared as of the last day of the business year. Therefore, it corresponds to the end of the time period covered by the income statement.

To understand the balance sheet, its purpose, and its contents, several accounting concepts need to be examined. First of all, the balance sheet represents the *accounting equation* for a company. The accounting equation is a mathematical expression that states the following:

$$Assets = Liabilities + Owners' Equity$$

Stated more fully, this means that the dollar total of the assets equals the dollar total of the liabilities plus the dollar total of the owners' equity. The balance sheet presents a company's resources (i.e., assets, or anything the company owns that has monetary value) and the origin or source of these resources (i.e., through borrowing or through the contributions of the owners). By expressing the same dollar amount twice (once as the dollar total of the assets, then as the dollar total of where the assets came from or who has an equity interest in them), we see that the two amounts must be equal or balance at any given point in time.

An interesting observation about the balance sheet is the valuation at which assets are presented. The average person would assume that the assets listed on the balance sheet would be shown at their current market values. In actuality, generally accepted accounting principles require that most assets be recorded and disclosed at their historical cost, or the original amount that the company paid to obtain ownership or control of the assets. As time passes, however, the current value of certain assets will drift further and further away from their historical cost. In an attempt to present useful information, financial statements show some assets (for which there is a definite market value) at their current market value. When there is no specific market value, historical values are used. An expanded discussion of this concept will follow.

A simple example of a balance sheet appears in Table 1.

ASSETS

As a category, assets include current assets, fixed or long-term assets, property, intangible assets, and other assets.

CURRENT ASSETS. Assets can be viewed as company-owned or controlled resources, from which the organization expects to gain a future benefit. Examples of assets for a typical company include cash, receivables from customers, inventory to be sold, land, and buildings. In order to make the balance sheet more readable, assets are grouped together based on similar characteristics and presented in totals, rather than as a long list of minor component parts.

The first grouping of assets is *current assets*. Current assets consist of cash, as well as other assets that will probably be converted to cash or used up within one year. The one-year horizon is the crucial issue in classifying assets as current. The concern is to

Table 1				
Sample Balance Sheet				
Assets			**Liabilities and Owners' Equity**	
Current assets	600,000		Current liabilities	280,000
Fixed Assets	90,000		Long-term debt	500,000
Property	800,000		Owners' equity	900,000
Intangible assets	50,000			
Other assets	140,000			
TOTAL ASSETS	1,680,000		TOTAL LIABILITIES AND OWNERS' EQUITY	1,680,000

present assets that will provide liquidity in the near future. Current assets should be listed on the balance sheet in the order of most liquid to least liquid. Therefore, the list of current assets begins with cash. Cash includes monies available in checking accounts and any cash on-hand at the business that can be used immediately as needed. Any cash funds or temporary investments that have restrictions on their withdrawals, or that have been set up to be spent beyond one year, should not be included in current assets.

Temporary investments known as trading securities are short-term investments that a company intends to trade actively for profit. These types of investments—common to the financial statements of insurance companies and banks—are shown on the balance sheet at their current market value as of the date of the balance sheet. Any increase or decrease in market value since the previous balance sheet is included in the calculation of net income on the income statement.

The next category on the list of current assets is accounts receivable, which includes funds that are to be collected within one year from the balance sheet date. *Accounts receivable* represent the historical amounts owed to the company by customers as a result of regular business operations. Many companies are unable to collect all of the receivables due from customers. In order to disclose the amount of the total receivables estimated to be collectible, companies deduct what is known as a *contra account*. A contra account has the opposite balance of the account from which it is subtracted. The specific account title might be "allowance for uncollectible accounts" or "allowance for bad debts," and its balance represents the portion of the total receivables that will probably not be collected. The expense related to this is shown on the income statement as *bad debt expense*. The net amount of accounts receivable shown is referred to as the *book value*. Other receivables commonly included on the balance sheet are notes receivable (due within one year) and interest receivable.

Inventory is shown next in the current asset section of the balance sheet. If the company is a retailer or wholesaler, this asset represents goods that a com-

pany has purchased for resale to its customers. If the company is a manufacturer, it will have as many as three different inventory accounts depending on the extent to which the goods have been completed. Inventory classified as *raw materials* represents the basic components that enter into the manufacture of the finished product. For a tractor manufacturer, raw materials would include the engine, frame, tires, and other major parts that are directly traceable to the finished product. The second type of inventory for a manufacturer would be *goods in process*. As the name implies, this category represents products that have been started but are not fully completed. After the goods are completed, they are included in the final inventory classification known as *finished goods*. The value assigned to inventory is either its current market price or its cost to the manufacturer, whichever is lower. This is a conservative attempt to show inventory at its original cost, or at its lower market value if it has declined in value since it was purchased or manufactured.

The final group in the current assets section of the balance sheet is *prepaid expenses*. This group includes prepayments for such items as office supplies, postage, and insurance for the upcoming year. The total for these items is shown at historical cost.

FIXED OR LONG-TERM ASSETS. These assets differ from those listed under current assets because they are not intended for sale during the year following the balance sheet date; that is, they will be held for more than one year into the future. Such asset investments are classified under the headings of *held to maturity* for investments in debt instruments such as corporate or government bonds, and *available for sale* for investments in equity (stock) instruments of other companies or debt securities that will not be held to maturity. Held-to-maturity investments are disclosed in the balance sheet at their *carrying value*. The carrying value is initially equal to the historical cost of the investment; this amount is adjusted each accounting period so that, when the investment matures, its carrying value will then be equal to its maturity value. These adjustments are included in the calculation of income for each accounting period. Available-for-sale investments are adjusted to market value at the end of each accounting period, and these adjustments are included in the calculation of owners' equity.

PROPERTY. Sometimes listed under the expanded heading *property, plant, and equipment,* this section of the balance sheet includes long-term, tangible assets that are used in the operation of the business. These assets have a long-term life and include such things as land, buildings, factory and office equipment, and computers. Land is listed first because it has an unlimited life, and it is shown at its historical cost. The other assets, such as buildings and equipment, are shown at book value. Book value is the original cost of the asset reduced by its total depreciation since being placed into service by a company. This net amount is frequently called net book value, and it represents the remaining cost of the asset to be depreciated over the remaining useful life of the asset.

Several methods are used to calculate depreciation (e.g., straight-line and accelerated), and each uses a mathematical formula to determine the portion of the original cost of the asset that is associated with the current year's operations. Note that depreciation is not an attempt to reduce a long-lived asset to its market value. Accountants use market value on the balance sheet when it is readily available and required for use by generally accepted accounting principles. However, in the case of many property items an unbiased estimate of market value may not be available. As a result, accountants use the asset's historical cost, reduced by the depreciation taken to date, as an indication of its remaining useful service potential.

INTANGIBLE ASSETS. Some long-lived assets of a company represent legal rights or intellectual property protections that are intangible by nature. Examples of this type of asset include a company's patents, copyrights, and trademarks. Each of these assets has a legally specified life and expires at the end of that period, although a few can be renewed. Accountants attempt to measure this decline in usefulness by amortizing the historical costs of these assets. This concept is the same as recording depreciation for items of tangible property discussed above.

One special type of intangible asset is known as *goodwill.* Goodwill is acquired when one company purchases another company and pays more than the estimated market value of the net assets held by the purchased company. The buying company might do this for a number of reasons, but it is often necessary in order to encourage the previous owners to sell, and to guarantee that the acquisition is successful. The difference between the purchase price and the market value of the assets also can be attributed to intangible factors in the purchased company's success, such as proprietary processes or customer relationships. Like other intangible assets, the historical cost of goodwill is amortized over its future years. Accounting rules set a maximum life of 40 years for goodwill, but this rule will be reduced to 20 years in the future.

OTHER ASSETS. This final section covering the disclosure of assets on the balance sheet is a miscellaneous category that includes any long-lived asset that does not fit in any of the categories defined above. This category might include such assets as long-lived receivables (from customers or related companies) and long-lived prepaid insurance premiums (those paid for coverage beyond the next year from the balance sheet date). Another example is a deferred charge (such as a deferred tax asset), or an amount that has been prepaid based on generally accepted accounting principles and holds future benefit for the company.

LIABILITIES

Liabilities include current liabilities, as well as long-term debt.

CURRENT LIABILITIES. Current liabilities are debts that come due within one year following the balance sheet date. These debts usually require cash payments to another entity, and they often have the word "payable" as part of their name. *Accounts payable* are amounts owed to suppliers by a company that has purchased inventory or supplies on a credit basis. *Interest payable* represents interest that has accrued on notes payable or other interest-bearing payables since the last payment was made by a company; this type of payable might be included in a general group known as accrued expenses. Other current liabilities include estimated warranty payments, taxes payable, and the current year's portion of long-term debt that is coming due within one year from the balance sheet date.

LONG-TERM DEBT. Long-term debts are those that come due more than one year following the balance sheet date. They include bonds payable, mortgage payable, and long-term notes payable, all of which have a specific maturity date. *Deferred income taxes payable* might also be disclosed in this category. The latter item is rather technical and controversial; it arises when accounting rules used in preparing the financial statements for reporting to owners differ from rules used on income tax returns for income tax authorities. Deferred income taxes payable typically result from an item being deducted on the income tax return (as allowed by tax rules) before it is reported as an expense on the income statement (as allowed by generally accepted accounting principles). When these timing differences reverse in future years, the deferred income taxes payable category is removed as the actual payment to tax authorities is made.

OWNERS' EQUITY

This final section of the balance sheet is one of the most difficult to comprehend. It is known as *stockholders' equity* for a corporation and consists of several possible subdivisions: paid-in capital, adjustments for changes in value of certain investments in stocks of other companies, and retained earnings. The paid-in capital section discloses the investment made in the corporation by the stockholder-owners. It will include the amount paid into the corporation by the stockholders for different types of equity instruments that have been issued by the corporation, such as preferred stock equity and common stock equity. Paid-in capital usually is separated into two parts—the par value of the stock and the amount paid in excess of the par value—as required by generally accepted accounting principles.

Adjustments for market value changes in available-for-sale investments in other companies are shown as a component of owners' equity. These adjustments also are reported in comprehensive income, because they reflect a change in owners' equity that is not a part of net income. Changes in the value of trading securities, which are short-term investments, are included in the calculation of net income, whereas changes in value of available-for-sale securities are reported only in owners' equity and the statement of comprehensive income.

The last category usually found under the heading of owners' equity is retained earnings. This amount represents any earnings (or the difference between total net income and net loss) since the inception of the business that have not been paid out to stockholders as dividends.

Returning to the aforementioned accounting equation, a user of financial statements can better understand that owners' equity is the balancing amount. If assets are considered a company's resources, they must equal the "sources" from which they came. The sources for assets are a company's creditors (as seen in the total of the liabilities) and its owners (as seen in the total for owners' equity). As such, retained earnings does not represent a fund of cash; instead it represents the portion of each asset that is owned by the stockholders. The remaining portion of each asset is owed to creditors in the form of liabilities.

It is important to keep in mind that the balance sheet does not present a company's market value. While some assets are presented at market value, others cannot be disclosed at market value because no such specific market value exists. The changes in the value of the assets that are required to be adjusted to market value for each balance sheet are included in either net income or comprehensive income, depending on the nature of the asset and the purpose for which management chose to acquire it.

Another important consideration about the balance sheet is the manner in which both assets and liabilities are separated into current and noncurrent groups. While not all companies will have all of the classifications discussed above, all will have both current and noncurrent items. This separation allows the user of the balance sheet to compare a company's current liquidity needs and resources to its long-term solvency status.

In conclusion, balance sheets are an important tool to help managers, lenders, and investors analyze a company's financial status and capabilities. They are particularly useful in helping to identify trends in the areas of payables and receivables. However, it is vital to remember that the document only presents a company's financial situation at a given point in time. It does not provide any information about the past decisions that helped the company to arrive at that point, or about the company's future direction or potential for success. For this reason, the balance sheet should be considered along with other required financial statements, as well as historical data, when evaluating a company's performance.

SEE ALSO: Cash Flow Analysis and Statement; Financial Issues for Managers; Financial Ratios; Income Statements

John M. Alvis
Revised by Laurie Hillstrom

FURTHER READING:

"Balance Sheets." *Business Owner's Toolkit.* 2005. CCH Tax and Accounting. Available from <http://www.toolkit.cch.com/text/P06_7035.asp>.

BusinessTown.com. "Basic Accounting: Balance Sheets." Available from <http://www.businesstown.com/accounting/basic-sheets.asp>.

Byrnes, Nanette. "The Downside of Disclosure: Too Much Data Can Be a Bad Thing. It's Quality of Information That Counts, Not Quantity." *Business Week,* 26 August 2002, 100.

Davenport, Todd. "The Uneven Evolution of Accounting Standards." *American Banker,* 28 July 2004.

BALANCED SCORECARD

The balanced scorecard is a performance measurement tool developed in 1992 by Harvard Business School professor Robert S. Kaplan and management consultant David P. Norton. Kaplan and Norton's research led them to believe that traditional financial measures, like return on investment, could not provide an accurate picture of a company's performance in the innovative business environment of the 1990s. Rather than forcing managers to choose between "hard" financial measures and "soft" operational measures—such as customer retention, product development cycle times, or employee satisfaction—they developed a method that would allow managers to consider both types of measures in a balanced way. "The balanced scorecard includes financial measures that tell the results of actions already taken," Kaplan and Norton explained in the seminal 1992 *Harvard Business Review* article that launched the balanced scorecard methodology. "And it complements the financial measures with operational measures on customer satisfaction, internal processes, and the organization's innovation and improvement activities—operational measures that are the drivers of future financial performance."

The balanced scorecard provides a framework for managers to use in linking the different types of measurements together. Kaplan and Norton recommend looking at the business from four perspectives: the customer's perspective, an internal business perspective, an innovation and learning perspective, and the financial (or shareholder's) perspective. Using the overall corporate strategy as a guide, managers derive three to five goals related to each perspective, and then develop specific measures to support each goal. Ideally, the scorecard helps managers to clarify their vision for the organization and translate that vision

into measurable actions that employees can understand. It also enables managers to balance the concerns of various stakeholders in order to improve the company's overall performance. "The balanced scorecard is a powerful concept based on a simple principle: managers need a balanced set of performance indicators to run an organization well," Paul McCunn wrote in *Management Accounting.* "The indicators should measure performance against the critical success factors of the business, and the 'balance' is the balancing tension between the traditional financial and nonfinancial operational, leading and lagging, and action-oriented and monitoring measures."

The balanced scorecard concept has enjoyed significant success since its introduction. According to the *Financial Times,* it was adopted by 80 percent of large U.S. companies as of 2004, making it the nation's most popular management tool for increasing performance. In addition, it has increasingly been applied in the public sector since it was promoted by the National Partnership for Reinventing Government. Part of the balanced scorecard's popularity can be attributed to the fact that it is consistent with many common performance improvement initiatives undertaken by companies, such as continuous improvement, cross-functional teamwork, or customer-supplier partnering. It complements these initiatives by helping managers to understand the complex interrelationships among different business areas. By linking the elements of a company's competitive strategy in one report, the balanced scorecard points out situations

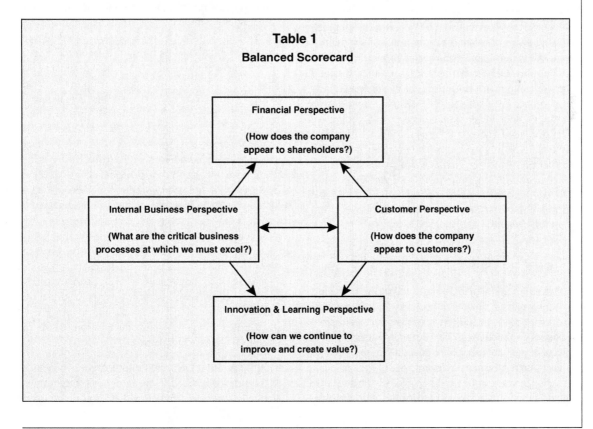

Table 1
Balanced Scorecard

Financial Perspective

(How does the company appear to shareholders?)

Internal Business Perspective

(What are the critical business processes at which we must excel?)

Customer Perspective

(How does the company appear to customers?)

Innovation & Learning Perspective

(How can we continue to improve and create value?)

where improvement in one area comes at the expense of another. In this way, the scorecard helps managers to make the decisions and tradeoffs necessary for success in today's fast-paced and competitive business environment.

HISTORY OF THE BALANCED SCORECARD APPROACH

In 1990 Robert S. Kaplan, a professor of accounting at the Harvard Business School, and David P. Norton, co-founder of a Massachusetts-based strategy consulting firm called Renaissance Worldwide Inc., conducted a year-long research project involving 12 large companies. The original idea behind the study, as Anita van de Vliet explained in *Management Today,* was that "relying primarily on financial accounting measures was leading to short-term decision-making, over-investment in easily valued assets (through mergers and acquisitions) with readily measurable returns, and under-investment in intangible assets, such as product and process innovation, employee skills, or customer satisfaction, whose short-term returns are more difficult to measure" (1997, pp.78).

Kaplan and Norton looked at the way these companies used performance measurements to control the behavior of managers and employees. They used their findings to devise a new performance measurement system that would provide businesses with a balanced view of financial and operational measures. Kaplan and Norton laid out their balanced scorecard approach to performance measurement in three *Harvard Business Review* articles beginning in 1992. Before long, the balanced scorecard had become one of the hottest topics at management conferences around the world. In fact, the *Harvard Business Review* called it one of the most important and influential management ideas of the past 75 years. In 1996 Kaplan and Norton expanded upon their original concept in a book titled *The Balanced Scorecard: Translating Strategy into Action.* They followed up with two other books that further developed the approach: *The Strategy-Focused Organization: How Balanced Scorecard Companies Thrive in the New Business Environment* (2001) and *Strategy Maps: Converting Intangible Assets into Tangible Outcomes* (2004).

THE FOUR PERSPECTIVES

Kaplan and Norton's basic balanced scorecard asks managers to view their business from four different perspectives: the customer perspective, an internal business perspective, an innovation and learning perspective, and the financial or shareholder perspective. These perspectives are relevant to all types of businesses. However, additional perspectives also may be important in certain types of businesses. For example, a company in the oil industry might wish to incorporate an environmental regulation perspective. In this way, the balanced scorecard maintains some flexibility for companies with special needs to add other perspectives.

CUSTOMER PERSPECTIVE. According to Kaplan and Norton, viewing a business from the customer perspective involves asking the question: "How do customers see us?" They contend that many companies in a wide range of industries have made customer service a priority. The balanced scorecard allows managers to translate this broad goal into specific measures that reflect the issues that are most important to customers. For example, Kaplan and Norton mention four main areas of customer concern: time, quality, cost, and performance. They recommend that companies establish a goal for each of these areas and then translate each goal into one or more specific measurements. Kaplan and Norton note that some possible measures, like percent of sales from new products, can be determined from inside the company. Other measures, like on-time delivery, will depend on the requirements of each customer. To incorporate such measures into the balanced scorecard, managers will need to obtain outside information through customer evaluations or benchmarking. Collecting data from outside the company is a valuable exercise because it forces managers to view their company from the customers' perspective.

INTERNAL BUSINESS PERSPECTIVE. The internal business perspective is closely related to the customer perspective. "After all, excellent customer performance derives from processes, decisions, and actions occurring throughout an organization," Kaplan and Norton wrote. "Managers need to focus on those critical internal operations that enable them to satisfy customer needs." Viewing a company from the internal business perspective involves asking the question, "What must we excel at?" Kaplan and Norton recommend focusing first on the internal processes that impact customer satisfaction, such as quality, productivity, cycle time, and employee skills. Using these critical processes as a base, managers should develop goals that will help the company to meet its customers' expectations. These goals should then be translated into measures that can be influenced by employee actions. It is important that internal goals and measures are broken down at the local level in order to provide a link between top management goals and individual employee actions. "This linkage ensures that employees at lower levels in the organization have clear targets for actions, decisions, and improvement activities that will contribute to the company's overall mission," the authors explained.

INNOVATION AND LEARNING PERSPECTIVE. In including the innovation and learning perspective in their balanced scorecard, Kaplan and Norton recognized that modern companies must make continual improvements in order to succeed in an intensely competitive global business environment. "A company's ability to innovate, improve, and learn ties directly to the company's value," they noted. That is, only through the ability to launch new products, create more value for customers, and improve operating efficiencies continually can a company penetrate new markets and increase revenues and margins—in short, grow and thereby increase shareholder value. Accordingly, viewing a business from the innovation and learning perspective involves asking the question, "How can we continue to improve and create value?" Managers should establish goals related to innovation and learning, and then translate the goals into specific measures—such as increasing the percentage of the company's sales derived from new products.

FINANCIAL PERSPECTIVE. Kaplan and Norton developed the balanced scorecard at a time when financial measures were increasingly coming under attack from management experts. Critics claimed that judging performance by financial measures encouraged companies to focus on short-term results and avoid taking actions that would create value over the long term. They also argued that financial measures looked backward at past actions rather than forward at future possibilities. Some experts told managers to focus solely on operational improvements and allow the financial performance to improve on its own.

Although these arguments convinced Kaplan and Norton to conduct their study of performance measurement, they found that financial controls are an important part of the puzzle. They claimed that managers need to know whether or not their operational improvements are reflected in the bottom line. If not, it may mean that management needs to reevaluate its strategy for the business. "Measures of customer satisfaction, internal business performance, and innovation and improvement are derived from the company's particular view of the world and its perspective on key success factors. But that view is not necessarily correct," Kaplan and Norton wrote. "Periodic financial statements remind executives that improved quality, response time, productivity, or new products benefit the company only when they are translated into improved sales and market share, reduced operating expenses, or higher asset turnover."

Thus, the fourth perspective in the balanced scorecard asks the question: "How do we look to shareholders?" Some of the goals a company might set in this area involve profitability, growth, and shareholder value. The measures attached to these goals might include traditional financial performance measures, such as return on assets or earnings per share. Although these measures can prove misleading when taken alone, when incorporated into a balanced scorecard they can provide managers with valuable infor-

mation about whether the strategy has contributed to bottom-line improvement. According to Kaplan and Norton, a common mistake for managers making large-scale operational improvements is failing to follow up with additional actions. For example, a company might undertake a quality improvement initiative which, when implemented successfully, creates excess capacity or makes certain employees redundant. Financial measurements will point out the need to make further changes.

DEVELOPING A BALANCED SCORECARD

Development of a balanced scorecard begins with the company's overall strategy or vision. It is important to consult with top management, rather than line managers, to obtain a clear picture of where the company wants to be in 3 to 5 years. The next step is to appoint a "scorecard architect" to establish the framework and methodology for designing the scorecard. With this framework in mind, the organization must define a linked set of strategic objectives that will lead the company toward top management's vision. These objectives should be true drivers of performance for the business as a whole, rather than a list of separate goals for business units or departments. It may be helpful to begin with the four perspectives included in the balanced scorecard model and then add more if needed, depending on the industry.

At this point, most companies will begin to involve line managers and staff members—and perhaps even customers—in establishing goals or objectives. The involvement might take the form of an executive workshop at which participants review and discuss the goals and appropriate measures. This approach builds consensus around the balanced scorecard and reduces the potential for unrealistic goals to be handed down from the top.

The strategic objectives provide a framework for managers to use in developing specific performance measures. "Most of the measures we use are not new, but they had been held in different silos, different boxes, in the organization," Rick Anderson, a performance analyst at BP Chemicals, told van de Vliet. "The [balanced scorecard] approach has brought existing measures onto one piece of paper, so everybody can relate to one area." The goals and measures in an organization's balanced scorecard can be broken down to provide custom scorecards for all business levels, even down to individual employees. These custom scorecards show how an employee's work activities link to the business's overall strategy. For incentive and compensation purposes, it is possible to assign weights to each measure based on its importance to the company and the individual's ability to affect it.

Once the balanced scorecard is in place, the next step is to collect and analyze the data for performance measurements. This data will enable the organization to see its strong performance areas, as well as areas for potential improvement. It is important to supply the performance data to employees, and to empower employees to find ways to sustain high performance and improve poor performance. Managers also must realize that the balanced scorecard is not set in stone. Experience in using the scorecard may point out areas that should be modified or adapted. In addition, managers may find ways to tie the scorecard into other areas, such as budgets, resource allocation, compensation, succession planning, and employee development.

AVOIDING POTENTIAL PITFALLS

Numerous organizations have implemented some version of the balanced scorecard since its introduction in 1992. However, professor Claude Lewy of the Free University of Amsterdam found that 70 percent of scorecard implementations failed. Many companies are attracted by the power and simplicity of the balanced scorecard concept, but then find implementation to be extremely time-consuming and expensive. Lewy admits that the balanced scorecard can be an effective way of translating an overall strategy to the many parts of an organization. However, he stresses that organizations must have a clear idea of what they want to accomplish, and be willing to commit the necessary resources in order to successfully implement the balanced scorecard. Along with Lex Du Mee of KPMG Management Consulting, Lewy conducted a study of seven European companies and came up with what he called the Ten Commandments of Balanced Scorecard Implementation.

In order to ensure an effective balanced scorecard implementation, Lewy and Du Mee recommended that organizations obtain the commitment of a top-level sponsor, as well as relevant line managers. The balanced scorecard initiative must be the organization's top priority if implementation is to succeed. They also emphasized the importance of putting strategic goals in place before implementing the scorecard. Otherwise, the goals and measures included in the scorecard are likely to drive the wrong behavior. Lewy and Du Mee also suggested that organizations try a pilot program before moving on to full-scale implementation. Testing the balanced scorecard in a few key business areas enables managers to make necessary changes and increase support for the initiative before involving the entire company. It also is important to provide information and training to employees prior to an organization-wide rollout.

Lewy and Du Mee also warn managers against using the balanced scorecard as a way to achieve extra top-down control. Employees are unlikely to support the goals and measures if the scorecard is used as a "gotcha" by management. Another potential pitfall, according to the researchers, is trying to use a standardized scorecard. Instead, they stress that each organization must devote the time and resources to develop its own customized program. Lewy and Du Mee found that balanced scorecard implementation was more likely to fail when companies underestimated the amount of training and communication required during the introductory phase, or the extra workload and costs involved with periodic reporting later on. Even though the balanced scorecard appears to be a simple idea, implementing it is likely to mean huge changes in an organization.

SOFTWARE AND SUPPORT

Once the balanced scorecard has been implemented successfully, the next significant task involves collecting and analyzing measurement data. Some companies found this process to be time-consuming and expensive, because the data was located on numerous different computer systems throughout the organization. However, by the 2000s a number of technological advances—such as data warehouses, enterprise resource planning systems, decision-support tools, groupware, and Internet technology—made data collection and analysis significantly easier. In fact, several software vendors created balanced scorecard applications for desktop computers. Typical software packages allow users to plug in the performance measures the company has chosen to monitor. The computer then collects the data and supplies performance grades according to formulas the company has determined. With the advent of electronic balanced scorecard applications, the process of performance measurement can be automated throughout a company.

In addition, Kaplan and Norton have used computer technology to provide information and support to organizations that adopt the balanced scorecard. For example, Norton's consulting firm, Renaissance Worldwide Inc., and Gentia Software formed the Balanced Scorecard Technology Council. This virtual users group sponsors a Web site (www.balancedscorecard.com) that provides research, product information, and a forum for ideas. Kaplan and Norton also founded an organization called the Balanced Scorecard Collaborative "to facilitate worldwide awareness, use, enhancement, and integrity of the Balanced Scorecard as a value-added management process." The collaborative also hosts a Web site at www.bsccol.com.

SEE ALSO: Performance Measurement; Strategy Formulation

Laurie Collier Hillstrom

FURTHER READING:

Cameron, Preston. "The Balancing Act: Even in Today's Volatile Economic Climate, Many Organizations Are Turning to the Balanced Scorecard to Help Steer Their Organization in the Right Direction." *CMA Management* 75, no. 10 (2002).

Kaplan, Robert S., and David P. Norton. "The Balanced Scorecard—Measures That Drive Performance." *Harvard Business Review* 70, no. 1 (1992): 71.

———. *The Balanced Scorecard: Translating Strategy into Action.* Boston: Harvard Business School Press, 1996.

———. "Putting the Balanced Scorecard to Work." *Harvard Business Review* 71, no. 5 (1993).

———. *The Strategy-Focused Organization: How Balanced Scorecard Companies Thrive in the New Business Environment.* Boston: Harvard Business School Press, 2001.

———. *Strategy Maps: Converting Intangible Assets into Tangible Outcomes.* Boston: Harvard Business School Press, 2004.

———. "Using the Balanced Scorecard as a Strategic Management System." *Harvard Business Review* 74, no. 1 (1996): 75.

Lester, Tom. "Measure for Measure: The Balanced Scorecard Remains a Widely Used Management Tool, but Great Care Must Be Taken to Select Appropriate and Relevant Metrics." *The Financial Times,* 6 October 2004.

Lewy, Claude, and Lex Du Mee. "The Ten Commandments of Balanced Scorecard Implementation." *Management Control and Accounting,* April 1998.

McCunn, Paul. "The Balanced Scorecard. . .the Eleventh Commandment." *Management Accounting* 76, no. 11 (1998): 34.

van de Vliet, Anita. "The New Balancing Act." *Management Today,* July 1997, 78.

Williams, Kathy. "What Constitutes a Successful Balanced Scorecard?" *Strategic Finance* 86, no. 5 (2004).

BAR CODING AND RADIO FREQUENCY IDENTIFICATION

A barcode is a series of parallel black bars and white spaces, both of varying widths. Bars and spaces together are called elements. Different combinations of the bars and spaces represent different characters, such as numbers or letters. Each combination or sequence of bars and spaces is a code that can be translated into information such as price, product type, place of manufacture, or origin of shipment.

Barcodes are simple to use, accurate, and quick. Almost everyone is familiar with their use in retail establishments. They are also often used in warehouses and manufacturing for selecting items from storage, receiving goods, and shipping.

The FDA requires that a product's national drug code be placed on the container label and outer wrapper on most prescription drugs and about 70 percent of over-the-counter drugs and on blood and blood components intended for transfusion. The U.S. Food and Drug Administration (FDA) estimates that this will prevent nearly 500,000 adverse events and blood transfusion errors and save $98 billion in reduced healthcare costs over a two year period.

HOW BARCODING WORKS

BARCODE READERS. The barcode itself does not actually contain detailed information. The barcode simply provides a reference number that cues a computer to access information. A barcode reader is required to read a barcode. Barcode readers may be fixed, portable batch, or portable RF. Fixed readers are attached to a host computer and terminal, and transmit one item at a time as the data is scanned. Battery-powered portable batch readers store data into memory for batch transfer into a host computer at a later time. The portable RF reader can transmit data in real-time, on-line.

SCANNERS AND DECODERS. The basic reader consists of a scanner and a decoder. Scanners capture the image of the barcode, and the decoder takes the digitized bar space patterns, decodes them, and transmits the decoded data to the computer.

There are several types of scanners. Laser scanners use a single spot of light to sweep across the barcode in a linear fashion. CCD scanners use an LED array with thousands of light detectors; the entire barcode image is captured and then transmitted. Automatic scanners are in a fixed position and read barcodes as they go by on a conveyor. Handheld scanners, such as wands, are portable and may be carried from place to place, as in a warehouse.

When a scanner is passed over the barcode, the dark bars absorb the scanner's light while the light spaces reflect it. A photocell detector receives the reflected light and converts it into an electrical signal. A low electrical signal is created for the reflected light and a high electrical signal is created for the dark bars. The width of the element determines the duration of the electrical signal. The decoder then decodes the signal into the characters represented by the barcode and passes it to a computer in traditional data format.

TYPES OF BARCODES

There are different types of barcodes. Some barcodes are entirely numeric, whereas others have numeric and alphabetic characters. The type used is dependent upon the implementation, the data that needs to be encoded, and how the barcode is to be printed. There are several barcode standards, called symbologies, each serving a different purpose. Each standard defines the printed symbol and how the scanner reads and decodes the printed symbol.

The Uniform Product Code (UPC) has been the North American standard for several decades. Others include the Automotive Industry Action Group (AIAG), the European Article Numbering System (EAN), and the Reduced Space Symbology (RSS)—an emerging standard for compressing barcodes so that they can fit into small spaces such as a prescription bottle, and the Global Trade Item Number (GTIN) or "Gee-tin," which can read and store other types of code.

RFID

Radio frequency identification (RFID) could become the most far-reaching wireless technology since the cell phone. RFID is a method of remotely storing and retrieving data using a small object attached to or incorporated into a product. Its purpose is to enable data to be transmitted via a portable device called a tag, read by a reader, and processed according to the needs of the particular application.

Transmitted data may provide information about product location, or specifics such as color, price, or purchase date. In some systems a return receipt can be generated. RFID tags contain far more detailed information than can be placed on a barcode. Some tags hold enough information to provide routing information for shipping containers, as well as a detailed inventory of what is inside the container.

An RFID system consists of tags, tag readers, tag programming stations, circulation readers, sorting equipment, and tag inventory wands. The tag is the key component. Data can be printed or etched on an electronic substrate and then embedded in a plastic or laminated paper tag.

Tags are classified according to their radio frequency: low-frequency, high-frequency, UHF, and microwave. Low-frequency tags are commonly used in automobile anti-theft systems and animal identification. High-frequency tags are used in library books, pallet tracking, building access, airline baggage tracking, and apparel tracking. Low- and high-frequency tags can be used without a license. UHF tags are used to track pallets, containers, trucks, and trailers. UHF cannot be used globally as there is no one global standard. Microwave tags are used in long-range access, such as General Motors' OnStar system.

While most RFID tags are write-once/read-only, there are some that offer read/write capability. These tags would allow tag data to be rewritten if need be.

Also, tags may be either passive or active. Passive tags do not have their own power supply. Their power comes from a minute electrical current induced by an incoming radio-frequency scan. Active tags have their own power source. The lack of a power source makes the passive tag much less expensive to manufacture and much smaller (thinner than a sheet of paper) than an active tag. As a result, the vast majority of RFID tags are passive. However, the response of a passive tag is typically just an ID number. Active tags have longer ranges, the ability to store more information, and are more accurate and reliable.

The tag contains a transponder with a digital memory chip with a unique electronic product code. A stationary or handheld device called an interrogator, consisting of an antenna, transceiver, and decoder, emits a signal creating an electromagnetic zone. When a tag comes within the range of a reader, it detects an activation signal that causes the tag to "wake up" and start sending data. The reader captures the data encoded in the tag's integrated circuit, decodes it, and sends it over a network to a host computer for processing.

THE ADVANTAGES OF RFID OVER BARCODING

RFID tags can contain far more detailed information than barcodes. Barcodes require a clear line of sight between the scanner and the barcode, a need that is absent from the RFID. It is also only possible to scan just one barcode at a time. Within the field of a reader, hundreds of RFID tags could be read within seconds. RFID codes are long enough that every RFID tag may have a unique code, allowing an individual item to be tracked as it changes location. Barcodes are limited to a single code for all stages of movement of a particular product.

Despite its advantages, it is unlikely that RFID will replace barcoding. The cost of tags is prohibitive in many situations, and there is less need to track individual products from origin to final consumer.

RFID USES

During WWII, RFID devices were used to distinguish British planes from inbound German planes. Modern uses include:

- Toll booths-RFID tags are used for electronic toll collection. Tags are read as vehicles pass causing debits from prepaid accounts.

- Electronic cash-cards imbedded with RFID chips can be used as electronic cash.

- Prisons-The Ohio Dept. of Rehabilitation and Correction requires inmates to wear transmitters. Prison computers are alerted if a prisoner tries to remove his tag.

- Food-Refrigerators will someday be able to track the expiration dates of the food it contains. SAP is working with Australian cattle ranchers to mark their animals with RFID tags and mark the cuts of meat derived from individual cows. This would allow companies to recall meat infected with contaminants such as bovine spongiform encephalopathy and avoid wholesale destruction of cattle.

- Humans-Medical information can be recorded on RFID tags implanted under human skin. This has already been approved by the FDA.

- Electronic keys-The majority of new cars come equipped with keys embedded with RFID tags containing unique identifiers. If a thief uses a key without the tag, the car will be immobilized within minutes. The same concept can be used to secure buildings and facilities.

- Merchandise-RFID tags can be used to track assets, manage inventory, and authorize payments. The Gap retail clothing chain uses shelves with RFID readers that monitor inventory by gathering information through layers of clothing. Wal-Mart, Home Depot, and other giant retailers are investing heavily in RFID technology to improve supply chain efficiency and track products. Wal-Mart has already mandated RFID use from its top 100 suppliers.

- Counterfeiting-The European Union is considering introducing RFID tags onto banknotes to prevent forgery. RFID tagged drugs can be monitored from factory to use, preventing drug counterfeiting. Branded merchandise tagged with unique serial numbers can be authenticated at various stages of its supply chain, thus thwarting potential counterfeiters.

CONTROVERSY OVER RFID USE

The use of RFID has caused some concern for privacy advocates. They feel that it may be a privacy violation for a consumer unaware of the presence an RFID tracking tag, or if they are unable to remove or deactivate it. Other concerns revolve around the ability to fraudulently or surreptitiously read a tag from a distance, and the ability to identify a purchaser through the use of a credit card or a loyalty card.

RFID advocates, however, feel that opposition will lessen as RFID use becomes more widespread and its use across a wide range of industries becomes apparent.

RFID usage is destined to continue and to expand, especially as costs decline and RFID technology is improved.

SEE ALSO: Distribution and Distribution Requirements Planning; Logistics and Transportation; Reverse Supply Chain Logistics; Supply Chain Management; Warehousing and Warehouse Management

R. Anthony Inman

FURTHER READING:

"Barcoding for Beginners & Bar Code FAQ." IDAutomation. com, Inc. Available from http://www.idautomation.com/barcoding4beginners.html.

Brewin, Bob. "Radio Frequency Identification." *ComputerWorld*, 16 December 2002.

Corcoran, Cate T. "Wal-Mart's Mandate: The Retailer's RFID Initiative Generates Mixed Signals." *Women's Wear Daily* 189, no. 8: 16B.

Coyle, John J., Edward J. Bardi, and C. John Langley, Jr. *The Management of Business Logistics.* Mason, OH: Thomson South–Western, 2003.

"FDA Issues Final Barcoding Rule for Drugs and Blood." *Healthcare Financial Management* 58, no. 4: 12.

Forcinio, Hallie. "Prepare for Barcoding." *Pharmaceutical Technology* 28, no. 5: 38–43.

Glover, Tony. "RFID Tags Could Be the Saviour of Supply Chain Management." *MicroScope,* 11 October 2004, 12.

In-Stat. "RFID Tag Market to Approach $3 Billion in 2009." Available from <http://www.instat.com/newmk.asp?ID=1206>.

Mayfield, Kendra. "Radio ID Tags: Beyond Barcodes." *Wired News,* 20 May 2002.

"Market Research into RFID." *Printing World,* 3 March 2005, 46.

"Organic RFID Tags." *R&D* 47, no. 2 (February 2005): 17.

Power, Denise. "RFID Eyed to Thwart Counterfeiting." *Women's Wear Daily* 189, no. 49: 16B.

"RFID Report." *Supply Chain Management Review* 9, no. 2 (March 2005): 60.

Spiegel, Robert. "Barcoding: An Extra Digit for Logistics." *Logistics Management* 442, no. 6: 44.

Worth Data. "Bar Code Basics." Available from <http://www.Barcodehq.com/primer.htm>.

BASES OF POWER

SEE: Leadership Styles and Bases of Power

Benchmarking is the process through which a company measures its products, services, and practices against its toughest competitors, or those companies recognized as leaders in its industry. Benchmarking is one of a manager's best tools for determining whether the company is performing particular functions and activities efficiently, whether its costs are in line with those of competitors, and whether its internal activities and business processes need improvement. The idea behind benchmarking is to measure internal processes against an external standard. It is a way of learning which companies are best at performing certain activities and functions and then imitating—or better still, improving on—their techniques.

Benchmarking focuses on company-to-company comparisons of how well basic functions and processes are performed. Among many possibilities, it may look at how materials are purchased, suppliers are paid, inventories are managed, employees are trained, or payrolls are processed; at how fast the company can get new products to market; at how the quality control function is performed; at how customer orders are filled and shipped; and at how maintenance is performed.

Benchmarking enables managers to determine what the best practice is, to prioritize opportunities for improvement, to enhance performance relative to customer expectations, and to leapfrog the traditional cycle of change. It also helps managers to understand the most accurate and efficient means of performing an activity, to learn how lower costs are actually achieved, and to take action to improve a company's cost competitiveness. As a result, benchmarking has been used in many companies as a tool for obtaining a competitive advantage.

Companies usually undertake benchmarking with a view towards the many improvements that it may offer. These benefits include reducing labor cost, streamlining the work flow through reengineered business processes and common administrative systems, improving data center operations through consolidation and downsizing, cooperative business and information technology planning, implementing new technology, outsourcing some assignments and functions, redesigning the development and support processes, and restructuring and reorganizing the information technology functions.

BENCHMARKING BASICS

The goal of benchmarking is to identify the weaknesses within an organization and improve upon them, with the idea of becoming the "best of the best." The benchmarking process helps managers to find gaps in performance and turn them into opportunities for improvement. Benchmarking enables companies to identify the most successful strategies used by other companies of comparable size, type, or regional location, and then adopt relevant measures to make their own programs more efficient. Most companies apply benchmarking as part of a broad strategic process. For example, companies use benchmarking in order to find breakthrough ideas for improving processes, to support quality improvement programs, to motivate staffs to improve performance, and to satisfy management's need for competitive assessments.

Benchmarking targets roles, processes, and critical success factors. Roles are what define the job or function that a person fulfills. Processes are what consume a company's resources. Critical success factors are issues that company must address for success over the long-term in order to gain a competitive advantage. Benchmarking focuses on these things in order to point out inefficiencies and potential areas for improvement.

A company that decides to undertake a benchmarking initiative should consider the following questions: When? Why? Who? What? and How?

WHEN. Benchmarking can be used at any time, but is usually performed in response to needs that arise within a company. According to C.J. McNair and Kathleen H.J. Leibfried in their book *Benchmarking: A Tool for Continuous Improvement,* some potential "triggers" for the benchmarking process include:

- quality programs
- cost reduction/budget process
- operations improvement efforts
- management change
- new operations/new ventures
- rethinking existing strategies
- competitive assaults/crises

WHY. This is the most important question in management's decision to begin the benchmarking process. McNair and Leibfried suggest several reasons why companies may embark upon benchmarking:

- to signal management's willingness to pursue a philosophy that embraces change in a proactive rather than reactive manner;
- to establish meaningful goals and performance measures that reflect an external/customer focus, foster "quantum leap" thinking, and focus on high-payoff opportunities;
- to create early awareness of competitive disadvantage; and

- to promote teamwork that is based on competitive need and is driven by concrete data analysis, not intuition or gut feeling.

WHO. Companies may decide to benchmark internally, against competitors, against industry performance, or against the "best of the best." Internal benchmarking is the analysis of existing practice within various departments or divisions of the organization, looking for best performance as well as identifying baseline activities and drivers. Competitive benchmarking looks at a company's direct competitors and evaluates how the company is doing in comparison. Knowing the strengths and weaknesses of the competition is not only important in plotting a successful strategy, but it can also help prioritize areas of improvement as specific customer expectations are identified. Industry benchmarking is more trend-based and has a much broader scope. It can help establish performance baselines. The best-in-class form of benchmarking examines multiple industries in search of new, innovative practices. It not only provides a broad scope, but also it provides the best opportunities over that range.

WHAT. Benchmarking can focus on roles, processes, or strategic issues. It can be used to establish the function or mission of an organization. It can also be used to examine existing practices while looking at the organization as a whole to identify practices that support major processes or critical objectives. When focusing on specific processes or activities, the depth of the analysis is a key issue. The analysis can take the form of vertical or horizontal benchmarking. Vertical benchmarking is where the focus is placed on specific departments or functions, while horizontal benchmarking is where the focus is placed on a specific process or activity. Concerning strategic issues, the objective is to identify factors that are of greatest importance to competitive advantage, to define measures of excellence that capture these issues, and to isolate companies that appear to be top performers in these areas.

HOW. Benchmarking uses different sources of information, including published material, trade meetings, and conversations with industry experts, consultants, customers, and marketing representatives. The emergence of Internet technology has facilitated the benchmarking process. The Internet offers access to a number of databases-like Power-MARQ from the nonprofit American Productivity and Quality Center-containing performance indicators for thousands of different companies. The Internet also enables companies to conduct electronic surveys to collect benchmarking data. How a company benchmarks may depend on available resources, deadlines, and the number of alternative sources of information.

TYPES OF BENCHMARKING

There are a number of different types of benchmarking, which are driven by different motivating factors and thus involve different comparisons. Some of the major types of benchmarking are as follows: Metric benchmarking is the use of quantitative measures as reference points for comparisons. Best-practice benchmarking focuses on identifying outstanding techniques. Information technology benchmarking includes data processing, systems analysis, programming, end-user support, and networks. Infrastructure benchmarking includes data centers, networks, data/ information, end-user support, and distribution remote centers. Application benchmarking includes system analysis, development and maintenance programming, and functionality. Strategy benchmarking includes skills assessment, information technology strategy, business-technology alignment, and delineation of roles and responsibilities.

There are many motivators that drive the different types of benchmarking. Application benchmarking and infrastructure benchmarking, for example, use such motivators as cost, quality, competition, and goal setting. An advantage of benchmarking is that it facilitates the process of change, clearly laying out the types of solutions external organizations have used and providing a global perspective on how part of the company affects the whole. It further helps focus improvement in the areas where actual gains can be made, which translates into value added to the company as well as its employees.

SUCCESSFUL BENCHMARKING

There are several keys to successful benchmarking. Management commitment is one that companies frequently name. Since management from top to bottom is responsible for the continued operation and evaluation of the company, it is imperative that management be committed as a team to using and implementing benchmarking strategies. A strong network of personal contacts as well as having an open mind to ideas is other keys. In order to implement benchmarking at all stages, there must be a well-trained team of people in order for the process to work accurately and efficiently. Based on the information gathered by a well-trained team, there must also be an effort toward continuous improvement. Other keys include a benchmarking process that has historical success, sufficient time and staff, and complete understanding of the processes to be benchmarked.

In almost any type of program that a company researches or intends to implement, there must be goals and objectives set for that specific program. Benchmarking is no different. Successful companies determine goals and objectives, focus on them, keep them simple, and follow through on them. As in any program, it is always imperative to gather accurate and consistent information. The data should be understood and able to be defined as well as measured. The data must be able to be interpreted in order to make comparisons with other organizations. Lastly, keys to successful benchmarking include a thorough follow-through process and assistance from consultants with experience in designing and establishing such programs.

THE FUTURE OF BENCHMARKING

Although early work in benchmarking focused on the manufacturing sector, it is now considered a management tool that can be applied to virtually any business. It has become commonplace for companies to use in order to compete in and lead their respective industries. It has helped many reduce costs, increase productivity, improve quality, and strengthen customer service.

In his book *Benchmarking the Information Technology Function,* Charles B. Greene noted that companies are increasingly interested in benchmarking for a number of activities, including:

- cost of supporting business driver (transaction costs, or cost per order)
- systems development activities, including maintenance, backlogs, development productivity and project management
- end-user support
- data centers/communication networks
- skills management
- business strategy alignment
- technology management
- customer/user satisfaction

According to a 2003 Bain and Company survey quoted in Financial Executive, benchmarking received the second-highest usage score (84 percent) among more than two dozen management tools used by senior executives around the world. The survey also reported that users tend to be highly satisfied (rated 3.96 on a 5-point scale) with the results benchmarking provides to their companies.

SEE ALSO: Competitive Advantage; Continuous Improvement; World-Class Manufacturer

James C. Koch
Revised by Laurie Hillstrom

FURTHER READING:

Engle, Paul. "World-Class Benchmarking." *Industrial Engineer* August 2004.

Greene, Charles B. *Benchmarking the Information Technology Function.* New York: The Conference Board, 1993.

Mard, Michael J., et al. *Driving Your Company's Value: Strategic Benchmarking for Value.* New Jersey: John Wiley, 2004.

McNair, C.J., and Kathleen H.J. Leibfried. *Benchmarking: A Tool for Continuous Improvement.* Harper Business, 1992.

Powers, Vicki. "Boosting Business Performance through Benchmarking." *Financial Executive* (November 2004).

Tirbutt, Edmund. "Brimming with Confidence: Benchmarking Your Perks against Your Rivals' Can Provide HR with Added Reassurance." *Employee Benefits* (November 2004).

BODY LANGUAGE

People in the workplace can convey a great deal of information without even speaking; this is called nonverbal communication. Nonverbal communication can convey just as much as written and verbal communication, and human beings read and react to these nonverbal signals in the workplace. Body language is nonverbal communication that involves body movement and gestures, which communications researchers call *kinesics*. There are hundreds of thousands of possible signs that can be communicated through body movements and gestures. In addition to body movements and gestures, the nonverbal cues given through facial expressions and eye contact, personal space, and touch, influence individual interactions in the workplace. While this body language is fairly well understood in general in each culture, there are major cultural differences in nonverbal communication.

BODY MOVEMENTS AND GESTURE

Gestures, or movements of the head, hands, arms, and legs can be used to convey specific messages that have linguistic translations. For example, a person might use a wave their hand rather than saying "hello", or nod his or her head in agreement, which means "yes" or "okay." These gestures can be very useful in the workplace because they are a quick way to convey thoughts and feelings without needing to speak or write. Additionally, many such gestures are generally widely understood, although they may carry different meanings in other cultures. For instance, although the "ok" sign that is made through touch of the thumb and forefinger with the remaining fingers extended is seen as a positive gesture in the U.S., in some other cultures, this is seen as a vulgar gesture.

In addition to the gestures that people use that have a particular meaning, people also use gestures that do not have specific, generally understood meanings. These gestures, called illustrators, add meaning to a verbal message. For instance, when giving a presentation, a person might use hand gestures to emphasize a point. Many people use gestures while speaking to others to accompany their words, and while these body movements may not have a meaning that can be pinpointed, they serve to embellish a person's words.

A person's body movements that convey feelings and emotions through facial expressions and body positions are called affect displays. These body movements may indicate whether a person is open and receptive, angry, distracted, or a number of other emotions. Many affect displays are commonly interpreted; for instance, individuals who sit in a slumped position and frown are believed to be disinterested or unhappy. Those who sit upright, smile, and have raised eyebrows, are seen as interested and happy. While these affect displays are often appropriately interpreted, they may not be related to the interaction with another person, and thus may be misread. For instance, if a person has a terrible headache, he may squint, look down, and grimace during a conversation, indicating to the speaker that he disagrees with her, even if he is receptive to and in agreement with the speaker.

Researchers also categorize certain nonverbal behaviors called *adaptors,* which are typically unconscious behaviors and are used when a person is tense or anxious. Examples of illustrators are adjusting one's clothes, biting one's nails, or fidgeting and toying with an object. Illustrators indicate to others that a person is upset or nervous, and behavior such as this during a job interview or a meeting with a coworker may be interpreted very negatively. A person who engages in such behavior may be seen as preoccupied, anxious, or even as dishonest. As with affect displays, such body language may not convey true feelings; a person who fidgets and bites her nails may be exhibiting such behaviors for innocuous reasons. Thus, while such behaviors are often interpreted correctly as presenting anxiety, they do not necessarily indicate that a person is in any way dishonest.

When listening to others, individuals often convey messages nonverbally. Therefore, care should be taken to avoid the following:

- Sitting or leaning back is a body movement that may convey disinterest in a speaker's words or disagreement with the speaker. Additionally, resting your chin on your hand may convey boredom. Conversely, leaning forward slightly, raising eyebrows, and making eye contact indicate that you are receptive to the speaker.

- Crossed arms often connote a defensive posture, which can indicate that a person is unhappy with the speaker, feels threatened by the speaker, or does not want to listen to the speaker.

- Adaptors, such as fidgeting or playing with objects, may indicate that you are nervous around the speaker or disinterested in the speaker's message.

FACIAL EXPRESSIONS AND EYE CONTACT

Although facial expressions and eye contact are not kinesics and therefore technically not body language, they are types of nonverbal communication that can have an effect on business relations. Researchers have found that people can identify with great accuracy seven separate human emotions, even after seeing only facial and eye expressions: sadness, happiness, anger, fear, surprise, contempt, and interest. Therefore, without speaking a word, a facial expression can convey a great deal of information to others. Similarly, eye contact or lack of eye contact can also indicate a person's attitudes and emotions.

Research indicates that people use four different facial management techniques to control our facial expressions. First, people intensify their facial expressions, or exaggerate them, in order to show strong emotion. For example, a saleswoman who just made a major sale might intensify her positive expression by smiling more broadly and raising her eyebrows. Second, people may deintensify their facial expressions when they control or subdue them. For instance, an employee who just found out that he got a raise might smile less or look less happy after finding out that his coworker did not get a raise. Third, a person neutralizes their expressions when they avoid showing any facial expression. A person might not show any emotion when being reprimanded in the workplace or when attempting to negotiate with another businessperson. Finally, humans mask their facial expressions. This occurs when a person hides his or her true emotions and conveys different emotions. For example, an employee might express enthusiasm to a manager who gives him an undesirable task in order to curry favor with that manager. Or, a customer service representative might express concern and caring in her facial expression, when in actuality she is annoyed by the customer. Each of these facial management techniques makes is possible for people to interact with one another in socially acceptable ways.

Making and maintaining eye contact can have positive outcomes in the workplace. Eye contact can be used to indicate to a person that you are receptive to what they have to say. Additionally, eye contact may indicate that you want to communicate with a person. Finally, eye contact can be used to express respect for a person by maintaining longer eye contact. Interestingly, refraining from making eye contact, such as looking down or away, may indicate a level of respect for someone of higher status. A lack of eye contact, or an unwillingness to maintain eye contact may indicate discomfort with a situation, a disinterest in the other person's words, or a dislike of the person. However, the degree to which a person does or does not make eye contact may be dependent on their own level of shyness or extraversion and cannot always be interpreted as a reaction to a particular person or situation.

PERSONAL SPACE

Researchers use the term *proxemic* to describe the way that a person uses space in communication. Each individual has a personal space, which is like an invisible bubble surrounding them. This bubble becomes larger or smaller, depending on the person with whom we interact. We are comfortable standing or sitting closer to someone we like and more comfortable with someone we dislike or don't know well standing or sitting at a distance. However, the amount of personal space that a person desires depends on many characteristics, including gender and age.

The personal space that a person prefers also depends on the situation. When interacting with friends, relatives, or conducting casual business, most people prefer a distance of one and a half to four feet. When conducting formal or impersonal business, most individuals prefer a personal space of 4 to 8 feet. Therefore, a person is likely to be more comfortable standing closely to a trusted coworker than to a new customer.

Although there are broad norms for a comfortable personal space, it is not uncommon for a person to feel that their personal space has been violated when another person sits or stands too closely. When personal space is violated, there are several reactions that people might have. First, they may withdraw by backing up or leaving the room. Second, if anticipating the possibility of a personal space violation, a person may avoid having their space violated. This could mean staying away from meetings, crowds, and parties. Third, people may insulate themselves from intrusion of personal space. A manager who puts her desk in her office in such a way that no one can sit near her is insulating. An employee who takes a seat at a the end of a table during a meeting might be doing so to prevent others from sitting near him. Finally, a person may fight to keep his personal space by asking the other person to back up or move away. In a business setting, it may be helpful to recognize the behaviors that others engage in when their personal space is violated. That is, if you notice that others step back from you when speaking, sit at more of a distance, or

if they seem physically uncomfortable, they may have a larger personal space, which should be respected.

TOUCH

In the workplace, people may use touch to communicate nonverbally. The functional-professional touch is businesslike and impersonal. The touch that a physician uses when conducting a physical examination is a functional-professional touch. However, touch is not a part of most professions, and thus, this type of touch is not used often in business settings. The social-polite touch, such as a handshake, is much more common. This type of touch is used to recognize other individuals. It is an expected touch in many business settings. Finally, the friendship-warmth touch shows that you value another as a person. A pat on the back or a hug is a friendship-warmth touch. In most workplaces, the social-polite touch is the only necessary touch, and most managers and employees are encouraged to avoid using touch (particularly the friendship-warmth touch) in the workplace. While many people see a hand on a shoulder or a pat on the back as a useful touch to convey encouragement or concern for another's well-being, sexual harassment fears have made many avoid all types of touch beyond handshakes.

CULTURAL DIFFERENCES

Across the U.S., most body language is consistently understood. However, in other nations and cultures, what is considered to be appropriate body language in one place, may be seen as highly inappropriate in others. As noted above, the American sign for "ok" may be seen as vulgar in other nations. Similarly, other types of gestures and body movements may convey unwanted negative meanings. Therefore, care should be taken before using gestures in other countries or with business partners from other countries. Body movements can also be misinterpreted based on culture. Although most people in the world understand the movement of the head up and down to mean "yes" or "I agree," this is not the case in all countries.

Norms and expectations regarding facial expressions and eye contact also differ across cultures. Because different cultures have different norms for respect, eye contact that is seen as relationship-building and respectful in the U.S. may be seen as challenging and disrespectful in other cultures.

Finally, personal space and touch are used differently in different nations. Americans tend to prefer larger amounts of personal space than do some Latin Americans, Italians, and Middle-Easterners. Germans, Chinese, and Japanese prefer larger amounts of personal space, similar to what Americans prefer. Thus, when conducting business with people from other cultures, it is important to understand and respect their personal space needs. Americans who do business with those who prefer less personal space may have to fight the urge to step back and therefore avoid insulting a business partner.

SEE ALSO: International Cultural Differences

Marcia J. Simmering

FURTHER READING:

Beall, Anne E. "Body Language Speaks." *Communication World* (March/April 2004): 18–20.

Knapp, M, L., and J.A. Hall. *Nonverbal Communication in Human Interaction.* 5th ed. Fort Worth, TX: Wadsworth, 2002.

Konnellan, Thomas K. "Great Expectations, Great Results." *HRMagazine* (June 2003): 155–158.

Ribbens, Geoff, and Richard Thompson. *Understanding Body Language.* Barron's Educational Series, 2001.

BRAINSTORMING

Brainstorming was developed by Alex F. Osborn in 1939 to enhance the ability of work groups to solve problems creatively. The participants in his early groups called his process "brainstorming" because it seemed to them that they were using their brains "to storm a creative problem and to do so in commando fashion, with each stormer audaciously attacking the same objective." According to David Whetten and Kim Cameron, there are four cardinal principles that govern effective brainstorming processes:

1. No evaluation of the effectiveness of any given alternative is to be undertaken while the group is generating alternatives. Evaluation of alternatives must come at a later stage in the problem-solving process.

2. The leader of the group must place no parameters upon the group regarding what kinds of alternatives or solutions should be suggested; in fact, the team leader should encourage the group to come up with novel ideas that normally would not receive consideration in the organization.

3. The quantity of ideas should initially take precedence over the quality of ideas; that is, the leader should push the group to produce a large number of ideas irrespective of their quality.

4. Participants should feel free to add to or modify previous ideas proposed by others; it

is often the case that marginal ideas that are added upon or altered in some fashion become transformed into powerful solutions. It should be emphasized that ideas do not belong to the individual who presents them, but to the group.

When generating ideas, it is best to have the members of a group first generate ideas individually and silently rather than shouting out ideas as an entire group. Research indicates that by having people work individually, they generate a greater number of unique ideas than when brainstorming as a group. After individual brainstorming, all ideas can be shared, and further brainstorming as a group can be used.

What topics should be addressed in brainstorming sessions? While theoretically it is possible to brainstorm around any topic, Osborn believed that the problem or topic should be specific rather than general; that is, it should be narrow enough so that the participants can easily comprehend its nature and target their responses to its solution. Also, multiple problems, such as brainstorming about what a new product should be named, how it should be packaged, and how it should be advertised, should not be set before a brainstorming group. The problems should be separated, and brainstormed in separate meetings that are devoted to one of the aforementioned topics.

Osborn believed the ideal size for a brainstorming group was between 5 and 10 people; however, he also contended that with the right kind of leader, large numbers of people of up to 100 could successfully participate in brainstorming sessions. However, research indicates that larger groups generally do not generate more ideas than small groups.

In order to facilitate success, leaders of brainstorming sessions should do the following:

1. Facilitators should teach the principles and objectives of brainstorming to the group before beginning the brainstorming session. Unless all group members understand these rules, the brainstorming effort will fail.

2. Facilitators must enforce the rules during the brainstorming session. Inevitably, people will begin evaluating suggestions during the "generation" phase of brainstorming or violate one of the other principles. When such violations occur, the leader must reteach the principle in question that has been violated, and relaunch the brainstorming process in the group.

3. Facilitators must ensure that the ideas are listed so that they can be referred to later when the group analyzes the ideas that it has generated. Idea records are often kept on flip charts, but an individual can record the information

and the results photocopied and distributed to the participants as well.

4. Facilitators should try to encourage all group members to get involved in the session and contribute ideas. Some group members may be reluctant to share their thoughts, which could lead to one or two participants dominating the session. A good facilitator finds ways to draw out ideas from all group members.

5. Facilitators need to keep the group focused and prevent participants from getting discouraged. Typically, participants offer several ideas at the beginning of a session; often these are the more obvious alternative solutions to the problem at hand. After these initial ideas are offered, the session might get bogged down as the quantity of ideas subsides. Facilitators should assist the group to push past this initial stage and continue working to come up with other alternatives, because it is at this point where truly creative solutions to problems may be offered.

6. Facilitators need to be able to restate and distill poorly articulated ideas in a way that clarifies without altering their meaning.

After a large set of ideas has been generated, they must then be evaluated and culled according to their efficacy. At this point, a large number of options are open to the leader in terms of how the ideas should be evaluated. However, generally it is advisable that the group who generated the ideas be accountable for evaluating them as well. During the analysis stage the leader must facilitate an evaluation of the ideas that the group generated. As the listed ideas are subtracted, merged, and refined in group discussion, it is common for a more comprehensive solution to the problem to be produced than what could have been generated individually or in other group problem-solving processes.

POTENTIAL PROBLEMS

Face-to-face brainstorming sessions may not always generate a large number of creative ideas for a variety of reasons. One problem with face-to-face sessions is called production blocking, which is basically anything that prevents a group member from verbalizing his or her ideas as they occur. Common production blocks are forgetting and distractions. Another problem with face-to-face sessions is evaluation apprehension, which simply means that individuals are afraid to vocalize their ideas. Evaluation apprehension might be caused because individuals are reluctant to share novel, but incompletely developed, ideas. Group members might also be afraid of how others will react if they suggest unpopular or politically sensitive alternatives.

Another potential problem with face-to-face brainstorming is social loafing, which occurs when individuals put forth less effort on a group project than they do working alone.

Electronic brainstorming sessions may reduce some of these problems. In online or network settings, participants can simultaneously contribute ideas, and can usually do so anonymously. Anonymity may make it more likely that individuals will contribute a larger number of creative alternatives. In fact, empirical research suggests that electronic sessions are generally more effective than face-to-face sessions in terms of the number of alternative ideas generated.

Although the anonymity offered by electronic brainstorming sessions may reduce the negative impact of some of the problems associated with face-to-face sessions, other research suggests that social loafing might still be a problem. One study published in the *Journal of Management Information Systems* found that allowing participants in electronic sessions to view and compare their participation rates against those of others in the group (e.g., a tally of how many ideas were suggested by each person) increased individuals' contributions of ideas, as everyone could readily see who was not participating much. In this study, electronic idea forums that allowed social comparison were the most productive, followed by anonymous electronic forums. Face-to-face sessions were the least productive in terms of the quantity of alternative solutions generated.

BRAINSTORMING AS CREATIVE DECISION MAKING

Because of its emphasis on group participation and creativity, brainstorming may also be seen as a tool for creative decision making. Creative decision making is a group decision-making technique in which group members attempt to generate as many alternative solutions as possible for a given problem. It is one of a number of decision-making tools that are used to ensure consideration of a diverse set of alternative solutions. Other common decision-making techniques include the nominal group technique and the Delphi technique.

SEE ALSO: Creativity; Decision Making; Group Dynamics; Problem Solving

Tim Barnett and Mark E. Mendenhall
Revised by Marcia J. Simmering

FURTHER READING:

Ditkoff, Mitchell. "Ten Skills for Brainstorming: Breakthrough Thinking." *Journal for Quality and Participation,* November/ December 1998, 30–32.

Ivancevich, John M., Robert Konopaske, and Michael T. Matteson. *Organizational Behavior and Management,* 7th ed. Boston: Irwin/McGraw-Hill, 2004.

Jones, Gareth R., Jennifer M. George, and Charles W.L. Hill. *Contemporary Management, 2nd edition.* Boston: Irwin/McGraw-Hill, 2000.

Osborn, Alex F. *Applied Imagination: Principles and Procedures of Creative Thinking.* New York: Scribner, 1953.

Shepherd, Morgan M., et al. "Invoking Social Comparison to Improve Electronic Brainstorming: Beyond Anonymity." *Journal of Management Information Systems* 12, no. 3 (1996): 155–168.

Whetten, David A., and Kim S. Cameron. *Developing Management Skills.* 6th ed. Upper Saddle River, NJ: Prentice Hall, 2005.

BREAK-EVEN POINT

A company's break-even point is the amount of sales or revenues that it must generate in order to equal its expenses. In other words, it is the point at which the company neither makes a profit nor suffers a loss. Calculating the break-even point (through break-even analysis) can provide a simple, yet powerful quantitative tool for managers. In its simplest form, break-even analysis provides insight into whether or not revenue from a product or service has the ability to cover the relevant costs of production of that product or service. Managers can use this information in making a wide range of business decisions, including setting prices, preparing competitive bids, and applying for loans.

BACKGROUND

The break-even point has its origins in the economic concept of the "point of indifference." From an economic perspective, this point indicates the quantity of some good at which the decision maker would be indifferent, i.e., would be satisfied, without reason to celebrate or to opine. At this quantity, the costs and benefits are precisely balanced.

Similarly, the managerial concept of break-even analysis seeks to find the quantity of output that just covers all costs so that no loss is generated. Managers can determine the minimum quantity of sales at which the company would avoid a loss in the production of a given good. If a product cannot cover its own costs, it inherently reduces the profitability of the firm.

MANAGERIAL ANALYSIS

Typically the scenario is developed and graphed in linear terms. Revenue is assumed to be equal for each unit sold, without the complication of quantity discounts. If no units are sold, there is no total revenue ($0). However, total costs are considered from two perspectives. Variable costs are those that increase with the quantity produced; for example, more materials will be required as more units are produced. Fixed costs, however, are those that will be incurred by the company even if no units are produced. In a company that produces a single good or service, this would include all costs necessary to provide the production environment, such as administrative costs, depreciation of equipment, and regulatory fees. In a multi-product company, fixed costs are usually allocations of such costs to a particular product, although some fixed costs (such as a specific supervisor's salary) may be totally attributable to the product.

Figure 1 displays the standard break-even analysis framework. Units of output are measured on the horizontal axis, whereas total dollars (both revenues and costs) are the vertical units of measure. Total revenues are nonexistent ($0) if no units are sold. However, the fixed costs provide a floor for total costs; above this floor, variable costs are tracked on a per-unit basis. Without the inclusion of fixed costs, all products for which marginal revenue exceeds marginal costs would appear to be profitable.

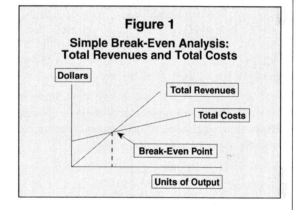

Figure 1

Simple Break-Even Analysis: Total Revenues and Total Costs

In Figure 1, the break-even point illustrates the quantity at which total revenues and total costs are equal; it is the point of intersection for these two totals. Above this quantity, total revenues will be greater than total costs, generating a profit for the company. Below this quantity, total costs will exceed total revenues, creating a loss.

To find this break-even quantity, the manager uses the standard profit equation, where profit is the difference between total revenues and total costs. Predetermining the profit to be $0, he/she then solves for the quantity that makes this equation true, as follows:

Let *TR* = Total revenues
TC = Total costs
P = Selling price
F = Fixed costs
V = Variable costs

Q = Quantity of output

$$TR = P \times Q$$
$$TC = F + V \times Q$$
$$TR - TC = \text{profit}$$

Because there is no profit ($0) at the break-even point, $TR - TC = 0$, and then $P \times Q - (F + V \times Q) = 0$. Finally, $Q = F(P - V)$.

This is typically known as the contribution margin model, as it defines the break-even quantity (Q) as the number of times the company must generate the unit contribution margin ($P - V$), or selling price minus variable costs, to cover the fixed costs. It is particularly interesting to note that the higher the fixed costs, the higher the break-even point. Thus, companies with large investments in equipment and/or high administrative-line ratios may require greater sales to break even.

As an example, if fixed costs are $100, price per unit is $10, and variable costs per unit are $6, then the break-even quantity is 25 ($100 ÷ [$10 – $6] = $100 ÷ $4). When 25 units are produced and sold, each of these units will not only have covered its own marginal (variable) costs, but will have also have contributed enough in total to have covered all associated fixed costs. Beyond these 25 units, all fixed costs have been paid, and each unit contributes to profits by the excess of price over variable costs, or the contribution margin. If demand is estimated to be at least 25 units, then the company will not experience a loss. Profits will grow with each unit demanded above this 25-unit break-even level.

While it is useful to know the quantity of sales at which a product will cease to generate losses, it may be even more useful to know the quantity necessary to generate a desired level of profit, say D.

$$TR - TC = D$$
$$P \times Q - (F + V \times Q) = D$$
$$\text{Then } Q = (F + D) \div (P - V)$$

This has the effect of regarding the desired profit as an increase in the fixed costs to be covered by sales of the product. As the decision-making process often requires profits for payback period, internal rate of return, or net present value analysis, this form may be more useful than the basic break-even model.

BASIC ASSUMPTIONS

There are several assumptions that affect the applicability of break-even analysis. If these assumptions are violated, the analysis may lead to erroneous conclusions.

It is tempting to the manager to set the contribution margin (and thus the price) by using the sales goal (or certain demand) as the quantity. However, sales goals and market demand are not necessarily equiva-

lent, especially if the customer is price-sensitive. Price-elasticity exists when customers will respond positively to lower prices and negatively to higher prices, and is particularly applicable to nonessential products. A small change in price may affect the sale of skis more than the sale of insulin, an inelastic-demand item due to its inherently essential nature. Therefore, using this method to set a prospective price for a product may be more appropriate for products with inelastic demand. For products with elastic demand, it is wiser to estimate demand based on an established, acceptable market price.

Typically, total revenues and total costs are modeled as linear values, implying that each unit of output incurs the same per-unit revenue and per-unit variable costs. Volume sales or bulk purchasing may incorporate quantity discounts, but the linear model appears to ignore these options.

A primary key to detecting the applicability of linearity is determining the relevant range of output. If the forecast of demand suggests that 100 units will be demanded, but quantity discounts on materials are applicable for purchases over 500 units from a single supplier, then linearity is appropriate in the anticipated range of demand (100 units plus or minus some forecast error). If, instead, quantity discounts begin at 50 units of materials, then the average cost of materials may be used in the model. A more difficult issue is that of volume sales, when such sales are frequently dependent on the ordering patterns of numerous customers. In this case, historical records of the proportionate quantity-discount sales may be useful in determining average revenues.

Linearity may not be appropriate due to quantity sales/purchases, as noted, or to the step-function nature of fixed costs. For example, if demand surpasses the capacity of a one-shift production line, then a second shift may be added. The second-shift supervisor's salary is a fixed-cost addition, but only at a sufficient level of output. Modeling the added complexity of nonlinear or step-function costs requires more sophistication, but may be avoided if the manager is willing to accept average costs to use the simpler linear model.

One obviously important measure in the break-even model is that of fixed costs. In the traditional cost-accounting world, fixed costs may be determined by full costing or by variable costing. Full costing assigns a portion of fixed production overhead charges to each unit of production, treating these as a variable cost. Variable costing, by contrast, treats these fixed production overhead charges as period charges; a portion of these costs may be included in the fixed costs allocated to the product. Thus, full costing reduces the denominator in the break-even model, whereas the variable costing alternative increases the denominator. While both of these methods increase the break-even point, they may not lend themselves to the same conclusion.

Recognizing the appropriate time horizon may also affect the usefulness of break-even analysis, as prices and costs tend to change over time. For a prospective outlook incorporating generalized inflation, the linear model may perform adequately. Using the earlier example, if all prices and costs double, then the break-even point $Q = 200 \div (20 - 12) = 200 \div 8 = 25$ units, as determined with current costs. However, weakened market demand for the product may occur, even as materials costs are rising. In this case, the price may shift downward to $18 to bolster price-elastic demand, while materials costs may rise to $14. In this case, the break-even quantity is 50 ($200 \div [18 - 14]$), rather than 25. Managers should project break-even quantities based on reasonably predictable prices and costs.

It may defy traditional thinking to determine which costs are variable and which are fixed. Typically, variable costs have been defined primarily as "labor and materials." However, labor may be effectively salaried by contract or by managerial policy that supports a full workweek for employees. In this case, labor should be included in the fixed costs in the model.

Complicating the analysis further is the concept that all costs are variable in the long run, so that fixed costs and the time horizon are interdependent. Using a make-or-buy analysis, managers may decide to change from in-house production of a product to subcontracting its production; in this case, fixed costs are minimal and almost 100 percent of the costs are variable. Alternatively, they may choose to purchase cutting-edge technology, in which case much of the variable labor cost is eliminated; the bulk of the costs then involve the (fixed) depreciation of the new equipment. Managers should project break-even quantities based on the choice of capital-labor mix to be used in the relevant time horizon.

Traditionally, fixed costs have been allocated to products based on estimates of production for the fiscal year and on direct labor hours required for production. Technological advances have significantly reduced the proportion of direct labor costs and have increased the indirect costs through computerization and the requisite skilled, salaried staff to support company-wide computer systems. Activity-based costing (ABC) is an allocation system in which managers attempt to identify "cost drivers" which accurately reflect the appropriate usage of fixed costs attributable to production of specific products in a multi-product firm. This ABC system tends to allocate, for example, the CEO's salary to a product based on his/her specific

time and attention required by this product, rather than on its proportion of direct labor hours to total direct labor hours.

EXTENSIONS OF BREAK-EVEN ANALYSIS

Break-even analysis typically compares revenues to costs. However, other models employ similar analysis.

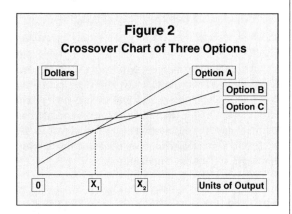

Figure 2
Crossover Chart of Three Options

In the crossover chart, the analyst graphs total-cost lines from two or more options. These choices may include alternative equipment choices or location choices. The only data needed are fixed and variable costs of each option. In Figure 2, the total costs (variable and fixed costs) for three options are graphed. Option A has the low-cost advantage when output ranges between zero and X units, whereas Option B is the least-cost alternative between X and X units of output. Above X units, Option C will cost less than either A or B. This analysis forces the manager to focus on the relevant range of demand for the product, while allowing for sensitivity analysis. If current demand is slightly less than X Option B would appear to be the best choice. However, if medium-term forecasts indicate that demand will continue to grow, Option C might be the least-cost choice for equipment expected to last several years. To determine the quantity at which Option B wrests the advantage from Option A, the manager sets the total cost of A equal to the total cost of B ($F_A + V_A \times Q = F_B + V_B \times Q$) and solves for the sole quantity of output (Q) that will make this equation true. Finding the break-even point between Options B and C follows similar logic.

The Economic Order Quantity (EOQ) model attempts to determine the least-total-cost quantity in the purchase of goods or materials. In this model, the total of ordering and holding costs is minimized at the quantity where the total ordering cost and total holding cost are equal, i.e., the break-even point between these two costs.

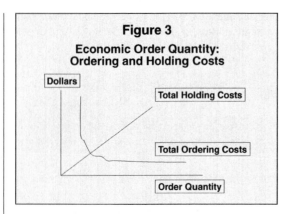

Figure 3
Economic Order Quantity:
Ordering and Holding Costs

As companies merge, layoffs are common. The newly formed company typically enjoys a stock-price surge, anticipating the leaner and meaner operations of the firm. Obviously, investors are aware that the layoffs reduce the duplication of fixed-cost personnel, leading to a smaller break-even point and thus profits that begin at a lower level of output.

APPLICATIONS IN SERVICE INDUSTRIES

While many of the examples used have assumed that the producer was a manufacturer (i.e., labor and materials), break-even analysis may be even more important for service industries. The reason for this lies in the basic difference in goods and services: services cannot be placed in inventory for later sale. What is a variable cost in manufacturing may necessarily be a fixed cost in services. For example, in the restaurant industry, unknown demand requires that cooks and table-service personnel be on duty, even when customers are few. In retail sales, clerical and cash register workers must be scheduled. If a barber shop is open, at least one barber must be present. Emergency rooms require round-the-clock staffing. The absence of sufficient service personnel frustrates the customer, who may balk at this visit to the service firm and may find competitors that fulfill the customer's needs.

The wages for this basic level of personnel must be counted as fixed costs, as they are necessary for the potential production of services, despite the actual demand. However, the wages for on-call workers might be better classified as variable costs, as these wages will vary with units of production. Services, therefore, may be burdened with an extremely large ratio of fixed-to-variable costs.

Service industries, without the luxury of inventoriable products, have developed a number of ways to provide flexibility in fixed costs. Professionals require appointments, and restaurants take reservations; when the customer flow pattern can be predetermined, excess personnel can be scheduled only when needed, reducing fixed costs. Airlines may shift low-demand flight legs to smaller aircraft, using less fuel and fewer attendants. Hotel and telecommunication managers advertise lower rates on weekends to smooth demand through slow business periods and avoid times when the high-fixed-cost equipment is underutilized. Retailers and banks track customer flow patterns by day and by hour to enhance their short-term scheduling efficiencies. Whatever method is used, the goal of these service industries is the same as that in manufacturing: reduce fixed costs to lower the break-even point.

Break-even analysis is a simple tool that defines the minimum quantity of sales that will cover both variable and fixed costs. Such analysis gives managers a quantity to compare to the forecast of demand. If the break-even point lies above anticipated demand, implying a loss on the product, the manager can use this information to make a variety of decisions. The product may be discontinued or, by contrast, may receive additional advertising and/or be re-priced to enhance demand. One of the most effective uses of break-even analysis lies in the recognition of the relevant fixed and variable costs. The more flexible the equipment and personnel, the lower the fixed costs, and the lower the break-even point.

It is difficult to overstate the importance of break-even analysis to sound business management and decision making. Ian Benoliel, CEO of management software developer NumberCruncher.com, said on Entrepreneur.com (2002):

> The break-even point may seem like Business 101, yet it remains an enigma to many companies. Any company that ignores the break-even point runs the risk of an early death and at the very least will encounter a lot of unnecessary headaches later on.

SEE ALSO: Activity-Based Costing; Cost Accounting; Cost-Volume-Profit Analysis; Financial Issues for Managers

Karen L. Brown
Revised by Laurie Hillstrom

FURTHER READING:

Benoliel, Ian. "Calculating Your Breakeven Point." Entrepreneur .com (25 March 2002). <http://www.entrepreneur.com/article/ 0,4621,298145,00.html>.

"Breakeven Analysis." Business Owner's Toolkit. Available from <http://www.toolkit.cch.com/text/P06_7530.asp>.

Deal, Jack. "The Break-Even Point and the Break-Even Margin." Business Know-How.com. Available from <http:// www.businessknowhow.com/money/breakeven.htm>.

Garrison, Ray H., and Eric W. Noreen. *Managerial Accounting*. Boston: Irwin/McGraw-Hill, 1999.

Horngren, Charles T., George Foster, and Srikant M. Datar. *Cost Accounting: A Managerial Emphasis.* Upper Saddle River, NJ: Prentice Hall, 1997.

Render, Barry, and Jay Heizer. *Principles of Operations Management.* Upper Saddle River, NJ: Prentice Hall, 1997.

BUDGETING

Organizations develop specific plans for saving and spending income and these plans, or budgets, are essential for developing spending and saving priorities. Properly preparing a budget also serves as a reference to check how well money is being managed during a period by allowing managers to see actual revenues and expenses compared to budgeted revenues and expenses. Corrective action can be taken earlier in a period when revenue shortfalls or expense excesses are identified.

The term "budget" can be dated back to medieval England, where it meant "leather purse" or "wallet." A budget allows businesses to meet specific goals by creating a system of saving and spending money efficiently. Simply defined, a budget is a plan for using corporate funds in a way that best meets the firm's wants and needs. The plan includes a recorded entry of expected income, expenses, and savings over a defined period of time.

A wide range of budgeting techniques exist, and although the fundamental purposes are similar, the specifics among various organizations are often different. One important aspect of budgeting is how organizations increase cash to finance ongoing operations and new opportunities. Large corporations, for example, may have the option of increasing cash by selling treasury stock (previously authorized shares of ownership that have never been offered for sale on the stock market). The liquidity of equity (stock) markets allows managers to implement these equity decisions fairly quickly to budget for projected needs. In addition, the debt-paying ability of large corporations is rated by several independent organizations. This creates a market for corporate debt, more commonly referred to as bonds. Corporations with favorable debt ratings have the ability to borrow money; that is, issue bonds, at lower interest rates than those with unfavorable debt ratings. Small businesses, in contrast, often do not have publicly traded shares of stock. Although these businesses can sell stock to investors, the process is more uncertain because the market for this type of stock is less liquid. Venture capital is also an option, but the number of small businesses seeking venture capital nearly always exceeds the amount of venture

capital available. Also, debt-rating agencies do not rate the debt-paying ability of many small businesses, limiting the extent to which these businesses can raise cash through bond issues. Without a ready market for debt, small businesses must often turn to the less liquid forms of debt financing such as bank loans, in some cases at higher interest rates than would be available from established credit markets available to larger corporations.

Budgets allow businesses to better utilize the financial resources available to them. To begin with, budgets help businesses operate within their means; that is, over the long term, budgets assist businesses in spending less money than they earn. Next, budgets help businesses achieve their financial goals by planning for the future and organizing money into categories such as income, expenses, and savings. In short, budgets help a business avoid credit problems, better prepare for financial emergencies, and build better money management skills by creating a structured plan.

There are several steps that should be followed to successfully implement a budget. These include setting financial goals, planning budget categories, maintaining financial records, and balancing and adjusting the budget. Setting financial goals is the starting point in the budgeting process. Questions managers should asked include: "What do we want accomplished within one month, one year, or ten years?" "What new products or services do we want to offer in the short- and long-term and how can we finance these?" "Will my operating expenses increase with inflation, and how will we increase revenue to meet these additional expenses?" Clearly, there are dozens of questions managers should ask to cover all the categories of revenue, expense, and debt and equity financing in addition to these, but these questions provide a starting point to spur additional questions. The answers to these questions should help determine how income should be spent and saved, but in general, budgeting questions should revolve around estimates of income and expenses. Categories include fixed expenses such as rent, insurance premiums, and taxes; estimates of variable expenses such as utilities and wages; and estimates that allow for uncertainties.

One way to budget is by comparing estimated financial figures created before a budgeting period with actual experience at the end of the budgeting period. The initial estimates are called pro forma financial statements. The three primary types of financial statements are a balance sheet, income statement, and statement of cash flows. The balance sheet shows assets owned, liabilities owed, and owners' equity (owners' financial stake in the businesses). The income statement details profit and loss for a given period. The statement of cash flows helps managers see where cash came from and where it went. By comparing pro forma financial statements to end-of-period financial statements, managers can judge whether or not their budgets are in line with estimates. Adjustments can then be made for future budgeting periods.

A budget must meet certain characteristics to successfully manage money. The budgeting should be specific enough to provide the needed information. It should be realistic as well as flexible. When unexpected expenses arise, the spending plan should be able to handle these costs. A budget is not a permanent plan and should be realigned when circumstances occur that alter budget categories. The budget should be carefully planned and organized, yet clear enough to be communicated to organizational stakeholders such as lenders and owners.

Companies create budgets for a mixture of reasons. They can serve a variety of functions, and thus many techniques can be implemented to develop them. Budgets can be used as a means of forecasting and planning for the future. Their creation can also be used as a motivational tool. The plan can be used as a means of evaluation and control as well as a resource for information and decision-making. Many different approaches to the budgeting process in addition to preparation or pro forma financial statements and comparison to actual financial statements can be used depending on the desired function of the company. Breakeven analysis, for instance, estimates the amount of sales required to cover a new product's or new service's expenses. Payback periods are similar, but add to breakeven analysis' focus on needed sales by adding the length of time needed to achieve those sales. This tells managers how long it will take to recoup initial expenses. Another type of budgeting is capital budgeting, in which large the estimated revenue from capital projects such as purchase of property, plants, and equipment is projected. Additional techniques include such as parametric, partial, zero-based, and equity budgeting. Each of these may be applied to organizations' financial situations depending on the needs of the individual businesses.

Whatever technique managers use, the important thing is that budgeting is essential. Businesses without budgets can quickly find themselves short of cash not only for new products and services, growth and expansion, and improvements in capital projects, but also in simply meeting short-term needs such as payroll, insurance, and tax expenses. Budgeting is thus a key element in all business planning.

SEE ALSO: Financial Issues for Managers; Zero-Based Budgeting

Kevin Nelson
Revised by Scott B. Droege

FURTHER READING:

Henry, David. "Loading Up on Junk." *Business Week,* 31 January 2005, 78–80.

Schick, Allen. "Twenty-Five Years of Budgeting Reform." *OECD Journal on Budgeting* 1, no, 4 (2004): 102–124.

U.S. Small Business Administration. *Small Business Startup Guide.* 2005. Available from <http://www.sba.gov/starting_business/startup/guide.html>.

BUNDLED GOODS AND SERVICES

Bundling is a marketing tactic that involves offering two or more goods or services as a package deal for a discounted price. Examples of bundling are as widespread as McDonald's value meals and automobiles with features such as air conditioning, sunroofs, and geographical systems. The most well-known example is the bundled computer package complete with a monitor, mouse, keyboard, and preloaded software for a single price. Alternatively, one could select and buy each component of the system separately. All components being equal, the differences are that the buyer doesn't have to purchase each item separately, and that the bundled package could cost as much as a third less than the each-sold-separately package. Bundling can be of products from one company, but cross-industry bundling is not uncommon—for example combining airline tickets with credit cards.

Bundling has been researched for over thirty-seven years. While it doesn't always pan out, bundling has been shown to be an effective and profitable marketing strategy under a variety of circumstances, including so-called pure bundling, in which a group of products are only available as a bundle and aren't sold separately, as well as mixed bundling, where the products are sold both as bundles and as individual units. Industries that have implemented bundling of goods and/or services include utilities, telecommunications services, software and computer companies, journal publishers, automobiles, vacation packages, and fast food restaurants, to name a few. Bundling usually saves the consumer from 7 percent to 15 percent over the cost of purchasing the items separately.

APPROACHES TO BUNDLING

Companies may choose to bundle goods for several reasons, including cost efficiency, market opportunities to enhance profits, and competitive strategy. Due to economies of scale, bundling may result in cost savings on the supply side. For instance, in some scenarios a company may save on packaging and inventory costs by bundling products rather than carrying them separately. There has been a fair amount of published research delving into what kinds of bundling practices are most likely to produce cost savings. Factors a company must consider include whether the bundled products compete with each other and whether the demand for the bundled products is positively or negatively correlated. And even though the tendency is to price bundles lower than the sum of their individual components, in some cases companies successfully pursue strategies in which the bundled price is actually higher. This is called 'premium bundles.'

As a competitive strategy, a marketer of a successful product may bundle a newer or less successful product with its stronger product as a means of edging its way into a new market. Perhaps the most famous example of this is Microsoft Corporation's bundling of various software applications. First they bundled Access and PowerPoint with Word and Excel. Later they bundled their Internet browser with their market-leading operating system. When they did this they increase their market share from 7 percent to 38 percent in one year. (In that example of bundling, which proved highly successful for Microsoft, the legality of the practice was the subject of protracted litigation, however, because it raised concerns about anti-competitive behavior.) In a broader marketing sense, bundling is often intended to entice value- and convenience-seeking customers who would otherwise buy from another supplier or multiple suppliers by offering unique or appealing combinations of goods relative to their competitors.

On the demand side, bundling is used to extract consumer surplus, or an economic value in excess of the purchase price, as suggested by Chuang and Sirbu. In the business-to-business market, for example, a national survey of telecommunications managers showed that 57 percent of businesses will subscribe to bundles of two or more services, while 19 percent of businesses would purchase bundled services if they were priced 10 percent lower.

As with most marketing practices, there is no exact formula for how to create a bundled package that will succeed in the marketplace. However, some observers have noted several qualities that appear common to many successful bundling strategies. According to a 1997 study by Mercer Management Consulting, Lexington, Massachusetts, good bundles have five qualities: (1) the package is worth more than the sum of its parts; (2) the bundle brings order and simplicity to a set of confusing or tedious choices; (3) the bundle solves a problem for the consumer; (4) the bundle is focused and lean in an effort to avoid carrying options the consumer has no use for; and (5) the bundle generates interest or even controversy.

INDUSTRY CASE STUDIES

UTILITIES AND TELECOMMUNICATIONS. In response to much of the deregulation or re-regulation in the utilities industry, companies are looking to bundle their services to provide their products with reduced costs to the consumer while using the power of free markets. According to a telecommunications bundling report published in *Utility Business,* 35 percent of telecom customers are as likely to purchase bundled services (local, long distance, and electric/gas services) from an electric/gas provider as they are from a local telephone service provider. According to another nationwide survey appearing in *Public Utilities Fortnightly,* residential consumers and small business owners are increasingly interested in purchasing bundled goods and services. These customers also want specialized packages that are offered at a discount of at least 5 percent with package increases directly proportional to the size of the discount. Overall, customers assume that bundling goods and services will add value and create economies of scale, according to a study in *Security Distributing & Marketing.*

COMPUTER HARDWARE AND SOFTWARE. In recent years, computer hardware and software companies have offered the bundling of their goods and services. Computer companies such as Gateway, Dell, and Compaq offer Microsoft products pre-installed on their hard drives as a prerequisite to a customer buying the product. These computer companies also offer extra software and peripherals as standard equipment with new desktop, laptop, or server models. Gateway, for example, offers a package including a mouse, mouse pad, wrist support, and maintenance kit for about $10 in addition to the purchase of a new machine. If these items were purchased separately, the cost could be as much as $40. In 1999, software publisher Corel Corporation began bundling its Word-Perfect Office Suite with a Hong Kong-based group, PC Chips Group, in order to appeal to smaller businesses looking for a computer with a large amount of software.

Computer hardware and software producers bundle their packages for several reasons. First, you cannot have a computer without software and vice-versa, and consumers would rather not incur the added expense of buying these two components separately. Secondly, it is very cost effective for both entities to enter into agreements to let their services co-exist with the consumer. Lastly, the bundling process gives these producers brand recognition in the market. Microsoft became the standard through selling its software products to the industry's largest computer producers such as IBM, Dell, Gateway, and Compaq.

UNBUNDLING TRENDS

Antitrust violations have forced some examples of unbundling. The European Court of First Instance ruled against Microsoft in December of 2004. Microsoft must provide the European market with a version of Windows operating system without their media player. The goal of this decision is to prevent Microsoft from having a monopoly.

There is some evidence that some consumers want unbundling. They want the option to buy exactly what they want, i.e., unbundled products. One example is pay-per-click advertising on Google and Yahoo. Advertisers would rather not pay based on an estimated audience, but are willing to pay for ads that actually are clicked on. Other examples include music (the consumer wants to download and pay for one song) or brokerage (buy one $5.00 stock) or pay for one periodical article rather than subscribe to the journal. This trend will not make bundling disappear, because for many consumers the package is easier and more convenient. However companies will need to carefully package bundles to meet consumer desires.

SEE ALSO: Service Industry; Service Operations; Service Process Matrix; Strategy Formulation

James C. Koch
Revised by Judith M. Nixon

FURTHER READING:

"Bundle Up, Electric Providers." *Public Utilities Fortnightly* 137, no. 2 (1999): 62.

"Bundling Survey Assesses Consumers' Interests." *Security Distributing and Marketing* 29, no. 1 (1999): 30.

"Business Unbundled: Microsoft." *The Economist* 374, 8407 (2005): 48.

Chuang, John Chung-I, and Marvin A. Sirbu. *Network Delivery of Information Goods: Optimal Pricing of Articles and Subscriptions.* 1997.

———. "Optimal Bundling Strategy for Digital Information Goods: Network Delivery of Articles and Subscriptions." *Information Economics and Policy* 11, no. 2 (1999): 147–76.

Fuerderer, R., A. Herrmann, and G. Wuebker, eds. *Optimal Bundling: Marketing Strategies for Improving Economic Performance.* New York: Springer, 1999.

Janiszewski, C., and M. Chuha, Jr. "The Influence of Price Discount Framing on the Evaluation of a Product Bundle." *Journal of Consumer Research* 30, no. 4 (2004): 534–547.

Mason, Charles. "The Future of Competition." *America's Network* 103, no. 3 (1999): S4–S5.

Mannes, G. "The Urge to Unbundle." *Fast Company* 91 (2005): 23–24.

Ovans, Andrea. "Make a Bundle Bundling." *Harvard Business Review* 75, no. 6 (1997): 18–20.

Porter, Anne Millen. "Electric Power Customers Prepare for Competition." *Purchasing,* 25 March 1999, S4–S11.

Salinger, Michael A. "A Graphical Analysis of Bundling." *Journal of Business* 68, no. 1 (1995): 85–98.

Solomon, Howard. "Corel Inks Office Suite Bundling Deal with PC Chips." *Computing Canada* 25, no. 15 (1999): 15–17.

"Utilities Pose Threat to Bundling." *Utility Business,* 28 February 1999, 72.

BUSINESS CONTINUITY PLANNING

Organizations are faced with a variety of threats and vulnerabilities, and these continue to evolve. Business disruptions can include natural disasters such as floods, fires, hurricanes, and power outages. Since 9/11, the threat of man-made disasters such as terrorist attacks has taken on a sense of urgency as well. The increasing density of our population further exacerbates the threats posed by both natural and man-made disasters. Although business continuity planning and disaster recovery planning are now generally recognized as vital, creating and maintaining a sound plan is quite complex.

Business continuity planning addresses the prospect that a disaster might interrupt an organization's business operations. Whether an organization is for-profit, non-profit, or governmental, the need to mitigate disaster risks has become especially salient. Firms should evaluate their degree of exposure to disaster, both externally (e.g., floods, fires, hurricanes) and internally (e.g., HVAC failure, sabotage).

A business impact analysis helps management to understand the criticality of different business functions, recovery time required, and the need for various resources. The question of which corporate functions receive top priority should be addressed. In selecting a strategy to protect the organization, cost-benefit comparisons are made with regard to the effects of doing without various services and functions (e.g., call centers, production locations, proprietary data) at specific points in time, and developing plans for optimum recovery periods for each service and function.

Thus, a business continuity plan includes the procedures and information about resources to help an organization recover from a disruption in its business operations. In the financial markets, major industry players have responded to the 9/11 terrorist attacks by attempting to deal with future risks, especially risks regarding trading operations. But because most networks rely on the open Internet, viruses or other service attacks remain potential threats.

A central office failure brought about by a fire or power outage can also affect trading operations.

Redundancy (including back-up sites and additional staff and technologies) is recommended, albeit expensive. An additional risk is that an entire network (such as AT&T) might go down. Jay Pultz, research vice-president at disaster and business continuity consultancy firm Gartner, Inc., is concerned that failures will increase because the companies that provide the networks are collapsing their infrastructure to a single backbone, as opposed to separate backbones for the Internet, phone, data, etc.

Business continuity and disaster recovery planning can demand a great deal of resources. For example, Voca (the United Kingdom direct debits clearing house) spends about 35 percent of its IT budget on these plans. But the alternative may be worse. Losses can mount quickly when firms cannot access data.

According to a study by Gartner, Inc., the average cost of computer-network downtime is $42,000 an hour. Technology-dependent firms such as online brokerages may incur costs of $1 million or more an hour. To ensure seamless service in case of disaster, Voca runs its business from a back-up site for up to five weeks a year. Off-site backups appear to be a favorite method for protecting data for 58 percent of solution providers, according to recent CRN poll data.

The Confederation of British Industry and security firm Qinetiq report that, even after overhauling business continuity plans, 60 percent of British companies are concerned about their preparation for disaster. Almost 70 percent of respondents to Information Week Research's Outlook 2005 survey ranked business continuity planning or disaster preparedness as a high priority. Still, according to analyst David Hill of Mesabi Group, most companies have neglected some operational needs, such as recovering data after a virus attack. Moreover, many business continuity plans are never even tested, and according to Peter Gerr of the Enterprise Strategy Group, one out of every five recovery efforts fails.

But forward-thinking enterprises are recognizing both external and internal signals for the need to formulate contingency plans. Externally, business continuity plans may be driven by regulation, as in the banking industry. Internal risk exposure, however, is a critical driver as well. A case in point is Madrid-based Banco Santander International, the largest commercial bank in South America and the tenth largest bank in the world. If operations stopped and trades or payments failed, the bank could be liable for compensation.

To maintain protection of business-critical customer data at its private banking center in Miami, Banco Santander chose a solution from VERITAS Software Corp. based on its compatibility with the bank's infrastructure. Data could then be replicated between Miami and New York sites over the IP network.

During the rash of hurricanes that hit Florida in 2004, every time a major warning was issued and facilities evacuated, primary operations were transferred to New York until the threat passed. The system is viewed as an insurance policy for the bank.

Oddly enough, smaller businesses have been found to lead many midsize businesses in implementing true disaster-recovery solutions. Small businesses often rely on value added resellers (VARs) for their solutions, and larger firms use internal IT departments. Midsize firms, however, are too complex to be relocated quickly, yet lack the internal staff to restore business processes rapidly, increasing opportunities for VARs to offer business continuity services to this market.

APPLICATIONS TO SUPPLY CHAIN MANAGEMENT

Outsourcing has become a standard practice among many organizations as a way to add flexibility to the supply chain. Often a particular task can be done more efficiently and/or effectively by an outside vendor. The advantage for the focal firm is that it can focus on its core competence, or at least those functions it does well, and outsource other functions so as to gain efficiency. Thus, rather than integrating all functions within the firm boundaries, the trend toward outsourcing and a variety of cooperative relationships continues. Ironically, the gains in efficiency and flexibility may often be outweighed by risks of being dependent on sole suppliers.

In a *Bank Technology News* article titled "Business Continuity Planning Must Extend to Vendors," John Hoge argues that client-vendor relationships are symbiotic and should lead to greater efficiency and productivity in a variety of industries. In banking, technology vendors are critical for the bank's basic business processes. But if the vendor's systems go down, the bank's systems can go down as well.

The implication is that vendors are increasingly compelled to include business continuity and disaster recovery as key aspects of their activities. Some vendors have adopted business impact analysis to tailor a recovery plan to meet the recovery requirements of specific units. An interesting twist regarding the benefits of "leaner" supply chains is the increased need for contingency plans in case of disruptions.

The "dark side" of supply chain management is discussed in a white paper appearing in a March 2005 issue of *Supply Chain Management Review*. The authors explore the notion of supply continuity planning, which is a comprehensive approach to managing supply risk. They state that by employing their supply continuity planning model, organizations can guard against a major supply disruption that could potentially delay orders and result in loss of customers.

Whereas companies previously relied on inventory buffers (safety stock, lead times, excess capacity) to protect them, today's competitive environment makes these buffers less attractive. A consequence is that today's lean supply chains are increasingly fragile, or more sensitive to shocks and disruptions.

The authors make a strong case for how devastating disruptions can be by citing several events, including a fire at a factory supplying valves to Toyota, resulting in estimated costs of $195 million; an earthquake in Taiwan, hampering the supply of computer chips and computer demand during the holiday season; a lightning strike at a radio-frequency chip plant in Albuquerque, NM, resulting in a fire, production delays, and the eventual withdrawal of Ericsson from mobile phone manufacturing-because the plant was its sole supplier; and the 9/11 terrorist attacks, resulting in loss of life and loss of information databases.

Based on case studies of four organizations that proactively manage inbound supply risk, the authors present a framework describing detailed efforts focused on four major activities: creating system awareness of supply risk, preventing the occurrence of supply disruptions, remediating supply interruptions, and managing knowledge.

BEING PREPARED

In a 2005 *Canadian Business* article titled "Always Be Prepared," an expert in enterprise risk presents a series of questions that managers should ask about the firm's state of readiness to continue business after a disruption. For example, does the business even have a plan? Is the plan tailor-made or "off the rack?" Are critical functions the basis of the plan? The maintenance of knowledge management, regular testing of the plan, and supplier preparedness are other important issues.

Being prepared for disaster is increasingly essential. The good news for those new to business continuity planning and disaster recovery planning is that information on how to prepare is proliferating. Business continuity and disaster recovery planning software explore the potential impacts of disaster, and underlying risks; constructing a plan; maintenance, testing, and auditing to ensure that the plan remains appropriate to the needs of the organization; and support infrastructure and services.

SEE ALSO: Contingency Approach to Management; Lean Manufacturing and Just-in-Time Production; Strategic Planning Tools; Strategy Formulation; Supply Chain Management

Bruce Walters

FURTHER READING:

Barnes, James C. *A Guide to Business Continuity Planning.* New York, NY: Wiley, 2001.

"The Business Continuity Planning & Disaster Recovery Planning Directory." Disaster Recovery World. Available from <http://www.disasterrecoveryworld.com>.

Garvey, Martin J. "From Good to Great (Maybe)." *Information-Week,* 3 January 2005, 45.

Gerson, Vicki. "Better Safe Than Sorry." *Bank Systems & Technology* 42, no. 1 (2005): 41.

Hanna, Greg. "How to Take a Computer Disaster in Stride." *Strategic Finance* 86, no. 7 (2005): 48–52.

Hofmann, Mark A. "Y2K Spurred Continuity Plan That Was Put to Test by 9/11." *Business Insurance* 39, no. 16 (2005): 71.

Hoge, John. "Business Continuity Planning Must Extend to Vendors." *Bank Technology News* 18, no. 2 (2005): 47.

Hood, Sarah B. "Always Be Prepared." *Canadian Business* 78, no. 6 (2005): 61–63.

Huber, Nick. "Business Continuity Plans Eat 35% of Clearing House's Core IT Spend." *ComputerWeekly,* 8 February 2005, 5.

Roberts, John, and Frank J. Ohlhorst. "Disaster Planning Promises Big Channel Profits." *CRN* 1130 (2005): 22.

Sisk, Michael. "Business Continuity: Still Not Entirely Ready For Disaster." *Bank Technology News* 17, no. 12 (2004): 41.

Zsidisin, George, A., Gary L. Ragatz, and Steven A. Melnyk. "The Dark Side of Supply Chain Management." *Supply Chain Management Review* 9, no. 2 (March 2005): 46–52.

BUSINESS PLAN

A business plan is a written document used to describe a proposed venture or idea. It typically includes the current state of a business, future vision for the business, target market analysis and challenges, sales and marketing strategies, and funding requirements to reach stated goals. Many business plans are designed with the intention of securing funding and investors to support a proposed idea; others are designed to assist with reorganization, takeovers, or to serve as an internal planning document. On its website, the U.S. Small Business Administration (SBA)(http://www.sba.gov) describes it this way:

A business plan precisely defines your business, identifies your goals, and serves as your firm's resume. . . It helps you allocate resources properly, handle unforeseen complications, and make good business decisions. Because it provides specific and organized information about your company and how you will repay borrowed money, a good business plan is a crucial part of any loan application. Additionally, it informs sales personnel, suppliers, and others about your operations and goals.

GETTING STARTED

The article "Write the Right Business Plan," lists ten things to consider before tackling the document:

1. Decide why you're writing your plan—what is your motivation?

2. Do your homework—read some books, explore web resources.

3. Compile your information—locate articles, financial statements.

4. Start typing—write down all your ideas, notes and questions in outline form.

5. Write a rough draft—Flesh out the outline with full sentences and paragraphs.

6. Do more research—support your case with data via Small Business Association contacts, annual reports, and competitors in the chosen industry.

7. Think about the numbers—develop pro forma financial statements.

8. Write a final draft—demonstrate attention to detail with accuracy and clarity.

9. Get feedback—have someone else read over your plan and offer advice.

10. Polish your plan to perfection—include a cover page, table of contents, nondisclosure form and an executive summary containing highlights.

Employees with the right skill set and expertise can collaborate to create the business plan. Alternatively, a consultant can be hired to assist with the process. A consultant can bring expertise and professionalism to the appearance and tone of your business plan, provide informed market analysis and research assistance, and supply educated projections for a market that the entrepreneur might be unfamiliar with or have little experience analyzing.

After determining who will be working on the plan, it is useful to decide on the scope of the plan and timeframe for completion of the plan. Once the team or consultant is in place, research and analysis can begin. Internal and external assessments should be conducted and then examined. The interpretations of these assessments will be the framework of the plan and will guide goal setting and strategies for the company. Once goals and strategies are determined, a solid

business plan can be formed toward fulfilling these goals.

From a management perspective, a business plan allows managers to set priorities and allocate resources effectively. It brings order and direction to an organization and provides a vision of the future that employees throughout the company can put energy into and get excited about. This shared vision and focus will benefit the company at every level and ensure that all constituents are working cooperatively and cohesively. Ideally, all employees will utilize the information from the business plan to assist in goal setting, and guide in decision making and performance assessments.

ELEMENTS OF A BUSINESS PLAN

The U.S. Small Business Administration recommends that a business plan describe four main elements of the proposed venture: an overview of the business, a marketing analysis, a financial plan, and a management plan. An executive summary and other supporting documents should also accompany the plan. These elements provide a solid starting point for a general plan, but there is no single formula to a business plan and a multitude of factors will impact the amount of content needed in a good business plan.

The executive summary is a synopsis of the entire business plan. It is critical that this summary be carefully crafted and compelling. This is the first and possibly the only information that a potential investor will read; if it is not informative enough or if it is lacking crucial data, the investor might not read beyond this summary component.

The business overview segment is a profile of the company and its primary industry. Projections, trends, and industry outlooks should be included. In this section the company describes the unique elements that make it a prime candidate for its proposed venture.

A market analysis details how the company will handle its sales and marketing strategies. This analysis includes information on the company's products or services and intended customers, and how customers will be made aware of the product or service. This section should also include a competitive analysis with a breakdown identifying Strengths, Weaknesses, Opportunities, and Threats (SWOT) to the company and the business proposed. A plan of action should explain how the company will address, exploit, or withstand each of these eventualities.

The financial section discusses the current financial state of the company and what types of financing will be required for the proposed venture. In this area, it is appropriate to discuss the specific dollar amounts required for the business venture, the cost to maintain and sustain the venture, and projections of income,

---

Element of a Business Plan

1. **Cover sheet**
2. **Statement of purpose**
3. **Table of contents**

I. The Business

A. Description of business
B. Marketing
C. Competition
D. Operating procedures
E. Personnel
F. Business insurance

II. Financial Data

A. Loan applications
B. Capital equipment and supply list
C. Balance sheet
D. Breakeven analysis
E. Pro-forma income projections (profit & loss statements)
　　Three-year summary
　　Detail by month, first year
　　Detail by quarters, second and third years
　　Assumptions upon which projections were based
F. Pro-forma cash flow

III. Supporting Documents

Tax returns of principals for the last three years Personal financial statement (all banks have these forms)
For franchised businesses, a copy of franchise contract and all supporting documents provided by the franchisor
Copy of proposed lease or purchase agreement for building space
Copy of licenses and other legal documents
Copy of resumes of all principals
Copies of letters of intent from suppliers, etc.

---

balance sheets, and cash flow. Statistics, facts, and research should support any financial projections listed.

The management plan section should discuss the strengths, experience, achievements, and expertise of the person or team undertaking the business venture. Investors want to know that they are offering their support to a person or team qualified and capable of handling the business proposed and the funds loaned.

A complete business plan will provide evidence to the lender that the entrepreneur has performed a thorough investigation of this new business venture, because it details how the business will generate cash flow, pay for operating expenses, and service debt repayment.

The accompanying table offers several elements for inclusion in designing a business plan.

CUSTOMIZING FOR INVESTOR-TYPE

Bankers, venture capital fund managers, and business angels each look at different features of a business plan when assessing it for investment. Bankers tend to focus on the financial aspects of the plan, and give little emphasis to marketing and management issues. Venture capital fund managers are typically most interested in both the marketing and the financial aspects of the plan. Business angels focus on entrepreneurial elements and "investor fit" considerations. Thus business plan writers should customize their proposals based on the audience they are trying to reach.

Bankers are interested in businesses that will be successful over the long term and entrepreneurs who will remain committed to the project as described in the business plan. When making their lending decisions, they are interested in collateral as security for the loan, and tend to support projects that are less risky. A banker's main interest is the repayment of the loan.

Venture capital fund managers invest for capital gain, and when a venture is successful, they also benefit. Likewise, if a business fails, venture capital fund managers stand to lose significantly-and at much cost to the outside investors whose funds they are managing. Therefore, venture capital fund managers focus on the uniqueness of the product or service, the status of the market, and the management team's potential for success. Venture capital fund managers' main interest is growth potential and potential returns.

Business angels interests align more closely with venture capital fund managers than with bankers. Business angels focus on how their interests match up with the entrepreneur's and how well they are able to work with the entrepreneur over the length of the project. They seek out entrepreneurs who have strong, positive qualities, such as integrity and responsibility, and with whom they feel a connection. Because the investment is personal for the business angel, he or she is interested in financial gains, but also enjoys the opportunity to participate in the venture itself. A business angel's main interest is potential returns, camaraderie with the entrepreneur(s), and personal involvement.

RECENT TRENDS

An article by A. Gome investigates a growing trend among certain entrepreneurs to move away from the old-style business plan that contains an extended, long-term outlook. They are opting instead to use an abbreviated, shorter-term document that better fits their business strategy.

Long-range planning documents don't work as well for some entrepreneurs because of the fast-changing markets they are entering into, which renders the business plan irrelevant within months. And, the short-term nature of some ventures preclude the need for a long-term plan. It is unnecessary to have a five-year plan if the entrepreneur expects to conclude his venture within a shorter time frame.

LIVING DOCUMENTS

Replacing the traditional business plan is what is called a "living document," typically one page in length and with a forward-looking range of one year. Goal-setting may be projected on three- to six-month timeframes, which are more easily monitored and attainable. The living document contains similar elements of a typical business plan-vision, values, objectives, methods toward reaching objectives-but abbreviated to fit on a single page. This document needs constant updating and adjusting, with ample flexibility to respond to customer and market fluctuations. Highly-tailored documents may also need to be prepared for each type of stakeholder, whether bankers, venture capital fund managers, or business angels.

RESOURCES

There are many resources for the entrepreneur looking to write a business plan. Local business organizations, public libraries, colleges and universities may offer useful workshops, seminars, or courses.

Local Small Business Administration (SBA) offices or websites (<http://www.sba.gov>) also offer resources. The SBA has sponsored more than 200,000 loans worth more than $45 billion, making it the largest single financial backer of U.S. businesses in the country. The SBA provides free online courses, e-mail guidance, print materials, and face-to-face consultations to small business owners.

The SBA also administers the Small Business Development Center Program to provide management assistance to current and prospective small business owners. This program provides a broad-based system of assistance for the small business community by linking the resources of federal, state and local governments with the resources of the educational community and the private sector.

There are also several books and software programs that assist with creating a business plan.

Business plans are useful documents for garnering funds for entrepreneurial ventures and evaluating progress in a business start-up. They are also useful for evaluating success in established companies, establishing steps for reorganizations or acquisitions, and for guiding the overall strategy of a company. Customizing the business plan for the intended investor type ensures that the proposal will mesh with the investor's interests and key considerations.

SEE ALSO: Entrepreneurship; Venture Capital

Monica C. Turner

FURTHER READING:

Bunderson, Gaye. "Have Your Business Plan in Hand Before Seeking $$$." *Idaho Business Review,* 31 January 2005.

Business Plans Handbook. Farmington Hills, MI: Gale Group, Inc., 2004.

Delmar, F. and Shane, S. "Does Business Planning Facilitate the Development of New Ventures?" *Strategic Management Journal* 24 (December 2004): 1165–1185.

Gome, A. "Plan Not to Plan." *BRW* 27 (February 2005): 72–73.

Lasher, William. *The Perfect Business Plan Made Simple.* New York, NY: Broadway Books, 2005.

Mason, Colin and Matthew Stark. "What Do Investors Look for in a Business Plan?" *International Small Business Journal* 22 (June 2005): 227–248.

McKeever, Mike P. *How to Write a Business Plan.* Berkeley, CA: Nolo, 2005.

Office of Small Business Development Centers. U.S. Small Business Administration. Available from http://www.sba.gov/sbdc/aboutus.html.

Pinson, Linda. *Anatomy of a Business Plan: A Step-By-Step Guide to Building a Business and Securing Your Company's Future.* Chicago, IL: Dearborn Trade Publishing, 2005.

U.S. Small Business Administration. "Elements of a Business Plan." Available from <http://www.sba.gov/starting_business/planning/writingplan.html>.

BUSINESS PROCESS REENGINEERING

Process reengineering is redesigning or reinventing how we perform our daily work, and it is a concept that is applicable to all industries regardless of size, type, and location.

While selected elements of process reengineering are well documented in the late 1800s and early 1900s, process reengineering as a body of knowledge or as an improvement initiative, takes the best of the historical management and improvement principles and combines them with more recent philosophies and principles, which make all people in an organization function as process owners and reinvent processes. It is this combination of the old and the new as well as the emphasis on dramatic, rapid reinvention that makes process reengineering an exciting concept. The differences between continuous process improvement and process reengineering are outlined in Figure 1.

The first question in process reengineering is: "Why are we doing this at all?" Answering this question is the beginning of the immediate, dramatic change and the application of supporting technical and behavioral concepts and tools that are necessary to implement process reengineering. To accomplish this, organizations must foster an environment that encourages quantum leaps in improvement by throwing out existing systems and processes and inventing new ones.

The intent of process reengineering is to make organizations significantly more flexible, responsive, efficient, and effective for their customers, employees and other stakeholders. According to field experts Michael Hammer and James Champy, process reengineering requires the "fundamental rethinking and radical redesign of business processes to achieve dramatic improvements in critical, contemporary measures of performance, such as cost, quality, service, and speed."

If process reengineering is to work, a business's priorities must change in the following ways: (1) from boss to customer focus; (2) from controlled workers to empowered, involved process owners and decision makers; (3) from activity-based work to a results orientation; (4) from scorekeeping to leading and teaching so that people measure their own results; (5) from functional (vertical) to process (horizontal or cross functional) orientation; (6) from serial to concurrent operations; (7) from complex to simple, streamlined processes; (8) from empire building and guarding the status quo to inventing new systems and processes and looking toward the future (i.e., from the caretaker mentality to visionary leadership).

As organizational priorities change, the culture will change as well. As people understand the vision for a better culture with better capabilities and results,

Figure 1

Area of Difference	Continuous Improvement	Reengineering
Reason for change	Desire to improve baselines	Compelling; (Rapid process re-design for survival)
Targets	Small improvement in every process; Cumulative effects	Aggressive (e.g., 10x or more, Six Sigma, etc.)
Approach	Non-structured	Structured and Disciplined
Scope	Evaluation of all steps in all processes	Broad cross functional processes
Focus	Parts of a system	Relations in system
Level of change	Incremental and continuous	Order of magnitude
Organizational structure	Vertical or horizontal	Flattened, horizontal
Involvement of executives	Important up-front; support throughout	Intensive long term involvement
Involvement of all employees	Gradual voluntary involvement	Non-voluntary
Use of teams	Work teams and cross-functional team	Cross functional teams
Role of information	Incidental	Cornerstone

Source: Mildred Golden Pryor and William Donald Pryor, *Process Reengineering*, Center for Excellence, A Partnership between Texas A&M University-Commerce and Raytheon-E-Systems, 1994.

they will be able-individually and as members of teams-to contribute positively to make the organizational vision a reality.

REASONS FOR PROCESS REENGINEERING

There are several reasons for organizations to reengineer their business processes: (1) to re-invent the way they do work to satisfy their customers; (2) to be competitive; (3) to cure systemic process and behavioral problems; (4) to enhance their capability to expand to other industries; (5) to accommodate an era of change; (6) to satisfy their customers, employees, and other stakeholders who want them to be dramatically different and/or to produce different results (7) to survive and be successful in the long term; and (8) to invent the "rules of the game."

Whatever the reason for reengineering, managers should ask themselves: What do our customers and other stakeholders want/require? How must we change the processes to meet customer and other stakeholder requirements and be more efficient and effective? Once streamlined, should the processes be computerized (i.e., how can information technology be used to improve quality, cycle time, and other critical baselines)? Processes must be streamlined (i.e., re-invented) before they are computerized. Otherwise, the processes may produce results faster, but those results may not be the ones needed.

REQUIREMENTS FOR SUCCESSFUL PROCESS REENGINEERING

Many experts indicate that there are essential elements of process reengineering, including:

- Initiation from the top by someone with a vision for the whole process and relentless deployment of the vision throughout the organization.

- Leadership that drives rapid, dramatic process redesign.

- A new value system which includes a greater emphasis on satisfying customers and other stakeholders.

- A fundamental re-thinking of the way people perform their daily work, with an emphasis on improving results (quality, cycle time, cost, and other baselines).

- An emphasis on the use of cross-functional work teams which may result in structural redesign as well as process redesign.

- Enhanced information dissemination (including computerization after process redesign) in order to enable process owners to make better decisions.

- Training and involvement of individuals and teams as process owners who have the knowledge and power to re-invent their processes.

- A focus on total redesign of processes with non-voluntary involvement of all internal constituents (management and non-management employees).

- Rewards based on results; and a disciplined approach.

Those same experts state there are many reasons that process reengineering fails, including:

- Not focusing on critical processes first.

- Trying to gradually "fix" a process instead of dramatically re-inventing it.

- Making process reengineering the priority and ignoring everything else (e.g., strategy development and deployment, re-structuring based on new strategies, etc.).

- Neglecting values and culture needed to support process reengineering and allowing existing culture, attitudes, and behavior to hinder reengineering efforts (e.g., short-term thinking, bias against conflict and consensus decision making, etc.).

- "Settling" for small successes instead of requiring dramatic results.

- Stopping the process reengineering effort too early before results can be achieved.

- Placing prior constraints on the definition of the problem and the scope for the reengineering effort.

- Trying to implement reengineering from the bottom up instead of top down.

- Assigning someone who doesn't understand Reengineering to lead the effort.

- Skimping on reengineering resources.

- Dissipating energy across too many Reengineering projects at once.

- Attempting to reengineer when the CEO is near retirement.

- Failing to distinguish reengineering from, or align it with, other improvement initiatives (e.g., quality improvement, strategic alignment, right-sizing, customer-supplier partnerships, innovation, empowerment, etc.)

- Concentrating primarily on design and neglecting implementation.

- Pulling back when people resist making reengineering changes (not understanding that resistance to change is normal).

Figure 2
Golden-Pryor Improvement Flowchart

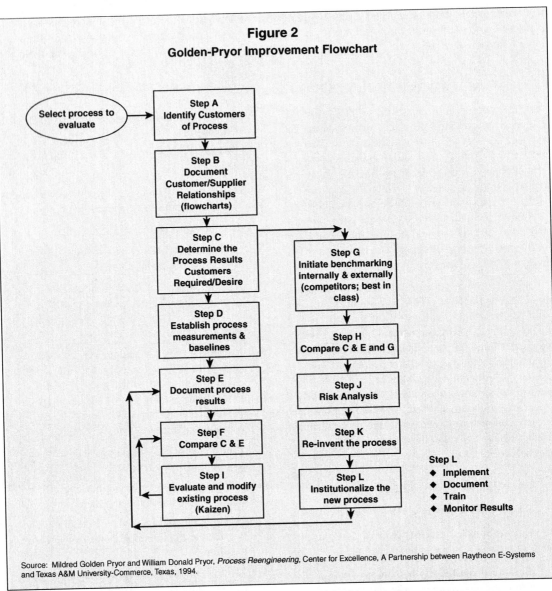

Source: Mildred Golden Pryor and William Donald Pryor, *Process Reengineering,* Center for Excellence, A Partnership between Raytheon E-Systems and Texas A&M University-Commerce, Texas, 1994.

Strategic approaches that are process-focused and that are extensions of process reengineering:

- Intensification-improving/re-inventing processes to better serve customers.

- Extension-using strong processes to enter new markets.

- Augmentation-expanding processes to provide additional services to existing customers.

- Conversion-using a process that you perform well and performing that process as a service for other companies.

- Innovation-applying processes that you perform well to create and deliver different goods and services.

- Diversification-creating new processes to deliver new goods or services.

Process reengineering is a valuable concept for organizations that are willing to undergo dramatic change and radical process redesign. It can co-exist with ongoing gradual process improvement efforts because not all processes can be radically redesigned at once.

In process reengineering, as in all improvement initiatives, assessments should be made in terms of cost/benefit analysis, and risk analysis. However, even the assessments should be done with a sense of urgency since process reengineering requires speed as well as radical redesign. Documentation of results will serve as the baseline for future improvements.

The various improvement methodologies (i.e., continuous improvement and process reengineering) should not be used as separate efforts but rather as two approaches within a single improvement initiative. In fact, a single flowchart can be used to make choices regarding both continuous process improvement and process reengineering (see Figure 2). Both gradual continuous improvement and process reengineering should be an integral part of process management.

SEE ALSO: Continuous Improvement; Product-Process Matrix

Mildred Golden Pryor

FURTHER READING:

Bossidy, Larry, and Ram Charan. *Execution: The Discipline of Getting Things Done.* New York, NY: Crown Publishing Group, Random House, 2002.

Champy, James. *Reengineering Management.* New York, NY: HarperCollins Publishers, 1995.

———. *X-Engineering the Corporation: Re-inventing Your Business in the Digital Age.* New York, NY: Warner Business Books, 2001.

Davenport, Thomas H. "Need Radical Innovation and Continuous Improvement? Integrate Process Reengineering and TQM." *Planning Review,* May-June 1993, 7–12.

———. *Process Innovation.* Boston, MA: Harvard Business School Press, 1993.

Hammer, Michael. *The Reengineering Revolution.* New York, NY: HarperCollins Publishing, 1996.

———. "Reengineering Work: Don't Automate, Obliterate." *Harvard Business Review,* July-August 1990, 104–112.

Hammer, Michael, and James Champy. *Reengineering the Corporation.* New York, NY: Harper Business Publisher, 1993.

Hengst, Marielle den, and Gert-Jan de Vreede. "Collaborative Business Engineering: A Decade of Lessons from the Field." *Journal Of Management Information Systems* 20, no. 4 (Spring 2004): 85–113.

Kinni, Theodore. "A Reengineering Primer." *Quality Digest,* January 1994, 26–30.

Kumar, Sameer, and Ralph Harris. "Improving Business Processes for Increased Operational Efficiency: A Case Study." *Journal Of Manufacturing Technology Management* 15, no. 7 (2004): 662.

Petroski, Henry. "Look First to Failure." *Harvard Business Review* 82, no. 10 (October 2004): 18.

Pryor, Mildred Golden, and Donald W. Pryor. "Process Reengineering as a Quality Strategy." *Israel Society For Quality Proceedings,* November 1994, 681–696.

———. *Process Reengineering Training Manual.* Commerce, TX: Center for Excellence, 1994.

Reijers, H.A., and S. Liman Mansar. "Best Practices in Business Process Redesign: An Overview and Qualitative Evaluation of Successful Redesign Heuristics" *OMEGA* 33, no. 4 (August 2005): 283.

Roberts, Lon. *Process Reengineering: The Key To Achieving Breakthrough Success.* Milwaukee, WI: ASQ Press, 1994.

Young, Martha, and Michael Jude. "Business Process Virtualization, Outsourcing and Process Reengineering." Cisco Press. Available from <http://www.informit.com/articles/article.asp?p=169681>.

BUSINESS STRUCTURE

When forming a new company, one of the first critical decisions is the formal structure that business will take. Issues such as liability, ownership, operating strategy, and taxation are all impacted by the formal structure of the business. Four different business structures are discussed below: partnership, corporation, Subchapter S, and limited liability corporation (LLC).

PARTNERSHIPS

A partnership is a business association where two or more individuals (or partners) share equally in profits and losses. As is the case with a sole proprietorship, partners have full legal responsibility for the business (including debts against the business). Persons entering into this type of business need a partnership agreement detailing how much each partner owns of the business, how much capital each person will contribute, and the percentage of profits to which they are entitled; how company decisions will be made; if the company is open to new/additional partners, and how they can join; and in what cases and how the company would be dissolved.

In a general partnership, all partners are liable for actions made on the company's behalf, including decisions make and actions taken by other partners. Profits (and loss) are shared by all partners, as are company assets and authority.

A limited partnership is a similar business arrangement with one significant difference. In a limited partnership, one or more partners are not involved in the management of the business and are not personally liable for the partnership's obligations. The extent to which the limited partner is liable is thus "limited" to his or her capital investment in the partnership.

In a limited partnership agreement, several conditions have to be met, the most important of which is that a limited partner or partners have no control or management over the daily operations of the organization. There must be at least two partners and one or more of these general partners manage the business and are liable for firm debts and financial responsibilities. If a limited partner becomes involved in the operation of the partnership, he or she stands to lose protection against liability. In addition, a limited partnership agreement, certificate, or registration has to be filed, usually with the secretary of state, but this varies by state. Such an agreement generally includes the names of general and limited partners, the nature of the business, and the term of the limited partnership or the date of dissolution. Since limited partnerships are often used to raise capital, there is a set term of duration for the agreement. Individual states may also have additional limited partnership requirements.

The most frequent use of the limited partnership agreement has been as an investment, removing the limited partner from financial liability but raising capital through his or her investments or contributions. Limited partnerships are common in real estate investments and, more recently, in entertainment business ventures.

Partnerships are not required to file tax returns for the company, but individual partners do have to claim their share of the company's income or loss on personal tax returns. The Internal Revenue Service (IRS) governs limited partnerships for tax purposes. IRS guidelines restrict limited partnership investments to 80 percent of the total partnership interests (see IRS Revenue Procedure 92-88 for information governing limited partnerships). Limited partnerships are also taxable under state revenue regulations.

CORPORATIONS

The major difference between a partnership and a corporation is that the corporation exists as a unique and separate entity from its owners, or shareholders. A corporation must be chartered by the state in which it is headquartered, and it can be taxed, sued, enter into contractual agreements, and is responsible for its own debts. The shareholders own the corporation, and they elect a board of directors to make major decisions and oversee corporate policy. The corporation files its own tax return and pays taxes on its income from operations. Unlike partnerships, which often dissolve when a partner leaves, a corporation can continue despite turnover in shareholders/ownership. For this reason, a corporate structure is more stable and reliable than a partnership.

There are several major advantages to choosing incorporation over partnership. Sale of stock can help raise large amounts of capital significantly faster and shareholders are only responsible for their personal financial investment in the company. Shareholders have only limited liability for debts and judgments made against the company. And the corporation can deduct the cost of benefits paid to employees from corporate tax returns.

Forming a corporation costs more money than a partnership, including legal and regulatory fees, which vary depending on the state in which the business is incorporated. Corporations are subject to monitoring by federal and state agencies, and some local agencies as well. More paperwork related to taxes and regulatory compliance is required. Taxes are higher for corporations, particularly if it pays dividends, which are taxed twice (once as corporation income, then again as shareholder income).

SUBCHAPTER S

Some small businesses are able to take advantage of the corporate structure and avoid double taxation. These companies must be small, domestic firms with seventy-five shareholders or less and only one class of stock, and all shareholders must meet eligibility requirements. If a company meets these requirements, they can treat company profits as distributions through shareholders' personal tax returns. This way the income is taxed to shareholders instead of the corporation, and income taxes are only paid once. Subchapter S corporations are also known as small business corporations, S-corps, S corporations, or tax-option corporations.

LIMITED LIABILITY CORPORATION

The limited liability corporation (LLC) structure combines the benefits of ownership with the personal protection a corporation offers against debts and judgments. One or more people can form an LLC, and business owner(s) can either choose to file taxes as a sole proprietorship/partnership or as a corporation. The process of forming an LLC is more extensive than a partnership agreement but still involves less regulatory paperwork than incorporation.

Major advantages offered by the LLC structure are that the business does not have to incorporate (or pay corporate taxes); one person alone can create an LLC; owners can be compensated through company profits; and business losses can be reported against personal income. Still, some may choose to file taxes as a corporate entity, particularly if owners want to keep corporate income within the business to aid its growth. According to the Small Business Administration, an LLC cannot file partnership tax forms if it meets more than two of the following four qualities that would classify it as a corporation: (1) limited liability to the extent of assets; (2) continuity of life; (3) centralization of management; and (4) free transferability of ownership to interests. If more than two of these apply, the LLC must file corporation tax forms.

An LLC that chooses to be taxed as an S corporation can also do the following, which the tradition S corporation cannot, according to David Meier in Entrepreneur:

- have more than seventy-five business owners

- include a nonresident alien as an owner

- have either a corporation or a partnership as an owner

- have more than 80 percent ownership in a separate corporate entity

- have disproportionate ownership—ownership percentages that are different from each respective owner's investment in the business

- flow-through business loss deductions in excess of each respective owner's investment in the business

- have owners/members that are active in the management of the business without losing limited personal liability exposure.

SEE ALSO: Entrepreneurship; Organizational Chart

Boyd Childress
Revised by Wendy H. Mason

FURTHER READING:

"Choosing the Best Ownership Structure for Your Business." On NOLO.com. Available from: <http://www.nolo.com/resource.cfm/catid/5de04e60-45bb-4108-8d757e247f35b8ab/111/182/>.

Gabriel, Michael Lynn. *Everyone's Partnership Book.* Available from <http://www.attorneyetal.com/Previews/Partnr.html>.

Hynes, Dennis L. *Agency, Partnership, and the LLC in a Nutshell.* St. Paul, MN: West Publishing, 1997.

Mancuso, Anthony. *LLC or Corporation?: How To Choose The Right Form For Your Business Entity.* Berkeley, CA: NOLO, 2005.

Meier, David. "The Many Benefits of Forming an LLC: A Closer Look at Why This Legal Structure Can Be Good for Business." *Entrepreneur,* 16 August 2004. Available from <http://www.entrepreneur.com/article/0,4621,316656,00.html>.

Small Business Administration. "Forms of Business Ownership." Available from <http://www.sba.gov/starting_business/legal/forms.html>.

C

A cafeteria plan, also called a flexible benefit plan, allows employees to choose from a menu of optional benefits the ones that best fit their individual needs. Thus, employees can customize their benefit packages. In a cafeteria plan, benefits required by law (e.g. Social Security, unemployment compensation, workers's compensation) and those mandated by company policies or labor agreements are supplemented by a list of other benefits to which employees can subscribe. Employees's choices of optional benefits are limited only by the total benefit dollars available and the variety of benefits offered by the employer. Optional benefits that are often part of cafeteria plans include dental insurance, vision care, group-term life insurance, child care, and disability insurance. Many companies offer some form of cafeteria benefit plan to their employees, although smaller companies are less likely to offer flexible benefits than larger companies.

Most cafeteria plans are compliant with Section 125 of the Internal Revenue Code. This means that they meet specific requirements set out by the Internal Revenue Service. Such plans offer the potential of cost savings to both employers and employees, particularly because amounts spent by either the employer or the employee are spent out of pre-tax earnings. Thus, both employers and employees may save on Federal Insurance Contributions Act payroll taxes and the employee may save on state and federal income taxes as well.

TYPES OF CAFETERIA PLANS

There are several variations of cafeteria plans, including core-plus plans and modular plans. Core-plus plans provide a set of mandatory benefits that are usually designed to meet the basic needs of all employees. In addition to legally-required benefits, medical insurance, long-term disability insurance, and retirement benefits are often included in the core. Optional benefits are offered to employees who spend benefit credits to select other benefits that best fit their needs. Modular plans usually package several different bundles of benefits that offer increasingly extensive arrays of benefits. The basic module might include only the legally-required benefits, basic health insurance, and life insurance. A second module might include everything in the basic module plus additional benefits. A third module might include everything in modules one and two and even more benefits. Employees would choose the module that best fits their needs and life situation.

PROBLEMS WITH CAFETERIA PLANS

Perhaps the largest problem with cafeteria plans, as opposed to one-size-fits-all benefit plans, is that cafeteria plans are more complicated to administer. Since employees choose individualized benefit packages, the company must take care to record and maintain each employee's benefit package accurately. The company must maintain adequate communication with employees about changes in the cost of benefits, their coverage, and their use of benefits. Employees must also be offered the opportunity to re-visit their benefit choices and make new selections as their needs and life situations change. Additionally, employers must be careful to comply with Internal Revenue Service (IRS) rules and regulations regarding cafeteria plans so that the plans retain their tax-favored status.

Another issue that arises with cafeteria plans is the adverse selection problem. This problem arises because employees are likely to choose the optional benefits they are most likely to use. If enough employees do this, the cost of the benefit will eventually be driven up, as the premiums received must cover the expenditures of the benefit. For example, suppose a company allows employees to change their cafeteria plan selections once each year. During this "free enrollment" period, an employee who knows (or suspects) that he or she faces extensive dental work in the coming year would be more likely to sign up for dental insurance than the employee who expects only routine dental care. Likewise, an employee who has begun having vision problems would probably be more likely to sign up for vision coverage than an employee with perfect eyesight. Sometimes, employers will place restrictions on certain benefits to try to alleviate the adverse selection problem. Modular plans may also reduce the adverse selection problem, as the employer can package benefits in a way that limits employees's opportunity to choose individual benefits, by requiring them to choose a broad package of benefits.

Given the increasing diversity of the labor force, the demand for benefit packages tailored to individual needs and circumstances is likely to remain strong. Thus, one would expect the number of companies offering flexible benefit plans to continue to increase, as well as the rate of employee participation in such plans.

SEE ALSO: Human Resource Management

Tim Barnett

FURTHER READING:

Gomez-Mejia, Luis R., David B. Balkin, and Robert L. Cardy. *Managing Human Resources.* 4th ed. Upper Saddle River, NJ: Prentice-Hall, 2004.

Henderson, Richard L. *Compensation Management in a Knowledge-Based World.* 9th ed. Upper Saddle River, NJ: Prentice-Hall, 2003.

CAPACITY PLANNING

Capacity planning has seen an increased emphasis due to the financial benefits of the efficient use of capacity plans within material requirements planning systems and other information systems. Insufficient capacity can quickly lead to deteriorating delivery performance, unnecessarily increase work-in-process, and frustrate sales personnel and those in manufacturing. However, excess capacity can be costly and unnecessary. The inability to properly manage capacity can be a barrier to the achievement of maximum firm performance. In addition, capacity is an important factor in the organization's choice of technology.

Capacity is usually assumed to mean the maximum rate at which a transformation system produces or processes inputs. Sometimes, this rate may actually be "all at once"—as with the capacity of an airplane. A more usable definition of capacity would be the volume of output per elapsed time and the production capability of a facility.

Capacity planning is the process used to determine how much capacity is needed (and when) in order to manufacture greater product or begin production of a new product. A number of factors can affect capacity—number of workers, ability of workers, number of machines, waste, scrap, defects, errors, productivity, suppliers, government regulations, and preventive maintenance. Capacity planning is relevant in both the long term and the short term. However, there are different issues at stake for each.

LONG-TERM CAPACITY PLANNING

Over the long term, capacity planning relates primarily to strategic issues involving the firm's major production facilities. In addition, long-term capacity issues are interrelated with location decisions. Technology and transferability of the process to other products is also intertwined with long-term capacity planning. Long-term capacity planning may evolve when short-term changes in capacity are insufficient. For example, if the firm's addition of a third shift to its current two-shift plan still does not produce enough output, and subcontracting arrangements cannot be made, one feasible alternative is to add capital equipment and modify the layout of the plant (long-term actions). It may even be desirable to add additional plant space or to construct a new facility (long-term alternatives).

SHORT-TERM CAPACITY PLANNING

In the short term, capacity planning concerns issues of scheduling, labor shifts, and balancing resource capacities. The goal of short-term capacity planning is to handle unexpected shifts in demand in an efficient economic manner. The time frame for short-term planning is frequently only a few days but may run as long as six months.

Alternatives for making short-term changes in capacity are fairly numerous and can even include the decision to not meet demand at all. The easiest and most commonly-used method to increase capacity in the short term is working overtime. This is a flexible and inexpensive alternative. While the firm has to pay one and one half times the normal labor rate, it foregoes the expense of hiring, training, and paying additional benefits. When not used abusively, most workers appreciate the opportunity to earn extra wages. If overtime does not provide enough short-term capacity, other resource-increasing alternatives are available. These include adding shifts, employing casual or part-time workers, the use of floating workers, leasing workers, and facilities subcontracting.

Firms may also increase capacity by improving the use of their resources. The most common alternatives in this category are worker cross training and overlapping or staggering shifts. Most manufacturing firms inventory some output ahead of demand so that any need for a capacity change is absorbed by the inventory buffer. From a technical perspective, firms may initiate a process design intended to increase productivity at work stations. Manufacturers can also shift demand to avoid capacity requirement fluctuation by backlogging, queuing demand, or lengthening the firm's lead times. Service firms accomplish the same results through scheduling appointments and reservations.

A more creative approach is to modify the output. Standardizing the output or offering complimentary services are examples. In services, one might allow customers to do some of the process work themselves (e.g., self-service gas stations and fast-food restaurants). Another alternative—reducing quality—is an undesirable yet viable tactic.

Finally, the firm may attempt to modify demand. Changing the price and promoting the product are common. Another alternative is to partition demand by initiating a yield or revenue management system. Utilities also report success in shifting demand by the use of "off-peak" pricing.

CAPACITY-PLANNING TECHNIQUES

There are four procedures for capacity planning; capacity planning using overall factors (CPOF), capacity bills, resource profiles, and capacity requirements planning (CRP). The first three are rough-cut approaches (involving analysis to identify potential bottlenecks) that can be used with or without manufacturing resource planning (MRP) systems. CRP is used in conjunction with MRP systems.

Capacity using overall factors is a simple, manual approach to capacity planning that is based on the master production schedule and production standards that convert required units of finished goods into historical loads on each work center. Bills of capacity is a procedure based on the MPS. Instead of using historical ratios, however, it utilizes the bills of material and routing sheet (which shows the sequence or work centers required to manufacture the part, as well as the setup and run time). Capacity requirements can then be determined by multiplying the number of units

required by the MPS by the time needed to produce each. Resource profiles are the same as bills of capacity, except lead times are included so that workloads fall into the correct periods.

Capacity requirements planning (CRP) is only applicable in firms using MRP or MRP II. CRP uses the information from one of the previous rough-cut methods, plus MRP outputs on existing inventories and lot sizing. The result is a tabular load report for each work center or a graphical load profile for helping plan-production requirements. This will indicate where capacity is inadequate or idle, allowing for imbalances to be corrected by shifts in personnel or equipment or the use of overtime or added shifts. Finite capacity scheduling is an extension of CRP that simulates job order stopping and starting to produce a detailed schedule that provides a set of start and finish dates for each operation at each work center.

A failure to understand the critical nature of managing capacity can lead to chaos and serious customer service problems. If there is a mismatch between available and required capacity, adjustments should be made. However, it should be noted that firms cannot have perfectly-balanced material and capacity plans that easily accommodate emergency orders. If flexibility is the firm's competitive priority, excess capacity would be appropriate.

SEE ALSO: Aggregate Planning; Manufacturing Resources Planning

R. Anthony Inman

FURTHER READING:

Cochran, Jeffery K., and Alberto Marquez Uribe. "A Set Covering Formulation for Agile Capacity Planning Within Supply Chains." *International Journal of Production Economics* 95, no. 2 (2005): 139–149.

Jonsson, Patrik, and Stig-Arne Mattsson. "Use and Applicability of Capacity Planning Methods." *Production and Inventory Management Journal* 43, no. 3-4 (2002): 89–95.

Meredith, Jack R., and Scott M. Shafer. *Operations Management for MBAs.* 2nd Edition. New York: John Wiley and Sons, Inc., 2002.

Vollmann, Thomas E., William L. Berry, D. Clay Whybark, and Robert F. Jacobs. *Manufacturing Planning and Control Systems.* Boston: McGraw-Hill, 2005.

CASE METHOD OF ANALYSIS

The case method of analysis involves studying actual business situations—written as an in-depth presentation of a company, its market, and its strategic decisions—in order to improve a manager's or a student's problem-solving ability. Cases typically investigate a contemporary issue in a real-life context. There are multiple issues to consider and many "correct" or viable alternatives to solve the case issues are presented. Case studies provide students with a "note of reality" that makes learning more relevant and enjoyable.

Cases are written and published in textbooks by students, faculty, or consultants. Cases may be based on actual company experiences, like a consulting project, or may be developed from articles and events in business periodicals and newspapers. Cases include actual information of a company's decisions and may include interviews, observations, or data from firm and industry records, as well as database records and published historical facts on the company and the industry. Barbazette identified five types of cases studies:

1. Identification cases studies help learners identify positive and negative characteristics of the situation.

2. Problem-solving case studies use systematic and creative problem-solving techniques.

3. Practice case studies require students to use a new idea or try a new skill.

4. Application cases studies are used at the end of a training program to summarize and review.

5. Serial case studies progressively add new elements.

HISTORY OF CASES

The case method was invented by the Harvard Business School over 80 years ago, where it still remains the foundation for teaching and research. By studying and examining actual cases, professors believed students could develop better insight as to how organizations reach conclusions. This method of study and analysis is seen as an effective way to train young business leaders to consider facts and present them more efficiently.

POPULARITY OF CASES TODAY

Today, cases remain a popular method of study in business schools—especially at Harvard and the University of Virginia, where they are used heavily in the Master of Business Administration (MBA) programs. While technology, computer simulations, and other learning methods continue to grow, cases fill a much-needed function in the educational process of students, future managers, and leaders. Cases are used in a wide variety of disciplines and areas of study. They are also popular for executive training and are used in weekend-format continuing education and professional development programs.

In their study of the skills of technologists, Birchall and Smith found that technologists are often seen as not having sufficient input into the strategic decision-making process of organizations. Thus, many turn to MBA programs to develop their knowledge, understanding, and personal competencies. The case method has traditionally been used to aid in this educational process. They also stress the use of multimedia tools and groupware to create enhanced learning opportunities based on a dynamic case analysis.

Many groups and organizations also publish cases for educational use. Sources for cases for business schools include:

- The Aspen Institute Business and Society Program

- The Batten Institute, Darden Graduate School of Business, University of Virginia

- Harvard Business School

- Richard Ivey School of Business, University of Western Ontario

- South-Western Publishing Company's CaseNet

- Stanford Graduate School of Business

The American Association for Business Communication, for example, included the best cases for teaching communications in a special issue of *Business Communication Quarterly.* Rogers and Rymer report that their reviewer panel of experienced instructors agreed that the best cases include the following attributes:

- Focus on the discipline

- Require decision making

- Furnish a business context

- Present an engaging story or scenario

- Provide sufficiently-realistic detail for analysis and response

- Function readily in a classroom setting

- Apply to a wide range of teaching philosophies and educational settings

- Relate to contemporary issues and problems

TEACHING WITH CASES

Cases rely almost exclusively upon discussion to elicit diverse ideas, experiences, and views about case material. Cases allow students to explore actual decisions made by companies. The case presents an account of what happened to a business or industry over a period of time, for example. It includes the events with which managers had to deal and charts various responses to these decisions. According to Hill and Jones, cases provide students with the experience of organizational problems they have not yet had the opportunity to experience first-hand. In a relatively short period of time, students have the chance to appreciate and analyze problems faced by many different companies and to understand how managers attempted to resolve them. Cases also illustrate underlying business theories.

To prepare a case analysis, students typically read the case several times before a classroom discussion. They first read for a general idea about the problem, the players in the case, the level of the decision, and the type of company or industry presented. On second and subsequent readings, students look for deeper problems and issues and try to differentiate symptoms from real case problems.

Some schools encourage students to research the company by locating articles on the company at the time the case situation occurred. Another research technique is to have students conduct a financial analysis of the company that might include ratio analysis or industry/competitor research. Many schools encourage students to discuss assigned cases in small groups or study teams before class. These teams may develop potential alternatives to solve the problems and ensure each member has considered the relevant facts in the case.

Class discussion occurs in either one large group or several smaller groups. In these groups, participants decide on the solution(s) and the proper course of implementation. They must also consider the time frame for implementation as well as evaluation and success measures. Class members or participants critique the various viable alternatives that are presented. The class is then presented with what the company under study actually did to solve the problem. Some cases are used as quizzes or exams.

Teaching with cases has changed relatively little over the years. However, a new approach, developed by Theroux, is called "real time case method.," In this method, a semester-long case is delivered in weekly installments and focuses on one company and the current events it faces. This method differs from the traditional case study method by its extended coverage and real-timeinteractivity.

STUDENTS'S PERCEPTIONS OF CASES

Although case method teaching has been used extensively in virtually all business schools for years, little research has been conducted to investigate the effectiveness and usefulness of the method. Among the few studies available is Weil's, which measures students's perceptions. Weil's study confirmed the usefulness of the case method.

Many students favor the case method because there are no "right" or "wrong" answers to the cases. Unlike solving a math or finance problem, there may be multiple ways to reach a successful solution for the case. Diversity of opinion and diversity of group make-up often bring unique solutions to cases. Students learn to respond quickly, formulate answers, speak up, and participate in class discussion. They learn to separate background information from the real problem. They learn to succinctly state problems, to recommend potential alternative solutions, and to explore the pros and cons of each solution. They learn to find hidden information in charts, graphs, tables, and financial data often included in cases.

Some students are discouraged by cases because they do not yield only one, clear answer. Students are forced to develop skills of critical thinking and these skills, while important to today's managers, take time to perfect. Students may also fear presenting their ideas to a large group. They may fear public speaking or presentation in general or they may fear their particular thoughts will be ridiculed by others. Some with limited work or life experience may not feel capable of critiquing a top-level manager's past decisions. However, these unique and fresh ideas often present interesting alternatives.

SEE ALSO: Business Plan; Training Delivery Methods

Marilyn M. Helms
Revised by Judith M. Nixon

FURTHER READING:

Barbazette, Jean. *Instant Case Studies: How to Design, Adapt, and Use Case Studies in Training.* San Francisco: Pfeiffer, 2004.

Barnes, Louis B., C.R. Christensen, and Abby J. Hansen. *Teaching and the Case Method.* 3rd ed. Boston: Harvard Business School Press, 1994.

Birchall, David, and Matty Smith. "Developing the Skills of Technologists in Strategic Decision Making—A Multi-Media Case Approach." *International Journal of Technology Management* 15, no. 8 (1998): 854–868.

Christensen, C.R. *Teaching by the Case Method.* Boston: Harvard Business School, 1983.

Copeland, M. "The Genesis of the Case Method in Business Administration." In *The Case Method at the Harvard Business School.* ed. Malcolm P. McNair. New York: McGraw-Hill, 1954.

Hill, Charles W.L., and Gareth R. Jones. *Strategic Management: An Integrated Approach.* 5th ed. Boston: Houghton/Mifflin Publishing Co., 2001.

Hunger, J.D., and Thomas L Wheelen. *Essential of Strategic Management.* 3rd ed. Upper Saddle River, NJ: Prentice Hall, 2003.

Klein, Hans E., ed. *The Art of Interactive Teaching with Cases, Simulations, Games, and other Interactive Methods.* Boston: The World Association for Case Method Research and Application, 1995.

Oyelere, Peter, Joanna Yeoh, Colin Firer, and Sidney Weil. "A Study of Students's Perceptions of the Usefulness of Case Studies for Development of Finance and Accounting-Related Skills and Knowledge." *Accounting Education* 10, no. 2 (2001): 123–146.

Rogers, Priscilla S., and Jone Rymer. "Business and Management Communication Cases: Challenges and Opportunities." *Business Communication Quarterly* 61, no. 1 (1998): 7–25.

Theroux, J., and C. Kilbane. "The Real-Time Case Method: A New Approach to an Old Tradition." *Journal of Education for Business* 79, no. 3 (2004): 163–167.

CASH FLOW ANALYSIS AND STATEMENT

Cash flow analysis is a method of analyzing the financing, investing, and operating activities of a company. The primary goal of cash flow analysis is to identify, in a timely manner, cash flow problems as well as cash flow opportunities. The primary document used in cash flow analysis is the cash flow statement. Since 1988, the Securities and Exchange Commission (SEC) has required every company that files reports to include a cash flow statement with its quarterly and annual reports. The cash flow statement is useful to managers, lenders, and investors because it translates the earnings reported on the income statement—which are subject to reporting regulations and accounting decisions—into a simple summary of how much cash the company has generated during the period in question. "Cash flow measures real money flowing into, or out of, a company's bank account," Harry Domash notes on his Web site, WinningInvesting.com. "Unlike reported earnings, there is little a company can do to overstate its bank balance."

THE CASH FLOW STATEMENT

A typical cash flow statement is divided into three parts: cash from operations (from daily business activities like collecting payments from customers or making payments to suppliers and employees); cash from investment activities (the purchase or sale of assets); and cash from financing activities (the issuing of stock or borrowing of funds). The final total shows the net increase or decrease in cash for the period.

Cash flow statements facilitate decision making by providing a basis for judgments concerning the profitability, financial condition, and financial management of a company. While historical cash flow statements facilitate the systematic evaluation of past cash flows, projected (or pro forma) cash flow statements provide insights regarding future cash flows.

Projected cash flow statements are typically developed using historical cash flow data modified for anticipated changes in price, volume, interest rates, and so on.

To enhance evaluation, a properly-prepared cash flow statement distinguishes between recurring and nonrecurring cash flows. For example, collection of cash from customers is a recurring activity in the normal course of operations, whereas collections of cash proceeds from secured bank loans (or issuances of stock, or transfers of personal assets to the company) is typically not considered a recurring activity. Similarly, cash payments to vendors is a recurring activity, whereas repayments of secured bank loans (or the purchase of certain investments or capital assets) is typically not considered a recurring activity in the normal course of operations.

In contrast to nonrecurring cash inflows or outflows, most recurring cash inflows or outflows occur (often frequently) within each cash cycle (i.e., within the average time horizon of the cash cycle). The cash cycle (also known as the operating cycle or the earnings cycle) is the series of transactions or economic events in a given company whereby:

1. Cash is converted into goods and services.

2. Goods and services are sold to customers.

3. Cash is collected from customers.

To a large degree, the volatility of the individual cash inflows and outflows within the cash cycle will dictate the working-capital requirements of a company. Working capital generally refers to the average level of unrestricted cash required by a company to ensure that all stakeholders are paid on a timely basis. In most cases, working capital can be monitored through the use of a cash budget.

THE CASH BUDGET

In contrast to cash flow statements, cash budgets provide much more timely information regarding cash inflows and outflows. For example, whereas cash flow statements are often prepared on a monthly, quarterly, or annual basis, cash budgets are often prepared on a daily, weekly, or monthly basis. Thus, cash budgets may be said to be prepared on a continuous rolling basis (e.g., are updated every month for the next twelve months). Additionally, cash budgets provide much more detailed information than cash flow statements. For example, cash budgets will typically distinguish between cash collections from credit customers and cash collections from cash customers.

A thorough understanding of company operations is necessary to reasonably assure that the nature and timing of cash inflows and outflows is properly reflected in the cash budget. Such an understanding becomes increasingly important as the precision of the cash budget increases. For example, a 360-day rolling budget requires a greater knowledge of a company than a two-month rolling budget.

While cash budgets are primarily concerned with operational issues, there may be strategic issues that need to be considered before preparing the cash budget. For example, predetermined cash amounts may be earmarked for the acquisition of certain investments or capital assets, or for the liquidation of certain indebtedness. Further, there may be policy issues that need to be considered prior to preparing a cash budget. For example, should excess cash, if any, be invested in certificates of deposit or in some form of short-term marketable securities (e.g., commercial paper or U.S. Treasury bills)?

Generally speaking, the cash budget is grounded in the overall projected cash requirements of a company for a given period. In turn, the overall projected cash requirements are grounded in the overall projected free cash flow. Free cash flow is defined as net cash flow from operations less the following three items:

1. Cash used by essential investing activities (e.g., replacements of critical capital assets).

2. Scheduled repayments of debt.

3. Normal dividend payments.

If the calculated amount of free cash flow is positive, this amount represents the cash available to invest in new lines of business, retire additional debt, and/or increase dividends. If the calculated amount of free cash flow is negative, this amount represents the amount of cash that must be borrowed (and/or obtained through sales of nonessential assets, etc.) in order to support the strategic goals of the company. To a large degree, the free cash flow paradigm parallels the cash flow statement.

Using the overall projected cash flow requirements of a company (in conjunction with the free cash flow paradigm), detailed budgets are developed for the selected time interval within the overall time horizon of the budget (i.e., the annual budget could be developed on a daily, weekly, or monthly basis). Typically, the complexity of the company's operations will dictate the level of detail required for the cash budget. Similarly, the complexity of the corporate operations will drive the number of assumptions and estimation algorithms required to properly prepare a budget (e.g., credit customers are assumed to remit cash as follows: 50 percent in the month of sale; 30 percent in the month after sale; and so on). Several basic concepts germane to all cash budgets are:

1. Current period beginning cash balances plus current period cash inflows less current period cash outflows equals current period ending cash balances.

2. The current period ending cash balance equals the new (or next) period's beginning cash balance.

3. The current period ending cash balance signals either a cash flow opportunity (e.g., possible investment of idle cash) or a cash flow problem (e.g., the need to borrow cash or adjust one or more of the cash budget items giving rise to the borrow signal).

RATIO ANALYSIS

In addition to cash flow statements and cash budgets, ratio analysis can also be employed as an effective cash flow analysis technique. Ratios often provide insights regarding the relationship of two numbers (e.g., net cash provided from operations versus capital expenditures) that would not be readily apparent from the mere inspection of the individual numerator or denominator. Additionally, ratios facilitate comparisons with similar ratios of prior years of the same company (i.e., intracompany comparisons) as well as comparisons of other companies (i.e., intercompany or industry comparisons). While ratio analysis may be used in conjunction with the cash flow statement and/or the cash budget, ratio analysis is often used as a stand-alone, attention-directing, or monitoring technique.

ADDITIONAL BENEFITS

In his book, *Buy Low, Sell High, Collect Early, and Pay Late: The Manager's Guide to Financial Survival,* Dick Levin suggests the following benefits that stem from cash forecasting (i.e., preparing a projected cash flow statement or cash budget):

1. Knowing what the cash position of the company is and what it is likely to be avoids embarrassment. For example, it helps avoid having to lie that the check is in the mail.

2. A firm that understands its cash position can borrow exactly what it needs and no more, there by minimizing interest or, if applicable, the firm can invest its idle cash.

3. Walking into the bank with a cash flow analysis impresses loan officers.

4. Cash flow analyses deter surprises by enabling proactive cash flow strategies.

5. Cash flow analysis ensures that a company does not have to bounce a check before it realizes that it needs to borrow money to cover expenses. In contrast, if the cash flow analysis indicates that a loan will be needed several months from now, the firm can turn down the first two offers of terms and have time for further negotiations.

LOAN APPLICATIONS

Potential borrowers should be prepared to answer the following questions when applying for loans:

1. How much cash is needed?
2. How will this cash help the business (i.e., how does the loan help the business accomplish its business objectives as documented in the business plan)?
3. How will the company pay back the cash?
4. How will the company pay back the cash if the company goes bankrupt?
5. How much do the major stakeholders have invested in the company?

Admittedly, it is in the best interest of the potential borrower to address these questions prior to requesting a loan. Accordingly, in addition to having a well-prepared cash flow analysis, the potential borrower should prepare a separate document addressing the following information:

1. Details of the assumptions underpinning the specific amount needed should be prepared (with cross-references to relevant information included in the cash flow analysis).
2. The logic underlying the business need for the amount of cash requested should be clearly stated (and cross-referenced to the relevant objectives stated in the business plan or some other strategic planning document).
3. The company should clearly state what potential assets would be available to satisfy the claims of the lender in case of default (i.e., the company should indicate the assets available for the collateralization of the loan).
4. Details of the equity interests of major stakeholders should be stated.

In some cases, the lender may also request personal guarantees of loan repayment. If this is necessary, the document will need to include relevant information regarding the personal assets of the major stakeholders available to satisfy the claims of the lender in case of default.

INADEQUATE CAPITALIZATION

Many businesses fail due to inadequate capitalization. Inadequate capitalization basically implies that there were not enough cash and/or credit arrangements secured prior to initiating operations to ensure that the company could pay its debts during the early stages of operations (when cash inflows are nominal, if any, and cash outflows are very high). Admittedly, it is extremely difficult to perform a cash flow analysis when the company does not have a cash flow history. Accordingly, alternative sources of information should be obtained from trade journals, government agencies, and potential lenders. Additional information can be solicited from potential customers, vendors, and competitors, allowing the firm to learn from others's mistakes and successes.

UNCONSTRAINED GROWTH

While inadequate capitalization represents a front-end problem, unconstrained growth represents a potential back-end problem. Often, unconstrained growth provokes business failure because the company is growing faster than their cash flow. While many cash flow problems are operational in nature, unconstrained growth is a symptom of a much larger strategic problem. Accordingly, even to the extent that cash flow analyses are performed on a timely basis, such analyses will never overcome a flawed strategy underpinning the unconstrained growth.

BANKRUPTCY

A company is said to be bankrupt when it experiences financial distress to the extent that the protection of the bankruptcy laws is employed for the orderly disposition of assets and settlement of creditors's claims. Significantly, not all bankruptcies are fatal. In some circumstances, creditors may allow the bankrupt company to reorganize its financial affairs, allowing the company to continue or reopen. Such a reorganization might include relieving the company from further liability on the unsatisfied portion of the company's obligations. Admittedly, such reorganizations are performed in vain if the reasons underlying the financial distress have not been properly resolved. Unfortunately, properly-prepared and timely cash flow analyses can not compensate for poor management, poor products, or weak internal controls.

SEE ALSO: Budgeting; Financial Issues for Managers; Financial Ratios; Strategic Planning Tools

Michael S. Luehlfing
Revised by Laurie Hillstrom

FURTHER READING:

Brahmasrene, Tantatape, C.D. Strupeck, and Donna Whitten. "Examining Preferences in Cash Flow Statement Format." *CPA Journal* 58 (2004).

Domash, Harry. "Check Cash Flow First." Winninginvesting. com. Available from http://www.winninginvesting.com/cash_flow.htm.

"Intro to Fundamental Analysis: The Cash Flow Statement." Investopedia.com. Available from http://www.investopedia.com/university/fundamentalanalysis/cashflow.asp.

Levin, Richard I. *Buy Low, Sell High, Collect Early, and Pay Late: The Manager's Guide to Financial Survival.* Englewood Cliffs, NJ: Prentice-Hall, 1983.

Mills, John, and Jeanne H. Yamamura. "The Power of Cash Flow Ratios." *Journal of Accountancy* 186, no. 4 (1998): 53–57.

"Preparing Your Cash Flow Statement." U.S. Small Business Administration, Online Women's Business Center. Available from http://www.onlinewbc.gov/docs/finance/cashflow.html.

Silver, Jay. "Use of Cash Flow Projections." *Secured Lender,* March/April 1997, 64–68.

Simon, Geoffrey A. "A Cash Flow Statement Says, 'Show Me the Money!'" *Tampa Bay Business Journal* 27 (2001).

CELLULAR MANUFACTURING

Cellular manufacturing is a manufacturing process that produces families of parts within a single line or cell of machines operated by machinists who work only within the line or cell. A cell is a small scale, clearly-defined production unit within a larger factory. This unit has complete responsibility for producing a family of like parts or a product. All necessary machines and manpower are contained within this cell, thus giving it a degree of operational autonomy. Each worker is expected to have mastered a full range of operating skills required by his or her cell. Therefore, systematic job rotation and training are necessary conditions for effective cell development. Complete worker training is needed to ensure that flexible worker assignments can be fulfilled.

Cellular manufacturing, which is actually an application of group technology, has been described as a stepping stone to achieving world class manufacturing status. The objective of cellular manufacturing is to design cells in such a way that some measure of performance is optimized. This measure of performance could be productivity, cycle time, or some other logistics measure. Measures seen in practice include pieces per man hour, unit cost, on-time delivery, lead time, defect rates, and percentage of parts made cell-complete.

This process involves placing a cluster of carefully selected sets of functionally dissimilar machines in close proximity to each other. The result is small, stand-alone manufacturing units dedicated to the production of a set or family of parts—or essentially, a miniature version of a plant layout.

While the machinery may be functionally dissimilar, the family of parts produced contains similar processing requirements or has geometric similarities. Thus, all parts basically follow the same routing with some minor variations (e.g., skipping an operation).

The cells may have no conveyorized movement of parts between machines, or they may have a flow line connected by a conveyor that can provide automatic transfer.

Cellular manufacturing is a hybrid system that links the advantages of a job shop with the product layout of the continuous flow line. The cell design provides for quick and efficient flow, and the high productivity associated with assembly lines. However, it also provides the flexibility of the job shop, allowing both similar and diverse products to be added to the line without slowing the process. Figures 1 and 2 compares a cellular layout to that of the typical job shop (process layout).

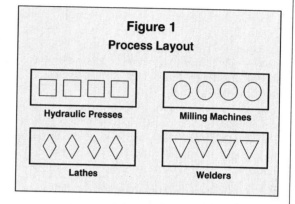

Figure 1
Process Layout

Hydraulic Presses   Milling Machines
Lathes   Welders

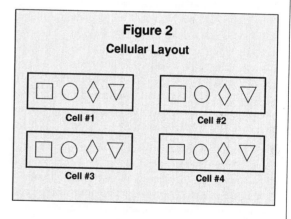

Figure 2
Cellular Layout

Cell #1   Cell #2
Cell #3   Cell #4

BENEFITS OF CELLULAR MANUFACTURING

Many firms utilizing cellular manufacturing have reported near immediate improvements in performance, with only relatively minor adverse effects. Cited improvements which seem to have occurred fairly quickly include reductions in work-in-process, finished goods, lead time, late orders, scrap, direct labor, and workspace.

In particular, production and quality control is enhanced. By breaking the factory into small, homogeneous and cohesive productive units, production and quality control is made easier. Cells that are not performing according to volume and quality targets can be easily isolated, since the parts/products affected can be traced to a single cell. Also, because the productive units are small, the search for the root of problems is made easier.

Quality parameters and control procedures can be dovetailed to the particular requirements of the parts or workpieces specific to a certain cell. By focusing quality control activity on a particular production unit or part type, the cell can quickly master the necessary quality requirements. Control is always enhanced when productive units are kept at a minimum operating scale, which is what cellular manufacturing provides.

When production is structured using cellular manufacturing logic, flow systematization is possible. Grouping of parts or products into sets or families reveals which ones are more or less amenable to continuous, coupled flow. Parts that are standardized and common to many products will have very low changeover times, and thus, are quickly convertible to continuous, line-flow production. Products that are low-volume, high-variety and require longer set-up times can be managed so that they evolve toward a line flow.

Cells can be designed to exploit the characteristics peculiar to each part family so as to optimize the flow for each cell and for groups of cells as a whole. Flow systematization can be done one cell at a time so as to avoid large disruptions in operations. Then the cells that were easy to systemize can provide experience that can be exploited when the more difficult systematization projects occur later. Cells that have been changed to a line flow will invariably show superior performance in the areas of quality, throughput time, and cost, which can lead to eventual plantwide benefit.

Work flow that is adapted to the unique requirements of each product or part allows the plant to produce high-volume and high-variety products simultaneously. Since the cell structure integrates both worker and product versatility into a single unit, it has the potential to attain maximum system flexibility while maintaining factory focus. Cells can be designed around single products, product groups, unique parts, part families, or whatever unique market requirements are identified. For the same part, there may be one high-volume, standardized design and one low-volume customized design. Cells can be built specifically for any of these with a focus on the individual marketing or production requirement called for by the individual product or part.

Systematic job rotation and training in multiple skills also make possible quick, flexible work assignments that can be used to alleviate bottlenecks occurring within the cell. Since normal cell operation requires the workers to master all the skills internal to the cell, little or no additional training should be needed when workers have to be redeployed in response to volume or sales mix changes. When it is routine for workers to learn new skills, they can be easily transferred to another job within the cell or possibly even to an entirely different production unit. Without this worker flexibility and versatility, there can be no real production system flexibility.

LIMITATIONS

While its benefits have been well documented, it should also be noted that some have argued that implementing cellular manufacturing could lead to a decrease in manufacturing flexibility. It is felt that conversion to cells may cause some loss in routing flexibility, which could then impact the viability of cell use. Obtaining balance among cells is also more difficult than for flow or job shops. Flow shops have relatively fixed capacity, and job shops can draw from a pool of skilled labor so balance isn't that much of a problem. By contrast, with cells, if demand diminishes greatly, it may be necessary to break up that cell and redistribute the equipment or reform the families.

Also, some researchers have warned that the benefits of cellular manufacturing could deteriorate over time due to ongoing changes in the production environment. Finally, it must be noted that conversion to cellular manufacturing can involve the costly realignment of equipment. The burden lies with the manager to determine if the costs of switching from a process layout to a cellular one outweigh the costs of the inefficiencies and inflexibility of conventional plant layouts.

THE IMPLEMENTATION PROCESS

A wide variety of methods for the implementation of cellular manufacturing have been proposed. These range from complex computer and mathematical models to straightforward applications, such as production flow analysis. A pattern for implementation is now presented.

The first step in implementing cellular manufacturing is to break down the various items produced by the company into a number of part sets or families. The grouping process (group technology) involves identifying items with similarities in design characteristics or manufacturing characteristics, and grouping them into part families. Design characteristics include size, shape, and function; manufacturing characteristics or process characteristics are based on the type and sequence of operations required. In many cases, though not always, the two kinds of characteristics are correlated. Therefore design families may be distinctly different from processing families.

Once identified, similar items can be classified into families. Then a system is developed that facilitates retrieval from a design and manufacturing database. For example, the system can be used to determine if an identical or similar part exists before a completely new part is designed. If a similar part is found, it may be that a simple modification would produce satisfactory results without the expense of new part design. Similarly, planning the manufacturing of a new part after matching it with an existing part family can eliminate new and costly processing requirements.

This grouping of part or product families requires a systematic analysis that often proves to be a major undertaking. Usually, there is a considerable amount of data to analyze, and this in turn can be quite time-consuming and costly. Three primary methods exist for accomplishing the grouping process: visual inspection, examination of design and production data, and production flow analysis. Visual inspection is the least accurate of the three but nonetheless the simplest and the least costly. The most commonly used method of analysis is the examination of design and production data. This method is more accurate but is also more time-consuming. Production flow analysis examines operation sequences and machine routing to uncover similarities (therefore, it has a manufacturing perspective rather than a design perspective). However, unless the operation sequencing and routings are verified, this method could be far from optimal.

The resulting number of families determines the number of cells required, as well as what machines are required within each cell. The cell usually includes all the processing operations needed to complete a part or subassembly. However, it is possible for a product to go from raw materials to packaging and be ready for shipment by the time it reaches the end of the cell.

The families will also help determine where within the cell each machine will be located for the most efficient flow, and how many employees are needed within each cell. After the product families are determined, the machines needed for the production process of a specific family are organized into cells according to processing requirements (e.g., the order of processing). Frequently, machines are grouped in an efficient U-shaped configuration. Since each machine operates on its own for much of the cycle, few workers may be needed, and even then only for a limited number of steps.

The optimal layout is one that minimizes the distance between cells, or the distance to the next production point. The resulting reduction in time and handling ultimately provides a reduction in processing costs. Some firms utilize "linked-cell manufacturing," which is the concept of arranging the manufacturing cells near the assembly cells. Again, this decreases travel distances while reducing materials handling.

Hopefully, the floor layout will also provide for the easy flow of a product to shipping, if shipping is located close to the cells in a streamlined flow.

Some plants in advanced stages of cellular manufacturing utilize what is known as a "mini-plant." The cell not only does the manufacturing, but also has its own support services, including its own industrial engineer, quality manager, accountant, and marketing representative and/or salesperson. Only research and development and human resource management are not dedicated to the mini-plant.

An entire facility can be broken down into a number of mini-plants, each of which operates as an independent profit center.

THE IMPACT OF CELLULAR MANUFACTURING ON WORKERS. Nancy Hyer and Urban Wemmerlov noted in *Mechanical Engineering* that while technology and processes represent the "hard side" of cells, people represent the "soft side." They state that the soft side factors are far more difficult to change than are the hard side factors. Most implementing firms spend most of their time struggling with soft issues. Cellular manufacturing calls for radical changes in the way industrial work is designed, structured, planned, controlled, and supervised. It makes worker self-management a reality, so management must be convinced that the workers can master all the required aspects of the work.

The decision to implement cellular manufacturing requires a deep commitment to excellence and a desire to permanently change the way factories are viewed and managed. Cellular manufacturing affects workers in a number of ways. Among the factors now discussed are issues of self-management, motivation, employee input, supervision, and group cohesiveness.

SELF-MANAGEMENT. Cell workers are encouraged to think creatively about production problems and are expected to arrive at pragmatic solutions to them. While they are free to seek advice from plant management and staff, the identified problems and subsequent analysis, and usually the solutions, are entirely their own. Workers have the authority and are encouraged to implement and follow up on action plans to improve their work. Some managers ask cells to set improvement targets for themselves and measure their performance in comparison to these targets. In addition, workers are given the freedom to plan, coordinate, and control their work within their cell as long as they meet company standards of quality, volume, time, and cost.

MOTIVATION. Behavioral psychology proposes that challenging work assignments keep employees motivated, satisfied, and productive. Flexible work assignments within the cells ensure that employees are constantly learning new tasks and constantly being challenged. Job rotation within the cell introduces variety in work patterns, thereby breaking the monotony (which has been known to cause absenteeism and problems in quality and productivity). Industrial work is productively accomplished in a group work setting. Cellular manufacturing can energize the group, attacking the lethargy found in many industrial situations.

EMPLOYEE INPUT. With the cell work group energized and motivated, the employees are more likely to actively and continually bring their mental capabilities to bear on job-related problems. Cell workers are the closest ones to the production process, so practical ideas are likely to instigate other ideas, which could then give rise to a continuous, almost self-sustaining chain reaction of improvement. As the workers see their own creative output being implemented, they begin to develop self-esteem and a stronger desire to succeed. They even begin to challenge each other to improve on their prior accomplishments.

The drive toward excellence is fueled by the human need to achieve until the desire to excel and continuously improve becomes part of the factory culture. Then as workers learn by doing more, they become more proficient at generating ideas which, perpetuates the cycle of improvement. Cellular manufacturing can be the structural catalyst that starts, contains, and sustains the improvement process.

SUPERVISION. The intense use of manufacturing cells tends to flatten the factory management structure and reduce overhead costs. When work group autonomy, worker versatility, and small group improvement activities converge, the need for supervision is drastically reduced, if not eliminated all together. Cell manufacturing perpetuates the idea that the work group should supervise itself. A workforce that is motivated, trained, and assigned specific clear responsibility for a product or part, coupled with simplified production planning and control, does not need to be minutely controlled or supervised in order to do a good job.

GROUP COHESIVENESS. The creation of small-scale productions dedicated to production of a few similar parts increases work group cohesiveness. Since each cell has few employees, typically less than fourteen, extensive interpersonal contact is unavoidable. The workers are now part of a single, identifiable unit with operating autonomy and responsibility for a specific product, linked by the common purpose of continually improving the productive unit for which they are responsible. The cell structure keeps problems at a level where they are manageable and gives employees the opportunity to exercise their creative potential in a pragmatic way. When problems calling for technical expertise beyond that of the workers, managers and production staff can be called on to provide assistance. Cell manufacturing builds a cohesive subculture within the wider social environment of the plant.

The use of flexible work assignments contributes even more to the group's cohesiveness and loyalty. Employees who regularly perform the work also done by coworkers are more likely to demonstrate empathy and support when dealing with each other on the job. If each worker has experienced each job firsthand, they are more able to offer encouragement and advice on how the work can be improved and each worker is more receptive to the input of his or her coworkers. Each worker can view and understand completely the task, responsibilities, and mission that top management has dedicated to the cell. The cross-fertilization process that emerges can generate some truly creative ideas for process improvement. As the expression goes, "as iron sharpens iron, so shall one man sharpen another."

Finally, work group cohesiveness, reinforced by the cell structure, facilitates total people management. Due to its small scale and mission focus, the cell can be easily mobilized. Top management is too far removed, spatially and socially, from the workers to be able to interact with them extensively enough to significantly control the socialization process. Management can shape corporate values and create a nurturing social environment, but it cannot instill these values into the minds of the lower level employees. Hence, corporate values are better communicated and instilled into daily work habits by small group processes.

The cell is better able to exercise social control over deviant workers since it can directly and immediately manipulate social rewards and punishment. Any worker who fails to conform may find his deviant behavior quickly detected and reacted to by the withdrawal of the social support of the cell. Deviant behavior that is hidden from management for long periods of time is very visible to the small group and can be dealt with quickly.

Conversely, high-performing group members are also quickly visible but are rewarded with esteem and respect from the other cell workers. Consequently, management can work through the cell to instill the corporation's values, attitudes, and philosophies. Once these are internalized by the group's key members, the group itself will take over the socialization process of indoctrinating these values into the mindset of each worker.

FOCUSED CELLULAR MANUFACTURING

In *International Journal of Operations and Production Management,* Fahad Al-Mubarak and Basheer M. Khumawala discuss a similar alternative to cellular manufacturing, focused cellular manufacturing (FCM). They define focused cellular manufacturing as a layout scheme that groups components by end-items and forms cell of machine for fabrication and assembly of the end-items. It differs from cellular manufacturing in that it does not attempt to take advantage of process similarities so as to reduce setup times.

The major advantage of FCM is the reduction of completion times for assembled end-items and work-in-process inventories while maintaining some degree of flexibility. In addition, it should be easy to install in a firm producing a few end-items in large volume or many end-items produced in small volume. Apparently, installing a single, focused cell for a few end-items is more practical than installation of many cells as required for a cellular layout.

The flow systematization and physical process integration of cellular manufacturing reinforce each other in potent ways. The underlying mechanisms can be collectively used to push manufacturing to higher performance levels. The result is an effectively designed cellular manufacturing structure, a production operation that integrates many concepts of superior manufacturing performance into a single small-scale production unit whose place in the large manufacturing system is clearly visible.

One final note is to distinguish cellular manufacturing from flexible manufacturing. A flexible manufacturing system is a more fully automated version of cellular manufacturing. A flexible manufacturing system utilizes a computer to control the start of work at each machine and to control the transfer of parts from machine to machine. While quite expensive, flexible manufacturing systems enable manufacturers to achieve some of the benefits of product layouts with small batch sizes provide greater flexibility because the system can operate with little or no human intervention.

SEE ALSO: Layout; World-Class Manufacturer

R. Anthony Inman

FURTHER READING:

Al-Mubarak, Fahad and Basheer M. Khumawala. "Focused Cellular Manufacturing: An Alternative to Cellular Manufacturing." *International Journal of Operations and Production Management* 23, no. 3 (2003): 277–299.

Hyer, Nancy and Urban Wemmerlov. "Cell Manufacturing: The Hard Part Is to Get People in Step with the Program." *Mechanical Engineering* 126, no. 3 (1 March 2004): E14–16.

Meredith, Jack R., and Scott M. Shafer. *Operations Management for MBAs.* Hoboken, NJ: John Wiley & Sons, Inc., 2004.

CENSUS—ECONOMIC

SEE: Economic Census

CHAIN OF COMMAND PRINCIPLE

The chain of command, sometimes called the scaler chain, is the formal line of authority, communication, and responsibility within an organization. The chain of command is usually depicted on an organizational chart, which identifies the superior and subordinate relationships in the organizational structure. According to classical organization theory the organizational chart allows one to visualize the lines of authority and communication within an organizational structure and ensures clear assignment of duties and responsibilities. By utilizing the chain of command, and its visible authority relationships, the principle of unity of command is maintained. Unity of command means that each subordinate reports to one and only one superior.

HISTORICAL BACKGROUND

The chain of command principle is ancient, but its application to the management of organizations was only systematized in the twentieth century. Two individuals—the French engineer and executive Henri Fayol and the German sociologist Max Weber—contributed much to our understanding of this principle. In his book, *General and Industrial Management,* Fayol presented what have come to be known as the fourteen principles of management. These principles include both the unity of command (his fourth principle) and the scalar chain (line of authority). Fayol's principle of the unity of command holds that a subordinate should report to one and only one supervisor. Fayol believed that this was necessary to provide the supervisor with clear position authority, and to prevent a subordinate from receiving conflicting orders. Fayol's scalar chain principle states that authority and responsibility flow, one level at a time, in a vertical line from the highest level in an organization to its lowest level. This line of authority establishes an organization's hierarchy. Fayol believed that it was a management error to abandon the chain of command for no reason, but he also allowed for circumstances in which the chain of command might be bypassed for the good of the company. For example, Fayol suggested that communication delays might sometimes be caused by blind adherence to the chain of command

and unity of command principles, and proposed what he called the "gangplank," which allows communications outside the chain of command as long as superiors are made aware. Weber also studied the problems inherent in large organizations, as organizations grew from family structures to much larger entities during the Industrial Revolution (1760–1850). Weber proposed the bureaucracy as a model of efficient organization. Bureaucratic characteristics have clearly defined hierarchies of authority and responsibility, consistent with the chain of command principle.

CURRENT STATUS

In many organizations, the chain of command principle is still very much alive. The manager's status is that of the deliverer of orders, and the employee enacts them under the monitoring of the manager. Both parties share responsibility for achievements. But, as Longnecker suggests in his book *Principles of Management and Organizational Behavior,* communication provides the underpinnings of this relationship. The discussions and meetings contact managers and their subordinates have may improve or harm the effectiveness of the direct report relationships in the chain of command.

A problem associated with the chain of command occurs when a subordinate bypasses a manager in either the giving of information or the requesting of a decision. This act undermines the authority and position of the manager who is bypassed. If this practice is allowed to continue in a bureaucratically-organized company, morale of the managers will decline. The urgency and frequency of these situations may, of course, mitigate the impact and inappropriateness of such contacts.

With the rapidly-changing environment and increasing uncertainty that organizations face in the twenty-first century, some adopt structures that emphasize flexibility and quick response to change. These types of organizations attempt to place decision-making authority in the organizational structure with those who can most effectively and efficiently respond to environmental imperatives. Thus, these organizations may have flatter hierarchies and communication and decision-making patterns that do not fully adhere to the chain of command or unity of command principles. In the case of matrix organizations, employees frequently have two managers or supervisors, violating the unity of command and chain of command principles. To be effective, individuals working in these organizations learn to share power, use open confrontation to resolve issues, and to utilize all directions in the organization to disseminate information. These more organic structures are not rigidly bound to the chain of command principle, although it is still an important organizing principle in most organizations.

SEE ALSO: Management Control; Management Functions; Organizational Chart; Organizational Structure

Denise Marie Tanguay
Revised by Tim Barnett

FURTHER READING:

Fayol, Henri. *General and Industrial Management.* trans. Constance Storrs. London: Pitman Publishing, Ltd., 1949.

Longnecker, Justin G. *Principles of Management and Organizational Behavior.* 4th ed. Columbus, OH: Charles E. Merrill Publishing Company, 1977.

Weber, Max. *The Theory of Social and Economic Organization.* trans. A.M. Henderson and T. Parsons. New York: Oxford University Press, 1947.

Wren, Daniel A. *The Evolution of Management Thought.* 4th ed. New York: John Wiley & Sons, Inc., 1994.

CHANGE—MANAGING

SEE: Managing Change

CHANGE—REACTIVE VS. PROACTIVE

SEE: Reactive vs. Proactive Change

CHANGE—TRENDS IN ORGANIZATIONS

SEE: Trends in Organizational Change

CHAOS THEORY

Chaos theory is a scientific principle describing the unpredictability of systems. Most fully explored and recognized during the mid-to-late 1980s, its premise is that systems sometimes reside in chaos, generating energy but without any predictability or direction. These complex systems may be weather patterns, ecosystems, water flows, anatomical functions, or organizations. While these systems's chaotic behavior may appear random at first, chaotic systems can be defined by a mathematical formula, and they are not without order or finite boundaries. This theory, in relation to organizational behavior, was somewhat discounted during the 1990s, giving way to the very similar complexity theory.

ORIGINS OF CHAOS THEORY

One of the first scientists to comment on chaos was Henri Poincaré(1854–1912), a late-nineteenth century French mathematician who extensively studied topology and dynamic systems. He left writings hinting at the same unpredictability in systems that Edward Lorenz (b. 1917) would study more than half a century later. Poincaré explained, "It may happen that small differences in the initial conditions produce very great ones in the final phenomena. A small error in the former will produce an enormous error in the latter. Prediction becomes impossible." Unfortunately, the study of dynamic systems was largely ignored long after Poincaré's death.

During the early 1960s, a few scientists from various disciplines were again taking note of "odd behavior" in complex systems such as the earth's atmosphere and the human brain. One of these scientists was Edward Lorenz, a meteorologist from the Massachusetts Institute of Technology (MIT), who was experimenting with computational models of the atmosphere. In the process of his experimentation he discovered one of chaos theory's fundamental principles— the Butterfly Effect. The Butterfly Effect is named for its assertion that a butterfly flapping its wings in Tokyo can impact weather patterns in Chicago. More scientifically, the Butterfly Effect proves that forces governing weather formation are unstable. These unstable forces allow minuscule changes in the atmosphere to have major impact elsewhere. More broadly applied, the Butterfly Effect means that what may appear to be insignificant changes to small parts of a system can have exponentially larger effects on that system. It also helps to dispel the notion that random system activity and disturbances must be due to external influences, and not the result of minor fluctuations within the system itself.

Another major contributor to chaos theory is Mitchell Feigenbaum (b. 1944). A physicist at the theoretical division of the Los Alamos National Laboratory starting in 1974, Feigenbaum dedicated much of his time researching chaos and trying to build mathematical formulas that might be used to explain the phenomenon Others working on related ideas (though in different disciplines) include a Berkeley, California mathematician who formed a group to study "dynamical systems"

and a population biologist pushing to study strangely-complex behavior in simple biological models. During the 1970s, these scientists and others in the United States and Europe began to see beyond what appeared to be random disorder in nature (the atmosphere, wildlife populations, etc.), finding connections in erratic behavior. As recounted by James Gleick (b.1954) in *Chaos,* a French mathematical physicist had just made the disputable claim that turbulence in fluids might have something to do with a bizarre, infinitely-tangled abstraction he termed a "strange attractor." Stephen Smale (b. 1930), at the University of California, Berkeley, was involved in the study of "dynamical systems." He proposed a physical law that systems can behave erratically, but the erratic behavior cannot be stable. At this point, however, mainstream science was not sure what to make of these theories, and some universities and research centers deliberately avoided association with proponents of chaos theory.

By the mid-1980s, chaos was a buzzword for the fast-growing movement reshaping scientific establishments, and conferences and journals on the subject were on the rise. Universities sought chaos "specialists" for high-level positions. A Center for Nonlinear Studies was established at Los Alamos, as were other institutes devoted to the study of nonlinear dynamics and complex systems. A new language consisting of terms such as *fractals, bifurcations,* and *smooth noodle maps* was born. In 1987, James Gleick published his landmark work, *Chaos: Making a New Science,* chronicling the development of chaos theory, as well as the science and scientists fueling its progress.

THE SCIENCE OF CHAOS THEORY

As stated by James Gleick, chaos is a science of the "global nature of systems," and so it crosses many disciplinary lines—from ecology to medicine, electronics, and the economy. It is a theory, method, set of beliefs, and way of conducting scientific research. Technically, chaos models are based on "state space," improved versions of the Cartesian graphs used in calculus. In calculus, speed and distance can be represented on a Cartesian graph as x and y. Chaos models allow the plotting of many more variables in an imaginary space, producing more complex imaginary shapes. Even this model assumes, however, that all variables can be graphed, and may not be able to account for situations in the real world where the number of variables changes from moment to moment.

The primary tool for understanding chaos theory (and complexity theory as well) is dynamic systems theory, which is used to describe processes that constantly change over time (e.g., the ups and downs of the stock market). When systems become dislodged from a stable state, they go through a period of oscillation, swinging back and forth between order and chaos. According to Margaret J. Wheatley in *Leadership and the New Science,* "Chaos is the final state in a system's movement away from order." When a system does reach that point, the parts of a system are manifest as turbulence, totally lacking in direction or meaning. Wheatley quotes researchers John Briggs and F. David Peat explaining the process of oscillation:

> Evidently familiar order and chaotic order are laminated like bands of intermittency. Wandering into certain bands, a system is extruded and bent back on itself as it iterates, dragged toward disintegration, transformation, and chaos. Inside other bands, systems cycle dynamically, maintaining their shapes for long periods of time. But eventually all orderly systems will feel the wild, seductive pull of the strange chaotic attractor.

In simpler terms, every system has the potential to fall into chaos.

The above "strange attractor" is the very same that a French mathematical physicist identified in the early 1960s. In complex systems, where all should fall apart, the attractor comes in, magnetically pulling system variables into an area and creating a visible shape. Because previous efforts to graph such phenomena could only be completed in two dimensions, this effect could not be visualized. However, computers now allow the phenomena of "strange attractors" to become visible, as images of multiple dimensions representing multiple variables can finally be created.

Part of the difficulty in studying chaos theory arises because complex systems are difficult to study in pieces. Scientists's efforts to separate pieces of dynamical systems often fall apart. The system depends on each minute part of that system and the way it interacts with all other components. As Briggs and Peat state, "The whole shape of things depends upon the minutest part. The part is the whole in this respect, for through the action of any part, the whole in the form of chaos or transformative change may manifest."

In the same breath, it is important to establish the importance of the autonomy the smallest parts of a system possess. Each component of a complex system has the ability to fluctuate, randomly and unpredictably, within the context of the system itself. The system's guiding principles (the attractors) allow these parts to cohere over time into definite and predictable form. This runs contrary to the impression many have of chaos theory, believing there is no order to be had in such a system. But chaotic movement does possess finite boundaries, within which is the capacity for infinite possibility. Even lacking direction, parts of a system can combine so that the system generates multiple configurations of itself, displaying "order without predictability." These systems never land in the same place twice, but they also never exceed certain boundaries.

PRACTICAL APPLICATION OF CHAOS THEORY

By the early 1980s, evidence accumulated that chaos theory was a real phenomenon. One of the first frequently-cited examples is a dripping water faucet. At times, water drops from a leaky faucet exhibit chaotic behavior (the water does not drip at a constant or orderly rate), eliminating the possibility of accurately predicting the timing of those drops. More recently, the orbit of Pluto was shown to be chaotic. Scientists took advantage of applications using chaos to their benefit; chaos-aware control techniques could be used to stabilize lasers and heart rhythms, among multiple other uses.

Another arena within which chaos theory is useful is that of organizations. Applying chaos theory to organizational behavior allows theorists to take a step back from the management of day-to-day activities and see how organizations function as unified systems. An organization is a classic example of a nonlinear system (i.e., a system in which minor events have the potential to set off grave consequences or chain reactions, and major changes may have little or no effect on the system whatsoever). In order to exploit the chaotic quality of an organization, one needs to try to see the organizational shape that emerges from a distance. Instead of pinpointing causes in the organization for organizational problems, the company is better served, according to chaos theory, by looking for organizational patterns that lead to certain types of behavior within the organization.

Organizational expectations for acceptable behavior, and the degree of freedom with which individuals are allowed to work, shape the way a company's problems and challenges are handled by its members. By allowing people and groups within an organization some autonomy, businesses encourage the organization to organize itself, enacting multiple iterations of its own functioning until the various pieces of the organization can work together most effectively. An organization that encourages this type of management has been termed a *fractal organization,* one that trusts in natural organizational phenomena to order itself.

However, applying chaos theory to organizational practice tends to go against the grain of most formal management patterns. Order can be confused with the more popular notion of control. Defined by organization charts and job descriptions, traditional management does not generally seek to add disorder to its strategic plan. As Wheatley states, "It is hard to open ourselves up to a world of inherentorderliness."

Organizations are focused on structure and design. Charts are drawn to illustrate who is accountable to whom or who plays what role and when. Business experts break down organizations into the smallest of parts. They build models of organizational practice and policy with hope that this atomizing yields better information on how to improve the organization's functioning. However, chaos theory implies that this is unnecessary, even harmful.

Self-organizing systems are those enabled to grow and evolve with free will. As long as each part of the system remains consistent with itself and the systems's past; these systems can harness the power of creativity, evolution, and free will—all within the boundaries of the organization's overall vision and culture. In this respect, chaos theory shows the need for effective leadership, a guiding vision, strong values, organizational beliefs, and open communication.

During the 1980s, chaos theory did begin to change decision-making processes in business. A good example is the evolution of high-functioning teams. Members of effective teams frequently recreate the role each member plays, depending on the needs of the team at a given point. Though not always the formally-designated manager, informal leaders emerge in an organization not because they have been given control, but because they have a strong sense of how to address the needs of the group and its members. The most successful leaders understand that it is not the organization or the individual who is most important, but the relationship between the two. And that relationship is in constant change.

One of the most influential business writers of the 1980s and 1990s, Tom Peters (b. 1942), wrote, *Thriving on Chaos: Handbook for a Management Revolution* in 1987. Peters offers a strategy to help corporations deal with the uncertainty of competitive markets through customer responsiveness, fast-paced innovation, empowering personnel, and most importantly, learning to work within an environment of change. In fact, Peters asserts that we live in "a world turned upside down," and survival depends on embracing "revolution." While not explicitly concerned with chaos theory, Peters's focus on letting an organization (and its people) drive itself is quite compatible with the central tenets of chaos theory.

As the global economy and technology continue to change the way business is conducted on a daily basis, evidence of chaos is clearly visible. While businesses could once succeed as "non-adaptive," controlling institutions with permanently-installed hierarchical structures, modern corporations must be able to restructure as markets expand and technology evolves. According to Peters, "To meet the demands of the fast-changing competitive scene, we must simply learn to love change as much as we have hated it in the past."

Organizational theorist Karl Weick (b. 1936) offers a similar theory to Peters's, believing that business strategies should be "just in time. . .supported by more investment in general knowledge, a large skill repertoire, the ability to do a quick study, trust in intuitions, and sophistication in cutting losses." Though he did not articulate his theories in terms of the explicit ideas offered by quantum physics and chaos theory, his statements support the general idea that the creation and health of an organization (or a system) depends on the interaction of various people and parts within that system. However, as Wheatley states in her book:

> Organizations lack this kind of faith, faith that they can accomplish their purposes in various ways and that they do best when they focus on direction and vision, letting transient forms emerge and disappear. We seem fixated on structures. . .and organizations, or we who create them, survive only because we build crafty and smart—smart enough to defend ourselves from the natural forces of destruction.

SEE ALSO: Complexity Theory; Trends in Organizational Change

Wendy H. Mason
Revised by Hal P. Kirkwood, Jr.

FURTHER READING:

Chen, Guanrong, and Xinghuo Yu, eds. *Chaos Control: Theory and Applications (Lecture Notes in Control and Information Sciences).* New York: Springer-Verlag, 2003.

Farazmand, Ali. "Chaos and Transformation Theories: A Theoretical Analysis with Implications for Organization Theory and Public Management." *Public Organization Review* 3, no. 4 (2003): 339–372.

Gleick, James. *Chaos: Making a New Science.* New York: Penguin Books, 1987.

Peters, Tom. *Thriving on Chaos.* New York: HarperCollins, 1987.

Sullivan, Terence J. "The Viability of Using Various System Theories to Describe Organisational Change." *Journal of Educational Administration* 42, no. 1 (2004): 43–54.

Wheatley, Margaret J. *Leadership and the New Science: Discovering Order in a Chaotic World Revised.* San Francisco: Berrett-Koehler Publishers, 2001.

CLOSED SYSTEMS

SEE: Open and Closed Systems

COALITION BUILDING

Coalitions refer to the temporary formation of persons, groups, or even nations for some type of joint or common action. It has been used as a term most often in relation to political or national issues, such as President George H. W. Bush's allied coalition during the Gulf War. In business, coalitions have been present for many years as a means of bringing together people, departments within an organization, entire companies, or industries with some common purpose. Examples of such purposes might include; achieving a common corporate goal, lowering insurance rates, regulating an industry action, or strategic planning. Coalitions are an exercise in power, whether in politics or business.

HISTORY OF COALITIONS

The concept of coalition building has too often been confused with interest groups and lobbying. The term refers to the formation of different interests, but not necessarily with the same intent as an interest group. From the French *coalascere,* the word is generally defined in political terms. Most early coalitions were temporary alliances formed among nontraditional allies to combat a common foe. Bush's Gulf coalition is one such example, and an example of a coalition that did not hold together even over a short span of time. Coalitions are also formed for election purposes. A historical example of this is the Republican Party, formed in the mid-nineteenth century from representatives from virtually all parties then existing on the American political scene—Whigs, Democrats, Free-Soilers, Abolitionists, Know-Nothings, members of the temperance movement, and others without a party allegiance. All of these elements did not survive the formation of the Republican Party as we know it today.

COALITIONS DEFINED

There are various definitions of a coalition that fit an organizational behavior setting. One simply states that a coalition occurs when members of a group organize to support their side of a particular issue. Another definition refers to a coalition as a relationship over a specific issue. Coalitions exist to preserve and even enhance self-interests, whether those of an individual or group, and achieve an adequate balance of power favorable to the coalition members's advantage. A more complete definition is a group formed to pursue a strategy that will be to the advantage of those most directly affected.

Another example of a coalition is one that forms over the issue of funding for management information systems within a single organization. Individuals express initial concern about a lack of resources to fully develop an integrated information system, yet have no formal way to share concerns with management. These individuals represent several units within the organization, including accounting, research, marketing, and distribution—few of whom commonly interact with the others. The issue focuses on management's budget control. But, as a group, membership serves on the overall organizational budget planning committee. At the point of decision making, the coalition acts in accord with common interests to recommend a comprehensive information system mutual to the needs of all units. Once this recommendation is forwarded to the organization's executive, the coalition disbands or continues, depending on the final decision on how the resources are to be used for information management.

Whatever definition of coalitions is accepted, understanding organizational coalitions helps to understand behavior in a complex organizational structures. Coalitions are a potent force in organizations. Organizational behavior literature is largely independent of the social psychology literature on coalitions, yet a closer tie between the two fields is building. Likewise, business and organization literature has not utilized the vast literature of political science that examines the unique formation of coalitions for mutual goals. The merging of these three independent disciplines into a body of coalition literature can only enhance our understanding of the formation of groups for common purposes.

COALITION BUILDING

A review of the business and behavioral science literature on coalitions suggests the following are common characteristics found in most coalitions:

1. Members act as a group.

2. They are formed for a specific purpose.

3. They contain a group of interacting individuals.

4. They are independent from the organization's formal structure.

5. They have no formal structure.

6. They are oriented to a specific issue to advance the group's purpose.

7. Perception of membership is mutual among members.

8. They have an external focus.

These characteristics may be common with other types of groups within organizations, but coalitions are separate and quite often powerful. As a part of an organizational power structure, coalitions are frequently seen as a manager's legitimate search for power, and as such, are used to increase personal power or to achieve organizational goals. When building a coalition, potential members will identify those individuals or groups who have a common interest or goal and who are most likely to join. Generally, coalitions take time to form as participants identify the common goal, the best manner to approach that goal, and the individuals or groups most likely to share the preferred strategy of goal-seeking. Borrowing from social psychology literature, "Coalitions form one person (or group) at a time."

Coalitions are used to increase a power base. Therefore, an understanding of coalition building is integral to a comprehensive knowledge of organizational behavior. As in politics, the emphasis on the word, "temporary" is closely associated with coalitions, but is not necessarily the rule in corporate life. Social psychologists Keith Murnigham and Danny Brass conclude that successful coalitions are fluid, form rather quickly, expand, burst at the moment of decision, and then rapidly disappear. Other types of relationships within the organization can include alliances, networks, cliques, a supportive managerial relationship, and other forms. Networks are a broad-based cooperative pursuit of general self interests, while alliances involve individuals or groups supporting each other. A clique is a group of individuals held together by a common interest. Cliques often form coalitions. Research indicates that some surreptitiousness (e.g., mobilizing quietly) may be essential to building a coalition. There is also research concluding that resistance, fear of retaliation, and insults often create ripe conditions for coalition building.

Several conditions have to be present for the formation of a coalition. First, there has to be an issue that requires addressing or interest in an issue that coalition members find they have in common. Second, potential members have to share a belief that they can achieve success through building a coalition. Third, there must be an understanding that the action taken has to be jointly performed. Once these criteria are met, the building of the coalition begins. Generally, coalition members form from a weakness—that is, individually they are not strong enough in the organization to achieve their goal.

When this collective action leads to a response, coalitions can take one of several directions. If initially successful, the coalition may grow. But the same is true if the coalition first encounters failure yet persists in reaching a collective goal. Disbanding the coalition is also a possibility in either scenario, resulting in the dormancy of the coalition. Coalitions may well be strengthened by success and continue to grow in power and influence. A dormant coalition may also be able to exercise power at a later time, but this is unlikely in most organizations. Coalitions may prevail and coalition goals may become the dominant organizational goal, although this alternative course of coalition action lacks adequate research findings from which to derive any solid conclusions. The stability of coalitions thus depends on goals, course of action, outcomes, and continued common interest.

COALITION GOALS

Coalition goals generally focus on the distribution of resources, always a source of contention in organizations. The lack of adequate resources, changes in the resource base, perceived inequitable resource distribution, and lack of a comprehensive understanding of resource allocation frequently result in the development of coalitions. Research also indicates that those with broader discretion and influence in job responsibilities and work activities are more likely to participate in coalition building. When the work environment is more rigidly controlled, coalitions are not as likely to be pursued as a strategy for addressing collective goals.

An example of a coalition and its effectiveness is found in the experience of Transworld Corporation's president Charles Bradshaw. As reported in *Business Week,* Bradshaw's fate as president was doomed by a coalition of forces within the company. At a finance committee meeting where Bradshaw opposed Transworld's acquisition of a nursing home corporation, the committee chair recited an endless list of facts and figures in support of the purchase. Bradshaw reflected, "Within two or three minutes I knew I had lost. No one was talking directly to me, but all statements addressed my opposition. I could tell there was general agreement around the board table." The finance committee assumed the form of a coalition for a common organizational purpose and Bradshaw was defeated on the acquisition issue. Although an example of a very powerful coalition, it includes most of the common characteristics of the coalition—an interacting group (the finance committee), a specific purpose (the nursing home corporation acquisition), a concentrated act (voting together in opposition to Bradshaw), no formal internal structure (a corporate committee), external focus (acquisition of an entity outside the organization), and orientation to advance the members's purpose (the corporate acquisition).

COALITION LITERATURE

The concept of coalitions has undergone differing applications and meanings within organizational theory. The earliest uses focus on conflicts within organizations and the presence of multiple goals within the same organization. Herbert Simon, former professor at Carnegie Mellon University and 1978 recipient of the Nobel Prize in economics, was one of the first researchers to identify the issue of conflict over goals in an organization. Simon, however, failed to mention coalitions arising within the organizations over this conflict. Simon's 1958 book, *Organizations,* which he co-authored with James G. March, mentioned coalitions between but not within organizations. March, also at Carnegie Mellon and later at Stanford, did draw a relationship between coalitions and organizations in a 1962 article in the *Journal of Politics*. March continued his work with Richard Cyert (also at Carnegie Mellon at that time and later president of the institution from 1972 to 1990) in works like the 1963, *A Behavioral Theory of the Firm.*

The second significant period of coalition research centered on James Thompson, who adopted the work of March and Cyert in his 1967 book, *Organizations in Action*, where he coined the term, "dominant coalition." Thompson (who was teaching business at Indiana University in 1967) concluded there were certain constraints on coalition building, mainly the organization's technology and environment. Thompson theorized that the more uncertainty in organizations due to technology and environment, the more power bases that exist. The coalition grows as the uncertainty increases.

Thompson also used the term, "inner circle" to describe the select few within an organization whose connections provide them with influence. Their role in coalition building is often one of leadership, but they seldom act alone in achieving goals. Their power is enhanced as the coalition strives to achieve a group goal; thus, the individual and coalition feed off each other. Carrying Thompson's point one step further, interdependency in an organization creates a greater likelihood for the formation of a coalition or coalitions.

A third phase of coalition scholarship was generated with the introduction of political science and social psychology methods and studies to organizational behavior. This led to the current divergent use of the term, and research from several disciplines points to how individual efforts at influence become the basis for coalition building. The application of different schools of research on coalitions led to more thorough study into the formation and operation of coalitions in the organization. In addition, game theory proponents contribute to understanding of the role of coalitions and their formation.

More recently, research into coalitions has moved away from the organizational environment to the political arena where coalitions have an impact on business. Periodical literature is highlighted with articles on how coalitions influence international business and economics, the health care industry, diversity and integration issues, foreign trade, the insurance market, and community activism. In the area of organizational behavior, research centers on the role of coalitions in organizational change, or how groups with seemingly dichotomous interests merge to exercise power on business strategy and decision making within an organization undergoing significant administrative and structural change.

In their seminal article on coalition research, William Stephenson, Jone Pearce, and Lyman Porter (of the University of California at Irvine) state that the study of coalitions has yet to produce any new way of understanding organizational processes. Considering the wide array of research from psychology, political science, game theory, sociology, and organizational behavior, their conclusion still begs an adequate answer. We can come to an understanding of the conditions necessary for the formation of a coalition, how they are built, how they exercise power and influence, and how they survive or disband, yet the question of the role of the coalition in organizational behavior remains unanswered and fertile for the researcher so inclined to look further for questions and answers.

SEE ALSO: Group Decision Making; Group Dynamics; Managing Change; Organizational Structure; Teams and Teamwork; Trends in Organizational Change

Boyd Childress
Revised by Wendy H. Mason

FURTHER READING:

Johns, Gary. *Organizational Behavior: Understanding and Managing Life at Work.* New York: HarperCollins, 1996.

March, James G., and Richard M. Cyert. *A Behavioral Theory of the Firm.* Englewood Cliffs, NJ: Prentice-Hall, 1963.

Murnigham, John Keith, and Daniel J. Brass. "Intraorganizational Coalitions." In *Research on Negotiation in Organizations.* eds. Max H. Bazerman, Roy J. Lewicki, and Blair H. Sheppard. Greenwich: JAI Press, 1991.

Pfeffer, Jeffrey. *New Directions for Organization Theory: Problems and Prospects.* New York: Oxford University Press, 1997.

Roberts, Joan M. *Alliances, Coalitions and Partnerships: Building Collaborative Organizations.* St. Paul, MN: New Society Publishers, 2004.

Simon, Herbert A., and James G. March. *Organizations.* New York: Wiley, 1958.

Stephenson, William B., Jone L. Pearce, and Lyman W. Porter. "The Concept of Coalition in Organization Theory and Research." *Academy of Management Review* (April 1985): 256–268.

Thompson, James D. *Organizations in Action: Social Science Bases of Administrative Theory.* New York: McGraw-Hill, 1967.

COMMUNICATION

Communication is the sharing or exchange of thought by oral, written, or nonverbal means. To function effectively, managers need to know and be able to apply strategically a variety of communication skills that match varying managerial tasks. These tasks might call for nonverbal, presentational, or written skills as the manager meets others, speaks at meetings, or prepares reports to be read by clients or those higher on the organizational ladder. To work effectively, managers also need to know sources of information. Finally, managers need to understand the different communication channels available.

UPWARD AND DOWNWARD COMMUNICATION

Information, the lifeblood of any organization, needs to flow freely to be effective. Successful management requires downward communication to subordinates, upward communication to superiors, and horizontal communication to peers in other divisions. Getting a task done, perhaps through delegation, is just one aspect of the manager's job. Obtaining the resources to do that job, letting others know what is going on, and coordinating with others are also crucial skills. These skills keep the organization working, and enhance the visibility of the manager and her division, thus ensuring continued support and promotion.

Downward communication is more than passing on information to subordinates. It may involve effectively managing the tone of the message, as well as showing skill in delegation to ensure the job is done effectively by the right person. In upward communication, tone is even more crucial, as are timing, strategy, and audience adaptation. In neither case can the manager operate on automatic as the messages are sent out.

THE COMMUNICATION PROCESS

At first glance the communication process, or the steps taken to get message from one mind to another, seems simple enough. As the definition at the opening suggested, the sender has an idea, which he transmits to the receiver through signs—physical sensations capable of being perceived by another. These signs might be a printed or spoken word, a gesture, a handshake, or a stern look, to name just a few. The receiver takes those signs, interprets them and then reacts with feedback.

The process is more complex, though. When communicating, the sender encodes the message. That is, she chooses some tangible sign (something which can be seen, heard, felt, tasted, or smelled) to carry the message to the receiver. The receiver, in turn, decodes that message; that is, he finds meaning in it. Yet the signs used in messages have no inherent meaning; the only meaning in the message is what the sender or receiver attributes to it.

To make sense out of a message, to determine the meaning to attribute to it, the receiver uses perception. With perception, the receiver interprets the signs in a communication interaction in light of his past experience. That is, he makes sense out of the message based on what those signs meant when he encountered them in the past. A firm, quick handshake, for example, may signal "businesslike" to someone because in the past he found people who shook hands that way were businesslike.

PERCEPTION

No person sees things exactly the same way as another; each has a unique set of experiences, a unique perceptual "filter," through which he or she compares and interprets messages. Making up this filter is the unique blend of education, upbringing, and all of the life experiences of the perceiver. Even in the case of twins, the perceptual filter will vary from between them. When communicating, each receiver uses that filter to give meaning to or make sense out of the experience.

Herein lies the challenge in communication, particularly for managers who need to be understood in order to get things done: getting the receiver to comprehend the message in a way similar to what was intended. While the word "communication" implies that a common meaning is shared between sender and receiver, this is not always the case. Under optimum circumstances, the meaning attributed to the message by the receiver will be close to what was intended by the sender. In most situations, however, the meaning is only an approximation, and may even be contrary to what was intended. The challenge of communication lies in limiting this divergence of meanings between sender and receiver.

While the wide range of potential experiences make communicating with someone from within the same culture a challenge, across cultures the possibilities are even wider and the challenge even greater. What one sign means in one culture might be taken in an entirely different way in another. The friendly Tunisian businessman who holds another man's hand as they walk down the street may be misunderstood in the North American culture, for example. Similarly, an intended signal may mean nothing to someone from another culture, while an unintended one may trigger an unexpected response.

Understanding the dynamics that underlie perception is crucial to effective and successful communication.

Because people make sense out of present messages based on past experiences, if those past experiences differ, the interpretations assigned may differ slightly or even radically depending on the situation. In business communication, differences in education, roles in the organization, age, or gender may lead to radical differences in the meaning attributed to a sign.

AUDIENCE ADAPTATION

The effective communicator learns early the value of audience adaptation and that many elements of the message can be shaped to suit the receiver's unique perceptual filter. Without this adaptation, the success of the message is uncertain. The language used is probably the most obvious area. If the receiver does not understand the technical vocabulary of the sender, then the latter needs to use terms common to both sender and receiver.

On the other hand, if the receiver has less education than the sender, then word choice and sentence length may need to be adapted to reflect the receiver's needs. For example, if the receiver is skeptical of technology, then someone sending a message supporting the purchase of new data processing equipment needs to shape it in a way that will overcome the perceptual blinders the receiver has to the subject. If the receiver is a superior, then the format of the message might need to be more formal.

COMMUNICATION BARRIERS

Communication barriers (often also called noise or static) complicate the communication process. A communication barrier is anything that impedes the communication process. These barriers are inevitable. While they cannot be avoided, both the sender and receiver can work to minimize them.

Interpersonal communication barriers arise within the sender or receiver. For example, if one person has biases against the topic under discussion, anything said in the conversation will be affected by that perceptual factor. Interpersonal barriers can also arise between sender and receiver. One example would be a strong emotion like anger during the interaction, which would impair both the sending and receiving of the message in a number of ways. A subtler interpersonal barrier is bypassing, in which the sender has one meaning for a term, while the receiver has another (for example, "hardware" could be taken to mean different things in an interchange).

Organizational barriers arise as a result of the interaction taking place within the larger work unit. The classic example is the serial transmission effect. As a message passes along the chain of command from one level to the next, it changes to reflect the person passing it along. By the time a message goes from bottom to top, it is not likely to be recognized by the person who initiated it.

Although communication barriers are inevitable, effective managers learn to adapt messages to counteract their impact. The seasoned manager, especially when in the role of sender, learns where they occur and how to deal with them. As receiver, she has a similar and often more challenging duty. The effort is repaid by the clearer and more effective messages that result.

COMMUNICATION REDUNDANCY

While audience adaptation is an important tool in dealing with communication barriers, it alone is not enough to minimize their impact. As a result, communication long ago evolved to develop an additional means to combat communication barriers: redundancy, the predictability built into a message that helps ensure comprehension. Every message is, to a degree, predictable or redundant, and that predictability helps overcome the uncertainty introduced by communication barriers. Effective communicators learn to build in redundancy where needed.

Communication redundancy occurs in several ways. One of the most obvious of these is through simple repetition of the message, perhaps by making a point early and again later into the same message. A long report, by contrast, might have its main points repeated in a variety of places, including the executive summary, the body, and the conclusion.

Another source of redundancy lies in the use of multiple media. Much spoken communication is repeated in the nonverbal elements of the message. A formal oral presentation is usually accompanied with slides, product samples, or videotaped segments to support the spoken word. A person interviewing for a job stresses his seriousness and sincerity with a new suit, a warm handshake, consistent eye contact, and an earnest tone in his voice.

A less obvious but more frequent source of redundancy lies in the grammar and syntax (roughly the word order used) of the message. These back up a message by helping the reader or listener predict the unknown from the known. For example, the role and meaning of an uncertain word at the beginning of a sentence can be determined partly by its placement after the word "the" and before a verb in the sentence, as well as by whether or not the verb takes the singular or plural.

In the previous example, the context in which the written message takes place, the collective meanings of the previous and following sentences, also adds to the predictability. Should noise garble one word of the message, the other words surrounding it can provide the clues needed for understanding, something that anyone familiar with speaking or reading a foreign language would know. Similarly, in a technical description, the context surrounding an unclear word or concept may be enough to determine its meaning, especially in a carefully constructed message.

A surprising source of communication redundancy lies in the way a message is formatted. In a business environment, format can help the receiver predict what will be in a message. A good example is the traditional annual report, which always carries the same type of information. Similarly, someone reading a memorandum from a colleague can reasonably expect that it will deal with internal business matters.

By contrast, the expectations inherent in a particular format can serve as a source of noise when it contains an unexpected message. For example, a company attempting to be innovative sends out its annual report as a videotape. Many of those receiving it might miss the point since it does not look like an annual report. On the other hand, since it might arouse attention, using a familiar format to package new material can be an effective marketing tool in another application.

As a result of redundancy, in whatever form it may appear, much of any message is predictable. The unpredictable element of the message, the new material that the receiver learns from the interaction, is the information that is inherent in the message. Everything else backs the message.

While managers need skill in all areas of communication, two areas, nonverbal communication and the corporate grapevine, are particularly relevant. Both are often misunderstood, and skill in strategically communicating through them is invaluable.

NONVERBAL COMMUNICATION

Nonverbal communication occurs when there is an exchange of information through nonlinguistic signs. In a spoken (and to some extent written) message, it consists of everything except the words. Nonverbal communication is a valid and rich source of information and merits close study. As with other elements of communication, the meaning of nonverbal signals depends upon perception. It does not have to be intentional in order to carry meaning to another person.

Nonverbal communication serves a variety of purposes, including sending first impressions such as a warm handshake. It also signals emotions (through tears or smiles), status (through clothing and jewelry), and when one wants to either take or relinquish a turn in conversation (using gestures or drawing a breath). Nonverbal signals can also signal when someone is lying; for example when being deceptive, vocal pitch often rises.

Many think of "body language" as synonymous with nonverbal communication. Body language is a rich source of information in interpersonal communication. The gestures that an interviewee uses can emphasize or contradict what he is saying. Similarly, his posture and eye contact can indicate respect and careful attention. Far subtler, but equally important, are the physical elements over which he has little control, but which still impact the impression he is making on the interviewer. His height, weight, physical attractiveness, and even his race are all sources of potential signals that may affect the impression he is making.

But nonverbal signals come from many other sources, one of which is time. If the interviewee in the previous example arrived ten minutes late, he may have made such a poor impression that his chances for hire are jeopardized. A second interviewee who arrives ten minutes early signals eagerness and promptness.

Haptics is a source of nonverbal communication that deals with touch. An interviewee with a weak handshake may leave a poor impression. The pat on the back that accompanies a verbal "well done" and a written commendation may strongly reinforce the verbal and written statements. Subconsciously, most managers realize that when the permissible level of haptic communication is exceeded, it is done to communicate a message about the state of the parties' relationship. It is either warmer than it had been, or one of the parties wishes it so. Unfortunately, explain Borisoff and Victor, conflict can arise when the two parties involved do not agree on an acceptable haptic level for the relationship.

Nonverbal communication also includes proxemics, a person's relationship to others in physical space. Most are familiar with the idea of a personal space "bubble" that we like to keep around ourselves. In the North American culture, this intimate space may be an 18-inch circle around the person, which only those closest are allowed to invade. Just beyond this space close friends may be tolerated, and acquaintances even farther out. Other cultures may have wider or narrower circles. Table 1 sets out the meanings typically attributed to personal spaces in the North American culture.

Managers also send nonverbal signals through their work environment. These signals can affect the communication process in obvious or subtle ways. For example, a manager may arrange the office so that she speaks to subordinates across a broad expanse of desk. Or, she may choose to be less intimidating and use a round table for conferences. The artifacts she uses in the office may say something about who the manager is, or how she wishes to be seen. The organization also speaks through the space it allots to employees. For example, the perception that a large, windowed, corner office may signal prestige while a tiny, sterile cubicle may convey (intentionally or unintentionally) low status.

Table 1

Proxemic Distances in the North America Culture

Zone	Distance	Persons Tolerated
Intimate	0 to 18'	Partner/spouse, parents, children
Personal	18' to 4"	Close friends
Social	4" to 12"	Business associates
Public	12" up	Strangers

Adapted from Smeltzer and Waltman et al., pp. 234-235

THE GRAPEVINE

The grapevine is the informal, confidential communication network that quickly develops within any organization to supplement the formal channels. The structure of the grapevine is amorphous; it follows relationship and networking patterns within and outside the organization, rather than the formal, rational ones imposed by the organization's hierarchy. Thus, members of a carpool, or people gathering around the water cooler or in the cafeteria, may be from different divisions of a company, but share information to pass the time. The information may even pass out of the organization at one level and come back in at another as people go from one network to another. For example, a member of a civic group might casually (and confidentially) pass on interesting information to a friend at a club, who later meets a subordinate of the first speaker at a weekend barbecue.

The grapevine has several functions in the organization. For one, it carries information inappropriate for formal media. Fearing legal repercussions, most would rarely use printed media to share opinions on the competence, ethics, or behavior of others. At the same time, they will freely discuss these informally on the grapevine. Similarly, the grapevine will carry good or bad news affecting the organization far more quickly than formal media can.

The grapevine can also serve as a medium for translating what top management says into meaningful terms. For example, a new and seemingly liberal policy on casual dress may be translated as it moves along the grapevine to clarify what the limits of casual dress actually are. As it informally fleshes out or clarifies what is also traveling in the formal channels, the grapevine can also serve as a source of communication redundancy. And when these corporate-sanctioned channels are inaccurate, especially in an unhealthy communication climate, what is on the grapevine is usually trusted far more by those using it than what passes on the formal channels.

Participants in the grapevine play at least one of several roles. The first of these, the liaison, is the most active participant since he both sends and receives information on the grapevine. This person often has a job with easy access to information at different levels of the organization (and often with little commitment to any level). This might be a secretary, a mailroom clerk, a custodian, or a computer technician. Often, too, the liaison is an extrovert and likable. While this role means that the liaison is in on much of what is going on in the organization, he also takes a chance since the information he passes on might be linked back to him.

Another role played in the grapevine is the deadender. This person generally receives information, but rarely passes it on. By far the most common participant in the grapevine, this person may have access to information from one or more liaisons. This role is the safest one to play in the grapevine since the deadender is not linked to the information as it moves through the organization. Many managers wisely play this role since it provides useful information on what is happening within the organization without the additional risk passing it on to others might entail.

The third role is the isolate. For one or more reasons, she neither sends nor receives information. Physical separation may account for the role in a few instances (the classic example is the lighthouse keeper), but the isolation may also be due to frequent travel that keeps the individual away from the main office. Frequently, the isolation can be traced to interpersonal problems or to indifference to what is happening in the organization (many plateaued employees fit in this category). Not surprisingly, top management often plays the role of isolate, although often unwillingly or unknowingly. This isolation may be owing to the kinds of information passing on the grapevine or to the lack of access others have to top management.

Of course, what is passing on the grapevine may affect a person's behavior or role played. The isolate who is close to retirement and indifferent to much of what is going on around him may suddenly become a liaison when rumors of an early retirement package or a cut in health benefits circulate. Meanwhile, the youngest members of the organization may not give a passing thought to this seemingly irrelevant information.

COMMUNICATION CHANNELS

Communication channels—or the media through which messages are sent—can have an influence on the success of communication. Typical channels used in business communication are face-to-face conversations, telephone conversations, formal letters, memos, or e-mails. Each channel has its own advantages and disadvantages in communicating a particular message.

Media richness theory indicates that the various communication channels differ in their capability to provide rich information. Face-to-face interaction is highest in media richness, because a person can perceive verbal and nonverbal communication, including posture, gestures, tone of voice, and eye contact, which can aid the perceiver in understanding the message being sent. Letters and e-mails have fairly low media richness; they provide more opportunity for the perceiver to misunderstand the sender's intent. Thus, messages should be communicated through channels that provide sufficient levels of media richness for their purpose. For instance, when managers give negative feedback to employees, discipline them, or fire them, it should be done in person. However, disseminating routine, nonsensitive information is properly done through memos or e-mails, where media richness is not critical.

A communication channel that has grown in popularity in business is electronic mail, or e-mail. E-mail provides almost instantaneous communication around the world, and is often a quick, convenient way to communicate with others. This is particularly true for workers in remote locations, such as telecommuters. E-mail may also allow individuals to get their work done more quickly and to manage communication more effectively, particularly by having a record of previous correspondence easily at hand on their computer.

Despite e-mail's many advantages, there are several problems associated with the increased use of e-mail in business. First, e-mail may not be private; e-mail messages may be accessed by people who were not intended to see the messages, and this may create problems related to keeping trade secrets or managing employee relations. Additionally, e-mail messages may be accessed long after they are sent; they may leave a "paper trail" that an organization would rather not have. A second problem with e-mail use is information overload. Because e-mail is easy and quick, many employees find that they have problems managing their e-mail communication or that their work is constantly interrupted by e-mail arrival. The third problem associated with e-mail is that it reduces the benefits that occur with more media-rich communication. Much of the socialization and dis-

semination of organizational culture that may occur through personal interactions may be lost with the increased reliance on electronic communication channels.

John L. Waltman
Revised by Marcia Simmering

FURTHER READING:

Athos, A.G., and R.C. Coffey. "Time, Space and Things." In *Behavior in Organizations: A Multidimensional View.* Englewood Cliffs, NJ: Prentice Hall, 1975.

Borisoff, Deborah, and David A. Victor. *Conflict Management: A Communication Skills Approach.* Englewood Cliffs, NJ: Prentice Hall, 1989.

Knapp, Mark L., and Judith A. Hall. *Nonverbal Communication In Human Interaction.* Belmont, CA: Wadsworth Publishing, 2001.

Smeltzer, Larry R., and John L. Waltman, et al. *Managerial Communication: A Strategic Approach.* Needham, MA: Ginn Press, 1991.

Timm, Paul R., and Kristen Bell DeTienne. *Managerial Communication.* Englewood Cliffs, NJ: Prentice Hall, Inc., 1991.

COMPETITIVE ADVANTAGE

Many firms strive for a competitive advantage, but few truly understand what it is or how to achieve and keep it. A competitive advantage can be gained by offering the consumer a greater value than the competitors, such as by offering lower prices or providing quality services or other benefits that justify a higher price. The strongest competitive advantage is a strategy that that cannot be imitated by other companies.

Competitive advantage can be also viewed as any activity that creates superior value above its rivals. A company wants the gap between perceived value and cost of the product to be greater than the competition.

Michael Porter defines three generic strategies that firm's may use to gain competitive advantage: cost leadership, differentiation, and focus. A firm utilizing a cost leadership strategy seeks to be the low-cost producer relative to its competitors. A differentiation strategy requires that the firm possess a "non-price" attribute that distinguishes the firm as superior to its peers. Firms following a focus approach direct their attention to narrow product lines, buyer segments, or geographic markets. "Focused" firms will use cost or differentiation to gain advantage, but only within a narrow target market.

COST ADVANTAGE RESULTING FROM EFFICIENCY

Efficiency is the ratio of inputs to outputs. Inputs can be any materials, overhead, or labor that is assigned to the product or service. The outputs can be measured as the number of products produced or services performed. The firm that can achieve the highest efficiency for the same service or product can widen the gap between cost and perceived value and may have greater profit margins.

There are many ways a company can increase efficiency. Efficiency is enhanced if, holding outputs constant, inputs are reduced; or if holding inputs constant, outputs are increased. Inputs can be reduced in many ways. Labor inputs can be reduced if employees are better trained so that time spent on each individual output is decreased.

Decreasing waste can decrease materials needed. If a method can be devised to decrease waste, it would increase efficiency. For instance, a bottling plant might determine that 10 gallons of liquid are spilled every day as a result of the bottling process. If the amount of lost liquid can be reduced, efficiency will increase.

Outputs can be increased by increasing the number of units a machine can produce in given period of time. Decreasing downtime can also increase outputs. For example, if a machine regularly breaks down and is out of order for two hours a day, finding a way to eliminate this downtime would increase the number of outputs.

It is often argued that large companies, by definition, are able to be more efficient because they can achieve economies of scale that others are not able to reach. Large companies usually offer more products in each product line, and their products may help to satisfy many different needs. If a consumer is not sure of the exact product he needs, he can go to the larger producer and be confident that the larger producer has something to offer. The consumer might believe that the smaller producer may be too specialized. Larger companies can cater to a larger population because of sheer size, while smaller companies have fewer resources and must specialize or fall victim to larger, more efficient companies.

PRODUCT DIFFERENTIATION

Product differentiation is achieved by offering a valued variation of the physical product. The ability to differentiate a product varies greatly along a continuum depending on the specific product. There are some products that do not lend themselves to much differentiation, such as beef, lumber, and notebook paper. Some products, on the other hand, can be highly differentiated. Appliances, restaurants, automobiles, and even batteries can all be customized and highly differ-

entiated to meet various consumer needs. In *Principles of Marketing* (1999), authors Gary Armstrong and Philip Kotler note that differentiation can occur by manipulating many characteristics, including features, performance, style, design, consistency, durability, reliability, or reparability. Differentiation allows a company to target specific populations.

It is easy to think of companies that have used these characteristics to promote their products. Maytag has differentiated itself by presenting "Old reliable," the Maytag repairman who never has any work to do because Maytag's products purportedly function without any problems and do not require repairs. The Eveready Battery Co./Energizer has promoted their products' performance with the Energizer Bunny® that "keeps going and going."

Many chain restaurants differentiate themselves with consistency and style. If a consumer has a favorite dish at her local Applebee's restaurant, she can be assured it will look and taste the same at any Applebee's restaurant anywhere in the country. And, the style of theme restaurants is the key to some establishments. Planet Hollywood and Hard Rock Cafe profit from their themes.

In the auto industry, durability is promoted by Chevrolet's "Like a Rock" advertising campaign.

SERVICE DIFFERENTIATION

Companies can also differentiate the services that accompany the physical product. Two companies can offer a similar physical product, but the company that offers additional services can charge a premium for the product. Mary Kay cosmetics offers skin-care and glamour cosmetics that are very similar to those offered by many other cosmetic companies; but these products are usually accompanied with an informational, instructional training session provided by the consultant. This additional service allows Mary Kay to charge more for their product than if they sold the product through more traditional channels.

In the personal computer business, Dell and Gateway claim to provide excellent technical support services to handle any glitches that may occur once a consumer has bought their product. This 24-hour-a-day tech support provides a very important advantage over other PC makers, who may be perceived as less reliable when a customer needs immediate assistance with a problem.

PEOPLE DIFFERENTIATION

Hiring and training better people than the competitor can become an immeasurable competitive advantage for a company. A company's employees are often overlooked, but should be given careful consideration. This human resource-based advantage is difficult for a competitor to imitate because the source of the advantage may not be very apparent to an outsider. As a *Money* magazine article reported, Herb Kelleher, CEO of Southwest Airlines, explains that the culture, attitudes, beliefs, and actions of his employees constitute his strongest competitive advantage: "The intangibles are more important than the tangibles because you can always imitate the tangibles; you can buy the airplane, you can rent the ticket counter space. But the hardest thing for someone to emulate is the spirit of your people."

This competitive advantage can encompass many areas. Employers who pay attention to employees, monitoring their performance and commitment, may find themselves with a very strong competitive advantage. A well-trained production staff will generate a better quality product. Yet, a competitor may not be able to distinguish if the advantage is due to superior materials, equipment or employees.

People differentiation is important when consumers deal directly with employees. Employees are the frontline defense against waning customer satisfaction. The associate at Wal-Mart who helps a customer locate a product may result in the customer returning numerous times, generating hundreds of dollars in revenue. Home Depot prides itself on having a knowledgeable sales staff in their home improvement warehouses. The consumer knows that the staff will be helpful and courteous, and this is very important to the consumer who may be trying a new home improvement technique with limited knowledge on the subject.

Another way a company can differentiate itself through people is by having a recognizable person at the top of the company. A recognizable CEO can make a company stand out. Some CEOs are such charismatic public figures that to the consumer, the CEO is the company. If the CEO is considered reputable and is well-liked, it speaks very well for the company, and consumers pay attention. National media coverage of CEOs has increased tremendously, jumping 21 percent between 1992 and 1997 (Gaines-Ross).

IMAGE DIFFERENTIATION

Armstrong and Kotler pointed out in *Principles of Marketing* that when competing products or services are similar, buyers may perceive a difference based on company or brand image. Thus companies should work to establish images that differentiate them from competitors. A favorable brand image takes a significant amount of time to build. Unfortunately, one negative impression can kill the image practically overnight. Everything that a company does must support their image. Ford Motor Co.'s former "Quality is Job 1" slogan needed to be supported in every aspect, including advertisements, production, sales floor presentation, and customer service.

Often, a company will try giving a product a personality. It can be done through a story, symbol, or other identifying means. Most consumers are familiar with the Keebler Elves and the magic tree where they do all of the Keebler baking. This story of the elves and the tree gives Keebler cookies a personality. When consumers purchase Keebler cookies, they are not just purchasing cookies, but the story of the elves and the magic tree as well. A symbol can be an easily recognizable trademark of a company that reminds the consumer of the brand image. The Nike "swoosh" is a symbol that carries prestige and makes the Nike label recognizable.

QUALITY DIFFERENTIATION

Quality is the idea that something is reliable in the sense that it does the job it is designed to do. When considering competitive advantage, one cannot just view quality as it relates to the product. The quality of the material going into the product and the quality of production operations should also be scrutinized. Materials quality is very important. The manufacturer that can get the best material at a given price will widen the gap between perceived quality and cost. Greater quality materials decrease the number of returns, reworks, and repairs necessary. Quality labor also reduces the costs associated with these three expenses.

INNOVATION DIFFERENTIATION

When people think of innovation, they usually have a narrow view that encompasses only product innovation. Product innovation is very important to remain competitive, but just as important is process innovation. Process innovation is anything new or novel about the way a company operates. Process innovations are important because they often reduce costs, and it may take competitors a significant amount of time to discover and imitate them.

Some process innovations can completely revolutionize the way a product is produced. When the assembly line was first gaining popularity in the early twentieth century, it was an innovation that significantly reduced costs. The first companies to use this innovation had a competitive advantage over the companies that were slow or reluctant to change.

As one of the first Internet service providers, America Online offered a unique innovation for accessing the nascent Internet—its unique and user-friendly interface. The company grew at a massive rate, leading the rapidly developing Internet sector as a force in American business. While most innovations are not going to revolutionize the way that all firms operate, the small innovations can reduce costs by thousands or even millions of dollars, and large innovations may save billions over time.

SUSTAINABLE COMPETITIVE ADVANTAGE

The achievement of competitive advantage is not always permanent or even long lasting. Once a firm establishes itself in an area of advantage, other firms will follow suit in an effort to capitalize on their similarities. A firm is said to have a "sustainable" competitive advantage when its competitors are unable to duplicate the benefits of the firm's strategy. In order for a firm to attain a "sustainable" competitive advantage, its generic strategy must be grounded in an attribute that meets four criteria. It must be:

- Valuable—it is of value to consumers.
- Rare—it is not commonplace or easily obtained.
- Inimitable—it cannot be easily imitated or copied by competitors.
- Non-substitutable—consumers cannot or will not substitute another product or attribute for the one providing the firm with competitive advantage.

SELECTING A COMPETITIVE ADVANTAGE

A company may be lucky enough to identify several potential competitive advantages, and it must be able to determine which are worth pursuing. Not all differentiation is important. Some differences are too subtle, too easily mimicked by competitors, and many are too expensive. A company must be sure the consumer wants, understands, and appreciates the difference offered.

The maker of expensive suits may offer its suits in the widest array of colors, but if 95 percent of the consumers wear only black and navy blue suits, then the wide array of colors adds little perceived value to the product. Variety would not become a competitive advantage, and would be a waste of resources. A difference may be worth developing and promoting, advise Armstrong and Kotler, if it is important, distinctive, superior, communicable, preemptive, affordable, and profitable.

A competitive advantage can make or break a firm, so it is crucial that all managers are familiar with competitive advantages and how to create, maintain, and benefit from them.

SEE ALSO: Economies of Scale and Economies of Scope; Porter's 5-Forces Model

Dena Waggoner
Revised by R. Anthony Inman

FURTHER READING:

Armstrong, Gary, and Philip Kotler. *Principles of Marketing.* 8th ed. Upper Saddle River, NJ: Prentice Hall, 1999.

Dess, Gregory G., G.T. Lumpkin, and Alan B. Eisner. *Strategic Management: Text and Cases.* Boston: McGraw-Hill Irwin, 2006.

Gaines-Ross, Leslie, and Chris Komisarjevsky. "The Brand Name CEO." *Across the Board* 36, no. 6, (1999): 26–29.

Kelleher, Herb, and Sarah Rose. "How Herb Keeps Southwest Hopping." *Money,* 28, 1999, 61–62.

Raturi, Amitabh S., and James R. Evans. *Principles of Operations Management.* Mason, OH: Thomson South-Western, 2005.

COMPETITIVE INTELLIGENCE

Intelligence is information that has been analyzed for decision making. It is important to understand the difference between information and intelligence. Information is the starting point; it is readily available numbers, statistics, bits of data about people, companies, products, and strategies. As a matter of fact, information overload is one of the leading problems of today's executive and the top reason for needing a competitive intelligence expert. Information becomes intelligence when is it distilled and analyzed. Combining this idea with those of competition or competitors leads to the concept of gathering and analyzing information about competitors for use in making management decisions. Competitive intelligence provides a link between information and business strategies and decisions. It is the process of turning vast quantities of information into action.

The field of competitive intelligence, as a profession, is relatively new in the U.S. An indication of the importance of competitive intelligence is the growth, since 1986, of the Society of Competitor Intelligence Professionals (SCIP), an organization committed to developing, improving, and promulgating the methods, techniques, and ethical standards of the group. SCIP defines competitive intelligence as "the legal and ethical collection and analysis of information regarding the capabilities, vulnerabilities, and intentions of business competitors conducted by using information databases and other 'open sources' and through ethical inquiry." The major research firm in the field, Fuld & Company, Inc., defines it as "information that has been analyzed to the point where you can make a decision and a tool to alert management to early warning of both threats and opportunities. Competitive intelligence offers approximations and best views of the market and the competition. It is not a peek at the rival's financial books." Competitive intelligence can help managers discover new markets or businesses, beat the competition to market, foresee competitor's actions, determine which companies to acquire, learn about new products and technologies that will affect the industry, and forecast political or legislative changes that will affect the company.

EXAMPLES

Examples of competitive intelligence include stock traders who analyze the data on prices and price movements to determine the best investments. These stock traders have the same data as other traders, but analysis of the data separates them from others. Another example is the Japanese automobile industry's analysis of the U.S.-automobile market in the 1970s. High gasoline prices and smaller families created a demand in the United States for smaller, more fuel-efficient cars. Japanese automakers employed competitive intelligence methods to determine this trend and then made manufacturing decisions based on it, beating the U.S. Big Three to market with high quality, fuel-efficient cars. Another example of successful use of competitive intelligence is AT&T's database of in-company experts. Part of this service is the monitoring of companies with which their own employees are most interested. This led to some early insights of emerging competitors. A final example is how Wal-Mart stores studied problems Sears had with distribution, and built a state-of-the art distribution system so that Wal-Mart customers were not frustrated by out-of-stock items, as were Sears's customers.

ETHICAL METHODS

Competitive intelligence is not spying on the competition. It has been associated in the past with the political and military intelligence used during the Cold War era. Because of this association, many people think that competitive intelligence uses illegal, shady, or unethical means to gather information about competitors. Visions of wiretapping, bribing competitor's employees, or stealing information come to mind. This is not true today. Such techniques can damage the reputation and image of corporations and are not worth the risk. SCIP takes a strong position on the importance of ethics and developed a code of ethics for members. Note the words, "legal and ethical," and the emphasis on retrieving data from "open sources." Competitive intelligence experts use openly-available

information. They do dig into public records and government databases and use the latest technology (such as satellite photoreconnaissance and software tools such as spiders) to help gather and analyze large datasets. However, the professionals and companies for which they work do not use illegal methods.

THE PROCESS

Today, competitive intelligence is an important activity within corporations, serving all areas of business functioning: research and development, human resources, sales, etc. A recent survey by The Futures Group found that 80 percent of large, U.S.-based organizations have a formal, in-house, competitive intelligence department. In the future, competitive intelligence activities will become standard. The wide availability of information on the Web makes competitive intelligence more accessible to medium-size and small firms. Software tools to analyze and disseminate intelligence also make it easier to implement competitive intelligence tools. The process of competitive intelligence is outlined in the following steps:

1. Setting intelligence objectives (i.e., designing the requirements)

2. Collecting and organizing data about the industry and competitors

3. Analyzing and interpreting the data

4. Disseminating the intelligence

SETTING THE OBJECTIVES. A clear statement of the intelligence needs of the organization should be outlined by management. If this step is ignored, the competitive intelligence department will be bogged down with too much information and possibly distracted by ad-hoc requests for data. This step is necessary regardless of where in the organization the competitive intelligence department is located. Some corporations have competitive intelligence report directly to the CEO; in others, it is located in marketing or in research and development. The role of any competitive intelligence program should be driven by the needs of the corporation, especially areas that have key performance consequences.

COLLECTING AND ORGANIZING THE DATA. The online revolution has enhanced ease in collecting and obtaining information, but the competitive intelligence expert must constantly be alert to new sources and places for finding information. The most obvious data collection sources include trade magazine and newspaper articles, company Web sites, newswires, chat forums, and Web search engines. Free information is available on industries via census data on government Web pages. Similarly, free public company information from U.S. Securities and Exchange Commission (SEC) filings, such as the 10-K and 10-Q report, can be easily obtained on the Web. These corporate reports yield detailed financial and product information and also identify mergers, acquisitions, and legal proceedings against the company. Other channels for fee-based data are information aggregators such as Factiva, Lexis Nexis, Hoover's Online, MergentOnline and Standard and Poors's databases. Analyst reports and market research reports from companies such as Jupiter, Forrester Research, and Frost and Sullivan, although usually quite expensive to acquire, provide detailed analyses on companies and industries.

ANALYZING AND INTERPRETING THE DATA. Analysis and interpretation is the real core of competitive intelligence. Collected data must be transformed into "qualitative" information (i.e., intelligence). One way to analyze data obtained from the Web is to use a Spider. There are competitive intelligence Spiders available that index and categorize documents found though Web searchers. Whether a Spider is used or not, the next step is to interpret the information. Lehmann and Winer outline four important aspects competitive intelligence professionals need to interpret about competitors: their current and future objectives, their current strategies, their resources, and their future strategies. Once this assessment is complete, competitive intelligence professionals measure their companies in comparison to competitors; this is known as benchmarking. From the benchmarking process, trend identification and prediction can be made.

DISSEMINATING THE INFORMATION. Dissemination is the delivery of current, real-time intelligence to the decision makers in the firm at the time they need it. Timely dissemination is essential if the intelligence is to be perceived as trustworthy. The current philosophy is that delivering to people at all levels in the organization enhances competitive advantages.

HISTORY AND LITERATURE

Competitive intelligence is, in part, an outgrowth of the military intelligence field. Within corporations, it is a direct outgrowth, or evolution, of market research, which uses investigation (especially understanding the strategies, capabilities, and options of competitors or rivals) to examine the marketplace. Examining marketing research books at the time competitive intelligence emerged helps identify the shift. Market research differs from competitive intelligence in that it is usually conducted when a new product is in the planning or development stage and often utilizes surveys, focus groups, and other research tools to study the market. Competitive intelligence requires a more continuous and structured scanning of competitors and the environment. William T. Kelly's work introduced the field of intelligence in his 1965 text. Michael E. Porter's books, aimed at practitioners, identify competitive

intelligence as a needed business function. Porter's books outline the tools for analyzing competitors and evaluating their strengths and weaknesses, which can then lead to opportunities. Leonard Fuld's work helped revolutionize and define the field. Fuld is a key writer and the founder of a major consulting firm that trains people in competitive intelligence methods and techniques.

THE COMPETITIVE INTELLIGENCE EXPERT

The competitive intelligence expert or analyst usually has a strong business background, combined with experience in the company. Likely candidates for the assignment are generally research-oriented people in sales, marketing, or research and development. Combining research skills with communication and writing skills is essential. Because of the research orientation of the job, people with library or information science backgrounds in the company are logical choices.

ORGANIZATIONS

THE SOCIETY OF COMPETITIVE INTELLIGENCE PROFESSIONALS (SCIP). The Society of Competitive Intelligence Professionals (SCIP), established in 1986, is a global, nonprofit, membership organization for everyone involved in creating and managing business knowledge. The mission of SCIP is to enhance the skills of knowledge professionals to help their companies achieve and maintain a competitive advantage. SCIP publishes the following influential periodicals:

- *Competitive Intelligence Magazine.* A bimonthly publication with articles by peers in the competitive intelligence profession.
- *Journal of Competitive Intelligence and Management.* A quarterly, international, blind-refereed journal covering all aspects of competitive intelligence and related management fields. This journal seeks to further the development of competitive intelligence and to encourage greater understanding of the management of competition.
- *Competitive Intelligence Review.* A journal archive for peer-reviewed research and case studies focused on the practice of competitive intelligence. Archive includes contents listings, summaries, and articles from past journal issues, dated 1990 to 2001.
- *SCIP Online.* SCIP's email newsletter, sent free to all members twice a month.

COMPETITIVE INTELLIGENCE DIVISION OF THE SPECIAL LIBRARIES ASSOCIATION (SLA). This organization was formed in 2004 as an association for corporate librarians and information professionals who have evolved beyond collecting and managing information, to provide examination of data that can help their organizations succeed. The Competitive Intelligence Division encompasses all aspects of competitive intelligence including: (1) planning, (2) identifying decision makers's intelligence needs, (3) collecting and analyzing information, (4) disseminating intelligence products and services, (5) evaluating intelligence activities, (6) promoting intelligence services among a client base, and (7) additional industry-specific issues. Competitive Intelligence Division members concentrate on developing their competitive intelligence skills to assist them in functioning more effectively as intelligence professionals within their respective organizations.

FULD & COMPANY, INC. Fuld & Company, Inc., is a research and consulting firm in the field of business and competitive intelligence. This company, founded by Leonard Fuld in 1979, is a full-service business intelligence firm providing: (1) research and analysis, (2) strategic consulting, (3) business intelligence process consulting, and (4) training to help clients understand the external competitive environment.

THE INSTITUTE FOR STRATEGY AND COMPETITIVENESS AT HARVARD SCHOOL OF BUSINESS. This Institute, led by Michael E. Porter, studies competition and its implications for company strategy; the competitiveness of nations, regions and cities; and solutions to social problems. Based at Harvard Business School, the Institute is dedicated to extending the research pioneered by Professor Porter and disseminating it to scholars and practitioners on a global basis.

Judith M. Nixon

FURTHER READING:

Boncella, Robert J. "Competitive Intelligence on the Web." *Communications of AIS* 12 (2003): 327–340.

Burwell, Helen P. *Online Competitive Intelligence: Increase Your Profits Using Cyber-Intelligence.* Tempe, AZ: Facts on Demand Press, 1999.

Chen, Hsinchun. "CI Spider." *Decision Support Systems* 34, no. 1 (2002): 1–17.

"Corporate CI 'Eagles.'" *Competitive Intelligence Magazine*, January 1998. Available from <http://www.scip.org>.

Fuld, Leonard M. *Competitive Intelligence: How To Get It; How To Use It.* New York: Wiley, 1985.

———. *Monitoring The Competition: Find Out What's Really Going on Over There.* New York: Wiley, 1988.

———. *The New Competitor Intelligence: The Complete Resource for Finding, Analyzing, and Using Information about Your Competitors.* New York: Wiley, 1995.

Gilad, Benjamin, and Tamar Gilad. *The Business Intelligence System: A New Tool for Competitive Advantage.* New York: American Management Association, 1988.

Kahaner, Larry. *Competitive Intelligence: How To Gather, Analyze, and Use Information to Move Your Business to the Top.* New York: Simon & Schuster, 1997.

Kelley, William Thomas. *Marketing Intelligence: The Management of Marketing Information.* London: Staples P., 1968.

Lehmann, Donald R., and Russell S. Winer. *Analysis for Marketing Planning.* 4th ed. Boston: Irwin, 1997.

Miller, Jerry, et al. *Millennium Intelligence: Understanding and Conducting Competitive Intelligence in the Digital Age.* Medford, NJ: CyberAge Books, 2000.

Porter, Michael E. *Competitive Advantage: Creating and Sustaining Superior Performance.* New York: Free Press, 1985.

———. *Competitive Strategy: Techniques for Analyzing Industries and Competitors.* New York: Free Press, 1980.

Snow, C.C. ed. *Strategy, Organization Design and Human Resources Management.* Greenwich, CT: JAI Press, 1989.

Tyson, Kirk W.M. *The Complete Guide to Competitive Intelligence.* 2nd ed. Chicago: Leading Edge Pub., 2002.

Vibert, Conor, ed. *Introduction to Online Competitive Intelligence Research: Search Strategies, Research Case Study, Research Problems, and Data Source Evaluations and Reviews.* Mason, Ohio: Thomson/Texere, 2004.

Walle, Alf H. "From Marketing Research to Competitive Intelligence: Useful Generalization or Loss of Focus?" *Management Decision* 37, no. 5/6 (1999): 519–525.

West, Chris. *Competitive Intelligence.* New York: Palgrave, 2001.

COMPLEXITY THEORY

The basic premise of complexity theory is that there is a hidden order to the behavior (and evolution) of complex systems, whether that system is a national economy, an ecosystem, an organization, or a production line. In business and finance, complexity theory places its focus on the ways a factory or company resemble an ecosystem or market, rather than a machine "whose parts and functions have been plucked out in advance," according to David Berreby. He maintains that the organization of systems is no accident, but "the results of laws of nature that we don't yet fully understand." Once understood, managers will learn that if left to function on their own, systems organize themselves, bringing about "order for free."

Proponents of complexity theory believe specific traits are shared by most complex systems. These systems are the combination of many independent actors behaving as a single unit. These actors respond to their environment, much as stock markets respond to news of changing economies, genes respond to natural selection, or the human brain responds to sensory input. All of these "networks" also act as a single system made of many interacting components. Complexity theory attempts to explain how even millions of independent actors can unintentionally demonstrate patterned behavior and properties that, while present in the overall system, are not present in any individual component of that system.

Complexity theory was founded on researchers's attempts to rationalize the behavior of large and complex systems, believing they cannot be explained by usual rules of nature. It attempts to discover how the many disparate elements of a system work with each other to shape the system and its outcomes, as well as how each component changes over time. It is also one way to express the perceived domination of systems over their myriad smaller influences.

While complexity theory is strikingly similar to chaos theory, complexity theorists maintain that chaos, by itself, does not account for the coherence of self-organizing, complex systems. Rather, complex systems reside at the edge of chaos—the actors or components of a system are never locked in to a particular position or role within the system, but they never fall completely out of control. As M. Mitchell Waldrop states in *Complexity*, "The edge of chaos is the constantly shifting battle zone between stagnation and anarchy, the one place where a complex system can be spontaneous, adaptive, and alive."

Sherry Turkle, author of *Life on the Screen* and professor of sociology of science at the Massachusetts Institute of Technology (MIT), feels that technology has helped bring the issues of complexity theory to life. She asserts that computers helped persuade us that knowing all the parts of a system (or a computer) cannot give anyone the ability to foresee all the complexity that can arise as all of those parts interact.

ORIGINS OF COMPLEXITY THEORY

Much of the research on complexity theory originates from the Sante Fe Institute in New Mexico, a mecca for those studying complexity theory. George A. Cowan, head of research at the Los Alamos nuclear laboratory, founded the Santa Fe Institute in the mid-1980s. Scientists at the institute claim that through the study of complexity theory, one can see not only the laws of chaos, but also those of order—through which a powerful explanation for how any collection of components will organize itself can be generated.

One of complexity theory's leading proponents is Stuart Kauffman, author of *At Home in the Universe: The Search for the Laws of Self-Organization and Complexity*. Also a member of the Santa Fe Institute, Kauffman states, "Life exists at the edge of chaos I suspect that the fate of all complex adapting systems in the biosphere—from single cells to economies—is to evolve to a natural state between order and chaos, a grand compromise between structure and surprise." Kauffman's theories originated during his pre-medicine days, when his studies of genetics began to inspire questions about DNA and genetic structures. Kauffman felt that there had to be some kind of built-in order, that trial and error was too much of a long shot to be responsible for the perfect biomolecular structure of the human genome.

Other researchers with a stronger focus on the business side of complexity theory are Howard Sherman and Ron Schultz, authors of *Open Boundaries* and fellows at Santa Fe Center for Emergent Strategies in collaboration with the Santa Fe Institute. They believe business today is faster and nonlinear (effects are not proportional to their causes), and that "experts" cannot predict which products or companies will succeed. Sherman and Schultz assert that competitive advantage is fleeting, and that change can rapidly turn assets into dead weight.

Another major contributor to complexity theory is John Holland, a computer scientist and professor at the University of Michigan. Holland designed the genetic algorithm based on the idea that components of complex systems can be broken down into building blocks, whose characteristics can then be represented in code. In simulations, units of code recombine to make "offspring"; the best of these offspring are allowed to reproduce, while the worst are discarded. As the algorithm works, better code evolves, and the results can be translated into real-world applications.

DETAILS OF COMPLEXITY THEORY

A complex system is defined as one in which many independent agents interact with each other in multiple (sometimes infinite) ways. This variety of actors also allows for the "spontaneous self-organization" that sometimes takes place in a system. This self-organization occurs without anyone being in charge or planning the organization. Rather, it is more a result of organisms/agents constantly adapting to each other. The complex systems are also adaptive (i.e., they always adapt in a way that benefits them). As an analogy, Waldrop suggests analogy to the way the human brain adapts to learn from experience.

Another important concept in complexity theory is that there is no master controller of any system. Rather, coherent system behavior is generated by the competition and cooperation between actors that is always present. And the components of a system do have different levels of organization—like an organization made up of divisions, which contain different departments, which are in comprised of different workers. But the important differentiation from this "organization," made by John Holland in *Complexity*, is that "complex adaptive systems are constantly revising and rearranging their building blocks as they gain experience. A firm will promote individuals who do well and (more rarely) will reshuffle its organizational chart for greater efficiency. Countries will make new trading agreements or realign themselves into whole new alliances."

Another important part of complexity theory is its assumption that there are principles underlying all "emergent properties," or traits that emerge from the interactions of many different actors. David Berreby uses the analogy of an ant colony that switches to a better food source. No individual ant made the decision; it was a result of their interactions.

One of the defining characteristics of complex systems is the inability to predict the outcome of any given change to the system. Because a system depends on so many intricate interactions, the number of possible reactions to any given change is infinite. Minor events can have enormous consequences because of the chain of reactions they might incite. Conversely, major changes may have an almost insignificant effect on the system as a whole. Because of this, strong control of any complex system may be impossible. While it may have order, no one absolutely governs a complex system.

Scientists create computer simulations that enable them to better identify emerging patterns in a system. They also write modification programs allowing system components to adapt to changes in the environment without the absolute necessity of radical changes to the overall structure. Computers can use these simulations to design production schedules and optimize assembly line performance.

COMPLEXITY THEORY IN BUSINESS

Complexity theory is used in business as a way to encourage innovative thinking and real-time responses to change by allowing business units to self-organize. Sherman and Schultz (as related by Hout) argue that modern business moves in a nonlinear fashion, with no continuity in the flow of competitive events, except when observed from hindsight. In order to effectively put complexity theory to work, however, organization leaders need to give up rigid control of these systems from above. Far more can be learned by stepping back from the day-to-day running of the organization and watching for emergent properties and organizational patterns. Those conditions or patterns that bring about the best solutions should be preserved whenever possible. Managers also need to allow organizations to evolve in response to ongoing messages from customers. As Hout states:

No intelligence from on high can match the quality of solutions to market problems that arise from players who are constantly communicating with one another on the ground level. The invisible hand of the marketplace should displace the visible hand of the manager. The markets can determine where one team or initiative or company ends and another begins. Managers interfere at their peril.

Efforts to downplay management, as related by Hout, claim that "management as we have known it is too cumbersome for today's fast, unpredictable pace. A new kind of company wins now. The best management models don't adapt to the new economy; they emerge from it. It's no longer the survival of the fittest; it's the arrival of the fittest." Even so, putting the ideas of complexity theory to work does not mean management need rest on its laurels. Hout asserts that organizations's leaders retain an obligation to formulate a guiding vision for the company, provide effective leadership, express and encourage strong values and organizational beliefs, and provide avenues for open communication. Managers need to manage the way that accident and law interact, knowing how and where to push to keep the system from neither descending into chaos nor becoming rigidly ordered.

Letting an organization self-organize does not negate the need for strategy. Rather, it means that organizational strategy should evolve based on feedback and change as it occurs. By establishing a corporate strategy first, an organization defines itself through conditions that were previously in place, and becomes non-adaptive to continuously-evolving market conditions. Sherman and Schultz recommend the "try something and see what happens" mentality.

CONTRARY BELIEFS

The idea that allowing complex systems to self-organize will yield the best solutions has validity, but complexity theory is not a panacea for all organizations. The notions of complexity theory assume that people in these companies are enthusiastic, intelligent, and can effectively work in teams—requiring less management than workers in more traditional, hierarchical, rigidly-controlled environments. Unfortunately, however, these fast-growing, evolutionary companies with bright, ambitious workers may need more management rather than less. Companies that are shaped and reshaped on such a frequent basis—constantly adapting to a changing business environment—lose some of the stability found at traditional corporate giants such as the industrial and automotive behemoths.

The modern corporation has a lot at stake. There are difficulties in teamwork and collaboration, with potential issues such as nonperforming team members, personality conflicts, opposing business styles, and the effects of stress on job performance. Organizational leaders need to effectively manage personnel and job performance, reward and groom talented performers, develop business relationships and networks, resolve conflict, and divest the company of nonperformers who may be holding the company back from adapting well to emerging trends and technologies. Other business leaders see emergent strategy as a problem, rather than a cure. According to Alan Kay, head of research and development at Disney Imagineering, "Most businesses do not move so fast that foresight, commitment, preemption, deterrence, and other traditional elements of strategy have lost their ability to build value. The best way to predict the future is to invent it."

Complexity theory and the Santa Fe Institute represent common ground where scientists and theorists from disciplines such as economics, physics, business management, and computer science can research behavior of complex systems and their various components. The complexity paradigm also offers a means of applying modern theories that an organization is more like a living organism than a machine. Organizations are conceptualized as evolving in response to complex interactions within and without the system.

Ron Schultz, co-author of *Open Boundaries,* explains that complexity theory "is about how our ideas shape our behaviors. If our ideas about the world in which we operate are machine-like and mechanical, our behaviors will be very different than if our ideas are based on that of complex adaptive systems, which are more evolutionary and organic." Rather than following more linear approaches to corporate decision making, complexity theory offers organizations a way to thrive on the ambiguity and unpredictability that characterize modern business.

Some of complexity theory's leading experts, such as J. Doyne Farmer and Norman Packard, make a living advising companies and practically applying the ideas behind complexity theory to business areas such as corporate investment. Organizations putting the theory into practice include Xerox's Palo Alto Research Center (PARC), Applied Biosystems, and the United States Marine Corps. Complexity theory offers companies the opportunity to create new markets and establish new ways to spread emerging knowledge throughout the company—enabling the organization, as a whole, to respond faster and better to ongoing change.

SEE ALSO: Chaos Theory; Managing Change; Organizational Behavior; Trends in Organizational Change

Wendy H. Mason

Revised by Hal P. Kirkwood, Jr

FURTHER READING:

Battram, Arthur. *Navigating Complexity: The Essential Guide to Complexity Theory in Business and Management.* London: Spiro Press, 2002.

Caldart, Adrián A., and Joan E. Ricart. "Corporate Strategy Revisited: A View from Complexity Theory." *European Management Review* 1, no. 1 (2004): 96–104.

Casti, John L. *Complexification: Explaining a Paradoxical World Through the Science of Surprise.* New York: HarperCollins, 1994.

Hout, Thomas M. "Books in Review: Are Managers Obsolete?" *Harvard Business Review* 77, no. 2 (1999): 161–168.

Okes, Duke. "Complexity Theory Simplifies Choices." *Quality Progress* 36, no. 7 (2003): 35–38.

Olsen, Edwin E., Glenda H. Eoyang, Richard Beckhard, and Peter Vaill. *Facilitating Organization Change: Lessons from Complexity Science.* San Francisco: Pfeiffer, 2001.

Sherman, Howard J., and Ralph Schultz. *Open Boundaries: Creating Business Innovation Through Complexity.* Reading, MA: Perseus Books, 1998.

Waldrop, Mitchell M. *Complexity: The Emerging Science at the Edge of Order and Chaos.* New York: Simon and Schuster, 1992.

COMPUTER-AIDED DESIGN AND MANUFACTURING

Computer-aided design (CAD), also known as computer-aided design and drafting (CADD), involves the entire spectrum of drawing with the aid of a computer—from straight lines to custom animation. In practice, CAD refers to software for the design of engineering and architectural solutions, complete with two- and three-dimensional modeling capabilities.

Computer-aided manufacturing (CAM) involves the use of computers to aid in any manufacturing process, including flexible manufacturing and robotics. Often outputs from CAD systems serve as inputs to CAM systems. When these two systems work in conjunction, the result is called CADCAM, and becomes part of a firm's computer-integrated manufacturing (CIM) process.

CADCAM systems are intended to assist in many, if not all, of the steps of a typical product life cycle. The product life cycle involves a design phase and an implementation phase. The design phase includes identifying the design needs and specifications; performing a feasibility study, design documentation, evaluation, analysis, and optimization; and completing the design itself. The implementation phase includes process planning, production planning, quality control, packaging, marketing, and shipping.

CAD systems can help with most of the design phase processes, while CAM systems can help with most of the implementation processes. The contributions of CAD and CAM systems are described below.

CAD SYSTEMS

CAD systems are a specialized form of graphics software, and thus must adhere to basic principles of graphics programming. All graphics programs work in the context of a graphics device (e.g., a window on a monitor, a printer, or a plotter). Graphics images are drawn in relation to a 2-D or 3-D coordinate system, of which there are several types.

A device coordinate system is 2-D and maps images directly to the points (pixels) of the hardware device. In order to facilitate device-independent graphics, a virtual device coordinate system abstracts the 2-D points into a logical framework.

Of course, the devices being designed are generally 3-D objects, which also require a world coordinate system for representing the space in which the objects reside, and a model coordinate system for representing each of the objects in that space. CAD software includes algorithms for projecting the 3-D models onto the 2-D device coordinate systems and vice versa.

CAD systems include several primitive drawing functions, including lines, polygons, circles and arcs, rectangles, and other simple shapes. From these primitives, 3-D composites can be constructed, and include cubes, pyramids, cones, wedges, cylinders, and spheres. These shapes can be drawn in any color, and filled with solid colors or other patterns (called hatching). In addition, basic shapes can be altered by filleting (rounding) or chamfering (line segmentation).

Based on the manipulation of basic shapes, designers construct models of objects. A skeletal wire form model is a 3-D representation that shows all edges and features as lines. A more realistic-looking model is called a solid model, which is a 3-D model of the object being designed as a unitary whole showing no hidden features. The solid model represents a closed volume. It includes surface information and data determining if the closed volume contains other objects or features.

Solid modeling involves functions for creating 3-D shapes, combining shapes (via union, intersection, and difference operations), sweeping (translational and rotational) for converting simple shapes into more complex ones, skinning (for creation of surface textures), and various boundary creation functions. Solid modeling also includes parameterization, in which the CAD system maintains a set of relationships between the components of an object so that changes can be propagated to following constructions.

Common shapes are constructed into features (e.g., slots, holes, pockets), which can then be included in a solid model of an object. Feature representation helps the user define parts. It also simplifies CAD software design because features are easier to parameterize than explicit interactions. Objects built from features are called parts. Since a product being designed is composed of several parts, many CAD systems include a useful assembly model, in which the parts are referenced and their geometric and functional relationships are stored.

CAD models can be manipulated and viewed in a wide variety of contexts. They can be viewed from any angle and perspective desired, broken apart or sliced, and even put through simulation tests to analyze for strengths and defects of design. Parts can be moved within their coordinate systems via rotation operations, which provide different perspectives of a part, and translation, which allows the part to move to different locations in the view space. In addition, CAD systems provide valuable dimensioning functionality, which assigns size values based on the designer's drawing.

The movement of these images is a form of animation. Often, CAD systems include virtual reality technology, which produces animated images that simulate a real-world interaction with the object being designed. For example, if the object is a building, the virtual reality system may allow you to visualize the scene as if you were walking around the inside and the outside of the building, enabling you to dynamically view the building from a multitude of perspectives. In order to produce realistic effects, the system must depict the expected effects of light reflecting on the surface as it moves through the user's view space. This process is called rendering.

Rendering technology includes facilities for shading, reflection, and ray tracing. This technique, which is also used in sophisticated video games, provides a realistic image of the object and often helps users make decisions prior to investing money in building construction. Some virtual reality interfaces involve more than just visual stimuli. In fact, they allow the designer to be completely immersed in the virtual environment, experiencing kinesthetic interaction with the designed device.

Some CAD systems go beyond assisting in parts design and actually include functionality for testing a product against stresses in the environment. Using a technique called finite element method (FEM), these systems determine stress, deformation, heat transfer, magnetic field distribution, fluid flow, and other continuous field problems.

Finite element analysis is not concerned with all design details, so instead of the complete solid model a mesh is used. Mesh generation involves computing a set of simple elements giving a good approximation of the designed part. A good meshing must result in an analytical model of sufficient precision for the FEM computation, but with a minimum number of elements in order to avoid unnecessary complexity.

In addition to FEM, some CAD systems provide a variety of optimization techniques, including simulated annealing and genetic algorithms (borrowed from the field of artificial intelligence). These methods help to improve the shape, thickness, and other parameters of a designed object while satisfying user-defined constraints (e.g., allowable stress levels or cost limitations).

When a designer uses CAD to develop a product design, this data is stored into a CAD database. CAD systems allow for a design process in which objects are composed of sub-objects, which are composed of smaller components, and so on. Thus CAD databases tend to be object-oriented. Since CAD designs may need to be used in CAM systems, or shared with other CAD designers using a variety of software packages, most CAD packages ensure that their databases conform to one of the standard CAD data formats. One such standard, developed by the American National Standards Institute (ANSI), is called Initial Graphics Exchange Specification (IGES).

Another data format is DXF, which is used by the popular AutoCAD software and is becoming a de facto industry standard. The capability to convert from one file format to another is called data exchange, and is a common feature of many CAD software packages.

Modern CAD systems offer a number of advantages to designers and companies. For example, they enable users to save time, money, and other resources by automatically generating standard components of a design, allowing the reuse of previously designed components, and facilitating design modification. Such systems also provide for the verification of designs against specifications, the simulation and testing of designs, and the output of designs and engineering documentation directly to manufacturing facilities. While some designers complain that the limitations of CAD systems sometimes serve to curb their creativity, there is no doubt that they have become an indispensable tool in electrical, mechanical, and architectural design.

CAM SYSTEMS

The manufacturing process includes process planning, production planning (involving tool procurement, materials ordering, and numerical control programming), production, quality control, packaging, marketing, and shipping. CAM systems assist in all but the last two steps of this process. In CAM systems, the computer interfaces directly or indirectly with the plant's production resources.

Process planning is a manufacturing function that establishes which processes and parameters are to be used, as well as the machines performing these processes. This often involves preparing detailed work instructions to machines for assembling or manufacturing parts. Computer-aided process planning (CAPP) systems help to automate the planning process by developing, based on the family classification of the part being produced, a sequence of operations required for producing this part (sometimes called a routing), together with text descriptions of the work to be done at each step in the sequence. Sometimes these process plans are constructed based on data from the CAD databases.

Process planning is a difficult scheduling problem. For a complex manufacturing procedure, there could be a huge number of possible permutations of tasks in a process requiring the use of sophisticated optimization methods to obtain the best process plan. Techniques such as genetic algorithms and heuristic search (based on artificial intelligence) are often employed to solve this problem.

The most common CAM application is numerical control (NC), in which programmed instructions control machine tools that grind, cut, mill, punch, or bend raw stock into finished products. Often the NC inputs specifications from a CAD database, together with additional information from the machine tool operator. A typical NC machine tool includes a machine control unit (MCU) and the machine tool itself. The MCU includes a data processing unit (DPU), which reads and decodes instructions from a part program, and a control loop unit (CLU), which converts the instructions into control signals and operates the drive mechanisms of the machine tool.

The part program is a set of statements that contain geometric information about the part and motion information about how the cutting tool should move with respect to the workpiece. Cutting speed, feed rate, and other information are also specified to meet the required part tolerances. Part programming is an entire technical discipline in itself, requiring a sophisticated programming language and coordinate system reference points. Sometimes parts programs can be generated automatically from CAD databases, where the geometric and functional specifications of the CAD design automatically translate into the parts program instructions.

Numerical control systems are evolving into a more sophisticated technology called rapid prototyping and manufacturing (RP&M). This technology involves three steps: forming cross sections of the objects to be manufactured, laying cross sections layer by layer, and combining the layers. This is a tool-less approach to manufacturing made possible by the availability of solid modeling CAD systems. RP&M is often used for evaluating designs, verifying functional specifications, and reverse engineering.

Of course, machine control systems are often used in conjunction with robotics technology, making use of artificial intelligence and computer controlled humanoid physical capabilities (e.g., dexterity, movement, and vision). These "steel-collar workers" increase productivity and reduce costs by replacing human workers in repetitive, mundane, and hazardous environments.

CAM systems often include components for automating the quality control function. This involves evaluating product and process specifications, testing incoming materials and outgoing products, and testing the production process in progress. Quality control systems often measure the products that are coming off the assembly line to ensure that they are meeting the tolerance specifications established in the CAD databases. They produce exception reports for the assembly line managers when products are not meeting specifications.

In summary, CAM systems increase manufacturing efficiency by simplifying and automating production processes, improve the utilization of production facilities, reduce investment in production inventories, and ultimately improve customer service by drastically reducing out-of-stock situations.

PUTTING IT ALL TOGETHER: COMPUTER INTEGRATED MANUFACTURING

In a CADCAM system, a part is designed on the computer (via CAD) then transmitted directly to the computer-driven machine tools that manufacture the part via CAM. Within this process, there will be many other computerized steps along the way. The entire realm of design, material handling, manufacturing, and packaging is often referred to as computer-integrated manufacturing (CIM).

CIM includes all aspects of CAD and CAM, as well as inventory management. To keep costs down, companies have a strong motivation to minimize stock volumes in their warehouses. Just-in-time (JIT) inventory policies are becoming the norm. To facilitate this, CIM includes material requirements planning (MRP) as part of its overall configuration. MRP systems help to plan the types and quantities of materials that will be needed for the manufacturing process. The merger of MRP with CAM's production scheduling and shop floor control is called manufacturing resource planning (MRPII). Thus, the merger of MRP with CADCAM systems integrates the production and the inventory control functions of an organization.

Today's industries cannot survive unless they can introduce new products with high quality, low cost,

and short lead time. CADCAM systems apply computing technology to make these requirements a reality, and promise to exert a major influence on design, engineering, and manufacturing processes for the foreseeable future.

SEE ALSO: Computer-Integrated Manufacturing; Manufacturing Resources Planning; Robotics

Michel Mitri
Revised by Rhoda L. Wilburn

FURTHER READING:

Bean, Robert. "CAD Should Enable Design Creativity: Engineers Need CAD Tools as Easy as the 'Paper Napkin.'" *Design News*, 10 January 2005.

Grabowski, Ralph, and R. Huber. *The Successful CAD Manager's Handbook.* Albany, NY: Delmar Publishers, 1994.

Lee, Kunwoo. *Principles of CAD/CAM/CAE Systems.* Reading, MA: Addison Wesley, 1999.

McMahon, Chris, and Jimmie Browne. *CAD/CAM: Principles, Practice, and Manufacturing Management.* 2d ed. Upper Saddle River, NJ: Prentice-Hall, 1999.

Port, Otis. "Design Tools Move into the Fast Lane." *Business Week*, 2 June 2003.

Sheh, Mike. "A Quantum Leap in Engineering Design." *Business Week*, 2 June 2003.

COMPUTER-AIDED MANUFACTURING

SEE: Computer-Aided Design and Manufacturing

COMPUTER-INTEGRATED MANUFACTURING

Computer-integrated manufacturing (CIM) is the use of computer techniques to integrate manufacturing activities. These activities encompass all functions necessary to translate customer needs into a final product. CIM starts with the development of a product concept that may exist in the marketing organization; includes product design and specification, usually the responsibility of an engineering organization; and extends through production into delivery and after-sales activities that reside in a field service or sales organization. Integration of these activities requires that accurate information be available when needed and in the format required by the person or group requesting the data. Data may come directly from the originating source or through an intermediate database according to Jorgensen and Krause. CIM systems have emerged as a result of the developments in manufacturing and computer technology. According to Kusiak the computer plays an important role integrating the following functional areas of a CIM system:

- Part and product design. There are four phases that are crucial in part and product design. They include preliminary design, refinement, analysis, and implementation.

- Tool and fixture design. Tooling engineers using computer-aided design (CAD) tools to develop the systems or fixtures that produce the parts.

- Process planning. The process planner designs a plan that outlines the routes, operations, machines, and tools required. He or she also attempts to minimize cost, manufacturing time, and machine idle time while maximizing productivity and quality.

- Programming of numerically controlled machines and material handling systems.

- Production planning. There are two concepts used here including materials requirement planning (MRP) and machine loading and scheduling.

- Machining. This is part of the actual manufacturing process, including turning, drilling, and face milling for metal removal operations.

- Assembly. After they are manufactured, parts and subassemblies are put together with other parts to create a finished product or subassembly.

- Maintenance. Computers can monitor, intervene, and even correct machine malfunctions as well as quality issues within manufacturing.

- Quality control. This involves three steps including system design, parameter design, and tolerance design.

- Inspection. This stage determines if there have been errors and quality issues during the manufacturing of the product.

- Storage and retrieval. These tasks involve raw materials, work-in-process inventory, finished goods, and equipment.

CIM ORIGIN

The term *computer-integrated manufacturing* was coined by Dr. Joseph Harrington in his 1974 book bearing that name. Until the 1970s, the most aggressive and successful automation was seen in production operations. Discrete parts manufacturing used highly mechanized machines that were driven and controlled by cams and complex devices such as automatic screw machines. Process manufacturers made use of these cam-driven controllers and limit switches for operations such as heat treating, filling and canning, bottling, and weaving states Robert Thacker of the Society of Manufacturing Engineers. The historical approach to automation focused on individual activities that result in the incorporation of large amounts of computerized activities. In the 1980s, managing information became an important issue.

CIM BENEFITS

According to the U.S. National Research Council, CIM improves production productivity by 40 to 70 percent, as well as enhances engineering productivity and quality. CIM can also decrease design costs by 15 to 30 percent, reduce overall lead time by 20 to 60 percent, and cut work-in-process inventory by 30 to 60 percent. Managers who use CIM believe that there is a direct relationship between the efficiency of information management and the efficiency and the overall effectiveness of the manufacturing enterprise. Thacker's view is that many CIM programs focus attention on the efficiency of information management and the problems that come with it instead of developing new and more sophisticated manufacturing machines, material transformation processes, manufacturing management processes, and production facilities. Computer-integrated manufacturing can be applied to nonmanufacturing organizations by changing the manufacturing focus toward a service orientation. CIM and Job Definition Format (JDF) are becoming increasingly beneficial to printing companies to streamline their production process.

THE CIM PLAN

A plan for a CIM system should provide a description of projects for automating activities, assisting activities with technology, and integrating the information flows among these activities. The planning process includes six crucial steps:

- project activation
- business assessment
- business modeling
- needs analysis
- conceptual design
- CIM plan consolidation and economic analysis

This process, according to Jorgensen and Krause, also acts as a building block for the future of the organization integrating these functions in order to diminish them as an impediment to integration.

CONCEPTUAL DESIGN

The conceptual design of a CIM environment consists of individual systems that fulfill the required capabilities, an overall architecture incorporating the systems and the communication links, and a migration path from the current systems architecture. Functional requirements must be compared to the current inventory of systems and available technology to determine system availability. Jorgensen and Krause state that the following techniques are used in satisfying system requirements:

- exploiting unused and available functional capabilities of current systems;

- identifying functional capabilities available for, but not installed on, current in-house systems;

- locating systems that are commercially available but not currently in-house;

- recognizing state-of-the-art technology that is not immediately commercially available on a system;

- foreseeing functional capabilities of systems on the technical horizon; and

- determining whether the requirement is beyond the capabilities of systems on the technical horizon.

MANAGING A CIM

Managers must understand that short-term goals must support the long-term goal of implementing a CIM. Top management establishes long-term goals for the company and envisions the general direction of the company. The middle management then creates objectives to achieve this goal. Upper management sees the focus as being very broad, whereas middle management must have a more narrow focus.

In deciding to implement a CIM, there are three perspectives that must be considered: the conceptual plan, the logical plan, and the physical plan. The conceptual plan is used to demonstrate a knowledgeable understanding of the elements of CIM and how they are related and managed. Thacker goes on to say that the conceptual plan states that by integrating the elements of a business, a manager will produce results better and faster than those same elements working independently.

The logical plan organizes the functional elements and logically demonstrates the relationships and dependencies between the elements. Thacker details that it further shows how to plan and control

the business, how to develop and connect an application, communications, and database network.

The physical plan contains the actual requirements for setting the CIM system in place. These requirements can include equipment such as hardware, software, and work cells. The plan is a layout of where the computers, work stations, robots, applications, and databases are located in order to optimize their use within the CIM and within the company. According to Thacker, sooner or later it becomes the CIM implementation plan for the enterprise.

CIM is challenged by technical and cultural boundaries. The technical challenge is first complicated by the varying applications involved. Thacker claims that it is also complicated by the number of vendors that the CIM serves as well as incompatibility problems among systems and lack of standards for data storage, formatting, and communications. Companies must also have people who are well-trained in the various aspects of CIM. They must be able to understand the applications, technology, and communications and integration requirements of the technology.

CIM cultural problems begin within the division of functional units within the company such as engineering design, manufacturing engineering, process planning, marketing, finance, operations, information systems, materials control, field service, distribution, quality, and production planning. CIM requires these functional units to act as whole and not separate entities. The planning process represents a significant commitment by the company implementing it. Although the costs of implementing the environment are substantial, the benefits once the system is in place greatly outweigh the costs. The implementation process should ensure that there is a common goal and a common understanding of the company's objectives and that the priority functions are being accomplished by all areas of the company according to Jorgensen and Krause.

SEE ALSO: Computer-Aided Design and Manufacturing; Flexible Manufacturing; Management Information Systems; Robotics

John C. Koch
Revised by Hal Kirkwood, Jr.

FURTHER READING:

Cagle, E. "Awaiting the Big Payoff." *Printing Impressions* 47, no. 6 (November 2004): 54–56.

Kusiak, Andrew. *Intelligent Manufacturing Systems.* Englewood Cliffs, NJ: Prentice Hall, 1990.

Mahmood, T. "Real-time Computer Integrated Manufacturing." *Circuits Assembly* 6, no. 3 (March 1995): 58–60.

Rehg, James A., and Henry W. Kraebber. *Computer Integrated Manufacturing.* Upper Saddle River, NJ: Pearson Prentice Hall, 2004.

Ruey-Chyi, W., C. Ruey-Shun, and C.R. Fan. "Design an Intelligent CIM System Based on Data Mining Technology for

New Manufacturing Processes." *International Journal of Materials and Product Technology* 2, no. 6 (2004): 487–504.

Thacker, Robert M. *A New CIM Model.* Dearborn, MI: Society of Manufacturing Engineers, 1989.

COMPUTER NETWORKS

For most businesses in the United States, computers are an essential part of their daily operations. Many businesses have come to rely on their computers to store and track information, communicate with customers and suppliers, design and manufacture products, and more. It is not uncommon for businesses of all sizes to have multiple computers in an office. Often, these computers are connected through networks that allow information to be shared between computers.

A computer network, as defined in the Merriam-Webster dictionary, is "a system of computers, peripherals, terminals, and databases connected by communications lines." In other words, networks are used to connect computers to other computers, as well as to other devices such as printers, scanners, and fax machines. Networks can be used to connect devices in the same building or they can be used to connect devices that are miles apart. Perhaps the most well known network in use today is the Internet. Many individuals and businesses around the world connect to the Internet on a daily basis. Other examples of networks include library card catalogs, the displays of flight arrival and departure times used at airports, and credit card readers at retail stores.

NETWORK CONFIGURATIONS

Networks can be set up in a number of different ways depending on the number of devices, the distances between those devices, the transmission speed requirements, and other factors. The most popular configurations, or topologies, include the bus, token ring, star, and star bus topologies.

BUS. With a bus configuration, each node is connected sequentially along the network backbone. A node is any device connected to the network, such as a computer, printer, or scanner. Backbone is the term used to describe the main cables to which the network segments are connected. Resistors are placed at each end of the network to ensure that the signal is terminated when it reaches the end. When one node sends information to another node through the network, the information travels along the backbone until it reaches the desired receiving node.

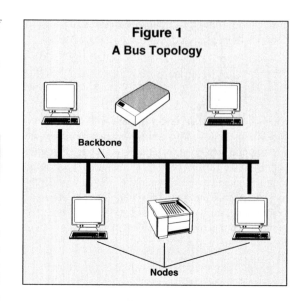

Figure 1
A Bus Topology

Backbone

Nodes

TOKEN RING. With a ring configuration, each node is connected sequentially along the network backbone. However, unlike the bus configuration, the end of the network connects to the first node, forming a circuit. Nodes on a token ring take turns sending and receiving information. In the token ring topology, a token travels along the backbone with the information being sent. The node with the token sends information to the next node along the backbone. The receiving node reads the information addressed to it and then passes the token and any additional information to the next node. This continues until the token and data make it back to the first node in the network.

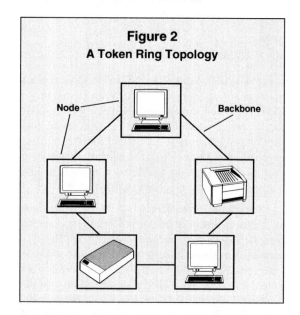

Figure 2
A Token Ring Topology

Node

Backbone

STAR. With a star configuration, each node is connected to a central hub via network segments. When one node sends information to another node, the information passes through the hub. The hub does not filter or route the information in any way; it simply serves as a connector between network segments.

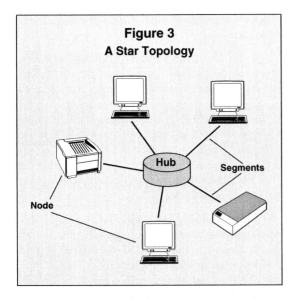

Figure 3
A Star Topology

Node
Hub
Segments

STAR BUS. With a star bus configuration, the hubs of multiple star networks are connected together via the backbone. This is the most common network configuration in use.

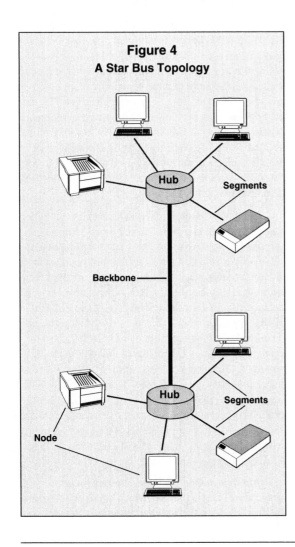

Figure 4
A Star Bus Topology

Hub
Segments
Backbone
Hub
Segments
Node

LOCAL AREA NETWORKS AND WIDE AREA NETWORKS

A local area network (LAN), as the name implies, is a network that connects devices that are local, or relatively close to each other. Nodes on a LAN are usually in the same building. A wide area network (WAN), on the other hand, is used to connect nodes that could be miles apart. LANs generally transmit data faster than WANs, and they are usually more reliable. Fiber-optic cables are used for both LANs and WANs.

ETHERNET NETWORKING. Ethernet is a LAN protocol (i.e., a set of rules that governs communications) developed in the mid-1970s by Bob Metcalfe and David Boggs at Xerox Corporation's Palo Alto Research Center. Today, Ethernet is the most widely used network technology in the world. The original Ethernet used a bus topology and provided for transfer rates of up to 10 million bits per second (Mbps). This Ethernet specification was modified slightly and became the Institute of Electrical and Electronics Engineering (IEEE) 802.3 standard, which helped solidify Ethernet as a widely-recognized, open international standard. The IEEE 802.3 specifies the physical networking interface and lower layers of software usually associated with Ethernet. Vendors ship an estimated total of 300 million Ethernet ports each year.

Although networks using Ethernet protocol generally connect devices over short distances, technological advances now allow Ethernet to connect devices that are miles apart. Ethernet is widely accepted and largely installed because it is simple and efficient and because network interface cards (NIC) for Ethernet can be easily installed in personal computers, workstations, or high-end computers. Furthermore, it can run on a variety of media, including fiber optics, twisted-pair, cable, and wireless connections.

REPEATERS. When Ethernet was first implemented, most people used a copper coaxial cable. However, the maximum length of this cable was 500 meters, which was not long enough for some networks. To address this problem, network engineers used repeaters to connect several Ethernet segments.

BRIDGES. Bridges provide a simple means for connecting LANs. A bridge is a device that connects physically separate LAN segments (such as different Ethernet cables) into one logical LAN segment. There are four categories of bridges: transparent, source routing, encapsulating, and translating. Transparent bridges are used for Ethernet, whereas source routing bridges are used for token ring networks. Encapsulating bridges connect two segments of the same media (such as token ring to token ring) over a medium. The receiving bridge removes the envelope, checks the destination, and sends the frame to the destination device. Translating bridges are used to connect different types of network media such as Ethernet and FDDI (fiber distributed data interface). FDDI is a set of protocols that uses a modified form of the token-passing method over fiber-optic cable.

ROUTERS. LAN segments joined by a router are physically and logically separate networks. In contrast to a bridge, when multiple network segments are joined by a router they maintain their separate logical identities (network address space), but constitute an internetwork.

Routers specify the destination and route for each packet, and they can be used to direct packets and interconnect a variety of network architectures. A major difference between a bridge and a router is that the bridge distinguishes packets by source and destination address, whereas a router can also distinguish packets by protocol type. Routers provide for the interfaces to WANs such as frame relay and packet switching services. Some new bridge products have added router capabilities; hence, the practical distinction is becoming blurred, giving rise to the term "brouter."

Routers can also be used to limit access to a network by the type of application (e.g., allowing electronic mail to pass, but not file transfer traffic). This capability provides a measure of security for the network, and is used extensively when creating firewalls. Firewalls are implemented to secure an organization's network when it is linked to the Internet.

SWITCHES. Ethernet communicates across the network using the Carrier Sense Multiple Access with Collision Detection (CSMA/CD) process. A protocol using CSMA/CD monitors, or listens to, the media for network traffic, or information traveling through the network from one node to another. If a node does not sense any traffic, it will send frames or packets of information onto the media. A network frame is like a mailed letter. The letter is put in an envelope that has a return address and the address of its destination. Data are like the letter and the frame is like the envelope. The data is placed in the frame and the frame has the addressing information and error-checking code. Each protocol has its distinctive frame. The device continues sending until it finishes or until a collision occurs.

A collision happens when more than one device transmits data at the same time. When a collision occurs, each device waits a random amount of time before trying to retransmit the data. By having each node wait a random amount of time, there is only a slim chance that the two devices will send out the data at the same time again. The collision detection and frame retransmission are part of the protocol.

One way to reduce the number of collisions is to add switches to the network. A switch, like a hub, connects nodes to each other. However, while a hub requires each node to share the bandwidth (i.e., the amount of simultaneous data traffic the network can

support), a switch allows each node to use the full bandwidth.

In a fully switched network, each node is connected to a dedicated segment of the network, which in turn is connected to a switch. Each switch supports multiple dedicated segments. When a node sends a signal, the switch picks it up and sends it through the appropriate segment to the receiving node. Ethernet protocol in a fully switched environment does not require collision detection because the switches can send and receive data simultaneously, thus eliminating the chance of collision.

Most companies do not use fully switched networks, as the cost of replacing each hub with a switch can be expensive. Instead, most use a mixed network configuration in which a combination of hubs and switches are used. For example, all of the computers in each department may be connected to their own departmental hub, and then all of the departmental hubs may be connected to a switch.

ETHERNET ADVANCEMENTS

The dominance of Ethernet as a LAN technology for desktop PCs has made it difficult for other technologies to gain acceptance. Ethernet technology continues to evolve as Ethernet vendors develop techniques to increase bandwidth and the support of more complex network configurations. For example, Fast Ethernet technology was developed to provide for increased bandwidth of up to 100 Mbps, ten times faster than the original Ethernet. When migrating from Ethernet to Fast Ethernet, a company may need to change network interface cards and the central wiring hub, and it may also need to upgrade the wiring.

In May 1996 eleven network vendors (including Cisco Systems and Sun Microsystems) formed the Gigabit Ethernet Alliance. The goal of the alliance was to develop a standard for 1 Gigabit per second (Gbps) Ethernet transmissions. Soon thereafter, network vendors were successful in designing networks that achieved the 1 Gbps transmissions goal, and in 2002 the IEEE approved the fibre-only 10 Gbps Ethernet. Throughout 2004 great progress was made in the development of l0 Gbps Ethernet technology and its infrastructure. The increased speed of the 10 Gbps Ethernet in terms of data storage, system backup, teleconferencing, and surveillance systems will prove beneficial to blade servers, networked enterprise switches, video servers, and other applications. The higher density, reduced power, and improved cost-effectiveness appeal to all of the major system developers.

Another development in Ethernet technology is power over Ethernet (POE), which the IEEE published in July 2003 as the 802.3af standard. PowerDsine

Table 1
Common Line Designations

Line Designation	Speed	Equivalents
DS0 (Digital Signal Zero)	64 Kbps	
ISDN	16 Kbps or 128 Kbps	Two DS0 lines plus signaling
T1	1.544 Mbps	24 DS0 lines
T3	43.232 Mbps	28 T1 lines
OC3 (Optical Carrier 3)	155 Mbps	84 T1 lines
OC12	622 Mbps	4 OC3 lines
OC48	2.5 Gbps	4 OC12 lines
OC192	9.6 Gbps	4 OC48 lines

Adapted from "How does a T1 line work?" How Stuff Works, Inc., 2005. Available from http://computer.howstuffworks.com/question372.htm

came up with the idea for POE in 1998 and convinced 3Com, Intel, Mitel, National Semiconductor, and Nortel Networks to promote this technology. One of the main purposes of POE is to standardize connections to portable and remote devices that no longer need AC line power. POE can be used for a number of applications, including digital cameras, security systems, and smart sensors.

NETWORK REMOTE ACCESS DEVICES

Network remote access devices are used to connect remote (off-site) users to an organization's network. There are many options available. See Table 1 for some of the common line designations.

MODEMS. A modem is a device that converts data from digital to analog signals so it can travel over the public switched telephone network (PSTN) to its destination. Once the signal reaches its destination, the modem converts it back to digital. As the PSTN was designed to carry voice (analog signals), it is not the best option for carrying data. Digital data networks (DDNs) are replacing the PSTN. DDNs are used to transmit both data and digitized voice. Because of their slow data transmission speeds, modems are no longer used in most business environments.

ISDN. Integrated services digital network (ISDN) is a switched, high-speed data service. ISDN is an international telecommunications standard for transmitting voice, video, and data over digital lines running at 64 Kbps, and reaches 1.5 Mbps in North America and 2 Mbps in Europe. ISDN uses the same copper telephone lines as modems do, but at a rate approximately five times faster. Furthermore, it is extremely reliable.

T1. A T1 line carries data approximately 60 times faster than a modem on a normal telephone line. The higher speed and extreme reliability make this a popular choice for many medium- to large-sized businesses. T1 lines can handle hundreds of users simultaneously for general browsing. However, it cannot handle that many users simultaneously downloading large files, such as MP3 files or video files. For very large companies, T1 lines may not be sufficient.

CABLE MODEMS. A cable modem is a device used to connect a computer to a coaxial cable, such as the kind used for cable television, in order to access online services. This device modulates and demodulates signals like a conventional modem. In addition, a cable modem functions like a router designed for installation on cable television networks. The most popular application for cable modems is high-speed Internet access, which provides much faster service than standard telephone-line modems, thus enabling users to access streaming audio, video, and other services.

WIRELESS TECHNOLOGY. Mobile telephones, laptop computers, and handheld computers are so affordable that they have become a part of everyday life for many people and businesses around the world. Advances in wireless technology have made it possible for people to access networks without having to physically connect to the network through cables. For example, it is not uncommon for business travelers to access networks on their wireless fidelity (Wi-Fi)-enabled laptop PCs or handheld computers while waiting at an airport.

Bluetooth is a wireless standard developed by a group of electronics manufacturers to allow any electronic device—such as computers, cell phones, keyboards, and headphones—to find and connect to other devices without any direct action from the user. The devices find one another and transmit data without any user input at all. Because Bluetooth technology is inexpensive and does not require the user to do anything special to make it work, it is gaining wide use around the world.

Wireless products are now affordable and very reliable. With wireless connections, it is possible for people to move around while connected to a network. This could be very useful in environments such as hospitals, so that health care professionals could access patient records from various locations around the campus. Many home and small-business users also use wireless networks to avoid the need to route twisted-pair wiring around their premises. In fact, domestic, small-office, and home-office networking accounts for most of the wireless Ethernet equipment sales in the United States.

In summary, computers connected with communications networks improve productivity and profitability by enabling people and organizations to develop closer relationships with coworkers, customers, business partners, and other people in general.

SEE ALSO: Computer Security; The Internet

Badie N. Farah
Revised by Rhoda L. Wilburn

FURTHER READING:

Black, Uyless. *ATM Volume III Internetworking with ATM.* Upper Saddle River, NJ: Prentice Hall, 1999.

FitzGerald, J., and A. Dennis. *Business Data Communications and Networking.* 6th ed. New York: John Wiley & Sons, 1999.

Franklin, Curt. "How Bluetooth Works." How Stuff Works, Inc. Available from <http://electronics.howstuffworks.com/bluetooth.htm>.

Horn, Keith. "10-Gbit Ethernet Is Ready, along with its Customers." *Electronic Design,* 23 August 2004, 18.

"How Does a T1 Line Work?" How Stuff Works, Inc. Available from <http://computer.howstuffworks.com/question372.htm>.

Marsh, David. "Ethernet Keeps Pumping the Data." *EDN,* 14 October 2004, 63.

———. "Power and Wireless Options Extend Ethernet's Reach." *EDN,* 11 November 2004, 67.

Panko, Raymond. *Business Data Communications and Networking.* 2nd ed. Upper Saddle River, NJ: Prentice Hall, 1999.

Pidgeon, Nick. "How Ethernet Works." How Stuff Works, Inc. Available from <http://computer.howstuffworks.com/ethernet.htm>.

Stamper, David A. *Business Data Communications.* 5th ed. New York: Addison-Wesley, 1999.

Tyson, Jeff. "How LAN Switches Work." How Stuff Works, Inc. Available from <http://computer.howstuffworks.com/lan-switch.htm>.

Vargo, J., and R. Hunt. *Telecommunications in Business.* Chicago: Irwin, 1996.

COMPUTER SECURITY

Computers have become such a big part of everyday life—both at work and at home—for many people around the world. These days, computers are an essential part of practically every type of business, from small, home-based businesses to large multinational corporations. In the business world, companies use computers to store information, design and manufacture products, run complex calculations, etc. On a personal level, many people rely on their home computers to store important information, watch movies, play games, communicate with others, and shop over the Internet.

Because so much valuable information is stored on computers, a new type of criminal has emerged in recent years. These criminals, sometimes called "hackers" or "scammers," use their computers to "break in" to companies' or other people's computers to steal information, such as credit card numbers. The incidence of identity theft is on the rise as computer criminals find increasingly sophisticated ways to obtain personal information and use it in malicious ways. However, not all hackers are interested in stealing information. Instead, some send viruses through websites or email to damage the receivers' computers.

RECORDS PROTECTION

Information stored in a computer system is subject to a variety of threats. It was not long ago that the biggest concern about computer data was protecting it from physical disasters such as floods and fires, technology failures, and human errors. Most organizations develop contingency plans whereby they examine the possibilities of losing computer operations, and formulate procedures for minimizing damage. A disaster recovery plan is typically adopted to outline how the organization will carry on business in the event of a catastrophic loss. Data backup is an essential element of disaster recovery and involves the regular, systematic backing up of data to media that may include floppy disks, removable hard disks, CD-ROMs, or magnetic tape. Ideally, the backup files are then stored in a safe that is fireproof, heatproof, waterproof, and preferably protected at an off-premise location.

While the threat to computer files from disasters is real, research shows that employees are frequent culprits in the destruction or alteration of company information. Customer information, new-product plans, company financial information, and legal information can be stolen and sold to other organizations. Former or disgruntled workers who want revenge on their employer or supervisor have been known to resort to computer crime. The victim of information theft rarely learns of the problem until afterward, since copying information does not alter the original in any way. For this reason, prosecution is rare and frequently results in mild treatment. In some cases, perpetrators have taken new jobs as security consultants after receiving minor punishments.

Although records protection is still of concern today, there are many more concerns about the safety of computer data, both at work and at home. Because so much business is now conducted over the Internet, computer criminals have discovered ways to steal that information. Terms such as spyware, phishing, pharming, viruses, firewalls, and spam are practically household words among computer users, especially those who use the Internet.

SPYWARE

Spyware is a term used to describe a program that is put on a computer without the user's permission, and usually without the user's knowledge. A spyware program runs in the background and keeps track of the programs the user runs and the websites the user visits. Some spyware tracks the user's keystrokes and extracts passwords and other information as they type. It then uses the information gathered to display certain advertisements or forces the user's browser to display certain websites or search results. Most spyware is written for the Windows operating system.

Spyware can be installed on an unsuspecting user's computer in any of the following ways:

- Piggybacked software installation: Some software applications install spyware as part of the program installation. This is especially true of "free" software that users download onto their computers.

- Drive-by download: Some websites automatically try to download and install spyware on the user's machine. Sometimes when this happens, the user's browser may display a standard popup message that tells the name of the software and asks if the user wants to install it. But if the user's security setting is low enough, his browser may not display the message.

- Browser add-ons: This type of spyware adds enhancements, such as a toolbar, an animated pal, or additional search boxes, to the user's web browser. While the user may like these enhancements, some of them embed themselves deep in the user's computer and are very hard to remove from the computer. These embedded spyware programs are also known as browser hijackers.

- Masquerading as anti-spyware: Some spyware claim to be anti-spyware software, but in reality are spyware programs themselves. They trick users into thinking that they remove spyware, when they actually install additional spyware of their own.

Not only does spyware infringe upon users' privacy, but it can also slow down their computers. Many spyware programs use up most of the computer's random access memory (RAM) and processor power, preventing other applications from using these resources. In addition, many spyware programs generate popup advertisements that slow down the user's web browser, reset the user's homepage to display advertisements every time she opens the web browser, and redirect the user's web searches. Some spyware programs even modify the user's Internet settings for modem connections to dial out to expensive, pay telephone numbers. Some of the more malicious spyware programs modify the user's firewall settings, increasing the opportunities for more spyware and viruses to enter the user's computer.

Spyware has become such a problem that many states are taking action to explicitly ban spyware. Several federal laws deal with spyware. These include the Computer Fraud and Abuse Act, which covers any unauthorized software installations; The Federal Trade Commission Act, which deals with deceptive trade practices; and the Electronic Communications Privacy Act, which makes it illegal for companies to violate the security of customers' personal information. Unfortunately, these laws are very hard to enforce.

PHISHING

Phishing is a term used to describe email scams that attempt to trick consumers into disclosing personal and/or financial information. The email messages appear to be from legitimate sources, such as banks, credit card issuers, or well-known Internet sites (such as America Online, Paypal, and eBay). The content of the messages varies, but often they tell the consumer that he needs to update personal information or that there is a problem with the consumer's account. The messages usually contain links to fake websites. When the user clicks the link, they are taken to websites that look official, and may even include images from the legitimate websites. These fake websites often instruct the unsuspecting user to enter credit card numbers, social security numbers, bank personal identification numbers (PINs), and other valuable information. Once the user enters that information, the violators use it or sell it. This leads to what is known as identity theft. The scammers use this information to assume the identity of the victims to make purchases in that person's name.

It is estimated that between July and October of 2004, the number of new phishing websites grew approximately 25 percent per month. The amount of money that phishers collected from victims in a twelve-month period (April 2003 through April 2004) is estimated to be $1.2 billion.

In an effort to stop phishing, U.S. Senator Patrick Leahy introduced the Anti-Phishing Act of 2005, which allows law enforcement officials to prosecute scammers before the actual fraud takes place. The bill also addresses pharming, which occurs when scammers redirect a user's browser to a fake banking or e-commerce site that asks for personal information. According to Leahy, "Some phishers and pharmers can be prosecuted under wire fraud or identity theft statutes, but often these prosecutions take place only when someone has been defrauded. For most of these criminals, that leaves plenty of time to cover their tracks. Moreover, the mere threat of these attacks undermines everyone's confidence in the Internet. When people cannot trust that websites are what they appear to be, they will not use the Internet for their secure transactions."

In December 2004 several financial institutions, Internet service providers (ISPs), online auctions, IT vendors, and law enforcement agencies came together to form an anti-phishing consortium. This group, called the Digital PhishNet group, includes big names such as Microsoft Corp.; America Online, Inc.; VeriSign, Inc.; EarthLink, Inc.; the Federal Bureau of Investigation (FBI); the Federal Trade Commission; and the U.S. Secret Service; the U.S. Postal Inspection Service. According to the consortium's website (<http://www.digitalphishnet.org>), it is a "joint enforcement initiative between industry and law enforcement" designed to catch phishing perpetrators.

The Anti-Phishing Working Group (APWG) also formed in response to the growing number of phishing complaints. According to the APWG website (<http://www.antiphishing.org>), the group is "the global pan-industrial and law enforcement association focused on eliminating the fraud and identity theft that result from phishing, pharming and email spoofing of all types." The APWG has more than 1,200 members, including nearly 800 companies and agencies, eight of the top ten U.S. banks, four of the top five U.S. Internet service providers, hundreds of technology vendors, and national and provincial law enforcement agencies worldwide.

SPAM

Spam is a term used to describe unsolicited email messages that usually contain an advertisement for some product or service, such as mortgage loans, pornography, or prescription drugs. Spammers send the messages to email addresses on wide-scale mailing lists, which could mean that each message is sent to thousands of people. Spam has become such an annoying problem for so many people that software programmers have developed spam filters to block or delete some email messages before they reach the recipient's email account. Most ISPs offer some level of spam filtering to their customers. However, even with these filters, hundreds of spam messages get through.

Practically everyone with a public email address receives spam every day. According to *BusinessWeek Online* (June 10, 2003), "in a single day in May [2003], No. 1 Internet service provider AOL Time Warner (AOL) blocked 2 billion spam messages—88 per subscriber—from hitting its customers' e-mail accounts. Microsoft, which operates No. 2 Internet service provider MSN plus e-mailbox service Hotmail, says it blocks an average of 2.4 billion spams per day."

Where do spammers get email addresses? Hundreds of companies compile lists of email address and put them on CDs, which they sell to anyone who is willing to pay for them. Each CD can contain millions of email addresses. These companies use programs to pull out screen names and email addresses from newsgroups and chat rooms or the Internet itself. Some spammers use spambots, which are programs that go through the web and look for the @ symbol and pull the email addresses associated with each one. Another method spammers use to obtain email addresses is to create websites specifically designed to attract web surfers. These websites may ask you to enter your email address to see what the site has to offer (for example, large amounts of money).

And finally, perhaps the most common method spammers use to get email addresses is to conduct a dictionary search of the mail servers and large ISPs. Dictionary searches use a program that establishes a connection with the target mail server and then submits millions of random email addresses. Often they will vary these email addresses very slightly (such as by adding a number somewhere in the address). The program then collects the email addresses for which the message actually goes through.

There are hundreds of companies around the world that have formed specifically to cater to spammers. They offer services for sending bulk email. Some of the larger companies can send billions of messages a day. Many of these companies are set up outside the United States to avoid U.S. laws. Some claim to be "spam free." This means that the email addresses they use are taken from the list of users who requested to receive bulk email, or "opt-in" email. A user's email address can be placed on an opt-in list when ordering something online. Many online stores include a checkbox near the bottom of the order page that asks the user to clear the checkbox if they do not want to receive email offers from their partners. If a user does not see that or misinterprets the checkbox, they may be placed on an opt-in list.

As mentioned above, there are many different spam filtering software programs on the market. These filters check email as it arrives in the user's electronic mailbox. The user can set up the filter to check for specific words or specific email addresses or specific types of attachments. If the filter detects any of these, it will either delete the message or place it in a separate folder. Unfortunately, spammers often find ways around these filters. Another problem with filters is that they sometimes filter out legitimate messages.

In 1998, Spamhaus.org was formed to track and stop spammers around the world. Australian-based Spamhaus (<http://www.spamhaus.org>) calls itself "an international non-profit organization whose mission is to track the Internet's Spam Gangs." Spamhaus.org also says it seeks to provide "dependable realtime anti-spam protection," works with law enforcement agencies to "identify and pursue spammers worldwide," and lobbies for "effective anti-spam legislation."

Today, Spamhaus continues to fight spam. The group publishes the Register Of Known Spam Operations (ROKSO), which lists the Internet Protocol (IP) addresses of the 200 worst spam gangs worldwide. ISPs can use this list to avoid signing up known spammers, and Law Enforcement Agencies can use the list to help target and prosecute spam gangs. Spamhaus also publishes two spam-blocking databases—the Spamhaus Block List (SBL) and the Exploits Block List (XBL).

VIRUSES

Computer viruses are programs that spread from one computer to another, causing problems on each computer it touches. As viruses propagate, they use up so much memory that it can slow down computer systems to the point that they are unusable. Some viruses actually attack files on the computer by deleting them or modifying them in some way that renders the computer unusable.

The extent of damage caused by a virus varies. Some affect a relatively small number of computers. Others have been so devastating that they can even cripple large companies. For example, in March 1999, when the Melissa virus hit, it was so destructive that it forced Microsoft and other large companies to completely shut down their email systems until the virus could be contained.

There are four general types of computer viruses:

1. Viruses. These are small programs that attach themselves to other programs. When a user runs the legitimate program, the virus program runs, too. Once on a computer, some viruses find other vulnerable programs and attach to them as well, causing even more damage. The virus spreads to other computers when the unknowing user shares or passes on an infected program via CD, for example.

2. Email viruses. These are viruses that are transmitted via email. When users open an email message or an email attachment containing a virus, they release it onto their computers. Some email viruses replicate themselves by emailing themselves to people listed in a victim's email address book.

3. Worms. These are small programs that usually take advantage of networks and spread to all computers on the network. Worms scan networks for computers with security holes in programs or operating systems, replicate themselves on those computers, and then start all over from there. Because worms usually spread through networks, they can affect multiple computers in a very short amount of time. The Slammer worm, released in January 2003, spread more rapidly than any other virus before it. Within 15 minutes, it had shut down cell phone and Internet service for millions of people around the world.

4. Trojan horses. These are computer programs that claim to be one thing but are actually viruses that damage the computer when the user runs it. Trojan horses cannot replicate automatically.

Because viruses have the potential to wreak havoc on computer networks and individual computers, many virus-protection products have been developed to prevent this. Most virus-protection software scans the computer when it is first turned on and looks for known viruses. As new viruses are discovered, virus protection providers have to update their virus definitions.

FIREWALLS

A firewall is basically a barrier that prevents damaging files or programs from reaching the user's computer. Many operating systems now include a built-in firewall. There are also many after-market firewall products available for purchase. Firewalls filter the data that comes through an Internet connection. If the firewall detects any suspicious information, it does not allow that information through. Most companies and many individuals who have Internet access use firewalls to protect their computers and networks. Although some firewalls protect against computer viruses, many experts recommend that companies and individuals invest in a separate anti-virus software package.

Firewalls control the flow of network traffic using one or more of the following methods:

- Packet filtering: The term "packet" is used to describe a small group of data. With the packet filtering method, a firewall compares the packets of incoming and outgoing data against a set of specific rules. If the packets meet the acceptable criteria, the firewall lets the data through. Any data that does not make it through the firewall is discarded.

- Proxy service: Proxy servers are used to access web pages by other computers. When a computer requests a web page, the proxy server retrieves the information and then sends it to the user's computer. With a proxy server, the computer hosting the website does not come into direct contact with the user's computer.

- Stateful inspection: This newer method compares only certain key parts of the packet to a database of trusted information. The firewall compares outgoing data against specific criteria and then compares incoming data against the same criteria. If the two comparisons match, the firewall lets the information through.

Several criteria that firewalls use to compare incoming and outgoing data are listed below:

- Internet Protocol (IP) addresses: Each computer on the Internet has a unique IP address, which consists of 32-bit numbers. If a firewall detects too many files being read by a certain IP address outside of the company, it may block all traffic to and from that IP address.

- Domain names: Each server on the Internet has its own domain name, which is the website address most people recognize (as opposed to the IP address). If a company knows that certain domain names are not "safe," they will set up the firewall to block access to that domain name. On the other hand, the company may set up the firewall to allow access to only certain domain names.

- Protocols: Protocol is a term used to describe the way a program communicates with a web browser. Some of the more common protocols include IP (Internet Protocol), which is the main delivery system for information over the Internet; TCP (Transmission Control Protocol), which breaks apart and rebuilds information from the Internet;

HTTP (Hyper Text Transfer Protocol), which is used for web pages; FTP (File Transfer Protocol), which is used to download and upload files; and many more. A company may set up a firewall that allows only one or two machines to handle certain protocol and prohibit that protocol on all other machines.

- Specific words or phrases: Companies can set up firewalls to search for specific words or phrases. If the firewall encountered packets containing any of those words, it would not allow the packet through.

As more people buy computers and connect to the Internet, the number of potential computer theft victims grows. However, as users become more well-informed about the dangers that exist, they will take precautions to avoid becoming a victim. And as governments and law enforcement agencies around the world are learning more about these crimes and how to deal with them, they are taking action to prosecute the perpetrators.

SEE ALSO: Computer Networks; Technology Management

Rhoda L. Wilburn

FURTHER READING:

Black, Jane. "Before Spam Brings the Web to Its Knees." *BusinessWeek* Online, 10 June 2003. Available from <http://www.businessweek.com/technology/content/jun2003/tc20030610_1670_tc104.htm>.

Boutin, Paul. "Slammed! An Inside View of the Worm that Crashed the Internet in 15 Minutes." *Wired Magazine,* July 2003.

Coustan, Dave. "How Spyware Works." How Stuff Works, Inc., 2005. Available from <http://computer.howstuffworks.com/spyware.htm>.

Gross, Grant. "U.S. Senator Introduces Phishing Penalties Bill." IDG News Service, 4 March 2005. Available from <http://www.infoworld.com/article/05/03/04/HNphishingbill_1.html>.

Jaikumar, Vijayan. "Fight Against Phishing Moves to a New Level: Consortium Brings Together Companies, Law Enforcement to Target e-Mail Scams." *Computerworld,* 13 December 2004, 10.

"Phishing Fraud." Available from <http://securities-fraud.org/phishing-attacks.htm>.

Tyson, Jeff. "How Firewalls Work." How Stuff Works, Inc., 2005. Available from <http://computer.howstuffworks.com/firewall.htm>.

CONCURRENT ENGINEERING

Concurrent engineering is a method by which several teams within an organization work simultaneously to develop new products and services. By engaging in multiple aspects of development concurrently, the amount of time involved in getting a new product to the market is decreased significantly. In markets where customers value time compression, fast-cycle developers have a distinct advantage. Additionally, in many high-technology areas such as electronics and telecommunications, product-technology performance is continuously increasing and price levels are dropping almost daily. In such areas, a firm's ability to sustain its competitive edge largely depends on the timely introduction of new or improved products and technologies. More and more, the time parameter makes the difference between mere survival and substantial profit generation. Concurrent engineering is a key method for meeting this need of shortening a new product's time-to-market.

SEQUENTIAL NEW PRODUCT DEVELOPMENT

In the past, commercial success was practically guaranteed for companies that could design, develop, and manufacture high-quality products that satisfied real needs at competitive prices. However, beginning in the early 1990s this traditional formula radically changed as time-to-market became a vital component of commercial success. Studies have demonstrated that being a few months late to market is much worse than having a 50 percent cost overrun when these overruns are related to financial performance over the lifecycle of a new product or service. In other words, time has become a key driver of competitive success, from design and development to the actual launch of a new product or service.

Traditional project planning and execution has been marked by the definition of objectives and milestones. These goals are met through a progression of networked activities, some of which must be performed sequentially, others of which may be conducted in parallel. Planning techniques such as Program Evaluation and Review Technique (PERT), Graphical Evaluation and Review Technique (GERT), and Critical Path Method (CPM) have been used to support this sequencing of tasks and activities. However, until the beginning of the 1990s time compression was not a major issue in the new product development environment. In the planning and scheduling of tasks and activities, any time compression concerns were only implicitly present.

CONCURRENT NEW PRODUCT DEVELOPMENT

Because time has become a competitive weapon, time pressures have become central to the project-based new product development organization. These pressures have led to the explicit understanding that time compression is a driver of project (and subsequent business) performance. As a consequence, methods, techniques, and organizational approaches have been designed and developed that allow for time compression needs to be handled in a proper manner. All time-centered approaches have one principle in common: they attempt to maximize the number of major design or development tasks that are performed concurrently, thus the concept of concurrent engineering.

In a concurrent engineering environment, even if certain tasks cannot be completely executed at the same time, designers and developers are encouraged to achieve maximum overlap between otherwise sequential activities. In other words, concurrent engineering aims at achieving throughput time reductions by planning and executing design and development activities in parallel, or by striving for maximum overlap between activities that cannot be completely executed in parallel (for example, when one of the tasks or activities requires information to be partially generated during a previous task or activity).

Therefore, concurrent engineering is based on the premise that the parallel execution of major design components will decrease the throughput time of projects, thus reducing the time-to-market for new products and services. For example, applying concepts of parallelism during the Boeing 777 transport design resulted in a time compression of 1.5 years as compared to its predecessor, the Boeing 767. Concurrent engineering allowed the Boeing Company to introduce the new airplane in time to limit the advantage of its competitor, Airbus Industrie.

Many companies have benefited from this same approach. Firms like Intel and Canon have been among the leaders in shortening their product development cycles through the implementation of concurrent engineering. However, this trend has not been limited to individual companies; complete industry sectors also have implemented concurrent engineering principles. At the beginning of the 1990s, the automotive industry pioneered many of the concurrent engineering concepts and their implementation. By early 2000s, many industries, including electronics and pharmaceuticals, were behaving in much the same manner.

IMPLEMENTING CONCURRENT ENGINEERING

In a concurrent engineering environment, teams of experts from different disciplines are formally encouraged to work together to ensure that design progresses smoothly and that all participants share the same, current information. The project and problem-solving methods and the technologies utilized make up the essential elements through which parallelism in new product design and development can be achieved. Following is a discussion of how each of these elements contributes to concurrent engineering implementation.

PROJECT METHODS. Project methods based on teamwork, milestone management, and target-oriented work definition and follow-up are paramount. These methods also must be supported by appropriate senior management commitment and incentive systems. Each team is granted a large degree of autonomy to solve design problems where and when they occur, without much hierarchical intervention. However management must ensure that the transfer of information between different activities or tasks is smooth and transparent. Also, the means of experimentation must allow the experts involved to rule out differences in interpretation on the functional and technical design parameters. In other words, for concurrent engineering to be successful, information and interpretation asymmetries between the experts involved must be avoided whenever possible.

PROBLEM-SOLVING METHODS. During design and development projects, methods are utilized that foster and support smooth interdisciplinary problem definition and problem solving. Methodologies such as brainstorming open the boundaries of the team to allow for wider ranges of alternative design definitions and solutions to be considered. The use of methodologies like Quality Function Deployment (QFD) further aids experts from different disciplinary backgrounds to jointly define a product's functional and technical requirements. Activity flow chart methods such as IDEF3 allow for detailed planning and monitoring of the different parallel and overlapping activities involved in project execution. Failure Mode and Effects Analysis (FMEA) allows for a systematic investigation of the occurrence and impact of possible flaws in the new product design. The use of Design of Experiments (DOE) enables the systematic identification of critical product/process parameters that influence performance. These are just a few of the many supportive methods that can be used in a concurrent engineering environment. The sources listed at the end of this essay provide more detailed and exhaustive overviews on these and other methodologies supporting concurrent engineering.

TECHNOLOGIES

In concurrent engineering, design technologies are utilized that foster efficient cross-disciplinary analysis, experimentation, and representation of new product designs. Some examples of these technologies include: three-dimensional (3-D) computer-aided design (CAD) systems, rapid prototyping techniques, rapid tooling and rapid testing techniques, as well as techniques that enable the representation of product designs in a virtual context. These design technologies are important because of the key information they convey: their 3-D character allows the expert to interpret design features in a more effective and efficient way.

All of these technologies contribute to the reduction of interpretation asymmetries between the experts involved, as well as to fast-cycle design and development, because they allow for high-speed iterations of analysis and experimentation on both concepts and models of the product. Thus, they modify traditional project management approaches by allowing for more systematic and flexible experimentation and iteration to be included throughout the project's design and development process. In fact, the time and cost incurred by the development and construction of prototypes generally are reduced by factors of 2 to 5 when using digital (e.g., 3-D CAD) and physical (e.g., rapid prototyping) technologies. These tools have become an important enabling factor in the concurrent engineering environment. Without their implementation and further upgrading, concurrent engineering might never be able to realize its full potential in terms of design cost and lead-time optimization.

This brief overview has provided a summary of the why, what, and how involved in implementing a concurrent engineering philosophy for the development of new products, services, and processes. It has outlined how introducing overlap during the execution of innovation project tasks and activities has become vital because of competitive pressures that force new product developers to be more time-conscious.

However, a final caveat is warranted. Although concurrent engineering is an important method for handling the time pressures that occur during new product development, rushing products to the market can sometimes be a mistake. First, markets need time to develop. Numerous examples exist where a new product was too early for the market to absorb it or where product variety has reached limits beyond which the product choice decision becomes too complicated for customers. Second, more revolutionary new product development, which often is based on significant technological advances, typically requires longer time horizons to reach completion. Putting too much emphasis on time compression may blind an organization to this basic fact. Third, the conceptual development of new product ideas requires time or "slack." In a high-speed development organization, time-compression imperatives may undermine this need. Therefore, both managers and new product developers need to find a balance between the paradoxical needs for speed and slack in their organizations. Despite its efficiency, concurrent engineering will only prove to be effective when this balance is achieved through the experience and leadership of an organization's senior management.

SEE ALSO: New Product Development; Time-Based Competition

Koenraad Debackere
Revised by Andrea A. Schurr

FURTHER READING:

Boothroyd, Geoffrey, Peter Dewhurst, and Winston Knight. *Product Design for Manufacture and Assembly*. 2nd ed. New York: Marcel Dekker, 2002.

Cooper, Robert G., and Scott J. Edgett. "Portfolio Management in New Product Development: Lessons from the Leaders—I." *Research Technology Management* 40, no. 5 (1997): 16–52.

Debackere, K. "Technologies to Develop Technology." *Nijmegen Innovation Lectures Monograph Series*. Antwerp: Maklu Publishers, 1999.

Iansiti, Marco. *Technology Integration: Making Critical Choices in a Dynamic World*. Boston: Harvard Business School Press, 1998.

ReVelle, Jack B., John W. Moran, and Charles A. Cox. *The QFD Handbook*. New York: John Wiley and Sons, 1998.

Ribbens, Jack. *Simultaneous Engineering for New Product Development: Manufacturing Applications*. New York: John Wiley and Sons, 2000.

Skalak, Susan Carlson. *Implementing Concurrent Engineering in Small Companies*. New York: Marcel Dekker, 2002.

Stalk, George, and Thomas M. Hout. *Competing against Time: How Time-Based Competition Is Reshaping Global Markets*. New York: The Free Press, 1990.

Ulrich, Karl T., and Steven D. Eppinger. *Product Design and Development*. 3rd ed. Boston: McGraw-Hill/Irwin, 2004.

Utpal, Roy, John M. Usher, and Hamid R. Parsaei, eds. *Simultaneous Engineering: Methodologies and Applications*. Amsterdam: Gordon and Breach Science Publishers, 1999.

CONFLICT MANAGEMENT AND NEGOTIATION

The term conflict refers to perceived incompatibilities resulting typically from some form of interference or opposition. Conflict management, then, is the employment of strategies to correct these perceived differences in a positive manner. For many decades, managers had been taught to view conflict as a negative force. However, conflict may actually be either functional or dysfunctional. Whereas dysfunctional conflict is destructive and leads to decreased productivity, functional conflict may actually encourage greater work effort and help task performance. Borisoff and Victor (1998) point out, "We have come to recognize and to acknowledge the benefits dealing with conflict affords. Because of our differences, we communicate, we are challenged, and we are driven to find creative solutions to problems."

THE EVOLUTION OF CONFLICT MANAGEMENT

The early approach to conflict management was based on the assumption that all conflict was bad and would always be counterproductive to organizational goals. Conflict management, therefore, was synonymous with conflict avoidance. This left the people experiencing the conflict with essentially only one outcome: a win-lose scenario. In such cases, the loser would feel slighted and this, in turn, would lead to renewed belligerence. Therefore, most managers viewed conflict as something they must eliminate from their organization. This avoidance approach to conflict management was prevalent during the latter part of the nineteenth century and continued until the mid-1940s.

Nevertheless, conflict avoidance is not a satisfactory strategy for dealing with most conflict. Conflict avoidance usually leaves those people who are being avoided feeling as if they are being neglected. Also, conflict avoidance usually fails to reconcile the perceived differences that originally caused the conflict. As a result, the original basis for the conflict continues unabated, held in check only temporarily until another confrontation arises to set the same unresolved tensions into motion again. Therefore, conflict avoidance strategies are not especially useful in the long run.

The human relations view of conflict management dominated from the late 1940s through the mid-1970s. This viewpoint argued that conflict was a natural and inevitable occurrence in any organizational setting. Because conflict was considered unavoidable, the human relations approach recommended acceptance of conflict. In other words, conflict cannot be eliminated and may even benefit the organization. It was during this time period that the term "conflict management" was introduced, according to Nurmi and Darling.

Since the mid-1970s a new position on organizational conflict has emerged. This theoretical perspective is the interactionist approach. This viewpoint espouses not only accepting conflict, but also encouraging it. Theorists are of the opinion that a conflict-free, harmonious, and cooperative organization tends to become stagnant and nonreponsive to market change and advancement. Therefore, it is necessary for managers to interject a minimum level of conflict to maintain an optimal level of organizational performance. For example, Shelton and Darling suggest conflict is a necessary condition for both individual and organizational progression. They encourage managers to "embrace conflict and use it for continuous transformation."

SOURCES OF CONFLICT

According to both Daft and Terry, several factors may create organizational conflict. They are as follows:

- Scarce Resources. Resources may include money, supplies, people, or information. Often, organizational units are in competition for scarce or declining resources. This creates a situation where conflict is inevitable.

• Jurisdictional Ambiguities. Conflicts may also surface when job boundaries and task responsibilities are unclear. Individuals may disagree about who has the responsibility for tasks and resources.

• Personality Clashes. A personality conflict emerges when two people simply do not get along or do not view things similarly. Personality tensions are caused by differences in personality, attitudes, values, and beliefs.

• Power and Status Differences. Power and status conflict may occur when one individual has questionable influence over another. People might engage in conflict to increase their power or status in an organization.

• Goal Differences. Conflict may occur because people are pursuing different goals. Goal conflicts in individual work units are a natural part of any organization.

• Communication Breakdown. Communication-based barriers may be derived from differences in speaking styles, writing styles, and nonverbal communication styles. These stylistic differences frequently distort the communication process. Faulty communication leads to misperceptions and misunderstandings that can lead to long-standing conflict. Additional barriers to communication may emerge from the cross-gender and cross-cultural differences of participants. Such fundamental differences may affect both the ways in which the parties express themselves and how they are likely to interpret the communication they receive. These distortions, in turn, frequently result in misreading by the parties involved. Moreover, it is common for the parties involved to be oblivious to these false impressions. The resultant misunderstandings subsequently lead the parties involved to believe that a conflict based on misunderstood behavior exists when, in fact, no conflict actually does exist. Miller and Steinberg call this misreading "pseudo-conflict," that is, perceived conflict rather than actual conflict. Much of what managers take to be an actual conflict is the product of such pseudo-conflict.

CONFLICT MANAGEMENT METHODOLOGIES

Management theorists have developed and suggested a range of options for handling organizational conflict. Figure 1 outlines the various components of the Conflict Resolution Grid, which is the result of widely accepted research presented by Thomas and Kilmann.

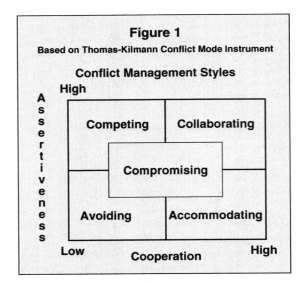

Figure 1
Based on Thomas-Kilmann Conflict Mode Instrument

Conflict Management Styles

Thomas and Kilmann identified a conflict-handling grid comprised of five conflict management styles based on two dimensions: assertiveness and cooperativeness. Assertiveness is the motivation of an individual to achieve his/her own goals, objectives, and outcomes, while cooperativeness assesses the willingness to allow or help the other party to achieve its goals or outcomes. Any of the five conflict resolution styles might be appropriate based on the circumstances of the situation and the personalities of the individuals involved.

1. Avoiding Conflict Resolution Style. The avoiding style is low on both assertiveness and cooperativeness. In other words, the manager is not very cooperative in helping the other individuals to achieve their goals, but neither is he/she aggressively pursuing his/her own preferred outcomes in the situation. The original problem, conflict, or situation is never directly addressed or resolved. However, avoiding behavior might be appropriate when the issue is perceived by the manager to be trivial. It might also be an appropriate approach to use when there is no chance of winning or when disruption would be very costly.

2. Competing Conflict Resolution Style. The competing style of resolving conflict is also known as the win-lose approach. A manager using this style, characterized by high assertiveness and low cooperativeness, seeks to reach his/her own preferred outcomes at the expense of other individuals. This approach may be appropriate when quick,

decisive action is needed, such as during emergencies. It can also be used to confront unpopular actions, such as urgent cost cutting.

3. Accommodating Conflict Resolution Style. This style reflects a high degree of cooperativeness. It has also been labeled as obliging. A manager using this style subjugates his/her own goals, objectives, and desired outcomes to allow other individuals to achieve their goals and outcomes. This behavior is appropriate when people realize that they are in the wrong or when an issue is more important to one side than the other. This conflict resolution style is important for preserving future relations between the parties.

4. Compromising Conflict Resolution Style. This style is characterized by moderate levels of both assertiveness and cooperativeness. Compromise can also be referred to as bargaining or trading. It generally produces suboptimal results. This behavior can be used when the goals of both sides are of equal importance, when both sides have equal power, or when it is necessary to find a temporary, timely solution. It should not be used when there is a complex problem requiring a problem-solving approach.

5. Collaborating Conflict Resolution Style. This approach, high on both assertiveness and cooperativeness, is often described as the win-win scenario. Both sides creatively work towards achieving the goals and desired outcomes of all parties involved. The collaboration style is appropriate when the concerns are complex and a creative or novel synthesis of ideas is required. The downside of this approach is that the process of collaborating mandates sincere effort by all parties involved and it may require a lot of time to reach a consensus.

Of the five modes described in the matrix, only the strategy employing collaboration as a mode of conflict management breaks free of the win-lose paradigm. It has become almost habitual to fall back on the win-win alternative, but this was not the authors' original intention. They did not reject win-lose configurations out of hand. Instead, strategic considerations for managing conflict according to varied circumstances were identified. For instance, in a conflict centered on bids by two alternative suppliers, the best choice might well be a competing strategy with a winner and loser. After all, the objective in such a situation is to win the contract for one's own company. In most cases, winning the contract can be accomplished only at the expense of the competing supplier, who by definition becomes the loser.

In contrast, a competing approach almost never works well in the interpersonal conflict of people working in the same office (or even the same organization). Unlike the case of competing suppliers, coworkers—both the winner and the loser—must go on working together. Indeed, in many conflicts revolving around office politics, an accommodating strategy may actually enable individuals to strengthen their future negotiating position through allowing themselves to lose in conflicts over issues they do not feel particularly strongly about. In such situations, accommodating can be seen as a form of winning through losing. For instance, a manager may choose to concede an issue to an employee who is experiencing considerable stress as a means to motivate him or her. Similarly, an individual might choose an accommodating strategy to add balance to negotiations in which one's counterpart has already had to give up several other points. Indeed, a winner in a win-lose scenario who fails to put forth some effort to accommodate the other party may even provoke a backlash in the form of lack of commitment or open resistance.

Even the traditional approach of conflict avoidance has its place as an occasionally acceptable strategy. While conflict avoidance has justly been the subject of considerable condemnation, it can be rather useful in allowing both parties to cool off or in buying time until all the facts of a matter have been gathered. A manager might choose to avoid an employee in the throes of an emotional outburst, for example, until the employee has had sufficient time to calm down.

Finally, compromise is often a useful strategy when dealing with relatively small concerns. This differs from an accommodating strategy, in which the conceding party finds an issue unimportant that the opposing party considers comparatively important. A manager might enlist a compromise approach most effectively when both parties consider the issue to be of moderate or little importance. In such cases, compromising saves both parties the time required to employ problem-solving techniques to address the fundamental core of the conflict.

While all of these modes have their place among the strategies available to the manager, the collaborating approach to conflict management represents the most beneficial mode for most types of conflict management. In the collaborating mode, conflict itself acts as a managerial tool. The manager utilizes the conflict to guide the conflicting parties to address what essentially are obstacles faced by the organization. Through collaborative behavior, the conflicting parties pool their creative energies to find innovative answers to old problems.

It is in this key respect that the collaborative mode of conflict management differs from the other four conflict-handling modes. Accommodating, avoiding, competing, and compromising—as permutations of the win-lose scenario—are simply forms of conflict interventions. Collaboration as a conflict-handling mode, on the other hand, represents an attempt to channel conflict in a positive direction, thus enabling the manager to use conflict as a tool to resolve otherwise incompatible objectives within the organization. In other words, this method of handling conflict acts less as a conflict intervention and more as true conflict management.

However, any of the five conflict resolution styles may be appropriate and effective depending on the specific situation, the parties' personality styles, the desired outcomes, and the time available, The key to becoming more prepared is to understand the advantages and disadvantages of each method.

THE FIVE A'S TECHNIQUE

Borisoff and Victor identify five steps in the conflict management process that they call the "five A's" of conflict management: assessment, acknowledgement, attitude, action, and analysis. They assert that these five steps allow for a sustained, ongoing process of problem-solving-oriented conflict management.

ASSESSMENT. In the assessment step, the parties involved collect appropriate information regarding the problem. The parties involved also choose which of the conflict-handling modes is most appropriate for the situation. The parties collectively decide what is and what is not central to the problem. The parties involved also indicate areas in which they may be willing to compromise, and what each party actually wants.

ACKNOWLEDGEMENT. The acknowledgement step is one in which each party attempts to hear out the other. Acknowledgement allows both parties to build the empathy needed for the motivation of a synergistic solution to the problem. The acknowledgement acts as feedback to the other party and it demonstrates that one understands (without necessarily agreeing with) the other party's position. Acknowledgement goes beyond merely responding to what is said, however; it involves actively encouraging the other party to openly communicate its concerns. This is aided by the use of active listening techniques and overt, nonverbal encouragement.

ATTITUDE. The attitude step tries to remove the foundation for pseudo-conflict. Stereotypical assumptions about different, culturally-based behaviors are uncovered. For example, a member of a high-context culture may misinterpret what a member of a low-context culture says as being needlessly blunt or even rude. Conversely, a member of a low-context culture may misinterpret what a person from a high-context culture says as being needlessly indirect or even outright deceptive. Such communication variations (as the works of Edward Hall have explained) have little to do with the actual intent or content of the messages, but represent instead culturally learned approaches to using implicit versus explicit communication styles. Similarly, in the attitude step, one acknowledges differences in the way that men and women are generally conditioned to communicate. Experts such as Borisoff and Merrill, for example, have delineated clearly differentiated communication styles between men and women, which are compounded by sex-trait stereotyping regarding issues of assertiveness, interruptive behavior, and perceptions of politeness. Finally, in the attitude step, one analyzes potentially problematic variations in styles of writing, speaking, and nonverbal mannerisms. Such differences may blur meanings. It is the role of the effective conflict participant to maintain an open mind toward all parties involved.

ACTION. The action step begins to actively implement the chosen conflict-handling mode. If the selected mode is the problem-solving approach, the manager conveys the opportunity for a conflict resolution based on trust and ongoing feedback on those points on which the parties have already agreed. Simultaneously, each individual evaluates the behavior of the other parties (often, little more than subtle hints) to ascertain where potential trouble spots might arise. Also, each individual must remain aware of his or her own communication style and general behavior. Finally, all parties must stay alert to new issues that are raised and look for productive solutions.

ANALYSIS. In this last step participants decide on what they will do, and then summarize and review what they have agreed upon. Part of the analysis step is to ascertain whether every participant's requirements have been addressed (and met, if possible). Finally, the analysis step initiates the impetus for approaching conflict management as an ongoing process. Analysis enables participants to monitor both the short-term and long-term results of the conflict resolution.

QUANTUM SKILLS

Shelton and Darling suggest a new set of management skills, more appropriate for the ever-changing, conflict-ridden contemporary organization. They refer to these skills as the quantum skills. The suggested managerial skills are derived from the field of quantum physics. They are as follows:

1. Quantum seeing. This skill is defined as the ability to see intentionally. When conflict occurs, managers must explore their own assumptions about the parties and search for the underlying intentions that are creating the conflict. Each party must then come to

recognize the relationship between individual thought processes and perceptions, and set clear intentions for positively resolving the situation.

2. Quantum thinking. This skill involves the ability to think paradoxically. Effective conflict resolution is a paradoxical process. "Win-win solutions require paradoxical thinking. They require the ability to find a fully acceptable solution to divergent points of view" (Shelton and Darling 2004, p. 30). In other words, collaborative solutions to conflicts that involve diametrically-opposed positions are unlikely to be achieved through linear problem-solving processes and thus require more unorthodox thinking.

3. Quantum feeling. This skill is defined as the ability to feel vitally alive. It is based on the premise that the level of organizational conflict is influenced by the negative emotions pervasive throughout the business world. As schedules have become more fast-paced and jobs have become more stressful, the level of organizational conflict has increased. Managers committed to the quantum feeling technique of conflict management must train themselves to view even negative events positively. They must challenge all parties in conflict to utilize creative, brain-storming techniques in an effort to construct "impossible" win-win solutions.

4. Quantum knowing. This skill is the ability to know intuitively. Managers wishing to develop this skill must integrate times of relaxation and reflection into their work routines. This skill focuses on staying mindful or aware of the organizational environment. Managers involved in conflict situations must guide all parties towards a more centered response to the negative emotions.

5. Quantum acting. This skill is based on the ability to act responsibly. Quantum acting is predicated on the belief that everything in the universe is a part of a complex whole in which each part is influenced by every other part. Therefore, a manager's thoughts affect the entire organizational unit. Thus, if managers want to encourage more creative responses to conflict, they must begin by modeling this behavior themselves.

6. Quantum trusting. This skill is the ability to trust life's process. It is derived from chaos theory. This theory suggests that without chaos organizations will become stagnant and, if left alone, they will return to a non-chaotic state. This skill may be appealing to managers experiencing conflict. It suggests that managers must simply "ride the rapids of conflict, fully participating in the dance without attempting to actively manage the course of resolution" (Shelton and Darling 2004, p. 37). The organizational unit will eventually self-organize.

7. Quantum being. This skill is the ability to be in a relationship, specifically, "the ability to literally become so connected to another that one can see the world through the other's eyes" (Shelton and Darling 2004, p.38). This skill provides the foundation for all parties to learn from and understand each other. It is a relationship of continuous learning.

This set of skills is grounded in a new science: worldview. These skills provide a whole-brained alternative for managing people and conflict.

Conflict management is an ongoing procedure. It entails continual communication and supervision. "Conflict-handling behavior is not a static procedure; rather it is a process that requires flexibility and constant evaluation to truly be productive and effective" (Borisoff and Victor 1998).

SEE ALSO: Diversity; Management Styles

David A. Victor
Revised by Patricia A. Lanier

FURTHER READING:

Borisoff, D., and D.A. Victor. *Conflict Management: A Communication Skills Approach.* 2nd ed. Boston: Allyn and Bacon, 1998.

Borisoff, D., and L. Merrill. *The Power to Communicate: Gender Differences and Barriers.* 3rd ed. Prospect Heights, IL: Waveland, 1998.

Daft, R.L. *Organizational Theory and Design.* St. Paul, MN: West, 1992.

Miller, G.R., and M. Steinberg. *Between People: A New Analysis of Interpersonal Communication.* Chicago: Science Research Associates, 1974.

Nurmi, R., and J. Darling. *International Management Leadership.* New York: International Business Press, 1997.

Shelton, C.D., and J.R. Darling. "From Chaos to Order: Exploring New Frontiers in Conflict Management." *Organization Development Journal* 22, no. 3 (2004): 22–41.

Terry, P.M. "Conflict Management." *Journal of Leadership Studies* 3, no. 2 (1996): 3–21.

Thomas, K.W., and R.H. Kilmann. *Thomas-Kilmann Conflict Mode Instrument.* Sterling Forest, NY: Xicom, Inc., 1974.

CONSULTING

Management consulting is generally a contract advisory service provided to organizations in order to identify management problems, analyze them, recommend solutions to these problems, and when requested, help implement the solutions. Although there are few formal educational or professional requirements to be a consultant, these services are ideally provided by individuals who are specially trained or qualified in a particular field, such as information technology or organizational change, and who strive to provide independent, objective advice to the client organization.

Only a moderate amount of research has been done on the management consulting industry, although the industry has experienced a phenomenal growth rate since essentially emerging during the 1980s. Management consultants perform a variety of services and use many different methods to complete their tasks. These external consultants do not take the place of managers and have no formal authority, although they are responsible for the value of their advice— occasionally in a legal sense.

The practice itself has existed since the early 1900s. Management consulting pioneers such as Arthur D. Little and Harrington Emerson contributed much to the foundations of the concept. The two were also involved with the founding of the first consulting firms. In the first half of the twentieth century, consultants began to expand on the earlier work. They began offering what was termed "business research" and introduced such business practices as budgeting, divisionalized organization, merit-based compensation schemes, and forecasting methods. During the early postwar years, and in many cases growing out of wartime experience, consulting experienced a big rush, with the formation of such firms as Cresap, McCormick & Paget, William E. Hill, Hay Associates, and Towers Perrin. In the 1960s, major accounting firms began to take notice of the growing market for consulting and began to offer consulting services of their own (however, by the late 1990s charges of conflicts of interest would cause some of these firms to distance their accounting practices from their consulting activities). Also at this time, with the formation of the Cambridge Research Institute and Management Analysis Center, consulting firms began to integrate methodology of the bigger firms and consolidate practices.

In the early 1980s there were an estimated 18,000 management consultants. Only 30 to 40 percent of these were employed in the large, institutionally organized firms. Since then the industry has experienced robust growth, with a particular surge during the 1990s dot.com period. *Money* magazine's February 1992 issue cited a 52 percent increase in the management consulting industry from 1978 to 1992. Today, management consulting is a $70 billion industry. There were an estimated 140,000 management consultants worldwide in 2000, with 70,000 residing in the United States alone. This can be compared to the estimated 150,000 American executives that management consultants interact with in the business world. For every executive, there are 0.5 management consultants, as opposed to 1980, when there were 0.1 for every executive. This exemplifies the dramatic growth the industry has undertaken in recent years.

There are four basic areas within the Consulting industry. Management Consulting consists of looking at a company's organization to assess its ability to achieve its goals. Strategic Consulting focuses on the direction and goals of a company as they relate to their specific industry. Information Technology (IT) Consulting brings technology advice to a company to improve its effectiveness and efficiency. Industry Specific Consulting brings expertise to highly specialized businesses.

E.H. Schein has divided the role of the management consultant into three categories. These roles are classified as purchase of expertise, doctor-patient, and process consultation. The purchase of expertise role is considered a "hands-off" approach in which the consultant brings his/her own views or opinions into the situation. The doctor-patient role is a more personal relationship between the client and consultant in which the consultant analyzes and assesses the threats to the company. In the process-consultation method, the consultant plays more of a facilitator role. The client provides the information necessary while the consultant defines the problems and creates the possible solutions. The client makes the final decision on how to resolve the problem.

D.B. Nees and L.E. Greiner have also divided the interaction between consultants and clients into five similar categories. The "mental adventurer" assesses long-term scenarios by using economic models and personal experience. The "strategic navigator" makes decisions based on quantitative data of the industry and makes choices without input from the client. The "management physician" makes decisions based on knowledge of the organization as opposed to the industry as a whole. The "system architect" directs the client by redefining and improving the routines and processes of the organization. Lastly, the "friendly copilot" acts as a counselor to senior management and does not offer any new ideas or knowledge to the client. The mental adventurer role correlates to Schein's expert model; the strategic navigator, management physician, and system architect to Schein's doctor-patient model; and the friendly co-pilot to Schein's process-consultation model.

Over the years, the relationship between the client and consultant has evolved into an intimate partnership. A.N. Turner has developed several task categories to describe management consulting approaches. These categories include supplying information to the client; figuring out clients' problems; making a diagnosis of the problem; producing proposals based on the diagnosis; aiding with the implementation of recommended actions; providing client learning; and perpetually improving organizational effectiveness. The first categories represent traditional roles of consultants, while the last represent newer, evolving tasks. Although the relationship is becoming more sophisticated and complex, it still has a long way to go. An executive is still more likely to be influenced by his or her own instincts, followed by the advice of the planning staff, board of directors, and investment bankers, before he or she is persuaded by management consultants.

The existence and phenomenal growth rate of the management consulting industry cannot be easily explained. However, Marvin Bower, of McKinsey & Company, a large consulting firm, offers six reasons why companies should hire consultants. First, consultants offer extensive knowledge and access to resources not available internally. Consultants also contribute broad experience in the field. Next, consultants possess the time to research and analyze the problem. Consultants are also professionals. They are also independent of their clients and are able to make objective decisions the client might not be able to make. Lastly, consultants have the ability to implement the recommendations they provide to their clients. In large organizations, many of the problems encountered should be able to be handled internally because they have dealt with them in the past. In this case, time would be the deciding factor on whether the problems were handled internally or outsourced to management consultants.

Depending on the respective firms, consultants most often have certain requirements for targeting potential clients. The level of engagement or difficulty is one factor to be considered. Some firms such as Gemini Consulting, another major player, are looking for "multidimensional engagements that address bottom-line business issues." These companies would rather deal with "high-end engagements" as opposed to routine supply chain work. The length of time involved is another factor to be considered. Some firms like to work with long-term engagements, where strategy can be developed and implemented over time. Other firms are content with taking on short-term discrete jobs. Larger firms tend to focus their attention on larger companies, and companies like McKinsey & Company tend to focus on engagements that "excite" their consultants. They enjoy making transformations and radical changes not only to the companies themselves, but to the industry as a whole.

Management consultants are becoming increasingly discriminating about the clients they accept in order to protect their reputations and ensure the success of the engagements. Some consultants base their evaluations on whether the proposed project will have a profound impact on the company. Some will only accept a client if they believe the project will be successful, while others look for clients that share their core values. It is not uncommon for prospective clients to ask for a proposal over the telephone. A work session is usually conducted to gather information and address problems. If the prospect states it does not have the time for a work session, the case is usually not taken. Consultants clearly avoid prospective clients who have already decided what they want to do before soliciting the consultant. It is estimated that up to 70 percent of clients begin the consulting process by asking the wrong questions. It is the consultant's responsibility to get the client's priorities in line and have the management focus on problems facing the company. This may explain the current rise in "relationship consulting" whereby a consultant works with a company for several years to see strategies implemented and changed as new challenges are faced by the company.

Kevin Nelson
Revised by Deborah Hausler

FURTHER READING:

Biswas, Sugata, and Daryl Twitchell. *Management Consulting: A Complete Guide to the Industry.* New York: John Wiley & Sons, 2002.

Canback, Staffan. "The Logic of Management Consulting." *Journal of Management Consulting,* November 1998, 3–

Fletcher, Winston. "The Grass Really Isn't Greener for the Consultants." *Marketing,* 26 November 1998, 7–8.

Plunkett, Jack W. *Plunkett's Consulting Industry Almanac.* Houston: Plunkett Research, Ltd., 2003.

CONSUMER BEHAVIOR

A consumer is the ultimate user of a product or service. The overall consumer market consists of all buyers of goods and services for personal or family use, more than 270 million people (including children) spending trillions of dollars in the United States as of the late 1990s.

Consumer behavior essentially refers to how and why people make the purchase decisions they do. Marketers strive to understand this behavior so they can better formulate appropriate marketing stimuli that will result in increased sales and brand loyalty. There are a vast number of goods available for purchase, but consumers tend to attribute this volume to the industrial world's massive production capacity. Rather, the giant known as the marketing profession is responsible for the variety of goods on the market. The science of evaluating and influencing consumer behavior is foremost in determining which marketing efforts will be used and when.

To understand consumer behavior, experts examine purchase decision processes, especially any particular triggers that compel consumers to buy a certain product. For example, one study revealed that the average shopper took less than 21 minutes to purchase groceries and covered only 23 percent of the store, giving marketers a very limited amount of time to influence consumers. And 59 percent of all supermarket purchases were unplanned. Marketers spend a great deal of time and money discovering what compels consumers to make such on-the-spot purchases. Market researchers obtain some of the best information through in-store research, and will often launch new products only in select small venues where they expect a reasonable test of the product's success can be executed. In this manner, they can determine whether a product's success is likely before investing excessive company resources to introduce that product nationally or even internationally.

CONSUMER NEEDS

Consumers adjust purchasing behavior based on their individual needs and interpersonal factors. In order to understand these influences, researchers try to ascertain what happens inside consumers' minds and to identify physical and social exterior influences on purchase decisions.

On some levels, consumer choice can appear to be quite random. However, each decision that is made has some meaning behind it, even if that choice does not always appear to be rational. Purchase decisions depend on personal emotions, social situations, goals, and values.

People buy to satisfy all types of needs, not just for utilitarian purposes. These needs, as identified by Abraham Maslow in the early 1940s, may be physical or biological, for safety and security, for love and affiliation, to obtain prestige and esteem, or for self-fulfillment. For example, connecting products with love or belonging has been a success for several wildly popular campaigns such as "Reach Out and Touch Someone," "Fly the Friendly Skies," and "Gentlemen Prefer Hanes." This type of focus might link products either to the attainment of love and belonging, or by linking those products with people similar to those with whom people would like to associate.

Prestige is another intangible need, and those concerned with status will pay for it. However, goods appealing to this type of need must be viewed as high-profile products that others will see in use. One benefit of targeting this type of market is that the demand curve for luxury products is typically the reverse of the standard; high-status products sell better with higher prices.

Some equate the type of need to be met with certain classes of goods. For instance, a need for achievement might drive people to perform difficult tasks, to exercise skills and talents, and to invest in products such as tools, do-it-yourself materials, and self-improvement programs, among others. The need to nurture or for nurturing leads consumers to buy products associated with things such as parenthood, cooking, pets, houseplants, and charitable service appeals.

Personality traits and characteristics are also important to establish how consumers meet their needs. Pragmatists will buy what is practical or useful, and they make purchases based more on quality and durability than on physical beauty. The aesthetically inclined consumer, on the other hand, is drawn to objects that project symmetry, harmony, and beauty. Intellectuals are more interested in obtaining knowledge and truth and tend to be more critical. They also like to compare and contrast similar products before making the decision to buy. Politically motivated people seek out products and services that will give them an "edge," enhancing power and social position. And people who are more social can best be motivated by appealing to their fondness for humanity with advertising that suggests empathy, kindness, and nurturing behavior. One successful way an insurance company targeted this market was through its "You're in good hands with Allstate" campaign.

Consumers also vary in how they determine whose needs they want to satisfy when purchasing products and services. Are they more concerned with meeting their own needs and buying what they want to, for their own happiness? Or do they rely on the opinions of others to determine what products and services they should be using? This determines, for example, whether or not they will make a purchase just because it's the newest, most popular item available or because it is truly what they need and/or want.

This also influences the way marketers will advertise products. For example, a wine distributor trying to appeal to people looking to satisfy their personal taste will emphasize its superior vintage and fine bouquet; that same distributor, marketing to those who want to please others, will emphasize how sharing the wine can improve gatherings with friends and family.

Cultural and social values also play large roles in determining what products will be successful in a given market. If great value is placed on characteristics such as activity, hard work, and materialism, then companies who suggest their products represent those values are more likely to be successful. Social values are equally important. If a manufacturer suggests their product will make the consumer appear more romantic or competitive in a place where those values are highly regarded, it is more likely consumers will respond.

PURCHASE PATTERNS

While all of this information might be helpful to marketers, it is equally important to understand what compels the consumer to actually make a purchase, as opposed to just generating interest. For example, some consumers respond based on how they are feeling, or more emotionally, while some are focused on making the wisest economic decision. Knowing the different elements that stimulate consumer purchase activity can help marketers design appropriate sales techniques and responses.

A study conducted by Susan Powell Mantel focused on analyzing the roles of "attribute-based processing" and "attitude-based processing" when analyzing consumer preference. According to the study, product attributes (qualities such as price, size, nutritional value, durability, etc.) are often compared disproportionately, i.e., one is the more focal subject of comparison, thus eliciting more consideration when the consumer decides which brand is the "best." The order of brand presentation in these cases is particularly important.

Adding to the complexity of the issue is the fact that purchase decisions are not always made on the basis of an "attribute-by-attribute" comparison (attribute-based processing). Consumers also make decisions based on an overall evaluation of their impressions, intuition, and knowledge based on past experience, or attitude-based processing. Learned attitudes also influence these decisions. For example, parents who drank Kool-Aid as children often buy it for their kids, either because they associate it with fond memories or just because of brand familiarity or loyalty.

There is time and effort associated with each of these strategies, though attribute-based processing requires significantly more effort on the consumer's part. To dedicate the time required for an attribute-by-attribute comparison, consumers need the combination of motivation and the time or opportunity to use such a strategy.

Other contributing factors were discussed in Mantel's study, such as personality differences and each individual's "need for cognition." Need for cognition reflects to what extent individuals "engage in and enjoy thinking." People with a high need for cognition tend to evaluate more and make more optimal in-store purchase decisions. This is in part because they do not react to displays and in-store promotions unless significant price reductions are offered. Low-need cognition people react easily when a product is put on promotion regardless of the discount offered.

Consumers are also affected by their perceived roles, which are acquired through social processes. These roles create individuals' needs for things that will enable them to perform those roles, improve their performance in those roles, facilitate reaching their goals, or symbolize a role/relationship, much in the way a woman's engagement ring symbolizes her taking on the role of a wife.

Other factors that influence purchase decisions include the importance attributed to the decision. People are not likely to take as much time doing brand comparisons of mouthwash as they are a new car. The importance of the purchase, as well as the risk involved, adds to how much time and effort will be spent evaluating the merits of each product or service under consideration. In cases of importance such as the purchase of a car or home appliance, consumers are more likely to use rational, attribute-based comparisons, in order to make the most informed decision possible.

In some cases, consumers make very little effort to evaluate product choices. "Habitual evaluation" refers to a state in which the consumer disregards marketing materials placed in a store, whether because of brand loyalty, lack of time, or some other reason. Indeed, evaluating all relevant marketing information can become time consuming if it is done every time a person shops.

On the opposite side of the coin, "extensive evaluation" is the state in which consumers consider the prices and promotions of all brands before making a choice. There are also in-between states of evaluation, depending again on the importance of the purchase and the time available to make a decision (some consumers, usually those who earn higher incomes, value their time more than the cost savings they would incur). Decisions on whether to compare various products at any given time may be a factor of the anticipated economic returns, search costs or time constraints, and individual household purchasing patterns.

When it comes time to actually make purchases, however, one person in the family often acts as an "information filter" for the family, depending on what type of purchase is being made and that person's expertise and interest. The information filter passes along information he or she considers most relevant when making a purchase decision, filtering out what is considered unimportant and regulating the flow of information. For example, men are more often the family members who evaluate which tools to purchase, while children pass along what they consider to be seminal information about toys. At times, family members may take on additional roles such as an "influencer," contributing to the overall evaluation of goods being considered for purchase. Or one person may act as the "decider," or the final decision-maker. Ultimately, purchase decisions are not made until consumers feel they know enough about the product, they feel good about what they're buying, and they want it enough to act on the decision.

INTERPRETING CONSUMER BEHAVIOR

When market researchers begin evaluating the behavior of consumers, it is a mistake to rely on conventional wisdom, especially when it is possible to study the actual activity in which consumers are engaged when using a product or service. Where are they when they buy certain items? When do they use it? Who is with them when they make the purchase? Why do they buy under certain circumstances and not others? Researchers need to determine the major needs being satisfied by that good or service in order to effectively sell it.

There are two principal ways to evaluate the motivation behind consumer purchases. These are by direction (what they want) and intensity (how much they want it). Direction refers to what the customer wants from a product. For example, if a customer is selecting pain reliever, they may like the idea is one pain reliever is cheaper than another, but what they really want is fast pain relief, and will probably pay more if they think the more expensive brand can do that more effectively. Marketers need to understand the principal motivation behind each type of product to correctly target potential customers.

The other way to evaluate consumer behavior, intensity, refers to whether a customer's interest in a product is compelling enough that they will go out and make the purchase. Good marketing can create that kind of intensity. A successful example of such a campaign was Burger King's "Aren't You Hungry?" campaign, which aired on late-night television and was compelling enough for people to leave their homes late at night to go out and buy hamburgers. Understanding consumer motivation is the best way to learn how to increase buyer incentive, as well as a better alternative to the easy incentive-decreasing the price.

While it is easy to speculate on all these elements of consumer motivation, it is much harder to actively research motivating factors for any given product. It is rare that a consumer's reasons for buying a product or service can be accurately determined through direct questioning. Researchers have had to develop other ways to get real responses. These include asking consumers "How do you think a friend of yours would react to this marketing material?" While consumers do not like to admit that marketing affects them at all, they are often willing to speculate on how it would affect someone else. And most often they answer with what would be their own responses.

Another tactic that has proven successful is to ask consumers "What kind of person would use this type of product?" By asking this question, market researchers can determine what the consumer believes buying the product would say about them, as well as whether or not they would want to be seen as that type of person.

INFLUENCING CONSUMER BEHAVIOR

One of the best ways to influence consumer behavior is to give buyers an acceptable motive. This is somewhat related to the idea of asking what type of person would buy a certain product in evaluating consumer behavior. Consumers want to feel they're doing something good, being a good person, eating healthy, making contacts, keeping up appearances, or that they just deserve to be spoiled a little bit. If marketers can convince consumers that they need a product or service for some "legitimate" reason, customers will be more likely to make a purchase.

In addition, sensory stimuli are important to marketing. When food packages are appealing or associated with other positive qualities, people often find that they "taste" better. For example, people often "taste" with their eyes, discerning differences in products where they do not see any difference during a blind taste test. One of the best examples of this was a test of loyal Coca-Cola customers who were totally unwilling to concede that any other soda was its equal. While able to see what they were drinking, they maintained this position. But during blind testing, some were unable to tell the difference between Coke and root beer.

Finally, another alternative for influencing customer behavior is by offering specialized goods. While commonality was once popular, more and more people are seeking diversity in taste, personal preferences, and lifestyle. Some successful campaigns touting the way their products stand out from the crowd include Dodge's "The Rules Have Changed" and Arby's "This is different. Different is good."

In fact, marketers are quite successful at targeting "rebels" and the "counterculture," as it is referred to in *Commodify Your Dissent*. As Thomas Frank writes, "Consumerism is no longer about 'conformity' but about difference. It counsels not rigid adherence to the taste of the herd but vigilant and constantly updated individualism. We consume not to fit in, but to prove, on the surface at least, that we are rock 'n' roll rebels, each one of use as rule-breaking and hierarchy-defying as our heroes of the 60s, who now pitch cars, shoes, and beer. This imperative of endless difference is today the genius at the heart of American capitalism, an eternal fleeing from 'sameness' that satiates our thirst for the New with such achievements of civilization as the infinite brands of identical cola, the myriad colors and irrepressible variety of the cigarette rack at 7-Eleven."

Wendy. H. Mason
Revised by Deborah Hausler

FURTHER READING:

Frank, Thomas. "Why Johnny Can't Dissent." In *Commodify Your Dissent: Salvos from The Baffler.* edited by Thomas Frank and Matt Weiland. New York: W.W. Norton & Co., 1997.

Hawkins, Delbert, Best, Roger, Coney, Kenneth. *Consumer Behavior: Building Marketing Strategy.* New York: McGraw-Hill/Irwin 9th Edition, March 2003.

Lack, Jennifer. "Meet You in Aisle Three." *American Demographics,* April 1999.

Mantel, Susan Powell, and Frank R. Kardes. "The Role of Direction of Comparison, Attribute-Based Processing, and Attitude-Based Processing in Consumer Preference." *Journal of Consumer Research,* March 1999.

Murthi, B.P.S., and Kannan Srinivasan. "Consumers' Extent of Evaluation in Brand Choice." *Journal of Business,* April 1999.

Solomon, Michael R. *Consumer Behavior.* New York: Prentice Hall 6th Edition, September 2003.

CONTINGENCY APPROACH TO MANAGEMENT

The contingency approach to management is based on the idea that there is no one best way to manage and that to be effective, planning, organizing, leading, and controlling must be tailored to the particular circumstances faced by an organization. Managers have always asked questions such as "What is the right thing to do? Should we have a mechanistic or an organic structure? A functional or divisional structure? Wide or narrow spans of management? Tall or flat organizational structures? Simple or complex control and coordination mechanisms? Should we be centralized or decentralized? Should we use task or people oriented leadership styles? What motivational approaches and incentive programs should we use?" The contingency approach to management (also called the situational approach) assumes that there is no universal answer to such questions because organizations, people, and situations vary and change over time. Thus, the right thing to do depends on a complex variety of critical environmental and internal contingencies.

HISTORICAL OVERVIEW

Classical management theorists such as Henri Fayol and Frederick Taylor identified and emphasized management principles that they believed would make companies more successful. However, the classicists came under fire in the 1950s and 1960s from management thinkers who believed that their approach was inflexible and did not consider environmental contingencies. Although the criticisms were largely invalid (both Fayol and Taylor, for example, recognized that situational factors were relevant), they spawned what has come to be called the contingency school of management. Research conducted in the 1960s and 1970s focused on situational factors that affected the appropriate structure of organizations and the appropriate leadership styles for different situations. Although the contingency perspective purports to apply to all aspects of management, and not just organizing and leading, there has been little development of contingency approaches outside organization theory and leadership theory. The following sections provide brief overviews of the contingency perspective as relevant to organization theory and leadership.

CONTINGENCY PERSPECTIVE AND ORGANIZATION THEORY

Environmental change and uncertainty, work technology, and the size of a company are all identified as environmental factors impacting the effectiveness of different organizational forms. According to the contingency perspective, stable environments suggest mechanistic structures that emphasize centralization, formalization, standardization, and specialization to achieve efficiency and consistency. Certainty and predictability permit the use of policies, rules, and procedures to guide decision making for routine tasks and problems. Unstable environments suggest organic structures which emphasize decentralization to achieve flexibility and adaptability. Uncertainty and unpredictability require general problem solving methods for nonroutine tasks and problems. Paul Lawrence and Jay Lorsch suggest that organizational units operating in differing environments develop different internal unit characteristics, and that the greater the internal differences, the greater the need for coordination between units.

Joan Woodward found that financially successful manufacturing organizations with different types of work technologies (such as unit or small batch; large-batch or mass-production; or continuous-process) differed in the number of management levels, span of management, and the degree of worker specialization. She linked differences in organization to firm performance and suggested that certain organizational forms were appropriate for certain types of work technologies.

Organizational size is another contingency variable thought to impact the effectiveness of different organizational forms. Small organizations can behave informally while larger organizations tend to become more formalized. The owner of a small organization may directly control most things, but large organizations require more complex and indirect control mechanisms. Large organizations can have more specialized staff, units, and jobs. Hence, a divisional structure is not appropriate for a small organization but may be for a large organization.

In addition to the contingencies identified above, customer diversity and the globalization of business may require product or service diversity, employee diversity, and even the creation of special units or divisions. Organizations operating within the United States may have to adapt to variations in local, state, and federal laws and regulations. Organizations operating internationally may have to adapt their organizational structures, managerial practices, and products or services to differing cultural values, expectations, and preferences. The availability of support institutions and the availability and cost of financial resources may influence an organization's decision to produce or purchase new products. Economic conditions can affect an organization's hiring and layoff practices as well as wage, salary, and incentive structures. Technological change can significantly affect an organization. The use of robotics affects the level and types of skills needed in employees. Modern information technology both permits and requires changes in communication and interaction patterns within and between organizations.

CONTINGENCY PERSPECTIVE AND LEADERSHIP

Dissatisfaction with trait-based theories of leadership effectiveness led to the development of contingency leadership theories. Fred Fiedler, in the 1960s and 1970s, was an early pioneer in this area. Various aspects of the situation have been identified as impacting the effectiveness of different leadership styles. For example, Fiedler suggests that the degree to which subordinates like or trust the leader, the degree to which the task is structured, and the formal authority possessed by the leader are key determinants of the leadership situation. Task-oriented or relationship oriented leadership should would each work if they fit the characteristics of the situation.

Other contingency leadership theories were developed as well. However, empirical research has been mixed as to the validity of these theories.

SEE ALSO: Decision Making; Leadership Styles and Bases of Power; Management Styles; Organizational Structure

Durward Hofler
Revised by Tim Barnett

FURTHER READING:

Burns, Tom, and G.M. Stalker. *The Management of Innovation.* London: Tavistock, 1961.

Fiedler, Fred E. *A Theory of Leadership Effectiveness.* New York: McGraw-Hill, 1967.

Gresov, Christopher, and Robert Drazin. "Equifinality: Functional Equivalence in Organizational Design." *Academy of Management Review,* April 1997.

Lawrence, Paul R., and Jay Lorsch. *Organizations and Environment: Managing Differentiation and Integration.* Homewood: Irwin, 1967.

Winfrey, Frank L., and James L. Budd. "Reframing Strategic Risk." *SAM Advanced Management Journal,* Autumn 1997.

Woodward, Joan. *Industrial Organization: Theory and Practice.* London: Oxford University Press, 1965.

Wren, Daniel A. *The Evolution of Management Thought.* 4th ed. New York: Wiley & Sons, 1994.

CONTINGENT WORKERS

As a category, contingent workers may include temporary employees, part-time employees, independent contract workers, employees of the temporary help industry ("temps"), consultants, seasonal employees, and interns. In contrast, full-time, permanent employees frequently are referred to as core employees. The U.S. Bureau of Labor Statistics (BLS) defines contingent workers in a more selective way. The BLS differentiates between workers with what it calls "alternative work arrangements" and contingent workers, who have no explicit or implicit contract and expect their jobs to last no more than a year.

TYPES OF CONTINGENT WORKERS

There is much discussion in the literature about just how the term *contingent worker* should be defined. Following are descriptions of common contingent worker categories.

TEMPS. Temporary employees, or temps, generally work for temporary employment agencies that place workers in companies for short-term assignments. While most temporary employees earn less than their full-time counterparts and do not receive benefits, that has changed for some job specialties, particularly in the computer and information systems areas. Milwaukee-based Manpower Inc. and Kelly Services Inc. of Troy, Michigan, are two of the largest temporary agencies.

PART-TIME EMPLOYEES. Part-time employees work fewer than 35 hours a week. They often receive fewer or no benefits from their employer, which results in a cost savings for the company. Additionally, these employees may be scheduled to meet particular peak needs of the organization. For example, clothing stores have higher night and weekend demand for staff than during the week daytime hours.

CONTRACT WORKERS. Contract workers are employees who negotiate a relationship directly with an employer for a particular piece of work or for a specific time period. Contract workers generally are self-employed and determine their own work hours. These employees may be more productive than in-house employees because they avoid much of the bureaucracy of day-to-day organizational life.

COLLEGE INTERNS. College interns are students who work for a company for either no salary or a reduced salary to gain work experience. These interns may work full-time or part-time, but they are likely to work for only a short time period, usually a semester or a summer. Interns are contingent workers because they provide a company with staffing flexibility. In addition, the company may choose to offer the intern full-time employment at the end of the internship.

TRENDS

After the fallout from downsizing during the 1980s, organizations have increasingly looked to various strategies for building more flexible workforces. Additionally, because of increasing and rapid changes in the world economy, including both competitive and regulatory forces, the ability to make low-cost staffing adjustments has become imperative. Factoring in the desire of many employees to have more flexible work arrangements, this has caused the contingent workforce to experience considerable growth during the 1990s and 2000s.

These variations in part-time, temporary, and/or contractual work arrangements certainly form a growing segment of the U.S. labor force. In 2001 the BLS estimated that contingent workers made up 24 percent of the American workforce. Approximately 22 million people worked part-time, 9 million were contract workers, and 1.2 million were temporary employees. This is a significant increase from BLS data in 1995, which estimated that between 2.7 and 6 million employees held contingent jobs. To some degree, contingent employment levels change due to unemployment levels. In a tight labor market, many employees find full-time core employment, but in times of higher unemployment there may be increases in contingent work.

ADVANTAGES AND DISADVANTAGES

Two of the major advantages of using contingent workers are staffing flexibility for the firm and reduced costs. Staffing becomes more flexible for a firm if it uses contingent workers because it can hire and fire new staff quickly, with few repercussions. For example, since temporary workers do not expect a long-term relationship with any one employer, the company can terminate employment at any time without causing harm to that employee, as the firm would if it were to lay off a core worker.

Additionally, having contingent workers provides the company with a buffer zone that protects its core workers. That is, in times of economic difficulty the firm always may have a group of contingent workers that it can lay off before reducing the ranks of its core employees. Another issue with improved staffing flexibility is that contingent work allows the company to hire employees who have skills that are not present in their core workforce. This is particularly likely to occur with contract or subcontract employees, who may be hired for a short-term project for which the company has no current staff.

The second major advantage that a firm has when using contingent workers is reduced costs. Contingent workers often are less expensive in terms of salary and benefits (most contingent workers receive no benefits). Additionally, many contingent workers are already trained, and therefore the company does not need to spend money on additional training. Furthermore, because the company only employs these workers when they are needed, there are fewer costs associated with carrying a large labor surplus.

There also are disadvantages associated with using contingent workers. First, many contingent workers lack commitment to the organization when compared to core workers. Contingent workers have a higher turnover rate and also may pose a security risk. Second, while some contingent employees have specialized skills, many are lacking in this regard. Thus, even when hiring from temporary agencies, a company may want to carefully screen temporary employees for needed job skills. A third problem associated with contingent workers is that they are likely to find it difficult to integrate into the company and may suffer from lower morale. Core workers may feel threatened by the presence of contingent employees, resent any lack of skill that they may have, or even overlook them due to their short employment. Thus, core and contingent workers may have more difficulty collaborating.

Historically, temporary employees have been used to substitute for employees who are on leave, to fill in for a short time while the company screens applicants to hire a new core employee, and to expand a company's short-term ability to handle an increased volume in jobs that are peripheral to core activities. This picture is changing in that, more often, contingent employees are being used in what previously were core organizational jobs. This can have an impact on morale because both contingent and core employees may be working side by side on the same job, but under different compensation and benefits terms. In addition, contingent workers may not get the same training, thereby affecting the risk level in some jobs, such as mining or petrochemical positions.

REASONS FOR CHOOSING CONTINGENT WORK

While many contingent workers may take contingent work because they prefer it to no work at all, work on a contingent basis may provide a transition to full-time employment and help workers to maintain current skills. However, contingent work may be an individual's preference for a number of reasons. Workers may choose contingent work because of preferences for certain types of work and/or flexible hours. Working parents may wish to schedule work time around child care or school hours. Some professional, technical, and managerial workers may find it advantageous to work on a contract basis. Older workers may wish to keep their earnings within the limit imposed by Social Security legislation. Additionally, some workers may choose contingent work because it provides for change and increased stimulation as they move from job to job.

Because there are many different types of contingent work and many different types of contingent workers, management must pay attention to how contingent work is used in their organization. Additionally, decisions about how to manage contingent workers and whether or not to integrate them into the core employee workforce may have a significant effect on the cost-benefit aspect of the contingent work arrangement.

SEE ALSO: Employee Compensation; Employee Recruitment Planning; Employee Screening and Selection; Employment Law and Compliance; Human Resource Information Systems; Human Resource Management

Denise Marie Tanguay
Revised by Marcia Simmering

FURTHER READING:

de Gilder, Dick. "Commitment, Trust, and Work Behaviour: The Case of Contingent Workers." *Personnel Review* 32, no. 5 (2003): 588–605.

Gómez-Mejía, Luis R., David B. Balkin, and Robert L. Cardy. *Managing Human Resources.* 4th ed. Upper Saddle River, NJ: Pearson/Prentice Hall, 2004.

Lachnit, Carroll. "HR Takes Charge of Contingent Staffing." *Workforce* 81, no. 3 (2002): 50–54.

McKie, W. Gilmore, and Laurence Lipsett. *The Contingent Worker: A Human Resources Perspective.* Alexandria, VA: Society for Human Resource Management, 1995.

Rice, Elizabeth M. "Capitalizing on the Contingent Workforce—Outsourcing Benefits Programs for Non-Core Workers Improves Companies' Bottom Line." *Employee Benefit Plan Review* 58, no. 8 (2004): 16–18.

U.S. Bureau of Labor Statistics. "Contingent and Alternative Employment Arrangements, February 2001." Available from <http://www.bls.gov/news.release/conemp.nr0.htm>.

CONTINUING EDUCATION AND LIFELONG LEARNING TRENDS

CONTINUING EDUCATION

Continuing Education, professional development and lifelong learning are all terms used to describe an educational or training process that is a key component for successful organizations. The term Continuing Education often elicits several definitions, however one of the most comprehensive and applicable is Liveright and Haygood's 1969 version, "a process whereby persons who no longer attend school on a regular full-time basis . . . undertake sequential and organized activities with the conscious intention of bringing about changes in information, knowledge undertaking, skill appreciation and attitudes or for the purpose of identifying or solving personal or community problems" (Courtenay, 1990).

Continuing Education and the adult education movement began with the twentieth century. As the world moved to an industrialized economy the need for continued education and improved access for adults challenged traditional educational venues and created opportunities for both professional and personal skill enhancement and enrichment. Several environmental factors are driving the demand for lifelong learning in the twenty-first century: abundant access to information, rapid technology changes, increased global interactions, industry shifts, as well as increasing entry level credentials and skill requirements.

Employers depend on continuing education as a tool for ensuring a highly skilled and knowledgeable workforce. Individuals use continuing education for upward career mobility, job enhancement and personal enrichment.

The Continuing education activity can take place at virtually any time or any place. The format for the continuing education learning should be driven by the content and learning goals. Internet and satellite technology allow employees to engage in educational coursework on the job or at home, which results in a tremendous savings of travel costs and time. Continuing Education courses are offered for academic or university level credit, as well as non-credit courses. Universities, community colleges, k-12 school districts, private consultants and corporations all participate in offering continuing education content and courses. Many organizations take advantage of "off-the shelf" or commission for customized content that is offered through their own employee training group.

LIFELONG LEARNING

Throughout the last decade the concept of lifelong learning has continued to gain popularity. Organizations in the twenty-first century are challenged to quickly adapt to industry changes and rapidly identify solutions for obstacles or barriers that the organization encounters. Through the lifelong learning process, individuals develop the capacity for addressing this organizational need. Key characteristics of lifelong learning include duration, learner-centered perspective, multi-level and multi-subject learning, and open access.

The core concept of lifelong learning is that individuals learn from cradle to grave and that each individual progresses from one learning level to the next throughout their lifetime. Each learning event is a continuous progression to the next learning event and never isolated or a means to an end in itself.

Lifelong learning also focuses on the learner rather than an instructor or trainer. The learning process often involves a facilitator but the facilitator should be skilled at providing an educational environment that allows the individual to enhance and engage in his or her own learning objectives. The learning format and content should be designed with the learner in mind. Lifelong learners require choices and educational experiences that fit within their lifestyle. The educational activity should balance the needs and convenience of the organization with individual learner's need in order to maximize the learning outcome. Lifelong learning activities are also designed for multiple learning styles. Experiential and applied learning as well as tutorials and self-directed content are often embraced by lifelong learners.

Lifelong learning encompasses all levels of educational acquisition and in an infinite number of subjects. It includes skill training, credential requirements, as well as social interests. This education may be in the form of formal education or training that is offered both as credit and non-credit in a variety of venues. It also occurs through non-formal means such as libraries, museums, manuals and mentors.

Lifelong learning should be accessible to all individuals regardless of age, race, ability, prior qualifications, workplace role or sociodemographics. Innovative delivery formats help to ensure that the learning activities are accessible to anyone that is interested in participating.

CONTINUING EDUCATION UNITS AND ACADEMIC CREDIT

Many industry boards, accreditation agencies and associations have established mandatory continuing professional education (CPE) requirements for licensure or certification. For example, the American Institute of Certified Public Accountants (AICPA) has established mandatory continuing professional education (CPE) for all members. Most state boards of accountancy have also phased in mandatory CPE as prerequisites for licensure of accounting and auditing practice units. Research has supported this trend. In an empirical study of the Texas State Board of Public Accountancy, researchers found evidence of an association between results of an employee's quality review and levels of continuing professional education in the profession (Thomas, Davis, and Seaman, 1998). Other organizations have established a certification process for their respective field such as the Society for Human Resource Management (SHRM), which has partnered with educational institutions to deliver the Professional Human Resource Management (PHRM) content and certification test nationally. Non-credit continuing education courses often carry state-board or association Continuing Education Units (CEU). Participants generally receive a certificate of completion and should maintain personal records of the units earned.

Post-secondary higher education also falls within the sphere of Continuing Education. As entry-level requirements continue to increase such as the 150 hour accounting program and demand for graduate level credentials, employers and employees search for flexible degree programs. Many employers offer a tuition reimbursement program for employees enrolled in college level degree programs when applicable to the workplace. Colleges and Universities recognize the growing demand from adult learners for academic degree programs, and many offer academic courses off campus, on-line or at the workplace in accelerated and non-traditional formats.

CORPORATE UNIVERSITIES

The corporate university is generally some blend of higher education and organizational training and development. "The first corporate colleges appeared almost 80 years ago, but their ranks have grown, relatively speaking by leaps and bounds" (Wilcox, 1987).

Corporate colleges or universities are characterized as institutions that may grant degrees, academic credit or non-credit training and are chartered by a parent company whose primary mission is not education. Some corporate universities have evolved from a mission to serve the corporation's training and development needs to a full-service private higher education institution. Northrop University began in 1942 as a training division of Northrop Aircraft and evolved to an institution offering undergraduate and postgraduate degrees. Kettering Institution (an independent university) grew out of General Motors. Many corporations identify a university or college partner to customize training and academic degree programs specifically to the corporation's business practices. Corporations are using these customized programs as a source for developing future corporate leaders and a means to focus on content areas that are critical to the company's strategic business plans. Multinational companies are developing corporate universities that allow employees around the world to participate in training and educational programs with cost effective delivery methods. The American Council on Education (ACE) consistently evaluates corporate college or university credits that are offered independent of a regionally accredited institution. ACE establishes recommendations for transfer credit to regionally accredited universities and colleges. Most of the individuals participating in corporate college or university programs are employed full-time which requires that the educational programs are offered in flexible formats. Generally, employees do not have the luxury of attending academic programs on a full-time basis or in a traditional fifteen to eighteen week semester format. Accelerated formats as well as weekend and distance education designs address the needs of working adult learners.

DISTANCE EDUCATION

Distance Education is an all-encompassing phrase for education and training that occurs away from the traditional classroom. Distance Education may occur in synchronous (real) or asynchronous time which allows both employers and learners to determine the best time for participation.

Distance Education began with correspondence study and has grown significantly as technology advancements create new opportunities for learning and content delivery. As computer technology became prevalent in business, the print based correspondence courses progressed to computer based training, which included simulations and ultimately interactive course content that provided participant feedback and enhanced learning. At the end of the twentieth century, educators and employers invested in telecommunication equipment that distributed educational or training activities from one video conferencing site to another. These interactive television programs allow companies to synchronously connect employee groups regardless of their physical distance. The tremendous growth of internet technology has created the most recent version of distance learning which is online or eLearning.

The internet is an information rich resource. Because the internet contains more information than any individual could ever process, it is important that individuals and organizations develop knowledge management strategies to sort, categorize and maximize the benefits the internet's wealth of information. Online learning is one component of knowledge management within the information technology environment.

Online learning content ranges from one-hour courses to complete bachelor, master or doctorate degree programs. Internet delivered courses have the benefits of serving multiple groups at multiple locations without the expense of equipment infrastructure at each location, and the course material can be delivered either synchronously or asynchronously which affords multinational operations the opportunity to connect individuals regardless of time zone or geographical location.

The online training and education market is very competitive offering many choices for organizations and learners. Colleges and Universities throughout the world are offering online courses as well as thousands of training and consulting groups. Organizations either select educational programs and courses ala carte or build a portfolio of eLearning options. Many large organizations have integrated eLearning into their corporate university entity. These groups generally have a planned web presence that includes a portal and learning management system (LMS) or course management system (CMS).

Online learning has created many new products and support options. In addition to the organization's web presence, portal and LMS, the organization also needs to assess the technology infrastructure that supports the eLearning initiative. The fundamental needs in this area are servers that provide redundancy and acceptable uptime. This is often referred to as hosting in the eLearning environment as well as technology support in the form of a help desk. Organizations interested in growing their own portfolio of online learning options should first develop a vision for their eLearning initiative prior to making any financial investments in equipment or software. Once the vision is established the organization should assess their existing technology capabilities and determine if there is capacity to support the eLearning initiative, or is it more cost effective to outsource all or some of the technology infrastructure. When the technology infrastructure has been addressed the organization should determine how content will be developed for the eLearning environment. Quality online courses are developed so that the technology optimizes the content. Many vendors offer digitized content and others specialize in specific areas of content development such as simulations or multimedia graphics and enhancements. Having a clear vision for the course content and understanding the learning needs will help to ensure that courses are developed efficiently and effectively.

Blended learning refers to online learning that is integrated with traditional classroom or training instruction. This blend provides the benefits of reduced travel costs and time with the positive relational aspects of face-to-face learning. Once an organization or an individual has established a clear vision for their educational needs they should consider all of the available online resources as tools to ensure that the "best fit" is created.

GLOBAL ECONOMY

The global economy has increased the need for organizations around the world to understand the culture and business practices of their peers, competitors and partners. Both foreign and domestic organizations abroad are implementing continuing education experiences in an effort to enhance cultural understanding and address skill and knowledge gaps. U.S. universities are partnering with both U.S. and foreign companies around the world to deliver educational courses and programs that are critical to organizational competitiveness. A central ministry of education in collaboration with a ministry of commerce generally drives these programs. For instance, China has placed a high priority on the field of Human Resource Development and Entrepreneurship as well as encouraging Chinese organizations to partner with foreign organizations in an effort to implement vocational and applied skill training. India has created a new industry as an outsource venue for customer service which creates customer service training opportunities in India. Korean manufacturers have a solid history of identifying corporate and educational partners that satisfy their organizational educational needs. Continuing Education helps global companies to connect the workforce with the organizational vision.

THE FUTURE OF CONTINUING EDUCATION

The abundant access of information, rapid technology changes, increased global interactions, industry shifts as well as increasing entry level credentials and skill requirements ensures that Continuing Education will remain a valuable resource for managers in the future.

Managers will continue to depend on continuing education as a tool for ensuring a highly skilled and knowledgeable workforce. Individuals will engage in lifelong learning as a means for upward career mobility, job enhancements and enriched quality of life.

The increased interest in lifelong learning coupled with rapid technology advancements and demands on individual personal time will guarantee that educational options will continue to be flexible and fit within the constraints of personal time and organizational priorities. The growing global economy will continue to drive the development of learning activities that span geographical regions and time zones allowing individuals around the world to collaborate and learn together.

Organizations around the world will depend on continuing education to maintain competitive positions and adopt current innovations. Managers will depend on lifelong learning to produce a workforce with the knowledge and solution based skill-set that is required for organizational growth.

Dawn Malone Gaymer

FURTHER READING:

American Society of Training and Development. "Interview: Marc Rosenberg is Positive About the Future." Available from <http://www.learning circuits.org/2005/mar2005/rosenb>.

Courtenay, S. "Defining Adult and Continuing Education." In *Handbook of Adult and Continuing Education*. San Francisco: Jossey-Bass, 1990.

"Create CPF Account for Lifelong Learning." *Business Times* (Singapore), 12 November 1998, 4.

Dooley, Kim, James Lindner, and Larry Dooley. "Advanced Methods in Distance Education: Applications and Practices for Educator, Trainers and Learners." *Information Management* 18, no. 1/2 (Spring 2005): 9.

Helms, Marilyn, and Judy Nixon. "Developing the Virtual Classroom: A Business School Alternative." *Education & Training* 39, no.9 (1997): 349–353.

Helms, Marilyn, Linda P. Fletcher, and Judy Nixon. "Integrating Team Teaching, Technology and Distance Learning in MBA Program: A Case Study". *Industrial and Commercial Training* 27, no. 7 (1997): 218–225.

Meister, Jeanne C. "Extending the Short Shelf-Life of Knowledge." *Training and Development,* June 1998, 52–9.

Thomas, C. William, Charles E. David, and Samuel L. Seaman. "Quality Review, Continuing Professional Education, Experience, and Substandard Performance: An Empirical Study." *Accounting Horizons* 12, no. 40 (1998): 340–362.

Walls, Michael. "Is CE Worth Continuing?" *Broker World* 25, no. 2 (February 2005): 46

Wilcox, John. "A Campus Tour of Corporate Colleges." *Training and Development Journal,* May 1987.

CONTINUOUS IMPROVEMENT

Continuous improvement in a management context means a never-ending effort to expose and eliminate root causes of problems. Usually, it involves many incremental or small-step improvements rather than one overwhelming innovation. From a Japanese perspective continuous improvement is the basis for their business culture. Continuous improvement is a philosophy, permeating the Japanese culture, which seeks to improve all factors related to the transformation process (converting inputs into outputs) on an ongoing basis. It involves everyone, management and labor, in finding and eliminating waste in machinery, labor, materials and production methods.

The Japanese word for continuous improvement, *kaizen,* is often used interchangeably with the term *continuous improvement.* From the Japanese character *kai,* meaning change, and the character *zen,* meaning good, taken literally, it means *improvement.*

Although kaizen is a Japanese concept, many U.S. firms have adopted it with considerable success by combining the best of traditional Japanese practices with the strengths of Western business practice, in other words, by merging the benefits of teamwork with the creativity of the individual. Some refer to its implementation in the West as lean manufacturing since, when combined with the principles of just-in-time (JIT), kaizen or continuous improvement forms the foundation for the concept of lean manufacturing.

HISTORY OF CONTINUOUS IMPROVEMENT

Following the defeat of Japan in World War II, America wanted to encourage the nation to rebuild. As with the Marshall Plan in Europe, General MacArthur asked a number of leading experts from the U.S. to visit Japan and advise them on how to proceed with the rebuilding process. As history would have it, one of these experts was Dr. W. Edwards Deming. Deming was a statistician with experience in census work, so he came to Japan to set up a census. While in Japan, he noticed some of the difficulties being experienced by some of the newly emerging industries. Many Japanese manufacturers were faced with huge difficulties stemming from a lack of investment funds, raw materials, and components, and from the low morale of the nation and the workforce. Based on his recent experience in reducing waste in U.S. war manufacture, he began to offer his advice.

By the mid-1950s, he was a regular visitor to Japan. He taught Japanese businesses to concentrate their attention on processes rather than results; concentrate the efforts of everyone in the organization on continually improving imperfection at every stage of the process. By the 1970s many Japanese organizations had embraced Deming's advice and were very quickly enjoying the benefits of their actions. Most notable is the Toyota Production System, which spawned several business improvement practices utilized heavily in Japan, including JIT and Total Quality Management (TQM).

Despite the fact that much of the foundation of continuous management and other Japanese concepts originated in the U.S., Western firms showed little interest until the late 1970s and early 1980s. By then the success of Japanese companies caused other firms to begin to reexamine their own approaches. Hence, kaizen or continuous management began to emerge in the U.S. concurrent along with the increasing popularity and use of Japanese techniques such as JIT and TQM. In fact, continuous improvement is a major principle of and a goal of JIT, while it is one of the two elements of TQM (the other is customer satisfaction). In some organizations, quality circles have evolved into continuous improvement teams with considerably more authority and empowerment than is typically given to quality circles. In fact, management consultants in the West have tended to use the term *kaizen* to embrace a wide range of management practices primarily regarded as Japanese and responsible for making Japanese companies strong in the areas of continual improvement rather than innovation.

KAIZEN ATTITUDES NECESSARY FOR IMPLEMENTATION

Most Japanese people are, by nature or by training, very attentive to detail and feel obligated to make sure everything runs as smoothly as possible, whether at work or at home. This attitude enhances the functionality of kaizen. However, this is not typically the case in the West. To encourage the kaizen attitude, organizations require a major change in corporate culture; one that admits problems, encourages a collaborative attitude to solving these problems, delegates responsibility and promotes continuous training in skills and development attitudes.

The driving force behind kaizen is dissatisfaction with the *status quo,* no matter how good the firm is perceived to be. Standing still will allow the competition to overtake and pass any complacent firm. The founder of Honda has been quoted as saying, "In a race competing for a split second, one time length on the finish line will decide whether you are a winner or a loser. If you understand that, you cannot disregard even the smallest improvement." Although continuous improvement involves making incremental changes that may not be highly visible in the short term, they can lead to significant contributions in the long term.

Organizational performance can improve from knowledge gained through experience. Lessons learned from mistakes mean those mistakes are less likely to be repeated, while successes encourage workers to try the same thing again or continue to try new things. While this learning process occurs throughout the system it is particularly important for accomplishing the long-term improvement associated with continuous improvement. In order for continuous improvement to be successful, the organization must learn from past experience and translate this learning into improved performance.

Part of the learning process is trying new approaches, exploring new methods and testing new ideas for improving the various processes. So experimentation can be an important part of this organizational learning. Naturally, many of these worker-led experiments will fail, so it is important to recognize that there is some risk associated with this experimentation. If management is uncomfortable with risk, it may be reluctant to allow any real degree of experimentation. Obviously, management cannot risk disabling the production process itself or endanger the well-being of the workforce, but the complete absence of risk can reduce the vision of those involved in the continuous improvement process. Improvements will generally come in modest increments of progress. Therefore, management must recognize that some experiments will fail as part of the learning process, and avoid the temptation to harshly judge the perpetrator as having new but unsuccessful ideas. Some even feel that it is critical to establish an environment that reinforces the notion that risk is good. Again, this involves consistency in management's attitude toward change and the empowerment of employees.

The achievement of continuous improvement requires a long-term view and the support of top management. But it is also important that all levels of management actively support and become involved in the process. Proper support structures of training, management, resource allocation, measurement, and reward and incentive systems must be in place for successful adoption. This includes a willingness to provide financial support and to recognize achievements. It is desirable to formulate goals with the workers' help, publicize the goals, and document the accomplishments. These goals give the workers something tangible to strive for, with the recognition helping to maintain worker interest and morale.

Kaizen also requires that all employees in the organization be involved in the process. Every employee must be motivated to accept kaizen as a means by which the firm can achieve a competitive advantage in the marketplace. All involved must push continuously at the margins of their expertise, trying to be better than before in every area. Japanese companies have been very successful with the use of teams composed of workers and managers. These teams routinely work together on problem solving. Moreover, the workers are encouraged to report problems and potential problems to the teams; their input is as important as that of management. In order to establish a problem-solving orientation, workers should receive extensive training in statistical process control, quality improvement, and problem solving.

Problem solving is the driving force behind continuous improvement. Actually, it can be said to become a way of life or a culture that must be assimilated into the thinking of management and workers alike. Workers are trained to spot problems that interrupt, or have the potential to interrupt, the smooth flow of work through the system. When such problems do occur, it is important to resolve them quickly. Also, workers are trained to seek improvements in the areas of inventory reduction, set-up time and cost reduction, increasing output rate, and generally decreasing waste and inefficiency.

Unfortunately, workers in a continuous improvement system have more stress than their counterparts in more traditional systems. This stress comes not only from the added authority and responsibility but also from the fast pace inherent in the system. There is little slack built into the system and a continual push to improve. For this reason, firms stressing continuous improvement have suffered severe criticism from some labor unions.

BENEFITS OF KAIZEN

The benefits of continuous improvement manifest themselves in numerous ways. In an August 2004 article, Perry Flint examined how American Airlines' Tulsa MRO base has seen dramatic improvements after implementing continuous improvement initiatives. The base is the largest such facility in the world with some 8,000 employees and 3 million square feet of docks and shops across 300 acres. Continuous Improvement teams in their components and avionics shop have helped reduce $1.5 million in inventory requirements while freeing 11,600 sq. ft. of shop space; repairing broken cargo door torque tubes in lieu of purchasing a new replacement has resulted in a savings of $250,000 per year; turnaround times for overhauls have improved more than 38 percent, and replacing parts only as needed on the 737NG has resulted in a savings of $100,000.

These improvements have been made possible through employee and union buy-in, the creation of employee-led work teams, and the realized benefits, after implementation, of employee-recommended improvements and streamlined procedures. The employee-driven improvements are integral to the success of the Continuous Improvement process. The changes are not force-fed by management, thus the employees are less resistant to the changes and recognize the necessity and value in implementing these alternative methods.

A case history of the kaizen training implementation at Pace Micro Technology details the improvements after an update to a continuous improvement program, including an overhaul of intranet support for continuous improvement activities. These improvements resulted in 238 ideas registered on the continuous improvement intranet that were either in action or waiting for teams to begin work, after just nine months. Of those, 39 teams had completed their work and realized a financial benefit of £1.1 million. In addition, there was 71 percent involvement across the organization. Leadership at all levels in the organization has led to the success at Pace, with individuals modeling behaviors, encouraging and enabling others to act, inspiring a shared vision, challenging the status quo and taking risks.

Through kaizen or continuous improvement, firms are able to produce better products and services at lower prices, thus providing greater customer satisfaction. In the long term, the final product will be more reliable, of better quality, more advanced, cheaper and more attractive to customers.

SEE ALSO: Japanese Management; Lean Manufacturing and Just-in-Time Production; Quality and Total Quality Management; Quality Gurus; Statistical Process Control and Six Sigma

R. Anthony Inman
Revised by Monica C. Turner

FURTHER READING:

Cane, Sheila. *Kaizen Strategies for Winning Through People.* London: Pitman Publishing, 1996.

"A Change of Pace: Refreshing Continuous Improvement and Developing Leaders at Pace." *Training Journal* (December 2004): 50–52.

de Jager, B., et al. "Enabling Continuous Improvement: A Case Study of Implementation." *Journal of Manufacturing Technology Management,* 15, no. 4 (2004): 315–324.

Dessinger, J., and J.L. Moseley. *Confirmative Evaluation: Practical Strategies for Valuing Continuous Improvement.* San Francisco, CA: Pfeiffer, 2004.

Etienne-Hamilton, E.C. *Operations Strategies for Competitive Advantage: Text and Cases.* Fort Worth, TX: The Dryden Press, 1994.

Flint, Perry. "Rewired for Success." *Air Transport World* 41, no. 9 (August 2004): 38–39.

Jorgensen, F., H. Boer, and F. Gertsen. "Development of a Team-Based Framework for Conducting Self-Assessment of Continuous Improvement." *Journal of Manufacturing Technology Management.* 15, no. 4 (2004): 343–349.

Maurer, Robert. *One Small Step Can Change Your Life: The Kaizen way.* New York, NY: Workman, 2004.

Rijnders, S., and H. Boer. "A Typology of Continuous Improvement Implementation Processes." *Knowledge and Process Management* 11, no. 4 (October-December 2004): 283–296.

Stevenson, William J. *Production Operations Management.* 6th ed. Boston, MA: Irwin McGraw-Hill, 1999.

Stonebraker, Peter W., and G. Keong Leong. *Operations Strategy: Focusing Competitive Excellence.* Boston, MA: Allyn and Bacon, 1994.

CORPORATE GOVERNANCE

Corporate governance is the responsibility of a firm's board of directors. While management runs the company and oversees day-to-day operations, it is the board of directors that "governs" the corporations by overseeing management and representing the interests of the firm's shareholders.

By law, a corporation of any size must have a board of directors elected by its shareholders. The directors have a fiduciary duty to the shareholders, who are the corporation's owners, and directors as well as corporate officers can be held liable for failing to meet their fiduciary duties to stockholders. A passive board can get into trouble by relying on an influential CEO.

Investors and the public are particularly interested in the financial reports that publicly-traded companies release, and boards of directors of these companies have a legal obligation to ensure that these reports are fair and accurate. Recent business failures, auditor malfeasance, and material deficiencies in financial disclosures, however, have caused a serious erosion of public confidence in the financial reporting of these companies.

Consequently, Congress enacted the Sarbanes-Oxley Act of 2002. Common law has traditionally held that corporate directors have a primary fiduciary duty to the corporation and a secondary duty the shareholders. Sarbanes-Oxley has essentially made directors primarily responsible to the shareholders. The mandates of Sarbanes-Oxley are both complex and extensive. Stated simply, however, they basically require that members of corporate boards must avoid any financial, family, employee, or business relationships with the companies on whose boards they serve.

Further, Sarbanes-Oxley limits the ability of employees of the independent auditing firm from going to work for companies the auditor performs audit services for, and it requires five-year rotation period for audit partners on a given company's assignments. In other words, Sarbanes-Oxley clearly emphasizes independences and avoidance of conflict of interest.

KEY GOVERNANCE ISSUES

Historically, corporate boards of directors have had a myriad of duties, most of them set by common law and the corporation's own by-laws. These duties often include: hiring, supervising, and sometimes firing the Chief Executive Officer; approving major strategic decisions; meeting with shareholders; establishing executive compensation; making decisions about mergers and acquisitions; assessing the viability of potential takeover bids; taking action if the corporation fails; overseeing financial reporting and audits; nominating board candidates; and refining board rules and policies.

One of the most difficult governance duties of the board of directors is the removal of the firm's CEO. This can occur when the board, representing the interests of the shareholders, disagrees with the strategic direction being pursued by the CEO, or if they merely want to show they are "doing their duty" as board members. For example, when Carly Fiorino was ousted as CEO of Hewlett-Packard (HP) in 2005, she was viewed by many to be hard-driving and fearless. The HP board of directors, however, had grown increasingly uncomfortable with her inability to deliver the profits that she promised she was going to deliver. Her refusal to relinquish some operating control, or to make any changes that the board requested, led to her downfall during a period of low profits and falling stock prices.

One measure of good governance is whether the company has a CEO who can maximize the company's performance. Whereas part of the governance function of the board of directors is to select the firm's CEO, another is to endorse the CEO's strategy—if it is the right one. For example, boards can support the CEO's strategic direction by endorsing proposed acquisitions. It can push the CEO to accomplish even more by encouraging him or her to think more broadly or by setting higher sales targets. The board can also support the CEO's leadership by making sure that the CEO is able to put together a strong management team to achieve those goals. In some cases the following CEO will be recruited from the management team built by the present CEO.

Another difficult time for boards occurs when the firm is the target of a takeover attempt. It is vitally important at such a time that the board have a clear sense of the value of the firm and that it is enabled to fully evaluate takeover offers. During a takeover it is the board's responsibility to accept or reject offers, and in so doing it must represent the shareholders' interests when negotiating the sale of the firm.

GOVERNANCE COMMITTEES

Boards often administer their governance responsibilities by establishing committees to oversee different areas of concern. Typical committees include audit, nominating, and compensation committees. This is largely in line with U.S. regulatory guidance. On August 16, 2002, the Securities and Exchange Commission (SEC) updated earlier proposals related to corporate governance that would recommend, but not mandate, that boards establish three oversight committees: a nominating committee, a compensation committee, and an audit committee. The SEC recommended that these oversight committees be composed entirely of independent directors.

Each committee oversees a specific area of corporate governance and reports to the full board. The nominating committee's area of oversight consists of issues related to management succession, including the CEO, and to the composition of the board of directors. The compensation committee oversees compensation of the firm's CEO and its officers, as well as director compensation. The audit committee is concerned with the company's financial condition, internal accounting controls, and issues relating to the firm's audit by an independent auditor.

Almost all publicly held corporate entities in the United States have an audit committee. Since 1978, the New York Stock Exchange (NYSE) has required corporations to have audit committees composed entirely of independent outside directors as a condition for being listed. The audit committees of corporate boards of directors are generally expected to serve as watchdogs for the investors and the creditors. Audit committees are expected to protect the interests of both investors and creditors, as well steward corporate accountability. Moreover, audit committees should make sure that management, the internal auditors, and the external auditors understand that the committee will hold them accountable for their actions (and in some cases, inaction).

The independent audit committee plays a key role in stewardship of the corporation it serves. The audit committee should help ensure that the financial statements are fairly stated, the internal controls are operating effectively, management risk is being reduced, and new processes are minimizing risks. Moreover, the audit committee members should be independent of management and maintain a close working relationship with the independent auditors.

In an article in the *Pennsylvania CPA Journal*, author John M. Fleming sets forth the primary responsibilities of the corporate audit committee: (1) Evaluating the processes in place to assess company risks and the effectiveness of internal controls, and assisting management in improving these processes where necessary; (2) monitoring the financial reporting process both internally and externally; and (3) monitoring and evaluating the performance of internal and external auditors.

A board will sometimes establish a fourth committee, the governance committee. The governance committee is concerned with overseeing how the company is being run, including evaluation of both management and the board of directors. In some cases the nominating committee will evolve into, or function as, a governance committee.

ACTIVE GOVERNANCE

Historically, corporate boards have been described as either active or passive. Some corporate CEOs relished having what they thought were "rubber stamp" boards of directors who would approve virtually any actions they chose to pursue. Sarbanes-Oxley has dramatically changed that dynamic. Corporate directors must now be much more independent, and their legal liability to shareholders has increased significantly.

One example in which a traditionally "quiet" board stepped up and became more active occurred with the Walt Disney Company. For years, Michael Eisner ruled the Disney empire with an allegedly brutal iron fist. After Roy E. Disney, Walt Disney's nephew, led a shareholder revolt of sorts and complained that investor votes were being ignored or circumvented, the Walt Disney Company board of directors finally decided to step in. In early 2004, the board took the chairmanship away from Eisner after more than 45 percent of votes cast at company's annual meeting opposed his board re-election. It was a resounding vote of no confidence. But the board then chose an Eisner ally, former U.S. Senator George Mitchell, as chairman, over the objections of several larger shareholders. Ironically, a year later, Eisner was easily re-elected to the board, with only 8.6 percent of voters withholding their support for him.

Boards can take simpler steps to ensure they are not passive without voting out the CEO. They can establish a non-executive chairman, a chairperson who is separate from the CEO. The board can also staff all board committees with independent outside directors, except the president and CEO.

THE ROLE OF INVESTOR ACTIVISM

Finding qualified people to serve on corporate boards of directors can be a challenging task. Corporate board members are learning in the current legal environment that serving on such board is can open them to a wide range of legal liability issues. The reforms of Sarbanes-Oxley and the SEC all seem well-intended, but will they make a difference for board members who get in over their heads or choose to look away?

Many critics argue that the proposed and enacted reforms do little to solve the real problems that exist with corporate boards. For example, one issue that has been repeatedly raised is the fact that corporate boards tend to only meet a couple of times a year. Yet it is further argued that more frequent meetings do little to solve the major problem, which is the fact that most corporate board members do not have enough access to information to fulfill their duties of stewardship to the shareholders.

Another issue that has been raised after continuous corporate failures revolves around the financial knowledge and competence of corporate board members. One proposed reform to remedy this problem has been to offer more generous pay for corporate board members, particularly those who serve on audit committees. The theory behind the increased pay is that it would help attract more chief financial officers and former chief executive officers from major accounting firms to serve on audit committees.

Proponents of such a move argue that former CFOs and CEOs are ideal audit committee members. But, there remains a limited pool of these professionals available to serve on audit committees. Furthermore, increased disclosure requirements are likely to raise liability for individual audit committee members, thus having a negative impact on their willingness to serve. Increased compensation may not persuade highly-qualified potential committee members to accept the burdensome legal responsibility of vouching for a multinational company's complex and intricate accounting system.

Finally, it is important to realize that having the best and most qualified corporate board of directors is no guarantee that financial reporting or other problems will not occur. Many of the corporate failures, large and small, that occur every year have arisen as a result of inattention, reckless disregard, or malfeasance. While some of the new and proposed regulations may address specific issues that have occurred in certain situations, they will never fully compensate for flaws in human nature. Many corporate failures would still have occurred under the new rules set by Congress and the SEC if board members found ways to ignore or circumvent them. As long as human judgment and discretion is permitted to operate within the corporate board function, there is room for error and wrongdoing.

Joanie Sompayrac

FURTHER READING:

Byron, Ellen. "Corporate Governance (A Special Report): Managers: Keep Out: Independent Directors Have a Lot More Power These Days, and a Lot More Responsibility." *Wall Street Journal,* 21 June 2004.

Fleming, John M. "Audit Committee: Roles, Responsibilities, and Performance." *Pennsylvania CPA Journal* 73 (Summer 2002): 29–32.

Hymowitz, Carol. "Corporate Governance (A Special Report); Experiments in Corporate Governance: Finding the Right Way to Improve Board Oversight Isn't Easy; But Plenty of Companies are Trying." *Wall Street Journal,* 21 June 2004.

Karmel, Roberta S. "Should a Duty to the Corporation Be Imposed on Institutional Shareholders?" *The Business Lawyer* 60 (November 2004): 1.

Raber, Roger. "What Has Really Changed in the American Boardroom." *Community Banker* 13 (October 2004): 60.

Saporito, Bill. "Why Carly's Out." *Time,* 21 February 2005, 34.

Sherman, Jay. "Eisner Still in Charge." *Television Week,* 14 February 2005, 3.

U.S. Securities and Exchange Commission. "NASD and NYSE Rulemaking: Relating to Corporate Governance." Available from <http://www.sec.gov/rules/sro/34–48745.htm>.

CORPORATE SOCIAL RESPONSIBILITY

Corporate social responsibility (CSR) can be defined as the "economic, legal, ethical, and discretionary expectations that society has of organizations at a given point in time" (Carroll and Buchholtz 2003, p. 36). The concept of corporate social responsibility means that organizations have moral, ethical, and philanthropic responsibilities in addition to their responsibilities to earn a fair return for investors and comply with the law. A traditional view of the corporation suggests that its primary, if not sole, responsibility is to its owners, or stockholders. However, CSR requires organizations to adopt a broader view of its responsibilities that includes not only stockholders, but many other constituencies as well, including employees, suppliers, customers, the local community, local, state, and federal governments, environmental groups, and other special interest groups. Collectively, the various groups affected by the actions of an organization are called "stakeholders." The stakeholder concept is discussed more fully in a later section.

Corporate social responsibility is related to, but not identical with, business ethics. While CSR encompasses the economic, legal, ethical, and discretionary responsibilities of organizations, business ethics usually focuses on the moral judgments and behavior of individuals and groups within organizations. Thus, the study of business ethics may be regarded as a component of the larger study of corporate social responsibility.

Carroll and Buchholtz's four-part definition of CSR makes explicit the multi-faceted nature of social responsibility. The economic responsibilities cited in the definition refer to society's expectation that organizations will produce good and services that are needed and desired by customers and sell those goods and services at a reasonable price. Organizations are expected to be efficient, profitable, and to keep shareholder interests in mind. The legal responsibilities relate to the expectation that organizations will comply with the laws set down by society to govern competition in the marketplace. Organizations have thousands of legal responsibilities governing almost every aspect of their operations, including consumer and product laws, environmental laws, and employment laws. The ethical responsibilities concern societal expectations that go beyond the law, such as the expectation that organizations will conduct their affairs in a fair and just way. This means that organizations are expected to do more than just comply with the law, but also make proactive efforts to anticipate and meet the norms of society even if those norms are not formally enacted in law. Finally, the discretionary responsibilities of corporations refer to society's expectation that organizations be good citizens. This may involve such things as philanthropic support of programs benefiting a community or the nation. It may also involve donating employee expertise and time to worthy causes.

HISTORY

The nature and scope of corporate social responsibility has changed over time. The concept of CSR is a relatively new one—the phrase has only been in wide use since the 1960s. But, while the economic, legal, ethical, and discretionary expectations placed on organizations may differ, it is probably accurate to say that all societies at all points in time have had some degree of expectation that organizations would act responsibly, by some definition.

In the eighteenth century the great economist and philosopher Adam Smith expressed the traditional or classical economic model of business. In essence, this model suggested that the needs and desires of society could best be met by the unfettered interaction of individuals and organizations in the marketplace. By acting in a self-interested manner, individuals would produce and deliver the goods and services that would earn them a profit, but also meet the needs of others. The viewpoint expressed by Adam Smith over 200 years ago still forms the basis for free-market economies in the twenty-first century. However, even Smith recognized that the free market did not always perform perfectly and he stated that marketplace participants must act honestly and justly toward each other if the ideals of the free market are to be achieved.

In the century after Adam Smith, the Industrial Revolution contributed to radical change, especially in Europe and the United States. Many of the principles espoused by Smith were borne out as the introduction of new technologies allowed for more efficient production of goods and services. Millions of people obtained jobs that paid more than they had ever made before and the standard of living greatly improved. Large organizations developed and acquired great power, and their founders and owners became some of the richest and most powerful men in the world. In the late nineteenth century many of these individuals believed in and practiced a philosophy that came to be called "Social Darwinism," which, in simple form, is the idea that the principles of natural selection and survival of the fittest are applicable to business and social policy. This type of philosophy justified cutthroat, even brutal, competitive strategies and did not allow for much concern about the impact of the successful corporation on employees, the community, or the larger society. Thus, although many of the great tycoons of the late nineteenth century were among the greatest philanthropists of all time, their giving was done as individuals, not as representatives of their companies. Indeed, at the same time that many of them were giving away millions of dollars of their own money, the companies that made them rich were practicing business methods that, by today's standards at least, were exploitative of workers.

Around the beginning of the twentieth century a backlash against the large corporations began to gain momentum. Big business was criticized as being too powerful and for practicing antisocial and anticompetitive practices. Laws and regulations, such as the Sherman Antitrust Act, were enacted to rein in the large corporations and to protect employees, consumers, and society at large. An associated movement, sometimes called the "social gospel," advocated greater attention to the working class and the poor. The labor movement also called for greater social responsiveness on the part of business. Between 1900 and 1960 the business world gradually began to accept additional responsibilities other than making a profit and obeying the law.

In the 1960s and 1970s the civil rights movement, consumerism, and environmentalism affected society's expectations of business. Based on the general idea that those with great power have great responsibility, many called for the business world to be more proactive in (1) ceasing to *cause* societal problems and (2) starting to participate in *solving* societal problems. Many legal mandates were placed on business related to equal employment opportunity, product safety, worker safety, and the environment. Furthermore, society began to expect business to voluntarily participate in solving societal problems whether they had caused the problems or not. This was based on the view that corporations should go beyond their economic and legal responsibilities and accept responsibilities related to the betterment of society. This view of corporate social responsibility is the prevailing view in much of the world today.

The sections that follow provide additional details related to the corporate social responsibility construct. First, arguments for and against the CSR concept are reviewed. Then, the stakeholder concept, which is central to the CSR construct, is discussed. Finally, several of the major social issues with which organizations must deal are reviewed.

ARGUMENTS FOR AND AGAINST CORPORATE SOCIAL RESPONSIBILITY

The major arguments for and against corporate social responsibility are shown in Exhibit 1. The "economic" argument against CSR is perhaps most closely associated with the American economist Milton Friedman, who has argued that the primary responsibility of business is to make a profit for its owners, albeit while complying with the law. According to this view, the self-interested actions of millions of participants in free markets will, from a utilitarian perspective, lead to positive outcomes for society. If the operation of the free market cannot solve a social problem, it becomes the responsibility of government, not business, to address the issue.

Exhibit 1

Arguments For and Against CSR

FOR	AGAINST
The rise of the modern corporation created and continues to create many social problems. Therefore, the corporate world should assume responsibility for addressing these problems.	Taking on social and moral issues is not economically feasible. Corporations should focus on earning a profit for their shareholders and leave social issues to others.
In the long run, it is in corporations' best interest to assume social responsibilities. It will increase the chances that they will have a future and reduce the chances of increased governmental regulation.	Assuming social responsibilities places those corporations doing so at a competitive disadvantage relative to those who do not.
Large corporations have huge reserves of human and financial capital. They should devote at least some of their resources to addressing social issues.	Those who are most capable should address social issues. Those in the corporate world are not equipped to deal with social problems.

The "competitive" argument recognizes the fact that addressing social issues comes at a cost to business. To the extent that businesses internalize the costs of socially responsible actions, they hurt their competitive position relative to other businesses. This argument is particularly relevant in a globally competitive environment if businesses in one country expend assets to address social issues, but those in another country do not. According to Carroll and Buchholtz, since CSR is increasingly becoming a global concern, the differences in societal expectations around the world can be expected to lessen in the coming years.

Finally, some argue that those in business are ill-equipped to address social problems. This "capability" argument suggests that business executives and managers are typically well trained in the ways of finance, marketing, and operations management, but not well versed in dealing with complex societal problems. Thus, they do not have the knowledge or skills needed to deal with social issues. This view suggests that corporate involvement in social issues may actually make the situation worse. Part of the capability argument also suggests that corporations can best serve societal interests by sticking to what they do best, which is providing quality goods and services and selling them at an affordable price to people who desire them.

There are several arguments in favor of corporate social responsibility. One view, held by critics of the corporate world, is that since large corporations create many social problems, they should attempt to address and solve them. Those holding this view criticize the production, marketing, accounting, and environmental practices of corporations. They suggest that corporations can do a better job of producing quality, safe products, and in conducting their operations in an open and honest manner.

A very different argument in favor of corporate social responsibility is the "self-interest" argument. This is a long-term perspective that suggests corporations should conduct themselves in such a way in the present as to assure themselves of a favorable operating environment in the future. This view holds that companies must look beyond the short-term, bottom-line perspective and realize that investments in society today will reap them benefits in the future. Furthermore, it may be in the corporate world's best interests to engage in socially responsive activities because, by doing so, the corporate world may forestall governmental intervention in the form of new legislation and regulation, according to Carroll and Buchholtz.

Finally, some suggest that businesses should assume social responsibilities because they are among the few private entities that have the resources to do so. The corporate world has some of the brightest minds in the world, and it possesses tremendous financial resources. (Wal-Mart, for example, has annual revenues that exceed the annual GNP of some countries.) Thus, businesses should utilize some of their human and financial capital in order to "make the world a better place."

THE STAKEHOLDER CONCEPT

According to Post, Lawrence, and Weber, stakeholders are individuals and groups that are affected by an organization's policies, procedures, and actions. A "stake" implies that one has an interest or share in the organization and its operations, per Carroll and Buchholtz. Some stakeholders, such as employees and owners, may have specific legal rights and expectations in regard to the organization's operations. Other stakeholders may not have specific rights granted by law, but may perceive that they have moral rights related to the organization's operations. For example, an environmental group may not have a legal right in regard to a company's use of natural resources, but may believe that they have a moral right to question the firm's environmental policies and to lobby the organization to develop environmentally friendly policies.

All companies, especially large corporations, have multiple stakeholders. One way of classifying stakeholder groups is to classify them as primary or secondary stakeholders. Primary stakeholders have some direct interest or stake in the organization. Secondary stakeholders, in contrast, are public or special interest groups that do not have a direct stake in the organization but are still affected by its operations. Exhibit 2 classifies some major stakeholder groups into primary and secondary categories.

Exhibit 2

Primary Stakeholders	Shareholders (Owners)
	Employees
	Customers
	Business Partners
	Communities
	Future Generations
	The Natural Environment
Secondary Stakeholders	Local, State, and Federal Government
	Regulatory Bodies
	Civic Institutions and Groups
	Special Interest Groups
	Trade and Industry Groups
	Media
	Competitors

Table based on Carroll and Buchholtz, 2003: p. 71

The owners of a firm are among the primary stakeholders of the firm. An organization has legal and moral obligations to its owners. These obligations include, but are not limited to, attempting to ensure that owners receive an adequate return on their investment. Employees are also primary stakeholders who have both legal and moral claims on the organization. Organizations also have specific responsibilities to their customers in terms of producing and marketing goods and services that offer functionality, safety, and value; to local communities, which can be greatly affected by the actions of resident organizations and thus have a direct stake in their operations; and to the other companies with whom they do business. Many social commentators also suggest that companies have a direct responsibility to future generations and to the natural environment.

An organization's responsibilities are not limited to primary stakeholders. Although governmental bodies and regulatory agencies do not usually have ownership stakes in companies in free-market economies, they do play an active role in trying to ensure that organizations accept and meet their responsibilities to primary stakeholder groups. Organizations are accountable to these secondary stakeholders. Organizations must also contend with civic and special interest groups that purport to act on behalf of a wide variety of constituencies. Trade associations and industry groups are also affected by an organization's actions and its reputation. The media reports on and investigates the actions of many companies, particularly large organizations, and most companies accept that they must contend with and effectively "manage" their relationship with the media. Finally, even an organization's competitors can be considered secondary stakeholders, as they are obviously affected by organizational actions. For example, one might argue that organizations have a social responsibility to compete in the marketplace in a manner that is consistent with the law and with the best practices of their industry, so that all competitors will have a fair chance to succeed.

CONTEMPORARY SOCIAL ISSUES

Corporations deal with a wide variety of social issues and problems, some directly related to their operations, some not. It would not be possible to adequately describe all of the social issues faced by business. This section will briefly discuss three contemporary issues that are of major concern: the environment, global issues, and technology issues. There are many others.

ENVIRONMENTAL ISSUES. Corporations have long been criticized for their negative effect on the natural environment in terms of wasting natural resources and contributing to environmental problems such as pollu-

tion and global warming. The use of fossil fuels is thought to contribute to global warming, and there is both governmental and societal pressure on corporations to adhere to stricter environmental standards and to voluntarily change production processes in order to do less harm to the environment. Other issues related to the natural environment include waste disposal, deforestation, acid rain, and land degradation. It is likely that corporate responsibilities in this area will increase in the coming years.

GLOBAL ISSUES. Corporations increasingly operate in a global environment. The globalization of business appears to be an irreversible trend, but there are many opponents to it. Critics suggest that globalization leads to the exploitation of developing nations and workers, destruction of the environment, and increased human rights abuses. They also argue that globalization primarily benefits the wealthy and widens the gap between the rich and the poor. Proponents of globalization argue that open markets lead to increased standards of living for everyone, higher wages for workers worldwide, and economic development in impoverished nations. Many large corporations are multinational in scope and will continue to face legal, social, and ethical issues brought on by the increasing globalization of business.

Whether one is an opponent or proponent of globalization, however, does not change the fact that corporations operating globally face daunting social issues. Perhaps the most pressing issue is that of labor standards in different countries around the world. Many corporations have been stung by revelations that their plants around the world were "sweatshops" and/or employed very young children. This problem is complex because societal standards and expectations regarding working conditions and the employment of children vary significantly around the world. Corporations must decide which is the responsible option: adopting the standards of the countries in which they are operating or imposing a common standard worldwide. A related issue is that of safety conditions in plants around the world.

Another issue in global business is the issue of marketing goods and services in the international marketplace. Some U.S. companies, for example, have marketed products in other countries after the products were banned in the United States.

TECHNOLOGY ISSUES. Another contemporary social issue relates to technology and its effect on society. For example, the Internet has opened up many new avenues for marketing goods and services, but has also opened up the possibility of abuse by corporations. Issues of privacy and the security of confidential information must be addressed. Biotechnology companies face questions related to the use of embryonic stem cells, genetic engineering, and cloning. All of these issues have far-reaching societal and ethical implications. As our technological capabilities continue to advance, it is likely that the responsibilities of corporations in this area will increase dramatically.

Corporate social responsibility is a complex topic. There is no question that the legal, ethical, and discretionary expectations placed on businesses are greater than ever before. Few companies totally disregard social issues and problems. Most purport to pursue not only the goal of increased revenues and profits, but also the goal of community and societal betterment.

Research suggests that those corporations that develop a reputation as being socially responsive and ethical enjoy higher levels of performance. However, the ultimate motivation for corporations to practice social responsibility should not be a financial motivation, but a moral and ethical one.

SEE ALSO: Ethics

Tim Barnett

FURTHER READING:

Arthaud-Day, M.L. "Transnational Corporate Social Responsibility: A Tri-Dimensional Approach to International CSR Research." *Business Ethics Quarterly* 15 (2005): 1–22.

Carroll, A.B., and A.K. Buchholtz. *Business and Society: Ethics and Stakeholder Management.* 5th ed. Australia: Thomson South-Western, 2003.

Garriga, E., and D. Mele. "Corporate Social Responsibility Theories: Mapping the Territory." *Journal of Business Ethics* 53 (2004): 51–71.

Marquez, A., and C.J. Fombrun. "Measuring Corporate Social Responsibility." *Corporate Reputation Review* 7 (2005): 304–308.

Post, J.E., A.T. Lawrence, and J. Weber. *Business and Society.* 10th ed. Boston: McGraw-Hill, 2002.

COST-VOLUME-PROFIT ANALYSIS

Cost-volume-profit (CVP) analysis expands the use of information provided by breakeven analysis. A critical part of CVP analysis is the point where total revenues equal total costs (both fixed and variable costs). At this breakeven point (BEP), a company will experience no income or loss. This BEP can be an initial examination that precedes more detailed CVP analyses.

Cost-volume-profit analysis employs the same basic assumptions as in breakeven analysis. The assumptions underlying CVP analysis are:

1. The behavior of both costs and revenues in linear throughout the relevant range of activity. (This assumption precludes the concept of volume discounts on either purchased materials or sales.)

2. Costs can be classified accurately as either fixed or variable.

3. Changes in activity are the only factors that affect costs.

4. All units produced are sold (there is no ending finished goods inventory).

5. When a company sells more than one type of product, the sales mix (the ratio of each product to total sales) will remain constant.

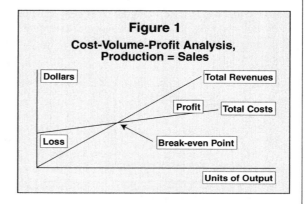

Figure 1
Cost-Volume-Profit Analysis,
Production = Sales

In the following discussion, only one product will be assumed. Finding the breakeven point is the initial step in CVP, since it is critical to know whether sales at a given level will at least cover the relevant costs. The breakeven point can be determined with a mathematical equation, using contribution margin, or from a CVP graph. Begin by observing the CVP graph in Figure 1, where the number of units produced equals the number of units sold. This figure illustrates the basic CVP case. Total revenues are zero when output is zero, but grow linearly with each unit sold. However, total costs have a positive base even at zero output, because fixed costs will be incurred even if no units are produced. Such costs may include dedicated equipment or other components of fixed costs. It is important to remember that fixed costs include costs of every kind, including fixed sales salaries, fixed office rent, and fixed equipment depreciation of all types. Variable costs also include all types of variable costs: selling, administrative, and production. Sometimes, the focus is on production to the point where it is easy to overlook that all costs must be classified as either fixed or variable, not merely product costs.

Where the total revenue line intersects the total costs line, breakeven occurs. By drawing a vertical line from this point to the units of output (X) axis, one can determine the number of units to break even.

A horizontal line drawn from the intersection to the dollars (Y) axis would reveal the total revenues and total costs at the breakeven point. For units sold above the breakeven point, the total revenue line continues to climb above the total cost line and the company enjoys a profit. For units sold below the breakeven point, the company suffers a loss.

Illustrating the use of a mathematical equation to calculate the BEP requires the assumption of representative numbers. Assume that a company has total annual fixed cost of $480,000 and that variable costs of all kinds are found to be $6 per unit. If each unit sells for $10, then each unit exceeds the specific variable costs that it causes by $4. This $4 amount is known as the unit contribution margin. This means that each unit sold contributes $4 to cover the fixed costs. In this intuitive example, 120,000 units must be produced and sold in order to break even. To express this in a mathematical equation, consider the following abbreviated income statement:

Unit Sales = Total Variable Costs + Total Fixed Costs + Net Income

Inserting the assumed numbers and letting X equal the number of units to break even:

$$\$10.00X = \$6.00X + \$480,000 + 0$$

Note that net income is set at zero, the breakeven point. Solving this algebraically provides the same intuitive answer as above, and also the shortcut formula for the contribution margin technique:

Fixed Costs ÷ Unit Contribution Margin = Breakeven Point in Units
$$\$480,000 ÷ \$4.00 = 120,000 \text{ units}$$

If the breakeven point in sales dollars is desired, use of the contribution margin ratio is helpful. The contribution margin ratio can be calculated as follows:

Unit Contribution Margin ÷ Unit Sales Price
= Contribution Margin Ratio
$$\$4.00 ÷ \$10.00 = 40\%$$

To determine the breakeven point in sales dollars, use the following mathematical equation:

Total Fixed Costs ÷ Contribution Margin Ratio
= Breakeven Point in Sales Dollars
$$\$480,000 ÷ 40\% = \$1,200,000$$

The margin of safety is the amount by which the actual level of sales exceeds the breakeven level of sales. This can be expressed in units of output or in dollars. For example, if sales are expected to be 121,000 units, the margin of safety is 1,000 units over breakeven, or $4,000 in profits before tax.

A useful extension of knowing breakeven data is the prediction of target income. If a company with the cost structure described above wishes to earn a target income of $100,000 before taxes, consider the condensed income statement below. Let X = the number of units to be sold to produce the desired target income:

Target Net Income = Required Sales Dollars
− Variable Costs − Fixed Costs
$$\$100,000 = \$10.00X − \$6.00X − \$480,000$$

Solving the above equation finds that 145,000 units must be produced and sold in order for the company to earn a target net income of $100,000 before considering the effect of income taxes.

A manager must ensure that profitability is within the realm of possibility for the company, given its level of capacity. If the company has the ability to produce 100 units in an 8-hour shift, but the breakeven point for the year occurs at 120,000 units, then it appears impossible for the company to profit from this product. At best, they can produce 109,500 units, working three 8-hour shifts, 365 days per year (3 X 100 X 365). Before abandoning the product, the manager should investigate several strategies:

1. Examine the pricing of the product. Customers may be willing to pay more than the price assumed in the CVP analysis. However, this option may not be available in a highly competitive market.

2. If there are multiple products, then examine the allocation of fixed costs for reasonableness. If some of the assigned costs would be incurred even in the absence of this product, it may be reasonable to reconsider the product without including such costs.

3. Variable material costs may be reduced through contractual volume purchases per year.

4. Other variable costs (e.g., labor and utilities) may improve by changing the process. Changing the process may decrease variable costs, but increase fixed costs. For example, state-of-the-art technology may process units at a lower per-unit cost, but the fixed cost (typically, depreciation expense) can offset this advantage. Flexible analyses that explore more than one type of process are particularly useful in justifying capital budgeting decisions. Spreadsheets have long been used to facilitate such decision-making.

One of the most essential assumptions of CVP is that if a unit is produced in a given year, it will be sold in that year. Unsold units distort the analysis. Figure 2 illustrates this problem, as incremental revenues cease while costs continue. The profit area is bounded, as units are stored for future sale.

Unsold production is carried on the books as finished goods inventory. From a financial statement perspective, the costs of production on these units are deferred into the next year by being reclassified as assets. The risk is that these units will not be salable in the next year due to obsolescence or deterioration.

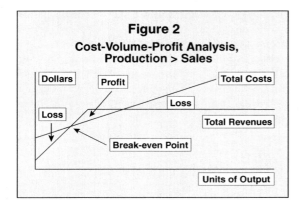

Figure 2
Cost-Volume-Profit Analysis, Production > Sales

While the assumptions employ determinate estimates of costs, historical data can be used to develop appropriate probability distributions for stochastic analysis. The restaurant industry, for example, generally considers a 15 percent variation to be "accurate."

APPLICATIONS

While this type of analysis is typical for manufacturing firms, it also is appropriate for other types of industries. In addition to the restaurant industry, CVP has been used in decision-making for nuclear versus gas- or coal-fired energy generation. Some of the more important costs in the analysis are projected discount rates and increasing governmental regulation. At a more down-to-earth level is the prospective purchase of high quality compost for use on golf courses in the Carolinas. Greens managers tend to balk at the necessity of high (fixed) cost equipment necessary for uniform spreadability and maintenance, even if the (variable) cost of the compost is reasonable. Interestingly, one of the unacceptably high fixed costs of this compost is the smell, which is not adaptable to CVP analysis.

Even in the highly regulated banking industry, CVP has been useful in pricing decisions. The market for banking services is based on two primary categories. First is the price-sensitive group. In the 1990s leading banks tended to increase fees on small, otherwise unprofitable accounts. As smaller account holders have departed, operating costs for these banks have decreased due to fewer accounts; those that remain pay for their keep. The second category is the maturity-based group. Responses to changes in rates paid for certificates of deposit are inherently delayed by the maturity date. Important increases in fixed costs for banks include computer technology and the employment of skilled analysts to segment the markets for study.

Even entities without a profit goal find CVP useful. Governmental agencies use the analysis to determine the level of service appropriate for projected revenues. Nonprofit agencies, increasingly stipulating fees for service, can explore fee-pricing options; in many cases, the recipients are especially price-sensitive due to income or health concerns. The agency can use CVP to explore the options for efficient allocation of resources.

Project feasibility studies frequently use CVP as a preliminary analysis. Such major undertakings as real estate/construction ventures have used this technique to explore pricing, lender choice, and project scope options.

Cost-volume-profit analysis is a simple but flexible tool for exploring potential profit based on cost strategies and pricing decisions. While it may not provide detailed analysis, it can prevent "do-nothing" management paralysis by providing insight on an overview basis.

SEE ALSO: Break-Even Point; Cost Accounting

John M. Alvis

FURTHER READING:

Bahe, Anita R. "Markets for High Quality Compost." *BioCycle* 37, no. 7 (1996): 83.

Caldwell, Charles W., and Judith K. Welch. "Applications of Cost-Profit-Volume Analysis in the Governmental Environment." *Government Accountants Journal,* Summer 1989, 3–8.

Clarke, Peter. "Bring Uncertainty into the CVP Analysis." *Accountancy,* September 1986, 105–107.

Davis, Joseph M. "Project Feasibility Using Breakeven Point Analysis." *Appraisal Journal* 65, no. 1 (1998): 41–45.

Greenberg, Carol. "Analyzing Restaurant Performance: Relating Cost and Volume to Profit." *Cornell Hotel & Restaurant Administration Quarterly* 27, no. 1 (1986): 9–11.

Hanna, Mark D., W. Rocky Newman, and Sri V. Sridharan. "Adapting Traditional Breakeven Analysis to Modern Production Economics: Simultaneously Modeling Economies of Scale and Scope." *International Journal of Production Economics* 29, no. 2 (1993): 187–201.

Harris, Peter J. "Hospitality Profit Planning in the Practical Environment: Integrating Cost-Volume-Profit Analysis with Spreadsheet Management." *International Journal of Contemporary Hospitality Management* 4, no. 4 (1992): 24–32.

Horngren, Charles T., George Foster, and Srikant M. Datar. *Cost Accounting: A Managerial Emphasis.* 9th ed. Upper Saddle River, NJ: Prentice Hall, 1997.

Kabak, Irwin W., and George J. Siomkos. "Adapting to a Changing System Procedure." *Industrial Engineering* 25, no. 4 (1993): 61–62.

Kuehn, Steven E. "Nuclear Power: Running with the Competition." *Power Engineering* 14, no. 1 (1994): 14.

Mathews, Ryan. "Rationalizing SKUs." *Progressive Grocer,* February 1996, 43–46.

McMahon, Seamus P. "Marketing Perspectives: Setting Retail Prices." *Bank Management,* January 1992, 46–49.

Sherman, Lawrence F., Jae K. Shim, and Mark Hartney. "Short Run Break-Even Analysis for Real Estate Projects." *Real Estate Issues,* Spring/Summer 1993, 15–20.

Weygandt, Jerry J., Donald E. Kieso, and Paul D. Kimmel. *Managerial Accounting: Tools for Business Decision Making.* Hoboken, NJ: John Wiley & Sons Inc., 2005.

COST ACCOUNTING

Cost accounting, often referred to as managerial or management accounting, is the branch of accounting that provides economic and financial information to decision makers within a company. The idea of providing information for use within the company (to aid management to plan, direct, and control operations) differentiates cost accounting from other segments of the accountancy profession. For example, financial accounting serves the public by providing financial reporting via financial statements, financial press releases and such. This public information is prepared and presented based on generally accepted accounting principles (GAAP), the broad rules that assure the user of the underlying framework supporting the information.

On the other hand, cost accounting is limited predominantly to use within the company to aid management in the process of making choices that will benefit the stockholders by maximizing company profits that translate into maximizing stockholder wealth. Since the information is used internally, the information may be presented on any logical basis just so long as it will aid the manager to reach an appropriate, informed decision.

A few concepts in cost accounting, however, form the bridge between financial and managerial accounting topics. One such concept is that of product costing for a manufacturing company. Not only is this information used internally in decision making (e.g., does a company make or buy a component?), product costing is also used to determine the historical basis to account for the cost of products sold during a period and the cost of the unsold inventory that remains as an asset on the statement of financial position at the end of the period.

OVERVIEW

Numerous cost accounting concepts can benefit management in decision-making, both for manufacturing and service companies. While many of the concepts discussed below are applicable to both types of companies, the basis for ease of discussion will be that of a manufacturing company. Therefore, some of the concepts to be discussed include understanding the distinction between manufacturing and non-manufacturing costs (and how these are disclosed in the financial statements), computing the cost of manufacturing a product (or providing a service), identifying cost behavior in order to utilize cost-volume-profit relationships, setting prices, budgeting and budgetary controls, and capital budgeting. These topics will be briefly discussed below.

MANUFACTURING VS. NON-MANUFACTURING COSTS

Manufacturing costs are those costs incurred by a producer of goods that are needed to transform raw materials into finished products, ready to sell. These costs consist of the cost of basic materials and components, plus the costs of labor and factory overhead needed to convert the materials into finished products.

Materials and labor can be classified as either direct or indirect in relation to the final product. Direct materials are those major components that can be easily traced to the finished good and are accounted for carefully due to their significance to the product. In the case of manufacturing a lawn mower, for example, these types of materials would include the engine, housing, wheels, and handle. Indirect materials would include those minor items that are essential but which cannot be easily traced to the finished product. Examples of these would be screws, nuts, bolts, washers, and lubricants. One might say that the cost of keeping an account of each of these indirect items exceeds the benefit derived from having the information. Consequently, the costs of these items are accumulated as part of factory overhead and prorated to products on some appropriate basis.

Direct labor refers to the efforts of factory workers that can be directly associated with transforming the materials into the finished product, such as laborers who assemble the product. Indirect laborers are those whose efforts cannot be traced directly or practically to the finished product. The indirect laborers would include maintenance personnel and supervisors.

Factory overhead includes all factory costs that can only be indirectly associated with the finished inventory, that is, all factory costs incurred in making a product other than the costs of direct materials and direct labor. In terms of cost behavior, some of these costs do not change in total even if the number of products manufactured increases or decreases from period to period; the behavior of these costs is said to be a fixed cost. For example, the amount of the monthly factory rent would not fluctuate based on the number of units produced during a particular month.

Other factory overhead costs that change in total in direct proportion to changes in the number of products manufactured are known as variable costs. For example, the number of nuts and bolts needed to assemble lawn mowers would increase and decrease exactly in proportion to the number of mowers produced and are therefore considered to be a variable cost. In summarizing this brief discussion of factory overhead costs, these costs include such things as depreciation of factory buildings and machinery, factory utilities, factory insurance, indirect materials, and indirect labor; some of these costs are variable while others are fixed in total for a specific time period.

All material, labor, and factory overhead costs are summarized into totals that represent the cost of the goods manufactured during a period of time. The cost of products that have been completed and sold during a time period are deducted from the related sales revenue total in order to determine the gross profit for the period. Thus it is logical that these manufacturing costs are referred to as product costs. The cost of unsold completed units at period's end is shown as finished goods on the balance sheet. Any costs of goods that are only partially completed at period's end are shown as work in process inventory, and any materials that have not yet entered into the manufacturing process are disclosed as raw materials inventory.

All the costs incurred by a manufacturing company other than the cost of factory operations are collectively known as non-manufacturing costs. These include all selling, administrative, and financing costs and these costs are deducted as expenses from sales revenues as they are incurred each period. Costs other than manufacturing costs are called period costs for this reason. None of the period costs are deferred to a future period because none of them represent an asset as defined by the accounting profession.

The discussion above has focused on the costs incurred by a manufacturer of goods. The discussion is also pertinent to a business that provides a service to its customers. Providers of services still incur material costs (such as cleaning supplies), labor costs, and general overhead related to providing the services. The major distinction is that, since no tangible product is created, no "product" costs can be deferred to a later period in which they will be sold.

COMPUTING THE COSTS OF PRODUCING A PRODUCT OR SERVICE

Manufacturing companies use a variety of production processes in creating goods. These processes include job shops, batch flows, machine-paced line flows, worker-paced line flow, continuous flows, and hybrids that consist of more than one of the previous separate flow process. The type of production process to a certain extent determines the type of product costing system that a company utilizes.

Job shops, such as machine shops, receive orders for products that are manufactured to the unique blueprint specifications of the requesting customer. As such, it would be rare for these products to meet the needs of any other customer. Thus each "job" must be accounted for separately as the goods are produced and no goods would be produced on a speculative basis. An appropriate method to determine the cost of each unique item produced is activity-based costing (ABC). This method is discussed in detail elsewhere in this publication; please see Activity-Based Costing. The essence of ABC costing is that the exact costs of materials and labor, and a highly accurate estimate of factory overhead costs based on the specific activities (cost drivers) incurred to produce the goods, are determined for each unique product.

Batch flow processes (such as clothing manufacturers use) and worker-paced line flows (such as found in fast food operations) can both use traditional product costing. This product costing system captures the exact costs of materials and labor while using some predetermined overhead rate to associate an appropriate amount of overhead with each product made. A very common basis for determining the overhead rate is the amount of labor time required to produce each unit of product. To determine the overhead rate, management must first estimate the total overhead costs for the upcoming year. Then an estimate of direct labor hours expected for the same period must be made. Finally the estimated overhead is divided by the estimated total direct labor hours and the resulting overhead rate per hour can be established. As each batch of products is completed and the total direct labor hours used is made known from time cards, the overhead rate is multiplied by the actual hours and the overhead is said to be "applied" to the products.

The traditional product costing method was especially popular in the United States until the mid-1980s when labor costs were still a significant portion of the total cost of products. However, with technological changes (such as computer-integrated manufacturing) and more capital intensive approaches to production (such as robotics), the use of a dwindling labor component of product cost as a basis to apply overhead cost was no longer adequate. This was the impetus for the development of ABC costing mentioned above.

Machine-paced line flow processes (such as used by automobile manufacturers) lend themselves to process cost accounting. In this system of product costing, products' costs are accumulated during each of the numerous processes through which the products flow. In the case of an automobile manufacturer, some of the processes might include subassembly stations that reside offline from the main conveyor system where engine assembly, dashboard assembly and the like occur. These major components and their related material, labor, and overhead costs are then carried forward to the next process and new material, labor, and overhead costs are added in each successive process until completion. Thus the individual costs incurred in each process and the total costs incurred are available for financial statements and decision-making purposes.

Companies that use a continuous flow process of production, such as a paper manufacturing company that operates 24/7, would likely use a standard costs system. This product costing system not only accumulates the actual costs incurred in manufacturing the product, but it also determines the standard costs that should have been incurred (based on predetermined standards for material, labor, and factory overhead). By allowing comparisons between actual and standard totals, any discrepancy or variance can be noted and investigated. In particular, any unfavorable costs being incurred can be corrected in a timely manner.

COST BEHAVIOR

One of the critical steps in decision-making is the estimation of costs to be incurred for the particular decision to be made. To be able to do this, management must have a good idea as to how costs "behave" at different levels of operations; i.e., will the cost increase if production increases or will the cost remain the same? A common use of cost behavior information is the attempt by management to predict the total production costs for units to be manufactured in the upcoming month. There are several methods used to estimate total product costs: the high-low method, a scatter-graph, and least-squares regression. Each of these methods attempts to separate costs into components that remain constant (fixed) in total regardless of the number of units produced and those that vary in total in proportion to changes in the number of units produced. Once the behavior of costs is known, predictive ability is greatly enhanced.

Use of the high-low method requires the use of only two past data observations: the highest level of activity (such as the number of units produced during a time period) and the associated total production cost incurred at that level, and the lowest level of activity and its associated cost. All other data points are ignored and even the two observations used must represent operations that have taken place under normal conditions. The loss of input from the unused data is a theoretical limitation of this method.

The scatter-graph method requires that all recent, normal data observations be plotted on a cost (Y-axis) versus activity (X-axis) graph. A line that most closely represents a straight line composed of all the data points should be drawn. By extending the line to where it intersects the cost axis, a company has a fairly accurate estimate of the fixed costs for the period. The angle (slope) of the line can be calculated to give a fairly accurate estimate of the variable cost per unit. The inclusion of the effect of all data points is a strength of this method, but the unsophisticated eye-balling of the appropriate line is a weakness.

The most robust method is the least-squares regression method. This method requires the use of thirty or more past data observations, both the activity level in units produced and the total production cost for each. This technique is known for its statistical strengths but its sophistication requiring the use of software packages can be a hindrance.

For a more detailed description of how the high-low method, a scatter-graph, and least-squares regression aid in separating costs into fixed and variable components, see Cost-Volume-Profit Analysis elsewhere in this publication. Included therein is also a discussion of break-even analysis, contribution margin, and profit/loss projections using cost behavior estimates.

Assuming that a company has used one of the techniques above and has separated costs of manufacturing its products into fixed and variable components, it can use the following general model and substitute derived fixed and variable amounts to create a specific model:

General Model: Total Cost = Fixed Costs for a Month + Variable Cost per Unit
Specific Model: Total Cost Expected = $10,000 per Month + $5.00 per Unit

Given this specific model, a prediction can easily be made of the total costs expected when any number of units are budgeted, as long as the number of units far within the normal range of operations for the company. For example, if 5,000 units are budgeted for the next month's production, the total expected cost would be:

$$\$10,000 + \$5.00 \ (5,000) = \text{Total Cost} = \$35,000$$

If the cost separation technique is fairly accurate, we are in a position to review whether actual costs are in line with our projected cost. Any significant variation between anticipated cost and actual costs should be investigated. The identification of any variances does not answer any questions; the variances merely note that investigation to ascertain the answers is needed.

One other idea is worth mentioning. Considering total production costs in the example above, the same techniques used to separate total costs into fixed and variable components can be utilized to separate any individual cost that isn't readily identifiable as being fixed or variable. A company could, for instance, take the past monthly factory electrical utility bills or the sales wages and use any of the three techniques to separate this individual cost into its fixed and variable components.

SETTING PRICES

Setting the price for goods and services involves an interesting interaction of several factors. The price must be sufficient to exceed the product and period costs and earn a desirable profit. For normal sales to external customers, most companies are unable to unilaterally set prices. Prices are typically set in these competitive markets by the laws of supply and demand. However, if a company manufactures a product unique to customer specifications, or if the company has a patent to its product, then the company can set its own price. One approach to accomplish this is cost-plus pricing. As discussed above, the company must have knowledge of the costs that it will incur. Then the company can apply the proper markup, given the competitive market conditions and other factors, to set its target-selling price.

Some companies add their markup to their variable costs, rather than using the full cost needed for cost-plus pricing. Variable cost pricing is especially useful in special instances such as in pricing special orders or when the company has excess capacity. In both of these cases, production and sales at normal prices to regular customers will be sufficient to cover the total fixed and variable costs for typical sales levels and the concern is only for the incremental units above normal sales levels.

Nissan Motors and other automobile manufacturers take what might be considered a "backward" approach to setting the prices of their vehicles relative to their expected costs. This approach is known as target costing. Once these companies determine what type of vehicle and market niche they wish to pursue, they test the market to see what "target price" the market will bear for their vehicle. From this number they deduct their "desired profit" in order to determine the "target cost" for their product. Then they gather the experts needed to ascertain if they will be able to produce the vehicle for this targeted cost.

If a company has two or more divisions and the output of one division can be used as input to a subsequent division, a price can be set for "sale" from one division to the next in order to measure profitability for each division. This internal transfer price should be set so as to encourage division managers to purchase and sell internally, thus maximizing overall company profits. Transfer prices can be determined based on negotiations between the affiliated divisions, based on the existence of excess capacity by the producing division, based on marking up the variable cost of the goods sold internally, or based on market prices for similar goods, and other approaches.

BUDGETING AND BUDGETARY CONTROLS

Managers use budgets to aid in planning and controlling their companies. A budget is a formal written expression of the plans for a specific future period stated in financial terms. Jerry Weygandt, Donald Kieso and Paul Kimmel's book, *Managerial Accounting: Tools for Business Decision Making* lists the following benefits of budgeting:

1. It requires all levels of management to plan ahead and formalize goals on a repetitive basis.

2. It provides definite objectives for evaluating performance at each level of responsibility.

3. It creates an early warning system for potential problems so that management can make changes before things get out of hand.

4. It facilitates the coordination of activities within the company by correlating segment/division goals with overall company goals.

5. It results in greater management awareness of the company's overall operations including the impact of external factors such as economic trends.

6. It motivates personnel throughout the company to meet planned objectives.

The master budget is the set of interrelated budgets for a selected time period. The specific parts to the master budget are the operating budgets and the financial budgets. The operating budgets begin with a sales budget derived from the sales forecasts provided by the marketing department, followed by the related unit production budget with detail budgets for direct materials, direct labor, and factory overhead. Finally a budget for selling and administrative expenses provides the final information needed for a budgeted income statement. The financial budgets, based on data from the budgeted income statement, are composed of a cash budget, a budgeted balance sheet, and a budget for capital expenditures.

Budgetary control is the process of comparing actual operating results to planned operating results and thereby identifying problem areas in order to take corrective actions. A starting point in this effort is the conversion of the master budget (determined at the start of the period and based on the most probable level of operations) into a flexible budget for the actual level of operations attained. Developing a flexible budget requires identifying the variable costs and the fixed costs for the period as discussed above. Once these cost behavior determinations have been made, total variable costs for the actual level of operations and the total fixed costs for the period can be combined into a flexible budget that discloses the costs that should have been incurred for the actual level of operations achieved.

In taking corrective actions, one must be aware of whether or not a manager is responsible for a particular cost that has been incurred. While all costs are controllable at some level of responsibility within a company, only the costs that a manager incurs directly are controllable by them. Any costs that are allocated to the manager's responsibility level are non-controllable at the manager's level.

The information above focused on budgetary controls for total costs, including product costs for units being produced and sold, general and administrative expenses, selling expenses, and any financial expenses incurred during the period. When considering comparing actual to standard costs for material, labor, and factory overhead costs, the use of a standard product costing system is needed to provide the detail to analyze each separate product cost component.

CAPITAL BUDGETING

Companies with excess funds must make decisions as to how to invest these funds in order to maximize their potential. The choices that involve long-term projects require the use the technique of capital budgeting, that is, choosing among many capital projects to find those that will maximize the return on the invested capital. Several methods of capital budgeting are available to management; among these are the payback period method, the net present value method, and the internal rate of return method. All of these methods require the use of estimated cash flow amounts.

The payback period method is especially simple if future inflows from the project being considered happen to be equal in amount each year. In this case, the formula for computing the payback period is:

Cost of Capital Project ÷ Net Annual Cash Inflow = Payback Period

If the project has uneven cash flows, creating a table with a cumulative net cash flow column will identify the year and an estimate of the portion of a year in which the project recoups its cost. A weakness of this method is that it does not consider the time value of money over the life of the project. However, the shorter the payback period is, the sooner the project's cost is recovered and the more attractive the project is.

A strength of the net present value method is that it uses the same cash flow information as described above and it requires that each cash flow be discounted by an appropriate discount rate to allow for the time value of money. The appropriate discount rate could

be the company's weighted average cost of capital or its required rate of return. After each cash inflow has been discounted to the point in time at which the investment is made, the total of the discounted cash inflows is compared to the cost of the capital project. If the present value of the net cash inflows equals the cost of the investment in the project, then the project is earning exactly the interest rate chosen for discounting. The exact discount rate at which the two values are equal is known as the internal rate of return. If the present value of the net cash inflows exceeds the cost of the capital project, the project is earning more than the discount rate. If the cost of the capital project exceeds the present value of the net cash inflows, that is, the net present value is negative; then the project is not earning at least the discount rate. While the project is profitable if the cash inflows exceed the cash outflows, it would be rejected since it is not earning the return that is needed.

Modern management theory stresses that setting and reaching goals requires that test readings and adjustments along the way are essential. The recent period of increased international competition has led to the need for cost cutting; some companies have been successful by downsizing, expanding globally, and capturing long-term contracts to minimize the increase in costs. Cost accounting can greatly benefit management by providing product or service cost information for use in planning, directing, and controlling the operations of the business.

SEE ALSO: Activity-Based Costing; Cost-Volume-Profit Analysis; Financial Ratios

John M. Alvis

FURTHER READING:

Eldenburg, Leslie G., and Susan K. Wolcott. *Cost Management: Measuring, Monitoring, and Motivating Performance.* John Wiley & Sons, 2004.

Hitt, Michael, Stewart Black, and Lyman Porter. *Management.* Prentice Hall. 2005.

Horngren, Charles T., Gary L. Sundem, and William O. Stratton. *Introduction to Management Accounting.* Prentice Hall, 2005.

Rasmussen, Nils H., and Christopher J. Eichom. *Budgeting: Technology, Trends, Software Selections, and Implementation.* John Wiley & Sons, 2004.

Robbins, Stephen P., and David A. DeCenzo. *Fundamentals of Management.* Prentice Hall, 2005.

Weygandt, Jerry J., Donald E. Kieso, and Paul D. Kimmel. *Managerial Accounting: Tools for Business Decision Making.* John Wiley & Sons, 2005.

Whitten, David A., and Kim Cameron. *Developing Management Skills.* Prentice Hall, 2005.

COVER LETTER TRENDS

SEE: Resumes and Cover Letter Trends

CREATIVITY

Creativity is an imaginative process that results in the creation of something new, be it a product, a service, or a technique. In his book *Managing Creativity,* John J. Kao of Harvard Business School observes that creativity is "a human process leading to a result which is novel (new), useful (solves an existing problem or satisfies an existing need), and understandable (can be reproduced)."

Creativity involves the merging or synthesis of differing concepts into a new concept that did not previously exist. Because creativity reflects the process of integrating diversity into new realities, many researchers have been interested in the skills necessary to be creative in one's work. Personality characteristics associated with people who are creative in nature include: openness to experience; being able to see things in unusual ways; curiosity; the ability to accept and reconcile apparent opposites; having a high tolerance for ambiguity; possessing an independence in thought and action; needing and assuming autonomy or self-reliance; a healthy level of nonconformity; a risk-taking orientation; persistence; sensitivity to problems; the ability to generate large numbers of ideas; flexibility; openness to unconscious phenomena; freedom from fear of failure; the ability to concentrate; and imagination. All of these skills reflect the complexity of trying to measure and predict the creative process. It is a multidimensional and often complex phenomenon that does not easily lend itself to social scientific investigation.

Many management scholars and social observers have argued that in order to stay on the cutting edge of an industry, companies must be able to respond quickly to market opportunities and threats, utilize the ideas of their people more comprehensively, and create new products and services more quickly and efficiently. All of these conditions require the creation of new ways of doing things within the company. Thus, some observers have argued that companies need to develop cultures that foster creativity rather than suppress it. Although this argument has been made by many management scholars since World War II, during the 2000s the rapid pace of technological change within the business world made the issue more cogent than in previous decades. In fact, an American Management Association survey of 500 CEOs, reported in *Psychology Today,* selected "practice creativity and innovation" as the top factor in ensuring corporate survival during the twenty-first century.

Kao notes that, in order to understand how to develop creativity in organizations, it is sometimes useful to study how *not* to facilitate creativity in organizations. He finds that the following organizational norms/behaviors suppress organizational creativity:

- Emphasizing bureaucratic structures and attitudes
- Requiring that decisions must always be made based on organizational tradition and culture
- Continually stressing the importance of standard operating procedures
- Suppressing people who attempt to be creative
- Blocking the flow of ideas with poor internal communication systems
- Tightly controlling systems that eliminate the slack necessary for unofficial initiatives
- Enforcing strict penalties for failure
- Omitting rewards for success
- Promoting values that inhibit risk taking and questioning
- Watching creative activity closely
- Emphasizing tight deadlines
- Stressing authority over responsibility

How, then, can managers foster creativity in the workplace? It requires an approach to managing that many managers find counterintuitive, and that goes against many values in traditional corporate cultures. Kao offers the following as requirements for enhancing creativity in organizations:

- Decentralizing organizational structure
- Promoting a culture that values creative experimentation
- Providing resources to new initiatives
- Encouraging experimental attitudes
- Providing the freedom to fail
- Ensuring that new ideas are not killed
- Removing bureaucracy from the resource allocation process
- Providing appropriate financial and nonfinancial rewards for success
- Encouraging risk taking and questioning

- Minimizing administrative interference in new initiatives and ideas

- Freeing the creative process from surveillance and evaluation

- Loosening deadlines

Managing creativity does not involve anarchy. Rather, it requires that organizational control systems—culture, norms, policies, programs, and reward systems—are loose enough to allow creativity to germinate and grow, while at the same time providing enough structure and overall control to ensure that the organization runs smoothly on a day-to-day basis.

In their article for *Psychology Today,* Stanley S. Gryskiewicz and Robert Epstein termed the optimal environment for organizational creativity "positive turbulence." The authors wrote: "The paradox of positive turbulence is one business leaders today cannot afford to ignore. The energizing, disparate, invigorating, unpredictable force that often feels like chaos is the same creative energy that can provide continuous success and organizational renewal. Without such risk-taking, without embracing uncertainty, many of today's leading businesses will be tomorrow's failures."

Gryskiewicz and Epstein describe sources of positive turbulence—which have the potential to help employees expand their horizons and gain a new perspective on their work—both within and outside of the company. Internal sources of positive turbulence include foreign assignments, cross-functional teams, and cross-generational teams. External sources of positive turbulence include conferences and training sessions, museum and gallery visits, presentations by outside experts, reading outside periodicals, and forging joint ventures and alliances.

In addition, Gryskiewicz and Epstein recommend a number of games and activities to stimulate creativity and innovation. These exercises are intended to develop four basic skills that employees need in order to express their creativity: capturing (noticing and preserving new ideas); challenging (looking beyond established ways of doing things and seeking out difficult problems); broadening (looking beyond one's area of expertise in order to make unusual connections); and surrounding (creating a diverse and interesting work environment).

SEE ALSO: Group Decision Making; Innovation

Mark E. Mendenhall
Revised by Laurie Hillstrom

FURTHER READING:

Gryskiewicz, Stanley S., and Robert Epstein. "Cashing In on Creativity at Work." *Psychology Today* 33, no. 5 (2000).

Kao, John J. *Managing Creativity.* Englewood Cliffs, NJ: Prentice-Hall, 1991.

Mauzy, Jeff, and Richard A. Harriman. *Creativity, Inc.: Building an Inventive Organization.* Boston: Harvard Business School Press, 2003.

Simon, Ethan S., et al. "How Do You Best Organize for Radical Innovation?" *Research Technology Management* 46, no. 5 (2003).

von Oetinger, Bolko. "From Idea to Innovation: Making Creativity Real." *Journal of Business Strategy* 25, no. 5 (2004).

Williams, Geoff, and Richard Florida. "Let's Get Creative." *Entrepreneur* 30, no. 10 (2002): 42.

CRITICAL PATH METHOD

SEE: Program Evaluation and Review Technique and Critical Path Method

CULTURE—INTERNATIONAL DIFFERENCES

SEE: International Cultural Differences

CULTURE—ORGANIZATIONAL

SEE: Organizational Culture

CUSTOMER RELATIONSHIP MANAGEMENT

Customer relationship management (CRM) is a combination of organizational strategy, information systems, and technology that is focused on providing better customer service. CRM uses emerging technology that allows organizations to provide fast and effective customer service by developing a relationship with each customer through the effective use of customer database information systems. The objectives of CRM are to acquire new customers, retain the right current customers, and grow the relationship with an organization's existing customers. An integrated business model that ties together technology, information systems, and business processes along the entire value chain of an organization is critical to the success of CRM.

CRM can also be considered a corporate strategy because it is a fundamental approach to doing business. The goal is to be customer-focused and customer-driven, running all aspects of the business to satisfy the customers by addressing their requirements for products and by providing high-quality, responsive customer service. Companies that adopt this approach are called customer-centric, rather than product-centric.

To be customer-centric, companies need to collect and store meaningful information in a comprehensive customer database. A customer database is an organized collection of information about individual customers or prospects. The database must be current, accessible, and actionable in order to support the generation of leads for new customers while supporting sales and the maintenance of current customer relationships. Smart organizations are collecting information every time a customer comes into contact with the organization. Based on what they know about the individual customer, organizations can customize market offerings, services, programs, messages, and choice of media. A customer database ideally would contain the customer's history of past purchases, demographics, activities/interests/opinions, preferred media, and other useful information. Also, this database should be available to any organizational units that have contact with the customer.

CRM has also grown in scope. CRM initially referred to technological initiatives to make call centers less expensive and more efficient. Now, a lot of organizations are looking at more macro organizational changes. Organizations are now asking how they can change their business processes to use the customer data that they have gathered. CRM is changing into a business process instead of just a technology process.

EVOLUTION OF CRM

Although there are now many software suppliers for CRM, it began back in 1993 when Tom Siebel founded Siebel Systems Inc. Use of the term CRM is traced back to that period. In the mid-1990s CRM was originally sold as a guaranteed way to turn customer data into increased sales performance and higher profits by delivering new insights into customer behaviors and identifying hidden buying patterns buried in customer databases. Instead, CRM was one of the biggest disappointments of the 1990s. Some estimates have put CRM failure rates as high as 75 percent. But more

than a decade later, more firms in the United States and Europe are appearing willing to give CRM another try. A 2005 study by the Gartner Group, found 60 percent of midsize businesses intended to adopt or expand their CRM usage over the next two years. Why the interest? Partially the renewed interest is due to a large number of CRM vendors that are offering more targeted solutions with a wider range of prices and more accountability.

Even though CRM started in the mid-1990s, it has already gone through several overlapping stages. Originally focused on automation of existing marketing processes, CRM has made a major leap forward to a customer-driven, business process management orientation.

The first stage began when firms purchased and implemented single-function client/server systems to support a particular group of employees such as the sales force, the call center representatives, or the marketing department. CRM initially meant applying automation to existing marketing activities and processes. However, automating poorly performing activities or processes did little to improve the quality of the return on investment.

In the second stage, organizations demanded more cross-functional integration to create a holistic view of their customers' relationships. Also, the integrated system's goal was to provide a single-face to the customer by enabling employees to work from a common set of customer information gathered from demographics, Web hits, product inquiries, sales calls, etc. Cross-functional integration allowed the whole organization to take responsibility for customer satisfaction and allowed for better predictive models to improve cross-selling and improved products and delivery options.

The third stage of CRM was heavily influenced by the Internet. Customer self-service and Internet-based systems became the next big thing in CRM. However, there were obstacles caused by a lack of seamless integration into the organization's operational systems and a lack of integration across customer touch points such as call centers, web transactions, and other various interactions. By rethinking the quality and effectiveness of customer-related processes, many organizations began to eliminate unnecessary activities, improve outdated processes, and redesign systems that had failed to deliver the desired outcomes. In this stage, the big CRM vendors used new Internet-based systems to extend the reach of CRM to thousands of employees, distribution partners, and even the customers themselves. Also, most organizations at this stage tie together their CRM systems with their ERP (Enterprise Resource Planning) system and other organizational operational systems.

The next stage of CRM will be when systems are designed based on what matters most to the customer and customers will have direct access to all of the information they need in order to do business with an organization. Customer driven CRM means that organizations first understand the customer, and then move inward to operations. The next generation of CRM will also focus more on financial results. Not all customer relationships are profitable and very few companies can afford to deliver an equal level of services to all customers. Organizations must identify existing profitable customer segments and develop the business requirements to support sustained relationships with these profitable segments. However, organizations also need to find cost effective alternatives for current non-buyers or low-margin customers.

PROBLEMS WITH CRM

One of the major problems with CRM is the large investment to build and maintain a customer database which requires computer hardware, database software, analytical programs, communication links, and skilled personnel. Also, there is the difficulty of getting everyone in the organization to be customer oriented and to get everyone to actually use the customer information that is available. Providing adequate training so that personnel feel comfortable using a new system is critical. Also, not all customers want a relationship with the company and some may resent the organization collecting information about them and storing it in a database. Another problem is the long wait for a return on investment. A three-year wait for ROI is still common. Research conducted by Helms in 2001 suggests that 45 percent of companies are unable to even compute ROI from their CRM investments and research conducted by Cap Gemini Ernst and Young (CGEY) found that two-thirds of companies could not provide any estimate of their ROI on CRM investments.

HOW TO SUCCEED WITH CRM

CRM projects require careful planning and implementation. To be successful, CRM involves major cultural and organizational changes that will meet with a lot of resistance. CRM should be enterprise-wide in scale and scope. However, it is usually better to take an incremental approach starting with a CRM pilot. Once the pilot succeeds, then introducing one CRM application at a time is recommended. Also, it is important to be skeptical of vendor claims and to know that user expectations for CRM are often unreasonable.

SEE ALSO: Marketing Communication; Strategy Implementation

Fraya Wagner-Marsh

FURTHER READING:

Beasty, Colin. "Tracking the Evolution of CRM." *Customer Relationship Management* 9, no. 2 (February 2005): 18.

Boardman, Richard. "Get a handle on CRM." *Computer Weekly,* 8 February 2005, 31.

Borck, James R. "CRM Meets Business Intelligence." *InfoWorld* 27, no. 2 (10 January 2005): 39.

Bull, Christopher. "Strategic Issues in Customer Relationship Management (CRM) Implementation." *Business Process Management Journal* 9, no. 5 (2003): 592–602.

Buttle, Francis. *Customer Relationship Management: Concepts and Tools.* Oxford: Elsevier Butterworth-Heinemann, 2004.

Cap Gemini Ernst and Young. "CGEY and Gartner Share Secrets of ROI." (2001). Available from http://www.crm-forum.com/library.

Cavenagh, Andrew. "What's the score? Is It All Hype, or Really the 'New Way' to Do Business?" *Power Economics,* 2 February, 2005, 8.

Chan, Joseph O. "Toward a Unified View of Customer Relationship Management." *Journal of American Academy of Business* 1 (March 2005): 32–39.

Dyche, Jill. *The CRM Handbook.* Boston:Addison-Wesley, 2002.

Freeland, John G., ed. *The Ultimate CRM Handbook.* New York: McGraw-Hill, 2003.

Gurau, Calin, Ashok Ranchhod, and Ray Hackney. "Customer-Centric Strategic Planning: Integrating CRM in Online Business Systems." *Information Technology and Management* 4, no. 2-3 (2003): 199–214.

Harris, Randy. "What is a Customer Relationship Management (CRM) System?" *Darwin Magazine,* December 2003.

Helms, C. "Promising ROI Keeps CRM Expenditures High." (2001) Available from http://www.1to1.com/inside1to1/19763.html.

Kale, Sudhir H. "CRM Failure and the Seven Deadly Sins." *Marketing Management* 13, no. 5 (2004): 42–46.

Kotler, Philip, Hoon Ang, Swee, Meng Leong, Siew, and Tiong Tan, Chin. *Marketing Management: An Asian Perspective.* Singapore: Pearson Education Asia Pte Ltd/Boardman, Prentice Hall, 2003.

Kotorov, Rado. "Customer Relationship Management: Strategic Lessons and Future Directions." *Business Process Management Journal* 9, no. 5 (2003): 566–571.

Neuborne, Ellen. "A Second Act for CRM." *Inc. Magazine,* March 2005, 40–41.

CYCLE TIME

Time has become a key success measure in business. Oftentimes, it is more important than other performance measures. For example, in marketing a product's success or failure often depends on "time-to-market," or how quickly a new product becomes available to the customer. One of many cycle time measures used in management, cycle time is the measure of a business cycle from beginning to end. Production cycle time refers to production activities, such as the total time required to produce a product. Order processing cycle time is used in the front office to determine the total time required to process an order. From a financial perspective, terms like cash-to-cash cycle time describe the amount of time a company takes to recover its financial investment. From a management perspective, cycle time is used to evaluate performance in all aspects of a business.

Cycle time has become the key measurement tool for the performance of a number of leading edge management concepts, including supply chain management (SCM), just-in-time (JIT) management, enterprise resources planning (ERP), theory of constraints management, and lean management. Cycle time improvements in any of these areas have been linked to reduced costs, reduced inventories, and increased capacity. The resource areas that are measured by cycle time include the measurement of financial flow, materials flow, and information flow. In each case, a delay or failure of any of these measures would indicate a failure of the entire business process.

Cycle time is best illustrated by a few examples. In marketing, time-to-market cycle time is the critical measure of success in the fashion, apparel, and technology industries. Companies that cannot get products to market quickly may get completely washed out. Time-to-market is the measure of time from idea inception through idea development, design and engineering, pilot, and finally production and customer availability. For example, the United States led the world in the idea phase of automotive air bag development. However, a slow design and engineering process enabled the Japanese to generally offer airbags in their vehicles several years before the United States.

Another example of cycle time is the production cycle time. This is the time from when an order is released on the production floor until completion and shipment to the customer. For the American automobile manufacturer this time is measured in weeks and, in some cases, months. For Toyota this time is approximately four hours. The repercussions for this are found is the staging of enormous amounts of work-in-process inventories. The actual "hands-on" production time in both cases is about the same. However, since the United States produces in large batch quantities, it effectively produces hundreds and thousands of cars at the same time. As a result, there is a lot of inventory staging and related work space requirements. This example illustrates the direct relationship between cycle time and inventory.

Another example of cycle time is order-processing time. Unfortunately, in far too many factories the paperwork time to process an order is longer than product production time. Order processing time starts when a phone call or fax initiates the order, and ends when the order is sent to production scheduling. This cycle time includes all paperwork-related steps, such as credit verification and order form completion.

In finance, performance measures such as cash-to-cash cycle time reflect a company's cash performance. This is the amount of time it takes from the time money is spent on a customer's product for the purchase of components until the "cash" is recovered from the customer in the form of a payment. In the computer industry the industry average cash-to-cash cycle time is 106 working days. For "best-in-class" companies this cash-to-cash cycle time is 21 working days, and for Dell Inc. it is a negative seven days. This example illustrates that the average computer company needs to finance its inventory investment for 106 days, whereas Dell has the advantage of being able to utilize its customers' cash to earn interest. Dell can then use this advantage to offer price incentives that the other computer manufacturers cannot.

A variant use of the term "cycle time" is found in industrial engineering. In this specific example, cycle time has a number of meanings—depending on the situation in which the term is used and the industry to which it is applied. It generally is considered to be a manufacturing term applied to an environment where a series of activities or tasks (each with a predetermined completion time known as task time) are performed in a specified sequence known as a "precedence relationship." However, the term can be used in the service sector if the rendering of the service requires a sequential series of tasks. As these tasks are completed at each operation or workstation, the product is passed on to the next workstation in the sequence until the product is complete and can be defined as a finished good.

The predetermined task times govern the range of possible cycle times. The minimum cycle time is equal to the longest task time in the series of tasks required to produce the product, while the maximum cycle time is equal to the sum of all the task times required for a finished good. For example, consider a product that requires five sequential tasks to manufacture. Task one takes 10 minutes to complete; task two, 12 minutes; task three, 20 minutes; task four, 8 minutes; and task five, 10 minutes. The minimum cycle time for this product would be 20 minutes (the longest time). Any cycle time less than 20 minutes would not allow the product to be made, because task three could not be completed. The maximum cycle time would be 60 minutes, or the sum of all task times in the sequence. This implies a range of possible cycle times of 20 to 55 minutes. However, the maximum cycle time would really only be feasible if there was no waste or non-value-added time in the process, such as delays between tasks. Some people refer to the sum of the task times as throughput time or the time required to move a product completely through the system.

However, in its more general usage cycle time is how long it takes for material to enter and exit a production facility. Depending on the industry, this definition is appropriate with slight modifications. For example, in the automobile collision repair industry cycle time refers to the time a car enters the facility for repair until the repair is completed.

SEE ALSO: Operations Management; Operations Scheduling

Gerhard Plenert

FURTHER READING:

Blackstone, John H. *Capacity Management.* Cincinnati, OH: South-Western Publishing Co., 1989.

Cox, James F., III, and John H. Blackstone, Jr., eds. *APICS Dictionary,* 9th ed. Falls Church, VA: American Production and Inventory Control Society Inc., 1998.

Plenert, Gerhard J. *International Operations Management,* Copenhagen, Denmark: Copenhagen Business School Press, 2002.

Stevenson, William J. *Production/Operations Management,* 6th ed. Boston: Irwin/McGraw-Hill, 1999.

D

Data processing and data management are critical components of business organizations.

DATA PROCESSING

Data processing refers to the process of performing specific operations on a set of data or a database. A database is an organized collection of facts and information, such as records on employees, inventory, customers, and potential customers. As these examples suggest, numerous forms of data processing exist and serve diverse applications in the business setting.

Data processing primarily is performed on information systems, a broad concept that encompasses computer systems and related devices. At its core, an information system consists of input, processing, and output. In addition, an information system provides for feedback from output to input. The input mechanism (such as a keyboard, scanner, microphone, or camera) gathers and captures raw data and can be either manual or automated. Processing, which also can be accomplished manually or automatically, involves transforming the data into useful outputs. This can involve making comparisons, taking alternative actions, and storing data for future use. Output typically takes the form of reports and documents that are used by managers. Feedback is utilized to make necessary adjustments to the input and processing stages of the information system.

The processing stage is where management typically exerts the greatest control over data. It also is the point at which management can derive the most value from data, assuming that powerful processing tools are available to obtain the intended results. The most frequent processing procedures available to management are basic activities such as segregating numbers into relevant groups, aggregating them, taking ratios, plotting, and making tables. The goal of these processing activities is to turn a vast collection of facts into meaningful nuggets of information that can then be used for informed decision making, corporate strategy, and other managerial functions.

DATA AND INFORMATION. Data consist of raw facts, such as customer names and addresses. Information is a collection of facts organized in such a way that it has more value beyond the facts themselves. For example, a database of customer names and purchases might provide information on a company's market demographics, sales trends, and customer loyalty/turnover.

Turning data into information is a process or a set of logically related tasks performed to achieve a defined outcome. This process of defining relationships between various data requires knowledge. Knowledge is the body or rules, guidelines, and procedures used to select, organize, and manipulate data to make it suitable for specific tasks. Consequently, information can be considered data made more useful through the application of knowledge. The collection of data, rules, procedures, and relationships that must be followed are contained in the knowledge base.

CHARACTERISTICS OF VALUABLE INFORMATION. In order for information to be valuable it must have the following characteristics, as adapted from Ralph M. Stair's book, *Principles of Information Systems:*

1. Accurate. Accurate information is free from error.

2. Complete. Complete information contains all of the important facts.

3. Economical. Information should be relatively inexpensive to produce.

4. Flexible. Flexible information can be used for a variety of purposes, not just one.

5. Reliable. Reliable information is dependable information.

6. Relevant. Relevant information is important to the decision-maker.

7. Simple. Information should be simple to find and understand.

8. Timely. Timely information is readily available when needed.

9. Verifiable. Verifiable information can be checked to make sure it is accurate.

DATA MANAGEMENT

Data are organized in a hierarchy that begins with the smallest piece of data used by a computer—for purposes of this discussion, a single character such as a letter or number. Characters form fields such as names, telephone numbers, addresses, and purchases. A collection of fields makes up a record. A collection of records is referred to as a file. Integrated and related files make up a database.

An entity is a class of people, objects, or places for which data are stored or collected. Examples include employees and customers. Consequently, data are stored as entities, such as an employee database and a customer database. An attribute is a characteristic of an entity. For example, the name of a customer is an attribute of a customer. A specific value of an attribute is referred to as a data item. That is, data items are found in fields.

The traditional approach to data management consists of maintaining separate data files for each application. For example, an employee file would be maintained for payroll purposes, while an additional employee file might be maintained for newsletter purposes. One or more data files are created for each application. However, duplicated files results in data redundancy. The problem with data redundancy is the possibility that updates are accomplished in one file but not in another, resulting in a lack of data integrity. Likewise, maintaining separate files is generally inefficient because the work of updating and managing the files is duplicated for each separate file that exists. To overcome potential problems with traditional data management, the database approach was developed.

The database approach is such that multiple business applications access the same database. Consequently, file updates are not required of multiple files. Updates can be accomplished in the common database, thus improving data integrity and eliminating

redundancy. The database approach provides the opportunity to share data, as well as information sources. Additional software is required to implement the database approach to data management. A database management system (DBMS) is needed. A DBMS consists of a group of programs that are used in an interface between a database and the user, or between the database and the application program. Advantages of the database approach are presented in Table 1. Disadvantages of the database approach are presented in Table 2.

DATA ORGANIZATION. Data organization is critical to optimal data use. Consequently, it is important to organize data in such a manner as to reflect business operations and practices. As such, careful consideration should be given to content, access, logical structure, and physical organization. Content refers to what data are going to be collected. Access refers to the users that data are provided to when appropriate. Logical structure refers to how the data will be arranged. Physical structure refers to where the data will be located.

One tool that database designers use to show the logical relationships among data is a data model, which is a map or diagram of entities and their relationships. Consequently, data modeling requires a thorough understanding of business practices and what kind of data and information is needed.

DATABASE MODELS. The structure of the relationships in most databases follows one of three logical database models: hierarchical, network, and relational.

A hierarchical database model is one in which the data are organized in a top-down or inverted tree-like structure. This type of model is best suited for situations where the logical relationships between data can be properly represented with the one-parent-many-children approach.

A network model is an extension of the hierarchical database model. The network model has an owner-member relationship in which a member may have many owners, in contrast to a one-to-many-relationship.

A relational model describes data using a standard tabular format. All data elements are placed in two-dimensional tables called relations, which are the equivalent of files. Data inquiries and manipulations can be made via columns or rows given specific criteria.

Network database models tend to offer more flexibility than hierarchical models. However, they are more difficult to develop and use because of relationship complexity. The relational database model offers the most flexibility, and was very popular during the early 2000s.

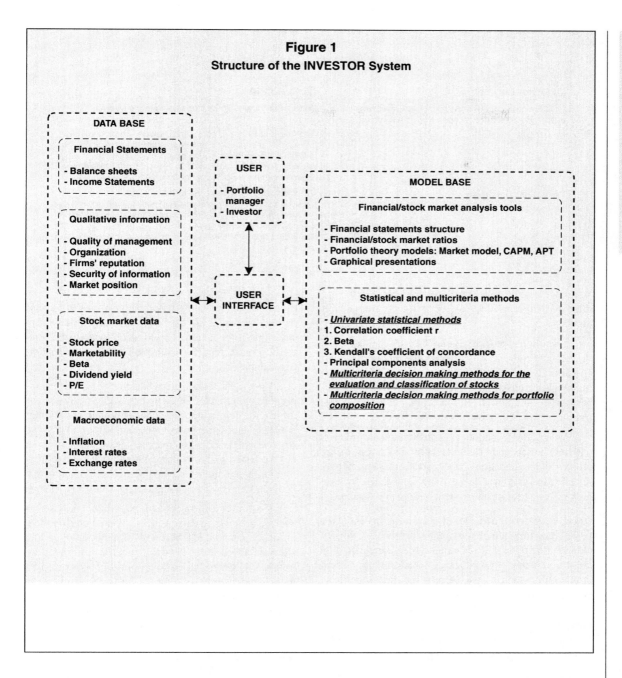

Figure 1
Structure of the INVESTOR System

DATABASE MANAGEMENT SYSTEMS. As indicated previously, a database management system (DBMS) is a group of programs used as an interface between a database and an applications program. DBMSs are classified by the type of database model they support. A relational DBMS would follow the relational model, for example. The functions of a DBMS include data storage and retrieval, database modifications, data manipulation, and report generation.

A data definition language (DDL) is a collection of instructions and commands used to define and describe data and data relationships in a particular database. File descriptions, area descriptions, record descriptions, and set descriptions are terms the DDL defines and uses.

A data dictionary also is important to database management. This is a detailed description of the structure and intended content in the database. For example, a data dictionary might specify the maximum number of characters allowed in each type of field and whether the field content can include numbers, letters, or specially formatted content such as dates or currencies. Data dictionaries are used to provide a standard definition of terms and data elements, assist programmers in designing and writing programs, simplify database modifications, reduce data redundancy,

Table 2

Disadvantage of the Database Approach

Disadvantages	Explanation
Relative high cost of purchasing and operating a DBMS in a mainframe operating environment	Some mainframe DBMSs can cost millions of dollars.
Specialized staff	Additional specialized staff and operating personnel may be needed to implement and coordinate the use of the database. It should be noted, however, that some organizations have been able to implement the database approach with no additional personnel.
Increased vulnerability	Even though databases offer better security because security measures can be concentrated on one system, they also may make more data accessible to the trespasser if security is breached. In addition, if for some reason there is a failure in the DBMS, multiple application programs are affected.

increase data reliability, and decrease program development time.

The choice of a particular DBMS typically is a function of several considerations. Economic cost considerations include software acquisition costs, maintenance costs, hardware acquisition costs, database creation and conversion costs, personnel costs, training costs, and operating costs.

Most DBMS vendors are combining their products with text editors and browsers, report generators, listing utilities, communication software, data entry and display features, and graphical design tools. Consequently, those looking for a total design system have many choices.

DATA WAREHOUSING. Data warehousing involves taking data from a main computer for analysis without slowing down the main computer. In this manner, data are stored in another database for analyzing trends and new relationships. Consequently, the data warehouse is not the live, active system, but it is updated daily or weekly. For example, Wal-Mart uses a very large database (VLDB) that is 4 trillion bytes (terabytes) in size. Smaller parts of this database could be warehoused for further analysis to avoid slowing down the VLDB.

FUTURE TRENDS. A private database is compiled from individual consumer or business customer names and addresses maintained by a company for use in its own marketing efforts. Such a database may have originated as a public database, but typically once the company begins adding or removing information it is considered a private database. By contrast, public databases are those names, addresses, and data that are complied for resale in the list rental market. This is publicly available data (i.e., any business can purchase it on the open market) rather than lists of specific customers or targets.

However, a new trend is combining features of the two approaches. Cooperative databases are compiled by combining privately held response files of participating companies so that costs are shared. Many consider this to be a future trend, such that virtually all catalog marketers, for example, would use cooperative databases.

Geographic Information Systems (GIS) are becoming a growing area of data management. GIS involves the combining demographic, environmental, or other business data with geographic data. This can involve road networks and urban mapping, as well as consumer buying habits and how they relate to the local geography. Output is often presented in a visual data map that facilitates the discovery of new patterns and knowledge.

Customer Resource Management (CRM) is another area where data process and data management is deeply involved. CRM is a set of methodologies and software applications for managing the customer relationship. CRM provides the opportunity for management, salespeople, marketers, and potentially even customers, to see sufficient detail regarding customer activities and contacts. This allows companies to provide other possible products or useful services, as well as other business options. Security of this information is of significant concern on both sides of the equation.

SEE ALSO: Computer Networks; Computer Security

Hal P. Kirkwood, Jr.

FURTHER READING:

Chu, Margaret Y. *Blissful Data: Wisdom and Strategies for Providing Meaningful, Useful, and Accessible Data for All Employees.* New York: American Management Association, 2003.

Churchill, Gilbert A. *Marketing Research: Methodological Foundations.* 8th ed. Cincinnati, OH: South-Western College Publishing, 2001.

Stair, Ralph M. *Principles of Information Systems: A Managerial Approach.* 4th ed. Cambridge, MA: Course Technology, 1999.

Wang, John. *Data Mining: Opportunities and Challenges.* Hershey, PA: Idea Group Publishing, 2003.

White, Ken. "DBMS Past, Present, and Future." *Dr. Dobb's Journal* 26, no. 8 (2001): 21–26.

DEBT VS. EQUITY FINANCING

Debt vs. equity financing is one of the most important decisions facing managers who need capital to fund their business operations. Debt and equity are the two main sources of capital available to businesses, and each offers both advantages and disadvantages. "Absolutely nothing is more important to a new business than raising capital," Steve Jefferson wrote in *Pacific Business News* (Jefferson, 2001). "But the way that money is raised can have an enormous impact on the success of a business."

DEBT FINANCING

Debt financing takes the form of loans that must be repaid over time, usually with interest. Businesses can borrow money over the short term (less than one year) or long term (more than one year). The main sources of debt financing are banks and government agencies, such as the Small Business Administration (SBA). Debt financing offers businesses a tax advantage, because the interest paid on loans is generally deductible. Borrowing also limits the business's future obligation of repayment of the loan, because the lender does not receive an ownership share in the business.

However, debt financing also has its disadvantages. New businesses sometimes find it difficult to make regular loan payments when they have irregular cash flow. In this way, debt financing can leave businesses vulnerable to economic downturns or interest rate hikes. Carrying too much debt is a problem because it increases the perceived risk associated with businesses, making them unattractive to investors and thus reducing their ability to raise additional capital in the future.

EQUITY FINANCING

Equity financing takes the form of money obtained from investors in exchange for an ownership share in the business. Such funds may come from friends and family members of the business owner, wealthy "angel" investors, or venture capital firms. The main advantage to equity financing is that the business is not obligated to repay the money. Instead, the investors hope to reclaim their investment out of future profits. The involvement of high-profile investors may also help increase the credibility of a new business.

The main disadvantage to equity financing is that the investors become part-owners of the business, and thus gain a say in business decisions. "Equity investors are looking for a partner as well as an investment, or else they would be lenders," venture capitalist Bill Richardson explained in *Pacific Business News* (Jefferson, 2001). As ownership interests become diluted, managers face a possible loss of autonomy or control. In addition, an excessive reliance on equity financing may indicate that a business is not using its capital in the most productive manner.

Both debt and equity financing are important ways for businesses to obtain capital to fund their operations. Deciding which to use or emphasize, depends on the long-term goals of the business and the amount of control managers wish to maintain. Ideally, experts suggest that businesses use both debt and equity financing in a commercially acceptable ratio. This ratio, known as the debt-to-equity ratio, is a key factor analysts use to determine whether managers are running a business in a sensible manner. Although debt-to-equity ratios vary greatly by industry and company, a general rule of thumb holds that a reasonable ratio should fall between 1:1 and 1:2.

Some experts recommend that companies rely more heavily on equity financing during the early stages of their existence, because such businesses may find it difficult to service debt until they achieve reliable cash flow. But start-up companies may have trouble attracting venture capital until they demonstrate strong profit potential. In any case, all businesses require sufficient capital in order to succeed. The most prudent course of action is to obtain capital from a variety of sources, using both debt and equity, and hire professional accountants and attorneys to assist with financial decisions.

SEE ALSO: Due Diligence; Financial Issues for Managers; Financial Ratios

Laurie Collier Hillstrom

FURTHER READING:

CCH Tax and Accounting. "Financing Basics: Debt vs. Equity." *CCH Business Owner's Toolkit.* Available from <http://www.toolkit.cch.com/text/P10_2000.asp/>.

Jefferson, Steve. "When Raising Funds, Start-Ups Face the Debt vs. Equity Question." *Pacific Business News,* 3 August 2001.

Tsuruoka, Doug. "When Financing a Small Business, Compare Options, Keep It Simple." *Investor's Business Daily,* 3 May 2004.

WomanOwned.com. "Growing Your Business: Debt Financing vs. Equity Financing." Available from <http://www.womanowned.com/growth/funding/financing.htm>.

DECISION MAKING

The essence of management is making decisions. Managers are constantly required to evaluate alternatives and make decisions regarding a wide range of matters. Just as there are different managerial styles, there are different decision-making styles. Decision making involves uncertainty and risk, and decision makers have varying degrees of risk aversion. Decision making also involves qualitative and quantitative analyses, and some decision makers prefer one form of analysis over the other. Decision making can be affected not only by rational judgment, but also by nonrational factors such as the personality of the decision maker, peer pressure, the organizational situation, and others.

Management guru Peter F. Drucker, as quoted in *Association Management,* identified eight "critically important" decision-making practices that successful executives follow. Each:

1. Ask "What needs to be done?"
2. Ask "What is right for the enterprise?"
3. Develop action plans
4. Take responsibility for decisions
5. Take responsibility for communicating
6. Focus on opportunities rather than problems
7. Run productive meetings
8. Think and say "we" rather than "I"

POSING THE PROBLEM CORRECTLY

According to Ralph L. Keeney, professor at the University of Southern California's Marshall School of Business and co-author of *Smart Choices: A Practical Guide to Making Better Decisions,* managers commonly consider too few alternatives when making difficult decisions. When approaching a problem, decision makers need to regularly consider, starting at the outset, "Is this what I really need to decide?" In addition, the nature of the problem may change during the decision-making process, as either the situation changes or the decision maker's insights into the situation change.

By not formulating the problem correctly, decision makers risk missing a whole range of other alternatives. Decision makers can improve the chances of

asking the right question by probing objectives, goals, interests, fears, and aspirations. They also need to consider very carefully the consequences of each alternative. They can devise new alternatives through brainstorming and imagining as many options as possible, keeping in mind objectives, but not necessarily being entirely practical at first. In practice, action-oriented decision makers tend to focus on solutions without considering whether they are working on the right problem. Instead of choosing from decisions selected by others, decision makers need to review what decisions they should be addressing.

Managers in a corporate setting tend to view decision making differently than entrepreneurs. Since they are typically given a fixed amount of budgeted resources to work with, managers tend to define a problem in terms of what can be done with the resources at hand. Entrepreneurs, on the other hand, will likely pose the problem in terms of an objective—"This is what I want to get done"—and then worry about finding the resources to accomplish that objective. As a result, entrepreneurial decision makers will lay out a wider range of alternatives from which to choose. They feel less constrained by a lack of resources. To develop more alternatives, decision makers should release themselves from existing constraints, think imaginatively, and brainstorm with others, all the while keeping objectives clearly in mind and being honest about what they really need or desire.

SYSTEMATIC ANALYSIS VS. INTUITIVE ANALYSIS

Entrepreneurs are famous for making "seat-of-the-pants" decisions, which means they make quick decisions based on a gut feeling or intuition. They are often forced to make decisions under conditions of uncertainty and without all of the necessary information. While some entrepreneurs are good decision makers, others need to be more cautious about the intuitive approach. One case against intuitive decision making comes from the credit industry. For example, some banks use scoring models for consumer and small business loans, but at times individual bankers override the automated system because they intuitively disagreed with the computer model's results. These loans, however, invariably have higher delinquency and charge off rates than loans approved by the computer model.

In some cases a person's intuition will be in conflict with the results of a more formal or systematic analysis, resulting in an uncomfortable feeling for the decision maker. What should a decision maker do then? Howard Raiffa, Harvard Business School professor emeritus, recommended in *Inc.:* "You should review both sides of the ledger to see if your intuition holds up when it is informed with some systematic analysis. And if your analysis seems wrong intuitively, don't accept the analysis, just keep on probing." The uncomfortable feeling may be sending a message to the decision maker that it's not quite time to act, that perhaps a little more thinking about the problem is required.

Emotions are one of several nonrational factors that play a role in decision making. According to Raiffa, decision makers should pay attention to emotions and feelings when making decisions. By partially committing to one alternative, decision makers can give themselves a chance to "sleep on it," which then becomes a way of testing different alternatives. In spite of practical recommendations to not let emotions play a part in decision making, emotions do come into play because the decision maker cares about the consequences that may occur as a result of any decision made.

Making quick decisions, something managers are often required to do, does not necessarily mean sacrificing systematic decision making. Managers can prepare themselves for making quick decisions by practicing pre-decision making. This involves keeping in mind a decision-making structure, such as a series of probing questions that must be answered, as a contingency plan in the event a quick decision is needed.

UNCERTAINTY AND RISK

Many decisions must be made in the absence of complete information. Decision makers often have to act without knowing for certain all of the consequences of their decisions. Uncertainty simply increases the number of possible outcomes, and the consequences of these outcomes should be considered. That is, it is important for the decision maker to identify what the uncertainties are, what the possible outcomes are, and what the consequences would be. Decision makers can sometimes clarify the problem they are working on by listing what could happen and assigning probabilities to each possible outcome (a formal representation of this is known as a *decision tree*).

Risk aversion is another nonrational factor affecting sound decision making. Studies have shown that people who exhibit risk-averse behavior in one setting will become risk-seekers when offered the same choice in a different setting. For example, most people will display risk-averse behavior by rejecting a fair gamble in favor of a certain gain. However, when the choice involves a fair gamble and a certain loss, most people display risk-seeking behavior by choosing the gamble over the certain loss, even though the risky choice may well result in an even greater loss.

The valuation of a risky alternative appears to depend more on the reference point from which a possible gain or loss will occur, than on the absolute gain to be realized. That is, the decision maker is motivated not by the absolute performance of a particular alternative, but whether that alternative will perform better or worse relative to a specific reference point. Consequently, decision makers can be easily influenced by shifting reference points.

DECISIONS BASED ON PRINCIPLES

Principled decision making can be a useful complement or alternative to analytical decision making. Principled decision making may or may not involve ethics. Ethical decision making uses ethical (moral) principles to make decisions, while principled decision making can employ all kinds of principles (i.e., including potentially unethical principles or decisions that lead to unethical outcomes). While not widely used, principled decision making is sometimes used by investment managers to manage risk and uncertain investments. Risk and portfolio managers may turn to principled decision making for complex risk management problems that cannot be modeled or solved.

Principled decision making emphasizes the process of decision making, with the end results of the decision being of secondary concern. It is essentially a two-step process, with the first step being to select and communicate the right principles to which decisions must adhere. The second step requires the decision maker to apply the appropriate principles. Principled decision making is easy to understand, and the principled decisions are easy to communicate to others in an organization.

Principles can be used to assist analytical decision making. For example, a portfolio manager may use principles as screens to segregate potential investments into acceptable and unacceptable categories. This effectively defines the search dimensions and reduces the sample space. Once principles have been used to reduce a problem to manageable size, then analytical techniques can be employed to make a final selection.

Principled decision making can be applied as an alternative to analytical decision making in such areas as organizational missions, goals, strategies, and codes of conduct. Sears, Roebuck and Co. was founded on the principle that the customer is always right, and that principle has served to guide corporate decisions over the years. Such principles, when used in decision making, can help the organization better cope with changes over time, shifts in leaders, fluctuating leadership styles, and changing market conditions.

THE ROLE OF INFORMATION: DECISION SUPPORT SYSTEMS

Armed with information, managers can make better decisions. Frontline managers, for example, who are supplied with direct activity cost information, can better manage revenues, margins, and costs. Organizations can achieve more consistency between upper management and lower-level managers by providing more information throughout the organization.

With Internet-hosted databases and user-friendly query tools becoming more common, corporations are turning to decision support systems (DSS) software to analyze the firm's databases and turn them into information useful for decision makers. DSS typically includes analytical and report-writing features, thus enabling users to translate raw data into a form useful for decision support.

Decision support technology is a relatively new development in software and may not yet be a high priority with the firm's information technology (IT) department. DSS, which offers users more flexible programming paradigms, can be compared to another type of software, enterprise resource planning (ERP), which enhances productivity by accelerating routine operations. DSS, on the other hand, slices and dices data that may be novel and complex into understandable chunks to facilitate shared consideration of multiple criteria.

One DSS technique is called analytic hierarchy process (AHP), which enables users to attack complex problems by reducing them to simpler pairwise comparisons between different combinations of options and criteria. When people are able to choose between pairs of options, their decisions are made more quickly and consistently than when larger sets of options must be considered. AHP was invented by Thomas Saaty, who cofounded Expert Choice Inc. (http://www.expertchoice.com) to provide AHP-related software and services.

DSS can result in significant time savings as well as improved decision making. Home products retailer Payless Cashways reported that its DSS software enabled it to realize a 70 percent time reduction in information and report gathering and a 30 percent rise in user productivity, along with reduced training time and better decisions on marketing, staffing, and warehousing. The company used DSS to extract and sort information related to sales volume, category performance, comparable-store sales, and in-stock figures.

DSS can speed collaboration when there are several decision makers who must be satisfied. By providing multiple users with access to the firm's data, DSS can clarify the decision-making process and enhance consistency among multiple decision makers. With electronic commerce competitors responding to strategic decisions within days or even hours, the speed with which decisions are made becomes more critical. DSS helps decision makers consider a wider range of alternatives in a shorter period of time. When more consideration is given to the probability and value of the competition's response, strategic decision making becomes more like game theory.

STRATEGIC DECISION MAKING

Strategic decisions are those that affect the direction of the firm. These major decisions concern areas such as new products and markets, acquisitions and mergers, subsidiaries and affiliates, joint ventures and strategic alliances, and other matters. Strategic decision making is usually conducted by the firm's top management, led by the CEO or president of the company.

In markets characterized by extreme competition and a rapid pace of change, companies are being forced to compete on the edge. Their strategic thinking can no longer be limited to identifying promising industries, core competencies, and strategic positions. Rather, top management is engaged in creating a continuing flow of temporary and shifting competitive advantages relative to other competitors and the market being served. As a result, greater emphasis is placed on efficient strategic decision making to create effective strategies.

Kathleen M. Eisenhardt, professor of strategy and organization at Stanford University, studied the strategic decision-making processes at different companies in high-velocity markets. Strategic decision makers at more effective firms were able to make quick, high-quality decisions that were widely supported throughout the firm. Her studies identified four areas in which effective strategic decision makers outperformed counterparts at less effective firms: (1) building collective intuition, (2) stimulating conflict, (3) maintaining a pace or schedule for decision making, and (4) defusing political behavior.

PREDICTIVE MARKETS

Also termed "betting markets" or "idea markets," prediction markets emerged during 2004 as a way to assess consensus opinion about questions of importance to corporate decision makers. As discussed by James M. Pethokoukis in *U.S. News & World Report,* companies such as Hewlett-Packard and Dentsu were exploring use of prediction markets to forecast corporate figures such as revenues, advertising demand, consumer trends, and employee retention. These markets enable companies to determine what products or decisions are more likely to be successful and where to focus resources. Firms were still researching how well this works and where it could best be applied. A senior manager at Dentsu explained, "The key value we see is that prediction markets have the potential to extract the best essence from group knowledge, as an alternative to majority decisions."

BUILDING COLLECTIVE INTUITION

Effective decision makers built a collective intuition by sharing information at "must-attend" meetings. They reviewed internal and external information, preferring real-time operational information over accounting-based data. At one firm each top manager was responsible for gathering and reporting data from a particular area. The managers gained an enhanced understanding of the data by discussing it from different perspectives at these meetings. The meetings also gave them a chance to get to know one another better, leading to open and direct interactions.

STIMULATING CONFLICT

Many decision makers tend to avoid conflict, fearing it will bog down the decision-making process and degenerate into personal attacks. However, Eisenhardt's studies found that in dynamic markets, conflict is a natural feature where reasonable managers will often diverge in assessments of how a market will develop. She found that conflict stimulates innovative thinking, creates a fuller understanding of options, and improves decision effectiveness. Without conflict, decision makers often overlooked key elements of a decision and missed opportunities to question assumptions.

Executives accelerated conflict by forming diverse executive teams made up of individuals who differed in age, gender, functional background, and corporate experience. Other techniques that can introduce conflict quicker include scenario planning, where teams systematically consider strategic decisions in light of several possible futures, and role playing, where executives advocate alternatives that they may or may not favor and play the role of competitors. Debate is encouraged and conflict stimulated when as broad a range of alternatives as possible is presented for discussion.

MAINTAINING A SCHEDULE

Strategic decision makers are faced with a dilemma when they feel that every strategic decision they make is unique, yet they feel pressured to make decisions as quickly as possible. Effective decision makers overcome this dilemma by focusing on the pace of decision making, not the speed with which a decision is made. By using general rules of thumb regarding how long a particular type of decision should take, they maintain decision-making momentum by launching the decision-making process promptly, keeping up the energy surrounding the process, and cutting off debate at the appropriate time.

In order to keep to a specific time frame, executives can alter or adjust the scope of a particular decision to fit the allotted timeframe by viewing it as part of a larger web of strategic choices. Eisenhardt's studies found that effective decision makers followed the natural rhythm of strategic choice. The rule for how long major decisions should take was a fairly constant two to four months. Decisions that would take less time were considered not important enough for the executive team, while those that appeared to take longer involved either too big an issue or management procrastination. By recognizing similarities among strategic decisions, such as those involving new products, new technologies, or acquisitions, executives could more easily gauge the scale of a decision.

One of the most effective methods for cutting off debate was a two-step method called "consensus with qualification." The decision-making process is conducted with consensus as a goal. If consensus is achieved, then the decision is made. However, if there is no consensus, then the deadlock can be broken by using a decision rule such as voting or, more commonly, letting the executive with the largest stake in the outcome make the final decision. By taking a realistic view of conflict as both valuable and inevitable, consensus with qualification helps maintain the pace of decision making. It helps managers plan progress and emphasizes that keeping to schedule is more important than forging consensus or developing massive data analyses.

DEFUSING POLITICS

The high stakes of strategic decision making can quickly turn the decision-making process into one of competition among ambitious managers. While less effective strategic decision makers view politics as a natural part of the decision-making process, effective strategic decision makers take a negative view of politicking. They not only see it as wasting valuable time, it can distort the information base, since politicking managers will tend to use information to their own advantage.

Politicking can be defused by emphasizing a collaborative, rather than competitive, environment, and by creating common goals. Rather than implying homogeneous thinking, common goals suggest that managers have a shared vision of where they want to be or who external competitors are. A balanced power structure, in which each key decision maker has a clear area of responsibility and the leader is recognized as the most powerful decision maker, can also defuse politicking among executives. The clear delineation of responsibility facilitates information sharing and other interaction, because each executive is operating from a secure power base. Finally, humor can defuse politicking and help build a collaborative outlook.

AN EIGHT-STEP APPROACH TO MAKING BETTER DECISIONS

The following list is adapted from Smart Choices by Hammond, et al.:

1. Work on the right decision problem. Be careful in stating the problem, and avoid unwarranted assumptions and option-limiting prejudices.

2. Specify your objectives. Determine what you want to accomplish, and which of your interests, values, concerns, fears, and aspirations are the most relevant.

3. Create imaginative alternatives. Alternatives represent different courses of action, and your decision can be no better than your best alternative.

4. Understand the consequences. Determine how well different alternatives satisfy all of your objectives.

5. Grapple with your tradeoffs. Since objectives frequently conflict with each other, it becomes necessary to choose among less-than-perfect possibilities.

6. Clarify your uncertainties. Confront uncertainty by judging the likelihood of different outcomes and assessing their possible impacts.

7. Think hard about your risk tolerance. In order to choose an alternative with an acceptable level of risk, become conscious of how much risk you can tolerate.

8. Consider linked decisions. Many important decisions are linked over time. The key to making a series of decisions is to isolate and resolve near-term issues while gathering information relevant to issues that will arise later.

SEE ALSO: Decision Rules and Decision Analysis; Decision Support Systems

David P. Bianco
Revised by Wendy H. Mason

FURTHER READING:

Amar, A.D. "Principled Versus Analytical Decision-Making: Definitive Optimization." *Mid-Atlantic Journal of Business,* June 1995, 119.

Crainer, Stuart. "The 75 Greatest Management Decisions Ever Made." *Management Review,* November 1998, 16.

Drucker, Peter F. "What Makes an Effective Executive." *Harvard Business Review,* 1 June 2004.

"Effective Executives Follow Eight Practices." *Association Management,* September 2004, 23.

Eisenhardt, Kathleen M. "Strategy as Strategic Decision Making." *Sloan Management Review,* Spring 1998, 65.

Ettore, Barbara. "Absolutely Great Decisions." *Management Review,* November 1998, 1.

Hammond, John, et al. *Smart Choices: A Practical Guide to Making Better Decisions.* Boston: Harvard Business School Press, 1999.

Hammond, John S., et al. "The Hidden Traps in Decision Making." *Harvard Business Review,* September-October 1998, 47.

Pethokoukis, James M. "All Seeing All Knowing (Creating Futures Markets to Aid in Corporate Decision Making)." *U.S. News & World Report,* 30 August 2004, 54.

Phillips-Wren, Gloria E., Eugene D. Hahn, and Guisseppi A. Forgionne. "A Multiple-Criteria Framework for Evaluation of Decision Support Systems." *Omega,* August 2004, 323.

DECISION RULES AND DECISION ANALYSIS

A decision rule is a logical statement of the type "if [condition], then [decision]." The following is an example of a decision rule experts might use to determine an investment quality rating:

If the year's margin is at least 4.27 percent and the year's ratio of shareholder funds to fixed assets is at least 35.2 percent, then the class of rating is at least lower investment grade (LIG).

The condition in this decision rule is "the year's margin is at least 4.27 percent and the year's ratio of shareholder funds to fixed assets is at least 35.2 percent," while "the class of rating is at least lower investment grade" is the decision part of the rule.

Decision rules give a synthetic, easily understandable, and generalized representation of the knowledge contained in a data set organized in an information table. The table's rows are labeled by objects, whereas columns are labeled by attributes; entries in the body of the table are thus attribute values. If the objects are exemplary decisions given by a decision maker, then the decision rules represent the preferential attitude of the decision maker and enable understanding of the reasons for his or her preference.

People make decisions by searching for rules that provide good justification of their own choices. However, a direct statement of decision rules requires a great cognitive effort from the decision maker, who typically is more confident making exemplary decisions than explaining them. For this reason, the idea of inferring preference models in terms of decision rules from exemplary decisions provided by the decision maker is very attractive. The induction of rules from examples is a typical approach of artificial intelligence. It is concordant with the principle of posterior rationality, and with aggregation-disaggregation logic. The recognition of the rules by the decision maker justifies their use as a powerful decision support tool for decision making concerning new objects.

There are many applications of decision rules in business and finance, including:

- Credit card companies use decision rules to approve credit card applications.

- Retailers use associative rules to understand customers' habits and preferences (market basket analysis) and apply the finding to launch effective promotions and advertising.

- Banks use decision rules induced from data about bankrupt and non-bankrupt firms to support credit granting decisions.

- Telemarketing and direct marketing companies use decision rules to reduce the number of calls made and increase the ratio of successful calls.

Other applications of decision rules exist in the airline, manufacturing, telecommunications, and insurance industries.

DESCRIBING AND COMPARING INFORMATION ATTRIBUTES

The examples (information) from which decision rules are induced are expressed in terms of some characteristic attributes. For instance, companies could be described by the following attributes: sector of activity, localization, number of employees, total assets, profit, and risk rating. From the viewpoint of conceptual content, attributes can be of one of the following types:

- Qualitative attributes (symbolic, categorical, or nominal), including sector of activity or localization

- Quantitative attributes, including number of employees or total assets

- Criteria or attributes whose domains are preferentially ordered, including profit, because a company having large profit is preferred to a company having small profit or even loss

The objects are compared differently depending on the nature of the attributes considered. More precisely, with respect to qualitative attributes, the objects are compared on the basis of an indiscernibility relation: two objects are indiscernible if they have the same evaluation with respect to the considered attributes. The indiscernibility relation is reflexive (i.e., each object is indiscernible with itself), symmetric (if object A is indiscernible with object B, then object B

also is indiscernible with object A), and transitive (if object A is indiscernible with object B and object B is indiscernible with object C, then object A also is indiscernible with object C). Therefore, the indiscernibility relation is an equivalence relation.

With respect to quantitative attributes, the objects are compared on the basis of a similarity relation. The similarity between objects can be defined in many different ways. For example, if the evaluations with respect to the considered attribute are positive, then the following statement may define similarity:

$$\frac{\text{Evaluation of A} - \text{Evaluation of B}}{\text{Evaluation of B}} \leq \text{Threshold}$$

For instance, with respect to the attribute "number of employees," fixing a threshold at 10 percent, Company A having 2,710 employees is similar to Company B having 3,000 employees. Similarity relation is reflexive, but neither symmetric nor transitive; the abandon of the transitivity requirement is easily justifiable, remembering, for example, Luce's paradox of the cups of tea (Luce, 1956). As for the symmetry, one should notice that the proposition yRx, which means "y is similar to x," is directional; there is a subject y and a referent x, and in general this is not equivalent to the proposition "x is similar to y."

With respect to criteria, the objects are compared on the basis of a dominance relation built using outranking relations on each considered criterion: object A outranks object B with respect to a given criterion if object A is at least as good as object B with respect to this criterion; if object A outranks object B with respect to all considered criteria then object A dominates object B. An outranking relation can be defined in many different ways. Oftentimes, it is supposed that outranking is a complete preorder (i.e., transitive and strongly complete). For each couple of objects, say object A and object B, at least one of the following two conditions is always verified: object A outranks object B and/or object B outranks object A. A dominance relation, built on the basis of the outranking relation being a complete preorder, is a partial preorder (i.e., it is reflexive and transitive, but in general not complete).

DECISION RULE SYNTAX

The syntax of decision rules is different according to the specific decision problem. The following decision problems are most frequently considered:

- Classification

- Sorting

- Choice

- Ranking

Following is a presentation of the syntax of decision rules considered within each one of the above decision problems.

CLASSIFICATION. Classification concerns an assignment of a set of objects to a set of predefined but non-ordered classes. A typical example of classification is the problem of market segmentation; in general there is no preference order between the different segments. The objects are described by a set of (regular) attributes that can be qualitative or quantitative. The syntax of decision rules specifies the condition part and the decision part.

With respect to the condition part, the following types of decision rules can be distinguished:

1. Decision rules based on qualitative attributes: "if the value of attribute q_1 is equal to r_{q1} and the value of attribute q_2 is equal to r_{q2} and . . . and the value of attribute q_p is equal to r_{qp}, then [decision]," where $r_{q1}, r_{q2}, \ldots, r_{qp}$ are possible values of considered attributes.

2. Decision rules based on quantitative attributes: "if the value of attribute q_1 is similar to r_{q1} and the value of attribute q_2 is similar to r_{q2} and . . . and the value of attribute q_p is similar to r_{qp}, then [decision]," where $r_{q1}, r_{q2}, \ldots, r_{qp}$ are possible values of considered attributes.

3. Decision rules based on qualitative and quantitative attributes: "if the value of attribute q_1 is equal to r_{q1} and the value of attribute q_2 is equal to r_{q2} and . . . and the value of attribute q_t is equal to r_{qt} and the value of attribute q_{t+1} is similar to r_{qt+1} and the value of attribute q_{t+2} is similar to r_{qt+2} and . . . and the value of attribute q_p is similar to r_{qp}, then [decision]," where $q_1 \, q_2 \ldots, q_t$ are qualitative attributes, $q_{t+1}, q_{t+2}, \ldots, q_p$ are quantitative attributes, and $r_{q1}, r_{q2}, \ldots, r_{qp}$ are possible values of considered attributes.

With respect to the decision part, the following types of decision rules can be distinguished:

1. Exact decision rule: "if [condition], then the object belongs to Y_j," where Y_j is a decision class of the considered classification.

2. Approximate decision rule: "if [condition], then the object belongs to Y_{j1} or Y_{j2} or . . . Y_{jk}," where $Y_{j1}, Y_{j2}, \ldots, Y_{jk}$ are some decision classes of the considered classification.

3. Possible decision rule: "if [condition], then the object could belong to Y_j," where Y_j is a decision class of the considered classification.

SORTING. Sorting concerns an assignment of a set of objects to a set of predefined and preference ordered classes. The classes are denoted by Cl_1 Cl_2 and so on,

and we suppose that they are preferentially ordered such that the higher the number the better the class (i.e., the elements of class Cl_2 have a better comprehensive evaluation than the elements of class Cl_1 the elements of class Cl_3 have a better comprehensive evaluation than the elements of class Cl_2 and so on. For example, in a problem of bankruptcy risk evaluation, Cl_1 is the set of unacceptable-risk firms, Cl_2 is a set of high-risk firms, Cl_3 is a set of medium-risk firms, and so on. The objects are evaluated by a set of attributes that generally include criteria and qualitative and/or quantitative (regular) attributes. The syntax of the condition depends on the type of attributes used for object description. If there are criteria only, then the following types of decision rules can be distinguished:

1. Exact D≥ decision rule: "if evaluation with respect to criterion q_1 is at least as good as r_{q1} and evaluation with respect to criterion q_2 is at least as good as r_{q2} and . . . evaluation with respect to criterion q_p is at least as good as r_{qp}, then the object belongs to at least class t," where $r_{q1}, r_{q2}, \ldots, r_{qp}$ are possible values of considered criteria.

2. Exact D≤ decision rule: "if evaluation with respect to criterion q_1 is at most as good as r_{q1} and evaluation with respect to criterion q_2 is at most as good as r_{q2} and . . . evaluation with respect to criterion q_p is at most as good as r_{qp}, then the object belongs to at most class t," where $r_{q1}, r_{q2}, \ldots, r_{qp}$ are possible values of considered criteria.

3. Approximate D≥≤ decision rule: "if evaluation with respect to criterion q_1 is at least as good as r_{q1} and evaluation with respect to criterion q_2 is at least as good as r_{q2} and . . . evaluation with respect to criterion q_h is at least as good as r_{qh} and evaluation with respect to criterion q_{h+1} is at most as good as r_{qh+1} and evaluation with respect to criterion q_{h+2} is at most as good as r_{qh+2} and . . . evaluation with respect to criterion q_p is at most as good as r_{qp}, then the object belongs to at least class t and at most to class t" where criteria $q_1 \, q_2 \ldots, q_k$ are not necessarily different from $q_{k+1}, q_{k+2}, \ldots, q_p$ and $r_{q1}, r_{q2}, \ldots, r_{qp}$ are possible values of considered criteria.

4. Possible D≥ decision rule: "if evaluation with respect to criterion q_1 is at least as good as r_{q1} and evaluation with respect to criterion q_2 is at least as good as r_{q2} and . . . evaluation with respect to criterion q_p is at least as good as r_{qp}, then the object could belong to at least class t," where $r_{q1}, r_{q2}, \ldots, r_{qp}$ are possible values of considered criteria.

5. Possible D≤ decision rule: "if evaluation with respect to criterion q_1 is at most as good as r_{q1} and evaluation with respect to criterion q_2 is at most as good as r_{q2} and . . . evaluation with respect to criterion q_p is at most as good as r_{qp}, then the object could belong to at most class t," where $r_{q1}, r_{q2}, . . ., r_{qp}$ are possible values of considered criteria.

CHOICE AND RANKING. Choice concerns selecting a small subset of best objects from a larger set, while ranking concerns ordering objects of a set from the best to the worst. In these two decision problems, the objects are evaluated by criteria and the decision is based on pairwise (relative) comparison of objects rather than on absolute evaluation of single objects. In other words, in these two cases the decision rules relate preferences on particular criteria with a comprehensive preference. The preferences can be expressed on cardinal scales or on ordinal scales: the former deal with strength of preferences and use relations like indifference, weak preference, preference, strong preference, absolute preference, while for the later the strength is meaningless.

Given objects x, y, w and z, and using a cardinal scale of preference, it always is possible to compare the strength of preference of x over y with the strength of preference of w over z and say whether the preference of x over y is stronger than, equal to, or weaker than the preference of w over z. Using an ordinal scale, the strengths of preference can be compared only if, with respect to the considered criterion, object x is at least as good as w and z is at least as good as y. Given an example of car selection, for any decision maker car x, with a maximum speed 200 kilometers per hour (124.28 miles per hour) is preferred to car y, with a maximum speed of 120 kilometers per hour (74.57 miles per hour) at least as much as car w, with a maximum speed 170 kilometers per hour (105.64 miles per hour) is preferred to car z, with a maximum speed 140 kilometers per hour (87 miles per hour). This is because it is always preferable to pass from a smaller maximum speed (car y versus z) to a larger maximum speed (car x versus w). The syntax of the decision rules in the choice and ranking problems depends on the distinction between cardinal and ordinal criteria:

1. Exact D≥ decision rule: "if with respect to cardinal criterion q 1, x is preferred to y with at least strength $h(q$ 1) and . . . and with respect to cardinal criterion qe, x is preferred to y with at least strength $h(qe)$ and with respect to ordinal criterion $qe + 1$, evaluation of x is at least as good as r_{qe+1} and evaluation of y is at most as good as s_{qe+1} and . . . and with respect to ordinal criterion q_{p+1}, evaluation of x is at least as good as r_{qp+1} and evaluation of y is at most as good as s_{qp+1}, then x is at least as good as y," where $h(q$ 1), . . ., $h(qe)$

are possible strengths of preferences of considered criteria and $r_{qe+1}, . . ., r_{qp}$, and $s_{qe+1}, . . ., s_{qp}$ are possible values of considered criteria. A more concise illustration: "if with respect to comfort (cardinal criterion) car x is at least strongly preferred to car y and car x has a maximum speed (ordinal criterion) of at least 200 kilometers per hour (124.28 miles per hour) and car y has a maximum speed of 160 kilometers per hour (99.42 miles per hour), then car x is at least as good as car y."

2. Exact D≤ decision rule: "if with respect to cardinal criterion q 1, x is preferred to y with at most strength $h(q$ 1) and . . . and with respect to cardinal criterion qe, x is preferred to y with at most strength $h(qe)$ and with respect to ordinal criterion $qe + 1$, evaluation of x is at most as good as r_{qe+1} and evaluation of y is at least as good as s_{qe+1} and . . . and with respect to ordinal criterion qp, evaluation of x is at most as good as r_{qp} and evaluation of y is at least as good as s_{qp+1}, then x is not at least as good as y," where $h(q$ 1), . . ., $h(qe)$ are possible strengths of preferences of considered criteria and $r_{qe+1}, . . ., r_{qp}$, and $s_{qe+1}, . . ., s_{qp}$ are possible values of considered criteria. An example of a D≤ decision rule: "if with respect to aesthetics (cardinal criterion) car x is at most indifferent with car y and car x consumes (ordinal criterion) at most 7.2 liters (1.90 gallons) of fuel per 100 kilometers (62.14 miles) and car y consumes at least at 7.5 liters (1.98 gallons) of fuel per 100 kilometers (62.14 miles), then car x is at most as good as car y."

3. Approximate D≥≤ decision rule: the "if" condition has the syntax composed of the "if" parts of the D≥ rule and the D≤ rule. The "then" decision represents a hesitation: "x is at least as good as y" or "x is not at least as good as y."

Using decision rules, it always is possible to represent all common decision policies. For instance, let us consider the lexicographic ordering: the criteria considered are ranked from the most important to the least important. Between two objects, the object preferred with respect to the most important criterion is preferred to the other; if there is an *ex aequo* (a tie) on the most important criterion, then the object preferred with respect to the second criterion is selected; if there is again an *ex aequo*, then the third most important criterion is considered, and so on. If there is an *ex aequo* on all the considered criteria, then the two objects are indifferent. The lexicographic ordering can be represented by means of the following D≤ decision rules:

1. If x is (at least) preferred to y with respect to criterion q 1, then x is preferred to y.

2. If x is (at least) indifferent with y with respect to criterion q 1 and x is (at least) preferred to y with respect to criterion q 2, then x is preferred to y.

3. If x is (at least) indifferent with y with respect to all the considered criteria except the last one and x is (at least) preferred to y with respect to criterion qn, then x is preferred to y.

4. If x is (at least) indifferent with y with respect to all the considered criteria, then x is indifferent to y.

Induction of decision rules from information tables is a complex task and a number of procedures have been proposed in the context of such areas like machine learning, data mining, knowledge discovery, and rough sets theory. The existing induction algorithms use one of the following strategies: (a) generation of a minimal set of rules covering all objects from a information table; (b) generation of an exhaustive set of rules consisting of all possible rules for a information table; (c) generation of a set of "strong" decision rules, even partly discriminant, covering relatively many objects each but not necessarily all objects from the information table.

CREDIBILITY OF DECISION RULES

Decision rules also can be considered from the viewpoint of their credibility. From this point of view, the following classes of decision rules can be distinguished:

1. Crisp, exact decision rules (i.e., the rules presented above whose "then" part is univocal).

2. Crisp, approximate decision rules, induced from an inconsistent part of a data set identified using the rough sets theory; the "then" part of approximate decision rules specifies several possible decisions that cannot be reduced to a single one due to inconsistent information.

3. Possible decision rules covering objects that may belong to the class suggested in the "then" part; the objects that may belong to a class are identified using the rough sets theory as objects belonging to so-called upper approximation of the class.

4. Fuzzy decision rules induced from a vague or imprecise data set using the fuzzy sets theory. Informally, a fuzzy set may be regarded as a class of objects for which there is a graduality of progression from membership to nonmembership: an object may have a grade of membership intermediate between one (full membership) and zero (nonmembership).

5. Probabilistic decision rules covering objects from the class suggested in the "then" part (positive objects), but also objects from other classes (negative objects); the ratio between the positive objects and the negative objects should be at least equal to a given threshold.

APPLICATIONS

Decision rules have been used for description of many specific decision policies, in particular for description of customers' decisions. The most well known decision rules of this type are the association rules, whose syntax is the following: for p percent of times if items $x_1 x_2 \ldots, x_n$ were bought, then items $y_1 y_2 \ldots, y_m$ were bought as well, and q percent of times $x_1 x_2 \ldots, x_n, y_1 y_2 \ldots, y_m$ were bought together. For example, 50 percent of people who bought diapers also bought beer; diapers and beer were bought in 2 percent of all transactions.

The following example illustrates the most important concepts introduced above. In Table 1, six companies are described by means of four attributes:

Warehouse	Attributes			
	A_1	A_2	A_3	A_4
C1	high	700	A	profit
C2	high	420	A	loss
C3	medium	530	B	profit
C4	medium	500	B	loss
C5	low	400	A	loss
C6	low	100	B	loss

Table 1
Sample Information Table

- A_1 capacity of the management
- A_2 number of employees
- A_3 localization
- A_4 company profit or loss

The objective is to induce decision rules explaining profit or loss on the basis of attributes $A_1 A_2$ and A_3 Let us observe that:

- Attribute A_1 is a criterion, because the evaluation with respect to the capacity of the management is preferentially ordered (high is better than medium and medium is better than low).

- Attribute A_2 is a quantitative attribute, because the values of the number of employees are not preferentially ordered (neither the high number of employees is generally better than the small number, nor the inverse). Similarity between companies is defined as follows: Company A is similar to Company B with respect to the attribute "number of employees" if:

$$\frac{\text{Employees of A} - \text{Employees of B}}{\text{Employees of B}} \leq 10\%$$

- Attribute A_3 is a qualitative attribute, because there is not a preferential order between types of localization: two companies are indiscernible with respect to localization if they have the same localization.

- Decision classes defined by attribute A_4 are preferentially ordered (trivially, profit is better than loss).

From Table 1, several decision rules can be induced. The following set of decision rules cover all the examples (within parentheses there are companies supporting the decision rule):

Rule 1. If the quality of the management is medium, then the company may have a profit or a loss (C3, C4).

Rule 2. If the quality of the management is (at least) high and the number of employees is similar to 700, then the company makes a profit (C1).

Rule 3. If the quality of the management is (at most) low, then the company has a loss (C5, C6).

Rule 4. If the number of employees is similar to 420 and the localization is B, then the company has a loss (C2).

Decision rules are based on elementary concepts and mathematical tools (sets and set operations, binary relations), without recourse to any algebraic or analytical structures. Principal relations involved in the construction of decision rules, like indiscernibility, similarity, and dominance, are natural and non-questioned on practical grounds. Decision rule representation of knowledge is not a "black box," or arcane methodology, because the rules represent relevant information contained in data sets in a natural and comprehensible language, and examples supporting each rule are identifiable. Because contemporary decision problems are associated with larger and larger data sets, induction of decision rules showing the most important part of the available information is increasingly in demand.

SEE ALSO: Decision Making; Decision Support Systems

Salvatore Greco, Benedetto Matarazzo, and Roman Slowinski

Revised by Wendy H. Mason

FURTHER READING:

Agrawal, Rakesh., Tomasz Imielinski, and Arun Swami. "Mining Association Rules Between Sets of Items in Large Databases." In *Proceedings of the 1993 ACM SIGMOD International Conference on Management of Data.* New York: ACM Press, 1993.

Greco, S., B. Matarazzo, and R. Slowinski. "The Use of Rough Sets and Fuzzy Sets in MCDM." In *Advances in Multiple Criteria Decision Making.* ed. T. Gal, T. Hanne, and T. Stewart. Dordrecht/Boston: Kluwer Academic Publishers, 1999.

Hu, Xiaohua, T.Y. Lin, and Eric Louie. "Bitmap Techniques for Optimizing Decision Support Queries and Association Rule Algorithms." *Proceedings of the 2003 International Database Engineering and Applications Symposium.* Hong Kong: SAR, July 2003.

Luce, R.D. "Semi-Orders and a Theory of Utility Discrimination." *Econometrica* 24 (1956): 178–191.

March, J.G. "Bounded Rationality, Ambiguity, and the Engineering of Choice." In *Decision Making: Descriptive, Normative, and Prescriptive Interactions.* ed. David E. Bell, Howard Raiffa, and Amos Tversky. Cambridge New York: Cambridge University Press, 1988.

Michalski, R.S., Ivan Bratko, and Miroslav Kubat, eds. *Machine Learning and Data Mining: Methods and Applications.* Chichester: J. Wiley & Sons, 1998.

Pawlak, Zdzislaw. *Rough Sets: Theoretical Aspects of Reasoning about Data.* Dordrecht/Boston: Kluwer Academic Publishers, 1991.

Pawlak, Zdzislaw, and Roman Slowinski. "Rough Set Approach to Multi-Attribute Decision Analysis." *European Journal of Operational Research* 72 (1994): 443–459.

Peterson, Martin. "Transformative Decision Rules." *Erkenntnis* 58, no. 1 (2003): 71–85.

Slovic, P. "Choice Between Equally Valued Alternatives." *Journal of Experimental Psychology, Human Perception and Performance* 1, no. 3 (1975): 280–287.

Slowinski, R. "Rough Set Processing of Fuzzy Information." In *Soft Computing: Rough Sets, Fuzzy Logic, Neural Networks,*

Uncertainty Management, Knowledge Discovery. ed. T.Y. Lin and A. Wildberger. San Diego: Simulation Councils Inc., 1995.

Slowinski, Roman, ed. *Fuzzy Sets in Decision Analysis, Operations Research, and Statistics.* Dordrecht/Boston: Kluwer Academic Publishers, 1998.

Slowinski, R., and J. Stefanowski. "Handling Various Types of Uncertainty in the Rough Set Approach." In *Rough Sets, Fuzzy Sets and Knowledge Discovery.* ed. W.P. Ziarko. London: Springer-Verlag, 1994.

Stefanowski, J. "On Rough Set Based Approaches to Induction of Decision Rules." In *Rough Sets in Data Mining and Knowledge Discovery, Vol. 1.* ed. L. Polkowski and A. Skowron. Heidelberg: Physica-Verlag, 1998.

Tversky, A. "Features of Similarity." *Psychological Review* 84, no. 4 (1977): 327–352.

Zadeh, Lofti. "Fuzzy Sets." *Journal of Information and Control* 8 (1965): 338–353.

DECISION SUPPORT SYSTEMS

Decision support systems (DSS) are computer information systems that perform complex data analysis in order to help users make informed decisions. In general, a DSS retrieves information from a large data warehouse, analyzes it in accordance with user specifications, then publishes the results in a format that users can readily understand and use. DSS find application in a wide range of business settings, including investment portfolio management.

Portfolio management is one of the most essential problems in modern financial theory. It involves the construction of a portfolio of securities (stocks, bonds, treasury bills, etc.) that maximizes the investor's utility. The process leading to the construction of such a portfolio consists of two major steps. In the first step the decision-maker (investor, portfolio manager) has to evaluate the securities that are available as investment instruments. The vast number of available securities, especially in the case of stocks, makes this step necessary, in order to focus the analysis on a limited number of the best investment choices. Thus, on the basis of this evaluation stage the decision-maker selects a small number of securities that constitute the best investment opportunities. In the second step of the process the decision maker must decide on the amount of the available capital that should be invested in each security, thus constructing a portfolio of the selected securities. The portfolio should be constructed in accordance with the decision-maker's investment policy and risk tolerance.

The portfolio theory assumes that the decision-maker's judgment and investment policy can be represented by a utility function that is implicitly used by the decision-maker in making his investment decisions. Thus, the maximization of this utility function will result in the construction of a portfolio that is as consistent as possible with the decision-maker's expectations and investment policy. However, it is quite difficult to determine the specific form of this utility function.

The founder of portfolio theory, Nobelist Harry Markowitz, has developed a framework according to which the decision-maker's utility is a function of two variables, the expected return of the portfolio and its risk. Thus, he formulated the maximization of the decision-maker's utility as a two-objective problem: maximizing the expected return of the portfolio and minimizing the corresponding risk. To consider the return and the risk, Markowitz used two well-known statistical measures, the *mean* of all possible returns to estimate the return of the portfolio, and the *variance* to measure its risk. On the basis of this mean-variance framework, Markowitz has developed a mathematical framework to identify the efficient set of portfolios that maximizes returns at any given level of allowable risk. Given the risk aversion policy of the investor, it is possible to select the most appropriate portfolio from the efficient set.

This pioneering work of Markowitz motivated financial researchers to develop new portfolio management techniques, and significant contributions have been made over the last decades. The most significant of the approaches that have been proposed for portfolio management include the capital asset pricing model (CAPM), the arbitrage pricing theory (APT), single and multi index models, as well as several optimization techniques. Elton and Gruber's 1995 book *Modern Portfolio Theory and Investment Analysis* provides a comprehensive discussion of the various approaches.

DECISION SUPPORT SYSTEMS IN PORTFOLIO MANAGEMENT

The concept of decision support systems (DSS) was introduced, from a theoretical point of view, in the late 1960s. DSS can be defined as computer information systems that provide information in a specific problem domain using analytical decision models and techniques, as well as access to databases, in order to support a decision maker in making decisions effectively in complex and ill-structured problems. Thus, the basic goal of DSS is to provide the necessary information to the decision-maker in order to help him or her get a better understanding of the decision environment and the alternatives available.

A typical structure of a DSS includes three main parts: the database, the model base, and the user interface. The database includes all the information and data that are necessary to perform the analysis on the decision problem at hand. Data entry, storage, and retrieval are performed through a database management system. The model base is an arsenal of methods, techniques, and models that can be used to perform the analysis and support the decision-maker. These models or techniques are applied to the raw data in order to produce analysis or more meaningful output for the decision-maker. A model base management system is responsible for performing all tasks that are related to model management, such as model development, updates, storage, and retrieval. Finally, the user interface is responsible for the communication between the user and the system, while it further serves as a link between the database and the model base. The appropriate design of the user interface is a key issue towards the successful implementation of the whole system, so as to ensure that the user can take full advantage of the analytical capabilities that the system provides. Advances in computer hardware and software have enabled user-friendly graphical user interfaces (GUIs) to serve this function.

During the last four decades DSS have been developed and implemented to tackle a variety of real world decision-making problems, including financial problems and portfolio management. The portfolio management process involves the analysis of a vast volume of information and data, including financial, stock market, and macroeconomic data. Analyzing a continuous flow of such a vast amount of information for every available security in order to make real time portfolio management decisions is clearly impossible with out the support of a specifically designed computer system that will facilitate not only the data management process, but also the analysis.

Thus, the contribution of DSS to portfolio management becomes apparent. They provide an integrated tool to perform real-time analyses of portfolio management related data, and provide information according to the decision-maker's preferences. Furthermore, they enable the decision-maker to take full advantage of sophisticated analytic methods, including multivariate statistical and econometric techniques, powerful optimization methods, advanced preference modeling, and multiple-criteria decision-making techniques. DSS incorporating multiple-criteria decision-making methods in their structure are known as multicriteria DSS, and they have found several applications in the field of finance. Zopounidis, Godefroid, and Hurson have presented the methodological framework for the design and development of a multicriteria DSS for portfolio management. The use of such innovative tools in portfolio management decision making, together with the tools provided by the modern portfolio theory (CAPM, APT, etc.), provide the basis for improving the portfolio management process. The

subsequent section illustrates the capabilities that a multicriteria DSS can provide in portfolio management through the presentation of the Investor system.

PORTFOLIO MANAGEMENT DSS IN PRACTICE: AN ILLUSTRATION OF THE INVESTOR SYSTEM

The Investor system is a DSS designed and developed to support the portfolio management process and to help construct portfolios of stocks. The system includes a combination of portfolio theory models, multivariate statistical methods, and multiple criteria decision-making techniques for stock evaluation and portfolio construction. The structure of the system is presented in Figure 1.

FINANCIAL DATA. The database of the system includes four types of information and data. The first involves the financial statements of the firms whose stocks are considered in the portfolio management problem. The balance sheet and the income statement provide valuable information regarding the financial soundness of the firms (e.g., sales, net profit, net worth, liabilities, assets, etc.). The system contains such financial data spanning a five-year period, so that users can reach informed conclusions about the firms' financial evolution.

QUALITATIVE INFORMATION. In addition to these financial data, information on some qualitative factors is also inserted in the database. The management of the firms, their organization, their reputation in the market, their technical facilities, and their market position affect directly the operation and the performance of the firms; thus, they constitute fundamental factors in the analysis of the firms whose stocks that are considered in the portfolio management problem.

MARKET DATA. The third type of information included in the database involves the stocks' market histories. This information involves the stock prices, the marketability of the stocks, their beta coefficient (a measure of risk representing the relationship between the changes in the price of individual stocks with the changes in the market), the dividend yield, the price/earnings ratio, and so forth.

MACROECONOMIC DATA. Finally, information regarding the macroeconomic environment is also included. Inflation, interest rates, exchange rates, and other macroeconomic variables have a direct impact on the performance of the stock market, thus potentially affecting any individual stock. The combination of this information with the financial and stock histories of individual firms enables portfolio managers to perform a global evaluation of the investment opportunities available, both in terms of their sensitivity and

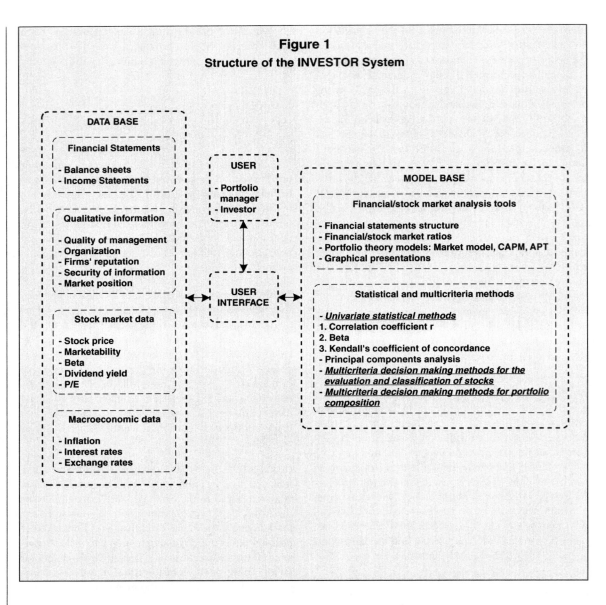

Figure 1
Structure of the INVESTOR System

DATA BASE

Financial Statements

- Balance sheets
- Income Statements

Qualitative information

- Quality of management
- Organization
- Firms' reputation
- Security of information
- Market position

Stock market data

- Stock price
- Marketability
- Beta
- Dividend yield
- P/E

Macroeconomic data

- Inflation
- Interest rates
- Exchange rates

USER

- Portfolio manager
- Investor

USER INTERFACE

MODEL BASE

Financial/stock market analysis tools

- Financial statements structure
- Financial/stock market ratios
- Portfolio theory models: Market model, CAPM, APT
- Graphical presentations

Statistical and multicriteria methods

- *Univariate statistical methods*
1. Correlation coefficient r
2. Beta
3. Kendall's coefficient of concordance
- Principal components analysis
- *Multicriteria decision making methods for the evaluation and classification of stocks*
- *Multicriteria decision making methods for portfolio composition*

risk with respect to the economic environment, and to their individual characteristics.

ANALYSIS TOOLS. The analysis of all this information is performed through the tools incorporated in the system's model base. Two major components can be distinguished in the model base. The first one consists of financial and stock market analysis tools. These can analyze the structure of the financial statements of the firms, calculate financial and stock market ratios, apply well-known portfolio theory models (e.g., the market model, the CAPM, the APT), and present several graphical summaries of the results obtained through these tools to facilitate drawing some initial conclusions about the stocks' performance.

The second component of the model base involves more sophisticated analysis tools, including statistical and multiple-criteria decision-making techniques.

More specifically, univariate statistical techniques are used to measure the stability of the beta coefficient of the stocks, while principal components analysis (a multivariate technique) is used to identify the most significant factors or criteria that describe the performance of the stocks, and to place the stocks into homogeneous groups according to their financial and stock market characteristics. The criteria identified as most crucial can be used to evaluate the stocks and thereby construct a portfolio that meets the investment policy of the investor/portfolio manager. Of course, the portfolio manager interacts with the system, and he or she can also introduce into the analysis the evaluation criteria that he or she considers important, even if these criteria are not found significant by principal components analysis.

The evaluation of the stocks' performance is completed through multiple-criteria decision-making

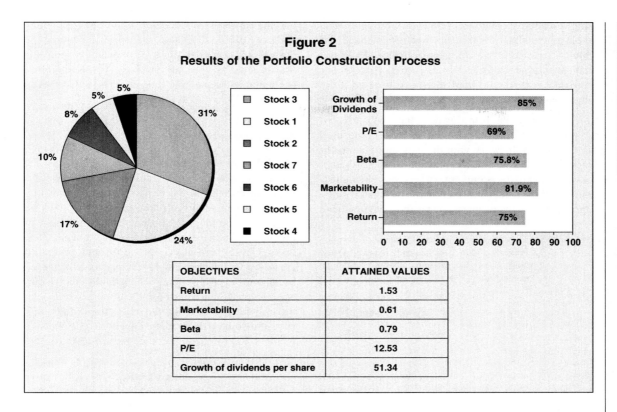

Figure 2
Results of the Portfolio Construction Process

OBJECTIVES	ATTAINED VALUES
Return	1.53
Marketability	0.61
Beta	0.79
P/E	12.53
Growth of dividends per share	51.34

methods. Multiple-criteria decision making is an advanced field of operations research that provides an arsenal of methodological tools and techniques to study real-world decision problems involving multiple criteria that often lead to conflicting results. The multiple-criteria decision-making methods that are incorporated in the model base of the Investor system enable the investor to develop an additive utility function that is fairly consistent with his or her investment policy, preferences, and experience. On the basis of this additive utility function a score (global utility) is estimated for each stock that represents its overall performance with respect to the selected evaluation criteria. The scores of the stocks are used as an index so they may be placed into appropriate classes specified by the user. Thus, the portfolio manager can develop an evaluation model (additive utility function) to distinguish, for instance, among the stocks that constitute the best investment opportunities, the stocks that do not have a medium-long term prospect but they can be considered only for the short run, and the stocks that are too risky and should be avoided. Of course, any other classification can be determined according to the objectives and the policy of the portfolio manager.

On the basis of this classification, the investor/portfolio manager can select a limited number of stocks to include in the actual portfolio, which represent the best investment opportunities. Constructing the portfolio is accomplished through multiple-criteria decision-making techniques that are appropriate for optimizing a set of objective functions subject to some

constraints. The objective functions represent the investor/portfolio manager's objectives on some evaluation criteria (return, beta, marketability, etc.), while constraints can be imposed to ensure that the constructed portfolio meets some basic aspects of the investment policy of the investor/portfolio manager.

For instance, the investor/portfolio manager can introduce constraints on the amount of capital invested in stocks of specific business sectors, the amount of capital invested in high-risk or low-risk stocks (high and low β coefficient, respectively), to determine a minimum level of return or a maximum level of risk, and so on. Once such details are determined, an interactive and iterative optimization procedure is performed that leads to the construction of a portfolio of stocks that meets the investor's investment policy and preferences. The results presented through the screen of Figure 2 show the proportion of each stock in the constructed portfolio, the performance of the portfolio on the specified evaluation criteria (attained values), as well as the rate of closeness (achievement rate) of the performance of the portfolio as opposed to the optimal values on each evaluation criterion (the higher this rate is, the closer the performance of the portfolio to the optimal one for each criterion).

Since the development of the portfolio theory in the 1950s, portfolio management has gained increasing interest within the financial community. Periodic turmoil in stock markets worldwide demonstrates the necessity for developing risk management tools that can be used to analyze the vast volume of information that is available. The DSS framework provides such tools that enable investors and portfolio managers to employ sophisticated techniques from the fields of statistical analysis, econometric analysis, and operations research to make and implement real-time portfolio management decisions.

Recent research in this field has been oriented towards combining the powerful analytical tools used in the DSS framework with the new modeling techniques provided by soft computing technology (neural networks, expert systems, fuzzy sets, etc.) to address the uncertainty, vagueness, and fuzziness that is often encountered in the financial and business environment.

SEE ALSO: Competitive Intelligence; Computer Networks; Computer-Aided Design and Manufacturing; Management Information Systems; Strategic Planning Tools

Constantin Zopounidis and Michael Doumpos
Revised by Laurie Hillstrom

FURTHER READING:

Elton, E.J., and M.J. Gruber. *Modern Portfolio Theory and Investment Analysis.* 5th ed. New York: John Wiley and Sons, 1995.

Markowitz, H. *Portfolio Selection: Efficient Diversification of Investments.* New York: John Wiley and Sons, 1959.

Phillips-Wren, Gloria E., et al., "A Multiple-Criteria Framework for Evaluation of Decision Support Systems." *Omega.* August 2004.

Turban, Efraim, et al. *Decision Support Systems and Intelligent Systems.* 7th ed. Englewood Cliffs, NJ: Prentice Hall, 2004.

Zopounidis, C., M. Godefroid, and C. Hurson. "Designing a Multicriteria DSS for Portfolio Selection and Management." In *Advances in Stochastic Modelling and Data Analysis.* edited by J. Janssen, C.H. Skiadas and C. Zopounidis. Dordrecht, Netherlands: Kluwer Academic Publishers, 1995, 261–292.

DELEGATION

Delegation is the process of giving decision-making authority to lower-level employees. For the process to be successful, a worker must be able to obtain the resources and cooperation needed for successful completion of the delegated task. Empowerment of the workforce and task delegation are closely intertwined. Empowerment occurs when upper-level employees share power with lower-level employees. This involves providing the training, tools and management support that employees need to accomplish a task. Thus, an enabled worker has both the authority and the capability to accomplish the work. Although authority can be delegated, responsibility cannot-the person who delegates a task is ultimately responsible for its success. The assigned worker is therefore accountable for meeting the goals and objectives of the task.

BENEFITS OF DELEGATION

Effective delegation can benefit the manager, the employee, and the organization. Perhaps the most important benefit for the company is a higher quality of work. Delegation can improve quality of work by allowing the employees who have direct knowledge of products and services to make decisions and complete tasks. Quality can also improve through enhanced employee motivation. Employees may do a better job because they feel a personal accountability for the outcome, even though responsibility ultimately rests with the individual who made the delegation. Motivation should also be enhanced as delegation enriches the worker's job by expanding the types of tasks that are involved in it.

Managers who delegate effectively also receive several personal benefits; most importantly, they have more time to do their own jobs when they assign tasks to others. Given the hectic nature of managerial work, time is a precious commodity. Effective delegation frees the manager to focus on managerial tasks such as planning and control. Managers also benefit from the development of subordinates' skills. With a more highly skilled workforce, they have more flexibility in making assignments and are more efficient decision makers. Managers who develop their workforce are also likely to have high personal power with their staff and to be highly valued by their organization.

DRAWBACKS OF DELEGATION

Although delegation can provide benefits to the organization, many managers lack the motivation or knowledge to delegate effectively, and thus delegation (or lack of delegation) may be detrimental to the company. Managers' lack of motivation to delegate may be associated with a number of fallacies associated with delegations. Many managers believe that "if you want it done right, you have to do it yourself." While this is at times untrue, because the ultimate responsibility for a task lies with the manager, this attitude often prevents delegation. Other reasons for a lack of motivation to delegate are lack of trust in subordinates, fear of being seen as lazy, reluctance to take risks, and fear of competition from subordinates. Some of these barriers are correctable through management training and development, but others may not be easily overcome. Mangers may also lack the competencies necessary to delegate effectively. They may choose the wrong tasks to delegate, the wrong subordinate to trust, or they may provide inadequate direction to the subordinate when delegating.

Improper delegation can cause a host of problems, primary of which is an incorrectly completed task, which may hurt the overall productivity of the organization. Additionally, the careers of the manager and subordinate may suffer. The manager is likely to take the blame for delegating the wrong task, delegating to the wrong person, or not providing proper guidance. The subordinate may also take the blame for doing the task incorrectly. Thus, poor delegation may detract from the personal success of managers and employees.

PLANNING

Delegation is not difficult. Anyone can give an assignment to someone. However, effective delegation (assigning a task to the correct person) is a highly skilled process that requires planning, thought, and managerial skill.

DEFINING SUCCESS. Two planning activities should be undertaken before delegating an assignment: defining success and assessing qualifications needed. Defining success requires a determination of what will constitute successful performance on the assigned task. An effective delegator assigns workers to tasks on which they have a high probability of succeeding. If a manager can't identify the successful outcome of a task, how can that manager determine if a worker is capable of performing it? The failure to define success turns delegation into a gamble, rather than a prediction. An effective delegator makes a prediction of success based on the match between job requirements and the worker's competencies. An ineffective delegator hopes that the worker will be successful but really has no basis for this hope, since success has not been defined. If success is well defined and communicated to the subordinate, the worker has a clear understanding of the task requirements and can focus his/her efforts on important activities. Similarly, clearly defining success helps the delegator coach the worker, which further enhances the probability of a positive outcome.

There are two components to defining success. The first is to define the successful outcome of the task, and the second is to determine the appropriate processes needed to complete the task. Both are needed in order to make an effective delegation. For example, a manager might be considering assigning a different salesperson to a particularly difficult client. Prior to making the delegation, the manager should reflect on the desired outcomes from this assignment (e.g., increased sales, decreased complaints) and the types of processes (e.g., better client education,

greater empathy) that might be needed to produce the desired result. Only after understanding what is needed can a rational delegation be made. Thus, managers should first ask themselves: "How will I judge the success of this delegation and what do I expect someone to do to be successful?"

ASSESSING QUALIFICATIONS NEEDED. The second step in planning delegation involves determining subordinate capabilities. There is always a choice in delegation, both as to which subordinates to delegate the assignment to, and whether to delegate the assignment at all. To make either decision, the manager needs to assess subordinate's capabilities. In making the assessment, a manager should ask, "What has this worker done to make me feel he or she will be effective on this assignment?" Managers should also ask themselves, "How do I think this person will perform on this assignment and why do I feel this way?" A worker could be effective in obtaining desired results, but could use an unacceptable process to obtain the results that negates the positive outcomes. Managers are very unlikely to make an accurate prediction of success for an assignment when they have no basis for the prediction. Thus, the better a manager knows a worker's past behaviors and accomplishments, the greater the chance of an effective future delegation. Often, however, managers have to delegate assignments to people who lack the relevant training or experience. The general process still applies in this situation, although the specific questions change. Here, the manager should carefully consider, "How has this person performed on previous assignments where he or she lacked training or experience?" Again, there must be a basis for the delegation, or it becomes a wild guess.

PROCESS

The process of delegation is as critical as the planning, because a poor process can reduce the effectiveness of the delegation in several ways. First, it can lower the worker's motivation to perform the task. A qualified worker who is not motivated to complete the assignment is not likely to produce the desired results. Second, lack of proper communication of standards for the task may lead to less than desirable outcomes. Finally, the delegation process may create some artificial barriers or fail to eliminate others barriers to performance. The failure to share information and discuss real or perceived problems can reduce efficiency and may lead to failure. To avoid these obstacles, the following items should be considered when making an assignment.

ALLOW EMPLOYEES TO PARTICIPATE IN THE DELEGATION PROCESS. Employees who accept their assignments are much more likely to be committed to their success. This acceptance is enhanced when employees have some say in the process. Thus, subordinates should be allowed to participate in determining when and how the delegated task will be accomplished and, when possible, what the assignment will be. At the most basic level, a manager can ask an employee if he or she is available to do a task, rather than telling him/her to do it. Participation can also increase supervisor/subordinate communication, which may minimize problems due to misunderstandings.

SPECIFY STANDARDS. Many communication problems occur because of the failure to clearly consider and specify the performance standards of the assignment. Some of the things to consider include the limitations of a subordinate's tasks, (e.g., gathering information only, or making a decision), their expected level of performance, their deadlines for reporting, and the constraints under which they will be operating. Where subordinates are given a choice in accepting the assignment, these issues should be discussed and negotiated prior to the delegation. Even when subordinates do not have the option of rejecting the assignment, these issues should be clearly described and subordinates should be asked for their input.

BALANCE RESPONSIBILITY AND AUTHORITY. A typical delegation error is to delegate work but avoid matching the responsibilities with the freedom to make decisions and the authority to implement them. This creates frustration, since the subordinate knows what needs to be done and how to do it, but is not given the opportunity to do it. Managers can avoid this problem by communicating to all individuals affected by the assignment that it has been delegated and who has the authority to complete the work. Managers can ask subordinates what resources they need for a task ad then empower them to secure those resources.

In addition to providing authority, managers should also provide adequate support for the delegated task. This might involve continually providing important information and feedback that are needed to accomplish the task. Finally, managers should publicly bestow credit when the task has been accomplished. This will enhance the subordinate's motivation and authority for future assignments. It also provides an important message to others that successful completion of tasks is acknowledged and rewarded.

DELEGATE CONSISTENTLY. Some managers delegate only when they are overworked or in a crisis. This can send a message to subordinates that they are being used since they only receive assignments when it benefits the manager. Ideally, delegation should benefit both the subordinate and the manager. Managers can send this message by delegating assignments that develop or stretch subordinates' talents and skills. Delegating to develop workers builds up a pool of talent for those inevitable crisis situations. It also enhances

worker motivation and confidence since they acquire experience and benefit from the new or improved skills. Care should be taken to assure that the employee has the capability to succeed in the assignment. Employees should not be set up to fail. Certainly some failure will occur. Managers must recognize this and provide helpful, developmental feedback in those situations. Emphasis should be placed on the positive things that were done on the assignment and what actions could have been taken to overcome the problems.

BALANCE THE ASSIGNMENTS. Managers need to ensure that delegation isn't viewed as getting someone else to do their dirty work. Thus, an effective manager should delegate the pleasant and the unpleasant, the challenging and the boring assignments. Similarly, assignments should be balanced across workers. For example, it is quite common for managers to delegate the most unpleasant task to the best worker since that person can be counted on to do a good job. Alternatively, a poor worker may avoid receiving an unpleasant assignment due to the poor quality of the final product. This type of situation quickly sends the message to the productive worker that the way to get out of receiving unpleasant assignments is to lower the quality of his/her work. One way to avoid this problem is to give the productive worker other rewards and/or to increase the number of unpleasant assignments to the unproductive worker until the quality of the result improves.

FOCUS ON RESULTS. Once the task has been delegated, managers need to allow subordinates the freedom to make the choices needed to accomplish the task. Managers should not supervise too closely for this may create frustration and make someone feel that the manager lacks confidence in their ability. Managers should review and evaluate the results of the assignment, not the means used to accomplish the task. However, managers are responsible for making sure that both the process and the outcome of the delegated task are consistent with the goals. As noted, one way to accomplish this is through the specification of clear standards prior to the delegation. The manager needs to remember these standards and intervene only when they have been violated. Managers should avoid the tendency to intervene simply due to style differences. One of the benefits of allowing subordinates to make their own choices is that this can be an important source of innovation for the organization. Sometimes employees really have a better way.

GROUP VS. INDIVIDUAL DELEGATION

A particular assignment can be delegated to an individual or a group of individuals. Additionally, a manager may not wish to delegate the whole task, but to participate as a member of the team. What are the considerations in individual versus group delegation or even participation? Perhaps the most important point is that all of the previous issues apply. Prior to making the assignment, the manager must define success and assess the capabilities of the individual or group. In making the assignment, the individual or group should be allowed to participate as much as possible, authority and responsibilities should be balanced, standards should be specified and the manager should focus on results.

One difference between individual and group delegation is that individual behavior is typically easier to control and monitor. One alternative to delegating the assignment and giving entirely to a subordinate is for a manager to participate in the process as a group member. The downside of this approach is that it may send the group an unintended message of a lack of trust. Employees may feel that the manager is not there to contribute, but to check on the quality of their work. Thus, managers should carefully review their own capabilities as a team member and answer the question, "What do I add to this group to accomplish this task?" The answer to this question should be clearly communicated to the group so they understand why the manager has undertaken a role in the group. Finally, a manager should carefully assess the group's past behavior and have a reason for predicting that the group can accomplish the task. Again, this should be a prediction, not a gamble or wish for success.

UPWARD DELEGATION

Many employees have become skilled in delegating to their supervisors. Upward delegation occurs when an employee shifts his or her assignment to a manager at a level above. This is not always easy, but is best done when a person feels that he or she lacks the skill or direction for a particular project, but that the manager above has the capabilities to perform the task. Upward delegation may start by asking the manager questions or asking for advice in help in solving a particular problem. If the manager feels that the employee has too many questions or needs too much assistance, the manager may rescind the delegation and remove task from the employee. If employees are avoiding delegated duties by overwhelming the manager with requests for assistance, the manager can require that the employee have at least one proposed solution to every problem brought to the manager. Additionally, this situation can be improved by the manager asking questions, which lead the worker to think through and resolve a problem. Questions like, "What would you do next? What do you see as our options?" and, "What do you see as the best approach?" communicate the message that the employee is expected to take the initiative to at least attempt to solve the assignment.

A manager who uses effective delegation across time and assignments will be more efficient and have more time for true managerial work and will reap the benefits of employee empowerment at the same time. This will occur because success will be clearly defined and communicated to a worker who will be matched with jobs based on his or her capabilities. When done correctly, the process of delegation empowers workers and enhances their motivation and commitment.

SEE ALSO: Management Styles; Motivation and Motivation Theory; Time Management

Richard R. Camp
Revised by Marcia Simmering

FURTHER READING:

Kreitner, Robert, and Angelo Kinicki. *Organizational Behavior* 6th ed. Boston, MA: McGraw-Hill/Irwin, 2004.

Malone, Thomas W. "Is Empowerment Just a Fad? Control Decision, Decision Making and IT." *Sloan Management Review.* 1997, 23–35.

Roebuck, Chris. *Effective Delegation.* New York: American Management Association, 1998.

Straub, Joseph T. *The Agile Manager's Guide to Delegating Work.* Bristol, VT: Velocity Business Publishing, 1998.

DEREGULATION

Deregulation refers to the deletion, abandonment, or relaxation of various laws, rules, and regulations that affect business and industry. However, the topic of deregulation is best understood by first understanding the purposes and effects of regulations.

REGULATION

It is often thought that individual firms lack the perspective and/or the incentive to protect society. Consequently, the regulation of business and industry by government is for the purposes of consumer protection and or the enhancement of business competition. Regulation is generally thought to also protect minorities, employees, investors, and the environment.

The railroad industry was one of the first industries that the federal government targeted. As a result, the Interstate Commerce Act was passed in 1887. As such, the Interstate Commerce Act created the first regulatory body in the United States—the Interstate Commerce Commission, which still regulates transportation rates, as well as establishes rules and regulations for interstate commerce.

The United States government expanded its control over industry by focusing on trusts, where a company is established for the purpose of controlling multiple companies. Consequently, the Sherman Antitrust Act was enacted in 1890 to control monopolies. In 1914, the Clayton Act amended the Sherman Act by forbidding specific business actions. For example, tying contracts interlocking directorates, and discriminatory pricing were made illegal if the results of these actions lessened competition.

The Federal Trade Commission Act, also enacted in 1914, formally established the Federal Trade Commission (FTC). Among other responsibilities, the FTC remains responsible for defining, detecting, and enforcing compliance with the Clayton Act. The Wheeler-Lea Act of 1938 expanded FTC jurisdiction to include any practice or practices that harm the public in general and those practices that harm competitors. The Robinson-Patman Act was enacted in 1938 due to the growth of large retailing conglomerates. This law covered discrimination against buyers as well as sellers.

In 1958 the National Traffic and Safety Act was enacted. This legislation provided for the creation of compulsory safety standards for automobiles and tires.

In 1966 the Fair Packaging and Labeling Act was passed. This act provided for the regulation of the packaging and labeling of consumer goods. It also required manufacturers to state package contents, the maker of the contents, and how much of individual contents are included.

The Antitrust Procedures and Penalties Act was enacted in 1974. This legislation increased fines for violation of the Sherman Act. Two years later, the Antitrust Improvement Act required firms to notify the FTC of merger plans. This act also gave state attorneys general the power to sue for the benefit of consumers.

GOVERNMENT PERMISSIVENESS

It is generally thought that the permissiveness of the federal government began during the presidency of Richard M. Nixon, which led the way for formal deregulation. During the 1980s the government turned its focus from laws, rules, and regulations to the creation of market incentives that were thought to motivate business.

Proponents of deregulation argue that government intervention impedes the natural laws of supply and demand and ultimately increases costs to consumers. In addition, the overregulation of business is thought to thwart innovation by creating delays and increased red tape. Thus in 1981 the Ronald Reagan administration created the Task Force on Regulatory Relief to review all proposed new regulations and review old regulations. The establishment of this task force also lead to the increased use of cost-benefit analysis, which compares the cost of all regulations to their benefit.

Other steps toward deregulation, as adapted from a summary in *Business Today,* by David Rachman and Michael H. Mescon (1987), are presented below.

1968. The Supreme Court allows non-AT&T equipment to be hooked up with the AT&T system (Carterfone decision).

1969. The Federal Communications Commission (FCC) lets MCI connect its long-distance network with local phone systems.

1970. The Federal Reserve lifts interest rate ceilings on bank deposits over $100,000 and with maturities less than six months.

1974. The Justice Department files an antitrust suit against AT&T.

1975. The Securities and Exchange Commission (SEC) stops stockbrokers from charging fixed commissions.

1977. Financial management and advice firm Merrill Lynch is allowed to enter into more direct competition with commercial banks with the debut of its cash management account.

1978. Congress deregulates the airline industry.

1979. The FCC permits AT&T to sell nonregulated services such as data processing.

1980. Congress deregulates the trucking and railroad industries.

1981. Sears Roebuck is allowed to offer one-stop financial shopping for insurance, brokerage services, and banking.

1982. Congress deregulates intercity bus services.

1984. AT&T is disbanded, leaving local telephone companies to operate separately from the long-distance company.

RECENT TRENDS

The debate over the advantages and disadvantages of deregulation continue to the present. For example, the future direction of U.S. aviation policy is continually debated, even though the United Stated deregulated the airline industry in 1978. Proponents of the Airline Deregulation Act of 1978 point to specific benefits of the free-market environment. For instance, the percentage of the population taking trips by air doubled between 1978 and 1997. In addition, the number of airlines operating in the United States more than doubled (from 43 to 90). Advocates of regulation, however, regularly refer to the bankruptcies of Pan American World Airways and Eastern Airlines as negative consequences of deregulation. Unfortunately, increased competition did not guarantee success for airlines, and many failed to adapt their business processes to the decrease in revenues from lower fare prices. Also, an already weak airline industry was severely affected by the September 11, 2001 terrorist attacks, and lead more of the major air carriers to financial trouble.

Telephone service deregulation, as a result of the Telecom Reform Act of 1996, also receives a great deal of attention. Proponents of telecommunications deregulation point to lower prices, better quality, and greater choices to users. However, advocates of regulation indicate that the larger long-distance carriers are still in control. Recent mergers and acquisitions support this trend towards larger long-distance carriers.

GLOBAL DEREGULATION

Deregulation is not limited to the United States. Europe has created a few low-cost, no-frills air carriers—a deregulation outcome cited by the United Kingdom's Civil Aviation Authority as the most "striking" development in European airline competition in years. Elsewhere in Europe, telecommunications, postal services, and railways have also undergone significant changes in recent years. The changes in these basic infrastructure services include reorganization reforms, as well as privatization of publicly owned industries.

DEREGULATION AND THE FUTURE

Deregulation issues continue to arise in transportation, energy, banking, broadcasting, and cable. Recent competition in the cable and telephone industries has warranted a backtracking of deregulation efforts by the FCC as potentially counterproductive to the market's development.

A chief concern with business legislation is the cost. That is, at what point does the cost of legislation outweigh the benefits? This cost-benefit question, first posed during the Reagan administration, is likely to persist. However, as products and services become more complex due to rapid technological change, various public constituencies are likely to ask for new regulations, and individual companies and industry groups will be required to maintain surveillance of current and pending legislation.

SEE ALSO: Economics

Gene Brown
Revised by Hal P. Kirkwood, Jr.

FURTHER READING:

"Deregulation." *Consumer Reports,* July 2002. Available from <http://www.consumerreports.org>.

"FCC Staff Stiffs Cable on Deregulation." *Multichannel News* 26, no. 6 (2005): 34.

Gorman, H. "Deregulation Increases Cash Flow, Profitability." *Electric Light & Power* 82, no. 5 (2004): 31–33.

Guasch, J. L. and Hahn, R. W. "The Costs and Benefits of Regulation: Implications for Developing Countries." *The World Bank Research Observer* 14, no. 1 (1999): 137–158.

Jackson, D. "A 2005 Focal Point." *Telephony* 245, no. 22 (2004): 50.

McDonald, M. "Changed Forever." *Air Transport World* 41, no. 7 (2004): 36–39.

Rachman, D. J., and M.H. Mescon. *Business Today.* New York: Random House, 1987.

DICTIONARY OF OCCUPATIONAL TITLES

SEE: Occupational Information Network

DISCRIMINATION

Discrimination, in an employment context, can be generally defined as treating an individual or group less well in recruiting, hiring, or any other terms and conditions of employment due to the person's or group's race, color, sex, religion, national origin, age, disability, or veteran's status. These categories are referred to as protected classifications because they are singled out for protection by equal employment opportunity (EEO) laws. Subcategories of people within each protected classification are referred to as protected groups. For example, male and female are the protected groups within the protected classification of sex. EEO legislation affords protection from illegal discrimination to all protected groups within a protected classification, not just the minority group. Thus, employment discrimination against a man is just as unlawful as that aimed at a woman. The lone exception to this rule concerns the use of affirmative action programs (discussed later), which, under certain circumstances, allow employers to treat members of certain protected groups preferentially.

In the U.S., effective federal legislation banning employment-related discrimination did not exist until the 1960s, when Congress passed Title VII of the Civil Rights Act (1964). In the years since, several other important federal laws have been passed. In addition to the myriad federal laws banning discrimination on the basis of race, color, sex, religion, national origin, age, disability, and veteran's status, almost all states have anti-discrimination laws affecting the workplace. Most of these laws extend the protections in federal law to employers that are not covered by the federal statutes because of their size (Title VII for example, applies only to employers with 15 or more employees). Some state laws also attempt to prevent discrimination against individuals and groups that are not included in federal law. For example, approximately 14 states have passed statutes protecting all workers in the states from employment discrimination based on sexual orientation and several others states prohibit public sector employers from discriminating on the basis of sexual orientation.

SPECIFIC ANTI-DISCRIMINATION LEGISLATION AFFECTING THE WORKPLACE

Title VII of the Civil Rights Act (CRA), passed in 1964, covers organizations that employ 15 or more workers for at least 20 weeks during the year. Specifically, the law states: "It shall be an unlawful employment practice for an employer to fail or refuse to hire or discharge any individual, or otherwise to discriminate against any individual with respect to his compensation, terms, conditions, or privileges of employment, because of such individual's race, color, religion, sex, or national origin." Interpretations of Title VII by courts have clarified the specific meaning of the prohibitions against discrimination. In general, it is safe to say that virtually any workplace decision involving personnel is subject to legal challenge on the basis of Title VII, including not only decisions made relative to recruiting and hiring, but also in relation to promotion, discipline, admission to training programs, layoffs, and performance appraisal. Harassment of applicants or employees because of their membership in a protected classification is also considered a violation of Title VII.

Title VII is probably the most valuable tool that employees have for remedying workplace discrimination because it covers the greatest number of protected classifications. If a court determines that discrimination has occurred, this law entitles the victim to relief in the form of legal costs and back pay (i.e., the salary the person would have been receiving had no discrimination occurred). For instance, suppose a woman sues a company for rejecting her application for a $35,000 per year construction job because the company unlawfully excludes women from this job. The litigation process takes two years and, ultimately, the court rules in the applicant's favor. To remedy this discrimination, the court could require the company to pay her legal fees and grant her $70,000 in back pay (two years' salary).

Title VII of the Civil Rights Act of 1964 has had an enormous impact on the human resource management (HRM) practices of many companies, by forcing them to take a close look at the way they recruit, hire, promote, award pay raises, and discipline their employees. As a result of this self-scrutiny, many firms have changed their practices, making them more systematic and objective. For instance, most firms now require their supervisors to provide detailed documentation to justify the fairness of their disciplinary actions, and many firms are now more cautious with regard to their use of employment tests that restrict the employment opportunities for certain protected groups.

A number of Supreme Court decisions in the mid-to late 1980s made discrimination claims under Title VII more difficult for employees to substantiate. To put more teeth into the law, Congress amended it by enacting the Civil Rights Act of 1991. This 1991 amendment expanded the list of remedies that may be awarded in a discrimination case-the employer now has more to lose if found guilty of discrimination. In addition to legal fees and back pay, an employer may now be charged with punitive and compensatory damages (for future financial losses, emotional pain, suffering, inconvenience, mental anguish, and loss of enjoyment of life). The cap for these damages ranges from $50,000 to $300,000 depending on the size of the company. Employees are entitled to such damages in cases where discrimination practices are "engaged in with malice or reckless indifference to the legal rights of the aggrieved individual" (e.g., the employer is aware that serious violations are occurring, but does nothing to rectify them).

Moreover, the CRA of 1991 adds additional bite to the 1964 law by providing a more detailed description of the evidence needed to prove a discrimination claim, making such claims easier to prove. The CRA of 1991 also differs from the 1964 law by addressing the issue of mixed-motives cases. The CRA of 1991 states that mixed-motive decisions are unlawful. That is, a hiring practice is illegal when a candidate's protected group membership is a factor affecting an employment decision, even if other, more legitimate factors are also considered. For instance, a company rejects the application of a woman because she behaves in an "unlady-like" manner-she is "too aggressive for a woman, wears no makeup, and swears like a man." The company is concerned that she would offend its customers. The employer's motives are thus mixed: its concern about offending customers is a legitimate motive; its stereotyped view of how a "lady" should behave is a discriminatory one.

OTHER MAJOR EEO LAWS

The Equal Pay Act of 1963 prohibits discrimination in pay on the basis of sex when jobs within the same company are substantially the same. The company is allowed to pay workers doing the same job differently if the differences are based on merit, seniority, or any other reasonable basis other than the workers' gender.

The Age Discrimination in Employment Act (ADEA) of 1967 bans employment discrimination on the basis of age by protecting applicants and employees who are 40 or older. The ADEA applies to nearly all employers of 20 or more employees. The ADEA protects only older individuals from discrimination; people under 40 are not protected. The act also prohibits employers from giving preference to individuals within the 40 or older group. For instance, an employer may not discriminate against a 50-year-old by giving preference to a 40-year-old. Except in limited circumstances, companies cannot require individuals to retire because of their age.

The Vocational Rehabilitation Act of 1973, a precursor to the 1990 passage of the Americans with Disabilities Act, requires employers who are federal contractors ($2,500 or more) to take proactive measures to employ individuals with disabilities. This law is limited in application since it only applies to federal agencies and businesses doing contract work with the government.

The Vietnam Veterans' Readjustment Assistance Act, passed in 1974, requires employers who are government contractors ($10,000 or more) to take proactive steps to hire veterans of the Vietnam era. The scope of this law is also limited by the fact that only government contractors must comply.

The Pregnancy Discrimination Act of 1978 amended the CRA of 1964 by broadening the interpretation of sex discrimination to include pregnancy, childbirth, or related medical conditions. It prohibits discrimination against pregnant job applicants or against women who are of child-bearing age. It states that employees who are unable to perform their jobs because of a pregnancy-related condition must be treated in the same manner as employees who are temporarily disabled for other reasons. It has also been interpreted to mean that women cannot be prevented from competing for certain jobs within a company just because the jobs may involve exposure to substances thought harmful to the reproductive systems of women.

The Immigration Reform and Control Act (IRCA) of 1986 prohibited discrimination based on national origin and citizenship. Specifically, the law states that employers of four or more employees cannot discriminate against any individual (other than an illegal alien) because of that person's national origin or citizenship status. In addition to being an anti-discrimination law, this act makes it unlawful to knowingly hire an unauthorized alien. At the time of hiring, an employer must require proof that the person offered the job is not an illegal alien.

The Americans with Disabilities Act (ADA) of 1990 was designed to eliminate discrimination against individuals with disabilities. The employment implications of the act, which are delineated in Titles I (private sector) and II (public sector) of the ADA, affect nearly all organizations employing 15 or more workers. According to the act, an individual is considered disabled if he or she has a physical or mental impairment which substantially limits one or more of the individual's major life activities, such as walking, seeing, hearing, breathing, and learning, as well as the ability to secure or retain employment. In the years since passage of the legislation, the courts have applied a fairly broad definition of disability. The ADA only protects qualified individuals with a disability. To win a complaint, an individual who has been denied employment because of a disability must establish that, with accommodation (if necessary), he or she is qualified to perform the essential functions of the job in question. To defend successfully against such a suit, the employer must demonstrate that, even with reasonable accommodation, the candidate could not perform the job satisfactorily, or it must demonstrate that the accommodation would impose an undue hardship. The ADA defines "undue hardship" as those accommodations that require significant difficulty to effect or significant expense on the part of the employer.

An example of an ADA case would be one in which an employee is fired because of frequent absences caused by a particular disability. The employee may argue that the employer failed to offer a reasonable accommodation, such as a transfer to a part-time position. The employer, on the other hand, may argue that such an action would pose an undue hardship in that the creation of such a position would be too costly.

INTERPRETING EEO LAW

It is clear from the preceding discussion that an employer may not discriminate on the basis of an individual's protected group membership. But exactly how does one determine whether a particular act is discriminatory? Consider the following examples:

Case 1: A woman was denied employment as a police officer because she failed a strength test. During the past year that test screened out 90 percent of all female applicants and 30 percent of all male applicants.

Case 2: A woman was denied employment as a construction worker because she failed to meet the company's requirement that all workers be at least 5 feet 8 inches tall and weigh at least 160 pounds. During the past year, 20 percent of the male applicants and 70 percent of the female applicants have been rejected because of this requirement.

Case 3: A female accountant was fired despite satisfactory performance ratings. The boss claims she has violated company policy by moonlighting for another firm. The boss was heard making the comment, "Women don't belong in accounting, anyway."

Case 4: A male boss fired his female secretary because he thought she was too ugly, and replaced her with a woman who, in his opinion, was much prettier.

The Civil Rights Acts of 1964 and 1991 prohibit sex discrimination. Yet, knowing that sex discrimination is unlawful provides very little guidance in these cases. For instance, how important are the intentions of the employer? And how important are the outcomes of the employment decisions? In the first two cases, the employer's intentions seem to be noble, but the outcomes of the employment decisions were clearly disadvantageous to women. In the third case, the employer's intentions appear questionable, but the outcome may be fair. After all, the employee did violate the company policy. In the fourth case, the employer's intentions are despicable, yet the outcome did not adversely affect women in the sense that another member of her sex replaced the discharged employee.

To determine whether an EEO law has been violated, one must know how the courts define the term *discrimination.* In actuality, there are two definitions: disparate treatment and disparate impact. Disparate treatment is intentional discrimination. It is defined as treating people unfairly based on their membership in a protected group. For example, the firing of the female accountant in Case 3 would be an example of disparate treatment if the discharge were triggered by the supervisor's bias against female accountants (i.e., if men were not discharged for moonlighting). However, the employer's actions in Cases 1 and 2 would not be classified as disparate treatment because there was no apparent intent to discriminate.

While disparate treatment is often the result of an employer's bias or prejudice toward a particular group, it may also occur as the result of trying to protect the group members' interests. For instance, consider the employer who refuses to hire women for dangerous jobs in order to protect their safety. While its intentions might be noble, this employer would be just as guilty of discrimination as one with less noble intentions.

What about Case 4, where a secretary was fired for being too ugly? Is the employer guilty of sex discrimination? The answer is no if the bias displayed by the boss was directed at appearance, not sex. Appearance is not a protected classification. The answer is yes if the appearance standard were being applied only to women; that is, the company fired women but not men on the basis of their looks.

Disparate impact is unintentional discrimination, defined as any practice without business justification that has unequal consequences for people of different protected groups. This concept of illegal discrimination was first established by the Griggs v. Duke Supreme Court decision, handed down in 1971. Disparate impact discrimination occurs, for instance, if an arbitrary selection practice (e.g., an irrelevant employment test) resulted in the selection of a disproportionately low number of females or African Americans. The key notion here is "arbitrary selection practice." If the selection practice were relevant or job-related, rather than arbitrary, the employer's practice would be legal, regardless of its disproportionate outcome. For example, despite the fact the women received the short end of the stick in Cases 1 and 2, the employer's actions would be lawful if the selection criteria (e.g., the strength test and height and weight requirements) were deemed job related. As it turns out, strength tests are much more likely to be considered job related than height and weight requirements. Thus, the employer would probably win Case 1 and lose Case 2.

AFFIRMATIVE ACTION

The aim of affirmative action is to remedy past and current discrimination. Although the overall aim of affirmative action is thus identical to that of EEO (i.e., to advance the cause of protected groups by eliminating employment discrimination), the two approaches differ in the way they attempt to accomplish this aim. EEO initiatives are color-blind, while affirmative action initiatives are color-conscious. That is, affirmative action makes special provisions to recruit, train, retain, promote, or grant some other benefit to members of protected groups (e.g., women, blacks).

In some cases, employers are legally required to institute affirmative action programs. For instance, Executive Order 11246, issued by President Lyndon Johnson, makes such programs mandatory for all federal government contractors. Affirmative action can also be court ordered as part of a settlement in a discrimination case. For example, in the 1970s, the state of Alabama was ordered by the Supreme Court to select one black applicant for each white hired as a state trooper. The purpose of this decree was to rectify the effects of past discrimination that had been blatantly occurring for several years.

Exhibit 1
Affirmative Action Options

Always Legal

1. Do nothing special, but make sure you always hire and promote people based solely on qualifications.

2. Analyze workforce for underutilization.

3. Set goals for increasing the percentage of minorities employed in jobs for which they are underutilized.

4. Remove artificial barriers blocking the advancement of minorities.

5. Create upward mobility training programs for minorities.

6. Advertise job openings in a way that ensures minority awareness (e.g., contact the local chapter of NOW or the NAACP).

7. Impose a rule that states that a manager cannot hire someone until there is a qualified minority in the applicant pool.

Sometimes Legal
(depends on the severity of the under-utilization problem)

8. Impose a rule that when faced with two equally qualified applicants (a minority and non-minority), the manager must hire the minority candidate.

9. Impose a rule that when faced with two qualified applicants (a minority and non-minority), hire the minority even if the other candidate has better qualifications.

10. Set a hiring quota that specifies one minority hiring for every non-minority hiring.

Never Legal

11. Do not consider any non-minorities for the position. Hire the most qualified minority applicant.

12. Fire non-minority employee and replace him or her with a minority applicant.

Most firms, however, are under no legal obligation to implement affirmative action programs. Those choosing to implement such programs do so voluntarily, believing it makes good business sense. These firms believe that by implementing affirmative action they can (1) attract and retain a larger and better pool of applicants, (2) avoid discrimination lawsuits, and (3) improve the firm's reputation within the community and its consumer base.

Affirmative action implementation consists of two steps. First, the organization conducts an analysis to identify the underutilized protected groups within its various job categories (e.g., officials and managers, professionals, service workers, sales workers). It then develops a remedial plan that targets these underutilized groups. A utilization analysis is a statistical procedure that compares the percentage of each protected group for each job category within the organization to that in the available labor market. If the organizational percentage is less than the labor-market percentage, the group is classified as being underutilized.

For example, the percentage of professionals within the organization who are women would be compared to the percentage of professionals in the available labor market who are women. The organization would classify women as being underutilized if it discovered, for instance, that women constitute 5 percent of the firm's professionals, and yet constitute 20 percent of the professionals in the available labor market.

The second step is to develop an affirmative action plan (AAP) that targets the underutilized protected groups. An AAP is a written statement that specifies how the organization plans to increase the utilization of targeted groups. The AAP consists of three elements: goals, timetables, and action steps.

An AAP goal specifies the percentage of protected group representation it seeks to reach. The timetable specifies the time period within which it hopes to reach its goal. For example, an AAP may state: "The firm plans to increase its percentage of female professionals from 5 to 20 percent within the next five years."

The action steps specify how the organization plans to reach its goals and timetables. Action steps typically include such things as intensifying recruitment efforts, removing arbitrary selection standards, eliminating workplace prejudices, and offering employees better promotional and training opportunities. An example follows of a set of action steps:

• Meet with minority and female employees to request suggestions.

• Review present selection and promotion procedures to determine job-relatedness

- Design and implement a career counseling program for lower level employees to encourage and assist in planning occupational and career goals.

- Install a new, less subjective performance appraisal system.

When a company initiates an AAP as a remedy for under-utilization, it attempts to bring qualified women or minorities into the workplace to make it more reflective of the population from which the employees are drawn. This practice sometimes involves the use of preferential treatment or giving members of underutilized groups some advantage over others in the employment process. The use of preferential treatment has triggered a storm of controversy, as detractors point to the seemingly inherent lack of fairness in giving preference to one individual over another based solely on that person's race or gender. Supporters, however, believe that preferential treatment is sometimes needed to level the playing field. The U.S. Supreme Court has ruled that preferential treatment is legal if engaged in as part of a bona fide affirmative action program that is designed to remedy underutilization. The AAP, however, must be temporary, flexible, and reasonable as noted in Exhibit 1.

SEE ALSO: Affirmative Action; Employee Recruitment Planning; Employee Screening and Selection; Employment Law and Compliance

Lawrence S. Kleiman
Revised by Tim Barnett

FURTHER READING:

Barnett, T., A. McMillan, and W. McVea. "Employer Liability for Harassment by Supervisors: An Overview of the 1999 EEOC Guidelines." *Journal of Employment Discrimination Law* 2, no. 4 (2000): 311–315.

Barnett, T. and W. McVea. "Preemployment Questions Under the Americans with Disabilities Act." *SAM Advanced Management Journal* 62 (1997): 23–27.

Clark, M. M. "Religion vs. Sexual Orientation." *HR Magazine* 49, no. 8 (2004): 54–59.

Dessler, G. *Human Resource Management.* 10th ed. Upper Saddle River, NJ: Prentice-Hall, 2005.

Kleiman, L.S. *Human Resource Management: A Tool for Competitive Advantage.* Cincinnati: South-Western College Publishing, 2000.

Kleiman, L.S., and R.H. Faley. "Voluntary Affirmative Action and Preferential Treatment: Legal and Research Implications." *Personnel Psychology* 77, no. 1 (1988): 481–496.

Smith, M.A., and C. Charles. "Title VII of the Civil Rights Act of 1964." *Georgetown Journal of Gender and the Law* 5, no. 1 (2004): 421–476.

Wolkinson, B.W., and R.N. Block. *Employment Law.* Cambridge, MA: Blackwell, 1996.

DISTRIBUTION AND DISTRIBUTION REQUIREMENTS PLANNING

A supply channel is composed of three structures. At one end of the channel is the manufacturer. The manufacturer focuses on the development and production of products and originates the distribution process. The terminal point in the channel is the retailer who sells goods and services directly to the customer for their personal, non-business use. In between the two lies a process called distribution, which is more difficult to define. One involved in the distribution process is labeled a "distributor." The *APICS Dictionary* describes a distributor as "a business that does not manufacture its own products but purchases and resells these products. Such a business usually maintains a finished goods inventory." The proliferation of alternative distribution forms, such as warehouse clubs, catalog sales, marketing channel specialists, and mail order, have blurred functional distinctions and increased the difficulty of defining both the distribution process and the term distributor.

One ultimately could maintain that distributors include all enterprises that sell products to retailers and other merchants—and/or to industrial, institutional, and commercial users—but do not sell in significant amounts to the ultimate customer. According to this definition, most companies that are involved with the disbursement of raw materials and finished products belong, in one sense or another, to the distribution industry. By adopting this definition, distribution is expanded to cover nearly every form of materials management and physical distribution activity performed by channel constituents, except for the processes of manufacturing and retailing.

Distribution involves a number of activities centered around a physical flow of goods and information. At one time the term distribution applied only to the outbound side of supply chain management, but it now includes both inbound and outbound. Management of the inbound flow involves these elements:

- Material planning and control

- Purchasing

- Receiving

- Physical management of materials via warehousing and storage

- Materials handling

Management of the outbound flow involves these elements:

- Order processing

- Warehousing and storage

- Finished goods management

- Material handling and packaging

- Shipping

- Transportation

Distribution channels are formed to solve three critical distribution problems: functional performance, reduced complexity, and specialization.

The central focus of distribution is to increase the efficiency of time, place, and delivery utility. When demand and product availability are immediate, the producer can perform the exchange and delivery functions itself. However, as the number of producers grows and the geographical dispersion of the customer base expands, the need for both internal and external intermediaries who can facilitate the flow of products, services, and information via a distribution process increases.

Distribution management also can decrease overall channel complexity through sorting and assistance in routinization. Sorting is the group of activities associated with transforming products acquired from manufacturers into the assortments and quantities demanded in the marketplace. Routinization refers to the policies and procedures providing common goals, channel arrangements, expectations, and mechanisms to facilitate efficient transactions. David F. Ross describes sorting as including four primary functions:

1. Sorting is the function of physically separating a heterogeneous group of items into homogeneous subgroups. This includes grading and grouping individual items into an inventory lot by quality or eliminating defects from the lot.

2. Accumulating is the function of combining homogeneous stocks of products into larger groups of supply.

3. Allocation is the function of breaking down large lots of products into smaller salable units.

4. Assorting is the function of mixing similar or functionally related items into assortments to meet customer demand. For example, putting items into kit form.

As the supply chain grows more complex, costs and inefficiencies multiply in the channel. In response, some channels add or contain partners that specialize in one or more of the elements of distribution, such as exchange or warehousing. Specialization then improves the channel by increasing the velocity of goods and value-added services and reducing costs associated with selling, transportation, carrying inventory, warehousing, order processing, and credit.

ROLE OF THE DISTRIBUTION FUNCTION

There are a number of critical functions performed by the channel distributor. Ross describes these functions as:

1. Product acquisition. This means acquiring products in a finished or semi-finished state from either a manufacturer or through another distributor that is higher up in the supply channel. These functions can be performed by independent channel intermediaries or by the distribution facilities of manufacturing companies.

2. Product movement. This implies significant effort spent on product movement up or down the supply channel.

3. Product transaction. Distributors can be characterized as selling products in bulk quantities solely for the purpose of resale or business use. Downstream businesses will then sell these products to other distributors or retailers who will sell them directly to the end customer, or to manufacturers who will consume the material/components in their own production processes.

Following are the separate elements contained within the three critical functions of distribution:

- Selling and promoting. This function is very important to manufacturers. One strategy involves the use of distribution channels to carry out the responsibilities of product deployment. In addition to being marketing experts in their industry, distribution firms usually have direct-selling organizations and a detailed knowledge of their customers and their expectations. The manufacturer utilizing this distributor can then tap into these resources. Also, because of the scale of the distributing firm's operations and its specialized skill in channel management, it can significantly improve the time, place, and possession utilities by housing inventory closer to the market. These advantages mean that the manufacturer can reach many small, distant customers at a relatively low cost, thus allowing the manufacturer to focus its expenditures on product development and its core production processes.

- Buying and building product assortments. This is an extremely important function for retailers. Most retailers prefer to deal with few suppliers providing a wide assortment of products that fit their merchandising strategy rather than many with limited product lines. This, of course, saves on purchasing, transportation, and merchandizing costs. Distribution firms have the ability to bring together related products from multiple manufacturers and assemble the right combination of these products in quantities that meet the retailer's requirements in a cost-efficient manner.

- Bulk breaking. This is one of the fundamental functions of distribution. Manufacturers normally produce large quantities of a limited number of products. However, retailers normally require smaller quantities of multiple products. When the distribution function handles this requirement it keeps the manufacturer from having to break bulk and repackage its product to fit individual requirements. Lean manufacturing and JIT techniques are continuously seeking ways to reduce lot sizes, so this function enhances that goal.

- Value-added processing. Postponement specifies that products should be kept at the highest possible level in the pipeline in large, generic quantities that can be customized into their final form as close as possible to the actual final sale. The distributor can facilitate this process by performing sorting, labeling, blending, kitting, packaging, and light final assembly at one or more points within the supply channel. This significantly reduces end-product obsolescence and minimizes the risk inherent with carrying finished goods inventory.

- Transportation. The movement of goods from the manufacturer to the retailer is a critical function of distribution. Delivery encompasses those activities that are necessary to ensure that the right product is available to the customer at the right time and right place. This frequently means that a structure of central, branch, and field warehouses, geographically situated in the appropriate locations, are needed to achieve optimum customer service. Transportation's goal is to ensure that goods are positioned properly in the channel in a quick, cost-effective, and consistent manner.

- Warehousing. Warehousing exists to provide access to sufficient stock in order to satisfy anticipated customer requirements, and to act as a buffer against supply and demand uncertainties. Since demand is often located far from the source (manufacturer), warehousing can provide a wide range of marketplaces that manufacturers, functioning independently, could not penetrate.

- Marketing information. The distribution channel also can provide information regarding product, marketplace issues, and competitors' activities in a relatively short time.

DRP

The need for more detailed distribution planning led to the emergence of distribution requirements planning (DRP) during the 1970s. DRP is a widely used and potentially powerful technique for helping outbound logistics systems manage and minimize inbound inventories. This concept extended the time-phase order point found in material requirements planning (MRP) logic to the management of channel inventory. By the 1980s DRP had become a standard approach for planning and controlling distribution logistics activities and had evolved into distribution resource planning. The concept now embraces all business functions in the supply channel, not just inventory and logistics, and is termed DRP II.

DRP is usually used with an MRP system, although most DRP models are more comprehensive than stand-alone MRP models and can schedule transportation. The underlying rationale for DRP is to more accurately forecast demand and then use that information to develop delivery schedules. This way, distribution firms can minimize inbound inventory by using MRP in conjunction with other schedules.

One of the key elements of DRP is the DRP table, which includes the following elements:

- Forecast demand for each stock-keeping unit (SKU)
- Current inventory level of the SKU
- Target safety stock
- Recommended replenishment quantity
- Replenishment lead time

The concept of DRP very closely mimics the logic of MRP. As with MRP, gross requirements consist of actual customer orders, forecasted demand, or some combination of both; scheduled receipts are the goods the distributor expects to receive from orders that already have been released, while goods that already are received and entered into inventory constitute the on-hand inventory balance. Subtracting scheduled receipts and on-hand inventory from gross requirements yields net requirements. Based upon the distributor's lot-sizing policy and receiving behavior, planned order receipts are generated. Firms may order only what they need for the next planning period or for a designated time period. Known as economic order quantity (EOQ), this involves a lot size based on a costing model. Alternatively, firms may be limited to multiples of a lot size simply because the supplying firm packages or palletizes their goods in standard quantities. Also, some distributors may require some

Figure 1
A DRP Calculation

Scheduled receipts: 1200, period 3
On-hand inventory balance: 1000
Lead time: 3 periods
Order receipt: period due
Lot size: 600 units per pallet

Periods	1	2	3	4	5	6	7	8
Gross Requirements	500	500	500	500	500	500	500	500
Scheduled Receipts			1200					
On Hand	500			200				
Net Requirements					300	200	100	
Planned Order Receipt					600	600	600	
Planned Order Release		600	600	600				

time interval between the arrival of goods on their docks and the entry of the goods into the inventory system. For example, a firm may have a staging area where goods remain for an average time period while awaiting quality or quantity verification. Hence, planned order receipt may be during the planning period when the goods are needed, or they may need to be received earlier depending on time requirements. Order release is then determined by offsetting the planned order receipt by the supplier's lead time. Figure 1 is a representation of a DRP calculation (ignoring possible safety stock requirements).

SEE ALSO: Forecasting; Logistics and Transportation; Reverse Supply Chain Logistics; Supply Chain Management; Warehousing and Warehouse Management

R. Anthony Inman

FURTHER READING:

Coyle, John J., Edward J. Bardi, and C. John Langley, Jr. *The Management of Business Logistics: A Supply Chain Perspective.* 7th ed. Mason, OH: South-Western/Thomson Learning, 2003.

Ross, David Frederick. *Distribution Planning and Control: Managing in the Era of Supply Chain Management.* 2nd ed. Boston: Kluwer Academic Publishers, 2004.

DIVERSIFICATION STRATEGY

Diversification strategies are used to expand firms' operations by adding markets, products, services, or stages of production to the existing business. The purpose of diversification is to allow the company to enter lines of business that are different from current operations. When the new venture is strategically related to the existing lines of business, it is called concentric diversification. Conglomerate diversification occurs when there is no common thread of strategic fit or relationship between the new and old lines of business; the new and old businesses are unrelated.

DIVERSIFICATION IN THE CONTEXT OF GROWTH STRATEGIES

Diversification is a form of growth strategy. Growth strategies involve a significant increase in performance objectives (usually sales or market share) beyond past levels of performance. Many organizations pursue one or more types of growth strategies. One of the primary reasons is the view held by many investors and executives that "bigger is better." Growth in sales is often used as a measure of performance. Even if profits remain stable or decline, an increase in sales satisfies many people. The assumption is often made that if sales increase, profits will eventually follow.

Rewards for managers are usually greater when a firm is pursuing a growth strategy. Managers are often paid a commission based on sales. The higher the sales level, the larger the compensation received. Recognition and power also accrue to managers of growing companies. They are more frequently invited to speak to professional groups and are more often interviewed and written about by the press than are managers of companies with greater rates of return but slower rates of growth. Thus, growth companies also become better known and may be better able, to attract quality managers.

Growth may also improve the effectiveness of the organization. Larger companies have a number of advantages over smaller firms operating in more limited markets.

1. Large size or large market share can lead to economies of scale. Marketing or production synergies may result from more efficient use of sales calls, reduced travel time, reduced changeover time, and longer production runs.

2. Learning and experience curve effects may produce lower costs as the firm gains experience in producing and distributing its product or service. Experience and large size may also lead to improved layout, gains in labor efficiency, redesign of products or production processes, or larger and more qualified staff departments (e.g., marketing research or research and development).

3. Lower average unit costs may result from a firm's ability to spread administrative expenses and other overhead costs over a larger unit volume. The more capital intensive a business is, the more important its ability to spread costs across a large volume becomes.

4. Improved linkages with other stages of production can also result from large size. Better links with suppliers may be attained through large orders, which may produce lower costs (quantity discounts), improved delivery, or custom-made products that would be unaffordable for smaller operations. Links with distribution channels may lower costs by better location of warehouses, more efficient advertising, and shipping efficiencies. The size of the organization relative to its customers or suppliers influences its bargaining power and its ability to influence price and services provided.

5. Sharing of information between units of a large firm allows knowledge gained in one business unit to be applied to problems being experienced in another unit. Especially for companies relying heavily on technology, the reduction of R&D costs and the time needed to develop new technology may give larger firms an advantage over smaller, more specialized firms. The more similar the activities are among units, the easier the transfer of information becomes.

6. Taking advantage of geographic differences is possible for large firms. Especially for multinational firms, differences in wage rates, taxes, energy costs, shipping and freight charges, and trade restrictions influence the costs of business. A large firm can sometimes lower its cost of business by placing multiple plants in locations providing the lowest cost. Smaller firms with only one location must operate within the strengths and weaknesses of its single location.

CONCENTRIC DIVERSIFICATION

Concentric diversification occurs when a firm adds related products or markets. The goal of such diversification is to achieve strategic fit. Strategic fit allows an organization to achieve synergy. In essence, synergy is the ability of two or more parts of an organization to achieve greater total effectiveness together than would be experienced if the efforts of the independent parts were summed. Synergy may be achieved by combining firms with complementary marketing, financial, operating, or management efforts. Breweries have been able to achieve marketing synergy through national advertising and distribution. By combining a number of regional breweries into a national network, beer producers have been able to produce and sell more beer than had independent regional breweries.

Financial synergy may be obtained by combining a firm with strong financial resources but limited growth opportunities with a company having great market potential but weak financial resources. For example, debt-ridden companies may seek to acquire firms that are relatively debt-free to increase the leveraged firm's borrowing capacity. Similarly, firms sometimes attempt to stabilize earnings by diversifying into businesses with different seasonal or cyclical sales patterns.

Strategic fit in operations could result in synergy by the combination of operating units to improve overall efficiency. Combining two units so that duplicate equipment or research and development are eliminated would improve overall efficiency. Quantity discounts through combined ordering would be another possible way to achieve operating synergy. Yet another way to improve efficiency is to diversify into an area that can use by-products from existing operations. For example, breweries have been able to convert grain, a by-product of the fermentation process, into feed for livestock.

Management synergy can be achieved when management experience and expertise is applied to different situations. Perhaps a manager's experience in working with unions in one company could be applied to labor management problems in another company. Caution must be exercised, however, in assuming that management experience is universally transferable. Situations that appear similar may require significantly different management strategies. Personality clashes and other situational differences may make management synergy difficult to achieve. Although managerial skills and experience can be transferred, individual managers may not be able to make the transfer effectively.

CONGLOMERATE DIVERSIFICATION

Conglomerate diversification occurs when a firm diversifies into areas that are unrelated to its current line of business. Synergy may result through the application of management expertise or financial resources, but the primary purpose of conglomerate diversification is improved profitability of the acquiring firm. Little, if any, concern is given to achieving marketing or production synergy with conglomerate diversification.

One of the most common reasons for pursuing a conglomerate growth strategy is that opportunities in a firm's current line of business are limited. Finding an attractive investment opportunity requires the firm to consider alternatives in other types of business. Philip Morris's acquisition of Miller Brewing was a conglomerate move. Products, markets, and production technologies of the brewery were quite different from those required to produce cigarettes.

Firms may also pursue a conglomerate diversification strategy as a means of increasing the firm's growth rate. As discussed earlier, growth in sales may make the company more attractive to investors. Growth may also increase the power and prestige of the firm's executives. Conglomerate growth may be effective if the new area has growth opportunities greater than those available in the existing line of business.

Probably the biggest disadvantage of a conglomerate diversification strategy is the increase in administrative problems associated with operating unrelated businesses. Managers from different divisions may have different backgrounds and may be unable to work together effectively. Competition between strategic business units for resources may entail shifting resources away from one division to another. Such a move may create rivalry and administrative problems between the units.

Caution must also be exercised in entering businesses with seemingly promising opportunities, especially if the management team lacks experience or skill in the new line of business. Without some knowledge of the new industry, a firm may be unable to accurately evaluate the industry's potential. Even if the new business is initially successful, problems will eventually occur. Executives from the conglomerate will have to become involved in the operations of the new enterprise at some point. Without adequate experience or skills (Management Synergy) the new business may become a poor performer.

Without some form of strategic fit, the combined performance of the individual units will probably not exceed the performance of the units operating independently. In fact, combined performance may deteriorate because of controls placed on the individual units by the parent conglomerate. Decision-making may become slower due to longer review periods and complicated reporting systems.

DIVERSIFICATION: GROW OR BUY?

Diversification efforts may be either internal or external. Internal diversification occurs when a firm enters a different, but usually related, line of business by developing the new line of business itself. Internal diversification frequently involves expanding a firm's product or market base. External diversification may achieve the same result; however, the company enters a new area of business by purchasing another company or business unit. Mergers and acquisitions are common forms of external diversification.

INTERNAL DIVERSIFICATION. One form of internal diversification is to market existing products in new markets. A firm may elect to broaden its geographic base to include new customers, either within its home country or in international markets. A business could also pursue an internal diversification strategy by finding new users for its current product. For example, Arm & Hammer marketed its baking soda as a refrigerator deodorizer. Finally, firms may attempt to change markets by increasing or decreasing the price of products to make them appeal to consumers of different income levels.

Another form of internal diversification is to market new products in existing markets. Generally this strategy involves using existing channels of distribution to market new products. Retailers often change product lines to include new items that appear to have good market potential. Johnson & Johnson added a line of baby toys to its existing line of items for infants. Packaged-food firms have added salt-free or low-calorie options to existing product lines.

It is also possible to have conglomerate growth through internal diversification. This strategy would entail marketing new and unrelated products to new markets. This strategy is the least used among the internal diversification strategies, as it is the most risky. It requires the company to enter a new market where it is not established. The firm is also developing and introducing a new product. Research and development costs, as well as advertising costs, will likely be higher than if existing products were marketed. In effect, the investment and the probability of failure are much greater when both the product and market are new.

EXTERNAL DIVERSIFICATION. External diversification occurs when a firm looks outside of its current operations and buys access to new products or markets. Mergers are one common form of external diversification. Mergers occur when two or more firms combine operations to form one corporation, perhaps with a new name. These firms are usually of similar size. One goal of a merger is to achieve management synergy by creating a stronger management team. This can be achieved in a merger by combining the management teams from the merged firms.

Acquisitions, a second form of external growth, occur when the purchased corporation loses its identity. The acquiring company absorbs it. The acquired company and its assets may be absorbed into an existing business unit or remain intact as an independent subsidiary within the parent company. Acquisitions usually occur when a larger firm purchases a smaller company. Acquisitions are called friendly if the firm being purchased is receptive to the acquisition. (Mergers are usually "friendly.") Unfriendly mergers or hostile takeovers occur when the management of the firm targeted for acquisition resists being purchased.

DIVERSIFICATION: VERTICAL OR HORIZONTAL?

Diversification strategies can also be classified by the direction of the diversification. Vertical integration occurs when firms undertake operations at different stages of production. Involvement in the different stages of production can be developed inside the company (internal diversification) or by acquiring another firm (external diversification). Horizontal integration or diversification involves the firm moving into operations at the same stage of production. Vertical integration is usually related to existing operations and would be considered concentric diversification. Horizontal integration can be either a concentric or a conglomerate form of diversification.

VERTICAL INTEGRATION. The steps that a product goes through in being transformed from raw materials to a finished product in the possession of the customer constitute the various stages of production. When a firm diversifies closer to the sources of raw materials in the stages of production, it is following a backward vertical integration strategy. *Avon's* primary line of business has been the selling of cosmetics door-to-door. *Avon* pursued a backward form of vertical integration by entering into the production of some of its cosmetics. Forward diversification occurs when firms move closer to the consumer in terms of the production stages. Levi Strauss & Co., traditionally a manufacturer of clothing, has diversified forward by opening retail stores to market its textile products rather than producing them and selling them to another firm to retail.

Backward integration allows the diversifying firm to exercise more control over the quality of the supplies being purchased. Backward integration also may be undertaken to provide a more dependable source of needed raw materials. Forward integration allows a manufacturing company to assure itself of an outlet for its products. Forward integration also allows a firm more control over how its products are sold and serviced. Furthermore, a company may be better able to differentiate its products from those of its competitors by forward integration. By opening its own retail outlets, a firm is often better able to control and train the personnel selling and servicing its equipment.

Since servicing is an important part of many products, having an excellent service department may provide an integrated firm a competitive advantage over firms that are strictly manufacturers.

Some firms employ vertical integration strategies to eliminate the "profits of the middleman." Firms are sometimes able to efficiently execute the tasks being performed by the middleman (wholesalers, retailers) and receive additional profits. However, middlemen receive their income by being competent at providing a service. Unless a firm is equally efficient in providing that service, the firm will have a smaller profit margin than the middleman. If a firm is too inefficient, customers may refuse to work with the firm, resulting in lost sales.

Vertical integration strategies have one major disadvantage. A vertically integrated firm places "all of its eggs in one basket." If demand for the product falls, essential supplies are not available, or a substitute product displaces the product in the marketplace, the earnings of the entire organization may suffer.

HORIZONTAL DIVERSIFICATION. Horizontal integration occurs when a firm enters a new business (either related or unrelated) at the same stage of production as its current operations. For example, Avon's move to market jewelry through its door-to-door sales force involved marketing new products through existing channels of distribution. An alternative form of horizontal integration that Avon has also undertaken is selling its products by mail order (e.g., clothing, plastic products) and through retail stores (e.g., Tiffany's). In both cases, Avon is still at the retail stage of the production process.

DIVERSIFICATION STRATEGY AND MANAGEMENT TEAMS

As documented in a study by Marlin, Lamont, and Geiger, ensuring a firm's diversification strategy is well matched to the strengths of its top management team members factored into the success of that strategy. For example, the success of a merger may depend not only on how integrated the joining firms become, but also on how well suited top executives are to manage that effort. The study also suggests that different diversification strategies (concentric vs. conglomerate) require different skills on the part of a company's top managers, and that the factors should be taken into consideration before firms are joined.

There are many reasons for pursuing a diversification strategy, but most pertain to management's desire for the organization to grow. Companies must decide whether they want to diversify by going into related or unrelated businesses. They must then decide whether they want to expand by developing the new business or by buying an ongoing business. Finally, management must decide at what stage in the production process they wish to diversify.

SEE ALSO: Strategic Planning Failure; Strategy Formulation; Strategy Implementation; Strategy in the Global Environment

Joe G. Thomas
Revised by Wendy H. Mason

FURTHER READING:

Amit, R., and J. Livnat. "A Concept of Conglomerate Diversification." *Academy of Management Journal* 28 (1988): 593–604.

Homburg, C., H. Krohmer, and J. Workman. "Strategic Consensus and Performance: The Role of Strategy Type and Market-Related Dynamism." *Strategic Management Journal* 20, 339–358.

Luxenber, Stan. "Diversification Strategy Raises Doubts." *National Real Estate Investor*, February 2004.

Lyon, D.W., and W.J. Ferrier. "Enhancing Performance With Product-Market Innovation: The Influence of the Top Management Team." *Journal of Managerial Issues* 14 (2002): 452–469.

Marlin, Dan, Bruce T. Lamont, and Scott W. Geiger. "Diversification Strategy and Top Management Team Fit." *Journal of Managerial Issues*, Fall 2004, 361.

Munk, N. "How Levi's Trashed a Great American Brand." *Fortune*, 12 April 1999, 83–90.

St. John, C., and J. Harrison, "Manufacturing-Based Relatedness, Synergy, and Coordination." *Strategic Management Journal* 20 (1999): 129–145.

DIVERSITY

The advent of equal employment opportunity (EEO) laws and affirmative action programs created new employment opportunities for members of protected groups that had previously been victimized by employment discrimination. The demographic mix within the twenty-first century workplace has consequently become much more diverse because many workers now entering the workforce are neither white, male, nor English speaking. People of color continue to increase their shares of the labor force. The rates of growth for these groups are projected to be faster than the rate for whites. Whereas the White non-Hispanics are projected to continue to decline as a percentage of the labor force, Hispanics are predicted to be the second largest group in 2025, accounting for 17 percent of the total labor force. Furthermore, as of 2000, Hispanics have a larger share of the market than African Americans, 13 percent versus 12.7 percent. The share of African Americans in the labor force is expected to increase by only 1.8 percent during the same time period. Asians and other people of color would account for approximately 8 percent of the labor force in 2025. Hispanics and Asians, therefore, will continue to be the two fastest growing groups.

The workforce is also becoming older and is experiencing a dramatic increase in the number of dual-income families (many of whom have young children), single-parent families, and families facing the demands of elder care. The projected labor market will continue to be significantly impacted by the aging of the baby-boom generation.

In the past, organizations ignored the impact that diversity had on the attitudes and behavior of employees. However, 25 years of political, social, and legal change brought new groups of employees into the workplace. At first, organizations attempted to handle these new groups through assimilation. People were expected to fit in. Equal treatment at the workplace meant the same treatment for each employee; individual differences were ignored. Consequently, assimilation often resulted in pressure to conform, exclusion and isolation, and reinforcement of the dominant group values. The problem became compounded as the number of diverse groups within the organization increased and the number of white males declined.

The failure to deal effectively with the diversity issue can hinder competitive advantage. For instance, firms choosing to do business as usual have been plagued with a high turnover among nontraditional employees, low morale within the organization, underutilization of employee skills, numerous intergroup conflicts, low productivity, and an inability to attract new workers. On the other hand, if diversity is dealt with effectively, competitive advantage can be enhanced. For instance, companies that value diversity can attract a larger and better pool of applicants than companies which limit themselves to a traditional workforce.

Accommodating the needs of the diverse workforce is more important to organizations now than ever before. When properly managed, such cultural diversity can represent a key strategic advantage. Diversity in age, gender, race, and viewpoint can offer organizations a number of benefits including additional knowledge, creative ideas and insights to aid in problem solving, enhanced product positioning, better development of strategic plans and objectives, and fresh opinions. These diverse workers can bring original ideas and approaches to the workplace that can help a firm target its products and services to a marketplace that is becoming more and more diverse. This adds economic importance to the issue of diversity since the combined African-American, Hispanic-American and Asian-American buying power is more than $750 billion dollars.

MINORITIES IN THE WORKPLACE

Although minorities have been entering the workforce in record numbers, their quests to reach the top of the corporate ladder have been thwarted. Many have topped out at entry- or mid-level management positions. Consider the following statistics:

- African Americans hold less than 1 percent of the senior-level corporate positions in America's 1000 largest companies despite EEO and affirmative action programs.

- Only 1.97 percent of Fortune 1000 board seats are held by Hispanics and Hispanic women hold only three tenths of all Fortune 1000 board seats. That is just 34 out of 10,314 seats. In addition, only seven Hispanic women serve as executive officers at Fortune 1000 companies.

- An examination of the Fortune 1000 companies reveals that only 3 percent have an African American on their Board of Directors.

Minorities have failed to reach the highest levels of management partly because many have only recently entered the managerial ranks; it takes time to climb the corporate ladder. However, this explanation does not account for the magnitude of the problem. For years minorities have faced invisible, subtle, yet very real institutional barriers to promotions into higher level executive positions. The belief that minority groups reach organizational plateaus consisting of artificial barriers that derail them from senior management opportunities has been alternately termed "the glass ceiling," or "the brick wall." These barriers found in the structure of many organizations have often stymied the advancement of these select employee groups.

How can the glass ceilings be cracked or the brick walls broken down? Effective diversity training that helps decision-makers overcome their biases would certainly help. But diversity training, by itself, is not enough, and diversity management must not be confused with affirmative action. The Society for Human Resource Management recommends the following components for a successful diversity initiative:

1. **Get executive commitment.** Enlisting the visible support and commitment of your organization's CEO is fundamental to a successful diversity initiative.

2. **Articulate the desired outcomes.** Be explicit about how support and commitment are to be shown and from whom it is expected.

3. **Assess the climate, needs and issues at your organization.** The use of focus groups can help clarify the obstacles. It will prove helpful to determine where your organization is currently on the diversity continuum before determining what interventions need to be taken.

4. **Create and maintain open channels of communication with employees at the launch of your diversity initiative and throughout the process.** Communication is crucial to the success of your diversity plan and should occur not only at the beginning of a diversity initiative, but also throughout the process.

5. **Consider forming a diversity taskforce to widen your support base.** This group can help analyze assessment data and make recommendations to top management.

6. **Develop a mechanism for dealing with systemic changes and procedural problems.** Once identified, obstacles and problems must be addressed. For example, your company may be committed to hiring persons outside of the dominant culture, but has difficulty promoting those same persons once they are with the organization.

7. **Design relevant, interactive applicable training.** The purpose of good training is to not just increase awareness and understanding about diversity, but to also develop concrete skills that employees can use to deal with workplace diversity, its implications and its effects.

8. **Evaluate and measure each component of your diversity initiative (training, taskforce, mentoring initiative, employee networks, etc.).** Set measurable criteria and determine what you would like to accomplish and how you will gather data.

9. **Ensure integration and accountability.** Integrate the concepts, skills and results of

your diversity efforts into the fabric of the organization and hold management accountable for encouraging diversity throughout the organization.

Dealing with diversity is a continuing process that enhances an organization's ability to adapt and capitalize on today's increasingly complex world and global marketplace. A well-managed diverse workforce can give your company the competitive advantage necessary to compete in a global economy.

SEE ALSO: Employment Law and Compliance; International Cultural Differences; Mentoring; Organizational Culture; Work-Life Balance

Patricia A. Lanier

FURTHER READING:

Bell, E.E., and S.M. Nkomo. *Our Separate Ways.* Boston, MA: Harvard Business School Press, 2001.

Counting Minorities. Available from <http://www.bls.gov/opub/rtaw/chapter1.htm>.

Fullerton, H.N., Jr. "Labor Force Participation: 75 Years of Change, 1950–98 and 1998–2025." *Monthly Labor Review* 122, no. 12 (1999): 3–12.

Fullerton, H.N., Jr., and M. Toossi. "Labor Force Projections to 2010: Steady Growth and Changing Composition." *Monthly Labor Review* 124, no. 11 (2001): 21–38.

Mitra, A. "Breaking the Glass Ceiling: African American Women in Management Positions." *Equal Opportunities International* 22, no. 2 (2003): 67–80.

Tatum, B.D. *Why Are All the Black Kids Sitting Together in the Cafeteria?* New York, NY: Basic Books, 2003.

Toossi, M. "Labor Force Projections to 2012: The Graying of the U.S. Workforce." *Monthly Labor Review* 127, no. 2 (2004): 37–57.

"What Are the Components of a Successful Diversity Initiative?" Available from <http://www.shrm.org/diversity/components.asp>.

DIVESTMENT

Divestment is a form of retrenchment strategy used by businesses when they downsize the scope of their business activities. Divestment usually involves eliminating a portion of a business. Firms may elect to sell, close, or spin-off a strategic business unit, major operating division, or product line. This move often is the final decision to eliminate unrelated, unprofitable, or unmanageable operations.

Divestment is commonly the consequence of a growth strategy. Much of the corporate downsizing of the 1990s has been the result of acquisitions and takeovers that were the rage in the 1970s and early 80s. Firms often acquired other businesses with operations in areas with which the acquiring firm had little experience. After trying for a number of years to integrate the new activities into the existing organization, many firms have elected to divest themselves of portions of the business in order to concentrate on those activities in which they had a competitive advantage.

REASONS TO DIVEST

In most cases it is not immediately obvious that a unit should be divested. Many times management will attempt to increase investment as a means of giving the unit an opportunity to turn its performance around. Portfolio models such as the Boston Consulting Group (BCG) Model or General Electric's Business Screen can be used to identify operations in need of divestment. For example, products or business operations identified as "dogs" in the BCG Model are prime candidates for divestment.

Decisions to divest may be made for a number of reasons:

MARKET SHARE TOO SMALL. Firms may divest when their market share is too small for them to be competitive or when the market is too small to provide the expected rates of return.

AVAILABILITY OF BETTER ALTERNATIVES. Firms may also decide to divest because they see better investment opportunities. Organizations have limited resources. They are often able to divert resources from a marginally profitable line of business to one where the same resources can be used to achieve a greater rate of return.

NEED FOR INCREASED INVESTMENT. Firms sometimes reach a point where continuing to maintain an operation is going to require large investments in equipment, advertising, research and development, and so forth to remain viable. Rather than invest the monetary and management resources, firms may elect to divest that portion of the business.

LACK OF STRATEGIC FIT. A common reason for divesting is that the acquired business is not consistent with the image and strategies of the firm. This can be the result of acquiring a diversified business. It may also result from decisions to restructure and refocus the existing business.

LEGAL PRESSURES TO DIVEST. Firms may be forced to divest operations to avoid penalties for restraint of trade. Service Corporation Inc., a large funeral home chain acquired so many of its competitors in some areas that it created a regional monopoly. The Federal Trade Commission required the firm to divest some of its operations to avoid charges of restraint of trade.

IMPLEMENTATION OF DIVESTMENT STRATEGIES

Firms may pursue a divestment strategy by spinning off a portion of the business and allowing it to operate as an independent business entity. Firms may also divest by selling a portion of the business to another organization. RJR Nabisco used both of these forms of divestment. In 1985 Nabisco Brands was bought by R.J. Reynolds, the manufacturer of Winston, Camel, and many other cigarette brands. Fueled in part by fears of legal liability resulting from tobacco lawsuits and by complaints from investors that the tobacco side of RJR Nabisco was dragging the food business down, in early 1999 the decision was made to spin-off the domestic tobacco operations into a separate company. Later in 1999 the decision was made to sell the overseas tobacco business to Japan Tobacco.

Another way to implement a divestment decision is to simply close a portion of the firm's operations. Faced with a decline in its market share of almost half in the 14 to 19 male age group and no introduction of a successful new product in years, and rising manufacturing costs, Levi Strauss has found it necessary to divest some of its operations. Since 1997 the company has announced plans to shut twenty-nine factories in North America and Europe and to eliminate 16,310 jobs. Selling many of the plants probably was not feasible as many other clothing manufacturers are also closing plants and moving operations overseas, depressing the price for clothing manufacturing facilities. Besides, the most likely buyers for the Levi's plants would be competitors and Levi Strauss probably would not want them to have the added capacity.

In 2004 Teleflex, a U.S. $2 billion industrial product manufacturer implemented a divestment and acquisition strategy to remove underperforming units while acquiring companies in markets where it intended to expand its business. Although a business may be identified as a target for divestment, the implementation of divestment is not always easy. First a buyer must be found. This may be difficult for a failing business unit. Once a buyer is found, then price must be negotiated. Many divestments are blocked by management's expectations for the operation. Firms may expect demand for the product to pick up. Management may also see the poor performance as a temporary setback that can be overcome with time and patience. Decisions to divest a business may be seen as an admission of failure on the part of management and may lead to escalating commitment to the struggling business as a way of protecting management's ego and public image. Robert Haas, president and CEO at Levi Strauss & Co., has certainly received bad publicity and has had his leadership abilities and judgment questioned as a result of his decision to close company plants and eliminate over 16,000 jobs.

Divestment is not usually the first choice of strategy for a business. However, as product demand changes and firms alter their strategies, there will almost always be some portion of the business that is not performing to management's expectations. Such an operation is a prime target for divestment and may well leave the company in a stronger competitive position if it is divested.

SEE ALSO: Downsizing and Rightsizing; Strategic Planning Failure; Strategy Implementation

Joe G. Thomas
Revised by Hal P. Kirkwood Jr.

FURTHER READING:

Badenhausen, K. "Breaking Up Is Good to Do." *Forbes*, 1 January 2005, 56–57.

Dranikoff, L., T. Koller, and A. Schneider. "Divestiture: Strategy's Missing Link." *Harvard Business Review* 80, no. 5 (May 2002): 75–83.

Grocer, S. "Teleflex Plans to Flex Its Divestiture Muscle." *Mergers & Acquisitions Report* 17, no. 45 (November 2004): 4–5.

Harding, D., and C. Tillen. "Getting Small to Grow Big." *Brandweek*, 24 January 2005, 20.

Munk, N. "How Levi's Trashed a Great American Brand." *Fortune*, 12 April 1999, 82–90.

Shimizu, K., and M.A. Hitt. "What Constrains or Facilitates Divestitures of Formerly Acquired Firms?" *Journal of Management* 31, no. 1 (February 2005): 50–73.

DOMESTIC MANAGEMENT SOCIETIES AND ASSOCIATIONS

Management societies and associations exist to promote greater professionalism within the field and provide educational opportunities for their members. Many societies and associations exist within the field of management. Some have members primarily from academia; others have members who are primarily practitioners; while still others have both. Although almost all associations within the field of management have some international members, the focus of the following paragraphs is on those societies and associations whose membership is predominantly in the United States.

The management associations discussed in this article all have similar organization structures and activities:

- All sponsor a variety of useful professional services available to their members.
- Most have local chapters that are affiliated with the national organization.

- Most have at least one and sometimes several conferences each year and sponsor publications designed to disseminate management research findings or to communicate helpful information to management practitioners.

- Some offer professional certification programs to allow members to demonstrate their competence within their area of specialty.

ACADEMY OF MANAGEMENT

The Academy of Management (AOM) is the preeminent professional organization for those involved or interested in management research and education in the United States. It was founded in 1936, and its membership consisted of about 12,000 individuals as of 2004. Most of its members are college professors teaching within the field of management or related disciplines. Most academy members have Ph.D.s in management or related disciplines. The academy also has some practitioner members. Although the academy has members from around the world, the overwhelming majority of its membership is in the United States.

AOM sponsors an annual conference each August. At this meeting, educational and professional development programs are held and scholarly research papers are presented and discussed. Other activities at the annual meeting include meetings of various divisions and interest groups and a job placement service that allows universities to recruit for qualified applicants to fill open faculty positions in management and related fields.

AOM publishes scholarly journals and a newsletter. The *Academy of Management Journal (AMJ)* features empirical papers, and the *Academy of Management Review (AMR)* features theoretical papers. The *Academy of Management Executive (AME)* publishes applied articles related to management practice and has a substantial readership among practitioners. There is also the *Academy of Management Learning and Education (AMLE)*.

AOM has a variety of divisions and interest groups that allow members with common interests to interact more closely. Some of these divisions include Business Policy & Strategy, Human Resource Management, Organizational Behavior, Operations Management, Social Issues in Management, Entrepreneurship, and Management History.

Within AOM, there are several associated organizations, including the Southern Management Association, the Eastern Academy of Management, the Southwest Academy of Management, the Midwest Academy of Management, and the Western Academy of Management. Each of these regional associations holds annual meetings of its own, with activities that are similar to those that take place at the national meeting of the academy. Many management scholars also hold memberships in one or more of these regional associations.

AOM has a significant presence online (http://www.aomonline.org). The site has information of interest to management scholars and researchers, news about upcoming conferences, and links to related divisions and groups.

AMERICAN MANAGEMENT ASSOCIATION

The American Management Association (AMA) is a large, nonprofit educational association that has as its goal the development of organizational effectiveness. AMA has programs related to many areas of management practice, including general and administrative services, strategic management, human resources, information systems, manufacturing, purchasing, research and development, and sales and marketing. Founded in 1923, AMA has about 80,000 members. Membership consists mainly of management practitioners based in the United States, although it does have a significant membership around the world.

AMA publishes about 80 business-related books each year. It also publishes several periodicals related to management, including *Management Review, The Take-Charge Assistant, Organizational Dynamics,* and *HR Focus.*

The association holds an annual conference and sponsors numerous seminars, workshops, and forums on various management-related topics.

AMA's web site (http://www.amanet.org) provides details about its programs, conferences, and seminars, as well as other useful information relevant to the practicing manager.

SOCIETY FOR HUMAN RESOURCE MANAGEMENT

The Society for Human Resource Management (SHRM), founded in 1948, is the largest professional association in its field. Its approximately 63,000 members are largely in the United States, and also belong to local professional chapters or college and university student chapters.

SHRM has several professional publications, most of which are free with membership in the organization. Its premiere publication is the monthly *HR Magazine. HR News, Workplace Visions,* and *Mosaics* are primarily of interest to practitioners. *HRM Journal* features academic research of interest to scholars in the field.

SHRM sponsors professional development and certification programs. Professional development activities include seminars and certificate programs, portfolio subscriptions, and certification preparation learning modules. A certification program is administered through the Human Resource Certification Institute (HRCI). Certification is available at two levels: Professional in Human Resources (PHR) and Senior Professional in Human Resources (SPHR). Certification requires several years of experience in an exempt HR position and the successful completion of a certification examination, which is offered twice a year.

SHRM funds human resources management academic research through its Foundation. It also conducts an annual HR salary survey.

The society holds an annual conference and exposition, an employment law and legislative conference, a leadership conference, and a diversity conference.

SHRM's web site (http://www.shrm.org) contains a wide variety of resources for the HR professional, including an information center, online publications, and a placement area. Although some of the internet services are available to the public, most are restricted to SHRM members.

APICS: THE ASSOCIATION FOR OPERATIONS MANAGEMENT

APICS: The Association for Operations Management (formerly Association for Production and Inventory Control) is a professional organization for those involved or interested in operations management, and production and inventory management. It provides professional certifications, educational programs, and publications. Founded in 1957, APICS has practitioner, academic, and student members. There are approximately 60,000 members worldwide, though concentrated in the United States.

APICS offers member discounts on educational materials, programs, and certification exam and review material. The organization also offers numerous national workshops and in-house training programs. Publications include *APICS—The Performance Advantage* and the *Production and Inventory Management Journal*.

APICS has two certification programs for professionals in the field: Certified in Production and Inventory Management (CPIM) and Certified in Integrated Resource Management (CIRM). CPIM certification was developed in 1973 to provide a means for individuals to assess their knowledge of production and inventory management relative to a common core of knowledge. CIRM certification was developed in 1991 and is designed to assess cross-functional knowledge of interrelated functions within an organization.

APICS holds an annual conference that allows members to learn about the latest management and manufacturing techniques. It also sponsors various research activities, including an undergraduate and graduate paper competition through its Educational and Research Foundation.

The APICS web site (http://www.apics.org) contains information about its services and the field.

WORLD AT WORK

Founded in 1955, WorldatWork (formerly the American Compensation Association) is a professional organization for those involved or interested in the management of employee compensation and benefits policies and procedures. WorldatWork provides information, training, research support, and networking opportunities to its 25,000 members. Specific benefits of membership include discounts on WorldatWork educational and training programs, career placement and networking opportunities, and updates in the field through various publications.

WorldatWork offers various educational and professional training programs. Seminars provide training in all areas of compensation and benefits management. In-house training programs allow organizations to sponsor training for their employees on-site.

WorldatWork sponsors a certification program that allows members to increase their credibility as a compensation and benefits management professional. Certification is available along two tracks: Certified Compensation Professional (CCP) and Certified Benefits Professional (CBP).

WorldatWork holds an annual conference and sponsors various research activities at leading U.S. universities. It publishes several journals and newsletters, including *Workspan* and *WorldatWork Journal*.

WorldatWork also attempts to increase linkages between practitioners and academia through its Academic Partnership Network. This concept is designed to foster increased communication between practitioners and academics.

WorldatWork's web site (http://www.worldatwork.org) includes information resources for the compensation and benefits professional.

INSTITUTE FOR SUPPLY MANAGEMENT

The Institute for Supply Management (ISM) is a professional association designed to advance the purchasing and supply management profession. Founded in 1915, it has approximately 45,000 members, mostly in the United States. To be eligible for membership, a person must be involved in the purchasing or materials process, be employed by an affiliated association, or be a full-time professor or administrator at a college or university whose academic responsibility includes purchasing or material management courses.

ISM offers a variety of educational and development programs and products. Conferences, seminars, and other educational activities allow purchasing and material managers to expand their professional skills.

ISM publishes *Inside Supply Management, International Journal of Purchasing and Materials Management,* and *Manufacturing ISM Report on Business,* a well-respected purchasing survey and indicator of economic trends.

ISM sponsors two certification programs: the Certified Purchasing Manager, which allows purchasing or materials management professionals to demonstrate their mastery of the requirements of the field; and the Accredited Purchasing Practitioner, designed primarily for entry-level buyers engaged in the operational side of purchasing and materials management.

ISM provides information about its conferences, seminars, professional forums, products, and other information of interest to the purchasing and materials management professional on its website at (http://www.ism.ws).

SEE ALSO: International Management Societies and Associations; Management and Executive Development

Tim Barnett
Revised by Judith M. Nixon

DOWNSIZING AND RIGHTSIZING

Downsizing refers to the permanent reduction of a company's workforce and is generally associated with corporate reorganization, or creating a "leaner, meaner" company. For example, the database developer Oracle Corporation reduced its number of employees by 5,000 after acquiring rival PeopleSoft. Downsizing is certainly not limited to the U.S.; Jamaica Air cut 15 percent of its workforce in an effort to trim expenses and anticipated revenue shortfalls.

Downsizings such as these are also commonly called reorganizing, reengineering, restructuring, or rightsizing. Regardless of the label applied, however, downsizing essentially refers to layoffs that may or may not be accompanied by systematic restructuring programs, such as staff reductions, departmental consolidations, plant or office closings, or other forms of reducing payroll expenses. Corporate downsizing results from both poor economic conditions and company decisions to eliminate jobs in order to cut costs and maintain or achieve specific levels of profitability. Companies may lay off a percentage of their employees in response to these changes: a slowed economy, merging with or acquiring other companies, the cutting of product or service lines, competitors grabbing a higher proportion of market share, distributors forcing price concessions from suppliers, or a multitude of other events that have a negative impact on specific organizations or entire industries. In addition, downsizing may stem from restructuring efforts to maximize efficiency, to cut corporate bureaucracy and hierarchy and thereby reduce costs, to focus on core business functions and outsource non-core functions, and to use part-time and temporary workers to complete tasks previously performed by full-time workers in order to trim payroll costs.

The following sections discuss trends in downsizing, the growth of downsizing, downsizing and restructuring, criticisms of downsizing, support for downsizing, and downsizing and management.

TRENDS IN DOWNSIZING

As a major trend among U.S. businesses, downsizing began in the 1980s and continued through the 1990s largely unabated and even growing. During this time, many of the country's largest corporations participated in the trend, including General Motors, AT&T, Delta Airlines, Eastman Kodak, IBM, and Sears, Roebuck and Company. In the twenty-first century, downsizing continued after a sharp decline in the stock market early in the century and followed by continued pressure on corporate earnings in the aftermath of the September 11, 2002, terrorist attacks. Downsizing affects most sectors of the labor market, including retail, industrial, managerial, and office jobs, impacting workers in a wide range of income levels. Table 1 compares the number of temporarily downsized workers with the number of permanently downsized workers.

While layoffs are a customary measure for companies to help compensate for the effects of recessions, downsizing also occurs during periods of economic prosperity, even when companies themselves are doing well. Consequently, downsizing is a controversial corporate practice that receives support and even praise from executives, shareholders, and some economists, and criticism from employees, unions, and community activists. Reports of executive salaries growing in the face of downsizing and stagnant wages for retained employees only fan the flames of this criticism. In contrast, announcements of downsizing are well received in the stock markets. It is not uncommon for a company's stock value to rise following a downsizing announcement.

Table 1
Number of U.S. Unemployed Workers by Month

Type of Downsizing	October 2004	November 2004	December 2004	January 2005	February 2005
Temporary downsizing	947,000	941,000	965,000	966,000	965,000
Permanent downsizing	3,127,000	3,124,000	3,144,000	3,082,000	3,015,000

Adapted from: U.S. Department of Labor, Bureau of Labor Statistics. 2005. Unemployed Persons by Reason of Unemployment. Employment Situation Summary

However, economists remain optimistic about downsizing and the effects of downsizing on the economy when the rate of overall job growth outpaces the rate of job elimination. A trend toward outsourcing jobs overseas to countries with lower labor costs is a form of downsizing that affects some U.S. employees. These jobs are not actually eliminated, but instead moved out of reach of the employees who lose their jobs to outsourcing. Some economists, however, suggest that the overall net effect of such outsourced jobs will actually be an increase in U.S. jobs as resulting corporate operating efficiencies allow for more employment of higher-tier (and thus higher-wage) positions. Regardless of whether downsizing is good or bad for the national economy, companies continue to downsize and the trend shows few signs of slowing down. For some sectors, this trend is projected to be particularly prevalent through 2012, as shown in Table 2.

Table 2
Projected Job Decline in Selected Occupations, 2002-2012

Occupation	Projected Decline
Chemical plant and system operators	-12%
Travel agents	-14%
Brokerage clerks	-15%
Fisheries workers	-27%
Textile workers	-34%
Word processors and typists	-39%
Telephone operators	-56%

Adapted from: U.S. Department of Labor, Bureau of Labor Statistics. 2005. Occupations with the Largest Job Decline, 2002-2012.

THE GROWTH OF DOWNSIZING

The corporate downsizing trend grew out of the economic conditions of the late 1970s, when direct international competition began to increase. The major industries affected by this stiffer competition included the automotive, electronics, machine tool, and steel industries. In contrast to their major competitors—Japanese manufacturers—U.S. companies had signifi-

cantly higher costs. For example, U.S. automobile manufacturers had approximately a $1,000 cost disadvantage for their cars compared to similar classes of Japanese cars. Only a small percentage of this cost difference could be attributed to labor costs, however, but labor costs were among the first to be cut despite other costs associated with the general structure of the auto companies and their oversupply of middle managers and engineers. Auto workers were among the first to be laid off during the initial wave of downsizing. Other U.S. manufacturing industries faced similar competitive problems during this period, as did some U.S. technology industries. Companies in these industries, like those in the auto industry, suffered from higher per-unit costs and greater overhead than their Japanese counterparts due to lower labor productivity and a glut of white-collar workers in many U.S. companies.

To remedy these problems, U.S. companies implemented a couple of key changes: they formed partnerships with Japanese companies to learn the methods behind their cost efficiencies and they strove to reduce costs and expedite decision-making by getting rid of unnecessary layers of bureaucracy and management. Nevertheless, some companies began simply to cut their workforce without determining whether or not it was necessary and without any kind of accompanying strategy. In essence, they downsized because they lacked new products that would have stimulated growth and because their existing product markets were decreasing.

DOWNSIZING AND RESTRUCTURING

Downsizing generally accompanies some kind of restructuring and reorganizing, either as part of the downsizing plan or as a consequence of downsizing. Since companies frequently lose a significant amount of employees when downsizing, they usually must reallocate tasks and responsibilities. In essence, restructuring efforts attempt to increase the amount of work output relative to the amount of work input. Consequently, downsizing often accompanies corporate calls for concentration on "core capabilities" or "core businesses," which refers to the interest in focusing on the primary revenue-generating aspects of a business. The jobs and responsibilities that are not considered part of the primary revenue-generating functions are the ones that are frequently downsized. These jobs might then be outsourced or handled by outside consultants and workers on a contract basis.

Eliminating non-core aspects of a business may also include the reduction of bureaucracy and the number of corporate layers. Since dense bureaucracy frequently causes delays in communication and decision-making, the reduction of bureaucracy may help bring about a more efficient and responsive corporate structure that can implement new ideas more quickly.

Besides laying off workers, restructuring efforts may involve closing plants, selling non-core operations, acquiring or merging with related companies, and overhauling the internal structure of a company. The seminal work on restructuring or reengineering, *Reinventing the Corporation,* by Michael Hammer and James Champy, characterizes the process as the "fundamental rethinking and radical redesign of business processes to achieve dramatic improvements in critical, contemporary measures of performance such as cost, quality, service, and speed." While discussion of reengineering is common and reengineering is often associated with downsizing, Hammer and Champy argue that reengineering efforts are not always as profound. Hence, these efforts frequently have mixed results.

Downsizing and reengineering programs may result from the implementation of new, labor-saving technology. For example, the introduction of the personal computer into the office has facilitated instantaneous communication and has thus reduced the need for office support positions, such as secretaries.

CRITICISM OF DOWNSIZING

While companies frequently implement downsizing plans to increase profitability and productivity, downsizing does not always yield these results. Although critics of downsizing do not rule out the benefits in all cases, they contend that downsizing is overapplied and often used as a quick fix without sufficient planning to bring about long-term benefits. Moreover, downsizing can lead to additional problems, such as poor customer service, low employee morale, and bad employee attitudes. Laying workers off to improve competitiveness often fails to produce the intended results because downsizing can lead to the following unforeseen problems and difficulties:

- The loss of highly-skilled and reliable workers and the added expense of finding new workers.

- An increase in overtime wages.

- A decline in customer service because workers feel they lack job security after layoffs.

- Employee attitudes that may change for the worse, possibly leading to tardiness, absenteeism, and reduced productivity.

- An increase in the number of lawsuits and disability claims, which tends to occur after downsizing episodes.

- Restructuring programs sometimes take years to bear fruit because of ensuing employee confusion and the amount of time it takes for employees to adjust to their new roles and responsibilities.

Some studies have indicated that the economic advantages of downsizing have failed to come about in many cases, and that downsizing may have had a negative impact on company competitiveness and profitability in some cases.

Downsizing has repercussions that extend beyond the companies and their employees. For example, governments must sometimes enact programs to help displaced workers obtain training and receive job placement assistance. Labor groups have reacted to the frequency and magnitude of downsizing, and unions have taken tougher stances in negotiations because of it.

Instead of laying employees off, critics recommend that companies eliminate jobs only as a last resort; not as a quick fix when profits fail to meet quarterly projections. Suggested alternatives to downsizing include early retirement packages and voluntary severance programs. Furthermore, some analysts suggest that companies can improve their efficiency, productivity, and competitiveness through quality initiatives such as Six Sigma, empowering employees through progressive human resource strategies that encourage employee loyalty and stability, and other such techniques.

SUPPORT FOR DOWNSIZING

Advocates of downsizing counter critics' claims by arguing that, through downsizing, the United States has maintained its position as one of the world's leading economies. Economists point out that despite the downsizing that has become commonplace since the 1970s, overall U.S. standards of living, productivity, and corporate investment have grown at a healthy pace. They reason that without downsizing, companies would not remain profitable and hence would go bankrupt when there is fierce competition and slow growth. Therefore, some executives and economists see downsizing as a necessary albeit painful task, and one that ultimately saves the larger number of jobs that would be lost if a company went out business.

Advocates of downsizing also argue that job creation from technological advances offsets job declines from downsizing. Hence, displaced workers are able find new jobs relatively easily, especially if those workers have skills that enhance the technological competence of prospective employers. In other words, despite the admitted discomfort and difficulties that downsizing has on displaced workers, some workers are able to locate new jobs and companies are able to achieve greater efficiency, competitiveness, and profitability. Moreover, even though downsizing may not solve all of a company's competitive problems or bolster a company's profits indefinitely, downsizing can help reduce costs, which can lead to greater short-term profitability. In addition, advocates of downsizing contend that staff-reduction efforts help move workers from mature, moribund, and obsolete industries to emerging and growing industries, where they are needed. Economists argue that this process strengthens the economy and helps it grow. This process also enables companies with growing competitive advantages to maintain their positions in the market in the face of greater domestic and global competition, and it is the difficult but necessary result of the transition toward a global economy.

DOWNSIZING AND MANAGEMENT

Downsizing poses the immediate managerial problem of dismissing a large number of employees in a dignified manner in order to help minimize the trauma associated with downsizing. Employees who are laid off tend to suffer from depression, anxiety, insomnia, high blood pressure, marital discord, and a host of other problems. Thus, when companies decide that downsizing is the best course of action, managers should do so in a way that does the least harm to employees and their families. This includes taking the time to allow dismissed employees to air their thoughts, instead of laying them off quickly and impersonally, and providing assistance in finding new jobs.

Because of the possible negative effects that occur after downsizing, managers may have to implement measures to counteract employee apathy, improve customer service, and restore employee trust. Analysts of downsized companies argue that managers should take steps immediately after workforce reductions to provide the remaining workers with the support and guidance they need. This involves providing employees with clear indications of what is expected of them and how they can meet increased productivity goals. Managers should confer with employees regularly to discuss performance and strategies for meeting the goals. In addition, managers should encourage employee initiative and communication and provide employees with rewards for excellent work. By promoting employee initiative and even employee involvement in decision-making, managers can help restore employee trust and commitment and help increase employee motivation.

The aftermath of downsizing also places greater demands on managers to make do with less. In other words, managers must strive to maintain or increase productivity and quality levels despite having a smaller workforce. Since downsizing often brings about a flatter corporate structure, the flow of information and communication no longer requires the effort needed prior to restructuring. Therefore, reports used for communication between layers of the old corporate hierarchy, for example, can be eliminated. If redundant but nonessential work cannot be completely eliminated, it perhaps can be reduced. By studying particular tasks and determining their essential components, managers can get rid of unnecessary tasks and eliminate unnecessary jobs altogether.

Downsizing appears to be an ongoing practice for the foreseeable future. Top managers with responsibility for making downsizing decisions are in a difficult predicament. Failure to downsize may result in inefficiencies, while downsizing clearly has a number of potentially negative effects on individuals and communities. Finding the balance between these outcomes is the primary challenge facing these managers.

SEE ALSO: Divestment; Quality and Total Quality Management; Strategic Planning Failure

Karl Heil
Revised by Scott B. Droege

FURTHER READING:

Hammer, Michael, and James Champy. *Reengineering the Corporation: A Manifesto for Business Revolution.* Harper Business Publications, 2004.

Mandel, Michael J. "Jobs: The Lull Will Linger." *Business Week,* 25 October 2004, 38–42.

Marks, M.L., and K.P. DeMeuse. "Resizing the Organization: Maximizing the Gain While Minimizing the Pain of Layoffs, Divestitures, and Closings." *Organizational Dynamics* 34, no. 1 (2004): 19–35.

Menn, Joseph. "Series of Layoffs Begins at PeopleSoft." *Los Angeles Times,* 15 January 2005, D1.

Weber, Joseph. "More Jobs—and More Layoffs." *Business Week Online,* 16 June 2004. Available at http://www.businessweek.com.

DUE DILIGENCE

Due diligence is a legal term that describes the level of care or judgment that a reasonable person would be expected to exercise in a given situation. The term finds application in a wide range of business settings, including mergers and acquisitions, occupational health and safety, environmental impact assessments, supplier and vendor relationships, asset purchase decisions, and employee hiring or promotion practices. Performing a due diligence analysis in such situations helps managers make informed decisions and reduce the risks incurred by the business. "Real due diligence analyzes and validates all the financial, commercial, operational, and strategic assumptions underpinning the decision," an analyst for Price Waterhouse Coopers told *Mondaq Business Briefing.* "Due diligence is a strategy to reduce the risk of failure, as well as the embarrassment of discovering what underlies spectacular success," Herrington J. Bryce added in *Nonprofit Times.*

In the area of workplace safety, employers have a responsibility to exercise due diligence in eliminating hazards and creating a work environment that minimizes the risk of accidents or injuries. In fact, due diligence is the legal standard used to determined whether employers can be held liable under occupational health and safety laws. Employers are generally not held liable for accidents if they can prove that they took reasonable precautions to protect workers from injury. Companies can establish due diligence by putting workplace safety policies and procedures in writing, providing appropriate training to employees, and holding managers accountable for following safety guidelines.

Due diligence also applies to the process of making investments, whether personal investments in shares of stock, corporate investments in technology, or the purchase of one company by another. In the area of mergers and acquisitions, a due diligence analysis is an important part of the process of evaluating potential investments and confirming basic information before entering into a transaction. "Quite often, a proposed merger or acquisition gets canned or valued down following conflicts over intellectual property rights, personnel, accounting discrepancies, or incompatibilities in integrating operating systems," wrote Lee Copeland in *Computer World.* "The process of researching, understanding and, in some cases, avoiding these risks is known as due diligence."

When a business makes a purchase offer of any kind, it is often a matter of policy to make the offer contingent on the results of a due diligence analysis. This analysis might include reviewing financial records, hiring experts to examine the assets in questions, and taking other reasonable steps to make sure that all questions are answered and expectations met. Experts suggest that sellers also perform due diligence analysis prior to entering into a transaction. Going through this process helps sellers be prepared for any questions that might arise out of the buyer's due diligence analysis, and also gives sellers a basis on which to evaluate the merits of potential purchase offers.

Although the legal concept of due diligence endured for half a century, it came under siege in the early 2000s following a spate of accounting scandals and revelations of deceit and ethical lapses by senior executives at major corporations. "The issue of due diligence arises whenever a financial transaction generates questions, such as: How could this have happened? How could this have gone undetected for so long?" Bryce noted. Rather than dismissing due diligence as an outdated concept, however, some analysts argued that such incidents underlined the importance of due diligence as way for managers to be informed about and exercise judgment over all transactions that affect the welfare of the business.

In a critique of traditional due diligence practices for *Mondaq Business Briefing,* Charles F. Bacon warned that traditional due diligence tends to be reactive. For example, senior management might order a due diligence analysis after making the decision to purchase a competitor. "In effect, they bought the car and now that the tires are getting kicked, they don't want to hear about the bad transmission or leaky gaskets because that would tarnish the fun of deal-making," Bacon explained. Instead, he recommended that businesses take a systemic approach to due diligence starting at the top and incorporating due diligence into all organizational decision-making. The ultimate goal is to create a culture of due diligence in which all employees are encouraged to question and explore the implications of financial and strategic decisions.

SEE ALSO: Entrepreneurship; Licensing and Licensing Agreements

Laurie Collier Hillstrom

FURTHER READING:

Bacon, Charles F. "Next Generation Due Diligence." *Mondaq Business Briefing* (1 October 2004).

Bryce, Herrington J. "Due Diligence: Evaluation of Financial Matters." *Nonprofit Times,* 15 October 2002.

Cecil, Mark. "Financial Services Players Rework Due Diligence." *Mergers and Acquisitions Report* (4 February 2002).

Cipra, Richard R. "There Is No Substitute for Due Diligence." *Los Angeles Business Journal* (8 November 2004).

Copeland, Lee. "Due Diligence." *Computer World,* 6 March 2000. Available from <http://www.computerworld.com/news/2000/story/0,11280,42836,00.html>.

Hallinan, Eric. "Due Diligence." *Reeves Journal* (June 2004).

Kroll, Luisa. "Gotcha: Pushing the Limits of Due Diligence." *Forbes,* 30 October 2000.

Nadler, Paul. "In Due Diligence, Numbers Are Just the Beginning." *American Banker* (23 June 2004).

E

SEE: Electronic Commerce

EAP

SEE: Employee Assistance Programs

ECONOMIC CENSUS

The U.S. economic census provides information about the structure and function of the nation's economy, from the national level to the local level, every five years. The Bureau of the Census is mandated by Title Thirteen of the United States Code (sections 131, 191, and 224) to develop an economic census every five years, covering years ending in two and seven. The 2002 Economic Census covers about 98 percent of the U.S. economy in its collection of establishment statistics. There are also several related census programs, including: censuses for outlying areas of Guam, Puerto Rico, U.S. Virgin Islands, and the Commonwealth of the Northern Mariana Islands; and additional reports on minority- and women-owned businesses (available in 2006), surveys of business expenditures, and nonemployer statistics. In addition, the Census of Agriculture and Census of Governments are conducted at the same time.

COLLECTING, COMPILING, AND ISSUING THE CENSUS DATA

With the exception of the Census of Agriculture, which is conducted by the Department of Agriculture, the 2002 Economic Census covered the entire economy of about 20 million business establishments. In December 2002, the Census Bureau mailed 600 versions of the census forms; these forms were tailored to the five-million businesses receiving them. Data for those not receiving forms—generally self-employed individuals with no paid employees—are obtained from other federal agencies.

The 2002 Economic Census consists of general statistics available for the nation, states, metropolitan areas, counties, places with 2,500 or more inhabitants, and zip code areas. All operations of a particular business location are summarized. Product statistics cover products, lines of merchandise, and lines of service provided by business establishments. For example, one can determine how much hardware is sold by all kinds of stores, not just hardware stores.

The Census Bureau compiles the data and issues report series on industry, geographic area, subject, and zip code. These reports are based on the North American Industry Classification System (NAICS). The new *Advance Report* presents economy-wide data at the national level. The *Industry Series* reports are issued only for individual industries in the goods-producing part of the economy—manufacturing, mining, and construction. They provide data primarily at the national level, although there is some state data. The *Geographic Area Series* will be issued separately for each of the twenty NAICS sectors. Within several sectors, there will be individual state-by-state reports. There will only be a few *Subject Series Reports,* primarily at the national level, that will provide additional analyses of industries. Of special significance are the *Merchandise Line Sales* report for retail businesses and *Commodity Line Sales* report for wholesale trade. Zip code statistics are issued for manufacturing, retail trade, and the service industries. The data for all components of the economic census generally include the number of establishments, number of employees, annual payroll, and measures of output such as sales or receipts. More detailed economic statistics vary by sector.

PRE-2002 ECONOMIC CENSUS DATA

The economic census is an integrated program collected in 5-year intervals since 1967, and before that for 1963, 1958, and 1954. In other words, the census provided comparable data across economic sectors using consistent time periods, definitions, classifications, and reporting units. Prior to 1954, the individual censuses were taken separately at varying time periods. The economic censuses were first incorporated in the 1810 Decennial Census, when questions dealing with manufacturing were included. The first census of business was taken in 1930 and included wholesale and retail trade. Industries continued to be added to the census. In 1933, some service industries were included; the census of transportation was added in 1963 and the census of construction began on a regular basis in 1967. Finally, the 1992 Economic Census included eight sectors: census of construction industries; census of finance, insurance, and real estate; census of manufactures; census of mineral industries; census of retail trade; census of service industries; census of transportation, communication, and utilities; and the census of wholesale trade.

NAICS AND THE 2002 ECONOMIC CENSUS

The North American Industry Classification System replaced the Standard Industrial Classification (SIC) system that began in the 1930s and was revised in 1967, 1972, 1987, and 2002. This new classification system organizes establishments into industries by type of producing and non-producing activities in which they are involved, rather than organizing business activities into a mixture of production and market-based categories (as in the past). The NAICS uses a numbering system of six digits instead of SIC's four digits, and increases the number of sectors of economic activity from ten to twenty. This allows more flexibility in designating subsectors and allows for expansion, especially for the service sector industries. With the NAICS, it is now possible to compare economic activity in the United States with that of Canada and Mexico.

The implementation of NAICS caused a major disruption when comparing data from the 1997 Economic Census with previous census data. NAICS data time series can go forward from 1997, but many

of the time series cannot go back in time because the NAICS categories require information not collected in earlier censuses; the hierarchy within the levels of classification and the scope for the sectors have changed. The 2002 Economic Census published data primarily on the basis of the 2002 North American Industry Classification System. Changes between the 1997 and 2002 NAICS were within construction and wholesale trade and did not effect sector totals. NAICS 2002 introduces a number of new industries—including residential remodelers, discount department stores, electronic shopping, electronic auctions, wholesale electronic markets, internet publishing and broadcasting, and web search portals. Economic Census comparisons are easier to make since 90 percent of all industries are comparable between 1997 and 2002. To facilitate comparisons, the 2002 Economic Census includes bridge tables and comparative statistics. *Advance Comparative Statistics for the United States 1997 NAICS Basis* will present 1997 and 2002 data at the national level.

USES OF THE ECONOMIC CENSUS

In summing up the importance of the census, Alan Greenspan (chairman of the Federal Reserve Board) stated that the census provides accurate statistics essential for sound economic policy and successful business planning. All levels of government, business, industry, and the general public use the statistical information from the economic census. It provides an essential framework for such measures as the production and price indexes, gross domestic product, input/output measures, and other key data that determine changes in the economy. Policymaking agencies of the federal government use these data to monitor and guide economic activity as well as to provide assistance to businesses. State and local governments use this information to assess business activities and tax bases within their jurisdictions.

According to the Census Bureau, individual businesses use the census data to gauge the competition, calculate market share, locate business markets, identify business site locations, design sales territories, set sales quotas, and evaluate new business opportunities. Trade associations study trends in their industries to keep members abreast of market changes. Consultants and researchers use census data to analyze market structure.

LEARNING ABOUT AND ACCESSING THE ECONOMIC CENSUS

The Census Bureau provides access to over 60,000 documents via its Web site. The *Census Catalog and Guide, Monthly Product Announcement,* and *Census and You* provide the latest information about Census Bureau products, programs, and future plans. Federal depository collections found in many public and academic libraries, Census Data Centers located in all states, and census data specialists are also available to assist local users. *The Guide to the 2002 Economic Census* is the best single source for learning about the 2002 Economic Census.

There were a number of significant changes in the 2002 Economic Census. The 2002 Economic Census includes "enterprise support" establishments, thus providing additional data on outsourcing activities that will impact comparisons between certain industries. The 2002 survey also gathered e-commerce information for the first time. New industries added in the 2002 Economic Census include Landscape Architectural Services, Veterinary Services, Landscaping Services, and Pet Care (except Veterinary) Services. The metropolitan statistical area concept is being supplemented with several hundred new, micropolitan, statistical areas, meaning data will be available for many new counties outside metropolitan areas. Selected data and reports are now available to the public on the *American FactFinder*'s site.

Most importantly, all components of the census will be available in database format on the Internet, DVD, and CD-ROM. This means faster publication and wider access along with fewer printed reports. Furthermore, the introduction of the new industry classification system provides a more accurate snapshot of the economy, and there will be greater integration of the census data economy-wide.

SEE ALSO: North American Industry Classification System

William W. Prince
Revised by Hal P. Kirkwood, Jr.

FURTHER READING:

"Economic Census 2002 Features Many Firsts" *CPA Journal* 73, no. 2 (2003): 16.

Parker, Robert P. "Economic Statistics: New Data Available in 2004." *Business Economics* 39, no. 2 (2004): 63–66.

U.S. Census Bureau. *American FactFinder.* Available from <http://factfinder.census.gov/servlet/SAFFBusiness?_sse=on>.

U.S. Census Bureau. *2002 Economic Census: Introduction.* Available from <http://www.census.gov/econ/census02/text/sector00/intro.htm>.

U.S. Census Bureau. 2002. *The Guide to the 2002 Economic Census.* Available from <http://www.census.gov/epcd/ec02/guide.html>.

U.S. Office of Management and Budget. 2002. *North American Industry Classification System–United States, 2002.* Washington: Government Printing Office. Available from: <http://www.census.gov/naics>.

ECONOMICS

The study of economics leads to the formulation of the principles upon which the economy is based. History, politics, and the social sciences cannot be understood without the basic understanding of economic principles. The science of economics is concerned with the scientific laws that relate to business administration, and attempts to formulate the principles that relate to the satisfaction of wants.

The term "economics" covers such a broad range of meaning that any brief definition is likely to leave out some important aspect of the subject. It is a social science concerned with the study of economies and the relationships between them. Economics is the study of how people and society choose to employ scarce productive resources, which could have alternative uses, to produce various commodities and distribute them for consumption. Economics generally studies problems from society's point of view rather than from the individual's. Finally, economics studies the allocation of scarce resources among competing ends.

OBJECTIVES

As a science, economics must first develop an understanding of the processes by which human desires are fulfilled. Second, economics must show how causes that affect production and consumption lead to various results. Furthermore, it must draw conclusions that will serve to guide those who conduct and, in part, control economic activity.

MICRO AND MACRO VIEWS OF THE ECONOMY

While there are numerous specialties within the academic field, at its most basic level economics is commonly divided into two broad areas of focus: microeconomics and macroeconomics. Microeconomics is the study of smaller levels of the economy, such as how an individual firm or a small group of firms operate. Macroeconomics is the study of whole economies or large sectors of economies.

MICROECONOMICS. Microeconomics is the social science dealing in the satisfaction of human wants using limited resources. It focuses on individual units that make up the whole of the economy. It examines how households and businesses behave as individual units, not as parts of a larger whole. For instance, microeconomics studies how a household spends its money. It also studies the way in which a business determines how much of a product to produce, how to make the best use of production factors, and what pricing strategy to use. Microeconomics also studies how individual markets and industries are organized, what patterns of competition they follow, and how these patterns affect economic efficiency and welfare.

MACROECONOMICS. Macroeconomics studies an economy at the aggregate level. It is concerned with the workings of the whole economy or large sectors of it. These sectors include government, business, and households. Macroeconomics deals with such issues as national economic output and growth, unemployment, recession, inflation, foreign trade, and monetary and fiscal policy.

BASIC ECONOMIC PRINCIPLES

Basic economic principles include the law of demand, demand determinants, the law of supply, supply determinants, market equilibrium, factors of production, the firm, gross product, as well as inflation and unemployment.

THE LAW OF DEMAND. When an individual want is expressed as an intention to buy, it becomes a demand. The law of demand is a theory about the relationship between the amount of a good that a buyer both desires and is able to purchase per unit of time, and the price charged for it. The ability to pay is as important as the desire for the good, because economics is interested in explaining and predicting actual behavior in the marketplace, not just intentions. At a given price for a good, economics is interested in the buyer's demand that can effectively be backed by a purchase. Thus, it is implied with demand that a consumer not only has the desire and need for a product, but also has the money to purchase it. The law of demand states that the lower the price charged for a product, resource, or service, the larger will be the quantity demanded per unit of time. Conversely, the higher the price charged, the smaller will be the quantity demanded per unit of time—all other things being constant. For example, the lower the purchase price for a six-pack of Coca-Cola, the more a consumer will demand (up to some saturation point, of course).

DEMAND DETERMINANTS. Movement along the demand curve—referred to as a change in quantity demanded—means that only the price of the good and the quantity demanded change. All other things are assumed to be constant or unchanged. These things include the prices of all other goods, the individual's income, the individual's expectations about the future, and the individual's tastes. A change in one or more of these things is called a change in demand. The entire demand curve will move as a result of a change in demand.

LAW OF SUPPLY. The law of supply is a statement about the relationship between the amount of a good that a supplier is willing and able to supply and offer for sale, per unit of time, and each of the different possible prices at which that good might be sold. This law further states that suppliers will supply larger quantities of a good at higher prices than at lower prices. In other words, supply generally is governed by profit-maximizing behaviors. The supply curve indicates what prices are necessary in order to give a supplier the incentive to provide various quantities of a good per unit of time. Just as with the demand curve, movement along the supply curve always assumes that all other things are constant.

SUPPLY DETERMINANTS. At the opportunity for sale at a certain price, a part of total supply becomes realized market supply. Economics emphasizes movement along the supply curve in which the price of the good determines the quantity supplied. As with the demand curve, the price of the good is singled out as the determining factor with all other things being constant. On the supply side, these things are the prices of resources and other production factors, technology, the prices of other goods, the number of suppliers, and the suppliers' expectations.

MARKET EQUILIBRIUM. Supply and demand interact to determine the terms of trade between buyers and sellers. In theory, supply and demand mutually determine the price at which sellers are willing to supply just the amount of a good that buyers want to buy. The market for every good has a demand curve and a supply curve that determine this price and quantity. When this price and quantity are established, the market is said to be in equilibrium. The price and quantity at which this occurs are called the equilibrium price and equilibrium quantity. In equilibrium, price and quantity have the tendency to remain unchanged.

FACTORS OF PRODUCTION

Factors of production are economic resources used in the production of goods, including natural, man-made, and human resources. They may be broken down into two broad categories: (1) property resources, specifically capital and land; and (2) human resources, specifically labor and entrepreneurial ability.

Managers often speak of capital when referring to money, especially when they are talking about the purchase of equipment, machinery, and other productive facilities. Financial capital is the more accurate term for the money used to make such purchases. An economist would refer to these purchases as investments. The economist uses the term *capital* to mean all the man-made aids used in production. It is sometimes referred to as investment goods. Capital consists of machinery, tools, buildings, transportation and distribution facilities, and inventories of unfinished goods. A basic characteristic of capital goods is that they are used to produce other goods. Capital goods satisfy wants indirectly by facilitating the production of consumable goods, while consumer goods satisfy wants directly.

To an economist, land is the fundamental natural resource that is used in production. This resource includes water, forests, oil, gas, and mineral deposits. These resources are rapidly becoming scarce. Land resources, which include natural resources above, on, and below the soil, are distinguished by the fact that man cannot make them.

Labor is a broad term that covers all the different capabilities and skills possessed by human beings. While this often this means direct production labor, it includes management labor as well. The term *manager* embraces a host of skills related to the planning, administration, and coordination of the production process.

Entrepreneurial ability also is known as enterprise. Entrepreneurs have four basic functions. First, they take initiative in using the resources of land, capital, and labor to produce goods and services. Second, entrepreneurs make basic business policy decisions. Third, they develop innovative new products, productive techniques, and forms of business organization. Finally, entrepreneurs bear the risk. In addition to time, effort, and business reputation, they risk their own personal funds, as well as those of associates and stockholders.

THE FIRM

The economic resources of land, capital, and labor are brought together in a production unit that is referred to as a business or a firm. The firm uses these resources to produce goods that are then sold. The money obtained from the sale of these goods is used to pay the economic resources. Payments to those providing labor services are called wages. Payments to those providing buildings, land, and equipment leased to the firm are called rent. Payments to those providing financial capital, such as loans, stocks, and bonds, are called dividends and interest. In other words, capital goods tend to increase the productivity of labor through being man-made and reproducible.

GROSS PRODUCT

The total dollar value of all the final goods produced by all the firms in an economy is called the gross product. This commonly is measured by one or both of the following:

1. Gross national product (GNP) includes the value of all goods and services produced by firms originating in a single nation. This means that foreign direct investment (FDI)— such as a Japanese auto plant in the United States—is not included in GNP, even though the plant might employ U.S. workers and sell its output exclusively to U.S. consumers. Conversely, the value of production by U.S.-based firms abroad would be considered part of the U.S. GNP.

2. Gross domestic product (GDP) includes the value of all goods and services produced within a nation, regardless of where the owners of production are based. In this case, FDI into the United States would contribute to U.S. GDP, while U.S. investment in other countries would contribute to those countries' GDP, not that of the United States.

GDP is the preferred measure of gross product for many kinds of economic analyses. This is because foreign investment has grown rapidly around the world, and because foreign-owned assets, such as a manufacturing facility, tend to have a greater net influence on the domestic economy in which they are situated. Both measures of gross product calculate the value of products and services on a value-added basis so that output is not double-counted, such as when products are resold through different phases of the supply and distribution chain.

In order to make comparisons, economists often use "real" GNP or GDP, which means the figure has been adjusted to hide the effects of inflation, or the general rise of prices relative to the quantity or quality of goods produced. Therefore, real gross product is commonly taken as an indictor of overall economic health. A rise at a moderate, sustainable pace is considered healthiest. However, if gross product is declining or rising at an unsustainably fast pace, it usually is interpreted as a negative signal.

INFLATION AND UNEMPLOYMENT

The economic health of a nation, of which gross product is one measure, is directly affected by two other important factors: inflation and unemployment.

INFLATION. Inflation is an ongoing general rise in prices without a corresponding rise in the quantity or quality of the underlying merchandise or services (i.e., getting "less for more"). Ultimately, inflation represents an economic imbalance and diminishes a currency's real and nominal purchasing power. The steeper the rise, the faster the decline of the currency's purchasing power. Rapid economic expansion is one factor that can lead to price inflation, as can lax or inconsistent control of the money supply (such as through central bank monetary policy). Leading measures of inflation in the United States are the Consumer Price Index (CPI) and the Producer Price Index (PPI).

When inflation data are used to adjust the estimate of GDP, it is known as the GDP deflator.

UNEMPLOYMENT. The unemployment rate measures the percentage of the total number of workers in the labor force who are actively seeking employment but are unable to find jobs. While this seems straightforward, there are some measurement issues to consider, such as what constitutes looking for a job, how part-time labor is interpreted (i.e., being underemployed rather than unemployed), and what happens when an individual is technically employable but not actively seeking employment for whatever reason.

Measurement difficulties aside, in general the higher the unemployment rate, the more the economy is wasting labor resources by allowing people to sit idle. Still, when unemployment rates are low there is a tendency toward wage inflation because new employees are harder to find and workers often require additional incentives in order to take or keep a job. Because having a moderate pool of unemployed workers serves as a buffer to rising labor costs, most economists view full employment (zero or negligible unemployment) as impractical and even undesirable. Structural unemployment seemingly allows human capital to flow more freely (and cheaply) when there are changes in demand for labor in various parts of the economy. Of course, this does not mean that high unemployment is viewed as positive.

SCHOOLS OF ECONOMIC THOUGHT

While many of the aforementioned basic economic principles and ideas are widely accepted by economists, there have been—and continue to be—differing theories about some areas of economic behavior. Following is a brief overview of the three most influential theoretical perspectives.

CLASSICAL ECONOMICS. Dating back to eighteenth-century Europe, classical economics posited the market system would ensure full employment of the economy's resources. Classical economists acknowledged that abnormal circumstances such as wars, political upheavals, droughts, speculative crises, and gold rushes would occasionally deflect the economy from the path of full employment. However, when these deviations occurred, automatic adjustments in prices, wages, and interest rates within the market would soon restore the economy to the full-employment level. A decrease in employment would reduce prices, wages, and interest rates. Lower prices would increase consumer spending, lower wages would increase employment, and lower interest rates would boost investment spending. Classical economists believed in Say's Law, which states that supply creates its own demand. Although more recent economic philosophies differ in some of the specifics, particularly on the role of governments, central banks, and international trade, many tenets of classical economics are still accepted today.

KEYNESIAN ECONOMICS. As a consequence of the 1936 publication of British economist John Maynard Keynes's *General Theory of Employment, Interest, and Money,* mainstream economists came to give less importance to the role of money in the economy than had classical economists. Keynes sought to explain why there was cyclical employment in capitalistic economies. It was Keynes's analysis of how total demand determines total income, output, and employment, and the potentially key role for fiscal policy in the process, that captured the attention of most economists.

Moreover, the General Theory seemed to make compelling arguments for the use of government fiscal policy to avoid such problems and to smooth out economic instability. Keynesian followers believe that savings must be offset by investment. They termed propensity to consume as a person's decision on how much of total income will be allocated to savings and how much will be spent. The Keynesian view sees the causes of unemployment and inflation as the failure of certain fundamental economic decisions, particularly saving and investment decisions. In short, the Keynesian view is one of a demand-based economy.

MONETARISM. More recently, the monetarists, led by Nobel laureate economist Milton Friedman, argued that money plays a much more important role in determining the level of economic activity than is granted to it by the Keynesians. Monetarism holds that markets are highly competitive and that a competitive market system gives the economy a high degree of macroeconomic stability. Monetarists argue that price and wage flexibility provided by competitive markets cause fluctuations in total demand rather than output and employment. Monetarism is thus concerned with controlling the money supply and not injecting excess liquidity into markets. This view is somewhat compatible with, but not identical to, the supply-side school of economics.

James C. Koch
Revised by Gerhard Plenert

FURTHER READING:

Bell, Carolyn Shaw. "Thinking about Economics." *American Economist* 23, no. 1 (1998): 18–33.

Curtis, Roy Emerson. *Economics: Principles and Interpretation.* Chicago: A.W. Shaw and Company, 1928.

Eggert, James. *What is Economics?* 4th ed. Mountain View, CA: Mayfield Publishing Company, 1997.

Samuelson, Paul A. *Economics.* 10th ed. New York: McGraw-Hill, 1976.

Stern, Gary H. "Do We Know Enough about Economics?" *Fedgazette* 11, no. 1 (1999): 12.

ECONOMIES OF SCALE
AND ECONOMIES OF SCOPE

Economies of scale are reductions in average costs attributable to production volume increases. They typically are defined in relation to firms, which may seek to achieve economies of scale by becoming large or even dominant producers of a particular type of product or service. A distinction can be made between internal and external economies of scales. Internal economies of scale occur when a firm reduces costs by increasing production. External economies of scale occur when an entire industry benefits from expansion; for example, through the creation of an improved transportation system, a skilled labor force, or by sharing technology.

Economies of scope are reductions in average costs attributable to an increase in the number of goods produced. For example, fast food outlets have a lowe+r average cost producing a multitude of goods than would separate firms producing the same goods. This occurs because the preparation of the multiple products can share storage, preparation, and customer service facilities (joint production).

ECONOMIES OF SCALE

The basic notion behind economies of scale is well known: As a plant gets larger and volume increases, the average cost per unit of output is expected to drop. This is partially because relative operating and capital costs decline, since a piece of equipment with twice the capacity of another piece does not cost twice as much to purchase or operate. If average unit production cost = variable costs + fixed costs/output, one can see that as output increases the fixed costs/output figure decreases, resulting in decreased overall costs.

Plants also gain efficiencies when they become large enough to fully utilize dedicated resources for tasks such as materials handling. The remaining cost reductions come from the ability to distribute non-manufacturing costs, such as marketing and research and development, over a greater number of products. This reduction in average unit cost continues until the plant gets so big that coordination of material flow and staffing becomes very expensive, requiring new sources of capacity.

This concept can be related to best operating levels by comparing the average unit cost of different sized firms. In many types of production processes, the most efficient types of production facilities are practicable only at high output levels. It is very expensive to build custom-made cars by hand, and would be equally or more expensive to use a large General Motors assembly plant to build just a few Chevrolets per year.

However, if the plant is used to build 6 million cars per year, the highly specialized techniques of the assembly line allow a significant reduction in costs per car.

Suppose, for example, that Honda were constrained to produce only 10,000 motorcycles a year instead of a possible 1 million. With this circumstance, the need for an assembly line would become obsolete. Each motorcycle could be produced by hand. Honda could rule out benefits that might be derived from the division and specialization of labor. In producing such a small number, the use of any production techniques that reduce average cost would become obsolete. In these two examples, Honda and General Motors would enjoy economies of scale with reduced average cost simply by increasing the scale of their operations.

More broadly, economies of scale can occur for a number of reasons, including specialization efficiencies, volume negotiating/purchasing benefits, better management of by-products, and other benefits of size that translate into savings or greater profitability for a large-scale producer.

SPECIALIZATION. In a small firm, labor and equipment must be used to perform a number of different tasks. It is more difficult for labor to become skilled at any one of them and thereby realize the gains in productivity and reduction in per-unit costs that specialization permits. In the same way, management functions cannot be as specialized in a smaller firm. Supervisors may have to devote time to screening job applicants, a task usually more efficiently handled by a personnel department in a larger firm. Executives may have to divide their attention between finance, accounting, and production functions that could be handled more proficiently by departments specializing in each of these areas in a larger firm.

According to Langlois, some economies of scale result from the specialization and division of labor. Mass production allows the use of specialized equipment and automation to perform repetitive tasks. The larger the output of a product, plant, or firm, the greater will be the opportunities for specialization of labor and capital equipment. Similarly, machinery and equipment cannot be used as efficiently when it has to be switched back and forth between tasks.

Increased specialization in the use of labor is feasible as a plant increases in size. Hiring more workers means that jobs can be divided and subdivided. Instead of performing five or six distinct operations in the productive process, each worker may now have just one task to perform. Workers can be used full-time on those particular operations at which they have special skills. In a small plant a skilled machinist may spend half his time performing unskilled tasks, resulting in higher production costs. Furthermore, the division of work operations made possible by large-scale operations gives workers the opportunity to become very proficient at the specific tasks assigned to them. Finally, greater specialization tends to eliminate the loss of time that accompanies the shifting of workers from one job to another.

VOLUME DISCOUNTS. Oftentimes, the suppliers of raw materials, machinery, and other inputs will charge a lower price per unit for these items if a firm buys in large quantities. When a firm produces at high output levels, it needs a large volume of inputs and can take advantage of the associated price discounts to reduce its per-unit costs; if the company is large enough it may have strong negotiating power on this point. There may be similar economies of scale for stocks of raw materials, and intermediate and final products, part of which may be held to meet interruptions to the supply of raw materials, a temporary breakdown of firms, and the uncertain flow of orders from customers.

ECONOMIC USE OF BY-PRODUCTS. The production of many types of goods gives rise to economically valuable by-products. Large-scale firms are often able to recycle "waste" by-products that smaller size firms simply have to throw away because it is not economical to do anything else with them. For example, a small sawmill may simply throw away sawdust and old wood scraps. Many processing firms find that the volume of these waste products is large enough to warrant their resale. For example, sawdust can be sold as a sweeping compound for cleaning floors and hallways in large buildings. Wood scraps may be packaged, processed, and sold as kindling wood and artificial logs for home barbecues and fireplaces. In this way, the sale of by-products effectively reduces the per-unit costs of producing lumber in large volumes. For the same reasons, large oil firms often produce a host of petroleum by-products, and meatpacking firms produce fertilizers, glue, leather, and other by-products of meat production.

EXTERNAL ECONOMIES OF SCALE. The growth of supporting facilities and services is encouraged by a firm's large scale of operation. As a firm's scale of operations gets larger, it often becomes worthwhile for other firms and local governments to provide it with unique services that result in direct or indirect cost advantages. If a firm builds a large plant in a particular area, an improvement in highways and expanded transportation services may soon follow. Smaller suppliers that find a large part of their sales going to the larger firm may move closer to reduce transportation costs. All of these developments could result in lower per-unit costs for the large firm.

LARGE ECONOMIES OF SCALE. Larger firms have a cost advantage over their competitors. Not only does a larger plant gain from economies of scale, it also will produce more. Companies often use this advantage as a competitive strategy by first building a large plant with substantial economies of scale, and then using its lower costs to price aggressively and increase sales volume. Large economies of scale cause the firm's long-run average total cost curve to fall over a sizeable range as output is increased. In industries where the technology of production leads to economies of scale, the long-run average total cost curve for a single firm may fall over almost the entire range of output covered by the industry demand curve. When long-run average total cost falls in this fashion, it is possible for a firm that gets into this market ahead of others to obtain a competitive advantage. The ever lower per-unit costs it realizes at higher and higher levels of output permit the firm to charge a price lower than the average per-unit costs that prevail at lower levels of output. In this way, the firm is able to satisfy the entire market demand at a price below that which potential new rival firms must charge when getting started. These new firms would thus not be able to charge a price low enough to compete for sales with the established firm. Therefore, the established firm is able to keep rivals out of the market and maintain a monopoly position.

ECONOMIES OF SCOPE

According to David Kass in his 1998 article, "Economies of Scope and Home Healthcare," economies of scope exist if a firm can produce several product lines at a given output level more cheaply than a combination of separate firms each producing a single product at the same output level. Economies of scope differ from economies of scale in that a firm receives a cost advantage by producing a complementary variety of products with a concentration on a core competency. While economies of scope and scale are often positively correlated and interdependent, strictly speaking the benefits from scope have little to do with the size of output.

For instance, in the paper products industry it is common for large firms to produce their own pulp, the primary ingredient in paper, before manufacturing the paper goods themselves. However, smaller firms may have to purchase pulp from others at a higher net cost than the large companies pay. The savings from producing both pulp and paper would be an economy of scope for the large producers, although the large companies probably also have economies of scale that make it feasible to invest in pulping operations in the first place.

In another example, banks have economies of scope when they offer a variety of related financial services, such as retail banking and investment services, through a single service infrastructure (i.e., their branches, ATMs, and Internet site). Clearly, the costs of providing each service separately would be much greater than the costs of using a single infrastructure to provide multiple services.

Research concerning hospitals has suggested that other types of services, such as pediatric care, may have economies of scope. With increasing competition and emphasis on service, economies of scope are necessary for hospitals to provide these services profitability.

DISECONOMIES OF SCALE

When a firm grows beyond the scale of production that minimizes long-run average cost, diseconomies of scale may result. When diseconomies of scale occur the firm sees an increase in marginal cost when output is increased. This can happen if processes become "out of balance," or when one process cannot produce the same output quantity as a related process. Diseconomies of scale also can occur when a firm becomes so large that:

- Transportation costs increase enough to offset the economies of scale

- Monitoring worker productivity becomes too imperfect or costly

- Coordinating the production process becomes too difficult

- Frequent breakdowns result

- Maintaining efficient flows of information becomes too expensive

- Workers feel alienated and become less productive

- The focus of the firm is reduced, leading to inefficiencies and loss of strategic position

SEE ALSO: Economics

James C. Koch
Revised by R. Anthony Inman

FURTHER READING:

Anupindi, Ravi, et al. *Managing Business Process Flows: Principles of Operations Management.* 2nd ed. Upper Saddle River, NJ: Pearson/Prentice Hall, 2004.

"Diseconomies of Scale." Available from <http://www.investopedia.com/terms/d/diseconimiesofscale.asp>.

"Diseconomies of Scale." Available from <http://www.tutor2u.net/economics/content/topics/buseconomics/diseconomies.htm>.

"Economies of Scope." Available from <http://www.tutor2u.net/economics/content/topics/buseconomics/economies_of_scope.htm>.

Kass, David I. "Economies of Scope and Home Healthcare." *Health Services Research* 33, no. 4 (1998).

Raturi, Amitabh S., and James R. Evans. *Principles of Operations Management.* Mason, OH: Thomson/South-Western, 2005.

"What Are Economies of Scale?" Available from <http://www.investopedia.com/printable.asp?a=articles/03/012703.asp>.

EFFECTIVENESS AND EFFICIENCY

Efficiency and effectiveness were originally industrial engineering concepts that came of age in the early twentieth century. Management theorists like Frederick Taylor and Frank and Lillian Gilbreth designed time and motion studies primarily to improve efficiency. Work simplification efforts again focused primarily on questions like "How fast can we do this task?" Work simplification also led to terminology like *streamlined processes* and *efficiency experts,* but the emphasis was still on time and motion. The concept of effectiveness, which takes into consideration creating value and pleasing the customer, became popular in the United States in the early 1980s when Americans perceived Japanese products such as cars and electronics to offer greater value and quality.

The words *efficiency* and *effectiveness* are often considered synonyms, along with terms like *competency, productivity,* and *proficiency.* However, in more formal management discussions, the words *efficiency* and *effectiveness* take on very different meanings. In the context of process reengineering, Lon Roberts (1994: 19) defines efficiency as "to the degree of economy with which the process consumes resources-especially time and money," while he distinguishes effectiveness as "how well the process actually accomplishes its intended purpose, here again from the customer's point of view."

Another way to look at it is this: efficiency is doing things right, and effectiveness is doing the right things. For example, think of a company that was successfully making buggy whips as automobiles became the mode of transportation. Assume that the processes used to make buggy whips were perfect. The relationships of internal and external suppliers and customers were perfect. The suppliers and customers teamed together to make perfect buggy whips. The buggy whips were delivered on or ahead of schedule at the lowest possible cost. This company was very efficient. However, the company and its strategists were not very effective. The company was doing the wrong things efficiently. If they had been effective, they would have anticipated the impending changes and gotten into a different market.

Let's consider a surgery example. A surgeon is very skilled, perhaps the best in the country. The impending job is to operate on the patient's left knee. However, the surgeon doesn't perform all the steps of the process leading up to the surgery. Someone else marks the right knee for surgery. However skilled this surgeon is, however fast he performs the surgery (i.e., however efficient he is), this process will not be effective. When the patient awakens from the surgery, he will not be a happy camper. And what about the HMO?

Who will pay for a surgery performed on the wrong knee?

Efficiency and effectiveness can both improve speed, on-time delivery, and various other process baselines. A travel application which has six signatures (as opposed to two) causes the travel application process to be inefficient and ineffective. Many of the people who sign the application are not effective in their job because they waste their time on things that don't add value for any of the stakeholders. They are not doing the right things. They are also inefficient because they are participating in a process that takes too long and therefore costs too much. Eliminating some of the signatures would make the process (and the signers) more efficient and more effective. People who sign all those travel applications might justify it by saying, "These people have to be here anyway. It does not cost us anything extra for them to be signing the travel applications." There's something terribly wrong with that type of thinking!

A process can also be inefficient and ineffective because the steps of the process are completed serially instead of simultaneously. Assume that a university curriculum/course approval process takes an average of two to three years. The steps of the serial process are identified as follows:

1. A professor suggests to the department chairman that a quality management course be added to the curriculum.

2. The department chairman reviews the course, agrees, and submits the suggestion to all the colleagues in the department.

3. The colleagues review the course, agree, and submit their recommendation to the department chairman.

4. The department chairman reviews their recommendation and submits it, along with all materials, to the dean of the business school.

5. The dean reviews the materials and recommendations, agrees, and submits them to all the department chairmen in the school.

6. The chairmen all agree, and submit the recommendations and materials back to the dean with their recommendation.

7. The dean submits the materials and recommendations to the entire faculty in the business school.

8. The faculty reviews all materials and sends recommendations back to the dean.

9. The dean submits all materials and recommendations to the associate vice president for academic affairs.

10. The associate vice president agrees and submits everything to the vice president.

11. The vice president agrees and submits everything back to the associate.

12. The associate submits everything to the faculty senate.

13. The faculty senate agrees and submits everything, with its recommendation, back to the vice president.

14. The vice president submits everything to the president.

15. The president signs the materials and submits them back to the associate vice president.

16. The associate vice president submits the recommendation for course approval to the coordinating board.

17. The coordinating board approves and submits the materials back to the associate vice president.

If the material were put in a shared computer file, the first 14 steps (or, at least steps 4 through 14) of this process could occur simultaneously. The first 14 steps of this process could be done in less than six weeks. Does the reader wonder why any person would ever recommend curriculum changes and get involved in such an inefficient and ineffective process? Professors and administrators don't want to do this work. They would prefer conducting research projects, writing articles, developing innovative teaching techniques, implementing improvement initiatives, working on strategic plans, and helping students. Instead, they are involved in meaningless work that does not add value for themselves or other stakeholders. Students and taxpayers would not want to pay for the extra time that it takes to do work serially instead of simultaneously.

Measures of efficiency, effectiveness, and capability for rapid adaptation are of great interest to all stakeholders: process owners, internal and external customers and suppliers, and executives. Inefficient processes are costly in terms of dollars, waste, rework, delays, resource utilization, and so on. Ineffective processes are costly as well because they are not reliable. They don't do what they are supposed to do. Processes that are not capable of rapid adaptation (flexibility and innovation) are costly because they are not capable of rapidly responding to customers' needs in terms of customization and rapid decision making. The greatest risk is that stakeholder loyalty will diminish.

In order to make processes more efficient, more effective, and more capable of rapid adaptations, people should ask themselves what, who, where, when, where, and how questions.

Perhaps the first question about a process is, why do it at all? Many steps exist simply because of organizational inertia ("We have always done it that way"). The second question might be, why do we do it this way?

Then you might consider questions like these: What is being done? What should be done? What can be done? When should it happen? and so forth. These questions, and the concepts of efficiency and effectiveness, apply to all processes, all jobs, all types of organizations, all industries.

Some process efficiency measures are:

• cycle time per unit, transaction, or labor cost;

• queue time per unit, transaction, or process step;

• resources (dollars, labor) expended per unit of output;

• cost of poor quality per unit of output;

• percent of time items were out of stock when needed;

• percent on-time delivery; and

• inventory turns.

Some effectiveness measures are:

• how well the output of the process meets the requirements of the end user or customer;

• how well the output of the sub process meets the requirements of the next phase in the process (internal customers); and

• how well the inputs from the external suppliers meet the requirements of the process.

By contrast, measures of ineffectiveness include:

• defective products;

• customer complaints;

• high warranty costs;

• decreased market share; and

• percent of activities that customers perceive to be non-value-added.

Some measures of adaptability are:

• the average time it takes to respond to special customer requests compared to routine requests;

• the percent of time special customer requests are denied compared to the denial of routine requests;

• the percent of special customer requests that have to be escalated to higher levels of management compared to the escalation of routine requests; and

• the capability to respond to product changes versus process changes.

Organizations should establish baselines for efficiency, effectiveness, and adaptability metrics. In other words, they should determine their current performance levels. Then they should benchmark best-in-class or world-class organizations and set aggressive goals or targets for improvement. Finally, they should determine root causes of problems and eliminate them or minimize their impact.

Generally, management and non-management employees have not had experience with the concepts and tools that will help them evaluate the processes which they own. In this case, training and opportunities to apply the concepts and tools should be provided. Examples of concepts and tools are:

• statistical process control, which measures variability in a process;

• trend charts, which measure performance over time;

• pie charts, which depict measurements compared to each other;

• process flow charts, which allow staff to quickly identify serial versus simultaneous processes, items which do not add value (like too many signatures, unnecessary travel and handling, long queues, etc.), and sub-processes that do not meet the needs of internal customers.

In addition to process concepts and tools, people should learn interrelationship concepts such as teamwork and communication as well as leadership skills in order to streamline relationships as well as processes and organizations.

Efficiency and *effectiveness* are often considered synonyms, but they mean different things when applied to process management. Efficiency is doing things right, while effectiveness is doing the right things. A third related concept is adaptability, which is flexibility or the capability to respond fast. In some respects, it is this capability for an organization to reinvent itself that ensures its long-term survival and success.

Organizational leaders can't comprehend the extent to which their organizations and processes are efficient, effective, and flexible unless they choose and use the right metrics. Of course, the results of those measurements should be fed back to the process owners so that they can improve the organization and the processes. This includes management processes as well as lower-level work processes. By their very nature, management processes can positively or negatively impact other work processes because they quite often deal with approvals (signature cycles) including requisitions for the purchase of essential equipment.

Answers to who, what, where, when, and how questions can be used to determine if the work should be done at all, who should do it, where and when it should be done, and how the work should be done. If these questions are answered truthfully, many activities in a process will be eliminated because they do not add value. Sometimes, entire processes will be eliminated.

Employees need to learn about and use various concepts and tools which will help them and their processes to be more efficient, effective, and flexible. For example, flow-charting the curriculum process mentioned above would have highlighted the need to replace serial sub-processes with sub-processes that were simultaneous and the need to eliminate duplications of effort and long waiting times. In addition, workers should learn interpersonal and leadership skills in order to be able to refine relationships as well as processes and organizations.

SEE ALSO: Time Management

Mildred Golden Pryor
Revised by Deborah Hausler

FURTHER READING:

"Efficiency or Effectiveness?" *Hindu* (20 January 2000).

Hammer, Michael. *Beyond Reengineering.* New York: HarperBusiness, 1996.

Pryor, Mildred Golden, J. Chris White, and Leslie A. Toombs. *Strategic Quality Management: A Strategic Systems Approach to Quality.* Houston, TX: Dame Publications, 1998.

Timothy, Allen. "Address Call of Effectiveness not Efficiency." *Precision Marketing* (17 October 2003): 18.

EFFICIENCY

SEE: Effectiveness and Efficiency

ELECTRONIC COMMERCE

Electronic commerce consists of the buying and selling of products and services via the Internet. It includes business-to-business, business-to-consumer, and consumer-to-consumer transactions. These transactions can include online retail sales, supplier purchases, online bill paying, and Web-based auctions. Electronic commerce utilizes a variety of technologies including electronic data interchange, electronic fund transfers, credit cards, and e-mail.

The term e-commerce is often used interchangeably with e-business. The common element is the effective implementation of business activities using Internet technologies. However, e-business is the broader, more encompassing strategy and related activities. In addition to retail sales it includes vendor-partner communication, electronic procurement, customer relationship management, data-mining, and numerous other business functions.

HISTORY

The development of the World Wide Web during the early 1990s dramatically changed the use of the Internet. The expansion of the Web, and along with it the Web browser, opened the Internet to anyone with basic computer experience and an online connection. As online activity increased, companies quickly saw the Internet's marketing potential. Subsequently, there was a rush to take products and services into this expanding electronic realm, and to redefine business itself.

According to studies demonstrating the growth of the Internet and electronic commerce:

- Fewer than 40 million people around the world were connected to the Internet during 1996. By the end of 2002, more than 605 million were connected.

- Approximately 627,000 Internet domain names had been registered as of December 1996. By the end of 2004 the number of domain names had reached 48 million.

- Internet traffic doubled approximately every 100 days for three consecutive years in the late 1990s. It is expected to grow between 100 and 150 percent annually through 2007.

To meet this demand, representatives from numerous industries—including consumer electronics companies, media corporations, telecommunications companies, hardware suppliers, software firms, satellite system designers, mobile phone networks, Internet service providers, television broadcasters and cable companies, and electric utilities—made aggressive Internet-related investments.

The downside of this impressive expansion was the Internet stock market bubble of 1999–2000, which had a significantly negative impact on the development of e-commerce on the Internet. Hundreds of companies with an idea and a business plan were able to gain access to a tremendous amount of venture capital and initial public offer funding. This resulted in many poor ideas being sold as profitable businesses, including pet food and grocery delivery services, as well as numerous application service providers just to name a few. The expansion, hype, and subsequent crash cooled many on the power and value in e-commerce. Coupled with the recession that followed the September 11, 2001 terrorist attacks, it was not until nearly 2005 that the e-commerce market began to exhibit a more realistic, normal, and steady rate of growth.

MARKET SIZE/OPPORTUNITY BASE

According to Forrester Research, the U.S. e-commerce market for retail sales was more than $95 billion in 2003, with five-year projections exceeding $200 billion. In Europe the retail segment totaled $53 billion in 2004. This amount was projected to reach $177 billion. The European and Asian markets show significant growth potential. North America does as well, but at a slower rate. China is viewed as an especially lucrative market for Western companies to penetrate with goods and services, in spite of the potential hurdles and hazards.

Based on U.S. Department of Commerce data, in May 2003 the market research firm eMarketer revealed that business-to-business e-commerce revenues were at approximately $720 billion in 2003, and were projected to hit $1.3 trillion by 2005. Computers and peripherals, aerospace and defense, and healthcare and pharmaceuticals were projected to be the largest industry segments.

Standard definitions of e-commerce must still be established. Current market research estimates of aggregate online retail trade generally purport to include only those transactions ordered and paid for online. However, they must rely on data supplied by individual companies that may not define it in the same way. Individual companies sometimes include as online sales transactions those that were conducted substantially online, but which also include a critical non-Internet component.

The Internet plays an important role in a much larger number of transactions than those completed online. In addition to the shoppers who choose items online but pay for them off-line, the Internet is an important source of research that influences off-line ordering and purchasing, particularly for big-ticket items such as automobiles. However, by the early 2000s, research indicated that consumers were beginning to visit brick-and-mortar stores and then go online to make their actual purchase. A September 2004 survey from the USC Annenberg Center for the Digital Future showed that approximately 69 percent of online shoppers browse traditional stores prior to making a purchase over the Internet.

STRATEGIES

One of the first challenges involved in moving to online commerce is how to compete with other e-commerce sites. A common problem in addressing this challenge is that e-commerce is often analyzed from a technical standpoint, not a strategic or marketing perspective. E-commerce provides several technical advantages over off-line commerce. It is much more convenient for the buyer and the seller, as there is no need for face-to-face interaction and Web-based stores are open 24 hours a day. Also, e-commerce purchasing decisions can be made relatively quickly, because a vendor can present all relevant information immediately to the buyer. These factors lend themselves to a transactional approach, where e-commerce is seen as a way to reduce the costs of acquiring a customer and completing a sale.

In contrast, most successful e-commerce Web sites take a relational view of e-commerce. This perspective views an e-commerce transaction as one step among many in building a lasting relationship with the buyer. This approach requires a long-term, holistic view of the e-commerce purchasing experience, so that buyers are attracted by some unique aspect of an e-commerce Web site, and not by convenience. Since consumers can easily switch to a competing Web site, customer loyalty is the most precious asset for an e-commerce site.

While the primary focus of most Internet activity is on the business-to-business and business-to-consumer facets of e-commerce, other transaction methods are included. The success of eBay and its consumer-to-consumer portal for auction-based transactions has dramatically changed how people and companies conduct business. In addition to having a significant effect on business-to-business transactions, retailers are beginning to tap into this new and dynamic approach to commerce. In a 2004 *Marketing* article, Amanda Aldridge reported that while eBay's revenue from collectibles was $1.4 billion, its total revenue was $2.2 billion.

BARRIERS TO SUCCESS

Despite the growing number of e-commerce success stories, plenty of e-commerce Web sites do not live up to their potential. There were three primary causes of e-commerce failures during the early 2000s.

First, most Web sites offer a truncated e-commerce model, meaning that they do not give Web users the capability to complete an entire sales cycle from initial inquiry to purchase. As analyzed by Forrester Research, the consumer sales cycle has four stages. First, consumers ask questions about what they want to buy. Second, they collect and compare answers. Third, the user makes a decision about the purchase. If the purchase is made, the fourth phase is order payment and fulfillment (delivery of the goods or services). The problem is that many Web sites do not provide enough information or options for all four phases. For example, a site may provide answers about a product, but not answers to the questions that the consumer has in mind. In other cases, the consumer gets to the point where he or she wants to make a purchase, but is not given an adequate variety of payment options to place the actual order.

The second problem occurs when e-commerce efforts are not integrated properly into the corporate organization. A survey by *Inter@ctiveWeek* magazine found that in most companies e-commerce is treated as part of the information system (IS) staff's responsibility, and not as a business function. While sales and marketing staff generally assist in the development of e-commerce Web sites, final profit and loss responsibility rests with the IS staff. This is a major source of breakdowns in e-commerce strategy because the units that actually make products and services do not have direct responsibility for selling them on the Web. One promising trend is that more companies are beginning to decentralize the authority to create e-commerce sites to individual business units, in the same way that each unit is responsible for its part of a corporate intranet.

SUCCESS FACTORS

After studying many aspects of electronic commerce, several consulting and analytic firms created guidelines on how to implement and leverage it successfully. In particular, two organizations have developed lists of critical success factors that seem to capture the state of thinking on this topic. First is the Patricia Seybold Group, which publishes trade newsletters and provides consulting services related to using information technology in corporations. This firm identified five critical e-commerce success factors:

1. Support customer self-service. If they so desire, Web users should be enabled to complete transactions without assistance.

2. Nurture customer relationships. Up-front efforts should focus on increasing customer loyalty, not necessarily on maximizing sales.

3. Streamline customer-driven processes. Firms should use Web technology to reengineer back-office processes as they are integrated with e-commerce systems.

4. Target a market of one. Each customer should be treated as an individual market, and personalization technology should be employed to tailor all services and content to the unique needs of each customer.

5. Build communities of interest. A company should make its e-commerce Web site a destination that customers look forward to visiting, not simply a resource people use because they have to conduct a transaction.

American Management Systems, a Vienna, Virginia, IT consulting firm, developed a list of recommendations that reflect similar thinking:

1. Focus on relationships and relationship pricing (price to maximize overall revenue per customer, not to maximize each transaction).

2. Create innovative bundles of products and services (including bundling products and services from other companies).

3. Provide superior customer service.

4. Develop a compelling experience for customers (use diverse and interesting content to make each transaction interesting and pleasurable).

5. Customize and personalize.

6. Convince customers that they need to return (make the site an information and/or entertainment resource, as well as a business tool).

7. Make routine tasks simple (reengineer so that customers can complete basic transactions and tasks with minimal effort).

8. Strive to match constant increases in customer expectations (utilize cutting-edge technology and benchmark the e-commerce Web site against those of all other firms, not simply those of direct competitors).

A quick review of two successful e-commerce sites, the Amazon.com bookstore site and Dell Computer's Web site, illustrate how many of these principles combine to help develop a strategic e-commerce capability.

Amazon.com, which has one of the highest sales volumes of any Web-based business, has optimized its site for the nature of its products and the preferences of its customers. The site is highly personalized; each visitor to the site, once registered, is greeted by name. The site content also is customized. Using software based on pattern recognition, Amazon.com compares a particular customer's purchase history to its overall record of transactions and generates a list of recommended books that seem to fit his or her interests and tastes. The company has a very integrated customer service support system, so that any customer service representative can access all data on the transactions, purchasing information, and security measures of each customer. The system also supports communications using e-mail, fax, and telephone.

Finally, Amazon.com helps to build a community of users through its Associates Program. Under this program, a Web site can host a hyperlink directly to the Amazon.com site. Any time that a visitor to that site buys books through Amazon.com, the Web site owner receives a share of the transaction revenues. This is a very inexpensive way for Amazon.com to extend its marketing and advertising reach across the Web.

Dell Computer also uses personalization and customization tools. For every major corporate customer, Dell creates a special Premier Page, which shows all products covered under purchasing contracts with that firm, as well as the special pricing under those contracts. This ensures that employees of that firm always get the right price for each purchase. Ford Motor Company reports that by encouraging employees to buy PCs from its Premier Page, the company saved $2 million in one year.

Dell also has integrated its e-commerce Web site with all back-office systems, so that when a customer orders a custom-configured PC, that information is automatically transferred to the production system to ensure that the unit is built according to specifications. This also improves customer service; Dell will proactively notify any customer if a production problem or inventory shortage will delay delivery.

These cases and analyses reflect some common lessons learned about the right way to approach electronic commerce:

1. First, no company can be successful in e-commerce by itself. Oftentimes, a firm must integrate its Web site with those of its trading partners, including suppliers, customers, and sometimes even competitors. Thus, each firm must create its own "value Web" that delivers the maximum benefit to its customers.

2. Second, site content is as important as product quality for firms engaging in e-commerce. A visit to an e-commerce site should create a lasting experience and strengthen a company's relationship with the customer. This involves much more than simply discussing the advantages of a company's products and services.

3. Third, firms must take advantage of all opportunities to use e-commerce for reengineering systems outside of the Web. One interesting consequence of this is that increased automation of business processes increases the value of human contact. If customers are used to completing transactions without human intervention, rapid and personal assistance during a problem will be much more memorable and valuable.

4. Finally, personalization is becoming an expectation of Web users. This does not mean that each Web site should be all things to all people. Instead of designing a Web site that appeals to a generic customer or a broad demographic segment, firms should create dynamic content that can target itself to match the tastes of each visitor separately. This maximizes the opportunity to use each Web visit to build the relationship with a particular customer, even if that visit does not result in a sale.

Electronic commerce, as used by U.S. firms, has already undergone several generations of evolution. Early experiences helped to stabilize e-commerce technology and set the development path for more sophisticated and useful technologies. Later experiences provided guidelines on strategic approaches and operational models that will help to improve e-commerce success.

There are two other key areas where more progress is needed to ensure the healthy growth of e-commerce. First, the emergence of the so-called digital economy is dependent on the creation of a robust infrastructure for all e-commerce, which in turn requires the development of standards. Second, government policy is having an increasing impact on e-commerce activities, and therefore policy needs to begin to catch up with the latest technology. Some of the policy issues that governments must address in regulating e-commerce, as identified by the U.S. government, are:

1. Financial issues, including customs and taxation, as well as electronic payment systems.

2. Legal issues, including the uniform commercial code for electronic commerce, intellectual property protection, privacy, and security.

3. Market access issues, including telecommunications infrastructure and interoperability, content, and technical standards.

Three key issues will determine the long-term viability of electronic commerce. These are:

1. Technological feasibility, or the extent to which technology—bandwidth availability and information reliability, tractability, and security—will be able to sustain exponentially increasing demands worldwide.

2. Socio-cultural acceptability, or the extent to which different global cultures and ways of doing business will accommodate this new mode of transacting, in terms of its nature (not face-to-face), speed, asynchronicity, and unidimensionality.

3. Business profitability, or the extent to which this way of doing business will allow for profit margins to exist at all (e.g., no intermediaries, instant access to sellers, global reach of buyers).

As technology continues to develop and mature, the ability to assess the impact of electronic commerce will become more cogent. Moreover, the significance of privacy, security, and intellectual property rights protection as prerequisites for the successful worldwide diffusion, adoption, and commercial success of Internet-related technologies—especially in places with less democratic political institutions and highly regulated economies—is continually increasing. The differentiation between the Internet (the global network of public computer networks) and intranets (corporate-based computer networks that involve well-defined communities and potentially more promising technology platforms for fostering Internet-related commerce) became significant in the late 1990s and early 2000s. Intranet development has surpassed the Internet in terms of revenue—by 2005 more than half of the world's Web sites were commercial in nature.

SEE ALSO: Consumer Behavior; Customer Relationship Management

Elias G. Carayannis and Jeffrey Alexander
Revised by Hal Kirkwood

FURTHER READING:

Barnatt, Christopher. "Embracing E-Business." *Journal of General Management* 30, no. 1 (2004): 79–97.

Domaracki, Gregory S., and Francois Millot. "The Dynamics of B2B E-Commerce." *AFP Exchange* 21, no. 4 (2001): 50–57.

Hof, Robert D. "The eBay Economy." *Business Week,* 25 August 2003, 124–129.

Lumpkin, G.T., and Gregory G. Dess. "E-Business Strategies and Internet Business Models: How the Internet Adds Value." *Organizational Dynamics* 33, no. 2 (2004): 161–173.

Mullaney, Timothy J., Heather Green, Michael Arndt, Robert D. Hof, and Linda Himelstein. "The E-biz Surprise." *Business Week,* 12 May 2003, 60–68.

U.S. Department of Commerce: Economics and Statistics Administration. "Digital Economy." Available from <https://www.esa.doc.gov/2003.cfm>.

Vulkan, Nir. *The Economics of E-Commerce: A Strategic Guide to Understanding and Designing the Online Marketplace.* Princeton, NJ: Princeton University Press, 2003.

ELECTRONIC DATA INTERCHANGE AND ELECTRONIC FUNDS TRANSFER

Electronic data interchange (EDI), or electronic data processing, is the electronic transmission of data between computers in a standard, structured format. Electronic funds transfer (EFT) is the term used for electronic data interchanges that involve the transfer of funds between financial institutions.

EDI has allowed companies to process routine business transactions, such as orders and invoices, more rapidly, accurately and efficiently than they could through conventional methods of transmission. While EDI has been around for decades, it wasn't until the late 1990s that this basic principle became a driving force in the rollout of electronic commerce, corporate extranets linking suppliers and customers, and related network-based technologies.

HISTORY

EDI has been present in the United States in some form since the mid-1960s. Businesses had been trying to resolve the difficulties intrinsic to paper-dependent commercial transactions. These difficulties include transmission speed (because of delays in entering the data onto paper and transporting the paper from sender to receiver); accuracy (because the data had to be recreated with each paper entry); and labor costs (labor-based methods of transmitting data are more expensive than computer-based methods).

In 1968 a group of railroad companies concerned with the accuracy and speed of intercompany transportation data transmissions formed an organization called the Transportation Data Coordinating Committee (TDCC) to study the problem and recommend solutions. Large companies such as General Motors and Kmart also reviewed the problems, which arose when they used their intracompany proprietary formats to send electronic data transmissions to outside parties. Because each company had its own proprietary format, there was no common standard among transmitting parties. A company doing business electronically with three other companies would need three different formats, one for each company.

By the 1970s several industries had developed common EDI programs for their companies within those industries, and a third-party network often administered these systems. Some examples of these systems include ORDERNET, which was developed for the pharmaceutical industry, and IVANS, which was developed for the property and casualty insurance industry. While these systems were standardized for each industry, they likewise could not communicate with other industries' proprietary systems. By 1973 the TDCC began developing set of standards for generic formats to handle this problem.

HOW EDI WORKS

EDI is quite different from other types of electronic communication. It is unlike a facsimile transmission (fax), which is the transfer of completely unstructured data through a digitized image. EDI also differs from other types of electronic communications among computers, such as electronic mail, network file sharing, or downloading information through a modem. In order to access electronic mail messages, shared network files, or downloaded information, the format of the computer applications of both the sender and the receiver must agree.

Since EDI uses a defined set of standards for transmitting business information, these standards allow data to be interpreted correctly, independent of the platforms used on the computers that transmit the data. When a sender transmits data, such as a purchase order, the EDI translation software converts the proprietary format of the sender's document processing software into a mutually recognized standard format. When the receiver obtains the data, the EDI translation software automatically converts the standard format into the receiver's proprietary document processing format. Because of the speed and accuracy of an EDI, users find that the system saves time and reduces costs over paper-based business transactions.

MODERN EDI

By the 2005, major retailers relied heavily on EDI to exchange purchase orders, invoices, and other information with their trading partners. In a June 2004 poll of 20 retailers, the majority said that they were either adding new trading partners or increasing the number of EDI transactions. It is estimated that between 80 and 90 percent of business-to-business traffic is conducted through EDI, and this number is growing 3 to 5 percent annually. Retail giants such as Wal-Mart Stores Inc., J.C. Penney Co., Supervalu Inc., and Hallmark Cards Inc. have been regular users of EDI. In fact, Wal-Mart has been one of the most influential companies driving new technology trends.

Since 2003, many companies have turned to a new technology in which data is transmitted over the Internet using the Applicability Statement 2 (AS2) protocol. The AS2 rules describe how to send data securely and ensure that the messages are received.

In September 2002, Wal-Mart asked its suppliers to switch from value-added networks (VANs) to AS2. Other companies have followed suit. One company claimed to have cut its costs by 70 percent after switching from a VAN to AS2. However, others have decided not to make the switch because of the costs involved.

Retailers are not the only businesses to take advantage of this technology. The healthcare industry also uses EDI to exchange patient information between medical providers and insurance companies. EDI is such a reliable means of transmitting data that a growing number of third-party payers, including Medicare, Medicaid, and commercial insurers, have started to require providers to submit claims electronically.

The Electronic Data Interchange rule was developed as part of the Health Insurance Portability and Accountability Act (HIPAA) and required compliance by October 16, 2003. This law requires all entities that transmit clinical data (including claims, referrals, and eligibility verification) to use the same electronic data file format. This can be accomplished by purchasing and maintaining a HIPAA-compliant practice management system (PMS) or by transmitting the data through a clearinghouse. The PMS is not the most cost-effective option for smaller entities, as it usually requires an administrator to maintain and upgrade the system as necessary. With the clearinghouse option, the entity sends data to a clearinghouse. The clearinghouse then sends the data to the appropriate recipients in the appropriate format.

ELECTRONIC FUNDS TRANSFER

An electronic funds transfer (EFT) is an EDI among financial institutions in which money is transferred from one account to another. Some examples of EFTs include electronic wire transfers; automatic teller machine (ATM) transactions; direct deposit of payroll; business-to-business payments; and federal, state, and local tax payments.

In general, EFT transactions are transferred through an automated clearing house (ACH) operator. An ACH operator is a central clearing facility operated by a private organization or a Federal Reserve bank on behalf of participating financial institutions, to or from which financial institutions transmit or receive ACH transactions. The ACH network is a nationwide system for interbank transfers of electronic funds. It serves a network of regional Federal Reserve banks processing the distribution and settlement of electronic credits and debits among financial institutions.

ACH transactions are stored in an ACH file, which is a simple ASCII-format file that adheres to ACH specifications. A single ACH file holds multiple electronic transactions, each of which carries either a credit or debit value. Typically, a payroll ACH file contains many credit transactions to employees' checking or savings accounts, as well as a balancing debit transaction to the employer's payroll account. An originating bank sends electronic payment instructions to a receiving bank. In those instances, the electronic transfers are processed in batches and settled within a few days.

The National Automated Clearing House Association (NACHA) oversees the ACH network and is primarily responsible for establishing and maintaining its operating rules. All financial institutions moving electronic funds through the ACH system are bound by the NACHA Operating Rules, which cover everything from participant relationships and responsibilities to implementation, compliance, and liabilities. While the NACHA rules are specific and quite detailed, adhering to a strict set of rules is crucial to the smooth and successful operation of the ACH system.

As the use of home computers becomes more and more a part of everyday life, the popularity of online banking and online bill payments continues to grow. Many banks allow their customers to access account information over the Internet and to transfer funds between accounts. Many credit card companies and utility companies allow customers to pay their bills online through EFTs. Online bill payments can save the consumer time and money. The customer can pay a bill in a matter of minutes over the Internet instead of spending money on postage to send a paper check and risking the chance that the bill may arrive past the due date.

On October 28, 2004, the Check Clearing for the 21st Century Act, also known as Check 21, took effect. This federal law allows banks to transmit checks electronically and substitute electronic images for original paper checks. Check 21 provides many advantages for banks and financial institutions. By transmitting checks electronically, banks can reduce the amount of time it takes to receive funds. This is because they no longer have to wait for another bank to receive paper checks before they send the funds. In addition to saving time, Check 21 saves banks millions of dollars in transportation and storage costs.

While Check 21 has made the banks happy, it has made many consumers unhappy. Many people write checks thinking that it will take at least two or three days for them to clear, thus giving them time to deposit the appropriate funds to cover the check. However, with Check 21 banks can clear checks within 24 hours of receiving them, cutting this safety net by days in many cases. In addition, although banks can process checks and debit the customer's accounts right away, they can still hold out-of-state checks for five days or more.

Consumer groups complain that this law increases the chances of fraud, error, bounced check fees, and inconvenience. There may be times when a bank cannot accept an electronic check image. In that case, the other bank could create a substitute check that has the same legal weight as the paper check. Having both the original check and a substitute check around could result in both checks being cashed, either fraudulently or by an honest mistake.

SEE ALSO: Distribution and Distribution Requirements Planning; Electronic Commerce; The Internet

Cindy Rhodes Victor
Revised by Rhoda L. Wilburn

FURTHER READING:

"Check it Out. Check Clearing for the 21st Century Act of 2003 Allows Banks to Transmit Cheques Electronically." *U.S. News & World Report,* 8 November 2004.

Mearian, Lucas. "First Horizon, SunTrust First Banks to Share Check Images; Southeastern Banks Overcome Technical Issues." *Computerworld,* 3 January 2005.

Sliwa, Carol. "EDI: Alive and Well After All These Years. Transactions Increase, Despite XML Option." *Computerworld,* 14 June 2004.

Stern, Linda. "That Check Won't Float." *Newsweek,* 20 September 2004.

ELECTRONIC FUNDS TRANSFER

SEE: Electronic Data Interchange and Electronic Funds Transfer

EMPATHY

Empathy is generally defined as the extent to which one has the ability to understand and accept another's feelings and emotions. Some view empathy simply as one's ability to "put themselves in another's shoes," or view an issue from another's perspective. However, some researchers suggest that perspective-taking is a cognitive process that precedes empathy, which is an affective or emotionally-based response to perspective-taking.

Empathy has been a subject of interest in a variety of different fields, but has only begun to be examined by those in the management area. Early childhood development researchers have concluded that empathy is a function of cognitive maturity; that is, the ability to take another's point of view requires a certain degree of cognitive complexity. Yet, from a moral development perspective, people are thought to progress from an egocentric form of morality toward a level of moral development where one examines issues from a variety of perspectives. Empathy is an attractive subject for researchers interested in the study of management because cognitive complexity and morality are generally considered to be important aspects of effective leadership.

Interest in empathy in the field of management stems from the growing popularity of the emotional intelligence concept, which has been popularized by Daniel Goleman's book *Emotional Intelligence.* According to Goleman, empathy—one of the basic components of emotional intelligence—is a critical part of social awareness, and, as such, key to success in life. Goleman extends the definition of empathy to include not only understanding others' feelings and behavior, but also intelligently using that understanding to forge stronger interpersonal relationships and make better decisions. Empathy is a particularly important factor in the success of those people who work in jobs where there is a high degree of interaction with other people—such as nursing, teaching, or management.

Although technical skills are considered less important as a person rises within an organizational hierarchy, the ability to empathize, on the other hand, is thought to be a more important determinant of success. Empathy is considered to be a quintessential managerial competence because it is a fundamental people skill.

Empathy is thought to have both a genetic and an experiential foundation. However, Goleman stresses that as a capability, empathy can be enhanced through desire and training. Research indicates that self-awareness is positively related to empathy, suggesting that empathy may be a function of the degree to which a person can read and manage his own emotions. Training that focuses on empathy building has been suggested as a means of fostering this social skill.

A person who is skillful at empathizing makes others feel respected and worthy of attention. The development of this skill requires effective communication. Thus, training managers in communication techniques such as active listening may contribute to building empathic competence.

Research examining empathy has largely been embedded within efforts to gain a greater understanding of emotional intelligence. Studies indicate that empathy is positively related to intrinsic motivation and effective problem-solving, supporting the view that empathy is an important aspect of effective leadership. The need for empathy is increasingly important in the workplace as the use of teams and self-directed work groups, where social competencies are a critical factor in success, are on the rise. Globalization, and the difficulties associated with intercultural relationships, also make empathy an increasingly critical managerial competence.

SEE ALSO: International Management; Teams and Teamwork

Jerry Bryan Fuller

FURTHER READING:

Goleman, Daniel. *Emotional Intelligence.* New York: Bantam Books, 1995.

EMPLOYEE ASSISTANCE PROGRAMS

Employee assistance programs (EAPs) are employer-sponsored benefit programs designed to improve productivity by helping employees to identify and resolve personal concerns. Most EAPs employ mental health professionals (usually on a contract basis) to provide confidential counseling and referral services to workers who are experiencing personal problems that interfere with their work attendance or productivity. For example, an EAP might help employees to resolve problems such as drug or alcohol abuse, emotional distress, child or elder care issues, anxiety, marital or family relationship concerns, emotional distress, depression, or financial difficulties. Employees may seek help on a voluntary, confidential basis, or may be referred by a supervisor who suspects that declining job performance is being caused by personal problems.

Companies that implement EAPs have documented improvements in worker health, functioning, productivity, and performance. They also have seen significant reductions in absenteeism, medical benefits costs, disability and worker's compensation claims, workplace accidents, and employee turnover. Surveys indicate that between 50 and 80 percent of large companies offer EAPs. The potential payoff of an EAP is evidenced by a study which found that every dollar spent on an EAP returned an estimated $3-$5 to the company in reduced absenteeism and greater productivity. "Divorce, drug addiction, alcohol abuse, caregiving for a disabled relative, and uncontrolled gambling can all cause employee disabilities and absences that exact a high workplace toll," wrote Kevin M. Quinley in *Compensation and Benefits Report.* "Addressing these problems—even if they are rooted in nonoccupational causes—can boost employee productivity and curb disability costs" (2003).

EAPs AND WELLNESS PROGRAMS

EAPs are often instituted as part of an employee wellness program. Employee wellness is a relatively new human resource management focus that seeks to eliminate certain debilitating health problems (e.g., cancer, heart disease, respiratory problems, hypertension) that can be caused by poor lifestyle choices (e.g., smoking, poor nutrition, lack of exercise, obesity, stress). Stress, for instance, is being called the fastest-growing occupational disease in the United States by some experts. Excessive amounts of stress can have debilitating health effects, leading to problems like ulcers, colitis, hypertension, headaches, lower back pain, and cardiac conditions. Stressed workers may perform poorly, quit their jobs, suffer low morale, generate conflicts among coworkers, miss work, or exhibit indifference toward coworkers and customers. These stress-induced outcomes cost U.S. businesses somewhere between $150 and $300 billion per year.

Lifestyle-related health problems have become quite prevalent: cancer, heart, and respiratory illnesses alone account for 55.5 percent of all hospital claims, and they can cause workplace problems such as absenteeism, turnover, lost productivity, and increased medical costs. For instance, people who have high blood pressure are 68 percent more likely than others to have medical claims of more than $5,000 per year, and the cost of medical claims for smokers is 18 percent higher than it is for nonsmokers.

To combat these problems, employee wellness programs provide employees with physical fitness facilities, on-site health screenings, and programs to help them quit smoking, manage stress, and improve nutritional habits. The employee wellness program at Apple Computer offers fitness facilities, health education, and preventative medicine that includes:

- A smoking cessation program

- Seminars on nutrition and weight management

- Health assessments that measure blood pressure and resting pulse

- Fitness evaluations that assess cardiopulmonary fitness level, strength, flexibility, body composition, and nutritional status

- Medical examinations that include physical exams and exercise strength tests to determine cardiovascular fitness

Employee wellness programs can be quite effective. Research indicates that participation in a wellness program increases productivity and reduces both absenteeism and turnover. A study conducted at Mesa Petroleum, for example, found that the productivity difference between participants and non-participants amounted to $700,000 in the program's first year and $1.3 million in the second.

If they are to work, wellness programs must successfully enlist "high-risk" individuals—those in greatest need of the program. Unfortunately, most employees who participate in wellness programs exhibit fewer risk factors to begin with, while employees at high-risk tend to stay away. Because at-risk individuals do not seek help, many employee wellness programs fail to meet their objectives.

Employers must, then, find some way to motivate high-risk individuals to participate. Some companies offer incentives such as cash bonuses to individuals who participate, while others impose certain penalties on non-participants. Examples of penalties include higher insurance premiums and deductibles.

OTHER FUNCTIONS OF EAPs

EAPs also play an important role in the prevention of and intervention in workplace violence incidents. Workplace violence and crisis intervention have received increased emphasis in EAPs since the terrorist attacks of September 11, 2001. Not only can counselors help employees to deal with the emotional impact of crises, they also can provide ongoing preparedness training for companies.

Many EAPs also provide management consultation services. In such cases, a supervisor may request assistance in dealing with a problem employee. EAP counselors might help the supervisor develop initiatives to change the employee's disruptive behavior. "Having an EAP sends a message to employees that the employer cares," noted Quinley. "Just knowing that can be a powerful incentive and hasten an employee's desire to return to work" (2003).

SEE ALSO: Human Resource Management; Safety in the Workplace; Stress

Lawrence S. Kleiman
Revised by Laurie Hillstrom

FURTHER READING:

Attridge, Mark, Tom Amaral, and Mark Hyde. "Completing the Business Case for EAPs: Research on EAP Organizational Services Shows They Save Money and Create Opportunities to Participate in Management Initiatives and Strategic Planning." *The Journal of Employee Assistance* 33, no. 3 (August 2003): 23.

Erfurt, J.C., A. Foote, and M.A. Heirich. "The Cost-Effectiveness of Worksite Wellness Programs for Hypertension Control, Weight Loss, Smoking Cessation, and Exercise." *Personnel Psychology* 45, no. 1 (1992): 5–27.

Kleiman, Lawrence S. *Human Resource Management: A Managerial Tool for Competitive Advantage.* 2nd ed. Cincinnati: South-Western College Publishing, 2000.

Mannion, Lawrence P. *Employee Assistance Programs: What Works and What Doesn't.* Westport, CT: Praeger, 2004.

Quinley, Kevin M. "EAPs: A Benefit That Can Trim Your Disability and Absenteeism Costs." *Compensation & Benefits Report* 17, no. 2 (February 2003): 6.

U.S. Department of Health and Human Services, Federal Occupational Health Service. "Documenting the Value of Employee Assistance Programs." Available from <http://www.foh.dhhs.gov>.

Van Den Bergh, Nan, ed. *Emerging Trends for EAPs in the 21st Century.* New York: Haworth Press, 2000.

EMPLOYEE BENEFITS

Employee benefits, sometimes called fringe benefits, are indirect forms of compensation provided to employees as part of an employment relationship. To compete for quality employees in today's marketplace, employers must do more than offer a "fair day's pay." Workers also want a good benefits package. In fact, employees have grown accustomed to generous benefits programs, and have come to expect them.

Employee benefits exist in companies worldwide, but the types and levels of benefits vary greatly from country to country. Generally speaking, companies in industrialized countries in Europe and North America offer employees the most generous benefit packages. Even within the industrialized world, however, employee benefits can vary significantly. For example, employees in Germany and other European countries receive more vacation days than the average U.S. employee. Conversely, most employers in the U.S. offer some form of medical/health insurance to employees. But most companies in European countries don't offer this employee benefit, because it is provided through government-sponsored socialized medicine programs.

HISTORICAL OVERVIEW

Employee benefits were not a significant part of most employees' compensation packages until the mid-twentieth century. In the U.S., for example, benefits comprised only about 3 percent of total payroll costs for companies in 1929. According to U.S. Chamber of Commerce, however, employee benefits in the U.S. now comprise approximately 42 percent of total payroll costs. Several things account for the tremendous increase in the importance of employee benefits in the U.S. In the 1930s, the Wagner Act significantly increased the ability of labor unions to organize workers and bargain for better wages, benefits, and working conditions. Labor unions from the 1930s to 1950s took advantage of the favorable legal climate and negotiated for new employee benefits that have since become common in both unionized and non-union companies. Federal and state legislation requires companies to offer certain benefits to employees. Finally, employers may find themselves at a disadvantage in the labor market if they do not offer competitive benefit packages.

LEGALLY REQUIRED BENEFITS

In the U.S., legislation requires almost all employers to offer the social security benefit, unemployment insurance, and workers' compensation insurance. Larger companies (those with 50 or more employees) are also required to offer employees an unpaid family and medical leave benefit. Each of these legally required benefits is discussed briefly below.

SOCIAL SECURITY. The Social Security Act of 1935, as amended, provides monthly benefits to retired workers who are at least 62 years of age, disabled workers, and their eligible spouses and dependents. Social Security is financed by contributions made by the employee and matched by the employer, computed as a percentage of the employee's earnings. As of 2005, the combined contribution of employer and employee for retirement, survivors', and disability benefits was 12.4 percent of the first $90,000 of employee income. Monthly benefits are based on a worker's earnings, which are adjusted to account for wage inflation. The Social Security Act also provides Medicare health insurance coverage for anyone who is entitled to retirement benefits. Medicare is funded by a tax paid by the employer and employee. The tax rate for Medicare is a combined 2.9 percent of the employee's total wage or salary income.

UNEMPLOYMENT INSURANCE. Unemployment compensation provides income to unemployed individuals who lose a job through no fault of their own. Eligible workers receive weekly stipends for 26 weeks. The specific amount of the stipend is determined by the wages the claimant was paid during the previous year. Unemployment compensation laws in most states disqualify workers from receiving benefits under the following conditions:

1. Quitting one's job without good cause. Workers who voluntarily quit their jobs are not eligible for unemployment compensation unless they can show good cause for quitting. Good cause exists only when the worker is faced with circumstances so compelling as to leave no reasonable alternative.

2. Being discharged for misconduct connected with work. If employees are discharged for misconduct, they are not eligible for unemployment, unless they can show that the discharge was unfair. To ensure fair discharges, employers should make employees aware of work rules through employee handbooks, posting of rules, and job descriptions. Employers must also provide workers with adequate warnings prior to discharge (unless a serious violation, such as stealing, has occurred).

3. Refusing suitable work while unemployed. Eligibility for unemployment compensation is revoked if an employee refuses suitable work while unemployed. Individuals must actively seek work and make the required number of search contacts each week. Benefits are terminated if the claimant refuses a bona fide job offer or job referral.

WORKERS' COMPENSATION INSURANCE. Millions of workers are hurt or become sick for job-related reasons each year. All 50 states have workers compensation insurance laws that are designed to provide financial protection for such individuals. Specifically, these laws require the creation of a no-fault insurance system, paid for by employers. When workers suffer job-related injuries or illnesses, the insurance system provides compensation for medical expenses; lost wages from the time of injury until their return to the job (employees are given a percentage of their income, the size of which varies from state to state); and death (paid to family members), dismemberment, or permanent disability resulting from job-related injuries.

Nationwide, payouts for workers' compensation are relatively high and curbing costs is a priority for many U.S. companies. The increase in costs is primarily due to rising medical costs that now account for as much as 60 percent of total workers' compensation costs in some states. Fraudulent claims also increase costs.

OPTIONAL EMPLOYEE BENEFITS

Other employee benefits are quite common, but are not required by federal law in the U.S. Some of the more significant optional benefits are summarized below.

HEALTH INSURANCE. Basic health-care plans cover hospitalization, physician care, and surgery. Traditional fee-for-service health care coverage became increasingly expensive in the late twentieth century. As a result, many U.S. companies adopted "managed care" health care plans. In general, managed care plans cut health care costs for employers by requiring them to contract with health care providers to perform medical services for their employees at an agreed upon fee schedule, in exchange for the employer encouraging (sometimes requiring) the employees to receive their medical care within the approved network of health care providers.

Health Maintenance Organizations (HMOs) are one type of managed care plan. HMOs are organizations of physicians and other health-care professionals who provide a wide range of services for a fixed fee. When participants need medical services, they pay a nominal per-visit charge of $5 or $10. Because members visit their health care facility more frequently, potential problems can be discovered and eliminated before they can become major health threats. Thus, HMOs can save money through preventative medicine. However, employees have a limited number of doctors from which to choose and must get approval from a primary care physician for specialized treatment.

Preferred Provider Organizations (PPOs) provide services at a discounted fee in return for the company's participation, which creates increased business for the health facility. Employees may choose any member facility of their choice. PPOs are somewhat less restrictive of patient choice than HMOs, since they allow employees to receive health care outside the approved network if the employee is willing to shoulder a higher percentage of their health care expenses.

Employers are not legally required to offer health insurance to employees. If they do, however, the Consolidated Omnibus Budget Reconciliation Act (COBRA) provides for a continuation of health insurance coverage for a period of up to three years for employees who leave a company through no fault of their own. Such employees are required to pay the premiums themselves, but at the company's group rate.

LONG-TERM DISABILITY (LTD) INSURANCE. This benefit provides replacement income for an employee who cannot return to work for an extended period of time due to illness or injury. An LTD program may be temporary or permanent. The benefits paid to employees are customarily set between 50 and 67 percent of that person's income.

PENSIONS. Pensions, or retirement incomes, may be the largest single benefit most employees receive. In most instances, employees become eligible to participate in company pension plans when they reach 21 years of age and have completed one year of service. After they have satisfied certain age and time requirements, employees become vested, meaning that the pension benefits they have earned are theirs and cannot be revoked. If they leave their jobs after vesting, but before retirement, employees may receive these benefits immediately or may have to wait until retirement age to collect them, depending on the provisions of their specific pension plan.

Employers may choose from two types of pension plans-defined benefit plans or defined contribution plans. Defined benefit plans specify the amount of pension a worker will receive on retirement. Defined contribution plans specify the rate of employer and employee contributions, but not the ultimate pension benefit received by the employee. If a defined benefit plan is chosen, an employer is committing itself to an unknown cost that can be affected by rates of return on investments, changes in regulations, and future pay levels. Consequently, most employers have adopted defined contribution plans.

Companies establish pension plans voluntarily, but once established, the Employee Retirement Income Security Act of 1974 (ERISA) requires that employers follow certain rules. ERISA ensures that employees will receive the pension benefits due them, even if the company goes bankrupt or merges with another firm. Employers must pay annual insurance premiums to a government agency in order to provide funds from which guaranteed pensions can be paid. Additionally, ERISA requires that employers inform workers what their pension-related benefits include.

LIFE INSURANCE PLANS. These employee benefits are very common. The premiums for basic life insurance plans are usually paid by the employer. Employee contributions, if required, are typically a set amount per $1,000 in coverage based on age. Employees are often given the opportunity to expand their coverage by purchasing additional insurance.

PERQUISITES AND SERVICES. A host of possible perquisites and services may be offered to employees as benefits, such as pay for time not worked (e.g., vacation, holidays, sick days, personal leave), reimbursement for educational expenses, discount on company products or services, automobile and homeowner insurance, employee savings plans, tax-sheltered annuities, employer-sponsored child day care and sick child care, stock options, and so forth. Executives are frequently offered a variety of perquisites not offered to other employees. The logic is to attract and keep good managers and to motivate them to work hard in the organization's interest.

BENEFITS ADMINISTRATION

Two issues that are crucial to the management of employee benefits are flexible benefit plans and cost containment. Many employers now offer flexible benefit plans, also known as cafeteria plans. These plans allow employees to choose among various benefits and levels of coverage. Under a cafeteria plan, employees may choose to receive cash or purchase benefits from among the options provided under the plan. Flexible benefit plans present a number of advantages:

- Such plans enable employees to choose options that best fit their own needs. New workers, for example, may prefer cash; parents may prefer to invest their benefit dollars in employer-sponsored childcare programs; and older workers may decide to increase their pension and health care coverage.

- Deciding among the various options makes employees more aware of the cost of the benefits, giving them a real sense of the value of the benefits their employers provide.

- Flexible benefit plans can lower compensation costs because employers no longer have to pay for unwanted benefits.

- Employers and employees can save on taxes. Many of the premiums may be paid with pretax dollars, thus lowering the amount of taxes to be paid by both the employee and the employer.

Because of these advantages, flexible benefit plans have become quite popular: such plans are now being offered by many U.S. companies. However, some companies are shying away from cafeteria plans because they create such an administrative burden. Moreover, the use of such plans can lead to increased insurance premiums because of adverse selection. Adverse selection means that people at high risk are more inclined than others to choose a particular insurance option. For instance, a dental plan option would be chosen primarily by employees with a history of dental problems. Consequently, insurance rates would increase because the number of low-risk individuals enrolled in the programs would be insufficient to offset the claims of high-risk individuals.

Companies can contain costs in several ways. Because an employer's workers' compensation premiums increase with each payout, firms can prevent unnecessary costs by scrutinizing the validity of each claim. Some employers cut costs by deleting or reducing some of the benefits they offer employees. This approach, however, can negatively affect both recruitment and retention. A more viable approach is to offer benefits that are less costly, but equally desirable. Companies can continue to offer attractive benefits by implementing some of the cost containment strategies discussed next.

Many companies implement utilization review programs in order to cut health care costs by ensuring that each medical treatment is necessary before authorizing payment, and ensuring that the medical services have been rendered appropriately at a reasonable cost. These programs require hospital pre-admission certification, continued stay review, hospital discharge planning, and comprehensive medical case management for catastrophic injuries or illnesses.

Employers also closely examine their firm's health insurance carriers in order to address the following questions:

1. Is the program tailored to company needs?

2. Are the prices competitive?

3. Will there be a good provider/vendor relationship?

4. Will payouts be accurate (e.g., will the correct amount be paid to the right person)?

5. How good is the customer service?

6. Is the insurance carrier financially secure?

Some employers have been able to increase the attractiveness of their benefit programs while holding costs constant, allowing an organization to get more of a "bang for its buck" from these programs.

SEE ALSO: Employee Assistance Programs; Employment Law and Compliance

Lawrence S. Kleiman
Revised by Tim Barnett

FURTHER READING:

Cornell Law School. Legal Information Institute. *U.S. Workers Compensation Law.* Ithaca, NY: 1999. Available from <www.law.cornell.edu/topics/workers_compensation.html>.

Kleiman, L.S. *Human Resource Management: A Tool for Competitive Advantage.* Cincinnati: South-Western College Publishing, 2000.

Newman, J.M. *Compensation.* 2nd ed. Boston: Irwin, 1999.

Social Security Administration. Available from <http://www.ssa.gov>.

U.S. Chamber of Commerce. Available from <http://www.uschamber.com>.

EMPLOYEE COMPENSATION

Employees receive compensation from a company in return for work performed. While most people think compensation and pay are the same, the fact is that compensation is much more than just the monetary rewards provided by an employer. According to Milkovitch and Newman in *Compensation,* it is "all forms of financial returns and tangible services and benefits employees receive as part of an employment relationship" The phrase "financial returns" refers to an individual's base salary, as well as short- and long-term incentives. "Tangible services and benefits" are such things as insurance, paid vacation and sick days, pension plans, and employee discounts.

An organization's compensation practices can have far-reaching effects on its competitive advantage. As compensation expert Richard Henderson notes, "To develop a competitive advantage in a global economy, the compensation program of the organization must support totally the strategic plans and actions of the organization." Labor costs greatly affect competitive advantage because they represent a large portion of a company's operating budget. By effectively controlling these costs, a firm can achieve cost leadership. The impact of labor costs on competitive advantage is particularly strong in service and other labor-intensive organizations, where employers spend between 40 and 80 cents of each revenue dollar on such costs. This means that for each dollar of revenue generated, as much as 80 cents may go to employee pay and benefits.

Compensation costs have risen sharply in recent years, primarily because of escalating benefit costs. Employers now spend more than $1 trillion on employee benefits. In 2003 the Society for Human Resource Management reported that benefit costs averaged 39 percent of total payroll in 2001, up from 37.5 percent in 2000. This means that, on average,

employers provide about $18,000 in benefits to each employee annually. The biggest cost increases have been in health benefits, which have been rising at an average of 12 percent annually for the past several years.

An organization must contain these spiraling costs if it is to get a proper return on its human resource investment, and thus gain a competitive advantage. When compensation-related costs escalate, the organization must find a way to offset them. In the past, companies passed along these increases in costs to the customer in the form of higher prices. However, most U.S. companies now find it very difficult to raise prices. Thus, to remain competitive in light of fierce domestic and foreign competition, unfavorable exchange rates, and cheaper foreign labor costs, it is imperative that companies find ways to control labor costs. Unless this can be done, organizations may be forced to implement such adverse actions as pay freezes, outsourcing/offshoring, and/or massive layoffs.

A host of laws such as the Equal Pay Act, Fair Labor Standards Act, and the Employment Retirement Income Security Act, regulate corporate compensation practices. Some pertain to pay issues such as discrimination, minimum wages, and overtime pay; others pertain to benefits, such as pensions, unemployment compensation, and compensation for work-related injuries. Organizations must understand and fully follow these laws in order to avoid costly lawsuits and/or government fines.

Pay and benefits are extremely important to both new applicants and existing employees. The compensation received from work is a major reason that most people seek employment. Compensation not only provides a means of sustenance and allows people to satisfy their materialistic and recreational needs, it also serves their ego or self-esteem needs. Consequently, if a firm's compensation system is viewed as inadequate, top applicants may reject that company's employment offers, and current employees may choose to leave the organization. With the aging of the U.S. workforce and the impending retirement of the "baby boomers," employers must be more concerned than ever before about retaining skilled, productive workers. Moreover, disgruntled employees choosing to remain with the organization may begin to behave unproductively (e.g., become less motivated, helpful, or cooperative).

INFLUENCE OF PAY ON EMPLOYEE ATTITUDES AND BEHAVIOR

Because compensation practices heavily influence recruitment, turnover, and employee productivity, it is important that applicants and employees view these practices in a favorable light. In the following section, we discuss how people form perceptions about a firm's compensation system and how these perceptions ultimately affect their behavior.

One would expect that an individual's satisfaction with his or her compensation would simply be a function of the amount of compensation received: the higher the compensation rate, the greater the satisfaction. However, in reality things are not that simple. In fact, the amount of pay is less important than its perceived fairness or equity. To put this finding in perspective, consider the behavior of many professional athletes when negotiating a new contract. The average NBA salary in 2003 was $4.9 million; the average baseball salary was $2.4 million; the average NFL salary was $1.3 million. Yet, ball players continue to ask for more money. In many instances, these demands stem from neither need nor greed. Rather, the demand for greater salaries often stems from perceptions of inequity. For instance, despite a $15 million salary, a player may feel that his pay is inequitable because a less capable player (or someone he perceives as being less capable) is earning an equal or greater salary.

Because equity is such an important concern, individuals responsible for developing a firm's compensation system need to understand how perceptions of equity are formed. Equity theory, formulated by J. Stacy Adams, attempts to provide such an understanding. The theory states that people form equity beliefs based on two factors: inputs and outcomes. Inputs (I) refer to the perceptions that people have concerning what they contribute to the job (e.g., skill and effort). Outcomes (O) refer to the perceptions that people have regarding the returns they get (e.g., pay) for the work they perform. People judge the equity of their pay by comparing their outcome-to-input ratio (O/I) with another person's ratio. This comparison person is referred to as one's "referent other." People feel equity when the O/I ratios of the individual and his or her referent other are perceived as being equal. A feeling of inequity occurs when the two ratios are perceived as being unequal. For example, inequity occurs if a person feels that he or she contributes the same input as a referent other, but earns a lower salary.

A person's referent other could be any one of several people. People may compare themselves to others:

- Doing the same job within the same organization

- Working in the same organization, but performing different jobs

- Doing the same job in other organizations

For example, an assistant manager at a Wal-Mart department store might compare her pay to other assistant managers at Wal-Mart, to Wal-Mart employees in other positions (either above or below her in the organizational hierarchy), or to assistant managers at Kmart department stores.

While the mechanism for choosing a referent other is largely unknown, one study found that people do not limit their comparisons to just one person; they have several referent others. Thus, people make several comparisons when they assess the fairness of their pay; perceived fairness is achieved only when all comparisons are viewed as equitable. When employees' O/I ratios are less than that of their referent others, they feel they are being underpaid; when greater, they feel they are being overpaid. According to equity theory, both conditions produce feelings of tension that employees will attempt to reduce in one of the following ways:

1. Decrease inputs by reducing effort or performance.

2. Attempt to increase outcomes by seeking a raise in salary.

3. Distort perceptions of inputs and/or outcomes by convincing themselves that their O/I ratio already is equal to that of their referent other.

4. Attempt to change the inputs and/or outcomes of their referent other(s). For example, they may try to convince their referent other(s) to increase inputs (e.g., work harder for their pay).

5. Choose a new referent other whose O/I ratio already is equal to their own.

6. Escape the situation. This response may be manifested by a variety of behaviors, such as absenteeism, tardiness, excessive work-breaks, or quitting.

While equity theory poses six possible responses to inequity, only two of them typically occur (namely, numbers 1 and 6). Research findings, for example, have linked underpayment to increases in absenteeism and turnover and to decreases in the amount of effort exerted on the job. These linkages are especially strong among individuals earning low salaries.

Contrary to equity theory's predictions, these responses occur only when employees believe they are underpaid. Overpaid individuals do not respond because they feel little, if any tension, and thus have no need to reduce it. (The research findings on the issue of overpayment find overpayment to be either just as satisfying as equity, or somewhat dissatisfying but not nearly as dissatisfying as underpayment.) When feeling underpaid, why do some people choose to decrease their inputs, while others choose to escape the situation? A recent study sheds some light on this issue. The study found that reaction to inequity depends on the source of the comparison; people react differently depending on whether they judge equity on the basis of external (referents outside of the organization) or internal (referents employed by the individual's own organization) comparisons. When perceptions of inequity are based on external comparisons, people are more likely to quit their jobs. For instance, a nurse working for Hospital A may move to Hospital B if the latter pays a higher salary. When based on internal comparisons, people are more likely to remain at work, but reduce their inputs (e.g., become less willing to help others with problems, meet deadlines, and/or take initiative).

From the previous discussion, one may conclude that employees will believe their pay is equitable when they perceive that it:

- Is fair relative to the pay received by coworkers in the same organization (internal consistency)

- Is fair relative to the pay received by workers in other organizations who hold similar positions (external competitiveness)

- Fairly reflects their input to the organization (employee contributions)

ACHIEVING INTERNAL CONSISTENCY

To achieve internal consistency, a firm's employees must believe that all jobs are paid what they are "worth." In other words, they must be confident that company pay rates reflect the overall importance of each person's job to the success of the organization. Because some jobs afford a greater opportunity than others to contribute, those holding such jobs should receive greater pay. For instance, most would agree that nurses should be paid more than orderlies because their work is more important; that is, it contributes more to patient care, which is a primary goal of hospitals.

For pay rates to be internally consistent, an organization first must determine the overall importance or worth of each job. A job's worth typically is assessed through a systematic process known as job evaluation. In general, the evaluation is based on "informed judgments" regarding such things as the amount of skill and effort required to perform the job, the difficulty of the job, and the amount of responsibility assumed by the jobholder.

Job evaluation judgments must be accurate and fair, given that the pay each employee receives is so heavily influenced by them. Most firms create a committee of individuals, called a job evaluation committee, for the purpose of making the evaluations. Because those serving on the committee represent the organization's various functional areas, collectively they are familiar will all the jobs being evaluated. Such individuals typically include department managers, vice presidents, plant managers, and HR professionals

(e.g., employee relations specialists and compensation managers). The committee chair usually is an HR professional or an outside consultant.

Perhaps the two most serious problems with job evaluation ratings are subjectivity and the rapidity with which jobs fundamentally change, both of which can cause inaccurate and unreliable ratings. In order to minimize subjectivity, the rating scales used to evaluate jobs must be clearly defined, and evaluators should be thoroughly trained on how to use them. Moreover, the evaluators should be provided with complete, accurate, and up-to-date job descriptions. The second issue is more difficult to address. Due largely to changes in technology, jobs now change so rapidly and so fundamentally that evaluation results quickly become out of date.

Job evaluation process is analogous to performance appraisal in that evaluators are asked to provide certain ratings on a form. Job evaluation ratings, however, focus on the requirements of the job rather than on the performance of the individual jobholder. Although several methods may be used to evaluate jobs, the most common approach is the point-factor method. Using this method, jobs are evaluated separately on several criteria, called compensable factors. These factors represent the most important determinants of a job's worth. A list of some commonly used factors and the criteria upon which they are judged appear in Exhibit 1.

The development of a point-factor rating scale consists of the following steps:

1. Select and carefully define the compensable factors that will be used to determine job worth.

2. Determine the number of levels or degrees for each factor. The only rule for establishing the number of degrees is that some jobs should fall at each level.

3. Carefully define each degree level. Each adjacent level must be clearly distinguishable.

4. Weight each compensable factor in terms of its relative importance for determining job worth.

5. Assign point values to the degrees associated with each compensable factor. Factors assigned greater weights in Step 4 would be allotted a greater number of possible points for each degree level.

When completing the job evaluation ratings, the evaluators use job descriptions to rate each job, one factor at a time until all jobs have been evaluated on all factors. They then calculate a total point value for a job by summing the points earned on each compensable factor.

Exhibit 1

**Compensable Factors Used in the
Point-Factor Method of Job Evaluation**

COMPENSABLE FACTOR	RATING CRITERIA
Skill/know-how	Education Experience Knowledge
Effort	Physical effort Mental effort
Responsibility	Judgement/decision-Making Internal business contacts Consequence of error Degree of influence Supervisory responsibilities Responsibility for independent action Responsibility for machinery/equipment Fiscal responsibility Responsibility for confidential information
Working conditions	Risks Comfort Physical demands Personal demands

This approach to job evaluation is difficult and time-consuming. However, most organizations believe that it is well worth the effort. If properly conducted, the overall score for each job should reflect its relative worth to the organization, thus enabling the firm to establish internal consistency.

When job evaluations have been completed, jobs are grouped into pay grades based on the total number of points received. Jobs with the same or similar point values are placed in the same grade. For example, consider jobs that are rated on a scale from one to one thousand. All jobs earning up to one hundred points could be assigned to pay grade one, jobs earning 101-200 to pay grade two, and so forth.

Administrators use pay grades because, without them, firms would need to establish separate pay rates for each job evaluation point score. Once jobs are classified into grades, all jobs within the same grade are treated alike for pay purposes; that is, the same range of pay applies to each job in a grade.

As companies develop pay grade systems, they must decide how many pay grades to establish. Most firms use thirty to fifty pay grades. However, some use as many as one hundred or more, while others use as few as five or six. The practice of limiting the number of pay grades eases the firm's administrative burdens. However, using a limited number of grades creates a situation in which jobs of significantly different worth fall into the same grade and receive the same pay. This outcome could lead to equity problems. For instance, registered nurses may feel underpaid if classified in the same pay grade as nursing aids.

ACHIEVING EXTERNAL COMPETITIVENESS

A firm achieves external competitiveness when employees perceive that their pay is fair in relation to what their counterparts in other organizations earn. To become externally competitive, organizations must first learn what other employers are paying and then make a decision regarding just how competitive they want to be. They then establish pay rates consistent with this decision. Following is an examination of how these steps are carried out.

The firm begins by conducting or acquiring a salary survey. This survey provides information on pay rates offered by a firm's competitors for certain benchmark jobs (i.e., jobs that are performed in a similar manner in all companies and can thus serve as a basis for making meaningful comparisons). Some firms gather this information from existing surveys already conducted by others, such as those produced by the Bureau of Labor Statistics. Trade associations also conduct surveys routinely for their members, or companies may hire consulting firms to gather such information. Salary surveys conducted by others should be used when they contain all the information needed by the company in question. When no such surveys exist, companies generally conduct their own.

After the pay practices of other companies have been identified, the organization must determine how competitive it wants to be (or can afford to be). Specifically, it must set a pay policy stipulating how well it will pay its employees relative to the market (i.e., what competitors pay for similar jobs). The determination of a pay policy is a crucial step in the design of a pay system. If pay rates are set too low, the organization is likely to experience recruitment and turnover problems. If set too high, however, the organization is likely to experience budget problems that ultimately may lead to higher prices, pay freezes, and layoffs.

The majority of firms pay at the market rate, which is the rate offered by most of the competitors for labor. Those paying above market are referred to as "market leaders." These typically are companies with the ability to pay and the desire to attract and retain top-notch employees (e.g., "cream of the crop"). Those paying below market ("market laggards") generally do so because they are unable to pay higher salaries. Such companies often attempt to attract employees by linking pay to productivity or profits so that the employees can earn more if the company does well.

When setting its pay policy, a company must consider its strategic plan. For example, if long-term employee commitment is a strategic goal, then the organization should attempt to develop compensation strategies that will enhance retention, such as establishing a generous retirement plan for long-service employees or adopting a profit-sharing system tied to tenure.

Once market rates for jobs are determined and a pay policy is established, an organization must price each of its jobs. Since market rates identified by a salary survey usually are restricted to benchmark jobs, how do organizations determine these rates for their non-benchmark jobs? Using the data collected on the benchmark jobs, an organization would determine the statistical relationship (i.e., simple linear regression) between job evaluation points and prevailing market rates. This regression line is referred to as the pay policy line. The appropriate pay rates for non-benchmark jobs are set based on this line.

ACHIEVING EMPLOYEE CONTRIBUTIONS EQUITY

Employee contributions equity is achieved when employees believe their pay fairly reflects their level of contribution to the organization. To achieve this aim, an organization must first establish a range of pay for each pay grade; it must then place each employee within that range based on his or her contribution to the organization.

A pay range specifies the minimum and maximum pay rates for all jobs within a grade. When establishing pay ranges, most employers set the market rate at the midpoint of the range. The spread from the midpoint usually varies, becoming larger as one progresses to higher pay grades. Most organizations establish a range spread of 10-25 percent for office and production work, 35-60 percent for professional and lower-level management positions, and 60-120 percent for top-level management positions.

The mechanism for recognizing employee contributions differs for new and existing employees. Contributions made by new employees are recognized by varying the level of starting pay they receive. New employees usually are paid at the minimum rate unless their qualifications exceed the minimum qualifications of the job. Those exceeding minimum qualifications are paid more because they can make a greater contribution, at least initially. Existing employees' contributions usually are recognized in the form of pay raises, typically granted on the basis of seniority and performance.

CONTEMPORARY COMPENSATION ISSUES

Modern organizations are making very significant changes in their compensation systems in order to better fit the dynamic, highly competitive business environment. Firms increasingly are using things such as skill-based pay, which compensates employees for the number and types of skills they possess instead of the type of job they have. Similarly, there is a strong movement to "at-risk" compensation, where employee pay is tied to performance. Under this system, the employee's bonus does not become part of his or her base pay. Instead, the bonus must be re-earned each year. These changes, and numerous others, are designed to help offset compensation costs by gains in productivity, and to develop more flexible workforces.

SEE ALSO: Employee Benefits; Employee Evaluation and Performance Appraisals; Human Resource Management

Lawrence S. Kleiman
Revised by G. Stephen Taylor

FURTHER READING:

Adams, J.S. "Injustices in Social Exchange." In *Advances in Experimental Social Psychology.* 2nd ed., ed. Berkowitz. New York: Academic Press, 1965.

Henderson, Richard I. *Compensation Management in a Knowledge-Based World.* 9th ed. Upper Saddle River, NJ: Prentice Hall, 2003.

Kleiman, Lawrence S. *Human Resource Management: A Tool for Competitive Advantage.* Cincinnati, OH: South-Western College Publishing, 2000.

Mathis, Robert L., and John H. Jackson. *Human Resource Management.* 11th ed. Mason, OH: Thomson/South-Western, 2006.

Milkovich, George T., and Jerry M. Newman. *Compensation.* 8th ed. New York: McGraw-Hill/Irwin, 2005.

U.S. Department of Labor, Bureau of Labor Statistics. "Compensation and Working Conditions." Available from <http://bls.gov/opub/cwc>.

EMPLOYEE EVALUATION AND PERFORMANCE APPRAISALS

Most companies have a formal performance appraisal system in which employee job performance is rated on a regular basis, usually once a year. A good performance appraisal system can greatly benefit an organization. It helps direct employee behavior toward organizational goals by letting employees know what is expected of them, and it yields information for making employment decisions, such as those regarding pay raises, promotions, and discharges.

Developing and implementing an effective system is no easy task, however. For instance, one study found that a majority of companies—65 percent—are dissatisfied with their performance appraisal systems. Analysts have found that a fairly low degree of reliability and validity remains a major bug in most appraisal systems. Many such systems are met with considerable resistance by those whose performance is being appraised, thus hampering the possibilities for effectiveness. While accurate and informative appraisal systems can be a major asset to a business, they are too often an unrealized goal.

There are three major steps in the performance appraisal process: identification, measurement, and management. With identification, the behaviors necessary for successful performance are determined. Measurement involves choosing the appropriate instrument for appraisal and assessing performance. Management, which is the ultimate goal, is the reinforcing of good performance and the correction of poor performance. Each step is described below. Additionally, management by objectives, which involves evaluating performance without a traditional performance appraisal, is described.

IDENTIFICATION

The organization must determine for each job family the skills and behaviors that are necessary to achieve effective performance. The organization should identify dimensions, which are broad aspects of performance. For instance, "quality of work" is a dimension required in many jobs. To determine which dimensions are important to job performance, the organization should rely on an accurate and up-to-date job analysis. Job descriptions written from job analyses should offer a detailed and valid picture of which job behaviors are necessary for successful performance.

In the identification stage, the company must also choose who will rate employee performance. Supervisors, peers, and the employees themselves may provide performance ratings. In most instances, performance appraisals are the responsibility of the immediate supervisor of an employee. Supervisors rate performance because they are usually the ones most familiar with the employee's work. Additionally, appraisals serve as management tools for supervisors, giving them a means to direct and monitor employee behavior. Indeed, if supervisors are not allowed to make the appraisals, their authority and control over their subordinates could be diminished.

While supervisory ratings can be quite valuable, some companies have added peer appraisals to replace or supplement those given by the supervisor. Naturally, peers and supervisors each view an individual's performance from different perspectives. Supervisors usually possess greater information about job requirements and performance outcomes. On the other hand, peers often see a different, more realistic view of the employee's job performance because people often behave differently when the boss is present. Using peer ratings to supplement supervisory ratings may thus help to develop a consensus about an individual's performance. It may also help eliminate biases and lead to greater employee acceptance of appraisal systems.

Potential problems may limit the usefulness of peer ratings, however, especially if they are used in lieu of supervisory ratings. First, the company must consider the nature of its reward system. If the system is highly competitive, peers may perceive a conflict of interest. High ratings given to a peer may be perceived as harming an individual's own chances for advancement. Second, friendships may influence peer ratings. A peer may fear that low ratings given to a colleague will harm their friendship or hurt the cohesiveness of the work group. On the other hand, some peer ratings may be influenced by a dislike for the employee being rated.

Some organizations use self-ratings to supplement supervisory ratings. As one might expect, self-ratings are generally more favorable than those made by supervisors and peers and therefore may not be effective as an evaluative tool. However, self-ratings may be used for employee development. Their use may uncover areas of subordinate-supervisor disagreement, encourage employees to reflect on their strengths and weaknesses, lead to more constructive appraisal interviews, and make employees more receptive to suggestions.

MEASUREMENT

Once the appropriate performance dimensions have been established for jobs, the organization must determine how best to measure the performance of employees. This raises the critical issue of which rating form to use. In the vast majority of organizations, managers rate employee job performance on a standardized form. A variety of forms exist, but they are not equally effective. To be effective, the form must be relevant and the rating standards must be clear. Relevance refers to the degree to which the rating form includes necessary information, that is, information that indicates the level or merit of a person's job performance. To be relevant, the form must include all the pertinent criteria for evaluating performance and exclude criteria that are irrelevant to job performance.

The omission of pertinent performance criteria is referred to as criterion deficiency. For example, an appraisal form that rates the performance of police officers solely on the basis of the number of arrests made is deficient because it fails to include other aspects of job performance, such as conviction record, court performance, number of commendations, and so on. Such a deficient form may steer employee behavior away from organizational goals; imagine if police officers focused only on arrests and neglected their other important duties.

When irrelevant criteria are included on the rating form, criterion contamination occurs, causing employees to be unfairly evaluated on factors that are irrelevant to the job. For example, criterion contamination would occur if an auto mechanic were evaluated on the basis of personal cleanliness, despite the fact that this characteristic has nothing to do with effective job performance.

Performance standards indicate the level of performance an employee is expected to achieve. Such standards should be clearly defined so that employees know exactly what the company expects of them. For instance, the standard "load a truck within one hour" is much clearer than "work quickly." Not only does the use of clear performance standards help direct employee behavior, it also helps supervisors provide more accurate ratings; two supervisors may disagree on what the term "quickly" means, but both attribute the same meaning to "one hour."

To meet the standards described in the previous section, a firm must use an effective rating form. The form provides the basis for the appraisal, indicating the aspects or dimensions of performance that are to be evaluated and the rating scale for judging that performance. Human Resources (HR) experts have developed a variety of instruments for appraising performance. A description of the most commonly used instruments, along with their strengths and weaknesses, is given in the following paragraphs. A summary of these instruments appears in Exhibit 1. It should be noted, however, that companies can create additional types of instruments. For instance, they can rate employees on job task performance using graphic or behavior rating scales.

EMPLOYEE COMPARISON SYSTEMS. Most appraisal instruments require raters to evaluate employees in relation to some standard of excellence. With employee comparison systems, however, employee performance is evaluated relative to the performance of other employees. In other words, employee comparison systems use rankings, rather than ratings. A number of formats can be used to rank employees, such as simple rankings, paired comparisons, or forced distributions. Simple rankings require raters to rank-order their employees from best to worst, according to their job performance. When using the paired comparison

---

Exhibit 1

Rating Errors and their Likely Causes

Errors	A	B	C	D	E	F
Leniency		X		X		X
Severity		X		X		
Central tendency	X	X				
Halo		X				X
Implicit personality theory					X	
Recency			X			

Key:
A administrative procedures
B poorly defined rating standards
C memory decay
D political considerations
E incomplete information
F rater's lack of conscientiousness

approach, a rater compares each possible pair of employees. For example, Employee 1 is compared to Employees 2 and 3, and Employee 2 is compared to Employee 3. The employee winning the most "contests" receives the highest ranking. A forced distribution approach requires a rater to assign a certain percentage of employees to each category of excellence, such as best, average, or worst. Forced distribution is analogous to grading on a curve, where a certain percentage of students get As, a certain percentage get Bs, and so forth.

Employee comparison systems are low cost and practical; the ratings take very little time and effort. Moreover, this approach to performance appraisal effectively eliminates some of the rating errors discussed earlier. Leniency is eliminated, for instance, because the rater cannot give every employee an outstanding rating. In fact, by definition, only 50 percent can be rated as being above average. By forcing raters to specify their best and worst performers, employment decisions such as pay raises and promotions become much easier to make.

Employee comparison systems are plagued with several weaknesses. Because the rating standards for judging performance are vague or nonexistent, the accuracy and fairness of the ratings can be seriously questioned. Moreover, employee comparison systems do not specify what a worker must do to receive a good rating and, thus, they fail to adequately direct or monitor employee behavior. Finally, companies using such systems cannot compare the performance of people from different departments fairly. For example, the sixth-ranked employee in Department A may be a better performer than the top-ranked employee in Department B.

GRAPHIC RATING SCALE. A graphic rating scale (GRS) presents appraisers with a list of dimensions, which are aspects of performance that determine an employee's effectiveness. Examples of performance dimensions are cooperativeness, adaptability, maturity, and motivation. Each dimension is accompanied by a multi-point (e.g., 3, 5, or 7) rating scale. The points along the scale are defined by numbers and/or descriptive words or phrases that indicate the level of performance. The midpoint of the scale is usually anchored by such words as "average," "adequate," "satisfactory," or "meets standards."

Many organizations use graphic rating scales because they are easy to use and cost little to develop. HR professionals can develop such forms quickly, and because the dimensions and anchors are written at a general level, a single form is applicable to all or most jobs within an organization. Graphic rating scales do present a number of problems, however. Such scales may not effectively direct behavior; that is, the rating scale does not clearly indicate what a person must do

to achieve a given rating, thus employees are left in the dark as to what is expected of them. For instance, an employee given a rating of 2 on "attitude" may have a difficult time figuring out how to improve.

Graphic rating scales also fail to provide a good mechanism for providing specific, non-threatening feedback. Negative feedback should focus on specific behaviors rather than on the vaguely defined dimensions the GRSs describe. For example, if told that they are not dependable, most employees would become angered and defensive; they would become less angry and defensive if such feedback were given in behavioral terms: "Six customers complained to me last week that you did not return their phone calls."

Another problem with GRSs concerns rating accuracy. Accurate ratings are not likely to be achieved because the points on the rating scale are not clearly defined. For instance, two raters may interpret the standard of "average" in very different ways. The failure to clearly define performance standards can lead to a multitude of rating errors (as noted earlier) and provides a ready mechanism for the occurrence of bias. U.S. courts consequently frown on the use of GRSs. One court noted that ratings made on a graphic rating scale amounted to no more than a "subjective judgment call," and ruled that such rating scales should not be used for promotion decisions because of the potential bias inherent in such a subjective process.

BEHAVIORALLY-ANCHORED RATING SCALES. A behaviorally-anchored rating scale (BARS), like a graphic rating scale, requires appraisers to rate employees on different performance dimensions. The typical BARS includes seven or eight performance dimensions, each anchored by a multi-point scale. But the rating scales used on BARS are constructed differently than those used on graphic rating scales. Rather than using numbers or adjectives, a BARS anchors each dimension with examples of specific job behaviors that reflect varying levels of performance.

The process for developing a BARS is rather complex. Briefly, it starts with a job analysis, using the critical incident technique. This involves having experts generate a list of critical incidents—or specific examples of poor, average, and excellent behaviors—that are related to a certain job. The incidents are then categorized by dimension. Finally, a rating scale is developed for each dimension, using these behaviors as "anchors" to define points along the scale.

When initially formulated, BARS were expected to be vastly superior to graphic rating scales. HRM experts thought the behavioral anchors would lead to more accurate ratings because they enabled appraisers to better interpret the meaning of the various points along the rating scale. That is, rather than having the rater try to pinpoint the meaning of a vague anchor such as "excellent," the rater would have improved accuracy by having a critical incident as an anchor. As we shall see, however, this expectation has not been met. Perhaps the greatest strength of BARS is its ability to direct and monitor behavior. The behavioral anchors let employees know which types of behavior are expected of them and gives appraisers the opportunity to provide behaviorally-based feedback.

The superiority of BARS over graphic rating scales has not been substantiated by research. In fact, the great majority of studies on this topic have failed to provide evidence that justifyies the tremendous amount of time and effort involved in developing and implementing BARS. The failures of BARS may lie in the difficulty raters experience when trying to select the one behavior on the scale that is most indicative of the employee's performance level. Sometimes an employee may exhibit behaviors at both ends of the scale, so the rater does not know which rating to assign.

BEHAVIOR OBSERVATION SCALES. A behavior observation scale (BOS) contains a list of desired behaviors required for the successful performance of specific jobs, which are assessed based on the frequency with which they occur. The development BOS, like BARS, also begins with experts generating critical incidents for the jobs in the organization and categorizing these incidents into dimensions. One major difference between BARS and BOS is that, with BOS, each behavior is rated by the appraiser.

When using BOS, an appraiser rates job performance by indicating the frequency with which the employee engages in each behavior. A multi-point scale is used ranging from "almost never" to "almost always." An overall rating is derived by adding the employee's score on each behavioral item. A high score means that an individual frequently engages in desired behaviors, and a low score means that an individual does not often engage in desired behaviors.

Because it was developed more recently, the research on BOS is far less extensive than that on BARS. The available evidence, however, is favorable. One study found that both managers and subordinates preferred appraisals based on BOS to both BARS and graphic rating scales. The same study found that equal employment opportunity attorneys believed BOS is more legally defensible than the other two approaches.

Because raters do not have to choose one behavior most descriptive of an employee's performance level, the problem noted earlier regarding BARS does not arise. Moreover, like BARS, BOS is effective in directing employees' behavior because it specifies what they need to do in order to receive high performance ratings. Managers can also effectively use BOS to monitor behavior and give feedback in specific behavioral terms so that the employees know what they are doing right and which behavior needs to be corrected. Like BARS, however, a BOS instrument takes a great deal of time to develop. Moreover, a separate instrument is needed for each job (since different jobs call for different behaviors), so the method is not always practical. Developing a BOS for a particular job would not be cost-efficient unless the job had many incumbents.

ACCURACY OF THE RATINGS. Accurate ratings reflect the employees' actual job performance levels. Employment decisions that are based on inaccurate ratings are not valid and would thus be difficult to justify if legally challenged. Moreover, employees tend to lose their trust in the system when ratings do not accurately reflect their performance levels, and this causes morale and turnover problems. Unfortunately, accurate ratings seem to be rare. Inaccuracy is most often attributable to the presence of rater errors, such as leniency, severity, central tendency, halo, and recency errors. These rating errors occur because of problems with human judgment. Typically, raters do not consciously choose to make these errors, and they may not even recognize when they do make them.

Leniency error occurs when individuals are given ratings that are higher than actual performance warrants. Leniency errors most often occur when performance standards are vaguely defined. That is, an individual who has not earned an excellent rating is most likely to receive one when "excellent" is not clearly defined. Why do appraisers distort their ratings in an upward or downward direction? Some do it for political reasons; that is, they manipulate the ratings to enhance or protect their self-interests. In other instances, leniency and severity come about from a rater's lack of conscientiousness. Raters may allow personal feelings to affect their judgments; a lenient rating may be given simply because the rater likes the employee.

Severity error occurs when individuals are given ratings that are lower than actual performance warrants. Severe ratings may be assigned out of a dislike for an individual, perhaps due to personal bias. A male appraiser may, for example, underrate a highly-performing female employee because she threatens his self-esteem; a disabled employee may receive an unduly low rating because the employee's presence makes the appraiser feel embarrassed and tense; or an appraiser may provide harsh ratings to minorities out of a fear and distrust of people with different nationalities or skin color. Alternately, a severe rating may be due to the very high standards of a rater, or to "send a message" to motivate employees to improve.

When raters make leniency and severity errors, a firm is unable to provide its employees with useful feedback regarding their performance. An employee who receives a lenient rating may be lulled into thinking that performance improvement is unnecessary. Severity errors, on the other hand, can create morale and motivation problems and possibly lead to discrimination lawsuits.

Central tendency error occurs when appraisers purposely avoid giving extreme ratings even when such ratings are warranted. For example, when rating subordinates on a scale that ranges from one to five, an appraiser would avoid giving any ones or fives. When this error occurs, all employees end up being rated as average or near average, and the employer is thus unable to discern who its best and worst performers are. Central tendency error is likely the result of administrative procedures. That is, it frequently occurs when an organization requires appraisers to provide extensive documentation to support extreme ratings. The extra paperwork often discourages appraisers from assigning high or low ratings. Central tendency errors also occur when the end points of the rating scale are unrealistically defined (e.g., a 5 effectively means "the employee can walk on water" and a 1 means "the employee would drown in a puddle").

Appraisals are also subject to the halo effect, which occurs when an appraiser's overall impression of an employee is based on a particular characteristic, such as intelligence or appearance. When rating each aspect of an employee's work, the rater may be unduly influenced by his or her overall impression. For example, a rater who is impressed by an employee's intelligence may overlook some deficiencies and give that employee all fives on a one-to-five scale; an employee perceived to be of average intelligence may be given all threes. The halo effect acts as a barrier to accurate appraisals because those guilty of it fail to identify the specific strengths and weaknesses of their employees. It occurs most often when the rating standards are vague and the rater fails to conscientiously complete the rating form. For instance, the rater may simply go down the form checking all fives or all threes.

Most organizations require that employee performance be assessed once a year. When rating an employee on a particular characteristic, a rater may be unable to recall all of the employee's pertinent job behaviors that took place during that rating period. The failure to recall such information is called memory decay. The usual consequence of memory decay is the occurrence of recency error; that is, ratings are heavily influenced by recent events that are more easily remembered. Ratings that unduly reflect recent events can present a false picture of the individual's job performance during the entire rating period. For instance, the employee may have received a poor rating because he or she performed poorly during the most recent month, despite an excellent performance during the preceding eleven months.

MANAGEMENT

In the management phase of performance appraisal, employees are given feedback about their performance and that performance is either reinforced or modified. The feedback is typically given in an appraisal interview, in which a manager formally addresses the results of the performance appraisal with the employee. Ideally, the employee will be able to understand his or her performance deficiencies and can ask questions about the appraisal and his or her future performance. The manager should give feedback in a way that it will be heard and accepted by the employee; otherwise, the appraisal interview may not be effective.

The appraisal interview may also have an appeals process, in which an employee can rebut or challenge the appraisal if he or she feels that it is inaccurate or unfair. Such a system is beneficial because it:

- allows employees to voice their concerns.

- fosters more accurate ratings—the fear of a possible challenge may discourage raters from assigning arbitrary or biased ratings.

- often prevents the involvement of outside third parties (e.g., unions, courts).

The downside of using an appeals system is that it tends to undermine the authority of the supervisor and may encourage leniency error. For example, a supervisor may give lenient ratings to avoid going through the hassle of an appeal.

MANAGEMENT BY OBJECTIVES

Management by objectives (MBO) is a management system designed to achieve organizational effectiveness by steering each employee's behavior toward the organization's mission. MBO is often used in place of traditional performance appraisals. The MBO process includes goal setting, planning, and evaluation. Goal setting starts at the top of the organization with the establishment of the organization's mission statement and strategic goals. The goal-setting process then cascades down through the organizational hierarchy to the level of the individual employee. An individual's goals should represent outcomes that, if achieved, would most contribute to the attainment of the organization's strategic goals. In most instances, individual goals are mutually set by employees and their supervisors, at which time they also set specific performance standards and determine how goal attainment will be measured.

As they plan, employees and supervisors work together to identify potential obstacles to reaching goals and devise strategies to overcome these obstacles. The two parties periodically meet to discuss the employee's progress to date and to identify any changes in goals necessitated by organizational circumstances. In the evaluation phase, the employee's success at meeting goals is evaluated against the agreed-on performance standards. The final evaluation, occurring annually in most cases, serves as a measure of the employee's performance effectiveness.

MBO is widely practiced throughout the United States. The research evaluating its effectiveness as a performance appraisal tool has been quite favorable. These findings suggest that the MBO improves job performance by monitoring and directing behavior; that is, it serves as an effective feedback device, and it lets people know what is expected of them so that they can spend their time and energy in ways that maximize the attainment of important organizational objectives. Research further suggests that employees perform best when goals are specific and challenging, when workers are provided with feedback on goal attainment, and when they are rewarded for accomplishing the goal.

MBO presents several potential problems, however, five of which are addressed here.

1. Although it focuses an employee's attention on goals, it does not specify the behaviors required to reach them. This may be a problem for some employees, especially new ones, who may require more guidance. Such employees should be provided with action steps specifying what they need to do to successfully reach their goals.

2. MBO also tends to focus on short-term goals, goals that can be measured by year's end. As a result, workers may be tempted to achieve short-term goals at the expense of long-term ones. For example, a manager of a baseball team who is faced with the goal of winning a pennant this year may trade all of the team's promising young players for proven veterans who can win now. This action may jeopardize the team's future success (i.e., its achievement of long-term goals).

3. The successful achievement of MBO goals may be partly a function of factors outside the worker's control. For instance, the baseball manager just described may fail to win the pennant because of injuries to key players, which is a factor beyond his control. Should individuals be held responsible for outcomes influenced by such outside factors? For instance, should the team owner fire the manager for failing to win the pennant? While some HRM experts (and baseball team owners) would say "yes," because winning is ultimately the responsibility of

the manager, others would disagree. The dissenters would claim that the team's poor showing is not indicative of poor management and, therefore, the manager should not be penalized.

4. Performance standards vary from employee to employee, and thus MBO provides no common basis for comparison. For instance, the goals set for an "average" employee may be less challenging than those set for a "superior" employee. How can the two be compared? Because of this problem, the instrument's usefulness as a decision-making tool is limited.

5. MBO systems often fail to gain user acceptance. Managers often dislike the amount of paperwork these systems require and may also be concerned that employee participation in goal setting robs them of their authority. Managers who feel this way may not properly follow the procedures. Moreover, employees often dislike the performance pressure that MBO places on them and the stress that it creates.

SEE ALSO: Human Resource Management; Job Analysis

Lawrence S. Kleiman
Revised by Marcia J. Simmering

FURTHER READING:

Gomez-Mejia, Luis R., David B. Balkin, and Robert L. Cardy. *Managing Human Resources.* 4th ed. Upper Saddle River, NJ: Prentice Hall, 2004.

Grote, Richard C. *The Performance Appraisal Question and Answer Book: A Survival Guide for Managers.* New York: AMACOM Books, 2002.

Kleiman, L.S. *Human Resource Management: A Tool for Competitive Advantage.* Cincinnati: South-Western College Publishing, 2000.

Latham, G.P., and K.N. Wexley. *Increasing Productivity Through Performance Appraisal.* 2nd ed. Reading, MA: Addison-Wesley, 1994.

Noe, Raymond A., John R. Hollenbeck, Barry Gerhart, and Patrick M. Wright. *Human Resource Management: Gaining a Competitive Advantage.* 5th ed. Boston: McGraw-Hill/Irwin, 2006.

EMPLOYEE HANDBOOK AND ORIENTATION

The employee handbook is a document compiled by an organization that is used to inform employees of rules, regulations, and policies. It is a consistent, formalized way in which organizations can communicate with employees, and it is one of the most important forms of information that the company can provide its employees. Employees can refer to the handbook to answer basic questions throughout their tenure with the organization. Additionally, managers in the organization can use the handbook to help them make uniform and consistent decisions regarding employees. By avoiding arbitrary or uninformed decisions by managers, the company may prevent problems that stem from the unfair or even illegal treatment of employees, such as reduced worker motivation, lower performance, or even litigation.

Orientation is a training program that introduces new employees to the company, their work units, and their particular jobs; it is used to familiarize employees with the organization's rules, policies, and procedures. Often the employee handbook is used as a reference during a company's orientation sessions. The typical elements of both the employee handbook and orientation are described in detail below.

THE EMPLOYEE HANDBOOK

Employee handbooks are likely to include information on the following topics: employee compensation and benefits, performance appraisal procedures, smoking restrictions, drug-testing procedures, leave policies, dress codes, sexual harassment, workplace dating, disciplinary procedures, and safety rules.

COMPENSATION AND BENEFITS. An employee handbook should provide information about compensation and benefits, and in particular, fringe benefits. Employees need to know how often they will receive paychecks and when and if pay raises will be given. Any variable pay (e.g., merit pay or incentive pay) should also be explained, since this pay is dependent upon employee performance. Employees should also be informed about who is eligible for which fringe benefits, what options they have, and when they are allowed to make changes to their benefits package. Additionally, detailed information about the benefits that are available is often included in employee handbooks.

PERFORMANCE APPRAISAL PROCEDURES. Employee handbooks should inform the employee about the procedure for performance appraisal. In addition to providing details about the instruments and required documentation in general, several questions should be answered. First, when will the appraisals be conducted? Some organizations conduct appraisals annually, and others do so more often (e.g., every six months). Additionally, will appraisals take place on a common date for everyone in a work unit (or company-wide) or are they conducted on the anniversary of an employee's hire date? Second, who will conduct the appraisal? Third, when and how will results be communicated to the employee? That is, will there be an appraisal meeting in which the employee is told the results of the performance appraisal? Fourth, what options are available to employees who disagree with their appraisal? These questions and any other details about the procedure should be addressed in this section of the handbook.

SMOKING RESTRICTIONS. Most organizations have a policy on smoking that indicates whether smoking is allowed in the physical facility, outside of the physical facility (and how far away from the building smokers must be), or outside of work altogether. Any restrictions on smoking should be detailed in the employee handbook. In some organizations, smoking inside or around physical facilities may be hazardous, such as when flammable substances are present. In other organizations, smoking may be prohibited within a building for the comfort of non-smokers. While restrictions on smoking in the workplace are fairly common, some employers are now prohibiting smoking even when employees are not on the job. This is in response to average increased health care costs for smokers and this restriction is legal in some states.

DRUG TESTING PROCEDURES. If a company tests its employees for illegal drug use, then the policies and procedures associated with the tests should be included in the employee handbook. The organization should inform employees of the type of test—urinalysis, hair analysis, or blood analysis—and of the specific sample collection procedures. Additionally, the handbook should indicate when tests will be used. Testing may occur before employment begins, or it may occur randomly, for a cause, or after an accident. Finally, details about possible actions associated with positive test results, and procedures to appeal test results, should be provided.

LEAVE POLICIES. Paid leave—such as sick leave, vacation days, and personal days—requires rules for administration. The employee handbook should detail the number of sick or personal days available to each employee; the reasons for which this leave may be taken; any documentation or verification that may be required to take a sick day; and who to contact in the event of an illness.

Employees must also be informed as to how and when vacations can be scheduled, how the time can be taken (e.g., intermittently or all at once), and whether days not taken in one year are carried over into the next year, or lost, or paid back to the employee in the form of cash. Additionally, the handbook should inform employees about the number of vacation days they have, particularly if the number increases with an employee's tenure.

The handbook should also detail information about who is eligible for unpaid leave under the Family and Medical Leave Act (FMLA), and what the

<hr>

Exhibit 1

Sample Casual Friday Dress Code

Although professional dress is required at the workplace Monday through Thursday, on Fridays employees may wear more casual clothing. Please follow these guidelines when deciding how to dress on Fridays.

All casual Friday clothing should be clean, unwrinkled, and conservative in nature. Men may wear slacks, khaki pants, or high quality blue jeans. Men's shirts must have a collar, but may be short- or long-sleeved. Men may wear loafers, but may not wear athletic shoes or sandals. As with the professional dress code, men may not wear earrings.

Women may wear slacks, khaki pants, high quality jeans, skirts (high quality denim skirts are acceptable), or dresses. Women may wear sleeveless tops, but may not wear spaghetti straps, halter tops, or strapless tops. Women may wear open-toed shoes, but may not wear flip-flop sandals or athletic shoes.

No employees, male or female, may wear the following items: shorts, athletic clothing (e.g., track pants, sweat pants, sweatshirts), t-shirts, hats, flip-flop sandals, or athletic shoes.

Even on Fridays, clothing should still be office appropriate. It should not be dirty, stained, have tears or holes, or be threadbare. Additionally, clothes should not have unprofessional prints (e.g., animal prints, neon colors) or advertisements on them. Finally, clothing should not be too revealing. Women's skirts must not be too short, and no employee's clothing should be too tightly fitted to their body.

If you are unsure about whether a clothing item is appropriate for this office, please consult with your manager or with a member of the human resources management department before you wear it.

<hr>

procedure is for requesting such leave. Some organizations may not be covered by this act because of their size, but for those that are, informing employees of their rights under this law is important. Some employers require that employees exhaust their other paid leave (e.g., sick days and vacation days) before taking FMLA leave, and if this is the case, it should be detailed in the employee handbook.

DRESS CODE. Many employee handbooks include a dress code that informs employees which type of clothing is appropriate for the office. This is particularly important if an employer has a "casual Friday" policy that allows employees to dress less formally on Fridays. Employees are often confused or unsure as to what is appropriate for casual Friday, so a detailed dress code is important. A dress code should provide specific detailed information about what employees may and may not wear in the workplace. See Exhibit 1 for a sample, casual Friday dress code.

SEXUAL HARASSMENT POLICY. A typical sexual harassment policy includes definitions as to what constitutes sexual harassment, a procedure for reporting claims of sexual harassment within the company, the process the organization follows for investigating a sexual harassment claim, and the penalties for engaging in sexual harassment. First, the policy should explain the two types of sexual harassment: quid pro quo and hostile environment. This will help employees to understand which behaviors are acceptable or unacceptable in the workplace. Second, the policy should indicate reporting procedures, or how an employee should go about reporting a claim of sexual harassment. Typically, employees are encouraged to report to their direct supervisor and to present

evidence of the alleged harassment. However, the organization should have an exception in the policy for those employees who are being harassed by their supervisor and therefore do not want to report to that person. Third, the details of the investigation of sexual harassment claims should be included in the policy: what evidence is necessary, which parties will be involved, the steps taken to resolve the problem. Finally, the policy should detail the disciplinary procedures for sexual harassment violations as some types of sexual harassment may be punishable by immediate dismissal.

WORKPLACE DATING. Many organizations are creating workplace dating policies that may restrict personal relationships between employees. Workplace dating has increased dramatically due to a number of factors, including the presence of more women in the workforce, an older average age for first marriage in the U.S., and the longer working hours of many employees. Companies often choose to limit workplace romance because of concerns of favoritism and/or sexual harassment. Despite their legality, many workplace dating policies have come under fire because some employees feel that these policies are an invasion of privacy. Additionally, because some couples may keep their relationship secret while other couples do not, there are concerns that such policies may be enforced inconsistently.

There are many different forms of workplace dating policies; they range in degree of restrictiveness. The least restrictive allows dating between anyone at any level of the organization. A slightly more strict policy would require that, if a relationship is established, a manager must be informed of such a relationship.

Some policies allow for dating employees in other work units or at the same level of hierarchy, but prohibit relationships between a supervisor and subordinate. The most restrictive policies prohibit any dating relationships whatsoever between any employees of the company.

DISCIPLINARY PROCEDURES. The employee handbook should include information about the disciplinary procedures that will be used if work rules are broken. This means that specific work rules will need to be listed, if they are not presented elsewhere in the employee handbook. Then, the company must identify actions that result in immediate termination, such as proof of theft, drug use on the job, quid pro quo sexual harassment, violence toward an employee or customer, or other types of extreme behavior. Additionally, the company must detail the procedures by which it will discipline less severe rule infractions.

Many organizations use progressive discipline, in which harsher punishments are given for each subsequent rule violation. The typical progression of punishments is a verbal warning, a written warning, a short suspension, then termination of employment. Progressive disciplinary procedures allow the employee to change his or her behavior on minor issues before they result in termination; thus, this type of discipline provides appropriate due process for employees. Managers find the prescribed steps of a progressive discipline procedure easy to follow, particularly because they do not have to determine the punishment to give.

One element of a successful disciplinary procedure, which should be documented in the employee handbook, is the right to appeal disciplinary decisions. If an employee feels that he or she has been unfairly disciplined, the organization should have a procedure by which the employee can have others examine the process to make sure that it is free from bias. Two of the most useful procedures for an appeals process are an open-door management policy and the use of an employee relations representative.

SAFETY RULES. Any rules related to safety and security need to be detailed in the employee handbook, not only to inform employees of proper procedures but also to protect the company from liability. This section of the handbook should identify any required safety clothing or equipment, proper use of machinery and other equipment, and any necessary security measures (e.g., locking exterior doors of the building).

LEGAL CONCERNS WITH EMPLOYEE HANDBOOKS

There are two major legal concerns associated with the employee handbook: (1) when organizations do not follow their own documented policies and procedures, and (2) a possible implied contract exception to employment-at-will. When an employee handbook details procedures for discipline, for investigation of sexual harassment or other topics on which improper procedures may result in litigation from employees, it is crucial that managers closely follow the handbook procedures. If managers deviate from procedures, they may be susceptible to claims of wrongful discharge or sexual harassment. For instance, if an employee is fired after only one minor rule violation, yet the handbook indicates that the first step with such a violation is a verbal warning, the employee is likely to have a viable claim for wrongful discharge. Similarly, if managers do not follow their own printed policies for the investigation of sexual harassment claims and an employee suffers continued harassment, the organization is likely to be found liable for that harassment. Thus, it is critical that managers be aware of the policies and procedures documented in the employee handbook particularly if there has been a recent change to them.

The second major legal issue associated with employee handbooks is the possibility that they may be seen as implied contracts and thus exempt employees from employment-at-will. Employment-at-will is a common employment agreement that allows employers to release an employee from the organization at any time for any non-discriminatory reason, and allows the employee to quit at any time. Most U.S. workers are at-will employees; those who are not have employment contracts that specify job duties, the length of employment, and possible reasons for termination of employment.

There are three major exceptions to the employment-at-will doctrine for which the employer is not legally able to terminate employment at their discretion. One is the implied contract exception in which an employee is led to believe that he or she has an employment contract with the employer and is therefore not an at-will employee. This issue comes into play with the employee handbook because the handbook details specific, possible rule violations and because many employers now ask employees to sign a document indicating that they have read and understand the information provided in the employee handbook. By requiring a signature, the company can indicate at a later date that the employee was aware of certain rules and regulations that they violated, thus protecting the company from employee claims of ignorance. However, while requiring a signature on the employee handbook has become very popular in many organizations, the company must make evident that the signature does not create an employment contract. That is, an employee may perceive their signature to indicate that he or she is no longer an at-will employee and will only be terminated if the rules in the handbook are violated. If the employer does not intend that an employment contract exist, then a statement such as "I understand that I am an at-will employee and can be terminated for any reason at any time" can be useful to protect the employer from claims of wrongful discharge.

ORIENTATION

Orientation is a training session intended to familiarize an employee with the workplace and its rules. An orientation session typically takes place within the first few working days that an employee is on the job, although it may occur before the job begins. A typical orientation program includes information about the company, the work unit, and other miscellaneous areas. To be effective, the orientation program should provide key information without overwhelming individuals and prepare them for their first work experience with the company. The employee handbook is a key supporting document throughout orientation.

COMPANY-LEVEL ORIENTATION INFORMATION. Orientation programs often include information about the company as a whole. This information may be a company overview, such as the origination and history of the company, its mission, and its values. This allows the employee to put the information about the current organization into its historical context.

Policies and procedures (regarding work rules, disciplinary procedures, etc.) should be reviewed in the orientation session so that employees are sure to be aware of them and so that they can ask questions if necessary.

Compensation and benefits should be reviewed, from the basics of when paychecks are issued to more detailed information about incentives and benefits. Many organizations provide detailed information about fringe benefits because new employees often need guidance in understanding their benefits or in selecting from a list of benefit options.

Safety and accident prevention should be addressed in orientation and depending on the type of work done in the company, further safety training programs may also be required. In many office settings, safety regulations are brief and easy to cover. However, in manufacturing settings, a great deal of time may need to be spent on educating employees about safe behaviors and the proper use of equipment. In such circumstances, orientation is likely to provide only an overview of safety issues before further training is offered.

Employee relations information should cover any employee assistance programs or wellness plans. It should also review employee rights, such as the right to appeal disciplinary actions or other managerial decisions related to human resources.

Orientation often includes an overview of the company's physical facilities and may include a tour of those facilities. New employees need to know which entrances and exits to use, how to maintain building security, where to park vehicles, where different work units are located, and even where the restrooms are. Such information will reduce new employees' anxiety and may prevent other problems—having a car towed, leaving an exterior door unlocked, or getting lost in a large building.

WORK UNIT ORIENTATION INFORMATION. In orientation, employees need to know specific information about the particular work unit in which they will be employed. This portion of the orientation may begin with an overview of the departmental functions and continue with information about the new employee's specific job duties and responsibilities, and the performance expectations of that position. Employees should then be told any policies or procedures that may be specific to the work unit. Finally, work unit orientation should include a tour of the department (where offices are, where supplies are kept, etc.), and an introduction to other employees and managers.

MISCELLANEOUS INFORMATION. Many orientation programs go beyond company and work unit information to provide new employees with details about the community, housing options, or other issues associated with adjusting a new location. This is particularly important if the organization hires employees who relocate from a distance, especially if new employees arrive from overseas.

NEWCOMER SOCIALIZATION

Both the employee handbook and the orientation session aid the organization in socializing newcomers. Socialization is the process by which new employees learn the values, norms, and necessary behaviors to effectively participate as members of the organization. Socialization may begin even before a person is hired and may continue for weeks or even months after the person is on the job. Formal socialization occurs when employees review the employee handbook and attend new employee orientation. Socialization continues informally through advice from co-workers, the employee's observation of the workplace, and by trial-and-error.

Socialization involves three phases: anticipatory socialization, encounter phase, and settling in. Anticipatory socialization occurs before an individual begins work at an organization. Through interactions with representatives of the company during the recruitment and selection process, the job applicant learns a lot about an organization. The encounter phase of socialization starts when an employee begins the new job, and typically the employee learns a great deal of new information. Regardless of how well-prepared an employee may feel to begin a new job with a new employer, there is likely to be something unexpected or even shocking that occurs when the employee is actually on the job. Finally, when the employee reaches the settling in stage of socialization, he or she begins to feel comfortable with both the job demands and the interpersonal relationships with others in the workplace.

The employee handbook and new employee orientation training are critical elements in preparing employees to be effective members of an organization. Thus, it is important that the handbook and orientation sessions include information that employees need to know about workplace policies and procedures In addition, attention to the stages of newcomer socialization will help managers to ease the difficulties in transition that new employees may face.

SEE ALSO: Employee Assistance Programs; Employee Benefits; Employee Compensation; Employee Evaluation and Performance Appraisals; Employee Recruitment Planning; Employee Screening and Selection; Employment Law and Compliance; Human Resource Management

Marcia J. Simmering

FURTHER READING:

Felsberg, Eric J. "Composing Effective Employee Handbooks." *Employment Relations Today* 31, no. 2 (Summer 2004): 117.

Goldstein, Irwin L., and J. Kevin Ford. *Training in Organizations.* 4th ed. Belmont, CA: Wadsworth Group, 2002.

Gomez-Mejia, Luis R., David B. Balkin, and Robert L. Cardy. *Managing Human Resources.* 4th ed. Upper Saddle River, NJ: Pearson Prentice Hall, 2004.

Klein, Howard J., and Natasha A. Weaver. "The Effectiveness of an Organizational-Level Orientation Training Program in the Socialization of New Hires." *Personnel Psychology* 53 (2000): 47–66.

Noe, Raymond A. *Employee Training and Development.* Boston: Irwin/McGraw-Hill, 1999.

Noe, Raymond A., John R. Hollenbeck, Barry Gerhart, and Patrick M. Wright. *Human Resource Management: Gaining a Competitive Advantage.* 5th ed. Boston: McGraw-Hill/Irwin, 2006.

EMPLOYEE RECRUITMENT PLANNING

Recruitment is the process used by an organization to locate and attract job applicants in order to fill a position. An effective approach to recruitment can help a company successfully compete for lim-ited human resources. To maximize competitive advantage, a company must choose the recruiting method that produces the best pool of candidates quickly and cost effectively. There are five steps to the process.

STEP 1: IDENTIFY THE JOB OPENING

This step would appear to be an easy one-just wait until an employee turns in a notice of resignation. Many job openings are, in fact, identified in this way. A major problem with this approach is that it may take the company a long time to fill the opening. For instance, it usually takes six to eight weeks to notify and screen applicants, and a week or more to make a decision regarding a job offer. After the decision is made, the selected candidate must give notice (usually about two weeks) to his or her previous employer. Thus, the job in question is likely to remain vacant for months, even if the process runs smoothly.

Ideally, organizations should attempt to identify job openings well in advance of an announced resignation. The HRM department should plan for future openings in both the short and long term. The projection of future openings provides organizations with the time needed to plan and implement recruitment strategies so that they do not fall prey to the "must-hire-by-last-week" syndrome. The HR plan should answer at least the following questions:

- Are any newly budgeted positions opening soon?

- Is a contract under negotiation that may result in the need for additional hires?

- What is the amount of expected turnover in the next several months?

STEP 2: DECIDE HOW TO FILL THE JOB OPENING

The first question to ask after determining that an opening exists is "Do we need to find a new person to fill the vacant position?" Sometimes it is unnecessary to staff a vacant position because the firm can rely on other alternatives. For instance, it may be more prudent to provide overtime opportunities to current workers to complete the needed work. Other alternatives include job elimination and job redesign (i.e., incorporating the tasks of the vacant position into currently existing positions). If the firm chooses to fill the vacancy, it must address two issues: (1) whether to outsource, and (2) in the absence of outsourcing, whether to recruit candidates internally or externally.

STEP 3: IDENTIFY
THE TARGET POPULATION

Now the organization must determine what types of individuals it is looking for to fill the vacant positions. To address this question, an organization must define its target population. Two issues arise here: (1) specifying worker requirements and (2) deciding whether to target a certain segment of the applicant population.

An organization must identify specific requirements of the job: the duties, reporting relationships, salary range for hiring, and competencies required of a new worker (e.g., education, experience, knowledge, skills, and abilities). Ideally, much of this information will have been gathered during a job analysis and thus be contained in the job description. If not, the recruiter should gather it from the hiring manager. An organization must also decide at this point whether to target all qualified applicants or to focus its recruitment efforts on certain segments of the qualified applicant population.

When recruiting internally, the issue is this: Should the company post the job so that all qualified employees can be considered? Or should the company select certain high-potential employees and groom them for the position? When recruiting externally, the company must decide whether to inform all potential applicants or target certain types. Companies may reap advantages when they target members of certain groups. Another strategy is to target graduates of specific schools that have exceptionally strong programs in the functional areas of concern. Additionally, some companies target top-performing employees working for other companies. Recruitment of such individuals poses some unique problems, however; these individuals may be difficult to reach because they are not actively seeking a new job. Moreover, the practice of pirating employees from other firms raises some serious ethical questions.

STEP 4: NOTIFY
THE TARGET POPULATION

Once an applicant population has been targeted, the company must determine how to notify these individuals of the vacant position. A variety of recruitment methods may be used for communicating vacancies. A firm can benefit from both low-involvement and high-involvement strategies at this stage of the recruitment process. Low-involvement strategies are things such as corporate sponsorship or advertisements of the company's product or service may influence applicants' positive perceptions of that firm and therefore increase applicant attraction, but do not specifically identify a job opening. High-involvement recruitment strategies involve things such as detailed recruitment advertisements or employee endorsements, which occur when potential applicants meet with current employees to hear more about their experiences with that company. Both low-involvement and high-involvement strategies have a positive effect on the number of applicants who apply for jobs with an organization and on the quality of the applicants who apply.

When choosing a specific way to notify the target population, different recruitment methods may be used. Some popular options are internal job postings; newspaper, radio, and television advertisements; trade magazine advertisements; Internet job sites; college campus interviews; and current employee referrals. The choice of which to use depends on the number of positions to be filled, the cost of each recruitment method, the characteristics of the target audience, and economic conditions.

The more positions to be filled, the more widely the firm may choose to advertise, perhaps using a newspaper or radio advertisement. Costs differ for recruitment methods and a firm may be willing to invest more in recruitment when suitable applicants are difficult to find or when poor hiring decisions may be costly. The characteristics of the target audience influence recruitment method; for example, using an Internet posting would be fruitless if most of the applicant pool is unlikely to have access to a computer. Poor economic conditions, where unemployment is high, will result in higher numbers of job applicants and possibly a lower average level of quality of applicants. In this situation, to avoid spending an inordinate amount of time weeding through applications, firms must discourage all but the best applicants from applying.

STEP 5: MEET WITH THE CANDIDATES

Finally, the most qualified candidates are brought in for interviews and other assessment procedures. These serve both selection and recruitment purposes. From a selection perspective, they give the firm a chance to further assess the candidates' qualifications. From a recruitment perspective, they provide the candidates with an opportunity to learn more about the employment opportunity.

Candidates should be provided with information about the company and the job. Failure to provide a sufficient amount of information could be detrimental to the recruiting process. For example, it may be interpreted by the candidates as an attempt to evade discussion of unattractive job attributes, or it may be viewed as an indication of the recruiter's disinterest in them. Without specific information, applicants might accept a job offer without knowing about aspects of it that might affect their long-term job satisfaction, or they may refuse an offer without knowing about some of the job's attractive attributes.

SEE ALSO: Employee Screening and Selection; Human Resource Management

Lawrence S. Kleiman

Revised by Marcia Simmering

FURTHER READING:

Barber, A.E. *Recruiting Employees: Individual and Organizational Perspectives.* Thousand Oaks: Sage Publications, 1998.

Collins, C.J., and J. Han. "Exploring Applicant Pool Quantity and Quality: The Effects of Early Recruitment Practice Strategies, Corporate Advertising, and Firm Reputation." *Personnel Psychology* 57 (2004): 684–717.

Kleiman, L.S. *Human Resource Management: A Tool for Competitive Advantage.* Cincinnati: South-Western College Publishing, 2000.

EMPLOYEE SCREENING AND SELECTION

According to R.D. Gatewood and H.S. Field, employee selection is the "process of collecting and evaluating information about an individual in order to extend an offer of employment." Employee selection is part of the overall staffing process of the organization, which also includes human resource (HR) planning, recruitment, and retention activities. By doing human resource planning, the organization projects its likely demand for personnel with particular knowledge, skills, and abilities (KSAs), and compares that to the anticipated availability of such personnel in the internal or external labor markets. During the recruitment phase of staffing, the organization attempts to establish contact with potential job applicants by job postings within the organization, advertising to attract external applicants, employee referrals, and many other methods, depending on the type of organization and the nature of the job in question. Employee selection begins when a pool of applicants is generated by the organization's recruitment efforts. During the employee selection process, a firm decides which of the recruited candidates will be offered a position.

Effective employee selection is a critical component of a successful organization. How employees perform their jobs is a major factor in determining how successful an organization will be. Job performance is essentially determined by the ability of an individual to do a particular job and the effort the individual is willing to put forth in performing the job. Through effective selection, the organization can maximize the probability that its new employees will have the necessary KSAs to do the jobs they were hired to do. Thus, employee selection is one of the two major ways

(along with orientation and training) to make sure that new employees have the abilities required to do their jobs. It also provides the base for other HR practices—such as effective job design, goal setting, and compensation—that motivate workers to exert the effort needed to do their jobs effectively, according to Gatewood and Field.

Job applicants differ along many dimensions, such as educational and work experience, personality characteristics, and innate ability and motivation levels. The logic of employee selection begins with the assumption that at least some of these individual differences are relevant to a person's suitability for a particular job. Thus, in employee selection the organization must (1) determine the relevant individual differences (KSAs) needed to do the job and (2) identify and utilize selection methods that will reliably and validly assess the extent to which job applicants possess the needed KSAs. The organization must achieve these tasks in a way that does not illegally discriminate against any job applicants on the basis of race, color, religion, sex, national origin, disability, or veteran's status.

AN OVERVIEW OF THE SELECTION PROCESS

Employee selection is itself a process consisting of several important stages, as shown in Exhibit 1. Since the organization must determine the individual KSAs needed to perform a job, the selection process begins with job analysis, which is the systematic study of the content of jobs in an organization. Effective job analysis tells the organization what people occupying particular jobs "do" in the course of performing their jobs. It also helps the organization determine the major duties and responsibilities of the job, as well as aspects of the job that are of minor or tangential importance to job performance. The job analysis often results in a document called the job description, which is a comprehensive document that details the duties, responsibilities, and tasks that make up a job. Because job analysis can be complex, time-consuming, and expensive, standardized job descriptions have been developed that can be adapted to thousands of jobs in organizations across the world. Two examples of such databases are the U.S. government's *Standard Occupational Classification* (SOC), which has information on at least 821 occupations, and the Occupational Information Network, which is also known as O*NET. O*NET provides job descriptions for thousands of jobs.

An understanding of the content of a job assists an organization in specifying the knowledge, skills, and abilities needed to do the job. These KSAs can be expressed in terms of a job specification, which is an

Exhibit 1

Selection Process

1. Job Analysis	The systematic study of job content in order to determine the major duties and responsibilities of the job. Allows the organization to determine the important dimensions of job performance. The major duties and responsibilities of a job are often detailed in the job description.
2. The Identification of KSAs or Job Requirements	Drawing upon the information obtained through job analysis or from secondary sources such as O*NET, the organization identifies the knowledge, skills, and abilities necessary to perform the job. The job requirements are often detailed in a document called the job specification.
3. The Identification of Selection Methods to Assess KSAs	Once the organization knows the KSAs needed by job applicants, it must be able to determine the degree to which job applicants possess them. The organization must develop its own selection methods or adapt methods developed by others. Selection methods include, but are not limited to, reference and background checks, interviews, cognitive testing, personality testing, aptitude testing, drug testing, and assessment centers.
4. The Assessment of the Reliability and Validity of Selection Methods	The organization should be sure that the selection methods they use are reliable and valid. In terms of validity, selection methods should actually assess the knowledge, skill, or ability they purport to measure and should distinguish between job applicants who will be successful on the job and those who will not.
5. The Use of Selection Methods to Process Job Applicants	The organization should use its selection methods to make selection decisions. Typically, the organization will first try to determine which applicants possess the minimum KSAs required. Once unqualified applicants are screened, other selection methods are used to make distinctions among the remaining job candidates and to decide which applicants will receive offers.

Source: Adapted from Gatewood and Field, 2001.

organizational document that details what is required to successfully perform a given job. The necessary KSAs are called job requirements, which simply means they are thought to be necessary to perform the job. Job requirements are expressed in terms of desired education or training, work experience, specific aptitudes or abilities, and in many other ways. Care must be taken to ensure that the job requirements are based on the actual duties and responsibilities of the job and that they do not include irrelevant requirements that may discriminate against some applicants. For example, many organizations have revamped their job descriptions and specifications in the years since the passage of the Americans with Disabilities Act to ensure that these documents contain only job-relevant content.

Once the necessary KSAs are identified the organization must either develop a selection method to accurately assess whether applicants possess the needed KSAs, or adapt selection methods developed by others. There are many selection methods available to organizations. The most common is the job interview, but organizations also use reference and background checking, personality testing, cognitive ability testing, aptitude testing, assessment centers, drug tests, and many other methods to try and accurately assess the extent to which applicants possess the required KSAs and whether they have unfavorable characteristics that would prevent them from successfully performing the job. For both legal

and practical reasons, it is important that the selection methods used are relevant to the job in question and that the methods are as accurate as possible in the information they provide. Selection methods cannot be accurate unless they possess reliability and validity.

VALIDITY OF SELECTION METHODS

Validity refers to the quality of a measure that exists when the measure assesses a construct. In the selection context, validity refers to the appropriateness, meaningfulness, and usefulness of the inferences made about applicants during the selection process. It is concerned with the issue of whether applicants will actually perform the job as well as expected based on the inferences made during the selection process. The closer the applicants' actual job performances match their expected performances, the greater the validity of the selection process.

ACHIEVING VALIDITY

The organization must have a clear notion of the job requirements and use selection methods that reliably and accurately measure these qualifications. A list of typical job requirements is shown in Exhibit 2. Some qualifications—such as technical KSAs and nontechnical skills—are job-specific, meaning that each job has a unique set. The other qualifications listed in the exhibit are universal in that nearly all employers consider these qualities important, regardless of the job. For instance, employers want all their employees to be motivated and have good work habits.

Exhibit 2
A Menu of Possible Qualities
Needed for Job Success

A. Technical KSAs or aptitude for learning them

B. Nontechnical skills, such as

   1. Communication

   2. Interpersonal

   3. Reasoning ability

   4. Ability to handle stress

   5. Assertiveness

C. Work habits

   1. Conscientiousness

   2. Motivation

   3. Organizational citizenship

   4. Initiative

   5. Self-discipline

D. Absence of dysfunctional behavior, such as

   1. Substance abuse

   2. Theft

   3. Violent tendencies

E. Job-person fit; the applicant

   1. is motivated by the organization's reward system

   2. fits the organization's culture regarding such things as risk-taking and innovation

   3. would enjoy performing the job

   4. has ambitions that are congruent with the promotional opportunities available at the firm

---

The job specification derived from job analysis should describe the KSAs needed to perform each important task of a job. By basing qualifications on job analysis information, a company ensures that the qualities being assessed are important for the job. Job analyses are also needed for legal reasons. In discrimination suits, courts often judge the job-relatedness of a selection practice on whether or not the selection criteria was based on job analysis information. For instance, if someone lodges a complaint that a particular test discriminates against a protected group, the court would (1) determine whether the qualities measured by the test were selected on the basis of job analysis findings and (2) scrutinize the job analysis study itself to determine whether it had been properly conducted.

SELECTION METHODS

The attainment of validity depends heavily on the appropriateness of the particular selection technique used. A firm should use selection methods that reliably and accurately measure the needed qualifications. The reliability of a measure refers to its consistency. It is defined as "the degree of self-consistency among the scores earned by an individual." Reliable evaluations are consistent across both people and time. Reliability is maximized when two people evaluating the same candidate provide the same ratings, and when the ratings of a candidate taken at two different times are the same. When selection scores are unreliable, their validity is diminished. Some of the factors affecting the reliability of selection measures are:

- *Emotional and physical state of the candidate.* Reliability suffers if candidates are particularly nervous during the assessment process.

- *Lack of rapport with the administrator of the measure.* Reliability suffers if candidates are "turned off" by the interviewer and thus do not "show their stuff" during the interview.

- *Inadequate knowledge of how to respond to a measure.* Reliability suffers if candidates are asked questions that are vague or confusing.

- *Individual differences among respondents.* If the range or differences in scores on the attribute measured by a selection device is large, that means the device can reliably distinguish among people.

- *Question difficulty.* Questions of moderate difficulty produce the most reliable measures. If questions are too easy, many applicants will give the correct answer and individual differences are lessened; if questions are too difficult, few applicants will give the correct answer and, again, individual differences are lessened.

- *Length of measure.* As the length of a measure increases, its reliability also increases. For example, an interviewer can better gauge an applicant's level of interpersonal skills by asking several questions, rather than just one or two.

In addition to providing reliable assessments, the firm's assessments should accurately measure the required worker attributes. Many selection techniques are available for assessing candidates. How does a company decide which ones to use? A particularly effective approach to follow when making this decision is known as the behavior consistency model. This model specifies that the best predictor of future job behavior is past behavior performed under similar circumstances. The model implies that the most effective selection procedures are those that focus on the candidates' past or present behaviors in situations that closely match those they will encounter on the job. The closer the selection procedure simulates actual work behaviors, the greater its validity. To implement the behavioral consistency model, employers should follow this process:

1. Thoroughly assess each applicant's previous work experience to determine if the candidate has exhibited relevant behaviors in the past.

2. If such behaviors are found, evaluate the applicant's past success on each behavior based on carefully developed rating scales.

3. If the applicant has not had an opportunity to exhibit such behaviors, estimate the future likelihood of these behaviors by administering various types of assessments. The more closely an assessment simulates actual job behaviors, the better the prediction.

ASSESSING AND DOCUMENTING VALIDITY

Three strategies can be used to determine the validity of a selection method. The following section lists and discusses these strategies:

1. Content-oriented strategy: Demonstrates that the company followed proper procedures in the development and use of its selection devices.

2. Criterion-related strategy: Provides statistical evidence showing a relationship between applicant selection scores and subsequent job performance levels.

3. Validity generalization strategy: Demonstrates that other companies have already established the validity of the selection practice.

When using a content-oriented strategy to document validity, a firm gathers evidence that it followed appropriate procedures in developing its selection program. The evidence should show that the selection devices were properly designed and were accurate measures of the worker requirements. Most importantly, the employer must demonstrate that the selection devices were chosen on the basis of an acceptable job analysis and that they measured a representative sample of the KSAs identified. The sole use of a content-oriented strategy for demonstrating validity is most appropriate for selection devices that directly assess job behavior. For example, one could safely infer that a candidate who performs well on a properly-developed typing test would type well on the job because the test directly measures the actual behavior required on the job. However, when the connection between the selection

device and job behavior is less direct, content-oriented evidence alone is insufficient. Consider, for example, an item found on a civil service exam for police officers: "In the Northern Hemisphere, what direction does water circulate when going down the drain?" The aim of the question is to measure mental alertness, which is an important trait for good police officers. However, can one really be sure that the ability to answer this question is a measure of mental alertness? Perhaps, but the inferential leap is a rather large one.

When employers must make such large inferential leaps, a content-oriented strategy, by itself, is insufficient to document validity; some other strategy is needed. This is where a criterion-related strategy comes into play. When a firm uses this strategy, it attempts to demonstrate statistically that someone who does well on a selection instrument is more likely to be a good job performer than someone who does poorly on the selection instrument. To gather criterion-related evidence, the HR professional needs to collect two pieces of information on each person: a predictor score and a criterion score.

• Predictor scores represent how well the individual fared during the selection process as indicated by a test score, an interview rating, or an overall selection score.

• Criterion scores represent the job performance level achieved by the individual and are usually based on supervisor evaluations.

Validity is calculated by statistically correlating predictor scores with criterion scores (statistical formulas for computing correlation can be found in most introductory statistical texts). This correlation coefficient (designated as r) is called a validity coefficient. To be considered valid, r must be statistically significant and its magnitude must be sufficiently large to be of practical value. When a suitable correlation is obtained ($r > 0.3$, as a rule of thumb), the firm can conclude that the inferences made during the selection process have been confirmed. That is, it can conclude that, in general, applicants who score well during selection turn out to be good performers, while those who do not score as well become poor performers.

A criterion-related validation study may be conducted in one of two ways: a predictive validation study or a concurrent validation study. The two approaches differ primarily in terms of the individuals assessed. In a predictive validation study, information is gathered on actual job applicants; in a concurrent study, current employees are used. The steps to each approach are shown in Exhibit 3.

Concurrent studies are more commonly used than predictive ones because they can be conducted

---

Exhibit 3
**Steps in the Predictive and
Concurrent Validation Processes**

Predictive Validation

1. Perform a job analysis to identify needed competencies.
2. Develop/choose selection procedures to assess needed competencies.
3. Administer the selection procedures to a group of applicants.
4. Randomly select applicants or select all applicants.
5. Obtain measures of the job performance for the applicant after they have been employed for a sufficient amount of time. For most jobs, this would be six months to a year.
6. Correlate job performance scores of this group with the scores they received on the selection procedures.

Concurrent Validation

1 and 2. These steps are identical to those taken in a predictive validation study.
3. Administer the selection procedures to a representative group of job incumbents.
4. Obtain measures of the current job performance level of the job incumbents who have been assessed in step 3.
5. Identical to step 6 in a predictive study.

---

more quickly; the assessed individuals are already on the job and performance measures can thus be more quickly obtained. (In a predictive study, the criterion scores cannot be gathered until the applicants have been hired and have been on the job for several months.) Although concurrent validity studies have certain disadvantages compared to predictive ones, available research indicates that the two types of studies seem to yield approximately the same results.

Up to this point, our discussion has assumed that an employer needs to validate each of its selection practices. But what if it is using a selection device that has been used and properly validated by other companies? Can it rely on that validity evidence and thus avoid having to conduct its own study? The answer is yes. It can do so by using a validity generalization strategy. Validity generalization is established by demonstrating that a selection device has been consistently found to be valid in many other similar settings. An impressive amount of evidence points to the validity generalization of many specific devices. For example, some mental aptitude tests have been found to be valid predictors for nearly all jobs and thus can be justified without performing a new validation study to demonstrate job relatedness. To use validity generalization evidence, an organization must present the following data:

- Studies summarizing a selection measure's validity for similar jobs in other settings.

- Data showing the similarity between the jobs for which the validity evidence is reported and the job in the new employment setting.

- Data showing the similarity between the selection measures in the other studies composing the validity evidence and those measures to be used in the new employment setting.

MAKING A FINAL SELECTION

The extensiveness and complexity of selection processes vary greatly depending on factors such as the nature of the job, the number of applicants for each opening, and the size of the organization. A typical way of applying selection methods to a large number of applicants for a job requiring relatively high levels of KSAs would be the following:

1. Use application blanks, resumes, and short interviews to determine which job applicants meet the minimum requirements for the job. If the number of applicants is not too large, the information provided by applicants can be verified with reference and/or background checks.

2. Use extensive interviews and appropriate testing to determine which of the minimally qualified job candidates have the highest degree of the KSAs required by the job.

3. Make contingent offers to one or more job finalists as identified by Step 2. Job offers may be contingent upon successful completion of a drug test or other forms of background checks. General medical exams can only be given after a contingent offer is made.

One viable strategy for arriving at a sound selection decision is to first evaluate the applicants on each individual attribute needed for the job. That is, at the conclusion of the selection process, each applicant could be rated on a scale (say, from one to five) for each important attribute based on all the information collected during the selection process. For example, one could arrive at an overall rating of a candidate's dependability by combining information derived from references, interviews, and tests that relate to this attribute.

Decision-making is often facilitated by statistically combining applicants' ratings on different attributes to form a ranking or rating of each applicant. The applicant with the highest score is then selected.

This approach is appropriate when a compensatory model is operating, that is, when it is correct to assume that a high score on one attribute can compensate for a low score on another. For example, a baseball player may compensate for a lack of power in hitting by being a fast base runner.

In some selection situations, however, proficiency in one area cannot compensate for deficiencies in another. When such a non-compensatory model is operating, a deficiency in any one area would eliminate the candidate from further consideration. Lack of honesty or an inability to get along with people, for example, may serve to eliminate candidates for some jobs, regardless of their other abilities.

When a non-compensatory model is operating, the "successive hurdles" approach may be most appropriate. Under this approach, candidates are eliminated during various stages of the selection process as their non-compensable deficiencies are discovered. For example, some applicants may be eliminated during the first stage if they do not meet the minimum education and experience requirements. Additional candidates may be eliminated at later points after failing a drug test or honesty test or after demonstrating poor interpersonal skills during an interview. The use of successive hurdles lowers selection costs by requiring fewer assessments to be made as the list of viable candidates shrinks.

SEE ALSO: Human Resource Management

Lawrence S. Kleiman
Revised by Tim Barnett

FURTHER READING:

Barrick, M.R., and R.D. Zimmerman. "Reducing Voluntary Turnover Through Selection." *Journal of Applied Psychology* 80, no. 1 (2005): 159–66.

Gatewood, R.D., and H.S. Field. *Human Resource Selection.* 5th ed. Fort Worth, TX: Dryden Press, 2001.

Hausknecht, J.P., D.V. Day, and S.C. Thomas. "Applicant Reactions to Selection Procedures: An Updated Model and Meta-Analysis." *Personnel Psychology* 57, no. 3: 639–83.

Kleiman, L.S. *Human Resource Management: A Tool for Competitive Advantage.* Cincinnati: South-Western College Publishing, 2000.

Occupational Information Network. Available at <http://online.onetcenter.org>.

Potosky, D., and P. Bobko. "Selection Testing Via the Internet: Practical Considerations and Exploratory Empirical Findings." *Personnel Psychology* 57, no. 4: 1003–1034.

Ryan, A.M., and N.T. Tippins. "Attracting and Selecting: What Psychological Research Tells Us." *Human Resource Management* 43, no. 4 (2004): 305–18.

EMPLOYMENT LAW AND COMPLIANCE

Employment law and compliance concerns the legal framework within which organizations must operate in their treatment of employees. Employers must comply with a myriad of federal and state laws and regulations. Laws and regulations exist covering a wide range of human resource practices, including recruiting, hiring, performance appraisal, compensation, health and safety, and labor relations.

The discussion that follows identifies and summarizes the major federal laws that comprise employment law.

MAJOR FEDERAL LAWS

Exhibit 1 provides a summary of some of the more important federal employment laws. The exhibit is divided into four sections: anti-discrimination law, compensation law, health and safety law, and labor relations law. The sections that follow provide additional information on each of these areas, with special emphasis on anti-discrimination laws, which probably have the greatest impact on employers.

ANTI-DISCRIMINATION LAWS

TITLE VII. Without a doubt, the most important anti-discrimination law is Title VII of the Civil Rights Act of 1964. Title VII was initially motivated by the U.S. government's desire to end workplace discrimination against African Americans, which was brought to national attention by the civil rights movement of the 1950s and 1960s. However, by the time the law was passed and signed into law in 1964, it had become a comprehensive workplace anti-discrimination law.

Title VII prohibits workplace discrimination on the basis of race, color, religion, national origin, and sex. Affected organizations must not discrimination in any employment decision or in regard to any term or condition of employment. Title VII applies to all U.S. organizations with fifteen or more employees, as well as labor unions and public sector employers. Only a few U.S. employers with more than fifteen employees are exempt from Title VII.

Title VII was amended in 1972 by the Equal Employment Opportunity Act. This law strengthened the enforcement of Title VII, which up to that time had been largely ineffective in changing workplace practices. The Equal Employment Opportunity Commission, a quasi-independent federal government agency, is in charge of enforcing Title VII, as well as many other anti-discrimination laws.

Exhibit 1

Sampling of Major Federal Employment Laws

Anti-Discrimination Laws	Major Provisions
Title VII of the Civil Rights Act 1964	Prohibits employment discrimination based on race, color, religion, national origin, and sex.
Age Discrimination in Employment Act 1967	Prohibits employment discrimination against applicants or employees aged 40 and older.
Americans with Disabilities Act 1990	Prohibits employment discrimination against qualified applicants or employees with a physical or mental disability.
Civil Rights Act 1991	Codifies the "adverse impact" theory of discrimination. Clarifies and strengthens rules for enforcement of the anti-discrimination provisions in Title VII.
Compensation Laws	
Fair Labor Standards Act 1938	Requires employers to pay a federal minimum wage to non-exempt workers. Requires employers to pay overtime pay to non-exempt workers.
Equal Pay Act 1963	Requires employers to pay men and women equally for doing substantially the same work, unless differences in pay are based on merit, quantity or quality of production, or any other factor other than sex.
Labor Laws	
Wagner Act 1935	Establishes the National Labor Relation Board. Lays out the framework for union organizing activities. Identifies and bans unfair management practices in regard to unionization.
Taft Hartley Act 1947	Identifies and bans unfair labor union practices in regard to union organizing efforts. Bans the closed shop and allows states to pass "right-to-work" laws that give workers the right to refuse to join a union. Allows the president to temporarily stop strikes that imperil the national interest.
Health and Safety Laws	
Occupational Safety and Health Act	Establishes general safety standards and standards for specific industries. Requires employers to record and report accidents that occur in the workplace. Lays out rules for federal workplace inspections and penalties for violations of the act.

Employees alleging workplace discrimination that falls under the purview of the EEOC must report the alleged discrimination to the EEOC or one of the state-level fair employment offices that exist in every state. The EEOC has the right to investigate claims of discrimination or to initiate investigations itself. Many times the EEOC will attempt to work out a solution with the affected organization, which may or may not involve an admission of guilt by the employer. If conciliation fails, the EEOC also has the right to bring class-action discrimination lawsuits against organizations on behalf of a "class" of employees who have allegedly suffered from discrimination.

If the EEOC's investigation does not reveal a strong case of discrimination, the agency can still issue a "right-to-sue" letter to a plaintiff, which gives that person the right to bring their charges of discrimination against an employer to state or federal court, whichever is appropriate in a given case. Some claims of discrimination filed with the EEOC do not have merit and the EEOC often issues findings to that effect—but such findings still do not prevent the individual plaintiff from filing his or her own lawsuit against an employer.

For many years, most discrimination claims filed under Title VII were race discrimination cases. However, with the advent of sexual harassment lawsuits in the late 1970s and 1980s, sex discrimination cases became quite common, as well. Sexual harassment has become such a major employment law issue that it deserves special attention, which is provided in the next section.

SEXUAL HARASSMENT. Sexual harassment at the workplace is a long-standing problem, affecting working women, as well as many men. Sexual harassment came to light during the mid-1970s and has since gained a great deal of national attention. The growing attention to the topic stems from a number of well-publicized cases in the 1990s—the Clarence Thomas hearings, the 1991 Tailhook Convention where several women were severely harassed by naval pilots, and the accusations made by Arkansas state employee Paula Jones about then-governor Bill Clinton.

Sexual harassment is a form of sex discrimination and therefore violates Title VII of the Civil Rights Act. The number of sexual harassment complaints filed with the Equal Employment Opportunity Commission (EEOC) has increased at an alarming rate; it rose from about 6,000 in 1991 to more than double this number in 2004. The majority of these complaints involve claims of unwanted physical contact, offensive language, sexual propositions, and socialization or date requests.

An employer should establish a written sexual harassment policy. The policy should specify grievance procedures by which employees can bring claims of harassment to management's attention. These procedures should provide employees with opportunities to bypass their supervisor if the supervisor is the one being accused. The company should also provide supervisory training that focuses on the legal definition of sexual harassment.

In addition to holding formal training sessions, top management should also meet with employees to emphasize management's strong commitment to keep the workplace free of harassment. The employer should also have investigative guidelines that maintain employee confidentiality. The EEOC recommends that a committee that consists of both men and women should investigate sexual harassment claims. Committee members should receive investigative training.

AGE DISCRIMINATION IN EMPLOYMENT ACT. The federal government added to employment law in 1967 by passing the Age Discrimination in Employment Act. This law prohibited discrimination in employment decisions on the basis of age, provided the person affected was between 40 and 70 years old. Initially, the law allowed mandatory retirement policies, but was later amended to remove the upper limit on age initially imposed by the law. Thus, as it stands today, the ADEA prohibits discrimination against applicants or employees who are aged 40 and older, with no upper age limit.

For many years, age discrimination suits have been more difficult to prove against organizations because the person alleging discrimination had to show that the employer had a specific intent to discriminate on the basis of age, that there was no other explanation for the employment decision other than age, and that there was a specific employer policy or procedures that was discriminatory. In short, the person had to prove what is called "disparate treatment" under employment law.

However, a 2005 Supreme Court decision involving public workers in the city of Jackson, Mississippi, appears to have changed the interpretation of the law. Although the ramifications of this case remain to be fully determined, and will probably depend on its use in future court rulings, it appears that those alleging age discrimination can now proceed under what is called the "disparate impact" theory of discrimination. This means that the person or persons alleging age discrimination would not have to prove discriminatory

intent. Instead, the person would only have to show that some action by the employer had a disproportionately negative effect on workers 40 and older. Once this was done, the employer would have the burden to show that the discriminatory action was job-related or consistent with business necessity. If this ruling's interpretation stands, it will probably increase the number of age discrimination cases filed against employers in the U.S.

AMERICANS WITH DISABILITIES ACT. The Americans with Disabilities Act of 1990 (ADA) prohibits discrimination in any employment decision against qualified applicants or employees with a disability. It also requires employers to reasonably accommodate the disabilities of applicants and employees. The ADA applies to the same set of companies covered by Title VII.

Three definitions are key to understanding the ADA. First, is the definition of disability, which is any physical or mental impairment that prevents the person from engaging in a major life activity. Covered disabilities include both physical and mental impairments. The extent of the disabilities covered is one of the more controversial aspects of the law. Some conditions are specifically excluded from coverage, including pyromania and kleptomania.

A second key definition is that of qualification. Under the ADA, a person with a disability is qualified for a job if he or she can perform the essential functions of the job with or without accommodation. This means that the person does not have to be able to do every single duty of the job, if they are very minor, but that he or she must be able to perform the major responsibilities of the job.

A third important definition under the law is reasonable accommodation. A reasonable accommodation is one that does not cause an undue hardship on the employer. Undue hardship would be determined on a case-by-case basis, and consider the cost and inconvenience to the employer of accommodating the disability.

The ADA has resulted in many disability discrimination complaints with the EEOC, as well as many lawsuits against employers. Although the law, like most, has had unintended consequences, its net effect appears to have been a positive one, as it seems to have increased opportunities for qualified, disabled workers.

CIVIL RIGHTS ACT OF 1991. In the late 1980s, the Supreme Court decided several employment discrimination cases that made it more difficult for employees to prove discrimination cases in court. Concerned about these cases, the U.S. Congress addressed several issues by passing the 1991 Civil Rights Act.

The law did several major things. First, it codified the "disparate impact" theory of discrimination, which means that employees alleging discrimination can sometimes more easily prove a discrimination case. Second, the law allowed plaintiffs to have jury trials under some circumstances, instead of "bench" trials decided by a federal judge. Juries tend to be sympathetic to plaintiffs, particularly those suing large corporations, so this was a major victory for employees. Third, the law extended Title VII of the Civil Rights Act to certain types of organizations that had not been covered before (for example, the law extended the reach of Title VII to the federal government, which prior to passage had been exempt). Finally, the law banned the "race norming" of employment test scores.

COMPENSATION LAWS

FAIR LABOR STANDARDS ACT. The most important compensation law is the Fair Labor Standards Act (FLSA), passed in 1938. This law provides the basic framework within which millions of U.S. workers are paid. These workers are called "non-exempt" workers. These workers are those that, by virtue of the type of jobs they hold, must be paid in accordance with the FLSA. Exempt workers, who are not covered by the law, are primarily executive, managerial, professional, and highly-paid technical workers.

One important provision of the law is the federal minimum wage provision. Non-exempt workers must be paid a basic minimum wage, which has periodically been raised to higher levels. Non-exempt workers must also be paid overtime for hours worked in excess of a standard workweek, which in most industries is 40 hours per week.

A final provision of the act does not involve compensation directly, but the employment of minors. The law prevents the employment of minors in almost all jobs before the age of fourteen, and places fairly stringent restrictions on the employment of children between the ages of fourteen and eighteen.

EQUAL PAY ACT. The Equal Pay Act was passed in 1963 as an amendment to the FLSA. The Equal Pay Act requires a single employer to pay men and women equally for doing "substantially" the same job for the employer. An employer is allowed to pay men and women differently if the difference is based on merit, quantity of production, quality of production, or any other factor other than gender. Thus, the law does not mean that men and women doing the same work can't be paid differently, only that the difference must not be based on the sex of the worker.

LABOR RELATIONS LAWS

THE WAGNER ACT. The Wagner Act, otherwise known as the National Labor Relations Act, provides the basic framework within which labor union and management interact in the United States. The law was passed in 1935. It guarantees workers' basic right to organize. It created the National Labor Relations Board to oversee union-management relations. It provided for an election process for unionization efforts in U.S. businesses. It prohibited five major "unfair labor practices" on the part of U.S. employers.

THE TAFT-HARTLEY ACT. In 1947, the U.S. Congress enacted the Taft-Hartley Act by overriding President Harry Truman's veto. Whereas the Wagner Act is "pro-labor" in its effect, the Taft-Hartley Act is most decidedly "pro-business" in its provisions.

The Taft-Hartley Act banned the union security arrangement known as the closed shop. In a closed shop, individuals must belong to the appropriate union before they can be hired by a company. This arrangement is now banned in all but a handful of situations.

Taft-Hartley also gave the states the right to pass what are called "right-to-work" laws, which create "open shops." An open shop exists when no individual can be compelled to join a union before or after they are hired, even if the employer's workforce is organized. Labor unions detest open shops, as they make it difficult for unionization efforts to succeed. Twenty-two states are "right-to-work" states; most in the South and Southwest.

Taft-Hartley also laid out several "unfair practices" of labor unions and banned them. Finally, the act gave the U.S. president authority to issue an injunction temporarily stopping a strike, if the strike is deemed to be causing a threat to national security or creating an emergency detrimental to the national interest.

HEALTH AND SAFETY LAWS

The primary law relating to the health and safety of U.S. workers is the Occupational Safety and Health Act , passed in 1970. This law is controversial because it imposes very complex and detailed safety standards on thousands of U.S. businesses. The Occupational Safety and Health Administration (OSHA) was created to administer and enforce the law.

OSHA has general safety standards for almost all employers and specific standards for certain industries. It has workplace inspectors who have the right to, with a search warrant, inspect the conditions in almost any business in the United States. OSHA has the right to respond to employee complaints of unsafe conditions and in fact, the highest priority for OSHA inspections are those situations that pose an imminent threat to the health and safety of workers.

OSHA has the power to impose penalties on employers who violate its provisions. The severity of the penalties will vary based on the seriousness of the violation, a first or repeat offense, the cooperation of the business, and the size of the business. Although many U.S. companies do not like dealing with OSHA, it does appear that the law and its enforcement has resulted in improvements in the health and safety conditions in U.S. businesses.

OTHER MAJOR LAWS

THE FAMILY AND MEDICAL LEAVE ACT. The Family and Medical Leave Act (FMLA) of 1993 requires all employers with fifty or more employees to grant workers up to twelve weeks of unpaid leave per year for the care of a newborn child, an ill family member, or their own illness. Employees may take the leave all at once or in increments.

While it helps employees, the FMLA can be quite costly to employers when they must replace workers on leave. Because women are more likely to use these leaves, companies that employ a majority of women are especially hard-hit. Consider the case of Sibley Memorial Hospital of Washington, D.C.: The hospital ran into difficulty when trying to replace an employee on leave. Because she worked in an extremely specialized position, the hospital could not find a replacement locally. In addition to paying the on-leave employee's medical benefits, Sibley had to pay for the replacement worker's round-trip airfare, weekly housing, car rental, and salary. At the end of the original employee's leave, she informed the hospital that she would not be returning to work.

The FMLA protects employers from this type of problem in two ways: (1) it allows employers to exempt workers with highest earnings, and (2) it requires employees to reimburse the employer for insurance premiums paid during the leave if they are able to return to work, yet choose not to do so. While Sibley Memorial Hospital was not able to utilize the first protection (the employee's salary was not among the top 10 percent), it was reimbursed for its insurance payments.

EMPLOYEE PRIVACY LAWS. Privacy has become one of the most important workplace issues of the twenty-first century. Privacy concerns surface at the workplace when organizations attempt to collect and/or disseminate information about employees in ways that intrude upon their privacy. Privacy issues also surface when employee behavior is constrained by certain workplace rules and policies, denying employees the right to be "let alone," or to do as they please.

Employees may justifiably lodge an invasion of a privacy claim if the information collected by an employer is irrelevant to the employer's business needs. A company should have a clear business reason for each piece of information collected and maintained on an individual. For example, a company should not collect information about an employee's spouse unless that information is needed for benefits administration or some other useful purpose.

As a general rule, information pertaining to such personal issues as home ownership, previous marriages, sexual orientation, parents' occupations, and previous arrest records are usually of no concern to employers, and efforts to collect such information could pose legal threats to the company.

PRIVACY ACT. Should employees have access to data kept on them? According to the Privacy Act of 1974, public-sector employees must be given access to any information in their files. Specifically, the act states that employees have the right to:

- Determine what information is being kept on them by their employers.
- Review that information.
- Correct erroneous information.
- Prevent the information from being used for a purpose other than that for which it was collected.

While the Privacy Act does not cover private-sector employees, most companies do allow employees to access to their own records as a good employee-relations gesture. Prohibiting employees from seeing their own files may create doubts and suspicions regarding the company's good faith efforts to create business-relevant personnel files.

FREEDOM OF INFORMATION ACT. The release of information maintained by government agencies is regulated by the Freedom of Information Act of 1966. The purpose of the act is to make most government records available to the public. Specifically, the act states that any individual may gain access to these records with proper authorization.

The act makes exceptions for personnel files and medical information. However, the public may still be given access to this information if its right to know outweighs the individual's right to privacy. In the private sector, legal constraints in this area stem from the common law of defamation. When releasing information about an employee, the employer must ensure that the information is given in good faith, no malice is intended, and the receiving party has a legitimate reason for the information.

SEE ALSO: Diversity; Employment Law and Compliance; Human Resource Management; Quality of Work Life; Safety in the Workplace

Lawrence S. Kleiman
Revised by Tim Barnett

FURTHER READING:

Bennett-Alexander, Dawn, and Laura Pincus. *Employment Law for Business.* Boston, MA: Irwin McGraw-Hill, 1998.

Kleiman, Lawrence S. *Human Resource Management: A Tool for Competitive Advantage*. Cincinnati, OH: South-Western College Publishing, 2000.

U.S. Equal Employment Opportunity Commission (EEOC). Available from <www.eeoc.gov>.

Wolkinson, Benjamin W., and Richard N. Block. *Employment Law: The Workplace Rights of Employees and Employers*. Cambridge, MA: Blackwell, 1996.

EMPOWERMENT

A primary goal of employee empowerment is to give workers a greater voice in decisions about work-related matters. Their decision-making authority can range from offering suggestions to exercising veto power over management decisions. Although the range of decisions that employees may be involved in depends on the organization, possible areas include: how jobs are to be performed, working conditions, company policies, work hours, peer review, and how supervisors are evaluated.

Many experts believe that organizations can improve productivity through employee empowerment. This occurs in one of two main ways. First, empowerment can strengthen motivation by providing employees with the opportunity to attain intrinsic rewards from their work, such as a greater sense of accomplishment and a feeling of importance. In some cases, intrinsic rewards such as job satisfaction and a sense of purposeful work can be more powerful than extrinsic rewards such as higher wages or bonuses. Motivated employees clearly tend to put forth more effort than those who are less motivated. The second means by which employee empowerment can increase productivity is through better decisions. Especially when decisions require task-specific knowledge, those on the front line can often better identify problems.

Empowering employees to identify problems—combined with higher-level management involvement in coordinating solutions across departmental boundaries within the firm—can enhance the overall decision-making process and increase organizational learning. For example, Toyota Motor Company empowers some of its employees to identify and help remedy problems occurring during product assembly. An automobile coming off Toyota's assembly line with a paint defect is seen as an opportunity to delve into the root cause of the defect, as opposed to merely fixing the defect and passing it on to distributors for resale. Solutions resulting from employee involvement tend to have more employee buy-in when it comes to implementation. Because such solutions are generated from the front lines, this further enhances the potential for productivity improvements by reducing the attitude that solutions are "passed down from above."

A number of different human resource management programs are available that grant employee empowerment to some extent. A number of these are discussed in the following sections, including informal participative decision-making programs, job enrichment, continuous improvement, and self-managed work teams.

INFORMAL PARTICIPATIVE DECISION-MAKING PROGRAMS

Informal participative decision-making programs involve managers and subordinates making joint decisions on a daily basis. Employees do not enjoy blanket authority to make all work-related decisions; managers decide just how much decision-making authority employees should have in each instance. The amount of authority varies depending on such situational factors as decision complexity and the importance of employee acceptance of the decision. While it may seem obvious, one key to empowerment is choosing under what conditions to empower employees. Employees should be empowered in situations where they can make decisions that are as good as, or better than, those made by their managers.

One possible problem is that the interests of workers may not align with those of the organization. For example, at one university a department head delegated the task of determining job performance standards to the faculty. Because the faculty believed that it was not in their own best interest to develop challenging standards, the standards they eventually developed were easily attainable. The success of empowerment also often hinges on whether employees want to participate in decision making. Some employees, for instance, have no desire to make work-related decisions. Suggestions for increasing employee participation levels include work situations where:

1. All possible solutions are equally effective. For example, consider employee vacation schedules. If one solution is as good as another, employee groups can be empowered to work out the scheduling.

2. Managers do not possess sufficient information or expertise to make a quality decision without employee input. Managers should at least consult their employees before a decision is reached to prevent overlooking solutions

that may appear obvious to front-line employees, but which may be more evasive for higher-level managers who are unfamiliar with front-line practices.

3. Managers do not know exactly what information is needed or how to find it. Again, managers should at least consult their employees before a decision is reached to determine whether employees have the information required to make an effective decision.

4. The group's acceptance of or commitment to effective implementation is crucial and the group is unlikely to accept a manager's unilateral decision. If employees' acceptance is crucial, participative decision-making should be used. As alluded to previously, employees tend to accept decisions more willingly if they have had a voice in the decision-making process. One caveat is that the participation should be genuine; managers should not ask for employee input simply to give the appearance of participation. Employees can usually recognize this ploy and, if they do, feelings of distrust will likely develop.

5. Employees' goals are aligned with those of management. If employees do not share management's goals, participative decision-making would be inappropriate, because the two parties would be at odds.

Several studies have examined the effects of informal participative decision-making programs. While the results have been mixed and thus cannot be considered definitive, most studies have found that informal participative decision-making programs do, in fact, have a positive impact on productivity.

JOB ENRICHMENT

Sometimes, employees are not motivated because of the way their jobs are designed. For example, consider the job of an assembly-line worker who does nothing but place a screw in a hole as the product passes by on the production line. Such a job provides little opportunity for workers to gain intrinsic rewards. Job enrichment aims to redesign jobs to be more intrinsically rewarding. Certain job characteristics help managers to build enrichment into jobs. These characteristics (summarized in Exhibit 1) include:

- Skill variety—The various skills needed to perform a given task, where increased skill requirements are associated with increased motivation

- Task identity—The degree to which employees perceive how their job impacts the overall production of a product or service

- Task significance—Whether the task is meaningful beyond the task itself

- Autonomy—Employee discretion over how to perform a task

- Feedback—Input from peers and supervisors regarding the quality of an employee's work

When these characteristics are present in a job, employees tend to be more motivated than when these characteristics are not present. However, there is not a "silver bullet" for motivating employees through empowerment; there is considerable variation in the degree to which each of these empowerment factors motivates individuals. On the other hand, it is a mistake

---

Exhibit 1

Job Characteristics That Enhance Intrinsic Motivation

1. **Skill Variety:** The degree to which a job requires a variety of different activities to carry out the work. A job has high skill variety if it requires a number of different skills and talents.

2. **Task Identity:** The degree to which a job requires completion of the whole and identifiable piece of work. A job has high task identity, if the worker does the job from the beginning to end with a visible outcome.

3. **Task Significance:** The degree to which the job has a substantial impact on the lives of other people, whether these people are in the immediate organization or in the world at large. A job has a task significance if people benefit greatly from results of the job.

4. **Autonomy:** The degree to which the job provides the workers with autonomy. A job has high autonomy if workers are given substantial freedom, independence, and discretion in scheduling the work and determining the procedures to be used in carrying it out.

5. **Job Feedback:** The degree to which the job provides the worker with knowledge of results. A job has high job feedback if carrying out the work activities required by the job provides the individual with direct and clear information about the effectiveness of his or her performance.

to think that because certain individuals do not respond equally to such job designs, overall productivity will not increase as a result of empowerment through proper job design and enrichment. In general, productivity tends to increase despite the inherent variation of specific effects.

Once a job has been identified as needing enrichment, the organization must redesign it to incorporate these characteristics: skill variety, task identity, task significance, autonomy, and feedback. Some specific job enrichment techniques include:

- Combining tasks. This involves assigning tasks performed by different workers to a single individual. For example, in a furniture factory, rather than working on just one part of the production process, each person could assemble, sand, and stain an entire table or chair. This change would increase skill variety, as well as task identity, as each worker would be responsible for the job from start to finish.

- Establish client relationships. Client relationships could be established by putting the worker in touch with customers. For example, an auto dealership service department could allow its mechanics to discuss service problems directly with customers, rather than going through the service manager. By establishing client relationships, skill variety is increased because workers have a chance to develop interpersonal skills. It also provides them with a chance to do a larger part of the job (task identity), to see how their work impacts customers (task significance), and to have more decision-making authority (autonomy).

- Reduce direct supervision. Workers gain autonomy when they are given responsibility for doing things previously done by supervisors. For instance, clerks could be allowed to check for their own errors or be allowed to order supplies directly.

Many organizations have successfully enriched otherwise dull jobs, thereby empowering employees to have greater control over their work and the decisions affecting them. In addition to increased productivity, empowerment also may lead to improvements in product or service quality, reduced absenteeism rates, and increased employee retention. In situations where enriched jobs become less automated, however, production may become less efficient. Job enrichment would thus be ill-advised in situations where the loss in efficiency cannot be offset by productivity gains stemming from increased motivation. Moreover, employees preferring highly automated, easy jobs are likely to oppose job enrichment efforts.

CONTINUOUS IMPROVEMENT

Companies adopting continuous improvement attempt to build quality into all phases of product or service design, production, and delivery. Often referred to as total quality management, these programs empower workers to trace product or service problems to their root causes and redesign production processes to eliminate them using various problem-solving and statistical techniques. In these situations, empowerment arises from the need to involve employees at nearly all organizational levels in continuous improvement efforts. The use of continuous improvement programs have grown rapidly, built on the successful experiences of numerous companies. Xerox, for example, was able to decrease the number of customer complaints it received by 38 percent after implementing continuous improvement methods, and Motorola reduced the number of defects in its products by 80 percent. Proponents of self-managed work teams claim they succeed because they are customer-focused and promote sound management practices like teamwork, continuous learning, and continuous improvement.

SELF-MANAGED WORK TEAMS

Self-managed work teams have the authority to manage themselves. Rather than having managers control their work, self-managed work teams incorporate group norms to regulate activities. They plan, organize, coordinate, and take corrective actions. Some can hire, fire, and discipline team members with little intervention from higher levels of management. In short, self-managed work teams are given responsibilities usually held by managers, but control comes from the concertive influence of the team rather than from more formal means. Not surprisingly, managers' jobs are minimized and group norms are maximized when self-managed work teams are used. Self-managed work teams are not for all organizations; characteristic needed for success include:

- Technical skills. Cross-training, which allows team members to move from job to job within the team, is essential. Thus, team members should receive training in the specific skills that will broaden their personal contributions to the overall effort.

- Interpersonal skills. Team members must communicate effectively, both one-on-one and in groups. Cooperative decision-making within and among teams demands the skills of group problem solving, influencing others, and resolving conflicts. Team members must learn problem-solving skills that assist in zeroing in on problem areas, gathering facts, analyzing causes, generating alternatives, selecting solutions, and other related facets.

- Administrative skills. Self-managed work teams must perform tasks formerly handled by supervisors. The team must learn how to keep records, report procedures, budget, schedule, monitor, and appraise the performance of team members.

Research findings concerning self-managing teams have been largely positive. Proponents claim that self-managed work teams are effective because they empower employees to make decisions that affect their day-to-day business lives. Thus, these teams radically change the way that employees value and think about their jobs. Other benefits associated with self-managed teams include greater flexibility to respond to market changes and competitive pressures.

However, there are a number of drawbacks. As noted previously, self-managed teams are not for every organization. Some may be better served by other ways of empowerment, rather than the dramatic empowerment seen with self-managed teams. Drawbacks can include:

- Rivalry within and across teams

- A shortage of time and skills on the team to deal with conventional management concerns like hiring, training, and resolving interpersonal disputes

- Difficulty appraising employees in the absence of a traditional management figure

In addition to these concerns, one of the most difficult issues companies face with self-directed work teams is deciding how to effectively implement them. A number of obstacles must be overcome. Sometimes, managers are reluctant to relinquish control and employees are reluctant to accept new responsibilities. To prepare team members f\or self-management, the organization must provide a considerable amount of training. Without proper training, teams are likely to become bogged down permanently in mid-process.

As the previous discussion suggests, empowerment is not a single event or process, but rather takes a variety of forms. The degree of empowerment ranges from asking employees for input to allowing total discretion. Informal participative decision-making programs, job enrichment, continuous improvement, and self-managed work teams are some of the ways that organizations empower employees, giving them more control, but at the same time increasing overall organizational productivity.

SEE ALSO: Continuous Improvement; Human Resource Management; Quality and Total Quality Management; Teams and Teamwork

Lawrence S. Kleiman
Revised by Scott B. Droege

FURTHER READING:

Druskat, Vanessa Urch, and Jane V. Wheeler. "How to Lead a Self-Managing Team." *MIT Sloan Management Review* 45, no. 4 (2004): 65–72.

Hawley, Casey Fitts. *201 Ways to Turn Any Employee into a Star Performer.* New York: McGraw-Hill, 2004.

Langfred, C.W., and Neta A. Moye. "Effects of Task Autonomy on Performance: An Extended Model Considering Motivational, Informational, and Structural Mechanisms." *Journal of Applied Psychology* 89, no. 6 (2004): 934–946.

Meyer, John P., Thomas E. Becker, and Christian Vandenberghe. "Employee Commitment and Motivation: A Conceptual Analysis and Integrative Model." *Journal of Applied Psychology* 89, no. 6 (2004): 991–998.

Pfeffer, Jeffrey. "How Companies Get Smart." *Business 2.0* 6, no. 1 (2005): 74.

Seibert, Scott E., Seth R. Silver, and W. Alan Randolph. "Taking Empowerment to the Next Level: A Multiple-Level Model of Empowerment, Performance, and Satisfaction." *Academy of Management Journal* 47, no. 3 (2004): 332–350.

ENTERPRISE RESOURCE PLANNING

Enterprise resource planning (ERP) refers to a computer information system that integrates all the business activities and processes throughout an entire organization. ERP systems incorporate many of the features available in other types of manufacturing programs, such as project management, supplier management, product data management, and scheduling. The objective of ERP is to provide seamless, real-time information to all employees throughout the enterprise. Companies commonly use ERP systems to communicate the progress of orders and projects throughout the supply chain, and to track the costs and availability of value-added services.

ERP systems offer companies the potential to streamline operations, eliminate overlap and bottlenecks, and save money and resources. But ERP systems are very expensive and time-consuming to implement, and surveys have shown that not all companies achieve the desired benefits. According to the online business resource *Darwin Executive Guides,* it is "a tall order, building a single software program that serves the needs of people in finance as well as it does the people in human resources and the warehouse. . . To do ERP right, the ways you do business will need to change and the ways people do their jobs will need to change too. And that kind of change doesn't come without pain."

EVOLUTION OF ERP

ERP is a part of an evolutionary process that began with material requirements planning (MRP). MRP is a computer-based, time-phased system for planning and controlling the production and inventory function of a firm-from the purchase of materials to the shipment of finished goods. It begins with the aggregation of demand for finished goods from a number of sources (orders, forecasts, and safety stock). This results in a master production schedule (MPS) for finished goods. Using this MPS and a bill-of-material (a listing for all component parts that make up the finished goods), the MRP logic determines the gross requirements for all component parts and subassemblies. From an inventory status file, the MRP logic deducts the on-hand inventory balance and all open orders to yield the net requirements for all parts. Then all requirements are offset by their lead times to provide a date by which an order must be released in order to avoid delaying the production of finished goods.

From this MRP logic evolved manufacturing resource planning (MRP II). Before MRP II, many firms maintained a separate computer system within each functional department, which led to the overlap in storage of much of the firm's information in several different databases. In some cases, the firm did not even know how many different databases held certain information, making it difficult, if not impossible, to update it. This could also cause confusion throughout the firm if different units (such as engineering, production, sales, and accounting) held different values for the same variables. MRP II expands the role of MRP by linking together such functions as business planning, sales and operations planning, capacity requirements planning, and all related support functions. The output from these MRP II functions can be integrated into financial reports, such as the business plan, purchase-commitment report, shipping budget, and inventory projections. MRP II is capable of addressing operational planning in units or financial planning in dollars, and has a simulation capacity that allows its users to analyze the potential consequences of alternative decisions.

The next step in the evolutionary process was enterprise resource planning (ERP), a term coined by the Gartner Group of Stamford, Connecticut. ERP extends the concept of the shared database to all functions within the firm. By entering information only once at the source and making it available to all employees, ERP enables each function to interact with one centralized database and server. Not only does this eliminate the need for different departments within the firm to reenter the same information over and over again into separate computer systems, but it also eliminates the incompatibility that was created by past practice.

FEATURES OF ERP

ERP is a hybrid of many different types of software, incorporating many of the features available in other programs. ERP provides a way to keep track of materials, inventory, human resources, billing, and purchase orders. It is also useful for managing various types of orders, from mass-customized orders where daily or weekly shifts occur within the plant or multiple plants, to products that are made-to-stock, made-to-order, or assembled-to-order.

Higher-level ERPs employ design engineering and engineering change control modules. These modules facilitate the development of new product-engineering information and provide for modification of existing bills of material, allowing engineers to support working models of items and bills of material prior to their production releases.

It is important to understand that ERPs are not cheap to implement and operate, nor can they be implemented overnight. Owens-Corning spent more than $100 million over the course of two years installing one of the most popular ERP systems, SAP AG's R/3 system. Microsoft spent $25 million over 10 months installing R/3. Chevron also spent $100 million on installation. Apparently, however, the benefits of ERP implementation and use can be enormous. Microsoft used it's ERP system to replace 33 different financial tracking systems used in 26 of its subsidiaries, with an expected savings of $18 million annually. In the same respect, Chevron expected to recoup its $100 million investment within two years.

Owens-Corning's aim was to offer buyers one-stop shopping for insulation, pipes, and roofing material. Use of the R/3 facilitated this goal by allowing sales representatives to quickly see what products were available at any plant or warehouse. Analog Devices use the R/3 to consolidate the products stored at its warehouse, thereby creating an international order-processing system that can calculate exchange rates automatically. ERP and supply chain management.

When ERP systems first appeared, they acted as the connection between front-office operations (e.g., sales and forecasting) and the day-to-day functions of manufacturing. As ERP technology has advanced, the systems have increasingly incorporated logistics and warehousing capabilities, further connecting them with the supply chain. Some ERP systems offer Internet functionality, which can provide real-time connectivity from suppliers to the end customer.

The result of ERP use is more than an automation of existing processes-it is a significantly new way of doing business that enables a firm to respond to market changes more rapidly and efficiently. This can apply to service firms as well as manufacturers. Many ERP packages also let the user track and cost service products in the same way they compute the cost of making, storing, and shipping physical products.

SEE ALSO: Management Information Systems; Manufacturing Resources Planning

R. Anthony Inman
Revised by Laurie Hillstrom

FURTHER READING:

"Enterprise Resource Planning." *Darwin Executive Guides* Available from <http://guide.darwinmag.com/technology/enterprise/erp>.

Hanson, J.J. "Successful ERP Implementations Go Far Beyond Software." *San Diego Business Journal* (5 July 2004).

Larson, Melissa. "Meet Customer Demands with New ERP Systems." *Quality* (February 1998): 80–81.

Millman, Gregory J. "What Did You Get from ERP and What Can You Get?" *Financial Executive* (May 2004).

O'Leary, Daniel F. *ERP: Systems, Life Cycle, E-Commerce, and Risk.* Cambridge University Press, 2000.

Olinger, Charles. "The Issues Behind ERP Acceptance and Implementation." *APICS: The Performance Advantage* (June 1998): 44–48.

Wallace, Thomas F., and Michael H. Kremzar. *ERP: Making It Happen-The Implementer's Guide to Success with ERP.* New York: John Wiley, 2001.

ENTREPRENEURSHIP

Entrepreneurship is the process of identifying opportunities, marshalling the resources needed to take advantage of the opportunities, and creating a new venture for the purposes of providing needed products/services to customers and achieving a profit. The word "entrepreneurship" is taken from the French word "entreprendre," which means "to undertake." A person who engages in entrepreneurship is called an entrepreneur. Entrepreneurship occurs all over the world, but it is a particular characteristic of free-market economies. Countries with the highest rates of entrepreneurship include the United States, Canada, Israel, Italy, and Great Britain.

Entrepreneurship involves considerable risk, as the failure rate for new ventures is very high. Thus, to be successful, an entrepreneur must be able to tolerate and even thrive under conditions of risk and uncertainty. Successful entrepreneurship also requires innovativeness and creativity, as well as self-confidence, high levels of energy, and a strong need for achievement.

Interest in entrepreneurship is at an all-time high. Most colleges and universities offer courses or even entire programs of study in entrepreneurship.

The process of entrepreneurship is complex and requires the aspiring entrepreneur to make many decisions. It begins with recognizing an opportunity and applying innovativeness and creativity to exploit the opportunity. The entrepreneur must engage in strategic thinking and identify a competitive advantage that will set the small business apart and provide customers a unique reason to patronize the business.

The outcomes of this strategic thinking should be a business plan, which is a written statement that provides a comprehensive blueprint for the new venture. Although every business plan should reflect the unique characteristics of the entrepreneur and the proposed new business, there are common elements that exist in most business plans. Typically, the business plan includes some or all of the following components:

• Executive Summary

• Description of the Firm's Product/Service

• Business Strategy

• Forecasted Financial Statement

• Loan or Investment Proposal

The executive summary provides a concise one to two page overview of the entire business plan. The description of the product or service should identify the key features and benefits of the product or service. The business strategy is the most detailed part of the business plan. Here, the plan provides the entrepreneur's vision and what he or she sees as the mission of the new venture. This section must also lay out key strategies in the areas of operations, marketing, and finance. The forecasted financial statements should include monthly and/or quarterly projected cash budgets, income statements, balance sheets, and capital expenditures. The loan or investment proposal should identify the type of financing required and a plan for repayment.

Entrepreneurship is an important, if not the most important, component of a successful market-based economy. Free economies require individuals who are willing to take risks by creating, organizing, and successfully running new businesses. Most entrepreneurs operate in the areas of small business and/or family-owned business. These are the engines of economic growth. If small businesses are defined as those having fewer than 100 employees, 99 percent of businesses in the U.S. are small. Ninety percent of these small businesses employ fewer than 20 employees. Yet, it is estimated that small businesses have created 85 percent of the new jobs in the U.S. since the early 1990s. Further, most of these small businesses are family-owned. Family-owned businesses employ more than 50 million people and generate more than 50 percent of the nation's GDP. Thus, much emphasis is placed on public policies that will encourage entrepreneurial activity and nurture and sustain new ventures, small businesses, and family-owned businesses.

As a way of life, entrepreneurship has several advantages. It offers individuals the chance to be their own boss and to enjoy an independent lifestyle. It provides individuals the opportunity to develop and grow a new business that makes an impact on their community. And, of course, successful new ventures offer the tantalizing prospect of almost unlimited profit potential. However, as a lifestyle, entrepreneurship also has its downside. It requires a tremendous amount of personal commitment and long work hours, particularly in the early stages of new business startup. Uncertainty of income and the potential for financial loss are also potential negatives.

SEE ALSO: Angels and Venture Capitalists; Business Plan; Initial Public Offering; Strategic Planning Tools; Strategy Formulation; Succession Planning; SWOT Analysis

Tim Barnet

FURTHER READING:

"Global Entrepreneurship Monitor." Available from <http://www.gemconsortium.org>.

Zimmerer, T.W., and N.M. Scarborough. *Essentials of Entrepreneurship ond Small Business Management.* Upper Saddle River, NJ: Prentice-Hall, 2002.

ERGONOMICS

According to the U.S. Occupational Safety and Health Agency (OSHA), ergonomics is the science of fitting the job to the worker. The term comes from the Greek words *ergon,* meaning "work," and *nomoi,* meaning "natural laws." The goal of ergonomics is apply scientific information about human capabilities and limitations to design of work environments, systems, and tools in order to make them as safe, comfortable, and efficient as possible. Ergonomics thus seeks to minimize the physical demands on workers and optimize system performance. An ergonomist is a scientist who studies physiological, psychological, and engineering design aspects of a job, including such factors as fatigue, lighting required, tools used, equipment layout, and placement of controls.

PRINCIPLES OF ERGONOMICS

Although ergonomics officially came into being just 50 years ago, the principles have been understood for thousands of years. One just has to look at ancient hand tools to see how our ancestors intuitively understood the concept of physical fit. Even in the early 1900s, scientific management pioneers in time and motion study—such as the Gilbreths—experimented with the design of tools to find the most effective ways to do things. The real impetus for the foundation of ergonomics, however, came during World War I. The rapid development of new technology exceeded the limits of human capabilities in some instances. For example, poor design of controls and instruments in aircraft cockpits meant that pilots often made fatal mistakes.

Today, there are three main areas of specialization within the field of ergonomics: physical (the study of postures, movements, etc.); cognitive (the study of workload, stress, decision making, etc.); and organizational (the study of policies and processes). Experts recommend that companies apply the following basic principles of ergonomics when designing jobs:

- workers should be able to adopt several different postures that are safe and comfortable

- when workers must exert muscular force, they should be encouraged to use the largest possible muscle groups

- whenever possible, workers should be able to perform regular work activities with their joints in the middle of the range of movement

ERGONOMICS PROBLEMS

With the increasingly automated workplace, ergonomics problems are relatively common. One growing area of concern for many organizations is the number of work-related musculoskeletal disorders (MSDs). MSDs represent more than 100 different injuries that occur when there is a mismatch between the physical requirements of the job and the physical capacity of the human body. In 2000, OSHA estimated that more than 600,000 American workers experienced serious injuries due to overexertion or repetitive motion on the job. Back pain and various cumulative trauma disorders (CTDs), such as wrist tendonitis and carpal tunnel syndrome, may all stem from work-related overuse. Specific risk factors associated with MSDs include repetitive motion, heavy lifting, forceful exertion, contact stress, vibration, awkward posture, and rapid hand and wrist movement. Designing the work and the work environment properly through ergonomics can prevent MSDs, or at least reduce their incidence and severity.

The federal government's involvement in ergonomics started in the early 1980s when OSHA began discussing ergonomic issues with labor unions, trade associations, and professional organizations. First focusing on reducing back injuries resulting from manual lifting, OSHA's efforts broadened during the late 1980s to include cumulative trauma disorders. Through the 1990s OSHA signed approximately 15 corporate settlement agreements to bring ergonomic programs to nearly half a million workers. Chrysler, Ford, and General Motors were the first three major companies to sign such agreements. In 1994 OSHA began to work on an ergonomics standard, but tremendous opposition developed that resulted in Congress prohibiting use of OSHA funds to publish any proposed standard during fiscal year 1998. Nonetheless, OSHA made certain ergonomics recommendations, launched an ergonomics page on the Internet, and held stakeholder meetings on ergonomics in several cities through out the country.

OSHA ERGONOMICS STANDARDS

OSHA continued holding discussions with stakeholders while also working to refine its proposed ergonomics standard. The new standard was officially announced in November 2000 and took effect in January 2001. Among more than 1,600 pages of findings and recommendations, OSHA defined repetitive stress as a workplace hazard and ordered employers to take action to protect workers. The standard stated that employees who suffered repetitive stress injuries on the job were entitled to up to 90 days of injury leave at up to 90 percent of their regular pay rate. Representatives of a number of companies and industries criticized the new OSHA ergonomics standard as an undue burden on employers, while worker advocates praised the rules.

OSHA has attempted to assist companies in complying with the rules. For example, it released a video entitled "Ergonomic Programs That Work." The four employers featured in the video are Navistar, Russell Corporation, Woodpro Cabinetry, and Sequins International. Navistar established an effective ergonomics program using educational seminars with the help of a consultant, employee input, and widespread management support. Navistar's program led to a 66 percent reduction in workers' compensation costs. Similarly, Woodpro saved $42,000 in workers' compensation costs by changing conveyor levels and adding additional conveyors to reduce worker lifting. Russell Corporation found that small changes—such as new, adjustable tables and chairs—combined with adequate ergonomic training reduced the number of injuries by 50 percent over a six-year period. At Sequins International, Inc., consultants, workers, management, and the union viewed videotapes of employees working and then discussed ways to improve conditions. By replacing old chairs with ergonomically correct chairs, using new tables with adjustable heights, and launching an extensive educational program to share ergonomic techniques to prevent and correct MSDs, Sequins cut its workers' compensation cost from $96,000 to $4,500, and employee production and satisfaction increased significantly.

Even though statistics show that MSDs occur in large numbers and are costly to businesses; ergonomics remains a complex and controversial issue. Some employer associations and organizations oppose mandated ergonomic guidelines, believe the seriousness of injuries is exaggerated, and question what causes these injuries. Other organizations, however, view ergonomics as a value-added business strategy that can reduce costs and increase productivity.

SEE ALSO: Human Resource Management; Safety in the Workplace

Fraya Wagner-Marsh
Revised by Laurie Hillstrom

FURTHER READING:

"Ergonomics," Ergonomics.org, undated. Available from ergonomics.org.

Fernberg, Patricia. "Healthy Returns from Ergonomics." *Occupational Health* (October 1998): 67–69.

Haddad, Charles. "OSHA's New Regulations Will Ease the Pain for Everyone." *Business Week,* 4 December 2000.

International Ergonomics Association. "The Discipline of Ergonomics." Available from <http://www.iea.cc/ergonomics>.

Kincaid, William H. "Add Value with a Comprehensive Approach to Ergonomics." *Occupational Hazards* (February 2004).

Kroemer, K.H.E. *Ergonomics: How to Design for Ease and Efficiency.* Englewood Cliffs, NJ: Prentice Hall, 2000.

Langford, Joe. "In Search of the Right Fit: What Is Ergonomics?" *Safety and Health Practitioner* (September 1998): 20–22.

Occupational Safety and Health Administration. "Ergonomics Programs Prevent Injuries, Save Money." *Ergonomics* (July 1998). Available from <http://www.osha-slc.gov/SLTC/ergonomics/index.html>.

Smith, S.L. "Ergonomics Is a Value-Added Strategy." *Occupational Hazards* (August 1998): 22.

Weiss, W.H. "Ergonomics: Major Health and Safety Issue." *Supervision* (April 1998): 3–6.

Wynn, Mike. "Establishing an Ergonomics Program." *Occupational Health and Safety* (August 1998): 106–108.

ETHICS

Webster's Collegiate Dictionary defines "ethics" as the "discipline dealing with what is good and bad and with moral duty and obligation," "a set of moral principles or value" or "a theory or system of moral values." Ethics assists individuals in deciding when an act is moral or immoral, right or wrong. Ethics can be grounded in natural law, religious tenets, parental and family influence, educational experiences, life experiences, and cultural and societal expectations.

Ethics in business, or business ethics as it is often called, is the application of the discipline, principles, and theories of ethics to the organizational context. Business ethics have been defined as "principles and standards that guide behavior in the world of business." Business ethics is also a descriptive term for the field of academic study in which many scholars conduct research and in which undergraduate and graduate students are exposed to ethics theory and practice, usually through the case method of analysis.

Ethical behavior in business is critical. When business firms are charged with infractions, and when employees of those firms come under legal investigation, there is a concern raised about moral behavior in business. Hence, the level of mutual trust, which is the foundation of our free-market economy, is threatened.

Although ethics in business has been an issue for academics, practitioners, and governmental regulators for decades, some believe that unethical, immoral, and/or illegal behavior is widespread in the business world. Numerous scandals in the late 1990s and early 2000s seemed to add credence to the criticism of business ethics. Corporate executives of WorldCom, a giant in the telecommunications field, admitted fraud and misrepresentation in financial statements. WorldCom's former CEO went on trial for alleged crimes related to this accounting ethics scandal.

A similar scandal engulfed Enron in the late 1990s and its former CEO, Ken Lay, also faced trial. Other notable ethical lapses were publicized involving ImClone, a biotechnological firm; Arthur Andersen, one of the largest and oldest public accounting firms; and Healthsouth, a large healthcare firm located in the southeast United States. These companies eventually suffered public humiliation, huge financial losses, and in some cases, bankruptcy or dissolution. The ethical and legal problems resulted in some corporate officials going to prison, many employees losing their jobs, and thousands of stockholders losing some or all of their savings invested in the firms' stock.

Although the examples mentioned involved top management, huge sums of money, and thousands of stakeholders, business ethics is also concerned with the day-to-day ethical dilemmas faced by millions of workers at all levels of business enterprise. It is the awareness of and judgments made in ethical dilemmas by all that determines the overall level of ethics in business. Thus, the field of business ethics is concerned not only with financial and accounting irregularities involving billions of dollars, but all kinds of moral and ethical questions, large and small, faced by those who work in business organizations.

The discussion that follows is organized into three parts: (1) the major theories or "moral philosophies" that are applied to business ethics; (2) a well-established model of ethical decision-making in business; and (3) the factors that affect individual ethical decision-making in the business context.

APPROACHES TO ETHICAL DECISION-MAKING

Philosophers have studied and written about ethics for thousands of years. The moral philosophies or ethical "theories" that have been developed form the foundation for ethics in business. Table 1 shows some of the major ethical philosophies that are applied to business ethics. Each of the ethical philosophies is briefly considered in this section.

TELEOLOGY. Teleological theories of ethics focus on the consequences caused by an action and are often referred to as "consequentalist" theories. By far the most common teleological theories are egoism and utilitarianism.

EGOISM. Egoism defines right and wrong in terms of the consequences to one's self. Egoism is defined by self-interest. An egoist would weigh an ethical dilemma or issue in terms of how different courses of action would affect his or her physical, mental, or emotional well being. Thus, an egoist, when faced with a business decision, would tend to choose the course of action that he or she believes would best serve self-interest.

Although it seems likely that egoism would potentially lead to unethical and/or illegal behavior, this philosophy of ethics is, to some degree, at the heart of a free-market economy. Since the time of political economist Adam Smith, advocates of a free market unencumbered by governmental regulation have argued that individuals, each pursuing their own self-interest, would actually benefit society at large.

This point of view is notably espoused by the famous economist Milton Friedman, who suggested that the only moral obligation of business is to make a profit and obey the law. However, it should be noted that Smith, Friedman, and most others who advocate unregulated commerce, acknowledge that some restraints on individuals' selfish impulses are required.

Table 1

Approaches to Ethics in Business

Teleological	Actions are judged as ethical or unethical based on their results.
Egoism	Actions are judged as ethical or unethical based on the consequences to one's self. Actions that maximize self-interest are preferred.
Utilitarianism	Actions are judged as ethical or unethical based on the consequences to "others." Actions that maximize the "good" (create the greatest good for the greatest number) are preferred.
Deontological	Actions are judged as ethical or unethical based on the inherent rights of individual and the intentions of the actor. Individuals are to be treated as means and not ends. It is the action itself that must be judged and not its consequences.
Justice	Actions are judged as ethical or unethical based on the fairness shown to those affected. Fairness may be determined by distributive, procedural, and/or interactional means.
Relativism	Actions are judged as ethical or unethical based on subjective factors that may vary from individual to individual, group to group, and culture to culture.

Adapted from: Ferrell, Fraedrich, and Ferrell, 2002, p. 57.

UTILITARIANISM. In the utilitarian approach to ethical reasoning, one emphasizes the utility, or the overall amount of good, that might be produced by an action or a decision. For example, companies decide to move their production facilities from one country to another. How much good is expected from the move? How much harm? If the good appears to outweigh the harm, the decision to move may be deemed an ethical one, by the utilitarian yardstick.

This approach also encompasses what has been referred to as cost-benefit analysis. In this, the costs and benefits of a decision, a policy, or an action are compared. Sometimes these can be measured in economic, social, human, or even emotional terms. When all the costs are added and compared with the results, if the benefits outweigh the costs, then the action may be considered ethical.

One fair criticism of this approach is that it is difficult to accurately measure costs and benefits. Another criticism is that the rights of those in the minority may be overlooked.

Utilitarianism is like egoism in that it advocates judging actions by their consequences, but unlike egoism utilitarianism focuses on determining the course of action that will produce the greatest good for the greatest number of people. Thus, it is the ends that determine the morality of an action and not the action itself (or the intent of the actor).

Utilitarianism is probably the dominant moral philosophy in business ethics. Utilitarianism is attractive to many business people, since the philosophy acknowledges that many actions result in good consequences for some, but bad consequences for others. This is certainly true of many decisions in business.

DEONTOLOGY. Deontological theories of ethics focus on (1) the rights of all individuals and (2) the intentions of the person(s) performing an action. Deontological theories differ substantially from utilitarian views on ethics and would not allow, for example, the harming of some individuals in order to help others. To the deontologist, each person must be treated with the same level of respect and no one should be treated as a means to an end.

Deontology proposes that the principles of ethics are permanent and unchanging—and that adherence to these principles is at the heart of ethical behavior. Many deontologists believe that the rights of individuals are grounded in "natural law." Deontology is most closely associated with the German philosopher Immanuel Kant.

JUSTICE. Justice-based theories of ethics concern the perceived fairness of actions. A just (ethical) action is one that treats all fairly and consistently in accord with ethical or legal standards. Justice theories of ethics are closely associated with the philosopher John Rawls.

To determine the fairness of an action, one often appeals to distributive, procedural, and/or interactional rules. Distributive fairness is based on the outcomes received by individuals and their perceptions of these outcomes. Procedural fairness is based on the processes (policies, procedures, rules) employed to reach decisions. Individuals evaluate the fairness of these processes in addition to (or instead of) the outcomes received.

Finally, interactional fairness relates to the personal treatment one receives in the administration of a decision-making process. Interpersonal fairness has to do with the respect and consideration shown in the administration of decisions. Informational fairness has to do with the explanations and accounts provided for the decisions made.

The study of organizational justice has become a major field within organizational behavior. To date, however, there has not been a complete integration between justice perceptions and ethical theory.

RELATIVISM. Teleological, utilitarian, and justice theories of ethics are all "universal" theories, in that they purport to advance principles of morality that are permanent and relatively enduring. Relativism states that there are no universal principles of ethics and that right and wrong must be determined by each individual or group.

The relativist believes that standards of right and wrong change over time and are different across cultures—and does not accept that some ethical standards or values are superior to others. The concept of relativism can probably be summarized as "What's right for one may not be right for another," or "When in Rome, do as the Romans do."

INDIVIDUAL ETHICAL DECISION-MAKING

There are many approaches to the individual ethical decision-making process in business. However, one of the more common was developed by James Rest and has been called the four-step or four-stage model of individual ethical decision-making. Numerous scholars have applied this theory in the business context. The four steps include: ethical issue recognition, ethical (moral) judgment, ethical (moral) intent, and ethical (moral) behavior.

ETHICAL ISSUE RECOGNITION. Before a person can apply any standards of ethical philosophy to an issue, he or she must first comprehend that the issue has an ethical component. This means that the ethical decision-making process must be "triggered" or set in motion by the awareness of an ethical dilemma. Some individuals are likely to be more sensitive to potential ethical problems than others. Numerous factors can affect whether someone recognizes an ethical issue; some of these factors are discussed in the next section.

ETHICAL (MORAL) JUDGMENT. If an individual is confronted with a situation or issue that he or she recognizes as having an ethical component or posing an ethical dilemma, the individual will probably form some overall impression or judgment about the rightness or wrongness of the issue. The individual may reach this judgment in a variety of ways, as noted in the earlier section on ethical philosophy.

ETHICAL (MORAL) INTENT. Once an individual reaches an ethical judgment about a situation or issue, the next stage in the decision-making process is to form a behavioral intent. That is, the individual decides what he or she will do (or not do) in regard to the perceived ethical dilemma.

According to research, ethical judgments are a strong predictor of behavioral intent. However, individuals do not always form intentions to behave that are in accord with their judgments, as various situational factors may act to influence the individual otherwise.

ETHICAL (MORAL) BEHAVIOR. The final stage in the four-step model of ethical decision-making is to engage in some behavior in regard to the ethical dilemma. Research shows that behavioral intentions are the strongest predictor of actual behavior in general, and ethical behavior in particular. However, individuals do now always behave consistent with either their judgments or intentions in regard to ethical issues. This is particularly a problem in the business context, as peer group members, supervisors, and organizational culture may influence individuals to act in ways that are inconsistent with their own moral judgments and behavioral intentions.

Some specific factors that influence the individual ethical decision-making process, as outlined above, are presented in the final section of this essay.

FACTORS AFFECTING ETHICAL DECISION-MAKING

In general, there are three types of influences on ethical decision-making in business: (1) individual difference factors, (2) situational (organizational) factors, and (3) issue-related factors.

INDIVIDUAL DIFFERENCE FACTORS. Individual difference factors are personal factors about an individual that may influence their sensitivity to ethical issues, their judgment about such issues, and their related behavior. Research has identified many personal characteristics that impact ethical decision-making. The individual difference factor that has received the most research support is "cognitive moral development."

This framework, developed by Lawrence Kohlberg in the 1960s and extended by Kohlberg and other researchers in the subsequent years, helps to explain why different people make different evaluations when confronted with the same ethical issue. It posits that an individual's level of "moral development" affects their ethical issue recognition, judgment, behavioral intentions, and behavior.

According to the theory, individuals' level of moral development passes through stages as they mature. Theoretically, there are three major levels of development. The lowest level of moral development is termed the "pre-conventional" level. At the two stages of this level, the individual typically will evaluate ethical issues in light of a desire to avoid punishment and/or seek personal reward. The pre-conventional level of moral development is usually associated with small children or adolescents.

The middle level of development is called the "conventional" level. At the stages of the conventional level, the individual assesses ethical issues on the basis of the fairness to others and a desire to conform to societal rules and expectations. Thus, the individual looks outside him or herself to determine right and wrong. According to Kohlberg, most adults operate at the conventional level of moral reasoning.

The highest stage of moral development is the "principled" level. The principled level, the individual is likely to apply principles (which may be utilitarian, deontological, or justice) to ethical issues in an attempt to resolve them. According to Kohlberg, a principled person looks inside him or herself and is less likely to be influenced by situational (organizational) expectations.

The cognitive moral development framework is relevant to business ethics because it offers a powerful explanation of individual differences in ethical reasoning. Individuals at different levels of moral development are likely to think differently about ethical issues and resolve them differently.

SITUATIONAL (ORGANIZATIONAL) FACTORS. Individuals' ethical issue recognition, judgment, and behavior are affected by contextual factors. In the business ethics context, the organizational factors that affect ethical decision-making include the work group, the supervisor, organizational policies and procedures, organizational codes of conduct, and the overall organizational culture. Each of these factors, individually and collectively, can cause individuals to reach different conclusions about ethical issues than they would have on their own. This section looks at one of these organizational factors, codes of conduct, in more detail.

Codes of conduct are formal policies, procedures, and enforcement mechanisms that spell out the moral and ethical expectations of the organization. A key part of organizational codes of conduct are written ethics codes. Ethics codes are statements of the norms and beliefs of an organization. These norms and beliefs are generally proposed, discussed, and defined by the senior executives in the firm. Whatever process is used for their determination, the norms and beliefs are then disseminated throughout the firm.

An example of a code item would be, "Employees of this company will not accept personal gifts with a monetary value over $25 in total from any business friend or associate, and they are expected to pay their full share of the costs for meals or other entertainment (concerts, the theater, sporting events, etc.) that have a value above $25 per person." Hosmer points out that the norms in an ethical code are generally expressed as a series of negative statements, for it is easier to list the things a person should not do than to be precise about the things a person should.

Almost all large companies and many small companies have ethics codes. However, in and of themselves ethics codes are unlikely to influence individuals to be more ethical in the conduct of business. To be effective, ethics codes must be part of a value system that permeates the culture of the organization. Executives must display genuine commitment to the ideals expressed in the written code—if their behavior is inconsistent with the formal code, the code's effectiveness will be reduced considerably.

At a minimum, the code of conduct must be specific to the ethical issues confronted in the particular industry or company. It should be the subject of ethics training that focuses on actual dilemmas likely to be faced by employees in the organization. The conduct code must contain communication mechanisms for the dissemination of the organizational ethical standards and for the reporting of perceived wrongdoing within the organization by employees.

Organizations must also ensure that perceived ethical violations are adequately investigated and that wrongdoing is punished. Research suggests that unless ethical behavior is rewarded and unethical behavior punished, that written codes of conduct are unlikely to be effective.

ISSUE-RELATED FACTORS. Conceptual research by Thomas Jones in the 1990s and subsequent empirical studies suggest that ethical issues in business must have a certain level of "moral intensity" before they will trigger ethical decision-making processes. Thus, individual and situational factors are unlikely to influence decision-making for issues considered by the individual to be minor.

Certain characteristics of issues determine their moral intensity. In general, the research suggests that issues with more serious consequences are more likely to reach the threshold level of intensity. Likewise, issues that are deemed by a societal consensus to be ethical or unethical are more likely to trigger ethical decision-making processes.

In summary, business ethics is an exceedingly complicated area, one that has contemporary significance for all business practitioners. There are, however, guidelines in place for effective ethical decision making. These all have their positive and negative sides, but taken together, they may assist the businessperson to steer toward the most ethical decision possible under a particular set of circumstances.

SEE ALSO: Goals and Goal Setting; Mission and Vision Statements

James H. Conley
Revised by Tim Barnett

FURTHER READING:

Barnett, Tim, and Sean Valentine. "Issue Contingencies and Marketers' Recognition of Ethical Issues, Ethical Judgments, and Behavioral Intentions." *Journal of Business Research* 57 (2004): 338–346.

Beauchamp, Tom L., and Norman E. Bowie. *Ethical Theory and Business.* Englewood Cliffs, NJ: Prentice Hall, 1993.

Ferrell, O.C., John Fraedrich, and Linda Ferrell. *Business Ethics.* Boston, MA: Houghton Mifflin Company, 2002.

Hosmer, LaRue Tone. *The Ethics of Management.* Homewood, IL: Irwin, 1991.

Kuhn, James W., and Donald W. Shriver, Jr. *Beyond Success.* New York, NY: Oxford University Press, 1991.

MacIntyre, Alasdair. *After Virtue.* Notre Dame, IN: University of Notre Dame Press, 1984.

Paine, Lynn Sharp. "Managing for Organizational Integrity." *Harvard Business Review* (March-April 1994).

Post, James E., William C. Frederick, Anne T. Lawrence, and James Weber. *Business and Society.* New York: McGraw-Hill, 1996.

Raiborn, Cecily A., and Dinah Payne. "Corporate Codes of Conduct: A Collective Conscience and Continuum." *Journal of Business Ethics* 9 (1990): 879–889.

Trevino, Linda K., and Michael E. Brown. "Managing to Be Ethical: Debunking Five Business Ethics Myths." *Academy of Management Executive* 18 (2004): 69–81.

EUROPEAN UNION

The European Union (EU) is an economic and political federation comprising 25 countries. The 15 original member nations are: Austria, Belgium, Denmark, Finland, France, Germany, Greece, Italy, Luxembourg, the Netherlands, Portugal, the Republic of Ireland, Spain, Sweden, and the United Kingdom. Ten new members as of May 2004 are: Cyprus, Czech Republic, Estonia, Hungary, Latvia, Lithuania, Malta, Poland, Slovakia, and Slovenia. The EU represents the latest and most successful in a series of efforts to unify Europe, including many attempts to achieve unity through force of arms such as those seen in the campaigns of Napoleon Bonaparte and World War II.

In the wake of the Second World War, which devastated the European infrastructure and economies, efforts began to forge political union through increasing economic interdependence. In 1951 the European Coal and Steel Community (ECSC) was formed to coordinate the production and trading of coal and steel within Europe. In 1957 the member states of the ECSC ratified two treaties creating the European Atomic Energy Community (Euratom) for the collaborative development of commercial nuclear power, and the European Economic Community (EEC), an international trade body whose role was to gradually eliminate national tariffs and other barriers to international trade involving member countries. Initially the EEC, or, as it was more frequently referred to at the time, the Common Market, called for a twelve to fifteen year period for the institution of a common external tariff among its members, but the timetable was accelerated and a common tariff was instituted in 1967.

Despite this initial success, participation in the EEC was limited to Belgium, France, Germany, Italy, Luxembourg, and the Netherlands. Immediately following the creation of the EEC a rival trade confederation known as the European Free Trade Association (EFTA) was created by Austria, Britain, Denmark, Finland, Norway, Portugal, Sweden, and Switzerland. Although its goals were less comprehensive than those of the EEC, the existence of the EFTA delayed European economic and political unity.

By 1961 the United Kingdom indicated its willingness to join the Common Market if allowed to retain certain tariff structures which favored trade between Britain and its Commonwealth. Negotiations between the EEC and the United Kingdom began, but insurmountable differences arose and Britain was denied access to the Common Market in 1963. Following this setback, however, the Common Market countries worked to strengthen the ties between themselves, culminating in the merger of the ECSC, EEC, and Euratom to form the European Community (EC) in 1967. In the interim the importance of the Commonwealth to the British economy waned considerably and by 1973 Britain, Denmark, and the Republic of Ireland had joined the EC. Greece followed suit in 1981, followed by Portugal and Spain in 1986 and Austria, Finland, and Sweden in 1995.

Even as it expanded the EC worked to strengthen the economic integration of its membership, establishing a European Monetary System (EMS), featuring the European Currency Unit (ECU, later known as the Euro), in 1979 and passing the Single European Act, which strengthened the EC's ability to regulate the economic, social, and foreign policies of its members, in 1987. The EC took its largest step to date toward true economic integration among its members with the 1992 ratification of the Treaty of European Union, after which the EC changed its name to the European Union (EU). The Treaty of European Union also created a central banking system for EU members, established the mechanisms and timetable for the adoption of the Euro as the common currency among members, and further strengthened the EU's ability to influence the public and foreign policies of its members.

Although the EU has accomplished a great deal in its first four years of existence, many hurdles must still be crossed before true European economic unity can be achieved. Many EU nations experienced great difficulty in meeting the provisions required by the EU for joining the EMS, although eleven countries met them by the 1 January 1999 deadline. Meeting these provisions forced several EU members, including Italy and Spain, to adopt politically unpopular domestic economic policies. Others, such as the United Kingdom, chose not to take politically unpopular action and thus failed to qualify for participation. Even though the Euro was introduced according to schedule, economic unity has far outstripped political cooperation among EU members to date and real and potential political disagreements within the EU remain a threat to its further development.

STRUCTURE

The EU maintains four administrative bodies dealing with specific areas of economic and political activity.

COUNCIL OF MINISTERS. The Council of Ministers comprises representatives, usually the foreign ministers, of member states. The presidency of the council rotates between the members on a semiannual basis. When issues of particular concern arise, members may send their heads of state to sit on the council. At such times the council is known as the European Council, and has final authority on all issues not specifically covered in the various treaties creating the EU and its predecessor organizations. The Council of Ministers also maintains the Committee of Permanent Representatives (COREPER), with permanent headquarters in Brussels, Belgium, to sit during the intervals between the council's meetings; and operates an extensive secretariat monitoring economic and political activities within the EU. The Council of Ministers and European Council decide matters involving relations between member states in areas including administration, agriculture and fisheries, internal market and industrial policy, research, energy, transportation, environmental protection, and economic and social affairs. Members of the Council of Ministers or European Council are expected to represent the particular interests of their home country before the EU as a whole.

EUROPEAN COMMISSION. The European Commission serves as the executive organization of the EU. Currently each country has one commissioner except for the five largest countries that have two. The Commission enlarges as more countries join. The European Commission seeks to serve the interests of Europe as a whole in matters including external relations, economic affairs, finance, industrial affairs, and agricultural policies. The European Commission maintains twenty-three directorates general to oversee specific areas of administration and commerce within the EU. It also retains a large staff to translate all EU documents into each of the EU's twenty official languages. Representatives sitting on the European Commission are expected to remain impartial and view the interests of the EU as a whole rather than the particular interests of their home countries.

EUROPEAN PARLIAMENT. The European Parliament comprises representatives of the EU member nations who are selected by direct election in their home countries. Although it serves as a forum for the discussion of issues of interest to the individual member states and the EU as a whole, the European Parliament has no power to create or implement legislation. It does, however, have some control over the EU budget, and can pose questions for the consideration of either the Council of Ministers or the European Commission.

COURT OF JUSTICE. The Court of Justice comprises thirteen judges and six advocates general appointed by EU member governments. Its function is to interpret EU laws and regulations, and its decisions are binding on the EU, its member governments, and firms and individuals in EU member states.

NOTABLE PROGRAMS

From its creation the EU has maintained the Economic and Social Committee (ESC), an appointed advisory body representing the interests of employers, labor, and consumers before the EU as a whole. Although many of the ESC's responsibilities are now duplicated by the European Parliament, the committee still serves as an advocacy forum for labor unions, industrial and commercial agricultural organizations, and other interest groups.

One ongoing area of contention among the members of the EU is agricultural policy. Each European nation has in place a series of incentives and subsidies designed to benefit its own farmers and ensure a domestically grown food supply. Often these policies are decidedly not beneficial to the EU as a whole, and lead to conflict between rival national organizations representing agricultural and fisheries industries. The degree of contention on agricultural and fisheries issues within the EU can be seen in the fact that nearly 70 percent of EU expenditures are made to address agricultural issues, even though agriculture employs less than 8 percent of the EU workforce. In an attempt to reduce conflict between national agricultural industries while still supporting European farmers, the EU adopted a Common Agricultural Policy (CAP) as part of the Treaty of European Union.

The CAP seeks to increase agricultural productivity, ensure livable wages for agricultural workers, stabilize agricultural markets, and assure availability of affordable produce throughout the EU. Although the

CAP has reduced conflicts within the EU, it has also led to the overproduction of many commodities, including butter, wine, and sugar, and has led to disagreements involving the EU and agricultural exporting nations including the United States and Australia.

The European Social Fund (ESF) and the European Regional Development Fund (ERDF) were established to facilitate the harmonization of social policies within EU member states. The ESF focuses on training and retraining workers to ensure their employability in a changing economic environment, while the ERDF concentrates on building economic infrastructure in the less-developed countries of the EU.

The European Investment Bank (EIB) receives capital contributions from the EU member states, and borrows from international capital markets to fund approved projects. EIB funding may be granted only to those projects of common interest to EU members that are designed to improve the overall international competitiveness of EU industries. EIB loans are also sometimes given to infrastructure development programs operating in less-developed areas of the EU.

LANGUAGES

The EU recognizes twenty official languages: Danish, Dutch, English, Finnish, French, German, Greek, Italian, Portuguese, Spanish, and Swedish. Other languages spoken in Europe, such as Irish Gaelic, are considered "treaty languages" or "working languages," while dialects such as Catalan are considered "minority languages." Treaty or working languages are those into which the EU translates only its basic legal texts; it is up to each member state to translate whatever EU documents it deems important into minority languages. All EU documents are available in the twenty official languages.

RECENT EVENTS

The EU added ten new members on May 1, 2004: Cyprus, the Czech Republic, Estonia, Hungary, Latvia, Lithuania, Romania, Poland, Slovakia and Slovenia. There are obstacles to inclusion of new members to the EU, however, in both the political and economic spheres. Any new members must conform to the national economic policy stipulations of the 1992 Treaty of European Union signed at Maastricht, and must also meet acceptable standards of internal political freedom. Turkey, for instance, was denied admission to the EU in 1997 due to its repression of its Kurdish minority, among other considerations. Similarly, Croatia was denied consideration for entrance due to its participation in ethnic cleansing activities during the Bosnian conflicts of the early to mid-1990s.

The major future event facing the EU since the adoption of the Treaty of European Union has been the adoption of the Euro as a single currency for members, which occurred in 2002.

THE EURO

The 1992 Maastricht Agreement established conditions that EU member nations would be expected to meet before they would be allowed to participate in the introduction of the single European currency. These conditions were designed to create a "convergence" among the various national economies of Europe to ease the transition to a single currency and ensure that no single country would benefit or be harmed unduly by its introduction. Such a convergence would also create greater uniformity among the various national economies of the EU, making administration of economic activity within the single-currency area more feasible. The conditions set for participation in the introduction of the Euro and inclusion in the single-currency area include:

- Maintaining international currency exchange rates within a specified range (called the Exchange Rate Mechanism or ERM) for at least two years prior to the introduction of the Euro.

- Maintaining long-term interest rates with 2 percent of the national inflation rate and within 1.5 percent of the three best-performing EU member states in terms of price stability.

- Maintaining public debt at no more than 3 percent of the gross domestic product.

- Maintaining total government debt at no more than 60 percent of gross domestic product.

These conditions have proven very difficult to meet for many EU members, and the United Kingdom was rejected for participation in the introduction of the Euro due to its failure to meet the provisions of the ERM in September 1992.

Despite these difficulties, implementation of the Euro has gone ahead on schedule through the three phases set forth at Maastricht. Phase one began in 1998 with an EU summit in Brussels, Belgium, that determined which of the fifteen member states had achieved sufficient convergence to participate in the introduction of the Euro. The selected participants were Austria, Belgium, Finland, France, Germany, Ireland, Italy, Luxembourg, the Netherlands, Portugal, and Spain (exceptions were Demark, Greece, Sweden and the UK). Phase two, which commenced on 1 January 1999, introduced the Euro as legal tender within the eleven selected countries, referred to as the single-currency area, although the new currency would only exist as a "currency of account," that is, it would exist only

Table A

Progress Toward Convergence
Number of Criteria Met (out of 5)

Country	1990	1991	1992	1993	1994	Approved for Participation in Euro Introduction
Austria	4	4	3	2	3	Y
Belgium	2	3	3	3	3	Y
Denmark	5	4	4	3	3	N
Finland	2	2	1	1	2	Y
France	5	5	4	4	4	Y
Germany	5	4	4	3	5	Y
Greece	0	0	0	0	0	N
Italy	0	0	0	0	0	Y
Luxembourg	5	5	5	4	5	Y
The Netherlands	3	4	3	3	3	Y
Portugal	0	0	0	0	0	Y
Republic of Ireland	4	4	4	3	3	Y
Spain	1	1	1	1	0	Y
Sweden	2	3	2	1	1	N
United Kingdom	3	3	2	2	3	N

on paper or for electronic transactions, as no Euro notes or coins were yet in circulation. Instead, the existing currencies of the participating countries functioned as fixed denominations of the Euro. Phase two also included the subordination of the eleven national banks in the single-currency area to the European Central Bank. Phase three, which began on 1 January 2002 set the Euro banknotes and coins into circulation and by July 2002 it became the legal tender of the EMU countries replacing the national currencies. At the time of introduction there were twelve countries in the Euro area are: Austria, Belgium, Finland, France, Germany, Ireland, Italy, Luxembourg, Netherlands, Portugal, Spain and Greece. Demark, Sweden and the UK are not using the Euro.

The initial introduction of the Euro as a currency of account began with a resounding success, as the new currency rose immediately to an exchange rate of 1.17 U.S. dollars to the Euro. Uncertainties about the further progress of European Union raised by conflicts in the Balkans in 1999 soon dampened investor interest in the Euro, however, and its value fell to 1.04 U.S. dollars per Euro by the summer of that year. In fact there was a steady decline of the value of the Euro compared to the dollar. On January 1999 the value of the Euro was set at U.S. $1.18, but by mid-1999 it had dropped to $1.08 and by the end of the year it dropped to $1.01 and by mid 2000 it had fallen to $0.95.

Future implications of the adoption of a single currency within the twelve selected EU countries are a matter of speculation, but a few general observations can be made. Surveys conducted by the international accounting firm KPMG in the late 1990s reveal that major European corporations feel that the introduction of the Euro will cause prices to fall and wages to rise within the single-currency area, since corporations will no longer have to allow for fluctuations in currency exchange rates when establishing their prices.

Other implications of the adoption of a single currency are also foreseeable. International trade within the single currency area will be greatly facilitated by the establishment of what amounts to a single market, complete with uniform pricing and regulation, in place of twelve national markets. The creation of a single market will also spur increased competition and the development of more niche products, and ease the acquisition of corporate financing, particularly in what would formerly have been international trade among members of the single currency area. Finally, in the long term, the establishment of the single currency area should simplify European corporate structures, since in time nearly all regulatory statutes within the single currency area should become uniform.

THE UNITED KINGDOM AND THE EURO

Another question regarding the Euro's future involves the exclusion of the United Kingdom from the single-currency area. Although the U.K. continues to attempt to meet the Maastricht provisions, its entry

Table B
Chronology

1952 Six countries - Belgium, France, the Federal Republic of Germany, Italy, Luxembourg and the Netherlands - create the European Coal and Steel Community (ECSC) by pooling their coal and steel resources in a common market controlled by an independent supranational authority.

1958 The Rome Treaties set up the European Economic Community (EEC) and the European Atomic Energy Community (Euratom), extending the common market for coal and steel to all economic sectors in the member countries.

1965 The Merger Treaty is signed in Brussels on April 8. It provides for a Single Commission and a Single Council of the then three European Communities.

1967 The Merger Treaty enters into force on July 1.

1973 The United Kingdom, Ireland, and Denmark join the European Community (EC).

1979 The European Parliament is elected, for the first time, by direct universal suffrage and the European Monetary System (EMS) becomes operative.

1981 Greece becomes the 10th member state.

1985 The program to complete the Single Market by 1992 is launched.

1986 Spain and Portugal become the 11th and 12th member states.

1987 The Single European Act (SEA) introduces majority voting on Single Market legislation and increases the power of the European Parliament.

1989 The Madrid European Council launches the plan for achievement of Economic and Monetary Union (EMU).

1990 East and West Germany are reunited after the fall of the Berlin Wall.

1991 Two parallel intergovernmental conferences produce the Treaty on European Union (Maastricht) which EU leaders approve at the Maastricht European Council.

1992 Treaty on European Union signed in Maastricht and sent to member states for ratification. First referendum in Denmark rejects the Treaty.

1993 The Single Market enters into force on January 1. In May, a second Danish referendum ratifies the Maastricht Treaty, which takes effect in November.

1994 The EU and the 7-member European Free Trade Association (EFTA) form the European Economic Area, a single market of 19 countries. The EU completes membership negotiations with EFTA members Austria, Finland, Norway and Sweden.

1995 Austria, Finland and Sweden join the EU on January 1. Norway fails to ratify its accession treaty. The EU prepares the 1996 Intergovernmental Conference on institutional reform.

1997 The Treaty of Amsterdam, resulting from the 1996 Intergovernmental Conference, is signed on October 2.

1999 The Euro is introduced on January 1 electronically in 12 participating member states, with complete introduction to occur in 2002. The Amsterdam Treaty enters into force on May 1.

2001 The Treaty of Nice results from the 2000 Intergovernmental Conference.

2002 The Euro is fully launched on January 1. The European Convention begins, as part of the debate on the future of Europe, to propose a new framework and structures for the European Union--geared to changes in the world situation, the needs of the citizens of Europe and the future development of the European Union. On October 9, the European Commission recommends that candidate countries Cyprus, the Czech Republic, Estonia, Hungary, Latvia, Lithuania, Malta, Poland, the Slovak Republic and Slovenia be the first to join the EU under the latest enlargement process, possibly in time for the elections to the European Parliament scheduled for June 2004.

2003 The Treaty of Nice enters into force on February 1.

2004 Ten countries (Cyprus, the Czech Republic, Estonia, Hungary, Latvia, Lithuania, Malta, Poland, the Slovak Republic and Slovenia) join the European Union on May 1. (Bulgarian and Romanian accession are anticipated for 2007. At the summit on December 16 and 17, the European Council decides whether Turkey is ready to begin accession negotiations. On June 18, the European Council accepted Croatia as a candidate country. On March 22, the Former Yugoslav Republic of Macedonia [FYROM] applied for EU membership.) A new European Parliament is elected on June 10 to 13. A new European Commission takes office on November 22.

Adpated from: http://www.eurunion.org/profile/brief.htm

into the single-currency area is unlikely in the near future. Having said this, British financial and insurance institutions, some of which are among the largest in the world, have already made provisions to trade in euros, as have many other financial institutions worldwide. Furthermore, the London and Frankfurt stock exchanges announced a planned alliance in 1998, to which the Spanish, Italian, and Dutch exchanges also

Table C
Member States

EU15 Member States:	Member States as of May 1, 2004: EU25:	Candidate Countries:
• Austria	• Cyprus	• Bulgaria
• Belgium	• Czech Republic	• Croatia
• Denmark	• Estonia	• Romania
• Finland	• Hungary	• Turkey
• France	• Latvia	**Application Pending:**
• Germany	• Lithuania	• Former Yugoslav Republic of Macedonia
• Greece	• Malta	
• Ireland	• Poland	
• Italy	• Slovakia	
• Luxembourg	• Slovenia	
• The Netherlands		
• Portugal		
• Spain		
• Sweden		
• United Kingdom		

expressed an interest in joining. As such, it appears clear that the United Kingdom will eventually join the single-currency area.

OBSTACLES FACING THE EU

Although the single-currency area, also referred to as "Euroland," represents a formidable force in international trade, the EU faces several grave challenges as it strives to form an ever closer linkage of its national constituents.

Among the most intractable problems faced by Euroland is the fact that while economic interconnection has gone forward at a rather rapid pace throughout the history of the EU, political integration has progressed relatively slowly. For example, despite the fact that the Treaty of European Union created a central bank to supercede the national banks of its members, responsibility for the creation of fiscal policies remains in the hands of each national government. As such, there is great potential for the central authority and national economic policy making agencies to adopt conflicting programs. Furthermore, national political institutions within the EU are likely to be more responsive to the desires of their national constituencies than to the well being of Euroland as a whole, especially in times of economic instability. It is difficult to see how voters in the nations of the EU will be able to put the good of Euroland ahead of their own particular interests, but it must also be said that the EU has surmounted similar obstacles in its history to date.

A second problem also arises out of the composition of Euroland. According to the optimal currency theory first posed by American Robert Mundell in 1961, in order for a single currency to succeed in a multinational area several conditions must be met. There should be no barriers to the movement of labor forces across national, cultural, or linguistic borders within the single-currency area; wage stability throughout the single currency area; and an area-wide system to stabilize imbalanced transfers of labor, goods, or capital within the single-currency area. These conditions do not exist in present-day Europe, where labor mobility is small and wages vary widely among EU member countries.

Furthermore, the present administrative structure of the EU is not powerful enough to redress imbalanced transfers, which are bound to occur periodically. Such imbalances would engage the sort of political response discussed previously, to the detriment of the EU as a whole.

Optimal currency theory also holds that for a single currency area to be viable it must not be prone to asymmetric shocks, that is, economic events that lead to imbalanced transfers. Ideally, a single-currency area should comprise similar economies that are likely to be on similar cycles, thus minimizing imbalances. Similarly, the need for a freely transferable labor force within the single-currency area is also necessary to minimize imbalances, since each national member of the area must be able to respond flexibly to changes in wage and price structures.

The EU has made remarkable progress during its first forty-seven years. Although the further strengthening of the EU, especially in political matters, faces major obstacles, the continued enhancement of economic ties binding members is likely to increase the political unity of EU members over time. That this is feasible is evidenced by the efforts of EU nations to conform to the stipulations of the Maastricht Agreement. Maintaining stable currency exchange rates, reducing public and overall government debt, and controlling long-term interest rates are all areas in which national governments and fiscal agencies had exercised complete autonomy in the past. Before the implementation of the Euro's second phase, many doubted that the EU member states could put aside their own internal interests to meet the Maastricht provisions; however, eleven of the fifteen managed to do so. Significantly, many had to experience economic slowdowns and increased unemployment in order to do so. Such resolve bodes well for continued strengthening of European unification in both political and economic areas. In fact, the history of the EU to date has been one of overcoming obstacles similar to those faced during the first two phases of the introduction of the Euro, and a unified Europe is and will remain a fact of international economic life for the foreseeable future.

SEE ALSO: Free Trade Agreements and Trading Blocs; International Business; International Management

Grant J. Eldridge

Revised by Judith M. Nixon

FURTHER READING:

Alesian, A., and R. Rerotti. "The European Union: A Politically Incorrect View." *Journal of Economic Perspectives* 18, no. 4 (2004): 27–48.

"Europe Ten Years from Now." *International Economy* 18, no. 3 (2004): 34–39.

"European Union in the U.S." Available from <http://www.eurunion.org>

McCormick, J. *Understanding the European Union: A Concise Introduction.* 2nd ed. New York: Palgrave, 2002.

Phinnemore, D., and L. McGowan. *A Dictionary of the European Union.* London and Chicago: Europa, 2002.

Pinder, J. *The European Union: A Very Short Introduction.* New York: Oxford University Press, 2001.

Reid, T.R. *The United States of Europe: The New Superpower and the End of American Supremacy.* New York: Penguin Press, 2004.

Vanthoor, W.F.V. *A Chronological History of the European Union, 1946–2001.* 2nd ed. Northampton, MA: Edward Elgar, 2002.

EXECUTIVE COMPENSATION

Executive employees, such as chief executive officers (CEOs), chief financial officers (CFOs), company presidents, and other upper level managers are often compensated differently than those at lower levels of an organization. Executive compensation consists of base salary, bonuses, long-term incentives, benefits, and perquisites. In addition to understanding the components of executive compensation, there are issues of pay equity and ethics associated with pay for these types of employees.

BASE SALARY OF EXECUTIVES

Base salary is the regular annual salary of the executive. While job evaluation is typically used to set employee pay in organizations, executive base salary levels are often more influenced by the opinion of the compensation committee (which consists of some or all of the members of the company's board of directors), which is often dependent on information from salary surveys of similar companies. Typically, pay of CEOs and other executives is set to be competitive with other executive salaries in the market and thus may be very high in comparison to the pay of employees in their own company. Recent data indicates that salaries for executives are on the rise. A survey of 100 major U.S. corporations conducted by Mercer Human Resource Consulting indicates that median total direct compensation for the chief executive officers in these corporations was $4,419,300 in 2004.

EXECUTIVE BONUSES

In the base salary of executives, most receive variable pay, a compensation that fluctuates according to some level of performance. The use of compensation beyond base salary is intended to motivate executives to reach certain organizational performance goals, for example, specific profit levels, and reward them for reaching these goals. One very popular type of variable pay is the executive bonus, which is a one-time payment tied to some short-term performance goal. The bonus may be based on any number of performance outcomes, ranging from judgments of executive performance by the board of directors, to levels of company profits or market share. Nearly all executives now receive some sort of bonus as a part of their compensation package. The Mercer study, described above, indicates that the CEOs of 100 major American corporations had a median bonus of $1.14 million in 2004, which equaled 141 percent of their annual salaries. In other words, bonuses accounted for more money than the CEO's annual salary in this sample.

LONG-TERM INCENTIVES

In recent years, incentives have become important for rewarding the performance of executives, and now make up about one half of total executive compensation. Incentives are rewards that are linked to specific long-term goals of the organization. The most common long-term incentive is the stock option, which either gives the executive free company stock, or allows him or her to purchase company stock at a reduced price for a period of time. These stocks become more valuable as the company improves financially, and therefore, ownership of stock is intended to encourage the executive to make the organization more profitable. Executives can then sell these stocks at a later time when they have appreciated in value, therefore providing compensation beyond the employee's tenure with the organization. Recent news stories detailing company failures in which unethical accounting practices and artificial inflation of stock prices caused lower-level employees to lose investments in company stock have raised concerns about the ethics of granting large numbers of stock options to executives.

EXECUTIVE BENEFITS AND PERQUISITES

Benefits for executive-level employees are also likely to be different than those offered to lower-level employees. Executives will often receive high levels of typical company fringe benefits, like health insurance, life insurance, and pension plans. Additionally, some executives may also have a contract for large severance packages, paying cash and stock options to a CEO fired from a company. Many executives negotiate generous severance packages at the time of hire, so that even if they are unable to deliver upon promises to the company, they can collect compensation upon exit.

Executive perquisites, or "perks," are special benefits and services for executives and other top employees of companies. Perks may be things such as a car service, an executive dining room, special parking, membership in clubs, and other such amenities. It is customary for many U.S. executives to receive perks as a part of their total compensation. Some of these perks, like car service or a company airplane, may serve to improve an executive's ability to do his or her job. Additionally, some perks bring with them a certain level of status, for example company-paid membership to an exclusive country club that is appealing to executive employees.

PAY EQUITY

Pay equity, or the fairness of pay, can be evaluated both internally and externally. These ideas are based on equity theory, a theory of motivation. Equity theory, briefly, indicates that a person examines what he brings to a job (inputs) and what he receives from a job (outcomes) and compares that to a reference person, evaluating the other person's inputs and outcomes. An employee might determine that she brings a certain level of education, experience, and effort to her job and that those inputs result in a certain level of salary and benefits. She would then compare this relationship to the education, experience, and effort, and the subsequent salary and benefits of another person. If these ratios are not equal, then the employee will feel unfairly treated. If this employee determines that her inputs are far greater than her counterpart's inputs, but their pay is the same, this employee will feel unfairly compensated.

External equity is the assessment of the fairness of pay in similar jobs in different organizations. Executives who compare their pay to executives in other similar firms are making an assessment of external equity. External equity can be determined through market pay surveys, in which companies share information about the pay and benefits in their jobs. Additionally, the pay levels of executives may be public knowledge, either in company publications to shareholders or in trade organizations. If an executive is compensated highly as compared to others in similar companies, he or she is likely to feel positively about this situation; however, executives who are compensated at a lower rate than comparable executives in other companies may attempt to have their salary raised or may look for another position.

Internal equity is an assessment of the fairness of pay in different jobs within the same organization. Executives and employees compare their inputs and their pay to one another's to determine if they are fairly treated. Internal equity is often referred to as pay structure, and there are two types of pay structures: egalitarian and hierarchical. In egalitarian pay structures, the range of pay from the lowest paid employee to the highest paid employee is not very big; there are not large differences in pay. Egalitarian structures tend to be preferred by the lower-paid employees, because they feel that executive pay is not too high. However, executives may become dissatisfied in organizations with egalitarian pay structures, because they feel that their pay may not be commensurate with their skills or job duties. Hierarchical pay structures, conversely, have a fairly wide range of pay between the lowest and highest paid employees. In hierarchical pay structures, upper-level employees are likely to be paid very high salaries, which they are likely to find satisfying. However, in hierarchical structures, employees in low-level jobs may feel unfairly treated because of their relatively lower pay rate.

The pay level of U.S. executives is very high as compared to the pay of executives in other countries, as compared to pay of U.S. executives in the past, and as compared to U.S. employees at lower levels of the organization. Currently, U.S. executives earn about 400 times the pay of the lowest paid workers in their own companies. In Europe and Asia, the pay of executives is about 10 times that of the lowest paid worker.

Additionally, many U.S. executives have generous stock option or severance packages that increase the value of their compensation. The high pay rates of American executives have garnered much media attention, particularly when organizations with high pay rates for CEOs and other top employees have lay-offs or plant closings. Many critics argue that executive pay is far too high, and that these pay rates invite ethical problems.

To examine the fairness of executive pay, several factors must be assessed. First, the executive pay package should be responsible to shareholders, which means that it is not so high that it detracts from company profits or that its incentives discourage unethical influence of stock prices. Second, pay packages must be competitive with those of other similar organizations so that executives can be recruited, rewarded, and retained successfully. If a pay package is not competitive, there may be motivation problems or turnover. Third, executive pay should fit with the company's strategy so that it encourages overall company success. This is particularly relevant in regards to short-term bonuses and long-term incentives which can be used to steer the performance of the executive and the organization. Finally, compensation for executives must be in compliance with regulations. There are a number of laws regarding retirement plans, stock options, and other compensation components which must be followed when designing executive pay plans.

ETHICAL CONCERNS WITH EXECUTIVE COMPENSATION

The base salary, bonuses, incentives, and benefits for executives have raised serious questions about the ethical implications of such pay. One concern about the high pay level for American executives is that they may encourage executives to make business decisions that benefit themselves rather than the organization in order to meet performance goals necessary to receive incentive pay. This is particularly likely if incentives are short-term in nature. For example, an executive may drive up short-term profits that cannot be sustained, only to collect a large bonus and leave the company before long-term financial problems are revealed.

A second concern with the ethics of high executive pay is the use of stock options as an incentive. Recent evidence of illegal practices in some high-profile American companies has prompted the enactment of the Sarbanes-Oxley Act of 2002. This act prevents executives of companies from keeping profits or bonuses acquired from selling company stock if they have misled the public about the financial health of the company to increase stock price.

Finally, some question the ethics of the high level of executive pay when lower-level employee pay has not risen at the same rate. There is a continually widening gap in compensation in different levels of organizations; for instance, the Mercer study described previously determined that CEOs enjoyed bonuses of 141 percent of salary in 2004, while other studies indicate that typical clerical and technical staff earn approximately 5 percent of salary as an annual bonus. Although some argue that executive level positions deserve high rates of pay due to the nature of the job and the high level of responsibility involved, others argue that the gap in executive versus typically employee pay has widened so dramatically that employees are under-compensated and may even be tempted to engage in unethical behavior, such as stealing from the company.

Executive compensation consists of base salary, bonuses, long-term incentives, benefits, and "perks." Total executive compensation has increased dramatically in recent years, which has led to concerns about pay equity and ethics. Because of the strong focus on external equity when determining executive compensation, internal equity is likely to be a concern. Additionally, as the gap between pay at lower and higher levels of the organization increasingly widens, many CEOs are perceived to be overcompensated. There are other ethical issues to be considered, such as the motivation of executives based on their bonuses, incentives, and stock option grants.

SEE ALSO: Human Resource Management

Marcia J. Simmering

FURTHER READING:

Chingos, Peter T., ed. *Responsible Executive Compensation for a New Era of Accountability.* Hoboken, N.J.: John Wiley & Sons, Inc., 2004.

"Executive Pay Trends: Looking Forward and Back." *Journal of Deferred Compensation* 10, no. 1 (2004): 24–35.

Lublin, Joann S. "CEO Bonuses Rose 46.4% at 100 Big Firms in 2004; Median Was $1.14 Million; Some Chiefs Under Fire Also Drew Sizable Extras." *Wall Street Journal,* 25 February 2005, A1.

Martocchio, Joseph J. *Strategic Compensation: A Human Resource Management Approach* 3rd ed. Upper Saddle River, NJ: Pearson Prentice Hall, 2004.

Milkovich, George T., and Jerry M. Newman. *Compensation.* 8th ed. New York: McGraw-Hill Irwin, 2005.

EXECUTIVE DEVELOPMENT

SEE: Management and Executive Development

EXPATRIATES

An expatriate is an employee sent by his or her employer to work in a foreign country. The firm is normally referred to as the parent company, while the country of employment is known as the host country. If General Motors sent one of its U.S. executives to oversee a new development in Brazil, the executive would be an expatriate, General Motors would be the parent company, and Brazil would be the host country. Equally, if an employee from Brazil was sent to the U.S. or an employee from Canada were sent to the People's Republic of China, they would be expatriates.

Many corporations are sending expatriates to their overseas operations. In fact, expatriates have and the need for internationally competent managers is expected to rise as more and more firms face global competition. Organizations need to understand the dynamic relationships between staffing and outcomes, and how these relationships change over time.

Expatriates provide a number of benefits for companies, including greater parent control and particular expertise. International experience is also seen as providing opportunities for personal and professional development and career advancement. Expatriates are very expensive, however, and this can discourage extensive use of expatriates. Many companies have also experienced relatively high failure rates, with failure often being attributed to the family's inability to adapt.

Surprisingly, give the high costs, and likelihood of failure, companies often make these expensive commitments with little or no preparation for the need for cross-cultural transition. Expatriate success and job performance is closely related to intercultural adjustment and the same is true of families.

Given this, it is critical that companies use a rigorous selection process to identify which employees would likely succeed as expatriates. The selection process should also include consideration of the family.

Several characteristics determine an expatriate's expected level of success: job skills, motivational state, language skills, relationship skills, and family situation. Technical competency is most often used as the selection criteria for expatriates, but that is rarely the best selection technique. The technical skills of an expatriate are of course important, but other skills can be as important. For example, an expatriate is likely to make more progress at the overseas location if he or she has effective managerial skills and administrative competencies. Strong relationships with the host country and headquarters' operations also make the expatriate's assignment more productive. Conflict resolution skills are also important to the expatriate. Expatriates must also have a strong belief in the assignment if it is to be a success, and they must believe that the assignment will be advantageous to their careers.

Motivation is likely to be higher if the person has an interest in the specific host country culture as well as in an overseas experience. To be successful the expatriate must be willing to acquire new behavior patterns and attitudes. The most successful expatriates enjoy the challenge of forging their way through new situations and are comfortable networking and initiating new social contacts. These are also critical for the families of expatriates. Training for expatriates and their families is therefore as important as proper selection.

To reduce the likelihood of premature termination of the assignment, companies should choose expatriates who have well-developed relationship skills. Some characteristics are crucial for a successful expatriate: tolerance for ambiguity, behavioral flexibility, strong interpersonal skills, and a nonjudgmental disposition. In addition, an effective expatriate would have high cultural empathy. Ethnocentrism is the belief that one's culture is superior. Ethnocentric expatriates are likely to have problems adjusting to a new culture, and the local people are likely to perceive them negatively. Communication is also key.

The expatriate needs to have some working knowledge of the host language. but it may be more important that the expatriate have outstanding nonverbal communication skills and an understanding that nonverbal communication varies between cultures. He or she should become familiar with common nonverbal protocol in the new culture.

Most expatriates take their families with them to the foreign country, and their family situation is one of the most critical factors in the successful completion of an overseas assignment. Family transition must be taken very seriously. An expatriate must be comfortable on a personal level. Major stress can be caused for the entire family by something as seemingly trivial as the transportation of a family pet. An expatriate's spouse must have a very strong willingness to live abroad. The spouse must be supportive as well as adaptive. Many firms have had expatriates' assignments terminated early because the spouse was unwilling or unable to make the necessary adjustments to the host country.

Predeparture training for the expatriate greatly increases the likelihood of success. The extent of training can depend on a variety of variables: previous overseas experience (if applicable), time until departure, and novelty of the new country. Cross-cultural training must be meaningful for the expatriate and family. Training should, at the minimum, inform the

Exhibit 1
Types of Allowances Given to Expatriates

Foreign Service Premiums

This is a sum of money that is simply a reward for being willing to move one's family to a new country. The sum is generally a percentage of one's base salary—usually between 10 to 25 percent.

Hardship Allowance

The hardship allowance is actually another foreign service premium added to the original one. It is based on not just having to go overseas, but where you go overseas. Hardship allowances are greatest when the expatriate is sent to places having poor living conditions, a vastly different culture, less access to good health care, etc.

Cost of Living Allowances

Cost of living allowances (COLAs) enable expatriates to maintain their standard of living. COLAs are given when the cost of living in the host country is greater than that in the United States.

Housing Allowances

The cost of housing in various parts of the world is much higher than it is in the United States. Large apartments in Tokyo or Hong Kong, for instance, can go for upwards of $10,000 a month. Housing allowances compensate expatriates for these higher costs.

Utility Allowances

Some companies give expatriates a fixed sum of money above their base salary to pay their utilities bills; other companies try to ascertain the difference in utility bills between the home and the host countries, and give an allowance based on that difference.

Furnishing Allowances

Some companies offer to ship all of the expatriate's furnishings overseas. A second approach is to pay for the lease or purchase of furnishings overseas by expatriates. A third approach is to just give the expatriate a fixed sum of money (usually between $8,000 to $10,000) to buy furnishings.

Education Allowances

Most expatriates send their children to private school overseas. Companies often pay the full cost of tuition, books, and supplies.

Home Leave Allowances

Companies usually provide expatriates and their families with round-trip, business-class airfare to visit the home country at least once a year.

Relocation Allowances

The allowance makes up for any mistakes made in any of the other allowances for unforeseen complications. Expatriates receive about one month's salary.

Medical Allowances

Companies usually pay for all medical expenses. In hardship countries where medical facilities are inadequate, this includes emergency trips to other countries to receive medical care.

Car and Driver Allowances

Most companies offer expatriate managers a car allowance. This enables the expatriate to lease, buy, or rent a car in the host country. In some cases, the expatriate is given funds to hire a chauffeur.

Club Membership Allowances

In some countries the only way an expatriate can gain access to recreational facilities (e.g., tennis courts, swimming pools, country clubs) is by joining clubs. Also, in many cultures these facilities are important places in which to develop contacts and conduct business. This type of allowance is usually made on a case-by-case basis.

Taxes

Many companies reimburse expatriates for taxes they pay in excess of what they would have paid had they remained in the United States.

---

expatriate about the new country, and at the best, it would immerse the expatriate into the new culture.

Low-interaction training is focused on information distribution. It generally takes the form of lectures, videos, and readings. The material should include general area studies and a company operational overview. A low-intensity training would be appropriate for someone who has been on an expatriate assignment before or someone familiar with the host country. Unfortunately, this is often the only training received by most expatriates whether they have previous experience or not. This lack of training is usually due to last-minute selection or no training budget.

Medium- to high-intensity training should have duration of one to two months. This training provides affective learning and cultural immersion. Medium-intensity training takes the intercultural experience workshop approach, offering cultural simulations, role plays, and case studies. Skill development can be culture-general or culture-specific. High-intensity training, most necessary for inexperienced expatriates entering a very different culture, provides sensitivity training and includes communication workshops and field exercises that focus on self awareness, listening skills, open-mindedness, and communication skills.

There are currently relatively few women expatriates (Stroh, Varma, Valy-Durbin, 2000), but their numbers are likely to increase in the future. Women expatriates and their male spouses present a different challenge for companies, and their special needs should be taken into account (Punnett, 2004). Similarly, there are situations where factors such as race, religion, disabilities, or sexual orientation may make it difficult for an individual to succeed in a particular location.

Given that expatriates are very expensive, it is in a firm's interest to make sure the assignment is successful. Proper expatriate selection and training, as well as attention to the needs of the family can be a productive investment.

SEE ALSO: Human Resource Management; International Business; International Cultural Differences; International Management; Japanese Management; Organizational Culture

Dena Waggoner
Revised by Betty Jane Punnett

FURTHER READING:

Ali, A., K. Van der Zee, and G. Sanders. "Determinants of Intercultural Adjustment Among Expatriate Spouses." *International Journal of Intercultural Relations* 27, no. 5 (2003): 563–580.

Gong, Y. "Towards a Dynamic Process Model of Staffing Composition and Subsidiary Outcomes in Multinational Enterprises." *Journal of Management* 29, no. 2 (2003): 259–280.

Punnett, B.J. *International Perspectives of Organizational Behavior and Human Resource Management.* Armonk, NY: M.E. Sharpe, 2004.

Schuler, R.S., P.S. Budhwar, and G.W. Florkowski. "International Human Resource Management." In *Handbook for International Management Research* ed. B.J. Punnett and O. Shenkar. Ann Arbor, MI: University of Michigan Press, 2004.

Stahl, G.K., E.L. Miller and R.L. Tung. "Toward the Boundaryless Career: A Closer Look at the Expatriate Career Concept and the Perceived Implications of an International Assignment." *Journal of World Business* 37, no. 3 (2002): 216–227.

Stroh, L.K., A. Varma, and S.J. Valy-Durbin. "Why are Women Left at Home: Are They Unwilling to Go on International Assignments?" *Journal of World Business* 35, no. 3 (2000): 241–255.

Tucker, M.F., R. Bonial and K. Lahti. "The Definition, Measurement and Prediction of Intercultural Adjustment and Job Performance Among Corporate Expatriates." *International Journal of Intercultural Relations* 28, no. 3-4 (2004): 221–251.

EXPERIENCE AND LEARNING CURVES

Experience and learning curve models are developed from the basic premise that individuals and organizations acquire knowledge by doing work. By gaining experience through repetition, organizations and individuals develop relatively permanent changes in behavior or learning. As additional transactions occur in a service, or more products are produced by a manufacturer, the per-unit cost often decreases at a decreasing rate. This phenomenon follows an exponential curve. The organization thus gains competitive advantage by converting this cost reduction into productivity gains. This learning competitive advantage is known as the experience curve, the learning curve, or the progress curve.

It is common for the terms *experience curve* and *learning curve* to be used interchangeably. They do, however, have different meanings. According to definitions by Hall and Starr, the experience curve is an analytical tool designed to quantify the rate at which experience of accumulated output, to date, affects total lifetime costs. Melnyk defined the learning curve as an analytical tool designed to quantify the rate at which cumulative experience of labor hours or cost allows an organization to reduce the amount of resources it must expend to accomplish a task. Experience curve is broader than learning curve with respect to the costs covered, the range of output during which the reductions in costs take place, and the causes of reduction.

The idea of "learning by doing" is intuitive. We often experience this effect when we take up a new sport or start to keyboard. Our skill levels increase rapidly with practice, up to a point, and then progress at a slower rate. Eventually, our golf score levels off around some value and our keystrokes per minute (without errors) levels off as well.

Organizational learning is complex in that we learn at many levels simultaneously. In organizations, procedures, norms, rules, and forms store knowledge. March states that managers of competitive organizations often find themselves in situations where relative position with regard to a competitor matters. This possible competitive advantage through enhanced learning is the essence of the study of experience and learning curves.

The analytical use of the concept for business purposes first surfaced in 1936 during airplane construction, when Wright observed that as the quantity of manufactured units doubled, the number of direct labor hours needed to produce each individual unit decreased at a uniform rate. The variation of labor cost with production quantity is illustrated by the following formula:

$$F = \log F/\log N$$

where F equals a factor of cost variation proportional to the quantity N. The reciprocal of F represents a direct percent variation of cost versus quantity.

This insight shows that experience-based learning is closely correlated with cumulative output, extending beyond changes in design and tooling. Wright found empirical evidence that as unit volume increases there are predictable corresponding reductions in cost. These data become central concepts for strategic and operational planning. There has been much discussion on the role of learning in business organizations. A seminal work in learning theory is the 1963 *A Behavioral Theory of the Firm* by Cyert and March. These authors viewed firms as adaptively-rational systems. This means that the firm learns from its experience. In its basic form, an adaptive system selects preferred states for use in the future. With experience, management uses decision variables that lead to goals and shuns those that do not lead to goals.

The learning curve model was expanded by Adler and Clark into a learning process model. A key conceptual difference from the prior model is that "a significant part of the effect of experience on productivity (captured in the learning curve model) might be due to the influence of identifiable managerial actions". The authors present two orders of learning. First-order learning refers to the classic learning curve model where productivity is an exponential function of experience. Second-order learning denotes that which is driven by changes in technology or human capital that lead to goal attainment.

FUNDAMENTALS OF EXPERIENCE AND LEARNING CURVES

Following a strategy of increasing market share, the experience curve focuses on cost leadership. Management attempts to increase market share while simultaneously reducing costs. This is a detriment to market entry as the firm can lower its price, which may further increase its market share and place added pressure on potential competitors, as found in a study by Lieberman. Learning through experience becomes an important component of the increased market share strategy.

Quality learning is enhanced through the shared experience at the worker and organizational levels. Quality increases as the firm moves further along the experience curve, thus increasing productivity and efficiency. As the individual employees and organization become more efficient, there should be a corresponding increase in productivity. More output for less input effectively increases capacity; taken together with the increased efficiency and productivity, this should lead to a reduction in unit cost. The business is investing in a cost-leadership posture based on the assumption that price is a basis for competition. If the firm is able to produce quality units and reduce market price, there is the opportunity for increased market share (the business strategy). Increased market share via reduced price may lead to the global goal of improving profits.

Use of a cost leadership strategy based on the experience curve implies several assumptions, according to Amit:

1. Price is a basis for competition.

2. If per unit cost is reduced, price may be reduced, which may lead to increased market share.

3. As cumulative output increases, the firm's average cost is reduced. Therefore, for any production rate, there is a reduction in the per-unit cost.

4. If market share is increased, profits will increase.

5. Another critical assumption of the experience curve, noted by Lieberman, is that learning can be kept within the organization. Where industry-wide dissemination of process technology is rapid, the benefits of organizational learning through the experience curve may be short-lived. The cost benefits, therefore, may not lead to increased market share even though industry costs are declining because all participants are learning at approximately the same rate.

LEARNING CURVE FORMULATION

The formula for the learning curve model is commonly shown either as a margin-cost model or as a direct-labor-hour model. The direct-labor-hours formula is more useful, as hourly compensation typically changes over time and there may be inflation considerations as well. However, both derivations will be presented here for clarity. Also, direct-labor hours may be easily converted into costs if necessary, according to Yelle. By convention, we refer to experience curves by the complement of the improvement rate. For example, a 90 percent learning curve indicates a 10 percent decrease in per-unit (or mean) time or cost, with each doubling of productive output. Experience and learning curves normally apply only to cost of direct labor hours.

MARGINAL COST MODEL. The cumulative-average learning curve formulation is:

$$Y_{cx} = ax^{-b}$$

where Y_{cx} = average cost of the first x units,

a = the first unit cost,

x = the cumulative unit number output,

and

b = the learning elasticity, which defines the slope of the learning curve.

This learning curve model indicates that as the quantity of units produced doubles, the average cost per unit decreases at a uniform rate.

DIRECT LABOR HOURS MODEL. The direct labor hour model of the learning curve is:

$$Y = KX^n$$

where Y = the number of direct labor hours required to produce the Xth unit,

K = the number of direct labor hours required to produce the first unit,

X = the cumulative unit number,

$n = \log \phi / \log 2$,

ϕ = the learning rate, and

$1 - \phi$ = the progress ratio.

These empirical models have been shown to fit many production situations very well. One criticism is that many other undocumented variables may be behind the benefits attributed to the experience curve. There are intermingling variables that also may account for cost reductions. Some of these variables might be economies of scale, product design decisions, tooling and equipment selections, methods analysis and layout, improved organizational and individual skills training, more effective production scheduling and control procedures, and improved motivation of employees. All of these variables play a role in decreasing cost and increasing capacity.

APPLICATIONS AND USES

There are three general areas for the application and use of experience curves; strategic, internal, and external to the organization. Strategic uses include determining volume-cost changes, estimating new product start-up costs, and pricing of new products. Internal applications include developing labor standards, scheduling, budgeting, and make-or-buy decisions. External uses are supplier scheduling, cash flow budgeting, and estimating purchase costs. The usefulness of experience and learning curves depends on a number of factors; the frequency of product innovation, the amount of direct labor versus machine-paced output, and the amount of advanced planning of methods and tooling. All lead to a predictable rate of reduction in throughput time.

Knowledge on the practical application of experience curves and learning curves has increased greatly since 1936. Interest was renewed in the early 1990s with the publication of *The Fifth Discipline* by Peter Senge. Senge melded theories on mental models, the systems approach, and learning curves in a way that made sense for executives.

These curves offer potential competitive advantage to managers who can capitalize on the cost reductions they offer. The experience and learning curves rely, however, on keeping the knowledge gained *within* their organization. Given rapid communication, high manager and engineer turnover, and skills in reverse engineering, this is harder to accomplish with each passing year. However, Hatch and Dyer found that in the case of the semiconductor manufacturing industry, in particular, skills acquired in one firm are not necessarily effectively transferable to another firm since knowledge is specific to the original work environment. Therefore, even if the employee is hired away, there is limited threat to the original firm.

Hatch and Dyer conclude that to truly maintain an advantage over the competition, firms must employ effective human resource selection, training, and deployment processes that facilitate learning by doing. Those firms that meet this challenge may enjoy the only truly sustainable advantage—the ability to learn (and improve) faster than competitors. As manufacturing and service product lives become shorter, management must be keenly on top of experience and learning curves to continue to enjoy the advantages.

SEE ALSO: Knowledge Management; Organizational Learning

James P. Gilbert
Revised by Monica C. Turner

FURTHER READING:

Abernathy, William J., and Kenneth Wayne. "The Limits of the Learning Curve." *Harvard Business Review* 52, no. 5 (1974): 109–119.

Adler, Paul S., and Kim B. Clark. "Behind the Learning Curve: A Sketch of the Learning Process." *Management Science* 37, no. 3 (1991): 267–281.

Amit, Raphael. "Cost Leadership Strategy and Experience Curves." *Strategic Management Journal* 7, no. 3 (1986): 281–292.

Cyert, Richard M., and James G. March. *A Behavioral Theory of the Firm.* Englewood Cliffs, NJ: Prentice-Hall, Inc., 1963.

Demeester, Lieven L., and Me Fontainebleu Qi. "Managing Learning Resources for Consecutive Product Generations." *International Journal of Production Economics* 95, no. 2 (2005): 265–283.

Hall, G., and S. Howell. "The Experience Curve from the Economist's Perspective." *Strategic Management Journal* 6, no. 3 (1985): 197–212.

Hatch, Nile W., and Jeffrey H. Dyer. "Human Capital and Learning as a Source of Sustainable Competitive Advantage." *Strategic Management Journal* 25, no. 12 (2004): 1155–1178.

Heizer, Jay, and Barry Render. *Operations Management.* 5th ed. Upper Saddle River, NJ: Prentice Hall, 1999.

Jaber, M. Y., and A. L. Guiffrida. "Learning Curves for Processes Generating Defects Requiring Reworks." *European Journal of Operational Research* 159, no. 3 (2004): 663–672.

Junginger, M., A. Faaij, and W. C. Turkenburg. "Global Experience Curves for Wind Farms." *Energy Policy* 33, no. 2 (2005): 133–150.

Lieberman, Marvin B. "The Learning Curve, Technology Barriers to Entry, and Competitive Survival in the Chemical Processing Industries." *Strategic Management Journal* 10, no. 5 (1989): 431–447.

Linton, Jonathan D., and Steven T. Walsh. "Integrating Innovation and Learning Curve Theory: An Enabler for Moving Nanotechnologies and Other Emerging Process Technologies into Production." *Research and Development Management* 34, no. 5 (2004): 517–526.

March, James G. "Exploration and Exploitation in Organizational Learning." *Organizational Science* 2, no. 1 (1991): 71–87.

Melnyk, Steven A., and David R. Denzler. *Operations Management: A Value-Driven Approach.* Chicago: Richard D. Irwin, 1996.

Senge, Peter M. *The Fifth Discipline: The Art and Practice of the Learning Organization.* New York: Doubleday Currency, 1990.

Smunt, Timothy L., and Charles A. Watts. "Improving Operations Planning with Learning Curves: Overcoming the Pitfalls of 'Messy' Shop Floor Data." *Journal of Operations Management* 21, no. 1 (2003): 93–107.

Starr, Martin K. *Operations Management: A Systems Approach.* Danvers, MA: Boyd & Fraser, 1996.

Teplitz, Charles J. *The Learning Curve Deskbook: A Reference Guide to Theory, Calculations, and Applications.* NY: Quorum Books, 1991.

Wright, T. P. "Factors Affecting the Cost of Airplanes." *Journal of the Aeronautical Sciences* 3, no. 4 (1936): 122–128.

Yelle, Louis E. "The Learning Curve: Historical Review and Comprehensive Survey." *Decision Sciences* 10, no. 2 (1979): 302–328.

EXPERT SYSTEMS

Expert systems are artificial intelligence (AI) tools that capture the expertise of knowledge workers and provide advice to (usually) non-experts in a given domain. Thus, expert systems constitute a subset of the class of AI systems primarily concerned with transferring knowledge from experts to novices.

KNOWLEDGE REPRESENTATION SYSTEMS

Knowledge representation systems, also called expert systems, are computerized models that capture the knowledge of one or more human experts and store it in the framework that is most appropriately suited to the reasoning processes that the experts use in their problem-solving behavior. Such systems are created by a specialized systems analyst called a knowledge engineer, whose task is to interview the expert and/or observe his problem-solving behavior, then determine the most appropriate form(s) of knowledge representation to model the expert's problem-solving techniques. This process, called knowledge acquisition, is perhaps the most difficult and time-consuming aspect of expert systems development. It requires both technical and people skills on the part of the knowledge engineer, who must establish rapport with the domain expert, maintain a productive relationship during the interviewing process, and recognize the required mapping from the expert's explanations to the appropriate knowledge representation. The knowledge engineer then encodes the expert's knowledge into a knowledge base, which is a repository of the expert's knowledge in a particular representational structure. Some of the most common knowledge representations are described below.

In addition to the knowledge base, an expert system includes an automated reasoning mechanism called an inference engine that performs calculations and/or logical processes to produce the results of a particular problem-solving session. The explanation facility of an expert system provides the user with an explanation of the reasoning process that was used to achieve the conclusion or recommendation. Each knowledge representation has a corresponding inference technique. Three very common knowledge representations are rule-based systems, frame-based systems, and case-based systems.

UNCERTAINTY IN ARTIFICIAL INTELLIGENCE

The types of problems that AI systems try to solve are often fraught with uncertainties. Sometimes experts are uncertain about the conclusions they may draw based on the facts that are presented to them. In addition, the facts themselves may not be clear-cut; they may be in error, incomplete, or ambiguous. Thus, AI systems must have the ability to reason and draw some inference even in the face of such uncertainties. AI systems do this in many ways. Two common approaches are described below.

RULES WITH CONFIDENCE FACTORS. This approach to uncertainty combines probability with logic. It enhances rule-based systems with probability-like numbers that represent the confidence in either a fact

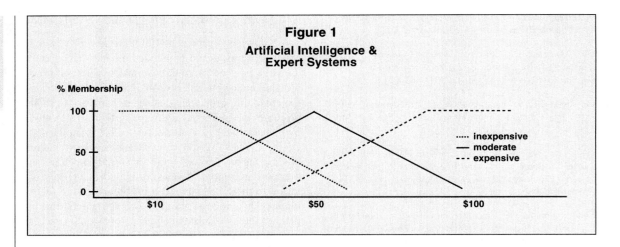

Figure 1
Artificial Intelligence & Expert Systems

or an inferred conclusion. For example, consider this rule:

> If the engine will not start but it will turn over, then the injection system is bad.

In some cases the facts are uncertain. Suppose the user is uncertain whether the engine starts or whether it turns over. If the user is 70 percent sure that the engine does not start and 80 percent sure that the engine turns over, then the conclusion of a bad injection system will be uncertain as well. A typical inference with this uncertainty is to multiply the two probabilities. In this case, 70 percent times 80 percent results in 56 percent confidence that the injection system is bad.

Furthermore, the rule itself may be uncertain. An expert may be only 60 percent sure that an unstartable engine that turns over implies a bad injection system. In this case, even if the user were 100 percent sure that the engine does not start but does turn over, the confidence in the conclusion of a bad injection system would be only 60 percent.

The inference process propagates the uncertainties through to the conclusions, so that the expert system tells the user not only what its recommendation is, but also the level of confidence in the recommendation.

An example of an expert system using rules can be found in the Department of Veterans Affairs within their OneVA initiative, which seeks to improve service by implementing improved information technology. A component of this initiative is the creation of an "expert system for the determination of potential benefits." This expert system utilizes a rule-based approach that analyzes customer data to determine proper eligibility levels.

FUZZY LOGIC SYSTEMS. Consider the question "Is this item expensive?" Here, "expensive" implies that the item costs a good deal of money. But how does one determine if an item is expensive? What is expensive to one person may be quite inexpensive to another.

This is a case of linguistic ambiguity, where one word may have different meanings depending on context.

Fuzzy logic deals with linguistic ambiguity by mapping precise values (e.g., price, temperature, age in years) onto imprecise concepts (e.g., expensive, cold, young) via a membership function. The imprecise concept is called a fuzzy set, and the membership function measures the degree to which a precise value belongs in the fuzzy set.

Consider Figure 1, which shows three fuzzy sets related to the price of a product: inexpensive, moderate, and expensive. The membership functions are the solid and dashed lines in the graph. The X-axis shows the crisp value (actual price) and the Y-axis shows the degree of membership of a particular crisp value in each of the fuzzy sets. The price of $10 has 100 percent membership in the inexpensive set and 0 percent membership in each of the others. By contrast, the $100 price has 100 percent membership in the expensive set and 0 percent in the others. The $50 price has some degree of membership in all of the sets; it has 100 percent membership in the moderate set, but also some small degree of membership in both the others.

Consider this rule:

> If the price is expensive then do not buy the product.

Such a rule will not fire at all if the price is $10. It will fire with 100 percent strength if the price is $100. It will fire with a much lower strength if the price is $50. This is the main idea behind fuzzy logic systems.

Fuzzy logic systems are used in many applications. They are commonly embedded in control systems, such as regulating automatic braking systems in cars and autofocusing in cameras.

IMPLEMENTATION

Expert systems are applied in banking and finance, forecasting, security, manufacturing, marketing, and many other business areas and industries.

Specifically, areas such as loan applications, fraud detection, inventory management, enterprise resource planning, and supply chain management find useful applications of expert systems. Significant growth is expected for the foreseeable future. According to Metaxiotis and Psarras in *Industrial Management & Data Systems,* France, Germany, Italy, and the United Kingdom are countries in which a high rate of growth is expected in the development of expert systems.

SEE ALSO: Artificial Intelligence

Michel Mitri
Revised by Hal P. Kirkwood, Jr.

FURTHER READING:

Bertino, E., G.P. Zarri, and B. Catania. *Intelligent Database Systems.* Boston: Addison-Wesley, 2001.

Jackson, P. *Introduction to Expert Systems.* Boston: Addison-Wesley, 1998.

Leondis, C.T. *Expert Systems: The Technology of Knowledge Management for the 21 Century.* vols. 1–6. Amsterdam: Elsevier Academic Press, 2001.

Metaxiotis, K., and J. Psarras. "Expert Systems in Business: Applications and Future Directions for the Operations Researcher." *Industrial Management & Data Systems* 103, no. 5/6 (2003): 361–68.

EXPORTING AND IMPORTING

Exporting is the act of producing goods or services in one country and selling or trading them to another country. The term *export* originates from the Latin words *ex* and *portare,* meaning to carry out. The counterpart to exporting is importing which is the acquisition and sale of goods from acquired from another country and selling them within the country. Although it is common to speak of a nation's exports or imports in the aggregate, the company that produces the good or service, as opposed to a national government, usually conducts exporting in terms of logistics and sales transactions. However, export and import levels may be highly influenced by government policies, such as offering subsidies that either restrict or encourage the sale of particular goods and services abroad. Certain exports, such as military technology, may be banned entirely, at least for certain recipients, in cases of trade embargoes or other government regulations (e.g., U.S. companies generally can't export to or import from Cuba). Exporting is just one method that companies use to establish their presence in economies outside their home country. Importing is the method used to acquire products not readily available from within the country or to acquire products at a less expensive cost than if it were produced in that country.

Countries may be in a favorable position to export for several reasons. A country may export goods if it is the world's sole supplier of a certain good, such as when it has access to natural resources others lack. Some countries are also able to manufacture products at a relatively lower cost than other countries, for example, when labor costs less. Other factors include the ability to produce superior quality goods or the ability to produce the goods in a season of the year when other countries need them (Branch, 1990).

BALANCE OF TRADE

A country's international trade consists of both importing and exporting goods and services. The difference between the amount exported and the amount imported equals the balance of trade. A trade surplus consists of exporting more than importing while a trade deficit consists of importing more than exporting.

BRIEF HISTORY OF U.S. EXPORTS AND IMPORTS

The United States has been heavily dependent upon exporting throughout its history. It has played an important role in global trade as well. Even before its Declaration of Independence, the United States relied heavily on the exportation of cotton, tobacco, and other agricultural products to Europe for much of its commerce. After the Revolutionary War, the United States endured English duties and restrictions in Europe and the West Indies. This caused the United States to form new trade ties with overseas buyers in Africa, India, and East Asia, helping to form a legacy of U.S. trading overseas.

Although the United States thrived in exporting during its first 100 years, it was not until the Industrial Revolution gained momentum in the late 19th century that exporting began to significantly increase. This occurred mainly due to the technological advancements in communications, manufacturing, transportation, and food preservation techniques. It was during this time that the United States made the transition from being a supplier of agricultural products to a manufacturer of industrial goods, such as ships, railroads, clothes and cars.

However, in the first decades of the twentieth century there was an increase in protective trade barriers and restrictions created by counties to further their own trade interests. As a result, many laws were created to protect domestic industries and give local firms an advantage in trade. The Sherman Antitrust Act of 1890, the Federal Trade Commission Act of 1914, the

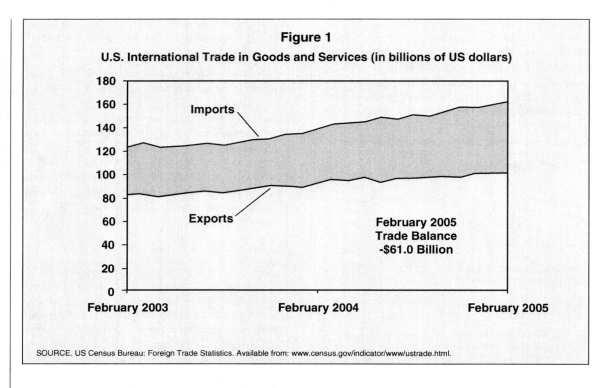

Figure 1

U.S. International Trade in Goods and Services (in billions of US dollars)

Imports

Exports

February 2005
Trade Balance
-$61.0 Billion

February 2003   February 2004   February 2005

SOURCE. US Census Bureau: Foreign Trade Statistics. Available from: www.census.gov/indicator/www/ustrade.html.

Trading with the Enemy Act of 1917, and the Smoot-Hawley Tariff Act of 1930 were some of the laws passed in the United States at this time. While not all of these were intended to reduce trade, and probably none were intended to devastate U.S. exports, the general pattern internationally was to raise protectionist trade barriers and tariffs in kind, creating an unfavorable climate for U.S. exports. This repressive trade environment is considered one of the causes of the Great Depression.

During the mid- and late 1930s, the United States and other nations cooperated to reduce trade barriers and create a smoother world trade climate. The U.S. Reciprocal Trade Agreements Act of 1934 helped to introduce lower tariffs and duties imposed on imports. As well, the most-favored-nation (MFN) trading program extended the benefits of any bilateral tariff reductions negotiated by the United States to all MFNs.

World War II helped to increase United States exports, as did reduced trade barriers. During the war, countries turned to the United States for supplies and the United States was increasingly perceived as an industrial power and a source of high-quality goods. In the postwar years, the United States emerged as the most powerful international trade leader, while the European and Japanese manufacturing sectors concentrated on rebuilding. From the 1940s to the 1960s, the U.S. trade surplus, the value of exports out of the country less the value of imports into the country, increased at a rate of 20 percent annually. U.S. exports continued to increase throughout the 1970s, growing from about $43 billion in 1970 to nearly $225 billion by 1980.

In the 1970s, however, increased competition from Western Europe and Japan wrested international market share from the United States. In the 1980s U.S. exports were outweighed by imports, as the national trade deficit grew to more than $160 billion annually by the late 1980s. Much of this deficit was due to oil imports; however, Japan's success at manufacturing quality goods for export, particularly autos and electronics, also contributed.

Despite this, increasing internationalization of markets and an ongoing effort to lower trade barriers greatly expanded global trading. From 1986 to 1990, U.S. merchandise exports contributed more than 40 percent of the rise in gross national product (GNP). In 1990, almost 84 percent of U.S. GNP growth was due to exports, which totaled a record high of $394 billion. The increase of U.S. exports in the late 1980s and early 1990s led to a significantly lower trade deficit and 2 million new jobs attributed to exports. The U.S. Department of Commerce estimates that for every $45,000 in export sales, one job is created, more than double the rate of jobs created by domestic sales. By calendar year 2004, annual U.S. exports of goods and services were around $1.147 trillion, leaving a $617 billion trade deficit, based on U.S. Census Bureau, Foreign Trade Statistics figures. According to World Trade Organization estimates, in 2004 the United States supplied about 9.6 percent of the world's merchandise exports by value. The United States was the world leader in imports claiming a 16.8 percent share of the world total imports.

CHARACTERISTICS OF EXPORTERS

Exports remain an important growth vehicle for U.S. companies, as many domestic product and service markets are saturated and offer only limited growth prospects. Today, many smaller firms export occasionally and seek to develop permanent, recurring business in foreign countries. Other companies only export to a few countries and want to increase the number of countries in which they do business. Fifteen percent of U.S. exporters account for 84 percent of the value of U.S. manufactured exports. One-half of all exporters sell in only one foreign market. Fewer than 20 percent of exporters, and fewer than 3 percent of U.S. companies overall, export to more than five markets.

METHODS OF EXPORTING

DIRECT EXPORTING. The typical exporting system is a company-owned export department, in which a manufacturer sells directly to companies or consumers in foreign countries. In this arrangement, the company has complete control over the marketing and distribution of its goods and services, distribution, sales, pricing, and other business choices. Most U.S. exporters, however, don't utilize this system. Many companies depend on one or several specialized export channels outside their organizations. Most companies choose direct and indirect routes. Direct exports are sold through foreign-based parties. Indirect exports are sold through home-based proxies or resellers. Both methods can be implemented through either merchants or agents. In these cases, merchants actually assume ownership of the goods, as opposed to agents, who only represent the manufacturer or owner. Bartering is another method that manufacturers may use to sell their goods abroad.

A direct merchant is an organization in a foreign country that buys goods in the United States, or another country, and then proceeds to sell the goods in their own country. The merchants usually offer complementary services to their buyers such as maintenance, parts sales, and technical support. A direct merchant often has a close relationship with the exporter, giving the merchant exclusive rights to sell and service the goods.

There are several different types of direct agents. Some direct agents, for example, are paid by U.S. firms on commission, have a contract, and usually do not sell competing products. The exporter trains the representative on the product and provides them with literature. Purchasing agents are similar to commission agents. They are sent to a foreign country by their company or homeland to purchase products for them. The agent is usually paid a fee or commission for this work. Purchasing agents are only in the target country for a short period of time and then leave.

INDIRECT EXPORTING. When a company uses a home-based merchant or agent to find and deliver goods to foreign buyers it utilizes indirect exporting. This method of exporting poses the least amount of risk and expense because it is relatively easy to start up and has a moderate up-front capital investment. Indirect agents act as intermediaries between the exporter and buyer and facilitate the flow of goods.

There are several different types of indirect agents. One is an export management company (EMC). EMCs usually represent several companies in one or more industries. The agent charges the domestic company a fee or commission and in return provides the manufacturer with access to foreign channels of distribution and knowledge of foreign markets. Another type of indirect agent is a Webb-Pomerene Association. There are about forty such associations in the United States. These associations are composed of competing manufacturers for the purpose of exporting. The associations are exempt from U.S. antitrust laws relating to price setting, discounting, and customer information. Export trading companies (ETCs) are another type of indirect agent. These were created in 1982 by the U.S. government to help U.S. manufacturers compete with powerful Japanese conglomerates. These companies are similar to EMCs and Webb-Pomerene Associations but are on a larger scale. Export commission houses are another form of indirect agent. In this case, commission agents represent buyers in foreign markets. The foreign buyer places an order and the commission agent solicits bids from domestic manufacturers. The lowest bidder is usually receives the order and is compensated by the foreign buyer with a fee or commission. This is an advantage for the exporter because the payment is usually received immediately and it takes little effort to complete the sale. Other forms of indirect trading include foreign freight forwarders, which manage overseas shipments for a fee; brokers, which bring buyers and sellers together, but do not handle or distribute the goods; and export agents, who represent the manufacturer, and act under their own name.

EXPORTING GUIDELINES

The international market is more than four times larger than the U.S. market. The growth rates in foreign countries are also much greater than domestic market growth. By exporting, companies can keep ahead of competition. Before implementing exporting, a company should measure the benefits against the costs and risks associated with it. The following are ten keys to keep in mind when exporting.

1. Obtain export counseling and create an international marketing plan before beginning to export. The plan should include goals, objectives, and expected problems.

2. Receive commitment from top management to correct initial problems and to meet financial requirements. Take a long-range view of exporting.

3. Carefully select foreign distributors. International distributors should act more independently than domestic ones, due to communication and transportation difficulties.

4. Establish a foundation for a profitable operation and growth.

5. Continue dedication to export effort even when U.S. market is booming. Many companies ignore their exporting plan when the U.S. economy picks up and subsequently fail.

6. Foreign distributors should be treated like domestic counterparts. Many companies implement advertising campaigns, discount offers, sales incentive programs, and so on to the U.S. market but don't make similar offers to their international distributors.

7. Do not assume that a marketing technique that works in one market will automatically work in others. Each market has to be treated separately to ensure success.

8. Be willing to make modifications to products to meet foreign regulations in other countries. Companies must take into account cultural preferences in other countries.

9. Messages pertaining to sale and warranties should be printed in languages locally understood. A company's foreign distributor may speak English, but it is unlikely that all sales and service personnel have this capability.

8. Readily available servicing for products should be provided. A company can earn a bad reputation when service support is not provided.

IMPORTING

Importing products into countries is often dependent on what product, commodity, or service is being imported. In the United States the Harmonized Tariff Schedule is the directory for determining what if any tariff is imposed on the product in question. Importing into any country should involve communicating with that country's customs agency to determine the necessary licensing and logistics issues. Often a customs broker is necessary to facilitate the smooth transfer of goods and services between countries. Inherently, importing involves exporting from one country; thus many of the issues involved in exporting are relevant and necessary for importing goods and services.

BARRIERS TO EXPORTS

Barriers to the export and import of goods have been widely established by governments. These barriers serve a number of purposes such as protecting industries, national employment levels, and improving trade balances. The United States and many other nations have made efforts to lower trade barriers, although many countries still have an intricate network of barriers that greatly impact the world export market.

The two major classes of trade restrictions are tariff and nontariff. Tariffs are duties imposed on goods leaving or coming into the country. Among other uses, tariffs are used to penalize other countries for trade or political actions. Nontariff barriers include quotas, taxes, and exchange rate controls. These can be broken down into six major categories that include specific trade limitations, customs and administrative entry restrictions, standards, government participation, import charges, and miscellaneous categories. Many governments offer various global export initiatives to encourage free trade. The General Agreement on Tariffs and Trade (GATT), which was signed by the United States and the majority of developed and developing countries, calls for a decrease of both tariff and nontariff barriers worldwide. Other important developments include the North American Free Trade Agreement of 1993, and the European Union's gradual evolution toward economic unity. These agreements significantly reduce trade barriers within the affected regions. In the United States, most governments support specific industries or companies through financial aid, lower tax rates, loans, and grants.

REASONS TO EXPORT

The most important reason a company begins exporting is to maximize profits by exploiting opportunities in foreign markets that are not available in domestic markets. A product may become obsolete in one country, but may be able to be sold abroad. By doing so, a manufacturer can reduce new product development costs and take advantage of learned efficiencies related to the product dealing with production, distribution, and marketing. When markets for products in the United States begin to mature and become saturated, producers can continue to receive continuous sales and profit gains through exporting. Markets in other countries are often less saturated and less competitive, allowing manufacturers to gain faster sales growth and higher profit margins. Foreign markets can provide shelter not only from maturing domestic markets, but also from increased competition in the home market. As manufacturing volume increases, benefits related to economies of scale aid the exporter's competitiveness in both foreign and domestic markets. Market risk diversification is also another benefit of exporting. A company can usually decrease its exposure to cyclical economic down-swings or regional problems by increasing its geographic opportunities. Exporting also decreases risks associated with seasonality of some products, e.g., warm-weather-related products might be marketed in the Southern Hemisphere when it's winter in the Northern Hemisphere.

As trade barriers continue to fall through the work of the World Trade Organization the value for a company to export their products will increase noticeably. The significant consumer buying power of many industrialized countries, especially the United States, is creating an ever expanding market for the exporting and importing of goods and services.

SEE ALSO: International Business; International Management; International Management

Kevin Nelson
Revised by Hal P. Kirkwood, Jr.

FURTHER READING:

Branch, Alan E. *Elements of Export Marketing and Management.* 2nd ed. London: Chapman and Hall, 1990.

Nelson, C.A. *Exporting: A Manager's Guide to the World Market.* New York: International Thomson Business Press, 1999.

Orton, C.W. "What Makes the U.S. Run Well?" *World Trade* 13, no. 10 (2000): 32–34.

Weiss, K.D. *Building an Import/Export Business.* Hoboken, NJ: Wiley, 2002.

F

FACILITATOR

A facilitator is a person who helps a group identify and solve problems by structuring the discussion and intervening when necessary to improve the effectiveness of the group's processes and outcomes. Facilitators, sometimes called moderators, maintain a neutral approach to topics and issues and serve the whole group in an unbiased manner.

The word *facilitator* is derived from the French word *faciliter,* which means to make easy or to simplify. Indeed, the goal of the facilitator is to make a group's decision-making process easy, efficient, and effective.

In the mid-1970s, Doyle and Strauss, authors of *How to Make Meetings Work,* argued that facilitators were "neutral servants" responsible for making sure participants were using the most effective approaches to problem solving and decision making while reaching consensus efficiently. The role of facilitators in business has grown dramatically in the past few years. A number of recent books published on the topic describe the responsibilities of a facilitator as well as approaches for developing facilitation skills. The distinction is often made between facilitators who are external to the organization or the group and facilitators who are internal. Both external and internal facilitators focus primarily on a group's process. In fact, some facilitators have minimal subject matter expertise.

THE ROLE OF THE FACILITATOR

Facilitators set the agenda for a group meeting or discussion, monitor the group's process in discussing agenda items, and help the group reach con-

sensus, make decisions, and set action plans. Effective facilitators bring out a variety of opinions and ideas, at the same time ensuring that all participants feel they are valued contributors to the discussion. Facilitators monitor how the group works together by encouraging participation, protecting individuals from attack, and minimizing dominance by one or two participants.

Facilitators begin by clearly defining the role they will play and the strategies they will use. In addition, facilitators help set ground rules for how group members will interact with each other, how long and when group members will speak, and how the group will make decisions.

Facilitators use a number of strategies to help groups achieve their goals. Focusing on consensus building, facilitators help participants discuss issues so that the end result is an outcome that all participants can support. Voting might be used to assess the depth of agreement or disagreement, but final group decisions are reached by consensus.

Facilitators can be most effective when groups are discussing future-oriented tasks such as developing mission statements, vision and value statements, or conducting strategic planning. Facilitation is also useful when groups are discussing complex or controversial issues that require an outsider's unbiased attention to structure and process.

Typically, facilitators use flip charts, electronic boards, and web conferencing tools to capture ideas generated by group participants as well as the flow of the discussion. This visual reminder of the group's ideas, decisions, and action plans provide a "recorded" memory for the group during the discussion and the notes following the group meeting.

ADVANTAGES AND DISADVANTAGES OF USING FACILITATORS

Advantages for groups that use facilitators include a well-structured meeting, focus on a common goal and a common process, record of the group's discussion and decisions, and an efficient way to reach consensus and productive outcomes. Facilitators provide strategies to handle conflicts between members as well as other nonproductive participant behaviors that impede the group's process. They also absolve group participants from the responsibility of handling the discussion or staying neutral.

Disadvantages can occur when facilitators are not effective. If a facilitator loses objectivity, the group may feel manipulated by the facilitator's approach. Also, if the facilitator does not manage the group's process effectively, the group will either waste time reaching consensus or in some cases may not meet their goals at all. Finally, groups can become overly dependent on a facilitator and may not learn the skills and strategies necessary to make decisions.

MANAGERS AS FACILITATORS

While facilitators are usually not members of the group since they are required to remain neutral, there is a trend toward managers and team members developing facilitation skills that they can use in meetings and discussions. Managers who assume the role of a facilitator, by definition, are not neutral. Yet, through facilitation managers can lead teams in managing change and achieving workrelated outcomes. Specifically, managers as facilitators provide clear expectations of the work to be done, monitor the team's process to increase team productivity, and manage the boundaries that can affect the work of the team. The manager as a facilitator empowers team members to make decisions and resolve problems.

For frequent, regular meetings, groups may rotate responsibility for acting as facilitator among team members or meeting participants. This spares any one person from always bearing the responsibility for focusing discussions, following the agenda, and enforcing time limits.

In a business world marked by rapid change, the role of facilitators will continue to expand as the need for managers and teams to solve complex problems also grows.

SEE ALSO: Management Styles; Teams and Teamwork

Mary V. Herman
Revised by Wendy Mason

FURTHER READING:

"GP Business: Resolve Conflict for the Best Team Effort." *General Practitioner* 12 November 2004, p. 30.

Kremer, Dennis. "Rules for Improved Meetings. (Viewpoint)" *Fairfield County Business Journal,* 20 December 2004, p. 38.

Rees, Fran. *How to Lead Work Teams: Facilitation Skills.* San Diego: Pfeiffer and Company, 1991.

Schwarz, Roger. *The Skilled Facilitator: Practical Wisdom for Developing Effective Groups.* San Francisco: Jossey–Bass, 1994.

Weaver, Richard, and John D. Farrell. *Managers as Facilitators: A Practical Guide to Getting Work Done in a Changing Workplace.* San Francisco: Berrett–Koehler, 1997.

FAMILY-FRIENDLY BUSINESS PRACTICES

SEE: Work-Life Balance

FEEDBACK

Feedback is the return of information about the result of a process, activity, or experience, usually relating to an individual's performance within a company. Feedback can be upward or downward in the organizational structure. Upward feedback is the process by which superiors or management are rated by employees or subordinates, while downward feedback is the flow of information from superiors or management to employees or subordinates.

In the past, feedback has been gathered from sources such as subordinates, peers, and internal or external customers. This is referred to as multi-source feedback when evaluations are collected from more than one source. In recent years, the majority of feedback has been collected for developmental purposes, but it seems that feedback is being used increasingly more in administrative decisions, including compensation and promotion. Such feedback is also being employed as a component of executive appraisals.

The impact of upward feedback is debatable, as is whether managers' responses to feedback are related to performance improvements over time. The major limitation of much research concerning feedback was that no one had examined whether managers' responses to such feedback were associated with performance improvement. It had been shown in the past that feedback alone was not the cause of behavior change; instead it was the goals that people set in response to feedback. A recent five-year study of upward feedback was conducted to answer some of these questions. The research covered more than 250 managers who received upward feedback annually over the five years. The results show that managers who were initially rated as being poor or moderate registered significant improvements in upward feedback ratings over the next five-year period. The results also show that managers who participated in discussions about their upward feedback improved more than managers who did not. It further showed that managers improved more in years when they discussed the previous year's feedback than in years when they did not. This study is important because it shows what managers do with upward feedback is related to its benefits.

In the past, it has been assumed that discrepancies between self-ratings and subordinate ratings raise self-awareness, highlight gaps between goals and job performance, and suggest areas of needed improvement. According to the self-consistency theory, when managers receive feedback showing that subordinates ratings are lower than self-ratings, the managers may question whether their behavior is consistent with their self-image. This should, in theory, motivate the managers to improve their performance and reduce discrepancies between how they look at themselves and how subordinates perceive them. However, if the feedback is consistent with self-ratings, managers may be satisfied and may not be motivated to improve their work ethic, even if their current performance level is low. Accordingly, the theory suggests that managers whose subordinate ratings exceed their self-rating have little incentive to improve their performance.

A recent study investigated whether performance improvement following upward feedback is related to self-other rating discrepancies. It also investigated how self-ratings change after feedback and whether agreement among raters influences performance improvement. The study determined that managers who overrated themselves compared to how others rated them tended to improve their performance from one year to the next, while the under raters tended to decline. These results are consistent with the self-consistency theory. Self-ratings tended to decrease for over raters and increase for under raters, but this was not constant throughout the range of self-ratings. Agreement with subordinate ratings was found to be negatively related to performance improvement.

An issue related to self-ratings of performance is the degree to which employees proactively seek feedback about their own performance from supervisors and/or coworkers. Some studies have linked employees' feedback seeking to increases in job performance. By asking more often how they are doing, employees tend to know how to perform better. Employees seek feedback in order to reduce their uncertainty, to manage impressions of themselves in the workplace, and to protect their own egos. They are more likely to seek feedback when they have a positive relationship with the manager from which they seek feedback, when they feel that their manager has expertise, and if they feel that their manager is supportive of them. Additionally, employees may be more likely to seek feedback in private, rather than when others are present.

Beyond its uses in performance appraisal, feedback may also be seen as a more general tool for communication within organizations. Many companies all over the world now use e-mail and toll-free numbers to solicit feedback from their employees. Many of these companies reward employees for their good ideas. In some instances, employees are paid for ideas that turn into new products and technologies, while other companies' reward with job opportunities. By implementing a suggestion system, there is a direct link between an employee's suggestion and the rewards that the employee receives for it. The majority of employee ideas focus on improving safety and operations within the company.

Kevin Nelson
Revised by Marcia Simmering

FURTHER READING:

Ashford, S.J., and L.L. Cummings. "Feedback as an Individual Resource: Personal Strategies of Creating Information." *Organizational Behavior and Human Performance* 32 (1983): 370–398.

Gordon, Jack. "If We Might Make a Suggestion." *Training,* July 1999, 20–21.

Johnson, Jeff. "The Effects of Interrater and Self-Other Agreement on Performance Improvement Following Upward Feedback." *Personnel Psychology,* Summer 1999, 271–303.

FINANCIAL ISSUES FOR MANAGERS

One of the most critical aspects of management pertains to the finances of running a firm. Although there are numerous issues facing modern managers with respect to financial management, the following sections will address three of the most ubiquitous— acquisition of outside capital for start-up and growth, management of working capital and cash flow, and the construction and implementation of a capital budgeting process. Accessing the capital markets is fundamental for procuring funds that allow the firm to grow. Working capital involves managing the current assets and liabilities of the firm. Capital budgeting is the process of making long-term fixed asset investments.

ACCESSING THE FINANCIAL MARKETS

In the initial start-up of any firm, management must procure the funds needed to get the business off the ground. These funds may come from a variety of sources, but managers should be aware that all assets are initially financed with either of two sources of capital—equity and debt. The capital markets represent the method by which external funds are made available to firms requiring outside capital infusions.

EQUITY MARKETS. The equity markets are the means by which managers may raise capital by selling portions of the firm's ownership. The most common method is selling common stock in the firm. Outside investors provide the firm with new investment capital in exchange for ownership rights in the firm. As owners, stockholders receive voting rights and may participate in the financial success of the firm. In corporations, stockholders are protected by limited liability, meaning they are liable only for losses limited to the amount invested in the firm's stock; personal assets are protected against liability. Other sources of equity capital include contributions by the individual owner or owners from their own resources, and those made by family and friends of originators of the business.

Another method of raising equity capital involves the sale of preferred stock in the firm. Preferred stock promises to pay investors a stated dividend amount, and may also offer the opportunity for eventual conversion into common shares, commonly called convertible preferred stock. Preferred stock is particularly important for larger corporations as a source of funds because current tax law subsidizes the investment by one corporation in another corporation's preferred stock by exempting a portion of dividend income from taxation.

Other methods of equity capital attainment include the selling of warrants and rights. Warrants are securities that grant the holder the right to purchase a fixed number of common shares in the firm at a specified price for a specified period of time. Because warrants are stand-alone securities that may be traded among investors, the firm may raise new capital immediately through the sale of warrants while delaying the dilution of existing stockholders's interests until the warrants are exercised.

Rights are similar to warrants in that firms issue rights as a method of raising new equity capital. In a rights offering, the firm issues additional common stock to raise new capital. Rights are then issued to all outstanding shareholders, giving them the right to purchase shares in the new offering to avoid dilution of their pro-rata ownership in the firm. Through the use of rights, the firm is able to directly access the group of investors who are already interested in the firm's financial success, namely existing shareholders. Because rights have value in that they allow the purchase of new shares at a set subscription price, they are desired by shareholders and may be sold to others if the shareholder decides not to use the rights.

DEBT MARKETS. The other major market for outside capital is the debt market. The debt market is often vital to the financial success of a firm and managers must be familiar with, and have access to, outside sources of debt capital to ensure the survival of the firm. A common method of debt financing is borrowing from financial institutions. Banks, finance companies, and other lenders offer loans of varying terms that are critical for financial management, particularly short-term debt to alleviate temporary cash flow problems. A firm that experiences seasonal sales or uneven production schedules will sometimes utilize an established line of credit to borrow during times of capital needs and repay during times of cash surplus. By arranging credit lines prior to the capital need, managers assure that the firm will not experience sales or production interruptions due to cash shortages. For longer-term needs, negotiated notes from lenders serve as an intermediate source of debt financing.

For longer-term capital, the bond markets represent the primary source of debt financing. Bonds are debt securities in which investors become creditors of the firm in exchange for the right to receive payments of interest at regular intervals. For firms desiring to grow beyond local or regional status, access to the bond markets is critical for long-term capital needs, especially when firms do not desire to dilute existing ownership by offering additional equity financing.

SHORT-TERM FINANCIAL ISSUES

Short-term financial issues for managers revolve around two primary areas; the management of current assets and current liabilities. Together, they constitute the overall management of cash flow for the firm. Cash flow management is absolutely critical to the financial survival of a firm, since a shortage of cash may result in a firm that shows a profit on its income statement actually going bankrupt by being unable to meet its financial obligations.

CURRENT ASSETS. Management of a firm's current assets starts with the management of cash. Cash provides the liquidity needed to meet everyday obligations owed to creditors and suppliers and the flexibility to take advantage of new opportunities that may arise. Managing cash is a tricky issue for many firms; cash is a necessary component of daily operations, yet cash is a non-earning asset. Dollars tied up in cash (checking accounts) could be earning higher rates of return if invested in other areas. Larger corporations spend considerable time and resources in cash management, whereby dollars are transferred back and forth between cash accounts and marketable securities that earn a higher rate of return. As previously mentioned, negotiated credit lines serve to supplement depleted cash during periods of shortage.

Another critical issue is the management of accounts receivable. Receivables are money owed to the firm that has not yet been collected. They represent an important investment for the firm, since dollars not yet received cannot earn a positive return. The management of accounts receivable involves the determination and implementation of the firm's credit policy such as how long customers are allowed to pay for merchandise or services received and cash discounts for immediate rather than deferred payment. These are important financial issues for any manager: to whom does the company extend credit, for how much, and for how long? A tight credit policy may result in missed sales opportunities, since fewer potential customers will qualify for credit sales. Conversely, liberal credit terms may result in longer average collection periods and greater uncollected accounts. There are real costs associated with these issues, and managers must work to find appropriate trade-offs that result not only in higher sales, but also in the greatest profitability.

A third aspect of current asset management involves the management of inventories. Like receivables, inventory represents an investment of resources by the firm that has yet to pay off. On one hand, adequate inventory levels are necessary to ensure uninterrupted production schedules and to meet unexpected sales demand. However, too much inventory means dollars tied up in non-earning assets that could be devoted to more profitable investments. Managers must decide whether to attempt to coordinate production with sales patterns, or maintain level production regardless of current demand. These decisions spill over into other areas such as employee morale, since uneven or random production scheduling may result in temporary layoffs or overtime requirements. Again, managers utilize negotiated credit lines to access capital to maintain needed inventory materials when production and sales patterns differ.

CURRENT LIABILITIES. Management of current liabilities involves accounts payable, short-term bank loans, lines of credit, and, for larger corporations, commercial paper. While the importance of short-term credit lines has already been discussed, accounts payable management is a critical issue, particularly for smaller firms. The longer a firm takes to pay its creditors, the longer it maintains access to and has the use of the funds. Thus, managers have every incentive to pay outstanding bills as slowly as possible. However, taking too long to pay may result in suppliers declining to offer future credit. Trade credit offered by sup-

pliers is one of the most important sources of short-term financing for small firms that have limited access to other capital market sources. It is incumbent on managers to seek and negotiate the most favorable trade credit terms possible, since longer payment periods reduce potential cash flow problems and provide greater financial flexibility.

Larger corporations are able to issue commercial paper to provide short-term financial liquidity. Commercial paper is a short-term, unsecured note backed only by the firm's ability to repay. As such, only large, established firms find a market for their commercial paper. Firms such as General Motors use commercial paper as a regular source of short-term debt financing to cover cash flow shortages and provide the firm with ready liquidity.

CASH BUDGET. Pulling together the management of current assets and liabilities results in the development of a cash budget. A cash budget is a schedule of expected cash inflows and outflows by a period that allows managers the ability to plan for and cover cash shortfalls and surpluses. A successful cash budget prevents the types of surprises or shortages that can result in financial crises such as the inability to pay creditors or purchase additional inventory to meet production needs.

Likewise, managers should work to monitor and manage the firm's cash conversion cycle. The cash conversion cycle consists, primarily, of three elements: the inventory conversion period, the receivable collections period, and the payables deferral period. The goal of effective cash management is to minimize the inventory conversion and receivables collection periods, and to maximize the payables deferral period. Through the successful management of current assets and liabilities, managers can maintain a cash conversion cycle that provides the firm with liquidity and profitability while avoiding the cash flow problems that so often result in financial distress.

CAPITAL BUDGETING ANALYSIS

The third major financial issue for managers involves long-term investments. This area, collectively known as capital budgeting, involves investment in fixed assets such as plant and equipment, new product and business analysis, and expansion and merger analysis. Capital budgeting is extremely important, because the decisions made involve the direction and opportunities for the future growth of the firm. The goal of corporate management is to maximize shareholder wealth; profitable capital projects result in increased firm value.

DISCOUNTED CASH FLOW. This process is also known as discounted cash flow analysis. The first step in evaluating a long-term investment opportunity is to estimate the net cash flows that would accrue to the firm. Managers should take care to use economically-sound techniques in cash flow analysis. All cash flows should be incremental (i.e., those that would otherwise not accrue to the firm unless this project or investment is undertaken). They should be on an after-tax basis; the only relevant cash flows are those that the firm will actually receive after all expenses and taxes are paid. Finally, sunk costs should not be included in the net cash flows associated with the project or investment. Only those cash flows associated with the future profitability of the investment should be included in the decision analysis. The proper economic decision is whether or not to invest today, and that decision is based on how the future cash flows will affect the present value of the firm. Past expenditures are not part of the analysis.

Once the project's net cash flows are determined, the timing of the cash flows should be considered. This is the discounted portion of discounted cash flow analysis. The decision of whether or not to invest is made in the present, so all dollars associated with the investment should be converted into present-value dollars. Managers must determine the proper interest rate at which to discount future cash flows. The discount rate should represent the opportunity cost of capital—the rate of return that could be earned on alternative investment projects of similar risk. Many firms set an internal "hurdle rate" for capital budgeting analysis, in effect saying no long-term investments will be undertaken that offer an expected rate of return lower than the hurdle rate. Normally, this rate is the weighted average cost of capital, which incorporates the firm's capital structure in determining the required rate of return on investment.

NET PRESENT VALUE ANALYSIS. Once the net cash flows are determined and the discount rate has been established, managers should utilize a discounted cash flow method to evaluate and rank investment alternatives. The most economically-sound technique is net present value analysis (NPV), which involves discounting all future project cash flows back to the present using the firm's discount rate, then subtracting the net cost of the investment project. If the present value of the future cash-flow stream exceeds the present cost, then undertaking the project would add value to the firm today. The NPV method is congruent with the idea of management's goal to maximize the present value, which represents shareholder wealth, of the firm.

INTERNAL RATE OF RETURN. Another popular technique is the internal rate of return (IRR) method. The IRR is actually a special case of the NPV method. The internal rate of return is the unique discount rate that equates the present value of the future cash flow stream to the net cost of the project. If the IRR of the project is greater than the firm's hurdle rate, then the project offers a chance to earn a profitable return on investment and should be undertaken.

PAYBACK METHOD. Finally, a third technique often used is the payback method. The payback method attempts to determine how long it will take for the project to recoup the total investment costs. Unlike the NPV and the IRR methods, the payback method is not a measure of profitability. Instead, it is a measure of time. Firms and managers often set a (subjective) hurdle period, such as no projects will be undertaken which do not recoup their initial costs in less than five years. The analysis then involves comparing the payback of the proposed investment to the firm's hurdle period. The payback method is popular because it provides an answer to a frequently-asked question—namely "how long before this investment pays for itself?" However, it is a flawed method because it does not consider all of the project's cash flows and does not consider the time value of money. Managers should employ the payback technique only in tandem with at least one of either the NPV or IRR discounted cash-flow methods.

Financial management is an integral aspect of managing a company. Accessing the capital markets to provide investment dollars, managing the working capital of the firm to ensure liquidity and flexibility, and making long-term investment decisions are all important issues that managers should address to allow the firm to grow and prosper.

Howard Finch
Revised by Scott B. Droege

FURTHER READING:

Block, Stanley B., and Geoffrey A. Hirt. *Foundations of Financial Management.* 11th ed. New York: McGraw-Hill, 2005.

Leach, J.C., and Ronald W. Melicher. *Entrepreneurial Finance.* 2nd ed. Mason, OH: Thomson South-Western, 2006.

Shapiro, Alan C. *Capital Budgeting and Investment Analysis.* Upper Saddle River, NJ: Prentice Hall, 2005.

FINANCIAL RATIOS

Financial ratios are one of the most common tools of managerial decision making. A ratio is a comparison of one number to another—mathematically, a simple division problem. Financial ratios involve the comparison of various figures from the financial statements in order to gain information about a company's performance. It is the interpretation, rather than the calculation, that makes financial ratios a useful tool for business managers. Ratios may serve as indicators, clues, or red flags regarding noteworthy relationships between variables used to measure the firm's performance in terms of profitability, asset utilization, liquidity, leverage, or market valuation.

USE AND USERS OF RATIO ANALYSIS

There are basically two uses of financial ratio analysis: to track individual firm performance over time, and to make comparative judgments regarding firm performance. Firm performance is evaluated using trend analysis—calculating individual ratios on a per-period basis, and tracking their values over time. This analysis can be used to spot trends that may be cause for concern, such as an increasing average collection period for outstanding receivables or a decline in the firm's liquidity status. In this role, ratios serve as red flags for troublesome issues, or as benchmarks for performance measurement.

Another common usage of ratios is to make relative performance comparisons. For example, comparing a firm's profitability to that of a major competitor or observing how the firm stacks up versus industry averages enables the user to form judgments concerning key areas such as profitability or management effectiveness. Users of financial ratios include parties both internal and external to the firm. External users include security analysts, current and potential investors, creditors, competitors, and other industry observers. Internally, managers use ratio analysis to monitor performance and pinpoint strengths and weaknesses from which specific goals, objectives, and policy initiatives may be formed.

PROFITABILITY RATIOS

Perhaps the type of ratios most often used and considered by those outside a firm are the profitability ratios. Profitability ratios provide measures of profit performance that serve to evaluate the periodic financial success of a firm. One of the most widely-used financial ratios is net profit margin, also known as return on sales.

$$\text{Net profit margin} = \frac{\text{net income}}{\text{net sales}}$$

Return on sales provides a measure of bottom-line profitability. For example, a net profit margin of 6 percent means that for every dollar in sales, the firm generated six cents in net income.

Two other margin measures are gross profit margin and operating margin.

$$\text{Gross profit margin} = \frac{\text{gross profit}}{\text{net sales}}$$

Gross margin measures the direct production costs of the firm. A gross profit margin of 30 percent would indicate that for each dollar in sales, the firm spent seventy cents in direct costs to produce the good or service that the firm sold.

$$\text{Operating margin} = \frac{\text{operating profit}}{\text{net sales}}$$

Operating margin goes one step further, incorporating nonproduction costs such as selling, general, and administrative expenses of the firm. Operating profit is also commonly referred to as earnings before interest and taxes, or EBIT. An operating margin of 15 percent would indicate that the firm spent an additional fifteen cents out of every dollar in sales on nonproduction expenses, such as sales commissions paid to the firm's sales force or administrative labor expenses.

Two very important measures of the firm's profitability are return on assets and return on equity.

$$\text{Return on assets} = \frac{\text{net income}}{\text{total assets}}$$

Return on assets (ROA) measures how effectively the firm's assets are used to generate profits net of expenses. An ROA of 7 percent would mean that for each dollar in assets, the firm generated seven cents in profits. This is an extremely useful measure of comparison among firms's competitive performance, for it is the job of managers to utilize the assets of the firm to produce profits.

$$\text{Return on equity} = \frac{\text{net income}}{\text{common shareholders equity}}$$

Return on equity (ROE) measures the net return per dollar invested in the firm by the owners, the common shareholders. An ROE of 11 percent means the firm is generating an 11-cent return per dollar of net worth.

One should note that in each of the profitability ratios mentioned above, the numerator in the ratio comes from the firm's income statement. Hence, these are measures of periodic performance, covering the specific period reported in the firm's income statement. Therefore, the proper interpretation for a profitability ratio such as an ROA of 11 percent would be that, over the specific period (such as fiscal year 2004), the firm returned eleven cents on each dollar of asset investment.

Table 1
Profitability Ratios

Gross profit margin	**Return on assets**
Operating margin	**Return on equity**
Net profit margin	

ASSET UTILIZATION RATIOS

Asset utilization ratios provide measures of management effectiveness. These ratios serve as a guide to critical factors concerning the use of the firm's assets, inventory, and accounts receivable collections in day-to-day operations. Asset utilization ratios are especially important for internal monitoring concerning performance over multiple periods, serving as warning signals or benchmarks from which meaningful conclusions may be reached on operational issues. An example is the total asset turnover (TAT) ratio.

$$\text{Total asset turnover} = \frac{\text{net sales}}{\text{total assets}}$$

This ratio offers managers a measure of how well the firm is utilizing its assets in order to generate sales revenue. An increasing TAT would be an indication that the firm is using its assets more productively. For example, if the TAT for 2003 was 2.2×, and for 2004 3×, the interpretation would follow that in 2004, the firm generated $3 in sales for each dollar of assets, an additional 80 cents in sales per dollar of asset investment over the previous year. Such change may be an indication of increased managerial effectiveness.

A similar measure is the fixed asset turnover (FAT) ratio.

$$\text{Fixed asset turnover} = \frac{\text{net sales}}{\text{net fixed assets}}$$

Fixed assets (such as plant and equipment) are often more closely associated with direct production than are current assets (such as cash and accounts receivable), so many analysts prefer this measure of effectiveness. A FAT of 1.6× would be interpreted as the firm generated $1.60 in sales for every $1 it had in fixed assets.

Two other asset utilization ratios concern the effectiveness of management of the firm's current assets. Inventory is an important economic variable for management to monitor since dollars invested in inventory have not yet resulted in any return to the firm. Inventory is an investment, and it is important for the firm to strive to maximize its inventory turnover. The inventory turnover ratio is used to measure this aspect of performance.

$$\text{Inventory turnover ratio} = \frac{\text{cost of goods sold}}{\text{average inventory}}$$

Cost of goods sold (COGS) derives from the income statement and indicates the expense dollars attributed to the actual production of goods sold during a specified period. Inventory is a current asset on the balance sheet. Because the balance sheet represents the firm's assets and liabilities at one point in time, an average figure is often used from two succes-

sive balance sheets. Managers attempt to increase this ratio, since a higher turnover ratio indicates that the firm is going through its inventory more often due to higher sales. A turnover ratio of 4.75×, or 475 percent, means the firm sold and replaced its inventory stock more than four and one-half times during the period measured on the income statement.

One of the most critical ratios that management must monitor is days sales outstanding (DSO), also known as average collection period.

$$\text{DSO} = \frac{\text{accounts receivable}}{\text{net sales}} \times 360 \text{ days}$$

This represents a prime example of the use of a ratio as an internal monitoring tool. Managers strive to minimize the firm's average collection period, since dollars received from customers become immediately available for reinvestment. Periodic measurement of the DSO will "red flag" a lengthening of the firm's time to collect outstanding accounts before customers get used to taking longer to pay. A DSO of thirty-six means that, on average, it takes thirty-six days to collect on the firm's outstanding accounts. This is an especially critical measure for firms in industries where extensive trade credit is offered, but any company that extends credit on sales should be aware of the DSO on a regular basis.

Table 2
Asset Utilization Ratios

Total asset turnover	Days sales outstanding
Inventory turnover	Fixed asset turnover

LEVERAGE RATIOS

Leverage ratios, also known as capitalization ratios, provide measures of the firm's use of debt financing. These are extremely important for potential creditors, who are concerned with the firm's ability to generate the cash flow necessary to make interest payments on outstanding debt. Thus, these ratios are used extensively by analysts outside the firm to make decisions concerning the provision of new credit or the extension of existing credit arrangements. It is also important for management to monitor the firm's use of debt financing. The commitment to service outstanding debt is a fixed cost to a firm, resulting in decreased flexibility and higher break-even production rates. Therefore, the use of debt financing increases the risk associated with the firm. Managers and creditors must constantly monitor the trade-off between the additional risk that comes with borrowing money and the increased opportunities that the new capital provides. Leverage ratios provide a means of such monitoring.

Perhaps the most straightforward measure of a firm's use of debt financing is the total-debt ratio.

$$\text{Total debt ratio} = \frac{\text{total debt}}{\text{total assets}}$$

It is important to recall that there are only two ways to finance the acquisition of any asset: debt (using borrowed funds) and equity (using funds from internal operations or selling stock in the company). The total debt ratio captures this idea. A debt ratio of 35 percent means that, for every dollar of assets the firm has, 35 cents was financed with borrowed money. The natural corollary is that the other 65 cents came from equity financing. This is known as the firm's capital structure—35 percent debt and 65 percent equity. Greater debt means greater leverage, and more leverage means more risk. How much debt is too much is a highly subjective question, and one that managers constantly attempt to answer. The answer depends, to a large extent, on the nature of the business or industry. Large manufacturers, who require heavy investment in fixed plant and equipment, will require higher levels of debt financing than will service firms such as insurance or advertising agencies.

The total debt of a firm consists of both long- and short-term liabilities. Short-term (or current) liabilities are often a necessary part of daily operations and may fluctuate regularly depending on factors such as seasonal sales. Many creditors prefer to focus their attention on the firm's use of long-term debt. Thus, a common variation on the total debt ratio is the long-term debt ratio, which does not incorporate current liabilities in the numerator.

$$\text{Long-term debt ratio} = \frac{\text{long-term debt}}{\text{total assets}}$$

In a similar vein, many analysts prefer a direct comparison of the firm's capital structure. Such a measure is provided by the debt-to-equity ratio.

$$\text{Debt-to-equity ratio} = \frac{\text{total debt}}{\text{total equity}}$$

This is perhaps one of the most misunderstood financial ratios, as many confuse it with the total debt ratio. A debt-to-equity ratio of 45 percent would mean that for each dollar of equity financing, the firm has 45 cents in debt financing. This does not mean that the firm has 45 percent of its total financing as debt; debt and equity percentages, together, must sum to one (100 percent of the firm's total financing). A little algebra will illustrate this point. Let x = the percent of equity financing (in decimal form), so $0.45x$ is the percent of debt financing. Then $x + 0.45$ $x = 1$, and $x = 0.69$. So, a debt to equity ratio of 45 percent indicates that each dollar of the firm's assets are financed with 69 cents of equity and 31 cents with debt. The point here is to caution against confusing the interpretation of the debt-to-equity ratio with that of the total debt ratio.

Two other leverage ratios that are particularly important to the firm's creditors are the times-interest-earned and the fixed-charge coverage ratios. These measure the firm's ability to meet its on-going commitment to service debt previously borrowed. The times-interest-earned (TIE) ratio, also known as the EBIT coverage ratio, provides a measure of the firm's ability to meet its interest expenses with operating profits.

$$\text{Times interest earned} = \frac{\text{EBIT}}{\text{interest charges}}$$

For example, a TIE of 3.6× indicates that the firm's operating profits from a recent period exceeded the total interest expenses it was required to pay by 360 percent. The higher this ratio, the more financially stable the firm and the greater the safety margin in the case of fluctuations in sales and operating expenses. This ratio is particularly important for lenders of short-term debt to the firm, since short-term debt is usually paid out of current operating revenue.

Similarly, the fixed charge coverage ratio, also known as the debt service coverage ratio, takes into account all regular periodic obligations of the firm.

$$\text{Fixed charge coverage} = \frac{\text{EBIT}}{(\text{Interest expense} + \frac{\text{Principal repayment}}{1 - \text{tax rate}})}$$

The adjustment to the principal repayment reflects the fact that this portion of the debt repayment is not tax deductible. By including the payment of both principal and interest, the fixed charge coverage ratio provides a more conservative measure of the firm's ability to meet fixed obligations.

Table 3

Leverage Ratios

Total debt ratio	Times interest earned
Long-term debt ratio	Fixed charge coverage
Debt-to-equity ratio	

LIQUIDITY RATIOS

Managers and creditors must closely monitor the firm's ability to meet short-term obligations. The liquidity ratios are measures that indicate a firm's ability to repay short-term debt. Current liabilities represent obligations that are typically due in one year or less. The current and quick ratios are used to gauge a firm's liquidity.

$$\text{Current ratio} = \frac{\text{current assets}}{\text{current liabilities}}$$

A current ratio of 1.5× indicates that for every dollar in current liabilities, the firm has $1.50 in current assets. Such assets could, theoretically, be sold and the proceeds used to satisfy the liabilities if the firm ran short of cash. However, some current assets are more liquid than others. Obviously, the most liquid current asset is cash. Accounts receivable are usually collected within one to three months, but this varies by firm and industry. The least liquid of current assets is often inventory. Depending on the type of industry or product, some inventory has no ready market. Since the economic definition of liquidity is the ability to turn an asset into cash at or near fair market value, inventory that is not easily sold will not be helpful in meeting short-term obligations. The quick (or acid test) ratio incorporates this concern.

$$\text{Quick ratio} = \frac{\text{current assets} - \text{inventories}}{\text{current liabilities}}$$

By excluding inventories, the quick ratio is a more strident liquidity measure than the current ratio. It is a more appropriate measure for industries that involve long product production cycles, such as in manufacturing.

Table 4

Liquidity Ratios

Current ratio	Quick ratio

MARKET VALUE RATIOS

Managers and investors are interested in market ratios, which are used in valuing the firm's stock. The price-earnings ratio and the market-to-book value ratio are often used in valuation analysis. The price/earnings ratio, universally known as the PE ratio, is one of the most heavily-quoted statistics concerning a firm's common stock. It is reported in the financial pages of newspapers, along with the current value of the firm's stock price.

$$\text{Price/earnings ratio} = \frac{\text{market price per share}}{\text{earnings per share}}$$

A note of caution is warranted concerning the calculation of PE ratios. Analysts use two different components in the denominator: trailing earnings and forecast earnings. Trailing earnings refer to the firm's reported earnings, per share, over the last twelve months of operation. Forecast earnings are based on security analyst forecasts of what they expect the firm to earn in the coming twelve-month period. Neither definition is more correct than the other; one should simply pay attention to which measure is used when consulting published PE ratios. A PE ratio of sixteen can be interpreted as investors are willing to pay $16 for $1

worth of earnings. PE ratios are used extensively, on a comparative basis, to analyze investment alternatives. In investment lingo, the PE ratio is often referred to as the firm's "multiple." A high PE is often indicative of investors's belief that the firm has very promising growth prospects, while firms in more mature industries often trade at lower multiples.

A related measure used for valuation purposes is the market-to-book value ratio. The book value of a firm is defined as:

$$\text{Book value per share} = \frac{\text{total shareholders equity}}{\text{common shares outstanding}}$$

Technically, the book value represents the value of the firm if all the assets were sold off, and the proceeds used to retire all outstanding debt. The remainder would represent the equity that would be divided, proportionally, among the firm's shareholders. Many investors like to compare the current price of the firm's common stock with its book, or break-up, value.

$$\text{Market-to-book ratio} = \frac{\text{market price per share}}{\text{book value per share}}$$

This is also known as the price/book ratio. If the ratio is greater than one, which is often the case, then the firm is trading at a premium to book value. Many investors regard a market-to-book ratio of less than one an indication of an undervalued firm. While the interpretation one draws from market ratios is highly subjective (do high PE or low PE firms make better investments?), these measures provide information that is valued both by managers and investors regarding the market price of a firm's stock.

Table 5

Market Value Ratios

Price/earnings ratio	Market-to-book ratio

CAUTIONS ON THE USE AND INTERPRETATION OF FINANCIAL RATIOS

Financial ratios represent tools for insight into the performance, efficiency, and profitability of a firm. Two noteworthy issues on this subject involve ratio calculation and interpretation. For example, if someone refers to a firm's "profit margin" of 18 percent, are they referring to gross profit margin, operating margin, or net profit margin? Similarly, is a quotation of a "debt ratio" a reference to the total debt ratio, the long-term debt ratio, or the debt-to-equity ratio? These types of confusions can make the use of ratio analysis a frustrating experience.

Interpreting financial ratios should also be undertaken with care. A net profit margin of 12 percent may be outstanding for one type of industry and mediocre to poor for another. This highlights the fact that individual ratios should not be interpreted in isolation. Trend analyses should include a series of identical calculations, such as following the current ratio on a quarterly basis for two consecutive years. Ratios used for performance evaluation should always be compared to some benchmark, either an industry average or perhaps the identical ratio for the industry leader.

Another factor in ratio interpretation is for users to identify whether individual components, such as net income or current assets, originate from the firm's income statement or balance sheet. The income statement reports performance over a specified period of time, while the balance sheet gives static measurement at a single point in time. These issues should be recognized when one attempts to interpret the results of ratio calculations.

Despite these issues, financial ratios remain useful tools for both internal and external evaluations of key aspects of a firm's performance. A working knowledge and ability to use and interpret ratios remains a fundamental aspect of effective financial management. The value of financial ratios to investors became even more apparent during the stock market decline of 2000, when the bottom dropped out of the soaring "dot.com" economy. Throughout the long run-up, some financial analysts warned that the stock prices of many technology companies—particularly Internet start-up businesses—were overvalued based on the traditional rules of ratio analysis. Yet investors largely ignored such warnings and continued to flock to these companies in hopes of making a quick return. In the end, however, it became clear that the old rules still applied, and that financial ratios remained an important means of measuring, comparing, and predicting firm performance.

SEE ALSO: Balance Sheets; Cash Flow Analysis and Statement; Financial Issues for Managers; Income Statements

Howard Finch
Revised by Laurie Hillstrom

FURTHER READING:

Fridson, Martin, and Fernando Alvarez. *Financial Statement Analysis: A Practitioner's Guide.* New York: John Wiley, 2002.

Harrington, Diana R. *Corporate Financial Analysis: Decisions in a Global Environment.* 4th ed. Chicago: Richard D. Irwin, Inc., 1993.

Helfert, Erich A. *Techniques of Financial Analysis: A Modern Approach.* 9th ed. Chicago: Richard D. Irwin, Inc., 1997.

NetMBA.com. "Financial Ratios." Available from <http://www.netmba.com/finance/financial/ratios>.

FIRST-MOVER ADVANTAGE

The idea of first-mover advantage is similar to the old adage, "the early bird gets the worm." In business, being the first company to sell a new product may provide long-lasting benefits or competitive advantages. Most researchers use the term, "first mover" to refer to the first company to enter a market, not the first company to develop a product (the inventor). First movers are also called market pioneers. The benefits of pioneering may result in market dominance and higher-than-average profitability over time. There are several reasons why these benefits may develop, but research has shown that being the first mover does not always provide advantages. Sometimes there are even first-mover disadvantages, where companies that enter a market later can achieve superior results to those attained by the first-mover firm.

For example, Amazon.com was the first major online bookstore, seizing a head start on later entrants. Established book retailers Barnes & Noble and Borders were quick to develop their own Web sites. Amazon maintained their first-mover advantage in two ways; by partnering with Borders and continuing to extend their product offerings into apparel, electronics, toys, and housewares. This negated any customer preference for purchasing from Barnes & Noble by becoming a much larger, one-stop-shopping destination. Company strategists need to decide if they are likely to benefit from being first, or whether it would be better to wait and follow the leader.

There are two stages to developing first-mover advantages. First, a company must have an opportunity to be first at something, either through skill or luck. Second, the firm must be able to capture the benefits of being first. In their award-winning article, professors Marvin Lieberman and David Montgomery of Stanford University described three benefits of being first: technology leadership, control of resources, and buyer switching costs.

TECHNOLOGY LEADERSHIP

First, early entrants can lead other companies in their understanding and use of technology in ways that are hard for later entrants to copy. One way this can happen is that the early entrant learns how to reduce the costs of producing a product through accumulated experience in producing it. This is called a "learning" or "experience" curve effect. Unless later entrants can learn how to produce at these lower costs faster than the first entrant did, the first entrant will have a cost advantage. Harvard University Professor Michael Porter discusses how Procter & Gamble developed an advantage in disposable diapers in the United States.

However, researchers have found that in most industries it is relatively easy for later entrants to learn new technology quickly and overcome the lead held by the first-mover firm.

Another way that a first mover may benefit from technology leadership is by applying for patents for their technology to try to prevent other companies from copying it. Patents appear to protect first-mover advantages in some industries, such as pharmaceuticals. In many industries, though, later entrants can invent their own technology quickly enough so that the first-mover's patent protection does not matter. A stronger advantage from technology leadership arises when the first mover can establish their product as the industry standard, making it more difficult for followers to gain customer acceptance.

CONTROL OF RESOURCES

The second type of first-mover benefit is the ability to control a resource necessary for the business that is better than resources later entrants must use. For example, the first company to open a new type of restaurant in town may obtain the best location. This is considered to be one of the advantages exploited by Wal-Mart when they were the first to locate discount stores in small towns. Other resources that a first entrant may be able to control include a supply of raw materials needed to make the product, or access to shelf space at the supermarket. First-mover firms also have the opportunity to build resources that may discourage entry by other companies. For example, the first mover may increase production capacity or broaden their product line, signaling that there is not enough room for followers to enter and profit.

BUYER-SWITCHING COSTS

The final type of benefit that first movers may enjoy comes from buyer-switching costs. If it is costly or inconvenient for a customer to switch to a new brand, the first company to gain the customer will have an advantage. Switching costs include adapting to a new product (e.g., employee training), and penalties associated with breaking a long-term contract. Especially for consumer products, the first mover has the opportunity to shape consumer preferences. The first company to offer a product of acceptable quality may earn brand loyalty. Satisfied consumers tend not to spend time seeking information about other products, and tend to avoid the risk of being dissatisfied if they switch. The pioneering brands in many product categories, such as Coca-Cola soft drinks and Kleenex facial tissues, often dominate their markets for a long time. These brand preferences appear to be more important for products purchased by consumers than for products purchased by businesses. Businesses buy products in larger volume and have more incentive to search for information about lower-cost options.

UNCERTAINTY OF FIRST-MOVER ADVANTAGE

Three types of benefits—technology leadership, control of resources, and buyer switching costs—can provide long-lasting first-mover advantages. However, researchers believe that in many industries, companies entering later can overcome these advantages. Sometimes there are even first-mover disadvantages, or advantages enjoyed by companies who enter later. For example, the first entrant may invest heavily in enticing customers to try a new type of product. Later entrants would benefit from informed buyers without having to spend as much on education. Later entrants may be able to avoid mistakes made by the first movers. If first movers become complacent, later entrants may take advantage of changing customer needs. As the Internet continues to develop, technology companies find themselves especially susceptible to second- or later-mover success. Follower companies are reverse-engineering many new products to develop competing products either faster or cheaper—negating much of the first-mover advantage.

Researchers are continuing to learn under what conditions first-mover advantages are most likely to occur. They are looking for differences across industries and geographic markets. For example, consumer product markets appear to offer more first-mover advantages than industrial markets, but more research is needed on service industries. Little is known about first-mover effects in countries other than the United States, though some evidence suggests that pioneering advantages may be stronger in other countries. Another important factor appears to be the ability of the first-mover firm to use their other resources to maintain the initial advantage of being first. For example, a firm that is already strong in marketing and distribution may be better able to sustain a lead with a new product than a newly-formed company. Researchers are also studying successful follower strategies.

Given the uncertainty about when first-mover advantages occur, companies need to carefully consider their strategy. Does the firm want to invest in seeking opportunities to be first? If opportunities arise, what is the best approach to market timing? Which of the three types of benefits are likely to be available to the first entrant in this market? Does the firm have the resources to sustain any initial benefits they gain from being first? If someone else enters first, how difficult will it be to follow? What advantages might later entry provide in better or lower-cost technology, or better adaptation to customer needs? Although first-mover advantages may be attractive, there are also advantages to being a follower. Company strategists need to decide which approach has the highest potential for long-term profits given their resources and market characteristics.

SEE ALSO: New Product Development; Product Life Cycle and Industry Life Cycle

Deborah R. Ettington
Revised by Hal P. Kirkwood, Jr.

FURTHER READING:

Boulding, William, and Markus Christen. "Sustainable Pioneering Advantage? Profit Implications of Market Entry Order." *Marketing Science* 22, no. 3 (2003): 371–392.

Kerin, Roger, P.R. Varadarajan, and Robert Peterson. "First-Mover Advantage: A Synthesis, Conceptual Framework, and Research Propositions." *Journal of Marketing* 56, no. 4 (1996): 33–52.

Lieberman, Marvin B., and David B. Montgomery. "First-Mover Advantages." *Strategic Management Journal* 9 (1998): 41–58.

————. "First-Mover (Dis)advantages: Retrospective and Link with the Resource-Based View." *Strategic Management Journal* 19, no. 12 (1998): 1111–1125.

Mittal, Sharad, and Sanjeev Swami. "What Factors Influence Pioneering Advantage of Companies?" *Vikalpa: The Journal for Decision Makers* 29, no. 3 (2004): 15–33.

Mueller, Dennis C. "First-Mover Advantage and Path Dependence." *International Journal of Industrial Organization* 15, no. 6 (1997): 827–850.

Nakata, Cheryl, and Kolachalam Sivakumar. "Emerging Market Conditions and Their Impact on First-Mover Advantages: An Integrative Review." *International Marketing Review* 14, no. 6 (1997): 461–485.

Rahman, Zillur, and Sanjay K. Bhattacharyya. "First Mover Advantages in Emerging Economies: A Discussion." *Management Decision* 41, no. 2 (2003): 141–147.

Robinson, William T., and Sungwook Min. "Is the First to Market the First to Fail? Empirical Evidence for Industrial Goods Businesses." *Journal of Marketing Research (JMR)* 39, no. 1 (2002): 120–129.

Sandberg, K. D. "Rethinking the First-Mover Advantage." *Harvard Management Update* 6, no. 5 (2001): 1–5.

FIVE S FRAMEWORK

The 5S framework was originally developed by just-in-time expert and international consultant Hiroyuki Hirano. The 5S framework is an extension of Hirano's earlier works on just-in-time production systems. The 5Ss represent a simple "good housekeeping" approach to improving the work environment consistent with the tenets of lean manufacturing systems. The focus on the concept is how the visual workplace can be utilized to drive inefficiencies out of the manufacturing process. This framework also improves workplace safety, which makes it attractive to businesses. According to Hirano, without the organization and discipline provided by successfully implementing the 5Ss, other lean manufacturing tools and methods are likely to fail. The "5Ss" stand for the Japanese words seiri, seiton, seiso, seiketsu, and shitsuke. These Japanese "S" words roughly translate into the English words organization, orderliness, cleanliness, standardized cleanup, and discipline. Alternative corresponding "Ss" have also been developed for the English language: sort, set in order, shine, standardize, and sustain.

Seiri, or sort, focuses upon reducing the amount of rarely used material or tools that tend to attract clutter. Only those things required for immediate production should be retained in the work area. *Seiton,* or orderliness, facilitates the reduction of clutter and efficient access to material or tools by following the old adage "a place for everything and everything in its place." Workers readily know when a tool is missing due to a visual signals (e.g., empty space on a signboard). *Seiso,* or cleanliness, focuses upon keeping the workplace, machinery, and tools clean. This includes keeping tools and machinery calibrated, performing preventive maintenance and the use of visual cues to signal when maintenance is needed. *Seiketsu,* or standardized cleanup, is essentially the condition that occurs when the first three pillars—the first 3Ss—are implemented well. However, it also includes institutionalizing the first three pillars. This includes developing rules, processes and procedures to ensure continuity and uniformity of achievements accrued by the first three pillars do not erode over time. Finally, *shitsuke,* or discipline, focuses upon putting procedures into place that sustain the psychological meaningfulness of the payoffs achieved by the overall framework. This may include periodic rewards for workers who excel in some facet of the framework or other visual signals that communicate the commitment of management to the continued implementation of 5S.

Use of color is a primary tool of the visual workplace. Examples include color-coded connections to mistake-proof and speed connections of all sorts of parts and colored boundary markers on shop floors. Information sharing is also an important aspect of the visual workplace. For example, processes can be designed to provide visual signals indicating that certain activities need to occur (e.g., empty inventory space on floor), or communicate productivity standards and output.

In recent years, many companies have utilized the simple guidelines provided by the 5S framework. However, implementing the framework is not always a simple task. It may require redesigning processes or buying new more reliable machinery. This difficulty has given rise to a burgeoning consulting business designed to help firms implement the 5S system including process design as well as employee training. Interestingly, while there appears to be a wide variety of firms utilizing the 5S framework, as of 2005, there is no published empirical research supporting its utility. There does however, appear to be some anecdotal evidence supporting the efficacy of the 5S framework.

SEE ALSO: Japanese Management; Lean Manufacturing and Just-in-Time Production; Quality and Total Quality Management

Jerry Bryan Fuller

FURTHER READING:

Doehrman, Marylou. "The Fives in 5S Apply to Every Industry." *Colorado Springs Business Journal,* February 2005.

Gerard, Alexis, and Bob Goldstein. *Going Visual: Using Images to Enhance Productivity, Decision Making, and Profits.* Hoboken, NJ: John Wiley & Sons, 2005.

Hirano, Hiroyuki. *5 Pillars of the Visual Workplace: The Source Book for 5S Implementation.* New York: Productivity Press, 1996.

Jusko, Jill. "Seeing is Believing: The Collins-Aikman Athens, Tennessee Operations Relies on Visual Signals, Good Housekeeping and Teamwork to Drive Its Lean Manufacturing Imperative." *Industry Week,* October 2002.

FLEXIBLE BENEFITS

SEE: Cafeteria Plan—Flexible Benefits

FLEXIBLE MANUFACTURING

Business firms generally choose to compete within one or two areas of strength. These areas of strength are often referred to as distinctive competencies, core competencies, or competitive priorities. Among the options for competition are price (cost), quality, delivery, service, and flexibility. An ever-increasing number of firms are choosing to compete in the area of flexibility. Generally, this has meant that the firm's major strength is flexibility of product (able to easily make changes in the product) or flexibility of volume (able to easily absorb large shifts in demand). Firms that are able to do this are said to have flexible capacity, the ability to operate manufacturing equipment at different production rates by varying staffing levels and operating hours, or starting and stopping at will. Specifically, manufacturing flexibility consists of three components: (1) the flexibility to produce a variety of products using the same machines and to produce the same products on different machines; (2) the flexibility to produce new products on existing machines; and (3) the flexibility of the machines to accommodate changes in the design of products.

FLEXIBLE MANUFACTURING SYSTEMS

A flexible manufacturing system (FMS) is a group of numerically-controlled machine tools, interconnected by a central control system. The various machining cells are interconnected, via loading and unloading stations, by an automated transport system. Operational flexibility is enhanced by the ability to execute all manufacturing tasks on numerous product designs in small quantities and with faster delivery. It has been described as an automated job shop and as a miniature automated factory. Simply stated, it is an automated production system that produces one or more families of parts in a flexible manner. Today, this prospect of automation and flexibility presents the possibility of producing nonstandard parts to create a competitive advantage.

The concept of flexible manufacturing systems evolved during the 1960s when robots, programmable controllers, and computerized numerical controls brought a controlled environment to the factory floor in the form of numerically-controlled and direct-numerically-controlled machines.

For the most part, FMS is limited to firms involved in batch production or job shop environments. Normally, batch producers have two kinds of equipment from which to choose: dedicated machinery or unautomated, general-purpose tools. Dedicated machinery results in cost savings but lacks flexibility. General purpose machines such as lathes, milling machines, or drill presses are all costly, and may not reach full capacity. Flexible manufacturing systems provide the batch manufacturer with another option—one that can make batch manufacturing just as efficient and productive as mass production.

OBJECTIVES OF FMS

Stated formally, the general objectives of an FMS are to approach the efficiencies and economies of scale normally associated with mass production, and to maintain the flexibility required for small- and medium-lot-size production of a variety of parts.

Two kinds of manufacturing systems fall within the FMS spectrum. These are assembly systems, which assemble components into final products and forming systems, which actually form components or final products. A generic FMS is said to consist of the following components:

1. A set of work stations containing machine tools that do not require significant set-up time or change-over between successive jobs. Typically, these machines perform milling, boring, drilling, tapping, reaming, turning, and grooving operations.

2. A material-handling system that is automated and flexible in that it permits jobs to move between any pair of machines so that any job routing can be followed.

3. A network of supervisory computers and microprocessors that perform some or all of the following tasks: (a) directs the routing of jobs through the system; (b) tracks the status of all jobs in progress so it is known where each job is to go next; (c) passes the instructions for the processing of each operation to each station and ensures that the right tools are available for the job; and (d) provides essential monitoring of the correct performance of operations and signals problems requiring attention.

4. Storage, locally at the work stations, and/or centrally at the system level.

5. The jobs to be processed by the system. In operating an FMS, the worker enters the job to be run at the supervisory computer, which then downloads the part programs to the cell control or NC controller.

BENEFITS OF FMS

The potential benefits from the implementation and utilization of a flexible manufacturing system have been detailed by numerous researchers on the subject. A review of the literature reveals many tangible and intangible benefits that FMS users extol. These benefits include:

- less waste
- fewer workstations
- quicker changes of tools, dies, and stamping machinery
- reduced downtime
- better control over quality
- reduced labor
- more efficient use of machinery

- work-in-process inventory reduced
- increased capacity
- increased production flexibility

The savings from these benefits can be sizable. Enough so that Ford has poured $4,400,000 into over-hauling its Torrence Avenue plant in Chicago, giving it flexible manufacturing capability. This will allow the factory to add new models in as little as two weeks instead of two months or longer. Richard Truett reports, in *Automotive News,* that the flexible manufacturing systems used in five of Ford Motor Company's plants will yield a $2.5 billion savings. Truett also reports that, by the year 2010, Ford will have converted 80 percent of its plants to flexible manufacturing.

LIMITATIONS OF FMS

Despite these benefits, FMS does have certain limitations. In particular, this type of system can only handle a relatively-narrow range of part varieties, so it must be used for similar parts (family of parts) that require similar processing. Due to increased complexity and cost, an FMS also requires a longer planning and development period than traditional manufacturing equipment.

Equipment utilization for the FMS sometimes is not as high as one would expect. Japanese firms tend to have a much higher equipment utilization rate than U.S. manufacturers utilizing FMS. This is probably a result of U.S. users' attempt to utilize FMS for high-volume production of a few parts rather than for a high-variety production of many parts at a low cost per unit. U.S. firms average ten types of parts per machine, compared to ninety-three types of parts per machine in Japan.

Other problems can result from a lack of technical literacy, management incompetence, and poor implementation of the FMS process. If the firm misidentifies its objectives and manufacturing mission, and does not maintain a manufacturing strategy that is consistent with the firm's overall strategy, problems are inevitable. It is crucial that a firm's technology acquisition decisions be consistent with its manufacturing strategy.

If a firm chooses to compete on the basis of flexibility rather than cost or quality, it may be a candidate for flexible manufacturing, especially if it is suited for low- to mid-volume production. This is particularly true if the firm is in an industry where products change rapidly, and the ability to introduce new products may be more important than minimizing cost. In this scenario, scale is no longer the main concern and size is no longer a barrier to entry.

However, an FMS may not be appropriate for some firms. Since new technology is costly and requires several years to install and become productive, it requires a supportive infrastructure and the allocation of scarce resources for implementation. Frankly, many firms do not possess the necessary resources. Economically justifying an FMS can be a difficult task—especially since cost accounting tends to be designed for mass production of a mature product, with known characteristics, and a stable technology. Therefore, it is difficult to give an accurate indication of whether flexible manufacturing is justified. The question remains of how to quantify the benefits of flexibility. In addition, rapidly-changing technology and shortened product life cycles can cause capital equipment to quickly become obsolete.

For other firms, their products may not require processes at the technological level of an FMS. IBM found that a redesigned printer was simple enough for high-quality manual assembly and that the manual assembly could be achieved at a lower cost than automated assembly. Potential FMS users should also consider that some of the costs traditionally incurred in manufacturing may actually be higher in a flexible automated system than in conventional manufacturing. Although the system is continually self-monitoring, maintenance costs are expected to be higher. Energy costs are likely to be higher despite more efficient use of energy. Increased machine utilization can result in faster deterioration of equipment, providing a shorter than average economic life. Finally, personnel training costs may prove to be relatively high.

For some firms, worker resistance is a problem. Workers tend to perceive automation as an effort to replace them with a tireless piece of metal that does not eat, take breaks, or go to the bathroom. To combat this perception, many firms stress that workers are upgraded as a result of FMS installation, and that no loss of jobs ensues. Despite any problems, use of flexible manufacturing systems should continue to grow as more firms are forced to compete on a flexibility basis and as technology advances. It has shown many advantages in low- to mid-volume, high-mix production applications. Future systems will probably see lower and lower quantities per batch. FMS can somewhat shift emphasis in manufacturing from large-scale, repetitive production of standard products to highly-automated job shops featuring the manufacture of items in small batches for specific customers. The increased availability of flexible manufacturing technology will also give multi-product firms more choices of how to design production facilities, how to assign products to facilities, and how to share capacity among products.

BEYOND FLEXIBLE MANUFACTURING: AGILE MANUFACTURING

Fliedner and Vokurka, in their *Production and Inventory Management Journal* article on agile manufacturing, define agile manufacturing as the ability to successfully market low-cost, high-quality products with short lead times (and in varying volumes) that provide enhanced customer value through customization. An agile firm manages change as a matter of routine. The difference between agility and flexibility is whether or not the change in market demand has been predicted. Flexibility refers to the capability of rapidly changing from one task to another when changing conditions are defined ahead of time. Agility refers to the ability to respond quickly to unanticipated marketplace changes. Fliedner and Vokurka present four, key dimensions of agile competition:

1. Enriching the customer. This requires a quick understanding of the unique requirements of individual customers and rapidly meeting those requirements.

2. Cooperating to enhance competitiveness. This includes better intraorganizational cooperation and may extend to interorganizational cooperation—such as supplier partnerships and virtual relationships.

3. Organizing to master change and uncertainty. This involves utilizing new organizational structures provided by such techniques as concurrent engineering and cross-functional teams.

4. Leveraging the impact of people and information. This places great emphasis on the development of employees through education, training, and empowerment.

IMPLEMENTING AGILE MANUFACTURING

Finally, the two authors prescribe a series of internal and external initiatives for successful implementation of agile manufacturing. The internal initiatives include the following:

1. Business process reengineering. This is the rethinking and radical redesign of business processes so that dramatic improvements in critical areas can be achieved.

2. Management planning and execution tools. This involves the use of such techniques as manufacturing resource planning, real-time manufacturing execution systems, production planning configurators, and real-time threaded scheduling.

3. Design for manufacturability/assembly. The results include modular products that allow for future upgrades, fewer parts for enhanced reliability, and recycling.

4. Reorganization processes. Process reorganization could include the use of flexible manufacturing systems or cellular manufacturing.

5. Intraorganizational cooperation. This form of cooperation calls for the use of employee empowerment/involvement techniques and employee education and training.

External initiatives include:

1. Interorganizational cooperation. This means early supplier involvement in product and process designs, training suppliers in such activities as vendor-managed inventories, and joint research efforts.

2. Supply chain practices. The use of outsourcing, schedule sharing, and postponement of product design are included.

3. Information technology. Some companies are using technology to improve supply chain improvement. For example, the move from centralized, mainframe computing to decentralized, client and server computing.

4. Point-of-sale data collection. Reductions in order entry time are being achieved with electronic data interchange (EDI), radio frequency communications tools, bar coding, and electronic commerce.

The authors feel that flexibility provided by agility may emerge as the most important competitive priority of the early twenty-first century, as competition is expected to ensure that manufacturers will increasingly need to adapt readily to market shifts. Ford Motor Company has reportedly invested $350 million in new, agile manufacturing equipment at its Cleveland Engine Plant. A Ford Vice President describes the move as the heart of lean manufacturing.

SEE ALSO: Cellular Manufacturing; Economies of Scale and Economies of Scope; Lean Manufacturing and Just-in-Time Production

R. Anthony Inman

FURTHER READING:

Chandra, Charu, Mark Everson, and Janis Grabis. "Evaluation of Enterprise-Level Benefits of Manufacturing Flexibility." *Omega* 33, no. 1 (2005): 17–31.

Fliedner, Gene, and Robert J. Vokurka. "Agility: Competitive Weapon of the 1990s and Beyond." *Production and Inventory Management Journal* 38, no. 3 (1997): 19–24.

"Ford Furthers Flexible Manufacturing Effort." *Manufacturing Engineering* 133, no. 1 (2004): 27.

Popely, Rick. "Ford Upgrades Chicago Plant to Meet Need for 'Flexible Manufacturing.'" *Knight Ridder Tribune Business News,* 9 June 2004.

Schonfeld, Erick. "The Customized, Digitized, Have-It-Your-Way Economy." *Fortune,* 28 September 1998, 114–124.

Truett, Richard. "Ford's Flexibility Reaps Rich Reward." *Automotive News* 78, no. 6106 (2004): 17.

Tseng, Mei-Chiun. "Strategic Choice of Flexible Manufacturing Technologies." *International Journal of Production Economics* 91, no. 3 (2004): 223–227.

FLEXIBLE SPENDING ACCOUNTS

Flexible spending accounts (FSAs), sometimes called reimbursement accounts, are accounts set up by employers. These accounts allow employees to make annual, pre-tax contributions that can be used to pay for certain health care and dependent care expenses that are not paid for by insurance companies. FSAs are offered under the umbrella of cafeteria benefit plans and are sometimes called cafeteria plans. FSAs must comply with all applicable rules and regulations governing benefits under cafeteria plans.

FLEXIBLE SPENDING ACCOUNTS IN PRACTICE

Employers must establish flexible spending accounts so that they comply with all applicable federal legislation. Once an FSA is established, employees have the opportunity to sign up for the plan during the annual "open enrollment" period. During the sign-up period that precedes the plan year, employees must estimate the relevant costs they are likely to incur during the year and indicate the amount of money they want set aside in the FSA for the year. Usually, the money is set aside using regular payroll deductions from the employee's paychecks. The deductions from employees' wages are pre-tax, thus reducing the employee's tax liability. Employees must carefully consider the amount they elect to contribute to the FSA, because amounts unused at the end of the plan year cannot be carried over to the next year and are forfeited by the employee if a balance remains at the end of the year. There is no legal limit to the annual amount that can be set aside, but employers can set their own limit if they wish.

As employees incur eligible expenses throughout the plan year, they must obtain and retain all receipts and documentation. Employees then provide required documentation that they have incurred eligible expenses (usually by providing receipts for the expenditures) and are reimbursed from the accumulated money in their account. Employees can turn in requests for reimbursement throughout the plan year or save all their documentation and turn in their request at the end of the plan year. Utilizing a flexible spending account requires employees to carefully plan and estimate their expenses. Flexible spending accounts can result in tax savings for both employers and participating employees, and can also result in greater understanding on the part of employees as to the cost of their health care and their responsibility for planning and budgeting to meet the cost. Recent innovations in FSAs include the introduction of debit cards by some employers. These debit cards allow employees to obtain immediate reimbursement for eligible expenses rather than compiling receipts and documentation, submitting the paperwork, and waiting for the employer to cut them a check.

EXPENSES ELIGIBLE FOR COVERAGE UNDER FSAS

Flexible spending accounts can be used to pay for eligible costs related to health care and dependent care for children or elderly parents. FSAs cover insurance premiums, deductibles, co-payments, prescription drugs, and many health-related expenses not covered by an employee's health insurance. For example, employees can pay for procedures and items such as laser eye surgery, orthodontia, hearing aids, and contact lenses with their FSAs. Flexible spending accounts can also be used to pay for certain expenses related to child and elder care. In 2003, the government expanded the drug coverage under FSAs to include certain types of over-the-counter drugs, such as pain relievers, cold medicines, nicotine patches, and allergy medications.

ORIGINATION OF FLEXIBLE SPENDING ACCOUNTS

The United States Congress passed Internal Revenue Code Section 125 in the late 1970s. Section 125 allows employers to offer cafeteria plans to their employees. Such a plan allows employees to choose, from among a menu of optional benefits, those that best fit their individual needs; thus, employees can customize their benefit packages. To be in compliance with Section 125, all the participants in the plan must be employees and the plan must allow employees to choose among cash and qualified benefits. When an employee elects to receive an optional benefit under a cafeteria plan, there are tax advantages to both the employer and employee. Since the employee's taxable income is reduced, the employer pays less Federal Insurance Contributions Act (FICA) tax. The employee subsequently pays less FICA and state/federal income tax. Employees' choices of optional benefits are limited only by the total benefit dollars available and the variety of benefits offered by the employer. Benefits that can be included in a Section 125 cafeteria plan include, among others:

- Group-term life insurance that meets certain guidelines

- Health insurance and/or accident insurance

- Legal services

- Deferred compensation plans, such as 401(k)s

- Flexible spending accounts for health care or dependent care expenses

Although flexible spending accounts have been available since the enactment of Section 125 in the late 1970s, for many years employers didn't offer them and only a small percentage of eligible employees utilized them. There were various reasons for their lack of popularity. Employers were initially put off by what they perceived as the complexity and administrative costs associated with cafeteria plans in general, and flexible spending accounts in particular. Employees were reluctant to participate because of the forfeiture rule, which requires a participating employee to "use or lose" the funds set aside in the FSA each year. The advent and spread of managed care plans, such as health maintenance organizations (HMOs) and preferred provider organizations (PPOs) in the 1980s and 1990s, also hampered the growth of flexible spending accounts. Managed care plans often included a low (or no) deductible, low co-payments, and coverage for preventive care. Employees' "out-of-pocket" health care expenses were often reduced; thus there was less incentive for employees to set aside money to cover non-reimbursed medical or dependent care expenses.

Rising health care costs and dissatisfaction with managed care plans in the 1990s and early 2000s however, caused many organizations to look for ways to cut health care costs. Many found it necessary to raise the premiums employees pay for health insurance, the deductible employees pay before health expenditures are covered, and the co-payments that employees pay once deductibles are met. Thus, employees' out-of-pocket expenses rose. The flexible spending account offers a way for employees to cover some of these extra expenses with pre-tax dollars, which lowers their out-of-pocket expenses. For example, if an employee had $2,500 a year of non-reimbursed medical expenses, and an FSA plan, they could set aside this amount from pre-tax earnings. Depending on the employee's overall tax rate, this could save the employee 25 to 35 percent in state and federal taxes, in addition to FICA savings. Employers offering FSAs also benefit, because employee contributions to an FSA reduce the amount of FICA taxes employers pay on their behalf. Because of this, a large percentage of employers now offer FSAs and similar types of accounts such as medical savings accounts and health savings accounts, with a large percentage of eligible employees taking part in this benefit.

A 2004 survey by the Society for Human Resource Management found that over 70 percent of member organizations offer flexible spending accounts as part of a cafeteria benefits plan. Small employers however, are much less likely to offer such plans. For example, one Bureau of Labor Statistics report estimated that only 4 percent of employers with fewer than 100 employees offer flexible spending accounts.

DIFFERENCES BETWEEN FLEXIBLE SPENDING ACCOUNTS AND HEALTH SAVINGS ACCOUNTS

Flexible spending accounts are similar to, but very different from, health savings accounts (HSAs). Flexible spending accounts have been available since the 1970s, although they have not always been widely utilized. Health savings accounts were created in 2003. Flexible spending accounts can be offered in conjunction with just about any type of medical insurance coverage because they are designed to cover expenses not otherwise covered. Health savings accounts, on the other hand, can only be offered as part of a "high deductible" insurance plan. The high-deductible plan must have a minimum $1,000 deductible for single employees and a $2,000 deductible for families. In addition, flexible spending plans basically allow employees to contribute up to an employer-specified maximum to their FSA each year. HSAs, limit employee contributions to the amount of the deductible in their health insurance plan. The contribution levels were initially capped at $2,600 for single employees and $5,150 for families. The deductible and contribution limits will increase over time, as they are tied to measures of inflation.

Perhaps the largest difference between flexible spending accounts and health savings accounts is in the way unused funds in the accounts are handled. Funds left unused in the FSA after the plan year ends are forfeited by the employee, which accounts for the largest drawback to their use. Health savings account contributions, in contrast, can be rolled over from year to year; thus, amounts left unused in one plan year can be applied to expenses incurred in a successive year. This is a major advantage of HSAs as opposed to FSAs.

Employers will likely continue to offer flexible spending accounts as a means to allow employees to better manage their health-care expenditures. However, the advent of health savings accounts in 2003, and another recent innovation—the health reimbursement account (HRA)—have both increased and complicated the choices available to employers and employees. Employers have the difficult choice of which plan to offer to employees, and employees have a difficult choice as to which of these plans best fit their needs. The federal government has provided guidance and illustration to employers to help them see the advantages and disadvantages of each plan. Employers have

the responsibility of fully communicating to employees the range of options available to them and the strengths and weaknesses of each. The Human Resources department in the organization should take the lead in educating employees as to the opportunities available to them so that employees can make informed choices as they attempt to maintain quality health coverage at an affordable cost.

SEE ALSO: Employee Benefits; Health Savings Accounts

Tim Barnett

FURTHER READING:

Gomez-Mejia, Luis R., David B. Balkin, and Robert L. Cardy. *Managing Human Resources.* 4th ed. Upper Saddle River, NJ: Prentice-Hall, 2004.

Gordon, Pat H., and Helen Box-Farnen. "Health Care Flexible Spending Accounts: An Old Benefit with New Appeal." *Compensation & Benefits Review* 36, no. 3 (2004): 38–44.

Henderson, Richard L. *Compensation Management in a Knowledge-Based World.* 9th ed. Upper Saddle River, NJ: Prentice-Hall, 2003.

Roberts, Sally. "Employers Seek Optimal Approach to Stacking Health Care Accounts." *Business Insurance* 39, no. 6 (2005): 1–4.

Zinkewicz, Phil. "Tax-Favored Flexible Savings Accounts (FSAs)...A Lid on Employer Health Costs." *Insurance Advocate* 114, no. 39 (2003): 2.

FOCUSED FACTORY

The term *focused factory,* was introduced in a 1974 *Harvard Business Review* article authored by Wickham Skinner. Responding to what the popular press called a "productivity crisis," Skinner introduced his solution to the problem. Skinner conducted a study of approximately fifty companies and found that the problem was not only productivity, but also the ability to compete. Manufacturing policies had not been designed, tuned, and focused (as a whole) on that one, key, strategic, manufacturing task essential to the company's success. Skinner urged manufacturers to learn to focus each plant on a limited, concise, manageable set of products, technologies, volumes, and markets. He also encouraged firms to learn to structure basic manufacturing policies and supporting services so that they focus on one, specific, manufacturing task instead of upon many inconsistent, conflicting, or implicit tasks.

Often, a conventional factory produces many products for many customers in many markets. This requires a multitude of simultaneous tasks from one group of resources. Managers in these plants may be striving for economies of scale and lower capital investment. Instead, they may end up with a hodgepodge of compromises, according to the focused-factory notion. Rather than designing the manufacturing policy around one, specific task, many possibly-contradictory objectives may coexist. The wage system may be established with an emphasis on high productivity, while production control may favor short lead times. Meanwhile, inventory control may want to minimize inventory levels, which means low order quantities. Production wants minimum setup time, which means large order quantities; all the while, plant engineers may want a plant layout that minimizes material handling and process design, which maximizes quality.

One way to compete effectively is to focus the entire manufacturing system on a limited task that is precisely defined by the company's strategy and its technological and economic limitations. A common objective can produce synergistic effects while minimizing power struggles between the departments. In his article, Skinner recommended that firms:

- Centralize the factory's focus on relative competitive ability.

- Avoid the common tendency to add staff and overhead in order to save on direct labor and capital investment.

- Let each manufacturing unit work on a limited task instead of the usual, complex mix of conflicting objectives, products, and technologies.

A factory focused on a narrow product mix for a particular market niche will outperform a conventional plant with a broad mission.

Because its equipment, supporting systems, and procedures can concentrate on a limited task for one set of customers, its overhead and other costs are likely to be lower than those of a conventional factory. A focused plant can become a competitive weapon because all its resources are focused on accomplishing the limited manufacturing task dictated by the company's overall strategy and marketing objectives. Simplicity, repetition, experience, and homogeneity of tasks breed competence. Remember, each key function area in manufacturing must have the same objective, one that is derived from corporate strategy. This task congruence can produce a manufacturing system that performs a limited number of tasks very well, thus creating a formidable competitive weapon.

If a firm wants to produce a number of entirely-different products with different technologies, markets, or volumes, it should do so in a number of separate plants. The implication here is the need for investment in new plants, new equipment, new tool-ing, training, and so forth—not the most practical idea for most firms. A more practical approach is Skinner's concept of a "plant within a plant," or PWP. Factories utilizing PWPs divide an existing facility, both physically and organizationally, into a number of PWPs. Each PWP has its own facilities within which to concentrate on its particular manufacturing task, use its own workforce approaches, production control, organizational structure, and so on.

The predicted results are as follows:

- Quality and volume are not mixed.

- Worker training and incentives have a clear focus.

- Engineering of processes, equipment, and materials handling are specialized as needed.

In an *Industry Week* Census of Manufacturers, a survey of the manufacturing practices currently most in favor among U.S. manufacturers, George Taninecz cross-tabulated plant practices against plant performance to determine practices most likely to produce the best performance. Of the plants, 61 percent surveyed had adopted a focused-factory approach that grouped employees, equipment, and support staff (engineering and marketing) into self-sustained operations. Focused factories reported major cuts in cycle time and better on-time delivery rates. Of the focused factories, 18.5 percent reduced cycle time by more than 50 percent over the previous five years, while 46 percent improved cycle time by more than 20 percent. A small number of practices showed strong correlation with productivity and cost reductions—among these was the focused factory approach.

The focused-factory concept is not limited to manufacturing only, but can be applied in service environments such as health care. From an inpatient perspective, witness the increase in specialty hospitals where staff, equipment and management attention is dedicated to one, particular type of disease or ailment. The current increase of ambulatory surgery centers (ASC) validates the use of a focused factory for outpatient care. Within the ASC, surgical equipment, staff, and scheduling are dedicated to a relatively-narrow range of procedures rather than being multipurpose. Fewer emergency interruptions and less down time between procedures allow physicians to perform more procedures within a given time frame. One example of focused-factory adoption is the Shouldice Hospital in Toronto, which performs only abdominal hernia operations. Eventually, we may observe facilities no longer organized by medical specialty but for the total needs of the patient. Focused factories are also cropping up in rehabilitation, long-term acute care, neonatal intensive care, cancer, AIDS, and orthopedic facilities.

Little empirical support has been offered to support the claims made by advocates of the focused factory.

However, a recent study by Robert Vokurka and Robert Davis found that focused plants have fewer final products with more standardization, and fewer variations, resulting in fewer required setups. They also found focused factories to have better flow, more automation, and less variation in customer delivery. The combination of these benefits then results in the need for fewer supporting staff. Vokurka and Davis also found focused factories to be superior to unfocused plants on such performance indicators as cost, quality, dependability, and speed. Of more significance was their finding that focused factories were superior in all financial measures—including profitability levels, returns, and growth. From a service perspective, a recent survey by Casalino, Devers, and Brewster found that specialized health care facilities experienced increased productivity and quality and decreased costs.

SEE ALSO: Product-Process Matrix; Strategy Formulation

R. Anthony Inman

FURTHER READING:

Casalino, Lawrence P., Kelly J. Devers, and Linda R. Brewster. "Focused Factories? Physician-Owned Specialty Facilities." *Health Affairs* 22, no. 6 (2003): 56.

Skinner, Wickham. "The Focused Factory." *Harvard Business Review* 52 (1974): 113–121.

Taninecz, George. "Best Practices & Performances." *Industry Week* 246, no. 22 (1997): 28–43.

Vokurka, Robert J., and Robert A. Davis. "Focused Factories: Empirical Study of Structural and Performance Differences." *Production and Inventory Management Journal* 41, no. 1 (2000): 44–55.

FORECASTING

Forecasting involves the generation of a number, set of numbers, or scenario that corresponds to a future occurrence. It is absolutely essential to short-range and long-range planning. By definition, a forecast is based on past data, as opposed to a prediction, which is more subjective and based on instinct, gut feel, or guess. For example, the evening news gives the weather "forecast" not the weather "prediction." Regardless, the terms forecast and prediction are often used interchangeably. For example, definitions of regression—a technique sometimes used in forecasting—generally state that its purpose is to explain or "predict."

Forecasting is based on a number of assumptions:

1. The past will repeat itself. In other words, what has happened in the past will happen again in the future.

2. As the forecast horizon shortens, forecast accuracy increases. For instance, a forecast for tomorrow will be more accurate than a forecast for next month; a forecast for next month will be more accurate than a forecast for next year; and a forecast for next year will be more accurate than a forecast for ten years in the future.

3. Forecasting in the aggregate is more accurate than forecasting individual items. This means that a company will be able to forecast total demand over its entire spectrum of products more accurately than it will be able to forecast individual stock-keeping units (SKUs). For example, General Motors can more accurately forecast the total number of cars needed for next year than the total number of white Chevrolet Impalas with a certain option package.

4. Forecasts are seldom accurate. Furthermore, forecasts are almost never totally accurate. While some are very close, few are "right on the money." Therefore, it is wise to offer a forecast "range." If one were to forecast a demand of 100,000 units for the next month, it is extremely unlikely that demand would equal 100,000 exactly. However, a forecast of 90,000 to 110,000 would provide a much larger target for planning.

William J. Stevenson lists a number of characteristics that are common to a good forecast:

- Accurate—some degree of accuracy should be determined and stated so that comparison can be made to alternative forecasts.

- Reliable—the forecast method should consistently provide a good forecast if the user is to establish some degree of confidence.

- Timely—a certain amount of time is needed to respond to the forecast so the forecasting horizon must allow for the time necessary to make changes.

- Easy to use and understand—users of the forecast must be confident and comfortable working with it.

- Cost-effective—the cost of making the forecast should not outweigh the benefits obtained from the forecast.

Forecasting techniques range from the simple to the extremely complex. These techniques are usually classified as being qualitative or quantitative.

QUALITATIVE TECHNIQUES

Qualitative forecasting techniques are generally more subjective than their quantitative counterparts. Qualitative techniques are more useful in the earlier stages of the product life cycle, when less past data exists for use in quantitative methods. Qualitative methods include the Delphi technique, Nominal Group Technique (NGT), sales force opinions, executive opinions, and market research.

THE DELPHI TECHNIQUE. The Delphi technique uses a panel of experts to produce a forecast. Each expert is asked to provide a forecast specific to the need at hand. After the initial forecasts are made, each expert reads what every other expert wrote and is, of course, influenced by their views. A subsequent forecast is then made by each expert. Each expert then reads again what every other expert wrote and is again influenced by the perceptions of the others. This process repeats itself until each expert nears agreement on the needed scenario or numbers.

NOMINAL GROUP TECHNIQUE. Nominal Group Technique is similar to the Delphi technique in that it utilizes a group of participants, usually experts. After the participants respond to forecast-related questions, they rank their responses in order of perceived relative importance. Then the rankings are collected and aggregated. Eventually, the group should reach a consensus regarding the priorities of the ranked issues.

SALES FORCE OPINIONS. The sales staff is often a good source of information regarding future demand. The sales manager may ask for input from each salesperson and aggregate their responses into a sales force composite forecast. Caution should be exercised when using this technique as the members of the sales force may not be able to distinguish between what customers say and what they actually do. Also, if the forecasts will be used to establish sales quotas, the sales force may be tempted to provide lower estimates.

EXECUTIVE OPINIONS. Sometimes upper-levels managers meet and develop forecasts based on their knowledge of their areas of responsibility. This is sometimes referred to as a jury of executive opinion.

MARKET RESEARCH. In market research, consumer surveys are used to establish potential demand. Such marketing research usually involves constructing a questionnaire that solicits personal, demographic, economic, and marketing information. On occasion, market researchers collect such information in person at retail outlets and malls, where the consumer can experience—taste, feel, smell, and see—a particular product. The researcher must be careful that the sample of people surveyed is representative of the desired consumer target.

QUANTITATIVE TECHNIQUES

Quantitative forecasting techniques are generally more objective than their qualitative counterparts. Quantitative forecasts can be time-series forecasts (i.e., a projection of the past into the future) or forecasts based on associative models (i.e., based on one or more explanatory variables). Time-series data may have underlying behaviors that need to be identified by the forecaster. In addition, the forecast may need to identify the causes of the behavior. Some of these behaviors may be patterns or simply random variations. Among the patterns are:

- Trends, which are long-term movements (up or down) in the data.

- Seasonality, which produces short-term variations that are usually related to the time of year, month, or even a particular day, as witnessed by retail sales at Christmas or the spikes in banking activity on the first of the month and on Fridays.

- Cycles, which are wavelike variations lasting more than a year that are usually tied to economic or political conditions.

- Irregular variations that do not reflect typical behavior, such as a period of extreme weather or a union strike.

- Random variations, which encompass all non-typical behaviors not accounted for by the other classifications.

Among the time-series models, the simplest is the naïve forecast. A naïve forecast simply uses the actual demand for the past period as the forecasted demand for the next period. This, of course, makes the assumption that the past will repeat. It also assumes that any trends, seasonality, or cycles are either reflected in the previous period's demand or do not exist. An example of naïve forecasting is presented in Table 1.

Table 1 Naïve Forecasting		
Period	**Actual Demand (000's)**	**Forecast (000's)**
January	45	
February	60	45
March	72	60
April	58	72
May	40	58
June		40

Another simple technique is the use of averaging. To make a forecast using averaging, one simply takes the average of some number of periods of past data by summing each period and dividing the result by the number of periods. This technique has been found to be very effective for short-range forecasting.

Variations of averaging include the moving average, the weighted average, and the weighted moving average. A moving average takes a predetermined number of periods, sums their actual demand, and divides by the number of periods to reach a forecast. For each subsequent period, the oldest period of data drops off and the latest period is added. Assuming a three-month moving average and using the data from Table 1, one would simply add 45 (January), 60 (February), and 72 (March) and divide by three to arrive at a forecast for April:

$$45 + 60 + 72 = 177 \div 3 = 59$$

To arrive at a forecast for May, one would drop January's demand from the equation and add the demand from April. Table 2 presents an example of a three-month moving average forecast.

Table 2
Three Month Moving Average Forecast

Period	Actual Demand (000's)	Forecast (000's)
January	45	
February	60	
March	72	
April	58	59
May	40	63
June		57

A weighted average applies a predetermined weight to each month of past data, sums the past data from each period, and divides by the total of the weights. If the forecaster adjusts the weights so that their sum is equal to 1, then the weights are multiplied by the actual demand of each applicable period. The results are then summed to achieve a weighted forecast. Generally, the more recent the data the higher the weight, and the older the data the smaller the weight. Using the demand example, a weighted average using weights of .4, .3, .2, and .1 would yield the forecast for June as:

$$60(.1) + 72(.2) + 58(.3) + 40(.4) = 53.8$$

Forecasters may also use a combination of the weighted average and moving average forecasts. A weighted moving average forecast assigns weights to a predetermined number of periods of actual data and computes the forecast the same way as described above. As with all moving forecasts, as each new period is added, the data from the oldest period is dis-carded. Table 3 shows a three-month weighted moving average forecast utilizing the weights .5, .3, and .2.

Table 3
Three–Month Weighted Moving Average Forecast

Period	Actual Demand (000's)	Forecast (000's)
January	45	
February	60	
March	72	
April	58	55
May	40	63
June		61

A more complex form of weighted moving average is exponential smoothing, so named because the weight falls off exponentially as the data ages. Exponential smoothing takes the previous period's forecast and adjusts it by a predetermined smoothing constant, α (called alpha; the value for alpha is less than one) multiplied by the difference in the previous forecast and the demand that actually occurred during the previously forecasted period (called forecast error). Exponential smoothing is expressed formulaically as such:

$$\text{New forecast} = \text{previous forecast} +$$
$$\text{alpha (actual demand} - \text{previous forecast)}$$
$$F = F + \alpha(A - F)$$

Exponential smoothing requires the forecaster to begin the forecast in a past period and work forward to the period for which a current forecast is needed. A substantial amount of past data and a beginning or initial forecast are also necessary. The initial forecast can be an actual forecast from a previous period, the actual demand from a previous period, or it can be estimated by averaging all or part of the past data. Some heuristics exist for computing an initial forecast. For example, the heuristic $N = (2 \div \alpha) - 1$ and an alpha of .5 would yield an N of 3, indicating the user would average the first three periods of data to get an initial forecast. However, the accuracy of the initial forecast is not critical if one is using large amounts of data, since exponential smoothing is "self-correcting." Given enough periods of past data, exponential smoothing will eventually make enough corrections to compensate for a reasonably inaccurate initial forecast. Using the data used in other examples, an initial forecast of 50, and an alpha of .7, a forecast for February is computed as such:

$$\text{New forecast (February)} = 50 + .7(45 - 50) = 41.5$$

Next, the forecast for March:

$$\text{New forecast (March)} = 41.5 + .7(60 - 41.5) = 54.45$$

This process continues until the forecaster reaches the desired period. In Table 4 this would be for the month of June, since the actual demand for June is not known.

Table 4		
Period	Actual Demand (000's)	Forecast (000's)
January	45	50
February	60	41.5
March	72	54.45
April	58	66.74
May	40	60.62
June		46.19

An extension of exponential smoothing can be used when time-series data exhibits a linear trend. This method is known by several names: double smoothing; trend-adjusted exponential smoothing; forecast including trend (FIT); and Holt's Model. Without adjustment, simple exponential smoothing results will lag the trend, that is, the forecast will always be low if the trend is increasing, or high if the trend is decreasing. With this model there are two smoothing constants, α and β with β representing the trend component.

An extension of Holt's Model, called Holt-Winter's Method, takes into account both trend and seasonality. There are two versions, multiplicative and additive, with the multiplicative being the most widely used. In the additive model, seasonality is expressed as a quantity to be added to or subtracted from the series average. The multiplicative model expresses seasonality as a percentage—known as seasonal relatives or seasonal indexes—of the average (or trend). These are then multiplied times values in order to incorporate seasonality. A relative of 0.8 would indicate demand that is 80 percent of the average, while 1.10 would indicate demand that is 10 percent above the average. Detailed information regarding this method can be found in most operations management textbooks or one of a number of books on forecasting.

Associative or causal techniques involve the identification of variables that can be used to predict another variable of interest. For example, interest rates may be used to forecast the demand for home refinancing. Typically, this involves the use of linear regression, where the objective is to develop an equation that summarizes the effects of the predictor (independent) variables upon the forecasted (dependent) variable. If the predictor variable were plotted, the object would be to obtain an equation of a straight line that minimizes the sum of the squared deviations from

the line (with deviation being the distance from each point to the line). The equation would appear as: $y = a + bx$, where y is the predicted (dependent) variable, x is the predictor (independent) variable, b is the slope of the line, and a is equal to the height of the line at the y-intercept. Once the equation is determined, the user can insert current values for the predictor (independent) variable to arrive at a forecast (dependent variable).

If there is more than one predictor variable or if the relationship between predictor and forecast is not linear, simple linear regression will be inadequate. For situations with multiple predictors, multiple regression should be employed, while non-linear relationships call for the use of curvilinear regression.

ECONOMETRIC FORECASTING

Econometric methods, such as autoregressive integrated moving-average model (ARIMA), use complex mathematical equations to show past relationships between demand and variables that influence the demand. An equation is derived and then tested and fine-tuned to ensure that it is as reliable a representation of the past relationship as possible. Once this is done, projected values of the influencing variables (income, prices, etc.) are inserted into the equation to make a forecast.

EVALUATING FORECASTS

Forecast accuracy can be determined by computing the bias, mean absolute deviation (MAD), mean square error (MSE), or mean absolute percent error (MAPE) for the forecast using different values for alpha. Bias is the sum of the forecast errors [$\Sigma(FE)$]. For the exponential smoothing example above, the computed bias would be:

$$(60 - 41.5) + (72 - 54.45) + (58 - 66.74) + (40 - 60.62) = 6.69$$

If one assumes that a low bias indicates an overall low forecast error, one could compute the bias for a number of potential values of alpha and assume that the one with the lowest bias would be the most accurate. However, caution must be observed in that wildly inaccurate forecasts may yield a low bias if they tend to be both over forecast and under forecast (negative and positive). For example, over three periods a firm may use a particular value of alpha to over forecast by 75,000 units (−75,000), under forecast by 100,000 units (+100,000), and then over forecast by 25,000 units (−25,000), yielding a bias of zero (−75,000 + 100,000 − 25,000 = 0). By comparison, another alpha yielding over forecasts of 2,000 units, 1,000 units, and 3,000 units would result in a bias of 5,000 units. If normal demand was 100,000 units per period, the first alpha would yield forecasts that were off by as much as 100 percent while the second alpha would be off by a maximum of only 3 percent, even though the bias in the first forecast was zero.

A safer measure of forecast accuracy is the mean absolute deviation (MAD). To compute the MAD, the forecaster sums the absolute value of the forecast errors and then divides by the number of forecasts (Σ |FE| $\div$ N). By taking the absolute value of the forecast errors, the offsetting of positive and negative values are avoided. This means that both an over forecast of 50 and an under forecast of 50 are off by 50. Using the data from the exponential smoothing example, MAD can be computed as follows:

$$(| 60 - 41.5 | + | 72 - 54.45 | + | 58 - 66.74 | + | 40 - 60.62 |)$$
$$\div \, 4 = 16.35$$

Therefore, the forecaster is off an average of 16.35 units per forecast. When compared to the result of other alphas, the forecaster will know that the alpha with the lowest MAD is yielding the most accurate forecast.

Mean square error (MSE) can also be utilized in the same fashion. MSE is the sum of the forecast errors squared divided by N-1 [(Σ(FE)) $\div$ (N-1)]. Squaring the forecast errors eliminates the possibility of offsetting negative numbers, since none of the results can be negative. Utilizing the same data as above, the MSE would be:

$$[(18.5) + (17.55) + (-8.74) + (-20.62)] \div 3 = 383.94$$

As with MAD, the forecaster may compare the MSE of forecasts derived using various values of alpha and assume the alpha with the lowest MSE is yielding the most accurate forecast.

The mean absolute percent error (MAPE) is the average absolute percent error. To arrive at the MAPE one must take the sum of the ratios between forecast error and actual demand times 100 (to get the percentage) and divide by N [(Σ | Actual demand − forecast | $\div$ Actual demand) $\times$ 100 $\div$ N]. Using the data from the exponential smoothing example, MAPE can be computed as follows:

$$[(18.5/60 + 17.55/72 + 8.74/58 + 20.62/48) \times 100] \div 4 = 28.33\%$$

As with MAD and MSE, the lower the relative error the more accurate the forecast.

It should be noted that in some cases the ability of the forecast to change quickly to respond to changes in data patterns is considered to be more important than accuracy. Therefore, one's choice of forecasting method should reflect the relative balance of importance between accuracy and responsiveness, as determined by the forecaster.

MAKING A FORECAST

William J. Stevenson lists the following as the basic steps in the forecasting process:

- Determine the forecast's purpose. Factors such as how and when the forecast will be used, the degree of accuracy needed, and the level of detail desired determine the cost (time, money, employees) that can be dedicated to the forecast and the type of forecasting method to be utilized.

- Establish a time horizon. This occurs after one has determined the purpose of the forecast. Longer-term forecasts require longer time horizons and vice versa. Accuracy is again a consideration.

- Select a forecasting technique. The technique selected depends upon the purpose of the forecast, the time horizon desired, and the allowed cost.

- Gather and analyze data. The amount and type of data needed is governed by the forecast's purpose, the forecasting technique selected, and any cost considerations.

- Make the forecast.

- Monitor the forecast. Evaluate the performance of the forecast and modify, if necessary.

SEE ALSO: Futuring; Manufacturing Resources Planning; Planning; Sales Management

R. Anthony Inman

FURTHER READING:

Finch, Byron J. *Operations Now: Profitability, Processes, Performance.* 2 ed. Boston: McGraw-Hill Irwin, 2006.

Green, William H. *Econometric Analysis.* 5 ed. Upper Saddle River, NJ: Prentice Hall, 2003.

Joppe, Dr. Marion. "The Nominal Group Technique." *The Research Process.* Available from <http://www.ryerson.ca/~mjoppe/ResearchProcess/841TheNominalGroupTechnique.htm>.

Stevenson, William J. *Operations Management.* 8 ed. Boston: McGraw-Hill Irwin, 2005.

FRANCHISING

When an individual has the desire and drive to run their own business but lacks a strong idea for a company, this person may look to franchising in order to be their own boss and run a proven business.

Franchising is an agreement or alliance between two organizations—the franchisor and the franchisee. The franchisor has the business model, training materials, and other materials for the business. The franchisee is the entrepreneur who agrees to operate a branch of the business in their location while paying the franchisor various fees and royalties for the use of the business idea or model.

TYPES OF FRANCHISING

Business-format franchising exists when a franchisor allows someone to market products or service, using the business name or trademark, in return for fess and royalties. When franchising is mentioned, most people think of this business-format franchising, like McDonald's, AAMCO Transmission, or Molly Maid. There is also product or trademark franchising. This is a limited franchise where a manufacturer may grant another party license to sell goods produced by the manufacturer. This might includes sales of cars through dealerships (e.g., Ford dealerships), sales of gasoline through service stations (e.g., Shell stations), and sales of soft drinks through local franchising (e.g., Coca Cola bottlers). A final type of franchising is conversion franchising. This franchising model is designed to bring formerly-independently-operating businesses together under the collective power of a national name and advertising. An example of the conversion franchising is Century 21 Realtors, an affiliation of previously-established real estate agents.

FRANCHISE START-UP

Franchise fees typically include a lump-sum entrance fee and other charges for regular services including royalties on sales, advertising fees, and marketing. In exchange for these licensing fees, the franchisor retains control over the delivery of the products and services, as well as marketing and the operational and quality standards of the franchise. The franchising company's revenue is generated through the franchisee that pays these on-going sales royalties, typically averaging 5 percent of sales. The contract, or franchise agreement, is signed by both parties and establishes the relationship between the franchisee and the franchisor. It also details the responsibilities of both sides.

Franchises include such popular names as Kentucky Fried Chicken (KFC), McDonald's, 7-Eleven, Body Shop, Tie Rack, Pizza Hut, and Jiffy Lube. These franchise operations have well-established names, brands, and reputations. The best franchises provide a strong brand or trademark of the concept, a proven business system, extensive training and product development, along with a number of initial and on-going managerial support services. Some help the franchisee secure funding and offer benefits, including discounted supplies. Typically, the franchised business is less risky than other forms of new venture creation because the business idea has been tested. There are mutual advantages to both parties to the agreement. The Service Corps of Retired Executives (SCORE), a volunteer group involved in counseling would-be entrepreneurs, report franchises are safer that other business forms and report less than a 5 percent failure rate compared to an 80 percent five-year failure rate for independent businesses and a 90 percent failure rate from independent restaurants. Banks are also supportive of the franchising business model and many will offer up to 70 percent of the initial capital costs.

WHY FRANCHISE?

Franchising allows a business to rapidly expand beyond its original owners. The franchisee pursues a new business, experiences the advantages of running their own business and being their own boss, and can gain wealth through a proven business idea. They provide the management skills to run the business, as well as contribute the capital to fund the opening and ongoing operations. The franchisor also benefits by the partnership and gains economy of scope advantages as more franchises are established. National or international advertising is then possible and the franchisor can more easily expand business locations with the help and capital from the franchisee. The franchisee helps to build brand awareness through market proliferation. The franchisee has a unique opportunity to run a business with a greater chance of success. There is experience from the franchisor for starting the business and many of the initial mistakes have been made and corrected.

The franchisee creates their own job and often creates a number of new jobs in the area as they hire employees. As the franchise becomes successful, the franchisee may chose to open other stores to create even more wealth. Franchising is popular in the United States as well as internationally. Franchising is at a mature level in the U.S., Europe and Australia, while Asia, South America, Mexico, and Central America report rapid growth. China, too, is experiencing franchise business growth.

RESEARCHING FRANCHISES

It is important to carefully perform initial due diligence to thoroughly examine the franchise offering. A Federal Trade Commission (FTC) rule was created and adopted in the mid-1970s that requires franchisors to disclose to franchisees very specific information including information about themselves, the business, and the terms of the relationship. This document is the Uniform Franchise Offering Circular (UFOC) and provides important legal information about the franchisor and its franchising program.

When deciding on a franchise, it is important to first gather information about an individual's personal goals for business ownership and to examine the franchise offering to find a compatible opportunity. While there are no guarantees in franchising, a well-developed operating plan is often an advantage. An entrepreneur should consider a number of issues regarding a possible franchise. For example, is the franchise in only a state or local market, or does it have a regional or national presence? Lower-risk franchises have a national presence and benefit from the size advantage. The franchisee will also want to consider if most of the existing outlets are profitable, and whether the franchise is the market leader with the largest market share among competitors. The entrepreneur should evaluate the presence of a national marketing and purchasing program. The lower-risk franchises also have documented training, manuals, field support, marketing and promotion, standardized operating procedures, and on-going feedback channels between the franchisor and the franchisees. The terms of the license agreement vary from less than ten years to more than twenty years and some have automatic renewal. Capital requirements for obtaining the franchise also vary. Other factors to consider include territory limitations, failure rates, and any relevant litigation history against the franchise. Investment requirements should also be clearly disclosed.

It is often a good idea to interview existing franchise owners to determine if start-up costs and processes are realistic. The expertise of a lawyer may be required to negotiate and interpret the franchise agreement contract. SCORE also recommends that potential franchising clients plan and analyze their options. This planning and analysis should include researching Chamber of Commerce and Better Business Bureau records for a given franchise. SCORE agrees the most important step for choosing a franchise is also considering the entrepreneur's interests, personal skills, and experience. It is easier to evaluate an established franchise than a new franchise. There may be few, if any, owners with whom to speak about the franchise. It is important that the new franchise have strong franchisee support and a proven business system. The business strategy should also be examined carefully.

FRANCHISING AND THE ECONOMY

A study by the International Franchise Association (IFA) revealed that more than 9.7 million people are employed by franchised businesses. This group of 767,483 franchises, ranging from automobile dealers to food operations, have a $506.6 billion U.S. payroll. These businesses are clearly important to the econ-

omy. The IFA also reports that the start-up costs for franchising can range from less than $5,000, to more than $500,000. IFA offers information on franchising—including news and events as well as discussion forums and education. It also includes information on government regulations for franchising.

In a 2004 study conducted by Pricewaterhouse-Coopers (for the International Franchise Association Educational Foundation) on the economic impact of franchised businesses, more than 760,000 franchised businesses exist in the United States and they generate some $1.53 trillion each year. This represents 9.5 percent of the private-sector economic output in the United States. These franchises generate one out of every seven jobs in America.

The IFA established a Franchise Index to track the market performance of the top fifty U.S. public franchisors. The index has increased steadily since January 2000, compared to a drop of 20.1 percent in the Standard and Poors (S&P) 500 Index over the same period. Interestingly, the franchise index has grown during tough economic times. Thus, franchising is a major economic force and franchising has a significant impact on the nation's economy.

The franchising business model attracts a number of qualified individuals, particularly in times of recession or slow business growth. Individuals are attracted to franchising through the opportunity to create their own jobs. While franchising is not a get-rich-quick proposition, many do have attractive returns on investment. Most analysts agree a three- to five-year period of hard work and dedication is needed before the franchised business is profitable. Over the years, more individuals are touting the advantages and value of franchising. These franchises are quick to pick up on key business trends, social and demographic changes, and changing lifestyles—healthy fast food, home health care for the elderly, pet care, education, personal services, home services, business services, automotive services, and travel services. Many also offer exclusive territories in a given market.

Additional advice on finding and comparing franchising opportunities is available on the franchise-broker websites (e.g., www.FranNet.com, www.FranChoice.com, and www.francorpconnect.com). FranNet.com is a franchise-broker website representing franchise consultants. Some potential franchisees prefer using a broker to find a franchise.

While there are many advantages to franchising, there are some disadvantages. Once a business grows beyond a certain size, it could make more money if it were wholly owned, since a percentage of the profit margin goes to the franchisor. Even if a franchise is capable of making strong profit figures, the individual running the franchise needs to enjoy the process of dealing with the franchisor as well as operating the business. The franchisee needs to be committed to the idea and the business model. The individual also needs to be supportive of the franchisor's system since the key to a successful product or service is the consistency of the offering. Customers expect a similar product or service from a franchise. Individuals who do not want to follow the predetermined structure and operating procedures of the franchise may not be successful.

The franchising arrangement is a balance of entrepreneurial spirit, standard business procedures, and following instructions. The venture, like other start-ups, will require a time and energy commitment as well. A disadvantage for the franchisor is the difficulty encountered in finding a franchisee with drive, energy, and business experience to run the business according to the franchise guidelines. The franchise also needs an appropriate location that must be researched to discern its current and future growth potential. Finally, the franchisee must provide some of their own funds for the start-up.

SEE ALSO: Business Plan; Due Diligence; Entrepreneurship; Strategy Formulation

Marilyn M. Helms

FURTHER READING:

Caplin, J. "How Do I Find the Right Franchise?" *Money* 33, no. 5 (2004): 55.

Doehrman, Marylou. "Pros and Cons of a Franchised Business." *Daily Record and the Kansas City Daily News-Press,* 3 January 2005: 1.

Inma, Chutarat. "Purposeful Franchising: Re-Thinking of the Franchising Rationale." *Singapore Management Review* 27, no. 1 (2005): 27–48.

Ng, L. "Unfolding Franchising." *Malaysian Business,* 1 September 2004, 50.

Timmons, Jeffry A., and Stephen Spinelli. *New Venture Creation: Entrepreneurship for the 21st Century.* Boston: McGraw-Hill Irwin, 2004.

Zaragoza, S. "Due Aims to Take Pain Out of Franchising." *Dallas Business Journal* 28, no. 17 (2004): 12.

FREE TRADE AGREEMENTS AND TRADING BLOCS

Sovereign nations join together, usually on a regional scale, to create free trade agreements. Free trade agreements are created to lower trade barriers and to stimulate trade between member countries. Member countries belonging to the free trade area trade freely with each other while maintaining trade barriers and tariffs for non-member countries. Free trade agreements are seen as having a positive impact on economic growth, especially for the smaller countries in the agreement. Trading blocs are groups of countries that have reached a common agreement to lower trade barriers throughout the group (e.g., NAFTA, ASEAN, and the European Union).

HISTORY

According to the Congressional Budget Office, since the end of World War II there has been significant support, especially from the United States, to eliminate artificial trade barriers and to support a greater liberalization of international trade. The General Agreement on Tariffs and Trade (GATT) was created shortly after World War II, between twenty-three countries, to facilitate and coordinate trade between the nations. In addition to creating a more liberal trade environment, it also had provisions and charters creating rules for employment, commodity agreements, restrictive business practices, international investments, and services. The process of creating a free trade agreement followed a pattern of discussion, negotiation, and eventual ratification. The full process was termed, "rounds." There were eight rounds in the GATT treaty. Despite numerous difficulties and differences between the involved countries, much was accomplished by GATT; although portions were never fully ratified by all of the countries.

In 1995, during the Uruguay round of GATT negotiations, the World Trade Organization (WTO) was created. The WTO became the official successor to the GATT. The WTO is the only international organization dealing with the global rules of trade between nations. Its main function is to ensure that trade flows as smoothly, predictably, and freely as possible. At the center of the WTO is its multilateral trading system that functions by seeking consensus between member nations (148 members). The notion of consensus facilitates cooperation and, potentially, an agreement that is most beneficial to all involved countries.

MOST FAVORED NATION

An important component of free trade agreements is the most favored nation status. The most favored nation status within a free trade agreement creates a situation where all countries are treated equally. Benefits, reduction of tariffs, and other trading privileges applied to one country will be applied to all countries with the most favored nation status.

TRADING BLOCS

Trading blocs are relationships between countries, generally in the same region, to facilitate free trade agreements. Trading blocs include: North

American Free Trade Agreement (NAFTA), Association of Southeast Asian Nations (ASEAN), European Union (EU), Mercado Comun del Sur (MERCOSUR), and Southern African Development Community (SADC). Southeast Asia has enjoyed unparalleled and astonishing economic growth in the past three decades since the establishment of ASEAN. In 1967, ASEAN's overall trade was worth $10 billion. In 2003, total trade reached a staggering $758 billion.

CRITICISM OF FREE TRADE

The expansion of free trade and the creation of trading blocs cause concern for some people. As reported by the Congressional Budget Office, the pursuit of free trade could "divert the world from multilateral negotiations and lead to the development of rival trading blocs." Other concerns include: the exploitation of developing countries by industrialized countries; environmental concerns as the production of goods overseas is not consistently regulated from country to country; and labor concerns over fair wages and the loss of jobs from industrialized countries to the developing countries, as well as political concerns that may influence the negotiations between trading partners.

BENEFITS OF FREE TRADE

Multilateral and free trade agreements create benefits by increasing imports and exports of goods. Countries are not the same in their production capabilities. Access to raw materials, necessary levels of technological development, and education of the workforce all have an impact on developing a product or service. Free trade agreements create the opportunity for countries to focus on what they do best, while being able to acquire goods and services at, potentially, the lowest price possible. By opening doors for other countries to compete fairly, without burdensome tariffs or trade policies, there is a belief that increased free trade is a deterrent to monopolistic activities.

FUTURE OF FREE TRADE AGREEMENTS

The most recent round of negotiations for multilateral trade in the World Trade Organization continues to drag on due to the increasing number of participants with their own views and requirements. The attractiveness of free trade agreements will remain high. Countries interested in increasing trade will circumvent the delays in the WTO by making their own agreements. The expansion of current trade agreements is also taking place—as with the expansion of NAFTA into the Free Trade Agreement for the Americas (FTAA). The U.S. market is extremely desirable and lucrative for smaller countries' exports, while also providing access to a wider variety of goods and services from the U.S. and other potential trading partners.

Hal P. Kirkwood, Jr.
Revised by Joo-Seng Tan

FURTHER READING:

"Economic and Budget Issue Brief: The Pros and Cons of Pursuing Free-Trade Agreements." *Congressional Budget Office* (2003) Avaliable from <http://www.cbo.gov>.

Magnusson, Paul. "States's Rights vs. Free Trade." *Business Week,* 7 March 2005, 102–103.

Mahmood, Amir. "WTO and Market Access in Non-Agricultural Products: Issues and Options for Developing Countries." *Journal of American Academy of Business, Cambridge* 6, no. 1 (2005): 1–11.

Poole, William. "Why are Economists and Noneconomists So Far Apart?" *Review (Federal Reserve Bank of Saint Louis)* 86, no. 5 (2004): 1–6.

Wirtz, Ronald A. "A Fork in the Free-Trade Road." *Region (Federal Reserve Bank of Minneapolis)* 18, no. 3 (2004): 6–9, 48–53.

FUTURING

Futuring is the field of using a systematic process for thinking about, picturing possible outcomes, and planning for the future. Futurists are people who actively view the present world as a window on possible future outcomes. They watch trends and try to envision what might happen. Futuring has its roots in the post–World War II era. Scientists, politicians, and academics began to consider ways of anticipating the future. This initial consideration led to a more cohesive and developed field of futuring in the mid-1960s. An association, the World Future Society, exists to provide a forum for further discussion and analysis.

Explorers often found themselves in situations where they had no idea what the future held for them. What was around the next bend; over the next mountain range; across the next river was a complete unknown. They were forced to make decisions that were literally life and death. Futurists can look to these explorers for guidance. Edward Cornish, former president of the World Future Society, highlights seven lessons that can be learned: (1) prepare for what you will face in the future; (2) anticipate future needs; (3) use poor information when necessary; (4) expect the unexpected; (5) think long term as well as short term; (6) dream productively; and (7) learn from your predecessors.

A major instigator of forecasting the future is the incredible rate of change that is taking place. Technologically, culturally, and environmentally change is all around and moving at a very fast rate. Mankind has lived through the Agricultural, Industrial and Cybernetic Revolutions. There will undoubtedly be another if not several more revolutions that will affect the planet. Futuring delves into this process of revolutions to attempt to forecast what might be the next one. Cornish discusses six current "super trends" that are dramatically affecting the present and the future.

Technological Progress. Improvements in computers, medicine, transportation, communications, and other industries all affected by technology.

Economic Growth. Impacted by technological progress the improvement of people's economic well-being continues to steadily improve over time.

Improving Health. Impacted by the aforementioned super trends—technological progress and economic growth—the average lifespan and overall health of the average person continues to improve over time.

Increased Mobility. Technological progress, economic growth, and improving health combine to improve mobility of people and products, creating both advantages and disadvantages as the world shrinks.

Environmental Decline. The scope of this progress and mobility and increasing population is impacting the earth with severe environmental issues that do not have a short-term solution.

Increasing De-culturation. Mankind has had a wide variety of cultures and races; due to some of the above trends, these cultures are being erased by poverty, migration, and tourism.

FORCES THAT AFFECT THE FUTURE

Futurists must account for several powerful forces that impact future events and trends. These forces are systems, chance, and chaos.

SYSTEMS. Systems exist in most every setting. Relationships between people, the human body, and cities sewage and transportation services are all examples of systems. Actions that impact one part of the system can inevitably affect other parts of the system.

CHANCE. Chance events occur continuously. These events can shape future outcomes. Small actions or details can have a profound effect that can cause major worldwide events.

CHAOS. Chaos is the idea that minor differences in something can have a profound effect on other things and then inevitably on the future. This means that there is always a wide array of possible outcomes; only extremely minor differences separate these possible outcomes from actually happening.

These three forces: systems, chance, and chaos, must all be considered at some level if a person is to try and forecast the future.

FUTURING METHODS

Futuring is accomplished by rather normal means of forecasting. There are four methods used in futuring to determine possible outcomes. These methods are: polling, gaming, modeling and simulation, and visioning.

POLLING. Polling is a method that involves consulting with others, preferably experts, who are knowledgeable on the topic in question. It consists of a series of questions to elicit responses that are then collated to determine what the overall perception of the group is. This is best performed when the participants cannot interact with each other and bias their answers.

GAMING. Another method of forecasting that is used by researchers, and especially by the government, is gaming. Gaming is a method of possible events where participants are placed in mock situations and are expected to make actual decisions based on the information and actions that are happening around them. Gaming possible events and situations with computer simulations is becoming more popular. Gaming assists with understanding how people will react in their roles and what possible outcomes of a given situation might be.

MODELING AND SIMULATION. Modeling is a method used in forecasting future outcomes. Modeling generally involves computer processing of data to provide possible outcomes. Data for the relevant variables is entered into the computer, with the model then run repetitively with minor variations to observe potential outcomes.

VISIONING. Many futurists use the visioning method to not only forecast, but to encourage potential futures. Visioning involves discussing and creating preferred futures. The result of visioning is a plan of action for following through with the ideas that are generated.

The different methods of forecasting the future can be used in a variety of settings depending on the people and information available. Other methods that are also used in futuring are:

Scanning—systematic survey of information sources focusing on trends

Trend Analysis—in-depth look at a specific trend and all of its related issues and elements

Trend Monitoring—continuous monitoring of important trends

Trend Projection—using numerical data to project where a trend should eventually end up

Brainstorming—generating new ideas by small group interaction

Historical Analysis—using historical events to anticipate current developments

Deja Viewing—reviewing the past to determine if anything similar has happened

Bringing the Future to the Present—looking ahead to the future and painting a picture of what you want to happen

Experience Hitchhiking—gaining experience by 'hitchhiking' with people who have gone through similar experiences already.

SCENARIOS

Scenarios are recognized as an effective method for forecasting the future. Scenarios are beneficial in forecasting because they deal with the uncertainty of a situation. Scenario creation focuses on identifying what might happen. This allows for analyzing the problem and determining what the consequences might be in light of the information available and in light of our own reactions to possible events. Futurists often use five different variations of scenario building: (1) *Continuation*—things will continue much as they are now; (2) *Optimistic*—things will get considerably better; (3) *Pessimistic*—things will get considerably worse; (4) *Disaster*—things will go terribly wrong; and (5) *Miracle*—things going stunningly well.

Each scenario is then given a percentage of probability on the likelihood that it will happen. Cost for each scenario in effort or outcome is important to consider. Scenarios assist in clarifying thinking about issues so that better decisions can be made.

WORLD FUTURE SOCIETY PREDICTIONS

The World Future Society brings together experts from around the world to report on future directions in their areas of expertise. The publication *Futurist* contained a two-part special report in 2005 on Trends Shaping the Future. A sampling of the trends is provided here:

- The world's population will grow to 9.2 billion by 2050. Implications for this trend include: (1) the need for global agriculture to produce more food than ever before; (2) migration will continue from the Southern hemisphere to the Northern hemisphere; and (3) in the developed countries potential retirees will need to continue working for a longer period of time.

- The global economy is growing more integrated. Implications for this trend include: (1) greater niche market competition as small companies have a greater reach using the Internet; and (2) demand for foreign language training may increase as workers are utilized across the globe.

- Consumerism is still growing rapidly. Implications for this trend include: (1) the increase in marketing and development of warehouse stores in Europe and Japan; (2) service and salesmanship will become a more decisive factor for purchases as price becomes more of a commodity; and (3) brands will continue to be important.

- Privacy is dying in many lands. Implications of this include: (1) the extension of terrorism-related surveillance measures; (2) an increase in privacy-related lawsuits in the U.S. as the struggle between security and privacy continues; and (3) encryption will become more widespread at the corporate and personal level.

- Water shortages will be a continuing problem for much of the world. Implications of this include: (1) the growth of famine and desertification in developing areas of the world; (2) water wars are possible in certain areas of the world; and (3) water impurities will become a growing problem.

- Advances in transportation technology will make travel and shipping faster, cheaper, and safer, by land, sea, and air. Implications of this include: (1) the further development of alternative-fuel vehicles; and (2) smart cars and other transportation developments will be used as congestion increases in urban areas.

- Consumers increasingly demand social responsibility from companies and each other. Implications of this trend will include: (1) increasing pressure for companies to adopt environmentally friendly practices; and (2) the Internet will help activists reach out to police and protest against companies' activities in other countries.

- Generation X and the "Millennials"—those born after 1981—will have major effects in the future. Implications will include: (1) the need for employers to adjust compensation and motivation for these groups; and (2) these groups will continue to expect and demand more advanced telecommunications and Internet services.

• Time is becoming the world's most precious commodity. Implications may include: (1) the need for companies to help employees balance their personal and work lives; and (2) Internet shopping will increase as the time for shopping at malls and stores will decrease.

Futurists are aware that random events can happen that can change the best forecasting; therefore, these techniques of trend-watching, reviewing past events, gaming, scenarios, and others all must allow for a certain amount of flexibility. Forces acting on any possible future include systems, chance, and chaos, as well as individual choice.

Developing the skills and techniques to see into the future is neither magic nor unattainable. Futurists are leading the way to envisioning possible futures. They believe that developing effective foresight can lead to better decision-making, greater discoveries, and an improved future. Futurists challenge the concept of fatalism—that the future is coming and there is nothing we can do about it. Using these forecasting methods individuals can change and guide their future. They are in a position to positively influence their future, which can potentially make things better for others and possibly change the world.

SEE ALSO: Brainstorming; Forecasting; Gap Analysis; Strategic Planning Tools; Strategy Implementation; Strategy in the Global Environment; Technological Forecasting; Technology Management; Technology Transfer

Hal P. Kirkwood, Jr.

FURTHER READING:

"The Art of Foresight." *Futurist* 38, no. 3 (2004): 31–37.

Cetron, M.J. "Trends Now Shaping the Future." *Futurist* 39, no. 2 (2005): 27–42.

———. "Trends Now Shaping the Future." *Futurist* 39, no. 3 (2005): 37–50.

Cornish, E. *Futuring: The Exploration of the Future.* Bethesda, MD: World Future Society, 2004.

May, T.A. "Tricks of the Futuring Trade." *Computerworld* 38, no. 12 (2004): 23.

Taylor, C. "Looking Ahead in a Dangerous World." *Time,* 11 October 2004, 60–61.

G

Gap analysis generally refers to the activity of studying the differences between standards and the delivery of those standards. For example, it would be useful for a firm to document differences between customer expectation and actual customer experiences in the delivery of medical care. The differences could be used to explain satisfaction and to document areas in need of improvement.

However, in the process of identifying the gap, a before-and-after analysis must occur. This can take several forms. For example, in lean management we perform a Value Stream Map of the current process. Then we create a Value Stream Map of the desired state. The differences between the two define the "gap". Once the gap is defined, a game plan can be developed that will move the organization from its current state toward its desired future state.

Another tool for identifying the gap is a step chart. With the step chart, various "classes" of performance are identified—including world-class status. Then, current state and desired future state are noted on the chart. Once again, the difference between the two defines the "gap".

The issue of service quality can be used as an example to illustrate gaps. For this example, there are several gaps that are important to measure. From a service quality perspective, these include: (1) service quality gap; (2) management understanding gap; (3) service design gap; (4) service delivery gap; and (5) communication gap.

Service Quality Gap. Indicates the difference between the service expected by customers and the service they actually receive. For example, customers may expect to wait only 20 minutes to see their doctor but, in fact, have to wait more than thirty minutes.

Management Understanding Gap. Represents the difference between the quality level expected by customers and the perception of those expectations by management. For example, in a fast food environment, the customers may place a greater emphasis on order accuracy than promptness of service, but management may perceive promptness to be more important.

Service Design Gap. This is the gap between management's perception of customer expectations and the development of this perception into delivery standards. For example, management might perceive that customers expect someone to answer their telephone calls in a timely fashion. To customers, "timely fashion" may mean within thirty seconds. However, if management designs delivery such that telephone calls are answered within sixty seconds, a service design gap is created.

Service Delivery Gap. Represents the gap between the established delivery standards and actual service delivered. Given the above example, management may establish a standard such that telephone calls should be answered within thirty seconds. However, if it takes more than thirty seconds for calls to be answered, regardless of the cause, there is a delivery gap.

Communication Gap. This is the gap between what is communicated to consumers and what is actually delivered. Advertising, for instance, may indicate to consumers that they can have their cars's oil changed within twenty minutes when, in reality, it takes more than thirty minutes.

IMPLEMENTING GAP ANALYSIS

Gap analysis involves internal and external analysis. Externally, the firm must communicate with customers. Internally, it must determine service delivery and service design. Continuing with the service quality example, the steps involved in the implementation of gap analysis are:

- Identification of customer expectations
- Identification of customer experiences
- Identification of management perceptions
- Evaluation of service standards
- Evaluation of customer communications

The identification of customer expectations and experiences might begin with focus-group interviews. Groups of customers, typically numbering seven to twelve per group, are invited to discuss their satisfaction with services or products. During this process, expectations and experiences are recorded. This process is usually successful in identifying those service and product attributes that are most important to customer satisfaction.

After focus-group interviews are completed, expectations and experiences are measured with more formal, quantitative methods. Expectations could be measured with a one to ten scale where one represents "Not At All Important" and ten represents "Extremely Important." Experience or perceptions about each of these attributes would be measured in a similar manner.

Gaps can be simply calculated as the arithmetic difference between the two measurements for each of the attributes. Management perceptions are measured much in the same manner. Groups of managers are asked to discuss their perceptions of customer expectations and experiences. A team can then be assigned the duty of evaluating manager perceptions, service standards, and communications to pinpoint discrepancies. After gaps are identified, management must take appropriate steps to fill or narrow the gaps.

THE IMPORTANCE OF SERVICE QUALITY GAP ANALYSIS

The main reason gap analysis is important to firms is the fact that gaps between customer expectations and customer experiences lead to customer dissatisfaction. Consequently, measuring gaps is the first step in enhancing customer satisfaction. Additionally, competitive advantages can be achieved by exceeding customer expectations. Gap analysis is the technique utilized to determine where firms exceed or fall below customer expectations.

Customer satisfaction leads to repeat purchases and repeat purchases lead to loyal customers. In turn, customer loyalty leads to enhanced brand equity and higher profits. Consequently, understanding customer perceptions is important to a firm's performance. As such, gap analysis is used as a tool to narrow the gap between perceptions and reality, thus enhancing customer satisfaction.

PRODUCT APPLICATIONS

It should be noted that gap analysis is applicable to any aspect of industry where performance improvements are desired, not just in customer service. For example, the product quality gap could be measured by (and is defined as) the difference between the quality level of products expected by customers and the actual quality level. The measurement of the product quality gap is attained in the same manner as above. However, while service delivery can be changed through employee training, changes in product design are not as easily implemented and are more time consuming.

Gap analysis can be used to address internal gaps. For example, it is also applicable to human resource management. There may be a gap between what employees expect of their employer and what they actually experience. The larger the gap, the greater the job dissatisfaction. In turn, job dissatisfaction can decrease productivity and have a negative effect on a company's culture.

Ford Motor Co., for example, utilized gap analysis while developing an employee benefit program. While management may believe it has a handle on employee perceptions, this is not always true. With this in mind, Ford's management set out to understand employee desires regarding flexible benefits. Their cross-functional team approach utilized focus groups, paper and pencil tests, and story boards to understand employee wants and needs. Their team, consisting of finance, human resources, line managers, benefits staff, and consultants, identified gaps in benefit understanding, coverage, and communications. As a result of gap analysis, Ford implemented a communications program that gained employee acceptance.

Gene Brown
Revised by Gerhard Plenert

FURTHER READING:

Chakrapani, Chuck. *The Informed Field Guide for Tools and Techniques: How to Measure Service Quality and Customer Satisfaction.* Chicago: American Marketing Association, 1998.

Frost, Julie. "Narrowing the Perception Gap: A Study in Employee Benefit Communications." *Compensation & Benefits Management* 14, no. 2 (1998): 22–28.

Fuller, Neil. "Service Quality Control." *Supply Management* 3, no. 19 (1998): 48.

Parasuraman, Valerie Z., and Leonard L. Berry. "SERVQUAL: A Multiple-Item Scale for Measuring Customer Perceptions of Service Quality." *Journal of Retailing* 64, no. 1 (1988): 12–40.

Plenert, Gerhard. *The eManager: Value Chain Management in an eCommerce World.* Dublin, Ireland: Blackhall Publishing, 2001.

———. *International Operations Management.* Copenhagen, Denmark: Copenhagen Business School Press, 2002.

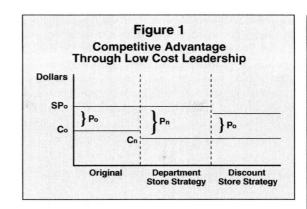

Figure 1

Competitive Advantage Through Low Cost Leadership

GENERIC COMPETITIVE STRATEGIES

Three of the most widely read books on competitive analysis in the 1980s were Michael Porter's *Competitive Strategy, Competitive Advantage,* and *Competitive Advantage of Nations.* In his various books, Porter developed three generic strategies that, he argues, can be used singly or in combination to create a defendable position and to outperform competitors, whether they are within an industry or across nations. Porter states that the strategies are generic because they are applicable to a large variety of situations and contexts. The strategies are (1) overall cost leadership; (2) differentiation; and (3) focus on a particular market niche. The generic strategies provide direction for firms in designing incentive systems, control procedures, and organizational arrangements. Following is a description of this work.

OVERALL COST LEADERSHIP STRATEGY

Overall cost leadership requires firms to develop policies aimed at becoming and remaining the lowest-cost producer and/or distributor in the industry. Company strategies aimed at controlling costs include construction of efficient-scale facilities, tight control of costs and overhead, avoidance of marginal customer accounts, minimization of operating expenses, reduction of input costs, tight control of labor costs, and lower distribution costs. The low-cost leader gains competitive advantage by getting its costs of production or distribution lower than those of the other firms in its market. The strategy is especially important for firms selling unbranded commodities such as beef or steel.

Figure 1 shows the competitive advantage firms may achieve through cost leadership. *C* is the original cost of production. *C* is the new cost of production. *SP* is the original selling price. *SP* is the new selling price. *P* is the original profit margin. *P* is the new profit margin.

If we assume our firm and the other competitors are producing the product for a cost of *C* and selling it at *SP,* we are all receiving a profit of *P.* As cost leader, we are able to lower our cost to *C* while the competitors remain at *C.* We now have two choices as to how to take advantage of our reduced costs.

1. Department stores and other high-margin firms often leave their selling price as *SP,* the original selling price. This allows the low-cost leader to obtain a higher profit margin than they received before the reduction in costs. Since the competition was unable to lower their costs, they are receiving the original, smaller profit margin. The cost leader gains competitive advantage over the competition by earning more profit for each unit sold.

2. Discount stores such as Wal-Mart are more likely to pass the savings from the lower costs on to customers in the form of lower prices. These discounters retain the original profit margin, which is the same margin as their competitors. However, they are able to lower their selling price due to their lower costs (*C*). They gain competitive advantage by being able to under-price the competition while maintaining the same profit margin.

Overall cost leadership is not without potential problems. Two or more firms competing for cost leadership may engage in price wars that drive profits to very low levels. Ideally, a firm using a cost leader strategy will develop an advantage that is not easily copied by others. Cost leaders also must maintain their investment in state-of-the-art equipment or face the possible entry of more cost-effective competitors. Major changes in technology may drastically change production processes so that previous investments in production technology are no longer advantageous. Finally, firms may become so concerned with maintaining low costs that needed changes in production or marketing are overlooked. The strategy may be more difficult in a dynamic environment because some of the expenses that firms may seek to minimize are research and development costs or marketing research costs, yet these are expenses the firm may need to incur in order to remain competitive.

DIFFERENTIATION STRATEGY

The second generic strategy, differentiating the product or service, requires a firm to create something about its product or service that is perceived as unique throughout the industry. Whether the features are real or just in the mind of the customer, customers must perceive the product as having desirable features not commonly found in competing products. The customers also must be relatively price-insensitive. Adding product features means that the production or distribution costs of a differentiated product may be somewhat higher than the price of a generic, non-differentiated product. Customers must be willing to pay more than the marginal cost of adding the differentiating feature if a differentiation strategy is to succeed.

Differentiation may be attained through many features that make the product or service appear unique. Possible strategies for achieving differentiation may include:

- warranties (e.g., Sears tools)

- brand image (e.g., Coach handbags, Tommy Hilfiger sportswear)

- technology (e.g., Hewlett-Packard laser printers)

- features (e.g., Jenn-Air ranges, Whirlpool appliances)

- service (e.g., Makita hand tools)

- quality/value (e.g., Walt Disney Company)

- dealer network (e.g., Caterpillar construction equipment)

Differentiation does not allow a firm to ignore costs; it makes a firm's products less susceptible to cost pressures from competitors because customers see the product as unique and are willing to pay extra to have the product with the desirable features. Differentiation can be achieved through real product features or through advertising that causes the customer to perceive that the product is unique.

Differentiation may lead to customer brand loyalty and result in reduced price elasticity. Differentiation may also lead to higher profit margins and reduce the need to be a low-cost producer. Since customers see the product as different from competing products and they like the product features, customers are willing to pay a premium for these features. As long as the firm can increase the selling price by more than the marginal cost of adding the features, the profit margin is increased. Firms must be able to charge more for their differentiated product than it costs them to make it distinct, or else they may be better off making generic, undifferentiated products. Firms must remain sensitive to cost differences. They must carefully monitor the incremental costs of differentiating their product and make certain the difference is reflected in the price.

Firms pursuing a differentiation strategy are vulnerable to different competitive threats than firms pursuing a cost leader strategy. Customers may sacrifice features, service, or image for cost savings. Customers who are price sensitive may be willing to forgo desirable features in favor of a less costly alternative. This can be seen in the growth in popularity of store brands and private labels. Often, the same firms that produce name-brand products produce the private label products. The two products may be physically identical, but stores are able to sell the private label products for a lower price because very little money was put into advertising in an effort to differentiate the private label product.

Imitation may also reduce the perceived differences between products when competitors copy product features. Thus, for firms to be able to recover the cost of marketing research or R&D, they may need to add a product feature that is not easily copied by a competitor.

A final risk for firms pursuing a differentiation strategy is changing consumer tastes. The feature that customers like and find attractive about a product this year may not make the product popular next year. Changes in customer tastes are especially obvious in the apparel industry. Polo Ralph Lauren has been a very successful brand in the fashion industry. However, some younger consumers have shifted to Tommy Hilfiger and other youth-oriented brands.

Ralph Lauren, founder and CEO, has been the guiding light behind his company's success. Part of the firm's success has been the public's association of Lauren with the brand. Ralph Lauren leads a high-profile lifestyle of preppy elegance. His appearance in his own commercials, his Manhattan duplex, his Colorado ranch, his vintage car collection, and private jet have all contributed to the public's fascination with the man and his brand name. This image has allowed the firm to market everything from suits and ties to golf balls. Through licensing of the name, the Lauren name also appears on sofas, soccer balls, towels, tableware, and much more.

COMBINATION STRATEGIES

Can forms of competitive advantage be combined? Porter asserts that a successful strategy requires a firm to aggressively stake out a market position, and that different strategies involve distinctly different approaches to competing and operating the business. An organization pursuing a differentiation strategy seeks competitive advantage by offering products or services that are unique from those offered by rivals, either through design, brand image, technology, features, or customer service. Alternatively, an organization pursuing a cost leadership strategy attempts to gain competitive advantage based on being the overall low-cost provider of a product or service. To be "all things to all people" can mean becoming "stuck in the middle" with no distinct competitive advantage. The difference between being "stuck in the middle" and successfully pursuing combination strategies merits discussion. Although Porter describes the dangers of not being successful in either cost control or differentiation, some firms have been able to succeed using combination strategies.

Research suggests that, in some cases, it is possible to be a cost leader while maintaining a differentiated product. Southwest Airlines has combined cost cutting measures with differentiation. The company has been able to reduce costs by not assigning seating and by eliminating meals on its planes. It has then been able to promote in its advertising that one does not get tasteless airline food on its flights. Its fares have been low enough to attract a significant number of passengers, allowing the airline to succeed.

Another firm that has pursued an effective combination strategy is Nike. When customer preferences moved to wide-legged jeans and cargo pants, Nike's market share slipped. Competitors such as Adidas offered less expensive shoes and undercut Nike's price. Nike's stock price dropped in 1998 to half its 1997 high. However, Nike reported a 70 percent increase in earnings for the first quarter of 1999 and saw a significant rebound in its stock price. Nike achieved the turnaround by cutting costs and developing new, distinctive products. Nike reduced costs by cutting some of its endorsements. Company research suggested the endorsement by the Italian soccer team, for example, was not achieving the desired results. Michael Jordan and a few other "big name" endorsers were retained while others, such as the Italian soccer team, were eliminated, resulting in savings estimated at over $100 million. Firing 7 percent of its 22,000 employees allowed the company to lower costs by another $200 million, and inventory was reduced to save additional money. While cutting costs, the firm also introduced new products designed to differentiate Nike's products from those of the competition.

Some industry environments may actually call for combination strategies. Trends suggest that executives operating in highly complex environments such as health care do not have the luxury of choosing exclusively one strategy over the other. The hospital industry may represent such an environment, as hospitals must compete on a variety of fronts. Combination (i.e., more complicated) strategies are both feasible and necessary to compete successfully. For instance, DRG-based reimbursement (diagnosis related groups) and the continual lowering of reimbursement ceilings have forced hospitals to compete on the basis of cost. At the same time, many of them jockey for position with differentiation based on such features as technology and birthing rooms. Thus, many hospitals may need to adopt some form of hybrid strategy in order to compete successfully, according to Walters and Bhuian.

FOCUS STRATEGY

The generic strategies of cost leadership and differentiation are oriented toward industry-wide recognition. The final generic strategy, focusing (also called niche or segmentation strategy), involves concentrating on a particular customer, product line, geographical area, channel of distribution, stage in the production process, or market niche. The underlying premise of the focus strategy is that a firm is better able to serve a limited segment more efficiently than competitors can serve a broader range of customers. Firms using a focus strategy simply apply a cost leader or differentiation strategy to a segment of the larger market. Firms may thus be able to differentiate themselves based on meeting customer needs, or they may be able to achieve lower costs within limited markets. Focus strategies are most effective when customers have distinctive preferences or specialized needs.

A focus strategy is often appropriate for small, aggressive businesses that do not have the ability or resources to engage in a nationwide marketing effort. Such a strategy may also be appropriate if the target market is too small to support a large-scale operation. Many firms start small and expand into a national organization. For instance, Wal-Mart started in small towns in the South and Midwest. As the firm gained in market knowledge and acceptance, it expanded throughout the South, then nationally, and now internationally. Wal-Mart started with a focused cost leader strategy in its limited market, and later was able to expand beyond its initial market segment.

A firm following the focus strategy concentrates on meeting the specialized needs of its customers. Products and services can be designed to meet the needs of buyers. One approach to focusing is to service either industrial buyers or consumers, but not both.

Martin-Brower, the third-largest food distributor in the United States, serves only the eight leading fast-food chains. With its limited customer list, Martin-Brower need only stock a limited product line; its ordering procedures are adjusted to match those of its customers; and its warehouses are located so as to be convenient to customers.

Firms utilizing a focus strategy may also be better able to tailor advertising and promotional efforts to a particular market niche. Many automobile dealers advertise that they are the largest volume dealer for a specific geographic area. Other car dealers advertise that they have the highest customer satisfaction scores within their defined market or the most awards for their service department.

Firms may be able to design products specifically for a customer. Customization may range from individually designing a product for a customer to allowing customer input into the finished product. Tailor-made clothing and custom-built houses include the customer in all aspects of production, from product design to final acceptance. Key decisions are made with customer input. However, providing such individualized attention to customers may not be feasible for firms with an industry-wide orientation.

Other forms of customization simply allow the customer to select from a menu of predetermined options. Burger King advertises that its burgers are made "your way," meaning that the customer gets to select from the predetermined options of pickles, lettuce, and so on. Similarly, customers are allowed to design their own automobiles within the constraints of predetermined colors, engine sizes, interior options, and so forth.

Potential difficulties associated with a focus strategy include a narrowing of differences between the limited market and the entire industry. National firms routinely monitor the strategies of competing firms in their various submarkets. They may then copy the strategies that appear particularly successful. The national firm, in effect, allows the focused firm to develop the concept, then the national firm may emulate the strategy of the smaller firm or acquire it as a means of gaining access to its technology or processes. Emulation increases the ability of other firms to enter the market niche while reducing the cost advantages of serving the narrower market.

Market size is always a problem for firms pursing a focus strategy. The targeted market segment must be large enough to provide an acceptable return so that the business can survive. For instance, ethnic restaurants are often unsuccessful in small U.S. towns, since the population base that enjoys Japanese or Greek cuisine is too small to allow the restaurant operator to make a profit. Likewise, the demand for an expensive, upscale restaurant is usually not sufficient in a small town to make its operation economically feasible.

Another potential danger for firms pursuing a focus strategy is that competitors may find submarkets within the target market. In the past, United Parcel Service (UPS) solely dominated the package delivery segment of the delivery business. Newer competitors such as Federal Express and Roadway Package Service (RPS) have entered the package delivery business and have taken customers away from UPS. RPS contracts with independent drivers in a territory to pick up and deliver packages, while UPS pays unionized wages and benefits to its drivers. RPS started operations in 1985 with 36 package terminals. By 1999 it was a $1 billion company with 339 facilities.

GENERIC STRATEGIES AND THE INTERNET

Porter asserts that these generic competitive strategies were not only relevant for the old economy, but are just as vital today. Indeed, he goes on to say that terms such as "old economy" and "new economy" may be misguided, and the concept of a firm's Internet operation as a stand-alone entity preclude the firm from garnering important synergies. Furthermore, the Internet may enhance a firm's opportunities for achieving or strengthening a distinctive strategic positioning. Therefore, effective strategy formulation at the business level should pay off, not in spite of the Internet, but in concert with it.

Porter describes how companies can set themselves apart in at least two ways: operational effectiveness (doing the same activities as competitors but doing them better) and strategic positioning (doing things differently and delivering unique value for customers). "The Internet affects operational effectiveness and strategic positioning in very different ways. It makes it harder for companies to sustain operational advantages, but it opens new opportunities for achieving or strengthening a distinctive strategic positioning." Although the Internet is a powerful tool for enhancing operational effectiveness, these enhancements alone are not likely to be sustained because of copying by rivals. This state of affairs elevates the importance of defining for the firm a unique value proposition. Internet technology can be a complement to successful strategy, but it is not sufficient. "Frequently, in fact, Internet applications address activities that, while necessary, are not decisive in competition, such as informing customers, processing transactions, and procuring inputs. Critical corporate assets—skilled personnel, proprietary product technology, efficient logistical systems—remain intact, and they are often strong enough to preserve existing competitive advantages."

Consistent with the earlier discussion regarding combination strategies, Kim, Nam, and Stimpert found in their study of e-businesses that firms pursuing a hybrid strategy of cost leadership and differentiation exhibited the highest performance. These authors concluded that cost leadership and differentiation must often be combined to be successful in e-business.

Porter's generic business strategies provide a set of methods that can be used singly or in combination to create a defendable business strategy. They also allow firms that use them successfully to gain a competitive advantage over other firms in the industry. Firms either strive to obtain lower costs than their competitors or to create a perceived difference between their product and the products of competitors. Firms can pursue their strategy on a national level or on a more focused, regional basis.

Clearly, Michael Porter's work has had a remarkable impact on strategy research and practice. The annual Porter Prize, akin to the Deming Prize, was established in 2001 in Japan to recognize that nation's leading companies in terms of strategy. Porter's ideas have stood the test of time and appear to be relevant both for profit-seeking enterprises and not-for-profit institutes in a variety of international settings. Torgovicky, Goldberg, Shvarts, and Bar Dayan have found a relationship between business strategy and performance measures in an ambulatory health care system in Israel, strengthening Porter's original theory about the non-viability of the stuck-in-the-middle strategy, and suggesting the applicability of Porter's generic strategies to not-for-profit institutes.

SEE ALSO: Strategic Planning Failure; Strategic Planning Tools; Strategy Formulation; Strategy Implementation; Strategy in the Global Environment; Strategy Levels

Joe G. Thomas
Revised by Bruce A. Walters

FURTHER READING:

Deephouse, D. "To Be Different, or To Be the Same? It's a Question (and Theory) of Strategic Balance." *Strategic Management Journal* 20 (1999): 147–66.

Harvard Business School Faculty Biography: Michael E. Porter. 2005. Available from <http://dor.hbs.edu/fi_redirect.jhtml?facInfo=bio&facEmId=mporter>.

Kim, E., D. Nam, and J.L. Stimpert. "Testing the Applicability of Porter's Generic Strategies in the Digital Age: A Study of Korean Cyber Malls." *Journal of Business Strategies* 21, no. 1 (2004): 19–45.

Kroll, M., P. Wright, and R. Heiens. "The Contribution of Product Quality to Competitive Advantage." *Strategic Management Journal* 20 (1999): 375–84.

Porter, Michael. *Competitive Advantage: Creating and Sustaining Superior Performance.* New York: Free Press, 1985.

———. *Competitive Advantage of Nations.* New York: Free Press, 1989.

———. *Competitive Strategy: Techniques for Analyzing Industries and Companies.* New York: Free Press, 1980.

———. "Strategy and the Internet." *Harvard Business Review* (March 2001): 63–78.

"Retrospective on Michael Porter's Competitive Strategy." *Academy of Management Executive* 16, no. 2 (2002): 40–65.

Sherer, P. "J&J in Talks to Purchase Centocor." *The Wall Street Journal,* 4 May 1999, A3.

Torgovicky, R., A. Goldberg, S. Shvarts, Y. Bar Dayan, et al. "Application of Porter's Generic Strategies in Ambulatory Health Care: A Comparison of Managerial Perceptions in Two Israeli Sick Funds." *Health Care Management Review* 30, no. 1 (2005): 17–23.

Walters, B.A., and S. Bhuian. "Complexity Absorption and Performance: A Structural Analysis of Acute-care Hospitals." *Journal of Management* 30 (2004): 97–121.

GLOBALIZATION

Globalization refers to the process of integration across societies and economies. The phenomenon encompasses the flow of products, services, labor, finance, information, and ideas moving across national borders. The frequency and intensity of the flows relate to the upward or downward direction of globalization as a trend.

There is a popular notion that there has been an increase of globalization since the early 1980s. However, a comparison of the period between 1870 and 1914 to the post-World War II era indicates a greater degree of globalization in the earlier part of the century than the latter half. This is true in regards to international trade growth and capital flows, as well as migration of people to America.

If a perspective starts after 1945—at the start of the Cold War—globalization is a growing trend with a predominance of global economic integration that leads to greater interdependence among nations. Between 1990 and 2001, total output of export and import of goods as a proportion of GDP rose from 32.3 percent to 37.9 percent in developed countries and 33.8 percent to 48.9 percent for low- to middle-income countries. From 1990 to 2003, international trade export rose by $3.4 to $7.3 trillion (see Figure 1). Hence, the general direction of globalization is growth that is unevenly distributed between wealthier and poorer countries.

RATIONALE

A primary economic rationale for globalization is reducing barriers to trade for the enrichment of all societies. The greater good would be served by leveraging

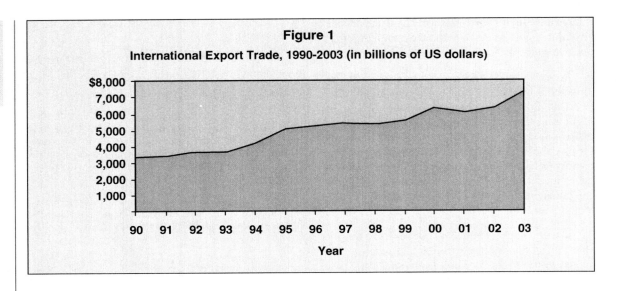

Figure 1

International Export Trade, 1990-2003 (in billions of US dollars)

comparative advantages for production and trade that are impeded by regulatory barriers between sovereignty entities. In other words, the betterment of societies through free trade for everyone is possible as long as each one has the freedom to produce with a comparative advantage and engage in exchanges with others.

This economic rationale for global integration depends on supporting factors to facilitate the process. The factors include advances in transportation, communication, and technology to provide the necessary conduits for global economic integration. While these factors are necessary, they are not sufficient. Collaboration with political will through international relations is required to leverage the potential of the supporting factors.

HISTORICAL BACKGROUND

Globalization from 1870 to 1914 came to an end with the World War I as various countries pursued isolationism and protectionism agendas through various treaties—the Treaty of Brest-Litovsk (1918), the Treaty of Versailles (1918), the Treaty of St. Germain (1919), and the Treaty of Trianon (1920). U.S. trade policies —the Tariff acts of 1921, 1922, 1924, 1926, and the Smooth Hawley Tariffs of 1930—raised barriers to trade. These events contributed to the implosion of globalization for more than forty years.

Toward the end of World War II, forty-four countries met in an effort to re-establish international trade. The milestone is referred to as Bretton Woods, named after the New Hampshire country inn where the meeting was held. Results of Bretton Woods included the creation of the International Monetary Fund (IMF), the World Bank, and subsequently, the General Agreements on Tariffs and Trade (GATT).

In 1948 the International Trade Organization (ITO) was established as an agency of the United Nations, with fifty member countries and the Havana Charter to facilitate international trade but it failed. As a result, GATT rose to fill the void as a channel for multilateral trade negotiations and recognition of "Most Favored Nation" status that applied the same trading conditions between members that applied to other trading partners with "most favored" partner standing.

GATT involved a number of different multilateral rounds of trade negotiations to reduce trade barriers and facilitate international trade. In the first round, the twenty-three founding members of GATT agreed to 45,000 tariff concessions affecting 20 percent of international trade worth $10 billion. Many of GATT's trade rules were drawn from the ITO charter. Subsequent trade rounds involved more members and additional issues, but the basic foundation of GATT remained the same.

In the second round, the Kennedy Round of the mid-1960s, the focus continued with tariff reductions.

In the third round, the Tokyo Round (1973–1979), 102 countries participated to reform the trading system, resulting in tariff on manufactured products reduced to 4.7 percent from a high of 40 percent at the inception of GATT. Important issues revolved around anti-dumping measures, and subsidies and countervailing measures. The reduction of trade barriers enabled about an average of 8 percent growth of world trade per year in the 1950s and 1960s.

In the fourth round, the Uruguay Round (1986 to 1993), 125 countries participated to develop a more comprehensive system.

On April 15, 1995, in Marrakesh, Morocco, a deal was signed to create the World Trade Organization (WTO), which replaced GATT with a permanent institution that required a full and permanent commitment.

The WTO encompasses trade in goods, services, and intellectual property related to trade with a more efficient dispute settlement system.

COMPLEXITIES AND CONTROVERSIES

The increase of globalization surfaced many complex and controversial issues as economies and societies became more interdependent with greater frequency of interactions between one another. A number of important trends make up globalization including: (1) location of integration activities; (2) impact upon poorer societies; (3) flow of capital; (4) migration of labor and work; (5) diffusion of technology; (6) sustainability of the natural environment; (7) reconfiguration of cultural dynamics; and (8) development of organizational strategies for global competition.

Many authors specialize in exploring each issue with much greater depth. The purpose of reviewing the different trends in this essay is to provide some highlight concerning the interrelated complexities underlying globalization.

LOCATION OF INTEGRATION ACTIVITIES. The extent of globalization unfolds in an uneven fashion to the degree that the question is raised whether international trade is more focused on regional rather than global integration. Trading blocs, such as the North American Free Trade Agreement (NAFTA), the European Union (EU), the Asia-Pacific Economic Co-operation (APEC), Mercosur (South American trading bloc), the Association of South East Asian Nations (ASEAN), and the East Africa Community (EAC), support regional cooperation between geographical neighbors.

Georgios Chortareas' and Theodore Pelagidis' research findings on openness and convergence in international trade indicate that intra-regional trade increased more than global trade in most situations. They stated that " . . . despite the positive international climate resulting from important reductions in transportation costs, the development of new technologies and trade liberalization markets continue to be determined, to a large extent, regionally and nationally. . ."

Within NAFTA, intra-regional exports rose from 34 percent in the 1980s to more than 56 percent in 2000; exports between Asian country members amounted to 48 percent in 2000; and exports within the EU were sustained at about 62 percent.

An example of limitations to fair market access for developing countries is that developed countries subsidize agricultural producers with about $330 billion per year, which creates a significant disadvantage for poorer economies without such subsidies. The impact is exacerbated because 70 percent of the world's poor population lives in rural communities and depends heavily on agriculture. Hence, one of the concerns with uneven distribution of globalization is its impact on poorer economies by perpetuating systems of inequality.

IMPACT ON POORER SOCIETIES. A challenge to globalization is that inequality arises from imbalances in trade liberalization where the rich gain disproportionately more than the poor. Ajit K. Ghose examined the impact of international trade on income inequality and found that inter-country inequality increased from 1981 to 1997, in a sample of ninety-six national economies, but international inequality measured by per capita GDP declined. The ratio of average income for the wealthiest 20 percent compared to the poorest 20 percent rose from 30 to 74 from the early 1960s to the late 1990s.

In 2004, one billion people owned 80 percent of the world's GDP, while another billion survives on a $1. However, during the same period, when average income is weighted by population, income inequality dropped by 10 percent in the same period. Also, global income distribution became more equal with other measures such as purchasing power parity or the number of people living in poverty.

The World Development Indicators for 2004 showed a drop in absolute number of people living on $1 per day from 1.5 billion in 1981 to 1.1 billion in 2001 with most of the achievements taking place in the East Asia region. Thus, the impact of globalization on inequality is a complex issue depending on the particular measures. More specific examination needs to account for other contributing factors, such as how regionalism increases concentration of trade between countries that are wealthier and leaving poorer countries at the margin.

FLOW OF CAPITAL. The flow of capital relates to both regionalism and inequality issues. Two forms of capital flow are foreign direct investments (FDI) made by business firms and investment portfolios, diversified with foreign assets or borrowers seeking foreign funding. Data from the World Bank indicated that FDI grew from an average of $100 billion per year in the 1980s to $370 billion in 1997. Net private capital flow amounts to about $200 billion in 2004.

Also, some economies have significant remittance flows from labor migration, which were approximately $100 billion in 2003 and $126 billion in 2004 for ninety developing countries. Some Caribbean countries receive more than 10 percent of their GDP from remittances. While developing countries are the primary recipients of remittances, transaction costs can amount to 10 to 15 percent per transaction. Reducing such obstacles would benefit poorer countries with heavy dependencies on remittances. The flow of money across national borders relates to the migration of both labor and work.

MIGRATION OF LABOR AND WORK. An important dimension of globalization is the migration of people. While the proportion of migration was greater during the earlier mercantilism period, sovereign border controls to a large extent create a filtration process for migration. About 175 million people lived in a different country than their birth country in 2000. They can be separated into three categories: 158 million international migrants, 16 million refugees, and 900,000 asylum seekers.

An important global trend in the future is the movement of labor from developing to developed countries because of the latter's need for labor with an aging population. Family-sponsored migration makes up 45 to 75 percent of international migrants who mainly originate from developing countries to countries in Europe and North America.

Even before 9/11, legal migration of labor needed to overcome substantial bureaucracy in the border control process. The number applying for entry into developed countries often far exceeds the number permitted. Due to extensive legal processes, some migrants enter illegally, while others become illegal with expiration of legal status.

Anti-terrorism measures imposed shortly after the 9/11 attacks resulted in a minor shift in the flow of migrants away from the United States toward other developed countries. With the aging of baby boomers in many developed countries, future globalization of migrant labor flows is receiving more attention, especially in education, health care, retirement funding, and housing, as well as meeting workforce needs to sustain business competitiveness.

Although migrant labor often entails the movement of people in search of work, a related globalization trend is the migration of work to different geographical location. While multinational corporations (MNCs) often seek low-cost labor, innovation advances in computer technology, satellite communication infrastructures, internet developments, and efficient transportation network enable companies to distribute work in ways not possible before.

Compression of time and space with internet technology allows for the distribution of work to take place around the world with global virtual teams. The phenomena of outsourcing and offshoring expand on the earlier sourcing of low-cost manufacturing. During the 1960s and 1970s, MNCs migrated to low-wage labor to manufacture products that entailed significant labor costs.

Expansion of MNCs in the 1990s encompassed highly skilled workers, service work, and global virtual teams. Firms started to outsource information technology (IT) functions as early as the 1970s, but a major wave of outsourcing started in 1989 with the shortage of skilled IT workers in developed countries. At the same time, the trend of shifting work around the globe to leverage the different time zones began with the financial industry's ability to shift trading between the various stock exchanges in New York, Tokyo, and Hong Kong, and London.

Technological innovations in computers and the internet enabled other industries, such as software engineering, data transcription, and customer service centers to also shift work around the globe. Higher education and high-skill health care jobs are also embarking on global outsourcing.

In 2001, outsourcing expenditures amounted to $3.7 trillion and the estimation for 2003 is $5.1 trillion. The impact of global outsourcing is not just a relocation of jobs, but also a dampening of employee compensation levels in more developed economies. For example, in 2000, salaries for senior software engineers were as high as $130K, but dropped to about $100K at the end of 2002; and entry-level computer help-desk staff salaries dropped from about $55K to $35K. For IT vendor firms in countries like India, IT engineering jobs command a premium Indian salary that is at a fraction of their U.S. counterparts. In sum, migration of labor and work create complex globalization dynamics.

DIFFUSION OF TECHNOLOGY. Innovations in telecommunication, information technology, and computing advances make up key drivers to support the increase of globalization. In 1995, the World Wide Web had 20 million users, exploded to 400 million by late 2000 and had an estimated one billion users in 2005. However, the rapid growth and adoption of information technology is not evenly diffused around the world.

The gap between high versus low adoption rates is often referred to as the digital divide. In 2002, the number of users per 1000 people was highest in Iceland at 647.9; others in the top five ranks of internet users included Sweden at 573.1, the United States at 551.4, Denmark and Canada both at 512.8, and Finland at 508.9. In comparison, countries at the low end of internet use were Tajikistan and Myanmar at 0.5 per 1000, Ethiopia at 0.7, the Congo at 0.9, Burundi at 1.2, and Bangladesh at 1.5.

The digital divide reflects other disparities of globalization. Globalization of computer technology also entails a growing trend of computer crimes on an international basis, which requires cross-border collaboration to address it. Additional globalization trends related to computer technology include developments in artificial intelligence, high-speed connections such as wireless applications, and integration with biotechnology.

SUSTAINABILITY OF THE NATURAL ENVIRONMENT. The impacts of globalization on environment sustainability are hotly contested, with major environmental protests held at international economic meetings or prominent multilateral trade forums. The United Nation's 1987 publication of the *Brundtland Report* (named for Gro Brundtland, Prime Minister of Norway), galvanized international attention on sustainable development. A major assumption was that the degradation of the environment in developing countries was due primarily to poverty.

Some advocates of globalization consider free trade to be a solution to alleviate poverty and subsequently, reduce pollution. However, the arguments depend upon corporate social responsibility, managerial knowledge of environmental sustainability, and a level of ignorance in the developing community.

Critics find that often large MNCs have greater financial resources than some developing countries, which can be used to compromise and derail regulatory regimes from protecting the environment. For example, while a MNC may not produce or sell certain environmentally damaging products in a country with tight regulatory controls, they may find their way to markets with fewer environmental regulatory constraints—"pollution havens." This line of logic leads to the notion of globalization becoming a "race to the bottom" as countries compete with lowering of environmental standards to attract foreign capital for economic development.

One of the landmarks on environmental globalization is the Kyoto Accord, an international treaty to reduce greenhouse gas emissions based on exchanging limited pollution credits between countries. After lengthy multilateral complex negotiations, the Kyoto Accord was concluded in December, 1997 for ratification by national governments. On February 16, 2005, the date for the Kyoto Protocol to take effect, 141 nations ratified the agreement. Even though the United States is the world's largest polluter in volume and per capita output of greenhouse gases, the Bush administration refused to ratify the Kyoto Accord.

RECONFIGURATION OF CULTURAL DYNAMICS. Culture is another area of complex controversies with globalization. Competing perspectives about how globalization affects cultures revolve around the debates of cultural homogenization versus cultural diversification. The optimistic view of cultural globalization is that cultural diversity focuses on freer cultural exchanges with broader choices and enrichment of learning from different traditions. People have greater choices of globally produced goods, in addition to local offerings, without being bound by their geographical location. Alternatively, critics of cultural globalization present evidence demonstrating the depletion of cultural diversity through processes referred to as "Disneyfication" or "McDonaldization."

Furthermore, not only is cultural diversity diminished but cultural quality is as well with mass produced goods being directed toward a common denominator. The criticisms are related to a sense of "Americanization" of the world, rather than globalization. The process involves a sense of far-reaching, anonymous cultural imperialism. Debates from each perspective are intense with substantial evidence that also reveals complex ties to social and political dynamics within and between national borders.

Cultural globalization continues into the foreseeable future with many more controversial dynamics related to three important issues: 1) the impact of extractive industries on the socio-economic, cultural exclusion and dislocation of indigenous peoples and their traditional knowledge; 2) international trading of cultural goods and knowledge; and 3) inflow of immigration impacts on national culture, which creates a tension between a sense of threat to the national culture and migrant demands for respect to their traditions in a multicultural society.

DEVELOPMENT OF ORGANIZATIONAL STRATEGIES FOR GLOBAL COMPETITION. The multiple dynamics of globalization—regionalism, inequality, financial flows, migration of labor and work, technological innovations, environmental sustainability, and cultural dynamics—form a turbulent and complex environment for managing business operations. While seven trends were highlighted to provide a brief sketch of interrelated complexities and controversies globalization, it also surfaced other significant issues.

Global concerns revolve around terrorism, rapid transmission of pandemic diseases and viruses, the rise of China's and India's economies, an aging population in wealthier northern countries versus younger growing populations in the southern hemisphere, and advances in biotechnology are intricately embedded in globalization processes.

COMPETING IN THE GLOBAL ECONOMY

Globalization entails both opportunities and threats for creating and sustaining competitive strategies. Emerging economies offer resources in terms of labor, as well as expanding market opportunities. However, geopolitical relationships and backlashes from perceptions of cultural imperialism, such as the tensions between the United States and the European Union during the Iraq war create challenges for business operations.

Global managers have a wide range of options to deal with globalization. Organizational strategies for international operations involve two related demands—the need for local orientation and the need for integration (as shown in Figure 2). Firms with low need for local orientation, but high need for integration require a global strategy that centralizes core operations with minor modifications for local adaptation. However, firms with a need for high local orientation, but low need for integration, require a multinational strategy that decentralizes significant operations to respond to local market conditions. Firms integrating a high need for both local orientation and organizational integration should strive for a transnational strategy.

In addition to selecting a strategy for global competition, managers also need to make decisions regarding the internationalization process. Two processes are important. First, the development of innovations in a home market and as products moves along the product life cycle stages, firms can take products entering into the plateau of a mature stage to new international markets. Often the flow moves from developed to developing countries.

Second, stages of internationalization with foreign entry modes that involve increasing resource commitment and risks start with exporting to licensing or joint ventures to wholly owned subsidiaries. The stage approach to internationalization takes time, which is a challenge within a global environment where information moves around the world in nanoseconds.

Alternatively, Kenichi Ohmae argued that the speed and complexities of globalization require firms to rethink their internationalization process because incremental stage models are too slow. Given the rate and quantity of knowledge flows in global competition, firms are likely to face competition in their home markets, with comparable innovations to their own before they are able to establish a foothold in the international market.

The incremental stage models are too slow for competing in an increasingly integrated global economy. Ohmae suggested that firms form global strategic alliances with partners established in three major markets—North America, Europe, and Asia, particularly Japan. Development of global competitive intelligence and innovation among the partners provide for rapid market development and the establishment of strategic positions in multiple locations.

Basically, globalization into the twenty-first century creates a fundamentally different competitive environment that shifted from incremental internationalization processes to almost simultaneous deployment of innovations. This internationalization process also shifts the work of global managers from managing a field of expatriates to collaborating with strategic partners across national borders and managing global offshore outsourcing vendors in multiple geographical locations.

Figure 2
Skill Profile of the Effective Global Manager

The ability to envision and implement the strategy of thinking globally while acting locally

Being able to manage change and transition

Being able to manage cultural diversity

The ability to design and function in flexible organizational structures

Being able to deal with stress and ambiguity

Having the skills required to work with others—especially in team setting

Being able to communicate well, and having a command of more than one language

Having the ability to learn and transfer knowledge in a organization

Entering into trusting alliances and operating with personal integrity and honesty

Being able to turn ideas into action

Having a stateless perception of the world

Being willing to take risks and to experiment

Globalization is a culmination of complex and controversial trends that include degree of geographical integration, inequalities, financial flows, labor and work, technological innovations, environmental sustainability, cultural dynamics, and organizational strategies for global competition. Given a historical perspective, globalization has fluctuated over time and many indicators support a trend of increasing globalization since the 1980s.

While the United States is the dominant superpower in the global economy, the rise of both China and India is an important consideration for international business. Global managers have options for strategies and structures, as well as different internationalization processes. In sum, globalization creates a competitive arena where MNCs evolve into global networks with collaboration and controversial differences as necessities to sustain a competitive strategy.

SEE ALSO: International Business; International Cultural Differences; International Management; Organizational Culture

Diana J. Wong-MingJi

FURTHER READING:

Agenor, Pierre-Richard. "Does Globalization Hurt the Poor?" *International Economics and Economic Policy* 1, no. 1 (2004): 21–51.

Chortareas, Georgios E., and Theodore Pelagidis. "Trade Flows: A Facet of Regionalism or Globalisation?" *Cambridge Journal of Economics* 28, no. 2 (March 2004): 353–271.

Clott, Christopher B. "Perspectives on Global Outsourcing and the Changing Nature of Work." *Business and Society Review* 109, no. 2 (2004): 153–170.

Corbett, M. "Outsourcing's Next Wave." *Fortune,* 14 June 2002.

Cowan, Tyler. *Creative Destruction: How Globalization is Changing the World's Culture.* Princeton, NJ: Princeton University Press, 2002.

Doyle, Michael W. "The Challenge of Worldwide Migration." *Journal of International Affairs* 57, no. 2 (Spring 2004): 1–5.

Ghose, Ajit K. "Global Inequality and International Trade." *Cambridge Journal of Economics* 28, no. 2 (March 2004): 229–252.

Johanson, J. and J.E. Vahlne. "The Internationalization Process of the Firm: A Model of Knowledge Development and Increasing Foreign Market Commitment." *Journal of International Business* 8 (1977): 23–32.

Keohane, Robert O., and Joseph S. Nye, Jr. "Globalization: What's New?" *Foreign Policy,* Spring, 104–119.

Minyard, Alan D. "The World Trade Organization: History, Structure, and Analysis." 1996. Available from <http://www2. netdoor.com/~aminyard/>.

Neal, Christopher. "Global Poverty Down by Half Since 1981 but Progress Uneven as Economic Growth Eludes Many Countries." The World Bank Group, 2004. Available from <http://web.worldbank.org>.

Ohmae, Kenichi. *The Borderless World.* New York, NY: Harper Business, 1990.

O'Neil, Tim. "Globalization: Fads, Fictions, and Facts." *Business Economics* 39 (January 2004): 16–27.

Palvia, Shallendra. "Global Outsourcing of IT and IT Enabled Services: Impact on U.S. and Global Economy." *Journal of Information Technology Cases and Applications* 5, no. 3 (2003): 1–11.

Simon, David. "Dilemmas of Development and the Environment in a Globalizing World: Theory, Policy and Praxis." *Progress in Development Studies* 3, no. 1 (2003): 5–41.

United Nations Development Program. *Human Development Report, 2004: Cultural Liberties in Today's Diverse World.* New York, NY: Oxford University Press, 2004.

United Nations Development Program. *Human Development Report, 2001: Making New Technologies Work for Human Development.* New York: Oxford University Press, 2001.

Wolf, Martin. *Why Globalization Works.* New Haven, CT: Yale University Press, 2004.

World Bank. *World Development Report, 2003: Sustainable Development in a Dynamic World.* New York, NY: Oxford University Press, 2003.

World Commission on Environment and Development. *Brundtland Report: Our Common Future.* New York, NY: Oxford University Press, 1987.

GOALS AND GOAL SETTING

Goals and objectives provide organizations with a blueprint that determines a course of action and aids them in preparing for future changes. A goal can be defined as a future state that an organization or individual strives to achieve. For each goal that an organization sets, it also sets objectives. An objective is a short-term target with measurable results. Without clearly-defined goals and objectives, organizations will have trouble coordinating activities and forecasting future events.

According to Barney and Griffin, organizational goals serve four basic functions; they provide guidance and direction, facilitate planning, motivate and inspire employees, and help organizations evaluate and control performance. Organizational goals inform employees where the organization is going and how it plans to get there. When employees need to make difficult decisions, they can refer to the organization's goals for guidance. Goals promote planning to determine how goals will be achieved. Employees often set goals in order to satisfy a need; thus, goals can be motivational and increase performance. Evaluation and control allows an organization to compare its actual performance to its goals and then make any necessary adjustments.

According to Locke and Latham, goals affect individual performance through four mechanisms. First, goals direct action and effort toward goal-related activities and away from unrelated activities. Second, goals energize employees. Challenging goals lead to higher employee effort than easy goals. Third, goals affect persistence. Employees exert more effort to achieve high goals. Fourth, goals motivate employees to use their existing knowledge to attain a goal or to acquire the knowledge needed to do so.

The elements of goal-setting theory are shown in Figure 1. The goal-setting model indicates that individuals have needs and values that influence what they desire. A need is defined as a lack of something desirable or useful. According to Maslow's hierarchy of needs, all individuals possess the same basic needs. Individuals do, however, differ in their values. Values are defined as a group of attitudes about a concept that contains a moral quality of like or dislike and acceptable or unacceptable. Values determine whether a particular outcome is rewarding. Employees compare current conditions to desired conditions in order to determine if they are satisfied and fulfilled. If an employee finds that he or she is not satisfied with the current situation, goal setting becomes a way of achieving what he or she wants.

Research suggests that individual differences play a role in determining goal effectiveness. Individuals may

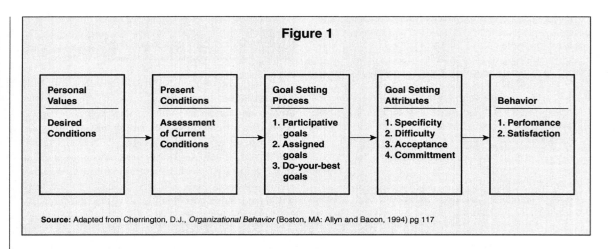

Figure 1

Personal Values Desired Conditions	Present Conditions Assessment of Current Conditions	Goal Setting Process 1. Participative goals 2. Assigned goals 3. Do-your-best goals	Goal Setting Attributes 1. Specificity 2. Difficulty 3. Acceptance 4. Committment	Behavior 1. Perfomance 2. Satisfaction

Source: Adapted from Cherrington, D.J., *Organizational Behavior* (Boston, MA: Allyn and Bacon, 1994) pg 117

differ in their goal orientations, priorities, and self-regulation ability. Research suggests that an individual's goal orientation may influence goal effectiveness. Employees with a learning orientation desire to acquire knowledge and skills, whereas employees with a performance goal orientation focus on the outcome rather than the achievement process. While employees with a learning goal orientation view goals as a challenge, employees with a performance goal orientation may view goals as a threat. Studies provide some support that assigned goals are more effective for individuals with a learning goal orientation. Personal and organizational goals are not always congruent. For example, as the number of two-income families increases, work-family conflicts increase. Employees now have to balance professional and personal goals. An employee's desire to achieve personal goals may affect his or her motivation to achieve organizational goals. When organizational and personal goals are not aligned, it may have a detrimental effect on performance. Self-regulation is also important in goal setting and goal achievement. Research has shown that employees improved self-regulation when they were trained in self-management. Self-regulation training can provide employees with an opportunity to set specific high goals, to monitor ways the environment may hinder goal attainment, and to identify and administer rewards for making goal progress, as well as punishments for failing to make progress.

GOAL ATTRIBUTES

Goal-setting attributes have been the subject of extensive research. The four attributes are; specificity, difficulty, acceptance, and commitment. Studies show that there is a direct relationship between goal specificity and employee performance. The more specific the goal, the less ambiguity involved and the higher the performance. When employees are given do-your-best goals, they do not have an external reference by which

they can measure their own performance. For example, telling a salesperson to "do the best you can" is an extremely vague goal that may not increase performance. However, "increase sales by 10 percent" is much more specific and encourages high performance because the employee has past sales as a reference point.

Goal difficulty also has a direct relationship with performance. Research shows that more difficult goals lead to higher performance, as long as the goals do not become so difficult that employees perceive them as impossible. Unreasonable goals frustrate, rather than motivate, employees. On the other hand, difficult but realistic goals lead to increased performance and motivation. Research suggests that employees are highly motivated when the probability of achieving a specific goal is 50 percent.

Goal acceptance is the degree to which employees accept a goal. Employees need to feel that the goal is fair and consistent in order to make it their own. Even if a goal is specific and attainable, individual acceptance is still necessary for effectiveness. Employees may reject goals for a multitude of reasons; they feel the work is meaningless, they do not trust the organization, or they do not receive feedback regarding their performance.

Finally, employees must be committed to the goal in order for it to be achieved. Commitment refers to the degree to which employees are dedicated to reaching the goal, and is determined by both situational and personal variables. Commitment to a goal can be increased by developing goals that appeal to employees's values and needs. Employees must be convinced that the goal is important. It should be relevant and significant to some personal value. For example, goals that are tied to company success, and therefore job security, often appeal to employees's need for security. It is also important that a leader or manager who is respected and credible convey the goal to employees. Goals must be attainable for employees to be committed. While goals may be challenging, employees should be convinced that goals are within reach. Research shows that commitment to goals increases when employees have the opportunity to participate in goal setting. Additionally, developing strategies is useful in helping employees achieve goals. Organizations that provide continuous training for employees build confidence and increase commitment to organizational goals.

TYPES OF GOALS AND OBJECTIVES

Goals should be closely tied to an organization's mission and vision statement. The strategic goals, tactical goals and objectives, and operational goals and objectives support the mission statement of the organization.

STRATEGIC GOALS. Strategic goals are set at the top of an organization and directly support the mission statement. Strategic goals are related to the entire organization instead of any one department. There are eight types of strategic goals found in organizations. The first type of strategic goal affects market standing, for example "to control 45 percent of the market share in the United States by the year 2011." Strategic goals regarding market standing help position a company as a market leader in any given industry. An example of the second strategic goal, innovation, is "to develop three new applications for use in businesses in the United States over the next three years." Productivity, the third type of strategic goal, involves reductions in manufacturing costs or increases in output. The fourth type of strategic goal is the efficient use of physical assets and financial resources, such as human resources. The fifth type of strategic goal involves the organization's profits and is usually defined in terms of return on assets or market value of stocks. Management development and performance is the sixth type of strategic goal, which concerns the conduct of managers as well as their continuing development. An example of this type of strategic goal is "to increase the number of hours offered in management training courses by 15 percent over the next year." The seventh type of strategic goal addresses the conduct of employees, as well as the concern for their attitudes and performance. An example of this type of strategic goal is "to reduce turnover by 12 percent over the next two years." Finally, the eighth type of strategic goal is concerned with the public and social responsibility of the organization. These types of goals might be concerned with reducing pollution or contributing to different charities.

TACTICAL GOALS. Tactical goals and objectives are directly related to the strategic goals of the organization. They indicate the levels of achievement necessary in the departments and divisions of the organization. Tactical goals and objectives must support the strategic goals of the organization. For example, if a strategic goal states that the organization is going to reduce total costs by 15 percent next year, then the different departments of the company would set tactical objectives to decrease their costs by a certain percentage so that the average of all departments equals 15 percent.

OPERATIONAL GOALS. Operational goals and objectives are determined at the lowest level of the organization and apply to specific employees or subdivisions in the organization. They focus on the individual responsibilities of employees. For example, if the department's tactical goal is related to an increase in return on assets by 5 percent, then the sales manager may have an operational objective of increasing sales by 10 percent.

SUPER-ORDINATE GOALS. Super-ordinate goals are those goals that are important to more than one party. They are often used to resolve conflict between groups. Through cooperating to achieve the goal, the tension and animosity between groups is often resolved. Feelings of camaraderie are created along with trust and friendship. Super-ordinate goals can be powerful motivators for groups to resolve their differences and cooperate with one another. In order for them to be successful, the parties must first perceive that there is mutual dependency on one another. The super-ordinate goal must be desired by everyone. Finally, all parties involved must expect to receive rewards from the accomplishment of the goal.

GOAL-SETTING APPROACHES

When choosing goals and objectives, there are several approaches an organization can take. Three common approaches are; the top-down approach, the bottom-up approach, and the interactive approach. In the top-down approach, goal setting begins at the top of the organization. Management by objectives (MBO) is a commonly-used top-down approach. This approach focuses on coordinating goal setting, incentives, and feedback. Studies suggest that approximately 50 percent of large organizations currently use or have used MBO. First, upper level managers (such as the CEO and other executives) establish the organizational mission and then determine strategic goals. The strategic goals determine the tactical goals and objectives as they are passed down to the next level of management.

The tactical goals in each department dictate the operational goals and objectives to individual employees. On the lowest level, the supervisor and employee agree upon performance objectives, as well as how goal attainment will be measured. This gives the supervisor a chance to address employee concerns or potential obstacles to goal achievement. When the next evaluation occurs, the supervisor and subordinate meet to assess to what extent performance objectives have been met. The top-down approach has several advantages. It helps guarantee that the goals and objectives of the organization are directly tied to and support the mission statement. It increases the likelihood that ambitious goals set by upper-level managers will trickle down to lower levels of the organization; thus, ambitious goals will be set for everyone in the organization. However, the top-down approach has several disadvantages. Oftentimes, members of upper-level management are so far removed from the day-to-day activities of the employees that the goals may be overly ambitious and unrealistic. Goals set at the top of the organization do not change as quickly with the organization, so they are not as flexible as goals set at the bottom of the organization. Finally, the top-down approach does not always involve employee participation in the goal-setting process. Thus, employees may not have a sense of ownership.

The bottom-up approach begins at the lower levels of the organization. Individuals at the bottom of the organization's chart set the goals and objectives for members directly above. Operational goals and objectives determine the tactical objectives, which in turn determine the strategic goals and objectives. Finally, the organizational mission is defined according to the guidelines set by the employees. Goals determined by bottom-up goal setting are likely to be more realistic than those set at the top of the organization. They are more flexible and reflect the current situation of the organization. Finally, goals created by all levels of the organization, and by all types of employees, are more likely to encourage employee commitment. There are disadvantages to bottom-up goal setting. Goals and objectives formulated by bottom-up goal setting are not always in line with the organization's mission. Often, organizations that use a bottom-up approach lack clear direction and focus. There is no hierarchical alignment with the goals of the organization. Another disadvantage of this type of goal setting is that the goals created by employees are not always challenging and ambitious. Studies have shown that challenging (yet realistic) goals are more motivational than those that are not.

The third approach to goal setting is interactive. It is a process by which employees at different levels of the organization participate in developing goals and objectives. Top levels of the organization begin by developing a mission statement. Managers at different levels and departments of the organization then come together and determine the strategic goals. Next, discussions regarding the tactical goals and objectives are decided upon by including lower-level managers and supervisors. Finally, individuals contribute to the process by defining their own operational goals and objectives.

This approach to goal setting involves the consensus of many different levels of management and frontline employees. Interactive goal setting involves discussion and cooperation among management and employees. The interactive approach enjoys the same advantages as bottom-up goal setting without many of the disadvantages. Goals are more realistic and current than in the top-down approach. Because it involves cooperation at all levels, employees feel valued and important. Their commitment to the organization, as well as the goals, is increased. Input from upper management helps to ensure that the goals are challenging and ambitious, which increases motivation. There are, however, a few disadvantages to the interactive approach. It is very time consuming because of the cooperation and consensus involved. It is also difficult to manage and maintain. If managers do not stay actively involved, it can quickly turn into a top-down or bottom-up approach with the disadvantages of each.

FEEDBACK AND EVALUATION

Employees should be provided with specific performance-related feedback to help them determine if they are achieving their goals. Frequent feedback is beneficial because it allows employees to adjust their level of effort to achieve their goals. Feedback from management should consistently be provided. However, feedback can also come from coworkers or customers. It may be in the form of tallies, charts, or graphs that depict performance over time. Feedback not only allows employees to assess their accomplishments, but it also provides them with the continued motivation to achieve their goals.

Not only should the employees be evaluated, but goals should be evaluated periodically. Because organizations face many changes, goals need to be flexible enough so that organizations can respond to dynamic environments. Goals that were set at the beginning of the year may not be realistic at the end of the year. When organizations set goals that are unattainable or unrealistic in the long or short run, employees become unmotivated. When evaluating the appropriateness of a goal, managers should determine whether or not the goal covers the most important aspects of performance. Are the goals realistic yet ambitious enough to motivate employees? Objectives should be measurable and specific. Objectives that are not measurable are often not directly tied to the organization's overall mission. They should be linked to rewards that are valued by employees and associated with specific time periods.

Goal setting is a commonly used motivational approach. Numerous studies have shown that that goal setting is related to profit and performance. In one study, goal setting led to improved productivity in 95 percent of the organizations. It also led to a 16 percent increase in worker productivity. Additionally, 61 percent of organizations surveyed used goal-setting theory specifically to increase performance. Organizations that set goals experienced higher levels of annual profit than those that did not. Therefore, goal setting is a powerful way to increase organizational effectiveness and employee performance.

While goal setting is advantageous to organizations, as well as employees, it is not an easy process to undertake. Managers sometimes underestimate the difficulty involved in setting goals. They are attracted to the benefits without understanding the limitations. Often beneficial are training courses on how to set goals, as well as a continuous follow-up process that involves all areas of the organization. Follow-up and refresher courses are often necessary to keep employees and managers focused on the goal-setting process. By offering courses that involve both managers and frontline employees, organizations are able to increase the level of consensus when it comes time to define goals.

SEE ALSO: Feedback; Management Styles; Mission and Vision Statements; Strategy Formulation; SWOT Analysis

Laura E. Marler

FURTHER READING:

Barney, Jay B., and Ricky W. Griffin. *The Management of Organizations.* Boston: Houghton Mifflin Company, 1992.

Cherrington, David J. *Organizational Behavior.* Boston: Allyn and Bacon, 1994.

Fried, Yitzhak, and Linda H. Slowik. "Enriching Goal-Setting Theory With Time: An Integrated Approach." *Academy of Management Review* 29, no. 3 (2004): 404–422.

Latham, Gary P. "The Motivational Benefits of Goal-Setting." *Academy of Management Executives* 18, no. 4 (2004): 126–129.

Locke, Edwin A., and Gary P. Latham. "Building a Practically Useful Theory of Goal Setting and Task Motivation: A 35-Year Odyssey." *American Psychologist* 57, no. 9 (2002): 705–717.

Terpstra, David E., and Elizabeth J. Rozell. "The Relationship of Goal Setting to Organizational Profitability." *Group & Organization Management* 19 (1994): 285–295.

Tubbs, Mark E. "Goal Setting Research in Industrial/ Organizational Psychology." *Multiple Perspectives on the Effects of Evaluation on Performance: Toward an Integration.* ed. Stephen Harkins. Boston: Kluwer Academic Publishers, 2001.

GOVERNMENT-UNIVERSITY-INDUSTRY PARTNERSHIPS

Since the 1970s the United States has seen the rise of various forms of collaboration among the sectors of government, academia, and industry. These forms include industry-specific inter-firm research consortia, government-industry technology transfer, and university-industry research centers. Yet the emergence of government-university-industry strategic partnerships is relatively recent, and often fostered by specific federal government programs. This new organizational form owes its development to recent trends in the U.S. research environment in industry, academia, and government.

Industrial research is facing pressures to decrease time-to-market for new inventions, and to conduct research aimed at specific, identifiable customer needs. As a result, traditional basic research activities in corporate laboratories have been scaled back. A survey conducted in 1997 by *R&D Magazine* found that much of this is directed basic research, closely linked to related applied research activities, rather than exploratory basic research aimed at the creation of new scientific knowledge.

To compensate, most U.S. firms now form extensive relationships with other organizations for research, including small businesses and universities. Partnerships are a way to identify and capture innovations produced by those organizations that have not been implemented by other companies.

The decline in federal research funding has had a great impact on universities, which are the major recipients of extramural federal research support. As a result, more universities have become interested in forming relationships with industry, such as conducting research for specific companies, housing collaborative research facilities, and licensing university inventions to firms.

The academic sector sees industry R&D funding as a potential replacement for federal funding, especially in view of the new interest among corporations in partnering with universities. Universities are also under pressure from another major funding source, the parents of undergraduate students, to address the perceived imbalance between research and teaching in academia. University administrators in turn are placing more pressure on professors to link research to their educational programs, and also to integrate real-world concerns into both teaching and research. These pressures may also force academia to become more applied in its research focus.

These developments mean that the United States government now shoulders more of the burden for funding fundamental, long-term research aimed at producing new knowledge. However, this responsibility is contradicted by calls from the Congress and from taxpayers for greater accountability for government, and formal measurements of program outcomes under the Government Performance and Results Act of 1993 (the GPRA).

One mechanism to link government R&D to tangible outcomes is to form closer relationships, including collaborative research efforts, with industrial and academic research organizations. Collaboration among these sectors brings many benefits, including:

- Sharing of risk and cost for long-term research.
- Access to complementary capabilities.
- Access to specialized skills.
- Access to new suppliers and markets.
- Access to state-of-the-art facilities.
- Creating new opportunities for technological learning.

U.S. agencies are becoming direct participants in R&D collaboration by forming partnerships between agency research facilities and external research organizations. This increase in collaboration calls for new mechanisms for R&D management that take into account the dynamics of working with extramural research organizations as partners rather than grantees or contractors.

SIGNIFICANCE OF GUI PARTNERSHIPS FOR INNOVATION

Government-university-industry (GUI) strategic research partnerships represent an organizational form designed to integrate disparate pools of intellectual capital. In these cases, participants in the partnership bring to the table very different skills, capabilities, and organizational contexts. The alliance evolves into a shared community of innovation, where each participant retains the legacy of its origins, but joins a network of researchers that evolves its own common values, norms, and vocabulary. The knowledge from each organization can then be integrated within the new context of a community of innovation, and applied by each participant toward its own learning goals.

GUI partnerships play a role of growing significance in national innovation systems. The total process model of innovation outlined by Professor Richard Rosenbloom of Harvard and Dr. William Spencer of SEMATECH emphasizes the importance of flows and linkages between firms and external sources of knowledge. As the global economy evolves toward knowledge-based competition, GUI partnerships are a mechanism for facilitating revolutionary innovation through knowledge fusion.

At the same time this diversity may mean that members lack a shared language of knowledge necessary for effective knowledge sharing. Viewed in the context of dynamic organizational learning, however, even such cultural gaps among GUISP participants can become an advantage. Organizations involved in successful strategic alliances engaged in learning not only at the level of technical knowledge, but also at the level of organizational structure, with participants adopting some of the organizational routines of their partners leading to greater efficiency in learning. Thus, as the gap in relative absorptive capacity narrows among participants in a GUI partnership, they face

greater potential to experience radical changes in organization and culture that can lead to more radical innovation.

GUI partnerships may also tend to foster the formation of trust more readily than purely private sector alliances. Multiple industry participants in a GUI partnership are not racing to gain strategic resources from the alliance, as occurs in some industry alliances. Two firms involved in a GUISP could receive the same knowledge from the partnership, but will use it to build very different firm-specific strategic capabilities.

One indication of the special significance of GUI partnerships is that this new organizational form is emerging in different nations and different economies. This suggests that there are strong driving forces motivating these partnerships that are common across different national cultures, political structures, and economic systems. While GUI partnerships in different countries have certain unique characteristics shaped by their national environment, they tend to share processes and structures of membership, governance, and interaction that point to the existence of universal critical success factors which apply to all such partnerships.

CASES OF GUI STRATEGIC RESEARCH PARTNERSHIPS

NSF ENGINEERING RESEARCH CENTERS PROGRAM. An illustrative case of a GUI research collaboration is the Engineering Research Centers (ERC) Program administered by the U.S. National Science Foundation. The ERC program was developed based on a 1983 study by the National Academy of Engineering, initiated at the request of the NSF Director at that time, which recommended the establishment of a new cooperative program with the following two goals:

- To improve engineering research so that U.S. engineers will be better prepared to contribute to engineering practice; and
- To assist U.S. industry in becoming more competitive in world markets.

Establishment of the ERC program was motivated by the perception that significant engineering advances were occurring through the integration of new developments across traditional disciplinary boundaries, and that engineering education in universities no longer prepared students properly for the way in which engineering research was conducted in industry. This required that the centers established by the programs share the following objectives:

- Provide continual interaction of academic researchers, students, and faculty with their peers, namely, the engineers and scientists in industry, to ensure that the research programs in the centers remain relevant to the needs of the engineering practitioner and that they facilitate and promote the flow of knowledge between the academic and industrial sectors;

• Emphasize the synthesis of engineering knowledge; that is, the research programs should seek to integrate different disciplines in order to bring together the requisite knowledge, methodologies, and tools to solve problems important to engineering practitioners; and

• Contribute to the increased effectiveness of all levels of engineering education.

The ERC Program is managed out of NSF's Engineering Education and Centers (EEC) Division of the Directorate for Engineering. The ERC Program issues solicitations for the establishment of ERCs, each with a specific technological focus, such as Data Storage Systems or Telecommunications Research. Universities submit proposals to host an ERC; these proposals are peer-reviewed by technical researchers and executives from academia and industry.

There were twenty-six ERCs in this program in 1999. Each ERC is funded by the NSF for eleven years, over which time each center is expected to generate funding from sources outside the NSF, so that the center is self-sufficient by the end of the grant period. To illustrate, in fiscal year 1994, the twenty-one centers then in the ERC program received $51.7 million from the ERC Program Office; $53.7 million from industry in cash, in-kind donations, and associated grants and contracts; and $73.5 million from university, nonprofit, and other U.S. government sources.

Each ERC forms several consortia involving university faculty, staff, and students, and multiple industrial firms (and on occasion government research facilities) to pursue specific research projects under the ERC's focus area. By this structure, projects tend to focus on more fundamental research of broad interest to industry, rather than on development of specific product technologies for individual firms.

The academic and industrial researchers exchange knowledge regarding the needs of industry in the research area, relevant developments across engineering disciplines, and the processes of academic and industrial research.

The outputs of the ERCs measured by the ERC Program include the numbers of partnerships formed, patents filed and awarded, licenses granted to industry, and undergraduate and graduate degrees awarded to students involved in ERC projects.

MARCO AND THE FOCUS CENTER RESEARCH PROGRAM. The Microelectronics Advanced Research Corporation (MARCO) is a not-for-profit research management organization chartered with the establishment and management of a new Focus Center Research Program (FCRP) to fund pre-competitive, cooperative, long-range, applied microelectronics research. This initiative was launched in cooperation with the Defense Advanced Research Projects Agency (DARPA) of the U.S. Department of Defense, the Semiconductor Industry Association, and SEMI/SEMATECH, an organization of semiconductor equipment manufacturers.

The FCRP concentrates on technical challenges very different from those addressed by firms and other organizations in the semiconductor industry. The parameters these challenges must meet include:

• Emphasis on the elimination of barriers via more revolutionary approaches, paradigm shifts, and the creation of multiple options.

• Long-range (beyond eight years to commercialization) research.

• Broader, less granular objectives.

• Fewer industrial business practices applied.

• Heavy emphasis on research efforts with faculty, post-docs, visiting scientists, and students.

The Focus Centers funded by the program will be virtual (or distributed) centers that span multiple universities. This will tap the best expertise across many institutions in order to build the greatest overall capability in a particular technology area.

Rather than depending on only one institution to manage research in a given technology area, the FCRP will create communities of innovation linking researchers at multiple universities. The research will be long-range but still linked directly to industry imperatives by setting priorities through the National Technology Roadmap for Semiconductors, an industry-wide strategic-planning process. Industry and government support can lead to direct interaction between the university researchers and the end-users of the knowledge generated under the FCRP, contributing to a common view of technical challenges and wider dissemination of new knowledge.

MEDEA. The Microelectronics Development for European Applications (MEDEA) initiative, based in Paris, was launched on July 1, 1996 as a collaborative project under the EUREKA program. The initiative integrates microelectronics into application systems to foster the market-oriented and industry-driven needs of the electronics systems industry.

Funding for MEDEA projects is split between the European Union Commission, the member states, and firms, with participating firms providing at least 50 percent of the program's budget. These member nations are Germany, France, The Netherlands, Italy, Belgium, and Austria. Nearly two-thirds of MEDEA funding will support development of applications.

The MEDEA structure ensures that governmental decision making on research priorities supports the needs of industry, cementing the link between the two through its cost-sharing requirements. Also, the moderate subsidy from the European Commission leverages that investment across national borders, encouraging further collaborative research. By involving multiple firms, universities, and research institutions in MEDEA, the program can facilitate the wide diffusion of new innovations.

THE FRAUNHOFER GESELLSCHAFT. The leading organization focused on applied research in Germany is the Fraunhofer Gesellschaft (FhG) and its 47 world-wide institutes. Founded in 1949, FhG conducts applied research for industry on a contract basis, using the facilities and personnel of regional polytechnics or universities.

By forging a stronger bond between academia and business, FhG aims to speed the commercial application of new technologies. The institutes receive all their financial support from industry and the German government, both paying equal shares. All contracts must be worth at least DM100,000 to receive government support. Furthermore, the exact level of funding is dependent upon the technical and economic risks of the proposal. Finally, the projects must be perceived as potentially profitable.

The FhG, as a contract research body partnering with sources of research capabilities, serves as a neutral organization for coordinating flows of knowledge among and between its clients and research affiliates. The Institutes of the FhG themselves comprise the transorganizational knowledge management infrastructure for each technical field by managing the interactions between diverse research partners. The FhG also has the influence to spark learning in a GUI setting through this interaction.

LESSONS LEARNED ABOUT GUI PARTNERSHIP MANAGEMENT

A cross-sectional analysis of empirical findings from representative case studies fields a preliminary list of key considerations and respective strategic management skills that firms must develop to participate in useful GUI alliances (see Table 1).

TASK DEFINITION. Government, university, and industry have different strengths in the conduct of R&D, and differing priorities that drive their participation in GUI alliances. Therefore, firms must recognize both the strengths and limitations of each type of partner in a GUI alliance, and negotiate appropriate roles for each. For example, a university-industry research center at Case Western Reserve University focusing on materials science met with success when industry partners asked their university counterparts to focus on long-term, fundamental research that still had practical importance to firms but were beyond their research

Table 1
Defining Attributes of the Key Sucess Factors in GUI Partnerships

Key Success Factors in GUI Partnerships	Focus (External vs. Internal)	Nature (People-vs. Technology-Driven)	Bias (Positive-sum vs. Zero-sum	Outlook (Strategic vs. Tactical)
Task Definition	Both	Both	Positive-sum	Tactical
Leadership & Authority	External	People-driven	Positive-sum	Strategic
Allocation of Benefits	External	People-driven	Positive-sum	Strategic
Stakeholder Management	External	People-driven	Positive-sum	Tactical
Lifecycle Management	Both	Both	Positive-sum	Strategic

time horizons. The center conducted research into biodegradable polymers, which had enormous long-term potential impact in the plastics industry, but which no firm could afford to pursue.

LEADERSHIP AND AUTHORITY. A GUI alliance also requires the identification of a lead player who has the authority and legitimacy to make fundamental decisions about the direction of the alliance and its operations. Although the lead player must enjoy the support and confidence of the other partners in the alliance, that entity must also be able to act without requiring the unanimous consent of the entire alliance for every operational decision.

GUI alliances operating as pure democracies will tend to degenerate into factions, due to the polarizing differences in organizational objectives among the partners. Often, the lead player emerges due to personalities and individual roles, not at the organizational level. For example, one GUI alliance organized under a Defense Department program ended up with a leader whose technical expertise garnered the respect of other researchers in the alliance, but whose organizational position also provided him with the authority and influence to work the management structures of the different partners.

ALLOCATION OF BENEFITS. A key issue for GUI alliance management is the creation of processes for the fair and appropriate allocation of the benefits from the alliances to the various partners. The most critical aspect of this is in the division of intellectual property rights from research.

A major stumbling block to numerous GUI alliances is the fundamental contradiction between the importance of well-defined and protected rights for industry partners, and the desire for the open dissemination of information by researchers. Today, the success of university technology transfer also means that some academic partners may want to own some of the IPRs that they can then market to outside organizations. For example, agreements that require universities to assign all patent rights from an alliance to the industry members will cause universities to at least hesitate, and often to refuse participation in an alliance. Creating processes for distributing these benefits to satisfy all partners is more art than science, given the competing priorities of the partners.

STAKEHOLDER MANAGEMENT. Related to the above point, firms that take a lead role in GUI alliances must be skilled at stakeholder management, especially in answering the concerns of stakeholders who are not direct members of the alliance. For example, one GUI alliance sponsored by the Defense Department required the lead industry partner to take into consideration how to communicate the benefits of the alliance to Congress. This helped to assure the alliance of continued funding

with minimal interference from the oversight committees involved in national security.

LIFE-CYCLE MANAGEMENT. Since GUI alliances are dynamic entities, industry participants must be sensitive to how the alliance and each of its members evolves over time, and how that evolution may change the motivations for the alliance. For example, alliances must have clear processes for members to enter and exit as needed, as the alliance expands or moves into new areas and away from old ones. Also, firms must recognize that GUI alliances in general are highly situation-specific.

Changes in the underlying conditions of the alliance may render the alliance obsolete or moot. Therefore, alliances must also be managed as a dynamic, evolutionary process, with the clear recognition up-front that the alliance may outlive its usefulness and therefore must have processes in place for the graceful termination of the alliance at such a time.

Using a framework developed by Carayannis and Alexander (1998), GUI partnerships can be categorized along four variables:

- R&D Agreement (R&DA), structured as a grant, cooperative agreement, or contract;
- R&D Focus (R&DF), looking at the time-frame and nature of research outputs;
- R&D Performer (R&DP), where research is primarily conducted (among university, industry, government, or other organizations);
- R&D Location (R&DL), at the program and project levels, in terms of geographic location and organizational location (centralized or decentralized).

The resulting categorization is shown in Table 2. This analysis shows that among these three examples, GUI partnerships are intended to leverage the capabilities and resources of different research performers to address research agendas of varying time horizons and using a range of governance mechanisms. The key design issue in structuring GUI partnerships is matching the governance mechanisms, and in particular the interface mechanisms for facilitating knowledge transfer, with the capabilities and research focus of the partnership.

Some pertinent factors to consider in the structure of GUI partnerships are the differing time horizons and cultures of partners from government, university, and industry. These examples of GUI collaborations raise two significant points about this new mode of research support and conduct.

First, global pressures on national and corporate innovation provide a common motivation for the formation of the collaborative efforts, indicating that the

Table 2
Characteristics of GUI Partnerships

	ERCs	MARCO	MEDEA	FhG
R&DA	Cooperative Agreement	Cooperative Agreement	Cooperative Agreement	Contract
R&DF	Long-range, applied	Long-range, basic	Medium-range, applied	Short-to-medium range, applied
R&DP	Primarily university	Primarily university	Primarily industry	For-profit independent institutes
D&DL: program project	US-centered Centralized	US-centered Distributed	EU-centered Distributed	Global Centralized

globalization of R&D has a comparable impact across nations. Implementing transorganizational knowledge management through GUI partnerships will reengineer some aspects of the national science and engineering enterprise, as barriers to knowledge sharing across economic sectors are broken down through repeated instances of collaboration.

Second, the design of GUI partnerships and their intelligent transorganizational knowledge interfaces is influenced by the past history and current structure of the science and engineering enterprise in each company. Therefore, cross-national comparisons are somewhat difficult, as knowledge-management practices in one culture may not apply in another setting. This suggests that further research is necessary to understand the extent to which GUI partnerships are a tool for international as well as national transorganizational innovation.

The lessons learned from GUI partnerships show that there are distinct skill sets that firms must develop if they are to derive the full benefits of the alliances from participation. GUI strategic R&D alliances constitute an ongoing process of learning, introspection, and discovery.

Case studies of GUI partnerships can show the importance of learning proper alliance management skills to firm success, particularly given the specific pressures and dynamics introduced by knowledge-based competition. It can also show how these alliances are useful tools in initiating and accelerating learning at all levels within and across organizations, enabling firms to maneuver more nimbly in the complete game of business.

For these partnerships to contribute effectively to firm-level and national competitiveness and innovation, the participants must develop new competencies in the mechanisms and processes for managing GUI partnerships, which are different from other forms of inter-organizational alliances.

SEE ALSO: Joint Ventures and Strategic Alliances; Licensing and Licensing Agreements; Product Life Cycle and Industry Life Cycle; Stakeholders; Strategy Formulation; Technology Management; Technology Transfer

Elias G. Carayannis and Jeffrey Alexander
Revised by Debbie Hausler

FURTHER READING:

Betz, Frederick. "Academic/Government/Industry Strategic Research Partnerships." *Journal of Technology Transfer* 22, no. 3 (1998): 9–16.

Branscomb, Lewis M., and J.H. Keller. *Investing in Innovation: Creating a Research and Innovation Policy That Works.* Cambridge, MA: The MIT Press, 1997.

EUREKA. "Project (E! 1535): MEDEA Project Summary: Summary of the Project." 1998. Available from <http://www.eureka.be/>.

Fraunhofer Institute. "Overview of the Fraunhofer Institute." Available from <http://www.fraunhofer.org>.

McGraw, Dan. "Building Strategic Partnerships." *ASEE Prism.* American Society for Engineering Education Online, 1999.

Rosenberg, Nathan, and Richard R. Nelson. "American Universities and Technical Advance in Industry." *Research Policy* 23 (1994): 323–348.

Schrieberg, D. "The Matchmakers." *Stanford Magazine,* January/February 1997.

U.S. House of Representatives Committee on Science. *Hearing on Defining Successful Partnership and Collaborations in Scientific Research.* Washington, DC: Government Printing Office, 1997.

U.S. National Science Foundation. *The Engineering Research Centers (ERC) Program: An Assessment of Benefits and Outcomes.* Arlington, VA: Engineering Education and Centers Division, Directorate for Engineering, NSF, 1997.

GROUP DECISION MAKING

Group decision making is a type of participatory process in which multiple individuals acting collectively, analyze problems or situations, consider and evaluate alternative courses of action, and select from among the alternatives a solution or solutions. The number of people involved in group decision-making varies greatly, but often ranges from two to seven. The individuals in a group may be demographically similar or quite diverse. Decision-making groups may be relatively informal in nature, or formally designated and charged with a specific goal. The process used to arrive at decisions may be unstructured or structured. The nature and composition of groups, their size, demographic makeup, structure, and purpose, all affect their functioning to some degree. The external contingencies faced by groups (time pressure and conflicting goals) impact the development and effectiveness of decision-making groups as well.

In organizations many decisions of consequence are made after some form of group decision-making process is undertaken. However, groups are not the only form of collective work arrangement. Group decision-making should be distinguished from the concepts of teams, teamwork, and self managed teams. Although the words teams and groups are often used interchangeably, scholars increasingly differentiate between the two. The basis for the distinction seems to be that teams act more collectively and achieve greater synergy of effort. Katzenback and Smith spell out specific differences between decision making groups and teams:

- The group has a definite leader, but the team has shared leadership roles

- Members of a group have individual accountability; the team has both individual and collective accountability.

- The group measures effectiveness indirectly, but the team measures performance directly through their collective work product.

- The group discusses, decides, and delegates, but the team discusses, decides, and does real work.

GROUP DECISION MAKING METHODS

There are many methods or procedures that can be used by groups. Each is designed to improve the decision-making process in some way. Some of the more common group decision-making methods are brainstorming, dialetical inquiry, nominal group technique, and the delphi technique.

BRAINSTORMING. Brainstorming involves group members verbally suggesting ideas or alternative courses of action. The "brainstorming session" is usually relatively unstructured. The situation at hand is described in as much detail as necessary so that group members have a complete understanding of the issue or problem. The group leader or facilitator then solicits ideas from all members of the group. Usually, the group leader or facilitator will record the ideas presented on a flip chart or marker board. The "generation of alternatives" stage is clearly differentiated from the "alternative evaluation" stage, as group members are not allowed to evaluate suggestions until all ideas have been presented. Once the ideas of the group members have been exhausted, the group members then begin the process of evaluating the utility of the different suggestions presented. Brainstorming is a useful means by which to generate alternatives, but does not offer much in the way of process for the evaluation of alternatives or the selection of a proposed course of action.

One of the difficulties with brainstorming is that despite the prohibition against judging ideas until all group members have had their say, some individuals are hesitant to propose ideas because they fear the judgment or ridicule of other group members. In recent years, some decision-making groups have utilized electronic brainstorming, which allows group members to propose alternatives by means of e-mail or another electronic means, such as an online posting board or discussion room. Members could conceivably offer their ideas anonymously, which should increase the likelihood that individuals will offer unique and creative ideas without fear of the harsh judgment of others.

DIALETICAL INQUIRY. Dialetical inquiry is a group decision-making technique that focuses on ensuring full consideration of alternatives. Essentially, it involves dividing the group into opposing sides, which debate the advantages and disadvantages of proposed solutions or decisions. A similar group decision-making method, devil's advocacy, requires that one member of the group highlight the potential problems with a proposed decision. Both of these techniques are designed to try and make sure that the group considers all possible ramifications of its decision.

NOMINAL GROUP TECHNIQUE. The nominal group technique is a structured decision making process in which group members are required to compose a comprehensive list of their ideas or proposed alternatives in writing. The group members usually record their ideas privately. Once finished, each group member is asked, in turn, to provide one item from their list until all ideas or alternatives have been publicly recorded on a flip chart or marker board. Usually, at this stage of the process verbal exchanges are limited to requests for clarification—no evaluation or criticism of listed ideas is permitted. Once all proposals are listed publicly, the group engages in a discussion of the listed alternatives, which ends in some form of ranking or rating in order of preference. As with brainstorming, the prohibition against criticizing proposals as they are presented is designed to overcome individuals' reluctance to share their ideas. Empirical research conducted on group decision making offers some evidence that the nominal group technique succeeds in generating a greater number of decision alternatives that are of relatively high quality.

DELPHI TECHNIQUE. The Delphi technique is a group decision-making process that can be used by decision-making groups when the individual members are in different physical locations. The technique was developed at the Rand Corporation. The individuals in the Delphi "group" are usually selected because of the specific knowledge or expertise of the problem they possess. In the Delphi technique, each group member is asked to independently provide ideas, input, and/or alternative solutions to the decision problem in successive stages. These inputs may be provided in a variety of ways, such as e-mail, fax, or online in a discussion room or electronic bulletin board. After each stage in the process, other group members ask questions and alternatives are ranked or rated in some fashion. After an indefinite number of rounds, the group eventually arrives at a consensus decision on the best course of action.

ADVANTAGES AND DISADVANTAGES OF GROUP DECISION MAKING

The effectiveness of decision-making groups can be affected by a variety of factors. Thus, it is not possible to suggest that "group decision making is always better" or "group decision making is always worse" than individual decision-making. For example, due to the increased demographic diversity in the workforce, a considerable amount of research has focused on diversity's effect on the effectiveness of group functioning. In general, this research suggests that demographic diversity can sometimes have positive or negative effects, depending on the specific situation. Demographically diverse group may have to overcome social barriers and difficulties in the early stages of group formation and this may slow down the group. However, some research indicates that diverse groups, if effectively managed, tend to generate a wider variety and higher quality of decision alternatives than demographically homogeneous groups.

Despite the fact that there are many situational factors that affect the functioning of groups, research through the years does offer some general guidance about the relative strengths and weaknesses inherent

in group decision making. The following section summarizes the major pros and cons of decision making in groups.

ADVANTAGES. Group decision-making, ideally, takes advantage of the diverse strengths and expertise of its members. By tapping the unique qualities of group members, it is possible that the group can generate a greater number of alternatives that are of higher quality than the individual. If a greater number of higher quality alternatives are generated, then it is likely that the group will eventually reach a superior problem solution than the individual.

Group decision-making may also lead to a greater collective understanding of the eventual course of action chosen, since it is possible that many affected by the decision implementation actually had input into the decision. This may promote a sense of "ownership" of the decision, which is likely to contribute to a greater acceptance of the course of action selected and greater commitment on the part of the affected individuals to make the course of action successful.

DISADVANTAGES. There are many potential disadvantages to group decision-making. Groups are generally slower to arrive at decisions than individuals, so sometimes it is difficult to utilize them in situations where decisions must be made very quickly. One of the most often cited problems is groupthink. Irving Janis, in his 1972 book *Victims of Groupthink,* defined the phenomenon as the "deterioration of mental efficiency, reality testing, and moral judgment resulting from in-group pressure." Groupthink occurs when individuals in a group feel pressure to conform to what seems to be the dominant view in the group. Dissenting views of the majority opinion are suppressed and alternative courses of action are not fully explored.

Research suggests that certain characteristics of groups contribute to groupthink. In the first place, if the group does not have an agreed upon process for developing and evaluating alternatives, it is possible that an incomplete set of alternatives will be considered and that different courses of action will not be fully explored. Many of the formal decision-making processes (e.g., nominal group technique and brainstorming) are designed, in part, to reduce the potential for groupthink by ensuring that group members offer and consider a large number of decision alternatives. Secondly, if a powerful leader dominates the group, other group members may quickly conform to the dominant view. Additionally, if the group is under stress and/or time pressure, groupthink may occur. Finally, studies suggest that highly cohesive groups are more susceptible to groupthink.

Group polarization is another potential disadvantage of group decision-making. This is the tendency of the group to converge on more extreme solutions to a problem. The "risky shift" phenomenon is an example of polarization; it occurs when the group decision is a riskier one than any of the group members would have made individually. This may result because individuals in a group sometimes do not feel as much responsibility and accountability for the actions of the group as they would if they were making the decision alone.

Decision-making in groups is a fact of organizational life for many individuals. Because so many individuals spend at least some of their work time in decision-making groups, groups are the subjects of hundreds of research studies each year. Despite this, there is still much to learn about the development and functioning of groups. Research is likely to continue to focus on identifying processes that will make group decision-making more efficient and effective. It is also likely to examine how the internal characteristics of groups (demographic and cognitive diversity) and the external contingencies faced by groups affect their functioning.

Tim Barnett

FURTHER READING:

Janis, I. *Victims of Groupthink.* Houghton Mifflin: Boston, 1972.

Hinsz, V.B., and G.S. Nickell. "Positive Reactions to Working in Groups in a Study of Group and Individual Goal Decision-Making." *Group Dynamics* 8 (2004): 253–264.

Luthans, F. *Organizational Behavior.* 10th ed. McGraw Hill Irwin: Boston, 2005.

Maznevski, M.L. "Understanding Our Differences: Performance in Decision-Making Groups with Diverse Members." *Human Relations* 47: 531–542.

Nelson, D.L., and J.C. Quick. *Organizational Behavior.* 3rd ed. Southwestern College Publishing: Australia, 2000.

Thomas-Hunt, M.C., and K.W. Phillips. "When What You Know is Not Enough: Expertise and Gender Dynamics in Task Groups." *Personality & Social Psychology Bulletin* 30 (2004): 1585–1598.

van de Ven, A. and A. Delbecq. "The Effectiveness of Nominal, Delphi, and Interacting Group Decision-Making Processes." *Academy of Management Journal* 17 (1974): 147–178.

van Knippenberg, D., C.K.W. De Dreu, and A.C. Homan. "Work Group Diversity and Group Performance: An Integrative Model and Research Agenda." *Journal of Applied Psychology* 89 (2004): 1008–1022.

GROUP DYNAMICS

A group can be defined as several individuals who come together to accomplish a particular task or goal. Group dynamics refers to the attitudinal and behavioral characteristics of a group. Group dynamics concern how groups form, their structure and process, and how they function. Group dynamics are relevant in both formal and informal groups of all types. In an organizational setting, groups are a very common organizational entity and the study of groups and group dynamics is an important area of study in organizational behavior.

The following sections provide information related to group dynamics. Specifically, the formation and development of groups is first considered. Then some major types or classifications of groups are discussed. Then the structure of groups is examined.

GROUP DEVELOPMENT

As applied to group development, group dynamics is concerned with why and how groups develop. There are several theories as to why groups develop. A classic theory, developed by George Homans, suggests that groups develop based on activities, interactions, and sentiments. Basically, the theory means that when individuals share common activities, they will have more interaction and will develop attitudes (positive or negative) toward each other. The major element in this theory is the interaction of the individuals involved.

Social exchange theory offers an alternative explanation for group development. According to this theory, individuals form relationships based on the implicit expectation of mutually beneficial exchanges based on trust and felt obligation. Thus, a perception that exchange relationships will be positive is essential if individuals are to be attracted to and affiliate with a group.

Social identity theory offers another explanation for group formation. Simply put, this theory suggests that individuals get a sense of identity and self-esteem based upon their membership in salient groups. The nature of the group may be demographically based, culturally based, or organizationally based. Individuals are motivated to belong to and contribute to identity groups because of the sense of belongingness and self-worth membership in the group imparts.

Group dynamics as related to development concerns not only why groups form but also how. The most common framework for examining the "how" of group formation was developed by Bruce Tuckman in the 1960s. In essence, the steps in group formation imply that groups do not usually perform at maximum effectiveness when they are first established. They encounter several stages of development as they strive to become productive and effective. Most groups experience the same developmental stages with similar conflicts and resolutions.

According to Tuckman's theory, there are five stages of group development: forming, storming, norming, performing, and adjourning. During these stages group members must address several issues and the way in which these issues are resolved determines whether the group will succeed in accomplishing its tasks.

1. Forming. This stage is usually characterized by some confusion and uncertainty. The major goals of the group have not been established. The nature of the task or leadership of the group has not been determined (Luthans, 2005). Thus, forming is an orientation period when members get to know one another and share expectations about the group. Members learn the purpose of the group as well as the rules to be followed. The forming stage should not be rushed because trust and openness must be developed. These feelings strengthen in later stages of development. Individuals are often confused during this stage because roles are not clear and there may not be a strong leader.

2. Storming. In this stage, the group is likely to see the highest level of disagreement and conflict. Members often challenge group goals and struggle for power. Individuals often vie for the leadership position during this stage of development. This can be a positive experience for all groups if members can achieve cohesiveness through resolution. Members often voice concern and criticism in this phase. If members are not able to resolve the conflict, then the group will often disband or continue in existence but will remain ineffective and never advance to the other stages.

3. Norming. This stage is characterized by the recognition of individual differences and shared expectations. Hopefully, at this stage the group members will begin to develop a feeling of group cohesion and identity. Cooperative effort should begin to yield results. Responsibilities are divided among members and the group decides how it will evaluate progress.

4. Performing. Performing, occurs when the group has matured and attains a feeling of cohesiveness. During this stage of development, individuals accept one another and conflict is resolved through group discussion. Members of the group make decisions through a rational process that is focused on relevant goals rather than emotional issues.

5. Adjourning. Not all groups experience this stage of development because it is characterized by the disbandment of the group. Some groups are relatively permanent (Luthans, 2005). Reasons that groups disband vary, with common reasons being the accomplishment of the task or individuals deciding to go their own ways. Members of the group often experience feelings of closure and sadness as they prepare to leave.

GROUP TYPES

One common way to classify group is by whether they are formal or informal in nature. Formal work groups are established by an organization to achieve organizational goals. Formal groups may take the form of command groups, task groups, and functional groups.

COMMAND GROUPS. Command groups are specified by the organizational chart and often consist of a supervisor and the subordinates that report to that supervisor. An example of a command group is an academic department chairman and the faculty members in that department.

TASK GROUPS. Task groups consist of people who work together to achieve a common task. Members are brought together to accomplish a narrow range of goals within a specified time period. Task groups are also commonly referred to as task forces. The organization appoints members and assigns the goals and tasks to be accomplished. Examples of assigned tasks are the development of a new product, the improvement of a production process, or the proposal of a motivational contest. Other common task groups are ad hoc committees, project groups, and standing committees. Ad hoc committees are temporary groups created to resolve a specific complaint or develop a process. Project groups are similar to ad hoc committees and normally disband after the group completes the assigned task. Standing committees are more permanent than ad hoc committees and project groups. They maintain longer life spans by rotating members into the group.

FUNCTIONAL GROUPS. A functional group is created by the organization to accomplish specific goals within an unspecified time frame. Functional groups remain in existence after achievement of current goals and objectives. Examples of functional groups would be a marketing department, a customer service department, or an accounting department.

In contrast to formal groups, informal groups are formed naturally and in response to the common interests and shared values of individuals. They are created for purposes other than the accomplishment of organizational goals and do not have a specified time frame. Informal groups are not appointed by the organization and members can invite others to join from time to time. Informal groups can have a strong influence in organizations that can either be positive or negative. For example, employees who form an informal group can either discuss how to improve a production process or how to create shortcuts that jeopardize quality. Informal groups can take the form of interest groups, friendship groups, or reference groups.

INTEREST GROUPS. Interest groups usually continue over time and may last longer than general informal groups. Members of interest groups may not be part of the same organizational department but they are bound together by some other common interest. The goals and objectives of group interests are specific to each group and may not be related to organizational goals and objectives. An example of an interest group would be students who come together to form a study group for a specific class.

FRIENDSHIP GROUPS. Friendship groups are formed by members who enjoy similar social activities, political beliefs, religious values, or other common bonds. Members enjoy each other's company and often meet after work to participate in these activities. For example, a group of employees who form a friendship group may have an exercise group, a softball team, or a potluck lunch once a month.

REFERENCE GROUPS. A reference group is a type of group that people use to evaluate themselves. According to Cherrington, the main purposes of reference groups are social validation and social comparison. Social validation allows individuals to justify their attitudes and values while social comparison helps individuals evaluate their own actions by comparing themselves to others. Reference groups have a strong influence on members' behavior. By comparing themselves with other members, individuals are able to assess whether their behavior is acceptable and whether their attitudes and values are right or wrong. Reference groups are different from the previously discussed groups because they may not actually meet or form voluntarily. For example, the reference group for a new employee of an organization may be a group of employees that work in a different department or even a different organization. Family, friends, and religious affiliations are strong reference groups for most individuals.

GROUP STRUCTURE

Group structure is a pattern of relationships among members that hold the group together and help it achieve assigned goals. Structure can be described in a variety of ways. Among the more common considerations are group size, group roles, group norms, and group cohesiveness.

GROUP SIZE. Group size can vary from 2 people to a very large number of people. Small groups of two to ten are thought to be more effective because each member has ample opportunity to participate and become actively involved in the group. Large groups may waste time by deciding on processes and trying to

decide who should participate next. Group size will affect not only participation but satisfaction as well. Evidence supports the notion that as the size of the group increases, satisfaction increases up to a certain point. In other words, a group of six members has twice as many opportunities for interaction and participation as a group of three people. Beyond 10 or 12 members, increasing the size of the group results in decreased satisfaction. It is increasingly difficult for members of large groups to identify with one another and experience cohesion.

GROUP ROLES

In formal groups, roles are usually predetermined and assigned to members. Each role will have specific responsibilities and duties. There are, however, emergent roles that develop naturally to meet the needs of the groups. These emergent roles will often replace the assigned roles as individuals begin to express themselves and become more assertive. Group roles can then be classified into work roles, maintenance roles, and blocking roles.

Work roles are task-oriented activities that involve accomplishing the group's goals. They involve a variety of specific roles such as initiator, informer, clarifier, summarizer, and reality tester. The initiator defines problems, proposes action, and suggests procedures.

The informer role involves finding facts and giving advice or opinions. Clarifiers will interpret ideas, define terms, and clarify issues for the group. Summarizers restate suggestions, offer decisions, and come to conclusions for the group. Finally, reality testers analyze ideas and test the ideas in real situations.

Maintenance roles are social-emotional activities that help members maintain their involvement in the group and raise their personal commitment to the group. The maintenance roles are harmonizer, gatekeeper, consensus tester, encourager, and compromiser. The harmonizer will reduce tension in the group, reconcile differences, and explore opportunities. Gatekeepers often keep communication channels open and make suggestions that encourage participation. The consensus tester will ask if the group is nearing a decision and test possible conclusions. Encouragers are friendly, warm, and responsive to other group members. The last maintenance role is the compromiser. This role involves modifying decisions, offering compromises, and admitting errors.

Blocking roles are activities that disrupt the group. They make take the form of dominating discussions, verbally attacking other group members, and distracting the group with trivial information or unnecessary humor. Often times the blocking behavior may not be intended as negative. Sometimes a member may share a joke in order to break the tension, or may question a decision in order to force group members to rethink the issue. The blocking roles are aggressor, blocker, dominator, comedian, and avoidance behavior. The aggressor criticizes members' values and makes jokes in a sarcastic or semi-concealed manner.

Blockers will stubbornly resist the group's ideas, disagree with group members for personal reasons, and will have hidden agendas. The dominator role attempts to control conversations by patronizing others. They often interrupt others and assert authority in order to manipulate members. Comedians often abandon the group even though they may physically still be a part. They are attention-getters in ways that are not relevant to the accomplishment of the group's objectives. The last blocking role, avoidance behavior, involves pursuing goals not related to the group and changing the subject to avoid commitment to the group.

Role ambiguity concerns the discrepancy between the sent role and the received role, as shown in Exhibit 1. Supervisors, directors, or other group leaders often send (assign) roles to group members in formal groups. Group members receive roles by being ready and willing to undertake the tasks associated with that role. Ambiguity results when members are confused about the delegation of job responsibilities. This confusion may occur because the members do not have specific job descriptions or because the instructions regarding the task were not clear. Group members who experience ambiguity often have feelings of frustration and dissatisfaction, which ultimately lead to turnover.

Role conflict occurs when there is inconsistency between the perceived role and role behavior. There are several different forms of role conflict. Interrole conflict occurs when there is conflict between the different roles that people have. For example, work roles and family roles often compete with one another and cause conflict. Intrarole conflict occurs when individuals must handle conflicting demands from different sources while performing the tasks associated with the same role.

GROUP NORMS. Norms are acceptable standards of behavior within a group that are shared by the members of the group. Norms define the boundaries of acceptable and unacceptable behavior. They are typically created in order to facilitate group survival, make behavior more predictable, avoid embarrassing situations, and express the values of the group. Each group will establish its own set of norms that might determine anything from the appropriate dress to how many comments to make in a meeting. Groups exert pressure on members to force them to conform to the group's standards. The norms often reflect the level of commitment, motivation, and performance of the group.

Performance norms determine how quickly members should work and how much they should produce. They are created in an effort to determine levels of individual effort. They can be very frustrating to managers because they are not always in line with the organization's goals. Members of a group may have the skill and ability to perform at higher levels but they don't because of the group's performance norms. For example, workers may stop working a production machine at 20 minutes before quitting time in order to wash up, even though they produced fewer items that day than management intended.

Reward-allocation norms determine how rewards are bestowed upon group members. For example, the norm of equality dictates equal treatment of all members. Every member shares equally so rewards are distributed equally to everyone. Equity norms suggest that rewards are distributed according to the member's contribution. In other words, members who contribute the most receive the largest share of the rewards. Members may contribute through effort, skill, or ability. Social responsibility norms reward on the basis of need. Members who have special needs therefore receive the largest share of the reward.

The majority of the group must agree that the norms are appropriate in order for the behavior to be accepted. There must also be a shared understanding

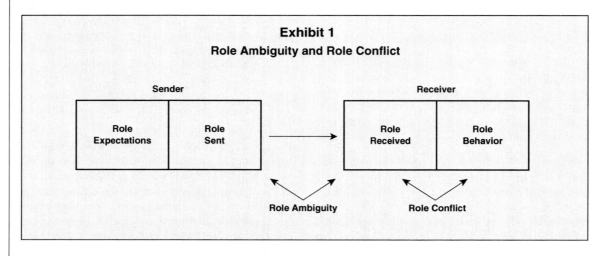

Exhibit 1
Role Ambiguity and Role Conflict

that the group supports the norms. It should be noted, however, that members might violate group norms from time to time. If the majority of members do not adhere to the norms, then they will eventually change and will no longer serve as a standard for evaluating behavior. Group members who do not conform to the norms will be punished by being excluded, ignored, or asked to leave the group.

GROUP COHESIVENESS. Cohesiveness refers to the bonding of group members and their desire to remain part of the group. Many factors influence the amount of group cohesiveness. Generally speaking, the more difficult it is to obtain group membership the more cohesive the group. Groups also tend to become cohesive when they are in intense competition with other groups or face a serious external threat to survival. Smaller groups and those who spend considerable time together also tend to be more cohesive.

Cohesiveness in work groups has many positive effects, including worker satisfaction, low turnover and absenteeism, and higher productivity. However, highly cohesive groups may be detrimental to organizational performance if their goals are misaligned with organizational goals. Highly cohesive groups may also be more vulnerable to groupthink. Groupthink occurs when members of a group exert pressure on each other to come to a consensus in decision making. Groupthink results in careless judgments, unrealistic appraisals of alternative courses of action, and a lack of reality testing. It can lead to a number of decision-making issues such as the following:

1. Incomplete assessments of the problem,
2. Incomplete information search,
3. Bias in processing information,
4. Inadequate development of alternatives, and
5. Failure to examine the risks of the preferred choice.

Evidence suggests that groups typically outperform individuals when the tasks involved require a variety of skills, experience, and decision making. Groups are often more flexible and can quickly assemble, achieve goals, and disband or move on to another set of objectives. Many organizations have found that groups have many motivational aspects as well. Group members are more likely to participate in decision-making and problem-solving activities leading to empowerment and increased productivity. Groups complete most of the work in an organization; thus, the effectiveness of the organization is limited by the effectiveness of its groups.

SEE ALSO: Brainstorming; Group Decision Making; Teams and Teamwork

Amy McMillan
Revised by Tim Barnett

FURTHER READING:

Cherrington, D.J. *Organizational Behavior.* Boston: Allyn and Bacon, 1994.

Frey, L.R., and S. Wolf. "The Symbolic & Interpretive Perspective on Group Dynamics." *Small Group Research* 35, no. 3 (2004): 277–316.

Greenberg, J., and R.A. Baron. *Behavior in Organizations.* 7th ed. Upper Saddle River, NJ: Prentice Hall, 2000.

Hellriegel, D., and J.W. Slocum, Jr. *Organizational Behavior.* 10th ed. Thomson South-Western, 2004.

Katz, D., and R. Kahn. *The Social Psychology of Organizations.* 2nd ed. New York: John Wiley & Sons, 1978, 196.

Luthans, F. *Organizational Behavior.* 10th ed. Boston: McGraw-Hill, 2005.

Robbins, S.P. *Essentials of Organizational Behavior.* Upper Saddle River, NJ: Prentice Hall, 1997.

H

HANDHELD COMPUTERS

Handheld computers—also known as personal digital assistants (PDAs)—are small, portable devices that offer users many of the same features and capabilities as desktop computers at a fraction of the size. Although the terms "handheld computer" and "PDA" are often used interchangeably, handhelds tend to be larger and feature miniature keyboards, while PDAs tend to be smaller and rely on a touch screen and stylus for data entry.

Since their introduction in the late 1990s, handheld computers have become standard equipment for many professionals, providing them with tiny, versatile electronic alternatives to paper day planners. "Once the domain of early adopting gadget lovers, handhelds now organize and update millions of mobile business professionals," reports Mike Brown at HandheldComputerDepot.com. Users have found PDAs to be particularly helpful tools for organizing and maintaining personal data, such as address books, appointment calendars, project lists, and expense reports. Later incarnations of the technology have also offered users mobile access to electronic mail, news, and entertainment through connectivity to the Internet.

When shopping for a handheld computer, experts recommend that users start by identifying their needs. They should consider, for example, whether they require only personal information management (PIM) functions, or whether they also wish to take notes during meetings, download e-mail and other information from the Internet, and connect with other users through a company computer network. Considering such needs, as well as the available budget, will help users decide among the basic options in handheld computers, including size, display, memory, operating system, and power source.

The size of handheld computers ranges from credit card to small notebook computer, and the available features and power generally increase with greater size. The most popular size for the devices is palm size-which falls somewhere between a calculator and a paperback book. Most handheld computers utilize a liquid crystal display (LCD), which acts as both an input and an output device. Only the larger PDAs feature keyboards, and most others require users to enter information on a touch screen, either by tapping letters with a stylus or by writing letters on the screen, which the device interprets using handwriting-recognition software. In the future, many handheld units are expected to incorporate voice-recognition technology.

Many handheld computers are designed to work closely with a desktop computer or network. In order to maintain up-to-date information in both places, a process known as synchronizing data must occur—users must perform frequent uploads and downloads between their PDA and desktop systems. This process can take place through cables, wireless connections, or over telephone lines via modem. Rather than downloading from PCs, however, some of the more sophisticated handheld devices allow users to connect directly to the Internet for downloading e-mail, Web magazines and news services, and audio programs.

In an article for *Computerworld,* Matt Hamblen and Sharon Gaudin warned that many corporate information technology (IT) managers were unprepared to deal with the proliferation of handheld computers among employees. They found that some companies ignored the devices, while others simply banned them from connecting to corporate networks. Instead, Hamblen and Gaudin recommended that IT managers embrace the new technology, helping employees choose products and find ways to use them to increase productivity. They argued that businesses should take an active role in deciding which handheld platforms and software applications their networks will support. They cautioned that businesses should also be aware of the security threats posed by handheld devices and take steps to protect the corporate network by establishing software synchronization standards.

Experts predict that the next evolution in handheld computers will be the "smartphone," which combines the most popular functions of PDAs (storing addresses and phone numbers, taking down notes or messages, and browsing the Internet remotely) with wireless phone service. Some analysts believe that the market for straightforward PDAs has become saturated. They claim that future growth will come in the form of phone units, because users will no longer be willing to carry both a PDA and a cellular phone.

SEE ALSO: Computer Security; Knowledge Management; Knowledge Workers; Technology Management; Technology Transfer; Telecommunications; Time-Based Competition; Virtual Organizations

Laurie Collier Hillstrom

FURTHER READING:

Brown, Mike. *"Handheld Buying Guide."* Handheld ComputerDepot.com. Available from <http://www. handheldcomputerdepot.com/buyingguide.html>.

Freundenrich, Craig C. "How PDAs Work." HowStuff Works. com. Available from <http://computer.howstuffworks.com/ pda.htm>.

Hamblen, Matt, and Sharon Gaudin. "IT Risks Chaos in Handheld Boom: Wireless Trend, Lack of Policies Feed Concern." *Computerworld*, 8 February 1999.

"PDA, RIP: The Next Big Thing that Wasn't—Or Was It?" *Economist*, 16 October 2003.

"The World at Your Fingertips: Handhelds that Deliver On Phone Calls, E-Mail, and Just Plain Fun." *Business Week*, 6 September 2004.

HEALTH SAVINGS ACCOUNTS

A health savings account (HSA) is an investment vehicle from which individuals can withdraw funds to pay qualified medical expenses as defined by the Internal Revenue Code. Accumulated funds can be used to pay current medical expenses or can be saved for medical expenses incurred in the future. The account can be set up by an employee in conjunction with his or her employer, but may also be set up by individuals through participating insurance companies and banks. To participate, an individual must have a high-deductible health insurance plan as their only form of health insurance and must not be eligible for Medicare. Generally, a high-deductible health care plan is one with at least a $1,000 deductible for an individual or $5,000 for a family. Participants contribute to the HSA and pay a premium for the high-deductible medical insurance, which is usually lower than the premium for conventional medical insurance. Also, an eligible individual cannot be a dependent of another taxpayer.

The individual's contributions to the account are tax deductible and, if an employer contributes to the account on behalf of an employee, the contribution is not taxable to the employee and the employer's taxable income is reduced by the amount of the contribution. Money placed in the account may be invested in a variety of investment vehicles, including stocks, bonds, and mutual funds. Investment gains are nontaxable, as long as money withdrawn from the fund is used for qualified medical expenses. There are maximum annual contributions, which are adjusted for inflation annually. In 2004, the maximum contribution is $2,000 for an individual plan and $5,150 for a family plan. However, those over age 55 are allowed to make so-called "catch-up" contributions.

PURPOSE

Most individuals in the United States who are not self-employed and who are not eligible for Medicare or Medicaid obtain their health insurance through their employers. There are two major problems with the current system of employer-sponsored health care coverage. First, since the employer usually pays some or all of the insurance premiums and bears the brunt of health care cost increases; the true cost of coverage is hidden from individuals, who therefore have little incentive to manage their health care efficiently. Second, employer-sponsored insurance creates a link between employment and health care that may be broken when an employee loses his or her job. These facts, combined with the tremendous increase in health-care costs in the U.S. experienced since the 1980s, has led the government and employers to look for ways to deliver health care insurance more efficiently and effectively.

Health maintenance organizations (HMOs), adopted by many employers in the 1980s, addressed the cost problem by allowing employers to make arrangements with health care providers to deliver health care services to their employees on a fixed-fee basis. In return for price concessions, employers essentially restricted the choices of participating employees to participating providers. HMOs were successful in reducing health care cost inflation, but their lack of flexibility and perceived over-emphasis on cost containment led to widespread dissatisfaction. Less restrictive preferred provider organizations, which allowed employees more freedom of choice if they were willing to pay a higher portion of costs, became the dominant form of employer-sponsored plan in the 1990s. But PPOs appear to be less successful in restraining health care costs. Thus, the government and employers continue to search for alternatives.

Attention focused on attempting to de-couple health insurance from employment and increasing consumer involvement in health care decisions. Such consumer-driven approaches place greater responsibility on individuals to choose and manage their health care. The goal of such approaches is to encourage individuals to be more careful consumers of health care. Flexible spending accounts and medical savings accounts are both consumer-driven approaches.

Health savings accounts overcome many of the difficulties with the earlier approaches to consumer-driven health care. For example, flexible spending accounts require the individual to use all contributed funds annually or lose the funds. Accumulated funds in HSAs carry over from year to year and can be held for life. Medical savings accounts are available only to the self-employed or those employed by small businesses. HSAs are available to anyone, regardless of employment status.

SEE ALSO: Employee Benefits; Employment Law and Compliance; Human Resource Management

Tim Barnett

FURTHER READING:

Moran, A.E. "HSAS: The New Consumer Health Plan: Is This the Real Thing?" *Employee Relations Law Journal* 30, no. 1 (2004): 101–111.

Gleckman, H., and L. Woellert. "Your New Health Plan." *Business Week*, 8 November 2004, 88–94.

HUMAN RESOURCE INFORMATION SYSTEMS

Human Resource Information Systems (HRIS) have become one of the most important tools for many businesses. Even the small, 20-person office needs to realize the benefits of using HRIS to be more efficient. Many firms do not realize how much time and money they are wasting on manual human resource management (HRM) tasks until they sit down and inventory their time. HRIS is advancing to become its own information technology (IT) field. It allows companies to cut costs and offer more information to employees in a faster and more efficient way. Especially in difficult economic times, it is critical for companies to become more efficient in every sector of their business; human resources (HR) is no exception.

HRIS refers to software packages that address HR needs with respect to planning, employee information access, and employer regulatory compliance. The following text begins with a discussion of human resource planning, followed by human resource management systems.

HUMAN RESOURCE PLANNING

American companies must now operate in a rapidly changing business environment. These changes have important implications for HRM practices. To ensure that management practices support business needs, organizations must continually monitor changing environmental conditions and devise HRM strategies for dealing with them. The procedure used to tie human resource issues to the organization's business needs is called human resource planning. Also known as HR planning, this procedure is defined as the "process of identifying and responding to [organizational needs] . . . and charting new policies, systems, and programs that will assure effective human resource management under changing conditions."

The purposes of HR planning are to enable organizations to anticipate their future HRM needs and to identify practices that will help them to meet those needs. HR planning may be done on a short- or long-term (three or more years) basis. Its aim is to ensure that people will be available with the appropriate characteristics and skills when and where the organization needs them. The use of HR planning enables companies to gain control of their future by preparing for likely events. That is, they can anticipate change and devise appropriate courses of action. When companies learn how to capitalize on future events, their own future improves.

As valuable as HR planning is, many companies ignore this opportunity. Some see it as too difficult and frustrating, while others simply do not see the need for it. However, when failing to properly plan for their human resources, employers are forced to respond to events after they occur, rather than before; they become reactive, rather than proactive. When this outcome occurs, an organization may be unable to correctly anticipate an increase in its future demand for personnel. At best, such a company would be forced to recruit personnel at the last minute and may fail to find the best candidates. At worst, the company may become seriously understaffed.

If a company remains understaffed for a prolonged period, it may ultimately suffer a variety of

Exhibit 1
HR Trend Analysis for a Manufacturing Firm

	2006	2007	2008	2009	2010
Projected sales (thousands of dollars)	10,200	8,700	7,800	9,500	10,000
Number of employees	240	200	165	215	?

consequences. For instance, the understaffing could cause existing employees to experience a great deal of stress as they attempt to meet additional demand without adequate resources and assistance. If required work is not getting done, the firm ultimately may experience an increase in back orders, which could cause a decrease in customer goodwill, an increase in competition, and a loss of market share.

When engaged in human resource planning, a company derives its human resource needs by first forecasting its demand for human resources (i.e., the number and types of people needed to carry out the work of the organization at some future point in time), and then its supply (i.e., the positions that are expected to be already filled). The difference between the two forecasts signifies the firm's HR needs. For example, if a firm estimates that it will demand 12 accountants during the next fiscal year and expects to retain its supply of nine who are already on staff, its HR need would be to hire three additional accountants. Following is a closer look at how a company can determine its HR needs and devise plans to meet them.

DEMAND FORECASTING

Demand forecasting involves predicting the number and types of people the organization will need at some future point in time. There are two general approaches to demand forecasting: statistical and judgmental. Using a statistical approach, an organization predicts its needed workforce size on the basis of certain business factors. A business factor is an attribute of the business, such as sales volume or market share, which closely relates to the size of the needed workforce. For example, a hospital could use the business factor of projected patient load to predict the number of nurses it would need at some point in time.

A statistical approach to demand forecasting typically is used when an organization operates in a stable environment, where an appropriate business factor can be predicted with some degree of certainty. For example, a statistical approach may be appropriate for a hospital located in an area with little population growth. Organizations operating in less stable environments (e.g., a hospital in an area experiencing explosive growth and change) are more likely to rely on a judgmental approach.

STATISTICAL APPROACHES. The most commonly used statistical methods of demand forecasting are trend, ratio, and regression analysis. In *trend analysis,* the future demand for human resources is projected on the basis of past business trends regarding a business factor. An example of a trend analysis is illustrated in Exhibit 1, which depicts the relationship between a business factor (namely, sales volume) and workforce size. As one can see from the exhibit, if the company expects its 2010 sales to be $10 million, it will need to increase its workforce to a size of nearly 240, which is the number of employees it had in 2006 when sales were $10.2 million.

Ratio analysis is the process of determining future HR demand by computing an exact ratio between the specific business factor and the number of employees needed. It thus provides a more precise estimate than trend analysis. For instance, the demand for professors at a university could be forecast on the basis of the student-faculty ratio. Suppose that a university has 10,000 students and 500 professors; the student-faculty ratio is thus 10,000:500 or 20:1. This ratio means that for every 20 students, the university needs 1 professor. If the university anticipates a student enrollment increase of 1,000 for next year, it would need to hire 50 (1000/20) new professors. This is in addition to any hiring needed to fill vacancies from existing faculty who might leave in the meantime.

Regression analysis is similar to both trend and ratio analyses in that forecasts are based on the relationship between a business factor and workforce size. However, this method is more statistically sophisticated. Using statistical software, the analyst first creates a scatter diagram depicting the relationship between the business factor and workforce size. The software can then calculate a regression line, which cuts right through the center of the points on the scatter diagram. (The regression line is mathematically determined using a formula found in most statistical texts.) By inspecting values along the regression line, one can see how many employees are needed at each value of the business factor. Both ratio analysis and regression analysis are aspects of human resource management systems (HRMS) packages, and therefore provide the business with the capabilities to calculate more accurate and timely forecasts.

An example of how regression analysis can be used to project HR demand is shown in Exhibit 2. In this example, the figures used in the trend analysis (Exhibit 1) are now depicted in the form of a scatter diagram. The line running through the center of the points plotted on the scatter diagram is the regression line. To determine the number of employees needed when the sales volume is $10 million, one would follow the path indicated by the dashed line. One would start at the point on the X axis reading "10,000," and then move up vertically until reaching the regression line. The value on the Y axis corresponding to that point (i.e., 230) reflects the needed workforce size.

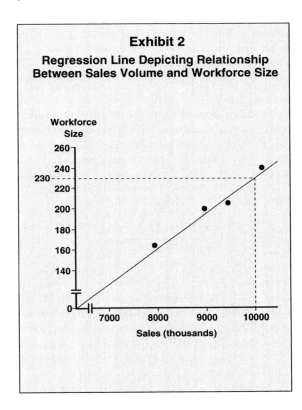

Exhibit 2

Regression Line Depicting Relationship Between Sales Volume and Workforce Size

Statistical methods of demand forecasting assume that the relationship between workforce size and the business factor remains constant over time. If this relationship were to change unexpectedly, the forecast would become inaccurate. For example, the forecast of needed professors based on the student-faculty ratio would be inaccurate if the university decided to change its teaching approach and institute distance learning classes. This approach to teaching involves the use of video equipment, which can beam the professor's lectures to many different locations, thus allowing many more students to enroll in the class. Consequently, the 20:1 ratio would no longer apply; the university would now be able to function with fewer professors (or at least more students per professor).

JUDGMENTAL APPROACHES. Judgmental approaches to demand forecasting involve the use of human judgment, rather than a manipulation of numbers. Two of the most commonly used judgmental techniques are group brainstorming and sales force estimates. The group brainstorming technique of demand forecasting uses a panel of experts (i.e., people within the organization who collectively understand the market, the industry, and the technological developments bearing on HRM needs). These experts are asked to generate a forecast through the process of brainstorming. A variety of brainstorming techniques exist. Most involve a face-to-face discussion among group members, who are asked to reach a consensus.

When using a *group brainstorming* technique to forecast human resources demand, participants must make certain assumptions regarding the future. That is, they must examine the firm's strategic plans for developing new products or services, expanding to new markets, and so forth, and then try to predict such things as:

- Future marketplace demands for the organization's products and services

- The percentage of the market that the organization will serve

- The availability and nature of new technologies that may affect the amounts and types of products or services that can be offered

The accuracy of the forecasts depends on the correctness of these assumptions. Of course, the future is very difficult to predict because it is subject to many uncertainties. Therefore, the organization must continually monitor its demand forecasts in light of any unexpected changes. HRMS packages facilitate the calculation and monitoring of demand forecasts.

The use of *sales force* estimates represents another judgmental approach for forecasting HR demand. This approach is most appropriately used when the need for additional employees arises from the introduction of new products. When a new product is launched, sales personnel are asked to estimate the demand for the product (i.e., expected sales volume) based on their knowledge of customer needs and interests. The organization then uses this information to estimate how many employees will be needed to meet this demand. One drawback of this approach is the possibility of bias. Some sales personnel may purposely underestimate product demands so they will look good when their own sales exceed the forecasts. Others may overestimate demand because they are overly optimistic about their sales potential.

SUPPLY FORECASTING

Once a demand forecast has been made, an organization has a relatively good idea of the number and nature of positions it will need to carry out its work at a particular point in time. It then estimates which of these positions will be filled at that time by individuals who already are employed by the company. The process used to make this estimation is called supply forecasting.

Supply forecasting is a two-step process. HRMS packages provide the employer with the means to automate much of these two steps. In the first step, the organization groups its positions by title, function, and responsibility level. These groupings should reflect levels of positions across which employees may be expected to advance. For instance, the HRM group might include the job titles of HR assistant, HR manager, and HR director. The secretarial group might include secretarial clerk, principal secretary, senior secretary, and administrative assistant.

The second step of supply forecasting is to estimate, within each job group, how many current employees will remain in their positions during the planning period, how many will move to another position (e.g., through transfer, promotion, or demotion), and how many will leave the organization. These predictions are partially based on past mobility trends (e.g., turnover and promotion rates). The organization also should consider any plans for mergers, acquisitions, unit or division divestitures, layoffs, retrenchments and downsizing, and even hostile takeovers. When making its supply forecast, the organization also should look at specific individuals. Some may have already announced, for instance, that they are retiring at the end of the year, returning to school in the fall, or getting married and planning on moving to a different part of the country.

Computerized statistical packages are available to help estimate the flow of employees through an organization. The estimates generated by these packages can be fairly accurate in stable environments. When the environment is unstable, of course, these estimates are suspect. For instance, an organization may base its estimates on past turnover rates, which have been about 10 percent during each of the past five years. If the turnover rate were to change drastically because of factors such as job dissatisfaction or downsizing, the organization would severely underestimate its future staffing needs.

ESTIMATING FUTURE HUMAN RESOURCE NEEDS

Combining the results of the supply and demand forecasts within each job group derives specific staffing needs. For example, consider a firm that currently employs twenty-five secretaries. As the result of its supply forecast, the firm predicts that five of these secretarial positions will become vacant by the end of the planning period because of retirements, promotions, and so forth. Its demand forecast predicts that three new secretarial positions will be needed during the coming period because of an increased demand for the company's product. By combining these two estimates, the firm now realizes that it must hire eight new secretaries (five to replace those expected to vacate their positions, plus three to fill the newly created positions).

OUTCOMES OF THE HR PLANNING PROCESS

When the HR planning process is completed, a firm must establish and implement HRM practices in order to meet its human resource needs. Following is a brief overview of how HRM practices can help organizations to deal with anticipated oversupplies and undersupplies of personnel.

The trend toward organizational restructuring usually results in a smaller workforce. Therefore, when an organization's strategic plan calls for restructuring, the HRM response usually is one of downsizing. Downsizing usually results in layoffs. Because of the negative outcomes that are often associated with layoffs, employers are encouraged to seek alternatives, such as hiring freezes, early retirements, restricted overtime, job sharing, and pay reductions.

When the results of demand and supply forecasting project an undersupply of personnel at some future point in time, the organization must decide how to resolve this problem. The solution may involve hiring additional staff, but there are other options. When HR plans indicate an undersupply of employees, firms can recruit personnel to staff jobs with anticipated vacancies. HRMS packages provide employers with capabilities to carry out recruitment in all of its steps. The first step is to conduct a job analysis to determine the qualifications needed for each vacant job.

The next step is to determine where and how to recruit the needed individuals. For instance, a company must decide whether to fill its vacancies externally (i.e., from the external labor market) or internally (i.e., from its own current workforce). When recruiting externally, an organization should first assess its attractiveness in the eyes of potential applicants; unattractive employers may have trouble generating a sufficiently large applicant pool. Such employers should attempt to increase the number of people who are attracted to the organization and thus interested in applying for a job there. This may be accomplished by increasing starting pay levels and/or improving benefit packages. Another option is to target certain protected groups whose members may be underemployed in the local labor market, such as older, disabled, or foreign-born individuals.

Internal recruitment efforts can be improved through the use of career development programs. When designing such a program, the organization should collect work history and skill level information on each of its employees. Such information would include age, education level, training, special skills (e.g., foreign language spoken), and promotion record, and should be stored on a computer. This employee information allows the organization to identify current employees who are qualified to assume jobs with greater responsibility levels. For instance, in departments where skilled managers are in short supply, a management replacement chart can be prepared that lists present managers, proposes likely replacements, and gives an estimate of when the replacement candidate will be trained and available to fill an open position.

Instead of hiring new workers to meet increasing demands, an organization may decide to improve the productivity of the existing workforce through additional training. Other options include the use of overtime, additional shifts, job reassignments, and temporary workers. Another option is to improve retention rates. When this aim is met, firms will have fewer job vacancies to fill.

Retention rates can be improved at the outset of the employer/employee relationship, when applicants are first recruited. Retention rates are likely to improve when applicants are given a realistic preview of what their jobs would actually be like (warts and all), rather than an overly glowing one.

Workers want to feel valued and needed by their organization. In a climate characterized by mergers, acquisitions, and layoffs, many workers feel very insecure about their jobs. Employees with such feelings often begin shopping around for other jobs. These fears can be eased by implementing HR plans for training and cross-training. Such plans allow workers to perform a variety of functions, thus ensuring that they have the necessary skills to continue making contributions to the firm. Management training also is crucial in this regard. Organizations must train managers to be good supervisors. Poor "people management" is a primary cause of voluntary turnover. Managers at all levels should know what is expected of them, in terms of managing people instead of just managing budgets.

Companies also can improve retention rates by creating a work environment that encourages employees to participate actively in the company's total welfare. Workers want recognition for their contributions to organizational progress, but this recognition must be tailored to the workers' individual needs. While some workers may be motivated by monetary rewards, others seek recognition by peers and managers, feelings of accomplishment, or job satisfaction.

Workers now demand more flexible schedules to best fit their lifestyles. Organizations can improve reten-

tion rates by implementing programs to accommodate these needs, such as job sharing, shortened workweeks, and telecommuting via computer and modem.

Finally, companies also can improve retention rates by offering attractive benefit packages, such as generous retirement plans, stock ownership, health and dental insurance, and employee discount programs. Many firms are now offering "cafeteria plan" benefit packages, which are tailored to the specific needs of each of their employees.

HUMAN RESOURCE MANAGEMENT SYSTEMS

Several major software companies provide HRMS packages. SAP, PeoleSoft, Oracle, and ADP are the largest. Depending on the company's needs and size, package options may include some or all of the following services:

- Employee career cycle management
- 24/7 data access to authorized managers
- Customized levels of access to confidential data
- Pre-populated forms and templates
- Access to real-time data—with instantaneous updates
- Employee administration
- Benefits administration
- Compliance
- Recruitment
- Performance and development
- Safety and health
- Succession planning
- Time-off management
- Organization management
- Payroll
- Training
- 401k plan administration

The opportunities to add more services are endless and continue to improve.

For most companies, the hardware and software needed to run these programs are fairly standard. Hardware and software is dependent on the complexity of the HRMS package; more complex HRMS packages require more hardware (e.g., server space and speed).

HRMS technology costs vary considerably, depending on the size of the company and its HR needs. Costs for deploying a comprehensive HRMS package include license fees, implementation, technology, training, and maintenance. Costs typically range from $300 to $700 per employee as an initial investment for companies with more than 1,000 employees. Smaller companies may decide it is better to rent the application than buy it. Research has found that most companies can recoup HRMS costs within three years of system launch, based on process efficiencies alone.

The value of HRMS results from a reduction in HR support costs, based on efficiency improvements. "Hackett's benchmark for the average annual cost of HR services per employee is approximately $1,900, with a best practice goal of less than $1,200" (Hamerman). By eliminating paper and process inefficiencies, companies can expect additional cost reductions while improving service and becoming more efficient. There are many other benefits of HRMS. Giga Information Group believes that HR departments can reduce time spent on administrative work by 40 percent to 50 percent, resulting in either the elimination of headcount or the redeployment of effort to higher value tasks, such as decision support and employee development.

Another benefit of HRMS includes allowing HR to transition from an administrative department to a strategic management department. The strategic value aspect of the HRMS investment focuses on managing human capital by supporting functions such as recruitment, performance/competency management, employee development, and employee customer service. By executing well in these areas, companies can reduce employee turnover, reduce hiring costs, and improve individual performance.

ADP offers a comprehensive suite of software that can run on almost all modern operating systems. A major player in the HRMS business is PeopleSoft. Acquired by Oracle Corp. in January 2005, PeopleSoft puts it focus on one complete HRM product line. This suite not only works in the HRM arena, it also allows employers to buy modules for CRM, SCM, and many other areas. There are three versions of the company's Enterprise suite: Enterprise, EnterpriseOne, and PeopleSoft World.

According to PeopleSoft, the Enterprise program is designed with the Internet in mind, and allows employers to:

- Plan the workforce needed to carry out an organization's business objectives, attract the right people, and provide them with the tools they need to be productive.

- Assess workforce skills and design learning and performance programs that develop people in alignment with their career paths and corporate objectives.

- Optimize a global workforce by putting the right people in the right jobs at the right time. This includes tracking the workforce and monitoring performance.

- Plan compensation and reward structures that align the workforce with corporate objectives. This includes linking the right employees with the right types of compensation, and rewarding them with a total package that maximizes efficiency, reduces costs, and increases overall performance.

EnterpriseOne works with the original Enterprise program and also let employers:

- Maintain a database of employee skill sets and competencies, as well as information about outside applicants.

- Track approved positions and headcount by company and department.

- Track recruitment data, such as where a company is finding employees, how long they stay, qualifications, and recruitment costs.

- Simplifying the employee evaluation process through automated workflow, which automatically alerts employees and managers about scheduled performance reviews.

- Helping managers to understand discrepancies between employees' expected and actual performance through built-in competency gap analysis tools.

- Providing true exception reporting with flexible reporting tools that summarize data, embed workflow messaging, and populate spreadsheets.

Finally, PeopleSoft's PeopleSoft World program was developed to help small businesses cope with the cost of changing hardware; it is built to work with the IBM iSeries. According to PeopleSoft, this system offers:

- Flexible and affordable pricing. Pre-integrated applications optimized on an IBM iSeries means lower implementation costs and ongoing IT needs. At the same time, users get a flexible architecture that enables them to tailor menus, security, and reporting to the specific needs of their business without costly modifications.

- Self-service capabilities: Web browser-based access to applications enables employees, customers, and suppliers to access relevant information quickly and easily, with less training.

- Full, robust solution: PeopleSoft World is a comprehensive, but low-maintenance solution for small businesses. It offers the same functionality available to larger enterprises, not a stripped-down version of a larger solution. It supports multicurrency, multi-language, and multi-company requirements and provides integration with other key PeopleSoft technologies.

All PeopleSoft Software is built on a Web-based platform, enabling "portal" technology. For both Enterprise and EnterpriseOne, portals are available to connect with employees over the Web. Technology continues to evolve, and HR is no exception. One of the fastest growing trends in HRMS is Web-based training/e-learning. E-learning tends to be far more affordable than classroom learning, and a higher degree of focus results in time savings. Not all e-learning is the same: some courses are self-paced with tutors available, some are instructor-led in real time, and some allow for student interaction.

Another HRMS trend is the use of online surveys. This allows companies to get fast information on their employees, policies, procedures, competition, and anything else they decide to survey. This also gives employees a sense of belonging and contributing to their company. Online employee surveys usually have an 80 percent return ratio, which is much higher than paper surveys.

Employees are becoming more self sufficient in the workplace because of HRMS and the growth of technology. They are able to answer questions, download forms, enroll in benefits, change payroll options, and complete training on their own. This saves both time and money. An employee does not have to make several phone calls in order to speak with the one person who knows the answer to their questions. Answers are readily available, usually on the company intranet. This also frees up HR to focus on more profitable activities for the company, such as recruiting and employee development.

Another growing trend includes improved methods for monitoring and managing employees' use of the Internet. This helps management to improve productivity, reduce legal liabilities, and control IT costs. Companies are blocking e-mail that may be offensive in order to reduce legal liabilities. They also are blocking Web sites that are inappropriate for workplace viewing. This has improved productivity by reducing non-productive activities.

HRMS providers have products for companies of all sizes. These providers profit by maximizing the services they offer. Therefore, they are going to target large companies that need more support. However, providers are still interested in small companies, and those that will need more support as they grow.

As the need for corporate cost-cutting, efficiency, and productivity becomes more important, the HRMS industry is going to continue to have strong growth potential. Not only can HRMS help with employee administration from recruiting to benefits, it can save companies thousands of dollars by lowering workforce and employee turnover levels. By 2005, the corporate world had only seen the beginning potential of HRMS.

SEE ALSO: Human Resource Management

Lawrence S. Kleiman
Revised by Badie N. Farah

FURTHER READING:

Dessler, Gary. *Human Resource Management.* 10th ed. Englewood Cliffs, NJ: Pearson/Prentice-Hall, 2004.

Gueutal, Hal G., and Dianna L. Stone, eds. *The Brave New World of eHR: Human Resources Management in the Digital Age.* San Francisco: Jossey-Bass, 2005.

Hamerman, Paul. "HR and Administrative B2E: Maturing and Expanding." Business.com, 2005. Available from <http://www.business.com/directory/human_resources/outsourcing/hrms_hris>.

———. "Justifying IT Investments: Human Resources Management Systems." Giga Information Group. Available from <http://www.majoraccounts.adp.com/news/art_hrms.htm>.

"Human Resource Information Systems (HRIS) Outsourcing." Business.com. Available from <http://www.business.com/directory/human_resources/outsourcing/hrms_hris>.

Losey, Mike, Sue Meisinger, and Dave Ulrich, eds. *The Future of Human Resource Management: 64 Thought Leaders Explore the Critical HR Issues of Today and Tomorrow.* New York: John Wiley & Sons, 2005.

Oracle Corp. "Products and Industries." Available from <http://www.peoplesoft.com/corp/en/products>.

HUMAN RESOURCE MANAGEMENT

Human resource management (HRM), also called personnel management, consists of all the activities undertaken by an enterprise to ensure the effective utilization of employees toward the attainment of individual, group, and organizational goals. An organization's HRM function focuses on the people side of management. It consists of practices that help the organization to deal effectively with its people during the various phases of the employment cycle, including pre-hire, staffing, and post-hire. The pre-hire phase involves planning practices. The organization must decide what types of job openings will exist in the upcoming period and determine the necessary qualifications for performing these jobs. During the hire phase, the organization selects its employees. Selection practices include recruiting applicants, assessing their qualifications, and ultimately selecting those who are deemed to be the most qualified.

In the post-hire phase, the organization develops HRM practices for effectively managing people once they have "come through the door." These practices are designed to maximize the performance and satisfaction levels of employees by providing them with the necessary knowledge and skills to perform their jobs and by creating conditions that will energize, direct, and facilitate employees' efforts toward meeting the organization's objectives.

HRM DEVELOPMENT AND IMPLEMENTATION RESPONSIBILITIES

While most firms have a human resources or personnel department that develops and implements HRM practices, responsibility lies with both HR professionals and line managers. The interplay between managers and HR professionals leads to effective HRM practices. For example, consider performance appraisals. The success of a firm's performance appraisal system depends on the ability of both parties to do their jobs correctly. HR professionals develop the system, while managers provide the actual performance evaluations.

The nature of these roles varies from company to company, depending primarily on the size of the organization. This discussion assumes a large company with a sizable HRM department. However, in smaller companies without large HRM departments, line managers must assume an even larger role in effective HRM practices.

HR professionals typically assume the following four areas of responsibility: establishing HRM policies and procedures, developing/choosing HRM methods, monitoring/evaluating HRM practices, and advising/assisting managers on HRM-related matters. HR professionals typically decide (subject to upper-management approval) what procedures to follow when implementing an HRM practice. For example, HR professionals may decide that the selection process should include having all candidates (1) complete an application, (2) take an employment test, and then (3) be interviewed by an HR professional and line manager.

Usually the HR professionals develop or choose specific methods to implement a firm's HRM practices. For instance, in selection the HR professional may construct the application blank, develop a structured interview guide, or choose an employment test. HR professionals also must ensure that the firm's HRM practices are properly implemented. This responsibility involves both evaluating and monitoring. For example, HR professionals may evaluate the usefulness of employment tests, the success of training programs, and the cost effectiveness of HRM outcomes such as

selection, turnover, and recruiting. They also may monitor records to ensure that performance appraisals have been properly completed.

HR professionals also consult with management on an array of HRM-related topics. They may assist by providing managers with formal training programs on topics like selection and the law, how to conduct an employment interview, how to appraise employee job performance, or how to effectively discipline employees. HR professionals also provide assistance by giving line managers advice about specific HRM-related concerns, such as how to deal with problem employees.

Line managers direct employees' day-to-day tasks. From an HRM perspective, line managers are mainly responsible for implementing HRM practices and providing HR professionals with necessary input for developing effective practices. Managers carry out many procedures and methods devised by HR professionals. For instance, line managers:

- Interview job applicants
- Provide orientation, coaching, and on-the-job training
- Provide and communicate job performance ratings
- Recommend salary increases
- Carry out disciplinary procedures
- Investigate accidents
- Settle grievance issues

The development of HRM procedures and methods often requires input from line managers. For example, when conducting a job analysis, HR professionals often seek job information from managers and ask managers to review the final written product. Additionally, when HR professionals determine an organization's training needs, managers often suggest what types of training are needed and who, in particular, needs the training.

HISTORICAL MILESTONES IN HRM DEVELOPMENT

Table 1 identifies some of the major milestones in the historical development of HRM. Frederick Taylor, known as the father of scientific management, played a significant role in the development of the personnel function in the early 1900s. In his book, *Shop Management,* Taylor advocated the "scientific" selection and training of workers. He also pioneered incentive systems that rewarded workers for meeting and/or exceeding performance standards. Although Taylor's focus primarily was on optimizing efficiency in manufacturing environments, his principles laid the groundwork for future HRM development. As Taylor was

Table 1

Milestones in the Development of Human Resource Management

1890-1910	Frederick Taylor develops his ideas on scientific management. Taylor advocates scientific selection of workers based on qualifications and also argues for incentive-based compensation systems to motivate employees.
1910-1930	Many companies establish departments devoted to maintaining the welfare of workers. The discipline of industrial psychology begins to develop. Industrial psychology, along with the advent of World War I, leads to advancements in employment testing and selection.
1930-1945	The interpretation of the Hawthorne Studies' begins to have an impact on management thought and practice. Greater emphasis is placed on the social and informal aspects of the workplace affecting worker productivity. Increasing the job satisfaction of workers is cited as a means to increase their productivity.
1945-1965	In the U.S., a tremendous surge in union membership between 1935 and 1950 leads to a greater emphasis on collective bargaining and labor relations within personnel management. Compensation and benefits administration also increase in importance as unions negotiate paid vacations, paid holidays, and insurance coverage.
1965-1985	The Civil Rights movement in the U.S. reaches its apex with passage of the Civil Rights Act of 1964. The personnel function is dramatically affected by Title VII of the CRA, which prohibits discrimination on the basis of race, color, sex, religion, and national origin. In the years following the passage of the CRA, equal employment opportunity and affirmative action become key human resource management responsibilities.
1985-present	Three trends dramatically impact HRM. The first is the increasing diversity of the labor force, in terms of age, gender, race, and ethnicity. HRM concerns evolve from EEO and affirmative action to "managing diversity." A second trend is the globalization of business and the accompanying technological revolution. These factors have led to dramatic changes in transportation, communication, and labor markets. The third trend, which is related to the first two, is the focus on HRM as a "strategic" function. HRM concerns and concepts must be integrated into the overall strategic planning of the firm in order to cope with rapid change, intense competition, and pressure for increased efficiency.

developing his ideas about scientific management, other pioneers were working on applying the principles of psychology to the recruitment, selection, and training of workers. The development of the field of industrial psychology and its application to the workplace came to fruition during World War I, as early vocational and employment-related testing was used to assign military recruits to appropriate functions.

The Hawthorne Studies, which were conducted in the 1920s and 1930s at Western Electric, sparked an increased emphasis on the social and informal aspects of the workplace. Interpretations of the studies emphasized "human relations" and the link between worker satisfaction and productivity. The passage of the Wagner Act in 1935 contributed to a major increase in the number of unionized workers. In the 1940s and 1950s, collective bargaining led to a tremendous increase in benefits offered to workers. The personnel function evolved to cope with labor relations, collective bargaining, and a more complex compensation and benefits environment. The human relations philosophy and labor relations were the dominant concerns of HRM in the 1940s and 1950s.

HRM was revolutionized in the 1960s by passage of Title VII of the Civil Rights Act and other anti-discrimination legislation—as well as presidential executive orders that required many organizations to undertake affirmative action in order to remedy past discriminatory practices. Equal employment opportu-

nity and affirmative action mandates greatly complicated the HRM function, but also enhanced its importance in modern organizations. As discussed more fully in a later section, these responsibilities continue to comprise a major part of the HRM job. Finally, changes in labor force demographics, technology, and globalization since the 1980s have had a major impact on the HRM function. These factors also are discussed in more detail in a later section.

PRE-HIRING, HIRING, AND POST-HIRING

PRE-HIRE PHASE. The major HRM activities in the pre-hire phase are human resource planning and job analysis. These activities form the cornerstone upon which other HRM practices are built. Human resource planning helps managers to anticipate and meet changing needs related to the acquisition, deployment, and utilization of employees. The organization first maps out an overall plan called a strategic plan. Then, through demand and supply forecasting it estimates the number and types of employees needed to successfully carry out its overall plan. Such information enables a firm to plan its recruitment, selection, and training strategies. For example, assume that a firm's HR plan estimates that 15 additional engineers will be needed during the next year. The firm typically hires recent engineering graduates to fill such positions. Because these majors are in high demand, the firm decides to begin its campus recruiting early in the academic year, before other companies can "snatch away" the best candidates.

Job analysis is the systematic process used for gathering, analyzing, and documenting information about particular jobs. The analysis specifies what each worker does, the work conditions, and the worker qualifications necessary to perform the job successfully. The job analysis information is used to plan and coordinate nearly all HRM practices, including:

- Determining job qualifications for recruitment purposes

- Choosing the most appropriate selection techniques

- Developing training programs

- Developing performance appraisal rating forms

- Helping to determine pay rates

- Setting performance standards for productivity improvement programs

For example, an organization may decide to use a mechanical aptitude test to screen applicants because a job analysis indicated that mechanical aptitude is an important job skill. Or, a firm may raise the pay of one of its employees because a job analysis indicated that the nature of the work recently changed and is now more demanding.

HIRING PHASE. The hiring phase of human resource management is also called staffing. Staffing involves policies and procedures used by organizations to recruit and select employees. Organizations use recruitment to locate and attract job applicants for particular positions. They may recruit candidates internally (i.e., recruit current employees seeking to advance or change jobs) or externally. The aim of recruitment practices is to identify a suitable pool of applicants quickly, cost-efficiently, and legally. Selection involves assessing and choosing among job candidates. To be effective, selection processes must be both legal and technically sound, accurately matching people's skills with available positions.

POST-HIRING PHASE. Training and development are planned learning experiences that teach workers how to effectively perform their current or future jobs. Training focuses on present jobs, while development prepares employees for possible future jobs. Training and development practices are designed to improve organizational performance by enhancing the knowledge and skill levels of employees. A firm must first determine its training needs and then select/develop training programs to meet these needs. It also must take steps to ensure that workers apply what they have learned on the job.

Through the performance appraisal process, organizations measure the adequacy of their employees' job performances and communicate these evaluations to them. One aim of appraisal systems is to motivate employees to continue appropriate behaviors and correct inappropriate ones. Management also may use performance appraisals as tools for making HRM-related decisions, such as promotions, demotions, discharges, and pay raises.

Compensation entails pay and benefits. Pay refers to the wage or salary employees earn, while benefits are a form of compensation provided to employees in addition to their pay, such as health insurance or employee discounts. The aim of compensation practices is to help the organization establish and maintain a competent and loyal workforce at an affordable cost.

Productivity improvement programs tie job behavior to rewards. Rewards may be financial (e.g., bonuses and pay raises) or nonfinancial (e.g., improved job satisfaction). Such programs are used to motivate employees to engage in appropriate job behaviors, namely those that help the organization meet its goals.

CONTEMPORARY ISSUES

HRM departments within organizations, just as the organizations themselves, do not exist in a vacuum. Events outside of work environments have far-reaching effects on HRM practices. The following paragraphs describe some of these events and indicate how they influence HRM practices.

As mentioned previously, the enactment of federal, state, and local laws regulating workplace behavior has changed nearly all HRM practices. Consider, for instance, the impact of anti-discrimination laws on firms' hiring practices. Prior to the passage of these laws, many firms hired people based on reasons that were not job-related. Today, such practices could result in charges of discrimination. To protect themselves from such charges, employers must conduct their selection practices to satisfy objective standards established by legislation and fine-tuned by the courts. This means they should carefully determine needed job qualifications and choose selection methods that accurately measure those qualifications.

Social, economic, and technological events also strongly influence HRM practices. These events include:

- An expanding cultural diversity at the workplace

- The emergence of work and family issues

- The growing use of part-time and temporary employees

- An increased emphasis on quality and teamwork

- The occurrence of mergers and takeovers

- The occurrence of downsizing and layoffs

- The rapid advancement of technology

- An emphasis on continuous quality improvement

- A high rate of workforce illiteracy

These events influence HRM practices in numerous ways. For example:

- Some firms are attempting to accommodate the needs of families by offering benefit options like maternity leave, child care, flex-time, and job sharing.

- Some firms are attempting to accommodate the needs of older workers through skill upgrading and training designed to facilitate the acceptance of new techniques.

- Some firms are educating their employees in basic reading, writing, and mathematical skills so that they can keep up with rapidly advancing technologies.

Unions often influence a firm's HRM practices. Unionized companies must adhere to written contracts negotiated between each company and its union. Union contracts regulate many HRM practices, such as discipline, promotion, grievance procedures, and overtime allocations. HRM practices in non-unionized companies may be influenced by the threat of unions. For example, some companies have made their HRM practices more equitable (i.e., they treat their employees more fairly) simply to minimize the likelihood that employees would seek union representation.

Legal, social, and political pressures on organizations to ensure the health and safety of their employees have had great impacts on HRM practices. Organizations respond to these pressures by instituting accident prevention programs and programs designed to ensure the health and mental well-being of their employees, such as wellness and employee assistance programs.

Today's global economy also influences some aspects of HRM. Many firms realize that they must enter foreign markets in order to compete as part of a globally interconnected set of business markets. From an HRM perspective, such organizations must foster the development of more globally-oriented managers: individuals who understand foreign languages and cultures, as well as the dynamics of foreign market places. These firms also must deal with issues related to expatriation, such as relocation costs, selection, compensation, and training.

EMPLOYMENT

Someone wishing to enter the HRM field may choose one of two routes: generalist or specialist. Entry-level HRM generalist positions are most often found in small or mid-sized organizations that employ few HR professionals—one or two people who must perform all functions. Because of their many responsibilities, HRM generalists have neither time nor resources to conduct in-depth studies or projects. They usually hire outside consultants who specialize in these kinds of services. For example, consultants might help the organization to revamp its compensation system, validate its selection practices, or analyze its training needs.

In larger organizations, each HR professional's area tends to be more focused, zeroing in on particular HRM tasks. Individuals holding these positions are called HRM specialists. Exhibits 1a and 1b describe some traditional and newer HRM specialty areas.

In most professions a direct path leads to entering the field. For instance, someone aspiring to be a lawyer, physician, accountant, or psychologist enrolls in appropriate educational programs and enters the field upon receiving a degree or license. HRM is atypical in this regard; people may enter the profession in a variety of ways. For instance, most of today's HR professionals enter the field through self-directed career changes. Approximately one-third of these individuals entered HRM by transferring from another part of the company; the remainder entered from other fields such as education, social services, accounting, sales, and administrative secretarial positions.

HR professionals entering the field directly out of college (about one-third of all HR professionals) traditionally come from a variety of academic backgrounds, including business, psychology, and liberal arts. More recently, however, HRM new hires have earned degrees in some area of business, such as HRM, management, or general business. For instance, when it hires recent graduates for entry-level HRM positions, Bell Atlantic considers business school graduates with concentrations in business administration, finance and commerce, management, or industrial relations. A survey of HR professionals revealed the following college majors: HRM (17 percent), business administration (23 percent), management (13 percent), psychology (12 percent), and labor/industrial relations (10 percent).

As one might expect, large organizations provide the greatest opportunities for HRM career growth. Most senior-level HR professionals take one of two paths up the corporate ladder. Some begin their careers as specialists and eventually become managers of their specialty units. To advance beyond this level, they must broaden their skills and become HRM generalists. The other path to securing a senior-level HRM position is to begin as an assistant HRM generalist at

Exhibit 1a
HRM Specialty Areas

TRADITIONAL SPECIALTY AREAS

Training/Development

Conducts training needs analysis; designs/conducts/evaluates training programs; develops/implements succession planning programs.

Compensation/Benefits

Develops job descriptions; facilitates job evaluation processes; conducts/interprets salary surveys; develops pay structure; designs pay-for-performance and/or performance improvement programs; administers benefits program.

Employee/Industrial Relations

Helps resolve employee relations problems; develops union avoidance strategies; assists in collective bargaining negotiations; oversees grievance procedures.

Employment/Recruiting

Assists in the HR planning process; develops/purchases HR information systems; develops/updates job descriptions; oversees recruiting function; develops and administers job posting system; conducts employment interviews, reference checks, and employment tests; validates selection procedures; approves employment decisions.

Safety/Health/Wellness

Develops accident prevention strategies; develops legal safety and health policies; implements/promotes EAP and wellness programs; develops AIDS and substance abuse policies.

EEO/Affirmative Action

Develops and administers affirmative action programs; helps resolve EEO disputes; monitors organizational practices with regard to EEO compliance; develops policies for ensuring EEO compliance, such as sexual harassment policies.

HRM Research

Conducts research studies, such as cost-benefit analysis, test validation, program evaluation, and feasibility studies.

(cont. Exhibit 1b)

---

a small plant or unit within the organization and advance into an HRM managerial role at successively larger plants or units. An HRM career in manufacturing might progress as follows:

1. The individual is hired as an HRM assistant at a manufacturing plant.

2. Within five or six years, the individual advances to the HRM manager's post at the plant.

3. Between six and ten years, the HR professional becomes the HRM manager at a larger plant.

4. During the eleven-to-fifteen-year range, the person reaches a senior-level HRM position at the divisional level and has several HRM

generalists and/or specialists reporting to him or her.

5. Between fifteen and twenty years, the person reaches a senior-level executive position, such as vice president of human resources.

ORGANIZATIONAL ETHICS

HR professionals primarily are responsible for developing HRM practices that enhance a firm's competitive advantage. HR professionals also have the responsibility to ensure that employees are treated ethically. Almost all HRM decisions have ethical consequences. Despite the abundance of laws designed to ensure fair treatment at the workplace, employees often are treated in an unethical manner. In some instances, employers skirt the law; in others, the letter of the law is followed, but employees are nonetheless

Exhibit 1b
HRM Specialty Areas (cont.)

NEW HRM SPECIALTY AREAS

Work and Family Programs

Develops and administers work and family programs including flextime, alternative work scheduling, dependent-care assistance, telecommuting, and other programs designed to accommodate employee needs; identifies and screen child- or elder-care providers; administers employer's private dependent-care facility; promotes work and family programs to employees.

Cross-Cultural Training

Translate the manners, mores, and business practices of other nations and cultures for American business people. Other cross-cultural trainers work with relocated employees' families, helping them adjust to their new environment.

Managed-Care

As a company's health-care costs continue to escalate, employers are embracing managed-care systems, which require employees to assume some of the costs. Employers hire managed-care managers to negotiate the best options for employees.

Managing Diversity

Develop policies and practices to recruit, promote, and appropriately treat workers of various ages, races, sexes, and physical abilities.

---

treated unfairly by management or by other employees. One survey revealed that the most serious ethical problems involve managerial decisions regarding employment, promotion, pay, and discipline that are based on favoritism, rather than ability or job performance.

HR professionals play three roles in the area of workplace ethics. One role is monitoring: they must observe the actions of organizational members to ensure that all individuals are treated fairly and legally. Second, HR professionals investigate complaints bearing on ethical issues, such as sexual harassment or violations of employees' privacy rights. Third, HR professionals serve as company spokespeople by defending the company's actions when confronted by a regulatory agency or the media.

Furthermore, HR professionals should act ethically themselves. When faced with ethical dilemmas, HR professionals must be willing to take a strong stand, even if it means putting their jobs at risk. If they choose to turn a blind eye, they become part of the problem and thus must assume some of the blame.

HR professionals should be guided by the Society for Human Resource Management Code of Ethics, which dictates that HR professionals should always:

- Maintain the highest standards of professional and personal conduct

- Encourage employers to make fair and equitable treatment of all employees a primary concern

- Maintain loyalty to employers and pursue company objectives in ways consistent with the public interest

- Uphold all laws and regulations relating to employer activities

- Maintain the confidentiality of privileged information

SEE ALSO: Human Resource Information Systems

Lawrence S. Kleiman
Revised by Tim Barnett

FURTHER READING:

Dessler, Gary. *Human Resource Managemen.* 10th ed. Englewood Cliffs, NJ: Pearson/Prentice-Hall, 2004.

Kleiman, Lawrence S. *Human Resource Management: A Managerial Tool for Competitive Advantage.* Cincinnati: South-Western College Publishing, 2000.

Lado, A.A., and M.C. Wilson. "Human Resource Systems and Sustained Competitive Advantage: A Competency-Based Perspective." *Academy of Management Review* 19, no. 4 (1994): 699–727.

Noe, Raymond A., et al. *Human Resource Management: Gaining a Competitive Advantage.* 5th ed. Boston: McGraw-Hill, 2006.

SHRM Online. Society for Human Resource Management. Available from <http://www.shrm.org>.

HYPOTHESIS TESTING

Social science research, and by extension business research, uses a number of different approaches to study a variety of issues. This research may be a very informal, simple process or it may be a formal, somewhat sophisticated process. Regardless of the type of process, all research begins with a generalized idea in the form of a research question or a hypothesis. A research question usually is posed in the beginning of a research effort or in a specific area of study that has had little formal research. A research question may take the form of a basic question about some issue or phenomena or a question about the relationship between two or more variables. For example, a research question might be: "Do flexible work hours improve employee productivity?" Another question might be: "How do flexible hours influence employees' work?"

A hypothesis differs from a research question; it is more specific and makes a prediction. It is a tentative statement about the relationship between two or more variables. The major difference between a research question and a hypothesis is that a hypothesis predicts an experimental outcome. For example, a hypothesis might state: "There is a positive relationship between the availability of flexible work hours and employee productivity."

Hypotheses provide the following benefits:

1. They determine the focus and direction for a research effort.

2. Their development forces the researcher to clearly state the purpose of the research activity.

3. They determine what variables will not be considered in a study, as well as those that will be considered.

4. They require the researcher to have an operational definition of the variables of interest.

The worth of a hypothesis often depends on the researcher's skills. Since the hypothesis is the basis of a research study, it is necessary for the hypothesis be developed with a great deal of thought and contemplation. There are basic criteria to consider when developing a hypothesis, in order to ensure that it meets the needs of the study and the researcher. A good hypothesis should:

1. Have logical consistency. Based on the current research literature and knowledge base, does this hypothesis make sense?

2. Be in step with the current literature and/or provide a good basis for any differences. Though it does not have to support the current body of literature, it is necessary to provide a good rationale for stepping away from the mainstream.

3. Be testable. If one cannot design the means to conduct the research, the hypothesis means nothing.

4. Be stated in clear and simple terms in order to reduce confusion.

HYPOTHESIS TESTING PROCESS

Hypothesis testing is a systematic method used to evaluate data and aid the decision-making process. Following is a typical series of steps involved in hypothesis testing:

1. State the hypotheses of interest

2. Determine the appropriate test statistic

3. Specify the level of statistical significance

4. Determine the decision rule for rejecting or not rejecting the null hypothesis

5. Collect the data and perform the needed calculations

6. Decide to reject or not reject the null hypothesis

Each step in the process will be discussed in detail, and an example will follow the discussion of the steps.

STATING THE HYPOTHESES. A research study includes at least two hypotheses—the null hypothesis and the alternative hypothesis. The hypothesis being tested is referred to as the null hypothesis and it is designated as H It also is referred to as the hypothesis of no difference and should include a statement of equality $(=, \geq, \text{ or } \leq)$. The alternative hypothesis presents the alternative to the null and includes a statement of inequality $(\neq)$. The null hypothesis and the alternative hypothesis are complementary.

The null hypothesis is the statement that is believed to be correct throughout the analysis, and it is the null hypothesis upon which the analysis is based. For example, the null hypothesis might state that the average age of entering college freshmen is 21 years.

H_0 The average age of entering college freshman = 21 years

If the data one collects and analyzes indicates that the average age of entering college freshmen is greater than or less than 21 years, the null hypothesis is rejected. In this case the alternative hypothesis could be stated in the following three ways: (1) the average age of entering college freshman is not 21 years (the average age of entering college freshmen $\neq 21$); (2) the average age of entering college freshman is less than 21 years (the average age of entering college freshmen < 21); or (3) the average age of entering college freshman is greater than 21 years (the average age of entering college freshmen > 21 years).

The choice of which alternative hypothesis to use is generally determined by the study's objective. The preceding second and third examples of alternative hypotheses involve the use of a "one-tailed" statistical test. This is referred to as "one-tailed" because a direction (greater than [>] or less than [<]) is implied in the statement. The first example represents a "two-tailed" test. There is inequality expressed (age ≠ 21 years), but the inequality does not imply direction. One-tailed tests are used more often in management and marketing research because there usually is a need to imply a specific direction in the outcome. For example, it is more likely that a researcher would want to know if Product A performed better than Product B (Product A performance > Product B performance), or vice versa (Product A performance < Product B performance), rather than whether Product A performed differently than Product B (Product A performance ≠ Product B performance). Additionally, more useful information is gained by knowing that employees who work from 7:00 a.m. to 4:00 p.m. are more productive than those who work from 3:00 p.m. to 12:00 a.m. (early shift employee production > late shift employee production), rather than simply knowing that these employees have different levels of productivity (early shift employee production ≠ late shift employee production).

Both the alternative and the null hypotheses must be determined and stated prior to the collection of data. Before the alternative and null hypotheses can be formulated it is necessary to decide on the desired or expected conclusion of the research. Generally, the desired conclusion of the study is stated in the alternative hypothesis. This is true as long as the null hypothesis can include a statement of equality. For example, suppose that a researcher is interested in exploring the effects of amount of study time on tests scores. The researcher believes that students who study longer perform better on tests. Specifically, the research suggests that students who spend four hours studying for an exam will get a better score than those who study two hours. In this case the hypotheses might be:

H_0 The average test scores of students who study 4 hours for the test = the average test scores of those who study 2 hours.
H_1 The average test score of students who study 4 hours for the test > the average test scores of those who study 2 hours.

As a result of the statistical analysis, the null hypothesis can be *rejected* or *not rejected*. As a principle of rigorous scientific method, this subtle but important point means that the null hypothesis cannot be *accepted*. If the null is rejected, the alternative hypothesis can be accepted; however, if the null is not rejected, we can't conclude that the null hypothesis is true. The rationale is that evidence that supports a hypothesis is not conclusive, but evidence that negates a hypothesis is ample to discredit a hypothesis. The analysis of study time and test scores provides an example. If the results of one study indicate that the test scores of students who study 4 hours are significantly better than the test scores of students who study two hours, the null hypothesis can be rejected because the researcher has found one case when the null is not true. However, if the results of the study indicate that the test scores of those who study 4 hours are not significantly better than those who study 2 hours, the null hypothesis cannot be rejected. One also cannot conclude that the null hypothesis is accepted because these results are only one set of score comparisons. Just because the null hypothesis is true in one situation does not mean it is always true.

DETERMINING THE APPROPRIATE TEST STATISTIC. The appropriate test statistic (the statistic to be used in statistical hypothesis testing) is based on various characteristics of the sample population of interest, including sample size and distribution. The test statistic can assume many numerical values. Since the value of the test statistic has a significant effect on the decision, one must use the appropriate statistic in order to obtain meaningful results. Most test statistics follow this general pattern:

$$\frac{\text{Sample statistic} - \text{Hypothesized parameter value}}{\text{Standard error of statistic}}$$

For example, the appropriate statistic to use when testing a hypothesis about a population means is:

$$Z = \frac{\overline{X} - \mu_0}{\sigma / \sqrt{\eta}}$$

In this formula Z = test statistic, $\overline{X}$ = mean of the sample, μ = mean of the population, σ = standard deviation of the sample, and η = number in the sample.

SPECIFYING THE STATISTICAL SIGNIFICANCE SEVEL. As previously noted, one can reject a null hypothesis or fail to reject a null hypothesis. A null hypothesis that is rejected may, in reality, be true or false. Additionally, a null hypothesis that fails to be rejected may, in reality, be true or false. The outcome that a researcher desires is to reject a false null hypothesis or to fail to reject a true null hypothesis. However, there always is the possibility of rejecting a true hypothesis or failing to reject a false hypothesis.

Rejecting a null hypothesis that is true is called a Type I error and failing to reject a false null hypothesis is called a Type II error. The probability of committing a Type I error is termed α and the probability of committing a Type II error is termed β. As the value of α increases, the probability of committing a Type I error increases. As the value of β increases, the probability of committing a Type II error increases. While one would like to decrease the probability of committing of both types of errors, the reduction of α results in the increase of β and vice versa. The best way to reduce the probability of decreasing both types of error is to increase sample size.

The probability of committing a Type I error, α, is called the level of significance. Before data is collected one must specify a level of significance, or the probability of committing a Type I error (rejecting a true null hypothesis). There is an inverse relationship between a researcher's desire to avoid making a Type I error and the selected value of α; if not making the error is particularly important, a low probability of making the error is sought. The greater the desire is to not reject a true null hypothesis, the lower the selected value of α. In theory, the value of α can be any value between 0 and 1. However, the most common values used in social science research are .05, .01, and .001, which respectively correspond to the levels of 95 percent, 99 percent, and 99.9 percent likelihood that a Type I error is not being made. The tradeoff for choosing a higher level of certainty (significance) is that it will take much stronger statistical evidence to ever reject the null hypothesis.

DETERMINING THE DECISION RULE. Before data are collected and analyzed it is necessary to determine under what circumstances the null hypothesis will be rejected or fail to be rejected. The decision rule can be stated in terms of the computed test statistic, or in probabilistic terms. The same decision will be reached regardless of which method is chosen.

COLLECTING THE DATA AND PERFORMING THE CALCULATIONS. The method of data collection is determined early in the research process. Once a research question is determined, one must make decisions regarding what type of data is needed and how the data will be collected. This decision establishes the bases for how the data will be analyzed. One should use only approved research methods for collecting and analyzing data.

DECIDING WHETHER TO REJECT THE NULL HYPOTHESIS. This step involves the application of the decision rule. The decision rule allows one to reject or fail to reject the null hypothesis. If one rejects the null hypothesis, the alternative hypothesis can be accepted. However, as discussed earlier, if one fails to reject the null he or she can only suggest that the null may be true.

EXAMPLE. XYZ Corporation is a company that is focused on a stable workforce that has very little turnover. XYZ has been in business for 50 years and has more than 10,000 employees. The company has always promoted the idea that its employees stay with them for a very long time, and it has used the following line in its recruitment brochures: "The average

tenure of our employees is 20 years." Since XYZ isn't quite sure if that statement is still true, a random sample of 100 employees is taken and the average age turns out to be 19 years with a standard deviation of 2 years. Can XYZ continue to make its claim, or does it need to make a change?

1. State the hypotheses.

$H_0 = 20$ years
$H_1 \neq 20$ years

2. Determine the test statistic. Since we are testing a population mean that is normally distributed, the appropriate test statistic is:

$$Z = \frac{\overline{X} - \mu_o}{\sigma / \sqrt{\eta}}$$

3. Specify the significance level. Since the firm would like to keep its present message to new recruits, it selects a fairly weak significance level ($\alpha = .05$). Since this is a two-tailed test, half of the alpha will be assigned to each tail of the distribution. In this situation the critical values of $Z = +1.96$ and -1.96.

4. State the decision rule. If the computed value of Z is greater than or equal to $+1.96$ or less than or equal to -1.96, the null hypothesis is rejected.

5. Calculations.

$$Z = \frac{31 - 30}{2 / 10}$$
$$= 2.5$$

6. Reject or fail to reject the null. Since 2.5 is greater than 1.96, the null is rejected. The mean tenure is not 20 years, therefore XYZ needs to change its statement.

SEE ALSO: Research Methods and Processes; Statistics

Donna T. Mayo
Revised by Marcia Simmering

FURTHER READING:

Anderson, David R., Dennis J. Sweeney, and Thomas A. Williams. *Statistics for Business and Economics.* 9th ed. Mason, OH: South-Western College Publishing, 2004.

Kerlinger, Fred N., and Howard B. Lee. *Foundations of Behavioral Research.* 4th ed. Fort Worth, TX: Harcourt College Publishers, 2000.

Pedhazur, Elazar J., and Liora Pedhazur Schmelkin. *Measurement, Design, and Analysis: An Integrated Approach.* Hillsdale, NJ: Lawrence Erlbaum Associates, 1991.

Schwab, Donald P. *Research Methods for Organizational Studies.* Mahwah, NJ: Lawrence Erlbaum Associates, 1999.

I

IPO

SEE: Initial Public Offering

IMPORTING

SEE: Exporting and Importing

INCOME STATEMENTS

The income statement is one of the three major financial statements that all publicly held firms are required to prepare annually. It provides a record of a company's revenues and expenses for a given period of time, and thus serves as the basic measuring stick of profitability. In fact, the income statement is often referred to as the profit-and-loss statement, with the bottom line literally revealing which result a company achieved. Along with the balance sheet and cash flow statement, the income statement provides important financial information to business managers, investors, lenders, and analysts.

"The income statement is simply a scorecard that summarizes the revenues and expenses of an organization for a specific period of time," Jayson Orr wrote in *CMA Management*. "It reveals critical information

about the operations and profitability of a business unit. It also reveals little secrets that may not be so obvious. In short, the income statement tells how successfully a business unit is fulfilling its prime directive—to generate profit."

Preparing an income statement is one of the basic responsibilities of the accounting function. Accounting is the process of recording and disclosing the financial information for a company so that operating results can be known and comparisons between different years and different companies can be made. Accounting has been described as the language of business. Because managers of all organizations use accounting information, perhaps on a daily basis, it is critical that they understand the language. One of the obstacles to the best use of accounting information is that its terminology is confusing, especially when some of the terms used in accounting have alternate meanings in other business settings.

One of the purposes of this essay is to provide logical definitions for key business terms from an accounting perspective; thus avoiding misunderstandings from applying an inappropriate definition. A second purpose is to describe the contents of the typical income statement prepared for a profit-seeking corporation.

ACCRUAL ACCOUNTING VS. CASH BASIS ACCOUNTING

An area of confusion for many people is the concept known as accrual accounting. When individuals and small companies spend money, the expenditure is generally considered to be an *expense*. This is what accountants refer as the *cash basis* of accounting. But larger companies, particularly publicly held corporations, are required to use the *accrual basis* of accounting. From the accrual accounting perspective, the purpose of the expenditure determines whether or not the expenditure is an expense at the time of payment. For example, if a business expends cash for office supplies, no expense occurs until the office supplies are used in business operations. The spending of cash is not the critical event. Thus, when a business buys postage stamps, it has purchased an *asset,* that is, an item that has a future potential to benefit the company. If the stamps are used to mail an invoice to a customer or supplier, then the *expense* occurs because the stamp (asset) has no further benefit for the company.

The same logic would apply to other expenditures wherein a company acquires an asset that offers future benefits on a long-term basis, such as a delivery truck. Identifying when the benefit occurs, and therefore when the expense occurs, is a more difficult task in this instance, and the point will be discussed later as the concept of *depreciation.* One unique aspect of an expense is that expenses are incurred in order to produce revenues.

The concept of revenues also proves confusing to some people. Revenues can be defined as the amount charged to customers for the services and products that are provided to them. When employees receive paychecks, they consider that they have earned their pay at that time. The paycheck represents the completion of labor for the previous work period. For a company that uses accrual accounting, however, the receipt of payment is not the critical event for determining when revenues have been earned. From an accrual accounting perspective, a company generally earns revenues at the time when a product or service is provided to the customer. Thus, whether a customer pays for the purchase of a product or service with cash (or check) or charges the purchase on a credit card, the company earns revenue when the product or service is provided. This concept is complicated because revenue is earned, and yet no cash might be paid to the company at the time that accounting says that revenue is earned. Using the paycheck example, employees actually earn their pay on a daily basis as they perform services for their company, but they do not receive payment until payday.

To merge the two concepts of revenues and expenses together, consider a rule accountants refer to as the *matching principle.* This rule can be summarized as follows: revenues are recorded in the time period when earned and expenses are matched (offset) against the revenues in the same time period that they cause revenues to be earned. More formal definitions can be summarized as follows: revenues can be defined as the total amount earned from providing goods and services to customers. Revenues are equal to (measured by) the amount of cash or legal claim to receive cash or other items of value to be received at a later date in payment from the customer. The receipt of payment might occur immediately or it might occur, say, 30 days after the invoice's date. In either case, the revenues are earned when the service or product is provided, not necessarily when the cash is received.

Expenses can be viewed as representing the use of the benefits that an employee or asset provides; the payment for the asset or services might or might not occur at the same time that the benefits are used. The important thing to remember is that expenses are incurred, and therefore matched with revenues, in the period in which the company earns the revenues.

THE INCOME STATEMENT

The income statement is considered by many to be a company's most important financial statement. It discloses the dollar amount of the profitability for a company during a specific period of time. Since published annual financial statements usually cover a 12-month period, which will be the assumption here.

The heading of the income statement should contain three crucial elements of information: the name of the company involved, the title of the statement identifying it as an income statement, and the specific 12-month period during which the income was earned. The basic format of the income statement is represented by the following equation: revenues minus expenses equal net income.

REVENUES. The income statement discloses total revenue and total expenses for the period in question. The amount of the revenues in excess of the expenses is the net income, or profit, earned by the company for the year covered by the statement. Notice that revenues are considered as a total or gross concept, whereas profit is considered a net concept, as in net income. Revenues represent the total amount that products and services are worth; expenses represent the amount that products or services cost the company; and the excess of the revenues over the expenses is the profit.

Consider a simple example: say that a company sells automobiles for profit. The company buys a car for a cost of $20,000 and sells it for $30,000 in revenue. Ignoring expenses other than the cost of the car, the profit can be determined by taking the $30,000 in revenue minus the $20,000 in expenses (the cost of the car), giving a figure of $10,000. If the total of all such sales for a year are shown and all related expenses incurred in that same year to produce the sales are deducted, the result is an income statement.

There are two basic formats of the income statement. The one summarized above is known as the *single-step income statement,* used by many service companies. All revenues are disclosed at the top of the statement, followed by all expenses of the company for the same time period. Some companies prefer to disclose their income tax expense after having deducted all other expenses from the revenues, since it doesn't relate directly to operations of the company, as do the other expenses. Net income is the bottom line, just as the expression says. However, for a company that is a corporation, an amount that is roughly the net income earned per share of corporate voting stock is disclosed last. This figure is entitled *earnings per share,* and when tracked over time it is used widely as an indicator of corporate performance from period to period.

The other format for the income statement is known as the *multiple-step income statement.* Its form is somewhat more complex; its purpose is to disclose in more detail certain relationships that many users of financial statements consider important. An abbreviated version of the multiple-step income statement is shown in Table 1.

Table 1

Sales Revenues	$1,000,000
Less Cost of Goods Sold	-600,000
Gross Profit on Sales	400,000
Less Operating Expenses	-250,000
Income Before Income Taxes	150,000
Less Income Tax Expense	-50,000
Net Income	$100,000
Earnings Per Share	$1.00

The following paragraphs examine each line in this hypothetical income statement. To begin with, revenues would follow the general description presented earlier; in other words, they would be recorded on an accrual basis as customers take delivery of products. Thus, in this sample the *sales revenue* refers to the revenue earned from providing products to the customer. Note, however, that a bank would not have sales revenue but, instead, would have interest revenue, while a car rental company would have rental revenue. The nature of the revenue would determine the adjective used to describe the source of the revenue. There are other points in time that revenue may be recorded as being earned, but point of sale is the dominant usage.

COST OF GOODS SOLD. *Cost of goods sold* (often abbreviated COGS) is the expense representing the cost that a company expends to manufacture a product, if it is a manufacturing firm, or to acquire a product for resale, if a wholesaler or retailer. This represents only the direct cost of providing the product to the customer; other costs of operating the business, such as management and sales staff salaries, are deducted as expenses in other locations of the income statement. Of course, a company that provides a service instead of a product would not have a COGS expense to be deducted on its income statement.

GROSS PROFIT ON SALES. *Gross profit on sales* (or simply gross profit or gross margin) represents the total profit on the sales, if only the cost of the product itself is considered. This amount is used in calculating numerous financial ratios, such as the gross margin percent; thus it is provided for the financial statement user's benefit to analyze operating performance and make comparisons with other firms in the same line of business.

OPERATING EXPENSES. *Operating expenses* are deducted next. Sometimes this category is divided into two major components: selling (marketing) expenses and general and administrative (G&A) expenses (or both together, SG&A). Selling expenses include any expense incurred in an attempt to sell the products. Expenses such as advertising, salaries of sales personnel, and sales commissions would be included. G&A expenses include all other expenses; these relate to the general administration activities needed to run the business for the current year covered by the income statement. Examples of G&A expenses include rent expense, insurance expense, and other expenses related to the general administration of the company.

A few special expenses in this category require added discussion. Based on the accrual accounting definition of expenses presented above, expenses are deducted when incurred to earn revenue, and this may not correspond with the point in time that cash is spent to pay for the expense. For example, one of the operating expenses might be *warranty expense.* A product might be sold with a two-year warranty to cover labor and parts needed for repairs. In the year that the product is sold and the revenue from the sale is recorded, the future two years of warranty expense must also be recorded. This might seem illogical except for two important reasons. First, accrual accounting requires that expenses be matched with related revenues when the revenues are earned. Second, the warranty expense was incurred to create the sale in the first place. The sale might not have occurred without the warranty made available to the customer. This means that the accountant, with management's approval, must estimate and currently deduct what the future sacrifice will be during the subsequent two-year period, long before any cash expenditures are made.

Another example of an estimated expense is an *uncollectible accounts expense* or *bad debt expense.* Any company that offers credit terms to its customers will experience a few instances when customers are unable to pay the balance of an account when it comes due. Since accrual accounting requires the disclosure of revenue when it is earned, even when on a credit basis, the company must deduct at the time the revenue is recorded an estimate of the total of the accounts that may prove to be uncollectible in the future.

The next example of an expense that must be estimated, but one that is common to many income statements, is *depreciation expense.* If a company owns a long-lived asset, such as a building, delivery truck, machine, or computer equipment, the company should not (and often cannot for tax purposes) deduct the total cost of the item in the year it is acquired and placed into service. Since the asset has potential benefit to the company in future years, the asset's cost must be allocated over the years of its estimated life as the company receives its benefits. When a long-lived asset is first acquired for use, therefore, management must make some good-faith estimates concerning the asset. The accountant can then calculate, by one of a number of mathematical formulas, the amount of the asset's cost that will be recorded as an expense each year of the asset's life. If, after a few years, it becomes clear that the original estimate was incorrect, an updated estimate is then used to calculate the new depreciation for the asset's remaining life. The total of all depreciation expensed over an asset's life should be equal to its cost less any amount for which it can be sold at the end of its useful life.

The final estimated expense that will be covered here is a *pension expense.* The nature of the pension expense is somewhat similar to the warranty expense. Pension expenses are also deducted before they are paid in cash. The main distinction is that a pension expense is much more difficult to estimate. Nonetheless, management must make a good-faith effort to determine the expense to be deducted each year. What makes the amount so difficult to estimate is that the actual payment to the employee might not occur for decades into the future. Meanwhile, management, with the assistance of actuaries, must make assumptions as to how long the employee will work for the company, how much the employee will earn in future years, how long the employee will live after retirement, and other such seemingly insurmountable hurdles. It will sound repetitive, but accrual accounting requires that expenses be deducted in the year that they are incurred to earn revenue. Since the employee is working currently to help the company earn revenues, the cost of all post-employment benefits must be deducted while the employee is currently employed. This is true for medical and dental benefits, just as it is for pension benefits.

INCOME BEFORE INCOME TAXES. *Income before income taxes* is the result of subtracting operating expenses from gross profit on sales. This amount is shown separately so that the profit from regular operations—before the impact of income taxes—can be seen easily.

INCOME TAX EXPENSE. The final expense normally shown as a deduction on the income statement is the *income tax expense.* The amount of the expense is the result of accrual accounting rules, which differ from rules required for filing tax returns. In other words, the income tax expense is matched to the revenues that give rise to that expense, regardless of the amount computed on the tax return or paid to the IRS.

NET INCOME. This is the "bottom line" amount that shows the excess of the revenue over all the expenses. It does not reflect the amount of cash left over at year-end. Because revenues are recorded when they are earned (and not necessarily when they are collected), and expenses are deducted from revenues when the expenses are incurred (and not necessarily when they are paid), net income is not correlated directly to cash left over at year-end. In the long run, however, all revenues should be collected in the form of cash and all expenses should be paid in the form of cash. In the short run, accrual accounting provides a more meaningful measurement of the profitability of the company than do mere cash receipts and expenditures.

EARNINGS PER SHARE. The final presentation on the income statement for a publicly held corporation is the amount of earnings per share of stock outstanding. In effect, this is the entire income statement condensed to show the amount of net income that each share of common voting stock earned for the income statement time period. If a stockholder owns 100 shares, the stockholder's investment earned 100 times this amount. This amount should not be confused with *dividends per share.* Dividends per share represents the amount of cash that the board of directors, as representatives of all stockholders, chooses to pay to the stockholders as a return on their investment in the company for the current period. Again, earnings and cash received do not mean the same thing.

OTHER SPECIAL ISSUES

A few other issues deserve some explanation. In the lower portion of many income statements (following operating expenses), there may be a different caption from income before income taxes. The caption income from operations is substituted when a company has experienced gains and losses. Gains and losses usually occur whenever a company sells an asset (other than inventory for which it is in business to sell) for more or less than the value of the asset in its records. The accounting concept here is to separate the disclosure of normal sales activities from the unusual disposal of other assets. (See also the discussion of *extraordinary items* below.)

There may also be up to three unique items that follow income tax expense at the end of the income statement. These items are *discontinued operations, extraordinary items,* and *cumulative effect of accounting changes.*

A company would include discontinued operations if it had disposed of a significant segment of its operations. This event would be of such a magnitude (usually defined in percentage terms) that the information on the income statement would be misleading if it were not separately disclosed from what the reader could consider to be regular recurring operations of the company.

Extraordinary items are major gains or losses that are defined to be both highly unusual in nature and infrequent in occurrence, such as expenses stemming from a natural disaster or the restructuring of long-term debt. These extremely rare gains and losses are disclosed apart from regular operations, including normal gains and losses as discussed above, so that the user of the income statement can better judge the results of normal recurring operations.

The last item disclosed as part of the income statement before the earnings per share data can be the cumulative effect of accounting changes. This caption is used only when the management of a company has decided that changing from one *generally accepted accounting principle* (as defined by independent standards organizations for the accounting profession) to a different generally accepted accounting principle will better disclose the results of operations for the users of the statements. This change is based on management's judgment, and the accounting firm that audits the company's financial statements reviews this change. Generally, any previous years' accounting data will be restated to use the new accounting rule so that comparisons of current and previous data will be made on the same basis.

COMPREHENSIVE INCOME

A relatively new concept that may be included at the end of the income statement is *comprehensive income*. Comprehensive income results from changes in certain assets and liabilities on the balance sheet (a financial statement of corporate assets and liabilities). These unique gains and losses are not included in calculating net income, but they may be added after net income is shown. They are excluded from net income itself because they would distort the basic purpose of the income statement: to disclose the results of operations. These particular gains and losses result, instead, from two main sources not related to operations. First, comprehensive income results from market value changes of certain investment securities that are reported in the financial statements at their current trading values. Second, these gains and losses also result from foreign exchange rate changes used to report the values of assets and liabilities in foreign subsidiaries. These items may be also be shown on other financial statements rather than as an addition to the income statement.

PROBLEMS WITH THE INCOME STATEMENT

Studying a company's income statement can help managers, investors, creditors, and analysts to form an understanding of the business's performance and profitability. Yet the income statement has come under criticism in recent years because the two main figures—income and expenses—are often obscured by accounting adjustments and subjective estimates. In the wake of accounting scandals at several major corporations, many analysts began pushing for expanded reporting standards that would limit companies' ability to overstate revenue or understate expenses. In any case, rather than relying on the income statement alone, users should examine all three major financial statements to gain further information about a company's results.

SEE ALSO: Balance Sheets; Cash Flow Analysis and Statement; Financial Issues for Managers

John M. Alvis
Revised by Laurie Hillstrom

FURTHER READING:

"Analyzing Company Reports: Understanding Income Statements." Ameritrade.com. Available from <http://www. ameritrade.com/educationv2/fhtml/learning/uincomestates. fhtml>.

"Income Statements." Inc.com. Available from <http://pf.inc. com/articles/2000/05/18739.html>.

Orr, Jayson. "Making Your Numbers Talk." *CMA Management*, November 2000.

Rappaport, Alfred. "Show Me the Cash Flow! The Income Statement Badly Needs an Overhaul. Here's a Way to Fix It." *Fortune*, 16 September 2002.

INDUSTRIAL RELATIONS

Most definitions of industrial relations acknowledge that industrial relations involves the complex interplay among management, workers and their representatives, and the government. Each of these three players has different needs and goals that determine how they interact with the other two parties. In general, management's goals center upon labor costs, productivity, and profitability. In contrast, workers and their representatives (i.e., unions) are concerned with securing high wages and benefits, safe working conditions, fulfilling work, and a voice in the workplace. Finally, as the representative of the members of the society in which employers and unions reside, the government's objectives include balancing the rights of both labor and management. Perhaps even more important, the government has the obligation to protect the rights of the members of society by maintaining relative harmony between workers and employers. In the U.S. private sector, industrial relations are governed by the National Labor Relations Act (1935, as amended).

There is a three-tier structure of industrial relations in the United States. Local unions deal with the daily interaction with employers at the workplace level. Typically, these local unions are affiliated with a national union such as the Service Employees International Union, which, as of 2005, is the largest national union in the United States. Labor federations, like the AFL-CIO, serve as umbrella organizations for national unions and provide overall direction for the labor movement, as well as services like training and government lobbying. However, the lack of advancement of organized labor in recent years has caused some national unions to leave the AFL-CIO and attempt to form a competing labor federation.

Industrial relations have changed substantially in the United States since 1980; there has been a change in the shared ideology among the three players. Prior to 1980, all three players acknowledged the legitimacy of the other players' roles. Employers kept their relationship with unions at arms length, neither embracing unions nor aggressively seeking to destroy them. This produced some level of stability within the industrial relations system. However, since 1980 employers have moved away from the "arms length" relationship with unions and have either pursued greater collaboration with labor or sought to aggressively suppress unionization, even to the point of intentionally violating U.S. labor law.

The percentage of workers represented by unions (i.e., union density) in the United States has decreased from a high of 35 percent in 1945 to 12.5 percent by 2005. Interestingly, union density is substantially greater in the public sector than in the private sector. In the public sector, approximately 36 percent of government workers are represented by unions, with the highest density being in local government (41 percent). This level of unionization in the public sector may decline in the future, however, given the trend toward privatizing government services. In the private sector, only 8 percent of workers are represented by unions, with the transportation industry and utilities maintaining the highest level of union density (25 percent). Union density in the private sector is approximately half of what it was in 1983. Union membership rates vary considerably by state. New York, Hawaii, Michigan, and Alaska have the highest membership rates—with 25 percent, 24 percent, 22 percent, and 20 percent, respectively—while North Carolina and South Carolina have the lowest rates (approximately 3 percent). As of 2005, full-time wage and salary workers who are represented by a union make more than those workers not represented by a union ($781 versus $612).

There are many reasons for the decline in union density other than the change in management attitudes toward unions. Employment has moved from manufacturing jobs and other jobs that have traditionally been represented by unions (e.g., railroads and mining) to more service and high technology jobs. There are more white collar and part-time jobs now than ever before, which has also contributed to the decline in union density because it is harder for unions to organize people in these jobs. Furthermore, employers have learned that using positive human resource management practices—like installing formal grievance systems, comprehensive benefit plans, and worker involvement programs—suppresses union organizing activity. Finally, in the past several decades the government has increasingly provided for the protection of workers' rights by passing a variety of legislative actions, including the Civil Rights Act (1964), the Occupational Safety and Health Act (1970), the Americans with Disabilities Act (1990), and the Family and Medical Leave Act (1993).

The number of strikes by unions has declined in the last two decades due to the fact that employees have a greater understanding of the impact of globalization on competition. Also, more employees are shareholders now than ever before. Some of these same factors appear to be reducing union density levels in other developed nations, although Canada is an exception; it has twice the union density of the United States.

In 1993 the Dunlop Commission was established by the Clinton Administration to propose ways to reform the labor policies set forth in the National Labor Relations Act. In general, the Commission concluded that labor law needed to be altered to make it easier for workers to seek union representation and to remove the constraints upon worker involvement. However, these recommendations have not been adopted, even though both labor and management acknowledge the need to change the antiquated labor laws that prevent closer, more trusting relations and hamper the flexibility needed by businesses to compete in the global economy. Consequently, there is a continuing need for labor law that reflects the changes that have occurred since the National Labor Relations Act was passed in 1935.

SEE ALSO: Employment Law and Compliance; Human Resource Management

Jerry Bryan Fuller

FURTHER READING:

Cutcher-Gershenfeld, Joel, and Thomas Kochan. "Taking Stock: Collective Bargaining at the Turn of the Century." *Industrial & Labor Relations Review* 58, no. 3 (2004).

Godard, John. "Do Labor Laws Matter? The Density Decline and Convergence Thesis Revisited." *Industrial Relations* 42, no. 3 (2003).

Kreisberg, Steven. "The Future of Public Sector Unionism in the United States." *Journal of Labor Research* 25, no. 2 (2004).

U.S. Department of Labor, Bureau of Labor Statistics. Available from <http://www.bls.gov>.

INDUSTRY LIFE CYCLE

SEE: Product Life Cycle and Industry Life Cycle

INITIAL PUBLIC OFFERING

An initial public offering (IPO) is the process through which a privately owned business sells shares of stock to the public for the first time. Also known as *going public,* an IPO provides a growing business with access to public capital markets and increases its credibility and exposure. It has long been considered a right of passage that marks an important phase in a business's development. At the same time, however, staging an IPO is both time consuming and expensive. It requires companies to navigate a complex Securities and Exchange Commission (SEC) registration process and disclose a great deal of confidential information to potential investors. Furthermore, the success of an IPO is not guaranteed, and depends in part upon industry, economic, and market conditions that are beyond a company's direct control. Overall, the decision to go public is a complicated one that requires careful management consideration and planning.

There is no doubt that becoming a public entity offers a number of advantages to a business. In addition to gaining immediate access to capital to fund expansion, it also makes it easier for the firm to obtain capital in the future. The IPO process provides a company with a great deal of publicity, which may help increase its credibility with suppliers and lenders, attract new customers, and create new business opportunities. Going public also offers an opportunity for the company's founders and venture capitalists to cash

out on their early investments, and provides a public valuation of the company to facilitate future mergers and acquisitions.

Some of the major disadvantages associated with going public include the high cost of staging an IPO (which may claim 15 to 20 percent of the proceeds from the stock sale), the demands on the time of managers (the process may take between six months and two years to complete), and the dilution of ownership and associated loss of management flexibility and control. In addition, the process of going public requires a private company to disclose confidential information about its strategy, capital structure, customers, products, competitors, profit margins, and employee compensation. Finally, becoming accountable to shareholders sometimes leads to an increased emphasis on short-term financial performance.

The first step in the IPO process involves applying to the SEC for permission to sell stock and preparing an initial registration statement according to SEC regulations. This statement includes a prospectus of detailed information about the company, financial statements, and a candid management analysis of the risks and benefits of investing in the company. The next step involves selecting an underwriter—usually an investment bank—to act as an intermediary between the company and the capital markets. The underwriter helps determine the valuation of the company and the suggested share price. It also helps assemble an underwriting team, which includes attorneys, accountants, and financial printers.

While the SEC completes its review of the registration statement—a period of time known as the *cooling off* or *quiet* period—the company undergoes an audit by independent accountants, files forms with the states where the stock will be sold, and begins marketing the investment to potential investors through *road shows* featuring top executives. Once the SEC review is complete, the company finalizes the registration statement, files a final amendment with the SEC, and agrees to an asking price for the shares of stock. Then the sale of stock finally takes place, overseen by the underwriter. Afterward, the underwriter meets with all involved parties to distribute funds from the sale, settle expenses, arrange for the transfer of stock, and file final reports with the SEC.

The pace of IPOs peaked in 1999, fueled by investor interest in Internet-related businesses. It declined markedly in 2000, as a drop in the value of technology stocks led to an overall drop in the stock market. Over the next few years, investors largely adopted a more cautious, back-to-basics approach toward IPOs. They increasingly demanded that companies demonstrate a proven business model, solid management team, large customer base, and strong revenue potential if they hoped to stage a successful

IPO. Another factor limiting the number of IPOs was the Sarbanes-Oxley Act (SOA) of 2002. Passed in the wake of several high-profile corporate accounting scandals, the act required the boards of public companies to include independent directors with financial experience. It also required public companies to form auditing committees chaired by an outside director. The SOA and similar regulations have made it more expensive for companies not only to go public, but also to be public, in the twenty-first century.

SEE ALSO: Cash Flow Analysis and Statement; Due Diligence; Entrepreneurship; Financial Issues for Managers; Strategy Implementation

Laurie Collier Hillstrom

FURTHER READING:

Evanson, David R. "Public School: Learning How to Prepare for an IPO." *Entrepreneur,* October 1997.

Kleeburg, Richard F. *Initial Public Offerings.* South-Western Publishing, 2005.

Quittner, Jeremy. "Private Matters: IPOs Move Further Out of Reach." *Business Week,* 1 November 2004.

Vallone, Paul. "IPO Checklist: Preparing Your Company for Public Markets." *San Diego Business Journal,* 23 February 2004.

Welch, Ivo. "IPO: The Initial Public Offerings Resource Page." Available from <http://www.iporesources.org/ipopage.html>.

INNOVATION

Innovation is the act of developing a new process or product and introducing it to the market. It is essentially an entrepreneurial act, whether it takes place in a start-up firm, a large organization, a not-for-profit, or a public-sector agency. Innovation means change: sometimes radical change, such as the development of the computer, and sometimes incremental change, such as the modification of existing computer software. In either case, managers must develop processes to encourage and guide the changes taking place.

Sources of, and opportunities for, innovation in organizations are described below. Finally, the management principles underlying an innovative organization are identified.

SOURCES OF INNOVATION

Innovation generally stems from the purposeful search for opportunities. Management guru Peter Drucker identified that opportunities for innovation exist both within and outside a company or industry. Opportunities internal to a company include unexpected events, incongruities in processes or between expectations and results, process needs, and changes in the marketplace or industry structure. Opportunities external to a company include demographic changes, changes in perception, and new knowledge.

UNEXPECTED EVENTS. Unexpected events can be failures as well as successes. For example, the failure of the technically superior Sony's Betamax VCR standard (and the success of the industry standard VHS format) led the firm to pay more attention to developing products in line with industry standards. Similarly, the development of the very successful Sony Walkman was the result of the CEO spending time in New York and noticing young people carrying portable radios on their shoulders. Progressive Insurance saw its business quadruple in size when it started sending claims adjusters in mobile offices to accident scenes.

INCONGRUITIES. Incongruities result from a difference between perception and reality. Federal Express was able to capitalize on consumer dissatisfaction with the U.S. Postal Service and demonstrate that individuals and companies were willing to pay a premium for overnight delivery of packages and documents.

Likewise, Southwest Airlines provided a dramatically different approach to airline service. Its low-fare, no-frills, first come-first seated approach has garnered devoted customers. Southwest Airlines has remained profitable for 31 straight years, even during the economic downturn following the terrorist attacks of 2001, when many airlines struggled to remain in business.

PROCESS NEEDS. Process need innovations are those which are created to support some other process or product. The development of the ATM (automatic teller machine) and now web-based and Internet banking options allow individuals to do their banking when the bank is closed and without relying on tellers being available. This has freed tellers from performing many routine functions such as cashing checks and has improved both efficiency and profit margins for banks.

MARKET AND INDUSTRY STRUCTURE CHANGES. Industry structures change in response to growth and changes in the marketplace. One of the most dramatic changes can be seen in the health care industry. The rise of HMOs (health maintenance organizations) and the decline of the traditional fee-for-service plans have impacted the health-care industry as a whole. The development of the personal computer also had a far-reaching impact on the computer industry as a whole. Until the personal computer, manufacturers of large mainframe computers, terminals, and software developed for specific uses within a firm dominated the computer industry. With the adoption of the personal computer and advent of the laptop computer, the composition of computer sales and marketing changed dramatically.

DEMOGRAPHIC CHANGES. Demographic changes are shifts in the makeup of the population. Increases in the Hispanic and Asian populations in the United States create opportunities for new products and services, such as cable television stations targeting these audiences. Innovations in prepared meals and takeout food are meeting the needs of busy two-income families and single-parent families.

CHANGES IN PERCEPTION. Americans have become more health conscious and we have seen the rise in popularity of stores such as GNC which cater to the demand for vitamins and other supplements. Similarly, stores such as Whole Foods provide organic produce, meats, dairy, and fish free from additives to satisfy a growing market demand for chemical-free products.

NEW KNOWLEDGE. New knowledge or technology is one of the strongest forces for innovation. Many companies, of all sizes and levels of sophistication, now have a web presence on the Internet with the capability of connecting their products with customers nearby or on the other side of the globe. No longer are consumers limited to the daytime hours for their activities; online stock trading, shopping, and banking are examples of services that are accessible at any time of day or night via the Internet. Other opportunities are being explored in the fields of genomics and nanotechnology. These technologies and systems will develop even further as consumers continue to demand new and innovative products and immediate access to information, goods and services.

MANAGING INNOVATION

Innovation must be seen as a process occurring within an organization, not a single event. This process can be managed. In general, the process follows five stages: (1) idea generation, (2) initial screening, (3) review, (4) seeking sponsorship, and (5) sponsorship and commercialization. At each of these stages the organization's culture must be designed to support the innovation process.

IDEA GENERATION. Idea generation requires a supportive organizational culture. Ideas, and the people who develop them, are fragile, and if the organization does not support them they will not develop. A supportive culture requires that the organization allow for experimentation and failure. In other words, not every idea will be commercially viable, but mistakes are to be learned from and learning should be celebrated. W.L. Gore is a company that celebrates learning and innovation. Each plant is kept small and everyone in the company is allowed to experiment with the products. In addition to the familiar GoreTex polymer coating, the company also manufactures products for the medical industry, NASA, and industrial use. The company operates internationally and holds hundreds of patents.

INITIAL SCREENING. The screening process can be made easier by assigning a facilitator from outside the organization who can help guide the initial idea through the organization's systems, as well as act as an advocate for the idea. At this stage the idea is evaluated and possibly revised before being sent on to a group to review for further development.

REVIEW. At this stage, the idea should be sufficiently developed to present to a group within the organization who will make a decision about funding further development. 3M has a long-standing process such as this. The Post-It notepads are probably the best-known illustration of the effectiveness of the process. Although no uses for the adhesive were initially found, the researcher was allowed to continue to spend time developing the product. The review process did not initially continue direct funding, but by allowing the researcher time, the company indirectly funded the development of a very successful product.

SEEKING SPONSORSHIP. In most organizations, an idea needs a sponsor to continue to move forward. The sponsor must be convinced of the value of the idea to the organization. Effective champions frequently are managers who know how to navigate the corporate structure for support and resources. In addition, they are effective at putting together a cross-functional team to help develop all aspects of the new idea. Both 3M and W.L. Gore have instituted systems that facilitate this process.

SPONSORSHIP AND COMMERCIALIZATION. At this stage the champion or sponsor takes the project forward through the final phases of corporate approval to commercialization. Many organizations, including Dow Corning, PepsiCo, 3M, and Black & Decker, spend a great deal of time interacting with customers at this stage. Customer input can help with final design issues, with searching out new uses for a product, and with simplifying processes. According to N. Radjou as quoted in *Industrial Management,* "Customers seek innovations that enhance their life cycle experience with a product—not the product-centric improvements in functionality and reliability that R & D engineers focus on." Utilizing consumer input can help companies focus their creativity on the products and improvements that will most satisfy consumer needs and wants.

INNOVATION IS WORK. Peter Drucker said, "Innovation is work." Successful organizations have internalized innovation as a strategic goal. As we move further into the information age, innovation, and the ability to manage it, becomes a crucial element of a successful corporate strategy. The speed at which information and ideas move throughout the global marketplace has forced organizations to internalize innovation as part of their processes and to develop cultures that encourage experimentation and new ideas.

SEE ALSO: Futuring; New Product Development

Stephanie Newell

Revised by Monica C. Turner

FURTHER READING:

Bate, J.D., and R.E. Johnston, Jr. "Strategic Frontiers: The Starting-Point for Innovative Growth." *Strategy and Leadership* 33, no. 1 (2005): 12–18.

Costin, H., ed. *Readings in Strategy and Strategic Planning.* Fort Worth, TX: The Dryden Press, 1998.

Francis, D., and J. Bessant. "Targeting Innovation and Implications for Capability Development." *Technovation* 25, no. 3 (2005): 171–183.

Frohman, A.L. "Building A Culture for Innovation." *Research-Technology Management* 41, no. 2 (1998): 9–12.

Henry, J., and D. Walker, eds. *Managing Innovation.* London: Sage Publications, 1991.

McDermott, B., and G. Sexton. *Leading Innovation: Creating Workplaces Where People Excel So Organizations Thrive.* Herentals, Belgium: Nova Vista Publishing, 2004.

Radjou, N. "Networked Innovation Drives Profits." *Industrial Management* 47, no. 1 (2005): 14–21.

Stefik, M., and B. Stefik. *Breakthrough: Stories and Strategies of Radical Innovation.* Cambridge, MA: MIT Press, 2004.

Tidd, J., J. Bessant, and K. Pavitt. *Managing Innovation: Integrating Technological, Market and Organizational Change.* Chichester, UK: John Wiley & Sons, 1997.

Verloop, J., and J.G. Wissema. *Insight in Innovation: Managing Innovation by Understanding the Laws of Innovation.* Boston, MA: Elsevier, 2004.

Von Stamm, B., and N. Nicholson. *Innovation: How to Create and Develop New Business Ideas.* Norwich: Format Publishing, 2005.

Yapp, C. "Innovation, Futures Thinking and Leadership." *Public Money and Management* 25, no. 1 (2005): 57–60.

INSTANT MESSAGING

Instant messaging (IM) is a general term encompassing a variety of software applications that enable users to have real-time text conversations, play turn-based games, and share pictures, music, and data files over the Internet. IM software allows users to maintain a list of contactsgmdash;sometimes referred to as a buddy list—with whom they can exchange messages whenever both parties are online. These messages appear in a small window on the computer screen that both the sender and the recipient can see. The most popular IM utilities—such as America Online Instant Messenger (AIM), Microsoft MSN Messenger, and Yahoo! Messenger—also offer a number of other features, including chat rooms for groups to exchange messages and the capability to use voice communication and view streaming content over the Internet.

While each different IM utility is proprietary, they all work on a client-server model. Client software resides on the user's computer and connects with a central server. Users open an IM session by logging into their account on the server. The server makes a record of the Internet address of the user's computer, then calls up the user's buddy list and checks to see who else is online. Once this information is provided to all connected clients, the buddies can exchange messages directly in real time.

IM has exploded in popularity since ICQ, the first free, public instant-messaging utility, was introduced in 1996. Many fans of IM took the technology to work with them, downloading IM client software onto corporate computer networks and using it as a tool to facilitate business communications. IM offers both advantages and disadvantages in the workplace. Proponents claim that it boosts employee productivity by allowing them to get immediate answers from co-workers and suppliers. Sales personnel and help desk technicians, in particular, find that it enables them to serve customers more effectively. Businesses can also use IM to conduct virtual meetings and facilitate collaboration on group projects. "Backers say IM, once dismissed as a plaything for the under-twenty set, dramatically speeds up the flow of information in and out of a company," Esther Shein wrote in *CFO.*

Most public IM utilities were created for personal use, however, which can create problems in a business setting. Most importantly, IT managers emphasize that public IM is not a secure form of communication. "When a user carries on a discussion with the person in the cube right next to him, if it's not a corporate IM utility, the message doesn't go from one computer right next door to the other one," network security consultant Dan Wooley explained in InstantMessagingPlanet.com. "It goes out of the corporate network and across different networks and then back to the other person's desk." As a result, anyone with access to the networks in between can intercept message traffic, potentially exposing confidential business information. IT managers also point out that the major public IM clients do not provide monitoring, virus protection, encryption, or other features usually associated with corporate IT applications. Finally, some business managers question whether IM conversations truly increase productivity or instead create a source of distraction for employees.

Despite such potential problems, however, many businesses are reluctant to block IM for fear of alienating employees who rely upon it. Instead, businesses have increasingly sought to manage its use through enterprise instant messaging (EIM) solutions. One approach involves implementing a software application called an IM gateway, which can intercept, log, and approve communication that takes place through the corporate network using public IM systems. Other companies choose to develop their own in-house IM systems, which can be designed to include such features as user authentication, network security, virus protection, message encryption, and message archiving. Logging and archiving of messages is particularly important in light of Securities and Exchange Commission rules that require companies to retain electronic correspondence that divulges key corporate information.

With proper management, IM technology seems likely to play an important role in future business communications. "Instant messaging is just one of a whole Swiss Army knife set of tools that will be used to conduct business," Nate Root of Forrester Research stated in *CFO*.

SEE ALSO: Communication; Handheld Computers

Laurie Collier Hillstrom

FURTHER READING:

Bird, Drew. "Managing IT's Role in Business." *Instant Messaging Planet,* July 2003. Available from <http://www.instantmessagingplanet.com/enterprise/article.php/2235591>.

Heck, Mike. "A Chat Checklist for IT Managers." *InfoWorld,* 26 August 2004.

Orzech, Dan. "Under IT's Radar, Instant Messaging Invades Corporate Desktops." *Instant Messaging Planet,* 14 July 2003. Available from <http://www.instantmessagingplanet.com/enterprise/article.php/2234871>.

Shein, Esther. "Will IM Pay? Backers Say Instant Messaging Will Revolutionize the Way Businesses Work." *CFO,* May 2004.

Spanbauer, Scott. "A Grown-Up's Guide to Instant Messaging." *PC World,* March 2004.

Tyson, Jeff. "How Instant Messaging Works." HowStuffWorks.com. Available from <http://computer.howstuffworks.com/instant-messaging.htm>.

INTELLECTUAL PROPERTY RIGHTS

Intellectual property is a term used to cover goods and services protected under the laws governing patents, trademarks, copyrights, and trade secrets. Although the legal rights concerning different kinds of intellectual property are similar in a general sense, they differ specifically in what they protect and in how the particular rights are established. Patents protect an inventor's right to exclude others from making, manufacturing, using, or selling an inventor's invention. Trademarks protect words, phrases, symbols, and designs. Copyrights protect original artistic, musical, and literary works, including software. Intellectual property rights can also encompass state trade secrets laws, which protect a company's proprietary and confidential information, such as methods of manufacturing, customer lists, supplier information, and the materials used during the manufacturing process.

PATENT RIGHTS

A patent is a grant of a property right by the United States government, through the Patent and Trademark Office (PTO), to the inventor of an invention. The term of this property right is 17 years from the date the patent is granted, as long as the holder of the patent pays maintenance fees. A patent is not a grant of the right to make, manufacture, use, or sell the invention, but rather the right to exclude others from making, manufacturing, using, or selling the invention.

The power to grant rights in patents arises from Article I, section 8 of the U.S. Constitution. The first patent law was passed in 1790, and the current law governing patents took effect in 1953. Since the first statute, over 5 million patents have been granted. The current statute set forth the subject matters for which patents may be granted and the conditions under which a patent will be issued. It also established the Patent and Trademark Office.

Under the law, anyone who "invents or discovers any new and useful process, machine, manufacture or composition of matter, or any new and useful improvements thereof, may obtain a patent." Courts have interpreted this language to include nearly anything that could be fabricated. One cannot, however, patent methods of doing business or printed matter, such as books. An invention must meet the test of being "new" under the standards in the law before a patent will be granted. The subject matter of an invention must be sufficiently different from what has been described before in a printed publication of some sort anywhere in the world, or on sale in the United States before the date of the application for the patent. In addition, the invention must not be obvious to a person who has ordinary skill in the relevant technical or scientific area at the time the inventor applies for the patent. Finally, an invention must be determined "useful" before a obtaining a patent, although this requirement is interpreted very broadly.

Only the inventor may apply for a patent, unless he has died or has been declared insane. An inventor applies for a patent by sending to the Commissioner of Patents and Trademarks a written specification, which is a description of the invention and of the process in which the invention is made and used. The specification must contain one or more claims about the subject matter that the applicant believes pertains to the invention, and include necessary drawings. The specification must be accompanied by a sworn oath or declaration by the inventor that he or she is the original and first inventor of the subject matter of the application, and the necessary filing fees.

TRADEMARK RIGHTS

A trademark is a word, name, phrase, symbol, or design, or a combination of these elements, which identifies and distinguishes the source of goods or services. The term *trademark* also encompasses service marks, which identify and distinguish the source of a service rather than a product. Trademark rights are used to prevent others from making, promoting, or selling goods or services which have a name, symbol, or design that is confusingly similar to that of an established trademark. It does not, however, prevent others from making or selling the same goods or services, as long as it is under a different, non-confusing mark.

There are two distinct types of rights in a trademark or service mark: the right to use the mark and the right to register the mark. These rights arise from either using the mark in actual commerce, or filing an application for registration of the mark with the PTO.

The Trademark Act of 1946, 15 U.S.C. Section 1051 et seq.; the Trademark Rules, 37 C.F.R. Part 2; and the Trademark Manual of Examining Procedure (2nd ed. 1993) control the registration of marks. The first party who either uses a mark in the course of commerce or business or files an application for registration with the PTO usually has the right to register that mark. A party can use a mark, or establish rights in it, without filing an application for registration. The registration, however, creates a presumption that the party who has registered the mark is the owner of the mark for the goods and services set forth in the registration application, and therefore has the right to use the mark anywhere in the country. This presumption can become important when two parties unintentionally begin using similar marks and become involved in a lawsuit over who has the right solely to use the mark. This is not determined by the PTO, but by a federal court, which has the power to issue an injunction to stop a party from using a mark, and to award damages for a party's improper use of another's mark.

Similarly, the owner of a mark may use the trademark (™) or service mark (ˢᴹ) designation with the mark to make it clear that the owner is claiming rights in the product or service so designated. The trademark or service mark designation may be used without the owner having registered the mark with the Patent and Trademark Office. If it is registered, however, the owner may use the registration symbol (®) with the mark.

Rights in a trademark, unlike rights in a copyright or a patent, can last for an indefinite period if the owner of the mark continuously uses the mark for its products or services. Federal registrations last for ten years, but between the fifth and sixth year after the date of the initial registration, the person who registered the mark must file an affidavit with information about the mark and ownership. If the registrant does not file this affidavit, the registration is cancelled. After the initial registration period, the mark can be renewed for successive ten-year terms. Registration of a mark with the PTO provides protection from others using the mark in the United States and its territories, but does not extend to its use in other countries.

COPYRIGHTS

A copyright gives an owner of "original works of authorship" the exclusive right to reproduce the work; prepare derivative works based on the copyrighted work; and distribute, perform, or display the work. The first Copyright Act was passed in 1790, and it has been revised many times, most recently in 1976. This act sets forth eight categories of works that can be copyrighted. These are

1. literary works
2. musical works, including lyrics
3. dramatic works, including music
4. pantomimes and choreographic works
5. pictorial, graphic, and sculptural works
6. motion pictures and other audiovisual works
7. sound recordings
8. architectural works

These categories are interpreted broadly, so that, for example, software is considered copyrightable as a literary work. However, the act does not protect an "idea, procedure, process, system, method of operation, concept, principal or discovery regardless of the form in which it is described, explained, illustrated or embodied in such work."

The term of a copyright is for the period of the life of the owner, plus 50 years. An entity or person can become the owner of a copyright in two ways, either by creating the work personally, or through owning a work for hire. Works for hire cover situations where an employee creates a work at the request of an employer (and the employer thereby owns the copyright), or where someone commissions the creation of a work, and the party commissioning the work and the creator have agreed in writing that the commissioning party shall be the owner and that the work shall be a work for hire.

In 1988, the United States became a signatory to the Berne Convention, by enacting the Berne Convention Implementation Act. The Berne Convention provides copyright protection for a copyright owner simultaneously in most countries in the world. To become a signatory country, the United States had to amend the Copyright Act to create a copyright in a work automatically upon completion of the creation. Now, as soon as a composer finishes a work or an author writes the last words of an article, there exists a copyright. However, if an owner wishes to sue for copyright infringement, the owner must register the copyright with the United States Copyright Office by completing an application, and sending it with two copies of the "best edition" of the work and the filing fee.

INTELLECTUAL PROPERTY IN THE INTERNET AGE

Efforts to protect intellectual property became vastly more complicated with the growth of Internet technology in the late 1990s and early 2000s. The global computer network gave people greater access to all kinds of creative works, and in many cases enabled them to copy such works without regard to legal protection. "Virtually all creative content can be digitized, even if it was not initially created on a computer, and the Internet has become the primary distribution channel for every kind of digital material," Jonathan Cohen explained in his article "Copyright and Intellectual Property in the Age of the Internet."

Since the Internet has an international reach, the digital age has also brought to light discrepancies in intellectual property laws between nations. Several attempts have been made to bring the protection granted by developed and developing nations in line. In 2002, for example, the World Intellectual Property Organization Copyright Treaty (WCT) was ratified by the United States, Japan, and the European Union. The WCT updated the Berne Convention to apply to the Internet age, setting international standards for the protection of literary and artistic works in digital form.

Simultaneously, major content providers have taken steps to protect their own intellectual property from unauthorized reproduction through digital rights management (DRM) technology. DRM systems involve anti-piracy measures that are built into software, video, and music files sold over the Internet to ensure that the owners of intellectual property are compensated for its use. DRM has proved cumbersome to consumers, however, because different content providers have established their own, usually incompatible, DRM systems—making it difficult for users to access content packaged and distributed with one DRM technology using a device that supports a different technology.

Some legal experts have also expressed concern that content providers will use DRM technology to erode the rights previously granted to the public under the "fair use" doctrine of copyright law. Whether a specific use of copyrighted material is determined to be fair depends on four factors: the purpose and character of the use; the nature of the work; the portion of the work used; and the effect of the use on the market for the work. Fair use protects such activities as videotaping a television program for later viewing, posting a newspaper cartoon on an office bulletin board, and quoting from a book in a report. In view of the rapidly evolving nature of intellectual property protection in the Internet age, business managers should seek legal advice in order to protect their own creative works as well as to avoid infringing on the rights of others.

Cindy Rhodes Victor
Revised by Laurie Hillstrom

FURTHER READING:

Cohen, Jonathan. "Copyright and Intellectual Property in the Age of the Internet." Jonathan Cohen and Associates. Available from <http://www.jcarchitects.com/IntellectualProperty.html>.

Dutfield, Graham. "Does One Size Fit All? The International Patent Regime." *Harvard International Review,* Summer 2004.

"Guarding Intellectual Property on the Internet." *PC World,* 7 December 2001.

Noble, Steve. "The Internet and Digital Copyright Issues." *Photo Marketing,* January 2005.

"Tide Turns in DRM Wars with Creation of Coral Consortium." *Online Reporter,* 9 October 2004.

Von Lohmann, Fred. "Fair Use and Digital Rights Management." Electronic Frontier Foundation. Available from <http://www.eff.org/IP/DRM/fair_use_and_drm.html>.

INTERNAL AUDITING

The Institute of Internal Auditors (2005) defines internal auditing as ". . .an independent, objective assurance and consulting activity designed to add value and improve an organization's operations. It helps an organization accomplish its objectives by bringing a systematic, disciplined approach to evaluate and improve the effectiveness of risk management, control and governance processes."

One way to distinguish between internal auditors and their more familiar counterparts, external auditors, is the intended audience of their reports. External auditors are hired by a company to audit that firm's financial statements and issue an opinion on the reliability of those financial statements. While external auditors are in a contractual relationship to the firm whose financial statements are being audited, external auditors owe their primary fiduciary responsibility to groups outside of the firm, such as investors and creditors. The external auditor's report or opinion is provided to groups outside of the firm that hired him to audit by including it in that firm's annual report. In contrast, internal auditors are employed by the organization that they are auditing. Similar to external auditors, the internal auditor might provide a written opinion based on his evaluation. However, in contrast to external auditors, the audience for that opinion will always be corporate management instead of investors and creditors.

Typically, the role of internal auditors is broader than that of external auditors. While a company's external auditors will focus on evaluating the firm's financial statements, internal auditors can provide financial, compliance, and operational auditing.

FINANCIAL AUDITS

The significance of the contribution of internal auditors to financial audits was dramatically increased with the passage of the Sarbanes-Oxley Act of 2002. That act made wide-spread changes in the responsibility of the parties involved in the financial reporting process.

One change that has enhanced the role of the internal auditor is the requirement in Section 302 of Sarbanes-Oxley that a firm's certifying officers (typically the chief executive officer and chief financial officer) must state that they are responsible for establishing and maintaining internal controls over financial reporting. As part of this certification, they must also indicate that the internal controls were designed to provide reasonable assurance regarding the reliability of financial reporting and the preparation of financial statements in accordance with generally accepted accounting principles in the United States. These Section 302 certifications are required to be included with the firm's annual financial statements. Most firms will rely extensively on the work of their internal auditors to provide the justification for the Section 302 certifications.

Section 404 of the Sarbanes-Oxley act also increased the responsibilities of internal auditors. This section requires that management include, in the firm's annual financial statements, a report on internal controls. The report must indicate that management is responsible for establishing and maintaining internal controls over financial reporting, and management's conclusions regarding the effectiveness of those internal controls. In most companies, the internal auditors will provide the documentation and testing of internal controls that will be necessary for management to make that report.

COMPLIANCE OR OPERATIONAL AUDITS

A compliance audit assures that the company's activities comply with relevant laws and regulations. An operational audit explores the effectiveness and efficiency of the firm's activities, seeking to reduce the risks faced by the specific firm. In performing an operational audit, performance standards may include a variety of criteria other than monetary measures, such as the percentage of late deliveries or idle labor time. It is the responsibility of the internal auditor to determine appropriate measures on the basis of experience and insight into the integrated functions of the company's activities. Typically, performance is measured against prior periods, industry standards, other operational units, or budgeted activity.

Internal auditing provides a broad-based, independent, value-adding function that is essential for the effective management of a firm. The value of internal audit has been greatly enhanced by the passage of the Sarbanes-Oxley Act of 2002.

SEE ALSO: Financial Issues for Managers

Karen L. Brown
Revised by Diana Franz

FURTHER READING:

Arens, Alvin A. *Auditing: An Integrated Approach.* 7th ed. Upper Saddle River, NJ: Prentice Hall, 1997.

Burke, Jacqueline, and Anthony N. Dalessio. "Highlights of SAS No. 82 for the Internal Auditor." *Internal Auditing,* November/December 1998, 40–44.

Financial Accounting Standards Board. "Facts About FASB-Mission Section." Available from <http://www.rutgers.edu/Accounting/raw/fasb/facts/fasfact1.html>.

Gauntt, James E., Jr., and G. William Glezen. "Analytical Auditing Procedures." *Internal Auditor,* February 1997, 56–60.

Grand, Bernard. "Theoretic Approaches to Audits." *Internal Auditing,* November/December 1998, 14–19.

"H.R. 3763 Sarbanes-Oxley Act of 2002." Available from <http://thomas.loc.gov/cgi-bin/query/z?c107:H.R.3763.ENR:>.

The Institute of Internal Auditors. Website. Available from <http://www.theiia.org>.

Jacka, J. Mike, and Paulette Keller. "The Building's On Fire!" *Internal Auditor,* February 1996, 46–50.

Ridley, Anthony J. "A Profession for the Twenty-First Century." *Internal Auditor,* October 1996, 20–25.

Simmons, Mark R. "COSO Based Auditing." *Internal Auditor,* December 1997, 68–73.

———. "The Standards and the Framework." *Internal Auditor,* April 1997, 50–55.

Taylor, Donald H., and G. William Glezen. *Auditing: An Assertions Approach.* 7th ed. New York: John Wiley and Sons, 1997.

Walz, Anthony. "Adding Value." *Internal Auditor,* February 1997, 51–54.

INTERNATIONAL BUSINESS

Today, business is acknowledged to be international and there is a general expectation that this will continue for the foreseeable future. International business may be defined simply as business transactions that take place across national borders. This broad definition includes the very small firm that exports (or imports) a small quantity to only one country, as well as the very large global firm with integrated operations and strategic alliances around the world. Within this broad array, distinctions are often made among different types of international firms, and these distinctions are helpful in understanding a firm's strategy, organization, and functional decisions (for example, its financial, administrative, marketing, human resource, or operations decisions). One distinction that can be helpful is the distinction between multi-domestic operations, with independent subsidiaries which act essentially as domestic firms, and global operations, with integrated subsidiaries which are closely related and interconnected. These may be thought of as the two ends of a continuum, with many possibilities in between. Firms are unlikely to be at one end of the continuum, though, as they often combine aspects of multi-domestic operations with aspects of global operations.

International business grew over the last half of the twentieth century partly because of liberalization of both trade and investment, and partly because doing business internationally had become easier. In terms of liberalization, the General Agreement on Tariffs and Trade (GATT) negotiation rounds resulted in trade liberalization, and this was continued with the formation of the World Trade Organization (WTO) in 1995. At the same time, worldwide capital movements were liberalized by most governments, particularly with the advent of electronic funds transfers. In addition, the introduction of a new European monetary unit, the euro, into circulation in January 2002 has impacted international business economically. The euro is the currency of the European Union, membership in March 2005 of 25 countries, and the euro replaced each country's previous currency. As of early 2005, the United States dollar continues to struggle against the euro and the impacts are being felt across industries worldwide.

In terms of ease of doing business internationally, two major forces are important:

1. technological developments which make global communication and transportation relatively quick and convenient; and

2. the disappearance of a substantial part of the communist world, opening many of the world's economies to private business.

DOMESTIC VS. INTERNATIONAL BUSINESS

Domestic and international enterprises, in both the public and private sectors, share the business objectives of functioning successfully to continue operations. Private enterprises seek to function profitably as well. Why, then, is international business different from domestic? The answer lies in the differences across borders. Nation-states generally have unique government systems, laws and regulations, currencies, taxes and duties, and so on, as well as different cultures and practices. An individual traveling from his home country to a foreign country needs to have the proper documents, to carry foreign currency, to be able to communicate in the foreign country, to be dressed appropriately, and so on. Doing business in a foreign country involves similar issues and is thus more complex than doing business at home. The following sections will explore some of these issues. Specifically, comparative advantage is introduced, the international business environment is explored, and forms of international entry are outlined.

THEORIES OF INTERNATIONAL TRADE AND INVESTMENT

In order to understand international business, it is necessary to have a broad conceptual understanding of why trade and investment across national borders take place. Trade and investment can be examined in terms of the comparative advantage of nations.

Comparative advantage suggests that each nation is relatively good at producing certain products or services. This comparative advantage is based on the nation's abundant factors of production—land, labor, and capital—and a country will export those products/services that use its abundant factors of production intensively. Simply, consider only two factors of production, labor and capital, and two countries, X and Y. If country X has a relative abundance of labor and country Y a relative abundance of capital, country X should export products/services that use labor intensively, country Y should export products/services that use capital intensively.

This is a very simplistic explanation, of course. There are many more factors of production, of varying qualities, and there are many additional influences on trade such as government regulations. Nevertheless, it is a starting point for understanding what nations are likely to export or import. The concept of comparative advantage can also help explain investment flows. Generally, capital is the most mobile of the factors of production and can move relatively easily from one country to another. Other factors of production, such as land and labor, either do not move or are less mobile. The result is that where capital is available in one country it may be used to invest in other countries to take advantage of their abundant land or labor. Firms may develop expertise and firm specific advantages based initially on abundant resources at home, but as resource needs change, the stage of the product life cycle matures, and home markets become saturated, these firms find it advantageous to invest internationally.

THE INTERNATIONAL BUSINESS ENVIRONMENT

International business is different from domestic business because the environment changes when a firm crosses international borders. Typically, a firm understands its domestic environment quite well, but is less familiar with the environment in other countries and must invest more time and resources into understanding the new environment. The following considers some of the important aspects of the environment that change internationally.

The economic environment can be very different from one nation to another. Countries are often divided into three main categories: the more developed or industrialized, the less developed or third world, and the newly industrializing or emerging economies. Within each category there are major variations, but overall the more developed countries are the rich countries, the less developed the poor ones, and the newly industrializing (those moving from poorer to richer). These distinctions are usually made on the basis of gross domestic product per capita (GDP/capita). Better education, infrastructure, technology, health care, and so on are also often associated with higher levels of economic development.

In addition to level of economic development, countries can be classified as free-market, centrally planned, or mixed. Free-market economies are those where government intervenes minimally in business activities, and market forces of supply and demand are allowed to determine production and prices. Centrally planned economies are those where the government determines production and prices based on forecasts of demand and desired levels of supply. Mixed economies are those where some activities are left to market forces and some, for national and individual welfare reasons, are government controlled. In the late twentieth century there has been a substantial move to free-market economies, but the People's Republic of China, the world's most populous country, along with a few others, remained largely centrally planned economies, and most countries maintain some government control of business activities.

Clearly the level of economic activity combined with education, infrastructure, and so on, as well as the degree of government control of the economy, affect virtually all facets of doing business, and a firm needs to understand this environment if it is to operate successfully internationally.

The political environment refers to the type of government, the government relationship with business, and the political risk in a country. Doing business internationally thus implies dealing with different types of governments, relationships, and levels of risk.

There are many different types of political systems, for example, multi-party democracies, one-party states, constitutional monarchies, dictatorships (military and nonmilitary). Also, governments change in different ways, for example, by regular elections, occasional elections, death, coups, war. Government-business relationships also differ from country to country. Business may be viewed positively as the engine of growth, it may be viewed negatively as the exploiter of the workers, or somewhere in between as providing both benefits and drawbacks. Specific government-business relationships can also vary from positive to negative depending on the type of business operations involved and the relationship between the people of the host country and the people of the home country. To be effective in a foreign location an international firm relies on the goodwill of the foreign government and needs to have a good understanding of all of these aspects of the political environment.

A particular concern of international firms is the degree of political risk in a foreign location. Political risk refers to the likelihood of government activity that has unwanted consequences for the firm. These consequences can be dramatic as in forced divestment, where a government requires the firm give up its assets, or more moderate, as in unwelcome regulations or interference in operations. In any case the risk occurs because of uncertainty about the likelihood of government activity occurring. Generally, risk is associated with instability and a country is thus seen as more risky if the government is likely to change unexpectedly, if there is social unrest, if there are riots, revolutions, war, terrorism, and so on. Firms naturally prefer countries that are stable and that present little political risk, but the returns need to be weighed against the risks, and firms often do business in countries where the risk is relatively high. In these situations, firms seek to manage the perceived risk through insurance, ownership and management choices, supply and market control, financing arrangements, and so on. In addition, the degree of political risk is not solely a function of the country, but depends on the company and its activities as well—a risky country for one company may be relatively safe for another.

The cultural environment is one of the critical components of the international business environment and one of the most difficult to understand. This is because the cultural environment is essentially unseen; it has been described as a shared, commonly held body of general beliefs and values that determine what is right for one group, according to Kluckhohn and Strodtbeck. National culture is described as the body of general beliefs and values that are shared by a nation. Beliefs and values are generally seen as formed by factors such as history, language, religion, geographic location, government, and education; thus firms begin a cultural analysis by seeking to understand these factors.

Firms want to understand what beliefs and values they may find in countries where they do business, and a number of models of cultural values have been proposed by scholars. The most well-known is that developed by Hofstede in1980. This model proposes four dimensions of cultural values including individualism, uncertainty avoidance, power distance and masculinity. Individualism is the degree to which a nation values and encourages individual action and decision making. Uncertainty avoidance is the degree to which a nation is willing to accept and deal with uncertainty. Power distance is the degree to which a national accepts and sanctions differences in power. And masculinity is the degree to which a nation accepts traditional male values or traditional female values. This model of cultural values has been used extensively because it provides data for a wide array of countries. Many academics and managers found this model helpful in exploring management approaches that would be appropriate in different cultures. For example, in a nation that is high on individualism one expects individual goals, individual tasks, and individual reward systems to be effective, whereas the reverse would be the case in a nation that is low on individualism. While this model is popular, there have been many attempts to develop more complex and inclusive models of culture.

The competitive environment can also change from country to country. This is partly because of the economic, political, and cultural environments; these environmental factors help determine the type and degree of competition that exists in a given country.

Competition can come from a variety of sources. It can be public or private sector, come from large or small organizations, be domestic or global, and stem from traditional or new competitors. For the domestic firm the most likely sources of competition may be well understood. The same is not the case when one moves to compete in a new environment. For example, in the 1990s in the United States most business was privately owned and competition was among private sector companies, while in the People's Republic of China (PRC) businesses were owned by the state. Thus, a U.S. company in the PRC could find itself competing with organizations owned by state entities such as the PRC army. This could change the nature of competition dramatically.

The nature of competition can also change from place to place as the following illustrate: competition may be encouraged and accepted or discouraged in favor of cooperation; relations between buyers and sellers may be friendly or hostile; barriers to entry and exit may be low or high; regulations may permit or prohibit certain activities. To be effective internationally, firms need to understand these competitive issues and assess their impact.

An important aspect of the competitive environment is the level, and acceptance, of technological innovation in different countries. The last decades of the twentieth century saw major advances in technology, and this is continuing in the twenty-first century. Technology often is seen as giving firms a competitive advantage; hence, firms compete for access to the newest in technology, and international firms transfer technology to be globally competitive. It is easier than ever for even small businesses to have a global presence thanks to the internet, which greatly expands their exposure, their market, and their potential customer base. For economic, political, and cultural reasons, some countries are more accepting of technological innovations, others less accepting.

INTERNATIONAL ENTRY CHOICES

International firms may choose to do business in a variety of ways. Some of the most common include exports, licenses, contracts and turnkey operations, franchises, joint ventures, wholly owned subsidiaries, and strategic alliances.

Exporting is often the first international choice for firms, and many firms rely substantially on exports throughout their history. Exports are seen as relatively simple because the firm is relying on domestic production, can use a variety of intermediaries to assist in the process, and expects its foreign customers to deal with the marketing and sales issues. Many firms begin by exporting reactively; then become proactive when they realize the potential benefits of addressing a market that is much larger than the domestic one.

Effective exporting requires attention to detail if the process is to be successful; for example, the exporter needs to decide if and when to use different intermediaries, select an appropriate transportation method, preparing export documentation, prepare the product, arrange acceptable payment terms, and so on. Most importantly, the exporter usually leaves marketing and sales to the foreign customers, and these may not receive the same attention as if the firm itself undertook these activities. Larger exporters often undertake their own marketing and establish sales subsidiaries in important foreign markets.

Licenses are granted from a licensor to a licensee for the rights to some intangible property (e.g. patents, processes, copyrights, trademarks) for agreed on compensation (a royalty payment). Many companies feel that production in a foreign country is desirable but they do not want to undertake this production themselves. In this situation the firm can grant a license to a foreign firm to undertake the production. The licensing agreement gives access to foreign markets through foreign production without the necessity of investing in the foreign location. This is particularly attractive for a company that does not have the financial or managerial capacity to invest and undertake foreign production. The major disadvantage to a licensing agreement is the dependence on the foreign producer for quality, efficiency, and promotion of the product—if the licensee is not effective this reflects on the licensor. In addition, the licensor risks losing some of its technology and creating a potential competitor. This means the licensor should choose a licensee carefully to be sure the licensee will perform at an acceptable level and is trustworthy. The agreement is important to both parties and should ensure that both parties benefit equitably.

Contracts are used frequently by firms that provide specialized services, such as management, technical knowledge, engineering, information technology, education, and so on, in a foreign location for a specified time period and fee. Contracts are attractive for firms that have talents not being fully utilized at home and in demand in foreign locations. They are relatively short-term, allowing for flexibility, and the fee is usually fixed so that revenues are known in advance. The major drawback is their short-term nature, which means that the contracting firm needs to develop new business constantly and negotiate new contracts. This negotiation is time consuming, costly, and requires skill at cross-cultural negotiations. Revenues are likely to be uneven and the firm must be able to weather periods when no new contracts materialize.

Turnkey contracts are a specific kind of contract where a firm constructs a facility, starts operations, trains local personnel, then transfers the facility (turns over the keys) to the foreign owner. These contracts are usually for very large infrastructure projects, such as dams, railways, and airports, and involve substantial financing; thus they are often financed by international financial institutions such as the World Bank. Companies that specialize in these projects can be very profitable, but they require specialized expertise. Further, the investment in obtaining these projects is very high, so only a relatively small number of large firms are involved in these projects, and often they involve a syndicate or collaboration of firms.

Similar to licensing agreements, franchises involve the sale of the right to operate a complete business operation. Well-known examples include independently owned fast-food restaurants like McDonald's and Pizza Hut. A successful franchise requires control over something that others are willing to pay for, such as a name, set of products, or a way of doing things, and the availability of willing and able franchisees. Finding franchisees and maintaining control over franchisable assets in foreign countries can be difficult; to be successful at international franchising firms need to ensure they can accomplish both of these.

Joint ventures involve shared ownership in a subsidiary company. A joint venture allows a firm to take an investment position in a foreign location without taking on the complete responsibility for the foreign investment. Joint ventures can take many forms. For example, there can be two partners or more, partners can share equally or have varying stakes, partners can come from the private sector or the public, partners can be silent or active, partners can be local or international. The decisions on what to share, how much to share, with whom to share, and how long to share are all important to the success of a joint venture. Joint ventures have been likened to marriages, with the suggestion that the choice of partner is critically important. Many joint ventures fail because partners have not agreed on their objectives and find it difficult to work out conflicts. Joint ventures provide an effective international entry when partners are complementary, but firms need to be thorough in their preparation for a joint venture.

Wholly-owned subsidiaries involve the establishment of businesses in foreign locations which are owned entirely by the investing firm. This entry choice puts the investor parent in full control of operations but also requires the ability to provide the needed capital and management, and to take on all of the risk. Where control is important and the firm is capable of the investment, it is often the preferred choice. Other firms feel the need for local input from local partners, or specialized input from international partners, and opt for joint ventures or strategic alliances, even where they are financially capable of 100 percent ownership.

Strategic alliances are arrangements among companies to cooperate for strategic purposes. Licenses and joint ventures are forms of strategic alliances, but are often differentiated from them. Strategic alliances can involve no joint ownership or specific license agreement, but rather two companies working together to develop a synergy. Joint advertising programs are a form of strategic alliance, as are joint research and development programs. Strategic alliances seem to make some firms vulnerable to loss of competitive advantage, especially where small firms ally with larger firms. In spite of this, many smaller firms find strategic alliances allow them to enter the international arena when they could not do so alone.

International business grew substantially in the second half of the twentieth century, and this growth is likely to continue. The international environment is complex and it is very important for firms to understand this environment and make effective choices in this complex environment. The previous discussion introduced the concept of comparative advantage, explored some of the important aspects of the international business environment, and outlined the major international entry choices available to firms. The topic of international business is itself complex, and this short discussion serves only to introduce a few ideas on international business issues.

Betty Jane Punnett
Revised by Monica C. Turner

FURTHER READING:

Allen, D., and M.E. Raynor. "Preparing for a New Global Business Environment: Divided and Disorderly or Integrated and Harmonious?" *Journal of Business Strategy* 25, no. 5 (September 2004): 16–25.

Buckley, P.J., ed. *What is International Business?* Basingstoke, Hampshire; New York, NY: Palgrave Macmillan, 2005.

Daniels, J.D., and L.H. Radebaugh. *International Business: Environments and Operations.* Reading, MA: Addison-Wesley, 1997.

"Exploiting Opportunity." *Business Mexico* 15, no. 2 (February 2005): 54–57.

Hofstede, G. *Culture's Consequences: Individual Differences in Work Related Values.* Beverly Hills, CA: Sage Publications, 1980.

Kauser, S. and V. Shaw. "The Influence of Behavioural and Organisational Characteristics on the Success of International Strategic Alliances." *International Marketing Review* 21, no. 1 (2004): 17–52.

Kluckhohn, F., and F.L. Strodtbeck. *Variations in Value Orientations.* Evanston, IL: Row, Peterson, 1961.

London, T., and S.L. Hart. "Reinventing Strategies for Emerging Markets: Beyond the Transnational Model." *Journal of International Business Studies* 35, no. 5 (September 2004): 350–370.

Punnett, B.J., and D. Ricks. *International Business.* Cambridge, MA: Blackwell Publishers, 1997.

"Trade: At Daggers Drawn." *Economist* 351, no. 8118 (1999): 17–20.

Welch, C. and I. Wilkinson. "The Political Embeddedness of International Business Networks." *International Marketing Review* 21, no. 2 (2004): 216–231.

World Trade Organization. "Trade and Investment Statistics". Available from <http://www.wto.org/english/res_e/booksp_e/anrep_e/anrep99_e.pdf>.

INTERNATIONAL CULTURAL DIFFERENCES

Culture in a global economy is a critical factor in international business. While many business transactions make economic sense, the ability to successfully fulfill profitable relationships often depends on being able to reconcile international differences arising from separate cultures. Understanding cultural differences is an initial step, but managers also need to engage in learning processes to develop international cultural competence. Cross-cultural training enables managers to acquire both knowledge and skills to fulfill the role of cultural agents. Advancing cultural intelligence and international cultural competence is critical to the future success of managers and leaders working in a global context.

Culture, as defined in Kroeber and Kluckhohn's classic, *Culture: A Critical Review of Concepts and Definitions,* is the "patterned ways of thinking, feeling, and reacting, acquired and transmitted mainly by symbols, constituting the distinctive achievements of human groups, including their embodiments in artifacts; the essential core of culture consists of traditional (i.e., historically derived and selected) ideas and especially their attached values" (1952). In international management research, Hofstede defined culture as ". . .the collective programming of the mind which distinguishes the members of one group or category of people from those of another" (1991). Many other definitions of culture are available. Common elements in the definitions are the shared and dynamic nature revolving around norms, values, and beliefs that are expressed in different behaviors, artifacts, and interactions.

Within the context of international business, culture involves multiple levels that span from broad to narrow and different dimensions. On a broad level, supranational culture differences span multiple countries and include regional, ethnic, religious, and linguistic dimensions. On a national level, governments create sovereign boundaries to distinguish different nations with political and legal regulatory systems. In the business literature, most research on culture uses the nation-state as a proxy for culture. Other levels of analysis for culture include subcultures, as well as professional and organizational groups. In addition to various levels, culture also involves different dimensions.

Four major classifications schemes provide frameworks for identifying international differences in culture. First, anthropologist Edward T. Hall (b. 1914) classified cultural differences along five different dimensions: time, space, things, friendships, and agreements. Second, Kluckhohn and Strodtbeck developed a cultural orientations framework that identified six issues, with variations in each one: relation to nature, relationships among people, mode of human activity, belief about basic human nature, orientation to time, and use of space. Third, Hofstede's framework is one of the most prominent one in international management. He identified four major dimensions of cultural values—individualism-collectivism, power distance, uncertainty avoidance, and masculinity-femininity— along with a fifth dimension subsequently identified as Confucian Dynamism, or long-term orientation. Finally, Trompenaars and Hampden-Turner extended Hofstede's classification with seven dimensions that include universalism versus particularism, collectivism versus individualism, affective versus neutral relationships, specificity versus diffuseness, achievement versus ascription, orientation toward time, and internal versus external control. The four different classifications provide different and overlapping approaches to organize the many complex dimensions that make up culture. A major premise underlying the need for organizing different cultural dimensions is a means to avoid costly mistakes in conducting international business.

The different classifications provide a map to make sense of the complex nature of culture. Important caveats to keep in mind are that each classification is not exhaustive and each one originates from a particular cultural perspective. Managers have to engage in learning processes with cross-cultural training to develop both cultural intelligence and international cultural competence. Cross-cultural training for international assignments encompasses a broad range of methods that may include area briefings, readings, lecture/discussions, language lessons, films, self-assessment exercises, role plays, field trips, sensitivity training, and cross-cultural simulations. Cross-cultural training also needs to be coordinated in multiple phases to maximize the learning effectiveness for individual managers and organizational performance. The three phases are predeparture orientation, in-country socialization, and country exit debriefing. The exit debriefing is important for organizational learning, and a knowledge management system can support the capture of the cultural lessons that are learned.

Kim and Ofori-Dankwa described four major delivery methods for cross-cultural training: the intellectual model, the area simulation model, the self-awareness model, and the cultural awareness model. The intellectual model involves the traditional classroom approach of general readings and lecture. The area simulation model incorporates culture-specific activities (e.g., working in Japan or Mexico) with games and exercises. The self-awareness training method focuses on having participants identify their strengths and weaknesses in dealing with different cultures, especially taken-for-granted assumptions about intercultural situations. The cultural awareness model focuses on the theoretical foundation for behavioral differences across cultures. The key to effective cross-cultural training is the integration of multiple methods that allow a participant to move from simple to complex levels of learning with increasing levels of training rigor.

The purpose of using multiple methods in cross-cultural training is to advance the learning process through the learning stages to develop cultural intelligence and international cultural competence. Cultural intelligence integrates the three interrelated elements of knowledge, mindfulness, and behavioral skills. International cultural competence goes a step further with a more complex skill set that integrates cognitive, affective, and behavioral learning to effectively engage in successful cross-cultural relationships. International cultural competence is very similar to intercultural communication competence, which integrates three components: culture-specific understanding of the other, culture-general understanding, and positive regard of the other. Increasing one's ability to work effectively across cultures also provides positive support to address a range of adjustment issues for expatriates who often face culture shock in the acculturation process. Overall, the most important key of cultural intelligence and intercultural competence is the integration of multiple spheres of cross-cultural learning to effectively engage in international business situations. Effectiveness in reconciling cross-cultural differences often leads to creativity, innovation, and synergy for productive workplace performances.

Although cross-cultural training supports global managers' ability to be effective, the learning process often moves through different stages of development. The different development stages of cultural intelligence are: (1) reactivity to external stimuli, (2) recognition of other cultural norms and motivation to learn more about them, (3) accommodation of other cultural norms and rules, (4) assimilation of diverse cultural norms into alternative behaviors, and (5) proactiveness in cultural behavior based on recognition of change cues that others do not perceive.

Global managers with high levels of cultural intelligence and competence play important strategic roles as cultural agents (c-agents), helping their organizations to span international boundaries. C-agents require both the ability to navigate different cultures and the legitimacy from different cultural perspectives, including organizational and within the local community. Organizations have increasing needs for global managers to fill the role of c-agents because demands of globalization increasingly depend on successful relationships with strategic alliance partners, international vendors, and global customers.

Within the global arena, national borders often form the defining entity for a culture. However, analysis of cultural differences needs to account for a range of diversity within a national culture. On a continuum of cultural diversity that ranges from homogenous to heterogeneous, Japan, Norway, and Poland are relatively more homogeneous when compared to India, Papua New Guinea, Australia, Britain, and Canada. The more heterogeneous societies encompass more distinctions between subcultures within the national borders. However, it is important to account for the fact that "almost no country is entirely homogeneous. The world's nearly 200 countries contain some 5000 ethnic groups. Two-thirds have at least one substantial minority—an ethnic or religious group that makes up at least 10 percent of the population."

In many ways, how a society addresses issues of multiculturalism creates an orientation that enables its citizens to live and work together in a global community. Cultural norms shaped by national government policies will need to avoid and dismantle policies for separation (keeping different cultural identities but not integrated) or assimilation (forced rejection of traditional cultural identity to integrate into dominant identity) in order to adopt new approaches of multiculturalism. Important principles for multicultural policies center on promoting tolerance and cultural understanding to respect diversity, recognize multiple identities, and build common bonds of membership to the local community.

In the future globalization will continue to increase the flow and interactions of people across cultures, which surfaces even more international differences. Understanding the different dimensions of culture provides an initial knowledge base to develop cultural intelligence and competence for effective international business relationships. However, global managers require cross-cultural training to advance their learning and growth in cultural intelligence and competence as they take on international assignments. More importantly, organizations will have an increasing need for global managers to become c-agents to develop effective international relationships. In addition, government leaders have opportunities to shape their national culture and support international competitiveness with new multiculturalism policies that promote both the inclusion of multiple cultural identities and the development of local communities in an era of globalization.

SEE ALSO: International Business; International Management; Organizational Culture

Diana J. Wong-MingJi

FURTHER READING:

Black, J. Stewart, and Mark Mendenhall. "A Practical but Theory-based Framework for Selecting Cross-Cultural Training Methods." *Human Resource Management* 28, no. 4 (1989): 511–539.

Earley, P. Christopher, and Randall S. Peterson. "The Elusive Cultural Chameleon: Cultural Intelligence as a New Approach to Intercultural Training for the Global Manager." *Academy of Management Learning & Education* 3, no. 1 (2004): 100–115.

Hall, Edward T. "The Silent Language in Overseas Business." *Harvard Business Review,* May-June, 1960.

Harris, Hilary, and Savita Kumra. "International Manager Development." *Journal of Management Development* 19, no. 7 (2000): 602–614.

Hofstede, Geert H. *Cultures and Organizations: Software of the Mind.* London: McGraw-Hill, 1991.

Human Development Report 2004: Cultural Liberty in Today's Diverse World. New York: United Nations Development Programme, 2004.

Kim, Pan S., and Joseph Ofori-Dankwa. "Utilizing Cultural Theory as a Basis for Cross-Cultural Training: An Alternative Approach." *Public Administration Quarterly* 18, no. 4 (1995): 478–500.

Kluckhohn, Florence Rockwood, and Fred L. Strodtbeck. *Variations in Value Orientations.* New York: Row, Petersen & Company, 1961.

Kroeber, A.L., and Clyde Kluckhohn. *Culture; A Critical Review of Concepts and Definitions.* Cambridge, MA: The Museum, 1952.

Maznevski, Martha L., Joseph J. DiStefano, Carolina B. Gomez, Niels G. Noorderhaven, and Fei-Chuan Wu. "Cultural Dimensions at the Individual Level of Analysis: The Cultural Orientations Framework." *International Journal of Cross Cultural Management* 2, no. 3 (2002): 275–295.

Thomas, David C., and Kerr Inkson. *Cultural Intelligence: People Skills for Global Business.* San Francisco, CA: Berrett-Koehler Publishers, 2004.

Trompenaars, Alfons, and Charles Hampden-Turner. *Riding the Waves of Culture: Understanding Cultural Diversity in Global Business.* 2nd ed. New York: McGraw Hill, 1998.

Zakaria, Norhayati. "The Effects of Cross-Cultural Training on the Acculturation Process of the Global Workforce." *International Journal of Manpower* 21, no. 6 (2000): 492–510.

INTERNATIONAL MANAGEMENT

During the 1990s and early 2000s, many companies took advantage of a world market that was increasingly open to international expansion and trade. Obstacles to free trade were eased through the

General Agreement on Tariffs and Trade (GATT), the North American Free Trade Agreement (NAFTA), and the Association of South East Asian Nations (ASEAN).

Economies opened, and due to technological developments in communication, transportation, and finance, there were fewer difficulties with the practical issues of conducting business across national borders. Communications technology showed exponential growth, including innovations that facilitated doing business anywhere at anytime, such as remote access and net conferencing.

As shown in Table 1, the number of Internet users in the world grew from 30 million to over 562 million over six years, and by 2002 almost 10 percent of the world population used the Internet.

Table 1
Internet Users 1996-2002

Year	Internet Users (millions)	Internet Users a Percentage of World Population
Jan 1996	30	.73
Jan 1997	57	1.41
Jan 1998	102	2.49
Jan 1999	153.5	3.75
Jan 2000	254.29	4.27
Jan 2001	455.55	7.5
Jan 2002	562.47	9.43

Accompanying all of these changes was an increase in need for international management for people who understand business and cultural issues well enough to manage and grow an international business effectively. Among those issues are:

- Business Structure
- Competition
- Political and economic environments
- Finance and business issues such as contracts, taxation, intellectual property, and risk
- Employment and leadership
- Cultural norms and values
- Technology

BUSINESS STRUCTURE

An international manager has the task of reopening business in a radically different environment. He or she must determine the overall structure of the business and its workflow. In a functional-based business (i.e., the new location needs to be able to perform standardized tasks that comply with overall corporate practices), skilled labor and ability to perform these tasks is key.

Technological infrastructure could be a crucial factor. For an area-based business, location is key, and detailed knowledge of the country and its culture is critical. Products may have to be adapted to the host market.

A global-based structure may have a varied set of product lines, each of which can be made and marketed across locations. These approaches can be mixed, but choosing the structure of the business should support the firm's primary goals.

Many businesses start by first establishing the new office or facility as an "export division" that falls under the umbrella of Operations or Marketing—which may eventually become an "International Division." How this new entity best fits within the parent organization's overall structure depends on the purpose for the new location and how much the parent company plans to grow the business.

Other options include opening a wholly-owned subsidiary or an overseas joint venture, contracting from an international company (IC) to manufacture products to specification, or purchasing supplies and/or materials from an IC manufacturer.

Other considerations include the additional costs of globalization, such as international freight, insurance, packing (up to 12 percent of manufacturing prices), sales terms, import duties, broker's fees, inventory costs, and international travel.

COMPETITION

Competition in the global marketplace continues to grow, particularly between the United States, the European Union, and Asian nations. For this reason, companies need to evaluate the competitive landscape of the host country. First, it is helpful to understand that the nature of competition varies by region and industry. Some nations support an atmosphere of pure competition; for example, there may be any number of sellers, each with relatively small market share, with competition based solely on price. Others may be more monopolistic. Understanding the type of environment in which a firm will participate in its host country ensures the use of appropriate business practices.

More specific threats to companies comes from existing competitors, new competitors who may also enter the market, and the bargaining power of suppliers and buyers in the host country or region. Also, some countries' business environments make entering the marketplace harder than others. For example, foreign businesses find it hard to compete with industry in Japan, where groups of firms are connected financially and rarely do business outside of that group (called "keiretsu").

When investigating the competitive climate, it is also helpful to understand the power wielded by many of the world's transnational corporations (TNCs). Many of the world's top TNCs earn more in revenues each year than most nations, as shown in Table 2. While this does not mean other companies cannot compete with the products and services offered by these companies, it helps to know that these TNCs are involved in establishing direction, lobbying industry, and other activities that have direct impact on the laws and regulations that affect entire industries and how smaller companies can conduct international business.

Table 2

Top Revenue Earners from the Global Fortune 500 (in billions of US$) Nations/States vs. Transnational Corporations

2003 Total Revenues

1. United States (Total of 189 companies), $5,841
2. Japan (82), $2,181
3. Germany (34), $1,363
4. France (37), $1,246
5. Britain (35), $1,079
6. Netherlands (12), $388
7. Switzerland (12), $382
8. China (15), $358
9. Italy (8), $300
10. South Korea (11), $266
11. Wal-Mart Stores (U.S.), $263
12. Britain/Netherlands (2), $250
13. BP (Britain), $232.5
14. Exxon Mobil (U.S.), $222.8
15. Royal Dutch/Shell Group (Britain/Netherlands), $201.7
16. General Motors (U.S.), $195.3
17. Canada (13), $185
18. Ford Motor Co.(U.S.), $164.5
19. Spain (7), $162
20. Daimler Chrysler (Germany), $156.6
21. Toyota Motor (Japan), $153.1
22. General Electric (U.S.), $134.1

Source: Compiled by Wendy H. Mason, Data from *Fortune's Global 500*, June 2004

Finally, understanding of international anti-trust laws and when they are enforced is critical to assessing the risks to an international business. The United States is the toughest nation in regard to anti-trust, even trying to enforce laws outside the country. The European Union is lax on enforcing anti-trust laws, but does use them as a means to levy fines on cartels. In Japan, enforcement of anti-trust legislation, which was enacted only under great pressure from outside the country, is weak at best, and usually nonexistent. Learning how "fair competition" is viewed in foreign business environments better prepares a manager to protect his or her own business.

ENVIRONMENTAL FACTORS

Both the economic and political environments of countries and regions have great impact on the managing of international operations. A few of the economic factors that impact international business are:

- Host nation's economy: free-market vs. centrally planned, or mixed.
- Gross Domestic Product (GDP), Gross National Product (GNP), and per capita income—all are gauges to consumer buying power.
- Spending patterns of host population.
- Variation in degree of development or industrialization.
- Infrastructure and technology available to business.
- Differences in available education and health care.

Some economies are less hospitable to job creation than others. For example, in Western Europe high minimum wages, healthy unemployment benefits, and employment protection laws are significant barriers to companies hoping to produce job growth in this part of the world. This and other issues also have an impact on finding employees to help staff and manage international operations.

The political environment plays a large role in determining how international companies will be able to manage business operations. Examples of political forces affecting international corporations include:

- Governments, political parties, and ideological beliefs (communism, capitalism, socialism, liberal, conservative, etc.).
- Nature of government-business relationships.
- Laws and attitude toward business.
- Tariffs and quotas.
- Currency controls (limits on the amount of money entering or leaving a country).

All businesses must abide by the laws, regulations, and bureaucracy in the host nation, including the United States and other capitalist countries. Examples of the obstacles an international corporation may encounter include complying with government restrictions on regulated professions and industries such as law, medicine, banking, insurance, transportation, and utilities. State and local governments may also require specific licenses for business and restrict foreign use of buildings. For all of these, proper compliance takes knowledge, time to learn, and expense.

While all of the above factors have significant impact on multi-national corporations, perhaps the most important factor for an international manager is awareness of the degree of risk associated with various political forces in the host region. In addition to weighing the stability of the established government in the region in which it conducts business, governments can seize property owned by foreigners within its borders. This is known as expropriation in cases where the government follows up with quick, adequate compensation for former owners of the property. However, some governments may confiscate property, meaning former owners do not receive proper compensation.

CONTRACTS

When parties representing different nations enter into a contract, dispute resolution becomes especially complicated. The United Nations (UN) Convention on Contracts for the International Sale of Goods (CISG) established legal rules for international sales contracts, including rights and obligations for both buyer and seller. Unless the parties to the contract expressly exclude the CISG, it applies to all contracts signed by companies from the countries that ratified the Convention. In the European Union (EU), the Rome Convention (1991) also applies to contracts formed between EU residents. Outside of these two agreements, companies must rely on private solutions and arbitration (which is used with increasing frequency).

INTELLECTUAL PROPERTY

Intellectual property is well protected in the United States, with patents, trademarks, and copyrights. But when companies engage in business with other countries, they take risks. For example, product counterfeiting, common in Asia, costs industries more than $200 billion worldwide, according to the U.S. Department of Commerce.

Other risks to business included trade secrets and industrial espionage. Most often, competitive information is obtained from inside the company, from published business materials, customers, competitor employees, and sometimes through direct observation.

Each nation has its own laws to protect intellectual property, but which products those laws protect differs as well. The UN's World Intellectual Property Organization (WIPO) was created to administer international property treaties, as was TRIPS, a World Trade Organization (WTO) agency.

The United States adopted its Foreign Corruption Practices Act (FCPA), which unfortunately acts as a barrier to United States companies. The FCPA was not adopted in Europe, or elsewhere, and compliance with the FCPA means American exporters lose business. Most importantly, international managers need to be aware piracy and counterfeiting, particularly in certain markets, and take steps to protect proprietary corporate information.

LIABILITY

Product liability is a much bigger issue in the United States than in other countries. For example, the United States is the only country that conducts jury trials or pays punitive damages in cases of product liability. There was a principle of strict liability adopted in Europe, but company defense is strong and some countries cap damages.

The United States places many burdens upon its own companies, which impacts how well American companies can conduct business internationally and what it costs them to do so. Like the FCPA, boycott legislation often applies only to the United States. These become significant obstacles to international competition when other countries do not follow suit.

FINANCE

Financial management of international corporations is particularly challenging, as countries change in value in terms of each other based on currency exchange rates. Companies must comply with financial laws and regulations in the host country. International managers need to:

- Understand how fluctuations in currency value change international business transactions.

- Learn about financial tools such as derivatives, hedges, payment timing, exposure netting, price adjustments, balance sheet neutralizing, and swaps, and how they affect business performance.

- Meet, network, and cooperate with counterparts in other organizations to protect and/or benefit the organization.

- Learn when and how to pay exporters in forms other than money; buyers frequently prefer payment rendered in the form of goods or services (countertrade).

- Differentiate between two types of currency: hard, convertible currency is accepted around the world at uniform rates; soft, nonconvertible currency is rarely of value outside the host country.

- Use international finance centers as a resource—these accumulate expertise and information to conduct financial transaction for international company units most profitably and at the lowest cost.

EMPLOYMENT AND LABOR FORCES

Investigation of the available labor force should be performed before a company chooses to expand its business to a given region. Managers should determine whether there are enough people of the right skill level for a company to run the business effectively, and whether or not they will want to work for a foreign employer.

When staffing international operations, managers must be able to fill positions from a pool of labor with the right education and skill to maintain and grow the business. Hiring options include choosing from the parent company, choosing people from the host country, or hiring from a local subsidiary. Refugees are often pulled into operations. However, they may lack the skills, health, or education to work. Guest workers may also provide labor, and are particularly helpful in times of rapid growth—when native workers are not willing or able to fill all positions and they do not feel displaced. However, even in times of growth, bringing in large numbers of guest workers (foreigners) often causes friction with citizens of the host country.

Proper planning also helps a company to recognize other forces that cannot be controlled (but must be managed) and plan accordingly. Managers of international operations need to understand the effects of price and wage controls, labor laws, and currency exchange in the host country. In Europe, the government plays a very active role in legislating wages and working conditions, particularly in Germany and France. In Japan, unions align more with specific companies than with industry, so union members have a stake in how well the company does and how much money it makes. They often work with company management.

Understanding cultural issues is critical to international management in general, but culture plays a particularly important role in building a labor force outside the United States. Though U.S. businesses have come to see women as part of the employment pool, women are less accepted as part of the workforce in many other countries.

Another consideration is race, which is still a source of conflict and discrimination in many areas, as is social status. Religious, tribal, racial, and other cultural factors have an impact, not just on employment, but on how an international company will be viewed by the host culture (and how many people will buy products made by the company). However, if managers are well informed and handle cultural issues properly, people from different cultures, speaking different languages, and possessing various abilities and levels of experience can strengthen the overall management of an international company.

Many corporations have particular difficulty finding qualified executives to effectively manage international companies. Successful leaders of international companies need to understand motivation, leadership, communication, conflict, and other behavioral issues that arise in cross-national and cross-cultural context. The ability to address these issues depends on an understanding of the host culture's values. Other skills cited as keys to successful international management include:

- Technical competence.
- Ability to speak, or willingness to learn, the host language.
- Tolerance for ambiguity and ability to manage uncertainty.
- Nonjudgmental attitude.
- Ability to emotionally connect with people from diverse cultures and backgrounds, and to understand differing viewpoints.
- Personal integrity.
- Strong commitment to personal and company standards.
- Inquisitive mindset/continuous learning.

Managers of international operations need to be adaptable and have a high tolerance for change and ambiguity. They are most successful when given autonomy and discretion in the workplace. Overall business savvy on the part of executives helps to ensure an international company will run well.

Thorough understanding of both the company and industry is important, along with an ability to leverage that understanding when planning, organizing, and implementing ideas. On a more practical level, international managers need to be able to manage accounting and auditing, business plans, policies and procedures, information systems, and corporate culture—all of which vary based on the infrastructure and culture of the host country.

CULTURAL ISSUES

Defined as the body of beliefs, norms, and values shared by a group of people, culture presents the biggest challenge to businesses working internationally. It is a key factor in how all other areas of business work together. As stated by Geert Hofstede, "Culture is more often a source of conflict than of synergy. Cultural differences are a nuisance at best and often

Table 3
Hofstede's 5 Cultural Dimensions

Value Dimension	Value Description	High Score	Low Score
Power Distance Index (PDI)	The degree of equality, or inequality, between people in the country's society	Indicates that inequalities of power and wealth have been allowed to grow within the society. These societies are more likely to follow a caste system that does not allow significant upward mobility of its citizens.	Indicates the society de-emphasizes the differences between citizen's power and wealth. In these societies equality and opportunity for everyone is stressed.
Individualism (IDV)	Degree to which a society reinforces individual or collective achievement and interpersonal relationships.	Indicates that individuality and individual rights are paramount within the society. Individuals may tend to form a larger number of looser relationships.	Typifies societies of a more collectivist nature with close ties between individuals. Reinforce extended families and collectives where everyone takes responsibility for fellow members of their group.
Masculinity (MAS)	Degree to which a society reinforces, or does not reinforce, the traditional masculine work role model of male achievement, control, and power	Indicates the country experiences a high degree of gender differentiation. Males dominate a significant portion of the society and power structure, with females being controlled by male domination.	Indicates the country has a low level of differentiation and discrimination between genders. Females are treated equally to males in all aspects of the society.
Uncertainty Avoidance Index (UAI)	Level of tolerance for uncertainty and ambiguity within the society - i.e. unstructured situations.	Indicates the country has a low tolerance for uncertainty and ambiguity. Creates a rule-oriented society that institutes laws, rules, regulations, and controls in order to reduce the amount of uncertainty.	Indicates the country has less concern about ambiguity and uncertainty and has more tolerance for a variety of opinions. Reflected in a society that is less rule-oriented, more readily accepts change, and takes more and greater
Long-Term Orientation (LTO)	Degree to which a society embraces, or does not embrace, long-term devotion to traditional, forward thinking values.	Indicates the country prescribes to the values of long-term commitments and respect for tradition. This is thought to support a strong work ethic where long-term rewards are expected as a result of today's hard work. However, business may take longer to develop in this society, particularly for an "outsider".	Indicates the country does not reinforce the concept of long-term, traditional orientation. In this culture, change can occur more rapidly as long-term traditions and commitments do not become impediments to change.

Source: Adapted from Geert Hofstede Cultural Dimensions website, http://www.geert-hofstede.com/

a disaster." A summary of Hofstede's major factors impacting international business relationships that also influence the practice of international management are shown in Table 3.

Managers of international operations should be aware of the importance of context in various countries. Context indicates the level in which communication occurs outside of verbal discussion. High-context communication depends heavily on gestures, body language, and other nonverbal cues. Much of what is communicated is implicit, or unspoken, and assumed to be understood through other cues. Low-context communication is explicit and precise, relying little on nonverbal embellishment for meaning. Many of these, and other cultural practices, is learned through socialization.

Culture influences management practices as well, including negotiation tactics, decision making, and rewards and recognition programs. For example, when conducting business, members of some cultures sit right down to business after shaking hands. In other countries, it is considered rude to mention business at all until after both parties have spent a significant amount of time establishing a relationship. Other management soft skills, such as motivation, making decisions, and rewarding employees, depend on cultural factors as well.

TECHNOLOGY

Technology is an important factor that can vary significantly, depending on the purpose of foreign investment and how important it is for technology to be standardized across business divisions. While some business leaders may choose to expand internationally to take advantage of cheaper labor or manufacturing costs, particularly in developing nations, they may also need to plan for "intermediate and appropriate technology."

The production processes used may vary from advanced to primitive, depending on the economic, cultural, and political variables of the host nation. Some governments urge investors to consider intermediate technology rather than the highly-automated equipment and processes of industrialized countries, in part because less advanced countries lack the infrastructure to support such technology. Companies may respond by searching for an appropriate technology that matches a country's resources, or it may choose to invest elsewhere.

Technology has also contributed significantly to the spread of globalization and international expansion. Advances in technology enable international businesses to conduct international financial transactions, purchase products, analyze data rapidly, make capital improvements, and streamline communications, transportation, and distribution channels.

The summaries above are brief introductions to broad issues to which entire semesters are devoted in business programs. International management requires a broad knowledge base in many areas, as well as an ability to adapt to working conditions in which the only constants are change and a devotion to continuous learning.

Most critical to international management is the desire and ability to work well with people of various cultures, interests, degrees of education, and intelligence—from employees to colleagues to government officials, with home country and host country, and across national and industrial borders.

SEE ALSO: International Cultural Differences; International Management

Wendy H. Mason

FURTHER READING:

Ball, Donald, et al. *International Business: The Challenge of Global Competition.* New York, NY: Irwin/McGraw-Hill, 2003.

Deresky, Helen. *International Management: Managing Across Borders and Cultures.* Upper Saddle River, NJ: Prentice-Hall, 2003.

"Geert Hofstede Cultural Dimensions." Available from <http://www.geert-hofstede.com>.

Harris, Philip R., and Robert T. Moran. *Managing Cultural Differences.* Houston, TX: Gulf Professional Publishing, 2000.

Hjelt, Paola. "The Fortune Global 500." *Fortune,* 26 July 2004, 159.

Holt, David H., and Karen Wiggington. *International Management.* Cincinnati, OH: Thomson South-Western, 2001.

Punnett, B.J., and D. Ricks. *International Business.* Cambridge, MA: Blackwell Publishers, 1997.

INTERNATIONAL MANAGEMENT SOCIETIES AND ASSOCIATIONS

One of the most noteworthy developments in business in the second half of the twentieth century was the rise of the professional business manager. Whereas previously individuals with a wide range of training, usually including experience in a given business, rose to management positions within corporations, in the present managers are often graduates of general business administration and related programs. Accompanying the rise of business management as a profession has been the development of management societies and associations.

International organizations exist to represent business managers engaged in a multitude of economic enterprises. These organizations serve many purposes, including the coordination of members' activities, facilitating exchange of information and the spread of new findings of interest to business managers, disseminating business information to members and other interested parties, monitoring trends in specific industries and areas of business management, and gathering and compiling statistics. Thus, business management associations and societies generally seek to encourage the professional advancement of their members, the economic advancement of specific industries or areas of business, and the development of more effective business management practices. In many cases their activities are closely linked to those of management institutes. The following list of some of the leading international management organizations shows both their diversity of scope and the similarity of their activities.

LEADING INTERNATIONAL MANAGEMENT ASSOCIATIONS

ASSOCIATION OF MANAGEMENT/INTERNATIONAL ASSOCIATION OF MANAGEMENT (AOM/IAOM). The Association of Management (AoM) and the International Association of Management (IAoM) were founded in 1975 as professional organizations representing business academicians and business management practitioners. The organization was first known as the Association of Human Resources Management and Organizational Behavior (HRMOB), and the name was change to AoM/IAoM in 1993. According to their mission, both organizations seek to bridge the gap between theory and practice in management, education, technology, and leadership across multiple disciplines. A primary goal is the continuing professional development of individual business managers. In this regard they are closely related to national business management associations worldwide. Both organizations also sponsor regularly scheduled meetings and issue publications to facilitate exchange of information among their members and between members and the wider business community and the public.

AMERICAN MANAGEMENT ASSOCIATION (AMA). In 1923, the National Personnel Association changed its name to the American Management Association. The AMA's mission is to be "a global, not-for-profit, membership-based association that provides a full range of management development and educational services to individuals, companies, and government agencies worldwide". The organizational serves as a forum for information and ideas on management practices and business trends, disseminated worldwide through multiple distribution channels.

ALL INDIA MANAGEMENT ASSOCIATION (AIMA). The All India Management Association (AIMA) claims to be the one Indian body helping to equip Indian managers to make the most of opportunities arising from transition. Begun in 1957 with support from the Indian government and industry, AIMA now has over 30,000 Professional Individual Members and over 3,000 Corporate/Institutional Members. Activities include management education and development, publications, and testing services. AIMA is represented on a number of committees involved with policy making in the Indian government, and is associated with the Asian Association of Management Organizations and the World Management Council, among other groups.

EUROPEAN FEDERATION OF MANAGEMENT CONSULTING ASSOCIATIONS (FEACO). Founded in 1960, FEACO comprises national associations representing management consultants. In addition to formulating standards of ethics and practice for the field, FEACO conducts industry surveys and compiles statistics on the performance of management consultancy companies in Europe.

INTERNATIONAL PROJECT MANAGEMENT ASSOCIATION (IPMA). Initiated in 1965 as an informal discussion group involving managers of international projects, the IPMA held its first official congress in 1967. In 1999 the association comprised 26 national organizations representing more than 12,000 project managers, and is the prime international promoter of project management. The IPMA confers professional certification upon qualified individuals, serves as a forum for information exchange within the project management field, conducts research and disseminates information on project management, and sponsors continuing professional education programs for project managers.

CENTRAL AND EAST EUROPEAN MANAGEMENT DEVELOPMENT ASSOCIATION (CEEMAN). CEEMAN's function is somewhat different from those of other management societies, given the relatively short time that the profession of business manager has existed in countries formerly under communist rule. As such, the organization is primarily concerned with advancing business and management education in Eastern Europe, and providing for information exchange among members.

ASSOCIATION OF INTERNATIONAL MANAGEMENT SALES EXECUTIVES (AIMSE). This group represents management sales personnel, pension fund managers, and marketers at money market management firms worldwide. AIMSE seeks to advance the management sales profession, and encourages the professional development of its members by conducting educational programs, gathering and disseminating management sales information, and facilitating exchange of information among members at its annual meeting.

AUSTRALIAN INSTITUTE OF MANAGEMENT (AIM). This is Australia's largest professional body for managers and is well known for providing management training and consulting. AIM maintains a network of bookshop and library facilities dedicated to applied management information. AIM membership is around 25,000 personal members and 6,000 key corporate members.

EUROPEAN ASSOCIATION OF PERSONNEL MANAGEMENT (EAPM). Founded in 1962, the EAPM represents a specific constituency within business management, namely, personnel managers. The association functions as the European representative of national personnel management organizations, and formulates standards of conduct and practice for personnel managers.

EUROPEAN WOMEN'S MANAGEMENT DEVELOPMENT NETWORK (EWMD). Founded in 1984, the EWMD represents women in business management in thirty countries regardless of their specific field of endeavor. The network works for the professional advancement of its members, serves as a forum for the exchange of information regarding women in management, and seeks to ensure gender equity in the business management professions.

INSTITUTE OF MANAGEMENT SPECIALISTS (IMS). Founded in 1971, the IMS comprises business managers and commercial business and technical professionals in thirty-nine countries. The institute formulates standards of practice for management specialists, and conducts examinations and bestows professional certification upon qualified individuals.

LATIN AMERICAN AND CARIBBEAN COUNCIL FOR SELF-MANAGEMENT (LACCSM). Founded in 1977, LACCSM comprises national management organizations, research centers, and businesses practicing self-management. The council serves as a forum for the exchange of information among its members, and gathers and disseminates self-management information to all interested parties.

MANAGEMENT PROFESSIONALS ASSOCIATION (MPA). Founded in 1981, the association comprises 26,000 individuals in 161 countries. The MPA seeks to represent the professional interests of business managers in all fields. In an effort to improve business management practice, the MPA develops model profiles describing successful personality traits shared by effective managers, and conducts research and educational programs in the field of business management. The MPA also makes available consulting services to corporations experiencing management problems.

WORLD MANAGEMENT COUNCIL (WMC). Rapid advances in the field of business management, and the perception of increased international trade, led U.S. president Herbert Hoover to convene the first International Management Congress in Prague, Czechoslovakia, in 1924. Attendees found the proceedings so informative that it was decided to form an international management organization to carry on some of the research, information exchange, and management practice initiatives developed during the Congress. The WMC was subsequently founded in 1926, and serves as an umbrella organization for associations representing business managers of every type worldwide. Its mission is to facilitate the exchange of business management information and the development and dissemination of new management practices and techniques among its membership. The WMC also operates national management associations in many countries, and has several regional affiliates, including the European Council of Management, Asian Association of Management Organizations, North American Management Council and the Pan American Council, which function as autonomous international business associations in their own right.

In addition to its functions as a research organization and a forum for the exchange of management information, the WMC maintains close relationships with international trade and development agencies, including the United Nations Economic and Social Council, the United Nations Industrial Development Organization, the United Nations Institute for Training and Research, and the International Labour Organization. Working both directly with these international bodies and through its regional affiliates, the WMC plays an active role in the development and implementation of national and international projects designed to improve management policies and practice.

The WMC brings its members together each year at its annual congress. The WMC congress features presentations of research and opinion and panel discussions on a variety of management topics selected by international industrial, government, and academic leaders.

PERFORMANCE MANAGEMENT ASSOCIATION (PMA). Founded in 1985, the PMA represents project managers in all fields of business activity. The association works to improve understanding of the techniques and value of performance measurement among business managers, and conducts educational programs for managers interested in learning more about this topic.

UNIVERSITY MANAGEMENT INSTITUTES

A somewhat related category of organizations concerns university management institutes. These organizations are similar to management societies and associations, but they generally pursue somewhat different goals. University management institutes are closely related to business management societies and organizations. Management institutes exist worldwide, and although they are primarily engaged in educational activities, they also occasionally work with management associations and industrial groups to gather data on specific industries or areas of economic activity. The Manufacturing 2000 Project (M2000) undertaken by the International Institute for Management Development provides an example of this sort of cooperation between academia, industry, and business management associations.

M2000, a ten-year project begun in 1990, brought together an operating team comprising researchers, professors, business managers, and corporate board members representing sixteen large manufacturing firms. Each firm participating in the project submitted their plans for managing change and developing best practices for consideration and revision by the entire M2000 operating team. Corporate, managerial, and academic participants in M2000 found that the project facilitated information exchange and had a positive influence on all concerned. Keeping in touch with the realities of everyday business management helped academicians develop more useful research projects, while remaining familiar with academic developments proved useful for managers wishing to make changes in corporate procedure or structure. Thus, although it is essentially an academic program, the International Institute of Management Development fulfills a function similar to that of leading business management associations.

Similarly the Decision Analysis Society (DAS), operated by the Fuqua School of Business at Duke University, is an organization comprising business academicians and researchers, managers, and other corporate representatives. DAS seeks to promote and develop the use of logical methods for the improvement of the decision-making process in both public and private enterprises. The society develops model procedures, risk analysis and assessment techniques, and expert systems for decision support.

Another example of a university management institute, the Federation for Enterprise Knowledge Development (FEND), is a collaborative effort involving representatives of leading corporations and business academics. FEND serves as a think tank, analyzing business management tools and methods and researching new management strategies. The federation also develops business management software applications, conducts educational programs for business managers, and provides assistance to businesses wishing to improve their management practices.

Other international university management institutes include the European Foundation for Management Development, through which academicians, corporations, managers, and educational institutions in forty-five countries work to address current issues in management development; the Institute for Administrative Management, an organization of professional managers and business management students united to identify and disseminate new trends and techniques in administrative management; and the Strategic Planning Society, through which educational institutions, government officials, business executives, and corporations of all sizes work to improve public policies regulating the practice of business management.

In a somewhat separate category is the International Academy of Management (IAM), an organization comprising fellows elected for their contributions to the field of management. The IAM is in large measure an educational organization whose main goal is to identify and objectively evaluate new hypotheses in the study and practice of business management.

THE ROLE OF MANAGEMENT ASSOCIATIONS AND SOCIETIES

As the above examples suggest, management associations, as distinct from university management institutes, exist primarily to advance their members' interests, or to advance a particular class or type of business manager. They can be active in the formulation of professional standards of ethics and practice, the development of national and international public policies pertaining to business and trade, business and management education, and the gathering and dissemination of information on the entire spectrum of business and management topics. They may also serve as certification bodies and sources of ethical and practice standards within a particular business management field. International management associations and societies all share one common function: facilitating the exchange of information among professionals from different countries. As such, they play a vital role in stimulating global trade, and promoting the advancement of business management as a profession.

SEE ALSO: Domestic Management Societies and Associations

Grant J. Eldridge
Revised by Bruce Walters

FURTHER READING:

All India Management Association. Available from <http://www.aima-ind.org>.

Australian Institute of Management. Available from <http://www.aim.com.au/about/about.html>.

"Corporate Governance Confab Set." *BusinessWorld,* 11 March 2005, 1.

International Association of Management. Available from <http://www.aom-iaom.org>.

Pina, Michael. "Helping Members Shine Overseas." *Association Management* 57, no. 3 (2005): 61.

Stimpson, Jeff. "Strengths of Associations, Networks and Alliances." *The Practical Accountant* 38, no. 2 (2005): 26–32.

Stone, Florence. "AMA Building Management Excellence for 80 Years." *MWorld,* Fall 2003.

Sugerman, Dale S. "Encouraging the "I" in ICMA." *Public Management* 87, no. 2 (2005): 34–36.

Wagner, R. "Contemporary Marketing Practices in Russia." *European Journal of Marketing* 39 (2005): 199–215.

INTERNATIONAL MONETARY FUND

The International Monetary Fund, widely known as the IMF, is an international cooperative institution headquartered in Washington, D.C., whose main mission is to promote and assist in international monetary stability. With its initial organization coming at the end of World War II, for many years the main goal of the IMF was to oversee a system of stable, fixed exchange rates among the currencies of member nations. Since 1971, the exchange rates of the world's currencies have been allowed to float, with supply and demand market forces determining their value. As of 2004 the IMF consisted of 184 member countries, which pay an initial quota subscription to become members. The organization works to achieve and enhance a stable world economy through the promotion of open financial disclosure among member nations, the provision of loans during periods of economic crises, and technical assistance provided through educational and promotional means.

The IMF has come under criticism from some sources for its role in high-profile assistance offered to the Mexican, South Korean, and Russian economies, among others. The member nations, however, continue to support the organization in its efforts to sustain international economic stability and promote international trade.

HISTORY

The events that ultimately led to the creation of the IMF had their origins in the conclusion of World War I. The economic terms of surrender were negotiated at the 1919 peace conference in Paris. As part of the peace treaty, known as the Treaty of Versailles, England and France demanded large amounts of war reparation payments from Austria and Germany to help rebuild their war-torn economies. However, the Austrian and German economies were depleted, too. This forced them to rely on foreign imports for goods and services unable to be produced locally. When a country imports more than it exports, it runs a balance of payments deficit. Together with other factors, the result may be a devaluation of the currency, since foreign sellers often demand to be repaid in their own currencies. The addition of war reparations on top of a large balance of payments deficit exacerbated the economic crisis, resulting in hyperinflation and political instability in Germany.

The great British economist John Maynard Keynes had participated in the peace conference following World War I and foresaw the scenario described above. Indeed, his book *The Economic Consequences of the Peace* predicted a second world war as an inevitable consequence of the severe penalties and lack of political and economic cooperation following the conclusion of World War I.

THE CREATION OF THE IMF

Keynes was determined to avoid repeating the mistakes made in the Treaty of Versailles. As World War II came to a close in 1944, an international conference was held at the resort community of Bretton Woods, New Hampshire. Forty-four nations were represented at the conference, with the chief negotiators being Keynes from Great Britain and Harry Dexter White from the United States. The result of their deliberations was the creation of the International Monetary Fund. The original goals of the fund were to aid members needing foreign exchange to conduct international trade and to promote a system of fixed exchange rates.

The original plan called for the U.S. dollar to be pegged to gold at a rate of $35 per ounce. Other currencies were set at fixed exchange rates to the dollar, and thus indirectly tied to gold. Countries participating agreed to set a "par" value for their currency based on this fixed exchange rate, allowing for a 1 percent fluctuation band. Should a country experience problems maintaining its par value, the IMF stood ready to lend foreign exchange to aid the cause. Member nations made an initial deposit into the fund known as a quota subscription. These deposits formed a pool from which the IMF could extend loans to members. As a special provision, if a member nation experienced chronic problems maintaining its par value, it would be allowed a one-time devaluation of its currency of up to 10 percent.

SPECIAL DRAWING RIGHTS

In 1969 the IMF created a new hybrid asset to serve as a reserve currency. The new financial asset was named a special drawing right, or SDR. The value of an SDR is a function of the current value of five different currencies from which it is comprised. They include the U.S. dollar, the Japanese yen, the United Kingdom pound sterling, and the respective euro values of Germany and France. The respective weights of the currencies, which constitute SDRs value, are revised every five years.

Member nations may use SDRs in a variety of ways. These include exchanging SDRs for other monetary assets or for maintaining operations, and exchanging SDRs directly with other members in exchange for foreign currencies to address a balance of payments problem. Since part of the mission of the IMF is to promote and enhance international trade, the board of governors has the option to decide on periodic special allocations of SDRs to augment members' existing reserve accounts.

THE IMF AND THE WORLD BANK

In addition to the IMF, the Bretton Woods Agreement resulted in the formation of the World Bank. Formally known as the International Bank for Reconstruction and Development, the World Bank's primary goal is to promote economic growth among the world's developing nations. It does so by effectively serving an investment-banking role, issuing bonds and notes to raise new investment capital, which it in turn lends to poor nations to finance specific projects. Typical projects include those associated with enhanced transportation routes, electric power development, and increased agricultural production.

As they share the ancestry of the Bretton Woods conference plus related economic roles, confusion between the IMF and the World Bank is common among the general public. They remain, however, two distinct organizations with their own individual goals and agendas aimed at promoting economic health and development among the world's nations.

THE END OF BRETTON WOODS

The system of fixed exchange rates created by the Bretton Woods Agreement and overseen by the IMF lasted from 1946 until 1971. For much of that period, the system worked very well. The U.S. dollar was pegged to gold and most other currencies were pegged to the dollar. During much of this period the United States ran a trade surplus, exporting more goods and services than it imported. Thus, the amount of U.S. dollars held domestically on net increased, causing little strain on the international monetary system.

This scenario changed during the 1960s. As the United States expanded its level of imports and increased industrial output during the Vietnam War, the amount of dollars held overseas expanded greatly. These dollars were deposited in foreign banks, allowing the banks to extend U.S. dollar denominated loans. The supply of U.S. dollars outstanding expanded significantly. At the same time, as more dollars were presented for redemption, the U.S. gold supply was being depleted. By the end of the decade, there were more dollars outstanding than there was gold to back them. In August 1971 the Nixon administration acknowledged the situation by closing the gold window, refusing to allow foreign central banks to exchange U.S. dollars for gold.

The Smithsonian Agreement of that year began the process of ending the Bretton Woods system of fixed foreign exchange rates. The initial agreement called for expanded fluctuation of exchange rates from 1 percent to 2.25 percent; subsequent economic activity made these bands unfeasible. Governments then decided to let their respective currencies float relative to each other, and the world moved to a floating exchange rate system.

THE ROLE OF THE IMF EVOLVES

In 1978, the IMF formally amended its constitution to alter its role in the world economy. It now plays a number of roles in its overall mission of promoting international stability and growth. These roles fall generally under three areas: surveillance, technical assistance, and financial assistance.

In its surveillance function, the IMF serves as a watchdog over member nations' economic policies. Each nation consults with IMF staffers on a regular basis regarding current and potential policy changes that may affect both the domestic economy and that of other nations. In this role, the IMF attempts to promote coordination and transparency in international economic policy, with the belief that open communication and mutual consideration of new policy initiatives will result on net in more robust international stability and trade.

Technical assistance to member nations takes up a large amount of daily operations at the fund. With a staff of approximately 2,700 experts from 140 countries, including many economists and statisticians, the IMF provides expertise and consultation on matters involving the implementation of both fiscal and monetary policy, trade laws and tariff measures, and programs aimed at strengthening and stabilizing local currency values. The technical staff produces numerous articles and publications designed to inform and educate policymakers on international economic affairs. Included are statistical compilations on trade, capital flows, employment, and other economic data. The technical area extends to educational training sessions, which are provided both at the IMF and jointly with other economic institutes throughout the world.

Perhaps the one area that has brought the IMF the most attention and raised its image among the general public has been its role of providing financial assistance to nations experiencing economic crises. This involves providing credits or arranging loans for nations experiencing such problems as severe balance of payments deficits or a sudden devaluation of their currency.

The 1990s saw the IMF make global headlines with several widely publicized financial assistance programs. The first occurred in 1995 with the crisis in Mexico. Faced with a severe devaluation of its currency due to a rapid loss of confidence in its policies, the Mexican government turned to the IMF for what was then a record $17.8 billion financial assistance package. While attempting to move towards a market-oriented economy, Russia required financial assistance several times during the 1990s. Included were large loans in both 1996 and 1998. And, in 1997, an extended crisis throughout much of east Asia resulted in the IMF arranging financial assistance for South Korea, Indonesia, and Thailand.

These financial assistance programs, which have grown successively larger in amount, have met with severe criticism from some sources. The IMF has been labeled a "bailout" source for poorly run economies, serving as a safety net for policymakers unable or unwilling to make difficult decisions which market discipline demanded. In addition, critics claim that IMF policies encourage poor nations to carry huge amounts of international debt, forcing them to use a large proportion of their annual revenues to make interest payments. The IMF has responded to its critics by actively working with both the public and private sectors to promote better information flow and legislation designed to prevent additional financial crises from taking place. The organization continues to develop systems and procedures designed to limit such crises from spreading to other countries and enveloping entire geographical regions.

The modern International Monetary Fund remains a major player on the global economic stage. The fund continues to grow and expand in its new roles within a world of floating exchange rates and rapid capital flows. The modern IMF wears a number of hats, including overseer and communicator of national policies and legislation, consultant and educator on numerous fiscal and monetary issues, and intermediary and lender for nations whose currencies come under pressure.

Critics continue to denounce the IMF for forcing nations in need to adopt its policy recommendations as a condition of assistance. In addition, the fund raises concerns among those who claim it acts as a safety net to alleviate poor or ineffective domestic monetary and trade policies. The IMF is also frequently charged with favoring bankers and elite classes, obstructing debt reduction for the world's poorest countries, and ignoring human rights violations. "Street protesters have it exactly right, for example, when they argue that the economic policies imposed on developing nations by the International Monetary Fund and World Bank have hammered the poor," Eric Pooley wrote in Time. "Using loans and the threat of default as levers, the IMF has pushed more than 90 countries to accept its brand of free-market shock therapy: lowering trade barriers, raising interest rates, devaluating currencies, privatizing state-owned industries, eliminating subsidies and cutting health, education, and welfare spending." While such programs attract foreign investment and stimulate the economy, they also tend to increase the cost of living and hurt small, local businesses.

Such criticisms are not likely to dissipate soon. Nevertheless, the 184 member nations continue to support the IMF in the belief that open communication and coordinated policies will lead to greater stability and promote a climate which fosters growth in international trade and development.

Howard Finch
Revised by Laurie Hillstrom

FURTHER READING:

International Monetary Fund. "Common Criticisms of the IMF." Available from <http://www.imf.org/external/np/exr/ccrit/eng/cri.htm>.

International Monetary Fund. "The IMF at a Glance." Available from <http://www.imf.org/external/np/exr/facts/glance.htm>.

Pooley, Eric. "The IMF: Dr. Death? A Case Study of How the Global Banker's Shock Therapy Helps Economies but Hammers the Poor." *Time,* 24 April 2000.

INTERNATIONAL ORGANIZATION FOR STANDARDIZATION

The International Organization for Standardization (ISO) is a non-governmental organization based in Geneva, Switzerland, that works to develop technical standards for products and services sold around the world. The steady rise in international trade that began in the mid-19th century and has persisted until the present day provided impetus for the global standardization of goods and services. Companies with overseas operations must know that products or services they contract for outside their home country will conform to their needs, and the only way to ensure this is for both parties in the transaction to meet a single set of standards. Thus, as economic interdependence increased among nations on all continents, the need for an authoritative international standards body became increasingly apparent. To address this need, the International Organization for Standardization (ISO) was founded in 1947.

The ISO comprises national standards bodies representing 148 countries and serves a variety of functions. It facilitates communication and cooperation among its members, eases the distribution of scientific and technical information on standards and standardization, operates over 2,850 technical groups devoted to standards and other commercial and industrial research, and maintains online databases covering international standards and other organizational activities. The ISO also seeks to ensure that standards are not used as a nontariff barrier to international trade by formulating international standards applicable to the full scope of commercial activity in any locale worldwide.

Although the majority of standards promulgated by the ISO are the result of the internal activities of its technical committees and working groups, ISO standards are not necessarily handed down to companies from the central organization. Companies often send their own internal standards to the ISO for consideration as international standards. Similarly, national standards organizations work with the ISO to make accepted national standards internationally applicable.

Adherence to standards formulated by ISO is completely voluntary, but companies that do conform to them have a distinct advantage over those that do not, particularly when trading overseas. ISO standards cover the entire spectrum of scientific, industrial, and commercial activities, including computer operating systems, manufacturing processes, product quality, safety, management technique, and environmental protection. In addition to its specific quality standards, the ISO has issued two sets of general standards, ISO 9000 and ISO 14000, to govern manufacturing and organizational processes and environmental protection, respectively.

THE ISO 9000 QUALITY STANDARDS SERIES

Released in 1987 and updated in 2000, the ISO 9000:2000 standards series governs general international quality assurance for products and services. It is divided into five specific areas. ISO 9000 is an overview, which includes guidelines for the selection, and use of quality management and quality assurance standards, provides definitions of quality concepts, and serves as a guide for the selection of ISO quality models applicable to specific industries. ISO 9001 provides a model for quality assurance in design and development, production, installation, and services. ISO 9002 provides a model for quality assurance in production and installation. ISO 9003 provides a model for quality assurance in final inspection and testing of products. Finally, ISO 9004 sets forth guidelines for developing and implementing internal corporate quality management programs and quality systems.

Each facet of the ISO 9000 standards series is general and can be applied to any industrial activity. In fact, the series' lack of specificity has led critics to note that two companies complying with ISO 9000 could conceivably produce goods that were radically different in terms of quality. The U.S. Department of Defense holds this view, stating that the ISO 9000 standards "are not adequate for use without significant supplementation." Despite these limitations, many corporations worldwide choose to adhere to the ISO 9000 standards. Under the General Agreement on Tariffs and Trade (GATT) companies may demand that their suppliers or other trading partners achieve ISO 9000 certification, and this demand will not be considered an illegal restraint of trade under GATT. Regardless of corporate opinions regarding ISO 9000, many countries are mandating that the foreign companies with which they trade achieve certification. For example, overseas producers of computer switches and pacemakers must be certified under ISO 9000 to

trade with the European Union, as must computer software producers wishing to sell their goods in Japan.

Companies wishing to attain ISO 9000 certification must first register with the ISO. Prior to registration, a third-party registrar must be found to audit and evaluate the company's operations and recommend changes that must be made to ensure conformation. Prior to this audit, companies must prepare a quality assurance program; define, document, and implement new procedures; and compile a corporate quality manual and preassess the manual with the selected auditor. Many adherents to the ISO 9000 standards have found that several components are necessary to ensure certification. First, companies must carefully evaluate their trading relationships to determine whether adherence to the ISO 9000 standards will result in increased profitability. If this is judged to be the case, management must be completely committed to achieving certification and a competent registrar must be secured. Staff must be carefully educated regarding the changes in processes and products required for conformation, and a core cadre of employees must be trained to constantly audit procedures following certification and conduct the periodic audits required to ensure that standards are being maintained.

In its early years, the ISO 9000 series of standards was not adopted as readily as had been anticipated, but by the early 1990s the standards were beginning to receive more widespread use. The U.S. Commerce Department finally endorsed global acceptance of ISO 9000 in 1994, and the formation of the International Accreditation Forum during the same year also provided an impetus to ISO 9000 certification. By 2005 more than half a million organizations in over 60 countries had either implemented or were in the process of implementing the quality management framework outlined in ISO 9000. QS-90000, a separate series of standards for the many automotive industry suppliers and has be updated an recently replaced by ISO/TS 16949:2002.

Although the ISO 9000 series eventually caught on and began to fulfill its role in regulating international industrial, commercial, and management activity, even its staunchest adherents found that the series did not account for environmental protection. This oversight allowed too much latitude for differences in process between companies in different countries, particularly those in the chemical industries. The Global Environmental Initiative held in Rio de Janeiro, Brazil, in 1992 further established the need for an internationally recognized set of standards governing industrial and commercial environmental protection policies and processes. In response to this need, ISO began work on a new series of standards designed to govern environmental protection.

THE ISO 14000 SERIES OF STANDARDS

Released in 1996, the ISO 14000 series of standards is designed to supplement the ISO 9000 series, and adherence to ISO 14000 assures customers that a company has sound environmental protection policies and processes. ISO 14000 is divided into ten separate areas of standardization:

1. ISO 14001 provides a model framework for the establishment of an environmental management system.

2. ISO 14004 offers a checklist for companies wishing to implement ISO 14001, and is not mandatory for ISO 14000 certification.

3. ISO 14010 is also voluntary and establishes guidelines for corporate environmental auditing procedures, including definition of quality audit evidence.

4. ISO 14011 provides guidance for the voluntary formation of corporate environmental auditing procedures, including a general outline of an effective environmental audit.

5. ISO 14012 delineates qualification criteria for environmental auditors.

6. ISO 14020 establishes standards for scientific evidence presented in corporate environmental management audits

7. ISO 14021 allows companies to self-declare environmental claims under certain circumstances.

8. ISO 14024 provides guidelines for verifying corporate environmental management claims and delineates the criteria which must be met for companies to use ISO-recognized labels advertising their compliance with ISO 14000 environmental standards.

9. ISO 14031 establishes standards for corporate review of existing environmental management systems.

10. ISO 14040 provides guidelines and criteria for long-range environmental assessments, which are required to determine whether or not certain commercial activities can be considered environmentally sustainable.

Although the ISO 9000 standards are currently viewed favorably in the corporate world, ISO 14000 has proven more controversial. ISO 14000 does not stipulate standards of corporate environmental performance, but rather governs only the means a company must employ to make its production activities environmentally sustainable. National standards for compliance with ISO 14000 also differ widely, as the third-party audits required to attain certification are conducted differently in different countries, and with differing criteria for compliance. Finally, while the GATT agreements allow companies to stop doing business with trading partners that fail to achieve ISO 9000 certification, refusing to do business with a company that failed to achieve ISO 14000 certification could be considered an illegal restraint of trade under the GATT provisions. Companies based in the United States have been particularly unwilling to secure ISO 14000 certification, given the amount of time, money, and effort they already expend in meeting the standards of environmental performance and practice set by the federal Environmental Protection Agency (EPA). In fact, U.S. and Canadian steelmakers went on record in 1996 against ISO 14000 compliance, stating that complying with ISO 9000 should become the sole recognized method for international standardization and that adding a new series of standards would create "standards gridlock."

Although widespread corporate compliance with ISO 14000 did not occur in the series' initial years, increased awareness of environmental concerns among both government agencies and the public worldwide will provide an impetus for ISO 14000 certification in the future. For instance, the rigorous Eco-Management and Audit Scheme (EMAS) promulgated by the European Union in 1992 has proven difficult for many companies to implement, yet compliance with EMAS may become essential for firms wishing to trade in Europe. Compliance with ISO 14000 standards will automatically make a company also eligible for EMAS certification. Similarly, compliance with ISO 14000 will provide a powerful marketing tool for companies wishing to sell products to environmentally conscious consumers. Compliance with ISO 14000 also provides legal evidence of due diligence, which would mitigate in favor of any ISO 14000-certified company which was sued for creating environmental damage or hazards. Finally, ISO 14000 certification removes barriers to international trade in the same manner as does ISO 9000 compliance.

THE FUTURE

Since its founding in 1947, the ISO has published more than 13,700 international standards, covering everything from dimensions of freight containers to symbols that provide danger warnings. ISO has addressed the standardization of protocols to allow different types of computers to communicate with one another, as well as the standardization of interfaces and connections to ensure the interoperability of various technologies. Although the majority of ISO standards are specific to individual products, materials, or processes, the ISO 9000 and 14000 series provide generic management system standards that can be applied to any product or service, by any type of organization.

ISO standards are not without their critics in the business world. Critics claim that the standards can be costly and time-consuming to implement, for example. But proponents point out that ISO certification enables businesses to increase knowledge of their capabilities, improve their processes and performance, ensure consumer and stockholder confidence, and gain a source of competitive advantage. As a result, the ISO seems likely to play an increasingly important role in international trade in the future. The general lowering of tariff barriers worldwide in recent years has led to a contradictory rise in the use of standards to exclude products of certain countries or regions, a practice which global adoption of ISO standards would eradicate. Furthermore, in the case of the ISO 14000 series, increased public environmental consciousness will provide a powerful incentive for corporate compliance and in the long run will also result in the passage of public policies mandating environmental sustainability such as the EMAS.

Grant J. Eldridge
Revised by Laurie Collier Hillstrom

FURTHER READING:

Babicz, Gillian. "Implementing ISO Isn't Easy." *Quality,* July 2000.

Hasek, Glenn. "ISO's Green Standard Takes Root." *Industry Week,* 16 February 1998.

International Organization for Standardization. "ISO: Introduction." Available from <http://www.iso.org/iso/en/aboutiso/introduction>.

Lally, Amy Pesapane. "ISO 14000 and Environmental Cost Accounting." *Law and Policy in International Business,* Summer 1998.

McLoughlin, Bill. "Just What Is ISO?" *HFN,* 20 October 1997.

Petry, Corinna C. "U.S. Seen Ill Prepared for Global Standards." *American Metal Market,* 3 April 1997.

Showalter, Kathy. "Trading in Green." *Business First-Columbus,* 21 February 1997.

Spearin, John. "An ISO Primer." *Detroiter,* December 2002.

THE INTERNET

The Internet is the world's largest computer network. It is a global information infrastructure comprised of millions of computers organized into hundreds of thousands of smaller, local networks. The term "information superhighway" is sometimes used to describe the function that the Internet provides: an international, high-speed telecommunications network that offers open access to the general public.

The Internet provides a variety of services, including electronic mail (e-mail), the World Wide Web (WWW), Intranets, File Transfer Protocol (FTP), Telnet (for remote login to host computers), and various file-location services.

E-MAIL

Electronic mail, or e-mail, is the most widely used function used on the Internet today. Millions of messages are passed via Internet lines every day throughout the world. Compared to postal service, overnight delivery companies, and telephone conversations, e-mail via the Internet is extremely cost-effective and fast. E-mail facilities include sending and receiving messages, the ability to broadcast messages to several recipients at once, storing and organizing messages, forwarding messages to other interested parties, maintaining address books of e-mail partners, and even transmitting files (called "attachments") along with messages.

Internet e-mail messages are sent to an e-mail address. The structure of an e-mail address is as follows: PersonalID@DomainName

The personal identifier could be a person's name or some other way to uniquely identify an individual. The domain is an indicator of the location of that individual, and appears to the right of the "at" (@) sign. A domain name is the unique name of a collection of computers that are connected to the Internet, usually owned by or operated on the behalf of a single organization (company, school, or agency) that owns the domain name. The domain name consists of two or more sections, each separated by a period.

From right-to-left, the portions of the domain name are more general to more specific in terms of location. In the United States, the rightmost portion of a domain is typically one of the following:

- com—indicating a commercial enterprise
- edu—indicating an educational institution
- gov—indicating a governmental body
- mil—indicating a military installation
- net—indicating a network resource
- org—indicating a nonprofit organization

In November of 2000 seven new domain names were created and made available: biz, .info, .name, .pro, .aero, .coop, and .museum.

In non-U.S. countries, the rightmost portion of a domain name is an indicator of the geographic origin of the domain. For example, Canadian e-mail addresses end with the abbreviation "ca."

SPAM. Commercial abuse of e-mail continues to be problematic as companies attempt to e-mail millions of online users in bulk. This technique is called "spam," so named after a skit by the comedy troupe Monty Python that involved the continuous repetition of the word. Online users are deluged with a massive amount of unwanted e-mail selling a wide array of products and services. Spam has become a network-wide problem as it impacts information transfer time and overall network load. Several organizations and governments are attempting to solve the spam problem through legislation or regulation.

VIRUSES. Computer viruses spread by e-mail have also grown as the Internet has grown. The widespread use of e-mail and the growing numbers of new, uninformed computer users has made it very easy to spread malicious viruses across the network. Security issues for both personal computers and for network servers will continue to be a crucial aspect of the ongoing development of the Internet and World Wide Web.

WORLD WIDE WEB

The World Wide Web (WWW) is a system and a set of standards for providing a graphic user interface (GUI) to Internet communications. The WWW is the single most important factor in the popularity of the Internet, because it makes the technology easy to use and gives attractive and entertaining presentation to users.

Graphics, text, audio, animation, and video can be combined on Web pages to create dynamic and highly interactive access to information. In addition, Web pages can be connected to each other via hyperlinks. These hyperlinks are visible to the user as highlighted text, underlined text, or images that the user can click to access another Web page.

BROWSERS. Web pages are available to users via Web browsers, such as Mozilla/Firefox, Netscape Navigator, or Microsoft's Internet Explorer. Browsers are programs that run on the user's computer and provide the interface that displays the graphics, text, and hyperlinks to the user. Browsers recognize and interpret the programming language called Hypertext Markup Language (HTML). HTML includes the ability to format and display text; size and position graphics images for display; invoke and present animation or video clips; and run small programs, called applets, for more complex interactive operations. Browsers also implement the hyperlinks and allow users to connect to any Web page they want.

SEARCH ENGINES. Sometimes a user knows what information she needs, but does not know the precise Web page that she wants to view. A subject-oriented search can be accomplished with the aid of search engines, which are tools that can locate Web pages based on a search criterion established by the user. Commonly used search engines include Google, Yahoo, Teoma, and Alta Vista.

BLOGS. The ease with which users can publish their own information using the World Wide Web has created an opportunity for everyone to be a publisher. An outcome from this is that every topic, hobby, niche, and fetish now has a thriving community of like-minded people. The ease of publishing information on the Web became easier with the advent of Web logs or "blogs," online diaries that opened the floodgates to an even greater level of individual participation in information sharing and community.

UNIFORM RESOURCE LOCATORS (URL)

A Uniform Resource Locator (URL) is a networked extension of the standard filename concept. It allows the user to point to a file in a directory on any machine on the Internet. In addition to files, URLs can point to queries, documents stored deep within databases, and many other entities. Primarily, however, URLs are used to identify and locate Web pages.

A URL is composed of three parts:

PROTOCOL. This is the first part of the address. In a Web address, the letters "http" stand for Hypertext Transfer Protocol, signifying how this request should be dealt with. The protocol information is followed by a colon. URL protocols usually take one of the following types:

- http—for accessing a Web page
- ftp—for transferring a file via FTP
- file—for locating a file on the client's own machine
- gopher—for locating a Gopher server
- mail—for submitting e-mail across the Internet
- news—for locating a Usenet newsgroup

RESOURCE NAME. This is the name of the server/machine at which the query should be directed. For an "http" request, the colon is followed by two forward slashes, and this indicates that the request should be sent to a machine.

PATH AND FILE NAME. The rest of a URL specifies the particular computer name, any directory tree information, and a file name, with the latter two pieces of information being optional for Web pages. The computer name is the domain name or a variation on it (on the Web, the domain is most commonly preceded by a machine prefix "www" to identify the computer that is functioning as the organization's Web server, as opposed to its e-mail server, etc.).

If a particular file isn't located at the top level of the directory structure (as organized and defined by whoever sets up the Web site), there may be one or more strings of text separated by slashes, representing the directory hierarchy.

Finally, the last string of text to the right of the rightmost slash is the individual file name; on the Web, this often ends with the extension "htm" or "html" to signify it's an HTML document. When no directory path or file name is specified (e.g., the URL http://www.domain.com), the browser is typically pointed automatically to an unnamed (at least from the user's perspective) default or index page, which often constitutes an organization's home or start page.

Thus, a full URL with a directory path and file name may look something like this:

http://www.mycompany.com/files/myfile.html

Lastly, a Web URL might also contain, somewhere to the right of the domain name, a long string of characters that does not correspond to a traditional directory path or file name, but rather is a set of commands or instructions to a server program or database application. The syntax of these URLs depends on the underlying software program being used. Sometimes these can function as reusable URLs (e.g., they can be bookmarked and retrieved repeatedly), but other times they must be generated by the site's server at the time of use, and thus can't be retrieved directly from a bookmark or by typing them in manually.

INTERNET SERVICE PROVIDERS

To gain access to the Internet a user typically subscribes to an Internet Service Provider (ISP). ISPs are companies that have permanent connection to the Internet. Subscribers to ISPs can connect to the ISP's server computer, and through that connection can gain access to the Internet. Some well-known commercial ISPs include America Online, MSN, and Earthlink, although there are hundreds of such services.

An alternative access to the Internet is provided via academic institutions (i.e. colleges or universities) and government agencies. Most students and faculty in colleges have accounts on the school's computer system, through which they can gain access to the Internet.

TRANSMISSION CONTROL PROTOCOL/ INTERNET PROTOCOL (IP)

The Internet is a network of computers, or more accurately, a vast network of networks. These networks are connected to each other via a high-speed backbone, a communication link that joins the major Internet host computers. These hosts are primarily mainframe computers at academic institutions. The communication along the Internet follows the Transmission Control Protocol (TCP)/Internet Protocol (IP) communications standard.

TCP is called a connection-based protocol, which enables two hosts to establish a direct connection and exchange streams of data. TCP guarantees delivery of data and also guarantees that packets of data will be delivered in the same order in which they were sent. In this regard, TCP acts like a telephone conversation.

IP is a connectionless protocol, acting something like the postal system. It allows you to address a data packet and drop it in the system, but there's no direct link between you and the recipient.

Each node (or computer) on the Internet is assigned a unique IP address. IP addresses are 32-bit numbers, normally written as 4 octets (in decimal), e.g., 128.8.4.5. These identify the particular network and host. IP addresses are numeric values. However, most users prefer symbolic names to identify the hosts they want to access. Thus, the Internet provides the Domain Name Service (DNS), which allows users to use symbolic names to locate Internet hosts.

INTRANETS

Internet technology has become extremely beneficial for businesses and other organizations as a cost-effective means of implementing their corporate-wide telecommunications needs. However, the public nature of the Internet poses a challenge to any company wishing to take advantage of its potential. The TCP/IP protocol does not provide adequate security for commercial institutions. It is relatively easy to eavesdrop on transmissions, and there is no inherent authentication mechanism. Thus, many companies adopt intranets, private networks based on Internet technology.

Intranets use the company's existing network infrastructure, together with the TCP/IP protocol, Web browsers, Web server technologies, and HTML-formatted Web pages. The key distinction between an intranet and the Internet is the use of a firewall, which is a security system with specialized software and/or hardware that can prevent unauthorized users from gaining access to the company's intranet server.

Intranets have many advantages over other corporate-wide network implementations. They are comparatively inexpensive to implement and easily allow different types of computers to communicate with each other, which overcomes a major obstacle to corporate-wide information sharing.

Most companies have a wide variety of computer platforms, including PCs, mainframes, and minicomputers, spread throughout the organization. Web technology and TCP/IP communications standards enable these diverse platforms to maintain a consistent user interface, thus reducing the amount of time it takes users to become proficient on the network.

Intranets are used for many business purposes, ranging from distribution of corporate documents to facilitating group collaboration via groupware and teleconferencing, to full-blown transaction-processing applications.

FILE TRANSFER PROTOCOL

The File Transfer Protocol (FTP) is a method of moving files between two Internet sites. Files can contain software, text, graphics, or other file formats.

Early Internet users developed FTP so researchers could copy files from one place to another across the Internet. Until 1995 and the popularization of the World Wide Web, FTP accounted for more traffic on the Internet than any other service. Nowadays, the bulk of traffic is done via the Web. However, even when downloading files via an Internet browser, FTP is the protocol involved. In this case, the URL begins with the protocol "ftp://" instead of "http://".

Although using FTP to transfer files from one system to another usually requires a user ID on both systems, many host systems provide anonymous FTP services. Anonymous FTP lets anyone in the world have access to a certain area of disk space on the host system and allows some files to be publicly available. Some systems have dedicated entire disks or even entire computers to maintaining extensive archives of source code and information. These sites are called anonymous FTP servers.

Once a user logs onto an FTP server, he or she can transfer data to or from that server using common FTP commands. The basic syntax for FTP commands is based on the UNIX operating system; however, many software products are available that provide graphic interfaces to FTP and thus simplify the file transfer process.

ARCHIE, GOPHER, AND VERONICA

As FTP sites proliferated over the Internet, it became necessary to create directories and indexes to allow Internet users to quickly locate desired information. Three commonly used tools exist for this purpose. An Archie is a database server that provides keyword search to locate relevant FTP files. Gophers, originally developed at the University of Minnesota, are menu-oriented directories to FTP files and sites. The menus are arranged in hierarchical structure based on topics, and are hyperlinked to FTP sites and even to other Gopher sites. Finally, a Veronica (Very Easy Rodent-Oriented Netwide Index) is a keyword-search tool that searches Gopher sites for relevant subject material.

Although these three tools are useful, their use has declined with the advent of the World Wide Web. One can think of the Archies, Gophers, and Veronicas of the world as being precursors to the modern search engines of the Web. In fact, Gophers are themselves accessible from the Web, and have their own URL protocol.

TELNET

Telnet is the Internet standard protocol for remote terminal connection, allowing a user at one site to interact with a remote timesharing system at another site as if the user's terminal were connected directly to the remote computer. A Telnet program is the terminal emulation software you use to log in to an Internet host; the host has similar Telnet software. Thus, via Telnet, your computer becomes a terminal connected to the host computer, and your interaction with that computer is the same as it would be if you were sitting at a terminal wired directly to that computer.

Telnet is a text-based connection protocol, providing only character-based communications capabilities with the host. Thus, Telnet has been greatly overshadowed by the Web, as there is limited content available by Telnet and it requires knowledge of various system commands. However, there are still many Telnet sites available. Most Internet browsers allow access to Telnet sites by specifying the Telnet protocol as the first part of a URL.

PEER-TO-PEER (P2P)

The peer-to-peer (P2P) protocol began to gain in popularity in the late 1990s and early 2000s. This protocol allows for the sharing of individual computer hard drives and storage devices. P2P spreads the network usage and downloading across all of the linked computers distributing the load more evenly. It also allows for a lack of accountability in serving and acquiring data. It has been extremely popular for downloading music, videos, and books.

The first and most well-known instance of P2P was Napster in 1999, a file sharing application for exchanging music files between users without regard to copyright restrictions or royalties. A significant amount of litigation took place between Napster and the Recording Industry Association of America to stop promoting copyright infringements. Napster eventually acquiesced to the legal actions; however P2P downloading continues to be a corporate issue.

USENET NEWSGROUPS

Usenet is an Internet news/discussion group forum that allows ongoing conversations on a given topic to occur over an extended period of time (weeks, months, and even years). These newsgroups are organized in a bulletin board framework, so that any Internet user can read or post messages to any topic area. Although Usenet newsgroups existed long before the WWW, they are still in wide use and accessible from the Web via their own URL protocol.

HISTORY OF THE INTERNET

The idea for the Internet began in the early 1960s as a military network developed by the U.S. Department of Defense's Advanced Research Project Agency (ARPA). At first, it was a small network called ARPANET, which promoted the sharing of super-computers amongst military researchers in the United States. A few years later, ARPA began to sponsor research into a cooperative network of academic time-sharing computers. By 1969, the first ARPANET hosts were constructed at Stanford Research Institute, University of California Los Angeles (UCLA), University of California Santa Barbara, and the University of Utah.

In the early 1970s, use of ARPANET expanded dramatically. Although it was originally designed to allow scientists to share data and access remote computers, e-mail quickly became ARPANET's most popular application, as researchers across the country used it for collaborating on research projects and discussing topics of interests.

In 1972, the InterNetworking Working Group (INWG) was established as the first standards-setting organization to govern the growing network. Under the leadership of Vinton Cerf, known as the "father of the Internet," INWG began to address the need for establishing agreed-upon protocols and enforce standardization in ARPANET functionality. Two early protocols, Telnet and FTP, are still in use today.

By 1973, ARPANET crossed national boundaries, establishing connections to University College in London, England, and the Royal Radar Establishment in Norway. In 1974, a commercial version of ARPANET, called Telenet, was developed by Bolt, Beranek, and Newman, Inc. (BBN), one of the original ARPA contractors that had helped get ARPANET running. It began a move away from the military/research roots of the original ARPANET.

In 1979, faculty members and graduate students at Duke University and the University of North Carolina created the first Usenet newsgroups, enabling users from all over the world join discussion groups on a myriad of subjects including politics, religion, computing, and even less-than-savory topics. Usenet influenced a continuing wave of growth.

Between 1981 and 1988, ARPANET grew from around 200 hosts to more than 60,000. Many factors influenced this explosive growth. First was the boom in the personal computer industry. With more people using inexpensive desktop machines, and with the advent of powerful, network-ready servers, many companies began to join this vast computer network for the first time, using it to communicate with each other and with their customers.

A second factor in growth was the National Science Foundation's NSFNET, built in 1986 for the purpose of connecting university computer science departments. NSFNET combined with ARPANET to form a huge backbone of network hosts. This backbone became what we now think of as the Internet (although the term "Internet" was used as early as 1982).

The third factor in growth was the concept of internetworking, which began to appear in popular culture in the 1980s. William Gibson's 1984 novel *Neuromancer* coined the ubiquitous term "cyberspace" to describe the new virtual communities, cultures, and geographies that the Internet provides.

The explosive growth of the Internet came with major problems, particularly related to privacy and security in the digital world. Computer crime and malicious destruction became a paramount concern. One dramatic incident occurred in 1988 when a program called the "Morris worm" temporarily disabled approximately 10 percent of all Internet hosts across the country. The Computer Emergency Response Team (CERT) was formed in 1988 to address such security concerns.

In 1990, as the number of hosts approached 300,000, the ARPANET was decommissioned, leaving only the Internet with NSFNET as its sole backbone. The 1990s saw the commercialization of the Internet, made possible when the NSF lifted its restriction on commercial use and cleared the way for the age of electronic commerce.

Electronic commerce was further enhanced by new applications being introduced to the Internet. For example, programmers at the University of Minnesota developed the first point-and-click method of navigating the Internet files in 1991. This program, which was freely distributed on the Internet, was called Gopher, and gave rise to similar applications such as Archie and Veronica.

An even more influential development, also started in the early 1990s, was Tim Berners-Lee's work on the World Wide Web, in which hypertext-formatted pages of words, pictures, and sounds promised to become an advertiser's dream come true. At the same time, Marc Andreessen and colleagues at the National Center for Supercomputing Applications (NCSA), located on the campus of University of Illinois at Urbana-Champaign, were developing a graphical browser for the World Wide Web called Mosaic (released in 1993), which would eventually evolve into Netscape.

By 1995, the Internet had become so commercialized that most access to the Internet was handled through Internet service providers (ISPs), such as America Online and Netcom. At that time, NSF relinquished control of the Internet, which was now dominated by WWW traffic.

Partly motivated by the increased commercial interest in the Internet, Sun Microsystems released an Internet programming language called Java, which promised to radically alter the way applications and information can be retrieved, displayed, and used over the Internet.

By 1996, the Internet's twenty-fifth anniversary, there were 40 million Internet users, and Internet-based electronic commerce had reached major proportions, with more than $1 billion in Internet shopping mall transactions.

DIRECTION OF THE INTERNET

The Internet is now truly global, with 150 countries connected. In less than 30 years, the Internet migrated from an American military information management tool to an information superhighway serving the entire world.

The Internet revolutionized late twentieth and early twenty-first century society as dramatically as the railroads and the Industrial Revolution of the nineteenth century. Telecommuting, e-commerce, blogs, and virtual communities have broken geographic boundaries and brought people closer together.

At the same time, the internet has introduced significant social challenges. There is a danger of creating a second-class citizenship among those without access. Privacy and security are a continuing concern. The workplace is drastically altering society as the information age makes industrial-era skills obsolete. The twenty-first century will be strongly influenced by the dispersion of information technology, and the Internet promises to be the conduit of this technology.

SEE ALSO: Computer Networks; Computer Security; Electronic Commerce; Electronic Data Interchange and Electronic Funds Transfer; Electronic Data Interchange and Electronic Funds Transfer

Michel Mitri
Revised by Hal P. Kirkwood, Jr.

FURTHER READING:

Berners-Lee, Tim. *Weaving the Web: The Original Design and Ultimate Destiny of the World Wide Web.* New York, NY: HarperBusiness, 2000.

Grauer, Robert, and Gretchen Marx. *Essentials of the Internet.* Upper Saddle River, NJ: Prentice Hall, 1997.

Hafner, Katie. *Where Wizards Stay Up Late: The Origin of the Internet.* New York, NY: Simon & Schuster, 1998.

Kalakota, Ravi, and Andrew B. Whinston. *Electronic Commerce: A Manager's Guide.* Reading, MA: Addison-Wesley, 1996.

INTRAPRENEURSHIP

Intrapreneurship describes the process of developing new products, services, and lines of business within an existing company. It is perhaps best understood as a form of internal entrepreneurship that takes place with the encouragement and support of management. An employee who takes responsibility for developing an innovative idea into a marketable product is known as an intrapreneur. Management consultants Gifford and Elizabeth Pinchot coined the term in 1976 and helped popularize the concept of intra-corporate entrepreneurship in their pioneering book *Intrapreneuring: Why You Don't Have to Leave the Corporation to Become an Entrepreneur* (1985).

The Pinchots and other experts recognized that entrepreneurial ventures often lost their innovative edge as they grew into established companies. In order to help organizations remain creative and competitive as they grew, the consultants came up with guidelines and models to foster this entrepreneurial spirit among employees. "There are many advantages in working with intrapreneurs in any organization. Given the business environment in this day, any organization needs people who can bring in new ideas and see them through," Emily Hwengere wrote in the Financial Gazette. "Without intrapreneurs who can identify and exploit new opportunities, organizations will naturally die." One of the most commonly cited intrapreneurship success stories is 3M Corporation, which has a policy that allows employees to spend 15 percent of their working hours developing their own business or product ideas. This policy led to the creation of Post-It-Notes and other successful products by 3M employees.

Experts recommend that business organizations create a culture that provides employees with both freedom and encouragement to develop new ideas. They emphasize that support for intrapreneurship must start with top executives and work its way down in the form of policies, programs, and reward systems. "The real challenge for any company trying to unleash new businesses is that people have to believe that this is not an unnatural act," Gary Hamel explained in Inc. "This is what's going to have to happen in companies-bringing ideas, capital, and talent together from all across the corporate entities. Companies have to learn how to leverage the competencies and the assets that they already have within." Some companies foster intrapreneurship by encouraging employees to form competing teams that function like small businesses or internal vendors. Other companies create formal innovation programs to ensure that every new idea receives a fair hearing. In some companies, upper management behaves like a venture capital firm, evaluating and providing financial support for promising new ideas.

Employees who succeed as intrapreneurs tend to possess many of the same talents and traits as traditional entrepreneurs as well as a commitment to the organization and its goals. Working within an existing company—rather than launching an independent start-up business—offers a number of advantages to such individuals. Access to the company's resources increases their chances of success, for example, while maintaining a salaried position provides them with added security in case of failure. Intrapreneurs also gain experience that they can apply to future entrepreneurial ventures, as well as a stimulating work environment. In this way, supporting intrapreneurship can help companies retain valuable employees. "One of the most wonderful things organizations have going for them is that people already have an intrinsic desire to go beyond-to learn, to grow, and to aspire to possibilities within themselves," according to Jacqueline Byrd and Paul Lockwood Brown, authors of *The Innovation Equation.*

Numerous books, articles, Web sites, and workshops exist to provide advice for companies and employees hoping to take advantage of the opportunities presented by intrapreneurship. In general, such sources recommend that intrapreneurs be willing to take risks, find an internal champion from senior management, negotiate measures of success for their project, ensure that the project is given adequate time to succeed, and select fellow employees who can contribute needed skills. Some of the major factors that inhibit intrapreneurship include resistance to change in organizations, a corporate bureaucracy that slows down project approval, a refusal to allocate resources to new ideas, a lack of training and support for employees, low rewards for success coupled with high costs of failure, and performance evaluation based solely on job descriptions. "When you set up a new unit, be careful that you steer a line between two paths," Hamel explained. "Totally isolating it, which is fine if it isn't at all related to what you're doing, and giving it a bear hug, where you hold on to it so tight that it can never escape the gravitational pull of old beliefs."

SEE ALSO: Creativity; Entrepreneurship

Laurie Hillstrom

FURTHER READING:

Byrd, Jacqueline, and Paul Lockwood Brown. *The Innovation Equation: Building Creativity and Risk-Taking in Your Organization.* Pfeiffer, 2002.

Fattal, Tony. "Intrapreneurship at Work: Championing Projects to Push Innovation in Your Company." *CMA Management,* November 2003.

Hwengere, Emily. "Factors that Inhibit Intrapreneurship." *Financial Gazette,* 30 May 2002.

"Intrapreneurship: Spinning Off a New Company." *Inc.,* September 2000. Available from <http://pf.inc.com/articles/2000/09/20222.html>.

King, Carla. "Intrapreneurship: Heady Business." Sun Microsystems. Available from <http://developers.sun.com/toolkits/articles/intrapreneur.html>.

Pinchot, Gifford, and Ron Pellman. *Intrapreneuring in Action.* Berrett-Kohler, 2000.

"Small Business Notes: Intrapreneurship." SmallBusinessNotes.com. Available from <http://www.smallbusinessnotes.com/choosing/intrapreneurship.html>.

INVENTORY MANAGEMENT

Inventory management, or inventory control, is an attempt to balance inventory needs and requirements with the need to minimize costs resulting from obtaining and holding inventory. There are several schools of thought that view inventory and its function differently. These will be addressed later, but first we present a foundation to facilitate the reader's understanding of inventory and its function.

WHAT IS INVENTORY?

Inventory is a quantity or store of goods that is held for some purpose or use (the term may also be used as a verb, meaning to take inventory or to count all goods held in inventory). Inventory may be kept "in-house," meaning on the premises or nearby for immediate use; or it may be held in a distant warehouse or distribution center for future use. With the exception of firms utilizing just-in-time methods, more often than not, the term "inventory" implies a stored quantity of goods that exceeds what is needed for the firm to function at the current time (e.g., within the next few hours).

WHY KEEP INVENTORY?

Why would a firm hold more inventory than is currently necessary to ensure the firm's operation? The following is a list of reasons for maintaining what would appear to be "excess" inventory.

Table 1

	January	February	March	April	May	June
Demand	50	50	0	100	200	200
Produce	100	100	100	100	100	100
Month-end inventory	50	100	200	200	100	0

MEET DEMAND. In order for a retailer to stay in business, it must have the products that the customer wants on hand when the customer wants them. If not, the retailer will have to back-order the product. If the customer can get the good from some other source, he or she may choose to do so rather than electing to allow the original retailer to meet demand later (through back-order). Hence, in many instances, if a good is not in inventory, a sale is lost forever.

KEEP OPERATIONS RUNNING. A manufacturer must have certain purchased items (raw materials, components, or subassemblies) in order to manufacture its product. Running out of only one item can prevent a manufacturer from completing the production of its finished goods.

Inventory between successive dependent operations also serves to decouple the dependency of the operations. A machine or workcenter is often dependent upon the previous operation to provide it with parts to work on. If work ceases at a workcenter, then all subsequent centers will shut down for lack of work. If a supply of work-in-process inventory is kept between each workcenter, then each machine can maintain its operations for a limited time, hopefully until operations resume the original center.

LEAD TIME. Lead time is the time that elapses between the placing of an order (either a purchase order or a production order issued to the shop or the factory floor) and actually receiving the goods ordered.

If a supplier (an external firm or an internal department or plant) cannot supply the required goods on demand, then the client firm must keep an inventory of the needed goods. The longer the lead time, the larger the quantity of goods the firm must carry in inventory.

A just-in-time (JIT) manufacturing firm, such as Nissan in Smyrna, Tennessee, can maintain extremely low levels of inventory. Nissan takes delivery on truck seats as many as 18 times per day. However, steel mills may have a lead time of up to three months. That means that a firm that uses steel produced at the mill must place orders at least three months in advance of their need. In order to keep their operations running in the meantime, an on-hand inventory of three months' steel requirements would be necessary.

HEDGE. Inventory can also be used as a hedge against price increases and inflation. Salesmen routinely call purchasing agents shortly before a price increase goes into effect. This gives the buyer a chance to purchase material, in excess of current need, at a price that is lower than it would be if the buyer waited until after the price increase occurs.

QUANTITY DISCOUNT. Often firms are given a price discount when purchasing large quantities of a good. This also frequently results in inventory in excess of what is currently needed to meet demand. However, if the discount is sufficient to offset the extra holding cost incurred as a result of the excess inventory, the decision to buy the large quantity is justified.

SMOOTHING REQUIREMENTS. Sometimes inventory is used to smooth demand requirements in a market where demand is somewhat erratic. Consider the demand forecast and production schedule outlined in Table 1.

Notice how the use of inventory has allowed the firm to maintain a steady rate of output (thus avoiding the cost of hiring and training new personnel), while building up inventory in anticipation of an increase in demand. In fact, this is often called anticipation inventory. In essence, the use of inventory has allowed the firm to move demand requirements to earlier periods, thus smoothing the demand.

CONTROLLING INVENTORY

Firms that carry hundreds or even thousands of different part numbers can be faced with the impossible task of monitoring the inventory levels of each part number. In order to facilitate this, many firm's use an ABC approach. ABC analysis is based on Pareto Analysis, also known as the "80/20" rule. The 80/20 comes from Pareto's finding that 20 percent of the populace possessed 80 percent of the wealth. From an inventory perspective it can restated thusly: approximately 20 percent of all inventory items represent 80 percent of inventory costs. Therefore, a firm can control 80 percent of its inventory costs by monitoring and controlling 20 percent of its inventory. But, it has to be the correct 20 percent.

The top 20 percent of the firm's most costly items are termed "A" items (this should approximately represent 80 percent of total inventory costs). Items that are extremely inexpensive or have low demand are termed "C" items, with "B" items falling in between A and C items. The percentages may vary with each firm, but B items usually represent about 30 percent of the total inventory items and 15 percent of the costs. C items generally constitute 50 percent of all inventory items but only around 5 percent of the costs.

By classifying each inventory item as an A, B or C the firm can determine the resources (time, effort and money) to dedicate to each item. Usually this means that the firm monitors A items very closely but can check on B and C items on a periodic basis (for example, monthly for B items and quarterly for C items).

Another control method related to the ABC concept is cycle counting. Cycle counting is used instead of the traditional "once-a-year" inventory count where firms shut down for a short period of time and physically count all inventory assets in an attempt to reconcile any possible discrepancies in their inventory records. When cycle counting is used the firm is continually taking a physical count but not of total inventory.

A firm may physically count a certain section of the plant or warehouse, moving on to other sections upon completion, until the entire facility is counted. Then the process starts all over again.

The firm may also choose to count all the A items, then the B items, and finally the C items. Certainly, the counting frequency will vary with the classification of each item. In other words, A item may be counted monthly, B items quarterly, and C items yearly. In addition the required accuracy of inventory records may vary according to classification, with A items requiring the most accurate record keeping.

BALANCING INVENTORY AND COSTS

As stated earlier, inventory management is an attempt to maintain an adequate supply of goods while minimizing inventory costs. We saw a variety of reasons companies hold inventory and these reasons dictate what is deemed to be an adequate supply of inventory. Now, how do we balance this supply with its costs? First let's look at what kind of costs we are talking about.

There are three types of costs that together constitute total inventory costs: holding costs, set-up costs, and purchasing costs.

HOLDING COSTS. Holding costs, also called carrying costs, are the costs that result from maintaining the inventory. Inventory in excess of current demand frequently means that its holder must provide a place for its storage when not in use. This could range from a small storage area near the production line to a huge warehouse or distribution center. A storage facility requires personnel to move the inventory when needed and to keep track of what is stored and where it is stored. If the inventory is heavy or bulky, forklifts may be necessary to move it around.

Storage facilities also require heating, cooling, lighting, and water. The firm must pay taxes on the inventory, and opportunity costs occur from the lost use of the funds that were spent on the inventory. Also, obsolescence, pilferage (theft), and shrinkage are problems. All of these things add cost to holding or carrying inventory.

If the firm can determine the cost of holding one unit of inventory for one year (H) it can determine its annual holding cost by multiplying the cost of holding one unit by the average inventory held for a one-year period. Average inventory can be computed by dividing the amount of goods that are ordered every time an order is placed (Q) by two. Thus, average inventory is expressed as $Q/2$. Annual holding cost, then, can be expressed as $H(Q/2)$.

SET-UP COSTS. Set-up costs are the costs incurred from getting a machine ready to produce the desired good. In a manufacturing setting this would require the use of a skilled technician (a cost) who disassembles the tooling that is currently in use on the machine. The disassembled tooling is then taken to a tool room or tool shop for maintenance or possible repair (another cost). The technician then takes the currently needed tooling from the tool room (where it has been maintained; another cost) and brings it to the machine in question.

There the technician has to assemble the tooling on the machine in the manner required for the good to be produced (this is known as a "set-up"). Then the technician has to calibrate the machine and probably will run a number of parts, that will have to be scrapped (a cost), in order to get the machine correctly calibrated and running. All the while the machine has been idle and not producing any parts (opportunity cost). As one can see, there is considerable cost involved in set-up.

If the firm purchases the part or raw material, then an order cost, rather than a set-up cost, is incurred. Ordering costs include the purchasing agent's salary and travel/entertainment budget, administrative and secretarial support, office space, copiers and office supplies, forms and documents, long-distance telephone bills, and computer systems and support. Also, some firms include the cost of shipping the purchased goods in the order cost.

If the firm can determine the cost of one set-up (S) or one order, it can determine its annual setup/ order cost by multiplying the cost of one set-up by the number of set-ups made or orders placed annually. Suppose a firm has an annual demand (D) of 1,000 units. If the firm orders 100 units (Q) every time it places and order, the firm will obviously place 10 orders per year (D/Q). Hence, annual set-up/order cost can be expressed as $S(D/Q)$.

PURCHASING COST. Purchasing cost is simply the cost of the purchased item itself. If the firm purchases a part that goes into its finished product, the firm can determine its annual purchasing cost by multiplying the cost of one purchased unit (P) by the number of finished products demanded in a year (D). Hence, purchasing cost is expressed as PD.

Now total inventory cost can be expressed as:

Total = Holding cost + Set-up/Order cost + Purchasing cost
or
Total = $H(Q/2) + S(D/Q) + PD$

If holding costs and set-up costs were plotted as lines on a graph, the point at which they intersect (that is, the point at which they are equal) would indicate the lowest total inventory cost. Therefore, if we want to minimize total inventory cost, every time we place an order, we should order the quantity (Q) that corresponds to the point where the two values are equal. If we set the two costs equal and solve for Q we get:

$$H(Q/2) = S(D/Q)$$
$$Q = 2\ DS/H$$

The quantity Q is known as the economic order quantity (EOQ). In order to minimize total inventory cost, the firm will order Q every time it places an order. For example, a firm with an annual demand of 12,000 units (at a purchase price of $25 each), annual holding cost of $10 per unit and an order cost of $150 per order (with orders placed once a month) could save $800 annually by utilizing the EOQ. First, we determine the total costs without using the EOQ method:

$Q = \$10(1000/2) + \$150(12,000/1000) + \$25(12,000) = \$306,800$

Then we calculate EOQ:

EOQ = $2(12,000)(\$150)/\$10 = 600$

And we calculate total costs at the EOQ of 600:

$Q = \$10(600/2) + \$150(12,000/600) + \$25(12,000) = \$306,000$

Finally, we subtract the total cost of Q from Q to determine the savings:

$\$306,800 - 306,000 = \$800$

Notice that if you remove purchasing cost from the equation, the savings is still $800. We might assume this means that purchasing cost is not relevant to our order decision and can be eliminated from the equation. It must be noted that this is true only as long as no quantity discount exists. If a quantity discount is available, the firm must determine whether the savings of the quantity discount are sufficient to offset the loss of the savings resulting from the use of the EOQ.

There are a number of assumptions that must be made with the use of the EOQ. These include:

- Only one product is involved.
- Deterministic demand (demand is known with certainty).
- Constant demand (demand is stable throughout the year).
- No quantity discounts.
- Constant costs (no price increases or inflation).

While these assumptions would seem to make EOQ irrelevant for use in a realistic situation, it is relevant for items that have independent demand. This means that the demand for the item is not derived from the demand for something else (usually a parent item for which the unit in question is a component). For example, the demand for steering wheels would be derived from the demand for automobiles (dependent demand) but the demand for purses is not derived from anything else; purses have independent demand.

OTHER LOT-SIZING TECHNIQUES

There are a number of other lot-sizing techniques available in addition to EOQ. These include the fixed-order quantity, fixed-order-interval model, the single-period model, and part-period balancing.

FIXED-ORDER-QUANTITY MODEL. EOQ is an example of the fixed-order-quantity model since the same quantity is ordered every time an order is placed. A firm might also use a fixed-order quantity when it is captive to packaging situations. If you were to walk into an office supply store and ask to buy 22 paper clips, chances are you would walk out with 100 paper clips. You were captive to the packaging requirements of paper clips, i.e., they come 100 to a box and you cannot purchase a partial box. It works the same way for other purchasing situations. A supplier may package their goods in certain quantities so that their customers must buy that quantity or a multiple of that quantity.

FIXED-ORDER-INTERVAL MODEL. The fixed-order-interval model is used when orders have to be placed at fixed time intervals such as weekly, biweekly, or monthly. The lot size is dependent upon how much inventory is needed from the time of order until the next order must be placed (order cycle). This system requires periodic checks of inventory levels and is used by many retail firms such as drug stores and small grocery stores.

SINGLE-PERIOD MODEL. The single-period model is used in ordering perishables, such as food and flowers, and items with a limited life, such as newspapers.

Unsold or unused goods are not typically carried over from one period to another and there may even be some disposal costs involved. This model tries to balance the cost of lost customer goodwill and opportunity cost that is incurred from not having enough inventory, with the cost of having excess inventory left at the end of a period.

PART-PERIOD BALANCING. Part-period balancing attempts to select the number of periods covered by the inventory order that will make total carrying costs as close as possible to the set-up/order cost.

When a proper lot size has been determined, utilizing one of the above techniques, the reorder point, or point at which an order should be placed, can be determined by the rate of demand and the lead time. If safety stock is necessary it would be added to the reorder point quantity.

Reorder point =
Expected demand during lead time + Safety stock

Thus, an inventory item with a demand of 100 per month, a two-month lead time and a desired safety stock of two weeks would have reorder point of 250. In other words, an order would be placed whenever the inventory level for that good reached 250 units.

Reorder point =
100/month × 2 months + 2 weeks' safety stock = 250

OTHER SCHOOLS OF THOUGHT IN INVENTORY MANAGEMENT

There are a number of techniques and philosophies that view inventory management from different perspectives.

MRP AND MRP II. MRP and MRP II are computer-based resource management systems designed for items that have dependent demand. MRP and MRP II look at order quantities period by period and, as such, allow discrete ordering (ordering only what is currently needed). In this way inventory levels can be kept at a very low level; a necessity for a complex item with dependent demand.

JUST-IN-TIME (JIT). Just-in-time (JIT) is a philosophy that advocates the lowest possible levels of inventory. JIT espouses that firms need only keep inventory in the right quantity at the right time with the right quality. The ideal lot size for JIT is one, even though one hears the term "zero inventory" used.

THEORY OF CONSTRAINTS (TOC). Theory of constraints (TOC) is a philosophy which emphasizes that all management actions should center around the firm's constraints. While it agrees with JIT that inventory should be at the lowest level possible in most instances, it advocates that there be some buffer inventory around

any capacity constraint (e.g., the slowest machine) and before finished goods.

THE FUTURE OF INVENTORY MANAGEMENT

The advent, through altruism or legislation, of environmental management has added a new dimension to inventory management-reverse supply chain logistics. Environmental management has expanded the number of inventory types that firms have to coordinate. In addition to raw materials, work-in-process, finished goods, and MRO goods, firms now have to deal with post-consumer items such as scrap, returned goods, reusable or recyclable containers, and any number of items that require repair, reuse, recycling, or secondary use in another product. Retailers have the same type problems dealing with inventory that has been returned due to defective material or manufacture, poor fit, finish, or color, or outright "I changed my mind" responses from customers.

Finally, supply chain management has had a considerable impact on inventory management. Instead of managing one's inventory to maximize profit and minimize cost for the individual firm, today's firm has to make inventory decisions that benefit the entire supply chain.

SEE ALSO: Aggregate Planning; Inventory Types; Lean Manufacturing and Just-in-Time Production; Manufacturing Resources Planning; Reverse Supply Chain Logistics; Supply Chain Management

R. Anthony Inman

FURTHER READING:

Biederman, David. "Reversing Inventory Management." *Traffic World* (12 December 2004): 1.

Stevenson, William J. *Production Operations Management.* Boston, MA: Irwin/McGraw-Hill, 2005.

Sucky, Eric. "Inventory Management in Supply Chains: A Bargaining Problem." *International Journal of Production Economics* 93/94: 253.

INVENTORY TYPES

Inventory is defined as a stock or store of goods. These goods are maintained on hand at or near a business's location so that the firm may meet demand and fulfill its reason for existence. If the firm is a retail establishment, a customer may look elsewhere to have his or her needs satisfied if the firm does not have the required item in stock when the customer arrives. If the firm is a manufacturer, it must maintain some inventory of raw materials and work-in-process in order to keep the factory running. In addition, it must maintain some supply of finished goods in order to meet demand.

Sometimes, a firm may keep larger inventory than is necessary to meet demand and keep the factory running under current conditions of demand. If the firm exists in a volatile environment where demand is dynamic (i.e., rises and falls quickly), an on-hand inventory could be maintained as a buffer against unexpected changes in demand. This buffer inventory also can serve to protect the firm if a supplier fails to deliver at the required time, or if the supplier's quality is found to be substandard upon inspection, either of which would otherwise leave the firm without the necessary raw materials. Other reasons for maintaining an unnecessarily large inventory include buying to take advantage of quantity discounts (i.e., the firm saves by buying in bulk), or ordering more in advance of an impending price increase.

Generally, inventory types can be grouped into four classifications: raw material, work-in-process, finished goods, and MRO goods.

RAW MATERIALS

Raw materials are inventory items that are used in the manufacturer's conversion process to produce components, subassemblies, or finished products. These inventory items may be commodities or extracted materials that the firm or its subsidiary has produced or extracted. They also may be objects or elements that the firm has purchased from outside the organization. Even if the item is partially assembled or is considered a finished good to the supplier, the purchaser may classify it as a raw material if his or her firm had no input into its production. Typically, raw materials are commodities such as ore, grain, minerals, petroleum, chemicals, paper, wood, paint, steel, and food items. However, items such as nuts and bolts, ball bearings, key stock, casters, seats, wheels, and even engines may be regarded as raw materials if they are purchased from outside the firm.

The bill-of-materials file in a material requirements planning system (MRP) or a manufacturing resource planning (MRP II) system utilizes a tool known as a product structure tree to clarify the relationship among its inventory items and provide a basis for filling out, or "exploding," the master production schedule. Consider an example of a rolling cart. This cart consists of a top that is pressed from a sheet of steel, a frame formed from four steel bars, and a leg assembly consisting of four legs, rolled from sheet steel, each with a caster attached. An example

of this cart's product structure tree is presented in Figure 1.

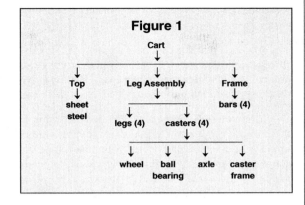

Figure 1

Generally, raw materials are used in the manufacture of components. These components are then incorporated into the final product or become part of a subassembly. Subassemblies are then used to manufacture or assemble the final product. A part that goes into making another part is known as a component, while the part it goes into is known as its parent. Any item that does not have a component is regarded as a raw material or purchased item. From the product structure tree it is apparent that the rolling cart's raw materials are steel, bars, wheels, ball bearings, axles, and caster frames.

WORK-IN-PROCESS

Work-in-process (WIP) is made up of all the materials, parts (components), assemblies, and subassemblies that are being processed or are waiting to be processed within the system. This generally includes all material—from raw material that has been released for initial processing up to material that has been completely processed and is awaiting final inspection and acceptance before inclusion in finished goods.

Any item that has a parent but is not a raw material is considered to be work-in-process. A glance at the rolling cart product structure tree example reveals that work-in-process in this situation consists of tops, leg assemblies, frames, legs, and casters. Actually, the leg assembly and casters are labeled as subassemblies because the leg assembly consists of legs and casters and the casters are assembled from wheels, ball bearings, axles, and caster frames.

FINISHED GOODS

A finished good is a completed part that is ready for a customer order. Therefore, finished goods inventory is the stock of completed products. These goods have been inspected and have passed final inspection requirements so that they can be transferred out of work-in-process and into finished goods inventory. From this point, finished goods can be sold directly to their final user, sold to retailers, sold to wholesalers, sent to distribution centers, or held in anticipation of a customer order.

Any item that does not have a parent can be classified as a finished good. By looking at the rolling cart product structure tree example one can determine that the finished good in this case is a cart.

Inventories can be further classified according to the purpose they serve. These types include transit inventory, buffer inventory, anticipation inventory, decoupling inventory, cycle inventory, and MRO goods inventory. Some of these also are know by other names, such as speculative inventory, safety inventory, and seasonal inventory. We already have briefly discussed some of the implications of a few of these inventory types, but will now discuss each in more detail.

TRANSIT INVENTORY

Transit inventories result from the need to transport items or material from one location to another, and from the fact that there is some transportation time involved in getting from one location to another. Sometimes this is referred to as pipeline inventory. Merchandise shipped by truck or rail can sometimes take days or even weeks to go from a regional warehouse to a retail facility. Some large firms, such as automobile manufacturers, employ freight consolidators to pool their transit inventories coming from various locations into one shipping source in order to take advantage of economies of scale. Of course, this can greatly increase the transit time for these inventories, hence an increase in the size of the inventory in transit.

BUFFER INVENTORY

As previously stated, inventory is sometimes used to protect against the uncertainties of supply and demand, as well as unpredictable events such as poor delivery reliability or poor quality of a supplier's products. These inventory cushions are often referred to as safety stock. Safety stock or buffer inventory is any amount held on hand that is over and above that currently needed to meet demand. Generally, the higher the level of buffer inventory, the better the firm's customer service. This occurs because the firm suffers fewer "stock-outs" (when a customer's order cannot be immediately filled from existing inventory) and has less need to backorder the item, make the customer wait until the next order cycle, or even worse, cause the customer to leave empty-handed to find another supplier. Obviously, the better the customer service the greater the likelihood of customer satisfaction.

ANTICIPATION INVENTORY

Oftentimes, firms will purchase and hold inventory that is in excess of their current need in anticipation of a possible future event. Such events may include a price increase, a seasonal increase in demand, or even an impending labor strike. This tactic is commonly used by retailers, who routinely build up inventory months before the demand for their products will be unusually high (i.e., at Halloween, Christmas, or the back-to-school season). For manufacturers, anticipation inventory allows them to build up inventory when demand is low (also keeping workers busy during slack times) so that when demand picks up the increased inventory will be slowly depleted and the firm does not have to react by increasing production time (along with the subsequent increase in hiring, training, and other associated labor costs). Therefore, the firm has avoided both excessive overtime due to increased demand and hiring costs due to increased demand. It also has avoided layoff costs associated with production cut-backs, or worse, the idling or shutting down of facilities. This process is sometimes called "smoothing" because it smoothes the peaks and valleys in demand, allowing the firm to maintain a constant level of output and a stable workforce.

DECOUPLING INVENTORY

Very rarely, if ever, will one see a production facility where every machine in the process produces at exactly the same rate. In fact, one machine may process parts several times faster than the machines in front of or behind it. Yet, if one walks through the plant it may seem that all machines are running smoothly at the same time. It also could be possible that while passing through the plant, one notices several machines are under repair or are undergoing some form of preventive maintenance. Even so, this does not seem to interrupt the flow of work-in-process through the system. The reason for this is the existence of an inventory of parts between machines, a decoupling inventory that serves as a shock absorber, cushioning the system against production irregularities. As such it "decouples" or disengages the plant's dependence upon the sequential requirements of the system (i.e., one machine feeds parts to the next machine).

The more inventory a firm carries as a decoupling inventory between the various stages in its manufacturing system (or even distribution system), the less coordination is needed to keep the system running smoothly. Naturally, logic would dictate that an infinite amount of decoupling inventory would not keep the system running in peak form. A balance can be reached that will allow the plant to run relatively smoothly without maintaining an absurd level of inventory. The cost of efficiency must be weighed against the cost of carrying excess inventory so that there is an optimum balance between inventory level and coordination within the system.

CYCLE INVENTORY

Those who are familiar with the concept of economic order quantity (EOQ) know that the EOQ is an attempt to balance inventory holding or carrying costs with the costs incurred from ordering or setting up machinery. When large quantities are ordered or produced, inventory holding costs are increased, but ordering/setup costs decrease. Conversely, when lot sizes decrease, inventory holding/carrying costs decrease, but the cost of ordering/setup increases since more orders/setups are required to meet demand. When the two costs are equal (holding/carrying costs and ordering/setup costs) the total cost (the sum of the two costs) is minimized. Cycle inventories, sometimes called lot-size inventories, result from this process. Usually, excess material is ordered and, consequently, held in inventory in an effort to reach this minimization point. Hence, cycle inventory results from ordering in batches or lot sizes rather than ordering material strictly as needed.

MRO GOODS INVENTORY

Maintenance, repair, and operating supplies, or MRO goods, are items that are used to support and maintain the production process and its infrastructure. These goods are usually consumed as a result of the production process but are not directly a part of the finished product. Examples of MRO goods include oils, lubricants, coolants, janitorial supplies, uniforms, gloves, packing material, tools, nuts, bolts, screws, shim stock, and key stock. Even office supplies such as staples, pens and pencils, copier paper, and toner are considered part of MRO goods inventory.

THEORETICAL INVENTORY

In their book *Managing Business Process Flows: Principles of Operations Management,* Anupindi, Chopra, Deshmukh, Van Mieghem, and Zemel discuss a final type of inventory known as theoretical inventory. They describe theoretical inventory as the average inventory for a given throughput assuming that no WIP item had to wait in a buffer. This would obviously be an ideal situation where inflow, processing, and outflow rates were all equal at any point in time. Unless one has a single process system, there always will be some inventory within the system. Theoretical inventory is a measure of this inventory (i.e., it represents the minimum inventory needed for goods to flow through the system without waiting). The authors formally define it as the minimum amount of inventory necessary to maintain a process throughput of R, expressed as:

$$\text{Theoretical Inventory} = \text{Throughput} \times \text{Theoretical Flow Time}$$
$$I_{th} = R \times T_{th}$$

In this equation, theoretical flow time equals the sum of all activity times (not wait time) required to process one unit. Therefore, WIP will equal theoretical inventory whenever actual process flow time equals theoretical flow time.

Inventory exists in various categories as a result of its position in the production process (raw material, work-in-process, and finished goods) and according to the function it serves within the system (transit inventory, buffer inventory, anticipation inventory, decoupling inventory, cycle inventory, and MRO goods inventory). As such, the purpose of each seems to be that of maintaining a high level of customer service or part of an attempt to minimize overall costs.

SEE ALSO: Inventory Management; Theory of Constraints

R. Anthony Inman

FURTHER READING:

Anupindi, Ravi, et al. *Managing Business Process Flows: Principles of Operations Management.* 2nd ed. Upper Saddle River, NJ: Pearson Prentice Hall, 2004.

Cox, James F., III, and John H. Blackstone, Jr. *APICS Dictionary.* 9th ed. Falls Church VA: American Production and Inventory Control Society, 1998.

Meredith, Jack R., and Scott M. Shafer. *Operations Management for MBAs.* 2nd ed. New York: John Wiley & Sons Inc., 2002.

Stevenson, William J. *Production/Operations Management.* 8th ed. Boston: Irwin/McGraw-Hill, 2005.

J

The Japanese have had phenomenal impact on world markets. Many industries, such as electronics, cameras, watches, motorcycles, machine tools, automotive products, shipbuilding, and even some aspects of aerospace are either dominated by Japanese firms or are heavily impacted by them.

Many people mistakenly attribute this phenomenon strictly to cultural differences. The vision of dedicated Japanese workers giving their life to the company for substandard wages surely accounts for the difference, they reason. Of course, this view doesn't always square with reality. First, Japanese factories have some of the highest wage structures seen outside the United States. Second, this "Japanese miracle" is also happening outside Japan. Most Japanese automobile manufacturers have successful plants located within the United States; all of them manufacturing quality automobiles utilizing American workers. When Matsushita bought a U.S. television plant in Chicago, they managed to maintain the 1,000 hourly employees while trimming the indirect labor by half. Utilizing the same workers employed by the U.S. firm, Matsushita doubled daily production while improving quality 40-fold. Outside warranty costs fell from $16 million per year to $2 million per year while selling twice as many sets.

Word of these success stories soon aroused considerable interest from U.S. firms. Interest in Japanese management was first generated in the U.S. with the appearance of a book by William Ouchi entitled "Theory Z", and later a book by Richard J. Schonberger entitled "Japanese Manufacturing Techniques: Nine Hidden Lessons in Simplicity", and the broadcast of an NBC television white paper entitled "If Japan Can, Why Can't We?"

William Ouchi's book "Theory Z" detailed much of the success being realized by the Japanese manufacturing firms. The Japanese style of management (as opposed to McGregor's Theory X and Theory Y) mystified many U.S. businessmen with its talk of cultural differences and notions such as lifetime employment.

In his book "Japanese Manufacturing Techniques: Nine Hidden Lessons in Simplicity", Richard Schonberger presented nine "lessons" the world could learn from the Japanese. These lessons included:

1. Management technology is a highly transportable technology.

2. Just-in-time production exposes problems otherwise hidden by excess inventories and staff.

3. Quality begins with production, and requires a company-wide "habit of improvement."

4. Culture is no obstacle; techniques can change behavior.

5. Simplify, and goods will flow like water.

6. Flexibility opens doors.

7. Travel light and make numerous trips, like the water beetle.

8. More self-improvement, fewer programs, less specialist intervention.

9. Simplicity is the natural state.

For many American business executives this was their first encounter with the concepts (and even just the terms) of just-in-time, kanban, Total Quality Management, and quality circles.

The NBC documentary "If Japan Can Why Can't We?" introduced Americans to the progress made in Japanese manufacturing and served as a "wake-up call" for American businesses that manufacturing had entered a new generation. For many viewers, this was their first introduction to W. Edwards Deming, statistical process control (SPC), and quality circles.

By the early 1980s it was evident that Japan was well on its way to the position as a worldwide dominant force in manufacturing that it enjoys today. Japan's rise to economic dominance sent ripples throughout the industrialized world. Since the early 1960s Japan has systematically increased its share of world trade in industrial and consumer goods, although persistent economic problems during the 1990s have arrested its rapid growth.

A number of reasons have been tendered to explain the success of the Japanese. When Japanese automobile manufacturers' market position began to strengthen in the 1970s it was easy to suppose that the 1973 Arab oil embargo and subsequent escalation in gas prices was the antecedent. Customers were sent searching for small fuel-efficient vehicles. Since the Japanese were already entrenched in the small car market, they had a considerable natural competitive advantage. However, it was expected that this advantage would wane as the Big Three automakers had time to react by incorporating small cars into their product line and as oil prices began to decrease.

However, as the Big Three were able to produce smaller cars and gas prices fell, the Japanese market share of the automobile industry continued to increase. Nor did this reasoning account for the simultaneous surge in Japanese market share in areas such as steel, consumer electronics, copiers and heavy equipment. After all, if the oil embargo was responsible for the increase in Japanese market share why didn't other traditional small car manufacturers such as Renault and Volkswagen have comparable success? Manufacturers began to realize that the Japanese success story was more than simply a matter of timing.

HISTORY

When Japanese industry was in its infancy stage, the Japanese market was too small to absorb the increasing domestic production. Japan needed a global market in order to further develop. By creating an export market, Japan was able to structurally transform its economy, thereby granting it access to the technology it needed to develop.

The Japanese goal became one of full employment through industrialization. This called for dominating the market in very select product areas. They carefully chose areas in which they had the confidence to dominate and concentrated on them rather than splitting their efforts over many areas.

A number of tactics were utilized to support this strategy. First of all, the Japanese imported their technology, thus avoiding the risks involved with major R&D expenditures. Instead, they negotiated license agreements to make workable new products. Then the best engineering talent was directed to the plant floor rather than to the product design department, thereby concentrating their ingenuity on high productivity and low cost rather than innovative design. Finally, they strove continuously to improve quality and reliability to the highest possible levels and then beyond; to levels competitors could not or would not supply. Implementation of these tactics was guided by a solid respect for people and the belief that waste must be eliminated (these two areas are discussed in depth below).

The Japanese example of success shows that neither massive research and development investment nor abundant natural resources is necessary for sustainable industrial development. For years Japan was well known as an imitator not an innovator as they copied, borrowed, and licensed technology from other countries. By building competence in adapting existing product designs and speeding up the processes the Japanese were able to manufacture superior quality at competitive prices, giving them a distinct advantage in world markets.

Japan showed the world that efficient production and quality control methods could overcome transportation cost disadvantages and tariff costs. They proved that cultural differences could be overcome and that the critical cultural points necessary for successful production could be transferred across national boundaries.

Japan's success as an economic superpower strongly implied that the West might lose its world dominance as the leader in technology. Emboldened by the success of the Japanese, other Pacific Rim countries began to follow their example, thus accelerating the diffusion of innovative technology throughout the industrial world. Actually, new centers of industrial superiority were created as a result.

Japan's success is also an indicator of the importance of quality as a strategic variable. When it looked like Japan could only hope to carve out a niche as a producer of outdated Western goods for the Asian market, Japanese leadership came to the conclusion that it could play a leading role in global industry by changing its quality image; a change made by producing quality goods for a sustained period of time. The Japanese learned from the price they paid for their reputation for inferior-quality products. They learned that quality reputations are built by producing quality products with a painstaking attention to detail and craftsmanship. They were also willing to make the necessary investment in human resources and technology needed to improve their quality image.

Synonymous with the improvement in quality was a profound improvement in Japan's position in global markets. From a weak position in the television market in the 1960s, Japan became the world's largest producer and exporter of household television sets in the world. They are sure to dominate the market for the coming revolution in high-resolution television. They totally dominate the VCR market and are challenging companies such as Intel in the market for large-scale integrated circuits.

In the early 1960s North American, British, and German motorcycle manufacturers lead the market. Today, Harley-Davidson is the only serious competitor for Japanese made motorcycles. In fact, Harley-Davidson teetered on the brink of nonexistence until wholeheartedly adopting Japanese manufacturing techniques, most notably just-in-time and Total Quality Management. Another example, Xerox, suffered embarrassing market share losses to Japanese manufacturers Canon, Sharp, and Minolta.

The emphasis placed on quality by Japanese manufacturers has been continuous since the inspiration derived from the first visit of Dr. W. Edwards Deming. Today, Japan is certainly seen as the worldwide symbol of quality. While Western firms measure quality in parts per thousand (the acceptable quality level or AQL), the leading Japanese manufacturers are achieving defects that are barely measurable, perhaps 3.4 defective parts per million. The Japanese turnaround in quality can clearly be attributed to such variables as worker training, employee involvement, and firm wide delegation of authority and responsibility for quality. A change in attitude and vision on the part of Japanese top management brought quality to the forefront as a strategic mission, one that allowed them to liberate the creative talent and resources necessary for long-term improvement and the eventual mastery of the quality concept.

RESPECT FOR PEOPLE

There are a number of facets to the Japanese respect for and treatment of workers. One of the most prominent is lifetime employment, which gained notoriety from William Ouchi's book "Theory Z". When many Japanese workers are hired for permanent positions in major industrial firms, they can generally consider it a job for life. However, this kind of benefit applies only to permanent workers, about one-third of the Japanese workforce. It is felt that if workers can stay with one firm for life, they more easily identify with the firm's goals and objectives.

Unlike the case for American labor unions, workers who are members of Japanese labor unions identify more with the company than the type of work they are doing. Also, Japanese unions tend to share the management's view. The better the company performs, the more the worker benefits. As a result, Japanese management believes in giving the workers more opportunity to expand their job boundaries rather than waiting until the worker proves himself. The Japanese also spend more on education and training, for all levels, than any other industrial nation. Also, because the Japanese believe that robots free people for more important tasks, they have invested heavily in robotics and automated equipment, making theirs perhaps the most automated manufacturing sector in the world.

Another area in which Japanese management has successfully tapped into worker potential is in the use of small group improvement activities (SGIA). One example is quality circles, a small group of volunteer employees who meet once a week, on a scheduled basis, to discuss their functions and the problems they are encountering. They then propose solutions and make a sincere attempt to implement real change.

Finally, the Japanese believe in what they call "bottom round" management. This concept, sometimes called consensus management or committee management, is an innate part of Japanese culture. It involves a slow decision-making process that attempts to reach a true consensus rather than a compromise. While the decision-making process is slow the implementation process is quite fast.

ELIMINATION OF WASTE

When the Japanese say elimination of waste they mean anything other than the absolutely essential minimum amount of workers, equipment, and materials necessary to meet demand. This means no safety stock, no inventory stored for use in smoothing production requirements, and so forth. If it can't be used right now it is considered waste.

A number of concepts are central to this idea of waste elimination. Instead of building a large manufacturing plant that does everything, the Japanese tend to build small plants that are highly specialized and form them into focused factory networks. It is difficult to manage a large facility; the bigger it is the more bureaucratic it tends to be. Bureaucracy is not conducive to the Japanese style of management. Also, a specialized plant can be more economically constructed and operated.

Along with the idea of smaller plants, the Japanese make considerable use of group technology. Japanese engineers examine each operation required to make a part and attempt to group dissimilar machines into clusters designed to be work centers for a given part or family of parts, thus eliminating or at least greatly shortening the time necessary for set-up and changeover.

Just-in-time (JIT) production is an important part of waste elimination. In fact, JIT has often been defined as the elimination of waste. JIT is the production of precisely the necessary unit in the correct quantity at the correct time in order to maintain perfect performance to schedule. Over producing is considered just as bad as under producing since unnecessary inventory would be wasteful.

In order for JIT to work effectively, production must flow smoothly. Any changes can cause disturbances in the flow, which can be amplified throughout the supply chain, causing disruptions and delays. In order to ensure a more uniform flow, the Japanese adopt a uniform plant load. This means that they simply plan to build the same mix of products each day. If you run some of everything you need each day, it only takes one day before you have more (as opposed to large lot sizes which tie up capacity for lengthy periods, causing delays in shipping).

Uniform plant loading requires that everything be produced in small lot sizes, implying that the number of set-ups required will increase. The principle of economic order quantity (EOQ) states that as lot sizes increase set-up costs decrease but as lot sizes decrease set-up costs increase. Therefore, this emphasis on small lots requires that set-up times be minimized. Instead of taking established set-up times as a given, the Japanese have managed to reduce set-up times tremendously, often to the point of single digits (i.e., less than ten minutes).

The Japanese also use a self-regulating system for production control known as *kanban*. It uses dedicated containers and recycles traveling requisitions/cards (often known as kanbans themselves) to regulate the system. It is also referred to as a "pull" system since the authority to produce or supply comes from downstream operations.

Finally, the Japanese utilize a number of quality control techniques to ensure maximized quality and minimized waste. Among these are *jidoka, bakayoke,* and poka-yoke.

Jidoka is a quality concept that means "stop everything" whenever an error occurs. It is controlling quality at the source. Instead of using inspectors to find problems someone else created, the Japanese worker is his own inspector, responsible for his/her own quality. When an error or defect is discovered, the worker has the authority and the responsibility to halt the production process. Usually, this is controlled by some mechanism such as push buttons. When the line stops, lights flash, bell ring, and flags wave as all attention is directed at the problem.

The Japanese also believe that, whenever possible, inspection should be performed by a machine, for the sake of speed and accuracy. A technique known as bakayoke is used for this purpose. Bakayokes are devices that are attached to machines to automatically check for abnormalities in the process, such as malfunction or tool wear, as well as measuring dimensions and warning when tolerances are close to being exceeded. For manual assembly, the Japanese utilize poka-yoke or mistake proofing.

Today, all these Japanese techniques have been repackaged and are now know as "Lean" management techniques. Even though JIT, kanban, and other tools have not changed in their application, the new "lean" label has removed some of the Japanese stigma and has made the tools more palatable. With the introduction of the lean label has also come a broader application of these principles to where they are now being used in the service sector and in the front office, with the same high degree of success.

JAPANESE KEIRETSU

A *keiretsu* is an organizational structure unique to Japanese major corporations. While not all major Japanese businesses are keiretsu, most of Japan's major corporate entities are. Moreover, the influence of the keiretsu on the Japanese business world is important even to non-keiretsu organizations. There are two types of keiretsu: the classical keiretsu and the vertically integrated keiretsu.

The so-called Big Six Japanese business groups are all examples of classical keiretsu. These are the Fuyo/Fuji Group, Sumitomo, Sanwa, Mitsui, Mitsubishi, and Daiichi-Kangyo Ginko. Classical keiretsu are bank-centered with no specific central industry.

While not considered classic keiretsu, many major single-industry companies in Japan are increasingly becoming viewed as vertical keiretsu. These include Hitachi, Toyota, Nissan, Toshiba, and Matsushita. These keiretsu are more pyramid-shaped, with a single industry or company at the pinnacle of the pyramid and the member companies collected beneath.

KEIRETSU DEFINED

Japan's keiretsu are not single entities. Each keiretsu is formed of an interdependent collection of individual firms woven into a common enterprise. In this, the keiretsu are similar to the Korean *chaebol,* but there the similarities stop.

The keiretsu form a type of family of member companies, each connected to the others through cross-shareholdership. In other words, each company within the keiretsu holds significant shares of stock in each of the other keiretsu members. The companies remain independent of each other, and are not subsidiaries of holding companies, as holding companies were out-lawed after World War II.

Additionally, the size of the keiretsu corporate families can be deceptive. Most keiretsu have well over 100 members, while many far exceed that amount. Hitachi alone has over 680 member firms and subsidiaries. While shareholder control is coordinated, technically the stock of each member firm in the keiretsu can be traded independently.

CLASSICAL KEIRETSU

In the classical keiretsu, member firms share in the compositions of their boards of directors or council of presidents. While legally independent of each other, the boards of directors for each member firm are largely made up of the same members.

Although a coordinating role may be given to the head of the central bank around which the keiretsu is formed, there is no central president in a classical keiretsu. For example, its Twenty Presidents Council governs Sumitomo. This is the council made up of the presidents of many companies that bear the name Sumitomo, such as the Sumitomo Bank, Sumitomo Chemical, Sumitomo Metal Industries, Sumitomo Metal Mining, and so forth. Yet not all members of the Twenty Presidents Council run companies with the name Sumitomo in it. Thus, both the Japanese giants NEC and Nippon Sheet Glass are central members of the Sumitomo keiretsu, despite the name difference. In addition to the twenty member firms whose heads comprise Sumitomo's Twenty Presidents Council, the Sumitomo keiretsu has reach through its affiliated companies. These are often giant industrial concerns who have strong relationships to the Sumitomo keiretsu's central members or which have close ties to Sumitomo Bank. Among Sumitomo's affiliate companies are some of the most important companies in Japan, including Mazda Motors, Daishowa Paper, Asahi Breweries, Sanyo Electric, and Daikin Industries, among others. The relationships can be even more confusing when one takes into account that some companies bear the name Sumitomo that are not members of the central twenty Sumitomo keiretsu members. Instead, these companies are affiliated companies only despite names such as Sumitomo Precision Products, Sumitomo Rubber Industries, or Sumitomo Seika products.

Nor is Sumitomo exceptional among classical keiretsu. Indeed, it is considered the most closely unified of the Big Six classical keiretsu. A popular saying in corporate Japan is "Sumitomo for unity," indicating that the ties and connections of Sumitomo's member companies are the most closely knit (which also makes them the most transparent).

At the other extreme, Daiichi-Kangyo Ginko, itself formed only in 1978 through the merger of two major bank-centered keiretsu, is highly complicated and is still in a state of settling its affairs out. Nevertheless, Daiichi-Kangyo is clearly run by its own Council of Forty-Seven Presidents centered around Daiichi-Kangyo Bank.

In any case, it is the coordination of shareholder-ships and directorships that allows the members of the classical keiretsu to act in concert financially, since members use the keiretsu's select bank and insurance companies. The banks, in turn, give favored treatment to keiretsu members, enabling comparatively easy access to financing of keiretsu projects.

Classical keiretsu often have no single industry on which they focus their output. Yet is their goal to create what is called a "one-set" principle. In the "one-set" principle, keiretsu members attempt to create a situation in which they would never have to rely on non-keiretsu firms to produce an end-product.

VERTICALLY INTEGRATED KEIRETSU

More common than the classical keiretsu is the vertically integrated corporate giant that focuses on a single industry. Technically these giant companies may not be viewed as keiretsu, since they have no central bank and do tend to have a specific company with a single leader as their chairperson. Yet these corporate giants are increasingly beginning to resemble keiretsu in most other respects. As a result, it is unclear as to what is and is not an actual keiretsu.

Giant Japanese companies such as Toyota have begun to control enough subsidiary companies to attain a "one-set" principle. These large companies have become a sort of vertically-organized keiretsu that have grown out of a central manufacturing company. Thus companies like Toyota can be viewed as a single-industry keiretsu.

For example, beneath the central Toyota Motor Corporation are 12 direct group companies each tied only to a specialized function in the production of Toyota automobiles. These include Toyota Central R&D Laboratories, Kanto Auto Works (car assembly), Toyota Auto Body, Toyoda Machine Works, Toyoda Automatic Loom Works (which despite its name produces car engines), Aichi Steel Works, Toyoda Gosei (resin and rubber products), Toyoda Boshoku (air filters), Toyota Tsusho Corporation (the keiretsu's wholesaler), Towa Real Estate, Aisin Seiki (auto parts), and the giant Nippondenso (electronics).

Many of these twelve direct group companies, in turn, control several of their own subsidiaries. Thus, Nippondenso controls Nippon Wiperblade, Asmo, Tsuda Industries, and Anjo Denki, and so on. Similarly, Aisin Seiki controls Aichi Giken, Aisin Takaoka, and Aisin-AW.

In this way, Toyota's orientation is vertical and spreads downward in a pyramid of related companies. Like the classical keiretsu, Toyota also has many closely affiliated companies it does not control directly. Thus several companies are part of the greater Toyota Group without formally being part of its actual structure. These are controlled not by bank loans, as in the classical keiretsu, but by supplier dependence. Among the many major Japanese firms affiliated in this way as part of a greater Toyota keiretsu are Kyoho Machine Works, Chuo Spring, Trinity Industrial, Tokai Rika, Aisan Industries, and many others.

Nor is Toyota in any way atypical for vertically structured single-industry keiretsu. Similar relationships exist for Nippon Steel, Nissan, Hitachi, and Toshiba, and dozens of other large Japanese concerns.

RELATIVE INDEPENDENCE OF MEMBER FIRMS

Most keiretsu member firms act with considerably greater independence than subsidiary firms of large U.S., Canadian, or European companies. The Japanese firm that is a keiretsu member is highly specialized, and thus less able to stand as self-sufficient than its non-Japanese counterparts. Yet while this dependence in effect coordinates their actions with the keiretsu as a whole, the leaders of the keiretsu member firms make agreements and arrangements far separate from their central bank or parent company.

Indeed, several vertically organized keiretsu members, far from acting in the subservient role of the Western corporation's subsidiary, have grown to be the dominant members of their keiretsu. Toyota Motor Corporation, for instance, grew from a dependent member of the Toyoda Automatic Loom keiretsu in 1937 to become the dominant member of today's Toyota keiretsu, under whose umbrella its former parent company now stands.

Because so many keiretsu members act independently, there is considerable overlap of commitments within industries. This is compounded by the fact that most keiretsu have strong commitments to reaching beyond the borders of Japan to integrate more fully into the global economy. Perhaps this is nowhere better illustrated than in the automotive industry. For example, IBC Vehicles is a joint venture between Isuzu Motors and the U.S. automaker General Motors. Subaru-Isuzu Automotive is a joint venture between Fuji Heavy Industries and Isuzu Motors. Fuji Heavy Industry, to point out just one cross-affiliation, is a major components supplier to the Italian company Fiat. Fiat is a supplier to Mazda while Mazda is tied closely to the U.S. automaker Ford. This brings one around full circle since Ford and General Motors are

major competitors. The web of relationships can go on for dozens of other ties as well.

ORIGINS OF THE KEIRETSU

Whatever the direction of the classical and vertically integrated keiretsu, it is in the past that the keiretsu as an organizational structure has its source. The keiretsu have a long history in Japanese society. The keiretsu evolved directly from Japan's pre-World War II industrial groups called *zaibatsu*. These zaibatsu were family-dominated, and resembled the chaebol structures that dominate South Korean industry today. Most of the leading zaibatsu families came to power during Japan's rapid industrialization following the Meiji Restoration in 1868; however, the companies' corporate organization and even some of the key families had their roots in Japan's feudal period. By 1945, four zaibatsu (Mitsui, Mitsubishi, Sumitomo, and Yasuda) controlled fully one-fourth of all Japanese business.

After World War II, U.S. occupation forces dismantled the four main zaibatsu as well as six smaller ones, blaming them for Japan's militarism. The zaibatsu members, in turn, simply came together again to form new entities centered on common business needs and relationships. The keiretsu that took their place were essentially identically to the pre-war zaibatsu with one main difference: the keiretsu centered on a bank and common financial resources in place of the earlier kinship ties of key individuals. Ironically, when reformed as keiretsu, the former zaibatsu members were given an excuse to drop the less profitable member firms, thus making the punitive measures imposed by the American occupation forces a sort of blessing in disguise. Three of the four leading pre-war zaibatsu reformed under the same name. The last of the four great pre-war zaibatsu, Yasuda, joined with many firms from the smaller dismantled zaibatsu (such as the Asano and Nezu zaibatsu) to form the Fuyo Group centered around Fuji Bank.

NEGATIVES OF JAPANESE MANAGEMENT

Despite their success, some do not see Japanese management techniques as the panacea others credit them as being. Even though research has shown that management techniques developed in Japan can be successfully applied in other countries with remarkable results, critics claim that their success comes not from catering to intrinsic values but to an array of stifling constraints unlikely to be tolerated in the West. Rather than a carefully nurtured atmosphere of trust and common enterprise, they see a restrictive system of internal controls. Much of this criticism has come from labor unions. It has been noted that workers in JIT systems have more stress than their counterparts in more traditional systems. Stress is seen to originate not only from additional authority and responsibility, but also from the fast-paced system where there is little slack and a continual push to improve. Apparently, some see the authority and responsibility delegated to the worker as a way for management to further burden the worker without a comparable increase in take-home pay. Constant improvement through use of *kaizen,* just-in-time, and Total Quality Management is felt to be within the purview of management not the worker.

There is really no mystery to the success attributed to Japanese management. The Japanese were convinced that a shift, caused by natural competitive forces, was taking place worldwide. They then rode this change, which was international in scope, to financial success by becoming the premier producer of products known for quality. They were prepared to sacrifice short-term financial results in order to invest for the long-term in superior quality; a variable consumers would soon demand.

Consumers are still showing their confidence in Japanese goods by purchasing what they see as commensurate quality at a fair price. Japanese produced television sets, for example, have an average life span that is twice that of similar sets produced in North America. Any country that can manage to achieve this kind of quality and parlay it into a strategic weapon should continue to have a competitive position within the markets in which it competes.

R. Anthony Inman and David A. Victor
Revised by Gerhard Plenert

FURTHER READING:

Bazargan, Darius. "Is Japanese Management Technique Best for Africa?" *African Business,* May 1997, 18–19.

Clark, Rodney. *The Japanese Company.* New Haven, CT: Yale University Press, 1979.

Crawford, Robert J. "Reinterpreting the Japanese Economic Miracle." *Harvard Business Review,* January/February 1998, 179–184.

Entienne-Hamilton, E.C. *Operations Strategies for Competitive Advantage: Text and Cases.* Fort Worth: The Dryden Press, 1994.

Ghinato, Paulo. "Quality Control Methods: Towards Modern Approaches Through Well Established Principles." *Total Quality Management* 9, no. 6 (August 1998).

Khol, Ronald. "Maybe We Can Learn Something from Japanese Managers After All." *Machine Design* 70, no. 8 (7 May 1998).

Murdoch, Adrian. "Eastern Promise." *Accountancy* 122, no. 1262 (October 1998): 43–44.

Ohsono, Tomokazu. *Charting Japanese Industry: A Graphical Guide to Corporate and Market Structures.* London: Cassell, 1995.

Plenert, Gerhard. *The eManager: Value Chain Management in an eCommerce World.* Dublin, Ireland: Blackhall Publishing, 2001.

———. *International Operations Management.* Copenhagen, Denmark: Copenhagen Business School Press, 2002.

Schonberger, Richard J. *Japanese Manufacturing Techniques: Nine Hidden Lessons in Simplicity.* New York: The Free Press, 1982.

Stevenson, William J. *Production Operations Management.* 6th ed. Boston: Irwin/McGraw-Hill, 1999.

JOB ANALYSIS

A job analysis is a step-by-step specification of an employment position's requirements, functions, and procedures. Just as a seed cannot blossom into a flower unless the ground is properly prepared, many human resource management (HRM) practices cannot blossom into competitive advantage unless grounded on an adequate job analysis.

Successful HRM practices can lead to outcomes that create competitive advantage. Job analyses, properly performed, enhance the success of these HRM practices by laying the foundation. Job analysis information can be applied to a variety of HRM practices. We now take a brief look at some of them.

ESTABLISHING FAIR AND EFFECTIVE HIRING PRACTICES

An employer's recruitment and selection practices seek to identify and hire the most suitable applicants. Job analysis information helps employers achieve this aim by identifying selection criteria, such as the knowledge, skills, and abilities (KSAs) needed to perform a job successfully. A firm's managers and human resource (HR) professionals can then use this information to choose or develop the appropriate selection devices (e.g., interview questions, tests). This approach to selection is legally required.

An employer facing discrimination charges must demonstrate to the courts that its selection criteria are job-related. To support this type of claim-relatedness, a firm must demonstrate that the challenged selection practice was developed on the basis of job analysis information. As one judge noted during a discrimination hearing, without a job analysis on which to base selection practices, an employer "is aiming in the dark and can only hope to achieve job-relatedness by blind luck."

In the 1990s, the need for firms to base selection criteria on job analysis information became even more important due to the passage of the Americans with Disabilities Act. This law states that employment decisions concerning disabled candidates must be based on their ability to perform the essential functions of the job. For instance, if report reading were an essential job function, then applicants whose disabilities prevented them from reading could be lawfully denied employment (assuming there was no way to accommodate them). If, however, report reading were not an essential function, the inability to read could not lawfully serve as a basis for denial. The determination of which job functions are essential is made during a job analysis.

DEVELOPING TRAINING AND APPRAISAL PROGRAMS

Firms can also use job analysis information to assess training needs and to develop and evaluate training programs. Job analyses can identify tasks a worker must perform. Then, through the performance appraisal process, supervisors can identify which tasks are being performed properly or improperly. The supervisor can next determine whether improperly performed work can be corrected through training.

HR professionals also use job analysis information to develop relevant training programs. The job analysis specifies how each job is performed, step by step, allowing HR professionals to develop training materials to teach trainees how to perform each task. To evaluate the effectiveness of a training program, the organization must first specify training objectives or the level of performance expected of trainees when they finish the program. The success of a training program is judged on the basis of the extent to which those performance levels have been reached. Expected performance levels are often specified during a job analysis.

Information obtained from a job analysis can be used to develop performance appraisal forms. An example of a job analysis-based form would be one that lists the job's tasks or behaviors and specifies the expected performance level for each. The role of job analysis is crucial here. Without job analysis information, organizations typically use a single, generalized form in which all workers are appraised on the basis of a common set of characteristics or traits that are presumed to be needed for all jobs (e.g., cooperation, dependability, leadership).

Job analysis-based appraisal forms are superior to the generalized forms because they do a better job of communicating performance expectations and because they provide a better basis for giving feedback and for making HRM decisions.

Most companies base pay rates, in part, on the relative worth or importance of each job to the organ-

ization. Job worth is typically determined by evaluating or rating jobs based on important factors such as skill level, effort, responsibility, and working conditions. The information provided by a job analysis serves as the basis for job worth evaluations.

Job analysis also plays an important role in the development of productivity improvement programs. Various pay-for-performance programs provide rewards to employees who perform their jobs at or above some desired level. Job analysis is used to identify that level of performance.

REMEDIAL USES

Managers must sometimes discipline employees for their failure to properly carry out their job responsibilities. For instance, workers may be disciplined for refusing to perform tasks that they believe are not part of their jobs. If the responsibilities and limits of authority of a job are delineated in a job analysis, this information may be used to help resolve such problems.

Job analysis information can also be useful from a safety and health point of view. While conducting a job analysis, an employer may uncover potential dangers or hazards of a job. The job analysis may also identify unsafe practices, such as tasks that are performed in a way that could cause injury.

DETERMINING THE TYPE OF INFORMATION TO BE COLLECTED

A wealth of information may be gathered during a job analysis. Job analysis information may be divided into three categories: job content, job context, and worker requirements. Job content refers to workers' job activities or what workers actually do on the job. Job context refers to the conditions under which the work is performed and the demands such jobs impose on the worker. Worker requirements refer to the worker qualifications needed to perform the job successfully. The specific information falling within each category is described next.

CONTENT. When gathering information about tasks, the job analyst seeks to determine what the worker does, the purpose of the action, and the tools, equipment, or machinery used in the process. The analyst may also gather additional information about tasks, such as their relative importance, the expected performance levels, and the type of training needed by a new worker to perform tasks satisfactorily. Job content can be described in a number of ways, depending on how specific one wants (or needs) to be. The different types of job content information are described in Exhibit 1.

Exhibit 1

The Different Types of Job Content Information

Broad Level

Function or Duty
- Definition: The major areas of the job-holder's responsibility.
- Example: A professor's functions are teaching, research, and service to the university/community.

Intermediate Level

Task
- Definition: What a worker does when carrying out a function of the job; it is an activity that results in a specific product or service.
- Example: The function of teaching requires a professor to perform several tasks like lecturing, giving/grading exams, and meeting with students.

Work Behavior
- Definition: An important activity that is not task specific; such behavior is engaged in when performing a variety of tasks.
- Example: "Communicating"—a professor engages in this behavior when performing several tasks, such as lecturing and meeting with students.

Specific Level

Subtasks
- Definition: The steps carried out in the completion of a task.
- Example: The task of providing lectures consists of several subtasks, such as reading the text and other relevant materials, deciding on what information to convey, and determining how this information can be communicated in a clear and interesting manner.

Critical Incidents
- Definition: Specific activities that distinguish effective from ineffective job performance.
- Example: "The professor uses several examples when explaining difficult concepts."

CONTEXT. Job context refers to the conditions under which work is performed and the demands such work imposes on employees. Specific types of job context information typically identified during a job analysis include reporting relationships, supervision received, judgment, authority, personal contacts, working conditions, and the physical and mental demands on the worker.

REQUIREMENTS. Worker requirements refer to the knowledge, skill, ability, personal characteristics, and credentials needed for effective job performance. These terms are defined as:

- Knowledge—the body of information one needs to perform the job.

- Skill—the capability to perform a learned motor task, such as forklift operating skills and word-processing skills.

- Ability—the capability needed to perform a non-motor task, such as communication abilities, mathematical abilities, and reasoning or problem-solving abilities.

- Personal characteristics—an individual's traits (e.g., tact, assertiveness, concern for others, objectivity, work ethic) or their willingness/ability to adapt to the circumstances in the environment (e.g., ability to withstand boredom, willingness to work overtime, willingness to treat others cordially).

- Credentials—proof or documentation that an individual possesses certain competencies, such as diplomas, certifications, and licenses.

The sheer amount of information that can be uncovered during a job analysis may be overwhelming, but it is usually unnecessary to gather all possible data. The purpose or intended use of the job analysis dictates the particular information to be gathered. Therefore, the analyst must decide how the job analysis will be used before deciding what information to seek.

For instance, if a job analysis were to be used to develop a technical training program for new employees, the analyst should focus on information about subtasks (a step-by-step description of how the job is carried out) and the specific knowledge, skills, and abilities (KSAs) one would need to do well on that job. If the purpose were to develop a written employment test to assess applicants' knowledge of the job, the analyst should target information about the specific tasks of the job and the knowledge required to perform each task (i.e., the facts, theories, principles, etc., one must know to be able to perform tasks satisfactorily).

DETERMINING HOW TO COLLECT THE INFORMATION

HR professionals often gather job analysis information. However, because these individuals lack sufficient expertise in the jobs being analyzed, they must enlist the actual job incumbents and their supervisors to gather and interpret the pertinent information. Job analysis information may be gathered by interviewing these individuals, observing them at work, and/or having them complete job analysis questionnaires. The appropriateness of each approach depends, in part, on the type of information sought.

INTERVIEWS. Job analysis interviews are structured conversations between the job analyst and one or more subject-matter experts. Interviews are typically held with both job incumbents and their supervisors. Interviews with incumbents tend to focus on job content and job context information. That is, incumbents are asked to describe what they do, how they do it, and the conditions under which they perform their jobs.

The typical role of the supervisor is to review and verify the accuracy of the incumbents' responses, and to provide further information concerning task importance, expected performance levels, training needs of new workers, and worker requirements.

As the most frequently used job analysis method, interviews provide a potential wealth of information. However, one-on-one interviews can be quite time-consuming. An interview usually takes between one and eight hours, depending on the amount and depth of information sought. Thus, interviewing can take a great deal of time, especially when the analyst must interview several people. When time constraints pose a problem, the best alternative is to conduct a group interview, where several subject-matter experts are interviewed simultaneously.

OBSERVATIONS. Sometimes a job analyst will supplement interviews with job analysis observations. As the name suggests, observation means watching the incumbent perform the job. Observation is most useful when jobs are complex and difficult to accurately describe. When analyzing such jobs, the analyst observes or videotapes the job and then interviews the worker for clarification or explanation. The observation allows the analyst to gain a better understanding of how the work is done and the KSAs needed to perform it.

While observation is usually used as a supplement to the interview, HR professionals sometimes base job analysis solely on observation. Whether or not observation yields sufficient data for the analysis depends on the type of information being collected.

For instance, it is an excellent method for identifying subtasks performed in routine/repetitive types of jobs, such as assembly-line work. When using this approach, however, analysts should be alert to the possibility that some workers may behave atypically when observed. For instance, they may increase their speed to impress the observer, or slow down in an effort to demonstrate how difficult their jobs are.

QUESTIONNAIRES. Job analysis questionnaires ask subject-matter experts—workers and/or supervisors—to record job information in writing. Job analysis questionnaires contain either open-ended or closed-ended questions. Open-ended questions ask respondents to provide their own answers to the questions. Closed-ended questions ask respondents to select an answer from a list provided on the questionnaire. Closed-ended questions are more commonly used because they provide greater uniformity of responses and are more easily scored.

A job analysis questionnaire containing only closed-ended questions is called a job analysis inventory. An inventory containing a list of task statements is called a task inventory; one containing a list of worker ability requirements is called an ability inventory. Job analysis inventories ask respondents to rate each item in terms of its importance to the job. Task inventories also request information regarding the frequency or time spent performing each task.

Companies use job analysis inventories when information is needed from several people (e.g., when many people hold the same job title). Compared to interviews, information can be collected much more quickly using this approach. Companies also use inventories as a means of grouping jobs. Grouping refers to categorizing jobs based on the similarity of tasks performed or skills needed; a group would consist of jobs in which all workers performed similar tasks or needed similar skills.

Once groups are established, the organization can determine selection criteria, training needs, and evaluation criteria applicable to all jobs within a group. Job analysis inventories are also used to determine workers' training needs. Workers are presented with a list of tasks or abilities and are asked to indicate those for which they need training. A five-point rating scale, ranging from "great need" to "no need," is typically used.

DETERMINING HOW JOB ANALYSIS INFORMATION WILL BE RECORDED

Once HR professionals have collected job analysis information, it must be recorded in some systematic way to produce a job description (i.e., a summary of job analysis findings). The format of job descriptions may be general purpose or special purpose.

GENERAL PURPOSE JOB DESCRIPTION. A general purpose job description is one that contains a variety of information that can be used for several purposes, such as communicating job responsibilities to employees and specifying minimum job requirements. For instance, a manager would pull out a job description to review essential functions and worker requirements prior to developing interview questions for a job applicant.

The particular information contained in the job description varies depending on company preference and the intended use of the instrument. A typical general purpose job description contains the following sections: job identification, job summary, essential functions, and worker requirements.

General purpose job descriptions used by most companies provide only a brief summary of job analysis information, and thus lack sufficient detail for some HRM applications. For instance, many fail to indicate subtasks, performance standards, and job context. Subtask information may serve as a basis for developing training programs; performance standards may serve as a basis for developing certain types of performance appraisal forms; and job context information may serve as a basis for making job evaluation ratings that are needed to establish pay rates.

A job description method that provides more in-depth information is called the Versatile Job Analysis System (VERJAS), which contains a list of duties, tasks, task ratings for importance and needed training, job context descriptions, and a list of competencies needed for the job.

SPECIAL PURPOSE JOB DESCRIPTIONS. Several special purpose job descriptions have been developed by a variety of HRM experts during the past 30 years. A key difference between general and special purpose job descriptions lies in the amount of detail they include. Special purpose formats cover fewer topics, but the topics covered are analyzed in more depth. Some of the more commonly used special purpose approaches are described next.

Functional job analysis (FJA) focuses primarily on recording job content information. Each task is analyzed separately on a worksheet that contains a task statement (specifying what the worker does, how it is done, and the results or final product of the worker's actions), the performance standards and training needs associated with the task, and seven rating scales. Three of the scales are known as worker function scales, indicating the level of worker involvement with data, people, and things. The other four scales indicate the level of ability needed in the areas of reasoning, mathematics, language, and following instructions.

Another special purpose method of job analysis is called the critical incident technique (CIT). It originated in the military during World War II and was used to identify critical factors in human performance in a variety of military situations. Critical factors are those that have been demonstrated to make the difference between success and failure in performing a job.

The critical incident technique requires the job analyst to collect critical incidents from people familiar with the job. The incidents are usually collected in the form of stories or anecdotes that depict successful and unsuccessful job behaviors. The stories are then condensed to a single statement that captures the essence of the story. The CIT has several useful HRM applications. For instance, it is a good tool for identifying selection criteria and training needs and for developing performance appraisal forms.

Job analysis is a key component of the HRM process. While the performance of comprehensive job analyses can be time consuming, ultimately employers will benefit from the many uses that a thorough job analysis can provide. From hiring and training to salary justification to remedial uses, job analysis will make the HR manager's job easier, protect an organization from claims of discrimination, and can give the overall organization a competitive advantage.

SEE ALSO: Employee Recruitment Planning; Employee Screening and Selection; Employment Law and Compliance; Occupational Information Network

Lawrence S. Kleiman
Revised by Andrea A. Schurr

FURTHER READING:

Brannick, Michael T., and Edward. L. Levine. *Job Analysis: Methods, Research, and Applications for Human Resource Management in the New Millennium.* Thousand Oaks, CA: Sage Publications, 2002.

Cooper, Kenneth C. *Effective Competency Modeling and Reporting: A Step-by-Step Guide for Improving Individual and Organizational Performance.* New York, NY: AMACOM, 2000.

Fine, Sidney A., and Steven F. Cronshaw. *Functional Job Analysis: A Foundation for Human Resources Management.* Mahwah, NJ: Lawrence Erlbaum Associates, 1999.

Gatewood, Robert D., and Hubert S. Field. *Human Resource Selection.* Fort Worth, TX: Harcourt College Publishers, 2001.

Kleiman, Lawrence S. *Human Resource Management: A Managerial Tool for Competitive Advantage.* Cincinnati, OH: Atomic Dog Publishing, 2004.

Schippmann, Jeffrey S. *Strategic Job Modeling: Working at the Core of Integrated Human Resources.* Mahwah, NJ: Lawrence Erlbaum Associates, 1999.

JOINT VENTURES AND STRATEGIC ALLIANCES

As economies become more globalized, more and more firms are participating in foreign markets. The most popular participation strategies include exporting, licensing, strategic alliances, joint ventures, and direct foreign investment. Each of these involves different levels of risk, capital, and returns.

The use of strategic alliances and joint ventures is rapidly becoming popular with a growing number of multinational firms. According to Cullen, an international strategic alliance is an "agreement between two or more firms from different countries to cooperate in any value-chain activity from R&D to sales". Hitt offered this definition, "joint venture is when an independent firm is created by at least two other firms".

Strategic alliances gained increased popularity in the 1990s, Harbison and Pekar reported that from 1987 to 1992 more than 20,000 new alliances were formed in the U.S, up from 5100 between 1980 and 1987. By 1999, U.S. corporations were involved in over 2,000 alliances with companies in Europe alone, according to Cullen. These cooperative strategies offer many potential advantages to the participant, but they are also pitted with special problems.

ADVANTAGES

Firms may have many motivations to form strategic alliances, and most of these reasons are based on the logic that each partner can bring complementary strengths to the table, resulting in a competitive advantage for the participants collectively. Partners in a strategic alliance can benefit from many aspects of a cooperative relationship: access to unfamiliar or untapped markets, risk sharing, economies of scale, shared technology, and decreased costs.

A partner's knowledge of the local market can be invaluable to a firm if it wants to get its services and products into a new market. This advantage is most easily achieved when the local firm is in a related industry with related products. The local partner knows the buying habits and preferences of the local buyers and suppliers, and he should also have knowledge of the existing channels of distribution. These relationships with others in the value chain may be otherwise unobtainable to an outside firm.

Consider a company that is contemplating entering foreign markets. Local governments often require, as a condition of entry, that entering companies allow some local ownership. This stipulation is found more often in developing countries than in more developed nations because the developing countries are trying to avoid being exploited for their resources. Through a joint venture the outside company can meet this requirement; in fact, the government of a developing country is often the partner in a joint venture.

Joint ventures and strategic alliances force companies to share revenues and profits, but they also share the risk of loss and failure. Thus, the popularity of the cooperative strategies increases as projected risk increases, because joint ventures allow firms to take on projects that are otherwise too risky or too costly.

Economies of scale can be achieved when two or more firms pool their resources together, maximizing efficiency based on the project's needs. Cooperative strategies also allow small companies to join together to compete against an industry giant. Companies of different sizes may also benefit from joining together. The large company offers its capital and resources in exchange for the efficiencies or innovations found at the smaller company. An article by Shafer describes how Abrakadoodle—a company that offers creative art classes for children in schools, day care centers, and community programs—established a strategic alliance with Binney and Smith, known for its Crayola brand art products. Abrakadoodle founder Mary

Rogers was seeking products of high quality that would be safe for children and that would be available nationally, so all locations could use the same materials in their classes. Since she was already using Crayola products in her classes, she states, "We realized that once we started franchising, the number of Crayola products used in Abrakadoodle classes would grow enormously." After months of negotiation, agreement was reached between the two companies. Crayola products will be featured exclusively in Abrakadoodle classes, Abrakadoodle will be allowed to use the Crayola trademark for advertising purposes and will be eligible for discounts on Crayola products. Both companies are benefiting from their shared vision for encouraging children's artistic creativity.

In cases where firms do not have the same strengths, creating alliances can allow them to share technology. This, in turn, can help firms produce more efficiently or at a higher quality. Firms must learn to recognize which other companies can offer complementary skills or technology.

When companies from developed countries cooperate with companies in less developed countries, they usually realize huge cost savings by seeking cheaper labor and untapped reserves of material. The company from the less developed country benefits from advanced technology and increased access to capital. Both companies benefit from the cooperative alliance. Many U.S. firms have been attacked for taking their manufacturing plants "south of the border" to Mexico and thereby harming American workers. The firms are criticized because they join with governments in developing nations so that they can obtain cheaper labor in less developed countries, thus lowering their production costs. Many argue that it harms American workers, but opponents often overlook the advantages that the developing country receives. Often, the large American company provides jobs to areas with alarmingly high unemployment rates and offers them infrastructure and support that they never had before.

SELECTING AN ALLIANCE PARTNER

In order to realize such benefits, many considerations must go into choosing a partner for a joint venture or a strategic alliance. Choosing a strategic alliance or joint venture partner is very important and can prove to be very difficult. Inherent in partner selection is the understanding of potential partners' goals. For one thing, a potential partner must have complementary strategic objectives. A venture will not succeed if the objectives are in conflict, but the objectives do not need to be identical. For example, a Korean radio manufacturer has advanced technology and this technology is attractive to the largest radio manufacturer in Germany. The German firm controls 80 percent of the German market. These firms have complementary objectives. The Korean firm will provide the German firm with the advanced technology, and the German firm will provide the Korean firm accesses into a new market. It is important that each partner understand and accept the other's objectives.

Potential partners should also possess complementary skills. Each partner must contribute more than capital to the project, bringing other competencies into the venture. One firm may bring technical skills and another may bring knowledge of the market. There are many skills that a firm can bring into the relationship: managerial expertise, production facilities, or access to limited resources. Skills are most easily meshed when partners have similar, but not identical, products. If both produce an identical product it may be difficult for them to work together. Even if skills are complementary competition may drive them apart and cause the venture to fail.

While the partners must offer complementary objectives and skills, both partners must believe that they can trust each other and that mutual commitment is a reality. As Cullen explained, "A common theme among managers from both failed and successful strategic alliances is the importance of building mutual trust and commitment among partners. No matter how mutually beneficial and logical the venture may seem ... without trust and commitment the alliance will fail entirely, or it will fail to reach its strategic potential". There are a variety of ways that a company can attain and sustain commitment and trust in cooperative ventures. Goal and intent revelation is a crucial step toward building trust.

MANAGEMENT STRUCTURE

The management structures that control cooperative efforts are varied, and they are usually unique to each relationship. Cullen identified five typical management structures used by companies for their joint ventures and strategic alliances: dominant parent, shared management structure, split-control management structure, independent management structure, and rotating management.

The dominant parent is generally the majority owner of a joint venture. In cases where there is no majority owner, the dominant parent may be the company that contributes the most valuable resources. When there is a dominant parent, this company makes more operational and strategic decisions. In many instances, a joint venture is treated as a subsidiary of the dominant parent. Often when large multinational firms have cooperative alliances with firms in small countries, the multinational firm comes in as the dominant parent.

The shared management structure and the split-control management structure are very similar. In these structures, both parent companies share deci-

sion-making responsibilities. In the shared structure, there are an equal number of managers in controlling positions from each company (board of directors, top management, and functional management). In split-control structures, there are not equal numbers of managers from each company at the functional level. In areas of expertise, one company may hold most or all of these positions. This can be because of differences in expertise or because one firm may insist on this type of arrangement if they do not want to share their knowledge or technology.

Independent management structures are found when the management of a joint venture, acts independently of either parent firm. Because a joint venture is a separate, legal entity, this is possible, but it is highly unlikely with new joint ventures. It is more common to see the independent management structure as a joint venture matures and begins to act as an independent firm. If the independent management structure is found in a young joint venture, it is often because the parents agreed to recruit externally for management positions.

In a rotating management structure, key positions of the hierarchy rotate between firms. Each firm assigns a person for their term. This structure is popular when an alliance partner is from a less developed country. With this type of management, local management can be trained so that technology and expertise are transferred to the community, according to Cullen.

DOMESTIC JOINT VENTURES AND ALLIANCES

Not all joint ventures and strategic alliances cross international boundaries. Companies in the same country can achieve many of the same benefits found in an international cooperative agreement. For instance, Zuber reported that in 1999, CKE Restaurants, the parent of Carl's Jr. and Hardee's fast-food restaurants, entered into a joint venture with Houston-based Equilon Enterprises and Motiva Enterprises, owners of Shell and Texaco gas station franchises. Under the plan, full-size CKE restaurants would be built next to the gas stations, as opposed to having smaller, more limited outlets operating from within the gas stations' convenience stores. This would enable CKE to get into new markets, and they will do so paired with two established gasoline brands. The gas stations hoped to benefit from increased traffic because they now would offer a single place to fill a gas tank and fill a customer's stomach.

Just as the companies that come together are quite varied, so are their reasons for doing so. There is, however, one best reason for bringing two firms together: synergy. Synergy is the realization that the whole may be greater than the sum of the parts, according to Hitt.

Often, when two firms are combined, they find that their new venture is greater than the sum of what each could have done independently. Many of the reasons presented create synergy, but one must analyze the venture to make sure that it creates something greater than the two companies could have been on their own. When there is synergy, new products are created for the market quicker or better than they would have been if the companies had kept their resources to themselves. If there is synergy, everyone benefits.

SEE ALSO: Competitive Advantage; Diversification Strategy; International Business; Strategy Formulation

Dena Waggoner
Revised by Monica C. Turner

FURTHER READING:

Cullen, J. *Multinational Management: A Strategic Approach.* Cincinnati: South-Western College Publishing, 1999.

Geringer, J.M. *Joint Venture Partner Selection.* Westport, CT: Quorum Books, 1988.

Harbison, J.R., and P. Pekar, Jr. *A Practical Guide to Alliances: Leapfrogging the Learning Curve.* Los Angeles, CA: Booz-Allen and Hamilton, Inc., 1998.

Hitt, M.A., R.D. Ireland., and R.E. Hoskisson. *Strategic Management: Competitiveness and Globalization.* 2nd ed. Minneapolis/St. Paul, MN: West Publishing, 1996.

Reuer, J.J. *Strategic Alliances: Theory and Evidence.* New York, NY: Oxford University Press, 2004.

Shafer, R. "Developing Strategic Partnerships." *Franchising World* 37, no. 1 (2005): 79–81.

Wallace, R.L. *Strategic Partnerships: An Entrepreneur's Guide to Joint Ventures and Alliances.* Chicago, IL: Dearborn Trade Publishers, 2004.

Zuber, A. "CKE Inks Pact for Texaco, Shell Sites." *Nation's Restaurant News* 33, no. 28 (1999): 1.

JUST-IN-TIME PRODUCTION

SEE: Lean Manufacturing and Just-in-Time Production

K

KNOWLEDGE MANAGEMENT

Knowledge management refers to an organization's strategic efforts to gain a competitive advantage by capturing and using the intellectual assets held by its employees and customers. Efforts to archive best practices and lessons learned, and to make better use of information stored in databases, also fall under the rubric of knowledge management. Advocates of knowledge management believe that capturing, storing, and the distributing knowledge will help employees work smarter, reduce duplication, and ultimately produce more innovative products and services that meet the customers' needs and offer a good value.

If a company knows something (e.g., changing tastes of the customers, innovative solutions to international tax issues, or how to use information systems to better monitor production processes) that its competitors do not, then that company has an opportunity to offer a distinguishing product or service. Knowledge management, as a business practice, impacts the entire organization by helping employees, managers, and executives share information and best practices that positively impact collective performance. Unlike downsizing, which emphasizes the reduction and control of costs (often through attrition and layoffs), knowledge management is a value-adding practice that seeks to enhance profits, innovation, and decision making by providing more and better information to every member of the organization.

To better understand why knowledge has become a critical factor in businesses, we need to understand that the United States and many other industrial countries are moving toward a knowledge economy. A knowledge economy is one where a majority of workers spend their day applying know-how to the production of goods and delivery of services. In a knowledge economy, employees work to improve decision-making, design, and delivery processes, while only a limited number of people are involved with the actual manufacturing of goods. Important questions that we might ask about a knowledge economy include:

- How many people now spend their day applying knowledge?

- How did the change to a knowledge economy come about?

- How do organizations go about managing knowledge?

American labor trends indicate that the percentage of people working in an information-intensive capacity is increasing while the number of people working in agriculture, manufacturing, nonprofessional service industries is decreasing.

As another indicator of the shift, during the second half of the twentieth century, knowledge-intensive companies (those that have 40 percent or more knowledge workers) account for 28 percent of the total U.S. employment and produced 43 percent of all new employment growth.

The rapid increase in knowledge-intensive work is often attributed to communication technologies, and especially digital technologies, that allow employees to transfer or access large amounts of data in minutes. Since the end of World War II, the world has seen the invention of the first programmable computer, satellite technology, fax machines, microprocessors, floppy disks, portable computers, cellular telephones and pagers, and the World Wide Web. All of these technologies are historically important because they allow great quantities of information to be shared with partners who are geographically separated from us and who, using earlier technologies, might have had to wait hours, days, or even weeks to receive information. Technology has, in effect, brought people closer together by allowing voice, text, and images to be rapidly transmitted across great distances.

In 1969, the Department of Defense launched the Advanced Research Project Agency, which created a distributed network (precursor to the Internet) that allowed researchers to share information and connect with other computers on the network. Later, researchers added e-mail bulletin boards to the system so that messages could be transmitted back and forth. This broad digital network took information sharing to an entirely new level. Whereas a fax machine might be able to transfer 2,000 words from New York to Los Angeles in a matter of minutes, this new digital network—today represented by the World Wide Web—allows information to be transmitted at the speed of light. Current statistics indicate that an ever-increasing number of people are using the Web to communicate and gather information. In 1983, there were an estimated 2,000 people using the Arpanet. In 1990, the count increased to just over 1 million users. By 2005, it was estimated that more than 900 million people worldwide would be using the Internet that year to gather and transmit information, and this figure was expected to more than double within five years. The consequence of all this growth is that decision makers now have almost instant access to large quantities of data that can be used to improve decision-making, strategic planning, and product design, and customer service.

Recognizing that knowledge systems are usually based on local area network (LAN) or Internet technology, several critical questions arise when an organization attempts to implement a knowledge management system. First, how do you measure the value of a knowledge management system? Like soft-skills training, many organizations and experts are struggling to measure the value added by a knowledge management system. For example, the value of new technology in a manufacturing plant can be measured with relative accuracy and be said to decrease production costs by a certain amount per unit. Knowledge management systems, however, commonly do not have such a direct impact on operations. How can we accurately measure value of having immediate access to information that improves decision-making or strategy?

Another problem is, how do you create an organizational culture that values sharing? The old adage "Information is power" exemplifies the cultural reasons why knowledge management systems can be challenging to implement. Traditionally in the United States, employees have been recognized and rewarded for individual effort and achievement. Collaborative effort and cooperation have not traditionally been rewarded. Consequently, implementing a knowledge management system may likely require that an organization reassess the values by which business is con-

ducted, the performance evaluation instruments, and the pay/bonus structures so that employees see ample incentive to share knowledge and cooperate throughout the organization.

How much information is too much? Information overload is a concern in organizations that are developing a knowledge management system. What information do we attempt to capture and make available? What information do we overlook? In large organizations, the answers to such questions can have a dramatic impact on the quantity and quality of information available to employees.

Finally, can knowledge really be captured? Knowledge managers assume that knowledge can be captured, replicated, and made useful for other members of an organization. Much knowledge, however, is tacit. It is unexpressed. For example, how do we capture the knowledge that an operations manager develops after years of working in manufacturing plants? How do we capture the sense of history, the habitual patterns of thinking, or the principles for good decision making that have proven effective over the years? If explicit knowledge is framed by tacit knowledge, how do we capture and share both forms of knowledge so that the user of the knowledge management system does not feel like the recipient of baseless or de-contextualized facts and figures?

SEE ALSO: Electronic Commerce; Electronic Data Interchange and Electronic Funds Transfer

Michael A. Netzley
Revised by Hal P. Kirkwood, Jr.

FURTHER READING:

Harvard Business Review on Knowledge Management. Boston: Harvard Business School Press, 1998.

Huotari, M.L., and M. Iivonen. *Trust in Knowledge Management and Systems in Organizations.* Hershey, PA: Idea Group Publishing, 2003.

Malhotra, Y. "Integrating Knowledge Management Technologies in Organizational Business Processes: Getting Real Time Enterprises to Deliver Real Business Performance." *Journal of Knowledge Management* 9, no. 1 (2005): 7–28.

Stewart, Thomas A. *Intellectual Capital: The New Wealth of Organizations.* New York: Doubleday/Currency, 1997.

Vouros, G.A. "Technological Issues Towards Knowledge-Powered Organizations." *Journal of Knowledge Management* 7, no. 2 (2003): 114–127.

KNOWLEDGE WORKERS

Knowledge workers, alternatively termed knowledge entrepreneurs, free agents, or human capital, constitute the fastest growing sector of the workforce in the world. Peter Drucker, the eminent management writer credited with coining the term knowledge worker, defines these individuals as "high level employees who apply theoretical and analytical knowledge, acquired through formal education, to develop new products or services". Knowledge workers are those who acquire, manipulate, interpret, and apply information in order to perform multidisciplinary, complex and unpredictable work. They analyze information and apply expertise in a variety of areas to solve problems, generate ideas, or create new products and services.

Examples of knowledge workers include professionals, scientists, educators, and information system designers. Knowledge work is characterized by the use of information, by unique work situations, and by creativity and autonomy. Knowledge workers make decisions rather than physical items and work with ideas rather than with objects. Their work focuses on mental rather than muscle power and is characterized by non-repetitive tasks. Knowledge workers use different methods and techniques to solve problems and have the authority to decide what work methods to use in order to complete their varying job tasks.

CATEGORIZATION OF KNOWLEDGE WORKERS

Knowledge workers can be grouped into various categories, based on the amount of time spent on individual tasks or on the type of information or skills possessed. The fact that knowledge workers can be classified in different ways is indicative of the variety of jobs they hold.

Knowledge workers can be categorized according to the amount of time engaged in routine versus innovative behaviors. On one end of the scale, workers perform tasks that are primarily repetitive and routine in nature but occasionally use complex information to make independent decisions, often with regard to customer service issues. Employees at the spectrum's opposite end spend most of their time accessing information and making independent decisions with regard to that information.

A second way to categorize those whose work focuses on information and ideas is as follows: specialty knowledge workers, portable knowledge workers, and creation of knowledge workers. Specialty knowledge workers possess a significant amount of knowledge related to a specific company's products or services. These individuals can be thought of as housing vital corporate assets in their heads. Portable knowledge workers possess information of wide and immediate utility. They are familiar with knowledge that is in demand by a variety of organizations. Software programmers, librarians, and persons with business degrees are examples of portable knowledge workers. Creation of knowledge workers focuses the majority of their efforts on innovative behaviors, such as product design and development. Examples of creation of knowledge workers include scientists and information systems designers.

KNOWLEDGE WORKER CHARACTERISTICS

Knowledge work is complex, and those who perform it require certain skills and abilities as well as familiarity with actual and theoretical knowledge. These persons must be able to find, access, recall, and apply information, interact well with others, and possess the ability and motivation to acquire and improve these skills. While the importance of one or more of these characteristics may vary from one job to the next, all knowledge workers need these basic qualifications. More jobs now require college degrees than ever before and a shortage of knowledge workers is imminent. Another future concern is the retirement of experienced plant managers, research scientists, and other knowledge workers that will lead to reduced capacity to innovate and pursue growth strategies as well as increase costly operational errors and decrease efficiency in the management of resources and productivity.

POSSESSING FACTUAL AND THEORETICAL KNOWLEDGE Knowledge workers are conversant with specific factual and theoretical information. Schoolteachers possess information regarding specialized subject matter, teaching strategies, and learning theories. The sales representative commands factual knowledge concerning the product he or she sells and theoretical knowledge about how to interest customers in that product. Prospective knowledge workers may need years of formal education to master the information needed to enter a particular field of work. Because knowledge is always being created, this type of employee will be acquiring additional information on a continual basis.

FINDING AND ACCESSING INFORMATION. At a time when the operations of today's information society depends on knowledge that is continually growing and changing, distribution of information within organizations has become problematic due to the massive amount of information with which employees need to be familiar. Knowledge workers must therefore know how to independently identify and find such material. Such employees need to know which sources provide the information they need and how to use these sources in order to locate information successfully.

ABILITY TO APPLY INFORMATION. Knowledge workers use information to answer questions, solve problems, complete writing assignments, and generate ideas. Use of analogical reasoning and relevance judgment enables employees to address successfully personal and customer service-related issues. Analogical reasoning is a knowledge-based problem-solving process in which persons apply information from precedents to new situations. Relevance judgment is the process by which individuals decide whether or not a precedent is applicable to the problem at hand. The non-repetitive nature of knowledge workers' jobs makes crucial the ability to apply information to new situations.

COMMUNICATION SKILLS. Knowledge work is characterized by close contact with customers, supervisors, subordinates, and team mates. Successful knowledge workers present clearly, in spoken and written word, both factual and theoretical information. These employees listen with understanding and ask for clarification when they do not understand what is being said to them.

Knowledge workers must be able to speak, read, write, and listen in one-on-one and group settings. Emphasis on quality customer service and customization of goods and services to meet individual customer needs and wants brings knowledge workers into close contact with customers. The goals of organizational effectiveness and continual improvement of products, together with the need to continually consider new information in order to accomplish work, require communication between supervisor and supervised and among team mates or colleagues. Knowledge workers possess communications skills that enable them to collaborate with one another for goal-setting, decision-making, and idea generating purposes.

MOTIVATION. The nature of knowledge work requires continual growth, in terms of mastery of information and skill development, on the part of those who do this type of work. Knowledge workers must become and remain interested in finding information, memorizing that information, and applying it to their work. Because new technological developments call on knowledge workers to change continuously the way they accomplish their work, these individuals must maintain a desire to apply their talents toward incorporating new information and new technologies into their work.

INTELLECTUAL CAPABILITIES. Knowledge workers must have the intellectual capabilities to acquire the skills discussed above. Such intellectual capacities include those concerned with the understanding, recall, processing and application of specialized information. Persons who perform knowledge work must possess the abilities needed to acquire appropriate communication skills and to learn how to figure out where and how information can be located. Knowledge workers are able to learn how to read and write at post-secondary levels and to perform abstract reasoning. They also have the intellectual capacity to understand

the value of acquiring and maintaining the knowledge and skills needed to accomplish their work.

HISTORICAL BACKGROUND

Some occupations have always centered on the use of specialized information. Only recently, however, have persons employed in these types of occupations begun to outnumber those employed in jobs that do not require intensive use of specialized knowledge. In the late 1950s and early 1960s, writers such as Fritz Machlup and Peter Drucker first identified and described the reasons behind this phenomenon. Today the increase in knowledge work professions concerns business administrators, professors, management consultants and others interested in learning how to increase business profits or improve life's quality.

Recently, the number of persons employed in traditional types of knowledge work professions has escalated while new types of knowledge work have appeared. Throughout history, people such as writers, teachers, and ministers, for example, have engaged themselves in intellectual activity. Their numbers grew as the population of Europeans in North America increased in the 1700s and early 1800s. Industrialization then fostered the creation of new categories of employees who used information to make their livings: inventors, consultants, and managers. As the population continued to grow, so did the economy, which became able to support greater numbers of knowledge workers.

In the 1950s, computer science and other knowledge based professions rapidly expanded. Economist Fritz Machlup examined the distribution, use, and creation of information in the United States. He used statistical information to show that manual workers' share of the labour force was decreasing while the white-collar share was increasing. He tried to differentiate among various types of knowledge workers. Machlup showed that knowledge-producing occupations were growing much faster than manual labour occupations, and he redefined the word "work" in terms of a way to manage and use knowledge.

Peter Drucker wrote extensively on the subject of the knowledge worker. Drucker identified and described the reasons for the decline of the blue collar worker and the rise of the knowledge worker, and he made what are now considered accurate predictions about the knowledge worker's future place in society. He described how knowledge-based positions evolved from manufacturing and agricultural jobs as automation changed the way these jobs were accomplished. Drucker argued that service sector activities had increased, expanded, and diversified, causing the number of knowledge workers to grow. He explained how emphasis on and developments in science and technology fostered the creation of new knowledge professions while an expanding economy enabled their growth.

Information continues to influence work and alter the way it is accomplished. Technology makes possible computerized databases to manage and access such information. In turn, the introduction of new technologies creates jobs for those who design, manage, and utilize these technologies. Organizational expansion, brought on by the use of new knowledge, also creates this type of work, as employees turn their attention toward coordinating additional work. Information's importance in the workplace continues to make crucial its accessibility.

KNOWLEDGE WORKER SHORTAGE

The information society requires a highly qualified workforce. As compared to the past, a larger proportion of the population should attend college and participate in formal training programs designed to teach specialized information and specific skills associated with knowledge work. The fact that traditional blue-collar workers cannot acquire easily the knowledge and skills needed to become knowledge workers will create a shortage of these types of workers. Although colleges and universities may adapt their curriculum's to prepare students for various types of knowledge work, it is unlikely that significantly greater percentages of the population will attend college. The American Society for Training and Development maintains that, while nine-tenths of all new jobs now require post-secondary levels of reading, writing, and math, only half of those entering the workforce for the first time have attained these skills. When the traditional blue-collar worker cannot make the transition to knowledge work, society will face problems caused by both unemployment and understaffing.

HIRING AND RETAINING THE KNOWLEDGE WORKER

The shortage of knowledge workers makes employers concerned with attracting and retaining these employees. In order to hire and retain knowledge workers, employers may offer higher salaries, attractive work environments, and continuing educational opportunities. Employers take actions designed to attract and retain knowledge workers by creating a free-agent community, respecting knowledge workers as new bosses, and providing growth opportunities. In a free-agent community, employees have the freedom to choose their work methods and work in the environments in which they function best. Treating knowledge workers as the new bosses means that management operates as a facilitator rather than as a controller of work. This gives knowledge workers the autonomy they need to complete their work as they see fit. Employers

make work attractive and rewarding by providing growth opportunities, such as those that are associated with ongoing training and development, special assignments, and rotation of jobs and job responsibilities. In such ways, employers attempt to address the knowledge worker shortage.

IMPROVING KNOWLEDGE WORKER PRODUCTIVITY

Knowledge worker productivity influences success in today's competitive work economy, and businesses are focusing on increasing this productivity. Management facilitates the knowledge worker's job performance by providing access to relevant information; environments that promote this information's desired use, continuing educational opportunities, and a balance between guidance and autonomy.

Employers use costly technologies to facilitate access to and manipulation of information. The term information technology refers to computer equipment and programs used to access, process, store, and disseminate information. Examples of information technologies include word processing, spreadsheet, and electronic mail programs, and a variety of other software programs designed to process information in specific ways. Information technologies are designed to reduce the amount of time employees spend on information access, management and manipulation and to increase the accuracy of these processes. Information technology is important because it helps make information accessible and manageable in a time when accessibility and manipulation of information are crucial to the world economy.

THE WORKPLACE

The characteristics of each individual knowledge worker's workplace depend on the type of work accomplished and what the employer is willing and able to provide. Workplace arrangements range from traditional physical office space occupied by employees between the hours of 9:00 A.M. to 5:00 P.M. each workday to virtual office space which can exist just about anywhere.

The traditional clerk or manual labourer's workspace may remain basically the same as it was in the past, altered slightly in order to bring employees into closer contact with one another and with their customers or to permit the introduction of new equipment. This being the physical aspects of this type of workplace center on the completion of repetitive tasks and job duties.

Knowledge workers who work exclusively with ideas and information may operate in a non-traditional workplace situated anywhere that employees have access to needed computer and communication equipment. Individuals who work in such "virtual offices" may utilize physical office space as necessary or use "hoteling" to visit customers. Hoteling is a process by which those who work out of virtual offices schedule physical office space for meetings with colleagues, customers, clients, and sales representatives. Writers, researchers, outside sales representatives, and product designers are examples of knowledge workers who might utilize non-traditional workspaces.

CHALLENGES AND OPPORTUNITIES

The increasing demand for employees who use their skills and talents to perform complex and non-repetitive work presents both challenges and opportunities. The challenges include attainment and maintenance of a well educated, highly skilled, and efficient workforce. Opportunities include chances for greater numbers of working age people to hold more rewarding jobs than previously possible and for employees to be judged according to their unique talents and abilities rather with regard to how quickly they complete repetitive tasks or how well they conform to pre-established work standards.

Education of a properly skilled workforce will take special effort. Society will need to convince its members to pursue educational and training opportunities that will qualify them for knowledge work. Businesses and educational institutions may work together to determine exactly what skills and knowledge students need to enter the workforce and how to educate students accordingly. Educators and employers will need to ensure that those who need to know how to use certain technologies are able to do so and will not become disconnected because they are unable to use advanced computer programs or telecommunications equipment. While potential knowledge workers will require familiarity with specialized information related to the type of work they plan to undertake, it will be important that their educational backgrounds give them a common basis for understanding one another.

Hiring, retention, and productivity of knowledge workers will remain important issues. As the shortage of persons qualified to perform knowledge work increases, employers will be challenged to find more effective ways to hire and retain these individuals. In order to improve productivity, employers will try to figure out how to promote teamwork among knowledge workers, how to best design the workplace, and how to keep knowledge workers from becoming overwhelmed with the information they need to do their jobs.

The use of information technology to manage and manipulate information presents a series of challenges. Employees will need to find ways to fund these technologies and to provide training on their use. In order to maximize the value of information technologies, employers will want to determine how and when information technologies increase knowledge worker productivity and performance, how to best match a particular technology with a specific job, and how computer programs can be best used to locate, process, and create information. Employers will also need to know how to evaluate employee use of information technologies and how to cope with underutilization of and resistance to these technologies. With this user-oriented infrastructure, mission critical business news, financial and research data is now available upon demand to the user's desktop. In fact, the availability of critical information via the web has created a new breed of telecommuting knowledge workers with anytime/anyplace capabilities.

The shift from blue-collar jobs to knowledge work presents new opportunities. Greater numbers of people will be able to hold jobs that enable them to develop their talents and use their creativity. These new knowledge workers will have greater job mobility. Employers will respect them as individuals who bring unique talents and abilities to their jobs as opposed to workers who perform repetitive tasks. Leadership opportunities will be open to increasingly greater numbers of people.

The twenty-first century has brought a new challenge in the form of outsourcing knowledge workers in several sectors of the economy. Business process outsourcing services are now flowing to countries such as India, the Philippines, Russia and China. Consultant A.T. Kearney predicts that analysis and research, regulatory reporting, human resources, and accounting will be the next generation of financial industry jobs migrating overseas. Concern about high costs and poor quality resulting from cultural and communication issues due to outsourcing, has been expressed. Under utilization and cost demands of business worldwide are influencing the changes in knowledge worker skills, requirements, and work location. Identifying and utilizing the knowledge worker in an effective and cost efficient manner is a challenge for business and for the economy today.

William W. Prince

FURTHER READING:

Cortada, James W., ed. *Rise of the Knowledge Worker.* Boston: Butterworth-Heinemann, 1998.

Donlan, Thomas G. "Catch a Tiger by the Tail." *Barron's,* 14 February 2005. Available from http://proquest.umi.com

Drucker, Peter F. *Managing in a Time of Great Change.* New York: Truman Talley Books/Dutton, 1995.

"Knowledge-Worker Productivity: The Biggest Challenge." *California Management Review* 41, no. 2 (1999): 41–57.

Goldsmith, Marshall. "Retain Your Top Performers." *Executive Excellence* 14, no. 11 (1997): 10–11.

Gordon, Edward E. "The New Knowledge Worker." *Adult Learning* 8, no. 4 (1997): 14–18.

Gould, Susan B., and Barbara R. Levin. "Building a Free Agent Community." *Compensation and Benefit Management* 14, no. 3 (1998): 24–30.

"High Cost of Lost Knowledge." *IIE Solutions* (June 2002).

Krebsbach, Karen. "Outsourcing: Fighting a Giant Sucking Sound: Banks Face Backlash on IT Job Exports Overseas." *Bank Technology News* (August 2003). Available from http://infotrac.galegroup.com

Munk, Nina. "The New Organization Man." *Fortune,* 137, no. 5 (1998): 34–41.

Price, Steven M. "Facilities Planning: A Perspective for the Information Age." *IIE Solutions* 29, no. 8 (1997): 20–23.

L

In manufacturing, facility layout consists of configuring the plant site with lines, buildings, major facilities, work areas, aisles, and other pertinent features such as department boundaries. While facility layout for services may be similar to that for manufacturing, it also may be somewhat different—as is the case with offices, retailers, and warehouses. Because of its relative permanence, facility layout probably is one of the most crucial elements affecting efficiency. An efficient layout can reduce unnecessary material handling, help to keep costs low, and maintain product flow through the facility.

Firms in the upper left-hand corner of the product-process matrix have a process structure known as a jumbled flow or a disconnected or intermittent line flow. Upper-left firms generally have a process layout. Firms in the lower right-hand corner of the product-process matrix can have a line or continuous flow. Firms in the lower-right part of the matrix generally have a product layout. Other types of layouts include fixed-position, combination, cellular, and certain types of service layouts.

PROCESS LAYOUT

Process layouts are found primarily in job shops, or firms that produce customized, low-volume products that may require different processing requirements and sequences of operations. Process layouts are facility configurations in which operations of a similar nature or function are grouped together. As such, they occasionally are referred to as functional layouts. Their purpose is to process goods or provide services that involve a variety of processing requirements. A manufacturing example would be a machine shop. A machine shop generally has separate departments where general-purpose machines are grouped together by function (e.g., milling, grinding, drilling, hydraulic presses, and lathes). Therefore, facilities that are configured according to individual functions or processes have a process layout. This type of layout gives the firm the flexibility needed to handle a variety of routes and process requirements. Services that utilize process layouts include hospitals, banks, auto repair, libraries, and universities.

Improving process layouts involves the minimization of transportation cost, distance, or time. To accomplish this some firms use what is known as a Muther grid, where subjective information is summarized on a grid displaying various combinations of department, work group, or machine pairs. Each combination (pair), represented by an intersection on the grid, is assigned a letter indicating the importance of the closeness of the two (A = absolutely necessary; E = very important; I = important; O = ordinary importance; U = unimportant; X = undesirable). Importance generally is based on the shared use of facilities, equipment, workers or records, work flow, communication requirements, or safety requirements. The departments and other elements are then assigned to clusters in order of importance.

Advantages of process layouts include:

- Flexibility. The firm has the ability to handle a variety of processing requirements.

- Cost. Sometimes, the general-purpose equipment utilized may be less costly to purchase and less costly and easier to maintain than specialized equipment.

• Motivation. Employees in this type of layout will probably be able to perform a variety of tasks on multiple machines, as opposed to the boredom of performing a repetitive task on an assembly line. A process layout also allows the employer to use some type of individual incentive system.

• System protection. Since there are multiple machines available, process layouts are not particularly vulnerable to equipment failures.

Disadvantages of process layouts include:

• Utilization. Equipment utilization rates in process layout are frequently very low, because machine usage is dependent upon a variety of output requirements.

• Cost. If batch processing is used, in-process inventory costs could be high. Lower volume means higher per-unit costs. More specialized attention is necessary for both products and customers. Setups are more frequent, hence higher setup costs. Material handling is slower and more inefficient. The span of supervision is small due to job complexities (routing, setups, etc.), so supervisory costs are higher. Additionally, in this type of layout accounting, inventory control, and purchasing usually are highly involved.

• Confusion. Constantly changing schedules and routings make juggling process requirements more difficult.

PRODUCT LAYOUT

Product layouts are found in flow shops (repetitive assembly and process or continuous flow industries). Flow shops produce high-volume, highly standardized products that require highly standardized, repetitive processes. In a product layout, resources are arranged sequentially, based on the routing of the products. In theory, this sequential layout allows the entire process to be laid out in a straight line, which at times may be totally dedicated to the production of only one product or product version. The flow of the line can then be subdivided so that labor and equipment are utilized smoothly throughout the operation.

Two types of lines are used in product layouts: paced and unpaced. Paced lines can use some sort of conveyor that moves output along at a continuous rate so that workers can perform operations on the product as it goes by. For longer operating times, the worker may have to walk alongside the work as it moves until he or she is finished and can walk back to the workstation to begin working on another part (this essentially is how automobile manufacturing works).

On an unpaced line, workers build up queues between workstations to allow a variable work pace. However, this type of line does not work well with large, bulky products because too much storage space may be required. Also, it is difficult to balance an extreme variety of output rates without significant idle time. A technique known as assembly-line balancing can be used to group the individual tasks performed into workstations so that there will be a reasonable balance of work among the workstations.

Product layout efficiency is often enhanced through the use of line balancing. Line balancing is the assignment of tasks to workstations in such a way that workstations have approximately equal time requirements. This minimizes the amount of time that some workstations are idle, due to waiting on parts from an upstream process or to avoid building up an inventory queue in front of a downstream process.

Advantages of product layouts include:

• Output. Product layouts can generate a large volume of products in a short time.

• Cost. Unit cost is low as a result of the high volume. Labor specialization results in reduced training time and cost. A wider span of supervision also reduces labor costs. Accounting, purchasing, and inventory control are routine. Because routing is fixed, less attention is required.

• Utilization. There is a high degree of labor and equipment utilization.

Disadvantages of product layouts include:

• Motivation. The system's inherent division of labor can result in dull, repetitive jobs that can prove to be quite stressful. Also, assembly-line layouts make it very hard to administer individual incentive plans.

• Flexibility. Product layouts are inflexible and cannot easily respond to required system changes—especially changes in product or process design.

• System protection. The system is at risk from equipment breakdown, absenteeism, and downtime due to preventive maintenance.

FIXED-POSITION LAYOUT

A fixed-position layout is appropriate for a product that is too large or too heavy to move. For example, battleships are not produced on an assembly line. For services, other reasons may dictate the fixed position (e.g., a hospital operating room where doctors, nurses, and medical equipment are brought to the patient). Other fixed-position layout examples include construction (e.g., buildings, dams, and electric or nuclear power plants), shipbuilding, aircraft, aerospace, farming, drilling for oil, home repair, and automated car washes. In order to make this work, required resources must be portable so that they can be taken to the job for "on the spot" performance.

Due to the nature of the product, the user has little choice in the use of a fixed-position layout. Disadvantages include:

- Space. For many fixed-position layouts, the work area may be crowded so that little storage space is available. This also can cause material handling problems.

- Administration. Oftentimes, the administrative burden is higher for fixed-position layouts. The span of control can be narrow, and coordination difficult.

COMBINATION LAYOUTS

Many situations call for a mixture of the three main layout types. These mixtures are commonly called combination or hybrid layouts. For example, one firm may utilize a process layout for the majority of its process along with an assembly in one area. Alternatively, a firm may utilize a fixed-position layout for the assembly of its final product, but use assembly lines to produce the components and subassemblies that make up the final product (e.g., aircraft).

CELLULAR LAYOUT

Cellular manufacturing is a type of layout where machines are grouped according to the process requirements for a set of similar items (part families) that require similar processing. These groups are called cells. Therefore, a cellular layout is an equipment layout configured to support cellular manufacturing.

Processes are grouped into cells using a technique known as group technology (GT). Group technology involves identifying parts with similar design characteristics (size, shape, and function) and similar process characteristics (type of processing required, available machinery that performs this type of process, and processing sequence).

Workers in cellular layouts are cross-trained so that they can operate all the equipment within the cell and take responsibility for its output. Sometimes the cells feed into an assembly line that produces the final product. In some cases a cell is formed by dedicating certain equipment to the production of a family of parts without actually moving the equipment into a physical cell (these are called virtual or nominal cells). In this way, the firm avoids the burden of rearranging its current layout. However, physical cells are more common.

An automated version of cellular manufacturing is the flexible manufacturing system (FMS). With an FMS, a computer controls the transfer of parts to the various processes, enabling manufacturers to achieve some of the benefits of product layouts while maintaining the flexibility of small batch production.

Some of the advantages of cellular manufacturing include:

- Cost. Cellular manufacturing provides for faster processing time, less material handling, less work-in-process inventory, and reduced setup time, all of which reduce costs.

- Flexibility. Cellular manufacturing allows for the production of small batches, which provides some degree of increased flexibility. This aspect is greatly enhanced with FMSs.

- Motivation. Since workers are cross-trained to run every machine in the cell, boredom is less of a factor. Also, since workers are responsible for their cells' output, more autonomy and job ownership is present.

OTHER LAYOUTS

In addition to the aforementioned layouts, there are others that are more appropriate for use in service organizations. These include warehouse/storage layouts, retail layouts, and office layouts.

With warehouse/storage layouts, order frequency is a key factor. Items that are ordered frequently should be placed close together near the entrance of the facility, while those ordered less frequently remain in the rear of the facility. Pareto analysis is an excellent method for determining which items to place near the entrance. Since 20 percent of the items typically represent 80 percent of the items ordered, it is not difficult to determine which 20 percent to place in the most convenient location. In this way, order picking is made more efficient.

While layout design is much simpler for small retail establishments (shoe repair, dry cleaner, etc.), retail stores, unlike manufacturers, must take into consideration the presence of customers and the accompanying opportunities to influence sales and customer attitudes. For example, supermarkets place dairy products near the rear of the store so that customers who run into the store for a quick gallon of milk must travel through other sections of the store. This increases the chance of the customer seeing an item of interest and making an impulse buy. Additionally, expensive items such as meat are often placed so that the customer will see them frequently (e.g., pass them at the end of each aisle). Retail chains are able to take advantage of standardized layouts, which give the customer more familiarity with the store when shopping in a new location.

Office layouts must be configured so that the physical transfer of information (paperwork) is optimized. Communication also can be enhanced through the use of low-rise partitions and glass walls.

A number of changes taking in place in manufacturing have had a direct effect on facility layout. One apparent manufacturing trend is to build smaller and more compact facilities with more automation and robotics. In these situations, machines need to be placed closer to each other in order to reduce material handling. Another trend is an increase in automated material handling systems, including automated storage and retrieval systems (AS/AR) and automated guided vehicles (AGVs). There also is movement toward the use of U-shaped lines, which allow workers, material handlers, and supervisors to see the entire line easily and travel efficiently between workstations. So that the view is not obstructed, fewer walls and partitions are incorporated into the layout. Finally, thanks to lean manufacturing and just-in-time production, less space is needed for inventory storage throughout the layout.

SEE ALSO: Lean Manufacturing and Just-in-Time Production; Product-Process Matrix

R. Anthony Inman

FURTHER READING:

Finch, Byron J. *Operations Now: Profitability, Processes, Performance.* 2nd ed. Boston: McGraw-Hill/Irwin, 2006.

Stevenson, William J. *Operations Management.* 8th ed., Boston: McGraw-Hill/Irwin, 2005.

LEADERSHIP STYLES AND BASES OF POWER

Studies of leadership styles are diverse in nature and multiple definitions have been offered. However, leadership style can be defined broadly as the manner and approach of providing direction, implementing plans, and motivating people.

Bases of power refer to the methods that managers and leaders utilize to influence their employees. When examining bases of power, the concept of authority must also be considered. These two are interconnected attributes tied to the behavior of superiors over subordinates. In their article, "Are There No Limits To Authority?", David Knights and Darren McCabe explain that "power should be understood to be a condition of social relations. Thus, it is erroneous to ask who has power. Instead, it is necessary to explore how power is exercised."

In turn, the nature of how power is exercised is a workable definition for authority. In short, authority and power are intertwined, with power being the ability to do things or have others do what one has ordered while authority is the foundation on which that power is built.

STYLES OF LEADERSHIP

Three different styles of leadership were identified by Kurt Lewin, renowned social scientist, in 1939: authoritarian, democratic, and laissez-faire. His results indicated that the democratic style is superior to the other two styles. Attributes of each style are outlined below

- The *authoritarian* makes all decisions, independent of member's input. The authority figure dictates direction, leaving members in the dark about future plans. The authority figure selects which members will work collaboratively and determines solely the work tasks for the teams. This leader type is very personal in his praise and criticisms of each member, but does not actively participate with the group, unless demonstrating to the group. The authority figure is friendly and/or impersonal, but not openly hostile.

- The *democratic* leader welcomes team input and facilitates group discussion and decision making. This leader type shares plans with the group and offers multiple options for group consideration. Encourages members to work freely with each other and leaves division of tasks to the group. This leader is objective in praise and criticism, and joins group activities without over-participating.

- The *laissez-faire* leader allows the group complete freedom for decision-making, without participating himself. This leader type provides materials and offers to assist only by request. The laissez-faire leader does not participate in work discussions or group tasks. This leader does not offer commentary on members' performance unless asked directly, and does not participate or intervene in activities.

Since 1939, Lewin's research has been the basis for many further research studies and articles on organizational behavioral in theory and in action. Each leadership style can be appropriate depending on the environment within which it is implemented, the members of the group (employees), and the goals or tasks that are being undertaken by the group. Leaders may adjust their style of leadership to fit certain tasks, groups, or settings.

An authoritarian leadership style can be effective when a situation calls for expedited action or decision-making. Group members who are not self-motivated, who prefer structure, and appreciate significant direction and monitoring may thrive under this style.

A democratic leadership style allows for multiple viewpoints, inputs, and participation, while still maintaining control and the leadership role. A quality democratic leader recognizes each member's strengths and effectively elicits the best performance from each member, all the while guiding and leading effectively. A challenge for the democratic leader is to recognize that not all tasks need to be handled by the group; that the leader should appropriately address some issues alone.

A laissez-faire leadership style works best when group members are highly skilled and motivated, with a proven track record of excellence. This hands-off approach can allow these capable members to be productive and effective. The laissez-faire style is interpreted by the members as a sign of confidence and trust in their abilities and further empowers them to be successful and motivated.

BASES OF POWER

Five bases of power were identified by French and Raven in 1960, which laid the groundwork for most discussions of power and authority in the latter half of the twentieth century. These five types of power are coercive, legitimate, reward, referent, and expert. Power can be manifested through one or more of these bases.

COERCIVE POWER. Coercive power rests in the ability of a manager to force an employee to comply with an order through the threat of punishment. Coercive power typically leads to short-term compliance, but in the long-run produces dysfunctional behavior.

Coercion reduces employees' satisfaction with their jobs, leading to lack of commitment and general employee withdrawal. In the United States, Canada, and Western Europe, coercive power has seen a decline in the last 50 years. Several reasons contribute to this, ranging from the legal erosion of employment-at-will and the awareness of employee violence or other forms of retaliatory behavior.

Equally important as an effect on the receding popularity of coercion as a basis of power has been the influence of quality management theorists, such as Philip Crosby and W. Edwards Deming. They suggested that there is a decline in productivity and creativity when coercive power is employed. The use of coercive power results in an atmosphere of insecurity or fear. In spite of this insight, coercion as a base of power continues to play a role even in those organizations influenced by theories of quality management.

In times of economic crisis or threats to the survival of the organization at large, coercion may come to the forefront. Coercive power may also materialize as organizations attempt to streamline their operations for maximum efficiency. If employees must be fired, those who fail to conform to the organizational goals for survival will be the most likely candidates for termination. The threat of termination for failure to comply, in turn, is coercive power.

LEGITIMATE POWER. Legitimate power rests in the belief among employees that their manager has the right to give orders based on his or her position. For example, at the scene of a crime, people usually comply with the orders of a uniformed police officer based simply on their shared belief that he or she has the predetermined authority to give such orders. In a corporate setting, employees comply with the orders of a manager who relies on legitimate power based on the position in the organizational hierarchy that the manager holds. Yet, although employees may comply based on legitimate power, they may not feel a sense of commitment or cooperation.

REWARD POWER. Reward power, as the name implies, rests on the ability of a manager to give some sort of reward to employees. These rewards can range from monetary compensation to improved work schedules. Reward power often does not need monetary or other tangible compensation to work when managers can convey various intangible benefits as rewards.

Huey describes Sam Walton, founder of Wal-Mart Stores, Inc., as an active user of reward power. Walton relies heavily on these intangible awards, indicating that "nothing else can quite substitute for a few well-chosen, well-timed, sincere words of praise. They are absolutely free-and worth a fortune".

When reward power is used in a flexible manner, it can prove to be a strong motivator, as Crosby, Deming, and others have shown. Still, when organizations rely too rigidly on rewards, the system can backfire. Employees may be tempted to unethically or even illegally meet the quotas to which overly rigid reward systems may be tied.

Another problem associated with rewards as a base for power is the possibility that the rewards will divert employees' attention from their jobs and focus their attention instead on the rewards dangled before them.

REFERENT POWER. Referent power derives from employees' respect for a manager and their desire to identify with or emulate him or her. In referent power, the manager leads by example. Referent power rests heavily on trust. It often influences employees who may not be particularly aware that they are modeling their behavior on that of the manager and using what they presume he or she would do in such a situation as a point of reference.

The concept of empowerment in large part rests on referent power. Referent power may take considerable time to develop and thus may not prove particularly effective in a workforce with a rapid turnover of personnel.

One common error in applying referent power in cross-cultural situations, however, comes in misunderstanding the ways in which employees identify with their superiors. Since identification with one's superior in the United States is hampered by symbols of legitimate power (for example, titles or dress), those who advocate its use encourage managers to dress down to the level of their employees and use terms such as "facilitator" and "coach" coupled with "associates" and "group members" rather than "boss" and "subordinates."

In societies such as Argentina or Mexico, symbols of legitimate power may not readily hamper identification, whereas American-style egalitarianism may diminish the respect employees feel for the manager. In short, U.S. employees are likely to identify with managers by personally liking them and feeling liked in return, whereas Argentine and Mexican employees are likely to identify with managers by respecting them and feeling respected in return. Thus, referent power may be more cross-culturally variable than the other four bases of power laid out by French and Raven.

Imberman describes how specialized training is now used in the grocery industry to train Latino immigrants in the democratic supervisory techniques of U.S. managers. In the past, when these men and women were promoted to supervisory positions, they tended to rely heavily on the Latino model of authoritarianism under which they were raised. The managerial style hindered their ability to effectively supervise employees or to garner the respect they were seeking. To remedy this situation, specialized training programs are now utilized. The end result is effective and confident supervisors, motivated workers, higher productivity, less waste, and better customer service.

EXPERT POWER. Expert power rests on the belief of employees that an individual has a particularly high level of knowledge or highly specialized skill set. Managers may be accorded authority based on the perception of their greater knowledge of the tasks at hand than their employees.

Interestingly, in expert power, the superior may not rank higher than the other persons in a formal sense. Thus, when an equipment repair person comes to the CEO's office to fix a malfunctioning piece of machinery, no question exists that the CEO outranks the repair person; yet regarding the specific task of getting the machine operational, the CEO is likely to follow the orders of the repair person.

Expert power has within it a built-in point of weakness: as a point of power, expertise diminishes as knowledge is shared. If a manager shares knowledge or skill instruction with his or her employees, in time they will acquire a similar knowledge base or skill set. As the employees grow to equal the manager's knowledge or skills, their respect for the superiority of his expertise diminishes.

The result is either that the manager's authority diminishes or that the manager intentionally chooses not to share his or her knowledge base or skill set with the employees. The former choice weakens the manager's authority over time, while the latter weakens the organization's effectiveness over time.

MULTIDIMENSIONAL POWER

Traditional theories such as those of French and Raven, as well as the empowerment advocates of the 1980s, such as Crosby and Deming, have tended to approach power and authority as one-dimensional. By contrast, several experts have more recently begun to reconfigure how power is viewed to a more multidimensional interweaving of relations or conflicting needs.

For example, Robert Grant et al. described TQM's consumer-focused goals and traditional management's economic model of the firm as two inherently opposed paradigms. Because these two paradigms are grounded in two independent sources of authority, they produce different but coexisting dimensions of power.

It has also been argued that authority is culturally based. Geert Hofstede, in one of the most thorough empirical surveys on cross-cultural influences on work-related values, delineated marked differences in what he called "power distance."

For Hofstede, power distance is the degree to which members of a culture feel comfortable with inequalities in power within an organization; that is, the extent to which one's boss is seen as having greater power than oneself. Thus, views regarding both power and leadership shape the conception of authority within an organization. And because both these facets of authority conception differ drastically from culture to culture, authority itself is conceived of differently from society to society.

Consequently, no single dimension of authority and power is likely to hold equally for all managers and employees in a multicultural domestic setting or in the multicultural milieu of the multinational corporation.

Finally, one can also argue against the one-dimensional view of authority and power when they are viewed not as independent elements in the abstract, but as intrinsically derived from relations within the organization. Power and authority are multidimensional because relationships are by nature multidimensional.

The ways in which managers influence their employees and encourage them to be productive depend on many variables, including the personality of the leader, the skills of the group/employees, the task or assignment at hand, or the group dynamics and personalities of group members. As with leadership styles, each base of power has its place in management and can prove effective in the right setting and right circumstances.

Along with leadership styles, there is much similarity and terminology crossover in the study of leadership theories; researchers should examine both terms in the available literature to access the full spectrum of knowledge on the topic of leadership.

SEE ALSO: Chain of Command Principle; Leadership Theories and Studies; Management Styles; Organizational Culture; Span of Control

David A. Victor
Revised by Monica C. Turner

FURTHER READING:

Alanazi, F.M., and Arnoldo Rodrigues. "Power Bases and Attribution in Three Cultures." *The Journal of Social Psychology* 143, no. 3 (June 2003): 375–395.

Carson, Paula Phillips, Kerry D. Carson, E. Leon Knight, Jr., and C. William Roe. "Power in Organizations: A Look Through the TQM Lens." *Quality Progress* 28, no. 11 (November 1995): 73–78.

Crosby, Philip B. *Quality Is Free: The Art of Making Quality Certain.* New York, NY: McGraw-Hill, 1979.

Deming, W. Edwards. *Out of the Crisis.* Cambridge, MA: Massachusetts Institute of Technology Press, 1986.

French, J.P.R., Jr., and B. Raven. "The Bases of Social Power." In *Studies in Social Power.* Dorwin Cartwright, ed. Ann Arbor, MI: University of Michigan Press, 1959.

Grant, Robert M., Rami Shani, and R. Krishnan. "TQM's Challenge to Theory and Practice." *Sloan Management Review* 35, no. 2 (Winter 1994): 25–35.

Heller, T. "Changing Authority Patterns: A Cultural Perspective." *Academy of Management Review* 10, no. 3 (July 1985): 488–495.

Huey, John. "Sam Walton in His Own Words." *Fortune,* 29 June 1992, 98–106.

Imberman, Woodruff. "Managing the Managers." *Progressive Grocer* 84, no. 3 (2005): 26–27.

Knights, David, and Darren McCabe. "Are There No Limits to Authority?: TQM and Organizational Power." *Organization Studies* 20, no. 2 (March 1999): 197–224.

Lewin, Kurt, R. Lippitt, and R.K. White. "Patterns of Aggressive Behavior in Experimentally Created 'Social Climates'." *Journal of Social Psychology* 10, no. 2 (May 1939): 271–301.

O'Regan, N., and A. Ghobadian. "Leadership and Strategy: Making it Happen." *Journal of General Management* 29, no. 3 (Spring 2004): 76–92.

Steensma, H., and F. van Milligen. "Bases of Power, Procedural Justice and Outcomes of Mergers: The Push And Pull Factors Of Influence Tactics." *Journal of Collective Negotiations* 30, no. 2 (2003): 113–134.

Victor, David A. *International Business Communication.* New York, NY: HarperCollins, 1992.

LEADERSHIP THEORIES AND STUDIES

Leadership can be defined as a process by which one individual influences others toward the attainment of group or organizational goals. Three points about the definition of leadership should be emphasized. First, leadership is a social influence process. Leadership cannot exist without a leader and one or more followers. Second, leadership elicits voluntary action on the part of followers. The voluntary nature of compliance separates leadership from other types of influence based on formal authority. Finally, leadership results in followers' behavior that is purposeful and goal-directed in some sort of organized setting. Many, although not all, studies of leadership focus on the nature of leadership in the workplace.

Leadership is probably the most frequently studied topic in the organizational sciences. Thousands of leadership studies have been published and thousands of pages on leadership have been written in academic books and journals, business-oriented publications, and general-interest publications. Despite this, the precise nature of leadership and its relationship to key criterion variables such as subordinate satisfaction, commitment, and performance is still uncertain, to the point where Fred Luthans, in his book *Organizational Behavior* (2005), said that "it [leadership] does remain pretty much of a 'black box' or unexplainable concept."

Leadership should be distinguished from management. Management involves planning, organizing, staffing, directing, and controlling, and a manager is someone who performs these functions. A manager has formal authority by virtue of his or her position or office. Leadership, by contrast, primarily deals with influence. A manager may or may not be an effective leader. A leader's ability to influence others may be based on a variety of factors other than his or her formal authority or position.

In the sections that follow, the development of leadership studies and theories over time is briefly traced. Table 1 provides a summary of the major theoretical approaches.

Table 1
Leadership Perspectives

Historical Leadership Theories

Leadership Theory	Time of Introduction	Major Tenets
Trait Theories	1930s	Individual characteristics of leaders are different than those of nonleaders.
Behavioral Theories	1940s and 1950s	The behaviors of effective leaders are different than the behaviors of ineffective leaders. Two major classes of leader behavior are task-oriented behavior and relationship-oriented behavior.
Contingency Theories	1960s and 1970s	Factors unique to each situation determine whether specific leader characteristics and behaviors will be effective.

Historical Leadership Theories

Leadership Theory	Time of Introduction	Major Tenets
Leader-Member Exchange	1970s	Leaders from high-quality relationships with some subordinates but not others. The quality of leader-subordinates relationship affects numerous workplace outcomes.
Charismatic Leadership	1970s and 1980s	Effective leaders inspire subordinates to commit themselves to goals by communicating a vision, displaying charismatic behavior, and setting a powerful personal example.
Substitutes foe Leadership	1970s	Characteristics of the organization, task, and subordinates may substitute for or negate the effects of leadership behaviors.

HISTORICAL DEVELOPMENT

Three main theoretical frameworks have dominated leadership research at different points in time. These included the trait approach (1930s and 1940s), the behavioral approach (1940s and 1950s), and the contingency or situational approach (1960s and 1970s).

TRAIT APPROACH. The scientific study of leadership began with a focus on the traits of effective leaders. The basic premise behind trait theory was that effective leaders are born, not made, thus the name sometimes applied to early versions of this idea, the "great man" theory. Many leadership studies based on this theoretical framework were conducted in the 1930s, 1940s, and 1950s.

Leader trait research examined the physical, mental, and social characteristics of individuals. In general, these studies simply looked for significant associations between individual traits and measures of leadership effectiveness. Physical traits such as height, mental traits such as intelligence, and social traits such as personality attributes were all subjects of empirical research.

The initial conclusion from studies of leader traits was that there were no universal traits that consistently separated effective leaders from other individuals. In an important review of the leadership literature published in 1948, Ralph Stogdill concluded that the existing research had not demonstrated the utility of the trait approach.

Several problems with early trait research might explain the perceived lack of significant findings. First, measurement theory at the time was not highly sophisticated. Little was known about the psychometric properties of the measures used to operationalize traits. As a result, different studies were likely to use different measures to assess the same construct, which made it very difficult to replicate findings. In addition, many of the trait studies relied on samples of teenagers or lower-level managers.

Early trait research was largely atheoretical, offering no explanations for the proposed relationship between individual characteristics and leadership.

Finally, early trait research did not consider the impact of situational variables that might moderate the relationship between leader traits and measures of leader effectiveness. As a result of the lack of consistent findings linking individual traits to leadership effectiveness, empirical studies of leader traits were largely abandoned in the 1950s.

LEADER BEHAVIOR APPROACH. Partially as a result of the disenchantment with the trait approach to leadership that occurred by the beginning of the 1950s, the focus of leadership research shifted away from leader traits to leader behaviors. The premise of this stream of research was that the behaviors exhibited by leaders are more important than their physical, mental, or emotional traits. The two most famous behavioral leadership studies took place at Ohio State University and the University of Michigan in the late 1940s and 1950s. These studies sparked hundreds of other leadership studies and are still widely cited.

The Ohio State studies utilized the Leader Behavior Description Questionnaire (LBDQ), administering it to samples of individuals in the military, manufacturing companies, college administrators, and student leaders. Answers to the questionnaire were factor-analyzed to determine if common leader behaviors emerged across samples. The conclusion was that there were two distinct aspects of leadership that describe how leaders carry out their role.

Two factors, termed consideration and initiating structure, consistently appeared. Initiating structure, sometimes called task-oriented behavior, involves planning, organizing, and coordinating the work of subordinates. Consideration involves showing concern for subordinates, being supportive, recognizing subordinates' accomplishments, and providing for subordinates' welfare.

The Michigan leadership studies took place at about the same time as those at Ohio State. Under the general direction of Rensis Likert, the focus of the Michigan studies was to determine the principles and methods of leadership that led to productivity and job satisfaction. The studies resulted in two general leadership behaviors or orientations: an employee orientation and a production orientation. Leaders with an employee orientation showed genuine concern for interpersonal relations. Those with a production orientation focused on the task or technical aspects of the job.

The conclusion of the Michigan studies was that an employee orientation and general instead of close supervision yielded better results. Likert eventually developed four "systems" of management based on these studies; he advocated System 4 (the participative-group system, which was the most participatory set of leader behaviors) as resulting in the most positive outcomes.

One concept based largely on the behavioral approach to leadership effectiveness was the Managerial (or Leadership) Grid, developed by Robert Blake and Jane Mouton. The grid combines "concern for production" with "concern for people" and presents five alternative behavioral styles of leadership. An individual who emphasized neither production was practicing "impoverished management" according to the grid. If a person emphasized concern for people and placed little emphasis on production, he was terms a "country-club" manager.

Conversely, a person who emphasized a concern for production but paid little attention to the concerns of subordinates was a "task" manager. A person who tried to balance concern for production and concern for people was termed a "middle-of-the-road" manager.

Finally, an individual who was able to simultaneously exhibit a high concern for production and a high concern for people was practicing "team management." According to the prescriptions of the grid, team management was the best leadership approach. The Managerial Grid became a major consulting tool and was the basis for a considerable amount of leadership training in the corporate world.

The assumption of the leader behavior approach was that there were certain behaviors that would be universally effective for leaders. Unfortunately, empirical research has not demonstrated consistent relationships between task-oriented or person-oriented leader behaviors and leader effectiveness. Like trait research, leader behavior research did not consider situational influences that might moderate the relationship between leader behaviors and leader effectiveness.

CONTINGENCY (SITUATIONAL) APPROACH. Contingency or situational theories of leadership propose that the organizational or work group context affects the extent to which given leader traits and behaviors will be effective. Contingency theories gained prominence in the late 1960s and 1970s. Four of the more well-known contingency theories are Fiedler's contingency theory, path-goal theory, the Vroom-Yetton-Jago decision-making model of leadership, and the situational leadership theory. Each of these approaches to leadership is briefly described in the paragraphs that follow.

Introduced in 1967, Fiedler's contingency theory was the first to specify how situational factors interact with leader traits and behavior to influence leadership effectiveness. The theory suggests that the "favorability" of the situation determines the effectiveness of task- and person-oriented leader behavior.

Favorability is determined by (1) the respect and trust that followers have for the leader; (2) the extent to which subordinates' responsibilities can be structured and performance measured; and (3) the control the leader has over subordinates' rewards. The situation is most favorable when followers respect and trust the leader, the task is highly structured, and the leader has control over rewards and punishments.

Fiedler's research indicated that task-oriented leaders were more effective when the situation was either highly favorable or highly unfavorable, but that person-oriented leaders were more effective in the moderately favorable or unfavorable situations. The theory did not necessarily propose that leaders could adapt their leadership styles to different situations, but that leaders with different leadership styles would be more effective when placed in situations that matched their preferred style.

Fiedler's contingency theory has been criticized on both conceptual and methodological grounds. However, empirical research has supported many of the specific propositions of the theory, and it remains an important contribution to the understanding of leadership effectiveness.

Path-goal theory was first presented in a 1971 *Administrative Science Quarterly* article by Robert House. Path-goal theory proposes that subordinates' characteristics and characteristics of the work environment determine which leader behaviors will be more effective. Key characteristics of subordinates identified by the theory are locus of control, work experience, ability, and the need for affiliation. Important environmental characteristics named by the theory are the nature of the task, the formal authority system, and the nature of the work group. The theory includes four different leader behaviors, which include directive leadership, supportive leadership, participative leadership, and achievement-oriented leadership.

According to the theory, leader behavior should reduce barriers to subordinates' goal attainment, strengthen subordinates' expectancies that improved performance will lead to valued rewards, and provide coaching to make the path to payoffs easier for subordinates. Path-goal theory suggests that the leader behavior that will accomplish these tasks depends upon the subordinate and environmental contingency factors.

Path-goal theory has been criticized because it does not consider interactions among the contingency factors and also because of the complexity of its underlying theoretical model, expectancy theory. Empirical research has provided some support for the theory's propositions, primarily as they relate to directive and supportive leader behaviors.

The Vroom-Yetton-Jago decision-making model was introduced by Victor Vroom and Phillip Yetton in 1973 and revised by Vroom and Jago in 1988. The theory focuses primarily on the degree of subordinate participation that is appropriate in different situations. Thus, it emphasizes the decision-making style of the leader.

There are five types of leader decision-making styles, which are labeled AI, AII, CI, CII, and G. These styles range from strongly autocratic (AI), to strongly democratic (G). According to the theory, the appropriate style is determined by answers to up to eight diagnostic questions, which relate to such contingency factors as the importance of decision quality, the structure of the problem, whether subordinates have enough information to make a quality decision, and the importance of subordinate commitment to the decision.

The Vroom-Yetton-Jago model has been criticized for its complexity, for its assumption that the decision makers' goals are consistent with organizational goals, and for ignoring the skills needed to arrive at group decisions to difficult problems. Empirical research has supported some of the prescriptions of the theory.

The situational leadership theory was initially introduced in 1969 and revised in 1977 by Hersey and Blanchard. The theory suggests that the key contingency factor affecting leaders' choice of leadership style is the task-related maturity of the subordinates. Subordinate maturity is defined in terms of the ability of subordinates to accept responsibility for their own task-related behavior. The theory classifies leader behaviors into the two broad classes of task-oriented and relationship-oriented behaviors. The major proposition of situational leadership theory is that the effectiveness of task and relationship-oriented leadership depends upon the maturity of a leader's subordinates.

Situational leadership theory has been criticized on both theoretical and methodological grounds. However, it remains one of the better-known contingency theories of leadership and offers important insights into the interaction between subordinate ability and leadership style.

RECENT DEVELOPMENTS

Although trait, behavioral, and contingency approaches have each contributed to the understanding of leadership, none of the approaches have provided a completely satisfactory explanation of leadership and leadership effectiveness. Since the 1970s, several alternative theoretical frameworks for the study of leadership have been advanced. Among the more important of these are leader-member exchange theory, transformational leadership theory, the substitutes for leadership approach, and the philosophy of servant leadership.

LEADER-MEMBER EXCHANGE THEORY. Leader-member exchange (LMX) theory was initially called the vertical dyad linkage theory. The theory was introduced by George Graen and various colleagues in the 1970s and has been revised and refined in the years since. LMX theory emphasizes the dyadic (i.e., one-on-one) relationships between leaders and individual subordinates, instead of the traits or behaviors of leaders or situational characteristics.

The theory's focus is determining the type of leader-subordinate relationships that promote effective outcomes and the factors that determine whether leaders and subordinates will be able to develop high-quality relationships.

According to LMX theory, leaders do not treat all subordinates in the same manner, but establish close relationships with some (the in-group) while remaining aloof from others (the out-group). Those in the in-group enjoy relationships with the leader that is marked by trust and mutual respect. They tend to be involved in important activities and decisions. Conversely, those in the out-group are excluded from important activities and decisions.

LMX theory suggests that high-quality relationships between a leader-subordinate dyad will lead to positive outcomes such as better performance, lower turnover, job satisfaction, and organizational commitment. Empirical research supports many of the proposed relationships (Steers et al., 1996).

TRANSFORMATIONAL LEADERSHIP THEORIES. Beginning in the 1970s, a number of leadership theories emerged that focused on the importance of a leader's charisma to leadership effectiveness. Included within this class of theories are House's theory of charismatic leadership, Bass's transformational leadership theory, and Conger and Kanungo's charismatic leadership theory.

These theories have much in common. They all focus on attempting to explain how leaders can accomplish extraordinary things against the odds, such as turning around a failing company, founding a successful company, or achieving great military success against incredible odds. The theories also emphasize the importance of leaders' inspiring subordinates' admiration, dedication, and unquestioned loyalty through articulating a clear and compelling vision.

Tranformational leadership theory differentiates between the transactional and the transformational leader. Transactional leadership focuses on role and task requirements and utilizes rewards contingent on performance. By contrast, transformational leadership focuses on developing mutual trust, fostering the leadership abilities of others, and setting goals that go beyond the short-term needs of the work group.

Bass's transformational leadership theory identifies four aspects of effective leadership, which include charisma, inspiration, intellectual stimulation, and consideration. A leader who exhibits these qualities will inspire subordinates to be high achievers and put the long-term interest of the organization ahead of their own short-term interest, according to the theory. Empirical research has supported many of the theory's propositions.

SUBSTITUTES FOR LEADERSHIP THEORY. Kerr and Jermier introduced the substitutes for leadership theory in 1978. The theory's focus is concerned with providing an explanation for the lack of stronger empirical support for a relationship between leader traits or leader behaviors and subordinates' satisfaction and performance. The substitutes for leadership theory suggests that characteristics of the organization, the task, and subordinates may substitute for or negate the effects of leadership, thus weakening observed relationships between leader behaviors and important organizational outcomes.

Substitutes for leadership make leader behaviors such as task-oriented or relationship-oriented unnecessary. Characteristics of the organization that may substitute for leadership include formalization, group cohesiveness, inflexible rules, and organizational rewards not under the control of the leader. Characteristics of the task that may substitute for leadership include routine and repetitive tasks or tasks that are satisfying. Characteristics of subordinates that may substitute for leadership include ability, experience, training, and job-related knowledge.

The substitutes for leadership theory has generated a considerable amount of interest because it offers an intuitively appealing explanation for why leader behavior impacts subordinates in some situations but not in others. However, some of its theoretical propositions have not been adequately tested. The theory continues to generate empirical research.

SERVANT LEADERSHIP. This approach to leadership reflects a philosophy that leaders should be servants first. It suggests that leaders must place the needs of subordinates, customers, and the community ahead of their own interests in order to be effective. Characteristics of servant leaders include empathy, stewardship, and commitment to the personal, professional, and spiritual growth of their subordinates. Servant leadership has not been subjected to extensive empirical testing but has generated considerable interest among both leadership scholars and practitioners.

Leadership continues to be one of the most written about topics in the social sciences. Although much has been learned about leadership since the 1930s, many avenues of research still remain to be explored as we enter the twenty-first century.

SEE ALSO: Contingency Approach to Management; Leadership Styles and Bases of Power; Management Styles

Tim Barnett

FURTHER READING:

Bass, Bernard M., Bruce J. Avolio, Dong I. Jung, and Yair Berso. "Predicting Unit Performance by Assessing Transformational and Transactional Leadership." *Journal of Applied Psychology* 88 (2003): 207–218.

Blank, Warren, John R. Weitzel, and Stephen G. Green. "A Test of the Situational Leadership Theory." *Personnel Psychology* 43 (1990): 579–597.

Fiedler, Fred E. *A Theory of Leadership Effectiveness*. New York, NY: McGraw-Hill, 1967.

Graeff, Claude L. "The Situational Leadership Theory: A Critical View." *Academy of Management Review* 8 (1983): 285–291.

Graen, George, and William Schiemann. "Leader-Member Agreement: A Vertical Dyad Linkage Approach." *Journal of Applied Psychology* 63 (1978): 206–212.

Greenberg, Jerald, and Robert A. Baron. *Behavior in Organizations: Understanding and Managing the Human Side of Work.* Upper Saddle River, NJ: Prentice-Hall, 2000.

House, Robert J. "A Path-Goal Theory of Leader Effectiveness." *Administrative Science Quarterly* 16 (1971): 321–339.

House, Robert J., and Ram N. Aditya. "The Social Scientific Study of Leadership: Quo Vadis?" *Journal of Management* 23 (1997): 409–473.

Kirkpatrick, Shelley A., and Edwin A. Locke. "Leadership: Do Traits Matter?" *Academy of Management Executive* 5 (1991): 48–60.

Kinicki, Angelo, and Robert Kreitner. *Organizational Behavior.* Boston, MA: McGraw-Hill Irwin, 2006.

Luthans, Fred. *Organizational Behavior.* Boston, MA: McGraw-Hill Irwin, 2005.

Podsakoff, Philip M., et al. "Do Substitutes for Leadership Really Substitute for Leadership? An Empirical Examination of Kerr and Jermier's Situational Leadership Model." *Organizational Behavior and Human Decision Processes* 54 (1993): 1–44.

Steers, Richard M., Lyman W. Porter, and Gregory A. Bigley. *Motivation and Leadership at Work.* New York: McGraw-Hill, 1996.

Stogdill, Ralph M. "Personal Factors Associated with Leadership: A Survey of the Literature." *Journal of Psychology* 25 (1948): 335–71.

Stogdill, Ralph M., and Bernard M. Bass. *Handbook of Leadership: A Survey of Theory and Research.* New York, NY: Free Press, 1974.

Vroom, Victor H., and Phillip W. Yetton. *Leadership and Decision Making.* Pittsburgh, PA: University of Pittsburgh Press, 1973.

Wren, Daniel A. *The Evolution of Management Thought.* New York, NY: Wiley, 1994.

Yukl, Gary. *Leadership in Organizations.* Englewood Cliffs, NJ: Prentice-Hall, 1994.

LEAN MANUFACTURING AND JUST-IN-TIME PRODUCTION

Associated with Japanese management techniques, just-in-time production (JIT) is a set of principles and practices based on the philosophy that firms should hold little or no inventory beyond that required for immediate production or distribution. That is, a manufacturer should receive raw materials or parts from its suppliers perhaps just hours before they will be used in production, and the firm's output should be shipped to its customers as soon after completion as possible—without holding onto a stock of either raw goods or finished products.

In practice, JIT has often been expressed as a holistic management system aimed at reducing waste, maximizing cost efficiency, and securing a competitive advantage. Thus, a number of additional conditions are considered necessary for the successful implementation of JIT. These include small lot sizes, short setup and changeover times, efficient and effective quality controls, and perhaps most of all, designing the whole production process to minimize backups and maximize the efficiency of human and machine labor.

Lean manufacturing encompasses a number of things. It essentially is a Westernized version of JIT and Japanese *kaizen,* or continuous improvement. Lean manufacturing is a process for measuring and reducing inventory and streamlining production. It is a means for changing the way a company measures plant performance. A knowledge-based system, lean manufacturing takes years of hard work, preparation, and support from upper management. Lean manufacturing is so named because it purports to use much less of certain resources (space, inventory, workers, etc.) than is used by normal mass-production systems to produce comparable output. The term came into widespread use with the 1990 publication of the book *The Machine That Changed the World* by James P. Womack, Daniel T. Jones, and Daniel Roos.

The *APICS Dictionary* defines lean manufacturing as a philosophy of production that emphasizes minimizing the amount of all resources (including time) used in various enterprise activities. It involves identifying and eliminating non-value-adding activities in design, production, supply chain management, and customer relations. Lean producers employ teams of multiskilled workers at all levels of the organization and use highly flexible, increasingly automated machines to produce volumes of products in potentially enormous variety. In effect, they incorporate the advantages of both mass production (high volume, low unit cost) and craft production (variety and flexibility). Quality is higher than in normal mass production. Compensation and rewards are based on meeting the total cost equation rather than on labor, overhead, or individual quality measures.

Lean manufacturing and JIT (lean/JIT) share most of the same characteristics, goals, and philosophy. In fact, the terms are often used interchangeably.

HISTORY OF LEAN MANUFACTURING/JIT

Lean/JIT have roots in both Japan and the United States.

JAPAN. Since Japan is a physically small country with minimal resources and a large population, the Japanese have always been careful not to waste resources such as time, labor, and space. Waste is seen as abhorrent to the Japanese because they have so little space and so few natural resources. Hence, it has been necessary for the Japanese to maximize the yield from minimally available resources. Also, dense population has made it necessary for the Japanese people to maintain mutual respect in order to work and live together.

Under this *wa* (harmony) culture, everyone tries to maintain the best possible human relationship and is reluctant to be involved in any confrontations. Additionally, most Japanese firms have a *rentai* relationship, which entails maintaining a "joint responsibility" between management and workers. Under this relationship, management should treat all workers equally. In exchange, each worker respects management's leadership position and follows orders exactly without mistakes, cooperates with coworkers, and generates ideas and creativity to improve the firm's competitiveness. This type of culture reinforces the basic tenets of lean/JIT: waste minimization, continuous improvement, and respect for all workers.

This concept was originally developed in Japan in the mid-1970s by the Toyota Motor Corporation. In fact, many firms continue to refer to lean/JIT as the Toyota system. The concept emphasized the avoidance of waste of materials, space, and labor. Significant attention was paid to identifying and correcting potential problems that could lead to any form of waste. Operations were constantly being improved and fine-tuned so as to further eliminate waste and thereby increase productivity and yield. In addition, equal respect was paid to all workers, while minimizing the trappings of status. As a result, by using lean/JIT, Toyota was able to reduce the time needed to produce a car from fifteen days to one day.

UNITED STATES. In 1924 Henry Ford's Highland Park plant, and later the River Rouge operation, mass-produced Model T parts just-in-time for assembly while assembly lines pulled work forward to the next assembly stations just-in-time. One hundred freight cars of material were unloaded daily, with materials flowing through fabrication, subassembly, final assembly, and back onto the freight cars. The production cycle was twenty-one days. At River Rouge the cycle was only four days, and that included processing ore into steel at the on-site steel mill.

Unfortunately, this "just-in-time" type manufacturing soon gave way to the large lot sizes and lengthy cycle times dictated by the economies of scale of mass production, mass markets, and standard designs with interchangeable parts. U.S. manufacturers held on to this paradigm until the early 1980s, when the development of the Toyota production system caused it to shift. U.S. manufacturers initially greeted lean/JIT with a great deal of ambivalence, thinking that the concept would never work in the United States due to its reliance on the cultural aspects of the Japanese work environment. However, this view changed when firms such as Hewlett-Packard and Harley-Davidson yielded significant benefits from its use.

MANUFACTURING

The idea behind lean/JIT is a concept called ideal production. Simply produce and deliver finished goods just in time to be sold, subassemblies just in time to go into subassemblies, and purchased materials just in time to be transformed into fabricated parts. The goal of lean/JIT is to find practical ways to create the effect of an automated industry that will come as close as possible to this concept of ideal production.

While the prevailing view of lean/JIT is that of an inventory control system, lean/JIT goes much further. It is an operational philosophy that incorporates an improved inventory control system in conjunction with other systems. These systems include:

- A setup improvement system
- A maintenance improvement system
- A quality improvement system
- A productivity improvement system

INVENTORY CONTROL SYSTEM. When larger quantities are ordered or produced, average inventory obviously is larger. This larger inventory results in increased inventory-carrying charges. If a reduction in carrying costs is desired, smaller quantities should be ordered and orders should be placed more often. However, the practice of ordering smaller quantities can have the side effect of increasing ordering costs. To balance these two costs, the concept of economic order quantity (EOQ) was developed. The EOQ formula derives the point, or order quantity, where inventory carrying costs and ordering or setup costs are the same. An order of this quantity will minimize the sum of the two costs.

However, the EOQ formula is flawed. While carrying costs and ordering/setup costs are obvious, other costs that can significantly affect lot size are not considered. The user of the formula often fails to consider quality, scrap, productivity, and worker motivation and responsibility. In addition, the EOQ formula user frequently fails to consider that even though setup costs are significant, they are not unalterable. American manufacturing managers traditionally considered setup costs as a necessary evil and made little or no effort to reduce them.

The lean/JIT philosophy suggests that a firm should eliminate any reliance upon the EOQ formula and seek the ideal production quantity of one. Of course, a lot size of one is not always feasible, but it is a goal used to focus attention on the concept of rapid adjustments and flexibility. Naturally, a reduction in inventory levels means an increase in setups or orders, so the responsibility rests with production to make every effort to reduce setup time and setup costs. It should be noted that this assumes setup time and cost are positively related. This is not always true because the cost to reduce setup time could be very high if retooling or equipment redesign were involved.

SETUP COST REDUCTION SYSTEM. Toyota began a campaign to reduce setup times in 1971. Five years later, the time required to set up presses to form fenders and hoods had fallen from 1 hour to 12 minutes, while U.S. manufacturers needed 6 hours to perform the same task. Toyota continues to strive for a concept it calls "single setup," which means less than 10 minutes for performing a setup. As the company continued to emphasize reduction of setup times, its operations became capable of "one-touch" setups, which take less than 1 minute.

Setup time can be divided into two phases: external time and internal time. External time includes activities that can take place while the machine is running, such as transporting dies between storage and the machines. These items are external to the run time and do not interrupt it. Internal time includes activities that can only be conducted when the machine is stopped, such as mounting and removing dies. These are items that will interrupt the run time. External time can be eliminated by ensuring that appropriate tools are ready before changeover begins. Internal time can be reduced by addressing the question, "How can operations be quickened?" Appropriate responses could include the use of locating pins and hand levers to replace bolts, the standardization of any remaining bolts, permanent installation of wrenches to adjusting nuts, and the use of an air driver instead of a ratchet.

Management sometimes tends to analyze the large, obvious costs such as direct labor, but then treat setup as an inherent cost that must be accepted. However, only by reducing setup time and costs can lot sizes be reduced toward the ideal lot size of one.

PREVENTIVE MAINTENANCE SYSTEM. Most arguments against preventive maintenance (PM) suggest that PM programs are more expensive than programs that only repair broken equipment. The flaw in this line of thought arises from the unpredictable nature of equipment breakdown. This reaction mode of maintenance usually means that the maintenance personnel must temporarily patch the equipment and defer the substantive repair until time allows. Unfortunately, since the equipment already has suffered lost time due to the initial breakdown, the likelihood of finding repair time decreases. The result often is a circular process of "adjust and tinker," with an increased risk of unexplained defects in the output.

A proposed requirement for lean/JIT is that machinery be in top running condition at all times. When using small lot sizes, management can ill afford unexpected downtime in production flow. Equipment must be in condition to produce whatever is needed, whenever it is needed. Therefore, a little time should be scheduled each day to ensure that machinery is capable of producing top quality results. Preventive maintenance is necessary for continuous, long-term improvement in the quality of the production process.

QUALITY IMPROVEMENT SYSTEM. In order for companies to successfully produce goods while receiving only minimum deliveries, no room can be allowed for poor quality. This requires an overhaul in the thinking of management, which traditionally sought the so-called acceptable quality level (AQL). After receipt, delivered goods are randomly inspected to see how many defective parts there are within a predetermined sample size. If the number of defects exceeds a certain amount (the AQL), the entire batch is rejected. No such provision is made under lean/JIT; all parts must be good. The Japanese use the term *zero defects* to describe this philosophy.

Zero defects certainly cannot be obtained overnight, nor can it be expected from all of a firm's current suppliers. To facilitate the receipt of high quality goods, a firm must offer more than the usual short-term contract or purchase order to the lowest bidder. A firm also may have to eliminate or decrease the use of multiple sourcing, or purchasing the same part from several sources as a backup in case one source experiences quality or delivery problems. By issuing long-term contracts to a single source, the lean/JIT firm gives its supplier the confidence and incentive to spend time and money on ensuring near perfect quality and constantly improving the product. Frequently, this makes for a captive supplier who must maintain the required quality in order to survive. The lean/JIT firm should then work constantly and directly with the supplier to monitor quality and provide technical support.

The use of lean/JIT improves the quality of suppliers, as well as the lean/JIT firm's internal quality. When lot sizes are drastically reduced, defect discovery is naturally enhanced. If a worker produces a lot size of one and passes it to the next station, the quality of feedback will be immediate. In this way, defects are discovered quickly and their causes can be corrected immediately. Production of large lots with high defect rates is avoided.

U.S. manufacturers traditionally allowed lot sizes and inventory levels to remain high "just in case" a quality problem, an equipment problem, or a delivery problem should arise. This "just in case" inventory, commonly called buffer stock, allowed the firm to maintain its production flow while the problem was being corrected. When a quality problem emerged and inventory was ample, the search for the source of the problem was postponed until a more suitable time. This suitable time may have never occurred. When lot sizes are minimal, one worker's problem threatens to bring subsequent processes to a halt. This means that all production workers and management must collaborate to find an immediate solution. The benefits here are twofold. First, the firm avoids the production of large quantities of defective parts. Secondly, good managers will be able to use this as motivation for unity of purpose within the workforce.

PRODUCTIVITY IMPROVEMENT SYSTEM. Productivity can be defined as good output divided by required input. The productivity facet of lean/JIT been described as nothing sitting idle, which wastes time. If equipment is operated only for productive purposes, then energy waste is eliminated. If all inventory is converted into product, then material waste is eliminated. If errors are not allowed, then rework is eliminated.

A number of productivity improvements may result from lean/JIT implementation. Among these are lower inventory levels, lower scrap rates, reductions in rework costs, reduction inventory carrying costs, smaller floor space requirements, reduced material handling, simpler inventory accounting, and more positive inventory control. All of these lower the input component or increase the good output of the productivity ratio.

Reductions in idle inventories allow the firm to reduce internal lead times—from the purchase of raw materials to the shipping of finished goods—allowing quicker changes in product mix and production quantities. Furthermore, the firm's ability to forecast is enhanced because the forecast horizon is shortened.

TEN STEPS TO LEAN/JIT PRODUCTION

Steve L. Hunter lists ten steps to implement a lean/JIT production system:

1. Reengineer the manufacturing system

2. Reduce setup

3. Integrate quality control

4. Integrate preventive maintenance

5. Level and balance the system

6. Integrate a pull system

7. Control inventory

8. Implement a vendor program

9. Utilize computer integrated manufacturing (CIM) benefits

While it was noted that inventory reduction is not the sole goal of lean/JIT implementation, it is a very obvious benefit. Less workspace is now needed due to the use of smaller lot sizes and reduced inventory levels. Much of this inventory was stored between and within work centers. By reducing inventory, firms have been able to actually move work centers closer together, freeing up space and reducing material handling distances. This results in a neater, more organized facility that provides for speedy identification of bottlenecks and fewer lost parts.

Additionally, this reduction in inventory and lot sizes promotes rapid feedback from downstream work centers when there is a quality problem. This feedback results in a reduction in scrap and rework, and ultimately a higher level of overall quality.

Reduced inventory and lot sizes also result in increased inventory turns. Inventory turn increases have been noted at Haworth (a twofold increase), Hewlett-Packard (a threefold increase), Richardson-Vicks Homecare Products (a threefold increase), IBM, Raleigh (a fourfold increase), and Harley-Davidson (a sixfold increase).

The introduction of preventive maintenance and the use of smaller, more flexible machinery combine to yield increased equipment utilization. One major firm was able to change from three lines running three shifts to two lines running one shift with no change in output.

The lean/JIT producer combines the advantages of craft and mass production, while avoiding the high cost of the former and the rigidity of mass production. Lean/JIT producers set their sights explicitly on perfection: continually declining costs, zero defects, zero inventories, and endless product variety. Lean/JIT manufacturing is the new paradigm for manufacturing, replacing a mass-production system that has existed for more than 70 years.

SEE ALSO: Cellular Manufacturing; Continuous Improvement; Flexible Manufacturing; Japanese Management; Poka-Yoke; Quality and Total Quality Management; World-Class Manufacturer

R. Anthony Inman

FURTHER READING:

Cox, James F., III, and John H. Blackstone, Jr. *APICS Dictionary.* 9th ed. Falls Church, VA: American Production and Inventory Control Society, 1998.

Hunter, Steve L. "The 10 Steps to Lean Production." *FDM* 76, no. 5 (2004): 22–25.

Stevenson, William J. *Operations Management.* 8th ed. Boston: Irwin/McGraw-Hill, 2005.

Womack, James P., Daniel T. Jones, and Daniel Roos. *The Machine That Changed the World: Based on the Massachusetts Institute of Technology 5-Million Dollar 5-Year Study on the Future of the Automobile.* New York: Rawson Associates, 1990.

Womack, James P., and Daniel T. Jones. *Lean Thinking: Banish Waste and Create Wealth in Your Corporation.* New York: Simon & Schuster, 1996.

LEVERAGED BUYOUTS

A leveraged buyout (LBO) is a restructuring of the capitalization and ownership of a company. The term *leveraged* refers to the use of debt as the primary method of financing the restructuring. The *buyout* portion refers to the fact that the method is often used to transform a publicly held company into one that is privately held. There are a number of reasons why this type of transaction might take place. These include cost savings, managerial incentives, decreasing the total number of owners, tax benefits, flexibility, and control. Oftentimes, the group pursuing the buyout includes the publicly held firm's upper management. This type of action is known as a management buyout (MBO).

Among the multiple parties involved when a public firm is taken private, there normally are both winners and losers. Existing shareholders who have their shares purchased in the buyout often win big. This is because most LBOs involve the payment of a premium over the market price at which the shares were trading prior to the announcement of the takeover. Similarly, the parties taking control of the firm gain managerial control and the enhanced flexibility normally associated with privately run firms. The new owners also have access to the firm's assets and cash flows, which formerly were part of the public corporation.

The biggest losers in an LBO are the firm's existing creditors. Because the buyout is financed primarily with debt capital, existing bondholders become creditors of a much riskier firm. This drives down the market value of outstanding bonds and makes future debt service much more uncertain. During the 1980s a number of institutional investors who held large bond positions in firms that were the subject of MBOs sued the management of the firms. They claimed that managers knowingly engaged in activities that harmed their economic investment as creditors of the corporation. These suits resulted in settlements and damage awards in several instances.

HISTORY OF LEVERAGED BUYOUTS

When a public firm experiences an LBO, its entire equity is purchased by a small group of investors. This group often includes the firm's current upper management. In order to entice existing shareholders to sell the firm's outstanding shares, the group often offers a premium above the stock's prevailing market value. The capital they need to purchase the shares is obtained by issuing debt, in the form of bonds, against the firm's assets and cash flows. From a balance-sheet perspective, the action all takes place on the right-hand side.

That is, the transaction involves the exchange of debt for equity. The result is that creditors have a larger claim, and owners a smaller claim, on the firm's assets. Note that the assets on the left-hand side of the firm's balance sheet do not change. Instead, what changes is how they are financed.

During the 1980s leveraged buyouts became a huge part of America's corporate landscape. This largely was the result of a single investment banking firm, Drexel Burham Lambert, and the efforts of one of its principals, Michael Milken. It was Milken who determined that high-yield bonds could fill an existing funding gap in corporate financing. The bonds, commonly referred to as junk bonds because of their riskiness, would be enticing to investors who otherwise might not be willing to take an equity position in high-risk firms. Drexel developed a market for junk bonds and served as the investment bank for corporate raiders and management groups interested in taking over existing corporations. The market flourished for several years, before Milken was prosecuted and convicted of securities violations. Drexel Burham Lambert ultimately went bankrupt, but the firm's legacy lives on in the active market for high-yield debt.

REASONS FOR TAKING A FIRM PRIVATE

The junk bond market enabled small investor groups to raise large sums of money in order to take public companies private. A number of reasons motivated managers and investors to pursue LBOs.

One advantage that a private firm has over a public one is administrative cost savings. A publicly traded company must produce annual reports, 10-K reports, comply with numerous regulations required by the Securities and Exchange Commission, hold annual shareholder meetings, and respond to shareholder requests. The management of publicly held firms must meet regularly with security analysts who follow the firm's stock, and maintain a shareholder relations department to deal with investor concerns. These costs are not required of a privately held firm.

In a private firm, managers no longer have to answer to the shareholder constituency. Lack of public accountability translates into greater management flexibility, since managers no longer have to focus as strongly on short-term operating results. The intense interest in reported quarterly earnings can bias managers in public firms to devote a great amount of effort and resources on short-term performance. Thus, managers of private firms have the luxury of being able to engage in investment activity that takes longer to produce tangible rewards. This greater flexibility and freedom from having to answer to shareholders is very enticing to upper-level management.

In addition, the process of buying up existing shares of the firm's stock severely diminishes the absolute number of shareholders. Because of their large capital investment and the fact that they now answer to themselves, the shareholders that remain after an LBO are highly interested in the firm's operations. These shareholders play an active role in the firm's management, as opposed to the hundreds of thousands of passive investors that hold a publicly traded firm's common stock.

The new entity's management has enhanced incentives to operate efficiently and profitably. This is because the high amount of debt service resulting from an LBO leaves little room for corporate perks and excess. The combination of having to pay the large interest expense on the debt and working for themselves, as opposed to anonymous shareholders, results in much greater motivation for management to perform. Equity holders remaining after an LBO often have some special expertise or talent that they bring to the firm, such as access to additional capital sources. Shareholders in the new private firm who are not part of active management also have much greater incentive to monitor active management, since their personal stake in the firm is typically high.

Corporate tax shields are another potential advantage of restructuring with debt financing. The corporate tax code in the United States allows companies to deduct the interest paid on debt as an expense for tax purposes. No such deduction is allowed for dividends paid on equity shares. Thus, increased use of debt results in lower tax obligations owed to the Internal Revenue Service. Firms facing large tax liabilities may reap considerable benefits from the tax savings that result from debt financing.

Finally, large publicly held corporations in mature industries typically have access to large amounts of free cash flow. These dollars are valuable, because they can be used to develop new products and markets or invest in other firms. In a public corporation, these cash flows may be used for perquisites such as corporate travel to conventions and trade shows, company cars, membership in clubs, and other types of nonmonetary rewards. By taking the firm private, remaining shareholders gain access to the firm's free cash flow and can put it to use, thereby reaping direct benefits.

THE 1990S

With the demise of Drexel Burnham Lambert and the default on several prominent junk bond issues associated with 1980s restructurings, leveraged buyout activity slowed considerably in the 1990s. The appetite of investors for new junk bond issues decreased, and some of the firms that had previously gone private subsequently were recapitalized as public corporations.

THE 2000S

After a lull in the 1990s, leveraged buyouts began to regain some of their charm in the early part of the twenty-first century. According to Dealogic, a New York-based deal tracker, LBO firms accounted for 10 percent of the $540 billion in mergers and acquisitions announced in the United States, double the average of 5 percent over the previous 10 years. Europe also showed a significant increase in LBO activities throughout the early 2000s.

Although leveraged buyouts relinquished the center stage they once held in American corporate finance, the concept of restructuring by replacing equity with debt and continuing under private management remains a significant opportunity for investors. Management in the modern corporation has greater incentive to operate efficiently and pay attention to shareholder concerns, lest the threat of a buyout cost them their positions with the firm.

SEE ALSO: Financial Issues for Managers; Shareholders

Howard Finch
Revised by Hal P. Kirkwood, Jr.

FURTHER READING:

Amihud, Yakov, ed. *Leveraged Management Buyouts: Causes and Consequences.* Washington, DC: Beard Books, 2002.

Berstein, Peter L. *Capital Ideas: The Improbable Origins of Modern Wall Street.* New York: Free Press, 1992.

Dolbeck, Andrew. "The Return of the Leveraged Buyout Deal." *Weekly Corporate Growth Report,* 23 August 2004, 1–3.

Higgins, Robert C. *Analysis for Financial Management.* 7th ed. Boston: Irwin/McGraw-Hill, 2004.

Rickertsen, Rick, and Robert E. Gunther. *Buyout: The Insider's Guide to Buying Your Own Company.* New York: AMACOM, 2001.

Thornton, Emily, Ronald Grover, and Tom Lowry. "Those Bulging Buyouts." *Business Week,* 9 February 2004, 74.

LICENSING AND LICENSING AGREEMENTS

A license provides the legal authority to engage in certain acts. Some licenses are required for the protection of the public. For example, a physician is licensed to assure professional competence, and the owner of a bar and restaurant is licensed to prove moral fitness. Some licenses are designed to raise government revenue (e.g., automobile licenses) or to grant some other party permission to make use of land (e.g., land easement). In business, a license is the granting of permission to use a property right in a limited capacity, while still allowing the licensor to retain ownership. For example, under a licensing agreement a U.S. clothing manufacturer may allow a foreign producer to use its designs and specifications to make clothes.

For a license to exist, there must be a contract between two or more parties giving an explanation as to what property rights the licensor is agreeing to give up to the licensee. This agreement or contract is known as the licensing agreement. These agreements have been in existence since the first copyrights and patents were issued in the late 1700s.

The licensing agreement is a complex legal document that begins by identifying parties to the agreement, as well as the dates of the agreement. It specifies the subject matter to be licensed, including patents and trade secrets. Also specified are the provisions or rights of the license, such as whether it grants exclusive rights or is subject to other agreements. Any limitations, such as territorial and quantity restrictions, are also specified. A final section can specify duration, termination, and related provisions of the agreement.

In business, licensing agreements or arrangements are mutually beneficial. The licensor provides his or her property right and the licensee contributes expertise in the particular industry or territory covered by the license. The resulting relationship becomes much the same as a joint venture or partnership. Licensing agreements include several types, including copyright licensing, patent licensing, merchandise licensing, trademark licensing, and software licensing.

BENEFITS OF LICENSING

Typically, a trademark owner will grant a license in order to exploit the trademark rights in areas where he or she does not have the appropriate expertise, infrastructure, or capital resources to maximize the value of the right. While the licensor is exploiting the trademark right, the licensee is betting that the name or symbol recognition of the property will influence consumers and motivate them to buy a particular item. Characters that have enjoyed popularity from trademark licensing relationships include Mickey Mouse, Barbie, and the Lion King. A major trend has been for manufacturers and retailers to build the core of their business with trademark-licensed products.

When granting a license, copyright owners are motivated by the prospect of receiving royalties for each product, performance, or copy of their work. In the case of a publication, the copyright is an exclusive right given to an author of an original work. Books, plays, magazines, photography, paintings, sculpture, articles, musical compositions, and radio and television programs are additional commodities that can be copyrighted. The exclusive right also allows copyright owners to reproduce their own work or allow others to do so.

LICENSING AS A GLOBALIZATION STRATEGY

In its most general sense, licensing is a key mode of entry for firms considering international expansion. A licensing agreement gives a foreign company the rights to produce and/or sell another firm's goods in their country. The agreement also may include production and sales in more than one country. The licensee takes the risks and makes the investment in facilities for handling the manufacturing of the goods, as well as managing other supply chain linkages to deliver and even sell the goods to the final consumer. The licensor is normally paid a royalty on each unit produced and sold. Because there is little investment for the licensor, this method is seen as an easier way to become an international or global company.

Licensing is growing as manufacturers and retailers build their core businesses and change their strategies to include more licenses. For example, Merck and Upjohn have licensed organizations in other parts of the world to manufacture and sell their pharmaceutical products. Other firms using licensing agreements in this way include McDonald's, Nestlé, Anheuser-Busch, and KFC.

The release of hot movies like the *Lord of the Rings* trilogy also triggers many license agreements and ties between mass merchandisers and licensors for toys, games, and children's apparel. Some retailers go so far as to demand exclusive agreements for licensed apparel and movie tie-in products in order to pursue marketplace differentiation strategies.

Service-based businesses also can benefit from licensing arrangements. Within the airline industry, many of the code-sharing arrangements that allow airlines to sell each other's seats are much like licensing agreements. Airlines and other firms enter such agreements when they need help commercializing a new technology, expanding a brand franchise globally, or building a marketing image. Rather than entering a new or international market alone, licensing is a faster way to grow a market and achieve market-share dominance. It also may allow firms to gain a larger market for their non-licensed products.

In the early 2000s a growing number of technology companies began launching intellectual property (IP) licensing programs in order to turn dormant projects into revenue, penetrate new markets, and evaluate potential business partners. These firms conducted inventories of their knowledge bases and patent families, and identified technologies that were outside the core business yet still offered some potential for development. They then sought to license these technologies to other firms.

In *Licensing Journal,* George A. Frank explained: "Patents that some corporations had obtained for reasons not directly related to the development or transfer of technology were proving to be a vast untapped resource. IP licensing has now become a tremendous income source, and indeed is not an important benchmark by which a corporation's success is measured" (2004). IBM, for example, earns more than $1 billion per year from its IP licensing program.

RISKS TO LICENSING

There are some risks and disadvantages to licensing. The firm may lose control over the manufacture and marketing of its goods in other countries. As a mode of international market entry, licensing also may be less profitable than other choices because returns must be shared between two parties. There even is a risk that the foreign licensee may sell a similar competitive product after the license agreement expires. Other risks and issues involve selecting a partner, as well as all of the general uncertainties in doing business with an international partner, including language, culture, political risk, and currency fluctuations. Alternatives to licensing include exporting, acquisitions, establishing a wholly owned international subsidiary, franchising, and forming strategic alliances.

SEE ALSO: Franchising; Intellectual Property Rights

Laurie Collier Hillstrom
Revised by Marilyn M. Helms

FURTHER READING:

Bradbury, Danny. "Breaking the Licensing Mould: Software Licensing Models Have Gone Through Some Changes in Recent Years, but None Are as Controversial as Microsoft's Latest Initiative." *MicroScope* 32, no. 3 (2002).

Ferraro, Neil P. "Poetic License? Caveats for Buying or Selling Technology: A Well-Crafted License Agreement Helps Maximize Financial and Technological Profits and Reduce Risk." *Contract Management* 44, no. 7 (2004).

Frank, George A. "Licensing IP Rights: Why, How, What, and When—A Corporate Perspective." *Licensing Journal* 24, no. 6 (2004).

Nanayakkara, Tamara. "Negotiating Technology Licensing Agreements." *International Trade Forum* April 2002. Available from <http://www.tradeforum.org/news>.

O'Haver, R. Russ. "Management Intangibles: Capitalizing on Your IP Assets." *Journal of Internet Law* 7, no. 6 (2003).

Pitts, Robert A., and David Lei. *Strategic Management: Building and Sustaining Competitive Advantage.* 2nd ed. Cincinnati: South-Western College Publishing, 2000.

LIFELONG LEARNING TRENDS

SEE: Continuing Education and Lifelong Learning Trends

LINE-AND-STAFF ORGANIZATIONS

Organizational structure involves, in addition to task organizational boundary considerations, the designation of jobs within an organization and the relationships among those jobs. There are numerous ways to structure jobs within an organization, but two of the most basic forms include simple line structures and line-and-staff structures.

In a line organization, top management has complete control, and the chain of command is clear and simple. Examples of line organizations are small businesses in which the top manager, often the owner, is positioned at the top of the organizational structure and has clear "lines" of distinction between him and his subordinates.

The line-and-staff organization combines the line organization with staff departments that support and advise line departments. Most medium and large-sized firms exhibit line-and-staff organizational structures. The distinguishing characteristic between simple line organizations and line-and-staff organizations is the multiple layers of management within line-and-staff organizations. The following sections refer primarily to line-and-staff structures, although the advantages and disadvantages discussed apply to both types of organizational structures.

Several advantages and disadvantages are present within a line-and-staff organization. An advantage of a line-and-staff organization is the availability of technical specialists. Staff experts in specific areas are incorporated into the formal chain of command. A disadvantage of a line-and-staff organization is conflict between line and staff personnel.

LINE-AND-STAFF POSITIONS

A wide variety of positions exist within a line-and-staff organization. Some positions are primary to the company's mission, whereas others are secondary—in the form of support and indirect contribution. Although positions within a line-and-staff organization can be differentiated in several ways, the simplest approach classifies them as being either line or staff.

A line position is directly involved in the day-to-day operations of the organization, such as producing or selling a product or service. Line positions are occupied by line personnel and line managers. Line personnel carry out the primary activities of a business and are considered essential to the basic functioning of the organization.

Line managers make the majority of the decisions and direct line personnel to achieve company goals. An example of a line manager is a marketing executive.

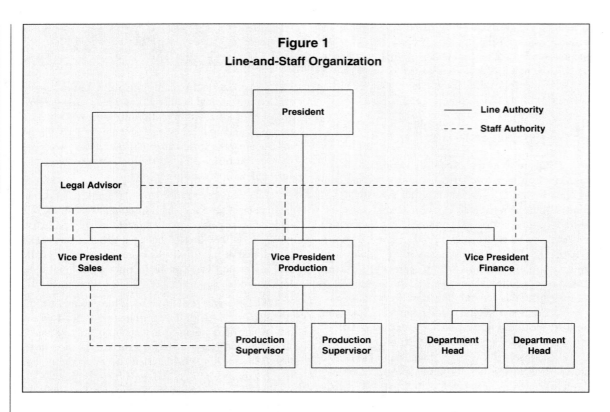

Figure 1
Line-and-Staff Organization

Although a marketing executive does not actually produce the product or service, he or she directly contributes to the firm's overall objectives through market forecasting and generating product or service demand. Therefore, line positions, whether they are personnel or managers, engage in activities that are functionally and directly related to the principal workflow of an organization.

Staff positions serve the organization by indirectly supporting line functions. Staff positions consist of staff personnel and staff managers. Staff personnel use their technical expertise to assist line personnel and aid top management in various business activities. Staff managers provide support, advice, and knowledge to other individuals in the chain of command.

Although staff managers are not part of the chain of command related to direct production of products or services, they do have authority over personnel. An example of a staff manager is a legal adviser. He or she does not actively engage in profit-making activities, but does provide legal support to those who do. Therefore, staff positions, whether personnel or managers, engage in activities that are supportive to line personnel.

LINE-AND-STAFF AUTHORITY

Authority within a line-and-staff organization can be differentiated. Three types of authority are present: line, staff, and functional. Line authority is the right to carry out assignments and exact performance from other individuals.

LINE AUTHORITY. Line authority flows down the chain of command. For example, line authority gives a production supervisor the right to direct an employee to operate a particular machine, and it gives the vice president of finance the right to request a certain report from a department head. Therefore, line authority gives an individual a certain degree of power relating to the performance of an organizational task.

Two important clarifications should be considered, however, when discussing line authority: (1) line authority does not ensure effective performance, and (2) line authority is not restricted to line personnel. The head of a staff department has line authority over his or her employees by virtue of authority relationships between the department head and his or her directly-reporting employees.

STAFF AUTHORITY. Staff authority is the right to advise or counsel those with line authority. For example, human resource department employees help other departments by selecting and developing a qualified workforce. A quality control manager aids a production manager by determining the acceptable quality level of products or services at a manufacturing company, initiating quality programs, and carrying out statistical analysis to ensure compliance with quality standards. Therefore, staff authority gives staff personnel the right to offer advice in an effort to improve line operations.

FUNCTIONAL AUTHORITY. Functional authority is referred to as limited line authority. It gives a staff person power over a particular function, such as safety or accounting. Usually, functional authority is given to specific staff personnel with expertise in a certain area. For example, members of an accounting department might have authority to request documents they need to prepare financial reports, or a human resource manager might have authority to ensure that all departments are complying with equal employment opportunity laws. Functional authority is a special type of authority for staff personnel, which must be designated by top management.

LINE-AND-STAFF CONFLICT

Due to different positions and types of authority within a line-and-staff organization, conflict between line and staff personnel is almost inevitable. Although minimal conflict due to differences in viewpoints is natural, conflict on the part of line and staff personnel can disrupt an entire organization. There are many reasons for conflict. Poor human relations, overlapping authority and responsibility, and misuse of staff personnel by top management are all primary reasons for feelings of resentment between line and staff personnel. This resentment can result in various departments viewing the organization from a narrow stance instead of looking at the organization as a whole.

Fortunately, there are several ways to minimize conflict. One way is to integrate line and staff personnel into a work team. The success of the work team depends on how well each group can work together in efforts to increase productivity and performance. Another solution is to ensure that the areas of responsibility and authority of both line and staff personnel are clearly defined. With clearly defined lines of authority and responsibility, each group may better understand their role in the organization. A third way to minimize conflict is to hold both line and staff personnel accountable for the results of their own activities. In other words, line personnel should not be entirely responsible for poor performance resulting from staff personnel advice.

Line-and-staff organizations combine the direct flow of authority present within a line organization with staff departments that offer support and advice. A clear chain of command is a consistent characteristic among line-and-staff organizational structures. Problems of conflict may arise, but organizations that clearly delineate responsibility can help minimize such conflict.

SEE ALSO: Leadership Styles and Bases of Power; Organizational Chart; Organizational Structure; Organizing

Tami L. Knotts
Revised by Scott B. Droege

FURTHER READING:

Hitt, Michael, Stewart Black, and Lyman W. Porter. *Management.* Englewood Cliffs, NJ: Prentice Hall, 2004.

Jones, Gareth R. *Organizational Theory, Design, and Change.* Upper Saddle River, NJ: Prentice Hall, 2004.

Judge, Timothy A., and Herbert G. Heneman, III. *Staffing Organizations.* Boston, MA: McGraw-Hill-Irwin, 2006.

Young, Gary J., Martin P. Charns, and Timothy C. Heeren. "Product-Line Management in Professional Organizations: An Empirical Test of Competing Theoretical Perspectives." *Academy of Management Journal* 47, no. 5: 723–735.

LISTENING

Listening is a critical part of communication, and poor listening can contribute to a host of interpersonal and organizational problems. Because a great deal of communication time is spent listening, errors are often costly. Communications research indicates that listening errors are common; organizational members often listen inadequately, hindering personal and organizational success.

There are two major types of listening: recall listening and empathic listening. With recall listening, a person attempts to correctly interpret and remember the content of what another person says. Recall listening can be improved greatly by minimizing distractions and practicing other good listening habits. Empathic listening involves expressing certain attitudes toward the speaker, such as openness to their message, enthusiasm, and concern. A good empathic listener will use nonverbal signals like nodding and eye contact to indicate a willingness to hear the message.

There are a number of ways to improve listening. These include avoiding distractions, listening for the speaker's emotions and controlling one's own emotions, recognizing gender differences in communication style, and engaging in active listening. By mastering techniques for improved listening, managers can better communicate with their supervisors, subordinates, coworkers, and customers.

AVOIDING DISTRACTIONS

The most basic approach to improving listening in the workplace is to avoid distractions that prevent one from concentrating on what is being said. Even when distractions cannot be completely eliminated, they can be minimized in order to improve concentration. In an office setting, listeners can close their office door to minimize outside noise, or move to a more quiet location such as an empty meeting room. Additionally, it may be necessary to ignore telephone calls and newly arrived e-mail in order to fully concentrate. Finally, interruptions from others, including coworkers, should be dealt with quickly so that attention can be returned to the speaker.

Not all distractions come from others in the organization; listeners are often distracted by work or other thoughts when they should be listening. Therefore, when it is important to listen, individuals should stop working, stop reading, and stop using their computers. When distracted by thoughts, listeners should focus their minds on what the speaker is saying. Mental wanderings are as distracting as physical interruptions.

Concentration and eye contact can minimize distractions and improve listening. To better concentrate, it is important to look the speaker in the eyes and sit at a proper distance. Listeners should sit close enough that the speaker knows that he or she has their attention. Listeners should also look at the speaker so that they are better able to follow his or her words. Finally, it is important to maintain eye contact when the other person is speaking.

One major threat to effective listening is speaking too often, and especially interrupting the speaker. If listeners do not allow the speaker time to finish his thoughts, they will miss the full meaning of his words. Additionally, if listeners are concerned with their response to the speaker, they likely are thinking about their own words and not listening properly. Thus, it may be useful for speakers to pause after the speaker has finished, making sure that she has said all that she intends to say. Furthermore, this is courteous to the speaker, and allows listeners time to gather their thoughts before responding.

MANAGING EMOTIONS

To listen effectively, it is important for listeners to read the speaker's emotions and manage their own feelings. Any anger, frustration, or hostility from either party can hinder the ability to listen properly. When listening to a person who is expressing negative emotion, listeners should try to show that these feelings have been recognized. Oftentimes, speakers want their feelings to be acknowledged before they are reading to discuss the content of their concern. This is particularly true with customers or clients; discussing a problem with an angry customer is likely to be futile if the listener does not first show that their feelings have been recognized and understood.

If listeners are unable to diffuse a speaker's negative emotions in a discussion, they are likely to be the target of hostile words. In this case there are several ways for listeners to respond: ignore the remark and continue listening to the speaker, make an issue of the comment, or respond to the comment in passing and continue with the original conversation. The response

of choice will often depend on the situation, but in all cases should be made deliberately and not based on emotion. Responding with anger is not likely to improve the situation.

In addition to reading the speaker's emotions, listeners must recognize their emotional reaction to the speaker and to his or her words. First, it is important to recognize the things that trigger negative emotions; listeners often are aware of topics and opinions that they have a strong reaction to. Knowing these can help listeners to step back from a conversation and minimize the emotional reaction to a particular topic. Second, people may have negative reactions to particular coworkers or customers that can impede effective listening. Again, advance recognition of feelings about a person may allow the listener to set them aside more easily when it is important to listen. Finally, when negative emotions occur unpredictably, listeners must remember that highly emotional communication is rarely effective in a business context. It may be necessary for listeners to physically excuse themselves for a short time to control their emotions before resuming discussion.

GENDER DIFFERENCES

Gender differences in communication can cause problems. By understanding these differences, listeners can improve their effectiveness when they are addressed by someone of the opposite sex. The major difference in communication is that women prefer to give many details before coming to a conclusion, while men prefer to give "the bottom line" with few details. This may lead male listeners to think that a female speaker is rambling or avoiding her opinion. Subsequently, the female speaker may believe that the male is not listening because he does not consider the details to be important. Conversely, a female listener may find a male speaker's comments too abrupt, or may believe the speaker is hiding details that he does not want others to know. On average, males and females may be different in the way that they communicate. However, not all individuals fit these generalized characteristics. Thus, in order to listen effectively it is important to recognize the way each person communicates, beyond mannerisms related to gender.

ACTIVE LISTENING

One specific technique to improve listening is called active listening. Active listening involves asking questions, using nonverbal cues, giving feedback, and using reflective listening to more effectively understand the speaker.

Oftentimes, a speaker may give incomplete information or speak in a way that the listener cannot understand. To understand the speaker, the listener may need to ask questions to elicit the information that has not been received. This can involve the use of closed questions, which require only a yes or no answer, and open questions, which require the speaker to elaborate. There are different times in which each is appropriate. For instance, assume a subordinate comes to a manager's office to discuss a lack of progress on a project and says, "There are some interpersonal issues with my team members." This would best be followed by an open question, such as, "What are some of the things that have been going on that are leading to these interpersonal issues?" A closed question, such as, "Is your team leader causing problems?" is unlikely to elicit the necessary information. Conversely, there are times when closed questions are most appropriate, particularly as follow-ups to open questions. After discussing the team problems with the subordinate, the aforementioned manager might confirm: "So, you'd like for me to meet with the team tomorrow to clarify each person's responsibilities?" Closed questions can often help to come to conclusions after a discussion.

Active listening also involves reading a speaker's tone of voice and body language, both of which may convey a different message than that of the words used. A person's tone of voice may reveal feelings that contradict his words; an employee who assures that she is excited to tackle a difficult task, but speaks in a flat, dull voice, may be hiding her hesitance to attempt that task. Body language can also convey more than words. A speaker who does not make eye contact and looks down may be conveying embarrassment or discomfort. A speaker who leans forward and gestures often may be excited or enthusiastic. Some commonly held beliefs about body language are not necessarily accurate. Crossed arms from a listener, often believed to be a sign of resistance to the speaker's words, may only be a sign of the listener's most comfortable sitting position. Some people believe that unwillingness to make eye contact indicates lying. However, many people can look others in the eye and lie, or may lack eye contact due to shyness or other reasons.

Feedback is a critical part of active listening; both nonverbal and verbal responses can improve listening. To show that they understand the listener, a speaker may nod their head, smile, or raise their eyebrows. Verbal responses to show comprehension include saying, "uh huh," "I agree," and "yes." To indicate a lack of understanding or the need for further information when listening, a listener might furrow his eyebrows or cock her head to one side. Replying, "I don't understand" or "Can you explain?" can improve a listener's ability to understand the speaker. One previously discussed element of feedback is acknowledging the speaker's feelings, particularly when the speaker is emotional. Before listeners can effectively understand the topic of discussion, they should recognize any negative feelings that the speaker appears to have.

Reflective listening is a hallmark of active listening and is a special type of feedback. With reflective listening, the listener takes the message that the speaker says and returns it to him or her for confirmation. For example, an employee may say, "I'm feeling very frustrated with our weekly staff meetings. We just seem to talk around all the same issues and I never get much out of them except the feeling that no one knows what anyone else is working on." In this case, a manager might respond, "It sounds as if you feel that the staff meetings are disorganized and not a good use of time." By rephrasing the speaker's words, the manager confirms that they are understood, which makes the speaker feel as if he has been heard correctly. One concern with reflective listening is that the speaker may feel as if the listener has just agreed with or validated his or her feelings. In some cases, the listener may disagree with the speaker's opinion, but still wants to indicate understanding of the message. In this circumstance, it is important to preface the reflective comment with, "I hear you saying that. . ." or "It seems you are. . ." to indicate that the message is the speaker's and not necessarily the listener's.

Listening is a critical business skill, and it can be improved by avoiding distractions, recognizing the speaker's emotions, understanding gender differences in communication style, and using active listening. By improving listening, problems associated with miscommunication in the workplace may be minimized.

SEE ALSO: Communication

Marcia J. Simmering

FURTHER READING:

"Be a Better Listener." *The Hindu Business Line* 9 June 2003.

Biech, Elaine. "The Lucrative Art of Authentic Listening." *Successful Meetings* 54, no. 1 (2005): 32–33.

Brody, Marjorie, and Danine Alati. "Learn to Listen." *Incentive* 178, no. 5 (2004): 57–58.

Colombo, George. "Are You Really Listening to Your Customers?" *Business Credit* 106, no. 6 (2004): 66–67.

Cooper, Lynn O. "Listening Competency in the Workplace: A Model for Training." *Business Communication Quarterly* 60, no. 4 (1997): 75–84.

Cousins, Roland B. "Active Listening Is More Than Just Hearing." *SuperVision* 61, no. 9 (2000): 14–15.

DiSanza, James R., and Nancy J. Legge. *Business and Professional Communication: Plans, Processes, and Performance.* Boston, MA: Allyn and Bacon, 2000.

Wilkie, Helen. *Writing, Speaking, Listening. The Essentials of Business Communication.* Oxford, United Kingdom: How To Books Ltd., 2001.

LOCATION STRATEGY

Being in the right location is a key ingredient in a business's success. If a company selects the wrong location, it may have adequate access to customers, workers, transportation, materials, and so on. Consequently, location often plays a significant role in a company's profit and overall success. A location strategy is a plan for obtaining the optimal location for a company by identifying company needs and objectives, and searching for locations with offerings that are compatible with these needs and objectives. Generally, this means the firm will attempt to maximize opportunity while minimizing costs and risks.

A company's location strategy should conform with, and be part of, its overall corporate strategy. Hence, if a company strives to become a global leader in telecommunications equipment, for example, it must consider establishing plants and warehouses in regions that are consistent with its strategy and that are optimally located to serve its global customers. A company's executives and managers often develop location strategies, but they may select consultants (or economic development groups) to undertake the task of developing a location strategy, or at least to assist in the process, especially if they have little experience in selecting locations.

Formulating a location strategy typically involves the following factors:

1. Facilities. Facilities planning involves determining what kind of space a company will need given its short-term and long-term goals.

2. Feasibility. Feasibility analysis is an assessment of the different operating costs and other factors associated with different locations.

3. Logistics. Logistics evaluation is the appraisal of the transportation options and costs for the prospective manufacturing and warehousing facilities.

4. Labor. Labor analysis determines whether prospective locations can meet a company's labor needs given its short-term and long-term goals.

5. Community and site. Community and site evaluation involves examining whether a company and a prospective community and site will be compatible in the long-term.

6. Trade zones. Companies may want to consider the benefits offered by free-trade zones, which are closed facilities monitored by customs services where goods can be brought without the usual customs requirements. The

United States has about 170 free-trade zones and other countries have them as well.

7. Political risk. Companies considering expanding into other countries must take political risk into consideration when developing a location strategy. Since some countries have unstable political environments, companies must be prepared for upheaval and turmoil if they plan long-term operations in such countries.

8. Governmental regulation. Companies also may face government barriers and heavy restrictions and regulation if they intend to expand into other countries. Therefore, companies must examine governmental—as well as cultural—obstacles in other countries when developing location strategies.

9. Environmental regulation. Companies should consider the various environmental regulations that might affect their operations in different locations. Environmental regulation also may have an impact on the relationship between a company and the community around a prospective location.

10. Incentives. Incentive negotiation is the process by which a company and a community negotiate property and any benefits the company will receive, such as tax breaks. Incentives may place a significant role in a company's selection of a site.

Depending on the type of business, companies also may have to examine other aspects of prospective locations and communities. Based on these considerations, companies are able to choose a site that will best serve their needs and help them achieve their goals.

COMPANY REQUIREMENTS

The initial part of developing a location strategy is determining what a company will require of its locations. These needs then serve as some of the primary criteria a company uses to evaluate different options. Some of the basic requirements a company must consider are:

- Size. A company must determine what size property or facility it needs.

- Traffic. If it is in the service business, a company must obtain statistics on the amount of traffic or the number of pedestrians that pass by a prospective location each day.

- Population. Whether a service or manufacturing operation, a company must examine the population of prospective locations to ensure that there is a sufficient number of potential customers (if a service business) or a sufficient number of skilled or trainable workers. In addition, manufacturers also benefit from being close to their customers, because proximity to customers reduces shipment time and increases company responsiveness to customers.

- Total costs. Companies must determine the maximum total costs they are willing to pay for a new location. Total costs include distribution, land, labor, taxes, utilities, and construction costs. More obscure costs also should be considered, such as transportation costs to ship materials and supplies, and the loss of customer responsiveness if moving further away from the customer base.

- Infrastructure. Companies must consider what their infrastructure requirements will be, including what modes of transportation they will need and what kinds of telecommunications services and equipment they will need.

- Labor. Companies must establish their labor criteria and determine what kind of labor pool they will need, including the desired education and skilled levels.

- Suppliers. Companies must consider the kinds of suppliers they will need near their locations. In addition, having suppliers nearby can help companies reduce their production costs.

Besides these basic requirements, companies must take into consideration their unique requirements of prospective locations. These requirements may correspond to their overall corporate strategy and corporate goals and to their particular industries.

LOCATION SELECTION TECHNIQUES

MANUFACTURING. Several techniques exist that can be used as part of a location strategy to determine the merits of prospective sites. Location strategists often divide assessment of prospective locations into macro analysis and micro analysis. Macro analysis encompasses the evaluation of different regions and communities, whereas micro analysis includes the evaluation of particular sites. The main macro analysis techniques are factor-rating systems, linear programming, and center of gravity.

Factor-rating systems are among the most commonly used techniques for choosing a location, because they analyze diverse factors in an easily comprehensible manner. Factor-rating systems simply consist of a weighted list of the factors a company considers the most important and a range of values for each factor (see Table 1). A company can rate each site with a value from the range based on the costs and benefits offered by the alternative locations, and multiply this

value by the appropriate weight. These numbers are then summed to get an overall "factor rating." Then a company can compare the overall ratings of alternative sites. This technique enables a company to choose a location systematically based on the best rating.

Table 1
Sample Factor-Rating System

Factor	Rating (1-100)	Weight	Factor-Rating
Energy availability	60	.3	18
Labor availability	80	.2	16
Transportation	40	.2	8
Supplies	90	.1	9
Taxes and regulations	70	.1	7
Infrastructure	70	.1	7
Overall Factor-Rating	—	—	65

Linear programming provides a method for evaluating the cost of prospective locations within a production/distribution network. This technique uses a matrix of production facilities and warehouses that shows the unit shipping costs from a manufacturing location designated by a variable, such as X, to prospective destinations, such as warehouses designated by other variables—E, F, and G—and the total amount of goods the prospective manufacturer, X, could produce. Other prospective manufacturing locations and the same information for each are also included in the matrix. After computing the total costs for each prospective location, a company can determine which one has lower total costs in terms of the entire production/distribution network.

The center of gravity method is useful for identifying an individual location by considering existing locations, the distances between them, and the volume of products to be shipped. Companies use this method mostly for locating distribution warehouses. To use this technique, companies plot their existing locations on a grid with a coordinate system (the particular coordinate system used does not matter). The idea behind this technique is to identify the relative distances between locations. After the existing locations are placed on the grid, the center of gravity is determined by calculating the X and Y coordinates that would have the lowest transportation costs.

SERVICES. Since service businesses generally must maintain a number of sites to remain close to customers, the location selected should be close to the targeted segment of the market. The market also can influence the number of new locations, as well as their size and features.

A simple technique for determining service locations is to establish a set of minimum criteria for opening new outlets. These criteria should be developed so that the locations selected have strong chances of success. A company could assess the potential of prospective locations based on primary criteria such as:

- The population of the community should more than 100,000.

- The annual per capita income should be more than $35,000.

After selecting locations that satisfy these criteria, a company might further evaluate the potential locations based on a set of criteria that considers the location's industrialization, person/car ratio, labor availability, population density, and infrastructure.

TRENDS IN LOCATION STRATEGY

Globalization and technology have been the biggest drivers of change in the location decision process over the last thirty years. Location activity has been very high in recent decades as a result of technology improvements, economic growth, international expansion and globalization, and corporate restructuring, mergers and acquisitions.

The top five location factors for global companies are costs, infrastructure, labor characteristics, government and political issues, and economy. Key sub-factors are the availability and quality of the labor force, the quality and reliability of modes of transportation, the quality and reliability of utilities, wage rates, worker motivation, telecommunication systems, record of government stability, and industrial relations laws. Other sub-factors—protection of patents, availability of management resources and specific skills, and system and integration costs—are of increasing importance.

Whereas wages and the industrial relations environment are significant factors in multinational location decisions, by far the main determinant is the host country market size. Furthermore, global economic considerations have become paramount in location strategy as companies contemplate the advantages afforded by various locations in terms of positioning in international markets and against competitors.

When companies seek new sites they generally strive to keep operating and start-up costs low, and so they often choose locations in collaboration with economic development groups to achieve these goals. Companies also now expect to move into new facilities more quickly than in the past, so they tend to focus more on leasing facilities than purchasing land and building new facilities. Also, by leasing facilities, companies can relocate every few years if the market requires it.

Technology, especially communications technology, has not only been a driver of change, but has facil-itated the site selection process. Managers can obtain initial information on alternative locations via the Internet and promotional software. Site selections agencies increasingly use geographical information system (GIS) technology, and e-mail has become a dominant mode of communication in location research and negotiation.

Location databases have enabled companies to do initial screening themselves, hence reducing their need to rely on economic developers to providing only very specific information and details on locations—such as commuting patterns and workforce characteristics.

Telecommunications technology has created the "virtual office" of employees working from remote locations. The growth of the virtual office has impacted location strategy in that some companies no longer need as much workspace because many employees work from remote sites. When these employees need to work at the office, they can call and reserve office space for themselves. The decrease in facility size can lead to millions of dollars worth of savings each year, while increasing productivity.

SEE ALSO: Globalization; International Business

Karl Heil
Revised by R. Anthony Inman

FURTHER READING:

Bognanno, Mario F., Michael P. Keane, and Donghoon Yang. "The Influence of Wages and Industrial Relations Environments on the Production Location Decisions of U.S. Multinational Corporations." *Industrial and Labor Relations Review* 58, no. 2 (2005): 171.

MacCarthy, B.L., and W. Atthirawong. "Factors Affecting Location Decisions in International Operations—A Delphi Study." *International Journal of Operations and Production Management* 23, no. 7 (2003): 794–828.

Spee, Roel, and Wim Douw. "Cost-Reduction Location Strategies." *Journal of Corporate Real Estate* 6, no. 1 (September 2003): 30–38.

Talley-Seijn, Margaret. "30 Years of Location Strategies." *Plants, Sites and Parks* 31, no. 3 (July 2004): 26–29.

LOGISTICS AND TRANSPORTATION

According to the Council of Supply Chain Management Professionals (CSCMP), logistics management can be defined as, "that part of supply chain management that plans, implements, and controls the efficient, effective forward and reverse flow and storage of goods, services and related information between the point of origin and the point of consumption in order to meet customers' requirements."

The history of logistics is rooted in its military application. Since WWII it has developed into an important function of business as it became evident that logistics and transportation add place and time value to products and enhance the form and possession value added by manufacturing and marketing.

The concept of logistics as a business discipline began to appear in the business-related literature in the 1960s when it was called physical distribution. At that time its focus was on the outbound side of the logistics system. With the emerging importance of Supply Chain Management, logistics and transportation has become even more crucial as supply chain managers realize that the coordination and integration of the logistics systems of all organizations with the supply chain are requirements for success.

According to Coyle, Bardi and Langley there are four subdivisions of logistics:

- Business logistics—this is the same as the definition from the CSCMP and approach we are adopting in our discussion.

- Military logistics—all that is necessary to support the operational capability of military forces and their equipment in order to ensure readiness, reliability, and efficiency.

- Event logistics—management of all involved (activities, facilities, and personnel) in organizing, scheduling, and deploying the resources necessary to ensure the occurrence of an event and efficient withdrawal afterwards.

- Service logistics—acquisition, scheduling, and management of facilities, personnel, and materials need to support and sustain a service operation.

Within the context of this essay we will be addressing the concept of business logistics. Business logistics systems can be classified into four categories:

Balanced System. Firms with a balanced system have reasonably balanced inbound and outbound flows.

Heavy inbound. These firms have a very heavy inbound flow but a very simple outbound flow. Firms with heavy inbound flow typically do not warehouse their finished goods, for example, aircraft manufacturers.

Heavy outbound. These firms have a complex outbound flow and a very simple inbound flow. Their inbound flow is usually raw material from a relatively short distance. Typically their outbound shipments are a wide variety of packaged finished goods

requiring storage and transportation to the final consumer.

Reverse system. Reverse supply chain logistics systems have reverse flows on the outbound side of their system. Durable products are returned for credit, trade-in, repair, salvage or disposal or the firm utilized returnable or reusable containers.

Coyle, Bardi and Langley list a number of activities that lie within the realm of logistics:

- Order fulfillment—activities involved with completing customer orders. Obviously, transportation and logistics would be an integral part of completing the orders since they directly impact delivery.

- Traffic and transportation—the physical movement of goods.

- Warehousing and storage—a number of warehousing decisions directly impact logistics and transportation. For example, how many warehouses are needed, where should they be located, how large should they be, how much inventory should be held in each?

- Plant and warehouse site location—location can alter time and place relationships between the warehouse and the customer. Frequently transportation cost is a major factor in plant and warehouse location.

- Materials handling—the placement of goods and the movement of goods within a warehouse, factory or other facility. This includes incoming movement of goods and the movement of goods from storage to order-picking areas to dock areas for shipment.

- Industrial packaging—transportation directly impacts the type packaging needed. Fast methods of transport, such as air, generally require little in the way of packaging while the slower modes, such as water or rail, require substantial packaging expenditures to ensure safe shipment.

- Purchasing—quantities purchased directly affect transportation costs. Also, transportation relates directly to the distance or location of goods purchased by the firm. Purchasing and logistics are increasingly integrated in many major firms.

- Demand forecasting—accurate and reliable forecasting is essential for effective inventory control purposes, especially within firms utilizing lean manufacturing and JIT.

- Inventory control—this is directly related to transportation and warehousing. If transportation is slow higher levels of inventory are needed, ergo, more warehouse capacity is needed.

- Production planning—production planning must operate in close coordination with logistics in order to ensure adequate market coverage. Production planning and logistics are increasingly integrated within large corporations.

- Parts and service support—the effectiveness of parts and service support depend upon speed of transportation, location of warehouses, and forecasting of support function needs. Obviously, parts and service support have a direct impact on customer service levels.

- Return goods handling—reverse supply chain logistics is an increasingly important but frequently overlooked dimension in logistics.

- Salvage and scrap disposal—disposal is an integral part of the reverse supply chain. There is an increasing interest, in the logistics literature, in the impact of the location of evaluation and disposal facilities for returned goods.

- Customer service levels—logistics plays an extremely important role in ensuring that customers get the right products at the right place at the right time. Transportation, warehousing, forecasting, inventory control, and production planning all have a direct impact on customer satisfaction.

The two most obvious aspects of logistics are warehousing and transportation.

WAREHOUSING AND STORAGE. Warehousing is defined as the storage of goods: raw materials, semi-finished goods, or finished goods. This includes a wide spectrum of facilities and locations that provide warehousing. Since this is a point in the logistics system where goods are held for varying amounts of time, the flow is interrupted or stopped, thereby creating additional costs to the product.

In a macroeconomic sense, warehousing creates time utility for raw materials, industrial goods and finished products. It also increases the utility of goods by broadening their time availability to prospective customers.

TRANSPORTATION. Transportation involves the physical movement or flow of goods. The transportation system is the physical link that connects customers, raw material suppliers, plants, warehouses and channel members. These are the fixed points in a logistics supply chain.

The basic modes of transportation are water, rail, motor carrier, air and pipeline. Water being the slowest mode with rail, motor carrier, and air following in order of speed of delivery. Generally, the order is reversed when looking at costs.

Selection of the appropriate carrier has several steps. First the firm selects a transportation mode. The shipper must compare the service desired with the rate or cost of service. Service usually means transit time or the time that elapses from the time the consignor makes the goods available for dispatch until the carrier delivers to the consignee. Pickup and delivery, terminal handling and movement between origin and destination account for the time involved in transporting goods.

The firm must balance the "need for speed" with the costs inherent in the mode of transport. This includes the rate charged for the service, minimum weight requirements, loading and unloading facilities, packaging, possible damage in transit, and any special services that may be desired or required. If next day delivery is imperative, the shipper will utilize an air freight carrier but will pay a premium price for such rapid service. If time is not a particularly critical element the shipper may elect to use rail or a motor carrier, or may even utilize a water carrier if time is inconsequential. Water-based modes of transportation are the least expensive and are used for commodity type products such as grain, coal, and ore. Some firms even utilize more than one mode of transportation, called intermodal transport, to move their goods.

Once a mode is selected, the shipper must decide the legal classification or type of carrier they wish to utilize: common, regulated, contract, exempt or private.

Common carriers serve the general public at reasonable prices and without discrimination. They cannot refuse to carry a particular commodity or refuse to serve a particular point with the scope of the carrier's operation. Common carriers are liable for all goods lost, damaged, or delayed unless caused by an act of God, an act of a public enemy, an act of public authority, an act of the shipper, or some defect within the good itself.

Regulated carriers are required to provide safe and adequate service and facilities upon reasonable request and are liable for damage up to limits established by the carrier. Regulated carriers can be motor carriers or water carriers and are subject to minimal federal controls.

A contract carrier does not serve the general public, but, rather serves one or a limited number of contracted customers. They have no legal service obligation. They often provide a specialized service and usually have lower rates than common or regulated carriers.

Exempt carriers are exempt from regulation regarding rates and services. Exempt status comes from the type commodity hauled or the nature of the carrier's operation. Exempt motor carriers are usually local and typically transport such items as agricultural goods, newspapers, livestock, and fish. Exempt water carriers transport bulk commodities such as coal, ore, grain, and liquid. Exempt rail carriers transport piggyback shipments and exempt air carriers haul cargo.

A firm's own transportation is termed a private carrier. Private carriers are not "for-hire" and not subject to the same federal regulations as other types of transport. However, the carrier's primary business must be something other than transportation.

Once the mode and type of carrier is determined a final decision can be made based on other factors. Accessibility is one such factor. Some firms have geographic limits to their routing network. Others may not possess physical access to needed facilities or have the ability to provide the equipment and facilities that movement of a particular commodity may require. Reliability, the consistency of the transit time a carrier provides, is also a key factor. Finally, convenience and communication are other important considerations when selecting a carrier.

Measures that a transportation firm would use to judge its performance include: orders shipped on time, orders shipped complete, order preparation time, product availability, and transit time. From the customer perspective performance can be gauged from orders received on time, orders received complete, orders received damage free, orders filled accurately, and orders billed accurately.

GLOBAL LOGISTICS

The expansion of the global marketplace puts the concept of global logistics into the limelight. Logistics experts must now manage all of the aforementioned logistics activities within a world-wide arena spanning a multitude of countries, languages, cultures, governments, and regulations. Along with this expansion of the marketplace comes the need for global channel intermediaries. Today's global logistics manager would be familiar with the role of each of the following:

- Foreign freight forwarders—handlers of a myriad of foreign freight services: rate quotes, vessel chartering, booking of vessel space, handling of documentation and cargo insurance, tracing and expediting, arranging inland transportation and providing translation services.

- Export management companies —suppliers of expertise to those wishing to sell products overseas but lacking the necessary resources.

- Export trading companies—locaters of overseas buyers. They also handle export docu-

mentation, transportation and the meeting of foreign government requirements.

- Customs house brokers—overseers of the movement of goods through customs. They also ensure that accompanying documents are complete and accurate.

- Ship brokers—sales representatives for ship owners and purchasing representatives for the shipper.

- Ship agents—local representative of the ship operator that handles the ship's arrival, berthing, clearance, loading and unloading.

- Export packers—suppliers of export packaging services.

- Port authorities—owner and operator of the port. They provide wharf, dock, and other terminal facilities at port locations.

SEE ALSO: Exporting and Importing; Forecasting; Lean Manufacturing and Just-in-Time Production; Reverse Supply Chain Logistics; Warehousing and Warehouse Management

R. Anthony Inman

FURTHER READING:

Coyle, John J., Edward J. Bardi, and C. John Langley, Jr. *The Management of Business Logistics: A Supply Chain Perspective.* Mason, OH: South-Western Thomson Learning, 2003.

LONGITUDINAL SCENARIOS

Strategic planning and forecasting tend to use projections of past events to develop future plans. Such approaches rely on historical data and assume a continuation of past business practices and environmental stability. Scenarios are used to develop plans for significant changes in products, personnel, or processes for which data are limited and uncertain. The premise is that the best way to prepare for radically different situations is to think through various events that could occur and consider alternatives for responding to those situations if they should happen.

One early application of this technique was a 1968 forecast for the Royal Dutch Shell Group that foresaw the 1973 OPEC oil price rise. By thinking through this possibility, Shell executives were able to respond more rapidly than their competitors. This allowed Shell to move from its position as the eighth-largest oil producer to the second-largest in two years time. Businesses in energy intensive industries like trucking or airlines could benefit by considering what would happen and how should they respond if gas prices were to reach extremely high levels.

Scenarios typically look at potential situations from one of two perspectives. Some firms approach scenario development by looking at possible chain reactions resulting from a possible change. For example, new medical technology could raise average life expectancies beyond 100 years. In this case, one might ask what the impact would be on labor markets, health care, retirement programs, and housing. In other words, how would the change in average life expectancy change business?

An alternative approach is to look at a desired future state and proceed backward to consider the precursor developments that would be necessary to achieve the desired state. Firms could look at what changes in immunology, surgery, and drug development would be necessary to make it possible for life expectancies to reach 100. The question becomes what could the business do to make this possibility a reality?

There are many different approaches firms can use to develop meaningful scenarios. In their 2001 article, "The Essentials of Scenario Writing," Steven Schnaars and Paschalina Ziamou suggested the following:

1. Optimistic vs. best guess vs. pessimistic scenarios. This approach looks at the most likely (best guess) future situation based on current information. The optimistic scenario introduces questions regarding what things would or could happen to result in a better than anticipated outcome, and how the organization can make those things actually happen. The pessimistic scenario looks at many of the things that could go wrong and tries to help decision makers plan responses to deal with these problems should they arise.

2. Good vs. bad scenarios. This approach avoids the tendency to focus on the most likely alternative of the "best guess" and forces managers to give more attention to both extremes.

3. Arrayed scenarios. These scenarios look at alternatives associated with a continuum along a single criterion or dimension. Firms could plan their response to a slight, moderate, or severe change in the price of gasoline or another key resource.

4. Independently themed scenarios. This approach looks at different aspects of the future. One scenario could look at possible technological breakthroughs, another at environmental concerns, and a third at potential market changes. Each scenario is conceptually independent of the others.

Firms can use scenarios to develop a variety of strategies. Some firms strive to develop strategies that perform equally well across all scenarios, while others try to develop strategies that would work well in response to each possible scenario. A third approach is to develop a strategy to postpone commitment and keep options open as long as possible.

Scenario development allows firms to deviate from a linear projection of past business practices. This is accomplished by developing potential situations that question traditional assumptions about the firm's relevant industry, processes, markets, and people that may make it necessary to significantly alter the current strategy. Great strategists are more attuned to their environment and notice small changes in it before their less attentive counterparts. Scenario analysis allows firms to recognize some of these possible changes before their competitors and plan responses accordingly.

SEE ALSO: Contingency Approach to Management; Forecasting; Strategic Planning Tools

Joe Thomas

FURTHER READING:

Mitchell, Donald W., and Carol Bruckner Coles. "Establishing a Continuing Business Model Innovation Process." *Journal of Business Strategy* 25, no. 3 (2004): 39–49.

Mitroff, Ian I. *Crisis Leadership: Planning for the Unthinkable.* Hoboken, NJ: Wiley, 2004.

Nutt, Paul C. "Expanding the Search for Alternatives During Strategic Decision-Making." *Academy of Management Executive* 18, no. 4 (2004): 13–28.

Roney, Curtis W. "Planning for Strategic Contingencies." *Business Horizons* 46, no. 2 (2003): 35–42.

Schnaars, Steven, and Paschalina Ziamou. "The Essentials Of Scenario Writing." *Business Horizons* 44, no. 4 (2001): 25–31.

von Oetinger, Bolko. "A Plea for Uncertainty: Everybody Complains about Uncertainty, but It Might Be a Good Thing." *Journal of Business Strategy* 25, no. 1 (2004): 57–59.

M

MIS

SEE: Management Information Systems

MACROECONOMICS

SEE: Economics

MACROENVIRONMENTAL FORCES

An organization's macroenvironment consists of nonspecific aspects in the organization's surroundings that have the potential to affect the organization's strategies. When compared to a firm's task environment, the impact of macroenvironmental variables is less direct and the organization has a more limited impact on these elements of the environment.

Macroenvironmental variables include sociocultural, technological, political-legal, economic, and international variables. A firm considers these variables as part of its environmental scanning to better understand the threats and opportunities created by the variables and how strategic plans need to be adjusted so the firm can obtain and retain competitive advantage.

The macroenvironment consists of forces that originate outside of an organization and generally cannot be altered by actions of the organization. In other words, a firm may be influenced by changes within this element of its environment, but cannot itself influence the environment. The curved lines in Figure 1 indicate the indirect influence of the environment on the organization.

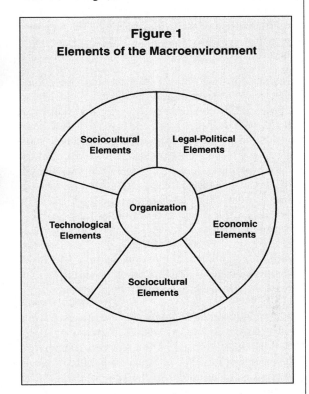

Figure 1
Elements of the Macroenvironment

SOCIOCULTURAL FACTORS

The sociocultural dimensions of the environment consist of customs, lifestyles, and values that characterize the society in which the firm operates. Sociocultural components of the environment influence the ability of the firm to obtain resources, make its goods and services, and function within the society. Sociocultural factors include anything within the context of society that has the potential to affect an organization. Population demographics, rising educational levels, norms and values, and attitudes toward social responsibility are examples of sociocultural variables.

POPULATION CHANGES. Changes in population demographics have many potential consequences for organizations. As the total population changes, the demand for products and services also changes. For instance, the decline in the birthrate and improvement in health care have contributed to an increase in the average age of the population in the United States. Many firms that traditionally marketed their products toward youth are developing product lines that appeal to an older market. Clothing from Levi Strauss & Co. was traditionally popular among young adults. While its popularity in this market has waned, the firm has been able to develop a strong following in the adult market with its Dockers label.

Other firms are developing strategies that will allow them to capitalize on the aging population. Firms in the health-care industry and firms providing funeral services are expected to do well given the increasing age of the U.S. population. They are projected as a growth segment of U.S. industry simply because of the population demographics.

RISING EDUCATIONAL LEVELS. Rising educational levels also have an impact on organizations. Higher educational levels allow people to earn higher incomes than would have been possible otherwise. The increase in income has created opportunities to purchase additional goods and services, and to raise the overall standard of living of a large segment of the population. The educational level has also led to increased expectations of workers, and has increased job mobility. Workers are less accepting of undesirable working conditions than were workers a generation ago. Better working conditions, stable employment, and opportunities for training and development are a few of the demands businesses confront more frequently as the result of a more educated workforce.

NORMS AND VALUES. Norms (standard accepted forms of behavior) and values (attitudes toward right and wrong), differ across time and between geographical areas. Lifestyles differ as well among different ethnic groups. As an example, the application in the United States of Japanese-influenced approaches to management has caused firms to reevaluate the concept of quality. Customers have also come to expect increasing quality in products. Many firms have found it necessary to reexamine production and marketing strategies to respond to changes in consumer expectations.

SOCIAL RESPONSIBILITY. Social responsibility is the expectation that a business or individual will strive to improve the welfare of society. From a business perspective, this translates into the public expecting businesses to take active steps to make society better by virtue of the business being in existence. Like norms and values, what is considered socially responsible behavior changes over time. In the 1970s affirmative action was a high priority. During the early part of the twenty-first century prominent social issues were environmental quality (most prominently, recycling and waste reduction) and human rights, in addition to general social welfare. More than just philanthropy, social responsibility looks for active participation on the part of corporations to serve their communities.

The stakeholder approach to social responsibility demonstrates some of the complexities of incorporating socially responsible issues into a firm's strategies. Stakeholders are anyone with a stake in the organization's existence. Highly visible stakeholders are stockholders, employees, customers, and the local community. Decisions to be responsible and maximize the return to stockholders may require closing an unprofitable plant. However, employees and members of the local community could view this move as socially irresponsible since the move would not benefit the community.

TECHNOLOGICAL FACTORS

Technology is another aspect of the environment a firm should consider in developing strategic plans. Changing technology may affect the demand for a firm's products and services, its production processes, and raw materials. Technological changes may create new opportunities for the firm, or threaten the survival of a product, firm, or industry. Technological innovation continues to move at an increasingly rapid rate.

DEMAND. Technology can change the lifestyle and buying patterns of consumers. Recent developments in the field of microcomputers have dramatically expanded the potential customer base and created innumerable opportunities for businesses to engage in business via Internet. Whereas computers were traditionally used only by large organizations to handle data processing needs, personal computers are commonly used by smaller firms and individuals for uses not even imagined fifteen years ago. Similarly, new developments in technology led to a reduction in prices for computers and expanded the potential market. Lower prices allow computers to be marketed to the general public rather than to business, scientific, and professional users—the initial market.

Technology may also cause certain products to be removed from the market. Asbestos-related illnesses have severely limited asbestos as a resource used in heat-sensitive products such as hair dryers. Further, a number of chemicals that have been commonly used by farmers to control insects or plants are prohibited from use or require licensure as a consequence of those chemicals appearing in the food chain.

PRODUCTION PROCESSES. Technology also changes production processes. The introduction of products based on new technology often requires new production techniques. New production technology may alter production processes. Robotics represents one of the most visible challenges to existing production methods. Robots may be used in positions considered hazardous for people or that require repetitive, detailed activities.

The consequences for other jobs currently occupied by people are not clear. When production was first automated, although some workers were displaced, new jobs were created to produce and maintain the automated equipment. The impact of robotics on jobs is in large part a function of the uses made of the technology and the willingness of workers to learn to use new technology.

In some industries, use of robots during the early 2000s increased production and efficiency but resulted in significant numbers of job losses. However, technological innovation can also result in increased job growth. For example, Ford Motor Company's $375-million technology update to its Norfolk assembly plant to build its 2004 F-150 resulted in the ability to build more models on its assembly line and consequently created about 270 new jobs, an 11 percent increase.

EVALUATING TECHNOLOGICAL CHANGES. There is little doubt that technology represents both potential threats and potential opportunities for established products. Products with relatively complex or new technology are often introduced while the technology is being refined, making it hard for firms to assess their market potential. When ballpoint pens were first introduced, they leaked, skipped, and left large blotches of ink on the writing surface. Fountain pen manufacturers believed that the new technology was not a threat to existing products and did not attempt to produce ballpoint pens until substantial market share had been lost.

Another technology, the electric razor, has yet to totally replace the blade for shaving purposes. Perhaps the difference is that the manufacturers of blades have innovated by adding new features to retain customers. Manufacturers of fountain pens did not attempt to innovate until the ballpoint pen was well established.

It is quite difficult to predict the impact of a new technology on an existing product. Still, the need to monitor the environment for new technological developments is obvious. Attention must also be given to developments in industries that are not direct competitors, since new technology developed in one industry may impact companies and organizations in others.

POLITICAL AND LEGAL FACTORS

The political-legal dimension of the general environment also affects business activity. The philosophy of the political parties in power influences business practices. The legal environment serves to define what organizations can and cannot do at a particular point in time.

ATTITUDES TOWARD BUSINESS

A pro-business attitude on the part of government enables firms to enter into arrangements that would not be allowed under a more anti-business philosophy. The numerous joint ventures between U.S. and Japanese automobile manufacturers could have been termed anticompetitive by a less pro-business administration. The release of many acres of government land for business use (logging, mining) angered many environmentalists who had been able to restrict business use of the land under previous administrations.

Changes in sentiments toward smoking and its related health risks have altered the public's attitude toward the tobacco industry. These changes have been reflected in many organizations by limiting smoking to designated areas or completely prohibiting it at work. The transformation in attitude has also caused firms within the tobacco industry to modify marketing strategies, encouraging many to seek expansion opportunities abroad.

LEGISLATION. The legal environment facing organizations is becoming more complex and affecting businesses more directly. It has become increasingly difficult for businesses to take action without encountering a law, regulation, or legal problem. A very brief listing of significant laws that affect business would include legislation in the areas of consumerism, employee relations, the environment, and competitive practices.

Many of the laws also have an associated regulatory agency. Powerful U.S. regulatory agencies include the Environmental Protection Agency (EPA), the Occupational Safety and Health Administration (OSHA), the Equal Employment Opportunity Commission (EEOC), and the Securities and Exchange Commission (SEC).

Estimates of the cost of compliance vary widely, but could well exceed $100 billion annually. Many of these costs are passed to consumers. However, costs of legal expenses and settlements may not be incurred for years and are not likely to be paid by consumers of the product or owners of the company when the violation occurred. Still, potential legal action often results in higher prices for consumers and a more conservative attitude by business executives.

LEVELS OF GOVERNMENT INFLUENCE. We generally speak about "the government" as referring to the federal government. It is the federal government that passes and enforces legislation concerning the entire country. Actions by the federal government affect a large number of firms and are consistent across state boundaries. Environmental analysis, however, should not overlook actions by both state and local governments.

Regulations concerning many business practices differ between states. Tax rates vary widely. Laws regarding unionization (e.g., right-to-work states) and treatment of homosexual workers differ between states.

Local governments have the potential to affect business practices significantly. Some local governments may be willing to provide incentives to attract business to the area. Some may build industrial parks, service roads, and provide low-interest bonds to encourage a desirable business to move into the community.

Regulatory measures such as building codes and zoning requirements differ significantly between communities. Infrastructure such as electric and sewer services, educational facilities, and sewage treatment capabilities may not be able to accommodate the increased demand associated with certain industries, making that locale unsuitable for establishing some businesses.

ECONOMIC FACTORS

Economic factors refer to the character and direction of the economic system within which the firm operates. Economic factors include the balance of payments, the state of the business cycle, the distribution of income within the population, and governmental monetary and fiscal policies. The impact of economic factors may also differ between industries.

BALANCE OF PAYMENTS. The balance of payments of a country refers to the net difference in value of goods bought and sold by citizens of the country. To decrease the dollar value of goods imported into a country, it is common practice to construct barriers to entry for particular classes of products. Such practices reduce competition for firms whose products are protected by the trade barriers.

Mexico has limited the number of automobiles that can be imported. The purpose of this practice is to stimulate the domestic automobile market and to allow it to become large enough to create economies of scale and to create jobs for Mexican workers. A side effect of the import restriction, however, has been an increase in the price and a decrease in the quality of automobiles available to the public.

Another potential consequence of import restrictions is the possibility of reciprocal import restrictions. Partially in retaliation to import restriction on Japanese televisions and automobiles by the United States, the Japanese have limited imports of agricultural goods from the United States.

Lowering trade restrictions as a means of stimulating the economy of a country may meet with mixed results. The North American Free Trade Agreement (NAFTA) has opened the borders between the United States, Canada, and Mexico for the movement of many manufacturers. Government officials in the United States argue the results have been positive, but many local communities that have lost manufacturing plants question the wisdom of the agreement.

As discussed in an article by Susan Schmidt in *World Trade* magazine, issues that stemmed from regulatory agencies and national security measures were barriers to free trade during the early part of the twenty-first century, demonstrating that NAFTA alone could not clear the path for companies and countries to take advantage of free trade benefits.

BUSINESS CYCLE. The business cycle is another economic factor that may influence the operation of a firm. Purchases of many durable goods (appliances, furniture, and automobiles) can be postponed during periods of recession and depression, as can purchases of new equipment and plant expansions. Economic downturns result in lower profits, reductions in hiring, increased borrowing, and decreased productivity for firms adversely affected by the recession. Positive consequences of recessions may include reductions in waste, more realistic perceptions of working conditions, exit of marginally efficient firms, and a more efficient system.

Some organizations may benefit from an economic downturn. Postponed purchases may result in the need to service existing products. An owner electing to keep a used automobile rather than buying a new one may need to have it repaired, thus creating an increased demand for automobile mechanics and replacement parts. Limited job opportunities during downturns also encourage individuals unable to get satisfactory jobs to consider going to college or joining the armed services.

INCOME DISTRIBUTION. The distribution of income may differ between economic systems. Two countries with the same mean (per capita) income levels may have dramatically different distributions of income. The majority of persons in the United States are considered middle income, with only a relatively small number of persons having exceptionally high or low incomes.

Many developing countries have citizens who are either extremely wealthy or extremely poor. Only a few persons would qualify as middle class. Therefore, although both countries had the same mean income, opportunities to market products to the middle class would be greater in the United States.

TRANSFER PAYMENTS. Transfer payments (e.g., welfare, social security) within the United States change the distribution of income. Transfer payments provide money to individuals in the lower income brackets and enable them to purchase goods and services they otherwise could not afford. Such a redistribution of income may not be the practice in other economic systems. Thus, large numbers of people in need of basic goods and services do not assure that those people will be able to purchase such goods and services.

MONETARY AND FISCAL POLICIES. Monetary and fiscal policies utilized by the federal government also influence business operations. Monetary policies are controlled by the Federal Reserve System and affect the size of the money supply and interest rates. Fiscal policies represent purchases made by the federal government.

For example, allocation of funds to defense means expenditures for weapons and hardware. If appropriations had gone to the Health and Human Services and Education Departments instead, much of the money would have constituted transfer payments. The primary beneficiaries of such a fiscal policy would be firms in the basic food and shelter businesses. No matter how government expenditures are reallocated, the result is lost sales and cut budgets for some companies, and additional opportunities for others.

Though unpopular in the United States, another aspect of government fiscal policy is deficit spending, which may allow government expenditures to rise, but can also influence interest rates, exchange rates, and other economic trends.

INTERNATIONAL FACTORS

A final component of the general environment is actions of other countries or groups of countries that affect the organization. Governments may act to reserve a portion of their industries for domestic firms, or may subsidize particular types of businesses to make them more competitive in the international market.

Some countries may have a culture or undergo a change in leadership that limits the ability of firms to participate in the country's economy. As with the other elements of the macroenvironment, such actions are not directed at any single company, but at many firms.

ECONOMIC ASSOCIATIONS. One of the most recent joint efforts by governments to influence business practices was NAFTA. The agreement between the United States, Canada, and Mexico was intended to facilitate free trade between the three countries. The result has been a decrease in trade barriers between them, making it easier to transport resources and outputs across national boundaries. The move has been beneficial to many businesses, and probably to the economies of all three countries. In most economic associations, preference is also given to products from member countries at the expense of products from nonmembers.

Probably the best-known joint effort by multiple countries to influence business practices is the Organization of Petroleum Exporting Countries (OPEC). The formation of OPEC, an oil cartel including most major suppliers of oil and gas, led to a drastic increase in fuel prices. Rising fuel prices had a significant effect on the demand for automobiles worldwide. The increases in oil prices also contributed to inflation all over the world. OPEC's early success encouraged countries producing other basic products (coffee beans, sugar, bananas) to attempt to control the prices of their products.

A more recent example of an economic association serving multiple countries was the International Coffee Organization (ICO). The United States rejoined the ICO 2004 in hopes of fostering sustainability and competition across countries and the industry. The United States works with the Honduras, Mexico, and Nicaragua, among others, as part of this organization.

INTERGOVERNMENTAL RELATIONS. Changing relationships between the United States and other countries may alter the ability of firms to enter foreign markets. The United States' establishment of trade relations with China in the 1970s created opportunities for many firms to begin marketing their products in China.

The rise of Ayatollah Ruhollah Khomeini to power in Iran altered the lives of many Iranian citizens. Wine, vodka, music, and other forms of entertainment were prohibited. Black markets provided certain restricted items. Other products, such as wine, began to be produced at home. Anti-American sentiments throughout the country showed the hostility of many citizens. Non-American firms thus had an opportunity to capitalize on the anti-American sentiments and to provide goods and services formerly provided by U.S. firms.

CULTURAL DIFFERENCES. In different countries, sometimes even within a country, there are substantial differences in attitudes, beliefs, motivation, morality, superstition, and perception, as well as other characteristics. Geert Hofstede (b. 1928) developed a model in which worldwide differences in culture are categorized according to five dimensions. These dimensions include:

- Power distance—the degree of inequality among people which the population of a country considers normal.

- Individualism vs. collectivism—the degree to which people in a country prefer to act as individuals or as members of a group.

- Masculinity vs. femininity—the degree to which values like assertiveness, performance, success, and competitiveness are used to guide decisions versus values like the quality of life, warm personal relationships, service, and solidarity.

- Uncertainty avoidance—the degree to which citizens of a country prefer structured over unstructured situations, rigidity of procedures, or willingness to accept risk and potential failure.

- Time orientation—the extent to which decisions are based on long-term orientation versus short-term orientation, past versus present versus future, and punctuality.

Hofstede argues that U.S. management theories contain a number of idiosyncrasies that are not necessarily shared by managers in other cultures. Approaches to motivation and leadership, for example, differ widely throughout the world. Citizens of Japan tend to put greater importance on collective effort and working as a team member. Individual recognition is not desired. It is viewed as contradictory to being a good team member.

Similarly, in other countries, high tax rates may make bonuses and other forms of monetary compensation less attractive and less motivating than in the United States. Hofstede argues that employees and products are more readily transferred between countries sharing similar cultures.

The macroenvironment consists of forces that originate outside of an organization and generally cannot be altered by actions of the organization. Dimensions of the macroenvironment consist of sociocultural factors, technological factors, political-legal elements, economic factors, and international elements. A firm needs to study these elements of its environment, as they have the potential to affect how the organization should operate to attain and maintain its competitive advantage.

SEE ALSO: Economics; SWOT Analysis

Joe G. Thomas
Revised by Wendy H. Mason

FURTHER READING:

David, Michael. "Increased Productivity Can Depress Job Growth." *The Virginian-Pilot,* 30 January 2005.

Ghumann, Mushtaq. "Accountability Towards the Community." *Business Recorder,* 7 February 2005.

Hofstede, Geert. "Cultural Constraints in Management Theories." *Academy of Management Executive* 7 (1993): 81–94.

Munk, Nina. "How Levi's Trashed a Great American Brand." *Fortune,* 12 April 1999, 83–90.

Pan, Yigang, and Peter S.K. Chi. "Financial Performance and Survival of Multinational Corporations in China." *Strategic Management Journal* 20 (1999): 359–374.

"Research and Markets: Ethics and Corporate Social Responsibility in Retail Financial Service." *Business Wire,* 2 Febrary 2005.

Schmidt, Susan M. "Think It's a Breeze Moving Goods Between the U.S. and Mexico? Think Again—Regulatory Regimes Are the Hidden Pitfalls in NAFTA and Other Free Trade Agreements." *World Trade,* January 2005, 52.

"U.S. to Rejoin International Coffee Organization." *Tea & Trade Coffee Journal,* 20 November 2004, 60.

Vogelstein, Fred. "The Barbarians Are No Longer at the Gate." *U.S. News & World Report,* 22 March 1999, 50.

MAINTENANCE

Maintenance is the combination of all technical and associated administrative actions intended to retain an item in, or restore it to, a state in which it can perform its required function. Many companies are seeking to gain competitive advantage with respect to cost, quality, service and on-time deliveries. The effect of maintenance on these variables has prompted increased attention to the maintenance area as an integral part of productivity improvement. Maintenance is rapidly evolving into a major contributor to the performance and profitability of manufacturing systems. In fact, some see maintenance as the "last frontier" for manufacturing.

In their article "Make Maintenance Meaningful" P.K. Kauppi and Paavo Ylinen describe the bulk of maintenance procedures as being as:

- Preventive maintenance—the prevention of equipment breakdowns before they happen. This includes inspections, adjustments, regular service and planned shutdowns.

- Repair work—repairing equipment and troubleshooting malfunctions in an effort to return the equipment to its previous condition. These repairs may be reactive or preventive.

- Improvement work—searching for better materials and improved design changes to facilitate equipment reliability. Repair work is often a part of improvement work.

As shown in Figure 1, six maintenance programs are identified within the maintenance hierarchy, each representing an increased level of sophistication.

Figure 1
Maintenance Hierarchy

Reliability-Centered Maintenance

Total Productive Maintenance

Preventative Maintenance

Predictive Maintenance

Scheduled Maintenance

Reactive Maintenance

REACTIVE MAINTENANCE

Reactive maintenance (also known as corrective maintenance) involves all unscheduled actions performed as a result of system or product failure. Basically, it is an attempt to restore the system/product to a specified condition. The spectrum of activities within this level are (1) failure identification, (2) localization and isolation, (3) disassembly, (4) item removal and replacement or repair in place, (5) reassembly, and (6) checkout and condition verification. This approach is mainly a response to machine breakdowns. Unfortunately, many manufacturers are still in a reactive mode of operation. Their main objective is to ship the product. If their manufacturing equipment breaks down, they fix it as quickly as possible and then run it until it breaks down again. This is an extremely unreliable process and is not the best way to maximize the useful life span of one's assets. It leaves machine tools in a state of poor repair and can cause the production of out-of-tolerance parts and scrap. Because of its unpredictable nature it can easily cause disruptions to the production process.

SCHEDULED MAINTENANCE

Scheduled maintenance utilizes a previously developed maintenance schedule for each machine tool. This is much like an oil change on an automobile that takes place every three months or 3,000 miles, whichever comes first. While this is a broadly practiced technique in many manufacturing organizations, it does possess some distinct disadvantages. The scheduled maintenance may take place too soon, while the machine still operates well (15-20 percent of all components fail after a predictable time), or it may come too late if the machine fails before the scheduled maintenance time. In some cases, the machine may still be running but producing unacceptable parts. Scheduled maintenance can be considered a part of preventive maintenance known as fixed-time maintenance (FTM). Preventive maintenance is discussed later.

PREDICTIVE MAINTENANCE

Predictive maintenance involves performing maintenance on a machine in advance of the time a failure would occur if the maintenance were not performed. Of course, this means that one must calculate when a machine is predicted to fail. In order to do this, the firm must collect data on variables that can be used to indicate an impending failure (vibration, temperature, sound, color, etc.). This data is then analyzed to approximate when a failure will occur and maintenance is then scheduled to take place prior to this time. By seeking the correct level of maintenance required, unplanned downtime is minimized.

PREVENTIVE MAINTENANCE

Preventive maintenance encompasses activities, including adjustments, replacement, and basic cleanliness, that forestall machine breakdowns. Preventive activities are primarily condition based. The condition of a component, measured when the equipment is operating, governs planned/scheduled maintenance. Typical preventive maintenance activities include periodic inspections, condition monitoring, critical item replacements, and calibrations. In order to accomplish this, blocks of time are incorporated into the operations schedule. One can easily see that this is the beginning of a proactive mode rather than a reactive one. The purpose of preventive maintenance is to ensure that production quality is maintained and that delivery schedules are met. In addition, a machine that is well cared for will last longer and cause fewer problems.

Current trends in management philosophy such as just-in-time (JIT) and total quality management (TQM) incorporate preventive maintenance as key factors in their success. JIT requires high machine availability, which in turn requires preventive maintenance. Also, TQM requires equipment that is well maintained in order to meet required process capability.

Preventive maintenance is also seen as a measure of management excellence. It requires a long-term commitment, constant monitoring of new technology, a constant assessment of the financial and organizational tradeoffs in contracting out versus in-house maintenance, and an awareness of the impact of the regulatory and legal environment.

The resulting benefits of preventive maintenance are many. Some of them are listed below:

- Safety. Machinery that is not well-maintained can become a safety hazard. Preventive maintenance increases the margin of safety by keeping equipment in top running condition.

- Lower cost. A modern and cost-effective approach to preventive maintenance shows that there is no maintenance cost optimum. However, maintenance costs will decrease as the costs for production losses decreases. Obviously, no preventive maintenance action is performed unless it is less costly that the resulting failure.

- Reduction in failures and breakdowns. Preventive maintenance aims at reducing or eliminating unplanned downtime, thereby increasing machine efficiency. Downtime is also reduced when the preventive maintenance process gives maintenance personnel sufficient warning so repairs can be scheduled during normal outages.

- Extension of equipment life. Obviously, equipment that is cared for will last longer than equipment that is abused and neglected.

- Improved trade-in/resale value of equipment. If the equipment is to be sold or traded in, a preventive maintenance program will help keep the machine in the best possible condition, thereby maximizing its used value.

- Increased equipment reliability. By performing preventive maintenance on equipment, a firm begins to build reliability into the equipment by removing routine and avoidable breakdowns.

- Increased plant productivity. Productivity is enhanced by the decrease in unexpected machine breakdown. Also, forecast shutdown time can allow the firm to utilize alternate routings and scheduling alternatives that will minimize the negative effect of downtime.

- Fewer surprises. Preventive maintenance enables users to avoid the unexpected. Preventive maintenance does not guarantee elimination of all unexpected downtime, but empirically it has proven to eliminate most of it caused by mechanical failure.

- Reduced cycle time. If process equipment is incapable of running the product, then the time it takes to move the product through the factory will suffer. Taninecz found, from an *Industry Week* survey, that there is a strong correlation between preventive maintenance and cycle-time reductions as well as near-perfect on-time delivery rates. Also, approximately 35 percent of the surveyed plants who widely adopted preventive maintenance achieved on-time delivery rates of 98 percent, compared to only 19.5 percent for non-adopters.

- Increased service level for the customer and reduction in the number of defective parts. These have a positive direct effect on stockouts, backlog, and delivery time to the customer.

- Reduced overall maintenance. By not allowing machinery to fall into a state of disrepair, overall maintenance requirements are greatly decreased.

TOTAL PRODUCTIVE MAINTENANCE

Total productive maintenance (TPM) is preventive maintenance plus continuing efforts to adapt, modify, and refine equipment to increase flexibility, reduce material handling, and promote continuous flows. It is operator-oriented maintenance with the involvement of all qualified employees in all maintenance activities. TPM has been described as preventive maintenance with these three factors added: (1) involving machine operators in preliminary maintenance activities by encouraging them to keep machines clean and well lubricated; (2) encouraging operators to report indications of incipient distress to the maintenance department; and (3) establishing a maintenance education and training program.

Developed in Japan, TPM places a high value on teamwork, consensus building, and continuous improvement. It is a partnership approach among organizational functions, especially production and maintenance. TPM means total employee involvement, total equipment effectiveness, and a total maintenance delivery system. In order to achieve this, machine operators must share the preventive maintenance efforts, assist mechanics with repairs when equipment is down, and work on equipment and process improvements within team activities. Tennessee Eastman found that another employee, such as an equipment operator, with minimal training, could do 40 percent of the traditional maintenance mechanic's work. Another 40 percent could be performed with additional training, but still below the certified level. Only 20 percent of the maintenance tasks actually required a certified mechanic's skills. They also reported that as much as 75 percent of maintenance problems can be prevented by operators at an early stage. This frees maintenance personnel to be responsible for the tasks that require their critical skills, such as breakdown analysis, overhaul, corrective maintenance and root cause analysis. This places them in a "consultant" role with the operators allowing them to:

- help the operator diagnose problems and restore equipment to like-new condition;

- use appropriate technologies and standards to verify that the equipment is in like-new condition after repair, overhaul, or replacement;

- use this knowledge to assess the root cause of the problem so that changes may be made to the design, operation, or maintenance practices in the future;

- work with purchasing, engineering, operations, and maintenance to modify procurement standards to assure maximum reliability in future equipment.

Of course, for all of this to work, the firm must have an organizational culture which supports a high level of employee involvement. Businesses must be willing to provide the necessary training in order to allow production personnel to perform the required tasks.

TPM's focus is on elimination of the major losses or inefficiencies incurred in production activities. These losses include those due to obstruction of equipment efficiency, manpower efficiency, and material and energy efficiency. Based on their link to corporate goals, targets for eliminating or reducing these losses are developed. Just as in activity-based cost accounting where cost drivers are identified, the objective of TPM is to identify variables that can demonstrate improved performance. All major equipment losses are functionally related to availability, performance, efficiency and/or quality rate so the improvement resulting from the maintenance system can be measured by its impact on overall equipment effectiveness (see below).

Beneficial results of TPM include:

- Overall equipment effectiveness and overall efficiency are maximized.

- It takes the guesswork out of determining which machine needs major repairs or rebuilding.

- It provides objectivity by converting the operator's intuition into quantifiable values.

- It pinpoints exact maintenance requirement. The operator carries out only the needed corrective actions so no unnecessary work, beyond routine maintenance, is done.

- It rapidly verifies the effectiveness of major corrective work.

- Operators improve their job skills.

- Operators are motivated by involvement in maintaining their own machines and by involvement in team-based concepts.

- Operator involvement in the process gives them ownership of making the project a success.

- A preventive maintenance program for the lifecycle of the equipment is developed.

- By getting everyone involved in equipment design and selection, a better understanding of why certain decisions and trade-offs are necessary results.

- Equipment and maintenance management (inherent in a reliability strategy) result.

- Capacity is maximized.

- Costs are minimized.

- Product quality is improved.

- Improved safety.

- The manufacturing process is continually improved.

As a final note on TPM, another school of thought holds that TPM can be adopted by continuous diagnostic monitoring of a machine's conditions and establishing a trend line for it. Trend lines approaching or veering into the domain that identifies poor operating conditions will trigger maintenance action.

RELIABILITY-CENTERED MAINTENANCE

It has been assumed that preventive maintenance programs help to ensure reliability and safety of equipment and machinery. However, tests performed by airlines in the mid-1960s showed that scheduled overhaul of complex equipment had little or no positive effect on the reliability of the equipment in service. These tests revealed the need for a new concept of preventive maintenance, which later became known as reliability-centered maintenance (RCM).

The concept of RCM is rooted in a 1968 working paper prepared by the Boeing 747 Maintenance Steering Group. A refined version appeared in 1970. Continued studies at the Department of Defense led to the 1986 publication of the "Reliability Centered Maintenance Requirements for Naval Aircraft, Weapons Systems and Support Equipment," a set of maintenance standards and procedures that certain military maintenance personnel were expected to follow. The RCM methodology was further developed and found application not only in the military and aviation, but also in the energy, manufacturing, foundry, and transport industries.

According to Bulmer, the RCM process can be considered as three separate but associated analyses: failure mode and effects analysis, consequence analysis, and task analysis. These analyses consider the specific characteristics and consequences of a failure and attempt to arrive at the optimal solution based on this information.

OVERALL EQUIPMENT EFFECTIVENESS

Total productive maintenance provides a systematic procedure for linking corporate goals to maintenance goals. This procedure calls for the consideration of external and internal corporate environments, and then the development of a basic maintenance policy congruent with the environments. Next key points for maintenance improvement are identified, which result in the definition of target values for maintenance performance. These values, referred to as overall equipment effectiveness (OEE), are a function of equipment availability, quality rate, and equipment performance efficiency, and provide a starting point for developing quantitative variables for relating maintenance measurement and control to corporate strategy.

Essentially, OEE offers a measurement tool that helps identify the real areas of opportunity within an operation. These areas have been termed the "six big losses." OEE allows the firm to break these losses into smaller components to better evaluate the impact the maintenance program is making on the operation. The six losses are:

1. Breakdowns from equipment failure (unplanned downtime)

2. Setup and adjustments from product changes and minor adjustments necessary to get the equipment operating properly after the line change

3. Idling and minor stoppages due to abnormal operation of the equipment causing momentary lapses in production, but not long enough to track as downtime

4. Reduced speeds, the discrepancy between design and actual speed the equipment operates

5. Process defects due to scrapped production and defects needing rework

6. Reduced yield and lost materials during the manufacturing process, from start-up to end of production run

If a company has an OEE of 85 percent or more, then it is considered to be a world-class company.

TRENDS IN MAINTENANCE

Two major trends in the development of maintenance management research have been identified: (1) emerging developments and advances in maintenance technology, information and decision technology, and maintenance methods; and (2) the linking of maintenance to quality improvement strategies and the use of maintenance as a competitive strategy.

The first major trend has to do with the impact of artificial intelligence techniques, such as expert systems and neural networks, on the formation of maintenance knowledge in industrial organizations. There is a diverse application of expert systems within the maintenance area. A number of these systems and their applications are listed below:

- CATS—an expert maintenance system for detecting sudden failures in diesel-electric locomotive systems

- INNATE—an expert system used for electronic circuit diagnosis

- FSM—an expert system used by Boeing for continuous condition monitoring of aircraft alarms

- RLA—an expert system developed by Lockheed for repair-level analysis for major parts in an aerospace system

- GEMS-TTS—an expert system used by AT&T maintenance specialists to isolate faults in communication links

- TOPAS—an expert system that diagnoses transmission and signaling problems in real time that may arise on switched circuits.

- CHARLEY—an expert system used by General Motors to diagnose problems with broken machine tools and to instruct less experienced individuals by providing explanations

- XCON—an expert system developed by Digital Equipment Corporation (now part of Compaq) for product configuration

The second major trend is typified by the emergence of total productive maintenance, which must be incorporated into the firm's strategy. In the quest for world-class manufacturing, many industries are appreciating the need for efficient maintenance systems that have been effectively integrated with corporate strategy. It is vital that maintenance management becomes integrated with corporate strategy to ensure equipment availability, quality products, on-time deliveries, and competitive pricing. Managerial attitudes have changed toward maintenance because of the emergence of new management philosophies. In addition, social trends such as lack of capital, fluctuations in currencies, competition, quality, and environmental consciousness, have also encouraged a new focus on maintenance.

Maintenance will continue to be a major area of concern for manufacturers and other forms of business. A study of some seventy manufacturing plants found that over 50 percent of the maintenance work performed by these firms was reactive (run to failure, emergency breakdown). The balance of maintenance work was preventive or period based (25 percent), predictive or condition based (15 percent), and proactive or root-caused based (10 percent). A strong correlation has been found to exist between manufacturing cost reduction and preventive/predictive maintenance. Over a five-year period a study group of companies found that productivity improvements correlated strongly with a number of variables, one of which was preventive/predictive maintenance.

Mike Laskiewicz recommends that organizations recognize maintenance as a key department that needs to be well managed. In addition, the maintenance department should be led by a strong-minded individual who is a good motivator, technically competent, experienced and familiar with advanced industry practices. Finally Laskiewicz notes that maintenance planning must be a top priority.

SEE ALSO: Continuous Improvement; Lean Manufacturing and Just-in-Time Production; Operations Strategy; Organizational Culture

R. Anthony Inman

FURTHER READING:

Chan, F.T.S., H.C.W. Lau, R.W.L. Ip, H.K. Chan, and S. Kong. "Implementation of Total Productive Maintenance: A Case Study." *International Journal of Production Economics* 95 (2005): 71.

Cox, James F., John H. Blackstone, Jr., and Michael S. Spencer, eds. *APICS Dictionary.* 8th ed. Falls Church, VA: APICS, 1995.

Laskiewicz, Mike. "4 Paths to Engineering, Maintenance Integration." *Control Engineering* 52, no. 2 (2005): 10.

Lee, Hsu-Hua. "A Cost/Benefit Model for Investments in Inventory and Preventive Maintenance in an Imperfect Production System." *Computers and Industrial Engineering* 48, no. 1 (2005): 55.

Oke, S.A. "An Analytical Model for the Optimisation of Maintenance Profitability." *International Journal of Productivity and Performance Management* 54, no. 1/2 (2005): 113–134.

Taninecz, George. "Best Practices and Performances." *Industry Week,* 1 December 1997, 28–43.

MAKE-OR-BUY DECISIONS

The make-or-buy decision is the act of making a strategic choice between producing an item internally (in-house) or buying it externally (from an outside supplier). The buy side of the decision also is referred to as outsourcing. Make-or-buy decisions usually arise when a firm that has developed a product or part—or significantly modified a product or part—is having trouble with current suppliers, or has diminishing capacity or changing demand.

Make-or-buy analysis is conducted at the strategic and operational level. Obviously, the strategic level is the more long-range of the two. Variables considered at the strategic level include analysis of the future, as well as the current environment. Issues like government regulation, competing firms, and market trends all have a strategic impact on the make-or-buy decision. Of course, firms should make items that reinforce or are in-line with their core competencies. These are areas in which the firm is strongest and which give the firm a competitive advantage.

The increased existence of firms that utilize the concept of lean manufacturing has prompted an increase in outsourcing. Manufacturers are tending to purchase subassemblies rather than piece parts, and are outsourcing activities ranging from logistics to administrative services. In their 2003 book *World Class Supply Management,* David Burt, Donald Dobler, and Stephen Starling present a rule of thumb for outsourcing. It prescribes that a firm outsource all items that do not fit one of the following three categories: (1) the item is critical to the success of the product, including customer perception of important product attributes; (2) the item requires specialized design and manufacturing skills or equipment, and the number of capable and reliable suppliers is extremely limited; and (3) the item fits well within the firm's core competencies, or within those the firm must develop to fulfill future plans. Items that fit under one of these three categories are considered strategic in nature and should be produced internally if at all possible.

Make-or-buy decisions also occur at the operational level. Analysis in separate texts by Burt, Dobler, and Starling, as well as Joel Wisner, G. Keong Leong, and Keah-Choon Tan, suggest these considerations that favor making a part in-house:

- Cost considerations (less expensive to make the part)
- Desire to integrate plant operations
- Productive use of excess plant capacity to help absorb fixed overhead (using existing idle capacity)
- Need to exert direct control over production and/or quality
- Better quality control
- Design secrecy is required to protect proprietary technology
- Unreliable suppliers
- No competent suppliers
- Desire to maintain a stable workforce (in periods of declining sales)
- Quantity too small to interest a supplier
- Control of lead time, transportation, and warehousing costs
- Greater assurance of continual supply
- Provision of a second source
- Political, social or environmental reasons (union pressure)
- Emotion (e.g., pride)

Factors that may influence firms to buy a part externally include:

- Lack of expertise
- Suppliers' research and specialized know-how exceeds that of the buyer

- cost considerations (less expensive to buy the item)

- Small-volume requirements

- Limited production facilities or insufficient capacity

- Desire to maintain a multiple-source policy

- Indirect managerial control considerations

- Procurement and inventory considerations

- Brand preference

- Item not essential to the firm's strategy

The two most important factors to consider in a make-or-buy decision are cost and the availability of production capacity. Burt, Dobler, and Starling warn that "no other factor is subject to more varied interpretation and to greater misunderstanding" Cost considerations should include all relevant costs and be long-term in nature. Obviously, the buying firm will compare production and purchase costs. Burt, Dobler, and Starling provide the major elements included in this comparison. Elements of the "make" analysis include:

- Incremental inventory-carrying costs

- Direct labor costs

- Incremental factory overhead costs

- Delivered purchased material costs

- Incremental managerial costs

- Any follow-on costs stemming from quality and related problems

- Incremental purchasing costs

- Incremental capital costs

Cost considerations for the "buy" analysis include:

- Purchase price of the part

- Transportation costs

- Receiving and inspection costs

- Incremental purchasing costs

- Any follow-on costs related to quality or service

One will note that six of the costs to consider are incremental. By definition, incremental costs would not be incurred if the part were purchased from an outside source. If a firm does not currently have the capacity to make the part, incremental costs will include variable costs plus the full portion of fixed overhead allocable to the part's manufacture. If the firm has excess capacity that can be used to produce the part in question, only the variable overhead caused by production of the parts are considered incremental. That is, fixed costs, under conditions of sufficient idle capacity, are not incremental and should not be considered as part of the cost to make the part.

While cost is seldom the only criterion used in a make-or-buy decision, simple break-even analysis can be an effective way to quickly surmise the cost implications within a decision. Suppose that a firm can purchase equipment for in-house use for $250,000 and produce the needed parts for $10 each. Alternatively, a supplier could produce and ship the part for $15 each. Ignoring the cost of negotiating a contract with the supplier, the simple break-even point could easily be computed:

$$\$250,000 + \$10Q = \$15Q$$
$$\$250,000 = \$15Q - \$10Q$$
$$\$250,000 = \$5Q$$
$$50,000 = Q$$

Therefore, it would be more cost effective for a firm to buy the part if demand is less than 50,000 units, and make the part if demand exceeds 50,000 units. However, if the firm had enough idle capacity to produce the parts, the fixed cost of $250,000 would not be incurred (meaning it is not an incremental cost), making the prospect of making the part too cost efficient to ignore.

Stanley Gardiner and John Blackstone's 1991 paper in the *International Journal of Purchasing and Materials Management* presented the contribution-per-constraint-minute (CPCM) method of make-or-buy analysis, which makes the decision based on the theory of constraints. They also used this approach to determine the maximum permissible component price (MPCP) that a buyer should pay when outsourcing. In 2005 Jaydeep Balakrishnan and Chun Hung Cheng noted that Gardiner and Blackstone's method did not guarantee a best solution for a complicated make-or-buy problem. Therefore, they offer an updated, enhanced approach using spreadsheets with built-in liner programming (LP) capability to provide "what if" analyses to encourage efforts toward finding an optimal solution.

Firms have started to realize the importance of the make-or-buy decision to overall manufacturing strategy and the implication it can have for employment levels, asset levels, and core competencies. In response to this, some firms have adopted total cost of ownership (TCO) procedures for incorporating non-price considerations into the make-or-buy decision.

SEE ALSO: Break-Even Point

R. Anthony Inman

FURTHER READING:

Balakrishnan, Jaydeep, and Chun Hung Cheng. "The Theory of Constraints and the Make-or-Buy Decision: An Update and Review." *Journal of Supply Chain Management: A Global Review of Purchasing & Supply* 41, no. 1 (2005): 40–47.

Burt, David N., Donald W. Dobler, and Stephen L. Starling. *World Class Supply Management: The Key to Supply Chain Management.* 7th ed. Boston: McGraw-Hill/Irwin, 2003.

Gardiner, Stanley C., and John H. Blackstone, Jr. "The 'Theory of Constraints' and the Make-or-Buy Decision." *International Journal of Purchasing & Materials Management* 27, no. 3 (1991): 38–43.

Wisner, Joel D., G. Keong Leong, and Keah-Choon Tan. *Principles of Supply Chain Management: A Balanced Approach.* Mason, OH: Thomson South-Western, 2005.

MANAGEMENT: ART VS. SCIENCE

SEE: The Art and Science of Management

MANAGEMENT AUDIT

The term *management audit* is commonly used for examination and appraisal of the efficiency and effectiveness of management in carrying out its activities. Areas of auditor interest include the nature and quality of management decisions, operating results achieved, and risks undertaken.

The management audit focuses on results, evaluating the effectiveness and suitability of controls by challenging underlying rules, procedures, and methods. Management audits, which are generally performed internally, are both compliance reviews and goals-and-effect analyses. When performed correctly, they are potentially the most useful of evaluation methods, because they result in change.

The management audit is a process of systematically examining, analyzing, and appraising management's overall performance. The appraisal is composed of ten categories, examined historically and in comparison with other organizations. The audit measures a company's quality of management relative to those of other companies in its particular industry, as well as the finest management in other industries. The ten categories of the management audit are (1) economic function, (2) corporate structure, (3) health of earnings, (4) service to stockholders, (5) research and development, (6) directorate analysis, (7) fiscal policies, (8) production efficiency, (9) sales vigor, and (10) executive evaluation. These categories do not represent single functions of management.

ECONOMIC FUNCTION

The economic function category in the management audit assigns to management the responsibility for the company's importance to the economy. In essence, the public value of the company is determined. The value is based on what the company does, what products or services it sells, and how it goes about its business in a moral and ethical sense. It includes the company's reputation as well as management's view of the purpose of the company.

The public is defined in this sense not only as the consumers of the company's products or services and its shareholders, but also a number of groups that the company must seek to satisfy. These groups include its employees, suppliers, distributors, and the communities in which it operates. A company cannot have achieved maximum economic function unless it has survived trade cycles, met competition, developed and replaced management, and earned a reputation among its various publics.

CORPORATE STRUCTURE

The corporate structure review evaluates the effectiveness of the structure through which a company's management seeks to fulfill its aims. An organization's structure must strengthen decision-making, permit control of the company, and develop the areas of responsibility and authority of its executives. These requirements must be met regardless of the type of company. Companies that have established product divisions or other forms of organization have maximized the delegation of authority, but have not reduced the need for a clear understanding of authority.

Companies are generally decentralized after the lines of authority have been established; but even large

Exhibit 1
Replacement Chart for the Position of District Manager

Candidates	S. Jones	B. Smith	H. Johnson
Performance in present job	4	3	5
When qualified to advance	2 yrs	2 yrs	Now
Advancement potential score	85	78	87
Rank	2	3	1

companies have endured conflicts as the result of a breakdown in the acceptance of authority. An example of this is General Motors in the early 1920s, when the company endured an $85 million inventory loss because division leaders did not accept the authority of principal executives.

HEALTH OF EARNINGS

The health of earnings function analyzes corporate income in a historical and comparative aspect. The question this function seeks to answer is whether assets have been employed for the full realization of their potential. This can be assessed by a study of the risk assumed in the employment of resources, in the profit returns upon employment, and the distribution of assets among various categories. The actual value of the assets may not be able to be determined, but a company can trace the cost of acquisitions, rate of depreciation, and the extent to which assets have been fully profitable or not. The information needed for this category can usually be found within the company's annual reports.

SERVICE TO STOCKHOLDERS

The evaluation of a company's service to its shareholders can be assessed in three areas: (1) the extent to which stockholders' principal is not exposed to unnecessary risks; (2) whether the principal is enhanced as much as possible through undistributed profits; and (3) whether stockholders receive a reasonable rate of return on their investment through the form of dividends.

The evaluation also covers the quality of service provided by the company to its stockholders, mainly in the form of information and advice about their holdings. Although companies and industries vary widely on the amount of earnings they can pay out in the form of dividends, the rate of return and capital appreciation are the most important indicators of fairness to stockholders.

RESEARCH AND DEVELOPMENT

The evaluation of research and development is essential because R&D is often responsible for a company's growth and improvement in its industry. Analyzing research results can show how well research dollars have been utilized, but it does not show whether management has realized the maximum from it potential. Just like health of earnings, research should be examined from a historical and comparative standpoint in dollars expended; the number of research workers employed; the ratio of research costs and staff to total expenses; and new ideas, information, and

products turned out. The examination of these figures compared with past results show management's willingness to employ research for future growth and health.

The American Institute of Management's evaluation attempts to determine what part of the company's past progress can properly be credited to research and how well research policies are preparing the company for future progress.

DIRECTORATE ANALYSIS

Directorate analysis covers the quality and effectiveness of the board of directors. Three principal elements are considered in the evaluation of the board. First, the quality of each director is assessed along with the quality and quantity of the contributions he or she makes to the board. Second, how well the directorate works together as a team is evaluated. Third, the directors are assessed to determine if they truly act as trustees for the company and act in the shareholders' best interest. This can best be examined in areas where a conflict of interest exists between a company's executives and its owners and public. One of the best areas to evaluate is corporate incentives. The manner in which a board handles conflicts of compensation provides a good key to its value.

FISCAL POLICY

The fiscal policy function of the management audit expresses the past and present financial policies. This function includes the company's capital structure; its organizations for developing fiscal policies and controls; and the application of these policies and controls in different areas of corporate activity.

PRODUCTION EFFICIENCY

Production efficiency is an important function for manufacturing companies as well as non-manufacturing companies. Production efficiency is divided into two parts. The first part, machinery and material management, evaluates the mechanical production of the company's products. The second aspect, manpower management, includes all personnel policies and practices for non-sales and non-executive employees developed by management. Only when both parts are analyzed can an overall evaluation of production be effectively performed.

SALES VIGOR

Sales vigor can be evaluated even though sales practices vary widely among industries. This can be accomplished after marketing goals have been determined and assessed. The goals must be assessed in terms of the overall goals of the company. Historical and comparative data are then analyzed to evaluate how well past sales potential has been realized and how well present company sales policies prepare the organization to realize future potential.

EXECUTIVE EVALUATION

Executive evaluation is the most important function of the management audit. The other nine functions indirectly evaluate the organization's management, since they represent the results of management's decisions and actions. This function addresses the quality of the executives and their management philosophy.

The American Institute of Management has found that the three essential elements in a business leader are ability, industry, and integrity. These elements provide a framework for the executive's evaluation in the management audit and should also be the criteria used in selecting and advancing executives. As a group, executives must regard the continuity of the organization as an important goal, assuring it by sound policies of executive selection, development, advancement, and replacement.

The most important management audit activity is an internal audit function. Each enterprise must have an independent source for developing and verifying controls, above and beyond what the external auditors might do in a financial audit.

The functions of the management audit remain the same regardless of the type of business. In order to get good results, companies must observe principles of sound management; the degree to which they succeed can be appraised by systems such as the one outlined here.

SEE ALSO: Effectiveness and Efficiency

Kevin Nelson
Revised by Charalambos Spathis, Eugenia Petridou,
and Constantine Zopounidis

FURTHER READING:

Craig-Cooper, Michael, and Philippe De Backer. *The Management Audit: How to Create an Effective Management Team.* Alexandria, VA: Financial Times Pitman Publishing, 1993.

Sayle, Allan J. *Management Audits: The Assessment of Quality Management Systems.* Brighton, MI: Allan Sayle Associates, 1997.

Torok, Robert M., and Patrick J. Cordon. *Operational Profitability: Conducting Management Audits.* Hoboken, NJ: John Wiley & Sons Inc., 1997.

MANAGEMENT AWARDS

One indicator of the growing recognition of management as a field of great importance has been the proliferation in the late twentieth century of prizes that various governments award their most outstanding organizations. Such official recognition of management practice, quality, and contribution to business reflects the belief at the highest levels that good management practice can be learned and nurtured through promoting awareness of best practices and innovative techniques.

THE FIVE MAJOR AWARDS

The five most prestigious management awards are Japan's Deming Prizes, the United States' Malcolm Baldrige National Award, the European Quality Awards, the Canada Awards for Excellence, and the AKAO Prize.

The first widely esteemed management award, Japan's Deming Prize, was only established in 1950. For nearly three decades, the Deming Prize stood essentially alone as a major prize for business management practice.

With the enormous success of Japanese industry in the late twentieth century, interest in Japanese business practices grew, including Japan's recognition of business successes. By the 1980s, Japan's successes in competing worldwide were admired worldwide and Japanese business began to find emulators. Subsequently, the United States and Europe set up their own equivalents to the Deming Prize to honor their own businesses. The United States established the Malcolm Baldrige National Quality Award in 1989, and soon after the 12 nations of the European Community (now the European Union) jointly created the European Quality Awards in 1990, awarding the first recipient in 1992.

To date, only one company—Xerox—has won all three major quality awards. Xerox was one of the first non-Japanese companies to win the Deming Application Prize (in 1980). Xerox then won the Baldrige Award in 1989, and (in the first year the prize was given out) a European Quality Award in 1992.

THE DEMING PRIZE. The Japanese Union of Scientists and Engineers (JUSE) created the first major management award, the Deming Prize, to recognize "contributions to quality and dependability of product." The award is still generally held as the most prestigious of all management awards, and is generally recognized as the most highly esteemed business award offered in Japan. The JUSE instituted the award in 1950, and began awarding the prize annually in 1951.

Interestingly, this most significant of Japan's business awards honors an American, Dr. W. Edwards Deming. Many Japanese government and academic leaders credit Deming with revolutionizing Japanese postwar industry through his advocacy in Japan of quality control and managerial efficiency.

The JUSE's Deming Prize Committee administers two types of awards honoring Deming: the Deming Prize and the Deming Application Prize. The Deming Prize is given to a person or group of people who have advanced the practice and furthered awareness of TQC. The Deming Application Prize, in turn, goes only to companies based on successes attributable to implementing TQC.

Beginning in 1970, the JUSE began to offer the Japan Quality Control Medal. Only those who have formerly won a Deming Application Prize five years or more earlier are eligible for the Quality Control Medal. The medal is intended to upgrade the quality control of former prize recipients. To this end, the criteria for the Quality Control Medal remain the same as the Deming Application Prize and the Medal is awarded at the same time as the other Deming Prize awards. The current aim of the examination is to find out how well a company implements total quality control by assessing its quality-assurance policies and activities, and by measuring the company's results in the areas of productivity improvement, quality improvement, cost reduction, expanded sales, and increased profits.

Non-Japanese companies were allowed to apply for and receive the Deming Prize starting in 1984; the categories that remain unavailable to non-Japanese companies include the individual prize and the factory award.

MALCOLM BALDRIGE NATIONAL QUALITY AWARD. The U.S. Congress created the Malcolm Baldrige National Quality Award in 1987 largely as a counterpart to Japan's Deming Prize. The specific goal of the Baldrige Award is to heighten U.S. awareness of TQM and to formally recognize successful quality management systems. The award is named for the U.S. Secretary of Commerce from 1981 to 1987. Baldrige was actually helping in drafting the creation of the award at the time of his death in a rodeo accident.

The U.S. Commerce Department's National Institute of Standards and Technology (NIST) administers the Baldrige Award. The NIST presents up to two awards each in three divisions: manufacturing, service, and small business. The NIST gave its first awards in 1988.

The Baldrige Award judges results companies have shown through management practices in seven specific areas. These are (1) leadership, (2) information and analysis, (3) strategic planning, (4) human resource focus, (5) process management, (6) business results and company performance, and (7) customer focus and satisfaction.

The Baldrige Award is open to any for-profit business in the United States. Like the Deming Prize, the award may be won by a foreign-owned company, but unlike the Deming Prize only those foreign-owned companies with more than 50 percent of their employees or physical assets located in the United States are eligible.

In addition to its more parochial focus, the Baldrige differs from the Deming Prize in three significant ways. First, the Baldrige Award emphasizes customer perceptions and the bottom line emphasizing clear-cut results through its seven specific areas. This makes the Baldrige more objective-oriented than the more systemic focus of the Deming Prize.

Second, while the NIST is an independent agency, the Baldrige relies on a wide array of professional groups to decide on its winners, while from its inception the Deming Prize has relied solely on the JUSE. The Baldrige is consequently able to draw on a wider range of expertise among its judges than the Deming Prize, but may be more open to charges of conflict of interest among the reviewers.

Finally, the Baldrige Award has a stated objective of sharing information while the Deming Prize does not. Consequently, the Baldrige is more likely to make known to other companies how the winners have achieved their success so that others may emulate them; the Deming Prize is more proprietary, allowing winners more readily to keep company secrets if they wish, thus widening the field of companies which may wish to participate but simultaneously limiting the benefit to other companies and to the dissemination of TQM principles in general.

THE EUROPEAN QUALITY AWARDS. By 1990, the European Community (now the European Union) felt that it had fallen behind Japan and the United States in the recognition of quality management. In that year, the European Foundation for Quality Management, with support from the European Organization for Quality and the European Commission, set about to create its own Deming or Baldrige equivalent, The European Quality Awards. The first winners were announced in October 1992.

The initial awards favored larger, for-profit companies, so by 1996 the European Commission began to give out additional awards for public sector organizations and for small- to mid-sized enterprises. The awards also have a category for operational units of companies, such as factories, research units, or assembly plants.

The European Quality Awards, regardless of category, judges applicants on nine criteria: (1) leadership; (2) people management; (3) policy and strategy,

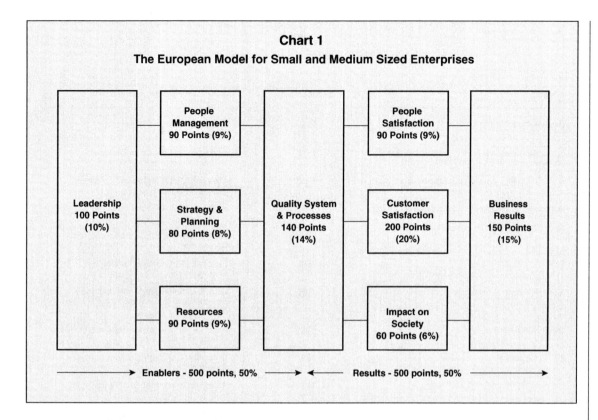

Chart 1

The European Model for Small and Medium Sized Enterprises

People Management 90 Points (9%)		People Satisfaction 90 Points (9%)	

Leadership 100 Points (10%)

Strategy & Planning 80 Points (8%)

Quality System & Processes 140 Points (14%)

Customer Satisfaction 200 Points (20%)

Business Results 150 Points (15%)

Resources 90 Points (9%)

Impact on Society 60 Points (6%)

→ Enablers - 500 points, 50% → ← Results - 500 points, 50% →

(4) resource management, (5) process management, (6) customer satisfaction, (7) people satisfaction (defined as the perception of people toward the organization), (8) impact on society, and (9) business results.

While the categories essentially copy those of the Baldrige Award, the emphasis on people's perceptions of the organization and of the organization's impact on society are unique to the European Quality Awards and add a societal element lacking in either the Deming or Baldrige Awards. The European Quality Awards also differ from the Deming and Baldrige, as noted earlier, in the various categories for eligible organizations. The European Quality Awards also differ in the nature of their awards jury, which is made up of business leaders as well as academics. Finally, by its nature, the European Union is more international than either Japan or the United States, and from the start, the award has been open to companies outside the European Union. Still, the award is limited to those companies that have at least 50 percent of their activities in Europe.

Applications to the program are examined by a team of six assessors, each of whom undergo training to ensure a high level of consistency in scoring. Assessors include some academics and quality professionals, but the majority are drawn from the ranks of experienced practicing managers from European countries. The application is assessed and scored on a scale from 0 to 1,000 points. Chart 1 illustrates the scoring system for the small- and medium-sized company award.

THE CANADA AWARDS FOR EXCELLENCE. After Japan established the Deming Prize, Canada was the next major industrialized nation to establish an award honoring managerial practice. Even then, it was not until 1983 that the federal government of Canada created the Canada Awards for Excellence. For the first ten years, the Canada Awards for Excellence were administered by the Canadian government directly. In 1993, Canada handed the administration of the award over to the National Quality Institute, a Canadian nonprofit organization.

From the beginning, the Canada Awards for Excellence differed from the Deming Prizes in significant ways that in some respects laid the foundation of the Baldrige and European Quality Awards. The Canada Awards for Excellence were from their inception more results-oriented than the Deming Prize and in this respect served as a blueprint for the Baldrige Award's results orientation. Indeed, the Canada Awards for Excellence have been judging nominees on their "Seven Drivers" as the criteria for excellence six years before the first Baldrige Award was given for its seven factors. Indeed, most of the Canadian Awards' Seven Drivers are the same as what the Baldrige Award would later adopt. The Canadian Seven Drivers are (1) leadership, (2) planning, (3) customer focus, (4) people focus, (5) process management, (6) supplier focus, and (7) organizational performance.

Similarly, the Canada Awards for Excellence foreshadowed the broader reach of the European Quality Awards. From their beginning, the Canadian

Figure 1
Major Management Prizes

Prize	Year Established	Administrating Organization
Deming Prize	1951	Japanese Union of Scientists and Engineers (JUSE)
Franz Edelman Award for Management Science Achievement	1975	Institute for Operations Research and the Management Sciences
Canada Quality Awards for Excellence	1983	National (Canadian) Quality Institute (since 1993)
Shingo Prize for Excellence in Manufacturing	1988	National (US) Association of Manufacturers
Malcolm Baldridge National Quality Award	1989	National Institute of Standards and of the Technology (NIST) US Department of Commerce
European Quality Awards	1990	European Foundation for Quality Management
ESCAP Human Resources Development Award	1990	United Nations Economic and Social Commission for Asia and the Pacific (ESCAP)
INFORMS Award	1991	Institute for Operations Research and the Management Sciences
EUCUSA Award	1997	European Customer Satisfaction Association
Canada Healthy Workplace Award	1999	National (Canadian) Quality Institute

Awards have been open to both public and private sector organizations that contribute to the nation's economic success. In this respect, the Canada Awards for Excellence foreshadow the decision in Europe over a decade later to expand the scope of the European Quality Awards from solely for-profit companies to include public sector organizations.

In many respects, the Canada Awards for Excellence are as significant as their better known counterparts in Japan, the United States, and Europe, but remain more limited in scope simply because of Canada's relatively small population. Still, the Canada Awards for Excellence are highly regarded within Canada itself, and since their founding over 300 people and organizations have received the award.

Until 1999, Canada offered only one Award for Excellence: the Quality Award. Beginning in 1999, Canada broke new ground by offering a second award previously unprecedented elsewhere in national awards, the Healthy Workplace Award. The Healthy Workplace Award recognizes organizations that "promote, encourage, support and offer exemplary health-related programs in the workplace," judging the organization in five areas: (1) leadership, (2) planning, (3) people focus, (4) process management, and (5) outcomes.

AKAO PRIZE. In 1996, the QFD Institute established the Akao Prize to recognize individuals who have made an "outstanding contribution to the advancement of QFD." The award roughly follows the pattern of the Deming award but differs from other quality awards not only in focusing exclusively on QFD, but in recognizing only individuals, and not organizations as a whole. The prize was named for Dr. Yoji Akao, himself a Deming Award winner and one of the seminal developers of the field of QFD. Dr. Akao personally hands out the award at the annual ceremony.

OTHER QUALITY AWARDS

The success of the major awards in attracting attention to management excellence in Japan, the United States, the European nations and Canada has promoted widespread interest in other nations as well as state awards within the United States, provincial awards within Canada, and individual national awards within Europe (as shown in Figure 1).

AUSTRALIA. Australia established its Australian Quality Awards for Business Excellence in 1991. The award is somewhat unique in that it has four tiers of recognition, nurturing companies to maintain ongoing quality management excellence. The first tier is the Business Improvement Level, giving first-level recognition for Progress or Foundation in Business Excellence. The next level, The Australian Quality Award for Business Excellence, is a best practices achievement award. The third level is the Australian Quality for Business Excellence Gold Award, open only to past award winners and intended to demonstrate ongoing improvement. The highest level is the

Table 1
Award Websites

American Society for Training and Development	http://www.astd.org/astd
Australian Business Excellence Awards	http://www.sai-global.com/AWARDS
Connecticut Quality Improvement Award	http://www.ctqualityaward.org/
Deming Prize	http://www.deming.org/demingprize/
The ESCAP Human Resources Development Award	http://www.escap-hrd.org/
European Customer Satisfaction Association	http://www.eucusa.org/de/index.php non-English
European Foundation for Quality Management	http://www.efqm.org/ or http://www.efqm.org/model_awards/eqa/intro.asp
Japanese Union of Scientists and Engineers	http://www.juse.or.jp/e/
Kwaliteit op Internet	http://www.leren.nl/rubriek/computers_en_internet/ internetten/zoeken_op_het_web/ non-English site
Malcolm Baldridge National Quality Award	http://www.quality.nist.gov/
Margaret Chase smith Quality Association	http://www.workforce-excellence.net/html/ stateawards/state-me.htm
Massachusetts Council for Quality	http://www.massexcellence.com/ AboutMax/stakeholders.html
National Quality Institute of Canada	http://www.nqi.ca/CAEAwards/default.aspx or http://www.nqi.ca/
President's Quality Award	http://www.opm.gov/pqa/
Shingo Prize	http://www.flex.net/~mcgovern/shingo.html
Society for Human Resource Management	http://www.shrm.org/
QFD Institute Akao Prize	http://www.qfdi.org/akaoprize.htm
Quality Texas Foundation	http://www.texas-quality.org/
UK Quality Award for Business Excellence	http://www.quality-foundation.co.uk/

Figure 2
The Hierarchy of Recognition

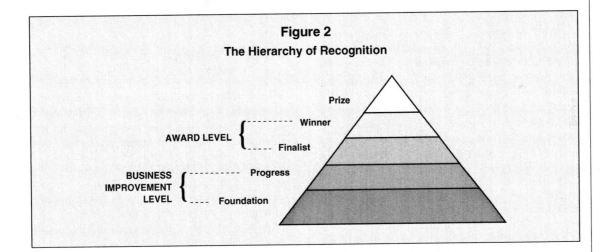

Australian Quality Prize, also open only to former winners and represents best practices internationally throughout the company.

At the awards, organizations can receive kudos via recognition either as a finalist or a winner. Figure 2 depicts the hierarchy of recognition. Winners gain the right to use the Australian Quality Awards for Business Excellence logo for three years.

NEW ZEALAND. The New Zealand Quality Foundation established the New Zealand Excellence Award in the late 1990s. Like its Australian counterpart, it is a tiered award, although with three rather than four tiers.

EUROPE. Several European countries have national prizes honoring business excellence and quality management in their nation. Among these are Denmark's Den *Danske Kvalitets Pris* (the Finnish Quality Award), the Dutch *Nederlandse Kwaliteitprijs* (Netherlands Quality Award), Ireland's Business Excellence Award, and Switzerland's *Esprix* award, also known as the *Schweizer Qualitätspreis für* Business Excellence (Swiss Quality Award for Business Excellence). The United Kingdom Quality Award for Business Excellence, established in 1994 by the president of the U.K. Board of Trade, was extended beyond for-profit organizations in 1995 to include categories not only for public organizations but, somewhat uniquely, also for voluntary services.

Even some regions within European nations (for example, Northern Ireland within the United Kingdom, and Flanders within Belgium) have begun to offer their own quality management prizes. Most of these competitions use the same guidelines as those used in the European Quality Awards.

UNITED STATES. Soon after the introduction of the Baldrige awards, a majority of the states began to offer their own awards. The oldest of these was the Connecticut Quality Improvement Award, begun in 1987, and so actually preceding the Baldrige Award by a year. Yet within ten years, Connecticut was just one of 41 states offering their own awards for excellence, most based at least in part on the Baldrige Award criteria. Several of these awards modified the Baldrige qualifications to include government, educational, or nonprofit organizations. Several awards from the larger states such as the Texas Quality Award and California's Eureka Award for Quality have tiered levels similar to the Australian Quality Awards described above.

Also notable is the Massachusetts Quality Award, established in 1992. The Massachusetts award is named for Armand Feigenbaum, the Massachusetts native whose book *Total Quality Control* (1951) founded the TQM movement. Most of the state awards are at least partially and usually entirely government funded. Maine's Margaret Chase Smith Maine State Quality Award, however, is unique in that it is entirely privately funded, which its organizers argue makes it freer from political considerations.

In addition to state-sponsored awards, several federal departments offer quality awards. For example, the U.S. Department of Energy Quality Accomplishment Award, begun in 1995, uses the Baldrige Award as its guidelines. The DOE Quality Accomplishment Award is administered by the Department of Commerce (and so independent of the DOE itself).

Similarly, the federal Office of Personnel Management annually offers the President's Award for Quality. The OPM's President's Award also uses the Baldrige Award criteria. The award recognizes federal agencies that have successfully implemented total quality management programs.

CANADA. In addition to the national Canada Awards for Excellence, the provinces of Manitoba and British Columbia offer their own awards. Additionally, Ontario's Durham region also offers its own award.

OTHER COUNTRIES

The Singapore Productivity and Standards Board in 1994 began the Singapore Quality Award to recognize organizations in Singapore for outstanding quality management practices and to enhance Singapore's competitiveness in the global market. Its model uses seven categories for comparing best practices and performances.

In 1995 the Japan Productivity Center for Socio-Economic Development established the Japan Quality Award to be awarded to companies excelling through strong customer focus, competitiveness, employee orientation and social responsibility.

The Costa Rica Excellence Award, a joint effort of the Costa Rican Chamber of Industries and Baxter, Firestone, and Intel, evaluates companies the parameters of ISO 9000 and ISO 14000 standards.

The South African Excellence Award focuses on companies attaining customer satisfaction and is awarded by the South African Excellence Foundation.

The Jordan's King Abdullah II Award for Excellence is the highest level recognition for companies in Jordan. It is aimed at increasing competitiveness by promoting quality awareness, performance and achievement.

AWARDS FOR OTHER MANAGEMENT AREAS

Many awards exist for other areas besides quality management. These awards range from teamwork issues to customer satisfaction and from manufacturing excellence to operations research management.

AQP NATIONAL TEAM EXCELLENCE AWARD. The Association for Quality and Participation annually awards teams within organizations for improving quality through participative teamwork for problem-solving, innovation, or improvement of an existing product, service, or process. The focus of the award is primarily for the United States.

THE INFORMS PRIZE. Since 1991, The Institute for Operations Research and the Management Sciences (INFORMS) has annually awarded their INFORMS Prize to a selected organization for pioneering efforts in the innovation of operations research/management sciences. In 1994, the award took its present name; from 1991 to 1994 the prize had been known as the ORSA Prize.

...tion to the INFORMS ...ations Research and the ...as since 1975 annually given ...elman Award for Management ...ement to reward "outstanding exam-...nagement science and operations research ...ce in the world." Though several Edelman .wards are given each year, the first-place prize carries a substantial $10,000 purse.

FRANK P. RAMSEY MEDAL. The Decision Analysis Society awards the Frank P. Ramsey Medal annually to recognize major contributions to the field of decision analysis. The medal is the most recognized decision analysis award, and takes its name from the Cambridge University probability expert who helped found the field.

SHINGO PRIZE. In 1988, the National Association of Manufacturers established the Shingo Prize for Excellence in Manufacturing. The Shingo Prize is administered by the NAM through the Utah State University College of Business, but is not linked substantively to the state of Utah. Also, while the prize has traditionally been awarded to U.S. companies, it is open to Canadian and Mexican manufacturers as well. The prize honors manufacturers for excellence in productivity and process improvement, quality enhancement, and customer satisfaction. The Shingo Prize rewards "focused improvements in core manufacturing processes, implementing lean, just-in-time philosophies and systems, eliminating waste, and achieving zero defects, while continuously improving products and costs."

EUCUSA AWARD. The European Customer Satisfaction Association (EUCUSA) began in 1997 to give awards annually to recognize European organizations and companies for achievements in improving customer satisfaction. The award categories are for large and small enterprises, nonprofit organizations, and cities or communities.

ISHIKAWA PRIZE. The Ishikawa Prize has been awarded annually since 1970 to recognize companies that have applied new methods or systems of management. The award is given by the same organization that gives the Deming Prize, the JUSE. Ichiro Ishikawa, for whom the award is named, was the first chairman of the JUSE's Board of Directors.

ESCAP AWARD. The United Nations Economic and Social Commission for Asia and the Pacific (ESCAP) in accordance with the Jakarta Plan of Action on Human Resources Development created the ESCAP Human Resources Development Award in 1990. The award is open to organizations in over 50 Asian or Pacific Island nations or territories belonging to the United Nations. The award annually recognizes exceptional work in the field of human resources development (HRD). In addition to the annual honoring ceremony in Bangkok, the winner receives $30,000 for the continuance of their project.

The ESCAP HRD Award has a theme each year. Some years the theme is less closely related to business initiatives than in others. For example, the theme in 1990 emphasized environmental management; the theme in 1992, drug abuse management; and the theme in 1998, education. Still, in most years, the award has recognized HRD for business initiatives. For example, the theme in 1994 was for "Human Resource Development for Women in Extreme Poverty," which was won by the Dhaka Ahsania Mission of Bangladesh. Similarly, the theme in 1995 had a primarily business focus, "HRD for Productive Employment of Youth," and was won by the "Barefoot College" of India's Social Work and Research Centre. In 1996 the theme was "People's Participation in Community Development," won by the Sungi Development Foundation of Pakistan; and in 1997, the theme was "Empowering the Urban Poor," won by Thailand's Human Development Centre.

SHRM AWARDS FOR PROFESSIONAL EXCELLENCE. The Society for Human Resource Management annually gives out four Awards for Professional Excellence. The four categories are for educators and for large, medium, and small organizations.

ASTD AWARDS. The American Society for Training and Development offers several awards in three different categories annually. The three categories are (1) Advancing Workplace Learning and Performance; (2) Excellence in Practice; and (3) Advancing ASTD's Vision.

The Advancing Workplace Learning and Performance Awards category includes awards for Distinguished Contribution, for Lifetime Achievement, for Champion of Workplace Learning and Performance, for Research, for Dissertation, and for Public Policy. Recipients have been of very high caliber, including in 1997 alone such figures as management authors Peter Senge and Peter Drucker, General Electric CEO Jack Welch, Senator Patrick Moynihan (New York), Senator William Roth (Delaware), Congressman Clay Shaw (Florida), and Congressman Sander Levin (Michigan).

The Excellence in Practice Awards category covers contributions in applied training in development in different areas including learning technologies, performance improvement, managing change, valuing differences, career development, organizational learning and technical training. The Vision Awards category covers contributions to the ASTD as an organization.

SEE ALSO: Quality and Total Quality Management; Quality Gurus

David A. Victor and James C. Koch
Revised by Judith M. Nixon

FURTHER READING:

Brown, M. G. *Baldrige Award Winning Quality: How to Interpret the Baldrige Criteria for Performance Excellence.* 13th ed. Portland, OR: Productivity Press Inc, 2004.

Funk, V. "Quality Awards Listing." *Quality Progress* 37, no. 8 (2004): 54–58.

Gabor, A. *The Man Who Discovered Quality: How W. Edwards Deming Brought the Quality Revolution to America: The Stories of Ford, Xerox, and GM.* New York : Times Books, 1990.

Hui, K.H., and T.K. Chuan. "Nine Approaches to Organizational Excellence." *Journal of Organizational Excellence* 22, no. 1 (2002): 53–65

Khoo, H.H., and K.C. Tan. "Managing for Quality in the USA and Japan: Differences between the MBNQA, DP and JQA." *TQM Magazine* 15, no. 1 (2003): 14–24.

Stading, G.L., and R.J. Vokurka. "Building Quality Strategy Content Using the Process from National and International Quality Awards." *TQM & Business Excellence* 14, no. 8 (2003): 931–946.

Tan, K.C. et al. "Factors Affecting the Development of National Quality Awards." *Business Excellence* 7, no. 3 (2003): 37–45.

Vukurka, R.J. "A Comparative Analysis of National and Regional Quality Awards." *Quality Progress* 33, no. 8 (2000): 41–49.

MANAGEMENT CONTROL

Management control describes the means by which the actions of individuals or groups within an organization are constrained to perform certain actions while avoiding other actions in an effort to achieve organizational goals. Management control falls into two broad categories—regulative and normative controls—but within these categories are several types.

Table 1
Types of Control

Regulative Controls	Normative Controls
Bureaucratic Controls	Team Norms
Financial Controls	Organizational Cultural Norms
Quality Controls	

The following section addresses regulative controls including bureaucratic controls, financial controls, and quality controls. The second section addresses normative controls including team norms and organization cultural norms.

REGULATIVE CONTROLS

Regulative controls stem from standing policies and standard operating procedures, leading some to criticize regulative controls as outdated and counterproductive. As organizations have become more flexible in recent years by flattening organizational hierarchies, expanding organizational boundaries to include suppliers in inventory management and customers in new product development, forging cooperative alliances with competitors, and developing virtual organizations in which employees are geographically dispersed and may meet only a few time each year, critics point out that regulative controls may prevent rather promote goal attainment.

There is some truth to this. Customer service representatives at Holiday Inn are limited in the extent to which they can correct mistakes involving guests. They can move guests to a different room if there is excessive noise in the room next to the guest's room. In some instances, guests may get a gift certificate for an additional night at another Holiday Inn if they have had a particularly bad experience. In contrast, customer service representatives at Tokyo's Marriott Inn have the latitude to take up to $500 off a customer's bill to solve complaints.

The actions of customer service representatives at both Holiday Inn and Marriott Inn must follow policies and procedures, yet those at Marriott are likely to feel less constrained and more empowered by Marriott's policies and procedures compared to Holiday Inn customer service representatives. The key in terms of management control is matching regulative controls such as policies and procedures with organizational goals such as customer satisfaction. Each of the three types of regulative controls discussed in the next few paragraphs has the potential to align or misalign organizational goals with regulative controls. The challenge for managers is striking the right balance between too much control and too little.

BUREAUCRATIC CONTROLS

Bureaucratic controls stem from lines of authority and this authority comes with one's position in the organizational hierarchy. The higher up the chain of command, the more an individual will have authority to dictate policies and procedures. Bureaucratic controls have gotten a bad name and often rightfully so. Organizations placing too much reliance on chain of command authority relationships inhibit flexibility to deal with unexpected events. However, there are ways managers can build flexibility into policies and procedures that make bureaucracies as flexible and able to quickly respond to customer problems as any other form of organizational control.

Consider how hospitals, for example, are structured along hierarchical lines of authority. The Board

Table 2

Definition and Examples of Regulative Controls

Type of Regulative Control	Definition	Example
Bureaucratic Controls	Policies and operating procedures	Employee handbook
Financial Controls	Key financial targets	Return on investment
Quality Controls	Acceptable levels of product or process variation	Defects per million

of Directors is at the top, followed by the CEO and then the Medical Director. Below these top executives are vice presidents with responsibility for overseeing various hospital functions such as human resources, medical records, surgery, and intensive care units. The chain of command in hospitals is clear; a nurse, for example, would not dare increase the dosage of a heart medication to a patient in an intensive care unit without a physician's order. Clearly, this has the potential to slow reaction times—physicians sometimes spread their time across hospital rounds for two or three hospitals and also their individual office practice. Yet, it is the nurses and other direct care providers who have the most contact with patients and are in the best position to rapidly respond to changes in a patient's condition.

The question bureaucratic controls must address is: How can the chain of command be preserved while also building flexibility and quick response times into the system? One way is through standard operating procedures that delegate responsibility downward. Some hospital respiratory therapy departments, for example, have developed standard operating procedures (in health care terms, therapist-driven protocols or TDPs) with input from physicians.

TDPs usually have branching logic structures requiring therapists to perform specific tests prior to certain patient interventions to build safety into the protocol. Once physicians approve a set of TDPs, therapists have the autonomy to make decisions concerning patient care without further physicians' orders as long as these decisions stay within the boundaries of the TDP. Patients need not wait for a physician to make the next set of rounds or patient visits, write a new set of orders, enter the orders on the hospitals intranet, and wait for the manager of respiratory therapy to schedule a therapist to perform the intervention. Instead, therapists can respond immediately because protocols are established that build in flexibility and fast response along with safety checks to limit mistakes.

Bureaucratic control is thus not synonymous with rigidity. Unfortunately, organizations have built rigidity into many bureaucratic systems, but this need not be the case. It is entirely possible for creative managers to develop flexible, quick-response bureaucracies.

FINANCIAL CONTROLS

Financial controls include key financial targets for which managers are held accountable. These types of controls are common among firms that are organized as multiple strategic business units (SBUs). SBUs are product, service, or geographic lines having managers who are responsible for the SBU's profits and losses. These managers are held responsible to upper management to achieve financial targets that contribute to the overall profitability of the corporation.

Managers who are not SBU executives often have financial responsibility as well. Individual department heads are typically responsible for keeping expenses within budgeted guidelines. These managers, however, tend to have less overall responsibility for financial profitability targets than SBU managers.

In either case, financial controls place constraints on spending. For SBU managers, increased spending must be justified by increased revenues. For departmental managers, staying within budget is typically one key measure of periodic performance reviews. The role of financial controls, then, is to increase overall profitability as well as to keep costs in line. To determine which costs are reasonable, some firms will benchmark other firms in the same industry. Such benchmarking, while not always an "apples-to-apples" comparison, provides at least some evidence to determine whether costs are in line with industry averages.

QUALITY CONTROLS

Quality controls describe the extent of variation in processes or products that is considered acceptable. For some companies, zero defects—no variation at all—is the standard. In other companies, statistically insignificant variation is allowable.

Quality controls influence the ultimate product or service outcome offered to customers. By maintaining consistent quality, customers can rely on a firm's product or service attributes, but this also creates an interesting dilemma. An overemphasis on consistency where variation is kept to the lowest levels may also reduce response to unique customer needs. This is not a problem when the product or service is relatively standardized such as a McDonald's hamburger, but

Table 3

Definition and Examples of Normative Controls

Type of Normative Control	Definition	Example
Team Norms	Informal team rules and responsibilities	Task delegation based on team member expertise
Organizational Cultural Norms	Shared organizational values, beliefs, and rituals	Collaboration may be valued more than individual "stars"

may pose a problem when customers have nonstandard situations for which a one-size-fits-all solution is inappropriate. Wealth managers, for example, may create investment portfolios tailored to a single client, but the process used to implement that portfolio such as stock market transactions will be standardized. Thus, there is room within quality control for both creativity; e.g., wealth portfolio solutions, and standardization; e.g., stock market transactions.

NORMATIVE CONTROLS

Rather than relying on written policies and procedures as in regulative controls, normative controls govern employee and managerial behavior through generally accepted patterns of action. One way to think of normative controls is in terms how certain behaviors are appropriate and others are less appropriate. For instance, a tuxedo might be the appropriate attire for an American business awards ceremony, but totally out of place at a Scottish awards ceremony, where a formal kilt may be more in line with local customs. However, there would generally be no written policy regarding disciplinary action for failure to wear the appropriate attire, thus separating formal regulative controls for the more informal normative controls.

TEAM NORMS

Teams have become commonplace in many organizations. Team norms are the informal rules that make team members aware of their responsibilities to the team. Although the task of the team may be formally documented and communicated, the ways in which team members interact are typically developed over time as the team goes through phases of growth. Even team leadership be informally agreed upon; at times, an appointed leader may have less influence than an informal leader. If, for example, an informal leader has greater expertise than a formal team leader, team members may look to the informal leader for guidance requiring specific skills or knowledge. Team

norms tend to develop gradually, but once formed, can be powerful influences over behavior.

ORGANIZATIONAL CULTURE NORMS

In addition to team norms, norms based on organizational culture are another type of normative control. Organizational culture involves the shared values, beliefs, and rituals of a particular organization. The Internet search firm, Google, Inc. has a culture in which innovation is valued, beliefs are shared among employees that the work of the organization is important, and teamwork and collaboration are common. In contrast, the retirement specialty firm, VALIC, focuses on individual production for its sales agents, de-emphasizing teamwork and collaboration in favor of personal effort and rewards. Both of these example are equally effective in matching norms with organizational goals; the key is thus in properly aligning norms and goals.

The broad categories of regulative and normative controls are present in nearly all organizations, but the relative emphasis of each type of control varies. Within the regulative category are bureaucratic, financial, and quality controls. Within the normative category are team norms and organization cultural norms. Both categories of norms can be effective and one is not inherently superior to the other. The managerial challenge is to encourage norms that align employee behavior with organizational goals.

SEE ALSO: Organizational Culture; Quality and Total Quality Management; Teams and Teamwork

Scott B. Droege

FURTHER READING:

Barry, L.L. "The Collaborative Organization: Leadership Lessons from Mayo Clinic." *Organizational Dynamics* 33, no. 3 (2004): 228–242.

Lalich, J. "Watch Your Culture." *Harvard Business Review* 82, no. 1 (2004): 34–39.

Rollag, K., S. Parise, and R. Cross. "Getting New Hires Up to Speed Quickly". *MIT Sloan Management Review* 46, no. 2 (2005): 35–41.

MANAGEMENT FUNCTIONS

The functions of management uniquely describe managers' jobs. The most commonly cited functions of management are planning, organizing, leading, and controlling, although some identify additional functions. The functions of management define the process of management as distinct from accounting, finance, marketing, and other business functions. These functions provide a useful way of classifying information about management, and most basic management texts since the 1950s have been organized around a functional framework.

DEVELOPMENT OF THE FUNCTIONAL APPROACH TO MANAGEMENT

Henri Fayol was the first person to identify elements or functions of management in his classic 1916 book *Administration Industrielle et Generale*. Fayol was the managing director of a large French coal-mining firm and based his book largely on his experiences as a practitioner of management. Fayol defined five functions, or elements of management: planning, organizing, commanding, coordinating, and controlling. Fayol argued that these functions were universal, in the sense that all managers performed them in the course of their jobs, whether the managers worked in business, military, government, religious, or philanthropic undertakings.

Fayol defined planning in terms of forecasting future conditions, setting objectives, and developing means to attain objectives. Fayol recognized that effective planning must also take into account unexpected contingencies that might arise and did not advocate rigid and inflexible plans. Fayol defined organizing as making provision for the structuring of activities and relationships within the firm and also the recruiting, evaluation, and training of personnel.

According to Fayol, commanding as a managerial function concerned the personal supervision of subordinates and involved inspiring them to put forth unified effort to achieve objectives. Fayol emphasized the importance of managers understanding the people who worked for them, setting a good example, treating subordinates in a manner consistent with firm policy, delegating, and communicating through meetings and conferences.

Fayol saw the function of coordination as harmonizing all of the various activities of the firm. Most later experts did not retain Fayol's coordination function as a separate function of management but regarded it as a necessary component of all the other management functions. Fayol defined the control function in terms of ensuring that everything occurs within the parameters of the plan and accompanying principles. The purpose of control was to identify deviations from objectives and plans and to take corrective action.

Fayol's work was not widely known outside Europe until 1949, when a translation of his work appeared in the United States. Nevertheless, his discussion of the practice of management as a process consisting of specific functions had a tremendous influence on early management texts that appeared in the 1950s.

Management pioneers such as George Terry, Harold Koontz, Cyril O'Donnell, and Ralph Davis all published management texts in the 1950s that defined management as a process consisting of a set of interdependent functions. Collectively, these and several other management experts became identified with what came to be known as the process school of management.

According to the process school, management is a distinct intellectual activity consisting of several functions. The process theorists believe that all managers, regardless of their industry, organization, or level of management, engage in the functions of management. The process school of management became a dominant paradigm for studying management and the functions of management became the most common way of describing the nature of managerial work.

CRITICISM OF THE FUNCTIONAL APPROACH TO MANAGEMENT

By the early 1970s, some experts suggested that the functions of management as described by Fayol and others of the process school of management were not an accurate description of the reality of managers' jobs. Chief among the critics of the functional approach was Henry Mintzberg.

Mintzberg argued that the functional or process school of management was "folklore" and that functions of management such as planning, organizing, leading, and controlling did not accurately depict the chaotic nature of managerial work. He felt that the functional approach to the managerial job falsely conveyed a sense that managers carefully and deliberately evaluated information before making management decisions.

Based upon an observational study of five executives, Mintzberg concluded that the work managers actually performed could best be represented by three sets of roles, or activities: interpersonal roles, informational roles, and decision-making roles. He described the interpersonal roles as consisting of figurehead, leader, and liaison. He identified three informational roles: monitor, disseminator, and spokesperson. Finally, he described four decision-making roles that included entrepreneur, disturbance handler, resource allocator, and negotiator.

Mintzberg's challenge to the usefulness of the functions of management and the process school attracted a tremendous amount of attention and generated several empirical studies designed to determine whether his or Fayol's description of the managerial job was most accurate. While this research did indicate that managers performed at least some of the roles Mintzberg identified, there was little in the findings that suggested that the functions of management were not a useful way of describing managerial work.

Scholars continue to debate this question. Research by David Lamond suggests that both approaches had some validity, with Fayol's approach describing the ideal management job and Mintzberg describing the day-to-day activities of managers. Thus, the general conclusion seems to be that while Mintzberg offered a genuine insight into the daily activities of practicing managers, the functions of management still provides a very useful way of classifying the activities managers engage in as they attempt to achieve organizational goals.

PLANNING

Planning is the function of management that involves setting objectives and determining a course of action for achieving these objectives. Planning requires that managers be aware of environmental conditions facing their organization and forecast future conditions. It also requires that managers be good decision-makers.

Planning is a process consisting of several steps. The process begins with environmental scanning, which simply means that planners must be aware of the critical contingencies facing their organization in terms of economic conditions, their competitors, and their customers. Planners must then attempt to forecast future conditions. These forecasts form the basis for planning.

Planners must establish objectives, which are statements of what needs to be achieved and when. Planners must then identify alternative courses of action for achieving objectives. After evaluating the various alternatives, planners must make decisions about the best courses of action for achieving objectives. They must then formulate necessary steps and ensure effective implementation of plans. Finally, planners must constantly evaluate the success of their plans and take corrective action when necessary.

There are many different types of plans and planning.

STRATEGIC PLANNING. Strategic planning involves analyzing competitive opportunities and threats, as well as the strengths and weaknesses of the organization, and then determining how to position the organization to compete effectively in their environment. Strategic planning has a long time frame, often three years or more. Strategic planning generally includes the entire organization and includes formulation of objectives. Strategic planning is often based on the organization's mission, which is its fundamental reason for existence. An organization's top management most often conducts strategic planning.

TACTICAL PLANNING. Tactical planning is intermediate-range planning that is designed to develop relatively concrete and specific means to implement the strategic plan. Middle-level managers often engage in tactical planning. Tactical planning often has a one- to three-year time horizon.

OPERATIONAL PLANNING. Operational planning generally assumes the existence of objectives and specifies ways to achieve them. Operational planning is short-range planning that is designed to develop specific action steps that support the strategic and tactical plans. Operational planning usually has a very short time horizon, from one week to one year.

ORGANIZING

Organizing is the function of management that involves developing an organizational structure and allocating human resources to ensure the accomplishment of objectives. The structure of the organization is the framework within which effort is coordinated. The structure is usually represented by an organization chart, which provides a graphic representation of the chain of command within an organization. Decisions made about the structure of an organization are generally referred to as "organizational design" decisions.

Organizing also involves the design of individual jobs within the organization. Decisions must be made about the duties and responsibilities of individual jobs as well as the manner in which the duties should be carried out. Decisions made about the nature of jobs within the organization are generally called "job design" decisions.

Organizing at the level of the organization involves deciding how best to departmentalize, or cluster jobs into departments to effectively coordinate effort. There are many different ways to departmentalize, including organizing by function, product, geography, or customer. Many larger organizations utilize multiple methods of departmentalization. Organizing at the level of job involves how best to design individual jobs to most effectively use human resources.

Traditionally, job design was based on principles of division of labor and specialization, which assumed that the more narrow the job content, the more proficient the individual performing the job could become.

However, experience has shown that it is possible for jobs to become too narrow and specialized. When this happens, negative outcomes result, including decreased job satisfaction and organizational commitment and increased absenteeism and turnover.

Recently many organizations have attempted to strike a balance between the need for worker specialization and the need for workers to have jobs that entail variety and autonomy. Many jobs are now designed based on such principles as job enrichment and teamwork.

LEADING

Leading involves influencing others toward the attainment of organizational objectives. Effective leading requires the manager to motivate subordinates, communicate effectively, and effectively use power. If managers are effective leaders, their subordinates will be enthusiastic about exerting effort toward the attainment of organizational objectives.

To become effective at leading, managers must first understand their subordinates' personalities, values, attitudes, and emotions. Therefore, the behavioral sciences have made many contributions to the understanding of this function of management. Personality research and studies of job attitudes provide important information as to how managers can most effectively lead subordinates.

Studies of motivation and motivation theory provide important information about the ways in which workers can be energized to put forth productive effort. Studies of communication provide direction as to how managers can effectively and persuasively communicate. Studies of leadership and leadership style provide information regarding questions such as, "What makes a manager a good leader?" and "In what situations are certain leadership styles most appropriate and effective?"

CONTROLLING

Controlling involves ensuring that performance does not deviate from standards. Controlling consists of three steps, which include establishing performance standards, comparing actual performance against standards, and taking corrective action when necessary. Performance standards are often stated in monetary terms such as revenue, costs, or profits, but may also be stated in other terms, such as units produced, number of defective products, or levels of customer service.

The measurement of performance can be done in several ways, depending on the performance standards, including financial statements, sales reports, production results, customer satisfaction, and formal performance appraisals. Managers at all levels engage in the managerial function of controlling to some degree.

The managerial function of controlling should not be confused with control in the behavioral or manipulative sense. This function does not imply that managers should attempt to control or manipulate the personalities, values, attitudes, or emotions of their subordinates. Instead, this function of management concerns the manager's role in taking necessary actions to ensure that the work-related activities of subordinates are consistent with and contributing toward the accomplishment of organizational and departmental objectives.

Effective controlling requires the existence of plans, since planning provides the necessary performance standards or objectives. Controlling also requires a clear understanding of where responsibility for deviations from standards lies. Two traditional control techniques are the budget and the performance audit. Although controlling is often thought of in terms of financial criteria, managers must also control production/operations processes, procedures for delivery of services, compliance with company policies, and many other activities within the organization.

The management functions of planning, organizing, leading, and controlling are widely considered to be the best means of describing the manager's job as well as the best way to classify accumulated knowledge about the study of management. Although there have been tremendous changes in the environment faced by managers and the tools used by managers to perform their roles, managers still perform these essential functions.

SEE ALSO: Management Control; Management Styles; Organizing; Planning

Tim Barnett

FURTHER READING:

Anderson, P., and M. Pulich. "Managerial Competencies Necessary in Today's Dynamic Health Care Environment." *Health Care Manager* 21, no. 2 (2002): 1–11.

Carroll, Stephen J., and Dennis J. Gillen. "Are the Classical Management Functions Useful in Describing Managerial Work?" *Academy of Management Review* 12, no. 1 (1980): 38–51.

Fayol, Henri. *General and Industrial Administration*. London: Sir Issac Pitman & Sons, Ltd., 1949.

Koontz, Harold, and Cyril O'Donnell. *Principles of Management: An Analysis of Managerial Functions*. New York: McGraw-Hill Book Co., 1955.

Lamond, David. "A Matter of Style: Reconciling Henri and Henry." *Management Decision* 42, no. 2 (2004): 330–356.

Mintzberg, Henry. *The Nature of Managerial Work*. New York: Harper & Row, 1973.

Robbins, Stephen P. and Mary Coulter. *Management*. Upper Saddle River, NJ: Prentice Hall, 1999.

MANAGEMENT INFORMATION SYSTEMS

All businesses share one common asset, regardless of the type of business. It does not matter if they manufacture goods or provide services. It is a vital part of any business entity, whether a sole proprietorship or a multinational corporation. That common asset is information.

Information enables us to determine the need to create new products and services. Information tells us to move into new markets or to withdraw from other markets. Without information, the goods do not get made, the orders are not placed, the materials are not procured, the shipments are not delivered, the customers are not billed, and the business cannot survive.

But information has far lesser impact when presented as raw data. In order to maximize the value of information, it must be captured, analyzed, quantified, compiled, manipulated, made accessible, and shared. In order to accomplish those tasks, an information system (IS) must be designed, developed, administered, and maintained.

INFORMATION SYSTEMS

An information system is a computer system that provides management and other personnel within an organization with up-to-date information regarding the organization's performance; for example, current inventory and sales. It usually is linked to a computer network, which is created by joining different computers together in order to share data and resources. It is designed to capture, transmit, store, retrieve, manipulate, and or display information used in one or more business processes. These systems output information in a form that is useable at all levels of the organization: strategic, tactical, and operational.

Systems that are specifically geared toward serving general, predictable management functions are sometimes called management information systems (MIS). A good example of an MIS report is the information that goes into an annual report created for the stockholders of a corporation (a scheduled report). The administration of an information system is typically the province of the MIS or information technology (IT) department within an organization.

Some applications have infringed on the familiar MIS landscape. Enterprise resource planning (ERP) software and executive information systems (EIS) both provide packaged modules and programs that perform the same functions as traditional MIS, but with greater functionality, flexibility, and integration capabilities.

MAINFRAMES. The original computerized information systems were based on mainframes. "Mainframe" is a term originally referring to the cabinet containing the central processor unit or "main frame" of a room-filling computer. After the emergence of smaller mini-computer designs in the early 1970s, the traditional large machines were described as "mainframe computers," or simply mainframes. The term carries the connotation of a machine designed for batch rather than interactive use, though possibly with an interactive time-sharing operating system retrofitted onto it.

It has been conventional wisdom in most of the business community since the late 1980s that the mainframe architectural tradition is essentially dead, having been swamped by huge advances in integrated circuit design technology and low-cost personal computing. Despite this, mainframe sales in the United States enjoyed somewhat of a resurgence in the 1990s, as prices came down and as large organizations found they needed high-power computing resources more than ever. Supporters claim that mainframes still house 90 percent of the data major businesses rely on for mission-critical applications, attributing this to their superior performance, reliability, scalability, and security compared to microprocessors.

THE INTERNET. The Internet has opened up further developments in information systems and the exchange of information via web-based e-mail, intranets, and extranets. These technologies allow for much faster data and information exchange and greater access for more users. Web-casting and videoconferencing allow for real-time information exchanges. Mobile computing technologies accessed by handheld devices, such as multi-functional mobile phones, personal digital assistants, and podcasting (via iPods), are offering further modes of communication.

INFORMATION SYSTEM DESIGN AND ADMINISTRATION

The design of an information system is based on various factors. Cost is a major consideration, but there certainly are others to be taken into account, such as the number of users; the modularity of the system, or the ease with which new components can be integrated into the system, and the ease with which outdated or failed components can be replaced; the amount of information to be processed; the type of information to be processed; the computing power required to meet the varied needs of the organization; the anticipated functional life of the system and/or components; the ease of use for the people who will be using the system; and the requirements and compatibility of the applications that are to be run on the system.

There are different ways to construct an information system, based upon organizational requirements, both in the function aspect and the financial sense. Of course, the company needs to take into consideration that hardware that is purchased and assembled into a network will become outdated rather quickly. It is almost axiomatic that the technologies used in information systems steadily increase in power and versatility on a rapid time scale. Perhaps the trickiest part of designing an information system from a hardware standpoint is straddling the fine line between too much and not enough, while keeping an eye on the requirements that the future may impose.

Applying foresight when designing a system can bring substantial rewards in the future, when system components are easy to repair, replace, remove, or update without having to bring the whole information system to its knees. When an information system is rendered inaccessible or inoperative, the system is considered to be "down."

A primary function of the maintaining an information system is to minimize downtime, or hopefully, to eradicate downtime altogether. The costs created by a department, facility, organization, or workforce being idled by an inoperative system can become staggering in a short amount of time. The inconvenience to customers can cost the firm even more if sales are lost as a result, in addition to any added costs the customers might incur.

Another vital consideration regarding the design and creation of an information system is to determine which users have access to which information. The system should be configured to grant access to the different partitions of data and information by granting user-level permissions for access. A common method of administering system access rights is to create unique profiles for each user, with the appropriate user-level permissions that provide proper clearances.

Individual passwords can be used to delineate each user and their level of access rights, as well as identify the tasks performed by each user. Data regarding the performance of any user unit, whether individual, departmental, or organizational can also be collected, measured, and assessed through the user identification process.

The OSI seven-layer model attempts to provide a way of partitioning any computer network into independent modules from the lowest (physical/hardware) layer to the highest (application/program) layer. Many different specifications can exist at each of these layers.

A crucial aspect of administering information systems is maintaining communication between the IS staff, who have a technical perspective on situations, and the system users, who usually communicate their concerns or needs in more prosaic terminology. Getting the two sides to negotiate the language barriers can be difficult, but the burden of translation should fall upon the IS staff. A little patience and understanding can go a long way toward avoiding frustration on the part of both parties.

There is more to maintaining an information system than applying technical knowledge to hardware or software. IS professionals have to bridge the gap between technical issues and practicality for the users. The information system should also have a centralized body that functions to provide information, assistance, and services to the users of the system. These services will typically include telephone and electronic mail "help desk" type services for users, as well as direct contact between the users and IS personnel.

INFORMATION SYSTEM FUNCTIONS

DOCUMENT AND RECORD MANAGEMENT. Document and record management may well be the most crucial aspect of any information system. Some examples of types of information maintained in these systems would be accounting, financial, manufacturing, marketing, and human resources. An information system can serve as a library. When properly collected, organized, and indexed in accordance with the requirements of the organization, its stored data becomes accessible to those who need the information.

The location and retrieval of archived information can be a direct and logical process, if careful planning is employed during the design of the system. Creating an outline of how the information should be organized and indexed can be a very valuable tool during the design phase of a system. A critical feature of any information system should be the ability to not only access and retrieve data, but also to keep the archived information as current as possible.

COLLABORATIVE TOOLS. Collaborative tools can consist of software or hardware, and serve as a base for the sharing of data and information, both internally and externally. These tools allow the exchange of information between users, as well as the sharing of resources. As previously mentioned, real-time communication is also a possible function that can be enabled through the use of collaborative tools.

DATA MINING. Data mining, or the process of analyzing empirical data, allows for the extrapolation of information. The extrapolated results are then used in forecasting and defining trends.

QUERY TOOLS. Query tools allow the users to find the information needed to perform any specific function. The inability to easily create and execute functional queries is a common weak link in many information systems. A significant cause of that inability, as noted earlier, can be the communication difficulties between a management information systems department and the system users.

Another critical issue toward ensuring successful navigation of the varied information levels and partitions is the compatibility factor between knowledge bases. For maximum effectiveness, the system administrator should ascertain that the varied collection, retrieval, and analysis levels of the system either operate on a common platform, or can export the data to a common platform. Although much the same as query tools in principle, intelligent agents allow the customization of the information flow through sorting and filtering to suit the individual needs of the users. The primary difference between query tools and intelligent agents is that query tools allow the sorting and filtering processes to be employed to the specifications of management and the system administrators, and intelligent agents allow the information flow to be defined in accord with the needs of the user.

KEY POINTS

Managers should keep in mind the following advice in order to get the most out of an information system:

- Use the available hardware and software technologies to support the business. If the information system does not support quality and productivity, then it is misused.

- Use the available technologies to create and facilitate the flow of communication within your organization and, if feasible, outside of it as well. Collaboration and flexibility are the key advantages offered for all involved parties. Make the most of those advantages.

- Determine if any strategic advantages are to be gained by use of your information system, such as in the areas of order placement, shipment tracking, order fulfillment, market forecasting, just-in-time supply, or regular inventory. If you can gain any sort of advantage by virtue of the use of your information system, use it.

- Use the quantification opportunities presented by your information system to measure, analyze, and benchmark the performances of an individual, department, division, plant, or entire organization.

An information system is more than hardware or software. The most integral and important components of the system are the people who design it, maintain it, and use it. While the overall system must meet various needs in terms of power and performance, it must also be usable for the organization's personnel. If the operation of day-to-day tasks is too daunting for the workforce, then even the most humble of aspirations for the system will go unrealized.

A company will likely have a staff entrusted with the overall operation and maintenance of the system and that staff will be able to make the system perform in the manner expected of it. Pairing the information systems department with a training department can create a synergistic solution to the quandary of how to get non-technical staff to perform technical tasks. Oft times, the individuals staffing an information systems department will be as technical in their orientation as the operative staff is non-technical in theirs. This creates a language barrier between the two factions, but the communication level between them may be the most important exchange of information within the organization. Nomenclature out of context becomes little more than insular buzzwords.

If a company does not have a formal training department, the presence of staff members with a natural inclination to demonstrate and teach could mitigate a potentially disastrous situation. Management should find those employees who are most likely to adapt to the system and its operation. They should be taught how the system works and what it is supposed to do. Then they can share their knowledge with their fellow workers. There may not be a better way to bridge the natural chasm between the IS department and non-technical personnel. When the process of communicating information flows smoothly and can be used for enhancing and refining business operations, the organization and its customers will all profit.

SEE ALSO: Knowledge Management

Jeffrey A. Moga
Revised by Monica C. Turner

FURTHER READING:

Caldelli, A., and M.L. Parmigiani. "Management Information System: A Tool for Corporate Sustainability." *Journal of Business Ethics* 55, no.2 (December 2004): 159–171.

Denton, D.K. "Focus on Data Context, Not Content." *Communications News* 40, no. 12 (December 2003): 50.

Lail, P.W. "Improving IT's Support of Business Strategy." *Pulp & Paper* 79, no.1 (January 2005): 23.

Lawrence, F.B., D.F. Jennings, and B.E. Reynolds. *ERP in Distribution.* Mason, OH: Thomson/South-Western, 2005.

Pawlowski, S. D. and D. Robey. "Bridging User Organizations: Knowledge Brokering and the Work of Information Technology Professionals." *MIS Quarterly* 28, no. 4 (December 2004): 645–672.

Zehir, C. and H. Keskin. "A Field Research on the Effects of MIS on Organizational Restructuring." *Journal of American Academy of Business* 3 (September 2003): 270–279.

MANAGEMENT LEVELS

Managers are organizational members who are responsible for the work performance of other organizational members. Managers have formal authority to use organizational resources and to make decisions. In organizations, there are typically three levels of management: top-level, middle-level, and first-level. These three main levels of managers form a hierarchy, in which they are ranked in order of importance. In most organizations, the number of managers at each level is such that the hierarchy resembles a pyramid, with many more first-level managers, fewer middle managers, and the fewest managers at the top level. Each of these management levels is described below in terms of their possible job titles and their primary responsibilities and the paths taken to hold these positions. Additionally, there are differences across the management levels as to what types of management tasks each does and the roles that they take in their jobs. Finally, there are a number of changes that are occurring in many organizations that are changing the management hierarchies in them, such as the increasing use of teams, the prevalence of outsourcing, and the flattening of organizational structures.

TOP-LEVEL MANAGERS

Top-level managers, or top managers, are also called senior management or executives. These individuals are at the top one or two levels in an organization, and hold titles such as: Chief Executive Officer (CEO), Chief Financial Officer (CFO), Chief Operational Officer (COO), Chief Information Officer (CIO), Chairperson of the Board, President, Vice president, Corporate head.

Often, a set of these managers will constitute the top management team, which is composed of the CEO, the COO, and other department heads. Top-level managers make decisions affecting the entirety of the firm. Top managers do not direct the day-to-day activities of the firm; rather, they set goals for the organization and direct the company to achieve them. Top managers are ultimately responsible for the performance of the organization, and often, these managers have very visible jobs.

Top managers in most organizations have a great deal of managerial experience and have moved up through the ranks of management within the company or in another firm. An exception to this is a top manager who is also an entrepreneur; such an individual may start a small company and manage it until it grows enough to support several levels of management. Many top managers possess an advanced degree, such as a Masters in Business Administration, but such a degree is not required.

Some CEOs are hired in from other top management positions in other companies. Conversely, they may be promoted from within and groomed for top management with management development activities, coaching, and mentoring. They may be tagged for promotion through succession planning, which identifies high potential managers.

MIDDLE-LEVEL MANAGERS

Middle-level managers, or middle managers, are those in the levels below top managers. Middle managers' job titles include: General manager, Plant manager, Regional manager, and Divisional manager.

Middle-level managers are responsible for carrying out the goals set by top management. They do so by setting goals for their departments and other business units. Middle managers can motivate and assist first-line managers to achieve business objectives. Middle managers may also communicate upward, by offering suggestions and feedback to top managers. Because middle managers are more involved in the day-to-day workings of a company, they may provide valuable information to top managers to help improve the organization's bottom line.

Jobs in middle management vary widely in terms of responsibility and salary. Depending on the size of the company and the number of middle-level managers in the firm, middle managers may supervise only a small group of employees, or they may manage very large groups, such as an entire business location. Middle managers may be employees who were promoted from first-level manager positions within the organization, or they may have been hired from outside the firm. Some middle managers may have aspirations to hold positions in top management in the future.

FIRST-LEVEL MANAGERS

First-level managers are also called first-line managers or supervisors. These managers have job titles such as: Office manager, Shift supervisor, Department manager, Foreperson, Crew leader, Store manager.

First-line managers are responsible for the daily management of line workers—the employees who actually produce the product or offer the service. There are first-line managers in every work unit in the organization. Although first-level managers typically do not set goals for the organization, they have a very strong influence on the company. These are the managers that most employees interact with on a daily basis, and if the managers perform poorly, employees may also perform poorly, may lack motivation, or may leave the company.

In the past, most first-line managers were employees who were promoted from line positions (such as production or clerical jobs). Rarely did these employees have formal education beyond the high school level. However, many first-line managers are now graduates of a trade school, or have a two-year associates or a four-year bachelor's degree from college.

MANAGEMENT LEVELS AND THE FOUR MANAGERIAL FUNCTIONS

Managers at different levels of the organization engage in different amounts of time on the four managerial functions of planning, organizing, leading, and controlling.

Planning is choosing appropriate organizational goals and the correct directions to achieve those goals. Organizing involves determining the tasks and the relationships that allow employees to work together to achieve the planned goals. With leading, managers motivate and coordinate employees to work together to achieve organizational goals. When controlling, managers monitor and measure the degree to which the organization has reached its goals.

The degree to which top, middle, and supervisory managers perform each of these functions is presented in Exhibit 1. Note that top managers do considerably more planning, organizing, and controlling than do managers at any other level. However, they do much less leading. Most of the leading is done by first-line managers. The amount of planning, organizing, and controlling decreases down the hierarchy of management; leading increases as you move down the hierarchy of management.

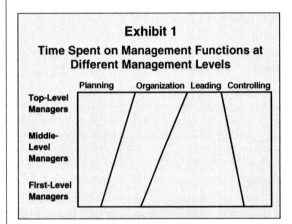

Exhibit 1

Time Spent on Management Functions at Different Management Levels

MANAGEMENT ROLES

In addition to the broad categories of management functions, managers in different levels of the hierarchy fill different managerial roles. These roles were categorized by researcher Henry Mintzberg, and they can be grouped into three major types: decisional, interpersonal, and informational.

DECISIONAL ROLES. Decisional roles require managers to plan strategy and utilize resources. There are four specific roles that are decisional. The *entrepreneur* role requires the manager to assign resources to develop innovative goods and services, or to expand a business. Most of these roles will be held by top-level managers, although middle managers may be given

some ability to make such decisions. The *disturbance handler* corrects unanticipated problems facing the organization from the internal or external environment. Managers at all levels may take this role. For example, first-line managers may correct a problem halting the assembly line or a middle level manager may attempt to address the aftermath of a store robbery. Top managers are more likely to deal with major crises, such as requiring a recall of defective products. The third decisional role, that of *resource allocator*, involves determining which work units will get which resources. Top managers are likely to make large, overall budget decisions, while middle mangers may make more specific allocations. In some organizations, supervisory managers are responsible for determine allocation of salary raises to employees. Finally, the *negotiator* works with others, such as suppliers, distributors, or labor unions, to reach agreements regarding products and services. First-level managers may negotiate with employees on issues of salary increases or overtime hours, or they may work with other supervisory managers when needed resources must be shared. Middle managers also negotiate with other managers and are likely to work to secure preferred prices from suppliers and distributors. Top managers negotiate on larger issues, such as labor contracts, or even on mergers and acquisitions of other companies.

INTERPERSONAL ROLES. Interpersonal roles require managers to direct and supervise employees and the organization. The *figurehead* is typically a top of middle manager. This manager may communicate future organizational goals or ethical guidelines to employees at company meetings. A *leader* acts as an example for other employees to follow, gives commands and directions to subordinates, makes decisions, and mobilizes employee support. Managers must be leaders at all levels of the organization; often lower-level managers look to top management for this leadership example. In the role of *liaison,* a manger must coordinate the work of others in different work units, establish alliances between others, and work to share resources. This role is particularly critical for middle managers, who must often compete with other managers for important resources, yet must maintain successful working relationships with them for long time periods.

INFORMATIONAL ROLES. Informational roles are those in which managers obtain and transmit information. These roles have changed dramatically as technology has improved. The *monitor* evaluates the performance of others and takes corrective action to improve that performance. Monitors also watch for changes in the environment and within the company that may affect individual and organizational performance. Monitoring occurs at all levels of management, although managers at higher levels of the organization are more likely to monitor external threats to the environment than are middle or first-line managers. The role of *disseminator* requires that managers inform employees of changes that affect them and the organization. They also communicate the company's vision and purpose.

Managers at each level disseminate information to those below them, and much information of this nature trickles from the top down. Finally, a *spokesperson* communicates with the external environment, from advertising the company's goods and services, to informing the community about the direction of the organization. The spokesperson for major announcements, such as a change in strategic direction, is likely to be a top manager. But, other, more routine information may be provided by a manager at any level of a company. For example, a middle manager may give a press release to a local newspaper, or a supervisor manager may give a presentation at a community meeting.

MANAGEMENT SKILLS

Regardless of organizational level, all managers must have five critical skills: technical skill, interpersonal skill, conceptual skill, diagnostic skill, and political skill.

TECHNICAL SKILL. Technical skill involves understanding and demonstrating proficiency in a particular workplace activity. Technical skills are things such as using a computer word processing program, creating a budget, operating a piece of machinery, or preparing a presentation. The technical skills used will differ in each level of management. First-level managers may engage in the actual operations of the organization; they need to have an understanding of how production and service occur in the organization in order to direct and evaluate line employees. Additionally, first-line managers need skill in scheduling workers and preparing budgets. Middle managers use more technical skills related to planning and organizing, and top managers need to have skill to understand the complex financial workings of the organization.

INTERPERSONAL SKILL. Interpersonal skill involves human relations, or the manager's ability to interact effectively with organizational members. Communication is a critical part of interpersonal skill, and an inability to communicate effectively can prevent career progression for managers. Managers who have excellent technical skill, but poor interpersonal skill are unlikely to succeed in their jobs. This skill is critical at all levels of management.

CONCEPTUAL SKILL. Conceptual skill is a manager's ability to see the organization as a whole, as a complete entity. It involves understanding how organizational units work together and how the organization fits into its competitive environment. Conceptual skill is crucial for top managers, whose ability to see "the big picture" can have major repercussions on the success of the business. However, conceptual skill is still necessary for middle and supervisory managers, who must use this skill to envision, for example, how work units and teams are best organized.

DIAGNOSTIC SKILL. Diagnostic skill is used to investigate problems, decide on a remedy, and implement a solution. Diagnostic skill involves other skills—technical, interpersonal, conceptual, and politic. For instance, to determine the root of a problem, a manager may need to speak with many organizational members or understand a variety of informational documents. The difference in the use of diagnostic skill across the three levels of management is primarily due to the types of problems that must be addressed at each level. For example, first-level managers may deal primarily with issues of motivation and discipline, such as determining why a particular employee's performance is flagging and how to improve it. Middle managers are likely to deal with issues related to larger work units, such as a plant or sales office. For instance, a middle-level manager may have to diagnose why sales in a retail location have dipped. Top managers diagnose organization-wide problems, and may address issues such as strategic position, the possibility of outsourcing tasks, or opportunities for overseas expansion of a business.

POLITICAL SKILL. Political skill involves obtaining power and preventing other employees from taking away one's power. Managers use power to achieve organizational objectives, and this skill can often reach goals with less effort than others who lack political skill. Much like the other skills described, political skill cannot stand alone as a manager's skill; in particular, though, using political skill without appropriate levels of other skills can lead to promoting a manager's own career rather than reaching organizational goals. Managers at all levels require political skill; managers must avoid others taking control that they should have in their work positions. Top managers may find that they need higher levels of political skill in order to successfully operate in their environments. Interacting with competitors, suppliers, customers, shareholders, government, and the public may require political skill.

CHANGES IN MANAGEMENT HIERARCHIES

There are a number of changes to organizational structures that influence how many managers are at each level of the organizational hierarchy, and what tasks they perform each day.

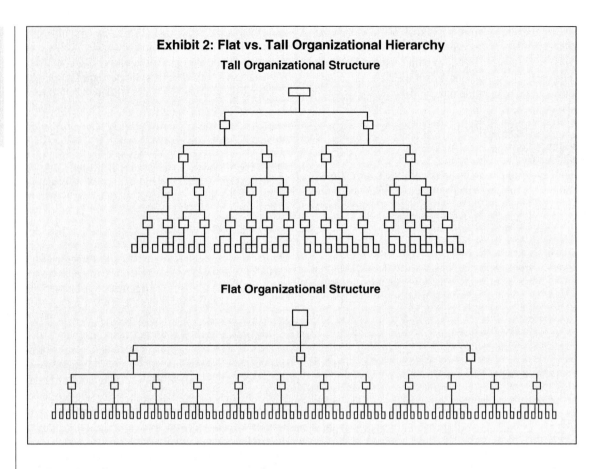

Exhibit 2: Flat vs. Tall Organizational Hierarchy

Tall Organizational Structure

Flat Organizational Structure

FLATTER ORGANIZATIONAL STRUCTURES. Organizational structures can be described by the number of levels of hierarchy; those with many levels are called "tall" organizations. They have numerous levels of middle management, and each manager supervises a small number of employees or other managers. That is, they have a small span of control. Conversely, "flat" organizations have fewer levels of middle management, and each manager has a much wider span of control. Examples of organization charts that show tall and flat organizational structures are presented in Exhibit 2.

Many organizational structures are now more flat than they were in previous decades. This is due to a number of factors. Many organizations want to be more flexible and increasingly responsive to complex environments. By becoming flatter, many organizations also become less centralized. Centralized organizational structures have most of the decisions and responsibility at the top of the organization, while decentralized organizations allow decision-making and authority at lower levels of the organization. Flat organizations that make use of decentralization are often more able to efficiently respond to customer needs and the changing competitive environment.

As organizations move to flatter structures, the ranks of middle-level managers are diminishing.

This means that there a fewer opportunities for promotion for first-level managers, but this also means that employees at all levels are likely to have more autonomy in their jobs, as flatter organizations promote decentralization. When organizations move from taller to flatter hierarchies, this may mean that middle managers lose their jobs, and are either laid off from the organization, or are demoted to lower-level management positions. This creates a surplus of labor of middle level managers, who may find themselves with fewer job opportunities at the same level.

INCREASED USE OF TEAMS. A team is a group of individuals with complementary skills who work together to achieve a common goal. That is, each team member has different capabilities, yet they collaborate to perform tasks. Many organizations are now using teams more frequently to accomplish work because they may be capable of performing at a level higher than that of individual employees. Additionally, teams tend to be more successful when tasks require speed, innovation, integration of functions, and a complex and rapidly changing environment.

Another type of managerial position in an organization that uses teams is the team leader, who is sometimes called a project manager, a program manager, or task force leader. This person manages the team by acting as a facilitator and catalyst. He or she may also engage in work to help accomplish the team's goals. Some teams do not have leaders, but instead are self-managed. Members of self-managed teams hold each other accountable for the team's goals and manage one another without the presence of a specific leader.

OUTSOURCING. Outsourcing occurs when an organization contracts with another company to perform work that it previously performed itself. Outsourcing is intended to reduce costs and promote efficiency. Costs can be reduced through outsourcing, often because the work can be done in other countries, where labor and resources are less expensive than in the United States. Additionally, by having an outsourcing company aid in production or service, the contracting company can devote more attention and resources to the company's core competencies. Through outsourcing, many jobs that were previously performed by American workers are now performed overseas. Thus, this has reduced the need for many first-level and middle-level managers, who may not be able to find other similar jobs in another company.

There are three major levels of management: top-level, middle-level, and first-level. Managers at each of these levels have different responsibilities and different functions. Additionally, managers perform different roles within those managerial functions. Finally, many organizational hierarchies are changing, due to changes to organizational structures due to the increasing use of teams, the flattening of organizations, and outsourcing.

SEE ALSO: Management and Executive Development; Management Functions; Organizational Chart; Organizational Structure; Outsourcing and Offshoring; Teams and Teamwork

Marcia J. Simmering

FURTHER READING:

DuBrin, Andrew J. *Essentials of Management.* 6th ed. Peterborough, Ontario: Thomson South-Western, 2003.

Jones, Gareth R., and Jennifer M. George. *Contemporary Management.* 4th ed. New York, NY: McGraw-Hill Irwin, 2006.

Mintzberg, Henry. "The Manager's Job: Folklore and Fact." *Harvard Business Review,* July-August 1975, 56–62.

———. *The Nature of Managerial Work.* New York: Harper & Row, 1973.

Rue, Leslie W., and Lloyd L. Byars. *Management: Skills and Applications.* 10th ed. New York, NY: McGraw-Hill Irwin, 2003.

Williams, Chuck. *Management.* Cincinnati, OH: South-Western College Publishing, 2000.

MANAGEMENT SCIENCE

Management science generally refers to mathematical or quantitative methods for business decision making. The term "operations research" may be used interchangeably with management science.

HISTORY

Frederick Winslow Taylor is credited with the initial development of scientific management techniques in the early 1900s. In addition, several management science techniques were further developed during World War II. Some even consider the World War II period as the beginning of management science.

World War II posed many military, strategic, logistic, and tactical problems. Operations research teams of engineers, mathematicians, and statisticians were developed to use the scientific method to find solutions for many of these problems.

Nonmilitary management science applications developed rapidly after World War II. Based on quantitative methods developed during World War II, several new applications emerged. The development of the simplex method by George Dantzig in 1947 made application of linear programming practical. C. West Churchman, Russell Ackoff, and Leonard Arnoff made management science even more accessible by publishing the first operations research textbook in 1957.

Computer technology continues to play an integral role in management science. Practitioners and researchers are able to use ever-increasing computing power in conjunction with management science methods to solve larger and more complex problems. In addition, management scientists are constantly developing new algorithms and improving existing algorithms; these efforts also enable management scientists to solve larger and more complex problems.

BREADTH OF MANAGEMENT SCIENCE TECHNIQUES

The scope of management science techniques is broad. These techniques include:

- mathematical programming
- linear programming
- simplex method
- dynamic programming
- goal programming
- integer programming
- nonlinear programming

- stochastic programming
- Markov processes
- queuing theory/waiting-line theory
- transportation method
- simulation

Management science techniques are used on a wide variety of problems from a vast array of applications. For example, integer programming has been used by baseball fans to allocate season tickets in a fair manner. When seven baseball fans purchased a pair of season tickets for the Seattle Mariners, the Mariners turned to management science and a computer program to assign games to each group member based on member priorities.

In marketing, optimal television scheduling has been determined using integer programming. Variables such as time slot, day of the week, show attributes, and competitive effects can be used to optimize the scheduling of programs. Optimal product designs based on consumer preferences have also been determined using integer programming.

Similarly, linear programming can be used in marketing research to help determine the timing of interviews. Such a model can determine the interviewing schedule that maximizes the overall response rate while providing appropriate representation across various demographics and household characteristics.

In the area of finance, management science can be employed to help determine optimal portfolio allocations, borrowing strategies, capital budgeting, asset allocations, and make-or-buy decisions. In portfolio allocations, for instance, linear programming can be used to help a financial manager select specific industries and investment vehicles (e.g., bonds versus stocks) in which to invest.

With regard to production scheduling, management science techniques can be applied to scheduling, inventory, and capacity problems. Production managers can deal with multi-period scheduling problems to develop low-cost production schedules. Production costs, inventory holding costs, and changes in production levels are among the types of variables that can be considered in such analyses.

Workforce assignment problems can also be solved with management science techniques. For example, when some personnel have been cross-trained and can work in more than one department, linear programming may be used to determine optimal staffing assignments.

Airports are frequently designed using queuing theory (to model the arrivals and departures of aircraft) and simulation (to simultaneously model the traffic on multiple runways). Such an analysis can yield information to be used in deciding how many runways to build and how many departing and arriving flights to allow by assessing the potential queues that can develop under various airport designs.

MATHEMATICAL PROGRAMMING

Mathematical programming deals with models comprised of an objective function and a set of constraints. Linear, integer, nonlinear, dynamic, goal, and stochastic programming are all types of mathematical programming.

An objective function is a mathematical expression of the quantity to be maximized or minimized. Manufacturers may wish to maximize production or minimize costs, advertisers may wish to maximize a product's exposure, and financial analysts may wish to maximize rate of return.

Constraints are mathematical expressions of restrictions that are placed on potential values of the objective function. Production may be constrained by the total amount of labor at hand and machine production capacity, an advertiser may be constrained by an advertising budget, and an investment portfolio may be restricted by the allowable risk.

LINEAR PROGRAMMING

Linear programming problems are a special class of mathematical programming problems for which the objective function and all constraints are linear. A classic example of the application of linear programming is the maximization of profits given various production or cost constraints.

Linear programming can be applied to a variety of business problems, such as marketing mix determination, financial decision making, production scheduling, workforce assignment, and resource blending. Such problems are generally solved using the "simplex method."

MEDIA SELECTION PROBLEM. The local Chamber of Commerce periodically sponsors public service seminars and programs. Promotional plans are under way for this year's program. Advertising alternatives include television, radio, and newspaper. Audience estimates, costs, and maximum media usage limitations are shown in Exhibit 1.

If the promotional budget is limited to $18,200, how many commercial messages should be run on each medium to maximize total audience contact? Linear programming can find the answer.

SIMPLEX METHOD

The simplex method is a specific algebraic procedure for solving linear programming problems. The simplex method begins with simultaneous linear

Exhibit 1

Constraint	Television	Radio	Newspaper
Audience per ad	100,000	18,000	40,000
Cost per ad	2,000	300	600
Maximum usage	10	20	10

equations and solves the equations by finding the best solution for the system of equations. This method first finds an initial basic feasible solution and then tries to find a better solution. A series of iterations results in an optimal solution.

SIMPLEX PROBLEM. Georgia Television buys components that are used to manufacture two television models. One model is called High Quality and the other is called Medium Quality. A weekly production schedule needs to be developed given the following production considerations.

The High Quality model produces a gross profit of $125 per unit, and the Medium Quality model has a $75 gross profit. Only 180 hours of production time are available for the next time period. High Quality models require a total production time of six hours and Medium Quality models require eight hours. In addition, there are only forty-five Medium Quality components on hand.

To complicate matters, only 250 square feet of warehouse space can be used for new production. The High Quality model requires 9 square feet of space while the Medium Quality model requires 7 square feet.

Given the above situation, the simplex method can provide a solution for the production allocation of High Quality models and Medium Quality models.

DYNAMIC PROGRAMMING

Dynamic programming is a process of segmenting a large problem into a several smaller problems. The approach is to solve the all the smaller, easier problems individually in order to reach a solution to the original problem.

This technique is useful for making decisions that consist of several steps, each of which also requires a decision. In addition, it is assumed that the smaller problems are not independent of one another given they contribute to the larger question.

Dynamic programming can be utilized in the areas of capital budgeting, inventory control, resource allocation, production scheduling, and equipment replacement. These applications generally begin with a longer time horizon, such as a year, and then break down the problem into smaller time units such as months or weeks. For example, it may be necessary to determine an optimal production schedule for a twelve-month period.

Dynamic programming would first find a solution for smaller time periods, for example, monthly production schedules. By answering such questions, dynamic programming can identify solutions to a problem that are most efficient or that best serve other business needs given various constraints.

GOAL PROGRAMMING

Goal programming is a technique for solving multi-criteria rather than single-criteria decision problems, usually within the framework of linear programming. For example, in a location decision a bank would use not just one criterion, but several. The bank would consider cost of construction, land cost, and customer attractiveness, among other factors.

Goal programming establishes primary and secondary goals. The primary goal is generally referred to as a priority level 1 goal. Secondary goals are often labeled level 2, priority level 3, and so on. It should be noted that trade-offs are not allowed between higher and lower level goals.

Assume a bank is searching for a site to locate a new branch. The primary goal is to be located in a five-mile proximity to a population of 40,000 consumers. A secondary goal might be to be located at least two miles from a competitor. Given the no trade-off rule, we would first search for a target solution of locating close to 40,000 consumers.

BLENDING PROBLEM. The XYZ Company mixes three raw materials to produce two products: a fuel additive and a solvent. Each ton of fuel additive is a mixture of 2/5 ton of material A and 3/5 ton of material C. A ton of solvent base is a mixture of 1/2 ton of material A, 1/5 ton of material B, and 3/10 ton of material C. Production is constrained by a limited availability of the three raw materials. For the current production period XYZ has the following quantities of each raw material: 20 tons of material A, 5 tons of material B, and 21 tons of material C. Management would like to achieve the following priority level goals:

Goal 1. Produce at least 30 tons of fuel additive.

Goal 2. Produce at least 15 tons of solvent.

Goal programming would provide directions for production.

INTEGER PROGRAMMING

Integer programming is useful when values of one or more decision variables are limited to integer values. This is particularly useful when modeling production processes for which fractional amounts of products cannot be produced. Integer variables are often limited to two values—zero or one. Such variables are particularly useful in modeling either/or decisions.

Areas of business that use integer linear programming include capital budgeting and physical distribution. For example, faced with limited capital a firm needs to select capital projects in which to invest. This type of problem is represented in Table 1.

As can be seen in the table, capital requirements exceed the available funds for each year. Consequently, decisions to accept or reject regarding each of the projects must be made and integer programming would require the following integer definitions for each of the projects.

x1 = 1 if the new office project is accepted; 0 if rejected

x2 = 1 if the new warehouse project is accepted; 0 if rejected

x3 = 1 if the new branch project is accepted; 0 if rejected

A set of equations is developed from the definitions to provide an optimal solution.

NONLINEAR PROGRAMMING

Nonlinear programming is useful when the objective function or at least one of the constraints is not linear with respect to values of at least one decision variable. For example, the per-unit cost of a product may increase at a decreasing rate as the number of units produced increases because of economies of scale.

STOCHASTIC PROGRAMMING

Stochastic programming is useful when the value of a coefficient in the objective function or one of the constraints is not know with certainty but has a known probability distribution. For instance, the exact demand for a product may not be known, but its probability distribution may be understood. For such a problem, random values from this distribution can be substituted into the problem formulation. The optimal objective function values associated with these formulations provide the basis of the probability distribution of the objective function.

MARKOV PROCESS MODELS

Markov process models are used to predict the future of systems given repeated use. For example, Markov models are used to predict the probability that production machinery will function properly given its past performance in any one period. Markov process models are also used to predict future market share given any specific period's market share.

COMPUTER FACILITY PROBLEM. The computing center at a state university has been experiencing computer downtime. Assume that the trials of an associated Markov Process are defined as one-hour periods and that the probability of the system being in a running state or a down state is based on the state of the

Table 1
Integer Programming Example

Project	Estimated Net Return	Year 1	Year 2	Year 3
New office	25,000	10,000	10,000	10,000
New warehouse	85,000	35,000	25,000	25,000
New branch	40,000	15,000	15,000	15,000
Available funds		50,000	45,000	45,000

system in the previous period. Historical data in Table 2 show the transition probabilities.

MANAGEMENT SCIENCE

Table 2

		To	
		Running	Down
From	Running	.9	.1
	Down	.3	.7

The Markov process would then solve for the following: if the system is running, what is the probability of the system being down in the next hour of operation?

QUEUING THEORY/WAITING LINE THEORY

Queuing theory is often referred to as waiting line theory. Both terms refer to decision making regarding the management of waiting lines (or queues). This area of management science deals with operating characteristics of waiting lines, such as:

- the probability that there are no units in the system
- the mean number of units in the queue
- the mean number of units in the system (the number of units in the waiting line plus the number of units being served)
- the mean time a unit spends in the waiting line
- the mean time a unit spends in the system (the waiting time plus the service time)
- the probability that an arriving unit has to wait for service
- the probability of n units in the system

Given the above information, programs are developed that balance costs and service delivery levels. Typical applications involve supermarket checkout lines and waiting times in banks, hospitals, and restaurants.

BANK LINE PROBLEM. XYZ State Bank operates a drive-in-teller window, which allows customers to complete bank transactions without getting out of their cars. On weekday mornings arrivals to the drive-in-teller window occur at random, with a mean arrival rate of twenty-four customers per hour or 0.4 customers per minute.

Delay problems are expected if more than three customers arrive during any five-minute period. Waiting line models can determine the probability that delay problems will occur.

TRANSPORTATION METHOD

The transportation method is a specific application of the simplex method that finds an initial solution and then uses iteration to develop an optimal solution. As the name implies, this method is utilized in transportation problems.

TRANSPORTATION PROBLEM. A company must plan its distribution of goods to several destinations from several warehouses. The quantity available at each warehouse is limited. The goal is to minimize the cost of shipping the goods. An example of production capacity can be found in Table 3. The forecast for demand is shown in Table 4.

The transportation method will determine the optimal amount to be shipped from each warehouse and determine the optimal destination.

Table 3

Origin	Warehouse Location	3 month capacity
1	Houston	2,000
2	Dallas	2,500
3	San Antonio	2,800
		Total 7,300

Table 4

Destination	Location	3 month forecast
1	New Orleans	1,800
2	Little Rock	3,200
3	Las Vegas	2,300
		Total 7,300

SIMULATION

Simulation is used to analyze complex systems by modeling complex relationships between variables with known probability distributions. Random values from these probability distributions are substituted into the model and the behavior of the system is observed. Repeated executions of the simulation model provide insight into the behavior of the system that is being modeled.

SEE ALSO: Operations Management; Operations Scheduling; Operations Strategy; Production Planning and Scheduling

Gene Brown
Revised by James J. Cochran

FURTHER READING:

Anderson, David R., Dennis J. Sweeney, and Thomas A. Williams. *Quantitative Methods for Business.* Cincinnati, OH: South-Western Publishing, 2004.

Blumenfrucht, Israel, and Joel G. Segal. "Updating the Accountant on Financial Advisory Services: Financial Models, Latest Quantitative Techniques, and Other Recent Developments." *National Public Accountant,* September 1998, 20–23.

Camm, D. Jeffrey, and James R. Evans. *Management Science & Decision Technology.* Cincinnati, OH: South-Western Publishing, 2000.

McCulloch, C.E., B. Paal, and S.P. Ashdown. "An Optimisation Approach to Apparel Sizing." *Journal of the Operational Research Society,* May 1998, 492–499.

MANAGEMENT SOCIETIES AND ASSOCIATIONS: DOMESTIC

SEE: Domestic Management Societies and Associations

MANAGEMENT SOCIETIES AND ASSOCIATIONS: INTERNATIONAL

SEE: International Management Societies and Associations

MANAGEMENT STYLES

A manager's style is determined by the situation, the needs and personalities of his or her employees, and by the culture of the organization. Organizational restructuring and the accompanying cultural change has caused management styles to come in and go out of fashion. There has been a move away from an authoritarian style of management in which control is a key concept, to one that favors teamwork and empowerment. Managerial styles that focus on managers as technical experts who direct, coordinate and control the work of others have been replaced by those that focus on managers as coaches, counselors, facilitators, and team leaders.

Successful management styles involve building teams, networks of relationships, and developing and motivating others. There is a greater emphasis on participative management styles and people management skills. Management theorists have repeatedly found evidence to support the advantages of management styles such as participative management; Theory Y versus Theory X; Theory Z; Total Quality Management (TQM); Management by Walking Around; Management by Objectives; and employee empowerment.

PARTICIPATIVE MANAGEMENT

Participative management involves sharing information with employees and involving them in decision-making. Employees are encouraged to run their own departments and make decisions regarding policies and processes. It has often been promoted as the quick cure for poor morale and low productivity. It is not, however, appropriate in every organization and at every level.

Employees must have the skills and abilities to participate. Employees must have the technical background, communication skills, and intelligence to make decisions and communicate those decisions effectively. The organization's culture must support employee involvement and the issues in which employees get involved must be relevant to them.

Representative participation allows workers to be represented by a small group who actually participate. The goal of representative participation is to redistribute power within the organization. Employees' interests become as important as those interests of management and stockholders.

According to Stephen P. Robbins, author of *Essentials of Organizational Behavior,* the two most popular forms of representative participation are works councils and board representatives. Works councils are groups of employees who have been elected by their peers and who must be consulted by management when making personnel decisions. Board representatives are employees that sit on the board of directors and represent labor interests.

As with participative management, representative participation is a poor choice for improving performance or morale. Evidence suggests that the overall influence of representative participation is small. The employees involved in representing personnel receive more benefit than those who they represent.

THEORY X AND THEORY Y

Douglas McGregor's Theory X assumes that people are lazy, they don't want to work, and it is the job of the manager to force or coerce them to work. McGregor's Theory X makes three basic assumptions: (1) The average human being dislikes work and will do anything to get out of it; (2) most people must be coerced, controlled, directed, and threatened or punished to get them to work toward organizational objectives; and (3) the average human being prefers to be directed, wishes to avoid responsibility, has relatively little ambition, and places job security above ambition. According to this theory, responsibility for demonstrating initiative and motivation lies with the employee and failure to perform is his or her fault. Employees are motivated by extrinsic rewards such as money, promotions, and tenure.

Theory Y suggests employees would behave differently if treated differently by managers. Theory Y assumes that higher-order needs dominate individuals. The set of assumptions for Theory Y is (1) the average human does not dislike work and it is as natural as play; (2) people will exercise self-direction and self-control in order to achieve objectives; (3) rewards of satisfaction and self-actualization are obtained from effort put forth to achieve organizational objectives; (4) the average human being not only accepts but also seeks responsibility; (5) human beings are creative and imaginative in solving organizational problems; and (6) the intellectual potential of the average human is only partially realized. If productivity is low and employees are not motivated, then it is considered failure on the manager's part.

THEORY Z

William Ouchi studied management practices in the United States and Japan and developed Theory Z. Theory Z combines elements of both U.S. and Japanese management styles and is sometimes called Japanese Management. It assumes that the best management style involves employees at all levels of the organization. Specific characteristics included in Theory Z are long-term employment, less specialized career paths, informal control, group decision making, and concern for the individual rises above work-related issues. This theory satisfies both lower order and higher order needs.

Looking out for employees' well being satisfies the lower-level needs. Incorporating group processes in decision making satisfy middle-level needs and encouraging employees to take responsibility for their work and decisions satisfy higher-level needs. Many firms are increasing productivity by placing more emphasis on group decision-making and teams. Firms are also showing more concern for family-related issues like childcare, flexible work schedules, and telecommuting.

TOTAL QUALITY MANAGEMENT

Total Quality Management (TQM) is a management style that integrates of all functions of a business to achieve a high quality of product. The major hallmarks are customer satisfaction, quality as the responsibility of all employees, and teamwork. As an integrated method, it involves every aspect of the company. The entire workforce, from the CEO to the line worker, must be involved in a shared commitment to improving quality.

TQM encourages employees to grow and learn and to participate in improvements, so it exemplifies a participative management style. TQM also encourages an ever-changing or continuous process, and emphasizes the ideas of working constantly toward improved quality.

Americans W. Edward Deming and Joseph M. Juran were the pioneers of the quality movement. Both did their major work in post-World War II Japan, and are credited with the major turnaround in the quality of Japanese products by the 1970s. In the 1980s both men were highly influential in the quality management movement in the United States.

MANAGEMENT BY WALKING AROUND

Management by Walking Around (MBWA) is a classic technique used by good managers who are proactive listeners. Managers using this style gather as much information as possible so that a challenging situation doesn't turn into a bigger problem. Listening carefully to employees' suggestions and concerns will help evade potential crises. MBWA benefits managers by providing unfiltered, real-time information about processes and policies that is often left out of formal communication channels. By walking around, management gets an idea of the level of morale in the organization and can offer help if there is trouble.

A potential concern of MBWA is that the manager will second-guess employees' decisions. The manager must maintain his or her role as coach and counselor, not director. By leaving decision-making responsibilities with the employees, managers can be assured of the fastest possible response time.

According to Max Messmer, another mistake managers make is to inadvertently create more work for employees. By offering suggestions that may be interpreted as assignments, managers can increase the workload and slow down progress.

Messmer illustrates an example of a team working on a project that needs a supplier of plastic molding. When the manager shows up, the team has reviewed three companies and selected the best one. The manager also knows of a good company, and suggests that team members give this company a call. They may not feel comfortable in saying that the decision has already been made, and will take the extra time to call the company in order to please the manager.

MANAGEMENT BY OBJECTIVES

Management by Objectives (MBO) is a company-wide process in which employees actively participate in setting goals that are tangible, verifiable, and measurable. Management theorist Peter Drucker pioneered this style in his 1954 book, *The Practice of Management.*

MBO provides a systematic method of assuring that all employees and work groups set goals that are in alignment with achieving the organization's goals. Xerox, Intel, and Du Pont are just a few examples of companies that use MBO at all levels of the organization. Overall organizational objectives are converted into specific objectives for employees. Objectives at each level of the organization are linked together through a "bottom up" approach as well as a "top down" approach. In this manner, if each individual achieves his/her goals, then the department will achieve its goals and the organization objectives will in turn be met.

There are four steps involved in the MBO process: setting goals, participative decision-making, implementing plans, and performance feedback. Top managers work with middle managers and middle managers work with lower level managers to set goals for their departments. Each manager then works with employees in the department to set individual performance goals. The participative decision-making step allows managers and employees to jointly set goals, define responsibility for achieving those goals, and set the evaluation process.

Managers are allowed to implement their plans and control their own performance. This step of MBO utilizes every manager's expertise to benefit the organization and permits managers to continuously improve their skills.

The final step is to continuously provide feedback on performance and achievement of objectives. By periodically reviewing employees' performance goals can be modified or new goals can be set. This step complements the formal appraisal system because the continuous feedback throughout the year keeps individuals informed of their progress.

As with any other management style, the organization's culture must be conducive for MBO to work.

Top management must be committed and involved in the MBO program for it to be beneficial. This management style is not without its problems. Managers often set their departmental goals and objectives too narrowly at the expense of the organization's strategic goals or objectives.

Another problem arises when managers are not flexible in setting up the goal setting and evaluation processes and employees lose the ability to respond to issues quickly. Unrealistic expectations about results are often a problem with MBO programs as well as the unwillingness of management to allocate rewards based on the accomplishment of individual goals.

EMPLOYEE EMPOWERMENT

Employee empowerment is a style of management that puts managers in the role of coach, adviser, sponsor, or facilitator. Decision-making is being pushed down to the lowest levels of the organization. The way work is designed and the way organizations are structured are changing.

Empowerment involves delegating the decision-making authority regarding the action to be taken on a task that is considered to be important to both the manager and employee. The main reasons for implementing an empowerment program are to provide fast solutions to business problems; to provide growth opportunities for employees and; to lower organizational costs while allowing the manager to work on multiple projects.

Employee empowerment is the most effective when management has set clear obtainable goals and defined specific accountability standards. The success of employee empowerment relies on the ability of management to provide resources such as time and money; to provide support by way of legitimacy; and to provide relevant and factual information so employees can make educated decisions. Training employees to take responsibility and make sound decisions that are supported by upper management as well as lower level managers are other areas that are important to the success of empowerment programs.

Employees benefit from empowerment because they have more responsibility in their jobs. Employee empowerment increases the level of employee involvement and therefore creates a deeper sense of satisfaction and higher levels of motivation. There are potential problems with empowerment programs that often result in unfavorable outcomes.

Many times managers delegate trivial, unimportant and boring tasks to employees and they retain the complicated and important tasks for themselves. Empowerment will not work unless the authority and decision-making tasks are perceived as meaningful by the employee.

Another problem arises when managers not only assign meaningless tasks to their employees but also then expect the employee to continuously consult them for approval. Managers must evaluate their employees' skills and abilities and determine if the organization's culture can support an empowerment program before beginning.

SELF-MANAGED WORK TEAMS

Employee empowerment led to the development of self-managed work teams. This management style delegates the authority to make decisions such as how to spend money, whom to hire, and what projects to undertake. Self-managed work teams are generally composed of 10 to 15 people and require minimal supervision. Xerox, General Motors, PepsiCo, Hewlett-Packard, and M&M/Mars are just a few organizations that have implemented self-managed work teams. According to Stephen P. Robbins, one in every five companies uses self-managed work teams.

Managers must select a management style that is best suited for them, their department, their subordinates, and finally the organization they work for. The situations managers encounter may require varying management styles depending on a specific assignment, the employees being managed, or the manager's personality. Management style can ultimately determine the performance outcome of employees and a company's growth depends on the management styles of its executives. Therefore, in order to determine the most appropriate management style, it is necessary to first review previous results produced as a result of a particular management approach.

Management positions require a certain degree of authority and therefore managers may often find themselves in leadership positions. However, not all leaders are managers and not all managers are leaders. Managers who possess good leadership skills influence and motivate employees to achieve organizational goals. It is therefore noteworthy to mention that certain leadership styles lend themselves to effective management styles as well.

SEE ALSO: Leadership Styles and Bases of Power; Leadership Theories and Studies; Quality and Total Quality Management; Theory X and Theory Y; Theory Z

Amy McMillan

FURTHER READING:

Cherrington, D.J. *Organizational Behavior: The Management of Individual and Organizational Performance.* 2nd ed. Needham Heights, MA: Allyn and Bacon, 1994.

Deming, W.E. *Out of the Crisis.* Cambridge, MA: MIT Press, 1986.

Juran, Joseph M. *Juran on Leadership for Quality.* New York: Free Press, 1989.

————. *Juran on Planning for Quality.* New York: Free Press, 1988.

Matejka, K., R.J. Dunsing, and C. McCabe. "The Empowerment Matrix." *Manage* 50, no. 2 (1999): 14–16.

McGregor, Douglas. *The Human Side of Enterprise.* New York: McGraw-Hill Book Co., 1960.

Mescon, M.H., C.L. Bovee, and J.V. Thill. *Business Today.* 10th ed. Upper Saddle River, NJ: Prentice Hall, 2002.

Miller, D., J. Hartwick, and I.L. Breton-Miller. "How to Detect a Management Fad—And Distinguish It from a Classic." *Business Horizons* 47 no. 4 (2004): 7–16.

Ouchi, William G. *Theory Z: How American Business Can Meet the Japanese Challenge.* Reading, MA: Addison-Wesley, 1981.

Robbins, Stephen P. *Essentials of Organizational Behavior.* 7th ed. Upper Saddle River, NJ: Prentice Hall, 2002.

MANAGEMENT THOUGHT

The schools of management thought are theoretical frameworks for the study of management. Each of the schools of management thought are based on somewhat different assumptions about human beings and the organizations for which they work. Since the formal study of management began late in the 19th century, the study of management has progressed through several stages as scholars and practitioners working in different eras focused on what they believed to be important aspects of good management practice. Over time, management thinkers have sought ways to organize and classify the voluminous information about management that has been collected and disseminated. These attempts at classification have resulted in the identification of management schools.

Disagreement exists as to the exact number of management schools. Different writers have identified as few as three and as many as twelve. Those discussed below include (1) the classical school, (2) the behavioral school, (3) the quantitative or management science school, (4) the systems school, (5) and the contingency school. The formal study of management is largely a twentieth-century phenomenon, and to some degree the relatively large number of management schools of thought reflect a lack of consensus among management scholars about basic questions of theory and practice.

Table 1 provides a brief summary of five major schools of management thought, their approximate dates of origin, and their relative areas of emphasis. The following sections discuss each of the management

Table 1
Five Major Schools of Management Thought

MANAGEMENT SCHOOLS	Beginning Dates	Emphasis
CLASSICAL SCHOOL		Managing workers and organizations more efficiently.
Scientific Management	1880s	
Administrative Management	1940s	
Bureaucratic Management	1920s	
BEHAVIORAL SCHOOL		Understanding human behavior in the organization.
Human Relations	1930s	
Behavioral Science	1950s	
QUANTITATIVE SCHOOL		Increasing quality of managerial decision-making through the application of mathematical and statistical methods.
Management Science	1940s	
Operations Management	1940s	
Management Information Systems	1950s—1970s	
SYSTEMS SCHOOL	1950s	Understanding the organization as a system that transforms inputs into outputs while in constant interaction with its' environment.
CONTINGENCY SCHOOL	1960s	Applying management principles and processes as dictated by the unique characteristics of each situation.

schools in more detail. In addition, three contemporary management perspectives are discussed.

THE CLASSICAL SCHOOL

The classical school is the oldest formal school of management thought. Its roots pre-date the twentieth century. The classical school of thought generally concerns ways to manage work and organizations more efficiently. Three areas of study that can be grouped under the classical school are scientific management, administrative management, and bureaucratic management.

SCIENTIFIC MANAGEMENT. In the late 19th century, management decisions were often arbitrary and workers often worked at an intentionally slow pace. There was little in the way of systematic management and workers and management were often in conflict. Scientific management was introduced in an attempt to create a mental revolution in the workplace. It can be defined as the systematic study of work methods in order to improve efficiency. Frederick W. Taylor was its main proponent. Other major contributors were Frank Gilbreth, Lillian Gilbreth, and Henry Gantt.

Scientific management has several major principles. First, it calls for the application of the scientific method to work in order to determine the best method for accomplishing each task. Second, scientific management suggests that workers should be scientifically selected based on their qualifications and trained to perform their jobs in the optimal manner. Third, scientific management advocates genuine cooperation between workers and management based on mutual self-interest. Finally, scientific management suggests that management should take complete responsibility for planning the work and that workers' primary responsibility should be implementing management's plans. Other important characteristics of scientific management include the scientific development of difficult but fair performance standards and the implementation of a pay-for-performance incentive plan based on work standards.

Scientific management had a tremendous influence on management practice in the early twentieth century. Although it does not represent a complete theory of management, it has contributed to the study of management and organizations in many areas, including human resource management and industrial engineering. Many of the tenets of scientific management are still valid today.

ADMINISTRATIVE MANAGEMENT. Administrative management focuses on the management process and principles of management. In contrast to scientific management, which deals largely with jobs and work at the individual level of analysis, administrative management provides a more general theory of management. Henri Fayol is the major contributor to this school of management thought.

Fayol was a management practitioner who brought his experience to bear on the subject of management functions and principles. He argued that management was a universal process consisting of functions, which he termed planning, organizing, commanding, coordinating, and controlling. Fayol believed that all managers performed these functions and that the functions distinguished management as a separate discipline of study apart from accounting, finance, and production. Fayol also presented fourteen principles of management, which included maxims related to the division of work, authority and responsibility, unity of command and direction, centralization, subordinate initiative, and team spirit.

Although administrative management has been criticized as being rigid and inflexible and the validity of the functional approach to management has been questioned, this school of thought still influences management theory and practice. The functional approach to management is still the dominant way of organizing management knowledge, and many of Fayol's principles of management, when applied with the flexibility that he advocated, are still considered relevant.

BUREAUCRATIC MANAGEMENT. Bureaucratic management focuses on the ideal form of organization. Max Weber was the major contributor to bureaucratic management. Based on observation, Weber concluded that many early organizations were inefficiently managed, with decisions based on personal relationships and loyalty. He proposed that a form of organization, called a bureaucracy, characterized by division of labor, hierarchy, formalized rules, impersonality, and the selection and promotion of employees based on ability, would lead to more efficient management. Weber also contended that managers' authority in an organization should be based not on tradition or charisma but on the position held by managers in the organizational hierarchy.

Bureaucracy has come to stand for inflexibility and waste, but Weber did not advocate or favor the excesses found in many bureaucratic organizations today. Weber's ideas formed the basis for modern organization theory and are still descriptive of some organizations.

THE BEHAVIORAL SCHOOL

The behavioral school of management thought developed, in part, because of perceived weaknesses in the assumptions of the classical school. The classical school emphasized efficiency, process, and principles. Some felt that this emphasis disregarded important aspects of organizational life, particularly as it related to human behavior. Thus, the behavioral school focused on trying to understand the factors that affect human behavior at work.

HUMAN RELATIONS. The Hawthorne Experiments began in 1924 and continued through the early 1930s. A variety of researchers participated in the studies, including Clair Turner, Fritz J. Roethlisberger, and Elton Mayo, whose respective books on the studies are perhaps the best known. One of the major conclusions of the Hawthorne studies was that workers' attitudes are associated with productivity. Another was that the workplace is a social system and informal group influence could exert a powerful effect on individual behavior. A third was that the style of supervision is an important factor in increasing workers' job satisfaction. The studies also found that organizations should take steps to assist employees in adjusting to organizational life by fostering collaborative systems between labor and management. Such conclusions sparked increasing interest in the human element at work; today, the Hawthorne studies are generally credited as the impetus for the human relations school.

According to the human relations school, the manager should possess skills for diagnosing the causes of human behavior at work, interpersonal communication, and motivating and leading workers. The focus became satisfying worker needs. If worker needs were satisfied, wisdom held, the workers would in turn be more productive. Thus, the human relations school focuses on issues of communication, leadership, motivation, and group behavior. The individuals who contributed to the school are too numerous to mention, but some of the best-known contributors include Mary Parker Follett, Chester Barnard, Abraham Maslow, Kurt Lewin, Renais Likert, and Keith Davis. The human relations school of thought still influences management theory and practice, as contemporary management focuses much attention on human resource management, organizational behavior, and applied psychology in the workplace.

BEHAVIORAL SCIENCE. Behavioral science and the study of organizational behavior emerged in the 1950s and 1960s. The behavioral science school was a natural progression of the human relations movement. It focused on applying conceptual and analytical tools to the problem of understanding and predicting behavior in the workplace. However, the study of behavioral science and organizational behavior was also a result of criticism of the human relations approach as simplistic and manipulative in its assumptions about the relationship between worker attitudes and productivity. The study of behavioral science in business schools was given increased credence by the 1959 Gordon and Howell report on higher education, which emphasized the importance to management practitioners of understanding human behavior.

The behavioral science school has contributed to the study of management through its focus on personality, attitudes, values, motivation, group behavior, leadership, communication, and conflict, among other issues. Some of the major contributors to this school include Douglas McGregor, Chris Argyris, Frederick

Herzberg, Renais Likert, and Ralph Stogdill, although there are many others.

THE QUANTITATIVE SCHOOL

The quantitative school focuses on improving decision making via the application of quantitative techniques. Its roots can be traced back to scientific management.

MANAGEMENT SCIENCE AND MIS. Management science (also called operations research) uses mathematical and statistical approaches to solve management problems. It developed during World War II as strategists tried to apply scientific knowledge and methods to the complex problems of war. Industry began to apply management science after the war. George Dantzig developed linear programming, an algebraic method to determine the optimal allocation of scarce resources. Other tools used in industry include inventory control theory, goal programming, queuing models, and simulation. The advent of the computer made many management science tools and concepts more practical for industry. Increasingly, management science and management information systems (MIS) are intertwined. MIS focuses on providing needed information to managers in a useful format and at the proper time. Decision support systems (DSS) attempt to integrate decision models, data, and the decision maker into a system that supports better management decisions.

PRODUCTION AND OPERATIONS MANAGEMENT. This school focuses on the operation and control of the production process that transforms resources into finished goods and services. It has its roots in scientific management but became an identifiable area of management study after World War II. It uses many of the tools of management science.

Operations management emphasizes productivity and quality of both manufacturing and service organizations. W. Edwards Deming exerted a tremendous influence in shaping modern ideas about improving productivity and quality. Major areas of study within operations management include capacity planning, facilities location, facilities layout, materials requirement planning, scheduling, purchasing and inventory control, quality control, computer integrated manufacturing, just-in-time inventory systems, and flexible manufacturing systems.

SYSTEMS SCHOOL

The systems school focuses on understanding the organization as an open system that transforms inputs into outputs. This school is based on the work of a biologist, Ludwig von Bertalanffy, who believed that a general systems model could be used to unite science. Early contributors to this school included Kenneth Boulding, Richard Johnson, Fremont Kast, and James Rosenzweig.

The systems school began to have a strong impact on management thought in the 1960s as a way of thinking about managing techniques that would allow managers to relate different specialties and parts of the company to one another, as well as to external environmental factors. The systems school focuses on the organization as a whole, its interaction with the environment, and its need to achieve equilibrium. General systems theory received a great deal of attention in the 1960s, but its influence on management thought has diminished somewhat. It has been criticized as too abstract and too complex. However, many of the ideas inherent in the systems school formed the basis for the contingency school of management.

CONTINGENCY SCHOOL

The contingency school focuses on applying management principles and processes as dictated by the unique characteristics of each situation. It emphasizes that there is no one best way to manage and that it depends on various situational factors, such as the external environment, technology, organizational characteristics, characteristics of the manager, and characteristics of the subordinates. Contingency theorists often implicitly or explicitly criticize the classical school for its emphasis on the universality of management principles; however, most classical writers recognized the need to consider aspects of the situation when applying management principles.

The contingency school originated in the 1960s. It has been applied primarily to management issues such as organizational design, job design, motivation, and leadership style. For example, optimal organizational structure has been theorized to depend upon organizational size, technology, and environmental uncertainty; optimal leadership style, meanwhile, has been theorized to depend upon a variety of factors, including task structure, position power, characteristics of the work group, characteristics of individual subordinates, quality requirements, and problem structure, to name a few. A few of the major contributors to this school of management thought include Joan Woodward, Paul Lawrence, Jay Lorsch, and Fred Fiedler, among many others.

CONTEMPORARY "SCHOOLS" OF MANAGEMENT THOUGHT

Management research and practice continues to evolve and new approaches to the study of management continue to be advanced. This section briefly reviews two contemporary approaches: total quality management (TQM) and the learning organization. While neither of these management approaches offer a complete theory of management, they do offer additional insights into the management field.

TOTAL QUALITY MANAGEMENT. Total quality management (TQM) is a philosophy or approach to management that focuses on managing the entire organization to deliver quality goods and services to customers. This approach to management was implemented in Japan after World War II and was a major factor in their economic renaissance. TQM has at least four major elements. Employee involvement is essential in preventing quality problems before they occur. A customer focus means that the organization must attempt to determine customer needs and wants and deliver products and services that address them.

Benchmarking means that the organization is always seeking out other organizations that perform a function or process more effectively and using them as a standard, or benchmark, to judge their own performance. The organization will also attempt to adapt or improve the processes used by other companies. Finally, a philosophy of continuous improvement means that the organization is committed to incremental changes and improvements over time in all areas of the organization. TQM has been implemented by many companies worldwide and appears to have fostered performance improvements in many organizations. Perhaps the best-known proponent of this school of management was W. Edwards Deming.

LEARNING ORGANIZATION. The contemporary organization faces unprecedented environmental and technological change. Thus, one of the biggest challenges for organizations is to continuously change in a way that meets the demands of this turbulent competitive environment. The learning organization can be defined as one in which all employees are involved in identifying and solving problems, which allows the organization to continually increase its ability to grow, learn, and achieve its purpose. The organizing principle of the learning organization is not efficiency, but problem solving. Three key aspects of the learning organization are a team-based structure, empowered employees, and open information. Peter Senge is one of the best-known experts on learning organizations.

SEE ALSO: Knowledge Management; Management Functions; Management Information Systems; Management Science; Management Styles; Organizational Behavior; Organizational Development; Organizational Learning; Organizing; Quality and Total Quality Management

Tim Barnett

FURTHER READING:

Daft, Richard L. *Management.* 7th ed. Australia: Thomson/ South-Western, 2005.

Fayol, Henri. *General and Industrial Administration.* London: Sir Issac Pitman & Sons, Ltd., 1949.

Griffin, Ricky W. *Management.* 8th ed. Boston: Houghton Mifflin Company.

Lewis, Pamela S., Stephen H. Goodman, and Patricia M. Fandt. *Management.* 2nd ed. Cincinnati: South-Western College Publishing, 1998.

Locke, Edwin A. "The Ideas of Frederick W. Taylor: An Evaluation." *Academy of Management Review* 7, no. 1 (1982): 14–24.

O'Connor, Ellen S. "The Politics of Management Thought: A Case Study of the Harvard Business School and the Human Relations School." *Academy of Management Review* 24, no. 1 (1999): 117–131.

Robbins, Stephen P., and Mary Coulter. *Management.* 6th ed. Upper Saddle River, NJ: Prentice Hall, 1999.

Senge, Peter. *The Fifth Discipline: The Art and Practice of Learning Organizations.* New York: Doubleday/Currency, 1990.

Warner, Malcolm. "Organizational Behavior Revisited." *Human Relations* 47, no. 10 (1994): 1151–1164.

Wren, Daniel. *The Evolution of Management Thought.* 3rd ed. New York: John Wiley and Sons, 1987.

MANAGEMENT AND EXECUTIVE DEVELOPMENT

Manager effectiveness has an enormous impact on a firm's success. Therefore, companies must provide instruction for managers and high-potential management candidates in order to help them perform current and future jobs with the utmost proficiency. Management development has long been an important component of corporate strategic planning. In fact, many companies consider the identification and development of next-generation managers to be their top human resource challenge.

Management development is important for new managers because these individuals really need instruction on how to perform their new supervisory jobs. Even so, companies often allow employees to make the transition to management with little or no training, leaving them with feelings of frustration, inadequacy, and dismay. More experienced managers also benefit from management development. A majority of first-line managers have their sights set on higher-level management jobs. Given these ambitions, companies need to provide lower-level and mid-level managers with formal development programs in order to help them climb the corporate ladder.

Management instruction programs should bridge gaps between what individuals already know and what they need to know for their new positions. Managers need different skills at each managerial level. The instructional programs needed to produce these skills are shown in Table 1.

Table 1

Instructional Needs at Different Managerial Levels

First-line managers need training in
- basic supervision
- motivation
- career planning
- performance feedback

Middle managers need training in
- designing and implementing effective group and intergroup work and information systems
- defining and monitoring group-level performance indicators
- diagnosing and resolving problems within and among work groups
- designing and implementing reward systems that support cooperative behavior

Executives need training in
- broadening their understanding of how factors such as competition, world economies, politics, and social trends influence the effectiveness of the organization

---

A variety of approaches are used to teach these subjects. Some are in traditional classroom-type settings, while others are taught outside of the classroom via career resource centers, job rotation, mentoring, and special projects.

CLASSROOM INSTRUCTION

Classroom training takes place within the organization or outside at seminars and universities. The subjects typically covered in these programs are briefly described in Table 2.

LECTURE. Most training experts criticize lectures because they are passive learning devices, focusing on one-way communication to learners who do not have the opportunity to clarify material. Lectures generally fail to gain and maintain learner attention unless they are given by someone who is able to make the material meaningful and promote questions and discussions. Lectures are most appropriate for situations where simple knowledge acquisition is the goal (e.g., describing company history during a new employee orientation session). However, lectures are not well suited to serve as the sole training method for teaching management skills, because the format does not provide trainees with feedback or the opportunity for practice.

Table 2

Content Areas of Classroom Instruction

Job Duties and Responsibilities. Trainees learn what they must do to fulfill the company's expectations of them.

Policies and Procedures. Trainees learn company police and procedures.

Employee Familiarization. Trainees become familiar with the job functions of their employees. The training provides specific instructions on how to review job descriptions, performance standards, personnel files, and so forth.

Attitudes and Confidence. The training attempts to establish new attitudes toward the job employees, and the manager, and to build the confidence necessary for managers to be effective on the job.

Handling Employee Interactions. Trainees are taught how to handle interpersonal problems effectively through such techniques as behavior modeling.

Career Development. Trainees learn about career opportunities in higher levels of management and how they may advance in the future.

General Management Training. These courses typically cover labor relations, management theory and practice, labor economics, and general management functions.

Human Relations/Leadership Programs. These topics are narrower than general management programs. They focus on the human relations problems of leadership, supervision, attitude toward employees, and communication.

Self-Awareness Program. The content of these programs is understanding one's own behavior and how that behavior is viewed by others, identifying the so-called games people play, and learning about one's strengths and weaknesses.

Problem-Solving/Decision-Making Programs. The emphasis is on teaching generalized problem-solving and decision-making skills that would be applicable to the wide range of work problems that managers encounter.

CASE METHOD. As the name suggests, the case method requires management trainees to analyze cases or scenarios depicting realistic job situations. Cases often are structured like a play that opens in the middle of a story and uses flashbacks to describe the action that led up to the opening scene, where an employee has just made a key decision. The rest of the case lays out the documentation and data available to the decision maker at the time of the decision. Questions are posed at the end of the case that ask the trainees to analyze the situation and recommend a solution. For instance, they may be asked to state the nature of the problem, identify the events that led to the problem, and indicate what the individual should do to resolve the problem.

The case method rests on the assumption that people are most likely to retain and use what they learn if they reach an understanding through "guided discovery." Trainers act as guides or facilitators. Cases typically do not have right or wrong answers. Therefore, the aim of the method is not to teach trainees the "right" answer, but rather to teach them how to identify potential problems and recommend realistic actions.

Critics of this method balk at the lack of direction trainees receive when analyzing a case. What if they arrive at a poor decision? Moreover, trainees do not get the opportunity to practice their skills. For instance, after analyzing a case involving a subordinate who has repeatedly arrived at work late, the trainees may conclude that the manager should have said something sooner and must now provide counsel. However, the case method does not afford trainees the opportunity to practice their counseling skills.

ROLE-PLAYING. As an instructional technique, role-playing presents a hypothetical problem involving human interaction. Trainees spontaneously act out that interaction face-to-face. Participants are then given feedback by the trainer and the rest of the group on their performance so they may gain insight regarding the impact of their behavior on others. The issues addressed during feedback typically revolve around these types of questions:

- What was correct about the participant's behavior?

- What was incorrect about the participant's behavior?

- How did the participant's behavior make the other participants feel?

- How could the trainee have handled the situation more effectively?

Role-playing may be used to develop skill in any area that involves human interaction. The method is most often used for teaching human relations skills and sales techniques. Role-playing provides management trainees with an opportunity to practice the skill being taught. It thus goes beyond the case method, which merely requires the trainee to make a decision regarding how to handle a situation. These two methods are often used in conjunction with one another. That is, after analyzing a case and recommending a solution, trainees are asked to act out the solution in the form of a role-play.

Critics of the role-playing method point out that role-players are often given little guidance beforehand on how to handle transactions. This may cause them to make mistakes, resulting in embarrassment and a loss of self-confidence. When their mistake-ridden role-play is finished, they sit, never getting the opportunity to do it correctly.

BEHAVIOR MODELING. Behavior modeling is based on the idea that workers learn best when they see how a task should be performed and then practice the task with feedback until they are competent. This method is similar to role-playing in that the trainees act out situations playing certain roles. However, the methods differ in two important ways. First, behavior modeling teaches trainees a preferred way to perform a task. Second, the interactions occurring during behavior modeling are practice sessions, not role plays. The trainees practice only the right way. If they make a mistake, the trainer immediately corrects them and asks them to repeat the step correctly.

A behavior modeling program typically consists of the following steps:

1. Present an overview of the material. This usually consists of a brief lecture that describes training objectives and the importance of the skill to be learned.

2. Describe the procedural steps. The trainee learns the one best way (or at least an effective way) to handle a situation. Case and role-playing methods, on the other hand, stress the variety of effective ways to handle a situation and do not emphasize any one particular approach.

3. Model or demonstrate the procedural steps. The trainee is shown a "model" of how the task is to be performed correctly. The model usually is presented in the form of a videotape or live demonstration.

4. Allow guided practice. Trainees then practice the modeled behaviors. As previously stated, these sessions are similar to role-plays, except that trainees are given feedback by the instructor (or classmates) during the skill practice session, rather than after. This procedure forces trainees to correct mistakes as soon as they are made, assuring them an opportunity to practice the correct way of performing the task. Practice sessions start with simple problems, similar to those depicted in the model. Later practice sessions are made more realistic by adding complexity to the situation.

5. Provide on-the-job reinforcement. Participants' managers often go through identical training programs to ensure that they will understand what their employees are learning and, hence, support these new behaviors back on the job.

Behavior modeling has become very popular. Research examining its effectiveness has been quite favorable. Behavior modeling works because it successfully incorporates each of the aforementioned learning principles: it captures and maintains trainees' attention and provides ample opportunity for practice and feedback.

NONCLASSROOM METHODS

Nonclassroom methods include career resource centers, job rotation, coaching and mentoring, and special assignments.

CAREER RESOURCE CENTERS. Some organizations make learning opportunities available to interested candidates by establishing career resource centers, which usually include an in-house library with relevant reading material. In some companies, candidates simply are given recommended readings lists. Other companies provide management candidates with comprehensive career-planning guides that contain company-related information about available resources, career options, and counseling contacts. These individuals also may be given workbooks that provide written assignments.

JOB ROTATION. Job rotation exposes management trainees to various organizational settings by rotating them through a number of departments. Thus, trainees have an opportunity to gain an overall perspective of the organization and learn how various parts interrelate. Additionally, they face new challenges during these assignments that may foster new skill development. Trainees usually have full management responsibility during these assignments. For example, in one hospital new department supervisors rotate through all major departments on a monthly basis, serving in a managerial capacity during their "tours." Although they often learn a lot from such training, they also may make harmful mistakes during their learning period because they lack knowledge of the functional area that they are supervising.

COACHING AND MENTORING. Coaching is a method of management development that is conducted on the job, in which experienced managers or peers advise and guide trainees in solving managerial problems. Typically, less experienced managers are coached by their direct supervisor or a coworker on their specific performance of managerial tasks. An upper-level manager is likely to coach several lower-level managers at once, offering feedback, helping them to find expert advice, and providing resources.

Mentoring is different from coaching in several ways. Mentors are experienced supervisors who establish close, one-on-one relationships with new managers, called protégés. A mentor usually is someone two or three levels higher in the organization than the protégé who teaches, guides, advises, counsels, and serves as a role model; the mentor is not necessarily the protégé's direct supervisor. Mentoring can help the protégé to form common values with the organization's senior leadership and better understand his or her role in the company. Additionally, protégés are often advocated for and protected by a mentor. A mentor may ensure that the protégé is assigned high-

visibility projects, or even change negative opinions about the protégé that may be held by others in the company. While a coach focuses on job-specific advice, a mentor is likely to give advice on a broader range of topics related to the protégé's career success.

SPECIAL ASSIGNMENT. Companies sometimes assign special, nonroutine job duties to trainees in order to prepare them for future assignments. One such special project is called action learning, which derives its name from the fact that the trainees can learn by doing. Candidates are given real problems generated by management. Trainees might be given a written assignment that specifies objectives, action plans, target dates, and the name of the person responsible for monitoring the completion of the assignment. For instance, trainees might be asked to study the company's budgeting procedures and submit a written critique.

Another type of special project is the task force, where trainees are grouped together and asked to tackle an actual organizational problem. For example, the task force may be asked to develop a new performance appraisal form, solve a quality problem, or design a program to train new employees. Trainees not only gain valuable experience by serving on a task force, they also have the opportunity to "show their stuff" to others within the organization.

MANAGEMENT SUCCESSION PLANNING

Most organizations base their management development and training efforts on succession planning, a systematic process of defining future management requirements and identifying the candidates who best meet them. Unfortunately, many companies take a very informal approach to succession planning. Identification of high-potential candidates is largely subjective, based on the opinions of the nominating managers, who choose "fast-track" or "superstar" employees with little consideration of the actual requirements of future positions. Research has found that promotions within the management ranks are often based on employee behaviors that have no bearing on managerial effectiveness; specifically, networking had the greatest influence on managerial promotions, even though networking made no contribution to actual performance. Additionally, ill-conceived succession planning activities can have disastrous consequences; as many as 30 percent of all newly placed executives are unprepared for their jobs and ultimately fail to meet company expectations.

Elements of an effective succession planning program involve human resource planning, defining qualifications for positions, identifying career paths, and developing replacement charts. The first step in succession planning is human resource planning, in which forecasting is used to determine projected staffing needs for the next several years. Based on these needs, management succession plans should specify key management positions for which staffing should be targeted. Succession plans should next define pertinent individual qualifications needed for each targeted position, which are based on information derived from a job analysis. A firm then identifies individuals with high potential for promotion into or through the management ranks. This is accomplished by assessing employee abilities and career interests through records of career progress, experience, past performance, and self-reported interests regarding future career steps.

Following the above steps, an organization identifies a career path for each high-potential candidate (i.e., those who have the interest and ability to move upward in the organization). A career path typically appears as a flow chart, indicating the sequencing of specific jobs that may lead one up the organizational ladder to a targeted job. The final step is to develop replacement charts that indicate the availability of candidates and their readiness to step into the various management positions. Such charts usually are depicted as diagrams superimposed onto the organizational chart. These show possible replacement candidates, in rank order, for each management position. Rank orders are often based on the candidates' "overall potential scores," derived on the basis of their past performance, experience, test scores, and so on.

SEE ALSO: Employee Evaluation and Performance Appraisals; Human Resource Management

Lawrence S. Kleiman
Revised by Marcia Simmering

FURTHER READING:

Blanchard, P. Nick, and James W. Thacker. *Effective Training: Systems, Strategies, and Practices.* 2nd ed. Upper Saddle River, NJ: Pearson Prentice Hall, 2003.

Goldstein, Irwin L., and J. Kevin Ford. *Training in Organizations.* 4th ed. Belmont, CA: Wadsworth Group, 2002.

Kleiman, Lawrence S. *Human Resource Management: A Managerial Tool for Competitive Advantage.* Cincinnati: South-Western College Publishing, 2000.

Noe, Raymond A. *Employee Training and Development.* Boston: Irwin/McGraw-Hill, 1999.

MANAGING CHANGE

One of the concepts discussed, written about, and analyzed most frequently in recent years has been organizational change and the related concepts of resistance to change and management of change.

Change has been variously defined as making a material difference in something compared to an earlier state, transforming or converting something, or simply becoming different. All of these definitions can be applied to change as it occurs within organizations and businesses. Organizational change may mean changing technological infrastructures (e.g., moving from a mainframe environment to distributed computing), marketing strategies (targeting a new customer base), or management and decision-making practices.

Organizational change is not new to the American business landscape. Since the nineteenth century and the Industrial Revolution, corporations have had to deal with change on an increasingly rapid scale. The greater the technological developments and the greater the amount of products and information generated, the more necessary it becomes for corporations to provide effective management and develop solid organizational practices. The most revered business professionals of the United States have been those who were best able to exploit changes in business and the economy. For example, in the late nineteenth century, Andrew Carnegie greatly expanded his empire by purchasing the very businesses he depended on for his steel business, making his company one of the first successful examples of vertical integration.

Beginning in the 1990s, change came at an exponentially faster rate due to factors such as increased competition in a global economy, expanding markets, new ways of doing business (such as e-commerce), and the omnipresent task of keeping up with the latest technology. Management guru Peter F. Drucker devoted his book *Management Challenges of the 21 Century* to that very topic. As a result, businesses had to revise (or devise) corporate missions and goals, management practices, and day-to-day business functions. Companies routinely began redesigning business strategies, often replacing traditional hierarchical organization charts with flatter structures centered around "empowered" teams.

The ultimate goal for most organizations is to change corporate climate and culture. An organization's climate can be defined by how its employees view the organization's fundamental reason for being, specifically, the company's overall mission and goals and how important the employees' sense of well-being is to those goals. The corporate climate then breeds an organizational culture that consists of what employees see as management's beliefs and value systems. These two things, climate and culture, then determine how each manager and employee shapes his or her own performance, usually in order to most successfully meet company goals and hopefully ensuring his or her own success as well as the company's. These factors affect every aspect of each person's job, including decision-making processes, communication patterns within the organization, and individual accountability and responsibility.

INDICATORS OF CHANGE

There are four primary indicators of major workplace change. They are a change to the organizational structure, a new product or service, new management, and new technology. Organizational structure may change through major downsizing, outsourcing, acquisitions, or mergers. These actions are often accompanied by layoffs, particularly as certain positions become redundant. A new product or service has implications for changes in production, sales, and customer service. Additionally, by changing product or service the organization may face new competitors or new markets. New management, such as a change in chief executive officer or president, often brings a period of transition during which upper-level managers are likely to alter existing business processes and personnel policies. Finally, new technology can create vast changes to the organization. Technology can change the production process or the working conditions (i.e., telecommuting), and these changes may influence the skills that employees use on the job.

ROUTINE VERSUS NON-ROUTINE CHANGE

There are changes in organizations that are routine (e.g., they are commonplace and often expected), and there are those that are not routine (e.g., unique and unexpected). Examples of routine changes are organizational turnover and staffing replacements, small changes to products or services, or changes in human resources policies. Routine changes are the easiest to manage, and employees are somewhat accustomed to routine changes. There is typically little concern over implementing such changes. However, if not handled properly by management, even routine change can prove to be difficult. If changes are not implemented properly or not well communicated, problems may arise. For example, a small change to the company vacation policy may seem insignificant to management, but if employees are not properly apprised of the change it could result in considerable difficulty if employees do not follow the new policy.

Non-routine change is much more difficult than routine change; it can be unpredictable, significant, or even radical, and employees are much less likely to adapt well to non-routine change. In general, a non-routine change is seen as threatening, and employees are likely to be resistant. For instance, if a company announces a merger with a former competitor, this non-routine change is very likely to create anxiety about compensation and job security.

TYPES OF CHANGE

In addition to some of the major indicators of organizational change and the broad distinction of routine versus non-routine change, change can be categorized even more specifically into four categories: structural change, cost change, process change, and cultural change. Structural change occurs when there is an alteration to the company's organizational structure. This reorganization may occur due to a merger or acquisition, or it may be the result of a restructuring. For instance, an organization that is intent on increasing its innovation may reorganize its traditional functional structure into a more flexible matrix structure that uses small, self-managed teams. Or, an organization that is expanding into new markets may adopt a divisional structure in which different geographic locations operate nearly independently of one another.

Cost changes are those that occur when an organization attempts to reduce costs in order to improve efficiency or performance. Major adjustments may be made to departments to cut costs; reducing budgets, laying off employees in redundant positions, and eliminating nonessential activities may all be a result of cost change.

Process changes are implemented to improve efficiency or effectiveness of organizational procedures. This may occur in production settings; there may be changes to how a product is created, assembled, packaged, or shipped. Or, in a service organization, there may be changes to the procedures used to accomplish work; new computer systems may create the need to change how paperwork is completed, or a new manager may modify the process used to handle customer complaints.

Cultural changes are the least tangible of all the types of change, but they can be the most difficult. An organization's culture is its shared set of assumptions, values, and beliefs. A prototypical culture is the very bureaucratic, top-down style in which stability and standard processes are valued. When such an organization tries to adopt a more participative, involved style, this requires a shift in many organizational activities. Primarily, manager-employee relations are altered with a change in culture.

IMPLEMENTING CHANGE

To properly implement change, management must take a number of steps: involving key people, developing a plan, supporting the plan, and communicating often.

1. The first step in implementing change is involving the key people; this typically means upper-level management and other

executives whose processes and employees will be affected by the change. For instance, if a new computer system is to be installed in all areas of a company, key people would be not only top managers, but also lower-level managers who supervise the employees' use of the new technology. A different set of key people would be involved in a cost-cutting change. If the company is reducing its operating budget in a specific division, the managers of that division and also human resources personnel should be involved. In any circumstance in which there is a change to personnel policies or in which demotions, transfers, or layoffs occur, the human resources department should be involved to manage this change.

2. After key personnel have been identified and properly involved, the second step in implementing change is to develop a plan for effective transformation. The plan should help to define the responsibilities of the key people involved while also laying out short-term and long-term objectives for the changes. Because change can be unpredictable, the plan should also be flexible enough to accommodate new occurrences.

3. The third step in implementing change is to support the plan; this means that management follows through on the plan it created. Key to this step is enabling employees to adapt to the change. Employees may need training, reward systems may need to be adapted, or hiring may be required. If the organization does not provide the support necessary for the plan to take effect, it is unlikely to succeed.

4. The final step in successful change implementation should occur throughout the change process. Communicating with employees about what is occurring, why the changes are being made, and how they will develop is critical. Because change can create a lot of fear, increased communication can be used to calm employees and encourage their continued support. In addition to downward communication, managers should pay attention to any upward communication that occurs. They should be available to take suggestions or answer questions that employees might have. Creating opportunities for employee feedback, such as holding meetings or having an open-door management policy, may facilitate change more successfully.

RESISTANCE TO CHANGE

As a general rule, it is not the proposed changes that people resist, but the impact that the changes will have on them, personally. People become comfortable in their jobs, in their areas of expertise, and in their relationships with coworkers and managers. Even when personnel are not very satisfied with the current workplace and therefore welcome change, they may find change to be stressful. Helping employees anticipate difficulties and informing employees of how these challenges will be handled can be a source of comfort to them. When an organization proposes large-scale change, those affected begin to worry about how their jobs will change, what new skills they will need, if their responsibilities will change, how established lines of communication will be altered, and how working relationships will change. The most successful members of a company may feel threatened because they were able to perform so well under the old organizational structure. Some common employee reactions to change include confusion, denial, loss of identity, and anger. And this resistance is not limited to employees—managers and executives may be just as prone as employees to experiencing problems with radical organizational change.

In their article "Challenging 'Resistance to Change,'" Eric B. Dent and Susan Galloway Goldberg discuss their research on the origins of this concept and the prevalent idea that managers must overcome this resistance or are doomed to failure. Kurt Lewin, the mid-twentieth-century social psychologist, introduced the term "resistance to change" as a systems concept affecting managers and employees equally. The term, and not its original context, was adopted and used as a psychological concept placing employees against managers. Dent and Goldberg feel that letting go of the term and its associations could help more useful models of change dynamics move forward.

There are theories of handling resistance to change that are related to this idea. While not explicitly questioning the use of the term, changing how organizations view resistance allows change to become an opportunity and not just a potential threat. Change is a personally challenging issue for everyone affected, but it also carries with it new possibilities. How corporate management responds to employee resistance can determine the fate of the organization. For example, a sense of confusion—usually represented by constant questioning from management and/or employees—usually means that not enough information has been provided. This can become an opportunity to convey additional information to employees, such as reiterating the big picture and why the company is working so hard to redefine its corporate culture. This is also a good time to provide assurances that management is going to take the time to address concerns.

Another common reaction is doubt or denial that actual change will occur. This reaction occurs sometimes because employees do not want change, and at other times because they do not believe management is fully committed to the idea. In any case, these reactions can also represent an opportunity for management to identify issues that may be present across the organization and address them. They can also alert management and higher-ups that actual implementation is not consistent with the plan that was put forth. A possibly related reaction is anger, sometimes accompanied by attempts to sabotage the company's efforts to change. Again, there can be benefits to this type of behavior. Employees who so visually make their feelings known let organizational leaders in on which impediments to change are likely to occur, and management can then formulate ways to address them. It also opens up areas for negotiation.

Peter Senge and his co-authors identified ten "challenges of change" (preferring the term "challenges" to "resistance") in the 1999 work *The Dance of Change: The Challenges to Sustaining Momentum in Learning Organizations.* As reported in *Fast Company,* he formalized these challenges as common excuses that are offered as reasons for resistance. These excuses can then be countered by addressing the real concerns behind them. For example, "This stuff isn't relevant" indicates the need for continuous and open communication from people who can convince others of the driving need for change in an organization. "This stuff isn't working" indicates a need for management to provide measurable criteria for success and clear expectations. "They. . .never let us do this stuff" indicates that, while management may be claiming to offer groups and teams more autonomy, they are really having trouble letting go of their control.

Another concern is the fact that people who consider themselves specialists or experts in a given area are often asked to start over (e.g., working in a different functional area or using different technology), sometimes more than once when companies make cross-training one of their goals. Again, this threatens the comfort zone for many people at all levels of an organization. Having proven themselves once, they are being asked to do so over again. In order to allay these fears, management needs to encourage people to ask questions, take initiative, and take risks. Fear of failure is possibly one of the strongest reasons for resisting change. Companies that hope change will be embraced need to view risks and failures as tools through which the organization can learn and grow.

Along these same lines, resistance need not be a dirty word. Whereas organizations once felt it was most important to put a positive spin on everything, corporate management is realizing that showing their own concerns about organizational change helps other personnel to deal with theirs. It also affords them the opportunity to teach others how to identify best practices under less than ideal circumstances, and to let employees know they empathize with their concerns.

Resistance to change, as put forth by Kurt Lewin, affects managers and employees equally when systems undergo change. As such, resistance is a naturally occurring phenomenon that can be dealt with in a constructive manner. In a sense, resistance is a sign that radical change is indeed occurring and that an organization is not just redefining the status quo. Management can help by anticipating common reactions and using them to their best advantage. For instance, if an employee is able to make requested changes to his or her performance but not willing to do so, some negotiation might be all that is required to convince that person to follow along with the company's new direction. For those who buy into the need for change but lack some of the necessary skills, targeted training could be all that is needed to quell the fears of those people. Whatever the resistance an organization encounters, it is almost a guaranteed part of change, which has become a constant in the business landscape. With the globalization of markets and speeding technological innovation, an organization cannot afford to rest on its laurels.

SEE ALSO: Organizational Culture; Trends in Organizational Change

Wendy H. Mason
Revised by Marcia J. Simmering

FURTHER READING:

Champy, James, and Nitin Nohria, eds. *Fast Forward: The Best Ideas on Managing Change.* New York: McGraw-Hill, 1996.

Dent, Eric B., and Susan Galloway Goldberg. "Challenging 'Resistance to Change.'" *Journal of Applied Behavioral Science* (March 1999): 25.

DuBrin, Andrew J. *Essentials of Management.* 6th ed. Thomson South-Western, 2003.

Hampton, John J., ed. *AMA Management Handbook.* 3rd ed. New York: American Management Association, 1994.

Managing Change and Transition. Boston: Harvard Business School Press, 2003.

Ristino, Robert J. *The Agile Manager's Guide to Managing Change.* Bristol, VT: Velocity Business Publishing, 2000.

Senge, Peter M., Art Kleiner, Charlotte Roberts, George Roth, Rick Ross, and Bryan Smith. *The Dance of Change: The Challenges to Sustaining Momentum in Learning Organizations.* New York: Doubleday, 1999.

Sims, Ronald R. *Changing the Way We Manage Change.* Westport, CT: Praeger, 2002.

Williams, Chuck. *Management.* Cincinnati: South-Western College Publishing, 2000.

MANUFACTURING RESOURCES PLANNING

Manufacturing resource planning, also known as MRP II, is a method for the effective planning of a manufacturer's resources. MRP II is composed of several linked functions, such as business planning, sales and operations planning, capacity requirements planning, and all related support systems. The output from these MRP II functions can be integrated into financial reports, such as the business plan, purchase commitment report, shipping budget, and inventory projections. It has the capability of specifically addressing operational planning and financial planning, and has simulation capability that allows its users to conduct sensitivity analyses (answering "what if" questions).

The earliest form of manufacturing resource planning was known as material requirements planning (MRP). This system was vastly improved upon until it no longer resembled the original version. The newer version was so fundamentally different from MRP, that a new term seemed appropriate. Oliver Wight coined the acronym MRP II for manufacturing resource planning.

In order to best understand MRP II, one must have a basic understanding of MRP, so we will begin with a look at MRP and then expand into MRP II.

MATERIAL REQUIREMENTS PLANNING

Material requirements planning (MRP) is a computer-based, time-phased system for planning and controlling the production and inventory function of a firm from the purchase of materials to the shipment of finished goods. All MRP systems are computer based since the detail involved and the inherent burden of computation make manual use prohibitive. MRP is time phased because it not only determines what and how much needs to be made or purchased, but also when.

Material requirements planning first appeared in the early 1970s and was popularized by a book of the same name by Joseph Orlicky. Its use was quickly heralded as the new manufacturing panacea, but enthusiasm slowed somewhat when firms began to realize the difficulty inherent in its implementation.

The MRP system is composed of three primary modules, all of which function as a form of input. These are the master production schedule, the bill-of-materials, and the inventory status file. Each module serves a unique purpose that is inter-related with the purpose of the other modules, and produces several forms of usable output.

MASTER PRODUCTION SCHEDULE. The master production schedule (MPS) is basically the production schedule for finished goods. This schedule is usually derived from current orders, plus any forecast requirements. The MPS is divided into units of time called "buckets." While any time frame may be utilized, usually days or weeks is appropriate. The MPS is also said to be the aggregate plan "disaggregated." In other words, the plan for goods to be produced in aggregate is broken down into its individual units or finished goods.

BILL-OF-MATERIALS. The bill-of-materials is a file made up of bills-of-material (BOM). Each BOM is a hierarchical listing of the type and number of parts needed to produce one unit of finished goods. Other information, such as the routings (the route through the system that individual parts take on the way to becoming a finished good), alternate routings, or substitute materials may be also be contained with the BOM.

A tool known as a product structure tree is used to clarify the relationship among the parts making up each unit of finished goods. Figure 1 details how a product structure tree for a rolling cart might appear on a bill-of-material. This cart consists of a top that is pressed from a sheet of steel; a frame formed from four steel bars; and a leg assembly consisting of four legs, each with a caster attached. Each caster is made up of a wheel, a ball bearing, an axle, and a caster frame.

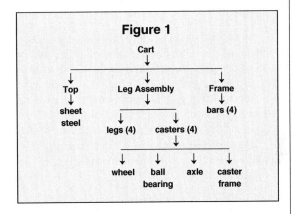

Figure 1

Cart

Top / Leg Assembly / Frame

Top → sheet steel

Frame → bars (4)

Leg Assembly → legs (4)   casters (4)

casters → wheel   ball bearing   axle   caster frame

The bill-of-material can be used to determine the gross number of component parts needed to manufacturer a given number of finished goods. Since a gross number is determined, safety stock can be reduced because component parts may be shared by any number of finished goods (this is known as commonality).

The process of determining gross requirements of components is termed the "explosion" process, or "exploding" the bill-of-material. Assuming we need 100 rolling carts, we can use our example product structure tree to compute the gross requirements for each rolling cart component. We can easily see that in order to produce 100 rolling carts, we would need 100 tops, which would require 100 sheets of steel; 100 leg assemblies, which would require 400 legs and 400 casters (requiring 400 wheels, 400 ball bearings, 400 axles, and 400 caster frames); and 100 frames, which would require 400 bars.

INVENTORY STATUS FILE. The inventory status file, or inventory records file, contains a count of the on-hand balance of every part held in inventory. In addition, the inventory status file contains all pertinent information regarding open orders and the lead time (the time that elapses between placing an order and actually receiving it) for each item.

Open orders are purchase orders (orders for items purchased outside the firm) or shop orders (formal instructions to the plant floor to process a given number of parts by a given date) that have not been completely satisfied. In other words, they are items that have been ordered, but are yet to be received.

THE MRP PROCESS. The MRP logic starts at the MPS, where it learns the schedule for finished goods (how many and when). It takes this information to the BOM where it "explodes" the gross requirements for all component parts. The MRP package then takes its knowledge of the gross requirements for all components parts to the inventory status file, where the on-hand balances are listed. It then subtracts the on-hand balances and open orders from the gross requirements for components yielding the net requirements for each component.

Of course, we now know not only how many components are needed but when they are needed in order to complete the schedule for finished goods on time. By subtracting the lead time from the due date for each part, we now see when an order must be placed for each part so that it can be received in time to avoid a delay in the MPS. A manual version of MRP for a part with requirements of 100 in period 3 and 250 in period 6 and with a two-period lead time is shown in Figure 2.

Notice that in order for the firm to meet demand on time (the MPS), they must place an order for 25 in Period 1 and an order for 200 in Period 4. The reader should be aware that this is an overly simplified version of MRP, which does not include such relevant factors as lot sizing and safety stock.

EXPANDING INTO MRP II

With MRP generating the material and schedule requirements necessary for meeting the appropriate sales and inventory demands, more than the obvious manufacturing resources for supporting the MRP plan was found to be needed. Financial resources would have to be generated in varying amounts and timing. Also, the process would require varying degrees of marketing resource support. Production, marketing, and finance would be operating without complete knowledge or even regard for what the other functional areas of the firm were doing.

In the early 1980s MRP was expanded into a much broader approach. This new approach, manufacturing resource planning (MRP II), was an effort to expand the scope of production resource planning and to involve other functional areas of the firm in the planning process, most notably marketing and finance, but also engineering, personnel, and purchasing. Incorporation of other functional areas allows all areas of the firm to focus on a common set of goals. It also provides a means for generating a variety of reports to help managers in varying functions monitor the process and make necessary adjustments as the work progresses.

When finance knows which items will be purchased and when products will be delivered, it can accurately project the firm's cash flows. In addition, personnel can project hiring or layoff requirements, while marketing can keep track of up-to-the-minute changes in delivery times, lead times, and so on. Cost accounting information is gathered, engineering input

Figure 2

	1	2	3	4	5	6
Gross Requirements			100			250
Scheduled Receipts (open orders)			50		50	
On Hand (inventory balance)	25	25	25	0	0	50
Net Requirements			25			200
Planned Order Receipt			25			200
Planned Order Release	25			200		

is recorded, and distribution requirements planning is performed.

An MRP II system also has a simulation capability that enables its users to conduct sensitivity analyses or evaluate a variety of possible scenarios. The MRP II system can simulate a certain decision's impact throughout the organization, and predict its results in terms of customer orders, due dates, or other "what if" outcomes. Being able to answer these "what if" questions provides a firmer grasp of available options and their potential consequences.

As with MRP, MRP II requires a computer system for implementation because of its complexity and relatively large scale. Pursuit of MRP or MRP II in a clerical fashion would prove far too cumbersome to ever be useful.

In addition to its efficient performance of the data processing and file handling, a computer also allows the system to run remarkably quick, providing near-immediate results and reports when asked to simulate a decision.

CLASSES OF FIRMS USING MRP AND MRP II

MRP and MRP II users are classified by the degree to which they utilize the various aspects of these systems. Class D companies have MRP working in their data processing area, but utilize little more than the inventory status file and the master production schedule, both of which may be poorly used and mismanaged. Typically, these firms are not getting much return for the expense incurred by the system.

Class C firms use their MRP system as an inventory ordering technique but make little use of its scheduling capabilities.

Class B companies utilize the basic MRP system (MPS, BOM, and Inventory file) with the addition of capacity requirements planning and a shop floor control system. Class B users have not incorporated purchasing into the system and do not have a management team that uses the system to run the business, but rather see it as a production and inventory control system.

Class A firms are said use the system in a closed loop mode. Their system consists of the basic MRP system, plus capacity planning and control, shop floor control, and vendor scheduling systems. In addition, their management uses the system to run the business. The system provides the game plan for sales, finance, manufacturing, purchasing, and engineering. Management then can use the system's report capability to monitor accuracy in the BOM, the inventory status file, and routing, as well as monitor the attainment of the MPS and capacity plans.

Class A firms have also tied in the financial system and have developed the system's simulation capabilities to answer "what if" questions. Because everyone is using the same numbers (e.g., finance and production), management has to work with only one set of numbers to run the business.

DEVELOPMENTS

With the advent of lean manufacturing and just-in-time (JIT), MRP and MRP II have fallen into disfavor with some firms, with some feeling that the systems are obsolete. However, research has found that in certain environments with advance demand information, MRP-type push strategies yield better performance in term of inventories and service levels than did JIT's kanban-based pull strategies.

A further extension of MRP and MRP II has been developed to improve resource planning by broadening the scope of planning to include more of the supply chain. The Gartner Group of Stamford, Connecticut, coined the term "enterprise resource planning" (ERP) for this system.

The authors of *Manufacturing Planning and Control for Supply Chain Management* note that MRP and ERP have become so entrenched in businesses that they no longer provide a source of competitive advantage. They feel that a sustaining competitive advantage will now require that manufacturing planning and control (MPC) systems to cross organizational boundaries and coordinate company units that have traditionally worked independently.

It is recommended that in the near future organizations will need to work in pairs or dyads. This means that pairs, or dyads, of firms will jointly develop new MPC systems that allow integrated operations. Organizations will learn as much as possible from each dyad and then leverage what they have learned into other dyads. They term this approach the "next frontier" for manufacturing planning and control systems.

SEE ALSO: Competitive Advantage; Enterprise Resource Planning; Inventory Types; Lean Manufacturing and Just-in-Time Production; Quality and Total Quality Management

R. Anthony Inman

FURTHER READING:

Krishnamurthy, Ananth, Rajan Suri, and Mary Vernon. "Re-Examining the Performance of MRP and Kanban Material Control Strategies for Multi-Product Flexible Manufacturing Systems." *International Journal of Flexible Manufacturing Systems* 16, no. 2 (2004): 123.

Orlicky, Joseph. *Material Requirements Planning.* New York, NY: McGraw-Hill, 1975.

Stevenson, William J. *Production Operations Management.* Boston, MA: Irwin/McGraw-Hill, 2004.

Vollmann, Thomas E., William L. Berry, D. Clay Whybark, and F. Robert Jacobs. *Manufacturing Planning and Control for Supply Chain Management*. Boston, MA: McGraw-Hill, 2005.

Wight, Oliver. *Manufacturing Resource Planning: MRP II*. Essex Junction, VT: Oliver Wight Ltd., 1984.

Zhou, Li, and Robert W. Grubbstrom. "Analysis of the Effect of Commonality in Multi-Level Inventory Systems Applying MRP Theory." *International Journal of Production Economics* 90, no. 2 (2004): 251.

MARKET SHARE

Firms are always concerned with the size of the potential market for their products or services and the proportion of that market they actually reach—often referred to as a company's market share. Market share is the percentage of the total market (or industry) sales made by one firm. As a formula, Market Share = Firm's Sales ÷ Total Market Sales. Share can be reflected as either percentage of sales dollars, percentage of units sold or percentage of customers. Percentage of sales dollars is the most common reference.

Market share is one of the most commonly quoted measures of success in any industry. To correctly determine market share, one must clearly define the market. Having a small share of a large market can be as profitable as a large share of a small market. A producer of leather horse saddles must determine if his market is made up of saddle sales, equestrian sales, or all leather goods sales. Obviously, his market share in the saddle industry is much larger than his share in the leather goods market.

There are two sources for measuring market share: competitors and consumers. Surveying competitors gives a more accurate and reliable picture of market share. It is possible to interview 100 percent of competitors, but not all consumers. To get a reliable figure from consumers, a large number of people would have to be interviewed. For many industries, sales and market share figures may already be compiled by government agencies, trade associations, or private research firms.

MARKET PLAYERS

Market share defines the roles played by various firms in an industry. The firm with the largest market share is the market leader. The market leader usually has the highest marketing expenditures, distribution, price changes, and new product innovations. Market challengers are the firms working to increase their market share. Firms in an industry that are content

with their share of the market or doing little to increase sales are considered the market followers. The market niche brand is the player that targets its business toward serving smaller, overlooked segments that are often ignored by the larger players. The niche marketer can be very profitable, opting for high margins over higher volume.

MARKET STRATEGIES

The leader must constantly monitor the market because the challenger is constantly trying to take away market share. The market leader has three options to keep its market position: expand the total market, protect market share, or expand market share. Creating more usage, new uses, or users expands markets. Leaders can protect market share by monitoring their position and rushing to remedy any weaknesses. Continuous innovation is the best way to protect market share. When leaders become complacent with their products or services, it becomes easier for the challenger to make progress. In large markets, small increases in market share can translate into very large sales increases; a one-point gain in market share can be worth hundreds of millions of dollars.

The market challenger must attempt to gain market share from the leader. The challenger must have some sustainable competitive advantage to attack the leader's market share. The challenger can attack other competitors through a direct attack by altering price, promotion, or distribution, or indirectly by diversifying or catering to underserved segments. Followers must keep quality high and prices low to maintain their positions. As Armstrong and Kolter point out in *Principles of Marketing* (1999), the market follower must "find the right balance between following closely enough to win customers from the market leader but . . . at enough of a distance to avoid retaliation."

Niche marketers have many options available to them. The company must find a niche that is safe and profitable. It must be large enough to sustain growth but small enough that it does not look attractive to the market's larger players. Targeting multiple niches is an option that offers the niche marketer a higher chance of survival because the firm is not dependent on one segment.

Across segments, attempts to affect market share take place across the four "P's" of the marketing mix: product, price, place, and promotion. However, there are instances in which increasing market share is not necessarily desirable. The costs to increase production, or improve the product, may not be covered by the incremental profits.

Market share is easily understood by most managers, employees, and shareholders; therefore, it is often used as a primary measure of success. It is critical to understand market share, how it is used to identify market participants, and how the different participants use it to determine their market strategy.

SEE ALSO: Generic Competitive Strategies

Dena Waggoner
Revised by Deborah Hausler

FURTHER READING:

Armstrong, Gary and Philip Kotler. *Principles of Marketing.* 8th ed. Upper Saddle River, NJ: Prentice Hall, 1999.

Davenport, Todd. "Focusing on Share? Wise Up, Analysts Say." *American Banker* (1 November 2004): 9.

"Marketing: Market Share." QuickMBA.com. <http://www.quickmba.com/marketing/market-share/>.

MARKETING COMMUNICATION

As the term suggests, marketing communication functions within a marketing framework. Traditionally known as the promotional element of the four Ps of marketing (product, place, price, and promotion), the primary goal of marketing communication is to reach a defined audience to affect its behavior by informing, persuading, and reminding. Marketing communication acquires new customers for brands by building awareness and encouraging trial. Marketing communication also maintains a brand's current customer base by reinforcing their purchase behavior by providing additional information about the brand's benefits. A secondary goal of marketing communication is building and reinforcing relationships with customers, prospects, retailers, and other important stakeholders.

Successful marketing communication relies on a combination of options called the promotional mix. These options include advertising, sales promotion, public relations, direct marketing, and personal selling. The Internet has also become a powerful tool for reaching certain important audiences. The role each element takes in a marketing communication program relies in part on whether a company employs a push strategy or a pull strategy. A pull strategy relies more on consumer demand than personal selling for the product to travel from the manufacturer to the end user. The demand generated by advertising, public relations, and sales promotion "pulls" the good or service through the channels of distribution. A push

strategy, on the other hand, emphasizes personal selling to push the product through these channels.

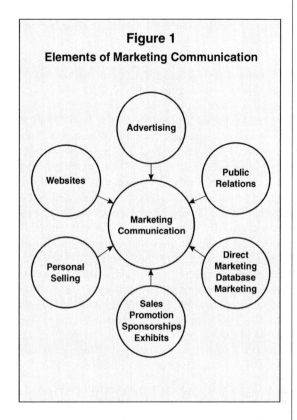

Figure 1
Elements of Marketing Communication

For marketing communication to be successful, however, sound management decisions must be made in the other three areas of the marketing mix: the product, service or idea itself; the price at which the brand will be offered; and the places at or through which customers may purchase the brand. The best promotion cannot overcome poor product quality, inordinately high prices, or insufficient retail distribution.

Likewise, successful marketing communication relies on sound management decisions regarding the coordination of the various elements of the promotional mix. To this end, a new way of viewing marketing communication emerged in the 1990s. Called integrated marketing communication, this perspective seeks to orchestrate the use of all forms of the promotional mix to reach customers at different levels in new and better ways.

INTEGRATED MARKETING COMMUNICATION

The evolution of this new perspective has two origins. Marketers began to realize that advertising, public relations, and sales were often at odds regarding responsibilities, budgets, management input and myriad other decisions affecting the successful marketing of a brand. Executives in each area competed with the others for resources and a voice in decision making. The outcome was inconsistent promotional efforts, wasted money, counterproductive management decisions, and, perhaps worst of all, confusion among consumers.

Secondly, the marketing perspective itself began to shift from being market oriented to market driven. Marketing communication was traditionally viewed as an inside-out way of presenting the company's messages. Advertising was the dominant element in the promotional mix because the mass media could effectively deliver a sales message to a mass audience. But then the mass market began to fragment. Consumers became better educated and more skeptical about advertising. A variety of sources, both controlled by the marketer and uncontrolled, became important to consumers. News reports, word-of-mouth, experts' opinions, and financial reports were just some of the "brand contacts" consumers began to use to learn about and form attitudes and opinions about a brand or company, or make purchase decisions. Advertising began to lose some of its luster in terms of its ability to deliver huge homogeneous audiences. Companies began to seek new ways to coordinate the multiplicity of product and company messages being issued and used by consumers and others.

Thus, two ideas permeate integrated marketing communication: relationship building and synergy. Rather than the traditional inside-out view, IMC is seen as an outside-in perspective. Customers are viewed not as targets but as partners in an ongoing relationship. Customers, prospects, and others encounter the brand and company through a host of sources and create from these various contacts ideas about the brand and company. By knowing the media habits and lifestyles of important consumer segments, marketers can tailor messages through media that are most likely to reach these segments at times when these segments are most likely to be receptive to these messages, thus optimizing the marketing communication effort.

Ideally, IMC is implemented by developing comprehensive databases on customers and prospects, segmenting these current and potential customers into groups with certain common awareness levels, predispositions, and behaviors, and developing messages and media strategies that guide the communication tactics to meet marketing objectives. In doing this, IMC builds and reinforces mutually profitable relationships with customers and other important stakeholders and generates synergy by coordinating all elements in the promotional mix into a program that possesses clarity, consistency, and maximum impact.

Practitioners and academics alike, however, have noted the difficulty of effectively implementing IMC. Defining exactly what IMC is has been difficult. For example, merely coordinating messages so that speaking "with one clear voice" in all promotional efforts does not fully capture the meaning of IMC. Also, changing the organization to accommodate the integrated approach has challenged the command and control structure of many organizations. However, studies suggest that IMC is viewed by a vast majority of marketing executives as having the greatest potential impact on their company's marketing strategies, more so than the economy, pricing, and globalization.

ADVERTISING

Advertising has four characteristics: it is persuasive in nature; it is non-personal; it is paid for by an identified sponsor; and it is disseminated through mass channels of communication. Advertising messages may promote the adoption of goods, services, persons, or ideas. Because the sales message is disseminated through the mass media—as opposed to personal selling—it is viewed as a much cheaper way of reaching consumers. However, its non-personal nature means it lacks the ability to tailor the sales message to the message recipient and, more importantly, actually get the sale. Therefore, advertising effects are best measured in terms of increasing awareness and changing attitudes and opinions, not creating sales. Advertising's contribution to sales is difficult to isolate because many factors influence sales. The contribution advertising makes to sales are best viewed over the long run. The exception to this thinking is within the internet arena. While banner ads, pop-ups and interstitials should still be viewed as brand promoting and not necessarily sales drivers, technology provides the ability to track how many of a website's visitors click the banner, investigate a product, request more information, and ultimately make a purchase.

Through the use of symbols and images advertising can help differentiate products and services that are otherwise similar. Advertising also helps create and maintain brand equity. Brand equity is an intangible asset that results from a favorable image, impressions of differentiation, or consumer attachment to the company, brand, or trademark. This equity translates into greater sales volume, and/or higher margins, thus greater competitive advantage. Brand equity is established and maintained through advertising that focuses on image, product attributes, service, or other features of the company and its products or services.

Cost is the greatest disadvantage of advertising. The average cost for a 30-second spot on network television increased fivefold between 1980 and 2005. Plus, the average cost of producing a 30-second ad for network television is quite expensive. It is not uncommon for a national advertiser to spend in the millions of dollars for one 30-second commercial to be produced. Add more millions on top of that if celebrity talent is utilized.

Credibility and clutter are other disadvantages. Consumers have become increasingly skeptical about advertising messages and tend to resent advertisers' attempt to persuade. Advertising is everywhere, from network television, to daily newspapers, to roadside billboards, to golf course signs, to stickers on fruit in grocery stores. Clutter encourages consumers to ignore many advertising messages. New media are emerging, such as DVRs (digital video recorders) which allow consumers to record programs and then skip commercials, and satellite radio which provides a majority of its channels advertising free.

PUBLIC RELATIONS

Public relations is defined as a management function which identifies, establishes, and maintains mutually beneficial relationships between an organization and the publics upon which its success or failure depends. Whereas advertising is a one-way communication from sender (the marketer) to the receiver (the consumer or the retail trade), public relations considers multiple audiences (consumers, employees, suppliers, vendors, etc.) and uses two-way communication to monitor feedback and adjust both its message and the organization's actions for maximum benefit. A primary tool used by public relations practitioners is publicity. Publicity capitalizes on the news value of a product, service, idea, person or event so that the information can be disseminated through the news media. This third party "endorsement" by the news media provides a vital boost to the marketing communication message: credibility. Articles in the media are perceived as being more objective than advertisements, and their messages are more likely to be absorbed and believed. For example, after the CBS newsmagazine *60 Minutes* reported in the early 1990s that drinking moderate amounts of red wine could prevent heart attacks by lowering cholesterol, red wine sales in the United States increased 50 percent. Another benefit publicity offers is that it is free, not considering the great amount of effort it can require to get out-bound publicity noticed and picked up by media sources.

Public relations' role in the promotional mix is becoming more important because of what Philip Kotler describes as an "over communicated society." Consumers develop "communication-avoidance routines" where they are likely to tune out commercial messages. As advertising loses some of its cost-effectiveness, marketers are turning to news coverage, events, and community programs to help disseminate their product and company messages. Some consumers may also base their purchase decisions on the image of the company, for example, how environmentally responsible the company is. In this regard, public relations plays an important role in presenting, through news reports, sponsorships, "advertorials" (a form of advertising that instead of selling a product or service promotes the company's views regarding current issues), and other forms of communication, what the company stands for.

DIRECT MARKETING AND DATABASE MARKETING

DIRECT MARKETING. Direct marketing, the oldest form of marketing, is the process of communicating directly with target customers to encourage response by telephone, mail, electronic means, or personal visit. Users of direct marketing include retailers, wholesalers, manufacturers, and service providers, and they use a variety of methods including direct mail, telemarketing, direct-response advertising, online computer shopping services, cable shopping networks, and infomercials. Traditionally not viewed as an element in the promotional mix, direct marketing represents one of the most profound changes in marketing and promotion in the last 25 years. Aspects of direct marketing, which includes direct response advertising and direct mail advertising as well as the various research and support activities necessary for their implementation, have been adopted by virtually all companies engaged in marketing products, services, ideas, or persons.

Direct marketing has become an important part of many marketing communication programs for three reasons. First, the number of two-income households has increased dramatically. About six in every ten women in the United States work outside the home. This has reduced the amount of time families have for shopping trips. Secondly, more shoppers than ever before rely on credit cards for payment of goods and services. These cashless transactions make products easier and faster to purchase. Finally, technological advances in telecommunications and computers allow consumers to make purchases from their homes via telephone, television, or computer with ease and safety. These three factors have dramatically altered the purchasing habits of American consumers and made direct marketing a growing field worldwide.

Direct marketing allows a company to target more precisely a segment of customers and prospects with a sales message tailored to their specific needs and characteristics. Unlike advertising and public relations, whose connections to actual sales are tenuous or nebulous at best, direct marketing offers accountability by providing tangible results. The economics of direct marketing have also improved over the years as more information is gathered about customers and prospects. By identifying those consumers they can serve more effectively and profitably, companies may be more efficient in their marketing efforts. Whereas network television in the past offered opportunities to reach huge groups of consumers at a low cost per thousand, direct marketing can reach individual consumers and develop a relationship with each of them.

Research indicates that brands with strong brand equity are more successful in direct marketing efforts than little-known brands. Direct marketing, then, works best when other marketing communication such as traditional media advertising supports the direct marketing effort.

Direct marketing has its drawbacks also. Just as consumers built resistance to the persuasive nature of advertising, so have they with direct marketing efforts. Direct marketers have responded by being less sales oriented and more relationship oriented. Also, just as consumers grew weary of advertising clutter, so have they with the direct marketing efforts. Consumers are bombarded with mail, infomercials, and telemarketing pitches daily. Some direct marketers have responded by regarding privacy as a customer service benefit. Direct marketers must also overcome consumer mistrust of direct marketing efforts due to incidents of illegal behavior by companies and individuals using direct marketing. The U.S. Postal Service, the Federal Trade Commission, and other federal and state agencies may prosecute criminal acts. The industry then risks legislation regulating the behavior of direct marketers if it is not successful in self-regulation. The Direct Marketing Association, the leading trade organization for direct marketing, works with companies and government agencies to initiate self-regulation. In March of 2003 the National Do Not Call Registry went into affect whereby consumers added their names to a list that telemarketers had to eliminate from their out-bound call database.

DATABASE MARKETING. Database marketing is a form of direct marketing that attempts to gain and reinforce sales transactions while at the same time being customer driven. Successful database marketing continually updates lists of prospects and customers by identifying who they are, what they are like, and what they are purchasing now or may be purchasing in the future. By using database marketing, marketers can develop products and/or product packages to meet their customers' needs or develop creative and media strategies that match their tastes, values, and lifestyles. Like IMC, database marketing is viewed by many marketers as supplanting traditional marketing strategies and is a major component of most IMC programs.

At the core of database marketing is the idea that market segments are constantly shifting and changing. People who may be considered current customers, potential customers, and former customers and people who are likely never to be customers are constantly changing. By identifying these various segments and developing a working knowledge of their wants, needs, and characteristics, marketers can reduce the cost of reaching non-prospects and build customer loyalty. Perhaps the most important role of database marketing is its ability to retain customers. The cumulative profit for a five-year loyal customer is between seven and eight times the first-year profit.

Since database marketing is expensive to develop and complex to implement effectively, companies considering database marketing should consider three important questions. First, do relatively frequent purchasers or high dollar volume purchasers for the brand exist? Secondly, is the market diverse enough so that segmenting into subgroups would be beneficial? Finally, are there customers that represent opportunities for higher volume purchases?

SALES PROMOTION/SPONSORSHIPS/ EXHIBITIONS

SALES PROMOTION. Sales promotions are direct inducements that offer extra incentives to enhance or accelerate the product's movement from producer to consumer. Sales promotions may be directed at the consumer or the trade. Consumer promotions such as coupons, sampling, premiums, sweepstakes, price packs (packs that offer greater quantity or lower cost than normal), low-cost financing deals, and rebates are purchase incentives in that they induce product trial and encourage repurchase. Consumer promotions may also include incentives to visit a retail establishment or request additional information. Trade promotions include slotting allowances ("buying" shelf space in retail stores), allowances for featuring the brand in retail advertising, display and merchandising allowances, buying allowances (volume discounts and other volume-oriented incentives), bill back allowances (pay-for-performance incentives), incentives to salespeople, and other tactics to encourage retailers to carry the item and to push the brand.

Two perspectives may be found among marketers regarding sales promotion. First, sales promotion is supplemental to advertising in that it binds the role of advertising with personal selling. This view regards sales promotion as a minor player in the marketing communication program. A second view regards sales promotion and advertising as distinct functions with objectives and strategies very different from each other. Sales promotion in this sense is equal to or even more important than advertising. Some companies allocate as much as 75 percent of their advertising/ promotion dollars to sales promotion and just 25 percent to advertising. Finding the right balance is often a difficult task. The main purpose of sales promotion is to spur action. Advertising sets up the deal by developing a brand reputation and building market value. Sales promotion helps close the deal by providing incentives that build market volume.

Sales promotions can motivate customers to select a particular brand, especially when brands appear to be equal, and they can produce more immediate and measurable results than advertising. However, too heavy a reliance on sales promotions results in "deal-prone" consumers with little brand loyalty and too much price sensitivity. Sales promotions can also force competitors to offer similar inducements, with sales and profits suffering for everyone.

SPONSORSHIPS. Sponsorships, or event marketing, combine advertising and sales promotions with public relations. Sponsorships increase awareness of a company or product, build loyalty with a specific target audience, help differentiate a product from its competitors, provide merchandising opportunities, demonstrate commitment to a community or ethnic group, or impact the bottom line. Like advertising, sponsorships are initiated to build long-term associations. Organizations sometimes compare sponsorships with advertising by using gross impressions or cost-per-thousand measurements. However, the value of sponsorships can be very difficult to measure. Companies considering sponsorships should consider the short-term public relations value of sponsorships and the long-term goals of the organization. Sports sponsorships make up about two-thirds of all sponsorships.

EXHIBITS. Exhibits, or trade shows, are hybrid forms of promotion between business-to-business advertising and personal selling. Trade shows provide opportunities for face-to-face contact with prospects, enable new companies to create a viable customer base in a short period of time, and allow small and midsize companies that may not be visited on a regular basis by salespeople to become familiar with suppliers and vendors. Because many trade shows generate media attention, they have also become popular venues for introducing new products and providing a stage for executives to gain visibility.

PERSONAL SELLING

Personal selling includes all person-to-person contact with customers with the purpose of introducing the product to the customer, convincing him or her of the product's value, and closing the sale. The role of personal selling varies from organization to organization, depending on the nature and size of the company, the industry, and the products or services it is marketing. Many marketing executives realize that both sales and non-sales employees act as salespeople for their organization in one way or another. One study that perhaps supports this contention found that marketing executives predicted greater emphasis being placed on sales management and personal selling in their organization than on any other promotional mix element. These organizations have launched training sessions that show employees how they act as salespeople for the organization and how they can improve their interpersonal skills with clients, customers, and prospects. Employee reward programs now reward employees for their efforts in this regard.

Personal selling is the most effective way to make a sale because of the interpersonal communication between the salesperson and the prospect. Messages can be tailored to particular situations, immediate feedback can be processed, and message strategies can be changed to accommodate the feedback. However, personal selling is the most expensive way to make a sale, with the average cost per sales call ranging from $235 to $332 and the average number of sales calls needed to close a deal being between three and six personal calls.

Sales and marketing management classifies salespersons into one of three groups: creative selling, order taking, and missionary sales reps. Creative selling jobs require the most skills and preparation. They are the "point person" for the sales function. They prospect for customers, analyze situations, determine how their company can satisfy wants and needs of prospects, and, most importantly, get an order. Order takers take over after the initial order is received. They handle repeat purchases (straight rebuys) and modified rebuys. Missionary sales reps service accounts by introducing new products, promotions, and other programs. Orders are taken by order takers or by distributors.

INTERNET MARKETING

Just as direct marketing has become a prominent player in the promotional mix, so too has the Internet. Virtually unheard of in the 1980s, the 1990s saw this new medium explode onto the scene, being adopted by families, businesses and other organizations more quickly than any other medium in history. Web sites provide a new way of transmitting information, entertainment, and advertising, and have generated a new dimension in marketing: electronic commerce. E-commerce is the term used to describe the act of selling goods and services over the Internet. In other words, the Internet has become more that a communication channel; it is a marketing channel itself with companies such as Amazon.com, CDNow, eBay, and others selling goods via the Internet to individuals around the globe. In less than 10 years advertising expenditures on the Internet will rival those for radio and outdoor. Public relations practitioners realize the value that web sites offer in establishing and maintaining relationships with important publics. For example, company and product information can be posted on the company's site for news reporters researching stories and for current and potential customers seeking information. Political candidates have web sites that provide information about their background and their political experience.

The interactivity of the Internet is perhaps its greatest asset. By communicating with customers, prospects, and others one-on-one, firms can build databases that help them meet specific needs of individuals, thus building a loyal customer base. Because the cost of entry is negligible, the Internet is cluttered with web sites. However, this clutter does not present the same kind of problem that advertising clutter does. Advertising and most other forms of promotion assume a passive audience that will be exposed to marketing communication messages via the mass media or mail regardless of their receptivity. Web sites require audiences who are active in the information-seeking process to purposely visit the site. Therefore, the quality and freshness of content is vital for the success of the web site.

THE FUTURE OF MARKETING COMMUNICATION

Marketing communication has become an integral part of the social and economic system in the United States. Consumers rely on the information from marketing communication to make wise purchase decisions. Businesses, ranging from multinational corporations to small retailers, depend on marketing communication to sell their goods and services. Marketing communication has also become an important player in the life of a business. Marketing communication helps move products, services, and ideas from manufacturers to end users and builds and maintains relationships with customers, prospects, and other important stakeholders in the company. Advertising and sales promotion will continue to play important roles in marketing communication mix. However, marketing strategies that stress relationship building in addition to producing sales will force marketers to consider all the elements in the marketing communication mix. In the future new information gathering techniques will help marketers target more precisely customers and prospects using direct marketing strategies. New media technologies will provide businesses and consumers new ways to establish and reinforce relationships that are important for the success of the firm and important for consumers as they make purchase decisions. The Internet will become a major force in how organizations communicate with a variety of constituents, customers, clients, and other interested parties.

SEE ALSO: Communication; Marketing Concept and Philosophy; Marketing Research

Charles M. Mayo
Revised by Deborah Hausler

FURTHER READING:

Arens, William F. *Contemporary Advertising*. 7th ed. Boston: Irwin/McGraw-Hill, 1998.

Belch, George E., and Michael A. Belch. *Advertising and Promotion: An Integrated Marketing Communication Perspective*. 4th ed. Boston: Irwin/McGraw-Hill, 1998.

Cutlip, Scott M., Allen H. Center, and Glen M. Broom. *Effective Public Relations*. 8th ed. Upper Saddle River, NJ: Prentice-Hall, 1999.

Harris, Thomas L. *Value-Added Public Relations: The Secret Weapon in Integrated Marketing*. Chicago: NTC Books, 1998.

Manning, Gerald L. and Barry L. Reese. *Selling Today: Building Quality Partnerships*. 7th ed. Upper Saddle River, NJ: Prentice-Hall, 1998.

Weitz, Barton W., Stephen B. Castleberry, and John F. Tanner. *Selling: Building Partnerships*. 3rd ed. Boston: Irwin/McGraw-Hill, 1998.

MARKETING CONCEPT AND PHILOSOPHY

The marketing concept and philosophy is one of the simplest ideas in marketing, and at the same time, it is also one of the most important marketing philosophies. At its very core are the customer and his or her satisfaction. The marketing concept and philosophy states that the organization should strive to satisfy its customers' wants and needs while meeting the organization's goals. In simple terms, "the customer is king".

The implication of the marketing concept is very important for management. It is not something that the marketing department administers, nor is it the sole domain of the marketing department. Rather, it is adopted by the entire organization. From top management to the lowest levels and across all departments of the organization, it is a philosophy or way of doing business. The customers' needs, wants, and satisfaction should always be foremost in every manager and employees' mind. Wal-Mart's motto of "satisfaction guaranteed" is an example of the marketing concept. Whether the Wal-Mart employee is an accountant or a cashier, the customer is always first.

As simple as the philosophy sounds, the concept is not very old in the evolution of marketing thought. However, it is at the end of a succession of business philosophies that cover centuries. To gain a better understanding of the thought leading to the marketing concept, the history and evolution of the marketing concept and philosophy are examined first. Next, the marketing concept and philosophy and some misconceptions about it are discussed.

EVOLUTION OF THE MARKETING CONCEPT AND PHILOSOPHY

The marketing concept and philosophy evolved as the last of three major philosophies of marketing. These three philosophies are the product, selling, and marketing philosophies. Even though each philosophy has a particular time when it was dominant, a philosophy did not die with the end of its era of dominance. In fact, all three philosophies are being used today.

PRODUCT PHILOSOPHY. The product philosophy was the dominant marketing philosophy prior to the Industrial Revolution and continued to the 1920s. The product philosophy holds that the organization knows its product better than anyone or any organization. The company knows what will work in designing and producing the product and what will not work. For example, the company may decide to emphasize the low cost or high quality of their products. This confidence in their ability is not a radical concept, but the confidence leads to the consumer being overlooked. Since the organization has the great knowledge and skill in making the product, the organization also assumes it knows what is best for the consumer.

This philosophy of only relying on the organization's skill and desires for the product did not lead to poor sales. In much of the product philosophy era, organizations were able to sell all of the products that they made. The success of the product philosophy era is due mostly to the time and level of technology in which it was dominant. The product era spanned both the pre-Industrial Revolution era and much of the time after the Industrial Revolution.

The period before the Industrial Revolution was the time when most goods were made by hand. The production was very slow and few goods could be produced. However, there was also a demand for those goods, and the slow production could not fill the demand in many cases. The importance for management of this shortage was that very little marketing was needed.

An example illustrates the effects of the shortages. Today, the gunsmith shop in Williamsburg, Virginia, still operates using the product philosophy. The gunsmiths produce single-shot rifles using the technology available during the 1700s. They are only able to produce about four or five rifles every year, and they charge from $15,000 to $20,000 for each rifle. However, the high price does not deter the demand for the guns; their uniqueness commands a waiting list of three to four years. Today's Williamsburg Gunsmith Shop situation was typical for organizations operating before the Industrial Revolution. Most goods were in such short supply that companies could sell all that they made. Consequently, organizations did not need to consult with consumers about designing and producing their products.

When mass production techniques created the Industrial Revolution, the volume of output was greatly increased. Yet the increased production of goods did not immediately eliminate the shortages from the pre-industrial era. The new mass production techniques provided economies of scale allowing for lower costs of production and corresponding lower prices for goods. Lower prices greatly expanded the market for the goods, and the new production techniques were struggling to keep up with the demand. This situation meant that the product philosophy would work just as well in the new industrial environment. Consumers still did not need to be consulted for the organization to sell its products.

One of the many stories about Henry Ford illustrates the classic example of the product philosophy in use after the Industrial Revolution. Henry Ford pioneered mass production techniques in the automobile industry. With the techniques, he offered cars at affordable prices to the general public. Before this time, cars were hand made, and only the very wealthy could afford them. The public enthusiastically purchased all the Model T Fords that the company could produce. The evidence that the product philosophy was alive and well in Ford Motor Company came in Henry Ford's famous reaction to consumer requests for more color options. He was said to have responded that "you can have any color car you want as long as it is black." Realizing that different colors would increase the cost of production and price of the Model T's, Henry Ford, using the product philosophy, decided that lower prices were best for the public.

SELLING PHILOSOPHY. The selling era has the shortest period of dominance of the three philosophies. It began to be dominant around 1930 and stayed in widespread use until about 1950. The selling philosophy holds that an organization can sell any product it produces with the use of marketing techniques, such as advertising and personal selling. Organizations could create marketing departments that would be concerned with selling the goods, and the rest of the organization could be left to concentrate on producing the goods.

The reason for the emergence of the selling philosophy was the ever-rising number of goods available after the Industrial Revolution. Organizations became progressively more efficient in production, which increased the volume of goods. With the increased supply, competition also entered production. These two events eventually led to the end of product shortages and the creation of surpluses. It was because of the surpluses that organizations turned to the use of advertising and personal selling to reduce their inventories and sell their goods. The selling philosophy also enabled part of the organization to keep focusing on the product, via the product philosophy. In addition, the selling philosophy held that a sales or marketing department could sell whatever the company produced.

The Ford Motor Company is also a good example of the selling philosophy and why this philosophy does not work in many instances. Ford produced and sold the Model T for many years. During its production, the automobile market attracted more competition. Not only did the competition begin to offer cars in other colors, the styling of the competition was viewed as modern and the Model T became considered as old-fashioned. Henry Ford's sons were aware of the changes in the automobile market and tried to convince their father to adapt. However, Henry Ford was sure that his standardized low-price automobile was what the public needed. Consequently, Ford turned to marketing techniques to sell the Model T. It continued to sell, but its market share began to drop. Eventually, even Henry Ford had to recognize consumer desires and introduce a new model.

The selling philosophy assumes that a well-trained and motivated sales force can sell any product. However, more companies began to realize that it is easier to sell a product that the customer wants, than to sell a product the customer does not want. When many companies began to realize this fact, the selling era gave way to the marketing era of the marketing concept and philosophy.

MARKETING PHILOSOPHY. The marketing era started to dominate around 1950, and it continues to the present. The marketing concept recognizes that the company's knowledge and skill in designing products may not always be meeting the needs of customers. It also recognizes that even a good sales department cannot sell every product that does not meet consumers' needs. When customers have many choices, they will choose the one that best meets their needs.

MARKET CONCEPT AND PHILOSOPHY

The marketing concept and philosophy states that the organization should strive to satisfy its customers' wants and needs while meeting the organization's goals. The best way to meet the organization's goals is also by meeting customer needs and wants. The marketing concept's emphasis is to understand the customers before designing and producing a product for them. With the customer's wants and needs incorporated into the design and manufacture of the product, sales and profit goals are far more likely to be met.

With the customer's satisfaction the key to the organization, the need to understand the customer is critical. Marketing research techniques have been developed just for that purpose. Smaller organizations may keep close to their customers by simply talking with them. Larger corporations have established methods in place to keep in touch with their customers, be it consumer panels, focus groups, or third-party research studies. Whatever the method, the desire is to know the customers so the organization can better serve them and not lose sight of their needs and wants.

The idea of keeping close to the organization's customers seems simple. In reality, it is very easy to forget the customer's needs and wants. Sometimes the management is so involved with the product that their own desires and wants begin to take dominance, even though they have adopted the marketing concept.

Yet it is easy for managers to forget the marketing concept and philosophy. For example, many years ago—before there was a Subway on every corner—a college student opened a small submarine sandwich shop near his university's campus. The sub shop was an immediate success. By using the marketing concept, the young entrepreneuer had recognized an unmet need in the student population and opened a business that met that need.

Unfortunately, the story does not end at this point. The sub shop was so successful that it began to outgrow its original location after about three years. The shop moved to a larger location with more parking spaces, also near the university. At the new sub shop, waiters in tuxedos met the students and seated them at tables with tablecloths. Besides the traditional subs, the shop now served full meals and had a bar. Within a few months the sub shop was out of business. The owner of the shop had become so involved with his business vision that he forgot the customers' needs and wants. They did not want an upscale restaurant—there were other restaurants in the area that met that need, they just wanted a quick sub sandwich. By losing sight of the customers' wants and needs, the owner of the sub shop lost his successful business.

MEETING CUSTOMER NEEDS WHILE MEETING ORGANIZATIONAL GOALS

Sometimes in the zeal to satisfy a customer's wants and needs, the marketing concept is construed to mean that the customer is always right. However, the marketing concept also states that it is important to meet organizational goals as well as satisfy customer wants and needs. Satisfying customer needs and organizational goals may involve conflicts that sometimes cannot be resolved. The organization that adopts the marketing concept will do everything in its power to meet the needs of its customers, but it must also make a profit. Sometimes the wants of the customers may include a low price or features that are not attainable for the organization if it is to make a profit. Consequently, the organization must hope for a compromise between what the consumer wants and what is practical for the business to provide.

CRITICISM OF THE MARKETING CONCEPT

Interpreted literally, the marketing concept only advocates discovering consumers' wants and needs and satisfying them. Critics assert that consumers may not be aware of all of their wants and needs. In the 1950s, were consumers aware of a need to cook their food by sending microwaves through their food? In the 1960s, were consumers aware of a need to have personal computers in their homes? Critics argue that the marketing concept's concentration on consumers' wants and needs stifle innovation. Organizations will no longer concentrate on research and development in hopes that one product in ten might meet with consumer acceptance, and will less likely come up with innovative products such as microwaves and personal computers.

Supporters of the marketing concept have contended that it does not stifle innovation and that it does recognize that consumers cannot conceive of every product that they may want or need. However, need is defined in a very broad sense. In the microwave and personal computer examples, the need was not for the specific product, but there was a need to cook food faster and a need for writing and calculating. The microwave and personal computer satisfied those needs though the consumer never imagined these products. The marketing concept does not stifle creativity and innovation. It seeks to encourage creativity to satisfy customer needs.

The marketing concept is a relative newcomer as a philosophy of doing business. However, its evolution started before the Industrial Revolution. As time progressed, customer and business needs also evolved. The product and selling philosophies eventually evolved into the marketing concept and philosophy. Today, the marketing concept and philosophy stands as a formula for doing business and many believe it is a prescription for success. It aims to satisfy customers by guiding the organization to meet the customers' needs and wants while meeting the organization's goals.

SEE ALSO: Market Share; Marketing Communication; Marketing Research

James Henley
Revised by Deborah Hausler

FURTHER READING:

Kotler, Philip, and Gary Armstrong. *Principles of Marketing.* 8th ed. Upper Saddle River, NJ: Prentice Hall, 1999.

Perreault, William D., Jr., and E. Jerome McCarthy. *Basic Marketing: A Global-Managerial Approach.* 13th ed. Boston: Irwin/McGraw-Hill, 1999.

MARKETING RESEARCH

Marketing research is the function that links the consumer, customer, and public to the marketer through information. This information is used to identify and define marketing opportunities and problems; to generate, refine, and evaluate marketing actions; to monitor marketing performance; and to improve understanding of the marketing process. Marketing research specifies the information, manages and implements the data-collection process, analyzes the results, and communicates the findings and their implications. Marketing research is concerned with the application of theories, problem-solving methods, and techniques to identify and solve problems in marketing. In order to offset unpredictable consumer behavior, companies invest in market research.

Increased customer focus, demands for resource productivity, and increased domestic and international competition has prompted an increased emphasis on marketing research. Managers cannot always wait for information to arrive in bits and pieces from marketing departments. They often require formal studies of specific situations. For example, Dell Computer might want to know a demographic breakdown of how many and what kinds of people or companies will purchase a new model in its personal computer line. In such situations, the marketing department may not be able to provide from existing knowledge the detailed information needed, and managers normally do not have the skill or time to obtain the information on their own. This formal study, whether performed internally or externally, is called marketing research.

The marketing research process consists of four steps: defining the problem and research objectives, developing the research plan, implementing the research plan, and interpreting and reporting the findings.

DEFINING THE OBJECTIVES

The marketing manager and the researcher must work closely together to define the problem carefully and agree on the research objectives. The manager best understands the decision for which information is needed; the researcher best understands marketing research and how to obtain the information.

Managers must know enough about marketing research to help in the planning and to interpret research results. Managers who know little about the importance of research may obtain irrelevant information or accept inaccurate conclusions. Experienced marketing researchers who understand the manager's problem should also be involved at this stage. The researcher must be able to help the manager define the problem and to suggest ways that research can help the manager make better decisions.

Defining the problem and research objectives is often the hardest step in the research process. The manager may know that something is wrong without knowing the specific causes. For example, managers of a retail clothing store chain decided that falling sales were caused by poor floor set-up and incorrect product positioning. However, research concluded that neither problem was the cause. It turned out that the store had hired sales persons who weren't properly trained in providing good customer service. Careful problem definition would have avoided the cost and delay of research and would have suggested research on the real problem.

When the problem has been defined, the manager and researcher must set the research objectives. A marketing research project might have one of three types of objectives. Sometimes the objective is exploratory—to gather preliminary information that will help define the problem and suggest hypotheses. Sometimes the objective is descriptive—to describe things such as the market potential for a product or the demographics and attitudes of consumers who buy the product. Sometimes the objective is casual—to test hypotheses about cause-and-effect relationships.

DEVELOPING THE RESEARCH PLAN

The second step of the marketing research process calls for determining the information needed, developing a plan for gathering it efficiently, and presenting the plan to marketing management. The plan outlines sources of secondary data and spells out the specific research approaches, contact methods, sampling plans, and instruments that researchers will use to gather primary data.

A marketing researcher can gather secondary data, primary data, or both. Primary data consists of information collected for the specific purpose at hand. Secondary data consists of information that already exists somewhere, having been collected for another purpose. Sources of secondary data include internal sources such as profit and loss statements, balance sheets, sales figures, and inventory records; and external sources such as government publications, periodicals, books, and commercial data. Primary data collection requires more extensive research, more time, and more money. Secondary sources can sometimes provide information that is not directly available or would be too expensive to collect.

Secondary data also present problems. The needed information may not exist. Researchers can rarely obtain all the data they need from secondary sources. The researcher must evaluate secondary information carefully to make certain of its relevance (fits research project needs), accuracy (reliably collected and reported), currency (up to date enough for current decisions), and impartiality (objectively collected and reported). Researchers must also understand how secondary sources define basic terms and concepts, as different sources often use the same terms but mean slightly different things, or they attempt to measure the same thing but go about it in different ways. Either way, the result can be that statistics found in secondary sources may not be as accurate or as relevant as they appear on the surface.

RESEARCH APPROACHES

Observational research is the gathering of primary data by observing relevant people, actions, and situations. Observational research can be used to obtain information that people are unwilling or unable to provide. In some cases, observation may be the only way to obtain the needed information.

Survey research is the approach best suited for gathering descriptive information. A company that wants to know about people's knowledge, attitudes, preferences, or buying behavior can often find out by asking them directly. Survey research is the most widely used method for primary data collection, and it is often the only method used in a research study. The major advantage of survey research is its flexibility. It can be used to obtain many different kinds of information in many different marketing situations. In the early and mid-1980s, some cola companies created a taste test against their competitors. This is an example of survey research. Participants were allowed to taste different cola brands without knowing which was which. The participant then decided which brand was preferred.

Whereas observation is best suited for exploratory research and surveys for descriptive research, experimental research is best suited for gathering causal information. Experiments involve selecting matched groups of subjects, giving them different treatments, controlling unrelated factors, and checking for differences in group responses. Thus, experimental research tries to explain cause-and-effect relationships.

RESEARCH CONTACT METHODS

Research may be collected by mail, telephone, e-mail, fax, or personal interview. Mail questionnaires can be used to collect large amounts of information at a low cost per respondent. Respondents may give more honest answers to more personal questions on a mail questionnaire than to an unknown interviewer in person or over the phone. However, mail questionnaires lack flexibility in that they require simply worded questions. They can also take a long time to complete, and the response rate—the number of people returning completed questionnaires—is often very low.

Telephone interviewing is the best method for gathering information quickly, and it provides greater flexibility than mail questionnaires. Interviewers can explain questions that are not understood. Telephone interviewing also allows greater sample control. Response rates tend to be higher than with mail questionnaires. But telephone interviewing also has its drawbacks. The cost per respondent is higher than with mail questionnaires, people may regard a phone call as more of an inconvenience or an intrusion, and they may not want to discuss personal questions with an interviewer. In the latter part of the 1990s, laws were also passed to guard against the invasion of privacy. If a person wishes to be taken off a solicitation or interview list, companies can be sued if they persist in calling.

Personal interviewing consists of inviting several people to talk with a trained interviewer about a company's products or services. The interviewer needs objectivity, knowledge of the subject and industry, and some understanding of group and consumer behavior. Personal interviewing is quite flexible and can be used to collect large amounts of information. Trained interviewers can hold a respondent's attention for a long time and can explain difficult questions. They can guide interviews, explore issues, and probe as the situation requires. The main drawbacks of personal interviewing are costs and sampling problems. Personal interviews may cost three to four times as much as telephone interviews.

SAMPLING PLAN

Marketing researchers usually draw conclusions about large groups of consumers by studying a relatively small sample of the total consumer population. A sample is a segment of the population selected to represent the population as a whole. Ideally, the sample should be representative so that the researcher can make accurate estimates of the thoughts and behaviors of the larger population. If the sample is not representative, it may lead the company to draw the wrong conclusions and misuse its resources.

The marketing researcher must design a sampling plan, which calls for three decisions:

1. Sampling unit—determining who is to be surveyed. The marketing researcher must define the target population that will be sampled. If a company wants feedback on a new basketball shoe, it would be wise to target active players and even professional players.

2. Sample size—determining the number of people to be surveyed. Large samples give more reliable results than small samples. Samples of less than 1 percent of a population can often provide good reliability, given a credible sampling procedure. Most commercial samples consist of between several hundred and several thousand respondents.

3. Sampling procedure—determining how the respondents should be chosen. To obtain a representative sample, a probability (random) sampling of the population should be drawn. This is a means of determining who is reached by the survey to ensure they are indeed a valid cross-section of the sampling unit. Choosing passersby on a street corner, for example, would not produce a random sample, whereas allowing a computer to pick names randomly from a relevant calling list probably would (depending on how the list was compiled). Probability sampling allows the calculation of confidence limits for sampling error.

RESEARCH INSTRUMENTS

In collecting primary data, marketing researchers have a choice of two main research instruments—the questionnaire and mechanical devices. The questionnaire is by far the most common instrument. A questionnaire consists of a set of questions presented to a respondent for his or her answers. In preparing a questionnaire, the marketing researcher must decide what questions to ask, the form of the questions, the wording of the questions, and the ordering of the questions. Each question should be checked to see that it contributes to the research objectives.

Although questionnaires are the most common research instrument, mechanical instruments are also used. Two examples of mechanical instruments are people meters and supermarket scanners. These techniques are not widely used because they tend to be expensive, require unrealistic advertising exposure conditions, and are hard to interpret.

COLLECTING THE INFORMATION

The researcher must now collect the data. This phase is generally the most expensive and the most liable to error. In the case of surveys, four major problems arise. Some respondents will not be at home and will have to be replaced. Other respondents will refuse to cooperate. Still others will give biased or dishonest answers. Finally, some interviewers will occasionally be biased or dishonest.

CHARACTERISTICS OF GOOD MARKETING RESEARCH

Following are the characteristics of good marketing research

1. Scientific method. Effective marketing research uses the principles of the scientific

method: careful observation, formulation of hypotheses, prediction, and testing.

2. Research creativity. At its best, marketing research develops innovative ways to solve a problem.

3. Multiple methods. Competent marketing researchers shy away from over-reliance on any one method, preferring to adapt the method to the problem rather than the other way around. They also recognize the desirability of gathering information from multiple sources to give greater confidence.

4. Interdependence of models and data. Competent marketing researchers recognize that the facts derive their meaning from models of the problem. These models guide the type of information sought and therefore should be made as explicit as possible.

5. Value and cost of information. Competent marketing researchers show concern for estimating the value of information against its cost. Value/cost evaluation helps the marketing research department determine which research projects to conduct, which research designs to use, and whether to gather more information after the initial results are in. Research costs are typically easy to quantify, while the value is harder to anticipate. The value depends on the reliability and validity of the research findings and management's willingness to accept and act on its findings. In general, the most valuable information tends to cost the most because it requires more intensive methods, but of course it is easy to spend a great deal of money on poorly conceived research.

6. Healthy skepticism. Competent marketing researchers will show a healthy skepticism toward assumptions made by managers about how the market works.

7. Ethical marketing. Most marketing research benefits both the sponsoring company and its consumers. Through marketing research, companies learn more about consumers' needs, and are able to supply more satisfying products and services. However, the misuse of marketing research can also harm or annoy consumers. There are professional ethical standards guiding the proper conduct of research.

PRESENTING THE RESEARCH PLAN

The last step in market research is the presentation of a formal plan. At this stage, the marketing researcher should summarize the plan in a written pro-posal to management. A written proposal is especially important when the research project will be large and complex or when an outside firm carries it out. The proposal should cover the management problems addressed and the research objectives, the information to be obtained, the sources of secondary information or methods for collecting primary data, and the way the results will help management decision making. A written research plan or proposal makes sure that the marketing manager and researchers have considered all the important aspect of the research and that they agree on why and how the research will be done.

MANAGEMENT'S USE OF MARKETING RESEARCH

In spite of the rapid growth of marketing research, many companies still fail to use it sufficiently or correctly. Several factors can stand in the way of its greater utilization.

1. A narrow conception of marketing research. Many managers see marketing research as only a fact-finding operation. The marketing researcher is supposed to design a questionnaire, choose a sample conduct interviews, and report results, often without being given a careful definition of the problem or of the decision alternatives facing management. As a result, some fact finding fails to be useful. This reinforces management's idea of the limited usefulness of some marketing research.

2. Uneven caliber of marketing researchers. Some managers view marketing research as little better than a clerical activity and reward it as such. Poorly qualified marketing researchers are hired, and their weak training and deficient creativity lead to unimpressive results. The disappointing results reinforce management's prejudice against expecting too much from marketing research. Management continues to pay low salaries, perpetuating the basic difficulty.

3. Late and occasional erroneous findings by marketing research. Managers want quick results that are accurate and conclusive. But good marketing research takes time and money. If they can't perceive the difference between quality and shoddy research, managers become disappointed, and they lower their opinion of the value of marketing research. This is especially a problem in conducting marketing research in foreign countries.

4. Intellectual differences. Intellectual divergences between the mental styles of line

managers and marketing researchers often get in the way of productive relationships. The marketing researcher's report may seem abstract, complicated, and tentative, while the line manager wants concreteness, simplicity, and certainty. Yet in the more progressive companies, marketing researchers are increasingly being included as members of the product management team, and their influence on marketing strategy in growing.

SEE ALSO: Marketing Concept and Philosophy; Research Methods and Processes

James C. Koch
Revised by Deborah Hausler

FURTHER READING:

Higgins, Lexis F. "Applying Principles of Creativity Management to Marketing Research Efforts in High-Technology Markets." *Industrial Marketing Management,* May 1999, 305–317.

Malhotra, Naresh K., Mark Peterson, and Susan Bardi Kleiser. "Marketing Research: A State-of-the-Art Review and Directions for the Twenty-First Century." *Academy of Marketing Science,* Spring 1999, 160–183.

"Market Focus: Research-Instant Intelligence." *PR Week,* 7 February 2005, 17.

"Online Market Research Poised for Even Bigger Growth." *B&T Weekly,* 21 January 2005.

"Simply Wrong Assumptions." *Nilewide Marketing Review,* 13 February 2005.

MECHANISTIC ORGANIZATIONS

Nearly one-half century ago, Burns and Stalker noted that mechanistic organizations are often appropriate in stable environments and for routine tasks and technologies. In some ways similar to bureaucratic structures, mechanistic organizations have clear, well-defined, centralized, vertical hierarchies of command, authority, and control. Efficiency and predictability are emphasized through specialization, standardization, and formalization. This results in rigidly defined jobs, technologies, and processes. The term mechanistic suggests that organizational structures, processes, and roles are like a machine in which each part of the organization does what it is designed to do, but little else.

It is easy to confuse mechanistic organizations with bureaucracies due to the considerable overlap between these two concepts. Yet despite the overlaps, a primary difference between mechanistic organizations and bureaucracy is the rationale for utilizing each

of these. A goal of bureaucratic structures is to protect lower-level administrative positions from arbitrary actions of owners and higher-level managers. For example, an individual holding the job title of vice-president of production would, in a bureaucracy, be protected from indiscriminant changes in work hours, wages, and responsibilities through formal rules, regulations, and grievance procedures. The goal of the bureaucracy is protection of positions within the organization.

Mechanistic organizations, on the other hand, are utilized to increase efficiency when tasks and technologies are relatively stable. The vice-president of production in a mechanistic organization would employ production processes and techniques that minimize waste and maximize outputs for a given quantity of inputs. The goal of mechanistic structures is efficiency. Thus, the rationale for bureaucracy is protection while the rationale for mechanistic organizations is efficiency. Clearly, the two are not mutually exclusive; an organization could be structured as a bureaucracy and also be mechanistic. On the other hand, many examples of inefficient bureaucracies can quickly come to mind, suggesting that while there is overlap between the concepts, there are distinctions as well.

Mechanistic structures are highly formalized, which simply means that nearly all processes and procedures have been administratively authorized. The organization considers processes and procedures outside these established protocols as variances that must be brought under control. Such formalization is driven by efficiency; reduction in variance increases predictability, and increases in predictability allow for improvements in efficiency. Examples pertinent to product or service distribution include the processes a store clerk uses when presented with a customer's credit card or how returns of products by customers are to be handled. Examples pertinent to product or service production and assembly include how a book publisher manages the workflow from completed manuscripts to final bookbinding and how Dell Computer manages assembly of made-to-order personal computers. Decision making is largely concerned with application of the appropriate predetermined rule, policy, procedure, or criteria.

Environmental and technological stability allow work to be clearly defined and differentiated. The work of the organization is divided into specific, precise tasks. Created from one or more such specific tasks, specialized job positions rigidly define skills needed, task methodology and procedures to be used, and specific responsibilities and authority. In effect, lower-level managers and other employees simply follow procedures, and while this may have the side effect of stifling creativity, it also increases efficiency of established processes. In stable environments, however, stifling creativity may be worth the improvements in efficiency. Few customers, for instance, would want a McDonald's employee to use creativity in preparing their hamburger. Instead, the repetitiveness and stability of the procedures needed to cook a hamburger are more efficient when the employee follows established procedures and customers can trust that each hamburger they purchase will taste the same.

However, specialized tasks are repetitive and can sometimes be boring. For example, at a Sam's Club store, one person stands at the door to perform the single task of marking customer receipts. Because employees often work separately with little interaction, it is often hard for them to see how one's small, specialized task relates to overall organizational objectives. Also, the work of mechanistic organizations tends to be impersonal. Jobs are designed around the task rather than the individual. Personnel selection, assignment, and promotion are based on the possession of skills required for specific tasks. Other people, like interchangeable parts of a machine, can replace people in a position.

Specialization carries throughout the organization. Positions are grouped together into specialized work units and, ultimately, into specialized functional departments such as production, marketing, or finance. Each organizational unit has clear and specific responsibilities and objectives. Communication is primarily vertical, with more emphasis on downward directives than on upward communication. Thus, such matters as goals, strategies, policies, and procedures are determined by top-level management and communicated downward as instructions and decisions to be implemented.

Upward communication usually involves transmittal of reports and other information for management to consider, usually at the request of management. Coordination is maintained through the chain of command. For example, top-level management is responsible for coordination across functional departments such as integrating marketing sales forecasts with production schedules. Within a department, the department manager is responsible for coordination across department subunits; production managers, for example, coordinate raw inventory requirements with work-in-process inventory.

At least two criticisms are generally made about mechanistic organizations. First, while focusing on task concerns such as efficiency and standardization, mechanistic organizations tend to ignore human needs and dynamics. Second, creativity, and thus innovation, are restricted by the rigidity of standardized and formalization. Thus, the appropriate environment for mechanistic organizations is a stable environment, while rapidly changing environments require more flexibility. Highly mechanized organizations operating in rapidly changing environments run the risk of becoming obsolete as competitors sacrifice maximum efficiency in exchange for flexibility to tackle new environmental conditions.

SEE ALSO: Effectiveness and Efficiency; Organic Organizations; Organization Theory; Organizational Behavior; Organizational Structure

Durward Hofler
Revised by Scott B. Droege

FURTHER READING:

Burns, T., and G.M. Stalker. *The Management of Innovation.* London: Tavistock, 1961.

Cardinal, L.B., S.B. Sitkin, and C.P. Long. "Balancing and Rebalancing in the Creation and Evolution of Organizational Control." *Organization Science* 15, no. 4 (2004): 411–432.

Martin P., and T.C. Heeren. "Product-Line Management in Professional Organizations: An Empirical Test of Competing Theoretical Perspectives." *Academy of Management Journal* 47, no. 5 (2004): 723–735.

McAdam R., and B. Lafferty. "A Multilevel Case Study Critique of Six Sigma: Statistical Control or Strategic Change?" *International Journal of Operations and Production Management* 24, no. 5 (2004): 530–549.

MEETING MANAGEMENT

Most organizations use meetings in the course of their work, and these meetings can be successful or unsuccessful, depending on whether they are managed properly. Managers must learn to properly organize and conduct meetings to contribute to organizational effectiveness. There are several important principles to meeting management: determining situations that require a meeting, understanding types of meetings, planning a meeting, running a meeting, closing the meeting, and managing people after the meeting.

SITUATIONS REQUIRING A MEETING

Before calling a meeting, it is important to know if one is needed. Some situations benefit from having a meeting, and in other situations, one is unnecessary. There are some common situations in which a meeting is needed.

First, you are likely to need to meet if you are managing a project. Because projects involve multiple people and a lot of information, you will likely need to meet with individuals at various stages: at the beginning of the project, throughout the project, and at the end of the project. Meetings may change in terms of content and frequency, depending on the stage of the project.

A second reason that a meeting is often called is when a supervisor needs to manage people. Managers need to meet with staff as a group or one-on-one to direct employees effectively. Typically, meetings to manage people are held at regular intervals.

A third reason to meet is when a manager must interact with a client. Client relationships may require meetings to pitch ideas, update the client on progress, or present a completed product or service.

A fourth situation in which a meeting is preferable is when written communication, such as interoffice memos or email, is burdensome. If issues are too complex for memos or email, a meeting may be a more efficient way to communicate.

Finally, managers may call meetings to address workplace problems. If a project is on the wrong course, or if there are interpersonal problems, a meeting may be the best way to address such problems.

While a meeting is often the best way to accomplish work objectives, there are times in which a meeting is simply a waste of people's time. There may be situations in which bringing a large group together to address an issue may only cause confusion or conflict. Additionally, there are some tasks that may be accomplished more easily and quickly, but just as effectively, by a smaller group (subcommittee) or an individual, then presented to the larger group for approval. Thus, while meetings can be very useful in the workplace, managers should take care to determine whether they are truly necessary.

TYPES OF MEETINGS

The reasons for calling the meeting should help to determine how the meeting should be formatted, or whether a meeting is really necessary. The length and formality of a meeting will differ depending on what type of meeting it is. There are six basic types of meeting: standing meeting, topical meeting, presentation, conference, emergency meeting, and seminar.

1. A *standing meeting* is a regularly scheduled meeting, such as a weekly check-in with employees or a project meeting that occurs every month. Because these meetings are recurring, they are easier to manage, with similar formats and agendas. Typically, these meetings are held on the same day and time, but they may be rescheduled if necessary.

2. A *topical meeting* is one that is called to discuss one specific subject. This may be a work issue or a project task. The invitees and format are dependent on the subject being addressed.

3. A *presentation* occurs when one or more people speak, and one moderator leads the meeting. Presentation meetings tend to be highly structured, and there purpose is usually to inform. It may be to inform clients, employees, or managers.

4. A *conference* is also highly structured, but it is used to solicit contributions from participants on a particular topic.

5. An *emergency meeting* is used to address a crisis, and they are often called with very little advance notice. These meetings may be used to address internal problems, such as a theft in the building, or external problems, such as a natural disaster.

6. A *seminar* is typically educational—someone with expertise provides participants with specific information.

The type of meeting will dictate who is invited to participate and how the participants are arranged in the meeting room. Topical meetings, conferences, and emergency meetings are best run in seating arrangements in which participants can all see one another and therefore be more likely to engage in discussion.

Conversely, presentations and seminars require a different seating arrangement where all participants can see the speaker, but do not need to see one another. These arrangements are presented in Figure 1, in which the ovals represent meeting participants and the shaded oval is the presenter or facilitator.

Standing meetings may vary in seating, depending on what is discussed; if a supervisor is giving information, then there is no need for participants to group themselves in order to see one another. Some standing meetings may literally be "standing" if participants only need to meet briefly to get information from a supervisor or team leader.

PLANNING A MEETING

The most critical part of planning a meeting is determining whether a meeting is actually necessary. There are many organizational issues that can be addressed without needing to hold a meeting. Meetings are time-consuming, and because they require many different people to leave their work to meet, they can hinder productivity if they are called when unnecessary. Additionally, some standing meetings are kept without any assessment as to whether or not that weekly or monthly meeting is actually productive and useful.

To determine whether a meeting is necessary, consider the problem that needs to be solved or the issue that must be addressed. If all that is required is dissemination of information, then a memo or email may be sufficient. If you need information, decide if you can get that information from one person or if a

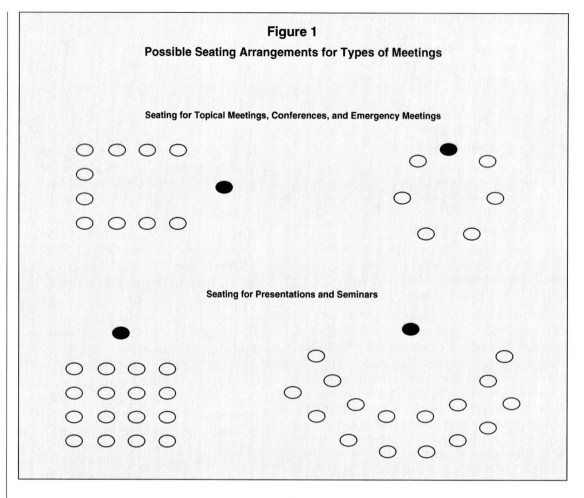

Figure 1

Possible Seating Arrangements for Types of Meetings

Seating for Topical Meetings, Conferences, and Emergency Meetings

Seating for Presentations and Seminars

meeting with several people is necessary. It is appropriate to call a meeting if you have to solicit information or feedback from a group of people, if a group decision must be made, or if a group will have questions regarding the information being given.

Once you have determined that a meeting is necessary, you must decide who should participate. Consider the goal or purpose of the meeting and be sure to invite those members of the organization who have the information or opinions necessary for the meeting. It may be helpful to ask others for their opinions as to who should attend the meeting, since you may not have all of the necessary information.

After the list of participants has been compiled, the participants should be contacted as soon as possible to ensure that all of the necessary people can attend. When contacting individuals about the meeting, let them know the time, place, and purpose of the meeting.

Additionally, if the meeting participants need to bring any documents or information to the meeting, be sure to ask them specifically for these things. It will be a waste of time to call a meeting without properly preparing yourself and the participants. Finally, if you have scheduled a meeting in advance, give participants a reminder of the meeting time and place as the meet-

ing draws nearer. A quick email or telephone call can remind participants of the meeting.

The final step in preparing for a meeting is to develop a meeting agenda. The agenda should indicate the desired outcome of the meeting, the major topics to address, and the type of action needed. You may also want to list a name of a participant next to an agenda item. For example, an agenda item might be: "Update on monthly sales numbers (Linda Smith)."

By determining which participants will need to be involved with each meeting agenda item, you may discover that a critical person has been overlooked and must be invited to the meeting. If possible, distribute the agenda to the meeting participants before the meeting so that they know what will be discussed and what they will be responsible for doing before and during the meeting. This agenda will also give you and the participants a better idea of how long the meeting should last.

RUNNING A MEETING

Deciding a meeting's purpose and preparing to hold the meeting are critical steps for an effective meeting. However, if the actual meeting is not properly run, it can be a waste of time and resources for everyone involved. The first and easiest step in running a meeting properly is to start the meeting on time. This indicates respect for meeting participants and their time.

When beginning the meeting, be sure to thank the participants for taking time to attend, and thank those who have done prior preparation for the meeting. Review the purpose of the meeting with the participants and determine who will take minutes of the meeting (if necessary). It may also be necessary to clarify your role in the meeting, which is dependent on the purpose of the meeting.

For instance, if the purpose of the meeting is to come to a group decision on a topic, your role may be to facilitate discussion and decision-making. If the meeting's purpose is to provide information on a new organizational policy and answer questions about that policy, your role will be quite different. You will be an information provider and a representative of the organization. Thus, to ensure smooth interactions in the meeting, it may be helpful to inform participants of your role.

Once the meeting is underway, you may need to establish some guidelines or rules for how the meeting should progress. Many of these guidelines for interaction are understood by members of the organization, but how strong unwritten rules are may depend on the people who attend the meeting. Therefore, there may be times in which it is necessary to establish or reiterate ground rules.

Ground rules might include: meeting attendees must participate in the meeting by providing information or opinions; participants must listen when others are speaking and not interrupt; members must maintain the momentum of the meeting and not get distracted with tangential topics. In some meetings it may be necessary to request that participants maintain confidentiality about what was discussed in the meeting.

Facilitating the meeting can be a daunting task. First, as meeting facilitator, you may have to enforce the established ground rules. For instance, if one participant is dominating discussion and preventing others from voicing opinions, you may need to ask that person to give others a chance to participate. Second, you are responsible for managing the time used in the meetings. It can be very difficult to keep a meeting's momentum and accomplish the tasks set forth in the agenda.

Be mindful of the time, and if necessary, get a meeting participant to help monitor the time. If the time seems to be getting out of hand, you may choose to table a certain topic to be addressed at a later time, or you may ask participants for their suggestions to resolve the impasse and move on.

While it is often difficult to encourage meeting participants to stop discussing a particularly interest-ing or controversial topic, this is often necessary. At times, you may be able to ask certain participants to gather more information related to a difficult topic, which will be shared in a later meeting and discussed further at that time.

CLOSING THE MEETING

Try to end the meeting on time; if necessary, schedule another meeting to address agenda items that need more time. At the close of the meeting, reiterate any conclusions, decisions, or assignments to participants, so that you are sure that you have summarized the meeting properly. Any meeting minutes should reflect these outcomes of the meeting, so that there is a record of tasks and responsibilities that were decided. Often during the course of the meeting, it is easy to forget specific issues that have been resolved.

In closing the meeting, you may also want to ask participants to evaluate the effectiveness of the meeting. Participants may be able to identify issues that should be addressed in a memo or another meeting. Additionally, participants may tell you that the meeting was unnecessary, which will aid in future meeting planning. Without such evaluation, unnecessary meetings may continue to be scheduled, or you may have some participants who are absent from future meetings, believing them to be a waste of time.

Regardless of the purpose of the meeting or the way in which it progressed, you should try to close the meeting on a positive note. Even if a meeting has involved difficult discussion or disagreements, try to find something positive to mention. This may be a conclusion that has been reached or a decision about the need for more information, or that all participants have voiced their concerns and that those concerns have been heard.

Finally, be sure to thank all participants for coming to the meeting.

AFTER THE MEETING

After the meeting, the most critical task is to disseminate information about the conclusions reached in the meeting. This is easily done by distributing the meeting minutes. However, if minutes have not been taken, you should record important outcomes of the meeting as soon as possible after the meeting. The distribution of information regarding the outcomes of the meeting helps participants know that their voices were heard and that the tasks accomplished in the meeting are recognized.

If tasks were assigned for people to complete after the meeting, distribute those via email, memo, or personal request. It is helpful to remind people of the tasks they were asked to do.

Post-meeting follow-up tasks should be carried out as soon as possible. To keep the momentum of the meeting and of the agenda, it is useful to provide information quickly.

TECHNOLOGY-ENABLED MEETINGS

Technology now allows people in remote locations to meet in a way that is similar to face-to-face meetings. Conference telephone calls and videoconferencing are alternatives when parties cannot meet in person.

Conference calls are made via telephone, and all parties are able to listen to and speak to one another. Many workplace telephones have the ability to place conference calls, and these calls are relatively inexpensive, especially when compared to the cost of an employee or client traveling long distances to attend a meeting.

The major difficulty associated with conference calls is the participants' inability to see one another. Because of this, participants may not know who is speaking; therefore, it is important that individuals identify themselves before speaking. Another problem with not seeing others is that interruptions are common in conference calls; care must be taken to wait for each person to speak in turn. Finally, as with all telephone conversations, facial expressions and eye contact are not possible, and thus, the meaning of a person's words may be lost.

Videoconferencing is done through an Internet connection, and it allows participants to see and hear one another through a video or computer screen. Because participants can see one another, many of the limitations associated with telephone conference calls are eliminated. However, many videoconferences have a short time delay; a person speaking in one location must wait for the others in the other location to receive the message. This means that reactions to speaker may lag such that the speaker cannot easily understand the reaction to his or her words.

Another major drawback to videoconferencing is that, with increasing use of technology, there is a possibility that others will not have adequate or compatible technology, or that the technology will fail. However, despite potential problems, videoconferencing provides much richer information than a conference call and is still less expensive in many cases than having all participants travel to one location.

TROUBLESHOOTING MEETINGS

There are a number of problems that can occur in meeting planning and facilitating. However, if you can determine the cause of the problems, avoiding or eliminating them may lead to more effective meetings.

The first problem that you may encounter in meeting management is when participants do not attend meetings consistently. If participants who need to attend meetings are not coming to them, there may be a number of different reasons why, and as a meeting planner, you need to ask the participant his or her reasons for not attending. If participants are forgetting to come to meetings, you may have to provide more reminders of upcoming meetings or schedule them further in advance. In severe cases, you may even have to personally approach participants immediately before a meeting to remind them of their need to attend.

A more serious problem occurs when participants choose not to attend meetings. It could be that participants feel that meetings are a waste of their time, or perhaps they feel that their contributions are not valued, or they may even dislike other participants enough to not attend. Although difficult, resolving interpersonal problems may be necessary to get needed participants to attend meetings.

A second problem associated with meeting management is when meetings become sidetracked by tangential topics or discussions with no resolution. This problem can be addressed either by improving meeting planning or meeting facilitation. In planning a meeting, if the agenda is not specific enough or if participants do not bring proper information to the meeting, it is easy to get bogged down in discussion that does not result in problem solving. Thus, when meetings become sidetracked, try to determine what the problem is either by observing participants comments or by specifically asking participants what could be done to better focus meetings before they occur.

If the problem is not in the meeting planning, then it is in the facilitation. The facilitator must keep meeting participants on track and speak up if discussion meanders. If a facilitator is unwilling to ask participants to save unrelated comments until a later time, or unable to maintain control over the meeting, it will turn into an unproductive session.

Another problem associated with meeting management is when members do not participate appropriately, either by dominating the discussion or not contributing to the discussion. The facilitator may need to remind participants of meeting etiquette or ground rules or specifically ask some participants to voice their opinions. If a meeting participant is particularly disruptive, it may be necessary for the facilitator to speak to the person outside of the meeting and request that they allow others more opportunity to contribute. In the worst case, a meeting participant may need to be replaced, particularly if bad behavior is detracting from organizational effectiveness.

Successful meeting management is an important management competency. Managers must understand situations that require meetings; the types of meetings;

how to plan, run, and close meetings; and how to manage activities after meetings. Furthermore, managers should be able to troubleshoot problems that arise from organizational meetings and know options for technology-enabled meetings.

SEE ALSO: Group Dynamics; Teams and Teamwork

Marcia J. Simmering

FURTHER READING:

Micale, Frances A. *Not Another Meeting!: A Practical Guide for Facilitating Effective Meetings.* Central Point, OR: Oasis, 2002.

Moscovick, Roger K., and Robert B. Nelson. *We've Got to Start Meeting Like This: A Guide to Successful Meeting Management.* Indianapolis, IN: Jist Publishing, 1996.

Streibel, Barbara J. *The Manager's Guide to Effective Meetings.* New York, NY: McGraw-Hill, 2002.

MENTORING

Mentors are individuals with advanced experience and knowledge who take a personal interest in helping the careers and advancement of their protégés. Mentors may or may not be in their protégés' chain of command, be employed in the same organization as their protégés, or even be in the same field as their protégés. Mentoring relationships may range from focusing exclusively on the protégé's job functions to being a close friendship that becomes one of the most important relationships in the protégé's life.

Most mentoring relationships are informal, and develop on the basis of mutual identification and the fulfillment of career needs. The mentor may see the protégé as a "diamond in the rough" or a younger version of him or herself, while the protégé, may view the mentor as a competent role model with valued knowledge, skills and abilities. Members of mentoring relationships often report a mutual attraction or chemistry that sparks the development of the relationship.

According to Kathy Kram, mentors provide two primary types of behaviors or roles. First, they provide career development roles, which involve coaching, sponsoring advancement, providing challenging assignments, protecting protégés from adverse forces, and fostering positive visibility. Second, mentors provide psychosocial roles, which involve personal support, friendship, counseling, acceptance, and role modeling. A given mentor may engage in some or all of these roles and these roles may not only vary from relationship to relationship, but may also vary over time in a given relationship.

Kram observes that mentoring relationships pass through four phases: initiation, cultivation, separation, and redefinition. The relationship develops during the initiation and cultivation stages. In initiation, the mentor and protégé meet and first begin to know a little about each other. The real learning occurs in the cultivation stage, where the mentor helps the protégé to grow and develop. The separation stage is typically reached after two to five years, and the relationship may terminate because of physical separation, or because the members no longer need one another. Research indicates that the majority of mentoring relationships end because of physical separation. After separation, the members of the relationship may redefine their relationship as a peer relationship, or may terminate their relationship entirely.

POSITIVE OUTCOMES OF MENTORING RELATIONSHIPS

Mentoring relationships are related to a variety of positive organizational and career outcomes. A number of different research studies indicate that mentored individuals have higher levels of mobility on the job, recognition, promotion, and compensation. Also, employees with mentors report higher levels of learning on the job than those without mentors. Additionally, research indicates that employees with positive mentoring experiences typically feel higher levels of pay satisfaction, career satisfaction, and organizational commitment. Finally, research indicates that the lower levels of turnover that occur with mentored individuals are due, in part, to their higher levels of organizational commitment that may be brought about by the mentoring relationship.

A recent meta-analysis (a statistical technique that combines results from numerous studies to give an "average" finding) conducted by Allen, Eby, Poteet, Lentz, and Lima in 2004 supports these findings. In their analysis of 43 individual studies, they found that individuals who had been mentored had better career outcomes from both career-related and psychosocial mentoring; they were more satisfied with their careers, believed strongly that they would advance in their careers, and were committed to their careers. The meta-analysis indicated that mentored individuals also had better compensation and more promotions that those employees without mentors.

Mentoring relationships may also be beneficial for the mentor. Mentors have reported more benefits than costs to being a mentor, research indicates that key benefits to mentors included a sense of satisfaction and fulfillment, recognition from others, career and job renewal, and support from their protégés.

Finally, mentoring relationships may be beneficial for the organization. Mentoring relationships are a powerful tool for socializing new employees, for increasing organizational commitment, and for reducing unwanted turnover. Mentoring relationships can foster innovation and revitalize mentors who have reached career plateaus. Because members of the relationship may share different insights and perspectives regarding organizational and societal cultures, mentoring relationships may also be useful in mergers and in international organizations.

GENDER, DIVERSITY, AND MENTORING

Although mentoring relationships are important for all organizational members, they are essential for women and employees of color. Mentors can help these individuals overcome barriers to advancement in organizations and break through the "glass ceiling," the invisible barrier to advancement based on gender biases. Research indicates that a full 91 percent of the female executives surveyed in a Catalyst study reported having a mentor, and the majority of respondents identified mentoring as a key strategy used to break through the glass ceiling.

A mentor can buffer women and people of color from both overt and covert forms of discrimination, and help them navigate the obstacle course to the executive suite. By conferring legitimacy on their female and minority protégés, mentors can alter stereotypic perceptions and send the message that the protégé has the mentor's powerful support and backing. Research indicates that mentors provide "reflected power" to their protégés, and use their influence to build their protégé's power in the organization. Mentors can train their female and minority protégés in the "ins and outs" of corporate politics and provide valuable information on job openings and changes in the organization-information that is typically provided in the "old boys' network."

Although most research indicates that women and people of color are as likely as their majority counterparts to have mentors, women reported greater barriers to getting a mentor than men. Research showed that women were more likely than men to report that mentors were unwilling to mentor them, that supervisors and coworkers would disapprove of the relationship, that they had less access to mentors, and that they were hesitant to initiate the relationship for fear that their efforts would be misconstrued as being sexual by either the mentor or others in the organization. In spite of these reported barriers, women were as likely as men actually to have a mentor, suggesting that women overcame these barriers in order to develop these important relationships. Similarly, other mentoring research indicates that African American protégés were more likely than Caucasian protégés to go outside their departments and formal lines of authority to develop mentoring relationships with higher ranking mentors of the same race. These studies indicate that women and minorities recognize the importance of mentors and are willing to overcome barriers to gaining this critical developmental relationship.

Another obstacle faced by female and minority protégés is that they are more likely than their majority counterparts to be in a "diversified mentoring relationship." Diversified mentoring relationships are composed of mentors and protégés who differ on one or more group memberships associated with power. Because of the scarcity of female and minority mentors at higher organizational ranks, female and minority protégés are more likely than their majority counterparts to be in cross-gender or cross-race relationships. These relationships provide limited role modeling functions, functions that are particularly important for women and employees of color. In addition, individuals in cross-gender relationships are less likely to engage in close friendship and social roles that involve after-work networking activities because of the threat or appearance of romantic involvement.

Female and minority protégés face a certain catch 22: even if they find a female or minority mentor who can provide role modeling functions these mentors may be restricted in helping them advance since women and people of color has less power in organizations than their majority counterparts. In sum, majority protégés obtain mentors who can provide more functions than minority or female protégés, and these functions in turn lead to increased power and more promotions, thus perpetuating the cycle.

One area of diversity that has received recent research attention is the role of age in mentoring relationships. Age has become a more important workplace issues as the large group of American baby boomers ages. Experts suggest that mentors be 8-15 years (a half generation) older than their protégés, so that the age difference is not as large as that of parent and child, and not so small that the mentor and protégé act more as peers. However, not all mentoring relationships have this age span. Research indicates that the mentoring experience differs for protégés based on their age, with younger protégés receiving more career-related mentoring than older protégés.

FORMAL MENTORING RELATIONSHIPS

In recognition of the benefits of mentoring relationships, many organizations attempt to replicate informal mentoring relationships by creating formal mentoring programs. One key difference between formal and informal mentoring relationships is that informal relationships develop spontaneously, whereas formal mentoring relationships develop with organizational assistance or intervention-usually in the form of voluntary assignment or matching of mentors and protégés. A second distinction is that formal relationships are usually of much shorter duration than informal relationships; formal relationships are usually contracted to last less than a year.

Although many organizations assume that formal relationships are as effective as informal relationships, existing research indicates that this is not the case. Georgia Chao and her associates found that protégés with formal mentoring relationships received less compensation than protégés with informal relationships. Other studies suggest that formal protégés not only received less compensation than informal protégés, but they also reported less psychosocial and career development functions and less satisfaction with their mentors than informal protégés. In fact, individuals with formal mentors did not receive more compensation or promotions than individuals who were not mentored. These researchers also found that women received fewer benefits from formal mentors than men did, indicating that female protégés may have the least to gain form entering a formal mentoring relationship. This research indicates that formal mentors are not a substitute for informal mentoring relationships.

In conclusion, organizations can create an environment that fosters mentoring relationships by structuring diverse work teams that span departmental and hierarchical lines and by increasing informal opportunities for networking and interaction. Organizations can increase the pool of diverse mentors by structurally integrating women and minorities into powerful positions across ranks and departments, and by rewarding these relationships in performance appraisals and salary decisions.

NEGATIVE MENTORING EXPERIENCES

Although there are numerous potential benefits for both the mentor and protégé from the mentoring relationship, it is not always a positive experience. Researchers have identified dysfunctional mentoring relationships in which the needs of either the mentor or protégé are not being met, or the relationship is causing some distress to either of the parties. Negative experiences that have been identified:

- Mentor delegates too much work to the protégé

- Mentor abuses his/her power over the protégé

- Mentor inappropriately takes credit for the protégé's work

- Mentor attempts to sabotage the protégé

- Mentor intentionally deceives the protégé

- Mentor intentionally is unavailable to or excludes protégé

- Mentor neglects protégé's career, or does not provide support

- Mentor is too preoccupied with his/her own career progress

- Mentor lacks technical competence and cannot guide protégé

- Mentor lacks interpersonal competence and cannot interact with protégé

- Poor fit in personality between mentor and protégé

- Poor fit in work styles between mentor and protégé

- Mentor has a bad attitude about the organization or job

- Mentor cannot mentor effectively due to problems in his/her personal life

- Mentor sexually harasses protégé

SEE ALSO: Diversity; Knowledge Management; Training Delivery Methods; Women and Minorities in Management

Belle Rose Ragins
Revised by Marcia Simmering

FURTHER READING:

Allen, Tammy D., Lillian T. Eby, Mark L. Poteet, Elizabeth Lentz, and Lizette Lima. "Career Benefits Associated with Mentoring for Protégés: A Meta-Analysis." *Journal of Applied Psychology* 89, no. 1 (2004): 127–136.

Chao, Georgia, Pat Walz, and Philip Gardner. "Formal and Informal Mentorship's: A Comparison on Mentoring Functions and Contrast with No Mentored Counterparts." *Personnel Psychology* 45 (1992): 619–636.

Dreher, George, and Ronald Ash. "A Comparative Study of Mentoring Among Men and Women in Managerial, Professional, and Technical Positions." *Journal of Applied Psychology* 75 (1990): 539–546.

Eby, Lillian, Marcus Butts, Angie Lockwood, and Shana A. Simon. "Protégés' Negative Mentoring Experiences: Construct Development and Nomological Validation." *Personnel Psychology* 57 (2004): 411–447.

Kram, Kathy. *Mentoring at Work.* Glenview, IL: Scott, Foresman & Co., 1985.

Ragins, Belle Rose. "Diversified Mentoring Relationships in Organizations: A Power Perspective." *Academy of Management Review* 22 (1997): 482–521.

———. "Mentor Functions and Outcomes: A Comparison of Men and Women in Formal and Informal Mentoring Relationships." *Journal of Applied Psychology* 1999.

Scandura, Terri. "Mentorship and Career Mobility: An Empirical Investigation." *Journal of Organizational Behavior* 13 (1992): 169–174.

Thomas, David. "The Impact of Race on Managers' Experiences of Developmental Relationships (Mentoring and Sponsorship): An Intra-Organizational Study." *Journal of Organizational Behavior* 11 (1990): 479–492.

MERGERS AND ACQUISITIONS

A merger takes place when two companies decide to combine into a single entity. An acquisition involves one company essentially taking over another company. While the motivations may differ, the essential feature of both mergers and acquisitions involves one firm emerging where once there existed two firms. Another term frequently employed within discussions on this topic is *takeover*. Essentially, the difference rests in the attitude of the incumbent management of firms that are targeted. A so-called friendly takeover is often a euphemism for a merger. A hostile takeover refers to unwanted advances by outsiders. Thus, the reaction of management to the overtures from another firm tends to be the main influence on whether the resulting activities are labeled friendly or hostile.

MOTIVATIONS FOR MERGERS AND ACQUISITIONS

There are a number of possible motivations that may result in a merger or acquisition. One of the most oft cited reasons is to achieve economies of scale. Economies of scale may be defined as a lowering of the average cost to produce one unit due to an increase in the total amount of production. The idea is that the larger firm resulting from the merger can produce more cheaply than the previously separate firms. Efficiency is the key to achieving economies of scale, through the sharing of resources and technology and the elimination of needless duplication and waste. Economies of scale sounds good as a rationale for merger, but there are many examples to show that combining separate entities into a single, more efficient operation is not easy to accomplish in practice.

A similar idea is economies of vertical integration. This involves acquiring firms through which the parent firm currently conducts normal business operations, such as suppliers and distributors. By combining different elements involved in the production and delivery of the product to the market, acquiring firms gain control over raw materials and distribution outlets. This may result in centralized decisions and better communications and coordination among the various business units. It may also result in competitive advantages over rival firms that must negotiate with and rely on outside firms for inputs and sales of the product.

A related idea to economies of vertical integration is a merger or acquisition to achieve greater market presence or market share. The combined, larger entity may have competitive advantages such as the ability to buy bulk quantities at discounts, the ability to store and inventory needed production inputs, and the ability to achieve mass distribution through sheer negotiating power. Greater market share also may result in advantageous pricing, since larger firms are able to compete effectively through volume sales with thinner profit margins. This type of merger or acquisition often results in the combining of complementary resources, such as a firm that is very good at distribution and marketing merging with a very efficient producer. The shared talents of the combined firm may mean competitive advantages versus other, smaller competition.

The ideas above refer to reasons for mergers or acquisitions among firms in similar industries. There are several additional motivations for firms that may not necessarily be in similar lines of business. One of the often-cited motivations for acquisitions involves excess cash balances. Suppose a firm is in a mature industry, and has little opportunities for future investment beyond the existing business lines. If profitable, the firm may acquire large cash balances as managers seek to find outlets for new investment opportunities. One obvious outlet to acquire other firms. The ostensible reason for using excess cash to acquire firms in different product markets is diversification of business risk. Management may claim that by acquiring firms in unrelated businesses the total risk associated with the firm's operations declines. However, it is not always clear for whom the primary benefits of such activities accrue. A shareholder in a publicly traded firm who wishes to diversify business risk can always do so by investing in other companies shares. The investor does not have to rely on incumbent management to achieve the diversification goal. On the other hand, a less risky business strategy is likely to result in less uncertainty in future business performance, and stability makes management look good. The agency problem resulting from incongruent incentives on the part of management and shareholders is always an issue in public corporations. But, regardless of the motivation, excess cash is a primary motivation for corporate acquisition activity.

To reverse the perspective, an excess of cash is also one of the main reasons why firms become the targets of takeover attempts. Large cash balances make for attractive potential assets; indeed, it is often implied that a firm which very large amount of cash is not being efficiently managed. Obviously, that conclusion is situation specific, but what is clear is that cash is attractive, and the greater the amount of cash the greater the potential to attract attention. Thus, the presence of excess cash balances in either acquiring or

...ung influence in
...tivity.

... makes firms attractive as
...ers is the presence of unused tax
...orate tax code allows for loss carry-
... firm loses money in one year, the loss
...rried forward to offset earned income in sub-
...ent years. A firm that continues to lose money,
however, has no use for the loss carry-forwards.
However, if the firm is acquired by another firm that is
profitable, the tax shields from the acquired may be
used to shelter income generated by the acquiring
firm. Thus the presence of unused tax shields may
enhance the attractiveness of a firm as a potential
acquisition target.

A similar idea is the notion that the combined
firm from a merger will have lower absolute financing
costs. Suppose two firms, X and Y, have each issued
bonds as a normal part of the financing activities. If
the two firms combine, the cash flows from the activities of X can be used to service the debt of Y, and vice
versa. Therefore, with less default risk the cost of new
debt financing for the combined firm should be lower.
It may be argued that there is no net gain to the combined firm; since shareholders have to guarantee debt
service on the combined debt, the savings on the cost
of debt financing may be offset by the increased return
demanded by equity holders. Nevertheless, lower
financing costs are often cited as rationale for merger
activity.

One rather dubious motivation for merger activity is to artificially boost earnings per share. Consider
two firms, A and B. Firm A has earnings of $1,000,
100 shares outstanding, and thus $10 earnings per
share. With a price-earnings ratio of 20, its shares are
worth $200. Firm B also has earnings of $1,000, 100
shares outstanding, but due to poorer growth opportunities its shares trade at 10 times earnings, or $100. If
A acquires B, it will only take one-half share of A for
each share of B purchased, so the combined firm will
have 150 total shares outstanding. Combined earnings
will be $2,000, so the new earnings per share of the
combined firm are $13.33 per share. It appears that the
merger has enhanced earnings per share, when in fact
the result is due to inconsistency in the rate of increase
of earnings and shares outstanding. Such manipulations were common in the 1960s, but investors have
learned to be more wary of mergers instigated mainly
to manipulate per share earnings. It is questionable
whether such activity will continue to fool a majority
of investors.

Finally, there is the ever-present hubris hypothesis concerning corporate takeover activity. The main
idea is that the target firm is being run inefficiently,
and the management of acquiring firm should certainly be able to do a better job of utilizing the target's

assets and strategic business opportunities. In addition, there is additional prestige in managing a larger
firm, which may include additional perquisites such as
club memberships or access to amenities such as corporate jets or travel to distant business locales. These
factors cannot be ignored in detailing the set of factors
motivating merger and acquisition activity.

TYPES OF TAKEOVER DEFENSES

As the previous section suggests, some merger
activity is unsolicited and not desired on the part of the
target firm. Often, the management of the target firm
will be replaced or let go as the acquiring firm's management steps in to make their own mark and implement their plans for the new, combined entity. In
reaction to hostile takeover attempts, a number of
defense mechanisms have been devised and used to
try and thwart unwanted advances.

To any offer for the firm's shares, several actions
may be taken which make it difficult or unattractive to
subsequently pursue a takeover attempt. One such
action is the creation of a staggered board of directors.
If an outside firm can gain a controlling interest on the
board of directors of the target, it will be able to influence the decisions of the board. Control of the board
often results in de facto control of the company. To
avoid an outside firm attempting to put forward an
entire slate of their own people for election to the
target firm's board, some firms have staggered the
terms of the directors. The result is that only a portion
of the seats is open annually, preventing an immediate
takeover attempt. If a rival does get one of its own
elected, they will be in a minority and the target firm's
management has the time to decide how to proceed
and react to the takeover threat.

Another defense mechanism is to have the board
pass an amendment requiring a certain number of
shares needed to vote to approve any merger proposal.
This is referred to as a supermajority, since the
requirement is usually set much higher than a simple
majority vote total. A supermajority amendment puts
in place a high hurdle for potential acquirers to clear if
they wish to pursue the acquisition.

A third defensive mechanism is a fair price
amendment. Such an amendment restricts the firm
from merging with any shareholders holding more
than some set percentage of the outstanding shares,
unless some formula-determined price per share is
paid. The formula price is typically prohibitively high,
so that a takeover can take place only in the effect of a
huge premium payment for outstanding shares. If the
formula price is met, managers with shares and stockholders receive a significant premium over fair market
value to compensate them for the acquisition.

Finally, another preemptive strike on the part of
existing management is a poison pill provision.

A poison pill gives existing shareholders rights that may be used to purchase outstanding shares of the firms stock in the event of a takeover attempt. The purchase price using the poison pill is a significant discount from fair market value, giving shareholders strong incentives to gobble up outstanding shares, and thus preventing an outside firm from purchasing enough stock on the open market to obtain a controlling interest in the target.

Once a takeover attempt has been identified as underway, incumbent management can initiate measures designed to thwart the acquirer. One such measure is a dual-class recapitalization; whereby a new class of equity securities is issued which contains superior voting rights to previously outstanding shares. The superior voting rights allow the target firm's management to effectively have voting control, even without a majority of actual shares in hand. With voting control, they can effectively decline unsolicited attempts by outsiders to acquire the firm.

Another reaction to undesired advances is an asset restructuring. Here, the target firm initiates the sale or disposal of the assets that are of primary interest to the acquiring firm. By selling desirable assets, the firm becomes less attractive to outside bidders, often resulting in an end to the acquisition activity. On the other side of the balance sheet, the firm can solicit help from a third party, friendly firm. Such a firm is commonly referred to as a "white knight," the implication being that the knight comes to the rescue of the targeted firm. A white knight may be issued a new set of equity securities such as preferred stock with voting rights, or may instead agree to purchase a set number of existing common shares at a premium price. The white knight is, of course, supportive of incumbent management; so by purchasing a controlling interest in the firm unwanted takeovers are effectively avoided.

One of the most prominent takeover activities associated with liability restructuring involves the issuance of junk bonds. "Junk" is used to describe debt with high default risk, and thus junk bonds carry very high coupon yields to compensate investors for the high risk involved. During the 1980s, the investment-banking firm Drexel Burnham Lambert led by Michael Milken pioneered the development of the junk-bond market as a vehicle for financing corporate takeover activity. Acquisition groups, which often included the incumbent management group, issued junk bonds backed by the firm's assets to raise the capital needed to acquire a controlling interest in the firm's equity shares. In effect, the firm's balance sheet was restructured with debt replacing equity financing. In several instances, once the acquisition was successfully completed the acquiring management subsequently sold off portions of the firm's assets or business divisions at large premiums, using the proceeds to retire some or all of the junk bonds. The takeover of RJR Nabisco by the firm Kohlberg Kravis Roberts [...] 1980s was one of the most celebrated tak[...] involving the use of junk-bond financing.

VALUING A POTENTIAL MERGER

There are several alternative methods that may be used to value a firm targeted for merger or acquisition. One method involves discounted cash flow analysis. First, the present value of the equity of the target firm must be established. Next, the present value of the expected synergies from the merger, in the form of cost savings or increased after-tax earnings, should be evaluated. Finally, summing the present value of the existing equity with the present value of the future synergies results in a present valuation of the target firm.

Another method involves valuation as an expected earnings multiple. First, the expected earnings in the first year of operations for the combined or merged firm should be estimated. Next, an appropriate price-earnings multiple must be determined. This figure will likely come from industry standards or from competitors in similar business lines. Now, the PE ratio can be multiplied by the expected combined earnings per share to estimate an expected price per share of the merged firm's common stock. Multiplying the expected share price by the number of shares outstanding gives a valuation of the expected firm value. Actual acquisition price can then be negotiated based on this expected firm valuation.

Another technique that is sometimes employed is valuation in relation to book value, which is the difference between the net assets and the outstanding liabilities of the firm. A related idea is valuation as a function of liquidation, or breakup, value. Breakup value can be defined as the difference between the market value of the firm's assets and the cost to retire all outstanding liabilities. The difference between book value and liquidation value is that the book value of assets, taken from the firm's balance sheet, are carried at historical cost. Liquidation value involves the current, or market, value of the firm's assets

Some valuations, particularly for individual business units or divisions, are based on replacement cost. This is the estimated cost of duplicating or purchasing the assets of the division at current market prices. Obviously, some premium is usually applied to account for the value of having existing and established business in place.

Finally, in the instances where firms that have publicly traded common stock are targeted, the market value of the stock is used as a starting point in acquisition negotiations. Earlier, a number of takeover defense activities were outlined that incumbent management may employ to restrict or reject unsolicited takeover bids. These types of defenses are not always in the best interests of existing shareholders. If the firm's existing managers take seriously the corporate goal of maximizing shareholder wealth, then a bidding war for the firm's stock often results in huge premiums for existing shareholders. It is not always clear that the shareholders interests are primary, since many of the takeover defenses prevent the use of the market value of the firm's common stock as a starting point for takeover negotiations. It is difficult to imagine the shareholder who is not happy about being offered a premium of 20 percent or more over the current market value of the outstanding shares.

CURRENT TRENDS IN MERGERS AND ACQUISITIONS

Mergers and Acquisitions were at an all-time high from the late 1990s to 2000. They have slowed down since then—a direct result of the economic slowdown. The reason is simple, companies did not have the cash to buy other companies. In 2005, however, we are seeing a robust economy and corporate profits, which means that businesses have cash. This cash is being used to buy companies—mergers and acquisitions. The end of 2004 saw several deals: Sprint is combining with Nextel, K-Mart Holding Corp is buying Sears, Roebuck & Co., Johnson & Johnson is planning to buy Guidant. These big corporation deals are spurring on an environment triggering more acquisitions. The telecom industry, the banking industry, and the software industry are potential areas for big mergers.

SEE ALSO: Financial Ratios

Howard Finch
Revised by Judith M. Nixon

FURTHER READING:

Brealey, R.A., and S.C. Myers. *Principles of Corporate Finance.* 7th ed. Boston, MA: McGraw-Hill/Irwin, 2003.

Bruner, R.F. *Applied Mergers and Acquisitions.* Hoboken, NJ: J. Wiley, 2004.

Coy, P., et al. "Shake, Rattle, and Merge." *Business Week,* 10 January 2005, 32.

Harrington, D.R. *Corporate Financial Analysis in a Global Environment.* 7th ed. Mason, Ohio: Thomson/South-Western, 2004.

MICROECONOMICS

SEE: Economics

MILES AND SNOW TYPOLOGY

In their 1978 book *Organization Strategy, Structure, and Process,* Raymond E. Miles and Charles C. Snow argued that different company strategies arise from the way companies decide to address three fundamental problems: entrepreneurial, engineering (or operational), and administrative problems. The entrepreneurial problem is how a company should manage its market share. The engineering problem involves how a company should implement its solution to the entrepreneurial problem. The administrative problem considers how a company should structure itself to manage the implementation of the solutions to the first two problems. Although businesses choose different solutions to these problems, Miles and Snow suggested that many companies develop similar solutions. As a result, they postulated that there are four general strategic types of organizations: prospector, defender, analyzer, and reactor organizations.

Prospector organizations face the entrepreneurial problem of locating and exploiting new product and market opportunities. These organizations thrive in changing business environments that have an element of unpredictability, and succeed by constantly examining the market in a quest for new opportunities. Moreover, prospector organizations have broad product or service lines and often promote creativity over efficiency. Prospector organizations face the operational problem of not being dependent on any one technology. Consequently, prospector companies prioritize new product and service development and innovation to meet new and changing customer needs and demands and to create new demands. The administrative problem of these companies is how to coordinate diverse business activities and promote innovation. Prospector organizations solve this problem by being decentralized, employing generalists (not specialists), having few levels of management, and encouraging collaboration among different departments and units.

Defender organizations face the entrepreneurial problem of how to maintain a stable share of the market, and hence they function best in stable environments. A common solution to this problem is cost leadership, and so these organizations achieve success by specializing in particular areas and using established and standardized technical processes to maintain low costs. In addition, defender organizations tend to be vertically integrated in order to achieve cost efficiency. Defender organizations face the administrative problem of having to ensure efficiency, and thus they require centralization, formal procedures, and discrete functions. Because their environments change slowly, defender organizations can rely on long-term planning.

Analyzer organizations share characteristics with prospector and defender organizations; thus, they face the entrepreneurial problem of how to maintain their shares in existing markets and how to find and exploit new markets and product opportunities. These organizations have the operational problem of maintaining the efficiency of established products or services, while remaining flexible enough to pursue new business activities. Consequently, they seek technical efficiency to maintain low costs, but they also emphasize new product and service development to remain competitive when the market changes. The administrative problem is how to manage both of these aspects. Like prospector organizations, analyzer organizations cultivate collaboration among different departments and units. Analyzer organizations are characterized by balance—a balance between defender and prospector organizations.

Reactor organizations, as the name suggests, do not have a systematic strategy, design, or structure. They are not prepared for changes they face in their business environments. If a reactor organization has a defined strategy and structure, it is no longer appropriate for the organization's environment. Their new product or service development fluctuates in response to the way their managers perceive their environment. Reactor organizations do not make long-term plans, because they see the environment as changing too quickly for them to be of any use, and they possess unclear chains of command.

Miles and Snow argued that companies develop their adaptive strategies based on their perception of their environments. Hence, as seen above, the different organization types view their environments in different ways, causing them to adopt different strategies. These adaptive strategies allow some organizations to be more adaptive or more sensitive to their environments than others, and the different organization types represent a range of adaptive companies. Because of their adaptive strategies, prospector organizations are the most adaptive type of company. In contrast, reactor organizations are the least adaptive type. The other two types fall in between these extremes: analyzers are the second most adaptive organizations, followed by defenders.

Since business environments vary from organization to organization, having a less adaptive strategy may be beneficial in some environments, such as highly regulated industries. For example, a study of the airline industry in the 1960s and 1970s indicated that the defender airlines were more successful than the prospector airlines in that the business environment changed slowly during this period because of the heavy regulation. Hence, the emphasis on efficiency by the defender airlines worked to their advantage.

On the other hand, prospector organizations clearly have an advantage over the other types of organizations in business environments with a fair amount of flux. Companies operating in mature markets in particular benefit from introducing new products or services and innovations to continue expanding. As Miles and Snow note, no single strategic orientation is the best. Each one—with the exception of the reactor organization—can position a company so that it can respond and adapt to its environment. What Miles and Snow argue determines the success of a company ultimately is not a particular strategic orientation, but simply establishing and maintaining a systematic strategy that takes into account a company's environment, technology, and structure.

FURTHER STUDIES

Scholars have attempted to verify the reliability and validity of the Miles and Snow typology. Such a study by Shortell and Zajac indicated that this typology of strategic orientations and its predictions generally were accurate. They found that prospectors are likely to be the first organizations to adopt new products and services, analyzers are likely to be the first organizations to adopt new managerial procedures and systems, and defenders are usually the first organizations to adopt new production-related technology. Moore carried Miles and Snow's framework to the retail environment, and concluded that the typology is generally applicable to retail contexts.

Other researchers further broadened the scope and applicability of Miles and Snow's typology, relating the strategic approaches strategic decision processes, international strategies, and functional areas within organizations. Subramanian, Fernandes, and Harper found that strategic types differed in terms of how managers perform environmental scanning. Prospectors tended to be more proactive in their scanning, followed by analyzers; defenders tended to be less proactive or "ad hoc."

As an example of the effects of functional expertise in an international context, Naranjo-Gil explored the impact of sophisticated accounting information systems on strategic performance among hospitals in Spain. Findings indicated that performance was enhanced primarily through sophisticated accounting information systems' role in implementing the prospector strategy.

Clearly, the Miles and Snow typology has contributed to our understanding of organizational behavior in a variety of settings. As demonstration for its further applicability, Peng, Tan, and Tong studied firms in the emerging Chinese economy. These authors concluded that the type of firm ownership can help predict strategic group membership. Specifically, state-owned enterprises tended to adopt defender strategies, and privately-owned enterprises tended to adopt prospector strategies. The analyzer orientation was also represented, most commonly under collective and foreign ownership. Future research efforts aimed at the extension of Miles and Snow's typology to international settings appears warranted.

SEE ALSO: First-Mover Advantage; Generic Competitive Strategies; Innovation; Technology Management

Karl Heil
Revised by Bruce Walters

FURTHER READING:

Fox-Wolfgramm, Susan J., Kimberly B. Boal, and James G. Hunt. "Organizational Adaptation to Institutional Change: A Comparative Study of First-Order Change in Prospector and Defender Banks." *Administrative Science Quarterly,* March 1998, 87.

Ghobadian, Abby, et al. "Evaluating the Applicability of the Miles and Snow Typology in a Regulated Public Utility Environment." *British Journal of Management,* 15 September 1998, S71.

Miles, Raymond E., and Charles C. Snow. *Organizational Strategy, Structure, and Process.* New York: McGraw-Hill, 1978.

Moore, M. "Towards aConfirmatory Model of Retail Strategy Types: An Empirical Test of Miles and Snow." *Journal of Business Research* 58 (2005): 696–704. .

Naranjo-Gil, D. "The Role of Sophisticated Accounting Systems in Strategy Management." *International Journal of Digital Accounting Research* 4, no. 8 (2004): 125–144.

Peng, M. W., J. Tan, and T.W. Tong. "Ownership Types and Strategic Groups in Emerging Economies." *The Journal of Management Studies* 41 (2004): 1105–1129.

Ramaswamy, Kannan, Anisya S. Thomas, and Robert J. Litschert. "Organizational Performance in a Regulated Environment: the Role of Strategic Orientation." *Strategic Management Journal,* January 1994, 63.

Shortell, Stephen M., and Edward J. Zajac. "Perceptual and Archival Measures of Miles and Snow's Strategic Types: A Comprehensive Assessment of Reliability and Validity." *Academy of Management Journal* (1990): 817.

Subramanian, R., N. Fernandes, and E. Harper. "An Empirical Examination of the Relationship Between Strategy and Scanning." *Mid-Atlantic Journal of Business* 29 (1993): 315–330.

MISSION AND VISION STATEMENTS

An organizational mission is an organization's reason for existence. It often reflects the values and beliefs of top managers in an organization. A mission statement is the broad definition of the organizational mission. It is sometimes referred to as a creed, purpose, or statement of corporate philosophy and values.

A good mission statement inspires employees and provides a focus and direction for setting lower level objectives. It should guide employees in making decisions and establish what the organization does. Mission statements are crucial for organizations to prosper and grow. While studies suggest that they have a positive impact on profitability and can increase shareholder equity, they also support that almost 40 percent of employees do not know or understand their company's mission.

Not only large corporations benefit from creating mission statements but small businesses as well. Entrepreneurial businesses are driven by vision and high aspirations. Developing a mission statement will help the small business realize their vision. Its primary purpose is to guide the entrepreneur and assist in refining the planning process. By developing a strategic plan that incorporates the mission statement, entrepreneurs are more likely to be successful and stay focused on what is important. The mission statement encourages managers and small business owners alike to consider the nature and scope of the business. *Business Week* attributes 30 percent higher return on several key financial measure for companies with well-crafted mission statements.

COMMON ELEMENTS

While mission statements vary from organization to organization and represent the distinctness of each one, they all share similar components. Most statements include descriptions of the organization's target market, the geographic domain, their concern for survival, growth and profitability, the company philosophy, and the organization's desired public image. For example:

> Our mission is to become the favorite family dining restaurant in every neighborhood in which we operate. This will be accomplished by serving a variety of delicious tasting and generously portioned foods at moderate prices. Our restaurants will be clean, fun, and casual. Our guests will be served by friendly, knowledgeable people that are dedicated to providing excellent customer service.

This mission statement describes the target market, which are families and the geographic domain of neighborhoods. It clearly states how it expects to be profitable by offering excellent customer service by friendly, knowledgeable people. When defining the mission statement it is important to take into account external influences such as the competition, labor conditions, economic conditions, and possible government regulation. It is important to remember however, that mission statements that try to be everything to everybody end up being nothing to anybody.

Companies should have mission statements that clearly define expected shareholder returns and they should regularly measure performance in terms of those expected returns. If the major reason for a business's existence is to make a profit then it stands to reason that expectations of profit should be included in the organization's mission. This means that management should reach a consensus about which aspects of the company's profit performance should be measured. These might include margin growth, product quality, market share changes, competitive cost position, and capital structure efficiency.

A mission statement sets the boundaries for how resources should be allocated and what strategic and operational goals should be set. The mission statement should acknowledge the company's strengths and then inform employees where to direct their efforts in order to take advantage of those strengths. Before writing a mission statement organizations should take a look at how they are different from the competition, whether it is in technology, image and name brand, or employees. It can often be thought of as a recipe for success because it not only defines the organization's accomplishments but it also provides employees with directions to help them develop plans and look for opportunities for improvement.

The organization defines what is acceptable behavior through the mission statement. Values and beliefs are the core of a strong mission statement. For example:

> Quality and values will secure our success. We will live by our values, have fun, and take pride in what we do. Our values are to maintain a work environment where people enjoy coming to work, to serve our guests and exceed their expectations, and to be profitable and result oriented.

This mission statement is simple and straightforward. It does not, however, specify the products or target market. The mission statement also provides meaning to the organization by stating not only what goals the company wants to achieve but also why it wants to achieve these goals. It is not effective unless it is challenging and forces workers to establish goals and means to measure the achievement of those goals. A mission statement should inspire employees and get them involved in the organization. It has been called the glue that holds the organization together through shared values and standards of behavior. A mission statement should be relevant to the history, culture, and values of the company.

Many statements refer to the social responsibility of the organization. For example, a company can show their concern for the community in the following:

> To be involved as good corporate citizens wherever we are around the world. We will treat customers and distributors with honesty, courtesy, and respect. We will respect and preserve the environment. Through all of this we will prove to be the worldwide leader in industry trade.

One important issue in organizations today is the concern with diversity. While it is not a traditional point included in mission statements, more and more companies are including it because of the globalization of the economy and the increased diversity of the workforce.

Before writing a mission statement, leaders in the organization must have an idea of what is in store for the future. This vision is the foundation for the mission statement. The vision provides a strategic direction, which is the springboard for the mission and its related goals. A vision statement differs from a mission statement. Vision statements are a view of what an organization is striving to become. For example:

> To bring back to neighborhoods all over America the importance of family unity. We will view ourselves as a family so these attributes will be carried over into our service.

They guide an organization into the future while mission statements are a reflection of the present. Because vision statements are a glimpse into the future, they are often not realized for several years. Organizations go through many changes and can face times of confusion and uncertainty. Changes are not always expected or easy, so a well thought out vision statement will help everyone stay focused and meet the organization's goals.

Some examples of well-known companies' mission statements:

- Wal-Mart: "To give ordinary folk the chance to buy the same thing as rich people."
- 3M: "To solve unsolved problems innovatively."
- Walt Disney: "To make people happy."

Historically, these may have seemed arrogant. But consider the outcome of the following mission statements from each company's early days:

- Ford Motor Company: "Ford will democratize the automobile."
- Sony: "Become the company most know for changing the world-wide poor-quality image of Japanese products."
- Wal-Mart: "Become a $125 billion company by the year 2000."

WRITING A MISSION STATEMENT

When creating a mission statement there are a few simple guidelines that can be followed. It is important to remember the basics so the mission statement stays simple and straight to the point. Some researchers agree that it should be kept to between 30 and 60 words, while others believe it does not necessarily have to be that brief. Some organizations have mission statements that are only one sentence, while others are a paragraph. An example of a mission statement that is limited to one sentence is "Our business is selling houses and our mission is total customer satisfaction." At a minimum, each mission statement should answer the following three questions: (1) What are the opportunities or needs the organization addresses? (2) What does the organization do to address those needs? and (3) What principles and values guide the organization? In other words, defining the organization's purpose, business and values.

Avoiding jargon and buzzwords will keep the mission statement clear and easy to understand. It should be universal and simple to comprehend for all employees in the organization. It should be unique and identify the organization. A mission statement is often what sets one company apart from the competition. It should outline the organization's competitive advantages and differentiate it from everyone else. Specific products/services offered as well as markets or customers should be included. Also a general business definition, behavioral standards, and desired competitive position can be added to a strong mission statement.

EMPLOYEE INVOLVEMENT

It is often helpful to allow company-wide input when creating a mission statement. This "bottom up" approach results in greater commitment to the organization and a better understanding of the organization. Employees from throughout the organization can help identify the core values of the company. In order to encourage employee participation, many companies have created competitions inviting employees to submit suggestions. Cash prizes are sometimes provided as an incentive for creative and inspirational statements. Some companies find it useful to invite customers to assist in writing a mission statement because they can provide an honest perspective. Another option is to review mission statements from other companies. This can help provide ideas as the writing process begins.

It is important to keep in mind that there will be a draft process involved in creating the mission statement. Employees can often provide invaluable insight on how to improve on each draft. In the end, the mission statement should reflect the personality of the organization. Thus, each company should be creative and unique in developing its own statement. Creating a mission committee that consists of members of management, frontline employees, and customers is another way to begin writing a mission statement. The major benefit of this strategy is the inclusion of all areas of the organization to ensure that everyone is represented. Another benefit is that employees will be more willing to work toward accomplishing the mission if they know they had a voice in its creation.

A "top down" approach can be effective in smaller organizations or even sole proprietorships. There is less time involved in creating a mission statement when it comes from the top. Also, many times frontline employees and lower level managers lack the insight necessary to see the big picture. They may not be able to conceptualize the entire organization and therefore miss important aspects of the business. Participation may not always be a good option for small businesses. In small businesses that are started by entrepreneurs the mission statement is generally a vision of an individual and therefore may not be negotiable. When the mission statement comes from upper management, employees are more assured of the organization's commitment to the statement.

A word of caution should be noted when deciding whether to adopt a "top down" approach or a "bottom up" approach. If the mission statement is to be created with a wide variety of input from both employees and customers then it will take longer than a "top down" approach. There must be a sharing of views and ideas with compromises made. A consensus should be developed without the problems associated with groupthink. There is always the possibility that too much compromise will distort the mission statement and the end result is something different from the original intent. The "top down" approach is not always effective because it rarely consults employees when making important decisions. Therefore, although it is the fastest route to take it isn't always the most effective. While the mission statement should be able to change with the times it is also understood to have a certain degree of permanence. As new businesses begin to grow and hire more employees the mission statement should provide a strong sense of stability and a clear definition of the culture.

A mission statement is worthless unless it has the support of the employees in the organization. It will only be successful if each employee commits to its success and internalizes it. Once the statement is completed it is extremely important that the organization not put it on the shelf to collect dust. It should be shared with the entire company. The introduction of the mission statement should come directly from top management in order to set the example. Organizations should be creative in making employees aware of the mission statement. Placing it strategically in locations where employees gather will increase awareness and remind them of the goals of the organization. Videos outlining the details of the new mission statement are often useful; however, it is critical that employees have the opportunity to discuss the statement with members of management. Setting up meetings with members of management and frontline employees can often help uncover areas where the company does not meet the standards set by the mission statement. Communicating the mission statement to customers will make them feel valued and important. It can be sent to customers in a mass mailing or posted on signs in areas those customers frequent. It sets forth the goals of the organization so customers know what to expect when doing business with the company.

SWOT ANALYSIS

SWOT is an acronym for strengths, weaknesses, opportunities, and threats. SWOT analysis is a strategic planning tool that helps an organization match its internal strengths and weaknesses with external opportunities and threats. SWOT analysis is important and useful in creating and executing the organization's mission statement. Often the best strategies for accomplishing the organization's mission are revealed through the SWOT analysis. The best strategies are those that take advantage of strengths and opportunities, offset threats, and improve weaknesses.

Organizations should first begin by reviewing internal strengths and weaknesses. When analyzing an organization's strengths it is important to identify distinctive competencies or strengths possessed by only a few competing firms. These distinctive competencies often become the competitive advantages that are included in the mission statement. Distinctive competencies can be found in financial resources, quality products and services, proprietary technology, or cost advantages. Organizational weaknesses are skills and capabilities that prevent an organization from implementing strategies that achieve its mission. They can be problems with facilities, lack of a clear strategic direction, internal operating problems, too narrow a product line, weak market image, or the inability to finance changes.

The next step is to identify external opportunities and threats. Organizational opportunities are circumstances in an organization's environment that if capitalized on will result in above normal increases in economic performance. Examples of opportunities are related to the possibility of adding a new product line, increasing market growth, or diversifying into related products. Threats are viewed as circumstances that give rise to normal or below normal economic performance. They can be found in the ease of entry of competitors, increased sales of substituted products, demographic changes, slowed market growth, or increased competition.

EVALUATION

Evaluation of the mission statement is necessary to ensure the organization is meeting its goals. If needed, new goals may have to be created in order to accommodate changes in the organization. It may be time to reevaluate what the organization is doing or where it is headed. This is a good time to think about entering into new areas or to begin doing things differently by rewriting part or all of the mission and vision statements.

In evaluating an organization's performance, management must look at several different aspects of the organization. First, managers need to determine if the organization's plans are clearly linked to its mission statement and related goals. Plans should be developed for both the short run and long run. Secondly, assigning jobs that are directly related to the achievement of organizational goals will help ensure they are attained. The goals should be communicated clearly so employees understand what tasks need to be carried out and what the rewards will be. Finally, when evaluating individual performance, the information gathered should be recent and compared to established standards.

Mission statements are often difficult to evaluate because they are written in a somewhat abstract form. They are, many times, not directly measurable and vaguely worded. Figure 1 presents an example of how mission statements can be measured from the top of the organization to the bottom. Strategic goals are directly tied to the organization's mission statement and apply to the organization as a whole. Tactical goals are departmental goals that support the strategic goals. Finally, operational goals are written at the individual level. Each one of these makes it possible to measure the organization's mission statements. An organization's likelihood of accomplishing its mission is increased as it creates strong and measurable goals at each level.

It is not necessary that the mission statement be measured in quantifiable terms. It may also be measured qualitatively. For example, "We will answer all of our customers' questions and if we don't know the answer, we will find out." While this is not a quantitative statement it can be measured by monitoring customer service calls and setting operational goals for employees that revolve around follow up and thoroughness.

Mission and vision statements give organizations a focus and a strategy for the future. According to Bart and Tabone, they have become the cornerstones of organizations. They contribute to organizations' success and can lead to increases in productivity and performance. They do not have to be reserved for the entire organization—each department or division can benefit from developing a mission statement, as long as they are not in contradiction to the company's overall mission. Preferably, an individual department's mission links it to the fulfillment of the overall company mission. Mission statements for functional

Figure 1

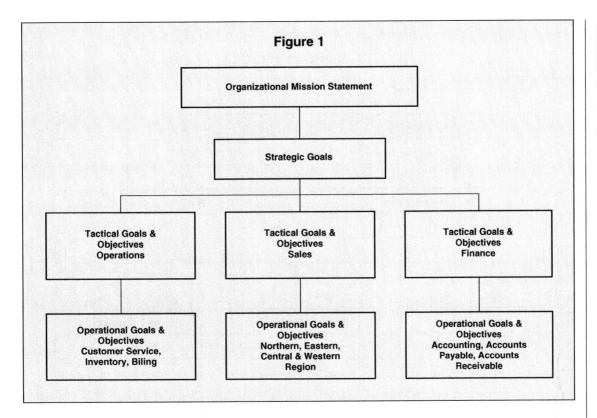

departments provide the same benefits as they do for the entire organization.

In conclusion, mission statements provide a sense of direction and purpose. In times of change and growth they can be an anchor and a guide in decision making. The benefits far outweigh the disadvantages and challenges when looking at the potential for increases in profitability and returns. Defining an organization by what it produces and who it satisfies are major steps towards creating a sound and stable mission statement. Setting a company apart from the competition is probably one of the biggest advantages.

SEE ALSO: Strategic Planning Failure; Strategic Planning Tools; Strategy Formulation; Strategy Implementation; SWOT Analysis

Amy McMillan

Revised by Deborah Hausler

FURTHER READING:

Bart, C.K., and J.C. Tabone. "Mission Statement Rationales and Organizational Alignment in the Not-For-Profit Health Care Sector." *Health Care Management Review,* Fall 1998, 54–69.

David, Forest R., and Fred B. David. "It's Time to Redraft Your Mission Statement." *Journal of Business Strategy,* January/February 2003, 11–14.

"Does Your Mission Statement Generate Results or Laughs?" *Pay for Performance Report,* October 2002, 6.

The Drucker Foundation Self-Assessment Tool: Process Guide. San Francisco: Jossey-Bass Publishers, 1999.

Karcher, J.N., et al. "The Bottom-Up Mission Statement: A Competitive Strategy for Midsized Accounting Firms." *CPA Journal,* June 1997, 36–40.

Miller, P.F., Jr. "Needed: A Mission Statement for Directors." *Directors & Boards,* Summer 1997, 27–30.

"Mission Statement Mypoia." *Training,* December 2004, 16.

Radtke, Janel M. *Strategic Communications for Nonprofit Organizations: Seven Steps to Creating a Succesful Plan.* Indianapolis: John Wiley & Sons, Inc., 1998.

Robbins, S.P. *Essentials of Organizational Behavior.* Upper Saddle River, NJ: Prentice Hall, 1997.

Wickman, P.A. "Developing a Mission for an Entrepreneurial Venture." *Management Decision,* May-June 1997, 373–381.

Yeargin, B. "Creating the Mission Statement." *Boating Industry,* May 1996, 47.

MODELS AND MODELING

A model is an abstraction of reality or a representation of a real object or situation. In other words, a model presents a simplified version of something. It may be as simple as a drawing of house plans, or as complicated as a miniature but functional representation of a complex piece of machinery. A model airplane may be assembled and glued together from a kit by a child, or it actually may contain an engine and a rotating propeller that allows it to fly like a real airplane.

Figure 1

Types of Models

PHYSICAL	
Iconic	Analog

SCHEMATIC	
Graphs & Charts	Diagrams & Drawings

VERBAL

MATHEMATICAL					
Use		Degree of Randomness		Degree of Specificity	
description	optimization	deterministic	probabilistic	specific	general

A more useable concept of a model is that of an abstraction, from the real problem, of key variables and relationships. These are abstracted in order to simplify the problem itself. Modeling allows the user to better understand the problem and presents a means for manipulating the situation in order to analyze the results of various inputs ("what if" analysis) by subjecting it to a changing set of assumptions.

MODEL CLASSIFICATIONS

Some models are replicas of the physical properties (relative shape, form, and weight) of the object they represent. Others are physical models but do not have the same physical appearance as the object of their representation. A third type of model deals with symbols and numerical relationships and expressions. Each of these fits within an overall classification of four main categories: physical models, schematic models, verbal models, and mathematical models.

PHYSICAL MODELS. Physical models are the ones that look like the finished object they represent. Iconic models are exact or extremely similar replicas of the object being modeled. Model airplanes, cars, ships, and even models of comic book super-heroes look exactly like their counterpart but in a much smaller scale. Scale models of municipal buildings, shopping centers, and property developments such as subdivisions, homes, and office complexes all hopefully look exactly as the "real thing" will look when it is built. The advantage here is the models' correspondence with the reality of appearance. In other words, the model user can tell exactly what the proposed object will look like, in three dimensions, before making a major investment.

In addition to looking like the object they represent, some models perform as their counterparts would. This allows experiments to be conducted on the model to see how it might perform under actual operating conditions. Scale models of airplanes can be tested in wind tunnels to determine aerodynamic properties and the effects of air turbulence on their outer surfaces. Model automobiles can be exposed to similar tests to evaluate how wind resistance affects such variables as handling and gas mileage. Models of bridges and dams can be subjected to multiple levels of stress from wind, heat, cold, and other sources in order to test such variables as endurance and safety. A scale model that behaves in a manner that is similar to the "real thing" is far less expensive to create and test than its actual counterpart. These types of models often are referred to as prototypes.

Additionally, some physical models may not look exactly like their object of representation but are close enough to provide some utility. Many modern art statues represent some object of reality, but are so different that many people cannot clearly distinguish the object they represent. These are known as analog models. An example is the use of cardboard cutouts to represent the machinery being utilized within a manufacturing facility. This allows planners to move the shapes around enough to determine an optimal plant layout.

SCHEMATIC MODELS. Schematic models are more abstract than physical models. While they do have some visual correspondence with reality, they look much less like the physical reality they represent. Graphs and charts are schematic models that provide pictorial representations of mathematical relationships. Plotting a line on a graph indicates a mathematical linear relationship between two variables. Two such lines can meet at one exact location on a graph to indicate the break-even point, for instance. Pie charts, bar charts, and histograms can all model some real situation, but really bear no physical resemblance to anything.

Diagrams, drawings, and blueprints also are versions of schematic models. These are pictorial representations of conceptual relationships. This means that the model depicts a concept such as chronology or sequence. A flow chart describing a computer program is a good example. The precedence diagrams used in project management or in assembly-line balancing show the sequence of activities that must be maintained in order to achieve a desired result.

VERBAL MODELS. Verbal models use words to represent some object or situation that exists, or could exist, in reality. Verbal models may range from a simple word presentation of scenery described in a book to a complex business decision problem (described in words and numbers). A firm's mission statement is a model of its beliefs about what business it is in and sets the stage for the firm's determination of goals and objectives.

Verbal models frequently provide the scenario necessary to indicate that a problem is present and provide all the relevant and necessary information to solve the problem, make recommendations, or at least determine feasible alternatives. Even the cases presented in management textbooks are really verbal models that represent the workings of a business without having to take the student to the firm's actual premises. Oftentimes, these verbal models provide enough information to later depict this problem in mathematical form. In other words, verbal models frequently are converted into mathematical models so that an optimal, or at least functional, solution may be found utilizing some mathematical technique. A look in any mathematics book, operations management book, or management science text generally provides some problems that appear in word form. The job of the student is to convert the word problem into a mathematical problem and seek a solution.

MATHEMATICAL MODELS. Mathematical models are perhaps the most abstract of the four classifications. These models do not look like their real-life counterparts at all. Mathematical models are built using numbers and symbols that can be transformed into functions, equations, and formulas. They also can be used to build much more complex models such as matrices or linear programming models. The user can then solve the mathematical model (seek an optimal solution) by utilizing simple techniques such as multiplication and addition or more complex techniques such as matrix algebra or Gaussian elimination. Since mathematical models frequently are easy to manipulate, they are appropriate for use with calculators and computer programs. Mathematical models can be classified according to use (description or optimization), degree of randomness (deterministic and stochastic), and degree of specificity (specific or general). Following is a more detailed discussion of mathematical model types.

TYPES OF MATHEMATICAL MODELS

DESCRIPTIVE MODELS. Descriptive models are used to merely describe something mathematically. Common statistical models in this category include the mean, median, mode, range, and standard deviation. Consequently, these phrases are called "descriptive statistics." Balance sheets, income statements, and financial ratios also are descriptive in nature.

OPTIMIZATION MODELS. Optimization models are used to find an optimal solution. The linear programming models are mathematical representations of constrained optimization problems. These models share certain common characteristics. Knowledge of these characteristics enables us to recognize problems that can be solved using linear programming.

For example, suppose that a firm that assembles computers and computer equipment is about to start production of two new types of computers. Each type will require assembly time, inspection time, and storage space. The amounts of each of these resources that can be devoted to the production of the computers is limited. The manager of the firm would like to determine the quantity of each computer to produce in order to maximize the profit generated by their sale. In order to develop a suitable model, the manager has obtained the information in Table 1.

Table 1		
	Type 1	**Type 2**
Profit per unit	$60	$50
Assembly time per unit	4 hours	10 hours
Inspection time per unit	2 hours	1 hour
Storage space per unit	3 cm^3	3 cm^3
Resource	**Amount available**	
Assembly time	100 hours	
Inspection time	22 hours	
Storage space	39 cm^3	

In this problem, the total impact of each type of computer on the profit and each constraint is a linear function of the quantity of that variable. By completing the model with the relevant constraints, the user has a suitable model for determining the quantity of each computer to produce in order to maximize (the optimum) the firm's profit. Optimization also can mean minimization when referring to financial losses, scrap, rework, time, or distance. Again, optimization models may be used in this sense.

DETERMINISTIC MODELS. Deterministic models are those for which the value of their variables is known with certainty. In a previous example, the manager knew profit margins and constraint values with certainty. This makes the linear programming model a deterministic optimization model.

Models that have values that are not known with certainty are said to be *stochastic or probabilistic models*. For example, a manufacturer that is having trouble deciding whether to build a large or small facility knows that the solution to this capacity problem depends upon the volume of demand that materializes. High demand would require a large facility while low demand would require a small facility. While the manufacturer has no way of knowing with certainty what demand will be, it can at least determine the probability of the occurrence of each. For example, if the manufacturer estimates that the probability of the occurrence of high demand is 70 percent and the occurrence of low demand is 30 percent, it can use this information along with the monetary value (expected payoff) of each situation to construct mathematical models such as payoff matrices or decision trees to find an optimal decision (see Table 2).

Table 2

	High demand (70%)	Low demand (30%)
Large facility	$5,000.00	(-$2,000.00)
Small facility	$3,000.00	$3,000.00

This type of model can be said to be a stochastic optimization model. Some models can even be very similar with the degree of randomness being the key differentiator. For example, in project management techniques, program evaluation and review technique (PERT) and the critical path method (CPM) are very similar except that CPM is used whenever the required time to complete the activities is known and PERT is used whenever the required activity times are not known but can be estimated. CPM is considered to be deterministic while PERT generally is said to be probabilistic. Once the activity times are established, the two techniques are virtually the same throughout the remainder of the problem's completion.

SPECIFIC MODELS. Specific models apply to only one situation or model one unique reality. The previous examples of profit function (descriptive), objective function (optimization), and payoff matrix (probabilistic) are all specific models. In other words, the values established in the model are relevant for that one unique situation. Linear programming models can be said to be deterministic specific, while decision trees can be called probabilistic specific models.

GENERAL MODELS. General models can be utilized in more than one situation. For example, the question of how much to order is determined by using an economic order quantity (EOQ) model. EOQ models identify the optimal order quantity by minimizing the sum of certain annual costs that vary with order size. On the other hand, the question of how much should be ordered for the next (fixed) interval is determined by the fixed order interval (FOI) model, which is used when orders must be placed at fixed time intervals (weekly, twice, etc.).

USING THE CLASSIFICATIONS

Knowing the type of model that is required provides the user with some advantage when converting a verbal model to a mathematical model. For example, if the decision maker reads the verbal model and determines that the situation is probabilistic and uses situation-specific variables, he or she might seek to convert the verbal model to a payoff matrix or a decision tree (both examples of stochastic/probabilistic specific models).

BENEFITS OF MODEL USE

The goal of modeling use is to adequately portray realistic phenomenon. Once developed properly, a great deal can be learned about the real-life counterpart by manipulating a model's variables and observing the results.

Real-world decisions involve an overwhelming amount of detail, much of which may be irrelevant for a particular problem or decision. Models allow the user to eliminate the unimportant details so that the user can concentrate on the relevant decision variables that are present in a situation. This increases the opportunity to fully understand the problem and its solution.

In his book, *Operations Management,* William J. Stevenson lists nine benefits of models:

1. Models generally are easy to use and less expensive than dealing with the actual situation.

2. Models require users to organize and sometimes quantify information and, in the process, often indicate areas where additional information is needed.

3. Models provide a systematic approach to problem solving.

4. Models increase understanding of the problem.

5. Models enable managers to analyze "what if" questions.

6. Models require users to be very specific about objectives.

7. Models serve as a consistent tool for evaluation.

8. Models enable users to bring the power of mathematics to bear on a problem.

9. Models provide a standardized format for analyzing a problem.

MODEL CONSTRUCTION

The accuracy of the results of the model analysis is dependent upon how well the model represents reality. The closer the model is to its actual counterpart, the more accurate the conclusions drawn and the predictions made about the object of attention. Hence, the model user must strive for the most accurate representation possible. Model users also must be careful to identify the decision variable values that provide the best output for the model. This is referred to as the model's optimal solution. However, the model user also must be careful not to include irrelevant variables that may cloud the picture and cause inaccurate conclusions or force the model user to spend an unnecessary amount of time in analysis.

In their book *Operations Management: Concepts, Methods, and Strategies,* Mark Vonderembse and Gregory White present a step-by-step process for successfully building a useful model:

1. Define the problem, decision, situation, or scenario and the factors that influence it.

2. Select criteria to guide the decision, and establish objectives. A perfect example of this is the use of heuristics in assembly-line balancing to guide the decision and the criteria of maximizing efficiency/minimizing idle time as an objective.

3. Formulate a model that helps management to understand the relationships between the influential factors and the objectives the firm is trying to achieve.

4. Collect relevant data while trying to avoid the incorporation of superfluous information into the model.

5. Identify and evaluate alternatives. Once again, the example of assembly-line balancing is appropriate. The user can manipulate

the model by changing the heuristics and comparing the final results, ultimately finding an optimal solution through trial-and-error. However, the production of alternatives may not be necessary if the model in use initially finds an optimal solution.

6. Select the best alternative

7. Implement the alternative or reevaluate

If the user is not familiar with models and their use, he or she would be wise to study the variety of models that are available for use and seek to understand their purpose and how each is used to generate results. Additionally, the user would be well served to learn how the individual model's results are interpreted and used, and what assumptions and limitations apply to each.

ADVANTAGES AND DISADVANTAGES

Models provide the most effective means developed for predicting performance. It is hard to conceive a prediction system that is not finally a model. To construct a model of a real process or system, careful consideration of the system elements that must be abstracted is required. This in itself usually is a profitable activity, for it develops insights into the problem. When building a model, we are immediately struck with the magnitude of our ignorance. What do we really know? Where are the gaps in available data? It is often impractical or impossible to manipulate the real world system in order to determine the effect of certain variables. Business systems are typical, for in order to use the business system itself as a laboratory could be disastrous and very costly. The dangers in using predictive models lie in the possibility of oversimplifying problems to keep models in workable form. The decision maker may place too much faith in a seemingly rigorous and complete analysis.

It is important for the model user to realize that model development and model solution are not completely separable. While the most accurate representation possible may seem desirable, the user still must be able to find a solution to the modeled problem. Model users need to remember that they are attempting to simplify complex problems so that they may be analyzed easily, quickly, and inexpensively without actually having to perform the task. Also desirable is a model that allows the user to manipulate the variables so that "what if" questions can be answered.

Models come in many varieties and forms, ranging from the simple and crude to the elegant and exotic. Whatever category they are in, all models share the distinction of being simplifications of more complex realities that should, with proper use, result in a useful decision-making aid.

Models are important and widely used in management. Marketing managers utilize the product life cycle model to facilitate understanding of the phases of product life. Accounting managers use ratios, such as the current ratio and the quick ratio, to quickly grasp the ability of an organization to pay its bills in the short term. Information systems managers have flow diagrams to depict the logic needed to develop a computerized order-entry system. Financial managers use net present value and internal rate of return in analyzing investment alternatives. Operations managers have precedence diagrams, decision trees, lot sizing models, material requirements planning, assembly-line balancing, and a host of other models they can use to make better decisions. Organizational performance is a result of the decisions that management makes. Models make these decisions easier to understand and often can lead to an optimal choice.

SEE ALSO: Decision Making; Decision Rules and Decision Analysis; Decision Support Systems

Kyriaki Kosmidou and Constantin Zopounidis

FURTHER READING:

Buffa, Elwood S. *Operations Management: Problems and Models.* 3rd ed. New York: Wiley, 1972.

Meredith, Jack R., and Scott M. Shafer. *Operations Management for MBAs.* New York: John Wiley & Sons, 1999.

Stevenson, William, J. *Operations Management.* 7th ed. Boston: McGraw-Hill/Irwin, 2002.

Vonderembse, Mark A., and Gregory P. White. *Operations Management: Concepts, Methods, and Strategies.* 3rd ed. Minneapolis/St. Paul, MN: West Publishing Company, 1996.

MORALE

From a managerial perspective, morale embodies the collective spirit and motivation of a group of employees. Other terms used to designate this concept include *espirit* and *espirit de corps.* In fact, espirit de corps was one of the first management principles identified by Henri Fayol in the early 1900s. Employee morale is how employees actually feel about themselves as workers, their work, their managers, their work environment, and their overall work life. It incorporates all the mental and emotional feelings, beliefs, and attitudes that individuals and groups hold regarding their job.

Consideration of employee morale and job satisfaction was a major emphasis of the behavioral school of management that started with the famous Hawthorne Experiments in the late 1930s. The behavioral school held that employee morale influences employee productivity. Theorists, such as Hertzberg, conducted research in the 1950s and 1960s indicating that employees' satisfaction and motivation were influenced more by how employees felt about their work than the specific attributes of their job, including pay and workplace surroundings.

Some organizations try to measure morale on a formal basis by conducting morale audits or attitude surveys that indicate the level of employee job satisfaction. Such measures, however, are fraught with ambiguities; it is difficult, if not impossible, to determine the level of truthfulness of employees' answers or the complexity of the variables. For instance, employees may have a very different level of job satisfaction regarding their company, their pay, their benefits, their profession, and their specific department's policies. Getting a true overall measure of what employees are feeling about their work is therefore difficult to obtain and to interpret. Since there are many variables at play, morale is not always directly linked to productivity, absenteeism, turnover, sales, etc. Nonetheless, morale is widely accepted as important to motivation and team building. The challenge for managers, then, is to negotiate these disparate factors in the manner that most contributes to the overall spirit of the employees.

The major determinant of morale is, in fact, the manager. Employees form their attitudes about work based primarily on their interactions with the supervisors and managers they work with every day. Since no two employees or companies are the same, it isn't easy to construct a stable model of managerial techniques that will consistently contribute to high morale across the board. Nevertheless, most employees respond positively to certain managerial practices. Some suggested morale-boosters include:

- practicing of fairness and consistency
- bestowing praise in public while leveling criticism in private
- encouraging humor and fun in the workplace
- communication, communication, communication
- listening and remaining receptive to new ideas
- getting to know something about employees' personal lives and treating them as individuals
- creating opportunities for employees to learn and grow
- sharing decision making and offering employees choices
- promoting from within
- leading by example

Organizations have tried scores of techniques to increase morale. The National Alliance for Youth Sports believes creating an atmosphere of fun and camaraderie goes a long way toward maintaining a high level of morale. Every Friday morning the first 30 minutes of the workday is spent with the 35-member staff broken into five teams to compete in different types of games, including miniature golf and Frisbee football. After the games, the workday begins with smiles all around. Symbiosis Corporation, a fast-growing Miami-based producer of medical products, uses mentors to build morale of nonexempt hourly employees by supporting personal growth and promoting a sense of belonging. After the pilot project recorded improvements in attitudes, productivity, and morale, Symbiosis expanded the program. Illinois Trade, located in Glenview, Illinois, surveyed its employees and found that many of its workers were interested in alternative remedies not covered by conventional medical insurance. To respect its workers' interests, Illinois Trade agreed to pay for herbal therapy and other forms of alternative medical care, and allows employees to receive a free massage on company time once a month.

In order to allow employees a sense of balance in their lives, some companies provide benefits that help employees run a household and put in a productive day at the office. Employees at Wilton Connor Packaging in Charlotte, North Carolina, can take their laundry to work and have it washed, dried, and folded for the cost of the soap; while at PepsiCo's headquarters employees are provided an on-site dry cleaning drop-off. Some companies offer concierge services that run errands and send someone to be at an employee's home for a delivery. Many companies also provide on-site child care, elder care, and fitness centers for their employees and their families.

To retain employees in an increasingly competitive marketplace, organizations must reinforce managerial techniques that foster a high degree of employee morale. Managers can make a difference by following common morale-boosting strategies, trying to provide their employees with supportive working environments, and incorporating creative techniques that make employees feel fulfilled personally and as part of a larger entity in which he or she feels integrated. The best managers take care of their employees so their employees can take care of business.

SEE ALSO: Human Resource Management; Quality of Work Life

Fraya Wagner-Marsh
Revised by Deborah Hausler

FURTHER READING:

Acland, Holly. "Morale Boosters." *Marketing,* 24 September 1998, 36–38.

Dolan, Kerry. "When Money Isn't Enough." *Forbes,* 18 November 1996, 164–170.

Ensman, Richard, Jr. "Morale Audit." *Incentive,* October 1998, 177–178.

Gillette, Becky. "Employee Morale Investments Often Pay Big Dividends." *Mississippi Business Journal,* 29 March 2004, 22.

"Have Fun Improving Morale." *Association Management,* July 1996, 24.

Johnson, Gail. "Retention Reality Check." *Training,* September 2004, 17.

MOTIVATION AND MOTIVATION THEORY

The term *motivation* is derived from the Latin word *movere,* meaning "to move." Motivation can be broadly defined as the forces acting on or within a person that cause the arousal, direction, and persistence of goal-directed, voluntary effort. Motivation theory is thus concerned with the processes that explain why and how human behavior is activated.

The broad rubric of motivation and motivation theory is one of the most frequently studied and written-about topics in the organizational sciences, and is considered one of the most important areas of study in the field of organizational behavior. Despite the magnitude of the effort that has been devoted to the study of motivation, there is no single theory of motivation that is universally accepted. The lack of a unified theory of motivation reflects both the complexity of the construct and the diverse backgrounds and aims of those who study it. To delineate these crucial points, it is illuminating to consider the development of motivation and motivation theory as the objects of scientific inquiry.

HISTORICAL DEVELOPMENT

Early explanations of motivation focused on instincts. Psychologists writing in the late 19th and early twentieth centuries suggested that human beings were basically programmed to behave in certain ways, depending upon the behavioral cues to which they were exposed. Sigmund Freud, for example, argued that the most powerful determinants of individual behavior were those of which the individual was not consciously aware.

According to *Motivation and Leadership at Work* (Steers, Porter, and Bigley, 1996), in the early twentieth century researchers began to examine other possible explanations for differences in individual motivation. Some researchers focused on internal drives as an explanation for motivated behavior. Others studied the effect of learning and how individuals base current behavior on the consequences of past behavior. Still others examined the influence of individuals' cognitive processes, such as the beliefs they have about future events. Over time, these major theoretical streams of research in motivation were classified into two major schools: the content theories of motivation and the process theories of motivation.

MAJOR CONTENT THEORIES

Content (or need) theories of motivation focus on factors internal to the individual that energize and direct behavior. In general, such theories regard motivation as the product of internal drives that compel an individual to act or move (hence, "motivate") toward the satisfaction of individual needs. The content theories of motivation are based in large part on early theories of motivation that traced the paths of action backward to their perceived origin in internal drives. Major content theories of motivation are Maslow's hierarchy of needs, Alderfer's ERG theory, Herzberg's motivator-hygiene theory, and McClelland's learned needs or three-needs theory.

MASLOW'S HIERARCHY OF NEEDS. Abraham Maslow developed the hierarchy of needs, which suggests that individual needs exist in a hierarchy consisting of physiological needs, security needs, belongingness needs, esteem needs, and self-actualization needs. Physiological needs are the most basic needs for food, water, and other factors necessary for survival. Security needs include needs for safety in one's physical environment, stability, and freedom from emotional distress. Belongingness needs relate to desires for friendship, love, and acceptance within a given community of individuals. Esteem needs are those associated with obtaining the respect of one's self and others. Finally, self-actualization needs are those corresponding to the achievement one's own potential, the exercising and testing of one's creative capacities, and, in general, to becoming the best person one can possibly be. Unsatisfied needs motivate behavior; thus, lower-level needs such as the physiological and security needs must be met before upper-level needs such as belongingness, esteem, and self-actualization can be motivational.

Applications of the hierarchy of needs to management and the workplace are obvious. According to the implications of the hierarchy, individuals must have their lower level needs met by, for example, safe working conditions, adequate pay to take care of one's self and one's family, and job security before they will be motivated by increased job responsibilities, status, and challenging work assignments. Despite the ease of application of this theory to a work setting, this theory has received little research support and therefore is not very useful in practice.

ALDERFER'S ERG THEORY. The ERG theory is an extension of Maslow's hierarchy of needs. Alderfer suggested that needs could be classified into three categories, rather than five. These three types of needs are existence, relatedness, and growth. Existence needs are similar to Maslow's physiological and safety need categories. Relatedness needs involve interpersonal relationships and are comparable to aspects of Maslow's belongingness and esteem needs. Growth needs are those related to the attainment of one's potential and are associated with Maslow's esteem and self-actualization needs.

The ERG theory differs from the hierarchy of needs in that it does not suggest that lower-level needs must be completely satisfied before upper-level needs become motivational. ERG theory also suggests that if an individual is continually unable to meet upper-level needs that the person will regress and lower-level needs become the major determinants of their motivation. ERG theory's implications for managers are similar to those for the needs hierarchy: managers should focus on meeting employees' existence, relatedness, and growth needs, though without necessarily applying the proviso that, say, job-safety concerns necessarily take precedence over challenging and fulfilling job requirements.

MOTIVATOR-HYGIENE THEORY. Frederick Herzberg developed the motivator-hygiene theory. This theory is closely related to Maslow's hierarchy of needs but relates more specifically to how individuals are motivated in the workplace. Based on his research, Herzberg argued that meeting the lower-level needs (hygiene factors) of individuals would not motivate them to exert effort, but would only prevent them from being dissatisfied. Only if higher-level needs (motivators) were met would individuals be motivated.

The implication for managers of the motivator-hygiene theory is that meeting employees lower-level needs by improving pay, benefits, safety, and other job-contextual factors will prevent employees from becoming actively dissatisfied but will not motivate them to exert additional effort toward better performance. To motivate workers, according to the theory, managers must focus on changing the intrinsic nature and content of jobs themselves by "enriching" them to increase employees' autonomy and their opportunities to take on additional responsibility, gain recognition, and develop their skills and careers.

MCCLELLAND'S LEARNED NEEDS THEORY. McClelland's theory suggests that individuals learn needs from their culture. Three of the primary needs in this theory are the need for affiliation (n Aff), the need for power (n Pow), and the need for achievement (n Ach). The need for affiliation is a desire to establish social relationships with others. The need for power reflects a desire to control one's environment and influence others. The need for achievement is a desire to take responsibility, set challenging goals, and obtain performance feedback. The main point of the learned needs theory is that when one of these needs is strong in a person, it has the potential to motivate behavior that leads to its satisfaction. Thus, managers should attempt to develop an understanding of whether and to what degree their employees have one or more of these needs, and the extent to which their jobs can be structured to satisfy them.

MAJOR PROCESS THEORIES

Process (or cognitive) theories of motivation focus on conscious human decision processes as an explanation of motivation. The process theories are concerned with determining how individual behavior is energized, directed, and maintained in the specifically willed and self-directed human cognitive processes. Process theories of motivation are based on early cognitive theories, which posit that behavior is the result of conscious decision-making processes. The major process theories of motivation are expectancy theory, equity theory, goal-setting theory, and reinforcement theory.

EXPECTANCY THEORY. In the early 1960s, Victor Vroom applied concepts of behavioral research conducted in the 1930s by Kurt Lewin and Edward Tolman directly to work motivation. Basically, Vroom suggested that individuals choose work behaviors that they believe lead to outcomes they value. In deciding how much effort to put into a work behavior, individuals are likely to consider:

- Their expectancy, meaning the degree to which they believe that putting forth effort will lead to a given level of performance.

- Their instrumentality, or the degree to which they believe that a given level of performance will result in certain outcomes or rewards.

- Their valence, which is the extent to which the expected outcomes are attractive or unattractive.

All three of these factors are expected to influence motivation in a multiplicative fashion, so that for an individual to be highly motivated, all three of the components of the expectancy model must be high. And, if even one of these is zero (e.g., instrumentality and valence are high, but expectancy is completely absent), the person will have not motivation for the task. Thus, managers should attempt, to the extent possible, to ensure that their employees believe that increased effort will improve performance and that performance will lead to valued rewards.

In the late 1960s, Porter and Lawler published an extension of the Vroom expectancy model, which is known as the Porter-Lawler expectancy model or simply the Porter-Lawler model. Although the basic premise of the Porter-Lawler model is the same as for Vroom's model, the Porter-Lawler model is more complex in a number of ways. It suggests that increased effort does not automatically lead to improved performance because individuals may not possess the necessary abilities needed to achieve high levels of performance, or because they may have an inadequate or vague perception of how to perform necessary tasks. Without an understanding of how to direct effort effectively, individuals may exert considerable effort without a corresponding increase in performance.

EQUITY THEORY. Equity theory suggests that individuals engage in social comparison by comparing their efforts and rewards with those of relevant others. The perception of individuals about the fairness of their rewards relative to others influences their level of motivation. Equity exists when individuals perceive that the ratio of efforts to rewards is the same for them as it is for others to whom they compare themselves. Inequity exists when individuals perceive that the ratio of efforts to rewards is different (usually negatively so) for them than it is for others to whom they compare themselves. There are two types of inequity— under-reward and over-reward. Under-reward occurs when a person believes that she is either puts in more efforts than another, yet receives the same reward, or puts in the same effort as another for a lesser reward. For instance, if an employee works longer hours than her coworker, yet they receive the same salary, the employee would perceive inequity in the form of under-reward. Conversely, with over-reward, a person will feel that his efforts to rewards ratio is higher than another person's, such that he is getting more for putting in the same effort, or getting the same reward even with less effort. While research suggests that under-reward motivates individuals to resolve the inequity, research also indicates that the same is not true for over-reward. Individuals who are over-rewarded often engage in cognitive dissonance, convincing themselves that their efforts and rewards are equal to another's.

According to the equity theory, individuals are motivated to reduce perceived inequity. Individuals may attempt to reduce inequity in various ways. A person may change his or her level of effort; an employee who feels under-rewarded is likely to work less hard. A person may also try to change his or her rewards, such as by asking for a raise. Another option is to change the behavior of the reference person, perhaps by encouraging that person to put forth more effort. Finally, a person experiencing inequity may change the reference person and compare him or herself to a different person to assess equity. For managers, equity theory emphasizes the importance of a reward system that is perceived as fair by employees.

GOAL-SETTING THEORY. The goal-setting theory posits that goals are the most important factors affecting the motivation and behavior of employees. This motivation theory was developed primarily by Edwin Locke and Gary Latham. Goal-setting theory emphasizes the importance of specific and challenging goals in achieving motivated behavior. Specific goals often involve quantitative targets for improvement in a behavior of interest. Research indicates that specific performance goals are much more effective than those in which a person is told to "do your best." Challenging goals are difficult but not impossible to attain. Empirical research supports the proposition that goals that are both specific and challenging are more motivational than vague goals or goals that are relatively easy to achieve.

Several factors may moderate the relationship between specific and challenging goals and high levels of motivation. The first of these factors is goal commitment, which simply means that the more dedicated the individual is to achieving the goal, the more they will be motivated to exert effort toward goal accomplishment. Some research suggests that having employees participate in goal setting will increase their level of goal commitment. A second factor relevant to goal-setting theory is self-efficacy, which is the individual's belief that he or she can successfully complete a particular task. If individuals have a high degree of self-efficacy, they are likely to respond more positively to specific and challenging goals than if they have a low degree of self-efficacy.

REINFORCEMENT THEORY. This theory can be traced to the work of the pioneering behaviorist B.F. Skinner. It is considered a motivation theory as well as a learning theory. Reinforcement theory posits that motivated behavior occurs as a result of reinforcers, which are outcomes resulting from the behavior that makes it more likely the behavior will occur again. This theory suggests that it is not necessary to study needs or cognitive processes to understand motivation, but that it is only necessary to examine the consequences of behavior. Behavior that is reinforced is likely to continue, but behavior that is not rewarded or behavior that is punished is not likely to be repeated. Reinforcement theory suggests to managers that they can improve employees' performance by a process of behavior modification in which they reinforce desired behaviors and punish undesired behaviors.

SEE ALSO: Goals and Goal Setting; Operant Conditioning; Organizational Behavior; Reinforcement Theory; Theory X and Theory Y; Theory Z

Tim Barnet
Revised by Marcia Simmering

FURTHER READING:

Adams, J. Stacy. "Toward an Understanding of Equity." *Journal of Abnormal and Social Psychology,* November 1963, 422–436.

Alderfer, Clayton P. *Existence, Relatedness, and Growth: Human Needs in Organizational Settings.* New York: Free Press, 1972.

Gordon, Judith R. *Organizational Behavior: A Diagnostic Approach.* 7th ed. Upper Saddle River, NJ: Prentice Hall, 2001.

Herzberg, Frederick, B. Mausner, and B. Snyderman. *The Motivation to Work.* New York: McGraw-Hill, 1959.

Jones, Gareth R., Jennifer M. George, and Charles W.L. Hill. *Contemporary Management.* 2nd ed. Boston: Irwin/McGraw-Hill, 2000.

Locke, Edwin A. "Toward a Theory of Task Motivation and Incentives." *Organizational Behavior and Human Performance,* May 1968, 157–189.

Maslow, Abraham H. *Motivation and Personality.* New York: Harper & Row, 1954.

McClelland, David C. "Business Drive and National Achievement." *Harvard Business Review,* July-August 1962, 99–112.

Mitchell, Terence R. "Matching Motivational Strategies with Organizational Contexts." *Research in Organizational Behavior* 19 (1997): 57–149.

Porter, Lyman W., Gregory Bigley, and Richard M. Steers. *Motivation and Work Behavior.* 7th ed. New York: McGraw-Hill/Irwin, 2002.

Robbins, Stephen P., and Mary Coulter. *Management.* 8th ed. Upper Saddle River, NJ: Prentice Hall, 2004.

Steers, Richard M., Lyman W. Porter, and Gregory A. Bigley. *Motivation and Leadership at Work.* 6th ed. New York: McGraw-Hill, 1996.

Vroom, Victor H. *Work and Motivation.* New York: John Wiley & Sons, 1964.

MULTIMEDIA

Multimedia is the term used to describe two or more types of media combined into a single package—usually denoting a combination of some or all of the following: video, sound, animation, text, and pictures. Multimedia gives the user the opportunity to influence the presentation of material. The selection and manipulation of various aspects of the presentation material is the interactive aspect of a multimedia presentation. Interactive features could range from a question-and-answer function to choosing from a menu of particular subjects or aspects of a presentation. One application of multimedia, for example, involves presenting the user with a "what if" scenario, in which the choices the user makes affect the outcome of the presentation. This affords the user a degree of control, not unlike directing a motion picture and having the opportunity to make changes to the plot at various junctures.

The advent and ascension of the personal computer as well as the development and proliferation of CD-ROMs have played significant roles in affording business the ability to affordably create multimedia computer presentations. Potential uses of multimedia that were previously confined within the province of computer science experts are now within the reach of a large segment of the business and public communities. Today a relative neophyte can potentially create a polished multimedia presentation with a computer and a commercially available presentation program. As computer-processing power increases and the capacity of data-storage media like the CD-ROM or DVD-ROM formats continues to grow, the ability of the average user to create multimedia presentations will grow as well.

THE MECHANICS OF MULTIMEDIA

The CD-ROM and its successor, the DVD-ROM, store data in the form of a binary code. The binary code is placed onto the discs by a stamping process that impresses lands (flat areas that represent the zero in binary code) and hollows (pits that represent the one in binary code) onto the surface of the disc. When the discs are placed into a player or computer drive, the playing mechanism spins the disc and flashes a laser beam over the surface of the disc. The reflected light patterns caused by the embossed data contained on the surface of the disc are then decoded by the reader/player and translated back into audio and video. The storage capacity of a CD-ROM disc is 635 megabytes, while the storage capacity of a DVD-ROM disc can be as great as 5.2 gigabytes. Since sound, graphics, and other visuals take up considerably more data space than text alone, the increased storage capacities of the CD-ROM and DVD-ROM discs have played an integral part in making the use of multimedia more commonplace. The durability, portability, and relatively low manufacturing cost of the discs also play a critical role in their proliferation. While the Read Only Memory (ROM) format is still the most common for both CDs and DVDs, today recordable disc drives are widely available to enable users to "burn" data (write, erase, and/or rewrite data) to a disc on their own.

USES OF MULTIMEDIA

Multimedia devices have an almost innumerable variety of applications. They are used in home-entertainment systems and can be extremely powerful educational tools. Educators, for example, have been exceptionally creative in combining some of the exciting elements of video-game applications with select features of educational material. By doing this, the concept of "edutainment" was created. The goal of using the multimedia edutainment approach is to entertain the user so effectively that the user remains unaware that he or she is actually learning in the process.

Multimedia can also offer critical services in the business world. While information can certainly be conveyed adequately by the singular use of still pictures, video, film, audio, or text, multimedia potentially multiplies the degree of effectiveness, in no small part due to the added entertainment value and the extent to which the viewers feel a part of the action. Such benefits can't easily be matched by the application of a singular medium. The effectiveness of teaching, selling, informing, entertaining, promoting, and presenting are all dependent upon one factor: the ability of the presented material to hold the attention of the desired audience. A dynamic multimedia presentation can usually be more effective than earlier methods at accomplishing this task with an audience that was raised on television and motion pictures. The computerized multimedia presentation offers the added benefit of cost-effective flexibility, allowing easy editing of the basic materials in order to tailor them to specific target audiences.

Training, informational and promotional materials, sales presentations, and point-of-sale displays that allow for customer interaction and communication both within and outside the organization are all common applications of multimedia in the business world. Multimedia presentations for many such applications can be highly portable, particularly in the cases of the CD-ROM, DVD-ROM, and videotape. The equipment required to produce these presentations is relatively commonplace or otherwise easy to access.

Perhaps the vanguard application of multimedia is virtual reality, a combination of video, stereo, and computer graphics that attempts to create an interactive three-dimensional environment that immerses the user within the simulation. Virtual reality has been employed in a wide range of practical applications: to train military troops, to streamline manufacturing and architectural design processes, to create simulated test environments for industry, and as a form of public entertainment.

One should still keep in mind, however, that even if rendered in a highly advanced multimedia format, an ineffectual presentation is still an ineffectual presentation. One should remain focused on the message being conveyed while shaping the choice and use of materials in accordance with that message.

SEE ALSO: Technology Management; Training Delivery Methods

Jeffrey A. Moga
Revised by Deborah Hausler

FURTHER READING:

Li, Nian-Ze, and Mark S. Drew. *Fundamentals of Multimedia.* New York: Prentice Hall, 2003.

Mayer, Richard E. *Multimedia Learning.* Cambridge: Cambridge University Press, 2001.

MULTINATIONAL CORPORATIONS

Multinational corporations have existed since the beginning of overseas trade. They have remained a part of the business scene throughout history, entering their modern form in the 17th and 18th centuries with the creation of large, European-based monopolistic concerns such as the British East India Company during the age of colonization. Multinational concerns were viewed at that time as agents of civilization and played a pivotal role in the commercial and industrial development of Asia, South America, and Africa. By the end of the 19th century, advances in communications had more closely linked world markets, and multinational corporations retained their favorable image as instruments of improved global relations through commercial ties. The existence of close international trading relations did not prevent the outbreak of two world wars in the first half of the twentieth century, but an even more closely bound world economy emerged in the aftermath of the period of conflict.

In more recent times, multinational corporations have grown in power and visibility, but have come to be viewed more ambivalently by both governments and consumers worldwide. Indeed, multinationals today are viewed with increased suspicion given their perceived lack of concern for the economic well-being of particular geographic regions and the public impression that multinationals are gaining power in relation to national government agencies, international trade federations and organizations, and local, national, and international labor organizations.

Despite such concerns, multinational corporations appear poised to expand their power and influence as barriers to international trade continue to be removed. Furthermore, the actual nature and methods of multinationals are in large measure misunderstood by the public, and their long-term influence is likely to be less sinister than imagined. Multinational corporations share many common traits, including the methods they use to penetrate new markets, the manner in which their overseas subsidiaries are tied to their headquarters operations, and their interaction with national governmental agencies and national and international labor organizations.

WHAT IS A MULTINATIONAL CORPORATION?

As the name implies, a multinational corporation is a business concern with operations in more than one country. These operations outside the company's home country may be linked to the parent by merger, operated as subsidiaries, or have considerable autonomy. Multinational corporations are sometimes perceived as large, utilitarian enterprises with little or no regard for the social and economic well-being of the countries in which they operate, but the reality of their situation is more complicated.

There are over 40,000 multinational corporations currently operating in the global economy, in addition to approximately 250,000 overseas affiliates running cross-continental businesses. In 1995, the top 200 multinational corporations had combined sales of $7.1 trillion, which is equivalent to 28.3 percent of the world's gross domestic product. The top multinational corporations are headquartered in the United States, Western Europe, and Japan; they have the capacity to shape global trade, production, and financial transactions. Multinational corporations are viewed by many as favoring their home operations when making difficult economic decisions, but this tendency is declining as companies are forced to respond to increasing global competition.

The World Trade Organization (WTO), the International Monetary Fund (IMF), and the World Bank are the three institutions that underwrite the basic rules and regulations of economic, monetary, and trade relations between countries. Many developing nations have loosened trade rules under pressure from the IMF and the World Bank. The domestic financial markets in these countries have not been developed and do not have appropriate laws in place to enable domestic financial institutions to stand up to foreign competition. The administrative setup, judicial systems, and law-enforcing agencies generally cannot guarantee the social discipline and political stability that are necessary in order to support a growth-friendly atmosphere. As a result, most multinational corporations are investing in certain geographic locations only. In the 1990s, most foreign investment was in high-income countries and a few geographic locations in the South like East Asia and Latin America. According to the World Bank's 2002 World Development Indicators, there are 63 countries considered to be low-income countries. The share of these low-income countries in which foreign countries are making direct investments is very small; it rose from 0.5 percent 1990 to only 1.6 percent in 2000.

Although foreign direct investment in developing countries rose considerably in the 1990s, not all developing countries benefited from these investments.

Most of the foreign direct investment went to a very small number of lower and upper middle income developing countries in East Asia and Latin America. In these countries, the rate of economic growth is increasing and the number of people living at poverty level is falling. However, there are still nearly 140 developing countries that are showing very slow growth rates while the 24 richest, developed countries (plus another 10 to 12 newly industrialized countries) are benefiting from most of the economic growth and prosperity. Therefore, many people in the developing countries are still living in poverty.

Similarly, multinational corporations are viewed as being exploitative of both their workers and the local environment, given their relative lack of association with any given locality. This criticism of multinationals is valid to a point, but it must be remembered that no corporation can successfully operate without regard to local social, labor, and environmental standards, and that multinationals in large measure do conform to local standards in these regards.

Multinational corporations are also seen as acquiring too much political and economic power in the modern business environment. Indeed, corporations are able to influence public policy to some degree by threatening to move jobs overseas, but companies are often prevented from employing this tactic given the need for highly trained workers to produce many products. Such workers can seldom be found in low-wage countries. Furthermore, once they enter a market, multinationals are bound by the same constraints as domestically owned concerns, and find it difficult to abandon the infrastructure they produced to enter the market in the first place.

The modern multinational corporation is not necessarily headquartered in a wealthy nation. Many countries that were recently classified as part of the developing world, including Brazil, Taiwan, Kuwait, and Venezuela, are now home to large multinational concerns. The days of corporate colonization seem to be nearing an end.

ENTRY OF MULTINATIONAL CORPORATIONS INTO NEW MARKETS

Multinational corporations follow three general procedures when seeking to access new markets: merger with or direct acquisition of existing concerns; sequential market entry; and joint ventures.

Merger or direct acquisition of existing companies in a new market is the most straightforward method of new market penetration employed by multinational corporations. Such an entry, known as foreign direct investment, allows multinationals, especially the larger ones, to take full advantage of their size and the economies of scale that this provides. The rash of mergers within the global automotive industries during the late 1990s are illustrative of this method of gaining access to new markets and, significantly, were made in response to increased global competition.

Multinational corporations also make use of a procedure known as sequential market entry when seeking to penetrate a new market. Sequential market entry often also includes foreign direct investment, and involves the establishment or acquisition of concerns operating in niche markets related to the parent company's product lines in the new country of operation. Japan's Sony Corporation made use of sequential market entry in the United States, beginning with the establishment of a small television assembly plant in San Diego, California, in 1972. For the next two years, Sony's U.S. operations remained confined to the manufacture of televisions, the parent company's leading product line. Sony branched out in 1974 with the creation of a magnetic tape plant in Dothan, Alabama, and expanded further by opening an audio equipment plant in Delano, Pennsylvania, in 1977.

After a period of consolidation brought on by an unfavorable exchange rate between the yen and dollar, Sony continued to expand and diversify its U.S. operations, adding facilities for the production of computer displays and data storage systems during the 1980s. In the 1990s, Sony further diversified it U.S. facilities and now also produces semiconductors and personal telecommunications products in the United States. Sony's example is a classic case of a multinational using its core product line to defeat indigenous competition and lay the foundation for the sequential expansion of corporate activities into related areas.

Finally, multinational corporations often access new markets by creating joint ventures with firms already operating in these markets. This has particularly been the case in countries formerly or presently under communist rule, including those of the former Soviet Union, eastern Europe, and the People's Republic of China. In such joint ventures, the venture partner in the market to be entered retains considerable or even complete autonomy, while realizing the advantages of technology transfer and management and production expertise from the parent concern. The establishment of joint ventures has often proved awkward in the long run for multinational corporations, which are likely to find their venture partners are formidable competitors when a more direct penetration of the new market is attempted.

Multinational corporations are thus able to penetrate new markets in a variety of ways, which allow existing concerns in the market to be accessed a varying degree of autonomy and control over operations.

CONCERNS ABOUT MULTINATIONAL CORPORATIONS

While no one doubts the economic success and pervasiveness of multinational corporations, their motives and actions have been called into question by social welfare, environmental protection, and labor organizations and government agencies worldwide.

National and international labor unions have expressed concern that multinational corporations in economically developed countries can avoid labor negotiations by simply moving their jobs to developing countries where labor costs are markedly less. Labor organizations in developing countries face the converse of the same problem, as they are usually obliged to negotiate with the national subsidiary of the multinational corporation in their country, which is usually willing to negotiate contract terms only on the basis of domestic wage standards, which may be well below those in the parent company's country.

Offshore outsourcing, or offshoring, is a term used to describe the practice of using cheap foreign labor to manufacture goods or provide services only to sell them back into the domestic marketplace. Today, many Americans are concerned about the issue of whether American multinational companies will continue to export jobs to cheap overseas labor markets. In the fall of 2003, the University of California-Berkeley showed that as many as 14 million American jobs were potentially at risk over the next decade. In 2004, the United States faced a half-trillion-dollar trade deficit, with a surplus in services. Opponents of offshoring claim that it takes jobs away from Americans, while also increasing the imbalance of trade.

When foreign companies set up operations in America, they usually sell the products manufactured in the U.S. to American consumers. However, when U.S. companies outsource jobs to cheap overseas labor markets, they usually sell the goods they produce to Americans, rather than to the consumers in the country in which they are made. In 2004, the states of Illinois and Tennessee passed legislation aimed at limiting offshoring; in 2005, another 16 states considered bills that would limit state aid and tax breaks to firms that outsource abroad.

Insourcing, on the other hand, is a term used to describe the practice of foreign companies employing U.S. workers. Foreign automakers are among the largest insourcers. Many non-U.S. auto manufacturers have built plants in the United States, thus ensuring access to American consumers. Auto manufacturers such as Toyota now make approximately one third of its profits from U.S. car sales.

Social welfare organizations are similarly concerned about the actions of multinationals, which are presumably less interested in social matters in countries in which they maintain subsidiary operations. Environmental protection agencies are equally concerned about the activities of multinationals, which often maintain environmentally hazardous operations in countries with minimal environmental protection statutes.

Finally, government agencies fear the growing power of multinationals, which once again can use the threat of removing their operations from a country to secure favorable regulation and legislation.

All of these concerns are valid, and abuses have undoubtedly occurred, but many forces are also at work to keep multinational corporations from wielding unlimited power over even their own operations. Increased consumer awareness of environmental and social issues and the impact of commercial activity on social welfare and environmental quality have greatly influenced the actions of all corporations in recent years, and this trend shows every sign of continuing. Multinational corporations are constrained from moving their operations into areas with excessively low labor costs given the relative lack of skilled laborers available for work in such areas. Furthermore, the sensitivity of the modern consumer to the plight of individuals in countries with repressive governments mitigates the removal of multinational business operations to areas where legal protection of workers is minimal. Examples of consumer reaction to unpopular action by multinationals are plentiful, and include the outcry against the use of sweatshop labor by Nike and activism against operations by the Shell Oil Company in Nigeria and PepsiCo in Myanmar (formerly Burma) due to the repressive nature of the governments in those countries.

Multinational corporations are also constrained by consumer attitudes in environmental matters. Environmental disasters such as those which occurred in Bhopal, India (the explosion of an unsafe chemical plant operated by Union Carbide, resulting in great loss of life in surrounding areas) and Prince William Sound, Alaska (the rupture of a single-hulled tanker, the Exxon Valdez, causing an environmental catastrophe) led to ceaseless bad publicity for the corporations involved and continue to serve as a reminder of the long-term cost in consumer approval of ignoring environmental, labor, and safety concerns.

Similarly, consumer awareness of global issues lessens the power of multinational corporations in their dealings with government agencies. International conventions of governments are also able to regulate the activities of multinational corporations without fear of economic reprisal, with examples including the 1987 Montreal Protocol limiting global production and use of chlorofluorocarbons and the 1989 Basel Convention regulating the treatment of and trade in chemical wastes.

In fact, despite worries over the impact of multinational corporations in environmentally sensitive and economically developing areas, the corporate social performance of multinationals has been surprisingly favorable to date. The activities of multinational corporations encourage technology transfer from the developed to the developing world, and the wages paid to multinational employees in developing countries are generally above the national average. When the actions of multinationals do cause a loss of jobs in a given country, it is often the case that another multinational will move into the resulting vacuum, with little net loss of jobs in the long run. Subsidiaries of multinationals are also likely to adhere to the corporate standard of environmental protection even if this is more stringent than the regulations in place in their country of operation, and so in most cases create less pollution than similar indigenous industries.

THE FUTURE FOR MULTINATIONAL CORPORATIONS

Current trends in the international marketplace favor the continued development of multinational corporations. Countries worldwide are privatizing government-run industries, and the development of regional trading partnerships such as the North American Free Trade Agreement (a 1993 agreement between Canada, Mexico, and United States) and the European Union have the overall effect of removing barriers to international trade. Privatization efforts result in the availability of existing infrastructure for use by multinationals seeking to enter a new market, while removal of international trade barriers is obviously a boon to multinational operations.

Perhaps the greatest potential threat posed by multinational corporations would be their continued success in a still underdeveloped world market. As the productive capacity of multinationals increases, the buying power of people in much of the world remains relatively unchanged, which could lead to the production of a worldwide glut of goods and services. Such a glut, which has occurred periodically throughout the history of industrialized economies, can in turn lead to wage and price deflation, contraction of corporate activities, and a rapid slowdown in all phases of economic life. Such a possibility is purely hypothetical, however, and for the foreseeable future the operations of multinational corporations worldwide are likely to continue to expand.

SEE ALSO: Free Trade Agreements and Trading Blocs; International Business; International Management; International Management; Transnational Organization

Grant J. Eldridge
Revised by Rhoda L. Wilburn

FURTHER READING:

Barton, Ron, and Michael Bishko. "Global Mobility Strategy." *HR Focus,* March 1998.

Burton, Daniel F., Jr., Erich Bloch, and Mark S. Mahomey. "Multinationals." *Challenge,* September-October 1994.

Chang, Sea-Jin, and Philip M. Rosenzweig. "Industry and Regional Patterns in Sequential Foreign Market Entry." *Journal of Management Studies,* November 1998.

Choucri, Nazli. "The Global Environment and Multinational Corporations." *Technology Review,* April 1991.

Dobbs, Lou. "The Myth of Insourcing." *U.S. News & World Report,* 3 May 2004, 56

Francis, Diane. "The New Love Affair with Transnationals." *Maclean's,* 20 December 1993.

Hatfield, John. "At the Mercy of the Monsters." *CA Magazine,* September 1998.

Jane, Wills. "Taking on the CosmoCorps?" *Economic Geography,* April 1998.

Mataloni, Raymond J. "U.S. Multinational Companies Operations in 1996." *Survey of Current Business,* September 1998.

Miller, William H. "A Force for Good." *Industry Week,* 19 April 1999.

Nuruzzaman, Mohammed. "Economic Liberalization and Poverty in the Developing Countries." *Journal of Contemporary Asia,* March 2005, 109.

Prahalad, C.K., and Kenneth Lieberthal. "The End of Corporate Imperialism." *Harvard Business Review,* July-August 1998.

Stopford, John. "Multinational Corporations." *Foreign Policy,* Winter 1998.

"Time to Bring it Back Home?" *The Economist,* 5 March 2005, 63.

Tsang, Eric W.K. "Internationalization as a Learning Process: Singapore MNCs in China." *Academy of Management Executives,* February 1999.

Tyler, Gus. "The Nation-State vs. the Global Economy." *Challenge,* March-April 1993.

Woollacott, Martin. "Are Businesses Forced to Keep Bad Company." *Business and Society Review,* Fall 1995, 45.

"Worldbeater Inc." *Economist,* 22 November 1997.

Zhao, Laixun. "Labour-Management Bargaining and Transfer Pricing in Multinational Corporations." *Canadian Journal of Economics,* October 1998.

MULTIPLE-CRITERIA DECISION MAKING

Real-world decision-making problems are usually too complex and ill-structured to be considered through the examination of a single criterion, attribute, or point of view that will lead to the optimum decision. In fact, such a unidimensional approach is merely an oversimplification of the actual nature of the problem at hand, and it can lead to unrealistic decisions. A more appealing approach would be the simultaneous consideration of all pertinent factors that are related to the problem. However, through this approach some very essential issues/questions emerge: how can several and often conflicting factors be aggregated into a single evaluation model? Is this evaluation model a unique and optimal one? Researchers from a variety of disciplines have tried to address the former question using statistical approaches, artificial intelligence techniques, and operations research methodologies. The success and usefulness of these attempts should be examined with regard to the second question. Obviously, a decision problem is not addressed in the same way by all decision makers. Each decision maker has his or her own preferences, experiences, and decision-making policy; thus one person's judgment is expected to differ from another's. This is a significant issue that should be considered during the development of decision-making models.

Addressing such issues constitutes the focal point of interest in multiple-criteria decision making (MCDM). MCDM constitutes an advanced field of operations research that is devoted to the development and implementation of decision support tools and methodologies to confront complex decision problems involving multiple criteria, goals, or objectives of conflicting nature. The tools and methodologies provided by MCDM are not just some mathematical models aggregating criteria, points of view, or attributes, but furthermore they are decision-support oriented. Actually, support is a key concept in MCDM, implying that the models are not developed through a straightforward sequential process where the decision maker's role is passive. Instead, an iterative process is employed to analyze the preferences of the decision maker and represent them as consistently as possible in an appropriate decision model. This iterative and interactive preference modeling procedure constitutes the underlying basis of the decision-support orientation of MCDM, and it is one of the basic distinguishing features of the MCDM as opposed to statistical and optimization decision-making approaches.

HISTORICAL OVERVIEW

From the very beginning of mankind, decision making always involved multiple criteria that have been treated either implicitly or explicitly, although no specific mathematical framework existed for this purpose. Pareto was the first to study, in an axiomatic way, the aggregation of conflicting criteria into a single evaluation index. He was also the first to introduce the concept of efficiency, one of the key aspects of the modern MCDM theory. Several decades later,

Koopmans extended Pareto's work introducing the notion of efficient vector, i.e., the non-dominated set of alternatives. During the same period (1940s to 1950s) von Neumann and Morgenstern introduced the expected utility theory, thus setting the foundations of another MCDM approach. In the 1960s the concepts and procedures described in these early works were extended by Charnes and Cooper and Fishburn. By the end of the 1960s significant research started to be undertaken in this field by the European operational research community. Roy, the founder of the European stream of MCDM, developed a new theoretical approach based on the concept of outranking relations. From the 1970s to the 1990s, MCDM evolved rapidly, scientific MCDM associations were formed, and numerous advances were published in the international literature, both on the theoretical aspects of MCDM as well as on its practical implementation. The field has benefited significantly from the widespread use of personal computers, which enabled the development of software packages employing MCDM methods. These software packages, known as multi-criteria decision support systems, provide the means to implement the theoretical advances in MCDM in user-friendly systems that enable real-time decision making through interactive and iterative procedures that enhance the decision maker's perception of the problem and his or her judgment and decision-making policy.

THEORETICAL APPROACHES TO MCDM

Among the MCDM methods and tools, several approaches and theoretical disciplines can be defined, although their distinctions and boundaries are often difficult to determine. This discussion adopts the classification of MCDM approaches proposed by Pardalos et al. It distinguishes four categories: (1) multi-objective mathematical programming, (2) multi-attribute utility theory, (3) outranking relations approach, and (4) preference disaggregation approach.

The multi-objective mathematical programming (MMP) is an extension of the well-known single-objective mathematical programming framework. It involves the optimization of a set of objectives that are expressed in the form of linear or nonlinear functions of some decision variables. The optimization of these objectives is performed subject to constraints imposed either by the decision environment or by the decision maker. The conflicting nature of the objectives in real-world decision problems makes impossible their simultaneous optimization. Thus, the decision maker cannot obtain an optimum solution, but has to consider finding a satisfying one. The determination of this satisfying solution depends on the decision maker's preferences, judgment, and decision policy. The MMP techniques that have been developed aim to determine initially the set of efficient solutions (solutions that are not dominated by any other solution with respect to the specified objectives) and then to identify a specific solution that meets the decision maker's preferences, through an interactive and iterative procedure. More details on this category of methods can be found in the books of Zeleny and Steuer.

The multi-attribute utility theory (MAUT) is an extension of the classical utility theory. Its aim is to represent/model the decision maker's preferences through a utility function $u(g)$ aggregating all the evaluation criteria: $u(g) = u(g_1, g_2, \ldots, g_n)$, where g is the vector of the evaluation criteria $g_1, g_2, \ldots, g_n$. In general, it is possible to decompose a multicriteria utility function in real functions $u_1, u_2, \ldots, u_n$ concerning the independence of criteria. Thus, different utility function models are obtained. The most studied form of utility function, from a theoretical point of view, is the additive form: $u(g_1, g_2, \ldots, g_n) = u_1(g_1) + u_2(g_2) + \cdots + u_n(g_n)$, where $u_1, u_2, \ldots, u_n$ are the marginal utilities defined on the scales of criteria. On the basis of the utilities of the alternatives that are determined through the developed utility function, the decision maker can rank them from the best alternatives (alternatives with the higher utility) to the worst ones (alternatives with the lower utility), classify them into appropriate classes through the definition of appropriate utility thresholds, or select the alternative with the higher utility as the best one. The books of Zeleny and Keeney and Raiffa provide a comprehensive discussion of MAUT, its axiomatic foundations, and the forms of utility functions that are commonly employed in decision-making problems, both under certainty and uncertainty.

The outranking relations approach was developed in Europe with the presentation of the ELECTRE methods (ELimination Et Choix Traduisant la REalité) by Roy. An outranking relation allows one to conclude that an alternative a outranks an alternative b if there are enough arguments to confirm that a is at least as good as b, while there is no essential reason to refuse this statement. To develop the outranking relation, the decision maker, in collaboration with the decision analyst, must specify the weights of the evaluation criteria, as well as some technical parameters (preference, indifference, and veto thresholds). The definition of these parameters enables the examination of whether there is a sufficient majority of criteria for which a is better than b (concordance) and if the unfavorable deviations for the rest of the criteria (discordance) are not too high. In this case it is possible to conclude that alternative a outranks alternative b. Furthermore, through this modeling procedure it is possible to identify the cases where the performances of two alternatives on the evaluation criteria differ significantly, thus making impossible their comparison (incomparability). A detailed presentation of all outranking methods can be found in the works of Vincke and Roy and Bouyssou.

The preference disaggregation approach refers to the analysis (disaggregation) of the global preferences (judgment policy) of the decision maker in order to identify the criteria aggregation model that underlies the preference result (ranking or classification/sorting). Similar to MAUT, preference disaggregation analysis uses common utility decomposition forms to model the decision maker's preferences. Nevertheless, instead of employing a direct procedure for estimating the global utility model (MAUT), preference disaggregation analysis uses regression-based techniques (indirect estimation procedure). More specifically, in preference disaggregation analysis the parameters of the utility decomposition model are estimated through the analysis of the decision maker's overall preference on some reference alternatives, which may involve either examples of past decisions or a small subset of the alternatives under consideration. The decision-maker is asked to provide a ranking or a classification of the reference alternatives according to his or her decision policy (global preferences). Then, using regression-based techniques the global preference model is estimated so that the ranking or classification specified by the decision maker can be reproduced as consistently as possible through the developed decision model. A rather exhaustive bibliography of the methods of the disaggregation of preferences can be found in the works of Jacquet-Lagrèze and Siskos and Pardalos, Siskos and Zopounidis.

Except for the functional and methodological differences among the four aforementioned MCDM approaches, their differences with regard to the types of decision problems that they address should also be pointed out. Real-world decision problems can be categorized into two groups:

1. Problems where the decision maker must evaluate a finite set of alternatives in order to select the most appropriate one, to rank them from the best to the worst, to classify them into predefined homogeneous classes, or to describe them. Typical examples involve the selection among different investment projects, personnel evaluation (ranking problem), and financial distress prediction (classification problem; i.e., discrimination between healthy and financially distressed firms). These type of problems are referred to as discrete MCDM problems.

2. Problems where there is an infinite set of alternatives. Thus the decision maker must construct the most appropriate one according to his or her goals or objectives. Recourse allocation problems are typical example of this kind. For instance, a portfo-

lio manager faces the problem of constructing a portfolio of securities according to his specific investment policy and objectives. Different combinations of securities can result to numerous portfolios. Thus, it is impossible to define an exhaustive set of portfolios for evaluation and selection of the most appropriate one. Instead, the portfolio manager must construct the most appropriate portfolio through the determination of the amount of capital that should be invested in each security. These type of problems are referred to as continuous MCDM problems.

Discrete MCDM problems are addressed through the multiattribute utility theory (MAUT), the outranking relations approach, and preference disaggregation, while continuous MCDM problems are addressed through MMP.

MCDM APPLICATIONS

In the international literature on management science and operations research there is an increasing number of real-world applications of MCDM. Of course, in the limited space here it would be impossible to provide an extensive bibliography regarding these applications. However, it is possible to outline some of the most significant areas to which MCDM has contributed. The following list reports some of these areas:

1. Finance and economics
   - Business failure prediction
   - Credit risk assessment
   - Portfolio selection and management
   - Company mergers and acquisitions
   - Financial planning
   - Country risk evaluation
   - Regional economic policy specification

2. Environmental Management and Energy planning
   - Forest management
   - Waste management
   - Power plant siting
   - Water resources planning
   - Nuclear power management
   - Energy intensity evaluation

3. Marketing
   - Customer satisfaction
   - Design of market penetration strategies
   - Retail evaluation

4. Transportation
   - Highway planning
   - Subway design

5. Human resources management
   - Job evaluation
   - Personnel selection

6. Education

7. Agriculture

Extensive information on these applications can be found in the books of Vincke, Pardalos et al., and Roy.

The complexity of real-world decisions and the plethora of factors and criteria that are often involved necessitate the implementation of a sound theoretical framework to structure and model the decision-making process. MCDM provides such a framework, as well as a wide variety of sophisticated methodological tools that are oriented towards the support of the decision makers in facing real-world decision problems. This decision-support orientation of MCDM, in combination with the focus given by researchers in this field to develop advanced and realistic preference modeling techniques, is its main distinguishing feature as opposed to statistical analysis and optimization theory. The advances in the field continue rapidly. According to Fishburn and Lavalle, they involve foundation aspects of MCDM such as the interface between behavioral decision theory and prescriptive practice and the underlying assumptions of MCDM methods, methodological aspects involving the development of more effective methods, and implementation aspects through the development of multicriteria decision-support systems. Along with these advances, researchers are also exploring the application of MCDM to other fields, including artificial intelligence (neural networks, expert systems, genetic algorithms) and fuzzy sets. The integration of the diverse nature of these fields within the MCDM framework increases the potentials regarding the development of advanced decision-support tools to confront the complexity of real-world decisions

SEE ALSO: Decision Making; Decision Rules and Decision Analysis; Decision Support Systems

Constantin Zopounidis and Michael Doumpos
Revised by Hal P. Kirkwood, Jr.

FURTHER READING:

Brugha, C.M. "Structure of Multi-Criteria Decision-Making." *The Journal of Operational Research Society* 55, no. 11 (2004): 1156–1169.

Figueira, J., S. Greco, and M. Ehrgott, eds. *Multiple Criteria Decision Analysis: State of the Art Surveys.* New York: Springer, 2004.

Fishburn, P.C., and I.H. Lavalle. "MCDA: Theory, Practice and the Future." *Journal of Multi-criteria Decision Analysis* 8, no. 1 (1999): 1–2.

Keeney, R.L., and H. Raiffa. *Decisions with Multiple Objectives: Preferences and Value Trade-Offs.* Cambridge: Cambridge University Press, 1993.

Pardalos, P.M., Y. Siskos, and C. Zopounidis. *Advances in Multicriteria Analysis.* Dordrecht: Kluwer Academic Publishers, 1995.

Roy, B. *Multicriteria Methodology for Decision Aiding.* Dordrecht: Kluwer Academic Publishers, 1996.

Vincke, P. *Multicriteria Decision Aid.* New York: John Wiley and Sons, 1992.

Zopounidis, C., and M. Doumpos. *Multicriteria Decision Aid Classification Methods.* New York: Springer, 2002.

N

NAICS

SEE: North American Industry Classification System

NEGOTIATION

SEE: Conflict Management and Negotiation

NEPOTISM

Nepotism describes a variety of practices related to favoritism; it can mean simply hiring one's own family members, or it can mean hiring and advancing unqualified or under qualified family members based simply on the familial relationship. The word nepotism stems from the Latin word for nephew, especially the "nephews" of the prelates in medieval times. While attitudes toward nepotism vary according to cultural background, nepotism is a sensitive issue in American business. Many companies and individuals consider the practice to be unethical, largely due to its conflict with traditional American values of self-reliance and fairness.

In Western societies nepotism raises legal concerns. Although U.S. laws do not specifically prohibit hiring one's relatives, studies show that between 10 and 40 percent of U.S. companies maintain formal policies prohibiting such a practice. Many of these anti-nepotism rules were instituted in the 1950s with the aim of preventing the hiring of incompetent male relatives of male employees. In the 1960s and 1970s the same rules applied but failed to reflect the change in the workforce as more women entered the job market; females were often the victims of these rules, however, and many were forced to quit.

Nepotism is also tied to discrimination issues and pragmatic concerns. There is substantial debate over whether employers with any form of biased preferences for hiring, including nepotism, can even survive in the business market, ethical issues notwithstanding. On the other hand, approximately 40 percent of Fortune 500 firms are family-owned, and the success of these businesses can be viewed as an implicit endorsement of nepotism.

Larry Singell and James Thornton identify four levels of anti-nepotism rules. They note that companies may institute policies that prohibit the employment of a current employee's relatives

- anywhere in the organization,

- at the same facility,

- in the same department or work group, or

- in positions where one may immediately influence the compensation, promotion, or work situation of the other.

Even if a company has a clearly stated policy, complications may follow in its enforcement. For example, the increase in dual-career marriages increased legal challenges to nepotism issues. Employees occasionally meet at work, socialize, fall in love, and eventually marry. In some cases, couples have had to decide which spouse has to quit, as company policy would not allow them to work for the same organization. Do practices such as hiring, or even not firing, family actually constitute discrimination?

Further, even if there is no complication between the two individuals as a result of marriage, there is sometimes pressure from in-laws and even close friends of in-laws for favoritism in hiring. There appear to be differences in nepotism practices between family-owned businesses and publicly owned businesses. Most family-owned businesses simply expect family to be involved in the future, as do the in-laws who join the family. However, there are usually more formal rules for publicly held companies; these companies must therefore be cautious, since they are open to outside scrutiny over their hiring and promotion practices.

ADVANTAGES

If practiced fairly (itself a contentious term in this regard), nepotism can be a true asset, Sharon Nelton suggests, citing the example of Thomas Publishing Company. In 1998 there were seven third- and fourth-generation family members working for the company. The third-generation president, Tom Knudson, encouraged nepotism among their independent sales contractors because he believed it resulted in high performance, stability, and long-term commitment.

Chad Kaydo also writes that nepotism may be viable. For example, a top salesperson's relative may have many of the same qualities that make the representative successful. Recruiting family members can therefore boost both performance as well as retention. For instance, one senior contractor began working for Thomas in 1940. By 1998 his wife and three of his adult children (two daughters and a son) all worked for the company. The son encountered a challenge when calling on a client at odds with the senior contractor. He easily and politely diffused the situation using the diplomacy techniques he had gleaned from his father, the very senior contractor the client disliked, and gained a larger-than-usual sale.

In the 2000s the tide in business seemed to be turning toward policies that encouraged hiring qualified relatives and spouses, with idea that good people tend to associate with good people. Jacquelyn Lynn noted that such policies can promote employee satisfaction by aiding individual efforts to balance professional and personal lives. Hiring family members can also provide benefits to companies, for example by reducing their health insurance costs.

DISADVANTAGES

There are, to be sure, nepotism disasters. Lines Brothers in Britain, once a highly successful maker of Triang toys, was rendered worthless in a just a few years by its second generation of leadership. Yale Express, a U.S. delivery company, was bankrupt within five years of the second generation assuming the presidency. The Great Atlantic and Pacific Tea Company (A&P) was once the largest supermarket chain in the United States, but went bankrupt under its heir.

Linda Wong and Brian Kleiner suggest that trouble arises most often when family and business needs conflict. A family's purpose is to care for and nurture family members; a business must produce quality goods and/or services as efficiently and as profitably as possible. If a company hires or promotes an incompetent family member, other employees may see this is a gross injustice and many complications may result. More directly, the unqualified heir may simply instill policies that drive the company into the ground.

Nepotism can also publicize family disagreements and prejudices to those within the company. It may even cause a company to lose valued executives and make it very difficult to attract and retain high-quality newcomers.

INTERNATIONAL ASPECTS

Abdalla Hayajenh, Ahmen Maghrabi, and Taher Al-Dabbagh note that nepotism has maintained a particularly strong footing in the Arab world. They indicate that the major factors behind nepotism in Arab countries include:

- socio-cultural structure (tribal and kinship relations);
- economic structure (a tight labor market making it difficult to find a job in other ways);
- educational structure (poor preparation of workers for economic development); and
- political structure (governments' assignation of educated tribal chiefs and their sons to key positions in return for loyalty).

In Asia the majority of entrepreneurs look to the family, rather than the broader populace, for the succession of the business. Studying Asian nepotism practices, Leon Richardson holds that nepotism works as well as any other management choice as long as one never tolerates incompetence. He notes that the Japanese successfully use nepotism, with senior men and women enjoying power and not hesitating to fire an incompetent "nephew."

In addition, many Latin American counties accept nepotism as the norm and are baffled by the oftennegative U.S. attitude toward the practice. As one South American executive commented, "If I cannot hire and trust my own family, just who can I trust?"

GUIDELINES

Craig Aronoff and John Ward argue that the key to the successful use of nepotism is clear communication of the rules before they are needed and fair application of the rules as needed. They believe in holding relatives to at least three standards in hiring:

1. appropriate education for the job;

2. three to five years of outside work experience; and

3. entry into an already existing and vital position with determined pay and performance expectations.

Many experts believe that outside experience is vital to the potential family-member hire. They feel the family member should establish their own competence and professional sense of worth before assuming work responsibilities within the family's firm. Testing and honing their skills and abilities allows them to bring expertise to the enterprise.

In the first sixteen years of business, CAM Specialty Products practiced a strict policy of not hiring family members. However, in 1997 an opportunity to invest in Deckare appeared and co-owner Gordon Hammett hired his son as work crew chief to handle on-site fieldwork. Hammett interviewed his son like all other candidates and honestly felt his son was a perfect fit for the job; he was familiar with his son's work ethic and knew his son enjoyed the type of work. As a result, the decision met with great success. The key was to have clear criteria for the job and to apply them consistently for all candidates, neither favoring nor discriminating against family members.

Nepotism is not a new phenomenon in business, but it is of particular interest as the world of business shrinks due to rapid travel and convenient and fast technological communication. As business becomes increasingly globalized, it is crucial to understand how cultural attitudes toward nepotism vary between the different countries in which a business operates. Furthermore, as more families rely on multiple incomes for their standard of living, the ethical and pragmatic considerations regarding nepotism must be carefully negotiated to ensure the most effective overall business strategy. While certain guidelines have been known to effect a smooth incorporation of nepotism into a successful business, there are no definitive strategies. Clearly, however, nepotism can lead to success if applied appropriately, or to disaster if applied without careful consideration of the all variables involved.

SEE ALSO: Employee Recruitment Planning; Entrepreneurship; Human Resource Management; Succession Planning; Work-Life Balance

Jean L. Bush-Bacelis
Revised by Laurie Collier Hillstrom

FURTHER READING:

Aronoff, Craig E., and John L. Ward. "Rules for Nepotism." *Nation's Business,* January 1993.

Bellow, Adam. *In Praise of Nepotism.* New York: Doubleday, 2003.

Hayajenh, Abdalla F., Ahmed S. Maghrabi, and Taher H. Al-Dabbagh. "Research Note: Assessing the Effects of Nepotism on Human Resource Managers." *International Journal of Manpower* 15, no. 1 (1994).

Kaydo, Chad. "Does Nepotism Work?" *Sales & Marketing Management,* July 1998.

Lynn, Jacquelyn. "Lawful Wedded Employees." *Entrepreneur,* April 2000.

Nelton, Sharon. "The Bright Side of Nepotism." *Nation's Business,* May 1998.

Padgett, Margaret Y., and Kathryn A. Morris. "Keeping it 'All in the Family': Does Nepotism in the Hiring Process Really Benefit the Beneficiary?" *Journal of Leadership and Organizational Studies* (Winter 2005).

Richardson, Leon. "Family Planning Can Work Wonders." *Asian Business,* September 1993, 72.

Sanderson, Rhonda. "Father & Son Pair Up for Deckare." *Franchising World,* May-June 1998.

Singell, Larry D., Jr., and James Thornton. "Nepotism, Discrimination and the Persistence of Utility-Maximizing, Owner-Operated Firms." *Southern Economic Journal* 63, no. 4 (1997).

Wong, Linda C., and Brian H. Kleiner. "Nepotism." *Work Study,* September-October 1994.

NEW PRODUCT DEVELOPMENT

The dynamics of markets, technology, and competition have brought changes to virtually every market sector and have made new product development one of the most powerful business activities. The monumental changes that constantly impact commerce have forced companies to innovate with increasing speed, efficiency, and quality. In turn, this has made new product development one of the most complex and difficult business functions. However, firms must innovate in order to survive. The power of innovation is revealed in numerous studies, which show that companies leading their industries attribute about half of their revenues to products developed in the most recent five years. By comparison, companies at the bottom of their industries achieve approximately one-tenth of their sales from new products.

A firm's new product development efforts are shaped by its size, as well as the nature of the industry in which it operates. New products may be defined as any product, service, or idea not currently made or marketed by a company, or which the consumer may perceive as new. Many types of new products exist, from never-seen-before products like Apple's personal communicator, to repositioned standards like Sears' shift to Sears Brand Central. Various studies suggest that between 50 and 80 percent of new products fail—the greater the rate of new product development, the higher the failure rate. *New Product News* predicts that more than 36,000 new products will be brought to market in 2005. Although there are numerous reasons why new products fail, faulty management and planning are at the core of most failures. Therefore, managing the new product development process is a key to a healthy organization.

HISTORY

The history of product innovation can be divided into three stages, beginning with the product-oriented or technology-pushed stage. In the post-World War II era Americans were coming off wartime shortages and were in the mood to buy the many goods that manufacturers produced. Engineers, who were more product-oriented than consumer oriented, designed new products that might or might not find places in consumers' hearts and minds. This was a product-oriented process in which the market was considered the receptacle for products that emerged from the firm's research and development efforts.

However, competition escalated and consumers became more skeptical and selective about the types of products they purchased. Marketers found it increasingly difficult to rely on persuasive sales techniques to move products. Retailers grew restless when these products did not move off shelves as quickly as planned. Companies had to know more about their target markets. What were the wants and needs of the people who were buying their products? How could their firm satisfy these wants and needs?

The second stage was marked by the emergence of the market as the driver of innovation. Instead of being technology-driven, new product development evolved into a market-led process in which new products emerged from well-researched customer needs. The new product development process was placed in the hands of marketers who knew consumers' wants and needs. Customer demand "pulled" the product through the development process.

Modern new product development is a blending of these two orientations into a "dual-drive" approach to innovation. Companies recognize that innovation is a complex process that requires sound investment in research and development, as well as significant marketing expertise that focuses on satisfying consumers' wants and needs.

The rapid pace of change that engulfed businesses toward the end of the twentieth century put an even greater burden on companies to build adaptive capabilities into their organizations. Global competition means there are more competitors capable of world-class performance. This has made competition more intense, rigorous, and aggressive than ever before. Fragmenting and more sophisticated markets mean that consumers demand more from products in terms of quality, differentiation, and "meaningfulness."

New technologies have had two important outcomes in regards to innovation. First, new technologies are responsible for this new market sophistication in which consumers have more choices and are thus more demanding. Secondly, new technology has increased manufacturers' capabilities for rapid response to shifting market needs.

Finally, product life cycles have become more compressed as the skills required for developing new products increase in complexity. For example, consider the development of a new type of computer software. The expertise needed to develop the software from conception to commercialization might take years. The product's life cycle in such a competitive and turbulent environment might last only a few months. Therefore, companies have embraced the view that new products are transient, whereas the skills and expertise needed to develop these products are a much more persistent requirement for success. Instead of the mono-approach, in which technology or markets drive innovation, new product development now requires a convergence of technology, marketing, product design, engineering, and manufacturing capabilities. Speed, efficiency, and quality in product development are the challenges that new product development faces in today's intense competitive environment.

TYPES AND SOURCES OF NEW PRODUCTS

There are five categories of new products. New-to-the-world products or services are new inventions like in-line skates and health maintenance organizations. New category entries, such as sport utility vehicles, are products or services that are new to a firm. Additions to product lines add products or services to a firm's current markets. For example, when a powder laundry detergent offers a liquid version it is considered a line extension. Product improvements are another type of new product and are common to every product category. Repositionings target products to new markets or for new uses.

Firms can obtain new products internally or externally. External sourcing means the company acquires the product or service, or obtains the rights to market the product or service, from another organization. Internal development means the firm develops the new product itself. This is riskier than external development because the company bears all of the costs associated with new product development and implementation. Collaborations, which include strategic partnerships, strategic alliances, joint ventures, and licensing agreements, occur when two or more firms work together on developing new products.

NEW PRODUCT DEVELOPMENT PROCESS

Historically, the new product development process has been conceived in discreet terms with a beginning and an end. Different companies and different industries may alter this seven-step process for different products, or the steps themselves may become blurred as companies become engaged in several stages at the same time.

The process begins with idea generation. For every successful new product, many new product ideas are conceived and discarded. Therefore, companies usually generate a large number of ideas from which successful new products emerge.

Idea screening, the second step, considers all new product ideas in the idea pool and eliminates ones that are perceived to be the least likely to succeed. Not only should the firm's manufacturing, technology, and marketing capabilities be evaluated at this stage, but also how the new idea fits with the company's vision and strategic objectives.

The third stage, concept development and testing, requires formal evaluations of the product concept by

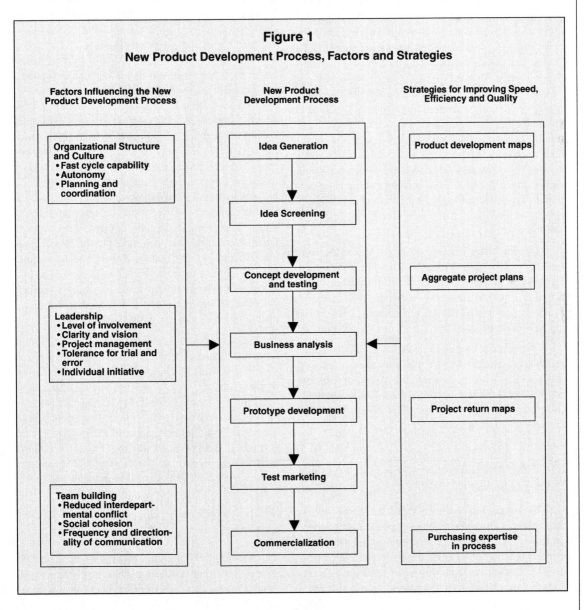

Figure 1
New Product Development Process, Factors and Strategies

Factors Influencing the New Product Development Process

Organizational Structure and Culture
• Fast cycle capability
• Autonomy
• Planning and coordination

Leadership
• Level of involvement
• Clarity and vision
• Project management
• Tolerance for trial and error
• Individual initiative

Team building
• Reduced interdepartmental conflict
• Social cohesion
• Frequency and directionality of communication

New Product Development Process

Idea Generation
↓
Idea Screening
↓
Concept development and testing
↓
Business analysis
↓
Prototype development
↓
Test marketing
↓
Commercialization

Strategies for Improving Speed, Efficiency and Quality

Product development maps

Aggregate project plans

Project return maps

Purchasing expertise in process

consumers, usually through some form of marketing research. New product ideas with low concept test scores are discarded or revised. While the Internet is making it easier to gather consumer data, there are limitations. As people get deluged with an increasing number of surveys and solicitations, it is possible that they will grow tired of helping marketers.

The business analysis stage is next. At this point the new product idea is analyzed for its marketability and costs. After passing the first three stages an idea may be discarded once marketing and manufacturing costs are analyzed, due to limited potential for profitability or commercial success. Throughout these four stages, the new idea has remained on paper with a relatively small investment required.

The fifth stage, prototype development, is the first stage where new product costs begin to escalate. Because of this, many companies have placed greater emphasis on the first four stages and reduced the proportion of new products that reach the prototype stage from about 50 percent to around 20 percent. At this stage the concept is converted into an actual product. A customer value perspective during this phase means the product is designed to satisfy the needs expressed by consumers. Firms may use quality function deployment (QFD) as they develop the prototype. QFD links specific consumer requirements such as versatility, durability, and low maintenance with specific product characteristics (for example, adjustable shelves, a door-mounted ice and water dispenser, and touch controls for a refrigerator). The customer value perspective requires the new product to satisfy customer needs and meet desired quality levels at specified production costs.

Test marketing tests the prototype and marketing strategy in simulated or actual market situations. Because of the expense and risks associated with actual test markets, marketers use them with caution. Products that test poorly are pulled back and reconceptualized or discarded.

Commercialization, the final stage, is when the product is introduced full scale. The level of investment and risk are highest at this stage. Consumer adoption rates, timing decisions for introduction, and coordinating efforts with production, distribution, and marketing should be considered.

FACTORS INFLUENCING NEW PRODUCT DEVELOPMENT

The seven-step process assumes a definite beginning and end. However, studies suggest that what goes on before and after new products are introduced is as important as the process itself. Organizational structure, leadership, and team building influence the speed and efficiency with which new products are introduced.

Structure influences efficiency, autonomy, and coordination. New product innovation requires structure that optimizes direction and guidance. Structure that facilitates internal information exchange, decision making, and materials flow is essential. A "fast-cycle" structure allows more time for planning and implementing activities to gain competitive advantage. This type of structure also cuts costs because production materials and information collect less overhead and do not accumulate as work-in-process inventory. Autonomy refers to the amount of decision making allowed at lower levels of management. The coordination of the engineering, product design, manufacturing, and marketing functions in the new product development process is vital.

Leadership influences strategy, culture, and the firm's overall ability to undertake new product development. Top management can demonstrate involvement in the development process by providing career advancement for entrepreneurial skills and encouraging broad employee participation. Clarity and vision are crucial to ensuring that new product ideas are good strategic fits for the company. The degree to which leadership allows trial and error and promotes individual initiative positively influences the development of new products. This acceptance of risk and support for an entrepreneurial spirit within the organization are crucial in order for innovation to flourish. New products emerge in a variety of ways and their development does not always proceed in rational and consistent manners. It is necessary for leadership to view the process as iterative and dynamic, and to foster adaptation and flexibility. Management flexibility and responsiveness to change also are needed. This type of leadership is particularly important to the project manager who must coordinate and integrate the various parts of the new product development process so that a coherent system emerges that produces a product with compelling value. Initiative encourages creativity and problem-solving skills.

Teams provide mechanisms for breaking down functional biases created by a strict adherence to structure. The amount of interdepartmental conflict in the organization, the social cohesion among team members, and the frequency and directionality of interdepartmental communication influence team building. Through shared understanding of the objectives and purposes of the project, as well as the tasks required in the development process, teams can shape the project and influence how work gets done in the organization.

IMPROVING SPEED, EFFICIENCY, AND QUALITY

New products often fail because of unanticipated market shifts that result in missed opportunities and misused channels of distribution. Failures also occur because companies miscalculate their own technological strengths or the product's technological challenges. These potential problems often crop up in the latter stages and result in delays, redesigns, or poor quality products.

Companies are constantly seeking ways to avoid these pitfalls. One solution is new product development maps that chart the evolution of a company's product lines. This historical perspective helps the firm to identify and analyze functional capabilities in a systematic, repetitive fashion that allows for the development of linkages and the identification of resources for new endeavors. These maps can direct the firm to new market opportunities and point out technological challenges.

Aggregate plans for projects offer another solution. Rather than viewing each new product development project individually, they consider all of the new product development projects under consideration by the firm. This is particularly important in firms with hundreds of new product development projects going on at the same time. Projects are categorized according to resources required and contribution to the firm's bottom line. Aggregate project plans enable management to improve the management of new product development by providing greater control over resource allocation and utilization. These plans help to point out where capabilities need to be improved, how sequencing projects may help, and how projects fit with the firm's development strategies.

Return maps graphically represent the contributions of all team members to product success in terms of time and money. Their focus is on the point at which product sales generate sufficient profit so that the firm's initial investment in development is returned. Return maps show team members the time and money needed to complete their tasks in the development process so that they may estimate and re-estimate their investment in the process. In doing this return maps illustrate the impact of their actions on the project's overall success.

Another way to improve the speed and efficiency with which new products are introduced is to involve purchasing in the development process. When purchasing expertise is introduced into the development project team, quality may increase, time to market entry may decrease, investment in inventory may diminish, and costs may significantly decrease.

Technology continues to change and create new opportunities and threats. Customer requirements and expectations continue to shift and create new demands. Old channels of distribution are becoming obsolete and new channels are opening new opportunities. Some competitors are falling by the wayside while others are surging to the forefront by making new and unexpected moves to gain advantage. The very structure of industry is changing. A key to success in this tumultuous environment will continue to be the ability to sustain a competitive advantage through innovation. However, speed, efficiency, and quality in product development will be paramount. Building capabilities in all aspects of product creation and implementation, overcoming uncertainty and facilitating decision-making, ensuring these innovations are strategically linked to the firm's vision, and doing this on a continuous basis is the challenge of new product development in the next century.

SEE ALSO: Innovation; Product Design; Product Life Cycle and Industry Life Cycle

Charles M. Mayo
Revised by Deborah Hausler

FURTHER READING:

Cooper, Robert G., Scott J. Edgett, and Elko J. Kleinschmidt. "Benchmarking Best NPD Practices." *Research-Technology Management* 47, no. 6 (2004): 43.

Crawford, C. Merle. *New Products Management.* 5th ed. Chicago: Irwin, 1997.

"Making NPD Work." *Nilewide Marketing Review,* 10 October 2004.

Moorman, Christine, and Anne S. Miner. "The Convergence of Planning and Execution: Improvisation in New Product Development." *Journal of Marketing* 62, no. 3 (1998): 1–20.

Poolton, Jenny, and Ian Barclay. "New Product Development from Past Research to Future Applications." *Industrial Marketing Management* 27, no. 3 (1998): 197–212.

Steenkamp, Jan-Benedict E.M., Frenkelter Hofstede, and Michel Wedel. "A Cross-National Investigation into the Individual and National Cultural Antecedents of Consumer Innovativeness." *Journal of Marketing* 63, no. 2 (1999): 55–69.

Wells, Melanie. "Have It Your Way." *Forbes Global* 8, no. 3 (2005): 16.

NON-COMPETE AGREEMENTS

A non-compete agreement, or covenant not to compete, generally is a contract in which one party agrees not to compete with another party in exchange for payment of some consideration. Non-compete agreements are most commonly found in employment contracts, particularly with management or sales employees; in agreements among shareholders or partners of a business; in contracts for the sale of a business; and in agreements for the funding of a business. Non-compete agreements are difficult to enforce, and must be carefully drafted to conform to the regulations of the state in which the agreement is to be performed.

NON-COMPETE AGREEMENTS IN EMPLOYMENT CONTRACTS

In an employment setting, a non-compete agreement is a contract between an employer and an employee, which prevents the employee from working for a competing company and from divulging to third parties, including new employers, the confidential business and proprietary information, trade secrets, customer lists, and technical and manufacturing processes of the contracting employer. A non-compete agreement must seek to protect a company's legitimate business interests and property. Without such an agreement, employees can leave a company, and subject to state protection against misappropriating a company's trade secrets and federal intellectual property statutes, freely compete with their former employers.

With some exceptions, most states recognize non-compete agreements or restrictive covenants in employment contracts, either through specific provision in a state statute or through the state courts' application of a common law "rule of reason" analysis. The "rule of reason" analysis weighs the company's interest in protecting its proprietary and confidential information in a geographic area for a period of time against the employee's need to have a way in which to earn a living. However, the specific provisions and types of non-compete agreements that the state will recognize varies among the states, and quite often, a non-compete agreement which is found valid in one state is determined by the courts in another state to be unenforceable because, for example, it is too broad in scope or time. Courts are generally not eager to enforce broadly such agreements because they may restrict an individual's ability to earn a living. Courts will also not enforce agreements that are merely broad-based attempts to prevent all competition. As a result, non-compete agreements must be drafted with care to conform with each state's requirements for a valid non-compete agreement. Non-compete agreements in and of themselves do not change the nature of the employment relationship. If it is an at-will relationship, either party can terminate it at any time, and the drafter of a non-compete agreement must be careful, in the attempt to restrict competition, that there is not instead a promise made that the employee will have a job with the employer for life.

One question regarding the at-will employment relationship when a non-compete agreement is in place is whether an employer can discharge an employee for refusing to sign a non-compete agreement, even if that agreement is deemed to be unreasonable. There is concern that such a discharge violates the public policy exception to employment at will; the non-compete agreement may have negative societal effects on the freedom of employees to seek or change jobs and limits to technological advancements. Whether a court will deem a discharge as a violation of public policy depends on the nature of that state's public policy exception and the nature of the state's laws regarding non-compete agreements. California and North Dakota prohibit non-compete agreements in employment relationships, and Oklahoma, Louisiana, Texas, Colorado, and Florida, have all placed limits on the use of non-compete agreements. Thus, the legality and enforceability of the non-compete agreement varies by state.

There are some common provisions in non-compete agreements that are required in all the states that have enforced such agreements. All contractual provisions that seek to restrict competition must be in writing. An oral contract between an employer and an employee, under which the employee promised to not work for a competing company, is not enforceable. As with any contract, there must be "valuable consideration" for the non-compete agreement. The definition of what is sufficient to constitute "valuable consideration" differs by locale, but generally if the non-compete provisions are part of the employment contract at the time of hire, being hired itself has been held to be sufficient consideration for a contract preventing competition if the employment relationship ends. If a non-compete agreement is presented to an employee after employment has commenced, there must be some payment, or at least the promise of a raise or promotion, to the employee in order for the agreement to be found to be based on sufficient consideration. While an employer could claim that continued employment itself was sufficient consideration, and that the employee would have been fired if he or she had signed the contract, such arguments are not favored by courts.

Most importantly, the provisions of the non-compete agreement regarding the geographic territory which the agreement covers, the areas of competition which the agreement protects, and the length of the time of the period of non-competition must be restricted. No court will enforce a contract that attempts to prevent an employee from ever working again. Accordingly, a non-compete agreement should include in very specific terms the interests which the employer wishes to protect from competition, such as technology, research and development efforts, customer lists, pricing information, suppliers, prospective customers and projects, the company's strategic planning efforts, and other confidential and proprietary business information. Companies commonly refer to these interests as "trade secrets."

Courts are most willing to set aside non-compete agreements, or at least modify them, on the issues of the length of the period of non-competition, and the geographic area which it covers. The basis for the time and geographic restrictions is that they must be "reasonable." This determination differs from state to state, and within a state, from industry to industry. However, anyone attempting to enforce a non-compete agreement must be aware that the agreement will not be looked upon with favor if the amount of time it extends or the geographic area it covers is too broad, based on the type of business, the location of the customer base, and the job duties of the employee restrained by the non-compete agreement. Recent court rulings indicate that the following time periods are likely to be upheld: up to five years for agreements regarding trade secrets, up to three years for agreements regarding sale of a business, and up to six months for other types of agreements (e.g., use of client lists).

NON-COMPETE PROVISIONS IN SHAREHOLDER/PARTNER, FUNDING, OR SALE OF A BUSINESS AGREEMENTS

Agreements among shareholders of or partners in privately held companies often contain non-compete provisions. These protect each of the parties to the agreement from competitive activities of another that would damage the business, since each of the shareholders or partners has access to the company's trade secrets and confidential and proprietary information. Similarly, in agreements to provide funds to a business, particularly where the funding is provided by a venture capital source, there regularly appear non-compete provisions. The funding source includes these provisions because it wants to ensure the likelihood of the business's success by preventing competition by the owners or key managers of the business. In a sale of a business, the former owners are often restrained from setting up a new business, within some geographic area, which will compete with the business they just sold, for a specified period of time, again so that the business which was sold can have a chance to survive without competition from those who have information about the company's strengths and weaknesses. There is usually a separately negotiated payment for the non-compete provisions in a sale of a business agreement, and often the sold business will retain the former owners as consultants during the pendency of the non-compete period. Courts are more willing to enforce these types of non-compete agreements, as opposed to those in employment contracts, since the parties have received something of value-an ownership interest, proceeds of a sale, or funding-that is more than just continued employment.

NON-SOLICITATION AGREEMENTS

A non-solicitation contract, which is similar to an agreement not to compete, prevents one party to the contract from seeking business from clients of the other party to the contract. These kinds of contracts can also restrict one party from recruiting for hire people who work for the other party.

SEE ALSO: Employment Law and Compliance; Entrepreneurship

Cindy Rhodes Victor
Revised by Marcia Simmering

FURTHER READING:

"10 Mistakes to Avoid in Non-Compete Agreements." *HR Focus* 79, no. 10: 2.

Garrison, Michael J., and Charles D. Stevens. "Sign This Agreement Not to Compete or You're Fired! Noncompete Agreements and the Public Policy Exception to Employment at Will." *Employee Responsibilities and Rights Journal* 15, no. 3 (2003): 103–126.

Wirtz, David. "Tip the Scales on Non-compete Agreements." *HRMagazine,* November 47, no. 11 (2002): 107–115.

NONPROFIT ORGANIZATIONS

In the United States, nonprofit organizations (NPOs) are organizations that qualify for tax-exempt status under the U.S. Internal Revenue Code. About half are public charities, to which donors can deduct contributions from their taxes. Private foundations also are charitable organizations, but they are not public charities. They exist primarily to fund charities or individuals. Other types of tax exempt organizations include social welfare, labor or agricultural organizations, business leagues, and fraternal beneficiary societies. Nonprofit organizations are not prohibited from earning a profit or paying salaries and wages, but they must devote any surplus to the organization.

Nonprofit organizations also are known as not-for-profit organizations, or as the "independent sector," as opposed to business or government. Nonprofits constitute about 10 percent of U.S. employees. These organizations play a unique role in society, falling between the concepts of public and private entities. Public agencies provide goods and services that are considered to be universally desirable (such as national security or infrastructure). Private enterprises serve individual tastes and preferences and depend on market-based competition to prosper. By contrast, nonprofit organizations supply services that are considered good for the community as a whole or for specific community members, but which do not elicit widespread taxpayer support for direct provision. The distinction may be characterized as the difference between "it is right" that these services should exist, and the idea all members of society "have a right" to such services.

While the nonprofit organization exists in many countries, the focus here is on the American NPO. The primary factors unique to this American sector are volunteers, contributions, and tax-exempt status.

THE ROLE OF NONPROFITS IN THE AMERICAN ECONOMY

Nonprofit organizations play a large role in the American economy. It is difficult to get an accurate count of nonprofits, because only organizations with more than $5,000 in annual gross receipts must register with the IRS and only those with receipts in excess of $25,000 must file with the IRS. According to the National Center for Charitable Statistics (NCCS), in 2001 there were 1.33 million tax exempt organizations in the United States. This figure includes those registered and filing with the IRS. Of these, 783,436 were registered charitable nonprofits, including 264,674 that filed with the IRS and 56,582 that were foundations. Human services organizations make up more than 30 percent of the charitable nonprofits; education is the second largest field with 17 percent, and healthcare/mental health is the third with 13 percent. The remaining nonprofit organizations (486,295) fall under the areas of social welfare, labor/agriculture, business leagues, and other. While hospitals represented less than 2 percent of the reporting charitable nonprofits, they had 41 percent of the total expenditures.

It is estimated that there are twice as many organizations not required to file with the IRS because they did not take in $5,000 annually. This would include such familiar organizations as PTAs and Little Leagues. No statistics are available regarding these organizations.

The NCCS collects and disseminates statistics on the U.S. nonprofit sector. This data is gathered from the IRS and other government agencies, private sector service organizations, and the scholarly community. The NCCS builds compatible national, state, and regional databases and develops uniform standards for reporting on the activities of charitable organizations. Excellent charts representing these data are presented in *The United States Nonprofit Sector 2001,* which is available from The National Council of Nonprofit Associations.

In 2004 nonprofit organizations contributed about 5 percent of the gross domestic product. In 2001 more than 12.5 million people were actively involved in NPO activity, representing approximately 9.5 percent of total U.S. employment. Employment in the nonprofit sector is growing more rapidly than in the business sector; 2.5 percent versus 1.8 percent. The number of Americans employed in the nonprofit sector has doubled in the last 25 years. According to the Council of

Foundations, the average annual turnover rate for associations is 24 percent, but there appears to be wide variation among nonprofit subsectors. For example, employee turnover in child welfare agencies shows rates between 100 percent and 300 percent.

The nonprofit sector relies heavily on volunteers, which can be a problem for nonprofit managers. Volunteers are motivated to support a particular cause, and not by pay and benefits. Thus, managers must provide creative incentives in "psychic income," such as recognition. In addition, attendance may be sporadic, leading to variable levels of capacity at any given time. Some organizations in this sector exist primarily to supply employment to those who have traditionally been considered unemployable, with the goal of boosting both morale and self-sufficiency.

FINANCIAL INFORMATION

To generate revenue, NPOs rely on direct appeal to those individuals, corporations, and other entities that value the underlying cause represented by the organization. Fundraising events, including door-to-door appeals and mass mailings, are highly visible means of garnering funds. Charitable nonprofits had about $822 billion in expenditures in 2001, representing approximately 8 percent of the Gross Domestic Product. This revenue came primarily from fees, government grants and contracts, and investments. About 14 percent came from contributions. Competition for funds is more complex than in the corporate world, as there is no financial reward for the contributor. Each year, the American Association of Fundraising Counsel (AAFRC) publishes national giving estimates in its *Giving USA* report. For 2000, *Giving USA* reported the following national totals:

- Individuals: $152.07 billion (75.0%)
- Foundations: $24.50 billion (12.0%)
- Bequests: $16.02 billion (7.8%)
- Corporations: $10.86 billion (5.3%)

Some organizations rely heavily on competitive grants from governmental or philanthropic institutions. Nationally generated funds may be redistributed to local communities on the basis of need, as is done by the United Way and the Red Cross. Increasingly, nonprofits have relied on participant dues, fees, or charges. Such charges can range from the minimal "suggested contribution" for a senior center lunch to the bill for costly medical procedures at a major hospital.

Of the reporting charitable nonprofit institutions in 2001, hospitals had the greatest percentage of total sector assets (about 30 percent), followed by higher education with approximately 20 percent. Human services, healthcare (excluding hospitals), and lower education, each had about 10 percent. Interestingly, only 6.5 percent of the reporting charitable nonprofits had annual expenditures greater than $5 million.

However, these organizations accounted for more than 82 percent of total assets and more than 87 percent of total expenditures.

The accuracy of financial information about this sector of the economy is limited. First, the ongoing initiative to collect and computerize data in standardized form began in the late 1980s to early 1990s. While the Bureau of Labor Statistics tabulates employment figures, the financial information lags due to attempts to standardize and code the data. Second, while all tax-exempt organizations must apply for such status, only those with total annual revenues of at least $25,000 are required to file a Form 990 with the Internal Revenue Service. These non-filers represent about two-thirds of all registered nonprofit organizations. Third, churches are not required to file a Form 990, leaving this data estimation to private sources. Fourth, pass-through contributions (for example, revenues to both the United Way and the local charities it supports) may be double-counted. Therefore, financial figures are at best an estimate.

There is no single agency with oversight for nonprofit organizations. The IRS serves as one control, but some states have instituted more rigorous guidelines than those at the federal level. The Financial Accounting Standards Board, a private self-regulatory body for the accounting profession, developed Financial Accounting Standards 116 and 117 covering nonprofits, but these prescriptions allow a different form of generally accepted accounting practices (GAAP) from private organizations with similar functions. The BBB Wise Giving Alliance collects and distributes information on national nonprofit organizations. It routinely asks such organizations for information about their programs, governance, fund-raising practices, and finances. Although The BBB Wise Giving Alliance does not recommend charities, it does select charities for evaluation based on the volume of donor inquiries about individual organizations. The BBB Wise Giving Alliance was formed in 2001 with the merger of the National Charities Information Bureau and the Council of Better Business Bureaus Foundation and its Philanthropic Advisory Service. The BBB Wise Giving Alliance is a nonprofit charitable organization, affiliated with the Council of Better Business Bureaus.

TAX-EXEMPT STATUS

In exchange for the supply of quasi-public goods and services, nonprofit organizations are exempt from federal taxation on the excess of revenues over costs within the fiscal year. This practice was established in 1913 with the passage of the first federal income tax law. In addition, they also may be forgiven state and local property taxes, and may receive discount postal privileges. Thus, these organizations are publicly subsidized while not directly supported by all taxpayers.

To qualify for tax-exempt status, the nonprofit organization must satisfy a variety of prerequisites. Among these is the declaration of a primary purpose or cause that qualifies under the Internal Revenue Service code. There is no ownership of assets or income other than that of the organization itself. Externally, this implies that there is no income distribution in the form of dividends or other such payments. Internally, there is the further requirement that the organization does not exist for the benefit of individual employees or board members; payment to such individuals in the form of salary, rent, or contractual arrangement is scrutinized by the IRS. However, the only available penalty is the withdrawal of tax-exempt status, and the IRS has historically delivered this blow only rarely.

Examples of nonprofit organizations include such well-known giants as the United Way, the Red Cross, and the Boy Scouts and Girl Scouts. At the other end of the spectrum are local volunteer fire departments, churches, crisis intervention centers, and civic centers. Many hospitals and universities function as nonprofit institutions.

Figure 1 lists the full range of categories of American NPOs as defined by the National Taxonomy

---

Figure 1

National Taxonomy of Exempt Entities Summary

A - Arts, Culture & Humanities
B - Education
C - Environment
D - Animal-Related
E - Health Care
F - Mental Health & Crisis Intervention
G - Diseases, Disorders & Medical Disciplines
H - Medical Research
I - Crime & Legal-Related
J - Employment
K - Food, Agriculture & Nutrition
L - Housing & Shelter
M - Public Safety, Disaster Preparedness & Relief
N - Recreation & Sports
O - Youth Development
P - Human Services
Q - International, Foreign Affairs & National Security
R - Civil Rights, Social Action & Advocacy
S - Community Improvement & Capacity Building
T - Philanthropy, Voluntarism & Grantmaking Foundations
U - Science & Technology
V - Social Science
W - Public & Societal Benefit
X - Religion-Related
Y - Mutual & Membership Benefit
Z - Unknown

Figure 2

10 broad categories of the National Taxonomy of Exempt Entities

I.   Arts, Culture, and Humanities A

II.   Education B

III.   Environment and Animals C, D

IV.   Health E, F, G, H

V.   Human Services I, J, K, L, M, N, O, P

VI.   International, Foreign Affairs Q

VII.   Public, Societal Benefit R, S, T, U, V, W

VIII. Religion Related X

IX.   Mutual/Membership Benefit Y

X.   Unknown, Unclassified Z

---

of Exempt Entities. This classification system offers a definitive classification system for nonprofit organizations recognized as tax exempt under the Internal Revenue Code. Figure 2 lists the major categories by which summaries relating to this sector are frequently reported.

From 1940 to the early 1990s, human services and health accounted for approximately half of the NPOs in the United States. In some NPOs, benefits are limited to a select group, such as senior citizens (local agencies on aging) or those suffering from a specific disease (the American Cancer Society). Other groups have relatively open membership for those willing to pay the fee; an example is the YMCA, which provides recreational facilities.

CHALLENGES FOR NONPROFIT MANAGEMENT

Management must contend with the unique aspects of nonprofit organizations: volunteer labor, solicited contributions, and maintaining tax-exempt status. In addition, Herzlinger suggests that NPOs are highly antithetical to business in other important ways: they lack ownership, competition, and the profit motive. Without these incentives, it may be difficult to maintain effectiveness and efficiency. Even measurement of customer satisfaction may prove elusive, as customers may have no alternatives against which to compare the services received. Some controversy exists over several aspects of nonprofit organizations:

1. For example, some question the rationale of the tax-exempt status of open-membership

---

Table 1

Websites

Alliance for Nonprofit Management	Association of providers of support services to nonprofits	http://www.allianceonline.org
ARNOVA	International membership organization fostering research. Aimed at the academics, provides publications and organizes an annual meeting	http://www.arnova.org
BoardSource (formerly the National Center for Nonprofit Boards)	Practical information for board members	http://www.boardsource.org
Foundation Center	Information for grant makers, criteria for awarding grants and lists of grants.	http://www. fdcenter.org
GuideStar.org	Provides access to IRS filings by nonprofits	http://www.guidestar.org
Internet Nonprofit Center	Disseminates information, advice and statistics	http://www.nonprofits.org
National Center for Charitable Statistics	Collects and disseminates data on nonprofits. Publishes New Nonprofit Almanac & Desk Reference	http://nccs.urban.org
National Council of Nonprofit Organization	An association of state and regional associations of non profits that has the goal of making resources available	http://www.ncna.org
Society for Nonprofit Organizations	National association of nonprofit member organizations providing education and training. Publishes Nonprofit World, a bi-monthly magazine.	http://danenet.wicip.org/snpo/newpage2.htm

---

facilities, such as the YMCA. For-profit providers of similar services submit that the subsidy of NPOs diminishes the for-profit organization's ability to compete. This situation has led to as yet unsuccessful legislative attempts to level the playing field.

2. Some people question how much nonprofits spend on programs. The BBB Wise Giving Alliance (a nonprofit organization itself) recommends that nonprofits spend at least 50 percent on program activity. Other organizations set this level as high as 80 percent. The remainder is to be spent on non-program expenses, such as administrative and fundraising costs. The amount spent on fundraising can vary widely based upon whether the nonprofit is new or established with many donors. However, no regulation exists to ensure that the majority of revenues are spent on the cause for which the funds were collected.

3. Others question how nonprofits are regulated, and who regulates them. State agencies are increasingly requiring reports from active NPOs to monitor fundraising activity; the agency in turn responds to individual inquiries about the NPO's self-reported record. As in the corporate and governmental groups, administrative salaries occasionally make the news, encouraging contributors to reconsider how their contributions are being used.

Nonprofit organizations are a valuable part of the economy in America and many other countries, providing a broad range of services that might not otherwise be affordable or available without the subsidy of tax exemption. As NPOs grow in number and scope, there is increasing pressure to report on financial activity and performance fulfillment in this sector. The future of nonprofits may rely on disclosure and accountability.

SEE ALSO: Balance Sheets; Financial Issues for Managers; Income Statements

Karen L. Brown
Revised by Judith M. Nixon

FURTHER READING:

BBB Wise Giving Alliance. "BBB Wise Giving Alliance." Available from <http://Give.org>

Council of Economic Advisors. *2005 Economic Report of the President.* Washington, D.C.: Government Printing Office, 2005. Available from <http://www.gpoaccess.gov/eop/>

Herzlinger, R.E. "Can Public Trust in Nonprofits and Governments be Restored?" *Harvard Business Review* 74, no. 2 (1996): 97–107.

Langer, Stephen. "How Much Are You Really Worth? Here's the Latest on Nonprofit Salaries." *Nonprofit World* 23, no. 1 (2005): 27.

Lewis, Robert L. *Effective Nonprofit Management: Essential Lessons for Executive Directors.* Gaithersburg, MD: Aspen Publishers, 2001.

The National Center for Charitable Statistics at the Urban Institute. "Number of Nonprofit Organizations in the United States 1996–2004." Available from <http://nccsdataweb.urban.org/PubApps/profile1.php?state=US>

National Council of Nonprofit Associations, and The National Center for Charitable Statistics at the Urban Institute. "The United States Nonprofit Sector 2001." Available from <http://www.ncna.org/_uploads/documents/live//us.nonprofit.sector.report.pdf>

The New Nonprofit Almanac & Desk Reference. Washington, D.C.: Independent Sector/Urban Institute, 2002.

The Non-Profit Sector in a Changing Economy. Paris: Organisation for Economic Co-operation and Development, 2003.

Pidgeon, Walter P. *The Not-for-Profit CEO: How to Attain and Retain the Corner Office.* New York: John Wiley, 2004.

Taylor, Barbara E., Richard P. Chait, and Thomas P. Holland. "The New Work of the Nonprofit Board." *Harvard Business Review* 74, no. 5 (1996): 36–46.

White, Gary W. "Nonprofit Organizations." *Journal of Business & Finance Librarianship* 9, no. 1 (2003): 49–80.

———. "Nonprofit Organizations Part II." *Journal of Business & Finance Librarianship* 10, no. 1 (2004): 63–79.

NORTH AMERICAN INDUSTRY CLASSIFICATION SYSTEM

The North American Industry Classification System or NAICS (pronounced "nakes") is a system for organizing data on industries and companies for standardized reporting. Implemented in 1997 for the United States and Canada and in 1998 for Mexico, the classification system replaces the U.S. Standard Industrial Classification (SIC) system, as well as the respective classification systems of the other two nations.

The system provides common industry definitions for Canada, Mexico, and the United States. It replaces the three countries' separate classification systems with essentially one uniform system, while allowing for nation-specific customization at the finest level of detail. This means at the broadest levels of the NAICS hierarchy the three countries share common industry codes, but at the most detailed level (represented by six-digit codes) each country may choose to recognize additional sub-industries that are of particular importance to their national economies while remaining within the broader framework of the cross-national system.

The NAICS and previous SIC systems are administered by the U.S. Office of Management and Budget, but are used by numerous government agencies along with private firms and nonprofit organizations. The systems describe a company or organization, often termed an establishment, using a numerical code based on its type of economic activity—i.e., the kinds of products or services a company provides. Groups of firms in similar lines of business are thus grouped together under the same classification number. Companies are assigned a four-digit to six-digit code, with each additional code number adding more specific data to identify the exact activities of the organization. The first two digits indicate the broad business sector, the third digit designates the sub sector, the fourth digit identifies the industry group, the fifth digit indicates the industry, and the sixth digit designates national industries. For example, the broad category of "information" is winnowed down to groups such as "publishers" and "broadcasters," which are further narrowed to highly specific industry designations like "software publishers" and "radio stations." In light of such specific categories, many large and diversified firms fall into multiple NAICS categories; hence, the category that accounts for the largest share of sales is sometimes known as the company's "primary" industry classification.

Major libraries or the U.S. Government Printing Office in Washington, D.C., maintain detailed information to help researchers determine a particular firm's classification codes. Private publishers also produce listings and rankings of companies by their SIC and NAICS codes. The official NAICS codes assigned to specific companies by government agencies, such as the Census Bureau in its economic censuses, are usually considered confidential, although for the typical company the correct codes can be readily surmised based on public information.

Problems with the SIC system, including the underreporting of services, led to the adoption of the NAICS system. When the SIC system was created in the 1930s, the U.S. economy was heavily dependent on manufacturing. By 2000, however, services had grown to represent 80 percent of the U.S. Gross Domestic Product (GDP). As a result, the SIC codes were replaced in part to provide better information on service firms. However, the service-oriented data is not as detailed as it is for manufacturers and does not have the detailed historical data that is available for manufacturers. The NAICS system was also created to recognize developments in high technology—particularly Internet-related businesses—and increases in international trade following the North American Free Trade Agreement (NAFTA). The revised version known as NAICS 2002 included such new industries as Internet Service Providers, Data Processing Services, and Web Search Portals.

The expanded and standardized coding system aids business reporting as well as assists researchers gathering and studying data across industries. The system provides a consistent framework for industrial statistics and can benefit anyone who uses industry-based data. According to the NAICS Web page sponsored by the Georgetown University Library, the system will most benefit economists, regulators, marketers, and publishers. Because the three governments designed the system jointly, it is expected to provide better standardization and comparability for nearly all North American industry data. However, the Georgetown library cautions that the new NAICS classifications do not always correlate directly with the previous SIC codes. In fact, 358 additional industry codes are included in the newer NAICS system that was not represented in the old system.

There are many uses of NAICS data. A firm can compare its own sales data in a particular NAICS classification to the total sales of all companies in the classification in order to estimate its market share and growth potential, or to gauge its general performance. If competitors have a larger market share, the firm may need to make adjustments in its strategy or target other subgroups within an industry that offer more sales or growth potential. Many organizations use these classifications; for example, Dun & Bradstreet publishes a plant list based on these codes that might be used by marketers or industry analysts to target particular types of firms.

Typical government census data arranged by NAICS classification include the number of establishments in a given category, the number of employees, payroll data, hours worked, value added by manufacturing, the quantity and value of products shipped, materials consumed, and even capital expenditures. Marketers can use the data to determine if categories are growing or not, and thus discover new opportunities. Data will also aid in determining where particular industries are clustered.

The NAICS Association, a private company that markets NAICS-related information, lists four key questions that can be answered using their data:

- Who are potential customers?

- What industries should be targeted?

- How are lists of potential customers obtained?

- What are the NAICS or SIC codes of customers?

Manuals of NAICS information released by the U.S. government are available and include alphabetized lists of NAICS and SIC codes. Data is also available on CD-ROM format for ease of database referencing.

SEE ALSO: Free Trade Agreements and Trading Blocs

Marilyn M. Helms

FURTHER READING:

Garritt, Fran. "Whatever Happened to the NAICS?" *RMA Journal,* May 2002.

Georgetown University. "North American Industry Classification System (NAICS)." Available from <http://www.gulib.lausun.georgetown.edu/swr/business/naics.htm>.

NAICS Association. "North American Industry Classification System." Available from <www.naics.com>.

Sabrosk, Suzanne. "NAICS Codes: A New Classification System for a New Economy." *Searcher,* November 2000.

U.S. Census Bureau. "North American Industry Classification System (NAICS)." Available from <http://www.census.gov/epcd/www/naics.html>.

SEE: Occupational Information Network

OBJECT-ORIENTED PROGRAMMING

Object-oriented programming (OOP) focuses on grouping, simplification, streamlining, and standardization. For example, it would seem unreasonable if every time someone traveled between two cities that they would experiment and do it by trial and error. A more reasonable methodology would be to develop maps and identify a standardized shortest route to travel, thereby simplifying the traveling process. However, this type of simplification has not always been obvious and even today we find many instances where it is not used. For example, in manufacturing there are numerous instances in which the same exact part was designed from scratch several times. It has separate drawings, separate part numbers, and is stored in separate places. Until recently, no grouping methodology existed to identify opportunities for part standardization. The grouping process that was finally developed is called group technology and comes from Russia. However, most manufacturers still do not use the technique.

OOP can be found in the modularization and interchangeability of computer hardware. You can open the box of almost any personal computer (PC) and interchangeably replace storage drives, memory, peripherals, and so on. This standardization was driven by competition and by the speed at which the technology has changed, but it has significantly simplified and streamlined the computer hardware updating and servicing process.

OOP has also made its way into management practices. For example, the implementation of change is always traumatic. One of the reasons for this is that no one seems to have a standard, objective measure for the success of the change process. By utilizing tools such as total quality management (TQM) for the standardization of the change process, which incorporates systematic problem solving (SPS), the implementation process becomes grouped and streamlined so that anyone can review the status of a change process.

The term *object-oriented programming* originally comes from the systems development and computer programming world. After years of programming and systems development, someone realized that there are many repetitive functions. For example, file adds, changes, and deletes occur frequently and during multiple processes. It would seam reasonable that one add-change-delete routine could be developed in a modular form that could be accessed any time an add-change-delete process needed to occur. Developers grouped these functions into accessible and executable modules that became known as objects. Developing programs using objects became known as object-oriented programming (OOP).

OOP significantly reduced the level of confusion between software developers. For example, when multiple developers were working on the same project, they did not need to thoroughly understand each other's code in order to develop their piece of the project. Similarly, in software maintenance, developers did not need to relearn the previous code in order to make changes. Understanding the OOP modules was sufficient to focus the change appropriately.

The design of the OOP process came partially out of a reaction to the slow development time for computer programs, and partly because of the high demand for computer developers. Using object-oriented programming, fewer people can accomplish more.

Operationally, OOP attempts to lead software development away from the abstract and refocus it on real-world objects. Examples of objects that could be the focus of a programming effort would be a user, display screen, and local-area network (LAN), not bits, bytes, and files. These objects become the focus of OOP programming attention.

In OOP the various properties of an object are analyzed. Understanding the properties assists in developing efficient modules. These properties include:

1. State—the properties of the object that cause a specific reaction to any specific event. For example, a terminal has several states: off; on and running; on and idle; and under maintenance.

2. Behavior—the way an object reacts to interactions from and with other objects. Behavior is determined by the set of operations defined as functional for that object. For example, an invalid entry from the person object is reacted to by an error message by the application package object.

3. Identity—objects are unique, merely because they exist separately. Objects are not grouped with other objects because of similar behavior. Nor can any object have more than one identity or name.

4. Encapsulation—this is where data and functionality are combined. Data and corresponding programs are elements that are isolated together. This prevents the corruption of their internal state.

5. Messaging—objects send messages to each other in order to access each other and to request a response. The object responds back to the requestor based on its defined behavior.

6. Collaboration—objects use each other to accomplish tasks. They share the responsibility for task completion.

7. Information hiding—this is where the activities within the object are hidden from other objects on the outside. This prevents corruption of the object or interference between objects.

8. Inheritance—this is a process of building objects by combining other objects together.

By linking one object to another, one often inherits the properties of the other.

We are in an increasingly complex world. Traditionally, systems did not require interaction much beyond the traditional keyboard, screen, user, and disk drive. Now we have massive networks, servers, firewalls, storage units, intranets, e-mail, e-commerce, electronic data interchange (EDI), and so on. OOP reduces the complexity of these massive systems by reducing them into object interactions. OOP offers:

1. Real-world modeling—natural, real-world modularization of systems. We take events and group them into real-world steps that then become objects. We no longer need to deal in the abstractions of computer developers.

2. Large-scaled systems—natural decomposition of real-world problems. We can decompose problems into realistic pieces that make sense.

3. Reusability in the software—software objects can be shared and reused.

4. Iterative development cycles—stages of the development process can be prototyped, allowing for feedback, earlier interaction, and early correction and testing.

OOP has allowed some specific features to be developed that have grown out of the benefits of OOP environment. These include:

1. Graphical user interface (GUI)—the user interface (for example, the screen display) is customizable independent of the software objects.

2. Client/server computing—this allows for the encapsulation of computer information objects, allowing them to be treated as building blocks for both expansion and downsizing.

3. Software reengineering—this allows for the reengineering of some objects while maintaining the integrity and the investment of other objects that do not require change. Entire systems do not need to be altered because a minor change, like a forms change or a new tax law, is enacted. Only the object associated with the change needs to be updated or replaced. Additionally, if pieces of a system become obsolete, they can simply be dropped from the system.

The benefits of OOP include:

• OOP offers usability and reusability of programming code without complete overhaul and replacement.

- OOP has significantly increased the speed of the programming process, both in development and in maintenance.

- OOP offers easier understanding of programming code for co-developers and outsiders trying to understand the code.

- OOP makes it easier to break down complex systems into components and then allows for the prototyping of these systems.

- OOP offers simplified implementation in that basic objects can be independently debugged and do not require as much testing.

- OOP is flexible and highly adaptable to changing business requirements

SEE ALSO: Complexity Theory; Computer Networks; Knowledge Management; Technological Forecasting; Technology Management; Technology Transfer

Gerhard Plenert
Revised by Wendy H. Mason

FURTHER READING:

Chisholm, Al. "Object-Oriented Programming: a Primer." *Control Engineering* (February 2004).

Korah, John. *Object Oriented Methodology: A Primer.* Dearborn, MI: SME Blue Book Series, 1994.

Plenert, Gerhard. *World Class Manager.* Rocklin, CA: Prima Publishing, 1995.

OCCUPATIONAL INFORMATION NETWORK

O*NET, or the Occupational Information Network, is an electronic replacement for the *Dictionary of Occupational Titles* (DOT). Like the DOT, which was last published in 1991, O*NET provides a comprehensive database of worker attributes and job characteristics. By describing the tasks to be performed and the levels of education that must be achieved, the O*NET database can be used as a tool for training and education, career guidance, employment counseling, and for writing job descriptions.

The U.S. Department of Labor developed the *Dictionary of Occupational Titles* (DOT) in the mid-1930s, soon after the federal-state employment service system was established. O*NET was also developed by and is supported by the U.S. Department of Labor. The main difference between the DOT and the O*NET database is the flexibility of the new database and its depth of information. Rather than having information for 12,000 occupations, as the DOT did, the O*NET database has 974 occupations which are related to a

common framework describing job requirements and worker characteristics, the content, and the context of work. A second difference between the DOT and the O*NET database is that O*NET can be updated more frequently; the Department of Labor uses a data collection program that provides for an update to the database twice annually. The most recent update was in December 2004. Additionally, there is now a Spanish-language version of the O*NET database available.

O*NET USES

O*Net can be used by many different people for a variety of reasons. Some of the uses for managers are:

- Writing and updating job descriptions and job specifications.

- Develop criteria for recruitment and selection.

- Develop criteria for performance appraisal systems.

- Structuring training and development activities.

- Structuring compensation systems.

- Improve career counseling.

O*NET DEVELOPMENT: COMMON LANGUAGE AND THE CONTENT MODEL

The O*NET database provides a common language that can be used to communicate in different areas of the economy and in workforce development efforts. This common language provides definitions and concepts for describing worker attributes and workplace requirements that can be widely understood and accepted. Knowledge, skills, and abilities (KSAs), interests, content, and context of work are described in comprehensive terms, and there is a common frame of reference in O*NET for understanding how these characteristics relate to successful job performance. O*NET's common language is intended to aid those who communicate about jobs in understanding one another, even when operating in different segments of the economy. The goal is for job descriptions and worker requirements to have the same meaning for human resources professionals, employees, educators, and students.

The conceptual foundation of the O*NET database is the Content Model; it provides a framework that identifies the most important types of information about work, integrating them into one system. Information in the model reflects both the character of occupations and of people, and it allows for information to be applied across jobs, sectors, or industries and within occupations. The Content Model was developed using research on job and organizational analysis, and thus has a strong theoretical and empirical foundation.

The Content Model has six domains:

1. Worker Characteristics—enduring characteristics that might influence job performance and the ability to acquire knowledge and skills used for effective work performance; this includes abilities, interests, values, and work styles.

2. Worker Requirements—work-related attributes gained and/or developed through a worker's education or experience; this includes knowledge, experience, and skills (basic skills and cross-functional skills).

3. Experience Requirements—previous activities, linked specifically to certain types of work activities, that are required for effective job performance; this includes formal education, certifications, licensures, and training.

4. Occupational Characteristics—global contextual characteristics that define and describe occupations and that may influence requirements for that occupation.

5. Occupational Requirements—detailed information regarding typical activities required in various occupations; generalized work activities (GWAs), or dimensions that summarize the kinds of tasks that may be performed within a single occupation are identified; additionally, information about the context, such as physical and social elements of the work, that may create specific demands on the worker are included.

6. Occupation-Specific Information—elements that apply only to a single occupation or a narrowly defined job family; this domain provides related information available in other areas of the Content Model, but is used when developing specific applications of O*NET information, such as writing a job description.

SEE ALSO: Job Analysis

Marcia Simmering

FURTHER READING:

O*NET Consortium. "About O*NET." Available from <http://www.onetcenter.org/overview.html>.

OFFSHORING

SEE: Outsourcing and Offshoring

OPEN AND CLOSED SYSTEMS

A system is commonly defined as a group of interacting units or elements that have a common purpose. The units or elements of a system can be cogs, wires, people, computers, and so on. Systems are generally classified as open systems and closed systems and they can take the form of mechanical, biological, or social systems. Open systems refer to systems that interact with other systems or the outside environment, whereas closed systems refer to systems having relatively little interaction with other systems or the outside environment. For example, living organisms are considered open systems because they take in substances from their environment such as food and air and return other substances to their environment. Humans, for example, inhale oxygen out of the environment and exhale carbon dioxide into the environment. Similarly, some organizations consume raw materials in the production of products and emit finished goods and pollution as a result. In contrast, a watch is an example of a closed system in that it is a relatively self-contained, self-maintaining unit that has little interacts or exchange with its environment.

All systems have boundaries, a fact that is immediately apparent in mechanical systems such as the watch, but much less apparent in social systems such as organizations. The boundaries of open systems, because they interact with other systems or environments, are more flexible than those of closed systems, which are rigid and largely impenetrable. A closed-system perspective views organizations as relatively independent of environmental influences. The closed-system approach conceives of the organization as a system of management, technology, personnel, equipment, and materials, but tends to exclude competitors, suppliers, distributors, and governmental regulators. This approach allows managers and organizational theorists to analyze problems by examining the internal structure of a business with little consideration of the external environment. The closed-system perspective basically views an organization much as a thermostat; limited environmental input outside of changes in temperature is required for effective operation. Once set, thermostats require little maintenance in their ongoing, self-reinforcing function. While the closed-system perspective was dominant through the 1960s, organization scholarship and research subsequently emphasized the role of the environment. Up through the 1960s, it was not that managers ignored the outside environment such as other organizations, markets, government regulations and the like, but that their strategies and other decision-making processes gave relatively little consideration to the impact these external forces might have on the internal operations of the organization.

Open-systems theory originated in the natural sciences and subsequently spread to fields as diverse as computer science, ecology, engineering, management, and psychotherapy. In contrast to closed-systems, the open-system perspective views an organization as an entity that takes inputs from the environment, transforms them, and releases them as outputs in tandem with reciprocal effects on the organization itself along with the environment in which the organization operates. That is, the organization becomes part and parcel of the environment in which it is situated. Returning for a moment to the example of biological systems as open-systems, billions of individual cells in the human body, themselves composed of thousands of individual parts and processes, are essential for the viability of the larger body in which they are a part. In turn, "macro-level" processes such as eating and breathing make the survival of individual cells contingent on these larger processes. In much the same way, open-systems of organizations accept that organizations are contingent on their environments and these environments are also contingent on organizations.

As an open-systems approach spread among organizational theorists, managers began incorporating these views into practice. Two early pioneers in this effort, Daniel Katz and Robert Kahn, began viewing organizations as open social systems with specialized and interdependent subsystems and processes of communication, feedback, and management linking the subsystems. Katz and Kahn argued that the closed-system approach fails to take into account how organizations are reciprocally dependent on external environments. For example, environmental forces such as customers and competitors exert considerable influence on corporations, highlighting the essential relationship between an organization and its environment as well as the importance of maintaining external inputs to achieve a stable organization.

Furthermore, the open-system approach serves as a model of business activity; that is, business as a process of transforming inputs to outputs while realizing that inputs are taken from the external environment and outputs are placed into this same environment. Companies use inputs such as labor, funds, equipment, and materials to produce goods or to provide services and they design their subsystems to attain these goals. These subsystems are thus analogous to cells in the body, the organization itself is analogous to the body, and external market and regulatory conditions are analogous to environmental factors such as the quality of housing, drinking water, air and availability of nourishment.

The production subsystem, for example, focuses on converting inputs into marketable outputs and often constitutes a primary purpose of a company. The boundary subsystem's goal is to obtain inputs or resources, such as employees, materials, equipment, and so forth, from the environment outside of the company, which are necessary for the production subsystem. This subsystem also is responsible for providing an organization with information about the environment. This adaptive subsystem collects and processes information about a company's operations with the goal of aiding the company's adaptation to external conditions in its environment. Another subsystem, management, supervises and coordinates the other subsystems to ensure that each subsystem functions efficiently. The management subsystem must resolve conflicts, solve problems, allocate resources, and so on.

To simplify the process of evaluating environmental influences, some organizational theorists use the term "task environment" to refer to aspects of the environment that are immediately relevant to management decisions related to goal setting and goal realization. The task environment includes customers, suppliers, competitors, employees, and regulatory bodies. Furthermore, in contrast to closed-systems, the open-system perspective does not assume that the environment is static. Instead, change is the rule rather than the exception. Consequently, investigation of environmental stability and propensity to change is a key task of a company, making the activities of an organization contingent on various environmental forces. As an open system, an organization maintains its stability through feedback, which refers to information about outputs that a system obtains as an input from its task environment. The feedback can be positive or negative and can lead to changes in the way an organization transforms inputs to outputs. Here, the organization acts as a thermostat, identified previously as an example of a relatively closed-system. The difference between closed-systems and open-systems, then, is in the complexity of environmental interactions. Closed-systems assume relatively little complexity; a thermostat is a simple device dependent mainly on temperature fluctuations. Conversely, open-system such as the human body and modern organizations are more intricately dependent on their environments. The point is that closed-systems versus open-systems do not represent a dichotomy, but rather a continuum along which organizations are more open or less open to their environments. The key defining variable governing this degree of openness is the complexity of the environment in which the organization is situated.

Managers must take into consideration their organization's position along the open-closed continuum. The Linux computer operating system, for instance, is "open-source" and Red Hat, Inc., the corporation selling the bundled revisions-the multiple inputs from geographically dispersed users-represents an organization that would cease to exist if it were not for an open-systems perspective. Thus, stable environments with low complexity are more consistent with a relatively closed-system or mechanistic management style, while rapidly-changing environments are more consistent with flexible, decentralized, or "organic" management styles.

SEE ALSO: Managing Change; Reactive vs. Proactive Change

Karl Heil
Revised by Scott B. Droege

FURTHER READING:

Chesbrough, H.W. *Open Innovation: The New Imperative for Creating and Profiting from Technology.* Boston: Harvard Business School Press, 2003.

Katz, D., and R.L. Kahn. *The Social Psychology of Organizations.* New York: John Wiley & Sons, 1978.

Prahalad, C.K., and V. Ramaswamy. *The Future of Competition: Co-Creating Unique Value with Customers.* Boston: Harvard Business School Press, 2004.

OPERANT CONDITIONING

Simply put, operant conditioning refers to a systematic program of rewards and punishments to influence behavior or bring about desired behavior. Operant conditioning relies on two basic assumptions about human experience and psychology: (1) a particular act results in an experience that is a consequence of that act and (2) the perceived quality of an act's consequence affects future behavior. In addition, a central idea of operant conditioning holds that the main influences on behavior are external—that is, it is in a person's external environment that his or her behavior is programmed.

The Harvard psychologist B.F. Skinner pioneered the field of behaviorism in the late 1930s and continued to contribute to it through the mid-1970s. Operant conditioning is one of the key concepts of this school of psychology. Skinner called his brand of conditioning operant conditioning to distinguish it from the conditioning theory developed by the Russian physiologist Ivan Pavlov, now referred to as classical conditioning. Classical conditioning primarily concerned itself with reflexive or unlearned behavior such as the jerking of a knee upon being tapped with a hammer. In a famous experiment, Pavlov training dogs to salivate in expectation of food at the sound of a bell. Operant conditioning, however, deals with learned, not reflexive behavior; it works by reinforcing (rewarding) and punishing behavior based on the consequences it produces. Reinforcement is used to increase the probability that behavior will occur in the future, whereas

punishment aims to decrease that probability. In addition, the process of removing reinforcement from an act is called *extinction.*

Organizational management literature often refers to operant conditioning as part of reinforcement theory and work behavior modification. Unlike other theories of management and motivation, operant conditioning does not rely on attitudes, beliefs, intentions, and motivation for predicting and influencing behavior, although Skinner and other behaviorists do not suggest that these factors do not exist. Instead, they posit that these notions find their genesis in external conditions and reinforcement. Hence, organizational management theorists who adopt this approach look to external factors—the environment—to explain and influence behavior within the work place. For example, this approach to management views motivation as a product of workers' environments, not as an internal quality of each individual worker's psychological makeup. Therefore, employees are highly motivated because that quality is reinforced with pay raises, promotions, etc. that employees find desirable.

Since most of the behavior taking place in a business is learned rather than reflexive, operant conditioning can be applied to organizational management. Workers learn various kinds of behavior before and after joining a company, and they encounter a host of stimuli in a company setting that can cause them to behave in certain ways with certain consequences. These kinds of behaviors are rewarded and punished depending on their value to a company. The stimuli in the workplace include schedules, corporate structures, company policies, telephone calls, managers, and so on. The consequences of work-place behavior include approval or disapproval from managers and coworkers, promotions, demotions, pay increases, etc. When consequences are directly linked to certain kinds of behavior, they are contingent on these kinds of behavior. The classic example is touching a hot stove and experiencing the immediate consequence of being burned. However, most consequences in a company are only partially contingent on the behavior (performance) of employees, and thus there are often entire networks of relationships between employee behavior and its consequences. These relationships are called schedules of reinforcement, and applying operant conditioning to the work place means controlling these schedules.

Reinforcement schedules are either continuous or intermittent, or partial. Continuous reinforcement schedules are those situations in which every occurrence of an act is reinforced. In contrast, intermittent schedules are those situations in which only some instances of an act are reinforced. Continuous reinforcement schedules generally facilitate new learning or the acquisition of new skills at the fastest rate. New employees learning how to process customer orders, for example, will learn the proper procedure the fastest if they are reinforced every time they take an order correctly. However, if a continuous schedule is suspended outright after being implemented for any substantial period, the behavior being reinforced might stop altogether. In addition, after a certain kind of behavior has been learned, it will occur more often if reinforced intermittently. Hence, employees who have learned the proper procedure for taking customer orders have the greatest likelihood of continuing to do so correctly if managers adopt an intermittent schedule after the behavior has been learned.

Moreover, reinforcement can be positive (adding something new, such as a raise or a promotion) or negative (the removal of something from the work environment, such as constant supervision) after new employees demonstrate they have sufficiently learned their jobs. Negative reinforcement, however, should not be confused with punishment, which involves undesirable or aversive consequences and decreases the probability of an act being repeated. Negative reinforcement, rather, is a kind of a reward that removes constraints or other elements from the work environment to encourage employee behavior.

Events or actions that increase the probability that certain behavior will occur in the future are called reinforcers, which can be divided into primary and secondary reinforcers. Primary reinforcers are things such as food, water, and shelter that are rewarding all by themselves, while secondary reinforcers are things such as money that have a reinforcing effect because of their relationship with primary reinforcers (for example, money can buy food, etc.). However, reinforcers may not always succeed in reinforcing behavior. If a person is not thirsty, for example, water may not serve as an effective reinforcer.

Because some behavior is so complex that it does not occur all at once, managers must reinforce progressive approximations of the desired behavior. This process begins with the reinforcement of behavior that may barely resemble the desired behavior, using a continuous reinforcement schedule with a progressive standard. Consequently, behavior must show improvement or greater approximation of the desired behavior to receive reinforcement as time goes on.

When managers wish to discourage certain kinds of behavior or decrease the probability of their occurrence, they can implement a schedule of punishment along the lines of a schedule of reinforcement. Punishment involves the application of undesirable consequences or the removal of positive consequences following undesired behavior. However, negative consequences must be meted out with consideration of how it will affect individual workers, because what constitutes punishment for one worker may not for another. Ultimately, these consequences or stimuli must be linked to the undesired behavior and decrease the probability of it reoccurring in order for them to constitute punishment in the technical sense of the operant conditioning approach. Moreover, effective punishment usually embodies the following qualities: it is consistent, immediate, impersonal, and contingent on specific behavior. Finally, punishment should be informative—letting employees know why they are being punished—and employees should recognize that future punishment can be avoided by refraining from the undesired behavior.

RECENT STUDY

A research article in 2004 by Timothy R. Hinkin and Chester A. Schriesheim found that in a study of 243 employees of two different hospitality organizations, those employees who received feedback from their managers, whether positive feedback or negative/corrective feedback, showed improved performance. This study also found that omission of commentary on good performance diminished worker effectiveness and reduced worker satisfaction. This supports the theory of operant conditioning that suggests a behavior that is totally ignored will eventually be extinguished.

Operant conditioning has been successfully applied in many settings: clinical, for individual behavior modification, teaching, for classroom management, instructional development, for programmed instruction, and management, for organizational behavior modification.

SEE ALSO: Motivation and Motivation Theory; Organizational Behavior

Karl Heil
Revised by Monica C. Turner

FURTHER READING:

Geiser, Robert L. *Behavior Mod and the Managed Society.* Boston: Beacon Press, 1976.

Hinkin, T.R., and C.A. Schriesheim. "If You Don't Hear From Me You Know You Are Doing Fine: The Effects of Management Nonresponse to Employee Performance." *Cornell Hotel & Restaurant Administration Quarterly,* November, 2004, 362–372.

Lutz, J. *Learning and Memory.* 2nd ed. Long Grove, IL: Waveland Press, 2004.

Malott, R.W., and E.A. Trojan. *Principles of Behavior.* 5th ed. Upper Saddle River, NJ: Pearson/Prentice Hall, 2004.

Nadler, Leanard, and Zeace Nadler. *The Handbook of Human Resource Development.* 2nd ed. New York, NY: John Wiley & Sons, 1990.

Pinder, Craig C. *Work Motivation: Theory, Issues, and Applications.* Glenview, IL: Scott, Foresman and Company, 1984.

Skinner, B.F. *About Behaviorism.* New York, NY: Alfred A. Knopf, 1974.

Smith, P., and A. Dyson. "Get with the Programme." *The Safety and Health Practitioner,* December 2004, 38–40.

OPERATING SYSTEMS

A computer's operating system is one of the most important "parts" of the computer. Almost every type of computer, including cellular telephones, needs an operating system in order to operate properly. When one turns on a computer, the operating system tells the computer what to do by controlling the system resources such as the processor, memory, disk space, etc. The operating system allows the user to work on the computer without having to know all the details about how the hardware works.

When choosing an operating system for a business, the primary considerations should be the hardware platform used, the number of users and attendant system security requirements, the ease of administration, the adaptability toward different uses, and the different applications that will be employed.

TYPES OF OPERATING SYSTEMS

Most simple, single-function computers (such as in microwave ovens with digital keypads) do not require an operating system. In fact, trying to implement an operating system in these computers would be overkill. On the other hand, all personal desktop and laptop computers and servers do require an operating system. While there are hundreds of operating systems available, the most popular by far are the Microsoft Windows family of operating systems, the Macintosh operating system, and the Unix family of operating systems.

There are four general types of operating systems. Their use depends on the type of computer and the type of applications that will be run on those computers.

1. Real-time operating systems (RTOS) are used to control machinery, scientific instruments, and industrial systems. In general, the user does not have much control over the functions performed by the RTOS.

2. Single-user, single task operating systems allow one user to do one thing at a time. And example of a single-user, single task operating system is the operating system used by personal digital assistants (PDAs), also known as handheld computers.

3. Single-user, multi-tasking operating systems allow a single user to simultaneously run multiple applications on their computer. This is the type of operating system found on most personal desktop and laptop computers. The Windows (Microsoft) and Macintosh (Apple) platforms are the most popular single-user, multi-tasking operating systems.

4. Multi-user operating systems allow multiple users to simultaneously use the resources on a single computer. Unix is an example of a multi-user operating system.

WHAT DO OPERATING SYSTEMS DO?

One of the operating system's main tasks is to control the computer's resources—both the hardware and the software. The operating system allocates resources as necessary to ensure that each application receives the appropriate amount. In addition to resource allocation, operating systems provide a consistent application interface so that all applications use the hardware in the same way. This is particularly important if more than one type of computer uses the operating system or if the computer's hardware is likely to change. By having a consistent application program interface (API), software written on one computer and can run on other types of computers. Developers face the challenge of keeping the operating system flexible enough to control hardware from the thousands of different computer manufacturers.

Operating systems must accomplish the following tasks:

1. Processor management. The operating system needs to allocate enough of the processor's time to each process and application so that they can run as efficiently as possible. This is particularly important for multitasking. When the user has multiple applications and processes running, it is up to the operating system to ensure that they have enough resources to run properly.

2. Memory storage and management. The operating system needs to ensure that each process has enough memory to execute the process, while also ensuring that one process does not use the memory allocated to another process. This must also be done in the most efficient manner. A computer has four general types of memory. In order of speed, they are: high-speed cache, main memory, secondary memory, and disk storage. The operating system must balance the

needs of each process with the different types of memory available.

3. Device management. Most computers have additional hardware, such as printers and scanners, connected to them. These devices require drivers, or special programs that translate the electrical signals sent from the operating system or application program to the hardware device. The operating system manages the input to and output from the computer. It often assigns high-priority blocks to drivers so that the hardware can be released and available for the next use as soon as possible.

4. Application interface. Programmers use application program interfaces (APIs) to control the computer and operating system. As software developers write applications, they can insert these API functions in their programs. As the operating system encounters these API functions, it takes the desired action, so the programmer does not need to know the details of controlling the hardware.

5. User interface. The user interface sits as a layer above the operating system. It is the part of the application through which the user interacts with the application. Some operating systems, such as Microsoft Windows and Apple Macintosh, use graphical user interfaces. Other operating systems, such as Unix, use shells.

WHICH OPERATING SYSTEMS ARE AVAILABLE?

Windows is the name of a family of operating systems created by the Microsoft Corporation for use with personal computers. Windows employs a graphical user interface (GUI), which eliminates the need for the user to learn complex commands. With a GUI, the user instructs the operating system by using a mouse to point and click icons that are displayed on the screen. Microsoft Windows, first released in 1985, was originally designed as a GUI for DOS, which uses the command-line approach. In order to communicate with the computer, DOS users must type commands or instructions at the command prompt, and then the command-line interpreter executes those commands. The term "DOS" can refer to any operating system, but it is frequently used as a synonym for Microsoft Disk Operating System (MS-DOS). DOS has limited use with modern computer systems and applications because it does not support multiple users or multitasking. Some of the other operating systems, including Windows, can also execute DOS-based applications. Today, most DOS systems have been replaced by more user-friendly systems that use a GUI.

Windows 3.1 was released in 1991. By then, Windows had gained in market share. Microsoft released Windows 95 in August 1995. It was so well marketed and in such high demand that people bought the operating system, even if they didn't own a home computer. With each new release, from Windows 98 to Window 2000 to Windows XP, Microsoft gained popularity. Today, almost every new personal computer comes preloaded with the Windows operating system. Windows can be run on practically any brand of personal computers. It is estimated that 90 percent of personal computers run the Windows operating system. The remaining 10 percent run the Macintosh operating system.

UNIX is a multi-user, multitasking operating system, and was designed to be a small, flexible system used by computer programmers. Since UNIX was designed to be used by programmers, it is not considered to be very user-friendly for the average person. However, graphical user interfaces have been developed for UNIX to help alleviate the ease-of-use issue.

Linux is a UNIX variant that runs on several different hardware platforms. Linus Torvalds, a student at the University of Helsinki in Finland, initially created it as a hobby. The kernel, at the heart of all Linux systems, is developed and released under the General Public License (GNU), and its source code is freely available to everyone. There are now hundreds of companies, organizations, and individuals that have released their own versions of operating systems based on the Linux kernel.

Because of its functionality, adaptability, and robustness, Linux is able to compete against the Unix and Microsoft operating systems. IBM, Hewlett-Packard, and other computer giants have embraced Linux and support its ongoing development. More than a decade after its initial release, Linux is being adopted worldwide mainly as a server platform. More and more people are starting to use Linux as a home and office desktop operating system. The operating system can also be incorporated directly into microchips in a process called "embedding." Many appliances and devices are now starting to use operating systems in this way.

SEE ALSO: Computer Networks; Computer Security; Computer-Integrated Manufacturing; Data Processing and Data Management; Management Information Systems

Rhoda L. Wilburn

FURTHER READING:

Coustan, Dave, and Curt Franklin. *How Operating Systems Work.* How Stuff Works, Inc., 2005. Available from <http://computer.howstuffworks.com/operating-system.htm>.

What is Linux? Linux Online. Available from <http://www.linux.org>.

OPERATIONS MANAGEMENT

One may generally consider that there are three distinct areas inherent in any business: marketing, finance, and operations; all other business disciplines fit somewhere under one or more of these areas. For example, finance could include investing, real estate, insurance or banking. While management is considered an academic discipline unto itself it is actually a part of all three areas: financial management, marketing management, and operations management. Operations management is the area concerned with the efficiency and effectiveness of the operation in support and development of the firm's strategic goals. Other areas of concern to operations management include the design and operations of systems to provide goods and services. To put it succinctly, operations management is the planning, scheduling, and control of the activities that transform inputs (raw materials and labor) into outputs (finished goods and services). A set of recognized and well-developed concepts, tools, and techniques belong within the framework considered operations management. While the term operations management conjures up views of manufacturing environments, many of these concepts have been applied in service settings, with some of them actually developed specifically for service organizations.

Operations management is also an academic field of study that focuses on the effective planning, scheduling, use, and control of a manufacturing or service firm and their operations. The field is a synthesis of concepts derived from design engineering, industrial engineering, management information systems, quality management, production management, inventory management, accounting, and other functions.

The field of operations management has been gaining increased recognition over the last two decades. One major reason for this is public awareness of the success of Japanese manufacturers and the perception that the quality of many Japanese products is superior to that of American manufacturers. As a result, many businesses have come to realize that the operations function is just as important to their firm as finance and marketing. In concert with this, firms now realize that in order to effectively compete in a global market they must have an operations strategy to support the mission of the firm and its overall corporate strategy.

Another reason for greater awareness of operations management is the increased application of operations management concepts and techniques to service operations. Finally, operations management concepts are being applied to other functional areas such as marketing and human resources. The term *marketing/operations interface* is often used.

HISTORY OF OPERATIONS MANAGEMENT

Until the end of the 18th century, agriculture was the predominant industry in every country. The advent of the steam engine and Eli Whitney's concept of standardized parts paved the way for the Industrial Revolution with its large manufacturing facilities powered by steam or water. A number of countries (the United States included) evolved from an agricultural economy to an industrial economy. But for a time, manufacturing was more of an art than a science. This changed with the introduction of Frederick W. Taylor's systematic approach to scientific management at the beginning of the twentieth century. The introduction of Taylor's method of scientific management and Henry Ford's moving assembly line brought the world into an age where management was predominantly centered around the production of goods.

In the late 1950s and early 1960s scholars moved from writing about industrial engineering and operations research into writing about production management. Production management had itself become a professional field as well as an academic discipline. As the U.S. economy evolved into a service economy and operations techniques began to be incorporated into services the term *production/operations management* came into use. Today, services are such a pervasive part of our life that the term *operations management* is used almost exclusively.

WHAT DO OPERATIONS MANAGERS DO?

At the strategic level (long term), operations managers are responsible for or associated with making decisions about product development (what shall we make?), process and layout decisions (how shall we make it?), site location (where will we make it?), and capacity (how much do we need?).

At the tactical level (intermediate term), operations management addresses the issues relevant to efficiently scheduling material and labor within the constraints of the firm's strategy and making aggregate planning decisions. Operations managers have a hand in deciding employee levels (how many workers do we need and when do we need them?), inventory levels (when should we have materials delivered and should we use a chase strategy or a level strategy?), and capacity (how many shifts do we need? Do we need to work overtime or subcontract some work?).

At the operational level, operations management is concerned with lower-level (daily/weekly/monthly) planning and control. Operations managers and their subordinates must make decisions regarding scheduling (what should we process and when should we process it?), sequencing (in what order should we process the orders?), loading (what order to we put on what machine?), and work assignments (to whom do we assign individual machines or processes?).

Today's operations manager must have knowledge of advanced operations technology and technical knowledge relevant to his/her industry, as well as interpersonal skills and knowledge of other functional areas within the firm. Operations managers must also have the ability to communicate effectively, to motivate other people, manage projects, and work on multidisciplinary teams. Sunil Chopra, William Lovejoy, and Candace Yano describe the scope of operations management as encompassing these multi-disciplinary areas:

- Supply Chains—management of all aspects of providing goods to a consumer from extraction of raw materials to end-of-life disposal.

- Operations Management/Marketing Interface—determining what customers' value prior to product development.

- Operations Management/Finance Interface—Capital equipment and inventories comprise a sizable portion of many firms' assets.

- Service Operations—Coping with inherent service characteristics such as simultaneous delivery/consumption, performance measurements, etc.

- Operations Strategy—Consistent and aligned with firm's other functional strategies.

- Process Design and Improvements—Managing the innovation process.

Mark Davis, Nicolas Aquilano and Richard Chase (1999) have suggested that the major issues for operations management today are:

- reducing the development and manufacturing time for new goods and services

- achieving and sustaining high quality while controlling cost

- integrating new technologies and control systems into existing processes

- obtaining, training, and keeping qualified workers and managers

- working effectively with other functions of the business to accomplish the goals of the firm

- integrating production and service activities at multiple sites in decentralized organizations

- working effectively with suppliers at being user-friendly for customers

- working effectively with new partners formed by strategic alliances

As one can see, all these are critical issues to any firm. No longer is operations management considered subservient to marketing and finance; rather, it is a legitimate functional area within most organizations. Also, operations management can no longer focus on isolated tasks and processes but must be one of the architects of the firm's overall business model.

SEE ALSO: Operations Strategy; Product Design; Production Planning and Scheduling; Product-Process Matrix; Service Operations; Supply Chain Management

R. Anthony Inman

FURTHER READING:

Anupindi, Ravi, Sunil Chopra, Sudhakar D. Deshmukh, Jan A. Van Mieghem, and Eitan Zemel. *Managing Business Process Flows: Principles of Operations Management.* Upper Saddle River, NJ: Pearson Prentice Hall, 2006.

Davis, Mark M., Nicholas J. Aquilano, and Richard B. Chase. *Fundamentals of Operations Management.* 3rd ed. Boston: Irwin McGraw-Hill, 1999.

Finch, Byron. *Operations Now.* 2nd ed., Boston: McGraw-Hill Irwin, 2006.

Rainbird, Mark. "A Framework for Operations Management: The Value Chain." *International Journal of Operations and Production Management* 34, no. 3/4 (2004): 337–345.

Raturi, Amitabh, and James R. Evans. *Principles of Operations Management.* Mason, OH: Thomson Southwestern, 2005.

OPERATIONS SCHEDULING

OPERATIONS SCHEDULING

Scheduling pertains to establishing both the timing and use of resources within an organization. Under the operations function (both manufacturing and services), scheduling relates to use of equipment and facilities, the scheduling of human activities, and receipt of materials.

While issues relating to facility location and plant and equipment acquisition are considered long term and aggregate planning is considered intermediate term, operations scheduling is considered to be a short-term issue. As such, in the decision-making hierarchy, scheduling is usually the final step in the transformation process before the actual output (e.g., finished goods) is produced. Consequently, scheduling decisions are made within the constraints established by these longer-term decisions. Generally, scheduling objectives deals with tradeoffs among conflicting goals for efficient utilization of labor and equipment, lead time, inventory levels, and processing times.

Byron Finch notes that effective scheduling has recently increased in importance. This increase is due in part to the popularity of lean manufacturing and just-in-time. The resulting drop in inventory levels and subsequent increased replenishment frequency has greatly increased the probability of the occurrence of stockouts. In addition, the Internet has increased pressure to schedule effectively. "Business to customer" (B2C) and "business to business" (B2B) relationships have drastically reduced the time needed to compare prices, check product availability, make the purchase, etc. Such instantaneous transactions have increased the expectations of customers, thereby, making effective scheduling a key to customer satisfaction. It is noteworthy that there are over 100 software scheduling packages that can perform schedule evaluation, schedule generation, and automated scheduling. However, their results can often be improved through a human scheduler's judgment and experience.

There are two general approaches to scheduling: forward scheduling and backward scheduling. As long as the concepts are applied properly, the choice of methods is not significant. In fact, if process lead times (move, queue and setup times) add to the job lead time and process time is assumed to occur at the end of process time, then forward scheduling and backward scheduling yield the same result. With forward scheduling, the scheduler selects a planned order release date and schedules all activities from this point forward in time.

With backward scheduling, the scheduler begins with a planned receipt date or due date and moves backward in time, according to the required processing times, until he or she reaches the point where the order will be released.

Of course there are other variables to consider other than due dates or shipping dates. Other factors which directly impact the scheduling process include: the types of jobs to be processed and the different resources that can process each, process routings, processing times, setup times, changeover times, resource availability, number of shifts, downtime, and planned maintenance.

LOADING

Loading involves assigning jobs to work centers and to various machines in the work centers. If a job can be processed on only one machine, no difficulty is presented. However, if a job can be loaded on multiple work centers or machines, and there are multiple jobs to process, the assignment process becomes more complicated. The scheduler needs some way to assign jobs to the centers in such a way that processing and setups are minimized along with idle time and throughput time.

Two approaches are used for loading work centers: infinite loading and finite loading. With infinite loading jobs are assigned to work centers without regard for capacity of the work center. Priority rules are appropriate for use under the infinite loading approach. Jobs are loaded at work centers according to the chosen priority rule. This is known as vertical loading.

Finite loading projects the actual start and stop times of each job at each work center. Finite loading considers the capacity of each work center and compares the processing time so that process time does not exceed capacity. With finite loading the scheduler loads the job that has the highest priority on all work centers it will require. Then the job with the next highest priority is loaded on all required work centers, and so on. This process is referred to as horizontal loading. The scheduler using finite loading can then project the number of hours each work center will operate. A drawback of horizontal loading is that jobs may be kept waiting at a work center, even though the work center is idle. This happens when a higher priority job is expected to arrive shortly. The work center is kept idle so that it will be ready to process the higher priority job as soon as it arrives. With vertical loading the work center would be fully loaded. Of course, this would mean that a higher priority job would then have to wait to be processed since the work center was already busy. The scheduler will have to weigh the relative costs of keeping higher priority jobs waiting, the cost of idle work centers, the number of jobs and work centers, and the potential for disruptions, new jobs and cancellations.

If the firm has limited capacity (e.g., already running three shifts), finite loading would be appropriate since it reflects an upper limit on capacity. If infinite loading is used, capacity may have to be increased through overtime, subcontracting, or expansion, or work may have to be shifted to other periods or machines.

SEQUENCING

Sequencing is concerned with determining the order in which jobs are processed. Not only must the order be determined for processing jobs at work centers but also for work processed at individual work stations. When work centers are heavily loaded and lengthy jobs are involved, the situation can become complicated. The order of processing can be crucial when it comes to the cost of waiting to be processed and the cost of idle time at work centers.

There are a number of priority rules or heuristics that can be used to select the order of jobs waiting for processing. Some well known ones are presented in a list adapted from Vollmann, Berry, Whybark, and Jacobs (2005):

- Random (R). Pick any job in the queue with equal probability. This rule is often used as a benchmark for other rules.

- First come/first served (FC/FS). This rule is sometimes deemed to be fair since jobs are processed in the order in which they arrive.

- Shortest processing time (SPT). The job with the shortest processing time requirement goes first. This rule tends to reduce work-in-process inventory, average throughput time, and average job lateness.

- Earliest due date (EDD). The job with the earliest due date goes first. This seems to work well if the firm performance is judged by job lateness.

- Critical ratio (CR). To use this rule one must calculate a priority index using the formula (due date–now)/(lead time remaining). This rule is widely used in practice.

- Least work remaining (LWR). An extension of SPT, this rule dictates that work be scheduled according to the processing time remaining before the job is considered to be complete. The less work remaining in a job, the earlier it is in the production schedule.

- Fewest operations remaining (FOR). This rule is another variant of SPT; it sequences jobs based on the number of successive operations remaining until the job is considered complete. The fewer operations that remain, the earlier the job is scheduled.

- Slack time (ST). This rule is a variant of EDD; it utilizes a variable known as slack. Slack is computed by subtracting the sum of setup and processing times from the time remaining until the job's due date. Jobs are run in order of the smallest amount of slack.

- Slack time per operation (ST/O). This is a variant of ST. The slack time is divided by the number of operations remaining until the job is complete with the smallest values being scheduled first.

- Next queue (NQ). NQ is based on machine utilization. The idea is to consider queues (waiting lines) at each of the succeeding work centers at which the jobs will go. One then selects the job for processing that is going to the smallest queue, measured either in hours or jobs.

- Least setup (LSU). This rule maximizes utilization. The process calls for scheduling first the job that minimizes changeover time on a given machine.

These rules assume that setup time and setup cost are independent of the processing sequence. However, this is not always the case. Jobs that require similar setups can reduce setup times if sequenced back to back. In addition to this assumption, the priority rules also assume that setup time and processing times are deterministic and not variable, there will be no interruptions in processing, the set of jobs is known, no new jobs arrive after processing begins, and no jobs are canceled. While little of this is true in practice, it does make the scheduling problem manageable.

GANTT CHARTS

Gantt charts are named for Henry Gantt, a management pioneer of the early 1900s. He proposed the use of a visual aid for loading and scheduling. Appropriately, this visual aid is known as a Gantt chart. This Gantt chart is used to organize and clarify actual or intended use of resources within a time framework. Generally, time is represented horizontally with scheduled resources listed vertically. Managers are able to use the Gantt chart to make trial-and-error schedules to get some sense of the impact of different arrangements.

There are a number of different types of Gantt charts, but the most common ones, and the ones most appropriate to our discussion, are the load chart and schedule chart. A load chart displays the loading and idle times for machines or departments; this shows when certain jobs are scheduled to start and finish and where idle time can be expected. This can help the scheduler redo loading assignments for better utilization of the work centers. A schedule chart is used to monitor job progress. On this type of Gantt chart, the vertical axis shows the orders or jobs in progress while the horizontal axis represents time. A quick glance at the chart reveals which jobs are on schedule and which jobs are on time.

Gantt charts are the most widely used scheduling tools. However, they do have some limitations. The chart must be repeatedly updated to keep it current. Also, the chart does not directly reveal costs of alternate loadings nor does it consider that processing times may vary among work centers.

SCHEDULING SERVICE OPERATIONS

The scheduling of services often encounters problems not seen in manufacturing. Much of this is due to the nature of service, i.e., the intangibility of services and the inability to inventory or store services and the fact that demand for services is usually random. Random demand makes the scheduling of labor extremely difficult as seen in restaurants, movie theaters, and amusement parks. Since customers don't like to wait, labor must be scheduled so that customer wait is minimized. This sometimes requires the use of queuing theory or waiting line theory. Queuing theory uses estimate arrival rates and service rates to calculate an optimum staffing plan. In addition, flexibility can often be built into the service operation through the use of casual labor, on-call employees, and cross-training.

Scheduling of services can also be complicated when it is necessary to coordinate and schedule more than one resource. For example, when hospitals schedule surgery, not only is the scheduling of surgeons involved but also the scheduling of operating room facilities, support staff, and special equipment. Along with the scheduling of classes, universities must also schedule faculty, classrooms, labs, audiovisual and computer equipment, and students. To further complicate matters, cancellations are also common and can add further disruption and confusion to the scheduling process.

Instead of scheduling labor, service firms frequently try to facilitate their service operations by scheduling demand. This is done through the use of appointment systems and reservations.

SEE ALSO: Aggregate Planning; Capacity Planning; Operations Management; Product-Process Matrix

R. Anthony Inman

FURTHER READING:

Finch, Byron. *Operations Now: Profitability, Processes, Performance.* Boston: McGraw-Hill Irwin, 2006.

Hurtubise, Stephanie, Claude Olivier, and Ali Gharbi. "Planning Tools for Managing the Supply Chain." *Computers & Industrial Engineering* 46 (2004): 763–779.

Kreipl, Stephan and Michael Pinedo. "Planning and Scheduling in Supply Chains: An Overview of Issues in Practice." *Production and Operations Management* 13, no. 1 (2004): 77–92.

Raturi, Amitabh S., and James R. Evans. *Principles of Operations Management.* Mason, OH: Thomson South-Western, 2005.

Stevenson, William J. *Production and Operations Management.* 8th ed. Boston: Irwin/McGraw-Hill, 2005.

Vollmann, Thomas E., William L. Berry, D. Clay Whybark, and F. Robert Jacobs. *Manufacturing Planning and Control for Supply Chain Management.* 5th ed. Boston: McGraw-Hill Irwin, 2005.

OPERATIONS STRATEGY

After collectively considering the products and services demanded by customers, strengths and weaknesses of competitors, the environment, and the firm's own strengths, weaknesses, cultures, and resources, proficient firms can formulate their vision as expressed through the mission statement. This statement expresses the organization's values and aspirations; basically its reason or purpose for existence. Based on this mission statement the firm will formulate its business strategy. This business strategy is a long-term plan for accomplishing the mission set forth in the mission statement. Each function within the business can then derive its own strategy in support of the firm's overall business strategy (financial strategy, marketing strategy, and operations strategy).

Operations strategy is the collective concrete actions chosen, mandated, or stimulated by corporate strategy. It is, of course, implemented within the operations function. This operations strategy binds the various operations decisions and actions into a cohesive consistent response to competitive forces by linking firm policies, programs, systems, and actions into a systematic response to the competitive priorities chosen and communicated by the corporate or business strategy. In simpler terms, the operations strategy specifies how the firm will employ its operations capabilities to support the business strategy.

Operations strategy has a long-term concern for how to best determine and develop the firm's major operations resources so that there is a high degree of compatibility between these resources and the business strategy. Very broad questions are addressed regarding how major resources should be configured in order to achieve the firm's corporate objectives. Some of the issues of relevance include long-term decisions regarding capacity, location, processes, technology, and timing.

The achievement of world-class status through operations requires that operations be integrated with the other functions at the corporate level. In broad terms, an operation has two important roles it can play in strengthening the firm's overall strategy. One option is to provide processes that give the firm a distinct advantage in the marketplace. Operations will provide a marketing edge through distinct, unique technology developments in processes that competitors cannot match.

The second role that operations can play is to provide coordinated support for the essential ways in which the firm's products win orders over their competitors, also known as distinctive competencies. The firm's operations strategy must be conducive to developing a set of policies in both process choice and infrastructure design (controls, procedures, systems, etc.) that are consistent with the firm's distinctive competency. Most firms share access to the same processes and technology, so they usually differ little in these areas. What is different is the degree to which operations matches its processes and infrastructure to its distinctive competencies.

KEY SUCCESS FACTORS

Industries have characteristics or strategic elements that affect their ability to prosper in the marketplace (i.e., attributes, resources, competencies, or capabilities). The ones that most affect a firm's competitive abilities are called key success factors (KSFs). These KSFs are actually what the firm must be competent at doing or concentrating on achieving in order to be competitively and financially successful; they could be called prerequisites for success. In order to determine their own KSFs, a firm must determine a basis for customer choice. In other words, how do customers differentiate between competitors offering the same or similar products or services and how will the firm distinguish itself from these competitors? Once this is determined, the firm has to decide what resources and competitive capabilities it needs in order to compete successfully, and what will it take to achieve a sustainable competitive advantage. These KSFs can be related to technology, operations, distribution, marketing, or to certain skills or organizational capability. For example, the firm may derive advantages from superior ability to transform material or information (technology or operations), to quickly master new technologies and bring processes online (technology or organizational capability), or to quickly design and introduce new products, service a broad range of products, customize products or services on demand, or provide short lead times (skills).

The set of KSFs that are delegated totally or substantially to the operations function has been termed the *manufacturing mission*. It represents what top management expects from operations in terms of its strategic contribution. All decisions made relative to system design, planning, control and supervision must aim at accomplishing the manufacturing mission. As such, the manufacturing mission is the principal driver of the operations function and gives it its reason for existence. All world-class manufacturers have an explicit, formal manufacturing mission.

From the manufacturing mission the operations function derives its distinctive competencies (also called competitive priorities or competitive weapons). Distinctive competence is defined as the characteristic of a given product/service or its producing firm that causes the buyer to purchase it rather than the similar product/service of a competitor. It is generally accepted that the distinctive competencies are cost/price, quality, flexibility, and service/time. Various experts include other competencies, such as location, but these can usually be categorized within one of the generally accepted four. Some experts also feel that innovation is quickly becoming a fifth distinctive competency, if it hasn't already. It should be noted that a firm's position on the product-process matrix is a controlling factor for the manufacturing mission and the firm's competitive priority or priorities.

DISTINCTIVE COMPETENCIES

Details relative to each distinctive competency are provided, along with the implications of each and some examples.

PRICE/COST. A firm competing on a price/cost basis is able to provide consumers with an in-demand product at a price that is competitively lower than that offered by firms producing the same or similar good/service. In order to compete on a price basis, the firm must be able to produce the product at a lesser cost or be willing to accept a smaller profit margin. Firms with this competency are generally in a position to mass produce the product or service, thereby giving the firm economies of scale that drive the production cost per unit down considerably. Commodity items are mass-produced at such volume that they utilize a continuous process, thus deriving tremendous economies of scale and very low prices Consumers purchasing commodity-type products are usually not greatly aware of brand difference, and will buy strictly on the basis of price; e.g., as long as it is a major brand of gasoline and location is not a factor, consumers will opt for the lowest price. Wal-Mart is able to offer low prices by accepting a lower profit margin per unit sold. Their tremendous volume more than makes up for the lower profit margin.

QUALITY. David Garvin lists eight dimensions of quality as follows:

- Performance. Performance refers to a product's primary operating characteristics. For an automobile this could mean fast acceleration, easy handling, a smooth ride or good gas mileage. For a television it could mean bright color, clarity, sound quality or number of channels it can receive. For a service this could merely mean attention to details or prompt service.

- Conformance. Conformance is the degree to which a product's design and operating characteristics meet predetermined standards. When a manufacturer utilizing coils of steel receives a shipment from the mill, it checks the width of the coil, the gauge (thickness) of the steel, the weight of the coil, and puts a sample on a Rockwell hardness tester to check to ensure that the specified hardness has been provided. Receiving inspection will also check to see if specified characteristics are met (e.g., hot-rolled, pickled, and oiled). Services may have conformance requirements when it comes to repair, processing, accuracy, timeliness, and errors.

- Features. Features are the bells and whistles of a product or service. In other words, characteristics that supplement the basic function of the product or service. Desirable, but not absolutely necessary, features on a VCR include four heads, slow-motion capability, stereo or surround sound, split screens or inset screens, and 365-day programming ability. Service examples include free drinks on an airline flight or free delivery of flowers.

- Durability. Durability is defined as mean time until replacement. In other words, how long does the product last before it is worn out or has to be replaced because repair is impossible? For some items, such as light bulbs, repair is impossible and replacement is the only available option. Durability may be had by use of longer life materials or improved technology processes in manufacturing. One would expect home appliances such as refrigerators, washer and dryers, and vacuum cleaners to last for many years. One would also hope that a product that represents a significant investment, such as an automobile, would have durability as a primary characteristic of quality.

- Reliability. Reliability refers to a product's mean time until failure or between failures. In other words, the time until a product breaks down and has to be repaired, but not replaced. This is an important feature for products that have expensive downtime and maintenance. Businesses depend on this characteristic for items such as delivery trucks and vans, farm equipment and copy machines since their failure could conceivably shut down the business altogether.

- Serviceability. Serviceability is defined by speed, courtesy, competence and ease of repair. This is can be an extremely important characteristic as witnessed by the proliferation of toll-free hot lines for customer service. A number of years ago, a major television manufacturer advertised that its product had its "works in a box." This meant that the television set was assembled out of modular units. Whenever there were problems with the set, a repairman making a house call simply had to replace the problem module, making the product easily and quickly serviceable.

- Aesthetics. A product's looks, feel, smell, sound, or taste are its aesthetic qualities. Since these characteristics are strictly subjective and captive to preference, it is virtually impossible to please everyone on this dimension.

- Perceived Quality. Perceived quality is usually inferred from various tangible and intangible aspects of the product. Many consumers assume products made in Japan are inherently of high quality due to the reputation of Japanese manufacturers, whereas 50 years ago, the perception was the complete opposite. Other characteristics such as high price or pleasing aesthetics may imply quality.

Firms competing on this basis offer products or services that are superior to the competition on one or more of the eight dimensions. Obviously, it would be undesirable if not impossible for firms to compete on all eight dimensions of quality at once. This would be prohibitively expensive, and there are some limitations imposed by trade-offs that must be made due to the nature of the product. For example, a firm may sacrifice reliability in order to achieve maximum speed.

SERVICE. Service can be defined in a number of ways. Superior service can be characterized by the term customer service or it could mean rapid delivery, on-time delivery, or convenient location.

FLEXIBILITY. Firms may compete on their ability to provide either flexibility of the product or volume. Firms that can easily accept engineering changes (changes in the product) offer a strategic advantage to their customers. This can also apply to services. A number of years ago, a well-known fast food restaurant advertised "hold the pickles, hold the lettuce, special orders don't upset us," which meant that ordering a nonstandardized version of the product would not slow down the delivery process. Also, some firms are able to absorb wide fluctuations in volume allowing customers with erratic demand the luxury of not holding excessive inventories in anticipation of change in demand.

TRADEOFFS. Firms usually focus on one distinctive competency (rarely more than two). For some competencies there are tradeoffs involved. An automobile manufacturer producing a product that is considered to be of high quality (leather seats, real wood trim, and an outstanding service package) will not be able to compete on a cost/price basis as the cost of manufacture prohibits it. An automotive parts house would like to keep their customers happy by offering the lowest prices possible. However, if the automotive parts house also wants to be able to fill almost every single order from walk-in customers, it must maintain an extensive inventory. The expense of this inventory could preclude the parts house from offering prices competitive with other similar firms not choosing to provide this level of service. Therefore, one parts house is competing on the basis of service (but not cost/price) while the other is competing of the basis of cost/price (but not service). The customer may have to wait a few days to get the desired part; if the customer cannot wait, he or she can pay more and purchase the part immediately from the competitor.

ORDER WINNERS/QUALIFIERS

Operations strategist and author Terry Hill introduced the terms qualifier and order winner (1989). A qualifier is a competitive characteristic a firm or product must be able to exhibit to be a viable competitor in the marketplace. An order winner is a competitive characteristic of a product or service that causes a customer to choose this firm's product or service rather than that of a competitor (distinctive competence). For example, say a consumer in the market for a new automobile has a predetermined level of quality that the automobile must possess before being considered for purchase. The consumer has narrowed his or her choice down to five models of automobile that all meet this minimum quality requirement. From this point the consumer, with all else being equal, will probably purchase the automobile that he or she can get for the least cost. Therefore, quality is the qualifier (must be present to be considered) and cost/price is the order winner (basis for the final choice).

THE NEED FOR AN OPERATIONS STRATEGY

In too many instances, a firm's operations function is not geared to the business's corporate objectives. While the system itself may be good, it is not designed to meet the firm's needs. Rather, operations is seen as a neutral force, concerned solely with efficiency, and has little place within the corporate consciousness. Steven C. Wheelwright and Robert H. Hayes described four generic roles that manufacturing can play within a company, from a strategic perspective. While they specifically discuss the manufacturing function, the term operations can be substituted with no loss in relevance. These generic roles are labeled stages 1 to 4, as explained below.

Stage 1 firms are said to be internally neutral, meaning that the operations function is regarded as being incapable of influencing competitive success. Management, thereby, seeks only to minimize any negative impact that operations may have on the firm. One might say that operations maintain a reactive mode. When strategic issues involving operations arise, the firm usually calls in outside experts.

Stage 2 firms are said to be externally neutral, meaning they seek parity with competitors (neutrality) by following standard industry practices. Capital investments in new equipment and facilities are seen as the most effective means of gaining competitive advantage.

Stage 3 firms are labeled internally supportive, that is, operations' contribution to the firm is dictated by the overall business strategy but operations has no input into the overall strategy. Stage 3 firms do, however, formulate and pursue a formal operations strategy.

Stage 4 firms are at the most progressive stage of operations development. These firms are said to be externally supportive. Stage 4 firms expect operations to make an important contribution to the competitive success of the organization. An operation is actually involved in major marketing and engineering decisions. They give sufficient credibility and influence to operations so that its full potential is realized. Firms within Stage 4 are known for their overall manufacturing capability.

Since the bulk of many, if not all, firms have the bulk of their labor force and assets tied to the operations function, it makes sense for most firms to strive for a position in Stage 3 or Stage 4. Firms can, of course, evolve from one stage to the next with few, if any, skipping a stage. In fact, most outstanding firms are in Stage 3, as Stage 4 is extremely difficult to reach.

The need for an operations strategy that reflects and supports the corporate strategy is not only crucial for the success of the corporate strategy but also because many decisions are structural in nature. In other words, the results are not easily changed. The firm could be locked into a number of operations decisions, which could take years to change if the need arose. These could range from process investment decisions to human resource management practices. Too often, marketing-led strategies leave operations to resolve the resulting issues from their unilateral view of what is best for the business as a whole. If corporate management cannot fully appreciate the issues and consequences of relegating operations to a tactical status it could find itself needing to make structural changes that are costly, time consuming, and much too late to make the competitive impact necessary to compete effectively.

Firms that fail to fully exploit the strategic power of operations will be hampered in their competitive abilities and vulnerable to attack from those competitors who do exploit their operations strategy. To do this effectively, operations must be involved throughout the whole of the corporate strategy. Corporate executives have tended to assume that strategy has only to do with marketing initiatives. They erroneously make the assumption that operation's role is strictly to respond to marketing changes rather than make inputs into them. Secondly, corporate executives assume that operations have the flexibility to respond positively to changing demands. These assumptions place unrealistic demands upon the operations function. A recent article by Michael A. Lewis in the *International Journal of Operations and Production Management* warns firms a practical operations strategy is iterative and will require market compromise. While corporate management perceives corporate improvement as coming through broad decisions concerning new markets, takeovers, and so on, it overlooks the idea that building blocks of corporate success can be found in the creative and effective use of operations strategy to support the marketing requirement within a well-conceived corporate strategy.

Operations management's attention must increasingly be toward strategy. The balance and direction of its activity should reflect its impact on the firm's performance toward achieving its goals through its strategy, and on the performance of operations itself, recognizing that both need to be done well. Linda Nielsen-Englyst recommends a four-phase process for formulating and updating operations strategy: learning, reviewing, aligning, and redirecting. Phase one is a learning stage where alternatives to the intended strategy are evaluated in practice. Phase two involves reviewing alternatives over time, allowing ideas to grow and mature. Phase three, the alignment stage, is an analytical process where the firm attempts to identify and document financial rationale for changing the intended strategy. Finally, in the redirecting phase, the firm tests its ideas in practice through local initiatives.

SEE ALSO: Mission and Vision Statements; Operations Management; Order-Winning and Order-Qualifying Criteria; Quality and Total Quality Management; Strategy Formulation

R. Anthony Inman

FURTHER READING:

Garvin, David A. "Competing on the Eight Dimensions of Quality." *Harvard Business Review,* November-December 1987, 101–109.

Hill, Terry. *Manufacturing Strategy: Text and Cases 3rd ed.* Homewood, IL: Irwin, 2000.

Lewis, Michael A., "Analysing Organisational Competence: Implications for the Management of Operations," International Journal of Operations and Production Management, Vol. 23, No. 7, 2003, 731–756.

Neilslen-Englyst, Linda, "Operations Strategy Formation—A Continuous Process," Integrated Manufacturing Systems, Vol. 14, No. 8, 2003, 677–685.

Wheelwright, Steven C., and Robert H. Hayes. "Competing Through Manufacturing." *Harvard Business Review,* January-February 1985, 99–109.

OPPORTUNITY COST

An opportunity cost is defined as the value of a forgone activity or alternative when another item or activity is chosen. Opportunity cost comes into play in any decision that involves a tradeoff between two or more options. It is expressed as the relative cost of one alternative in terms of the next-best alternative. Opportunity cost is an important economic concept that finds application in a wide range of business decisions.

Opportunity costs are often overlooked in decision making. For example, to define the costs of a college education, a student would probably include such costs as tuition, housing, and books. These expenses are examples of accounting or monetary costs of college, but they by no means provide an all-inclusive list of costs. There are many opportunity costs that have been ignored: (1) wages that could have been earned during the time spent attending class, (2) the value of four years' job experience given up to go to school, (3) the value of any activities missed in order to allocate time to studying, and (4) the value of items that could have purchased with tuition money or the interest the money could have earned over four years.

These opportunity costs may have significant value even though they may not have a specific monetary value. The decision maker must often subjectively estimate Opportunity costs. If all options were purely financial, the value of all costs would be concrete, such as in the example of a mutual fund investment. If a person invests $10,000 in Mutual Fund ABC for one year, then he forgoes the returns that could have been made on that same $10,000 if it was placed in stock XYZ. If returns were expected to be 17 percent on the stock, then the investor has an opportunity cost of $1,700. The mutual fund may only expect returns of 10 percent ($1,000), so the difference between the two is $700.

This seems easy to evaluate, but what is actually the opportunity cost of placing the money into stock XYZ? The opportunity cost may also include the peace of mind for the investor having his money invested in a professionally managed fund or the sleep lost after watching his stock fall 15 percent in the first market correction while the mutual fund's losses were minimal. The values of these aspects of opportunity cost are not so easy to quantify. It should also be noted that an alternative is only an opportunity cost if it is a realistic option at that time. If it is not a feasible option, it is not an opportunity cost.

Opportunity-cost evaluation has many practical business applications, because opportunity costs will exist as long as resource scarcity exists. The value of the next-best alternative should be considered when choosing among production possibilities, calculating the cost of capital, analyzing comparative advantages, and even choosing which product to buy or how to spend time. According to Kroll, there are numerous real-world lessons about opportunity costs that managers should learn:

1. Even though they do not appear on a balance sheet or income statement, opportunity costs

are real. By choosing between two courses of action, you assume the cost of the option not taken.

2. Because opportunity costs frequently relate to future events, they are often difficult to quantify.

3. Most people will overlook opportunity costs.

Because most finance managers operate on a set budget with predetermined targets, many businesses easily pass over opportunities for growth. Most financial decisions are made without the consultation of operational managers. As a result, operational managers are often convinced by finance departments to avoid pursuing value-maximizing opportunities, assuming that the budget simply will not allow it. Instead, workers slave to achieve target production goals and avoid any changes that might hurt their short-term performance, for which they may be continually evaluated.

People incur opportunity costs with every decision that is made. When you decided to read this article, you gave up all other uses of this time. You may have given up a few minutes of your favorite television program or a phone call to a friend, or you may have even forgone the opportunity to invest or earn money. All possible costs should be considered when making financial or economic decisions, not simply those that can be concretely measured in terms of dollars or rates of return.

SEE ALSO: Balance Sheets; Economics; Strategic Planning Failure

Dena Waggoner
Revised by Laurie Collier Hillstrom

FURTHER READING:

Internet Center for Management and Business Administration. "Opportunity Cost." NetMBA.com. Available from <http://www.netmba.com/econ/micro/cost/opportunity>

Kroll, Karen. "Costly Omission." *Industry Week,* 6 July 1998, 20.

"Opportunities Lost Because 'There Isn't the Budget'?" *Management Accounting,* June 1998, 7.

Sikora, Martin. "Trying to Recoup the Cost of Lost Opportunities." *Mergers and Acquisitions Journal,* March 2000.

ORDER-QUALIFYING CRITERIA

SEE: Order-Winning and Order-Qualifying Criteria

ORDER-WINNING AND ORDER-QUALIFYING CRITERIA

The terms "order winners" and "order qualifiers" were coined by Terry Hill, professor at the London Business School, and refer to the process of how internal operational capabilities are converted to criteria that may lead to competitive advantage and market success. In his writings, Hill emphasized the interactions and cooperation between operations and marketing. The operations people are responsible for providing the order-winning and order-qualifying criteria—identified by marketing—that enable products to win orders in the marketplace. This process starts with the corporate strategy and ends with the criteria that either keeps the company in the running (i.e., order qualifiers) or wins the customer's business.

COMPETITIVE ADVANTAGE AND COMPETITIVE PRIORITIES

Many factors shape and form the operations strategy of a corporation, for example, the ever increasing need for globalizing products and operations and thus reducing the unit cost, creating a technology leadership position, introducing new inventions, taking advantage of mass customization, using supplier partnering, and looking for strategic sourcing solutions. All of these factors require an external or market-based orientation; these are the changes that take place in the external environment of the company.

Traditionally, strategic decisions were thought of as "big decisions" made by general managers. However, big strategic decisions may not be the only source of competitive advantage for the firm. Jay Barney wrote, "Recent work on lean manufacturing suggests that it is the simultaneous combination of several factors that enables a manufacturing facility to be both very high quality and very low cost. This complicated system of numerous interrelated, mutually supporting small decisions is difficult to describe, and even more difficult to imitate, and thus a source of sustained competitive advantage." Barney contrasted big and small decisions further, "Recognizing that small decisions may be more important for understanding competitive advantages than big decisions suggests that the study of strategy implementation—the process by which big decisions are translated into operational reality—may be more important for understanding competitive advantage than the study of strategy formulation."

The strategy expressed as a combination of a few big and hundreds of small decisions leads to setting up competitive priorities for improving operational practices through investments in various programs. These competitive priorities place different and diverse demands on manufacturing. These demands, sometimes called manufacturing tasks, can be organized into three distinctly different groups: product-related demands, delivery-related demands, and cost demands.

The emphasis given to these priorities and the state of the organization determine the nature and level of investments deemed necessary to implement the operations strategy. These investments in operational practices are expected to lead to better operational performance, as measured and evaluated internally using indicators like reject rates in the manufacturing process, production schedule fulfillment, and others. Through investments firms create and acquire resources that can isolate them from negative market influences and can serve as a source of competitive advantage for them. These investments can be made in tangible assets (e.g., machinery and capital equipment) and intangible assets (e.g., brand names and the skills of individual employees).

A distinction has to be made between investments aimed at creating resources and those aimed at creating capabilities. Few resources on their own are productive. Productive activity requires the cooperation and coordination of teams of resources. An operational capability is the capacity for a team of resources to perform some task or activity.

While resources are the source of a firm's capabilities, capabilities are the main source of its competitive advantage. Capabilities are not evaluated in themselves, and they cannot be thought of as absolute values. They have to be evaluated relative to the capabilities of competitors. This is the reason for distinguishing between competitiveness dimensions (like the 3 Ps from the marketing mix: price, place, and product) and capability-based dimensions (like cost-time-quality measures). They show the two sides of the same coin: the internal capabilities and their evaluation in the market.

ORDER QUALIFIERS AND ORDER WINNERS

Terry Hill argues that the criteria required in the marketplace (and identified by marketing) can be divided into two groups: order qualifiers and order winners. An order qualifier is a characteristic of a product or service that is required in order for the product/service to even be considered by a customer. An order winner is a characteristic that will win the bid or customer's purchase. Therefore, firms must provide the qualifiers in order to get into or stay in a market. To provide qualifiers, they need only to be as good as their competitors. Failure to do so may result in lost sales. However, to provide order winners, firms must be better than their competitors. It is important to note that order qualifiers are not less important than order winners; they are just different.

Firms must also exercise some caution when making decisions based on order winners and qualifiers. Take, for example, a firm producing a high quality product (where high quality is the order-winning criteria). If the cost of producing at such a high level of quality forces the cost of the product to exceed a certain price level (which is an order-qualifying criteria), the end result may be lost sales, thereby making "quality" an order-losing attribute.

Order winners and qualifiers are both market-specific and time-specific. They work in different combinations in different ways on different markets and with different customers. While, some general trends exist across markets, these may not be stable over time. For example, in the late 1990s delivery speed and product customization were frequent order winners, while product quality and price, which previously were frequent order winners, tended to be order qualifiers. Hence, firms need to develop different strategies to support different marketing needs, and these strategies will change over time. Also, since customers' stated needs do not always reflect their buying habits, Hill recommends that firms study how customers behave, not what they say.

When a firm's perception of order winners and qualifiers matches the customer's perception of the same, there exists a "fit" between the two perspectives. When a fit exists one would expect a positive sales performance. Unfortunately, research by Sven Horte and Hakan Ylinenpaa, published in the *International Journal of Operations and Production Management,* found that for many firms a substantial gap existed between managers' and customers' opinions on why they did business together. The researchers found that favorable sales performance resulted when there was a good fit between a firm's perception of the strengths of a product and customer perception of the product. Conversely, when firms with high opinions about their competitive strengths had customers who did not share this opinion, sales performance was negative.

PRODUCT LIFE CYCLE

Over time product sales follow a pattern called the product life cycle. The different stages of the product life cycle also influence a product's set of order winners and order qualifiers. The length of and the sales at each stage of the cycle, as well as the overall length of the life cycle, vary from product to product and depend on such factors as the rate of technological change, the amount of competition in the industry, and customer preferences.

In the early portion of a product's life, product design is critical. A product's early users are almost always more interested in product performance than in price. This stage is characterized by a large number of product innovations. A considerable amount of product design is undertaken to make the product more useful and desirable for its users. Abernathy referred to this early phase of product technology as the search for dominant design. Dominant designs are those that "make a market," such as Ford's Model T car, the DC-3 airplane, and the IBM PC. At this stage, the production process is most likely to be a job shop or close to a job shop.

As the dominant design gets more accepted, cost reduction becomes increasingly important. Thus, process innovation—geared primarily toward lowering costs, increasing yield, and improving throughput time—becomes more important. Changes become less radical as the product, the process, and the organization become more standardized. The production process moves closer to the continuous flow end of the process spectrum. When this happens, both the product and the process become increasingly vulnerable to the introduction of new offerings of similar function (i.e., substitute products) by other producers. Then, the company has to decide when and how to abandon the product and process that they perfected and in which they invested so much.

As the product moves through its life cycle, the requirements for the product and for the production process change. During the early part of the life cycle a production facility with high flexibility (i.e., a job shop) can generate order winners such as customization. For a mature product a dedicated facility (i.e., a flow shop) can produce high quality and low cost, which are the order winners for many, but not all, mature products.

Terry Hill noted that different product characteristics require different production processes, and without communication between marketing, which identifies the order winners and qualifiers, and operations, which develops the operational capabilities to deliver these characteristics, market success cannot be achieved. Hill developed a tool—product profiling—to ascertain a certain level of fit between process choices and the order-winning criteria of the products. The purpose of profiling is to provide comparison between product characteristics required in the market and the process characteristics used to manufacture the products and make the necessary adjustments.

SEE ALSO: Competitive Advantage; Operations Strategy; Product Life Cycle and Industry Life Cycle

Gyula Vastag
Revised by R. Anthony Inman

FURTHER READING:

Barney, Jay. "Organizational Culture: Can It Be a Source of Sustained Competitive Advantage?" *Academy of Management Review* 11 (1986): 656–65.

Barney, Jay. "Firm Resources and Sustained Competitive Advantage." *Journal of Management* 17 (1991): 99–120.

Hill, Terry. *Manufacturing Strategy: Text and Cases.* 3rd ed. Boston: Irwin McGraw-Hill, 2000.

Horte, Sven Ake, and Hakan Ylinenpaa. "The Firm's and Its Customers' Views on Order-Winning Criteria." *International Journal of Operations and Production Management* 17, no. 10 (1997): 1006–1019.

Vastag, G., and Ram Narasimhan. "An Investigation of Causal Relationships Among Manufacturing Strategic Intent, Practices and Performance." In *Performance Measurement.* eds. A.D. Neely and D.B. Waggoner. Cambridge, UK: Centre for Business Performance, 1998: 679–86.

ORGANIC ORGANIZATIONS

The term "organic" suggests that, like living things, organizations change their structures, roles, and processes to respond and adapt to their environments. Burns and Stalker noted in *The Management of Innovation* that organic structures are appropriate in unstable, turbulent, unpredictable environments and for non-routine tasks and technologies. For organizations coping with such uncertainty, finding appropriate, effective, and timely responses to environmental challenges is of critical importance. Organic organizations are characterized by:

- decentralization

- flexible, broadly defined jobs

- interdependence among employees and units

- multi-directional communication

- employee initiative

- relatively few and broadly defined rules, regulations, procedures, and processes

- employee participation in problem solving and decision making, often interactively and in groups

In organic organizations, the emphasis is on effectiveness, problem solving, responsiveness, flexibility, adaptability, creativity, and innovation. Such an organization is able to respond in a timely manner to environmental change because employees are empowered to be creative, to experiment, and to suggest new ideas. The process of innovation is triggered by employees throughout the organization in a "bottom-up" manner. The following four sections explain how these characteristics fit together in a cohesive organizational structure that allows for flexibility and ongoing change.

MEETING CHALLENGES

An unstable external environment increases the uncertainty and complexity with which an organization must contend. An organization is continually confronted with a variety of new and unexpected problems and opportunities, of which the nature and relevant factors are initially unclear and for which appropriate responses are not immediately obvious. Further, since the environment changes rapidly, responses to today's problems and opportunities may need to be modified or may even be inappropriate or irrelevant to tomorrow's challenges. In short, the organization cannot keep doing the same old things in the same old ways. Under conditions of uncertainty and complexity, the organization must design its structures and processes to be flexible and responsive to changes in customer desires, technology, governmental regulations, and economic conditions.

FLEXIBILITY AND SHARED AUTHORITY

The need for flexibility and responsiveness leads to the decentralization of decision-making authority in organic organizations. As a result, rules, regulations, procedures, and policies tend to be few, are defined broadly rather than precisely, loosely rather than rigidly, and are often informal rather than written. Employees are allowed to exercise a great deal of discretion. The authority to identify problems and opportunities and to devise responses is delegated to those best able to respond, regardless of their position, unit, or level in the organization. Emphasis is placed more on individual and group control than on managerial, hierarchical control. Top-level managers in organic organizations are more concerned with coordination and integration as opposed to passing directives down a vertical hierarchy, which is a common task of top-level managers in mechanistic organizations.

The need for flexibility and responsiveness also affects how work is designed and performed in organic organizations. Jobs are not clearly or precisely defined in these organizations. Positions, roles, job descriptions, and standard operating procedures are broad and generalized rather than specific and specialized. Employees accept general responsibility for getting things done, but the manner in which they accomplish their tasks is dictated more by autonomous or semi-autonomous teams than by standard operating procedures. Because the work of organic organizations is often interdependent, specific tasks and responsibilities vary from one situation to another and are refined through direct interaction and mutual adjustment among employees and work units. Too much direction from top-level management may hinder rather than assist the accomplishment of tasks.

A key issue in organic organizations is determining who has the knowledge, perspective, experience, expertise, or skills required to identify opportunities or find solutions to problems. Rather than assuming that top management is the fountainhead of all knowledge and wisdom, organic organizations assume that various people in the organization may have crucial insights or capabilities. Thus, communication is multidirectional, decentralized, and informal rather than hierarchical and formalized. In order to facilitate the sharing of information and ideas, employees are frequently empowered to communicate across traditional organizational boundaries regardless of position or level or unit.

Going one step further, pharmaceutical firms, for example, may collaborate across corporations and with academic researchers to conduct basic research leading to new drug development. Jack Welch, former CEO of General Electric, referred to this type of company as a "boundaryless organization." Coordination and integration with multiple constituencies beyond traditional organizational boundaries is a necessary component for success, especially in multinational organizations.

Diversity of information and perspectives is often the key to the development of creative responses to vague, complex problems and opportunities. Thus, in organic organizations, much work is done in groups composed of employees with different backgrounds and from different levels, units, or functional areas. Such teams are among the main coordination mechanisms in organic organizations.

THE HUMAN ELEMENT

Human needs and dynamics play an important role in organic organizations. The empowerment and participation of employees is motivational because it meets the human need for autonomy, responsibility, challenge, esteem, social interaction, and personal development. Furthermore, this empowerment and participation helps the organization develop and capitalize on its intellectual capital, which is becoming increasingly valued by many organizations. By emphasizing initiative, direct interaction, open communication, and the creation of teams composed of various members of the organization, organic organizations are able to utilize their internal diversity to foster innovative responses to environmental challenges and changes.

MIXING STYLES

The organic organization is not entirely without hierarchy or formalized rules, regulations, procedures, and processes. Indeed, structural parameters, even if loosely or broadly defined, are necessary to prevent the chaos that would result from absolute decentralization (i.e., where everyone in the organization is completely free to decide what they want to do or not do). As an example of such structural parameters, while employees of Minnesota Mining and Manufacturing (3M) are encouraged to take the initiative in suggesting new products and seeking support from others in the organization, new product teams must still meet specific financial measures at each stage of product development. Nonetheless, the real control is found in constant interaction among peers and the normative rules that develop informally among them.

It is not always necessary for an entire organization to be organic. Some units, such as research and development departments, may benefit from an organic structure because they face an unstable environment. Units that have a more stable environment, such as routine, administrative departments, may favor a mechanistic structure. Some units may borrow from both models. Customer service departments, for example, can build flexibility into responding to exceptional circumstances while maintaining standardized protocols for more typical situations.

The structures of organic organizations are informal, fluid, and constantly changing to identify and develop responses to new problems and opportunities. Authority and responsibility shifts from one situation to another. Groups are established, complete their work, and disband, and a single employee may belong to several temporary teams at the same time. In organic organizations there is diminished emphasis on superior-subordinate roles in favor of dispersed initiative. Roles, tasks, and responsibilities are not limited by rigid, vertical boundaries of hierarchy for decision-making, communication, coordination, and control. Relations and interactions between personnel and units continually change, and managers and other employees must figure out which relations and interactions will be most effective for each particular problem or opportunity.

SEE ALSO: Effectiveness and Efficiency; Mechanistic Organizations; Organization Theory

Durward Hofler
Revised by Scott B. Droege

FURTHER READING:

Berry, L. "The Collaborative Organization: Leadership Lessons from Mayo Clinic." *Organizational Dynamics* 33, no. 3 (2004): 228–42.

Burns, T., and G.M. Stalker. *The Management of Innovation.* London: Tavistock, 1961.

Cardinal, Laura B., Sim B. Sitkin, and Chris P. Long. "Balancing and Rebalancing in the Creation and Evolution of Organizational Control." *Organization Science* 15, no. 4 (2004): 411–32.

Gooderham, P.N., and O. Nordhaug. *International Management: Cross-Boundary Challenges.* Malden, MA: Blackwell Publishing, 2004.

Hansen, M.T., and N. Nohria. "How to Build Collaborative Advantage." *MIT Sloan Management Review* 46, no. 1 (2004): 22–31.

Pearce, C.L. "The Future of Leadership: Combining Vertical and Shared Leadership to Transform Knowledge Work." *Academy of Management Executive* 18, no. 1 (2004): 47–58.

ORGANIZATION THEORY

Organization theory is a broad field with roots in sociology. Anthropologists, philosophists, and political scientists have contributed greatly to the field. Organization theory as a topic for managers, as opposed to scholars, has come about fairly recently. For example, political scientists trace many ideas back to Ancient Rome or even before. Philosophers reach even farther back in time, and anthropologists have been interested in organization in terms of how groups arrange social systems and status systems as long as there has been a field of anthropology.

Although it is difficult to pinpoint when managers became interested in theories of organization, some suggest it was around the 1940s, when the writings of the German sociologist and engineer, Max Weber, were translated into English. Although Weber's lifework was spent trying to understand why capitalism arose first in Western Europe rather than in Asia, American managers lifted Weber's notion of bureaucracy out of these studies to explain then-modern forms of organizations that coincided with what Weber had described among Western European organizations. These organizations had reduced the influence of patriarchal styles of management to systems in which job positions, rather than the people in those positions, provided the source of authority.

Phillip Selznick became well known for studying goal conflict and power struggles during the U.S. government's subsidy of the Tennessee Valley Authority, which was an effort to put unemployed Americans to work producing electricity for the Tennessee Valley area. In the 1950s Herbert Simon studied how managers make decisions when information is complex but incomplete. The 1960s brought about research elaborating why the closed-system mentality of organizations—the idea that organizations have little reciprocal interaction with their environments—was not accurate. The result was a shift to viewing organizations as open systems that are intertwined with their environments in such a way that reciprocal interdependence is created. Managers began to realize that society has a profound effect on organizations, as organizations also have a profound effect on society.

Taken in total, then, organization theory as a management topic of interest was born out of non-management research. Bureaucracy, authority, goal conflict, power, managerial decision-making, and interaction between organizations and their environments are all topics of concern among today's organization theorists, but none of these ideas arose from management research.

Management research has borrowed from these various fields to attempt to answer two questions that are of specific interest to managers: Why do organizations exist and how do they function? With respect to the first question, it seems reasonable to argue that organizations exist to provide society with a level of goods and services that would otherwise be unattainable. With respect to the second, how organizations function, organizations combine human skills, knowledge, technology, and material resources to produce goods and services.

The broadest variant of organization theory looks at the relationship between organizations and their social and natural environments, as originated by open-system theorists. One branch of Western moral philosophy conceives of organizations as having a social contract with society, whereby they are granted legitimacy for the purpose of serving the social good. This constructive purpose includes the production of goods and services and their fair allocation. Yet organizations can also cause negative social outcomes. Negative externalities include the social problems associated with monopolies, unsafe products, and the unfair treatment of employees, as well as the ecological problems posed by industrial accidents and industry-related pollution of the natural environment.

Because of the existence of negative externalities, organization theory is influenced by the concept of social control that can be found in political science, economics, and sociology. Social control refers to the laws, regulations, and social customs that are meant to minimize the negative impacts of organizational activities. Because organization theorists address social control, they also examine the nature of the relationship between organizations and their regulatory agencies.

The anthropological view derives from the knowledge that standards of social control reflect the underlying assumptions, values, and beliefs of cultures. The restraints or expectations placed on organizations, therefore, can vary across societies. The stakeholder model of organizations is useful for demonstrating this form of cultural relativism. The stakeholder model depicts an organization as surrounded by a variety of constituent groups, such as customers, social activists, regulators, the media, stockholders, and regulatory agencies.

Stakeholder expectations, in turn, can depend upon cultural affiliations. For example, employees in the United States tend to expect more active participation in the work contract than do employees in Japan. Thus, a Japanese firm with operations in the United States may face employment laws and employee views of justice and fairness that differ from those of the home country. When the scope of organization theory is widened to include international issues such as the activities of multinational corporations in host environments, the impact of cultural relativism must be acknowledged.

Although organization theory never loses sight of the importance of the organizational-societal interface (and this is one distinguishing feature between organization theory and organization behavior), it also deals with what goes on inside organizations. Weber's classical theory of bureaucracy, for example, was followed by research on the more informal aspects of organizational life. This line of inquiry is strongly influenced by the insight that organizational activity can involve less-than-rational processes that yield unexpected consequences, including the negative externalities mentioned above. Hence, although organizations ideally exist as tools for constructive social purposes, these purposes can be subverted by the constraints on rational decision processes within organizations.

Contemporary theorists use many metaphors to guide their investigations into the suboptimal and even non-rational decisions enacted in organizations. These metaphors include those that suggest organizations are systems of power and political intrigue, miniature cultures, chaos, temples, theaters, machines, families, and jungles. These metaphors arise through shared meaning that has been socially constructed and generally agreed upon, thus subconsciously institutionalizing the specific, agreed-upon metaphor for certain organizations.

Organization theorists are interested in why organizations exist and how these social systems function. This interest has yielded a body of research on the organizational-societal relationship and the formal and informal aspects of organizational life, yet there is no single answer to either of these root issues.

SEE ALSO: Mechanistic Organizations; Organic Organizations; Organizational Analysis and Planning

Diane L. Swanson
Revised by Scott B. Droege

FURTHER READING:

Brown-Johnson, N., and S.B. Droege. "Reflections on the Generalization of Agency Theory: Cross-cultural Considerations." *Human Resource Management Review* 14, no. 3 (2004): 325–35.

Vázquez, X.H. "Allocating Decision Rights on the Shop Floor: A Perspective from Transaction Cost Economics and Organization Theory." *Organization Science* 15, no. 4 (2004): 463–81.

Zajac, E.J., and Westphal, J.D. "The Social Construction of Market Value: Institutionalization and Learning Perspectives on Stock Market Reactions." *American Sociological Review* 69, no. 3 (2004): 433–58.

ORGANIZATIONAL ANALYSIS AND PLANNING

Organizational analysis and planning focuses on cultivating and maintaining an efficient workforce through the design and structure of an organization, as well as the relationships and behavior of individuals within organizations. Specifically, organizational analysis is concerned with developing models and theories that accurately capture the functioning and development of organizations and that account for the ways in which organizations respond to and bring about changes. Organizational planning, on the other hand, involves designing an organization's structure and dividing up the responsibilities of an organization. The goals of organizational analysis and planning typically have been to determine the best way to view and organize a company in order to manage it successfully and to bring about greater efficiency.

MODELS OF ORGANIZATIONAL ANALYSIS

One of the basic techniques of organizational analysis is modeling—developing models of organizations that delineate the way they function and evolve in order to identify the best way of managing each one. Modeling enables managers to determine the crucial variables in particular circumstances so they can experiment with different combinations of variables to achieve their desired results. For example, managers can determine the best combination of technology and organizational structure for their company by using organizational models.

Organizational models typically focus on behavior, structure, or technology. In consideration of these variables, four general models of organizational analysis exist: the rational (also called the classical model), the natural system (also called the participative model), the sociotechnical, and the cognitive model.

RATIONAL MODEL. A pioneer of the rational model of organization was Frederick Taylor, who was influential near the start of the twentieth century. Taylor's background in engineering prompted his organizational analysis on efficiency. In Taylor's view, there was one best way—the most efficient way—to perform a task. Scientific management sprang from his work, with resultant time and motion studies in which tasks were timed and employee motions were gauged for efficiency. The best way to perform a task, in Taylor's view, was the way that accomplished the task in the least amount of time. He extended this view from employees to management, suggesting that nearly all organizational tasks could become more efficient if scientific principles were applied.

This was at the dawn of the introduction of the automobile to America. Although many Western European nations began manufacturing automobiles before the early 1900s, production efficiencies still had a long way to go. Applying scientific management principles helped Ford Motor Company develop the first American, mass-produced automobile. Frederick Taylor, then, was correct. Scientific management did work, but it was not without problems. The main problem was that it ignored the boredom that repetitive tasks created for workers. Workers became simply replaceable parts in the organizational machine.

In addition, the rational model of organization presupposes that decisions about an organization's structure are reached because of the rational assessment of an organization's needs, goals, and external influences. And like Taylor's scientific management, this is true in some situations, but is not comprehensive enough to tell the whole story of how needs, goals and external influences affect organizational analysis and planning.

The rational model assumes that deviations from rationality result from errors in judgment and calculation as well as from ignorance. This model treats organizations as mechanical groups because it conceives of the organization as having structure of different parts, and all of these parts can be modified and manipulated in order to improve the efficiency of the entire organization. Furthermore, individual parts of the organization are viewed as modifiable through deliberate effort. Finally, this model sees the long-term development of the organization as modifiable and controllable through planned modification in order to accomplish definite goals.

The rational model is still pervasive among managers and corresponds to the pyramidal organizational structure, in which top managers are at the apex and employees are at the bottom. Managers possess the authority in this model, defining and assigning tasks to the employees, who are charged with completing the tasks. They must begin by giving employees clear and detailed instructions. After that, managers must evaluate employee performance and distribute rewards and punishments based on the way employees performed their tasks.

Managers assume that worker motivation is directly correlated with economic rewards and punishments meted out by the managers. Motivation, from a rational perspective, simply involves increasing pay or threatening workers with various punishments. Hence, according to this model, managers rely on pay and related forms of compensation to motivate workers to complete their tasks efficiently in order to achieve company goals.

The problem with this assumption is that there are many motivators other than money, there can be many ways to perform a given task, and there are many organizational goals that are not rational. The rational model is thus a starting point for thinking about organizational analysis, but certainly not encompassing enough to provide a complete picture.

NATURAL SYSTEM MODEL. In contrast to the rational model, the natural system model views organizations holistically, that is, as systems. The natural system model sees an organization as not only striving to accomplish its own goals, but also other important goals. An organizational structure is regarded as an institution in its own right that has needs of its own. Hence, according to this model, an organization seeks to maintain a balance of its various needs and goals, which may restrict the way it pursues other goals.

Unlike the rational model of organization, the natural system model sees the modification of an organization as unplanned and adaptive reactions to unstable conditions that threaten the balance of the organization as an entire system. The way an organization responds to problems is characterized as a defense mechanism and as being influenced by the common values ensconced in the members of the organization. This model concentrates on threats to an organization's equilibrium, that is, on events and activities with the potential of disrupting an organization's balance.

When deviations from organizational plans and goals occur, they are seen not as the product of error or ignorance, but as the result of limitations brought about by an organization's social structure. This model generally is based on the concept of organizations as organisms in which all the parts are interconnected and interdependent. Consequently, changes in one part of an organization are thought to have an impact on other parts of the organization, and so planned modification of the organization is difficult.

In practical terms, the natural system model strives to balance the needs of all the members of the organization as well as other stakeholders, such as customers, shareholders, and suppliers. This model holds that organizations function best when members belong to at least one effective work group (department, committee, or staff group), thereby contributing to the goals of organizations. Members who belong to more than one work group help link the different units of the organization together and facilitate communication and the exchange of information throughout the organization.

The natural system model views change as affecting the entire organization, not just individuals or individual units. Consequently, managers cannot change just one small part of an organization; rather, they must change the whole organization. As a result, planning for change must be comprehensive and systematic. Theoretically, the natural system model helps prevent conflicts in that changes take place only with the involvement of each member of the organization. Therefore, commitment to change is greatly increased and conflict over change is limited.

SOCIOTECHNICAL MODEL

Because of the limitations of the previous models of organization, theorists have developed other models to capture the essence and functioning of modern organizations. The sociotechnical model does not rely on the mechanical and biological analogies of the rational and natural system models. Instead, the sociotechnical model views organizations as having a greater ability to modify their form and structure. Nevertheless, like the natural system model, the sociotechnical model sees organizations as evolving. An organization changes when the expectations of its members change as a result of their collaboration with other members and the exchange of information.

This model views organizations as systems that interact with their environments. Through the course of this interaction, organizational behavior is affected by human, social, technological, and organizational inputs. These inputs are all interdependent, thus a change in one causes a change in the others. The basic tenets of the sociotechnical model include the belief that behavior in organizations can have a number of causes, that organizations are systems, and that informal social systems are different from formal social systems.

An organization's main task is accomplished through the process of inputs being converted into outputs. The organization is designed around these tasks. Similarly each unit of the organization is designed around its specific subtask. The sociotechnical model assumes that an organization's effectiveness is determined by its design to perform its main task. Organizations have differentiated, yet integrated, units based on three primary factors: technology (including techniques, skills, and materials), geographic location, and time (work shifts). According to this model, if an organization is effectively designed around its main task and if its units are differentiated and integrated effectively, then the number of conflicts will be reduced.

COGNITIVE MODEL

The cognitive model of organization consists of three primary components: cognition, the decision-making or problem-solving process, and an organizational setting. Cognition refers to the information-processing units of an organization and its organizational units. The decision-making or problem-solving component is a series of steps, operations, and procedures that an organizational unit uses to make decisions or solve problems. The organizational setting component is the arrangement of the organization, that is, the way tasks are distributed and the way processes are coordinated.

Although the rational model of organization focuses on clarifying and assigning tasks, it does not address the other aspects of organizations. In particular, it provides little in terms of the ways organizations solve problems once tasks are clarified and assigned. The cognitive model moves beyond this level of organizational analysis by focusing on the processes through which organizations assign specific activities and times for the activities to be performed.

The cognitive model focuses on the decision-making process of an organization. An organization makes decisions in accordance with its objectives and based on available information. Since this model views individuals as having the capacity to do only a few things at a time, the organization functions as the combination of these limited capacities and facilitates the overall completion of a number of complex tasks, which are broken down into a series of subtasks so that individuals can perform them. These subtasks are the areas of specialization within an organization. Specialization, in turn, brings about the flow of specific information to and from specialized units.

This model provides several key insights into the workings of organizations. It conceives of an organization as a process that develops from the interaction of human cognition, organizational structure, and the types of decisions that need to be made. Because of these characteristics, the cognitive model focuses on the development and adaptation of organizations in different circumstances. Furthermore, this model accounts for the way in which specialization affects organizational behavior and coordination.

In conclusion, because each different organization model has its advantages and disadvantages, managers must decide which one (or ones) best captures the workings of their company by evaluating the assumptions and key processes of each, as well as by determining which one can solve the kinds of problems they need to solve.

TYPES OF ORGANIZATIONAL PLANNING STRUCTURES

Organizational planning involves designing an organization's structure to maximize efficiency. This includes dividing a company up into different units, departments, and teams. Prior to this division, managers must consider a company's goals and business obstacles as well as alternative company structures.

Business goals may include, for example, increasing the flow of information, promoting teamwork, and reducing redundancy. Next, managers must consider the different organizational structures and select the one that holds the greatest potential for eliminating problems with the current corporate structure or for bringing about the desired structural environment. The selection may be made by taking different organizational models into consideration, as well.

Managers and executives generally divide an organization into different units based on one of the following six criteria:

FUNCTION. A manufacturing firm typically includes functional units such as engineering, production, finance, sales, and personnel. These different functions are controlled by managers who head each function. In this organizational structure, each function primarily focuses on its core tasks (e.g., production or finance).

PRODUCT. Large, diversified companies may find it advantageous to divide their tasks based on product groups, such as foodstuffs, farm chemicals, and pharmaceuticals. This organizational structure has the benefit of enabling each business unit to produce desired results. However, it can lead to high administrative costs and redundancy.

CUSTOMERS. Companies may be divided into different units based on target customers. For example, a book publisher may be organized by retail bookstores, mail-order book stores, online book stores, and school system tier, such as elementary, middle school, high school, and higher education.

GEOGRAPHIC LOCATION. Many sales and service companies use geographic location as the basis for creating departments within the organization. This organizational structure calls for members of each group to concentrate on particular locations for which they are responsible.

PROCESS. Some companies are organized by process. Process organization is common in manufacturing and clerical companies. For example, natural gas companies have different units for exploration, production, and distribution. This type of organizational structure enables each unit to have its own specialists.

MATRIX. Matrix organizational structures include not only general functional units like production, sales, and finance, but also product or geographic units. Company executives frequently oversee the product units directly. The product units, in turn, collaborate with and coordinate the functional units. By adopting the matrix arrangement, companies attempt to reap the benefits of the functional and the product or geographic structures, while bypassing the inefficient and redundant aspects of the product structure. A company with a matrix organizational structure has functional units such as development, production, and sales matched in a matrix by product or geographic location.

Company executives and managers must strive to select the organizational structure that best suits their fields of business, that offers the optimal amount of control, specialization, and cooperation, and that facilitates key business activities while also taking into consideration concerns for efficiency and effectiveness.

SEE ALSO: Organizational Chart; Organizational Development; Organizational Structure

Karl Heil
Revised by Scott B. Droege

FURTHER READING:

French, W., C.H. Bell, and R.A. Zawacki. *Organization Development and Transformation: Managing Effective Change*, 6th ed. McGraw-Hill, 2005.

Goodman, P.S., and D.M. Rousseau. "Organizational Change that Produces Results: The Linkage Approach." *Academy of Management Executive* 18, no. 3 (2004): 7–20.

Roberts, John. *The Modern Firm: Organizational Design for Performance and Growth.* Oxford University Press, 2004.

Wall, S.J. "The Protean Organization: Learning to Love Change." *Organizational Dynamics* 34, no. 1 (2004): 37–46.

ORGANIZATIONAL BEHAVIOR

Organizational behavior is a misnomer. It is not the study of how organizations behave, but rather the study of individual behavior in an organizational setting. This includes the study of how individuals behave alone, as well as how individuals behave in groups.

The purpose of organizational behavior is to gain a greater understanding of those factors that influence individual and group dynamics in an organizational setting so that individuals and the groups and organizations to which they belong may become more efficient and effective. The field also includes the analysis of organizational factors that may have an influence upon individual and group behavior. Much of organizational behavior research is ultimately aimed at providing human resource management professionals with the information and tools they need to select, train, and retain employees in a fashion that yields maximum benefit for the individual employee as well as for the organization.

Organizational behavior is a relatively new, interdisciplinary field of study. Although it draws most heavily from the psychological and sociological sciences, it also looks to other scientific fields of study for insights. One of the main reasons for this interdisciplinary approach is because the field of organizational behavior involves multiple levels of analysis, which are necessary to understand behavior within organizations because people do not act in isolation. That is, workers influence their environment and are also influenced by their environment.

INDIVIDUAL LEVEL OF ANALYSIS

At the individual level of analysis, organizational behavior involves the study of learning, perception, creativity, motivation, personality, turnover, task performance, cooperative behavior, deviant behavior, ethics, and cognition. At this level of analysis, organizational behavior draws heavily upon psychology, engineering, and medicine.

GROUP LEVEL OF ANALYSIS

At the group level of analysis, organizational behavior involves the study of group dynamics, intra- and intergroup conflict and cohesion, leadership, power, norms, interpersonal communication, networks, and roles. At this level of analysis, organizational behavior draws upon the sociological and socio-psychological sciences.

ORGANIZATION LEVEL OF ANALYSIS

At the organization level of analysis, organizational behavior involves the study of topics such as organizational culture, organizational structure, cultural diversity, inter-organizational cooperation and conflict, change, technology, and external environmental forces. At this level of analysis, organizational behavior draws upon anthropology and political science.

Other fields of study that are of interest to organizational behavior are ergonomics, statistics, and psychometrics.

A number of important trends in the study of organizational behavior are the focus of research efforts. First, a variety of research studies have examined topics at the group level of analysis rather than exclusively at the individual level of analysis. For example, while empowerment has largely been investigated as an individual-level motivation construct, researchers have begun to study team empowerment as a means of understanding differences in group performance. Similar research has focused on elevating the level of analysis for personality characteristics and cooperative behavior from the individual level to the group level.

Another research trend is an increasing focus on personality as a factor in individual- and group-level performance. This stems from the movement toward more organic organization designs, increased supervisory span of control, and more autonomous work designs. All of these factors serve to increase the role that personality plays as a determinant of outcomes such as stress, cooperative or deviant behavior, and performance.

Personality traits that are related to flexibility, stress hardiness, and personal initiative are also the subject of research. Examples of these personality traits include a tendency toward individualism or collectivism, self-monitoring, openness to experience, and a proactive personality. Forms of behavior that are constructive and change-oriented in nature are also studied. These forms of behavior are proactive in nature and act to improve situations for the individual, group, or organization. Examples of these behaviors include issue selling, taking initiative, constructive change-oriented communication, innovation, and proactive socialization.

Other topics of interest in the field of organizational behavior include the extent to which theories of behavior are culturally bound, unethical decision-making, self-management and self-leadership, and work/family conflict.

SEE ALSO: Motivation and Motivation Theory; Organic Organizations; Organizational Culture; Organizational Development

Jerry Bryan Fuller

ORGANIZATIONAL CHART

An organizational chart is a pictorial representation of a company's structure and reporting relationships. This chart can provide a great deal of information and may help organizational members understand the overall structure of the organization and its strategy. This entry describes how organizational charts are constructed, including the software that can be used to create them; what information the organizational chart provides; the benefits of making the chart available inside and outside of the organization; and the circumstances under which a chart is likely to change.

CONSTRUCTING AN ORGANIZATIONAL CHART

All organizational charts have similar elements that allow them to be easily interpreted and understood by people inside and outside of the organization. Charts consist of shapes and lines that represent work units and their hierarchy. See Figure 1 for an example of an organizational chart.

The basic building block of an organizational chart is the rectangle, which can represent a person or a work unit (e.g., a department). For example, as shown in figure 1, the CEO position has a separate rectangle that denotes one person, but the entire Public and Community Relations Department is also represented by one rectangle. If the outline of the rectangle is dashed, this means that a position is open and must be filled, as with one of the manager positions. If a rectangle is divided, and two or more names are in it, this may indicate job sharing or that multiple people are responsible for the outcomes associated with this position. In the figure, W. Allen and P. Lloyd are comanagers in one area of the Production and Services Marketing Department, where they have a job sharing arrangement and each works part-time hours.

The boxes may contain as much or as little information as the organization prefers. They may include a job title, an employee's name, an employee's department, or even information such as job tenure, education, or salary. Alternatively, a chart may be created without rectangles, with names or titles standing alone. The three employees in the Public and Community Relations Department are listed with their names not in rectangles. This often is done to save space on the chart.

Rectangles on an organizational chart are linked with solid or dashed lines. A solid line indicates a formal, direct relationship and a dashed line indicates that one employee or department advises another or has some other sort of indirect relationship. Note that all but one of the reporting relationships in figure 1 are formal. L. Jiminez has a dashed line to the Product and Services Marketing Department, which means that she sometimes will work for that department or will report to that department's manager. When lines represent a tree structure—when two or more rectangles are linked to another with multiple lines—this indicates that several individuals or departments report to one supervisor. For instance, the tree structure represents the relationship between the CEO and the three top managers who report to the CEO. Finally, a rectangle that is attached horizontally outside of the vertical hierarchy typically indicates an assistant or staff person. In the example, this is represented by the executive secretary to the CEO.

While organizational charts can be created by hand, most are created using computer software. Although it may be labor intensive, organizational charts can be created using drawing tools in a word processing program. Microsoft's PowerPoint presentation software allows for the creation of organizational charts, although there is little space available to create large charts. Specific software exists for creating

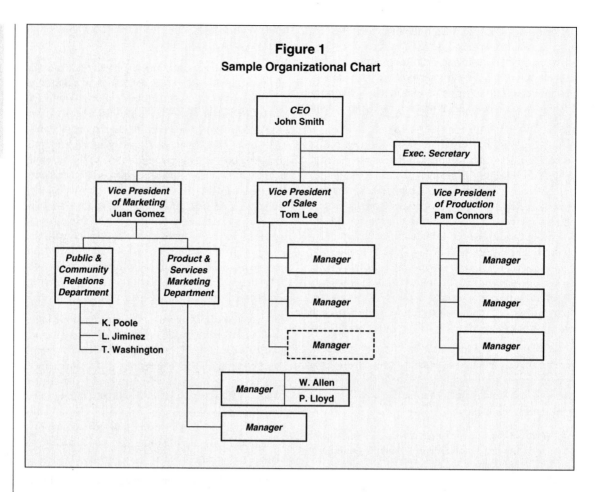

Figure 1

Sample Organizational Chart

larger, more complex charts, and there are many different packages available for purchase. Some examples are OrgPlus5, ConceptDraw V, SmartDraw, and Abra OrgChart. These software programs allow for quick and easy chart creation with point-and-click menus and automatic resizing and alignment. Many of these software programs also allow one to easily download charts into a word processing document, a presentation, or a Web site. Other features available in these programs include the ability to insert employee photographs, as well as information from other human resources computer programs, directly into charts.

INFORMATION IN THE ORGANIZATIONAL CHART

The organizational chart provides a great deal of information about the organization as a whole and the interaction of its parts. From a chart, one can see the organization's structure, its hierarchy, the degree to which it is centralized or decentralized, and its chain of command. Each of these is summarized below.

ORGANIZATIONAL STRUCTURE. First, organizational charts detail an organization's structure. It may be functional, in which work units are divided based on what they do and named after those functions (e.g.,

research and development, marketing, sales, etc.). The structure may be divisional, based on product, customers served, or geographic location. Finally, an organizational chart may represent a matrix structure, in which work units are organized by both function and division.

ORGANIZATIONAL HIERARCHY AND CENTRALIZATION. In addition to outlining the type of organizational structure, the organizational chart also indicates the number of management levels, whether the organizational structure is tall or flat, and the span of control at each level. Tall organizations have many levels of middle management and small spans of control. Each manager supervises and directs few employees, and the chain of command has many managers. Conversely, a flat organization has fewer management levels and larger spans of control. Because managers supervise more employees, employees tend to have more autonomy and discretion in their jobs.

Organizational hierarchy and the number of management levels often indicates the degree of centralization within an organization. Centralized organizations are those in which most of the decision making occurs by a few people at the top of the hierarchy. This typically creates a top-down management structure, in which top-level managers strongly control the direction of the workplace through their decisions and supervision. Conversely, an organization with a decentralized structure allows greater decision-making and authority at lower organizational levels. Highly decentralized companies may have units that operate nearly independently of one another. The degree of hierarchy on an organization's chart normally will help one to determine the degree of centralization or decentralization within its structure. Typically, the taller the organization, the more centralized it is; flatter organizations generally require more decentralization, because managers each have broader spans of control and cannot direct and closely supervise so many people. Additionally, as previously described, the organization's structure may indicate the degree of centralization. Functional structures tend to be more centralized than do divisional structures.

CHAIN OF COMMAND. The vertical and horizontal lines connecting the rectangles on an organizational chart indicate reporting relationships and chain of command. That is, they indicate which employees are directly responsible for the supervision of others and who has ultimate accountability for a group of employees.

AVAILABILITY OF THE ORGANIZATIONAL CHART

Many companies make their organizational chart available to their employees and to the public. The members of the public who may have an interest in a company's organizational chart include company shareholders, investors, distributors and suppliers, customers, potential job applicants, and even community members.

Employees typically have access to the organizational chart through materials provided by the organization (e.g., the employee handbook) or through a company Web site. Providing the organizational chart to employees allows them to see the structure of the organization and to better understand the entirety of the organization and how their position or work unit fits into it. Additionally, the observable chain of command can help an employee to understand to whom they are accountable. This may aid the company in diagnosing organizational problems by being able to pinpoint accountability.

Many organizations now make their organizational charts available for viewing by the general public, either online or in corporate literature for shareholders and prospective employees. By providing this information, these external stakeholders and other interested parties may gain a better understanding of the organization. The chart may give them a sense of the organization's operations, workforce, or even its strategy.

CHANGES TO THE ORGANIZATIONAL CHART

There are a number of reasons that an organizational chart might change since the chart must reflect any alterations to the organizational structure. The structure may change due to a company's growth, decline, or restructuring.

GROWTH OR DECLINE. All organizations progress through a life cycle of growth, maturity, and decline, and in each stage the organizational structure is likely to be different. In the growth stage, the company is expanding rapidly, gaining customers and market share. Growth will occur when a company is just beginning and products and services are gaining a foothold. It may also occur when an organization develops a new product or expands into new markets, perhaps in other countries. With growth, the organizational chart will change. Levels of management may be added, along with new departments.

In maturity, an organization is no longer growing at a rapid rate and is stable in its production and sales. The organization may introduce minor changes to a product or service, but there are unlikely to be major changes to its structure.

In the decline stage, the organization is losing ground in the marketplace. It may be that its products or services are becoming obsolete or that its competitors are taking over the market. In decline, the organization may shed levels of management or positions in all divisions. Additionally, it may outsource work in some areas and thus remove those departments from its structure. Or, as certain products or services are dropped from the organization, the work units needed for these products and services also may be eliminated. Thus, in the decline stage the organizational chart is likely to be streamlined or shrunken.

RESTRUCTURING. Restructuring occurs when an organization reduces its workforce by eliminating large numbers of management and line employees. Restructuring typically occurs when information technology can be used to achieve the same productivity outcomes with fewer people. With restructuring, management levels may be eliminated entirely, or entire departments may be removed. This particularly is true if outsourcing accompanies the restructuring.

SEE ALSO: Management Levels; Organizational Structure

Marcia J. Simmering

FURTHER READING:

DuBrin, Andrew J. *Essentials of Management.* 7th ed. Cincinnati, OH: Thomson/South-Western, 2004.

Jones, Gareth R., and Jennifer M. George. *Contemporary Management.* 4th ed. New York: McGraw-Hill/Irwin, 2006.

Rue, Leslie W., and Lloyd L. Byars. *Management: Skills and Application.* 10th ed. New York: McGraw-Hill/Irwin, 2003.

Williams, Chuck. *Management.* 3rd ed. Mason, OH: Thomson/South-Western, 2005.

ORGANIZATIONAL CULTURE

As people work together to accomplish goals, groups develop into organizations. As goals become more specific and longer-term, and work more specialized, organizations become both more formal and institutionalized. Organizations tend to take on a life of their own and widely held beliefs, values, and practices develop, differentiating one organization from another and often affecting the organization's success or failure. In the early 1980s, management scholars began attempting to describe these belief systems, which they referred to as organizational or corporate cultures.

Interest in organizational cultures was further created by William Ouchi's 1981 best-seller, *Theory Z: How American Business Can Meet the Japanese Challenge.* Ouchi considered organizational culture to be a key determinant of organizational effectiveness. In 1982 two other best-sellers, Terrance Deal and Allan Kennedy's *Corporate Cultures: The Rites and Rituals of Corporate Life* and Thomas Peters and Robert Waterman's *In Search of Excellence,* supported the idea that excellent companies tended to have strong cultures.

An organizational culture is defined as the shared assumptions, values, and beliefs that guide the actions of its members. Organizational culture tends to be shaped by the founders' values, the industry and business environment, the national culture, and the senior leaders' vision and behavior. There are many dimensions or characteristics of organizational culture that have been defined. For example, a research study conducted by J.A. Chatman and K.A. Jehn in 1994, identified seven primary characteristics that define an organization's culture: innovation, stability (maintaining the status quo versus growth), people orientation, outcome orientation, easygoingness, detail orientation, and team orientation.

Large organizations usually have a dominant culture that is shared by the majority of the organization and subcultures represented by groups of individuals with unique values or beliefs that may or may not be consistent with the dominant culture. Subcultures that reject the dominant culture are called countercultures. Strong organizational cultures are those where the core values of the dominant culture are strongly believed by the great majority of organizational members. A strong culture tends to increase behavior consistency and reduce turnover. However, strong cultures may be less adaptive to change, may create barriers to diversity, and may create barriers to successful acquisitions and mergers.

CULTURAL FIT BETWEEN ORGANIZATION AND MEMBERS

There are many practices within an organization that tend to keep a culture alive and measure the cultural fit between the organization and its employees. Many of the human resource practices such as selection, performance appraisal, training, and career development reinforce the organization's culture. Organizational beliefs also tend to influence the work norms, communication practices, and philosophical stances of employees. Organizations use a process called socialization to adapt new employees to the organization's culture. If employees do not adapt well, they feel increasing pressure from supervisors and from coworkers who are better acculturated. They might stay and fight, stay and become isolated, or leave the organization, voluntarily or involuntarily, and look for a different organization whose culture they fit better.

In contrast, employees who understand and share the organization's values have a better basis for making choices that match the firm's goals. Many organizations compete through innovation. When most employees understand and support the organization's expectations, less time is spent explaining, instructing, and building consensus before trying something innovative. Moreover, the error level will be lower in most cases. Employees who are well acculturated also find their work more meaningful: They are part of, and contributing to, something larger than themselves. Thus, a good cultural fit between employees and the organization contributes to employee retention, organizational productivity, and profit.

MEANS OF CONVEYING CULTURE

Organizations often convey cultural values explicitly by means of mission statements or corporate credos, or to a lesser extent through slogans, logos, or advertising campaigns. Leaders and managers also show what the organization values by what they say and do, what they reward, who they make allies, and how they motivate compliance. Other elements of culture appear tacitly in symbols and symbolic behavior: For instance, meeting protocols, greeting behavior, allocation and use of space, and status symbols are a few areas where organizational norms often develop. Culture can regulate social norms as well as work or task norms.

The new-employee orientation typically offered by organizations conveys selected cultural elements of which management is both aware and proud. Some cultural elements might be initially unpalatable, however, and some others might be hard to put into words. For instance, an orientation would rarely say outright that the culture rewards neglect of one's personal life and demands a 60-hour work week, although these expectations are not unknown in corporate life. Perceptive new employees learn about tacit cultural elements through observation and through questioning trusted employees or mentors. This is not one-time learning; employees must continue to watch for signs that the rules are changing.

These organizational rules include explicit policy statements, but also a much larger and less evident set of unwritten organizational expectations. Attentive employees figure them out sooner than others. They listen to the metaphors, images, and sayings that are common in the organization. They watch, for example, the consequences of others' mistakes to reach conclusions about appropriate behavior.

Organizations also communicate values and rules through displayed artifacts. For example, in some organizations, the CEO's office displays many symbols of wealth, such as expensive original art or antiques. In others, the CEO's workspace is very Spartan and differs little from that of other executives and higher-level managers. In the former case, a manager with other sources of income might be able to afford similar status symbols but would be unwise to display them since this might be perceived as competing with the CEO. In the latter case, display of personal wealth by people in general would probably be counter to organizational values.

Even the way a physical plant is laid out communicates cultural messages: Is it an open area where everyone can see everyone? Are there cubicles? Are there private offices? Is it easy or difficult to move and communicate between functional areas? Have ergonomics and convenience been considered or ignored? Are there adequate neutral spaces for people to meet to make decisions and solve problems? Do the break rooms and lunch rooms invite or discourage use?

SOME COMPONENTS OF CULTURE

The idea that organizations have cultures came originally from ethnography, the study and description of human social cultures. Researchers in organizational culture have borrowed some of that language. Individuals in societies took on specific "roles," such as ruler, priest, historian, or teacher. In organizations, similar roles emerge. The historian or storyteller, for instance, is usually a longtime employee who narrates inspirational stories about the company's early years

or its evolution. Embodied in the stories are many of the core values that permeate the organization. This "organizational folklore" includes oft-repeated stories about the founder, a long-term CEO, a dramatic firing, or an individual who rose through the ranks very quickly owing to some attribute highly valued by the firm. The stars of an organization are comparable to a social culture's heroes. An organization's success stories yield "role models" for the ambitious.

Organizations develop "rites and rituals" comparable to traditional activities within an ethnic culture. Whereas some organizations might emphasize award ceremonies, others might de-emphasize explicit recognition and affiliation behaviors. Still others might foster "management by walking around," whereby managers spend frequent one-on-one time away from their desks giving praise or criticism to individuals. As another example, lunch with the president might be a longstanding tradition, although the amount of actual communication will vary from organization to organization according to unwritten rules about who talks to whom.

Although all organizations have both formal and informal communication networks, organizational culture strongly affects the content, reliability, and influence of the informal network or "grapevine." When information through formal channels is scarce, the grapevine carries heavier traffic. Leaders aware of culture's importance try to find ways to tap and monitor the grapevine and sometimes use the grapevine by adding information to it.

CULTURE CHANGE

An organization's culture is composed of relatively stable characteristics that are based on deeply held values that are reinforced by many organizational practices. However, an organizational culture can be changed. Cultural changes are most likely to occur when there is a dramatic setback such as a financial crisis or when there is a turnover in top leadership. Also, younger and smaller organizations and organizations with a weak culture are more amenable to change.

Deliberate and major culture change occurs by executive fiat, by implementation of a plan, or a combination of these means. When leadership changes or when existing leadership commits to change, employees learn that the old assumptions which they were comfortable are no longer safe. After a merger or acquisition, for example, "how we do things here" will change, sometimes quickly and radically. A wise leadership team implements a planned culture-change process. The process usually consists of a series of two-way communications that elicit the prevailing assumptions, reassure employees that the changes can benefit them, introduce (sometimes gradually) the new vision, and work to gain employees' commitment and support. Leaders also must model the new culture for others and change the organization's structure and management practices to support the new culture. If the leaders skip the process or do an inadequate job, employees at all levels experience stress, confusion, and anger. When change is introduced so as not to arouse fear and resentment, however, transition may be relatively smooth.

A 1992 research study by J.P. Kotter and J.L. Heskett showed that long-term financial performance was highest for organizations with an adaptive culture. One example of when organizations must adapt their culture is when organizations become multinational. With the increase in global organizations, it has become clear that national cultures impinge on organizational cultures. Besides language differences, employees bring to the job many radically different assumptions about such aspects as the dignity of work, the proper relationship between employee and supervisor, the value of initiative, the treatment of unwelcome information, and the voicing of complaints. Organizations with international customers, and even more, those with global operations have needed to learn how to adapt to a multicultural environment. Failure to adapt jeopardizes an organization's chance of success abroad.

To summarize, organizational culture is the shared assumptions, beliefs and values held by most members of an organization. Culture is conveyed in both explicit and implicit ways. Newcomers to an organization must quickly assimilate a great deal about the culture. Veteran employees must remain aware of cultural change too, especially when the leadership changes. A strong culture that is aligned with the organization's strategic context and is adaptive to environmental changes can enhance an organization's long-term financial performance.

SEE ALSO: International Cultural Differences

Jeanette W. Gilsdorf
Revised by Dr. Fraya Wagner-Marsh

FURTHER READING:

Chatman, J.A. and K.A. Jehn. "Assessing the relationship between industry characteristics and organizational culture: How different can you be?." *Academy of Management Journal* 37 (1994): 522–553.

David, Stanley M. *Managing Corporate Culture.* Cambridge, MA: Ballinger Pub. Co., 1984.

Deal, Terrence E., and Allan A. Kennedy. *Corporate Cultures: The Rites and Rituals of Corporate Life.* Reading, MA: Addison-Wesley, 1982.

Frost, Peter J., Larry F. Moore, Meryl R. Louis, Craig C. Lundberg, and Joanne Martin, eds. *Organizational Culture.* Beverly Hills, CA: Sage, 1985.

Graf, Alan B. "Building Corporate Cultures." *Chief Executive,* March 2005, 18.

Hofstede, Geert. *Cultures and Organizations: Software of the Mind.* New York: McGraw-Hill, 1991.

Kilman, Ralph H., M.J. Saxton, and Roy Serpa, eds. *Gaining Control of the Corporate Culture.* San Francisco: Jossey-Bass, 1985.

Kotter, J.P. and J.L. Heskett. *Corporate Culture and Performance.* New York: Free Press, 1992.

LaRue, Bruce, and Robert R. Ivany. "Transform Your Culture." *Executive Excellence,* December 2004, 14–15.

LeFranc, Fred. "A Dynamic Culture Can Make a Franchise System Successful." *Franchising World,* February 2005, 75–77.

Oden, Howard W. *Managing Corporate Culture, Innovation, and Intrapreneurship.* Westport, CT: Quorum Books, 1997.

Ouchi, William G. "Theory Z: How American Business Can Meet the Japanese Challenge." Reading, MA: Addison-Wesley Publishing, 1982.

Panico, C. Richard. "Culture's Competitive Advantage." *Global Cosmetic Industry* 172, no. 12 (December 2004): 58–60.

Peters, Thomas J., and Robert H. Waterman, Jr. *In Search of Excellence: Lessons from America's Best Run Companies.* New York: Harper & Row, 1982.

Schein, Edgar H. *Organizational Culture and Leadership: A Dynamic View.* San Francisco: Jossey-Bass, 1995.

Schneider, Benjamin, ed. *Organizational Climate and Culture.* San Francisco: Jossey-Bass, 1990.

Weick, Karl E. *Sensemaking in Organizations.* Thousand Oaks, CA: Sage, 1995.

Wright, Gordon. "Realigning the Culture." *Building Design & Construction* 46, no. 1 (January 2005): 26–34.

ORGANIZATIONAL DEVELOPMENT

Organizational development is an ongoing, systematic process to implement effective change in an organization. Organizational development is known as both a field of applied behavioral science focused on understanding and managing organizational change and as a field of scientific study and inquiry. It is interdisciplinary in nature and draws on sociology, psychology, and theories of motivation, learning, and personality.

HISTORY OF ORGANIZATIONAL DEVELOPMENT

In the late 1960s organizational development was implemented in organizations via consultants, but was relatively unknown as a theory of practice and had no common definition among its practitioners. Richard Beckhard, an authority on organizational development and change management, defined organizational development as "an effort, planned, organization-wide, and managed from the top, to increase organization effectiveness and health through planned interventions in the organization's processes, using behavioral-science knowledge" (Beckhard 1969).

Throughout the 1970s and 1980s organizational development became a more established field with courses and programs being offered in business, education, and administration curricula. In the 1990s and 2000s organizational development continued to grow and evolve and its influences could be seen in theories and strategies such as total quality management (TQM), team building, job enrichment, and reengineering.

RATIONALE AND IMPLEMENTATION

Organizational development takes into consideration how the organization and its constituents or employees function together. Does the organization meet the needs of its employees? Do the employees work effectively to make the organization a success? How can the symbiotic relationship between employee satisfaction and organizational success be optimized? Organizational development places emphasis on the human factors and data inherent in the organization-employee relationship. Organizational development strategies can be used to help employees become more committed and more adaptable, which ultimately improves the organization as a whole.

The organizational development process is initiated when there is a need, gap, or dissatisfaction within the organization, either at the upper management level or within the employee body. Ideally, the process involves the organization in its entirety, with evidenced support from upper management and engagement in the effort by all members from each level of the organization.

To launch the process, consultants with experience in organizational development and change management are often utilized. These consultants may be internal to the company or external, with the cautionary understanding that internal consultants might be too entrenched in the existing company environment to effectively coordinate and enforce the action plans and solutions required for successful change.

Data analysis through task forces, interviews, and questionnaires can illuminate likely causes for disconnects throughout an organization. These gaps can then be analyzed, an action plan formed, and solutions employed. This is by no means a linear process, nor is it a brief one. Feedback from all constituents should be elicited throughout the process and used to make adjustments to the action plan as necessary. Constant monitoring during the entire implementation effort is important for its success and acceptance.

THE FUTURE OF ORGANIZATIONAL DEVELOPMENT

There are contradictory opinions about the status and future prospects of organizational development. Is it a theory whose time has come and gone? Does its basis in behavioral science, a "soft" science, make it unappealing? What are the challenges for the future?

An article by Bunker, Alban, and Lewicki proposes six areas that could revitalize the field of organizational development in the future: virtual teams, conflict resolution, work group effectiveness, social network analysis, trust, and intractable conflict. These authors suggest that focusing on these areas will help bridge the gap between research theory (i.e., academics) and practice (i.e., consultants). Getting these two groups to communicate with each other will benefit both groups and promote organizational development efforts.

In a survey conducted by Church, Waclawski, and Berr, twenty individuals involved in the study and practice of organizational development were questioned about their perspectives and predictions on the future of the field. The most in-demand services, according to those polled, are:

• executive coaching and development

• team building and team effectiveness

• facilitating strategic organizational change

• systemic integration

• diversity and multiculturalism.

They list the daily challenges in the field as the need for speed, resistance to change, interpersonal skills and awareness, and differentiating organizational development, which refers to the variety of definitions of organizational development among practitioners and how this impacts consultants, clients, and the clients' needs.

The opinions on the future direction of the field vary among its practitioners. Nevertheless, the continuing interest in and value of optimizing an organization's needs and goals with the needs, wants, and personal satisfaction of its employees indicate that organizational development will continue to be relevant to and vital for organizational reform in the future, either in its present form or through evolution into other theories and practices.

SEE ALSO: Organization Theory; Organizational Learning; Quality and Total Quality Management; Teams and Teamwork

Monica C. Turner

FURTHER READING:

Beckhard, Richard. *Organization Development: Strategies and Models.* Reading, MA: Addison-Wesley, 1969.

Brown, D.R., and D.F. Harvey. *An Experiential Approach to Organization Development.* Upper Saddle River, NJ: Pearson Prentice Hall, 2004.

Bunker, B.B., B.T. Alban, and R.J. Lewicki. "Ideas in Currency and OD Practice: Has the Well Gone Dry?" *Journal of Applied Behavioral Science* 40, no. 4 (December 2004): 403–22.

Burke, W.W. "Internal Organization Development Practitioners: Where Do They Belong?" *Journal of Applied Behavioral Science* 40, no. 4 (December 2004): 423–31.

Cummings, T.G., and C.G. Worley. *Organization Development and Change.* 8th ed. Mason, OH: Thomson/South-Western, 2005.

French, W.L., C. Bell, and R.A. Zawacki. *Organization Development and Transformation: Managing Effective Change.* 6th ed. New York: McGraw-Hill/Irwin, 2005.

Massarik, F., and M. Pei-Carpenter. *Organization Development and Consulting: Perspectives and Foundations.* San Francisco: Pfeiffer, 2002.

Shifo, R. "OD in Ten Words or Less: Adding Lightness to the Definitions of Organizational Development." *Organizational Development Journal* 22, no. 3 (Fall 2004): 74–85.

Waclawski, J., and A.H. Church. *Organization Development: A Data-driven Approach to Organizational Change.* San Francisco: Jossey-Bass, 2002.

Wheatley, M., R. Tannenbaum, P.Y. Griffin, and K. Quade. *Organization Development at Work: Conversations on the Values, Applications, and Future of OD.* San Francisco: Pfeiffer, 2003.

ORGANIZATIONAL LEARNING

The importance of learning in organizations has been recognized since the early twentieth century. Organizational learning was implicitly applied by Henry Ford in developing the Model T. This work demonstrated the existence of learning curves, whereby the time and cost needed to assemble products decreased by a constant percentage—usually 20 to 30 percent—for every doubling of output.

The phenomenon of learning curves, also called experience curves, progress curves, or learning by doing, became very popular in the 1960s and 1970s. At that time, many managers were held up to (and fired for not reaching) the 80 percent mark, meaning, with each doubling of output, costs were expected to decrease to 80 percent of the prior cost level. This overly simplistic view of learning curves resulted in disgruntlement with them in the 1980s.

Modern scholars realize that, although the learning curve is present in many organizations, there is great variation in the slope of those learning curves. The disparity in organizational learning rates clearly indicates that productivity rates are not guaranteed to improve as experience increases. Other factors are at play.

The goal of much research on organizational learning is to determine which characteristics of an organization cause it to be able to continually learn and adapt to new circumstances. Those that are able to do so are called "learning organizations" because they are uniquely capable of improving themselves by learning from experience. Peter Senge popularized the concept of the learning organization in his 1993 book *The Fifth Discipline,* and he identified the following as its core ingredients:

1. Mental models—everyone sets aside old ways of thinking.

2. Personal mastery—everyone becomes self-aware and open to others.

3. Systems thinking—everyone learns how the whole organization works.

4. Shared vision—everyone understands and agrees to a plan of action.

5. Team learning—everyone works together to accomplish the plan.

Organizations that meet Senge's criteria offer work settings in which members develop their abilities to learn and are encouraged and helped to make that learning continuously available to everyone else. These organizations have value-driven organizational cultures that emphasize information sharing, teamwork, empowerment, participation, and learning. Importantly, the leaders of learning organizations set an example for others by embracing change and communicating enthusiasm for solving problems and growing with new opportunities. Jack Welch, formerly the CEO of General Electric, communicated his enthusiasm for the learning organization when he stated in General Electric's 1999 annual report that this was the company's only competitive advantage.

The imperative for improved learning derives from the emerging global, knowledge-based economy, which focuses on collective, entrepreneurial learning to create continual innovations in products, processes, and services. It is driven by the continuing growth of new technological knowledge. This, in turn, leads to newly definable markets for this knowledge and to changing organizational and network structures, thus enabling organizations to apply new technology in both old and new markets.

SEE ALSO: Knowledge Management; Organizational Culture; Trends in Organizational Change

Michael J.C. Martin
Revised by Rebecca J. Bennett

FURTHER READING:

Argote, Linda. *Organizational Learning: Creating, Retaining & Transferring Knowledge.* The Netherlands: Kluwer Academic Publishing, 1999.

Argyris, C., and D. Schon. *Organizational Learning II.* London: Addison-Wesley, 1996.

Garvin, David A. "Building a Learning Organization." *Harvard Business Review* 71 (1993).

Kline, Peter, and Bernard Saunders. *Ten Steps to a Learning Organization.* Green River Books, 1997.

Senge, Peter M. *The Fifth Discipline: The Art and Practice of Learning Organization.* London: Century Business, 1993.

ORGANIZATIONAL STRUCTURE

Organizational structure refers to the way that an organization arranges people and jobs so that its work can be performed and its goals can be met. When a work group is very small and face-to-face communication is frequent, formal structure may be unnecessary, but in a larger organization decisions have to be made about the delegation of various tasks. Thus, procedures are established that assign responsibilities for various functions. It is these decisions that determine the organizational structure.

In an organization of any size or complexity, employees' responsibilities typically are defined by what they do, who they report to, and for managers, who reports to them. Over time these definitions are assigned to positions in the organization rather than to specific individuals. The relationships among these positions are illustrated graphically in an organizational chart (see Figures 1a and 1b). The best organizational structure for any organization depends on many factors including the work it does; its size in terms of employees, revenue, and the geographic dispersion of its facilities; and the range of its businesses (the degree to which it is diversified across markets).

There are multiple structural variations that organizations can take on, but there are a few basic principles that apply and a small number of common patterns. The following sections explain these patterns and provide the historical context from which some of them arose. The first section addresses organizational structure in the twentieth century. The second section provides additional details of traditional, vertically-arranged organizational structures. This is followed by descriptions of several alternate organizational structures including those arranged by product, function, and geographical or product markets. Next is a discussion of combination structures, or matrix organizations. The discussion concludes by addressing emerging and potential future organizational structures.

ORGANIZATIONAL STRUCTURE DURING THE TWENTIETH CENTURY

Understanding the historical context from which some of today's organizational structures have developed helps to explain why some structures are the way they are. For instance, why are the old, but still operational steel mills such as U.S. Steel and Bethlehem Steel structured using vertical hierarchies? Why are newer steel mini-mills such as Chaparral Steel structured more horizontally, capitalizing on the innovativeness of their employees? Part of the reason, as this section discusses, is that organizational structure has a certain inertia—the idea borrowed from physics and chemistry that something in motion tends to continue on that same path. Changing an organization's structure is a daunting managerial task, and the immensity of such a project is at least partly responsible for why organizational structures change infrequently.

At the beginning of the twentieth century the United States business sector was thriving. Industry was shifting from job-shop manufacturing to mass production, and thinkers like Frederick Taylor in the United States and Henri Fayol in France studied the new systems and developed principles to determine how to structure organizations for the greatest efficiency and productivity, which in their view was very much like a machine. Even before this, German sociologist and engineer Max Weber had concluded that when societies embrace capitalism, bureaucracy is the inevitable result. Yet, because his writings were not translated into English until 1949, Weber's work had little influence on American management practice until the middle of the twentieth century.

Management thought during this period was influenced by Weber's ideas of bureaucracy, where power is ascribed to positions rather than to the individuals holding those positions. It also was influenced by Taylor's scientific management, or the "one best way" to accomplish a task using scientifically-determined studies of time and motion. Also influential were Fayol's ideas of invoking unity within the chain-of-command, authority, discipline, task specialization, and other aspects of organizational power and job separation. This created the context for vertically-structured organizations characterized by distinct job classifications and top-down authority structures, or what became known as the traditional or classical organizational structure.

Job specialization, a hierarchical reporting structure through a tightly-knit chain-of-command, and the subordination of individual interests to the superordinate goals of the organization combined to result in organizations arranged by functional departments with order and discipline maintained by rules, regulations, and standard operating procedures. This classical view, or bureaucratic structure, of organizations was the dominant pattern as small organizations grew increasingly larger during the economic boom that occurred from the 1900s until the Great Depression of the 1930s. Henry Ford's plants were typical of this

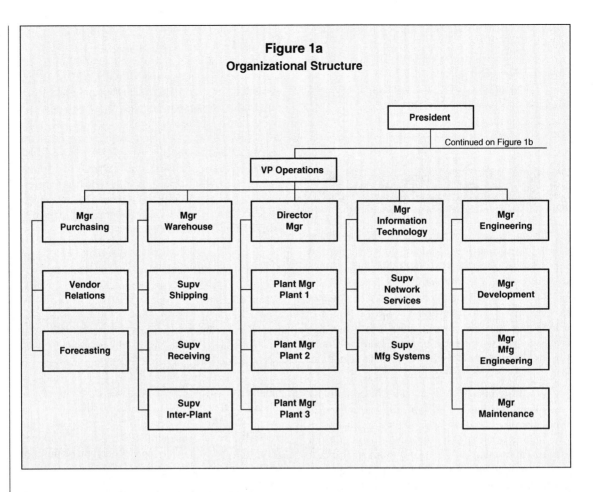

Figure 1a
Organizational Structure

President

Continued on Figure 1b

VP Operations

Mgr Purchasing | Mgr Warehouse | Director Mgr | Mgr Information Technology | Mgr Engineering

Vendor Relations | Supv Shipping | Plant Mgr Plant 1 | Supv Network Services | Mgr Development

Forecasting | Supv Receiving | Plant Mgr Plant 2 | Supv Mfg Systems | Mgr Mfg Engineering

Supv Inter-Plant | Plant Mgr Plant 3 | Mgr Maintenance

growth, as the emerging Ford Motor Company grew into the largest U.S. automaker by the 1920s.

The Great Depression temporarily stifled U.S. economic growth, but organizations that survived emerged with their vertically-oriented, bureaucratic structures intact as public attention shifted to World War II. Postwar rebuilding reignited economic growth, powering organizations that survived the Great Depression toward increasing size in terms of sales revenue, employees, and geographic dispersion. Along with increasing growth, however, came increasing complexity. Problems in U.S. business structures became apparent and new ideas began to appear. Studies of employee motivation raised questions about the traditional model. The "one best way" to do a job gradually disappeared as the dominant logic. It was replaced by concerns that traditional organizational structures might prevent, rather than help, promote creativity and innovation—both of which were necessary as the century wore on and pressures to compete globally mounted.

TRADITIONAL ORGANIZATIONAL STRUCTURE

While the previous section explained the emergence of the traditional organizational structure, this section provides additional detail regarding how this affected the practice of management. The structure of every organization is unique in some respects, but all organizational structures develop or are consciously designed to enable the organization to accomplish its work. Typically, the structure of an organization evolves as the organization grows and changes over time.

Researchers generally identify four basic decisions that managers have to make as they develop an organizational structure, although they may not be explicitly aware of these decisions. First, the organization's work must be divided into specific jobs. This is referred to as the division of labor. Second, unless the organization is very small, the jobs must be grouped in some way, which is called departmentalization. Third, the number of people and jobs that are to be grouped together must be decided. This is related to the number of people that are to be managed by one person, or the span of control—the number of employees reporting to a single manager. Fourth, the way decision-making authority is to be distributed must be determined.

In making each of these design decisions, a range of choices are possible. At one end of the spectrum, jobs are highly specialized with employees performing a narrow range of activities, while at the other end of the spectrum employees perform a variety of tasks. In

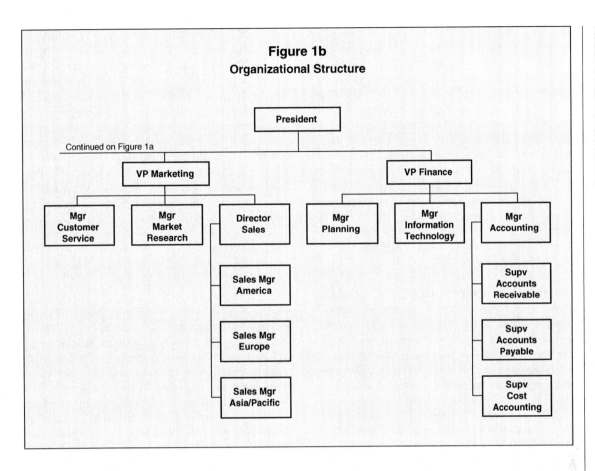

Figure 1b
Organizational Structure

Continued on Figure 1a

traditional bureaucratic structures, there is a tendency to increase task specialization as the organization grows larger. In grouping jobs into departments, the manager must decide the basis on which to group them. The most common basis, at least until the last few decades, was by function. For example, all accounting jobs in the organization can be grouped into an accounting department, all engineers can be grouped into an engineering department, and so on. The size of the groupings also can range from small to large depending on the number of people the managers supervise. The degree to which authority is distributed throughout the organization can vary as well, but traditionally structured organizations typically vest final decision-making authority by those highest in the vertically structured hierarchy. Even as pressures to include employees in decision-making increased during the 1950s and 1960s, final decisions usually were made by top management. The traditional model of organizational structure is thus characterized by high job specialization, functional departments, narrow spans of control, and centralized authority. Such a structure has been referred to as traditional, classical, bureaucratic, formal, mechanistic, or command and control. A structure formed by choices at the opposite end of the spectrum for each design decision is called unstructured, informal, or organic.

The traditional model of organizational structure is easily represented in a graphical form by an organizational chart. It is a hierarchical or pyramidal structure with a president or other executive at the top, a small number of vice presidents or senior managers under the president, and several layers of management below this, with the majority of employees at the bottom of the pyramid. The number of management layers depends largely on the size of the organization. The jobs in the traditional organizational structure usually are grouped by function into departments such as accounting, sales, human resources, and so. Figures 1a and 1b illustrate such an organization grouped by functional areas of operations, marketing and finance.

BASIS FOR DEPARTMENTALIZATION

As noted in the previous section, many organizations group jobs in various ways in different parts of the organization, but the basis that is used at the highest level plays a fundamental role in shaping the organization. There are four commonly used bases.

FUNCTIONAL DEPARTMENTALIZATION. Every organization of a given type must perform certain jobs in order do its work. For example, key functions of a manufacturing company include production, purchasing, marketing, accounting, and personnel. The functions of a hospital include surgery, psychiatry, nursing, housekeeping, and billing. Using such functions as the basis for structuring the organization may, in some instances, have the advantage of efficiency. Grouping jobs that require the same knowledge, skills, and resources allows them to be done efficiently and promotes the development of greater expertise. A disadvantage of functional groupings is that people with the same skills and knowledge may develop a narrow departmental focus and have difficulty appreciating any other view of what is important to the organization; in this case, organizational goals may be sacrificed in favor of departmental goals. In addition, coordination of work across functional boundaries can become a difficult management challenge, especially as the organization grows in size and spreads to multiple geographical locations.

GEOGRAPHIC DEPARTMENTALIZATION. Organizations that are spread over a wide area may find advantages in organizing along geographic lines so that all the activities performed in a region are managed together. In a large organization, simple physical separation makes centralized coordination more difficult. Also, important characteristics of a region may make it advantageous to promote a local focus. For example, marketing a product in Western Europe may have different requirements than marketing the same product in Southeast Asia. Companies that market products globally sometimes adopt a geographic structure. In addition, experience gained in a regional division is often excellent training for management at higher levels.

PRODUCT DEPARTMENTALIZATION. Large, diversified companies are often organized according to product. All the activities necessary to produce and market a product or group of similar products are grouped together. In such an arrangement, the top manager of the product group typically has considerable autonomy over the operation. The advantage of this type of structure is that the personnel in the group can focus on the particular needs of their product line and become experts in its development, production, and distribution. A disadvantage, at least in terms of larger organizations, is the duplication of resources. Each product group requires most of the functional areas such as finance, marketing, production, and other functions. The top leadership of the organization must decide how much redundancy it can afford.

CUSTOMER/MARKET DEPARTMENTALIZATION. An organization may find it advantageous to organize according to the types of customers it serves. For example, a distribution company that sells to consumers, government clients, large businesses, and small businesses may decide to base its primary divisions on these different markets. Its personnel can then become proficient in meeting the needs of these different customers. In the same way, an organization that provides services such as accounting or consulting may group its personnel according to these types of customers. Figure 2 depicts an organization grouped by customers and markets.

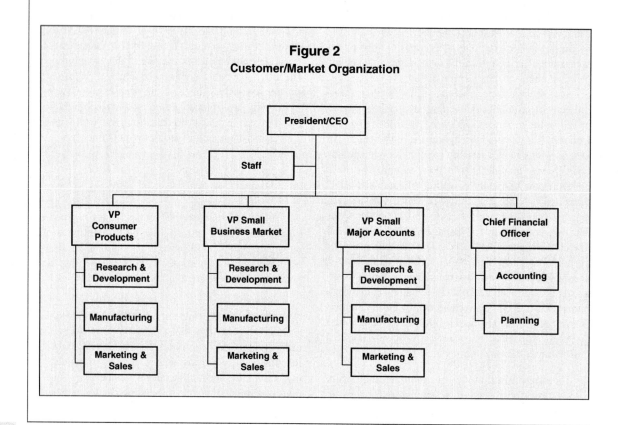

Figure 2
Customer/Market Organization

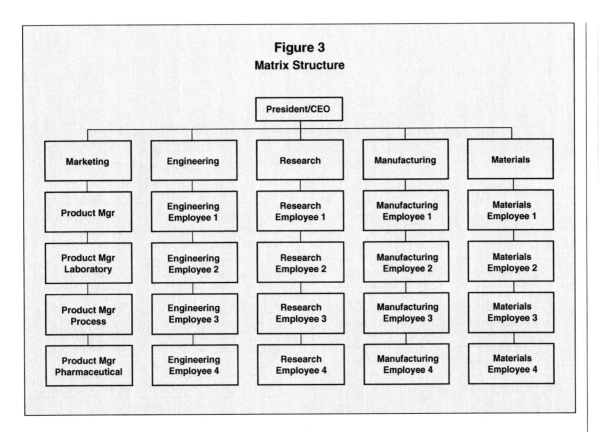

Figure 3
Matrix Structure

President/CEO

Marketing	Engineering	Research	Manufacturing	Materials
Product Mgr	Engineering Employee 1	Research Employee 1	Manufacturing Employee 1	Materials Employee 1
Product Mgr Laboratory	Engineering Employee 2	Research Employee 2	Manufacturing Employee 2	Materials Employee 2
Product Mgr Process	Engineering Employee 3	Research Employee 3	Manufacturing Employee 3	Materials Employee 3
Product Mgr Pharmaceutical	Engineering Employee 4	Research Employee 4	Manufacturing Employee 4	Materials Employee 4

MATRIX ORGANIZATIONAL STRUCTURE

Some organizations find that none of the afore-mentioned structures meet their needs. One approach that attempts to overcome the inadequacies is the matrix structure, which is the combination of two or more different structures. Functional departmentaliza-tion commonly is combined with product groups on a project basis. For example, a product group wants to develop a new addition to its line; for this project, it obtains personnel from functional departments such as research, engineering, production, and marketing. These personnel then work under the manager of the product group for the duration of the project, which can vary greatly. These personnel are responsible to two managers (as shown in Figure 3).

One advantage of a matrix structure is that it facilitates the use of highly specialized staff and equipment. Rather than duplicating functions as would be done in a simple product department struc-ture, resources are shared as needed. In some cases, highly specialized staff may divide their time among more than one project. In addition, maintaining func-tional departments promotes functional expertise, while at the same time working in project groups with experts from other functions fosters cross-fertilization of ideas.

The disadvantages of a matrix organization arise from the dual reporting structure. The organization's top management must take particular care to establish proper procedures for the development of projects and to keep communication channels clear so that poten-tial conflicts do not arise and hinder organizational functioning. In theory at least, top management is responsible for arbitrating such conflicts, but in prac-tice power struggles between the functional and prod-uct manager can prevent successful implementation of matrix structural arrangements. Besides the product/ function matrix, other bases can be related in a matrix. Large multinational corporations that use a matrix structure most commonly combine product groups with geographic units. Product managers have global responsibility for the development, manufacturing, and distribution of their own product or service line, while managers of geographic regions have responsi-bility for the success of the business in their regions.

STRATEGIC BUSINESS UNITS

As corporations become very large they often restructure as a means of revitalizing the organization. Growth of a business often is accompanied by a growth in bureaucracy, as positions are created to facilitate developing needs or opportunities. Continued changes in the organization or in the external business environ-ment may make this bureaucracy a hindrance rather than a help, not simply because of the size or complex-ity of the organization but also because of a sluggish bureaucratic way of thinking. One approach to encour-age new ways of thinking and acting is to reorganize parts of the company into largely autonomous groups,

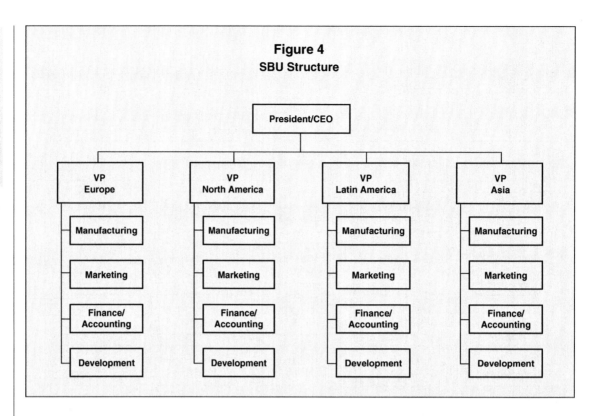

Figure 4
SBU Structure

called strategic business units (SBUs). Such units generally are set up like separate companies, with full profit and loss responsibility invested in the top management of the unit—often the president of the unit and/or a senior vice president of the larger corporation. This manager is responsible to the top management of the corporation. This arrangement can be seen as taking any of the aforementioned departmentalization schemes one step further. The SBUs might be based on product lines, geographic markets, or other differentiating factors. Figure 4 depicts SBUs organized by geographic area.

EMERGING TRENDS IN ORGANIZATIONAL STRUCTURE

Except for the matrix organization, all the structures described above focus on the vertical organization; that is, who reports to whom, who has responsibility and authority for what parts of the organization, and so on. Such vertical integration is sometimes necessary, but may be a hindrance in rapidly changing environments. A detailed organizational chart of a large corporation structured on the traditional model would show many layers of managers; decision making flows vertically up and down the layers, but mostly downward. In general terms, this is an issue of interdependence.

In any organization, the different people and functions do not operate completely independently. To a greater or lesser degree, all parts of the organization need each other. Important developments in organiza-

tional design in the last few decades of the twentieth century and the early part of the twenty-first century have been attempts to understand the nature of interdependence and improve the functioning of organizations in respect to this factor. One approach is to flatten the organization, to develop the horizontal connections and de-emphasize vertical reporting relationships. At times, this involves simply eliminating layers of middle management. For example, some Japanese companies—even very large manufacturing firms—have only four levels of management: top management, plant management, department management, and section management. Some U.S. companies also have drastically reduced the number of managers as part of a downsizing strategy; not just to reduce salary expense, but also to streamline the organization in order to improve communication and decision making.

In a virtual sense, technology is another means of flattening the organization. The use of computer networks and software designed to facilitate group work within an organization can speed communications and decision making. Even more effective is the use of intranets to make company information readily accessible throughout the organization. The rapid rise of such technology has made virtual organizations and boundarlyless organizations possible, where managers, technicians, suppliers, distributors, and customers connect digitally rather than physically.

A different perspective on the issue of interdependence can be seen by comparing the organic model of organization with the mechanistic model.

The traditional, mechanistic structure is characterized as highly complex because of its emphasis on job specialization, highly formalized emphasis on definite procedures and protocols, and centralized authority and accountability. Yet, despite the advantages of coordination that these structures present, they may hinder tasks that are interdependent. In contrast, the organic model of organization is relatively simple because it de-emphasizes job specialization, is relatively informal, and decentralizes authority. Decision-making and goal-setting processes are shared at all levels, and communication ideally flows more freely throughout the organization.

A common way that modern business organizations move toward the organic model is by the implementation of various kinds of teams. Some organizations establish self-directed work teams as the basic production group. Examples include production cells in a manufacturing firm or customer service teams in an insurance company. At other organizational levels, cross-functional teams may be established, either on an ad hoc basis (e.g., for problem solving) or on a permanent basis as the regular means of conducting the organization's work. Aid Association for Lutherans is a large insurance organization that has adopted the self-directed work team approach. Part of the impetus toward the organic model is the belief that this kind of structure is more effective for employee motivation. Various studies have suggested that steps such as expanding the scope of jobs, involving workers in problem solving and planning, and fostering open communications bring greater job satisfaction and better performance.

Saturn Corporation, a subsidiary of General Motors (GM), emphasizes horizontal organization. It was started with a "clean sheet of paper," with the intention to learn and incorporate the best in business practices in order to be a successful U.S. auto manufacturer. The organizational structure that it adopted is described as a set of nested circles, rather than a pyramid. At the center is the self-directed production cell, called a Work Unit. These teams make most, if not all, decisions that affect only team members. Several such teams make up a wider circle called a Work Unit Module. Representatives from each team form the decision circle of the module, which makes decisions affecting more than one team or other modules. A number of modules form a Business Team, of which there are three in manufacturing. Leaders from the modules form the decision circle of the Business Team. Representatives of each Business Team form the Manufacturing Action Council, which oversees manufacturing. At all levels, decision making is done on a consensus basis, at least in theory. The president of Saturn, finally, reports to GM headquarters.

THE FUTURE

Industry consolidation—creating huge global corporations through joint ventures, mergers, alliances, and other kinds of interorganizational cooperative efforts—has become increasingly important in the twenty-first century. Among organizations of all sizes, concepts such as agile manufacturing, just-in-time inventory management, and ambidextrous organizations are impacting managers' thinking about their organizational structure. Indeed, few leaders were likely to blindly implement the traditional hierarchical structure common in the first half of the century. The first half of the twentieth century was dominated by the one-size-fits-all traditional structure. The early twenty-first century has been dominated by the thinking that changing organizational structures, while still a monumental managerial challenge, can be a necessary condition for competitive success.

SEE ALSO: Line-and-Staff Organizations; Organizational Chart; Organizational Development

Howard Distelzweig
Revised by Scott B. Droege

FURTHER READING:

Brews, Peter J., and Christopher L. Tucci. "Exploring the Structural Effects of Internetworking." *Strategic Management Journal* 25, no. 5 (2004): 429–452.

Hansen, Morten T., and Nitin Nohria. "How to Build Collaborative Advantage." *MIT Sloan Management Review* 46, no. 1 (2004): 22–31.

Lumpkin, G.T., and Gregory G. Dess. "E-Business Strategies and Internet Business Models: How the Internet Adds Value." *Organizational Dynamics* 33, no. 2 (2004): 161–173.

O'Reilly, Charles A., III, and Michael L. Tushman. "The Ambidextrous Organization." *Harvard Business Review* 82, no. 4 (2004): 74–82.

Ticoll, David. "Get Self-Organized." *Harvard Business Review* 82, no. 9 (2004): 18–20.

ORGANIZING

Organizing is the managerial function of arranging people and resources to work toward a goal. The purposes of organizing include but are not limited to determining the tasks to be performed in order to achieve objectives, dividing tasks into specific jobs, grouping jobs into departments, specifying reporting and authority relationships, delegating the authority necessary for task accomplishment, and allocating and deploying resources in a coordinated fashion.

Henri Fayol first identified organizing as a function of management in his classic monograph *General and Industrial Administration*. This book was published in France in 1916 but was not translated into English until the 1920s, and it was not published in the United States until 1949. Fayol's monograph has had a profound effect on the teaching and practice of management in the years since. Early "principles of management" texts published in the 1950s generally were organized around management functions, including organizing, as are most basic management texts in the late 1990s.

Organizing plays a central role in the management process. Once plans are created the manager's task is to see that they are carried out. Given a clear mission, core values, objectives, and strategy, the role of organizing is to begin the process of implementation by clarifying jobs and working relationships. It identifies who is to do what, who is in charge of whom, and how different people and parts of the organization relate to and work with one another. All of this, of course, can be done in different ways. The strategic leadership challenge is to choose the best organizational form to fit the strategy and other situational demands.

ORGANIZING DECISIONS

When organizing, managers must make decisions about the division of labor and work specialization, departmentalization, chain of command, span of management, centralization, and formalization. Collectively, these decisions are often called organizational design.

DIVISION OF LABOR OR SPECIALIZATION. More than two centuries ago Adam Smith concluded that division of labor contributes to increased productivity and efficiency by allowing workers to specialize and become proficient at a specific task. This principle, coupled with technological advances, made possible the tremendous productivity of industrial companies during most of the twentieth century. By the 1940s most manufacturing jobs in developed nations were highly specialized, with workers performing specific, standardized, and repetitive tasks. This resulted in reduced staffing, training, and compensation costs, since highly skilled workers were often not necessary. In addition, since employees were doing the same task repetitively, they tended to become very good at it.

Despite the improvements in productivity made possible by the division of labor, managers must be aware of the negative aspects of specialization: fatigue, stress, boredom, low quality products, absenteeism, and turnover. Such problems have led to programs geared toward job enlargement and job enrichment.

DEPARTMENTALIZATION. After the work to be completed is organized into identifiable jobs through a process of dividing labor, jobs are then combined into logical sections or departments. Doing so allows for effective coordination of effort. There are many ways to departmentalize, each of which has important advantages and disadvantages. One of the most common forms is functional departmentalization, which involves grouping similar jobs into a common department, such as accounting, sales, human resources, and engineering. Another form is product departmentalization, which involves organizing around an enterprise's various product lines. Other ways of departmentalizing include organizing by customer and by geographic territory. In practice, most large companies use a hybrid form of departmentalization, which means they combine one or more of the above methods to form their organizational structure.

CHAIN OF COMMAND. The chain of command is a line of authority extending from the top to the bottom of the organizational structure. Classic principles of organizing emphasize that one must be aware of the need to define the extent of managers' responsibility and authority by specifying their place in the chain of command. Another principle of organizing related to the chain of command is called the unity of command, which states that a person should have only one superior to whom he or she must report.

SPAN OF MANAGEMENT. The span of management, often called the span of control, is the number of individuals who are directly responsible to a particular manager. A classic principle of organizing suggests that there are definite limits to the number of subordinates one manager can supervise effectively. When organizing, managers must keep these limits in mind. Wide spans of management lead to flatter organizational structures with fewer layers of management, and are thus considered more efficient. However, if spans become too wide managers may not be able to provide adequate direction to subordinates. Narrow spans of management lead to tall organizational structures with many layers of management. Although narrower spans of management allow for closer supervision of subordinates they have many drawbacks, including cost, communication problems, and difficulty in developing the initiative and autonomy of subordinates.

In general, the trend is toward wider spans of management, with an accompanying decrease in management hierarchy. Technological advances in information processing and communication have made wider spans of management more feasible.

DEGREE OF CENTRALIZATION. Another organizing decision is the degree of centralization in the organizational structure. If decision-making authority in an organization is highly centralized, then most major decisions are made at the upper levels of the structure. Conversely, if decision-making authority is decentralized, important decisions are often made at lower levels of the hierarchy. The degree of centralization that is appropriate for a given organization depends upon many factors, including the nature of the environmental conditions that face the enterprise, the characteristics and abilities of lower-level employees, and the size of the enterprise. Many organizations are favoring a greater degree of decentralization of their decision-making authority.

FORMALIZATION. The degree of formalization in an enterprise refers to the degree to which there are standardized rules and procedures governing the activities of employees. A company with a high degree of formalization is characterized by detailed job descriptions and clearly defined policies and procedures covering a wide variety of employee behaviors. Conversely, a company with a low level of formalization is characterized by non-structured jobs and fewer explicit policies and procedures.

As companies grow larger, a certain amount of formalization is inevitable. Employees require some direction in their job responsibilities and in the procedures required for consistency within the organization's production schema. When organizing, however, managers should be aware of the costs of excessive formalization, which may include stifling employee creativity and innovation as well as slowing the organization's responsiveness to critical issues and problems.

FACTORS AFFECTING ORGANIZING DECISIONS

There is no standard formula for the best way to organize an enterprise. Several factors have been shown to influence organizing decisions. Among the most important of these factors are strategy, size, environmental conditions, and technology.

STRATEGY. Managers organize in order to achieve the objectives of the enterprise for which they work. Thus, the strategy of the enterprise affects organizing decisions. Changes in strategy frequently necessitate changes in the way the enterprise is organized.

SIZE. Small enterprises tend to exhibit less formalization, centralization, and complexity in their organizational structure. Nevertheless, enterprises of the same size may be organized quite differently because of differences in strategy, environmental conditions, and technology.

ENVIRONMENTAL CONDITIONS. The key factor in the external environment that is relevant to organizing is uncertainty. Some enterprises face competitive environments that change rapidly and are quite complex, while others face relatively stable conditions. Generally, turbulent environments call for organizing decisions that lead to less formalization and centralization in the organizational structure.

TECHNOLOGY. The processes by which an enterprise transforms inputs into outputs may also affect organizing decisions. Some research suggests that organizing decisions that lead to high degrees of formalization, centralization, and work specialization are more appropriate for routine technologies and that the converse is true for non-routine technologies.

SEE ALSO: Management Functions; Organizational Chart; Organizational Structure

Tim Barnett

Revised by Rebecca J. Bennett

FURTHER READING:

Fayol, Henri. *General and Industrial Administration.* London: Sir Issac Pitman & Sons, Ltd., 1949.

Robbins, Stephen P., and Mary Coulter. *Management.* 10th ed. Upper Saddle River, NJ: Prentice Hall, 2003.

Schermerhorn, J. *Management.* 8th ed. John Wiley & Sons, 2004.

OUTSOURCING AND OFFSHORING

Outsourcing refers to a firm's practice of paying another firm to perform a function or produce a product that could be done or made in-house by the paying firm. It usually involves more information exchange, coordination, and trust than a mere vendor relationship, since a certain amount of management control is transferred to the supplier. Products and services can be outsourced domestically or to a foreign company. Outsourcing is increasingly associated with firms located overseas, where salaries are markedly lower.

Offshoring refers to business processes—as opposed to product production—being relocated to a lower-cost location, usually overseas. Related practices are near-sourcing and out-tasking. Near-sourcing is the relocation of business processes to lower-cost locations that are in close proximity to the United States, specifically in Mexico or Canada. Out-tasking means turning over a narrowly-defined segment of a business to another firm, on an annual basis or shorter, with continued direct or indirect management and decision making functions retained by the client.

Outsourcing and offshoring began in the 1960s and 70s with the transfer of physical manufacturing processes to lower-cost areas. For example, some U.S. companies shifted production to factories in Mexico that were part of a *maquiladora* system. Offshoring of physical products then moved to other low-cost locations such as China, India, the Philippines, and Eastern Europe.

Despite increased transportation, dock, duty, and broker costs and loss of supply chain speed, firms found that a 30 to 50 percent reduction in labor costs more than compensated for these increases.

The information technology revolution has made location much less important since inputs and outputs can be transmitted digitally. This has facilitated the offshoring of many white-collar functions. For example, the computer manufacturer Dell has outsourced its technical support for residential customers. When customers dial the number for technical support they are connected with technicians in India. With the costs of establishing sufficient bandwidth, compatible software connections, and video hookups decreasing rapidly, more employers may embrace the opportunity to replace employees located in the United States with lower-cost workers overseas.

Some analysts foresee a new global division of labor emerging. They propose that the West will focus on the highest levels of product creation, the part that entails artistry, creativity, and empathy with the customer, and the jobs involving turning these concepts into actual products and services will be sent overseas. However, outsourcing is also used for the process of innovation. Some American firms feel that their current spending on research and development is not yielding a sufficient return, so they are turning to "original design manufacturers" (ODMs). These ODMs completely design products that are then sold to firms such as Dell, Motorola and Philips, who tweak them to their own specifications and label them with their own brand names. Approximately 30 percent of digital cameras, 65 percent of MP3 players, and 70 percent of personal digital assistants (PDAs) are produced by ODMs.

Outsourcing and offshoring have caused considerable controversy in the United States, as the country has lost jobs to foreign nations. Forrester Research predicts that 3.3 million white-collar jobs and $136 billion in wages will shift from the United States to lower-wage countries by the year 2015. Despite possible backlash, some feel that outsourcing and offshoring are beneficial to the United States. Nineteenth-century economist David Ricardo proposed that the nation losing jobs will eventually recover its economic loss by developing worldwide markets for its products and services. Outsourcing can also enable firms to spend more time and resources on their core competencies, leading to more innovative goods and services to be sold globally.

SEE ALSO: International Business; International Management; International Management; Technology Management; Technology Transfer

R. Anthony Inman

FURTHER READING:

"40 Risks Purchasing Pros Must Address for Outsourcing Success." *Supplier Selection & Management Report,* March 2005, 406.

Economic Policy Institute. "EPI Issue Guide: Offshoring." Available from <http://www.epinet.org/>.

Engardio, Pete, and Bruce Einhorn. "Outsourcing Innovation." *Business Week* Online, 21 March 2005. Available from <http://www.businessweek.com/magazine/content/5_12/b39225601.htm>.

LaLonde, Bud. "From Outsourcing to 'Offshoring'-Part 1." *Supply Chain Management Review* 8, no. 2 (2004): 6–7.

Michel, Roberto. "Sorting Out Offshoring Versus Outsourcing." *MSI* 22, no. 1 (2004): 2.

P

PARTICIPATIVE MANAGEMENT

Participative (or participatory) management, otherwise known as employee involvement or participative decision making, encourages the involvement of stakeholders at all levels of an organization in the analysis of problems, development of strategies, and implementation of solutions. Employees are invited to share in the decision-making process of the firm by participating in activities such as setting goals, determining work schedules, and making suggestions. Other forms of participative management include increasing the responsibility of employees (job enrichment); forming self-managed teams, quality circles, or quality-of-work-life committees; and soliciting survey feedback. Participative management, however, involves more than allowing employees to take part in making decisions. It also involves management treating the ideas and suggestions of employees with consideration and respect. The most extensive form of participative management is direct employee ownership of a company.

Four processes influence participation. These processes create employee involvement as they are pushed down to the lowest levels in an organization. The farther down these processes move, the higher the level of involvement by employees. The four processes include:

1. Information sharing, which is concerned with keeping employees informed about the economic status of the company.

2. Training, which involves raising the skill levels of employees and offering development opportunities that allow them to apply new skills to make effective decisions regarding the organization as a whole.

3. Employee decision making, which can take many forms, from determining work schedules to deciding on budgets or processes.

4. Rewards, which should be tied to suggestions and ideas as well as performance.

BENEFITS OF PARTICIPATIVE MANAGEMENT

A participative management style offers various benefits at all levels of the organization. By creating a sense of ownership in the company, participative management instills a sense of pride and motivates employees to increase productivity in order to achieve their goals. Employees who participate in the decisions of the company feel like they are a part of a team with a common goal, and find their sense of self-esteem and creative fulfillment heightened.

Managers who use a participative style find that employees are more receptive to change than in situations in which they have no voice. Changes are implemented more effectively when employees have input and make contributions to decisions. Participation keeps employees informed of upcoming events so they will be aware of potential changes. The organization can then place itself in a proactive mode instead of a reactive one, as managers are able to quickly identify areas of concern and turn to employees for solutions.

Participation helps employees gain a wider view of the organization. Through training, development opportunities, and information sharing, employees can acquire the conceptual skills needed to become effective managers or top executives. It also increases the commitment of employees to the organization and the decisions they make.

Creativity and innovation are two important benefits of participative management. By allowing a diverse group of employees to have input into decisions, the organization benefits from the synergy that comes from a wider choice of options. When all employees, instead of just managers or executives, are given the opportunity to participate, the chances are increased that a valid and unique idea will be suggested.

REQUIREMENTS OF PARTICIPATIVE MANAGEMENT

A common misconception by managers is that participative management involves simply asking employees to participate or make suggestions. Effective programs involve more than just a suggestion box. In order for participative management to work, several issues must be resolved and several requirements must be met. First, managers must be willing to relinquish some control to their workers; managers must feel secure in their position in order for participation to be successful. Often managers do not realize that employees' respect for them will increase instead of decrease when they implement a participative management style.

The success of participative management depends on careful planning and a slow, phased approach. Changing employees' ideas about management takes time, as does any successful attempt at a total cultural change from a democratic or autocratic style of management to a participative style. Long-term employees may resist changes, not believing they will last. In order for participation to be effective, managers must be genuine and honest in implementing the program. Many employees will need to consistently see proof that their ideas will be accepted or at least seriously considered. The employees must be able to trust their managers and feel they are respected.

Successful participation requires managers to approach employee involvement with an open mind. They must be open to new ideas and alternatives in order for participative management to work. It is important to remember that although the manager may not agree with every idea or suggestion an employee makes, how those ideas are received is critical to the success of participative management.

Employees must also be willing to participate and share their ideas. Participative management does not work with employees who are passive or simply do not care. Many times employees do not have the skills or information necessary to make good suggestions or decisions. In this case it is important to provide them with information or training so they can make informed choices. Encouragement should be offered in order to accustom employees to the participative approach. One way to help employees engage in the decision-making process is by knowing their individual strengths and capitalizing on them. By guiding employees toward areas in which they are knowledgeable, a manager can help to ensure their success.

Before expecting employees to make valuable contributions, managers should provide them with the criteria that their input must meet. This will aid in discarding ideas or suggestions that cannot be implemented, are not feasible, or are too expensive. Managers should also give employees time to think about ideas or alternative decisions. Employees often do not do their most creative thinking on the spot.

Another important element for implementing a successful participative management style is the visible integration of employees' suggestions into the final decision or implementation. Employees need to know that they have made a contribution. Offering employees a choice in the final decision is important because it increases their commitment, motivation, and job satisfaction. Sometimes even just presenting several alternatives and allowing employees to choose from them is as effective as if they thought of the alternatives themselves. If the employees' first choice is not feasible, management might ask for an alternative rather than rejecting the employee input. When an idea or decision is not acceptable, managers should provide an explanation. If management repeatedly strikes down employee ideas without implementing them, employees will begin to distrust management, thus halting participation. The key is to build employee confidence so their ideas and decisions become more creative and sound.

CONCERNS

Participative management is not a magic cure for all that ails an organization. Managers should carefully weigh the pros and the cons before implementing this style of management. Managers must realize that changes will not take effect overnight and will require consistency and patience before employees will begin to see that management is serious about employee involvement. Participative management is probably the most difficult style of management to practice. It is challenging not only for managers but for employees as well.

While it is important that management allows employees to participate in decision making and encourages involvement in the organization's direction, managers must be cognizant of the potential for employees to spend more time formulating suggestions and less time completing their work. Upper-level management will not support a participative management program if they believe employees are not meeting their daily or weekly goals. Some suggestions for overcoming this potential problem are to set aside a particular time each week for workers to meet with management in order to share their ideas, or to allow them to work on their ideas during less busy times of the day or week. Another idea that works for some managers is to allow employees to set up individual appointments to discuss ideas or suggestions.

Managers should remember that participative management is not always the appropriate way to handle a given situation. Employees often respect a manager that uses his or her authority and makes decisions when it is necessary. There are times when, as a manager, it is important to be in charge, make a decision, and then accept the responsibility for the choices made. For example, participative management is probably not appropriate when disciplinary action is needed.

When managers look upon their own jobs as a privilege instead of as a responsibility, they will fail at making participative management work. They will be less willing to turn over some of the decision-making responsibility to subordinates. Another reason that participative management fails is that managers do not realize it is not the same as delegating or simply shifting responsibility. Participation alone has no value; it is only an effective tool if it is used to solve problems and meet goals. Some managers believe that inviting employees to join in meetings and form committees will create a successful participative management program. However, these measures are only successful when employees' ideas are accepted by management and implemented.

The larger the organization, the more difficult it becomes to institute a participative management style. Large organizations have more layers and levels, which complicate effective communication and make it difficult to register the opinions and suggestions of a diverse group of employees and managers. Critics argue that unions are often more effective than participative management in responding to employee needs because union efforts can cut through bureaucratic organizations more quickly.

Participative management programs can be threatened by office politics. Due to hidden agendas and peer pressure, employees may keep their opinions to themselves and refuse to tell a manager if they feel an idea will not work. Managers also play a part in politics when they implement participative management programs to impress their own bosses but have no intention of seeing them through.

Many companies have experienced the positive effects of participative management. Employees are more committed and experience more job satisfaction when they are allowed to participate in decision making. Organizations have reported that productivity improved significantly when managers used a participative style. Participative management is not an easy management style to implement. It presents various challenges and does not succeed overnight. Managers will be more successful if they remember that it will take time and careful planning before they will see

results. Starting with small projects that encourage and reward participation is one way to get employees to believe that management is sincere and trustworthy.

SEE ALSO: Empowerment; Human Resource Management; Management Styles; Motivation and Motivation Theory; Synergy; Teams and Teamwork

Amy McMillan
Revised by Debbie D. DuFrene

FURTHER READING:

Coleman, P.T. "Implicit Theories of Organizational Power and Priming Effects on Managerial Power-Sharing Decisions: An Experimental Study." *Journal of Applied Social Psychology* 34, no. 2 (2004): 297–321.

Coye, R.W., and J.A. Belohlav. "An Exploratory Analysis of Employee Participation." *Group and Organization Management* 20, no. 1 (1995): 4–17.

Greenfield, W.M. "Decision Making and Employee Engagement." *Employment Relations Today* 31, no. 2 (2004): 13–24.

Kaner, S., and L. Lind. *Facilitator's Guide to Participatory Decision-making.* Gabriola Island, BC, Canada: New Society Publishers, 1996.

Keef, L. "Generating Quality Interaction." *Occupational Health & Safety* 73, no. 5 (2004): 30–31.

McCoy, T.J. *Creating an Open Book Organization: Where Employees Think and Act Like Business Partners.* New York: Amacom, 1996.

Robbins, S.P. *Essentials of Organizational Behavior.* 8th ed. Upper Saddle River, NJ: Prentice Hall, 2005.

Sumukadas, N., and R. Sawhney. "Workforce Agility through Employee Involvement." *IIE Transactions* 36, no. 10 (2004): 1011–1021.

Vanderburg, D. "The Story of Semco: The Company that Humanized Work." *Bulletin of Science, Technology & Society* 24, no. 5 (2004): 430–34.

Weiss, W.H. "Improving Employee Performance: Major Supervisory Responsibility." *Supervision,* October 1998, 6–8.

PATENTS AND TRADEMARKS

Trademarks and patents, along with copyrights, constitute the major forms of legal protection for what is commonly referred to as intellectual property. Although the rights in these three kinds of intellectual property protection are somewhat similar, trademarks, patents, and copyrights differ in what they protect. Patents protect inventions, while trademarks protect words, phrases, symbols, and designs. Copyrights protect original artistic, musical, and literary works, including software.

PATENTS

A patent is a grant of a property right by the United States government, through the Patent and Trademark Office, to the inventor of an invention. The term of this property right is twenty years from the date the patent is granted, as long as the holder of the patent pays maintenance fees. A patent is not a grant of a right to make, manufacture, use, or sell the invention; rather it secures the right to exclude others from making, manufacturing, using, or selling the invention for the duration of the patent.

A patented invention is no guarantee of future commercial success. Statistically, although millions of patents have been granted, the number of successful inventions is minuscule. One avenue of commercialization open to a patentee is licensing his or her patent to a company, or a number of companies, provided he or she is able to locate a firm that is willing to risk investing in a wholly untried product or process. Upon licensing the patent, however, the patent holder cannot demand that royalties from the product continue beyond the stipulated 20-year patent period, nor can the patentee set the product's price or determine its use.

CREATION OF PATENT RIGHTS

The power to grant rights in patents arises from Article I, section 8 of the United States Constitution, which provides that "Congress shall have power . . . to promote the progress of science and useful arts, by securing for limited times to authors and inventors the exclusive right to their respective writings and discoveries." The first patent law was passed in 1790, and the current law governing patents was enacted in 1952 and became effective 1 January 1953. Since the first statute, over five million patents have been granted. The current statute sets forth the subject matters for which patents may be granted and the conditions under which a patent will be issued. It also established the Patent and Trademark Office.

Under the law, anyone who "invents or discovers any new and useful process, machine, manufacture or composition of matter, or any new and useful improvements thereof, may obtain a patent." Courts have interpreted this language to include nearly anything that could be fabricated, although they have not allowed methods of doing business or printed matter, such as books, to be patented. An invention must meet the test of being new under the standards in the law before a patent will be granted. The subject matter of an invention must be sufficiently different from what has been described in a printed publication of some sort anywhere in the world, or sold in this country, before the date of the application for the patent. In addition, the invention must go beyond what would seem a commonsense or obvious advancement, even to a practitioner or expert in the field. Finally, an invention must be determined "useful" before a patent will issue; this requirement, however, is interpreted very broadly.

Only the inventor may apply for a patent, with two exceptions: (1) if the inventor has died before applying for a patent, the inventor's estate may do so, and (2) if the inventor is insane, the inventor's guardian may apply for the patent.

An inventor applies for a patent by sending to the Commissioner of Patents and Trademarks, at the Patent and Trademark Office, a written specification, which is a description of the invention and of the process in which the invention is made and used. The specification must contain one or more claims about the subject matter that the applicant believes constitute an invention. The specification must be accompanied by a sworn oath or declaration by the inventor that he or she is the original and first inventor of the subject matter of the application. The application must also include drawings, where necessary, and the appropriate filing fee, which the patent statute and rules have established.

THE PATENT AND TRADEMARK OFFICE

The Patent and Trademark Office carries out the patent laws by examining the applications to determine if the inventor is entitled to a patent. The office publishes the specifications and drawings of all patents on the day they are issued. It records assignments of any patents to entities other than the inventors. It maintains a search room for the public to look at issued patents and the office's records.

TRADEMARKS

A trademark is a word, name, phrase, symbol, or design, or a combination of these elements, that identifies and distinguishes the source of goods or services. The term also encompasses service marks. Service marks are the same as trademarks except that they identify and distinguish the source of a service rather than a product. Trademark rights are used to prevent others from making, promoting, or selling goods or services which have a name, symbol, or design that is confusingly similar to that of the trademark. It does not, however, prevent others from making or selling the same goods or services, as long as it is under a different, non confusing mark.

CREATION OF TRADEMARK RIGHTS

There are two distinct types of rights in a trademark or service mark: the right to use the mark and the right to register the mark. These rights arise either from using the mark in actual commerce or from filing an application for registration of the mark with the Patent and Trademark Office.

The registration of marks is controlled under the Trademark Act of 1946; the Trademark Rules, 37 C.F.R. Part 2; and the *Trademark Manual of Examining Procedure.* The act covers not only trademarks and service marks, but also certification marks, collective trademarks, and collective membership marks.

The first party who either uses a mark in the course of commerce or business or files an application for registration with the Patent and Trademark Office usually has the right to register that mark. A party can use a mark, or establish rights in it, without filing an application for registration. The registration, however, creates a presumption that the party who has registered the mark is the owner of the mark for the goods and services set forth in the registration application, and therefore has the right to use the mark anywhere in the country. This presumption can become important when two parties unintentionally begin using similar marks and become involved in a lawsuit over who has the sole right to use the mark. The Patent and Trademark Office does not determine this, rather it is the decision of a court, which has the power to issue an injunction to stop a party from using a mark and to award damages for a party's improper use of another's mark.

Similarly, the owner of a mark may use the trademark (™) or service mark (SM) designation with the mark to make it clear that the owner is claiming rights in the product or service so designated. The ™ and SM designation may be used without the owner having registered the mark with the Patent and Trademark Office. If it is registered, however, the owner may use the registration symbol (®) with the mark.

Rights embodied in a trademark, unlike those of a copyright or a patent, can last for an indefinite period if the owner of the mark continuously uses the mark for its products or services. Federal registrations last for ten years, but between the fifth and sixth year after the date of the initial registration, the person who registered the mark must file an affidavit with information about the mark and ownership. If the registrant does not file this affidavit, the registration is cancelled. After the initial registration period, the mark can be renewed for successive ten-year terms. Registration of a mark with the Patent and Trademark Office provides protection from others using the mark in the United States and its territories, but does not extend to its use in other countries.

PATENTS AND TRADEMARKS IN THE INTERNET AGE

The growth of Internet technology has affected patent and trademark protection in a number of different ways. For instance, the Internet has made it significantly easier for individuals and companies to conduct searches of patent and trademark databases, whether they are looking to patent an invention or license someone else's invention. The global reach of the Internet has also spurred efforts to harmonize international patent and trademark protection, which may eventually offer firms greater protection in worldwide markets. In other ways, however, the Internet has made it more difficult for owners to protect their intellectual property rights. The widespread availability of intellectual property in digital form has led to illegal copying of technology, software, music, and other protected materials.

In the early 2000s, a growing number of technology companies began launching intellectual property licensing programs in order to turn their accumulated patent bases into revenue. These firms conducted inventories of their patents and identified technologies that were outside the core business yet still offered some potential for development. They then sought to license these technologies to other firms. IP licensing has proven quite lucrative for a number of large technology firms. IBM, for example, earns over one billion dollars per year from its IP licensing program.

SEE ALSO: Entrepreneurship; Intellectual Property Rights; Licensing and Licensing Agreements

Cindy Rhodes Rhode
Revised by Laurie Hillstrom

FURTHER READING:

Ambrogi, Robert J. "The Top Internet Sites for Patents, Trademarks." *Palm Beach Daily Business Review,* 24 March 2004.

Brown, Marc E. "New Kinds of Protection for Intellectual Property." *Electronic Business,* 1 April 2003.

Geffken, Carl. "Protecting Your Intellectual Property: Understanding Your Rights Regarding Patents, Copyrights, and Trademarks Is Vital in Protecting Your Company's Offerings across the Globe." *Global Cosmetic Industry* (January 2004).

O'Haver, R. Russ. "Management Intangibles: Capitalizing on Your IP Assets." *Journal of Internet Law* (December 2003).

U.S. Patent and Trademark Office. "General Information Concerning Patents." January 2005. Available from <http://www.uspto.gov/web/offices/pac/doc/general/index.html>.

U.S. Small Business Administration. "Protecting Your Ideas." Available from <http://www.sba.gov/starting_business/startup/ideas.html>.

PERFORMANCE APPRAISALS

SEE: Employee Evaluation and Performance Appraisals

PERFORMANCE MEASUREMENT

Improvement in individual, group, or organizational performance cannot occur unless there is some way of getting performance feedback. Feedback is having the outcomes of work communicated to the employee, work group, or company. For an individual employee, performance measures create a link between their own behavior and the organization's goals. For the organization or its work unit's performance measurement is the link between decisions and organizational goals.

It has been said that before you can improve something, you have to be able to measure it, which implies that what you want to improve can somehow be quantified. Additionally, it has also been said that improvement in performance can result just from measuring it. Whether or not this is true, measurement is the first step in improvement. But while measuring is the process of quantification, its effect is to stimulate positive action. Managers should be aware that almost all measures have negative consequences if they are used incorrectly or in the wrong situation. Managers have to study the environmental conditions and analyze these potential negative consequences before adopting performance measures.

TYPES OF PERFORMANCE MEASURES

Performance measures can be grouped into two basic types: those that relate to results (outputs or outcomes such as competitiveness or financial performance) and those that focus on the determinants of the results (inputs such as quality, flexibility, resource utilization, and innovation). This suggests that performance measurement frameworks can be built around the concepts of results and determinants.

Measures of performance of a business usually embrace five fundamental, but interlinking areas:

1. Money, usually measured as profit
2. Output/input relationships or productivity
3. Customer emphasis such as quality
4. Innovation and adaptation to change
5. Human resources

Within the operations area, standard individual performance measures could be productivity measures, quality measures, inventory measures, lead-time measures, preventive maintenance, performance to schedule, and utilization. Specific measures could include:

1. Cost of quality: measured as budgeted versus actual.

2. Variances: measured as standard absorbed cost versus actual expenses.

3. Period expenses: measured as budgeted versus actual expenses.

4. Safety: measured on some common scale such as number of hours without an accident.

5. Profit contribution: measured in dollars or some common scale.

6. Inventory turnover: measured as actual versus budgeted turnover.

While financial measures of performance are often used to gauge organizational performance, some firms have experienced negative consequences from relying solely on these measures. Traditional financial measures are better at measuring the consequences of yesterday's actions than at projecting tomorrow's performance. Therefore, it is better that managers not rely on one set of measures to provide a clear performance target. Many firms still rely on measures of cost and efficiency, when at times such indicators as time, quality, and service would be more appropriate measures. To be effective, performance yardsticks should continuously evolve in order to properly assess performance and focus resources on continuous improvement and motivating personnel. In order to incorporate various types of performance measures some firm's develop performance measurement frameworks. These frameworks appear in the literature and vary from Kaplan and Norton's balanced scorecard to Fitzgerald's framework of results and determinants.

Kaplan and Norton's balanced scorecard approach operates from the perspective that more than financial data is needed to measure performance and that nonfinancial data should be included to adequately assess performance. They suggest that any performance measurement framework should allow managers to ask the following questions:

- How do we look to our shareholders? (financial perspective)
- What must we excel at? (internal business perspective)
- How do our customers see us? (customer perspective)
- How can we continue to improve and create value? (innovation and learning perspective)

However, the balanced scorecard is flawed as it does not allow for one of the most important questions of all:

- What are our competitors doing? (the competitor perspective)

Keegan proposed a similar, but lesser known, performance measurement framework titled the "performance matrix." The performance matrix is more flexible, as it is able to integrate different dimensions of performance, and employs generic terms such as internal, external, cost, and noncost.

DESIGNING THE PERFORMANCE MEASUREMENT SYSTEM

A number of suggestions have been offered by various experts on the subject of designing performance measurement systems. Below is a list of suggestions derived from a number of these experts. Some of these apply to all measures and some apply to a limited number of a firm's measures. A firm's performance measures should:

- Be simple and easy to use.

- Have a clear purpose.

- Provide fast feedback.

- Cover all the appropriate elements (internal, external, financial and nonfinancial).

- Relate to performance improvement, not just monitoring.

- Reinforce the firm's strategy.

- Relate to both long-term and short-term objectives of the organization.

- Match the firm's organization culture.

- Not conflict with one another.

- Be integrated both horizontally and vertically in the corporate structure.

- Be consistent with the firm's existing recognition and reward system.

- Focus on what is important to customers.

- Focus on what the competition is doing.

- Lead to identification and elimination of waste.

- Help accelerate organizational learning.

- Help build a consensus for change when customer expectations shift or strategies and priorities call for the organization to behave differently.

- Evaluate groups not individuals for performance to schedule.

- Establish specific numeric standards for most goals.

- Be available for constant review.

Other recommendations for organizations that are developing performance measures include:

1. Data collection and methods of calculating the performance measure must be clearly defined.

2. Objective performance criteria are preferable to subjective ones.

3. Recognize that measures may vary between locations; avoid a "one size fits all" mentality.

Wisner and Fawcett provide a nine-step process for developing a performance measurement system:

1. Clearly define the firm's mission statement.

2. Identify the firm's strategic objectives using the mission statement as a guide (profitability, market share, quality, cost, flexibility, dependability, and innovation).

3. Develop an understanding of each functional area's role in achieving the various strategic objectives.

4. For each functional area, develop global performance measures capable of defining the firm's overall competitive position to top management.

5. Communicate strategic objectives and performance goals to lower levels in the organization. Establish more specific performance criteria at each level.

6. Assure consistency with strategic objectives among the performance criteria used at each level.

7. Assure the compatibility of performance measures used in all functional areas.

8. Use the performance measurement system to identify competition, locate problem areas, assist the firm in updating strategic objectives and making tactical decisions to achieve these objectives, and supply feedback after the decisions are implemented.

9. Periodically reevaluate the appropriateness of the established performance measurement system in view of the current competitive environment.

Finally, it is important that the performance measurement systems used by managers be continually reviewed and revised as the environment and economy changes. Failure to make the necessary modifications can inhibit the ability of the organization to be an effective and efficient global competitor.

SEE ALSO: Balanced Scorecard; Employee Evaluation and Performance Appraisals; Human Resource Management; Quality and Total Quality Management

R. Anthony Inman
Revised by Marcia Simmering

FURTHER READING:

Boyd, Lynn H., and James F. Cox, III. "A Cause-and-Effect Approach to Analyzing Performance Measures." *Production and Inventory Management Journal* 38, no. 3 (1997): 25–32.

Denton, D. Keith. "Effective Measurement Involves Asking the Right Questions." *Production and Inventory Management Journal* (1995): 65–67.

Gunasekaran, A., H. James Williams, and Ronald E. McGaughey. "Performance Measurement and Costing System in New Enterprise." *Technovation* 25, no. 5 (May 2005): 523.

Hinton, Matthew, and David Barnes. "Towards a Framework for Evaluating the Business Process Performance of E-Business Investments." *International Journal of Business Performance Management* 7, no. 1 (2005): 87.

Kaplan, R.S., and D.P. Norton. "The Balanced Scorecard-Measures That Drive Performance." *Harvard Business Review,* January-February 1992, 71–79.

Keegan, D.P., R.G. Eiler, and C.R. Jones. "Are Your Performance Measures Obsolete?" *Management Accounting,* June 1989, 38–43.

Robson, Ian. "Implementing a Performance Measurement System Capable of Creating a Culture of High Performance." *International Journal of Productivity and Performance Management* 54, no. 1-2 (2005): 137–145.

Tangen, Stefan. "Performance Measurement: From Philosophy to Practice." *International Journal of Productivity and Performance Management* 53, no. 8 (2004): 726.

Vokurka, Robert, and Gene Fliedner. "Measuring Operating Performance: A Specific Case Study." *Production and Inventory Management Journal* 36, no. 1 (1995): 38–43.

Wisner, J.D., and S.E. Fawcett. "Link Firm Strategy to Operating Decisions through Performance Measurement." *Production and Inventory Management Journal* 32, no. 3 (1991): 5–11.

PERSONALITY AND PERSONALITY TESTS

Personality is a set of enduring traits and characteristics that relate to a person's emotions, motivations, interpersonal interactions, and attitudes. Personality is different from ability. Whereas personality may dictate attitudes towards situations or people, attitudes are transient and personality is enduring.

Personality is meaningful to management, because employees' personalities may dictate how well they perform their jobs. Personality may indicate how hard a person will work, how organized they are, how well they will interact with others, and how creative they are.

In recent years, more organizations have been using self-reporting personality tests to identify personality traits as part of their hiring or management development processes. Employers recognize that experience, education, and intelligence may not be the only indicators of who the best hire might be. Additionally, understanding one's own personality characteristics may improve one's ability to develop as an employee and manager. Therefore, it is important to understand the different facets of personality and the ways in which they can be measured.

Research into the human personality has been conducted for many decades, and much of this work has focused on defining personality and understanding how many dimensions of personality there are. One primary area of agreement about personality is that it is a trait. That is, personality is enduring and unlikely to change substantially in one's adult life.

Because personality is a trait, this also means that a person is likely to behave similarly in a variety of situations. This does not mean that a person cannot or will not adapt to a change in circumstances (e.g., behavior at work versus behavior in social situations), but that, on average, a person demonstrates similar personality across all situations and may behave differently from those with dissimilar personality characteristics.

A major debate in the area of personality research is where personality originates, which is often described as the "nature vs. nurture" argument. Researchers who believe that individuals are born with a personality that is determined by genetics and remains unchanged regardless of environment, subscribe to the "nature" theory of the origin of personality. The "nurture" perspective is that personality is not determined by genetics, but rather by a host of environmental forces and personal experiences, such as geography, socio-economic status, and parental upbringing. Most scholars now agree that personality is determined by a combination of both genetics and environment, and that neither is solely responsible for personality.

There are a number of different ways in which personality has been categorized, and different opinions exist about the number of dimensions of personality. Early tests of personality were developed to diagnose mental illness, and while some of these tests were used in employment settings, their acceptability and applicability were questionable. However, there are now tests specifically for use in normal adult populations, each of which is based on different conceptions of the dimensionality of personality.

MINNESOTA MULTIPHASIC PERSONALITY INVENTORY AND CALIFORNIA PSYCHOLOGICAL INVENTORY

Some of the earlier tests used to assess the personality of job applicants and employees were the Minnesota Multiphasic Personality Inventory (MMPI) and the California Psychological Inventory (CPI), which is based on the MMPI.

The MMPI was developed for psychological clinical profiling and includes ten clinical scales. While some of these scales may be applicable to predicting job performance in a selection tool, others are not. Additionally, the items used in the MMPI may be off-putting to job applicants. However, before the availability of personality tests commercially available for use in a business setting, organizations often used the MMPI to assess the personality characteristics of applicants and employees.

Using the psychological basis of the MMPI, the CPI was created to assess the personality of normal adult populations. It assesses seventeen different dimensions of performance, including dominance, responsibility, empathy, and sociability. The CPI is much more appropriate for business settings than the MMPI, but was not created for use in business hiring.

FIVE-FACTOR MODEL

A different conception of personality is captured in the Sixteen Personality Factor Questionnaire, also called the 16 PF. It yields scores of sixteen different personality traits, including dominance, vigilance, and emotional stability. These sixteen factors can be combined to express five "global factors" of personality. These five global factors are often called the Big Five or the Five-Factor Model.

Most researchers agree that while more than five dimensions of personality are present in human beings, nearly all of them can be subsumed within five: emotional stability, conscientiousness, agreeableness, extraversion, and openness to experience. They are summarized in Table 1.

EMOTIONAL STABILITY. Emotional stability (also called neuroticism, when scored oppositely) involves a person's ability to remain stable and balanced. A person who is high in emotional stability is even-tempered, calm, and somewhat resistant to stress. A person who is low in emotional stability tends to be moody, depressed, and very susceptible to stress. In most professions, a person who is high in emotional stability is preferred. Employees with low emotional stability are more likely to be distracted from work by stress, deadlines, or situations in their personal lives, whereas those with high levels of this trait are more able to control their emotions and feelings at work.

CONSCIENTIOUSNESS. Conscientiousness is a person's ability to be dependable, organized, punctual, and to persist in the face of setbacks. Research indicates that conscientiousness is the personality characteristic that is most related to job performance across a variety of jobs. Thus, in nearly every situation, a person who is high in conscientiousness will be better suited to perform a job. Individuals who are low in conscientiousness do not give much attention to detail, are likely to overlook deadlines, or may lose important documents. Additionally, individuals low in conscientiousness are more likely to give up when faced with challenges or difficulties in their work, whereas employees with high conscientiousness will continue to persist.

AGREEABLENESS. Agreeableness, when high, indicates that a person is warm, friendly, and tactful. Low agreeableness is demonstrated when employees are cold, abrasive, and unfriendly. Preference on whether an employee high in agreeableness or low in agreeableness is somewhat dependent on the type of job.

In general, a person with high agreeableness can be easier to work with, because they tend to be easier to

---

Table 1

Personality Factor	Characteristics of Individuals High in Factor	Characteristics of People Low in Factor
Emotional Stability	• Calm • Resistant to stress • Secure • Stable	• Anxious • Depressed • Insecure • Susceptible to stress
Conscientiousness	• Dependable • Organized • Persevering • Punctual	• Disorganized • Easily discouraged • Unpredictable • Unreliable
Agreeableness	• Amiable • Cooperative • Flexible • Trusting	• Aloof • Contrary • Suspicious • Unfriendly
Extraversion	• Active • Assertive • Excitable • Sociable	• Apprehensive • Dull • Shy • Timid
Openness to Experience	• Creative • Curious • Insightful • Intellectual	• Bored • Intolerant • Routine-oriented • Uninterested

---

talk to and interact with in a group setting. And, in some jobs, being highly agreeable is an advantage, such as in sales, or in other jobs that require patient and friendly interactions with people. However, there are some jobs in which being too warm and friendly can be a detriment, such as a collections agent; and in these jobs, being low in agreeableness could be advantageous.

EXTRAVERSION. Extraversion is how outgoing and social a person is. Someone high in extraversion enjoys crowds, social gatherings, and working in groups. A person low in extraversion is more comfortable working on his or her own and is less gregarious. As with agreeableness, the level of extraversion that is desired in an employee is dependent on the job. In jobs that involve interacting with others, such as sales, teaching, or public relations, high extraversion may be helpful. However, if a job requires independent work and solitude, such as computer programming, having a person high in extraversion may be difficult, and thus a person lower in extraversion would be preferred.

OPENNESS TO EXPERIENCE. Openness to experience refers to how open-minded a person is. An individual who is high in openness to experience is curious, imaginative, open-minded, and enjoys trying new things. People who are low in openness to experience are routine-oriented, close-minded, literal, and prefer not to try new things.

As with agreeableness and extraversion, the degree to which an employee is benefited by openness depends on the job. High openness is important in jobs that require creativity and flexibility; you would definitely prefer to have high openness in advertising or research positions. However, some jobs reward routine work, and in those jobs in which creativity is not needed or desired, a person low in openness may find these jobs more rewarding.

In summary, high emotional stability and conscientiousness are desirable in nearly all jobs, and the level of agreeableness, extraversion, and openness to experience are dependent on the job duties and requirements. While personality can relate to how well a person performs a job, it is not the only characteristic upon which a hiring decision should be made. Ideally, a person's education, experience, and intelligence should be evaluated for a position, with personality being part of the criteria considered.

REVISED NEO PERSONALITY INVENTORY

In addition to the 16 PF instrument, the Revised NEO Personality Inventory (NEO PI-R), developed by Costa and McCrae, assesses the five personality dimensions of the Five-Factor Model and thirty additional traits used to create the scores on these dimensions. For instance, to determine scores on the Neuroticism (i.e., Emotional Stability) scale, the following facets are

measured: anxiety, angry hostility, depression, self-consciousness, impulsiveness, and vulnerability. This NEO PI-R was developed specifically for use in business settings.

MYERS-BRIGGS TYPE INDICATOR

The Myers-Briggs Type Indicator (MBTI) is a very popular test, primarily used in organizations to develop managers and build teams. It is very different from the other personality tests. Rather than tapping the Big Five personality characteristics, the MBTI is based on the work of Jung and addresses four areas of personality to create sixteen distinct types.

The four areas of personality are perception (sensing vs. intuiting), judgment (thinking vs. feeling), extraversion (extraversion vs. introversion), and orientation towards the outer world (perceiving vs. judging). The scores along these four dimensions can be combined to create sixteen different "types." The scores on each dimension represent the strength of dimension; so a person might be "sensing, thinking, introverted, and perceiving" and very strong in sensing, but somewhat less strong in thinking.

While the other personality inventories are often used as a selection tool in the organization, the MBTI is best used for career development, counseling, and team selection. Another difference between the MBTI and other personality tests is that strengths on the different dimensions are all seen as valuable. So, a person who is strong in "thinking" is seen as just as skilled an employee as one who is strong in "feeling," but is believed to be more suited to different types of tasks and duties. Contrast this with the NEO-PI: on that instrument, a low score on some dimensions, like conscientiousness, would be undesirable to an organization.

While the Myers-Briggs Type Indicator is used in many organizations and is very popular among employers and employees, there is not as much empirical evidence of its validity compared to other personality inventories. Thus, it is typically not recommended as a tool for employee selection, but rather is best suited for employee and managerial development and team-building.

USING PERSONALITY TESTS FOR SELECTION

When employers first began to learn about personality and the impact that it could have on job performance, they did not have specific employment tests to measure personality. Therefore, many turned to psychologists and existing personality tests (e.g., the MMPI) to determine the characteristics of job applicants. Unfortunately, the purpose of some of these tests was to diagnose mental illness or psychological disorders, and although they could provide some information related to personality, the test items were likely to seem strange and intrusive to job applicants.

Furthermore, because the tests were not written in an employment context, the information that they provided typically went beyond what was needed to make an informed hiring decision. For these reasons, many managers had negative experiences with personality testing in the workplace and thought it to be inappropriate and useless.

However, there are now tests designed specifically for business hiring needs. These tests tap into the Big Five personality characteristics and are written in such a way as to not offend the average job applicant. Therefore, human resources departments should investigate which tests are available and most appropriate to their company before adopting personality testing.

To use a personality test for selection, its reliability, validity, and acceptability must be evaluated.

RELIABILITY. Reliability, or the degree to which a test measures some characteristic consistently, is a necessary requirement for a selection test. If a test does not measure consistently, then it cannot be valid; thus, assessing the reliability of personality tests is crucial for accurate selection. In general, most commercial personality tests have demonstrated high reliability.

Reliability can be assessed in several different ways. The test-retest method of assessing reliability involves giving one group the same test twice and statistically evaluating the consistency of scores. Because personality tests are intended to measure stable, enduring personality traits, the test-retest reliability of these tests should be high.

The equivalent measures method of determining reliability involves creating two tests that evaluate the same content domains, giving them to the same group, and statistically comparing the scores of each individual. If the two tests truly are equal in content, then high reliability will be indicated by very similar scores on both tests.

Finally, internal consistency is one of the most used measures of reliability. An assessment of internal consistency only requires one version of a test and one sample of people; the test is then broken into two parts, and the consistency of responses on the two parts is determined. A well-known form of the internal consistency approach, called coefficient alpha, averages the correlations between all possible splits of a test, and therefore results in a highly accurate assessment of reliability.

VALIDITY. The validity, or accuracy, of personality tests has been measured in a number of research studies and can be assessed in two main ways: content validity and criterion-related validity. Additionally, meta-analysis has been used to understand the validity of personality tests.

Content validity is an assessment of the degree to which the items on a test capture the domain of interest. This assessment is made by subject matter experts, such as trained psychologists or expert managers. While content validity is an important assessment of the usefulness of a selection test, criterion-related validity provides empirical evidence as to a test's accuracy.

Criterion-related validity indicates how well a test predicts job performance, and it can be evaluated concurrently or predictably. In a concurrent criterion-related validity study of a personality test, job incumbents are given the personality test, and their job performance is measured at the same time. A correlation between test scores and job performance indicates the level of validity of the new test.

With predictive criterion-related validity, job applicants are given the new personality test, but it is not used when making the hiring decisions. After a certain time period, the scores on the personality test are correlated with job performance scores of the new employees to determine the validity of the test. While concurrent validity studies are often preferred because they can be done quickly, the motivation of current employees to do well on these tests may not be high, or at least not as high as the motivation of job applicants.

With predictive validity, the benefit occurs with the use of actual job applicants; however, the time lag involved is often a major drawback.

In both cases, a big concern is range restriction; that is, because the full range of scores on the test is not evaluated (since not all applicants are hired and, presumably, current employees would have high scores on the personality test), the actual validity of a test may be underestimated.

Meta-analysis is a statistical technique that can be used to further explore the validity of selection tests. Meta-analysis combines individual research studies to indicate an overall average validity for most jobs; using this, the general validity of selection tests can be estimated. Based on information from meta-analysis, most personality tests have low to moderate validity, as compared to other selection methods such as intelligence tests, work samples, and structured interviews. However, they are still useful for hiring in many jobs because the information they provide is unique.

Intelligence tests and work samples cannot indicate a person's level of different personality traits, and although structured interview questions may be written to capture some elements of personality, such as conscientiousness, or agreeableness, typically, a personality test will provide information above and beyond other employment tests. Therefore, the inclusion of a validated personality test may increase the overall validity of the selection battery for certain jobs.

There are three major threats to the validity of personality tests: faking, socially desirable responding, and careless responding. While all occur for different reasons, the effects of these types of responses can reduce the validity of personality tests.

Faking occurs when a job applicant purposely attempts to score more positively than he or she would if answering items truthfully. Because many personality inventories include response choices that are easily seen as more desirable than others, applicants may be able to deliberately misrepresent themselves to look more favorable, or "fake good."

Although most personality tests include instructions that request that applicants answer truthfully, they may choose not to follow these instructions. There are no firm conclusions on the amount of faking that occurs, or its effect on test scores, but many researchers argue that when faking occurs, it is unlikely to skew test appreciably.

Socially desirable responding is similar to faking in that the applicant answers items falsely in order to look better; however, unlike faking, socially desirable responding is not deliberate. These unconscious and unintended responses are chosen in order to conform with social norms. For instance, an applicant may overestimate his punctuality or organization skills on a personality test because these are skills that the employer wants. However, this decision would not be conscious, but instead would represent a generous view of one's own habits.

Response carelessness occurs when an applicant does not pay careful enough attention to the items on the test and therefore responds incorrectly. This occurs when the applicant has poor reading skills, is in a hurry, is bored, or is not motivated to take the test. Careless responses can harm the reliability and the validity of the test because they lack consistency and accuracy.

To avoid these problems, many personality inventories now include scales to detect faking, socially desirable responding, and response carelessness from which scores can be used to adjust the scores on the other scales. Thus, most published personality inventories have the means to avoid and/or correct for these threats to validity.

ACCEPTABILITY. Acceptability is an assessment made by job applicants. Their reaction to taking the personality test may have an influence on their motivation to take the test, their continuation in the hiring process, or their opinions about the company. For example, if a job applicant is asked a number of questions on a personality test that she believes to be invasive and too personal, she may be offended and therefore not accept a job offer. She may then complain to friends about the company's selection tests—reducing the number of people who might have applied for jobs with the organization.

Any of these outcomes are likely to hurt recruitment and selection efforts, and thus, only tests with high levels of acceptability should be used.

Understanding personality can be useful in the workplace. There are many commercial personality tests available that can be used for selection. Many of these are high in reliability and have low to moderate validity. Many tests are written specifically for business settings and are likely to be deemed acceptable by job applicants.

Research supports the use of tests based on the Five-Factor Model of personality for selection. The Myers-Briggs Type Indicator, a very popular inventory, can be useful for development and team-building in the organization.

SEE ALSO: Employee Screening and Selection; Employment Law and Compliance; Human Resource Management; Leadership Theories and Studies; Management Styles

Marcia J. Simmering

FURTHER READING:

Anastasi, Anne, and Susana Urbina. *Psychological Testing.* Upper Saddle River, NJ: Prentice Hall, 1997.

Barrick, Murray R., and Michael K. Mount. "The Big Five Personality Dimensions and Job Performance: A Meta Analysis." *Personnel Psychology* 44 (1991): 1–26.

Gardner, William L., and Mark J. Martinko. "Using the Myers-Briggs Type Indicator to Study Managers: A Literature Review and Research Agenda." *Journal of Management* 22, no. 1 (1996): 45–83.

McCrae, Robert R., and Paul T. Costa, Jr. "Validation of the Five-Factor Model of Personality Across Instruments and Observers." *Journal of Personality and Social Psychology* 52, no. 1 (1987): 81–90.

McFarland, Lynn A., and Ann Marie Ryan. "Variance in Faking Across Noncognitive Measures." *Journal of Applied Psychology* 85, no. 5 (2000): 812–821.

Schneider, Benjamin, and D. Brent Smith. *Personality and Organizations.* Mahwah, NJ: Lawrence Erlbaum Associates, 2004.

PIONEERS OF MANAGEMENT

The study of management as a discipline is relatively new, especially when compared with other scientific disciplines. Yet, to truly understand current management thought, it is necessary to examine the historical links. It is best to consider not only management pioneers' management theories, but also the contextual and environmental factors that helped to clarify the developmental process behind the theories. Therefore, management pioneers may be easily placed along a historical timeline.

Using the work of Daniel Wren as a guide, the following categories are employed: (1) early management thought; (2) the scientific management era; (3) the social man era; and (4) the modern era.

EARLY MANAGEMENT THOUGHT: THE ECONOMIC FACET

Adam Smith and James Watt have been identified as the two men most responsible for destroying the old England and launching the world toward industrialization. Adam Smith brought about the revolution in economic thought and James Watt's steam engine provided cheaper power that revolutionized English commerce and industry. In doing so, they also laid the foundation for modern notions of business management theory and practice.

ADAM SMITH. Adam Smith (1723–1790) was a Scottish political economist. His *Wealth of Nations,* published in 1776, established the "classical school" and with its publication, he became the father of "liberal economics." Smith argued that market and competition should be the regulators of economic activity and that tariff policies were destructive. The specialization of labor was the mainstay of Smith's market system. According to Smith, division of labor provided managers with the greatest opportunity for increased productivity.

JAMES WATT AND MATTHEW BOULTON. James Watt (1736–1819), aided by Matthew Boulton (1728–1809), and building on the work of his predecessors, developed his first workable steam engine in 1765. Together the partners founded the engineering firm of Boulton, Watt, and Sons.

Recognized as Watt's greatest breakthrough, in 1971 he developed a steam engine with rotary, rather than the traditional up-and-down, movement. This made the engine more adaptable to factory uses as the engine replacing water wheel power for grinding grain, driving textile machines, and operating bellows for iron works.

Steam power lowered production costs, lowered prices, and expanded markets. In 1800 the sons of Boulton and Watts took over the management of the company and instituted one of the first complete applications of scientific management. In this plant there is evidence of market research, including machine layout study involving workflow, production standards, cost accounting, employee training, employee incentives, and employee welfare programs.

EARLY MANAGEMENT THOUGHT: MANAGEMENT PIONEERS IN THE FACTORY SYSTEM

The division of labor, combined with the advances in technology, provided the economic rationale for the factory system. However, the factory system brought new problems for owners, managers, and society. Four management pioneers proposed solutions for coping with the pressures of the new large-scale industrial organizations. They were Robert Owens, Charles Babbage, Andrew Ure, and Charles Dupin.

ROBERT OWENS. Robert Owens (1771–1858) was a successful Scottish entrepreneur and a utopian socialist who sowed the first seeds of concern for the workers. He was repulsed by the working conditions and poor treatment of the workers in the factories across Scotland. Owen became a reformer. He reduced the use of child labor and used moral persuasion rather than corporal punishment in his factories. He chided his fellow factory owners for treating their equipment better than they treated their workers.

Owen deplored the evils of the division of labor and in his ideal system believed each man would do a number of different jobs switching easily from one job to another. Additionally, Owen hated the modern factory system, so he decided to revolutionize it. In 1813 he proposed a factory bill to prohibit employment of children under the age of ten and to limit hours for all children to $10^1/_2$ hours per day with no night work. The bill became law six years later, but was limited to cotton mills, reduced the age limit to nine, and included no provision for inspections; therefore, the law had little impact.

Feeling frustrated in his attempts to reform Britain, Owen traveled to America in 1824. He continued on to New Harmony, Indiana, where he had purchased a large plot of land. New Harmony was the first and most famous of sixteen U.S.-based Owenite communities appearing between 1825 and 1829. None, however, lasted more than a few years as full-fledged socialist communities.

CHARLES BABBAGE. Charles Babbage (1792–1871) is known as the patron saint of operations research and management science. Babbage's scientific inventions included a mechanical calculator (his "difference engine"), a versatile computer (his "analytical engine"), and a punch-card machine. His projects never became a commercial reality; however, Babbage is considered the originator of the concepts behind the present day computer.

Babbage's most successful book, *On the Economy of Machinery and Manufacturers,* described the tools and machinery used in English factories. It discussed the economic principles of manufacturing, and analyzed the operations; the skills used and suggested improved practices.

Babbage believed in the benefits of division of labor and was an advocate of profit sharing. He developed a method of observing manufacturing that is the same approach utilized today by operations analysts and consultants analyzing manufacturing operations.

ANDREW URE AND CHARLES DUPIN. Andrew Ure (1778–1857) and Charles Dupin (1784–1873) were early industrial educators. Ure provided academic training at Anderson's College in Glasgow for managers in the early factory system. He published a text in 1835 that dealt mainly with the technical problems of manufacturing in the textile industry, but also dealt with problems of managing.

Obviously pro-management, Ure advocated an "automatic plan" to provide harmony and to keep any individual worker from stopping production. He was a defender of the factory system and believed workers must recognize the benefits of mechanization and not resist its introduction.

Dupin was a French engineer and professor who pioneered industrial education in France. He is credited with having a great influence on the writings of Henri Fayol. Dupin published *Discours sur le Sort Des Ouvriers,* translated Discourse on the Condition of the Workers, in 1831. This manuscript included concepts such as time study and the need to balance workloads after introducing division of labor. He wrote of the need for workers to receive concise instructions and the need to discover and publish the best way to perform work with the least amount of worker energy.

THE SCIENTIFIC MANAGEMENT ERA

Since management relied heavily on engineers for advice in the new factories, it is not surprising that associations of engineers were some of the first to examine and write about management problems. The American Society of Mechanical Engineers (ASME) was founded in 1880 and was one of the first proponents of the search for scientific management.

HENRY TOWNE. Henry Towne, president of the Yale and Towne Manufacturing Company, began applying systematic management practices as early as 1870. In 1866 he wrote a paper, *The Engineer as an Economist,* that suggested that ASME become a clearinghouse for information on managerial practices, since there was no management association.

Towne also published several papers and a book, *Evolution of Industrial Management,* on the use of "gain sharing" to increase worker productivity. In his last book Towne contrasted the status of scientific management in 1886 and in 1921, noting the establishment of industrial management courses,

and crediting Frederick Taylor as the apostle of the scientific movement.

FREDERICK A. HALSEY. Frederick A. Halsey was another engineer who wrote papers presented to ASME outlining his ideas about wages. He attacked the evils of profit sharing and proposed a special "premium plan" for paying workers based on time saved. Halsey proposed incentives based on past production records, including a guaranteed minimum wage and a premium for not doing work. Halsey's plan, along with Taylor's ideas on piece rates, had a major influence in the United States and Great Britain on the design of pay schemes.

HENRY METCALFE. Another early application of the scientific principles of management occurred when Captain Henry Metcalfe developed a system of controls that he applied to the management of the Frankford Arsenal. In 1885, Metcalfe published *The Cost of Manufactures and the Administration of Workshops, Public and Private.* This book is considered a pioneer work in the area of management science.

DANIEL McCALLUM. Unlike many industries, the railroad industry forced managers to develop special ways of managing a labor force that was dispersed over a wide geographical area. Daniel McCallum (1815–1878) became general superintendent of the Erie Railroad in 1854. He developed principles of management that included discipline, division of labor, detailed job descriptions, promotion and pay based on merit, frequent and accurate reporting of worker performance, and a clearly defined chain of command.

McCallum also designed a formal organizational chart and a sophisticated information management system using the telegraph. His system and rules, however, ran afoul of the militant union and he resigned after a six-month strike. Later, McCallum successfully ran the Northern railroads during the Civil War. He also served as a management consultant for several railroads after the war.

FREDERICK TAYLOR. Probably the most famous management pioneer of all is Frederick W. Taylor (1856–1915), the father of scientific management. Taylor rose from common laborer to chief engineer in six years, and completed a home study course to earn a degree in mechanical engineering in 1883.

In trying to overcome soldiering by the workers, Taylor began a scientific study of what workers ought to be able to produce. This study led to the beginnings of scientific management. Taylor used time studies to break tasks down into elementary movements, and designed complementary piece-rate incentive systems.

Taylor believed management's responsibility was in knowing what you want workers to do and then seeing that they do it in the best and cheapest way.

He developed many new concepts such as functional authority. In other words, Taylor proposed that all authority was based on knowledge, not position. He wrote *Shop Management* in 1903, became the president of the American Society of Mechanical Engineers in 1906, and was a widely traveled lecturer, lecturing at Harvard from 1909 to 1914.

In 1911, Taylor published *Principles of Scientific Management* in 1911. Its contents would become widely accepted by managers worldwide. The book described the theory of scientific management. Scientific management was defined as methods aimed at determining the one best way for a job to be done.

During this same period organized labor waged an all-out war on Taylorism resulting in a congressional investigation. In February of 1912, however, the committee reported finding no evidence to support abuses of workers or any need for remedial legislation. Taylor did not neglect the human side of work, as often suggested. He simply emphasized the individual worker not the group. Taylor called for a revolution that would fuse the interests of labor and management into a mutually rewarding whole.

HENRY GANTT. Henry Gantt (1861–1919) worked with Taylor at the Midvale Steel Company and was considered a Taylor disciple. Gantt felt the foreman should teach the workers to be industrious and cooperative which, in turn, would facilitate the acquisition of all other knowledge.

Gantt also designed graphic aids for management called Gantt charts using horizontal bars to plan and control work. Similar to Taylor, Gantt called for the scientific study of tasks, movements, working conditions, and worker cooperation. He also focused on the connection between the involvement of management and financial interests.

FRANK GILBRETH. Frank Gilbreth (1868–1924) and Lillian Gilbreth (1878–1972) were a husband and wife team that brought many significant contributions, as well as color, to scientific management. Frank began working at age seventeen as an apprentice bricklayer, and later became a chief superintendent and independent contractor. Frank's early work parallels Taylor's and, in later years, Frank formed his own management consulting company, which was closely associated with scientific management methods.

Frank Gilbreth published a series of books describing the best way of laying bricks, handling materials, training apprentices, and improving methods while lowering costs and paying higher wages.

In 1907, Frank Gilbreth met Frederick Taylor and soon became one of Taylor's most devoted advocates. Frank turned his attention away from construction, and extended his interest in motion study (similar to Taylor's time study) to the general field of management.

In order to supplement the human eye, Gilbreth used motion picture cameras, lights, and clocks calibrated in fractions of minutes to create "micromotion" study. Gilbreth also developed a list of seventeen basic motions he called "therbligs" (Gilbreth spelled backwards) to help analyze any worker movement. Unfortunately, the partnership of Frank and Lillian came to an end in 1924 when Frank died of a heart attack. Lillian continued their work through motion study seminars and consulting, later becoming a professor of management at Purdue University (1935–1948).

LILLIAN GILBRETH. Dr. Lillian Gilbreth, known as the first lady of management, played an important role in Frank's research and made many contributions of her own. Lillian pursued a degree in psychology, and in addition to her marriage and family of twelve, she assisted Frank with his work. Lillian's thesis-turned-book, *The Psychology of Management,* is one of the earliest contributions to understanding the human side of management.

Lillian faced many incidents of discrimination during her life, including the fact that her book could only be published if her initials were used so readers would not know she was a woman. Dr. Gilbreth's work was always more management than psychology. Her work illustrated concern for the worker and attempted to show how scientific management would benefit the individual worker, as well as the organization. Lillian wrote about reduction of worker fatigue, how to retool for disabled veteran workers returning to the workplace, and how to apply principles of scientific management to the home.

HARRINGTON EMERSON. Harrington Emerson (1853–1931) was educated in Germany and symbolized a new breed of "efficiency engineers" who were bringing new methods of time and cost savings to American industry. Emerson practiced his system as general manager of the Burlington Railroad, but saw the need for applications of his system in other industries.

The Engineering Magazine published a series of articles by Emerson in 1908 and 1909 that were later issued as a single volume. To Emerson, organization was one of the greatest problems that led to inefficiency. Emerson embraced the general staff concept where each firm was to have a chief of staff and four major sub groupings of staff under him: one for employees, one for machines, one for materials, and one for methods. Staff advice was available to all levels and focused on planning.

Emerson made other contributions in the areas of cost accounting and in setting standards for judging workers and shop efficiency. In 1913, Emerson published *Twelve Principles of Efficiency*. This publication became a landmark in the history of management thought. Harrington Emerson achieved renown in his time and his legacy lives on today.

MORRIS COOKE. While Taylor, the Gilbreths, Gantt, and Emerson were working with industrial enterprises, Morris Cooke (1872–1960) was extending the gospel of efficiency in non-industrial organizations. Cooke focused his attention on educational and municipal organizations.

Cooke conducted a study of administration in educational organizations funded by the Carnegie Foundation for the Advancement of Teaching. The resulting study was a bombshell in the academic world. Cooke's findings included, among other things, widespread use of inbreeding (hiring your own graduates), inefficient committee management, autonomous departments working against university coordination, and pay based on tenure.

In 1911, Cooke was selected as director of public works and brought scientific management to the governance of Philadelphia. In four years he saved the city over $1 million in garbage collection costs alone. Cooke wrote *Our Cities Awake* (1918) to put forth his case for using scientific management for better-managed municipalities.

Cooke became a close friend of Samuel Gompers, president of the American Federation of Labor, and tried to bring labor and management together in a time when they were becoming more antagonistic.

HUGO MUNSTERBERG. While the efficiency engineers studied mechanical efficiency, the industrial psychologists studied human efficiency, with the same goal in mind of improving productivity. The father of industrial psychology was Hugo Munsterberg (1863–1916). In 1892, Munsterberg established his psychological laboratory at Harvard, which was to become the foundation stone in the industrial psychology movement.

Munsterberg published *Psychology and Industrial Efficiency* (1913), which included theories directly related to Taylor's scientific management. The book contained three parts. Part one, the "best possible man," was a study of the demand jobs made on people, and the importance of finding people whose mental capabilities made them well-matched for the work. Part two, the "best possible work," described the psychological conditions under which the greatest output might be obtained from every worker. Part three, the "best possible effect," examined the necessity of creating the influences on human needs that were desirable for the interests of business.

Munsterberg's proposals were based on his own evidence from studies involving telephone operators, trolley drivers, and naval officers.

WALTER DILL SCOTT. Walter Dill Scott (1869–1955) taught at Northwestern University from 1901 to 1920 and then served as president of the university for nineteen years. Scott was interested in employee attitudes and motivation in production and devised a system,

adopted by the army, for classifying personnel and testing officer candidates. In fact, he was awarded the Distinguished Service Medal for his work.

From March 1910 till October 1911, Scott wrote a series of articles entitled *The Psychology of Business* later published in *System* magazine. These articles were based on actual business cases and represented one of the earliest applications of the principles of psychology to motivation and productivity in industry.

THE EMERGENCE OF ADMINISTRATIVE THEORY

HENRI FAYOL. Two contributors to the administrative theory of management are Henri Fayol (1841–1925) and Max Weber (1864–1920). Both wrote during the scientific management era in America, but neither was accorded the full measure of his contribution until some decades after his death.

Fayol was trained as a mining engineer and became the managing director of a coal-mining and iron foundry combine. From his own experience, he formulated and wrote papers about his ideas of administrative theory as early as 1900. His first mention of the "elements" of administration came in a book published in 1916. However, America was not thoroughly exposed to Fayol's theory until the book was translated in 1949 and entitled *General and Industrial Management.*

Fayol identified the major elements or functions of management as planning, organization, command, coordination, and control. Planning and organization received the majority of his attention in his writings. Fayol believed that management could be taught, that managerial ability was sorely needed as one moved up the ladder, and that management was a separate activity applicable to all types of undertakings.

Fayol's fourteen principles of management included: division of labor, authority, discipline, unity of command, unity of direction, subordination of individual interests to the general interest, remuneration, centralization, scalar chain, order, equity, stability of tenure of personnel, initiative, and *espirit de corps* (morale).

MAX WEBER. The work of Max Weber (1864–1920) runs chronologically parallel to that of Fayol and Taylor. Weber was a German intellectual with interests in sociology, religion, economics, and political science. He was a professor, editor, government consultant, and author. Weber used the concept of "bureaucracy" as an ideal organizational arrangement for the administration of large-scale organizations. His work was not translated into English until 1947.

Weber's concept of the best administrative system was actually similar to Taylor's. Some of Weber's essential elements included division of labor, and chain of command. He also believed that selection should be based on technical qualifications, officials'/managers' appointments should be based on qualifications, managers should not be owners, and impersonal and uniform rules should be applied.

PETER DRUCKER. Peter Drucker (b. 1909) made an enduring contribution to understanding the role of manager in a business society. Unlike the previous Fayolian process texts, Drucker developed three broader managerial functions: (1) managing a business; (2) managing managers; and (3) managing workers and work. He proposed that in every decision the manager must put economic considerations first. Drucker recognized that there may be other non-economic consequences of managerial decision, but that the emphasis should still be placed on economic performance.

THE SOCIAL MANERA

The behavioral school of management thought began late in the scientific management era, but did not achieve large-scale recognition until the 1930s. The real catalyst for the emergence of the behavioral school was a series of research studies conducted at the Hawthorne plant of Western Electric between 1924 and 1932. This research became known as the Hawthorne experiments.

ELTON MAYO AND THE HAWTHORNE STUDIES. Elton Mayo (1880–1949) joined the Harvard faculty in 1926 as associate professor of industrial research, and two years later was asked to work with Western Electric, as part of the Harvard research group, to continue the Hawthorne studies.

Mayo was intrigued by the initial results of the early illumination studies that showed output had increased upon changes in illumination—either brighter or darker—but no one knew why. Mayo believed the increased output came from a change in mental attitude in the group as the workers developed into a social unit.

Other experiments included the piecework experiment, the interviewing program, and the bank wiring room experiments. From these experiments the Mayoists concluded that employees have social needs as well as physical needs, and managers need a mix of managerial skills that include human relations skills.

MARY PARKER FOLLETT. Another contributor to the behavioral school of thought was Mary Parker Follett. Follett (1868–1933) was trained in philosophy and political science, and became interested in vocational guidance and the emerging field of social psychology. She had an international reputation as a political philosopher and in 1924 published *Creative Experience,* a book that was widely read by businessmen of the day.

Follett advocated a business philosophy that embraced integration as a way to reduce conflict without compromise or domination. She also proposed the "law of the situation," where parties agree to take their orders from the situation instead from an individual.

Another facet of her philosophy focused on coordination as a fundamental principle of organization. Follett believed the primary leadership task was to define the purpose of the organization and integrate that purpose with individual and group purposes. In other words, she thought that organizations should be based on a group ethic rather than individualism. Thus, managers and employees should view themselves as partners rather than adversaries.

CHESTER BARNARD. Chester Barnard (1886–1961) was a self-made scholar who attended Harvard on a scholarship, but never graduated because he lacked a laboratory science course. He joined the AT&T system in 1909 and became the president of New Jersey Bell in 1927.

Barnard's best known work, *The Functions of the Executive* (1938), was a collection of eight lectures in which he described a theory of organizations in order to stimulate others to examine the nature of cooperative systems. Looking at the disparity between personal and organizational motives, Barnard described an "effective-efficient" dichotomy.

According to Barnard, effectiveness deals with goal achievement, and efficiency is the degree to which individual motives are satisfied. He viewed formal organizations as integrated systems where cooperation, common purpose, and communication are universal elements, whereas the informal organization provides communication, cohesiveness and maintenance of feelings of self-worth. Barnard also developed the "acceptance theory of authority" based on his idea that bosses only have authority if subordinates accept that authority.

THE MODERN ERA: TOTAL QUALITY MANAGEMENT

A quality revolution swept through the business sector during the latter part of the twentieth century. The universal term used to describe this phenomenon was "total quality management" or TQM. This revolution was led by a small group of quality gurus, the most well-known were W. Edwards Deming (1900–1993) and Joseph Juran (b. 1904).

W. EDWARDS DEMING. Deming, an American, is considered to be the father of quality control in Japan. In fact, Deming suggested that most quality problems are not the fault of employees, but the system. He emphasized the importance of improving quality by suggesting a five-step chain reaction. This theory proposes that when quality is improved, (1) costs decrease because of less rework, fewer mistakes, fewer delays, and better use of time and materials; (2) productivity

Table 1

Deming's 14 Points

1. Create consistency of purpose toward the improvement of product and service, and communicate this goal to all employees.
2. Adopt the new philosophy of quality throughout all levels with the organization.
3. Cease dependence on inspection to achieve quality; understand that quality comes from improving processes.
4. No longer select suppliers based solely on price. Move towards developing a long-term relationship with a single supplier.
5. Processes, products, and services should be improved constantly; reducing waste.
6. Institute extensive on-the-job training.
7. Improve supervision.
8. Drive out fear of expressing ideas and concerns.
9. Break down barriers between departments. People should be encouraged to work together as a team.
10. Eliminate slogans and targets for the workforce.
11. Eliminate work quotas on the factory floor.
12. Remove barriers that rob workers of their right to pride of workmanship.
13. Institute a program of education and self-improvement.
14. Make sure to put everyone in the company to work to accomplish the transformation.

improves; (3) market share increases with better quality and prices; (4) the company increases profitability and stays in business; and (5) the number of jobs increases. Deming developed a 14-point plan to summarize his teachings on quality improvement. These fourteen points are listed in Table 1.

JOSEPH M. JURAN. Joseph Juran's experience led him to conclude that more than 80 percent of all quality defects are caused by factors within management's control. He referred to this as the "Pareto principle." From this theory, he developed a management trilogy that included quality planning, control, and improvement. Juran suggested that an area be selected which has experience chronic quality problems. It should be analyzed, and then a solution is generated and finally implemented.

The quality work of Joseph Juran and W. Edwards Deming changed the way people looked at business.

THE MODERN ERA: CONTEMPORARY MANAGEMENT HISTORIANS

The following group of individuals have proven themselves to be great teachers and intellectual leaders in matters of fundamental concern to management history. Their leadership and research have contributed greatly to our understanding of the evolution of management.

ARTHUR BEDEIAN. Arthur Bedeian, a management professor at Louisiana State University, is a management historian with universal interests. He has written on a variety of management-related topics, many of which fall within the area of management history. Bedeian has made several significant contributions to management history. These include his research into specific areas of inquiry such as scientific management and his bibliographic investigations and memoriams. However, perhaps his most important contribution to the field is his editorship of the four volumes of the *Management Laureates: A Collection of Autobiographical Essays.*

ALFRED BOLTON. Alfred Bolton was born in Canada in 1926. At the age of fifty-four, he began work on his doctorate at Nova University. It was during this time that he developed an interest in management history. His most significant contribution to the body of management history knowledge is his work with Ron Greenwood regarding the Hawthorne study participants. The work resulting from this collaborative effort has provided a unique glimpse into the groundbreaking experiments at Western Electric.

DANIEL WREN. Daniel Wren (b. 1932) is considered one of the leading authorities on the history of management thought. He is one of the most prolific writers in this field. His textbook, *The Evolution of Management Thought,* focuses on describing management history by providing a conceptual framework for understanding the evolution of management. Both his research and teaching in this area have led many to consider Wren as one of the management history gurus of the twentieth century.

SEE ALSO: Management Thought; Quality and Total Quality Management; Quality Gurus

Fraya Wagner-Marsh
Revised by Patricia A. Lanier

FURTHER READING:

Deming, W. Edwards. *Out of the Crisis.* Cambridge, MA: Massachusetts Institute of Technology, 2000.

Duncan, W. Jack. *Great Ideas in Management: Lessons from the Founders and Foundations of Managerial Practice.* San Francisco, CA: Jossey-Bass, 1989.

Gazell, J.A. "Drucker on Effective Public Management." *Journal of Management History* 6, no. 1 (2000): 48–62.

Gibson, Jane Whitney, Richard M. Hodgetts, and Jorge M. Herrer. "Management History Gurus of the 1990s: Their Lives, Their Contributions." *Journal of Management History* 5, no. 6 (1999): 380–397.

Lewis, P.S., S. H. Goodman, and P.M. Fandt. *Management: Challenges for Tomorrow's Leaders.* Cincinnati, OH: Thompson South-Western, 2005.

Robbins, Stephen R., and David A. DeCenzo. *Fundamentals of Management.* Upper Saddle River, NJ: Pearson Prentice Hall, 2004.

Spigener, J.B. "What Would Deming Say?" *Quality Progress* 34, no. 3 (2001): 61–64.

Wrege, Charles D., Ronald G. Greenwood, and R. Greenwood. "A New Method Of Discovering Primary Management History: Two Examples Where 'Little Things Mean A Lot.'" *Journal of Management History* 3, no. 1 (1997): 59–92.

Wren, Daniel A. *The Evolution of Management Thought.* New York, NY: John Wiley & Sons, 2004.

Wren, Daniel A., Arthur G. Bedeian, and J.D. Breeze. "The Foundations of Henri Fayol's Administrative Theory." *Management Decision* 40, no. 9 (2002): 906–918.

Wren, Daniel A., and Ronald G. Greenwood. *Management Innovators.* New York, NY: Oxford University Press, 1998.

PLANNING

Planning is the management function that involves setting goals and deciding how to best achieve them. Setting goals and developing plans helps the organization to move in a focused direction while operating in an efficient and effective manner. Long-range planning essentially is the same as strategic planning; both processes evaluate where the organization is and where it hopes to be at some future point. Strategies or plans are then developed for moving the organization closer to its goals. Long-range plans usually pertain to goals that are expected to be met five or more years in the future.

People often confuse the role of planning and scheduling. They are different methodologies and utilize a different set of tools. Planning takes a futuristic view and sets anticipated timelines, while scheduling focuses on an organization's day-to-day activities. For example, most enterprise resource planning (ERP) systems are good at the planning function, but are very poor at the scheduling function. A tool like finite capacity scheduling (FCS) is necessary to facilitate the daily tracking of material and labor movements.

LONG-RANGE PLANNING AND STRATEGIC MANAGEMENT

Since the purpose of strategic management is the development of effective long-range plans, the concepts often are used interchangeably. The traditional process models of strategic management involve planning organizational missions; assessing relationships between the organization and its environment; and identifying, evaluating, and implementing strategic alternatives that enable the organization to fulfill its mission.

One product of the long-range planning process is the development of corporate-level strategies. Corporate strategies represent the organization's long-term direction. Issues addressed as part of corporate strategic planning include questions of diversification, acquisition, divestment, and formulation of business ventures. Corporate strategies deal with plans for the entire organization and change relatively infrequently, with most remaining in place for five or more years.

Long-range plans usually are less specific than other types of plans, making it more difficult to evaluate the progress of their fulfillment. Since corporate plans may involve developing a research-intensive new product or moving into an international market, which may take years to complete, measuring their success is rarely easy. Traditional measures of profitability and sales may not be practical in evaluating such plans.

Top management and the board of directors are the primary decision makers in long-range planning. Top management often is the only level of management with the information needed to assess organization-wide strengths and weaknesses. In addition, top management typically is alone in having the authority to allocate resources toward moving the organization in new and innovative directions.

WHY ENGAGE IN LONG-RANGE PLANNING?

Research has found that firms engaged in strategic planning outperform firms that do not follow this approach. Managers also appear to believe that strategic planning leads to success, as the number of firms using strategic planning has increased in recent years. Because planning helps organizations to consider environmental changes and develop alternative responses, long-range planning seems particularly useful for firms operating in dynamic environments.

A review of studies regarding long-range and strategic planning and performance allows a number of generalizations to be made about how long-range planning can contribute to organizational performance.

1. Long-range plans provide a theme for the organization. This theme is useful in formulating and evaluating objectives, plans, and policies. If a proposed objective or policy is not consistent with the existing theme, it can be changed to better fit the organization's strategies.

2. Planning aids in the anticipation of major strategic issues. It enhances the ability of a firm to recognize environmental changes and begin courses of action to prevent potential problems. Rewarding employees for recognizing and responding to environmental changes sensitizes employees to the need for planning.

3. Planning assists in the allocation of discretionary resources; future costs and returns from various alternatives can be more easily anticipated. Strategies also reflect priorities resulting from multiple objectives and business-unit interdependencies.

4. Plans guide and integrate diverse administrative and operating activities. The relationship between productivity and rewards is clarified through strategic planning, guiding employees along the path to the desired rewards. Strategies also provide for the integration of objectives, avoiding the tendency for subunit objectives to take precedence over organizational objectives.

5. Long-range planning is useful for developing prospective general managers. Strategic planning exposes middle managers to the types of problems and issues they will have to face when they become general managers. Participation in strategic planning also helps middle managers to see how their specialties fit into the total organization.

6. Plans enable organizations to communicate with groups in the environment. Plans incorporate the unique features of the product or company that differentiate it from its competitors. Branding communicates to the public an image of product attributes (e.g., price, quality, and style). Similarly, dividend policies make a difference in the attractiveness of a stock to blue-chip, growth, and speculative investors.

THE STRATEGIC MANAGEMENT/ LONG-RANGE PLANNING PROCESS

The first basic step in long-range planning is the definition of the organization's mission. Essentially, the mission is what differentiates the organization from others providing similar goods or services. Strategies are developed from mission statements to aid the organization in operationalizing its mission.

Long-range planning primarily is the responsibility of boards of directors, top management, and corporate planning staffs. Strategic decision makers are responsible for identifying and interpreting relevant information about the business environment. Thus, a key part of strategic management involves identifying threats and opportunities stemming from the external environment and evaluating their probable impact on the organization.

Environmental analysis, another key component of long range-planning, identifies issues to be considered when evaluating an organization's environment. The environment consists of two sets of factors. These include the macro-environment, consisting of factors with the potential to affect many businesses or business segments, and the task environment, with elements more likely to relate to an individual organization. Industry analysis is an especially important part of analyzing the specific environment of an organization.

Internal characteristics of an organization must be thoroughly identified and accounted for in order to effect long-term planning. Internal factors can represent either strengths or weaknesses. Internal strengths provide a basis upon which strategies can be built. Internal weaknesses represent either current or potential problem areas that may need to be corrected or minimized by appropriate strategies. Internal planning issues commonly involve the functional areas of finance, marketing, human resource management, research and development, operations/production, and top management.

Once the organization's mission is determined and its internal and external strengths and weaknesses are identified, it is possible to consider alternative strategies that provide the organization with the potential to fulfill its mission. This process essentially involves the identification, evaluation, and selection of the most appropriate alternative strategies. Strategic alternatives include strategies designed to help the organization grow faster, maintain its existing growth rate, reduce its scope of operations, or a combination of these alternatives. Corporate grand strategies are evaluated later in this discussion.

Strategy implementation is another important part of long-range planning. Once a strategic plan has been selected, it must be operationalized. This requires the strategy to be implemented within the existing organizational structure, or the modification of the structure so that it is consistent with the strategy. Implementing a strategy also requires integration with the organization's human component.

A final element of long-range planning is strategic control, which evaluates the organization's current performance and compares this performance to its mission. Strategic control essentially brings the strategic management process full circle in terms of comparing actual results to intended or desired results.

CORPORATE-LEVEL PLANS

Corporate-level plans are most closely associated with translating organizational mission statements into action. In a multi-industry or multiproduct organization, managers must juggle the individual businesses to be managed so that the overall corporate mission is fulfilled. These individual businesses may represent operating divisions, groups of divisions, or separate legal business entities. Corporate-level plans primarily are concerned with:

1. Scope of operations. What businesses should we be in?

2. Resource allocation. Which businesses represent our future? Which businesses should be targeted for termination?

3. Strategic fit. How can the firm's businesses be integrated to foster the greatest organizational good?

4. Performance. Are businesses contributing to the organization's overall financial picture as expected, in accordance with their potential? The business must look beyond financial performance to evaluate the number and mix of business units. Has the firm been able to achieve a competitive advantage in the past? Will it be able to maintain or achieve a competitive advantage in each business in the future?

5. Organizational structure. Do the organizational components fit together? Do they communicate? Are responsibilities clearly identified and accountabilities established?

CORPORATE PORTFOLIO ANALYSIS

The Boston Consulting Group (BCG) Model is a relatively simple technique for helping managers to assess the performance of various business segments and develop appropriate strategies for each investment within the corporate portfolio.

The BCG Model classifies business unit performance on the basis of the unit's relative market share and the rate of market growth. Products and their respective strategies fall into one of four quadrants. The typical starting point for a new business is as a *question mark*. If the product is new, it has no market share but the predicted growth rate is good. What typically happens is that management is faced with a number of these types of products, but with too few resources to develop all of them. Thus, long-range planners must determine which of the products to attempt to develop into commercially viable products and which ones to drop from consideration. Question marks are cash users in the organization. Early in their life, they contribute no revenues and require expenditures for market research, test marketing, and advertising to build consumer awareness.

If the correct decision is made and the product selected achieves a high market share, it becomes a *star* in the BCG Model. Star products have high market share in a high growth market. Stars generate large cash flows for the business, but also require large infusions of money to sustain their growth. Stars often are the targets of large expenditures for advertising and research and development in order to improve the product and to enable it to establish a dominant industry position.

Cash cows are business units that have high market share in a low-growth market. These often are products in the maturity stage of the product life cycle. They usually are well-established products with wide consumer acceptance and high sales revenues. Cash cows generate large profits for the organization because revenues are high and expenditures are low. There is little the company can do to increase product sales. The plan for such products is to invest little money into maintaining them, and to divert the large profits generated into products with more long-term earnings potentials (i.e., question marks and stars).

Dogs are businesses with low market share in low-growth markets. These often are cash cows that have lost their market share or are question marks the company has elected not to develop. The recommended strategy for these businesses is to dispose of them for whatever revenue they will generate and reinvest the money in more attractive businesses (question marks or stars).

CORPORATE GRAND STRATEGIES

Corporate strategies can be classified into three groups or types. Collectively known as grand strategies, these involve efforts to expand business operations (growth strategies), maintain the status quo (stability strategies), or decrease the scope of business operations (retrenchment strategies).

GROWTH STRATEGIES. Growth strategies are designed to expand an organization's performance, usually as measured by sales, profits, product mix, or market coverage. Typical growth strategies involve one or more of the following:

1. Concentration strategy, in which the firm attempts to achieve greater market penetration by becoming very efficient at servicing its market with a limited product line.

2. Vertical integration strategy, in which the firm attempts to expand the scope of its current

operations by undertaking business activities formerly performed by one of its suppliers (backward integration) or by undertaking business activities performed by a business in its distribution channel.

3. Diversification strategy, in which the firm moves into different markets or adds different products to its mix. If the products or markets are related to its existing operations, the strategy is called *concentric diversification*. If the expansion is in products and markets unrelated to the existing business, the diversification is called *conglomerate*.

STABILITY STRATEGIES. When firms are satisfied with their current rate of growth and profits, they may decide to employ a stability strategy. This strategy basically extends existing advertising, production, and other strategies. Such strategies typically are found in small businesses in relatively stable environments. The business owners often are making a comfortable income operating a business that they know, and see no need to make the psychological and financial investment that would be required to undertake a growth strategy.

RETRENCHMENT STRATEGIES. Retrenchment strategies involve a reduction in the scope of a corporation's activities. The variables to be considered in such a strategy primarily involve the degree of reduction. Retrenchment strategies can be subdivided into the following:

1. Turnaround strategy, in which firms undertake a temporary reduction in operations in an effort to make the business stronger and more viable in the future. These moves are popularly called downsizing or rightsizing. The hope is that a temporary belt tightening will allow the firm to pursue a growth strategy at some future point.

2. Divestment, in which a firm elects to spin off, shut down, or sell a portion of its business. This strategy would commonly be used with a business unit identified as a dog by the BCG Model. Typically, a poor performing unit is sold to another company and the money is reinvested in a business with greater potential.

3. Liquidation strategy, which is the most extreme form of retrenchment. Liquidation involves the selling or closing of the entire business operation, usually when there is no future for the business. Employees are released, buildings and equipment are sold, and customers no longer have access to the product. This generally is viewed as a strategy of last resort, and is one that most managers work hard to avoid.

The purpose of an organization is its role as defined by those who maintain authority over it. How the organization elects to fulfill this role constitutes its plan. Mission statements differentiate the organization from other organizations providing similar goods or services. Objectives are the intermediate goals or targets to be completed as the organization fulfills its mission. Plans outline how a firm intends to achieve its mission. Policies provide guidelines or parameters within which decisions are made so that decisions are integrated with other decisions and activities.

SEE ALSO: Forecasting; Government-University-Industry Partnerships; Strategic Planning Tools; Strategy Formulation; Strategy in the Global Environment; Strategy Levels

Joe G. Thomas
Revised by Gerhard Plenert

FURTHER READING:

Plenert, Gerhard. *The eManager: Value Chain Management in an eCommerce World.* Dublin, Ireland: Blackhall Publishing Ltd., 2001.

———. *International Operations Management.* Copenhagen, Denmark: Copenhagen Business School Press, 2002.

Plenert, Gerhard Johannes, and Bill Kirchmier. *Finite Capacity Scheduling: Management, Selection, and Implementation.* New York: John Wiley & Sons Inc., 2000.

POISON PILL STRATEGIES

Poison pill strategies are defensive tactics that allow companies to thwart hostile takeover bids from other companies. Many companies may find themselves unprepared when facing such bids. By adopting a poison pill strategy, a company can be somewhat reassured that acquiring companies will approach its board of directors, not the shareholders. Poison pill strategies are also known as shareholders' protection rights plans.

HISTORY

During the late 1950s and early 1960s, several large corporations began acquiring other companies to diversify their operations. Diversification allowed them to offset their losses in a failing industry with profits from other unrelated, successful industries. Such phenomena caused concerns about the potential of conglomerates to concentrate excessive economic power in the hands of a few corporations. This led to the passage of the Williams Act in 1968, which required the acquiring company to fully disclose the terms of an impending acquisition and to allow a period for competing offers for the target company to be made. By the late 1970s, the pace of acquisition nearly came to a halt. In 1982, however, the U.S. Supreme Court passed a landmark ruling in the case of *Edgar v. MITE Corp.* that invalidated the basis for anti-takeover laws in thirty-seven states. Furthermore, under the Reagan administration, the U.S. Department of Justice followed a lax policy towards enforcing anti-takeover laws. No longer able to shelter themselves against unfriendly takeover bids, many companies opted to devise anti-takeover strategies. At that time there was a significant increase in poison pill adoptions. However, in light of recent corporate scandals and an overall perception of poor corporate ethics poison pills began to show a decline between 2002 to 2004.

TYPES OF POISON PILL STRATEGIES

"FLIP-OVER" RIGHTS PLAN. Most poison pill strategies involve some form of discrimination against the acquiring company. The most commonly used strategy is called the "flip over" or the shareholder rights plan. Under this strategy, the holders of common stock of a company receive one right for each share held, which allows them an option to buy more shares in the company. The rights have a set expiration date and do not carry voting power. They are worthless at the time of the offering because the exercise price is set well above the going market price of common shares. A shareholder cannot sell these rights independently as they trade together with the shares. When a suitor company makes an unwelcome bid, the rights begin trading separately from the shares. If the takeover bid is successful, the shareholder rights may be exercised to purchase shares at a discount of as much as fifty percent from the going market price. All the shareholders except the acquirer can exercise their rights to purchase shares at discount. This results in a significant dilution in the share holdings of the acquirer, possibly placing the control of the firm in jeopardy. The attempted takeover bid becomes expensive. If the takeover bid is abandoned, the company might redeem the rights, usually at five cents per share.

"FLIP-IN" RIGHTS PLAN. A variation of the flip over is the "flip-in" plan. The plan allows the rights holder to purchase shares in the target company at a discount upon the mere accumulation of a specified percentage of stock by a potential acquirer. For example, the rights become exercisable to purchase the target company's common stock at 50 percent discount from market price in the event the acquirer purchases more than, say, 30 percent ownership in the target company. The acquirer is precluded from exercising flip-in rights. This strategy allows more power than the "flip-over" rights plan and, therefore, has become a common form of poison pill adopted by many U.S. corporations.

POISON DEBT. The target company issues debt securities on certain stipulated terms and conditions in order to discourage a hostile takeover bid. Examples include covenants that severely restrict the company's ability to sell assets, an increase in the interest rates, an acceleration of the maturity date, a conversion of debt to equity at favorable rates, and rights to buy notes at a substantial premium to the prevailing market price at the time of the takeover bid.

"PUT RIGHTS" PLAN. Under this plan, the target company issues rights to its stockholders in the form of a dividend. When an acquirer purchases a specified percentage ownership in the target company, the target shareholders, excluding the acquirer, are entitled to sell their common stock back to the company for a specified sum of cash, debt securities, preferred stock, or some combination thereof. This form of poison pill strategy is rarely used by the U.S. corporations.

VOTING POISON PILL PLAN. This poison pill strategy is designed to dilute the controlling power of the acquirer. Under this plan, the target company issues a dividend of securities, conferring special voting privileges to its stockholders. For example, the target company might issue shares that do not have special voting privileges at the outset. When a potential hostile bid occurs, the stockholders, other than the acquiring party, receive super voting privileges. Alternately, the target company's stockholders might receive securities with voting rights that increase in value over period.

EXAMPLES OF RIGHTS PLANS. On 5 November 1998, Motorola, Inc. adopted a new rights plan to replace an existing plan. Under the plan, one right attaches to each existing share of common stock. If a person or group acquires a ten percent stake, all other right holders will be entitled to purchase the company's stock at a fifty percent discount. Motorola may redeem the new rights at one cent per right at any time before a person or group takes a ten percent stake.

On 13 October 1998, Baldwin Piano & Organ Company announced a shareholder rights plan by declaring a dividend of one stock purchase right for each share of common stock owned. Unlike rights plans adopted by other companies, Baldwin's innovative plan would permit a qualified offer to go forward without the board's approval. A qualified offer must be all cash, made to all shareholders, contain a firm financing commitment, and a fairness opinion from an investment bank. A qualified offer must result in the acquirer gaining at least seventy-percent of Baldwin's then outstanding shares.

In late 2004 PeopleSoft management attempted to use a poison pill that would be triggered when twenty percent of the company was acquired however shareholder interest in accepting the takeover by Oracle Corp. led to an eventual merger of the two companies.

Cisco had implemented a poison pill plan triggered when an individual or group acquired more than fifteen percent of the company. The plan was set to expire in 2008 however, in March 2005 Cisco decided to end the shareholder rights' program citing revision of its corporate governance procedures.

THE NET EFFECTS OF POISON PILL STRATEGIES

The net effect of a poison pill strategy is to make it prohibitively expensive for an acquirer to buy the control of a company. The underlying assumption is that the board will always act in the best interest of the shareholders, a view that is explicitly rejected by agency theorists. Agency theorists have argued that the practice of allowing management to adopt poison pill strategy has reduced the number of potential offers and actual takeovers. In doing so, they have protected incumbent management at the expense of shareholders. It is argued that poison pills have the effect of perpetuating inefficiencies and poor management that ultimately is reflected in lower stock values.

Boards of directors invariably argue that poison pill strategies have exactly the opposite effect on stock values. They help maintain their independent decision making power to run their companies in the best interests of the shareholders. Poison pill strategies also provide bargaining strength to the board in order to extract the most value for the stock from a potential acquirer.

While there are merits to the arguments on both sides, an efficient allocation of resources through merger and acquisition activities can only enhance shareholders' wealth no matter how hostile the tender offers of corporate raiders. Many of the defensive tactics of management should be opposed by the shareholders as they might cause a loss of their wealth, although other defensive actions-for example, by soliciting competitive bids-can increase their wealth.

SEE ALSO: Diversification Strategy; Leveraged Buyouts; Mergers and Acquisitions

Ramesh C. Garg
Revised by Hal P. Kirkwood, Jr.

FURTHER READING:

Dolbeck, A. "Hard to Swallow: Poison Pills on the Decline." *Weekly Corporate Growth Report*, 22 March 2004, 1–3.

Lowry, J.P. "Poison Pills in U.S. Corporations-A Re-examination." *Journal of Business Law*, May 1992, 337–341.

Simon, C.E., and J.M. Bryan. *Corporate Anti-Takeover Defenses: The Poison Pill Device*. St. Paul, MN: Thomson West., 2004.

Velasco, J. "The Enduring Illegitimacy of the Poison Pill" *Journal of Corporation Law* 27, no. 3 (Spring 2002): 381–423.

POKA-YOKE

Poka-yoke is a technique for avoiding simple human error in the workplace. Also known as mistake-proofing, goof-proofing, and fail-safe work methods, poka-yoke is simply a system designed to prevent inadvertent errors made by workers performing a process. The idea is to take over repetitive tasks that rely on memory or vigilance and guard against any lapses in focus. Poka-yoke can be seen as one of the three common components of Zero Defect Quality Control performed by Japanese companies (source inspection and feedback are the other two).

Dr. Shigeo Shingo, a renowned authority on quality control and efficiency, originally developed the mistake-proofing idea. Realizing its value as an effective quality control technique, he formalized its use in Japanese manufacturing as the poka-yoke system. One hundred percent inspections catch unacceptable products but do nothing to improve the process. Shingo was emphatic that the purpose of this system be to improve the process not sort out defective parts.

Today, this concept is in wide use in Japan. Toyota Motor Corporation, whose production system Shingo helped design, averages twelve poka-yoke devices per machine in their manufacturing plants, thus validating the concept as beneficial to industry. Patel, Dale, and Shaw, in the article "Set-Up Time Reduction and Mistake Proofing Methods: An Examination in Precision" list the potential benefits as:

- elimination of set-up errors and improved quality
- decreased set-up times with associated reduction in production time and improved production capacity
- simplified and improved housekeeping
- increased safety
- lower costs
- lower skill requirements
- increased production flexibility
- improved operator attitudes.

In a *Quality* magazine article, Melissa Larson provides interesting details about benefits resulting from the implementation of poka-yoke systems at the Supply Support Activity (SSA) at Fort Carson, Colorado, a military retail supply operation of the U.S. Army.

Inventory, receipt, and batch processing all improved quantifiably. Location survey accuracy was approximately sixty-five percent prior to implementation. After implementing the use of the bar-code readers location accuracy increased to ninety-eight percent.

Inventory adjustments averaged $3000 a month. Inventory adjustments dropped to an average of $250 per month.

The rate of incorrect receipt closures to the supplier had been ninety percent. This rate dropped to zero percent. Batch processing was also significantly improved. Traditionally, the SSA had approximately fifteen to twenty batch processing failures per month, and a myriad of system file failures due to operators performing the process out of proper sequence. Since the poka-yoke implementations, there have been zero batch process failures.

Catalog update improvements also resulted. The error rate was twenty-two percent but dropped to zero percent. Original request processing time was 12.5 days, but with the new request processing time is 1.6 days. Actual dollars invested in these activities totaled less than $1000.

TYPES OF POKA-YOKES

Poka-yoke is based on prediction and detection. That is, recognizing that a defect is about to occur or recognizing that a defect has occurred. Consequently, there are two basic types of poka-yoke systems. The control poka-yoke does not allow a process to begin or continue after an error has occurred. It takes the response to a specific type of error out of the hands of the operator. For example, a fixture on a machine may be equipped with a sensing device that will not allow the process to continue unless the part is properly inserted. A 3.5-inch floppy disk will not work if inserted backwards or upside down. As a matter of fact, it won't fit into the drive at all unless properly inserted. A second type of poka-yoke provides some type of warning when an error occurs. This does not prevent the error, but immediately stops the process when an error is detected. This type of poka-yoke is useful for mass production environments with rapid processing as the device prevents mass production of scrapped material. For environments where large losses of time or resources do not result, a warning poka-yoke is warranted. All that is needed is a way to ensure that the error is investigated and corrected in a timely manner.

Poka-yokes can be as simple as a steel pin on a fixture that keeps incorrectly placed parts from fitting properly, or they can be as complex as a fuzzy logic neural network used to automatically detect tool breakage and immediately stop the machine. Surprisingly, the simple low-cost devices tend to be in the majority. Regardless of degree of simplicity, all poka-yokes fall into one of three categories: contact methods, fixed-value methods, and motion-step methods. Each is briefly discussed.

CONTACT METHODS. Contact methods are based on some type of sensing device which detects abnormalities in the product's shape or dimension and responds accordingly. Interference pins, notches with matching locator pins, limit switches and proximity switches are sometimes used to ensure that a part is positioned correctly before work occurs. Asymmetric parts with matching work fixtures can also alleviate incorrect positioning. If orientation is not critical, symmetrical designs can then be used to prevent defects.

Contact methods are useful in situations which encourage mistakes. Such situations involve rapid repetition, infrequent production, or environmental problems such as poor lighting, high or low heat, excess humidity, dust, noise, or anything which distracts a worker. Paul Dvorak, in "Poka-Yoke Designs Make Assemblies Mistakeproof," an article appearing in *Machine Design,* recommends that the maintenance engineer investigate at least four areas for potential problems that require contact method solutions:

1. Look for where the product will fail if parts are assembled incorrectly.

2. Look for small features critical to proper assembly.

3. Beware of relying on subtle differences to determine top from bottom or front from back, especially if the parts are painted dark colors.

4. Beware of designs so complicated that they confuse inexperienced operators.

FIXED-VALUE METHODS. Fixed-value methods are used in processes where the same activity is repeated several times, such as tightening of bolts. This method frequently involves very simple techniques, such as methods that allow operators to easily track how often this activity has been performed. Dvorak gives the example of an operator who is responsible for tightening down six bolts on a product. Before passing the product on, the tightening process is performed a fixed number of times (six). A simple poka-yoke device would incorporate the use of a wrench dipped in diluted paint. Since untightened bolts will not have paint on them, the operator can easily see if he or she has performed the process the required number of times. A second example (from Dvorak) would be the use of packaged material in the exact (fixed) quantities needed to complete the process. If the bolts were stored in containers of six, the operator could easily see when the process was still incomplete as the box would still contain one or more bolts.

MOTION-STEP METHOD. The motion-step method is useful for processes requiring several different activities performed in sequence by a single operator. This is similar to the fixed-value situation in that the operator is responsible for multiple activities but instead of performing the same activity multiple times the operator performs different activities. First, each step in the

Table 1

Examples of Poka-Yokes

	Contact Type	Warning Type
Contact Method	A steel pin on a fixture keeps incorrectly placed parts from fitting properly.	A device on a drill counts the number of holes drilled in a work piece; a buzzer sounds if the work piece is removed before the correct number of holes have been drilled.
Fixed-value Type	Light sensors determine if each crayon is present in each box; if a crayon is missing, the machines will stop automatically.	Bolts are tightened with a wrench dipped in paint. Bolts with no paint on them are still un-tightened.
Motion-Step Method	A simple proximity switch opens after all components are loaded in the proper order.	A device detects when each component is removed from a dispenser; if a component is not removed, the device alerts the assembler before he can move on to another unit.

process is identified by the specific motions needed to complete it. Then devices are created to detect whether each motion is performed and then alert the operator when a step is skipped. An assembly process could utilize a device that senses when all required components are present at the start of the process for each unit. The devices could then detect when each component is removed from its dispenser, If a component is not removed, the sensing device alerts the assembler before he/she can move on to another unit.

SELF CHECKS

Poka-yoke devices which provide the fastest possible feedback about defects and allow workers to assess the quality of their own work are referred to as self-checks. Self-checks can be used to allow workers to rapidly identify slips or work errors such as incomplete or omitted operations and to verify the existence or absence of an attribute. For example, at Brigham and Women's Hospital, a computer system is used to check and process doctors' prescriptions.

EXAMPLES. A number of "real world" applications are presented in the business and engineering literature. Below are a list of examples of poka-yoke applications. James R. Evans and William M. Lindsay present these examples in their book *The Management and Control of Quality:*

- Color-coding a wiring template to assist the worker.

- Installing a device on a drill to count the number of holes drilled in a work piece; a buzzer sounds if the work piece is removed before the correct number of holes has been drilled.

- Cassette covers were frequently scratched when the screwdriver slipped out of the screw

slot and slid against the plastic covers. The screw design was changed as shown in Table 1 to prevent the screwdriver from slipping.

- A metal roller is used to laminate two surfaces bonded with hot melted glue. The glue tended to stick to the roller and cause defects in the laminate surface. An investigation showed that if the roller were dampened the glue would not stick. A secondary roller was added to dampen the steel roller during the process, preventing the glue from sticking.

- One production step at Motorola involves putting alphabetic characters on a keyboard, then checking to make sure each key is placed correctly. A group of workers designed a clear template with the letters positioned slightly off center. By holding the template over the keyboard, assemblers can quickly spot mistakes.

John Grout presented these examples in "Mistake-Proofing Production," an article written for *Production and Inventory Management Journal:*

- Trinity Industries Railcar Division workers created a layout jig to avoid having to use a tape measure and chalk to position subassemblies on each car individually. The jig has tops that allow it to be quickly positioned correctly on the car's chassis. Each component that is to be attached to the car has a corresponding cutout on the jig. The jig eliminates two modes of worker error. It eliminates incorrect measurements and inaccurate positioning of parts. It also eliminates the worker vigilance required to ensure all of the components are attached. Omitted parts are made very obvious because an empty space exists on the layout jig. Without the jig, there would be no indication that anything is missing. Once parts are spot welded in place the jig is lifted off and welding is completed. Not only is dependence on worker vigilance reduced, cost savings result from the simplified, accelerated process.

- Binney and Smith, maker of Crayola Crayons, uses light sensors to determine if each crayon is present in each box of crayons they produce. If a crayon is missing, the machines will stop automatically. Producing complete boxes of crayons right the first time is the preferred outcome.

- A mail-order computer company has designed its boxes and packing material to avoid mistakes. The inner flaps of the box bottom have a large brightly colored warning to "Stop! Open the other side." When the correct side is opened, a book titled "Setting Up Your Computer" is on top of the packing material. The sequence of the book matches the arrangement of the contents of the box. Each instruction involves the next item from the box.

- Airplane lavatory lights come on only when the door lock is engaged. This keeps customers from failing to lock the door.

- John Deere produced a gearbox that was assembled without oil, mounted on a machine, and required replacement after factor tests. A team streamlined production with a simple proximity switch that opens after all components were loaded into an assembly fixture. The switch prevents workers from using air wrenches to tighten bolts on the assembly until they cycle an oil gun into the gearbox. After filling the gearbox a solenoid releases the interlock sending air to the wrench. Then workers can tighten cover bolts and send the box to the next station.

- The electrical connectors in one machine control formerly used only three-pin connectors to join each in a series. Labels instructed assemblers which boards went where and which connectors should be joined. But in the field, assemblers connecting and disconnecting them wear or bend the pins, which meant putting on a new plug. Soon the label was gone. The simple solution involved three, four and five-pin connectors that cannot join others and demand a single assembly sequence.

- Ficarra's solution to labels that come off is to machine them into parts, especially when the function is to determine the correct orientation.

- On Varian machines, assemblers are guided by small machined-in pictures that cannot wear off.

SERVICE APPLICATIONS

Poka-yoke can also be applied to service-based organizations. The following is summarized from the paper "Using Poka-Yoke Concepts to Improve a Military Retail Supply System," which was printed in *Production and Inventory Management Journal*.

While manufacturing typically only considers errors made by the producer, service industries must consider errors from both the server and the customer. Additionally, service organizations interface in many different ways to transfer a service to the customer. Because of the possibility that service errors can be created by both the customer and the server, service poka-yokes are grouped into two categories: fail-safing the server and fail-safing the customer.

SERVER POKA-YOKES

There are three types poka-yoke systems that can be used to fail-safe the server: task poka-yokes, treatment poka-yokes, and tangible poka-yokes.

TASK POKA-YOKES. Task poka-yokes focus on server tasks and common mistakes servers make while performing the service/task for the customer. A good example of a control-oriented, task poka-yoke is the coin return machine used in may fast-food restaurants. The coin portion of a customer's change from payment is returned automatically through these machines. This takes the control out of the hands of the cash register operator, eliminating errors and speeding up the processing of customers.

TREATMENT POKA-YOKES. Treatment poka-yokes focus on the social interaction between the customer and the server (i.e., eye contact, greeting). By mistake-proofing/standardizing what servers say and do to customers, managers can reasonably ensure that customers receive proper, fair and consistent treatment. Burger King utilized warning-oriented, treatment poka-yokes by placing "cue cards" at the service point ensuring that servers know what to say the minute they interface with the customer.

TANGIBLE POKA-YOKES. Tangible poka-yokes attempt to improve the tangible, physical impression and experience for the customer in addition to the direct task of the server (i.e., dirty office, unkempt server, sloppy documents). Motorola uses a control-oriented poka-yoke in the legal department by having a second lawyer inspect all legal work for spelling, presentation, and arithmetic. In this way, the legal department is ensuring that the "tangibles" of the service are satisfactory in addition to the task of the service (legal work).

CUSTOMER POKA-YOKES

Fail-safeing the customer also consists of three of poka-yoke systems: preparation poka-yokes, encounter poka-yokes, and resolution poka-yokes.

PREPARATION POKA-YOKES. Preparation poka-yokes attempt to fully prepare the customer before they even enter the service. An example of a warning-oriented, preparation poka-yoke is the notice a university sends to each student prior to registration for the next semester detailing the courses he needs to finish his degree. This system could be converted to a control system by having an automated registration process which would not allow students to sign up for classes out of sequence or until all prerequisites are met.

ENCOUNTER POKA-YOKES. Encounter poka-yokes attempt to fail-safe a customer at a service who may misunderstand, ignore, or forget the nature of the service or their role in it. A good example of a control-oriented, encounter poka-yoke is the use of concrete curbing at an oil& lube shop that directs customers so that they do not/cannot pull the wrong way into the station. This system also assists in the selection process so that customers are not served out of order.

RESOLUTION POKA-YOKES. Resolution poka-yokes attempt to remind customers of the value of their input to the continuous improvement of a service. A hotel which uses an automated check-out system through the television in each room could attach a few questions to the check-out process to ensure the customer provides feedback on key issues. This would be a control-oriented resolution poka-yoke. Obviously, one of the keys to the success of any customer-oriented poka-yoke is to obtain willing customer participation.

BARRIERS TO IMPLEMENTATION AND RECOMMENDATIONS

Patel, Dale and Shaw note that there are a number of barriers a firm may face when implementing poka-yoke devices within their system. These include:

- Difficulty in accepting change
- Justification of the investment
- Using inappropriate and ineffective methods
- Time requirements
- Difficulty encountered as a result of continuous process

Stewart and Grout, in an article entitled "The Human Side of Mistake-Proofing," make the following recommendations for the implementation of poka-yoke devices:

1. The outcome of the process or routine must be known in advance so as to have a standard for comparison.

2. The process must be stable, i.e., outcomes are not changing.

3. There must be an ability to create a break between cause and effect in the process so as to provide an opportunity to insert a poka-yoke.

4. Environments requiring substantial operator skill are prime locations for poka-yoke devices.

5. Environments where training or turnover cost is high are prime locations for poka-yoke devices.

6. Environments with frequent interruptions and distractions are prime locations for poka-yoke devices.

7. Environments with a consistent set of mixed products are prime locations fopoka-yoke devices.

8. The beginning of any process where there are multiple other possible processes that could be initiated are a prime location for poka-yoke devices.

9. Locations in the process with similarly positioned or configured parts, controls or tools are prime locations for poka-yoke devices.

10. Any point in the process requiring replacement or orientation of parts in order to prevent mispositioning is a prime location for poka-yoke devices.

11. Any point in the process where adjustments are made for machine or process setups is a prime location for poka-yoke devices.

John Grout attributed defects to three sources: variance, mistakes, and complexity. Complexity requires techniques which simplify the process while managing variance can be accomplished by utilizing statistical process control (SPC). However, if quality problems are the result of mistakes, poka-yoke devices are the appropriate technique to use. In this case, poka-yoke provide an even more effective quality improvement tool than SPC. Other poka-yoke benefits include reduced training costs and the advantage of freeing workers' time and minds for more creative and value-adding activities.

Circumstances where poka-yoke is not the appropriate response are situations involving high speed production, situations where X-bar ($\bar{X}$) & R charts are effective, and use in destructive testing. Other situations, however, provide opportunities for simple, inexpensive, and fail-safe devices to improve performance. Grout relates the example of Lucent Technologies, which reported that half of their 3,300 mistake-proof devices cost less than $100. However, they estimate a net savings of $8.4 million or about $2,545 per device. Poka-yoke is a most impressive and powerful tool.

SEE ALSO: Japanese Management; Quality and Total Quality Management

R. Anthony Inman

FURTHER READING:

Dvorak, Paul. "Poka-Yoke Designs Make Assemblies Mistake-proof." *Machine Design,* 10 March 1998, 181–184.

Evans, James R., and William M. Lindsay. *The Management and Control of Quality.* South-Western Publishing, 2004.

Ghinato, Paulo. "Quality Control Methods: Towards Modern Approaches Through Well Established Principles." *Total Quality Management* 9, no. 6 (August 1998).

Grout, John R. "Mistake-Proofing Production." *Production and Inventory Management Journal* 38, no. 3 (3rd Quarter 1997): 33–37.

Larson, Melissa, "Drill Template Illustrates 'Poka-Yoke.'" *Quality* 10, no. 6 (June 1998).

Patel, S., B.G. Dale and P. Shaw. "Set-up Time Reduction and Mistake Proofing Methods: An Examination in Precision Component Manufacturing." *The TQM Magazine* 13, no. 3 (2001): 175–179.

Snell, Todd, and J. Brian Atwater. "Using Poka-Yoke Concepts to Improve a Military Retail Supply System." *Production and Inventory Management Journal* 37, no. 4 (1996).

Stewart, Douglas M., and John R. Grout. "The Human Side of Mistake-Proofing." *Production and Operations Management* 10, no. 4 (2001): 440–459.

Stewart, Douglas M. and Steven A. Melnyk. "Effective Process Improvement: Developing Poka-Yoke Processes." *Production and Inventory Management Journal* 41, no. 4 (2000): 48–55.

POPULAR PRESS MANAGEMENT BOOKS

The past several decades have witnessed a profusion of management books published in the popular press, many becoming best sellers. This trend began during economic hard times when managers were searching for some easy-to-understand cures for their organizations' financial woes. While the economy greatly improved during the 1990s, managers continue to look for new insights that might help them improve their own or their organizations' fortunes. When the economy slowed in the early part of the twenty-first century, managers again began searching for the golden elixir that would save their jobs.

Despite their enormous sales, popular management books must weather a rather severe image problem. They are quite often perceived as hastily assembled tracts attempting to capitalize on a hot (and usually short-lived) management fad, borne of managers' frazzled attempts to overcome obstacles and challenges that do not generalize well for a wide audience, but which hide these faults behind hyperbolic and trendy word spinning. Typically relying as much on their style as on their substance, popular management books are criticized for lacking both empirical and rational justification, assuming factors that one would be ill-advised to assume, and excessively simplifying very complex problems. Lastly, critics skeptically eye the sheer volume of such books, along with the frequency with which new ones arrive in bookstores before sliding into the background, typically just in time for a new generation of popular books to detail the next fad.

On the other hand, fads do indeed become fads for a reason; some observers emphasize that fads (and the books that extol them) need not be dismissed out of hand. In fact, it is those managers and organizations that are able to spot and expediently capitalize on fads while they are useful that end up excelling over time. Moreover, due to the recognizability and popularity of fads, organizations can utilize the hype surrounding them as a springboard to more general and useful organizational learning and management techniques. In other words, a fool will follow a popular management book to the letter simply because the fad it details is hot; a successful manager will utilize fads for what they are worth, no more and no less, and will avoid inflating the wisdom (or lack thereof) of a popular management book. A confluence of the best and most useful elements of fads past can result in increased quality, productivity, and profitability. The important thing is for managers and organizations to remain focused on their actual concerns-what does the organization do? what elements or techniques are and are not appropriate to its goals? and so on. Simply hammering a useless fad into an organization not suited to it, of course, can be disastrous.

Since a systematic analysis of popular-press management books would be an endless odyssey, what follows are brief summaries of six quite popular titles. The purpose is not so much to critically examine the books, since the criticisms, like the books themselves, do not generalize reliably; rather, the more modest goal is to lay the foundation for what a reader can expect from popular-press management books, from which one can deduce the degree of usefulness therein for one's own purposes.

COMPETITIVE ADVANTAGE THROUGH PEOPLE

Stanford professor Jeffrey Pfeffer in his book *Competitive Advantage Through People* has described the potential impact of human resource management practices on competitive advantage. Based on his study of popular and academic business literature and interviews with people from a wide range of the business community, Pfeffer identified 16 human resource management practices that, in his opinion, can enhance a firm's competitive advantage:

1. *Employment security.* A guarantee of employment stating that no employee will be laid off for lack of work.

2. *Selectivity in recruiting.* Carefully selecting the right employees in the right way.

3. *High wages.* Wages that are higher than required by the market (i.e., than those paid by competitors).

4. *Incentive pay.* Allowing employees who are responsible for enhanced levels of performance and profitability to share in the benefits.

5. *Employee ownership.* Giving the employees ownership interests in the organization by providing them with such things as shares of company stock and profit-sharing programs.

6. *Information sharing.* Providing employees with information about operations, productivity, and profitability.

7. *Participation and empowerment.* Encouraging the decentralization of decision making, broader worker participation, empowerment in controlling their own work process.

8. *Teams and job redesign.* The use of interdisciplinary teams that coordinate and monitor their own work.

9. *Training and skill development.* Providing workers with the skills necessary to do their jobs.

10. *Cross-utilization and cross-training.* Train people to perform several different tasks.

11. *Symbolic egalitarianism.* Equality of treatment among employees established by such actions as eliminating executive dining rooms and reserved parking spaces.

12. *Wage compression.* Reducing the size of the pay differences among employees.

13. *Promotion from within.* Filling job vacancies by promoting employees from jobs at lower organizational levels.

14. *Long-term perspective.* The organization must realize that achieving competitive advantage through the workforce takes time to accomplish, and thus a long-term perspective is needed.

15. *Measurement of practices.* Organizations should measure such things as employee attitudes, the success of various programs and initiative, and employee performance levels.

16. *Overarching philosophy.* An underlying management philosophy that connects the various individual practices into a coherent whole.

THE ONE MINUTE MANAGER

Written by Kenneth Blanchard and Spencer Johnson, *The One Minute Manager* warns managers of the perils of treating employees too harshly or too softly. In the first instance, the employer wins; in the latter, the employee wins. The ideal is to manage employees in a way that both parities win. This aim can be accomplished if managers use three techniques: goal setting, positive reinforcement, and verbal reprimand, each of which can be implemented within one minute.

The use of one-minute goals helps clarify the employees' specific responsibilities and lets them know performance standards to which they will be held. The manager should then frequently review the employees' goal achievements to ensure they remain on target. Moreover, managers should focus their time on catching their employees doing something right, rather than something wrong. Immediate praise should accompany these behaviors. Finally, when seen doing something wrong, employees should receive immediate feedback, indicating exactly what was done wrong and how the manager feels about it. Following the reprimand, the manager should praise the individual as a person, thus establishing a clear separation between the person and the problem behavior.

WHO MOVED MY CHEESE?

Written by Spencer Johnson, M.D., *Who Moved My Cheese?* is a simple parable that reveals profound truths about change. It is an amazing and enlightening story of four characters that live in a "Maze" and look for "Cheese" to nourish them and make them happy. Two mice are named Sniff and Scurry—nonanalytical and nonjudgmental, they just want cheese and are willing to do whatever it takes to get it. Hem and Haw are "little people," mouse-size humans who have an entirely different relationship with cheese. It's not just sustenance to them; it's their self-image. Their lives and belief systems are built around the cheese they've found.

Most of us reading the story will see the cheese as something related to our livelihoods—our jobs, our career paths, the industries we work in—although it can stand for anything, from health to relationships. In the story, the characters are faced with unexpected change. Eventually, one of them deals with it successfully, and writes what he has learned from his experience on the maze walls. When the reader sees the "handwriting on the wall," he or she can discover for him or herself how to deal with change more effectively. One of the most eloquent of the wall sayings is "what would you do if you weren't afraid?" The point of the story is that we have to be alert to changes in the cheese, and be prepared to go running off in search of new sources of cheese when the cheese we have runs out.

GUNG HO!

Blanchard (*The One Minute Manager*, 1984), along with co-author Bowles (*Raving Fans*, Morrow, 1993), recounts an organizational turnaround based on three Native American lessons. This inspirational story of business leaders Peggy Sinclair and Andy Longclaw uses allegory to explain fundamental techniques to boost enthusiasm and performance.

Meet Peggy Sinclair, the newly promoted factory manager who was sent to the worst plant in the thirty-two owned by the company with the expectation to shut it down in 6 months. And Andy Longclaw, who is pointed out to her the first day, in spite of his area's remarkable performance, as a "troublemaker" by one of her executive staff. Sinclair Longclaw patiently shows Sinclair Native American principles that help turn Walton Works #2 from the worst in the company to a workplace recognized by the White House as one of the nation's finest workplaces. Those three important principles are:

1. "The Spirit of the Squirrel" teaches a lesson of the power of worthwhile work.

2. "The Way of the Beaver" showcases empowerment.

3. "The Gift of the Goose" shows the exponential factor of motivation.

GOOD TO GREAT

Jim Collins' book, *Good to Great*, is based on extensive research on a set of companies that moved from mediocre performance to great results and sustained those results for at least fifteen years. (The good-to-great companies generated cumulative stock returns that beat the general stock market by an average of seven times in fifteen years.)

The research team contrasted the good-to-great companies with a carefully selected set of comparison companies that failed to make the leap from good to great. What was different? Why did one set of companies become truly great performers while the other set remained only good? The team spent five years analyzing the histories of all twenty-eight companies in the study. After 15,000 hours of digging through mountains of data, Collins and his team discovered the key determinants of greatness—why some companies make the leap and others don't. The findings of the Good to Great study:

1. Level 5 Leaders: During the transition years, all of the companies were led by humble individuals who channel their ego needs away from themselves and into the larger goal of building a great company. It is not that Level 5 leaders have no ego or self-interest. Indeed, they are incredibly ambitious—but their ambition is first and foremost for the institution, not themselves. Ten out of eleven of those profiled came up from inside the company whereas the mediocre comparison companies turned to outsiders six times more often.

2. First Who Then What: The good-to-great leaders began the transformation by first getting the right people on the bus (and the wrong people off the bus) and then figured out where to drive it. The comparison companies frequently followed the "genius with a thousand helpers" model where the leader sets a vision and then enlists a crew of highly capable "helpers" to make the vision happen. This model fails when the genius departs.

3. Confront the Brutal Facts (Yet Never Lose Faith): Create a culture where people have a tremendous opportunity to be heard, and, ultimately, for the truth to be heard. Leadership begins with getting people to confront the brutal facts and to act on the implications. Retain absolute faith that you can and will prevail in the end, regardless of the difficulties.

4. Hedgehog Concept: See what is essential and ignore the rest. Hedgehog companies understand what they can be the best at, what they can feel passionate about and that is what they focus on.

5. A Culture of Discipline: Good-to-great firms have a high ethic of responsibility and a high culture of discipline. Get disciplined people to engage in discipline thought and take disciplined action.

6. Technology Accelerators: Good-to-great companies avoid technology fads and yet they become pioneers in the application of carefully selected, relevant technologies.

7. The Flywheel and the Doom Loop: Good-to-great companies follow a pattern of buildup leading to breakthrough. They accumulate successes and use the cumulative

consistent momentum to push them yet further out in front. There is no dramatic, revolutionary event.

PRIMAL LEADERSHIP

Business leaders who maintain that emotions are best kept out of the work environment do so at their organization's peril. Bestselling author Daniel Goleman's theories on emotional intelligence (EI) have radically altered common understanding of what "being smart" entails, and in *Primal Leadership,* he and his coauthors present the case for cultivating emotionally intelligent leaders. Since the actions of the leader apparently account for up to seventy percent of employees' perception of the climate of their organization, Goleman and his team emphasize the importance of developing what they term "resonant leadership." Focusing on the four domains of emotional intelligence—self-awareness, self-management, social awareness, and relationship management—they explore what contributes to and detracts from resonant leadership, and how the development of these four EI competencies spawns different leadership styles. The best leaders maintain a style repertoire, switching easily between "visionary," "coaching," "affiliative," and "democratic," and making rare use of less effective "pace-setting" and "commanding" styles. The authors' discussion of these methods is informed by research on the workplace climates engendered by the leadership styles of more than 3,870 executives. Indeed, the experiences of leaders in a wide range of work environments lend real-life examples to much of the advice Goleman et al. offer, from developing the motivation to change and creating an improvement plan based on learning rather than performance outcomes, to experimenting with new behaviors and nurturing supportive relationships that encourage change and growth. The book's final section takes the personal process of developing resonant leadership and applies it to the entire organizational culture.

SEE ALSO: Management Styles; The Art and Science of Management

Lawrence S. Kleiman
Revised by Rebecca Bennett

FURTHER READING:

Blanchard, K., and S. Bowles. *Gung Ho!* Morrow, 1998.

Blanchard, K., and S. Johnson. *The One-Minute Manager.* New York: Morrow, 1982.

Collins, J. *Good to Great.* Harper Business, 2001.

Goleman, D., R. Boyatzis, and A. McKee. *Primal Leadership.* Harvard Business School Press, 2002.

Johnson, S., M.D. *Who Moved My Cheese?* Putnam, 1998.

Pfeffer, J. *Competitive Advantage Through People.* Boston: Harvard Business School Press, 1994.

PORTER'S 5-FORCES MODEL

A means of providing corporations with an analysis of their competition and determining strategy, Porter's five-forces model looks at the strength of five distinct competitive forces, which, when taken together, determine long-term profitability and competition. Porter's work has had a greater influence on business strategy than any other theory in the last half of the twentieth century, and his more recent work may have a similar impact on global competition.

Michigan native Michael Porter was born in 1947, was educated at Princeton, and earned an MBA (1971) and Ph.D. (1973) from Harvard. He was promoted to full professor at Harvard at age 34 and is currently C. Roland Christensen Professor of Business Administration at the Harvard Business School. He has published numerous books and articles, the first *Interbrand Choice, Strategy and Bilateral Market Power,* appearing in 1976. His best known and most widely used and referenced books are *Competitive Strategy* (1980) and *Competitive Advantage* (1985). *Competitive Strategy* revolutionized contemporary approaches to business strategy through application of the five-forces model. In *Competitive Advantage,* Porter further developed his strategy concepts to include the creation of a sustainable advantage. His other model, the value chain model, centers on product added value. Porter's work is widely read by business strategists around the world as well as business students. Any MBA student recognizes his name as one of the icons of business literature. The Strategic Management Society named Porter the most important living strategist in 1998, and Kevin Coyne of the consulting firm McKinsey and Co. called Porter "the single most important strategist working today, and maybe of all time."

The five-forces model was developed in Porter's 1980 book, *Competitive Strategy: Techniques for Analyzing Industries and Competitors.* To Porter, the classic means of developing a strategy—a formula for competition, goals, and policies to achieve those goals—was antiquated and in need of revision. Porter was searching for a solution between the two schools of prevailing thought-the Harvard Business School's urging firms to adjust to a unique set of changing circumstances and that of the Boston Consulting Group, based on the experience curve, whereby the more a company knows about the existing market, the more its strategy can be directed to increase its share of the market.

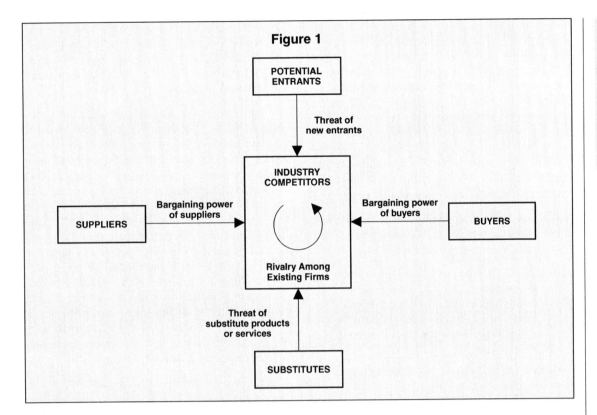

Figure 1

POTENTIAL
ENTRANTS

Threat of
new entrants

INDUSTRY
COMPETITORS

Bargaining power
of suppliers

SUPPLIERS

Bargaining power
of buyers

BUYERS

Rivalry Among
Existing Firms

Threat of
substitute products
or services

SUBSTITUTES

Porter applied microeconomic principles to business strategy and analyzed the strategic requirements of industrial sectors, not just specific companies. The five forces are competitive factors which determine industry competition and include: suppliers, rivalry within an industry, substitute products, customers or buyers, and new entrants (see Figure 1).

Although the strength of each force can vary from industry to industry, the forces, when considered together, determine long-term profitability within the specific industrial sector. The strength of each force is a separate function of the industry structure, which Porter defines as "the underlying economic and technical characteristics of an industry." Collectively, the five forces affect prices, necessary investment for competitiveness, market share, potential profits, profit margins, and industry volume. The key to the success of an industry, and thus the key to the model, is analyzing the changing dynamics and continuous flux between and within the five forces. Porter's model depends on the concept of power within the relationships of the five forces.

THE FIVE FORCES

INDUSTRY COMPETITORS. Rivalries naturally develop between companies competing in the same market. Competitors use means such as advertising, introducing new products, more attractive customer service and warranties, and price competition to enhance their standing and market share in a specific industry. To Porter, the intensity of this rivalry is the result of

factors like equally balanced companies, slow growth within an industry, high fixed costs, lack of product differentiation, overcapacity and price-cutting, diverse competitors, high-stakes investment, and the high risk of industry exit. There are also market entry barriers.

PRESSURE FROM SUBSTITUTE PRODUCTS. Substitute products are the natural result of industry competition, but they place a limit on profitability within the industry. A substitute product involves the search for a product that can do the same function as the product the industry already produces. Porter uses the example of security brokers, who increasingly face substitutes in the form of real estate, money-market funds, and insurance. Substitute products take on added importance as their availability increases.

BARGAINING POWER OF SUPPLIERS. Suppliers have a great deal of influence over an industry as they affect price increases and product quality. A supplier group exerts even more power over an industry if it is dominated by a few companies, there are no substitute products, the industry is not an important consumer for the suppliers, their product is essential to the industry, the supplier differs costs, and forward integration potential of the supplier group exists. Labor supply can also influence the position of the suppliers. These factors are generally out of the control of the industry or company but strategy can alter the power of suppliers.

BARGAINING POWER OF BUYERS. The buyer's power is significant in that buyers can force prices down, demand higher quality products or services, and, in essence, play competitors against one another, all resulting in potential loss of industry profits. Buyers exercise more power when they are large-volume buyers, the product is a significant aspect of the buyer's costs or purchases, the products are standard within an industry, there are few changing or switching costs, the buyers earn low profits, potential for backward integration of the buyer group exists, the product is not essential to the buyer's product, and the buyer has full disclosure about supply, demand, prices, and costs. The bargaining position of buyers changes with time and a company's (and industry's) competitive strategy.

POTENTIAL ENTRANTS. Threats of new entrants into an industry depends largely on barriers to entry. Porter identifies six major barriers to entry:

- Economies of scale, or decline in unit costs of the product, which force the entrant to enter on a large scale and risk a strong reaction from firms already in the industry, or accepting a disadvantage of costs if entering on a small scale.

- Product differentiation, or brand identification and customer loyalty.

- Capital requirements for entry; the investment of large capital, after all, presents a significant risk.

- Switching costs, or the cost the buyer has to absorb to switch from one supplier to another.

- Access to distribution channels. New entrants have to establish their distribution in a market with established distribution channels to secure a space for their product.

- Cost disadvantages independent of scale, whereby established companies already have product technology, access to raw materials, favorable sites, advantages in the form of government subsidies, and experience.

New entrants can also expect a barrier in the form of government policy through federal and state regulations and licensing. New firms can expect retaliation from existing companies and also face changing barriers related to technology, strategic planning within the industry, and manpower and expertise problems. The entry deterring price or the existence of a prevailing price structure presents an additional challenge to a firm entering an established industry.

In summary, Porter's five-forces models concentrates on five structural industry features that comprise the competitive environment, and hence profitability, of an industry. Applying the model means, to be profitable, the firm has to find and establish itself in an industry so that the company can react to the forces of competition in a favorable manner. For Porter, *Competitive Strategy* is not a book for academics but a

blueprint for practitioners-a tool for managers to analyze competition in an industry in order to anticipate and prepare for changes in the industry, new competitors and market shifts, and to enhance their firm's overall industry standing.

Throughout the relevant sections of *Competitive Strategy,* Porter uses numerous industry examples to illustrate his theory. Since those examples are now over twenty years old, changes in technology and other industrial shifts and trends have made them somewhat obsolete. Although immediate praise for the book and the five-forces model was exhaustive, critiques of Porter have appeared in business literature. Porter's model does not, for example, consider nonmarket changes, such as events in the political arena that impact an industry. Furthermore, Porter's model has come under fire for what critics see as his under-evaluation of government regulation and antitrust violations. Overall, criticisms of the model find their nexus in the lack of consideration by Porter of rapidly changing industry dynamics. In virtually all instances, critics also present alternatives to Porter's model.

Yet, in a *Fortune* interview in early 1999, Porter responded to the challenges, saying he welcomed the "fertile intellectual debate" that stemmed from his work. He admitted he had ignored writing about strategy in recent years but emphasized his desire to reenter the fray discussing his work and addressing questions about the model, its application, and the confusion about what really constitutes strategy. Porter's *The Competitive Advantage of Nations* (1990) and the more recent *On Competition* (1998) demonstrate his desire to further stimulate discussion in the business and academic worlds.

SEE ALSO: Competitive Advantage; Generic Competitive Strategies; Product Life Cycle and Industry Life Cycle; Strategy Formulation

Boyd Childress
Revised by Hal P. Kirkwood, Jr.

FURTHER READING:

Competitive Advantage: Creating and Sustaining Superior Performance. New York: Free Press, 1998.

Competitive Strategy: Techniques for Analyzing Industries and Competitors. New York: Free Press, 1998.

Mahon, J. F., and R.A. McGowan. "Modeling Industry Political Dynamics." *Business and Society* 37, no. 4 (1998, December): 390–413.

Porter, M.E. *Michael Porter on Competition.* Boston, MA: Harvard Business School Press, 1998.

"Professor Porter Ph.D.: Management Theorists." *Economist, 333* (1994, October): 75.

Siaw, I. and A. Yu. "An Analysis of the Impact of the Internet on Competition in the Banking Industry, Using Porter's Five

Forces Model". *International Journal of Management* 21, no. 4 (2004, December): 514–524.

Slater, S. F. and E.M.A. Olson. "Fresh Look at Industry and Market Analysis." *Business Horizons* 45. no. 1, (2002, January/February): 15–23.

Surowiecki, J. "The Return of Michael Porter." *Fortune* 139, no. 2 (1999, February): 135–138.

PRICING POLICY AND STRATEGY

Managers should start setting prices during the development stage as part of strategic pricing to avoid launching products or services that cannot sustain profitable prices in the market. This approach to pricing enables companies to either fit costs to prices or scrap products or services that cannot be generated cost-effectively. Through systematic pricing policies and strategies, companies can reap greater profits and increase or defend their market shares. Setting prices is one of the principal tasks of marketing and finance managers in that the price of a product or service often plays a significant role in that product's or service's success, not to mention in a company's profitability. Generally, pricing policy refers how a company sets the prices of its products and services based on costs, value, demand, and competition. Pricing strategy, on the other hand, refers to how a company uses pricing to achieve its strategic goals, such as offering lower prices to increase sales volume or higher prices to decrease backlog. Despite some degree of difference, pricing policy and strategy tend to overlap, and the different policies and strategies are not necessarily mutually exclusive.

After establishing the bases for their prices, managers can begin developing pricing strategies by determining company pricing goals, such as increasing short-term and long-term profits, stabilizing prices, increasing cash flow, and warding off competition. Managers also must take into account current market conditions when developing pricing strategies to ensure that the prices they choose fit market conditions. In addition, effective pricing strategy involves considering customers, costs, competition, and different market segments.

Pricing strategy entails more than reacting to market conditions, such as reducing pricing because competitors have reduced their prices. Instead, it encompasses more thorough planning and consideration of customers, competitors, and company goals. Furthermore, pricing strategies tend to vary depending on whether a company is a new entrant into a market or an established firm. New entrants sometimes offer products at low cost to attract market share, while incumbents' reactions vary. Incumbents that fear the new entrant will challenge the incumbents' customer base may match prices or go even lower than the new entrant to protect its market share. If incumbents do not view the new entrant as a serious threat, incumbents may simply resort to increased advertising aimed at enhancing customer loyalty, but have no change in price in efforts to keep the new entrant from stealing away customers.

The following sections explain various ways companies develop pricing policy and strategy. First, cost-based pricing is considered. This is followed by the second topic of value-based pricing. Third, demand-based pricing is addressed followed by competition-based pricing. After this, several strategies for new and established pricing strategies are explained.

COST-BASED PRICING

The traditional pricing policy can be summarized by the formula:

$$\text{Cost} + \text{Fixed profit percentage} = \text{Selling price.}$$

Cost-based pricing involves the determination of all fixed and variable costs associated with a product or service. After the total costs attributable to the product or service have been determined, managers add a desired profit margin to each unit such as a 5 or 10 percent markup. The goal of the cost-oriented approach is to cover all costs incurred in producing or delivering products or services and to achieve a targeted level of profit.

By itself, this method is simple and straightforward, requiring only that managers study financial and accounting records to determine prices. This pricing approach does not involve examining the market or considering the competition and other factors that might have an impact on pricing. Cost-oriented pricing also is popular because it is an age-old practice that uses internal information that managers can obtain easily. In addition, a company can defend its prices based on costs, and demonstrate that its prices cover costs plus a markup for profit.

However, critics contend that the cost-oriented strategy fails to provide a company with an effective pricing policy. One problem with the cost-plus strategy is that determining a unit's cost before its price is difficult in many industries because unit costs may vary depending on volume. As a result, many business analysts have criticized this method, arguing that it is no longer appropriate for modern market conditions. Cost-based pricing generally leads to high prices in weak markets and low prices in strong markets, thereby impeding profitability because these prices are the exact opposites of what strategic prices would be if market conditions were taken into consideration.

While managers must consider costs when developing a pricing policy and strategy, costs alone should not determine prices. Many managers of industrial goods and service companies sell their products and services at incremental cost, and make their substantial profits from their best customers and from short-notice deliveries. When considering costs, managers should ask what costs they can afford to pay, taking into account the prices the market allows, and still allow for a profit on the sale. In addition, managers must consider production costs in order to determine what goods to produce and in what amounts. Nevertheless, pricing generally involves determining what prices customers can afford before determining what amount of products to produce. By bearing in mind the prices they can charge and the costs they can afford to pay, managers can determine whether their costs enable them to compete in the low-cost market, where customers are concerned primarily with price, or whether they must compete in the premium-price market, in which customers are primarily concerned with quality and features.

VALUE-BASED PRICING

Value pricers adhere to the thinking that the optimal selling price is a reflection of a product or service's perceived value by customers, not just the company's costs to produce or provide a product or service. The value of a product or service is derived from customer needs, preferences, expectations, and financial resources as well as from competitors' offerings. Consequently, this approach calls for managers to query customers and research the market to determine how much they value a product or service. In addition, managers must compare their products or services with those of their competitors to identify their value advantages and disadvantages.

Yet, value-based pricing is not just creating customer satisfaction or making sales because customer satisfaction may be achieved through discounting alone, a pricing strategy that could also lead to greater sales. However, discounting may not necessarily lead to profitability. Value pricing involves setting prices to increase profitability by tapping into more of a product or service's value attributes. This approach to pricing also depends heavily on strong advertising, especially for new products or services, in order to communicate the value of products or services to customers and to motivate customers to pay more if necessary for the value provided by these products or services.

DEMAND-BASED PRICING

Managers adopting demand-based pricing policies are, like value pricers, not fully concerned with costs. Instead, they concentrate on the behavior and characteristics of customers and the quality and characteristics of their products or services. Demand-oriented pricing focuses on the level of demand for a product or service, not on the cost of materials, labor, and so forth.

According to this pricing policy, managers try to determine the amount of products or services they can sell at different prices. Managers need demand schedules in order to determine prices based on demand. Using demand schedules, managers can figure out which production and sales levels would be the most profitable. To determine the most profitable production and sales levels, managers examine production and marketing costs estimates at different sales levels. The prices are determined by considering the cost estimates at different sales levels and expected revenues from sales volumes associated with projected prices.

The success of this strategy depends on the reliability of demand estimates. Hence, the crucial obstacle managers face with this approach is accurately gauging demand, which requires extensive knowledge of the manifold market factors that may have an impact on the number of products sold. Two common options managers have for obtaining accurate estimates are enlisting the help from either sales representatives or market experts. Managers frequently ask sales representatives to estimate increases or decreases in demand stemming from specific increases or decreases in a product or service's price, since sales representatives generally are attuned to market trends and customer demands. Alternatively, managers can seek the assistance of experts such as market researchers or consultants to provide estimates of sales levels at various unit prices.

COMPETITION-BASED PRICING

With a competition-based pricing policy, a company sets its prices by determining what other companies competing in the market charge. A company begins developing competition-based prices by identifying its present competitors. Next, a company assesses its own product or service. After this step, a company sets it prices higher than, lower than, or on par with the competitors based on the advantages and disadvantages of a company's product or service as well as on the expected response by competitors to the set price. This last consideration-the response of competitors-is an important part of competition-based pricing, especially in markets with only a few competitors. In such a market, if one competitor lowers its price, the others will most likely lower theirs as well.

This pricing policy allows companies to set prices quickly with relatively little effort, since it does not require as accurate market data as the demand pricing. Competitive pricing also makes distributors more receptive to a company's products because they are priced within the range the distributor already handles. Furthermore, this pricing policy enables companies to select from a variety of different pricing strategies to achieve their strategic goals. In other words, companies can choose to mark their prices above, below, or on par with their competitors' prices and thereby influence customer perceptions of their products. For example, if a Company A sets its prices above those of its competitors, the higher price could suggest that Company A's products or services are superior in quality. Harley Davidson used this with great success. Although Harley-Davidson uses many of the same parts suppliers as Honda, Kawasaki, Yamaha, and Honda, they price well above the competitive price of these competitors. Harley's high prices combined with its customer loyalty and mystique help overcome buyer resistance to higher prices. Production efficiencies over the last two decades, however, have made quality among motorcycle producers about equal, but pricing above the market signals quality to buyers, whether or not they get the quality premium they pay for.

STRATEGIES FOR NEW AND ESTABLISHED PRODUCTS

Product pricing strategies frequently depend on the stage a product or service is in its life cycle; that is, new products often require different pricing strategies than established products or mature products.

NEW PRODUCT PRICING STRATEGY. Entrants often rely on pricing strategies that allow them to capture market share quickly. When there are several competitors in a market, entrants usually use lower pricing to change consumer spending habits and acquire market share. To appeal to customers effectively, entrants generally implement a simple or transparent pricing structure, which enables customers to compare prices easily and understand that the entrants have lower prices than established incumbent companies.

Complex pricing arrangements, however, prevent lower pricing from being a successful strategy in that customers cannot readily compare prices with hidden and contingent costs. The long-distance telephone market illustrates this point; large corporations have lengthy telephone bills that include numerous contingent costs, which depend on location, use, and service features. Consequently, competitors in the corporate long-distance telephone service market do not use lower pricing as the primary pricing strategy, as they do in the consumer and small-business markets, where telephone billing is much simpler.

Another example is the computer industry. Dell, Fujitsu, HP, and many others personal computer makers offer bundles of products that make it more difficult for consumers to sort out the true differences among these competitors. For example, consumers purchasing an HP computer from the retailer, Best Buy, will have not only the computer itself, but also six months of "free" Internet access bundled into the price. Comparing the absolute value of each personal computer become more difficult as an increasing number of other products such as Quicken, Adobe's Photoshop Elements, and other software are sold together with the purchase. For Macintosh users or for those who might consider switching from a personal computer to a Macintosh, Apple announced in 2005 that it would begin selling the Mac Mini, a Macintosh that, as with PC makers, bundles its iLife® software into the mix. By extending its brand to non-premium price tiers, Apple will compete head-to-head with established firms. And although the Mac Mini is at a low price point, starting at $499, it will be difficult for consumers to directly compare the bundled products of PCs directly with the bundled products of Apple's Mac Mini. The complexity of these comparisons is what can make such new product pricing successful.

ESTABLISHED PRODUCT PRICING STRATEGY. Sometimes established companies need not adjust their prices at all in response to entrants and their lower prices, because customers frequently are willing to pay more for the products or services of an established company to avoid perceived risks associated with switching products or services.

However, when established companies do not have this advantage, they must implement other pricing strategies to preserve their market share and profits. When entrants are involved, established companies sometimes attempt to hide their actual prices by embedding them in complex prices. This tactic makes it difficult for customers to compare prices, which is advantageous to established companies competing with entrants that have lower prices. In addition, established companies also may use a more complex pricing plan, such as a two-part pricing tactic. This tactic especially benefits companies with significant market power. Local telephone companies, for example, use this strategy, charging both fixed and per-minute charges.

MARKET SEGMENTATION

Because all customers do not have the same needs, expectations, and financial resources, managers can improve their pricing strategies by segmenting markets. Successful segmentation comes about when managers determine what motivates particular markets and what differences exist in the market when taken as a whole. For example, some customers may be motivated largely by price, while others are motivated by functionality and utility. The idea behind segmentation is to divide a large group into a set of smaller groups that share significant characteristics such as age, income, geographic location, lifestyle, and so on. By dividing a market into two or more segments, a company can devise a pricing scheme that will appeal to the motivations of each of the different market segments or it can decide to target only particular segments of the market that best correspond to its products or services and their prices.

Managers can use market segmentation strategically to price products or services in order to attain company objectives. Companies can set prices differently for different segments based on factors such as location, time of sale, quantity of sale, product design, and a number of others, depending on the way companies divide up the market. By doing so, companies can increase their profits, market share, cash flow, and so forth.

SEE ALSO: Product Design; Product Life Cycle and Industry Life Cycle; Product-Process Matrix; Strategy Formulation

Karl Heil
Revised by Scott B. Droege

FURTHER READING:

Kardes, F.R., M.L. Cronley, J.J. Kellaris, and S.S. Posavac. "The Role of Selective Information Processing in Price-Quality Inference." *Journal of Consumer Research* 31, no. 2 (2004): 368–375.

Meyvis, T. and C. Janiszewski. "When Are Broader Brands Stronger Brands? An Accessibility Perspective on the Success of Brand Extensions." *Journal of Consumer Research* 31, no. 2 (2004): 346–358.

Potter, D. "Confronting Low-End Competition." *MIT Sloan Management Review* 45, no. 4 (2004): 73–79.

Smagalla, D. "Does Promotion Pricing Grow Future Business?" *MIT Sloan Management Review* 45, no. 4 (2004): 9.

PROBLEM SOLVING

A managerial problem can be described as the gap between a given current state of affairs and a future desired state. Problem solving may then be thought of as the process of analyzing the situation and developing a solution to bridge the gap. While it is widely recognized that different diagnostic techniques are appropriate in different situations, problem solving as a formal analytical framework applies to all but the simplest managerial problems. The framework is analogous to the scientific method used in chemistry, astronomy, and the other physical sciences. In both cases, the purpose underlying the analytic process is to minimize the influence of the investigator's personal biases, maximize the likelihood of an accurate result, and facilitate communication among affected parties.

Problem solving was popularized by W. Edwards Deming and the expansion of the total quality management movement in the 1980s. While Deming described what he called the Shewhart cycle, the technique is more commonly known as the Deming Wheel or simply as the PDCA cycle. Regardless of the name, a problem solver is urged to follow a step-by-step approach to problem solving-plan, do, check, act (hence the PDCA acronym).

In the planning stage, a manager develops a working hypothesis about why a given problem exists and then develops a proposed solution to the problem. The second step is to implement, or do, the proposed remedy. Next, the manager studies or checks the result of the action taken. The focus of this review is to determine whether the proposed solution achieved the desired result-was the problem solved? The fourth step then depends upon the interpretation of the check on results. If the problem was solved, the manager acts to institutionalize the proposed solution. This might mean establishing controls or changing policy manuals to ensure that the new way of doing business continues. However, if the check indicates that the problem was not solved or was only partially corrected, the manager acts by initiating a new cycle. Indeed, the technique is represented as a cycle based on the belief that many problems are never fully solved. For example, suppose that the problem in a given manufacturing facility is determined to be that labor productivity is too low. A change in processing methods may be found to successfully increase labor productivity. However, this does not preclude additional increases in labor productivity. Therefore, the PDCA cycle suggests that managers should pursue a course of continuous improvement activity.

The problem-solving framework can be used in a wide variety of business situations, including both large-scale management-change initiatives and routine improvement or corrective activity. Indeed, management consultants may be thought of as professional problem solvers. By relying on the proven problem-solving framework, external consultants are often able to overcome their lack of specific industry experience or knowledge of an organization's internal dynamics to provide meaningful analysis and suggestions for improvement. To more fully explore the issues presented by problem solving, the four-step PDCA cycle is expanded to a nine-step framework in the next section.

Perhaps the only generalizable caveat regarding problem solving is to guard against overuse of the framework. For example, Florida Power & Light became well known for their problem-solving ability in the late 1980s. One of their most successful initiatives was to institute an aggressive tree-trimming program to anticipate and prevent power failure due to downed limbs falling on electrical lines during storms. They were so successful that they integrated the problem-solving framework into their day-to-day managerial decision making and organizational culture. While this resulted in well reasoned decisions, it also meant that implementing even simple changes like moving a filing cabinet closer to the people using it required an overly bureaucratic approval process. This phenomenon is commonly referred to as paralysis of analysis. Therefore, managers should remain aware of the costs in both time and resources associated with the problem-solving framework. Accordingly, the nine-step framework described below is offered as a suggested guide to problem solving. Managers should feel free to simplify the framework as appropriate given their particular situation.

THE PROBLEM-SOLVING FRAMEWORK

PROBLEM IDENTIFICATION. Although business problems in the form of a broken piece of machinery or an irate customer are readily apparent, many problems present themselves in a more subtle fashion. For example, if a firm's overall sales are increasing, but its percentage of market share is declining, there is no attention-grabbing incident to indicate that a problem exists. However, the problem-solving framework is still helpful in analyzing the current state of affairs and developing a management intervention to guide the firm toward the future desired state. Therefore, a solid approach to problem solving begins with a solid approach to problem identification. Whatever techniques are used, a firm's approach to problem identification should address three common identification shortfalls. First and most obviously, the firm wants to avoid being blindsided. Many problems develop over time; however, unless the firm is paying attention, warning signals may go unheeded until it is too late to effectively respond. A second common error of problem identification is not appropriating properly. This means that although a firm recognizes that an issue exists, they do not recognize the significance of the problem and fail to dedicate sufficient resources to its solution. It can be argued that not prioritizing properly has kept many traditional retail firms from responding effectively to emerging internet-based competitors. Finally, a third common error in problem identification is overreaction-the Chicken Little syndrome. Just as every falling acorn does not indicate that the sky is falling, neither does every customer complaint indicates that a crisis exists. Therefore, a firm's problem identification methods should strive to present an accurate assessment of the problems and opportunities facing the firm.

While no specific problem-identification technique will be appropriate for every situation, there are several techniques that are widely applicable. Two of the most useful techniques are statistical process control (SPC) and benchmarking. SPC is commonly used in the repetitive manufacturing industries, but can also prove useful in any stable production or service-delivery setting. A well formulated SPC program serves to inform managers when their operational processes are performing as expected and when something unexpected is introducing variation in process outputs. A simplified version of SPC is to examine performance outliers-those instances when performance was unusually poor or unusually good. It is believed that determining what went wrong, or conversely what went right, may inspire process or product modifications. Competitive benchmarking allows managers to keep tabs on their competition and thereby gauge their customers' evolving expectations. For instance, benchmarking might involve reverse engineering-disassembling a competitor's product-to study its design features and estimate the competitor's manufacturing costs. Texas Nameplate Company, Inc., a 1998 Malcolm Baldrige National Quality Award winner, uses competitive benchmarking by periodically ordering products from their competitors to compare their delivery-time performance.

Additional listening and problem identification techniques include the time-tested management-by-walking-around, revamped with a Japanese influence as going to gemba. The technique suggests that managers go to where the action is-to the production floor, point of delivery, or even to the customer's facilities to directly observe how things are done and how the product is used. Other methods include active solicitation of customer complaints and feedback. Bennigan's Restaurants offer a five-dollar credit toward future purchases to randomly selected customers who respond to telephone surveys on their satisfaction with their most recent restaurant visit. Granite Rock Company, a 1992 Baldrige Award winner, goes even farther by allowing customers to choose not to pay for any item that fails to meet their expectations. All that Granite Rock asks in return is an explanation of why the product was unsatisfactory.

PROBLEM VERIFICATION. The amount of resources that should be dedicated to verification will vary greatly depending upon how the problem itself is manifested. If the problem is straightforward and well-defined, only a cursory level of verification may be appropriate. However, many business problems are complex and ill defined. These situations may be similar to the case of a physician who is confronted with a patient that has self-diagnosed his medical condition. While considering the patient's claim, the doctor will conduct her own analysis to verify the diagnosis. Similarly, the need for verification is especially important when a manager is asked to step in and solve a problem that has been identified by someone else. The introduction of the manager's fresh perspective and the possibility of a hidden agenda on the part of the individual who initially identified the issue under consideration suggests that a "trust, but verify" approach may be prudent. Otherwise, the manager may eventually discover she has expended a great deal of time and effort pursuing a solution to the wrong problem.

In the case of particularly ambiguous problems, McKinsey & Company, a management-consulting group, uses a technique they call Forces at Work. In this analysis, McKinsey's consultants review the external pressures on the client firm arising from suppliers, customers, competitors, regulators, technology shifts, and substitute products. They then attempt to document the direction and magnitude of any changes in the various pressures on the firm. In addition, they review any internal changes, such as shifts in labor relations or changes in production technology. Finally, they look at how the various factors are impacting the way the firm designs, manufactures, distributes, sells, and services its products. Essentially, McKinsey attempts to create comprehensive before-and-after snapshots of their client's business environment. Focusing on the differences between the two, they hope to identify and clarify the nature of the challenges facing the firm.

PROBLEM DEFINITION. The next step in problem solving is to formally define the problem to be addressed. This is a negotiation between the individuals tasked with solving the problem and the individuals who oversee their work. Essentially, the parties need to come to an agreement on what a solution to the problem will look like. Are the overseers anticipating an implementation plan, a fully operational production line, a recommendation for capital investment, or a new product design? What metrics are considered important-cycle time, material costs, market share, scrap rates, or warranty costs? Complex problems may be broken down into mutually exclusive and collectively exhaustive components, allowing each piece to be addressed separately. The negotiation should recognize that the scope of the problem that is defined will drive the resource requirements of the problem solvers. The more focused the problem definition, the fewer resources necessary to generate a solution. Finally, the time frame for problem analysis should also be established. Many business problems require an expedited or emergency response. This may mean that the problem solvers need to generate a temporary or interim solution to the problem before they can fully explore the underlying causes of the problem. Ensuring that the overseers recognize the limitations inherent in an interim solution serves to preserve the credibility of the problem solvers.

ROOT-CAUSE ANALYSIS. Now that the problem has been formally defined, the next step is for the problem solvers to attempt to identify the causes of the problem. The ultimate goal is to uncover the root cause or causes of the problem. The root cause is defined as that condition or event that, if corrected or eliminated, would prevent the problem from occurring. However, the problem solver should focus on potential root causes they are within the realm of potential control. For example, finding that a particular weight of motor oil is insufficient to protect an engine from overheating readily leads to an actionable plan for improvement. Finding that the root cause of a problem is gravity does not.

A common technique for generating potential root causes is the cause-and-effect diagram (also known as the fishbone or Ishikawa diagram). Using the diagram as a brainstorming tool, problem solvers traditionally review how the characteristics or operation of raw materials, labor inputs, equipment, physical environment, and management policies might cause the identified problem. Each branch of the diagram then becomes a statement of a causal hypothesis. For example, one branch of the diagram might suggest that low salaries are leading to high employee turnover, which in turn results in inexperienced operators running the machinery, which leads to a high scrap rate and ultimately higher material costs. This analysis suggests that to address the problem of high material costs, the firm may have to address the root cause of insufficient salaries.

Collection and examination of data may also lead the problem solver toward causal hypotheses. Check sheets, scatter plots, Pareto diagrams, data stratification, and a number of other graphical and statistical tools can aid problem solvers as they look for relationships between the problems identified and various input variables. Patterns in the data, changes in a variable over time, or comparisons to similar systems may all be useful in developing working theories about why something is happening. The problem solver should also consider the possibility of multiple causes or interaction effects. Perhaps the problem manifests only when a specific event occurs and certain conditions are met-the temperature is above 85 degrees or the ambient humidity is abnormally low.

Once the problem solver has identified the likely root causes of the problem, an examination of the available evidence should be used to confirm or disconfirm which potential causes actually are present and impacting the performance under consideration. This might entail developing an experiment where the candidate cause is controlled to determine whether its manipulation influences the presence of the problem. At this stage of the analysis, the problem solver should remain open to disconfirming evidence. Many elegant theories fail to achieve the necessary confirmation when put to the test. At this stage of the analysis it is also common for the problem solver to discover simple, easily implemented actions that will solve all or part of the problem. If this occurs, then clearly the problem solver should grasp the opportunity to "pick the low hanging fruit." Even if only a small component of the problem is solved, these interim wins serve to build momentum and add credibility to the problem-solving process.

ALTERNATIVE GENERATION. Once the root causes of the problem have been identified, the problem solver can concentrate on developing approaches to prevent, eliminate, or control them. This is a creative process. The problem solver should feel free to challenge assumptions about how business was conducted in the past. At times, an effective approach is to generalize the relationship between the cause and the problem. Then the problem solver can look for similar relationships between other cause and effects that might provide insight on how to address the issues at hand. In general, it is useful to attempt to generate multiple candidate solutions. By keeping the creative process going, even after a viable solution is proposed, the problem solver retains the possibility of identifying a more effective or less expensive solution to the problem.

EVALUATION OF ALTERNATIVES. Assuming that the problem was well defined, evaluation of the effectiveness of alternative solutions should be relatively straightforward. The issue is simply to what extent each alternative alleviates the problem. Using the metrics previously identified as important for judging success, the various alternatives can generally be directly compared. However, in addition to simply measuring the end result, the problem solvers may also want to consider the resources necessary to implement each solution. Organizations are made up of real people, with real strengths and weaknesses. A given solution may require competencies or access to finite resources that simply do not exist in the organization. In addition, there may be political considerations within the organization that influence the desirability of one alternative over another. Therefore, the problem solver may want to consider both the tangible and intangible benefits and costs of each alternative.

IMPLEMENTATION. A very common problem-solving failure is for firms to stop once the plan of action is developed. Regardless of how good the plan is, it is useless unless it is implemented. Therefore, once a specific course of action has been approved, it should continue to receive the necessary attention and support to achieve success. The work should be broken down into tasks that can be assigned and managed. Specific milestones with target dates for completion should be established. Traditional project management techniques, such as the critical path method (CPM) or the program evaluation and review technique (PERT) are very useful to oversee implementation efforts.

POST-IMPLEMENTATION REVIEW. Another common failure is for firms to simply move on after a solution has been implemented. At a minimum, a post-implementation evaluation of whether or not the problem has been solved should be conducted. If appropriate and using the metrics that were established earlier, this process should again be relatively straightforward-were the expected results achieved? The review can also determine whether additional improvement activities are justified. As the PDCA cycle suggests, some problems are never solved, they are only diminished. If the issue at hand is of that nature, then initiating a new cycle of problem-solving activity may be appropriate.

A secondary consideration for the post-implementation review is a debriefing of the problem solvers themselves. By its very nature, problem solving often presents managers with novel situations. As a consequence, the problem-solving environment is generally rich in learning opportunities. To the extent that such learning can be captured and shared throughout the organization, the management capital of the firm can be enhanced. In addition, a debriefing may also provide valuable insights into the firm's problem-solving process itself. Given the firm's unique competitive environment, knowing what worked and what did not may help focus future problem-solving initiatives.

INSTITUTIONALIZATION AND CONTROL. The final step in problem solving is to institutionalize the results of the initiative. It is natural for any system to degrade over time. Therefore, any changes made as a result of the problem-solving effort should be locked in before they are lost. This might entail amending policy manuals, establishing new control metrics, or even rewriting job descriptions. In addition, the firm should also consider whether the problem addressed in the initiative at hand is an isolated incident or whether the solution can be leveraged throughout the organization. Frequently, similar problems are present in other departments or other geographic locations. If this is the case, institutionalization might involve transferring the newly developed practices to these new settings.

SEE ALSO: Project Management

Daniel R. Heiser
Revised by Badie N. Farah

FURTHER READING:

Deming, W. Edwards. *Out of the Crisis*. Cambridge: Massachusetts Institute of Technology, Center for Advanced Engineering Study, 1992.

Ketola, Jeanne and Kathy Roberts. *Correct! Prevent! Improve!: Driving Improvement Through Problem Solving and Corrective and Preventive Action*. Milwaukee: ASQ Quality Press, 2003.

National Institute of Standards and Technology. "Award Recipients." Malcolm Baldrige National Quality Award Program, 1999. Available from <www.quality.nist.gov>.

Rasiel, Ethan M. *The McKinsey Mind: Using the Techniques of the World's Top Strategic Consultants to Help You and Your Business*. New York: McGraw-Hill, 2001.

———. *The McKinsey Way—Understanding and Implementing the Problem-Solving Tools and Management Techniques of the World's Top Strategic Consulting Firm*. New York: McGraw-Hill, 1999.

Smith, Gerald F. *Quality Problem Solving*. Milwaukee: ASQ Quality Press, 1998.

PROCESS MANAGEMENT

Process management is a concept that integrates quality/performance excellence into the strategic management of organizations. It is Category 6.0 of the Malcolm Baldrige National Quality Award. Process management includes (1) process design or engineering, which is the invention of new processes; (2) process definition, which requires the description of existing processes; (3) process documentation; (4) process analysis and control; and (5) process improvement.

Process design and definition include describing what must be done and how it is to be accomplished. After defining a process, it must be documented using a flowchart, a process map, or even a simple checklist. Until the process is described and documented, one cannot be assured that a process is in place. At that point, the process can be analyzed and improved.

There are many process analysis tools, including cause-and-effect diagrams, statistical process control, and trend analyses. Process improvement may result from gradual, continuous improvement or a dramatic reinvention or reengineering of the process.

HISTORICAL PERSPECTIVE

Process management can trace its roots back to the early days of industrial engineering and quality management (quality control and quality engineering). The earliest focus was on streamlining factory processes to increase productivity. However, process management concepts are now used in all types of organizations to improve process baselines (safety, quality, cycle time, productivity, on-time delivery, etc.), as well as to improve financial and operational results.

In 1911, Frederick Taylor published *The Principles of Scientific Management*. Some of his ideas are the predecessors for modern industrial engineering tools and concepts that are used to reduce cycle time and/or improve productivity. Frank and Lillian Gilbreth also used time and motion studies to improve processes and to increase productivity by evaluating how much time it took to do each task within a process, and the best way to do each task (the motions involved). Their work and personal lives were publicized in the book, *Cheaper by the Dozen*.

One of the world's leading experts on improving the manufacturing process, Shigeo Shingo, created with Taiichi Ohno, many of the features of just-in-time (JIT) manufacturing methods, systems, and processes that constitute the Toyota Production System. Much of Shingo's work is documented in books he has written, such as *A Study of the Toyota Production System From An Industrial Engineering Viewpoint* (1989).

Experts in the field of quality developed many process-management concepts and tools:

1. Dr. W. Edwards Deming (1900–1993) is famous for his work in Japan in the 1950s and for theories such as his Fourteen Points and Plan-Do-Check-Act (PDCA) Cycle (also referred to as the Shewhart Cycle). He also refined and publicized other concepts and tools, including statistical process control. Many of Dr. Deming's theories are contained in his book, *Out of the Crisis.*

2. Dr. Joseph Juran (b.1904) also worked with the Japanese beginning in the 1950s. Some of his theories supporting process management are Juran's Trilogy (process planning, process control, and process improvement); Big Q (the quality department is responsible for quality) vs. Little Q (everyone is responsible for quality); and the Quality Planning Roadmap. Juran's books include *Juran's Quality Control Handbook* and *A History of Managing for Quality.*

3. Dr. Kaoru Ishikawa, author of *Guide to Quality Control,* invented the cause-and-effect diagram and taught people involved in teams (quality circles) to ask what caused each effect.

4. Dr. Walter Shewhart, a statistician who worked at Western Electric, Bell Laboratories and who used statistics to explain process variability, first published his theories in his book *Economic Control of Quality of Manufactured Product* (1931).

PROCESS THINKING

Examples of simple, essential questions in process thinking are:

1. What is a process?

2. Who are the internal and external customers of a process?

3. Who are the process owners?

4. Who improves processes-process owners, customers, suppliers?

5. How do you improve processes?

6. What might not add value for customers?

7. What role does measurement play?

WHAT IS A PROCESS?

A process is a series of connected steps or actions with a beginning and an end that can be replicated. Organizations should be viewed as a set or hierarchy of processes that produce outputs of value to a customer, as well as a set of functions such as engineering, manufacturing, accounting, and marketing.

The most successful organizations are managed from a horizontal (process) perspective, as well as from a vertical (function) perspective. Understanding an organization from the process perspective will cause changes in the way one thinks about people and processes as depicted in Figure 1.

Figure 1

Functional Focus	Cross-Funcitonal (Process) Focus
Employees are the problem.	The process is the problem.
Measure individuals.	Measure process results.
Motivate people.	Remove process barriers and constraints.
Who made this error?	What caused the error?
Evaluate employees.	Evaluate the process.
Vertical organizations.	Cross-functional (horizontal) organizations.

Examples of processes in various organizations are included in the following list. Please note that many of the processes could be found in all the various organization types.

1. University
   - Teaching Students
   - Paying for Classes
2. Hospital
   - Emergency Care
   - Payroll
3. Factory
   - Purchasing Material
   - Training Workers
4. Federal Agency
   - Procurement
   - Hiring New Employees
5. Retail Store
   - Selling Products
   - Employee Scheduling
6. Bank
   - Opening New Accounts
   - Statement Distribution
7. Church
   - Recruiting Members
   - Maintaining Facilities
8. Restaurant
   - Preparing Meals
   - Advertising
9. Construction
   - Budgeting
   - Managing Subcontractors
10. Not for Profit
    - Distribution of Funds
    - Employee Recruitment

A process involves the steps or stages by which inputs such as people, materials, methods, machines, and environment are transformed into outputs (products and services).

WHO ARE THE CUSTOMERS OF A PROCESS?

Because a transformation process exists to satisfy customer requirements, process owners need to understand who their customers are, what they want, and how to provide what they want. The customers of a process are the people who require the products and services that are the result of the process or one phase of the process. They are classified as: (1) external customers-people who ultimately use the products and/or services (process outputs or work results) of an organization; and (2) internal customers—the owners of the next phases in the process who must wait for the delivery of a product or service before completing work.

External and internal customers must be satisfied if organizations are to experience the highest levels of success. Individuals and teams must understand their roles as suppliers to internal and external customers if customer satisfaction is to be a reality. At the same time, individuals and teams must act as internal customers who communicate requirements to internal suppliers.

CUSTOMER/SUPPLIER RELATIONSHIPS. Concepts relating to customer/supplier relationships and satisfaction are as follows:

- Customers (internal and external) have a right to expect quality products and services.

- Every member of an organization has an internal customer—the next phase in the process.

- If each team member treats other team members like valuable customers, relationships and work results (individual and team performance) will improve.

- The customer determines if the product or service is what he or she ordered and if it has the value expected and promised by the supplier.

Individuals and team members should ask internal customers and suppliers, "How am I doing?" and "What did you expect compared to what I gave you?" The answer will assist in improving processes, products, services, and relationships.

Basically, customers want to be their suppliers' first priority. They want (and deserve) perfect products and services delivered on or ahead of schedule at the lowest possible cost. They expect suppliers to be in the improvement mode of operation so that the customers are assured of paying a competitive price.

Perfection is the aspiration, level-improvement is the goal. Whatever today's standard is, tomorrow's customers will require more. It is the responsibility of the supplier to remain on a journey toward perfection; to determine current baselines for important customer requirements such as safety, quality, schedule, and cost; and to determine what process and relationship improvements are necessary to improve those baselines.

RELATIONSHIPS AMONG QUALITY, SCHEDULE, AND COST. One of the things that must be done when evaluating and improving processes is to establish process baselines. The baselines for quality, schedule, and cost are so interwoven that it is difficult to measure and improve one of them without considering the other. This is as it should be since customers want the highest quality products and services on or ahead of schedule and at the lowest possible price.

If you improve the quality of processes and relationships, you can expect other baselines (e.g., quality, schedule, and cost) to improve. While quality, schedule, and cost are measured as separate baselines, long-term improvement is interdependent and process focused.

Customers expect speed of delivery as well as quality. Therefore, objectives of process management are customer satisfaction and retention through the improvement of quality and cycle time. In order to satisfy and retain external customers, suppliers should:

1. Be competitive based on speed as well as quality.

2. Provide real-time information to internal and external customers.

3. Design and streamline processes so that they are free of defects, constraints, and activities that do not add value for the customer.

4. Eliminate procrastination.

5. Change paradigms based on sequential decision making to paradigms that include concurrent decision making, as well as concurrent engineering.

6. Empower workers to dismantle time-wasting bureaucracy.

WHO ARE THE PROCESS OWNERS?

The process owners (the people who actually do the jobs) are the most knowledgeable about the processes by which they accomplish their work. Therefore, if process evaluation and improvement becomes an integral part of daily work, safety improvement, defect prevention, and cycle-time reduction can become a reality. Process owners are those empowered to do work, improve how they do the work, and accept accountability as process owners.

PROCESS EVALUATION AND IMPROVEMENT. An essential concept in process management is that all processes have improvement potential. If organizations only focus on current processes, current problems, and doing the things that are currently done, they may eventually encounter a variety of problems, such as:

- They may continue making a product (e.g., buggy whips) long after the market is gone. These perfect products may have no customers.

- They may do everything in a process perfectly, but they may be doing many things that do not need to be done at all (efficient, not effective).

- They may be focusing only on quality, when speed is also important.

- They may miss opportunities to improve products, services, processes, and relationships.

WHO IMPROVES PROCESSES?

People who know the most about processes and who are most capable of evaluating and improving them are process owners—people who are accountable for process output or results. However, feedback from customers and suppliers contributes a great deal to improvement.

Examples of data a customer could provide include (1) whether the product or service meets the customer's needs/expectations; (2) whether there are any defects or discrepancies; and (3) whether the product or service is delivered on-time or early.

Examples of data suppliers could provide are (1) whether the customer's requirements (e.g., purchase orders) were clear and understandable; and (2) whether

Figure 2

Area of Difference	Continuous Improvement	Reengineering
Reason for change	Desire to improve baselines	Compelling (rapid process redesign for survival)
Targets	Small improvement in every process; cumulative effects	Aggressive (e.g., 10 times or more, six sigma, etc.)
Approach	Nonstructured	Structured and disciplined
Scope	Evaluation of all steps in all processes	Broad cross-functional processes
Focus	Parts of a system	Relations in system
Level of change	Incremental and continuous	Order of magnitude
Organizational structure	Vertical or horizontal	Flattened, horizontal
Involvement of executives	Important up-front; support throughout	Intensive long-term involvement
Involvement of all employees	Gradual voluntary involvement	Nonvoluntary
Use of terms	Work teams and cross-functional team	Cross-functional teams
Role of information	Incidental	Cornerstone

customers met lead-time requirements when placing orders.

HOW DO YOU IMPROVE PROCESSES?

Improvement may be gradual and continuous (i.e., kaizen, continuous process improvement), or it may be dramatic process redesign (i.e., process reengineering). The differences between the two are depicted in Figure 2.

Both gradual, continuous improvement and process reengineering should be an integral part of process management and improvement.

The following are some of the things people can do to improve processes:

- Use a structured methodology such as the Golden-Pryor Improvement Checklist.

- Eliminate activities that do not add value for the customer. Ask yourself: "Would the customer want to pay for this activity?" If the answer is no, ask yourself: "Why are we doing this? Is it a federal law? A state law?" If the answer is no, ask yourself: "What benefit do we gain by doing this?" At this point, you are coming close to eliminating the activity.

- Eliminate constraints—things that frustrate employees and slow processes.

- Streamline/simplify processes. It is difficult to document and teach people complex processes.

- Once processes are streamlined, computerize them if feasible.

- Provide leadership in a positive direction. Function as a strategist. Envision and invent the future with streamlined processes and relationships.

- Act empowered; be accountable. As individuals and members of teams, function as process owners and consider process management and improvement an integral part of daily work. Don't say, "They won't let us . . ." Make decisions, not excuses.

- Document and publicize improvements. Success breeds success.

- Continue to monitor and evaluate processes to identify additional opportunities for improvement.

- Ask (and teach others to ask) what, where, why, who, when, and how questions about each step in a process (or job).

PROCESS QUESTIONS.

What:

- is there to do?
- is being done?
- should be done?
- can be done?
- constraints keep us from doing it?

Who:

- does this job?
- should do this job?
- knows how to do it?
- should know how to do it?

Where:

- is this job done?
- should it be done?

• can it be done?

When:

• is this job done?

• should it be done?

• can it be done?

When process-improvement efforts fail, it is generally because people have a deficiency in knowledge—they do not know what actions to take. They should be trained on specific improvement methodologies, and they should be held accountable for documenting improvement results.

Improvement team members generally need a model that provides them common knowledge about what they are required to do individually and as a team, such as the Golden Pryor Improvement Checklist in Figure 3.

WHAT MIGHT NOT ADD VALUE?

The concept of value implies worth; value is something that a customer would expect to pay for, such as labor to design, build, and deliver a product or service. Customers want to pay for perfect products and services delivered on or ahead of schedule at the lowest reasonable cost. They only want to pay for activities that add value to products and services, and to processes and relationships that impact the products and services.

WHAT ROLE DOES MEASUREMENT PLAY?

Organizational leaders are accustomed to measuring things that are important to themselves. They also need to measure items that are important to customers. Improving process results does not require sophisticated measurements. It requires systematic identification and elimination of root causes of problems, process constraints, and activities that do not add value. It is as much continuous learning as it is continuous improvement. Improvement results from learning that is fed back and used as the basis for the next decisions.

Quality products and services are the result of quality processes that exist because of quality people who build quality relationships and streamline processes. Specific measurements must be established for individual phases of a process in addition to the final process output. The following can apply in any organization in any industry:

• Quality—first pass yield, scrap, rework, repair.

Figure 3

Golden Pryor Process Improvement Checklist

I. Determine what work processes you Own and list them. Classify them as critical or ancillary.

II. Describe and flowchart each process.
   A. Choose which process to evaluate first.
      1. Identify and list process and decision steps.
      2. Identify and remove non-value-added steps.
      3. Identify and remove process constraints for each phrase of the process.
      4. If flowcharts do not reflect requirements, change the process or change the requirement documents (directives, procedures, etc.)
   B. Using flowcharts, determine the customer and suppliers for each process.

III. Establish quality measurements. Define quality for the output(s) of each process and identify data sources.

IV. Establish time measurements (cycle-time, on-time delivery, etc.)
   A. Determine static cycle time (process flow time).
      1. Compute cycle time for sub-processes and total process cycle time.
      2. Identify slack time/queue time.
      3. Establish perfect cycle times (no constraints, bottlenecks, or excess queue time).
      4. Search a second time for non-value-added-activities and eliminate those that still exist. Examples: Redundant Inspection, unnecessary documentation, unnecessary handling, meetings without agendas.
   B. Identify other measurements relating to time and establish process baselines.

V. Establish other baselines and measurements.
   A. Safety (e.g., classrooms, discipline problems, acts of violence).
   B. Customer satisfaction (e.g., level of satisfaction with products or services and trends).
   C. Human resources (hours of training, % multiple skills/job rotations, absenteeism, etc.)

VI. Identify process baselines with greatest improvement potential.

VII. Use TQM/SPC tools to determine system improvement/problem resolution options.

VII. Select best improvement option(s) and implement.

IX. Measure—monitor/track and feedback results to process owners, management, et al. Determine whether process baselines—safety, quality, cycle time are getting better or worse, Analyze the trends, and do root cause analysis.

X. Continue improvement efforts.

XI. Publicize improvements

- Productivity/Use of Time—cycle time, on-time delivery, non-value-added activities, overtime.
- Environmental and Safety—injuries, compliance, ergonomics, discipline problems, incidents of violence.
- People Issues—absenteeism, turnover, morale, grievances, skill levels, stakeholder satisfaction.
- Customer Satisfaction—new and repeat business, customer returns, warranty costs, field service reports/data, involvement.
- Supplier Performance—rating system, quality, capabilities, conformance to requirements.

ESSENTIAL ELEMENTS

This essay focused on process management as it relates to existing processes, not the invention of new processes, products, and services. Process management requires process design (new processes) or definition (existing processes); process documentation; process analysis and control; and process improvement.

Essential elements in process management include: (1) Understanding process thinking, including process ownership; (2) Identifying and satisfying customers' requirements; (3) Establishing process baselines and measurement; (4) Analyzing and improving processes through the use of quality and industrial engineering concepts and tools; and (5) Understanding how to use gradual, continuous process improvement and rapid, dramatic process redesign or reengineering.

Process management is the job of every employee of every organization in every industry.

SEE ALSO: Continuous Improvement; Japanese Management; Managing Change; Product-Process Matrix; Trends in Organizational Change

Mildred Golden Pryor
Revised by Wendy H. Mason

FURTHER READING:

Burlton, Roger. *Business Process Management: Profiting From Process*. Indianapolis, IN: Sams Publishing, May 2001.

Crosby, Philip. *Quality without Tears*. New York: McGraw-Hill, 1984.

Deming, W. Edwards. *The New Economics*. Cambridge, MA: MIT Center for Advanced Engineering Study, 1993.

———. *Out of the Crisis*. Cambridge, MA: MIT Center for Advanced Engineering Study, 1986.

Garvin, David A. *Managing Quality: The Strategic and Competitive Edge*. New York, NY: Free Press, 1988.

Hammer, Michael, and James Champy. *Reengineering the Corporation: A Manifesto for Business Revolution*. New York, NY: HarperCollins Publishers, 1993.

Harrington, H.J. *Business Process Improvement: The Breakthrough Strategy for Total Quality, Productivity, and Competitiveness*. New York, NY: McGraw-Hill, 1991.

———. *The Improvement Process: How America's Leading Companies Improve Quality*. New York, NY: McGraw-Hill, 1987.

Imai, Masaaki. *Kaizen: The Key to Japan's Competitive Success*. New York, NY: McGraw-Hill, 1986.

Ishikawa, Kaoru. *Guide to Quality Control*. Tokyo, Japan: Asian Productivity Organization, 1982.

———. *What Is Total Quality Control?* Englewood Cliffs, NJ: Prentice-Hall, 1985.

Juran, Joseph M. *A History of Managing for Quality*. Milwaukee, WI: ASQ Quality Press, 1995.

Juran, Joseph M., and Frank M. Gryna. *Juran's Quality Control Handbook*. New York, NY: McGraw-Hill, 1988.

———. *Quality Planning and Analysis: From Product Development Through Use*. New York, NY: McGraw-Hill, 1993.

Mizuno, Shigeru. *Management for Quality Improvement: The 7 New QC Tools*. Cambridge, MA: Productivity Press, 1979.

Pryor, Mildred Golden, and Brian D. Cullen. "Learn to Use TQM As Part of Everyday Work." *Industrial Management*, May-June 1993, 10–14.

Pryor, Mildred Golden, and J. Chris White. *Strategic Quality Management*. Dallas, TX: ASQ, Texas Quality EXPO, October 1996.

Pryor, Mildred Golden, J. Chris White, and Leslie A. Toombs. *Strategic Quality Management: A Strategic Systems Approach to Quality*. Houston, TX: Dame Publications, 1998.

Pryor, Mildred Golden, and Leslie A. Toombs. *Total Quality Management*. Commerce, TX: Center for Excellence, 1993.

Pryor, Mildred Golden, and W. Donald Pryor. *Process Reengineering*. Commerce, TX: Center for Excellence, 1994.

Senge, Peter M. *The Fifth Discipline: The Art & Practice of The Learning Organization*. New York, NY: Doubleday/Currency, 1990.

Shingo, Shigeo. *Revolution in Manufacturing: The SMED (Single Minute Exchange of Die) System*. Cambridge, MA: Productivity Press, Inc., 1985.

———. *A Study of the Toyota Production System*. Cambridge, MA: Productivity Press, Inc., 1989.

Smith, Howard, and Peter Fingar. *Business Process Management (BPM): The Third Wave*. Tampa, FL: Meghan-Kiffer Press, 2003.

PROCUREMENT

SEE: Purchasing and Procurement

PRODUCT-PROCESS MATRIX

The product-process matrix is a tool for analyzing the relationship between the product life cycle and the technological life cycle. It was introduced by Robert H. Hayes and Steven C. Wheelwright in two classic management articles published in *Harvard Business Review* in 1979, entitled "Link Manufacturing Process and Product Life Cycles" and "The Dynamics of Process-Product Life Cycles." The authors used this matrix to examine market-manufacturing congruence issues and to facilitate the understanding of the strategic options available to a company. The matrix itself consists of two dimensions, product structure/product life cycle and process structure/process life cycle. The production process used to manufacture a product moves through a series of stages, much like the stages of products and markets, which begins with a highly flexible, high-cost process and progresses toward increasing standardization, mechanization, and automation, culminating in an inflexible but cost-effective process. The process structure/process life cycle dimension describes the process choice (job shop, batch, assembly line, and continuous flow) and process structure (jumbled flow, disconnected line flow, connected line flow and continuous flow) while the product structure/product life cycle describes the four stages of the product life cycle (low volume to high volume) and product structure (low to high standardization). Later writers on the subject sometimes insert an additional stage in the extreme upper-left corner of the matrix: the project.

A company can be characterized as occupying a particular region on the matrix (see accompanying Figure). This region is determined by the firm's stage in the product life cycle and the firm's choice of production process. At the upper left extreme, firms are characterized as process oriented or focused while the lower right extreme holds firms that are said to be product focused. The decision of where a firm locates on the matrix is determined by whether the production system is organized by grouping resources around the process or the product. Note from the figure that the vertices of the matrix result in four distinct types of operations (described by the appropriate process choice) located on the diagonal of the matrix.

PROCESS CHOICES

PROJECT. Projects are briefly included in the discussion since they are sometimes found at the extreme upper-left corner of the matrix (depending on the author). These include large-scale, one-time, unique products such as civil-engineering contracts, aerospace programs, construction, etc. They are also customer-specific and often too large to be moved, which practically dictates that project is the process of choice.

JOB SHOP. If a manufacturer had broken a large cog on an outdated (i.e., replacement parts are no longer available) but still useful machine, she would take the

Product-Process Matrix

Process structure Process life cycle stage ↓	Product structure Product life cycle stage →	Low volume Unique (one of a kind)	Low volume Multiple Products	Higher volume Standardized product	Very high volume Commodity product
	(Project)				
Jumbled flow (job shop)		Job shop			
Disconnected line flow (batch)			Batch		
Connected line flow (assembly line)				Assembly line	
Continuous flow (continuous)					Continuous

broken cog to a machine shop where they would manufacture a new one from scratch. This machine shop (along with tool and die manufacturers) is probably the primary example of manufacturing job shops. A job shop is the producer of unique products; usually this product is of an individual nature and requires that the job shop interpret the customer's design and specifications, which requires a relatively high level of skill and experience. Once the design is specified, one or a small number of skilled employees are assigned to the task and are frequently responsible for deciding how best to carry it out. Generally, resources for processing have limited availability with temporary in-process storage capability needed while jobs wait for subsequent processing. If the product is not a one-time requirement, it is at least characterized by irregular demand with long periods of time between orders. Efficiency is difficult since every output must be treated differently.

In a job shop, the outputs differ significantly in form, structure, materials and/or processing required. Each unique job travels from one functional area to another according to its own unique routing, requiring different operations, using different inputs, and requiring varying amounts of time. This causes the flow of the product through the shop to be jumbled, following no repetitive pattern.

Job shops and batch operations (upper-left quadrant of the matrix) are usually organized around the function of the individual machines. In other words, machinery is grouped according to the purpose it serves or the capabilities it possesses. For example, in a machine shop, hydraulic presses would be grouped in one area of the shop, lathes would be grouped into another area of the shop, screw machines in another area, heat or chemical treatment in still another, and so on (also contributing to the jumbled flow). This is labeled a *process layout*.

In addition to machine shops and tool and die manufacturers, job shops are also appropriate for use in service operations, since the product is customized and frequently requires different operations. Service examples include law offices, medical practices, automobile repair, tailor shops, and so forth.

BATCH. Firms utilizing batch processes provide similar items on a repeat basis, usually in larger volumes than that associated with job shops. Products are sometimes accumulated until a lot can be processed together. When the most effective manufacturing route has been determined, the higher volume and repetition of requirements can make more efficient use of capacity and result in significantly lower costs.

Since the volume is higher than that of the job shop, many processes can be utilized in repetition, creating a much smoother flow of work-in-process throughout the shop. While the flow is smoother, the work-in-process still moves around to the various machine groupings throughout the shop in a somewhat jumbled fashion. This is described as a disconnected line flow or intermittent flow.

Examples of batch processing operations include printing and machine shops that have contracts for higher volumes of a product. Services utilizing batches could be some offices (processing orders in batches), some operations within hospitals, classes within universities (how many classes have only one pupil?), and food preparation.

LINE. When product demand is high enough, the appropriate process is the assembly line. Often, this process (along with continuous; both are in the lower-right quadrant of the matrix) is referred to as mass production. Laborers generally perform the same operations for each production run in a standard and hopefully uninterrupted flow. The assembly line treats all outputs as basically the same. Firms characterized by this process are generally heavily automated, utilizing special-purpose equipment. Frequently, some form of conveyor system connects the various pieces of equipment used. There is usually a fixed set of inputs and outputs, constant throughput time, and a relatively continuous flow of work. Because the product is standardized, the process can be also, following the same path from one operation to the next. Routing, scheduling, and control are facilitated since each individual unit of output does not have to be monitored and controlled. This also means that the manager's span of control can increase and less skilled workers can be utilized.

The product created by the assembly-line process is discrete; that is, it can be visually counted (as opposed to continuous processes which produce a product that is not naturally divisible). Almost everyone can think of an example of assembly-line manufacturing (automobile manufacturing is probably the most obvious). Examples of assembly lines in services are car washes, class registration in universities, and many fast food operations.

Because the work-in-process equipment is organized and sequenced according to the steps involved to produce the product and is frequently connected by some sort of conveyor system, it is characterized as flowing in a line. Even though it may not be a straight line (some firms utilize a U-shaped assembly line) we say that it has a connected line flow. Also, firms in the lower-right quadrant (line and continuous) are classified as having a *product layout*.

Continuous manufacturing involves lot-less production wherein the product flows continuously rather than being divided. A basic material is passed through successive operations (i.e., refining or processing) and eventually emerges as one or more products. This process is used to produce highly standardized outputs in extremely large volumes. The product range is usually so narrow and highly standardized that it can be characterized as a commodity.

Considerable capital investment is required, so demand for continuous process products must be extremely high. Starting and stopping the process can be prohibitively expensive. As a result, the processes usually run 24 hours a day with minimum downtime (hence, continuous flow). This also allows the firm to spread their enormous fixed cost over as large a base as possible.

The routing of the process is typically fixed. As the material is processed it usually is transferred automatically from one part of the process to the next, frequently with self-monitoring and adjusting. Labor requirements are low and usually involve only monitoring and maintaining the machinery.

Typical examples of industries utilizing the continuous process include gas, chemicals, electricity, ores, rubber, petroleum, cement, paper, and wood. Food manufacture is also a heavy user of continuous processing; especially water, milk, wheat, flour, sugar and spirits.

USING THE MATRIX

The product-process matrix can facilitate the understanding of the strategic options available to a company, particularly with regard to its manufacturing function. A firm may be characterized as occupying a particular region in the matrix, determined by the stages of the product life cycle and its choice of production process(es) for each individual product. By incorporating this dimension into its strategic planning process, the firm encourages more creative thinking about organizational competence and competitive advantage. Also, use of the matrix provides a natural way to involve manufacturing managers in the planning process so they can relate their opportunities and decisions more effectively with those of marketing and of the corporation itself, all the while leading to more informed predictions about changes in industry and the firm's appropriate strategic responses.

Each process choice on the matrix has a unique set of characteristics. Those in the upper-left quadrant of the matrix (job shop and batch) share a number of characteristics, as do those in the lower-right quadrant (assembly line and continuous). Upper-left firms employ highly skilled craftsmen (machinists, printers, tool and die makers, musical instrument craftsmen) and professionals (lawyers, doctors, CPAs, consultants). Hence upper-left firms can be characterized as labor intensive. Since upper-left firms tend to utilize general-purpose equipment, are seldom at 100 percent capacity, and employ workers with a wide range of skills, they can be very flexible. However, there is a difficult trade-off between efficiency and flexibility of operations. Most job shops tend to emphasize flexibility over efficiency. Since efficiency is not a strong point of upper-left firms, neither is low-cost production. Also, the low volume of production does not allow upper-left firms to spread their fixed costs over a wide enough base to provide for reduced costs. Finally, upper-left firms are also more likely to serve local markets.

Lower-right firms require production facilities that are highly specialized, capital intensive, and interrelated (therefore, inflexible). Labor requirements are generally unskilled or semi-skilled at most. Much of the labor requirement deals with merely monitoring and maintaining equipment. Lower-right firms are also more likely to serve national markets and can be vertically integrated.

Hayes and Wheelwright relate three areas affected by the use of the product-process matrix: distinctive competence, management, and organization.

DISTINCTIVE COMPETENCE. Distinctive competence is defined as the resources, skills, and organizational characteristics that give a firm a comparative advantage over its competitors. Simply put, a distinctive competence is the characteristic of a given product that causes the buyer to purchase it rather than the similar product of a competitor. It is generally accepted that the distinctive competencies are cost/price, quality, flexibility and service/time. By using the product-process matrix as a framework, a firm can be more precise about its distinctive competence and can concentrate its attention on a restricted set of process decisions and alternatives and a restricted set of marketing alternatives. In our discussion, we have seen that the broad range of worker skills and the employment of general-purpose equipment give upper-left firms a large degree of flexibility while the highly specialized, high-volume environment of lower-right firms yields very little in the way of flexibility. Therefore, flexibility would be a highly appropriate distinctive competence for an upper-left firm. This is especially true when dealing with the need for flexibility of the product/service produced. Lower-right firms find it very difficult to sidetrack a high-volume operation because of an engineering change in the product. An entire line would have to be shut down while tooling or machinery is altered and large volumes of possibly obsolete work-in-process are accounted for. Upper-left firms, however, would have none of these problems with which to contend. It must be noted though that lower-right firms may possess an advantage regarding flexibility of volume.

Quality may be defined a number ways. If we define quality as reliability, then lower-right firms could claim this as a distinctive competence. Lower-right firms would have the high volume necessary to quickly find and eliminate bugs in their product, yielding more reliability to the end user. However, if we define quality as quality of design (that is, "bells and whistles"—things that embody status, such as leather seats in an automobile or a handcrafted musical instrument), then quality would be seen as a possible distinctive competence of upper-right firms.

Service may also be defined in more ways than one. If one defines service as face-to-face interaction and personal attention, then upper-left firms could claim service as a distinctive competence. If service is defined as the ability to provide the product in a very short period of time (e.g., overnight), then service as a distinctive competence would belong to lower-right firms.

Finally, remember that high volume, economies of scale, and low cost are characteristics of firms in the lower-right quadrant of the matrix. Upper-left firms produce low volumes (sometimes only one) and cannot take advantage of economies of scale. (Imagine, for instance, what you would have to pay for a handcrafted musical instrument.) Therefore, it is obvious that price or cost competitiveness is within the domain of lower-right firms.

MANAGEMENT. In general, the economics of production processes favor positions along the diagonal of the product-process matrix. That is, firms operating on or close to the diagonal are expected to outperform firms choosing extreme off-diagonal positions. Hayes and Wheelwright provide the example of a firm positioned in the upper-right corner of the matrix. This would appear to be a commodity produced by a job shop, an option that is economically unfeasible. A firm positioned in the lower-left corner would represent a unique one-time product produced by a continuous process, again not a feasible option. Both examples are too far off the diagonal. Firms that find themselves too far off the diagonal invite trouble by impairing their ability to compete effectively. While firms operating in the near vicinity, but not exactly on the diagonal, can be niche players, positions farther away from the diagonal are difficult to justify. Rolls Royce makes automobiles in a job shop environment but they understand the implications involved. Companies off the diagonal must be aware of traps it can fall into and implications presented by their position.

Also, a firm's choice of product-process position places them to the right or left of competitors along the horizontal dimension of the matrix and above or below its competitors along the vertical dimension of the matrix. The strategic implications are obvious. Of course, a firm's position on the matrix may change over time, so the firm must be aware of the implications and maintain the capability to deal with them appropriately. The matrix can provide powerful insights into the consequences of any planned product or process change.

Use of the product-process matrix can also help a firm define its product. Hayes and Wheelwright relate the example of a specialized manufacturer of printed circuit boards who produced a low-volume, customized product using a highly connected assembly-line process. Obviously, this would place them in the lower-left corner of the matrix; not a desirable place to be. This knowledge forced the company to realize that what they were offering was not really circuit boards after all, but design capability. So, in essence, they were mass-producing designs rather than the boards themselves. Hence, they were not far off the diagonal at all.

ORGANIZATION. Firms organize different operating units so that they can specialize on separate portions of the total manufacturing task while still maintaining overall coordination. Most firms will select two or more processes for the products or services they produce. For example, a firm may use a batch process to make components for products, which are constructed on assembly lines. This would be especially true if the work content for component production or the volume needed was not sufficient for the creation of a dedicated line process. Also, firms may need separate facilities for different products or parts, or they may simply separate their production within the same facility. It may even be that a firm can produce the similar products through two different process options. For example, Fender Musical Instruments not only mass produces electric guitars (assembly line) but also offers customized versions of the same product through the Fender Custom Shop (job shop). Again, the matrix provides a valuable framework for diagnostic use in these situations.

OTHER USES OF THE PRODUCT-PROCESS MATRIX

Additional uses of the matrix include:

- Analyzing the product entry and exit.

- Determining the appropriate mix of manufacturing facilities, identifying the key manufacturing objectives for each plant, and monitoring progress on those objectives at the corporate level.

- Reviewing investment decisions for plants and equipment in terms of their consistency with product and process plans.

- Determining the direction and timing of major changes in a company's production processes.

- Evaluating product and market opportunities in light of the company's manufacturing capabilities.

- Selecting an appropriate process and product structure for entry into a new market.

It should be noted that recent empirical research by Sohel Ahmad and Roger G. Schroeder found the proposed relationship between product structure and process structure to be significant but not strong. In general terms, they found that as the product life cycle changes the process life cycle also shifts in the consistent direction, but not necessarily along the diagonal. Some 60 percent of the firms studied did not fall on the diagonal. The researchers propose that this occurred because new management and technological initiatives have eliminated or minimized some of the inherent trade-offs found on the Product-Process Matrix. They classify these initiatives as processing technology, product design and managerial practice (e.g., TQM and JIT). Therefore, Ahmad and Schroeder recommend that the matrix be conceptualized as having three axes instead of two. They propose an x-axis (product life cycle stages), a y-axis (process life cycle stages), and a z-axis that represents an organization's proactive effort towards adopting and implementing these innovative initiatives. As a firm moves away from the origin along the z-axis, it becomes able to minimize some of the trade-offs seen in the Product-Process Matrix framework.

SEE ALSO: Operations Strategy; Process Management

R. Anthony Inman

FURTHER READING:

Ahmad, Sohel, and Roger G. Schroeder. "Refining the Product-Process Matrix." *International Journal of Operations and Production Management* 22, no. 1 (2002): 103–124.

Anupindi, Ravi, Sunil Chopra, Sudhakar D. Deshmukh, Jan A. Van Mieghem, and Eitan Zemel. *Managing Process Business Flows.* 2nd ed. Upper Saddle River, NJ: Pearson Prentice Hall, 2006.

"The Dynamics of Process-Product Life Cycles." *Harvard Business Review,* March-April 1979, 27–136.

Finch, Byron. *Operations Now.* 2nd ed. Boston: McGraw-Hill Irwin, 2006.

Hayes, Robert, and Steven C. Wheelwright. "Link Manufacturing Process and Product Life Cycles." *Harvard Business Review,* January-February 1979, 133–140.

PRODUCT DESIGN

Product design is cross-functional, knowledge-intensive work that has become increasingly important in today's fast-paced, globally competitive environment. It is a key strategic activity in many firms because new products contribute significantly to sales revenue. When firms are able to develop distinctive products, they have opportunities to command premium pricing. Product design is a critical factor in organizational success because it sets the characteristics, features, and performance of the service or good that consumers demand. The objective of product design is to create a good or service with excellent functional utility and sales appeal at an acceptable cost and within a reasonable time. The product should be produced using high-quality, low-cost materials and methods. It should be produced on equipment that is or will be available when production begins. The resulting product should be competitive with or better than similar products on the market in terms of quality, appearance, performance, service life, and price.

THE INCREASING IMPORTANCE OF PRODUCT DESIGN

Product design is more important than ever because customers are demanding greater product variety and are switching more quickly to products with state-of-the-art technology. The impacts of greater product variety and shorter product life cycles have a multiplicative effect on the number of new products and derivative products that need to be designed. For example, just a few years ago, a firm may have produced four different products and each product may have had a product life cycle of ten years. In this case, the firm must design four new products every ten years. Today, in order to be competitive, this firm may produce eight different products with a life cycle of only five years; this firm must introduce eight new products in five years. That represents sixteen new products in ten years or one product every seven and one-half months. In this fast-paced environment, product design ceases to be an ad hoc, intermittent activity and becomes a regular and routine action. For an organization, delays, problems, and confusion in product design shift from being an annoyance to being life threatening.

PRODUCT DESIGN AND SUPPLY CHAIN MANAGEMENT

Product design can also be an important mechanism for coordinating the activities of key supply chain participants. As organizations outsource the production of sub-assemblies and components, they also may be asking suppliers to participate in product design. As they outsource design capabilities it is essential that they manage and coordinate the flow of information among the supply chain participants. This can be especially important as firms outsource components to two or more suppliers. Now, there may be important design interfaces among two, three, or more suppliers. These interfaces must be properly managed to ensure cost effective and timely designs. Clearly, information and communication technologies become important parts of this effort.

PRODUCT DESIGN: A KEY TO ORGANIZATIONAL SUCCESS

Product design is an essential activity for firms competing in a global environment. Product design drives organizational success because it directly and significantly impacts nearly all of the critical determinants for success. Customers demand greater product variety and are quick to shift to new, innovative, full-featured products. In addition, customers make purchase decisions based on a growing list of factors that are affected by product design. Previously, customers made purchase decisions based primarily on product price and/or quality. While these factors are still important, customers are adding other dimensions such as customizability, order-to-delivery time, product safety, and ease and cost of maintenance. Environmental concerns are expanding to include impacts during production, during the product's operating life, and at the end of its life (recycle-ability). In addition, customers demand greater protection from defective products, which leads to lower product liability losses. Safer and longer lasting products lead to enhanced warrantee provision, which, in turn, impact customer satisfaction and warrantee repair costs.

Programs and activities are being put in place so organizations can cope with these dimensions. Organizations are embracing concepts such as *mass customization, design for manufacturing and assembly, product disposal, quality function deployment, and time-based competition.* They are using technology such as *rapid prototyping* and *computer-aided design* to examine how products function, how much they may cost to produce, and how they may impact the environment. Firms are searching for and implementing new technologies to determine ways to design better products. They are examining legal and ethical issues in product design as well as the impact of product design on the environment.

MASS CUSTOMIZATION

Mass customization is the low-cost, high-quality, large volume delivery of individually customized products. It is the ability to quickly design and produce customized products on a large scale at a cost comparable to non-customized products. Customization, cost effectiveness is the ability to produce highly differentiated products without increasing costs, significantly. Consumers expect to receive customized products at close to mass-production prices. Customization volume effectiveness is the ability to increase product variety without diminishing production volume. As markets become more and more segmented and aggregate demand remains constant or increases, firms must continue to design and produce high volumes across the same fixed asset base. Customization responsiveness is the ability to reduce the time required to deliver

customized products and to reorganize design and production processes quickly in response to customer requests. It would be counter-productive to pursue mass customization if a customized product takes too long to produce. Speed in product design and production is an indispensable criterion for evaluating an organization's mass customization capability.

DESIGN FOR MANUFACTURING AND ASSEMBLY

Improving manufacturability is an important goal for product design. A systems approach to product design that was developed by two researchers from England, Geoffrey Boothroyd and Peter Dewhurst, is called design for manufacturability and assembly (DFMA). It can be a powerful tool to improve product quality and lower manufacturing cost. The approach focuses on manufacturing issues during product design. DFMA is implemented through computer software that identifies designs concepts that would be easy to build by focusing on the economic implications of design decisions. These decisions are critical even though design is a small part of the overall cost of a product because design decisions fix 70 to 90 percent of the manufacturing costs. In application, DFMA has had some startling successes. With the DFMA software, Texas Instruments reduced assembly time for an infrared sighting mechanism from 129 minutes to 20 minutes. IBM sliced assembly time for its printers from thirty minutes to three minutes.

Firms are recognizing that the concept behind DFMA can also be extended beyond cost control to design products that are easy to service and maintain. To do this effectively, service and maintenance issues should be considered at the earliest stages of the design. Also, firms will be required to examine disposal during product design as they become liable for recycling the products they make. It can be easier to recycle products if those factors are part of the product design paradigm.

DISPOSAL AND PRODUCT DESIGN

Disposal is becoming an increasingly important part of product design. The European Union is taking the lead by requiring that most of an automobile is recycled by the year 2010. This requirement has a major impact on product design. The most obvious effect is to change the notion that a consumer is the final owner for a product. With this approach, the product returns to the manufacturer to be recycled and the recycling process should begin in product design. Vehicles should be designed so they can be disassembled and recycled easily. The designers should avoid exotic materials that are difficulty to recycle. For example, parts that have plastic and metal fused together should not be used in applications where they are difficult to separate. The designers should determine which parts will be designed to be refurbished and reused, and which will be designed to be discarded, broken down, and recycled. All this should be done without adding costs or reducing product quality.

QUALITY AND QUALITY FUNCTION DEPLOYMENT

Product design shapes the product's quality. It defines the way that good and service functions. Quality has at least two components. First, the product must be designed to function with a high probability of success, or reliability; that is, it will perform a specific function without failure under given conditions. When product reliability increases, the firm can extend the product's warrantee without increasing customer claims for repairs or returns. Warrantees for complex and expensive items such as appliances are important selling points for customers. Second, quality improves when operating or performance characteristics improve even though reliability does not. The goals of product design should be greater performance, greater reliability, and lower total production and operating costs. Quality and costs should not be viewed as a trade-off because improvements in product and process technologies can enhance quality and lower costs.

Quality function deployment is being used by organizations to translate customer wants into working products. Sometimes referred to as the house of quality, quality function deployment (QFD) is a set of planning and communication routines that focus and coordinate actions and skills within an organization. The foundation of the house of quality is the belief that a product should be designed to reflect customers' desires and tastes. The house of quality is a framework that provides the means for inter-functional planning and communications. Through this framework, people facing different problems and responsibilities can discuss various design priorities.

PROTOTYPING

Engineering and operations combine to develop models of products called prototypes. These may be working models, models reduced in scale, or mock-ups of the products. Where traditional prototype development often takes weeks or months, the technology for rapid prototyping has become available. Some companies are using the same technology that creates virtual reality to develop three-dimensional prototypes. Other firms employ lasers to make prototypes by solidifying plastic in only a few minutes; this process can produce prototypes with complex shapes. Prototyping should increase customer satisfaction and improve design

stability, product effectiveness, and the predictability of final product cost and performance.

COMPUTER-AIDED DESIGN

Currently, business managers and engineers perceive computer-aided design (CAD) as a tool to assist engineers in designing goods. CAD uses computer technology and a graphic display to represent physical shapes in the same way that engineering drawings have in the past. It is used in the metalworking industry to display component parts, to illustrate size and shape, to show possible relationships to other parts, and to indicate component deformation under specified loads. After the design has been completed, the engineer can examine many different views or sections of the part and finally send it to a plotter to prepare drawings. This capability greatly reduces engineering time and avoids routine mistakes made in analysis and drawing. It significantly increases productivity and reduces design time, which allows faster delivery.

Applications of CAD systems are not limited to producing goods. While it's true that services do not have physical dimensions, the equipment and facilities used to produce services do. For example, the service stalls in an automotive center or rooms in an emergency medical center have physical characteristics that can be represented by the interactive graphics capabilities of a CAD system.

LEGAL AND ETHICAL ISSUES IN PRODUCT DESIGN

What is the responsibility of an organization and its managers to see that the goods and services they produce do not harm consumers? Legally, it is very clear that organizations are responsible for the design and safe use of their products. Consumers who believe they have been damaged by a poorly designed good or service have legal recourse under both civil and criminal statutes. Often, however, only the most serious and obvious offenses are settled in this way. More difficult ethical issues in product design result when the evidence is not as clear. For example, what responsibilities does a power tool manufacturer have with respect to product safety? Does a power saw manufacturer have the responsibility to design its product so that it is difficult for a child to operate? Suppose a parent is using a power saw and is called away to the telephone for a few minutes. A ten-year old may wander over, press the trigger and be seriously injured. Designing the saw so it has a simple and inexpensive lockout switch that would have to be pressed simultaneously when the trigger is pressed would make it more difficult for the accident to happen. What is the responsibility of the parent? What is the responsibility of the company?

PRODUCT DESIGN
AND THE ENVIRONMENT

Organizations consider product design a critical activity to the production of environmentally friendly products. Organizations increasingly recognize that being good corporate citizens increases sales. Fast-food restaurants have begun recycling programs and redesigned packaging materials and systems in response to customer concerns. In other cases, being a good corporate citizen and protecting a company's renewable resources go well together; there are win-win opportunities where an organization can actually design products and processes that cut costs and increase profits by recapturing pollutants and reducing solid waste.

OVERVIEW OF PRODUCT
DESIGN PROCESS

Product design time can be reduced by using a team approach and the early involvement of key participants including marketing, research and development, engineering, operations, and suppliers. Early involvement is an approach to managing people and processes. It involves an upstream investment in time that facilitates the identification and solution of downstream problems that would otherwise increase product design and production costs, decrease quality, and delay product introduction.

Time-based competitors are discovering that reducing product design time improves the productivity of product design teams. To reduce time, firms are reorganizing product design from an "over-the-wall" process to a team-based concurrent process. Over-the-wall means to proceed sequentially with the limited exchange of information and ideas. When this approach is used, problems are often discovered late because late-stage participants are excluded from decisions made early in the process. As a result, poor decisions are often made.

Product design is a labor-intensive process that requires the contribution of highly trained specialists. By using teams of specialists, communications are enhanced, wait time between decisions is reduced, and productivity is improved. Participants in this team-based process make better decisions faster because they are building a shared knowledge base that enhances learning and eases decision-making. By sharing development activities, design decisions that involve interdependencies between functional specialists can be made more quickly and more effectively. This reorganized process creates a timely response to customer needs, a more cost-effective product design process, and higher-quality products at an affordable price.

There are several reasons why early involvement and concurrent activities bring about these improve-ments. First, product design shifts from sequential, with feedback loops that occur whenever a problem is encountered, to concurrent, where problems are recognized early and resolved. The ability to overlap activities reduces product design time. Second, when a team of functional specialists works concurrently on product design, the participants learn from each other and their knowledge base expands. People are better able to anticipate conflicts and can more easily arrive at solutions. As a result, the time it takes to complete an activity should decline. Third, fewer changes later in the process results in faster and less expensive product design. When problems are discovered late, they take more time and money to solve.

Product design requires the expertise and decision-making skills of all parts of the organization. Marketing, engineering, operations, finance, accounting, and information systems all have important roles. Marketing's role is to evaluate consumer needs, determine potential impact of competitive pressure, and measure the external environment. Engineering's role is to shape the product through design, determine the process by which the product will be made, and consider the interface between the product and the people. Operations' role is to ensure that the product can be produced in full-scale production. Finance's role is to develop plans for raising the capital to support the product in full-scale production and to assist in the evaluation of the product's profit potential. Accounting and information systems provide access to information for decision making. Cross-functional teamwork and knowledge sharing are thus keys to success.

SEE ALSO: Computer-Aided Design and Manufacturing; Pricing Policy and Strategy; Product Life Cycle and Industry Life Cycle; Product-Process Matrix; Quality and Total Quality Management; Reverse Supply Chain Logistics; Supply Chain Management

Mark Vonderembse

FURTHER READING:

Corswant, F, and C. Tunälv. "Coordinating Customers and Proactive Suppliers: A Case Study of Supplier Collaboration in Product Development." *Journal of Engineering and Technology Management* 19, no. 3-4 (2002): 249–261.

Droge, C., J. Jayaram, and S. Vickery. "The Ability to Minimize the Timing of New Product Development and Introduction: An Examination of Antecedent Factors in the North American Automobile Supplier Industry." *Journal of Product Innovation Management* 17 (2000): 24–40.

Gerwin, D., and N.J. Barrowman. "An Evaluation of Research on Integrated Product Development." *Management Science* 48, no. 7 (2002): 938–953.

Hong, S.K., and M.J. Schniederjans. "Balancing Concurrent Engineering Environmental Factors for Improved Product Development Performance." *International Journal of Production Research* 38, no. 8 (2000): 1779–1800.

Koufteros, X.A., M. Vonderembse, and J. Jayaram. "Internal and External Integration for Product Development: The Contingency Effects of Uncertainty, Equivocality, and Platform Strategy." *Decisions Sciences* 36, no. 1 (2005): 977–133.

Koufteros, X.A., M. Vonderembse, and W. Doll. "Concurrent Engineering and Its Consequences." *Journal of Operations Management* 19 (2001): 97–115.

Krishnan, V., and K.T. Ulrich. "Product Development Decisions: A Review of the Literature." *Management Science* 47, no. 1 (2001): 1–21.

McDermott, C.M., and G.C. O'Connor. "Managing Radical Innovation: An Overview of Emergent Strategy Issues." *Journal of Product Innovation Management* 19, no. 6 (2002): 424–438.

Meyer, M.H., and A.P. Lehnerd. *The Power of Product Platforms.* New York: The Free Press.

Reinertsen, D.G. *Managing the Design Factory.* New York: The Free Press.

Song, X. M., and M. Montoya-Weiss. "The Effect of Perceived Technological Uncertainty on Japanese New Product Development." *Academy of Management Journal* 44 (2001): 61–80.

Tu, Q., M. Vonderembse, and T.S. Ragu-Nathan. "The Impact of Time-Based Manufacturing Practices on Mass Customization and Value to Customer." *Journal of Operations Management* 19 (2001): 201–217.

Vonderembse, M.A., and G.P. White. *Operations Management: Concepts, Methods, and Strategies.* Danvers, MA: John Wiley & Sons, 2004.

PRODUCT LIFE CYCLE AND INDUSTRY LIFE CYCLE

Recognizing that all living things go through a cycle of birth, growth, maturity, and death, the inspiration for the concepts of product life cycle and industry life cycle comes from biology. The life-cycle concept is an appropriate description of what happens to products and industries over time. When applied to organizations, the product life cycle and industry life cycle contain the four stages of introduction, growth, maturity, and decline.

This concept is much more than an interesting analogy of business and biology. In biology, a living organism's position in its life cycle leads to different courses of action concerning the organism's future. An industry's position and a product's position in their life cycles also lead to very different decisions concerning their futures. Consequently, the life-cycle concept was adopted from biology for use as a strategic planning tool for products and industries.

The following sections define the terms, explain why products have a life cycle, describe the stages of the product life cycle, and examine the strategic implications of the product life cycle.

DEFINITIONS

The life cycle can be used to observe the behavior of many concepts in business. In its classic form, which is described in a later section, it is best applied to products and industries. Used in this form, a product is not individual but a group of similar products. For example, the Chevrolet Malibu, Ford Taurus, and Honda Accord are a product group of mid-sized sedans.

Industry is a much broader classification than product; an industry consists of many similar groups of products. The product groups of mid-size sedan, pickup truck, and sport-utility vehicle all belong to the automobile industry.

Generally, industries have longer life cycles than products. The automobile industry has lasted more than 100 years and shows no signs of declining. However, the large family-sedan appears to be well into the decline stage. After decades of dominance in the automobile industry, only a few large cars, such as Ford's Crown Victoria, are being manufactured.

The life-cycle concept also describes individual brand products, such as the Ford Taurus. However, individual products in a group of products usually have much shorter life cycles, and they do not always follow the classic shape of the product life cycle. They may be introduced and die, and then be reintroduced again at a latter point. For example, the Chevrolet Nova has had more than one life cycle. Consequently, products are defined as groups of similar products, and industries defined as a collection of comparable product groups.

The discussion that follows is applicable to both industries and products. The terms product life cycle and industry life cycle both refer to the four stages of introduction, growth, maturity, and decline. To simplify the discussion, both the product life cycle and industry life cycle will be combined and simply called the product life cycle.

RATIONALE FOR THE PRODUCT LIFE CYCLE

Since products are not living beings, why do they have life cycles? The reason is that society accepts products at different rates, but all go through similar stages of societal acceptance. This acceptance of innovations by societies is called the diffusion of innovations. As society begins to adopt and accept an innovation, the new product grows, eventually reaching maturity. When there is a better alternative to the product or when public preference changes, the products will enter a decline, possibly ending with the death of the product.

The diffusion-of-innovations concept categorizes society by the speed with which the individual members adopt a new product. It classifies people into the five categories of innovators, early adopters, early majority, late majority, and laggards.

INNOVATORS. The first people in a society to adopt a new product are the innovators. These people are risk takers and may be looking for new products to try. They represent only 2.5 percent of the population. Though these people are the first to try a product, they are not usually opinion leaders. Consequently, they do not pass information about the product to the rest of the population.

EARLY ADOPTERS. The early adopters have many opinion leaders in their ranks. They are the first people in the neighborhood to try a new product, and many of them willingly pass the information about the product onto other people. Their experiences can determine whether a product will have a long or short life cycle. They represent about 13.5 percent of the population.

EARLY MAJORITY. Once the early adopters have tried and given their approval to a product, the early majority will begin to follow. Thirty-four percent of the population is in this category. Since they represent such a large percent of the population, the adoption by the early majority causes the new product to enter a period of rapid growth.

LATE MAJORITY. After a significant portion of the population has adopted a product, the late majority will consider its use. These people are not risk takers; they typically wait until they see the product approved by others. They also represent about 34 percent of the population. Once they have adopted the product, the innovators, early adopters, early majority, and late majority represent a total of about 84 percent of the population. By this point, the new product will have reached its maturity.

LAGGARDS. The last category of society to adopt a new product is generally fearful about trying new things. Often, they wait until being forced to adopt because the alternate product is no longer being produced. The laggards represent about 16 percent of the population.

NEW-PRODUCT DEVELOPMENT

Although product development is not usually recognized as a formal stage in the product life cycle, many ideas for long-term product planning are derived from the concepts that are generated through this preliminary process. Product development is defined as a strategy for company growth by offering modified or new products to current market segments. Additionally, product development focuses on turning product concepts into a physical product, while ensuring that that the idea can be turned into a workable product through each stage.

In the product development stage, costs begin to accumulate due to the investment in proposed concepts and ideas. Before introduction, a successful product in the marketplace will go through the following eight distinct stages of new product development:

idea generation, idea screening, concept development, marketing strategy, business analysis, product development, test marketing, and commercialization.

Idea generation usually stems from the organization's internal sources (R&D, engineering, marketing). Company employees will brainstorm new ideas to generate viable product concepts. Additionally, a company may also analyze their competition's new product offerings with the intention of differentiating and improving on existing designs.

Ideas are ultimately screened, reducing the number of unrealistic concepts and focusing on realistic, attainable concepts. A single idea is developed into a product concept. Concepts are then tested to measure how appealing the product might be to consumers from the anticipated target market. Testing may range from focus groups to random surveys.

After concept testing, a marketing strategy is needed to define how the product will be positioned in the marketplace. Identifying the product's anticipated target market, financial expectations, distribution channels, and pricing strategy are also determined at this time.

Business analysis, including sales forecasting, determines if the product will be profitable to manufacturer. Many factors are considered when judging the products anticipated profitability. Managers will look at the length of time it takes for the product to be profitable, cost of capital, and other financial considerations when deciding weather to proceed with development. If the concept is approved, a prototype is created from the product concept.

The prototype undergoes rigorous testing to ensure safety and effectiveness of the product. These tests are a good measure for determining whether or not a product is safe and if it should if the designers should move forward with the creation of the product.

Once a successful prototype is developed, companies perform test marketing on the product. Typically, a company will conduct formal research on a product concept to see if the proposed idea has validity with the targeted audience. Again, customer surveys and focus groups are conducted with the intention of testing the product on a sample of the targeted demographic. The testing is then analyzed to measure consumer reaction to the product. Once all the information is available and the company decides to introduce the product, high commercialization costs are incurred.

STAGES OF THE PRODUCT LIFE CYCLE

As stated above, the product life cycle consists of four stages: introduction, growth, maturity, and decline. Figure A illustrates the product life cycle. Determination of a product's stage in its life cycle is not based on age, but on the relationship of sales, costs, profits, and number of competitors. Each of these stages is described below.

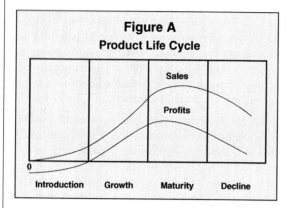

Figure A
Product Life Cycle

INTRODUCTION. When a new product is introduced to a market, the innovators may be the only people aware of the new product. If the product is a new product class, the innovators may not know what the product uses are. Recalling that the innovators represent only a small percent of the population, the sales of the new product will be low. However, there is an advantage in this situation in that the new product does not yet have any competition. During the introduction stage of a new product, the developer enjoys a monopoly.

Unfortunately, the product monopoly does not usually translate to immediate profits. The product may have been in development for a long time and considerable development costs are still in the recovery phase. Also, an expensive marketing effort may be needed to introduce the product to the public. With low sales and high expenses, the introduction stage of the life cycle is usually a money loser for the company. However, the hope is for the future of the product, and the company usually is more than willing to incur the losses.

GROWTH. As the early adopters begin to try the product, a sale begins to grow and profits usually start to follow. This is a great time for a company introducing a new product because the company still enjoys a monopoly early in the growth stage. The company is reaping all the sales and profits of the new product. When Chrysler introduced the idea of the minivan, they were in this enviable position of having the only minivan on the market.

As the early adopters begin influencing the early majority, sales and profits sore. The competition has also been watching from the new product's inception. Unfortunately for the original firm, the competition has also noticed the new product's success. Although they cannot be the first, the competition races to offer their own products and gain a share of a growing market. Chrysler's minivan did not maintain its monopoly for long; soon, the other major automobile manufacturers offered models to compete with Chrysler. Although total

sales and profits continue to grow throughout the growth stage, they are divided among many manufacturers.

MATURITY. By the end of the growth stage of the life cycle, the market is beginning to become very competitive, and this trend continues into the early period of the maturity stage. Besides many more manufacturers offering their products, the producers continue the product-differentiation process begun in the growth stage. The result is a market saturated with many manufacturers offering many models of the product. These manufacturers produce a multitude of models, from desktop computers to notebooks.

With so many companies now in the market, the competition for customers becomes fierce. Although total sales continue to grow during the first part of the maturity stage, the increased competition causes profits to peak at the end of the growth stage and beginning of the maturity stage. Profits then decline during the remainder of the maturity stage. The declining profits mean that the market is not as attractive to companies as it was in the growth stage.

In the growth stage, even inefficient companies made money. However, only the best companies and their products survive in the maturity stage. Manufacturers begin to drop out as they see profits turn to losses. Though there is still competition in the computer industry, for example, companies such as Dell and Apple have emerged as the leaders in the market. During the later part of the maturity stage, even sales begin to dip, putting more pressure on the remaining manufacturers.

DECLINE. The number of companies abandoning the market continues and accelerates in the decline stage. Not only does the efficiency of the company play a factor in the decline, but also the product category itself now becomes a factor. By this time, the market may perceive the product as "old," and it may no longer be in demand. For example, the public replaced their preference for station wagons with their desire for minivans. Advancing technology may also bypass and replace a product, as when tapes and CDs replaced the vinyl record.

The product will continue to exist as long as a few manufacturers can maintain profitability. The laggards will resist switching to the alternative, and manufacturers who can profitably serve this niche will continue to do so. Eventually, even the laggards will switch, and the last companies producing the product will be forced to withdraw, thereby killing the product group.

PRODUCT STRATEGIES DURING THE PRODUCT LIFE CYCLE

Depending on the stage of the product life cycle, the marketing strategy should vary to meet the changing conditions. The marketing mix consists of the product, promotion, price, and distribution. Each element must change with the product life cycle if the company expects to maximize sales and profits. It is important to note that as products move through each stage of the life cycle, they should be monitored and re-evaluated in terms of reducing both production costs and the time it takes to make a product or service profitable with its new position.

Strategic options for products during the product life cycle are examined below.

INTRODUCTION STAGE. In the introduction stage, the product's novelty and lack of competition dominate the marketing strategy. The public is not aware of the product and does not know what benefits it offers them.

Product strategy is focused on introducing one model. Since the public is unaware of the product, to offer more models could confuse them as they learn the purpose of the product. This model may offer various options, but there are usually no major variations on the basic idea of the product. The cost of development may also prohibit the company from developing more models for introduction. With no competition yet in the product category, one model is adequate for introduction.

Since the product is new, persuading the market to buy the product is of secondary importance to informing the public that the product exists. It is the innovators who will begin to buy the product, and they need to be informed. With only one company offering the product, those innovators that decide to purchase the product have only one company from which they can purchase the product. Consequently, the promotion efforts concentrate on informing the public of the product benefits and the company producing the product. Persuasion to buy a particular brand is not needed in the introduction stage.

The pricing policy offers the company an opportunity to regain some development costs. Since the company's product is not only new to the company, but also introduces a new product, the company can use a skimming pricing strategy; that is, a very high price for the new product. Though the high price of the new product may deter some potential customers, many innovators and early adopters will pay the high price to own the new product. The first electronic calculators, for example, were quite expensive. If the product is easily copied, however, the developer may want to use a low-price penetration policy to deter future competition.

Since there are few purchasers in the introduction stage, the distribution does not need to be widespread. The innovators are risk takers and desire to purchase something new. Consequently, they may seek out the distributors carrying the new product, and only a few distributors will suffice.

GROWTH STAGE. In the growth stage, the early adopters, followed by the early majority, begin to consume the product in growing numbers. The increasing sales result in the emergence of profits rather than losses.

During the early part of the growth stage, the company can continue its product policy of offering one basic model. However, if the new product group is successful, eventually competitors will offer their own products to compete in the new category. At that point, the original company will need to offer more models. The models should be differentiated from one another so that the company can continue to attract the new customers coming into the market.

Even with competition beginning to offer their products in the new category, the original company still dominates the market. However, as the market leader rather than a monopoly, the company will need to change its promotion policy of informing the public about their new product and new product category.

With an informing policy, the market leader would still receive the majority of new sales. Unfortunately for the original company, the competition will not be using an informative policy. They will be trying to persuade the public why their product is better than the market leader's product. Consequently, the market leader should switch to a persuasive promotion policy.

As the competition enters the market, they will probably be offering products at prices lower than the price of the original product. This is a penetration pricing policy designed to take sales away from the market leader. If the original company used a skimming pricing policy, its continued use would surely lead to rapid lost sales to the competition unless it is altered. Prices should be lowered so that sales can continue to grow, and the competition kept at bay.

In a growing market, the company's exclusive distribution policy would limit the potential growth for the firm, and sales would go to the competition. Consequently, the company must increase its product distribution to maintain its leadership in the market.

MATURITY STAGE. Many competitors characterize the maturity stage. With the large number of firms producing products, the competition for customers becomes quite intense, and profits decline. The strategy for firms during the maturity stage becomes one of survival, as many competitors will eventually withdraw from the market.

With many companies offering several models of the product, the number of products on the market becomes tremendous. The original company must continue differentiating their models so that the market is aware of the differences in the company's products and the competitors' products. The customers are going to ask why they should buy a particular company's product; just because the product was the first on the market is not going to persuade the customers to continue buying the product. Quality, styling, and product features are a few of the means of differentiating the product from the competition.

During the maturity stage, the need to inform the public has long since passed. Now, the promotion strategy focus is on continuing the persuasion tactics started during the growth stage. The purpose of persuasion is to position the product to the market, which involves creating an image for a product. The image should not be an advertiser's creation, but based on the reality of the product.

The differentiation methods of quality, styling, and features are excellent means of positioning a product. For example, a Chevrolet Corvette and Porsche Boxster are both sports cars, but consumers see the different positions of the cars. The company differentiates its products and uses promotion to create the different position image. Each company hopes that its position is preferred by the consumers.

With the intense competition, management keeps the price of the product to its lowest possible level. For example, the competition for entry-level personal computers has now shifted to offering the lowest price. All of the companies in a mature market must now watch costs carefully.

Every aspect from development through production through marketing is designed to offer the lowest cost possible. A cost and a price advantage over competitors in this stage are significant competitive advantages. Consumers are aware of prices and will reward the company with the lower price, all else being equal. The firm that does not have a significant cost advantage risks losing customers and going out of business.

The absence of a company's product in a particular location may result in lost sales during the maturity period. Widespread distribution is essential. If the company's product is not in a particular location, one or more of the competitors' products are likely to be there. The firm cannot risk losing sales simply because their products were not available.

DECLINE STAGE. During the decline stage, sales and profits begin an even sharper drop, and the number of competitors is reduced even further. With public preference for this product waning, the decline stage continues until the last of the producers cannot make a profit, and the product category dies.

The product strategy now becomes one of reducing the number of models offered. With the public abandoning the product and competition declining, the need for many models is no longer there. The company now focuses its attention on the costs and profitability of the remaining models. Costs, such as research and development and production, are cut to the minimal amount necessary. After the cost cuts, management eliminates those products that are no longer profitable.

The promotion efforts also include an examination of costs. Only the minimal amount of promotion necessary to keep the product selling is done. The remaining people in the market want the product and do not need to be convinced that they should buy the product. They only need to know that the product is still available. Consequently, the promotion effort shifts to reminder promotion.

Products' prices are also kept as low as possible during the decline stage. Since the number of competitors has dropped, it may seem that a company could raise prices. If the remaining customers maintain strong brand loyalty, this policy might be possible. However, the product has fallen out of favor, and customers have other product alternatives. A price increase that could not be justified by cost increases runs the risk of alienating even the few customers left purchasing the product. Consequently, the strategy should be to keep the prices as low as possible.

Cost is also an overriding factor in the distribution of the product during the decline stage. The declining sales may not justify the widespread distribution reached during the maturity stage. Only those areas or markets that are still profitable should be covered, and the unprofitable distribution outlets eliminated. Hopefully for the last companies producing the product, the brand-loyal customers or laggards will seek out the limited locations of the products and continue purchasing it.

DECLINE STAGE TRAP. Just because a product's sales begin to decline does not mean that the product life cycle has reached the decline stage. However, if the company believes that the product is in a decline, the implementation of the decline stage strategies may lead to the death of the product long before its time.

Before the strategies for declining products are tried, the company should definitely establish that the product is in decline. The company should first follow strategies to boost sales and not resign themselves to the cost-cutting strategies of the decline stage. For example, Arm & Hammer could have easily decided that their baking soda was dying, and implemented decline stage strategies. However, they chose to fight for its life. They differentiated the product by finding new uses—such as a deodorizer and an ingredient in toothpaste. They so successfully repositioned the product that many people now think about baking soda as a deodorizer first and disregard its original use in baking.

Borrowed from biology, the life-cycle concept has been adapted and applied to products and industries. The product life cycle maintains that products and industries move through the stages of introduction, growth, maturity, and decline. By viewing a product from the perspective of its product-life-cycle position, management can use the product life cycle as a valuable decision-making tool. As the product moves through its life cycle, the appropriate strategies for its future development vary greatly. Knowledge of the appropriate strategies can help guide management actions.

SEE ALSO: Product Design; Product-Process Matrix; Strategic Planning Tools; Strategy Formulation; Strategy Implementation

James Henley
Revised by Matthew Ross

FURTHER READING:

Hawkins, Del I., Roger J. Best, and Kenneth A. Coney. *Consumer Behavior: Building Marketing Strategy.* Boston, MA: McGraw-Hill, 1998.

Kotler, Philip, and Gary Armstrong. *Principles of Marketing.* Upper Saddle River, NJ: Prentice Hall, 2001.

Perreault, William D., Jr., and E. Jerome McCarthy. *Basic Marketing: A Global-Managerial Approach.* Boston, MA: Irwin McGraw-Hill, 1999.

Teresko, John. "Making a Pitch for PLM." *Industry Week* 253, no. 8 (August 2004): 57.

PRODUCTION PLANNING AND SCHEDULING

Production planning is the function of establishing an overall level of output, called the production plan. The process also includes any other activities needed to satisfy current planned levels of sales, while meeting the firm's general objectives regarding profit, productivity, lead times, and customer satisfaction, as expressed in the overall business plan. The managerial objective of production planning is to develop an integrated game plan where the operations portion is the production plan. This production plan, then, should link the firm's strategic goals to operations (the production function) as well as coordinating operations with sales objectives, resource availability, and financial budgets.

The production-planning process requires the comparison of sales requirements and production capabilities and the inclusion of budgets, pro forma financial statements, and supporting plans for materials and workforce requirements, as well as the production plan itself. A primary purpose of the production plan is to establish production rates that will achieve management's objective of satisfying customer demand. Demand satisfaction could be accomplished through the maintaining, raising, or lowering of inventories or backlogs, while keeping the workforce relatively stable. If the firm has implemented a just-in-time philosophy, the firm would utilize a chase strategy, which would mean satisfying customer demand while keeping inventories at a minimum level.

The term *production planning* is really too limiting since the intent is not to purely produce a plan for the operations function. Because the plan affects many firm functions, it is normally prepared with information from marketing and coordinated with the functions of manufacturing, engineering, finance, materials, and so on. Another term, *sales and operations planning,* has recently come into use, more accurately representing the concern with coordinating several critical activities within the firm.

Production planning establishes the basic objectives for work in each of the major functions. It should be based on the best tradeoffs for the firm as a whole, weighing sales and marketing objectives, manufacturing's cost, scheduling and inventory objectives, and the firm's financial objectives. All these must be integrated with the strategic view of where the company wants to go.

The production-planning process typically begins with an updated sales forecast covering the next 6 to 18 months. Any desired increase or decrease in inventory or backlog levels can be added or subtracted, resulting in the production plan. However, the production plan is not a forecast of demand. It is planned production, stated on an aggregate basis. An effective production-planning process will typically utilize explicit time fences for when the aggregate plan can be changed (increased or decreased). Also, there may be constraints on the degree of change (amount of increase or decrease).

The production plan also provides direct communication and consistent dialogue between the operations function and upper management, as well as between operations and the firm's other functions. As such, the production plan must necessarily be stated in terms that are meaningful to all within the firm, not just the operations executive. Some firms state the production plan as the dollar value of total input (monthly, quarterly, etc.). Other firms may break the total output down by individual factories or major product lines. Still other firms state the plan in terms of total units for each product line. The key here is that the plan be stated in some homogeneous unit, commonly understood by all, that is also consistent with that used in other plans.

PRODUCTION SCHEDULING

The production schedule is derived from the production plan; it is a plan that authorized the operations function to produce a certain quantity of an item within a specified time frame. In a large firm, the production schedule is drawn in the production planning department, whereas, within a small firm, a production schedule could originate with a lone production scheduler or even a line supervisor.

Production scheduling has three primary goals or objectives. The first involves due dates and avoiding late completion of jobs. The second goal involves throughput times; the firm wants to minimize the time a job spends in the system, from the opening of a shop order until it is closed or completed. The third goal concerns the utilization of work centers. Firms usually want to fully utilize costly equipment and personnel.

Often, there is conflict among the three objectives. Excess capacity makes for better due-date performance and reduces throughput time but wreaks havoc on utilization. Releasing extra jobs to the shop can increase the utilization rate and perhaps improve due-date performance but tends to increase throughput time.

Quite a few sequencing rules (for determining the sequence in which production orders are to be run in the production schedule) have appeared in research and in practice. Some well-known ones adapted from Vollmann, Berry, Whybark and Jacobs (2005) are presented in Operations Scheduling.

THE PRODUCTION PLANNING AND PRODUCTION SCHEDULING INTERFACE

There are fundamental differences in production planning and production scheduling. Planning models often utilize aggregate data, cover multiple stages in a medium-range time frame, in an effort to minimize total costs. Scheduling models use detailed information, usually for a single stage or facility over a short term horizon, in an effort to complete jobs in a timely manner. Despite these differences, planning and scheduling often have to be incorporated into a single framework, share information, and interact extensively with one another. They also may interact with other models such as forecasting models or facility location models.

It should be noted that a major shift in direction has occurred in recent research on scheduling methods. Much of what was discussed was developed for job shops. As a result of innovations such as computer-integrated manufacturing (CIM) and just-in-time (JIT), new processes being established in today's firms are designed to capture the benefits of repetitive manufacturing and continuous flow manufacturing. Therefore, much of the new scheduling research concerns new concepts and techniques for repetitive manufacturing-type operations. In addition, many of today's firms cannot plan and schedule only within the walls of their own factory as most are an entity with an overall supply chain. Supply chain management requires the coordination and integration of operations in all stages of the chain. If successive stages in a supply belong to the same firm, then these successive stages can be incorporated into a single planning and scheduling model. If not, constant interaction and information sharing are required to optimize the overall supply chain.

SEE ALSO: Aggregate Planning; Operations Management; Operations Scheduling; Product-Process Matrix; Supply Chain Management

R. Anthony Inman

FURTHER READING:

Hurtubise, Stephanie, and Claude Olivier, and Ali Gharbi. "Planning Tools for Managing the Supply Chain." *Computers & Industrial Engineering* 46 (2004): 763–779.

Kreipl, Stephan, and Michael Pinedo. "Planning and Scheduling in Supply Chains: An Overview of Issues in Practice." *Production and Operations Management* 13, no. 1 (2004): 77–92.

Vollmann, Thomas E., William L. Berry, Clay D. Whybark, and F. Robert Jacobs. *Manufacturing Planning and Control for Supply Chain Management.* 5th ed. New York: Irwin McGraw-Hill, 2005.

PRODUCTIVITY CONCEPTS AND MEASURES

Productivity is an overall measure of the ability to produce a good or service. More specifically, productivity is the measure of how specified resources are managed to accomplish timely objectives as stated in terms of quantity and quality. Productivity may also be defined as an index that measures output (goods and services) relative to the input (labor, materials, energy, etc., used to produce the output). As such, it can be expressed as:

$$\text{Productivity} = \frac{\text{Output}}{\text{Input}}$$

Hence, there are two major ways to increase productivity: increase the numerator (output) or decrease the denominator (input). Of course, a similar effect would be seen if both input and output increased, but output increased faster than input; or if input and output decreased, but input decreased faster than output.

Organizations have many options for use of this formula, labor productivity, machine productivity, capital productivity, energy productivity, and so on. A productivity ratio may be computed for a single operation, a department, a facility, an organization, or even an entire country.

Productivity is an objective concept. As an objective concept it can be measured, ideally against a universal standard. As such, organizations can monitor productivity for strategic reasons such as corporate planning, organization improvement, or comparison to competitors. It can also be used for tactical reasons such as project control or controlling performance to budget.

Productivity is also a scientific concept, and hence can be logically defined and empirically observed. It can also be measured in quantitative terms, which qualifies it as a variable. Therefore, it can be defined and measured in absolute or relative terms. However, an absolute definition of productivity is not very useful; it is much more useful as a concept dealing with relative productivity or as a productivity factor.

Productivity is useful as a relative measure of actual output of production compared to the actual input of resources, measured across time or against common entities. As output increases for a level of input, or as the amount of input decreases for a constant level of output, an increase in productivity occurs. Therefore, a "productivity measure" describes how well the resources of an organization are being used to produce input.

Productivity is often confused with efficiency. Efficiency is generally seen as the ratio of the time needed to perform a task to some predetermined standard time. However, doing unnecessary work efficiently is not exactly being productive. It would be more correct to interpret productivity as a measure of effectiveness (doing the right thing efficiently), which is outcome-oriented rather than output-oriented.

Productivity is usually expressed in one of three forms: partial factor productivity, multifactor productivity, and total productivity. Each one is now discussed.

PARTIAL-FACTOR PRODUCTIVITY

The standard definition of productivity is actually what is known as a partial factor measure of productivity, in the sense that it only considers a single input in the ratio. The formula then for partial-factor productivity would be the ratio of total output to a single input or:

$$\text{Productivity} = \frac{\text{Total output}}{\text{Single input}}$$

Managers generally utilize partial productivity measures because the data is readily available. Also, since the total of multifactor measures provides an aggregate perspective, partial factor productivity measures are easier to relate to specific processes. Labor-based hours (generally, readily available information) is a frequently used input variable in the equation. When this is the case, it would seem that productivity could be increased by substituting machinery for labor. However, that may not necessarily be a wise decision. Labor-based measures do not include mechanization and automation in the input; thus when automation replaces labor, misinterpretation may occur.

Other partial factor measure options could appear as output/labor, output/machine, output/capital, or output/energy. Terms applied to some other partial factor measures include capital productivity (using machine hours or dollars invested), energy productivity (using kilowatt hours), and materials productivity (using inventory dollars).

MULTIFACTOR PRODUCTIVITY

A multifactor productivity measure utilizes more than a single factor, for example, both labor and capital. Hence, multifactor productivity is the ratio of total output to a subset of inputs:

$$\text{Multifactor productivity} = \frac{\text{Total output}}{\text{Subset of inputs}}$$

A subset of inputs might consist of only labor and materials or it could include capital. Examples include:

$$\frac{\text{Output}}{\text{Labor + Machine}}$$

or

$$\frac{\text{Output}}{\text{Labor + Capital + Energy}}$$

or

$$\frac{\text{Quantity of production at standard price}}{\text{Labor cost + Materials cost + Overhead}}$$

Obviously, the different factors must be measured in the same units, for example dollars or standard hours.

TOTAL FACTOR PRODUCTIVITY

A broader gauge of productivity, total factor productivity is measured by combining the effects of all the resources used in the production of goods and services (labor, capital, raw material, energy, etc.) and dividing it into the output. As such the formula would appear as:

$$\text{Total productivity} = \frac{\text{Total output}}{\text{Total input}}$$

or

$$\text{Total productivity} = \frac{\text{Goods or services produced}}{\text{All inputs used to produce them}}$$

One example, is a ratio computed by adding standard hours of labor actually produced, plus the standard machine hours actually produced in a given time period divided by the actual hours available for both labor and machines in the time period.

Total output must be expressed in the same unit of measure and total input must be expressed in the same unit of measure. However, total output and total input need not be expressed in the same unit of measure. Resources are often converted to dollars or standard hours so that a single figure can be used as an aggregate measure of total input or output. For example, total output could be expressed as the number of units produced, and total input could be expressed in dollars, such as tons of steel produced per dollar input. Other varieties of the measure may appear as dollar value of good or service produced per dollar of input, or standard hours of output per actual hours of input.

Total productivity ratios reflect simultaneous changes in outputs and inputs. As such, total productivity ratios provide the most inclusive type of index for measuring productivity and may be preferred in making comparisons of productivity. However, they do not show the interaction between each input and output separately and are thus too broad to be used as a tool for improving specific areas.

Total Factor Productivity is a measure favored by the Japanese, whereas labor productivity is the measure favored by the United States. As such, the individual "productivity" of the American employee tends to be the best in the world, in that an American employee can purchase more eggs per one hour of work than anyone else in the world. But as a measure of national productivity, the Japanese have, in the past, tended to be better performers.

PRODUCTIVITY MEASURES

It has been said that the challenge of productivity has become a challenge of measurement. Productivity is difficult to measure and can only be measured indirectly, that is, by measuring other variables and then calculating productivity from them. This difficulty in measurement stems from the fact that inputs and outputs are not only difficult to define but are also difficult to quantify.

Any productivity measurement system should produce some sort of overall index of productivity. A smart measurement program combines productivity measurements into an overall rating of performance. This type of system should be flexible in order to accommodate changes in goals and policies over time. It should also have the ability to aggregate the measurement systems of different units into a single system and be able to compare productivity across different units.

The ways in which input and output are measured can provide different productivity measures. Disadvantages of productivity measures have been the distortion of the measure by fixed expenses and also the inability of productivity measures to consider quality changes (e.g., output per hour might increase, but it may cause the defect rate to skyrocket). It is easier to conceive of outputs as tangible units such as number of items produced, but other factors such as quality should be considered.

Experts have cited a need for a measurement program that gives an equal weight to quality as well as productivity. If quality is included in the ratio, output may have to be defined as something like the number of defect-free units of production or the number of units which meet customer expectations or requirements.

The determination of when productivity measures are appropriate performance measures depends on two criteria. The first is the independence of the transformation process from other processes within the organization. Second is the correspondence between the inputs and outputs in the productivity measurement process.

USE OF PRODUCTIVITY MEASURES

Productivity is a required tool in evaluating and monitoring the performance of an organization, especially a business organization. When directed at specific issues and problems, productivity measures can be very powerful. In essence, productivity measures are the yardsticks of effective resource use.

Managers are concerned with productivity as it relates to making improvements in their firm. Proper use of productivity measures can give the manager an indication of how to improve productivity: either increase the numerator of the measure, decrease the denominator, or both.

Managers are also concerned with how productivity measures relate to competitiveness. If two firms have the same level of output, but one requires less input thanks to a higher level of productivity, that firm will be able to charge a lower price and increase its market share or charge the same price as the competitor and enjoy a larger profit margin.

Within a time period, productivity measures can be used to compare the firm's performance against industry-wide data, compare its performance with similar firms and competitors, compare performance among different departments within the firm, or compare the performance of the firm or individual departments within the firm with the measures obtained at an earlier time (i.e., is performance improving or decreasing over time?).

Productivity measures can also be used to evaluate the performance of an entire industry or the productivity of a country as a whole. These are aggregate measures determined by combining productivity measures of various companies, industries, or segments of the economy.

PRODUCTIVITY INDEX

Since productivity is a relative measure, for it to be meaningful or useful it must be compared to something. For example, businesses can compare their productivity values to that of similar firms, other departments within the same firm, or against past productivity data for the same firm or department (or even one machine). This allows firms to measure productivity improvement over time, or measure the impact of certain decisions such as the introduction on new processes, equipment, and worker motivation techniques.

In order to have a value for comparison purposes, organizations compute their productivity index. A productivity index is the ratio of productivity measured in some time period to the productivity measured in a base period. For example, if the base period's productivity is calculated to be 1.75 and the following period's productivity is calculated to 1.93, the resulting productivity index would be 1.93/1.75 = 1.10. This would indicate that the firm's productivity had increased 10 percent. If the following period's productivity measurement fell to 1.66 the productivity index of 1.66/1.75 = 0.95 it would indicate that the organization's productivity has fallen to 95 percent of the productivity of the base period. By tracking productivity indexes over time, managers can evaluate the success, or lack thereof, of projects and decisions.

FACTORS AFFECTING PRODUCTIVITY

There is quite a variety of factors which can affect productivity, both positively and negatively. These include:

1. capital investments in production

2. capital investments in technology

3. capital investments in equipment

4. capital investments in facilities

5. economies of scale

6. workforce knowledge and skill resulting from training and experience

7. technological changes

8. work methods

9. procedures

10. systems

11. quality of products

12. quality of processes

13. quality of management

14. legislative and regulatory environment

15. general levels of education

16. social environment

17. geographic factors

The first 12 factors are highly controllable at the company or project level. Numbers 13 and 14 are marginally controllable, at best. Numbers 15 and 16 are controllable only at the national level, and 17 is uncontrollable.

IMPROVING PRODUCTIVITY

Productivity improvement can be achieved in a number of ways. If the level of output is increased faster than that of input, productivity will increase. Conversely, productivity will be increased if the level of input is decreased faster than that of output. Also,

an organization may realize a productivity increase from producing more output with the same level of input. Finally, producing more output with a reduced level of input will result in increased productivity.

Any of these scenarios may be realized through improved methods, investment in machinery and technology, improved quality, and improvement techniques and philosophies such as just-in-time, total quality management, lean production, supply chain management principles, and theory of constraints.

A firm or department may undertake a number of key steps toward improving productivity. William J. Stevenson (1999) lists these steps to productivity improvement:

- Develop productivity measures for all operations; measurement is the first step in managing and controlling an organization.

- Look at the system as a whole in deciding which operations are most critical, it is overall productivity that is important.

- Develop methods for achieving productivity improvement, such as soliciting ideas from workers (perhaps organizing teams of workers, engineers, and managers), studying how other firms have increased productivity, and reexamining the way work is done.

- Establish reasonable goals for improvement.

- Make it clear that management supports and encourages productivity improvement. Consider incentives to reward workers for contributions.

- Measure improvements and publicize them.

- Don't confuse productivity with efficiency. Efficiency is a narrower concept that pertains to getting the most out of a given set of resources; productivity is a broader concept that pertains to use of overall resources. For example, an efficiency perspective on mowing the lawn given a hand mower would focus on the best way to use the hand mower; a productivity perspective would include the possibility of using a power mower.

As a cautionary word, organizations must be careful not to focus solely on productivity as the driver for the organization. Organizations must consider overall competitive ability. Firm success is categorized by quality, cycle time, reasonable lead time, innovation, and a host of other factors directed at improving customer service and satisfaction.

PRODUCTIVITY AT THE NATIONAL LEVEL

Since productivity is one of the basic variables governing economic production activity some mention of national productivity concerns would be appropriate.

As a matter of fact, productivity may be the most important variable governing economic production activity. It is the fundamental controllable factor in wealth production. Since other economic variables depend on it, increasing productivity tends to have a beneficial multiplying effect on other economic variables. This is generally true at every level of economic aggregation.

Productivity growth in the United States lagged that of other leading industrial countries in the 1970s and 1980s. This caused some concern among American government officials and business leaders. Although, the United States' productivity was still among the world's highest, it was losing ground to other nations, most notably Japan, Korea, the United Kingdom, and West Germany.

Concern was especially great in the area of manufacturing; a significant portion of American productivity could be attributed to high agricultural productivity, whereas manufacturing tended to be lower. Productivity in services lagged that of both agriculture and manufacturing. However, the picture may be changing. While the United States' productivity growth slowed during the late twentieth century, it has since increased. With the aspect of automation within service industries, service sector productivity is continually on the increase.

Improving productivity is of national importance because, for a society to increase its standard of living, it must first increase productivity. Overall productivity for individual countries is calculated by dividing output, as measured by GDP or GNP, by the country's total population. Thus, productivity is measured as the dollar value per capita outputs. An increase in this measure of productivity means that each person in the country, on average, produced more goods and services. Also if productivity increases, then profits increase. The resulting profits can then be used to pay for wage increases (inherent in inflation) without having to raise prices. In this way, productivity gains actually help curb inflation.

It has been estimated that technology was responsible for at least half of the growth in productivity in the United States between 1948 and 1966. It would appear, then, that if the United States wants to continue to increase productivity, technology may be the key. Extensive press attention has focused on the factory of the future, where factory workers are being replaced in order to improve flexibility and productivity. Apparently, the role and importance of productivity will not diminish any time soon.

SEE ALSO: Economies of Scale and Economies of Scope; Effectiveness and Efficiency; Experience and Learning Curves; Financial Issues for Managers; Financial Ratios

R. Anthony Inman
Revised by Gerhard Plenert

FURTHER READING:

Plenert, Gerhard. *The eManager: Value Chain Management in an eCommerce World.* Dublin, Ireland: Blackhall Publishing, 2001.

———. *International Operations Management.* Copenhagen, Denmark: Copenhagen Business School Press, 2002.

Stevenson, William J. *Production and Operations Management.* Boston, MA: Irwin McGraw-Hill, 1999.

Vora, Jay A. "Productivity and Performance Measures: Who Uses Them." *Production and Inventory Management Journal* 33, no. 1 (1992): 46-49.

PROFESSIONAL READINGS FOR MANAGERS

"Information was once a sought-after and treasured commodity like a fine wine. Now, it's regarded more like crabgrass, something to be kept at bay," observes Richard Saul Wurman in his book *Information Anxiety2.* Professional reading, like every other aspect of a manager's professional activities, must be well thought out. Today's manager is surrounded, even bombarded, by information, but the shape, scope and delivery method of this professional literature changes daily. To keep up with general trends or focus in-depth on one industry, it is not sufficient to read traditional print titles. Information savvy managers monitor a variety of information streams. The Internet, e-mail, cell phones, seminars, webinars, blogs, television, radio, industry DVDs, popular business magazines, newsletters, e-zines, scholarly journals, newspapers, books, and technical reports compete continuously for the busy manager's time and attention.

THE INTERNET

By its nature, the Internet is too much for one manager to take on. Guides are needed to make the most of the incredible wealth of information available online. The Business Reference and Services Section (BRASS) of the American Library Association's (ALA) Best of the Best Business Web Sites product (http://www.ala.org/ala/rusa/rusa.htm) is an excellent guide. This free service identifies and categorizes significant Web sites within broad business categories such as "general management," "human resource management and labor relations," and "MIS and knowledge management." Each category then contains lists of topic-based, content-rich Web sites. For example under "human resource management" one might find a link to the Society for Human Resource Management (http://www.shrm.org/) or Workindex.com (www.workindex.com), a site sponsored by and prepared as a joint venture between Cornell University and *Human*

Resource Executive Magazine. Other sites that have been listed include hrvillage (www.hrvillage.com) and Workplace via WorkNet@ILR (www.ilr.cornell.edu/workplace.html).

Like BRASS, About.com (www.about.com) has a central philosophy that "people are the best guides to the Internet." Therefore, the site recruits enthusiastic experts in nearly 500 fields of endeavor who create online informational guides that are well organized, focused, and practical. About.com's management section (www.management.about.com) allows one to choose from basic information, links to other articles, what links are most popular on the site, as well as a section of links on hot topics.

Bpubs (www.bpubs.com) speaks to the busy manager with the tagline "No homepages. No indexes. No surfing. . . just content. Because your time is worth something." This free site allows the busy professional to read articles online at no cost. There is a search engine to provide access by specific subject, or the site can be searched by navigating through established categories such as "management science" and "human resources." Under "management science" one can focus further on such issues as "total quality management" or "change management," among others.

The Institute of Management and Administration (IOMA) Web site (www.ioma.com) is an example of a site that charges a fee for access to certain resources, but allows free searching along with some free, full-text information.

BLOGS

As the Internet grows and matures, new types of communication are being introduced. With these new avenues of expression comes another choice in the panoply of choices for the information-seeking manager to consider. In 2001 the term "blog" was barely a blip on the screen of the general reader, but by 2005 blogs had become an important and sometimes powerful method of discovering and disseminating information. Blogging is on the rise and corporate blogging adds another publishing platform for businesses to get their message out to internal and external customers. Corporate executives at Boeing, Sun Microsystems, General Motors, and others are publishing these online journals, discussing issues, trends, products, and business philosophies.

MAGAZINES AND NEWSPAPERS

Traditional trade magazines and newspapers still play an important role in keeping managers informed of current issues in the business world. Familiar titles such as *Forbes* (www.forbes.com), *Fortune* (www.fortune.com), *Business Week* (www.businessweek.com), and *Inc.* (www.inc.com), as well as newer entries into this field such as *Fast Company* (www.fastcompany.com), all have Web sites that serve as companions to their print publications. Major newspapers, such as *The New York Times* (www.nytimes.com), *The Wall Street Journal* (www.wsj.com), and *The Washington Post* (www.washingtonpost.com), are all accessible via the Internet. Each of these Web sites offers at least a selection of articles at no cost. Some require paid subscriptions for access to "premium content" and some offer pay-per-view services that allow access to single articles for a one-time fee. All include features that are not available in the print versions, and some include features in print that are not available online. Some newspapers require readers to register—for free—before gaining access to the site.

Workforce Management is the latest incarnation of a venerable title in the area of human resource management. Formerly titled *Workforce, Personnel Journal,* and *Journal of Personnel Research,* this publication continues to include articles on practical topics facing managers, including compensation and benefits, employee training, supervision, communications, and other relevant subjects. Like any serious business publication, *Workforce Management* has a Web version (www.workforce.com). Like other resources the Web site contains access to free content, as well as articles and services that are restricted to paid subscribers.

PROFESSIONAL ASSOCIATIONS

Professional associations are one of the richest veins of business information, offering a variety of resources. The three associations outlined below represent the tip of the iceberg in the large sea of management associations. However, they are time-honored, all-encompassing organizations that have served managers of every stripe for a long time.

The American Management Association (www.amanet.org) provides individual and corporate members with "access to the latest and the best management thinking and practice." Members receive association publications including *AMA Management Update,* a monthly electronic newsletter that emphasizes current topics, strategies, and trends; *Executive Matters,* a print newsletter focusing on management issues; and *MWorld: The American Management Association Journal,* a quarterly print journal with articles written by executives and educators that focuses on inventive solutions to management problems, as well as best practices and emerging trends.

The Academy of Management (www.aomonline.org) is a leading professional association that focuses on disseminating knowledge about management and organizations. The academy publishes four, well-established scholarly journals dedicated to the theory, research, education, and practice of management.

These journals, *The Academy of Management Review* (AMR), *Academy of Management Journal* (AMJ), *Academy of Management Learning and Education* (AMLE), and *Academy of Management Executive* (AME) are included in the organization's membership cost. Academic journals like these generally include articles that are longer than professional magazine literature. The articles are documented with notes, tables, charts, or graphs. As a general rule, authors are college or university professors. Article content usually provides extensive analysis of a topic or issue.

The Society for Human Resource Management's (SHRM) (www.shrm.org) mission is "to serve the needs of HR Professionals by providing the most essential and comprehensive resources available." This mission is accomplished in part through a variety of publications, most notably *HR Magazine*—formerly *Personnel Administrator* and *Journal for Personnel Administration.* This well-established monthly magazine covers a wide variety of articles on topics related to human resources management, including global issues, training and development, outsourcing, and technology trends.

SUBSCRIPTION DATABASES

While online business databases come in a variety of formats, they all consist of a data collection that is organized around a subject or group of subjects and made electronically available and searchable through an interface provided by the database developer. Online databases can be the product of one company or the aggregation of information collected from a variety of content providers. Access to electronic databases is almost always through subscription, and the cost is generally significant. However, libraries of all kinds— college and university, public, and corporate—subscribe to the databases that are most appropriate for their patrons. Many states also have launched statewide library projects that provide citizens with electronic access to business/management databases through libraries. Although the look and feel of each database is different, searching can be done by author, title, keyword, publication title, words in an abstract, product names, and a variety of other key data points.

ABI/INFORM, a product of ProQuest Information and Learning, is advertised as "one of the world's first electronic databases" and has been a leading source of business information for more than thirty years. ABI/INFORM indexes more than one thousand journals covering articles on business conditions, trends, management techniques, and corporate strategies. Approximately 50 percent of titles covered in the database are presented in full-text on a user's desktop. Thomson Gale, a business of The Thomson Corp., offers a variety of business-related databases including Business and Company Profile ASAP and Business &

Management Practices. Business and Company Profile ASAP gives searchers a broad, deep collection from which to choose, including journals, newspapers, a company directory, hard to find private company data, and newswire releases. Business & Management Practices is a more highly focused product, containing information on management, planning, production, finance, information technology, and human resources. Both Thomson Gale products offer substantial full-text coverage of articles.

Factiva, a joint venture between Dow Jones and Company and Reuters Group, includes coverage of Dow Jones and Reuters newswires and *The Wall Street Journal,* plus more than 7,000 other sources from around the world. In addition to current news, Factiva offers access to historical articles going back 30 years. Many articles are available in languages other than English.

LexisNexis Academic is an interdisciplinary, full-text database providing searchable access to more than 5,600 sources including national and regional newspapers, non-English language sources, journals, wire services, newsletters, company reports, SEC filings, U.S federal and state case law, codes, regulations, legal news, law reviews, international legal information, transcripts of broadcasts, and selected reference works.

Emerald is a leading publisher of journals in the management arena. Emerald currently publishes more than 150 titles including *Management Decision, TQM Magazine, Journal of Documentation,* and *Journal of Consumer Marketing.* Emerald also offers a variety of products aimed at making journal content easily accessible. Emerald Fulltext provides the ability to search more than 40,000 articles from more than 100 Emerald journals. Emerald Management Reviews (formerly Anbar) gives subscribers access to article reviews from "the world's leading 400 journals and periodicals as determined by an independent Accreditation Panel." Key titles reviewed include the *Harvard Business Review, Journal of Marketing, Sloan Management Review,* and *The Economist.* Emerald also offers a "support resource" called Management First, which is aimed at the "working manager." This product includes articles, interviews, case studies, discussion forums, and an electronic newsletter.

BOOKS

Bookstores, newsstands, the Internet, and libraries—whether they are public, academic, or corporate—all offer a wealth of information, inspiration, and guidance for today's manager. Investing time and energy into professional reading should be a personal commitment for every manager and a corporate-level commitment for any company interested in successfully riding the wave of information that threatens to drown the unprepared.

SEE ALSO: Domestic Management Societies and Associations; International Management Societies and Associations; Popular Press Management Books

Sheila Delacroix

FURTHER READING:

Moss, Rita W. *Strauss's Handbook of Business Information: A Guide for Librarians, Students, and Researchers.* 2nd ed. Westport, CT: Libraries Unlimited, 2004.

White, Gary W. *The Core Business Web: A Guide to Key Information Resources.* New York: The Haworth Information Press, 2003.

Wurman, Richard Saul. *Information Anxiety 2.* Indianapolis, IN: Que, 2001.

PROFIT SHARING

Profit sharing is an organizational incentive plan whereby companies distribute a portion of their profits to their employees in addition to prevailing wages. Profit sharing can generate benefits to the company by fostering greater employee cooperation, reducing labor turnover, raising productivity, cutting costs, and providing retirement security. Profit sharing gives employees a direct stake in the profitability of a company, creating an atmosphere in which employees want the business to succeed as much as management does. The annual U.S. Chamber of Commerce *Employee Benefits Survey* shows that approximately 19 to 23 percent of U.S. companies have offered some form of profit sharing since 1963. According to the Profit Sharing/401(k) Council of America, 700,000 American businesses offered defined contribution plans (including profit sharing and 401(k) plans) to their employees in 2003. These plans covered 62.5 million American workers and contained $2.4 trillion in assets.

HISTORY

Profit sharing was quite common in primitive fishing and farming economies; in fact, it still persists among fisherman in many parts of the world. Albert Gallatin, Secretary of the Treasury under Presidents Jefferson and Madison, introduced profit sharing into his New Geneva, Pennsylvania, glassworks in the 1790s. Profit-sharing plans as we know them today were developed in the 19th century, when companies such as General Foods and Pillsbury distributed a percentage of their profits to their employees as a bonus. The first deferred profit-sharing plan was developed in 1916 by Harris Trust and Savings Bank of Chicago. Profit sharing was also instrumental during World War II, enabling wartime employers to provide additional compensation to their employees without actually raising their wages.

FORMS OF PROFIT SHARING

There are three basic types of profit-sharing plans:

1. Cash plans distribute cash or stock to employees at the end of the year. The main drawback of this plan is that employee profit-sharing bonuses are taxed as ordinary income. Even if the distribution takes the form of stock or some other payment, it becomes taxable as soon as the employee receives it.

2. Deferred plans direct profit shares into a trust fund on behalf of individual employees and distribute them at a later date, often at retirement. The Internal Revenue Service allows immediate taxation to be avoided in this plan. The deferred profit-sharing plan is a type of defined-contribution plan. A separate account is established for every employee. The accounts increase as contributions are made to them, earning interest or capital gains. Qualified deferred profit-sharing plans give employees a variety of investment choices for their accounts; these choices are common when outside firms manage the accounts.

3. Combination plans pay part of the profit share out directly in cash and defer the remainder into a trust fund.

VESTING REQUIREMENTS

It is becoming less common for companies to manage their own accounts, due to the fiduciary responsibilities and liabilities involved with them. Instead, companies typically contract the responsibility to financial management firms. The amount of future benefits depends on the performance of the account. The balance of the account will include the employer's contributions from profits, any interest earned, any capital gains or losses, and possibly any forfeiture from other plan participants, which may occur when participants leave the company before they are vested (that is, eligible to receive the funds in their accounts); the funds in their accounts are then distributed to the other employees' accounts.

The time required to become fully vested varies from company to company. Immediate vesting means employees are entitled to the funds in their accounts as soon as their employer makes the contribution.

Some companies utilize partially vested schedules, entitling employees to, say, 20 percent of the account before gradually becoming fully vested over a period of time. Establishing a vesting schedule is one way to limit access to the account. Another way is to create strict rules as to when payments can be made from employees' accounts, such as at retirement, death, disability, or termination of employment.

CONTRIBUTION LIMITS

The IRS also limits the amount that employers may contribute to their profit-sharing plans. Tax laws allow employers to contribute a maximum of 15 percent of an employee's salary to his or her account. If a company contributes less than 15 percent to an account in a particular year, they can make up the difference in a following year, up to a maximum of 25 percent of an employee's salary.

Individual companies may determine the amount of their contributions in one of two ways. One is a set formula written into the plan document. Formulas are commonly based on the company's pre-tax net profits, earnings growth, or another measure of profitability. Some companies determine a certain amount to contribute each year, settled on by the board of directors.

Many companies incorporate profit-sharing plans when economic times are hard and they are unable to provide guaranteed wage increases. Chrysler Corporation, for example, developed a profit-sharing plan for its union and non-union employees in the economic recession of 1988. The plan was incorporated into the union contract in exchange for wage concessions made by its workers. Although harsh economic times made contributions small, by 1994 (when the economy had recovered) Chrysler was paying an average bonus of $4,300 per person to 81,000 employees, for a total of about $348 million.

Many companies are also encouraged to develop profit-sharing programs because they provide significant tax advantages, which can benefit higher-paid as well as lower-paid employees. IRS regulations allow the deductibility of the employer's profit-sharing contributions as a business expense and also allow the deferral of this money into a trust without any tax liabilities until the money is received (usually at retirement, disability, death, severance of employment, or under withdrawal provisions), at which point the employee is usually in a lower tax bracket.

The Employee Retirement Income Security Act (ERISA), which was passed on September 2, 1974, is the primary legislation regulating the standards for pension plans and other employee-benefit plans. The intent of the ERISA was to protect employee rights under plans such as corporate pensions, deferred profit

sharing, stock-bonus plans, and welfare. ERISA does not mandate companies to establish a profit-sharing plan, nor does it require any minimum benefit levels. ERISA did, however, establish guidelines for participation, vesting, funding, fiduciary standards, reporting/disclosing, and plan-termination insurance.

ADVANTAGES AND DISADVANTAGES

Profit sharing has become one of a new breed of incentives called *total system incentives*. These incentives link all of the employees of a company to the pursuit of organizational goals. A common misconception of profit sharing is that it is more suited for smaller companies where employees can more easily see the connection between their efficiency and company contributions. In actuality, profit sharing is being successfully utilized in large and small companies, labor-intensive and capital-intensive industries, mass production and job-shop situations, and industries with volatile profits as well as those with stable profits. Profit sharing can reward employee performance, seniority, and thrift, depending on the design of the plan.

Although the concept has experienced a tremendous growth rate, profit-sharing plans do not always work. Roughly 2 percent of deferred plans are terminated annually—some as a result of mergers, others because companies are liquidated or sold. The majority of terminations tend to occur after consecutive years of losses, when investment performance is poor, or when ineffective communication has resulted in lack of employee understanding, appreciation, or interest. Profit sharing may also entail some disadvantages for a company. Such plans may limit the company's ability to reward the performance of individual employees, for example, since the pay for all employees moves up or down according to a formula. At smaller companies, tying employee compensation to often-uncertain profits may result in drastic income swings from one year to the next. Finally, some critics claim that profit sharing may encourage employees to focus only on increasing profitability, perhaps at the expense of quality or other goals.

Kevin Nelson
Revised by Laurie Collier Hillstrom

FURTHER READING:

Girard, Bryan. "Is There an ESOP in Your Company's Future? An Employee Stock Ownership Plan Could Enhance Your Company's Bottom Line." *Strategic Finance* May 2002.

HR Guide to the Internet. "Profit Sharing." 1999. Available from <http://www.hr-guide.com/data/G444.htm>.

Metzger, Bert L. *How to Motivate with Profit Sharing*. Evanston, IL: Profit Sharing Research Foundation, 1978.

Profit Sharing/401(k) Council of America. "45th Annual Survey of Profit Sharing and 401(k) Plans." *Pension Benefits* (December 2002).

PROGRAM EVALUATION AND REVIEW TECHNIQUE AND CRITICAL PATH METHOD

Program Evaluation and Review Technique (PERT) and Critical Path Method (CPM) are tools widely used in project scheduling. Both are based on network diagrams applicable for both the planning and control aspects of production. Visual display of the network enhances the communication and highlights the interdependency of the various activities required for project completion. Perhaps the greatest contribution of these tools is the identification of sequentially time-critical activities that require the closest monitoring.

BACKGROUND

In the early 1900s the Gantt chart was widely hailed as the reason that ships were built in record time. Developed by an engineer named Henry Gantt, this horizontal bar chart shows the scheduled times for individual jobs to be accomplished by specific resources. However, this tool is static in nature, and requires frequent manual updating, especially when activities are sequentially dependent.

In Figure 1, the Gantt chart shows the prospective times for five activities in a project, but does not show an underlying dependency of Activity D on the completion of Activity B.

In the 1950s, two groups independently developed what has become known as the PERT/CPM method of project scheduling. Each of these techniques improved on the Gantt chart by building into the tool the explicit sequencing of activities.

PERT was developed by the U.S. Navy, the Lockheed Corporation, and the consulting firm of Booz, Allen and Hamilton to facilitate the Polaris missile project. As time was a primary issue, this technique used statistical techniques to assess the probability of finishing the project within a given period of time.

By contrast, CPM was created in the environment of industrial projects, where costs were a major factor. In addition to the identification of the time-critical path of activities, representatives from the Du Pont Company and Sperry-Rand Corporation also developed a time-cost tradeoff analysis mechanism called crashing.

These two tools differ in the network diagram display. PERT historically uses the activity-on-arrow (AOA) convention, while CPM uses activity-on-node (AON). For most purposes, these two conventions are interchangeable; however some propriety software requires the logic of a specific convention. Both forms of network diagrams use arrows (lines implying direction) and nodes (circles or rectangles) to define the set of project activities or tasks. The flow of logic is from left to right. To simplify the diagram, letters are frequently used to represent individual activities. Figures 2 and 3 illustrate the differences for the same simple project.

Figure 2 illustrates the AOA convention, in which arrows depict activity requiring time and resources. The node represents an event, which requires neither time nor resources; this event is actually recognition that prior tasks are completed and the following tasks can begin. While the length of the arrow is not necessarily related to the duration of the task, there may be a tendency on the part of the analyst to sketch longer arrows for longer activities. To maintain the integrity of the network, there may be need for a dummy activity, as it is not acceptable to have two tasks that share the same beginning and ending nodes.

In Figure 3, the AON uses nodes to represent activities. The arrows have no implication of time, used only to indicate sequential flow. Since the AOA

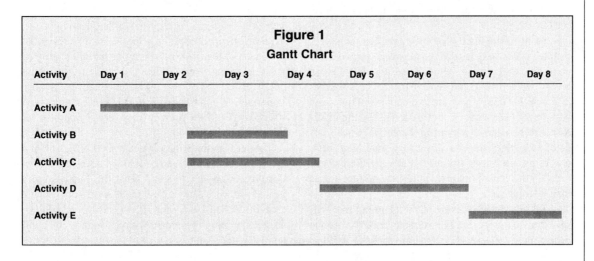

Figure 1

Gantt Chart

Activity	Day 1	Day 2	Day 3	Day 4	Day 5	Day 6	Day 7	Day 8

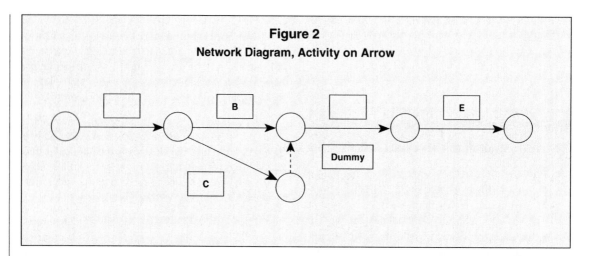

Figure 2

Network Diagram, Activity on Arrow

convention requires the use of dummy activities, the simpler AON convention will be used here to illustrate an example.

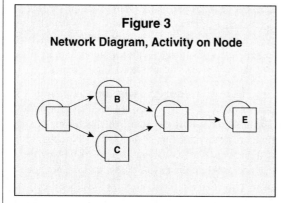

Figure 3

Network Diagram, Activity on Node

USING CPM TO SCHEDULE AND CONTROL A PROJECT

Scheduling is an important part of the planning of any project. However, it is first necessary to develop a list of all the activities required, as listed in the work breakdown structure. Activities require both time and the use of resources. Typically, the list of activities is compiled with duration estimates and immediate predecessors.

To illustrate the use of CPM, we can imagine a simple cookie-baking project: the recipe provides the complete statement of work, from which the work breakdown structure can be developed. The resources available for this project are two cooks and one oven with limited capacity; the raw materials are the ingredients to be used in preparing the cookie dough. As listed in Table 1, the activities take a total of 80 minutes of resource time. Because some activities can run parallel, the cooks should complete the project in less than 80 minutes.

Table 1 displays some of the planning that will save time in the project. For example, once the oven is turned on, it heats itself, freeing the cooks to perform other activities. After the dough is mixed, both batches of cookies can be shaped; the shaping of the second batch does not have to wait until the first batch is complete. If both cooks are available, they can divide the dough in half and each cook can shape one batch in the same four-minute period. However, if the second cook is not available at this time, the project is not delayed because shaping of the second batch need not be completed until the first batch exits the oven.

Table 1

List of Project Activities (CPM)

Description of Activity	Duration (minutes)	Immediate Predecessor(s)
A. Preheat oven	15 minutes	—
B. Assemble, measure ingredients	8 minutes	—
C. Mix dough	2 minutes	B
D. Shape first batch	4 minutes	C
E. Bake first batch	12 minutes	A, D
F. Cool first batch	10 minutes	E
G. Shape second batch	4 minutes	C
H. Bake second batch	12 minutes	E, G
I. Cool second batch	10 minutes	H
J. Store cookies	3 minutes	F, I
Total time	**80 minutes**	

Some expertise is required in the planning stage, as inexperienced cooks may not recognize the independence of the oven in heating or the divisibility of the dough for shaping. The concept of concurrent engineering makes the planning stage even more important, as enhanced expertise is needed to address which stages of the project can overlap, and how far this overlap can extend.

After beginning the project at 8:00 A.M., the first batch of dough is ready to go into the oven at 8:14, but the project cannot proceed until the oven is fully heated—at 8:15. The cooks actually have a one-minute cushion, called slack time. If measuring, mixing, or shaping actually take one additional minute, this will not delay the completion time of the overall project.

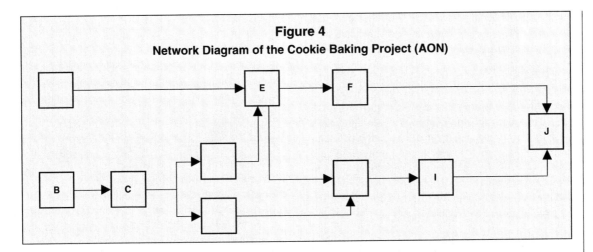

Figure 4
Network Diagram of the Cookie Baking Project (AON)

Figure 4 illustrates the network diagram associated with the cookie-baking project. The set of paths through the system traces every possible route from each beginning activity to each ending activity. In this simple project, one can explicitly define all the paths through the system in minutes as follows:

A-E-F-J = 15 + 12 + 10 + 3 = 40
A-E-H-I-J = 15 + 12 + 12 + 10 + 3 = 52
B-C-D-E-F-J = 8 + 2 + 4 + 12 + 10 + 3 = 39
B-C-D-E-H-I-J = 8 + 2 + 4 + 12 + 12 + 10 + 3 = 51
B-C-G-H-I-J = 8 + 2 + 4 + 12 + 10 + 3 = 39

The critical path is the longest path through the system, defining the minimum completion time for the overall project. The critical path in this project is A-E-H-I-J, determining that the project can be completed in 52 minutes (less than the 80-minute total of resource-usage time). These five activities must be done in sequence, and there is apparently no way to shorten these times. Note that this critical path is not dependent on the number of activities, but is rather dependent on the total time for a specific sequence of activities.

The managerial importance of this critical path is that any delay to the activities on this path will delay the project completion time, currently anticipated as 8:52 A.M. It is important to monitor this critical set of activities to prevent the missed due-date of the project. If the oven takes 16 minutes to heat (instead of the predicted 15 minutes), the project manager needs to anticipate how to get the project back on schedule. One suggestion is to bring in a fan (another resource) to speed the cooling process of the second batch of cookies; another is to split the storage process into first- and second-batch components.

Other paths tend to require less monitoring, as these sets of activities have slack, or a cushion, in which activities may be accelerated or delayed without penalty. Total slack for a given path is defined as the difference in the critical path time and the time for the given path. For example, the total slack for B-C-G-

H-I-J is 13 minutes (52–39 minutes). And the slack for B-C-D-E-H-I-J is only one minute (52–51), making this path near critical. Since these paths share some of the critical path activities, it is obvious that the manager should look at the slack available to individual activities.

Table 2 illustrates the calculation of slack for individual activities. For projects more complex than the simplistic cookie project, this is the method used to identify the critical path, as those activities with zero slack time are critical path activities. The determination of early-start and early-finish times use a forward pass through the system to investigate how early in the project each activity could start and end, given the dependency on other activities.

Table 2
Calculation of Slack Time

Activity	Early Start	Early Finish	Late Start	Late Finish	Slack
A	8:00	8:15	8:00	8:15	0
B	8:00	8:08	8:01	8:09	1
C	8:08	8:10	8:09	8:11	1
D	8:10	8:14	8:11	8:15	1
E	8:15	8:27	8:15	8:27	0
F	8:27	8:37	8:39	8:49	12
G	8:10	8:14	8:23	8:27	13
H	8:27	8:39	8:27	8:39	0
I	8:39	8:49	8:39	8:49	0
J	8:49	8:52	8:49	8:52	0

The late-time calculations use the finish time from the forward pass (8:52 A.M.) and employ a backward pass to determine at what time each activity must start to provide each subsequent activity with sufficient time to stay on track.

Slack for the individual activities is calculated by taking the difference between the late-start and early-start times (or, alternatively, between the late-finish and early-finish times) for each activity. If the difference is zero, then there is no slack; the activity is totally defined as to its time-position in the project and must therefore be a critical path activity. For other activities, the slack defines the flexibility in start times, but only assuming that no other activity on the path is delayed.

CPM was designed to address time-cost trade-offs, such as the use of the fan to speed the cooling process. Such crashing of a project requires that the project manager perform contingency planning early in the project to identify potential problems and solutions and the costs associated with employing extra resources. Cost-benefit analysis should be used to compare the missed due-date penalty, the availability and cost of the fan, and the effect of the fan on the required quality of the cookies.

This project ends with the successful delivery of the cookies to storage, which brings two questions to mind: First, should the oven be turned off? The answer to this depends on the scheduling of the oven resource at the end of this project. It might be impractical to cool the oven at this point if a following project is depending on the heating process to have been maintained. Second, who cleans up the kitchen? Project due dates are often frustrated by failure to take the closeout stages into account.

USING PERT TO SCHEDULE AND CONTROL A PROJECT

In repetitive projects, or in projects employing well-known processes, the duration of a given activity may be estimated with relative confidence. In less familiar territory, however, it may be more appropriate to forecast a range of possible times for activity duration. Using the same cookie-baking project example, Figure 4 still accurately represents the sequencing of activities.

Table 3 illustrates the project with three time estimates for each activity. While m represents the most likely time for the activity, a suggests the optimistic

estimate and b is the pessimistic estimate. The estimated time and or standard deviation for each activity (E) are calculated from the formula for the flexible beta distribution. With a reasonably large number of activities, summing the means tends to approximate a normal distribution, and statistical estimates of probability can be applied.

The mean is calculated as $[(a + 4m + b) \div 6]$, an average heavily weighted toward the most likely time, m. The standard deviation for an activity is $[(b - a) \div 6]$, or one-sixth of the range. Managers with a basic understanding of statistics may relate this to the concept of the standard deviation in the normal distribution. Since ± 3 standard deviations comprise almost the entire area under the normal curve, then there is an intuitive comparison between a beta standard deviation and the normal standard deviation.

Using these new estimates for activity duration, the activity paths through the system have not changed, but the estimates of total time (T) are as follows:

A-E-F-J = 40.66 minutes
A-E-H-I-J = 53 minutes
B-C-D-E-F-J = 40.66 minutes
B-C-D-E-H-I-J = 53 minutes
B-C-G-H-I-J = 40.66 minutes

There are two factors that should be considered coincidental to the comparison of PERT and CPM in the example. First, there are two critical paths of $T = 53$ minutes each in the PERT analysis. Second, all the other paths have the same duration of $T = 40.66$ minutes. These concepts are neither more nor less likely to happen under PERT as opposed to CPM; they are strictly a function of the numbers in the estimates. However, the serendipity of two critical paths allows us to address the issue of which would be considered the more important of the two.

In Table 4, each of the critical paths is considered. Relevant to this analysis is the sum of the variances on the critical path; note that summing variances

---

Table 3
List of Project Activities (PERT)

Description of Activity	Duration (minutes)					
	a	m	b	E_t	V_t	S_t
A. Preheat oven	12	15	18	15.00	1	1
B. Assemble, measure ingredients	6	8	12	8.33	1	1
C. Mix dough	2	2	2	2.00	0	0
D. Shape first batch	3	4	9	4.67	1	1
E. Bake first batch	10	12	16	12.33	1	1
F. Cool first batch	5	10	11	9.33	1	1
G. Shape second batch	3	4	9	4.67	1	1
H. Bake second batch	10	12	16	12.33	1	1
I. Cool second batch	5	10	11	9.33	1	1
J. Store cookies	2	3	10	4.00	1.78	1.33
Total times	58	90	114			

Table 4
Variability of Project Activities (PERT)

Path = A–E–H–I–J	Duration (minutes)					
Description of Activity	a	m	b	E_t	V_t	S_t
A. Preheat oven	12	15	18	15.00	1	1
E. Bake first batch	10	12	16	12.33	1	1
H. Bake second batch	10	12	16	12.33	1	1
I. Cool second batch	5	10	11	9.33	1	1
J. Store cookies	2	3	10	4.00	1.78	1.33
Total variance					5.78	
Standard deviation					2.40	

Path = B–C–D–E–H–I–J	Duration (minutes)					
Description of Activity	a	m	b	E_t	V_t	S_t
B. Assemble, measure ingredients	6	8	12	8.33	1	1
C. Mix dough	2	2	2	2.00	0	0
D Shape first batch	3	4	9	4.67	1	1
E. Bake first batch	10	12	16	12.33	1	1
H. Bake second batch	10	12	16	12.33	1	1
I. Cool second batch	5	10	11	9.33	1	1
J. Store cookies	2	3	10	4.00	1.78	1.33
Total variance					6.78	
Standard deviation					2.60	

is mathematically valid, while summing standard deviations is not. Path A-E-H-I-J has a total variance of 5.78 minutes, while path B-C-D-E-H-I-J has a variance of 6.78. Thus, path B-C-D-E-H-I-J, with the larger variance, is considered the riskier of the two paths and should be the primary concern of the project manager. We assign the entire project a variance of 6.78 minutes, and the standard deviation (the square root of the project variance) is 2.60 minutes.

Armed with this project standard deviation, the next step is to estimate the probability of finishing the project within a defined period. Applying the critical path time of 53 minutes to the normal distribution, the probability of finishing in exactly $T = 53$ minutes is 50/50. The relevant formula for calculating the number of standard normal distributions is as follows:

$$Z = (C - T) \div S \text{ where}$$

T = total time of the critical path ($T = 53$)
S = standard deviation of the project ($S = 2.60$)
C = arbitrary time for end of project

If $C = 9:00$ a.m., then $Z = [(9:00 - 8:53) \div 2.60] = 7 \div 2.60 = 2.69$ standard normal deviations. Referring to a cumulative standard normal table, we find that $Z = 0.99632$, or a 99.632 percent chance of finishing by 9:00 A.M.

If $C = 8:50$ A.M., then $Z = [(8:50 - 8:53) \div 2.60] = -3 \div 2.60 = -1.15$. In this case, we use $(1 - \text{table value})$ for the probability = $1 - 0.87493 = 0.1251$, or a 12.51

percent chance of finishing 3 minutes earlier than predicted.

From a managerial viewpoint, it should be reiterated that there is only a 50/50 chance of completing the project within the sum of the activity-time estimates on the critical path (T). This perspective is not emphasized in the CPM analysis, but is likely relevant in that context also. Adding a buffer to the promised due date (where $C > T$) enhances the probability that the project will be completed as promised.

There may be competitive advantages to bidding a project on the basis of a nearer-term completion date (where $C < T$), but managers can assess the risks involved using PERT analysis. In the cookie example, there may be a promised delivery time riding on this project estimate, or the resources (cooks and oven) may be promised to other projects. By using PERT, managers can allocate the resources on a more informed basis.

Both PERT and CPM rely heavily on time estimates, as derived from local experts, to determine the overall project time. While the estimating process may intimidate local managers, this may suffice to produce an estimate that becomes a *fait accompli,* as managers strive to meet the goal rather than explain why they failed to do so.

These two project management tools, frequently used together, can assist the project manager in establishing contract dates for project completion, in estimating the risks and costs of contingencies, and in monitoring project progress. Many commercial software packages exist to support the project manager in tracking both costs and time incurred to date throughout the project duration.

SEE ALSO: Operations Scheduling; Project Management

Karen L. Brown
Revised by Badie N. Farah

FURTHER READING:

Mantel, Samuel J., Jr., Jack R. Meredith, Scott M. Shafer, and Margaret M. Sutton. *Core Concepts: Project Management in Practice.* New York, NY: John Wiley & Sons, Inc., July 2004.

Meredith, Jack R., and Samuel J. Mantel, Jr. *Project Management: A Managerial Approach.* New York, NY: John Wiley & Sons, Inc., 2002.

Ragsdale, Cliff T. *Spreadsheet Modeling and Decision Analysis.* Cincinnati, OH: Thomson/South-Western College Publishing, 2004.

Stevenson, William J. *Operations Management.* Boston, MA: McGraw-Hill, 2005.

Taylor, Bernard W., III. *Introduction to Management Science.* Englewood Cliffs, NJ: Prentice-Hall, 2004.

PROJECT MANAGEMENT

Project management is the application of relevant logic and tools to planning, directing, and controlling a temporary endeavor. While some organizations specialize in projects, others may require project management skills only occasionally to effect a change, either physical or sociological in nature, from the norm.

BACKGROUND

The origin of project management is in the construction industry, going back as far as the construction of the pyramids. A pharaoh "contracted" for the construction of his personal resting place, assigned to a project manager. This manager was responsible for the logical development of the physical structure, including quarrying and transport of stone, marshalling of labor, and construction of the pyramid as envisioned by the monarch.

Today, directives come from corporations and municipal agencies, from prospective home-owners and nonprofit organizations. Modern construction firms employ an updated model of project management, using visual tools and software to help manage the sequencing of materials delivery, equipment usage, and labor specialization. Frequently, a single firm will have multiple projects under way at a given time, complicating the need for precise timing of resource availability to complete each task effectively and efficiently.

Some professionals have recognized a similarity to construction firms in operational style. For example, legal and public accounting firms, while not requiring steel beams or earth-moving equipment, have multiple legal cases or professional audits in progress simultaneously. For these firms, it is necessary to allocate the availability of professional specialists.

Almost all companies encounter the need for project management at some point. The need may arise for a new physical plant, an expansion, or a move to a new location. Reengineering may suggest a change in processes, with an accompanying equipment rearrangement and retraining to ensure the effectiveness of the change. The speed at which technology changes, forces companies to adopt new hardware and software to stay current. Softer issues, such as the implementation of quality programs, also are within the project management purview.

NATURE OF A PROJECT

A project is typically defined as a set of interrelated activities having a specific beginning and ending, and leading to a specific objective. Probably the most important concept in this definition is that a project is intended as a temporary endeavor, unlike ongoing, steady state operations. Secondary is the uniqueness of the output.

To ensure that a project is temporary, it is necessary to define the ending explicitly. The outputs of the project, or deliverables, may be tangible (a new heating system) or intangible (a retrained workgroup), but in either case should be defined in measurable terms (completed installation or documented level of expertise). While the reason for undertaking the project may have been to reduce utility costs by 10 percent or to increase productivity by 20 percent, achieving such goals may be outside the scope of the project.

Each project requires specific definition of its goals. In a training project example, the project manager may be given responsibility for identifying and implementing a training system that will enhance productivity by 15 percent; in this case, the project is not complete until the 15 percent goal is reached. If the initial training program enhances productivity by only 12 percent, the project manager is obligated to provide additional training, or the project may be terminated as a failure. Note that a 12 percent increase in productivity was something to celebrate, but did not meet the

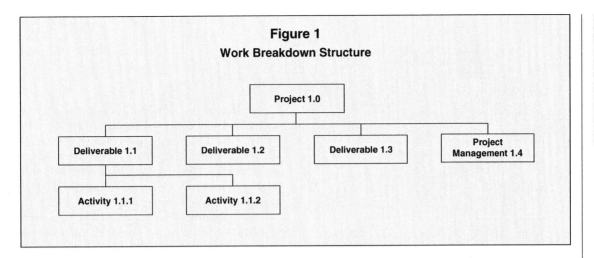

Figure 1
Work Breakdown Structure

Project 1.0

Deliverable 1.1 | Deliverable 1.2 | Deliverable 1.3 | Project Management 1.4

Activity 1.1.1 | Activity 1.1.2

hurdle rate of acceptability. If instead the project is to implement a previously identified training program, known to achieve excellent results, then the project is finished when the trainees achieve the test scores known to correlate with a specified level of improvement in productivity. At this point, the project manager has achieved the deliverable, as measured in specific terms; the project is a success. Whether or not the desired improvement in productivity follows is outside the scope of the project.

Obviously, it behooves the project manager to have a well-defined scope for the project. The more nebulous the assignment, the more the project is subject to "scope-creep," or the tendency for the project to acquire additional duties. A "statement of work" document or charter, outlining the relevant specifications of deliverables, helps to keep a project clearly defined. Once the work is completely specified, the requisite activities can be identified and assigned.

The work breakdown structure (WBS) is one of the tools used by project managers to ensure that all activities have been included in planning. By numbering the project "1.0." the implication is that this is the first project for the company; subsequent projects would be numbered sequentially. In the illustrated example, the deliverables are specified on the second layer of the WBS, along with an overhead allocation for the project management team. Under each deliverable is an increasingly specified description of the activities involved in achieving the deliverable. Alternatively, the second line may be functional headings (finance, marketing, operations) or time periods (January, February, March). The objective of the WBS is to clarify that all activities have been addressed and assigned.

While the definition of a project also tends to include the word *unique,* this may be true only in a narrowly defined sense. A company that builds a new branch location (first project) has a template for the construction of a second branch location (second project). In the marketing field, subsequent product rollouts can learn from the initial product introduction. To the extent that the project is repetitive, the planning process, WBS, and cost estimates can provide a valuable template for future projects.

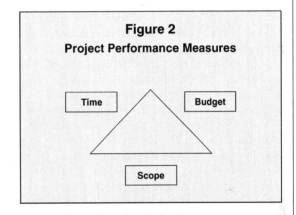

Figure 2
Project Performance Measures

Time | Budget

Scope

PROJECT PERFORMANCE MEASURES

The traditional measures for judging project success are: the fulfillment of scope, time and within budget. This is frequently depicted as a triangle.

Increasing any of the triangle's sides inherently changes at least one of the other sides. Thus, increasing the scope of the project will necessarily increase either the time required to complete the project or the budget allocated to the project. Unfortunately, the expanded scope can cause both time and budget to escalate simultaneously, as constrained resources come into conflict. Some project contracts have penalty clauses that elicit hefty payments if the project completion is past the contract date. Similarly, when the scope is decreased, the requisite time and budget may be reduced; resources may be assigned elsewhere.

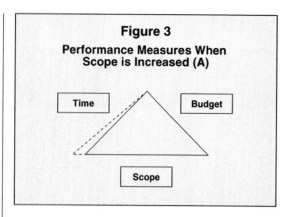

Figure 3

Performance Measures When Scope is Increased (A)

Time

Budget

Scope

The triangle analogy breaks down when the time factor is reduced, i.e., the project completion date is moved up. An unexpected deadline change may necessitate the use of overtime resources. Overtime hours strain the budget, and may still be insufficient to complete the project within the specified time. Managers attempting to respond to deadline changes should note the relative costs of time-intensive expenses (such as weekly rental of equipment) and of resource-intensive expenses (wages).

The schedule and budget are developed subsequent to the work breakdown structure, so that all activities and resources are identified. Scheduling requires that the project manager recognize two primary aspects of project activities. First, some activities must be done in sequence, while others may be done at the same time. Second, activities that could be run in parallel with multiple resources must be performed sequentially if the same limited resources are required for both activities. Gantt charts provide time-line displays, while network diagrams, such as Program Evaluation and Review Technique (PERT) or CPM diagrams, illustrate the sequentially dependency of activities. A baseline overview of the project is developed at this point for later comparison to actual progress.

From the beginning to the ending of the project, there is a critical path, or longest time-line path through the sequenced activities. This critical path determines the minimum time required for the project, and is the focus of the project manager's attention. If any of these activities are delayed, the on-time delivery of the project is at risk. To track this risk, milestones are established; the project review process addresses the actual progress as compared to the scheduled progress.

The budget is typically developed by estimating expenses at the bottom layer of the WBS, then rolling up the expenses to a project total. The numbering system in the WBS can be tailored to form a chart of accounts for tracking expenses associated with each activity. The project management heading is appropriate

under any of these alternatives to ensure that staff salaries/wages are suitably allocated to the project. Earned value analysis incorporates both on-time and within-budget concepts of tracking the costs incurred to date on a project.

While customer satisfaction is sometimes added as a fourth factor in the list of project performance measures, this complicates the evaluation. If the project manager brings in the project according to scope specifications, on time, within budget, then customer dissatisfaction may be due to the customer's inability to define the scope in terms that would achieve the objective. Customer service in the project management context should include adequate discussion of alternative outcomes at the scope development stage.

ROLES IN THE PROJECT MANAGEMENT ENVIRONMENT

Who is the customer of a project? Generically, the customer is the entity to which the deliverables are actually delivered. In an externally contracted project, the customer is easily identified. In an in-house project, the customer is the executive authorizing both the initiation of the project and the money allocated to it. In either case, the customer is the one with the right to complain when the performance measures of scope, time, and budget are not met.

Ideally, a project will have a sponsor, an intermediary between the customer and the project manager. This individual can help to define the scope for optimal delivery of results, to allocate appropriate funding, to resolve conflicts during the execution of the project.

The project champion is the source of the idea for the project. While the champion is frequently an individual, the idea may originate with the board of directors or the safety committee in a company. The project champion, however, may not be the ideal choice for project manager.

The project manager is in charge of the work to be accomplished. This is not to say that the manager actually does the work, but rather that he/she is the coordinator of all relevant activities through delegation. In many cases, this manager may not possess expertise in the field, but rather possesses the skills to oversee a large number of diverse tasks and to identify the best-qualified employees to carry out the tasks. The manager should exercise judgment in assigning tasks; seasoned professionals will expect to accomplish the tasks according to their knowledge and experience, while others may require much definition and direction. In some cases, the project manager's ability to accomplish the job depends on negotiating and persuasive skills.

The authority of the project manager depends heavily on the organizational structure. In the "projectized" organization, resources are assigned exclusively to the project, then returned to a pool and assigned to a new project. The manager has near absolute authority and responsibility. In the functional organization (finance, marketing, operations, etc.), the project manager must negotiate with the functional manager for resources obtained from the department. Individuals tend to feel a greater responsibility to the functional manager. In this organization, the project manager has responsibility for the project, but relatively little authority without interference by the sponsor. The matrix organization is a managerial attempt to compromise these extremes by transferring some extent of authority from the functional manager to the project manager; thus, there are both strong-form and weak-form matrix organizations.

The project manager should be a master of many skills. Organization, negotiation, and teambuilding are desirable, while technical expertise may be less important. An expert whose intense focus on technical detail excludes the broader aspects of the project can undermine projects. Communication skills are of prime importance, as written and oral reports are mandatory. In addition, clarity of the initial assignment can reduce the amount of conflict management required in later stages of the project.

Surrounding the project manager is a team with the goal of supporting the planning, directing, and controlling functions. Typically, a full-time (or nearly full-time) team member is assigned responsibility for traditional office functions, such as communication coordination. This member may also be in charge of fielding reports and recording the responses for comparison to the baseline schedule. Other members exercise delegated authority in project oversight, up to and including direct responsibility for sub-projects within the larger project context.

PROJECT MANAGEMENT INSTITUTE

The primary professional organization in this field is the Project Management Institute (PMI). Founded in 1969, PMI has more than 40,000 worldwide members including representatives of government, industry, and academia. This body publishes standards for the profession of project management and awards certification as a Project Management Professional (PMP) on the basis of examination; continuing certification is dependent on continuing education and service to the field of project management.

The Standards Committee of PMI has continually updated versions of the generically worded Guide to the Project Management Body of Knowledge

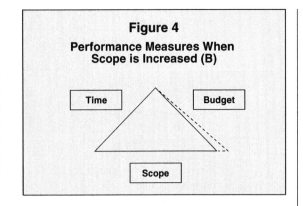

Figure 4
Performance Measures When Scope is Increased (B)

Time | Budget

Scope

(PMBOK). As project management is widely applicable, the membership is diverse, with a large number of specific interest groups, and the standards are of necessity generically stated. However, the Standards Committee has agreed in the focus on nine primary areas of requisite knowledge for project managers.

These knowledge areas cover the obvious concerns of scope, time, cost, and quality, conforming to

Table 1

PMI Specific Interest Groups (SIGS)
Aerospace & Defense
Automation Systems
Automotive
Configuration Management
Consulting
Design-Procurement-Construction
Diversity
eBusiness
Education & Training
Financial Services
Government
Healthcare Project Management
Human Resources
Information Systems
Information Technology & Telecommunications
International Development
Manufacturing
Marketing & Sales
Metrics
New Product Development
Oil, Gas & Petrochemical
Pharmaceutical
Program Management Office
Quality in Project Management
Retail
Risk Management
Service & Outsourcing
Students of PM
Troubled Projects
Utility
Women in Project Management

Table 2

**Project Management Knowledge
Areas (PMBOK)**

Integration Management

Scope Management

Time Management

Cost Management

Quality Management

Human Resource Management

Communication Management

Risk Management

Procurement Management

the performance measures applied to projects. In addition, the softer issues of communication and human resource management are addressed; procurement management is included, as this concept is of major importance to many of the industries involved. Of particular note, however, are the areas of project integration and risk management.

PROJECT INTEGRATION MANAGEMENT

Management of project integration includes the process of synthesis and response to change. The overall project employs five basic processes: *initiating, planning, executing, controlling, and closing.*

The initiating process incorporates development of the idea for the project and justification based on a feasibility study. It is at this stage that the boundaries of the project should be defined. To return to the earlier training example, the responsibility for identifying a specific training program should be determined.

Project planning addresses the specific timeframe and budget for the project. Activities are identified and assigned. Planning is considered a most important process because without excellent planning the ensuing activities are unlikely to succeed. Executing involves carrying out the assigned activities, while controlling monitors the activity for scope, time, and budget concerns.

Perhaps the most ignored process of projects in general is the closing process. Toward the end of a project, enthusiasm can wane, and it is the responsibility of the project manager to maintain active collaboration until the end of the project. Phased-out employees should be evaluated and returned to the pool/function from which they were recruited. A series of meetings should be held to review the degree to which the performance measures were met, from both the defined scope and the satisfaction of the customer. If these are not in agreement, then the reasons should be documented. Areas of success and failure are both important to note, as these can be the basis for company-wide learning. Even dissimilar projects can provide some learning opportunities, as the company understands, for instance, its tendency to underestimate costs or scheduling requirements.

While these processes, initiating through closing, appear to be linear in nature, they instead define a feedback system. The specifics of the Planning process may indicate that the initiating idea was flawed. Execution may encounter problems with planning. controlling may indicate a return to planning, or even to the earlier initiating idea process. And closing may determine that the entire project was doomed from the outset. Failure to recognize the iterative nature of these processes can be costly, as a project may be adjusted or abandoned at early stages to prevent loss.

Within the company, the project life-cycle stages of the project should be identified. Generically, these may be identified as definition, design, test, implementation, and retirement stages, or some variation on this theme. Interestingly, each of these stages employs each of the processes described above. For example, in the definition life-cycle stage, there is an initiation process, progressing to a feasibility study. As the definition stage reaches its conclusion, it "delivers" the project to the design stage, but only if the mini-project of definition has been successful. Many projects have lingered when a rational analysis would suggest that revision or abandonment would be less costly. The iterative nature of project management logic suggests a stringent review at frequent stages to ensure that both the project itself and the environment to which the project was to respond are in agreement. Management of the integration of project stages is especially important in a rapidly changing environment.

PROJECT RISK MANAGEMENT

Among the project management knowledge areas, risk management is likely the activity that best defines project management. This umbrella concept addresses the risks in all aspects of managing a project.

First are the traditional performance measures. Was the scope well defined? If the customer assumed that a specific aspect was included, then the contracting firm's reputation may be damaged when the aspect was not specified in the charter. Were the costs estimated correctly? Underestimating can undermine profits, while overestimating can lose an opportunity for business or in-house improvement. Were the time estimates reasonable? Past-due penalties can be significant.

Other risks can include the insolvency of the customer and/or a subcontractor, or the lack of in-house expertise to accomplish the tasks involved in the project. Weather, economic changes, and governmental regulations can change the feasibility of any project. Above all is the risk that the project is not sufficient to respond to changes in the environmental circumstances that triggered the project's initiation, especially in a project of long duration.

Project management is a structured approach to solving a problem with a temporary, unique solution. Project planning is a most important stage, setting the stage on which the rest of the project must play out. The project manager should be heavily involved in this planning process to ensure his/her understanding of scope, time, and cost, the primary performance measures by which project success is measured. Monitoring of the activities enhances the probability that the project will stay on track for all of these measures. Each stage and process of project management should address the minimization of risk to the firm, in terms of both money and reputation.

SEE ALSO: Product-Process Matrix; Program Evaluation and Review Technique and Critical Path Method; Program Evaluation and Review Technique and Critical Path Method

Karen L. Brown
Revised by Wendy H. Mason

FURTHER READING:

Gido, Jack, and James P. Clements. *Successful Project Management.* Cincinnati: South-Western College Publishing, 1999.

Kerzner, Harold. *Project Management: A Systems Approach to Planning, Scheduling, and Controlling.* 8th ed. Hoboken, NJ: John Wiley & Sons, Inc., 2003.

Martin, Paula. *The Project Management Memory Jogger: A Pocket Guide for Project Teams (Growth Opportunity Alliance of Lawrence).* Salem, NH: GOAL/QPC, 1997.

Meredith, Jack R., and Samuel J. Mantel, Jr. *Project Management: A Managerial Approach.* 5th ed. New York: John Wiley & Sons, Inc., 2002.

PMI Standards Committee. *A Guide to the Project Management Body of Knowledge (PMBOK Guide).* 2000 ed. Upper Darby, PA: Project Management Institute, 2000.

PURCHASING AND PROCUREMENT

Purchasing and procurement is used to denote the function of and the responsibility for procuring materials, supplies, and services. Recently, the term "supply management" has increasingly come to describe this process as it pertains to a professional capacity. Employees who serve in this function are known as buyers, purchasing agents, or supply managers. Depending on the size of the organization, buyers may further be ranked as senior buyers or junior buyers.

HISTORY

Prior to 1900, there were few separate and distinct purchasing departments in U.S. business. Most pre-twentieth-century purchasing departments existed in the railroad industry. The first book specifically addressing institutionalized purchasing within this industry was *The Handling of Railway Supplies—Their Purchase and Disposition,* written by Marshall M. Kirkman in 1887.

Early in the twentieth century, several books on purchasing were published, while discussion of purchasing practices and concerns were tailored to specific industries in technical trade publications. The year 1915 saw the founding of The National Association of Purchasing Agents. This organization eventually became known as the National Association of Purchasing Management (NAPM) and is still active today under the name The Institute for Supply Management (ISM).

Harvard University offered a course in purchasing as early as 1917. Purchasing as an academic discipline was furthered with the printing of the first college textbook on the subject, authored by Howard T. Lewis of Harvard, in 1933.

Early buyers were responsible for ensuring a reasonable purchase price and maintaining operations (avoiding shutdowns due to stockouts). Both World Wars brought more attention to the profession due to the shortage of materials and the alterations in the market. Still, up until the 1960s, purchasing agents were basically order-placing clerical personnel serving in a staff-support position.

In the late 1960s and early 1970s, purchasing personnel became more integrated with a materials system. As materials became a part of strategic planning, the importance of the purchasing department increased.

In the 1970s the oil embargo and the shortage of almost all basic raw materials brought much of business world's focus to the purchasing arena. The advent of just-in-time purchasing techniques in the 1980s, with its emphasis on inventory control and supplier quality, quantity, timing, and dependability, made purchasing a cornerstone of competitive strategy.

By the 1990s the term "supply chain management" had replaced the terms "purchasing," "transportation," and "operations," and purchasing had assumed a position in organizational development and management. In other words, purchasing had become responsible for acquiring the right materials, services, and technology from the right source, at the right time, in the right quantity.

Only in small firms is purchasing still viewed as a clerical position. When one notes that, on average, purchasing accounts for over half of most organizations' total monetary expenditures, it is no wonder that purchasing is marked as an increasingly pivotal position.

FACTORS FOR PURCHASING

The importance of purchasing in any firm is largely determined the four factors: availability of materials, absolute dollar volume of purchases, percent of product cost represented by materials, and the types of materials purchased. Purchasing must concern itself with whether or not the materials used by the firm are readily available in a competitive market or whether some are bought in volatile markets that are subject to shortages and price instability. If the latter condition prevails, creative analysis by top-level purchasing professionals is required.

If a firm spends a large percentage of its available capital on materials, the sheer magnitude of expense means that efficient purchasing can produce a significant savings. Even small unit savings add up quickly when purchased in large volumes. When a firm's materials costs are 40 percent or more of its product cost (or its total operating budget), small reductions in material costs can increase profit margins significantly. In this situation, efficient purchasing and purchasing management again can make or break a business.

Perhaps the most important of the four factors is the amount of control purchasing and supply personnel actually have over materials availability, quality, costs, and services. Large companies tend to use a wide range of materials, yielding a greater chance that price and service arrangements can be influenced significantly by creative purchasing performance. Some firms, on the other hand, use a fairly small number of standard production and supply materials, from which even the most seasoned purchasing personnel produce little profit, despite creative management, pricing, and supplier selection activities.

THE ROLE OF PURCHASING

There are two basic types of purchasing: purchasing for resale and purchasing for consumption or transformation. The former is generally associated with retailers and wholesalers. The latter is defined as industrial purchasing.

Purchasing can also be seen as either strategic or transactional. Also, the words "direct" and "indirect" have been used to distinguish the two types. Strategic (direct) buying involves the establishment of mutually beneficial long-term relationship relationships between buyers and suppliers. Usually strategic buying involves purchase of materials that are crucial to the support of

the firm's distinctive competence. This could include raw material and components normally used in the production process. Transactional (indirect) buying involves repetitive purchases, from the same vendor, probably through a blanket purchase order. These orders could include products and services not listed on the bill of materials, such as MRO goods, but are used indirectly in producing the item.

Some experts relate that the purchasing function is responsible for determining the organization's requirements, selecting an optimal source of supply, ensuring a fair and reasonable price (for both the purchasing organization and the supplier), and establishing and maintaining mutually beneficial relationships with the most desirable suppliers. In other words, purchasing departments determine what to buy, where to buy it, how much to pay, and ensure its availability by managing the contract and maintaining strong relationships with suppliers.

In more specific terms, today's purchasing departments are responsible for:

- coordinating purchase needs with user departments
- identifying potential suppliers
- conducting market studies for material purchases
- proposal analysis
- supplier selection
- issuing purchase orders
- meeting with sales representatives
- negotiating
- contract administration
- resolving purchasing-related problems
- maintenance of purchasing records

These functions obviously entail no insignificant amount of responsibility.

As the role of purchasing grows in importance, purchasing departments are being charged with even more responsibilities. Newer responsibilities for purchasing personnel, in addition to all purchasing functions, include participation in the development of material and service requirements and related specifications, conducting material and value-analysis studies, inbound transportation, and even management of recovery activities such as surplus and scrap salvage, as well as its implications for environmental management.

In the 1970s and 1980s purchasing fell under the rubric of "materials management." Many corporations and individual facilities employed executives who held the title "materials manager," responsible for purchasing and supply management, inventory management, receiving, stores, warehousing, materials handling, production planning, scheduling and control, and traffic/transportation. Today, the term materials management has expanded to include all activities from raw material procurement to final delivery to the customer, to management of returns; hence, the newer title supply chain management.

As purchasing personnel became even more central to the firm's operations they became known as "supply managers." As supply managers, they are active in the strategic-planning process, including such activities as securing partnering arrangements and strategic alliances with suppliers; identification of threats and opportunities in the supply environment; strategic, long-term acquisition plans; and monitoring continuous improvement in the supply chain.

A study by found that strategic purchasing enables firms to foster close working relationships with a limited number of suppliers, promotes open communication among supply chain partners, and develops a long-term strategic relationship orientation for achievement of mutual goals. This implies that strategic purchasing plays a synergistic role in fostering value-enhancing relationships and knowledge exchange between the firm and its suppliers, thereby creating value. In addition, supply managers are heavily involved in cross-functional teams charged with determining supplier qualification and selection, as well ensuring early supplier involvement in product design and specification development.

A comprehensive list of objectives for purchasing and supply management personnel would include:

- to support the firm's operations with an uninterrupted flow of materials and services;
- to buy competitively and wisely (achieve the best combination of price, quality and service);
- to minimize inventory investment and loss;
- to develop reliable and effective supply sources;
- to develop and maintain healthy relations with active suppliers and the supplier community;
- to achieve maximum integration with other departments, while achieving and maintaining effective working relationships with them;
- to take advantage of standardization and simplification;
- to keep up with market trends;
- to train, develop and motivate professionally competent personnel;
- to avoid duplication, waste, and obsolescence;
- to analyze and report on long-range availability and costs of major purchased items;

- to continually search for new and alternative ideas, products, and materials to improve efficiency and profitability; and
- to administer the purchasing and supply management function proactively, ethically, and efficiently.

DETERMINING REQUIREMENTS

In progressive firms, purchasing has a hand in new product development. As a part of a product development team, purchasing representatives have the opportunity to help determine the optimal materials to be used in a new product, propose alternative or substitute materials, and assist in making the final decision based on cost and material availability. Purchasing representatives may also participate in a make-or-buy analysis at this point. The design stage is the point at which the vast majority of the cost of making an item can be reduced or controlled.

Whether or not purchasing had an impact on a product's design, the purchasing agent's input may certainly be needed when defining the materials-purchase specifications. Specifications are detailed explanations of what the firm intends to buy in order to get its product to market.

Generally specified is the product itself, the material from which it is to be made, the process for making it, minimum levels of quality, tolerances (a range in which a specified characteristic is acceptable, e.g., an outer diameter must be a certain size, ±25 millimeters), inspection and test standards, and a specific function the product must perform.

If the product requires a standardized component, the specifications are easily communicated by specifying a trade or brand name. However, a custom part can complicate the situation considerably; if incorrectly manufactured, such a product can severely damage a relationship, resulting in unnecessary costs and possible legal action. It is the buyer's responsibility to adequately communicate the specifications to the supplier so that there is no misunderstanding.

SUPPLY SOURCING

Part of the sourcing decision involves determining whether to purchase a part from an outside supplier or produce the part internally. This is typically known as a make-or-buy decision. If the buyer chooses to purchase the part externally, then he must find qualified suppliers who are willing to make and sell the product to his or her firm under the specified conditions.

Buyers have a number of places to go to locate sources of supply, some obvious and some indirect. The most obvious sources would include the Yellow

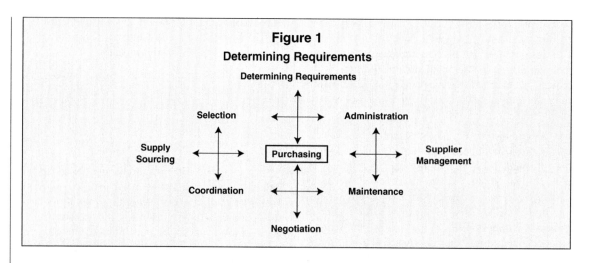

Figure 1
Determining Requirements

Pages, other purchasing departments, and direct marketing. Purchasing departments typically have a number of trade publications to which they subscribe, such as *Purchasing, Iron Age,* and *Purchasing World,* which are filled with advertisements for a multitude of suppliers. Also, being a subscriber usually puts the buyer's name on a mailing list so that flyers, postcards, and other varieties of direct marketing find their way into the purchasing department's hands.

Other sources of supply include manufacturer directories and trade registers. The best known of these is *Thomas' Register of American Manufacturers,* frequently referred to simply as the *Thomas Register.* With 125,000 trade and brand names, 151,000 U.S. and Canadian company listings, and 6,000 catalogs, it is a valuable tool for buyers. Practically every purchasing department has access to this source, either through the 34-volume book series or CD-ROMs.

Suppliers also may be found at trade exhibits, in supplier catalogs, or via recommendations from other knowledgeable sources, such as salesmen and engineers. Probably the most important and frequently used source will soon be the World Wide Web; countless firms maintain Web pages and are listed in online catalogs and directories.

Many firms find themselves in a situation where a suitable supplier cannot be found. In this situation, the firm is forced to develop a supplier. Supplier development is sometimes referred to as "reverse marketing," which entails finding the supplier with the most potential for success and providing the resources necessary for the supplier to manufacture the needed product. This could include training in production processes, quality, and management assistance, as well as providing temporary personnel, tooling, and even financing.

When the product being purchased is fairly standard and readily available, most firms choose to utilize the competitive bidding process of supplier selection. This involves little or no negotiation. A request for bids is sent to a limited number of qualified suppliers asking for a price quote for the product, given the terms and conditions of the contract. The contract generally goes to the lowest bidder. For government bid requests, the contract legally must go to the lowest bidder qualified to fulfill the contract.

NEGOTIATION

When competitive bidding is not the appropriate mechanism for reaching the purchasing department's objectives, the buyer turns to the process of negotiation. This does not indicate a second-choice alternative, since the negotiation process is more likely to lead to a complete understanding of all issues involved between the supplier and the purchasing firm. This improved understanding can greatly reduce the number and impact of unseen problems that may arise later.

A number of circumstances dictate the use of negotiation. When a thorough analysis is required to solve a difficult make-or-buy decision, or when the risks and costs involved cannot be accurately predetermined, negotiation should be used. Also, when a buyer is contracting for a portion of the seller's production capacity rather than a product, negotiation is typically appropriate.

Other circumstances where negotiation is favored include: when early supplier involvement is employed, when tooling and setup costs represent a large percentage of the supplier's costs, when production is interrupted frequently for change orders, or when a long time is required to produce the purchased products.

If successful negotiation is to occur, the buyer must have a reasonable knowledge of what is being purchased, the process involved, and any factors that may affect cost, quality, delivery, and service. A thorough cost and/or price analysis is essential. The negotiating buyer must also know the strengths and weaknesses of the negotiating supplier, as well as his own. Also, in light of today's global marketplace, strong cultural awareness is a must. Through proper preparation and some negotiating skill, the purchasing agent should be able to secure a contract that fulfills his/her company's needs and is adequately beneficial to the supplier as well.

SUPPLIER MANAGEMENT

After locating proper suppliers and securing contracts, it then falls to the purchasing function to monitor and control the suppliers' performance until the contracts are fulfilled—and beyond, if further business is to be conducted. All purchasing organizations need some vehicle for assessing supplier performance. Many firms have formal supplier-evaluation programs that effectively monitor supplier performance in a number of areas, including quality, quantity delivery, on-time delivery, early delivery (just-in-time users do not like early deliveries), cost, and intangibles.

For some firms, consistent supplier performance results in certification. Supplier certification generally implies (or in some cases formally asserts) that the supplier has been a part of a formal education program, has demonstrated commitment to quality and delivery, and has proven consistency in his processes. Frequently, organizations are able to take delivery from certified suppliers and completely bypass the receiving inspection process.

The buyer is also responsible for maintaining a congenial relationship with the firm's suppliers. If the buyer is an unreasonable negotiator, and does not allow the supplier to make an adequate profit, future dealings may be endangered. The supplier may refuse to deal with the buyer in the future, or the supplier may greatly increase the price of a product the buyer could not obtain elsewhere. Also, relations can become strained when the buyer consistently asks for favored treatment such as expediting or constantly changing a particular order's delivery schedule.

E-PURCHASING AND E-PROCUREMENT

The Internet and e-commerce is drastically changing the way purchasing is done. Internet use in buying has led to the terms "e-purchasing" or "e-procurement." Certainly, communication needed in competitive bidding, purchase order placement, order tracking, and follow-up are enhanced by the speed and ease afforded by establishing online systems. In addition, negotiation may be enhanced and reverse auctions facilitated. Reverse auctions allow buying firms to specify a requirement and receive bids from suppliers, with the lowest bid winning.

E-procurement is considered one of the characteristics of a world-class purchasing organization. The use of e-procurement technologies in some firms has resulted in reduced prices for goods and services, shortened order-processing and fulfillment cycles, reduced administrative burdens and costs, improved control over off-contract spending, and better inventory control. It allows firms to expand into trading networks and virtual corporations.

Criteria for e-purchasing include:

- Supporting complete requirements of production (direct) and non-production (indirect) purchasing through a single, internet-based, self-service system.

- Delivering a flexible catalog strategy.

- Providing tools for extensive reporting and analysis.

- Supporting strategic sourcing.

- Enhancing supply-chain collaboration and coordination with partners.

SEE ALSO: Distribution and Distribution Requirements Planning; Quality and Total Quality Management; Supply Chain Management

R. Anthony Inman

FURTHER READING:

Burt, David N., Donald W. Dobler, and Stephen L. Starling. *World Class Supply Management: The Key to Supply Chain Management.* Boston, MA: McGraw-Hill Irwin, 2003.

Caridi, Maria, Sergio Cavalieri, Giorgio Diazzi, and Cristina Pirovano. "Assessing the Impact of e-Procurement Strategies Through the Use of Business Process Modelling and Simulation Techniques." *Production Planning and Control* 15, no. 7 (2004): 647–661.

Chang, Yoon, Harris Markatsoris, and Howard Richards. "Design and Implementation of an e-Procurement System." *Production Planning & Control* 15, no. 7 (2004): 634–646.

Chen, Injazz J., Antony Paulraj, and Augustine A. Lado. "Strategic Purchasing, Supply Management, and Firm Performance." *Journal of Operations Management* 22 (2004): 505–523.

Inside Supply Management: Resources to Create Your Future. Tempe, AZ: Institute for Supply Management.

Mehra, Satish, and R. Anthony Inman. "Purchasing Management and Business Competitiveness in the Coming Decade." *Production Planning and Control* 15, no. 7 (2004): 710–718.

"Procurement Head Reveals Keys to Achieve World-Class Status." *Supplier Selection & Management Report* 5, no. 2 (2005): 1–4.

Q

The Quality Gurus—Dr. W. Edwards Deming, Dr. Joseph Juran, Philip Crosby, Armand V. Feigenbaum, Dr. H. James Harrington, Dr. Kaoru Ishikawa, Dr. Walter A. Shewhart, Shigeo Shingo, Frederick Taylor, and Dr. Genichi Taguchi—have made a significant impact on the world through their contributions to improving not only businesses, but all organizations including state and national governments, military organizations, educational institutions, healthcare organizations, and many other establishments and organizations.

DR. W. EDWARDS DEMING (1900–1993)

Dr. W. Edward Deming is best known for reminding management that most problems are systemic and that it is management's responsibility to improve the systems so that workers (management and non-management) can do their jobs more effectively. Deming argued that higher quality leads to higher productivity, which, in turn, leads to long-term competitive strength. The theory is that improvements in quality lead to lower costs and higher productivity because they result in less rework, fewer mistakes, fewer delays, and better use of time and materials. With better quality and lower prices, a firm can achieve a greater market share and thus stay in business, providing more and more jobs.

When he died in December 1993 at the age of ninety-three, Deming had taught quality and productivity improvement for more than fifty years. His Fourteen Points, System of Profound Knowledge, and teachings on statistical control and process variability are studied by people all over the world. His books include: *Out of the Crisis* (1986), *The New Economics* (1993), and *Statistical Adjustment of Data* (1943).

In emphasizing management's responsibility, Deming noted that workers are responsible for 10 to 20 percent of the quality problems in a factory, and that the remaining 80 to 90 percent is under management's control. Workers are responsible for communicating to management the information they possess regarding the system. Deming's approach requires an organization-wide cultural transformation.

Deming's philosophy is summarized in his famous fourteen points, and it serves as a framework for quality and productivity improvement. Instead of relying on inspection at the end of the process to find flaws, Deming advocated a statistical analysis of the manufacturing process and emphasized cooperation of workers and management to achieve high-quality products.

Deming's quality methods centered on systematically tallying product defects, analyzing their causes, correcting the causes, and recording the effects of the corrections on subsequent product quality as defects were prevented. He taught that it is less costly in the long-run to get things done right the first time then fix them later.

THE RISE OF DEMING'S INFLUENCE

The son of a small-town lawyer, Deming (a teacher and consultant in statistical studies) attended the University of Wyoming, University of Colorado, and Yale University, where he earned his Ph.D. in mathematical physics. He then taught physics at several universities, worked as a mathematical physicist at the U.S. Department of Agriculture and was a statistical adviser for the U.S. Census Bureau.

From 1946 to 1993 he was a professor of statistics at New York University's graduate school of business administration, and he taught at Columbia University. Deming became interested in the use of statistical analysis to achieve better quality control in industry in the 1930s.

In 1950 Deming began teaching and consulting with Japanese industrialists through the Union of Japanese Scientists and Engineers (JUSE). In 1960, he received the Second Order Medal of the Sacred Treasure from the Emperor of Japan for improvement of quality and the Japanese economy. In 1987 he received the National Medal of Technology from U. S. President Ronald Reagan because of his impact on quality in the United States.

From 1946 to 1993, he was an international teacher and consultant in the area of quality improvement based on statistics, leadership, and customer satisfaction. The Deming Prize for quality was established in 1951 in Japan by JUSE and in 1980 in the United States by the Metropolitan Section of the American Society for Quality.

American companies ignored Deming's teachings for years. In 1980, NBC aired the program "If Japan Can, Why Can't We?," highlighting Deming's contributions in Japan and American companies began to discover Deming. His ideas were used by major U.S. corporations as they sought to compete more effectively against foreign manufacturers.

As a consultant, Deming continued to conduct Quality Management seminars until just days before his death in 1993.

DEMING'S SYSTEM OF PROFOUND KNOWLEDGE

One of Deming's essential theories is his System of Profound Knowledge, which includes appreciation for a system, knowledge about variation (statistics), theory of knowledge, and psychology (of individuals, groups, society, and change). Although the Fourteen Points are probably the most widely known of Dr. Deming's theories, he actually taught them as a part of his System of Profound Knowledge. His knowledge system consists of four interrelated parts: (1) Theory of Optimization; (2) Theory of Variation; (3) Theory of Knowledge; and (4) Theory of Psychology.

THEORY OF OPTIMIZATION. The objective of an organization is the optimization of the total system and not the optimization of the individual subsystems. The total system consists of all constituents—customers, employees, suppliers, shareholders, the community, and the environment. A company's long-term objective is to create a win-win situation for all of its constituents.

Subsystem optimization works against this objective and can lead to a suboptimal total system. According to Deming, it is poor management, for example, to purchase materials or service at the lowest price or to minimize the cost of manufacturing if it is at the expense of the system. Inexpensive materials may be of such inferior quality that they will cause excessive costs in adjustment and repair during manufacturing and assembly.

THEORY OF VARIATION. Deming's philosophy focuses on improving the product and service uncertainty and variability in design and manufacturing processes. Deming believed that variation is a major cause of poor quality. In mechanical assemblies, for example, variations from specifications for part dimensions lead to inconsistent performance and premature wear and failure. Likewise, inconsistencies in service frustrate customers and hurt companies' reputations. Deming taught Statistical Process Control and used control charts to demonstrate variation in processes and how to determine if a process is in statistical control.

There is a variation in every process. Even with the same inputs, a production process can produce different results because it contains many sources of variation, for example the materials may not be always be exactly the same; the tools wear out over time and they are subjected to vibration heat or cold; or the operators may make mistakes. Variation due to any of these individual sources appears at random; however, their combined effect is stable and usually can be predicted statistically. These factors that are present as a natural part of a process are referred to as common (or system) causes of variation.

Common causes are due to the inherent design and structure of the system. It is management's responsibility to reduce or eliminate common causes. Special causes are external to the system, and it is the responsibility of operating personnel to eliminate such causes. Common causes of variation generally account for about 80 to 90 percent of the observed variation in a production process. The remaining 10 to 20 percent are the result of special causes of variation, often called assignable causes. Factors such as bad material from a supplier, a poorly trained operator or excessive tool wear are examples of special causes. If no operators are trained, that is system problem, not a special cause. The system has to be changed.

THEORY OF KNOWLEDGE. Deming emphasized that knowledge is not possible without theory, and experience alone does not establish a theory. Experience only describes—it cannot be tested or validated—and alone is no help for management. Theory, on the other hand, shows a cause-and-effect relationship that can be used for prediction. There is a lesson here for the widespread benchmarking practices: copying only an example of success, without understanding it in theory, may not lead to success, but could lead to disaster.

THEORY OF PSYCHOLOGY. Psychology helps to understand people, interactions between people and circumstances, interactions between leaders and employees, and any system of management. Consequently, managing people requires knowledge of psychology. Also required is knowledge of what motivates people. Job satisfaction and the motivation to excel are intrinsic. Reward and recognition are extrinsic. Management needs to create the right mix of intrinsic and extrinsic factors to motivate employees.

DEMING'S SEVEN DEADLY DISEASES

Deming believed that traditional management practices, such as the Seven Deadly Diseases listed below, significantly contributed to the American quality crisis.

1. Lack of constancy of purpose to plan and deliver products and services that will help a company survive in the long term.

2. Emphasis on short-term profits caused by short-term thinking (which is just the opposite of constancy of purpose), fear of takeovers, worry about quarterly dividends, and other types of reactive management.

3. Performance appraisals (i.e., annual reviews, merit ratings) that promote fear and stimulate unnecessary competition among employees.

4. Mobility of management (i.e., job hopping), which promotes short-term thinking.

5. Management by use of visible figures without concern about other data, such as the effect of happy and unhappy customers on sales, and the increase in overall quality and productivity that comes from quality improvement upstream.

6. Excessive medical costs, which now have been acknowledged as excessive by federal and state governments, as well as industries themselves.

7. Excessive costs of liability further increased by lawyers working on contingency fees.

DEMING'S FOURTEEN POINTS

Deming formulated the following Fourteen Points to cure (eliminate) the Seven Deadly Diseases and help organizations to survive and flourish in the long term:

1. Create constancy of purpose toward improvement of product and service. Develop a plan to be competitive and stay in business. Everyone in the organization, from top management to shop floor workers, should learn the new philosophy.

2. Adopt the new philosophy. Commonly accepted levels of delays, mistakes, defective materials, and defective workmanship are now intolerable. We must prevent mistakes.

3. Cease dependence on mass inspection. Instead, design and build in quality. The purpose of inspection is not to send the product for rework because it does not add value. Instead of leaving the problems for someone else down the production line, workers must take responsibility for their work. Quality has to be designed and built into the product; it cannot be inspected into it. Inspection should be used as an information-gathering device, not as a means of "assuring" quality or blaming workers.

4. Don't award business on price tag alone (but also on quality, value, speed and long term relationship). Minimize total cost. Many companies and organizations award contracts to the lowest bidder as long as they meet certain requirements. However, low bids do not guarantee quality; and unless the quality aspect is considered, the effective price per unit that a company pays its vendors may be understated and, in some cases, unknown. Deming urged businesses to move toward single-sourcing, to establish long-term relationships with a few suppliers (one supplier per purchased part, for example) leading to loyalty and opportunities for mutual improvement. Using multiple suppliers has been long justified for reasons such as providing protection against strikes or natural disasters or making the suppliers compete against each other on cost. However, this approach has ignored "hidden" costs such as increased travel to visit suppliers, loss of volume discounts, increased set-up charges resulting in higher unit costs, and increased inventory and administrative expenses. Also constantly changing suppliers solely on the base of price increases the variation in the material supplied to production, since each supplier's process is different.

5. Continuously improve the system of production and service. Management's job is to continuously improve the system with input from workers and management. Deming was a disciple of Walter A. Shewhart, the developer of control charts and the continuous cycle of process improvement known as the Shewhart cycle. Deming popularized the Shewhart Cycle as the Plan-Do-Check-Act (PDCA) or Plan-Do-Study-Act (PDSA) cycle; therefore, it is also often referred to as the Deming cycle.

In the planning stage, opportunities for improvement are recognized and operationally defined. In the doing stage, the theory and course of action developed in the previous stage is tested on a small scale through conducting trial runs in a laboratory or prototype setting. The results of the testing phase are analyzed in the check/study stage using statistical methods. In the action stage, a decision is made regarding the implementation of the proposed plan. If the results were positive in the pilot stage, then the plan will be implemented. Otherwise alternative plans are developed. After full scale implementation, customer and process feedback will again be obtained and the process of continuous improvement continues.

6. Institute training on the job. When training is an integral part of the system, operators are better able to prevent defects. Deming understood that employees are the fundamental asset of every company, and they must know and buy into a company's goals. Training enables employees to understand their responsibilities in meeting customers' needs.

7. Institute leadership (modern methods of supervision). The best supervisors are leaders and coaches, not dictators. Deming highlighted the key role of supervisors who serve as a vital link between managers and workers. Supervisors first have to be trained in the quality management before they can communicate management's commitment to quality improvement and serve as role models and leaders.

8. Drive out fear. Create a fear-free environment where everyone can contribute and work effectively. There is an economic loss associated with fear in an organization. Employees try to please their superiors. Also, because they feel that they might lose their jobs, they are hesitant to ask questions about their jobs, production methods, and process parameters. If a supervisor or manager gives the impression that asking such questions is a waste of time, then employees will be more concerned about pleasing their supervisors than meeting long-term goals of the organization. Therefore, creating an environment of trust is a key task of management.

9. Break down barriers between areas. People should work cooperatively with mutual trust, respect, and appreciation for the needs of others in their work. Internal and external organizational barriers impede the flow of information, prevent entities from perceiving organizational goals, and foster the pursuit of subunit goals that are not necessarily consistent with the organizational goals. Barriers between organizational levels and departments are internal barriers. External barriers are between the company and its suppliers, customers, investors, and community. Barriers can be eliminated through better communication, cross-functional teams, and changing attitudes and cultures.

10. Eliminate slogans aimed solely at the work force. Most problems are system-related and require managerial involvement to rectify or change. Slogans don't help. Deming believed that people want to do work right the first time. It is the system that 80 to 90 percent of the time prevents people from doing their work right the first time.

11. Eliminate numerical goals, work standards, and quotas. Objectives set for others can force sub-optimization or defective output in order to achieve them. Instead, learn the capabilities of processes and how to improve them. Numerical goals set arbitrarily by management, especially if they are not accompanied by feasible courses of action, have a demoralizing effect. Goals should be set in a participative style together with methods for accomplishment. Deming argued that the quota or work standard system is a short-term solution and that quotas emphasize quantity over quality. They do not provide data about the process that can be used to meet the quota, and they fail to distinguish between special and common causes when seeking improvements to the process.

12. Remove barriers that hinder workers (and hinder pride in workmanship). The direct effect of pride in workmanship is increased motivation and a greater ability for employees to see themselves as part of the same team. This pride can be diminished by several factors: (1) management may be insensitive to workers' problems; (2) they may not communicate the company's goals to all levels; and (3) they may blame employees for failing to meet company goals when the real fault lies with the management.

13. Institute a vigorous program of education and self improvement. Deming's philosophy is based on long-term, continuous process improvement that cannot be carried out without properly trained and motivated employees. This point addresses the need for ongoing and continuous education and self-improvement for the entire organization.

This educational investment serves the following objectives: (1) it leads to better motivated employees; (2) it communicates the company goals to the employees; (3) it keeps the employees up-to-date on the latest techniques and promotes teamwork; (4) training and retraining provides a mechanism to ensure adequate performance as the job responsibilities change; and (5) through increasing job loyalty, it reduces the number of people who "job-hop."

14. Take action to accomplish the transformation. Create a structure in top management that will promote the previous thirteen points. It is the top management's responsibility to create and maintain a structure for the dissemination of the concepts outlined in the first thirteen points. Deming felt that people at all levels in the organization should learn and apply his Fourteen Points if statistical process control is to be a successful approach to process improvement and if organizations are to be transformed. However, he encouraged top management to learn them first. He believed that these points represent an all-or-nothing commitment and that they cannot be implemented selectively.

THE DEMING CYCLE

Known as the Deming Plan-Do-Check-Act (PDCA) Cycle, this concept was invented by Shewhart and popularized by Deming. This approach is a cyclic process for planning and testing improvement activities prior to full-scale implementation and/or prior to formalizing the improvement. When an improvement idea is identified, it is often wise to test it on a small scale prior to full implementation to validate its benefit. Additionally, by introducing a change on a small scale, employees have time to accept it and are more likely to support it. The Deming PDCA Cycle provides opportunities for continuous evaluation and improvement.

The steps in the Deming PDCA or PDSA Cycle as shown in Figure 1 are as follows:

1. Plan a change or test (P).

2. Do it (D). Carry out the change or test, preferably on a small scale.

3. Check it (C). Observe the effects of the change or test. Study it (S).

4. Act on what was learned (A).

5. Repeat Step 1, with new knowledge.

6. Repeat Step 2, and onward. Continuously evaluate and improve.

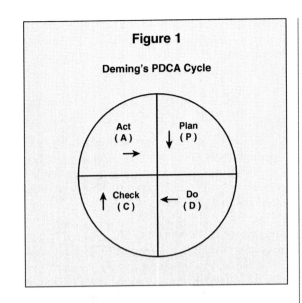

Figure 1

Deming's PDCA Cycle

Deming was trained as a mathematical physicist, and he utilized mathematical concepts and tools (Statistical Process Control) to reduce variation and prevent defects. However, one of his greatest contributions might have been in recognizing the importance of organizational culture and employee attitudes in creating a successful organization. In many ways, his philosophies paralleled the development of the resource-based view of organizations that emphasized that employee knowledge and skills and organizational culture are very difficult to imitate or replicate, and they can serve as a basis of sustainable competitive advantage.

DR. JOSEPH JURAN (B. 1904)

Dr. Juran was born on December 24, 1904 in Braila, Romania. He moved to the United States in 1912 at the age of 8. Juran's teaching and consulting career spanned more than seventy years, known as one of the foremost experts on quality in the world.

A quality professional from the beginning of his career, Juran joined the inspection branch of the Hawthorne Co. of Western Electric (a Bell manufacturing company) in 1924, after completing his B.S. in Electrical Engineering. In 1934, he became a quality manager. He worked with the U. S. government during World War II and afterward became a quality consultant. In 1952, Dr. Juran was invited to Japan. Dr. Edward Deming helped arrange the meeting that led to this invitation and his many years of work with Japanese companies.

Juran founded the Juran Center for Quality Improvement at the University of Minnesota and the Juran Institute. His third book, *Juran's Quality Control Handbook,* published in 1951, was translated into Japanese. Other books include *Juran on Planning for Quality* (1988), *Juran on Leadership for Quality*

(1989), *Juran on Quality by Design* (1992), *Quality Planning and Analysis* (1993), and *A History of Managing for Quality* (1995). *Architect of Quality* (2004) is his autobiography.

SELECTED JURAN QUALITY THEORIES

Juran's concepts can be used to establish a traditional quality system, as well as to support Strategic Quality Management. Among other things, Juran's philosophy includes the Quality Trilogy and the Quality Planning Roadmap.

JURAN'S QUALITY TRILOGY. The Quality Trilogy emphasizes the roles of quality planning, quality control, and quality improvement. Quality planning's purpose is to provide operators with the ability to produce goods and services that can meet customers' needs. In the quality planning stage, an organization must determine who the customers are and what they need, develop the product or service features that meet customers' needs, develop processes which are able to deliver those products and services, and transfer the plans to the operating forces. If quality planning is deficient, then chronic waste occurs.

Quality control is used to prevent things from getting worse. Quality control is the inspection part of the Quality Trilogy where operators compare actual performance with plans and resolve the differences. Chronic waste should be considered an opportunity for quality improvement, the third element of the Trilogy. Quality improvement encompasses improvement of fitness-for-use and error reduction, seeks a new level of performance that is superior to any previous level, and is attained by applying breakthrough thinking.

While up-front quality planning is what organizations should be doing, it is normal for organizations to focus their first quality efforts on quality control. In this aspect of the Quality Trilogy, activities include inspection to determine percent defective (or first pass yield) and deviations from quality standards. Activities can then focus on another part of the trilogy, quality improvement, and make it an integral part of daily work for individuals and teams.

Quality planning must be integrated into every aspect of the organization's work, such as strategic plans; product, service and process designs; operations; and delivery to the customer. The Quality Trilogy is depicted below in Figure 2.

JURAN'S QUALITY PLANNING ROAD MAP. Juran's Quality Planning Road Map can be used by individuals and teams throughout the world as a checklist for understanding customer requirements, establishing measurements based on customer needs, optimizing

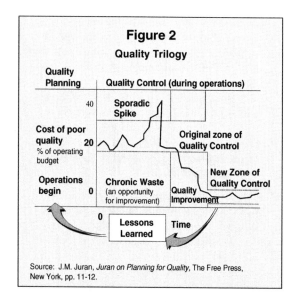

Figure 2
Quality Trilogy

Source: J.M. Juran, *Juran on Planning for Quality*, The Free Press, New York, pp. 11-12.

product design, and developing a process that is capable of meeting customer requirements. The Quality Planning Roadmap is used for Product and Process Development and is shown in Figure 3.

Juran's Quality Trilogy and Quality Roadmap are not enough. An infrastructure for Quality must be

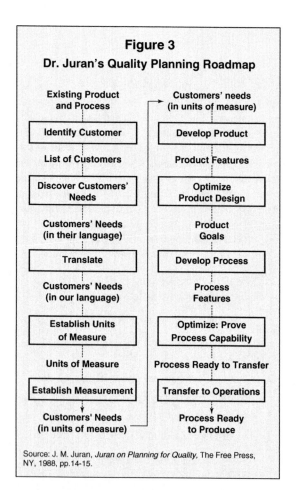

Figure 3
Dr. Juran's Quality Planning Roadmap

Source: J. M. Juran, *Juran on Planning for Quality*, The Free Press, NY, 1988, pp.14-15.

developed, and teams must work on improvement projects. The infrastructure should include a quality steering team with top management leading the effort, quality should become an integral part of the strategic plan, and all people should be involved. As people identify areas with improvement potential, they should team together to improve processes and produce quality products and services.

Under the "Big Q" concept, all people and departments are responsible for quality. In the old era under the concept of "little q," the quality department was responsible for quality. Big "Q" allows workers to regain pride in workmanship by assuming responsibility for quality.

PHILIP CROSBY (1926–2001)

Philip Bayard Crosby was born in Wheeling, West Virginia, in 1926. After Crosby graduated from high school, he joined the Navy and became a hospital corpsman. In 1946 Crosby entered the Ohio College of Podiatric Medicine in Cleveland. After graduation he returned to Wheeling and practiced podiatry with his father. He was recalled to military service during the Korean conflict, this time he served as a Marine Medical Corpsman.

In 1952 Crosby went to work for the Crosley Corp. in Richmond, Indiana, as a junior electronic test technician. He joined the American Society for Quality, where his early concepts concerning Quality began to form. In 1955, he went to work for Bendix Corp. as a reliability technician and quality engineer. He investigated defects found by the test people and inspectors.

In 1957 he became a senior quality engineer with Martin Marietta Co. in Orlando, Florida. During his eight years with Martin Marietta, Crosby developed his "Zero Defects" concepts, began writing articles for various journals, and started his speaking career.

In 1965 International Telephone and Telegraph (ITT) hired Crosby as vice president in charge of corporate quality. During his fourteen years with ITT, Crosby worked with many of the world's largest industrial and service companies, implementing his pragmatic management philosophy, and found that it worked.

After a number of years in industry, Crosby established the Crosby Quality College in Winter Park, Florida. He is well known as an author and consultant and has written many articles and books. He is probably best known for his book *Quality is Free* (1979) and concepts such as his *Absolutes of Quality Management, Zero Defects, Quality Management Maturity Grid, 14 Quality Improvement Steps, Cost of Quality,* and *Cost of Nonconformance.* Other books he has written include *Quality Without Tears* (1984) and *Completeness* (1994).

Attention to customer requirements and preventing defects is evident in Crosby's definitions of quality and "non-quality" as follows: "Quality is conformance to requirements; non-quality is nonconformance."

CROSBY'S COST OF QUALITY. In his book *Quality Is Free,* Crosby makes the point that it costs money to achieve quality, but it costs more money when quality is not achieved. When an organization designs and builds an item right the first time (or provides a service without errors), quality is free. It does not cost anything above what would have already been spent. When an organization has to rework or scrap an item because of poor quality, it costs more. Crosby discusses Cost of Quality and Cost of Nonconformance or Cost of Nonquality. The intention is spend more money on preventing defects and less on inspection and rework.

CROSBY'S FOUR ABSOLUTES OF QUALITY. Crosby espoused his basic theories about quality in four Absolutes of Quality Management as follows:

1. Quality means conformance to requirements, not goodness.

2. The system for causing quality is prevention, not appraisal.

3. The performance standard must be zero defects, not "that's close enough."

4. The measurement of quality is the price of nonconformance, not indexes.

To support his Four Absolutes of Quality Management, Crosby developed the Quality Management Maturity Grid and Fourteen Steps of Quality Improvement. Crosby sees the Quality Management Maturity Grid as a first step in moving an organization towards quality management. After a company has located its position on the grid, it implements a quality improvement system based on Crosby's Fourteen Steps of Quality Improvement as shown in Figure 4.

Crosby's Absolutes of Quality Management are further delineated in his Fourteen Steps of Quality Improvement as shown below:

Step 1. Management Commitment

Step 2. Quality Improvement Teams

Step 3. Quality Measurement

Step 4. Cost of Quality Evaluation

Step 5. Quality Awareness

Step 6. Corrective Action

Figure 4
Crosby's Quality Management Maturity Grid

Rater _____ Unit _____

Measurement Categories	Stage I: Uncertainty	Stage II: Awakening	Stage III Enlightenment	Stage IV: Wisdom	Stage V: Certainty
Management understanding and attitude	No comprehension of quality as a management tool. Tend to blame quality department for "quality problems."	Recognizing that quality management may be of value but not willing to provide money or time to make it all happen.	While going through quality improvement program, learn more about quality management. Becoming supportive and helpful.	Participating. Understand absolutes of quality management. Recognize their personal role in continuing emphasis.	Consider quality management an essential part of company system.
Quality organization status	Quality is hidden in manufacturing or engineering departments. Inspection probably not part of organization. Emphasis on appraisal and sorting.	A stronger quality leader is appointed but main emphasis is still on appraisal and moving the product. Still part of manufacturing or other organization.	Quality department reports to top management, all appraisal is incorporated and manager has role in management of company.	Quality manager is an officer of company; effective status reporting and preventive action. Involved with consumer affairs and special assignments.	Quality manager on board of directors. Prevention is main concern. Quality is a thought leader.
Problem handling	Problems are fought as they occur; no resolution; inadequate definition; lots of yelling and accusations.	Teams are set up to attack major problems. Long-range solutions are not solicited.	Corrective action communication established. Problems are faced openly and resolved in an orderly way.	Problems are identified early in their development. All functions are open to suggestion and improvement.	Except in the most unusual cases, problems are prevented.
Cost of quality as % of sales	Reported: unknown Actual: 20%	Reported: 3% Actual: 18%	Reported: 8% Actual: 12%	Reported: 6.5% Actual: 8%	Reported: 2.5% Actual: 2.5%
Quality improvement actions	No organized activities. No understanding of such activities.	Trying obvious "motivational" short-range efforts.	Implementation of 14-step program; thorough understanding and establishment of each step.	Continuing the 14-step program and starting Make Certain.	Quality improvement is a normal and continued activity.
Summation of company quality posture	"We don't know why we have problems with quality."	"Is it absolutely necessary to always have problems with quality?"	"Through management commitment and quality improvement we are identifying and resolving our problems."	"Defect prevention is a routine part of our operation."	"We know why we do not have problems with quality."

Source: Philip B. Crosby, Quality Is Free, McGraw-Hill Book Company, New York, 1979, pp. 38-39.

Step 7. Zero-Defects Planning

Step 8. Supervisory Training

Step 9. Zero Defects

Step 10. Goal Setting

Step 11. Error Cause Removal

Step 12. Recognition

Step 13. Quality Councils

Step 14. Do It All Over Again

ARMAND V. FEIGENBAUM

Feigenbaum was still a doctoral student at the Massachusetts Institute of Technology when he completed the first edition of *Total Quality Control* (1951).

An engineer at General Electric during World War II, Feigenbaum used statistical techniques to determine what was wrong with early jet airplane engines. For ten years he served as manager of worldwide manufacturing operations and quality control at GE. Feigenbaum serves as president of General Systems Company, Inc., Pittsfield, Massachusetts, an international engineering firm that designs and installs integrated operational systems for major corporations in the United States and abroad.

Feigenbaum was the founding chairman of the International Academy for Quality and is a past president of the American Society for Quality Control, which presented him its Edwards Medal and Lancaster Award for his contributions to quality and productivity. His Total Quality Control concepts have had a very positive impact on quality and productivity for many organizations throughout the industrialized world.

DR. H. JAMES HARRINGTON

An author and consultant in the area of process improvement, Harrington spent forty years with IBM. His career included serving as Senior Engineer and Project Manager of Quality Assurance for IBM, San Jose, California. He was President of Harrington, Hurd and Reicker, a well-known performance improvement consulting firm until Ernst & Young bought the organization. He is the international quality advisor for Ernst and Young and on the board of directors of various national and international companies.

Harrington served as president and chairman of the American Society for Quality and the International Academy for Quality. In addition, he has been elected as an honorary member of six quality associations outside of North America and was selected for the Singapore Hall of Fame. His books include *The Improvement Process, Business Process Improvement, Total Improvement Management, ISO 9000 and Beyond, Area Activity Analysis, The Creativity Toolkit, Statistical Analysis Simplified, The Quality/Profit Connection,* and *High Performance Benchmarking.*

DR. KAORU ISHIKAWA (1915–1989)

A professor of engineering at the University of Tokyo and a student of Dr. W. Edwards Deming, Ishikawa was active in the quality movement in Japan, and was a member of the Union of Japanese Scientists and Engineers. He was awarded the Deming Prize, the Nihon Keizai Press Prize, and the Industrial Standardization Prize for his writings on quality control, and the Grant Award from the American Society for Quality Control for his educational program on quality control.

Ishikawa's book, *Guide to Quality Control* (1982), is considered a classic because of its in-depth explanations of quality tools and related statistics. The tool for which he is best known is the cause and effect diagram. Ishikawa is considered the Father of the Quality Circle Movement. Letters of praise from representatives of companies for which he was a consultant were published in his book *What Is Total Quality Control?* (1985). Those companies include IBM, Ford, Bridgestone, Komatsu Manufacturing, and Cummins Engine Co.

Ishikawa believed that quality improvement initiatives must be organization-wide in order to be successful and sustainable over the long term. He promoted the use of Quality Circles to: (1) Support improvement; (2) Respect human relations in the workplace; (3) Increase job satisfaction; and (4) More fully recognize employee capabilities and utilize their ideas. Quality Circles are effective when management understands statistical techniques and act on recommendations from members of the Quality Circles.

DR. WALTER A. SHEWHART (1891–1967)

A statistician who worked at Western Electric, Bell Laboratories, Dr. Walter A. Shewhart used statistics to explain process variability. It was Dr. W. Edward Deming who publicized the usefulness of control charts, as well as the Shewhart Cycle. However, Deming rightfully credited Shewhart with the development of theories of process control as well as the Shewhart transformation process on which the Deming PDCA (Plan-Do-Check or Study-Act) Cycle is based. Shewhart's theories were first published in his book *Economic Control of Quality of Manufactured Product* (1931).

SHIGEO SHINGO (1919–1990)

One of the world's leading experts on improving the manufacturing process, Shigeo Shingo created, with Taiichi Ohno, many of the features of just-in-time (JIT) manufacturing methods, systems, and processes, which constitute the Toyota Production System. He has written many books including *A Study of the Toyota Production System From An Industrial Engineering Viewpoint* (1989), *Revolution in Manufacturing: The SMED (Single Minute Exchange of Die) System* (1985), and *Zero Quality Control: Source Inspection and the Poka Yoke System* (1986).

Shingo's greatness seems to be based on his ability to understand exactly why products are manufactured the way they are, and then transform that understanding into a workable system for low-cost, high quality production. Established in 1988, the Shingo Prize is the premier manufacturing award in the United States, Canada, and Mexico. In partnership with the National Association of Manufacturers, Utah State University administers the Shingo Prize for

Excellence in Manufacturing, which promotes world class manufacturing and recognizes companies that excel in productivity and process improvement, quality enhancement, and customer satisfaction.

Rather than focusing on theory, Shingo focused on practical concepts that made an immediate difference. Specific concepts attributed to Shingo are:

- Poka Yoke requires stopping processes as soon as a defect occurs, identifying the source of the defect, and preventing it from happening again.

- Mistake Proofing is a component of Poka Yoke. Literally, this means making it impossible to make mistakes (i.e., preventing errors at the source).

- SMED (Single Minute Exchange of Die) is a system for quick changeovers between products. The intent is to simplify materials, machinery, processes and skills in order to dramatically reduce changeover times from hours to minutes. As a result products could be produced in small batches or even single units with minimal disruption.

- Just-in-Time (JIT) Production is about supplying customers with what they want when they want it. The aim of JIT is to minimize inventories by producing only what is required when it is required. Orders are "pulled" through the system when triggered by customer orders, not pushed through the system in order to achieve economies of scale with the production of larger batches.

FREDERICK TAYLOR (1856–1915)

An industrial (efficiency) engineer, manager, and consultant, Frederick Taylor is known as the Father of Scientific Management. In 1911, he published *The Principles of Scientific Management.* Taylor believed in task specialization and is noted for his time and motion studies. Some of his ideas are the predecessors for modern industrial engineering tools and concepts that are used in cycle time reduction.

While quality experts would agree that Taylor's concepts increase productivity, some argue that his concepts are focused on productivity, not process improvement and as a result could cause less emphasis on quality. Dr. Joseph Juran said that Taylor's concepts made the United States the world leader in productivity. However, the Taylor system required separation of planning work from executing the work. This separation was based on the idea that engineers should do the planning because supervisors and workers were not educated. Today, the emphasis is on transferring planning to the people doing the work.

DR. GENICHI TAGUCHI (B. 1924)

Dr. Genichi Taguchi was a Japanese engineer and statistician who defined what product specification means and how this can be translated into cost effective production. He worked in the Japanese Ministry of Public Health and Welfare, Institute of Statistical Mathematics, Ministry of Education. He also worked with the Electrical Communications Laboratory of the Nippon Telephone and Telegraph Co. to increase the productivity of the R&D activities.

In the mid 1950s Taguchi was Indian Statistical Institute visiting professor, where he met Walter Shewhart. He was a Visiting Research Associate at Princeton University in 1962, the same year he received his Ph.D. from Kyushu University. He was a Professor at Tokyo's Aoyama Gakuin University and Director of the Japanese Academy of Quality.

Taguchi was awarded the Deming Application prize (1960), Deming awards for literature on quality (1951, 1953, and 1984), Willard F. Rockwell Medal by the International Technologies Institute (1986).

Taguchi's contributions are in robust design in the area of product development. The Taguchi Loss Function, The Taguchi Method (Design of Experiments), and other methodologies have made major contributions in the reduction of variation and greatly improved engineering quality and productivity. By consciously considering the noise factors (environmental variation during the product's usage, manufacturing variation, and component deterioration) and the cost of failure in the field, Taguchi methodologies help ensure customer satisfaction.

Robust Design focuses on improving the fundamental function of the product or process, thus facilitating flexible designs and concurrent engineering. Taguchi product development includes three stages: (1) system design (the non-statistical stage for engineering, marketing, customer and other knowledge); (2) parameter stage (determining how the product should perform against defined parameters; and (3) tolerance design (finding the balance between manufacturing cost and loss).

SEE ALSO: Quality and Total Quality Management

Mildred Golden Pryor

FURTHER READING:

Crosby, Philip. *Completeness.* New York, NY: Penguin Books, 1994.

———. *Quality is Free.* New York, NY: McGraw-Hill, 1979.

———. *Quality & Me: Lessons from an Evolving Life.* San Francisco, CA: Jossey-Bass, 1999.

———. *Quality without Tears.* New York, NY: McGraw-Hill, 1984.

Deming, W. Edwards. *The New Economics.* Cambridge, MA: MIT Center for Advanced Engineering Study, 1993.

———. *Out of the Crisis.* Cambridge, MA: MIT Center for Advanced Engineering Study, 1986.

———. *Quality, Productivity, and Competitive Position.* Cambridge, MA: MIT Center for Advanced Engineering Study, 1982.

Feigenbaum, Armand V. *Total Quality Control.* New York, NY: McGraw-Hill, 1991.

Gitlow, Howard S., Alan J. Oppenheim, Rosa Oppenheim, and David M. Levine. *Quality Management.* New York, NY: McGraw-Hill/Irwin, 2005.

Harrington, H. James. "The $7,000 SNAFU: Confronting the 'Not My Problem' Response to Customer Service." *Quality Digest,* February 2004.

———. *Business Process Improvement: The Breakthrough Strategy for Total Quality, Productivity, and Competitiveness.* New York, NY: McGraw-Hill, 1991.

———. *High Performance Benchmarking.* New York, NY: McGraw-Hill, 1996.

———. *The Improvement Process: How America's Leading Companies Improve Quality.* New York, NY: McGraw-Hill, 1987.

Ishikawa, Kaoru. *Guide to Quality Control.* Tokyo, Japan: Asian Productivity Organization, 1982.

———. *What Is Total Quality Control?* Englewood Cliffs, NJ : Prentice-Hall, 1985.

Juran, Joseph M. *Architect of Quality.* New York, NY: McGraw-Hill, 2004.

———. "A Call to Action—The Summit: Carlson School of Management, University of Minnesota, Minneapolis, Minnesota." *Measuring Business Excellence* 6, no. 3 (2002): 4–9.

———. "A Close Shave." *Quality Progress* 37, no. 5 (May 2004): 41–44.

———. *A History of Managing for Quality.* Milwaukee, WI: ASQ Quality Press, 1995.

———. *Juran on Leadership for Quality.* London, England: Collier Macmillan, 1989.

———. *Juran on Planning for Quality.* London, England: Collier Macmillan, 1988.

———. *Juran on Quality by Design.* New York, NY: Maxwell Macmillan International, 1992.

Juran, Joseph M., and Frank M. Gryna. *Juran's Quality Control Handbook.* New York, NY: McGraw-Hill, 1988.

———. *Quality Planning and Analysis: From Product Development through Use.* New York, NY: McGraw-Hill, 1993.

Pryor, Mildred Golden, and Brian D. Cullen. "Learn to Use TQM as Part of Everyday Work." *Industrial Management* 35, no. 3 (May-June 1993): 10–14.

Pryor, Mildred Golden, J. Chris White, and Leslie A. Toombs. *Strategic Quality Management: A Strategic, Systems Approach to Continuous Improvement.* Thomson Learning Custom Publishing, 1998.

Shewhart, Walter A. *Economic Control of Quality Manufactured Product.* New York, NY: Van Nostrand, 1931.

Shingo, Shigeo. *Revolution in Manufacturing: The SMED (Single Minute Exchange of Die) System.* Cambridge, MA: Productivity Press, Inc., 1985.

———. *A Study of the Toyota Production System.* Cambridge, MA: Productivity Press, Inc., 1989.

———. *Zero Quality Control: Source Inspection and the Poka Yoke System.* Cambridge, MA: Productivity Press, Inc., 1986.

Stimson, William A. "A Deming Inspired Management Code of Ethics." *Quality Progress* 38, no. 2 (2005): 67–75.

Taylor, Frederick W. *The Principles of Scientific Management.* New York, NY: W.W. Norton & Co., 1911.

QUALITY AND TOTAL QUALITY MANAGEMENT

Although quality and quality management does not have a formal definition, most agree that it is an integration of all functions of a business to achieve high quality of products through continuous improvement efforts of all employees. Quality revolves around the concept of meeting or exceeding customer expectation applied to the product and service. Achieving high quality is an ever changing, or continuous, process therefore quality management emphasizes the ideas of working constantly toward improved quality. It involves every aspect of the company: processes, environment and people. The whole workforce from the CEO to the line worker must be involved in a shared commitment to improving quality.

Therefore, in brief, quality and total quality management (TQM) in particular can be defined as directing (managing) the whole (total) production process to produce an excellent (quality) product or service.

It differs from other management techniques in the attitude of management toward the product and toward the worker. Older management methods focused on the volume of production and the cost of the product. Quality was controlled by using a detection method (post production inspection), problems were solved by management and management's role was defined as planning, assigning work, controlling the production. Quality management, in contrast, is focused on the customer and meeting the customer's needs. Quality is controlled by prevention, i.e., quality is built in at every stage. Teams solve problems and everyone is responsible for the quality of the product. Management's role is to delegate, coach, facilitate and mentor. The major quality management principles are: quality, teamwork, and proactive management philosophies for process improvement.

The U.S. Department of Defense's Definition of Total Quality

Total Quality (TQ) consists of continuous improvement activities involving everyone in the organization—managers and workers—in a totally integrated effort toward improving performance at every level. This improved performance is directed toward satisfying such cross-functional goals as quality, cost, schedule, missing, need, and suitability. TQ integrates fundamental management techniques, existing improvement efforts, and technical tools under a disciplined approach focused on continued process improvement. The activities are ultimately focused on increasing customer/user satisfaction.

ORIGINS

Quality management in is not derived from a single idea or person. It is a collection of ideas, and has been called by various names and acronyms: TQM, total quality management; CQU, continuous quality improvement; SQC, statistical quality control; TQC, total quality control, etc. However each of these ideas encompasses the underlying idea of productivity initiatives that increase profit by improving the product.

Though most writers trace the quality movement's origins to W. Edward Deming, Joseph M. Juran and Philip B. Crosby, the roots of quality can be traced even further back, to Frederick Taylor in the 1920s. Taylor is the "father of scientific management." As manufacturing left the single craftsman's workshop, companies needed to develop a quality control department. As manufacturing moved into big plants, between the 1920s and the 1950s, the terms and processes of *quality engineering* and *reliability engineering* developed. During this time productivity was emphasized and quality was checked at the end of the line. As industrial plants became larger, post-production checks became more difficult and statistical methods began to be used to control quality. This was called *reliability engineering* because it moved quality control toward building quality into the design and production of the product. Taylor was the pioneer of these methods. Although some writers consider Taylor's methods part of classical management in opposition to the quality management system, both Deming and Juran both used statistical methods for quality assurance at Bell Telephone laboratories.

In the decades that followed World War II, the U.S. had no trouble selling everything made. This demand had the effect in the U.S. of driving industry to increase production, which resulted in less quality control. U.S. manufacturers became complacent, thinking that they could sell any product and that the consumer did not want or demand quality. The post World War II situation in Japan was just the opposite. The war had left the country devastated, and it needed to rebuild its means of production. In addition, Japanese manufacturers needed to counteract the shoddy reputation they had that products "made in Japan" were of low quality.

Japan began focusing on serious quality efforts. Japanese teams went abroad to visit foreign countries to learn how other countries managed quality, and they invited foreign experts to lecture in Japan on quality management. Two of these foreign experts were Americans W. Edward Deming and Joseph Juran. They each had a profound influence on Japanese quality processes, encouraging quality and design, *built in,* and zero defect programs. It took twenty years of concerted effort to revamp Japan's industrial system. The strategies used involved high-level managers as leaders, all levels and functions were trained in managing for quality, continuous progress was undertaken, quality circles were used, and the entire workforce was enlisted. By the early 1980s Japanese products, particularly automobiles and electronic products, were superior in quality to U.S. products. U.S. companies lost markets in the U.S. and in the western world to the Japanese and went in search of the *Japanese secret.* They found W. Edward Deming.

DEMING'S CONTRIBUTIONS

Deming was an American who worked in the 1930s with Walter A. Shewhart at Bell Telephone Company. Shewhart was a statistician who had the theory that product control could best be managed by statistics. He developed a statistical chart for the control of product variables. Deming developed a process, based on Shewhart's, using statistical control techniques that alerted managers of the need to intervene in the production process.

He then utilized these techniques during World War II while working on government war production. In 1947 Douglas MacArthur and the U.S. State Department sent Deming to Japan to help the war-devastated Japanese manufacturing plants. He introduced these "statistical process control" methods in a series of lectures on statistical methods to Japanese businessmen and engineers. The Japanese were an attentive audience and utilized Deming's ideas readily. They found him charming and considerate and listened to his ideas. His concept of employees working toward quality fit well into their personal ideas. His philosophy went beyond statistical quality control and encouraged building quality into the product at all stages.

Deming developed the chain reaction: as quality improves, costs go down and productivity goes up; this leads to more jobs, greater market share, and long-term survival. He stressed worker pride and satisfaction and considered it management's job to improve the process, not the worker. Quality circles, a central Deming theme, are based on the importance of employees meeting regularly in groups to comprehensively discuss product quality. The GDP in Japan rose steadily from 1960s by more than 10 percent per year. By 1951 the Japanese had named their quality prize in his honor. Deming's book, *Out of the Crisis*, emphasized improving quality of the product as more important than short-term financial goals. He de-emphasized quantity, and emphasized quality. He believed that "statistical process control" was an invaluable instrument in the quest for quality. Deming developed fourteen points for management which can be summarized as:

1. Create a plan; publish the aims and purposes of the organization.

2. Learn and adopt the new philosophy of quality.

3. Understand the purpose of inspection; stop depending on inspection.

4. Stop awarding business based on price alone.

5. Improve the system constantly.

6. Institute training.

7. Teach and institute leadership.

8. Drive out fear, create trust, and create a climate for innovation.

9. Optimize the efforts of teams, groups and staff areas.

10. Eliminate exhortations, and targets for the work force; provide methods of achievement.

11. Eliminate numerical quotas for the work force.

12. Remove barriers that rob people of pride for workmanship.

13. Encourage education and self improvement for everyone.

14. Make action to accomplish the transformation, make it everyone's job.

Besides the fourteen points, Deming is known for the *Deming Cycle* and the *Seven Deadly Diseases*. The Deming Cycle is illustrated in Figure 1. It involves five steps: consumer research and planning of the product (plan), producing the product (do), checking the product (check), marketing the product (act), and analyzing how the product is received (analyze.)

The Seven Deadly Diseases can be summarized as:

1. Lack of constancy of purpose to plan products and services.

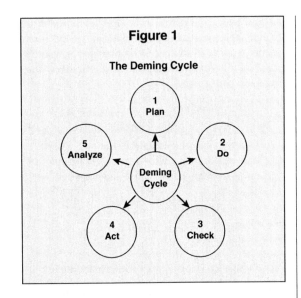

Figure 1

The Deming Cycle

1 Plan

5 Analyze

2 Do

Deming Cycle

4 Act

3 Check

2. Emphasis on short-term profits.

3. Personal review systems for managers and management by objectives.

4. Job hopping by managers.

5. Using only visible data in decision making.

6. Excessive medial costs.

7. Excessive costs of liability driven up by lawyers that work on contingency.

JURAN'S CONTRIBUTIONS

Joseph M. Juran, like Deming, went to Japan in 1954 and assisted the Japanese in their quest to achieve quality. Like Deming, Juran emphasized planning, organizing and controlling. However he emphasized customer satisfaction more than Deming did and focused on management and technical methods rather than worker satisfaction. Juran was a prolific author, publishing over a dozen books. His most influential book *Quality Control Handbook* (later called *Juran's Quality Handbook*)was published in 1951 and became a best seller.

By 1960 Japan was using quality control circles and simple statistical techniques learned and applied by Japanese workers. Juran developed basic steps that companies must take, however he believed there was a point of diminishing return, a point at which quality goes beyond the consumer needs. For example, if the consumer trades his car in after 50,000 miles, the car need only be built to perform trouble-free for 60,000 miles. Building a better car would drive up costs without delivering the expected product. This is called the *Pareto Principle,* or the Juran 80/20 rule: 80 percent of the trouble comes from 20 percent of the problems. The rule is named for Vilfredo Pareto, an economist, but it was Juran that applied the idea to management. It can be expressed as: "concentrate on the 'vital few' sources of problems; don't be distracted by less important problems." Juran's trilogy involves:

1. Quality planning (determine customer needs, develop product in response to needs).

2. Quality control (assess performance, compare performance with goals, act on differences between performance and goals).

3. Quality improvement (develop infrastructure, identify areas of improvement and implement projects, establish project team, provide teams with what they need).

Juran's ten steps to quality improvement are:

1. Build awareness of opportunities to improve.

2. Set goals.

3. Organize to reach goals.

4. Provide training.

5. Carry out projects to solve problems.

6. Report progress.

7. Give recognition.

8. Communicate results.

9. Keep score.

10. Maintain momentum by making annual improvement part of the systems and processes of the company.

The Union of Japanese Scientists and Engineers (JUSE) considered Juran's vision of top-to-bottom quality management even more important to their quality turnaround than Deming's insights. JUSE asked Juran if it could name its top-level award, a 'super-Deming award' after him, but he declined. This medal is called the Japan Quality Control Medal.

CROSBY'S CONTRIBUTIONS

Philip Crosby, author of *Quality is Free,* founded the Quality College in Winter Park, Florida. Crosby emphasized meeting customer requirements by focusing on prevention rather than correction. He claimed that poor quality costs about 20 percent of the revenue; a cost that could be avoided by using good quality practices. He pushed for zero defects. His "absolutes" are: (1) quality is defined as conformance to requirements, not *goodness;* (2) the system for achieving quality is prevention, not appraisal; (3) the performance standard is zero defects, not *that's close enough;* and (4) the measure of quality is the price of non-conformance, not indexes.

Crosby's method does not dwell on statistical process control and problem solving techniques that the Deming method uses. He stated that quality is free because prevention will always be lower than the costs of detection, correction and failure. Like Deming, Crosby had fourteen points:

1. Manage commitment, that is, top level management must be convinced and committed and communicated to the entire company.

2. Quality improvement team composed of department heads, oversee improvements.

3. Quality measurement are established for every activity.

4. Cost of quality is estimated to identify areas of improvement.

5. Quality awareness is raised among all employees.

6. Corrective action is taken.

7. Zero defects is planned for.

8. Supervisor training in quality implementation.

9. Zero defects day is scheduled.

10. Goal setting for individuals.

11. Error causes are removed by having employees inform management of problems.

12. Recognition is given, but it is non-financial, to those who meet quality goals.

13. Quality councils meet regularly.

14. Do it all over again (i.e., repeat steps one through thirteen).

Looking at the history of quality management, we see several stages of development. The first was *quality control,* which involved setting up product specifications and then inspect the product fore for leaves the plant. The second state is *quality assurance,* which involved identifying the quality characteristics and procedures for quantitatively evaluating and controlling them. The next phase is the true *total quality control,* a term actually coined by Feingenbaum in 1983. At this stage the quality became a total organization effort. It effected production, profit, human interaction and customer satisfaction. The fourth stage is *total quality management.* In TQM the customer is the center and quality is an organization-wide effort.

QUALITY PRIZES

The top three quality prizes are the Deming Prize, the Baldrige Award and the European Quality Awards. Union of Japanese Scientists and Engineers have annually awarded the Deming Prize since 1951. For three decades it was *the* quality award and is still the

---

Figure 2

Chronology

1931	Walter A. Shewhart of Bell Laboratories publishes Economic Control of Quality of Manufactured Products and introduces statistical quality control.
1950	W. Edwards Deming addressed Japanese scientists, engineers, and corporate executive on subject of quality.
1951	First Deming Prize awarded by the Union of Japanese Scientists and Engineers (JUSE).
1952	Joseph M. Juran publishes the Quality Control Handbook.
1970	Philip Crosby introduces the concept of zero defects.
1979	Crosby publishes Quality is Free.
1980	Ford Motor Company invites Deming to speak to executives.
1981	Bob Galvin, Motorola's chairman starts quality improvement, which leads to the six sigmas.
1982	Deming publishes Quality, Productivity, and Competitive Position.
1984	Crosby publishes Quality without Tears: The Art of Hassle-Free Management.
1987	Congress creates the Malcolm Baldrige National Quality Award.
1992	First European Quality Awards named, which is sponsored by the Foundation for Quality Management with support from the European Organization for Quality and the European Commission.

---

most prestigious award. The Deming Prize is given to a person or group of people who have advanced the practice and furthered awareness of TQC. The Deming Application Prize goes only to companies based on successes attributable to implementing TQC. The second major quality prizes was established by Congress in 1987 (Public Law 100-107) and is called the Baldrige Award. The award set a national standard for quality and companies use the criteria as a management guide. Applicants must address seven specific categories: leadership, strategic planning, customer and market focus, information and analysis, human resource focus, process management, and business results. Winners are required to share their successful strategies. U.S. Department of Commerce's National Institute of Standards and Technology administer the Malcolm Baldrige National Quality Award. The third award is the awarded by The Foundation for Quality Management with support from the European Organization for Quality and the European Commission. It is called the European Quality Award and was first awarded in 1992.

QUALITY IN THE U.S.

The U.S. was slow to see the advantages of TQM, although the American Society for Quality Control (now known as American Society for Quality) was formed in 1946. Huge markets for American-made products after World War II kept American industries producing products with little change in manufacturing methods. It wasn't until the late 1970s that U.S. manufacturing came up against foreign competition and the trade deficit, and at that time it became obvious that Japanese companies were far ahead of U.S. companies in quality.

One of the first companies in the U.S. to grasp and utilize TQM was Motorola. In 1981 Bob Galvin, Motorola's chairman, called for an across-the-board improvement of 10:1 in five years. To accomplish this they needed a breakthrough technique. This breakthrough is detailed in the Six Sigma process:

- Faith that the improvement target could be achieved.

- Total customer satisfaction.

- Powerful new tools, especially design of experiments.

- Cycle-time reduction.

- Designing for ease of manufacturing.

- Manufacturing innovations.

- True partnerships with key suppliers.

- Training for all employees.

Within five years Motorola had achieved their goal. In 1988 they were awarded the Malcolm Baldrige National Quality Award for their impressive Six Sigma process. Keki R. Bhote nurtured the Six Sigma project for eleven years at Motorola and then went on to consult with other companies.

In the early 1980s when Donald Petersen was CEO of Ford, Ford executives were investigating the secret of the Japanese success. They discovered W. Edwards Deming's holistic blend of statistics and management. Deming's ideas came to Detroit. Ford was in serious trouble because of Japanese competition.

Deming introduced the statistical methods needed to improve processes. These are the foundation of what became known as Six Sigma, a statistical measure that refers to 3.4 defects per million. Besides this scientific method of improving quality, Deming emphasized that all employees needed to work toward quality. He advocated teamwork and cross-department collaboration, close work with suppliers and employee training. Other companies that adopted the Deming quality methods were General Motors, Florida Power & Light, and Procter and Gamble.

Not all U.S. attempts at quality improvement have been successful. Frequently cited reasons for failure are poor leadership, team-mania (setting up teams before management or employee have been trained in team work), and lack of integration of quality efforts into the whole organization. Obstacles and barriers to success have been researched by Robert J. Masters. He lists eight common problems that lead to failure:

1. Lack of management commitment. Management must commit time and resources and clearly communicate the importance and goals to all personnel.

2. Inability to change the organizational culture. Change takes time and effort. In order for the culture to change, the employees need to want change and be willing to participate. This requires reasons that management must convey. The change will only occur if the employees trust the management. It cannot occur from a state of fear.

3. Improper planning. Planning must involve all parts of the organization and be communicated clearly to employees.

4. Lack of training. The most effective training comes from senior management. Informal training needs to occur on a continual basis.

5. Organizational structure problems and isolated individuals or departments. Multifunctional teams will help break down some of these barriers. Restructuring is another method.

6. Ineffective measurement and lack of data. Effective decisions require that the employees have access to the necessary data.

7. Inadequate attention to internal and external customers.

8. Inadequate empowerment, lack of teamwork. Teams require training. Their recommendations should be followed whenever possible. Individuals need to be empowered to make decisions.

IMPLEMENTING TQM

Although different authorities on total quality management emphasize different techniques and use different terminology, all share three common ideas: quality, teamwork and process improvement. Although many books have been written to guide U.S. companies through TQM, one of the major writers was Joseph Jablonski. In *Implementing TQM,* he identified three characteristics: (1) participative management; (2) continuous process improvement; and (3) utilization of teams.

Participative management is the opposite of the hierarchical management style of the early twentieth century businesses. It involves all employees in the management process and decision making by having managers set policies and make key decisions based upon the advice and ideas of subordinates. This method provides management with more information from the front line and motivates the workers as they have some control of the decisions. Continuous process improvement is one of Deming's major ideas and involves small steps toward the ultimate goal. This involves patience on the part of management. Teamwork refers to cross-functional teams of workers that share in problem solving.

Jablonski went on to list six attributes necessary for success: (1) customer focus; (2) process focus; (3) prevention versus inspection; (4) employee empowerment and compensation; (5) fact-based decision making; and (6) receptiveness to feedback.

U.S. companies have long relied upon company organization by functions. TQM emphasizes a decentralized structure to encourage leadership and creativity. The purpose of this change in structure is to change the behavior of the employees. This is a major change for most U.S. companies. However, successful companies have more functional integration and fewer layers of hierarchy.

QUALITY AND THE 1990S AND BEYOND

In the 1980s many U.S. companies implemented total quality management systems in order to be competitive in the global market place. Successes lead them to be interested in hiring managers and engineers with some TQM training. This prompted universities to start teaching quality methods. To help universities in this, the University Challenge program was developed by a group of companies that had implemented TQM successfully. Their goal was to encourage universities to commit to integrating TQM in their own operations and courses. Initially eight universities with both business and engineering schools were chosen. Milliken worked with North Carolina State University and Georgia Institute of Technology. IBM worked with Massachusetts Institute of Technology and Rochester Institute of Technology. Motorola worked with Purdue University. Procter & Gamble Company worked with University of Wisconsin at Madison and Tuskegee University. Xerox worked with Carnegie Mellon.

Another area of transformation by TQM since 1990 is in human resources. Numerous studies have indicated that human resource practices that improve the corporate culture lead to better profits. Therefore many companies have extended TQM to the HR department. Yet another area of development of TQM in American firms is in the area of ethical philosophy and behavior of top management. Recent corporate scandals have increased interest from the public in corporate responsibility and accountability. Corporate responsibility is defined as how a company's operating practices affect its stakeholders, such as consumers, and the natural environment. This is new quality movement is being called total responsibility management. It involves responsible vision and values, leadership build on these values.

TQM has had a wide acceptance in the U.S., which has been growing since the 1970s. Quality management principles have had a remarkable influence on every sector of American business and are spreading to non-profit organizations and universities. It is essential that this trend continue for U.S. companies to be competitive in the global market and to meet consumer demands.

SEE ALSO: Continuous Improvement; Japanese Management; Management Awards; Participative Management; Quality Gurus; Teams and Teamwork

Judith M. Nixon

FURTHER READING:

Besterfield, D., C. Besterfield-Michna, G.H. Besterfield., and M. Besterfield-Sacre. *Total Quality Management.* 2nd ed. Upper Saddle River, NY: Prentice-Hall, 1999.

Bou, J.C., and I. Beltran. "Total Quality Management, High-Commitment Human Resource Strategy and Firm Performance: An Empirical Study." *Total Quality Management* 16, no. 1 (2005): 71–86.

Chen, A.Y.S., and J.L. Rodgers. "Teaching the Teachers TQM." *Management Accounting* 76 (1995): 42–46.

Creech, B. *The Five Pillars of TQM.* New York: Truman Talley Books/Dutton.

Davids, M. "W. Edwards Deming (1900–1993) Quality Controller." *Journal of Business Strategy* 20, no. 5 (1999): 31–32.

Deming, W.E. *Out of the Crisis.* Cambridge, MA: MIT Press, 1986.

Gallear, D., and A. Ghobadian. "An Empirical Investigation of the Channels That Facilitate a Total Quality Culture." *Total Quality Management* 15, no. 8 (2004): 1043–1967.

Goetsch, D.L., and S.B. Davis. *Total Quality Handbook.* Upper Saddle River, NJ: Prentice Hall, 2001.

Hoyer, R.W., and B.Y. Hoyer. "What Is Quality? Learn How Each of the Eight Well-Known Gurus Answers This Question." *Quality Progress* 34, no. 7 (2001): 52–62.

Jablonski, J.R. *Implementing TQM.* 2nd ed. Albuquerque: Technical Management Consortium, 1992.

Juran, J. M. *Juran on Leadership for Quality.* New York: Free Press, 1989.

———. *Juran on Planning for Quality.* New York: Free Press, 1988.

Masters, R.J. "Overcoming the Barriers to TQM's Success." *Quality Progress* 29, no. 5 (1996): 53–55.

Mouradian, G. *The Quality Revolution.* New York: University of Press of America, 2002.

Port, O. "The Kings of Quality." *Business Week,* 2004.

Ross, J.E., and S. Perry. *Total Quality Management: Text, Cases and Readings.* 3rd ed. Boca Raton, St. Lucie Press, 1999.

Saad, G. H., and S. Siha. "Managing Quality: Critical Links and a Contingency Model." *International Journal of Operations & Production Management* 20, no. 10 (2000): 1146–1163.

Strach, P., and A. Everett. "Is There Anything Left to Learn From Japanese Companies?" *SAM Advanced Management Journal* 69, no. 3 (2004): 4–13.

Waddock, S., and C. Bodwell. "Managing Responsibility: What Can Be Learned From the Quality Movement." *California Management Review* 47, no. 1 (2004): 25–37.

Washbush, J.B. "Deming: A New Philosophy or Another Voice?" *Management Decision* 40, no. 10 (2002): 1029–1036.

QUALITY OF WORK LIFE

In today's high tech, fast-paced world, the work environment is very different than it was a generation ago. According to the Institute of Industrial Engineers, it is not uncommon for a person to change careers an average of six times in his or her lifetime. It is now rare for a person to stay with a single company his or her entire working life. Because employees are often willing to leave a company for better opportunities, companies need to find ways not only to hire qualified people, but also to retain them.

Unfortunately, many employees these days feel they are working harder, faster, and longer hours than ever before. Job-related employee stress can lead to lack of commitment to the corporation, poor productivity, and even leaving the company; all of which are of serious concern to management. Many employees bring work home with them on a regular basis, especially now that it is so easy for them to do that. With the wide availability of cell phones, pagers, personal digital assistants (PDAs), and computers, employees find it harder to get away from the office.

One of the more stressful professions today is in the Information Technology (IT) field. Not long ago, IT professionals were extremely well respected and in demand. As technology advanced rapidly, there was a high demand for programmers and engineers. Most had their choice of high-paying jobs as technology companies competed to recruit the best of them.

This is not the case today. In June 2004, Meta Group, Inc. surveyed 650 companies and found that nearly 75 percent of the companies acknowledged morale problems among their IT staffs. This number was up from the year before, which showed that two-thirds cited poor worker morale as an issue. Perhaps this is because the U.S. technology sector experienced widespread layoffs during the third quarter of 2004. In general, when layoffs happen the remaining employees are forced to pick up the workload of those who were laid off. This leads to added responsibility and longer work hours, often without additional compensation. This in turn leads to stress, burnout, and resentment. Other causes of employee dissatisfaction include low wages, lack of challenges, insufficient resources, unrealistic expectations, pressure to produce, willfully blind management, unreasonable policies and procedures, difficulty balancing family and work, and increased health benefit costs.

As employers try to address employee turnover and job satisfaction issues, they must first determine what the issues are. Several companies have convened focus groups and conducted employee-satisfaction surveys to find out how their employees feel and to determine what they can do to make their employees happy.

There are also a number of independent organizations that conduct employee surveys to gather this information. One such organization is the Families and Work Institute (www.familiesandwork.org), a nonprofit research center "that provides data to inform decision-making on the changing workforce and workplace, changing family and changing community. Founded in 1989, FWI is known for ahead of the curve, non-partisan research into emerging work-life issues; for solutions-oriented studies addressing topics of vital importance to all sectors of society; and for fostering connections among workplaces, families, and communities."

Every five years FWI conducts the National Study of the Changing Workforce (NSCW), a nationally representative sample of employed workers designed to collect and compile information on the work and personal/family lives of the U.S. workforce. The study is widely used by policy makers, employers, the media, and all those interested in the widespread impacts of the changing conditions of work and home life.

The 2002 NSCW showed a slight increase from 1992 in the number of companies that offer work-life supports on the job—both specific benefit entitlements and less formal policies and practices. Despite this, the survey showed a large increase in the number of employees with families who felt there was interference between their jobs and their family lives, than employees 25 years ago. The NSCW also found "the importance of supportive work-life policies and practices, such as flexible work arrangements, is clear—when they are available, employees exhibit more positive work outcomes, such as job satisfaction, commitment to employer, and retention, as well as more positive life outcomes, such as less interference between job and family life, less negative spillover from job to home, greater life satisfaction, and better mental health."

What does this mean to the employer? As more companies start to realize that a happy employee is a productive employee, they have started to look for ways to improve the work environment. Many have implemented various work-life programs to help employees, including alternate work arrangements, on-site childcare, exercise facilities, relaxed dress codes, and more. Quality-of-work-life programs go beyond work/life programs by focusing attention less on employee needs outside of work and realizing that job stress and the quality of life at work is even more direct bearing on worker satisfaction. Open communications, mentoring programs, and fostering more amicable relationships among workers are some of the ways employers are improving the quality of work life.

ALTERNATE WORK ARRANGEMENTS

Many employers have found it beneficial to allow alternate work arrangements for their employees. This is one way to improve employee productivity and morale. There are three alternate arrangements that are widely used today.

Telecommuting is the term used to describe the work situation in which the employee works outside of the office, usually at home or at a location closer to home. In general, when one telecommutes, he or she communicates with the office via telephone and email, and may go into the office periodically to touch base with the employer and to attend meetings. Advancements in technology have made this possible for many people to telecommute. The telecommuting employee may be able to access files on the office's network from remote locations. And with conference call, videoconferencing, and WebEx capabilities, the employee can *attend* meetings from other locations. With WebEx technology, meeting attendees can sit at their own computers and view the meeting organizer's computer desktop via the Internet. As the meeting organizer opens applications and moves the mouse on his or her computer, the remote attendees can see those same applications and movements as if they were running them on their own computers.

Flextime is another name for flexible work hours. Although most employees with flextime do work a full eight-hour day, they can start and end the workday at a time agreeable to both the employer and the employee, rather than the traditional 8:00 a.m. to 5:00 p.m. work day. Most employers require their employees to be in the office during "core hours," such as 10:00 a.m. to 2:00 p.m. but do not mandate the start and end times.

Alternate work schedules, like flexible schedules, involve working outside of the traditional 8 to 5 workday. However, alternate schedules have a fixed start and end time, whereas flextime allows the employee to vary start and end as long as they are there during the core hours. An alternate schedule may be 6:00 a.m. to 3:00 p.m. or 11:00 a.m. to 8:00 p.m. five days a week, or it may be four 10-hour days, or any other *different* schedule.

The advantages of these alternate work arrangements to the employee include flexible work hours, shorter or no commute, and a comfortable working environment. The advantages to the employer include less need for office space, increased productivity, lower use of sick leave, and improved employee morale.

While there are many advantages to these alternatives, there are also several disadvantages that the employer must consider. These include problems maintaining adequate staffing coverage, difficulty scheduling meetings, lack of interpersonal dynamics, and concerns about safety and security (for flextime and alternate schedule employees that come in early or leave late). It is up to the employer to weigh the advantages against the disadvantages to determine if any of these alternatives will work.

To improve the quality of work life and eliminate job stress, employers can also make efforts to be more aware of the workload and job demands. Employers need to examine employee training, communication, reward systems, coworker relationships, and work environment. Employees often are able to give employers the best advice on reducing work stress.

Employees in the future will likely be looking for corporations that have a new work environment, one that encourages each employee to work toward improvement in the product or service; gives employees the responsibility and authority to make decisions, provides timely feedback, and rewards employees based upon the quality of the product and efforts.

Team effort will assume central importance, especially that of self-directed work teams. Employees will choose employers who have aims and values that match theirs and who value balance in their employees' lives. Employees want to learn and advance, so opportunities for professional growth will attract employees.

Companies will seek employees with technical skills, vision, and the ability to organize and persuade in presentation of ideas and information. Strong communication skills and the ability to learn will be high on employers' demand list for employees. There are a great number of common elements between the employee list and the employer list. To attract and retain employees, companies need to be exploiting those points of convergence and continuously work with employees to redesign the work, eliminate job stress, increase job autonomy, provide learning and training opportunities, and improve the quality of work life.

SEE ALSO: Contingent Workers; Employee Assistance Programs; Human Resource Management; Safety in the Workplace; Work-Life Balance

Rhoda L. Wilburn

FURTHER READING:

"Alternate Work Arrangements: A Manager's Guide." University of California-Davis. Available from <http://www.hr.ucdavis.edu/Pubs/All/Altwork/Alternate_Work>.

Bond, James T., et al. "The 2002 National Study of the Changing Workforce." Families and Work Institute, 2002. Executive Summary available from <http://www.familiesandwork.org/announce/2002NSCW.html/>.

Brown, T. "Sweatshops of the 1990s: Employees Who "Survived" Downsizing Are Working Harder and Longer These Days." *Management Review,* August 1996, 13–18.

Caproni, P.J. "Work/Life Balance: You Can't Get There from Here." *Journal of Applied Behavioral Science,* March 1997, 46–56.

Caudron, S. "On the Contrary, Job Stress Is in the Job Design." *Workforce,* September 1998, 21.

Cole, J. "Building Heart and Soul: Increased Employer Concern for Employees." *HR Focus,* September 1998, 9.

Herman, R.E., and J.L. Gioia. "Making Work Meaningful: Secrets of the Future-Focus Corporation." *Futurist,* December 1998, 24.

Jackson, Lee Anna. "When the Love is Gone: How to Reignite Passion for the Job." *Black Enterprise,* January 2005, 54

King, Julia. "Going Down Fast: Slashed Resources and Impossible Demands Have Caused IT Morale to Disintegrate." *Computerworld,* 8 November 2004, 51

Lau, R.S.M., and B.E. May. "A Win-Win Paradigm for Quality of Work Life and Business Performance." *Human Resource Development Quarterly* 9, no. 3 (1998): 211–226.

Manley, Will. "The Manley Arts: Labor, Work, and Happiness." *Booklist,* 1 November 2002, 454

McManus, Kevin. "Should I Stay or Should I Go?" *IIE (Institute of Industrial Engineers, Inc.) Solutions,* July 2002, 17.

Melymuka, K. "Frazzled? Let's Party." *Computerworld,* 16 June 1998, 6.

Sevice, R. "Get a Life: Importance of a Balanced Professional and Personal Life." *Business & Health,* July 1998, 6.

"Work/Life Balance a Key to Productivity." *Employee Benefit Plan Review,* September 1998, 30–31.

R

REACTIVE VS. PROACTIVE CHANGE

Workplace change occurs rapidly and often in many businesses. This change may take place in order to respond to a new opportunity or to avoid a threat to the company. Regardless of the reason, change can be difficult for all involved; managers and employees face new challenges with change, and managers must learn to ease the difficulty of the transition. One of the major issues associated with managing change is reactive versus proactive responses to change. This entry will discuss proactive and reactive responses to change, the major models of organizational change, and the responsibilities of change managers with special emphasis on the roles of transitional management teams and change agents.

PROACTIVE AND REACTIVE RESPONSES TO CHANGE

Proactive change involves actively attempting to make alterations to the work place and its practices. Companies that take a proactive approach to change are often trying to avoid a potential future threat or to capitalize on a potential future opportunity. Reactive change occurs when an organization makes changes in its practices after some threat or opportunity has already occurred. As an example of the difference, assume that a hotel executive learns about the increase in the number of Americans who want to travel with their pets. The hotel executive creates a plan to reserve certain rooms in many hotel locations for travelers with pets and to advertise this new amenity, even before travelers begin asking about such accommodations. This would be a proactive response to change because it was made in anticipation of customer demand. However, a reactive approach to change would occur if hotel executives had waited to enact such a change until many hotel managers had received repeated requests from guests to accommodate their pets and were denied rooms.

MODELS OF CHANGE

There are a number of theoretical models of change. Each attempts to describe the process through which organizations successfully alter their business practices, their organizational structure, or their organizational climate. The models of change which will be discusses in this section are summarized in Exhibit 1.

LEWIN'S THREE-STEP MODEL FOR CHANGE. In the late 1940s social psychologist Kurt Lewin developed a three-step model for implementing change based on the concept of force field analysis. Force field analysis addresses the driving and resisting forces in a change situation. Driving forces must outweigh resisting forces in a situation if change is to occur. Thus, managers must be willing to advocate change strongly in order to overcome resistance from employees.

There are three steps in Lewin's model. The first step is "unfreezing," which involves dismantling those

Exhibit 1

Models of Change

Model/Approach	Summary
Lewin's three-step model	Old activities must be unfrozen, a new concept introduced, then new activities must be frozen
Bullock and Batten's planned change	Exploration, planning, action, and integration
Kotter's eight steps	Establish a sense of urgency, form a powerful guiding coalition, create a vision, communicate the vision, empower others to act on the vision, plan for and create short-term wins, consolidate improvements and produce still more change, institutionalize new approaches
Beckhard and Harris's change formula	$C = [ABD] > X$, Where C = change, A = level of dissatisfaction with the status quo, B = Desirability of the proposed change or end state, D = practicality of the change, and X = cost of changing
Nadler and Tushman's congruence model	Organization is a system that draws inputs from internal and external sources and transforms them into outputs through four components: the work itself, the people, the informal organization, and the formal organization
Bridges's managing the transition	Transition, which differs from change, consists of three phases: ending, neutral zone, and new beginning
Carnall's change management model	Change depends on level of management skills in managing transitions effectively, dealing with organizational cultures, and managing organizational politics
Senge et al.'s systematic model	Start small; grow steadily; don't plan everything; expect challenges
Stacey and Shaw's complex responsive process	Change emerges naturally from communication and conflict; and mangers are a part of the whole environment

things that support or maintain the previous behavior. In an organization, these elements of the old could be the compensation system or the approach to performance management. In the second step, the organization "presents a new alternative." This means introducing a clear and appealing option for a new pattern of behavior. The final step in this model is "freezing" which requires that changed behavior be reinforced both formally and informally in the organization. It is in this step that managers can have a great amount of influence through their use of positive reinforcement.

Lewin's model does not explicitly state the notion that simply introducing change will result in the change being adopted or being sustained over the long run. If an attempt to create change in the organization is unsuccessful, it means that there is a problem in one of the three steps in the model.

BULLOCK AND BATTEN'S PHASES OF PLANNED CHANGE. R.J. Bullock and D. Batten derived their ideas from project management and they recommend using exploration, planning, action, and integration for planned change. Exploration occurs when managers confirm the need for change and secure resources needed for it. These resources may be physical or they may be mental, such as managers' expertise. The next step, planning, occurs when key decision makers and experts create a change plan that they then review and approve. Next, action occurs with enactment of the plan. There should be opportunities for

feedback during the action phase. Finally, integration begins when all actions in the change plan have taken place. Integration occurs when the changes have been aligned with the organization and there is some degree of formalization, such as through policies and procedures in the organization.

KOTTER'S EIGHT STEPS. John P. Kotter identified eight steps every organization must follow in order to reap long-term benefits from organizational change: establish a sense of urgency; form a powerful guiding coalition; create a vision and strategy; communicate the vision; empower others to act on the vision; generate short-term wins; consolidate improvements and produce still more change; and institutionalize the new approach (i.e., make it a part of the organizational culture).

The first step, establishing a sense of urgency, involves selling the need for change to managers and employees. Kotter recommends creating a "felt-need" for change in others. The second step is for managers to create a powerful group of people who can work together to enact change. Their power will be a driving force in encourages others to adopt change. Third, the organization must have a vision that will guide the entirety of the change effort, and this vision must be communicated repeatedly (step four)—as much as ten times as often as one would expect to.

Steps five through eight occur after the sense of urgency is created, and these steps are easier to delegate or decentralize. In step five, others in the organization are empowered to act on the vision. Managers should assist in this process by eliminating barriers such as old systems or structures. Step six asks managers to plan for and to create short-term wins. This means that small improvements should be recognized and celebrated publicly. In step seven, the current improvements are built upon with new projects and resources. Finally, in step eight, the new approaches should be institutionalized; that is, they should become a routine path to organizational success.

BECKHARD AND HARRIS'S CHANGE FORMULA. The change formula is a mathematical representation of the change process (see Exhibit 1). The basic notion is that, for change to occur, the costs of change (X) must be outweighed by dissatisfaction with the status quo (A), the desirability of the proposed change (B), and the practicality of the change (D). There will be resistance to change if people are not dissatisfied with the current state of the organization (A), or if the changes are not seen as an improvement (B), if the change cannot be done in a feasible way (D), or the cost is far too high (X).

This formula can also be conceptualized as $(A \times B \times D) > X$. The multiplicative nature of this formula indicates that if any variable is zero or near zero, resistance to change will not be overcome. In other words, the variables of A, B, and D do not compensate for one another, and when one is very low, the cost of change is likely to be too high.

NADLER AND TUSHMAN'S CONGRUENCE MODEL. Nadler and Tushman's model presents the dynamics of what occurs in an organization when we try to change it. The foundation of this model is that of the organization as an open system, in which organizational subsystems are influence by the external environment. The organizational system draws inputs from internal and external sources—such as the organization's own strategy, its resources, and its environment—and transforms them into outputs, such as behavior and performance. This transformation from inputs to outputs occurs through four organizational elements: the work, the people, and the formal and informal organization. The work involves the daily activities carried out by individuals in the organization. The skills and capabilities of the people involved in the organization are critical. The formal organization is characterized by its structure, its standard procedures, and its policies. The informal organization encompasses things such as norms, values, and political behavior.

In this model, effective change occurs when all four components (work, people, formal, and informal organization) are managed, because they are all interrelated. A change in the work procedures themselves may not be effective if the people do not have the capabilities to engage in the new practices. A change to the formal organization may not be effective if the beliefs and values of people (i.e., the informal organization) do not support it. If there is a lack of congruence among these four elements, then there is resistance to change. Furthermore, there may be control issues in which there is confusion over who regulates the new structures and processes. Finally, power problems may occur as managers and employees feel threatened that their current power may be removed by the change.

WILLIAM BRIDGES'S MANAGING THE TRANSITION. William Bridges distinguished planned change from transition. He believes that transition is more complex because it requires abandoning old practices and adopting new behaviors or ways of thinking, whereas planned change is about changing physical locations or organizational structures. Bridges believes that transition often lags behind planned change because it is more complex and more difficult to achieve. Because it is psychological, it is harder to manage.

Bridges describes three phases of transition: ending, neutral zone, and new beginning. Ending is similar to Lewin's concept of unfreezing in that you must end a current situation before you can begin something new. So, in this phase, old structures, practices, and behaviors must be stopped. Ideally, this ending can be commemorated or marked in some way. In the second phase, the neutral zone, the old practices have been stopped, but new ones have not yet been adopted. In this phase, many employees will feel disoriented and anxious; nevertheless, it may be a time in which creativity rises. Finally, new beginnings are not planned and predicted, but must evolve as organizational members psychologically adjust to transition. Managers can encourage, support, and reinforce these new beginnings. Bridges recommends that four key elements be communicated to people during a new beginning: the purpose behind the change; a picture of how the organization will be after the change; a step-by-step plan to get to that stage; and the part they can play in that outcome.

CARNALL'S CHANGE MANAGEMENT MODEL. Carnall's view of change is focused on managers and the skills they can use to manage change. Carnall describes three skills that must be present at all levels of management: (1) managing transitions effectively; (2) dealing with organizational cultures; and (3) managing organizational politics. Managing transitions involves helping employees learn as they change and supporting a culture of openness and risk-taking. Managing organizational cultures involves creating a "more adaptable culture." This is an organizational culture in which people are more open, there is greater information flow, and perhaps greater autonomy. Finally, to manage organizational politics, the manager should recognize and understand different organizational groups and their political agendas. The manager should be able to build coalitions and control the agenda through his or her political skill.

SENGE'S SYSTEMIC MODEL. Senge and colleagues encourage managers to think like biologists when approaching organizational change. That is, to better understand how organizations react to change, one should view them as systems bound by many interrelated actions that may affect each other over a long period of time. To enact change, Senge et al recommend that managers start small, grow steadily, do not plan the whole thing, and expect challenges. Furthermore, Senge et al offer a number of issues related to the challenges of first initiating change, then sustaining that change, and finally redesigning and rethinking change.

CHANGE MANAGERS

In both proactive and reactive responses to change and in every model of change, one element remains the same: the need for change managers. There are different types of change managers and their roles encompass a variety of duties. Managers may have responsibility for change that is not ever formally dictated or outlined, or a person or group may be specifically chosen to enact or facilitate change. Described below are two formal ways in which change managers can be identified: transition management teams and change agents. Some responsibilities of change managers are then described.

TRANSITION MANAGEMENT TEAMS. In some organizations that are experiencing change, a specific group of managers is chosen to coordinate change throughout an organization. This transition management team typically consists of eight to twelve people whose full-time responsibilities are to manage and facilitate the change process in the organization. Transition management teams are responsible not only for the structural and procedural changes that occur, but also for managing emotions and resistance to change. These teams typically report to the chief executive officer of the company on a regular basis.

Transition management teams do the day-to-day work involved in change management, and they are not simply another layer of management between top management and line employees. Furthermore, they are not the planning committee; these teams do not develop the plans for the change, they only facilitate the change that is being enacted. Neither are they responsible for determining when and where change is needed, or how it will be brought about. Instead, they manage changes that have been identified and implemented by upper management. Finally, these teams are not permanent. They exist only while the organization is in flux, and they are dissolved once the company has successfully changed.

CHANGE AGENTS. A change agent is one person who is formally in charge of guiding a change effort. The change agent is typically a part of organizational development, which is a set of planned change interventions intended to improve a company's long-term performance and survival. A change agent may be appointed from within the ranks of current company managers, or the agent may be an outside consultant who is brought in during the period of change. Unlike the transition management team, which only facilitates a change that has been identified and planned by others, the change agent is involved in all steps of organizational change. The agent helps to clarify problems, gather relevant information, assist managers in creating a plan, evaluate the plan's effectiveness, and implement the plan. After change has been successfully enacted, the change agent either returns to his or her normal duties (if this person is from within the organization), or ends his or her work with the company (if this person is a consultant).

There are advantages and disadvantages to choosing either an organizational member or an outside consultant to be a change agent. Outside consultants can be more costly and there is a greater risk for trade secrets to be leaked. Additionally, the consultant is unlikely to have the knowledge of the organization that an employee has, nor is this person likely to be trusted by others in the organization, as they would trust one of their own organizational members. However, consultants do have a more unbiased view of the organization and its problems. They may also bring more innovative or creative ideas to the company. Finally, they may be used as a scapegoat when change is implemented. That is, the negative emotions of organizational members may be directed towards the outsider rather than at the company's management, which may make for a smoother transition during the change process.

RESPONSIBILITIES OF CHANGE MANAGERS. Change managers are responsible for garnering support for change and overcoming resistance to change. There are ten techniques that change managers can use to accomplish this:

1. Plan well. Appropriate time and effort must go into planning change before implementation begins.

2. Allow for discussion and negotiation. Employees must have some input into the changes. This two-way communication can help reduce employee concerns.

3. Allow for participation. If employees participate in changes that affect them, they are more likely to support those changes.

4. Emphasize the financial benefits. If employees can earn higher compensation through organizational change, telling them about this possibility will help to increase support for the change.

5. Avoid too much change. Employees can only handle a certain amount of change before there are negative repercussions from stress, so changes should be introduced slowly and over time.

6. Gain political support. For change to be successful, certain key employees (those with informal power in the organization) must support it.

7. Let employees see successful change. Employees will be more willing to support change if they see that it has worked successfully in other companies or other areas of their company.

8. Reduce uncertainty. Uncertainty about the change effort can cause negative emotions and actions, and any information that change managers can give to reduce uncertainty can reduce resistance to change.

9. Ask questions to involve workers. Change managers should ask workers questions that move them toward a goal or objective or that reinforce positive accomplishments.

10. Build strong working relationships. Better working relationships in general will aid in change management; trust and mutual respect are critical elements of good working relationships.

Managing change can be a reactive or a proactive process, and there are a number of different models of organizational change. Each model emphasizes different approaches to understanding and managing change. In many of these models, the role of the change manager is emphasized. The change manager may be a part of a transitional management team or may be a change agent. This person facilitates the changes to the organization and is often a critical element in the success or failure of the change.

SEE ALSO: Managing Change; Organizational Development; Trends in Organizational Change

Marcia J. Simmering

FURTHER READING:

Beckhard, R.F., and R.T. Harris. *Organizational Transitions: Managing Complex Change.* Reading, MA: Addison-Wesley, 1987.

Bridges, W. *Managing Transitions.* Reading, MA: Perseus, 1991.

Bridges, W., and S. Mitchell. "Leading Transition: A New Model for Change." In *On Leading Change.* F. Hesselbein and R. Johnston, eds. New York: Jossey-Bass, 2002.

Bullock, R.J., and D. Batten. "It's Just a Phase We're Going Through." *Group and Organizational Studies* 10 (1985): 383–412.

Cameron, Esther, and Mike Green. *Making Sense of Change Management: A Complete Guide to the Models, Tools, & Techniques of Organizational Change.* Sterling, VA: Kogan Page, 2004.

Carnall, C.A. *Managing Change in Organizations.* London: Prentice Hall, 1990.

DuBrin, Andrew J. *Essentials of Management.* 7th ed. Cincinnati: Thomson South-Western, 2004.

Kotter, John P. *Leading Change.* Boston: Harvard Business School Press, 1996.

Lewin, Kurt. *Field Theory in Social Science.* New York: Harper and Row, 1951.

Luecke, Richard. *Managing Change and Transition.* Boston: Harvard Business School Press, 2003.

Nadler, David, Michael L. Tushman, and Mark B. Nadler. *Competing by Design: The Power of Organizational Architecture.* New York: Oxford University Press, 1997.

Ristino, Robert J. *The Agile Manager's Guide to Managing Change.* Bristol, VT: Velocity Business Publishing, 2000.

Senge, Peter. *The Fifth Discipline.* London: Century Business, 1993.

Senge, Peter M., et al. *The Dance of Change: The Challenges to Sustaining Momentum in Learning Organizations.* New York: Doubleday, 1999.

Sims, Ronald R. *Changing the Way We Manage Change.* Westport, CT: Praeger, 2002.

Stacey, Ralph D. *Strategic Management and Organisational Dynamics: The Challenge of Complexity.* London: Pitman Publishing, 1993.

———. *Complex Responsive Processes in Organizations: Learning and Knowledge Creation.* London: Routledge, 2001.

Williams, Chuck. *Management.* 3rd ed. Mason, Ohio: Thomson/South-Western, 2005.

REINFORCEMENT THEORY

Reinforcement theory is the process of shaping behavior by controlling the consequences of the behavior. In reinforcement theory a combination of rewards and/or punishments is used to reinforce desired behavior or extinguish unwanted behavior. Any behavior that elicits a consequence is called *operant behavior,* because the individual operates on his or her environment. Reinforcement theory concentrates on the relationship between the operant behavior and the associated consequences, and is sometimes referred to as operant conditioning.

BACKGROUND AND DEVELOPMENT OF REINFORCEMENT THEORY

Behavioral theories of learning and motivation focus on the effect that the consequences of past behavior have on future behavior. This is in contrast to classical conditioning, which focuses on responses that are triggered by stimuli in an almost automatic fashion. Reinforcement theory suggests that individuals can choose from several responses to a given stimulus, and that individuals will generally select the response that has been associated with positive outcomes in the past. E.L. Thorndike articulated this idea in 1911, in what has come to be known as the *law of effect*. The law of effect basically states that, all other things being equal, responses to stimuli that are followed by satisfaction will be strengthened, but responses that are followed by discomfort will be weakened.

B.F. Skinner was a key contributor to the development of modern ideas about reinforcement theory. Skinner argued that the internal needs and drives of individuals can be ignored because people learn to exhibit certain behaviors based on what happens to them as a result of their behavior. This school of thought has been termed the behaviorist, or radical behaviorist, school.

REINFORCEMENT, PUNISHMENT, AND EXTINCTION

The most important principle of reinforcement theory is, of course, reinforcement. Generally speaking, there are two types of reinforcement: positive and negative. Positive reinforcement results when the occurrence of a valued behavioral consequence has the effect of strengthening the probability of the behavior being repeated. The specific behavioral consequence is called a reinforcer. An example of positive reinforcement might be a salesperson that exerts extra effort to meet a sales quota (behavior) and is then rewarded with a bonus (positive reinforcer). The administration of the positive reinforcer should make it more likely that the salesperson will continue to exert the necessary effort in the future.

Negative reinforcement results when an undesirable behavioral consequence is withheld, with the effect of strengthening the probability of the behavior being repeated. Negative reinforcement is often confused with punishment, but they are not the same. Punishment attempts to decrease the probability of specific behaviors; negative reinforcement attempts to

increase desired behavior. Thus, both positive and negative reinforcement have the effect of increasing the probability that a particular behavior will be learned and repeated. An example of negative reinforcement might be a salesperson that exerts effort to increase sales in his or her sales territory (behavior), which is followed by a decision not to reassign the salesperson to an undesirable sales route (negative reinforcer). The administration of the negative reinforcer should make it more likely that the salesperson will continue to exert the necessary effort in the future.

As mentioned above, punishment attempts to decrease the probability of specific behaviors being exhibited. Punishment is the administration of an undesirable behavioral consequence in order to reduce the occurrence of the unwanted behavior. Punishment is one of the more commonly used reinforcement-theory strategies, but many learning experts suggest that it should be used only if positive and negative reinforcement cannot be used or have previously failed, because of the potentially negative side effects of punishment. An example of punishment might be demoting an employee who does not meet performance goals or suspending an employee without pay for violating work rules.

Extinction is similar to punishment in that its purpose is to reduce unwanted behavior. The process of extinction begins when a valued behavioral consequence is withheld in order to decrease the probability that a learned behavior will continue. Over time, this is likely to result in the ceasing of that behavior. Extinction may alternately serve to reduce a wanted behavior, such as when a positive reinforcer is no longer offered when a desirable behavior occurs. For example, if an employee is continually praised for the promptness in which he completes his work for several months, but receives no praise in subsequent months for such behavior, his desirable behaviors may diminish. Thus, to avoid unwanted extinction, managers may have to continue to offer positive behavioral consequences.

SCHEDULES OF REINFORCEMENT

The timing of the behavioral consequences that follow a given behavior is called the reinforcement schedule. Basically, there are two broad types of reinforcement schedules: continuous and intermittent. If a behavior is reinforced each time it occurs, it is called continuous reinforcement. Research suggests that continuous reinforcement is the fastest way to establish new behaviors or to eliminate undesired behaviors. However, this type of reinforcement is generally not practical in an organizational setting. Therefore, intermittent schedules are usually employed. Intermittent reinforcement means that each instance of a desired behavior is not reinforced. There are at least four types of intermittent reinforcement schedules: fixed interval, fixed ratio, variable interval, and variable ratio.

Fixed interval schedules of reinforcement occur when desired behaviors are reinforced after set periods of time. The simplest example of a fixed interval schedule is a weekly paycheck. A fixed interval schedule of reinforcement does not appear to be a particularly strong way to elicit desired behavior, and behavior learned in this way may be subject to rapid extinction. The fixed ratio schedule of reinforcement applies the reinforcer after a set number of occurrences of the desired behaviors. One organizational example of this schedule is a sales commission based on number of units sold. Like the fixed interval schedule, the fixed ratio schedule may not produce consistent, long-lasting, behavioral change.

Variable interval reinforcement schedules are employed when desired behaviors are reinforced after varying periods of time. Examples of variable interval schedules would be special recognition for successful performance and promotions to higher-level positions. This reinforcement schedule appears to elicit desired behavioral change that is resistant to extinction.

Finally, the variable ratio reinforcement schedule applies the reinforcer after a number of desired behaviors have occurred, with the number changing from situation to situation. The most common example of this reinforcement schedule is the slot machine in a casino, in which a different and unknown number of desired behaviors (i.e., feeding a quarter into the machine) is required before the reward (i.e., a jackpot) is realized. Organizational examples of variable ratio schedules are bonuses or special awards that are applied after varying numbers of desired behaviors occur. Variable ratio schedules appear to produce desired behavioral change that is consistent and very resistant to extinction.

REINFORCEMENT THEORY APPLIED TO ORGANIZATIONAL SETTINGS

Probably the best-known application of the principles of reinforcement theory to organizational settings is called behavioral modification, or behavioral contingency management. Typically, a behavioral modification program consists of four steps:

1. Specifying the desired behavior as objectively as possible.

2. Measuring the current incidence of desired behavior.

3. Providing behavioral consequences that reinforce desired behavior.

4. Determining the effectiveness of the program by systematically assessing behavioral change.

Reinforcement theory is an important explanation of how people learn behavior. It is often applied to organizational settings in the context of a behavioral modification program. Although the assumptions of reinforcement theory are often criticized, its principles continue to offer important insights into individual learning and motivation.

SEE ALSO: Leadership Styles and Bases of Power; Motivation and Motivation Theory; Operant Conditioning

Tim Barnett
Revised by Marcia Simmering

FURTHER READING:

Ivancevich, John M., Robert Konopaske, and Michael T. Matteson. *Organizational Behavior and Management.* 7th ed. Boston: Irwin/McGraw-Hill, 2004.

Porter, Lyman W., Gregory Bigley, and Richard M. Steers. *Motivation and Work Behavior.* 7th ed. New York: McGraw-Hill/Irwin, 2002.

Skinner, B.F. *Science and Human Behavior.* New York: Macmillan, 1953.

Thorndike, E.L. *Animal Intelligence: Experimental Studies.* New York: Macmillan, 1911.

RESEARCH METHODS AND PROCESSES

In any organization, managers at all levels need accurate and timely information for managerial decision making. Whether the decisions made are at technical, tactical, or strategic levels, good, accurate, and timely information always leads to a better decision. Gathering of information is done through a sound and scientific research process. Each year organizations spend enormous amounts of money for research and development in order to maintain their competitive edge. Accurate information obtained through research leads to enormous benefits.

APPLIED VERSUS PURE RESEARCH

Research can be defined as scientifically and methodically delving into the unknown in order to provide information for solving problems. The heart of this definition is the concept of problem solving. Both applied and pure (also known as basic) research attempt to solve problems. In applied research, the researcher attempts to solve a known problem and find answers to specific questions. In other words, the emphasis of applied research is on practical problem solving. For instance, when a paper recycling company wants to determine whether or not their recycled papers meet the required specification as to the thickness of the paper across the roll, they might design a systematic procedure for answering this specific question. The research in such a situation represents applied research. Another example of applied research might be that of prediction. As an example, consider a trucking company that is interested in predicting the tonnage of material shipped in the next quarter. The practical problem is predicting the tonnage and determining which variables are good predictors of tonnage for the next quarter.

Applied research can help make a decision about the following, including a variety of other business and management decisions:

- pricing a new product

- where to locate a new retail store

- how many employees to hire

- how many products to offer

- what to pay employees

Applied research can be used to collect information about markets, competitors, and customers. For example, research can help pinpoint the optimal business location and the size of markets. It can also be used to monitor competitive actions. Customer research determines customer loyalty, customer satisfaction, and customer preferences.

On the other hand, pure, or basic, research does not necessarily try to answer specific questions or solve specific problems. Pure or basic research is done in order to expand knowledge and probe into the unknown. For example, when a researcher is interested in determining how employee demographics and tenure on the job relate to preference for flexible work schedules may represent pure research. Both pure and applied research deals with problem definition and problem solving. Most basic research is conducted by professors in academic institutions (i.e. colleges and universities), by the government, or by consulting firms. Few business organizations will engage in pure research related to business problems. However, understanding the process and methods used for both applied and basic research are important to interpreting research results.

RESEARCH PROCESS

Any research involves several chronological steps, but that does not mean each step must be completed before the next step is undertaken. Furthermore, the process of research is dynamic and the process may change as the research progresses. The steps involved in most research endeavors are shown in Figure 1.

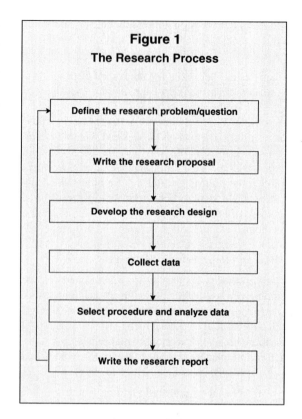

Figure 1
The Research Process

- Define the research problem/question
- Write the research proposal
- Develop the research design
- Collect data
- Select procedure and analyze data
- Write the research report

THE RESEARCH QUESTION

Managers' needs for information are the primary source of problem definition and the research question. Managers need information to make educated decisions arising from unanticipated as well as planned changes. As such, managers must select between different alternatives and thus require information about the organization and its environment. The question to be answered or the problem to be solved must first be clearly defined. Questions to be answered could be very specific or extremely broad. The more specific the questions, the easier it will be to answer the research questions. There might be hypotheses that could be tested scientifically. Once the questions to be answered are clearly defined then the value of the research must be assessed. Clearly, if the costs of performing the research project exceed the value that the research will provide, then the project should not be continued.

THE RESEARCH PROPOSAL

Research endeavors require a proposal that explains the problem to be address and the procedure by which the questions will be answered. The researcher's proposal tells the managers what they should expect from the research. It is a contract between the managers and the researcher. For instance, if a company wants to know the degree to which its new incentive program is effective in improving employee performance, then the consultant or employee conducting the research will create a proposal that indicates to that company how the question will be addressed and what specific information the company will have at the end of the research process. The proposal may indicate, for example, that the research will indicate the level of satisfaction of employees with the new incentive plan, the increased firm performance with the plan, and the individual increases in performance (as measured by managers) with the incentive plan. The purpose of the research proposal is to effectively guide the researchers in their development of the research design and data collection to answer the specific research questions.

RESEARCH DESIGN

Once the proposal is approved, the researcher has a foundation for development of the research design. The plan for conducting the research is the research design. There are two general forms of research design, namely non-experimental (ex-post-facto) and experimental. In a non-experimental design, the researcher does not control or alter any of the independent variables. The researcher merely studies existing situations, variables, and the interrelation among variables and reports the results of his or her findings. The two major non-experimental designs are field studies and surveys. Field studies combine literature review and possibly analysis of some case studies. For example, if one is interested in determining the effectiveness of total quality management (TQM), there will be a thorough literature search on the topic as well as a study of the firms that have applied TQM and have been successful. A literature review means that a researcher identifies previous writings and research on a topic, summarizes the current knowledge on the topic, and assesses the value of that prior research on the current problem. On the other hand, surveys deal with the formulation of a questionnaire (survey instrument) by which one can measure the magnitude of the desired variables as well as the interrelation among the variables. Non-experimental designs are primarily exploratory in nature and provide descriptive measures and can also be used for predictive purposes.

There are two broad categories of experimental designs: field and laboratory. In both field experiments and laboratory experiments, the researcher controls and may alter and introduce some variables in order to determine the effect of a given variable. Field experiments are done in a natural setting, whereas laboratory experiments are undertaken in a simulated setting. Studies on the effectiveness of different configurations of teams and their level of effectiveness can be undertaken in both field and office settings. In an office setting, a researcher might organize workplace teams, using different criteria to establish each, then measure the success of their group interactions and their productivity on real work tasks. This would be a natural setting, except for the way in which teams were organized. Team composition could also be studied in a laboratory in which the researchers had complete control over more variables. To study team effectiveness in a laboratory setting, individuals would be placed in teams using different criteria, then asked to perform a series of tasks specially designed to measure team interactions and performance. This laboratory setting would allow the researcher more control, because the types of individuals involved could be chosen, rather than using only the employees available in a field setting; by designing tasks specific to the study, rather than using existing work tasks; and by having more ability to watch and measure team performance without hindering organizational performance.

DATA COLLECTION

Data collection is the process of gathering the specific information used to answer the research questions. There are a number of issues associated with data collection, including the use of primary or secondary data, survey design, sampling, survey administration, and increasing response rates.

PRIMARY DATA AND SECONDARY DATA. Data can be primary or secondary, and whether one or both are used, and which is used, depends largely on the research question and the availability of these data sources. Secondary data refer to data gathered by others or from other studies. Secondary data is generally less costly and less time consuming than gathering primary data, typically is accumulated before primary data is gathered, and may even help determine the course by which primary data is pursued. An example of secondary data is if a company uses data from the U.S. Census or data collected for another organizational activity (e.g., performance information for individuals from the company's annual performance appraisal). While secondary data can be used for background information about specific research, it may also answer some specific research questions. However, because secondary data was collected for another purpose, it may not adequately address the new research question. In today's world of rapidly growing information technologies, secondary data are available from numerous sources. A researcher should explore the existing data before starting the research process, since there are datasets for many different types of information currently available. There are abundant data available in literature, company records, government publications, trade associations, and through the Internet.

Primary data is that which is collected by the researcher to address the current research question. Types of primary data include subject demographics, lifestyle characteristics, attitudes, knowledge, intentions, motivations, and behavior. Demographic data includes statistics regarding populations, such as age, sex, income, level of education, and so forth. Lifestyle characteristics describe a respondent's activities, interests, and opinions. Attitudes refer to views and opinions about things, events, or ideas. Knowledge is the degree to which respondents are aware of these things, events, or ideas. Intentions generally refer to a respondent's planned future behavior. Motivations describe the reasons behind a respondent's behavior. Behavior is related to what respondents do.

Primary data can be collected in the field or the laboratory through communication and observation. Communication generally requires the direct questioning of respondents via a paper-and-pencil survey (i.e., questionnaire) or telephone survey. Observation involves the direct recording of respondent behavior. Surveys are probably the most common design in business research. For instance, if one is interested in determining the success of TQM, a survey can be designed that encompasses questions regarding elements of success, strengths, weaknesses, and other questions dealing with TQM. Then the survey can be sent to companies that have been successful in implementing TQM. The survey results could shed light on many aspects of TQM.

SURVEY DESIGN. Survey design is of major importance, because is a survey is poorly designed, it will not provide the researchers with the data that addresses the research question. Survey questions, called items, must be properly chosen to in order to elicit appropriate respondent answers. The steps involved include determining the information that will be sought, the type of questionnaire, the method of administration, the content of individual questions, the form of response to each question, the wording of each question, the sequence of questions, the physical characteristics of the questionnaire, and, finally, pretesting the questionnaire.

Some items for certain areas of interest already exist. For instance, there are existing surveys that measure employees' satisfaction with pay and benefits. If survey items do not already exist in the published literature, the researchers must create their own items, based on their review of the existing literature and their own expertise. Often, a focus group of experts can also help to create items. For example, if a company wants to assess its employees' attitudes towards an intended change in work rules, the researcher may lead a focus group of several experienced company managers to capture all of the relevant ideas that need to be addressed by the survey. Before

the survey instrument is sent out, it must be tested for reliability and validity. Reliability refers to how consistently the instrument measures, and validity refers to whether the instrument is measuring.

One concern when designing a survey is how to word the items. One of the most popular ways to measure attitudes on a survey is by using the Likert scale. This method presents a series of statements to respondents for which they are asked to indicate the degree to which they agree with the statements. An example of a statement might be "The sales people are helpful." Respondents are asked to indicate the degree to which they agree with the statements by checking either SA (strongly agree), A (agree), N (neither agree nor disagree), D (disagree), or SD (strongly disagree). Respondents' answers would then be scored where SA = 5, A = 4, N = 3, D = 2, and SD = 1. A total score would be computed by average or summing scores on related items.

SAMPLING. When administering a questionnaire there are two options as to who should complete the survey. Option one is to give the questionnaire to everyone in the targeted population. This is called a census. However, a census is usually not practical or cost effective. For instance, you may not be able to survey every one of your customers from last year to determine levels of customer satisfaction with your products. Consequently, in order to save time and money, only a sample or subset of the target population receives the questionnaire.

When selecting individuals for a sample, either a probability approach or a nonprobability approach can be used. Probability samples are those where each element of the population has a known probability of being selected. A random sample, for example, is the case where each element has the same probability of being selected. There are some specific types of nonprobability samples: convenience samples, judgment samples, and quota samples. Convenience samples are chosen at the convenience of the researcher. For example, a researcher might distribute a survey to all customers who enter one retail store in a one-week period to determine their level of customer satisfaction with the company's products. This sample is rather easy to select, but it may not represent the full range of customers who have used that product. In a judgment sample, individuals are selected by the researcher because they are believed to represent the population under study. Quota samples attempt to make the sample representative of the population under study where quotas are set for specific groups of people, which are generally selected on the basis of demographic characteristics.

The chief advantage of a probability sample over a nonprobability sample is the ability to assess the reliability and the amount of sampling error in the results.

For example, if the goal were to estimate the annual household income for a given county, probability sampling would allow an accuracy assessment of the estimate. This could not be accomplished with a nonprobability sample.

SURVEY ADMINISTRATION. After the survey has been designed and its reliability and validity assessed, the company must decide the administration method that it will use. Each administration method has its own advantages and disadvantages in terms of cost, information control, sampling control, and administrative control. Information control refers to the possible variation in responses to questions. Sampling control is the ability to select cooperative respondents. Administrative control refers to factors affecting the efficiency of the survey, including timing, quality control, and standardization.

Personal interviews are generally the most expensive means of data collection. In a company, this would mean having researchers meet with employees one-on-one to ask them the survey questions and record their responses. One of the main advantages of the personal interview is the ability to ask any type of question, including an open-ended question, and to adapt to the respondent's answers. However, in addition to being expensive and time consuming, this method is not anonymous, and therefore respondents may be reluctant to answer questions that they feel are sensitive or invasive.

The mail questionnaire is usually the least expensive method of data collection. Besides cost savings, another advantage of the mail questionnaire is its wide distribution potential. However, mail questionnaires cannot control the speed of responses, and the researcher cannot explain ambiguous questions. Mail questionnaires are probably best utilized when asking personal or sensitive questions, particularly if the survey can be made anonymous. Questionnaires can be circulated using various methods, such as post, electronic mail, and fax.

The telephone interview is associated with relatively low cost and higher response rates, and is one of the fastest methods of data collection. While there are methods to address the problem, unlisted numbers make it more difficult to obtain representative samples. Establishing rapport is also more difficult in telephone interviewing than in the personal interview.

One survey administration method that is growing in popularity is the Internet survey, in which respondents answer items on a survey that is located on a web site. Newer, specialized software products are making it easier to conduct online surveys, even for those people with little to no computer programming skills. Studies indicate that Internet research can result in faster responses, lower costs, higher response rates, and better flexibility. Additionally, this method aids in data administration, since survey responses can be directly inserted into a data spreadsheet by the web survey software.

INCREASING RESPONSE RATES. One of the main concerns of survey research is the response rate, or the number of people who are asked to complete a survey who actually do. Nonresponse error is a source of bias because of the failure to get answers from some of the sample. "Not-at-homes" plague the telephone survey and uncooperative respondents affect telephone, mail, Internet, and personal interview surveys. While research results are mixed regarding effective means for increasing response rates, the following represent some ideas for increasing response rates:

- give respondents advance notice of the survey
- guarantee confidentiality or anonymity
- provide monetary incentives
- provide a postage-paid return envelope for mail surveys
- personalize outgoing envelopes

DATA ANALYSIS

Research provides data, and it is the task of the researcher to transform the collected data into useful information for management. The first step in data analysis is preparing the data by editing it for several factors, including:

- completeness—checking for any omissions
- legibility—making sure that handwriting is understandable so that answers will be coded correctly
- comprehensibility—making sure the answer is understandable
- consistency—checking for consistent answers from the respondent
- uniformity—checking to see that responses are recorded in the same manner

Once the data is edited it is ready for coding, which is determining how survey responses will be transformed into numerical data. The first step in coding is the development of a codebook. The codebook formalizes the coding process by listing answers and their accompanying codes. After the data is coded and entered into a data spreadsheet, statistical analyses can be performed to create useful information for the researchers. If there are hypotheses to be tested, the researcher is in a position to use the gathered data to test the hypotheses. Data analysis could be as simple as reporting descriptive statistics such as averages, measures of variability, and percentages, or if needed, advance statistical techniques could be applied.

RESEARCH REPORT

The research report can be as simple as a short report of a few pages giving the overall findings of the research, or it can be a long report with numerous parts. The degree of formality required by management dictates the type of report to prepare. Figure 2 presents the order of inclusion of the various parts of a long formal report.

Figure 2

Parts of a Complete Research Report

Research report parts

I. Prefatory section
   A. Title fly
   B. Title page
   C. Letter of authorization
   D. Letter of transmittal
   E. Table of contents
   F. Synopsis or executive summary

II. Introduction to the research
   A. Background comments
   B. Statement of the problem (research question)
   C. Objectives of the research

III. Methodology
   A. Research design
   B. Instrument used and data collection
   C. Data analysis and statistical procedures used
   D. Limitations of the study

IV. Findings

V. Summary, conclusions and recommendations

VI. Appendices

VII. Bibliography

PREFATORY SECTION. In this part of the report, first a title fly needs to be prepared. The title fly only includes the title of the report. The title should be carefully worded so it tells the reader exactly what the report is about. Following the title fly is the title page. The title page should include the title of the report, the name and the title of the recipient of the report, and the name and the title of the individual who prepared the report and the date. The letter that authorized the undertaking of the research project, followed by a letter of transmittal indicating the completion of the research report are the next items included in the report. Include a table of contents followed by an executive summary. The executive summary, summarizing the report's major findings, should be brief and to the point. This summary should briefly explain the conclusions.

INTRODUCTION TO THE RESEARCH. This section of the report provides a clear background and statement of the research question and provides information about the objectives of the research. Included in this section would be a literature review about previous studies with the same or similar problem. If there are hypotheses to be tested, population parameters to be estimated, theories to be considered, they will be incorporated into this section of the report

RESEARCH METHOD. This section will provide a detailed explanation of research design and will provide answers to many questions. What type of design was used? What instruments were used for the collection of data? Were there any subjects involved in the study? What did the subjects do? How was the sample selected? What kind of statistical or non-statistical techniques were used for data analysis? Finally, in this section of the report the limitations encountered in the study should be presented.

FINDINGS. This section is probably one of the most important parts of the research report. Provided in this section would be the results of the data analyses and explanation of all the findings. At this point, all the raw data have been analyzed and converted to meaningful information for management's use. This is the section where the original research question is answered.

SUMMARY, CONCLUSIONS, AND RECOMMENDATIONS. A concise yet precise summary of major findings will be included in this section, followed by any recommendations that the researcher considers important and meaningful.

APPENDICES AND BIBLIOGRAPHY. Statistical tests, large tables of information, copies of measurement instruments, and supporting documents should be included in the appendices. Finally, the report should end by providing a bibliography of all sources of information.

SEE ALSO: Hypothesis Testing; Statistics

Mo Ahmadi
Revised by Marcia J. Simmering

FURTHER READING:

Babbie, Earl R. *The Practice of Social Research.* 10th ed. Belmont, CA: Thomson/Wadswoth, 2004.

Cooper, Donald R., and Pamela S. Schindler. *Business Research Methods.* 8th ed. New York: McGraw-Hill, 2003.

Davis, Duane. *Business Research for Decision Making.* 6th ed. South-Western College Publishing, 2005.

Hoover, Kenneth R., and Todd Donovan. *The Elements of Social Scientific Thinking.* 8th ed. Belmont, CA: Thomson/Wadswoth, 2004.

Kerlinger, Fred N., and Howard B. Lee. *Foundations of Behavioral Research.* 4th ed. Fort Worth, TX: Harcourt College Publishers, 2000.

Pedhazur, Elazur, and Llora Pedhazur Schmelkin. *Measurement, Design, and Analysis.* Hillsdale, NJ: Lawrence Erlbaum Associates, 1991.

Salkind, Neil J. *Exploring Research*. 6th ed. Upper Saddle River, NJ: Prentice Hall, 2006.

Schwab, Donald P. *Research Methods for Organizational Studies*. Mahwah, NJ: Lawrence Erlbaum Associates, 1999.

RESUMES AND COVER LETTER TRENDS

Employment is the goal of applying for a position. The applicant has specific tools that should be used to achieve this desired goal. The standard tools in the application process include the cover letter and the resume, as well as, in some cases, a completed application form. To use these tools effectively the applicant must know their purpose, their structure and how to transmit them to the employer with the best possible chance of employment.

THE COVER LETTER

Writing the cover letter is a difficult task. It is like an introduction to who you are, what you are seeking, and why you are applying for the position. The cover letter should create an initial impression and communicate skills and abilities—the added value that the applicant will bring to the job. It should be persuasive, showing why you are the right candidate, highlighting key work experience and education from the resume, thus encouraging the employer to read the resume. In general, the cover letter has three or four paragraphs, but it is not stylised to the extent that all cover letters have the same format. The beginning paragraph identifies the position you are seeking and gives a general statement connecting the position with your experience and background. The second paragraph is open to your development of related skills, experiences, education, and personal traits that demonstrate why you are the best candidate for the opening. The third paragraph may continue this area, but it also may illustrate your advantages for the position with special traits, other experiences, or training that strengthen the match between the position listed and you as the most suitable candidate. The information and the style of conveying yourself on paper should lead to a favorable opinion of you as an applicant and a desire to review your resume. The closing paragraph offers information for contact, availability, and desire for further interaction.

The format and content of the cover letter will vary widely depending on the corporate culture. For example, a cover letter to a law firm will be conservative in nature while a letter to an advertising firm will be more creative or unusual. The applicant's name, address, and phone number should be at the top of each page. The cover letter should be addressed to a particular person in the company, or the salutation should be eliminated. Generally it should be brief, direct, preferably one page in length and have ample white space. If there is a strong interest in the job, then follow up with a hard copy of the cover letter and resume. Finally, the candidate should be sure to proof read the letter several times to eliminate grammar and spelling errors. Employers frequently eliminate a candidate due to a careless error in spelling or typing format. The envelope is important because it should be addressed directly to the person listed in the job announcement. If these initial pieces are in good form, the applicant can proceed to develop the resume and transmit these elements of the application process to the prospective employer. In some cases there may be an application form that must carefully be completed and included with the application. Even the most appropriate letter, resume, and completed application do not insure an interview or employment. However, follow up with the prospective employer may benefit the applicant.

INTRODUCTION TO RESUME CONCEPTS

In the professional application process, a resume serves to introduce and identify the applicants who apply for openings within an organization. Changes in the resume have occurred over time and the advent of electronic communication has brought new approaches to the process. Delineating the resume structure and function as well as the method of submission is important to today's job seeker. Clearly, there are elements, which are the same and new options open to the applicant such as presenting an online resume to a potential employer.

A resume is typically a one to three page summary of a person's skills, accomplishments, experiences, and education designed to help a person obtain a job. The resume may include a list of references and other data. It is the primary tool of the job search and may take several drafts to prepare effectively.

Before the resume is written, applicant should first identify skills and abilities as well as special needs relating to the work environment, salary, geographic location, and people environment. This will help the person develop a career objective and the types and locations of companies to which the person will apply. It will be helpful to list at least several skills that have been developed in the education, work, and internships, volunteer or extracurricular areas. These skills should be emphasized and any other relevant work talents should be included as well. A list of three great accomplishments and the personal qualities that helped reach the goals should be noted.

Individuals with a varied work history and people in some professions may require extended resumes. For example, college/university teaching, research and service requirements for faculty promotion and tenure means that faculty members applying for a position will submit resumes listing extensive publications and service involvement that may result in resumes in excess of five pages.

RESUME TYPE AND CONSTRUCTION

Resumes can be divided into two types: chronological and functional or skills resumes. The reverse chronological resume organizes the candidate's work and education experience with the most recent listed first. The reverse chronological resume is mostly preferred by employers and recruiters and is by far the most frequently used resume format. It is especially useful for individuals who have demonstrated continuous progress in their work history and are seeking a position of increased responsibilities.

The functional resume emphasizes transferable skills acquired through formal education and in non-related work experiences that would be applicable to the professional position being applied for. The employment history is generally minimized. This type of resume is suitable for the recent graduate with little relevant work experience, individuals with unexplained gaps of employment and others who have been job-hopping. With this type of resume, the applicant exhibits the relevant transferable skills and knowledge that he or she would bring to the position. Another approach is to combine a functional resume with a brief reverse chronological work history.

The information regarding the required skills and qualifications of occupations of interest is an extremely important step. This will help to decide if and how these requirements relate to one's own skills and needs. As the resume is organized, the applicant should keep in mind the specific needs of the employer. The candidate should consider what the employer seeks in a candidate and make it easy for the employer to pick out those skills by selecting appropriate categories—using underlining, boldfacing, or capitalizing, and presenting relevant experience and skill areas higher on the page. It will help to remember that you are selling yourself. Create a good first impression by highlighting skills and abilities appropriate to the position. The candidate should also use active language and articulate marketable skills acquired through one's experience or education.

The candidate should feel free to develop his or her own categories to highlight relevant special experiences and skills. For individuals with relatively little relevant work experience, it is frequently useful to separate professional experiences from other work experiences (e.g., part-time jobs, non-career work) by creating separate categories for these content areas. In this way, more attention can be given to relevant skills by putting them in categories closer to the top of the resume so they are read first. Several categories can be used as guidelines to assist in organizing a resume. In constructing a rough draft, the candidate should not be concerned with length. Categories can be omitted or added in later revisions. There is no absolutely correct way to organize a resume.

The resume should be consistent throughout. It should follow a standard pattern of spacing, formatting, and overall presentation. The candidate should normally present information in reverse chronological order within categories, listing education and work experiences starting with the most recent first. Grammar and spelling should be checked carefully (including looking for things that automatic spell-checking would miss) because misspellings and poorly constructed sentences communicate negative impressions about a candidate. Social security numbers, marital status, race, or date of birth can be excluded from the resume. The candidate should also ensure that the resume is neat and visually appealing. In general, unusual fonts and excess graphics on the resume are not considered professional. The candidate should choose high-quality paper in white, off-white, or other conservative colors and have the final version printed at high resolution (basic laser printer or better).

RESUME FORMAT

The candidate's name, address, telephone number and email are typically listed first in the resume. Candidates should present themselves with the name they use in their personal and business life; nicknames should be avoided. If the candidate has a campus address that does not apply during vacations or after graduation, the candidate should present both a current and a permanent address. Candidates should use their permanent home address, a post office box, or someone who will know where to contact them at all times. Also, phone numbers should always include area codes. If the candidate has an e-mail address, he or she might want to include that as well.

The objective is one of the most important parts of a resume and should not be overlooked. It informs potential employers that you are moving in a certain direction, relates your work preference, and serves as a focal point from which to review and analyse the resume. It should be brief, clearly stated, and consistent with the accomplishments and demonstrated skills as documented on the resume. If the candidate is considering more than one professional goal, the person should consider developing more than one resume, each presenting a different objective. The profile is an alternative to an objective statement. It gives the candidates the opportunity to present their strengths at the very beginning of the resume.

In writing the major areas of the resume, it is important to emphasize one's abilities and accomplishments more than past duties. The candidate may also want to indicate how well he or she has performed. This will help infuse personal qualities such as character and personality into the resume. The education category is particularly important if the candidate has not had a great deal of work experience. The highest level of education attained should be listed first. Candidates should include their degrees (A.S., B.S., B.A., etc.), major institutions attended, dates of graduation, minors or concentrations, and any special workshops, seminars, related coursework, or special projects. A G.P.A. of higher than a 3.0 (either overall or in major) should also be noted here.

Many young applicants may have limited paid work experience, but have been involved in volunteer work, internships, practicums, or student-teaching work experiences. The important point to the employer is what the candidate's skills are and what the candidate can do on the job. This type of candidate may want to use a skills or functional format. The candidate should include the title of the position, the name of the organization, location of work, and dates. The work responsibilities should be described with an emphasis on achievements using action words to communicate the candidate's skills. The most important and related responsibilities should be listed first. Candidates should identify the most relevant work experiences and link them to the current position. They should be brief with the irrelevant experiences or not list the information. It is sometimes useful to divide the work experience into two categories, relevant experience and other experience.

The additional information category is useful for displaying information that doesn't fit into any other category. Although personal interests, computer knowledge, and activities can be separate categories, especially if they are very strong, they can be listed here as well. Language proficiency, or any other relevant information can be placed here. A personal interest category can sometimes be used to evaluate candidate's suitability to a geographic area or to understand their personality type. Social or civic activities, health and fitness or sports activities, or hobbies that indicate how the candidate spends leisure time could be included. If using computers is a necessary skill for the job, the candidate's knowledge should be emphasized. Activities, honors, and leadership are also important categories to include. If the activities involve work responsibility, note it in some detail. The employer is interested in the skills the candidate has developed whether through volunteer or paid experiences. Recognition and demonstration of leadership roles are valuable and should be accentuated.

REFERENCES

The candidate should ask individuals if they would be willing to be listed as references, prior to mentioning their names to prospective employers. Names of individuals are not usually listed on the resume unless there is space available at the end, but a typed list of three references should be prepared to provide at the interview. This list should include name, employer, title, address, and business email and phone numbers. *References furnished upon request* may also be stated at the bottom of the resume.

THE RESUME IN THE ELECTRONIC ERA

In the last several years transmittal of the resume and cover letter has changed substantially due to the increased use of the Internet. (Some companies still prefer regular mail to e-mail.) Due to ease of use in a 24/7 environment, rapid response time, and low expense, recruiters and job seekers are increasingly using this mode of transmittal. In the past, the cover letter and resume were mailed to the prospective employer, but more and more mega and niche job boards as well as corporate websites are being used. With few exceptions, the email cover letter and resume will remain very similar to the cover letter and resume that was mailed through the post office.

In the online environment the applicant can incorporate the cover letter as an attachment or as part of the e-mail. The salutation, body and closing of the cover letter should be formatted in the same manner as if it were being sent through the mail. Excessive formatting and the use of HTML should be avoided if the cover letter is part of the e-mail. This could result in line breaks, tabs and other formatting changes. Instead, it is wiser to use plain text or rich text format (rtf) to avoid these issues. The applicant should indicate the name and the position being applied for in the email subject line. Today the point of the resume has become more about getting the interview rather than providing a job history. Since Human Resource (HR) Departments may be reviewing hundreds of resumes for a given position, the traditional objective statement at the beginning of a resume is being replaced by an attention getting headline relating the applicant to the position to entice the HR personnel to continue reading the application.

Today a large majority of all resumes and cover letters are transmitted via the Internet utilizing several formats with various capabilities. It is now described as an E-resume, electronic resume or online resume. Due to the intended needs as well as relative advantages and disadvantages, there are a number of formats used to transmit the documents, including plain text, rich text file, Microsoft Word, image scanned PDF files, web sites, and Macromedia Flash. The list of options for transmitting a resume will change with the introduction of new technologies/methodologies such as web logs or *blogs.*

The plain text file incorporated into an e-mail message is the simplest method of electronically submitting a resume. (However, formatting capabilities are not available unless rich text formatting is used.) The email recipient can then easily migrate plain text or rich text into Microsoft Word or Word Perfect. Attaching a Word file is widely used for transmitting a resume since the applicant can email the actual formatted resume with the ability to select a wide range of formatting capabilities. However, some organizations are hesitant to open the attached document because of a possible virus. Adobe Acrobat provides a software program to scan the document into a PDF format so that the document will remain unchanged. The employer can then view the document using a free Adobe program.

Web portfolios provide the most flexibility of all the options. It can combine the print and hyperlinks as well as stills, sound, and animation through the use of Macromedia Flash. In other words, it can be equivalent to a small website that can display graphs, charts, project activities, and work samples to showcase the applicant's capabilities. Artists, teachers, architects, and other professionals requiring a multimedia format can use it. Macromedia Flash is rapidly becoming the accepted standard for integrating various mediums in a small file size that leads to a high speed of transfer. However, the software requires a tech savvy user to create the multimedia hyper-linked portfolio or Flash application and requires some skill to access it. The latest Internet innovation has been the use of weblogs or web diaries that, to date, have seen limited use in the application process. The weblog provides the employer with information about the applicants' work experiences, business ideas, thoughts, and testimonials. Recently, sales and marketing personnel have been successfully incorporated web blogs into their resumes.

POSTING RESUMES TO AN ONLINE DATABANK

The applicant has a number of options when looking for a position. The resume can be submitted to the company website doing the hiring or posted on massive job boards such as Monster (http://www.monster.com) or Workopolis (http://www.workopolis.com). Due to identity theft on some job banks, individual job seekers submit resumes directly to individual corporate websites. There are a few safety guidelines that should be adhered to when posting your resume to searchable databases: omit personal information such as your social security number; never pay a fee up front for use of a resume bank;

never agree to a pre-screening background check online; and be wary of companies located outside the United States. In addition the applicant should use standard fonts such as *Times New Roman*, *Helvetica*, or *Arial*; avoid elaborate stylising and graphics; always maintain a professional e-mail address; and do not password protect your attached resume document.

Online resumes and job applications are exploding on the Internet. In 2002, there were 36 million resumes transmitted online. This online traffic results from applicants to individual corporate websites; to the three mega job board online portals such as Monster, HotJobs (http://hotjobs.yahoo.com) and CareerBuilder (http://www.careerbuilder.com/) and niche job boards such as association and college alumni sites; to federal government positions via the U. S. Office of Personnel Management's USA Jobs website (which posted 600,000 new online resumes and logged more than 66 million visits in the 9 months prior to June 2004) which can also post applicants of future jobs; to the 40,000 employment-related sites such as CA Source (http://www.casource.com) for chartered accountants. Gerry Crispin, co-author of *CareerXRoads,* estimates that in 15 percent of new hires are coming from the fast growing niche boards. In addition to identifying key websites for certain job openings, valuable information can be gleaned from e-networking through profession-related discussion boards, listservs, and instant messaging, as well as researching companies online.

Online resume banks will either be form-based or allow the applicant to paste the resume into a plain-text field. When the applicant enters the resume in either of these formats, it is critical that the applicant use words from the job posting as well as variations of the term in the resume. For example, if the applicant is a personnel officer, then personnel and human resources should both be used. If the applicant is an administrator, then use director, administrator or supervisor also. Because of the large number of applications, employers are now using applicant-tracking systems (ATS) to screen applications for identifying the top applicants for a job. Therefore, it can be important for the applicant to use key words from the job description and his or her qualifications to ensure that the applicant tracking system retrieves the application.

In the highly competitive environment of the workplace, the resume and the cover letter are the first steps to gaining an interview and ultimately the position. Being aware of effective cover letters and resume construction is highly important to all job seekers. Knowing the impact of the electronic medium is essential because it shows that an applicant is knowledgeable of the web and its impact on job advertising and applications. Evaluators of applications are seeking the most qualified and capable person for their organization. A well-developed resume and cover letter shows a savvy candidate with the potential to contribute to the organization of interest.

SEE ALSO: Employee Recruitment Planning; Employee Screening and Selection; Human Resource Management

Bill Prince and Nancy Ryan Prince

FURTHER READING:

Brinkmeyer, Jessalyn. "Beyond the Resume: Use Weblogs to Differentiate Yourself in the Eyes of the Recruiters." *Sales and Marketing Management,* March 2005, 47.

Buck, Joseph. "Writing Winning Resumes." *NAPM Insights,* December 1995, 9.

"CA Source Online Database a Hit with CAs and Employers." *CA Magazine,* October 2002.

Casalino, Christie. "PR Technique: Recruitment—Creating a First Impression that Lasts." *PR Week,* 14 February 2005.

Chyna Julie T. "Crafting an Electronic Resume." *Healthcare Executive,* November/December 2003.

Crispin, Gerry, and Mark Mehler. *CareerXRoads.* 8th ed. Kendall Park, NJ: MMC Group, 2003.

Noble, David F. *Gallery of Best Cover Letters.* 2nd ed. Indianapolis, IN: Jist Works, 2004.

"Resume Styles: Chronological versus Functional? Best Selling Author Richard H. Beatty Joins in the Resume Discussion." *Internet Wire,* 5 November 2002.

Whitcomb, Susan B., and Pat Kendall. *eResumes.* New York: McGraw Hill, 2002.

REVERSE SUPPLY CHAIN LOGISTICS

Consumer awareness, enhanced by legally imposed green law constraints, have lead to the need for safe return of products from the field as well as more environmentally friendly products. As a result, logistics planning must now consider both forward and return flows of products, parts, subassemblies, scrap and containers. It seems that an entirely new spectrum of goods has emerged at what was once considered the end of the supply chain. These goods include:

- Products that have failed, but can be repaired or reused.

- Products that are obsolete but still have value.

- Unsold products from retailers.

- Recalled products.

- Parts repaired in the field that still have value.

- Items that have secondary usage, i.e. items that have another usage after they have exhausted their original use.

- Waste that must be accounted for and disposed of or used for energy production.

- Containers that must be returned to their origin or some sort of consolidation facility.

In their *Harvard Business Review* article, Guide and Wassenhove describe a reverse supply chain as "the series of activities required to retrieve a used product from a customer and either dispose of it or reuse it."

Donald F. Blumberg describes reverse logistics as the "coordination and control, physical pickup and delivery of the material, parts, and products from the field to processing and recycling or disposition, and subsequent returns back to the field where appropriate." This may include the services related to receiving the returns from the field, and the processes required to diagnose, evaluate, repair, and/or dispose of the returned units, products, parts, subassemblies, and material, either back to the direct/forward supply chain or into secondary markets or full disposal.

As a point of contrast, Blumberg describes forward logistics as "the overall management and coordination and control of the full direct service logistics pipeline, including the flow of the original material, parts and the final products to the central warehouse and distribution system, as well as the initial physical flow down to regional and local supply points to the end user or purchaser."

A number of forces seem to be influencing this increase in need for reverse logistics activities. These include:

- The previously mentioned *green* forces such as legislation and consumer awareness and concern. Frequently, due to legislation, the original manufacturer is now responsible for final disposal of the product. The increasing value of return products increases the need for safe return from the field.

- Increased number of customer goods returned for credit as a result of increased demand for customer service and satisfaction. Large retail chains usually have an agreement with suppliers allowing them to return goods. While originally intended to cover failed products, it has expanded to cover perfect goods that simply have not sold. From the consumer perspective, the buyer may return a good simply because they have decided not to keep it.

- Shortened product life cycles. As products become obsolete more quickly the possibility of and potential for returns increases.

- The drive to reduce costs. Firms are striving to reuse potentially good items through reuse, recycling or secondary usage. For example, Ford Motor Company has a program for recycling plastic bumpers into tail light housings.

- Increase in e-commerce sales. The massive increase of sales made via the Internet is conducive to increased returns as consumers buy merchandise *"sight unseen"* only to be disillusioned or dissatisfied with their purchase.

- Increased demand for repairs, re-manufacturing, upgrades, or re-calibration.

- Potentially valuable products that are no longer viewed as such by the current user. Consumers may purchase a new TV or washer/dryer even though the one they own still has a useful life.

- Increased use of returnable or reusable containers.

- Warranty returns. For many items with warranties, the good is first returned and then its disposition determined.

- Rental returns. The proliferation of rental businesses ensures the return of used but still valuable furniture and appliances.

- Product recalls. Products may be recalled by the manufacturer due to potential failure in the field or safety concerns.

Guide and Van Wassenhove list five key components to the reverse supply chain:

1. Product Acquistion. The used product must be retrieved.

2. Reverse Logistics. Once collected, used products are transported to some sort of facility for inspection, sorting, and disposition.

3. Inspection and Disposition. The returned products are tested, sorted, and graded. Diagnostic tests may be performed to determine a disposal action that recovers the most value from the returned product. If a product is new it may be returned to the forward supply chain. Others may be eligible for some form or reconditioning while others may be sold for scrap or recycling.

4. Reconditioning. Some products may be reconditioned or completely remanufactured.

Most people have seen products labeled *factory reconditioned* which implies it is used but like new and may have a warranty. Some products may have parts that can be extracted for reuse or as spare parts. Others go for salvage or recycling.

5. Distribution and sales. Reconditioned or remanufactured products may be sold in secondary markets where customers are unwilling to purchase a new product. In other instances the firm may need to create a new market if demand is not currently present. Of course, there are distribution needs in getting the product to the secondary market.

Blumberg lists a number of important characteristics that need to be managed coordinated, and controlled if the reverse supply chain is to be economically viable:

- Uncertain flow of materials—firms often do not know when a return item will arrive nor are they certain of its condition. The item may be *like new* or may require substantial repair or even disposal. Field service engineers often try a new part in a field failure, assuming the old part is bad. Subsequently, the old part is returned. When it turns out that the new part did not fix the problem, the old part is still returned as *bad*, thus creating a flow of mixed good and bad parts. Typically, 30 to 35 percent of high tech returns are perfectly good.

- Customer diversity—the return flow can be quite diverse and dependent upon the specific customer or end user. This may require considerable knowledge of specific customers and their use of the product.

- Time—from a cost or service perspective it may be desirable to return/repair/process an item as quickly as possible so that it may be quickly disposed of or reused.

- Value improvement—the firm will of course want to maximize the value of its return goods by transforming them into the state that will provide the most revenue or least cost.

- Flexibility—where demands fluctuate, the facility, transportation or other services may need to be flexible to support the firm's goals for the returned material.

- Multiparty coordination—since reverse logistics almost always involves multiple parties, an efficient and rapid real-time communication system or network is needed.

CLOSED LOOP SUPPLY CHAIN

Increasingly, it is found that the original supplier is in the best position to control the return process. The basic reverse supply chain logistics model operates independently of the forward supply chain that delivered the original product. When a firm controls the full process of forward and backward shipment the result is called a closed loop supply chain.

The closed loop supply chain generally involves a manufacturer, although sometimes it is the buyer, taking responsibility directly for the reverse logistics process. The products, parts, etc. are returned and recovered directly by the original manufacturer or through indirect (dealer) channels representing the original manufacturer's own field service force. The primary difference in this and the reverse supply chain is that in this model the entire direct and reverse flow can be and usually is controlled by the original manufacturer.

Within a closed loop system involving a consumer market the primary interaction is between the retailer and the original manufacturer. Returns can be failed products or simply those purchased and returned. In this model there are two reverse linkages, consumer to retailer and retailer to original manufacturer.

Closed loop systems allow firms to track the product and its failure and repair experience, thereby revealing how to cost-effectively service and support field service. Also, the close control and rapid recovery provided by a closed loop system allows minimum inventory for field support. Blumberg states that inventory value is maximized through:

- Rapid returns to the manufacturer for reuse.

- Ability to liquate products, parts, and sub-assemblies with value to secondary markets.

- Controlled recycling or disposition within environmental and other legal requirements.

- Ability to efficiently process returns back into the original direct supply chain.

Reducing inventory often produces significant additional efficiencies and results to the firm including:

- Simplifying processes of retail and whole-sale return, reducing labor cost.

- Reducing undesirable shrinkage and damage from returns.

- Improving the database and visibility of products throughout their life cycle.

- Reducing disposition cycle times, thereby, increasing cash flow.

Blumberg also states that the strategic value of closed loop reverse logistics management operations will have a very positive effect in terms of:

- Reducing cost of returns.

- Increasing the value of the salvage merchandise.

- Capturing vital information and reliability, maintainability, and dependability of products supported.

- Reducing transportation and warehousing expenses and time including the partial or full elimination of small package shipments.

- Automating and fully controlling the total returns process.

General experience dictates that the introduction of closed loop supply chain management can result in the bottom line direct savings of 1 to 3 percent or more of total revenues, particularly for organizations in a mature or stagnating market.

RESPONSIVE VS. EFFICIENT

By strategic design, forward supply chains generally strive to be either efficient, that is, designed to deliver the product at a low cost, or responsive, meaning designed for speed of response. Obviously, there is a trade-off between the two structures; the quest for low-cost (efficiency) would tend involve foregoing actions that would increase responsiveness, while striving for increased responsiveness almost always involves an increase in cost (or a decrease in efficiency).

Blackburn, Guide, Souza and Van Wassenhove suggest that reverse supply chains follow a similar structure even though most currently strive to be efficient. They propose that reverse supply chains may be structured as efficient or responsive depending upon the type of product returned. Their research indicates that for reverse supply chains, the most influential product characteristic is marginal value of time (MVT). They also propose that efficient reverse supply chains can achieve processing economies by delaying testing, sorting, and grading until the products have been collected at a central location. This works well for products that have a low marginal value of time. However, for items with a high marginal value of time, for example, PCs, a responsive reverse supply chain is appropriate. Early diagnosis, for example by field testing, can maximize asset recovery value by accelerating returns to their ultimate disposition, a process they call *preponement* (as opposed to the postponement tactic prevalent in forward supply chains). Also, by diverting new and scrap products from the main flow, flow time for items requiring additional work, repair and reconditioning, is reduced. Therefore if efficiency is the objective, then the reverse supply chain should be designed to centralize the evaluation activity. If responsiveness is the goal, a decentralized evaluation activity would be appropriate in order to minimize time delays in processing returns.

The total value of returned products in the U.S. alone is estimated at $100 billion per year. With this kind of volume the importance of the reverse supply chain can only go up.

SEE ALSO: Inventory Management; Inventory Types; Logistics and Transportation; Production Planning and Scheduling; Purchasing and Procurement; Quality and Total Quality Management; Supply Chain Management

R. Anthony Inman

FURTHER READING:

Blackburn, Joseph D., et al. "Reverse Supply Chains for Commercial Returns." *California Management Review* 46, no. 2: 6–22.

Blumberg, Donald F. *Introduction to Management of Reverse Logistics and Closed Loop Supply Chain Processes.* Boca Raton, FL: CRC Press, 2005.

Guide, V. Daniel R., Jr., and Luk N. Van Wassenhove. "The Reverse Supply Chain." *Harvard Business Review* 80, no. 2: 25–26.

RIGHTSIZING

SEE: Downsizing and Rightsizing

RISK MANAGEMENT

Risk management is a systematic process of identifying and assessing company risks and taking actions to protect a company against them. Some risk managers define risk as the possibility that a future occurrence may cause harm or losses, while noting that risk also may provide possible opportunities. By taking risks, companies sometimes can achieve considerable gains. However, companies need risk management to analyze possible risks in order to balance potential gains against potential losses and avoid expensive mistakes. Risk management is best used as a preventive measure rather than as a reactive measure. Companies benefit most from considering their risks when they are performing well and when markets are growing in order to sustain growth and profitability.

The task of the risk manager is to predict, and enact measures to control or prevent, losses within a company. The risk-management process involves identifying exposures to potential losses, measuring these exposures, and deciding how to protect the company from harm given the nature of the risks and the company's goals and resources. While companies face a host of different risks, some are more important than others. Risk managers determine their importance and ability to be affected while identifying and measuring exposures. For example, the risk of flooding in Arizona would have low priority relative to other risks a company located there might face. Risk managers consider different methods for controlling or preventing risks and then select the best method given the company's goals and resources. After the method is selected and implemented, the method must be monitored to ensure that it produces the intended results.

THE EVOLUTION OF RISK MANAGEMENT

The field of risk management emerged in the mid-1970s, evolving from the older field of insurance management. The term *risk management* was adopted because the new field has a much wider focus than simply insurance management. Risk management includes activities and responsibilities outside of the general insurance domain, although insurance is an important part of it and insurance agents often serve as risk managers. Insurance management focused on protecting companies from natural disasters and basic kinds of exposures, such as fire, theft, and employee injuries, whereas risk management focuses on these kinds of risks as well as other kinds of costly losses, including those stemming from product liability, employment practices, environmental degradation, accounting compliance, offshore outsourcing, currency fluctuations, and electronic commerce. In the 1980s and 1990s, risk management grew into vital part of company planning and strategy and risk management became integrated with more and more company functions as the field evolved. As the role of risk management has increased to encompass large-scale, organization-wide programs, the field has become known as enterprise risk management.

TYPES OF RISK MANAGERS AND TYPES OF RISK

Company managers have three general options when it comes to choosing a risk manager:

1. Insurance agents who provide risk assessment services and insurance advice and solutions to their clients;

2. Salaried employees who manage risk for their company (often chief financial officers or treasurers); and

3. Independent consultants who provide risk-management services for a fee.

Because risk management has become a significant part of insurance brokering, many insurance agents work for fees instead of for commissions. To choose the best type of risk manager for their companies, managers should consider the company's goals, size, and resources.

Managers also should be aware of the types of risks they face. Common types of risks include automobile accidents, employee injuries, fire, flood, and tornadoes, although more complicated types such as liability and environmental degradation also exist. Furthermore, companies face a number of risks that stem primarily from the nature of doing business. In *Beyond Value at Risk,* Kevin Dowd sums up these different types of risks companies face by placing them in five general categories:

1. Business risks, or those associated with an organization's particular market or industry;

2. Market risks, or those associated with changes in market conditions, such as fluctuations in prices, interest rates, and exchange rates;

3. Credit risks, or those associated with the potential for not receiving payments owed by debtors;

4. Operational risks, or those associated with internal system failures because of mechanical problems (e.g., machines malfunctioning) or human errors (e.g., poor allocation of resources); and

5. Legal risks, or those associated with the possibility of other parties not meeting their contractual obligations.

In addition, environmental risks constitute a significant and growing area of risk management, since reports indicate the number and intensity of natural disasters are increasing. For example, the periodical *Risk Management* reported that there were about five times as many natural disasters in the 1990s as in the 1960s. The year 2004 was one of the worst in history, with three major hurricanes hitting the state of Florida and a tsunami causing death and devastation in the Pacific Rim. Some observers blame the rising number of natural disasters on global warming, which they believe will cause greater floods, droughts, and storms in the future.

Furthermore, any given risk can lead to a variety of losses in different areas. For example, if a fire occurs, a company could lose its physical property

such as buildings, equipment, and materials. In this situation, a company also could lose revenues, in that it could no longer produce goods or provide services. Furthermore, a company could lose human resources in such a disaster. Even if employees are not killed or injured, a company would still suffer losses because employers must cover benefits employees draw when they miss work.

ASSESSING RISKS ASSOCIATED WITH DOING BUSINESS

One way managers can assess the risks of doing business is by using the risk calculator developed by Robert Simons, a professor at the Harvard Business School. Although the risk calculator is not a precise tool, it does indicate areas where risks and potential losses exist, such as the rate of expansion and the level of internal competition. Using the risk calculator, managers can determine if their company has a safe or dangerous amount of risk. The risk calculator measures three kinds of internal pressures: risk stemming from growth, corporate culture, and information management. Rapid growth, for example, could be a risk and lead to losses, because if a company grows too quickly, it may not have enough time to train new employees adequately. Hence, unchecked growth could lead to lost sales and diminished quality.

Managers can assess the increased risk associated with growth by determining if sales goals are set by top management without input from employees. If a company sets sales goals in this manner, then it has a high level of risk in that the goals may be too difficult for employees to meet. In cases where employees feel extreme pressure in trying to achieve goals, they may take unnecessary risks. Similarly, companies that rely heavily on performance-based pay also tend to have higher levels of risk.

To assess risk arising from corporate culture, managers should determine what percentage of sales comes from new products or services developed by risk-taking employees. If the percentage is high, then the amount of risk is also high, because such a company depends significantly on new products and the related risks. In addition, a corporate culture that allows or encourages employees to work independently to develop new products increases company risk, as does a high rate of new product or service failures.

Finally, managers can determine business risks resulting from information management by determining if they and their subordinates spend a lot of time gathering information that should already be available. Another way of assessing these risks is by managers considering whether they look at performance data frequently and whether they notice if reports are missing or late.

RISK MANAGEMENT METHODS

Risk managers rely on a variety of methods to help companies avoid and mitigate risks in an effort to position them for gains. The four primary methods include exposure or risk avoidance, loss prevention, loss reduction, and risk financing. A simple method of risk management is exposure avoidance, which refers to avoiding products, services, or business activities with the potential for losses, such as manufacturing cigarettes. Loss prevention attempts to root out the potential for losses by implementing such things as employee training and safety programs designed to eradicate risks. Loss reduction seeks to minimize the effects of risks through response systems that neutralize the effects of a disaster or mishap.

The final option risk managers have is to finance risks, paying for them either by retaining or transferring their costs. Companies work with risk managers insofar as possible to avoid risk retention. However, if no other method is available to manage a particular risk, a company must be prepared to cover the losses—that is, to retain the losses. The deductible of an insurance policy is an example of a retained loss. Companies also may retain losses by creating special funds to cover any losses.

Risk transferring takes place when a company shares its risk with another party, such as an insurance provider, by getting insurance policies that cover various kinds of risk that can be insured. In fact, insurance constitutes the leading method of risk management. Insurance policies usually cover (a) property risks such as fire and natural disasters, (b) liability risks such as employer's liability and workers' compensation, and (c) transportation risks covering air, land, and sea travel as well as transported goods and transportation liability. Managers of large corporations may decide to manage their risks by acquiring an insurance company to cover part or all of their risks, as many have done. Such insurance companies are called captive insurers.

Risk managers also distinguish between preloss and postloss risk financing. Preloss risk financing includes financing obtained in preparation for potential losses, such as insurance policies. With insurance policies, companies pay premiums before incurring losses. On the other hand, postloss financing refers to obtaining funds after losses are incurred (i.e., when companies obtain financing in response to losses). Obtaining a loan and issuing stocks are methods of postloss financing.

During the implementation phase, company managers work with risk managers to determine the company goals and the best methods for risk management. Generally, companies implement a combination of methods to control and prevent risks effectively, since these methods are not mutually exclusive, but complementary. After risk management methods have been implemented, risk managers must examine the risk management program to ensure that it continues to be adequate and effective.

EMERGING AREAS OF RISK MANAGEMENT

In the 1990s, new areas of risk management began to emerge that provide managers with more options to protect their companies against new kinds of exposures. According to the Risk and Insurance Management Society (RIMS), the main trade organization for the risk management profession, among the emerging areas for risk management were operations management, environmental risks, and ethics.

As forecast by RIMS, risk managers of corporations started focusing more on verifying their companies' compliance with federal environmental regulations in the 1990s. According to *Risk Management,* risk managers began to assess environmental risk such as those arising from pollution, waste management, and environmental liability to help make their companies more profitable and competitive. Furthermore, tighter environmental regulations also goaded businesses to have risk managers check their compliance with environmental policies to prevent possible penalties for noncompliance.

Companies also have the option of obtaining new kinds of insurance policies to control risks, which managers and risk managers can take into consideration when determining the best methods for covering potential risks. These nontraditional insurance policies provide coverage of financial risks associated with corporate profits and currency fluctuation. Hence, these policies in effect guarantee a minimum level of profits, even when a company experiences unforeseen losses from circumstances it cannot control (e.g., natural disasters or economic downturns). Moreover, these nontraditional policies ensure profits for companies doing business in international markets, and hence they help prevent losses from fluctuations in a currency's value.

Risk managers can also help alleviate losses resulting from mergers. Stemming from the wave of mergers in the 1990s, risk managers became a more integral part of company merger and acquisition teams. Both parties in these transactions rely on risk management services to determine and control or prevent risks. On the buying side, risk managers examine a selling company's expenditures, loss history, insurance policies, and other areas that indicate a company's potential risks. Risk managers also suggest methods for preventing or controlling the risks they find.

Finally, risk managers have been called upon to help businesses manage the risks associated with increased reliance on the Internet. The importance of online business activities in maintaining relationships with customers and suppliers, communicating with employees, and advertising products and services has offered companies many advantages, but also exposed them to new security risks and liability issues. Business managers need to be aware of the various risks involved in electronic communication and commerce and include Internet security among their risk management activities.

ENTERPRISE RISK MANAGEMENT

As the field of risk management expanded to include managing financial, environmental, and technological risks, the role of risk managers grew to encompass an organization-wide approach known as enterprise risk management (ERM). This approach seeks to implement risk awareness and prevention programs throughout a company, thus creating a corporate culture able to handle the risks associated with a rapidly changing business environment. Practitioners of ERM incorporate risk management into the basic goals and values of the company and support those values with action. They conduct risk analyses, devise specific strategies to reduce risk, develop monitoring systems to warn about potential risks, and perform regular reviews of the program.

In the United States, the Sarbanes-Oxley Act of 2002 provided the impetus for a number of large firms to implement enterprise risk management. Passed in the wake of scandals involving accounting compliance and corporate governance, the act required public companies to enact a host of new financial controls. In addition, it placed new, personal responsibility on boards of directors to certify that they are aware of current and future risks and have effective programs in place to mitigate them. "Fueled by new exchange rules, regulatory initiatives around the globe, and a bevy or reports that link good corporate governance with effective risk management, attention is turning to ERM," Lawrence Richter Quinn noted in *Financial Executive.* "[Some executives believe that it] will save companies from any number of current and future ills while providing significant competitive advantages along the way."

In late 2004 the London-based Treadway Commission's Committee of Sponsoring Organizations (COSO) issued *Enterprise Risk Management-Integrated Framework,* which provided a set of "best practice" standards for companies to use in implementing ERM programs. The COSO framework expanded on the work companies were required to do under Sarbanes-Oxley and provided guidelines for creating an organization-wide focus on risk management. According to *Financial Executive,* between one-third and one-half of Fortune 500 companies had launched or were considering launching ERM initiatives by the end of 2004.

SEE ALSO: Business Continuity Planning; Strategic Planning Tools; Succession Planning

Karl Heil
Revised by Laurie Collier Hillstrom

FURTHER READING:

Braunstein, Adam. "Strategies for Risk Management." *CIO* (24 February 2005). Available from <http://www2.cio.com/analyst/report2268.html>.

D'Arcangelo, James R. "Beyond Sarbanes-Oxley: Section 404 Exercises Can Provide the Starting Point for a Comprehensive ERM Program." *Internal Auditor* (October 2004).

Dowd, Kevin. *Beyond Value at Risk.* New York: Wiley: 1998.

Lam, James. *Enterprise Risk Management: From Incentives to Controls.* Hoboken, NJ: John Wiley, 2003.

Mills, Evan. "The Coming Storm: Global Warming and Risk Management." *Risk Management* (May 1998): 20.

Quinn, Lawrence Richter. "ERM: Embracing a Total Risk Model." *Financial Executive* (January-February 2005).

Risk and Insurance Management Society, Inc. "(RIMS) Website." Available from <www.rims.org>.

Simons, Robert. "How Risky Is Your Company?" *Harvard Business Review* (May 1999): 85.

Telegro, Dean Jeffery. "A Growing Role: Environmental Risk Management in 1998." *Risk Management* (March 1998): 19.

White, Larry. "Management Accountants and Enterprise Risk Management." *Strategic Finance* (November 2004).

ROBOTICS

Today's manufacturers in numerous industries are gaining rapid increases in productivity by taking advantage of automation technologies. One of these automation technologies, robotics, is a key factor leading the way in the twenty-first century. Firmly established as a critical manufacturing technology, robotics is gaining acceptance by the workforce, garnering praise for its reliability, and being utilized more extensively in medium and small companies.

As manufacturing assembly has grown increasingly complex, the need for new and expanded capabilities, particularly in automated assembly systems, has become evident. As components get smaller, as in micro-manufacturing, it is required that greater precision, more flexibility and higher throughput are achieved. Manual assembly no longer suffices for a great many of manufacturing's current requirements. Functions formerly performed by humans, especially difficult, dangerous, monotonous, or tedious tasks, are now often assumed by robots or other mechanical devices that can be operated by humans or computers. Robots can take the place of humans in extreme settings or life threatening situations involving nuclear contaminants, corrosive chemicals, or poisonous fumes.

While the automotive industry is the largest market for robot manufacturers, other industries are increasing their use of robotics. According to reports from the Robotics Industries Association, industries such as semiconductors and electronics, metals, plastics and rubber, food and consumer goods, life sciences and pharmaceuticals, and aerospace are all finding ways that their services can be enhanced and improved through robotics.

Some of these manufacturers are also improving the quality of their products by using robots with powerful machine-vision inspection equipment or by linking their robots to statistical process control systems. Robot fixtures can move quickly and fluidly without sacrificing accuracy. Servo-driven positioners can be programmed to handle more than one model on the same line, something especially important to lean organizations. This programmability also allows its users to set up the systems again and again for different applications. In most cases, converting robots from one application to another can be completed with minimal downtime, requiring only programming changes. Benefits include reduced capital expenses (you don't have to buy new fixtures for new applications), floor space requirements, lead-time, component expenses, and training investment.

A BRIEF HISTORY OF ROBOTICS

Despite the fact that robotics technology was developed in the United States, Japan became the first nation to actually embrace robotics; many observers view this as a significant factor in Japan's emergence as a global manufacturing power. Today Japan is not only one of the major users of manufacturing robotics but it is also the dominant manufacturer of industrial robots.

In the early 1980s, 70 percent of robot orders were for use in the automotive industry. During this time, robot manufacturers simultaneously improved their reliability and performance and sought to lessen their dependence on the automotive industry by focusing on specific niche markets. By concentrating on applications other than spot welding, painting, and dispensing, the robotics industry was able to develop products that could successfully handle not only assembly, but also material handling and material removal. Spot welding, which for a long time was the major application of robotics, eventually was eclipsed by materials handling. This was a clear indication that

the robotics industry was indeed becoming less dependent on the automotive industry, since materials handling is used in a wide and varied range of industries. Additionally, non-manufacturing applications started to become viable in such areas as security, health care, environmental cleanup, and space and undersea exploration.

Advances in robot control technology, simulation, and offline programming made robots easier to program, maintain, and use. Simulation use allowed for the discovery of potential problems before the robots were actually installed.

CURRENT USE OF INDUSTRIAL ROBOTS

Though less dependent on the automotive industry than in the past, the robotics industry still finds its widest application in that market. However, driven by the need for increased manufacturing efficiency, the automakers and automotive-related industries are moving away from hard automation in favor of flexible automation. Analysts predict greater use of robots for assembly, paint systems, final trim, and parts transfer in the automotive industry. Realistic robot simulation is making an impact by integrating vehicle design and engineering into manufacturing.

One reason for increased practicality of robots is the availability to control machinery and systems through personal or laptop computers. According to Waurzyniak, some advances in computer-guided systems are robots with force sensing capabilities and 3-D and 2-D vision-guidance capabilities. NASA is using sophisticated computer-guided robot controllers for its Space Shuttle Endeavor and the Mars landing craft. Each of these systems utilize computer control of some sort, ranging from simple machine-specific tracking, to shop-wide data collection across a variety of machinery and instruments, to galactic monitoring and control in a unique, outer space environment.

The Robotic Industries Association reports that an estimated 144,000 industrial robots are in use in the United States in 2004, up from 82,000 in 1998. In 2004, North American manufacturers purchased 14,838 robots, valued at nearly $1 billion, a 20 percent increase from 2003 and the industry's second best unit total ever. There has been a 152 percent increase in new robots ordered and a 78 percent increase in revenue in 2004 as well.

The key factors driving this growth in robotics are mass customization of electronic goods (specifically communications equipment), the miniaturization of electronic goods and their internal components, and the re-standardization of the semiconductor industry. The food and beverage industry is also in the midst of an equipment-spending boom in an effort to improve operating efficiencies. Robot installations for such tasks as packaging, palletizing, and filling are expected to see continued growth. In addition, increases are anticipated in the aerospace, appliance, and non-manufacturing markets.

THE FUTURE OF ROBOTICS

To some, the future of robotics has never looked brighter. Production of bipedal robots that mimic human movement are being created around the globe. Honda Motor Company's ASIMO (Advanced Step in Innovative Mobility) robot is considered the world's most advanced humanoid robot. It can climb stairs, kick, walk, talk, dance and even communicate and interact via its voice and facial recognition systems. Honda plans to one day market the robot as an assisted-living companion for the disabled or elderly.

Other robots that simulate human movement have been created at Cornell University, Massachusetts Institute of Technology (MIT), and Holland's Delft University of Technology. In a March 2005 article in *Machine Design,* the creators of the three robots describe the mechanics utilized in their designs and detail how their robots use less energy than ASIMO, although they do not have the range of capabilities of the ASIMO robot. These variations in mobility indicate promise and potential in a variety of robotic applications for the future.

Chip Walter's article, "You, robot", discusses renowned robotics researcher, Hans Moravec, Carnegie Mellon University scientist and cofounder of the university's Robotics Institute. Moravec is known for his longstanding prediction that super-robots that can perceive, intuit, adapt, think, and even simulate feelings, much like humans, will be practicable before the year 2050. His confidence in his predictions led him to open his own robotics firm in 2003, the Seegrid Corporation, to assist him in fulfilling his claims. His path toward that vision is to start simply—to create mobile carts with software and vision systems that can be 'taught' to follow paths and navigate independently. Moravec believes that machines will evolve in small steps, eventually reaching the levels of human intelligence and movement. His bedrock belief, on which he bases his technology, is ". . . if robots are going to succeed, the world cannot be adapted to them; they have to adapt to the world, just like the rest of us."

Stuart Brown reports that navigation technologies such as the global positioning system (GPS) are allowing industrial robots to move around in the world. GPS in conjunction with inertial navigation systems (INS) and the booming field of silicon micro-electromechanical systems (MEMS) are impacting robotics from simple automated lawn mowers to complex airplane control systems. Robotics are reaching the micro-level with the exploration of robotic water 'insects' equipped with biomechanical sensors that could be used as environmental monitors. The current prototype weighs less than a gram and draws power from ultra-thin electrical wires. An affordable and time-saving alternative to locating gas leaks has been developed in a pipe-inspecting robot crawler; equipped with multiple joints and video cameras, it easily navigates sharp turns and narrow pipes while projecting images of pipe integrity to a monitor. Plans for the future include a sensor that will detect corrosion and cracks in the pipes that do not appear in the video images.

Robots have come of age. While they were initially used for fairly simple tasks such as welding and spray-painting automobiles, these machines have increased tremendously in ability over the last decade, reaching further and broader than simple auto applications. Robotics will remain vital in the decades to come due to expanding scientific fields and increasing demand for more affordable and sophisticated methods of accomplishing common tasks.

SEE ALSO: Lean Manufacturing and Just-in-Time Production; Quality and Total Quality Management; Simulation

R. Anthony Inman
Revised by Monica C. Turner

FURTHER READING:

Bing, J., M. Simson, and J. Zaleski. "Robot: From Mere Machine to Transcendent Mind." *Publishers Weekly,* 5 October 1998, 65.

Brown, S. F. "Send in the Robots!" *Fortune* (Industrial Management Version), 24 January 2005, 140C–146C.

Brown, T. "Robot Helper Struts Stuff at Purdue." *Journal and Courier,* 11 March 2005. Available from <http://www.boilerstation.com/planet/stories/200503112purdue_planet1110517953.shtml>.

Ichbiah, D. *Robots: From Science Fiction to Technological Revolution.* New York, NY: Harry N. Abrams, Inc, 2005.

Meredith, J.R., and S.M. Shafer. *Operations Management for MBAs.* New York, NY: John Wiley & Sons, Inc, 1999.

Robotic Industries Association. "North American Robotics Orders Rise 20 Percent in 2004." Robotics Online. Available from <http://www.roboticsonline.com/public/articles/articlesdetails.cfm?id=1848>.

Robotic Industries Association. "Robotics Market Remains Hot in North America." Robotics Online. Available from <http://www.roboticsonline.com/public/articles/articlesdetails.cfm?id=1597>.

Rubenstein, C. "Industry Focus: Robotics in Electronic Assembly." *Robotics World* 16, no. 4 (1998): 35–39.

"Six Degrees of Robotic Fixturing." *Automotive Manufacturing & Production* 110, no. 11 (1998): 80.

Vincent, D.A. "Leading the Charge to a Productive 21st Century." *Robotics World* 16, no. 4 (1998): 19–26.

Walter, C. "You, Robot." *Scientific American* 292, no. 1 (2005): 36–37.

Waurzyniak, P. "Automating the Factory." *Manufacturing Engineering* 134, no. 2 (2005): 93–99.

"Your Standard Robot." *Machine Design* 70, no. 15 (1998): 56.

S

Organizational strategies are the means through which companies accomplish their missions and goals. Successful strategies address four elements of the setting within which the company operates: (1) the company's strengths, (2) its weaknesses, (3) the opportunities in its competitive environment, and (4) the threats in its competitive environment. This set of four elements—strengths, weaknesses, opportunities, and threats—when used by a firm to gain competitive advantage, is often referred to as a SWOT analysis. SWOT was developed by Ken Andrews in the early 1970s. An assessment of strengths and weaknesses occurs as a part of organizational analysis; that is, it is an audit of the company's internal workings, which are relatively easier to control than outside factors. Conversely, examining opportunities and threats is a part of environmental analysis—the company must look outside of the organization to determine opportunities and threats, over which it has lesser control.

Andrews's original conception of the strategy model that preceded the SWOT asked four basic questions about a company and its environment: (1) What can we do? (2) What do we want to do? (3) What might we do? and (4) What do others expect us to do?

The answers to these questions provide the input for an effective strategic management process. While Andrews' original conception of this analysis has been developed and changed to the more streamlined SWOT analysis that we know today, his work is the foundation of this activity.

STRENGTHS, WEAKNESSES, OPPORTUNITIES, AND THREATS

Strengths, in the SWOT analysis, are a company's capabilities and resources that allow it to engage in activities to generate economic value and perhaps competitive advantage. A company's strengths may be in its ability to create unique products, to provide high-level customer service, or to have a presence in multiple retail markets. Strengths may also be things such as the company's culture, its staffing and training, or the quality of its managers. Whatever capability a company has can be regarded as strength.

A company's weaknesses are a lack of resources or capabilities that can prevent it from generating economic value or gaining a competitive advantage if used to enact the company's strategy. There are many examples of organizational weaknesses. For example, a firm may have a large, bureaucratic structure that limits its ability to compete with smaller, more dynamic companies. Another weakness may occur if a company has higher labor costs than a competitor who can have similar productivity from a lower labor cost. The characteristics of an organization that can be strength, as listed above, can also be a weakness if the company does not do them well.

Opportunities provide the organization with a chance to improve its performance and its competitive advantage. Some opportunities may be anticipated, others arise unexpectedly. Opportunities may arise when there are niches for new products or services, or when these products and services can be offered at different times and in different locations. For instance, the increased use of the Internet has provided numerous opportunities for companies to expand their product sales.

Threats can be an individual, group, or organization outside the company that aims to reduce the level of the company's performance. Every company faces threats in its environment. Often the more successful companies have stronger threats, because there is a desire on the part of other companies to take some of that success for their own. Threats may come from new products or services from other companies that aim to take away a company's competitive advantage. Threats may also come from government regulation or even consumer groups.

A strong company strategy that shows how to gain competitive advantage should address all four elements of the SWOT analysis. It should help the organization determine how to use its strengths to take advantage of opportunities and neutralize threats. Finally, a strong strategy should help an organization avoid or fix its weaknesses. If a company can develop a strategy that makes use of the information from SWOT analysis, it is more likely to have high levels of performance.

Nearly every company can benefit from SWOT analysis. Larger organizations may have strategic-planning procedures in place that incorporate SWOT analysis, but smaller firms, particularly entrepreneurial firms may have to start the analysis from scratch. Additionally, depending on the size or the degree of diversification of the company, it may be necessary to conduct more than one SWOT analysis. If the company has a wide variety of products and services, particularly if it operates in different markets, one SWOT analysis will not capture all of the relevant strengths, weaknesses, opportunities, and threats that exist across the span of the company's operations.

LIMITATIONS OF SWOT ANALYSIS

One major problem with the SWOT analysis is that while it emphasizes the importance of the four elements associated with the organizational and environmental analysis, it does not address how the company can identify the elements for their own company. Many organizational executives may not be able to determine what these elements are, and the SWOT framework provides no guidance. For example, what if a strength identified by the company is not truly a strength? While a company might believe its customer service is strong, they may be unaware of problems with employees or the capabilities of other companies to provide a higher level of customer service. Weaknesses are often easier to determine, but typically after it is too late to create a new strategy to offset them. A company may also have difficulty identifying opportunities. Depending on the organization, what may seem like an opportunity to some, may appear to be a threat to others. Opportunities may be easy to overlook or may be identified long after they can be exploited. Similarly, a company may have difficulty anticipating possible threats in order to effectively avoid them.

While the SWOT framework does not provide managers with the guidance to identify strengths, weaknesses, opportunities, and threats, it does tell managers what questions to ask during the strategy development process, even if it does not provide the answers. Managers know to ask and to determine a strategy that will take advantage of a company's strengths, minimize its weaknesses, exploit opportunities, or neutralize threats.

Some experts argue that making strategic choices for the firm is less important than asking the right questions in choosing the strategy. A company may mistakenly solve a problem by providing the correct answer to the wrong question.

USING SWOT ANALYSIS TO DEVELOP ORGANIZATIONAL STRATEGY

SWOT analysis is just the first step in developing and implementing an effective organizational strategy. After a thorough SWOT analysis, the next step is to rank the strengths, weaknesses, opportunities, and threats and to document the criteria for ranking. The company must then determine its strategic fit given its internal capabilities and external environment in a two-by-two grid (see Figure 1). This fit, as determined

Figure 1

		Internal	
		Strengths	**Weaknesses**
External	**Opportunities**	**Quadrant 1** **Possible Strategies**	**Quadrant 2** **Possible Strategies**
	Threats	**Quadrant 3** **Possible Strategies**	**Quadrant 4** **Possible Strategies**

in the grid, will indicate what strategic changes need to be made. The quadrants in this grid are as follows:

- *Quadrant 1*—internal strengths matched with external opportunities;
- *Quadrant 2*—internal weaknesses relative to external opportunities;
- *Quadrant 3*—internal strengths matched with external threats; and
- *Quadrant 4*—internal weaknesses relative to external threats.

Quadrant 1 lists the strategies associated with a match between the company's strengths and its perceived external opportunities. It represents the best fit between the company's resources and the options available in the external market. A strategy from this quadrant would be to protect the company's strengths by shoring up resources and extending competitive advantage. If a strategy in this quadrant can additionally bolster weaknesses in other areas, such as in Quadrant 2, this would be advantageous.

Quadrant 2 lists the strategies associated with a match between the company's weaknesses with external opportunities. Strategies in this quadrant would address the choice of either improving upon weaknesses to turn them into strengths, or allowing competitors to take advantage of opportunities in the marketplace.

Quadrant 3 matches the company's strengths and external threats. Strategies in this quadrant may aim to transform external threats into opportunities by changing the company's competitive position through use of its resources or strengths. Another strategic option in this quadrant is for the company to maintain a defensive strategy to focus on more promising opportunities in other quadrants.

Quadrant 4 matches a company's weaknesses and the threats in the environment. These are the worst possible scenarios for an organization. However, because of the competitive nature of the marketplace, any company is likely to have information in this quadrant. Strategies in this quadrant may involve using resources in other quadrants to exploit opportunities to the point that other threats are minimized. Additionally, some issues may be moved out of this quadrant by otherwise neutralizing the threat or by bolstering a perceived weakness.

Once a strategy is decided on in each quadrant for the issues facing the company, these strategies require frequent monitoring and periodic updates. An organization is best served by proactively determining strategies to address issues before they become crises.

An example of how a firm can develop strategies using these quadrants is as follows. Generic Corporation produces high-quality; high-priced specialty kitchen items in a catalog and in stores and is known for their excellent customer service. This strength has been able to offset its major weaknesses, which are having few stores and no current capabilities for Internet sales. Its major opportunities come from the explosion of Internet shopping, and its threats are other more high-profile competitors, operating primarily on the Internet, and the concerns of identity theft in Internet sales that many customers have. Matching Generic's strengths to its opportunities (Quadrant 1), the firm may choose to enhance its Internet site to allow online purchases, still providing its excellent 24-hour telephone customer service. Ideally, this strategy will offset the weakness of not having an Internet presence, which addresses the concerns of Quadrant 2. Additionally, by bolstering the strength of excellent customer service by applying it to the online shopping site, the company may be able to alleviate customer concerns about identity theft (Quadrant 3). A strategy for Quadrant 4, which matches the company's weaknesses and threats, is that Generic may consider selling its online business to a competitor. Certainly, the Quadrant 4 strategy is the least preferred, but a proactive strategy that plans for managing such a situation is favored over a crisis situation in which the company is forced to sell with no planning.

A SWOT analysis is a first, but critical, step in developing an organizational strategy. By examining the company's internal capabilities—its strengths and weaknesses and its external environment—opportunities and threats, it helps to create strategies that can proactively contend with organizational challenges.

SEE ALSO: Strategic Planning Tools; Strategy Formulation

Marcia J. Simmering

FURTHER READING:

Andrews, K. *The Concept of Corporate Strategy.* Homewood, IL: R.D. Irwin, 1971.

Barney, Jay. *Gaining and Sustaining Competitive Advantage.* 2nd ed. Upper Saddle River, NJ: Prentice Hall, 2002.

Fleisher, Craig S., and Babette E. Bensoussan. *Strategic and Competitive Analysis: Methods and Techniques for Analyzing Business Competition.* Upper Saddle River, NJ: Prentice Hall, 2003.

Jackson, Susan E., and Randall S. Schuler. *Managing Human Resources: A Partnership Perspective.* 7th ed. Cincinnati, OH: South-Western College Publishing, 2000.

SAFETY IN THE WORKPLACE

One of the biggest issues facing employers today is the safety of their employees. Workplace accidents are increasingly common. In 2003, for instance, the Bureau of Labor Statistics (BLS) reported a total of

4.4 million nonfatal workplace injuries in private industries. Organizations have a moral responsibility to ensure the safety and well-being of their members. Organizational practices that promote safety can also help a company establish competitive advantage by reducing costs and complying with safety laws.

Workplace safety can be quite expensive. Unintentional injuries alone cost more than $146.6 billion per year for medical and insurance costs, workers' compensation, survivor benefits, lost wages, damaged equipment and materials, production delays, other workers' time losses, selection and training costs for replacement workers, and accident reporting.

State and federal governments strictly regulate organizational safety practices. The government views safety violations very seriously, and the penalties for violating safety laws can be quite severe. In addition to being issued large fines, employers who violate safety regulations can be held liable for criminal charges. The following examples illustrate the types of penalties associated with such violations:

- In November of 2004, OSHA fined General Motors (GM) Powertrain plant in Massena, NY for six serious safety violations, including an obstructed exit route, inadequate guarding of moving machine parts, and the failure to assess the need for personal protective equipment for workers. There were additional fines for recordkeeping violations, specifically underreporting injuries and illnesses. The penalty was $160,000.

- In September of 2004, a Weyerhaeuser plant in West Virginia was cited for improper reporting of injuries and illnesses to OSHA. The fine was $77,000 and the company had nine months to undergo an independent audit of their recordkeeping practices.

- In July of 2004, OSHA issued a proposed fine against Fru-Con Construction Corp in the amount of $280,000 for the company's negligence which resulted in the deaths of four employees. An improperly secured 2 million pound, 315 foot long launching truss collapsed, killing the four employees.

GOVERNMENT REGULATION OF SAFETY PRACTICES AT THE WORKPLACE

Federal laws regulate the safety practices of most organizations. We limit our discussion to laws that affect a majority of organizations, but note that several additional laws exist which cover particular segments of the workforce. For instance, numerous laws pertain to government contractors, to specific states, and to specific industries (e.g., transportation, nuclear power, food, and drug).

The Occupational Safety and Health Act of 1970 is probably the most comprehensive and wide-ranging legislation in this area. It applies to nearly all U.S. workplaces. The act aims to ensure safe working conditions for every American worker by:

1. Setting and enforcing workplace safety standards;

2. Promoting employer-sponsored educational programs that foster safety and health; and

3. Requiring employers to keep records regarding job-related safety and health matters.

Three separate agencies were created by the act:

1. The Occupational Safety and Health Administration (OSHA) develop and enforce health and safety standards.

2. The Occupational Safety and Health Review Commission hear appeals from employers who wish to contest OSHA rulings.

3. The National Institute for Occupational Safety and Health conducts health and safety research to suggest new standards and update previous ones.

The following discussion focuses on the safety standards imposed by OSHA and how they are enforced. OSHA has issued literally thousands of safety and health standards. Areas of basic concern include fire safety, personal protection equipment, electrical safety, basic housekeeping, and machine guards. Each standard specifies such things as permissible exposure limit, monitoring requirements, methods of compliance, personal protective equipment, hygiene facilities, training, and record-keeping.

To comply with these standards, most mid- to large-sized organizations employ safety professionals to keep up with them and ensure that each is being met. These professionals face too many specific issues to mention here, but some of the most important issues they must address appear in Figure 1.

Figure 1
OSHA – Employee Responsibilities

- Read the OSHA poster at the jobsite.
- Comply with all applicable OSHA standards.
- Follow all lawful employer safety and health rules and regulations, and wear or use prescribed protective equipment while working.
- Report hazardous conditions to the supervisor.
- Report any job-related injury or illness to the employer, and seek treatment promptly.
- Exercise rights under the Act in a responsible manner.

Companies with more than ten employees are subject to routine OSHA inspections. Companies with fewer than ten employees are exempt from such inspections, but can be investigated if a safety-related problem is brought to the attention of OSHA. High-hazard industries, such as manufacturing firms, chemical companies, and construction companies, are subject to inspections regardless of the number of employees.

OSHA conducts inspections based on the following priority classifications, which are listed in order of importance:

1. *Imminent danger.* OSHA gives top priority to workplace situations that present an "imminent danger" of death or serious injury to employees. The company must take immediate corrective action.

2. *Fatality or catastrophe investigations.* The second highest priority is given to sites that have experienced an accident that has caused at least one employee to die or three or more to be hospitalized. Employers must report these events within 8 hours. The inspection aims to determine the cause of the accident and whether any violation of OSHA standards contributed to it.

3. *Employee complaint investigations.* OSHA responds third to employee complaints about hazards or violations. The speed with which OSHA responds depends on the seriousness of the complaint. Employees may request to remain anonymous.

4. *Referrals from other sources.* Consideration is given to referrals of hazard information from federal, state and local agencies, individuals, organizations, and the media.

5. *Follow-ups.* OSHA sometimes will return to verify that violations have been corrected.

6. *General programmed inspections.* OSHA will also inspect an organization if it is a high-hazard industry or has a lost workday injury rate that is above the national norm for that industry.

When an OSHA inspection reveals that an employer has violated one of its standards, it issues a citation. The citation, posted near the site of the violation, lists the nature of the violation, the abatement period (i.e., the time frame within which the company must rectify the problem), and any penalty levied against the employer. Willful violations (i.e., those that an employer intentionally and knowingly commits) carry a penalty of up to $70,000 for each offense. If a death occurs because of a willful violation, the employer may be both fined and imprisoned.

Congress enacted the Hazard Communication Standard (more commonly referred to as the Employee Right-to-Know Law) in 1984. This law gives workers the right to know what hazardous substances they are dealing with on the job. A substance is considered hazardous if exposure to it can lead to acute or chronic health problems. Federal and state agencies have compiled lists of more than 1,000 substances deemed hazardous under this law. The law requires all organizations to (1) develop a system for inventorying hazardous substances, (2) label the containers of these substances, and (3) provide employees with needed information and training to handle and store these substances safely.

Employers typically violate the OSHA Hazard Communication Standard more frequently than any other OSHA standard. The majority of companies are cited for failing to have:

- written hazard communication programs

- an up-to-date hazardous chemical inventory list

- properly labeled chemical containers

- material safety data at the work site, in the form of material safety data sheets (MSDS)

- training programs for teaching employees about the chemicals they work with

Government fines for right-to-know violations may be as high as $1000 per chemical for first violations and $10,000 per chemical for second violations. Additional penalties for environmental crimes include fines up to $75,000 per day and imprisonment.

Another law affecting organizational safety and health practices is the Americans with Disabilities Act (ADA). An individual is protected by the ADA if he or she is disabled, that is, if the individual has a physical or mental impairment that substantially limits one or more of the individual's major life activities. According to the ADA regulations, temporary, non-chronic impairments that are short in duration and have little or no long-term impact are usually not considered disabilities under the act. For example, broken limbs, sprains, concussions, appendicitis, or influenza are not disabilities. However, if a broken leg did not heal properly and resulted in permanent impairment that significantly restricted walking or other major life activities, it could then be considered a disability.

In 2004, there were 15,376 total charges filed as ADA violations with the Equal Employment Opportunity Commission (EEOC). From July 1992 (when the law first took effect) through the end of September 2004, employees filed 204,997 complaints with the EEOC. Employees who became disabled as the result of workplace conditions or injuries filed about half of these charges. Individuals with back impairments have lodged the greatest number of charges. People also frequently claimed emotional, neurological, and extremity impairments.

Penalties for ADA violations may be as high as $50,000 for initial violations and up to $100,000 for each subsequent violation. In addition, the Civil Rights Act of 1991 allows claimants to collect up to $300,000 in punitive damages for "willful" violations.

ACCIDENTS AND ACCIDENT PREVENTION

Despite laws designed to ensure safety at the workplace, U.S. companies' accident rates are alarmingly high. According to one estimate, employees lost eighty million workdays in 2002 from workplace injuries, and more than 3.7 million people suffered disabling injuries on the job that year.

What causes all of these industrial injuries? These causes can be divided into three categories: employee error, equipment insufficiency, and procedure insufficiency. Examples of causes falling within each category are listed here:

- Employee error—misjudged situations; distractions by others; neuromuscular malfunctions; inappropriate working positions; and knowingly using defective equipment;

- Equipment insufficiency—use of inappropriate equipment; safety devices being removed or inoperative; and the lack of such things as engineering controls, respiratory protection, and protective clothing;

- Procedure insufficiency—failure of procedure for eliciting warning of hazard; inappropriate procedure for handling materials; failure to lock out or tag out; and a lack of written work procedures.

Workplace accidents pose serious problems for employees and for a firm's competitive advantage, but employers can prevent most of them. Many preventive strategies work.

Some people just seem to be accident prone. If some people do have inherent tendencies toward accidents, then organizations should be able to lower their accident rates by screening out accident-prone applicants. Research studies have discovered that individuals with certain personality characteristics are more likely than others to be involved in industrial accidents. For instance, one study found that people with higher accident rates tend to be impulsive and rebellious, and they tend to blame outside forces, rather than themselves, for their mishaps. Another study identified the following four "high-risk" personality characteristics:

- Risk taking: high risk-takers actually seek out danger rather than trying to minimize or avoid it.

- Impulsiveness: impulsive individuals fail to think through the consequences of their actions.

- Rebelliousness: rebellious individuals tend to break established rules, including safety rules.

- Hostility: hostile individuals tend to lose their tempers easily and thus engage in aggressive acts, such as kicking a jammed machine.

Many organizations now use personality tests to screen out individuals with accident-prone tendencies. For example, some companies use a test (called the Personnel Selection Inventory-Form 3S) to assess applicants' safety consciousness. One part of the test measures the degree to which individuals perceive a connection between their own behavior and its consequences. As noted earlier, individuals unable to see this connection are at greater risk for accidents.

Employers who provide all new employees with training on safe and proper job procedures experience fewer accidents. Employees should learn how to perform each of their tasks as safely as possible. Training should be very specific, as illustrated in the example that follows. This example covers the procedures to be followed by employees working at a large food manufacturing plant:

- When picking up pans from the conveyor belt, pick up no more than two pans before you place them on the pan rack.

- Stack roll pans no higher than the rear rail of the pan rack.

- When you lift or lower the dough, keep both hands on the dump chain.

- When you pull the dough trough away from the dough mixer, hold both hands on the front rail and not on the rail sides.

While safety training is essential, employees do not always apply what they have learned. Just as many automobile drivers know it is wrong to exceed legal speed limits, but do it anyway, workers may choose to ignore instructions and carry out procedures in their own, unsafe way. One way to mitigate this problem is to implement a safety incentive program. Such programs aim to motivate safe behavior by providing workers with incentives for avoiding accidents. The organization formulates safety goals (usually on a department-wide basis) and rewards employees if these goals are met. For example, a particular department may establish the goal of reducing lost-time accidents by 50 percent over the next three months.

If this goal were to be met, all employees within that department would receive an incentive reward, usually in the form of a cash bonus or merchandise.

Safety incentive programs often work quite well. For example, Willamette Industries implemented a program because it was experiencing an average of thirty accidents per year that caused people to miss work. As a result of the program, the company went 450 days without a lost-time accident.

Two problems often arise with safety incentive programs, however. In some cases, workers get so caught up in trying to win incentive rewards that they conceal their injuries and do not report them. When injuries go unreported, injured workers relinquish their rights to workers' compensation and firms remain unaware of safety problems. Second, workers may continue to perform in an unsafe manner (e.g., take risky shortcuts) because they remain unconvinced that such behavior is likely to result in accidents. Unfortunately, these employees are grievously mistaken; unsafe behaviors are a leading cause of accidents. According to one estimate, for every 100,000 unsafe behaviors there are 10,000 near-miss accidents, 1,000 recordable accidents, 100 lost-time accidents, and 1 fatality.

SAFETY AUDITS

Because employees who "know better" often continue to engage in accident-causing behavior, many employers have redirected their focus from accident prevention to the prevention of unsafe acts that could lead to an accident. To do so, firms conduct safety audits. A safety committee or supervisors who observe employees on the job and correct unsafe behaviors generally conduct such audits.

Each employee should be monitored according to a planned schedule, generally on a weekly basis, as follows:

STEP 1: OBSERVATION. Stop in the work area for a few moments and observe worker's activities, looking for both safe and unsafe practices. Use the following guide:

- Be alert to unsafe practices that the employee corrects immediately upon seeing you enter the area (putting on protective equipment, such as gloves or goggles).
- Note whether appropriate protective clothing is being worn.
- Observe how employees use tools.
- Scrutinize the safety of the work area. For instance, is the floor slippery?
- Determine whether rules, procedures, and operating instructions are being followed.

STEP 2: EMPLOYEE DISCUSSION. These discussions should help employees recognize and correct their unsafe acts. When engaging in them, adhere to the following advice:

- If you spot an unsafe act, be non-confrontational. Point out the violation and ask the worker to state what he or she was doing and what safety-related consequences may arise if such behavior continues. Your goal is to help, not blame. Audits should not result in disciplinary actions unless an individual consistently violates safety rules.
- As you observe your employees, encourage them to discuss any safety concerns they may have and ask them to offer any ideas for safety improvement.
- Commend any good performance that you observe.

STEP 3: RECORDING AND FOLLOW-UP. Findings should be recorded in writing. Pursue any item discussed during the audit that requires follow-up.

Accident investigations determine accident causes so that changes can be made to prevent the future occurrence of similar accidents. "Near misses" should also be investigated so that problems can be corrected before serious accidents occur. Supervisors always play a key role in accident investigations. For minor accidents, investigation may be limited to the supervisor meeting with the injured worker and filing a report. In large-scale investigations, the supervisor is usually part of a team of experts, which may also include an engineer, maintenance supervisor, upper-level manager, and/or safety professional.

Accident investigations should be performed in the following manner. When an accident occurs, the investigator's first responsibility is to ensure the safety of all employees by:

- making sure the injured are cared for and receive medical attention, if necessary;
- guarding against a more dangerous secondary event by removing danger sources and evacuating other personnel from the area if necessary; and
- restricting access to the area so no one else will be harmed, and so the scene will not be disturbed.

You should then begin an investigation to identify both the immediate and underlying causes of the accident. The immediate cause is the event that directly led to the accident, such as a slippery floor, failure to wear safety gear, or failure to follow proper procedures.

Immediate causes, while easily found, are not always very helpful in suggesting how future incidents of this nature can be avoided. To accomplish this aim, the investigator must discover the underlying cause of the accident. For example, suppose a worker slips and falls on spilled oil. The oil on the floor is the immediate cause of the accident, but you need to know why it was not cleaned up and why a machine was leaking oil in the first place. Poor training, lack of rule enforcement, low safety awareness, poor maintenance, or crowded work areas commonly underlie accidents.

The investigator should ensure the accident scene is kept intact until the investigation is finished, as this will be the only chance to view the scene exactly as it was at the time of the accident. If a camera is available, photographs of the scene should be taken. Nothing related to the incident should be destroyed or discarded. The investigator should inspect the location (e.g., check for chemicals, broken pieces of machinery) and interview injured or affected workers, eyewitnesses, and anyone else who may be familiar with the accident area. Interviews should be conducted immediately, while the incident is still fresh in everyone's mind. Individuals should give their own account of the incident; by letting them tell their stories without interruption, the investigator can determine if the various responses corroborate one another. Continue asking why until the underlying causes surface. Once the causes are identified, the investigator should recommend any changes indicated by the findings.

Safety committees often oversee organizations' safety functions. Consisting of both management and non-management personnel, committees perform the following tasks:

1. Assist with inspections and accident investigations.

2. Conduct safety meetings.

3. Answer workers' questions about safety programs.

4. Bring workers' safety concerns to management's attention.

5. Help develop safety incentive programs.

6. Develop ideas to improve workplace safety.

7. Prepare evacuation plans.

8. Prepare procedures for disasters such as tornadoes, hurricanes, etc. and contingency plans following the disaster.

Safety in the workplace works most effectively with a combination of employer attentiveness and employee responsibility. Costs, both financial and physical, can be decreased and injuries reduced with proper training, employer involvement and company-wide adherence to OSHA rules and guidelines. Ensuring safety is important for not only each individual company and worksite, but for industries and national concerns as well.

SEE ALSO: Employment Law and Compliance

Lawrence S. Kleiman
Revised by Monica C. Turner

FURTHER READING:

Cho, A. "OSHA Report Cites Contractor in Fatal Ohio Collapse." *ENR—Engineering News Record* 253, no. 6 (2004): 12.

Juergens, J. "Safety First." *Occupational Health & Safety* 73, no. 6 (2004): 94–96.

Kleiman, L.S. *Human Resource Management: A Tool for Competitive Advantage.* Cincinnati: South-Western College Publishing, 2000.

Nash, J.L. "OSHA Fines General Motors Corp. $160,000 for Recordkeeping, Safety Violations." *Occupational Hazards* 66, no. 11 (2004): 8.

———. "Weyerhaeuser Subsidiary Fined $77,000 for Failing to Record Injuries." *Occupational Hazards* 66, no. 9 (2004): 12–14

Stewart, R. "The Challenge of Creating a Culture of Safety." *Canadian HR Reporter* 18, no. 6 (2005): 11.

Taylor, B., Jr. *Effective Environmental Health and Safety Management Using theTeam Approach.* Hoboken, NJ: Wiley & Sons, 2005.

Williams, H.A.H. "10 Steps to a Safer Workplace." *HR Focus* 74, no. 2 (1997): 9–10.

SALES MANAGEMENT

In today's global marketplace, managers face many challenges related to fulfilling the customer's ever-changing needs and expectations. The concept of customer service has recently become more complex as a result of globalization of goods and services. Customers are now well-informed decision makers as a result of the abundance of information that is available online and in the media. In addition, today's consumer is most concerned with how a salesperson can solve basic problems and ultimately add value to a product or service. The role of sales intermediaries is now, more than ever, important to success in this new competitive global marketplace. As a result, sales managers have a new challenge of responding to this new environment with innovative techniques for managing and motivating the sales force. The following sections define general sales management terms, examine the role of a sales manager, and focus on methods used to mange, lead and motivate employees.

SALES MANAGEMENT DEFINED

Sales management can be most easily defined as planning, implementing, and controlling personal contact programs designed to achieve the sales and profit objectives of the firm. Overall, sales managers are responsible for directing the firm's sales program. In carrying out this objective, a sales manager assigns territories, sets goals, and establishes training programs. In addition to setting individual goals, sales managers monitor the performance of their salespeople and continually offer direction and leadership on ways to improve their performance.

The organizational structure for sales management varies depending on the firm's size and strategy. In field sales management, the structure consists of the unit manager, district manager, regional manager, general manager and vice president of sales. The unit manager is often referred to as the manager-in-training with interaction taking place at the customer level. Key responsibilities for the unit manager include training new salespeople, recruiting, selling to small accounts, and running district meetings. District managers, a step up from unit managers, have 5 to 10 years of management experience and generally manage 8 to 10 salespeople. District managers typically report to the regional manager, who is responsible for managing multiple districts in a given geographic area. The general manager is sometimes referred to the vice president of sales and marketing. This position is traditionally at the top of the sales organizational chart, with the VP of Marketing and Sales driving the sales strategy of the firm.

There are distinct differences in bottom and top-level managers. The main difference is the amount of time they spend on each of their tasks. Lower-level managers spend the majority of their time on staffing, directing and monitoring salespeople. Top-level managers generally focus on planning, organizing and coordinating their sales strategy with overall corporate objectives. They also forecast sales, set objectives, develop strategies and policies, and establish budgets.

SALES MANAGEMENT STRATEGIES

Sales managers are confronted with several challenges when designing an effective sales strategy. How should a sales force be structured? How large a sales force is needed? What methods should the sales force use to deliver their message? Strategies vary based on the number of products that the firm offers and if the firm sells to one particular type of customer versus selling to many different types of customers.

When selling one product line to a single industry, with customers in many locations, a territorial sales strategy is used. With this strategy, a sales manager will assign sales representatives to exclusive territories in a given region. These representatives will sell full product lines consisting of multiple products to customers in that territory. A good example of this strategy is food equipment sales. A sales representative for a commercial food equipment company will

typically promote the companies full line of products when selling to restaurants, schools, and cafeterias in their defined territory.

A product sales force strategy is often used when a firm sells along product lines. Using this strategy, a sales manger will require their representatives to focus on selling a single product or small select group of products. This strategy is used by managers when products are numerous and complex. This strategy is widely used in healthcare sales where a salesperson focuses on selling doctors and healthcare providers specific products that are integral to their specialized area of medicine.

Finally, sales managers may use a customer focused sales force strategy where salespeople specialize in matching target customers to specific products or services. This strategy helps a company to concentrate more on building strong, long-term relationships with key customers.

MOTIVATING THE SALES FORCE

A topic of particular interest in sales management is motivation. Motivation is quite possibly the most important aspect of sales management. If a sales force is properly screened, selected and trained, and the product is right, then motivation becomes critical for success. There are many reasons why motivating a sales force is an important part of the sales process. First, salespeople must cope with acceptance and rejection on a continual basis. They go from being exhilarated as the result of a big sale to the disappointment that results from being turned down. Often, salespeople will spend many hours on the road, away from their families, which may affect their overall morale. This, paired with the fact that salespeople usually operate without managerial supervision, indicates that these individuals require a high level of self motivation in order to consistently produce good results. And finally, motivation directly influences the level of enthusiasm a salesperson has in presenting the product or service to the customer. If a sales representative is passionate and enthusiastic about a product or service, it can directly influence the customer's decision to purchase, as well as building strong relationships for future purchases. With that said, it is important to note that sales managers are responsible for instilling and maintaining an effective level of motivation in their staff. In addition to providing strong leadership, a sales manager must motivate a sales force in order to achieve pre-determined sales goals.

Managers can use a variety of tools to successfully motivate their sales force. The most powerful motivator is a well-designed compensation package. Sales managers can effectively motivate salespeople by designing a compensation formula that is a good balance of salary, bonuses, and commissions. Managers define selling objectives in the form of quotas, established compensation levels, and an effective incentive portion. There are a variety of formulas for compensating salespeople; the formula depends on linking the firm's overall performance expectations to each salesperson.

Straight commission is used by sales managers to reward salespeople for their accomplishments, rather than their time or efforts. Straight commission compensation fosters independence for the salesperson. It is a strong motivator in that payout only occurs if a sale is made, resulting in lower costs for the company. It is favorable program for organizations that want to minimize compensation costs; especially for new and growing companies. There are some disadvantages of straight commission, which include the inability of sales managers to control selling activities, as well as high employee turnover.

Another compensation program frequently used by organizations is salary plus bonus. Essentially, the salary plus bonus formula includes base salary with a performance-based bonus paid when sales goals and quotas are achieved. Sales reps may also be evaluated on factors, including creation of new accounts, average gross margin, and after sales servicing. Unlike straight commission, this program helps to reduce the rate of employee turnover. The plan also encourages salespeople to build long-term relationships with their customers. By having the security of a consistent income, salespeople can be patient with their customers and allow them to take the time needed to make an informed decision. This is particularly important when buying cycles are long and when sales representatives need time to get acclimated with the buying cycle of the customer.

When selling complex products or services, a salary plus commission structure may be used to compensate the sales force. Under this program, a salesperson is guaranteed a base salary and is awarded a commission based on factors determined by the organization. Typically, a salary plus commission program is structured around upper and lower thresholds related to sales volume. For example, a salesperson may earn 4 percent on the first $20,000 of sales volume each month, 5 percent on an additional $15,000 and 6 percent on sales over $40,000. Other firms may use different criteria, such as reaching sales quotas on the number of individual products sold in each product category. The advantages to this method are related to the flexibility of program. Firms are able to customize the program to meet corporate objectives as they relate to the sales force. Commissions can be spread out over a given period to ensure reps will continue to offer the customer a high level of service, and to discourage the reps from leaving the company after a big sale.

Salary plus commission and a bonus is a combination of the aforementioned programs. This plan combines the stability of a salary, the incentive of a commission, as well as special bonus awards. Every activity of a salesperson is financially recognized by this program and is favored by salespeople because of the earning potential of the plan. The plan is not as popular as the others because of the complexity involved to administer the program.

Short-term incentive programs are often used by firms to motivate salespeople beyond standard compensation packages. Sales contests are the most common incentive used to generate excitement about selling products and services. The contests usually run for a limited time and include cash prizes or travel to those salespeople who achieve a certain level of sales. Timing of the contests is crucial. Typically, contests should be rolled out during the slower seasons of a given industry in order to boost sales and to generate incremental revenue.

RECRUITING A SUCCESSFUL SALES FORCE

The sales manager is responsible for recruiting salespeople by identifying sources for new employees, screening applicants, conducting interviews, contacting references, and recommending candidates to the regional manger. Typically, the regional sales manager recruits and selects new salespeople when needed. Often, candidates are found through universities, Internet sites, or applicants who formally apply to the company through cold-calling efforts.

Managers should identify certain key qualities when recruiting candidates for employment. Personality is an important factor when considering a candidate for a sales position. Empathy, ego and optimism are good personality attributes to consider when screening candidates for a sales position. Each of these attributes has a strong correlation to success in sales. Empathy is the ability to sense the reactions of another person and ego refers to the inner need to persuade another individual for one's own satisfaction. Both of these traits combined are predictors of a good salesperson and are strongly considered when recruiting and interviewing job applicants. Additionally, it is important to consider the applicant's level of optimism as it relates to personal achievement. Optimism and enthusiasm are good indicators of the ability of a salesperson to manage adversity and is a trait that is often needed to overcome rejection and slow sale months.

Although most companies have their own selection procedures, a typical candidate selection process will resemble the following:

1. First interview by district sales manager (Candidate is accepted and given a formal application or they are not accepted and sent a rejection letter.)

2. Candidates that submit an application are invited to a second interview with the district manager.

3. Candidates may spend a day in the field with a salesperson and the district manager receives feedback from the salesperson on the candidate's level of enthusiasm.

4. District manager checks the candidate's references and criminal background.

5. Regional sales manager interviews the candidate.

6. Regional manager and district manager discuss the candidate via telephone conference or personal meeting. (Decision is made whether to offer the candidate the position)

7. Regional sales manager formally offers the job to the candidate.

8. Physical examination is needed if offer is accepted by the candidate.

TOTAL QUALITY MANAGEMENT AND CUSTOMER SATISFACTION

A primary responsibility of a sales manager is managing relations with customers. The emergence of a global market for products and services has spurred new theories regarding management of products as they relate to the customer. Total quality management (TQM) is defined as a management process and set of disciplines that are coordinated to ensure that the organization consistently meets customer expectations. Originally defined as a manufacturing theory, TQM is now being applied to sales in particular. In the sales and marketing context, TQM defines the quality of the sales and service effort in terms of customer satisfaction. The goal of TQM is to sell service and quality driven value (rather than price), to create loyal customers, and long-term profits. Sales and service systems that link individuals, departments, suppliers and customers are central to TQM. Each department within an organization has a direct responsibility to the customer in some capacity. Marketing designs its new products with the customer in mind. Manufacturing focuses on achieving the highest level of product quality. Under TQM, challenging, but reasonable improvement goals are set for sales and service quality. Innovation and continuous improvement of the sales and servicing process is paramount to the idea of TQM.

The customer is considered from every aspect of TQM. By focusing on customer expectations and questioning them using formal techniques, TQM can discover previous misconceptions and new opportunities. Some fundamental ideas behind TQM are making continuous improvements to products and services,

eliminating defects, doing things right the first time, and understanding that employees closest to the process know how to improve the process. As a function of sales and service, TQM focuses on the exchange between the buyer and the seller. Intangible issues such as responsiveness to varying customer needs, empathy for customer concerns, reliable service performance, and assurance of service capabilities are considered when managing relationships with customers. This process is somewhat more difficult than actual management of product quality because customers are required to be participative in the process. They are expected to offer feedback to the company on products and services to allow for continuous improvement to the process.

Customer satisfaction is central to the philosophy of total quality management. In sales management, TQM suggests that organizations need to have the majority of employees in customer support functions, with fewer staff positions. This will help to eliminate costs associated with management and reduces levels in the decision making process. Fewer levels of management also allows for the organization to be flexible enough to change quickly to support new sales opportunities. Continuous improvement for all products and improvement in the selling process allows firms to consistently move forward with innovative products and services in order to remain competitive in the new global market.

CAREER PATHS

Sales management jobs are found in both consumer and commercial industries, in positions ranging from district manager, to vice president of marketing and sales, to top sales management of the firm. Competition for sales management jobs can be intense. Sales managers typically start out as salespeople, working their way to the top with strong leadership and organizational abilities. The progression of salespeople into management positions is gradual, with representatives moving into more executive positions by taking on more responsibility with larger, national accounts. It is likely that a sales representative will spend a portion of their career as a district or regional sales trainer, before moving into a senior sales management role. The progression of salespeople into management positions vary based on the size and organizational structure of the organization.

SEE ALSO: Customer Relationship Management; Employee Compensation; Employee Recruitment Planning; Human Resource Management; Motivation and Motivation Theory; Quality and Total Quality Management

Matthew Ross

FURTHER READING:

Dalrymple, Douglas J., and William L. Cron. *Sales Management: Concepts and Cases.* 6th ed. New York, NY: John Wiley and Sons, 1998.

Hughes, G. David, Daryl McKee, Charles H. Singler. *Sales Management: A Career Path Approach.* Cincinnati, OH: South-Western College Publishing, 1999.

Kotler, Philip, and Gary Armstrong. *Principles of Marketing.* 9th ed. Upper Saddle River, NJ: Prentice Hall, 1999.

SCENARIO PLANNING

Strategic planning and forecasting tend to use projections of past events to develop future plans. These approaches rely on historical data and assume a continuation of past business practices and environmental stability. Scenarios are used to develop plans for significant changes in the environment, personnel, or processes for which data are limited and uncertain. The premise is that the best way to prepare for radically different situations is to think through various events that could occur and consider alternatives for responding to those situations if they should happen, (von Oetinger, 2004).

Major corporations such as Shell and General Electric redefined scenario planning in the 1970s to meet specific company needs. These companies realized that traditional planning, which is based on forecasts, was becoming strategically dangerous as they moved out of the relatively stable 1950s and 1960s. Traditional planning assumes that tomorrow's business world will be quite like yesterday's.

Scenario planning simply defined means creating a variety of possible future scenarios. Firms can then respond in one of two ways. First, firms may examine each scenario and determine whether the organization's current strategy would help them survive and succeed in those situations. Or, firms can examine a desired future state and see what they must do to get to that point. The purpose of this planning is to try to understand how the underlying dynamics of an industry can and how the organization could best respond to a change that could happen or to make a desired situation occur. The organization identifies certain events that could change the industry's structure and studies the present and future driving forces that might come into play that could cause such events. Scenario planning is effective for large organizations and small organizations alike. The organizations that utilize the plan the best are the ones that make scenarios relevant to long-term needs, which may require a more focused approach. The ultimate purpose of this method seems to be the same for large and small organizations: to analyze the consequences of present actions and decisions; to identify and avoiding problems before they occur; to identify the present consequences of future events; and to envision aspects of possible or desired futures.

Scenario planning is different from other forms of strategic planning, such as forecasts and trend analysis. Scenario planning, in fact, uses both of these techniques, but also identifies how these can be upset and thus cause different outcomes. Some scenarios may seem nonsensical or highly improbable, but actually help organizations deal with major changes. Levi-Strauss uses the method to analyze the impact of everything from cotton deregulation to the total worldwide extinction of cotton. Similarly, businesses in energy intensive industries like trucking or airlines could benefit from considering what would happen to their business and how should they respond if gas prices were to reach $2.50 or $3.00 per gallon.

Scenario planning helps organizations understand that business decisions are not just about submitting numbers and creating budgets, but about recognizing a wider context of events that might happen. Scenarios are created around uncertainties in the business or its environment. The goal is to move from one predicted outcome to understanding how multiple uncertainties will impact an organization. Although every organization is different, success is higher when the company's strategy is correlated to changes in the environment, which can create opportunities for prepared organizations while creating threats to those less prepared.

In creating a scenario plan, these driving forces can be categorized into external and internal factors. External factors could include: market forces, which shape the needs and behaviors of consumers and suppliers; cost forces, which depend on the economics of the business; government forces, which are out of the hands of individual organizations but set the rules of the game; and, most importantly, competitive forces and uncertain strategic considerations. The need to match or beat competitors can determine the opportunities and threats of an organization. Internal factors could include planning for turnover of critical top managers, responding to major accidents, or significant changes in stock prices.

One pitfall of scenario planning is that organizations tend to make scenarios too broad or too narrow. When scenarios are too broad, people tend to dismiss them because they feel the scenarios are unrealistic or highly improbable. When they are too narrow, scenarios are usually minor variations of the existing strategy or the same theme.

There are many different approaches firms can use to develop meaningful scenarios. Schnaars and Ziamou suggest the following:

- Optimistic vs. best guess vs. pessimistic scenarios. This approach looks at the most likely (best guess) future situation based on current information. The optimistic scenario introduces question as to what things would or could happen to result in a better than anticipated outcome and how can the organization make those things happen? The pessimistic scenario looks at many of the things that could go wrong and tries to help decision makers plan responses to deal with these problems should they happen.

- Good vs. bad scenarios. This approach avoids the tendency to focus on the most likely alternative of the "best guess" and forces managers to give more attention to both extremes.

- Arrayed scenarios. These scenarios look at alternatives associated with a continuum along a single criterion or dimension. For example firms could plan their response to a slight, moderate, or severe change in the price for gasoline, or other key resource.

- Independently themed scenarios. This approach looks at different aspects of the future. One scenario could look at possible technological breakthroughs, another at environmental concerns, and a third at potential market changes. Each scenario is conceptually independent of the others.

After scenarios are created, strategies are developed by first determining the direction in which the organization should (or wants to) be going. The group then decides on the events that support this vision and the outcomes the organization wants for this event. This is sometimes difficult because the world is rapidly changing, and one designs his or her organization to deal with the change. Scenario planning is a valuable tool for an organization because it gathers the clues a company has and puts them together in different ways to allow people to think about them without making judgments.

Why should organizations implement scenario planning as opposed to other planning techniques? First, the company can use the method as an approach to risk management. The method attempts to answer questions like, "How do we come up with a strategy that's possible in a wide range of different futures?" The organization can also use the method to upset the rules that everybody understands, to create new rules of competition. Scenario development causes firms to deviate from a linear projection of past business practices by developing potential situations that question traditional assumptions about the firm's relevant industry, processes, markets, and people that may make it necessary to significantly alter the current strategy.

Scenario planning is effective when used properly by managers with good business judgment; it is not a substitute for business judgment. The process does not help an organization become better than they might be ordinarily, but helps utilize professional judgment across a wider range of alternatives.

SEE ALSO: Forecasting; Longitudinal Scenarios; Planning; Strategic Planning Tools

Kevin Nelson
Revised by Joe Thomas

FURTHER READING:

Epstein, Jeffery H. "Scenario Planning: An Introduction." *The Futurist* 32, no. 6 (1998): 50–51.

Gupta, M., L. Boyd, and L. Sussman. "To Better Maps: A T.O.C. Primer For Strategic Planning." *Business Horizons* 47, no. 2 (2004): 15–26.

Mitchell, Donald, and Carol Coles. "Establishing a Continuing Business Model Innovation Process." *Journal of Business Strategy* 25, no. 3 (2004): 39–49.

Mitroff, Ian. *Crisis Leadership: Planning for the Unthinkable.* New York: John Wiley. 2003.

Nutt, Paul. "Expanding the Search for Alternatives During Strategic Decision Making." *Academy of Management Executive* 18, no. 4 (2004): 13–28.

Roney, Curtis. "Planning for Strategic Contingencies." *Business Horizons* 46, no. 2 (2003): 35–42.

Schnaars, Steven, and Paschalina Ziamou. "The Essentials of Scenario Writing." *Business Horizons* 44, no. 4 (2001): 25–31.

Von Oetinger, Bolko. "A Plea For Uncertainty." *Journal of Business Strategy* 25, no. 1 (2004): 57–59.

SECURITIES AND EXCHANGE COMMISSION

The U.S. Securities and Exchange Commission (SEC) is an independent, nonpartisan, quasi-judicial regulatory agency that is responsible for administering federal securities laws. The main objective of these laws is to protect investors in securities markets in the United States from fraud and other dishonest activities. The laws are designed to ensure that securities markets operate fairly and that investors have access to disclosures of all material information concerning publicly traded securities.

Congressional investigations of the collapse of the stock market in 1929 and the subsequent Depression found that investors suffered heavy losses for two major reasons. First, many companies had failed to disclose relevant information. Second, many misrepresentations of financial information had been made to the investors. The SEC was created to provide oversight in an attempt to prevent such a situation from arising again.

The SEC regulates firms engaged in the purchase and sale of securities, people who provide investment advice, and investment companies. The SEC may also provide the means to enforce securities laws through the appropriate sanctions. The commission may also serve in an advisory capacity to the federal courts in Chapter 11 cases (e.g., corporate reorganization proceedings under Chapter 11 of the Bankruptcy Reform Act of 1978).

ORGANIZATION

The SEC was established by Congress in 1934 under the Securities Exchange Act. The commission is made up of five commissioners, all of whom are appointed by the president of the United States with the advice and consent of the Senate. Each commissioner is appointed to a fixed five-year term; terms are staggered so that one expires on June 5 of every year. One of the commissioners is designated as chair by the president. As a matter of policy, no more than three of the five commissioners may be from the same political party. The commission employs financial analysts and examiners, accountants, lawyers, economists, investigators, and other professionals to carry on its responsibilities. The following description provides a listing of the principal divisions of the commission.

DIVISION OF CORPORATION FINANCE. Corporation Finance has the overall responsibility of ensuring that disclosure requirements are met by publicly held companies registered with the SEC. Its responsibilities include reviewing registration statements for publicly traded corporate securities, as well as documents concerning proxies, mergers and acquisitions, tender offers, and solicitations.

DIVISION OF MARKET REGULATION. This division is responsible for overseeing the securities markets and their self-regulatory organizations (such as the nation's stock exchanges), for registering and regulating brokerage firms, and for overseeing other market participants, such as transfer agents and clearing organizations. It also sets financial responsibility standards and regulates trading and sales practices affecting operation of the securities markets.

DIVISION OF ENFORCEMENT. The Enforcement Division has the responsibility of enforcing federal securities laws. These responsibilities include investigating possible violations of the federal securities laws and recommending appropriate remedies for consid-

eration by the Securities and Exchange Commission. The SEC typically brings between 400 and 500 civil enforcement actions per year against companies and individuals that it suspects of breaking securities laws.

DIVISION OF INVESTMENT MANAGEMENT. This division has the responsibility of administering three statutes: the Investment Company Act of 1940; the Investment Advisers Act of 1940; and the Public Utility Holding Company Act of 1935. The Division of Investment Management ensures compliance with regulations regarding the registration, financial responsibility, sale practices, and advertising of investment companies and investment advisers. New products offered by these entities are also reviewed by the staff in this division. The staff reviews and processes investment company registration statements, proxy statements, and periodic reports as per the laws specified under the Securities Act.

OFFICE OF COMPLIANCE INSPECTIONS AND EXAMINATIONS. This office conducts and coordinates all compliance inspection programs of brokers, dealers, self-regulatory organizations, investment companies and advisers, clearing agencies, and transfer agents. It determines whether these entities are in compliance with the federal securities laws, with the goal of protecting investors.

SECURITIES LAWS ADMINISTERED BY THE SEC

The Securities and Exchange Commission is responsible for enforcing the following seven major securities laws:

SECURITIES ACT OF 1933. The Securities Act imposes mandatory disclosure requirements on companies that sell their new securities through the securities markets. The act's base philosophy is to let the issuer disclose and to let the investor beware. This act is often referred to as the "truth in securities" law. The act requires that investors receive financial and other significant information concerning securities being offered for public sale. The act also prohibits deceit, misrepresentations, and other fraud in the sale of securities.

In 1975, Congress amended the Securities Act of 1933. The major focus of the amendment was the requirement that the SEC move towards establishing a single nationwide securities market. The law did not specify the structure of a national securities market, but it is assumed that any national market would make extensive use of computers and electronic communication devices.

SECURITIES EXCHANGE ACT OF 1934. The Securities Exchange Act of 1934 extends the disclosure concepts to securities already outstanding. The major provisions of the Securities Exchange Act of 1934 are as follows:

1. The act created the Securities and Exchange Commission as a watchdog for the securities business.

2. It required listed companies to file registration statements and periodic financial reports with both the SEC and the exchange.

3. It gave the SEC the power to prohibit market manipulation, misrepresentation, and other unfair practices.

4. It required all national securities exchanges to register with the SEC and to be under its effective supervision and regulation.

5. It gave the Board of Governors of the Federal Reserve System the authority to control margin requirements.

6. It granted the SEC the power to control short selling, trading techniques, and the procedures of the exchanges.

7. It required officers, directors, and major stockholders to file monthly reports of any changes in their stockholdings.

PUBLIC UTILITY HOLDING ACT OF 1935. Interstate holding companies engaged, through subsidiaries, in the electric utility business or in the retail distribution of natural or manufactured gas are subject to regulation under this act. These companies, unless specifically exempted, are required to submit reports providing detailed information concerning the organization, financial structure, and operations of the holding company and its subsidiaries. Holding companies are subject to SEC regulations on such matters as system structure, acquisitions, combinations, and issue and sale of securities.

THE TRUST INDENTURE ACT OF 1939. Under the scrutiny of the SEC, this act applies to debt securities, including bonds, debentures and notes, and similar debt instruments offered for public sale and issued under trust indentures with more than $7.5 million in securities outstanding at any one time. Even though such securities may be registered under the Securities Act, they may not be offered for sale to the public unless a formal agreement between the issuer of bonds and bondholder, known as the trust indenture, conforms to the statutory standards of this act.

INVESTMENT COMPANY ACT OF 1940. Under this act, activities of companies—including mutual funds—engaged primarily in investing, reinvesting, and trading in securities, and whose own securities are offered to the investing public, are subject to certain statutory pro-

hibitions and to Securities and Exchange Commission regulation. Public offerings of investment companies' securities must also be registered under the Securities Act of 1933. In this context, it should be noted that although the SEC serves as a regulatory agency in these cases, the SEC does not supervise the company's investment activities. The mere presence of the SEC as a regulatory agency does not in itself guarantee a safe investment for potential investors.

INVESTMENT ADVISERS ACT OF 1940. The Investment Advisers Act of 1940 establishes a pattern of regulating investment advisers. The main purpose of this act is to ensure that all persons, or firms, that are compensated for providing advising services to anyone about securities investments are registered with the SEC and conform to the established standards designed to protect investors. The SEC has the authority to strip an investment adviser of his or her registration should he or she be found guilty of committing a statutory violation or securities fraud.

SARBANES-OXLEY ACT OF 2002. The Sarbanes-Oxley Act, signed into law by President George W. Bush on July 30, 2002, marked the first significant reform of American business practices in decades. Passed in the wake of several financial scandals at major corporations, the Act was intended to enhance corporate responsibility, combat accounting fraud, and clarify financial disclosures. It also created the Public Company Accounting Oversight Board (PCAOB) to guarantee that the auditing profession remained unbiased in performing its vital role of ensuring corporate compliance with financial reporting standards.

U.S. government leaders hoped that the Sarbanes-Oxley Act would serve to clean up American capital markets, improve corporate governance, and restore investor confidence. High-profile cases of insider trading and fraud at such companies as Enron and WorldCom—which took place either under the noses or with the implicit approval of the major public accounting firms hired to audit them—has led to a movement to increase the power of the SEC.

SEE ALSO: Business Continuity Planning; Due Diligence; Ethics; Financial Issues for Managers; Financial Ratios

Ramesh C. Garg
Revised by Laurie Collier Hillstrom

FURTHER READING:

Barber, Marc. "U.S. Clean-Up Operation: Regulators in the U.S. are as Determined as Ever to Restore Faith After the Series of Accounting Scandals in Recent Years." *Accountant* May 2004.

Garg, Ramesh, et al. *Basics of Financial Management.* Acton, Massachusetts: Copley Publishing Group, 1997.

U.S. Securities and Exchange Commission. "The Investor's Advocate: How the SEC Protects Investors and Maintains Market Integrity." 12 January 2005. Available from <http://www.sec.gov/about/whatwedo. html>.

SENSITIVITY TRAINING

Sensitivity training is often offered by organizations and agencies as a way for members of a given community to learn how to better understand and appreciate the differences in other people. It asks training participants to put themselves into another person's place in hopes that they will be able to better relate to others who are different than they are. Sensitivity training often specifically addresses concerns such as gender sensitivity, multicultural sensitivity, and sensitivity toward those who are disabled in some way. The goal in this type of training is more oriented toward growth on an individual level. Sensitivity training can also be used to study and enhance group relations, i.e., how groups are formed and how members interact within those groups.

HISTORY

The origins of sensitivity training can be traced as far back as 1914, when J.L. Moreno created "psychodrama," a forerunner of the group encounter (and sensitivity-training) movement. This concept was expanded on later by Kurt Lewin, a gestalt psychologist from central Europe, who is credited with organizing and leading the first T-group (training group) in 1946. Lewin offered a summer workshop in human relations in New Britain, Connecticut. The T-group itself was formed quite by accident, when workshop participants were invited to attend a staff-planning meeting and offer feedback. The results were fruitful in helping to understand individual and group behavior.

Based on this success, Lewin and colleagues Ronald Lippitt, Leland Bradford, and Kenneth D. Benne formed the National Training Laboratories in Bethel, Maine, in 1947 and named the new process sensitivity training. Lewin's T-group was the model on which most sensitivity training at the National Training Laboratories (NTL) was based during the 1940s and early 1950s. The focus of this first group was on the way people interact as they are becoming a group. The NTL founders' primary motivation was to help understand group processes and use the new field of group dynamics, to teach people how to function better within groups. By attending training at an off-site venue, the NTL provided a way for people to

remove themselves from their everyday existence and spend two to three weeks undergoing training, thus minimizing the chances that they would immediately fall into old habits before the training truly had time to benefit its students. During this time, the NTL and other sensitivity-training programs were new and experimental. Eventually, NTL became a nonprofit organization with headquarters in Washington, D.C. and a network of several hundred professionals across the globe, mostly based in universities.

During the mid-1950s and early 1960s, sensitivity training found a place for itself, and the various methods of training were somewhat consolidated. The T-group was firmly entrenched in the training process, variously referred to as encounter groups, human relations training, or study groups. However, the approach to sensitivity training during this time shifted from that of social psychology to clinical psychology. Training began to focus more on interpersonal interaction between individuals than on the organizational and community formation process, and with this focus took on a more therapeutic quality. By the late 1950s, two distinct camps had been formed-those focusing on organizational skills, and those focusing on personal growth. The latter was viewed more skeptically by businesses, at least as far as profits were concerned, because it constituted a significant investment in an individual without necessarily an eye toward the good of the corporation. Thus, trainers who concentrated on vocational and organizational skills were more likely to be courted by industry for their services; sensitivity trainers more focused on personal growth were sought by individuals looking for more meaningful and enriching lives.

During the 1960s, new people and organizations joined the movement, bringing about change and expansion. The sensitivity-training movement had arrived as more than just a human relations study, but as a cultural force, in part due to the welcoming characteristics of 1960s society. This social phenomenon was able to address the unfilled needs of many members in society, and thus gained force as a social movement. The dichotomy between approaches, however, continued into the 1960s, when the organizational approach to sensitivity training continued to focus on the needs of corporate personnel.

The late 1960s and 1970s witnessed a decline in the use of sensitivity training and encounters, which had been transformed from ends in themselves into traditional therapy and training techniques, or simply phased out completely. Though no longer a movement of the scale witnessed during the 1960s, sensitivity-training programs are still used by organizations and agencies hoping to enable members of diversified communities and workforces to better coexist and relate to each other.

GOALS OF SENSITIVITY TRAINING

According to Kurt Back, "Sensitivity training started with the discovery that intense, emotional interaction with strangers was possible. It was looked at, in its early days, as a mechanism to help reintegrate the individual man into the whole society through group development. It was caught up in the basic conflict of America at mid-century: the question of extreme freedom, release of human potential or rigid organization in the techniques developed for large combines." The ultimate goal of the training is to have intense experiences leading to life-changing insights, at least during the training itself and briefly afterwards.

Sensitivity training was initially designed as a method for teaching more effective work practices within groups and with other people, and focused on three important elements: immediate feedback, here-and-now orientation, and focus on the group process. Personal experience within the group was also important, and sought to make people aware of themselves, how their actions affect others, and how others affect them in turn. Trainers believed it was possible to greatly decrease the number of fixed reactions that occur toward others and to achieve greater social sensitivity. Sensitivity training focuses on being sensitive to and aware of the feelings and attitudes of others.

By the late 1950s another branch of sensitivity training had been formed, placing emphasis on personal relationships and remarks. Whether a training experience will focus on group relationships or personal growth is defined by the parties involved before training begins. Most individuals who volunteer to participate and pay their own way seek more personal growth and interpersonal effectiveness. Those who represent a company, community service program, or some other organization are more likely ready to improve their functioning within a group and/or the organization sponsoring the activity. Some training programs even customize training experiences to meet the needs of specific companies.

IN PRACTICE

An integral part of sensitivity training is the sharing, by each member of the group, of his or her own unique perceptions of everyone else present. This, in turn, reveals information about his or her own personal qualities, concerns, emotional issues, and things that he or she has in common with other members of the group. A group's trainer refrains from acting as a group leader or lecturer, attempting instead to clarify the group processes using incidents as examples to clarify general points or provide feedback. The group action, overall, is the goal as well as the process.

Sensitivity training resembles group psychotherapy (and a technique called psychodrama) in many respects, including the exploration of emotions, personality, and relationships at an intense level. Sensitivity training, however, usually restricts its focus to issues that can be reasonably handled within the time period available. Also, sensitivity training does not include among its objectives therapy of any kind, nor does it pass off trainers/facilitators as healers of any sort. Groups usually focus on here-and-now issues; those that arise within the group setting, as opposed to issues from participants' pasts. Training does not explore the roots of behavior or delve into deeper concepts such as subconscious motives, beliefs, etc.

Sensitivity training seeks to educate its participants and lead to more constructive and beneficial behavior. It regards insight and corrective emotional or behavioral experiences as more important goals than those of genuine therapy. The feedback element of the training helps facilitate this because the participants in a group can identify individuals' purposes, motives, and behavior in certain situations that arise within the group. Group members can help people to learn whether displayed behavior is meaningful and/or effective, and the feedback loop operates continuously, extending the opportunity to learn more appropriate conduct.

Another primary principle of sensitivity training is that of feedback; the breakdown of inhibitions against socially repressed assertion such as frankness and self-expression are expected in place of diplomacy. Encounters that take place during sensitivity training serve to help people practice interpersonal relations to which they are likely not accustomed. The purpose is to help people develop a genuine closeness to each other in a relatively short period of time. Training encounters are not expected to take place without difficulty. Many trainers view the encounter as a confrontation, in which two people meet to see things through each other's eyes and to relate to each other through mutual understanding.

There is a difference between the scientific study of group dynamics (a branch of social psychology) and the human relations/group workshop aspect. The popularity of sensitivity training during the 1960s was due in large part to the emotional, experiential aspect. Yet many pragmatic advocates of sensitivity training felt it was necessary to avoid working with the most emotional converts, and conducted experiments in a laboratory in as realistic a situation as could be approximated, seeking a scientific approach more characteristic of psychological studies.

Other programs, not so concerned with the scientific validity of their studies or with freedom from distraction, offer full-time training programs during the day. Participants can choose on their own whether or not to maintain contact with the office for the duration of training. Others offer part-time sessions for several hours a day, and the participants' daily routine is otherwise uninterrupted. Sensitivity-training programs generally last a few days, but some last as many as several weeks.

T-GROUPS

Within most training groups (T-groups), eight to ten people meet with no formal leader, agenda, or books-only a somewhat passive trainer. Trainers do not necessarily direct progress, just help participants to understand what is happening within the group. In defining a T-group, Robert T. Golembiewski explains the major distinguishing features as follows: "it is a learning laboratory; it focuses on learning how to learn; and it distinctively does so via a 'here-and-now' emphasis on immediate ideas, feelings, and reactions."

The learning takes place within a group's struggle to create something meaningful for itself in an essentially unstructured setting. Issues that traditionally arise in such a setting include developing group norms and cohesion, reasons for scape-goating, selective communication channels, struggles for leadership, and collective decision-making patterns. Power struggles and decision-making conflict are the most prevalent problems as groups work toward establishing an identity and meet individual member needs. More specifically, group members can help each other identify when they are: attempting to control others or, conversely, when they are seeking support; punishing themselves or other group members; withdrawing from the group; trying to change people rather than accepting them; reacting emotionally to a given situation; and ignoring, rather than scrutinizing, behavior between group members.

Ultimately, T-groups were not a tremendously successful part of the sensitivity-training movement. This was in part because T-group trainers do not actually teach, but help people learn by assuming a more passive role. This sometimes confuses and upsets those who expect and desire more guidance. Another reason is that despite the intensity of the learning experience, most participants have difficulty quantifying exactly what they have learned and why it matters.

IN ORGANIZATIONS

Organizational goals appear to be the antithesis of those of sensitivity training. Sensitivity training is fueled on emotional outbursts in group settings, possibly leading to a change in attitude toward another individual. Desired results include more openness, spontaneity, and sensitivity to others. And while organizations are made up of people who interact and could benefit from such training, the goals of an organization are often more

related to increased production or higher profit margins than modifying means of interpersonal communication. To make sensitivity training work in organizational settings, the training must be adapted to the goals of the particular organization.

In its orientation as a study of group dynamics, sensitivity training is similar to the general concept of organizational development, a process by which organizations educate themselves in order to achieve better problem-solving capabilities. However, most sensitivity programs do focus on individual behavior within groups, while organizational development focuses on the group and how it works as a whole. Also, sensitivity-training groups are often composed entirely of people who are strangers to each other, while organizational-development programs seek to educate groups of people with shared working histories and experiences. Finally, the end goals of these training programs differ significantly. Sensitivity training, if successful, leads to self-awareness and insight that will help its participants in all aspects of life (including the workplace). Organizational development places more of its focus on becoming aware of one's role within workplace dynamics, leading to more effective group functioning (one of sensitivity training's goals, but with a more defined group in which to function).

POLITICAL CORRECTNESS AND THE RESPONSE TO SENSITIVITY TRAINING

The development of sensitivity training has led many critics to claim that such training is not really designed to help people be more sensitive to other people's ideas and feelings, but it is really crafted to change one's attitudes, standards and beliefs. These critics argue that sensitivity training merely wears people down until they conform to the mentality of the group, and agree that views of the group are acceptable, regardless of the value of the group idea or belief. These critics further assert that sensitivity training is often misused to force people into complying with community directives to conform to standards of political correctness. Political correctness has been defined as "avoidance of expressions or actions that can be perceived to exclude or marginalize or insult people who are socially disadvantaged or discriminated against" or the "alteration of language to redress real or alleged injustices and discrimination or to avoid offense." For example, the politically correct (PC) word for someone who is crippled would be *disabled,* and the PC word for someone who is blind would be *visually impaired.* While political correctness seems like a good thing, opponents of the political correctness movement argue that it represents a totalitarian movement toward an ideological state in which citizens will be terrorized into conforming with the PC movement or risk punishment by the State.

This friction between advocates for sensitivity training and opponents of the PC movement has resulted in an emotional reaction to sensitivity training the workplace. In spring, 2000, the Environmental Protection Agency announced to its Washington-area employees that it was planning a series of sensitivity training seminars to "create understanding, sensitivity and awareness of diversity issues and provide a forum for exchanging information and ideas." The course failed miserably. The EPA employees complained the course literature was condescending and one-sided. Many employees seemingly felt that only certain ones of them were being asked to *be sensitive* to the others.

Proponents of the PC movement assert that it merely makes each of us a bit more sensitive to the challenges that our fellow citizens may face on a day-by-day basis. Clearly, the debate will continue. Sensitivity training will continue, and employers and other organizations will continue to assess whether its effectiveness warrants the costs.

SEE ALSO: Continuous Improvement; Feedback; Group Decision Making; Group Dynamics; Human Resource Management; Teams and Teamwork; Training Delivery Methods

Wendy H. Mason
Revised by Joanie Sompayrac

FURTHER READING:

Back, Kurt W. *Beyond Words: The Story of Sensitivity Training and the Encounter Movement.* 2nd ed. New Brunswick, NJ: Transaction Books, 1987.

Golembiewski, Robert T., and Arthur Blumberg, eds. *Sensitivity Training and the Laboratory Approach: Readings about Concepts and Applications.* 2nd ed. Itasca, IL: F.E. Peacock Publishers, Inc., 1973.

Green, Thad B., and Raymond T. Butkus. *Motivation, Beliefs and Organizational Transformation.* Westport, CT: Quorum Books, 1999.

Hornestay, David. "Sensitivity Training Can Strike A Nerve." *Government Executive* 33, no. 2 (February 2001): 73.

Lakin, Martin. *Interpersonal Encounter: Theory and Practice in Sensitivity Training.* New York: McGraw-Hill Book Co., 1972.

Lind, Bill. *The Origins of Political Correctness: An Address.* 2002. Available from <http://www.academia.org/lectures/lind1.html>.

Schloss, Gilbert A., et al. "Some Contemporary Origins of the Personal Growth Group." In *Sensitivity Training and Group Encounter.* edited by Robert W. Siroka, Ph.D., et al. New York: Grosset & Dunlap, 1971.

"Sensitivity Training." In *Encyclopedia of World Problems and Human Potential.* Brussels: Union of International Associations, 1994.

Weiss, Tracey B., PhD, and Franklin Hartle. *Reengineering Performance: Breakthroughs in Achieving Strategy Through People.* Boca Raton, FL: St. Lucie Press, 1997.

SERVICE FACTORY

The term *service factory,* coined by Richard B. Chase and Warren J. Erikson, represents the idea that the factory can be a source of customer service in addition to a place where products are manufactured. Since those who make products (factory workers) are often more knowledgeable about them than those in field service, it stands to reason that they can contribute to sales and marketing efforts. In addition, factory workers can be a resource for installation, maintenance and troubleshooting issues involving the products they had a hand in producing.

Richard B. Chase and David A. Garvin identify four (although there can be more) roles that the service factory can play in strengthening a firm's marketing efforts. These roles are (1) laboratory, (2) consultant, (3) showroom, and (4) dispatcher.

LABORATORY. The service factory can easily serve as a laboratory for testing new products and processes thereby enhancing potential quality and manufacturability of the new products. In addition, the laboratory can serve as a test site for traditional to high-risk experiments to modify or improve existing operations. Chaparral Steel claims that their research and development is done right on the factory floor.

CONSULTANT. The service factory can also serve as a consultant, solving problems out in the field. Since they have worked extensively with both the firm's products and processes, factory workers are a natural source of technical expertise when problems arise. Tektronix serves as a service factory consultant by providing a postcard with a toll-free number to a phone on the shop floor. In addition, factory floor workers can also serve as trainers for use of the product and quality control.

SHOWROOM. As a showroom, the service factory can serve as a working demonstration of the systems and processes the firm uses to manufacturer products as well as a showcase for the factory's products themselves. Nissan in Smyrna, Tennessee offers weekly tours, open to the public, where visitors ride a small train, complete with tour guide, through the manufacturing facility. Throughout the tour the train stops at points of interest, such as robots painting car bodies, where the tour guide emphasizes the quality and superiority of Nissan's processes. Frito-Lay's Vancouver, Washington plant offers three different factory tours, one for wholesalers, one for retailers, and one for the public.

DISPATCHER. As a dispatcher the service factory serves as the linchpin of after-sales support. The service factory can help their customers avoid stock-outs and the resulting downtime by quickly providing replacement parts. This responsiveness can then be emphasized by the company's sales force. Of course, this requires that the dispatcher firm be able to anticipate demand surges.

In order to make the service factory work, manufacturing and marketing personnel must work well together. Shop floor employees will need to be trained in communication skills. In addition to marketing personnel, factory managers and workers must understand customer needs.

There is evidence that the service factory concept can be applied in countries other than the U.S. as examples have been explored in the U.K., Germany and Hungary. In addition there are recommendations that the service factory concept be applied throughout global supply chains and not just limited to single factory use.

SEE ALSO: Service Industry; Service Operations; Service Process Matrix

R. Anthony Inman

FURTHER READING:

Chase, Richard B., and David A. Garvin. "The Service Factory." *Harvard Business Review,* July-August 1989: 61–69.

———. "The Service Factory." *Academy of Management Executive* 2, no. 3 (1988): 191–196.

Chickan, Attila, and Krisztina Demeter. "Services Provided by Manufacturing—The Hungarian Case." *International Journal of Production Economics* 46-47 (December 1996): 489–495.

Lin, Binshan, Christopher L. Martin, and John A Vassar. "Strategic Implications of the Service Factory." *Human Systems Management* 14, no. 3 (1995): 219–226.

Lin, Binshan, and John A. Vassar. "The Service Factory: Implications for Manufacturing Managers." *Industrial Management and Data Systems* 92, no. l: 18–22.

Seuring, Stefan. "Outsourcing into Service Factories: An Exploratory Analysis of Facility Operators in the German Chemical Industry." *International Journal of Operations and Production Management* 23, no. 10 (2003): 1207–1233.

Turley, Lou W., and Douglas L. Fugate. "The Multi-Dimensional Nature of Service Facilities: Viewpoints and Recommendations." *The Journal of Services Marketing* 6, no. 3 (1992): 37–45.

Voss, Chris. *Applying Service Concepts in Manufacturing.* 12, no. 4 (1992): 93–99.

Youngdahl, William E., and Arvinder P.S. Loomba. "Service-Driven Global Supply Chains." *International Journal of Service Industry Management* 11, no. 4 (2000): 329.

SERVICE INDUSTRY

The growth of the service industry in the past two decades has prompted a number of questions about this sector of the American economy and the reasons for this trend. Some questions about the growth of the service industry include: What is the service industry and what types of businesses operate in it? What are the trends in growth for the service industry and the reasons underlying its growth? How is the service sector affected by recessions and economic downswings? What are the human resources issues associated with the service industry? How is offshoring affecting American service jobs? What is expected in the future for the service industry?

DEFINITION OF THE SERVICE INDUSTRY

In the U.S. economy, jobs can be categorized into sectors, which can then be split into divisions, each of which include various industries. There are two major sectors in the U.S. economy, as identified by the U.S. Standard Industry Classification System: the goods-producing sector and the service-producing sector. The goods-producing sector includes agriculture, forestry, and fishing; mining; construction; and manufacturing. The service-producing sector includes the divisions of (1) transportation, communications, and utilities; (2) wholesale trade; (3) retail trade; (4) finance, insurance, and real estate; (5) public administration; and (6) services. This sixth group—the services division—includes a number of industries (see Table 1).

Table 1
Main Groups of Industries in the Services Division

- Some agricultural services (including landscaping and horticulture)
- Hotels and other places of lodging
- Personal services (including dry cleaning, tax preparation, and hair cutting)
- Business services (including temporary agencies and business software developers)
- Automotive services
- Miscellaneous repairs
- Motion pictures
- Amusements and recreation
- Healthcare
- Legal services
- Private education
- Social services
- Museums, zoos, and botanical gardens
- Membership organizations (including houses of worship and clubs)
- Engineering and management services (including consulting)
- Other miscellaneous services

The service sector is difficult to define and to encompass. There are a number of ways to identify the sector, its divisions, its industries, and the types of jobs within them. The general category of the service division includes a wide variety of industries, but can be categorized into primarily consumer-oriented (providing a service directly to a consumer), primarily business-oriented (providing a service directly to another business) or mixed (providing services to both businesses and individual consumers).

Alternately, the services division activities can be described by their economic activities as physical, intellectual, aesthetic, and other experiential activities. Physical activities involve working with objects; examples include repairing cars, landscaping, cutting hair, or preparing a meal. Intellectual activities involve providing education or training, such as at a university or trade school. The aesthetic activities entail providing consumers with artistic or visual experiences; museums, theater performances, art shows, and musical performances are examples. Finally, other experiential activities involve providing customers with recreation, such as in amusement and theme parks, zoos, or campgrounds.

A final way in which to categorize services is by what is transformed through the service. A service may transform a physical object, which occurs when something is repaired, altered, or improved. Having an article of clothing custom-made, a room remodeled, or an appliance repaired would involve transforming a physical object. Service division jobs may also change a consumer. Examples of changes to consumers are education, whereby the consumer learns knowledge or skills; health care, in which a person's health is improved; or personal services, such as when a hairstylist cuts a consumer's hair. A change to an organization is a third type of transformation involved in the service industry. For instance, a management consulting firm may make changes to an organization's structure or business processes to improve it. The final set of jobs in this categorization captures those professions in which there is no apparent object. For example, when an attorney provides legal representation to a client, or in professional sports competitions a service is provided, even though no specific object can be identified.

GROWTH IN THE SERVICES DIVISION

Data from the U.S. Bureau of Labor Statistics indicates that more than 97 percent of the jobs added to U.S. payrolls from 1990 to 2002 were provided by the service-producing sector. In 1984, the number of jobs in manufacturing was relatively comparable to the number of jobs in the services, but by 1999, the service industry employed about twice as many individuals as manufacturing or government.

The three industries within the services division that experienced the most growth in the last decade have been (1) business services, (2) health care, and (3) social services. The business services areas in which the largest number of jobs were gained were personnel supply and computer services. The personnel supply area includes organizations such as temporary employment agencies, traditional employment agencies, and other organizations that supply labor to other companies. The computer services industry includes mass-produced software, custom programming, custom computer systems design, and computer leasing. The primary reason for growth in both of these areas has been changes in business processes.

In the health care industry, there were four components that added large numbers of jobs: offices of physicians and other practitioners, nursing and personal care facilities, hospitals, and home health care. These components gained 430,000 to 1.2 million jobs each between 1990 and 2002. Two main reasons for this increase are new medical procedures, with which additional personnel are required to perform them, and because of the increased number of elderly persons in the U.S. and their requisite health care needs.

The third industry that gained the most jobs in the services division is social services. Social services encompass daycare for children, residential care for the elderly, and other family services; engineering and management services; private education; recreation and amusement; and membership organizations (e.g., houses of worship).

The reasons for growth in the largest growth area of the services division—the business-oriented services—can be linked to three broad economic developments relevant to those services: contractual arrangements, increased construction activity, and changes in technology.

First, contractual labor arrangements, such as outsourcing, have created opportunities in the field of personnel supply (e.g., temporary agencies and employee leasing). This is due primarily to the increased demand for temporary employees from U.S. businesses that want more flexibility in staffing and more control over labor costs. Additionally, as temporary and leasing agencies provide more training for the employees that they place with companies, this has made use of such agencies more attractive to many companies. A related reason for increased demand of such agencies is that many core employees are hired after a stint as temporary employees, which reduces recruitment and staffing costs for the companies utilizing temporary agencies. These contractual labor arrangements have also contributed to the growth of management services, such as consulting and facilities support. Finally, engineering services have changed; many engineers now operate under these new contractual arrangements rather than working for one employer as an employee.

The second major economic development that has led to growth in jobs in business-oriented services is the increase in construction activity. More construction brings higher demand for engineering, architecture, surveying, landscaping, and horticultural services. The third major economic development, improved technology, has driven a higher demand for computer services, such as computer repair, technical support, and software development. Management and engineering services, in the form of consulting, have also grown with this improved computer technology.

RECESSIONS AND THE SERVICES DIVISION

The U.S. Bureau of Labor Statistics (BLS) has studied the effects of economic recessions and expansions on the industries in the services division. The common wisdom has been that the service industry resists economic recessions; and to some extent that is true. Typically, the services do not show a decline in employment during the course of a recession. However, the BLS has found that some areas of the service sector are affected by economic downturns, indicated by a slowing of job growth.

Most areas of the services division are cyclical, which means that they are likely to experience slow growth or may even lose jobs during a recession. Engineering and management are the most cyclical areas of the services division and typically lose jobs in the average quarter of a recession. One reason for this is that these types of companies (e.g., management consulting firms, architectural firms) depend heavily on projects, not on ongoing production, which are likely to be cut back in times of economic recession. Business services are also cyclical, particularly with personnel supply (e.g., employment agencies) and computer services (e.g., custom software creation). Other cyclical areas are in agricultural services, because of the landscaping and horticultural component; automotive services, such as car rentals and repairs; miscellaneous repairs; the lodging industry; personal services, such as laundry, cleaning, and garment services; and motion pictures.

There are five areas of the services division that are deemed at least minimally counter-cyclical—that is, they gain jobs more quickly during a recession than in normal times. Health care services are the most counter-cyclical, gaining jobs rapidly during an economic downturn. This is likely due to the nature of this industry; health care is unaffected by recession because consumers see it as a necessity rather than something that can be used less often depending on the economy. Moreover, because much of U.S. health care costs are supplemented by Medicare, Medicaid, and private insurance, this funding is not susceptible to competition

with other types of purchases, and the benefits continue to be available to Americans during times of recession and unemployment.

The health care industry is one that is truly counter-cyclical; however, there is no strong consensus as to why this is. There is some evidence that health actually improves during economic recessions in the reduced use of tobacco and through improvements in diet an exercise. Thus, the demand for health care is unlikely to be driving the growth of this industry. Rather, some experts believe that the health care industry benefits from higher unemployment rates during a recession, because more people are likely to pursue jobs in the health care industry when unemployment is high. Because this industry tends to have many job vacancies, a recession may create a higher supply of employees to fill these jobs.

The other counter-cyclical service sector groups, as identified by the U.S. Bureau of Labor Statistics, are not truly counter-cyclical, in that they do not show statistical significance of this characteristic. However, they are likely to be less cyclical than the other areas of the service sector. One of these ostensibly counter-cyclical areas is private education, which is in higher demand when more people are unemployed due to an economic recession. That is, if people can't find jobs, they tend to go back to school, resulting in higher demand for teachers and administrators in public education. The other areas—child day care, amusements and recreations, and private colleges—exhibit their counter-cyclical tendencies because they tend to have fairly unattractive, low-paying jobs, which people are less likely to take in strong economic conditions, but more likely to take when the unemployment rate is high. A higher unemployment rate means that more attractive job opportunities in other industries are less available, and people must turn to less attractive jobs. Labor shortages in these lower paying industries are likely to be high in times of economic expansions, and thus these areas are less likely to be cyclical in their nature.

HUMAN RESOURCES IN THE SERVICES DIVISION

As jobs in the U.S. economy shift from the goods-producing sector to the services sector, so do many of the tasks involved in successful human resource management. Job analysis, recruitment and selection, training, performance appraisal, compensation, and labor relations are all likely to be affected by this current trend towards increased services jobs. There are a few specific concerns for human resources in the service industry:

Job analysis, which involves gathering information to understand how to successfully perform a job, is likely to be conducted differently in service jobs than in manufacturing jobs. Because much of service work is knowledge work, in which job activities are less observable, this may mean differences in the way that job analysis is conducted. In service jobs, observation of job tasks may not be as useful as interviewing job incumbents or using a standardized form such as the Position Analysis Questionnaire.

Recruitment and selection practices in the services sector are as varied as the types of positions in this sector. The areas that are counter-cyclical or non-cyclical, however, may require stronger or more creative recruitment practices. As mentioned previously, many of the job areas that grow during economic recessions do so because there are fewer attractive job options available. Thus, during strong economic conditions, these areas (i.e., health care, day care, amusement and recreation, and private colleges) may have difficulty recruiting job applicants, and may need to be more innovative in their approach. During strong economic times, this may also mean that these counter-cyclical areas may find a lack of suitable job candidates, which may mean that selection criteria are changed, such that some skills are trained by the organization rather than having them present upon hire.

Training in the services sector may require increased attention to technology skills, as many service sector jobs now require the use of computers. Even entry-level retail jobs make use of computer technology for inventory and sales, and the ability to use these machines is critical. Additionally, customer-service skills are a crucial training need in many service industry jobs; thus, this type of training is likely to increase in value in service jobs.

Performance appraisal in the service sector is likely to be different than in the goods producing sector. While a physical accounting of performance through measuring production is possible in manufacturing and similar industries, it is less possible in service jobs. There may not be observable outcomes in service sector jobs. Thus, appraising performance by measuring behaviors is more appropriate for this sector. Additionally, outcomes other than production can be measured in service jobs: customer satisfaction, sales in a retail location, or other outcomes can be meaningful ways to measure performance.

Compensation in the goods-producing sector can be specifically linked to productivity (e.g., actual goods produced), but tying compensation to outcomes in the services sector may be more difficult. Some outcomes are easy to measure, such as in the number and value of homes sold by a real estate agent, but others are more difficult to assess, such as the degree to which a customer service representative has successfully resolved a customer's problem. Thus, compensation that effectively rewards and motivates employees must be based on a performance appraisal that reliably and accurately captures performance. Human resources managers should use caution when developing rewards based on outcomes; a poorly designed incentive system may result in employees aiming for outcomes at the expense of customers. For instance, if a car repair shop pays employees for each new set of brakes they install, employees may begin to try to sell brakes to customers who don't need them in order to receive extra pay.

Labor unions originally grew in prominence in goods-producing jobs but now also represent many employees in the service industry. Although labor union membership has declined overall in recent decades, unions are still a presence in both manufacturing and service jobs. For instance, the Service Employees International Union (SEIU) is the largest and fastest growing union in North America, representing employees in areas of health care (e.g., nurses and nursing home employees), public services (e.g., schoolteachers and other government employees), building services (e.g., janitors and security guards), and industrial and allied employees (i.e., services in industrial companies). The SEIU has actually grown in membership over the years, from 625,000 members in 1980 to over 1.8 million today, and this growth has coincided with the increase of jobs in the services industry. Many service sector employees seek representation from a union due to concerns about pay, benefits, and job security that may not be as strong as in some other areas of the economy.

OFFSHORING

One topic that is becoming increasingly important to the services division of the U.S. economy is offshoring. Offshoring occurs when U.S. jobs and production are relocated to a foreign country. Offshoring can be contrasted with outsourcing, which occurs when a company contracts with another company to perform part of their work, but does not necessarily shift to a foreign country.

While offshoring has received a great deal of recent media attention and increasing in the U.S., levels of job losses in the service sector due to offshoring are small relative to total U.S. employment. McCarthy indicates that an estimated 103,000 jobs moved offshore in 2000, and Mark Zandi estimates that the loss in service jobs due to offshoring was about 75,000 per year from February 2001 to October 2003. U.S. employment statistics further indicate the small risk for offshoring of service jobs, with approximately 14 million jobs currently at risk for offshoring, but about 96 million jobs at low risk for offshoring in 2000. However, these estimates may either understate or overstate the total effect of offshoring on U.S. employment. New jobs may have been created overseas by U.S. companies, rather than shifting existing jobs away from the U.S.

Offshoring of service jobs has increased and is likely continue to do so, experts believe. Research indicates that offshoring has increased pace in recent years. This trend is worrisome, because of the possible impact on the U.S. economy. Some analysts believe that the service sector taking longer to rebound from the 2001 recession is partly due to offshoring. McCarthy estimates that a cumulative job loss of 3.4 million jobs and respective wage loss of about $151 billion will occur by 2015. The increase in offshoring has caught the attention of U.S. lawmakers, as Congress and state legislators have focused attention on the issue and have even introduced legislation to limit offshoring.

India has gained many U.S. service sector jobs through offshoring in recent years. Much of this is due to India's focus on becoming more prominent in the world in their information technology capabilities. Additionally, many Indians now pursue higher education to give them skills that prepare them for jobs in which there is a labor shortage. For instance, many U.S. employers are now hiring Indian call center agencies to provide customer service to clients in North America. Calls from overseas (e.g., American) customers are routed to an Indian call center, where an Indian employee who speaks English (often with little Indian accent) assists the customer with his or her computer problem or other customer service need. Because skilled Indian employees cost far less than similarly skilled American employees, offshoring for this job is very attractive to American companies wanting to cut costs. Author Paul Davies notes that the annual cost in 2003 of an American employee in a U.S. call center was about $43,000 but that a similarly skilled Indian employee cost about $6200.

THE FUTURE OF THE SERVICE INDUSTRY

As detailed above, the U.S. economy has experienced a shift from goods-producing jobs to service-sector jobs. Projections by the U.S. Department of Labor's Bureau of Labor Statistics expects this trend to continue with service jobs accounting for approximately 20.8 million of the 21.6 million new jobs from 2002 to 2012. In particular, jobs in the education and health services areas are expected to grow the fastest, adding more jobs than any other area of this sector at an estimated 31.8 percent Additionally, professional and businesses services (e.g., employment services; professional, scientific, and technical services; computer systems design; management jobs) will grow at a high rate (30.4 percent). Jobs in information will increase by an estimated 18.5 percent; this area includes jobs related to software and Internet publishing and broadcasting, and Internet service providers. Another area that will increase is leisure and hospitality, with

employment growing by 17.8 percent due to an increased demand for leisure activities, accommodations, and food services. Trade, transportation, and utilities will increase by 14.1 percent in jobs related to transportation and warehousing; the retail trade; and water, sewage, and other utilities. A 12.3 percent growth is expected in employment in financial activities, with increases in jobs in real estate, finance, and insurance. Governmental service jobs should also grow at a rate of 11.8 percent, with jobs in public education and hospitals, state and local governments, and the federal government increasing in number. Finally, other non-governmental services that should increase at a predicted 15.7 percent are jobs in religious organizations, personal care services (e.g., hair stylists), and private household employment (e.g., cleaning services).

The services sector is distinct from the goods-producing sector in the U.S. economy, and includes a very wide variety of industries and jobs. The number of jobs in the services sector has been growing in recent years, and data from the U.S. government indicate that this trend will continue. While many service sector jobs are believed to be recession-proof, only some areas of that sector are truly counter-cyclical, and some are simply noncyclical, meaning that they resist job loss during times of economic downturn. As service sector jobs increase in number, there are new concerns for managing human resources, one of which is the issue of offshoring, which is increasingly slowly.

SEE ALSO: Human Resource Management; Outsourcing and Offshoring; Service Factory; Service Operations; Service Process Matrix

Marcia J. Simmering

FURTHER READING:

Davies, Paul. *What's This India Business?: Offshoring, Outsourcing, and the Global Services Revolution.* Yarmouth, ME: Nicholas Brealy Publishing, 2004.

Garner, C. Alan. "Offshoring in the Service Sector: Economic Impact and Policy Issues." *Economic Review—Federal Reserve Bank of Kansas City* 89, no. 3 (2004): 5–37.

Goodman, Bill, and Reid Steadman. "Services: Business Demand Rivals Consumer Demand in Driving Job Growth." *Monthly Labor Review,* April 2002.

Goodman, William C. "Employment in Services Industries Affected by Recessions and Expansions." *Monthly Labor Review,* October 2001.

McCarthy, John C. "3.3 Million U.S. Service Jobs to Go Offshore." *WholeView TechStrategy Research,* 11 November 2002.

————. "Near-Term Growth of Offshoring Accelerating." *Trends,* 14 May 2004.

U.S. Department of Labor, Bureau of Labor Statistics. "Tomorrow's Jobs." *Occupational Outlook Handbook* 2004-05 ed. Available from <www.bls.gov>.

Zandi, Mark. "OffShoring Threat." 24 October 2003.

SERVICE OPERATIONS

Services lie at the hub of economic activity in the United States. Service jobs account for almost 80 percent of total U.S. employment. As such, we say that the U.S. has a service economy. Within this service economy, the term service has several meanings when paired with other words. For example, a service firm is defined as one that derives more than 50 percent of its sales from providing services. RCA's service revenues now exceed its revenues from electronic manufacturing. A service package is a bundle of explicit and implicit benefits performed with a supporting facility and using facilitated goods. When you eat at a fast food restaurant (supporting facility), you may purchase a hamburger (facilitating good) that someone else cooked for you (service). The service concept is the perception and expectations of the service itself in the minds of the customers, employers, shareholders, and lenders. The service system is the equipment, layout, and procedures used to provide the service and maintain quality and delivery standards. The service revolution relates to the shift in the United States to a service economy and the proliferation of service automation.

A service operation is an open transformation process of converting inputs (consumers) to desired outputs (satisfied consumers) through the appropriate application of resources (family, material, labor, information, and the consumer as well). More simply, services are economic activities that produce time, place, form, or psychological utility. A meal in a fast food restaurant saves time. A meal with a date in an elegant restaurant with superior service provides a psychological boost. Wal-Mart attracts millions of customers because they can find department store merchandise, groceries, gasoline, auto service, dry cleaning, movie rental, hair styling, eyeglasses and optical services, and nursery items all in one place.

The U.S. economy consists of sectors producing goods and services. The goods-producing sector consists of manufacturing, construction, and extractive industries such as agriculture, mining, forestry, and fishing. Different types of services include business services such as consulting, banking and financial services; trade services such as retailing, maintenance and repair; social/personal services such as restaurants and healthcare; public services such as government and education; and infrastructure services such as transportation and communication.

SERVICES IN THE UNITED STATES

Services are not peripheral activities, but are an integral part of society. Except for basic subsistence living, services are an absolute necessity for a functional economy and enhancement of the quality of life. While an industrial society defines the standard of living by the quantity of goods, a service society sees the standard of living through quality of life as measured by health, education, and recreation. The central figure in this society is the professional who can provide information rather than energy or physical strength. In addition, infrastructure services (communication and transportation) are seen as essential links between sectors of the economy. These infrastructure services are prerequisites for the industrialization of an economy, so no advanced society can be without them.

The United States, like most societies, began as an agricultural economy. As manufacturing became dominant, the economy became centered around industry. In the early part of the twentieth century, only 30 percent of those employed in the United States were working in services, with the rest in industry or agriculture. However, by 1950, half of the workforce was employed in services. In 1956, for the first time in the history of our industrial society, the number of white-collar workers exceeded the number of blue-collar workers. The United States can no longer be characterized as an industrial society, but rather as a postindustrial or service society. Services now account for approximately 70 percent of the national income and 80 percent of the jobs.

A traditional lack of productivity in the service sector is one reason for its increasing growth. Generally, productivity in services lags that in manufacturing and agriculture. As productivity grows faster in some segments (manufacturing and agriculture) these segments will invariably shed jobs that will then be picked up by the less productive sector (services). Also, during the past four recessions in the United States, service-industry employment actually increased as jobs in manufacturing decreased or were lost to other countries. This suggests that consumers will postpone purchases of hard goods but are not willing to give up services such as education, telephone service, banking, healthcare, and public services (such as fire and police protection). Finally, countries with successful manufacturing histories are the ones that now have the ability to create service jobs. There is a ripple effect from manufacturing to the creation of services, along with a continual stream of newly invented services for sale. Also, services can now be bought in greater quantities than in the past.

The fact is that the service sector has replaced the goods-producing sector as the economy's dominant force. This shift in the economic locus has variously been called the service sector revolution, the postindustrial revolution, the information age, and the technotronic age.

CHARACTERISTICS OF SERVICES

While the variety of services is endless, there are a number of characteristics that most services share. Services are generally performed with an open-systems perspective, that is, the system is not closed or isolated from the consumer as it is in manufacturing. The consumer is said to be within the service's "factory." There is a high degree of customer contact throughout the service process, with the customer frequently participating in the process itself. Customer participation within the process means that there is simultaneous production and consumption; thus, the service cannot be stored for later use, possibly as a buffer to absorb fluctuations in demand.

Although services can have tangible (high goods content) and intangible (low goods content) attributes, services are generally regarded as intangible, that is, you can't see, feel, or test a service's performance before purchasing it. Hence, reputation is extremely important. Since services are intangible, it makes sense that they can't be patented. The intangibility of services sometimes makes it difficult for the service firm to identify their product. Is the product at a restaurant the food itself, the service, or the atmosphere? Another problem, due to intangibility, is the difficulty in measuring output. Service output tends to be variable and nonstandard, making quality control and productivity measurement a problem. In fact, quality control is usually limited to process control. Even this is difficult since a high degree of personal judgment by the individual performing the service makes homogeneous input a near impossibility. Measures of effectiveness and efficiency are also subjective.

Services are time perishable. An empty seat on an airline means that that seat on that flight will never be available again. The same holds true for an empty hotel room. The empty room will never again be available on that particular night. The usefulness of service capacity is time-dependent—another reason that services cannot be inventoried and held for a later date. This means that services cannot be transferred or resold but must be sold directly to the customer. It also means that services cannot be mass produced.

Labor intensity is another characteristic of services. In fact, labor is usually the most important determinant of service organization effectiveness.

Site selection for services is usually dictated by the location of consumers. Preferably, services will utilize decentralized facilities within close proximity to customers.

Services can also have very weak barriers to entry. Though not true for all services, many require little in the way of capital investment, proprietary technology, or multiple locations.

CLASSIFYING SERVICE FIRMS

Service firms can be classified according to their various characteristics. This allows clarification of the relationships between firms and customers and of potential strategies for competition.

A simple classification of services is by capital intensity and labor skills. This allows services to be grouped into equipment-based services and people-based services. Equipment-based services can then be subdivided into automatic services such vending machines and automated car washes; services monitored by unskilled labor, such as dry cleaning and movie theaters; and services operated by skilled labor, such as excavating, airlines, and computer services. People-based services are subdivided into those utilizing unskilled labor, such as lawn care, security guards, and janitorial service; those utilizing skilled labor, such as appliance repair, plumbing, catering, electrical work, and auto body repair; and professional services such as law, medicine, accounting, and consulting.

Though generally thought of as a manufacturing tool, Wheelwright and Hayes's product-process matrix also provides a basis for classifying services. This framework groups firms based on their position on the product life cycle and product structure and their stage within the process life cycle and process structure, yielding the classifications of project, job shop, batch, repetitive-assembly, and continuous-flow manufacturing. Projects include professional services in which the process is characterized by a number of interrelated, well-defined activities, accomplished in a sequence. Doctors, lawyers, and architects typically manage a number of projects. Job shops and batches define services that are tailored to the customers' specifications. Repetitive assembly has a line flow, as do services that can be standardized and divided into routine tasks such as university registration, license renewal, and military medical examinations.

Richard Chase has argued that service delivery systems can be improved by separating them into high- and low-contact operations and managing them accordingly. High-contact services must have their operations near the customer and must be able to interact well with the public, since quality is often subjective (in the eye of the beholder). Output is variable, so wages have to be time-based. Low-contact services can place their operations near their suppliers, labor, or transportation, since the customer is not in the environment. The workforce is required to have only technical skills, as work would be performed on a customer surrogate. This also allows wages to be output-based.

Roger Schmenner expanded this concept by including the degree of labor intensity and customization with the contact (interaction) classification. Service firms with low interaction/customization utilize standard operating procedures and pay less attention to physical surroundings. Firms with high interaction/customization strive to maintain quality, react to customer intervention and gain employee loyalty. Low labor-intensive firms concentrate on capital decisions, technological advances, maintaining a high utilization rate, and scheduling service delivery. Highly labor-intensive services emphasize workload scheduling, managing growth, hiring, training, and employee welfare.

In his 1986 article, "How Can Service Businesses Survive and Prosper," Shemenner provided a framework for understanding services and utilizing them strategically. This framework, which resembles Wheelwright and Hayes's Product-Process Matrix and is used in similar fashion, is called the Service Process Matrix. Within this matrix service firms are classified by their position on a graph with two dimensions. The horizontal dimension is the degree of labor intensity, which is defined as the ratio of labor cost to capital cost. The vertical dimension of the matrix measures the degree of customer interaction and customization. Firms that have a high degree of labor intensity and a high degree of interaction/customization are termed professional services. Service firms with a high degree of labor intensity but a low degree of interaction/customization are called mass services. Low labor intensity and a high degree of interaction/customization characterize the service shop, while firms with both low labor intensity and a low degree of interaction/customization constitute a service factory.

As with the product-process matrix, firms on the service matrix have strategic implications dependent upon where they fit within the matrix. Again like the product process matrix, service firms are generally more effective if they stay in close proximity to a diagonal running from the upper-left corner to the lower-right corner of the matrix.

SERVICES AND MANUFACTURING

Theodore Levitt, in his classic article, "Production-Line Approach to Service," describes how service managers can design their operations to achieve the economics of production. The design and conversion processes of services are sometimes called the "technical core." By insulating the technical core such that the customer has essentially no personal contact with the service providers, the business can operate more efficiently. The technical core can be insulated by restricting the offerings (fast food restaurants have very limited menus); customizing at delivery (as computers are); structuring the service in such a way that the customer has to go where the service is offered (like banks); trying to incorporate self-service so that customers can shop at their own pace; and separating services that lend themselves to automation (ATMs and vending machines). By insulating the technical core one can essentially apply to services what has been learned in manufacturing, namely standardization and mass delivery. Levitt uses the example of McDonald's to provide a picture of a service that utilizes manufacturing techniques to the point that the end product results in what he terms the "technocratic hamburger." McDonald's makes use of a limited menu, division of labor, a standardized product (food preparers at McDonald's have little or no discretion when it comes to making the product), task grouping to allow specialized skills, and an assembly-line approach, all applied to the technical core that is insulated (away from the ordering and seating area) from the consumer.

LOCATION AND LAYOUT IN SERVICES

Location selection in services is a macro decision, while site selection is a micro decision. As with manufacturing, service location decisions involve such variables as expansion, impact on the environment, and governmental regulation. However, services also factor in such variables as access, visibility, traffic, competition and parking.

Service layout requirements are somewhat different from manufacturing but the same terminology is used. In both services and manufacturing we find the fixed-position layout, process layout, and product, or in this case, service-based layout. The fixed-position layout is the simplest. In this situation, the customer remains in one place throughout the service as materials and labor are brought to that location. If the customer or item being serviced must remain in one location, the service must relocate there, as with pool cleaning, landscaping, or home decorator consulting. In other cases, the nature of the equipment dictates a fixed position. Examples include dialysis machines, beauty salons, or psychiatric counseling.

In process layouts, similar machines, such as hair dryers in a beauty salon, are grouped together to produce batches of services (much the same as in the batch or disconnected line-flow process of the product-process matrix). University classrooms and movie theaters provide excellent examples of a process layout in a service environment.

If the equipment required to serve the customer is sequentially arranged according to the steps of the service process, the layout is said to be service-based (or product layout). As in manufacturing, the product layout can be continuous (without interruption) and is usually lacking in flexibility. Drivers license renewal, registration for university classes, and cafeterias are examples of a service or product layout.

SERVICE OPERATIONS STRATEGY

As with manufacturing, service operations require a strategic approach. Metters, King-Metters, Pullman and Walton describe the strategic planning process as a hierarchy consisting of strategic positioning, service strategy, and tactical execution

STRATEGIC POSITIONING. Strategic positioning involves first defining the firm's target market. In other words, what is the set of customers the firm seek to serve. Next, the firm must determine its core competence or what will distinguish it from other service firms, i.e., cost leadership, differentiation, or focus. At this point, the firm then must make decisions regarding its mission and high-level goals and objectives.

SERVICE STRATEGY. At the service strategy level, the service firm must define its service concept, operating system and service delivery system. The service strategy links the firm's strategic position with tactical execution. The firm begins by determining its competitive priorities, and its order winners and order qualifiers. Competitive priorities are the characteristics of the firm or things that it does better than other service firms (e.g., low cost, quality, service, or flexibility). The firm's competitive priority(s) must be both an order qualifier and an order winner. The order qualifier is a characteristic that the service must possess in order to compete in the market. If the firm lacks this then the consumer will not even consider purchasing the firm's service. The order winner is the characteristic that will cause the consumer to purchase the firm's service over its competitors. The service concept then is the set of competitive priorities that the target market values.

The operating strategy describes how the firm's different functions (marketing, finance, and operations) will support the service concept. If the firm's order winning competitive priority is quality, what will operations do to ensure quality of the service and how will marketing promote this characteristic?

The service delivery system defines the components of the system necessary to execute the service concept. Examples of the needed variables are capacity requirements, quality management systems, and management policies. Each of these should support the firm's competitive priorities so that the firm is clearly distinct from its competitors.

TACTICAL EXECUTION. Finally, the firm approaches tactical execution issues. Tactical execution involves the day-to-day activities required to function and support the service strategy. Included are capacity management, facility location, inventory management, facility layout, supplier selection, operations scheduling, staffing, and productivity improvement.

Decisions that are made in the above strategic planning process are heavily influenced by their position on Marc McCluskey's service maturity model. This model divides service maturity into four stages:

Stage 1: Baseline service—the focus is mainly on responding to requests in a timely manner.

Stage 2: Operational efficiency—the focus is on cost reduction

Stage 3: Customer support excellence—the focus is on efficiency

Stage 4: The focus is on changing the concept of service and growing market opportunity

McCluskey notes that most firms are still in stage 1, moving into the second.

AUTOMATION IN SERVICES

A recent phenomenon in services is the application of automation. Often services lag manufacturing and agriculture in productivity. One way to improve productivity in services is to remove the customer from the process as much as possible by whatever means possible. One way is the use of automation. Many of these applications are things we see everyday but give little consideration; most were introduced in fairly recent times.

Financial services have seen the proliferation of ATMs and the use of electronic funds transfer. Education makes use of PCs, audio-visual equipment, calculators, translation computers and electronic library cataloguing. Restaurants and supermarkets make wholesale use of optical scanning. If you have been to Las Vegas or an airport you have probably stood on a moving sidewalk. Hotels utilize electronic reservation systems, electronic locks, electronic wake-up calls, and message services. Other fields such as government, communication, healthcare, and the leisure industry have all benefited from the automation of services. As technology advances, we are likely to see more and more services being automated as service productivity increases.

SEE ALSO: Inventory Management; Layout; Operations Scheduling; Operations Strategy; Order-Winning and Order-Qualifying Criteria; Product-Process Matrix; Purchasing and Procurement; Service Process Matrix; Vendor Rating

R. Anthony Inman

FURTHER READING:

Levitt, Theodore J. "Production-Line Approach to Service." *Harvard Business Review,* September-October 1972, 41–52.

McCluskey, Marc. "How Mature is Your Service Operation?" *Supply Chain Management Review* 8, no. 5 (2004): 17–20.

Metters, Richard, Kathryn King-Metters, Madeleine Pullman, and Steve Walton. *Successful Service Operations Management.* Mason, OH: Thomson South-Western, 2006.

Schmenner, Roger W. "How Can Service Businesses Survive and Prosper." *Sloan Management Review,* Spring 1986, 21–32.

————. *Service Operations Management.* Englewood Cliffs, NJ: Prentice Hall, Inc., 1995.

SERVICE PROCESS MATRIX

The Service Process Matrix is a classification matrix of service industry firms based on the characteristics of the individual firm's service processes. The matrix was derived by Roger Schmenner and first appeared in 1986. Although considerably different, the Service Process Matrix can be seen somewhat as a service industry version of Wheelwright and Hayes' Product-Process Matrix. The Service Process Matrix can be useful when investigating the strategic changes in service operations. In addition, there are unique managerial challenges associated with each quadrant of the matrix. By paying close attention to the challenges associated with their related classification, service firms may improve their performance.

The classification characteristics include the degree of labor intensity and a jointly measured degree of customer interaction and customization. Labor intensity can be defined as the ratio of labor cost to plant and equipment. A firm whose product, or in this case service, requires a high content of time and effort with comparatively little plant and equipment cost would be said to be labor intense. Customer interaction represents the degree to which the customer can intervene in the service process. For example, a high degree of interaction would imply that the customer can demand more or less of some aspects of the service. Customization refers to the need and ability to alter the service in order to satisfy the individual customer's particular preferences.

The vertical axis on the matrix, as shown in Figure 1, is a continuum with high degree of labor intensity on one end (bottom) and low degree of labor intensity on the other end (top). The horizontal axis is a continuum with high degree of customer interaction and customization on one ends (right) and low degree of customer interaction and customization on the other end (left). This results in a matrix with four quadrants, each with a unique combination of degrees of labor intensity, customer interaction and customization.

Figure 1
The Service Process Matrix

Adapted from Schmenner, Roger W. *Service Operations Management,* Englewood Cliffs, NJ: Prentice Hall, 1995, page 11

The upper left quadrant contains firms with a low degree of labor intensity and a low degree of interaction and customization. This quadrant is labeled "Service Factory." Low labor intensity and little or no customer interaction or customization makes this quadrant similar to the lower right area of the Product-Process Matrix where repetitive assembly and continuous flow processes are located. This allows service firms in this quadrant to operate in a fashion similar to factories, hence the title "Service Factory." These firms can take advantage of economies of scale and may employ less expensive unskilled workers as do most factories. Firms classified as service factories include truck lines, hotels/motels, and airlines.

The upper right quadrant contains firms with a low degree of labor intensity but a high degree of interaction and customization. The upper right quadrant is labeled "Service Shop." Hospitals, auto repair shops and many restaurants are found in this quadrant.

The lower left quadrant contains firms with a high degree of labor intensity but a low degree of interaction and customization. This quadrant is labeled "Mass Service." Mass service providers include retail/wholesale firms and schools.

Finally, the lower right quadrant contains firms with a high degree of labor intensity and a high degree of interaction and customization. The lower right quadrant is labeled "Professional Service." This quadrant is similar to the upper left section of the Product-Process

Matrix where job shops and batch processes are found. Doctors, lawyers, accountants, architects, and investment bankers are typical service providers that tend to be labor intense and have a high degree of customer interaction and customization.

In 1994, Dotchin and Oakland proposed that in addition to the four categories: service factory, service shop, mass service and professional service, a fifth category should be added: personal service. They justify the inclusion by describing personal services as those directed at people, thereby high contact, as opposed to professional services which are directed to things, thereby, achieved with little contact time.

MOVEMENT WITHIN THE MATRIX

On Wheelwright and Hayes' Product-Process Matrix processes appear on a diagonal running from the upper left corner to the lower right corner. Firms that position themselves directly on the diagonal are seen to be the most efficient. Similarly, a notional diagonal can be said to run from the upper left corner to the lower right corner of the Service Process Matrix. Schmenner states that many of the segmentation steps taken by service firms have been toward the diagonal. The attraction seems to be better control. From the perspective of the matrix, need for control would be greater for service shops, which lie completely above the diagonal, and mass services, which lie below the diagonal. The need for control is not as great for service factories and professional services, as evidenced by the fact that the diagonal transverses each of those quadrants.

Schmenner also states that most services that have changed their positions within the matrix over time have tended to move up the diagonal. This, of course, implies a decrease in the degree of interaction and customization and a decrease in labor intensity. Those firms most affected by a move up the diagonal would be found in the professional services where labor intensity and interaction/customization was high. Obviously, any move up the diagonal, be it with professional services, mass service, or service shops, would be a movement toward the service factory.

The legal field, a Professional Service, is a prime example of "up the diagonal" movement. Most have surely noticed the increase of television advertising on the part of some in the legal profession. Other than personal injury, the most prolific amount of advertising seems to come from lawyers seeking cases involving bankruptcy and uncontested divorces. Obviously, these are the cases that require the least amount of customization. By handling this case "in bulk" the attorney also lowers the labor intensity by handling multiple cases in one trip to the court house and enjoys economies of scale just like a factory, a Service Factory.

The traditional restaurant had a considerable degree of customization, customer interaction putting it into the Service Shop category. The fast food industry has taken restaurants into the Service Factory area through the dramatic elimination of customization and lowering of labor intensity. However, the degree of standardization may vary.

Witness Wendy's where you can "hold the pickles; hold the lettuce, special orders don't upset us!" Also, hospitals have seen movement within the matrix. Consider Shouldice Hernia Centre in Canada, a hospital that specializes in one type of surgery so that customization is at it lowest, allowing them to run as a service factory rather than a service shop. Even banking has made movement toward the Service Factory with the universal use of ATMs.

Retailing has also seen changes within the Matrix. Warehouse stores such as Sam's Club and Internet sales have allowed retailers to move from Mass Service to Service Factory by drastically cutting labor intensity. However, some have gone in the opposite direction by becoming full-service boutiques and specialty stores stressing customer interaction, customization and labor intensity.

MANAGERIAL CHALLENGES

There are a number of proposed challenges for management that are inherent in a firm's position within the Service Process Matrix. For firms with low labor intensity, plant and equipment choices are extremely important, implying the need to closer monitor technological advances. Since capacity is somewhat inflexible, scheduling service delivery is more important so demand must be managed. For firms with high labor intensity, workforce issues such as hiring, training, employee development and control, employee welfare and workforce scheduling are critical. Firms with low customer interaction and customization face more marketing challenges than other firms.

The need to "warm up" the service dictates special attention to physical surroundings. For these firms standard procedures are safe to use. In addition, the classic managerial pyramid with many layers and a rigid relationship between layers is appropriate. Firms with high degrees of interaction and customization must manage higher costs resulting from lack of economies of scale. In addition, higher skilled labor costs more and demands more attention, benefits, quality of work life and benefits. The managerial hierarchy tends to be flatter and less rigid.

RECENT CHANGES

While the concept of the Service Process Matrix is conceptual or theoretical in nature, it should be noted that in 2000, Rohit Verma conducted an exploratory study, using a broad sample of quantitative data, in an attempt to validate the idea that management challenges do differ across the different types of services represented by the quadrants of the Matrix.

Verma's findings did not closely match the proposed expectations. Capital decisions, technological advances and scheduling service delivery are perceived to be more of a challenge in high interaction/customization. Conversely, hiring, training, employee scheduling, and loyalty were found to become less important at interaction/customization increases.

The importance of managing employee career advancement and marketing of services increases as labor intensity increases. Capital decisions and fighting cost increases were found to be more important for the service factory and the service shop than for mass service and professional service. Starting new operations, workforce scheduling and managing organizational hierarchy were found to be more important for service factory and service shops.

As such, only four of 22 management challenge relationships proposed by the Service Process Matrix were supported by the empirical analysis. Despite this, the Product Service Matrix continues to be the standard classification scheme utilized in service research.

In 2004, Schmenner updated the Service Process Matrix by redefining the axes and the resulting diagonal. He had earlier stated that the lure of the diagonal was the need for control but later changed his mind. He stated that in retrospect, the issue was not control, but productivity that results from "swift, even flow." The concept of Swift, Even Flow argues that productivity increases as the flow of products and information becomes faster and variability decreases. Hence the X axis of the Service Process Matrix changes from interaction and customization to degree of "variation," in the sense that variation occurs in providing the service not that the firm provides a variety of services. Of course, interaction and customization are sources of variation.

The Y axis changes from labor intensity to relative throughput time. Throughput time is the time that elapses between the services or facilitating good's initial availability until the service is complete. The Service Process Matrix is now represented by Swift, Even Flow: Swift = relative throughput time; Even Flow = degree of variation; rather than degree of labor intensity and degree of customer interaction and customization.

Redefining the axes of the Matrix then causes the classification of services to change from the type service itself to the provider of the service. For example, in the previous Matrix, restaurants appeared as service shops. With the new axes, traditional restaurants are still service shops but gourmet restaurants could be considered professional service and fast food restaurants

(with their quick throughput time) would be service factories. Hence, particular services may now be spread out in the Matrix.

In order to improve productivity then, firms would strive to move left and upward or up the diagonal. The previously noted challenges for managers remain the same. Consider Southwest Airlines whose turnarounds are done swiftly with little variation.

Although, not all services fit cleanly into these quadrants, it is instructive, providing insight into service productivity. It also provides insight into how service firms differentiate themselves from each other as well as helping to explain why successful service firms achieved their positions and maintained them.

SEE ALSO: Product-Process Matrix; Service Operations

R. Anthony Inman

FURTHER READING:

Dotchin, John, and John S. Oakland. "Total Quality Management in Services: Part 1: Understanding and Classifying Services." *International Journal of Quality and Reliability Management* 11, no. 3 (1994): 9–26.

Schmenner, Roger W. "How Can Service Businesses Survive and Prosper?" *Sloan Management Review,* Spring 1986, 21–32.

———. "Service Businesses and Productivity." *Decision Sciences* 35, no. 3 (2004): 333–347.

———. *Service Operations Management.* Englewood Cliffs, NJ: Prentice Hall, 1995.

Verma, Rohit. "An Empirical Analysis of Management Challenges in Service Factories, Service Shops, Mass Services, and Professional Services." *International Journal of Service Industry Management* 11, no. 1 (2000).

SHAREHOLDERS

Shareholders or stockholders own parts or shares of companies. In large corporations, shareholders are people and institutions that simply invest money for future dividends and for the potential increased value of their shares, whereas in small companies they may be the people who established the business or who have a more personal stake in it. When investors buy shares of companies, they receive certificates that say how many shares they own. Owning shares of a company often entitles an investor to a part of the company's profits, which is issued as a dividend. In addition, shareholders are typically offered a fixed payout per share if the company is bought out. Because they are partial owners of a company, shareholders are allowed to vote at shareholder meetings for certain company actions (such as approving or rejecting a merger proposal), review company accounts, and receive periodic reports on company performance. If shareholders cannot attend annual meetings, they are permitted to vote by proxy by mailing in their vote. Furthermore, if a company decides to issue more shares, current shareholders have the option to buy shares before they are offered to the public.

Shareholders are entitled to vote on a variety of issues, although the specific areas where shareholders have a say are determined by state laws and corporate bylaws. Generally, shareholders have the right to appoint a corporate president, elect members to a board of directors, and vote on significant changes in a corporation. These significant changes might include changes in the line of business, change of company name, and company divestments, acquisitions, and mergers. Boards of directors act on behalf of the shareholders and, in practice, make most decisions such as appointing corporate officers and reviewing corporate policies, finances, and strategies.

Shareholders may vote only during a corporation's annual shareholder meeting or at a special shareholder meeting, which would normally be called by the board of directors. A notice of the meeting and a notice of the agenda (the major points of the meeting) must be provided before each shareholder meeting. Shareholder voting power is proportionate to the number of shares each shareholder owns. For example, if a corporation had two shareholders—one with 400 shares and one with 100 shares—the one with 400 shares would wield far greater voting power.

Shareholders may own two kinds of stock: common stock and preferred stock. Owners of common stock have the last claim to company profits and assets and they may receive dividends at the discretion of a company's board of directors. In addition, common stock does not have a fixed value. Holders of common stock, therefore, profit when a company performs well and suffer losses when a company does not perform well. Nonetheless, common stockholders are typically the bulk of a publicly traded firm's shareholders and in many cases enjoy voting privileges that preferred stockholders lack. On the other hand, owners of preferred stock have first claim to a company's profits and assets. Investors may own three different kinds of preferred stock: (1) stock with preferred dividends that entitles them to a fixed dividend rate, (2) stock with preferred assets that allows them to receive to the first cut of the money from a company's sale, and (3) stock with both preferred dividends and preferred assets. Shareholders also may own redeemable and convertible stock. Redeemable stock allows a company to repurchase it at some point, whereas convertible stock enables stockholders to exchange preferred stock for common stock.

Companies sell their stocks to raise money. While they have other financing options such as loans and bonds, companies may choose to issue stocks because they need to raise more capital than they can readily borrow, because equity capital may be viewed as less costly than debt financing, or because favorable stock market conditions may present an opportunity for private owners to receive cash for part or all of their shares. Companies may sell their stocks either through private placement or public offerings. Private placement is usually limited to large institutions or a small group of individuals.

Before the rise of the publicly traded corporation, often the families that founded companies were the shareholders, managers, and members of the board of directors. But because these companies needed to raise increasing amounts of capital to expand, they eventually had to turn to outside investors. As a result, outside parties quickly became managers and members of the board. After offering shares to the public, founding family members still retained control of their corporations in many cases; however, shares also were dispersed among a variety of investors who had small holdings. This structure remained in place until the second half of the twentieth century when institutions such as banks, pension funds, and insurance companies began to accumulate large amounts of stocks in specific companies and became the major shareholders in the United States.

TYPES OF SHAREHOLDERS

Shareholders are generally classified as individual investors or institutional investors. Individual investors are individuals who invest their own money and institutional investors are organizations that invest the money of others. Institutional investors include insurance companies, banks, pension funds, and investment companies. The number of individual investors has risen over time, with slight decreases during periods of inflation or recession.

Table 1 Growth of Individual Shareholders	
Period Percentage of U.S. families owning shares	
1989	17
1992	19
1995	15
1998	19
2001	21

Adapted From: *Survey of Consumer Finance*, Federal Reserve Board

Institutional investors also have increased in number and influence. While they once concentrated on short-term investments by planning strategic stock trades, they since have become major players in the long-term investment market. Moreover, institutional investors have been clamoring for a voice in company operations and they are the largest shareholders in the United States. The major institutional investors are pension funds, which invest retirement money. As a result of the trend towards concentration of stock in the hands of institutional investors, companies have become more attentive to their needs.

SIGNIFICANT NATIONAL EVENTS IMPACTING SHAREHOLDERS

In recent years, significant events have occurred in the United States that have directly impacted shareholders: the terrorist attacks of September 11, 2001 and the accounting scandals that were revealed in late 2001.

SEPTEMBER 11. On September 11, 2001, terrorists hijacked four planes that targeted major emblematic and financial centers in the U.S, with three of the four planes impacting their targets, the World Trade Center Towers in New York City, NY and the Pentagon in Washington, D.C. The impact on the U.S. Stock Market was immediate; the exchanges were closed on September 11 and remained closed for four consecutive days. The economy had slowed down prior to the attacks, with a sharp rise in unemployment rates and sluggish GDP growth; these events, coupled with the attacks, did not bode well for the stock market and the economy. Despite best efforts to reassure shareholders and shore up financial markets, stock market prices plummeted 14percentage as investors reacted in the first weeks following the terrorist attacks.

ACCOUNTING SCANDALS. In mid-October 2001, Enron Corporation, one of the largest energy companies in the world, shocked Wall Street by reporting huge losses and a dramatic reduction in shareholder equity. The U.S. Securities and Exchange Commission launched a formal investigation. On December 2, 2001, Enron filed for Chapter 11 bankruptcy. In January 2002, the U.S. Justice Department began a criminal investigation which ultimately revealed accounting discrepancies in the form of overstated earnings, underreported losses, improper transactions and partnerships created to conceal liabilities from investors, as well as the illegal shredding of thousands of key accounting documents, emails, and memorandums by Enron and their accounting firm, Arthur Andersen LLP. Arthur Andersen LLP was indicted by the U. S. Justice Department in March 2002 making it the first major accounting firm ever to be criminally prosecuted.

Starting in 2002 and continuing throughout 2004, various officers of Enron Corp. were prosecuted for their part in the demise of the company. Also in 2004, the remaining accounting firms, now known as the "Big Four", were audited. The investigation into Enron and its fraudulent accounting acts spawned a flurry of similar investigations into Qwest, WorldCom, Global Crossing Ltd, and Tyco International Ltd, among others.

Shareholder confidence was sorely shaken which negatively impacted stock market prices, industry stability, and holdings in both personal and retirement accounts. In 2002, the government responded by passing regulations and safeguards designed to protect shareholder interests, the most impact being the Sarbanes-Oxley Act. The Sarbanes-Oxley Act provides accounting oversight in the form of the Public Company Accounting Oversight Board; requires chief executive officers to certify the accuracy of a company's financial statements, with harsh penalties for knowingly falsifying financial reports; institutes federal criminal penalties for executives and companies who defraud shareholders; prevents investment firms from retaliating against negative criticisms by analysts and protects employees who act as 'whistleblowers' to reveal company misconduct.

In 2004, companies are still coming into compliance with the Sarbanes-Oxley Act and feeling the affects financially. The regulation of corporate accounting will continue to be an issue for many years to come.

SHAREHOLDER CONTROL AND CORPORATE DECISION MAKING

Since shareholders elect a corporation's directors, they can exert a significant amount of influence on a company and its policies, because directors know that they might be fired if shareholders are not satisfied with their performance and their decisions. Nevertheless, shareholders traditionally have been interested mostly in return on investment and hence they have not played a major role in company operations or governance, which they have left to boards and management. However, in recent decades investors have at times bought stocks to seize control of companies.

The influential shareholders are usually institutional shareholders who own large quantities of a company's stock and wield proportionate power. In contrast, individual investors have much less control and can influence decisions only by rallying large numbers of investors to support their position. Consumer advocate Ralph Nader introduced this process—often called a proxy fight—in 1969 to influence General Motors' policies towards public transportation, women, and minorities. However, the Securities and Exchange

Commission issued a ruling in 1983 that helped prevent shareholders buying stocks solely to influence a company's operations. Despite this ruling, the practice of buying stocks to seize control of a company is common. When a company buys a significant share of stock of another company largely to influence its operations against its will, analysts refer to it as a hostile takeover. To prevent hostile takeovers, managers sometimes devote much effort to keeping stock prices high and other defensive tactics, although this strategy has harmed some companies ultimately.

One technique shareholders have used to link top management and shareholder goals has been issuing corporate executives stock options, which allow them to purchase stocks at some point in the future at a predetermined price. If the stock price rises significantly over time (that is, well beyond the predetermined level), these options can provide a substantial profit opportunity for their holders. Therefore, if stock prices rise, both top managers and shareholders benefit and, in theory, their interests are more closely aligned.

SHAREHOLDERS AND MANAGEMENT PERSPECTIVE

Two general perspectives on companies and social responsibility exist in the field of management, making successful management inherently difficult in that managers sometimes must choose between shareholder interests and employee interests. Nevertheless, the interests of shareholders, employees, customers, and other stakeholders ultimately are interconnected, not mutually exclusive.

SHAREHOLDER VALUE. Because of direct and indirect influence from shareholders and because of company dependence on shareholders, many companies make increasing shareholder value a key goal, if not the ultimate goal. Shareholder value refers to a company's value less its debt. In other words, companies create value for their shareholders when their investment returns are more than investment costs. Shareholders normally expect a minimum return on their investments that is equal to the going return on a low-risk investment (e.g., U.S. Treasury securities) plus a risk premium for the level of risk associated with a particular company. For example, a new Internet company is expected to deliver a higher return (higher premium) than IBM, but IBM is more certain of delivering its return (lower risk). As a company delivers such returns, in the form of dividends and share price appreciation, the company is said to be enhancing shareholder value or wealth. If a company is perceived as not increasing shareholder wealth over time, investors may lose confidence and either sells off its shares or pressure the company to take steps to improve its performance, such as by replacing the CEO or altering the corporate strategy.

Managers of a company that focuses on shareholder value will strive to remain abreast of shareholder interests. Consequently, Andrew Black et al. suggest in *In Search of Shareholder Value* that managers must think like entrepreneurs in order to meet shareholders' needs and add to shareholder value, which may require some refocusing if managers are accustomed to simply following the directions of their superiors.

To create additional shareholder value, managers must concentrate on a company's primary revenue-generating functions and running a company as efficiently as possible, which should help a company become a product or service leader and establish closer ties with consumers. Consequently, managers must begin their effort to increase shareholder value by identifying the key revenue-generating functions and then by promoting them. Furthermore, managers must distinguish between the interests of shareholders who have long-term interests in a company's worth and those who have short-term interests. Then they must strive to implement growth strategies that will benefit both kinds of investors insofar as possible, even though these interests may be in conflict with each other, according to J.P. Donlon and John Gutfreund.

However, this approach has come under the attack of employee advocates and other critics. In corporate theory, companies traditionally have been viewed according to the stakeholder model. This model suggests that a company can improve its financial conditions by attending to the needs and desires of its stakeholders, which include not only shareholders but also employees, distributors, customers, and so on. Shareholder and employee interests are sometimes viewed as being at odds with each other, especially around issues such as layoffs. According to the stakeholder model, managers should weigh the interests of one group of stakeholders against the interests of another in order to manage a company fairly. Hence, the shareholder value approach is controversial in that it gives priority to shareholder needs.

Supporters of the shareholder value approach defend their position by arguing that if a company is beholden to more than one interest group, then it will face the dilemma of having to decide between the different groups. If it must decide between competing interests, then the company must base this decision on some additional reason, but companies are hard-pressed to determine what the deciding criterion should be if not increasing shareholder value. The stakeholder model offers no suggestions. Without a decisive criterion, a company would constantly face this kind of dilemma, which would drastically slow-down the decision-making process. Such a dilemma could manifest itself, for example, as a proposal that would increase shareholder value and meet customer needs, but would result in the reducing the workforce.

However, a company does not ignore the interests of other stakeholders while concentrating on shareholder value. For example, employees will quit if their interests are not attended to and customers will patronize the competition if their needs are not met, and so management inevitably must take their needs into consideration. Finally, advocates of this approach contend that if a company fails to be profitable, then it will have to close, which would benefit none of the stakeholders.

EMPLOYEE/SHAREHOLDER PARTNERSHIPS AND THE STAKEHOLDER MODEL. However, not all analysts subscribe to the shareholder value approach to management. Instead, some insist on the stakeholder model, arguing that the needs of both major stakeholder groups—shareholders and employees—can be met if a corporate structure is adopted that breaks down the adversarial relationship between them. The idea is to establish partnerships that empower employees and allow them to play a more active role in company decisions, according to William McDonald Wallace in *Postmodern Management*. The partnership arrangement makes all members' income dependent on company performance, which makes a company's costs flexible and provides an impetus for members to be flexible. This type of relationship, Wallace argues, enables companies to weather recessions and adjust prices to meet pricing tactics of competitors. Consequently, this approach would benefit both shareholders and employees.

Furthermore, while the shareholder value approach can lead to gains and benefits for shareholders, it can also lead to layoffs and closures that adversely affect employees. Because of the ubiquity of shareholder-oriented practices of hostile takeovers, twenty-nine states passed laws to discourage such takeovers. These laws generally require corporate directors to consider the ramifications of their takeover plans on other stakeholders, especially employees. In addition, downsizing and layoffs are often attributed to too much emphasis on shareholder interests by management. Indeed, shareholders seem to encourage and applaud downsizing as stock prices typically increase on the announcement of impending layoffs alone.

Despite complaints from other stakeholders and despite alternative approaches, the shareholder orientation is forecast to remain the dominant bent of corporate management, according to William Beaver in his article "Is the Stakeholder Model Dead?" Beaver argues that three factors contribute to the institutionalization of the shareholder orientation: (1) the growing number of investors in the United States, (2) calls for the privatization of social security, and (3) the growth of using the stock market as a means for investing for retirement. If social security is privatized in part or in whole, investors will demand even more from companies in order to ensure that their stocks grow. Moreover, no opposing approach is gaining much

ground. The stakeholder model, for example, has no major driving force behind it; for instance, labor unions represent only ten percent of the country's workers. In addition, the Republican-controlled Congress of the late 1990s was reluctant to pass any legislation that would impede corporate profits.

Nevertheless, management must attend to the needs of other stakeholders besides shareholders—especially employees and customers—in order to attract and retain highly qualified employees and satisfy customers. Clearly, a company's competitive strategy and human assets underlie the kind of economic performance and profitability needed to sustain shareholder value creation; the two need not be seen as opposing interests. Moreover, management can improve shareholder value while meeting the needs of other stakeholders such as employees and customers.

CORPORATE MONITORS

Shareholders also have come to be seen as monitors of corporations and their management. As the former head of the U.S. Labor Department during the Reagan Administration, Robert Monks argued that shareholding was a responsibility, not the mere buying of favorable stocks and selling unfavorable ones. Instead, Monks argued that shareholders have the responsibility to intervene in a company's operations and help implement policies that will increase a company's worth.

SHAREHOLDER RELATIONS

Because shareholders are owners of the company and because they hold considerable power, the management of public companies faces two ongoing tasks: (1) meeting shareholder needs and providing shareholders with information on company performance and plans, and (2) maximizing the profit of shareholders. Providing shareholders with both of these is the essence of shareholder relations—and one without the other generally will fail to satisfy shareholder demands. Companies must develop information systems that provide shareholders with periodic reports on company performance, since receiving this information constitutes one of the basic rights of shareholders. While a company is required to provide basic information such as sales, profits, assets, and liabilities in annual and quarterly reports, the investors of the late 1980s and the 1990s began demanding more detailed, frequent, and understandable information. Financial analysts and institutional investors in particular have a need for additional information. The accounting scandals of the 2000s and resulting regulations are also demanding more comprehensive disclosure. Furthermore, Securities and Exchange Commission regulations require public companies to release complete and timely information to shareholders. Hence, managers must make sure that the information they provide is current and not misleading. Management also benefits from putting forth effort to cultivate a knowledgeable pool of shareholders who are informed about company activities and goals, who will support management decisions, and who have realistic expectations of the company's potential.

To meet the information needs of different types of investors, some companies have two separate investor relations programs: one for individual investors and one for institutional investors. An individual investor program might include issuing a magazine that highlights key aspects of a company, an annual report, quarterly reports, and a proxy statement seeking support for company proposals by proxy. On the other hand, an institutional investor program might include all the reports and information given to individual investors as well as meetings with these investors in various cities where they are concentrated, periodic conference calls to discuss current results and events, and tours of corporate properties.

Shareholder relations responsibilities cut across a company, extending from company executives on down through the corporate structure. Some companies develop special investor relations departments to handle these responsibilities, while others divide them among various departments. Either way, management must set specific goals when developing a shareholder relations program and management can establish these goals by determining what support it seeks from shareholders and what shareholders think of the company, according to H. Peter Converse in his article for *Investor Relations: The Company and Its Owners*. Since every company is unique to some extent, the goals and methods for achieving the goals will vary from company to company.

By implementing a successful shareholder and potential investor relations program, companies also can accomplish their business goals of advancing company growth and profitability. Through investor relations, companies can increase their ability to raise funds via stock offerings, offer a competitive stock option program to court talented executives, and prevent hostile takeovers.

SEE ALSO: Corporate Governance; Knowledge Management; Stakeholders

Karl Heil

Revised by Monica C. Turner

FURTHER READING:

Anderson, C.D., and J.W. Blood. *Investor Relations: The Company and Its Owners*. New York, NY: American Management Association, 1963.

Beaver, W. "Is the Stakeholder Model Dead?" *Business Horizons* 42, no. 2 (March/April 1999): 8–12.

Bebchuk, L.A. "The Case for Increasing Shareholder Power." *Harvard Law Review* 118, no. 3 (2005): 833–914.

Black, A.P., P. Wright, and J.E. Bachman. *In Search of Shareholder Value: Managing the Drivers of Performance*. London: Pitman Publishing, 1998.

Deakin, S. "The Coming Transformation of Shareholder Value." *Corporate Governance* 13, no. 1 (2005): 11–18.

Donlon, J.P., and J. Gutfreund. "Good for the Company, Good for the Shareholder?" *Chief Executive* 132 (March 1998): 50–59.

Hochhauser, M. "Smart Executives, Dumb Decisions." *Risk Management* 51, no. 9 (September 2004): 64.

Letza, S., S. Xiuping, and J. Kirkbride. "Shareholding Versus Stakeholding: A Critical Review of Corporate Governance." *Corporate Governance* 12, no. 3 (2004): 242–262.

Rose, C. "Stakeholder Orientation vs. Shareholder Value-A Matter of Contractual Failures." *European Journal of Law and Economics* 18, no. 1 (2004): 77–97.

Tipgos, M. A., and T.J. Keefe. "A Comprehensive Structure of Corporate Governance in Post-Enron Corporate America." *The CPA Journal* 74, no. 12 (2004): 46–51.

Wallace, W. M. *Postmodern Management: The Emerging Partnership Between Employees and Shareholders*. Westport, CT: Quorum Books, 1998.

SIMULATION

Simulation is used to model efficiently a wide variety of systems that are important to managers. A simulation is basically an imitation, a model that imitates a real-world process or system. In business and management, decision makers are often concerned with the operating characteristics of a system. One way to measure or assess the operating characteristics of a system is to observe that system in actual operation. However, in many types of situations the cost of direct observation can be very high. Furthermore, changing some of the relationships or parameters within a system on an experimental basis may mean waiting a considerable amount of time to collect results on all the combinations that are of concern to the decision maker.

In business and management, a simulation is a mathematical imitation of a real-world system. The use of computers to conduct simulations is not essential from a theoretical standpoint. However, most simulations are sufficiently complex from a practical standpoint to require the use of computers in running them. A simulation can also be considered to be an experimental process. In a set of experimental runs, the decision maker actively varies some of the parameters or relationships in the system. If the mathematical model behind the simulation is valid, the results of the simulation runs will imitate the results of the real system if it were to operate over some period of time.

In order to better understand the fundamental issues of simulation, an example is useful. Suppose a regional medical center seeks to provide air ambulance service to trauma and burn victims over a wide geographic area. Issues such as how many helicopters would be best and where to place them would be in question. Other issues such as scheduling of flight crews and the speed and payload of various types of helicopters could also be important. These represent decision variables that are to a large degree under the control of the medical center. There are uncontrollable variables in this situation as well. Examples are the weather and the prevailing accident and injury rates throughout the medical center's service region.

Given the random effects of accident frequencies and locations, the analysts for the medical center would want to decide how many helicopters to acquire and where to place them. Adding helicopters and flight crews until the budget is spent is not necessarily the best course of action. Perhaps two strategically placed helicopters would serve the region as efficiently as four helicopters of some other type scattered haphazardly about. Analysts would be interested in such things as operating costs, response times, and expected numbers of patients who would be served. All of these operating characteristics would be impacted by injury rates, weather, and any other uncontrollable factors as well as by the variables they are able to control.

The medical center could run their air ambulance system on a trial-and-error basis for many years before they had any reasonable idea what combinations of resources would work well. Not only might they fail to find the best or near-best combination of controllable variables, but also they might very possibly incur an excessive loss of life as a result of poor resource allocation. For these reasons, this decision-making situation would be an excellent candidate for a simulation approach. Analysts could simulate having any number of helicopters available. To the extent that their model is valid, they could identify the optimal number to have to maximize service, and where they could best be stationed in order to serve the population of seriously injured people who would be distributed about the service region. The fact that accidents can be predicted only statistically means that there would be a strong random component to the service system and that simulation would therefore be an attractive analytical tool in measuring the system's operating characteristics.

BUILDING THE MODEL

When analysts wish to study a system, the first general step is to build a model. For most simulation purposes, this would be a statistically based model that relies on empirical evidence where possible. Such a model would be a mathematical abstraction that approximates the reality of the situation under study. Balancing the need for detail with the need to have a model that will be amenable to reasonable solution techniques isa constant problem. Unfortunately, there is no guarantee that a model can be successfully built so as to reflect accurately the real-world relationships that are at play. If a valid model can be constructed, and if the system has some element that is random, yet is defined by a specific probability relationship, it is a good candidate to be cast as a simulation model.

Consider the air-ambulance example. Random processes affecting the operation of such a system include the occurrence of accidents, the locations of such accidents, and whether or not the weather is flyable. Certainly other random factors may be at play, but the analysts may have determined that these are all the significant ones. Ordinarily, the analysts would develop a program that would simulate operation of the system for some appropriate time period, say a month. Then, they would go back and simulate many more months of activity while they collect, through an appropriate computer program, observations on average flight times, average response times, number of patients served, and other variables they deem of interest. They might very well simulate hundreds or even thousands of months in order to obtain distributions of the values of important variables. They would thus acquire distributions of these variables for each service configuration, say the number of helicopters and their locations, which would allow the various configurations to be compared and perhaps the best one identified using whatever criterion is appropriate.

MONTE CARLO SIMULATION

There are several different strategies for developing a working simulation, but two are probably most common. The first is the Monte Carlo simulation approach. The second is the event-scheduling approach. Monte Carlo simulation is applied where the passage of time is not incorporated into the simulation model. Consider again the air ambulance example. If the simulation is set up to imitate an entire month's worth of operations all at once, it would be considered a Monte Carlo simulation. A random number of accidents and injuries would generate a random number of flights with some sort of average distance incorporated into the model. Operating costs and possibly other operating values sought by the analysts would be computed.

The advantage of Monte Carlo simulation is that it can be done very quickly and simply. Thus, many months of operations could be simulated in the ambulance example. From the many months of operational figures, averages and distributions of costs could readily be acquired. Unfortunately, there is also a potentially serious disadvantage to the Monte Carlo simulation approach. If analysts ignore the passage of time in designing the simulation, the system itself may be oversimplified. In the air ambulance example, it is possible to have a second call come in while a flight is in progress which could force a victim to wait for a flight if no other helicopter is available. A Monte Carlo simulation would not account for this possibility and hence could contribute to inaccurate results. This is not to say that Monte Carlo simulations are generally flawed. Rather, in situations where the passage of time is not a critical part of the system being modeled, this approach can perform very well.

EVENT-SCHEDULING METHOD

The event-scheduling method explicitly takes into account time as a variable. In the air ambulance example, the hypothetical month-long simulation of the service system would emerge over time. First, an incident or accident would occur at some random location, at some random time interval from the beginning point. Then, a helicopter would respond, weather permitting, the weather being another random component of the model. The simulated mission would require some random time to complete with the helicopter eventually returning to its base. While on that service mission, another call might come in, but the helicopter would probably need to finish its first mission before undertaking another. In other words, a waiting line or queue, a term often used in simulation analysis to indicate there are "customers" awaiting service, could develop. The event scheduling approach can account for complexities like this where a Monte Carlo simulation may not.

With a computer program set up that would imitate the service system, hundreds of months would be simulated and operating characteristics collected and analyzed through averages and distributions. This would be done for all the relevant decision-variable combinations the analysts wish to consider. In the air ambulance example, these would include various numbers of helicopters and various base location combinations. Once the analysts have collected enough simulated information about each of the various combinations, it is very likely that certain combinations will emerge as being better than others. If one particular design does not rise to the top, at least many of them can usually be eliminated, and those that appear more promising can be subjected to further study.

PROGRAMMING LANGUAGES

It was noted that while there is no theoretical need to computerize a simulation, practicality dictates that need. In the air ambulance example, analysts would require thousands of calculations to simulate just one month of operation for one set of decision-variable values. Multiply this by hundreds of monthly simulations, and the prospect of doing it somehow by hand becomes absolutely daunting. Because of this problem, programming languages have been developed that explicitly support computer-based simulation. Using such programs, analysts can develop either of the types of simulations mentioned here, a Monte Carlo simulation or an event-scheduling method simulation, or other types as well.

A particularly widely used language is called SIMSCRIPT. It is particularly well-suited to the event-scheduling method. The language itself has undergone several incarnations, so different versions, identified by Roman numeral, can be found on different computer systems. To apply this language, analysts would develop a logical flow diagram, or model, of the system they seek to study. SIMSCRIPT is a stand-alone language that can be used to program a wide variety of models. Thus, someone who uses simulation regularly on a variety of problem types might be well-served by having this type of language available.

Another widely used language is called GASP IV. It operates more as an add-in set of routines to other high-level programming languages such as FORTRAN or PL/1. With the rapid proliferation of personal computers in recent years, specific simulation software packages, simulation add-ins to other packages, and other capabilities have become widely available. For instance, a simple Monte Carlo simulation can be performed using a spreadsheet program such as Microsoft's Excel. This is possible because Excel has a built-in random number function. However, one must be aware that the validity of such random number functions is sometimes questionable.

One of the basic building blocks within any simulation language or other tool is the random number generator. Ordinarily, such a generator consists of a short set of programming instructions that produce a number that "looks" uniformly random over some numeric interval, usually a decimal fraction between zero and one. Of course, since the number comes from programming code, it is not really random; it only looks random. Any fraction between zero and one is theoretically as likely as any other. Such numbers can then be combined or transformed into apparently-random numbers that follow some other probability function, such as a normal probability distribution or a Poisson probability distribution.

This capability facilitates building simulations that have different types of random components within them. However, if the basic generator is invalid or not very effective, the simulation results may very well be invalid even though the analysts have developed a perfectly valid model of the system being studied. Thus, there is a need for analysts to be sure that the underlying random number generating routines produce output that at least 'looks' random. There is a need for external validity in a simulation model, a need for the model to accurately imitate reality. There is just as critical a need for the building blocks within the model to be valid, for internal validity which can be a problem when an untested random number generator is employed.

EXPERIENTIAL GAMES

One particularly fast-growing area of simulation applications lies in experiential games. Board games that we played as youngsters were basically simulations. Usually, some kind of race was involved. The winner was the player who could maneuver their playing pieces around the board, in the face of various obstacles and opponents' moves, the fastest. The basic random number generator was usually a pair of dice. Computer-based simulations have expanded the complexity and potential of such gaming a great deal.

Management and business simulations have been developed that are sufficiently sophisticated to use in the college classroom setting. Almost all of these consist of specialized computer programs that accept decision sets from the game's players. With their decision sets entered into the computer program, some particular period of time is simulated, usually a year. The program outputs the competitive results with financial and operating measures that would include such variables as dollar and unit sales, profitability, market shares, operating costs, and so forth. Some competitors fare better than others because their decisions proved to be more effective than others in the face of competition in the computer-simulated marketplace. An important difference between board games and business simulations lies in the complexity of outcomes. The board game traditionally has only one winner. A well-developed business simulation can have several winners with different players achieving success in different aspects of the simulated market that is the game's playing field. Hence, business simulations have become very useful and effective learning tools in classroom settings. A fundamental reason for this lies in the fact that simulation permits an otherwise complex system to be imitated at very low costs, both dollar and human.

Simulation will continue to prove useful in situations where timely decision making is important and when experimenting with multiple methods and variables are not fiscally possible or sound. Simulation allows for informative testing of viable solutions prior to implementation.

SEE ALSO: Models and Modeling

James H. Macomber
Revised by Monica C. Turner

FURTHER READING:

Laguna, M., and J. Marklund. *Business Process Modeling, Simulation, and Design.* Upper Saddle River, NJ: Pearson/Prentice Hall, 2005.

McLeish, D.L. *Monte Carlo Simulation and Finance.* Hoboken, NJ: Wiley, 2005.

Robert, C.P., and G. Casella. *Monte Carlo Stastical Methods.* 2nd ed. New York, NY: Springer, 2004.

Santos, M. "Making Monte Carlo Work." *Wall Street & Technology* 23, no. 3 (March 2005): 22–23.

Savage, S. "Rolling the Dice." *Financial Planning* 33, no. 3 (March 2003): 59–62.

Scheeres, J. "Making Simulation a Reality." *Industrial Engineer* 35, no. 2 (February 2003): 46–48.

SIX SIGMA

SEE: Statistical Process Control and Six Sigma

SPAN OF CONTROL

Span of control or span of management is a dimension of organizational design measured by the number of subordinates that report directly to a given manager. This concept affects organization design in a variety of ways, including speed of communication flow, employee motivation, reporting relationships, and administrative overhead. Span of management has been part of the historical discussion regarding the most appropriate design and structure of organizations.

HISTORICAL DISCUSSION OF SPAN OF CONTROL

A small, or narrow, span of control results in each manager supervising a small number of employees, while a wide span of management occurs when more subordinates report directly to a given manager. A small span of management would make it necessary to have more managers and more layers of management to oversee the same number of operative employees than would be necessary for an organization using a wider span of management. The narrower span of management would result in more layers of management and slower communications between lower level employees and top level managers of the firm. Recent moves to downsize organizations and to eliminate unnecessary positions has resulted in many organizations moving to wider spans of management and the elimination of layers of middle-level managers.

An argument for a narrow span of control was presented by V.A. Gaicunas, who developed a formula showing that an arithmetic increase in the number of a manager's subordinates resulted in a geometric increase in the number of subordinate relationships that a manager had to manage. According to Gaicunas, managers must manage not only one-to-one direct reporting relationships, but also relationships with various groups of subordinates and the relationships that exist between and among individual subordinates. The formula is shown below:

$$I = N(2N/2+N-1)$$

where I is the total number of interactions
and N is the number of subordinates.

Therefore, if a manager has two subordinates, there are 6 potential relationships to manage. However, if the manager's subordinates are increased to three, then the number of relationships is increased to 18. As the number of relationships increased, Gaicunas argued, the sheer number of interactions would exceed the abilities of the manager.

Researchers generally argue that a small span of management and a "tall" organization structure will be more expensive to operate because of the large number of managers and it may have communication problems resulting from the multiple levels of management. Such organizations are often seen as well suited for a stable, certain type of environment. A "flat" organization design resulting from a wider span of management would require managers to assume more administrative duties since those activities would be shared by fewer employees. It will also result in more employees reporting to each manager, increasing the managers' supervisory responsibilities. However, some research also suggests the wider span of management may cause employees to feel greater ownership of their work and increase their motivation, morale, and productivity. This type of organization design is often seen as effective in more uncertain environments.

FACTORS THAT MAY AFFECT SPAN OF CONTROL

While early discussions of span of control often centered on pinpointing the optimal number of subordinates, a number of factors may influence the span of control most appropriate for a given management position. Assuming that all other aspects of a manager's job are the same, these factors would likely alter the span of management as follows:

1. Job complexity. Subordinate jobs that are complex, ambiguous, dynamic or otherwise complicated will likely require more management involvement and a narrower span of management.

2. Similarity of subordinate jobs. The more similar and routine the tasks that subordinates are performing, the easier it is for a manager to supervise employees and the wider the span of management that will likely be effective.

3. Physical proximity of subordinates. The more geographically dispersed a group of subordinates the more difficult it is for a manager to be in regular contact with them and the fewer employees a manager could reasonably oversee, resulting in a narrower span of management.

4. Abilities of employees. Managers who supervise employees that lack ability, motivation, or confidence will have to spend more time with each employee. The result will be that the manager cannot supervise as many employees and would be most effective with a narrower span of management.

5. Abilities of the manager. Some managers are better organized, better at explaining things to subordinates, and more efficient in performing their jobs. Such managers can function effectively with a wider span of management than a less skilled manager.

6. Technology. Cell phones, email, and other forms of technology that facilitate communication and the exchange of information make it possible for managers to increase their spans of management over managers who do not have access to or who are unable to use the technology.

The trend in recent years has been to move toward wider spans of control to reduce costs, speed decision making, increase flexibility and empower employees. However, to avoid potential problems of wide spans of control, organizations are having to invest in training managers and employees and in technology enabling the sharing of information and enhancing communication between and among managers and employees.

SEE ALSO: Empowerment; Management Styles; Organizational Structure; Organizing

Joe Thomas

FURTHER READING:

Davison, Barbara. "Management Span of Control: How Wide Is Too Wide?" *Journal of Business Strategy.* 24 (2003): 22–29.

Griffin, Ricky. *Management.* Boston: Houghton Mifflin, 2005.

Hitt, Michael, J.S. Black, and Lyman, Porter. *Management.* Upper Saddle River: Pearson/Prentice Hall, 2005.

Klein, E.E. "Using Information Technology To Eliminate Layers Of Bureaucracy." *National Public Accountant.* 23 (2001): 46–48.

SPIRITUALITY IN LEADERSHIP

Before a definition of spirituality in leadership can be provided, one must first examine the meaning of the two key aspects of the phrase: the "spirit" and the "leader." One dictionary definition of spirit is "that which is traditionally believed to be the vital principle or animating force within living beings." Thus, the spirit relates to the deeper sense, meaning, or significance of something. A dictionary definition of the leader is "one who shows the way by going in advance; one who causes others to follow some course of action or line of thought." Thus, the leader is one who influences followers to think or behave in some way. Combining the two terms suggest that the leader who incorporates spirituality into his or her leadership will be one who causes others to seek out and understand their inner selves and who fosters a sense of meaning and significance among his or her followers. Thus, one definition of spirituality in leadership is a holistic approach to leadership in which the leader strives to encourage a sense of significance and interconnectedness among employees.

Spiritual leadership involves the application of spiritual values and principles to the workplace. The spiritual leader understands the importance of employees finding meaning in their work and demonstrates a genuine concern for the "whole" person, not just the employee. Spiritual leadership tries to assist others in finding meaning in their work by addressing fundamental questions such as:

- Who are we as a work team, department, or organization?

- Is our work worthy? What is our greater purpose?

- What are our values and ethical principles?

- What will be our legacy?

The spiritual leader strives for a workplace that is truly a community, consisting of people with shared traditions, values, and beliefs.

Spirituality in leadership implies that the focus will be less on formal position power and more on people; less on conformity and more on transformation and diversity; and less on controlling and more on partnership, collaboration, and inspiration. Spirituality in leadership does not require that the leader adhere to a particular religion or that he or she attempt to convince subordinates to pursue a specific set of religious principles. While leaders who emphasize spirituality may base their leadership approach in Christianity or another religious tradition, they may also have so-called "non-traditional" religious beliefs or may not adhere to any particular religion at all. Spirituality in leadership is more concerned with the development of employees as "whole people"—people who exhibit compassion to other employees, superiors, subordinates, and customers.

SPIRITUALITY IN THE WORKPLACE

Spirituality in leadership cannot be understood apart from the more general issue of spirituality in the workplace because spirituality plays an increasingly important part in the workplace. Many employees look to the workplace as a means of finding meaning in their lives. In today's world, many employees regard their workplace as a community—even as other "communities" that give meaning to people's lives are strained or ripped apart by modern styles of living. In the U.S. of the mid-twentieth century, for example, most people lived near, not only their immediate family, but also their extended family (i.e. grandparents, aunts, uncles, cousins). This is no longer the case, as many in the U.S. and around the world do not live in close proximity to their family of origin or extended family members. Thus, one's family is not an immediate and ready source of support for many individuals. This has led to a loss of identity and connectedness in people's lives, since people's families provide a rich context for self-understanding, personal growth, and maturity.

Similarly, the pattern of individuals' affiliation with formalized religion and religious institutions has undergone a dramatic change in recent years. Beginning in the 1960s, a general sense of dissatisfaction and skepticism about organized religion became common, particularly among younger people. In the subsequent years, rates of attendance at religious services and active involvement in religion declined worldwide. Although the majority of people today will self-identify as a member of some religious faith, many still do not attend formal religious services and have only a tenuous connection with a particular church, synagogue, etc. Thus, many people appear to be estranged from formal religion, which takes away another potential avenue to a sense of self-worth, identity and spiritual growth.

Likewise, many people used to find a sense of identity and connection in their neighborhoods and communities. This has changed as well. Many people relocate several times during their careers and spend relatively short periods of time in any one place. They do not put down roots in their local community, do not participate to a great degree in community events, and do not form strong relationships with neighbors. Anecdotal and survey evidence suggest that it is common for people to live next door or across the street from people and know almost nothing about them, even in small towns. In general, many people seem to be "drifting" without a strong connection to others or overall sense of purpose.

Within this context, it is easy to explain why so many people seek to derive great meaning from their work and their organizations. Most spend more time in the workplace with their coworkers than anywhere else. Close friendships, courtships, and marriages are common among coworkers. The modern workplace is not just a place where people work, but a place where they form friendships, socialize, and attempt to find a sense of fulfillment. It is also a place where people attempt to make sense of and derive meaning from the activities that comprise what we call "work" and how these activities fit within the greater fabric of individuals' lives. This quest for meaning has prompted the recognition that spirituality in the workplace and spiritual leadership are real issues affecting the quality of life in the modern organization.

THE ROLE OF LEADERSHIP IN DEVELOPMENT

The study of leadership is multi-faceted and definitions of leadership vary, but in general, all definitions of leadership agree that it involves exerting influence on other people. If a leader in the workplace possesses a strong sense of spirituality that affects his or her attitudes, emotions, and behaviors in a positive way, then the leader is likely to influence subordinates to pursue the development of spirituality in their own lives. This raises at least two questions: "What leadership approach or style effectively promotes spirituality in the workplace?" and "What benefits are derived from fostering spirituality in the workplace?"

There appears to be a shift in approaches to leadership in the workplace, with an increasing focus on more holistic approaches that focus on compassion, encouragement, empathy, and service. Some contend that the greatest aspects of leadership are assisting followers in finding meaning and purpose in their work and fostering a sense of community among followers. This point of view suggests that spirituality in leadership does not involve directives and the chain of command, but transformational leadership that defines the organization's values and helps followers perceive that

they are contributing to a valuable and worthwhile goal set.

Although there is little if any empirical evidence that any particular leadership approach or style would be more or less consistent with spirituality in the workplace, two leadership approaches seem to be more closely related to the concept of spiritual leadership than others: servant leadership and transformational leadership.

SERVANT LEADERSHIP. Servant leadership is not a full-fledged theory of leadership but can be thought of as a philosophy of leadership. It de-emphasizes the position of power or elite status of the leader. Instead, this approach to leadership suggests that the leader must first be a servant of others. It suggests that leaders must place the needs of subordinates, customers, and the community ahead of their own interests in order to be effective. Characteristics of servant leaders include empathy, stewardship, and commitment to the personal, professional, and spiritual growth of their subordinates. Servant leadership is consistent with aspects of Christianity, but is not a "Christian" theory per se. Servant leadership has not been subjected to extensive empirical testing but has generated considerable interest among both leadership scholars and practitioners.

TRANSFORMATIONAL LEADERSHIP. Beginning in the 1970s, a number of leadership theories emerged that focused on the importance of a leader's charisma to leadership effectiveness. Included within this class of theories are House's theory of charismatic leadership, Bass's transformational leadership theory, and Conger and Kanungo's charismatic leadership theory. These theories have much in common. They all focus on attempting to explain how leaders can accomplish extraordinary things against the odds, such as turning around a failing company, founding a successful company, or achieving great military success against incredible odds. The theories also emphasize the importance of leaders' inspiring subordinates' admiration, dedication, and unquestioned loyalty through articulating a clear and compelling vision.

Transformational leadership theory differentiates between the transactional and the transformational leader. Transactional leadership focuses on role and task requirements and utilizes rewards contingent on performance. By contrast, transformational leadership focuses on developing mutual trust, fostering the leadership abilities of others, and setting goals that go beyond the short-term needs of the work group. Bass's transformational leadership theory identifies four aspects of effective leadership, which include charisma, inspiration, intellectual stimulation, and consideration. A leader who exhibits these qualities will inspire subordinates to be high achievers and put the long-term interest of the organization ahead of their own short-term interest, according to the theory. Empirical research has supported many of the theory's propositions. Thus, transformational leadership styles would seem to be consistent with a spiritual approach to leadership.

THE BENEFITS OF SPIRITUALITY IN LEADERSHIP

Since there has been little empirical research regarding spirituality in the workplace or spiritual leadership, it is difficult to say precisely what the benefits (or costs) of spirituality in leadership will be. However, enough conceptual and empirical research has been conducted to suggest several potential benefits of incorporating a spiritual dimension into leadership. From the perspective of followers, incorporating spirituality into leadership has the potential to create a workplace that is more humane and that provides a sense of community and shared purpose. From the perspective of the organization, incorporating spirituality in leadership may lead to greater perceptions of trust, organizational support, and commitment among employees, which could have positive effects on organizational performance. However, spirituality in leadership should not be thought of as a "device" for developing positive organizational outcomes, but must instead be a genuine philosophical belief on the part of leaders.

SEE ALSO: Leadership Styles and Bases of Power; Leadership Theories and Studies

Tim Barnett

FURTHER READING:

Bolman, L.G., and T.E. Deal. "Reframing Ethics and Spirit." *Business Leadership*. San Francisco: Jossey-Bass, 2003.

Conger, J. "Our Search for Spiritual Community." In *Spirit at Work*. San Francisco: Jossey-Bass, 1994.

Covey, S.R. *Principle-Centered Leadership*. New York: Free Press, 1990.

Kinicki, A., and R. Kreitner. *Organizational Behavior.* Boston: McGraw-Hill Irwin, 2006.

Kotter, J. "Change Leadership." *Executive Excellence* 16, no. 4 (1999): 16–17.

McEnroe, J.J. "Portrait of Outstanding Leaders." *Trustee* 48, no. 2 (1995): 6–9.

Sanders, J. E. III, W.E. Hopkins, and G.D. Geroy. "Spirituality-Leadership-Commitment Relationships in the Workplace: An Exploratory Assessment." *Proceedings of the Academy of Management National Meeting* (2004): A1–A6.

Scott, K.T. "Leadership and Spirituality: A Quest for Reconciliation." In *Spirit at Work* New York: Jossey-Bass, 1994.

STAKEHOLDERS

A firm's stakeholders are the individuals, groups, or other organizations that are affected by and also affect the firm's decisions and actions. Depending on the specific firm, stakeholders may include governmental agencies such as the Securities and Exchange Commission, social activist groups such as Greenpeace, self-regulatory organizations such as the National Association of Securities Dealers, employees, shareholders, suppliers, distributors, the media and even the community in which the firm is located among many others. The following discussion divides the stakeholder perspective into three categorizations, but it is important to realize that firms do not always initially set out to establish one perspective over another. Instead, firms tend to develop their views of stakeholders and stakeholder management over time in reaction to events that unfold throughout the firm's history.

STAKEHOLDER PERSPECTIVE

Although numerous ways of viewing stakeholders exist, categorizing stakeholder perspectives into three broad categories helps elicit the basic underlying themes among these numerous views. These broad categorizations include the separation perspective, the ethical perspective, and the integrated perspective.

THE SEPARATION PERSPECTIVE. The separation perspective suggests that, because managers are agents of the firm's owners—the shareholders—managers should always strive to act in the best interest of the firm's owners. This view does not cause managers to ignore non-owner stakeholders; indeed, when taking actions that benefit stakeholders also benefit owners, the separation perspective would advise managers to do so. One facet that differentiates this perspective from the others, however, is the rationale behind such decisions; the reason managers make decisions and take actions benefiting non-owner stakeholders is ultimately to reward owners. Clearly, problems arise when a given decision would maximize the benefit to non-owners at the expense of owners, but that would serve the greater good of society in general. For example, suppose a new but relatively expensive technology was created that lowered pollution from steel mini-mills below the level required by the Environmental Protection Agency (EPA). In this case, there is no law requiring the steel mini-mills to purchase and implement the new technology, but doing so would benefit stakeholders such as the community in which the mini-mill had factories. Yet, due to the cost of the new technology, owners' profits would suffer. The separation perspective would direct managers in this situation to dismiss the benefit of lower pollution levels for the community in favor of maximizing owners' profits by meeting EPA requirements, but not by spending funds in excess of what the EPA requires.

THE ETHICAL PERSPECTIVE. The ethical perspective is that businesses have an obligation to conduct themselves in a way that treats each stakeholder group fairly. This view does not disregard the preferences and claims of shareholders, but takes shareholder interests in consideration only to the extent that their interests coincide with the greater good. Budweiser, for example, has modified its advertising over the years to discourage under-age drinking and driving while intoxicated. Social activist groups such as Mothers against Drunk Drivers have pressured Budweiser through their own advertising as well as media attention to maximize responsible alcohol consumption even though this may decrease overall sales for Budweiser. This approach focuses on ethics and suggests that managers have responsibilities apart from profit-oriented activities. While recognizing the claims shareholders have to profit in exchange for putting their capital at risk, the stakeholder perspective that holds ethics as the preeminent decision rule. Taken to an extreme, this perspective can minimize the right of owners to participate in financial gain in proportion to the risks they bear when doing what is ethically best for non-owner stakeholders runs counter to what is financially best for owners. A possible outcome in a capitalistic society could be that fewer and fewer owners place their capital at risk through firm ownership, a condition that may ultimately decrease the economic good of society in general and thus harm the very groups the ethical perspective intended to protect.

THE INTEGRATED PERSPECTIVE. The third approach, the integrated perspective, suggests that firms cannot function independently of the stakeholder environment in which they operate, making the effects of managerial decisions and actions on non-owner stakeholders part and parcel of decisions and actions made in the interests of owners. This view holds that managerial decisions and actions are intertwined with multiple stakeholder interests in such a way that breaking shareholders apart from non-owner stakeholders is not possible. Managers who, according to this approach, make decisions in isolation of the multitude of stakeholders and focus singly on shareholders overlook important threats to their own well-being as well as opportunities on which they might capitalize. For example, the National Association of Securities Dealers (NASD) is a self-regulatory organization that monitors and disciplines members such as insurance companies and brokerages. By incorporating NASD regulations into their management decisions and actions, insurance companies and brokerages, at least to some extent, preempt outside governmental action that may make compliance more restrictive or cumbersome. The NASD, in turn, answers to the governmental agency, the Securities and Exchange Commission

(SEC). The SEC reports to the U.S. Department of Justice. Each of these—insurance companies and brokerages, the NASD, SEC, and U.S. Department of Justice—are linked in such a way insurance companies and brokerages ignoring these stakeholders would quickly be unable to make a profit and thus fail to serve the interests of owners.

EMERGENCE OF THE STAKEHOLDER PERSPECTIVE

The conventional thinking dominating the early management literature with the rise of management as a "profession" separate from the firm's owners was that, as agents representing owners, top managers' responsibility was primarily and ultimately to these owners or shareholders. Increasingly, though, managers have come to view non-owner stakeholders as essential to firms' success, not only in financial terms, but also in societal terms (Rodgers and Gago, 2004). However, this has not eliminated managerial decisions that are overly concerned with financial performance at the expense of other stakeholder interests. The collapse of Enron and WorldCom early in the twenty-first century, charges of accounting fraud against firms such as Tyco and Time Warner, Medicare fraud by HealthSouth and United Healthcare illustrate that despite the apparent logic of an integrated perspective of stakeholder management, some managers still hold to the separation perspective. As shareholders of these and other firms have seen, however, is that sole regard to financial results is not always in the best interests of these shareholders. Those holding Enron and WorldCom stock, even those who knew nothing about illegal activities by the firm's top management, quickly came to realize that excluding non-owner stakeholders is not necessarily consistent with maximizing shareholder wealth. In fact, excluding non-owner stakeholders can inadvertently bring more pressure on managers when non-stakeholder interests are not respected. Consider, for instance, additional regulations to which firms must now comply in the wake of many of these situations. The Sarbanes-Oxley Act creates additional reporting requirements in attempts to prevent accounting abuses in the future. Estimates suggest that compliance will coast an average of $35 million per year for large firms with revenues in excess of $4 billion. Obviously, then, neglecting non-owner stakeholders is not always in the best interest of shareholders even if managers take the separation perspective to stakeholder management.

The separation perspective can be traced at least as far back as 1776 when Adam Smith wrote *An Inquiry into the Nature and Causes of the Wealth of Nations*. Among Smith's most quoted lines is in the work's preface and states: "It is not from the benevolence of the butcher, the brewer, or the baker, that we expect our dinner, but from their regard to their own interest." This reference to what has come to be known as laissez faire capitalism positions self-interest as the most prominent feature of national industrial development. Yet, even though he did not specifically use the term, Smith also realized that stakeholders outside the firm have an important part to play in industrialization. By making provision for what he called the "public good," Smith disseminated the idea of owners' self-interest as a critical variable promoting economic growth, while also realizing that unchecked self-interest must be balanced against the greater good. In this respect, then, the separation perspective and the integrated perspective, while not fully formed, both have their roots in early industrialism.

The ethical perspective stems at least back to the eighteenth-century writings of philosopher, Immanuel Kant. The focus of the ethical perspective is the firm's responsibility to stakeholders from a normative view; that is, the ethically correct action should supercede actions based solely on self-interest, thus making managerial decisions and actions that impact stakeholders based on universal standards of right and wrong the rule that managers should follow. This standpoint, though, suffers from shortcoming stemming from different standards of right and wrong. When right and wrong are apparent, decisions are easy, but management challenges are rarely so clear. Simply suggesting that managers do the "right thing" ignores conflicts of interest inherent in capitalistic competition, and doing the right thing can result in compromises that are not in the best interests of any of the stakeholders, but rather a way to satisfice or make decisions and take actions that are "good enough," but not optimal. The ethical view of stakeholders can result in managers overemphasizing the greater good to the point that they ignore the reality of self-interest, particularly as it pertains to maximize shareholder wealth.

Integrating the broad categorizations of separation and ethics allows room for both self-interest of owners and corporate responsibility to non-owner stakeholders. An integrated perspective of stakeholders positions the self-interests of managers as a key driver of economic growth, but tempers this with social responsibility toward non-owner stakeholders. Maytag, for instance, found that by balancing a plant closure with adequate notice, the reputation of the firm was held intact—a benefit to owners—at the same time that competing stakeholder interests were considered. In this situation, Maytag's Galesburg, Illinois refrigeration assembly plant announced it would be moving operations to a location with less expensive labor and other operational costs, but took the unusually move of giving the firm's 1,000 employees, its local suppliers and the small Galesburg community two years to prepare. Maytag allowed local employment

agencies to set up job training within the Maytag plant to prepare its employees for employment after the plant closure. This illustrates how integration of multiple stakeholder interests can move beyond only self-interest or only ethics by integrating both of these.

It is overly simplistic to suggest that managers should just do the right thing in all situations, because the "right thing" to do is not always clear. On the other hand, acting solely in the financial interests of shareholders can result in unintended consequences that ultimately cause shareholders harm. Integrating multiple perspectives allows room for managers to balance the interests of multiple stakeholders. Such stakeholder perspectives allow for competing dimensions, thus provide a framework to help managers harmonize the interests of multiple parties.

SEE ALSO: Corporate Governance; Ethics; Shareholders

Scott B. Droege

FURTHER READING:

Crane, Andrew, Dirk Matten, and Jeremy Moon. "Stakeholders as Citizens? Rethinking Rights, Participation, and Democracy." *Journal of Business Ethics* 53, no. 1-2 (2004): 107–123.

David, H., and A. Borrus. "No Escaping Sarbanes-Oxley." *Business Week* Online. Available from <www.businessweek.com>.

Dubbink, W. "The Fragile Structure of Free Market Society." *Business Ethics Quarterly* 14, no. 1 (2004): 23–47.

Heath, J., and W. Norman. "Stakeholder Theory, Corporate Governance and Public Management: What Can the History of State-Run Enterprises Teach Us in the Post-Enron Era?" *Journal of Business Ethics* 53, no. 3 (2004): 247–266.

Keep, W. "Adam Smith's Imperfect Invisible Hand: Motivations to Mislead." *Business Ethics: A European Review* 12, no. 4 (2003): 343–354.

Lea, D. "The Imperfect Nature of Corporate Social Responsibilities to Stakeholders." *Business Ethics Quarterly* 14, no. 2 (2004): 201–218.

Molyneaux, D. "Saints and CEOs: An Historical Experience of Altruism, Self-Interest and Compromise." *Business Ethics: A European Review* 12, no. 2 (2003): 133–144.

Reynolds, S.J., and N.E. Bowie. "A Kantian Perspective on the Characteristics of Ethics Programs." *Business Ethics Quarterly* 14, no. 2 (2004): 275–293.

Roberts, R.W., and L. Mahoney. "Stakeholder Conceptions of the Corporation: Their Meaning and Influence in Accounting Research." *Business Ethics Quarterly* 14, no. 3 (2004): 399–332.

Rodgers, W., and S. Gago. "Stakeholder Influence on Corporate Strategies Over Time." *Journal of Business Ethics* 52, no. 4 (2004): 349–364.

Wei-Skillern, J. "The Evolution of Shell's Stakeholder Approach: A Case Study." *Business Ethics Quarterly* 14, no. 4 (2004): 713–729.

STATISTICAL PROCESS CONTROL AND SIX SIGMA

SIX SIGMA

The term six sigma (6σ) originated as a performance measure or a measure of quality. Using six sigma, process goals are set in parts per million (PPM) in all areas of the production process. Since its origin, six sigma has now evolved into a methodology for improving business efficiency and effectiveness by focusing on productivity, cost reduction, and enhanced quality.

Six Sigma has its roots back with the efforts of Joseph Juran and W. Edwards Deming. Their programs for Zero Defects and Total Quality Management in Japan, lead to the adoption of the six sigma philosophy by Motorola. Motorola was able to achieve a 200-fold improvement in production quality and saved a reported $2.2 billion using this tool. General Electric has also become the strong proponent of six sigma where it claims extensive successes. GE used six sigma during the reign of Jack Welch, where he made it the biggest corporate initiative in GE's history and received global recognition. Other users include Texas Instruments and Allied Signal. Allied took six sigma to an even higher level by incorporating it not just in production but by making it a system of leadership. Other current users include JP Morgan Chase, Sun Microsystems, American Express, and Lloyds TSB. Today, six sigma is branded as a management methodology that utilizes measures as a foundational tool for business process reengineering.

The name six sigma comes from the statistical use of the sigma (σ) symbol, which denotes standard deviations. The six identifies the number of standard deviations around the mean. Hence, six sigma says that you have to go out beyond six standard deviations around the mean before you find failure. With a high enough number of sigmas (beyond six), you would approach the point of "zero defects." For example, a move from 3σ to 4σ represents an 11-fold improvement; a move from 4σ to 5σ represents another 27-fold improvement; and a move from 5σ to 6σ represents an additional 69-fold improvement. Thus the overall improvement from 3σ to 6σ is more than 20,000-fold.

At the 3σ level, the number of defects per million totals 66,807 (or 93.3 percent accuracy). At the 4σ level the number of defects drops to 6,210 (or 99.4 percent accuracy). At the 5σ level the number of defects drops still further to 233 (or 99.97 percent accuracy). At the 6σ level the number of defects would be 3.4 per million. This equates to a 99.9997 percent accuracy. In today's world, where 98 percent or 99 percent accuracy is considered excellent, 6σ is now becoming the universally recognized standard of quality.

THE PRINCIPLES OF SIX SIGMA

A key principle of six sigma is measurement. Unfortunately that also means that if you measure the wrong things, you'll get the wrong results. For example, measuring throughput may speed up production, but at the cost of quality. Measuring quality may increase quality, but decrease customer service. So one of the toughest challenges in six sigma measurement is to identify the measurement system that will trigger the correct collection of responses.

A second key principle of measures in the six sigma environment is that all the measures should be openly visible. Openly displaying all measures on charts and graphs is a primary motivator toward the correct response.

A third principle to remember is that the change curve applies. When change happens, performance will initially go down before it recovers and goes back up. This drop in performance is often scary, but a little patience will soon see its recovery.

A principle of success or failure in the six sigma world is the requirement for cultural change or change readiness. If the organization is not primed for change, then an environment for change must be instilled prior to starting six sigma, or the project is doomed to failure. This requires training, team bonding, and team based goal setting. The resistance that exists because of a lack of understanding of what the six sigma process is attempting to achieve, can be avoided with proper training.

Six sigma concentrates on measuring and improving those outputs that are critical to the customer. The tools to accomplish this include a range of statistical methodologies that are focused on continuous improvement using a statistical thinking paradigm. This paradigm includes the following principles:

- Everything is a process.

- All processes have variations that are inherent within them.

- Data analysis is a key tool in understanding the variations in the process and in identifying improvement opportunities.

It is in the management methodology where the key, underlying benefits of six sigma can be found, which includes a problem solving and process optimization methodology. Six sigma creates a leadership vision utilizing a set of metrics and goals to improve business results by using a systematic five-phased problem solving methodology. There are two common problem solving project management methodologies that are commonly associated with six sigma. The first is DMAIC (Define, Measure, Analyze, Improve, Control), and the second is DMADV (Define, Measure,

Analyze, Design, Verify). We will discuss the most common, DMAIC.

Six sigma is a measurement-based strategy that focuses on reducing variations through monitoring and measurement tools. It is based on a philosophy that holds that every process can and should be repeatedly evaluated and significantly improved, with a focus on time required, resources, quality, cost, etc. The philosophy prepares employees with the best available problem-solving tools and methodologies using the five-phased DMAIC process. Explaining each of the steps in the process in more detail we have:

- Define—At the first stages of the process we look for and identify poorly performing areas of a company. We then target the projects with the best return and develop articulated problem and objective statements that have a positive financial impact on the company.

- Measure—At this stage we are trying to tie down the process under consideration. Where does it start and end? What should we be measuring to identify the deviation? What data characteristics are repeatable and identifiable? What is the capability of the process? We use tools like process mapping, flow charting, and FEMA (Failure Model Effects Analysis). We develop a baseline for the targeted area and implement an appropriate measurement system.

- Analyze—Having identified the who and what of this problem, we now target the where, when, and why of the defects in the process. We use appropriate statistical analysis tools, scatter plots, SPC and SQC, Input / Output matrixes, hypothesis testing, etc., and attempt to accurately understand what is happening in the process.

- Improve—At this point we should have identified the critical factors that are causing failure in the process. And, through the use of experiments, we can systematically design a corrective process that should generate the desired level of improvement. This improvement will then be monitored to assure success.

- Control—In the control phase we implement process control tools that can manage and monitor the process on an ongoing basis. The DMAIC process is now in full operation, but it does not stop here. The continuous monitoring of the process will not only assure the success of this change process, but it will also identify future opportunities for improvement.

Six sigma is an organization-wide strategy that develops employees and gives them the tools and capabilities to solve complex problems in a rapid fashion. Employees now have the capabilities to improve overall performance through their step-by-step improvements, always from a customer and financial perspective. Six sigma helps employees use statistical and measurement tools to deliver breakthrough results throughout the organization.

Six sigma requires full participation, from senior management to the factory floor workers. Each assumes a specific role in the six sigma process. At the top of the pecking order we find the Champions. These individuals are responsible for coordinating the business goals and objectives, which are set towards achieving the six sigma standard within the organization. They are responsible for providing the logistics and informational resources that will be needed for the successful completion of the project. They also select the project and identify the scope of the projects to be worked on. They identify the team that should work on the project, and work to remove barriers that may block the success of the project.

Most companies go on to use a classification methodology similar to the one created by Motorola to describe the abilities of their six sigma user. For example, classifications like Green Belt (part-time user) or Black Belt (full-time user) are common. Each level requires an improved mastery of the six sigma tools and skill set, as well as the roles and responsibilities of the individual in the improvement process. The objective is to create a methodology for defining the skill set of the users.

The Master Black Belt is the guru of the six sigma methodology. This individual works as a coach, leader, and teacher for the other individuals on the team. The Black Belt is the change agent for the six sigma process. This individual is a high performer and has a dedicated position that is responsible for six sigma projects. The Green Belt is a specially trained member of the team and usually sits on a function-specific part of the organization. The Green Belt works under the Black Belt on specific aspects of the six sigma projects. The Yellow Belt represents the remainder of the organization, which has been trained on some of the basic skills. These individuals are working their way towards becoming knowledgeable in the six sigma process.

Each of the successful six sigma users have customized the process to fit their own culture and methodology. In order to accomplish this, it is important to identify the key business goals and objectives of the organization, and then to adapt the six sigma methodology and philosophy to fit this goal set. We need to develop an action plan identifying how we are going to focus the six sigma tool so as to focus on the big returns and avoid any waste in investment. Hence, it is useful to identify the areas where six sigma performs well. These include:

- Transformation of the level of customer awareness and expectation throughout all the employees of the organization.

- Improved customer-supplier relationship.

- Drives operational process improvements with savings in cost, improvements in service and productivity, and increased returns.

- Drives information flow improvements.

- Drives a deeper, organization wide understanding of the organization's operation.

- Improved sales force effectiveness.

- Introduces all employees to new tools that will enhance performance.

- Provides a vehicle for the development of a training program.

Six sigma is not an all or nothing venture. Six sigma is a collection of tools and you pick selectively from those tools in order to gain the desired result. It is also not an increase in the level of organization bureaucracy. In fact, if use properly, it will reduce the level of bureaucracy within the organization.

STATISTICAL PROCESS CONTROL

Statistical Process Control (SPC), and its companion Statistical Quality Control (SQC), are tools utilized by a six sigma process. They are not the invented creations of the Japanese or of Edward Deming. However, Ed Deming taught SPC techniques to Japanese manufacturing, and, as a result, has become the default father of the SPC process. The original objective of SPC is to provide productivity and quality information about a production process real-time. The focus was on process control and continuous improvement. The operators become their own inspectors and control their own processes.

The SPC process should collect data and report results as the process is occurring, so that immediate action can be taken. This should help a process, and its quality measures, avoid straying beyond acceptable limits and would avoid the production of bad parts. When appropriately applied, SPC can virtually eliminate the production of defective parts. Additionally, SPC creates visibility of the cause of the failure. Since an operator is able to immediately recognize that a failure is occurring, he would be able to react to that failure and observe the cause of the failure, and then take corrective action. As Peter Drucker emphasizes, the "operators become the 'owners' of not just the process, but also the parts they produce."

Because of its success, SPC has found application in other industries, including service industries, transportation industries, deliver services, and can even be found in fast food and baggage handling. For example, on-time delivery performance can be monitored on an SPC chart.

Within the SPC process there are several tools. These tools include a change management process, the collection of data, and the display of the data. In the change management process we find the use of PDCA (Plan-Do-Check-Act). The objective is to solve problems by trial and error. The process includes (P) planning a work change, (D) executing the change, (C) monitoring the effects of the change to assure that the desired results are occurring, and taking corrective (A) action in the event that the desired results are not occurring—in effect repeating the PDCA cycle. The PDCA cycle is repeated until the error is reduced to zero.

In the SPC data collection process, the objective is to collect the necessary data that will be needed to validate that a specific process is occurring correctly. The methodology for measurement is established at the point where the appropriate data is collected. Only the data that is required for the monitoring of the process is collected. An analysis of the specific reasons for collection the data is important because any additional, unnecessary data collection is considered to be a waste. The accuracy of the measurement process is also confirmed.

There are several tools available for the display of SPC data. These include:

1. Graphs and Charts are used to display trends or to summarize the data. These tend to be bar or line graphs that report on a specific parameter of performance.

2. Check Sheets or Tally Sheets are used to take the raw data and reorganize it into specific categories that are being observed.

3. Histograms or Frequency distribution charts are used to translate raw data into a pictorial display showing the performance of specific quality characteristics.

4. Pareto Principles are used to prioritize the contribution effect of specific quality problems. This tool assists in identifying which problems have the largest impact on a specific quality problem under study.

5. Brainstorming is used to generate ideas by taking advantage of the synergistic power of a team of people.

6. Ishikawa Diagrams (Fishbone Charts) are used to create problem and solution visibility by grouping problem causes into branches. Often this is referred to as a cause and effect

diagram. Using this tool in conjunction with the PDCA process helps to narrow down the root cause.

7. Control Charts are used to validate that the variation of measurement of a specific parameter is kept within a set of control limits.

In SPC, the most critical part of the process is the validation that you are measuring the right thing and thereby motivating the correct response. Additionally, if one measure can take the place of several measures, then that one measure should be identified, thereby simplifying the measurement process. Once a measurement has been selected, then we are ready to set up the data collection process and to establish control charts that will monitor the performance of this data.

The control charts are built around a specific product parameter that requires monitoring because of its impact on the over-all quality of the product. The following discussion is an extremely basic overview of the SPC process, and should not be considered to be sufficient for implementing an SPC process. Rather, this discussion is simply intended to give the reader and basic overview of the process.

The next step in the SPC process is to establish a set of control variables that includes an average (X) and a range (R). These can be established by going to the drawings are reviewing the initial part specifications using the expected value as X and the tolerance range as R. Or, these variables can be established using historical values and calculating the historical average (X) and range (R) for the data.

Having established an X and R value, we can calculate an Upper Control Limit (UCL) and a Lower Control Limit (LCL).

$$UCL = X + R$$
$$LCL = X - R$$

From these values, a pair of control charts is created. These charts are used to plot the SPC data as it occurs. They are used as a visual tool to monitor the process. Chart 1 is an example of two basic SPC charts which are monitoring a process. For these charts we will use X=1.23 and R=.45.

From Chart 1 we can see how the measurement data is recorded on the chart at the time each measurement occurs. The objectives behind this data collection process are several. One is to catch outliers in the

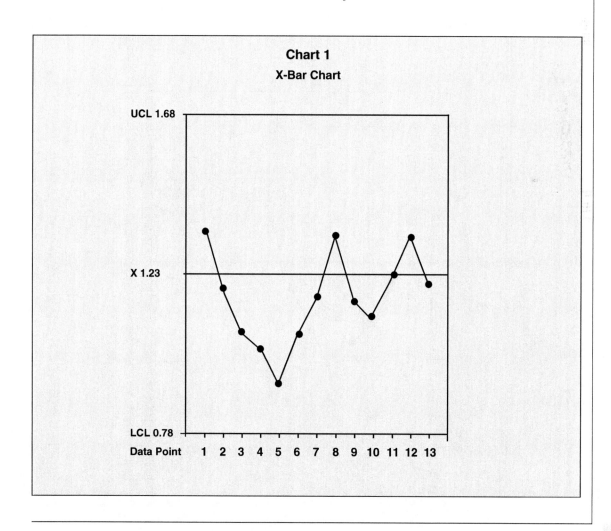

Chart 1

X-Bar Chart

UCL 1.68

X 1.23

LCL 0.78

Data Point   1   2   3   4   5   6   7   8   9   10   11   12   13 data (anything above the UCL or below the LCL). These outliers are quality failures and must immediately stop the process. Another purpose for the measures is to identify trends. For example data points 1 through 5 indicate a strong trend to failure approaching the LCL. Corrective action should be taken immediately to avoid the possibility of producing bad parts. Another objective can be seen in data points 7 through 13 which indicates that perhaps our LCL and UCL are too far and need to be brought in tighter, thereby giving us a higher level of performance and a higher level of quality.

Another methodology for applying SPC processes is by collecting data, not on every event, but on a random sampling of the event. This occurs when there is a large volume of activity and the time required to measure each event is too burdensome. A statistical sample is taken, and from that sample the average of the sample data (X) and the range of that sample (R = highest minus lowest measure) is calculated. For example, if our random sample size was 5 data points and our sample included the measures of 1.4, 1.45, 1.2, 1.3, and 1.65, then X = 1.4 and R = 1.65−1.2 = .45. This X value would then be the first data point plotted on Chart 1.

Using the statistical random sample, a Range chart would also need to be created. Chart 2 is an example of a range chart and the first data point of Chart would be the plot of the data corresponding to the example given. For this example, the lower limit is zero, which states that there is no deviation between each of the data points of that sample. The center point is R (.45) and the UCL is equal to 2 time R (.90).

In the example of the Range Chart (R Chart), the lower the value is better. A lot of vibration all over the chart suggests that the process may be going out of control. Also, a trend moving upwards as we see from data points 5 through 10 would indicate that a process is starting to go out of control and corrective action should be taken immediately.

With the X-Bar and R Charts, we can now create summarized reports, like the Histograms and Frequency Distributions that were discussed earlier. This allows a long term, summarized perspective of the process, rather than the chronological time-line that the X-Bar and R Charts offer.

There are systems and philosophies that go beyond SPC, which includes "Design of Experiments (DOE)" and "Concept Management." In DOE the

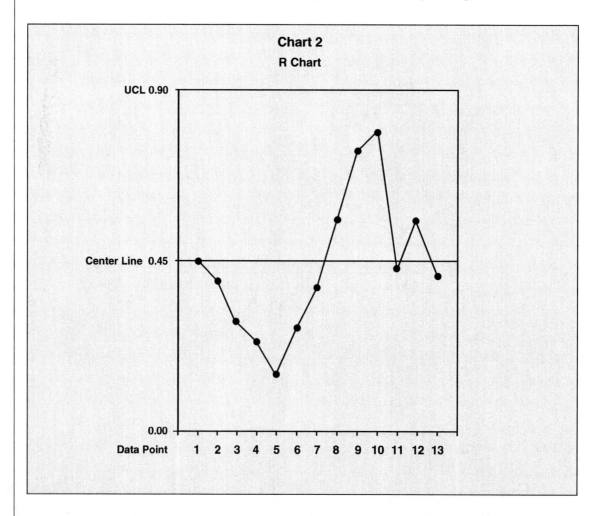

Chart 2

R Chart

focus is on front-end design work, rather than on SPC problem solving as you go. And Concept Management utilizes Total Quality Management (TQM) methodologies to implement continuous improvement change processes, once again in an attempt to identify and resolve potential problems before they occur. Additionally, Concept Management uses Breakthrough Thinking techniques rather than Root Cause Analysis to question the cause of problems.

Six Sigma, and one of it's primary tools SPC, have their roots in Japanese manufacturing process. But they have since become a key quality standard for the United States and Europe through their use of management principles and effective measurement tools.

SEE ALSO: Quality and Total Quality Management; Quality Gurus

Gerhard Plenert

FURTHER READING:

Antony, Dr. Jiju, and Mukkarram Bhaiji. "Key Ingredients for a Successful Six Sigma Program." Available from <onesixsigma.com>.

Bothe, Keki R. *World Class Quality.* NY: AMACOM, 1991.

Drucker, Peter. "The Emerging Theory of Manufacturing." *Harvard Business Review,* May/June 1990, 95.

Kullmann, John. "An Introduction to Six Sigma." Available from <onesixsigma.com>.

Plenert, Gerhard. *The eManager: Value Chain Management in an eCommerce World.* Dublin, Ireland: Blackhall Publishing, 2001.

———. *International Operations Management.* Copenhagen, Denmark: Copenhagen Business School Press, 2002.

Plenert, Gerhard, and Shozo Hibino. *Making Innovation Happen: Concept Management Through Integration.* DelRay Beach, FL: St. Lucie Press, 1997.

Pyzdek, Thomas. "Cargo Cult Six Sigma." *Quality Digest.*

Robustelli, Peter, and John Kullmann. "Implementing Six Sigma to Affect Lasting Change." Available from <onesixsigma.com>.

Ross, Joel E. *Total Quality Management.* Delray Beach, FL: St. Lucie Press, 1995.

Venturehaus. "An Introduction to Six Sigma." Available from <onesixsigma.com>.

STATISTICS

Statistics is a field of knowledge that enables an investigator to derive and evaluate conclusions about a population from sample data. In other words, statistics allow us to make generalizations about a large group based on what we find in a smaller group.

The field of statistics deals with gathering, selecting, and classifying data; interpreting and analyzing data; and deriving and evaluating the validity and reliability of conclusions based on data.

Strictly speaking, the term "parameter" describes a certain aspect of a population, while a "statistic" describes a certain aspect of a sample (a representative part of the population). In common usage, most people use the word "statistic" to refer to research figures and calculations, either from information based on a sample or an entire population.

Statistics means different things to different people. To a baseball fan, statistics are information about a pitcher's earned run average or a batter's slugging percentage or home run count. To a plant manager at a distribution company, statistics are daily reports on inventory levels, absenteeism, labor efficiency, and production. To a medical researcher investigating the effects of a new drug, statistics are evidence of the success of research efforts. And to a college student, statistics are the grades made on all the exams and quizzes in a course during the semester. Today, statistics and statistical analysis are used in practically every profession, and for managers in particular, statistics have become a most valuable tool.

A set of data is a population if decisions and conclusions based on these data can be made with absolute certainty. If population data is available, the risk of arriving at incorrect decisions is completely eliminated.

But a sample is only part of the whole population. For example, statistics from the U.S. Department of Commerce suggest that as of April 2005, 10.1 percent of rental homes and apartments were vacant. However, the data used to calculate this vacancy rate was not derived from all owners of rental property, but rather only a segment ("sample" in statistical terms) of the total group (or "population") of rental property owners. A population statistic is thus a set of measured or described observations made on each elementary unit. A sample statistic, in contrast, is a measure based on a representative group taken from a population.

QUANTITATIVE AND QUALITATIVE STATISTICS

Measurable observations are called quantitative observations. Examples of measurable observations include the annual salary drawn by a BlueCross/BlueShield underwriter or the age of a graduate student in an MBA program. Both are measurable and are therefore quantitative observations.

Observations that cannot be measured are termed qualitative. Qualitative observations can only be described. Anthropologists, for instance, often use qualitative statistics to describe how one culture varies from another. Marketing researchers have increasingly used qualitative statistical techniques to describe phenomena that are not easily measured, but can instead be described and classified into meaningful categories. Here, the distinction between a population of variates (a set of measured observations) and a population of attributes (a set of described observations) is important.

Values assumed by quantitative observations are called variates. These quantitative observations are further classified as either discrete or continuous. A discrete quantitative observation can assume only a limited number of values on a measuring scale. For example, the number of graduate students in an MBA investment class is considered discrete.

Some quantitative observations, on the other hand, can assume an infinite number of values on a measuring scale. These quantitative measures are termed continuous. How consumers feel about a particular brand is a continuous quantitative measure; the exact increments in feelings are not directly assignable to a given number. Consumers may feel more or less strongly about the taste of a hamburger, but it would be difficult to say that one consumer likes a certain hamburger twice as much as another consumer.

DESCRIPTIVE AND INFERENTIAL STATISTICS

Managers can apply some statistical technique to virtually every branch of public and private enterprise. These techniques are commonly separated into two broad categories: descriptive statistics and inferential statistics. Descriptive statistics are typically simple summary figures calculated from a set of observations. Suppose a professor computes an average grade for one accounting class. If the professor uses the statistic simply to describe the performance of that class, the result is a descriptive statistic of overall performance.

Inferential statistics are used to apply conclusions about one set of observations to reach a broader conclusion or an inference about something that has not been directly observed. In this case, a professor might use the average grade from a series of previous accounting classes to estimate, or infer, the average grade for future accounting classes. Any conclusion made about future accounting classes is based solely on the inferential statistics derived from previous accounting classes.

FREQUENCY DISTRIBUTION

Data is a collection of any number of related observations. A collection of data is called a data set. Statistical data may consist of a very large number of observations. The larger the number of observations, the greater the need to present the data in a summarized form that may omit some details, but reveals the general nature of a mass of data.

Frequency distribution allows for the compression of data into a table. The table organizes the data into classes or groups of values describing characteristics of the data. For example, students' grade distribution is one characteristic of a graduate class.

A frequency distribution shows the number of observations from the data set that fall into each category describing this characteristic. The relevant categories are defined by the user based on what he or she is trying to accomplish; in the case of grades, the categories might be each letter grade (A, B, C, etc.), pass/fail/incomplete, or grade percentage ranges. If you can determine the frequency with which values occur in each category, you can construct a frequency distribution. A relative frequency distribution presents frequencies in terms of fractions or percentages. The sum of all relative frequency distributions equals 1.00 or 100 percent.

Table 1 illustrates both a frequency distribution and a relative frequency distribution. The frequency distribution gives a break down of the number of

---

Table 1

Frequency Distribution for a Class of 25 M.B.A. Students

Grade Scale	Student/Grade Frequency	Relative Frequency
A	5	20%
B	12	48%
C	4	16%
D	2	8%
F	1	4%
I (Incomplete)	1	4%
TOTAL	25	100%

students in each grade category ranging from A to F, including "I" for incomplete. The relative frequency distribution takes that number and turns it into a percentage of the whole number.

The chart shows us that five out of twenty-five students, or 25 percent, received an A in the class. It is basically two different ways of analyzing the same data. This is an example of one of the advantages of statistics. The same data can be analyzed several different ways.

PARAMETERS

Decisions and conclusions can often be made with absolute certainty if a single value that describes a certain aspect of a population is determined. As noted earlier, a parameter describes an entire population, whereas a statistic describes only a sample. The following are a few of the most common types of parameter measurements used.

AGGREGATE PARAMETER. An aggregate parameter can be computed only for a population of variates. The aggregate is the sum of the values of all the variates in the population. Industry-wide sales is an example of an aggregate parameter.

PROPORTION. A proportion refers to a fraction of the population that possesses a certain property. The proportion is the parameter used most often in describing a population of attributes, for example, the percentage of employees over age fifty.

ARITHMETIC MEAN. The arithmetic mean is simply the average. It is obtained by dividing the sum of all variates in the population by the total number of variates. The arithmetic mean is used more often than the median and mode to describe the average variate in the population. It best describes the values such as the average grade of a graduate student, the average yards gained per carry by a running back, and the average calories burned during a cardiovascular workout. It also has an interesting property: the sum of the deviations of the individual variates from their arithmetic mean is always is equal to zero.

MEDIAN. The median is another way of determining the "average" variate in the population. It is especially useful when the population has a particularly skewed frequency distribution; in these cases the arithmetic mean can be misleading.

To compute the median for a population of variates, the variates must be arranged first in an increasing or decreasing order. The median is the middle variate if the number of the variates is odd. For example, if you have the distribution 1, 3, 4, 8, and 9, then the median is 4 (while the mean would be 5). If the number of variates is even, the median is the arithmetic mean of the two middle variates. In some cases (under a normal distribution) the mean and median are equal or nearly equal. However, in a skewed distribution where a few large values fall into the high end or the low end of the scale, the median describes the typical or average variate more accurately than the arithmetic mean does.

Consider a population of four people who have annual incomes of $2,000, $2,500, $3,500, and $300,000—an extremely skewed distribution. If we looked only at the arithmetic mean ($77,000), we would conclude that it is a fairly wealthy population on average. By contrast, in observing the median income ($3,000) we would conclude that it is overall a quite poor population, and one with great income disparity. In this example the median provides a much more accurate view of what is "average" in this population because the single income of $300,000 does not accurately reflect the majority of the sample.

MODE. The mode is the most frequently appearing variate or attribute in a population. For example, say a class of thirty students is surveyed about their ages. The resulting frequency distribution shows us that ten students are 18 years old, sixteen students are 19 years old, and four are 20 or older. The mode for this group would be the sixteen students who are 19 years old. In other words, the category with the most students is age 19.

MEASURE OF VARIATION

Another pair of parameters, the *range* and the *standard deviation,* measures the disparity among values of the various variates comprising the population. These parameters, called measures of variation, are designed to indicate the degree of uniformity among the variates.

The range is simply the difference between the highest and lowest variate. So, in a population with incomes ranging from $15,000 to $45,000, the range is $30,000 ($45,000 - $15,000 = $30,000).

The standard deviation is an important measure of variation because it lends itself to further statistical analysis and treatment. It measures the average amount by which variates are spread around the mean. The standard deviation is a versatile tool based on yet another calculation called the variance. The variance for a population reflects how far data points are from the mean, but the variance itself is typically used to calculate other statistics rather than for direct interpretation, such as the standard deviation, which is more useful in making sense of the data.

The standard deviation is a simple but powerful adaptation of the variance. It is found simply by taking the square root of the variance. The resulting figure can be used for a variety of analyses. For example, under a normal distribution, a distance of two standard deviations from the mean encompasses approximately 95 percent of the population, and three standard deviations cover 99.7 percent.

Thus, assuming a normal distribution, if a factory produces bolts with a mean length of 7 centimeters (2.8 inches) and the standard deviation is determined to be 0.5 centimeters (0.2 inches), we would know that 95 percent of the bolts fall between 6 centimeters (2.4 inches) and 8 centimeters (3.1 inches) long, and that 99.7 percent of the bolts are between 5.5 centimeters (2.2 inches) and 8.5 centimeters (3.3 inches). This information could be compared to the product specification tolerances to determine what proportion of the output meets quality control standards.

PROBABILITY

Modern statistics may be regarded as an application of the theory of probability. A set is a collection of well-defined objects called elements of the set. The set may contain a limited or infinite number of elements. The set that consists of all elements in a population is referred to as the universal set.

Statistical experiments are those that contain two significant characteristics. One is that each experiment has several possible outcomes that can be specified in advance. The second is that we are uncertain about the outcome of each experiment. Examples of statistical experiments include rolling a die and tossing a coin. The set that consists of all possible outcomes of an experiment is called a sample space, and each element of the sample space is called a sample point.

Each sample point or outcome of an experiment is assigned a weight that measures the likelihood of its occurrence. This weight is called the probability of the sample point.

Probability is the chance that something will happen. In assigning weights or probabilities to the various sample points, two rules generally apply. The first is that probability assigned to any sample point ranges from 0 to 1. Assigning a probability of 0 means that something can never happen; a probability of 1 indicates that something will always happen. The second rule is that the sum of probabilities assigned to all sample points in the sample space must be equal to 1 (e.g., in a coin flip, the probabilities are .5 for heads and .5 for tails).

In probability theory, an event is one or more of the possible outcomes of doing something. If we toss a coin several times, each toss is an event. The activity that produces such as event is referred to in probability theory as an experiment. Events are said to be mutually exclusive if one, and only one, can take place at a time. When a list of the possible events that can result from an experiment includes every possible outcome; the list is said to be collectively exhaustive. The coin toss experiment is a good example of collective exhaustion. The end result is either a head or a tail.

There are a few theoretical approaches to probability. Two common ones are the classical approach and the relative frequency approach. Classical probability defines the probability that an event will occur as the number of outcomes favorable to the occurrence of the event divided by the total number of possible outcomes. This approach is not practical to apply in managerial situations because it makes assumptions that are unrealistic for many real-life applications. It assumes away situations that are very unlikely, but that could conceivably happen. It is like saying that when a coin is flipped ten times, there will always be exactly five heads and five tails. But how many times do you think that actually happens? Classical probability concludes that it happens every time.

The relative frequency approach is used in the insurance industry. The approach, often called the relative frequency of occurrence, defines probability as the observed relative frequency of an event in a very large number of trials, or the proportion of times that an event occurs in the long run when conditions are stable. It uses past occurrences to help predict future probabilities that the occurrences will happen again.

Actuaries use high-level mathematical and statistical calculations in order to help determine the risk that some people and some groups might pose to the insurance carrier. They perform these operations in order to get a better idea of how and when situations that would cause customers to file claims and cost the company money might occur. The value of this is that it gives the insurance company an estimate of how much to charge for insurance premiums. For example, customers who smoke cigarettes are in higher risk group than those who do not smoke. The insurance company charges higher premiums to smokers to make up for the added risk.

SAMPLING

The objective of sampling is to select that part which is representative of the entire population. Sample designs are classified into probability samples and nonprobability samples. A sample is a probability sample if each unit in the population is given some chance of being selected. The probability of selecting each unit must be known. With a probability sample, the risk of incorrect decisions and conclusions can be measured using the theory of probability.

A sample is a non-probability sample when some units in the population are not given any chance of being selected, and when the probability of selecting any unit into the sample cannot be determined or is not known. For this reason, there is no means of measuring the risk of making erroneous conclusions derived from non-probability samples. Since the reliability of the results of non-probability samples cannot be measured, such samples do not lend themselves to statistical treatment and analysis. Convenience and judgment samples are the most common types of non-probability samples.

Among its many other applications, sampling is used in some manufacturing and distributing settings as a means of quality control. For example, a sample of 5 percent may be inspected for quality from a predetermined number of units of a product. That sample, if drawn properly, should indicate the total percentage of quality problems for the entire population, within a known margin of error (e.g., an inspector may be able to say with 95 percent certainty that the product defect rate is 4 percent, plus or minus 1 percent).

In many companies, if the defect rate is too high, then the processes and machinery are checked for errors. When the errors are found to be human errors, then a statistical standard is usually set for the acceptable error percentage for laborers.

In sum, samples provide estimates of what we would discover if we knew everything about an entire population. By taking only a representative sample of the population and using appropriate statistical techniques, we can infer certain things, not with absolute precision, but certainly within specified levels of precision.

SEE ALSO: Data Processing and Data Management; Forecasting; Models and Modeling; Planning

James C. Koch
Revised by Scott Droege

FURTHER READING:

Anderson, David, Dennis Sweeney, and Thomas Williams. *Essentials of Statistics for Business and Economics.* Thomson South-Western, 2006.

Hogg, Robert, and Elliot Tanas. *Probability and Statistical Inference.* 7th ed. Upper Saddle River, NJ: Prentice Hall, 2005.

STRATEGIC ALLIANCES

SEE: Joint Ventures and Strategic Alliances

STRATEGIC PARTNERSHIPS

SEE: Government-University-Industry Partnerships

STRATEGIC PLANNING FAILURE

Strategic management is the process of defining the purpose and pursuits of an organization and the methods for achieving them. Robert Grant emphasizes that competition provides the rationale for strategy because strategy is about winning. It follows then that the inter-dependence of competitors is the essence of strategy—actions of individual competitors and teams of competitors affect outcomes for other participants. In other words, organizational leaders must "play the game" strategically because their organizations are involved in a game of strategy (e.g., chess) not simply a game of chance (e.g., bingo) or a game of skill (e.g., tennis). Of course, the necessary skills must exist, and at times things will happen that were not predictable. However, each organization must have a strategic focus if it intends to survive and flourish in the long term.

The overall strategic management model can be broken into two major phases: strategy development and strategy deployment. Strategy development is the creation and establishment of an organization's overall mission and vision and the means to achieve them. Strategic development includes the following elements of the strategic management model:

• Mission —Why does the organization exist?

• Internal and External Assessments—What are the internal strengths and weaknesses and external threats and opportunities?

• Vision—Where does the organization want to be in the future?

• Goals and Objectives—What are the overall, high-level desired results as well as specific, measurable outcomes required to achieve the mission and vision?

• Strategy Formulation—What is the plan of how and when to achieve the goals and objectives? This includes strategies, tactics, and action plans (Who will do what and when?)

Strategy deployment, or implementation, is the translation of strategic plans into actions and results. It is the execution of the strategic plan at all levels in the organization. Development and deployment are considered separately because the best strategic plans will have no impact if not implemented well. Conversely, simple strategic plans that are deployed well can have major impact. The strategy deployment phase includes the following elements of the model:

• Strategy Implementation—execution or deployment of the strategic plans.

- Measurement and Feedback—the monitoring and feedback element answers the questions "How is the organization doing?" "What modifications and improvements are necessary?"

Other elements of strategic management that are required for strategic planning to be successful are:

- Core Competencies—What are our best capabilities?

- Distinctive Competencies —Which of our competencies are unique and not easily replicated?

- Core Values—What do we care about as an organization? What are our shared values?

- Critical Success Factors—What do we have to do right to be successful?

- Leadership Competencies—What leadership characteristics and competencies do we require of our managers and non-managers?

RECENT HISTORY OF STRATEGIC PLANNING

In the 1960s and 1970s, strategic planning was viewed by executives as the best way to ensure productivity and profits. The assumption was that everything that was of potential value to decision making and strategic planning could be measured, and that after subjecting those measurements to various quantitative models, results would show executives the best strategies.

In the early 1960s, professors Ken Andrews and C. Roland Christensen of the Harvard Business School contended that strategy could be a potentially powerful tool for linking business functions and assessing a company's weaknesses and strengths in relationship to its competitors' strengths and weaknesses. General Electric emerged as a pioneer in the area of corporate strategic planning and developed a high-powered staff of full-time strategic planners to direct GE's planning efforts. With the assistance of McKinsey and Company, GE was organized into strategic business units (SBUs) and strategic plans were developed for each SBU.

In 1963, the Boston Consulting Group pioneered a variety of strategic approaches that became popular with executives. Two of BCG's approaches were the "experience curve" and the "growth and market-share matrix." The trust of executives in strategic planning models increased throughout the 1970s, and perhaps peaked with the publication of "Competitive Strategy," by Harvard professor Michael E. Porter in 1980. Porter's books and articles continue to have a tremendous influence on many executives, university students, and professors.

By the early 1980s, some executives began to feel that the return on their investment in the development of large strategic planning departments had been a disappointment. Also, the increase in computer technology and globalization of industries caused increased complexity in those industries, and the strategic models of the 1960s and 1970s could not deal with the complex dynamics of the new marketplace.

The death knell for strategic planning began when General Electric chairman Jack Welch significantly downsized the GE operating units' planning departments. Many other executives followed Welch's example during the 1980s and 1990s. Strategic planning was replaced in the minds of executives with thoughts of improving quality and productivity through operational innovation. The most prominent of these approaches included total quality management (TQM) and the Quality philosophies of Deming, Juran, and Crosby. In the 1990s, corporations began to focus on process reengineering and downsizing as a way of increasing operational effectiveness even more. Process Reengineering, an idea authors Hammer and Champy espoused was accepted by many as an additional strategy toward increased productivity.

In the 1990s, strategic planning was reborn. New approaches for strategy focused on growth through mergers/acquisitions and joint ventures, generation of innovative ideas through decentralized strategic efforts within the company, emergent strategy, and the leveraging of core competencies to create strategic intent.

The dominant theme for organizations in the twenty-first century is strategic and organizational innovation, and issues include reconciling size with flexibility and responsiveness. New alliances mean cooperative strategies, complexity, changes in commitments of corporate social responsibility, etc. Today's strategic planning requires new models of leadership, less formal structures, and more commitment to self direction. Also, past strategic failures relating to ethical problems require renewed commitments to ethical standards. Strategic management has evolved from the 1950s when its theme was budgetary planning and control to the twenty-first century when its theme is strategic and organizational innovation. See Table 1.

WHY DID TRADITIONAL STRATEGIC MANAGEMENT/STRATEGIC PLANNING FAIL?

Sydney Finkelstein maps four circumstances in which strategic planning failure is most likely to occur: launching new ventures, promoting innovation and change, managing mergers and acquisitions and

Table 1
The Evolution of Strategic Management/Strategic Planning

Period	1950's	1960's and Early 1970's	Late 1970's and early 1980's	Late 1980's and early 1990's	2000+
Dominant Theme	Budgetary planning & control.	Corporate planning.	Strategic Positioning. Analysis of industry & competition.	Strategic competitive advantage.	Strategic and organizational innovation.
Main Focus and Issues	Financial control, especially through operating budgets.	Planning growth, especially diversification and Portfolio Planning.	Selecting industries and markets. Positioning for market leadership.	Focusing strategy around Sources of competitive advantage. Dynamic aspects of strategy.	Reconciling size with flexibility & responsiveness.
Principal Concepts & Techniques	Financial budgeting. Investment planning. Project appraisal.	Medium- and long-term forecasting. Corporate planning techniques. Synergy.	Industry Analysis. Competitor analysis. Segmentation. Experience curves. PIMS analysis. SBU's (Strategic Business Units). Portfolio Planning.	Resources and capabilities. Shareholder value. Knowledge management. Information Technology. Analysis of speed, responsiveness & first-mover advantage.	Cooperative strategies. Competing for standards. Complexity & self-organization Corporate social responsibility. Renewed commitment to ethics.
Organizational Implications	Systems of operational and capital budgeting become key mechanisms of coordination and control.	Creation of corporate planning departments & long-term planning processes. Mergers & acquisitions.	Multidivisional & multinational structures. Greater industry & market selectivity. Divestment of unattractive business units.	Restructuring. Continuous improvement & process reengineering. Refocusing. Outsourcing. E-business.	Alliances and networks. New models of leadership. Informal structures. Less reliance on direction, more on emergence.

Adapted from: Robert M. Grant, Contemporary Strategy Analysis, 5th and 2nd eds., Blackwell Publishers, Inc., Cambridge, Massachusetts, 2005 and 1995.

responding to new environmental pressures. So in this era of dramatic change, global alliances, and a variety of environmental pressures, the potential for failure is very real.

Henry Mintzberg believes that the strategic planning models of the 1960s and 1970s ultimately failed because they did not distinguish between strategic planning and strategic thinking. Traditional strategic planning models were heavily oriented to quantitative analysis, the results of which directed the executive towards what strategy should be taken. These planning models actually subverted strategic thinking that involves the synthesis of one's experience, intuition, and creativity, in addition to analysis. Traditional strategic planning was not useless, but it should have been done after strategic thinking and vision development had taken place.

Another problem with traditional strategic planning was that it did not include in the planning process those who had to implement the strategic plan. The strategic planning was done at the very top of the organization, or by expert consultants, and the strategic plan was handed down to managers in bound, published documents. People often felt less than committed to such plans, and the documents themselves often did not take into account the actual business challenges these managers faced on a day-to-day basis. At lower levels in the hierarchy, the problem was even more severe because planning was often used to exercise blatant control over people.

Mintzberg notes that another reason traditional strategic planning failed was because it was based on some fundamental flaws: (1) the fallacy of prediction; (2) the fallacy of detachment; and (3) the fallacy of formalization.

THE FALLACY OF PREDICTION. Traditional strategic planning was based on the assumption that one could measure all of the variables that were relevant to the future of a business, analyze the results, and construct strategies based upon the results that, if followed, would ensure future success. However, even the best strategies experience unforeseen economic, industry, social, and market shifts. The fallacy of prediction inevitably led to the downfall of traditional strategic planning, because the strategies could not deliver what they promised: predictable success.

THE FALLACY OF DETACHMENT. Traditional strategic planning assumed that it was better to be detached from the workers and from middle managers when analyzing data, in order to prevent bias in the planning process. However, this simply separated the strategy makers from the strategy implementers, which turned out to be a fatal mistake. When problems of implementation arose, both sides pointed fingers at each other as the cause for the failure. Additionally, traditional strategic planning was often based on inappropriately aggregated data, data that was no longer current, or data that did not have important contextual information linked to it. Also strategic planners often ignored qualitative data, thus creating huge blind spots in the final strategic plan.

THE FALLACY OF FORMALIZATION. This fallacy is based on the notion that formal systems are superior to human systems in terms of information processing and decision making. Mintzberg believes that though formal systems might be able to process larger amounts of data than humans can, formal systems cannot integrate, synthesize, or create new directions from such analyses—only humans can perform the latter processes. We think in order to act, but we also act in order to think. Our experiments that work converge gradually into viable strategies.

THE ICARUS PARADOX

Danny Miller offers another perspective as to why strategies often fail. In his landmark study, Miller investigated the decline of powerful corporations, and his findings have done much to help managers understand the causes of strategic and organizational failure.

Miller named the model he developed from his findings, the *Icarus Paradox* after the tragic figure from Greek mythology. Icarus's father, Daedalus, was an inventor, who was asked to build a labyrinth for King Minos. Upon completion of his task, King Minos would not allow Daedalus to leave. Determined to escape, Daedalus built wings for himself and his son, Icarus, by adhering the wings of birds onto long boards with wax. Icarus was fascinated with the invention and was eager to try flying. Daedalus taught Icarus how to fly using his invention, but cautioned Icarus to fly only at a moderate height—neither too low nor too high. The escape was a success, but Icarus, ignoring the advice of his father, began gaining confidence in his ability to fly and grew more daring. He ultimately flew too high—too close to the sun—and the heat from the sun caused the wax to melt. His wings disintegrated and he plummeted helplessly to his death. The paradox of Icarus was that his skill and technology, which led him to freedom, ultimately also led to his death.

Miller found in his research that the victories and strengths of companies can often be the cause of their future strategic failure. Miller delineated four major causes of strategic failure: leadership traps, monolithic cultures and skills, power and politics, and structural memories. All of these causes emerge while an organization is experiencing success-especially in its strategic initiatives.

LEADERSHIP TRAPS. Success can be a trap in and of itself. Miller found that consistent success tends to reinforce leaders' world views and ties them rigidly to the strategies and processes that brought about past successes. This causes, in turn, these same leaders to become:

- overconfident
- prone to excess and neglect
- prone to shape strategies based on their preferences rather than what data, changing business circumstances, customers, and technological shifts dictate
- conceited—true believers in the adulation heaped upon them by the press, subordinates, shareholders, and other admirers
- obstinate—prone to resent challenges to their way of thinking
- isolated from the reality of the marketplace

The impact of those tendencies on strategy making is very negative when strategy is developed from ego, preconceptions of what causes success, stubbornness, and old, worn conceptual models.

MONOLITHIC CULTURES AND SKILLS AND POWER AND POLITICS. Miller found that another reason for strategic failure in organizations that have been successful is due to the fact that these organizations tend to rely on "star" departments and the culture that builds up around them. When certain functions take precedence over others in an imbalanced manner, other business functions are seen as less important, and perhaps even unimportant, to the success of the organization. Over time, the evolution of organizational cultures in successful companies usually becomes monolithic, intolerant, and focused on a single goal or very limited goals. Additionally, the star department attracts the best and the brightest managers away from other departments, so that the organization has an imbalance of managerial talent throughout the organization. Conversely, talented managers in departments outside the star department usually join companies that can appreciate their skills. Over time, managerial talent is diluted (excepted for within the star department) and becomes imbalanced throughout the organization. The "star" departments have more power, and people in these departments are able to use their power to play politics and gain even more resources and success.

POWER AND POLITICS. As managers in the star departments increase their power, they become less inclined to adjust the way they have always conducted business. Programs, policies, and practices that in the past, have proven successful and given these managers such high status are loyally adhered to, and the ability to make organizational adjustments becomes limited. The ultimate consequence of this type of power build-up in a company is that past strategies are perpetuated, often without a careful evaluation of their current effectiveness.

STRUCTURAL MEMORIES. Past successful strategies engender policies, routines, systems, and programs in a company, and the institutionalization of these processes within a company creates a powerful organizational culture. Miller notes that "the more established and successful the strategy, the more deeply imbedded it will be in such programs, and the more it will be implemented routinely, automatically, and unquestioningly. Managers will rely on ingrained habits and reflex actions rather than deliberating and reflecting on new problems." In these situations, the past fashions how one sees the present, and is a powerful force for continually choosing the same, or similar, strategic courses of action, both within the organization and outside the organization.

DISRUPTIVE TECHNOLOGIES AS A CAUSE OF STRATEGIC FAILURE

Clayton M. Christensen, in his book *The Innovator's Dilemma* reported research findings that suggest that even when companies do follow sound management practices they still are exposed to events and problems that can cause strategic failure.

The innovator's dilemma is that "the logical, competent decisions of management that are critical to the success of their companies are also the reasons why they lose their positions of leadership." He contends that good management involves sustaining the success of products and processes, and that companies are generally good at this. However, such companies can be blind sided by the emergence of disruptive technologies. These disruptive technologies are products or processes that appear in the marketplace, but that look harmless to the successful company.

In the short term, they do not seem to pose much of threat, and thus they are ignored. However, over time, disruptive technologies can become a powerful force, and that when they do, successful companies are not organized or prepared to respond to what essentially is a new competitor in the market. Examples of disruptive technologies are the small, off-road motorcycles that were introduced by Japanese manufacturers into the United States. Over time, they threatened the product lines of Harley-Davidson and BMW. Health maintenance organizations (HMOs) strategically hurt traditional health insurers, and transistors killed the vacuum tube industry.

Successful companies miss seeing the threat of disruptive technologies because they are essentially caught in the routine of maintaining the status quo, i.e., their current success. To spot future disruptive technologies and plan for combat against them, a company would need to invest resources in the scanning for, and development of, disruptive technologies; be willing to enter into the market when a potentially disruptive technology emerges; be adept at developing new ways of analyzing emerging markets; and be aware that improving their product, and increasing its price, creates vacuums at the lower price range for emerging technologies to enter. The goal is to be able to both sustain successful products and processes, yet at the same time be able to see, evaluate, and develop disruptive technologies.

Strategic planning often fails for a variety of reasons such as:

1. Failure of merging organizations to understand either or both complementary competencies and synergies as well as areas that are not complementary and synergistic.

2. Failure to understand the culture of the organization.

3. Failure to adequately execute the strategic plans.

4. Failure to function as a team at the executive level or other levels.

5. Failure to develop values and culture to support the plans.

6. Failure to expeditiously do what is needed to be done.

7. Failure to trust and support each other at the various levels of the organization

8. Failure to prevent ethical and legal problems.

EXAMPLES OF STRATEGIC PLANNING FAILURE

HEWLETT PACKARD. CEO Carly Fiorina positioned HP as perhaps the widest-ranging technology company in the world, with offerings from digital cameras, to printers, to supercomputers. She staked her career on HP's acquisition of Compaq in 2002, and she lost. She was fired on February 7, 2005. The acquisition had been bitterly opposed by major shareholders including Walter Hewlett. Under Fiorina's direction, HP unsuccessfully battled IBM, Dell, Sony, EMC, and others. Today, the $80 billion HP is struggling in everything except its stellar printing business.

For months, Wall Street analysts have argued that HP's pieces/divisions would be worth far separately than they are together as a company. Fiorina fiercely resisting breaking up HP, and the Board of Directors insists that it will keep HP intact. HP has problems in enterprise computing. It is losing ground to EMC Corp. in storage and to Dell and IBM in servers. So much more is needed than simply replacing one or more top executives. How much HP energy was lost as Walter Hewlett and numerous employees and shareholders fought Fiorina's vision? How much more was lost as Hewlett was pushed off the board of the company his father founded? Fiorina was a decisive, gifted communicator. However, she fired or lost many executives, and she rigorously resisted changing strategies even as she made dramatic changes. She merged HP's 80-plus autonomous business units into a more centralized, four-division giant and eventually laid off thousands of workers. She had to also battle two cultures, HP and Compaq, both of which were very reluctant to change.

Why did the strategic planning based on the company vision fail? It was difficult for HP executives to rapidly understand complementary and non-complementary competencies, strategies, and synergies as well as differences in the respective cultures. From the outside, it would appear that most of the failure can be traced lack of trust and support among the players—the board members, some members of the board and Fiorina, the employees and the company, the shareholders and the board, and the shareholders and Fiorina. Also, Fiorina never had the loyalty of the employees. Some insist say it was failure of Fiorina to execute her ambitious strategic plan, and that is the reason she was fired. One *Business Week* article says Fiorina broke three key rules that CEO's must follow:

place the company's well-being above all else, including yourself; know your company from the inside out—some say that Fiorina did not fully comprehend the impact on operations of her vision to transform HP's structure and strategy; and hold people accountable, including yourself. Only history will tell whether HP will spin-off divisions or remain the one-stop shop that Carly Fiorina envisioned.

XEROX. The Xerox Board of Directors suddenly promoted Anne Mulcahy to president in May, 2000, after ousting G. Richard Thoman, who lasted thirteen months, and reinstalling Chairman Paul A. Allaire as CEO. The company was floundering after years of weak sales and high costs. Employees and customers were disgruntled. Then in October, Xerox reported its first quarterly loss in sixteen years. Debt was piling up, and the Securities & Exchange Commission began investigating whether Xerox used accounting tricks to boost income. Insiders and those outside of Xerox felt that Mulcahy had the strategic mind and toughness to serve as CEO. On July 26, 2004, Mulcahy was named CEO of Xerox. When Anne Mulcahy took over as CEO, Xerox was in terrible shape. It was fighting the Securities and Exchange Commission over accounting practices. It was $14 billion in debt, and bankruptcy was a real possibility. She was relentless in her efforts to stabilize Xerox. She made dramatic staff and business cuts. She brought in a new CFO. She met with numerous customers. Also, she got her people focused on turnaround and growth, which she says is the job of leadership.

What caused strategic plans prior to Mulcahy to fail? Six former senior executives of Xerox settled an SEC enforcement action charging them with fraud and agreed to pay over $22 Million in penalties, disgorgement and interest. Specific charges included securities fraud and aiding and abetting Xerox's violations of the reporting, books and records and internal control provisions of the federal securities laws. In other words, instead of relying on strategic plans to work (or changing the strategic plans) Xerox's senior management had apparently substituted accounting manipulations for the company's actual operational performance. Certainly there was a failure to develop values and culture to support the strategic plans, and there were legal and ethical problems related to the lack of appropriate shared core values. Apparently the strategic plans were also not appropriate, or they had not been fully executed since both customers and employees were unhappy, sales were weak, and costs were high.

SEE ALSO: Strategic Planning Tools; Strategy Formulation; Strategy Implementation; Strategy in the Global Environment; Strategy Levels

Mark E. Mendenhall
Revised by Mildred Golden Pryor

FURTHER READING:

"The Accidental CEO." *Fortune,* 23 June 2003, 58–65.

Baldrige, Malcolm. *National Quality Award Criteria.* Washington D.C.: National Institute of Standards and Technology, 2004.

"The Best Managers." *Business Week,* 10 January 2005, 56–67.

Christensen, Clayton M. *The Innovator's Dilemma: When New Technologies Cause Great Firms to Fail.* Cambridge, Boston, Massachusetts: Harvard Business School Press, 1997.

Christensen, Clayton M., and Michael E. Raynor. *The Innovator's Solution: Creating and Sustaining Successful Growth.* Boston: Harvard Business School Press, 2003.

Christensen, Clayton M., Scott D. Anthony, and Erik A Roth. *Seeing What's Next: Using the Theories of Innovation to Predict Industry Change.* Boston, MA: Harvard Business School Press, 2005.

Collis, David J., and Cynthia A. Montgomery. *Corporate Strategy.* New York: McGraw-Hill/Irwin, 2005.

Finkelstein, Sydney. *Why Smart Executives Fail and What You Can Learn from Their Mistakes.* New York: Penguin Group USA, 2003.

Grant, Robert M. *Contemporary Strategy Analysis.* 5th and 2nd eds. Cambridge, MA: Blackwell Publishers, Inc., 2003 and 1995.

Graves, Suzanne, and John Moran. "The Pitfalls Associated with Strategic and Operational Planning." *The Quality Management Forum* 20, no. 4 (Winter 1994): 1–4.

Henderson, Bruce. "The Origin of Strategy." *Harvard Business Review,* November-December 1989, 139–143.

Hitt, Michael A., R. Duane Ireland, and Robert E. Hoskisson. *Strategic Management: Competitiveness and Globalization.* Thomson South-Western, 2005.

Hofer, C.W., and D. Schendel. *Strategy Formulation: Analytical Concepts.* St. Paul, MN: West, 1978.

Kipp, Mike. "Why Head-in-the-Sand Leadership Sinks the Ship." *The Journal of Business Strategy* 25, no. 5 (2004): 63–64.

Miller, Danny. *The Icarus Paradox: How Exceptional Companies Bring About Their Own Downfall.* New York: HarperCollins, 1990.

Mintzberg, Henry. "The Fall and Rise of Strategic Planning." *Harvard Business Review,* January-February 1994, 107–114.

Neff, Thomas J., and James M. Citrin. *Lessons from the Top: The Search for America's Best Leaders.* New York: Doubleday, A Division of Random House, Inc., 2001.

Porter, Michael. *Competitive Advantage.* New York: The Free Press, 1985.

———. *Competitive Strategy: Techniques for Analyzing Industries and Competitors.* New York: The Free Press, A Division of McMillen, Inc., 1980 and 1998.

Pryor, Mildred Golden, J. Chris White, and Leslie A. Toombs. *Strategic Quality Management: A Strategic, Systems Approach to Continuous Improvement.* Thomson Learning, 1998.

"The Story of Kiely & Carly," *McClean's* 118, no. 9 (2005): 29.

"Three Simple Rules Carly Ignored." *Business Week,* 28 February 2005, 46.

U.S. Securities and Exchange Commission. *Litigation Release No. 18174.* and *Accounting and Auditing Enforcement Release No. 1796* 5 June 2003. Available from <http://www.sec.gov/litigation/litreleases/lr18174.htm>.

STRATEGIC PLANNING TOOLS

Strategic planning may be characterized as a systematic effort to produce fundamental decisions and actions that shape and guide what a business organization is, what it does, and why it does it. The objective of strategic planning is to develop a map by which to manage an organization's positioning.

Although some would suggest that strategic planning has lost some of its effectiveness, most managers continue to recognize the need for effective strategic planning and implementation. While strategic planning requires a significant amount of time and can be quite frustrating, if done properly, it can enable a firm to recognize its most effective position within its industry.

There are a variety of perspectives, models and approaches used in strategic planning. The development and implementation of these different tools depend on a large number of factors, such as size of the organization, nature and complexity of the organization's environment, and the organization's leadership and culture.

Five strategic planning tools are presented below: the Boston Consulting Group Matrix; the GE Market Growth/Market Share Matrix; SWOT Analysis; Porter's Generic Competitive Strategies; and Porter's Five Forces Model.

BOSTON CONSULTING GROUP MATRIX

In the late 1960s the Boston Consulting Group, a leading management consulting company, designed a four-cell matrix known as BCG Growth/Share Matrix. This tool was developed to aid companies in the measurement of all their company businesses according to relative market share and market growth. The BCG Matrix made a significant contribution to strategic management and continues to be an important strategic tool used by companies today. The matrix provides a composite picture of the strategic position of each separate business within a company so that the management can determine the strengths and the needs of

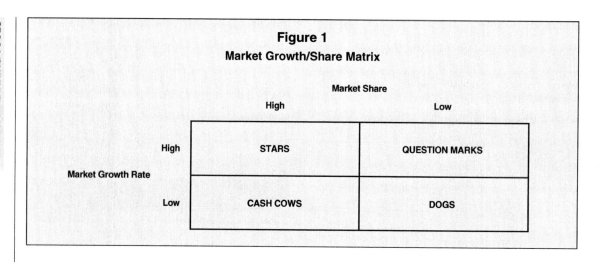

Figure 1
Market Growth/Share Matrix

all sectors of the firm. The development of the matrix requires the assessment of a business portfolio, which includes an organization's autonomous divisions (activities, or profit centers).

The BCG Matrix presents graphically the differences among these business units in terms of relative market share and industry growth rate. The vertical axis represents in a linear scale the growth rate of the market in which the business exists (see Figure 1). This is generally viewed as the expected growth rate for the next five years of the market in which a particular business competes. The values of the vertical axis are the relevant market growth rates (i.e., 5 percent, 10 percent, 15 percent, 20 percent, etc.). Usually a 10 percent cut-off level is selected in order to distinguish high from low market growth rate (a 10 percent value corresponds to doubling current experience in the next five to seven years).

The horizontal axis represents in a logarithmic scale the market share of a business within a firm relative to the market share of the largest competitor in the market. For example, Company A may have a 10 percent market share and Company B, the leading competitor, holds 40 percent of the market. Company A's market share relative to Company B's market share is 25 percent, or .25×. If Company A has a 40 percent share and Company B has a 10 percent share, Company A's market share is 400 percent, or 4.0×.

Relative market share is an indicator of organization's competitive position within the industry, and underlies the concept of experience curve. Thus, business organizations with high relative market share tend to have a cost leadership position.

Each of a company's products or business units is plotted on the matrix and classified as one of four types: question marks, stars, cash cows, and dogs. Question marks, located in the upper-right quadrant, have low relative market share in a high-growth market. These businesses are appropriately called

question marks because it is often uncertain what will happen to them. Careful examination by management can help determine how many resources (if any) should be invested in these businesses. If significant change can increase relative market share for a question mark, it can become a star and eventually gain cash-cow status. If relative market share can not be increased, the question mark becomes a dog.

The upper-left quadrant contains stars, businesses with high relative market share in high-growth markets. These businesses are very important to the company because they generate a high level of sales and are quite profitable. However, because they are in a high growth market that is very attractive to competitors, they require a lot of resources and investments to maintain a high market share. Often the cash generated by stars must be reinvested in the products in order to maintain market share.

When the market growth slows down, stars can take different paths, depending on their abilities to hold (or gain) market share or to lose market share. If a star holds or gains market share when the growth rate slows, stars become more valuable over time, or cash cows. However, if a star loses market share, it becomes a dog and has significantly less value (if any) to the company.

The lower-left quadrant contains businesses that have high relative market share in low-growth markets. These businesses are called cash cows and are highly profitable leaders in their industries. The funds received from cash cows are often used to help other businesses within the company, to allow the company to purchase other businesses, or to return dividends to stockholders.

Dogs generate low relative market share in a low-growth market. They generate little cash and frequently result in losses. Management should carefully consider their reasons for maintaining dogs. If there is a loyal consumer group to which these businesses appeal, and if the businesses yield relatively consistent cash that can cover their expenses, management may choose to continue their existence. However, if a dog consumes more resources than it's worth, it will likely be deleted or divested.

Strategic business units, which are often used to describe the products grouping or activities, are represented with a circle in the BCG Matrix. The size of the circle indicates the relative significance of each business unit to the organization in terms of revenue generated (or assets used).

Although the BCG Matrix is not used as often as it was in past years, one big advantage of the matrix is its ability to provide a comprehensive snapshot of the positions of a company's various business concerns. Furthermore, an important benefit of the BCG Matrix is that is draws attention to the cash flow, investment characteristics, and needs of an organization's business units, helping organizations to maintain a balanced portfolio.

Unfortunately, the BCG Matrix, like all analytical techniques, also has some important limitations. It has been criticized for being too simplistic in its use of growth rate and market share. Market growth rate is only one variable in market attractiveness and market share is only one variable in a business's competitive position. Furthermore, viewing every business as a star, cash flow, dog, or question mark is not always realistic. A four-cell matrix is too simple because strategic competitive positions are more complicated than "high" and "low".

Another disadvantage of using the BCG Matrix is that it is often difficult for a company to sufficiently divide its business units or product lines. Consequently, it is difficult to determine market share for the various units of concern.

GENERAL ELECTRIC MATRIX

In the 1980s General Electric, along with the McKinsey and Company Consulting group, developed a more involved method for analyzing a company's portfolio of businesses or product lines. This nine-cell matrix considers the attractiveness of the market situation and the strength of the particular business of interest. These two dimensions allow a company to use much more data in determining each business unit's position.

The key to the successful implementation of this strategic tool is the identification and measurement of the appropriate factors that define market attractiveness and business strength. Those individuals involved in strategic planning are responsible for determining the factors. The attractiveness of the market may be based on such factors as market growth rate, barriers

to entry, barriers to exit, industry profitability, power of the suppliers and customers, availability of substitutes, negotiating power of both customers and members of the channel of distribution, as well as other opportunities and threats.

The strength of a particular business may be based on such factors as market-share position, cost placement in the industry, brand equity, technological position, and other possible strengths and weaknesses. The development of General Electric (GE) Matrix requires assessing the criteria to evaluate both industry attractiveness and business strength. The calculation of scores for these dimensions is frequently based on a simple weighted sum formula.

To consider this approach as a matrix analysis, market attractiveness is placed on the vertical axis with the possible values of low, medium, and high (see Figure 2). Business strength is placed on the horizontal axis with the possible values of weak, average, and strong. A circle on the matrix represents each business unit (or product line). The size (area) of each circle represents the size of the relevant market in terms of sales. A portion of the circle is shaded to represent the market share of each business unit or product line within the market.

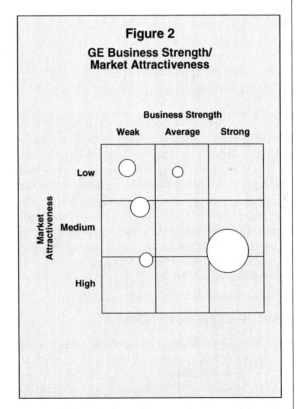

Figure 2
GE Business Strength/ Market Attractiveness

The nine cells of this matrix define three general zones of consideration for the strategic manager. According to this approach, the first zone contains businesses that are the best investments. These are units high in market attractiveness and strong in business strength, followed by those that are strong in business strength and medium in market attractiveness, and those that are medium in business strength and high in market attractiveness. Management should pursue investment and growth strategies for these units. Management should be very careful in determining the appropriate strategy for those business units located in any of the three cells in the diagonal of this matrix.

The second zone includes those business units that have moderate overall attractiveness and those units that have medium business strength and market attractiveness, weak business strength and high market attractiveness, and strong business strength and low market attractiveness. These businesses should be managed according to their relative strengths and the company's ability to build on those strengths. Moreover, possible changes in market attractiveness should be carefully considered.

Those businesses that fall in the last zone are low in overall attractiveness; these are a good investment only if additional resources can move the business from a low overall attractiveness position to a moderate or strong overall attractiveness position. If not, these businesses should be considered for deletion or harvest.

The GE Matrix may be considered as an improvement over the BCG Matrix. The major advantage of using this matrix design is that both a business' strength and an industry's attractiveness are considered in the company's decision. Generally, it considers much more information than BCG Matrix, it involves the judgments of the strategic decision-makers, and it focuses on competitive position.

A major disadvantage, however, is the difficulty in appropriately defining business strength and market attractiveness. Also, the estimation of these dimensions is a subjective judgment that may become quite complicated. Another disadvantage lies in the lack of objective measures available to position a company; managers making these strategic decisions may have difficulty determining their unit's proper placement. Too, some argue that the GE Matrix cannot effectively depict the positions of new products or business units in developing industries.

SWOT ANALYSIS MATRIX

One of the most widely used strategic planning tools is a SWOT (Strengths, Weaknesses, Opportunities, Threats) analysis. Most companies use, in one form or another, SWOT analysis as a basic guide for strategic planning. The worth of a SWOT analysis is often dependent on the objective insight of those management individuals who conduct the SWOT analysis. If management (or consultant management) is able to provide objective, relevant information for the analysis, the results are extremely useful for the company.

A SWOT analysis involves a company's assessment of its internal position by identifying the company's strengths and weaknesses. In addition, the company must determine its external position by defining its opportunities and threats.

Strengths represent those skills in which a company exceeds and/or the key assets of the firm. Examples of strengths are a group of highly skilled employees, cutting-edge technology, and high-quality products. Weaknesses are those areas in which a firm does not perform well; examples include continued conflict between functional areas, high production costs, and a poor financial position.

Opportunities are those current or future circumstances in the environment that might provide favorable conditions for the firm. Examples of opportunities include an increase in the market population, a decrease in competition and a legislation that is favorable to the industry. Threats are those current or future circumstances in the environment, which might provide unfavorable conditions for the firm. Examples of threats include increased supplier costs, a competitor's new product-development process, and a legislation that is unfavorable to the industry.

After a firm has identified its strengths and weaknesses, it should determine the significance of each factor. A management team should review all strengths and weaknesses to determine the level (minor or major) of each strength and weakness. The importance (low or high) of each strength and weakness should also be identified. As shown in Figure 3, the combination of level of performance and importance yields four possibilities.

Cell 1 contains important areas in which the company is exhibiting poor performance. When a company identifies these areas it becomes aware of the need to improve its efforts in order to strengthen its performance. Important areas in which the company is performing very well are located in Cell 2. A company should continue its current efforts in these areas. Cell 3 contains unimportant areas in which the firm is performing poorly. Since these areas are a low priority for the company, it need not pay a great deal of attention to these areas. The last category, Cell 4, includes areas in which the company is performing well, but which are unimportant. The firm may need to pull back some of its efforts in this area, depending on how unimportant the area is to the overall picture.

In order to be most effectively used, opportunities and threats must also be classified. One way to examine opportunities is to consider how attractive (low or high) an opportunity is to a particular company. A business might also consider its probability of success (low or high) in utilizing a particular opportunity. A company doesn't need to pursue an opportunity that is not particularly attractive to it, nor does it need to pursue an opportunity for which it does not possess the requisite

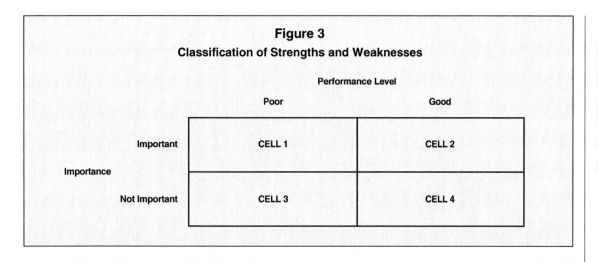

Figure 3
Classification of Strengths and Weaknesses

Performance Level

	Poor	Good
Important	CELL 1	CELL 2
Not Important	CELL 3	CELL 4

Importance

strengths. Threats should be evaluated according to their seriousness (low or high) and their probability of occurrence (low or high). A company must pay much more attention to a very serious threat that is quite likely to occur, than to a mild threat that is unlikely to occur.

Careful determination and classification of a company's strengths, weaknesses, opportunities, and threats provides an excellent way for a company to analyze its current and future situation. It is not necessary for a company to take advantage of all opportunities, nor is it necessary for a company to develop methods to deal with all threats. Additionally, a company need not strengthen all of its weaknesses or be too smug about all its strengths. All of these factors should be evaluated in the context of each other in order to provide the company with the most useful planning information.

PORTER'S GENERIC COMPETITIVE STRATEGIES

Michael Porter has suggested a method of categorizing the various types of competitive strategies. He identified two generic competitive strategies: overall lower cost and differentiation. These strategies are termed generic because they can be applied to any size or form of business. Overall lower cost refers to companies that can develop, manufacture, and distribute products more efficiently than their competitors. Differentiation refers to companies that are able to provide superior products based on some factor other than low cost. Differentiation can be based on customer service, product quality, unique style, and so on.

Porter also suggests that another factor affecting a company's competitive position is its competitive scope. Competitive scope defines the breadth of a company's target market. A company can have a broad (mass market) competitive scope or a narrow (niche market) competitive scope. The combination of broad scope and narrow scope with a low-cost strategy and differentiation results in the following generic competitive strategies: cost leadership, cost focus, differentiation, and focused differentiation (see Figure 4).

The implementation of these strategies requires different organizational arrangements and control processes. Larger firms with greater access to resources typically select a cost leadership or a differentiation

Figure 4
Porter's Generic Competition

Competitive Advantage

	Lower Cost	Differentiation
Broad Target	COST LEADERSHIP	DIFFERENTIATION
Narrow Target	COST FOCUS	FOCUSED DIFFERENTIATION

Competitive Scope

strategy, whereas smaller firms often compete on a focus basis.

Cost leadership is a low-cost, broad-based market strategy. Firms pursuing this type of strategy must be particularly efficient in engineering tasks, production operations, and physical distribution. Because these firms focus on a large market, they must also be able to minimize costs in marketing and R&D. A low-cost leader can gain significant market share enabling it to procure a more powerful position relative to both suppliers and competitors. This strategy is particularly effective in case of price-sensitive buyers in the market and small possibilities to achieve product differentiation.

A cost-focus strategy is a low-cost, narrowly focused market strategy. Firms employing this strategy may focus on a particular buyer segment or a particular geographic segment, and must locate a niche market that wants or needs an efficient product and is willing to do without the extras in order to pay a lower price for the product. A company's costs can be reduced by providing little or no service, providing a low-cost method of distribution, or producing a no-frills product.

A differentiation strategy involves marketing a unique product to a broad-based market. Because this type of strategy involves a unique product, price is not the significant factor. In fact, consumers may be willing to pay a high price for a product that they perceive as different. The product difference may be based on product design, method of distribution, or any aspect of the product (other than price) that is significant to a broad market group of consumers. A company choosing this strategy must develop and maintain a product that is perceived as different enough from the competitor's products to warrant the asking price.

Effective implementation of a differentiation strategy requires an analytical study of customer needs and preferences in order to offer a unique product. This usually helps business organizations to achieve customer loyalty, which can also serve as an entry barrier for new firms. Several studies have shown that a differentiation strategy is more likely to generate higher profits than a cost-leadership strategy, because differentiation creates stronger entry barriers. However, a cost-leadership strategy is more likely to generate increases in market share.

A differentiation-focus strategy is the marketing of a differentiated product to a narrow market, often involving a unique product and a unique market. This strategy is viable for a company that can convince consumers that its narrow focus allows it to provide better goods and services than its competitors.

None of these competitive strategies is guaranteed to achieve success, and some companies that have successfully implemented one of Porter's generic strategies have found that they could not sustain the strategy. Several risks associated with these strategies are based on evolved market conditions (buyer perceptions, competitors, etc).

Recent researchers argue that both cost-leadership and differentiation strategies can be simultaneously achieved. The principal condition for this situation is superior quality, which may lead to increased customer commitment on the one hand, and minimized quality costs (through learning effects, economies of scale, etc.) on the other.

PORTER'S FIVE-FORCES MODEL

Before a company enters a market or market segment, the competitive nature of the market or segment is evaluated. Porter suggests that five forces collectively determine the intensity of competition in an industry: threat of potential entrants, threat of potential substitutes, bargaining power of suppliers, bargaining power of buyers, and rivalry of existing firms in the industry. By using the model shown in Figure 5, a firm can identify the existence and importance of the five competitive forces, as well as the effect of each force on the firm's success.

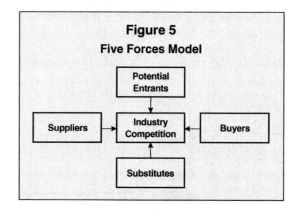

Figure 5
Five Forces Model

The threat of new entrants deals with the ease or difficulty with which new companies can enter an industry. When a new company enters an industry, the competitive climate changes; there is new capacity, more competition for market share, and the addition of new resources. Entry barriers and exit barriers affect the entrance of new companies into a marketplace. If entry barriers (capital requirements, economies of scale, product differentiation, switching costs, access to distribution channels, cost of promotion and advertising, etc.) are high, a company is less likely to enter a market. The same holds true for exit barriers.

The threat of substitutes affects competition in an industry by placing an artificial ceiling on the prices companies within an industry can charge. A substitute product is one that can satisfy consumer needs also targeted by another product; for example, lemonade can be substituted for a soft drink. Generally, competitive pressures arising from substitute products increase as the relative price of substitute products declines and as consumer's switching costs decrease.

The bargaining power of buyers is affected by the concentration and number of consumers, the differentiation of products, the potential switching costs, and the potential of buyers to integrate backwards. If buyers have strong bargaining power in the exchange relationship, competition can be affected in several ways. Powerful buyers can bargain for lower prices, better product distribution, higher-quality products, as well as other factors that can create greater competition among companies.

Similarly, the bargaining power of suppliers affects the intensity of competition in an industry, especially when there is a large number of suppliers, limited substitute raw materials, or increased switching costs. The bargaining power of suppliers is important to industry competition because suppliers can also affect the quality of exchange relationships. Competition may become more intense as powerful suppliers raise prices, reduce services, or reduce the quality of goods or services.

Competition is also affected by the rivalry among existing firms, which is usually considered as the most powerful of the five competitive forces. In most industries, business organizations are mutually dependent. A competitive move by one firm can be expected to have a noticeable effect on its competitors, and thus, may cause retaliation or counter-efforts (e.g. lowering prices, enhancing quality, adding features, providing services, extending warranties, and increasing advertising).

The nature of competition is often affected by a variety of factors, such as the size and number of competitors, demand changes for the industry's products, the specificity of assets within the industry, the presence of strong exit barriers, and the variety of competitors.

Recently, several researchers have proposed a sixth force that should be added to Porter's list in order to include a variety of stakeholder groups from the task environment that wield over industry activities. These groups include governments, local communities, creditors, trade associations, special interest groups, and shareholders.

The implementation of strategic planning tools serves a variety of purposes in firms, including the clear definition of an organization's purpose and mission, and the establishment of a standard base from which progress can be measured and future actions can be planned. Furthermore, the strategic planning tools should communicate those goals and objectives to the organization's constituents. Thus, the worth of these tools, as well as others, is often dependent on the objective insight of those who participate in the planning process. It is also important for those individuals who will implement the strategies to play a role in the strategic-planning process; this often requires a team effort that should allow a variety of inputs and should result in a better overall understanding of the company's current and future industry position.

SEE ALSO: Generic Competitive Strategies; Porter's 5-Forces Model; Strategic Planning Failure; Strategy Formulation; Strategy Implementation; Strategy in the Global Environment; Strategy Levels; SWOT Analysis

Donna T. Mayo
Revised by Evangelos Grigoroudis and Constantin Zopoundis

FURTHER READING:

Costin, Harry. *Readings in Strategy and Strategic Planning.* Fort Worth, TX: The Dryden Press, 1998.

David, R. Fred. *Strategic Management: Concepts and Cases.* Upper Saddle River, NJ: Prentice Hall, 2003.

Houlden, Brian. *Understanding Company Strategy: An Introduction to Analysis and Implementation.* Cambridge, MA: Blackwell Publishers, Inc., 1996.

Hunger, J. David, and Thomas L. Wheelen. *Essentials of Strategic Management.* Reading, MA: Addison Wesley, 1997.

Porter, Michael E. *Competitive Strategy.* New York, NY: The Free Press, 1980.

———. *Competitive Strategy of Nations.* New York, NY: The Free Press, 1990.

Stahl, J. Michael, and David W. Grigsby. *Strategic Management for Decision Making.* Massachusetts: PWS-KENT Publishing, 1992.

Wheelen, L. Thomas, and David J. Hunger. *Strategic Management and Business Policy: Entering 21st Century Global Society.* Reading, MA: Addison Wesley, 1998.

STRATEGY FORMULATION

Stated simply, strategy is a road map or guide by which an organization moves from a current state of affairs to a future desired state. It is not only a template by which daily decisions are made, but also a tool with which long-range future plans and courses of action are constructed. Strategy allows a company to position itself effectively within its environment to reach its maximum potential, while constantly monitoring that environment for changes that can affect it so as to make changes in its strategic plan accordingly.

In short, strategy defines where you are, where you are going, and how you are going to get there.

HISTORY

Strategic planning, as a formalized business process, has been in practice for almost 40 years. However, it is commonplace to find that a grand majority of organizations have no clear concept of how to effectively conduct the planning process. As a result, most strategic plans are poorly conceived and do nothing more than sit on a bookshelf; no real impact is ever made on the company and its activities. Fortunately, within the past decade or so, there have been attempts made to clarify the major components and processes of strategic planning. In this respect, it has become easier for ordinary an organization to effectively create and implement a first rate strategic plan.

STRATEGY FORMULATION

Basic strategic planning is comprised of several components that build upon the previous piece of the plan, and operates much like a flow chart. However, prior to embarking on this process, it is important to consider the players involved. There must be a commitment from the highest office in the organizational hierarchy. Without buy-in from the head of a company, it is unlikely that other members will be supportive in the planning and eventual implementation process, thereby dooming the plan before it ever takes shape. Commitment and support of the strategic-planning initiative must spread from the president and/or CEO all the way down through the ranks to the line worker on the factory floor.

Just as importantly, the strategic-planning team should be composed of top-level managers who are capable of representing the interests, concerns, and opinions of all members of the organization. As well, organizational theory dictates that there should be no more than twelve members of the team. This allows group dynamics to function at their optimal level.

The components of the strategic-planning process read much like a laundry list, with one exception: each piece of the process must be kept in its sequential order since each part builds upon the previous one. This is where the similarity to a flow chart is most evident, as can be seen in the following illustration.

The only exceptions to this are environmental scanning and continuous implementation, which are continuous processes throughout. This article will now focus on the discussion of each component of the formulation process: environmental scanning, continuous implementation, values assessment, vision and mission formulation, strategy design, performance audit analysis, gap analysis, action-plan development, contingency planning, and final implementation. After that, this article will discuss a Japanese variation to Strategy Formulation, Hoshin Planning, which has become very popular.

ENVIRONMENTAL SCANNING

This element of strategy formulation is one of the two continuous processes. Consistently scanning its surroundings serves the distinct purpose of allowing a company to survey a variety of constituents that affect its performance, and which are necessary in order to conduct subsequent pieces of the planning process. There are several specific areas that should be considered, including the overall environment, the specific industry itself, competition, and the internal environment of the firm. The resulting consequence of regular inspection of the environment is that an organization readily notes changes and is able to adapt its strategy accordingly. This leads to the development of a real advantage in the form of accurate responses to internal

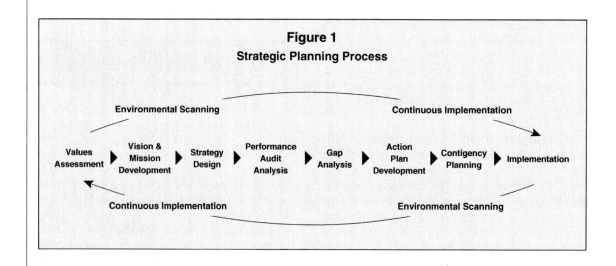

Figure 1
Strategic Planning Process

Environmental Scanning

Continuous Implementation

Values Assessment ▶ Vision & Mission Development ▶ Strategy Design ▶ Performance Audit Analysis ▶ Gap Analysis ▶ Action Plan Development ▶ Contigency Planning ▶ Implementation

Continuous Implementation

Environmental Scanning

and external stimuli so as to keep pace with the competition.

CONTINUOUS IMPLEMENTATION

The idea behind this continual process is that each step of the planning process requires some degree of implementation before the next stage can begin. This naturally dictates that all implementation cannot be postponed until completion of the plan, but must be initiated along the way. Implementation procedures specific to each phase of planning must be completed during that phase in order for the next stage to be started.

VALUES ASSESSMENT

All business decisions are fundamentally based on some set of values, whether they are personal or organizational values. The implication here is that since the strategic plan is to be used as a guide for daily decision making, the plan itself should be aligned with those personal and organizational values. To delve even further, a values assessment should include an in-depth analysis of several elements: personal values, organizational values, operating philosophy, organization culture, and stakeholders. This allows the planning team to take a macro look at the organization and how it functions as a whole.

Strategic planning that does not integrate a values assessment into the process is sure to encounter severe implementation and functionality problems if not outright failure. Briefly put, form follows function; the form of the strategic plan must follow the functionality of the organization, which is a direct result of organizational values and culture. If any party feels that his or her values have been neglected, he or she will not adopt the plan into daily work procedures and the benefits will not be obtained.

VISION AND MISSION FORMULATION

This step of the planning process is critical in that is serves as the foundation upon which the remainder of the plan is built. A vision is a statement that identifies where an organization wants to be at some point in the future. It functions to provide a company with directionality, stress management, justification and quantification of resources, enhancement of professional growth, motivation, standards, and succession planning. Porrus and Collins (1996) point out that a well-conceived vision consists of two major components: a core ideology and the envisioned future.

A core ideology is the enduring character of an organization; it provides the glue that holds an organi-

zation together. It itself is composed of core values and a core purpose. The core purpose is the organization's entire reason for being. The envisioned future involves a conception of the organization at a specified future date inclusive of its aspirations and ambitions. It includes the BHAG (big, hairy, audacious goal), which a company typically reaches only 50 to 70 percent of the time. This envisioned future gives vividly describes specific goals for the organization to reach.

The strategic results of a well formulated vision include the survival of the organization, the focus on productive effort, vitality through the alignment of the individual employees and the organization as a whole, and, finally, success. Once an agreed-upon vision is implemented, it is time to move on to the creation of a mission statement.

An explicit mission statement ensures the unanimity of purpose, provides the basis for resource allocation, guides organizational climate and culture, establishes organizational boundaries, facilitates accountability, and facilitates control of cost, time, and performance. When formulating a mission statement, it is vital that it specifies six specific elements, including the basic product or service, employee orientation, primary market(s), customer orientation, principle technologies, and standards of quality. With all of these elements incorporated, a mission statement should still remain short and memorable. For example, the mission statement of the American Red Cross, reads:

> "The mission of the American Red Cross is to improve the quality of human life; to enhance self-reliance and concern for others; and to help people avoid, prepare for, and cope with emergencies."

Other functions of a mission statement include setting the bounds for development of company philosophy, values, aspirations, and priorities (policy); establishing a positive public image; justifying business operations; and providing a corporate identity for internal and external stakeholders.

STRATEGY DESIGN

This section of strategy formulation involves the preliminary layout of the detailed paths by which the company plans to fulfill its mission and vision. This step involves four major elements: identification of the major lines of business (LOBs), establishment of critical success indicators (CSIs), identification of strategic thrusts to pursue, and the determination of the necessary culture.

A line of business is an activity that produces either dramatically different products or services or that are geared towards very different markets. When considering the addition of a new line of business, it should be based on existing core competencies of the organization, its potential contribution to the bottom line, and its fit with the firm's value system.

The establishment of critical success factors must be completed for the organization as a whole as well as for each line of business. A critical success indicator is a gauge by which to measure the progress toward achieving the company's mission. In order to serve as a motivational tool, critical success indicators must be accompanied by a target year (i.e. 1999, 1999–2002, etc.). This also allows for easy tracking of the indicated targets. These indicators are typically a mixture of financial figures and ratios (i.e. return on investment, return on equity, profit margins, etc.) and softer indicators such as customer loyalty, employee retention/turnover, and so on.

Strategic thrusts are the most well-known methods for accomplishing the mission of an organization. Generally speaking, there are a handful of commonly used strategic thrusts, which have been so aptly named *grand strategies*. They include the concentration on existing products or services; market/product development; concentration on innovation/technology; vertical/horizontal integration; the development of joint ventures; diversification; retrenchment/turnaround (usually through cost reduction); and divestment/liquidation (known as the final solution).

Finally, in designing strategy, it is necessary to determine the necessary culture with which to support the achievement of the lines of business, critical success indicators, and strategic thrusts. Harrison and Stokes (1992) defined four major types of organizational cultures: power orientation, role orientation, achievement orientation, and support orientation. Power orientation is based on the inequality of access to resources, and leadership is based on strength from those individuals who control the organization from the top. Role orientation carefully defines the roles and duties of each member of the organization; it is a bureaucracy. The achievement orientation aligns people with a common vision or purpose. It uses the mission to attract and release the personal energy of organizational members in the pursuit of common goals. With a support orientation, the organizational climate is based on mutual trust between the individual and the organization. More emphasis is placed on people being valued more as human beings rather than employees. Typically an organization will choose some mixture of these or other predefined culture roles that it feels is suitable in helping it to achieve is mission and the other components of strategy design.

PERFORMANCE AUDIT ANALYSIS

Conducting a performance audit allows the organization to take inventory of what its current state is. The main idea of this stage of planning is to take an

Figure 2
SWOT Analysis

Internal strengths should be matched or paired with external opportunitites →	Opportunitites (External)
Weaknesses (Internal)	Threats (External)

in-depth look at the company's internal strengths and weaknesses and its external opportunities and threats. This is commonly called a SWOT analysis.

Developing a clear understanding of resource strengths and weaknesses, an organization's best opportunities, and its external threats allows the planning team to draw conclusions about how to best allocate resources in light of the firm's internal and external situation. This also produces strategic thinking about how to best strengthen the organization's resource base for the future.

Looking internally, there are several key areas that must be analyzed and addressed. This includes identifying the status of each existing line of business and unused resources for prospective additions; identifying the status of current tracking systems; defining the organization's strategic profile; listing the available resources for implementing the strategic thrusts that have been selected for achieving the newly defined mission; and an examining the current organizational culture. The external investigation should look closely at competitors, suppliers, markets and customers, economic trends, labor-market conditions, and governmental regulations. In conducting this query, the information gained and used must reflect a current state of affairs as well as directions for the future. The result of a performance audit should be the establishment of a performance gap, that is, the resultant gap between the current performance of the organization in relation to its performance targets. To close this gap, the planning team must conduct what is known as a gap analysis, the next step in the strategic planning process.

GAP ANALYSIS

A gap analysis is a simple tool by which the planning team can identify methods with which to close the identified performance gap(s). All too often, however, planning teams make the mistake of making this step much more difficult than need be. Simply, the planning team must look at the current state of affairs

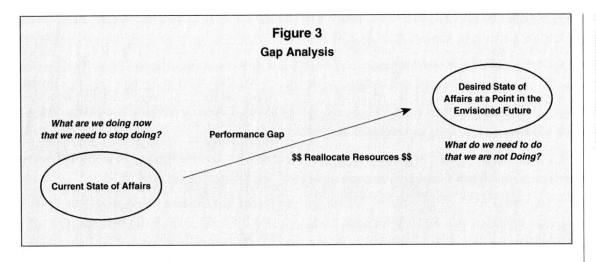

Figure 3
Gap Analysis

What are we doing now
that we need to stop doing?

Performance Gap

$$ Reallocate Resources $$

Current State of Affairs

Desired State of
Affairs at a Point in the
Envisioned Future

What do we need to do
that we are not Doing?

and the desired future state. The first question that must be addressed is whether or not the gap can feasibly be closed. If so, there are two simple questions to answer: "What are we doing now that we need to stop doing?" and "What do we need to do that we are not doing?" In answering these questions and reallocating resources from activities to be ceased to activities to be started, the performance gap is closed. If there is doubt that the initial gap cannot be closed, then the feasibility of the desired future state must be reassessed.

ACTION PLAN DEVELOPMENT

This phase of planning ties everything together. First, an action plan must be developed for each line of business, both existing and proposed. It is here that the goals and objectives for the organization are developed.

Goals are statements of desired future end-states. They are derived from the vision and mission statements and are consistent with organizational culture, ethics, and the law. Goals are action oriented, measurable, standard setting, and time bounded. In strategic planning, it is essential to concentrate on only two or three goals rather than a great many. The idea is that a planning team can do a better job on a few rather than on many. There should never be more than seven goals. Ideally, the team should set one, well-defined goal for each line of business.

Writing goals statements is often a tricky task. By following an easy-to-use formula, goals will include all vital components.

- Accomplishment/target (e.g., to be number one in sales on the East Coast by 2005)

- A measure (e.g., sales on the East Coast)

- Standards (e.g., number one)

- Time frame (e.g., long-term)

Objectives are near-term goals that link each long-term goal with functional areas, such as operations, human resources, finance, etc., and to key processes such as information, leadership, etc. Specifically, each objective statement must indicate what is to be done, what will be measured, the expected standards for the measure, and a time frame less than one year (usually tied to the budget cycle). Objectives are dynamic in that they can and do change if the measurements indicate that progress toward the accomplishment of the goal at hand is deficient in any manner. Simply, objectives spell out the step-by-step sequences of actions necessary to achieve the related goals.

With a thorough understanding of how these particular elements fit and work together, an action plan is developed. If carefully and exactly completed, it will serve as the implementation tool for each established goal and its corresponding objectives as well as a gauge for the standards of their completion.

CONTINGENCY PLANNING

The key to contingency planning is to establish a reactionary plan for high impact events that cannot necessarily be anticipated. Contingency plans should identify a number of key indicators that will create awareness of the need to reevaluate the applicability and effectiveness of the strategy currently being followed. When a red flag is raised, there should either be a higher level of monitoring established or immediate action should be taken.

IMPLEMENTATION

Implementation of the strategic plan is the final step for putting it to work for an organization. To be successful, the strategic plan must have the support of every member of the firm. As mentioned in the beginning, this is why the top office must be involved from the beginning. A company's leader is its most influential member. Positive reception and implementation of the strategic plan into daily activities by this office greatly increases the likelihood that others will do the same.

Advertising is key to successful implementation of the strategic plan. The more often employees hear about the plan, its elements, and ways to measure its success, the greater the possibility that they will undertake it as part of their daily work lives. It is especially important that employees are aware of the measurement systems and that significant achievements be rewarded and celebrated. This positive reinforcement increases support of the plan and belief in its possibilities.

HOSHIN PLANNING

Hoshin planning, or "hoshin kanri" in Japanese, is a planning method developed in Japan during the 1970s and adopted by some U.S. firms starting in the 1980s. Also known in the United States as policy deployment, management by policy, and hoshin management, it is a careful and deliberate process by which the few most important organizational goals are deployed throughout the organization. It consists of five major steps:

1. Development at the executive level of a long-term vision.

2. Selection of a small number of annual targets that will move the organization toward the vision.

3. Development of plans at all levels of the organization that will together achieve the annual targets.

4. Execution of the plans.

5. Regular audits of the plans. Among U.S. companies that utilize this method are Hewlett-Packard and Xerox.

HISTORY OF HOSHIN PLANNING

The literal meaning of "hoshin kanri" is helpful in understanding its use "hoshin" is made up of two characters that mean "needle" and "pointing direction," together meaning something like a compass "kanri" also is made up of two characters that mean "control" or "channeling" and "reason" or "logic." Together they mean managing the direction of the company, which is vitally important especially in times of rapid change.

Hoshin management was developed in Japan as part of the overall refinement of quality programs in that country after World War II. At one time, "made in Japan" was synonymous with shoddy quality, but with

the encouragement of the American occupation force, the Japanese Union of Scientists and Engineers (JUSE) made great efforts to improve Japanese manufacturing. An important element of the JUSE program between 1950 and 1960 was inviting W. Edwards Deming and Joseph M. Juran to train managers and scholars in statistical process control (SPC) and quality management. So significant were these visits, especially Deming's, that the highest Japanese award for quality is called the Deming Prize. Each company developed its own planning methodology, but the Deming Prize system involves the sharing of best practices, and common themes developed. In 1965 Bridgestone Tire published a report described the planning techniques used by Deming Prize winners, which were given the name hoshin kanri. By 1975 hoshin planning was widely accepted in Japan.

In the early 1980s hoshin planning began to gain acceptance in the United States, first in companies that had divisions or subsidiaries in Japan which won the Deming Prize: Yokagawa Hewlett-Packard, Fuji Xerox, and Texas Instruments' Oita plant. Florida Power and Light, the only company outside Japan to win the Deming Prize, was an early adopter. During the 1990s the practice spread. In 1994 Noriaki Kano, professor of management science at the University of Tokyo and member of the Deming Prize Committee, gave a presentation on the topic at the meeting of the American Society of Quality Control (now the American Society for Quality).

THE CONTEXT FOR HOSHIN PLANNING

Hoshin planning should be seen in the context of total quality management (TQM). Several elements of TQM are especially important for the effectiveness of hoshin planning. Most basic is a customer-driven master plan that encapsulates the company's overall vision and direction. Hoshin planning also assumes an effective system of daily management that keeps the company moving on course, including an appropriate business structure and the use of quality tools such as SPC. A third important element of TQM is the presence of cross-functional teams. Experience in problem solving and communications across and between levels of the organization are vital for hoshin planning.

A number of general principles underlie this method. Of utmost importance is participation by all managers in defining the vision for the company as well as in implementing the plans developed to reach the vision. Related to this is what the Japanese call "catchball," which means a process of lateral and vertical communication that continues until understanding and agreement is assured. Another principle is individual initiative and responsibility. Each manager sets his own monthly and yearly targets and then integrates them with others. Related to this principle is a focus on the process rather than strictly on reaching the target and a dedication to root cause analysis. A final principle that is applied in Japan-but apparently not in the United States-is that when applying hoshin planning, there is no tie to performance reviews or other personnel measures.

STEPS OF POLICY DEPLOYMENT

In its simplest form, hoshin planning consists of a plan, execution, and audit. In a more elaborated form it includes a long-range plan (five to ten years), a detailed one-year plan, deployment to departments, execution, and regular diagnostic audits, including an annual audit by the CEO.

FIVE- TO TEN-YEAR VISION. The long-range vision begins with the top executive and his staff, but is modified with input from all managers. The purpose is to determine where the company wants to be at that future point in time, given its current position, its strengths and weaknesses, the voice of the customer, and other aspects of the business environment in which it operates. Beyond stating the goal, this long-range plan also identifies the steps that must be taken to reach it. It focuses on the vital few strategic gaps that must be closed over the time period being planned.

Once the plan has been drafted, it is sent to all managers for their review and critique. The object is to get many perspectives on the plan. The review process also has the effect of increasing buy-in to the final plan. This process is easier in Japanese companies than in most U.S. firms because most Japanese companies have only four layers of management.

ANNUAL PLAN. Once the long-range vision is in place, the annual plan is created. The vital few areas for change that were identified in the vision are translated into steps to be taken this year. Again, this process involves lateral and vertical communication among managers. The targets are selected using criteria such as feasibility and contribution to the long-term goals. The targets are stated in simple terms with clearly measurable goals. Some companies and authors refer to such an annual target as a hoshin. Most companies set no more than three such targets, but others establish as many as eight. Not all departments are necessarily involved in every hoshin during a given year. The targets are chosen for the sake of the long-term goals, not for involvement for its own sake.

DEPLOYMENT TO LOWER LEVELS. Once the targets, including the basic metrics for each, are established, the plan is deployed throughout the company. This is the heart of hoshin planning. Each hoshin has some sort of measurable target. Top-level managers, having discussed it with their subordinates earlier in the process, commit to a specific contribution to that target, and then their subordinates develop their own plans to reach that contribution, including appropriate metrics. Plans are deployed to lower levels in the same way (see Figure 1). An important principle here is that those who have to implement the plan design the plan. In addition to the lower level targets, the means and resources required are determined. Catchball plays an important role here. A key element of the hoshin discipline is the horizontal and vertical alignment of the many separate plans that are developed. All ambiguities are clarified, and conflicting targets or means are negotiated.

The final step in deploying the hoshin is rolling up the separate plans and targets to ensure that they are sufficient to reach the company-wide target. If not, more work is done to reconcile the difference.

EXECUTION. The best-laid plans can come to naught if they are not properly executed. In terms of TQM, the execution phase is where hoshin management hands responsibility over to daily management. The strategies identified in the plan become part of the daily operation of the company. If the process has been done properly, all employees know what has to be done at their level to reach the top-level goals and thereby move the company toward the future described in the long-term vision.

AUDITING THE PLAN. Essential to hoshin planning is the periodic diagnostic audit, most often done on a monthly basis. Each manager evaluates the progress made toward his own targets, and these reports are rolled up the organization to give feedback on the process to the highest levels. Successes and failures are examined at every level, and corrective action is taken as necessary. If it becomes apparent that something is seriously amiss in the execution, because of a significant change in the situation or perhaps a mistake in the planning phase, the plan may be adjusted and the change communicated up and down the organizational structure as necessary. The audit is a diagnostic review, an opportunity for mid-course corrections and not a time for marking up a scorecard. At the end of the year, the CEO makes an annual diagnostic review of the entire plan, focusing not only on the overall success or failure, but also on the entire process, including the planning phase. The results of this audit become part of the input for the next annual plan, along with the five-to-ten-year plan and changes in the internal or external business environment.

EVALUATION

Although full implementation of hoshin planning in a large organization takes considerable effort, it is recognized as having many advantages over traditional business planning. The discipline of

Figure 4

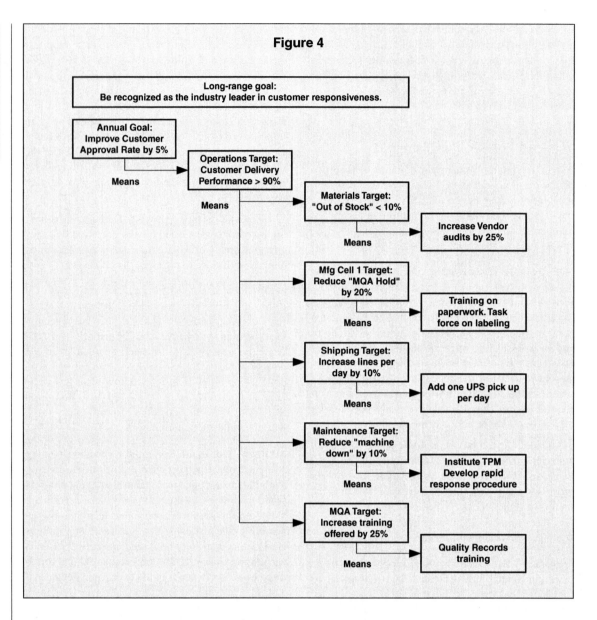

hoshin planning uncovers the vital few changes that need to be made and ties them to strategic action. It transmits the signals from top management to the rest of the organization in a form that can bring about change at every level. It is participative: the individuals that have to implement the plans have input into their design. Perhaps most importantly, it focuses on the process rather than just the result. This includes continual improvement of the hoshin planning process itself. Organizations that persist in this method over a period of a few years report great benefits from its use.

SEE ALSO: Continuous Improvement; Mission and Vision Statements; Strategic Planning Failure; Strategic Planning Tools; Strategy Implementation; Strategy in the Global Environment; Strategy Levels

Howard Distelzweig and Connie Clark
Revised by Gerhard Plenert

FURTHER READING:

Babich, Peter. *Hoshin Handbook.* 2nd ed. Poway, CA: Total Quality Engineering, Inc., 1996.

Bechtell, Michele L. *The Management Compass: Steering the Corporation Using Hoshin Planning.* New York: AMACOM, 1995.

———. "Navigating Organizational Waters with Hoshin Planning." *National Productivity Review,* Spring 1996.

Collins, Brendan, and Ernest Huge. *Management by Policy: How Companies Focus Their Total Quality Efforts to Achieve Competitive Advantage.* Milwaukee: ASQC Quality Press, 1993.

Collins, James C., and Jerry I. Porras. "Building Your Company's Vision." *Harvard Business Review,* September-October 1996, 65–90.

Goldstein, Leonard D., Timothy M. Nolan, and J. William Pfeiffer. *Applied Strategic Planning: How to Develop a Plan that Really Works.* New York: McGraw-Hill, Inc., 1993.

Harrison, Roger, and Herb Stokes. *Diagnosing Organizational Culture.* San Francisco: Pfeiffer, 1992.

King, Bob. *Hoshin Planning: the Developmental Approach.* Methuen, MA: GOAL/QPC, 1989.

Mellum, Mara Minerva, and Casey Collett. *Breakthrough Leadership: Achieving Organizational Alignment through Hoshin Planning.* Chicago: American Hospital Publishers, Inc., 1995.

Plenert, Gerhard. *The eManager: Value Chain Management in an eCommerce World.* Dublin, Ireland: Blackhall Publishing, 2001.

———. *International Operations Management.* Copenhagen, Denmark: Copenhagen Business School Press, 2002.

"Total Quality Engineering." *Hoshin Planning.* Poway, CA: Total Quality Engineering, Inc. Available from <http://www.tqe.com/hoshin.html>.

STRATEGY IMPLEMENTATION

A key role of a CEO's is to communicate a vision and to guide strategic planning. Those who have successfully implemented strategic plans have often reported that involving teams at all levels in strategic planning helps to build a shared vision, and increases each individual's motivation to see plans succeed.

Clarity and consistent communication, from mapping desired outcomes to designing performance measures, seem to be essential to success. Successful leaders have often engaged their teams by simply telling the story of their shared vision, and publicly celebrating large and small wins, such as the achievement of milestones. To ensure that the vision is shared, teams need to know that they can test the theory, voice opinions, challenge premises, and suggest alternatives without fear of reprimand.

Implementing strategic plans may require leaders who lead through inspiration and coaching rather than command and control. Recognizing and rewarding success, inspiring, and modeling behaviors is more likely to result in true commitment than use of authority, which can lead to passive resistance and hidden rebellion.

CREATING STRATEGIC PLANS

The senior management team must come together to review, discuss, challenge, and finally agree on the strategic direction and key components of the plan. Without genuine commitment from the senior team, successful implementation is unlikely.

Strategic group members must challenge themselves to be clear in their purpose and intent, and to push for consistent operational definitions that each member of the team agrees to. This prevents differing perceptions or turf-driven viewpoints later on. A carefully chosen, neutral facilitator can be essential in helping the team to overcome process, group dynamics, and interpersonal issues.

A common way to begin is to review the organization's current state and future possibilities using a SWOT (strength, weakness, opportunity, and threat) analysis. This involves identifying strengths and core capabilities in products, resources, people, and customers. These are what the organization is best at, and why it is in business. Many organizations have responded to this review by spinning off ventures that were not related to their core business. For example, Chrysler sold its interests in Maserati, Lambourghini, and Diamond Star and then concentrated on developing "great cars, great trucks." This sent a clear message to employees and other stakeholders, and triggered the company's renaissance.

Using SWOT, once strengths and core capabilities are defined the next step is to identify weaknesses or vulnerabilities. This is usually the most difficult for organizations and leaders to assess. The identification of gaps is often threatening. In some organizations it is not considered safe to admit to weakness; but an honest appraisal can make the difference between success and failure. Again, reviews should include a look at products, services, resources, customers, and employees. Do the right skills exist in the current staff? Are there enough resources to invest in areas of critical need? Are the appropriate systems and structures in place to support the needs of the team? Does the culture reinforce and connect with the mission and vision of the organization?

Now the review moves to the external environment. What opportunities exist for development and growth? Do these opportunities correspond to the organization's strengths? What are the critical changes the market faces over the next one, three, and five years? How well is the organization positioned for the anticipated market changes? Additional points for debate include the greatest innovation or change that needs to occur for the organization to be successful, and the values that will drive these changes.

Next, using the SWOT assessment process, threats in the current and future market are identified. How is the competition positioned relative to the opportunities for growth that have been identified, and how are they positioned relative to the organization's strengths and weaknesses?

With this information, organizations can finalize their strategy by defining the vision, creating a mission statement, and identifying their competitive advantages. The communication of the strategy will require a clear, consistent message. It is an ideal time for the leadership to operationally define each critical area of the plan to ensure agreement and commitment. Key stakeholders should be included in the process. Soliciting their input is often a valuable aide in implementation.

Finally, organizations should review each of the gaps that have been identified. Do the necessary resources exist to invest in shoring up the gaps? Are these resources allocated properly? It is usually not possible to address all of the gaps at once. Organizations should create a priority list for action so plans are realistic and focused on the greatest areas of need. These priorities will become a key focus of implementing the plan.

Once the senior leadership team has completed the top-level strategy, the next step is to break that overall goal down into functional areas or core strategies. Typically this will include service/operations management, technology management, product management, supplier management, people management, and financial management, or some variation on these areas. Each identifies how they contribute to achieving the overall strategic plan. They can model the steps taken by the senior team and conduct a SWOT analysis from their vantage point. Once the core strategies are defined, the senior team must ensure that the overall strategy will be achieved; that is, that the sum of the parts (functional strategies) will add up to the whole (overall strategy).

Strategy communication continues to be critical, so operational definitions should not be overlooked. Each functional area should create their own definitions to ensure agreement and commitment. A common source of problems in implementation is that divergent functional perspectives may not be aligned with the overall strategy. Unless these issues are addressed, each area may interpret the plan with a lens of "How does my area win?" rather than "How does the organization win?"

Key stakeholders can be engaged in different ways. Aside from events, publicity, and personification of the vision and strategy by key leaders, stakeholders can be engaged by soliciting their input on the current state of the organization and the vision (similar to the SWOT analysis described earlier). Involving stakeholders in this manner should be done seriously, with an intent to use their distinct perspectives; this can add to the soundness of the analysis. Asking for opinions and then ignoring them can arouse distrust and resentment.

As the strategic plan and performance measures are being created, the organization must make sure that they are aligned with the systems, structure, culture, and performance management architecture. The best plans may fail because the reward systems motivate different behaviors than those called for in the strategy map and measurement design. For example, if a team approach to business development is outlined in the plan, but sales commission remains individual, organizations will be hard pressed to see a team focus.

The career development, performance management and reward systems must be reviewed to ensure linkage to and support of the strategic intent. Many organizations have found they needed to link their strategic plan to their internal systems and structures to ensure overall alignment and to avoid confusion.

IMPLEMENTING STRATEGIC PLANS

Once strategies have been agreed on, the next step is implementation; this is where most failures occur. It is not uncommon for strategic plans to be drawn up annually, and to have no impact on the organization as a whole.

A common method of implementation is hoopla—a total communication effort. This can involve slogans, posters, events, memos, videos, Web sites, etc. A critical success factor is whether the entire senior team appears to buy into the strategy, and models appropriate behaviors. Success appears to be more likely if the CEO, or a very visible leader, is also a champion of the strategy.

Strategic measurement can help in implementing the strategic plan. Appropriate measures show the strategy is important to the leaders, provide motivation, and allow for follow-through and sustained attention. By acting as operational definitions of the plan, measures can increase the focus of the strategy, aligning the workforce around specific issues. The results can include faster changes (both in strategic implementation, and in everyday work); greater accountability (since responsibilities are clarified by strategic measurement, people are naturally more accountable); and better communication of responsibilities (because the measures show what each group's primary responsibility is), which may reduce duplication of effort.

Creating a strategic map (or causal business model) helps identify focal points; it shows the theory of the business in easily understood terms, showing the cause and effect linkages between key components. It can be a focal point for communicating the vision and mission, and the plan for achieving desired goals. If tested through statistical-linkage analysis, the map also allows the organization to leverage resources on the primary drivers of success.

The senior team can create a strategic map (or theory of the business) by identifying and mapping the critical few ingredients that will drive overall performance. This can be tested (sometimes immediately, with existing data) through a variety of statistical techniques; regression analysis is frequently used, because it is fairly robust and requires relatively small data sets.

This map can lead to an instrument panel covering a few areas that are of critical importance. The panel does not include all of the areas an organization measures, rather the few that the top team can use to guide decisions, knowing that greater detail is available if they need to drill down for more intense examination. These critical few are typically within six strategic performance areas: financial, customer/market, operations, environment (which includes key stakeholders), people, and partners/suppliers. Each area may have three or four focal points; for example, the people category may include leadership, common values, and innovation.

Once the strategic map is defined, organizations must create measures for each focal point. The first step is to create these measures at an organizational level. Once these are defined, each functional area should identify how they contribute to the overall measures, and then define measures of their own. Ideally, this process cascades downward through the organization until each individual is linked with the strategy and understands the goals and outcomes they are responsible for and how their individual success will be measured and rewarded.

Good performance measures identify the critical focus points for an organization, and reward their successful achievement. When used to guide an organization, performance measures can be a competitive advantage because they drive alignment and common purpose across an organization, focusing everyone's best efforts at the desired goal. But defining measures can be tricky. Teams must continue to ask themselves, "If we were to measure performance this way, what behavior would that motivate?" For example, if the desired outcome is world-class customer service, measuring the volume of calls handled by representatives could drive the opposite behavior.

CASCADING THE PLAN

In larger organizations, cascading the strategic plan and associated measures can be essential to everyday implementation. To a degree, hoopla, celebrations, events, and so on can drive down the message, but in many organizations, particularly those without extremely charismatic leaders, this is not sufficient.

Cascading is often where the implementation breaks down. For example, only sixteen percent of the respondents in a 1999 Metrus Group survey believed that associates at all levels of their company could describe the strategy. In a 1998 national survey of Quality Progress readers, cascading was often noted

as being a serious problem in implementing strategic measurement systems.

Organizations have found it to be helpful to ask each functional area to identify how they contribute to achieving the overall strategic plan ("functional area" designating whatever natural units exist in the organization-functions, geographies, business units, etc.). Armed with the strategic map, operational definitions and the overall organizational strategic performance measures, each functional area creates their own map of success and defines their own specific performance measures. They can follow the model outlined above starting with their own SWOT analysis.

For example, in the 1990s, Sears cascaded its strategic plan to all of its stores through local store strategy sessions involving all employees. The plan was shown graphically by a strategy map, and reinforced through actions such as the sale of financial businesses such as Allstate. Online performance measures helped store managers to gain feedback on their own performance, and also let them share best practices with other managers.

Functional area leaders may be more successful using a cascade team to add input and take the message forward to others in the area. Developing ambassadors or process champions throughout the organization to support and promote the plan and its implementation can also enhance the chances of success. These champions may be candidates for participation on the design or cascade teams, and should be involved in the stakeholder review process.

EXTERNAL CONSULTANTS

External consultants can play an important role in building and implementing strategic plans if they are used appropriately. Rather than creating or guiding an organization's strategy, the primary role of a consultant should be that of a facilitator, a source of outside perspective, and perhaps as a resource for guiding the process itself. This allows each member of the internal team to participate fully without having to manage the agenda and keep the team focused on the task at hand. Consultants can keep the forum on track by directing the discussion to ensure objective, strategic thinking around key issues, tapping everyone's knowledge and expertise, raising pertinent questions for discussion and debate, managing conflict, and handling groupthink and other group dynamics issues.

Consultants can extract the best thinking from the group, and ensure that the vision and mission are based on a sound, critical review of the current state and anticipated future opportunities. Once this is accomplished, consultants can facilitate the identification of desired outcomes and the drivers needed to achieve them. They can also help to assure that a true consensus is actually reached, rather than an appearance of a consensus due to fear, conformity, or other group effects.

During the cascading phase, consultants can help to avoid failure by facilitating the linkage from the over-arching corporate strategy, through the departmental and or functional level to the team and individual level. This is a point where turf interests can invade the thought process, coloring local measurement design to ensure local rewards. This may not align with the overall strategic intent, so care must be taken to continually link back to the over-arching vision of the organization.

Building and implementing winning strategic plans is a continuous journey, requiring routine reviews and refinement of the measures and the strategic plans themselves. By partnering with internal teams, stakeholders and trusted external consultants, leaders can develop better strategic plans and implement them more successfully.

STRATEGY IMPLEMENTATION ISSUES

Strategy implementation almost always involves the introduction of change to an organization. Managers may spend months, even years, evaluating alternatives and selecting a strategy. Frequently this strategy is then announced to the organization with the expectation that organization members will automatically see why the alternative is the best one and will begin immediate implementation. When a strategic change is poorly introduced, managers may actually spend more time implementing changes resulting from the new strategy than was spent in selecting it. Strategy implementation involves both macro-organizational issues (e.g., technology, reward systems, decision processes, and structure), and micro-organizational issues (e.g., organization culture and resistance to change).

MACRO-ORGANIZATIONAL ISSUES OF STRATEGY IMPLEMENTATION

Macro-organizational issues are large-scale, system-wide issues that affect many people within the organization. Galbraith and Kazanjian argue that there are several major internal subsystems of the organization that must be coordinated to successfully implement a new organization strategy. These subsystems include technology, reward systems, decision processes, and structure. As with any system, the subsystems are interrelated, and changing one may impact others.

Technology can be defined as the knowledge, tools, equipment, and work methods used by an organization in providing its goods and services. The tech-

nology employed must fit the selected strategy for it to be successfully implemented. Companies planning to differentiate their product on the basis of quality must take steps to assure that the technology is in place to produce superior quality products or services. This may entail tighter quality control or state-of-the-art equipment. Firms pursuing a low-cost strategy may take steps to automate as a means of reducing labor costs. Similarly, they might use older equipment to minimize the immediate expenditure of funds for new equipment.

Reward systems or incentive plans include bonuses and other financial incentives, recognition, and other intangible rewards such as feelings of accomplishment and challenge. Reward systems can be effective tools for motivating individuals to support strategy implementation efforts. Commonly used reward systems include stock options, salary raises, promotions, praise, recognition, increased job autonomy, and awards based on successful strategy implementation. These rewards can be made available only to managers or spread among employees throughout the organization. Profit sharing and gain sharing are sometimes used at divisional or departmental levels to more closely link the rewards to performance.

Questions and problems will undoubtedly occur as part of implementation. Decisions pertaining to resource allocations, job responsibilities, and priorities are just some of the decisions that cannot be completely planned until implementation begins. Decision processes help the organization make mid-course adjustments to keep the implementation on target.

Organizational structure is the formal pattern of interactions and coordination developed to link individuals to their jobs and jobs to departments. It also involves the interactions between individuals and departments within the organization. Current research supports the idea that strategies may be more successful when supported with structure consistent with the new strategic direction. For example, departmentalizations on the basis of customers will likely help implement the development and marketing of new products that appeal to a specific customer segment and could be particularly useful in implementing a strategy of differentiation or focus. A functional organizational structure tends to have lower overhead and allows for more efficient utilization of specialists, and might be more consistent with a low-cost strategy.

MICRO-ORGANIZATIONAL ISSUES OF STRATEGY IMPLEMENTATION

Micro-organizational issues pertain to the behavior of individuals within the organization and how individual actors in the larger organization will view strategy implementation. Implementation can be studied by looking at the impact organization culture and resistance to change has on employee acceptance and motivation to implement the new strategy.

Peters and Waterman focused attention on the role of culture in strategic management. Organizational culture is more than emotional rhetoric; the culture of an organization develops over a period of time is influenced by the values, actions and, beliefs of individuals at all levels of the organization.

Persons involved in choosing a strategy often have access to volumes of information and research reports about the need for change in strategies. They also have time to analyze and evaluate this information. What many managers fail to realize is that the information that may make one strategic alternative an obvious choice is not readily available to the individual employees who will be involved in the day-to-day implementation of the chosen strategy. These employees are often comfortable with the old way of doing things and see no need to change. The result is that management sees the employee as resisting change.

Employees generally do not regard their response to change as either positive or negative. An employee's response to change is simply behavior that makes sense from the employee's perspective. Managers need to look beyond what they see as resistance and attempt to understand the employee's frame of reference and why they may see the change as undesirable.

FORCE FIELD ANALYSIS

One technique for evaluating forces operating in a change situation is force field analysis. This technique uses a concept from physics to examine the forces for and against change. The length of each arrow as shown in Figure 1 represents the relative strength of each force for and against change. An equilibrium point is reached when the sum of each set of forces is equal. Movement requires that forces for the change exceed forces resisting the change. Reducing resisting forces is usually seen as preferable to increasing supporting forces, as the former will likely reduce tension and the degree of conflict.

This model is useful for identifying and evaluating the relative power of forces for and against change. It is a useful way of visualizing salient forces and may allow management to better assess the probable direction and speed of movement in implementing new strategies. Forces for change can come from outside the organization or from within. External forces for change may result from sociocultural factors, government regulations, international developments, technological changes, and entry or exit of competitors. Internal forces for change come from within the organization and may include changes in market share, rising production costs, changing financial conditions, new product development, and so on.

Similarly, forces resisting change may result from external or internal sources. Common external pressures opposing change are contractual commitments to other businesses (suppliers, union), obligations to customers and investors, and government regulations of the firm or industry. Internal forces resisting change are usually abundant; limited organizational resources (money, equipment, personnel) is usually one of the first reasons offered as to why change cannot be implemented. Labor agreements limit the ability of management to transfer and, sometimes, terminate employees. Organization culture may also limit the ability of a firm to change strategy. As the experience at Levi Strauss & Co. suggests, it is often hard to convince employees of the need for change when their peers and other members of the organization are not supportive of the proposed change.

The total elimination of resistance to change is unlikely because there will almost always remain some uncertainty associated with a change. Techniques that have the potential to reduce resistance to change when

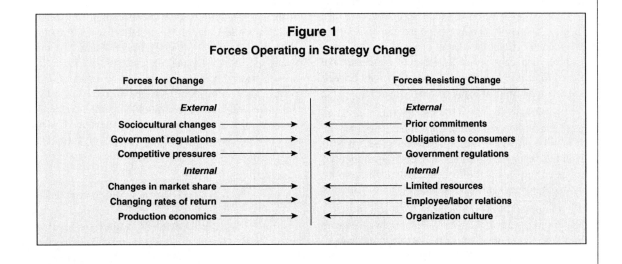

Figure 1
Forces Operating in Strategy Change

Forces for Change	Forces Resisting Change
External	*External*
Sociocultural changes →	← Prior commitments
Government regulations →	← Obligations to consumers
Competitive pressures →	← Government regulations
Internal	*Internal*
Changes in market share →	← Limited resources
Changing rates of return →	← Employee/labor relations
Production economics →	← Organization culture

implementing new strategies include participation, education, group pressure, management support, negotiation, co-optation and coercion.

Participation is probably the most universally recommended technique for reducing resistance to change. Allowing affected employees to participate in both the planning and implementation of change can contribute to greater identification with the need for and understanding of the goals of the new strategy. Participation in implementation also helps to counteract the disruption in communication flows, which often accompanies implementation of a change. But participation has sometimes been overused. Participation does not guarantee acceptance of the new strategy, and employees do not always want to participate. Furthermore, participation is often time consuming and can take too long when rapid change is needed.

Another way to overcome resistance to implementing a new strategy is to educate employees about the strategy both before and during implementation. Education involves supplying people with information required to understand the need for change. Education can also be used to make the organization more receptive to the need for the change. Furthermore, information provided during the implementation of a change can be used to build support for a strategy that is succeeding or to redirect efforts in implementing a strategy that is not meeting expectations.

Group pressure is based on the assumption that individual attitudes are the result of a social matrix of co-workers, friends, family, and other reference groups. Thus, a group may be able to persuade reluctant individuals to support a new strategy. Group members also may serve as a support system aiding others when problems are encountered during implementation. However, the use of a group to introduce change requires that the group be supportive of the change. A cohesive group that is opposed to the change limits the ability of management to persuade employees that a new strategy is desirable.

Management can take steps employees will view as being supportive during the implementation of a change. Management may extend the employees time to gradually accept the idea of change, alter behavior patterns, and learn new skills. Support might also take the form of new training programs, or simply providing an outlet for discussing employee concerns.

Negotiation is useful if a few important resistors can be identified, perhaps through force field analysis. It may be possible to offer incentives to resistors to gain their support. Early retirement is frequently used to speed implementation when resistance is coming from employees nearing retirement age.

Co-optation is similar to negotiation in that a leader or key resistor is given an important role in the implementation in exchange for supporting a change.

Manipulation involves the selective use of information or events to influence others. Such techniques may be relatively quick and inexpensive; however, employees who feel they were tricked into not resisting, not treated equitably, or misled may be highly resistant to subsequent change efforts. Distrust of management is often the result of previous manipulation.

Coercion is often used to overcome resistance. It may be explicit (resistance may be met with termination) or implicit (resistance may influence a promotion decision). Coercion may also result in the removal of resistors through either transfer or termination. Coercion often leads to resentment and increased conflict. However, when quick implementation of a change is needed or when a change will be unpopular regardless of how it is implemented, some managers feel coercion may be as good as most alternatives and faster than many others.

ROLE OF TOP MANAGEMENT

Top management is essential to the effective implementation of strategic change. Top management provides a role model for other managers to use in assessing the salient environmental variables, their relationship to the organization, and the appropriateness of the organization's response to these variables. Top management also shapes the perceived relationships among organization components.

Top management is largely responsible for the determination of organization structure (e.g., information flow, decision-making processes, and job assignments). Management must also recognize the existing organization culture and learn to work within or change its parameters. Top management is also responsible for the design and control of the organization's reward and incentive systems.

Finally, top management are involved in the design of information systems for the organization. In this role, managers influence the environmental variables most likely to receive attention in the organization. They must also make certain that information concerning these key variables is available to affected managers. Top-level managers must also provide accurate and timely feedback concerning the organization's performance and the performance of individual business units within the organization. Organization members need information to maintain a realistic view of their performance, the performance of the organization, and the organization's relationship to the environment.

SEE ALSO: Strategic Planning Failure; Strategic Planning Tools; Strategy Formulation; Strategy in the Global Environment; Strategy Levels

Carolyn Ott, David A. Zatz, and Joe G. Thomas
Revised by Gerhard Plenert

FURTHER READING:

Anthanassiou, N., and D. Nigh. "The Impact of U.S. Company Internationalization on Top Management Team Advice Networks." *Strategic Management Journal,* January 1999, 83–92.

Galbraith, J., and R. Kazanjian. *Strategy Implementation: Structure, Systems and Process.* 2nd ed. St. Paul, MN: West, 1986.

Harris, L. "Initiating Planning: The Problem of Entrenched Cultural Values." *Long Range Planning* 32, no. 1 (1999): 117–126.

Heskitt, J.L., W.E. Sasser, Jr., and L.A. Schlesinger. *The Service Profit Chain.* New York: The Free Press, 1997.

Hillman, A., A. Zardkoohi, and L. Bierman. "Corporate Political Strategies and Firm Performance." *Strategic Management Journal,* January 1999, 67–82.

Kaplan, R.S., and D.P. Norton. *The Balanced Scorecard: Translating Strategy Into Action.* Boston: The Harvard Business School Press, 1996.

Kotter, J., and L. Schlesinger. "Choosing Strategies for Change." *Harvard Business Review,* March-April 1979, 106–114.

Kouzes, J.M., and B.Z. Posner. *The Leadership Challenge: How to Keep Getting Extraordinary Things Done in Organizations.* New York: Jossey-Bass Publishers, 1995.

Lewin, K. Field. *Theory in Social Sciences.* New York: Harper & Row, 1951.

Morgan, B.S., and W.A. Schiemann. "Measuring People and Performance: Closing the Gaps." *Quality Progress* 1 (1999): 47–53.

Munk, N. "How Levi's Trashed a Great American Brand." *Fortune,* 12 April 1999, 83–90.

Peters, T., and R. Waterman. *In Search of Excellence.* New York: Harper & Row 1982.

Plenert, Gerhard, *The eManager: Value Chain Management in an eCommerce World.* Dublin, Ireland: Blackhall Publishing, 2001.

———. *International Operations Management.* Copenhagen, Denmark: Copenhagen Business School Press, 2002.

Rucci, A.J., S.P. Kirn, and R.T. Quinn. "The Employee-Customer-Profit Chain at Sears." *Harvard Business Review* 76, no. 1 (1998): 83–97.

Schiemann, W.A., and J.H. Lingle. *Bullseye: Hitting Your Strategic Targets Through Measurement.* Boston: The Free Press, 1999.

Thomas, J. "Force Field Analysis: A New Way to Evaluate Your Strategy." *Long Range Planning,* 1 December 1985, 54–59.

STRATEGY LEVELS

Although alignment of strategic initiatives is a corporate-wide effort, considering strategy in terms of levels is a convenient way to distinguish among the various responsibilities involved in strategy formulation and implementation. A convenient way to classify levels of strategy is to view corporate-level strategy as responsible for market definition, business-level strategy as responsible for market navigation, and functional-level strategy as the foundation that supports both of these (see Table 1).

CORPORATE-LEVEL STRATEGY

Corporate-level strategies address the entire strategic scope of the enterprise. This is the "big picture" view of the organization and includes deciding in which product or service markets to compete and in which geographic regions to operate. For multi-business firms, the resource allocation process—how cash, staffing, equipment and other resources are distributed—is typically established at the corporate level. In addition, because market definition is the domain of corporate-level strategists, the responsibility for diversification, or the addition of new products or services to the existing product/service line-up, also falls within the realm of corporate-level strategy. Similarly, whether to compete directly with other firms or to selectively establish cooperative relationships—strategic alliances—falls within the purview corporate-level strategy, while requiring ongoing input from

Table 1
Corporate, Business, and Functional Strategy

Level of Strategy	Definition	Example
Corporate strategy	Market definition	Diversification into new product or geographic markets
Business strategy	Market navigation	Attempts to secure competitive advantage in existing product or geographic markets
Functional strategy	Support of corporate strategy and business strategy	Information systems, human resource practices, and production processes that facilitate achievement of corporate and business strategy

business-level managers. Critical questions answered by corporate-level strategists thus include:

1. What should be the scope of operations; i.e.; what businesses should the firm be in?

2. How should the firm allocate its resources among existing businesses?

3. What level of diversification should the firm pursue; i.e., which businesses represent the company's future? Are there additional businesses the firm should enter or are there businesses that should be targeted for termination or divestment?

4. How diversified should the corporation's business be? Should we pursue related diversification; i.e., similar products and service markets, or is unrelated diversification; i.e., dissimilar product and service markets, a more suitable approach given current and projected industry conditions? If we pursue related diversification, how will the firm leverage potential cross-business synergies? In other words, how will adding new product or service businesses benefit the existing product/service line-up?

5. How should the firm be structured? Where should the boundaries of the firm be drawn and how will these boundaries affect relationships across businesses, with suppliers, customers and other constituents? Do the organizational components such as research and development, finance, marketing, customer service, etc. fit together? Are the responsibilities or each business unit clearly identified and is accountability established?

6. Should the firm enter into strategic alliances—cooperative, mutually-beneficial relationships with other firms? If so, for what reasons? If not, what impact might this have on future profitability?

As the previous questions illustrate, corporate strategies represent the long-term direction for the organization. Issues addressed as part of corporate strategy include those concerning diversification, acquisition, divestment, strategic alliances, and formulation of new business ventures. Corporate strategies deal with plans for the entire organization and change as industry and specific market conditions warrant.

Top management has primary decision making responsibility in developing corporate strategies and these managers are directly responsible to shareholders. The role of the board of directors is to ensure that top managers actually represent these shareholder interests. With information from the corporation's multiple businesses and a view of the entire scope of operations and markets, corporate-level strategists have the most advantageous perspective for assessing organization-wide competitive strengths and weaknesses, although as a subsequent section notes, corporate strategists are paralyzed without accurate and up-to-date information from managers at the business-level.

CORPORATE PORTFOLIO ANALYSIS

One way to think of corporate-level strategy is to compare it to an individual managing a portfolio of investments. Just as the individual investor must evaluate each individual investment in the portfolio to determine whether or not the investment is currently performing to expectations and what the future prospects are for the investment, managers must make similar decisions about the current and future performances of various businesses constituting the firm's portfolio. The Boston Consulting Group (BCG) matrix is a relatively simple technique for assessing the performance of various segments of the business.

The BCG matrix classifies business-unit performance on the basis of the unit's relative market share and the rate of market growth as shown in Figure 1.

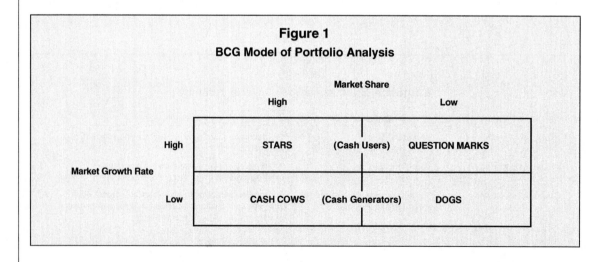

Figure 1
BCG Model of Portfolio Analysis

Products and their respective strategies fall into one of four quadrants. The typical starting point for a new business is as a question mark. If the product is new, it has no market share, but the predicted growth rate is good. What typically happens in an organization is that management is faced with a number of these types of products but with too few resources to develop all of them. Thus, the strategic decision-maker must determine which of the products to attempt to develop into commercially viable products and which ones to drop from consideration. Question marks are cash users in the organization. Early in their life, they contribute no revenues and require expenditures for market research, test marketing, and advertising to build consumer awareness.

If the correct decision is made and the product selected achieves a high market share, it becomes a BCG matrix star. Stars have high market share in high-growth markets. Stars generate large cash flows for the business, but also require large infusions of money to sustain their growth. Stars are often the targets of large expenditures for advertising and research and development to improve the product and to enable it to establish a dominant position in the industry.

Cash cows are business units that have high market share in a low-growth market. These are often products in the maturity stage of the product life cycle. They are usually well-established products with wide consumer acceptance, so sales revenues are usually high. The strategy for such products is to invest little money into maintaining the product and divert the large profits generated into products with more long-term earnings potential, i.e., question marks and stars.

Dogs are businesses with low market share in low-growth markets. These are often cash cows that have lost their market share or question marks the company has elected not to develop. The recommended strategy for these businesses is to dispose of them for whatever revenue they will generate and reinvest the money in more attractive businesses (question marks or stars).

Despite its simplicity, the BCG matrix suffers from limited variables on which to base resource allocation decisions among the business making up the corporate portfolio. Notice that the only two variables composing the matrix are relative market share and the rate of market growth. Now consider how many other factors contribute to business success or failure. Management talent, employee commitment, industry forces such as buyer and supplier power and the introduction of strategically-equivalent substitute products or services, changes in consumer preferences, and a host of others determine ultimate business viability. The BCG matrix is best used, then, as a beginning point, but certainly not as the final determination for resource allocation decisions as it was originally intended. Consider, for instance, Apple Computer. With a market share for its Macintosh-based computers below ten percent in a market notoriously saturated with a number of low-cost competitors and growth rates well-below that of other technology pursuits such as biotechnology and medical device products, the BCG matrix would suggest Apple divest its computer business and focus instead on the rapidly growing iPod business (its music download business). Clearly, though, there are both technological and market synergies between Apple's Macintosh computers and its fast-growing iPod business. Divesting the computer business would likely be tantamount to destroying the iPod business.

A more stringent approach, but still one with weaknesses, is a competitive assessment. A competitive assessment is a technique for ranking an organization relative to its peers in the industry. The advantage of a competitive assessment over the BCG matrix for corporate-level strategy is that the competitive assessment includes critical success factors, or factors that are crucial for an organizational to prevail when all organizational members are competing for the same customers. A six-step process that allows corporate strategist to define appropriate variables, rather than being locked into the market share and market growth variables of the BCG matrix, is used to develop a table that shows a businesses ranking relative to the critical success factors that managers identify as the key factors influencing failure or success. These steps include:

1. Identifying key success factors. This step allows managers to select the most appropriate variables for its situation. There is no limit to the number of variables managers may select; the idea, however, is to use those that are key in determining competitive strength.

2. Weighing the importance of key success factors. Weighting can be on a scale of 1 to 5, 1 to 7, or 1 to 10, or whatever scale managers believe is appropriate. The main thing is to maintain consistency across organizations. This step brings an element of realism to the analysis by recognizing that not all critical success factors are equally important. Depending on industry conditions, successful advertising campaigns may, for example, be weighted more heavily than after-sale product support.

3. Identifying main industry rivals. This step helps managers focus on one of the most common external threats; competitors who want the organization's market share.

4. Managers rating their organization against competitors.

5. Multiplying the weighted importance by the key success factor rating.

6. Adding the values. The sum of the values for a manager's organization versus competitors gives a rough idea if the manager's firm is ahead or behind the competition on weighted key success factors that are critical for market success.

A competitive strength assessment is superior to a BCG matrix because it adds more variables to the mix. In addition, these variables are weighted in importance in contrast to the BCG matrix's equal weighting of market share and market growth. Regardless of these advantages, competitive strength assessments are still limited by the type of data they provide. When the values are summed in step six, each organization has a number assigned to it. This number is compared against other firms to determine which is competitively the strongest. One weakness is that these data are ordinal: they can be ranked, but the differences among them are not meaningful. A firm with a score of four is not twice as good as one with a score of two, but it is better. The degree of "betterness," however, is not known.

CORPORATE GRAND STRATEGIES

As the previous discussion implies, corporate-level strategists have a tremendous amount of both latitude and responsibility. The myriad decisions required of these managers can be overwhelming considering the potential consequences of incorrect decisions. One way to deal with this complexity is through categorization; one categorization scheme is to classify corporate-level strategy decisions into three different types, or grand strategies. These grand strategies involve efforts to expand business operations (growth strategies), decrease the scope of business operations (retrenchment strategies), or maintain the status quo (stability strategies).

GROWTH STRATEGIES

Growth strategies are designed to expand an organization's performance, usually as measured by sales, profits, product mix, market coverage, market share, or other accounting and market-based variables. Typical growth strategies involve one or more of the following:

1. With a concentration strategy the firm attempts to achieve greater market penetration by becoming highly efficient at servicing its market with a limited product line (e.g., McDonalds in fast foods).

2. By using a vertical integration strategy, the firm attempts to expand the scope of its current operations by undertaking business activities formerly performed by one of its suppliers (backward integration) or by undertaking business activities performed by a business in its channel of distribution (forward integration).

3. A diversification strategy entails moving into different markets or adding different products to its mix. If the products or markets are related to existing product or service offerings, the strategy is called concentric diversification. If expansion is into products or services unrelated to the firm's existing business, the diversification is called conglomerate diversification.

STABILITY STRATEGIES

When firms are satisfied with their current rate of growth and profits, they may decide to use a stability strategy. This strategy is essentially a continuation of existing strategies. Such strategies are typically found in industries having relatively stable environments. The firm is often making a comfortable income operating a business that they know, and see no need to make the psychological and financial investment that would be required to undertake a growth strategy.

RETRENCHMENT STRATEGIES

Retrenchment strategies involve a reduction in the scope of a corporation's activities, which also generally necessitates a reduction in number of employees, sale of assets associated with discontinued product or service lines, possible restructuring of debt through bankruptcy proceedings, and in the most extreme cases, liquidation of the firm.

- Firms pursue a turnaround strategy by undertaking a temporary reduction in operations in an effort to make the business stronger and more viable in the future. These moves are popularly called downsizing or rightsizing. The hope is that going through a temporary belt-tightening will allow the firm to pursue a growth strategy at some future point.

- A divestment decision occurs when a firm elects to sell one or more of the businesses in its corporate portfolio. Typically, a poorly performing unit is sold to another company and the money is reinvested in another business within the portfolio that has greater potential.

- Bankruptcy involves legal protection against creditors or others allowing the firm to restructure its debt obligations or other payments, typically in a way that temporarily increases cash flow. Such restructuring allows the firm time to attempt a turnaround strategy. For example, since the airline hijackings and the subsequent tragic events of September 11, 2001, many of the airlines based in the U.S. have filed for bankruptcy to avoid liquidation as a result of stymied demand for air travel and rising fuel prices. At least one airline has asked the courts to allow it to permanently suspend payments to its employee pension plan to free up positive cash flow.

- Liquidation is the most extreme form of retrenchment. Liquidation involves the selling or closing of the entire operation. There is no future for the firm; employees are released, buildings and equipment are sold, and customers no longer have access to the product or service. This is a strategy of last resort and one that most managers work hard to avoid.

BUSINESS-LEVEL STRATEGIES

Business-level strategies are similar to corporate-strategies in that they focus on overall performance. In contrast to corporate-level strategy, however, they focus on only one rather than a portfolio of businesses. Business units represent individual entities oriented toward a particular industry, product, or market. In large multi-product or multi-industry organizations, individual business units may be combined to form strategic business units (SBUs). An SBU represents a group of related business divisions, each responsible to corporate headquarters for its own profits and losses. Each strategic business unit will likely have its' own competitors and its own unique strategy. A common focus of business-level strategies are sometimes on a particular product or service line and business-level strategies commonly involve decisions regarding individual products within this product or service line. There are also strategies regarding relationships between products. One product may contribute to corporate-level strategy by generating a large positive cash flow for new product development, while another product uses the cash to increase sales and expand market share of existing businesses. Given this potential for business-level strategies to impact other business-level strategies, business-level managers must provide ongoing, intensive information to corporate-level managers. Without such crucial information, corporate-level managers are prevented from best managing overall organizational direction. Business-level strategies are thus primarily concerned with:

1. Coordinating and integrating unit activities so they conform to organizational strategies (achieving synergy).

2. Developing distinctive competencies and competitive advantage in each unit.

3. Identifying product or service-market niches and developing strategies for competing in each.

4. Monitoring product or service markets so that strategies conform to the needs of the markets at the current stage of evolution.

In a single-product company, corporate-level and business-level strategies are the same. For example, a furniture manufacturer producing only one line of furniture has its corporate strategy chosen by its market definition, wholesale furniture, but its business is still the same, wholesale furniture. Thus, in single-business organizations, corporate and business-level strategies overlap to the point that they should be treated as one united strategy. The product made by a unit of a diversified company would face many of the same challenges and opportunities faced by a one-product company. However, for most organizations, business-unit strategies are designed to support corporate strategies. Business-level strategies look at the product's life cycle, competitive environment, and competitive advantage much like corporate-level strategies, except the focus for business-level strategies is on the product or service, not on the corporate portfolio.

Business-level strategies thus support corporate-level strategies. Corporate-level strategies attempt to maximize the wealth of shareholders through profitability of the overall corporate portfolio, but business-level strategies are concerned with (1) matching their activities with the overall goals of corporate-level strategy while simultaneously (2) navigating the markets in which they compete in such a way that they have a financial or market edge-a competitive advantage-relative to the other businesses in their industry.

ANALYSIS OF BUSINESS-LEVEL STRATEGIES

PORTER'S GENERIC STRATEGIES. Harvard Business School's Michael Porter developed a framework of generic strategies that can be applied to strategies for various products and services, or the individual business-level strategies within a corporate portfolio. The strategies are (1) overall cost leadership, (2) differentiation, and (3) focus on a particular market niche. The generic strategies provide direction for business units in designing incentive systems, control procedures, operations, and interactions with suppliers and buyers, and with making other product decisions.

Cost-leadership strategies require firms to develop policies aimed at becoming and remaining the lowest cost producer and/or distributor in the industry. Note here that the focus is on cost leadership, not price leadership. This may at first appear to be only a semantic difference, but consider how this fine-grained definition places emphases on controlling costs while giving firms alternatives when it comes to pricing (thus ultimately influencing total revenues). A firm with a cost advantage may price at or near competitors prices, but with a lower cost of production and sales, more of the price contributes to the firm's gross profit margin. A second alternative is to price lower than competitors and accept slimmer gross profit margins, with the goal of gaining market share and thus increasing sales volume to offset the decrease in gross margin. Such strategies concentrate on construction of efficient-scale facilities, tight cost and overhead control, avoidance of marginal customer accounts that cost more to maintain than they offer in profits, minimization of operating expenses, reduction of input costs, tight control of labor costs, and lower distribution costs. The low-cost leader gains competitive advantage by getting its costs of production or distribution lower than the costs of the other firms in its relevant market. This strategy is especially important for firms selling unbranded products viewed as commodities, such as beef or steel.

Cost leadership provides firms above-average returns even with strong competitive pressures. Lower costs allow the firm to earn profits after competitors have reduced their profit margin to zero. Low-cost production further limits pressures from customers to lower price, as the customers are unable to purchase cheaper from a competitor. Cost leadership may be attained via a number of techniques. Products can be designed to simplify manufacturing. A large market share combined with concentrating selling efforts on large customers may contribute to reduced costs. Extensive investment in state-of-the-art facilities may also lead to long run cost reductions. Companies that successfully use this strategy tend to be highly centralized in their structure. They place heavy emphasis on quantitative standards and measuring performance toward goal accomplishment.

Efficiencies that allow a firm to be the cost leader also allow it to compete effectively with both existing competitors and potential new entrants. Finally, low costs reduce the likely impact of substitutes. Substitutes are more likely to replace products of the more expensive producers first, before significantly harming sales of the cost leader unless producers of substitutes can simultaneously develop a substitute product or service at a lower cost than competitors. In many instances, the necessity to climb up the experience curve inhibits a new entrants ability to pursue this tactic.

Differentiation strategies require a firm to create something about its product that is perceived as unique within its market. Whether the features are real, or just in the mind of the customer, customers must perceive the product as having desirable features not commonly found in competing products. The customers also must be relatively price-insensitive. Adding product features means that the production or distribution costs of a differentiated product will be somewhat higher than the price of a generic, non-differentiated product. Customers must be willing to pay more than the marginal cost of adding the differentiating feature if a differentiation strategy is to succeed.

Differentiation may be attained through many features that make the product or service appear unique. Possible strategies for achieving differentiation may include warranty (Sears tools have lifetime guarantee against breakage), brand image (Coach handbags, Tommy Hilfiger sportswear), technology (Hewlett-Packard laser printers), features (Jenn-Air ranges, Whirlpool appliances), service (Makita hand tools), and dealer network (Caterpillar construction equipment), among other dimensions. Differentiation does not allow a firm to ignore costs; it makes a firm's products less susceptible to cost pressures from competitors because customers see the product as unique and are willing to pay extra to have the product with the desirable features.

Differentiation often forces a firm to accept higher costs in order to make a product or service appear unique. The uniqueness can be achieved through real product features or advertising that causes the customer to perceive that the product is unique. Whether the difference is achieved through adding more vegetables to the soup or effective advertising, costs for the differentiated product will be higher than for non-differentiated products. Thus, firms must remain sensitive to cost differences. They must carefully monitor the incremental costs of differentiating their product and make certain the difference is reflected in the price.

Focus, the third generic strategy, involves concentrating on a particular customer, product line, geographical area, channel of distribution, stage in the production process, or market niche. The underlying premise of the focus strategy is that the firm is better able to serve its limited segment than competitors serving a broader range of customers. Firms using a focus strategy simply apply a cost-leader or differentiation strategy to a segment of the larger market. Firms may thus be able to differentiate themselves based on meeting customer needs through differentiation or through low costs and competitive pricing for specialty goods.

A focus strategy is often appropriate for small, aggressive businesses that do not have the ability or resources to engage in a nation-wide marketing effort. Such a strategy may also be appropriate if the target market is too small to support a large-scale operation. Many firms start small and expand into a national organization. Wal-Mart started in small towns in the South and Midwest. As the firm gained in market knowledge and acceptance, it was able to expand throughout the

South, then nationally, and now internationally. The company started with a focused cost-leader strategy in its limited market and was able to expand beyond its initial market segment.

Firms utilizing a focus strategy may also be better able to tailor advertising and promotional efforts to a particular market niche. Many automobile dealers advertise that they are the largest-volume dealer for a specific geographic area. Other dealers advertise that they have the highest customer-satisfaction scores or the most awards for their service department of any dealer within their defined market. Similarly, firms may be able to design products specifically for a customer. Customization may range from individually designing a product for a customer to allowing the customer input into the finished product. Tailor-made clothing and custom-built houses include the customer in all aspects of production from product design to final acceptance. Key decisions are made with customer input. Providing such individualized attention to customers may not be feasible for firms with an industry-wide orientation.

FUNCTIONAL-LEVEL STRATEGIES. Functional-level strategies are concerned with coordinating the functional areas of the organization (marketing, finance, human resources, production, research and development, etc.) so that each functional area upholds and contributes to individual business-level strategies and the overall corporate-level strategy. This involves coordinating the various functions and operations needed to design, manufacturer, deliver, and support the product or service of each business within the corporate portfolio. Functional strategies are primarily concerned with:

- Efficiently utilizing specialists within the functional area.

- Integrating activities within the functional area (e.g., coordinating advertising, promotion, and marketing research in marketing; or purchasing, inventory control, and shipping in production/operations).

- Assuring that functional strategies mesh with business-level strategies and the overall corporate-level strategy.

Functional strategies are frequently concerned with appropriate timing. For example, advertising for a new product could be expected to begin sixty days prior to shipment of the first product. Production could then start thirty days before shipping begins. Raw materials, for instance, may require that orders are placed at least two weeks before production is to start. Thus, functional strategies have a shorter time orientation than either business-level or corporate-level strategies. Accountability is also easiest to establish with functional strategies because results

of actions occur sooner and are more easily attributed to the function than is possible at other levels of strategy. Lower-level managers are most directly involved with the implementation of functional strategies.

Strategies for an organization may be categorized by the level of the organization addressed by the strategy. Corporate-level strategies involve top management and address issues of concern to the entire organization. Business-level strategies deal with major business units or divisions of the corporate portfolio. Business-level strategies are generally developed by upper and middle-level managers and are intended to help the organization achieve its corporate strategies. Functional strategies address problems commonly faced by lower-level managers and deal with strategies for the major organizational functions (e.g., marketing, finance, production) considered relevant for achieving the business strategies and supporting the corporate-level strategy. Market definition is thus the domain of corporate-level strategy, market navigation the domain of business-level strategy, and support of business and corporate-level strategy by individual, but integrated, functional level strategies.

SEE ALSO: Generic Competitive Strategies; Porter's 5-Forces Model; Strategic Planning Failure; Strategic Planning Tools; Strategy Formulation; Strategy Implementation; Strategy in the Global Environment

Joe Thomas
Revised by Scott B. Droege

FURTHER READING:

D'Aveni, Richard A. "Corporate Spheres of Influence." *MIT Sloan Management Review* 45: 38–46.

Deephouse, D. "To Be Different, or to Be the Same? It's a Question (and Theory) of Strategic Balance." *Strategic Management Journal* 20 (1999): 147–166.

Digman, L. *Strategic Management.* Houston: Dame, 1997.

Dyer, J.H., P. Kale, and H. Singh. "When to Ally and When to Acquire." *Harvard Business Review* 82 (2004): 108–116.

Hambrick, D., I. MacMillan, and D. Day. "Strategic Attributes and Performance in the BCG Matrix." *Academy of Management Journal* (1982): 500–509.

Kroll, M., P. Wright, and R. Heiens. "The Contribution of Product Quality to Competitive Advantage: Impacts on Systematic Variance and Unexplained Variance in Returns." *Strategic Management Journal* 20 (1999): 375–384.

Porter, M. *Competitive Advantage: Creating and Sustaining Superior Performance.* New York: Free Press, 1985.

———. *Competitive Strategy: Techniques for Analyzing Industries and Companies.* New York: Free Press, 1980.

STRATEGY IN THE GLOBAL ENVIRONMENT

Globalization was the buzzword of the 1990s, and in the twenty first century, there is no evidence that globalization will diminish. Essentially, globalization refers to growth of trade and investment, accompanied by the growth in international businesses, and the integration of economies around the world. According to Punnett (2004) the globalization concept is based on a number of relatively simple premises:

- Technological developments have increased the ease and speed of international communication and travel.

- Increased communication and travel have made the world smaller.

- A smaller world means that people are more aware of events outside of their home country, and are more likely to travel to other countries.

- Increased awareness and travel result in a better understanding of foreign opportunities.

- A better understanding of opportunities leads to increases in international trade and investment, and the number of businesses operating across national borders.

- These increases mean that the economies around the world are more closely integrated.

Managers must be conscious that markets, supplies, investors, locations, partners, and competitors can be anywhere in the world. Successful businesses will take advantage of opportunities wherever they are and will be prepared for downfalls. Successful managers, in this environment, need to understand the similarities and differences across national boundaries, in order to utilize the opportunities and deal with the potential downfalls.

The globalization of business is easy to recognize in the spread of many brands and services throughout the world. For example, Japanese electronics and automobiles are common in Asia, Europe, and North America, while U.S. automobiles, entertainment, and financial services are also common in Asia, Europe, and North America. Moreover, companies have become transnational or multinational-that is, they are based in one country but have operations in others. For example, Japan-based automaker Honda operates the largest single factory in the United States, while U.S. based Coca-Cola operates plants in other countries including France and Belgium—with about 80 percent of that company's profits come from overseas sales.

During the early 1990s, there were reasons to feel that globalization was working. The economic success of Singapore, the rapid economic growth in the Asian Tigers (as the Asian countries that grew rapidly were called), the industrializing of countries, such as Brazil and Mexico, and a variety of other positive economic events around the world suggested that the results of globalization were indeed good for development in poorer countries, as well as in richer ones. During the 1990s, the United States experienced one of its most sustained periods of growth as well, and there was much talk of a "new economy", based on globalization, which was immune to economic shocks and recession.

Unfortunately, this rapid growth was not without consequences. The Seattle meetings of the World Trade Organization turned into a fiasco, with anti-globalization groups demonstrating against globalization on all fronts—from animal rights to environmental concerns, poverty alleviation, and jobs for Americans. The anti-globalization forces have not coalesced into a coherent whole because they represent such diverse and often contradictory views. The vehemence of their protests, however, make it clear that globalization is not a panacea for the world's problems. In addition, the Asian Tigers suffered major economic setbacks in the late 1990s. In 2002, Argentina's economy, which had been one of the stars of the 1990s, crashed, when the country could no longer maintain its currency at par with the U.S. dollar.

Further problems occurred in the Triad economies. Japan, Europe, and the United States, often referred to as the Triad, dominated international trade and investment for much of the second half of the twentieth century. The Japanese economy went into a severe period of recession and deflation in the late 1990s, and in 2001 both the European and the U.S. economies took a downward turn as well. In turn, the rest of the world was negatively affected by the economic situation in the Triad. The terrorist attacks in the United States in September, 2001, exacerbated this already negative economic situation.

In developing appropriate global strategies, managers need to take the benefits and drawbacks of globalization into account. A global strategy must be in the context of events around the globe, as well as those at home.

International strategy is the continuous and comprehensive management technique designed to help companies operate and compete effectively across national boundaries. While companies' top managers typically develop global strategies, they rely on all levels of management in order to implement these strategies successfully. The methods companies use to accomplish the goals of these strategies take a host of forms. For example, some companies form partnerships with companies in other countries, others acquire companies in other countries, others still develop products, services, and marketing campaigns designed to

Table 1
Differences Between Domestic and International Strategy

Factors	Domestic Conditions	Global Conditions
Culture	Homogeneous	Heterogeneous
Currency	Uniform	Different currencies and exchange rates
Economy	Stable and uniform	May be variable and unpredictable
Government	Stable	May be unstable
Labor	Skilled workers available	Skilled workers may be hard to find
Language	Generally a single language	Different languages and dialects
Marketing	Many media, few restrictions	May be fewer media and more restrictions
Transport	Several competitive modes	May be inadequate

Source: World Bank

appeal to customers in other countries. Some rudimentary aspects of international strategies mirror domestic strategies in that companies must determine what products or services to sell, where and how to sell them, where and how they will produce or provide them, and how they will compete with other companies in the industry in accordance with company goals.

The development of international strategies entails attention to other details that seldom, if ever, come into play in the domestic market. These other areas of concern stem from cultural, geographic, and political differences. Consequently, while a company only has to develop a strategy taking into account known governmental regulations, one language (generally), and one currency in a domestic market, it must consider and plan for different levels and kinds of governmental regulation, multiple currencies, and several languages in the global market.

The most recent wave of globalization by U.S. companies began in the 1980s, as companies began to realize that concentrating on the domestic market alone would lead to stagnant sales and profits and that emerging markets offered many opportunities for growth. Part of the motivation for this globalization stemmed from the lost market share in the 1970s to multinational companies from other countries, especially those from Japan. Initially, these U.S. companies tried to emulate their Japanese counterparts by implementing Japanese-style management structures and quality circles. After adapting these practices to meet the needs of U.S. companies and recapturing market share, these companies began to move into new markets to spur growth, enable the acquisition of resources (often at a cost advantage), and gain competitive advantage by achieving greater economies of scale.

The globalization of U.S. companies has not been without concerns and detractors. Exporting U.S. jobs, exploiting child labor, and contributing to poverty have all been charges laid at the doors of U.S. companies.

These charges have been accompanied by demonstrations and consumer boycotts.

Nor have U.S. companies been the only ones affected. Companies in the rest of the developed world have globalized along with U.S. companies, and they have also faced the sometimes negative consequences.

Interestingly, in the late twentieth and early twenty-first century, there has also been a growth in international companies from developing and transitional countries, and this trend can be expected to continue and increase. Exports and investment from the People's Republic of China are a notable example, but companies from Southeast Asia, India, South Africa, and Latin America, to name some countries and regions, are making themselves known around the world.

TYPES OF GLOBAL BUSINESS ACTIVITIES

Businesses may choose to globalize or operate in different countries in four distinct ways: through trade, investment, strategic alliances, and licensing or franchising. Companies may decide to trade tangible goods such as automobiles and electronics (merchandise exports and imports). Alternatively, companies may decide to trade intangible products such as financial or legal services (service exports and imports).

Companies may enter the global market through various kinds of international investments. Companies may choose to make foreign direct investments, which allow them to control companies and assets in other countries. In addition, companies may elect to make portfolio investments, by acquiring the stock of companies in other countries in order to gain control of these companies.

Another way companies tap into the global market is by forming strategic alliances with companies in other countries. While strategic alliances come in many forms, some enable each company to access the home market of the other and thereby market their products as being affiliated with the well-known host company. This method of international business also enables a company to bypass some of the difficulties associated with internationalization such as different political, regulatory, and social conditions. The home company can help the multinational company address and overcome these difficulties because it is accustomed to them.

Finally, companies may participate in the international market by either licensing or franchising. Licensing involves granting another company the right to use its brand names, trademarks, copyrights, or patents in exchange for royalty payments. Franchising, on the other hand, is when one company agrees to allow a company in another country to use its name and methods of operations in exchange for royalty payments.

OVERVIEW OF INTERNATIONAL STRATEGY DEVELOPMENT

Generally, a company develops its international strategy by considering its overall strategy, which includes its operations at home and abroad. we can consider four aspects of strategy: (1) scope of operations, (2) resource allocation, (3) competitive advantage, and (4) synergy. The first component encompasses the geographic locations—countries and regions—of possible operations as well as possible markets or niches in various regions. Since companies have limited resources and since different regions offer different advantages, managers must select the markets that offer the company the optimal opportunities.

The second component of the global strategy focuses on use of company resources so that a company can compete successfully in the chosen markets. This component of strategy planning also determines the relative importance of various company functions and bases the allocation of resources on the relative importance of each function. For instance, a company may decide to allocate its resources based on product lines or geographical locations.

Next, management must decide where the company can achieve competitive advantage over other companies in the industry. Management can identify their competitive advantage by determining what the company does better (or can do better) than its competitors. Companies may realize this advantage through a host of techniques such as using superior technology, implementing more efficient organizational practices and distribution systems, and cultivating well-known brands. This component of the strategy involves not only identifying existing or potential areas of competitive advantage but also developing a plan for sustaining areas of competitive advantage. Finally, global strategy should involve establishing a plan for the company that enables its various functions and operations to benefit

one another. For example, a company can use one line of products to encourage sales of another line of products and thereby enabling different parts of a business to benefit from each other.

Many companies are now outsourcing many of their operations internationally. For example, if you call to get information on your credit card, you may well be talking to someone in India or Mexico. Equally, manufacturers often outsource production to low labor cost countries. Concerns over ethical issues, such as slave and child labor, have led to companies outsourcing under controlled conditions—offshore production may be subject to surprise visits and searches and outsourced factories are required to conform to specific criteria.

STAGES OF INTERNATIONAL STRATEGY DEVELOPMENT

Strategy development itself generally takes places in two stages: strategy formulation and strategy implementation. When planning a strategy, companies identify their international objectives and put together a strategy that will enable them to realize their goals. During the planning stage managers propose, revise, and finally ratify plans for entering new markets and competing in them.

After a strategy has been agreed on, managers must take steps to have it implemented. Consequently, this stage involves determining when to begin global operations as well as actually starting operations and putting into action the other components of the global strategy.

More specifically, the first stage—strategy formulation—entails analysis of the company and its environment, establishing strategic goals, and developing plans to achieve goals as well as a control framework. By assessing itself and the global business environment, a company can determine what markets, products, services, etc. offer opportunities for growth. This process involves the collection of data on a company and its environment, including information on global markets, regulation, productivity, costs, and competitors. Therefore, the collection of data should supply managers with economic, financial, political, legal, and social information on various countries and their markets for different products or services. Based on this information, managers can determine what markets and products offer economically feasible opportunities for global expansion.

Once this analysis is complete, managers must establish strategic goals, which are the significant goals a company seeks to achieve through a particular pursuit such as entering a new regional market. These goals must be practicable, measurable, and limited to a specific time frame. After the strategic goals have been established, companies should develop plans that allow them to accomplish their goals, and these plans should concentrate on how to implement strategic plans. Finally, strategy formulation involves a control framework, which is a process management uses to help ensure that a company remains on the right course when implementing its strategic plans. The control framework essentially responds to various developments while the strategic plans are being implemented. For example, if sales are lower than the projected sales that are part of the strategic goals, then a company might increase its marketing efforts and temporarily lower its prices to stimulate additional sales.

INTERNATIONAL MARKET EVALUATION

While many aspects of international strategy and its formulation are similar to their domestic counterparts, some key aspects are not, and hence call for different methods and different kinds of information. Gaining knowledge of international markets is one of these key differences—and a crucial part of developing an international strategy. In order for a company to enter a new market, capture market share, and thereby increase sales and profits, it must know what that market is like. At a basic level, a company must examine different markets, evaluate the advantages and disadvantages of entering each, and select only the markets that show the greatest potential for entry and growth.

When examining different international markets, a company should consider the market potential, competition, regulation, and cultural factors of each. Company managers can assess market potential by collecting data on the gross domestic product (GDP), per capita GDP, population, transportation, and other figures of various countries. This kind of information will enable managers to determine the spending power of the consumers in each country and determine if that spending power allows them to purchase a company's

products or services. Managers also should consider the currency stability of the different markets, which can be done by using documents from the home countries to determine currency value and fluctuation over a period of years.

To select the best markets for entry, managers also should consider the degree of competition within different markets and should anticipate future competition in them as well. Determining the degree of competition involves the identification of all the companies competing in the prospective markets as well as their sizes, market shares, and prices. Managers then should evaluate a prospective market by considering the number of competitors and their characteristics as well as the market conditions—that is, whether the market is saturated with competition and cannot support any new entrants.

Next, managers should evaluate the regulatory environment of the prospective markets, since knowing tax, trade, other related policies is essential for a successful international business. This step entails determining the respective tariffs and trade barriers of prospective markets. Different types of trade barriers may influence the kind of business activity a company chooses for a particular market. For example, if a prospective market has trade barriers that restrict the entry of foreign-made goods, a company might decide to access the market through foreign direct investment and manufacture its products in that country itself. Ownership restrictions also may limit a company's interest in a particular market; some countries permit foreign companies to set up local operations only if they establish a partnership with a local company. In addition, managers should find out if prospective countries charge foreign companies higher taxes or if they offer tax breaks and incentive to encourage economic development. A final consideration companies must make concerning government is stability. Since some countries have rough government transitions resulting from coups and uprisings, companies must countenance the possibility of political turmoil that could substantially disrupt business.

The last step in international market evaluation is the assessment of cultural factors. To avoid difficulties associated with cultural differences, some managers look for new markets that have cultural similarities to their home market, especially for initial international market penetration endeavors. Unlike market potential, competition, and regulation, cultural differences are more difficult to evaluate. Nevertheless, managers must try to determine the consumer needs and preferences in the prospective markets. Managers must also account for cultural differences in labor relations such as worker motivation, compensation, hours, etc. if planning foreign direct investment in an overseas company. Moreover, a thorough understanding of a prospective country's culture will greatly facilitate any

Table 2 Differences Between Domestic and International Strategy	
Country	GDP per Capita (2003 Estimate in US$)
Luxembourg	55,100
United States	37,800
Norway	37,700
Bermuda	36,000
Cayman Islands	35,000
San Marino	34,600
Switzerland	32,800
Denmark	31,200
Iceland	30,900
Austria	30,000

kind of global business enterprise. This cultural knowledge should include a basic understanding of a prospective country's beliefs and attitudes, language and communication styles, dress, food preferences and customs, time and time consciousness, relationships, values, and work ethic. This kind of cultural information is essential for developing an effective and realistic global strategy.

Since conducting primary research is labor intensive and time consuming, managers may obtain preliminary information on prospective markets from books such as Dun & Bradstreet's *Guide to Doing Business Around the World* and *Business Protocol: How to Survive and Succeed in Business,* or the Economist's "Doing Business in. . ." series, which list potential trade opportunities, policies, etiquette, taxes, and so on for various countries.

After examining the prospective markets in this manner, managers are ready to evaluate the advantages and disadvantages of each potential market. One way of doing so is the determination of costs, advantages, and disadvantages of each prospective market. The costs of each market include direct costs and opportunity costs. Direct costs are those a company pays when establishing a business in a new market, such as costs associated with purchasing property and equipment and producing and shipping goods. Opportunity costs, on the other hand, refer to the costs associated with the loss of other opportunities, since entering one market rules out or postpones entering another because of a company's limited resources. Hence, the profits that could have been earned in the alternative market constitute the opportunity costs.

Each prospective market usually has a variety of advantages, such as the possibility for growth, which will lead to greater revenues and profits. Other advantages include relatively low material and labor costs, new technology gaining strategic advantage over competitors, and matching competitors' actions. However, each prospective market also usually has a number of disadvantages, including opportunity costs, greater business complexity, and potential losses stemming from unforeseen aspects of prospective markets and from currency fluctuations. Other disadvantages might result from potential losses associated with unstable political conditions.

ANALYSIS OF TWO INTERNATIONAL STRATEGIES

In the late 1990s after a significant amount of globalization had taken place, business analysts began to examine the success of various strategies for doing business in other countries. This examination led to the distinction between various orientations of international strategies. The main distinction was between

multi-domestic (also called multi-local) international strategies and global strategies. Multi-domestic international strategies refer to those that address competition in each country or region on an individual basis, whereas global strategy refers to addressing competition in an integrated and holistic manner across country and regional boundaries. Hence, multi-domestic international strategies attempt to appeal to the needs of customers in different countries or regions, while global strategies attempt to standardize products and marketing to work across boundaries. Instead of relying on one of these strategies, multinational companies might adopt a different strategy for different products or services. For example, a company might use a global strategy for its electronics and a multi-domestic strategy for its appliances.

Critics of the standardization approach argue that it makes two questionable assumptions: that consumers' needs are becoming more homogenous throughout the world and that consumers prefer high quality and low prices over advanced features and functions. Nevertheless, standardized global strategies have some significant benefits. Companies can reduce their marketing expenditures, for example, if they use the same ads in all their markets. PepsiCo, for example, uses the same televisions ads in all of its national markets, saving an estimated $10 million a year. Besides marketing savings, global strategies can lead to other kinds of benefits and advantages in areas such as design, packaging, manufacturing, distribution, customer service, and software development.

Some people argue that companies must customize their products or services to meet the needs of various international markets, and hence must use a multi-domestic strategy at least in part. For example, KFC planned a standardized approach to its foray into the Japanese market, but the company soon realized it had to change its strategy to meet the needs of Japanese consumers and customize its operations in Japan. Consequently, KFC introduced smaller pieces of foods to cater to a Japanese preference, and located restaurants in crowded areas along with other restaurants, moving away from independent sites. As a result of these changes, the fast-food restaurant experienced stronger demand in Japan.

The development of regional trading blocs has promoted an emphasis regional strategies as companies develop plans to take advantage of the conditions within various trading blocs such as the North American Free Trade Agreement (NAFTA), the European Union, the Asia-Pacific Economic Cooperation (APEC) and the Association of Southeast Asian Nations (ASEAN). In addition, the United States has signed 16 different trade agreements with South American countries, creating a foundation for a trading bloc consisting of all North and South American countries. Consequently, companies have been establishing regional strategies designed around these trading blocs. Nike, for example, established central warehouses for its European distribution, just as it has a central warehouse for its U.S. distribution. This strategy has enabled Nike to reduce its inventory, cut down on redundancy, reduce costs, and enhance availability. In addition, News Corporation originally relied on a global strategy with its STAR-TV satellite television network; attempting to provide the same television shows across Asia in English. The company quickly switched to a multi-domestic strategy, providing programming in local languages after receiving low ratings and advertising dollars with its first approach.

A variety of corporate collapses, and the revelation of unethical and illegal practices in many international companies, has led to a focus on Corporate Governance and Ethics in the early twenty first century. Issues of what constitutes socially responsible behavior are likely to be a major part of global strategy for the coming years.

SEE ALSO: International Business; International Management; International Management; Macroenvironmental Forces; Multinational Corporations; Strategic Planning Failure; Strategic Planning Tools; Strategy Formulation; Strategy Implementation; Strategy in the Global Environment; Strategy Levels; Transnational Organization

Karl Heil
Revised by Betty Jane Punnett

FURTHER READING:

Bartlett, C.A. and S. Ghoshal. "What is a Global Manager?" In *Annual Editions: International Business.* Dubuque, IL: Dushkin Publishers.

Feffer, J. *Power Trip: U.S. Unilateralism and Global Strategy after September 11.* New York: Seven Stories Press, 2003.

Florini, A. "Business and Global Governance." *Brookings Review,* Spring 2003, 5–8.

Gupta, A.K., and V. Gorindarajan. *Global Strategy and the Organization.* John Wiley & Sons Publishers, 2003.

Punnett, B.J. *International Perspectives on Organizational Behavior and Human Resource Management.* Armonk, N.Y.: MESharpe Inc., 2004.

STRESS

STRESS IN ORGANIZATIONS

As the pace at which our society operates increases, the pressures for every member of society to keep up with this pace also increase. Many of these pressures affect people through their jobs. Stress has become the "buzzword" that many people use to describe the impact that these pressures cause. In the short-term, stress can enable individuals to meet high levels of demand or pending deadlines. Prolonged stress, however, has been shown to cause illness and other conditions that can have detrimental effects on an employer's workforce. As Leon Warshaw noted in 1979 in his book on dealing with stress in the workplace: "Stress affects personality, modifying our perceptions, feelings, attitudes and behavior. And it reaches beyond its immediate victims to affect the political, social and work organizations whose activities they direct and carry out." In other words, the increasing rate of stress at work has wide-ranging effects—absenteeism, impaired teamwork, workplace violence, decreased efficiency, increased rates of physical and mental illness, employee burnout, risk of discrimination and growth in early retirement.

In his 2004 article "Workplace Stress Sucks $300 Billion Annually from Corporate Profits," Ron Ball cites a recent study by Ravi Tangi that establishes a formula for measuring the "hard costs" of stress on business as whole. This formula quantified stress as causing the following:

- 19 percent of absenteeism

- 40 percent of turnover

- 55 percent of employee assistance programs

- 30 percent of short- and long-term disability

- 10 percent of drug plan costs

- 60 percent of total workplace accidents

- 100 percent of workers compensation and litigation complaints

There are many factors that contribute to making a workplace stressful. Research clearly indicates that certain jobs are more stressful than others. For example, people who work as police officers, fire fighters, air traffic controllers, and elected officials are exposed to higher levels of stress that people who work as janitors, florists, medical records technicians, forklift operators, librarians and musical instrument repairers. The factors that contribute to making some jobs more stressful include: level of decision-making required; level of monitoring workers must endure; unpleasant or dangerous physical or emotional conditions; repeated exchange of information with others; and whether job tasks are generally structured or unstructured.

Understanding the factors that contribute to creating stress in the workplace can help employers begin to manage stress among the workforce. The rest of this section will describe some of the detrimental effects of stress on the workplace and offer potential solutions for employers to minimize the potential harm to employees and to the work environment as a whole.

CONTROLLING ABSENCES

In increasing numbers, employees are calling in "sick" when they are really suffering from stress. A 2005 survey reported in the Silicon Valley/San Jose Business Journal found that only 38 percent of the employees who called in sick were actually suffering from a physical illness. The other 62 percent of these workers who failed to show up were dealing with stress, family issues, morale issues, motivational issues, etc. These results indicate a need for employers to implement some type of absence control measures.

Research from a wide range of organizations from around the world indicates that about 5 percent of the workforce accounts for about one-third of the absences, or lost days of work. This same research indicates that younger workers often have more absence patterns than older workers. Also, workers with the best attendance records are not always the healthiest or most fit employees. In many instances, the workers with poor attendance records demonstrate poor irregular attendance problems at previous jobs, and within the first six months of any new job. Therefore, employers must take note of attendance patterns of prospective workers (when available) and pay close attention to attendance issues during probationary periods for new hires. Second, employers must set clear rules for attendance at work and identify disciplinary rules that will be enforced if workers fail to comply with the attendance rules. Supervisors must be adequately trained to set for these rules and enforce them for the employer. Further, the employer could examine monthly or quarterly budget reports that review the absenteeism statistics for each department of the company. If there is one department that seems to be experiencing higher-than-normal rates of absenteeism, it could be indicative of stress or morale problems that the employer may need to address.

TEAMWORK ISSUES

Traditional research has taught us that teamwork in the workplace is generally desirable and tends to produce positive results. It is important to note, however, that many workplace teams fail to produce positive results because people often prefer to worth with other people who are similar to them. These teams are often comprised of workers who come from diverse backgrounds, and they bring their own biases and cultural perceptions to the team dynamic. On some teams, this diversity can add richness and depth, and on other depths, this diversity facilitates the creation of barriers between team members. Employers can avoid breakdowns in teams by assigning manageable tasks to teams and setting reasonable deadlines for completion of these tasks. Also, employers should clearly define the charge and expectations for the team project and how it should undertake its mission. The less time teams have to get mired down in harmful infighting, the greater the chance of success.

WORKPLACE VIOLENCE

The following scenario is becoming increasingly typical: In December 2000, Michael McDermott, a software engineer at Edgewater Technology, selects and shoots co-workers in his Wakefield, Mass., office. Seven people die. Employers at the Internet solution provider had recently told McDermott that wages would be garnished from his paycheck to pay the IRS for back taxes.

Because of their increasing frequency, violent acts are now considered a major workplace safety and health threat. A 1999 study by Yale University's School of Management, which surveyed workers throughout the country asked, "How often are you angry at work?" and more than 20 percent of respondents answered, "All the time." That seed of dissatisfaction often grows as time passes. The Occupational Safety and Health Administration estimates that two million workers are victims of violent workplace acts each year. By 2003, workplace violence—including assaults and suicides—accounted for 16 percent of all work-related fatal occupational injuries. Homicides are annually among the top three causes of workplace fatalities for all workers.

Organizational interventions aimed at preventing workplace violence satisfy employers' moral and ethical obligations to provide their employees with safe work environments. Moreover, such interventions also help companies reduce their costs and comply with the law. Workplace violence can cost employers large sums of money. Employers must pay for victims' medical and psychiatric care, repairs and clean-up, insurance rate hikes, and increased security measures. Additional costs are incurred as the result of absenteeism, as the average victim misses 3.5 days of work following an incident.

Employers must also be concerned about workplace violence for legal reasons. The General Duty Clause of the Occupational Safety and Health Act states that employers can be cited for a violation if there is a recognized danger of workplace violence in their establishment, and they do nothing to prevent it. In addition to being fined by OSHA, employers can also be sued by victims of violence. The legal test for determining employer liability for violent acts committed by non-employees is as follows. The employer is liable if:

- it knew or should have known that a criminal act was probable (e.g., it was warned about threats made to an employee); and

- it could have reasonably protected the employee from criminal assault, but failed to do so; and

- its failure to protect the employee caused the subsequent injuries to occur (in other words, had the employer done its part, the injury would not have happened).

A similar legal test is used to determine employer liability for violent acts committed by employees. An employer is liable for negligent hiring if it knew or should have known of the applicant's violent tendencies, yet decided to hire that person anyway. In a similar vein, successful negligent retention suits can be filed when an employer retains a current employee despite knowledge of violent tendencies. Employers are liable in these situations if they had (or should have had) information signaling the danger of future violent acts, yet ignored this danger.

So what can a company do to minimize the occurrences of violent acts? In 2002, OSHA issued a set of guidelines listing some of the security measures that can be implemented to reduce the threat of violence. These measures include:

- provide improved lighting and employee escort services to and from parking lots

- ensure reception areas can be locked when no one is on duty

- create a policy stipulating that there are always at least two people on duty

- provide security systems, such as electronic access control systems, silent alarms, metal detectors, and video cameras

- establish policies regarding visitor access (sign-in, identification badges)

- equip field staff with cellular phones

- install curved mirrors at hallway intersections or concealed areas as well as bullet-proof glass

- provide safety education for employees so they know what conduct is unacceptable, and what to do if they witness or are subjected to workplace violence

- provide drop safes to limit the amount of cash on hand

- instruct employees not to enter any location where they feel unsafe.

An employer should consider these measures in light of the level of risk at a particular worksite. For example, metal detectors and bullet-proof glass would be appropriate for inner-city emergency departments, abortion clinics, and psychiatric facilities where violence is highest. In addition to implementing OSHA recommendations, an employer can further minimize violent acts through the use of pre-employment screening, strict anti-violence and anti-drug/alcohol policies, and training. All workers should be taught how to recognize early signs of a troubled or potentially violent person and how to respond to such persons. Managers should be further trained on how to properly handle terminations since such acts often trigger violence.

DECREASED EFFICIENCY AND INCREASED RATES OF PHYSICAL AND MENTAL ILLNESS

Excessive amounts of stress can have debilitating health effects, such as ulcers, colitis, hypertension, headaches, lower back pain, carpel tunnel syndrome and cardiac conditions. Stressed workers may perform poorly, quit their jobs, suffer low morale, generate conflicts among coworkers, miss work, or exhibit indifference toward coworkers and customers. These stress-induced outcomes now cost U.S. businesses somewhere between $200 and $500 billion per year.

Stress can sometimes cause workers to turn to drugs and alcohol. The use of drugs and alcohol is pervasive in the United States. For instance, nearly 10 percent of all full-time employees use illicit drugs (primarily marijuana and cocaine), and another 10 percent are alcoholics. An increasing number of U.S. workers are taking some type of stimulant—beyond caffeine. A 1999 Drug Enforcement Agency survey estimated that at least 15 percent of United States adults methamphetamine. Substance had tried abuse costs U.S. employers an estimated $75 billion a year in terms of lost productivity, accidents, workers' compensation, health insurance claims, and theft of company property.

While most organizations are taking steps to keep their workplaces drug-free voluntarily, government contractors are required to take such steps. The 1988 Drug-Free Workplace Act states that government contractors must ensure a drug-free workplace by notifying employees about:

- the dangers of drug abuse in the workplace;

- its policy of maintaining a drug-free workplace;

- any available drug counseling, rehabilitation, and employee assistance programs; and

- the penalties that may be imposed upon employees for drug abuse violations occurring in the workplace.

Employers can combat substance abuse at the workplace by screening out applicants and discharging employees who have been identified as substance abusers. Substance abuse is most commonly detected through urine and blood tests. About two-thirds of all corporations presently require drug testing of current or future employees. Supervisors can also detect substance abuse by observing their employees' behavior. Some of the symptoms to look for are mood swings, slurred speech, flushed cheeks, frequent absences on Mondays and Fridays, missing deadlines, and overreacting to criticism.

Detecting substance abuse early can be quite useful to a company, as illustrated by the findings of a U.S. Postal Service study. The Postal Service tested 5,465 applicants for drugs, but did not use these results in hiring decisions. About 4,000 of these applicants were eventually hired. In a three-year follow-up, employees who tested positive had a 66 percent higher absenteeism rate and a 77 percent greater termination rate than those testing negative. The Postal Service now estimates that had it not hired the drug-positive group, it could have saved $150 million in absenteeism, rehiring, retraining, and injury compensation costs.

When dealing with current employees with drug problems, some employers take a rehabilitative approach: they help abusers overcome their problem through remedial counseling. Employee assistance programs (EAPs) employ mental health professionals (usually on a contract basis) to provide services to workers who are experiencing substance abuse or other personal problems. For example, the EAP at the Chase Manhattan Bank helps employees resolve problems of drug or alcohol abuse, child care, elder care, marital or family relationship concerns, emotional distress, anxiety, depression, or financial difficulties. Employees may seek help on a voluntary, confidential basis, or may be referred by a supervisor who suspects that the employee's declining job performance is being caused by personal problems.

Many companies currently use EAPs. The potential payoff of an EAP is evidenced by a study that found that every dollar spent on an EAP returned an estimated $3 to $5 in lower absenteeism and greater productivity.

Employers must develop written substance abuse policies that specify their approach to handling these problems. The policy should specify the prohibited behaviors and note the consequences employees will face if they break the rules. Such policies serve two purposes: (1) to act as a deterrent and (2) to establish a sound legal basis for taking punitive action (e.g., suspension or discharge).

EMPLOYEE WELLNESS

Employee wellness is a relatively new human resource management focus that seeks to eliminate certain debilitating health problems (e.g., cancer, heart disease, respiratory problems, hypertension) that can be caused by a person's poor lifestyle choices (e.g., smoking, poor nutrition, lack of exercise, obesity). Such health problems have become quite prevalent: Cancer, heart, and respiratory illnesses alone account for 61 percent of all hospital claims. These ailments can cause workplace problems such as absenteeism, turnover, lost productivity, and increased medical costs. For instance, people who have high blood pressure are 70 percent more likely than others to have medical claims of more than $5,750 per year, and the cost of medical claims for smokers is 22 percent higher than it is for nonsmokers.

Many organizations attempt to help employees improve or maintain their overall health by offering them employee wellness programs. Such programs provide employees with physical fitness facilities, on-site health screening, and programs to help them quit smoking, manage stress, and improve nutritional habits. Employee wellness programs can be quite effective. Research indicates that participation in a wellness program reduces both absenteeism and turnover, and increases productivity. A study conducted at Mesa Petroleum, for example, found that the productivity difference between participants and non-participants amounted to $700,000 in the first year, and $1.3 million in the second year.

If they are to work, wellness programs must successfully enlist "high-risk" individuals—those in greatest need of the program. Unfortunately, most employees who participate in wellness programs are those who fall into a low-risk category. Because at-risk individuals do not seek help, many employee wellness programs fail to meet their objectives. Employers must, then, find some way to motivate high-risk individuals to participate. Some companies offer positive inducements (e.g., cash bonuses) to individuals who participate; other companies focus their efforts on non-participants by imposing certain penalties. For example, they may increase insurance premium contributions of non-participants or raise their deductible levels.

Companies can help eliminate, or at least minimize, job stress. A firm can eliminate many sources of employee stress by implementing effective HRM practices. For instance, the implementation of effective selection and training procedures can help ensure that workers are properly suited to the demands of their jobs. Providing clearly written job descriptions can reduce worker uncertainty regarding job responsibilities. The use of effective performance appraisal systems can relieve stress by clarifying performance expectations. And the implementation of effective pay-for-performance programs can relieve stress by reducing worker uncertainty regarding rewards.

Unfortunately, companies cannot always eliminate all sources of job stress; some stress may be inherent in the job. For instance, some jobs are dangerous (e.g., logging, police work, firefighting), and some place the worker in demanding interpersonal situations (e.g., customer relations specialists). When job stresses cannot be relieved, the worker must learn to cope with them. A firm can help by offering employees stress counseling or by providing them the opportunity to "work off" their stress through physical exercise. Some of the organizational interventions described earlier, such as the use of EAPs and wellness programs, can be helpful in this regard.

SEE ALSO: Contingent Workers; Employee Assistance Programs; Human Resource Management

Joanie Sompayrac

FURTHER READING:

Asworth, Susan. "Low Morale, Other Issues Push Absences to Five-Year High." *Silicon Valley/San Jose Business Journal,* 4 March 2005.

Ball, Ron. "Workplace Stress Sucks $300 Billion Annually From Corporate Profits." *Customer Inter@ction Solutions* 23, no. 5 (November 2004): 62.

Cooper, Cary L., and Roy Payne. *Stress at Work.* John Wiley & Sons, 1978.

Frost, Peter J., Walter R. Nord, and Linda A. Krefting. *HRM Reality: Putting Competence in Context.* Prentice Hall, Upper Saddle River, New Jersey, 2002.

Gunch, D. "Employees Exercise to Prevent Injuries." *Personnel Journal,* July 1993, 58–62.

Jex, Steve M. *Stress and Job Performance: Theory, Research and Implications for Managerial Practice.* SAGE Publications, 1998.

Kleiman, L.S. *Human Resource Management: A Tool for Competitive Advantage.* Cincinnati: South-Western College Publishing, 2000.

Newell, Sue. *Creating the Healthy Organization: Well-Being, Diversity and Ethics at Work.* Thomson Learning, Cincinnati, 2002.

U.S. Occupational Safety and Health Administration. "Fact Sheet, 2002." Available from <http://www.osha.gov/OshDoc/data_General_Facts/factsheet-workplace-violence.pdf>.

U.S. Occupational Safety and Health Administration. "OSHA Home Page." Available from <www.osha.gov>.

Warshaw, Leon J. *Managing Stress: Addison-Wesley Series on Occupational Stress.* Reading, MA: 1979.

SUCCESSION PLANNING

Succession planning is a critical part of the human resources planning process. Human resources planning (HRP) is the process of having the right number of employees in the right positions in the organization at the time that they are needed. HRP involves forecasting, or predicting, the organization's needs for labor and supply of labor and then taking steps to move people into positions in which they are needed.

Succession planning is the systematic process of defining future management requirements and identifying candidates who best meet those requirements. Succession planning involves using the supply of labor within the organization for future staffing needs. With succession planning, the skills and abilities of current employees are assessed to see which future positions they may take within the organization when other employees leave their positions. Succession planning is typically used in higher-level organizational positions, such as executive-level positions. For instance, if a company predicts that its Chief Executive Officer will retire in the near future, the organization may begin looking months or even years in advance to determine which current employee might be capable of taking over the position of the CEO.

Succession planning is aimed at promoting individuals within the organization and thus makes use of internal selection. Internal selection, as opposed to hiring employees from outside the organization, has a number of benefits and drawbacks. With internal selection, the organization is aware of current employees' skills and abilities, and therefore is often better able to predict future performance than when hiring from the outside. Because of access to annual performance appraisals and the opinions of the employee's current managers, the company can have a fairly accurate assessment of the employee's work capabilities. Additionally, the organization has trained and socialized the employee for a period of time already, so the employee is likely to be better prepared for a position within the organization than someone who does not have that organizational experience. Finally, internal selection is often motivating to others in the organization—opportunities for advancement may encourage employees to perform at a high level.

Despite its many advantages, internal selection can also have some drawbacks. While the opportunities for advancement may be motivating to employees who believe that they can move up within the organization at a future date, those employees who feel that they have been passed over for promotion or are at a career plateau are likely to become discouraged and may choose to leave the organization. Having an employee who has been trained and socialized by the organization may limit the availability of skills, innovation, or creativity that may be found when new employees are brought in from the outside. Finally, internal selection still leaves a position at a lower level that must be staffed from the outside, which may not reduce recruitment and selection costs.

Many companies organize their management training and development efforts around succession planning. However, not all organizations take a formal approach to it, and instead do so very informally, using the opinions of managers as the basis for promotion, with little consideration of the actual requirements of future positions. Informal succession planning is likely to result in managers who are promoted due to criteria that are unrelated to performance, such as networking within and outside of the organization. Organizations would be better served by promoting managers who were able to successfully engage in human resource management activities and communicate with employees. Poor succession planning, such as just described, can have negative organizational consequences. Research indicates that poor preparation for advancement into managerial positions leaves almost one-third of new executives unable to meet company expectations for job performance. This may have negative repercussions for the newly promoted manager, the other employees, and the company's bottom line.

STEPS IN SUCCESSION PLANNING

There are several steps in effective succession planning: human resources planning, assessing needs, developing managers, and developing replacement charts and identifying career paths.

HUMAN RESOURCES PLANNING. Engaging in human resources planning by forecasting the organization's needs for employees at upper levels is the first step in succession planning. Some staffing needs can be anticipated, such as a known upcoming retirement or transfer. However, staffing needs are often less predictable—organizational members may leave for other companies, retire unexpectedly, or even die, resulting in a need to hire from outside or promote from within. The organization should do its best to have staff available to move up in the organization even when unexpected circumstances arise. Thus, accurate and timely forecasting is critical.

ASSESSING NEEDS AND DEVELOPING REPLACEMENT CHARTS. The second major step for succession planning is to define and measure individual qualifications needed for each targeted position. Such qualifications should be based on information from a recent job analysis. Once these qualifications are defined, employees must be evaluated on these qualifications to identify those with a high potential for promotion. This may involve assessing both the abilities and the career interests of employees. If a lower-level manager has excellent abilities but little interest in advancement within the organization, then development efforts aimed at promotion will be a poor investment.

To determine the level of abilities of employees within the organization, many of the same selection tools that are used for assessing external candidates can be used, such as general mental ability tests, personality tests, and assessment centers. However, when selecting internally, the company has an advantage in that it has much more data on internal candidates, such as records of an employee's career progress, experience, past performance, and self-reported interests regarding future career steps.

DEVELOPING MANAGERS. The third step of succession planning, which is actually ongoing throughout the process, is the development of the managers who are identified as having promotion potential. In order to prepare these lower-level managers for higher positions, they need to engage in development activities to improve their skills. Some of these activities may include:

- Job rotation through key executive positions. By working in different executive positions throughout the organization, the manager gains insight into the overall strategic workings of the company. Additionally, the performance of this manager at the executive level can be assessed before further promotions are awarded.

- Overseas assignments. Many multinational companies now include an overseas assignment as a way for managers to both learn more about the company and to test their potential for advancement within the company. Managers who are successful at leading an overseas branch of the company are assumed to be prepared to take an executive position in the home country.

- Education. Formal courses may improve managers' abilities to understand the financial and operational aspects of business management. Many companies will pay for managers to pursue degrees such as Masters in Business Administration (MBAs), which are expected to provide managers with knowledge that they could not otherwise gain from the company's own training and development programs.

- Performance-related training and development for current and future roles. Specific training and development provided by the company may be required for managers to excel in their current positions and to give them skills that they need in higher-level positions.

DEVELOPING REPLACEMENT CHARTS AND IDENTIFYING CAREER PATHS. In the final step of succession planning, the organization identifies a career path for each high-potential candidate—those who have the interest and ability to move upward in the organization. A career path is the typical set of positions that an employee might hold in the course of his or her career. In succession planning, it is a road map of positions and experiences designed to prepare the individual for an upper-level management position. Along with career paths, the organization should develop replacement charts, which indicate the availability of candidates and their readiness to step into the various management positions. These charts are depicted as organizational charts in which possible candidates to replacement others are listed in rank order for each management position. These rank orders are based on the candidates' potential scores, which are derived on the basis of their past performance, experience, and other relevant qualifications. The charts indicate who is currently ready for promotion and who needs further grooming to be prepared for an upper-level position.

PROBLEMS WITH SUCCESSION PLANNING

Succession planning is typically useful to the organization in its human resource planning, and when done properly, can be beneficial to organizational performance. However, there are potential problems associated with the use of succession planning: the crowned prince syndrome, the talent drain, and difficulties associated with managing large amounts of human resources information.

CROWNED PRINCE SYNDROME. The first potential problem in succession planning is the crowned prince syndrome, which occurs when upper management only considers for advancement, those employees who have become visible to them. In other words, rather than looking at a wider array of individual employees and their capabilities, upper management focuses only on one person—the "crowned prince." This person is often one who has been involved in high-profile projects, has a powerful and prominent mentor, or has networked well with organizational leaders. There are often employees throughout the organization who are capable of and interested in promotion who may be overlooked because of the more visible and obvious "crowned prince," who is likely to be promoted even if these other employees are available. Not only are performance problems a potential outcome of this syndrome, but also the motivation of current employees may suffer if they feel that their high performance has been overlooked. This may result in turnover of high quality employees who have been overlooked for promotion.

TALENT DRAIN. The talent drain is the second potential problem that may occur in succession planning. Because upper management must identify only a small group of managers to receive training and development for promotion, those managers who are not assigned to development activities may feel overlooked

and therefore leave the organization. This turnover may reduce the number of talented managers that the organization has at the lower and middle levels of the hierarchy. Exacerbating this problem is that these talented managers may work for a competing firm or start their own business, thus creating increased competition for their former company.

MANAGING HUMAN RESOURCE INFORMATION. The final problem that can occur in succession planning is the concern with managing large amounts of human resources information. Because succession planning requires retention of a great deal of information, it is typically best to store and manage it on a computer. Attempting to maintain such records by hand may prove daunting. Even on the computer, identifying and evaluating many years' worth of information about employees' performance and experiences may be difficult. Add to that the challenges of comparing distinct records of performance to judge promotion capability, and this information overload is likely to increase the difficulty of successful succession planning.

Succession planning, which is identifying and preparing managers for future promotions within the organization is one element of successful human resource planning. Unfortunately, many organizations do a poor job of succession planning. Even when it is done properly, succession planning has some potential problems that can harm employee motivation and the company's bottom line. Effective succession planning, however, is likely to improve overall firm performance and to reward and motivate employees within the organization.

SEE ALSO: Employee Screening and Selection; Entrepreneurship; Human Resource Information Systems; Human Resource Management; Management and Executive Development

Marcia J. Simmering

FURTHER READING:

Dessler, Gary. *Human Resource Management*. 8th edition. Upper Saddle River, NJ: Prentice Hall, 2000.

Goldstein, Irwin L, and J. Kevin Ford. *Training in Organizations: Needs Assessment, Evaluation, and Development*. 4th edition. Belmont, CA: Wadsworth/Thomson Learning, 2002.

Gomez-Mejia, Luis R., David B. Balkin, and Robert L. Cardy. *Managing Human Resources*. 4th ed. Upper Saddle River, NJ: Prentice Hall, 2004.

Noe, Raymond A. *Employee Training and Development*. Boston, MA: Irwin/McGraw-Hill, 1999.

Noe, Raymond A., John R. Hollenbeck, Barry Gerhart, and Patrick M. Wright. *Human Resource Management: Gaining a Competitive Advantage*. 5th edition. Boston, MA: McGraw-Hill/Irwin, 2006.

SUPPLY CHAIN MANAGEMENT

Supply chain management (SCM) is a broadened management focus that considers the combined impact of all the companies involved in the production of goods and services, from suppliers to manufacturers to wholesalers to retailers to final consumers and beyond to disposal and recycling. This approach to managing production and logistics networks assumes all companies involved in the process of delivering goods to consumers are part of a network, pipeline, or supply chain. It encompasses everything required to satisfy customers and includes determining which products they will buy, how to produce them, and how to deliver them. The supply chain philosophy ensures that customers receive the right products at the right time at an acceptable price and at the desired location.

Increasing competition, complexity, and geographical scope in the business world have led to this broadened scope and continuing improvements in the capabilities of the personal computer have made the optimization of supply chain performance possible. Electronic mail and the Internet have revolutionized communication and data exchange, facilitating the necessary flow of information between the companies in the supply chain.

Companies that practice supply chain management report significant cost and cycle time reductions. For example, Wal-Mart Stores Inc. announced increases in inventory turns, decreases in out-of-stock occurrences, and a replenishment cycle that has moved from weeks to days to hours.

A fundamental premise of supply chain management is to view the network of facilities, processes, and people that procure raw materials, transform them into products, and ultimately distribute them to the customer as an integrated chain, rather than a group of separate, but somewhat interrelated, tasks. The importance of this integration cannot be overstated because the links of the chain are the key to achieving the goal. Every company has a supply chain, but not every company manages their supply chain for strategic advantage.

While easy to understand in theory, the chain management becomes more complex the larger the company and its range of products, and the more international the locations of its suppliers, customers, and distribution facilities. Supply chain management is also complex because companies may be part of several pipelines at the same time. A manufacturer of synthetic rubber, for example, can at the same time be part of the supply chains for tires, mechanical goods, industrial products, shoe materials and footwear, aircraft parts, and rubberized textiles.

LINKS WITHIN THE SUPPLY CHAIN

With supply chain management, information, systems, processes, efforts, and ideas are integrated across all functions of the entire supply chain. Supply chains become more complex as goods flow from more than one supplier to more than one manufacturing and distribution site. The possibility of outside sources for functions like assembly and packaging are also options in the chain.

The basic tasks of a company do not change, regardless of whether or not it practices supply chain management. Suppliers are still required to supply material, manufacturing still manufactures, distribution still distributes, and customers still purchase. All of the traditional functions of a company still take place. The ultimate difference in a company that manages its supply chain is their focus shifts from what goes on inside each of the links, to include the connections between the links.

A company practicing effective supply chain management also recognizes that the chain has connections that extend beyond the traditional boundaries of the organization. Managing the connections is where the integration of the supply chain begins. Any improvement in or disruption to the supply chain linkages affects the entire chain. The cumulative supply chain effect of uncertainty can be seen in this example. Suppose a manufacturer of integrated circuit boards receives a shipment of poor quality silicon. Because the manufacturer is dependent on its supplier for timely shipments, the poor quality lot results in a shipment delay to one of its customers. The computer manufacturer is forced to shut down its line because component circuit boards are not available. As a result, computer shipments to retailers are late. Finally, the customer goes to the retailer to purchase a new computer but is unable to find the desired brand. Frustrated, the customer decides to buy the product of a competitor. Consider too, the timing involved in this process. Because of production and transportation lead times, the actual receipt of the poor quality silicon probably occurred several months before the customer made a computer purchase.

A wide variety of events occurs in the supply chain that is largely unpredictable. Suppliers can make early or late deliveries. Customers can increase, decrease, or even cancel orders. New customers can place large orders. Machines or trucks can break down. Employees can get sick, go on strike, and quit. Supplier shipments or manufactured products can have quality problems. In the past, companies prepared for uncertainty and improved their levels of customer satisfaction by allowing inventory levels to rise. This is no longer an acceptable solution. High inventories translate to increased carrying costs and risks of obsolescence that can limit a company's flexibility.

Throughout the supply chain, inventory is traditionally created and held at many locations. Any time a portion of that inventory can be reduced or eliminated, the company decreases costs and increases profitability. Shortening the length of time it takes to move a product from one link of the chain to the next also shortens the cycle time of the entire chain and thereby increases competitiveness and customer satisfaction.

IMPORTANCE OF CHAIN VISIBILITY

SCM provides needed visibility along the chain to improve performance. Without visibility up and down the supply chain an effect known as the "bullwhip" can result. In reviewing the demand patterns at various points in their supply chain, Procter & Gamble (P&G) noticed that while the consumers, or in this case the babies, consumed diapers at a steady rate, the demand order variability in the supply chain was amplified as it moved up the supply chain. Without being able to see the sales of its product at the distribution channel stage, they had to rely on sales orders from resellers to make product forecasts, plan capacity, control inventory, and schedule production. This lack of visibility resulted in excessive inventory, inaccurate forecasts, excessive or constrained capacity, and reduced customer service levels. Each link in the supply chain stockpiled inventory to counteract the effects of demand uncertainty and variability. Various studies have shown that these inventory stockpiles can equal as much as 100 days' supply and by considering the effect on raw materials, the total chain could contain more than a year's supply of inventory.

Companies like P&G, Dell Computer, Hewlett-Packard, Campbell Soup, M&M/Mars, Nestlé, Quaker Oats, and many others have been able to control the bullwhip effect. Some of the methods used include innovative information flow for forecasting demand, revised price structures, or developing strategies to allow smaller batch sizes, while still maximizing transportation efficiency. By understanding the effects of supply chain integration, visibility and information, these companies were able to develop strategies that enabled them to overcome many problems.

SCM BENEFITS

In addition to helping to create an efficient, integrated company, supply chain management also plays a large part in reducing costs. A study by the A.T. Kearney management consulting company estimates that supply chain costs can represent more that eighty percent of the cost structure in a typical manufacturing company. These numbers indicate that even slight improvement in the process eventually can translate into millions of dollars on the bottom line. These costs include lost sales due to poor customer service or out of stock retail products. For every dollar of inventory in a system, there are one to two dollars of hidden supply chain costs: working capital costs, asset costs, delivery costs, write downs and so on. Leaner inventories free up a large amount of capital.

Depending on the industry, companies leading in supply chain performance achieve savings equal to three to seven percent of revenues compared with their median performing peers. One Efficient Consumer Response Study, sponsored by the Food Marketing Institute, estimated that forty two days could be removed from the typical grocery supply chain, freeing up $30 billion in current costs, and reducing inventories by forty-one percent.

REQUIREMENTS OF SCM

CUSTOMER FOCUS. All sources agree the fundamental focus of supply chain management begins by understanding the customer, their values, and requirements. This includes internal customers of the organization and the final customer as well. Companies must seek to know exactly what the customer expects from the product or service and must then focus their efforts on meeting these expectations. The process of suppliers must be aligned with the buying process of the customer. Even performance measurements must be customer driven, because the behavior of the final customer ultimately controls the behavior of the entire supply chain.

INFORMATION FLOW. Another requirement is increased information flow. Companies must invest in the technology that will provide access to greater amounts of timely information. Information makes it possible to move to more instantaneous merchandise replenishment and allow all parties in the chain to respond quickly to all changes. Information facilitates the decisions of the supply chain such as evaluation and exploration of alternatives. Information flow is key to the visibility of the product as it flows through the supply chain and is needed at every stage of the customer order. Improving the intelligence of where products are in the chain also improves inventory management and customer service capabilities. Issues of trust and security are fundamental to information integration. Many organizations are successfully dealing with these issues through the development of partnering relationships.

EMPLOYEE AND MANAGEMENT SUPPORT. As partners in the supply chain must also be highly flexible, supply chain strategies often require changes in processes and traditional roles. All members of the supply chain must be open to new methods and ideas. The flexibility and change required is often difficult for organizations and their employees. It is however, the ability to embrace necessary changes that will position a company to take advantage of the benefits of supply chain management. Because the supply chain is a dynamic entity, businesses are advised to organize for change. They must anticipate resistance and be prepared to deal with it. Training in the concepts of supply chain management will aid in this effort. Also, as with any organization change, the new ideas must be supported and embraced by all levels of management.

MEASUREMENT. Often companies undertake ways to improve themselves without also thinking about how to measure whether or not they have been successful. Performance measurement must consider the entire supply chain and be related to the effect on the ultimate goal of customer satisfaction. Therefore the final concept of supply chain management is ensuring measurement techniques are adequately considered during the implementation of supply chain management techniques.

ACHIEVING THE GOALS OF SUPPLY CHAIN MANAGEMENT

Methods being used to achieve the goals of supply chain management can be divided into two categories. Some methods seek to achieve the goals through improving the processes within the links of the chain. There are also methods that seek to achieve the goals by changing the roles or functions of the chain.

The methods used to improve the process include modeling various alternatives, effective measurement, improved forecasting, designing for the supply chain, cross-docking inventories, direct store delivery, and electronic data interchange (EDI) technology. Direct store delivery methods bypass the distribution center. Products using direct store delivery include bakeries, cosmetics, snack foods, and other items where product freshness or quick replenishment is required. Cross-docking is a process that keeps products from coming to rest as inventory in a distribution center. Products arrive at the center and are immediately off loaded, moved, and immediately reloaded on waiting delivery trucks.

EDI technology is the electronic exchange of information between the computer systems of two or more companies. It is used to process transactions like order entry, order confirmation, order changes, invoicing, and pre-shipment notices. The EDI movement was started by big retailers like Wal-Mart, Kmart, and Target. To do business with some of these large customers, EDI processing is a requirement. EDI delivers results by facilitating the constant and rapid exchange of information between companies. Customer order, invoice, and other information that would previously require hours of data entry can be done in minutes.

Point of sale data can be transmitted in a matter of minutes or hours instead of weeks.

Methods that use changing roles include postponement strategies, vendor managed inventory, and supplier integration. Postponement strategies delay the differentiation of products in order to gain flexibility to respond to changing customer needs. Product inventory is held in a generic form so that as specific demand becomes known, the product can be finished and shipped in a timely manner. Vendor managed inventory and continuous replenishment programs are ways in which organizations are reaching beyond their boundaries and integrating their efforts with suppliers and customers. Point of sale data is transferred from customer to supplier in real time so that automatic replenishments can occur. Companies can even surrender the responsibility for managing inventory to some of their suppliers. Supplier integration moves beyond partnering with suppliers and focuses on aligning with all critical suppliers the supply chain.

SCOR

The supply chain operations reference (SCOR) model is a process reference model, developed in 1996 by the Supply-Chain Council, as a cross-industry diagnostic, benchmarking, and process improvement tool for supply chain management. SCOR provides a complete set of supply chain performance metrics, industry best practices, and enabling systems' functionality that allows firms to thorough analyze all aspects of their current supply chain. A number of notable firms, such as IBM, Intel, 3M, and Siemens have used the model successfully.

The model separates supply chain operations into five distinct processes: plan, source, make, deliver, and return. Within these are three levels of process detail. Level I deals with process types, Level II is the configuration level and deals with process categories, and Level III is the process element level. The SCOR model endorses twelve performance metrics. The Levels II and III metrics are keys to the Level I metrics that fall within the five process categories. Empirical research by Archie Lockamy III and Kevin McCormack found while some of the practices found in the model did not have expected degree of impact, many of the practices did result in significant supply chain performance improvements.

SCM AND THE ENVIRONMENT

As environmental practices increase in importance supply chain strategies will do the same. Firms finding that release of waste into the biophysical environment is becoming more difficult or even impossible are saddled with a new responsibility, waste control.

This may have far-reaching implications for supply chain management. When source reduction is impossible or incomplete, the firm must deal with returned products as well as disassembly, recycling, reuse, repairwork or remanufacturing, all of which mean more movement of material. The supply chain is then extended beyond the final consumer to become a "reverse supply chain" (note that an earlier SCOR model contained only four processes; the "return" process was later added).

THE FUTURE

Supply chain management is an evolving process. It is much like the philosophies of total quality management (TQM) or business process reengineering in that there is no stopping point. Emerging technologies and successful supply chain management techniques used by companies today are the foundation of future improvements in techniques and technologies. Supply chain management can provide great payoffs in cost and efficiency to the organization.

Enabled with improving technology and a broader view of the organization, supply chain management addresses the issues of complexity and competition by exploiting and enhancing the chain to provide strategic, financial, and competitive advantage.

SEE ALSO: Distribution and Distribution Requirements Planning; Electronic Data Interchange and Electronic Funds Transfer; Reverse Supply Chain Logistics

Marilyn M. Helms
Revised by R. Anthony Inman

FURTHER READING:

Gunasekaran, A. and E.W.T. Ngai. "Virtual Supply-Chain Management." *Production Planning & Control* 15, no. 6 (2004): 584–595.

Handfield, Robert, Robert Sroufe, and Steven Walton. "Integrating Environmental Management and Supply Chain Strategies." *Business Strategy and the Environment* 14, no. 1 (2005): 1–18.

Huan, Samuel H., Sunil K. Sheoran, and Ge Wang. "A Review and Analysis of Supply Chain Operations Reference (SCOR) Model." *Supply Chain Management: An International Journal* 9, no. 1 (2004): 23–29.

Kannan, Vijay R., and Keah Choon Tan. "Just-In-Time, Total Quality Management, and Supply Chain Management: Understanding Their Linkages and Impact of Business Performance." *Omega* 33, no. 2 (2005): 153.

Lockamy, Archie, III, and Kevin McCormack. "Linking SCOR Planning Practices to Supply Chain Performance: An Exploratory Study." *International Journal of Operations & Production Management* 24, no. 11/12 (2004): 1192–1218.

Nagurney, Anna, and Fuminori Toyasaki. "Reverse Supply Chain Management and Electronic Waste Recycling: A Multitiered Network Equilibrium Framework for E-cycling."

Transportation Research. Part E, Logistics & Transportation Review 41E, no. 1 (2005).

New, Steve, and Roy Westbrook, eds. *Understanding Supply Chains: Concepts, Critiques & Futures.* Oxford University Press, 2004.

Supply Chain Council Website. Available from <www.supply-chain.org>.

Walker, William T. *Supply Chain Architecture.* Boca Raton: CRC Press, 2005.

Wisner, Joel D., G. Keong Leong, and Keah-Choon Tan. *Principles of Supply Chain Management: A Balanced Approach.* Mason, OH: Thomson South-Western, 2005.

SWEATSHOPS

Sweatshops are work environments that possess three major characteristics—long hours, low pay, and unsafe or unhealthy working conditions. Sweatshops have been a factor in the production of goods around the world for centuries, but the globalization of business has led increasing numbers of major corporations to take advantage of low-cost sweatshop labor in developing countries. Recent examples of sweatshop conditions in the garment industry have caused an international outcry by labor leaders, activists, and government officials. Although manufacturers tend to deny it, sweatshops still exist, even in the United States.

THE HISTORY OF SWEATSHOPS

One of the earliest examples of a sweatshop was in the crude textile mills of Ecuador. Spanish conquerors put the native population to work in sweatshop conditions in the manufacture of cloth, rough garments, and assorted textile goods. The use of the term is more recently traced to working conditions in England's emerging manufacturing industries, where women and children sweated in jobs performed under horrid conditions-the work being monotonous, the hours long, and the pay miserably low. The British government established a Select Committee of the House of Lords on the Sweating System in 1889, thus publicly exposing the conditions for the first time. With massive immigration into the United States, especially beginning in the late 1880s, sweatshops became common in American cities on the east coast.

Southern and eastern European immigrants were easy prey for manufacturers who paid low wages and provided poor working conditions in factories. In many instances, the newly arrived immigrants were glad to have these sweating jobs at any wage, no matter how low. The situation in many of the new industries was ripe for sweatshops to develop. Social and economic conditions in most cities produced a large population from which to find workers willing to accept any wage and management systems that neglected the workers, thus removing any consideration of the human factor in manufacturing. Generally, workers lacked access to the kind of knowledge and resources that would enable them to overcome the impossible working conditions, while governments, both local and national, were unwilling to intervene on their behalf. Other characteristics of sweatshops included overcrowding, lack of sanitary conditions, no worker breaks or relief, demands to complete a task within a limited period of time, and-as important to the continuance of the sweatshop-the total lack of job security.

EFFORTS TO IMPROVE SWEATSHOPS

Initial efforts to correct or improve sweatshops in the United States began in 1884 with legislation in the state of New York to eliminate the production of tobacco products in homes-a practice common in the cigar industry. Similar state labor laws proved generally ineffective before trade unions were able to bring about slight relief. But it took federal minimum wage and maximum-hours legislation in 1938 before sweatshops began to disappear.

Making matters worse for the workers, there were few if any advocates for improving sweatshop conditions. The immigrants had virtually no voice in management or government. Many could not read or write-much less read and write in English-and were essentially pawns of often unscrupulous, profit-driven manufacturers. Educational opportunities were seldom available, and moving up the corporate ladder was not an option.

Jacob Riis did much to call attention to the living conditions of many of these workers in 1903 with the publication of *How the Other Half Lives,* a photojournalistic account of the living conditions in New York's tenements. Although powerful, Riis's photographs did little to address working conditions in U.S. sweatshops. In the eighth edition of their classic study on the United States working class, *Labor Problems: A Text Book,* published in 1912, Thomas S. Adams and Helen Sumner outlined the three conditions in sweatshops and added a disturbing fourth-danger to the consumer's health from using goods manufactured in sweatshops. Few American consumers took notice, but union involvement in improving working conditions was quite evident beginning in the 1910s, especially in the garment industry.

Another industry where sweatshop conditions existed (and still do) was the agricultural industry, which employs a great many immigrants (both legal and illegal) for harvesting or picking fruits and vegetables. The working conditions included long daylight hours under a hot California or Florida sun with few or no breaks. Wages were just as miserable and women and children were especially abused. These workers seldom had the means or education to improve their plight, and all desperately needed the money. Once again unions attempted to bring some relief to the workers, and labor battles, including fights and even open warfare, were all too frequent.

SWEATSHOPS IN MODERN INDUSTRY

Sweatshops have not been abolished to this day, as is evident in numerous recent examples in the apparel industry that have brought national attention and government reaction to the issue. Garment manufacturers found new ways to finish goods in factories outside the United States, where labor costs were miniscule but sweatshops flourished. In countries in South and Central America and Asia, such companies found a ready labor supply where wage expectations were low and the sweatshop thrived. Companies like The Gap, Liz Claiborne, Kathie Lee Gifford, Nike, and Wal-Mart all came under criticism for marketing goods produced in sweatshops.

National attention was directed at these and other companies in the apparel industry through media outlets, and consumers were sometimes advised not to purchase certain brand names. Advocacy groups, particularly vibrant among college students (who got their start by refusing to buy college or university logo merchandise produced in sweatshops), organize consumer awareness of sweatshop conditions and attempt to pressure companies into ceasing their sweatshop-labor practices. A site was mounted on the Internet by Sweatshop Watc—a coalition of labor, community, civil rights, immigrant, and women's organizations (www.sweatshopwatch.com)—to further spread awareness and coalesce activist projects.

The U.S. government has lent its efforts toward eliminating the problem, proposing legislation aimed at ending the use of sweatshop labor in foreign countries. However, the most devastating blow to companies marketing sweatshop goods came in the form of lawsuits filed by the dozens.

Despite the concentrated efforts, negative publicity, and legislative action, the proliferation of sweatshops continues. Representatives of the New York-based National Labor Committee traveled to El Salvador during 1998 to see firsthand local working conditions. While visiting a factory that made jackets for Liz Claiborne, the group found workers reporting fifteen-hour days, two daily bathroom breaks, and appalling working conditions-all for sixty cents an hour. Women were routinely tested for pregnancy and fired if pregnant. Protestors were fired and overtime was enforced. Suspensions without pay were common. A jacket selling for $198 was manufactured for eight-four cents (leaving labor costs as 0.4 percent of the retail price). If sweatshops are illegal in the United States, critics ask, why are U.S. firms neglecting such offshore conditions among their suppliers of finished goods?

Does a remedy exist? In the United States, the courts are a possible avenue of relief. In May 1999, a Los Angeles court issued subpoenas to seventeen U.S. firms-including The Gap, Wal-Mart, Sears, Tommy Hilfiger, Jones Apparel Group, and Warnaco-seeking over one billion dollars in damages over apparel goods reportedly manufactured in Siapan sweatshops. In February 1999, U.S. garment firms announced support of another one billion dollar suit against sweatshop factories in the Mariana Islands.

Congress also joined the fight; while a 1997 bill aimed at curbing sweatshops in the garment industry failed, a 1998 House hearing was held to discourage the use of sweatshop labor in the garment industry. In early 1999, a presidential task force finally agreed on a foreign factory monitoring system. The task force-which included representatives of apparel manufacturers, labor unions, and human rights organizations-set forth a voluntary workplace code of conduct that included provisions prohibiting forced labor, harassment or abuse of workers, and discrimination, and provisions supporting worker rights to organize and participate in collective bargaining, minimum wage and benefit guarantees, and a safe and healthy work environment. While the Clinton administration and industry leaders praised the agreement as historic, some people criticized it for making participation voluntary and not addressing the need for workers to receive a basic living wage.

But the problem of sweatshops is likely to deepen. Structural adjustment programs, which are often imposed on developing countries by major financial institutions like the International Monetary Fund, are among the hallmarks of the emerging global economy. These programs, which derive from liberal capitalist economic theories, can act indirectly as barriers against labor laws and labor organization (under the logic that these constitute threats to free trade) while deregulating the flow of foreign investment. Hence, the prevailing social and economic climate makes sweatshop labor not only possible, but attractive (and for some industries, almost necessary).

In addition, the governments of many developing nations are reluctant to enforce strong worker-protection laws. They view cheap labor as one of the major assets they can offer to attract investment by multinational companies, which creates jobs and provides capital for development. These governments argue that all of the major developed nations limited worker rights early in their economic histories, and that they should be allowed to do so as well, with the goal of eventually achieving the prosperity that would enable them to eliminate sweatshops. They also claim that sweatshops often provide the best wages and working conditions available to workers in the developing world, who might otherwise be condemned to prostitution, begging, or subsistence farming.

Meanwhile, popular organizing against sweatshop labor is also gaining momentum. These groups try to capitalize on the knowledge that, if the general public were aware of the conditions in which certain consumer items were produced, they would refrain from buying them. Improved global communications, using such tools as satellite and the Internet, make it easy to disseminate information about the business activities of multinational corporations in developing nations. Activists hope that consumer pressure will force companies to become more socially responsible or face devastating negative publicity, like that experienced by Nike and The Gap.

Co-op America, sponsor of the "No Sweat!" program to end sweatshop labor, recommends that individuals and businesses take the following steps to aid the cause: organize local community groups to support a sweatshop-free purchasing law in local or state government; investigate companies with which you do business and insist they maintain good records on labor issues; use your clout as a shareholder to encourage companies to treat employees fairly; and purchase union-made, local, and fair-trade approved goods. Businesses can submit to workplace monitoring under programs run by the Fair Labor Association, Social Accountability International, or Worldwide Responsible Apparel Production.

SEE ALSO: Ethics; Globalization; International Management; Stress

Boyd Childress
Revised by Laurie Collier Hillstrom

FURTHER READING:

Balko, Radley. "Sweatshops and Globalization." A World Connected. Available from <http://www.aworldconnected.org>.

Barnes, Edward. "Slaves of New York." *Time,* 2 November 1998, 72–75.

Co-op America. "Ten Ways to End Sweatshops." Available from <http://www.sweatshops.org/tenways.html>.

Esbenshade, Jill. *Monitoring Sweatshops: Workers, Consumers, and the Global Apparel Industry.* Philadelphia: Temple University Press, 2004.

Greathead, Scott. "Making It Right: Sweatshops, Ethics, and Retailer Responsibility." *Chain Store Age,* May 2002.

Hartman, Laura P., ed. *Rising Above Sweatshops: Innovative Approaches to Global Labor Challenges.* New York: Praeger, 2003.

Kernaghan, Charles. "Sweatshop Blues: Companies Love Misery." *Dollars & Sense,* March-April 1999, 18–21.

"A World of Sweatshops." *Business Week,* 6 November 2000.

SYNERGY

Synergy, also known as synergism, refers to the combined effects produced by two or more parts, elements, or individuals. Simply stated, synergy results when the whole is greater than the sum of the parts. For example, two people can move a heavy load more easily than the two working individually can each move their half of the load. Synergy can be a positive or negative outcome of combined efforts.

According to the *American Heritage Dictionary,* the term "synergy" is derived from the Greek word *sunergos,* meaning "working together." Positive synergy is sometimes called the 2 + 2 = 5 effect. Operating independently, each subsystem can produce two units of output. However, by combining their efforts and working together effectively, the two subsystems can produce five units of output.

Negative synergy can be called the 2 + 2 = 3 effect. Again, individuals operating alone can each produce two units of output. However, with negative synergy, the combination of their efforts results in less output than what they would have achieved if they had each worked alone. Negative synergy can result from inefficient committees, business units that lack strategic fit, and from other poorly functioning joint efforts.

HISTORY OF SYNERGY

Synergy has origins as a theological term describing the cooperation of human effort with divine will. In recent years the term has most often been used in association with systems theory. Systems theory, as applied to biology and the physical sciences, describes the interdependence of various parts of an organism, such as the human body. The human body, as a system, is comprised of a set of interrelated subsystems, including the brain, skeleton, muscles, and others. To fully understand the larger system, one must examine the subsystems and the interrelationships. Systems theory was one of the first management theories to explicitly state that changing one of the subsystems could have an impact on the total system. Synergy was developed as a measure of the effectiveness of the joint efforts of various subsystems. Discussions of synergy also figure in medical literature, such as in research that addresses how the effects of medication on individuals are magnified when combined with a special diet or exercise.

INDIVIDUALS AND SYNERGY

One way to observe synergy in an organization is to observe the combined efforts of individuals working together. Synergy can result from the efforts of people serving on committees or teams. By combining their knowledge, insights, and ideas, groups often make better decisions than would have been made by the group members acting independently. Positive synergy resulting from group decisions may well include the generation of more ideas, more creative solutions, increased acceptance of the decision by group members, and increased opportunity for the expression of diverse opinions. Much of the current interest in teams and team building is an effort to achieve positive synergy through the combined efforts of team members.

Negative synergy occurs in groups, committees, and other joint efforts for a number of reasons. Groups commonly experience negative synergy because group decisions are often reached more slowly, and thus may be more expensive to make than individual decisions. The opportunity costs for having a group of high-paid executives spend an afternoon in a meeting rather than in more productive endeavors can be quite high. Negative synergy can also occur in group decisions if an individual is allowed to dominate and control the group decision. Also, groupthink—the pressure to conform—may cause the group to strive for harmony instead of evaluating information and alternative courses of action honestly and objectively.

SYNERGY AT THE ORGANIZATION LEVEL

Organizations strive to achieve positive synergy or strategic fit by combining multiple products, business lines, or markets. One way to achieve positive synergy is by acquiring related products, so that sales representatives can sell numerous products during one sales call. Rather than having two representatives make two sales calls to a potential customer, one sales representative can offer the broader mix of products.

Mergers and acquisitions are corporate-level strategies designed to achieve positive synergy. The 2004 acquisition of AT&T Wireless by Cingular was an effort to create customer benefits and growth prospects that neither company could have achieved on its own—offering better coverage, improved quality and reliability, and a wide array of innovative services for consumers.

Negative synergy is also possible at the corporate level. Downsizing and the divestiture of businesses is in part the result of negative synergy. For instance, Kimberly-Clark Corporation set out to sharpen its emphasis on consumer and health care products by divesting its tiny interests in business paper and pulp production. According to the company, the removal of the pulp mill will enhance operational flexibility and eliminate distraction on periphery units, thus allowing the corporation to concentrate on a single, core business activity.

The intended result of many business decisions is positive synergy. Managers expect that combining employees into teams or broadening the firm's product or market mix will result in a higher level of performance. However, the mere combination of people or business elements does not necessarily lead to better outcomes, and the resulting lack of harmony or coordination can lead to negative synergy.

SEE ALSO: Mergers and Acquisitions; Organizational Structure; Teams and Teamwork

Debbie D. DuFrene

FURTHER READING:

"Cingular Wins AT&T Wireless Bid." CNN.com. Available from <http://www.cnn.com/2004/BUSINESS/02/17/att.wireless/>.

Corning, P.A. "Synergy and Self-organization in the Evolution of Complex Systems." *Systems Research* 12, no. 2 (1995): 89–121.

Gupta, D., and Y. Gerchak. "Quantifying Operational Synergies in a Merger/Acquisition." *Management Science* 48, no. 4 (2002): 517–33.

Kreps, G.L. *Organizational Communication.* 2nd ed. Boston: Addison-Wesley, 1989.

Lehman, C.M., and D.D. DuFrene. *Business Communication.* 14th ed. Mason, OH: Thomson/South-Western, 2005.

Millman, G.J. "Desperately Seeking Synergy." *Financial Executive* 16, no. 2 (March 2000): 12.

Sikora, M. "IRS Hasn't Got Time for Pain of Forced Divestiture: Say Goodbye to Favorable Tax Treatment of Sell-offs Executed to Address Regulatory Objections to a Deal." *Mergers & Acquisitions: The Dealmaker's Journal,* 1 April 2004.

SYSTEMS ANALYSIS

Systems analysis is the process of examining a business situation for the purpose of developing a system solution to a problem or devising improvements to such a situation. Before the development of any system can begin, a project proposal is prepared by the users of the potential system and/or by systems analysts and submitted to an appropriate managerial structure within the organization.

PROJECT PROPOSAL

The project proposal is the attempt to respond to or take advantage of a particular situation and is an essential element for correctly launching the system analysis. Although there are no hard and fast rules as to the form and content of the project proposal, the proposal should address the following points:

- The specifics of the business situation or problem.
- The significance of the problem to the organization.
- Alternative solutions.
- The possible use of computer information systems to solve the problem.
- The various people interested in or possessing knowledge relevant to the problem.

System projects that are to be shared by a number of departments and users are usually approved by a committee rather than an individual. A project proposal is submitted to a committee that determines the merits of the proposal and decides whether or not to approve it. The committee is made up of people from various functional areas of the organization who have an interest in the operation and information of the proposed system.

THE SYSTEMS DEVELOPMENT LIFE CYCLE

The systems development life cycle (SDLC) describes a set of steps that produces a new computer information system. The SDLC is a problem-solving process. Each step in the process delineates a number of activities. Performing these activities in the order prescribed by the SDLC will bring about a solution to the business situation. The SDLC process consists of the following phases:

1. Preliminary investigation—the problem is defined and investigated.
2. Requirements definition—the specifics of the current system as well as the requirements of the proposed new system are studied and defined.
3. Systems design—a general design is developed with the purpose of planning for the construction of the new system.
4. Systems development—the new system is created.
5. System installation—the current operation is converted to run on the new system.

6. Systems evaluation and monitoring—the newly operational system is evaluated and monitored for the purpose of enhancing its performance and adding value to its functions.

7. Looping back from a later phase to an earlier one may occur if the need arises.

Each phase has a distinct set of unique development activities. Some of these activities may span more than one phase. The management activity tends to be similar among all phases.

The SDLC is not standardized and may be unique to a given organization. In other words, the names and number of phases may differ from one SDLC to the next. However, the SDLC discussed here is, to a large extent, representative of what is typically adopted by organizations.

At each phase certain activities are performed; the results of these activities are documented in a report identified with that phase. Management reviews the results of the phase and determines if the project is to proceed to the next phase.

The first two phases of the SDLC process constitute the systems-analysis function of a business situation. The following discussion will concentrate on phase one (Preliminary Investigation) and phase two (Requirements Definition) of the outlined SDLC process.

PRELIMINARY INVESTIGATION

The first phase of the systems development life cycle is preliminary investigation. Due to limited resources an organization can undertake only those projects that are critical to its mission, goals, and objectives. Therefore, the goal of preliminary investigation is simply to identify and select a project for development from among all the projects that are under consideration. Organizations may differ in how they identify and select projects for development. Some organizations have a formal planning process that is carried out by a steering committee or a task force made up of senior managers. Such a committee or task force identifies and assesses possible computer information systems projects that the organization should consider for development. Other organizations operate in an ad hoc fashion to identify and select potential projects. Regardless of the method used, and after all potential projects have been identified, only those projects with the greatest promise for the well-being of the organization, given available resources, are selected for development.

The objective of the systems-investigation phase is to answer the following questions: What is the business problem? Is it a problem or an opportunity? What are the major causes of the problem? Can the problem be solved by improving the current information system? Is a new information system needed? Is this a feasible information system solution to this problem?

The preliminary-investigation phase sets the stage for gathering information about the current problem and the existing information system. This information is then used in studying the feasibility of possible information systems solutions.

It is important to note that the source of the project has a great deal to do with its scope and content. For example, a project that is proposed by top management usually has a broad strategic focus. A steering committee proposal might have a focus that covers a cross-function of the organization. Projects advanced by an individual, a group of individuals, or a department may have a narrower focus.

A variety of criteria can be used within an organization for classifying and ranking potential projects. For planning purposes, the systems analyst—with the assistance of the stakeholders of the proposed project—collects information about the project. This information has a broad range and focuses on understanding the project size, costs, and potential benefits. This information is then analyzed and summarized in a document that is then used in conjunction with documents about other projects in order to review and compare all possible projects. Each of these possible projects is assessed using multiple criteria to determine feasibility.

FEASIBILITY STUDY

The feasibility study investigates the problem and the information needs of the stakeholders. It seeks to determine the resources required to provide an information systems solution, the cost and benefits of such a solution, and the feasibility of such a solution. The analyst conducting the study gathers information using a variety of methods, the most popular of which are:

- Interviewing users, employees, managers, and customers.

- Developing and administering questionnaires to interested stakeholders, such as potential users of the information system.

- Observing or monitoring users of the current system to determine their needs as well as their satisfaction and dissatisfaction with the current system.

- Collecting, examining, and analyzing documents, reports, layouts, procedures, manuals, and any other documentation relating to the operations of the current system.

- Modeling, observing, and simulating the work activities of the current system.

The goal of the feasibility study is to consider alternative information systems solutions, evaluate their feasibility, and propose the alternative most suitable to the organization. The feasibility of a proposed solution is evaluated in terms of its components. These components are:

1. Economic feasibility—the economic viability of the proposed system. The proposed project's costs and benefits are evaluated. Tangible costs include fixed and variable costs, while tangible benefits include cost savings, increased revenue, and increased profit. A project is approved only if it covers its cost in a given period of time. However, a project may be approved only on its intangible benefits such as those relating to government regulations, the image of the organization, or similar considerations.

2. Technical feasibility—the possibility that the organization has or can procure the necessary resources. This is demonstrated if the needed hardware and software are available in the marketplace or can be developed by the time of implementation.

3. Operational feasibility—the ability, desire, and willingness of the stakeholders to use, support, and operate the proposed computer information system. The stakeholders include management, employees, customers, and suppliers. The stakeholders are interested in systems that are easy to operate, make few, if any, errors, produce the desired information, and fall within the objectives of the organization.

REQUIREMENTS DEFINITION

This phase is an in-depth analysis of the stakeholders' information needs. This leads to defining the requirements of the computer information system. These requirements are then incorporated into the design phase. Many of the activities performed in the requirements definition phase are an extension of those used in the preliminary investigation phase. The main goal of the analyst is to identify what should be done, not how to do it. The following is a discussion of the activities involved in requirements definition.

INFORMATION NEEDS OF THE STAKEHOLDERS. Analysis of the information needs of the stakeholders is an important first step in determining the requirements of the new system. It is essential that the analyst understands the environment in which the new system will operate. Understanding the environment means knowing enough about the management of the organization, its structure, its people, its business, and the

current information systems to ensure that the new system will be appropriate.

THE CURRENT INFORMATION SYSTEM. A comprehensive and detailed analysis of the current system is essential to developing a quality, new information system. The analyst should understand and document how the current system uses hardware, software, and people to accept and manage input data and to convert such data into information suitable for decision making. The documentation should be detailed and complete. For example, the analyst should assess the quality of input and output activities that form the user's interface. In addition, the volume and timing of such activities may be documented.

THE CAPABILITIES OF THE NEW COMPUTER INFORMATION SYSTEM. Functional requirements include the necessary hardware and software configurations along with the appropriate human resources. Specific functional requirements often include the following:

• User interface requirements—the input and output needs of the user that must be provided for by the new computer information system. These needs include layouts and definitions of input and output, volume, frequency, origination of input, and destination for reports.

• Processing requirements—the activities required for converting input into output, including calculations, decision rules, database operations, and other processing operations. In addition, requirements concerning capacity, throughput, turnaround time, response time, and the system's availability time are established.

• Storage requirements—the organization, content, and size of databases, and types and frequency of updates and inquiries. Furthermore, backup procedures and the length of time and rationale for retention of backups are delineated.

• Control requirements—the accuracy, validity, security, and adaptability requirements for the system's input, processing, output, and databases. Crash recovery and auditing requirements of the organization are further specified in this stage.

The analysis team, at the end of this phase, produces a document containing the functional requirements of the new computer information system. Additionally, the document contains preliminary schedules and a budget for the next phase. The task force or committee responsible for the project studies the document for the purpose of approving or not approving the work of the analysis team. In addition, the analysis team provides the committee with a demonstration. In essence, the analysis team walks the committee members, step by step, through the requirements definition phase. If the committee approves this phase, then the analysis team is funded and given the go-ahead to proceed to the next phase. However, if the committee does not approve this phase, then either the project is canceled or, after appropriate modifications, the analysis team resubmits a new document to the committee.

A walk-through starts with a description of the project. From this point, the analysts delineate a set of well-defined goals, objectives, and benefits of the computer information system. Following that, the budgets and staffing requirements are articulated and the plans are shared with the committee. Specific, planned tasks are compared to actual accomplishments, and deviations, if any, are noted and accounted for. The plans for asset protection and business control are reviewed with the committee members. Finally, the analysts seek the committee's approval of the objectives, plans, time table, and budget for the next phase—systems design.

In summary, systems analysis is an essential starting point in the development of computer information systems projects. An organization generally follows a development pattern set up to meet its needs. Regardless of which methodology an organization uses, the objective of systems analysis is to fully understand the current environment and future requirements of a computer information systems project.

SEE ALSO: Business Process Reengineering; Data Processing and Data Management; Management Information Systems; Open and Closed Systems; Systems Design

Badie N. Farah

FURTHER READING:

Kendall, Kenneth, and Julia Kendall. *Systems Analysis and Design*. 6th ed. Englewood Cliffs, NJ: Prentice-Hall, 2005.

McLeod, Raymond, Jr., and George Schell Sumner. *Management Information Systems*. 9th ed. Englewood Cliffs, NJ: Prentice-Hall, 2004.

Valacich, Joseph, Joey George, and Jeffrey Hoffer. *Essentials of Systems Analysis and Design*. 2nd ed. Englewood Cliffs, NJ: Prentice-Hall, 2004.

SYSTEMS DESIGN

A system can be defined in several ways, including: (1) a set of interrelated parts that function as a whole to achieve a common purpose; (2) a piece of software that operates to manage a related collection of tasks; or (3) a design for an organization that perceives sets of processes as a related collection of tasks.

Systems can be open or closed. An open system is one that interacts with the external environment; a closed system has no external interactions. A system is normally thought to have inputs, outputs, and a transformation process by which the inputs are transformed to the desired outputs. The majority of systems are open, requiring interaction with the environment for the source of inputs and the destination for outputs.

Almost any collection of related items or tasks that take inputs and produce outputs can be characterized as a system. This also allows for subsystems that are contained by the suprasystem. For example, an airplane can be conceived of as a system. The airplane takes fuel, oxygen, and passengers at one point and transforms the fuel and oxygen to a motive force, thus transforming the passengers from people who wanted to travel to people who have arrived. However, an airplane is made up of many subsystems, such as the engine that takes the fuel inputs and the cargo area that accepts passengers. Individually, either of these two subsystems can function, but together they produce an output that is greater than the sum of the outputs from the two subsystems. In many cases, as in the one described here, systems and subsystems are mutually dependent for their survival, or their utility.

Subsystems need to communicate in order for the suprasystem to function effectively. The subsystems therefore require common language(s) for system integration. Language is of the utmost importance in system integration. This connects systems theory and information theory.

Normally, systems are shown as having a feedback loop. An adaptation from engineering control systems, this requires systems that are automatically controlled to have a feedback loop in order to direct the correction of inputs to result in the correct outputs. In organizational development theory, this feedback loop can be conceived of as business results, consumer comments, or market information.

For example, a thermostat is a simple system. The thermostat takes the temperature of the room as an input. If the temperature is below the set point, the furnace comes on to heat the room. As the room heats, the temperature that is read into the thermostat is compared against the set point. Once the room temperature reaches the set point, the furnace turns off. The input for this system is the room temperature. The transformation process is the heating of the room. The output is the warmed room. The feedback loop is the constant temperature measurement comparison to the set point.

HISTORY

In the late 1940s Norbert Wiener's *Cybernetics* set the stage for later development of the ideas of systems theory. In 1955, using ideas that were developed from the biological sciences, Bertanlanffy, Hempel, Bass, and Jonas wrote a seminal work on systems theory that presented the activities that occur within a corporation as being similar to a biological system. This was a dramatic shift from the mechanistic way of conceptualizing organizational activities that was popular during the first half of the twentieth century. In 1956 Kenneth E. Boulding presented an addition to systems theory that classified systems into hierarchies. He called this the hierarchy of levels. The hierarchy of levels indicated that systems are composed of a collection of systems that operate in a hierarchical manner. More recently, Wendell L. French and Cecil H. Bell offered a list of systems into which the typical organization can be separated, and the concept of systems was used for the development of business process reengineering activities, as described by Michael Hammer and James Champy.

SYSTEMS DESIGN AND DEVELOPMENT

Systems theory can be helpful in analyzing business processes and finding inefficiencies. Business processes can include a set of elements such as a purchasing agent, a supplier, the customer orders that request a part, and the final product that uses the part. Analyzing how well this system functions across functional lines can help reduce non-value-added activities such as cyclical flows of paperwork and unnecessary cross-checking for accuracy. Many systems such as the one described develop over time without a great deal of effort to design or develop systems with efficiency. They become cumbersome due to stop-gap solutions that increase the number of steps, circular flows, and a variety of other non-value-added activities that are usually implemented to minimize errors or solve a problem in service. As a company grows, these stop-gap fixes can cause bottlenecks and delays in the process. At times, the original purpose of the measure is forgotten or even becomes obsolete, but the process is performed this way by employees who do not understand the system and its goals.

Systems within companies are often not readily apparent because they cross functional borders, geographical borders, and hierarchical borders. Employees within the system can therefore be blind to the impact of their activities on the end result of the system. At times, they may not even be aware of the result itself, but simply their piece of the activity. In systems design, therefore, it is often necessary to look across these borders to identify the key activities of the system and eliminate paperwork or other activities that only serve to reduce overall productivity.

BUSINESS PROCESS REENGINEERING. Business process reengineering (BPR) was begun to help companies overcome these artificial barriers and see the whole system as a process that produces an end product, such as a bill, a satisfied customer, or a well-designed product. The popularity of BPR has waned somewhat because of the high number of failures to produce the promised results. In 1999 Hammer and Champy admitted that about 70 percent of the BPR efforts undertaken do not result in success.

BPR is the identification, analysis, and redesign of systems within a corporation in order to improve the efficiency of the operations. Much of the focus of BPR has been on the elimination of labor and employees, often at a fast pace. This has resulted in the phenomenon of downsizing. Downsizing is meant to eliminate all non-value-added activities as well as all nonessential employees of the system under evaluation. This concept attracted enthusiastic adherence in the early 1990s. However, it left some internal corporate systems changed with the expectation of improved efficiency, but the result was less than favorable. The interaction of other systems had been neglected in the analysis, as was sufficient time to retrain employees to adapt to the new system. The phenomenon of rehiring fired employees as consultants to keep the business running effectively was a direct result of over-enthusiastic downsizing. This, of course, reduced the expected savings and efficiencies, thus reducing the effectiveness of business process reengineering overall.

EXAMINING A SYSTEM. Systems design requires that all elements of the system be identified: inputs, outputs, feedback, and transformation. In addition, it is important to recognize that an organization consists of many different systems, all of which interact, and that the transitions between systems can be particularly difficult to manage. The use of systems design allows the compartmentalization of processes into understandable and measurable systems that can then be diagnosed, redesigned, and implemented. This is of great value to complex organizations that are seeking greater efficiency and profitability.

For example, the system of product delivery—including order receipt, production, materials acquisition, packaging, quality control, and delivery—can be seen as a separate system from the human resources system—which consists of the interviewing, hiring, training, development, and release of employees—although the two systems certainly interact. However, analysis of the efficiencies of the human resources system can be conducted separately from analysis of the efficiencies of the product delivery system. Separating the system into its component parts can assist in the diagnosis of problems in a system. For example, hiring employees is an input to the human resources system, the training and development is the transformation, and the release of employees through retirement, layoffs, or firing is an output, as is the delivery of trained and qualified workers.

It is one thing to conceive of an organization as the total system containing various subsystems in the abstract; in practice, however, identifying the suprasystem and the subsystems has no convention and depends entirely upon the arbitrary perspective of the observer. French and Bell identify five subsystems of a corporation that may be considered generic and applicable to most business entities. These five subsystems are technological, task, structural, human-social, and the external interface subsystems. Other observers might identify more subsystems in a completely different manner.

Simply stated, the diagram of a system can be separated into subsystems by tracing a line around the boundaries of related activities that have a common goal. The items that cross the boundary are then considered either inputs or outputs.

VALUE-ADDED AND NON-VALUE-ADDED ACTIVITIES. Systems design requires that one consider the value-added activities and minimize the non-value-added activities. Value-added activities are those that directly affect the product or service, such as assembly or delivery of a package. Non-value-added activities include such things as quality testing and writing a receipt. Normally this requires a cross-functional team that can examine the interfaces over which the system extends and ensure that these "hand-offs" occur efficiently. Various tools are used to develop a system, and several varieties of flow charts and diagrams can be used to develop a visual representation of the system. Team members may then analyze and discuss the activities represented on the flow chart and evaluate whether they are essential or can be minimized or eliminated.

Oftentimes, this is not immediately evident. For example, perhaps accounting policy once required that the account manager be called every time an order came in from a particular company with a spotty payment history. Over time, the computer systems were upgraded to check customer credit and whether a customer was current on its bills. At this point, the call to the account manager could have been eliminated. However, the customer service agent trained to call the account manager does not realize that these checks are occurring. The account manager receiving the calls may consider them important or trivial, but does not realize that at one time the calls were made to prevent over-selling to unreliable customers. During a discussion and analysis of this system, these two functional representatives should find that this activity is non-value-adding and, because of the improvements to the computer system, the calls are now completely unnecessary—a fact that may not have been uncovered otherwise.

In systems design, any activity that does not directly add to the value of the product is eliminated while value-added activities are made efficient. The related activities that must be done, as well as the activities that aid in the accounting, documentation, or delivery of the product, are examined together.

SYSTEM DEVELOPMENT. System development can be the development of a new system or improvement of an existing system. This can be approached much the same as system design and with much the same tools. However, current employees must be included in the development process and retrained to understand and help with the implementation. In addition, the goals or set points and the feedback loops are developed at this point in order to guide the system toward proper performance.

SYSTEM IMPLEMENTATION

Implementation of a new system design must include training employees to understand the new system and their role in achieving the goals the company has for it. Implementation times can vary depending upon the complexity of the system being implemented.

Computer systems have been developed to help organizations conduct, control, and document related tasks more efficiently. In this case, the design and development requires a study of the system to be modeled or controlled by the computer. Software and hardware are then acquired or developed to effectively handle the tasks. Implementation requires a verification stage that tests the computer system prior to actual use to verify that the system operates as envisioned. Modifications to fit the needs of the corporation are usually made over time as problems are identified with use. These systems tend to be expensive and development often requires significant effort to correctly handle the complexities of each individual company. Some computer systems can be purchased off the shelf that handle such typical tasks as accounting, inventory control, or transportation. Some of these are even developed for a particular industry. However, most off-the-shelf products still require technical modification to fit the needs of the individual company.

It should be apparent that computer systems closely parallel the organizational systems previously discussed. In this sense the two definitions are related, but not the same.

SEE ALSO: Business Process Reengineering; Open and Closed Systems; Systems Analysis

Terri Friel

Revised by Badie N. Farah

FURTHER READING:

Bertanlanffy, Ludwig von. *General Systems Theory: Foundations, Development, Applications.* rev. ed. New York: George Brazillers, 1976.

Boulding, Kenneth E. "General Systems Theory—The Skeleton of Science." *Management Science* 2 (April 1956): 197–208.

Flood, R.L., and E.R. Carson. *Dealing With Complexity: An Introduction to the Theory and Application of Systems Science.* 2nd ed. New York: Plenum, 1993.

Flood, R.L., and M.C. Jackson. *Creative Problem Solving: Total Systems Intervention.* Chichester, UK: Wiley, 1991.

———. *Critical Systems Thinking: Directed Readings.* Chichester, UK: Wiley, 1991.

French, Wendell L., and Cecil H. Bell, Jr. *Organizational Development: Behavioral Science Interventions for Organiza-tional Improvement.* 6th ed. Englewood Cliffs, NJ: Prentice Hall, 1999.

Hammer, Michael, and James Champy. *Reengineering the Corporation.* New York: Harper Business, 2003.

Kast, Fremont E., and Jamens E. Rosenzweig. "General Systems Theory: Applications for Organization and Management." *Academy of Management Journal,* December 1972, 447–465.

Laszlo, Ervin. *Introduction to Systems Philosophy.* New York: Gordon and Breach, Science Publishers, 1972.

Machol, R.E., ed. *Systems Engineering Handbook.* New York: McGraw-Hill, 1965.

Mingers, John, and Leslie P. Willcocks, eds. *Social Theory and Philosophy for Information Systems.* New York: John Wiley & Sons, 2004.

Wiener, Norbert. *Cybernetics.* New York: Wiley, 1948.

T

The definition of task analysis varies depending on the purpose for it and the context in which it is performed. Similarly, purposes for conducting task analyses vary, from using the process as an aid in designing job descriptions to using it to develop effective tools for human-computer interaction (e.g., analyzing user needs and behaviors to develop software). David H. Jonassen et al describe five general classes of task analysis: job or performance analysis, learning analysis, cognitive task analysis, content or subject-matter analysis, and activity-based methods, which is a relatively new category of the task-analysis discipline. Each approach requires different methods. In many cases, however, task analysis can most simply be described as the division of activity into its specific component levels in order to determine the value in solving particular performance problems.

Task analysis is a way of assessing what people, machines, or a combination thereof do and why they do it. Analyses examine how and where specific information flows, how it is modified at various stages (what is done to the information), who performs those modifications (a computer or person), and whether he, she, or it is the appropriate vehicle for efficient and effective completion of those tasks.

Task analysis is also studied in relation to group support systems (GSS). This type of analysis does not focus on the study of all tasks, but on those tasks typically encountered in organizational decision-making groups. Often such analysis is conducted in an effort to discern how the introduction of new elements, such as technology, can facilitate more effective group functioning and decision making.

Some workplaces emphasize tasks so heavily that they can be considered task environments, or may operate under task management. A task environment views tasks as behavior requirements. Required behaviors vary with the task(s) to be performed, and those tasks influence behavior in that each task is characterized by its purpose, that is, what group members must do to accomplish a certain task (e.g., creative tasks require that a group generates ideas). Behavior determination for each task includes deciding what needs to be accomplished and how each goal should be met. Leaders in these organizations focus on managing the work that needs to be performed, and they expect employees to fall in line behind them in order to meet the prescribed goals. More specifically, the leaders manage procedures for coordinating the sequence of procedures and materials for the completion of specific tasks. These types of situations provide much fodder for research into group support systems and organizational behavior.

ORIGINS OF TASK ANALYSIS

Task analysis has been studied almost since the Industrial Revolution, during which employers began to focus on breaking down jobs into the specific tasks required. One of the first true leaders of task analysis was Frederick Winslow Taylor, the author of *The Principles of Scientific Management*, first published in 1911. Taylor applied critical thinking to industry, seeking the most efficient way to perform tasks and/or jobs and rewarding workers who found ways to facilitate working toward that goal.

Taylor's theories were a precursor to Jonassen's first classification of task analysis: job or performance analysis. Originally meant to describe the simple behaviors performed on the job, analysis of this sort also became used as a way to plan technical training. During the 1950s and 1960s subject-matter analysis began to be used to plan curricula in educational facilities. This involved analyzing content into its most basic constructs and determining how they relate to other subject matter. The 1960s led to another revolution in learning psychology, and thus, to another form of analysis: learning analysis. This movement focused on people who learned processed information as they performed certain tasks. Cognitive task analysis evolved from this class, as did research in human-computer interaction. Finally, activity analysis studies how people perform in natural surroundings and which social and contextual factors affect that performance.

Task analysis was studied in organizational literature and as part of the group process in the mid- to late-1960s. Scholars of group behavior felt that tasks undertaken as part of the group process played particularly important roles in how group members interacted and performed. Group support systems (GSS) literature also emphasized the importance of tasks and, from the mid-1980s to the mid-1990s, developed a task classification scheme that has since been widely used. In the late 1990s theories were explored as to how tasks and technology worked together within GSS. The theory asserts that clear descriptions of tasks are an important part of any GSS environment, and that technology is linked specifically to the demands of the tasks to be performed.

MARKETPLACE TRENDS

The use of task analysis across various market segments is growing. Computer-supported cooperative work (CSCW) and GSS continue to increase in importance with the need to support interdisciplinary collaboration, telecommuting, and cultural challenges in the global workplace. The use of task analysis is making its way into the military as well. As described in an article by Pezzano and Burke in *Defense AT&L*, the U.S. Army used task analysis to identify requirements, increase flexibility, and reduce risk in maturing technological systems.

In the fields of occupational and organizational psychology, cognitive task analysis is being used in two ways. In the healthcare field, occupational therapists work to identify how people approach everyday tasks in order to better help patients learn to perform tasks. On a more organizational level, researchers examine the cognitive activity behind complex task performance to better train workers and design or improve manufacturing systems. The goal in these studies is to reduce error and mitigate risk in work settings. This is also referred to as "process tracing." While no dominant methodology has evolved yet for

this emerging trend, models are being developed and proposed as the popularity of the technique continues to grow.

DEFINING DATA AND ACTIVITY FLOW

A major part of task analysis is defining the data or information processed in an organization, as well as the flow of that organization's activity. This analysis helps an organization better understand its practices. Many professionals clarify ideas through the use of data-flow diagrams and activity-flow diagrams. Data-flow diagrams provide detail on information—where it goes and when, and which unit of a system handles it at which point. Activity-flow diagrams provide detail on the data processing and a system's communication needs.

DATA-FLOW DIAGRAMS

Specific elements included on data-flow diagrams (DFDs) include outside units such as customer needs, inside units such as the employees who actually manipulate data, and whether a data element inputs to an element or reads from an element. Data storage areas are also indicated on DFDs. Data-flow diagrams can be designed to illustrate existing processes as well as to document better and even ideal situations. Each type of element is denoted within a prescribed symbol (e.g., rectangles signify outside units) so that a simple glance at the chart is enough to differentiate each element.

DFDs are helpful in that they show exactly how data flow is initiated and by whom, who or which system receives the data, and what they do to the data. Diagrams can also be annotated to show the volume and frequency with which these changes occur. However, data-flow diagrams do not show specific processing details, nor are they a helpful representation of how the process fits onto a timeline.

ACTIVITY-FLOW DIAGRAMS

Activity-flow diagrams (AFDs) keep track of the people or systems that use data or information, and the time sequence in which that occurs. Activity-flow diagrams are similar to flow charts, with a special language and symbols specific to their purpose. They also note any activities that involve the transformation of data or materials.

Activities included on AFDs include the following:

1. Transportation of information—physically moving information from one place to the next. No transformation of data takes place.

2. Information transformation—changing information from one medium to another. The

location and content of that data does not change.

3. Algorithmic processing—sorting incoming data and making decisions about the information according to pre-programmed rules.

4. Judgmental processing—sorting information according to multiple, more complex dimensions than algorithmic processing may be capable of.

5. Correlating information—retrieving information from several sources and merging several aspects of each to form a new record.

6. Information analysis—looking for patterns, projections, and trends in the treatment of data.

7. Negotiation—persuading, teaching, and learning. It involves using more complex judgment and interpersonal communication.

8. Information generation—organizing, synthesizing, and adding new information.

The purpose of AFDs is to look for efficiencies and prescribe support in the most appropriate and effective way possible where it is lacking. Support may be required in a human capacity, or technological systems may be available to automate or support some activities. Processes are allocated to computers and/or personnel according to what each does best and what best suits the needs of the specific processes. Various options are analyzed using cost/benefit analysis, but tend to follow some general conditions:

• Data transport, transformation, and algorithmic processing can be highly automated.

• Judgment processing and correlation can be supported by technology.

• Analysis and creation of data requires human effort.

SEE ALSO: Human Resource Management; Job Analysis; Strategic Planning Tools

Wendy H. Mason

FURTHER READING:

Desberg, Peter, and Judson Taylor. *Essentials of Task Analysis.* Lanham, MA: University Press of America, 1986.

Hackos, JoAnn T., and Janice C. Redish. *User and Task Analysis for Interface Design.* New York: John Wiley & Sons, Inc., 1998.

Jonassen, David H., Wallace H. Hannum, and Martin Tessmer. *Handbook of Task Analysis Procedures.* Westwood, CT: Greenwood Publishing Group, 1989.

———. *Task Analysis Methods for Instructional Design.* Mahwah, NJ: Lawrence Erlbaum Associates, Inc., 1999.

Kirwan, B., and L.K. Ainsworth. *A Guide to Task Analysis.* Washington: Taylor & Francis, 1992.

Patrick, John, and Nic James. "Process Tracing of Complex Cognitive Work Tasks." *Journal of Occupational and Organizational Psychology* (June 2004): 259.

Pezzano, Anthony, and Peter Burke. "Flexible Contracting Approach: Mitigating the Challenges of Technology Maturation." *Defense AT&L,* July/August 2004, 20.

Watson, Diane E. *Task Analysis: An Individual and Population Approach.* 2nd ed. Bethesda, MD: American Occupational Therapy Assn., 2003.

TEAMS AND TEAMWORK

A team is a collection of individuals organized to accomplish a common purpose, who are interdependent, and who can be identified by themselves and observers as a team. Teams exist within a larger organization and interact with other teams and with the organization. Teams are one way for organizations to gather input from members, and to provide organization members with a sense of involvement in the pursuit of organizational goals. Further, teams allow organizations flexibility in assigning members to projects and allow for cross-functional groups to be formed.

TYPES OF TEAMS

There are six major types of teams: informal, traditional, problem solving, leadership, self-directed, and virtual. Table 1 describes some of the characteristics of these six types of teams.

INFORMAL TEAMS. Informal teams are generally formed for social purposes. They can help to facilitate employee pursuits of common concerns, such as improving work conditions. More frequently however, these teams form out of a set of common concerns and interests, which may or may not be the same as the organization's. Leaders of these teams generally emerge from the membership and are not appointed by anyone in the organization.

TRADITIONAL TEAMS. Traditional teams are the organizational groups commonly thought of as departments or functional areas. Leaders or managers of these teams are appointed by the organization and have legitimate power in the team. The team is expected to produce a product, deliver a service, or perform a function that the organization has assigned.

Table 1
Six Types of Teams

Informal
- Social in nature
- Leaders may differ from those appointed by the organization

Traditional
- Departments/functional areas
- Supervisors/managers appointed by the organization

Problem-Solving
- Temporary teams
- Frequently cross-functional
- Focused on a particular project

Leadership
- Steering committees
- Advisory councils

Self-Directed
- Small teams
- Little or no status differences among team members
- Have authority to decide how to get the work done

Virtual
- Geographically spread apart
- Meetings and functions rely on available technology

PROBLEM SOLVING TEAMS. Problem-solving teams or task forces are formed when a problem arises that cannot be solved within the standard organizational structure. These teams are generally cross-functional; that is, the membership comes from different areas of the organization, and are charged with finding a solution to the problem.

LEADERSHIP TEAMS. Leadership teams are generally composed of management brought together to span the boundaries between different functions in the organization. In order for a product to be delivered to market, the heads of finance, production, and marketing must interact and come up with a common strategy for the product. At top management levels, teams are used in developing goals and a strategic direction for the firm as a whole.

SELF-DIRECTED TEAMS. Self-directed teams are given autonomy over deciding how a job will be done. These teams are provided with a goal by the organization, and then determine how to achieve that goal. Frequently there is no assigned manager or leader and very few, if any, status differences among the team members.

These teams are commonly allowed to choose new team members, decide on work assignments, and may be given responsibility for evaluating team members. They must meet quality standards and interact with both buyers and suppliers, but otherwise have great freedom in determining what the team does. Teams form around a particular project and a leader emerges for that project. The team is responsible for carrying out the project, for recruiting team members, and for evaluating them.

VIRTUAL TEAMS. Technology is impacting how teams meet and function. Collaborative software and conferencing systems have improved the ability for employees to meet, conduct business, share documents, and make decisions without ever being in the same location. While the basic dynamics of other types of teams may still be relevant, the dynamics and management of virtual teams can be very different. Issues can arise with a lack of facial or auditory clues; participants must be taken at their word, even when video-conferencing tools are used.

Accountability is impacted by taking a team virtual. Each member is accountable for their tasks and to the team as a whole usually with minimal supervision. Key factors in the success of a virtual team are effective formation of the team, trust and collaboration between members, and excellent communication.

CHARACTERISTICS OF EFFECTIVE TEAMS

Some characteristics of effective teams are clear direction and responsibilities, knowledgeable members, reasonable operating procedures, good interpersonal relationships, shared success and failures, and good external relationships.

CLEAR DIRECTION. Clear direction means that the team is given a clear and distinct goal. The team may be empowered to determine how to achieve that goal, but management, when forming the team, generally sets the goal. A clear direction also means that team outcomes are measurable.

CLEAR RESPONSIBILITIES. Clear responsibilities means that each team member understands what is expected of her or him within the team. The roles must be clear and interesting to the team members. Each team member needs to be able to rely on all the other members to carry out their roles so that the team can function effectively. Otherwise, one or two team members come to feel that they are doing all the work. This is one of the reasons so many individuals are initially reluctant to join teams.

KNOWLEDGEABLE MEMBERS. An effective team will be comprised of individuals who have the skills and knowledge necessary to complete the team's task. Cooperation is essential at an early stage in inventorying the skills and knowledge each member brings to the team, and working to determine how to utilize those skills to accomplish the team task.

REASONABLE OPERATING PROCEDURES. All teams need a set of rules by which they operate. Sports teams for example, operate according to a clearly laid-out set of rules about how the game is played. Similarly, work teams need a set of procedures to guide meetings, decision making, planning, division of tasks, and progress evaluation. Setting, and sticking to, procedures helps team members become comfortable relying on one another.

INTERPERSONAL RELATIONSHIPS. Teams are composed of diverse individuals, each of whom comes to the team with his or her own set of values. Understanding and celebrating this diversity helps to make a stronger, more effective team.

SHARING SUCCESS AND FAILURES. Everyone wants to feel appreciated. Within a team, members should be willing to express their appreciation, as well their criticisms, of others' efforts. Similarly, the organization must be willing to reward the team for successful completion of a task and hold all members responsible for failure.

EXTERNAL RELATIONSHIPS. In the process of building a strong team, groups external to the team are frequently ignored. In order for the team to successfully complete its task, it cannot operate in isolation from the rest of the organization. Teams need help from people within the organization who control important resources. Establishing clear lines of communication with these people early on will facilitate the completion of the team's task.

TEAM BUILDING

The most successful teams go through five stages of development. Table 2 outlines these stages.

Table 2
Five Stages of Team Development

Forming
- Assess the ground rules
- Gather information about group goals

Storming
- Initiate conflict with other team members
- Find mutually acceptable resolutions

Norming
- Build cohesion
- Develop a consensus about norms

Performing
- Channel energy toward the task
- Apply problem-solving solutions generated in the previous stages

Adjournment
- Disengagement after successful completion of goals
- Regrets at team break-up

FORMING. Forming is the stage when team members become acquainted with one another. They also assess the group task and the ground rules that will apply to that task. At this stage everyone is typically very polite and willing to go along with suggestions made by other team members. Team members try to avoid making enemies and are frequently more patient with one another than they might be later in the process.

STORMING. As the novelty of being a member of the team wears off, conflict emerges. Members of the team emerge who want to exert greater influence over the process. Leadership struggles begin, as do interpersonal conflicts. Conflicts erupt over the task requirements and the best way to achieve that task. This is the stage at which listening and finding mutually acceptable resolutions to the conflict is most important. The team can either emerge united and ready to take on the assigned task, or divided, with some members taking a passive role.

NORMING. In the norming stage team members make an effort to discover what standards of performance are acceptable. What do deadlines really mean? How high a level of quality is necessary? Does every member have to be at every meeting? What about developing sub-teams? If the team can establish harmonious relationships at this stage, they are ready to move on to the performing stage. Some teams, however, disband at this stage.

PERFORMING. At this stage the team is ready to be productive and work on the task assigned. Team members' roles have been established and clarified. Group interaction should be relatively smooth as the team applies some of the problem-solving skills it learned in earlier stages to the task at hand. If the team has reached this stage without successfully working through the problems and issues of the earlier stages, it may disband or regress and work through those issues.

ADJOURNMENT. At some point almost all teams are disbanded, whether their task is completed or a team member leaves. On the one hand this can be a happy stage, with members congratulating one another on a job well done. On the other hand adjournment means the disruption of working arrangements that may have become comfortable and efficient, and possibly the end of friendships.

SELECTING THE TEAM MEMBERS

Forming an effective team is more complex than simply throwing a group of people together, assigning them a task, and hoping for the best. Potential team members need to be interviewed and their skills and knowledge should be assessed. Issues to consider in selecting team members include: the individual's motivation with respect to both the team and the task at hand; the attitudes and goals of potential team members;

potential problems with intragroup relationships; and potential problems with relationships with external groups.

The organization needs to first assess what the skills, knowledge, and attitudes of potential team members should be. What are the tasks that need to be accomplished for the team to be successful? Have managers analyzed the jobs and developed an inventory of required skills and knowledge?

Once these steps have been completed, potential team members can be interviewed. Among the issues the interview process should cover are:

- What strengths does the individual bring to the team?

- What is she or he is willing to work on improving?

- What problem solving style does the individual employ?

- Can she or he share information in an effective manner?

- Does the individual have good listening skills?

- Can the individual provide constructive feedback?

It is important to remember that effective teams are generally made up of a variety of personalities. The selection process needs to be structured so that it is not biased toward one personality type. An effective team needs both the thoughtful, detail-oriented individuals, as well as the outgoing, insightful individuals.

Additional considerations for building an effective team are being identified. There are four important factors to consider when selecting team members:

1. years of professional work experience;

2. frequency of team participation;

3. type of team training;

4. situational entry to team assignments (volunteered, assigned, requested).

These factors can be effectively utilized by management when selecting team members to increase the opportunity for overall success.

ORGANIZATIONAL BENEFITS OF TEAMS

The major impetus for organizations to embrace the team concept is the effort to improve productivity and quality. Teams are a key component of many total quality management programs. The QS 9000 program, which suppliers to the major automobile manufacturers have embraced, relies on the team approach to ensure quality while maintaining a low-cost approach to manufacturing.

In addition to improved productivity and quality, some of an organization's major benefits from the use of teams are improved quality of work life for employees, reduced absenteeism and turnover, increased innovation, and improved organizational adaptability and flexibility. Effective implementation of teams can also improve office politics by improving the communication and trust between the team members.

IMPROVED QUALITY OF WORK LIFE. Effective teams frequently improve the quality of work life for the employees. An effective team is generally one in which members are empowered to make decisions about how to get work done. Giving team members authority and control over the work processes reduces the amount of external control and increases the sense of ownership and accountability for the work being done. This helps to create a satisfying and rewarding work environment.

LOWER ABSENTEEISM AND TURNOVER. A satisfying and rewarding work environment helps to lower absenteeism and turnover. Teams are particularly effective in this area. Membership in a work team gives an employee a sense of belonging, interaction with others on a regular basis, and recognition of achievements. All of these help to eliminate a sense of isolation within the organization. Team members identify with and feel pride in the work they are doing and come to rely on one another being there. At some companies, employees are evaluated based on their contribution to their team's efforts.

INCREASED INNOVATION. W.L. Gore & Associates is an excellent example of a firm that utilizes the team concept and has a strong record of innovation. Gore is a multinational company structured around the concept of small plants (no more than 250 employees) where everyone works in teams. Everyone is allowed to experiment with the products and develop new uses. The result is that Gore has a continuous stream of patent applications and has been successful in developing new products in areas as diverse as clothing, surgical supplies, and coatings for industrial use.

ORGANIZATIONAL ADAPTATION AND FLEXIBILITY. During the 1980s Ford was able to reduce its automobile design cycle by implementing Team Taurus. Through the early involvement of employees from planning, designing, engineering, and manufacturing, the company was able to eliminate some of the bottlenecks that had delayed the design process. The involvement of suppliers and assembly workers helped to decrease the number of parts involved and lower costs. Reducing the time from design to manufacture helped Ford to be more responsive to market changes and increase its market share in the 1980s and '90s.

Teams are not appropriate for all organizations or in all types of businesses. Behavioral scientists are still working to determine exactly when teams will be most effective, what motivates team members, what types of business can best benefit from the implementation of teams, and so on. The study of the philosophy and psychology of teamwork is still in its infancy. While effective teams can produce extraordinary results, studies have found that an estimated 50 percent of self-directed work teams culminate in failure.

The introduction of effective and stable new technologies has greatly affected teams and teamwork. Collaborative software and other multimedia options are providing businesses with tools to conduct teamwork regardless of location or time. New issues of accountability, team structure, and team selection are arising for management to deal with and coordinate within the businesses overall goals and objectives.

But as more and more businesses introduce the team concept, the wrinkles in the process are being ironed out and team popularity is growing. An increasing number of organizations are using teams to improve productivity and quality, and to solve a range of managerial problems.

Improved quality of work life and a reduction in absenteeism and turnover all contribute to a positive impact on the bottom line. Involving employees in teams helps the organization remain open to change and new ideas. As long as teams are seen as a means of improving the organization's ability to meet competitive challenges, teams will be part of the business world.

SEE ALSO: Empowerment; Group Dynamics; Participative Management

Stephanie Newell
Revised by Hal P. Kirkwood, Jr.

FURTHER READING:

Carney, Steven H. *The Teamwork Chronicles: A Startling Look Inside the Workplace for Those Who Want Better Teamwork.* Austin, TX: Greenleaf Book Group, LLC, 2003.

Gold, N. *Teamwork: An Interdisciplinary Approach.* New York, NY: Palgrave Macmillan, 2005.

Huszczo, Gregory E. *Tools for Team Excellence: Getting Your Team into High Gear and Keeping It There.* Palo Alto, CA: Davies-Black Publishing, 1996.

Johnson, P., V. Heimann, and K. O'Neill. "The 'Wonderland' of Virtual Teams." *Journal of Workplace Learning* 13, no. 1 (2001): 24.

"Managing Virtual Teams is Fraught with Difficulty, Says New Report." *Training Journal* 5 (May 2003).

Maxwell, John C. *The 17 Indisputable Laws of Teamwork: Embrace Them and Empower Your Team.* Nashville, TN: Nelson Books, 2001.

Nemiro, Jill. *Creativity in Virtual Teams: Key Components for Success.* San Francisco, CA: Pfeiffer, 2004.

Stewart, Greg L., Charles C. Manz, and Henry P. Sims. *Team Work and Group Dynamics.* New York, NY: John Wiley & Sons, 2000.

Weiss, W.H. "Team Management." *SuperVision* 65 no. 11 (November 2004): 19–21.

TECHNOLOGICAL FORECASTING

Forecasting is defined by B.R. Martin as "the process involved in systematically attempting to look into the longer-term future of science, technology, the economy and society with the aim of identifying the areas of strategic research and emerging generic technologies likely to yield the greatest economic and social benefits."

Numerous techniques for forecasting technological developments were pioneered in the 1960s in both business and government (particularly military) applications, and the term "foresight studies" is now commonly used. The more important of the techniques are described here.

THE S-SHAPED LOGISTIC CURVE

The growth of a new technological capability typically follows an S-shaped curve that can be divided into three stages. The first is slow initial growth, as the new technology has to prove its superiority over existing technologies. Once this is demonstrated, a period of rapid growth follows. Finally, its growth is limited by technological or socioeconomic factors and levels off toward some upper limit. The commercially successful exploitation of technology often depends upon the astute perception and exploitation of this growth. Thus, forecasters pay significant attention to extrapolating the growth of the S-shaped curve of a technological capability at some relatively early stage of its life. In so doing, they use mathematical functions or models.

ENVELOPE CURVES AND TREND EXTRAPOLATION

Technological evolutions typically progress through successive generations of capabilities (e.g. 286, 386, 486, and Pentium microprocessors) and, as each capability is superseded by its technologically superior successor, overall functional performance continues to rise along an envelope curve generated by successive S-curves. This envelope curve defines a trend against time, which may be extrapolated forward to predict future capabilities.

Richard Foster focuses general management attention upon the importance of identifying S-curves while, for the mathematically sophisticated reader, Meade and Islam provide a critique of the relative merits of some of the numerous technological techniques available.

DELPHI METHOD

The Delphi method and its extensions provide the backbone of foresight studies. This method was originally funded by the U.S. Air Force and later developed by Olaf Helmer and coworkers at the Rand Corporation. It derives its name from the Oracle of Delphi, who was the prime source of prophecy in ancient Greece. The method is based upon the premise that the best sources of technological forecasts are the opinions of experts in the given technology. That is, the simplest way of making a forecast is to ask the experts in the field to do it. It is undesirable to base a forecast on a single oracle or expert, however distinguished, so the opinion of a sample or committee of experts is sought. The considered judgment or consensus of a committee of experts provides a viable approach to deriving a technological forecast, but suffers from the disadvantage that it may be biased toward the opinions of its dominant members. The Delphi approach avoids this disadvantage by requiring members to participate anonymously.

The Delphi method is usually conducted by one individual, known as the director. The panel's members are selected based upon expertise and availability, security considerations (e.g., commercial or military) and the avoidance of overall bias. Panel members can usually be selected from peer judgments, literature citations, honors and awards, patents, and professional society status. A typical panel consists of between ten and fifty members.

The approach is iterative, with each iteration called a round. In each round the members are interrogated individually and confidentially (usually by questionnaire) for their views on the likelihood and timing of the occurrences of certain future, technological breakthroughs or other events. Direct interactions among panel members is forbidden; this preserves anonymity between panel members, with controlled anonymous feedback. A unique feature of the Delphi method, as noted by Parenté et al, is that it provides feedback from earlier rounds between successive polls. The results of each round are summarized statistically as median-date and interquartile-range responses and circulated among panel members. In the first round, members often differ widely in their judgments, yielding a wide interquartile range. However, as members anonymously exchange the rationales of their judgments in successive rounds a consensus is reached, usually rather quickly—after about four rounds. The director then consolidates the results of this final round, which constitute the reported forecast. The panel's forecasts are usually presented in the form of the final median dates and interquartile ranges for each of the events considered.

These techniques—the S-shaped logistic curve, envelope curves and trend extrapolation, and the Delphi method—are a primary sampling of the tools used for technological forecasting. Advances in computer technology will continue to provide additional forecasting opportunities for years to come.

SEE ALSO: Futuring; Longitudinal Scenarios; Multiple-Criteria Decision Making

Michael J.C. Martin
Revised by Monica C. Turner

FURTHER READING:

Alsan, A., and M.A. Oner. "Comparison of National Foresight Studies by Integrated Foresight Management Model." *Futures* 36, no. 8 (October 2004): 889–902.

Foster, R. N. *Innovation: The Attacker's Advantage.* New York: Summit Books, 1986.

Grupp, H., and H.A. Linstone. "National Technology Foresight Activities Around the Globe: Resurrection and New Paradigms." *Technological Forecasting & Social Change* 60, no. 1 (2 January 1999): 85–94.

Kuwahara, T. "Technology Forecasting Activities in Japan." *Technological Forecasting & Social Change* 60, no. 1 (2 January 1999): 5–14.

Martin, B.R. "Foresight in Science and Technology." *Technology Analysis & Strategic Management* 7, no. 2 (June 1995): 139–68.

Meade, N., and T. Islam. "Technological Forecasting: Model Selection, Model Stability, and Combining Models." *Management Science* 44, no. 8 (August 1998): 1115–130.

Parenté, R.J., T.F. Hiöb, R.A. Silver, C. Jenkins, M.P. Poe, and R.J. Mullins. "The Delphi Method, Impeachment and Terrorism: Accuracies of Short-range Forecasts for Volatile World Events." *Technological Forecasting & Social Change* 72, no. 4 (May 2005): 401–11.

Porter, A.L., W.B. Ashton, G. Clar, J.F. Coates, K. Cuhls, S.W. Cunningham, et al. "Technology Futures Analysis: Toward Integration of the Field and New Methods." *Technological Forecasting & Social Change* 71, no. 3 (March 2004): 287–303.

Rowe, G., G. Wright, and A. McColl. "Judgment Change During Delphi-Like Procedures: The Role of Majority Influence, Expertise, and Confidence." *Technological Forecasting & Social Change* 72, no. 4 (May 2005): 377–99.

Salo, A., T. Gustafsson, and R. Ramanathan. "Multicriteria Methods for Technology Foresight." *Journal of Forecasting* 22, no. 2/3 (March/April 2003): 235–55.

TECHNOLOGY MANAGEMENT

Technology is a Greek word derived from the synthesis of two words: *techne* (meaning art) and *logos* (meaning logic or science). So loosely interpreted, technology means the art of logic or the art of scientific discipline. Formally, it has been defined by Everett M. Rogers as "a design for instrumental action that reduces the uncertainty in the cause-effect relationships involved in achieving a desired outcome". That is, technology encompasses both tangible products, such as the computer, and knowledge about processes and methods, such as the technology of mass production introduced by Henry Ford and others.

Another definition was put forth by J. Paap, as quoted by Michael Bigwood in *Research-Technology Management.* Paap defined technology as "the use of science-based knowledge to meet a need." Bigwood suggests this definition "perfectly describes the concept of technology as a bridge between science and new products." Technology draws heavily on scientific advances and the understanding gained through research and development. It then leverages this information to improve both the performance and overall usefulness of products, systems, and services.

In the context of a business, technology has a wide range of potential effects on management:

- Reduced costs of operations. For example, Dell Computer Corporation used technology to lower manufacturing and administrative costs, enabling the company to sell computers cheaper than most other vendors.

- New product and new market creation. For example, Sony Corporation pioneered the technology of miniaturization to create a whole new class of portable consumer electronics (such as radios, cassette tape recorders, and CD players).

- Adaptation to changes in scale and format. In the early part of the twenty-first century, companies addressed how small devices such as cell phones, personal digital assistants (PDAs), and MP3 players could practically become, as well as how each product could support various features and functions. For example, cell phones began to support email, web browsing, text messaging, and even picture taking as well as phone calls.

- Improved customer service. The sophisticated package-tracking system developed by Federal Express enables that company to locate a shipment while in transit and report its status to the customer. With the development of the World Wide Web, customers can find the location of their shipments without even talking to a Federal Express employee.

- Reorganized administrative operations. For example, the banking industry has reduced the cost of serving its customers by using technologies such as automated teller machines, toll-free call centers, and the Web. As of early 2005, the cost of a bank transaction

conducted by a human teller was approximately $2, compared to $1 for a telephone banking transaction, $.50-1.00 for an ATM transaction, and about ten cents for banking over the Internet. Automated Clearing House (ACH) or "checkless" check processing costs were $.25-.50 per transaction. This reduction in cost could be attributed primarily to reduction the amount of labor involved, which had a profound effect on employment and labor-management relations in banking.

Professor Michael Porter of Harvard Business School is one of many business analysts who believe that technology is one of the most significant forces affecting business competition. In his book *Competitive Advantage* (1985), Porter noted that technology has the potential to change the structure of existing industries and to create new industries. It is also a great equalizer, undermining the competitive advantages of market leaders and enabling new companies to take leadership away from existing firms. In a Grant Thorton LLP survey conducted during late 2004, 47 of 100 mid-size manufacturing businesses agreed that innovation had become increasingly import to the industry. As M.F. Wolff reported, corporate strategists were encouraging this by bringing product designers along on customer visits, offering rewards and recognition programs to employees with innovative ideas, including innovation as a priority in business strategies, setting revenue goals attributable to innovation, and looking for "willingness and ability to innovate" when making hiring decisions.

TECHNOLOGY MANAGEMENT

Since technology is such a vital force, the field of technology management has emerged to address the particular ways in which companies should approach the use of technology in business strategies and operations. Technology is inherently difficult to manage because it is constantly changing, often in ways that cannot be predicted. Technology management is the set of policies and practices that leverage technologies to build, maintain, and enhance the competitive advantage of the firm on the basis of proprietary knowledge and know-how.

The U.S. National Research Council in Washington, D.C., defined management of technology (MOT) as linking "engineering, science, and management disciplines to plan, develop, and implement technological capabilities to shape and accomplish the strategic and operational objectives of an organization" (National Research Council, 1987). While technology management techniques are themselves important to firm competitiveness, they are most effective when they complement the overall strategic posture adopted by the firm. The strategic management of technology tries to create competitive by incorporating technological opportunities into the corporate strategy.

Technology management needs to be separated from research and development (R&D) management. R&D management refers to the process by which a company runs its research laboratories and other operations for the creation of new technologies. Technology management focuses on the intersection of technology and business, encompassing not only technology creation but also its application, dissemination, and impact. Michael Bigwood suggests that New Technology Exploitation (NTE) lies somewhere between R&D and New Product Development, with characteristics of the cyclical learning process of scientific discovery and the more defined and linear process of product development.

Given these trends, a new profession, known as the technology manager, emerged. Defined as a generalist with many technology-based specializations and who possessed new managerial skills, techniques, and ways of thinking, technology managers knew company strategy and how technology could be used most effectively to support firm goals and objectives.

Educational programs supporting this career grew as well. Formal Technology Management programs became available in the 1980s and these were largely affiliated with engineering or business schools. Coursework was limited, and the field was just finding its own unique focus. During the 1990s, the increasing integration of technology into overall business function and strategy helped to align technology management more closely with business programs. Most graduate programs in the 2000s were offered through business schools, either as separate MBA tracks or as MBA concentrations. Coursework in these programs shifted emphasis from technology to management, centering around innovation management and technology strategy, while touching on other areas such as operations, new product development, project management, and organizational behavior, among others. There was still little specialization in any particular industry.

During the early 2000s, another shift took place. Global distribution, outsourcing, and large-scale collaboration impacted the nature of technology management (TM) and preparatory educational programs. At least two MBA programs were shifting their technology management focus to "innovation and leadership," with particular emphasis on real-world problem solving in partnership with large corporations.

TECHNOLOGY AND INNOVATION

Technological change is a combination of two activities invention and innovation. Invention is the development of a new idea that has useful applica-

tions. Innovation is a more complex term, referring to how an invention is brought into commercial usage. The distinction between the two is very important. As an example, Henry Ford did not invent the automobile; companies in Europe such as Daimler were producing cars well before Ford founded his company. Henry Ford instead focused on the innovation of automobiles, creating a method (mass production) by which cars could be manufactured and distributed cheaply to a large number of customers.

Figure 1
Examples of Technological Innovation and Market Growth

Products chosen by the Centre for Technology Management at the University of Cambridge. for "demonstrating one or more characteristics that assist in the analysis of modern innovation and new product introduction (NPI) processes."

- Microsoft Xbox
- Sendo mobile phones
- Crest SpinBrush (open innovation - 'connect and develop')
- yet2.com (virtual technology marketplace)
- Disney consumer electronics (brand expression through product design)
- IBM PC (dominant design, successful follower, market exit)
- Exertris exercise bike (start-up, short time-to-market)
- Palm Pilot (product vision; 'crossing the chasm')
- Pioneer digital sound projector PDSP-1 (technology licensing)
- smart car (lean manufacturing, supply chain partnering)
- ASML TWINSCAN (technology network)
- Airbus A380 (consortium, 're-integration')
- Linux (open-source software)
- Zara fashion (responsiveness, vertical integration)
- Chopper bicycle (design inspired by 'lead-users')
- IBM PC (dominant design, successful follower)
- Bowmar calculators (failure to capture value from innovation)
- Sinclair C5 (technology push, failed innovation)
- Ariane 5 flight 501 (catastrophic failure, software reuse)
- EMI CAT Scanner (failure to capture long-term value from innovation)
- Dasani (product launch, branding; misfortune-'sod's law')

Detailed case histories are available at the Centre's Product Case Histories page: http://www.betterproductdesign.net/npi/products/index.htm.

Source: Centre for Technology Management, 2005.

The practice of technology management and the development of technology strategy require an understanding of the different forms of innovation and the features of each form.

- Incremental innovations exploit the potential of established designs, and often reinforce the dominance of established firms. They improve the existing functional capabilities of a technology by means of small-scale improvements in the technology's value, adding attributes such as performance, safety, quality, and cost.

- Generational or next-generation technology innovations are incremental innovations that lead to the creation of a new but not radically different system.

- Radical innovations introduce new concepts that depart significantly from past practices and help create products or processes based on a different set of engineering or scientific principles and often open up entirely new markets and potential applications. They provide new functional capabilities unavailable in previous versions of the product or service. More specifically related to business, radical innovation has been defined as "the commercialization of new products and technologies that have strong impact on the market, in terms of offering wholly new benefits, and the firm, in terms of its ability to create new businesses." (O'Connor and Ayers)

- Architectural innovations serve to extend the radical-incremental classification of innovation and introduce the notion of changes in the way in which the components of a product or system are linked together.

There are two important steps required to properly manage corporate innovation. First is to correctly identify a project as a new product vs. a technological innovation, so a proper development process can be used (the first may be a more traditional stage-gate process; the second should be more cyclical and iterative). Second, managers need to identify what category an innovation falls under, since each type of innovation has its own challenges. In the aircraft industry, for example, an improvement in the construction of a wing is an incremental innovation. Such a new technology can be introduced relatively easily and integrated with existing products. An example of a generational innovation is the introduction of the Boeing 777, a new class of aircraft different from previous models. While similar in appearance to the 767 and its predecessor, the 777 introduced a whole new set of technologies and capabilities, requiring tremendous investment by Boeing and its business partners. A radical innovation in aircraft was the introduction of the jet engine, which completely changed the performance of aircraft compared to propeller-driven air-

planes. Finally, the concept of a flying machine as envisioned by the Wright Brothers exemplifies an architectural innovation. Prior to the Wright brothers, the concept of mechanical flight had been invented and discussed. The Wright brothers actually developed and demonstrated a design that made human flight a reality.

INNOVATION MANAGEMENT

Invention is an activity often identified with a single engineer or scientist working alone in a laboratory until he or she happens upon an idea that will change the world, like the light bulb. In reality, industrial invention, at least since the time of Edison, has involved many people working together in a collaborative setting to create new technology. Innovation requires an even broader set of people, including manufacturing engineers, marketing and sales managers, investors and financial managers, and business strategists. The methods for organizing this set of people to bring a new idea from the laboratory to the marketplace form the basis of the discipline of innovation management.

Innovation traditionally has been viewed as a linear process, which involves several stages in sequence: research, development, manufacturing, marketing, and ultimately, reaching the customer.

In each step, a group of employees take the idea as it is passed to them from the previous stage, modify it to accomplish a specific function, and pass it on to the next stage. Each team involved in the process has a clear function. Researchers are responsible for creating a working demonstration of the technology, developers and engineers turn it into something that can be produced, manufacturing engineers actually turn out the product, and marketers sell it to customers.

This linear model of innovation has proven to be a misconception of the process, however. For example, problems during the manufacturing process may require researchers to go back and change the technology to facilitate production. The technology may reach the marketing stage, only to turn out to be something no one wants to buy. Technology cannot be handed off between stages like a baton in a relay race. In any case, managing innovation in a sequential process would take a very long time, especially if each stage needs to perfect the technology before it can move on to the next stage. Some models simply add on to the linear stage-gate development approach, adding R&D discovery or planning phases to the front end of the process.

An alternative to the linear model of innovation was offered by the expanded, *chain-linked* model of innovation. This model captures the interactions between the different stages of innovation in a more complete fashion. Some of the important aspects of innovation highlighted by this model are:

- Technologies can move both forwards and backwards in the process, for example going back to the lab if further development is needed.

- Downstream stages (such as marketing) can be consulted for input at earlier stages (such as design and test).

- Scientific research and engineering knowledge contributes to every stage in the innovation process.

- Most firms create technology platforms, which are generic architectures that become the basis for a variety of technology-based products and services.

- The knowledge and skills needed for innovation are developed by communities of practitioners, not by individuals, and many of those communities exist outside of a particular firm (for example, in universities).

- Users of technology can be an important source of ideas for improvements or even new innovations with substantial market potential.

While the chain-linked model of innovation is more difficult to comprehend and analyze than the linear model, it is ultimately more rewarding as it tracks more closely to the way that innovations actually progress on their way from the laboratory to the marketplace.

Another innovation process suggested was new technology exploitation (NTE), as suggested by Bigwood, which resides somewhere between new product development and "pure science." He defined NTE as "the testing of novel technical approaches specifically aimed at achieving a pre-defined result (target performance, cost reduction, etc)." It is an iterative process, allowing for the more cyclical learning process of scientific discovery, but clearly working toward tangible goals and benefits.

Another technology management process, Strategic Technology Roadmapping (TRM) was discussed by Rachel Wells et al in *Research Technology Management*. Technology road mapping is both a process and a communication. TRM aims to "integrate technology issues considerations with the strategic business context, to identify those technologies that have the greatest potential to meet business goals, and to accelerate the transfer of technology into products." TRM makes use of visual aids to show links between R&D programs, capability targets, and requirements. It also seeks to help coordinate technology plans at a strategic level, and to help senior managers make better technology investment decisions. It also helps to manage conflicts between technology "push" and market "pull," which are discussed in more detail below.

INTERNAL FORCES AFFECTING INNOVATION

While users and other external organizations are important sources of ideas for innovations, the internal organization of a company has the greatest impact on its capability for creating innovation. The ideal work environment for innovation does not exist. Instead, innovation is facilitated through the tension and balance between various conflicting but necessary forces:

- Creativity and discipline. Creative employees are needed who challenge existing assumptions and develop new and radical approaches to solving key problems. That creativity must be tempered by the discipline to capture the ideas generated by creative employees and by systematically determining which ideas can be turned into innovations, and how.

- Individuality and teamwork. Creativity is considered an individual trait, with some people being more naturally creative than others. But innovation is clearly a team effort, often involving hundreds or thousands of people. While companies should allow employees to express their individuality as a way to facilitate creative thought, that freedom must be placed in the context of the firm as a collaborative environment, where even the most brilliant individual has to work well with others for the company to succeed.

- Exploration and focus. New ideas can come from a wide variety of sources, and it is hard to predict which paths of investigation will lead to the next breakthrough technology. Still, no firm has the resources to conduct research in every conceivable field at all times. The freedom to explore new domains of knowledge needs to be balanced by corporate decisions on what areas of investigation have the greatest promise of paying off, and focusing research in those areas.

- Long-term and short-term. Radical innovations often take years to progress from concept to tangible product. For example, the digital computer invented in the 1950s had its roots in research conducted in the mid-1800s on logic and mathematics. Unfortunately, most firms cannot spend money on research that will only begin generating revenues in ten or twenty years. Most innovative activity in firms by necessity is focused on short-term improvements and technologies. Still, firms should not lose sight of long-term innovations, as those are the technologies that can undermine existing market dominance.

One enduring debate in technology and innovation management is whether small firms are inherently more innovative than large ones. The answer appears to be different at different times. For example, the small firm Apple Computer appeared to turn out many more innovations in the 1980s than its large rival, IBM, but in the 1990s, IBM used its huge resources to regain technological dominance in computers while Apple floundered. During the 2000s, Apple came back strongly with innovative designs and technology, such as the iPod, and made big waves in the consumer arena. Also during 2004, IBM elected to sell its personal computing division to focus on information technology and software development. IBM appeared to be shedding some weight to focus on innovation and development in core business areas.

It may be more accurate to say that small firms are better organized to handle specific types of innovation compared to large firms. Small firms have very streamlined organizational structures that have few layers of management, and managers are multi-functional; i.e. they may handle business development as well as technical work, or they may be project leaders and handle company-wide finances. This cross-disciplinary approach favors flexibility and efficiency, which in turn is more conducive to radical innovation. The small firm model of organization is quite different from large established firms in which personnel in general have more narrow tasks and bureaucratic processes tend to suppress creativity and individual initiative.

Large companies are geared for production and distribution, which are large-scale undertakings that do not accommodate rapid change. Hence, the organizational structure of a large firm is quite matrix oriented engineering disciplines are assigned to projects, and a central laboratory supports research and development. Innovation is organized in a more linear fashion, and internal organization favors discipline and focus. This type of organization is better suited to incremental innovation, since it can identify problems and focus tremendous resources on solving them.

There are several ways in which small and large firms can overcome natural tendencies to gain proficiency in all types of innovation. Lockheed Martin, a large aerospace firm, was the originator of the Skunk Works, a lean, aggressive organization focused on R&D and rapid development of cutting-edge technologies. The group is kept completely isolated from the larger corporate organization, so that the engineers are unencumbered with overhead issues that are handled by other resources within the company at large. From the cultural point of view, aside from the infrastructure a large company has to handle regulatory matters as well as financial support. A small firm and a Skunk Works of a large firm can be very similar.

A small firm, in turn, can partner with a larger firm to gain access to the resources and infrastructure needed to address incremental as well as radical innovation. Carayannis et al. (1997) found that small firms tended to form technology-based strategic alliances as a source of financing. The funds gained through the alliance with a larger firm are then devoted to acquiring and developing tangible strategic assets such as proprietary technology, general working capital, and skills and know-how possessed by key managerial personnel. The large firm in the alliance receives technology-related intellectual property rights (IPRs) and marketing rights more often than equity, manufacturing rights, and so forth, in exchange for their capital infusion. An alliance with a large firm can create a powerful combination that benefits both the small company and its established partner.

Table 1

Technology vs. Market Push and Pull

The Technology Perspective

	Market Pull	Market Push
Technology Pull	*Market Satisfying*	*Technology Satisfying*
Technology Push	*Technology Satisfying*	*Market Seeding*

During the early 2000s, companies were still seeking ways to build radical innovation competencies into their own organization. O'Connor and Ayers reported on a three-year study of twelve large firms (such as GE, Corning, IBM, and Shell Chemicals, among others) who worked to develop this competency, and identified three key competencies that were critical to success:

- Discovery—creation, recognition, elaboration, and articulation of opportunities

- Incubation—experimentation, technical, as well as for market learning, market creation, and matching the innovation with company strategy

- Acceleration—exploiting the technology, investing to build new business and infrastructure, responding to market opportunities

Finally, O'Connor and Ayers concluded that no one model works for all companies. Of the twelve companies studies, four had very distinct but different approaches, each influenced by that company's corporate culture. But nearly all participants in the study acknowledged a need for cultural change within the organization before radical innovation could take place.

EXTERNAL FORCES AFFECTING INNOVATION

Various forces outside the direct control of the firm can also affect the innovation process. One set of forces relates to the tension between the demands of the market and the capabilities of the technology under development.

A conventional way of analyzing technology development is to contrast the influence of *technology push* with that of *market pull*. The primary difference between a push or pull scenario is between solving a problem and accommodating a solution. Technology push is the process of solving a problem by providing a technical answer to a market need (which can be either anticipated or existing). Market pull involves solving a problem to provide a market answer to a technical need, or accommodating a technical solution by finding market uses. The dynamic balancing act between technology push and market pull drives the speed and acceleration of technological change, and in the process creates significant windows of market opportunity as well as competitive threats to the established technologies.

The terms push and pull can be expanded to encompass either a technology or market point of view:

- Technology push has been historically defined by an innovation-cycle-driven culture focused on marketing/technology management analysis. In this context, a firm's R&D division brings an idea from the invention stage to its fruition in commercial markets.

- The not-so-traditional technology pull is best described as the reaction to demand in the market. The desire for more efficient technologies by customers creates incremental improvements in these technologies that may eventually lead to a critical mass of innovations and possibly to radical improvements.

- On the other hand, market pull has been historically defined by marketing. The marketplace dictates the products that are to be supplied by a firm. In order to meet demand, a firm must constantly strive to increase performance and customer satisfaction.

- Market push is a term that addresses the creation of markets through marketing-driven efforts that, along with technology pull, can lead to the creation of technological standards that define and enable the emergence of new markets (see Figures 1 and 2).

Table 2
Technology vs. Market Push and Pull

The Market Perspective

	Market Pull	Market Push
Technology Pull	*Reacting to Demand*	*Seeding Demand*
Technology Push	*Meeting Demand*	*Anticipating Demand*

Source: Carayannis, Elias and Samanta Roy, "Davids vs. Goliaths in the Small Satellite Industry: The Role of Technological Innovation Dynamics in Firm Competitiveness." *International Journal of Technovation,* under review

In Figures 1 and 2, we interpret the possible configurations combining market and technology push and pull from a technology and a market perspective. The emphasis swings from a reactive stance, through an accommodating one, to a proactive one (from reacting to demand and satisfying markets to seeding and anticipating demand). The relative strength of each of the four forces (technology push or pull and market push or pull) varies during the lifecycle of the technology.

Technologies, as they develop, often follow a pattern known as the technology S-curve. In the first phase of development, tremendous investment in the technology yields relatively little improvement in performance, since the investment is devoted to researching various aspects of the technology, many of which do not have useful results. At some point, the technology takes off when a key breakthrough is made. At this critical moment, called an inflection point, the performance of the technology improves rapidly. During this second, or growth, phase, additional investment is focused on the technological breakthrough, with rapid results. As that breakthrough technology is more fully understood and exploited, the rate of improvement begins to slow and the technology enters its third phase, maturity. Finally, the technology reaches a point where additional research yields little new knowledge and few results. At this point, the technology begins the final stage, decline, and often becomes obsolete as better technologies are developed and introduced to the market.

Technology and innovation management constitute a discipline of management that continues to gain importance, impact, and attention. As technology is a pervasive force in business and in society, management of technology helps to ensure that the development of new technology and its applications are aimed at useful purposes, and that the benefits of new technology outweigh the disruptions and difficulties that accompany innovation. While it is possible to specialize in technology management, this discipline also constitutes a set of skills that all managers should possess in the modern technology-intensive and technology-driven world of business.

SEE ALSO: Innovation; Management Information Systems; New Product Development; Organizational Learning; Technology Transfer

Elias G. Carayannis and Jeffrey Alexander
Revised by Wendy H. Mason

FURTHER READING:

Betz, Frederick. *Executive Strategy Strategic Management and Information Technology.* Wiley, 2001.

Bigwood, Michael P. "Managing the New Technology Exploitation Process." *Research-Technology Management,* November-December 2004, 38.

Burgelman, Robert A., Clayton M. Christensen, and Steven C. Wheelwright. *Strategic Management of Technology and Innovation.* McGraw-Hill/Irwin, 2003.

Carayannis, Elias, and Jeffrey Alexander. "The Wealth of KnowledgeConverting Intellectual Property To Intellectual Capital In Co-opetitive Research and Technology Management Settings." *International Journal of Technology Management* 17, no. 3/4 (1998).

Carayannis, Elias, S. Kassicieh, and R. Radosevich. "Financing Technological Entrepreneurship: The Role of Strategic Alliances in Procuring Early Stage Seed Capital." Paper presented at the 1997 Proceedings of the Portland International Conference on Management of Engineering and Technology, Portland, OR, July 1997.

"Fitch Ratings Comments on IBM's Sale of PC Business." *Business Wire,* 8 December, 2004.

Harrison, Norma, and Danny Samson. *Technology Management: Text and International Cases.* McGraw-Hill/Irwin, 2001.

Khalil, Tarek. *Management of Technology.* McGraw-Hill Science/Engineering/Math, 1999.

Miller, Roger, and Serghei Floricel. "Value Creation and Games of Innovation." *Research-Technology Management,* November-December 2004, 25.

Nambisan, Satish, and David Wilemon. "Industry Should Help Redefine the Agenda for Technology Management Education." *Research-Technology Management,* November-December 2004, 9.

O'Connor, Gina Colarelli, and Alan D. Ayers. "Building a Radical Innovation Competency." *Research-Technology Management,* January-February 2005, 23.

Porter, Michael. *Competitive Advantage.* New York: The Free Press, 1985.

Rivas, Rio, and David H. Gobeli. "Accelerating Innovation at Hewlett-Packard." *Research-Technology Management,* January-February 2005, 32.

Rogers, Everett M. *The Diffusion of Innovations.* New York: The Free Press, 1995.

Rosenberg, Nathan and Ralph Landau. "An Overview of Innovation." In *The Positive Sum Strategy.* Washington National Academy Press, 1986.

Rosenbloom, Richard and William Spencer, eds. *Engines of Innovation U.S. Industrial Research at the End of an Era.* Cambridge, MA: Harvard Business School Press, 1996.

Schilling, Melissa. *Strategic Management of Technological Innovation.* McGraw-Hill/Irwin, 2004.

U.S. National Research Council. *Management of Technology The Hidden Competitive Advantage.* Washington National Academy Press, 1987.

U.S. Office of Technology Assessment. "Innovation and Commercialization of Emerging Technologies." Report OTA-BP-ITC-165, Washington GPO, September 1995. Available from <www.ota.nap.edu>.

Wells, Rachel, et al. "Technology Roadmapping for a Service Organization." *Research-Technology Management,* March-April 2004, 46.

Wolff, M.F. "Manufacturers Seek More Innovation." *Research-Technology Management,* January-February 2005, 6.

TECHNOLOGY TRANSFER

Technology transfer is a fast-growing activity in the U.S. research and development system, and one which has received substantial attention from governments, industry, and universities. The exact nature of this activity is difficult to pin down, partly because the term has many different connotations. Some of the varieties of technology transfer commonly discussed in business periodicals (such as the *Wall Street Journal*) include:

- International technology transfer: the transfer of technologies developed in one country to firms or other organizations in another country. In the U.S., this issue is often associated with the undesired transfer of weapons technology to "hostile" nations.

- North-South technology transfer: activities for the transfer of technologies from industrial nations (the North) to less-developed countries (the South), usually for the purpose of accelerating economic and industrial development in the poor nations of the world.

- Private technology transfer: the sale or other transfer of a technology from one company to another.

- Public-private technology transfer: the transfer of technology from universities or government laboratories to companies.

While all four types of technology transfer are of concern to businesses, this overview will deal mostly with the first two types. International technology transfer and North-South technology transfer these activities tend to be driven directly by foreign policy and national defense concerns, while the other two types are driven by a balance of corporate and policy interests.

WHAT IS TECHNOLOGY TRANSFER?

Technology is information that is put to use in order to accomplish some task. Transfer is the movement of technology via some communication channel from one individual or organization to another. Technology is the useful application of knowledge and expertise into an operation.

Technology transfer usually involves some source of technology, group which posses specialized technical skills, which transfers the technology to a target group of receptors who do not possess those specialized technical skills, and who therefore cannot create the tool themselves (Carayannis et al., 1997). In the United States especially, the technology transfer experience has pointed to multiple transfer strategies, two of which are the most significant: the licensing of intellectual property rights and extending property rights and technical expertise to developing firms.

The major categories of technology transfer and commercialization involve the transfer of:

a. technology codified and embodied in tangible artifacts

b. processes for implementing technology

c. knowledge and skills that provide the basis for technology and process development.

WHY TRANSFER TECHNOLOGY?

Most technology transfer takes place because the organization in which a technology is developed is different from the organization that brings the technology to market. The process of introducing a technology into the marketplace is called technology commercialization. In many cases, technology commercialization is carried out by a single firm. The firm's employees invent the technology, develop it into a commercial product or process, and sell it to customers. In a growing number of cases, however, the organization that creates a technology does not bring it to the market. There are several potential reasons for this:

- If the inventing organization is a private company, it may not have the resources needed to bring the technology to market, such as a distribution network, sales organization, or simply the money and equipment for manufacturing the product (these resources are called complementary assets). Even if the company has those resources, the technology may not be viewed as a strategic product for that firm, especially if the technology was created as a byproduct of a research project with a different objective.

- If the inventing organization is a government laboratory, that laboratory is forbidden in general by law or policy (in the United States) from competing with the private sector by selling products or processes. Therefore, the technology can only be brought to market by a private firm.

- If the inventing organization is a university, the university usually does not have the resources or expertise to produce and market the products from that technology. Also, if the technology was developed with funding from the federal government, U.S. law strongly encourages the university to transfer the technology to a private firm for commercialization.

From a public policy perspective, technology transfer is important because technology can be utilized as a resource for shared prosperity at home and abroad. As a resource, technology (1) consists of a body of knowledge and know-how, (2) acts as a stimulant for healthy competitive international trade, (3) is linked with other nations' commercial needs, and (4) needs an effective plan for management and entrepreneurship from lab to market.

From a business perspective, companies engage in technology transfer for a number of reasons:

- Companies look to transfer technologies from other organizations because it may be cheaper, faster, and easier to develop products or processes based on a technology someone else has invented rather than to start from scratch. Transferring technology may also be necessary to avoid a patent infringement lawsuit, to make that technology available as an option for future technology development, or to acquire a technology that is necessary for successfully commercializing a technology the company already possesses.

- Companies look to transfer technologies to other organizations as a potential source of revenue, to create a new industry standard, or to partner with a firm that has the resources or complementary assets needed to commercialize the technology.

For government laboratories and universities, the motivations for technology transfer are somewhat different:

- Governments or universities may transfer technology from outside organizations if it is needed to accomplish a specific goal or mission (for example, universities may transfer in educational technologies), or if that technology would add value to a technology the government or university is hoping to transfer out to a company.

- Government laboratories and universities commonly transfer technologies to other organizations for economic development reasons (to create jobs and revenues for local firms), as an alternate source of funding, or to establish a relationship with a company that could have benefits in the future.

HOW DO YOU TRANSFER TECHNOLOGY?

The first requirement for an organization to transfer a technology is to establish legal ownership of that technology through intellectual property law. There are four generally recognized forms of intellectual property in industrialized nations:

- patents, dealing with functional and design inventions

- trademarks, dealing with commercial origin and identity

- copyrights, dealing with literary and artistic expressions

- trade secrets, which protect the proprietary capabilities of the firm

Under U.S. law, a patent is granted only by the federal government and lets the patentee exclude others from making, using, selling or offering an invention for a fixed term, currently 20 years from the date the patent application is filed. The number of patents granted by the U.S. government is up by 21 percent in 2003. A trademark, as defined under the Trademark Act of 1946 (The Lanham Act) is "any word, name, symbol, or device, or any combination thereof (1) used by a person, or (2) which a person has a bona fide intention to use in commerce. . .to identify and distinguish his or her goods, including a unique product, from those manufactured or sold by others, and to indicate the source of the goods, even if that source is unknown."

A copyright seeks to promote literary and artistic creativity by protecting, for a limited time, what the U.S. Constitution broadly calls writings of authors. The general rule in the United States for a work created on or after January 1, 1978, whether or not it is published, is that copyright lasts for the author's lifetime plus 50 years after the author's death. The copyright in a work made for hire or in an anonymous work lasts for 75 years from publication or 100 years from creation, whichever is shorter.

A trade secret is information that an inventor chooses not to disclose and to which the inventor also controls access, thus providing enduring protection. Trade secrets remain in force only if the holder takes reasonable precautions to prevent them from being revealed to people outside the firm, except through a legal mechanism such as a license. Trade secrets are governed by state rather than federal law.

The second step in technology transfer is finding a suitable recipient for that technology—one that can use the technology and has something of value to offer in return. Firms are now studying more systematically the process of licensing and technology transfer. There are five information activities needed to support technology transfer:

- technology scouting—searching for specific technologies to buy or license.

- technology marketing—searching for buyers for a technology, the inverse of tech scouting;

also searching for collaborators, joint venture or development partners, or for investors or venture capital to fund a specific technology.

- technology assessment—evaluating technology, aimed at answering the question "what is this technology worth?" Includes research of any intellectual properties, and market and competitor assessments.

- transfer-related activities—information about the transfer process itself, such as licensing terms and practices, contracts, conducting negotiations, and how to do the transfer most successfully.

- finding experts—to assist in any of the above areas. A common saying in the field is, "technology transfer is a contact sport."

These information needs are often supported by service companies, such as licensing consultants, and by electronic media, including databases and online networks. Some new online networks use the Internet to help firms in these information activities.

The information-transfer process is one of the most critical steps in technology transfer. New licensing practices are designed to address this process. For example, many licenses now bundle both the basic technology and the equipment needed to utilize that technology in a single agreement. A license may also include a "know-how" agreement, which exchanges relevant trade secrets (with appropriate protections) to the licensee to help in exploiting technology. In some industries, such as petroleum exploration, firms even practice wet licensing, whereby employees of the licenser are loaned out to the licensee to teach how a technology should be properly used.

The major barrier to the increase in technology transfer among firms is organizational behavior. In the past, cultural blocks such as the "not invented here" syndrome prevented firms from even showing interest in technology transfer. New concepts along the lines of knowledge management are changing behaviors and beliefs, leading firms to realize the enormous gains to be made through the active pursuit of licensing.

Once the organization has at least started to establish ownership of the technology, there are several possible legal and/or contractual mechanisms for transferring technology from one organization to another:

- licensing—the exchange of access to a technology and perhaps associated skills from one company for a regular stream of cash flows from another.

- cross-licensing—an agreement between two firms to allow each other use of or access to specific technologies owned by the firms.

- strategic supplier agreement—a long-term supply contract, including guarantees of future purchases and greater integration of activity than a casual market relationship. One prominent example is the second-source agreements signed between semiconductor chip manufacturers.

- contract R&D—an agreement under which one company or organization, which generally specializes in research, conducts research in a specific area on behalf of a sponsoring firm.

- joint or cooperative R&D agreement—an agreement under which two or more companies agree to cooperate in a specific area of R&D or a specific project, coordinating research tasks across the partner firms and with sharing of research results.

- R&D corporation or research joint venture—the establishment of a separate organization, jointly owned by two or more companies, which conducts research on behalf of its owners. A notable example is Bellcore, which originally was established by the seven Regional Bell Holding Companies of the United States and which would conduct research and set standards for the local telephone system.

- research consortium—any organization with multiple members formed to conduct joint research in a broad area, often in its own facilities and using personnel on loan from member firms and/or direct hires. The Microelectronics and Computer Technology Corporation (MCC) and Semiconductor Manufacturing Technology (SEMATECH) are examples of such organizations.

The choice of which mechanism to use in a particular technology transaction depends on many factors, including the stage of development for that technology, what the company receiving the technology is willing or able to pay, what technology or other assets it might be able to offer in place of money, the likely benefits of establishing a longer-lasting partnership between the organizations instead of a one-time transfer; and the exact legal status of ownership over that technology. For example, if a small firm simply wants to sell its technology to a large firm in exchange for money, it will probably choose to license the technology. If the small firm also wants access to the large firm's complementary assets, such as its production facilities and distribution network, it will try to negotiate a more substantial and permanent relationship, such as an R&D contract or a cooperative R&D agreement.

PRIVATE TECHNOLOGY TRANSFER

Technology transfer between private companies is most commonly accomplished through licensing, although other mechanisms such as joint ventures, research consortia, and research partnerships are also quite popular. Licensing is a big business by itself. In 2002 U.S. companies received over $66 billion in payments on technology licenses from other organizations, of which $58 billion was from domestic sources. Data from the U.S. Department of Commerce compiled in the mid-1990s indicated that international technology licensing was rising at approximately 18 percent per year, and domestic technology licensing was rising at 10 percent per year.

Another growing mode of private technology transfer is the formation of research joint ventures (RJVs) between companies in the United States. For years, such joint ventures were rare, mostly due to fears among companies that joint ventures would provoke antitrust litigation from the government. Passage of the National Cooperative Research Act (NCRA) in 1984 and the National Cooperative Research and Production Act in 1993 relaxed antitrust regulation of such partnerships, leading to a substantial increase in RJVs.

Studies of the filings of RJVs registered with the Department of Justice under the NCRA shows some interesting trends:

- Although multi-firm consortia such as SEMATECH and the Microelectronics and Computer Corporation (MCC) attract the most interest, about 85 percent of RJVs involve only two firms.

- Most RJVs focus on developing process technologies rather than product technologies, as processes are viewed as pre-competitive technologies in many industries.

- The largest concentration of RJVs focus on telecommunications, while software and computer hardware are also leading industries for RJV activity. These industries have significant impact on technological advances in other industries, and therefore attract much interest for partnering firms. Not surprisingly, RJVs are less common in the chemical and pharmaceutical industries, probably because process technologies have greater competitive impact in those industries than in others.

Research joint ventures are an advantageous means of acquiring high-risk technologies, for several reasons. First, joint ventures enable the risks and costs involved in early research in technology to be shared across multiple firms, reducing the burden on each individual company. Second, the resources and expertise needed to develop certain technologies may be distributed across multiple firms, so RJVs are the only way to combine those resources in one effort. Third, in industries where technology advances quickly, RJVs are an effective way to keep up with new developments. Finally, RJVs are often used to develop and set critical technical standards in certain industries, especially telecommunications. These reasons indicate that RJVs will continue to increase in significance as a tool for technology transfer.

TECHNOLOGY TRANSFER FROM GOVERNMENT TO INDUSTRY

In an effort to increase the application of government research results to industry technology problems (and therefore fuel technology-based economic growth), the United States government has passed a series of laws since 1980 to encourage the transfer of technologies from government laboratories to industry. Technology licensing was the earliest focus of activity, based on the notion that government laboratories were like treasure chests of available technologies that could easily be applied to corporate needs. In fact, government technology licensing activity is extremely limited, except in the National Institutes of Health. The NIH has been the source of several groundbreaking therapies and other medical technologies and enjoys close relations with the pharmaceutical industry, enabling the agency to gain large amounts of licensing revenue.

Other agencies face substantial difficulties in licensing technologies. Often, their technologies require substantial development before commercialization, reducing their value to firms. Also, most government laboratories do research in areas where there is no clear, consistent path to commercialization as exists in the pharmaceutical industry. The uncertainty of commercialization also diminishes the willingness of firms to purchase technology licenses from laboratories.

Instead, most agencies have focused on signing Cooperative Research and Development Agreements (CRADAs), a mechanism developed under the 1986 Federal Technology Transfer Act. CRADAs are contracts to conduct joint R&D projects, where the government laboratory contributes personnel and equipment, while the partner contributes these assets and funding as well. The number of CRADAs signed by government agencies has increase steadily in recent years.

There are several potential benefits and potential difficulties involved in CRADA research relationships:

- Transfer of product and process technologies can have a significant impact on recipient firms' business performance. For example, the invention of an improved method for delivering the medication paclitaxel was licensed by the National Institutes of Health to Bristol-Myers-Squibb as the product Taxol, which has since become a leading treatment for breast and ovarian cancer. However, there is no data to show what portion of transfers are successful versus those which are not.

- Technology transfer may or may not result in commercial products. A survey of 229 technology transfer projects at 29 federal laboratories, conducted by the Georgia Institute of Technology, found that 22 percent of the projects resulted in new commercial products, while 38 percent contributed to products under development. Interestingly, in 13 percent of the projects, new product development or product improvement was never a goal.

- Laboratories' views on technology transfer can affect success. Now that most of the legal barriers to technology transfer have apparently been eliminated by congressional legislation, the true barriers are generated by the culture of the laboratories and the attitudes of researchers and laboratory administrators. For example, in several cases firms have complained that laboratory researchers were not used to meeting the strict timetables on project completion that private sector researchers must observe.

- Technology transfer, especially in joint research, can aid the government laboratory as well. A report by the GAO examining ten CRADA projects found that the laboratories can also benefit from technology transfer, for example, through enhanced expertise for researchers, development of technologies that also support the laboratory's mission, acquisition of sophisticated equipment and infrastructure, and increased laboratory revenues from industrial sources.

UNIVERSITY-INDUSTRY TECHNOLOGY TRANSFER

One of the original pieces of U.S. technology-transfer legislation, the Bayh-Dole Act, directed government agencies to encourage universities and other research organizations to license out technologies developed with federal funding. Since 1980, this activity has become a small but growing source of revenue for universities. Technology transfer from academia and other research institutions to industry continues to grow, according to the annual survey of the Association of University Technology Managers. The 2003 survey shows that increasing numbers of research institutions are forging licensing agreements with commercial entities to bring newly developed technology and products to the market. In 2003, the 165 institutions of higher education responding to the survey reported receiving close to $1 billion in licensing revenue in 2003, a 1 percent increase over 2002.

Commercial institutions pay royalties for the right to put inventions and discoveries from universities to commercial use in products such as computer-imaging technology, medical diagnostic testing, and treatment of disease. Institutions of higher education, in turn, can use the revenue to increase investments in research and development. This technology transfer also leads to sponsored research agreements between firms and universities, often to undertake additional research needed to commercialize technologies. Universities now receive approximately 7 percent of all research funding from industry, compared to about 3 percent in the 1970s. Institutions of higher education also reported spinning off nearly 350 companies and receiving 3,450 U.S. patents for new technologies and inventions. Since fiscal year 1998 when the question was first asked, 178 U.S. survey respondents have reported a total of 2,230 new products introduced to the market place.

For industry, universities offer the best way to acquire basic technological research as those activities are curtailed within firms. Universities also house experts in very focused fields of study that are likely to have benefits to a small number of firms. Finally, joint industry-university research is viewed as an important recruiting tool in today's competition for scientific talent, since industry-funded projects are often carried out by graduate students who later go to work for their former sponsors.

Technology transfer is a valuable mechanism by which industry can accelerate its innovation activities and gain competitive advantage through cooperation. Technology transfer can also boost overall economic growth and regional economic development. While further study is needed to estimate the exact benefits gained from technology transfer and ways to achieve those benefits, it is clear that this is an activity that is becoming a central feature of the U.S. research and development system.

SEE ALSO: Joint Ventures and Strategic Alliances; Licensing and Licensing Agreements; Technology Management

Elias G. Carayannis and Jeffrey Alexander
Revised by Badie N. Farah

FURTHER READING:

Carayannis, Elias, Everett Rogers, K. Kurihara, and M. Albritton. "High-Technology Spin-offs from Government R&D Laboratories and Research Universities." *International Journal of Technovation* 18, no. 1 (1998): 1–11.

———. "Cooperative Research and Development Agreements (CRADAS) as Technology Transfer Mechanisms." *R&D Management,* Spring 1998.

Carayannis, Elias, and Jeffrey Alexander. "Secrets of Success and Failure in Commercializing U.S. Government R&D Laboratories Technologies: A Structured Case Studies Approach." *International Journal of Technology Management* 17, no. 3/4 (1998).

Geisler, E. "Technology Transfer: Toward Mapping the Field, a Review, and Research Directions." *Journal of Technology Transfer,* Summer-Fall 1993, 88–93.

Goldscheider, Robert, ed. *Licensing Best Practices: The LESI Guide to Strategic Issues and Contemporary Realities.* New York: John Wiley & Sons, 2002.

Ham, Rose Marie, and David C. Mowery. "Improving Industry-Government Cooperative R&D." *Issues in Science & Technology,* Summer 1995, 67–73.

Megantz, Robert C. *Technology Management: Developing and Implementing Effective Licensing Programs.* New York: John Wiley & Sons, 2002.

Muir, Albert E. *The Technology Transfer System.* Latham, NY: Latham Book Publishing, 1997.

Parr, Russell L., and Patrick H. Sullivan. *Technology Licensing: Corporate Strategies for Maximizing Value.* New York: John Wiley & Sons, 1996.

Shenkar, Oded. *The Chinese Century: The Rising Chinese Economy and Its Impact on the Global Economy, the Balance of Power, and Your Job.* New York: John Wiley & Sons, 2005.

TELECOMMUNICATIONS

Traditionally, telecommunications denoted the long-distance connections that linked television networks to their affiliates and the long-distance phone connections that linked telephone networks to local switching centers. Hence the term applied both to AT&T's long-distance telephone network and to the television industry's worldwide networks-but each used very different technologies to transmit voice or video. Now with the rapidly growing size of the Internet, telecommunications has expanded to include data networks. The newest technologies to join the telecommunications industry are wireless phones and wireless data businesses.

Telecommunications and information-related industries continue to enjoy a rapid growth in the Internet and the wireless phone sectors. Table 1 provides a summary of the major classes of telecommunications services and how they function.

Table 1
Telecommunications Providers and Data Networks

Local and Regional Telephone
- Regional or local phone services–from central office to residents
- Wireless phone services–from local towers to adjacent cell phones
- Commercial phone services–from central office to businesses

Long-Distance Telephone
- Phone/voice networks–backbone of the long-distance phone system

Internet and Data Networks
- Data/voice over the Internet backbone or private networks
- Internet content areas: Web sites, subscription content, private networks linked to Internet

Television
- Regional cable-TV companies–central office downloads TV programming and sends it out to residents
- Satellite TV companies–residents each have satellite dish
- Broadcast networks–content is beamed up to satellites, received by local stations, and retransmitted as conventional analog or digital signals to viewers

THE REGULATORY ENVIRONMENT

The concept of universal service has traditionally referred to the goal that all Americans should have access to affordable telephone service. Television access does not require that homes be wired, so that is less problematic; but there is increasing pressure for universal Internet access. Universal telephone access has been met by means of policies established by government regulatory bodies. Phone or Internet services in densely populated areas promise good revenue and profits, because the cost of wiring businesses and residences is lessened by the short distances. The regulations are needed to ensure that people in remote areas have access; as people continue to move further and further away from population centers, the cost of bringing phone wires can be prohibitively expensive. But the phone companies are nonetheless required to extend the wire to them. The quid pro quo for making the huge investment to wire homes and businesses was protection from competitors; this protection was usually provided by state public utility commissions or municipal government policies. As a practical matter, limiting competition and the number of wires strung along highways and into homes makes good sense, especially from an aesthetic perspective.

In 1996 the Federal Communication Commission (FCC) issued an extensive new set of regulations to increase the competition in the industry. The local phone companies take serious objection to competitors coming into their territories and grabbing business and residential customers in the densely populated urban and suburban locations. But that is what is happening; cable-TV companies are partnering with long-distance companies and using their cables to offer a package of phone, TV, premium TV, digital music, Internet access, and e-mail. The Regional Bell Operating companies have also engaged in a variety of mergers. The FCC appears to be ready to approve mergers that open up competition in the local phone and cable-TV markets (e.g., AT&T was allowed to acquire TCI and other cable services), but not always the mergers between local phone companies.

The National Telecommunications and Information Administration (NTIA), an agency of the United States Department of Commerce, is the executive branch's principal voice on domestic and international telecommunications and information technology issues. NTIA works to spur innovation, encourage competition, help create jobs, and provide consumers with more choices and better quality telecommunications products and services at lower prices. Now that a considerable portion of today's business, communication, and research takes place on the Internet, access to the computers and networks may be as important as access to traditional telephone services. The NTIA is preparing policy to ensure access to the Internet service.

THE FCC AND COMPETITION IN THE TELEPHONE INDUSTRY

In 1982 AT&T signed a consent decree agreeing to the break up of its business into the long-distance business, which it retained, and seven Regional Bell Operating Companies (RBOCs), which became separate business entities serving specified regions. The Telecommunications Act of 1996 was a major revision of policy regulating the industry. That act attempted "to promote competition and reduce regulation in order to secure lower prices and higher quality services for American telecommunications consumers and encourage rapid deployment of new telecommunications technologies." The act tried to stimulate competition by laying down the conditions for regional phone companies to move into the long-distance arena and for long-distance carriers to offer business and residential phone services. But little in the way of increased competition has occurred in the mainstream telephone industry, even less in the cable-TV industry.

In 1999 competition was heating up as businesses in all three sectors went after three major opportunities for growth and increased profits: (1) the rapidly growing market for Internet access, (2) the rapidly growing market for wireless phones, (3) the opportunity to grab a share in all sectors by offering customers a package rate on phone, wireless phone, cable-TV, and Internet services. The current situation in these markets is:

1. The long-distance market is rapidly expanding to serve both the increased number of long-distance phone calls and, especially, the greatly increased demand for Internet access. At the same time competition is increasing, and the amount of capacity is multiplying because of advances in fiber-optic technology. As a result, prices are declining and profits are squeezed because of the huge costs of upgrading the technology of the vast infrastructure

2. Cable-TV companies are in the best position to become profitable, because their cable systems can provide the full package of services into the home. Providing long-distance phone service and Internet service requires a partnership with a long-distance carrier. As a result, mergers in the business have become hot topics. The cable-TV sector is the least competitive telecommunication market, and cable companies have been able to increase their rates. But many companies carry a large debt load resulting from the costs of upgrading their cable systems; repayment of their debt is the justification for rate increases.

3. The regional phone carriers are poorly situated for long-term competition. Currently, most are protecting their profit margins and fending off competition. But direct competition from the cable-TV and AT&T companies in the local phone business could be catastrophic for them; AT&T is promising substantially lower monthly phone rates. The phone companies are impeded by their slow-speed wires and switches from providing high-speed Internet access-video over their system is impossible. They are being forced to consider the huge investment required by rewiring every home in order to stay competitive.

4. The wireless phone business is largely unregulated, highly competitive, and growing very rapidly. Having a national network, whereby long distance calls remain on a single carrier's infrastructure, has become a strong competitive edge. The result is that customers' phones work in every major city and that there are no roaming changes to cover long-distance changes from other inter-exchange carriers. Bigger is better in this environment, and large wireless companies are thus merging with long-distance carriers.

5. Internet access and e-mail are the fastest growing services in the telecommunications industry. The Internet-service business is made up of the linkages from homes and businesses to Internet service providers (ISPs), which in turn provide linkages to the major Internet backbone mostly provided by long-distance carrier MCI Worldcom. In 1999 most of the linkages from homes and businesses were carried by the local phone companies; while much faster speeds were available from the cable-TV firms, few were ready to provide data services. Competition for high-speed linkages from home or business to the Internet backbone will be intense. The cable-TV industry is much better positioned to capture business in the short term; eventually, digital lines into businesses and homes will probably be needed as voice, TV, data, and on-demand video are all delivered in a digital format as part of a package of services.

THE TELEPHONE INDUSTRY

A long-distance telephone call is the typical way in which most people experience the telephone network, which extends from home phones to a local switching center, then to another remote switching center, and finally to the home or business called. The term telecommunications primarily applies to the long-distance carriers, such as AT&T, MCI, and Sprint, which carry transmissions between switching centers. The local telephone markets are dominated by the Regional Bell Operating Companies (RBOCs), such as Verizon, BellSouth, and SBC Communications. The RBOCs bear the responsibility for universal access, for ensuring that every residence-no matter how remote-has affordable phone service. Often these rural and remote sites pay the minimum amount, approximately $15 per month, for the minimal service. The RBOCs claim that their costs for customers exceed $15 per month; the public utility commissions at the state level help the RBOCs subsidize those customers with revenue from urban and suburban customers, as well as access fees paid by long-distance carriers. The RBOCs are guaranteed a profit by the public utility commissions, but the rates have been virtually constant with little growth in the number of phones added. At present, this is a good business to be in, but it is expected to be a very bad business as competition from cable-TV companies drives down prices.

Each local telephone center is a hub from which copper wires extend to homes and businesses. This last mile of wiring is the window or portal into millions of homes and businesses, controlling-in some ways-the services provided and the revenues generated

from homes and businesses. The last mile of wiring is also the major bottleneck to providing better and faster services to those millions of sites. The twisted pair wires in virtually every home are the major problem with boosting the speed of Internet access over those lines. But those millions of miles of wires are extremely expensive to replace. In order for the regional phone companies to effectively compete agains the cable-TV companies, they will have to re-wire, thereby opening up the possibility of providing the full bundle of services to the home owners.

In every major Asian city, wireless phones are everywhere. This phenomenon will be repeated in the United States as more and more workers transact business away from their desks, and as less and less time is spent at home. It is quite possible that phone calls originating from wireless phones will surpass those from wired phones in the near future.

John Malone, a cable industry executive, coined the term convergence to describe the packaging of multiple services to customers, such as cable-TV, premium movie channels, Internet services, digital music channels, and phone service. Convergence is made possible by advances in transmission technology; all of those services can be provided to homes over a single cable. And that means that cable-TV companies can move into the phone business, phone companies can move into the TV business, etc. As convergence becomes a reality, competition in the telecommunications industry moves to new level.

TELECOMMUNICATIONS TECHNOLOGIES

All the major cable-TV companies have announced that they will provide high-speed Internet services alongside the regular TV and pay-per-view channels; TCI and Time Warner say they will also include telephone services. All these services will be offered over one coaxial cable (wire). The cable companies employ a transmission approach called broadband; Media One's logo includes the phrase "Broadband is the Future." Coaxial cable can carry high-speed data and/or multiple channels of video over an insulated central copper wire wrapped in another cylindrical conducting wire, which is then shielded and wrapped in a protective cover. This wire is split into many channels by breaking out the wiring spectrum into multiple frequencies and transmitting each channel on a separate frequency; this is what broadband means, it delivers an amazing amount of content by using frequency division multiplexing. Part of the available frequency spectrum is dedicated to data for Internet access and another part is dedicated to voice for telephony.

As great as broadband sounds, it has the inherent drawback of being an analog approach for sending digital TV signals, digital sound, and for sending and receiving digital data; at both ends of the cable, a digital-to-analog or analog-to-digital conversion is required. Another potential problem is that the data channel might become overloaded as more and more customers begin to interact with Internet services; broadband was designed as a transmission approach to send multiple channels of video one way only, while e-mail service is two way.

The unshielded, twisted pair of wires in virtually every home are the major impediment to boosting the speed of Internet access over phone lines. Speed for sending and receiving data is expressed in terms of how many bits (ones or zeros) per second can be moved. The maximum speed for a telephone modem is 56,000 bits per second; most people find that annoyingly slow. The phone companies are implementing a new service called digital subscriber line (DSL), which uses its four wires to carry both voice and data simultaneously in both directions. Data can be received or downloaded from the Internet at speeds up to 1.5 million bits per second, but data sent from the home moves at a much slower rate. DSL technology, however, is proving difficult and expensive to implement, especially at distances greater than two miles from the switching centers. The requisite DSL modems are also more expensive and difficult for users to install. DSL gives the phone companies voice and high-speed data services, it does not open up the lucrative premium TV market. In order for the regional phone companies to effectively compete against the cable-TV companies, they will have to re-wire, either with coaxial cables or fiber-optic cables. But that will make them competitive with the cable companies and open up the possibility of providing the full bundle of services to home owners.

Fiber-optic wiring is the preferred choice of the long distance companies and often the preferred choice of regional telephone companies as they upgrade in urban and suburban locations where demand for capacity is a concern. Fiber-optic media is much faster than electrical wires, it is unaffected by electrical interference, and much more secure. But it is much more expensive to install because these tiny glass filaments are very difficult to align and join together. Lasers transmit pulses of light, rather than electrical signals, to send data and photo-decoders to receive the data; hence the speed of the lasers is dependent on these devices. The hair-thin strands of fiber are made of very pure flexible glass or plastic filaments along which photons, the fundamental unit of light, move in waves or streams.

The speed and capacity of fiber-optic cables keeps on doubling and will continue to expand exponentially. In 1995 scientists introduced wavelength division multiplexing (WDM), a method of splitting (multiplexing) the cable into streams of color, each carrying 2.5 billion laser pulses per second. Initially each fiber carried eight streams of data at 2.5 gigabit speeds, the multiplexed total capacity being twenty gigabits per second. In 1997 new WDM devices doubled throughput with 16 color bands, and soon after it became possible to multiplex into 40 colors; in 1998 80-band systems were announced as were 160-band systems for the year 2000. At the same time, the lasers sending and receiving the data streams increased in speed from 2.5 gigabits to 10 gigabits. 400 gigabits-per-second speeds per fiber strand are commercially available, as well as, terabit speeds provide quite a contrast to the 56,000 bits per second modem speed.

So much additional capacity has become available that prices dropped by a substantial amount. Inexpensive high-speed communication links mean that distance is dead; instantaneous global transactions can become a reality.

WIRELESS PHONES

There is rapid growth (approximately 80 percent per year) in the wireless phone business. Prices continue to decline for both the phone devices and the monthly service charges. Sprint, AT&T, and Verizon (to name a few companies) are advertising hundreds of minutes of calls anytime and to anywhere in the United States for $49 per month; this is an example of a price incentive made possible because of these companies national networks. It would not be surprising to see mergers between other long-distance companies, following the lead of MCI WorldCom.

Wireless phones and wireless data services send and receive voice and data from their antennae to local towers, which are, in turn, linked to adjacent towers and long-distance lines. The area within range of any tower is called a cell; most are adjacent to other cells, forming a honeycomb pattern. As mobile wireless phones move from cell to cell, their calls are automatically switched from tower to tower. There are many dead spots-especially in rural areas-with no reception because there are no towers nearby.

The first cell phones were analog devices, with well-known security problems and often poor-quality reception. Cellular phones broadcast in the 800-900 MHz frequencies; which some scanners can hear. The newer digital phones provide better security and better quality sound, but they operate at lower voltages, have shorter ranges, and require more towers. The PCS standard for digital phones has been widely accepted in the United States, but Europeans have adopted another digital standard, GSM, making wireless communications during international travel difficult.

There is already a great deal of push to commercially provide wearable PCs, combinations of PDAs (personal digital assistants) and phones that handle both voice and data. A small single device would offer voice mail and e-mail, pager and beeper services, Internet access, word processing, spreadsheets, and graphics. Digital phones can handle digital data. The next generation, of wireless services, is available now; these Internet devices will feature 400,000 bps speeds, with more to come.

CONVERGENCE ON DIGITAL TRANSMISSION

Many of the long-distance companies have adopted and are implementing a data networking approach, now being called an IP standard from the UNIX TCP/IP protocol suite. Data, voice, and video are being sent digitally as packets of data, rather than as parts of an analog frequency. The digital approach promises faster, cheaper and better telecommunications services; it is especially well suited to the fiber-optic wiring. But it is the widespread acceptance of digital players, e.g., digital TV, digital phones, CD and DVD video and music players, not to mention PCs, which suggests that digital data networks make the most sense. And in the long-distance arena, with the amount of data surpassing the amount of voice, moving both voice and data to IP networking, as AT&T is, reduces complexity and duplication.

Cable-TV transmissions employ frequency division multiplexing to continuously send many channels one way to the TV tuners. Data and voice transmissions are two way, often short bursts from sender and receiver. This adds considerable complexity, as TCI and Time Warner discovered during the Implementation of phone and Internet services over their coaxial cables.

Phone conversations are semi-permanent sessions between sender and receiver. The phone companies use circuit-switching technology to connect the two parties by establishing a circuit, or connection, for the duration of the call for the exclusive use of the two parties. But that is preceded by establishing the linkage or circuit through the local switching center, the long-distance carrier, and the other switching center. Here again the wire capacity is broken up into circuits using frequency division multiplexing. The traditional T-1 line provides twenty-four separate telephone circuits over copper wire; each circuit is equivalent to 64,000 bits per second digital channel.

Data network standards were established as millions of local area networks were created in businesses all over the world. Data is sent and received in packets, called datagrams, defined by protocols, such as the dominant IP protocol. The packets have a "to" address, a "from" address, lots of digital data, and error-checking data; each packet also indicates that it is one of many in a group, to be assembled by the receiving computer. Data networks operate like the mail delivery system; data is put into the envelop, the to and from addresses contain both a single individual address as well as the area's zip code. Trucks (wires) take all the mail to central hubs, where it is again sorted and sent to further destinations and, eventually to the right zip code post office, which delivers the envelop to the right home address. Data networks use packet switching devices, typically routers, to truck the packets from router to router along the path.

Packet switching is much more efficient for little e-mail messages or slow phone conversations. With packet switching, an exclusive circuit need not be maintained-the entire bandwidth is always open to accept packets. The standard for fiber optic transmission is 2.5 Gbps (2.5 billion bits per second), so very large documents or books can be moved in the blink of an eye. Compressed video and compressed music take up lots of bandwidth; a CD holds 600 million bytes (4.8 billion bits), but that can be compressed by half into roughly 2.5 billion bits, and could be send and received in a second.

TURMOIL IN THE TELECOMMUNICATIONS INDUSTRY

The telecommunications industry is in turmoil because

1. data has surpassed voice as the predominant content to be transmitted,

2. the convergence of the telephone, cable TV, and data communications industries,

3. the rapidly increasing addition of transmission capacity and rapidly decreasing prices.

Traditionally, the industry was dominated by AT&T, which built a highly reliable infrastructure to carry phone messages. Much of the telecom infrastructure throughout the world is optimized for voice, and is poorly situated for carrying data. At the current time, data make up 98 percent of the telecommunication content. Every major organization has built its own data networks, and the quantity of traffic continues to grow. These internal data networks are fast and inexpensive because they are digital. By contrast, internal data networks routinely transmit and receive data at ten million bits of data per second; phone modems, which permit data to be carried over the phone lines, are limited to 56,000 bits per second. Businesses can lease high-speed (1 million bits per second) data lines from telecommunication providers, but these lines are expensive.

The fiber-optic technology described above promises huge advances in capacity resulting in potential decreases in transmission prices. The contrast between the speeds of the fiber cables compared to speeds experienced by most residential customers and many businesses using modems in untenable. Fiber-optic cables operate at billions of bits per second, and soon at trillions of bits per second. Local-area networks (LANs) linking PCs together operate at 10-100 million bits per second and higher, at very low costs. The slow speed of modems using phone wires is especially a problem as users attempt to download software or music, or even to access graphic-intensive Web sites.

Remaining profitable as prices drop is a difficult process. The PC industry is the clearest precedent; major computer companies, e.g., IBM, NCR, and Digital Equipment, Hewlett-Packard, were often at a disadvantage against newer companies such as Dell and Gateway. Similarly, it will be difficult for large telecommunications companies, such as AT&T, to compete against newer competitors such as Quest and ITCX. The larger long-distance carriers have worldwide operations and the economic benefits of huge scope and scale; they need not depend upon any other company's services. But these large long-distance companies have enormous investments in a now-profitable, but rapidly obsoleting, infrastructure. AT&T, for example, is battered by operating cost and price structures that reflect the past limitations of transmission capacity, which, in turn, resulted from slow-speed media and switching devices. It is much cheaper to maintain a single strand of fiber-optic cable and its switches than thousands of copper cables and their switches, when both carry the same amount of digital data/voice/video. The large traditional companies will be squeezed by the need to make major new investments in the latest fiber-optic switching technologies, while at the same time covering the costs of operating the old infrastructure as the prices are dropping.

Another problem for the established long-distance carriers is their requirement to pay access fees to the Regional Bell operating companies that complete their calls to customers. The rationale for the access fees is that the long-distance carriers need to contribute to the costs of providing universal service across the country, especially to the rural telephone companies, rather than have those costs shouldered only by local phone companies. The long-distance companies are saddled with $25 billion of subsidies to the local phone services. As AT&T broke up in 1984, the long-distance business was highly profitable; long-distance calls were billed at 50 cents per minute in 1984, with access fees at 15 cents per minute; now the average long distance charge is below 10 cents per minute, but the access fees remain high-above three cents per minute.

Despite growing pressures from businesses and residential customers, access to the Internet continues to be largely funneled through telephone modems, devices which translate digital computer data into analog signals that are then carried over phone lines.

The local telephone companies appear highly resistant to upgrading their technologies and wiring. They are trying to introduce high-speed 1.5 million bits per second (inbound only) Internet access using new modem technologies, but appear to be having problems rolling out these Internet services to residential customers. Cable-TV companies provide Internet access via cable modems in the major metropolitan areas. The phone companies offer high-speed Internet access via DSL modems, but only a very limited number of homes have been wired with DSL. The cable-TV providers and the local telephone services continue to be protected by the FCC from the competitive pressures assailing the long-distance companies; they have been protected from the need to deploy digital technology in order to remain competitive.

By contrast, newer wireless cellular phone companies require a relatively small investment for a regional phone system, serving a city and suburbs, for example. But many wireless phone customers abhor the roaming charges, which are costly because the regional wireless company has to subcontract with a long-distance carrier for calls outside its region.

The telecommunications industry is experiencing a whirlwind of activity. Rapid growth is occurring in every sector of the industry, but data networks to accommodate Internet traffic are growing as fast as companies can implement them. The industry competes globally, and having global reach appears to be a competitive edge. Bigger is indeed better if the goal is to connect businesses in the United States to their subsidiaries in other regions of the globe. At the same time, the ability to deploy technology that is smaller, faster, and cheaper gives advantage to smaller, more agile companies. Smaller is better if, and only if, government regulations permit smaller companies to take chunks of the more lucrative business segments from the established companies.

In the short term, the best telecommunications segment is the cable television business. Protected by municipal regulations, the cable companies have been able to raise prices for the traditional TV fare. But it turns out that broadband cable technology is the best way to provide a wide variety of services into millions of homes: TV, pay-per-view video, Internet access, e-mail, telephone, and digital tunes. The major cable companies could be sending millions of home bills for over $100 per month for such packages.

In the short term, the regional phone companies are in the worst strategic position. The barrier to entry to compete against the cable companies is the steep cost of rewiring millions of homes and businesses and replacing their circuit switching systems. The traditional technology is obsolete and neither ISDN nor

DSL can make telephone companies competitive against cable companies.

In the short term the wireless phone business will continue to grow and prosper. It is safe to predict continuing growth for the foreseeable future. The speculation that virtually every adult in the United States will own a wireless phone surprises very few people; virtually every adult in Singapore and Hong Kong already does. Here again, having a global or national network is a powerful competitive advantage to a wireless phone company; Sprint and AT&T are both trying to grab market share by advertising low prices for calls anywhere in the United States. Calls are handled by one carrier from end to end, resulting in less complexity, less cost, and better service. New digital phones already offer caller ID and voice mail; and by adding computing power these devices are also offering e-mail and access to business databases via the Internet. Sending and receiving wireless data is relatively easy in a digital environment.

"Distance is dead," claims Tom Peters in his book The Circle of Innovation, and that will be the single most important factor shaping the economy for the next 50 years. In the short term, demand for long-distance carriers will continue to grow at the same time that the capacity of every fiber strand is more than doubling every year. The Internet growth driving demand for backbone capacity is particularly high.

Laser pulses transmit data along the hair-thin glass fibers. Each strand of fiber-optic cable can now move data at a very high speed. Voice and data traffic on the North American long-distance backbone now approximates 1 terabit-each strand of new fiber-optic cable may be able to carry that much. Cables often contain ninety-six strands of fiber, but some have as many as 436 strands. Capacity should catch up with demand within the first decade of the twenty-first century. Indeed there should be a glut of capacity. And that means continually declining prices. The trick in this business segment will be to offer very low prices and have very low costs.

SEE ALSO: Computer Networks; Technology Management; Technology Transfer

James Perotti
Revised by Badie Farah

FURTHER READING:

Douskalis, Bill. *IP Telephony: The Integration of Robust VoIP Services.* Upper Saddle River, NJ: Prentice-Hall PTR, 2000.

Freeman, Roger L. *Fundamentals of Telecommunications.* 2nd ed. New York: John Wiley & Sons, 2005.

Schoning, Heinrich. *Business Management of Telecommunications.* Englewood Cliffs, NJ: Prentice-Hall, 2005.

THEORY X AND THEORY Y

Theory X and Theory Y represent two sets of assumptions about human nature and human behavior that are relevant to the practice of management. Theory X represents a negative view of human nature that assumes individuals generally dislike work, are irresponsible, and require close supervision to do their jobs. Theory Y denotes a positive view of human nature and assumes individuals are generally industrious, creative, and able to assume responsibility and exercise self-control in their jobs. One would expect, then, that managers holding assumptions about human nature that are consistent with Theory X might exhibit a managerial style that is quite different than managers who hold assumptions consistent with Theory Y.

The first section explains the development of Theory X and Theory Y. Second, the effect of Theory X and Theory Y on management functions is discussed. Third is a criticism of Theory Y followed by the concluding section, Theory X and Theory Y in the twenty-first century.

CONCEPTUALIZATION AND DEVELOPMENT

After the Hawthorne experiments and the subsequent behavioral research of the 1930s and 1940s, the human relations approach to management joined the classical perspective as a major school of management thought. Whereas the classical school as espoused by management pioneers such as Frederick Taylor and Henri Fayol focused on principles of management, scientific selection and training, and worker compensation, the human relations approach emphasized behavioral issues such as job satisfaction, group norms, and supervisory style.

The human relations model was hailed as a more enlightened management paradigm because it explicitly considered the importance of individual and how managers could increase productivity by increasing workers' job satisfaction. The end goal for management increased employee productivity; the assumption was that satisfied workers would be more productive compared with workers who felt antagonized by the companies they worked for.

In the 1950s, Douglas McGregor (1906-1964), a psychologist who taught at MIT and served as president of Antioch College from 1948-1954, criticized both the classical and human relations schools as inadequate for the realities of the workplace. He believed that the assumptions underlying both schools represented a negative view of human nature and that another approach to management based on an entirely different set of assumptions was needed. McGregor laid out his ideas in his classic 1957 article "The Human Side of Enterprise" and the 1960 book of the same name, in which he introduced what came to be called the new humanism.

McGregor argued that the conventional approach to managing was based on three major propositions, which he called Theory X:

1. Management is responsible for organizing the elements of productive enterprise-money, materials, equipment, and people-in the interests of economic ends.

2. With respect to people, this is a process of directing their efforts, motivating them, controlling their actions, and modifying their behavior to fit the needs of the organization.

3. Without this active intervention by management, people would be passive-even resistant-to organizational needs. They must therefore be persuaded, rewarded, punished, and controlled. Their activities must be directed. Management's task was thus simply getting things done through other people.

According to McGregor, these tenets of management are based on less explicit assumptions about human nature. The first of these assumptions is that individuals do not like to work and will avoid it if possible. A further assumption is that human beings do not want responsibility and desire explicit direction. Additionally, individuals are assumed to put their individual concerns above that of the organization for which they work and to resist change, valuing security more than other considerations at work. Finally, human beings are assumed to be easily manipulated and controlled. McGregor contended that both the classical and human relations approaches to management depended this same set of assumptions. He called the first style of management "hard" and identified its methods as close supervision, tight controls, and coercion.

The hard style of management led to restriction of output, mutual distrust, unionism, and even sabotage. McGregor called the second style of management "soft" and identified its methods as permissiveness and need satisfaction. McGregor suggested that the soft style of management often led to managers' failure to perform their managerial role. He also pointed out that employees often take advantage of an overly permissive manager by demanding more but performing at lower levels.

McGregor drew upon the work of Abraham Maslow (1908-1970) to explain why Theory X assumptions led to ineffective management. Maslow had proposed that man's needs are arranged in levels, with physical and safety needs at the bottom of the needs hierarchy and social, ego, and self-actualization needs at upper levels of the hierarchy. Maslow's basic point was that once a need is met, it no longer motivates behavior; thus, only unmet needs are motivational. McGregor argued that most employees already had their physical and safety needs met and that the motivational emphasis had shifted to the social, ego, and self-actualization needs. Therefore, management had to provide opportunities for these upper-level needs to be met in the workplace, or employees would not be satisfied or motivated in their jobs.

Such opportunities could be provided by allowing employees to participate in decision making, by redesigning jobs to make them more challenging, or by emphasizing good work group relations, among other things. According to McGregor, neither the hard style of management based on the classical school nor the soft style of management inspired by the human relations movement were sufficient to motivate employees. Thus, he proposed a different set of assumptions about human nature as it pertains to the workplace.

McGregor put forth these assumptions, which he believed could lead to more effective management of people in the organization, under the rubric of Theory Y. The major propositions of Theory Y include the following:

1. Management is responsible for organizing the elements of productive enterprise-money, materials, equipment, and people in the interests of economic ends.

2. People are not by nature passive or resistant to organizational needs. They have become so as a result of experience in organizations.

3. The motivation, potential for development, capacity for assuming responsibility, and readiness to direct behavior toward organizational goals are all present in people-management does not put them there. It is a responsibility of management to make it possible for people to recognize and develop these human characteristics for themselves.

4. The essential task of management is to arrange organizational conditions and methods of operation so that people can achieve their own goals by directing their efforts toward organizational objectives.

Thus, Theory Y has at its core the assumption that the physical and mental effort involved in work is natural and that individuals actively seek to engage in work. It also assumes that close supervision and the threat of punishment are not the only means or even the best means for inducing employees to exert productive effort. Instead, if given the opportunity, employees will display self-motivation to put forth the effort necessary to achieve the organization's goals. Thus, avoiding responsibility is not an inherent quality of human nature; individuals will actually seek it out under the proper conditions. Theory Y also assumes that the ability to be innovative and creative exists among a large, rather than a small segment of the population. Finally, it assumes that rather than valuing security above all other rewards associated with work, individuals desire rewards that satisfy their self-esteem and self-actualization needs.

Although McGregor did not believe that it was possible to create a completely Theory Y-type organization in the 1950s, he did believe that Theory Y assumptions would lead to more effective management. He identified several approaches to management that he felt were consistent with the precepts of Theory Y. These included decentralization of decision-making authority, delegation, job enlargement, and participative management. Job enrichment programs that began in the 1960s and 1970s also were consistent with the assumptions of Theory Y.

In the 1970s, 1980s, and 1990s, McGregor's conceptualization of Theory X and Theory Y were often used as the basis for discussions of management style, employee involvement, and worker motivation. Empirical evidence concerning the validity of Theory X and Theory Y, however, was mixed. Some writers suggested that organizations implementing Theory Y tended to revert back to Theory X in tough economic times.

Others suggested that Theory Y was not always more effective than Theory X, but that the contingencies of each managerial situation determined which of the approaches was more appropriate. Still others suggested extensions to Theory Y. One of these, William Ouchi's Theory Z, attempted to combine the strength of American management philosophies based on Theory Y with Japanese management philosophies.

Along with writers such as Argyris and Likert, McGregor was one of several important humanist writers of the mid-twentieth century who argued that traditional organizational hierarchies create a state of dependence between subordinates and their managers and served as a bridge between the human relations school and a new form of organizational humanism based on Theory Y.

EFFECT ON MANAGEMENT FUNCTIONS

In their well-known textbook, Harold Koontz and Cyril O'Donnell illustrated how the managerial functions of planning, leading, and controlling might be affected by Theory X and Theory Y assumptions. In regard to planning, Theory X assumptions might lead to the superior setting of objectives with little or no participation from subordinates. Theory Y assumptions, conversely, should lead to cooperative objectives designed with input from both employees and managers, resulting in a higher commitment by subordinates to accomplish these shared objectives.

Under Theory X, managers' leadership styles are likely to be autocratic, which may create resistance on the part of subordinates. Communication flow is more likely to be downward from manager to the subordinates. In contrast, Theory Y may foster leadership styles that are more participative, which would empower subordinates to seek responsibility and be more committed to goal achievement. Theory Y leadership should increase communication flow, especially in the upward direction.

In regard to control, Theory X is likely to result in external control, with the manager acting as a performance judge; the focus is generally on the past. Conversely, Theory Y should lead to control processes based on subordinates' self-control. The manager is more likely to act as a coach rather than a judge, focusing on how performance can be improved in the future rather than on who was responsible for past performance. Although the conceptual linkages between Theory X and Theory Y assumptions and managerial styles are relatively straightforward, empirical research has not clearly demonstrated that the relationship between these assumptions and managers' styles of planning, organizing, leading, and controlling is consistent with McGregor's ideas.

CRITICISM OF THEORY Y

The goal of managers using Theory X management styles was to accomplish organizational goals through the organization's human resources. McGregor's research suggested that when work was better aligned with human needs and motivations, employee productivity would increase. As a result, some critics have suggested that, rather than concern for employees, Theory Y style managers were simply engaged in a seductive form a manipulation. Even as managers better matched work tasks to basic human motivational needs through participative management, job rotation, job enlargement, and other programs that emerged at least partly from McGregor's work, managers were still focusing on measures of productivity rather than measures of employee well-being. In essence, critics charge that Theory Y is a condescending scheme for inducing increased productivity from employees, and unless employees share in the economic benefits of their increased productivity, then they have simply been duped into working harder for the same pay.

THEORY X AND THEORY Y
IN THE TWENTY-FIRST CENTURY

McGregor's work on Theory X and Theory Y has had a significant impact on management thought and practice in the years since he first articulated the concepts. In terms of the study of management, McGregor's concepts are included in the overwhelming majority of basic management textbooks, and they are still routinely presented to students of management. Most textbooks discuss Theory X and Theory Y within the context of motivation theory; others place Theory X and Theory Y within the history of the organizational humanism movement.

Theory X and Theory Y are often studied as a prelude to developing greater understanding of more recent management concepts, such as job enrichment, the job-characteristics model, and self-managed work teams. Although the terminology may have changed since the 1950s, McGregor's ideas have had tremendous influence on the study of management.

In terms of the practice of management, the workplace of the early twenty-first century, with its emphasis on self-managed work teams and other forms of worker involvement programs, is generally consistent with the precepts of Theory Y. There is every indication that such programs will continue to increase, at least to the extent that evidence of their success begins to accumulate.

SEE ALSO: Theory Z

Tim Barnett
Revised by Scott B. Droege

FURTHER READING:

Drach-Zahavy, A. "The Proficiency Trap: How to Balance Enriched Job Designs and the Team's Need for Support." *Journal of Organizational Behavior* 25, no. 8 (2004): 979–997.

Grandy, A. "Emotions at Work: Theory, Research and Applications for Management." *Human Relations* 57, no. 10 (2004): 1351–1356.

McGregor, D. *The Human Side of Enterprise.* New York: McGraw-Hill Book Company, 1960.

Spence-Laschinger, H.K., J.E. Finegan, J. Shamian, and P. Wilk. "A Longitudinal Analysis of the Impact of Workplace Empowerment on Work Satisfaction." *Journal of Organizational Behavior* 25, no. 4 (2004): 527–544.

THEORY Z

Theory Z is an approach to management based upon a combination of American and Japanese management philosophies and characterized by, among other things, long-term job security, consensual decision making, slow evaluation and promotion procedures, and individual responsibility within a group context. Proponents of Theory Z suggest that it leads to improvements in organizational performance. The following sections highlight the development of Theory Z, Theory Z as an approach to management including each of the characteristics noted above, and an evaluation of Theory Z. Realizing the historical context in which Theory Z emerged is helpful in understanding its underlying principles. The following section provides this context.

DEVELOPMENT OF THEORY Z

Theory Z has been called a sociological description of the humanistic organizations advocated by management pioneers such as Elton Mayo, Chris Argyris, Rensis Likert, and Douglas McGregor. In fact, the descriptive phrase, "Theory Z," can be traced to the work of Douglas McGregor in the 1950s and 1960s. McGregor, a psychologist and college president, identified a negative set of assumptions about human nature, which he called Theory X. He asserted that these assumptions limited the potential for growth of many employees.

McGregor presented an alternative set of assumptions that he called Theory Y and were more positive about human nature as it relates to employees. In McGregor's view, managers who adopted Theory Y beliefs would exhibit different, more humanistic, and ultimately more effective management styles. McGregor's work was read widely, and Theory Y became a well-known prescription for improving management practices.

But in the 1970s and 1980s, many United States industries lost market share to international competitors, particularly Japanese companies. Concerns about the competitiveness of U. S. companies led some to examine Japanese management practices for clues to the success enjoyed by many of their industries. This led to many articles and books purporting to explain the success of Japanese companies. It was in this atmosphere that Theory Z was introduced into the management lexicon.

Theory Z was first identified as a unique management approach by William Ouchi. Ouchi contrasted American types of organizations (Type A) that were rooted in the United States' tradition of individualism with Japanese organizations (Type J) that drew upon the Japanese heritage of collectivism. He argued that an emerging management philosophy, which came to be called Theory Z, would allow organizations to enjoy many of the advantages of both systems. Ouchi presented his ideas fully in the 1981 book, Theory Z: How American Companies Can Meet the Japanese Challenge. This book was among the best-selling management books of the 1980s.

Professor Ouchi advocated a modified American approach to management that would capitalize on the best characteristics of Japanese organizations while retaining aspects of management that are deeply rooted in U.S. traditions of individualism. Ouchi cited several companies as examples of Type Z organizations and proposed that a Theory Z management approach could lead to greater employee job satisfaction, lower rates of absenteeism and turnover, higher quality products, and better overall financial performance for U.S. firms adapting Theory Z management practices. The next section discusses Ouchi's suggestions for forging Theory Z within traditional American organizations.

THEORY Z AS AN APPROACH TO MANAGEMENT

Theory Z represents a humanistic approach to management. Although it is based on Japanese management principles, it is not a pure form of Japanese management. Instead, Theory Z is a hybrid management approach combining Japanese management philosophies with U.S. culture. In addition, Theory Z breaks away from McGregor's Theory Y. Theory Y is a largely psychological perspective focusing on individual dyads of employer-employee relationships while Theory Z changes the level of analysis to the entire organization.

According to Professor Ouchi, Theory Z organizations exhibit a strong, homogeneous set of cultural values that are similar to clan cultures. The clan culture is characterized by homogeneity of values, beliefs, and objectives. Clan cultures emphasize complete socialization of members to achieve congruence of individual and group goals. Although Theory Z organizations exhibit characteristics of clan cultures, they retain some elements of bureaucratic hierarchies, such as formal authority relationships, performance evaluation, and some work specialization. Proponents of Theory Z suggest that the common cultural values should promote greater organizational commitment among employees. The primary features of Theory Z are summarized in the paragraphs that follow.

LONG-TERM EMPLOYMENT

Traditional U.S. organizations are plagued with short-term commitments by employees, but employers using more traditional management perspective may inadvertently encourage this by treating employees simply as replaceable cogs in the profit-making machinery. In the United States, employment at will, which essentially means the employer or the employee can terminate the employment relationship at any time, has been among the dominant forms of employment relationships. Conversely, Type J organizations generally make life-long commitments to their employees and expect loyalty in return, but Type J organizations set the conditions to encourage this. This promotes stability in the organization and job security among employees.

CONSENSUAL DECISION MAKING

The Type Z organization emphasizes communication, collaboration, and consensus in decision making. This marks a contrast from the traditional Type A organization that emphasizes individual decision-making.

INDIVIDUAL RESPONSIBILITY

Type A organizations emphasize individual accountability and performance appraisal. Traditionally, performance measures in Type J companies have been oriented to the group. Thus, Type Z organizations retain the emphasis on individual contributions that are characteristic of most American firms by recognizing individual achievements, albeit within the context of the wider group.

SLOW EVALUATION AND PROMOTION

The Type A organization has generally been characterized by short-term evaluations of performance and rapid promotion of high achievers. The Type J organization, conversely, adopts the Japanese model of slow evaluation and promotion.

INFORMAL CONTROL WITH FORMALIZED MEASURES

The Type Z organization relies on informal methods of control, but does measure performance through formal mechanisms. This is an attempt to combine elements of both the Type A and Type J organizations.

MODERATELY SPECIALIZED CAREER PATH

Type A organizations have generally had quite specialized career paths, with employees avoiding jumps from functional area to another. Conversely, the Type J organization has generally had quite non-specialized career paths. The Type Z organization adopts a middle-of-the-road posture, with career paths that are less specialized than the traditional U.S. model but more specialized than the traditional Japanese model.

HOLISTIC CONCERN

The Type Z organization is characterized by concern for employees that goes beyond the workplace. This philosophy is more consistent with the Japanese model than the U.S. model.

EVALUATION OF THEORY Z

Research into whether Theory Z organizations outperform others has yielded mixed results. Some studies suggest that Type Z organizations achieve benefits both in terms of employee satisfaction, motivation, and commitment as well as in terms of financial performance. Other studies conclude that Type Z organizations do not outperform other organizations.

Difficulties in the Japanese economy in the 1990s led some researchers to suggest that the widespread admiration of Japanese management practices in the 1970s and 1980s might have been misplaced. As a result, Theory Z has also received considerable criticism. It is unclear whether Theory Z will have a lasting impact on management practices in the U. S. and around the world into the twenty-first century, but by positioning target research at the organizational level rather then the individual level, Ouchi will surely leave his mark on management practice for years to come.

SEE ALSO: Empowerment; Japanese Management; Theory X and Theory Y

Tim Barnett
Revised by Scott B. Droege

FURTHER READING:

Barney, J. "An Interview with William Ouchi." *Academy of Management Executive* 18, no. 4 (2004): 108–117.

Daft, R.L. "Theory Z: Opening the Corporate Door for Participative Management." *Academy of Management Executive* 18, no. 4 (2004): 117–122.

Leonard, D., and W.C. Swap. *Deep Smarts: How to Cultivate and Transfer Enduring Business Wisdom.* Boston: Harvard Business School Press, 2005.

Ouchi, W.G. *Theory Z: How American Business Can Meet the Japanese Challenge.* Reading, MA: Addison-Wesley, 1981.

THEORY OF CONSTRAINTS

The Theory of Constraints (TOC) is a management philosophy developed by Dr. Eliyahu Moshe Goldratt. According to Goldratt the strength of any chain, process, or system is dependent upon its weakest link. TOC is systemic and strives to identify constraints to system success and to effect the changes necessary to remove them. Dr. Goldratt and the TOC became widely known with the 1984 publication of Goldratt's novel *The Goal.*

HISTORY

In early 1979 Goldratt introduced a software-based manufacturing scheduling program known as Optimized Production Timetables (OPT), changed in 1982 to Optimized Production Technology. With the publication of *The Goal,* Goldratt used his Socratic teaching style to educate the world about managing bottlenecks (constraints) and his new ideas about performance. *The Goal,* is a love story set in the manufacturing industry (thrice revised) detailing the tribulations of a plant manager named Alex Rogo. Rogo is faced with the shutdown of his hometown manufacturing plant. Goldratt uses Rogo's predicament to introduce his principles, which result not only in the rescue of Rogo's plant, but also in the salvation of Rogo's marriage. Goldratt himself appears in the book as a character known as Jonah, Rogo's old college professor.

Goldratt used three additional novels to refine and develop the principles set forth in *The Goal. It's Not Luck,* a sequel to *The Goal,* addresses changing markets and introduces a number of methods of logical thinking that are used to make decisions, solve problems, and resolve conflict. *The Critical Chain* depicts a situation whereby TOC principles are effectively utilized in project management. *Necessary But Not Sufficient* contains Goldratt's most holistic expression of TOC and deals with the role of technology in organizations.

Goldratt also produced a number of nonliterary works that espouse his ideas. *The Race,* introduced the concept of the drum-buffer-rope and buffer management. *Essays on the Theory of Constraints, What Is This Thing Called Theory of Constraints and How Should It Be Implemented?* and *The Haystack Syndrome: Sifting Information Out of the Data Ocean* were used, among other publications, to introduce the thinking processes and other TOC concepts.

COMPONENTS OF THE THEORY OF CONSTRAINTS

Theory of constraints consists of separate, but related processes and interrelated concepts, including the following: the performance measures and five focusing steps, logical thinking processes, and logistics.

PERFORMANCE MEASURES. According to Goldratt there are three key performance measurements to evaluate: throughput, inventory and operating expense. TOC emphasizes the use of these three global operational measures rather than local measures (e.g., efficiency and utilization). Goldratt places the greatest importance on increasing throughput. Throughput is defined as the rate at which the system generates money through sales, not through production. Goods are not considered an asset until sold. This contradicts the common accounting practice of listing inventory as an asset even if it may never be sold. Goldratt has advocated a new accounting model as an alternative to traditional cost accounting procedures and measures. Inventory is defined as the money invested in goods that the firm intends to sell or material that the firm intends to convert into salable items. The concept of value-added and overhead are not considered. Operating expense includes all the money the firm spends converting inventory into throughput. The objective of the firm, therefore, is to increase throughput and/or decrease inventory and operating expense in such a way as to increase profit, return on investment, and cash flow (more global measures). In *The Goal*, Alex explains to Jonah that his plant's use of a robot has resulted in a thirty six percent improvement in one area. Jonah then asks if Alex is now able to ship more products, and if he has fired any employees or reduced inventory as a result (in other words, whether increased throughput, reduced operating expense, or reduced inventory resulted). When the reply was no, Jonah questions how there can be any real improvement; and of course, there can't.

Increasing throughput and/or decreasing inventory or operating expense should lead to the accomplishment of the firm's goal: to make money now as well as in the future. Anything that prevents a firm from reaching this goal is labeled as a constraint. Constraints may appear in the form of capacity, material, logistics, the market (demand), behavior, or even management policy. TOC thinking regards all progress toward the goal of making money as relating directly to management attention toward the constraint(s). The marginal value of time at a constraint resource is said to be equal to the throughput rate of the product processed at the constraint, while the marginal value of time at a non-constraint resource is said to be negligible.

FIVE FOCUSING STEPS. The five focusing steps are a tool Goldratt developed to help systems deal with constraints. These steps ensure improvement efforts remains on track towards system-level improvements. Dettmer believes that these are collectively the most important aspect of TOC. TOC's five focusing steps are:

Step 1: Identify the system's constraint(s).

Step 2: Decide how to exploit the system's constraint(s).

Step 3: Subordinate everything else to the decisions made in Step 2.

Step 4: Elevate the system's constraint(s)

Step 5: If a constraint is broken in Step 4, go back to Step 1, but do not allow inertia to cause a new constraint.

The orientation of TOC is toward the output of the entire system, rather than a look at a discrete unit or component. The five focusing steps assist with identifying the largest constraint that overshadows all of the others. These steps constitute an iterative process. As soon as one constraint is strengthened, the next weakest link becomes the priority constraint and should be addressed. Thus, a process of ongoing system improvement is applied to the business practice of the firm.

LOGICAL THINKING PROCESS. Goldratt introduced a staged logical thinking process to be used in conjunction with the five focusing steps. The thinking process assists with working through the change process by identifying the following: what to change, what to change to, and how to effect the change. The thinking processes consist of logic tools used to identify problems, then develop and implement solutions. These tools include effect-cause-effect (ECE) diagramming and its components: negative branch reservations, the current reality tree, the future reality tree, the prerequisite tree, the transition tree, the evaporating cloud, the negative branch reservation, and the ECE audit process. These tools allow an organization to analyze and to verbalize cause and effect.

The following is a brief description of the thinking process. A current reality tree, a cause-effect diagram, is drawn in order to discover the problems. These problems are known as undesirable effects. The cause of an undesirable effect is known as a root cause. The first goal is to find the causes of these undesirable effects. Each statement in a current reality tree that is not a derivative of another must be a root cause. If you build a tree that is comprehensive enough, at least one root cause will lead to most of the undesirable effects. This particular root cause is labeled a core problem, the major improvement target. The fewer root causes responsible for the undesirable effects, the better. The solution to this core problem is apparently not readily available. If it were, then the problem would have already been solved. Some conflict, therefore, must exist that prevents an immediate solution. This conflict becomes evident upon the construction of an evaporating cloud.

An evaporating cloud is a conflict-resolution tool. The process begins with a statement of the desired objective, one that is the opposite of the core problem. Then, the prerequisites necessary to achieve the requirements are listed. Any conflicts and assumptions that exist between the prerequisites are verbalized. For example, if one objective is to increase profit, then the requirements may be to improve the product and to decrease expenses. Prerequisites for each, respectively, might be to increase expenditures on capital equipment and to decrease expenditures, two obviously conflicting elements. The best solution is to remove the conflict; a compromise is not desirable. The next move involves finding an injection, a breakthrough idea that will evaporate the cloud. The "evaporating" refers to the tool's ability to dissipate conflict and to create a win-win solution. Usually, the original injection is not sufficient to fully solve the problem, but additional needed injections become clear when building the future reality tree.

A future reality tree is another cause-effect diagram. The tree starts with the proposed solution to the core problem and delineates the injection(s) and the ensuing desirable effects. The future reality tree is a "what if." It provides the opportunity to evaluate and to improve a solution before it is implemented. It is noted that one should be careful not to allow the solution to cause new undesirable effects.

A prerequisite tree describes the implementation of the injection(s) and is composed of an obstacle and an intermediate objective. This diagram breaks the implementation tasks into smaller increments, noting expected obstacles and intermediate objectives whose accomplishments will overcome the obstacles. The intermediate objectives are sequenced, displaying the necessary order of accomplishment and determining which ones can be achieved in parallel. This tool is powerful in that it does not ignore the obstacles. It uses them, rather, as the main vehicle for this phase.

Finally, a transition tree or implementation plan is constructed. This element presents a detailed description of the gradually evolving change envisioned. This task forces one to carefully examine which actions are really needed and if they are sufficient to guarantee the required change.

The thinking-process tools are powerful resources when used effectively. They have found successful use in the logistics and medicine areas of the United States Air Force, in primary education, and in the service sector. James Cox and Michael Spencer, both college professors and "Jonahs," state in *The Constraints Management Handbook* that the thinking processes may be the most important management tools developed this century.

LOGISTICS.

Logistics in TOC include drum-buffer-rope scheduling, buffer management, and VAT analysis.

DRUM-BUFFER-ROPE. Drum-buffer-rope is a TOC production application and the name given to the method used to schedule the flow of materials in a TOC facility. Srikanth and Umble (1997), define each component as follows:

- Drum. The drum is the constraint and therefore sets the pace for the entire system. The drum must reconcile the customer require-

ments with the system's constraints. In simpler terms, the drum is the rate or pace of production set by the system's constraint.

- Buffer. A buffer includes time or materials that support throughput and/or due date performance. A buffer establishes some protection against uncertainty so that the system can maximize throughput. A time buffer is the additional planned lead time allowed, beyond the required setup and run times, for materials to reach a specified point in the product flow. Strategically placed, time buffers are designed to protect the system throughput from the internal disruptions that are inherent in any process. A stock buffer is defined as inventories of specific products that are held in finished, partially finished, or raw material form, in order to fill customer orders in less than the normal lead-time. Stock buffers are designed to improve the responsiveness of the system to specific market conditions.

- Rope. The rope is a schedule for releasing raw materials to the floor. The rope is devised according to the drum and the buffer. The rope ensures that non-capacity constraint resources are subordinate to the constraint. Restated, the rope is a communication process from the constraint to the gating operation that checks or limits material released into the system to support the constraint.

BUFFER MANAGEMENT. Buffer management provides the means by which the schedule is managed on the shop floor. Buffer management is a process in which all expediting in a shop is motivated by what is scheduled to be in the buffers (constraint, shipping, and assembly buffers). Buffers can be maintained at the constraint, convergent points, divergent points, and shipping points. By expediting this material into the buffers, the system helps to avoid idleness at the constraint and missed customer due dates. Also, the causes of items missing from the buffer are identified, and the frequency of occurrences is used to prioritize improvement activities.

VAT ANALYSIS. VAT analysis determines the general flow of parts and products from raw materials to finished products. It conceptualizes an organization in terms of the interaction of its individual component parts, both products and processes. Three general categories of production structures result from this standpoint, each necessitating a unique approach to management planning and control. The logical structure is the sequence of operations through which each product must pass in order to manufacture and assemble a product or product family. A *V* logical structure starts with one or a few raw materials, and the product

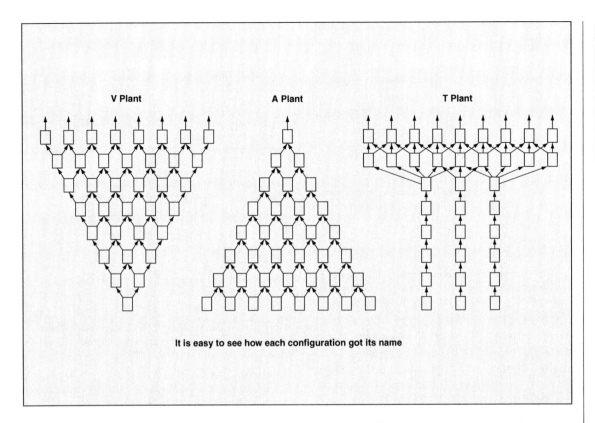

It is easy to see how each configuration got its name

expands into a number of different products as it flows through its routings. The shape of an *A* logical structure is dominated by converging points. Many raw materials are fabricated and assembled into a few finished projects. A *T* logical structure consists of numerous similar finished products assembled from common assemblies and subassemblies. The graph shows the general appearance of each structure. Once the general parts flow is determined, the system control points (gating operations, convergent points, divergent points, constraints, and shipping points) can be identified and managed. This determination focuses management's attention on a few control points where buffers can be used to protect and to maximize throughput. Five control points are used to manage the process: (1) the constraint, (2) the points of divergence (where a part or material is diverted to different routes in order to make different products), (3) the points of convergence (where two or more parts are combined in subassembly), (4) the gating operation (releases work into the shop), and (5) the shipping operation.

The shape of the structure determines which control points are utilized to manage production. A *T* structure focuses attention on the constraint and the gating operation. The five-step focusing process is used to manage the constraint with a buffer placed before the constraint to absorb variations in the process. The output from the gating operation is tied to the constraint; that is, since the constraint controls the amount of throughput; the gating operation cannot process more than the constraint.

A *V* structure also uses a buffer to protect the constraint and the gating operation releases orders at the same rate as the constraint as seen in the *T* structure. However, an additional control point exists in the *V* structure, the divergent point. The divergent point is controlled by a schedule derived from the shipping schedule. This derivation prevents misallocation of material to a product not currently in demand.

The *A* structure also manages the constraint and gating operation in a fashion similar to the *T* structure. Any diverging points are scheduled in accordance with the shipping schedule. In addition, an assembly buffer is used to maintain the flow into the convergent points. An additional schedule based on the shipping schedule (similar to that used in the *V* structure) is used to keep capacity from being misallocated to the wrong order. By using VAT analysis, significant improvements in the production process can result.

The unexpected and enormous success of *The Goal,* initially published in a small run of 3,000 copies and has now sold more than 2 million copies, and further development of TOC has lead many organizations to put TOC theory into practice. Over the past two decades a growing number of books, articles, and dissertations have appeared elaborating on Dr. Goldratt's philosophy and providing examples of TOC principles in use. Followers of Goldratt's philosophy, those who have completed an extensive training course conducted by Goldratt's educational firm, the Avraham Y. Goldratt Institute, refer to themselves as Jonahs. TOC materials are available in multiple languages and formats, including videotapes, audiotapes, and computer software.

SEE ALSO: Inventory Management; Inventory Types; Manufacturing Resources Planning; Operations Scheduling; Operations Strategy

R. Anthony Inman
Revised by Theresa Liedtka

FURTHER READING:

Cox, James F., and Michael S. Spencer. *The Constraints Management Handbook.* Boca Raton, FL: St. Lucie Press, 1998.

Dettmer, H. William. *Goldratt's Theory of Constraints: A Systems Approach to Continuous Improvement.* Milwaukee, WI: ASQC Quality Press, 1997.

Dugdale, David, and Colwyn Jones. "Accounting for Throughput: Techniques for Performance Measurement, Decisions and Control." *Management Accounting* 75, no. 11 (1997): 52–56.

Essays on the Theory of Constraints. Great Barrington, MA: The North River Press, 1990.

Gardiner, Stanley C., John H. Blackstone, and Lorraine R. Gardiner. "The Evolution of the Theory of Constraints." *Industrial Management* 36, no. 3 (1994): 13–16.

Goldratt Consulting Group. Available from <http://www.goldrattconsulting.com>.

Goldratt, Eliyahu M. *Critical Chain.* Great Barrington, MA: The North River Press, 1997.

———. *Haystack Syndrome: Sifting Information Out of the Data Ocean.* Croton-on-Hudson, NY: North River Press, 1990.

———. *It's Not Luck.* Croton-on-Hudson, NY: North River Press, 1994.

———. *Late Night Discussions on the Theory of Constraints.* Great Barrington, MA: The North River Press, 1992.

———. "What is the Theory of Constraints?" *APICS: The Performance Advantage,* June 1993, 18–20.

———. *What Is This Thing Called Theory of Constraints and How Should It Be Implemented?* Croton-on-Hudson, NY: North River Press, 1990.

Goldratt, Eliyahu M., Eli Schragenheim, and Carol A. Ptak. *Necessary But Not Sufficient: A Theory of Constraints Business Novel.* Great Barrington, MA: The North River Press, 2000.

Goldratt, Eliyahu M., and Jeff Cox. *The Goal: A Process of Ongoing Improvement.* 3rd ed. Great Barrington, MA: The North River Press, 2004

———. *The Goal: A Process of Ongoing Improvement.* 2nd ed. Croton-on-Hudson, NY: The North River Press, 1994.

———. *The Goal: Excellence in Manufacturing.* Croton-on-Hudson, NY: The North River Press, 1984.

Goldratt, Eliyahu M., and Robert E. Fox. *The Race.* Croton-on-Hudson, NY: The North River Press, 1986.

Kendall, Gerald I. *Securing the Future: Strategies for Exponential Growth Using the Theory of Constraints.* Boca Raton, FL: St. Lucie Press, 1998.

Mabin, Victoria, J., and Steven J. Balderstone. *The World of the Theory of Constraints: A Review of the International Literature.* Boca Raton, FL: St. Lucie Press, 2000.

McMullen, Thomas B., Jr. *Introduction to the Theory of Constraints (TOC) Management System.* Boca Raton, FL: St. Lucie Press, 1998.

Newbold, Robert C. *Project Management in the Fast Lane: Applying the Theory of Constraints.* Boca Raton, FL: St. Lucie Press, 1998.

Noreen, Eric, Debra Smith, and James T. Mackey. *The Theory of Constraints and its Implications for Management Accounting.* Great Barrington, MA: The North River Press, 1995.

Rahman, Shams-ur. "Theory of Constraints: A Review of the Philosophy and Its Applications." *International Journal of Operations and Production Management* 18, no. 4 (1998): 336–355.

Scheinkopf, Lisa J. *Thinking for a Change: Putting the TOC Thinking Processes to Use.* Boca Raton, FL: St. Lucie Press, 1999.

Schragenheim, Eli, and H. William Dettmer. *Manufacturing at Warp Speed: Optimizing Supply Chain Financial Performance.* Boca Raton, FL: St. Lucie Press, 2001.

Smith, Debra. *The Measurement Nightmare: How the Theory of Constraints Can Resolve Conflicting Strategies, Policies, and Measures.* Boca Raton, FL: St. Lucie Press, 2000.

Srikanth, Mokshagundam L., and Harold E. Cavallaro, Jr. *Regaining Competitiveness: Putting 'The Goal' To Work.* New Haven, CT: The Spectrum Publishing Company, 1987.

Srikanth, Mokshagundam L., and Michael M. Umble. *Synchronous Management: Profit-Based Manufacturing for the 21st Century.* 2 vols. Guilford, CT: The Spectrum Publishing Company, 1997.

Stein, Robert R. *Reengineering the Manufacturing System: Applying the Theory of Constraints.* 2nd ed. New York: Marcel Dekker, Inc., 2003.

Woeppel, Mark J. *The Manufacturer's Guide to Implementing the Theory of Constraints.* Boca Raton, FL: St. Lucie Press, 2001.

Womack, David E., and Steve Flowers. "Improving System Performance: A Case Study in the Application of the Theory of Constraints." *Journal of Healthcare Management* 44, no. 5 (1999): 397–407.

TIME-BASED COMPETITION

The widespread use of just-in-time production (JIT) and other advanced manufacturing techniques has been credited with providing such improvements as decreased inventories, set-up times, downtime and workspace. These decreases have yielded increases in inventory turns, equipment utilization, labor utilization, and ultimately, profit. Simply stated, this means that finished goods are produced and delivered just in time to be sold, subassemblies just in time to be assembled into finished goods, fabricated parts just in time to go into subassemblies and raw materials just in time to be transformed into fabricated parts. In effect, consumption of time has been reduced. While the JIT philosophy dictates that improvement in these areas be part of a continuous process, it does not have to stop there. Some firms have reduced the consumption of time, not only in the production area, but also throughout the system. Firms that manage this have gone beyond JIT and its competitive advantages. They have an advantage in time-based competition.

WHAT IS TIME-BASED COMPETITION?

JIT was the first manifestation of time-based competition. Time-based competition is the extension of JIT into every facet of the product delivery cycle, from research and development through marketing and distribution of the final product. Even quality, while still critical to success, is not the competitive advantage it once was in many industries. Manufacturing firms then have three strategic options: seek coexistence, retreat in the face of competitors, or attack (directly or indirectly). It has been said that strategy is and always has been a moving target. For some firms who choose to attack, this target has moved to speed and time-based competition.

The term *time-based competition* came into use with its appearance in a 1988 *Harvard Business Review* article entitled "Time-The Next Source of Competitive Advantage" by George Stalk, Jr. It was further defined in a series of articles and books written by consultants from the Boston Consulting Group.

Time-based competition is a broad-based competitive strategy which emphasizes time as the major factor for achieving and maintaining a sustainable competitive advantage. It seeks to compress the time required to propose, develop, manufacture, market and deliver its products.

In order to do this, the firm must change its current processes and alter the decision structures used to design, produce and deliver to the customer.

Time-based competition appears in two different forms: fast to market and fast to produce. Firms that compete with to-market speed emphasize reductions in design lead-time. In other words, the firm has the ability to minimize the time it takes to develop new products or make rapid design changes. Products fifty percent over budget but introduced on time have been found to generate higher profit levels than products brought to market within budget but six months late. Also, this form allows firms to gain a market edge by being able to consistently introduce more new products or large numbers of product improvements/variations faster than its competitors, thereby dominating the market. Sun Microsystems achieved leadership in engineering workstations by reducing (by fifty percent compared to competitors) the time required to design and introduce new systems. Additionally, these firms

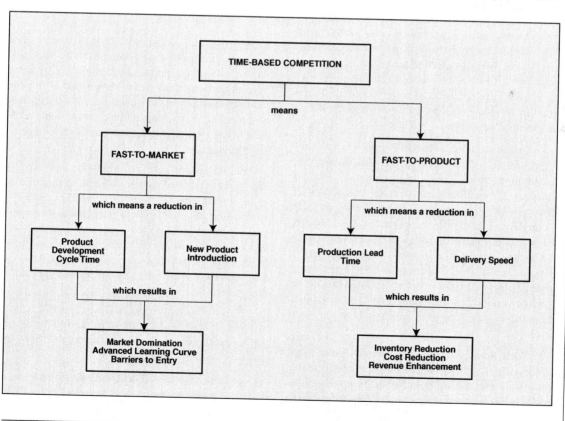

are now moving further along the learning curve than the competition. Both factors ultimately increase barriers to entry by competitors.

Fast-to-product firms emphasize speed in responding to customer demands for existing products. Wal-Mart has been able to dominate its industry by replenishing its stores twice as fast as its competitors. Firms competing in this area focus on lead-time reduction throughout the system, from the time the customer places an order until the customer ultimately receives the product. This includes the ability to reduce the time it takes to manufacture products (throughput time) as well as the ability to reduce the time between taking a customer's order and actually delivering the product (delivery speed). These reductions in lead-time are usually accompanied by significant reductions in inventory levels. As with JIT, there is less rework, fewer supervisors, lower carrying costs, less overhead, and so forth, as well as enhanced quality and on-time delivery performance. Some customers, known as impatient customers, place a great deal of value on reduced lead-time. These customers are willing to pay a premium to get their goods and services quickly. This combination of lower costs and higher revenues contributes significantly to an improved corporate performance.

While product development cycle time, new product introduction, production lead time, and delivery speed all contribute to improved business performance, not all contribute equally. A study by Shawnee Vickery, Cornelia Droge, James Yeomans, and Robert Markland found that the most consistent predictor of business performance was new product introduction. The second best predictor was product development cycle time. While production lead time and delivery speed were found to be related to business performance (respectively, in order of contribution), their relationship to business performance was not as significant as the other two factors.

The production cycle encompasses order entry through the completion of all paperwork, through finished goods all the way to distribution of the final product. JIT methods greatly reduce the amount of time consumption from initiation of the purchase order through the transformation process, but improvement in these other areas have much potential. Studies have shown that few companies have value-added time in excess of 10 percent of average order cycle times. In fact, 95 to 99 percent of the time a product or service is not receiving value, it is waiting. Hence, time can be removed from any part of the product cycle.

Some firms have traced the complete order entry process only to find that it took longer to complete the paperwork than it did to manufacture the product. One major manufacturer compressed its manufacturing processes but still took months to convert a customer order into an approved order for manufacture. Time reductions resulting from JIT success are worth much less when orders sit at the retailer for weeks, float in the mail for a week, sit at the distributor for a week, float in the mail for another week and then begin the now shortened transformation process at the factory.

Paperwork is subject to the same delays. When paperwork moves in batches (similar to manufacturing), several days of delay can develop while the order sits in a stack awaiting enough volume for the batch to move on to the next stage in processing. Time-based competitors begin by eliminating all unnecessary paperwork. Incoming mail is categorized as fast or slow track, allowing the fast track orders to be handled immediately. Also, some firms structure the paperwork process so that transactions are handled one at a time, eliminating the delay caused from batch movement. A door manufacturer managed to refine its process to the point that it could price and schedule 95 percent of incoming orders during the initial customer call.

Frequently, when delays occur, the delay time is made up at the end of the product cycle. Obviously, the last place to make up for lost time is at the distribution and transportation stage (similar to the way a delayed airline flight might make up for delayed takeoffs and manage to still land on time). If time can be reduced in these emergency situations, why not reduce it permanently and reap the benefits of time-based competition?

IMPLEMENTATION

George Stalk, Jr. relates that a firm becomes a time-based competitor by accomplishing four tasks: (1) understanding the rules of response, (2) making value-delivery systems two to three times as flexible and responsible as its competitors, (3) pricing how customers value these capabilities, and (4) implementing a strategy for surprising its competitors with time-based advantages.

Philip Carter, Steven Melnyk, and Robert Handfield identified seven process strategies for implementing time-based competition. These include: system simplification, system integration, standardization, parallel activities, variance control, automation and excess resources. They feel that by identifying these strategies, they have developed a linkage between lead-time reduction and the tactics needed to achieve this goal.

Shawnee Vickery, Cornelia Droge, James Yeomans and Robert Markland identified 10 steps to guide the implementation of time-based competition. They felt that implementing firms need to

1. perform a thorough process analysis to understand your current business operation;

2. develop measurement system that focuses on time;

3. increase the speed of new product introduction times by using methods such as concurrent engineering and cross-functional teams;

4. evaluate all managerial decision alternatives in terms of time;

5. embrace change and develop change-oriented management practices and methods;

6. understand the critical importance of top management support to sustain change;

7. treat bottlenecks, downtime, and other problems as opportunities to learn;

8. find ways to incorporate time reduction results into the employee reward structure;

9. give employees a better understanding of how their jobs contribute to time compression; and

10. balance improvements with work disruptions in order to keep customers happy.

Some time-based firms rely on technology (e.g., more productive machinery) to reduce lead times while others seek to streamline the system and its processes. For example, Japanese manufacturers focused on single-minute exchange of dies when setting up or changing machines. Still, others use techniques such as team building and alliance building to reduce time by focusing on integrating the various components of the supply chain. Hillman Willis and Anthony Jurkus, in a *Review of Business* article, note that some firms, such as Black and Decker, Ford and AT&T have found success by organizing teams to work, from the time of inception, on an entire family of new products. By bringing together people from product engineering, manufacturing, marketing, and purchasing throughout the development process and giving them the authority to make real decisions, enormous time and expense has been cut from new product efforts. Developing products and manufacturing processes simultaneously collapse time collapsed yet the manufacturability of the product is ensured. Also, this process facilitates the standardization of components across the family of products, thereby making them easier and less costly to assemble. Orders can then be filled by assembling the appropriate set of components, reducing both time and cost by as much as half. One firm has reported that an ad hoc cross-functional team took actions that reduced average cycle time from 18.1 hours to 9.4 hours. This 48 percent reduction in cycle time corresponds to a 92.5 percent increase in productivity.

Other firms are using cutting edge technologies, such as Stream-of-Variation Analysis (SOVA), to facilitate time-based competition. SOVA is a generic math model which integrates multivariate statistics, control theory and design/manufacturing knowledge into a unified framework to optimize manufacturing performance and identify and isolate causes of dimensional variation which occur during the pre-production stage of a product.

Time-based competition is a reality for many firms. Generally, these time-based competitors began by correcting their manufacturing techniques (often through JIT), then fixing sales and distribution, and finally adjusting their approach to innovation. Their strategy is based on the results of flexible manufacturing, rapid response, expanding variety, and increasing innovation. It is a metastrategy which improves performance through changes in the processes and structures used to design, manufacture and deliver products to the customer, thereby impacting overall firm performance (e.g., return on investment, return on assets). Motorola, Northern Telecom, and Toyota are but a few of the companies that have found ways to increase the overall value of their delivery systems through the compression of time.

One final word of caution: recent studies have suggested that time reductions that are not tied to viable business strategies can needlessly increase costs and dramatically reduce profits.

SEE ALSO: Cycle Time; Lean Manufacturing and Just-in-Time Production; New Product Development

R. Anthony Inman

FURTHER READING:

Carter, Philip L., Steven A. Melnyk and Robert B. Handfield. "Identifying the Basic Process Strategies for Time-Based Competition." *Production and Inventory Management Journal* 1st Quarter (1995): 65–70.

Ceglarek, D., W. Huang, S. Zhou, Y. Ding, R. Kumar, and Y. Zhou. "Time-Based Competition in Multistage Manufacturing: Stream-of-Variation Analysis (SOVA) Methodology—Review." *International Journal of Flexible Manufacturing Systems* 16 (2004): 11–44.

Choong, Y. Lee, Niwat Rittisakdanon, and Xiaomu Zhou. "Reengineering for Time-Based Competition: Reducing Time-to-Market by Reengineering." *International Journal of Management* 18, no. 1 (2001): 33.

Stalk, George, Jr. "The Time Paradigm." *Forbes,* 30 November 1998.

———. "Time—The Next Source of Competitive Advantage." *Harvard Business Review,* July-August 1988.

Vickery, Shawnee K., Cornelia L.M. Droge, James M. Yeomans, and Robert E. Markland. "Time-Based Competition in the Furniture Industry." *Production and Inventory Management Journal* 4th quarter (1995): 14–21.

Willis, T. Hillman, and A.F. Jurkus. "Product Development: An Essential Ingredient of Time-Based Competition." *Review of Business* 22, no. 1-2 (2001): 22–27.

TIME MANAGEMENT

Many business people struggle with time management and would like to accomplish more tasks in a day, or have more time for non-work activities. There are a number of tips and suggestions for improving time management in a person's workplace and home, and different approaches work for different people.

DELEGATE

Many of us attempt to accomplish tasks that can be easily assigned to or contracted out to someone else. By delegating a task, you can have more time to accomplish other important tasks. When can a task be delegated and when should you attempt it yourself? Some guidelines are as follows. A primary concern is that you should only delegate if there is a person who is skilled enough to do the task at hand. You can delegate to employees you supervise, those who are your colleagues, and even those above you. When you delegate a task to your subordinate—downward delegation—you have the authority to make sure that the task is done correctly, but assigning a task to an employee who lacks the skill to do it will often require more time than if you did the task yourself. Delegating to a peer, or a colleague, works well if you and the other person have complementary skills. You can trade responsibilities if you each have skills that are stronger than the other person's. Although most employees do not consider it, you can also delegate to employees above you in the organizational hierarchy—upward delegation. If you have been assigned a task that should not be yours or a task that is beyond your abilities, you can ask a superior for guidance or clarification. Your feedback may indicate to your supervisor that the task is better done by him or herself.

Another consideration when delegating is the type of task that can be delegated. There are three types of tasks that are best suited to being assigned to someone else: (1) tasks for which you do not have adequate skill or expertise, (2) tasks that you do not want to do but that others might, and (3) tasks that are easy to accomplish but detract from your value to the organization.

First, if someone else can do something more effectively than you can, you will spend too much time attempting to do it yourself. For instance, if you are planning a retirement party for a colleague, you could purchase, prepare, and arrange the food and beverages yourself. However, if you are not very good at preparing food or creating a buffet, it would be to use your time to hire a caterer for this task. In addition to saving the time it takes to purchase and prepare food and drinks, by hiring a reputable caterer, you would spend considerably less energy managing the task and thinking about it.

A second circumstance that benefits from delegation is if there is a task that another person might enjoy more than you. Again, consider the example of organizing a retirement party. Perhaps you do not enjoy party planning, but your colleague does. You can delegate this task to your colleague, perhaps taking on one of his tasks in return, creating a situation in which both of you feel satisfied with the work you are assigned.

A final situation in which you should delegate is if there is an easy task that takes little skill to accomplish. For instance, if you are sending a mass mailing, it is poor time management for you to stuff the envelopes yourself. A lower-level employee, like an assistant or secretary, might better do this. By allowing this other person to do a task that is easy to complete, you are freed to complete other tasks that require more skill and attention. Since the person to whom you have delegated this task is likely to complete it just as effectively as you would have, then there is no drawback to assigning the task to another.

When should you not delegate? First, you should accomplish your major job tasks. For instance, it may be appropriate for your secretary to stuff envelopes with a letter soliciting business from former clients, but it is not appropriate for this secretary to write the entirety of this letter without your help or final approval. If you consistently have others complete tasks that are supposed to be yours, then you may find yourself replaced by another employee. Second, you should not delegate tasks in which the outcome is critical. If you have tasks that, if not completed, can lose the company a client or money, you must be responsible for this task. If you are accountable for an important outcome, you should use caution when delegating. Finally, there are some tasks for which delegation is too expensive. While hiring a caterer for a party does not represent a large cost, there are other times in which hiring others to complete tasks (e.g., offer training or develop a web site) can be cost prohibitive to some organizations.

PRIORITIZE TASKS

Procrastination, or putting off a task that must be completed, is common to many people, even in business environments. Procrastination occurs for many reasons: you may not know where to start on a task, you may not understand a task, you may dislike the task, or you may worry that you cannot complete a task successfully. Often a person's anxiety about a task leads them to avoid it. Therefore, to accomplish more in a workday, it is best to tackle the most difficult or worrisome task first. This is a beneficial because it allows you to devote the time and mental energy that is necessary for a difficult or unpleasant task when you are most able to. Furthermore, by reducing the anxiety associated with this task in tackling it early, you will find that work becomes easier. When the unpleasant task is finished, it no longer creates anxiety and worry, which can save time.

If a person leaves unpleasant or difficult tasks until shortly before their deadlines or until the end of the workday, he or she will have less energy to complete this task. Additionally, the anxiety and dread associated with the completion of the task that has been procrastinated may affect a person's ability to complete other tasks throughout the day. The negative emotions associated with the anticipation an unpleasant task is likely to distract a person from the other tasks that they are trying to complete. This can make even easy tasks more time consuming to complete.

SET GOALS

Goals can be very effective ways to meet workplace demands in a timely manner. Goals are measurable, short-term objectives. Simply by setting an appropriate goal, you can better organize your day or week. Decades of research have supported the effectiveness of goal setting on performance in a variety of tasks. However, for a goal to be effective, it must be designed properly by being specific and difficult. Specific goals are much more effective than nonspecific goals, because your progress can be assessed. For instance, setting a goal of reading 20 pages of a report is a good goal because you can determine whether or not it was accomplished. If your goal was to "read a lot of the report" then you might determine 5 pages into it, that you had accomplished that goal, when in reality, you had not read enough. Goals should also be difficult, but not too challenging. A goal that is too easy, such as "respond to one e-mail today" are not motivating because they present no challenge at all. Overly difficult goals (e.g., "improve my sales by 50 percent in one month") are also not motivational; they are so challenging that a person may give up too soon, realizing they will never reach the goal. In addition to being appropriately specific and difficult, you are more likely to reach goals to which you are committed. A lack of interest or commitment in reaching the goal makes the goal-setting process futile.

One of the advantages of setting goals to improve time management is that, over time, you gain a more realistic understanding of what can be accomplished in a workday. People who do not often set goals may not be aware of what their capabilities are; however, those who have set goals more consistently have a good idea of which goals they have been able to meet and which were set too high or too low.

MEET DEADLINES EARLY

Some people thrive when working under deadlines. Newspaper reporters operate each day with a set of firm deadlines. However, many other people find deadlines to be daunting and stressful. Deadlines are set to help us manage time. By always meeting deadlines, or even by meeting them early, you can appropriately manage time. If you complete deadline work early, you reduce the stress associated with your schedule, and you have more self-confidence about completing work tasks. Additionally, a person's work is likely to be higher quality if deadlines are met; attention to detail can suffer when a person is hurrying to finish a project. To meet your deadlines early, you can break larger tasks into smaller ones and prioritize them. In addition, setting interim deadlines before a final deadline can help you to set goals and to make a large and seemingly unmanageable project seem easier to complete. Finally, tackling more difficult tasks first, as described previously, may increase your ability to meet deadlines.

STAY ORGANIZED

Organization and time management go hand in hand. Many people waste time looking for documents, messages, or other information necessary to complete tasks in a timely manner. There are a number of steps that can help you stay organized. First, arrange your workspace in a way that promotes organization. That is, have a place for everything, and put everything in its place. If you do not have a specific location for telephone messages, it is not surprising that you might spend time looking for a telephone message or even misplace one. Additionally, put the items that are most used closest to you. If you use a reference book (such as a dictionary or a computer programming language reference book) frequently, putting that book across the room wastes time. You want to minimize the amount of time you spend getting up from your desk retrieving or looking for items.

A second suggestion for staying organized is to spend a little time each day organizing your workspace. Discard paper and electronic documents that are no longer needed, file documents that will be needed at a later time, and write a to do list for tasks that must be accomplished that day or the next day. Some time management experts suggest that you only touch each piece of paper in your office once. That is, if you receive a memo, you should read it when you receive it and take action based on it only once, rather than reading the memo, putting it down, and having to reread it several times before acting on it.

A third suggestion it to use a calendar or day planner to stay organized; this will help you to remember important dates and deadlines. Without a calendar in which such dates are noted, some tasks or meetings may be forgotten; instead of planning the time you need to do certain tasks, you may have to drop everything to accomplish a task that must be done for a meeting that you forgot was later that day. For a calendar to be effective for time management, however, you must be sure to note important dates. An incomplete or inaccurate calendar is useless. This suggestion fits nicely with the recommendation to spend a little time each day organizing your workspace. If part of your organization effort includes documenting any important dates and times and reviewing events on a calendar scheduled fro the following days, this can aid time management.

FIND YOUR PRODUCTIVE TIME

Each person has a time of the day in which they are better able to concentrate or to do certain types of work. And, most people have a time of the day in which they have difficulty staying focused and getting things done. Some people are very productive in the mornings, but less able to concentrate in the afternoons. Others cannot tackle difficult tasks in the morning and prefer to wait until later in the day to do work that requires attention to detail. By determining when you are best able to do certain types of tasks, you can schedule them throughout your day so that you are most productive. For instance, if you are able to read and evaluate best in the morning, schedule those tasks for when you first arrive at work. If you find yourself getting sleepy in the afternoons, then reading quietly is not the best task for this time of day. Instead, you may choose to do tasks that involve a little bit of physical activity or that do not require as much mental concentration. Perhaps returning telephone calls or meeting with co-workers is better for afternoon tasks.

By scheduling tasks during the times of day when you are best able to do them, you are likely to be able to complete your work in a more time effective manner. Many people waste time trying to concentrate or solve difficult problems by doing so at a time that is ineffective for them. Re-reading a memo three times because you lack concentration in the late afternoon is a poor choice when you could read the memo once in the morning.

MINIMIZE STRESS

Stress is a major barrier to effective time management. Stress created by the workplace or by personal concerns can create anxiety and worry that are distracting from work. Even ineffective time management can lead to stress, since anxiety over completing tasks in a timely manner can hinder their accomplishment. To manage stress, it is important to first recognize

what is creating the stress. Is it worry over a particular task, a work situation, or an issue at home? Once the stressor is recognized, it can be better managed. If the source of stress is unidentified, then it cannot be managed.

Once the source of stress is identified, you must determine which parts of the situation can be controlled and which cannot. For instance, if the source of stress is a looming deadline for a project, tackling some elements of that project or scheduling some of the tasks may relieve stress. However, there may be parts of the project that are causing stress that cannot be managed. For instance, if part of the successful completion of the project depends on the work of another person, this may create stress that cannot be controlled unless you have some ability to monitor the work of the other person. For stressors that are out of your control, you must either find ways to exert more control or to ignore the issue and focus on those tasks that you can control.

Even when stressors have been identified and controlled to some extent, you may still experience stress. To reduce stress physically, you can get an appropriate amount of sleep, exercise regularly, and eat properly. Many Americans are sleep deprived, and skipping even a couple of hours of sleep each night can have noticeable consequences in the workplace. Some sleep experts liken working while sleep deprived to working while drunk. Although many people think that they will get more done by working more hours and sleeping less, getting appropriate amounts of sleep can instead make a person more productive during their working hours, requiring less time on the job. There are many suggestions for improving sleep, as detailed in Exhibit 1.

Exhibit 1
Tips for Improving Sleep

- Create an environment in a bedroom that reduces distractions; don't do work or watch TV in the bedroom
- Make your bedroom as dark and as quiet as possible
- Go to bed and wake up at the same times every day
- Avoid caffeine late in the day
- Relax before bedtime by taking a warm bath or listening to soothing music
- Reduce worry at bedtime by writing a list of things to do the next day before going to bed
- If you are in bed but cannot sleep, get up and do something boring until you are sleepy

---

Physical exercise can also reduce stress. Sports and other fitness activities can reduce a person's resting heart rate and blood pressure, which can help to alleviate the negative effects of stress. Many people forgo physical activity, believing that time invested in exercise will detract from a person's ability to complete other tasks. However, much like getting proper sleep, even minimal physical activity can make a person more effective during working hours due to decreased stress and anxiety.

LEARN TO SAY NO

Many people who struggle with time management do so because they have too many obligations. People agree to take on tasks or responsibilities, knowing that their time is limited, but feeling that they cannot say no. However, people agree to take on tasks that they have little time for because they want to help others, they feel guilty for saying no, feel obligated by a superior, or misjudge the time they have available. Saying yes to people who make requests can feel good, but not having time to accomplish tasks can be a letdown to the person and the organization. So, often times, saying no to a request is a better option than taking on a task for which there is not adequate time. Therefore, knowing the right time to decline a request is important.

How does a person know when to say yes or no to a request? First, you must consider what the actual commitment is; that is, how much time, effort, and energy it will take. If you do not fully explore the possible commitments required by a certain request, you may be agreeing to do something that takes much longer than you originally anticipated. Second, you must decide if agreeing to the request is a good use of your time. If you compare the proposed commitment to your normal duties, which is more important? Those tasks that have very meaningful outcomes may be worth agreeing to do even when time is limited.

Even when a person knows that they do not have the time available to say yes to a new commitment, saying no can be difficult. To decline a request more effectively, you should do four things. First, offer the person a reason for your answer of no. If you do not provide a good reason to decline the request, then others may assume that you are lazy or selfish. Second, be tactful when you turn someone down because the denial may make him or her angry or hurt. Third, suggest an alternative that takes less time. By giving the requester another option, such as a different employee who might do the task or another time when you can help, you show that you want to cooperate, while still protecting your time. Finally, tell the person "no" as soon as possible. By asking for time to think over a decision when you know that you will decline their request, you may cause more problems or even find yourself obligated to say yes.

REDUCE THE INTRUSION OF TECHNOLOGY

The availability of communication technology, such as e-mail and cellular telephones has done much to improve the ability of Americans to get work done. However, communication technology can also hinder your ability to get work done. Employees now have many interruptions while trying to get work done. If you find that the arrival of a new email message or the ringing of the telephone is interrupting your work, you may choose to ignore them. If you are able to postpone speaking with people or responding to email messages, it may be helpful to set aside a time period that is communication free. For instance, you might decide that from 1–3 p.m. each day, you must concentrate on getting specific tasks done, and during that time, you will not take calls or read e-mails. It is important, however, after this period of no communication to respond to work-related messages received during this time period.

ORGANIZATIONAL APPROACHES TO IMPROVING TIME MANAGEMENT

Because time management can have an effect on employees' productivity in the workplace, some employers are now offering information and assistance for employees who want to better manage their time. Some organizations now offer time management workshops that teach skills such as those listed above. Additionally, seminars may be developed around particular models of time management, such as those presented in Steven Covey's book *The Seven Habits of Highly Effective People.*

Another approach employers can use to assist employees in time management skills is through wellness programs. Wellness programs are opportunities offered or subsidized by the organization to promote physical and emotional health and well-being, thereby reducing stress. They are intended as preventative measures and aim to reduce health risks and/or emotional stress. One of the outcomes that may be associated with a wellness plan is the ability to better manage time—if people are more physically well, many of the stress-related barriers to time management are reduced. Wellness plans may involve free or reduced-cost health club memberships, on-site health clubs, relaxation courses, stress-reduction courses, smoking cessation courses, and even time management courses. Some organizations even take the step of reducing health insurance premiums for those employees who participate in a wellness plan.

Finally, many organizations now offer benefits and services intended to help employees manage non-work activities. Flexible work hours, on-site day care, leave banks, and even valet services are now being offered in some organizations. These types of services, while often improving employee recruitment and retention, may also help to reduce distractions at work, to reduce employee stress, and to assist employees in being more productive during working hours.

Time management is a challenge for many people, and there are a number of tips that can help employees to make better use of their time. By learning delegating skills, prioritizing tasks appropriately, setting goals, meeting deadlines early, staying organized, finding the most productive time of the day, minimizing stress, saying "no" to some requests, and reducing the intrusion of technology, employees may be able to improve their time management. Additionally, many organizations now offer programs to teach employees time-management skills in order to reduce stress and improve overall well-being, and to assist them in managing their non-work lives.

SEE ALSO: Goals and Goal Setting; Lean Manufacturing and Just-in-Time Production; Meeting Management; Organizing; Stress; Technology Management; Time-Based Competition

Marcia J. Simmering

FURTHER READING:

Covey, Steven R. *The Seven Habits of Highly Effective People.* New York, NY: Simon & Schuster, Inc., 1989.

Mancini, Marc. *Time Management.* New York: McGraw-Hill Professional, 2003.

Tracy, Brian. *Time Power: A Proven System for Getting More Done in Less Time Than You Ever Thought Possible.* New York: AMACON Books, 2004.

TOTAL QUALITY MANAGEMENT

SEE: Quality and Total Quality Management

TRADEMARKS

SEE: Patents and Trademarks

TRADING BLOCS

SEE: Free Trade Agreements and Trading Blocs

TRAINING DELIVERY METHODS

Training is a set of a systematic processes designed to meet learning objectives related to trainees' current or future jobs. These processes can be grouped into the following phases; needs analysis, design, development, implementation, and evaluation. The phases are sequential, with the outputs of the previous phases providing the inputs to those that follow. Figure 1 depicts the phases and their relationships. Training delivery methods consist of the techniques and materials used by trainers to structure learning experiences. Different training delivery methods are better or worse at achieving various learning objectives. During the design phase (see Figure 1) the different methods are examined to determine their appropriateness for the learning objectives. Once appropriate methods have been identified, they are applied to the training plan in the development phase.

There are three categories of learning objectives: knowledge, skills, and attitudes (KSAs). Knowledge objectives are of three types: declarative, procedural, and strategic. Declarative knowledge is the person's store of factual information. Procedural knowledge is the person's understanding about how and when to apply the facts. Strategic knowledge is used for planning, monitoring, and revising goal-directed activity. Skill reflects one's proficiency at specific tasks such as operating a piece of equipment, giving a presentation, or making a business decision. Attitudes are beliefs and/or opinions about objects and events and the positive or negative affect (feelings) associated with them. Attitudes affect motivation levels, which in turn influence a person's behavior. Most training programs have learning objectives for knowledge, skill, and attitudes; these programs need to combine several methods into an integrated whole because no single method can do everything well.

The various training delivery methods can be divided into cognitive and behavioral approaches. Cognitive methods provide information orally or in written form, demonstrate relationships among concepts, or provide the rules for how to do something. They stimulate learning through their impact on cognitive processes and are associated most closely with changes in knowledge and attitudes. The lecture, discussion, e-learning and, to some extent, case studies are cognitive methods. Though these types of methods can influence skill development, it is not their strength.

Conversely, behavioral methods allow the trainee to practice behavior in a real or simulated fashion. They stimulate learning through experience and are best at skill development and attitude change. Equipment simulators, business games, role plays, the in-basket technique, behavior modeling and, to some

Figure 1

Model of the Training Process

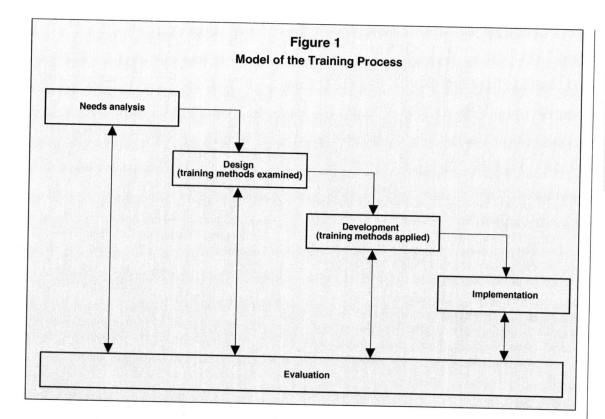

extent, case studies are behavioral methods. Both behavioral and cognitive methods can be used to change attitudes, though they do so through different means. On-the-job training is a combination of many methods and is effective at developing knowledge, skills, and attitudes, but is best at the latter two.

LECTURE METHOD

The lecture is best used for creating a general understanding of a topic. Several variations in the lecture format allow it to be more or less formal and/or interactive. In the pure lecture, communication is one way—from trainer to trainees. It is an extensive oral presentation of material. A good lecture begins with an introduction that lays out the purpose, the order in which topics will be covered, and ground rules about interruptions (e.g., questions and clarification). This is followed by the main body of the lecture in which information is given. The topic areas should be logically sequenced so that the content of preceding topics prepares trainees for the following topics. The lecture should conclude with a summary of the main learning points and/or conclusions.

During the pure lecture trainees listen, observe, and perhaps take notes. It can be useful in situations in which a large number of people must be given a limited amount of information in a relatively short period; however, it is not effective for learning large amounts of material in a short time period. Thus, an effective lecture should not contain too many learning points.

Trainees will forget information in direct proportion to the amount of information provided. Because the pure lecture provides only information, its usefulness is limited; when the only training objective is to have trainees acquire specific factual information, better learning can be achieved at less cost by putting the information into text. This allows trainees to read the material at their leisure and as often as necessary to retain the material. The only added value provided by the lecture is credibility that may be attached to the lecturer or the focus and emphasis provided by trainer presentation skills. Another major benefit of the lecture is that it is interactive, and that trainees can ask questions or have the presenter change the pace of the lecture if necessary.

DISCUSSION METHOD

The discussion method uses two-way communication between the lecturer and the trainees to increase learning opportunities. This method uses a short lecture (20 minutes or less) to provide trainees with basic information. This is followed by a discussion among the trainees and between the trainees and the trainer that supports, reinforces, and expands upon the information presented in the short lecture. Verbal and nonverbal feedback from trainees allows the trainer to determine if the desired learning has occurred. If not, the trainer may need to spend more time on this area and/or present the information again, but in a different manner.

Questioning (by trainees or the trainer) and discussions enhance learning because they provide clarification and keep trainees focused on the material. Discussions allow the trainee to be actively engaged in the content of the lecture, which improves recall and use in the future. Trainee questions demonstrate the level of understanding about the content of the lecture. Trainer questions stimulate thinking about the key learning points.

The pure lecture is most useful when trainees lack declarative knowledge or have attitudes that conflict with the training objectives. The discussion method is more effective than the pure lecture for learning procedural and strategic knowledge because of the discussion and questioning components. If the training objective is skill improvement, neither the lecture or discussion method is appropriate.

Both the lecture and discussion method are useful for changing or developing attitudes, though the discussion method is more effective. The lecture, and especially the discussion, modify employee attitudes by providing new insights, facts, and understanding.

E-LEARNING

Many companies have implemented e-learning, which encompasses several different types of technology assisted training, such as distance learning, computer-based training (CBT), or web-based training (WBT). Distance learning occurs when trainers and trainees are in remote locations; typically, technology is used to broadcast a trainer's lecture to many trainees in many separate locations. Distance learning provides many of the same advantages and disadvantages as the lecture method. Distance learning can be much less expensive than paying for trainees in multiple locations to travel for a lecture, but it may reduce motivation to learn because of the remoteness of the trainer.

Computer-based training and web-based training are virtually similar. With this type of training, content is delivered through the computer, using any combination of text, video, audio, chat rooms, or interactive assessment. It can be as basic as reading text on a screen or as advanced as answering quiz questions based on a computerized video that the trainee has viewed. The difference between CBT and WBT is that, with CBT, the training program is stored on a hard-drive, a CD-ROM, or diskette. This means that it is not easy to update and may be more difficult for employees to access. Conversely, WBT is housed online through either a company's intranet or through the World Wide Web. This increases accessibility of training; employees may even be able to train from their home computers. Additionally, updates to content are quick and relatively easy. For example, if an error in the training content is found, one update on the training program housed on a server updates the content for every trainee who accesses it after that point. For a change to made to CBT, new CD-ROMs or diskettes would have to be produced.

E-learning is an alternative to classroom-based training, and it can provide a number of advantages. E-learning can:

- reduce trainee learning time, by allowing trainees to progress at their own pace

- reduce the cost of training, particularly by reducing costs associated with travel to a training location

- provide instructional consistency, by offering the same training content to employees worldwide

- allow trainees to learn at their own pace thereby reducing any boredom or anxiety that may occur

- provide a safe method for learning hazardous tasks with computer simulations

- increase access to training to learners in locations around the world

E-learning is effective at developing declarative and, in particular, procedural knowledge. It can be useful in developing some types of skills and for modifying attitudes. E-learning develops declarative knowledge through repeated presentation of facts, using a variety of formats and presentation styles. It can do an excellent job of describing when and how to apply knowledge to various situations. Procedural knowledge is developed by allowing trainees to practice applying the knowledge to various situations simulated by the software. This training delivery method is valuable because it can automatically document trainee's responses, interpret them, and provide appropriate practice modules to improve areas of weakness.

Using e-learning, skill development is limited by the software's ability to mimic the trainee's job environment and context. For some situations, such as training employees in the use of word processing, spread sheet, and other computer-based software, e-learning is an appropriate choice for teaching skills. Here, the tasks and situations trainees will face on the job are easily simulated by the training software. On the other hand, it is very difficult to develop CBT software that realistically simulates interaction between two or more people or a person and an object in a dynamic environment. Other methods must be utilized for these situations.

E-learning can be effective at developing or modifying attitudes. The factual relationships among objects and events, and the consequences of particular courses of action, can be portrayed in many ways with e-learning technology. How objects, events and their relationships are perceived can be altered by the visual and textual presented in a CBT. However, since the objects and events are simulated, rather than real, the emotional or affective side of attitudes may not be activated. In addition, there is no opportunity during e-learning to discuss attitudes with others in a setting where a trainer can monitor, direct, and reinforce the discussion to support the desired attitude(s). This may be one reason many adult learners indicate a preference for e-learning to be combined with some form of instructor-based training. Trainees often prefer blended training, which is when both computer and face-to-face training are combined, and it is used by many organizations.

SIMULATIONS

Simulations are designed to mimic the processes, events, and circumstances of the trainee's job. Equipment simulators, business games, in-basket exercises, case studies, role playing, and behavior modeling, are types of simulations.

EQUIPMENT SIMULATORS. Equipment simulators are mechanical devices that incorporate the same procedures, movements and/or decision processes that trainees must use with equipment back on the job. Among those trained with this method are airline pilots, air traffic controllers, military personnel, drivers, maintenance workers, telephone operators, navigators, and engineers. To be effective the simulator and how it is used must replicate, as closely as possible, the physical and psychological (time pressures, conflicting demands, etc.) aspects of the job site. To facilitate this, the equipment operators and their supervisors should be involved in the simulation design and pre-testing. This reduces potential resistance to the training and, more importantly, increases the degree of fidelity between the simulation and the work setting.

BUSINESS GAMES. Business games attempt to reflect the way an industry, company, or functional area operates. They also reflect a set of relationships, rules, and principles derived from appropriate theory (e.g., economics, organizational behavior, etc.). Many business games represent the total organization, but some focus on the functional responsibilities of particular positions within an organization (e.g., marketing director, human resource manager). These are called *functional simulations*. Games that simulate entire companies or industries provide a far better understanding of the big picture. They allow trainees to see how their decisions and actions influence not only their immediate target but also areas that are related to that target.

Prior to starting the game trainees are given information describing a situation and the rules for playing the game. They are then asked to play the game, usually being asked to make decisions about what to do given certain information. The trainees are then provided with feedback about the results of their decisions, and asked to make another decision. This process continues until some predefined state of the organization exists or a specified number of trials have been completed. For example, if the focus is on the financial state of a company, the game might end when the company has reached a specified profitability level or when the company must declare bankruptcy. Business games involve an element of competition, either against other players or against the game itself. In using them, the trainer must be careful to ensure that the learning points are the focus, rather than the competition.

IN-BASKET TECHNIQUE. The in-basket technique simulates the type of decisions that would typically be handled in a particular position such as a sales manager or operations manager. It affords an opportunity to assess and/or develop decision-making skills and attitudes. To begin the exercise, trainees are given a description of their role (a current or future job) and general information about the situation. Trainees are then given a packet of materials (such as requests, complaints, memos, messages, and reports) which make up the in-basket. They are asked to respond to the materials within a particular time period (usually 2 to 4 hours). When the in-basket is completed, the trainer asks the trainee to identify the processes used in responding to the information and to discuss their appropriateness. The trainer provides feedback, reinforcing appropriate decisions and processes or asking the trainee to develop alternatives. A variation is to have trainees discuss their processes in a group format moderated by the trainer. Here the trainer should attempt to get the trainees to discover what worked well, what didn't and why.

CASE STUDY. Case studies are most often used to simulate strategic decision-making situations, rather than the day-to-day decisions that occur in the in-basket. The trainee is first presented with a history of the situation in which a real or imaginary organization finds itself. The key elements and problems, as perceived by the organization's key decision makers, may also be provided. Case studies range from a few pages in length to more than a hundred. Trainees are asked to respond to a set of questions or objectives. Responses are typically, though not always, in written form. Longer cases require extensive analysis and assessment of the information for its relevance to the decisions being made. Some require the trainee to gather information beyond what was in the case. Once individuals have arrived at their solutions, they discuss the diagnoses and solutions that have been generated in small groups, large groups, or both. In large groups a trainer should facilitate and direct the discussion. The trainer must guide the trainees in examining the possible alternatives and consequences without actually stating what they are.

Written and oral responses to the case are evaluated by the trainer. The trainer should convey that there is no single right or wrong solution to the case, but many possible solutions depending on the assumptions and interpretations made by the trainees. The value of the case approach is the trainees' application of known concepts and principles and the discovery of new ones. The solutions are not as important as the appropriateness with which principles are applied and the logic with which solutions are developed.

ROLE PLAY. The role play is a simulation of a single event or situation. Trainees who are actors in the role play are provided with a general description of the situation, a description of their roles (e.g., their objectives, emotions, and concerns) and the problem they face.

Role plays differ in the amount of structure they provide to the actors. A structured role play provides trainees with a great deal of detail about the situation that has brought the characters together. It also provides in greater detail each character's attitudes, needs, opinions, and so on. Structured role plays may even provide a scripted dialog between the characters. This type of role play is used primarily to develop and practice interpersonal skills such as communication, conflict resolution, and group decision making. Spontaneous role plays are loosely constructed scenarios in which one trainee plays herself while others play people that the trainee has interacted with in the past (or will in the future). The objective of this type of role play is to develop insight into one's own behavior and its impact on others. How much structure is appropriate in the scenario will depend on the learning objectives.

Whether structured or spontaneous, role plays may also differ based on the number of trainees involved. Single, multiple, and role-rotation formats provide for more or less participation in the role play. In a single role play, one group of trainees role plays while the rest of the trainees observe. While observing, other trainees analyze the interactions and identify learning points. This provides a single focus for trainees and allows for feedback from the trainer. This approach may cause the role players to be embarrassed at being the center of attention, leading to failure to play the roles in an appropriate manner. It also has the drawback of not permitting the role players to observe others perform the roles. Having non-trainees act out the role play may eliminate these problems, but adds some cost to the training.

In a multiple role play, all trainees are formed into groups. Each group acts out the scenario simultaneously. At the conclusion, each group analyzes what happened and identifies learning points. The groups may then report a summary of their learning to the other groups, followed by a general discussion. This allows greater learning as each group will have played the roles somewhat differently. Multiple role plays allow everyone to experience the role play in a short amount of time, but may reduce the quality of feedback. The trainer will not be able to observe all groups at once, and trainees are usually reluctant to provide constructive feedback to their peers. In addition, trainees may not have the experience or expertise to provide effective feedback. To overcome this problem, video tapes of the role plays can be used by the trainee and/or trainer for evaluation.

The role-rotation method begins as either a single or multiple role play. However, when the trainees have interacted for a period of time, the role play is stopped. Observers then discuss what has happened so far and what can be learned from it. After the discussion, the role play resumes with different trainees picking up the roles from some, or all, of the characters. Role rotation demonstrates the variety of ways the issues in the role play may be handled. Trainees who are observers are more active than in the single role play since they have already participated or know they soon will be participating. A drawback is that the progress of the role play is frequently interrupted, creating additional artificiality. Again, trainees may be inhibited from publicly critiquing the behavior of their fellow trainees.

BEHAVIOR MODELING. Behavior modeling is used primarily for skill building and almost always in combination with some other technique. Interpersonal skills, sales techniques, interviewee and interviewer behavior, and safety procedures are among the many types of skills that have been successfully learned using this method. While live models can be used, it is more typical to video tape the desired behavior for use in training. The steps in behavior modeling can be summarized as follows:

1. Define the key skill deficiencies

2. Provide a brief overview of relevant theory

3. Specify key learning points and critical behaviors to watch for

4. Have an expert model the appropriate behaviors

5. Have trainees practice the appropriate behaviors in a structured role play

6. Have the trainer and other trainees provide reinforcement for appropriate imitation of the model's behavior

Behavior modeling differs from role plays and games by providing the trainee with an example of what the desired behavior looks like prior to attempting the behavior. While this method is primarily behavioral, steps 2 and 3 reflect the cognitively oriented learning features of the technique. Feedback to the trainee is especially powerful when video is used to record both the model's and the trainee's performance. Through split screen devices, the performance of the model and the trainee can be shown side by side. This allows the trainee to clearly see where improvements are needed.

Simulations are not good at developing declarative knowledge. Some initial level of declarative and procedural knowledge is necessary before a simulation can be used effectively. Although some knowledge development can occur in simulations, usually other methods are required for this type of learning. Simulations provide a context in which this knowledge is applied. Improving the trainees' ability to apply knowledge (i.e., facts, procedures, strategies) is the focus of simulations. Simulations do a good job of developing skills because they:

- simulate the important conditions and situations that occur on the job
- allow the trainee to practice the skill
- provide feedback about the appropriateness of their actions

Each of the different formats has particular types of skills for which they are more appropriate:

- Mechanical, machine operation, and tool-usage skills are best learned through use of equipment simulators.
- Business decision-making skills (both day to day and strategic), planning, and complex problem solving can be effectively learned through the use of business games.
- The in-basket technique is best suited to development of strategic knowledge used in making day-to-day decisions.
- Case studies are most appropriate for developing analytic skills, higher-level principles, and complex problem-solving strategies. Because trainees do not actually implement their decision/solution, its focus is more on what to do (strategic knowledge) than on how to get it done (skills).
- Role plays provide a good vehicle for developing interpersonal skills and personal insight, allowing trainees to practice interacting with others and receiving feedback. They are an especially effective technique for creating attitude change, allowing trainees to experience their feelings about their behavior and others' reactions to it.

ON-THE-JOB TRAINING

The most common method of training, on-the-job training (OJT) uses more experienced and skilled employees to train less skilled and experienced employees. OJT takes many forms and can be supplemented with classroom training. Included within OJT are the job-instruction technique, apprenticeships, coaching, and mentoring. Formal OJT programs are typically conducted by employees who can effectively use one-on-one instructional techniques and who have superior technical knowledge and skills. Since conducting one-on-one training is not a skill most people develop on their own, *train-the-trainer* training is required for OJT trainers. In addition to training the trainers, formal OJT programs should carefully develop a sequence of learning events for trainees. The formalized instructional process that is most commonly used is called the job-instruction technique.

JOB-INSTRUCTION TECHNIQUE (JIT). The JIT was developed during World War II and is still one of the best techniques for implementation of OJT nearly forty years later. It focuses on skill development, although there are usually some factual and procedural-knowledge objectives as well. There are four steps in the JIT process: prepare, present, try out and follow up.

Prepare. Preparation and follow up are the two areas that are most often ignored in OJT programs. Preparation should include a written breakdown of the job. Ignoring this step will prevent the trainer from seeing the job through the eyes of the trainee. When the trainer is very skilled there are many things he does on the job without thinking about them. This can result in their being overlooked in training without a systematic analysis and documentation of the job tasks prior to beginning training.

Once the tasks have been documented, the trainer must prepare an instructional plan. Here, the trainer must determine what the trainee currently knows and does not know. This is the needs analysis phase of Figure 1. Interviewing the trainee, checking personnel records and previous training completed are among the many ways of determining what KSAs the trainee currently has. This is compared to the KSAs the trainee needs to perform the tasks. The instructional plan is then completed focusing on the trainee's KSA deficiencies.

Immediately prior to the training, the trainee should be provided with an orientation to the OJT/JIT learning process. The orientation should help trainees understand their role and the role of the trainer. The importance of listening effectively and feeling comfortable asking questions should be emphasized. The trainee should become familiar with the steps in the JIT process so he or she knows what to expect and when it will occur.

Present. In this stage of JIT there are four activities: tell, show, demonstrate, and explain. When telling and showing, the trainer provides an overview of the job while showing the trainee the different aspects of it. The trainer is not actually doing the job, but pointing out important items such as where levers are located, where materials are stored, and so on. The trainer then demonstrates how to do the job, explaining why it is done that particular way and emphasizing key learning points and important safety instructions. The components of the job should be covered one at a time, and in the order they would normally occur while performing the job.

Try Out. The trainee should be able to explain to the trainer how to do the job prior to actually trying to do the job. This provides a safe transition from watching and listening to doing. When the trainee first tries out the job the trainer should consider any errors to be a function of the training, not the trainee's learning ability. When errors are made they should be used to allow the trainee to learn what not to do and why. The trainer can facilitate this by questioning the trainee about his actions and guiding him or her in identifying the correct procedures.

Follow Up. During follow up the trainer should check the trainees' work often enough to prevent incorrect or bad work habits from developing. The trainer should also reassure the trainee that it is important to ask for help during these initial solo efforts. As trainees demonstrate proficiency in the job, progress checks can taper off until eventually they are eliminated.

APPRENTICESHIP TRAINING. Apprenticeship training dates back to the Middle Ages, when skilled craftsmen passed on their knowledge to others as a way of preserving the guilds. Today, apprenticeship programs are partnerships between labor unions, employers, schools, and the government. They are most often found in the skilled trades and professional unions such as boiler engineers, electrical workers, pipe fitters, and carpenters. The typical apprenticeship program requires two years of on-the-job experience and about 180 hours of classroom instruction, though requirements vary. An apprentice must be able to demonstrate mastery of all required skills and knowledge before being allowed to graduate to journeyman status. This is documented through testing and certification processes. Journeymen provide the on-the-job training, while adult education centers and community colleges typically provide the classroom training. Formal apprenticeship programs are regulated by governmental agencies that also set standards and provide services.

COACHING. Coaching is a process of providing one-on-one guidance and instruction to improve the work performance of the person being coached in a specific area. It differs from other OJT methods in that the trainee already has been working at the job for some time. Usually, coaching is directed at employees with performance deficiencies, but it can also serve as a motivational tool for those performing adequately.

Typically the supervisor acts as the coach. Like the OJT trainer, the coach must be skilled both in how to perform the task(s) and how to train others to do them. The amount of time supervisors devote to coaching activities steadily increased during the 1990s and will likely represent more than 50 percent of supervisors' time by the new millennium.

The coaching process, viewed from the coach's perspective, generally follows the outline below. Note the similarities between JIT and this process.

1. Understand the trainee's job, the KSAs and resources required to meet performance expectations, and the trainee's current level of performance.

2. Meet with the trainee and mutually agree on the performance objectives to be achieved.

3. Mutually arrive at a plan/schedule for achieving the performance objectives.

4. At the work site, show the trainee how to achieve the objectives, observe the trainee's performance, then provide feedback.

5. Repeat step 4 until performance improves.

MENTORING. pararing is a form of coaching in which an ongoing relationship is developed between a senior and junior employee. This technique focuses on providing the junior employee with political guidance and a clear understanding of how the organization goes about its business. Mentoring is more concerned with improving the employee's fit within the organization than improving technical aspects of performance, thus differentiating it from coaching. Generally, though not always, mentors are only provided for management-level employees.

SEE ALSO: Case Method of Analysis; Continuing Education and Lifelong Learning Trends; Employee Screening and Selection; Management and Executive Development; Mentoring

P. Nick Blanchard
Revised by Marcia J. Simmering

FURTHER READING:

Beer, Valorie. *The Web Learning Fieldbook: Using the World Wide Web to Build Workplace Learning Environments.* San Francisco, CA: Jossey-Bass/Pfeiffer, 2000.

Blanchard, P.N., and J.W. Thacker. *Effective Training: Systems, Strategies, and Practices.* 2nd ed. Englewood Cliffs, NJ: Prentice Hall, 2003.

Decker, P., and B. Nathan. *Behavior Modeling Training: Principles and Applications.* New York: Praeger, 1985.

Gold, L. "Job Instruction: Four Steps to Success." *Training and Development Journal,* September 1981, 28–32.

Goldstein, Irwin L., and Kevin J. Ford. *Training in Organizations.* 4th ed. Belmont, CA: Wadsworth Group, 2002.

Noe, R.A. *Employee Training and Development.* Boston: Irwin McGraw-Hill, 1999.

Rothwell, William J., and H.C. Kazanas. *Improving On the Job Training.* 2nd edition. San Francisco: Jossey-Bass, 2004.

Welsh, Elizabeth, Connie Wanberg, Kenneth G. Brown, and Marcia J. Simmering. "E-Learning: Emerging Uses, Empirical Results, and Future Directions." *International Journal of Training and Development* 7, no. 4 (2003): 245–258.

TRANSNATIONAL ORGANIZATION

Organizations competing on an international basis face choices in terms of resource allocation, the balance of authority between the central office and business units, and the degree to which products and services are customized in order to accommodate tastes and preferences of local markets. When employing a transnational strategy, the goal is to combine elements of global and multidomestic strategies. Each of these will now be briefly discussed.

A global strategy involves a high degree of concentration of resources and capabilities in the central office and centralization of authority in order to exploit potential scale and learning economies. Customization at the local level is thus necessarily low. The multidomestic strategy, on the other hand, represents the opposite view of international strategy. Resources are dispersed throughout the various countries where the firm does business, decision-making authority is pushed down to the local level, and each business unit is allowed to customize product and market offerings to specific needs. The corporation as a whole foregoes the benefits that could be derived from centralization and coordination of diverse activities.

A transnational strategy allows for the attainment of benefits inherent in both global and multidomestic strategies. The overseas components are integrated into the overall corporate structure across several dimensions, and each of the components is empowered to become a source of specialized innovation. It is a management approach in which an organization integrates its global business activities through close cooperation and interdependence among its headquarters, operations, and international subsidiaries, and its use of appropriate global information technologies (Zwass, 1998).

The key philosophy of a transnational organization is adaptation to all environmental situations and achieving flexibility by capitalizing on knowledge flows (which take the form of decisions and value-added information) and two-way communication throughout the organization. The principal characteristic of a transnational strategy is the differentiated contributions by all its units to integrated worldwide operations. As one of its other characteristics, a joint innovation by headquarters and by some of the overseas units leads to the development of relatively standardized and yet flexible products and services that can capture several local markets. Decision making and knowledge generation are distributed among the units of a transnational organization.

Structure follows strategy (Chandler, 1962), implying that a transnational strategy must have an appropriate structure in order to implement the strategy. Just as the transnational strategy is a combination or hybrid strategy between global and multidomestic strategies, the organizational structure of firms pursuing transnational strategies is a structure that draws on characteristics of the worldwide geographic structure and the worldwide product divisional structure. The combination of mechanisms needed is somewhat contradictory, because the structure need be centralized and decentralized, integrated and nonintegrated, and formalized and nonformalized. But firms that can successfully implement this strategy and structure often perform better than firms pursuing only multidomestic or global strategies.

Transnational companies often enter into strategic alliances with their customers, suppliers, and other business partners to save time and capital. As long-term partnerships, these alliances may bring to the firm specialized competencies, relatively stable and sophisticated market outlets that help in honing its products and services, or stable and flexible supply sources. This may result in a virtual corporation, consisting of several independent firms that collaborate to bring products or services to the market.

A transnational model represents a compromise between local autonomy and centralized decision making. The organization seeks a balance between the pressures for global integration and the pressures for local responsiveness. It achieves this balance by pursuing a distributed strategy which is a hybrid of the centralized and decentralized strategies. Under the transnational model, a multinational corporation's assets and capabilities are dispersed according to the most beneficial location for a specific activity. Simultaneously, overseas operations are interdependent, and knowledge is developed jointly and shared worldwide.

Transnational firms have higher degrees of coordination with low control dispersed throughout the organization. The five implementation tactics (Vitalari and Wetherbe, 1996) used for implementing the transnational model are:

- mass customization-synergies through global research and development (e.g., American Express, Time Warner, Frito-Lay, MCI)

- global sourcing and logistics (e.g., Benetton, Citicorp)

- global intelligence and information resources (e.g., Andersen Consulting, McKinsey Consulting)

- global customer service (e.g., American Express)

- global alliances (e.g., British Airways and US Air; KLM and Northwest)

STUDIES

In a study of SBUs in large U.S.-based multinational firms, Wasilewski (2002) reported positive associations between transnational marketing strategies and performance. Improvements apparently resulted both from efficiencies gained from global integration and flexibility inherent in national responsiveness.

King and Sethi (1999) define a comprehensive taxonomy of transnational strategy with five important dimensions of transnational strategy: the configuration of value-chain activities, which refers to the geographic dispersal of a firm's value-chain components; the coordination of value-chain activities; centralization; strategic alliances; and market integration, which refers to the extent to which the parent corporation views the international market as a single competitive arena.

Asea Brown Boveri (ABB) is an example of a successful transnational management model implementation. ABB, with home bases in Sweden and Switzerland, exemplifies the trend towards cross-national mergers that lead firms to consider multiple headquarters in the future. It is managed as a flexible network of units, and one of management's main functions is the facilitation of information/knowledge flows between units. ABB's subsidiaries have full responsibility for product categories on a worldwide basis. Operating transnationally brings the benefits of access to new markets and the opportunity to utilize and develop resources wherever they may be located.

Nestlè CEO Peter Brabeck recently questioned the idea of a so-called global consumer. The firm appears to be successfully implementing a transnational strategy by making centralization decisions based partly on whether value-chain activities are upstream or downstream. According to Brabeck: "The closer we come to the consumer, in branding, pricing, communication, and product adaptation, the more we decentralize. The more we are dealing with production, logistics, and supply-chain management, the more centralized decision making becomes. After all, we want to leverage Nestlè's size, not be hampered by it" (Wetlaufer, 2001).

SEE ALSO: International Business; International Management; International Management; Organizational Structure

Mike Raisinghani
Revised by Bruce Walters

FURTHER READING:

Bartlett, C.A., and S. Ghoshal. *Managing Across Borders. The Transnational Solution.* Boston: Harvard Business School Press, 1998.

———. "Managing Innovation in the Transnational Corporation." *Managing the Global Firm.* edited by C.A. Bartlett, Y. Doz, and G. Hedlund. London: Routledge, 1990.

Carillo, J. "Transnational Strategies and Regional Development: The Case of GM and Delphi in Mexico." *Industry and Innovation* 11 (2004): 127–153.

Child, J., and Y. Yan. "National and Transnational Effects in International Business: Indications from Sino-Foreign Joint Ventures." *Management International Review* 41, no. 1 (2001): 53–75.

Engle, A. D., and M.E. Mendenhall. "Transnational Roles, Transnational Rewards: Global Integration in Compensation." *Employee Relations* 26 (2004): 613–625.

Hitt, M.A., R.D. Ireland, and R.E. Hoskisson *Strategic Management: Competitiveness and Globalization: Concepts and Cases.* 6th ed., Mason, OH: South-Western Publishing, 2005.

Jones, M. "Globalization and Organizational Restructuring: A Strategic Perspective." *Thunderbird International Business Review* 44 (2002): 325–351.

King, William R., and Vikram Sethi. "An Empirical Assessment of the Organization of Transnational Information Systems." *Journal of Management Information Systems,* Spring 1999, 7–28.

Vitalari, Nicholas P., and James C. Wetherbe. "Emerging Best Practices in Global Systems Development." In *Global Information Technology and Systems Development.* edited by P.C. Palvia, S.C. Palvia, and E.M. Roche. Nashau, NH: Ivy League Publishing, Ltd., 1996.

Wasilewski, N. "An Empirical Study of the Desirability and Challenges of Implementing Transnational Marketing Strategies." *Advances in Competitiveness Research* 10, no. 1 (2002): 123–149.

Wetlaufer, S. "The Business Case Against Revolution: An Interview with Nestle's Peter Brabeck." *Harvard Business Review* 79, no. 2 (2001): 112–121.

Zwass, Vladimir. *Foundations of Information Systems.* New York: Irwin/McGraw-Hill, 1998.

TRANSPORTATION

SEE: Logistics and Transportation

TRENDS IN ORGANIZATIONAL CHANGE

Organizations have entered a new era characterized by rapid, dramatic and turbulent changes. The accelerated pace of change has transformed how work is performed by employees in diverse organizations. Change has truly become an inherent and integral part of organizational life.

Several emerging trends are impacting organizational life. Of these emerging trends, five will be examined: globalization, diversity, flexibility, flat, and networks. These five emerging trends create tensions for organizational leaders and employees as they go through waves of changes in their organizations. These tensions present opportunities as well as threats, and if these tensions are not managed well, they will result in dysfunctional and dire organizational outcomes at the end of any change process. These five trends and the specific tensions they produce are presented in Table 1.

GLOBALIZATION

Organizations operate in a global economy that is characterized by greater and more intense competition, and at the same time, greater economic interdependence and collaboration. More products and services are being consumed outside of their country of origin than ever before as globalization brings about greater convergence in terms of consumer tastes and preferences. Yet at the same time, in the midst of greater convergence, there is the opposite force of divergence at work where companies have to adapt corporate and business strategies, marketing plans, and production efforts to local domestic markets.

To stay competitive, more organizations are embracing offshore outsourcing. Many functions are being shifted to India, the Philippines, Malaysia, and other countries for their low labor costs, high levels of workforce education, and technological advantages. According to the 2002-2003 Society for Human Resource Management (SHRM) Workplace Forecast, companies such as Ford, General Motors, and Nestle employ more people outside of their headquarters countries than within those countries.

Almost any company, whether in manufacturing or services, can find some part of its work that can be done off site. Forrester Research projects that 3.3 million U.S. service- and knowledge-based jobs will be shipped overseas by the year 2015, 70 percent of which will move to India. Communication and information sharing are occurring across the globe in multiple languages and multiple cultures. Global competition and global cooperation coexist in the new world economy.

One major consequence of globalization is greater mobility in international capital and labor markets. This creates a global marketplace where there is more opportunity, because there are more potential customers. However, there is also more competition, as local companies have to compete with foreign companies for customers.

According to Dani Rodrik, professor of international political economy at Harvard's Kennedy School of Government, the processes associated with the global integration of markets for goods, services, and capital have created two sources of tensions.

First, reduced barriers to trade and investment accentuate the asymmetries between groups that can cross international borders, and those that cannot. In the first category are owners of capital, highly skilled workers, and many professionals. Unskilled and semi-skilled workers and most middle managers belong in the second category.

Second, globalization engenders conflicts within and between nations over domestic norms and the social institutions that embody them. As the technology for manufactured goods becomes standardized and diffused internationally, nations with very different sets of values, norms, institutions, and collective preferences begin to compete head on in markets for similar goods. Trade becomes contentious when it unleashes forces that undermine the norms implicit in local or domestic workplace practices.

Table 1	
Change–Trends and Tensions in Organizations	
Trends	**Tensions**
1. Globalization	Global versus Local
2. Diversity	Heterogeneity versus Homogeneity
3. Flexibility	Flexibility versus Stability
4. Flat	Centralization versus Decentralization
5. Networks	Interdependence versus Independence

Professor Rodrik concluded that "the most serious challenge for the world economy in the years ahead lies in making globalization compatible with domestic social and political stability" (Rodrik 1997, p. 2). This implies ensuring that international economic integration does not lead to domestic social disintegration. Organizations that are confronted with this challenge will have to manage the tension created by the global integration versus local disintegration dilemma.

The overall picture as a consequence of globalization is one of turbulence and uncertainty, in which a variety of contradictory processes present a wide range of both opportunities and threats that defy established ways of doing business and working in organizations. Integration and exclusion coexist uneasily side-by-side in organizations.

For example, many apparent dichotomies or paradoxes—competition versus collaboration, market forces versus state intervention, global actions versus local solutions—are losing their sharp edges as contradictory forces appear to converge and reinforce each other in organizations across the globe. Companies that compete fiercely in some markets form strategic alliances in others; government guidance and regulation are required to make markets work effectively; and "think globally, act locally" has been adopted as business strategy (or as a mantra) to deal with the challenges of doing business in the globalized economy. As organizations transform themselves to stay competitive, they will need to confront and resolve some, if not all, of these dichotomies or paradoxes.

On another level, because of globalization, the fates of people living and working in different parts of the world are becoming intertwined. Global events may have significant local impact. September 11, 2001 has been called the "day that changed the world". Heightened security concerns are changing expectations for people in organizations, and the role of organizations themselves. The threat of terrorism continues to be an ongoing concern worldwide. It has created a renewed focus on workplace security as employees experience a heightened sense of vulnerability in the workplace. Employee monitoring and screening are occurring more frequently. Concern over travel for business purposes is resulting in the increased use of alternate forms of communication such as teleconferencing and videoconferencing.

DIVERSITY

Globalization is impacting how organizations compete with each other. In combination with changing demographics, globalization is causing a rapid increase in diversity in organizations. Never before have people been required to work together with colleagues and customers from so many different cultures and countries.

Diversity is moving American society away from "mass society" to "mosaic society". Organizations reflect this "mosaic society" in their more diverse workforce (in terms of not only race, ethnic or culture but also in terms of age, sexual orientation, and other demographic variables). More than ever, people have to interact and communicate with others who come from diverse backgrounds. This in turn has meant that employees need new relational skills to succeed. An emerging stream of research in international management has called these new relational skills "cultural intelligence". Cultural intelligence is defined as the capability to adapt effectively across different national, organizational and professional cultures (Earley, Ang and Tan, 2005). More managers take up global work assignments in industries around the world. They learn how to work with people who not only think and communicate differently but also do things differently. Managers will need to develop their cultural intelligence to manage greater diversity in organizations.

Diversity in organizations will continue to increase. As indicated by the U.S Census Bureau National Population Projections, the Hispanic population will increase by 11.2 percent between 2000 and 2025 to become the largest minority group in the United States. All other minority groups will increase by about 9 percent, while the number of Caucasians will decrease by approximately 19 percent. The world population is growing at a high rate in developing countries, while remaining stable or decreasing in the developed world. The result will be income inequities and economic opportunity leading to increased immigration and migration within and between nations. More temporary workers will be used for specific tasks, and there will be a greater demand for highly skilled workers.

The aging American workforce population means more retirees and potential gaps in availability of experienced workers. According to American Association of Retired Persons (AARP), by 2015 nearly one in five U.S. workers will be age 55 or older. Retirees often want to keep a foot in the workplace. AARP's research shows that nearly 8 of 10 baby boomers envision working part time after retirement; 5 percent anticipate working full time at a new job or career; only 16 percent foresee not working at all.

People of different ethnic and cultural backgrounds possess different attitudes, values, and norms. Increasing cultural diversity in both public and private sector organizations focuses attention on the distinctions between ethnic and cultural groups in their attitudes and performance at work. This greater focus can result in the tension between finding similarities and accentuating differences in the face of greater diversity in organizations.

There is an on-going debate between the *heterogenists* and the *homogenists* concerning the impact of greater diversity in organizations. The *heterogenists* contend that diverse or heterogeneous groups in organizations have performance advantages over homogeneous groups while the *homogenists* take the opposing view—that homogeneous groups are more advantageous than heterogeneous or diverse groups in organizations.

According to the *heterogenists,* organizations with greater diversity have an advantage in attracting and retaining the best available human talent. The exceptional capabilities of women and minorities offer a rich labor pool for organizations to tap. When organizations attract, retain, and promote maximum utilization of people from diverse cultural backgrounds, they gain competitive advantage and sustain the highest quality of human resources.

Organizations with greater diversity can understand and penetrate wider and enhanced markets. Not only do these organizations embrace a diverse workforce internally, they are better suited to serve a diverse external clientele. Organizations with greater diversity also display higher creativity and innovation. Especially in research-oriented and high technology organizations, the array of talents provided by a gender- and ethnic-diverse organization becomes invaluable. Heterogeneous or diverse groups display better problem solving ability as they are more capable of avoiding the consequences of *groupthink,* compared to highly cohesive and homogeneous groups that are more susceptible to conformity.

On the other hand, greater organizational diversity has its drawbacks. With the benefits of diversity come organizational costs. Too much diversity can lead to dysfunctional outcomes. Diversity increases ambiguity, complexity, and confusion. Organizations with greater diversity may have difficulty reaching consensus and implementing solutions. In many organizations, diversity can produce negative dynamics such as ethnocentrism, stereotyping and cultural clashes.

The *homogenists* argue that homogeneous groups often outperform culturally diverse groups, especially where there is a serious communication problem. Cross-cultural training is necessary to enable culturally diverse groups to live up to their potential and overcome communication difficulties. The diversity movement, according to the *homogenists,* has the potential to polarize different social groups and harm productivity while breeding cynicism and resentment, heightening intergroup frictions and tensions, and lowering productivity, just the opposite of what managing diversity is intended to accomplish.

The challenge therefore is for management to manage the tension produced by heterogeneity versus homogeneity. If properly managed, organizations can reap the benefits of greater diversity. Aside from proper management, organizations need to learn to appreciate and value diversity before the benefits of diversity can be fully realized. To achieve this, diversity training programs may help people in organizations understand and value diversity.

FLEXIBILITY

Globalization and diversity trends are forcing organizations to become more flexible and adaptable. To be able to function globally and to embrace diversity, leaders and employees in organizations have to become more flexible and develop a wider repertoire of skills and strategies in working with diverse groups of people in the workplace as well as in the marketplace.

The response to increased diversity has, in many cases, been increased organizational flexibility. Some organizations allow workers to have very different work arrangements (e.g. flex-time) and payment schedules. Some organizations (and workers) have found it convenient to treat some workers as independent consultants rather than employees. In certain occupations, advances in communication and information technologies have enabled *telecommuting*—working at home via computer. One consequence of this is the blurring of boundaries between work and home, and where and when work occurs. The benefits of greater flexibility may be countered by the negative consequences of working 24/7 including higher stress and burnout.

The response to increased competition, however, has resulted in a tension generated by the demands to be flexible and yet maintain some stability as changes are implemented in organizations. To stay competitive, organizations are constantly changing and restructuring to increase flexibility and decrease costs. Business process reengineering, business process outsourcing, job redesign, and other approaches to optimize business processes have been implemented to increase operational and process efficiency while reducing the costs of doing business.

Changes in business and operational processes need time to stabilize for employees to learn the new processes, become familiar with them, and be able to operate effectively and efficiently. Yet, competitive pressures can cause organizations to go through a series of changes without giving employees adequate time for learning and training, and for the benefits of the change to be fully realized in the organization. This tension is well-captured by Columbia Business School professor Eric Abrahamson in his book, *Change Without Pain* (2004) in which he discussed how organizations can go through change overload and how employees can experience change fatigue and burnout. Professor Abrahamson proposes "creative recombination" as an alternative approach to the highly destructive, destabilizing and painful changes caused by "creative destruction".

FLAT

In a greater competitive marketplace, speed or response time is critical. How organizations response to customers and other stakeholders or be the first to market may make a significant difference as time is at a premium. Organizations that can develop new technologies faster or can adapt to changes in the market faster are the ones that will survive the competition. To maximize response time, organizations have been flattening their hierarchies and structures, in addition to other initiatives such as downsizing and networking. Flat organizations make decisions more quickly because each person is closer to the ultimate decision-makers. There are fewer levels of management, and workers are empowered to make decisions. Decision-making becomes decentralized.

However, flat organizations create a new tension between decentralization and centralization. Among the drivers of decentralization are communications technologies that allow companies to push decision-making away from the core. Proponents of decentralization emphasize the idea that less hierarchical organizations mirror the efficiencies of the networks that enable them: they are faster, more resilient, more responsive, more flexible and more innovative. Also, they argue, people who work within decentralized organizations feel empowered and energized. They do not need to focus on the chain of command and they do not feel constrained by it.

Organizations are caught between the opposing forces of centralization and decentralization. They want to leverage the opportunities offered by decentralization and create more nimble and forceful organizations, but they cannot always do so because the forces of centralization come into play. There are obvious benefits to centralization as control is comparatively tighter and accountability is clearer compared to a flatter, more decentralized organizational structure.

Take the example of IT operations. The key to a centralized organization's success is its responsiveness. If the centralized operation can be responsive to the needs of the business, then that approach can make sense. Several companies, such as DaimlerChrysler and PepsiCo, have migrated back to centralizing IT operations after attempts at decentralization.

The debate over the centralization versus decentralization of operations in organizations is an enduring one. It is an age-old battle of standardization versus autonomy, corporate efficiency versus local effectiveness and pressure on costs and resources versus accommodation of specific local needs.

Vacillation between centralization and decentralization is both non-productive and unnecessary. Organizations, as they desire to become flatter, will need to be clear about how they need to respond to the tension between centralization and decentralization.

NETWORKS

Organizations that flatten tend to encourage horizontal communication among workers. Rather than working through the organizational hierarchy, it is often faster for workers who need to coordinate with each other simply to communicate directly. Such organizations are highly networked.

Another meaning of networked organizations refers to their relations to other organizations. Organizations that have downsized to just their core competencies must then outsource all the functions that used to be done inhouse. To avoid losing time and effort managing contracts with suppliers, organizations have learned to develop close ties to their suppliers so that social mechanisms of coordination replace legal mechanisms, which are slow and costly. In many industries, such as the garment industry in Italy, strong relationships have developed between manufacturers and suppliers (and other manufacturers), so that considerable work is done without a contract and without even working out a firm price. For these networked organizations to work, high trust and social capital between organizations are key elements.

Networked organizations are particularly important in industries with complex products where technologies and customer needs change rapidly, such as in high technology industries. Close ties among a set of companies enables them to work with each other in ways that are faster than arms-length contracts would permit, and yet retains the flexibility of being able to drop the relationship if needed (as opposed to performing the function in-house). The trend towards networked organizations and structures create a new tension between interdependence and independence. The forces of aggregation and disaggregation throw up new challenges for organizations, for example, the use of independent contractors, joint ventures, strategic partnerships and alliances even with competitors.

One advantage of networks is that organizations have greater flexibility and thus they can become more competitive in the global marketplace. Another advantage is that organizations do not require that many resources such as employee benefits, office space, and financing for new business ventures.

On the other hand, networks have distinct disadvantages. Organizations may find it more difficult to control quality of goods or services as they now have to depend on their partners in the networks to deliver the quality that is desired. Legal and contracting expertise as well as negotiation expertise will also be important for networks. Alternative forms of control may need to be developed to control quality. Alternative mechanisms for coordination may also need to be developed to manage the growing constellation and sometimes tenuous nature of other partner organizations in the network.

All the five trends and the tensions they produce result in greater organizational or system complexity for both leaders and employees in organizations. The tensions produced by these trends cannot be solved. They have to be managed. Effective approaches in organizational change will involve not one strategy but many alternatives and will require leaders and employees to develop greater resilience in confronting these tensions.

SEE ALSO: Diversity; Globalization

Joo-Seng Tan

FURTHER READING:

Abrahamson, E. *Change Without Pain.* Boston: Harvard Business School Press, 2004.

Earley, P.C., Soon Ang, and Joo-Seng Tan. *CQ: Developing Cultural Intelligence in the Workplace.* Stanford, CA: Stanford University Press, 2005.

Rodrik, D. *Has Globalization Gone Too Far?* Washington, DC: Institute for International Economics, 1997.

SHRM Workplace Forecast: A Strategic Outlook 2000–2003. Alexandria: Society for Human Resource Management.

U.S. Census Bureau. *Current Population Survey.* Washington, DC: GPO, 2005. Available from <http://www.census.gov>

U

UNIFORM COMMERCIAL CODE

UNIFORM COMMERCIAL CODE

The Uniform Commercial Code (UCC) is a collection of recommended laws covering many different issues that arise during commercial transactions, such as sales contracts, leases, negotiable instruments, letters of credit, bank collections, and secured transactions. The impetus behind the creation of the UCC was the hope that each state would adopt it as a statute, thereby giving uniformity throughout the country to the area of commercial law.

HISTORY

The first draft of the UCC was created in the fall of 1951 by an editorial board consisting of representatives from the National Conference of Commissioners on Uniform State Laws and the American Law Institute. Pennsylvania adopted the draft as state law in 1953, but no other state enacted it until the editorial board issued a revised code in late 1956. After the revision, Massachusetts and Kentucky were the first to adopt the UCC. Today, all of the states (except Louisiana, which has only adopted certain parts) and the District of Columbia have adopted the UCC.

TOPICS COVERED BY THE UCC

Until 1987, the UCC consisted of nine articles. Each article was separate and distinct from the other articles, and covered a specific topic in commercial law.

Article 1 is entitled "General Provisions," and sets forth general definitions and principles of interpretation for all of the articles.

Article 2, "Sales," controls every stage of a transaction for the sale of goods, from general obligations, construction of a contract, and performance under that contract to breach, repudiation, and excuse of a sales contract. Article 2 also provides remedies for problems that may occur during a sales transaction.

Article 3 covers negotiable instruments, which include checks, cashiers' checks, travelers' checks, promissory notes, and certificates of deposit. This article regulates all transactions involving negotiable instruments, such as negotiation and endorsements; payment on the instruments; liability of parties such as the endorser, drawer, and acceptor; and dishonor of the instrument.

Article 4, "Bank Deposits and Collections," regulates collect items and post deposits, and governs the relationship among depository, collecting, and payer banks, and between a payer bank and its customer.

Article 5 addresses letters of credit, including the issuer's obligations, warranties that arise, and remedies that are provided for problems during the issuance process or after a letter of credit has issued.

In 1989, *Article 6* was revised and changed from covering bulk transfers to governing bulk sales. It regulates the obligations of a buyer of a bulk sale. A bulk sale generally involves the sale of more than half of the seller's inventory, not in the ordinary course of a seller's business, when the buyer has (or after inquiry would have had) notice that the seller is not going to continue to operate a similar business after the sale, including auction and liquidation sales. There are specific provisions for notice to claimants (such as creditors of the seller), distribution of the sale's proceeds, filing notices of bulk sales, and liability for noncompliance. This ensures that creditors are not bypassed when a company decides to end its business.

Article 7 governs warehouse receipts, bills of lading, and other such documents relating to ownership and transportation of goods.

Article 8, "Investment Securities," includes rules regulating the issuance of security certificates, the transfer and registration of securities, and the obligations of an intermediary who holds them.

Article 9 covers secured transactions, which occur when one party gives another a secured interest in a piece of property, usually to secure payment of a debt. The provisions of this article determine when a security interest may arise, the types of property that may be covered, the validity of the underlying security agreement, and the issue of default. Article 9 also covers the rights of third parties through a process called *perfection* of a security interest, which occurs when the holder of the security interest files notice of it with the state, so that other creditors know of the existence of the security interest.

Since the creation of the first nine articles, two more articles have been added to the UCC. Article 2A, approved in 1987, covers leases of personal property (not apartments or offices). Article 4A, added in 1989, regulates the issuance, acceptance, and payment of electronic funds transfers.

Article 2 of the UCC, which is widely considered to be the "bible" for contracts concerning the purchase or sale of goods in the United States, underwent a decade-long revision process that was finally completed in 2003. As of 2004, it appeared likely to be adopted by state legislatures and thus become the law of the land. The major impetus behind the changes was updating Article 2 to accommodate electronic commerce. When enacted, the revisions are expected to force both buyers and sellers to revisit their organizational contract management and administration policies.

SEE ALSO: Exporting and Importing; International Management

Cindy Rhodes Victor
Revised by Laurie Collier Hillstrom

FURTHER READING:

Hakes, Russell A. *The ABC's of the UCC, Article 9: Secured Transactions.* Chicago: American Bar Association, 1996.

Murray, John, Jr. "What the Updated UCC Means to You." *Purchasing,* 6 May 2004.

Rumbaugh, Charles E. "The New (and Improved) Article 2 to the UCC." *Contract Management,* December 2004.

Uniform Commercial Code. 14th ed. St. Paul, MN: West Publishing Co., 1996.

UTILITY THEORY

Utility theory provides a methodological framework for the evaluation of alternative choices made by individuals, firms and organizations. Utility refers to the satisfaction that each choice provides to the decision maker. Thus, utility theory assumes that any decision is made on the basis of the utility maximization principle, according to which the best choice is the one that provides the highest utility (satisfaction) to the decision maker.

UTILITY THEORY IN CONSUMER BEHAVIOR

Utility theory is often used to explain the behavior of individual consumers. In this case the consumer plays the role of the decision maker that must decide how much of each of the many different goods and services to consume so as to secure the highest possible level of total utility subject to his/her available income and the prices of the goods/services.

UTILITY THEORY AND DEMAND

In addition to providing an explanation of consumer disposition of income, utility theory is useful in establishing individual consumer demand curves for goods and services. A consumer's demand curve for a good or service shows the different quantities that consumers purchase at various alternative prices. Factors that are held constant are consumers' tastes and preferences, income, and price.

UTILITY FUNCTIONS

In all cases the utility that the decision maker gets from selecting a specific choice is measure by a utility function U, which is a mathematical representation of the decision maker's system of preferences such that: $U(x) > U(y)$, where choice x is preferred over choice y or $U(x) = U(y)$, where choice x is indifferent from choice y—both choices are equally preferred.

Utility functions can be either cardinal or ordinal. In the former case, a utility function is used to derive a numerical score for each choice that represents the utility of this choice. In this setting the utilities (scores) assigned to different choices are directly comparable. For instance, a utility of 100 units towards a cup of tea is twice as desirable as a cup of coffee with a utility level of 50 units. In the ordinal case, the magnitude of the utilities (scores) are not important; only the ordering of the choices as implied by their utilities matters. For instance, a utility of 100 towards a cup of tea and a utility level of 50 units for a cup of coffee simply state that a cup of coffee is preferred to a cup of tea, but it cannot be argued that a cup of tea is twice as desirable as a cup of coffee. Within this setting, it is important to note that an ordinal utility function is not unique, since any monotonic increasing transformation of an ordinal utility function will still provide the same ordering for the choices.

ASSUMPTIONS ON PREFERENCES

Irrespective of the type of utility function, utility theory assumes that preferences are complete, reflexive and transitive. The preferences are said to be complete if for any pair of choices x and y, one and only one of the following be stated: (1) x is preferred to y, (2) y is preferred to x, or (3) x and y are equally preferred. The preferences are said to be reflexive if for any pair of choices x and y such that x equally preferred to y, it is concluded that y is also equally preferred to x. Finally, the preferences are said to be transitive if for any three choices x, y, z such that x is preferred over y, and y is preferred over z, it is concluded that x is preferred over z. The hypotheses on reflexivity and transitivity imply that the decision maker is consistent (rational).

MARGINAL RATE OF SUBSTITUTION

A further assumption of utility theory is that decision makers are willing to trade one choice for another. The existing trade-offs define the marginal rate of substitution. As example suppose that two investment projects are considered by a decision maker. Project x has a return of 6 percent and a risk of 4 percent, whereas the return for project y is 5 percent and its risk is 2 percent. Furthermore assume that the decision maker considers both projects to be equally preferred. With this assumption it is clear that the decision maker is willing to increase the risk by 2 percent in order to improve return by 1 percent. Therefore, the marginal rate of substitution of risk for return is 2. In real world situations, the marginal rates of substitution are often decreasing. Such situations correspond to diminishing marginal utilities (marginal utility is defined as the change in total utility resulting from a one-unit change in consumption of the good or service). In the above example, we can assume that the decision maker is willing to take higher risks in order to get higher return, but only up to a specific point which is called saturation point. Once the risk has reached that point, the decision maker would not be willing to take any higher risk to increase return and therefore the marginal rate of substitution at this risk level would be zero.

MULTI-ATTRIBUTE UTILITY THEORY

The traditional framework of utility theory has been extended over the past three decades to the multi-attribute case, in which decisions are taken by multiple criteria. Multi-attribute utility theory has been evolved as one of the most important topics in multiple criteria decision making with many real world applications in complex real world problems.

The concept of utility can be used to analyze individual consumer behavior, to explain individual consumer demand curves as well as in modeling the decision makers' preferences. In all cases, it is assumed that some choices are evaluated and the best one is identified as the choice that maximizes the utility or satisfaction. The utility theory has been a research topic of major importance for the development of economics, decision theory, and management and it still attracts the interest of both practitioners and academic researchers.

SEE ALSO: Consumer Behavior; Economics

Michael Doumpos and Constantin Zopounidis

FURTHER READING:

Aleskerov, F., and B. Monjardet. *Utility Maximization, Choice and Preference.* Heidelberg: Springer Verlag, 2002.

Belton, V. and T.J. Stewart. *Multiple Criteria Decision Analysis: An Integrated Approach.* Dordrecht: Kluwer Academic Publishers, 2002.

Hammond, J.S, R.L. Keeney, and H. Raiffa. *Smart Choices: A Practical Guide to Making Better Decisions.* Boston: Harvard Business School Press, 2002.

Keeney, R.L. and H. Raiffa. *Decisions with Multiple Objectives: Preference and Value Tradeoffs.* Cambridge University Press, Cambridge, 1993.

V

VALUE-ADDED TAX

A value-added tax (VAT) is a fee assessed against businesses at each step of the production and distribution process, usually whenever a product is resold or value is added to it. A VAT is levied on the difference between the purchase cost of an asset and the price at which it can be sold (i.e., the amount of value added to it). Producers and distributors typically pass the cost of the VAT on to the final consumer in the form of price increases. Tax is added to a product's price each time it changes hands until delivery to the customer takes place, when the final tax is paid.

Value-added tax falls under the general category of a consumption tax, meaning taxes on what people buy rather than on their earnings, savings, or investments. VAT has also been referred to as a sort of national sales tax, though it functions very differently. Sales tax is imposed on the total retail price of the item sold, while VAT tax is imposed on the value added at each stage of production and distribution. And though more complicated than sales tax, value-added tax systems have more checks against tax fraud because the tax is assessed at more than one point in the distribution process.

THE VAT ASSESSMENT PROCESS

The process of assessing value-added tax occurs roughly as follows:

1. Manufacture adds value to a product; the amount of value added can be described as the difference between the cost of the materials used to make the product and the price charged to the customer (often a wholesaler).

2. The manufacturer pays value-added tax (a percentage of the value added), which is then included in the purchase price charged to the customer (wholesaler).

3. The manufacturer gets a rebate from the government for VAT paid on the materials.

4. The customer (wholesaler) pays a VAT on the value they add, which can be described as the difference between what they paid to the manufacturer and the price they at which they sell it to their customer (retailer). This VAT amount is included in the price charged to the retailer.

5. The wholesaler gets a rebate for VAT from the government for the VAT paid to the manufacturer.

6. The retailer pays value-added tax on the value they add, which can be described as the price charged to customers less the wholesale cost, and includes the VAT in the final sales price of the product.

7. The retail store collects value-added tax from the person buying the product (retail price thus includes all VATs collected at each stage of this process) and gets a rebate for the VAT paid to the wholesaler.

Value-added tax is a primary source of tax revenue in many European and other developed countries. With the exception of the United States, all countries of the Organization for Economic Cooperation and Development (OECD) use a VAT or similar tax on consumer expenditures. Though a value-added tax system has not been extensively used in United States, some presidents have examined the idea.

HISTORY OF VALUE-ADDED TAX

Value-added tax was first suggested in Germany during the post–World War I period as a replacement to the country's turnover tax. The turnover tax was similar to the value-added tax system but did not provide rebates for the taxes paid at each stage. Other proponents of VAT suggested that the United States adopt it as a substitute for excise taxes imposed after the War. However, it was not until 1953 that the value-added tax system was put in place in the United States or Europe. That year, Michigan adopted a modified VAT, termed a Business Activities Tax, and used the system for 14 years. France was the first country to begin using value-added tax to partially replace its own turnover tax system.

In 1967 the Council of European Economic Community (EEC) issued directives for widespread adoption of value-added tax to replace existing turnover taxes and link EEC members with a common tax system. The Council also hoped the new system would increase foreign trade, which was hindered by the complex regulatory practices of the turnover tax system. After the directive, countries outside the EEC such as Austria, Sweden, Brazil, Greece, and Peru also adopted some variation of the VAT, either in addition to or as a replacement for their own national tax structures.

A 1983 *U.S. News & World Report* article titled "What's Wrong with the System?" examined alternatives to the current tax system in the United States, citing problems such as complexity of tax laws, the expense of hiring professionals to prepare tax documents, and IRS backlog. One of the cited alternatives was value-added tax, by then widely used across Europe and other developed countries.

From 1987 to 1997, value-added tax was introduced in many eastern European countries, the former Soviet republics, and Asia. China, Thailand, the Philippines, and Bangladesh all implemented the policy during the mid-1990s. By the early 2000s, VAT had become the a key component of the tax systems in more than 120 countries, with tax rates varying from 5 to 25 percent. Writing in *Finance and Development,* Liam Ebrill claimed that "the rapid rise of the value-added tax was the most dramatic-and probably most important-development in taxation in the latter part of the twentieth century, and it still continues."

CHARACTERISTICS OF VALUE-ADDED TAX

There are three types of value-added tax used around the world, each different in the ways that taxes on investment (capital) expenditures are handled. The most common is the consumption method, which allows businesses to immediately deduct the full value of taxes paid on capital purchases. The second is the net income method, which allows gradual deduction of VAT paid on capital purchases over a number of years, much like depreciation. The third type, gross national product method of value-added tax, provides no allowance for taxes paid on capital purchases. The name of this type of tax is derived from the fact that the tax base is approximately equal to private GNP. The consumption method is most favored among general populations because it most equally taxes income from labor and capital and promotes capital formation.

In theory, value-added tax systems with a uniform rate are neutral to all forms of productive input. However, countries across the world have had to modify the VAT system with multiple rates and exemptions to meet political, economic, and social needs. Most nations do not assess any tax on necessities such as food, medicine, and shelter. And because of the difficulty in computing value added, professional services such as banking, accounting, and insurance are often exempt. The largest variation from uniform tax rates is the zero tax rate on exports. Since taxes will likely be assessed at a product's destination, many do not impose a tax on the final selling price of exports. To compensate, the VAT is applied to imported products. Working together, countries seek more balanced trade.

IMBALANCES IN THE VAT SYSTEM

Financial services have traditionally been exempt from value-added tax because no one has found a systematic, easy way to tax these services, partially because of the difficulty in determining the nature of services provided. Also, some wonder if it is fair to charge a tax on services often related to saving and investment.

Though some services are exempt from value-added tax, they must still pay the VAT on expenses such as office equipment; additionally, these business are ineligible for rebates on the VAT they pay. Therefore, exempt business sectors pay the total VAT on any good and service purchased. Often the cost of paying value-added tax is rolled into fees charged for the services offered. As a result of this imbalance, competition becomes greater, as companies can import services tax free, instead of buying services from a company whose price probably is inflated to absorb some or all of the hidden VAT taxes paid.

To remove such distortions in the economic effect of a value-added tax, a new method of taxing financial services would need to be devised. If these services were no longer exempt from value-added tax, they could reclaim prepaid VATs on equipment, etc., but they would also be required to charge VAT on any services offered. What complicates the matter further is categorizing which services are performed specifically on a customer's behalf and which are performed on the institution's behalf. Additionally, services performed for the institution as a whole still indirectly benefit consumers. These issues make for murky ground when computing the value a service provider should be taxed upon.

The benefit of staying with the current system is that people are used to it. The option of charging VAT to financial services means added resources must be committed to changing existing VAT coverage and finding a way to measure value added for financial institutions. A third option is to look for a distinct way of taxing services while remaining under the value-added tax system. As an example, the European Commission was exploring the idea of taxing services on a cash-flow basis, taxing cash movement.

THE BENEFITS OF VALUE-ADDED TAX

One of the best reasons for instituting a value-added tax, according to VAT proponents, is that the system encourages personal savings and investment—principal elements of a healthy economy—by taxing only consumption. In the current United States tax structure, citizens pay taxes twice on money they save—once when income tax is withdrawn from their paycheck, and again when they pay taxes on the interest earned from savings and gains from investments. Similarly, the tax system in place in the United States encourages corporations to use debt financing, in which interest payments made by the company are tax deductible. Any dividends earned are subject to double taxation. And because taxes on capital purchases cannot be immediately deducted (only later as depreciation expense), the costs of capital investment increase. If a company does have a large asset base, it must generate more income to increase investor returns, subjecting itself again to higher tax payments.

Another benefit touted by VAT supporters is a more constant revenue flow. Tax revenues under the current U.S. structure rise and fall as a result of changing economic conditions, decreasing during recessions and growing during an economic boom. During recessionary periods, revenues may fall enough that government financial requirements utilize all available funds, and economic recovery becomes further delayed. Proponents of value-added tax believe it results in more financial stability and revenue flow.

Supporters of VAT for the United States view the system as a supplementary tax that could help make up for revenue lost due to personal income taxes, and believe imposition of a VAT may also result in general lowering of income-tax rates. They also assert that items such as food, medicine, and shelter should be exempt (as they are in other countries with a value-added tax structure) in order to maintain fair practices for those who must expend the majority of their income on basic necessities. It would also mean people who save and invest money realize benefits. Finally, VAT advocates maintain that the current tax system in the United States cannot raise sufficient revenue to support minimal government expenses.

A value-added tax would in theory eliminate the need for federal tax expenditures, which are largely responsible for depletion of federal revenues and increases in the national debt. Also, since the VAT is a consumption tax, people will be more motivated to save and invest disposable income. Additionally, a VAT would in some way reduce bias toward those who earn higher incomes. Tax write-offs can usually be taken advantage of only by those who itemize—meaning that they are available only to a small percentage of U.S. citizens, usually those with the highest incomes.

DRAWBACKS OF VALUE-ADDED TAX

Dropping the current tax system in the United States in order to adopt a VAT would require additional taxes on state and local services and products as well. Because value-added tax is similar to implementing a national sales tax, it impinges on territory currently occupied by states and local governments, and could add to the expenses incurred by cities and states by making them responsible for collection and enforcing compliance to the VAT system. It would require that every state rewrite its tax code, and could also add another tax layer for cities already charging state and local sales taxes. And while some cities could benefit from nontaxable export sales, others that depend primarily on domestic industry could face large losses in sales, resulting in declining revenues and lost jobs.

The prospect of a value-added tax also raises questions such as: Which goods and services purchased by cities would be federally taxed? Which provided by cities would be federally taxed? There would be no provisions for tax-exempt municipal bonds, which could mean an increase of up to thirty percent of finance costs for some municipalities. Deductions for state and local taxes, mortgage interest, investment in enterprise zones, housing, and jobs would also be eliminated. And cities with citizens who have less disposable income could stand to lose significant revenues with a consumption tax, revenues that would affect the public infrastructure and its investment in schools, roads, and utilities. VAT critics feel a de facto national sales tax will also reduce the amount of local funding states can expect from the local sales tax.

Because those with higher incomes spend a lesser proportion of their total wealth on consumption, households with lower income would still realize disadvantages and pay more tax proportionately than those who make more. However, adjustments can be made to value-added taxes so that taxation of food, housing, clothing, and medicine are given a zero or low tax rate. Also affecting citizens with lower incomes would be the fact that charitable contributions would no longer be deductible expenses.

Adding to the drawbacks, some economists feel that instituting a value-added tax would result in increasing prices and, as a result, inflation. U.S. economists have estimated the net effect of a VAT implementation as a five percent price increase. Also, assumptions that administrative costs would decrease with a value-added tax system may be erroneous. VAT-compliance costs to business would be higher, especially with special exemptions and multiple rate levels to consider. And the VAT would not eliminate income or payroll taxes completely, meaning the VAT would only add to administrative costs incurred.

A fairly recent complication in the administration of VAT systems involves electronic commerce. Though the sales of online retailers accounted for an ever-increasing percentage of overall sales of software, videos, and music, such sales were not subject to VAT. Governments in the EU and elsewhere planned to implement a VAT for electronic commerce in order to protect traditional retailers from unfair competition and create a new source of revenues. "New technologies are steadily drawing VAT into the realms of competition between tax regimes and presenting its architects with the problem of how legislation can be redesigned to reflect previously unimagined transactions, while preserving neutrality with the existing ones," Graeme Ross wrote in *International Tax Review*.

VAT IN THE UNITED STATES

Though the concept of value-added tax has met with considerable success outside the United States, U.S. policy makers have not yet warmed to the idea. The topic has been debated by economists since the post–World War I period but attracts only mild, sporadic support. The suggestion to adopt a VAT policy in the United States has been formally proposed at least five times since the early 1970s. Supporters are firmly convinced problems with the existing tax structure could be corrected with its adoption through the generation of revenues and subsequent stimulation of production.

VAT would replace individual and corporate income tax, as well as the Internal Revenue Service (IRS) and the almost $500 billion in related annual federal tax expenditures. However, deductions for mortgage interest, state and local taxes, earned income credit, and so on would no longer apply. Establishment of a value-added tax structure would directly change how state and local revenues are taxed. A VAT would require a determination of whether any taxable base includes state and local taxes, i.e., whether the price of a good or service had been calculated before or after any state and local income, property, or other taxes were applied.

On the import/export front, the United States loses by its lack of participation in a VAT system. With such a system, the country's large trade deficit could be improved. As provided by the General Agreement on Tariffs and Trade (GATT), prices for export goods can be discounted for some taxes, but not for income and social security taxes. But countries that use the VAT system can reduce prices by the total amount of VAT paid, giving them an economic advantage over the corporate and payroll taxes U.S. firms must pay. By adopting a VAT system and reducing the level of corporate, income, and payroll taxes, the United States could increase its export volume and U.S. firms would not be forced to lower prices to compete with other countries.

SEE ALSO: Exporting and Importing; International Management; Product Design; Product Life Cycle and Industry Life Cycle; Production Planning and Scheduling

Wendy H. Mason

Revised by Laurie Collier Hillstrom

FURTHER READING:

Ebrill, Liam, et al. "The Allure of the Value-Added Tax." *Finance and Development*, June 2002.

"Get the VAT Out: Tax Refund." *U.S. News & World Report*, 28 April 1997.

Hooper, Paul, and Karen A. Smith. "A Value-Added Tax in the U.S.: An Argument in Favor." *Business Horizons*, May-June 1997.

"Introduce VAT to Halt Sales Tax War Among States." *Business Line*, 19 May 1999.

Ogley, Adrian. *Principles of Value-Added Tax—A European Perspective*. International Information Services, Inc., 1998.

Ross, Graeme. "Indirect Taxation—Designing Its Future." *International Tax Revenue*, October 2004.

Scott, Andrew. "Taxing Financial Services: A Future with Options." *OECD Observer*, January 1999.

"What's Wrong with the System?" *U.S. News & World Report*, 18 April 1983.

VALUE ANALYSIS

Lawrence D. Miles developed Value Analysis (VA) at General Electric in 1947. The technique simultaneously pursues two complimentary objectives: maximizing the utility provided by the product or service and minimizing or eliminating waste. Toward this end, the value content of the product or process realized by the consumer is defined. Using the user's definition of value as a filter, the product's components or the steps in the production or service-delivery process are classified as either value-added or non-value-added. The analyst's goal is to eliminate as much of the non-value-added elements as possible by reengineering the design of the product or process. Equally important, the analyst also considers the possibility of substituting functionally equivalent elements for the value-added elements of the product or process design. In the latter case, a substitution is justified when the functionality of the element is maintained or enhanced at a reduced cost to the producer.

Value analysis may be applied to the design and redesign of products, services, and processes. All that is required is that the item under analysis be capable of being divided into mutually exclusive and collectively exhaustive elements. In the case of a product design, the product's bill of materials provides the necessary list of components. In the case of a service delivery or production process, a list of the individual tasks performed to achieve the ultimate objective are sufficient. The function of each product or process element is then identified and classified. Then the analyst must operationally define value within the context established by the product or process under review. Using this definition, each function is analyzed to determine whether or not and how it adds value. Finally, design changes may be proposed to eliminate, reduce, or replace elements that fail to add sufficient value to the overall product or process.

DEFINING VALUE

The first task facing the value analyst is to operationally define value within the context of a particular product or process. In doing so it is important to acknowledge that value is subjective. Just as beauty lies in the eyes of the beholder, value is highly dependent upon perspective. Therefore, it is useful to recall that all products and processes have multiple stakeholders. Indeed, in operationally defining value, the analyst might consider the perspectives of end consumers, individuals making the purchasing decision, suppliers, employees, managers, creditors, investors, regulators, and even the local community. While not all of these potential stakeholders will be concerned with every product or process, an initial consideration of which perspectives to consider is helpful in identifying a robust definition of value to drive the extended analysis. Frequently, the analyst will discover that the different perspectives will lead to conflicting definitions of value. While this complicates the task at hand, honing in on an acceptable definition of value often requires balancing competing demands.

The value-definition phase begins with the gathering of information. The value analyst should have a clear idea of the scope of the review expected. Then each stakeholders' perspective should be explored to determine what they consider to be valuable. What are the utilities expected to be provided by the product or the objectives to be achieved by the process? Are there specific operational goals that should be considered? For example, is there an expectation that all telephone orders will be delivered within twenty-four hours? At this initial stage, each stakeholders experience with the product or process should be broadly considered in order to facilitate the consideration of integrating complimentary elements in the product or process design. Information regarding stakeholder requirements may be revealed through direct observation, focus groups, interviews, surveys or other methods.

IDENTIFYING THE CURRENT STATE

The next step is to identify the as-is state of the product or process under review. In the case of a product design, this may be as simple as developing a bill of materials detailing the relevant components. In the case of a service delivery or production process, a flowchart is commonly used to graphically illustrate the tasks performed to achieve the current output. One of the primary purposes of creating an as-is representation is to ensure that existing problems are not duplicated in a new design. Information about component failures, warranty claims, and customer complaints can be quite valuable at this stage. A physical walkthrough to observe the flow of a process or dismantling of a product may also provide useful information. Any deviations between the as-is documentation and what the analyst sees should be recorded. It is also useful to note any differences between how different employees perform the same task or any variation of the same component provided by different suppliers.

FUNCTION ANALYSIS

The next step of the analysis is to determine the function of each element (each product component or each process task) identified in the as-is documentation. The convention is to use a verb-noun pair to describe the intended result or objective for each element-essentially what contribution the element makes. The verb answers the question "What is to be done?" The verb sets the action to be taken. The noun answers the question "What is it being done to?" The noun signifies what is acted upon. The activity of generating these pairs is more complicated than it appears to be. In practice, it is common to generate several verb-noun pairs that describe the objective or intended result of that element. For example, the function of a light bulb filament might be alternatively described as "generate light" or "convert energy." Each function is then classified as either primary or secondary. The primary functions are the basic reasons that the product or process exists. Secondary functions are those that serve to support or make possible the primary functions. These secondary functions are generally a consequence of the specific design chosen to achieve the product or process' primary function. Therefore, the design elements that provide only secondary functions are prime candidates for elimination or improvement. They also provide a framework for evaluating the elements that provide the associated prime function. The analyst can examine the element providing the primary function to determine whether it can be replaced or redesigned in such a way that the need for the secondary support function is eliminated.

Distinguishing primary and secondary functions is sometimes difficult in practice. To address this concern, Charles Bytheway developed the Function Analysis System Technique (FAST) at Univac in 1964. FAST builds on the VA verb-noun pair analysis by linking those verb-noun pairs to describe complex systems. Bytheway's technique relied on a series of standardized fill-in-the-blank questions. By inserting the verb-noun functions identified through value analysis into the standardized questions, FAST seeks to identify the cause-and-consequence relationships among the various product or process elements. These relationships can then be graphed as a network diagram, with the verb-noun pairs representing the product or process elements as the nodes and the causal relationships represented as the arcs. FAST then identifies those elements that are essential to providing the product or process basic function as the critical path. Everything that falls outside this critical path is then considered as a prime candidate for elimination or improvement.

Bytheway's set of original questions for FAST includes the following:

1. What subject or problem would you like to address?

2. What are you really trying to do when you?

3. What higher level function has caused to come into being?

4. Why is it necessary to?

5. How is actually accomplished or how is it proposed to be accomplished?

6. Does the method selected to cause any supporting functions to come into being?

7. If you did not have to perform , would you still have to perform the other supporting functions?

8. When you , do apparent dependent functions come into existence as a result of the current design?

9. What or who actually?

VALUE-ADDED ASSESSMENT

The function of each design element is then reviewed against the operational definition of value to determine whether and how it contributes to the worth of the product or process. Although each situation is unique, several functions are commonly considered to be non-value-added. The following list is a small sample of highly suspect verbs:

- Administration: allocates, assigns, records, requests, or selects.
- Waiting or delay: files, sets up, stages, updates, or awaits.
- Motion or transportation: collates, collects, copies, delivers, distributes, issues, loads, moves, or receives.
- Oversight or control: approves, expedites, identifies, inspects, labels, maintains, measures, monitors, reviews, or verifies.
- Rework or repair: adjusts, changes, reconciles, repairs, returns, revises, or cancels.

However, identifying non-value-added design elements is only one aspect of the value assessment. The value-added elements should also be appraised. For example, assume that our evaluation has determined that the function of a bolt is to "attach-component." Our initial analysis reveals that this is a secondary function that supports the overall operation of our product and is therefore value-added. However, during the information-gathering phase of our analysis we discovered that several warranty claims can be traced to the failure of this bolt. Based upon this information we should then consider whether a substitute component might provide a higher level of value. In this situation we might consider a bigger, stronger bolt. If the revised design leads to fewer failures, our customers might experience fewer field failures. In addition, even though the new component presumably costs more than the original, we may find the overall product profitability improved if the reduced warranty claims offset the higher production costs. We might also choose to extend our analysis to consider other functionally equivalent components to the original bolt. Returning to our example, the function of the bolt was to "attach-component." Several other design elements might perform the same fastening function at either a reduced cost or improved performance level. A more complete analysis might consider substituting a screw, a rivet, adhesive, or even a weld for the troublesome bolt. Each potential substitution has its own implications for production costs and stakeholder satisfaction.

COMPARING ALTERNATIVE DESIGNS

A useful device for communicating the relative improvement of one design over another is to measure the value-added content of each product or process design. When evaluating alternative process designs, a common unit of measurement is elapsed time. This is generally accomplished by calculating the percentage of time allocated to performing value-added tasks relative to the total process throughput time. In general, the process with the higher percentage of value-added activity will also have the shortest total throughput time. If this is not true, it probably indicates that the process output is significantly improved in the longer, but more value-added, process. In these cases, the absolute values for value-added and non-value-added activity may be more relevant. Another common unit of measure is manufacturing costs. In general, the accounting techniques of activity-based costing are used to allocate the costs to specific design elements. Again, either percentage or absolute measures may be appropriate for evaluating alternative designs. A third common objective, particularly for comparing product designs, is weight. The underlying rationale is that a lower weight generally indicates less material used—hence lower manufacturing costs. In addition, handling, transportation, and operating costs are also commonly reduced in proportion to product weight. Ultimately, the appropriateness of any unit of measure is dependent upon the product or process under review and the intentions of the value analyst.

SEE ALSO: Competitive Advantage; New Product Development

Daniel Heiser
Revised by Badie N. Farah

FURTHER READING:

Akiyama, Kaneo. *Function Analysis: Systematic Improvement of Quality and Performance.* Cambridge, MA: Productivity Press, Inc., 1991.

Emblemsvag, Jan. *Life-Cycle Costing: Using Activity-Based Costing and Monte Carlo Methods to Manage Future Costs and Risks.* New York: John Wiley & Sons, 2003.

Fleisher, Craig S., and Babette Bensoussan. *Strategic and Competitive Analysis: Methods and Techniques for Analyzing Business Competition.* Englewood Cliffs, NJ: Prentice-Hall, 2002.

Have, Ten Steven. *Key Management Models.* Englewood Cliffs, NJ: Prentice-Hall, 2002.

Shillito, M. Larry, and David J. De Marle. *Value: Its Measurement, Design and Management.* New York: Wiley-Interscience, 1992.

Trischler, William E. *Understanding and Applying Value-Added Assessment: Eliminating Business Process Waste.* Milwaukee, WI: ASQC Quality Press, 1996.

VALUE CHAIN MANAGEMENT

Value chain management (VCM) is the integration of all resources starting with the vendor's vendor. It integrates information, materials, labor, facilities, logistics, etc. into a time-responsive, capacity-managed solution that maximizes financial resources and minimizes waste. In other words, efficient and effective value chain management optimizes value for the customers' customer. The following sections discuss the development of VCM, integrated supply chain planning and scheduling, full resource management, cycle time responsiveness, chain-wide resource optimization, and information integration.

DEVELOPMENT OF VALUE CHAIN MANAGEMENT

Using the previous definition as a basis, it is helpful to review how VCM was developed. Traditional industries focused on vertically integrated operations. For example, if you manufactured a product, you wanted to control the material sources, the transportation, the warehousing, the production, and possibly even the retailing of your product. The theory held that more vertical elements that were under your direct control, the more efficiently you were able to perform.

International competitive pressures caused organizations to realize that they simply were not good at everything; thus, they began to focus on what they did best. In other words, they focused on their core competencies. This shift away from vertical integration encouraged organizations to look outside of themselves for services. For example, a manufacturer would have a shipping company do all their packaging and shipping. This introduced more steps in the vendor-to-customer linkage, making the management of this process more complex.

The trend toward operational diversification focused organizations on developing a supply chain whereby an organization would establish a relationship with shippers, vendors, and customers so that all the linkages in the supply chain could be effectively integrated. These interrelationships became extremely complex to manage. Initially, the management of these relationships and linkages was primarily performance-based. Having too many linkages in the supply chain would often cause unresponsiveness to customer demands. Time-to-market became the buzzword of successful competitive positions; the organization that managed its supply chain most effectively tended to have the competitive advantage, at least in terms of customer responsiveness and order fulfillment.

Soon, managers realized that time responsiveness was not the only important element in customer satisfaction. The supply chain linkages-the links among upstream suppliers, manufacturers, and downstream distributors-also had a cost element and resource-efficiency element associated with them. This realization generated a need for value chain management, which is the management of all the linkages of the supply chain in the most efficient way. Sometimes this includes the elimination of elements of the supply chain; for example, Web marketing has eliminated the need for retail outlets.

Amazon.com is a well-known example of eliminating the need for physical "bricks-and-mortar" retail locations. Another example is Atomic Dog Publishing. This textbook company leases online textbooks to students for a semester. Because the texts are online, Atomic Dog has cut out an intermediary between text development and customers; in other words, Atomic Dog manages its value chain through disintermediation by eliminating the need for college bookstores.

Returning to the definition of value chain management, we can now look at the key aspects that are incorporated in VCM. These include:

- integrated supply chain planning and scheduling
- full resource management
- cycle-time responsiveness
- chain-wide resource optimization
- information integration

INTEGRATED SUPPLY CHAIN PLANNING AND SCHEDULING

The planning process for managing the supply chain is easy and has existed for many years. Systems like material requirements planning (MRP), manufacturing resource planning (MRP II), distribution requirements planning (DRP), theory of constraints (TOC), just-in-time (JIT), critical path method (CPM), and program evaluation and review technique (PERT) have performed the planning process effectively for the last 30 years. However, under these environments, capacity has been treated largely as an afterthought, and therefore scheduling has been plagued with performance challenges. The introduction of capacity management tools like finite capacity scheduling (FCS) into the existing planning environments has allowed the development of schedules that were optimizable both in timing and in cost. Most planning systems still do not include these scheduling elements, but rather focus on achieving delivery performance through the utilization of an overriding expedite process. FCS enhancements are a key piece in the development of efficient VCM environments.

FULL RESOURCE MANAGEMENT

Traditional environments focused on managing only the material resources, assuming all the other resources had an infinite capacity. This logical fallacy came from the limitations of the planning systems previously discussed. In a centrally-controlled environment where authoritarian rule existed, the expediting process could make this management style operational. Unfortunately, in a multi-stage supply chain integration, the scheduler needs to make sure that capacity limitations are considered at all steps in the supply chain. Expediting across the links of the supply chain was extremely difficult, if not impossible. For example, the constrained resource at one link in the supply chain may be entirely different than the constrained resource at another step in the supply chain. For one step, the constrained resource could be labor while at another step it could be truck capacity. Therefore, a scheduling system that analyzed and constrained all the resource elements at all steps became a critical piece in VCM.

CYCLE-TIME RESPONSIVENESS

Total cycle time measures are needed because they have, in many cases, become more important than cost when it comes to competitive advantage. Strategic positioning requires a supply chain to be able to supply a customized product at speeds quicker than anyone else, even if the product is not customized. Therefore, a measure of cycle-time performance, measuring the time from when the order for a customized product is placed until it is delivered to the customer, becomes as important as price.

CHAIN-WIDE RESOURCE OPTIMIZATION

Value chain management adds the evaluation not only of all the traditional resources like labor, materials, machinery, etc., but also the optimal management of time and financial resources. Realizing that the supply chain has more steps than existed in the traditional vertical model in which a single firm integrated many supply chain processes and functions within a single organization, the profit margins of each step have become smaller as firms became disintegrated in order to focus on one or only a few core competencies. This "disintegration" has created the need for profits to be available at multiple points throughout the value chain because each step in the chain needs to share a smaller piece of the overall margin pie. In order to accomplish this, value chain management focuses on value-added optimization (also referred to as waste elimination). Some organizations have interpreted this to include the elimination of steps in the supply chain, like the elimination of retailers at Amazon.com and elimination of the need for college bookstores by Atomic Dog Publishing. The efficient performance of all the remaining links in the supply chain is also carefully evaluated by each link.

INFORMATION INTEGRATION

VCM is meaningless if a near-total sharing of information does not exist among all elements of the supply chain. This incorporates multiple levels of information, from the operational information (which includes capacities and work loads), to the strategic levels (which include vision and mission statements). This sharing of information has to be fully accessible and interactive, which often suggests some sort of Web-based database. Each link of the supply chain will need to be able to evaluate the efficiencies and performances of all the other links in the supply chain. However, this information network should not be available to elements outside of the immediate supply chain, like competitors. The shared information within the chain will primarily be utilized by each of the elements of the supply chain for their specific planning and scheduling. It will also be utilized by the sales/marketing functions to generate realistic schedules for the customer and end-consumer of the supply chain process. An overall finite capacity scheduling process that projects realistic and feasible schedules while simultaneously optimizing cost and timing will be necessary.

In summary, value chain management increases the number of steps in the supply chain by focusing on core competencies. VCM attempts to optimize the integrated efficiency of these steps in the management of resources, including the response time and the cost resource. Going into the future, VCM will become increasingly important as pressures to globalize mount, competition shrinks industry profits, and new market entrants challenge existing competitors.

SEE ALSO: Cycle Time; Lean Manufacturing and Just-in-Time Production; Supply Chain Management; Cycle Time

Gerhard Plenert
Revised by Scott B. Droege

FURTHER READING:

Chopra, S., and M.S. Sodhi. "Managing Risk to Avoid Supply-Chain Breakdown." *MIT Sloan Management Review* 46, no. 1 (2004): 53–62.

Cooper, R., and R. Slagmulder. "Achieving Full-Cycle Cost Management." *MIT Sloan Management Review* 46, no. 1 (2004): 45–53.

Lee, H.L., M.L. Fisher, A. Raman, and V.G. Narayanan. "Smarter Supply Chains." In *Harvard Business Review (On Point Collection.* Boston: Harvard Business School Press, 2004.

Lejeune, M.A., and N. Yakova. "On Characterizing the 4 C's in Supply Chain Management." *Journal of Operations Management* 23, no. 1 (2005): 81–100.

Plenert, G. *Making Innovation Happen: Concept Management Through Integration.* Boca Raton, FL: St. Lucie Press, 1998.

VALUE CREATION

Value creation is the primary aim of any business entity. Creating value for customers helps sell products and services, while creating value for shareholders, in the form of increases in stock price, insures the future availability of investment capital to fund operations. From a financial perspective, value is said to be created when a business earns revenue (or a return on capital) that exceeds expenses (or the cost of capital). But some analysts insist on a broader definition of "value creation" that can be considered separate from traditional financial measures. "Traditional methods of assessing organizational performance are no longer adequate in today's economy," according to Value Based Management.net. "Stock price is less and less determined by earnings or asset base. Value creation in today's companies is increasingly represented in the intangible drivers like innovation, people, ideas, and brand."

When broadly defined, value creation is increasingly being recognized as a better management goal than strict financial measures of performance, many of which tend to place cost-cutting that produces short-term results ahead of investments that enhance long-term competitiveness and growth. As a result, some experts recommend making value creation the first priority for all employees and all company decisions. "If you put value creation first in the right way, your managers will know where and how to grow; they will deploy capital better than your competitors; and they will develop more talent than your competition," Ken Favaro explained in *Marakon Commentary.* "This will give you an enormous advantage in building your company's ability to achieve profitable and long-lasting growth."

The first step in achieving an organization-wide focus on value creation is understanding the sources and drivers of value creation within the industry, company, and marketplace. Understanding what creates value will help managers focus capital and talent on the most profitable opportunities for growth. "If customers value consistent quality and timely delivery, then the skills, systems, and processes that produce and deliver quality products and services are highly valuable to the organization," Robert S. Kaplan and David P. Norton wrote in their book *Strategy Maps: Converting Intangible Assets into Tangible Outcomes.* "If customers value innovation and high performance, then the skills, systems, and processes that create new products and services with superior functionality take on high value. Consistent alignment of actions and capabilities with the customer value proposition is the core of strategy execution."

Although the intangible factors that drive value creation differ by industry, some of the major categories of intangible assets include technology, innovation, intellectual property, alliances, management capabilities, employee relations, customer relations, community relations, and brand value. According to Kaplan and Norton, the link between these intangible assets and value creation is corporate strategy. It is important to note that investments made to enhance intangible assets (research and development, employee training, and brand building, for example) usually provide indirect

VALUE CREATION

rather than direct benefits. In this way, focusing on value creation forces an organization to adopt a long-term perspective and align all of its resources toward future goals.

SEE ALSO: Competitive Advantage; Entrepreneurship; Intrapreneurship; Value Analysis; Value Chain Management

Laurie Collier Hillstrom

FURTHER READING:

"Creating Value: Value Creation Index." Value Based Management.net. Available from <http://www.valuebasedmanagement.net/methods_valuecreationindex.html>.

Favaro, Ken. "Put Value Creation First (If You Want to Grow Your Way to Greatness)." *Marakon Commentary.* 1998. Available from <http://www.favaro.net/publications/pvcf/ken_pvcf.html>.

Kaplan, Robert S., and David P. Norton. "How Strategy Maps Frame an Organization's Objectives." *Financial Executive,* March-April 2004.

————. *Strategy Maps: Converting Intangible Assets into Tangible Outcomes.* Cambridge: Harvard Business School Press, 2004.

Kapoor, Amit. "Creating Value." *Financial Times,* 13 March 2003.

Madden, Jim. "Creating Corporate Value." *Financial Executive,* March-April 2004.

Perla, Michael L. "Financial Value Creation." *CFO Refresher,* 2003. Available from <http://www.refresher.com>.

VENDOR RATING

Vendor rating is the result of a formal vendor evaluation system. Vendors or suppliers are given standing, status, or title according to their attainment of some level of performance, such as delivery, lead time, quality, price, or some combination of variables. The motivation for the establishment of such a rating system is part of the effort of manufacturers and service firms to ensure that the desired characteristics of a purchased product or service is built in and not determined later by some after-the-fact indicator. The vendor rating may take the form of a hierarchical ranking from poor to excellent and whatever rankings the firm chooses to insert in between the two. For some firms, the vendor rating may come in the form of some sort of award system or as some variation of certification. Much of this attention to vender rating is a direct result of the widespread implementation of the just-in-time

concept in the United States and its focus on the critical role of the buyer-supplier relationship.

Most firms want vendors that will produce all of the products and services defect-free and deliver them just in time (or as close to this ideal as reasonably possible). Some type of vehicle is needed to determine which supplying firms are capable of coming satisfactorily close to this and thus to be retained as current suppliers. One such vehicle is the vendor rating.

In order to accomplish the rating of vendors, some sort of review process must take place. The process begins with the identification of vendors who not only can supply the needed product or service but is a strategic match for the buying firm. Then important factors to be used as criteria for vendor evaluation are determined. These are usually variables that add value to the process through increased service or decreased cost. After determining which factors are critical, a method is devised that allows the vendor to be judged or rated on each individual factor.

It could be numeric rating or a Likert-scale ranking. The individual ratings can then be weighted according to importance, and pooled to arrive at an overall vendor rating. The process can be somewhat complex in that many factors can be complementary or conflicting. The process is further complicated by fact that some factors are quantitatively measured and others subjectively.

Once established, the rating system must be introduced to the supplying firm through some sort of formal education process. Once the buying firm is assured that the vendor understands what is expected and is able and willing to participate, the evaluation process can begin. The evaluation could be an ongoing process or it could occur within a predetermined time frame, such as quarterly. Of course the rating must be conveyed to the participating vendor with some firms actually publishing overall vendor standings. If problems are exposed, the vendor should formally present an action plan designed to overcome any problems that may have surfaced. Many buying firms require the vendor to show continuing improvement in predetermined critical areas.

CRITERIA FOR EVALUATION

Vendor performance is usually evaluated in the areas of pricing, quality, delivery, and service. Each area has a number of factors that some firms deem critical to successful vendor performance.

Pricing factors include the following:

• Competitive pricing. The prices paid should be comparable to those of vendors providing similar product and services. Quote requests should compare favorably to other vendors.

- Price stability. Prices should be reasonably stable over time.

- Price accuracy. There should be a low number of variances from purchase-order prices on invoiced received.

- Advance notice of price changes. The vendor should provide adequate advance notice of price changes.

- Sensitive to costs. The vendor should demonstrate respect for the customer firm's bottom line and show an understanding of its needs. Possible cost savings could be suggested. The vendor should also exhibit knowledge of the market and share this insight with the buying firm.

- Billing. Are vendor invoices are accurate? The average length of time to receive credit memos should be reasonable. Estimates should not vary significantly from the final invoice. Effective vendor bills are timely and easy to read and understand.

Quality factors include:

- Compliance with purchase order. The vendor should comply with terms and conditions as stated in the purchase order. Does the vendor show an understanding of the customer firm's expectations?

- Conformity to specifications. The product or service must conform to the specifications identified in the request for proposal and purchase order. Does the product perform as expected?

- Reliability. Is the rate of product failure within reasonable limits?

- Reliability of repairs. Is all repair and rework acceptable?

- Durability. Is the time until replacement is necessary reasonable?

- Support. Is quality support available from the vendor? Immediate response to and resolution of the problem is desirable.

- Warranty. The length and provisions of warranty protection offered should be reasonable. Are warranty problems resolved in a timely manner?

- State-of-the-art product/service. Does the vendor offer products and services that are consistent with the industry state-of-the-art? The vendor should consistently refresh product life by adding enhancements. It should also work with the buying firm in new product development.

Delivery factors include the following:

- Time. Does the vendor deliver products and services on time; is the actual receipt date on or close to the promised date? Does the promised date correspond to the vendor's published lead times? Also, are requests for information, proposals, and quotes swiftly answered?

- Quantity. Does the vendor deliver the correct items or services in the contracted quantity?

- Lead time. Is the average time for delivery comparable to that of other vendors for similar products and services?

- Packaging. Packaging should be sturdy, suitable, properly marked, and undamaged. Pallets should be the proper size with no overhang.

- Documentation. Does the vendor furnish proper documents (packing slips, invoices, technical manual, etc.) with correct material codes and proper purchase order numbers?

- Emergency delivery. Does the vendor demonstrate extra effort to meet requirements when an emergency delivery is requested?

Finally, these are service factors to consider:

- Good vendor representatives have sincere desire to serve. Vendor reps display courteous and professional approach, and handle complaints effectively. The vendor should also provide up-to-date catalogs, price information, and technical information. Does the vendor act as the buying firm's advocate within the supplying firm?

- Inside sales. Inside sales should display knowledge of buying firms needs. It should also be helpful with customer inquiries involving order confirmation, shipping schedules, shipping discrepancies, and invoice errors.

- Technical support. Does the vendor provide technical support for maintenance, repair, and installation situations? Does it provide technical instructions, documentation, general information? Are support personnel courteous, professional, and knowledgeable? The vendor should provide training on the effective use of its products or services.

- Emergency support. Does the vendor provide emergency support for repair or replacement of a failed product.

- Problem resolution. The vendor should respond in a timely manner to resolve problems.

An excellent vendor provides follow-up on status of problem correction.

A 2001 article in *Supply Management* notes that while pricing, quality, delivery, and service are suitable for supplies that are not essential to the continued success of the buying firm, a more comprehensive approach is needed for suppliers that are critical to the success of the firm's strategy or competitive advantage. For firms that fall into the latter category performance may need to be measured by the following 7 C's.

1. Competency—managerial, technical, administrative, and professional competence of the supplying firm.

2. Capacity—supplier's ability to meet physical, intellectual and financial requirements.

3. Commitment—supplier's willingness to commit physical, intellectual and financial resources.

4. Control—effective management control and information systems.

5. Cash resources—financial resources and stability of the supplier. Profit, ROI, ROE, asset-turnover ratio.

6. Cost—total acquisition cost, not just price.

7. Consistency—supplier's ability to exhibit quality and reliability over time.

If two or more firms supply the same or similar products or services, a standard set of criteria can apply to the vendor's performance evaluation. However, for different types of firms or firms supplying different products or services, standardized evaluation criteria may not be valid. In this case, the buying firm will have to adjust its criteria for the individual vendor. For example, Honda of America adjusts its performance criteria to account for the impact of supplier problems on consumer satisfaction or safety. A supplier of brakes would be held to a stricter standard than a supplier of radio knobs.

AWARDS AND CERTIFICATION

Many buying firms utilize awards and certification programs to rate vendors. Attainment of certification status or an award serves as an indicator of supplier excellence. Certification and awards-program recognition represents a final step in an intense journey that involves rigorous data collection under the total-quality-management-rubric as well as multitudes of meetings with suppliers and purchasing internal customers. Serious buying firms view these programs as an integral part of their overall efforts to improve the total value of the company.

The attainment of a supplier award usually serves as an indication that the vendor has been rated as excellent. Intel awards their best suppliers the Supplier Continuous Quality Improvement Award (SCQI). Other firms may utilize a hierarchy of awards to indicate varying degrees of performance from satisfactory to excellent. DaimlerChrysler awards its best suppliers the Gold Pentastar Award. Several hundred vending firms receive this award per year. However, only a handful (less than a dozen) of DaimlerChrysler's vendors are good enough to garner the Platinum Pentastar Award.

For other firms, supplier certification is desirable. Supplier certification can be defined as a process for ensuring that suppliers maintain specific levels of performance in the areas of price, quality, delivery, and service. Certification implies that participating firms have reached a level of excellence that other firms were unable or unwilling to achieve. For example a quality certified firm maintains a level of quality such that customer-receiving inspection may be utilized with decreasing frequency up to the point where it is eliminated altogether. Theoretically, this will ensure that all of the supplier's products meet the customer's product specifications. In this case, the goal of supplier certification is quality at the source.

While it is uncertain whether individual firms are consistent in the manner in which they certify vendors, a quality certification would likely require that the vending firm be part of a formal education program, utilize statistical process control (SPC), and have a quality assurance plan (set written procedures).

BENEFITS

Benefits of vendor rating systems include:

- Helping minimize subjectivity in judgment and make it possible to consider all relevant criteria in assessing suppliers.

- Providing feedback from all areas in one package.

- Facilitating better communication with vendors.

- Providing overall control of the vendor base.

- Requiring specific action to correct identified performance weaknesses.

- Establishing continuous review standards for vendors, thus ensuring continuous improvement of vendor performance.

- Building vendor partnerships, especially with suppliers having strategic links.

- Developing a performance-based culture.

Vendor ratings systems provide a process for measuring those factors that add value to the buying firm through value addition or decreased cost. The process will continually evolve and the criteria will change to meet current issues and concerns.

For example, some feel that supplier evaluation must now reflect the strategic direction of the buying company's environmental initiatives. As a result, some firms have recently developed supplier evaluation systems that place significant weight on environmental criteria. It would seem that the concept will remain valid for some time.

SEE ALSO: Purchasing and Procurement; Quality and Total Quality Management; Supply Chain Management

R. Anthony Inman

FURTHER READING:

"Measure for Measure." *Supply Management,* 1 February 2001, 39.

Muralidharan, C., N. Anantharaman, and S.G. Deshmukh. "Vendor Rating in Purchasing Scenario: A Confidence Interval Approach." *International Journal of Operations and Production Management* 21, no. 9/10 (2001): 1305–1325.

Trent, Robert J., and Robert M. Monczka. "Purchasing and Supply Management: Trends and Changes Throughout the 1990s." *International Journal of Purchasing and Materials Management,* Fall 1998, 2–11.

Walton, Steve V., Robert B. Handfield, and Steven A. Melnyk. "The Green Supply: Integrating Suppliers Into Environmental Management Processes." *International Journal of Purchasing and Materials Management,* Spring 1998, 2–11.

VENTURE CAPITAL

Venture capital refers to money that is invested in companies during the early stages of their development. Such funds may come from wealthy individuals, government-backed Small Business Investment Companies (SBICs), or professionally managed venture capital firms. Since investing in an unproven business venture is highly speculative, venture capitalists generally target companies that they believe offer significant potential for growth, and therefore an opportunity to earn a high rate of return in a relatively short period of time. In exchange for providing capital, as well as a source of management assistance and industry contacts for growing firms, the investors usually require a percentage of equity ownership in the company, some measure of control over its strategic direction, and payment of assorted fees. "Private equity provides capital and access to a network that can transform a company into an industry player," Karen E. Klein noted in *Business Week.* "But the price is high: a chunk of your business."

Like other sources of equity financing, venture capital offers both advantages and disadvantages. The main advantage is that the business is not obligated to repay the money. For a start-up company, this frees up important cash flow that might otherwise be needed to service debt. The involvement of high-profile investors may also help increase the credibility of a new business. The main disadvantage to venture capital financing is that the investors become part owners of the business, and thus gain a say in business decisions. The company's founders face a dilution of their ownership positions and a possible loss of autonomy or control.

Even for business owners willing to make the tradeoff, venture capital is scarce and often difficult to obtain. Venture capitalists tend to be highly selective in choosing investments. Some will only consider investments in specific technologies, industries, or geographic areas. In fact, the larger venture capital firms typically reject more than 90 percent of the requests for funding that they receive. They evaluate the remaining requests thoroughly, and at considerable expense, before selecting a few that closely match the investors' areas of expertise and offer the best earnings potential. As a result, private equity financing is more likely to be an option for existing businesses with a solid track record and good prospects for future growth than for start-up companies. It is a particularly good choice for fast-growing companies that have few tangible assets to use as collateral for loans.

For a business owner, the process of obtaining venture capital begins with a formal proposal. The most important element of this proposal is a detailed business plan describing the company's goals and strategies. The proposal should also include recent financial statements, projections of future growth, a brief history of the company, biographies of key managers, the amount of money requested, and a description of how the funds will be used. Experts recommend that companies seeking equity financing evaluate several venture capital firms before entering into a deal. Managers should also hire professionals to help them understand the terms of the agreement to avoid giving away too much control.

On receiving a proposal of interest, a venture capital firm usually follows up with a thorough investigation of the company's investment potential. This process might include analyzing financial statements, interviewing customers and suppliers, and meeting with the management team. If the venture capital firm remains interested following the evaluation phase, it usually responds with a proposal of its own, known as a term sheet. The term sheet acts as a blueprint for the investment deal, with provisions covering such issues as the valuation of the investment, voting rights, and liquidation options.

The final terms are decided through negotiations between the business managers and the venture capital firm. One of the most important factors in the negotiation process is agreeing upon the valuation of the business, which determines the amount of equity that is required in exchange for the venture capital (a business with a low valuation must provide a high percentage of equity, and vice versa). As a general rule, venture capital firms seek to control between 30 and 40 percent of equity in the companies in which they invest. This amount allows the venture capital firm to exercise influence without assuming control or eliminating the management team's incentive to grow the business. The venture capital firm usually hopes to achieve a return of three to five times the original investment within five years, by selling its equity either to the company's management or on the public stock markets.

Overall, venture capital can provide a valuable source of financing for growing businesses. Because of its associated risks, however, experts generally suggest that it be viewed as one of a number of potential sources of financing and be used in combination with debt financing whenever possible. "Private equity isn't for the faint of heart," Klein acknowledged. "But then again, entrepreneurs aren't known for being timid."

SEE ALSO: Due Diligence; Entrepreneurship; Financial Issues for Managers; Financial Ratios

Laurie Collier Hillstrom

FURTHER READING:

Bartlett, Joseph W. *Fundamentals of Venture Capital.* Lanham, MD: Madison Books, 1999.

Cardis, Joe, et al. *Venture Capital: The Definitive Guide for Entrepreneurs, Investors, and Practitioners.* New York: Wiley & Sons, 2001.

Klein, Karen E. "A Private Equity Affair: Getting the Most from Venture Capital." *Business Week,* 1 November 2004, 47.

McKimmie, Kathy. "Funding Fundamentals: Where to Turn for Startup and Expansion Capital." *Indiana Business Magazine,* January 2004, 24–27.

Stancill, James McNeill. *Entrepreneurial Finance: For New and Emerging Businesses.* Mason, OH: Thomson/South-Western, 2004.

Weiss, Jeffrey M. "Venture Capital Tips." *Detroiter,* May 2002, 19.

Worrell, David. "Raising Money: All in the Delivery." *Entrepreneur,* May 2004.

VIDEOCONFERENCING

Videoconferencing is a communications system that allows people in separate locations to talk to and see each other using live audio and video. A point-to-point videoconference connects individuals at two separate sites, and a multi-point conference connects individuals at more than two sites simultaneously.

Equipment ranges from sophisticated room-based systems to laptop systems, future developments are occurring for use in 3G cell phones and wireless devices. The most common uses of videoconferencing in corporate environments relate to training activities and meetings, but videoconferencing is also used for sales, job interviews, customer service, product demonstrations, technical and engineering collaboration, and troubleshooting. Increasingly, corporations use videoconferencing in new areas to fit more specific needs, especially as technology make collaborative features easier to use.

There has been an upward trend in utilization of videoconferencing and web-conferencing software in the corporate setting since the terrorist attacks of 2001. Increases in travel costs, travel safety concerns, and the slow economy have all led to the employment of alternative methods of collaboration and communication. Lending increased interest to alternative methods are improvements in technology, declining product prices and the development of standards, which allows better communication among a variety of videoconferencing systems. Networks capable of offering high-speed broadband, both wired and wireless, and improved Voice over Internet Protocol (VoIP) are also contributing to increased usage in web and videoconferencing specifically.

KINDS OF PRODUCTS/SYSTEMS

Room-based videoconferencing generally involves a sophisticated system that is built into a conference room, often specially designed and wired for this purpose. Also known as a boardroom system or a conference room system, this option is appropriate for large groups because cameras can focus on an individual speaker as well as include the entire group. Equipment includes a screen or monitor, projectors, microphones, PCs, and cameras that focus on participants as well as documents or other prepared visual aids.

A *roll-about* or *roll-around* system is a portable system on wheels that can move around the office and be plugged into a socket. This system is appropriate for frequent communication between small groups. Such portable systems may provide functions similar to those of room-based videoconferencing, with the possibility of plugging in additional equipment according to the needs of users. Models are produced for use at both high and low bandwidths.

A *personal* or *desktop* system, uses a personal computer and includes a small video camera that can be positioned on the user's computer and monitor. Typically, a fixed-focus camera and headset provide audio and head-and-shoulder images-the "talking head"-to the other individual participating in the conference. On the screen, several windows show the image of the other participant(s) and any shared documents. Such systems are appropriate for individuals and small groups.

The availability of free services, via Yahoo Messenger, AOL Instant Messenger, and Microsoft NetMeeting/Messenger, allow even the smallest of companies/groups to utilize this increasingly popular medium. In addition to basic video feeds and/or audio feeds, these free services also provide document sharing, whiteboard usage, and URL sharing (each person looking at the same webpage together). These extended capabilities in communication and feedback are available to any user equipped with an internet connection, web camera, and microphone (sometimes bundled into the webcam equipment).

As an alternative to purchasing a system, some vendors offer the use of videoconference facilities or rent studio space.

VIDEOCONFERENCING IN USE

BENEFITS. Videoconferencing allows individuals to interact and communicate visually without having to gather at a single site. The most frequently cited benefits concern reduced travel and accommodation costs and saved time. Less easily quantifiable benefits relate to the opportunity this technology provides for collaborative work. It allows access to remote expertise and a wider range of individuals, and because it is interactive, it can lead to increased speed of decision making, cost-effective use of training time, group problem solving and the chance to establish rapport. Videoconferencing used for customer assistance has been linked to increased customer satisfaction.

LIMITS. Like any scheduled meeting, a videoconference, particularly one involving room-based systems and groups, requires organization and planning around the schedules of participants and technicians. Despite improvements in technology, barriers to increased use continue to be choppy images and poor audio, depending on the system used and its ability to maintain connection speed, which in turn depends on the kind of connection. Accommodations must be made if there is a possibility of delayed connections or if the resolution does not allow certain character sizes on visual aids to be distinguished. In some cases it may be necessary to overcome a lack of user acceptance.

Some new users report being uncomfortable with the unfamiliar technology and having trouble with nonverbal cues such as making eye contact; in these cases preparation or training may help. If customers or potential customers are involved, incentives or facilitators on the premises may be helpful until the customers get accustomed to this technology.

EFFECT ON HUMAN COMMUNICATION. Remote technology has been shown to affect human communication mainly due to the lack of cues normally present in face-to-face live interaction. For example, eye contact differs, and if the resolution is poor, it is not possible to look into people's eyes to gauge the degree of interest or attention. The feedback normally expected may be missing or delayed if there is a slight time lag. Turn-taking may also differ, even if the delay amounts to only a fraction of a second.

Preparation or training should be considered in terms of intended use (for example, a one-time meeting of groups of possible trading partners as opposed to regular team meetings) and the technical characteristics of the system (for example, whether or not audio can be simultaneously transmitted and received without any interference). New users and virtual teams need to be aware of factors that may lead to hesitancy or initial uneasiness, which in turn effect communication. Some experts recommend that people meet face-to-face before working remotely as a team in order to overcome possible effects of these factors. For example, if people know each other already, they can treat inadvertent interruptions lightly. On the other hand, videoconferencing can be used for introductory meetings; participants need only be aware of possible limits.

Some techniques enhance the use of video. Looking into the camera as much as possible will help maintain eye contact. If the camera is located close to the image on a screen, looking at the individual produces a similar effect. Notes can be inserted on the monitor with some software; otherwise a good position for note cards is next to the camera. Trainers recommend practicing, including speaking with an inanimate object to get used to speaking to a camera.

APPLICATIONS. As technology improves, applications are moving beyond the meetings and training activities usually associated with videoconferencing in business. Applications actually encompass a wide range of activities. For example, videoconferencing can be used for customer service and sales. Engineers or specialists can provide customer service and support using video images, and they can show new product applications. In the salesroom, it can provide customers with advice or explanations from specialists with the aim of complementing the activity of sales personnel. Many consumer websites, from online storefronts to financial institutions, host internet websites that offer video assistance combined with text-based chat to serve customer needs.

In the area of quality control, hand-held cameras can be used on the factory floor to discover problems or detect faults before they cause lengthy delays in production. These cameras can be used for troubleshooting, with a team of experts able to interact and reach a solution.

Videoconferencing is also used for trade promotion, with the conference itself conducted as a special event. Members of a business-related association in one area may meet with a group of businesspersons based in a different country to present their companies or products. Videoconferences are also used to provide investors with updates by the chief executive or the chief financial officer of public companies.

TECHNICAL CONCERNS

General concerns include interoperability: whether a system can interface with other conferencing systems via physical network facilities. Another factor includes ease of use. An easy to use interface is particularly important when built-in collaboration features are used. Video and audio quality must also be considered.

VIDEO AND AUDIO QUALITY. Although video quality has improved since the appearance of early systems, with some vendors comparing their products to television video, not all systems in use offer the video quality typical of television. This is in part due to the frame rate, which refers to the maximum amount of full-screen images transmitted per second. The frame rate for the full-motion video normally seen on television is about 30 frames per second. Roughly speaking, the lower the frame rate, the choppier the image. A system providing 15 frames per second will most likely exhibit some choppy images or jerky movements, but this frame rate may be considered sufficient for certain kinds of business meetings. The capability of a system to deal with excessive screen motion is also a factor in determining video quality, while image clarity relates to the number of pixels defined per image.

The synchronization of voice transmission and lip movement depends on whether or not there is a delay or lag in the time it takes to receive a video image and audio signals. If the audio is poorly synchronized, the speaker's lip movements will follow the sound after a fraction of a second or more.

NETWORKS/VIDEO TRANSPORT. A common network used for video transport is the Internet via DSL (digital subscriber line) or Cable. Other networks are ISDN, local area network (LAN), asynchronous transfer mode (ATM), and the plain old telephone system (POTS).

INTERNET VIA DSL AND CABLE. Systems allowing videoconferencing over the Internet are increasingly common, with compatibility and ease-of-use issues still encountered from time-to-time. Bandwidth is high enough to allow for continuous transmission of motion video and audio.

ISDN. ISDN is available from telephone companies, with charges to subscribers based on the amount of data transmitted. This network generally allows 15 to 25 frames of live video per second depending on image size. ISDN has been used for room-based conference systems, but it is also used for personal/desktop systems.

LAN. Videoconferencing over the local-area network (LAN) utilizes the system that already connects an organization's computers. With network video conferencing, software on a desktop or laptop PC or in a conference room can be used to make a video call on the premises or to a distant location. However, because of video's bandwidth requirements, certain kinds of traffic may suffer as a result of videoconferencing on a LAN. As a result, each call may impact the quality of service on a LAN (as well as on a wide-area network—WAN, which connects distant locations belonging to the same organization). Technical features that allow users to select how much bandwidth they want for a call result in a more efficient use of bandwidth.

ATM. ATM is a network technology based on transferring data in relatively small cells or packets of a constant size. This allows ATM equipment to transmit video, audio, and computer data over the same network without one kind of data monopolizing the line.

POTS. POTS allows 7 to 12 frames per second, which results in jerky images. It is mainly used for consumer applications. Video and sound quality and poorly synchronized audio remain sticking points for POTS technology.

STANDARDS FOR VIDEOCONFERENCING. Standards must be defined in order to allow different products to communicate with each other. The most frequently used standards are H.320 for video over ISDN and H.323 for video over IP (Internet Protocol). Improvements and advances in broadband and wireless, are increasing the usage of the H.323 standard. H.310/H.321 covers ATM for sites with an ATM network; H.234 covers POTS video, which is being used less and less as affordable consumer broadband and wireless options are being utilized.

OUTLOOK

With improved high-speed broadband becoming a common household amenity, the opportunities for business to be conducted in corporate and home office locations is now possible. Video, audio, data, and especially systems integrating all three are expected to take precedence over the larger, dedicated systems, especially when a hard-wired room is required.

Corporate video conferencing is the largest segment of the videoconferencing market and is projected to jump from $6 million in 2003 to nearly $180 million by 2008, according to Wainhouse Research. In 2004, according to Wainhouse's *Videoconferencing Endpoint Survey,* more than 70 percent of those surveyed claimed to use group videoconferencing as part of their job, and nearly 75 percent of respondents noted an increase in the use of videoconferencing in the past two years and anticipated an increase in usage in the coming years. Respondents indicated they believed that the future of videoconferencing would be primarily via web conferencing or instant-messaging services and secondarily via desktop video conferencing.

The growing use of videoconferencing is expected to lead to changes in approaches to teamwork, business communication practices, and presentation techniques. Face-to-face communication may take on greater significance if it becomes increasingly reserved for initial meetings, key relationships, and special situations. As more and more people use personal or desktop systems, videoconferencing will be seen as a normal on-the-job activity, involving a wide range of applications and benefits. Further developments in wireless technology and video-capable appliances will make this industry exciting for both personal and corporate usage.

SEE ALSO: Computer Networks; Virtual Organizations

Gina Poncini
Revised by Monica C. Turner

FURTHER READING:

Fitchard, K. "Conferencing Gets the Picture." *Telephony* 245, no. 13 (21 June 2004): 52–54.

Foley, T. "Supporting International Operations Through Technology." *Franchising* 37, no. 2 (February 2005): 38–40.

Leong, K.C. "Video E-mail Goes Corporate." *Computerworld* 39, no. 12 (March 2005): 23–24.

MacArthur, G. "Videoconferencing Over IP: The Switch is On." *Business Communications Review* 34, no. 9 (September 2004): 62.

"New Era of Communications." *SuperVision* 65, no. 1 (January 2004): 12–13.

Ohlhorst, F.J. "Videoconferencing Tailored for All." *CRN* 1105 (26 July 2004): 12A–14A.

Palmer, J. "Face Time." *Barron's* 85, no. 3 (January 2005): 16.

Romney, J. "Video Hits." *In The Black* 74, no. 10 (November 2004): 46–49.

Stowell, C. "Real-Time Collaboration with Flair." *Communications News* 42, no. 3 (March 2005): 40–42.

Videoconferencing Endpoint Survey. Wainhouse Research, May 2004. Available from <http://www.wainhouse.com/surveys/wrsurvey-rmc04v2.pdf>.

VIRTUAL ORGANIZATIONS

The term *virtual organization* is used to describe a network of independent firms that join together, often temporarily, to produce a service or product. Virtual organization is often associated with such terms as virtual office, virtual teams, and virtual leadership. The ultimate goal of the virtual organization is to provide innovative, high-quality products or services instantaneously in response to customer demands.

The term *virtual* in this sense has its roots in the computer industry. When a computer appears to have more storage capacity than it really possesses it is referred to as virtual memory. Likewise, when an organization assembles resources from a variety of firms, a virtual organization seems to have more capabilities than it actually possesses.

BACKGROUND

Traditional organizations integrated work vertically; that is, they delegated authority in a pyramidal, hierarchical structure. As the pyramid shape suggests, power was concentrated primarily among the handful of individuals at the top. This organizational form, shown in Figure 1, was first developed in the United States in the late 19th century with the advent of mass production.

The prominent theorist of traditional hierarchical organizations was the renowned industrial engineer, Frederick Winslow Taylor. His book, *Principles of Scientific Management,* introduced the principles for designing and managing mass-production facilities such as Ford's automobile factory in Michigan and Carnegie's steel works in Pittsburgh.

The hierarchical structure was designed to manage highly complex processes like automobile assembly where production could be broken down into a series of simple steps. Hierarchical corporations often controlled and managed all activities of a business from, the raw materials to their allocation to consumers. A centralized managerial hierarchy controlled the entire production process, with white-collar workers establishing rules and procedures to manage a blue-collar workforce.

From World War II until the early 1980s, the trend was to build increasing layers of management with more staff specialists. This centralized hierarchical structure

Figure 1
The Traditional Hierarchy

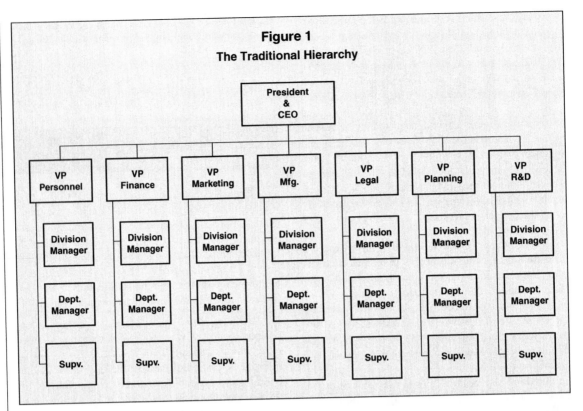

was seen as effective for managing large number of workers, but lacked agility and was unable to process information rapidly throughout the organization.

NEW DEMANDS ALTER ORGANIZATIONAL FORMS

Since the 1980s, many organizations have flattened their structures by shifting authority downward, giving employees increased autonomy and decision-making power. Advantages of flatter organization forms include a decreased need for supervisors and middle management, faster decision making, and the ability to process information faster because of the reduced number of layers in the organization.

A consequence of flatter organizations, though, is that employees tend to be more dispersed both geographically and organizationally. Responding to this problem of dispersion, many organizations have eliminated superfluous processes and begun focusing on their core, value-added business. Flat organizations using joint ventures and strategic alliances are providing increased flexibility and innovation, and are replacing many traditional hierarchies.

THE NEW BUSINESS FORM

Ray Grenier and George Metes discuss the shift to this new organizational structure as a response to unprecedented customer expectations and alternatives, global competition, time compression, complexity, rapid change, and increased use of technology.

They describe the virtual model as a lead organization that creates alliances with groups and individuals from different organizations who possess the highest competencies to build a specific product or service in a short period of time (see Figure 2).

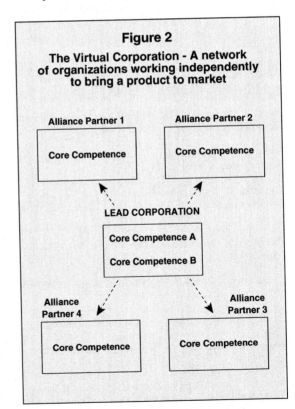

Figure 2
The Virtual Corporation - A network of organizations working independently to bring a product to market

Grenier and Meters further explain that these alliances are virtual because products and services are not produced in a single corporation whose purpose is longevity. Rather, these new virtual organizations consist of a hybrid of groups and individuals from different companies that might include customers, competitors, and suppliers who have a focused purpose of bringing a high-quality product or service to market as rapidly as possible. These alliances may be temporary with short concept-to-delivery cycles.

William Davidow and Michael Malone, authors of *The Virtual Corporation,* claim that virtual corporations will be central to the new business revolution. Their concept of the virtual corporation brings diverse innovations together such as just-in-time supply, work teams, flexible manufacturing, reusable engineering, worker empowerment, organizational streamlining, computer-aided design, total quality, and mass customization into a coherent vision for the twentieth century corporation.

The virtual corporation is more permeable than traditional organizational forms. Interfaces in a virtual organization between company, supplier, and customers continuously change, resulting in a blurring of traditional functions. Inside the office, work groups and job responsibilities may shift regularly. The virtual organization may not have a central office or an organizational chart. Suppliers, customers, and even competitors may spend time alongside one another in the virtual organization.

CHARACTERISTICS OF A VIRTUAL ORGANIZATION

Partners in virtual organizations share risks, costs, and rewards in pursuit of a global market. The common characteristics of these organizations include a purpose that is motivated by specific market opportunities, world-class core competence, information networks, interdependent relationships, and permeable boundaries.

Virtual organizations represent structures that are motivated by specific market opportunities. Once the alliance has been formed and the opportunity has been exploited, partners may move on to new partnerships and alliances.

Each partner in a virtual corporation contributes a world-class core competence, such as design, manufacturing, or marketing. This ability of multiple firms to create synergies among world-class functions and processes creates untold possibilities.

As organizations create these new linkages, advanced information technology becomes an important element, and key to the success of a virtual organization. Computerized information systems allow employees from geographically dispersed locations to link up with one another. The virtual office may use desktop videoconferencing, collaborative software, and intranet systems to enhance the flow of information among team members. Besides the need for instantaneous communication with one another, members of these autonomous virtual teams have increasing requirements regarding the amount and quality of information they need to do their work.

Members of the virtual organization, in turn, create a network of interdependent relationships. These relationships require firms to be much more dependent on one another than they have been in the past, demanding unprecedented levels of trust. Strong interdependencies cause organizations' boundaries to be blurred as competitors, suppliers, and customers enter into cooperative agreements. These new relationships among firms obligate organizations to use innovative management practices.

VIRTUAL TEAMS

Virtual teams are often the group structure used in virtual organizations. Jessica Lipnack and Jeffrey Stamps define virtual teams as "a group of people who interact through interdependent tasks guided by a common purpose." Unlike conventional teams, a virtual team performs work across space, time, and organizational boundaries connected by interactive communication technologies. Virtual teams may include employees, management, customers, suppliers, and government working together to achieve common goals. These teams often stay together only to perform its episodic task. They may work jointly on a new project, but when the product is designed and goes into production, the project is finished and the virtual team dissolves.

Lipnack and Stamps offer three key features for a successful virtual team. One is the choice of team members with the appropriate skills and knowledge for the task; second is the definition of a purpose to steer the group; and third is the effective linking of team members, including communication channels, interactions, and relationships.

Virtual team members are required to learn a new set of skills. One skill is the ability to interact with one another effectively despite infrequent or total lack of face-to-face contact. Another is the ability to assimilate quickly and effectively into new teams. Virtual team members should be technically adept to deal with the variety of required computer-based technologies. Additionally, virtual team members may need intercultural skills to work effectively in multi-national organizations.

VIRTUAL LEADERS

Greiner and Metes discuss the new leadership skills required to lead in the virtual environment, including the ability to manage a network of interdependent firms, to design virtual operations, to create and sustain virtual relationships with internal as well as external constituents, to support virtual teams, and to keep virtual teams focused. The leader of a virtual organization demands a new set of skills unlike the skills required in a traditional hierarchy.

VIRTUAL LEARNING

Another critical element to the success of the virtual organization is the ability of the organization to create world-class learning systems. These learning systems help leaders sustain or create world-class competencies. Effective learning systems can create pathways throughout the organization, in network fashion, enhancing the innovative capabilities of the organizational members. An organization's ability to sustain a leadership position in the world economy demands that organizations be on the cutting edge to develop rapid and elegant solutions to emerging consumer demands.

EXAMPLES OF VIRTUAL ORGANIZATIONS

An industry that is known for its use of partners and alliances is the entertainment industry, which has partnered with the computing, communications, consumer electronics, and publishing industries to convert movies, textbooks, and other software into digital formats.

Increasing numbers of firms are moving to these new organizational forms. Corning, the glass and ceramics maker, is one such firm known for making partnerships work to their advantage. Corning has partnered with such firms as Siemens, Germany's electronics conglomeration, and Vitro, Mexico's largest glassmaker. Alliances are so important to Corning's business strategy that the corporation has defined itself as a network of organizations.

Computer organizations that have successfully implemented forms of this new structure include Apple Computer and Sun Microsystems. When Apple Computer linked its easy-to-use software with Sony's manufacturing skills in miniaturization, Apple was able to get its product to market quickly and gain a market share in the notebook segment of the PC industry.

Sun Microsystems has been considered another highly decentralized organization comprised of independently operating companies. Sun positions information systems as a top priority, trying to achieve faster and better communication. With numerous "SunTeams," members operate across time, space, and organizations to address critical business issues. Sun managers identify key customer issues and then form teams with the critical skills and knowledge needed to address the issue. This team might include sales people, marketing personnel, finance, and operations from various places around the globe; customers and suppliers may become episodic members as necessary. Weekly meetings may take place via conference calls. Critical to the team's success is the selection of talent from the organization, defining a clear purpose for the team's efforts, and establishing communication links among the team members.

Sun has been working on further development of technologies such as EDI (Electronic Data Interchange) and RFID (Radio Frequency Identification technology). Both EDI and RFID will impact information exchange globally and across numerous industries.

CHALLENGES

Virtual organizations can be very complex and problematic; they fail as often as they succeed. Among the many challenges of the virtual organization are strategic planning dilemmas, boundary blurring, a loss of control, and a need for new managerial skills.

Strategic planning poses new challenges as virtual firms determine effective combinations of core competencies. Common vision among partners is quintessential to cooperating firms. Focused on a common goal, firms develop close interdependencies that may make it difficult to determine where one company ends and another begins. The boundary-blurring demands that these boundaries be managed effectively. Coordinating mechanisms are critical elements for supporting these loose collections of firms.

Virtual structures create a loss of control over some operations. This loss of control requires communication, coordination, and trust among the various partners, as well as a new set of managerial skills. Employees are exposed to increased ambiguity about organizational membership, job roles and responsibilities, career paths, and superior-subordinate relationships. This ambiguity requires management to rethink rewards, benefits, employee development, staffing and other employee-related issues. Developing leaders who are able to create and sustain these organizational forms is critical.

Les Pang offers a list of best practices, based on a review of successful implementations of virtual organizations.

- Foster cooperation, trust and empowerment.

- Ensure each partner contributes and identifiable strength or asset.

- Ensure skills and competencies are complementary, not overlapping.

- Ensure partners are adaptable.

- Ensure contractual agreements are clear and specific on roles and deliverables.

- If possible, do not replace face-to-face interaction entirely.

- Provide training that is critical to team success.

- Recognize that it takes time to develop the team.

- Ensure that technology is compatible and reliable.

- Provide technical assistance that is competent and available.

FUTURE OF VIRTUAL ORGANIZATIONS

The business environment will no doubt require firms to become even more flexible, more agile, and to bring products and services to market at an increasing rapid pace. Traditional organization forms are no longer capable of sustaining the needs of this relentless pace. New forms of organizing, such as the virtual organization, hold promise as organizational leaders experiment and learn new strategies for managing in the twenty-first century and beyond. These new structures, however, will require managers and leaders to face exciting challenges as they move into an environment of increased uncertainty and volatility.

SEE ALSO: Lean Manufacturing and Just-in-Time Production; Organizational Structure; Teams and Teamwork; Trends in Organizational Change

Gail Fann Thomas
Revised by Monica C. Turner

FURTHER READING:

Camarinha-Matos, L., H. Afsarmanesh, and M. Ollus, eds. *Virtual Organizations: Systems and Practices.* New York, NY: Springer, 2005.

Davidow, W.H., and M.S. Malone. *The Virtual Corporation: Structuring and Revitalizing the Corporation for the 21st Century.* New York, NY: Harper Collins Publishers, 1992.

Greiner, R., and G. Metes. *Going Virtual: Moving Your Organization into the 21st Century.* Upper Saddle River, New Jersey: Prentice Hall, Inc., 1995.

Hilty, L.M., E.K. Seifert, and R. Treibert, eds. *Information Systems for Sustainable Development.* Hershey, PA: Idea Group Publishing, 2005.

Kirkman, B.L., B. Rosen, P.E. Tesluk, and C.B. Gibson. "The Impact of Team Empowerment on Virtual Team Performance: The Moderating Role of Face-to-Face Interaction." *Academy of Management Journal* 47, no. 2 (April 2004): 175–192.

Levary, R.R., and R. Mathieu. "Supply Chain's Emerging Trends." *Industrial Management* 46, no. 4 (July/August 2004): 22–27.

Lipnack, J., and J. Stamps. *Virtual Teams: Reaching Across Space, Time and Organizations with Technology.* New York, NY: John Wiley and Sons, 1997.

Pang, Les. "Understanding Virtual Organizations." *Information Systems Control Journal* 6 (2001): 42–47.

Taylor, F.W. *The Principles of Scientific Management.* New York, NY: Harper, 1911.

Vakola, M., and I.E. Wilson. "The Challenge of Virtual Organization: Critical Success Factors in Dealing with Constant Change." *Team Performance Management* 10, no. 5-6 (2004): 112–120.

VISION STATEMENTS

SEE: Mission and Vision Statements

WAREHOUSING AND WAREHOUSE MANAGEMENT

Warehousing is the storage of goods for profit. The physical location, the warehouse, is a storage facility that receives goods and products for the eventual distribution to consumers or other businesses. A warehouse is also called a distribution center. Warehouse management is the process of coordinating the incoming goods, the subsequent storage and tracking of the goods, and finally, the distribution of the goods to their proper destinations.

HISTORY

Warehousing's roots go back to the creation of granaries to store food, which was historically available for purchase during times of famine. As European explorers began to create shipping-trade routes with other nations, warehouses grew in importance for the storage of products and commodities from afar. Ports were the major location for warehouses.

As railroads began to expand travel and transportation, the creation of rail depots for the storage of materials became necessary. In 1891 the American Warehousemen's Association was organized to challenge the railroad companies' control over freight depots. President Theodore Roosevelt significantly strengthened the Interstate Commerce Commission with passage of the Hepburn Act in 1906. Commercial warehousing began to grow after the government placed more restrictions on railroads.

World War II impacted warehousing in several ways, including the need to increase the size of warehouses and the need for more mechanized methods of storing and retrieving the products and materials. As mass production grew throughout manufacturing, the needs of efficient and effective warehousing capabilities grew with it.

MODERN ISSUES

The warehouse industry found itself recovering from a recession at the start of the twenty-first century, partially brought on by the hype of the dot-com bubble and the excess production created after it burst. It also coped with new methods of distribution, such as just-in-time (JIT) manufacturing—where warehousing is unnecessary because products are shipped directly to customers.

Warehousing companies are now striving to become more than simply storage facilities. They are transforming themselves into "third-party logistics providers" or "3PLs" that provide a wide array of services and functions. In addition to packing and staging pallets, contemporary warehousing facilities offer light manufacturing, call centers, labeling, and other non-storage options.

WAREHOUSE FUNCTIONS

Warehousing is a key component of the overall business supply chain. The supply chain consists of the facilities and distribution options for the procurement of materials from manufacturer to customer and all points in between. It includes the production of materials into components and finished products and then the distribution to customers.

Warehouse functions include:

- the storage of goods to permit managing product flow or to accommodate longer production runs;

Growth of Warehousing 1997–2002
Warehousing and Storage

	Establishments	Revenue	Annual Payroll($,000)	Paid employees
1997	6,497	10,657,925	2,926,119	109,760
2002	12,637	17,924,787	18,689,122	639,174

Source: U.S. Department of Commerce: Department of the Census: Economic Census

- serving as a mixing point where products from different suppliers are mixed and then distributed to fulfill customer orders;
- a sales branch and customer service location;
- a source of supplies for production;
- a staging area for final packaging or finishing.

WAREHOUSE OPERATIONS

Warehouses are operated in several ways. Public warehousing involves the client paying a standard fee for the storage of merchandise. Private warehousing is storage and operations controlled completely by a single manufacturer. Leased warehousing is an option for more stable inventory. Contract warehousing clients pay fees regardless of whether they are using the space or not; the space is always there for them to use, however. According to *Overview of Warehousing in North America,* contract warehousing accounts for more than 60 percent of the U.S. commercial market.

A warehouse stands empty without some form of product. Delivery of goods and materials takes place either by truck, rail, or boat on a dock or loading area. The goods are received, processed, and then sent into the warehouse for storage.

The storage of goods has been the primary function for warehouses. Once the goods have been received from the manufacturer and/or shipper, they are compactly stored to maximize space within the facility. Products are placed on pallets, which allow for more consistent stacking and moving within the facility.

Contract and public warehouses receive goods and products from a multitude of manufacturers and shippers. A crucial aspect of warehouse management is inventory control. Inventory control is the ability to locate and track a given product within the warehouse to facilitate quick selection and loading for order fulfillment. It is also the process of maintaining sufficient amounts of product to meet customer demands, while at the same time balancing the expense of keeping product in storage. Perpetual, annual, physical, and cycle counting are all methods of keeping track of inventory.

Order picking is the process of selecting products to fulfill an order. There are several types of picking methods:

- Discrete or pick-by-order: Specific products are selected on a per order basis.
- Batch or pick-by-article: Multiples of a product are selected to fulfill multiple orders. The products are sorted in the staging area and combined with other products to fulfill the orders.
- Wave: Involves gathering products based on specific routing or shipping criteria.
- Reverse-order: Used when part of an order is held to be combined with another order.

Reverse-order picking is related to cross-docking, another function of warehouses. Cross-docking is a direct flow of goods from receiving to shipping, with little if any storage. Cross-docking is contingent on the timely delivery of products, accurate management on the loading dock, and effective ordering by the customer.

Warehousing is also involved in the packaging and labeling of a product as it moves through the facility. Proper packaging is necessary for effective storage and to guard against damage. Labeling, or tagging, is an important element of the packaging. Proper labeling improves the ability to identify, track, store, and select the correct product for order fulfillment.

Once the product has been selected, or picked, it is brought to a staging area for final processing and shipment. The loading dock is a hub of activity as products are arriving for storage and being staged for distribution. Effective management of this area is crucial for warehouse success. It is here that cross-docking takes place.

The final stage of warehousing is the transportation facet of delivering and shipping goods.

WAREHOUSE MANAGEMENT

In the past warehouse management was very paper-intensive in its coordination of a multitude of activities. This has changed with the introduction of warehouse management system software.

Warehouse management systems (WMS) assist managers in tracking products throughout the entire storage and distribution process. These systems span from simple computer automation systems to high-end, feature-rich management programs that improve order picking, facilitate better dock logistics, and monitor inventory management.

TRENDS

According to a *Warehousing Management* survey, competition in warehousing has become extremely tight because businesses seek warehouse firms with extremely thin margins. Companies are succeeding by remaining flexible and investing in technology. The main issues or trends in warehousing include radio frequency identification (RFID), transportation management systems, pick-to-light technology, and voice-activated receiving and packaging.

Voice-activated receiving and packaging allows for warehouse personnel to speak requests into the WMS, thus speeding the entire process. Transportation management systems provide an advanced level of detail on goods prior to their arrival and also provide a more specific time of delivery. RFID has dramatically improved the ability to effectively manage inventory and track the location of specific goods within the warehouse. Pick-to-light technology improves order picking along warehouse conveyor belts by monitoring and identifying products for specific shipments.

A significant trend is the continuing growth of 3PL providers as companies try to cut costs and management issues by outsourcing their warehouse and distribution functions. An outcome of increased 3PL activity is a wave of mergers that are consolidating the industry. Customer demands for one-stop shopping and new technologies are a driving force behind this consolidation.

Warehousing is a mature industry seeking methods to maximize profits and striving to add services to compete for customers. The warehousing industry is a key component of the supply chain and will likely remain so as long as there are manufacturers and consumers.

SEE ALSO: Location Strategy; Logistics and Transportation; Supply Chain Management

Hal P. Kirkwood, Jr.

FURTHER READING:

Ackerman, K.B. *Practical Handbook of Warehousing.* New York, NY: Van Nostrand Reinhold, 1993.

Albright, B. "Recession Impacts Supply Chain Markets: WMS Growth Slows; Transportation and Events Software Picks Up Speed." *Frontline Solutions* 3, no. 6 (2002): 10–12.

Bolten, E.F. *Managing Time and Space in the Modern Warehouse.* New York, NY: American Management Association, 1997.

Forger, G. "Leading Trends in Manufacturing, Warehousing & Distribution." *Modern Materials Handling* 59, no. 13 (December 2004): 38.

Friedman, D. "How to Select the Best Warehouse Management System." *Material Handling Management* 60, no. 1 (January 2005): 28–29.

Harrington, L.H. "How to Solve the Warehousing Puzzle." *Logistics Today* 44, no. 9 (September 2003): 32–38.

Johnson, J.R. "Warehousing's Crystal Ball." *Warehousing Management* 9, no. 6 (July 2002): 24–28.

"An Overview of Warehousing in North America—Market Size, Major 3PLs, Benchmarking Prices and Practices." *North America Warehousing Market Report 2004.* Stoughton, WI: Armstrong & Associates, Inc., 2004.

Singer, T. "Trends in Warehousing and Distribution." *Industrial Maintenance & Plant Operation* 65, no. 11 (November 2004): 12–18.

WOMEN AND MINORITIES IN MANAGEMENT

The role of women and minorities in the twenty-first century American work place continues to develop.

For centuries, women have served their families—preparing food, making clothes, and performing other functions—to make homes for their husbands and children. As times changed and economic opportunities moved from the farms to the factories, the roles of women began to evolve. Instead of staying home and producing goods for the family, women began looking for jobs outside the home. While many women worked in traditionally "female" occupations such as teaching and nursing, many women began working in factories or low-paying clerical and labor jobs. The industrial revolution forever changed the way the American economy operated, and with that change, more women chose to work and supplement family income.

Additionally, the demographic mix within the twenty-first century workplace has become much more diverse because many workers now entering the workforce are neither white, male, nor English speaking. People of color continue to increase their share of the labor force. The rates of growth for these groups are projected to be faster than the rate for whites.

WOMEN AND MINORITIES IN THE LABOR FORCE

WOMEN. In 1950 only about one in three women participated in the labor force. By 1998, approximately three out of every five women of working age were in the labor force. By 2003, close to 60 percent of all women aged sixteen and older were in the labor force. The U.S. Department of Labor projects this figure will continue to increase at a slower rate reaching and is projected to reach nearly 63 percent by the year 2015.

At the beginning of the twentieth century, women made up less than 20 percent of the United State labor force. By 1950, this percentage increased to 33.9 percent. By the year 2000, women comprised more than 46 percent of the civilian labor force. Therefore, within the roughly the past fifty years the number of women in the American workforce has multiplied by more than 240 percent. As of February 2005, there were almost 67 million women employed in the civilian labor force. The U.S. Department of Labor estimates that women over the age of twenty participated in the workforce at a rate of 62 percent in 2004. Furthermore, the increase of women participating in the workforce will cover many racial groups, with women of color enjoying the fastest growth rate.

Interestingly, however, the rate of growth of women in the labor force has slowed somewhat during the last decade of the twentieth century. One cultural shift that appears to be contributing to this curiosity is the renewed emphasis on marriage and family. Tradition has held that men were expected to be the primary wage earners of the family, while women were expected to make the home. Renewed societal emphasis on these traditional roles for men and women during the 1990s has arguably placed greater pressure on men to work to support their families and placed greater pressure on women to stay at home. Some researchers attribute the slower growth rate to factors such as increased educational attainment by married women, the recession of the early 1990s, a rising birthrate, and a slowdown in women's return to work after giving birth. While these conditions have not led to lower unemployment rates for men or higher unemployment rates for women, it does appear they are be contributing to the slower employment growth rate for women.

MINORITIES. While the employment growth rate for women appears to be slowing, minority labor force participation is expected to continue to increase especially for non-white Hispanics. For example, Hispanics are predicted to be the second largest group in 2025, accounting for 17 percent of the total labor force. Furthermore, as of 2000, Hispanics have a larger share of the market than African Americans, 13 percent versus 12.7 percent. The share of African Americans in the labor force is expected to increase by only 1.8 percent during the same time period. Asians and other people of color would account for 8 percent of the labor force in 2025. Hispanics and Asians, therefore, will continue to be the two fastest growing groups.

UNEMPLOYMENT

Historically, women have endured higher rates of unemployment than men; however, this trend appears to be changing. Through the first quarter of 2005, the seasonally adjusted unemployment rate for women ages twenty and over was 3.9 percent, while the average rate for men in the same age range was 4.1 percent. The unemployment rate for African American women was higher, averaging 9.1 percent for the first quarter of 2005, while African American men were unemployed at a rate 10.9 percent.

OCCUPATIONS

The biggest percentage of women employed in the United States labor force are working in technical, sales, and administrative support occupations. Despite the increase of women working in professions that have traditionally been male-dominated, such as engineering, construction, athletics, truck driving, mortuary science, and law enforcement, most women still tend work in traditionally "female" occupations. However, one of the most significant changes that took place in the twentieth century was the rise of women managers. In 1900, only 4.4 percent of managers were women. By 2000, 46 percent of all managers were women, a tenfold increase. By 2002, 34 percent of working women were in a managerial or processional occupation. However, both women professionals and women managers are clustered in certain specialty areas. In 2002, nearly 50 percent of women workers were employed in three occupational groups—sales, services, and administrative support. As example, only 11 percent of engineers were women, but 98 percent of preschool and kindergarten teachers were women. Furthermore, only 19 percent of dentists were women, whereas 93 percent of registered nurses were women. Therefore, women are still underrepresented in many professions and overrepresented in others.

WOMEN ENTREPRENEURS

Businesses owned by women are increasing in terms of quantity, diversity, and impact on the American economy. In 2003, over 38 percent of self-employed persons were women and about almost 6 percent of employed women were self-employed. Furthermore, women-owned businesses employ over nineteen million people in the United States or 1 in every 7 employed persons nationwide according to figures published by the Center for Women's Business Research. As of 2004 there were 10.6 million women-owned businesses in the United States. Job growth provided by women-owned businesses has exceeded the national averages in almost every major industry. Between 1997 and 2004 the number of businesses owned by women increased by 24 percent compared to 12 percent for all firms. Among the industries that have experienced the most dramatic growth in women-owned businesses are construction, manufacturing, wholesale trade, transportation, and communication. This growth in businesses owned by women has exploded despite the fact that female entrepreneurs generally have lower levels of credit available to them than businesses owned by men.

Many of the businesses owned by women are home-based. By 2002, 66 percent of all home-based businesses were owned by women. These businesses are changing the face of business since they enable many women to balance work and family commitments at home while fulfilling their business objectives.

WOMEN AND MINORITIES ON CORPORATE BOARDS

The combination of increased cultural and governmental pressure for corporations to add women to their boards has resulted in an increase of women seated on corporate boards. As of 2003, 89 percent of the corporate boards in the *Fortune* 500 had at least one female director. Nonetheless, women still only accounted for 13.6 percent of all corporate board members in 2003. Further, the same women often hold several of these seats on different corporate boards.

Although minorities have been entering the workforce in record numbers, their attempts to reach the top of the corporate ladder have been disappointing. For example, an examination of the *Fortune* 1000 companies reveals that only 3 percent have an African American on their Board of Directors. Only 1.97 percent of *Fortune* 1000 board seats are held by Hispanics and Hispanic women hold only three tenths of all *Fortune* 1000 board seats. That is just 34 out of 10,314 seats. In addition, only seven Hispanic women serve as executive officers at *Fortune* 1000 companies.

LAWS AFFECTING EMPLOYMENT OF WOMEN AND MINORITIES

THE EQUAL PAY ACT OF 1963. The Equal Pay Act of 1963 was enacted as an amendment to the Fair Labor Standards Act. The Equal Pay Act forbids employers from paying employees different wages or salaries based on sex. The act mandates that employers may not pay men and women different wages if their jobs require equal skills, effort, and responsibilities and occur in the same work environment. If men and women in the same jobs do receive different pay, their pay must be equalized by raising the lower pay rather than lowering the higher pay. The Equal Pay act specifies four instances in which differences in pay are permitted: (1) under a seniority system; (2) under a merit system; (3) under a system that measures earnings by quantity or quality of production; or (4) under a differential system based on any other factor besides sex.

The act is administered by the Equal Employment Opportunity Commission (EEOC). To ensure enforcement, employers are required to keep records documenting employee hours, pay rates, job descriptions, and other relevant information. If employers violate the act, they may be required to pay back wages and possible punitive damages.

TITLE VII OF THE CIVIL RIGHTS ACT OF 1964. Title VII of the Civil Rights Act of 1964 prohibits discrimination in hiring, firing, promotion, assignment, and other treatment of persons in the workplace based on race, color, national origin, religion, or sex. Title VII applies to both public and private employers, employment agencies, and labor unions with fifteen or more employees or members. As with the Equal Pay Act, the EEOC administers enforcement of Title VII (Civil Rights Act of 1964).

In addressing claims, the courts have held that sex discrimination under Title VII refers to discrimination based on gender and not related to sexual orientation. In addition, while Title VII does not ban discrimination based on marital status, there are many state laws that forbid such discrimination.

SEXUAL HARASSMENT. Subjecting women to sexual harassment in the work place is considered a form of sex discrimination under Title VII. Generally, there are two primary forms of sexual harassment: quid pro quo, and hostile environment.Under the quid pro quo type of sexual harassment, a victim (usually a woman) is either promised a reward (i.e., pay raise, promotion, etc.) in exchange for sexual favors, or threatened with punishment for not complying with sexual requests. These requests can be expressed or implied.

Under the hostile environment theory, the employer is charged with creating conditions, or allowing others in the work place to create conditions, that make the work environment extremely unpleasant or hostile for the victimized employee(s) (usually women). The types of activities that may contribute to a hostile work environment include: displaying sexually suggestive pictures; using offensive or sexually suggestive language; discussing sexual activities; talking about a person's physical characteristics; inappropriate touching, etc.

Employers have a legal obligation to prevent either type of sexual harassment from occurring in the work place. Businesses usually establish detailed policies to try to prevent sexual harassment situations from arising in the work place.

PREGNANCY DISCRIMINATION ACT. Title VII of the Civil Rights Act was amended in 1978 by the Pregnancy Discrimination Act, which bans discrimination against women in employment because of pregnancy, childbirth, and related medical conditions. This act provides that women covered by the law "shall be treated the same for all employment-related purposes, including receipt of benefits under fringe benefit programs."

EXECUTIVE ORDER 11246. President Lyndon B. Johnson issued Executive Order 11246 in 1965. This order mandates that companies who do business ($10,000 or more annually) with the federal government must take affirmative actions to increase the representation of women and minorities in their employment ranks. If a company in question does more than $50,000 of annual business with the federal government, its affirmative action plan must be in writing.

FAMILY AND MEDICAL LEAVE ACT OF 1993. Enforced by the U.S. Department of Labor, the Family and Medical Leave Act applies to private employers with fifty or more employees and to all governmental employers, and requires employers to provide up to twelve weeks of unpaid leave to employees who have undergone childbirth; adoption; personal illness or injury; or illness or injury of a child, parent or spouse. During the leave period, the employee's health benefits must remain intact. Once the employee returns from the unpaid leave, the employee is entitled to return to the same or comparable position.

CONCERNS OF WOMEN AND MINORITY WORKERS

PAY DIFFERENCES. Despite the progress women made during the twentieth century, differences remain in the average pay of men and women. Although between 1979 and 2003 the earnings gap between women and men narrowed significantly, according to the Bureau of Labor Statistics, women still earned seventy-nine cents to every dollar earned by men in 2003. Women's earnings tend to rise with the level of education they possess; for example, in 2003 women with a college degree earned approximately $800 per week compared to $320 for those with less than a high school diploma.

In addition, white women earned 15 percent more than African American women and 38.3 percent more than Hispanic women as of 2003. Nevertheless, the gender gap in terms of earnings is not as dramatic among African Americans and Hispanics. Both African American and Hispanic women earned 88 percent of their male counterparts in 2003. Within different occupational categories, there are notable gender differences in terms of pay; for example, in professional specialty occupations have earnings that are about 75 percent of those of men. This difference is due partly to women's concentration in lower-paying professional occupations such as nursing and teaching. In the professional and related occupations, women are much less likely to work in some of the highest paying fields, such as engineering and computer and math related fields.

MATERNITY, PREGNANCY, CHILD BIRTH, AND CHILD CARE. According to the U.S. Department of Labor, 99 out of every 100 women will work for pay in the United States at some point in their lives. Further, the number of families in which a woman is the head of the household and no male spouse is present is continuing to rise. In 2003, women were the primary breadwinners in over 22 percent of all families in the United States, and 72 percent of these female heads of households were employed. Furthermore, the proportion of married-couple families in which only the wife worked rose to 6.8 percent in 2003. With so many women in the workforce—both single mothers and married women—many of these women were concerned with balancing work with pregnancy and child-care issues.

Despite the increasing need for child care as more mothers work outside the home, very few companies have policies for dealing with working parents who need outside child care. Although it is still common for women to quit their jobs or delay advancement at work because of child bearing, many women appear to be setting aside motherhood in pursuit of the executive suite. A 2001 nationwide survey of high-earning career women found that 33 percent of them are childless at ages 40–55. However, a survey of 187 of *Fortune* Magazine's Most Powerful Women in Business found that 72 percent were mothers. In fact, as of 2003 nearly three-quarters of all mothers were in the labor force including more than 60 percent of those women with children under the age of three. Therefore, working women continue to be plagued by the challenge of balancing work and family roles. Historically, women have taken less demanding, lower paying jobs, and it is often the case that the structures, habits, values, and atmospheres of work become organized around the availability of women whose top priority is their children.

In addition to the challenge of finding childcare, some working women are forced to face the issue of pregnancy discrimination. Despite the fact that the courts have banned pregnancy discrimination as a form of sex discrimination under Title VII of the Civil Rights Act, working women are still dealing with the problem. In 2004, 4,512 women who claimed that they were discriminated against as a result of pregnancy filed charges with the EEOC. Of the claims that were found to have merit, employers were forced to pay over $11 million in damages (not including litigation).

ALTERNATIVE WORK SCHEDULES. The increasing number of women in the work place has generated a demand for alternative work schedules. Since women have traditionally operated as managers of the household and primary caretakers for their children, they have often required greater flexibility in their work schedules to balance work and family obligations. Alternative work schedules have attempted to offer the dual benefit of providing women with flexible schedules to meet their family obligations while enabling employers to benefit from the work women have to offer. Generally, alternative work schedules can take several forms: (1) flexible work schedules, (2) compressed work schedules, and (3) job-sharing. Each of these types of work arrangements represents a departure from the traditional fixed schedule of 8 hours per day, 5 days per week, beginning and ending at the same time each day.

Flexible work schedules allow an employee to determine her own schedule within specified parameters. Employers may allow employees to vary their starting and ending time daily or to adhere to a predetermined fixed starting and ending time. Under a system of compressed work schedules, full-time employees may still work forty-hour weeks; however, they may work four 10-hour days and take one day a week off. Another arrangement may exist when an employee works four 9-hour days and one 4-hour day.

Job sharing is where two employees share the same job; these two employees may alternate days, or one may work mornings and the other works afternoons. Employers are under no obligation to offer alternative work schedules; however, many employers are recognizing that it is in their interest to offer some such arrangement in order to avoid alienating a valuable segment of the workforce. Alternative work schedules allow employers to attract female employees who can make significant contributions to the company while fulfilling their family commitments at the same time.

In 2003, 25 percent of all female salary workers worked fewer than 35 hours per week. In contrast, only 11 percent of employed men worked part time.

SEXUAL HARASSMENT AT WORK. Despite legislative and judicial efforts to minimize incidences of sexual harassment at work, it is still a significant problem for women in the work place. In 2004 a total of 13,136 claims of sexual harassment were filed with EEOC and with the state and local Fair Employment Practices agencies around the country that have a work-sharing agreement with the Commission. Of these complaints, women filed 84.9 percent of them. The damages awarded based on many of these claims (not including awards from litigation), totaled approximately $37.1 million.

Employers have clear incentives to prevent sexual harassment from occurring in the work place; the courts have determined that sexual harassment is a form of sex discrimination under Title VII of the Civil Rights Act of 1964. Employers found guilty of sexual harassment or allowing it to occur can be forced to pay substantial damages. Beyond the legal and monetary penalties, companies can suffer because sexual harassment can lead to lower productivity, absenteeism, employee turnover, poor morale, and devastating publicity for the company.

WOMEN AND MINORITIES IN MANAGEMENT

Despite the growing number of women in the labor force, women are still struggling to completely infiltrate the ranks of managers and executives. In the executive suite, women made up 15.7 percent of corporate officers in the *Fortune* 500 in 2002. In 2003, they held 13.6 percent of board seats in the same companies. But their actual numbers, compared to the percentage of women in the workforce, are still insignificant.

In a similar fashion, many minorities have topped out at entry or mid-level management positions. In 2003, African Americans hold less than 1 percent of the senior-level corporate positions in America's 1000 largest companies despite equal opportunity and affirmative action programs.

THE GLASS CEILING. While the numbers of women entering the workforce and rising to management are growing, women still have trouble advancing past middle-level management positions. Even many women who do rise above middle management find it difficult to secure a position at the top of the organizational structure. Many observers describe this as a "glass ceiling" acting as a barrier between women and the top-level positions they are striving for.

For years minorities have faced these same invisible, subtle, yet very real institutional barriers to promotions into higher level executive positions. The belief that minority groups reach organizational plateaus consisting of artificial barriers that derail them from senior management opportunities has been alternately termed "the brick wall." These barriers found in the structure of many organizations have often stymied the advancement of these select employee groups.

It has also been suggested that as a consequence of occupational sex segregation, many women confront "glass elevators" rather than "glass ceilings." Of the executive positions held by women most are in non-manufacturing companies and positions placing emphasis on employee relationships. In addition, recent research suggests that the "glass cliff" may have replaced the "glass ceiling" for some women. It is suggested that women managers in the public sector seem to be more at risk than their male counterparts.

Nonetheless, both women and businesses continue to wrestle with issues related to these "glass" phenomena. While the existence of these barriers has been acknowledged for at least a decade, their persistence indicates that efforts to break them have been largely unsuccessful. Among the advice that women have been given to help break through the glass ceiling are: exceed performance expectations; develop a style with which male managers are comfortable; look for challenging assignments; and find influential mentors. Additionally, removing these gender barriers may make good business sense. The "glass ceiling" may lead to disillusionment and higher turnover among very capable women. Also, if irrelevant factors are used to exclude women from the top management positions, all employees may begin to assume that similar extraneous factors would affect their future progress in an organization.

As more women reach the upper levels of management and start their own businesses, the odds increase that women will have increased opportunities at all levels of business. Nonetheless, U.S. corporations still have a tremendous distance to travel before women can say that they enjoy equal opportunity in the workplace.

SEE ALSO: Diversity; Entrepreneurship; Mentoring; Sensitivity Training; Work-Life Balance

Patricia A. Lanier

FURTHER READING:

Arfken, D.E., S.L. Bellar, and M.M. Helms. "The Ultimate Glass Ceiling Revisited: The Presence of Women on Corporate Boards." *Journal of Business Ethics* 50, no. 2 (2004): 177–186.

"Breaking Through the Glass Ceiling: Women in Management." Available from <http://www.ilo.org/public/english/dialogue/sector/techmeet/tmwm97/tmwm-com.htm>.

"Capturing the Impact: Women-Owned Businesses in the United States." Available from <http://www.nfwbo.org>.

"Catalyst Census of Women Board of Directors of Canada." Available from <http://www.catalystwomen.org/bookstore/files/fact/WBD03factsheetfinal.pdf>.

"Changes in Women's Labor Force Participation in the 20th Century." Available from <http://www.bls.gov/pub/ted/2000/feb/wk3/art03.htm>.

"Counting Minorities." Available from <http://www.bls.gov/opub/rtaw/chapter1.htm>.

Dreher, G. F. "Breaking the Glass Ceiling: The Effects of Sex Ratios and Work-Life Programs on Female Leadership at the Top." *Human Relations* 56, no. 5 (2003): 541–562.

"Employment Characteristics of Families Summary." Available from <http://www.bls.gov/news.release/famee.nr0.htm>.

"Facts on Working Women." Available from <http://permanent.access.gpo.gov/lps5585/millennium52000.htm>.

Fullerton, H.N., Jr., and M. Toosi. "Labor Force Participation: 75 Years of Change, 1950–98 and 1998–2025." *Monthly Labor Review* 122, no. 12 (2001): 3–12.

Goodman, J.S., D.L. Fields, and T.C. Blum "Cracks in the Glass Ceiling: In What Kinds of Organizations Do Women Make It to the Top?" *Group & Organization Management* 28, no. 4 (2003): 475–502.

Hewlett, S.A. *Creating a Life: Professional Women and the Quest for Children.* New York, NY: Miramax Books, 2002.

"Highlights of Women's Earnings in 2003." Available from <http://www.bls.gov/cps/cpswom2003.pdf>.

Hultin, M. "Some Take the Glass Excalarot, Some Hit the Glass Ceiling: Career Consequence of Occupational Sex Segregation." *Work and Occupations* 30, no. 1 (2003): 30–62.

Jalilvand, M. "Married Women, Work, and Values." *Monthly Labor Review* 123, no. 8 (2000): 26–31.

Mitra, A. "Breaking the Glass Ceiling: African American Women in Management Positions." *Equal Opportunities International* 22, no. 2 (2003): 67–80.

Nutley, S., and J. Mudd. "Has the Glass Cliff Replaced the Glass Ceiling for Women Employed in the Public Sector?" *Public Money & Management* 25, no. 1 (2005): 3–4.

"Pregnancy." Available from <http://www.eeoc.gov/types/pregnancy.html>.

"Self-Employed Women: 1976–2003." Available from <http://www.bls.gov/opub/ted/2004/apr/wk4/art04.htm>.

"Sexual Harassment." Available from <http://www.eeoc.gov/types/sexual_harassment.html>.

Tatum, B.D. *Why Are All the Black Kids Sitting Together in the Cafeteria?* New York, NY: Basic Books, 2003.

Tischler, L. "Where Are the Women? So What Happened?" *Fast Company* 79 (2004): 52–61.

"Women in the Labor Force: A Databook." Available from <http://www.bls.gov/cps/wlf–databook.htm>.

"Women at Work: A Visual Essay." Available from <http://www.bls.gov/opub/mlr/2003/10/ressum3.pdf>.

"Working the Twenty-First Century." Available from <http://www.bls.gov/opub/working/home.htm>.

WORK-LIFE BALANCE

Helping employees balance work and non-work responsibilities has been a growing concern of corporations for more than twenty years. The interest in work-life balance issues began in the 1980s as more women entered the workplace and focused primarily on helping employees balance work and family responsibilities by offering family-friendly benefits. These practices are now aimed a work-life balance, which is a more encompassing term that reflects the desire of nearly every employee for more flexibility in their work in order to mange the competing demands of work and life outside of work.

While many employees enjoy the benefits of work-family balance practices, many were inspired by changes in the workforce over the last two decades. These changes include increases in the number of employed women, especially mothers, single-parent families, and dual-income families. Additionally, many employees are now responsible for caring for elderly parents and other relatives. Corporate interest in family-friendly practices has steadily escalated as companies have realized the advantages of providing work-life balance benefits.

THE CHANGING WORKFORCE AND GROWING CORPORATE INTEREST

A number of changes in workforce demographics have brought work-life balance issues to the attention of companies. The major change related to the need for family-friendly benefits is the number of women in the U.S. workforce, which has more than doubled since 1970. Additionally, more women are remaining in the workforce after marriage and after having children, increasing the number of dual-career households in America. Add to this a larger number of single women with children in the workforce in the past two decades, and there is increased demand for family-friendly work policies.

Although the trend toward work-life balance practices began with demands from mothers in the workforce, the push now is coming from all employees: fathers and mothers, single parents, and employees with responsibilities for caring for aged relatives, and even employees who just want more flexibility in their daily lives. Nine out of ten workers in America live in households with family members, and nearly half of all employees have care-giving responsibilities. Recognizing these changes, corporations are creating work environments that make it possible for employees to be both good workers and good caregivers. However, the corporate motive for work-life balance policies is more than altruism and a desire to help and support employees. Employers have realized that it makes good business sense to provide such benefits. It helps with recruitment and retention of employees by creating an atmosphere of loyalty to the corporation.

Programs and benefits that directly address work-life balance issues include:

- dependent care (child-care and elder-care programs)

- flexible or alternative work schedules (flex-time, compressed work weeks, telecommuting, job sharing, and part time employment)

- leaves (paid and unpaid family care leaves, maternity phase-back, and so on)

Corporate America's growing concern for family issues is evidenced by the number of business journals that identify and rank family-friendly corporations. *Working Mother* was the first periodical to write a lead story on family-friendly companies. This article has appeared annually since 1986 and is called "Best Companies for Working Mothers." It identifies the top 100 work-life sensitive companies, assessing compensation, opportunities for women, child-care benefits, flexibility in work, and other benefits such as paid maternity and paternity leave. Additionally, *Business Week* magazine ran its first major cover story on "Work & Family" in 1993 at the time the Family and Medical Leave Act was enacted., and in 1996 *Business Week* launched in a major cover story issue a biannual ranking of the "Best Companies for Work and Family." Finally, the third major business periodical to rank companies was *Fortune.* Their "The 100 Best Companies to Work for in America" was first published in January 1998. Evidence from their study indicated that family-friendly polices help the bottom line.

TYPES OF WORK/LIFE BALANCE BENEFITS

CHILD AND DEPENDENT CARE PROGRAMS. In the last decade, there has been an increase in the number of day-care centers in America, and only about 28 percent of families with children had a parent who stayed home full time. This has prompted many organizations to either provide or subsidize day care for employees. Additionally, some companies provide assistance for child care for older children before and after school. This is an important concern of employees with school-age children because elementary school students typically spend 1,032 hours a year in school whereas full-time employees spend 2,025 hours per year at work. This leaves a 1,000-hour discrepancy. Employee concern about care before and after school is increasingly recognized as a drain on productivity and morale. Employers who provide this benefit report increased retention of employees who take advantage of it. The positive relationship between the availability of child-care centers and employees' performance was identified by a study done at the University of Michigan. Attitudes, recruitment and retention, and performance were all more positive when child-care centers were available.

However, not all companies can provide on-site child-care or after-school programs. In these instances the company can provide information about referral services and tax-free salary withholding for flexible spending accounts. Companies can also support community programs that provide care. Similar programs can be set up for elder care needs. Hewitt Associates determined in a 2003 study that 94 percent of large employers surveyed allowed employees to put aside pre-tax earnings for child care into flexible spending accounts that 13 percent of large corporations surveyed offered on-site or near-site child care, and 13 percent offered "backup emergency childcare" for when regular child care was temporarily unavailable.

FLEXIBLE WORK PROGRAMS. Flexible work programs accommodate employees by allowing variations on when and where they do their work. Flexible work programs consist of flextime, compressed workweeks, telecommuting, job sharing, paid time off, and other leave programs.

In the past, employees arrived at work at 8 a.m. or 9 a.m. and left at 5 p.m. But now changes in employees' personal lives make flexibility in work arrangements an important benefit. Flextime allows employees to vary the start and end times of their work day, and employees are typically required to be present during certain core hours (e.g., 10 a.m.–2 p.m.) but still working eight hours per day. This is one of the most frequently provided work/life balance benefit, and is well-liked by many different employees. Flextime allows all employees-those with children and those without-the ability to better manage their work and non-work lives. A 2003 poll of over 600 companies conducted by the Mellon Financial Corporation indicated that the number of employees who are allowed flexible work arrangements has doubled from 32 percent in 1996 to 71 percent in 2003.

The compressed workweek is a type of scheduling plan in which full-time hours are worked in fewer than five days. For instance, employees may work four 10-hour days and always have a three-day weekend. The compressed workweek is intended to allow employees more flexibility by having more days away from work; however the longer hours worked each day may actually detract from productivity and from work/life balance.

Telecommuting, or working out of one's home and communicating with the workplace through technology, is on the rise for a number of reasons. First, technology has improved steadily over the past few decades, allowing faster and higher quality communication from home. Access to the Internet is the primary reason that people can now work effectively out of their homes. Another reason for an increase in telecommuting is many employees' desire to commute less often. With dual-career families in which spouses work in different cities, or in large urban areas, employees may find some hours of their day taken up with a long commute. By telecommuting even a few days a week, employees can cut devote more time to work and/or family. Additionally, telecommuting can reduce pollution associated with driving to work. While telecommuting shares many of the advantages of other flexible work arrangements, it has some distinct disadvantages.

The primary disadvantage is the employee's lack of access to the workplace, supervisors, coworkers, and even customers. If a person's work is improved through the physical presence of the employee in the workplace, it may not be advisable to institute telecommuting. A second major concern with telecommuting is the inability to supervise the remote worker. While many employees are not allowed to telecommute until they have a record of effective performance in the workplace, performance problems resulting from a lack of supervision may arise in some cases. Finally, a major drawback is that the employee loses touch with the organizational culture; the patterns of behavior that one observes in a certain workplace are not as easy to learn when a person is absent from that workplace. This may be irrelevant in some workplaces, but crucial to meeting objectives in others. Additionally, by being absent and perhaps not learning the organizational culture, the employee may reduce his or her ability to be promoted.

Job sharing is allowing two employees with complementary schedules to split the responsibilities of a single traditional full-time job. This typically allows employees to keep the fringe benefits of a full-time position, while working fewer hours. Job-sharing may be used temporarily when an employee reduces hours, perhaps to continue working while managing childcare duties. A 2002 study conducted by Hewitt Associates studied the benefits provided by more than 1,000 companies and found that 28 percent of organizations offer job sharing. While job sharing accommodates the schedules of employees, having two people accountable for one position may result in conflict. Therefore, care should be taken when allowing employees to job share.

Paid time off, in the form of vacation days, sick days, and other forms of paid absences, are ways to help employees manage issues associated with health, school, leisure, or any other non-work activity. Many employers now allow employees to draw leave time from a single pool for any type of leave rather than allowing only a fixed number of days for each type of absence. Leaves and time-off programs include paid and unpaid authorized leaves such as sabbaticals, social service leaves, leaves for emergencies, paid leave banks, and family-care leaves. Many employees want and need leaves in addition to annual vacations for reasons such as care of newborns or sick family members and for personal interests or volunteer work. These leaves are different from flexible work schedules in that flextime addresses when and where the work gets done; time-off programs provide employees with leave during unusual or emergency times. Many companies provide this benefit by leave-sharing programs. These allow employees to voluntarily donate their paid time off to coworkers. Companies may also offer paid leave banks in which employees are given a single pool of time off to use for vacations, personal time, illnesses, and family emergencies. Employers using paid leave banks do so to provide flexibility to employees and to assist managers in scheduling time off. However, the availability of more flexibility for leave time may hinder the organization if key employees are absent when needed, and thus, these programs must be properly managed.

FAMILY AND MEDICAL LEAVE ACT

The Family and Medical Leave Act of 1993 (P.L. 103-3) brought a major change in the attitudes toward leaves in the business world. It requires businesses with 50 or more employees to provide employees with at least 12 weeks a year of unpaid leave for birth, adoption, or personal or family illnesses. Employers must pay health-care coverage during the leave and return employees to their same or equivalent jobs. Social and demographic changes were the impetus for this law; the law, along with pressure stemming from the same social and demographic changes, has driven the adoption of family-friendly benefits. Families may no longer have a full-time parent at home. Employees need time off to care for themselves or family members such as sick children, spouses, and elderly relatives. Impetus also came from other countries, primarily western European countries, Canada and Japan, all which have family leave policies more generous than those outlined in the Family and Medical Leave Act. In 1993 the United States was the only country of 188 surveyed by the International Labor Organization that had no mandatory parent leave law.

Most business groups opposed the FMLA on the grounds that it would reduce business efficiency and add administrative costs to employers. However, studies generally have found that it has not been a major burden or had a significant impact on employer costs. In a study conducted by Westat for the U.S. Department of Labor in 2000, respondents indicated that the FMLA had either no noticeable effect or a positive effect on the business productivity (83 percent), profitability (90 percent), and growth (90 percent) of their company. Further, respondents indicated that intermittent leave, which was posited to be most disruptive to organizations, had no impact on productivity (81 percent) or profitability (94 percent). Not only did businesses report few negative effects from the FMLA, nearly 79 percent of the employees surveyed in the study indicated that the leave had positive effects on their ability to care for family members.

WORK-LIFE BALANCE AND THE BOTTOM LINE

Companies often seek to add work-life balance benefits because it makes good business sense. The three top reasons are (1) recruitment/retention of employees, (2) commitment to the firm, and (3) productivity. Retention is important to employers, and will become more critical as baby boomers retire and are replaced by smaller generations. Additionally, employee retention is increasingly valued as corporations realize that the cost of recruiting and training is more expensive than providing work/life balance benefits.

Several research studies have been done to determine the effects of work-life balance benefits. Paul Osterman, in a major 1995 study, suggested three reasons for employers to adopt work/family programs: to lower absenteeism rates, to bolster recruitment and retention of employees, and to encourage commitment to the firm. In another study by Steven L. Grover and Karen J. Crooker, published in *Personnel Psychology,* the authors found a relationship between employee commitment and benefits such as parental leave, flexible scheduling, child-care assistance, and child-care information. An interesting aspect of this study was that employee commitment increased regardless of whether the employee was a user or nonuser of the benefits. In a more recent study done by Aeon Consulting in 1998, family-friendly benefits were again correlated with employee commitment. A study published in 2004, conducted by Wendy Caser and Louis Buffardi, indicated that flexible scheduling and dependent care assistance offered by organizations were related to applicants' intentions to pursue jobs at these companies.

Further, a report by the Families and Work Institute entitled *The 1997 National Study of the Changing Workforce* found that the quality of workers' jobs and the supportiveness of the workplace are predictors of productivity, job satisfaction, commitment, and retention. This study was based on 2,877 employees. In contrast to the positive effect of a supportive workplace, the study found that difficult and demanding jobs in nonsupportive environments tended to suffer from poorer job performance.

BACKLASH FROM CHILDLESS EMPLOYEES

One concern with the introduction of new family-friendly programs into the workplace is backlash from childless employees. These employees may feel that they are not getting the same level of benefits as their coworkers with children, because they cannot take advantage of the programs in which the organization has invested. As such, employees with children receive more total compensation (because of the added benefits) than do childless employees. This problem may be alleviated with a flexible benefits plan, in which those employees who do not choose family-friendly benefits may choose other types of benefits. Additionally, experts suggest that employers develop "work/life" programs that allow employees flexibility for any activity outside of work, rather than just "family-friendly" benefits for employees with children. Thus, if all employees are able to take advantage of flexible hours, telecommuting, or other types of work arrangements to better manage their lives, then the policies are likely to be accepted by all employees.

SEE ALSO: Employee Benefits; Employment Law and Compliance; Human Resource Management; Women and Minorities in Management

Judith M. Nixon
Revised by Marcia Simmering

FURTHER READING:

Caspar, Wendy J., and Louis C. Buffardi. "Work-Life Benefits and Job Pursuit Intentions: The Role of Anticipated Organizational Support." *Journal of Vocational Behavior* 65 (2004): 391–410.

Gomez-Mejia, Luis R., David B. Balkin, and Robert L. Cardy. *Managing Human Resources.* 4th ed. Upper Saddle River, NJ: Prentice Hall, 2004.

Grover, S.L., and K.J. Crooker. "Who Appreciates Family-Responsive Human Resource Policies: The Impact of Family-Friendly Policies on the Organizational Attachment of Parents and Non-Parents." *Personnel Psychology* 48, no. 2 (Summer 1995): 271–288.

Hammers, Maryann. "A 'Family-Friendly' Backlash." *Workforce Management,* August 2003, 77–79.

Kiger, Patrick. "Child-Care Models." *Workforce Management,* April 2004, 38.

Making Work Flexible: Policy to Practice. New York: Catalyst, 1996.

Mercer Work/Life and Diversity Initiatives Benchmarking Survey 1996. Louisville, KY: William M. Mercer Inc., 1996.

Nilles, J.M. *Managing Telework: Strategies for Managing the Virtual Workforce.* New York: John Wiley & Sons, 1998.

Osterman, P. "Work/Family Programs and the Employment Relationship." *Administrative Science Quarterly,* December 1995, 681.

Scott, M.B. "Flexibility Improves Workplace at Owens Corning, Dun & Bradstreet Information Systems." *Employee Benefit Plan Review,* September 1996, 30–31.

Seitel, S. *Work & Family: A Retrospective Research and Results from 1990 to 1995.* Minnetonka, MN: Work & Family Connection, Inc., 1997.

Waldfogel, J. "Family and Medical Leave: Evidence from the 2000 Surveys." *Monthly Labor Review,* September 2001.

WORLD-CLASS MANUFACTURER

The term "world-class manufacturer" is popularly used to denote a standard of excellence: the best of the best manufacturers at the international level. It came into prominence following the 1986 publication of *World Class Manufacturing: The Lessons of Simplicity Applied* by Richard J. Schonberger, which was his follow-up to *Japanese Management Techniques: Nine Hidden Lessons in Simplicity.*

World marketplace events during the 1970s and 1980s caused competition to grow to such an intense level that many firms were forced to re-examine their concept of manufacturing strategy, especially in terms of the tradeoffs among the four competitive priorities: cost, quality, delivery/service, and flexibility. Managers began to realize that they no longer had to make these tradeoffs but could instead compete on several competencies.

Some of those excited by the concept describe it as capturing the breadth and the essence of the fundamental changes taking place in larger industrial enterprises, with their overriding goal and underlying mindset of continual and rapid improvement. Others describe it as the culmination of the relentless pursuit of competitive excellence. Richard Schonberger states that the emphasis on world-class manufacturing may someday be chronicled as the third major event in the history of manufacturing management, following the use of standard methods and times espoused by Frederick Taylor and Frank Gilbreth, and the findings of the Hawthorne experiments at Western Electric, which held that motivation, to a significant degree, comes from recognition. For simplicity's sake, we will describe a world-class manufacturer as a company that is able to compete effectively in a global market.

Clearly, there are some demands placed on individuals and organizations that desire world-class status. Peter Stonebreaker and Keong Leong presented a hierarchy of steps, appearing as five levels, that lead to world-class operations (see Figure 1). This series of steps will be used to describe the characteristics of world-class manufacturers.

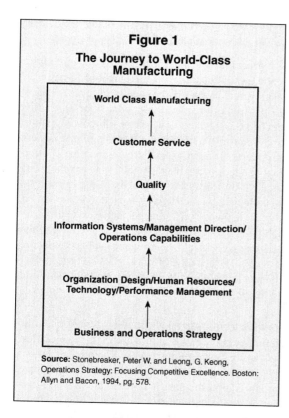

Figure 1
The Journey to World-Class Manufacturing

World Class Manufacturing

↑

Customer Service

↑

Quality

↑

Information Systems/Management Direction/
Operations Capabilities

↑

Organization Design/Human Resources/
Technology/Performance Management

↑

Business and Operations Strategy

Source: Stonebreaker, Peter W. and Leong, G. Keong,
Operations Strategy: Focusing Competitive Excellence. Boston:
Allyn and Bacon, 1994, pg. 578.

LEVEL ONE: BUSINESS AND OPERATIONS STRATEGY

All world-class manufacturers have an explicit, formal manufacturing mission. Within this mission is the operating goal to become world class. They use competitive information to establish organizational goals and objectives, which they communicate to all members of the enterprise. They regularly assess the appropriateness of these objectives to attaining and maintaining world-class status.

World-class manufacturing requires an overall willingness to establish closer connections with everyone, from suppliers to workers. It requires an unwavering commitment to self-analysis and improvement. It requires an aggressive approach to technology that can turn visionary strategies into reality. All of these must be reflected in the firm's business and operations strategy if world-class status is to be attained.

LEVEL TWO: ORGANIZATION DESIGN, HUMAN RESOURCES, TECHNOLOGY, AND PERFORMANCE MEASUREMENT

The following sections discuss how organization design, human resources, technology, and performance measurement factor into an organization's effort to become a world-class manufacturer.

ORGANIZATION DESIGN. World-class manufacturers integrate all elements of the manufacturing system in such a way that the needs and wants of its customers are satisfied in an effective, timely manner. This requires the commitment and the expenditure of efforts and resources by all elements within the system to ensure their proper integration. This commitment extends to outside elements as well, as the world-class manufacturer encourages and motivates its suppliers and vendors to become co-equals with the other elements of the manufacturing system.

World-class manufacturers work to eliminate organizational barriers to communication and to organize the firm in such a way that the core values needed to reach world-class status take precedence. In fact, most companies that have succeeded in implementing many of the world-class tools—such as just-in-time production (JIT), total quality management (TQM), manufacturing resource planning (MRP II) and total productive maintenance (TPM)—already had the core values well in place. Companies that are already world class are able to quickly absorb other world-class manufacturing concepts as they are developed and publicized.

HUMAN RESOURCES. World-class manufacturers recognize that employee involvement and empowerment are critical to achieving continuous improvement in all elements of the manufacturing system. The continuity of organizational development and renewal comes primarily through the involvement of the employee. World-class companies invest comparatively more in their relationships with their workers, providing significantly more training than their competitors. An *Industry Week* survey found that firms approaching world-class status were three to five times more likely to report "highly effective" human-resources programs than other firms. Some analysts note that combining lean manufacturing principles with employee participation can help firms become world-class manufacturers.

TECHNOLOGY. A great deal of emphasis is placed on technology, equipment, and processes by those trying to attain world-class status. World-class manufacturers view technology as a strategic tool for achieving and maintaining their world-class status. A high priority is placed on the discovery, development, and timely implementation of the most relevant technology available and the identification and support of those who can communicate and implement this technology. The most highly competitive firms have made significantly more progress than others in implementing TQM, reengineering, simultaneous engineering, group technology, computer-assisted manufacturing (CAM), material resources planning (MRP), and the use of local area networks (LANs).

PERFORMANCE MEASUREMENT. World-class manufacturers recognize the importance of measurement in defining the goals and performance expectations for their organization. They routinely adopt or develop the appropriate performance measurements needed to interpret and quantitatively describe the criteria used to measure the effectiveness of their manufacturing system and its interrelated components.

Use of the proper measurements allows world-class manufacturers to assess their performance against themselves (internal benchmarking), their competitors (competitive benchmarking), and against other world-class manufacturing firms that are not competitors (generic and functional benchmarking). World-class status is achieved through a relentless commitment to continuous improvement, which cannot be achieved without measurement.

LEVEL THREE: INFORMATION SYSTEMS, MANAGEMENT DIRECTION, AND OPERATIONS CAPABILITIES

The following sections discuss how information systems, management direction, and operations capabilities factor into an organization's effort to become a world-class manufacturer.

INFORMATION SYSTEMS. World-class manufacturers require world-class information systems for collecting, processing, and disseminating data and for providing the feedback mechanism that is necessary for meeting their objectives. Information systems are fully integrated into the business processes of firms that adhere to continuous improvement and TQM strategies. Capturing and analyzing customer feedback and designing, manufacturing, and delivering world-class quality products and services is rooted in superior information systems. Richard Schonberger states that functions within a world-class firm all have a common language and signaling system. World-class firms embrace computerized maintenance management and computer-integrated manufacturing. Additionally, organizational commitment to continuous improvement is supported by the strategic use of information systems.

MANAGEMENT DIRECTION. Management is responsible for directing the manufacturing organization's journey to world-class status and for creating an organizational culture committed to all that is necessary for achieving continuous improvement. Corporate culture and values are the foundation for superior manufacturing, which in turn reflects and is reflected by the caliber of corporate management. This implies that personal commitment, involvement, and a sense of direction by management are critical to the success of world-class firms.

The manufacturing excellence needed for world-class status is nurtured by direction from superior management, which must penetrate the manufacturing function, viewing and managing it as an integral, indivisible part of the firm. It cannot tolerate mediocrity or even average manufacturing performance.

Management must seek to describe and understand the interdependency of the multiple elements of their manufacturing system, to discover new relationships, to explore the consequences of alternative decisions, and communicate unambiguously within the organization and with the firm's customers and suppliers. Stimulating and accommodating continuous change forces management to experiment and assess outcomes. They must be able to translate knowledge acquired in this way into some sort of direction, framework, or model that leads to improved operational decision making, while incorporating a learning process into their fundamental operating philosophy. The objective of world-class status tests management's ability to learn, adapt, and innovate faster in the face of an intensely competitive global market.

OPERATIONS CAPABILITIES. World-class manufacturers are concerned with whether their operations systems have the ability to meet design specifications, rather than with evaluating the quality and quantity of products after the fact. In order to attain world-class status, the manufacturing firm has to be given the proper resources. With these resources, the firm must have the capability to produce the right quantity, the right quality, at the right time (often just in time), and at the right price. The proper technology must be on hand or readily attainable. In addition, the firm must have the necessary managerial capabilities to compete successfully on a global basis. For many firms, the necessary operational capability involves the ability to provide customers with a large degree of flexibility of either product or volume, or exceptional response time to orders, changes in orders, or new product development.

Beyond the firm itself, operations capability implies a superior interactive relationship with all vendors and suppliers. World-class firms have extensively implemented JIT, are heavily involved with programs that contractually commit suppliers to annual cost cuts, and are making efforts to involve the supplier early in the new product development process.

LEVEL FOUR: QUALITY

World-class manufacturers place an emphasis on quality. Firms in this category are usually in an advanced state of TQM implementation, continually seeking to enhance their business. All quality costs (prevention costs, appraisal costs, and cost of defects—both internal and external) are evaluated and held to the lowest reasonable sum. "Zero defects" is the goal of the world-class manufacturer. In order to achieve zero defects, the world-class firm is educated in and has fully implemented statistical quality control (SQC), sometimes called statistical process control (SPC) or quality at the source. Hence, quality is maintained and elevated through quality planning, quality control, and quality improvement. In conjunction with this effort to improve processes and products, world-class firms utilize an activity called benchmarking. This involves comparing the firm's performance, either overall or in a functional area, with that of other world-class organizations. The use of TQM techniques, according to some analysts, is the most striking differentiator between world-class and non-world-class firms. Quality has also been found to be the most important competitive differentiator in the eyes of the customer.

LEVEL FIVE: CUSTOMER SERVICE

World-class manufacturers instill within their organization and constantly reinforce the idea that all who are a part of the organization must know their customers and must seek to satisfy the wants and needs of not only the customers, but also all other stakeholders. The goal of satisfaction is pursued in regards to the product, order processing, delivery, quick response to changes, and service after the sale. After all, the goal of continuous improvement is to improve processes and add value to products and services in such a way as to increase customer satisfaction and loyalty and ensure long-term profitability.

LEVEL SIX: WORLD-CLASS MANUFACTURING

While world-class manufacturing may be difficult for manufacturers to define, many say they know it when they see it. Whatever it is, it must be from the customer's vantage point. An *Industry Week* survey found that, among factories approaching world-class status, a higher percentage were likely to belong to public companies; have corporate parents with revenues greater than $1 billion; participate in an automotive industry value chain; and employ 250 or more

people at the location. These firms reported large cost reductions over the previous three years, as well as increased revenues, higher capacity utilization, higher sales per employee, and returns on invested capital (ROIC) that exceeded that of other manufacturers. Daniel F. Baldwin states that truly world-class firms are always examining their business processes and continuously seeking solutions to improve in key areas, such as lead time reduction, cost cutting, exceeding customer expectations, streamlining processes, shortening time to market for new products, and managing the global operation.

World-class manufacturers are the ones that possess the knowledge and technology to provide products and services of continually improving quality. It is what separates practitioners of the new paradigm from the industrialist dinosaurs.

SEE ALSO: Benchmarking; Customer Relationship Management; Human Resource Management; Management Awards; Performance Measurement; Quality and Total Quality Management

R. Anthony Inman

FURTHER READING:

Baldwin, Daniel F. "Q&A: World-Class Manufacturing." *Surface Mount Technology* 18, no. 1 (2004): 23.

Schonberger, Richard J. *Japanese Manufacturing Techniques: Nine Hidden Lessons in Simplicity.* New York: The Free Press, 1982.

———. "The Right Stuff, Revisited." *MSI* 21, no. 9 (2003): 26–30.

———. *World Class Manufacturing: The Lessons of Simplicity Applied.* New York: The Free Press, 1986.

Stonebreaker, Peter W., and G. Keong Leong. *Operations Strategy: Focusing Competitive Excellence.* Boston: Allyn and Bacon, 1994.

Taninecz, George. "Long-Term Commitments: Practices and Performances Validate World-Class Plants." *Industry Week* 253, no. 2 (2004): 51–53.

Z

ZERO-BASED BUDGETING

The budgeting process is an essential component of management control systems and has been an effective system by which management can successfully plan, coordinate, and control. The process involves the creation and implementation of the broad objectives of an organization, the detailed objectives, and a short-term and long-term financial plan. The philosophy and procedures used to implement zero-base budgeting in industry and government settings are quite similar, only slightly differing with the mechanics to fit the specific needs of each organization.

The basic process of zero-based budgeting is to justify budget requests every budgeting cycle, regardless of prior period budgets. The following sections address the specifics including the history, implementation, drawbacks and solutions, and behavioral impacts of zero-based budgeting.

HISTORY OF ZERO-BASED BUDETING

Government budgeting was established in Great Britain in the late 17th century. The enactment of the 1689 Bill of Rights gave taxing authority to Parliament as opposed to the King. Parliament gradually established spending programs and by the 1820s published detailed annual financial statements showing revenues and expenditures and a projected surplus or deficit. The usage of budgets by the United States government did not begin until 1800 when a law was passed for the Secretary of the Treasury to submit an annual financial report to Congress. This action was not taken by the Treasury department, and instead, federal govern-ment agencies developed their own reports and sub-mitted them to the Treasury.

Several attempts were made in the early 1900s to implement federal budgeting and financial manage-ment, but each failed, even though 44 individual states had already passed laws concerning budgets. Congress passed the Budgeting and Accounting Act in 1921 along with the creation of a centralized Bureau of the Budget. Although created in 1921, it was not until the mid-1940s that the federal budget included identifica-tion of the major goals and program objectives, a sys-tematic analysis of supplies and needs for both military and civilian purposes, and a long-range plan of projects. In the 1960s, the Planning-Programming-Budgeting System (PPBS) was adopted by President Lyndon B. Johnson to be implemented throughout the federal government.

The PPBS was short-lived, however. In the 1970s, every federal department except for the Defense Department abandoned the system. The concept of zero-based budgeting gained notoriety in 1977 when President Jimmy Carter announced he was introduc-ing zero-based budgeting into the federal budgeting process. The term, "zero-based budgeting," and the techniques for carrying out these budgeting processes had been previously introduced in an article written by Peter A. Pyhrr in the Harvard Business Review in 1970, but former President Carter adopted this method at the federal level, zero-based budgeting began to spread more rapidly.

President Carter, while still governor of Georgia in 1973, contracted with Pyhrr to implement the system for the entire executive budget recommendations for the state of Georgia. However, when the system was applied to governmental budgeting, it failed due to the great amount of effort and time required development and implementation. With further refinement, however, zero-based budgeting was largely hailed as a success when introduced to Congress in 1977.

Early business budgets focused on controlling costs and little emphasis on measuring effectiveness. In the early 1900s, the use of budgets increased due to the necessity for industries to implement more careful factory planning. A systematic plan of budgeting arose from two areas: industrial engineering and cost accounting. Scientific methods were used by industrial engineers to arrive at production standards, which could then be used to estimate future operations and performance standards. Cost accountants used budgeting to establish standard costs and to estimate future expected costs in a budgetary form. Also at this time, texts on budgeting and managerial accounting began to emerge.

As zero-based budgeting gained traction in the 1970s among public budgeting constituents, it also gained popularity among private enterprises, and during this time a number of organizations modified and implemented the system. An example of an organization successfully implementing this system is the Florida Power and Light Company. In 1977 zero-based budgeting became required for all Florida Power and Light general office staff departments. Ben Dady, the company's director of management control, favored the system because when managers develop the zero-based budget, they begin with nothing in terms of budgeted dollars, and have to justify or prove why they need to spend money on each activity or project for all the dollars they expect to spend. New and old problems are treated equally. Every managerial activity is properly identified and then evaluated by analyzing more efficient ways and alternative levels of performing the same activity. These alternatives are then ranked and relative priorities are established.

The publicity in the 1970s surrounding zero-based budgeting gave the impression that the system was a relatively new technique, although the system was not new at all. Zero-based budgeting is quite similar to the Planning-Programming-Budgeting system, implemented in the 1960s. Both systems involve evaluating the inputs and outputs for specific activities, as opposed to the traditional line-item format.

IMPLEMENTATION OF ZERO-BASED BUDGETING

The zero-based budgeting system puts the burden of proof on the manager, and demands that each manager justify the entire budget in detail and prove why he or she should spend the organization's money in the manner proposed. A "decision package" must be developed by each manager for every project or activity, which includes an analysis of cost, purpose, alternative courses of action, measures of performance,

consequences of not performing the activity, and the benefits.

This approach is different than traditional budgeting techniques due to the analysis of alternatives. Managers must identify alternative methods of performing each activity first, such as evaluating the costs and benefits of making a project or outsourcing it, or centralizing versus decentralizing operations. In addition, managers must identify different levels for performing each alternative method of the proposed activity. This means establishing a minimum level of spending, often 75 percent of the current operating level, and then developing separate decision packages that include the costs and benefits of additional levels of spending for that particular activity. The different levels allow managers to consider and evaluate a level of spending lower than the current operating level, giving decision-makers the choice of eliminating an activity or the ability to choose from a selection of levels of effort including tradeoffs and shifts in expenditure levels among organizational units.

The decision packages must be ranked in order of importance once they have been created. This allows each manager to identify priorities, combine decision packages for old and new projects into one ranking, and allows top management to evaluate and compare the needs of individual units or divisions to make funding allocations. In this respect, zero-based budgeting is quite different than traditional rolling budgets. Rolling budgets often appeal to people who prepare budgets because they make budget development much easier. Managers can add an inflation factor to the previous year's budget and then include any adjustments for major changes. Rolling budgets also give management a concrete number to help make comparisons from year to year. However, traditional rolling budgets have a tendency to create conflict; they can create an incentive to spend money carelessly in order to justify the next year's budget. They can also create inefficient operations due to the fact that individual departments or units do not have to justify expenditures based on operations, but only on the prior year's expenditures.

Zero-based budgeting addresses such problems that can occur with traditional rolling budgets. In zero-based budgeting, each dollar spent by management must be justified with a detailed account of what will be purchased, how many labor hours are needed, what problems will be faced, and so forth. This allows management an opportunity to review operations in depth and make recommendations for changes to if necessary. The zero-based budgeting process helps managers identify redundancies and duplications among different departments, concentrating on the dollars needed for proposed programs as opposed to percentage increases or decreases form the previous year. Specific priorities of departments and divisions are identified more easily in zero-based budgeting.

The process also allows for the comparability of different departments as to the respective priorities funded. Zero-base budgeting enables a performance audit to determine whether each project or activity has been performed as efficiently as planned.

ZERO-BASED BUDGETING DRAWBACKS AND SOLUTIONS

One drawback to zero-based budgeting is cost in terms of managerial time; it takes a considerable amount of time to go through the process of reviewing operations in enough detail to justify costs each budget cycle without relying on past expenditures. One solution to this problem is to create a rolling budget every year and perform a zero-based budget every three to five years, or when a major change occurs within the operation. This allows an organization to benefit from the advantages of zero-based budgeting without an excessive amount of work. Likewise, traditional rolling budgets should never strictly rely on a prior-year budget plus a percentage; consideration should always be given to past numbers. In some cases, a zero-based budget may rely on some prior numbers where it is overwhelming to create a budget from scratch. Ultimately, the process gives top management the opportunity to judge the performance of managers in terms of allocating resources efficiently and effectively, and gives managers more responsibility in developing their budgets.

An organization should not feel that all budgets must be developed in entirely the same manner. Some departments can utilize an in-depth study of a zero-based budget while others can use a rolling budget. This is a way to spread the extensive work over a number of years instead of concentrating on one certain year. Many organizations have implemented the system in some form or another and found that it did not work. If properly implemented, however, the process could have a considerable improvement over traditional rolling budgets. The number and nature of decision packages varies from organization to organization; it is not uncommon for large organizations to identify several thousand packages. Furthermore, it is often hard or even impossible for top executives to have the necessary knowledge or time to develop and rank priorities for thousands of packages.

To alleviate this problem, managers, after ranking their own packages, can have their top executives rank the packages of all the managers that report to them. This approach is used by one of zero-based budgeting's pioneers, Texas Instruments. Another solution is for each level of management to rank a certain percentage of packages within its own area of responsibility. In this solution, the first level of management may rank 40 percent of the proposed packages; the next level may rank the next 40 percent of packages, while top management may concentrate on the remainder of the budget.

BEHAVIORAL IMPACTS OF ZERO-BASED BUDGETING

The impact of budgeting on organizations was probably first studied by Argyris in the 1950s. These studies show some of the behavioral effects resulting from the way budgets are used in organizations. The results of his research showed that the particular process used could cause dysfunctional behavior in subordinates, regardless of the degree of technical refinement of the budgetary system. In the 1970s, Hopwood's studies inquired into the effects of budgets on human behavior. These studies showed that the use by a superior of a budget-constrained style of evaluation gave rise to significant levels of job-related tension; had adverse effects on peer and subordinate-superior relationships, and was implicated in manipulative behavior on subordinates. A long line of studies have been performed since then to uncover an array of variables that govern the effects of reliance on budgets on behavioral outcomes, including managerial performance. Examples of these variables include budgetary participation, task uncertainty, environmental uncertainty, strategy, and culture.

Zero-based budgeting may require an extensive amount of time, money, and paper work; but it does provide a systematic method of addressing an organization's financial concerns, in turn enabling an organization to better allocate its resources. A combination of zero-based budgets with rolling budgets or some other form of budgeting that spreads the work of justifying new budgets each cycle is one way to incorporate zero-based budgeting without undo stress at the same time for all managers with budgetary responsibility.

Kevin Nelson
Revised by Scott B. Droege

FURTHER READING:

Hilton, R.W. *Managerial Accounting: Creating Value in a Dynamic Business Environment.* McGraw-Hill, 2005.

Warren, C.S., J.M. Reeve, and P.E. Fess. *Accounting.* 21st ed. Thomson South-Western, 2005.

ZERO SUM GAME

A zero-sum game is a term used in connection with game theory and management games. Game theory is a mathematical theory that applies to certain situations in which there are conflicts of interest between two or more individuals or groups. Management games are training or educational activities utilizing game theory models consisting of work situations. A zero-sum game is one type of management game in which all the payoffs for all players total zero; what one player or group gains, the other loses.

To better understand the term zero-sum game, it is beneficial to analyze game theory, as well as management games. Game theory is a significant branch of operations research and is closely related to decision theory and operational gaming. It attempts to answer the question, In a situation of conflict, what choice should the player make?

Game theory deals with abstract models of conflict situations or games of strategy. A game occurs when an individual or teams of people are in competition either against one another or against situations, or both.

A game can be represented by the following model:

1. there are *n* players (*n* being a certain number), each of whom is required to make one choice from a specified set of possible choices;

2. when every player has made a choice, the particular combination of choices they have made determines an outcome that, in some way, affects or interests all players;

3. each player knows what outcome results from each possible combination of choices;

4. each player has an order of preference for the possible outcomes (often each player assigns to each outcome a numerical value, called a payoff, which can be thought of as representing the number of points, or dollars, etc., that he gains or loses from the outcome);

5. each player knows the preferences of the other players (she knows what their payoffs are) and all players are assumed to act so as to gain the most they can from the game; but

6. each player makes his choice without knowing what choice the other players are making.

In the game, the competing players are identified as *persons* whether they are individuals, teams, or any other group representing a single set of interests. A *play* of a game is an exercise of the conflict model according to the rules; it consists of one or more *moves* by each player and may involve moves left to chance. The outcome of the game is represented by the payoff, a gain or loss of some utility to each of the players as a result of the positions reached at the end of the game. The *solution* of a game is comprised of the identification from among all the possible alternative courses of action, which ensures the player's expected payoff at a quantity called the *value* of the game.

In a business scenario, for example, the competition between two companies may be structured in game-theory terms. The persons are the companies, the play can be a determined period of time; and the rules are the discipline of the marketplace. Within the rules, management may make a variety of decisions upon which actions may be taken. These are known as the moves.

The firm's master plan is the strategy. In this example, the strategies of the companies would describe the companies' general decisions on such topics as advertising, mergers, and new product lines. The results of the interactions among the strategic choices made by the two firms are manifested by the payoff, which could be chosen to be annual gross sales, net profits, and so on. Only when a situation such as this is structured and quantified is it meaningful to address a solution and value for the game. The theory is used to calculate the optimum strategy that maximizes the winnings or minimizes the losses of one or more of the players.

Finite games, those in which each player has available a finite number of strategies, may be categorized according to the number of persons, relationships among payoffs, and whether cooperation among the players is allowed. The simplest form is the two-person zero-sum game, zero-sum denoting that the sum of the payoffs to the two players is zero.

A payoff matrix can be arranged to identify the payoffs for each player. The matrix is expressed in terms of the payoff to A, whereas B's payoffs are the negative of A's, thus satisfying the condition that their sum be zero. Positive entries indicate payments by B to A; negative ones, payments by A to B.

The solution can take two forms; the pure strategy case, in which a single strategy will be indicated as optimal; or a mixed strategy case, in which two or more strategies appear along with the relative frequencies with which they must be employed. An example of a two-person zero-sum game given by Derek French and Heather Saward, showing a pure strategy solution, is presented in Exhibit 1.

Exhibit 1
Matrix of a Two-Person Zero-Sum Game

		B's Strategies		
		B_1	B_2	B_3
A's Strategies	A_1	0	-1	7
	A_2	2	3	8
	A_3	9	5	6
	A_4	10	4	-2
		10	5	8

A's problem is to choose one of his four strategies; while B's is to choose one of his three. For example, the choices of A2 and B2 result in the payment by B to A of three units, while A4 and B3 lead to the payment by A to B of two units. First, consider A's analysis of his problem: A1 is a weak strategy because it nets A less than does the equally available strategy A2, regardless of B's choice. In this example, A1 is dominated by A2, and hence A1 from further consideration. By choosing A4 in an effort to realize the payoff of ten units at A4 and B1 could result in the loss of two units if B selects B3; similar dilemmas exist for the other choices.

Suppose that A takes a conservative point of view and examines the least his choice could produce; a gain of two for A2, a gain of five for A3, and a loss of two for A4. Of these options, A3 and its consequence appear the best choice; the five-unit gain represents an assured security level to A since he cannot be driven below this point by any action taken by B. In essence, A has examined the minimum gain that each row strategy could produce and, striving to maximize his gain has selected the greatest of these.

This is referred to as A's maximum strategy (R3 in Exhibit 1). At this point, B analyzes the greatest loss he might sustain as a result of his strategy choice; ten units for B1, five units for B2, and eight units for B3. Of these choices, B2 causes the smallest loss on B and establishes his security level by guaranteeing that no action of A's can cause his loss to be above five.

Summarizing, B has identified the maximum loss that each column strategy could produce and, wanting to minimize his loss has selected the least of these; known as B's minimax strategy. The most important feature of this result is the independently arrived-at agreement on the part of the players as to their security levels. This example also possesses a saddle-point, an element that is concurrently the greatest of the row minima and the least of the column maxima. The significance lies in the fact that if either player deviates from this choice; it will result in either decreased gain or increased loss.

The solution is that A always employs A3, B always employs B2, and the value of the game is five. This, of course, is not a fair game since A always wins five units at each play. It can be made fair, however, by requiring A to pay five units to B each time to induce B to play, or by reducing each element of the game matrix by five.

In recent years there has been opportunity to watch game strategies being used on the reality television shows that place teams, and eventually individuals, against each other. While ultimately a zero-sum game (in the end, one person wins everything), successful participants employed various strategies to cooperate with and exploit each other, all in an effort to win.

Although the most notorious use of game theory was utilized by the armed services in the Vietnam War for strategic purposes, the theory is noted today for its potential contribution to industrial affairs. Game theory is used to analyze economic policies and international agreements (e.g., whether economic sanctions act as practical incentives or build additional resentment). It is applied in management games, in which managers are grouped into teams representing a manager or the management of one of several competing organizations. The manager must take a sequence of decisions relating to a simulation of a real-life management problem, and is then presented with the results of each decision after it is made.

In the game, the result of an individual decision is the response, or the next move, of the other competitors. The games are used for several training purposes. They provide experience and they bring rapid feedback on the results of a decision. They also can show cause-and-effect relationships that may be blurred during longer time periods in real-life situations. The end result is to attain more personal involvement, greater attention, and greater retention of new concepts and ideas that have been acquired.

SEE ALSO: Decision Making

Kevin Nelson
Revised by Wendy H. Mason

FURTHER READING:

Finch, Frank, ed. *The Facts on File Encyclopedia of Management Techniques.* New York, NY: Facts on File, 1985.

French, Derek, and Heather Saward. *Dictionary of Management.* Aldershot, Hants, England: Gower, 1983.

"Game Theory." *Asia Africa Intelligence Wire,* 29 August 2004.

McMillan, John. *Games, Strategies and Managers.* New York, NY: Oxford University Press, 1996.

Poundstone, William. *Prisoners' Dilemma.* New York, NY: Anchor Books, Doubleday, 1993.

This index is sorted word-by-word.

Concurrent engineering, **112–115**
See also New product development; Time-based competition

Confidence factors, 279–280

Conflict management and negotiation, **115–119**, 163
See also Diversity; Management styles

Conglomerate diversification, 189

Consulting, **120–121**

Consumer behavior, **121–125**

Contextual influences, 17

Contingency approach to management, **125–126**, 447–448, 514

Contingent workers, **126–128**
See also Employee compensation; Employee recruitment planning; Employee screening and selection; Employment law and compliance; Human resource management

Continuing education and lifelong learning trends, **128–131**

Continuous improvement, **132–134**, 255
See also Japanese management; Lean manufacturing and just-in-time production; Quality and Total Quality Management; Quality gurus; Statistical process control and Six Sigma

Contracts, 384, 390

Contribution margin model, 46

Controlling, 496

Cooke, Morris, 654

Copyrights, 378–379

Corporate governance, **134–137**

Corporate-level strategy, 851–854

Corporate reorganization, 197–200

Corporate social responsibility, **137–141**
See also Ethics

Corporations (business structure), 62

Cost accounting, 1–3, **144–148**

Cost-based pricing, 673–674

Cost of goods sold, 369

Cost-volume-profit (CVP) analysis, **141–144**

Costs, 47, 410–411

Cover letters, 757–761

Creativity, **149–150**
See also Group decision making; Innovation

Critical path method. *See* Program evaluation and review technique and critical path method

Crosby, Philip, 731–733, 738

Crossover chart, 47

Current assets, 27–28, 289–290

Current liabilities, 29, 290

Customer relationship management (CRM), **150–152**

Customer service, 319–321

Cycle inventory, 415

Cycle time, **152–154**
See also Operations management; Operations scheduling

D

Data processing and data management, **155–159**

Database management systems (DBMS), 157–158

Database marketing, 530

Database models, 156

Debt *vs.* equity financing, **159–160**, 289
See also Due diligence; Financial issues for managers; Financial ratios

Decision making, **160–164**
empowerment, 253–256
ethics and, 261–264
group, 341–343
make-or-buy decisions, 479–481
multiple-criteria, 571–575
shareholder control, 803–804

Decision package, 986

Decision rules and decision analysis, **164–170**
See also Decision making; Decision support systems (DSS)

Decision support systems (DSS), 161–162, **170–174**
See also Competitive intelligence; Computer-aided design and manufacturing (CAD); Computer networks; Management information systems; Strategic planning tools

Decoupling inventory, 414–415

Delegation, **174–177**
See also Management styles; Motivation and motivation theory; Time management

Dell Computer, 216–217

Delphi method, 342, 892

Demand-based pricing, 674

Demand forecasting, 352–354

Deming, W. Edwards, 132, 418, 655–656, 725–729, 736–737

Deming Prize, 483–484, 739–740

Departmentalization, 631–632

Deregulation, **177–179**
See also Economics

Design for manufacturing and assembly (DFMA), 691

Dialetical inquiry, 341

Dictionary of Occupational Titles. *See* Occupational Information Network

Differentiation strategy, 90–92, 322

Digital rights management (DRM) technology, 379

Direct exporting, 283

Direct marketing, 529–530

Disaster recovery planning, 52–54

Disciplinary procedures, 239

Discounted cash flow, 291–292

Discrimination, **179–184**
See also Employee recruitment planning; Employee screening and selection; Employment law and compliance

Discussion method, 929–930

Distance education, 130–131

Distinctive competencies, 607–608

Distribution and distribution requirements planning, **184–187**
See also Forecasting; Logistics and Transportation; Supply chain management; Warehousing and warehouse management

Diversification strategy, **187–191**
See also Strategic planning failure; Strategy formulation; Strategy implementation; Strategy in the global environment

Group technology, 74–75

Growth strategy, 187–188, 854

Gung Ho! (Blanchard), 669

H

Halsey, Frederick A., 652

Handheld computers, **349–350**

Harrington, H. James, 733

Harvard Business School, 68, 95

Health insurance, 224, 350–351

Health savings accounts, 305, **350–351**

Heider, Fritz, 23

Hewlett Packard, 830

High-low method, 146

Hill, Terry, 611–613

Horizontal integration, 190

Hoshin planning, 842–843

Human resource information systems, **351–357**

Human resource management, **357–363,** 391, 792–793

The Human Side of Enterprise (McGregor), 911–914

Hypothesis testing, **364–366**

I

Icarus paradox, 828

Ideal production, 452

Importing, 281–285

Income statements, **367–371**
  See also Balance sheets; Cash flow analysis and statement; Financial issues for managers

Independent contract workers, 126–128

Indirect exporting, 283

Induction algorithms, 19–20

Industrial relations, **371–373**
  See also Employment law and compliance; Human resource management

Industry life cycle. *See* Product life cycle and industry life cycle

Inflation, 207–208

Initial public offering (IPO), **373–374**
  See also Cash flow analysis and statement; Entrepreneurship; Financial issues for managers; Strategy implementation

Innovation, 91–92, **374–376,** 894–899

Instant messaging, **376–377**
  See also Communication; Handheld computers

Institute for Supply Management (ISM), 196–197

Institute of Management Specialists (IMS), 395

Integrated marketing communication, 527–528

Intellectual property rights, **377–379,** 390, 641–643

Interactionist approach, 115

Internal auditing, **379–380**
  See also Financial issues for managers

Internal diversification, 189

Internal rate of return, 292

International business, **381–385,** 385–387, 467, 473–474, 568–571, 858–863

International cultural differences, **385–387,** 391–393, 473
  See also International business; International management; Organizational culture

International management, **387–393**
  See also International cultural differences

International management societies and associations, **393–396,** 705–706
  See also Domestic management societies and associations

International Monetary Fund (IMF), **396–399**

International Organization for Standardization (ISO), **399–402**

International Project Management Association (IPMA), 394

Internet, 379, **402–407,** 704–705
  See also Computer networks; Computer security; Electronic commerce; Electronic data interchange and electronic funds transfer

Internet marketing, 531–532

Internships, 11–12

Intranets, 404–405

Intrapreneurship, **407–408**
  See also Creativity; Entrepreneurship

Inventory management, **408–412,** 451
  See also Aggregate planning; Inventory types; Lean manufacturing and just-in-time production; Manufacturing resource planning; Reverse supply chain logistics; Supply chain management

Inventory types, **412–415**
  See also Inventory management; Theory of constraints

Investor system, 171–174

IPO, 373–374

Ishikawa, Kaoru, 733

ISO standards, 399–402

J

Japanese management, 132–134, 299–300, **417–423,** 450–453, 662–667, 842–843

Job analysis, **423–427**
  See also Employee recruitment planning; Employee screening and selection; Employment law and compliance; Occupational information network

Job-instruction technique (JIT), 933–934

Job rotation, 518

Job satisfaction, 25–26, 75–76, 562–563, 741–743

Johnson, Spencer, 668–669

Joint ventures and strategic alliances, 335–340, 384, **427–430**
  See also Competitive advantage; Diversification strategy; International business; Strategy formulation

Juran, Joseph M., 656, 729–731, 737–738

Just-in-time production, 450–453

K

Kaizen, 132–134

Kaplan, Robert S., 30–35

Keiretsu, 420–422

Key success factors (KSS), 607

Keynes, John Maynard, 208, 397

Kinesics, 40–43

Knowledge management, **431–432**
> *See also* Electronic commerce; Electronic data interchange and electronic funds transfer

Knowledge representation systems, 279–281

Knowledge workers, **432–437**

L

Labor relations, 251, 371–373

Latin American and Caribbean Council for Self-Management (LACCSM), 395

Layout, **439–442**
> *See also* Lean manufacturing and just-in-time production; Product-process matrix

Leader behavior approach, 446–447

Leader Behavior Description Questionnaire (LBDQ), 447

Leader-member exchange theory (LMX), 448–449

Leadership styles and bases of power, **442–445**
> *See also* Chain of command principle; Leadership theories and studies; Management styles; Organizational culture; Span of control

Leadership theories and studies, **445–450**
> *See also* Contingency approach to management; Leadership styles and bases of power; Management styles

Leading, 495

Lean manufacturing and just-in-time production, **450–453**
> *See also* Cellular manufacturing; Continuous improvement; Flexible manufacturing; Japanese management; Poka-Yoke; Quality and Total Quality Management; World class manufacturer

Learning curves, 276–279, 628

Learning organization, 515

Least-squares regression method, 146

Lecture method, 929

Level strategy, 5–6

Leverage ratios, 294–295

Leveraged buyouts, **454–455**
> *See also* Financial issues for managers; Shareholders

Lewin, Kurt, 442

Licensing and licensing agreements, 384, **455–457**
> *See also* Franchising; Intellectual property rights

Life insurance, 225

Lifelong learning trends, 129, **457–459**

Lilienthal, David E., 15

Limited Liability Corporations, 62–63

Line-and-staff organizations, **457–459**
> *See also* Leadership styles and bases of power; Organizational chart; Organizing

Liquidity ratios, 295–296

Listening, **459–461**
> *See also* Communication

Loading, 604

Loan applications, 72

Local area networks, 105–106

Location strategy, **462–464**
> *See also* Globalization; International business

Logistics and transportation, **464–467**, 918–919
> *See also* Exporting and importing; Forecasting; Lean manufacturing and just-in-time production; Reverse supply chain logistics; Warehousing and warehouse management

Long-range planning, 657–660

Long-term debt, 29

Long-term disability (LTD) insurance, 224

Longitudinal scenarios, **467–468**
> *See also* Contingency approach to management; Forecasting; Strategic planning tools

Lorenz, Edward, 79

Lot-sizing techniques, 411–412

M

Machine learning systems, 18

Macroenvironmental forces, **469–474**
> *See also* Economics; SWOT analysis

Magazines and newspapers, 705

Maintenance, **474–479**
> *See also* Continuous improvement; Lean manufacturing and just-in-time production; Operation strategy; Organizational culture

Make-or-buy decisions, **479–481**
> *See also* Break-even point

Malcolm Badridge National Quality Award, 484

Management and executive development, 194–197, **515–519**
> *See also* Employee evaluation and performance appraisals; Human resource management

Management audit, **481–482**
> *See also* Effectiveness and efficiency

Management awards, **483–490**
> *See also* Quality and total quality management; Quality gurus

Management books, 30–35, 667–670, 911–920

Management by objectives (MBO), 235–236, 510

Management by walking around (MBWA), 509–510

Management coefficients model, 7–8

Management control, **490–492**
> *See also* Organizational culture; Quality and total quality management; Teams and teamwork

Management functions, **493–495**, 500, 657–660
> *See also* Management control; Management styles; Organizing; Planning

Management information systems, **496–498**
> *See also* Knowledge management

Management levels, **498–503**
> *See also* Management and executive development; Management functions; Organizational chart; Organizational structure; Outsourcing and offshoring; Teams and teamwork

Management Professionals Association (MPA), 395

Management research, 15–17

Management science, **503–508**
> *See also* Operations management; Operations scheduling; Operations strategy; Production planning and scheduling

Management structure, 429

Management styles, **508–511**
    See also Leadership styles and bases of power; Leadership
       theories and studies; Quality and total quality management;
       Theory X and Theory Y; Theory Z

Management thought, **511–515**

Managerial accounting. *See* Cost accounting

Managing change, **519–522,** 745–749
    See also Organizational culture; Trends in organizational change

Manufacturing costs, 144–145

Manufacturing processes, 73–77

Manufacturing resource planning, 257, **523–526**
    See also Competitive advantage; Enterprise resource planning;
       Inventory types; Lean manufacturing and just-in-time
       production; Quality and total quality management

March, James G., 84

MARCO (Microelectronics Advanced Research Corp.), 337

Market pioneers, 297–299

Market segmentation, 675–676

Market share, **526–527**
    See also Generic competitive strategies

Market value ratios, 296

Marketing communication, **527–532**
    See also Communication; Marketing concept and philosophy;
       Marketing research

Marketing concept and philosophy, **532–535**
    See also Market share; Marketing communication; Marketing
       research

Marketing research, **535–539**
    See also Marketing concept and philosophy; Research methods
       and processes

Mass customization, 691

Material requirements planning (MRP), 186–187, 257, 523–525

Mathematical models, 559–560

Matrix structure, 633

Mayo, Elton, 655

McCallum, Daniel, 652

McGregor, Douglas, 911–915

Mechanistic organization, **539–540**
    See also Effectiveness and efficiency; Organic organizations;
       Organization theory; Organizational behavior; Organizational
       structure

MEDEA (Microelectronics Development for European Applications),
    337–338

Meeting management, **540–545**
    See also Group dynamics; Teams and teamwork

Mentoring, 518, **545–548,** 934
    See also Diversity; Knowledge management; Training delivery
       methods; Women and minorities in management

Mergers and acquisitions, **548–551**
    See also Financial ratios

Meta-analysis, 16

Metcalfe, Henry, 652

Microsoft Corp., 51–52

Miles, Raymond E., 551–553

Miles and Snow typology, **551–553**
    See also First-mover advantage; Generic competitive strategies;
       Innovation; Technology management

Miller, Danny, 828–829

Minorities in the workplace, 192, 546, 971–976

Mintzberg, Henry, 15, 493–494, 500, 827–828

Mission and vision statements, **553–557,** 839
    See also Strategic planning failure; Strategic planning tools;
       Strategy formulation; Strategy implementation; SWOT analysis

Models and modeling, 517, **557–562,** 617–619, 806–809
    See also Decision making; Decision rules and decision analysis;
       Decision support systems (DSS)

Monte Carlo simulation, 807–808

Morale, **562–563,** 741–743
    See also Human resource management; Quality of work life

Motivation and motivation theory, 25–26, 123–124, 253–256, **563–566**
    See also Goals and goal setting; Operant conditioning;
       Organizational behavior; Reinforcement theory; Theory X and
       Theory Y; Theory Z

MRO goods inventory, 415

Mulchy, Anne, 830

Multimedia, **566–568**
    See also Technology management; Training delivery methods

Multinational corporations, **568–571**
    See also Free trade agreements and trading blocs; International
       business; International management; Transnational organizations

Multiple-criteria decision making (MCOM), **571–575**
    See also Decision making; Decision rules and decision analysis;
       Decision support systems (DSS)

Munsterberg, Hugo, 654

Myers-Briggs Type Indicator (MBTI), 648

N

NAICS, 203–204, 589–591

Negotiation, 722–723

Nepotism, **577–579**
    See also Employee recruitment planning; Entrepreneurship; Human
       resource management; Succession planning; Work-life balance

Net present value analysis, 292

Network configurations, 104–105

Networked organizations, 940–941

Networks, computer, 104–108

Networks, neural, 18

New product development, 112–115, 374–376, **579–583,** 695
    See also Innovation; Product design; Product life cycle and
       industry life cycle

Niche strategy, 323–324

Nominal group technique, 341–342

Non-compete agreements, **583–585,** Employment law and compliance,
    Entrepreneurship

Nonprofit organizations, **585–589**
    See also Balance sheets; Financial issues for managers; Income
       statements

Nonverbal communication, 40–43, 87

Normative controls, 492

North American Industry Classification System (NAICS), 203–204,
    589–591
    See also Free trade agreements and trading blocs

Norton, David P., 30–35

O

Object-oriented programming (OOP), **593–595**
  See also Complexity theory; Computer networks; Knowledge management; Technological forecasting; Technology management; Technology transfer

Occupational information network (O*NET), **595–596**
  See also Job analysis

Occupational Safety and Health Administration (OSHA), 251–252, 259–260, 774–775

Offshoring, 793–794

Ohio State University, 447

On-the-job training, 933–934

One Minute Manager (Blanchard and Johnson), 668

O*NET, 595–596

Online learning, 130–131

Open and closed systems, **596–598**
  See also Managing change; Reactive *vs.* proactive change

Operant conditioning, **598–600**
  See also Motivation and motivation theory; Organizational behavior

Operating expenses, 369–370

Operating systems, **600–601**
  See also Computer-integrated manufacturing; Computer networks; Computer security; Data processing and data management; Management information systems

Operations management, **602–603**
  See also Operations strategy; Product design; Product-process matrix; Production planning and scheduling; Service operations; Supply chain management

Operations research, 503–508

Operations scheduling, **603–606,** 709–714
  See also Aggregate planning; Capacity planning; Operations management; Product-process matrix

Operations strategy, **606–610**
  See also Mission and vision statements; Operations management; Order-writing and order-qualifying criteria; Quality and total quality management; Strategy formulation

Opportunity cost, **610–611**
  See also Balance sheets; Economics; Strategic planning failure

Order-winning and order-qualifying criteria, **611–613**
  See also Competitive advantage; Operations strategy; Product life cycle and industry life cycle

Organic organizations, **613–615**
  See also Effectiveness and efficiency; Mechanistic organizations; Organization theory

Organization theory, **615–617**
  See also Mechanistic organizations; Organic organizations; Organizational analysis and planning

Organizational analysis and planning, **617–620**
  See also Organizational chart; Organizational development; Organizational structure

Organizational behavior, 80–84, **620–621**
  See also Motivation and motivation theory; Organic organizations; Organizational culture; Organizational development

Organizational change, 519–522

Organizational chart, **621–624,** 629–635
  See also Management levels

Organizational conflict, 115–119

Organizational culture, 492, **624–626**
  See also International cultural differences

Organizational development, **626–628**
  See also Organization theory; Organizational learning; Quality and total quality management; Teams and teamwork

Organizational learning, **628–629**
  See also Knowledge management; Organizational culture; Trends in organizational change

Organizational structure, 501–503, 621–624, **629–635,** 940
  See also Line-and-staff organizations; Organizational development

Organizing, 495, **635–637**
  See also Organizational chart; Organizational structure

Orientation, employee, 240

Osborn, Alex F., 43

OSHA, 251–252, 774–775

Ouchi, William, 417, 419, 509, 624, 914–915

Outsourcing and offshoring, 53, **637–638**
  See also International business; International management; Technology management; Technology transfer

Overall cost leadership, 321–322

Overall equipment effectiveness (OEE), 477–478

Owens, Robert, 651

Owners' equity, 30

P

Part-time workers, 126–128

Participative management, 253–256, 508–509, **639–641**
  See also Human resource management; Management styles; Motivation and motivation theory; Synergy; Teams and teamwork

Partnerships, 61–62

Patents and trademarks, 377–378, **641–643**
  See also Licensing and licensing agreements

Path-goal theory, 448

Pay equity, 227–228, 272–273

Payback method, 292

Pensions, 224

PeopleSoft, 356–357

Performance Management Association (PMA), 395

Performance measurement, 30–35, 231–236, 288–289, 334, **644–646**
  See also Balanced scorecard; Human resource management; Quality and total quality management; Strategy formulation

Person-organization fit (p-o fit), 17

Personal digital assistants (PDAs), 349–350

Personal selling, 531

Personal space, 42, 87–88

Personality and personality tests, **646–650**
  See also Employee screening and selection; Employment law and compliance; Human resource management; Leadership theories and studies; Management styles

PERT. *See* Program evaluation and review technique and critical path method

Peters, Tom, 81

Pfeffer, Jeffrey, 667–668

Phishing, 109–110